Summary of Financial Ratios

Short-Term Liquidity Ratios

1. $\text{Current Ratio} = \dfrac{\text{Current Assets}}{\text{Current Liabilities}}$

2. $\text{Quick Ratio} = \dfrac{\text{Cash} + \text{Short-Term Investments} + \text{Receivable}}{\text{Current Liabilities}}$

3. $\text{Cash Ratio} = \dfrac{\text{Cash} + \text{Short-Term Investments}}{\text{Current Liabilities}}$

4. $\text{Operating Cash Flow Ratio} = \dfrac{\text{Cash Flows from Operating Activities}}{\text{Current Liabilities}}$

Debt Management Ratios

5a. $\text{Times Interest Earned (\textit{Accrual basis})} = \dfrac{\text{Operating Income}}{\text{Interest Expense}}$

5b. $\text{Times Interest Earned (\textit{Cash basis})} = \dfrac{(\text{Cash Flows from Operations} + \text{Income Taxes Payable} + \text{Interest Payments})}{\text{Interest Payments}}$

6. $\text{Long-Term Debt-to-Equity Ratio} = \dfrac{\text{Long-Term Debt (including current portion)}}{\text{Total Equity}}$

7. $\text{Debt-to-Equity Ratio} = \dfrac{\text{Total Liabilities}}{\text{Total Equity}}$

8. $\text{Long-Term Debt-to-Total Assets Ratio} = \dfrac{\text{Long-Term Debt (including current portion)}}{\text{Total Assets}}$

9. $\text{Debt-to-Total Assets Ratio} = \dfrac{\text{Total Liabilities}}{\text{Total Assets}}$

Asset Efficiency Ratios

10. $\text{Accounts Receivable Turnover Ratio} = \dfrac{\text{Net Credit Sales or Net Sales}}{\text{Average Accounts Receivable}}$

11. $\text{Inventory Turnover Ratio} = \dfrac{\text{Cost of Goods Sold}}{\text{Average Inventory}}$

12. $\text{Asset Turnover Ratio} = \dfrac{\text{Net Sales}}{\text{Average Total Assets}}$

Profitability Ratios

13. $\text{Gross Profit Margin Percentage} = \dfrac{\text{Gross Profit}}{\text{Net Sales}}$

14. $\text{Operating Margin Percentage} = \dfrac{\text{Income from Operations}}{\text{Net Sales}}$

15. $\text{Net Profit Margin Percentage} = \dfrac{\text{Net Income}}{\text{Net Sales}}$

16. $\text{Return on Assets} = \dfrac{\text{Net Income} + [\text{Interest Expense} \times (1 - \text{Tax Rate})]}{\text{Average Total Assets}}$

17. $\text{Return on Equity} = \dfrac{\text{Net Income}}{\text{Average Equity}}$

Stockholder Ratios

18. $\text{Earnings per Share (EPS)} = \dfrac{(\text{Net Income} - \text{Preferred Dividends})}{\text{Average Number of Common Shares Outstanding}}$

19. $\text{Return on Common Equity} = \dfrac{\text{Net Income}}{\text{Average Common Equity}}$

20. $\text{Dividend Yield Ratio} = \dfrac{\text{Dividends per Common Share}}{\text{Closing Market Price per Share for the Year}}$

21. $\text{Dividend Payout Ratio} = \dfrac{\text{Common Dividends Paid}}{\text{Net Income}}$

22. $\text{Total Payout Ratio} = \dfrac{(\text{Common Dividends} + \text{Common Stock Repurchases})}{\text{Net Income}}$

23. $\text{Stock Repurchase Payout} = \text{Total Payout Ratio} - \text{Dividend Payout Ratio}$

Dupont Analysis

24. $\text{Return on Equity} = \left(\dfrac{\text{Net Income}}{\text{Sales}} \right) \times \left(\dfrac{\text{Sales}}{\text{Average Total Assets}} \right) \times \left(\dfrac{\text{Average Total Assets}}{\text{Average Equity}} \right)$

EXPERIENCE *MANAGERIAL ACCOUNTING* IN THE REAL WORLD WITH VIDEOS!

Developed by *Cornerstones* co-author Dan Heitger from Miami University, these videos center on cutting-edge success, showing how progressive companies use **managerial accounting** to fuel better business performance. Students will see both *manufacturing and service* examples to connect the text concepts to the business world. This series features top companies such as:

- **Hard Rock Café** — *Investments*
- **BP** — *Process Costing*
- **Washburn Guitar** — *Job Order Costing*
- **Cold Stone Creamery** — *Activity-Based Costing*
- **Buycostumes.com** — *Business Strategy*
- **Little Guys Electronics** — *Pricing*
- **The Second City** — *Overhead Analysis*
- **Zingerman's Deli** — *Cost Behavior*
- **Boyne Resorts** — *Cost-Volume-Profit Analysis*
- **High Sierra** — *Budgets and Profit Planning*
- **Herman Miller** — *Economic-Value-Added Analysis*
- **Navistar** — *Relevant Costs*

Critical thinking exercises accompany each video to test student comprehension and stimulate class discussion. The accompanying instructor guide offers you discussion questions, video synopses, learning goals, and experiential exercises to enhance your classroom experience!

2E

cornerstones
OF
FINANCIAL & MANAGERIAL ACCOUNTING

JAY S. RICH
Illinois State University

JEFFERSON P. JONES
Auburn University

DAN L. HEITGER
Miami University

MARYANNE M. MOWEN
Oklahoma State University

DON R. HANSEN
Oklahoma State University

SOUTH-WESTERN
CENGAGE Learning™

Australia • Brazil • Japan • Korea • Mexico • Singapore • Spain • United Kingdom • United States

**Cornerstones of Financial & Managerial
   Accounting, 2e**
Rich, Jones, Heitger, Mowen, and Hansen

Vice President of Editorial,
   Business: Jack W. Calhoun

Editor-in-Chief: Rob Dewey

Senior Acquisitions Editor: Matthew Filimonov

Associate Developmental Editor: Krista Kellman

Editorial Assistant: Ann Mazzaro

Marketing Manager: Natalie Livingston

Senior Content Project Manager: Tim Bailey

Media Editor: Bryan England

Senior Frontlist Buyer,
   Manufacturing: Doug Wilke

Senior Marketing Communications
   Manager: Libby Shipp

Production Service: LEAP Publishing Services, Inc.

Compositor: Knowledgeworks Global Limited

Senior Art Director: Stacy Jenkins Shirley

Cover and Internal Designer: Mike Stratton

Cover Image: © Doug Norman Crystals/Alamy

Senior Rights Acquisitions
   Specialist: Deanna Ettinger

For product information and technology assistance, contact us at
Cengage Learning Customer & Sales Support, 1-800-354-9706

For permission to use material from this text or product, submit all
requests online at **www.cengage.com/permissions**.
Further permissions questions can be emailed to
permissionrequest@cengage.com.

Exam*View*® is a registered trademark of eInstruction Corp. Windows is a
registered trademark of the Microsoft Corporation used herein under
license. Excel® spreadsheet software is a registered trademark of Microsoft
Corporation.

Library of Congress Control Number: 2010939894

ISBN-13: 978-0-538-47348-4
ISBN-10: 0-538-47348-7

South-Western Cengage Learning
5191 Natorp Boulevard
Mason, OH 45040
USA

Cengage Learning products are represented in Canada by Nelson
Education, Ltd.

For your course and learning solutions, visit **www.cengage.com**
Purchase any of our products at your local college store or at our preferred
online store **www.cengagebrain.com**

Printed in Canada
1 2 3 4 5 6 7 14 13 12 11

BRIEF CONTENTS

Get There with Cornerstones

Cornerstones **is an innovative text and technology solution that helps you achieve your desired grades.** The best part about this solution is that it was created by modern professors who understand the challenges you face every day. The authors of *Cornerstones* realized that their students were using textbooks differently than they had in the past. They found that because other books were not structured around helping students complete homework, they were spending too much of their classes going over homework in class. *Cornerstones* will help you learn more independently before attending lecture.

Cornerstones is all about giving you the tools you need to succeed. According to our research with students like you, this approach models the way that students use textbooks. Most admit that they attempt the homework before going into the text itself to learn, making clear and easy-to-find examples crucial. For this reason, we have linked the Cornerstone Exercises to the Cornerstone examples and created a multi-tiered approach to homework assignments.

The *Cornerstones* approach not only helps you get further with your homework so that you can comprehend the more technical aspects of accounting, but it also gives you the tools to understand analysis and decision-making.

> *"I found that after reading the material, the 'Cornerstones' helped reinforce the main points and overall understanding.... The professor can spend more time teaching other concepts and different examples."*
> —**Sarah Earnhart, Student at Eastern Illinois University**

SUPERIOR TEXT AND PEDAGOGY!

Carefully crafted in response to studies on student reading behavior, this innovative approach has been proven to increase student engagement and preparedness while improving grades. Each major concept is illustrated in a

Cornerstone, which supports accounting concepts with a compelling example, step-by-step calculations to solve a business problem, and a link to a brief video segment that reinforces and summarizes key concepts and procedures.

> *"With my current textbook, it is hard to find valuable material. With* Cornerstones, *finding important material is much quicker and more effective."*
> —**Joshua Marks, Student at St. Norbert College**

Focus on Decision Making

The new **You Decide** feature helps students actively practice decision making by playing the part of a manager or business owner. By considering the different factors of their decisions and how they will affect outcomes, *Cornerstones* is helping students prepare for the real world.

YOU DECIDE — Choosing Among Inventory Costing Methods

You are the owner and manager of Simply Fresh, a supermarket that specializes in selling fresh, organic food. You know that managing inventory is crucial to the company's success and that generally accepted accounting principles give you the freedom to choose between FIFO, LIFO, and average cost to report inventory and cost of goods sold.

What factors should you consider in selecting among the different inventory costing methods?

Three factors that should be considered are as follows:

- *Actual physical flow of inventory*: Because most companies sell their oldest merchandise first, FIFO will give the closest approximation to the physical flow of inventory. However, GAAP does not require that the choice of inventory costing method be consistent with the physical flow of goods.
- *Financial statement effects*: During periods of rising prices, the use of FIFO will result in the highest cost for ending inventory, the lowest cost of goods sold, and the highest net income. These positive financial results may be desirable to satisfy shareholders who demand higher stock prices or meet lending agreements that are tied to financial performance. In addition, if management's bonus plan is tied to reported income, the use of FIFO may result in higher bonuses for management.
- *Tax benefits*: During periods of rising prices, the use of LIFO will result in lower income and possibly create significant tax savings for the company.

If financial statement users wish to make good decisions, it is important to understand the differences that result from management's choice of inventory method.

MULTIPLE WAYS TO PRACTICE

Cornerstones offers a variety of question types and levels of difficulty in the end-of-chapter homework, including:

- Review Problems
- Discussion Questions
- Multiple-Choice Exercises
- Cornerstone Exercises*
- Exercises
- Problems
- Cases
- Continuing Problems (in the *Financial* volume)
- Making the Connection integrative exercises

* By offering Cornerstone Exercises that reference the Cornerstone examples in the text, students have a way to get started with the homework.

> *"The connectivity between topical content (LOs), calculations, and decisions are developed well in the end-of-chapter material."* —NOEL MCKEON, FLORIDA STATE COLLEGE

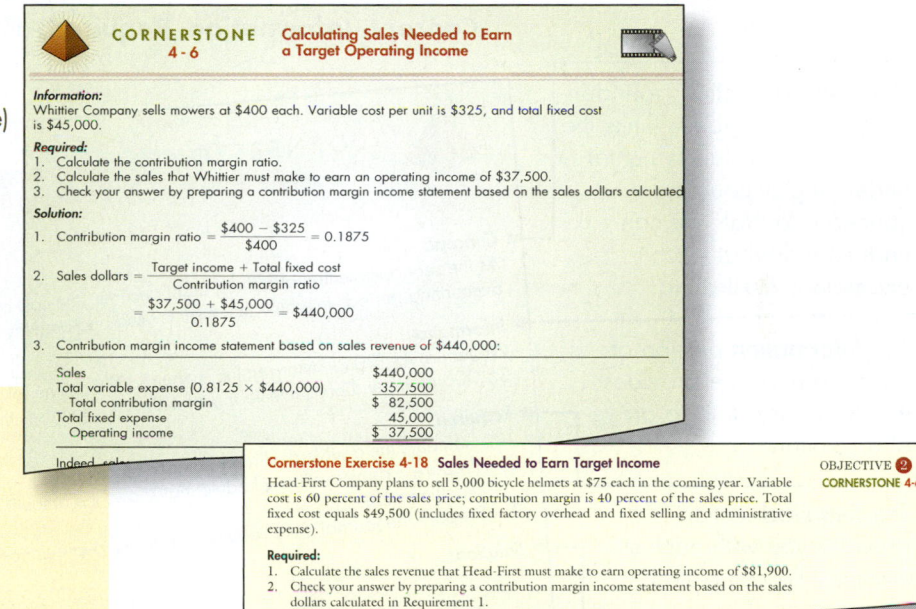

CORNERSTONE 4-6 Calculating Sales Needed to Earn a Target Operating Income

Information:
Whittier Company sells mowers at $400 each. Variable cost per unit is $325, and total fixed cost is $45,000.

Required:
1. Calculate the contribution margin ratio.
2. Calculate the sales that Whittier must make to earn an operating income of $37,500.
3. Check your answer by preparing a contribution margin income statement based on the sales dollars calculated.

Solution:

1. Contribution margin ratio $= \dfrac{\$400 - \$325}{\$400} = 0.1875$

2. Sales dollars $= \dfrac{\text{Target income} + \text{Total fixed cost}}{\text{Contribution margin ratio}}$

   $= \dfrac{\$37,500 + \$45,000}{0.1875} = \$440,000$

3. Contribution margin income statement based on sales revenue of $440,000:

Sales	$440,000
Total variable expense (0.8125 × $440,000)	357,500
Total contribution margin	$ 82,500
Total fixed expense	45,000
Operating income	$ 37,500

Indeed, sale...

Cornerstone Exercise 4-18 Sales Needed to Earn Target Income

OBJECTIVE ❷
CORNERSTONE 4-6

Head-First Company plans to sell 5,000 bicycle helmets at $75 each in the coming year. Variable cost is 60 percent of the sales price; contribution margin is 40 percent of the sales price. Total fixed cost equals $49,500 (includes fixed factory overhead and fixed selling and administrative expense).

Required:
1. Calculate the sales revenue that Head-First must make to earn operating income of $81,900.
2. Check your answer by preparing a contribution margin income statement based on the sales dollars calculated in Requirement 1.

> *"I have recently tried the problems in* Cornerstones *and found that the step-by-step examples that are placed within the text helped extremely.... I compared the chapters in* Cornerstones *to our textbooks and felt that* Cornerstones *was much easier to understand by just reading the chapter."*
> —KATIE HOGAN, STUDENT AT UNIVERSITY OF CINCINNATI

> *"It supports student learning in the beginning by giving them direction, then as they progress leads them to be more independent and learn to apply the concepts and knowledge. This should prepare them for testing and real-world better than if they are always given the appropriate learning objective to apply."*
> —BARBARA WOODS MCELROY, SUSQUEHANNA UNIVERSITY

- **More advanced exercises and problems** are presented that sometimes cover multiple Learning Objectives. These questions further challenge you since they do not list the corresponding Cornerstone example(s). These help you grasp more difficult concepts and see the big picture.

- **Conceptual Connection** analytical requirements within many end-of-chapter assignments help students understand the differences between alternative methods, how different decisions will yield different results, and articulate why this is the case.

- **Illustrating Relationships questions** help you understand the relationships between different variables and how they impact each other.

- For the *Financial* volume, a **continuing problem** using a hypothetical company called **"Front Row Entertainment"** is now included. You can connect concepts from each chapter by following Front Row Entertainment as it engages in various business transactions. In addition, three new chapter-spanning **Making the Connection assignments** present opportunities to integrate concepts from several chapters to analyze financial statement information in a broader context.

HOW TO USE THE CORNERSTONES

Cornerstone examples are clear, consistently formatted and step-by-step to help you understand concepts and complete homework. Each Cornerstone has four parts: **Concept**, **Information**, **Required**, and **Solution**.

The *Concept* section, found in the financial chapters, links the Cornerstone to fundamental underlying accounting concepts so that you can understand what each example is illustrating.

The *Information* portion of each Cornerstone provides the necessary data to arrive at a solution.

The *Required* section provides you with each step that must be completed.

The *Solution* ends each Cornerstone, showing the calculations for each of the required steps in the problem. You can use these solutions as a model to help you complete similar problems in the homework.

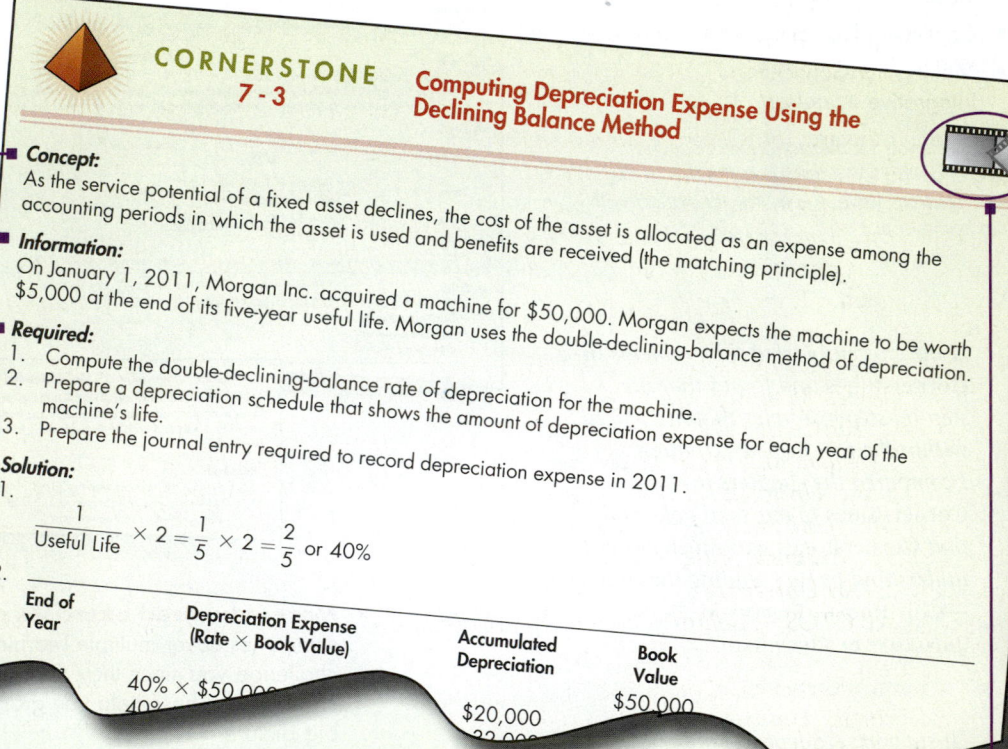

CORNERSTONE 7-3
Computing Depreciation Expense Using the Declining Balance Method

Concept:
As the service potential of a fixed asset declines, the cost of the asset is allocated as an expense among the accounting periods in which the asset is used and benefits are received (the matching principle).

Information:
On January 1, 2011, Morgan Inc. acquired a machine for $50,000. Morgan expects the machine to be worth $5,000 at the end of its five-year useful life. Morgan uses the double-declining-balance method of depreciation.

Required:
1. Compute the double-declining-balance rate of depreciation for the machine.
2. Prepare a depreciation schedule that shows the amount of depreciation expense for each year of the machine's life.
3. Prepare the journal entry required to record depreciation expense in 2011.

Solution:
1.
$$\frac{1}{Useful\ Life} \times 2 = \frac{1}{5} \times 2 = \frac{2}{5} \text{ or } 40\%$$

2.

End of Year	Depreciation Expense (Rate × Book Value)	Accumulated Depreciation	Book Value
	40% × $50,000 40%	$20,000	$50,000

Each Cornerstone has an online video offering a step-by-step presentation of each part of the Cornerstone example. These videos provide you with visual and auditory reinforcement of the content.

ACKNOWLEDGMENTS AND THANKS

We would like to thank the following reviewers and focus group participants whose valuable comments and feedback helped shape and refine this edition:

Joe Adamo, *Cazenovia College*

Janice Ammons, *Quinnipiac University*

Sheila Ammons, *Austin Community College*

Siti Arshad-Snyder, *Clarkson College*

Jane Austin, *Oklahoma City University*

Timothy Baker, *California State University – Fresno*

Eric Ball, *Wake Technical Community College*

Timothy Biggart, *Berry College*

Jennifer Blaskovich, *University of Nebraska*

Kevin Bosner, *Medaille College*

Anna M. Boulware, *St. Charles Community College*

Rachel Brassine, *East Carolina University*

Bob Braun, *Southern Louisiana University*

Linda Bressler, *University of Houston – Downtown*

Rada Brooks, *University of California – Berkeley*

Steven Buchheit, *Texas Tech University*

John Callister, *Cornell University*

Charles Carpenter, *Francis Marion University*

Amy Chataginer, *Mississippi Gulf Coast Community College*

Bea Chiang, *The College of New Jersey*

Star Ciccio, *Johnson and Wales University*

Norman Colter, *University of New Mexico*

Deb Cosgrove, *University of Nebraska*

Terry Dancer, *Arkansas State University*

Lee Daniel, *Troy University*

John Davis, *KCTCS – Ashland Community and Technical College*

Patricia Davis, *Keystone College*

Barbara Durham, *University of Central Florida*

Carol Dutton, *South Florida Community College*

Diane Eure, *Texas State University*

Amanda Farmer, *University of Georgia*

Virginia Fullwood, *Texas A&M University – Commerce*

Karen Geiger, *Arizona State University*

Alex Gialanella, *Iona College*

John Giles, *North Carolina State University*

Rajul Gokarn, *Clark Atlanta University*

Marina Grau, *Houston Community College*

John P. Gray, *Faulkner University – Montgomery*

Michael Hayden, *Purdue University*

Dell Ann Janney, *Culver-Stockton College*

Cindi Khanlarian, *University of North Carolina – Greensboro*

Rajabali Kiani, *California State University – Northridge*

Shirly A. Kleiner, *Johnson County Community College*

Mike Klickman, *University of Dallas*

Stephen M. Komer, *University of North Carolina – Charlotte*

David Krug, *Johnson Community College*

Janice Lawrence, *University of Nebraska – Lincoln*

Ron Lazer, *University of Houston*

Natasha Librizzi, *Milwaukee Area Technical College*

Ted Lynch, *Hocking College*

Linda Mallory, *Catawba Valley Community College*

David Marcinko, *Skidmore College*

Barbara Woods McElroy, *Susquehanna University*

Cynthia Miglietti, *Bowling Green State University*

April Mohr, *Jefferson Community and Technical College*

Sy Pearlman, *California State University – Long Beach*

Rama Ramamurthy, *College of William and Mary*

Barbara Reider, *University of Montana*

Barbara Rice, *Kentucky Community and Technical College*

Dana Roark, *Northwestern Oklahoma State University*

Pamela Rouse, *Butler University*

Maria Roxas, *Central Connecticut State University*

Robert Rutledge, *Texas State University*

Anwar Salimi, *California State University – Pomona*

Cathy Scott, *Navarro College*

Lewis Shaw, *Suffolk University*

John W. Shishoff, *University of Dayton*

Ron Singleton, *Western Washington University*

William R. Singleton, *Western Washington University*

Gerald Smith, *University of Northern Iowa*

Nancy Snow, *University of Toledo*

Naomi Soderstrom, *University of Colorado at Boulder*

Beverly Soriano, *Framingham State College*

Gloria Stuart, *Georgia Southern University*

John J. Surdick, *Xavier University*

Karen Tabak, *Maryville University*

Steve Teeter, *Utah Valley University*

Donald R. Trippeer, *SUNY – Oneonta*

Donna Veins, *Johnson and Wales University*

Charles Wellens, *Fitchburg State University*

Jean Wells, *Howard University*

Scott White, *Lindenwood University*

Terrence Willyard, *Baker College*

Tammy Wolf, *Purdue University*

Denise Wooten, *Erie Community College – North*

Jan Workman, *East Carolina University*

Judith Zander, *Grossmont College*

CONTENTS

CHAPTER 7
Operating Assets   328

CHAPTER 8
Current and Contingent Liabilities   384

CHAPTER 9
Long-Term Liabilities   422

CHAPTER 16
Job-Order Costing 808

CHAPTER 17
Process Costing 862

CHAPTER 18
Activity-Based Costing and Management 910

CHAPTER 22
Performance Evaluation, Variable Costing, and Decentralization   1102

CHAPTER 23
Short-Run Decision Making: Relevant Costing and Inventory Management   1146

ABOUT THE AUTHORS

Dr. Jay S. Rich is a Professor of Accounting at Illinois State University. He received his B.S., M.S., and Ph.D. from the University of Illinois. Prior to entering the Ph.D. program, Rich worked as an auditor at Price Waterhouse & Co. and earned his CPA. His primary teaching interest is financial accounting, and he has taught numerous courses at the undergraduate, masters, and doctoral levels. Rich has been awarded both the Outstanding Dissertation Award and Notable Contribution to the Literature Award by the Audit Section of the American Accounting Association. He has published articles in *The Accounting Review, Auditing: A Journal of Practice & Theory, Accounting Horizons, Organizational Behavior and Human Decision Processes, Accounting Organizations and Society*, and served on the editorial board of *Auditing: A Journal of Practice & Theory*. His outside interests include family, travel, reading, and watching sports, but he spends most of his free time driving his children to various activities. He also repeatedly develops plans to exercise and diet at some point in the future and has not been to a movie in years. By all accounts, he is a master at grilling meat, a mediocre skier, and a shameful golfer.

Dr. Jefferson P. Jones is the PricewaterhouseCoopers Associate Professor of Accounting at Auburn University. He received his Bachelor's and Master of Accountancy degrees from Auburn University and his Ph.D. in accounting from Florida State University. While earning his CPA, he worked for Deloitte & Touche. Jones has received numerous teaching awards, including the Outstanding Master of Accountancy Professor Award, the Beta Alpha Psi Outstanding Teaching Award (six times), the Auburn University College of Business McCartney Teaching Award, and the Auburn University School of Accountancy Teaching Award. In addition to an Intermediate Accounting text, his published articles appear in *Advances in Accounting, Review of Quantitative Finance and Accounting, Issues in Accounting Education, International Journal of Forecasting, The CPA Journal, Managerial Finance, Journal of Accounting and Finance Research*, and *The Journal of Corporate Accounting and Finance*. Jones has made numerous presentations around the country on research and pedagogical issues. He is a member of the American Accounting Association (AAA), the American Institute of Certified Public Accountants (AICPA), and the Alabama Society of CPAs (ASCPA). He is married, has two children, and enjoys playing golf.

Dr. Dan L. Heitger is Associate Professor of Accounting and Co-Director of the Center for Business Excellence at Miami University. He received his Ph.D. from Michigan State University and his undergraduate degree in accounting from Indiana University. He actively works with executives and students of all levels in developing and teaching courses in managerial and cost accounting, risk management, and business reporting. Heitger co-founded an organization that provides executive education for large international organizations. His interactions with business professionals through executive education and the Center allow him to bring a current and real-world perspective to his writing. His published research focuses on managerial accounting, governance, risk management, and sustainability issues and has appeared in *Harvard Business Review, Behavioral Research in Accounting, Issues in Accounting Education, Journal of Accountancy*, and *Management Accounting Quarterly*. His outside interests include hiking with his wife and three children in the National Park system.

Dr. Maryanne M. Mowen is Associate Professor of Accounting at Oklahoma State University. She received her Ph.D. from Arizona State University. With degrees in economics and history, she brings a unique interdisciplinary perspective to teaching and writing in both cost accounting and management accounting. Her research interests include management accounting, behavioral decision theory, and Sarbanes-Oxley compliance, and she teaches an ethics course about the impact of Sarbanes-Oxley on the accounting profession. Mowen has published articles in journals such as *Decision Science, Journal of Economic Psychology*, and *Journal of Management Accounting Research*. She has also served as a consultant to midsized and Fortune 100 companies and works with corporate controllers on management accounting issues. Outside the classroom, she enjoys hiking, traveling, reading mysteries, and solving crossword puzzles.

Dr. Don R. Hansen is Professor of Accounting at Oklahoma State University. He received his Ph.D. from the University of Arizona and has an undergraduate degree in mathematics from Brigham Young University. His research interests include activity-based costing and mathematical modeling. Hansen's published articles appear in *The Accounting Review, Journal of Management Accounting Research, Accounting, Organizations and Society, Accounting Horizons*, and *IIE Transactions*, and he served on the editorial board of *The Accounting Review*. His outside interests include taking part in family and church activities, reading, watching movies, watching sports, and studying Spanish.

1 Accounting and the Financial Statements

Doug Norman Crystals/Alamy

After studying Chapter 1, you should be able to:

1. Explain the nature of accounting.

2. Identify the forms of business organizations and the types of business activities.

3. Describe the relationships shown by the fundamental accounting equation.

4. Prepare a classified balance sheet and understand the information it communicates.

5. Prepare an income statement and understand the information it communicates.

6. Prepare the retained earnings statement and understand the information it communicates.

7. Understand the information communicated by the statement of cash flows.

8. Describe the relationships among the financial statements.

9. Describe other information contained in the annual report and the importance of ethics in accounting.

AP Photo/Paul Sakuma

EXPERIENCE FINANCIAL ACCOUNTING

with Apple

In 1976, Steve Jobs and Steve Wozniak, the founders of **Apple Inc.** began building personal computers in Jobs' parents' garage. By 1984, Apple had become a leader in the personal computing industry, and its Macintosh computer is regarded by many as a key contributor to the development of the desktop publishing market. Apple appeared invincible. However, the development of Microsoft's Windows operating system and several Apple product failures led many to predict the end of one of the computer industry's most prominent companies. How could a company with such a bright future experience failure? And, perhaps more remarkable, how could a company on the verge of extinction experience the kind of success that Apple has recently experienced? With the introduction of the iMac, the iPod, the iTunes Store, and the iPad, Apple's stock price increased from approximately $7 per share in June 1998 to more than $230 in March 2010.

What type of information can help someone predict the successes of a company like Apple? A good place to start is with the financial information contained in a company's annual report. This financial information is provided in the form of financial statements—a summary of the results of a company's operations. A study of a company's financial statements will help you determine how successful a company has been in the past as well as its prospects for the future. While this information is easily accessible and free of charge, your final judgment on a company's future prospects will be influenced by how well you understand the information contained in its financial statements.

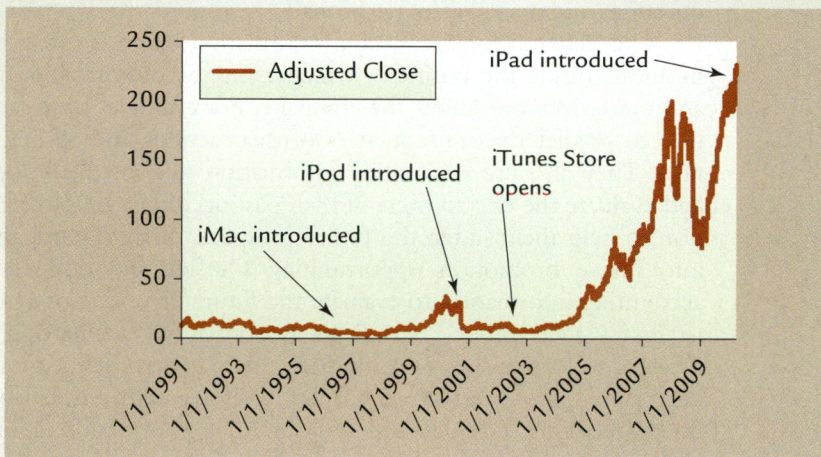

OBJECTIVE **1**
Explain the nature of accounting.

WHAT IS ACCOUNTING?

Our economy is comprised of many different businesses. Some companies, such as **Apple Inc.**, focus on providing goods, which for Apple take many forms including Macintosh computers, iPods, iPhones, and downloadable music. Other companies are primarily concerned with providing services. For example, **Walt Disney** offers a variety of entertainment services from theme parks to motion pictures. While most entities, like Apple and Disney, exist in order to earn a profit, some are organized to achieve some other benefit to society (for example, school districts exist to meet the educational needs of a community). Regardless of their objective, all entities use accounting to plan future operations, make decisions, and evaluate performance.

Accounting is the process of identifying, measuring, recording, and communicating financial information about a company's business activities so decision makers can make informed decisions. Accounting information is useful because it helps people answer questions and make better decisions.

The demand for accounting information comes from both inside and outside the business. Inside the business, managers use accounting information to help them plan and make decisions about the company. For example, they can use accounting information to predict the consequences of their actions and to help decide which actions to take. They also use accounting information to control the operations of the company and evaluate the effectiveness of their past decisions. Employees use accounting information to help them judge the future prospects of their company, which should translate into future promotion opportunities. Outside the business, investors (owners) use accounting information to evaluate the future prospects of a company and decide where to invest their money. Creditors (lenders) use accounting information to evaluate whether to loan money to a company. Even governments use accounting information to determine taxes owed by companies, to implement regulatory objectives, and to make policy decisions. This demand for accounting information is summarized by Exhibit 1-1.

Accounting is more than the process of recording information and maintaining accounting records—activities that are frequently called bookkeeping. Accounting is the "language of business." That is, accounting can be viewed as an information system that communicates the business activities of a company to interested parties. The focus of this book is on providing information that satisfies the needs of external decision-makers (outside demand) and is termed **financial accounting**. The objectives of financial accounting involve providing decision-makers with information that assists them in

Exhibit 1-1

The Demand for Accounting Information and Typical Questions

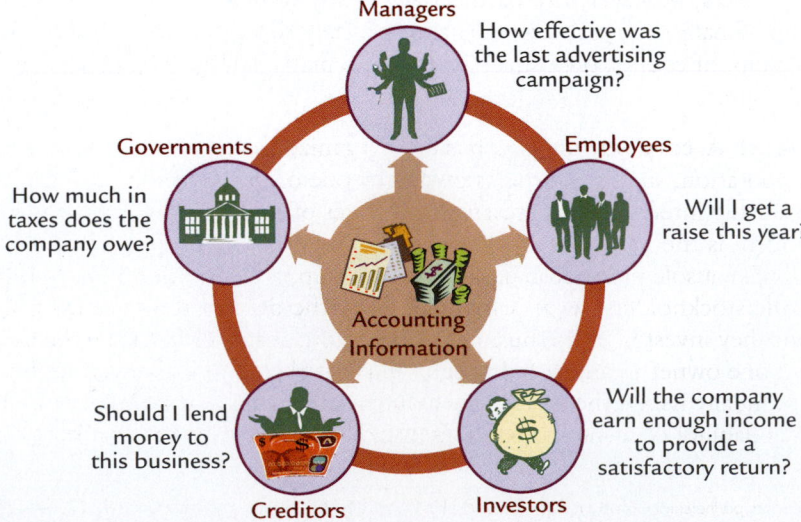

Managers — How effective was the last advertising campaign?

Employees — Will I get a raise this year?

Governments — How much in taxes does the company owe?

Investors — Will the company earn enough income to provide a satisfactory return?

Creditors — Should I lend money to this business?

Accounting Information

assessing the amounts, timing, and uncertainties of a company's future cash flows. This information is provided through four basic financial statements: the balance sheet, the income statement, the retained earnings statement, and the statement of cash flows.

In this chapter, we will discuss the basic functioning of the accounting system within a business. We will address the following questions:

- What forms do businesses take?
- What are the basic business activities?
- How does the accounting system report these activities?
- How can decision-makers use the information provided by the accounting system?

Regardless of your major or future plans, knowledge of accounting and the ability to use accounting information will be critical to your success in business.

Concept Q&A

How will accounting affect my life?

Answer:

Accounting will impact many aspects of your daily life. The business that sells you goods or services uses accounting to keep track of how much money it received as well as the cost of operating the business. Calculating the amount of tax that is due to the government requires accounting. When you invest your money, you should use accounting to understand a company's business and its prospects for the future. Plans that you make for the future often involve accounting to determine how much money you will need.

BUSINESSES: FORMS AND ACTIVITIES

Accounting identifies, measures, records, and communicates financial information about an accounting entity. An accounting entity is a company that has an identity separate from that of its owners and managers and for which accounting records are kept.

OBJECTIVE **2**

Identify the forms of business organizations and the types of business activities.

Forms of Business Organization

This text emphasizes accounting for entities which take one of three different forms: sole proprietorship, partnership, or corporation.

Sole Proprietorship
A **sole proprietorship** is a business owned by one person. Sole proprietorships, which account for more than 70 percent of all businesses, are usually small, local businesses such as restaurants, photography studios, retail stores, or website providers. This organizational form is popular because is it simple to set up and gives the owner control over the business. While a sole proprietorship is an accounting entity separate from its owner, the owner is personally responsible for the debt of the business. Sole proprietorships can be formed or dissolved at the wishes of the owner.

Partnership
A **partnership** is a business owned jointly by two or more individuals. Small businesses and many professional practices of physicians, lawyers, and accountants are often organized as partnerships. Relative to sole proprietorships, partnerships provide increased access to financial resources as well as access to the individual skills of each of the partners. Similar to sole proprietorships, partnerships are accounting entities separate from the partners; however, the partners are jointly responsible for all the debt of the partnership.[1] Finally, the partnership is automatically dissolved when any partner leaves the partnership; of course, the remaining partners may form a new partnership and continue to operate.

Corporation
A **corporation** is a business organized under the laws of a particular state. A corporation, such as **Apple**, is owned by one or more persons called *stockholders*, whose ownership interests are represented by shares of stock. A primary advantage of the corporate form is the ability to raise large amounts of money (capital) by issuing shares of stock. Unlike a sole proprietorship or a partnership, a corporation is an "artificial person" and the stockholders' legal responsibility for the debt of the business is limited to the amount they invested in the business. In addition, shares of stock can be easily transferred from one owner to another through capital markets without affecting the corporation that originally issued the stock. The ability to raise capital by selling new shares, the limited legal liability of owners, and the transferability of the shares give the corporation

---

[1] Many professional partnerships—including the largest public accounting firms—have been reorganized as *limited liability partnerships* (LLPs), which protect the personal assets of the partners from being used to pay partnership debts.

Exhibit 1-2

Forms of Business Organization

Sole Proprietorship	Partnership	Corporation
➕ Easily formed	➕ Access to the resources and skills of partners	➕ Easier to raise money
➕ Tax advantages	➕ Tax advantages	➕ Easier to transfer ownership
➕ Controlled by owner	➖ Shared control	➕ Limited liability
➖ Personal liability	➖ Personal liability	➖ More complex to organize
➖ Limited life	➖ Limited life	➖ Higher taxes

an advantage over other forms of business organization. However, the requirements to form a corporation are more complex relative to the other forms of business organization. In addition, corporations generally pay more taxes than owners of sole proprietorships or partnerships for two reasons:

- First, the corporate income tax rate is greater than the individual income tax rate.
- Second, a corporation's income is taxed twice—at the corporate level as income is earned, and at the individual level as earnings are distributed to stockholders. This is known as double taxation.

Exhibit 1-2 illustrates the advantages and disadvantages of each form of organization. While the combined number of sole proprietorships and partnerships greatly exceeds that of corporations, the majority of business in the United States is conducted by corporations. Therefore, this book emphasizes the corporate form of organization.

Business Activities

Regardless of the form of a business, all businesses engage in activities that can be categorized as financing, investing, or operating activities. These activities are illustrated in Exhibit 1-3.

Financing Activities A company's financing activities include obtaining the funds necessary to begin and operate a business. These funds come from either issuing stock or borrowing money. Most companies use both types of financing to obtain funds.

Exhibit 1-3

Business Activities

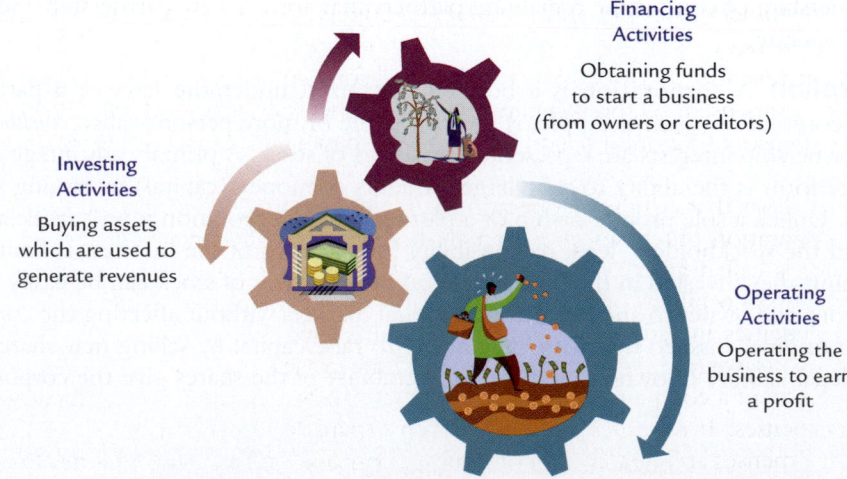

Financing Activities
Obtaining funds to start a business (from owners or creditors)

Investing Activities
Buying assets which are used to generate revenues

Operating Activities
Operating the business to earn a profit

When a corporation borrows money from another entity such as a bank, it must repay the amount borrowed. The person to whom the corporation owes money is called a **creditor**. This obligation to repay a creditor is termed a **liability** and can take many forms. A common way for a corporation to obtain cash is to borrow money with the promise to repay the amount borrowed plus interest at a future date. Such borrowings are commonly referred to as *notes payable*. A special form of note payable that is used by corporations to obtain large amounts of money is called a *bond payable*.

In addition to borrowing money from creditors, a corporation may issue shares of stock to investors in exchange for cash. The dollar amount paid to a corporation for these shares is termed *common stock* and represents the basic ownership interest in a corporation. As of September 26, 2009, **Apple** had issued 899,805,500 shares of common stock. The corporation is not obligated to repay the stockholder the amount invested; however, many corporations distribute a portion of their earnings to stockholders on a regular basis. These distributions are called *dividends*.

Creditors and stockholders have a claim on the **assets**, or economic resources, of a corporation. However, the claims on these resources differ. In the case of financial difficulty or distress, the claims of the creditors (liabilities) must be paid prior to the claims of the stockholders (called **stockholders' equity**). Stockholders' equity is considered a residual interest in the assets of a corporation that remain after deducting its liabilities.

Investing Activities Once a corporation has obtained funds through its financing activities, it buys assets that enable it to operate. For example, **Apple** has bought approximately $4.67 billion in land, buildings, machinery, and equipment that it uses in its operations. The corporation may also obtain intangible assets that lack physical substance, such as copyrights and patents. Apple reported $453 million of intangible assets that it uses in its operations. The purchase (and sale) of the assets that are used in operations (commonly referred to as property, plant, and equipment) are a corporation's investing activities.

Regardless of its form, assets are future economic benefits that a corporation controls. The assets purchased by a corporation vary depending on the type of business that the corporation engages in, and the composition of these assets is likely to vary across different companies and different industries. For example, in 2009, property, plant, and equipment made up approximately 6.2 percent of **Apple**'s total assets. This is typical of many technology companies. In contrast, property, plant, and equipment made up 74.5 percent of the total assets of **Southwest Airlines**, a company that relies heavily on airplanes to produce revenue.

Operating Activities Once a corporation has acquired the assets that it needs, it can begin to operate. While different businesses have different purposes, they all want to generate revenue. **Revenue** is the increase in assets that results from the sale of products or services. For example, **Apple** reported revenue of approximately $42.9 billion in 2009. In addition to revenue, assets such as *cash*, *accounts receivable* (the right to collect an amount due from customers), *supplies*, and *inventory* (products held for resale) often result from operating activities.

To earn revenue, a corporation will incur various costs or expenses. **Expenses** are the cost of assets used, or the liabilities created, in the operation of the business. Apple reported expenses of $25.683 billion related to the cost of iPods and other products sold in 2009.

The liabilities that arise from operating activities can be of different types. For example, if a corporation purchases goods on credit from a supplier, the obligation to repay the supplier is called an *account payable*. As of September 26, 2009, **Apple** reported approximately $5.6 billion of accounts payable. Other examples of liabilities created by operating activities include *wages payable* (amounts owed to employees for work performed) and *income taxes payable* (taxes owed to the government).

The results of a company's operating activities can be determined by comparing revenues to expenses. If revenues are greater than expenses, a corporation has earned **net income**. If expenses are greater than revenues, a corporation has incurred a **net loss**.

YOU DECIDE   Choice of Organizational Form

You are an entrepreneur who has decided to start a campus-area bookstore. In order to start your business, you have to choose among three organizational forms—sole proprietorship, partnership, or corporation. You have enough personal wealth to finance 40 percent of the business, but you must get the remaining 60 percent from other sources.

How does the choice of organizational form impact your control of the business and ability to obtain the needed funds?

The choice of organizational form can greatly impact many aspects of a business's operations. Each form has certain advantages and disadvantages that you should carefully consider.

- *Sole Proprietorship*: A sole proprietorship would give you the most control of your business. However, you would be forced to obtain the additional 60 percent of funds needed from a bank or other creditor. It often is difficult to get banks to support a new business.
- *Partnership*: If you choose to form a partnership, you would still have access to bank loans. In addition, you would also have the ability to obtain the additional funds from your partner or partners. In this situation, the partners would then have a 60 percent interest in the business, which may be an unacceptable loss of control.
- *Corporation*: If you choose to form a corporation, you could obtain the needed funds by issuing stock to investors. While a 60 percent interest may still be transferred to the stockholders, if the stock were widely dispersed among many investors, you might still retain effective control of the business with a 40 percent interest.

The choice of organizational form involves the consideration of many different factors.

OBJECTIVE
Describe the relationships shown by the fundamental accounting equation.

COMMUNICATION OF ACCOUNTING INFORMATION

The financing, investing, and operating activities of a company are recorded by accounting systems as detailed transactions. To effectively communicate a company's activities to decision-makers, these detailed transactions are summarized and reported in a set of standardized reports called **financial statements**. The role of financial statements is to provide information that will help investors, creditors, and others make judgments and predictions that serve as the basis for the various decisions they make. Financial statements help to answer questions such as those shown in Exhibit 1-4.

Exhibit 1-4

Questions Answered by Financial Statements

How much better off is the company at the end of the year than it was at the beginning of the year?

What are the economic resources of the company and the claims against those resources?

From what sources did a company's cash come and for what did the company use cash during the year?

The Four Basic Financial Statements

Companies prepare four basic financial statements:

- The **balance sheet** reports the resources (assets) owned by a company and the claims against those resources (liabilities and stockholders' equity) at a specific point in time.
- The **income statement** reports how well a company has performed its operations (revenues, expenses, and income) over a period of time.

- The **retained earnings statement** reports how much of the company's income was retained in the business and how much was distributed to owners over a period of time.[2]
- The **statement of cash flows** reports the sources and uses of a company's cash over a period of time.

While financial statements can be prepared for any point or period of time (e.g., monthly, quarterly, or annually), most companies prepare financial statements at the end of each month, quarter, and year. Note that the balance sheet is a point-in-time description, whereas the other financial statements are period-of-time descriptions that explain the business activities between balance sheet dates as shown in Exhibit 1-5.

Exhibit 1-5

Financial Statement Time Periods

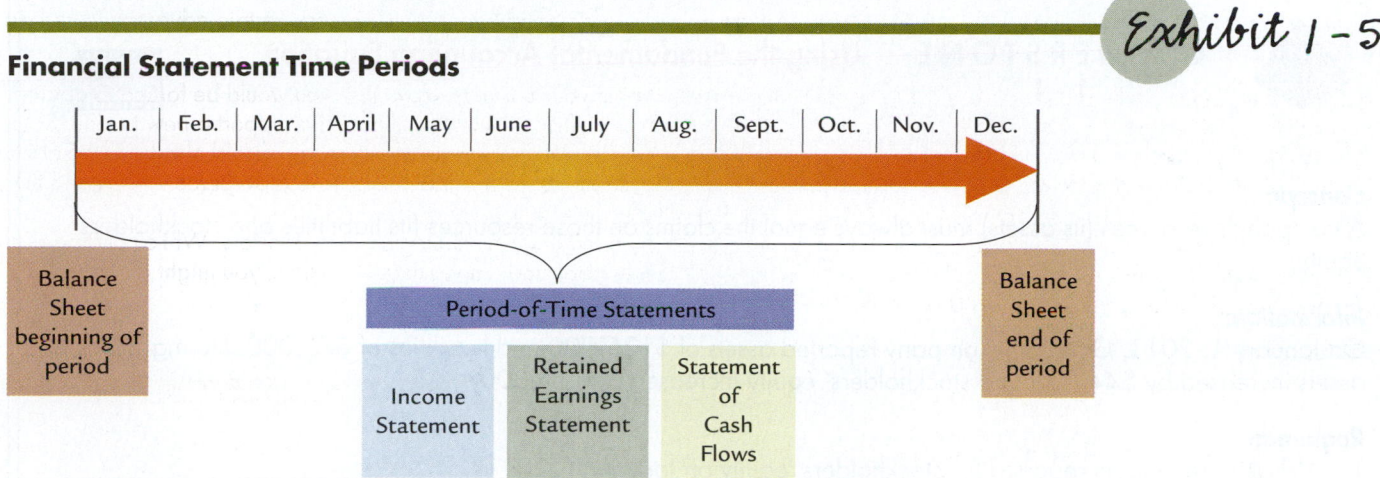

These four statements are prepared and issued at the end of an accounting period. While the accounting period can be a year, companies also issue statements monthly or quarterly to satisfy the users' needs for timely information. The financial statements are accompanied by supporting information and explanatory material called the notes to the financial statements.

In order to make it easier to use financial statements over time and across companies, a common set of rules and conventions have been developed to guide the preparation of financial statements. These rules and conventions, called **generally accepted accounting principles (GAAP)**, were developed by several different organizations over a number of years. In the United States, the **Securities and Exchange Commission (SEC)** has the power to set accounting rules for publicly traded companies. However, the SEC has delegated this authority to the **Financial Accounting Standards Board (FASB)**. While the FASB is the primary accounting standard setter in the United States, the FASB has been working closely with the **International Accounting Standards Board (IASB)** in its development of **international financial reporting standards (IFRS)**. While this text focuses on U.S. GAAP, the importance of IFRS cannot be ignored. Therefore, major differences between U.S. GAAP and IFRS are highlighted in margin notes throughout the text.

While financial statements prepared under GAAP provide the kind of information users want and need, the financial statements do not interpret this information. The financial statement user must use his or her general knowledge of business and accounting to interpret the financial statements as a basis for decision-making.

The Fundamental Accounting Equation

To understand financial statements, it is necessary that you understand how the accounting system records, classifies, and reports information about business activities. The **fundamental accounting equation** illustrates the foundation of the accounting system.

IFRS

IFRS describes an international set of generally accepted accounting standards used by over 100 countries in order to facilitate the conduct of business around the world.

IFRS

The fundamental accounting equation is the same under IFRS as under U.S. GAAP.

$$Assets = Liabilities + Stockholders' Equity$$

[2] Information contained in the retained earnings statement is often included in a more comprehensive statement of changes in stockholders' equity, which describes changes in all components of stockholders' equity. This statement is presented in Chapter 10.

The fundamental accounting equation captures two basic features of any company. The left side of the accounting equation shows the assets, or economic resources of a company. The right side of the accounting equation indicates who has a claim on the company's assets. These claims may be the claims of creditors (liabilities) or they may be the claims of owners (stockholders' equity). The implication of the fundamental accounting equation is that what a company owns (its assets) must always be equal to what it owes (its liabilities and stockholders' equity). **CORNERSTONE 1-1** illustrates this key relationship implied by the fundamental accounting equation.

 **CORNERSTONE 1-1**   **Using the Fundamental Accounting Equation**

Concept:
A company's resources (its assets) must always equal the claims on those resources (its liabilities and stockholders' equity).

Information:
On January 1, 2011, Gundrum Company reported assets of $125,000 and liabilities of $75,000. During 2011, assets increased by $44,000 and stockholders' equity increased by $15,000.

Required:
1.   What is the amount reported for stockholders' equity on January 1, 2011?
2.   What is the amount reported for liabilities on December 31, 2011?

Solution:
1.   Stockholders' equity on January 1, 2011, is $50,000. This amount is calculated by rearranging the fundamental accounting equation as follows:

$$\text{Assets} = \text{Liabilities} + \text{Stockholders' Equity}$$
$$\$125,000 = \$75,000 + \text{Stockholders' Equity}$$
$$\text{Stockholders' Equity} = \$125,000 - \$75,000 = \mathbf{\underline{\$50,000}}$$

2.   At December 31, 2011, liabilities are $104,000. This amount is computed by adding the change to the appropriate balance sheet elements and then rearranging the fundamental accounting equation as follows:

$$\text{Assets} = \text{Liabilities} + \text{Stockholders' Equity}$$
$$(\$125,000 + \$44,000) = \text{Liabilities} + (\$50,000 + \$15,000)$$
$$\text{Liabilities} = (\$125,000 + \$44,000) - (\$50,000 + \$15,000)$$
$$= \$169,000 - \$65,000 = \mathbf{\underline{\$104,000}}$$

The fundamental accounting equation will be used to capture all of the economic activities recorded by an accounting system.

OBJECTIVE
Prepare a classified balance sheet and understand the information it communicates.

THE CLASSIFIED BALANCE SHEET

The purpose of the balance sheet is to report the financial position of a company (its assets, liabilities, and stockholders' equity) at a specific point in time. The relationship between the elements of the balance sheet is given by the fundamental accounting equation:

$$\text{Assets} = \text{Liabilities} + \text{Stockholders' Equity}$$

Note that the balance sheet gets its name because the economic resources of a company (assets) must always equal, or be in balance with, the claims against those resources (liabilities and stockholders' equity).

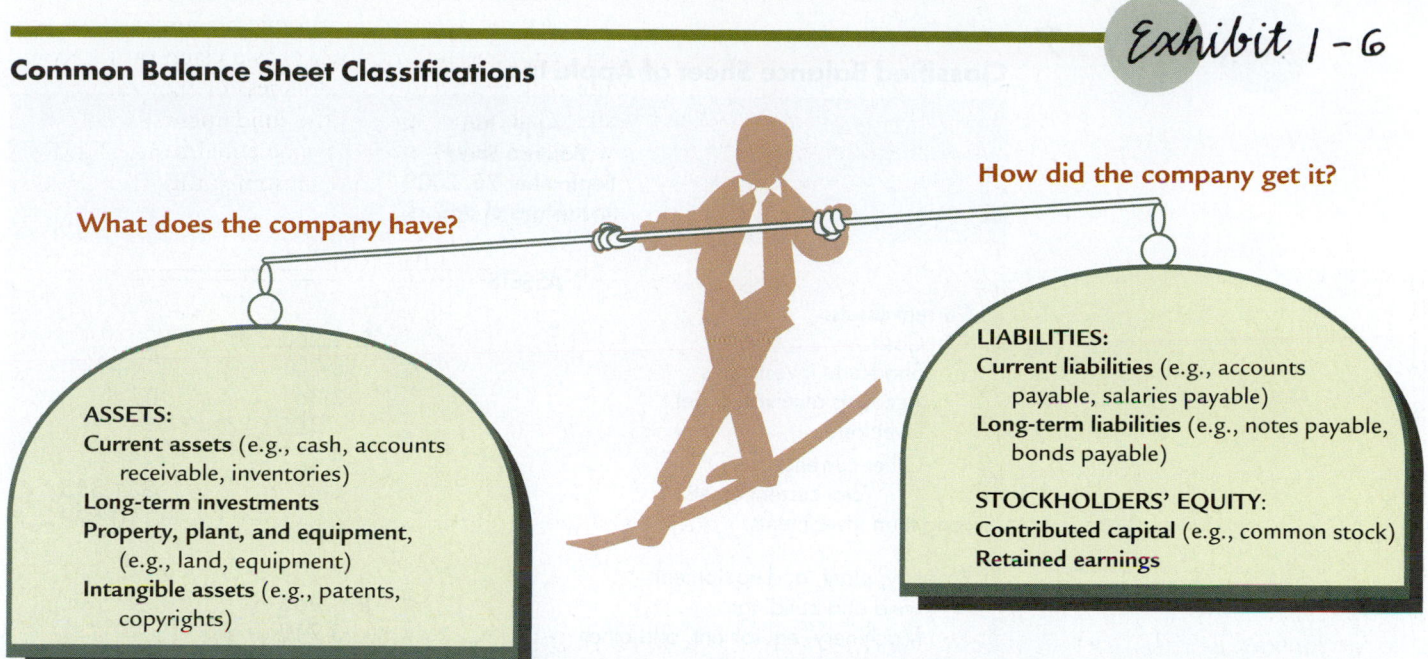

Exhibit 1-6

Common Balance Sheet Classifications

What does the company have?

How did the company get it?

ASSETS:
Current assets (e.g., cash, accounts receivable, inventories)
Long-term investments
Property, plant, and equipment, (e.g., land, equipment)
Intangible assets (e.g., patents, copyrights)

LIABILITIES:
Current liabilities (e.g., accounts payable, salaries payable)
Long-term liabilities (e.g., notes payable, bonds payable)

STOCKHOLDERS' EQUITY:
Contributed capital (e.g., common stock)
Retained earnings

The balance sheet is organized, or classified, to help users identify the fundamental economic similarities and differences between the various items within the balance sheet. These classifications help users answer questions such as:

- how a company obtained its resources
- whether a company will be able to pay its obligations when they become due

While companies often use different classifications and different levels of detail on their balance sheets, some common classifications are shown in Exhibit 1-6.

Let's examine the balance sheet classifications in more detail by looking at **Apple**'s balance sheet shown in Exhibit 1-7 (p. 12).

With regard to the heading of the financial statement, several items are of interest:

- *Company name*: The company for which the accounting information is collected and reported is clearly defined.
- *Financial statement type*: The title of the financial statement follows the name of the company.
- *Date*: The specific date of the statement is listed. **Apple** operates on a fiscal year that ends in September. A **fiscal year** is an accounting period that runs for one year. While many companies adopt a fiscal year that corresponds to the calendar year, others adopt a fiscal year that more closely corresponds with their business cycle.
- *Amounts*: **Apple** reports its financial results rounded to the nearest millions of dollars. Large companies often round the amounts presented to make for a more clear presentation. For Apple, the reported cash amount of $5,263 is actually $5,263,000,000.

IFRS

IFRS use the same balance sheet classifications, although terminology differences do exist. For example, stockholders' equity may be called "capital and reserves."

Current Assets

The basic classification of a company's assets is between current and noncurrent items. In a typical company, it is reasonable to designate one year as the dividing line between current and noncurrent items. However, if the operating cycle of a company is longer than one year, it may be necessary to extend this dividing line beyond one year so that it corresponds to the length of the operating cycle. The **operating cycle** of a company is the average time that it takes a company to purchase goods, resell the goods, and collect the cash from customers. In other words, **current assets** consist of cash and other assets that are reasonably expected to be converted into cash within one year or one operating

Exhibit 1-7

Classified Balance Sheet of Apple Inc.

Apple Inc.
Balance Sheet*
September 26, 2009
(in millions of dollars)

ASSETS

Current assets:		
Cash	$ 5,263	
Short-term investments	18,201	
Accounts receivable, net	3,361	
Inventories	455	
Other current assets	4,275	
Total current assets		$31,555
Long term investments		10,528
Property, plant, and equipment:		
Land and buildings	$ 955	
Machinery, equipment, and other	3,712	
Less: accumulated depreciation	(1,713)	
Total property, plant, and equipment		2,954
Intangible assets		453
Other assets		2,011
Total assets		$47,501

LIABILITIES AND STOCKHOLDERS' EQUITY

Current liabilities:		
Accounts payable	$ 5,601	
Salaries payable	357	
Unearned revenue	2,053	
Other current liabilities	3,495	
Total current liabilities		$11,506
Long-term liabilities		4,355
Total liabilities		$15,861
Stockholders' equity:		
Contributed capital	$ 8,210	
Retained earnings	23,353	
Other equity**	77	
Total stockholders' equity		31,640
Total liabilities and stockholders' equity		$47,501

*The balance sheet information was taken from the annual report of Apple Inc. and has been summarized and reformatted by the authors.

**The $77 million of other equity reported by Apple represents accumulated other comprehensive income. Accumulated other comprehensive income is discussed in Chapter 10.

cycle, whichever is longer. Because most companies have operating cycles less than one year, we will use the one-year dividing line to distinguish between current and noncurrent items. Common types of current assets are:

- Cash
- Short-term investments or marketable securities—investments in the debt and stock of other companies as well as government securities
- Accounts receivable—the right to collect an amount due from customers
- Inventories—goods or products held for resale to customers

- Other current assets—a "catch-all" category that includes items such as prepaid expenses (advance payments for rent, insurance, and other services) and supplies

Current assets are listed on the balance sheet in order of liquidity or nearness to cash. That is, the items are reported in the order in which the company expects to convert them into cash.

Noncurrent Assets

Assets that are not classified as current are classified as long-term or noncurrent assets. These include long-term investments; property, plant, and equipment; intangible assets; and other noncurrent assets.

Long-Term Investments
Long-term investments are similar to short-term investments, except that the company expects to hold the investment for longer than one year. This category also includes land or buildings that a company is not currently using in operations. **Apple** reported long-term investments of $10,528 million.

Property, Plant, and Equipment
Property, plant, and equipment represents the tangible, long-lived, productive assets used by a company in its operations to produce revenue. This category includes land, buildings, machinery, manufacturing equipment, office equipment, and furniture. **Apple** reported property, plant, and equipment of $2,954 million, representing 6.2 percent ($2,954 ÷ $47,501) of its total assets. Property, plant, and equipment is originally recorded at the cost to obtain the asset. Because property, plant, and equipment helps to produce revenue over a number of years, companies assign, or allocate, a portion of the asset's cost as an expense in each period in which the asset is used. This process is called *depreciation*. The *accumulated depreciation* shown on Apple's balance sheet represents the total amount of depreciation that the company has expensed over the life of its assets. Because accumulated depreciation is subtracted from the cost of an asset, it is called a *contra-asset*. The difference between the cost and the accumulated depreciation is the asset's book value (or carrying value).

Intangible Assets
Intangible assets are similar to property, plant, and equipment in that they provide a benefit to a company over a number of years; however, these assets lack physical substance. Examples of intangible assets include patents, copyrights, trademarks, and goodwill.

Other Noncurrent Assets
Other noncurrent assets is a catch-all category that includes items such as deferred charges (long-term prepaid expenses) and other long-term miscellaneous items.

Current Liabilities

Current liabilities are closely related to current assets. **Current liabilities** consist of obligations that will be satisfied within one year or the operating cycle, whichever is longer. These liabilities can be satisfied through the payment of cash or by providing goods or services. **Current liabilities are typically listed in the order in which they will be paid** and include:

- Accounts payable—an obligation to repay a vendor or supplier for merchandise supplied to the company
- Salaries payable—an obligation to pay an employee for services performed
- Unearned revenue—an obligation to deliver goods or perform a service for which a company has already been paid
- Interest payable—an obligation to pay interest on money that a company has borrowed
- Income taxes payable—an obligation to pay taxes on a company's income

Concept Q&A

Many classifications on the balance sheet are essentially subtotals. Is it really important to place accounts within the right category or is it enough to simply understand if they are assets, liabilities, or stockholders' equity?

Answer:
It is critical that you be able to identify accounts as assets, liabilities, or stockholders' equity accounts. However, the classifications are also important. Financial accounting is concerned with communicating useful information to decision-makers. These classifications provide decision-makers with information about the structure of assets, liabilities, and stockholders' equity that assists them in understanding a company's financial position.

IFRS

IFRS does not specify a particular order of the balance sheet classifications. International balance sheets often list noncurrent assets before current assets and stockholders' equity before noncurrent and current liabilities.

Long-Term Liabilities and Stockholders' Equity

Long-term liabilities are the obligations of the company that will require payment beyond one year or the operating cycle, whichever is longer. Common examples are:

- Notes payable—an obligation to repay cash borrowed at a future date
- Bonds payable—a form of an interest-bearing note payable issued by corporations in an effort to attract a large amount of investors

Stockholders' equity is the last major classification on a company's balance sheet. Stockholder's equity arises primarily from two sources:

- Contributed capital—the owners' contributions of cash and other assets to the company (includes the common stock of a company)
- Retained earnings—the accumulated net income of a company that has not been distributed to owners in the form of dividends

If a firm has been profitable for many years, and if its stockholders have been willing to forgo large dividends, retained earnings may be a large portion of equity. **Apple** reported approximately $23.353 billion of retained earnings, representing over 73 percent of its total stockholders' equity.

Together, a company's liabilities and equity make up the **capital** of a business. **Apple** has debt capital, capital raised from creditors, of approximately $15.8 billion (total liabilities). Of this, approximately $11.5 billion comes from current creditors, while approximately $4.3 billion comes from long-term creditors. Apple's equity capital, which is the capital of the stockholders, is approximately $31.6 billion (total stockholders' equity).

Using the fundamental accounting equation and the common classifications of balance sheet items, a company will prepare its balance sheet by following five steps:

Step 1. Prepare a heading that includes the name of the company, the title of the financial statement, and the time period covered.

Step 2. List the assets of the company in order of their liquidity or nearness to cash. Use appropriate classifications. Add the assets and double underline the total.

Step 3. List the liabilities of the company in order of their time to maturity. Use appropriate classifications.

Step 4. List the stockholders' equity balances with appropriate classifications.

Step 5. Add the liabilities and stockholders' equity and double underline the total.

In general, only the first items in a column as well as any subtotals or totals have dollar signs. Also when multiple items exist within a classification, these items are grouped together in a separate column (to the left of the main column) and their total is placed in the main column. **CORNERSTONE 1-2** illustrates the steps in the preparation of a classified balance sheet.

 **CORNERSTONE 1-2**   **Preparing a Classified Balance Sheet**

Concept:
The balance sheet reports the financial position of a company (its assets, liabilities, and stockholders' equity) at a specific point in time.

Information:
Hightower Inc. reported the following account balances at December 31, 2011:

Inventories	$ 2,300	Accounts receivable	$ 4,200	Accounts payable	$ 3,750
Land	12,100	Cash	2,500	Common stock	14,450
Salaries payable	1,200	Equipment	21,000	Patents	2,500
Retained earnings	11,300	Accumulated depreciation	5,800	Notes payable	8,100

(Continued)

Required:
Prepare Hightower's balance sheet at December 31, 2011.

**CORNERSTONE
1-2**
(continued)

Solution:

} Step 1

Hightower Inc. Balance Sheet December 31, 2011

ASSETS

Current assets:		
Cash	$ 2,500	
Accounts receivable	4,200	
Inventories	2,300	
Total current assets		$ 9,000
Property, plant, and equipment:		
Land	$12,100	
Equipment	21,000	
Less: accumulated depreciation	(5,800)	
Total property, plant, and equipment		27,300
Intangible assets:		
Patents		2,500
Total assets		$38,800

} Step 2

LIABILITIES AND STOCKHOLDERS' EQUITY

Current liabilities:		
Accounts payable	$ 3,750	
Salaries payable	1,200	
Total current liabilities		$ 4,950
Long-term liabilities:		
Notes payable		8,100
Total liabilities		$13,050
Stockholders' equity:		
Common stock	$14,450	
Retained earnings	11,300	
Total stockholders' equity		25,750
Total liabilities and stockholders' equity		$38,800

} Step 3

} Step 4

} Step 5

Using Balance Sheet Information

The balance sheet conveys important information about the structure of assets, liabilities, and stockholders' equity which is used to judge a company's financial health. For example, the relationship between current assets and current liabilities gives investors and creditors insights into a company's **liquidity**—the ability to pay obligations as they become due. Two useful measures of liquidity are *working capital* and the *current ratio*. Working capital and current ratios for a company are helpful when compared to other companies in the same industry. It is even more helpful to look at the trend of these measures over several years.

Working Capital   **Working capital** is a measure of liquidity, computed as:

Working Capital = Current Assets − Current Liabilities

Because current liabilities will be settled with current assets, **Apple**'s working capital of $20,049 million ($31,555 million − $11,506 million) signals that it has adequate funds with which to pay its current obligations. Because working capital is expressed in a dollar amount, the information it can convey is limited. For example, comparing Apple's working capital of $20,049 million to **Dell**'s working capital of $5,285 million would be misleading since Apple is almost $15 billion larger (in terms of net assets).

Current Ratio The **current ratio** is an alternative measure of liquidity that allows comparisons to be made between different companies and is computed as:

$$\text{Current Ratio} = \frac{\text{Current Assets}}{\text{Current Liabilities}}$$

For example, **Apple**'s current ratio of 2.74 ($31,555 million ÷ $11,506 million) can be compared with its competitors (e.g., Dell's current ratio is 1.28).[3] Apple's current ratio tells us that for every dollar of current liabilities, Apple has $2.74 of current assets. When compared to **Dell**, Apple is much more liquid.

YOU DECIDE Assessing the Creditworthiness of a Prospective Customer

You are the regional credit manager for Nordic Equipment Company. Thin Inc., a newly organized health club, has offered to purchase $50,000 worth of exercise equipment by paying the full amount plus 9 percent interest in six months. At your request, Thin provides the following figures from its balance sheet:

Current Assets		Current Liabilities	
Cash	$10,000	Accounts payable	$25,000
Accounts receivable	50,000	Notes payable	30,000
Supplies	4,000	Current portion of mortgage payable	18,000
Total	$64,000	Total	$73,000

Based on what you know about the company's current assets and liabilities, do you allow Thin to purchase the equipment on credit?

In making your decision, it is important to consider the relationship between a company's current assets and its current liabilities. Observe that Thin's current liabilities exceed current assets by $9,000 ($64,000 − $73,000) resulting in negative working capital. In addition, Thin's current ratio is 0.88 ($64,000 ÷ $73,000). By all indications, Thin is suffering from liquidity issues. Finally, there is no evidence presented that Thin's liquidity problem will improve. If Thin does fail to pay its liabilities, it is possible that the existing creditors could force Thin to sell its assets in order to pay off the debt. In such situations, it is possible that you will not receive the full amount promised. Unless Thin can demonstrate how it will pay its current short-term obligations, short-term credit should not be extended.

Allowing a company to purchase assets on credit requires evaluating the debtor's ability to repay the loan out of current assets.

OBJECTIVE 5

Prepare an income statement and understand the information it communicates.

THE INCOME STATEMENT

The income statement reports the results of a company's operations—the sale of goods and services and the associated cost of operating the company—for a given period. The long-term survival of a company depends on its ability to produce net income by earning revenues in excess of expenses. Income enables a company to pay for the capital it uses (dividends to stockholders and interest to creditors) and attract new capital necessary for continued existence and growth. Investors buy and sell stock and creditors loan money based on their beliefs about a company's future performance. The past income reported on a company's income statement provides investors with information about a company's ability to earn future income.

[3] Information for Dell was obtained from Dell's fiscal year that ended on January 29, 2010.

Elements of the Income Statement

The income statement consists of two major items: revenues and expenses. An income statement for **Apple** is presented in Exhibit 1-8.

Examining the heading of the income statement, you should notice that it follows the same general format as the balance sheet—it indicates the name of the company, the title of the financial statement, and the time period covered by the statement. However, the income statement differs from the balance sheet in that it covers a period of time instead of a specific date.

Revenues   Revenues are the increase in assets that result from the sale of products or services. Revenues can arise from different sources and have different names depending on the source of the revenue. *Sales revenue* (or *service revenue* for companies that provide services) arises from the principal activity of the business. For **Apple**, its sales revenue comes from sales of hardware (such as iPods, Macintosh computers, iPhones, iPads), software (operating systems), peripheral products and accessories, digital content (such as iTunes store sales), and service and support. Apple, like most other companies, generally recognizes sales revenue in the period that a sale occurs. Revenues also can be generated from activities other than the company's principal operations (nonoperating activities). For example, in addition to sales of its products, Apple also earns *interest income* from investments.

Expenses   Expenses are the cost of resources used to earn revenues during a period. Expenses have different names depending on their function. **Apple**'s income statement in Exhibit 1-8 reports five different expenses:

- *Cost of goods sold* (often called *cost of sales*)—the cost to the seller of all goods sold during the accounting period.[4]
- *Selling, general, and administrative expenses*—the expenses that a company incurs in selling goods, providing services, or managing the company that are not directly related to production. These expenses include advertising expenses; salaries paid to salespersons or managers; depreciation on administrative buildings; and expenses related to insurance, utilities, property taxes, and repairs.
- *Research and development expense*—the cost of developing new products.

Exhibit 1-8

Income Statement of Apple Inc.

Apple Inc. Income Statement* For the fiscal year ended September 26, 2009 (in millions of dollars)		
Revenues:		
Net sales	$42,905	
Interest income	407	$43,312
Expenses:		
Cost of goods sold	$25,683	
Selling, general, and administrative expenses	4,149	
Research and development	1,333	
Other expenses	81	
Income taxes expense	3,831	35,077
Net income		$ 8,235

*The income statement information was taken from the annual report of Apple Inc. and has been summarized and reformatted by the authors.

---

[4] We will discuss procedures for calculating cost of goods sold in Chapter 6.

- *Other expense*—a catch-all category used to capture other miscellaneous expenses incurred by the company.
- *Income taxes expense*—the income taxes paid on the company's pretax income.

Net Income   Net income, or net earnings, is the difference between total revenues and expenses. **Apple** reported net income of $8,235 million ($43,312 million – $35,077 million). If total expenses are greater than total revenues, the company would report a net loss.

Preparing an Income Statement

The preparation of an income statement involves four steps:

Step 1. Prepare a heading that includes the name of the company, the title of the financial statement, and the time period covered.

Step 2. List the revenues of the company, starting with sales revenue (or service revenue) and then listing other revenue items. Add the revenues to get total revenue.

Step 3. List the expenses of the company, usually starting with cost of goods sold. Add the expenses to get total expenses.

Step 4. Subtract the expenses from the revenues to get net income (or net loss if expenses exceed revenues). Double-underline net income.

In general, only the first items in a column as well as any subtotals or totals have dollar signs. Also when multiple items exist within a classification, these items are grouped together in a separate column (to the left of the main column) and their total is placed in the main column. **CORNERSTONE 1-3** shows how to prepare an income statement.

Income Statement Formats

Companies prepare their income statements in one of two different formats: single-step income statements or multiple-step income statements.

Single-Step Income Statement   The format that we illustrated in Cornerstone 1-3 is called a *single-step income statement*. In a single-step income statement, there are only two categories: total revenues and total expenses. Total expenses are subtracted from total revenues in a *single step* to arrive at net income. The advantage of a single-step income statement is its simplicity.

 **CORNERSTONE 1-3**   **Preparing an Income Statement**

Concept:
The income statement reports the results of a company's operations (revenues less expenses) for a given period of time.

Information:
Hightower Inc. reported the following account balances for the year ending December 31, 2011:

Cost of goods sold	$31,300	Interest expense	$ 540
Salaries expense	8,800	Sales revenue	50,600
Insurance expense	700	Depreciation expense	1,500
Interest income	1,200	Rent expense	2,100
Income taxes expense	2,000		

Required:
Prepare Hightower's income statement for the year ending December 31, 2011.

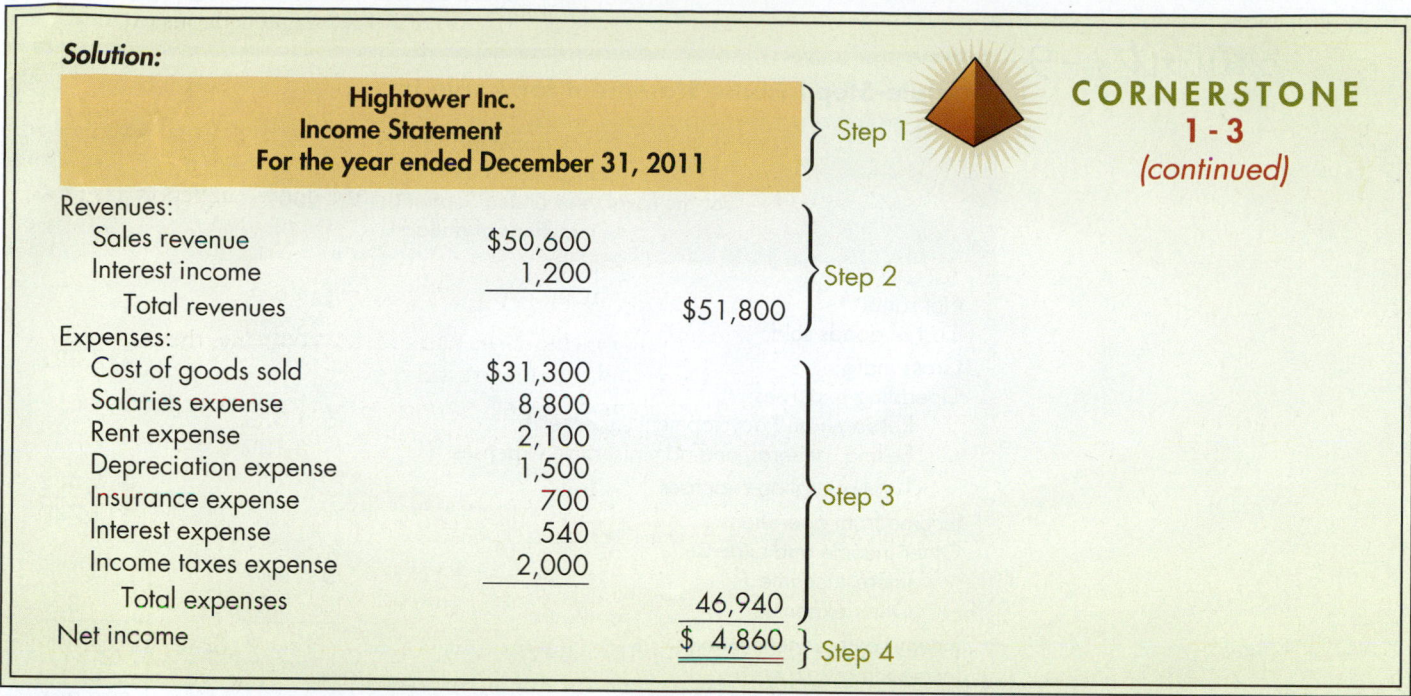

Solution:

CORNERSTONE
1-3
(continued)

Hightower Inc.
Income Statement
For the year ended December 31, 2011

} Step 1

Revenues:		
Sales revenue	$50,600	
Interest income	1,200	
Total revenues		$51,800

} Step 2

Expenses:		
Cost of goods sold	$31,300	
Salaries expense	8,800	
Rent expense	2,100	
Depreciation expense	1,500	
Insurance expense	700	
Interest expense	540	
Income taxes expense	2,000	
Total expenses		46,940
Net income		$ 4,860

} Step 3

} Step 4

Multiple-Step Income Statement

A second income statement format is the *multiple-step income statement*. The multiple-step income statement provides classifications of revenues and expenses that financial statement users find useful. A multiple-step income statement contains three important subtotals:

- **Gross margin (gross profit)**—the difference between net sales and cost of goods sold (or cost of sales)
- **Income from operations**—the difference between gross margin and operating expenses
- **Net income**—the difference between income from operations and any nonoperating revenues and expenses

A multiple-step income statement for **Apple** is shown in Exhibit 1-9 (p. 20).

Gross Margin

A company's *gross margin* or *gross profit* is calculated as:

Gross Margin = Net Sales − Cost of Goods Sold

Gross margin represents the initial profit made from selling a product, but it is *not* a measure of total profit because other operating expenses have not yet been subtracted. However, gross margin is closely watched by managers and other financial statement users. A change in a company's gross margin can give insights into a company's current pricing and purchasing policies, thereby providing insight into the company's future performance.

Income from Operations

Income from operations is computed as:

Income from Operations = Gross Margin − Operating Expenses

Operating expenses are the expenses the business incurs in selling goods or providing services and managing the company. Operating expenses typically include research and development expenses, selling expenses, and general and administrative expenses. Income from operations indicates the level of profit produced by the principal activities of the company. **Apple** can increase its income from operations by either increasing its gross margin or decreasing its operating expenses.

Nonoperating Activities

A multiple-step income statement reports nonoperating activities in a section which is frequently called *other income and expenses*. *Nonoperating activities* are revenues and expenses from activities other than the company's principal operations. They include gains and losses from the sale of equipment and other items

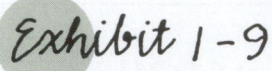

Exhibit 1-9

Multiple-Step Income Statement for Apple Inc.

Apple Inc.
Income Statement*
For the fiscal year ended September 26, 2009
(in millions of dollars)

Net sales	$42,905	
Cost of goods sold	25,683	
Gross margin		$17,222
Operating expenses:		
Research and development expense	$ 1,333	
Selling, general, and administrative expenses	4,149	
Total operating expenses		5,482
Income from operations		$11,740
Other income and expense:		
Interest income	$ 407	
Other expenses	(81)	326
Income before income taxes		$12,066
Income taxes expense		3,831
Net income		$ 8,235

*The income statement information was taken from the annual report of Apple Inc. and has been summarized and reformatted by the authors.

that were not acquired for resale. For many companies, the most important nonoperating item is interest. Exhibit 1-10 lists some common nonoperating items.

Net Income Nonoperating items are subtracted from income from operations to obtain income before taxes. Income taxes expense is then subtracted to obtain net income. Regardless of the format used, notice that there is no difference in the amount of the revenue or expense items reported. That is, net income is the same under either the single-step or the multiple-step format. The only difference is how the revenues and expenses are classified.

Using Income Statement Information

A company's ability to generate current income is useful in predicting its ability to generate future income. When investors believe that future income will improve, they will buy stock. Similarly, creditors rely on their judgments of a company's future income to make loans. Investors' and creditors' estimates of the future profitability and growth of a company are aided by a careful examination of how a company has earned its revenue and managed its expenses.

Exhibit 1-10

Typical Nonoperating Items

Other Revenues and Gains	Other Expenses and Losses
 Interest revenue on investments	 Interest expense from loans
Dividend revenue from investments in stock of other companies	Losses from sale of property, plant, and equipment
Rent revenue	Losses from accidents or vandalism
Gains on sale of property, plant, and equipment	Losses from employee strikes
	Income taxes expense

Net Profit Margin A useful measure of a company's ability to generate profit is its **net profit margin** (sometimes called return on sales). Net profit margin shows the percentage of profit in each dollar of sales and is computed as:

$$\text{Net Profit Margin} = \frac{\text{Net income}}{\text{Sales revenue}}$$

This ratio provides an indication of management's ability to control expenses. Future income depends on both maintaining (or increasing) market share while controlling expenses.

 **Assessing Future Profitability**

You are looking to invest in one of two companies in the same industry—Growth Inc. or Stagnation Company. Your initial examination revealed that both companies reported the same amount of net income for 2012. Further analysis produced the following five-year summary:

Growth Inc.

	2008	2009	2010	2011	2012
Sales revenues	$625,000	$750,000	$820,000	$920,000	$1,000,000
Net income	$ 30,000	$ 36,000	$ 40,000	$ 45,000	$ 50,000
Profit margin	4.8%	4.8%	4.9%	4.9%	5.0%

Stagnation Company

	2008	2009	2010	2011	2012
Sales revenue	$1,025,000	$975,000	$940,000	$1,020,000	$1,040,000
Net income	$ 51,000	$ 48,000	$ 46,000	$ 49,000	$ 50,000
Profit margin	5%	4.9%	4.9%	4.8%	4.8%

Which company is the better investment?

Investors seek those investments that will provide the largest return at the lowest risk. One factor associated with large returns is future profitability. Over the last five years, Growth's sales and net income have steadily increased while Stagnation's sales and net income have remained, on average, stable. Sales growth is an indicator of the possibility of increasing future income. Further, Growth's increasing profit margin (compared to a decreasing profit margin for Stagnation) indicates that Growth is doing a better job at controlling its expenses relative to Stagnation, enabling Growth to earn more profit on each dollar of sales. While the future never can be predicted with certainty, the data suggests that, if current trends continue, Growth will grow more rapidly than Stagnation. Therefore, an investment in Growth would probably yield the larger future return.

Accounting information can help you judge a company's potential for future profitability and growth.

RETAINED EARNINGS STATEMENT

The owners of a company contribute capital in one of two ways:

- directly, though purchases of common stock from the company, and
- indirectly, by the company retaining some or all of the net income earned each year rather than paying it out in dividends.

As noted earlier, the income earned by the company but not paid out in the form of dividends is called retained earnings. The retained earnings statement summarizes and explains the changes in retained earnings during the accounting period.[5] The beginning balance in retained earnings is increased by net income earned during the year and decreased by any dividends that were declared. Exhibit 1-11 (p. 22) shows the retained earnings statement for **Apple**.

OBJECTIVE
Prepare the retained earnings statement statement and understand the information it communicates.

---

[5] Some companies may choose to report a statement of changes in stockholders' equity, which explains the changes in all of the stockholders' equity accounts. This statement is discussed more fully in Chapter 10.

Retained Earnings Statement for Apple Inc.

Apple Inc. Retained Earnings Statement* For the fiscal year ended September 26, 2009 (in millions of dollars)	
Retained earnings, Sept. 27, 2008	$15,129
Add: Net income	8,235
	$23,364
Less: Dividends	0
Other**	(11)
Retained earnings, Sept. 26, 2009	$23,353

*The retained earnings statement was created by the authors from information contained in Apple Inc.'s 2009 annual report.
**The other item deducted in Apple's retained earnings statement is related to common stock issued under Apple's stock plans. This item is beyond the scope of this text.

Notice the heading is similar to the heading for the income statement in that it covers a period of time (the fiscal year ended September 26, 2009). In addition, **Apple** declared no dividends for 2009 but chose to keep the net income earned within the company. Many growing companies, such as Apple, choose not to pay dividends in order to reinvest its earnings and support future growth.

The preparation of the retained earnings statement involves four steps:

Step 1. Prepare a heading that includes the name of the company, the title of the financial statement, and the time period covered.
Step 2. List the retained earnings balance at the beginning of the period obtained from the balance sheet.
Step 3. Add net income obtained from the income statement.
Step 4. Subtract any dividends declared during the period. Double-underline the total, which should equal retained earnings at the end of the period as reported on the balance sheet.

The preparation of a retained earnings statement is detailed in **CORNERSTONE 1-4**.

CORNERSTONE 1-4   **Preparing a Retained Earnings Statement**

Concept:
The retained earnings statement summarizes and explains the changes in retained earnings during an accounting period.

Information:
Hightower Inc. reported the following account balances for the year ending December 31, 2011:

Net income	$4,860	Retained earnings, 1/1/2011	$ 9,440
Dividends	3,000	Retained earnings, 12/31/2011	11,300

Required:
Prepare Hightower's retained earnings statement for the year ending December 31, 2011.

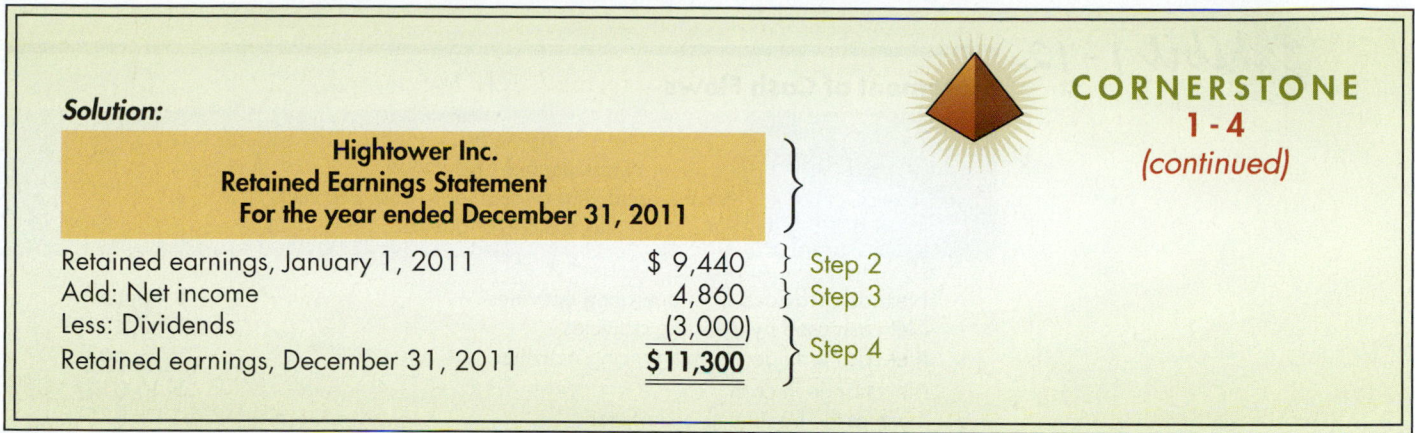

Solution:

Hightower Inc. Retained Earnings Statement For the year ended December 31, 2011		
Retained earnings, January 1, 2011	$ 9,440	Step 2
Add: Net income	4,860	Step 3
Less: Dividends	(3,000)	
Retained earnings, December 31, 2011	$11,300	Step 4

CORNERSTONE 1-4 (continued)

Use of the Retained Earnings Statement

The retained earnings statement is used to monitor and evaluate a company's dividend payouts to its shareholders. For example, some older investors seek out companies with high dividend payouts so that they will receive cash during the year. Other investors are more interested in companies that are reinvesting a sufficient amount of earnings that will enable them to pursue profitable growth opportunities. Finally, creditors are interested in a company's dividend payouts. If a company pays out too much in dividends, the company may not have enough cash on hand to repay its debt when it becomes due.

 **YOU DECIDE** **Dividend Policy Decisions**

You are the manager of a fast-growing software engineering firm. Over the last five years, your company has doubled the amount of its income every year. This tremendous growth has been financed through funds obtained from stockholders and cash generated from operations. The company has virtually no debt.

How would you respond to stockholders who have recently complained that the company's policy not to pay dividends is preventing them from sharing in the company's success?

Retained earnings can be an important source of financing for many companies. When companies feel that they have profitable growth opportunities, they should reinvest the earnings in the business instead of paying out the amount to stockholders as dividends. The reinvestment of these funds should result in higher stock prices (and increased wealth for the stockholders) as the company grows. If the company chose to pay a dividend, it would be forced to either abandon the growth opportunities or finance them through some other, more costly method (e.g., issuing debt).

When management feels that the company has growth opportunities that will increase the value of the company, the reinvestment of earnings is usually preferable.

STATEMENT OF CASH FLOWS

The last of the major financial statements, the statement of cash flows, describes the company's cash receipts (cash inflows) and cash payments (cash outflows) for a period of time. The statement of cash flows for **Apple** is shown in Exhibit 1-12 (p. 24).

 **OBJECTIVE 7**
Understand the information communicated by the statement of cash flows.

Exhibit 1-12

Statement of Cash Flows

| Apple Inc. |
| Statement of Cash Flows* |
| For the fiscal year ended September 26, 2009 |
| (in millions of dollars) |

Net cash provided from operating activities	$ 10,159
Net cash used by investing activities	(17,434)
Net cash provided from financing activities	663
Net change in cash	$ (6,612)
Cash at the beginning of the year	11,875
Cash at the end of the year	$ 5,263

*The statement of cash flows information was taken from the annual report of Apple Inc. and
 has been summarized and reformatted by the authors.

Elements of the Statement of Cash Flows

Cash flows are classified into one of three categories:

- **Cash flows from operating activities**—any cash flows directly related to earning income. This category includes cash sales and collections of accounts receivable as well as cash payments for goods, services, salaries, and interest.
- **Cash flows from investing activities**—any cash flow related to the acquisition or sale of investments and long-term assets such as property, plant, and equipment.
- **Cash flows from financing activities**—any cash flow related to obtaining capital of the company. This category includes the issuance and repayment of debt, common stock transactions, and the payment of dividends.

The preparation of the statement of cash flows will be discussed in Chapter 11.

Use of the Statement of Cash Flows

Because cash is the lifeblood of any company and is critical to success, the statement of cash flows can be an important source of information as users attempt to answer how a company generated and used cash during a period. Such information is helpful as users assess the company's ability to generate cash in the future. Creditors can use the statement of cash flows to assess the creditworthiness of a company. A company with healthy cash flow—particularly if it comes from operating activities—is in a good position to repay debts as they come due and is usually a low-risk borrower. Stockholders are also interested in the adequacy of cash flows as an indicator of the company's ability to pay dividends and to expand its business. The statement of cash flows is covered in more detail in Chapter 11.

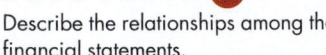

OBJECTIVE **8**
Describe the relationships among the
financial statements.

RELATIONSHIPS AMONG THE STATEMENTS

At this point, it is important to notice the natural relationships of the four basic financial statements and the natural progression from one financial statement to another. The accounting period begins with a balance sheet. During the year, the company earns net income from operating its business. Net income from the income statement increases retained earnings on the retained earnings statement. Ending retained earnings is then reported in the stockholders' equity section of the balance sheet at the end of the accounting period. Therefore, the income statement can be viewed as explaining, through the retained earnings statement, the change in the financial position during the year. Finally, the statement of cash flows explains the change in cash during the year. These relationships are shown in Exhibit 1-13.

Exhibit 1-13   Relationships Among the Financial Statements

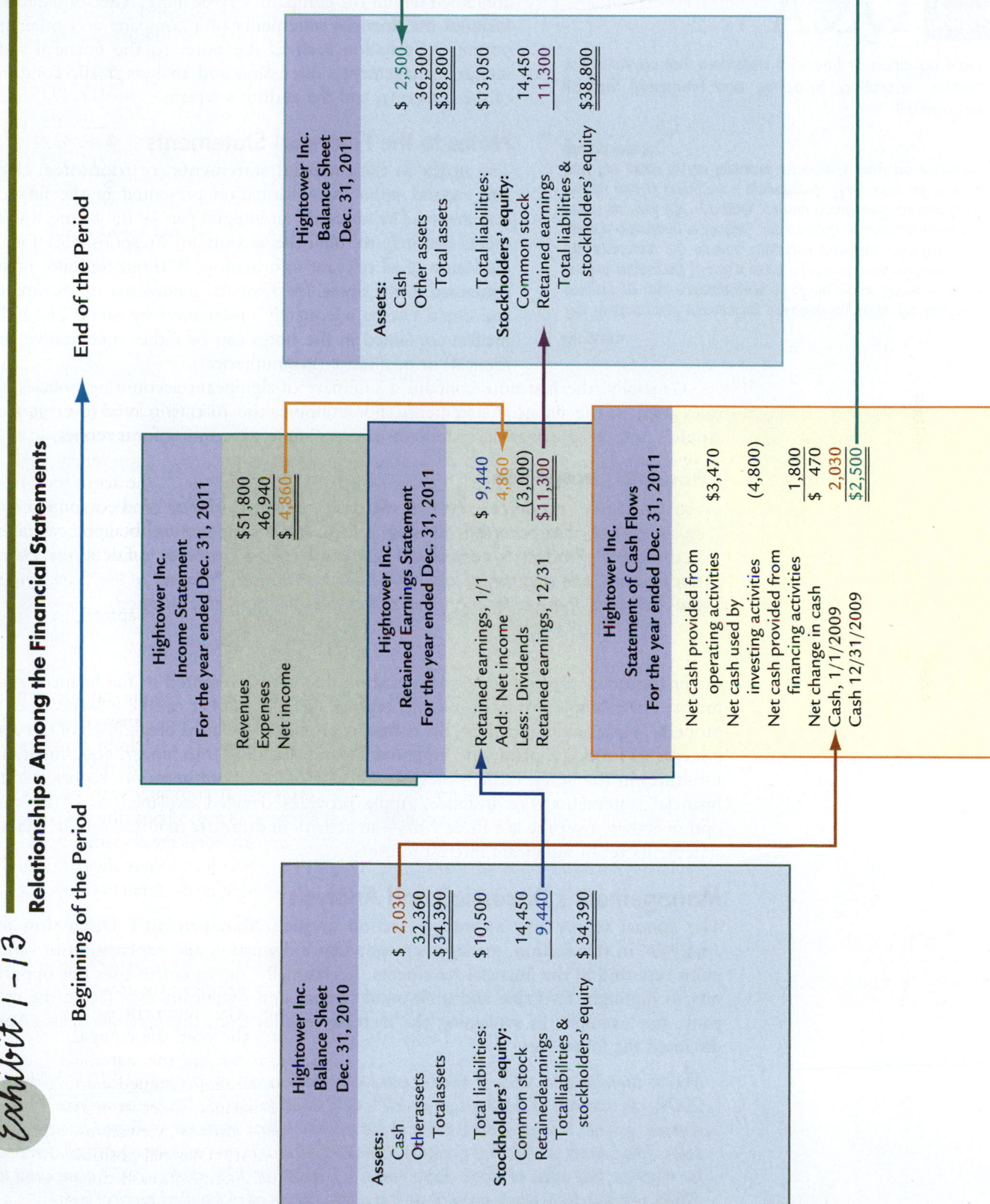

Beginning of the Period → **End of the Period**

Hightower Inc.
Income Statement
For the year ended Dec. 31, 2011

Revenues	$51,800
Expenses	46,940
Net income	$ 4,860

Hightower Inc.
Retained Earnings Statement
For the year ended Dec. 31, 2011

Retained earnings, 1/1	$ 9,440
Add: Net income	4,860
Less: Dividends	(3,000)
Retained earnings, 12/31	$11,300

Hightower Inc.
Statement of Cash Flows
For the year ended Dec. 31, 2011

Net cash provided from operating activities	$3,470
Net cash used by investing activities	(4,800)
Net cash provided from financing activities	1,800
Net change in cash	$ 470
Cash, 1/1/2009	2,030
Cash 12/31/2009	$2,500

Hightower Inc.
Balance Sheet
Dec. 31, 2010

Assets:	
Cash	$ 2,030
Other assets	32,360
Total assets	$34,390
Total liabilities:	$10,500
Stockholders' equity:	
Common stock	14,450
Retained earnings	9,440
Total liabilities & stockholders' equity	$34,390

Hightower Inc.
Balance Sheet
Dec. 31, 2011

Assets:	
Cash	$ 2,500
Other assets	36,300
Total assets	$38,800
Total liabilities:	$13,050
Stockholders' equity:	
Common stock	14,450
Retained earnings	11,300
Total liabilities & stockholders' equity	$38,800

Concept Q&A

Is there a single equation or financial statement that captures the business activities (operating, investing, and financing) that all companies engage in?

Answer:

The fundamental accounting equation captures the business activities of companies and encompasses all of the major financial statements. While certain statements provide more information on certain business activities (for example, the income statement provides information about a company's operating activities), information is also contained in other statements as well (for example, current assets and current liabilities provide insight into a company's operations). Therefore, all financial statements and the notes to the financial statements must be examined as an integrated whole.

OTHER ITEMS IN THE ANNUAL REPORT AND PROFESSIONAL ETHICS

The financial statements discussed in the previous sections were reported to users in an *annual report*. For publicly-traded companies that are required to file reports with the Securities and Exchange Commission, the annual report is contained within the company's 10-K filing. The annual report includes the financial statements of a company and other important information such as the notes to the financial statements, management's discussion and analysis of the condition of the company, and the auditor's report.

Notes to the Financial Statements

The **notes to the financial statements** (or **footnotes**) clarify and expand upon the information presented in the financial statements. The notes are an integral part of the financial statements and help to fulfill the accountant's responsibility for full disclosure of all relevant information. Without the information contained in the notes, the financial statements are incomplete and could not be adequately understood by users. The information contained in the notes can be either quantitative (numerical) or qualitative (nonnumerical).

Generally, the first note contains a summary of significant accounting policies and rules used in the financial statements. For example, the following is an excerpt from **Apple**'s notes to the financial statements concerning its accounting for revenues:

> ### Revenue Recognition
>
> *The Company recognizes revenue when persuasive evidence of an arrangement exists, delivery has occurred, the sales price is fixed or determinable, and collection is probable. Product is considered delivered to the customer once it has been shipped and title and risk of loss have been transferred. For most of the Company's product sales, these criteria are met at the time the product is shipped.*

Other footnotes provide additional detail on line items presented in the financial statements. For example, while **Apple** only reports a single number on the balance sheet for property, plant, and equipment, the company provides a detailed breakdown of the components of property, plant, and equipment (land, building, machinery, equipment, and furniture) in the notes. Other notes provide disclosures about items not reported in the financial statements. For instance, Apple provides detailed explanations of its stock option activity over the last three years—an activity not directly reported on the financial statements yet of significant interest to users.

Management's Discussion and Analysis

The annual report also includes a section entitled **Management's Discussion and Analysis**. In this section, management provides a discussion and explanation of various items reported in the financial statements. Additionally, management uses this opportunity to highlight favorable and unfavorable trends and significant risks facing the company. For example, in explaining the increase in sales from the previous years, **Apple** disclosed the following:

> *iPhone revenue and sales of related products and services amounted to $13.0 billion in 2009, an increase of $6.3 billion or 93% compared to 2008. The year-over-year iPhone revenue growth is largely attributable to the year-over-year increase in iPhone handset unit sales. This growth is attributed primarily to expanded distribution and strong overall demand for iPhones. Net sales of iPods decreased $1.1 billion or 12% during 2009 compared to 2008, resulting from lower average selling prices across all of the iPod product lines.*

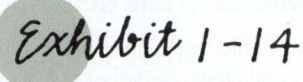

Auditor's Report for Apple Inc.

Report of Independent Registered Public Accounting Firm (partial)

The Board of Directors and Shareholders of Apple Inc.:

We have audited the accompanying consolidated balance sheets of Apple Inc. as of September 26, 2009, and the related consolidated statements of operations, shareholders' equity, and cash flows for the year then ended. These financial statements are the responsibility of the Company's management. Our responsibility is to express an opinion on these consolidated financial statements based on our audit.

We conducted our audits in accordance with the standards of the Public Company Accounting Oversight Board (United States). Those standards require that we plan and perform the audit to obtain reasonable assurance about whether the financial statements are free of material misstatement. An audit includes examining, on a test basis, evidence supporting the amounts and disclosures in the financial statements. An audit also includes assessing the accounting principles used and significant estimates made by management, as well as evaluating the overall financial statement presentation. We believe that our audits provide a reasonable basis for our opinion.

In our opinion, the financial statements referred to above present fairly, in all material respects, the consolidated financial position of Apple Inc. as of September 26, 2009, and the consolidated results of its operations and its cash flows for the year then ended, in conformity with U.S. generally accepted accounting principles.

We also have audited, in accordance with the standards of the Public Company Accounting Oversight Board (United States), Apple Inc.'s internal control over financial reporting as of September 26, 2009, based on criteria established in Internal Control—Integrated Framework issued by the Committee of Sponsoring Organizations of the Treadway Commission (COSO), and our report dated October 27, 2009 expressed an unqualified opinion thereon.

/s/ Ernst & Young LLP
San Jose, California
October 27, 2009

Report of Independent Accountants

An independent accountant (or auditor) is an accounting professional who conducts an examination of a company's financial statements. The objective of this examination is to gather evidence that will enable the auditor to form an opinion as to whether the financial statements fairly present the financial position and result of operations of the company. The auditor's opinion of the financial statements is presented in the form of an **audit report**. Exhibit 1-14 shows an excerpt from the audit report for **Apple**.

Because financial statement users cannot directly observe the company's accounting practices, companies hire auditors to give the users of the financial statements assurance or confidence that the financial statements are a fair presentation of the company's financial health. In performing an audit, it is impractical for an auditor to retrace every transaction of the company for the entire accounting period. Instead, the auditor performs procedures (e.g., sampling of transactions) that enable an opinion to be expressed on the financial statement as a whole.

 **Career Analysis**

As you consider various career options, keep in mind that virtually every organization must have an accounting system. Thus, accountants are employed in a wide range of businesses, including private companies, public accounting firms, governments, and banks. To help you evaluate whether an accounting career is right for you, consider the following question:

(Continued)

What skills and character traits are required for accountants?

Accountants must have well-developed analytical skills and must be effective communicators, both verbally and in writing. Most accounting assignments—whether in business, government, or public accounting—are team assignments in which team members must be able to communicate effectively and work quickly and cooperatively to a solution.

As a profession, accounting requires a high level of academic study and is subject to professional competence requirements. Most members of public accounting firms, and many management accountants and consultants, are (or are in the process of becoming) Certified Public Accountants (CPAs). Other valuable professional certifications are the Certified Management Accountant (CMA), the Certified Internal Auditor (CIA), and the Certified Fraud Examiner (CFE) designations. All of these designations are designed to ensure that the accountants who offer their services are properly qualified and maintain a high level of personal integrity and ethical behavior.

While the career opportunities for accountants are virtually boundless, even if you choose a different career path, the knowledge and experience that you can gain from accounting will prove invaluable in your career.

Accountants must possess strong analytical and communication skills, demonstrate professional competency, and behave ethically.

Professional Ethics

Confidence that standards of ethical behavior will be maintained—even when individuals have incentives to violate those standards—is essential to the conduct of any business activity. Owners of businesses must trust their managers, managers must trust each other and their employees, and the investing public must trust accountants to behave according to accepted ethical standards, which may or may not be reflected in formal written codes. The violation of ethical standards may bring clear and direct penalties but more often brings subtle and long-lasting negative consequences for individuals and companies.

For the economy to function effectively and efficiently, users must have faith that the information reported in financial statements is accurate and dependable. This can only be accomplished through ethical behavior of the accountants involved in the financial reporting process. The American Institute of Certified Public Accountants (AICPA), recognizing that its members have an obligation of self-discipline above and beyond the requirements of generally accepted accounting principles, has adopted a code of professional conduct which provides ethical guidelines for accountants in the performance of their duties. These ethical principles require accountants to serve the public interest with integrity. For example, auditors should fulfill their duties with objectivity, independence, and due professional care. In no situation should an auditor yield to pressure from management to report positively on financial statements that overstate the company's performance or prospects. Violation of these ethical standards can result in severe penalties, including revocation of an accountant's license to practice as a certified public accountant.

In recent years, there have been an increasing number of news reports about unethical behavior involving accounting practices. Acting ethically is not always easy. However, because of the important role of accounting in society, accountants are expected to maintain the highest level of ethical behavior. Throughout this book, you will be exposed to ethical dilemmas that we urge you to consider. As you analyze these cases, consider the guidelines in Exhibit 1-15.

Exhibit 1-15

Guidelines in Ethical Decision Making

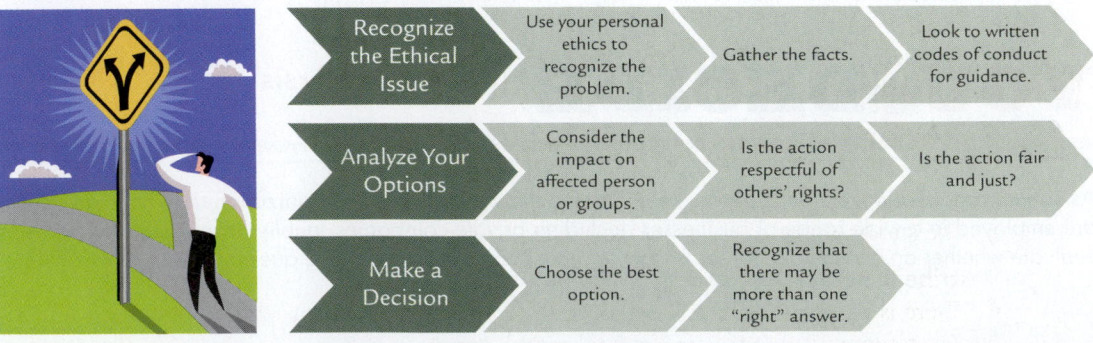

Recognize the Ethical Issue	Use your personal ethics to recognize the problem.	Gather the facts.	Look to written codes of conduct for guidance.
Analyze Your Options	Consider the impact on affected person or groups.	Is the action respectful of others' rights?	Is the action fair and just?
Make a Decision	Choose the best option.	Recognize that there may be more than one "right" answer.	

SUMMARY OF LEARNING OBJECTIVES

LO1. **Explain the nature of accounting.**
- Accounting is the process of identifying, measuring, recording, and communicating financial information.
- This information is used both inside and outside of the business to make better decisions.
- Accounting is also called the language of business.
- Financial accounting focuses on the needs of external decision-makers.

LO2. **Identify the forms of business organizations and the types of business activities.**
- The three forms of business organizations are the sole proprietorship (owned by one person), the partnership (jointly owned by two or more individuals), and the corporation (separate legal entity organized under the laws of a particular state).
- Regardless of the form of business, all businesses are involved in three activities. Financing activities include obtaining funds necessary to begin and operate a business. Investing activities involve buying the assets that enable a business to operate. Operating activities are the activities of a business that generate a profit.

LO3. **Describe the relationships shown by the fundamental accounting equation.**
- The fundamental accounting equation captures all of the economic activities recorded by an accounting system.
- The left side of the accounting equation shows the assets, or economic resources of a company.
- The right side of the accounting equation shows the claims on the company's assets (liabilities or stockholders' equity).

LO4. **Prepare a classified balance sheet and understand the information it communicates.**
- A balance sheet reports the resources (assets) owned by a company and the claims against those resources (liabilities and stockholders' equity) at a specific point in time.
- These elements are related by the fundamental accounting equation:
  Assets = Liabilities + Stockholders' Equity.
- In order to help users identify the fundamental economic similarities and differences between the various items on the balance sheet, assets and liabilities are classified as either current or noncurrent (long-term). Stockholders' equity is classified as either contributed capital or retained earnings.

LO5. **Prepare an income statement and understand the information it communicates.**
- The income statement reports how well a company has performed its operations over a period of time and provides information about the future profitability and growth of a company.
- The income statement includes the revenues and expenses of a company, which can be reported in either a single-step or multiple-step format.

LO6. **Prepare the retained earnings statement and understand the information it communicates.**
- The retained earnings statement reports how much of a company's income was retained in the business and how much was distributed to owners for a period of time.
- The retained earnings statement provides users with insights into a company's dividend payouts.

LO7. **Understand the information communicated by the statement of cash flows.**
- The statement of cash flows reports the sources of a company's cash inflow and the uses of a company's cash over time.
- The statement of cash flows can be used to assess the creditworthiness of a company.

LO8. **Describe the relationships among the financial statements.**
- There is a natural relationship among the four basic financial statements so that financial statements are prepared in a particular order.

- Starting with the balance sheet at the beginning of the accounting period, financial statements are generally prepared in the following order: income statement, the retained earnings statement, and the balance sheet at the end of the accounting period.
- The statement of cash flows explains the change in cash on the balance sheets at the beginning and end of the accounting period.

LO9. **Describe other information contained in the annual report and the importance of ethics in accounting.**

- The notes to the financial statements clarify and expand upon the information presented in the financial statements, and are considered an integral part of a company's financial statements.
- Management's discussion and analysis provides a discussion and explanation of various items reported in the financial statements.
- The auditor's report gives the auditor's opinion as to whether the financial statements fairly present the financial condition and results of operations of the company.
- Maintenance of standards of ethical behavior is essential to the conduct of any business activity. Violation of these standards often brings significant short- and long-term negative consequences for individuals and companies.
- The maintenance of a high ethical standard is necessary for users to have faith in the accuracy of the financial statements, which is a key factor in the effective and efficient functioning of the economy.

CORNERSTONES
FOR CHAPTER 1

CORNERSTONE 1-1 Using the fundamental accounting equation (p. 10)

CORNERSTONE 1-2 Preparing a classified balance sheet (p. 14)

CORNERSTONE 1-3 Preparing an income statement (p. 18)

CORNERSTONE 1-4 Preparing a retained earnings statement (p. 22)

KEY TERMS

Accounting (p. 4)
Assets (p. 7)
Audit report (p. 27)
Balance sheet (p. 8)
Capital (p. 14)
Cash flows from financing activities (p. 24)
Cash flows from investing activities (p. 24)
Cash flows from operating activities (p. 24)
Corporation (p. 5)
Creditor (p. 7)
Current assets (p. 11)
Current liabilities (p. 13)
Current ratio (p. 16)
Expenses (p. 7)
Financial accounting (p. 4)
Financial Accounting Standards Board (FASB) (p. 9)
Financial statements (p. 8)

Fiscal year (p. 11)
Footnotes (p. 26)
Fundamental accounting equation (p. 9)
Generally accepted accounting principles (GAAP) (p. 9)
Gross margin (gross profit) (p. 19)
Income from operations (p. 19)
Income statement (p. 8)
Intangible assets (p. 13)
International Accounting Standards Board (IASB) (p. 9)
International financial reporting standards (IFRS) (p. 9)
Liability (p. 7)
Liquidity (p. 15)
Long-term investments (p. 13)
Long-term liabilities (p. 14)

REVIEW PROBLEM

Preparing Financial Statements

Concept:

A company's business activities are summarized and reported in its financial statements. The balance sheet reports the company's financial position (assets, liabilities, and stockholders' equity) at a specific point in time. The income statement reports the results of a company's operations (revenues less expenses) for a given period of time. The retained earnings statement summarizes and explains the changes in retained earnings during the accounting period.

Information:

Enderle Company reported the following account balances at December 31, 2011:

Equipment	$19,800	Sales revenue	$82,500	Interest expense	$ 1,200
Retained earnings, 12/31/2011	15,450	Accumulated depreciation	5,450	Retained earnings, 1/1/2011	10,300
Copyright	1,200	Cash	2,900	Depreciation expense	3,500
Accounts payable	5,500	Salaries expense	18,100	Cost of goods sold	52,000
Interest income	2,300	Common stock	11,500	Inventory	5,600
Bonds payable	10,000	Land	15,000	Income taxes expense	3,000
Dividends	1,850	Accounts receivable	3,700	Interest payable	300

Required:

1. Prepare Enderle's single-step income statement for the year ending December 31, 2011.
2. Prepare Enderle's retained earnings statement for the year ending December 31, 2011.
3. Prepare Enderle's balance sheet at December 31, 2011.

Solution:

1.

Enderle Company
Income Statement
For the year ended December 31, 2011

Revenues:		
Sales revenue	$82,500	
Interest income	2,300	
Total revenues		$84,800
Expenses:		
Cost of goods sold	$52,000	
Salaries expense	18,100	
Depreciation expense	3,500	
Interest expense	1,200	
Income taxes expense	3,000	
Total expenses		77,800
Net income		$ 7,000

2.

Enderle Company
Retained Earnings Statement
For the year ended December 31, 2011

Retained earnings, January 1, 2011	$10,300
Add: Net income	7,000
Deduct: Dividends	(1,850)
Retained earnings, December 31, 2011	**$ 15,450**

3.

Enderle Company
Balance Sheet
December 31, 2011

ASSETS

Current assets:		
Cash	$ 2,900	
Accounts receivable	3,700	
Inventory	5,600	
Total current assets		$12,200
Property, plant, and equipment:		
Land	$15,000	
Equipment	19,800	
Less: accumulated depreciation	(5,450)	
Total property, plant, and equipment		29,350
Intangible assets:		
Copyright		1,200
Total assets		$42,750

LIABILITIES AND STOCKHOLDERS' EQUITY

Current liabilities:		
Accounts payable	$ 5,500	
Interest payable	300	
Total current liabilities		$ 5,800
Long-term liabilities:		
Bonds payable		10,000
Total liabilities		$15,800
Stockholders' equity:		
Common stock	$11,500	
Retained earnings	15,450	
Total stockholders' equity		26,950
Total liabilities and stockholders' equity		$42,750

DISCUSSION QUESTIONS

1. Define *accounting*. How does accounting differ from *bookkeeping*?
2. Why is there a demand for accounting information? Name five groups that create demand for accounting information about businesses, and describe how each group uses accounting information.
3. What is an accounting entity?
4. Name and describe three different forms of business organization.
5. Name and describe the three main types of business activities.

6. Define the terms *assets*, *liabilities*, and *stockholders' equity*. How are the three terms related?
7. Define the terms *revenue* and *expense*. How are these terms related?
8. Name and briefly describe the purpose of the four financial statements.
9. What types of questions are answered by the financial statements?
10. What is point-in-time measurement? How does it differ from period-of-time measurement?
11. Write the fundamental accounting equation. Why is it significant?
12. What information is included in the heading of each of the four financial statements?
13. Define current assets and current liabilities. Why are current assets and current liabilities separated from noncurrent assets and long-term liabilities on the balance sheet?
14. Describe how items are ordered within the current assets and current liabilities sections on a balance sheet.
15. Name the two main components of stockholders' equity. Describe the main sources of change in each component.
16. What equation describes the income statement?
17. How does the multiple-step income statement differ from the single-step income statement?
18. Explain the items reported on a retained earnings statement.
19. Name and describe the three categories of the statement of cash flows.
20. How is the retained earnings statement related to the balance sheet? How is the income statement related to the retained earnings statement?
21. Describe the items (other than the financial statements) found in the annual report.
22. Give an example of unethical behavior by a public accountant and describe its consequences.

MULTIPLE-CHOICE EXERCISES

1-1 Which of the following statements is *false* concerning forms of business organization?

a. A corporation has tax advantages over the other forms of business organization.
b. It is easier for a corporation to raise large sums of money than it is for a sole proprietorship or partnership.
c. A sole proprietorship is an easy type of business to form.
d. Owners of sole proprietorships and partnerships have personal liability for the debts of the business while owners of corporations have limited legal liability.

1-2 Which of the following statements regarding business activities is true?

a. Operating activities involve buying the assets that enable a company to generate revenue.
b. Financing activities include obtaining the funds necessary to begin and operate a business.
c. Investing activities center around earning interest on a company's investments.
d. Companies spend a relatively small amount of time on operating activities.

1-3 At December 31, Pitt Inc. has assets of $10,500 and liabilities of $5,800. What is the stockholders' equity for Pitt at December 31?

a. $4,700   c. $15,200
b. $5,800   d. $16,300

1-4 Which of the following is *not* one of the four basic financial statements?

a. income statement   c. balance sheet
b. auditor's report   d. statement of cash flows

1-5 What type of questions do the financial statements help to answer?

a. Is the company better off at the end of the year than at the beginning of the year?
b. What resources does the company have?
c. What did a company use its cash for during the year?
d. All of the above.

1-6 Which of the following is *not* shown in the heading of a financial statement?

a.   The title of the financial statement

b.   The name of the company

c.   The time period covered by the financial statement

d.   The name of the auditor

Use the following information for Multiple-Choice Exercises 1-7 and 1-8:
At December 31, Marker reported the following items: cash, $8,200; inventory, $3,700; accounts payable, $6,300; accounts receivable, $3,900; common stock, $5,900; property, plant, and equipment, $10,000; interest payable, $1,400; retained earnings, $12,200.

1-7 Refer to the information for Marker above. What is the total of Marker's current assets?

a. $10,100

b. $15,800

c. $16,000

d. $25,800

1-8 Refer to the information for Marker above. What is Marker's stockholders' equity?

a. $5,900

b. $12,200

c. $18,100

d. $25,800

1-9 Which of the following statements regarding the income statement is true?

a.   The income statement provides information about the future profitability and growth of a company.

b.   The income statement shows the results of a company's operations at a specific point in time.

c.   The income statement consists of assets, expenses, liabilities, and revenues.

d.   Typical income statement accounts include sales revenue, unearned revenue, and cost of goods sold.

1-10 For the most recent year, Grant Company reported revenues of $165,500, cost of goods sold of $92,100, inventory of $5,400, salaries expense of $43,850, rent expense of $15,000, and cash of $17,330. What was Grant's net income?

a. $9,150

b. $14,550

c. $19,950

d. $31,880

1-11 Which of the following statements concerning retained earnings is true?

a.   Retained earnings is the difference between revenues and expenses.

b.   Retained earnings is increased by dividends and decreased by net income.

c.   Retained earnings represents accumulation of the income that has not been distributed as dividends.

d.   Retained earnings is reported as a liability on the balance sheet.

1-12 Which of the following sentences regarding the statement of cash flows is *false*?

a.   The statement of cash flows describes the company's cash receipts and cash payments for a period of time.

b.   The statement of cash flows reconciles the beginning and ending cash balances shown on the balance sheet.

c.   The statement of cash flows reports cash flows in three categories: cash flows from business activities, cash flows from investing activities, and cash flows from financing activities.

d.   The statement of cash flows may be used by creditors to assess the creditworthiness of a company.

1-13 Which of the following statements is true?

a.   The auditor's opinion is typically included in the notes to the financial statements.

b.   The notes to the financial statements are an integral part of the financial statements that clarify and expand on the information presented in the financial statements.

c.   The management's discussion and analysis section does not convey any information that cannot be found in the financial statements themselves.

d.   The annual report is required to be filed with the New York Stock Exchange.

CORNERSTONE EXERCISES

Cornerstone Exercise 1-14 Using the Accounting Equation

OBJECTIVE ③
CORNERSTONE 1-1

Listed below are three independent scenarios.

Scenario	Assets	Liabilities	Equity
1	$ (a)	$33,000	$44,000
2	110,000	(b)	68,000
3	49,000	32,000	(c)

Required:
Use the fundamental accounting equation to find the missing amounts.

Cornerstone Exercise 1-15 Using the Accounting Equation

OBJECTIVE ③
CORNERSTONE 1-1

At the beginning of the year, Morgan Company had total assets of $440,000 and total liabilities of $285,000.

Required:
Use the fundamental accounting equation to answer the following independent questions:

a. What is total stockholders' equity at the beginning of the year?
b. If, during the year, total assets increased by $85,000 and total liabilities increased by $38,000, what is the amount of total stockholders' equity at the end of the year?
c. If, during the year, total assets decreased by $65,000 and total stockholders' equity increased by $45,000, what is the amount of total liabilities at the end of the year?
d. If, during the year, total liabilities increased by $95,000 and total stockholders' equity decreased by $75,000, what is the amount of total assets at the end of the year?

Cornerstone Exercise 1-16 Financial Statements

OBJECTIVE ④⑤⑥⑦
CORNERSTONE 1-2
CORNERSTONE 1-3
CORNERSTONE 1-4

Listed below are elements of the financial statements.

a. Liabilities
b. Net change in cash
c. Assets
d. Revenue

e. Cash flow from operating activities
f. Expenses
g. Stockholders' equity
h. Dividends

Required:
Match each financial statement item with its financial statement: balance sheet (B), income statement (I), retained earnings statement (RE), or statement of cash flows (CF).

Cornerstone Exercise 1-17 Balance Sheet

OBJECTIVE ④
CORNERSTONE 1-2

Listed below are items that may appear on a balance sheet.

Item	Classification
1. Accounts payable	a. Current assets
2. Machinery	b. Property, plant, and equipment
3. Inventory	c. Intangible assets
4. Common stock	d. Current liabilities
5. Notes payable (due in 5 years)	e. Long-term liabilities
6. Cash	f. Contributed capital
7. Copyright	g. Retained earnings
8. Net income less dividends	
9. Accumulated depreciation	
10. Accounts receivable	

Required:
Match each item with its appropriate classification on the balance sheet.

Cornerstone Exercise 1-18 Balance Sheet

OBJECTIVE ④
CORNERSTONE 1-2

An analysis of the transactions of Cavernous Homes Inc. yields the following totals at December 31, 2011: cash, $3,200; accounts receivable, $4,500; notes payable, $5,000; supplies, $8,100; common stock, $7,000; and retained earnings, $3,800.

(Continued)

Required:

Prepare a balance sheet for Cavernous Homes Inc. at December 31, 2011.

OBJECTIVE
CORNERSTONE 1-3

Cornerstone Exercise 1-19 Income Statement

An analysis of the transactions of Canary Cola Inc. for the year 2011 yields the following information: revenue, $78,000; supplies expense, $33,200; rent expense, $20,500; and dividends, $7,000.

Required:

What is the amount of net income reported by Canary Cola for 2011?

OBJECTIVE
CORNERSTONE 1-4

Cornerstone Exercise 1-20 Retained Earnings Statement

Parker Company has a balance of $25,000 in retained earnings on January 1, 2011. During 2011, Parker reported revenues of $74,000 and expenses of $57,000. Parker also paid a dividend of $8,000.

Required:

What is the amount of retained earnings on December 31, 2011?

EXERCISES

OBJECTIVE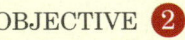

Exercise 1-21 Decisions Based on Accounting Information

Decision-makers use accounting information in a wide variety of decisions including the following:
1. Deciding whether or not to lend money to a business
2. Deciding whether or not an individual has paid enough in taxes
3. Deciding whether or not to place merchandise on sale in order to reduce inventory
4. Deciding whether or not to invest in a business
5. Deciding whether or not to demand additional benefits for employees

Required:

Match each decision with one of the following decision-makers who is primarily responsible for the decision: a government (G), an investor (I), a labor union (U), business managers (M), or a bank (B).

OBJECTIVE ❷

Exercise 1-22 Forms of Business Organizations

Listed below are definitions, examples, or descriptions related to business entities.

1. Owned by one person
2. Can make and sell goods (manufacturing)
3. Owned by more than one person
4. Can sell goods (merchandising)
5. Can provide and sell services
6. Legally, a separate entity from the owner(s)
7. A law firm owned by some of the employees, who are each liable for the financial obligations of the entity
8. The Coca-Cola Company

Required:

1. For each of the three types of business entities (sole proprietorship, partnership, and corporation), select as many of the definitions, examples, or descriptions as apply to that type of entity.

2. Explain the advantages and disadvantages of each type of business entity.

OBJECTIVE ❷

Exercise 1-23 Business Activities

Listed below are various activities that companies engage in during a period.

a. The purchase of equipment
b. The payment of a dividend
c. The purchase of supplies
d. The sale of equipment
e. The sale of goods or services
f. Borrowed money from a bank
g. Contribution of cash by owners

Required:

For each of the activities listed above, classify the activity as operating (O), investing (I), or financing (F).

Exercise 1-24 Business Activities

OBJECTIVE ❷

Bill and Steve recently formed a company that manufactures and sells high-end kitchen appliances. The following is a list of activities that occurred during the year.

a. Bill and Steve each contributed cash in exchange for common stock in the company.
b. Land and a building to be used as a factory to make the appliances were purchased for cash.
c. Machines used to make the appliances were purchased for cash.
d. Various materials used in the production of the appliances were purchased for cash.
e. Three employees were paid cash to operate the machines and make the appliances.
f. Running low on money, the company borrowed money from a local bank.
g. The money from the bank loan was used to buy advertising on local radio and television stations.
h. The company sold the appliances to local homeowners for cash.
i. Due to extremely high popularity of its products, Bill and Steve built another factory building on its land for cash.
j. The company paid a cash dividend to Bill and Steve.

Required:

Classify each of the business activities listed as either an operating activity (O), an investing activity (I), or a financing activity (F).

Exercise 1-25 Accounting Concepts

OBJECTIVE ❹ ❺ ❻

A list of accounting concepts and related definitions is presented below.

Concept		Definition
1. Revenue	a.	Owner's claim on the resources of a company
2. Expense	b.	The difference between revenues and expenses
3. Net income (loss)	c.	Increase in assets from the sale of goods or services
4. Dividend	d.	Economic resources of a company
5. Asset	e.	Cost of assets consumed in the operation of a business
6. Liability	f.	Creditors' claims on the resources of a company
7. Stockholders' equity	g.	Distribution of earnings to stockholders

Required:

Match each of the concepts with its corresponding definition.

Exercise 1-26 The Fundamental Accounting Equation

OBJECTIVE ❸

Financial information for three independent cases is given below.

	Assets	Liabilities	Equity
1.	$112,800	$ (b)	$51,000
2.	275,000	162,500	(c)
3.	(a)	15,000	43,200

Required:

Compute the missing numbers in each case.

Exercise 1-27 Balance Sheet Structure

OBJECTIVE ❹

The following accounts exist in the ledger of Higgins Company: accounts payable, accounts receivable, accumulated depreciation, bonds payable, building, common stock, cash, equipment, income taxes payable, inventory, notes payable (due in 5 years), prepaid insurance, retained earnings, trademarks, wages payable.

Required:

1. Organize the above items into a properly prepared classified balance sheet.
2. Which information might be helpful to assess liquidity?

Exercise 1-28 Identifying Current Assets and Liabilities

OBJECTIVE ❹

Dunn Sporting Goods sells athletic clothing and footwear to retail customers. Dunn's accountant indicates that the firm's operating cycle averages six months. At December 31, 2011, Dunn has the following assets and liabilities:

a. Prepaid rent in the amount of $8,500. Dunn's rent is $500 per month.
b. A $9,700 account payable due in 45 days.
c. Inventory in the amount of $46,230. Dunn expects to sell $38,000 of the inventory within three months. The remainder will be placed in storage until September 2012. The items placed in storage should be sold by November 2012.
d. An investment in marketable securities in the amount of $1,900. Dunn expects to sell $700 of the marketable securities in six months. The remainder are not expected to be sold until 2014.
e. Cash in the amount of $1,050.
f. An equipment loan in the amount of $60,000 due in March 2016. Interest of $4,500 is due in March 2012 ($3,750 of the interest relates to 2011, with the remainder relating to the first three months of 2012).
g. An account receivable from a local university in the amount of $2,850. The university has promised to pay the full amount in three months.
h. Store equipment at a cost of $9,200. Accumulated depreciation has been recorded on the store equipment in the amount of $1,250.

Required:

1. Prepare the current asset and current liability portions of Dunn's December 31, 2011, balance sheet.
2. Compute Dunn's working capital and current ratio at December 31, 2011.
3. As in investor or creditor, what do these ratios tell you about Dunn's liquidity?

OBJECTIVE ④

Exercise 1-29 Current Assets and Current Liabilities

Hanson Construction has an operating cycle of nine months. On December 31, 2011, Hanson has the following assets and liabilities:

a. A note receivable in the amount of $1,200 to be collected in six months.
b. Cash totaling $475.
c. Accounts payable totaling $1,800, all of which will be paid within two months.
d. Accounts receivable totaling $12,000, including an account for $8,000 that will be paid in two months and an account for $4,000 that will be paid in 18 months.
e. Construction supplies costing $8,800, all of which will be used in construction within the next 12 months.
f. Construction equipment costing $60,000, on which depreciation of $22,400 has accumulated.
g. A note payable to the bank in the amount of $7,600 is to be paid within the next year.

Required:

1. Calculate the amounts of current assets and current liabilities reported on Hanson's balance sheet at December 31, 2011.

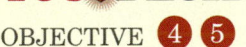

2. Comment on Hanson's liquidity.

OBJECTIVE ④ ⑤

Exercise 1-30 Depreciation

Swanson Products was organized as a new business on January 1, 2011. On that date, Swanson acquired equipment at a cost of $425,000, which is depreciated at a rate of $40,000 per year.

Required:

Describe how the equipment and its related depreciation will be reported on the balance sheet at December 31, 2011, and on the 2011 income statement.

OBJECTIVE ④

Exercise 1-31 Stockholders' Equity

On January 1, 2011, Mulcahy Manufacturing Inc., a newly formed corporation, issued 1,000 shares of common stock in exchange for $135,600 cash. No other shares were issued during 2011, and no shares were repurchased by the corporation. On November 1, 2011, the corporation's major stockholder sold 300 shares to another stockholder for $43,800. The corporation reported net income of $25,300 for 2011.

Required:

Prepare the stockholders' equity section of Mulcahy's balance sheet at December 31, 2011.

Exercise 1-32 Classified Balance Sheet

OBJECTIVE 4

College Spirit sells sportswear with logos of major universities. At the end of 2011, the following balance sheet account balances were available.

Accounts payable	$104,700	Income taxes payable	$ 11,400
Accounts receivable	6,700	Inventory	481,400
Accumulated depreciation	23,700	Long-term investment	110,900
Bonds payable	180,000	Note payable, short-term	50,000
Cash	13,300	Prepaid rent (current)	54,000
Common stock	300,000	Retained earnings, 12/31/2011	84,500
Furniture	88,000		

Required:

1. Prepare a classified balance sheet for College Spirit at December 31, 2011.
2. Compute College Spirit's working capital and current ratio at December 31, 2011.
3. Comment on College Spirit's liquidity as of December 31, 2011.

Exercise 1-33 Classified Balance Sheet

OBJECTIVE 4

Jerrison Company operates a wholesale hardware business. The following balance sheet accounts and balances are available for Jerrison at December 31, 2011.

Accounts payable	$ 65,100	Trucks	$106,100
Accounts receivable	95,500	Income taxes payable	21,600
Accumulated depreciation		Interest payable	12,600
(on data processing equipment)	172,400	Inventory	187,900
Accumulated depreciation		Land	41,000
(on building)	216,800	Investments (long-term)	32,700
Accumulated depreciation (on trucks)	31,200	Notes payable (due June 1, 2012)	150,000
Bonds payable (due 2015)	200,000	Prepaid insurance (for 4 months)	5,700
Building (warehouse)	419,900	Retained earnings, 12/31/2011	?
Cash	11,400	Salaries payable	14,400
Common stock	150,000	Investments (short-term)	21,000
Equipment, data processing	309,000		

Required:

1. Prepare a classified balance sheet for Jerrison at December 31, 2011.
2. Compute Jerrison's working capital and current ratio at December 31, 2011.
3. If Jerrison's management is concerned that a large portion of its inventory is obsolete and cannot be sold, how will Jerrison's liquidity be affected?

Exercise 1-34 Income Statement Structure

OBJECTIVE 5

The following accounts exist in the ledger of Butler Company: salaries expense, advertising expense, cost of goods sold, depreciation expense, interest expense, income taxes expense, sales revenue, and utilities expense.

Required:

1. Organize the above items into a properly prepared single-step income statement.
2. **Conceptual Connection:** What information would be helpful in assessing Butler's ability to generate future income?

Exercise 1-35 Income Statement

OBJECTIVE 5

ERS Inc. maintains and repairs office equipment. ERS had an average of 10,000 shares of common stock outstanding for the year. The following income statement account balances are available for ERS at the end of 2011.

Advertising expense	$24,200	Salaries expense (for	
Depreciation expense		administrative personnel)	$195,600
(on service van)	16,250	Service revenue	933,800
Income taxes expense	15,150	Supplies expense	66,400
Interest expense	10,100	Utilities expense	26,100
Rent expense	58,400	Wages expense (for service	
Insurance expense	11,900	technicians)	448,300

(Continued)

Required:

1. Prepare a single-step income statement for ERS for 2011.
2. **Conceptual Connection:** Compute net profit margin for ERS. If ERS is able to increase its service revenue by $100,000, what should be the effect on future income?
3. Assume that ERS net profit margin was 8.5% for 2010. As an investor, what conclusions might you draw about ERS' future profitability?

OBJECTIVE **5**

Exercise 1-36 Multiple-Step Income Statement

The following information is available for Bergin Pastry Shop.

Gross margin	$34,700
Income from operations	9,200
Income taxes expense (15% of income before taxes)	?
Interest expense	1,800
Net sales	85,300

Required:
Prepare a multiple-step income statement for Bergin.

OBJECTIVE **5**

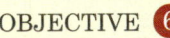

Exercise 1-37 Income Statement

The following information is available for Wright Auto Supply at December 31, 2011.

Cost of goods sold	$277,000	Rent expense	$ 18,000
Depreciation expense	29,000	Salaries (administrative)	32,000
Income taxes expense	38,085	Sales revenue	583,900
Interest expense	2,700	Wages expense (salespeople)	98,250

Required:

1. Prepare a single-step income statement for the year ended December 31, 2011.
2. Prepare a multiple-step income statement for the year ended December 31, 2011.
3. **Conceptual Connection:** Comment on the differences between the single-step and the multiple-step income statements.

OBJECTIVE **6**

Exercise 1-38 Retained Earnings Statement

At the end of 2010, Sherwood Company had retained earnings of $18,240. During 2011, Sherwood had revenues of $837,400 and expenses of $792,100, and paid cash dividends in the amount of $38,650.

Required:

1. Determine the amount of Sherwood's retained earnings at December 31, 2011.
2. Comment on Sherwood's dividend policy.

OBJECTIVE **7**

Exercise 1-39 Statement of Cash Flows

Walters Inc. began operations on January 1, 2011. The following information relates to Walters' cash flows during 2011.

Cash received from owners	$201,500	Cash paid to purchase machine	$32,000
Cash paid for purchase of land and building	128,700	Cash paid to employees for salaries	46,400
Cash paid for advertising	34,200	Cash paid for dividends to stockholders	37,500
Cash received from customers	139,800	Cash paid for supplies	28,700

Required:

1. Calculate the cash provided/used for each cash flow category.
2. Comment on Walters' creditworthiness.

OBJECTIVE **8**

Exercise 1-40 Relationships Among the Financial Statements

Zachary Corporation's December 31, 2010 balance sheet included the following amounts:

Cash	$ 17,400
Retained earnings	103,600

Zachary's accountant provided the following data for 2011:

Revenues	$ 673,900	Cash inflow from operating activities	$ 857,300
Expenses	587,100	Cash outflow for investing activities	(994,500)
Dividends	34,200	Cash inflow from financing activities	156,600

Required:
Calculate the amount of cash and retained earnings at the end of 2011.

Exercise 1-41 Relationships Among the Financial Statements

OBJECTIVE 8

The following information for Kellman Inc. is available at the end of 2011.

Total assets on 12/31/2010	$72,400	Common stock on 12/31/2010	$50,000
Total assets on 12/31/2011	78,500	Common stock on 12/31/2011	50,000
Total liabilities on 12/31/2010	12,100	Net income for 2011	14,300
Total liabilities on 12/31/2011	9,800		

Required:
Calculate the amount of dividends reported on the retained earnings statement for 2011.

Exercise 1-42 Relationships Among the Financial Statements

OBJECTIVE 8

During 2011, Moore Corporation paid $14,500 of dividends. Moore's assets, liabilities, and common stock at the end of 2010 and 2011 were:

	12/31/2010	12/31/2011
Total assets	$144,200	$178,100
Total liabilities	52,600	59,700
Common stock	60,000	60,000

Required:
Using the information provided, compute Moore's net income for 2011.

Exercise 1-43 Annual Report Items

OBJECTIVE 9

DeSalle Company's annual report includes the following items: financial statements, notes to the financial statements, management's discussion and analysis, and a report of independent accountants.

Required:
For each of the following items, where would you most likely find the information in the annual report?

a. A description of the risks associated with operating the company in an international market.
b. Detailed information on the outstanding debt of a company, including the interest rate being charged and the maturity date of the debt.
c. A description of the accounting methods used by the company.
d. The total resources and claims to the resources of a company.
e. A discussion of the sales trends of the company's most profitable products.
f. The amount of dividends paid to common stockholders.
g. An opinion as to whether the financial statements are a fair presentation of the company's financial position and results of operations.
h. The cost of operating a company over a period of time.

Exercise 1-44 Professional Ethics

OBJECTIVE 9

Ethical behavior is essential to the conduct of business activity. Consider each of the following business behaviors:

a. A manager prepares financial statements that grossly overstate the performance of the business.
b. A CPA resigns from an audit engagement rather than allow a business client to violate an accounting standard.
c. An internal auditor decides against confronting an employee of the business with minor violations of business policy. The employee is a former college classmate of the auditor.
d. An accountant advises his client on ways to legally minimize tax payments to the government.
e. A manager legally reduces the price of a product to secure a larger share of the market.

f. Managers of several large companies secretly meet to plan price reductions designed to drive up-and-coming competitors out of the market.

g. An accountant keeps confidential details of her employer's legal operations that would be of interest to the public.

h. A recently dismissed accountant tells competitors details about her former employer's operations as she seeks a new job.

Required:

Identify each behavior as ethical (E) or unethical (U).

PROBLEM SET A

OBJECTIVE ③

Problem 1-45A Applying the Fundamental Accounting Equation

At the beginning of 2011, Huffer Corporation had total assets of $226,800, total liabilities of $84,200, common stock of $80,000, and retained earnings of $62,600. During 2011, Huffer had net income of $42,750, paid dividends of $11,900, and issued additional common stock for $12,800. Huffer's total assets at the end of 2011 were $278,200.

Required:

Calculate the amount of liabilities that Huffer must have at the end of 2011 in order for the balance sheet equation to balance.

OBJECTIVE ④⑤⑥⑧

Problem 1-46A Accounting Relationships

Information for Beethoven Music Company is given below.

Total assets at the beginning of the year	$145,200	Equity at the beginning of the year	$ (b)
		Equity at the end of the year	104,100
Total assets at the end of the year	(a)	Dividends paid during the year	(c)
Total liabilities at the beginning of the year	92,600	Net income for the year	77,500
		Revenues	554,800
Total liabilities at the end of the year	126,900	Expenses	(d)

Required:

Use the relationships in the balance sheet, income statement, and retained earnings statement to determine the missing values.

OBJECTIVE ⑤

Problem 1-47A Arrangement of the Income Statement

Powers Wrecking Service demolishes old buildings and other structures and sells the salvaged materials. During 2011, Powers had $425,000 of revenue from demolition services and $137,000 of revenue from salvage sales. Powers also had $1,575 of interest income from investments. Powers incurred $243,200 of wages expense, $24,150 of depreciation expense, $48,575 of supplies expense, $84,000 of rent expense, $17,300 of miscellaneous expense, and $43,900 of income taxes expense.

Required:

Prepare a single-step income statement for Powers for 2011.

OBJECTIVE ④⑤⑥⑧

Problem 1-48A Income Statement and Balance Sheet Relationships

Each column presents financial information taken from one of four different companies, with one or more items of data missing.

Financial Statement Item	Company			
	Floyd	Slater	Wooderson	O'Bannion
Total revenue	$125	$ 715	$ (e)	$2,475
Total expense	92	(c)	54	(g)
Net income (net loss)	(a)	184	18	(600)
Total assets	905	1,988	(f)	8,140
Total liabilities	412	(d)	117	2,280
Total equity	(b)	823	80	(h)

Required:

Use your understanding of the relationships among financial statements and financial statement items to find the missing values (a–h).

Problem 1-49A Income Statement and Balance Sheet

OBJECTIVE 4 5

The following information for Rogers Enterprises is available at December 31, 2011, and includes all of Rogers' financial statement amounts except retained earnings:

Accounts receivable	$ 72,920	Property, plant, and equipment	$ 90,000
Cash	13,240	Rent expense	135,000
Common stock (10,000 shares)	70,000	Retained earnings	?
Income taxes expense	12,800	Salaries expense	235,200
Income taxes payable	4,150	Salaries payable	14,800
Interest expense	16,000	Service revenue	463,500
Notes payable (due in 10 years)	25,000	Supplies	42,000
Prepaid rent (building)	31,500	Supplies expense	34,400

Required:

Prepare a single-step income statement and a classified balance sheet for the year ending December 31, 2011, for Rogers.

Problem 1-50A Retained Earnings Statement

OBJECTIVE 6

Dittman Expositions has the following data available:

Dividends, 2011	$ 8,250	Retained earnings, 12/31/2010	$ 16,900
Dividends, 2012	9,910	Revenues, 2011	419,700
Expenses, 2011	386,500	Revenues, 2012	442,400
Expenses, 2012	412,600		

Required:

Prepare statements of retained earnings for 2011 and 2012.

Problem 1-51A Retained Earnings Statements

OBJECTIVE 6

The table below presents the statements of retained earnings for Bass Corporation for three successive years. Certain numbers are missing.

ILLUSTRATING RELATIONSHIPS

	2010	2011	2012
Retained earnings, beginning	$21,500	$ (b)	$33,600
Add: Net income	9,200	10,100	(f)
	$30,700	$ (c)	$ (g)
Less: Dividends	(a)	(d)	(3,900)
Retained earnings, ending	$27,200	$ (e)	$41,200

Required:

Use your understanding of the relationship between successive statements of retained earnings to calculate the missing values (a–g).

Problem 1-52A Income Statement, Retained Earnings Statement, and Balance Sheet

OBJECTIVE 4 5 6

The following information relates to Ashton Appliances for 2011.

Accounts payable	$ 16,800	Income taxes expense	$ 16,650
Accounts receivable	69,900	Income taxes payable	12,000
Accumulated depreciation (building)	104,800	Insurance expense	36,610
Accumulated depreciation (furniture)	27,600	Interest expense	15,500
Bonds payable (due in 7 years)	192,000	Inventory	59,850
Building	300,000	Other assets	92,800
Cash	41,450	Rent expense (store equipment)	80,800
Common stock	243,610	Retained earnings, 12/31/2010	54,000
Cost of goods sold	511,350	Salaries expense (administrative)	101,000
Depreciation expense (building)	11,050	Salaries payable	7,190
Depreciation expense (furniture)	12,000	Sales revenue	948,670
Furniture	130,000	Wages expense (store staff)	127,710

(Continued)

Required:

1. Prepare a single-step income statement for 2011, a retained earnings statement for 2011, and a properly classified balance sheet as of December 31, 2011.
2. **Conceptual Connection:** How would a multiple-step income statement be different from the single-step income statement you prepared for Ashton?

OBJECTIVE ⑧

Problem 1-53A Stockholders' Equity Relationships

Data from the financial statements of four different companies are presented in separate columns in the table below. Each column has one or more data items missing.

	Company			
Financial Statement Item	**Berko**	**Manning**	**Lucas**	**Corey**
Equity, 12/31/2010				
Common stock	$50,000	$35,000	$ (i)	$15,000
Retained earnings	12,100	(e)	26,400	21,900
Total equity	(a)	$44,300	$66,400	$36,900
Net income (loss) for 2011	$ 7,000	$ (1,800)	$ 6,000	(m)
Dividends during 2011	$ 2,000	$ 0	(j)	$ 1,400
Equity, 12/31/2011				
Common stock	$50,000	$35,000	$55,000	$15,000
Retained earnings	(b)	(f)	(k)	27,600
Total equity	(c)	(g)	$84,500	(n)
Total assets, 12/31/2011	$92,500	(h)	$99,200	(o)
Total liabilities, 12/31/2011	(d)	$14,800	(l)	$10,700

Required:

Use your understanding of the relationships among the financial statement items to determine the missing values (a–o).

OBJECTIVE ③ ⑧

Problem 1-54A Relationships Among Financial Statements

Carson Corporation reported the following amounts for assets and liabilities at the beginning and end of a recent year.

	Beginning of Year	**End of Year**
Assets	$392,500	$415,100
Liabilities	148,550	149,600

Required:

Calculate Carson's net income or net loss for the year in each of the following independent situations:

1. Carson declared no dividends, and its common stock remained unchanged.
2. Carson declared no dividends and issued additional common stock for $33,000 cash.
3. Carson declared dividends totaling $11,000, and its common stock remained unchanged.
4. Carson declared dividends totaling $17,000 and issued additional common stock for $29,000.

PROBLEM SET B

OBJECTIVE ③

Problem 1-45B Applying the Fundamental Accounting Equation

At the beginning of 2011, KJ Corporation had total assets of $553,700, total liabilities of $261,800, common stock of $139,000, and retained earnings of $152,900. During 2011, KJ had net income of $225,200, paid dividends of $74,400, and issued additional common stock for $94,000. KJ's total assets at the end of 2011 were $721,800.

Required:

Calculate the amount of liabilities that KJ must have at the end of 2011 in order for the balance sheet equation to balance.

Problem 1-46B The Fundamental Accounting Equation

OBJECTIVE 4 5 6 8

Information for TTL Inc. is given below.

Total assets at the beginning of the year	$ (a)	Equity at the end of the year	$ (c)
Total assets at the end of the year	758,150	Dividends paid during the year	35,500
Total liabilities at the beginning of the year	368,200	Net income for the year	(d)
Total liabilities at the end of the year	(b)	Revenues	929,440
Equity at the beginning of the year	272,900	Expenses	835,320

Required:

Use the relationships in the balance sheet, income statement, and retained earnings statement to determine the missing values.

Problem 1-47B Arrangement of the Income Statement

OBJECTIVE 5

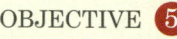

Parker Renovation Inc. renovates historical buildings for commercial use. During 2011, Parker had $763,400 of revenue from renovation services and $5,475 of interest income from miscellaneous investments. Parker incurred $222,900 of wages expense, $135,000 of depreciation expense, $65,850 of insurance expense, $109,300 of utilities expense, $31,000 of miscellaneous expense, and $61,400 of income taxes expense.

Required:

Prepare a single-step income statement for Parker for 2011.

Problem 1-48B Income Statement and Balance Sheet Relationships

OBJECTIVE 4 5 6 8

Each column presents financial information taken from one of four different companies, with one or more items of data missing.

Financial Statement Item	Company Crick	Company Pascal	Company Eiffel	Company Hilbert
Total revenue	$925	$ 533	$ (e)	$1,125
Total expense	844	(c)	377	(g)
Net income (net loss)	(a)	289	126	(340)
Total assets	709	1,810	(f)	3,150
Total liabilities	332	(d)	454	2,267
Total equity	(b)	950	98	(h)

Required:

Use your understanding of the relationships among financial statements and financial statement items to find the missing values (a–h).

Problem 1-49B Income Statement and Balance Sheet

OBJECTIVE 4 5

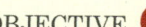

Ross Airport Auto Service provides parking and minor repair service at the local airport while customers are away on business or pleasure trips. The following account balances (except for retained earnings) are available for Ross Airport Auto Service at December 31, 2011.

Accounts payable	$ 17,200	Interest income	$ 4,100
Accounts receivable	39,200	Inventory (repair parts)	6,100
Accumulated depreciation		Investments (long term)	35,000
(equipment)	42,300	Notes payable (due May 2, 2018)	160,000
Cash	7,700	Prepaid rent (3 months)	27,300
Common stock (20,000 shares)	100,000	Rent expense	103,500
Depreciation expense (equipment)	12,450	Retained earnings, 12/31/2011	48,200
Dividends	6,300	Service revenue (parking)	232,600
Equipment	270,800	Service revenue (repair)	198,500
Income taxes expense	2,700	Supplies expense (repair parts)	36,900
Income taxes payable	1,100	Wages expense	246,100
Interest expense	21,300	Wages payable	12,500
Interest payable	4,800		

Required:

Prepare a single-step income statement and a classified balance sheet for the year ended December 31, 2011.

OBJECTIVE **6**

Problem 1-50B Retained Earnings Statement

Magical Experiences Vacation Company has the following data available:

Dividends, 2011	$ 13,200	Retained earnings, 12/31/2010	$ 47,100
Dividends, 2012	15,900	Revenues, 2011	244,900
Expenses, 2011	185,300	Revenues, 2012	391,400
Expenses, 2012	308,600		

Required:
Prepare statements of retained earnings for 2011 and 2012.

OBJECTIVE **6**

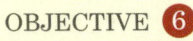

Problem 1-51B Retained Earnings Statements

The table below presents the statements of retained earnings for Dillsboro Corporation for three successive years. Certain numbers are missing.

	2010	2011	2012
Retained earnings, beginning	$ (a)	$19,500	$26,700
Add: Net income	11,100	(c)	9,500
	$ 26,900	$ (d)	$ (f)
Less: Dividends	(7,400)	(5,200)	(g)
Retained earnings, ending	$ (b)	$ (e)	$34,100

Required:
Use your understanding of the relationship between successive statements of retained earnings to calculate the missing values (a–g).

OBJECTIVE **4 5 6**

Problem 1-52B Income Statement, Retained Earnings Statement, and Balance Sheet

McDonald Marina provides docking and cleaning services for pleasure boats at its marina in southern Florida. The following account balances are available:

Accounts payable	$ 26,400	Interest expense	$ 236,000
Accounts receivable	268,700	Interest payable	18,000
Accumulated depreciation (building)	64,500	Land	875,000
Accumulated depreciation (equipment)	950,400	Rent expense	14,600
Bonds payable (due 2016)	2,000,000	Rent payable	2,400
Building	197,300	Retained earnings, 12/31/2010	128,600
Cash	22,300	Service revenue (cleaning)	472,300
Common stock (40,000 shares)	600,000	Service revenue (docking)	1,460,000
Depreciation expense (building)	21,500	Supplies expense	89,100
Depreciation expense (equipment)	246,300	Supplies	9,800
Dividends	25,300	Utilities expense	239,400
Equipment	2,490,000	Wages expense	987,200
Income taxes expense	21,700	Wages payable	21,600

Required:
1. Prepare a single-step income statement, a retained earnings statement, and a classified balance sheet for the year ended December 31, 2011.
2. **Conceptual Connection:** How would a multiple-step income statement be different from the single-step income statement you prepared for McDonald Marina?

OBJECTIVE **8**

Problem 1-53B Stockholders' Equity Relationships

Data from the financial statements of four different companies are presented in separate columns in the table below. Each column has one or more data items missing.

	Company			
Financial Statement Item	Stackhouse	Compton	Bellefleur	Merlotte
Equity, 12/31/2010				
Common stock	$45,000	$39,000	$ 80,000	$25,000
Retained earnings	18,800	15,300	6,900	(k)
Total equity	$63,800	$ (d)	$ 86,900	$38,900

Financial Statement Item	Company			
	Stackhouse	Compton	Bellefleur	Merlotte
Net income (loss) for 2011	$ (a)	$ 7,100	$ 9,700	$ (4,500)
Dividends during 2011	$ 2,100	$ 800	$ (h)	$ 0
Equity, 12/31/2011				
Common stock	$45,000	$39,000	$ 80,000	$25,000
Retained earnings	21,700	(e)	(i)	(l)
Total equity	$ (b)	$ (f)	$ 95,300	$ (m)
Total assets, 12/31/2011	$ (c)	$88,200	$113,400	$ (n)
Total liabilities, 12/31/2011	$14,400	$ (g)	$ (j)	$15,700

Required:

Use your understanding of the relationships among the financial statement items to determine the missing values (a–n).

Problem 1-54B Relationships Among Financial Statements

OBJECTIVE

Leno Corporation reported the following amounts for assets and liabilities at the beginning and end of a recent year.

	Beginning of Year	End of Year
Assets	$231,500	$348,100
Liabilities	84,550	125,900

Required:

Calculate Leno's net income or net loss for the year in each of the following independent situations:
1. Leno declared no dividends, and its common stock remained unchanged.
2. Leno declared no dividends and issued additional common stock for $12,000 cash.
3. Leno declared dividends totaling $8,000, and its common stock remained unchanged.
4. Leno declared dividends totaling $11,000 and issued additional common stock for $15,000.

CASES

Case 1-55 Using Accounting Information

James Hadden is a freshman at Major State University. His earnings from a summer job, combined with a small scholarship and a fixed amount per term from his parents, are his only sources of income. He has a new MasterCard that was issued to him the week he began classes. It is spring term, and Jim finds that his credit card is "maxed out" and that he does not have enough money to carry him to the end of the term. Jim confesses that irresistible opportunities for spring term entertainment have caused him to overspend his resources.

Required:

Describe how accounting information could have helped Jim avoid this difficult situation.

Case 1-56 Analysis of Accounting Periodicals

The accounting profession is organized into three major groups: (a) accountants who work in nonbusiness entities, (b) accountants who work in business entities, and (c) accountants in public practice. The periodical literature of accounting includes monthly or quarterly journals that are written primarily for accountants within each of these groups.

Required:

1. Use your library and identify one journal published for each of the three professional groups. Identify the publisher of each journal and describe its primary audience.
2. Choose two of the three audiences you have just described. Briefly explain how members of one audience would benefit by reading a journal published primarily for members of the other audience.

Case 1-57 Career Planning

A successful career requires us to take advantage of opportunities that are difficult to foresee. Success is also aided by having a plan or strategy by which to choose among career alternatives as they arise.

Required:

1. How do you want to be employed in five years, and what must you do to get there?
2. How do you want to be employed in ten years, and what must you do to get there?

Case 1-58 Financial Statement Analysis

Agency Rent-A-Car Inc. rents cars to customers whose vehicles are unavailable due to accident, theft, or repair ("Wheels while your car heals"). The company has a fleet of more than 40,000 cars located at 700 offices throughout the United States and Canada. Its balance sheets at January 31, 2011, and January 31, 2010, contain the following information (all dollar amounts are stated in thousands of dollars):

	1/31/2011	1/31/2010
Assets		
Cash	$ 4,850	$ 3,408
Accounts receivable	27,409	30,989
Supplies	6,864	7,440
Property and equipment	279,189	287,456
Other assets	15,666	14,441
	$333,978	$343,734
Liabilities and Stockholders' Equity		
Accounts payable	$ 18,602	$ 33,384
Other noncurrent liabilities	157,861	163,062
Stockholders' equity	157,515	147,288
	$333,978	$343,734

Required:

1. What is the dollar amount of current assets and current liabilities at January 31, 2011? At January 31, 2010? What does this information tell you about the company's liquidity?
2. Assume that stockholders were paid dividends of $18,100 during 2010 and that there were no other changes in stockholders' equity except for net income. How much net income did the business earn during the year?

Case 1-59 Financial Statement Analysis

Reproduced below are portions of the president's letter to shareholders and selected income statement and balance sheet data for the Wright Brothers Aviation Company. Wright Brothers is a national airline that provides both passenger service and package delivery service.

To Our Stockholders:

In 2011, the airline industry began to show some life. As fuel prices leveled and travelers showed an increased willingness to fly domestically, it was generally perceived that a gradual recovery was in place. The worldwide increase in the demand for air travel throughout the year translated into improved demand for the Company's services. In fact, revenues for both the passenger and package segments improved in every quarter of 2011. Most importantly, the Company started generating cash from operations in the last half of the year, and the passenger segments returned to generating profits in the third quarter....

With improved operating performance as the basis for negotiating a financial restructuring, the next critical step for the Company is to satisfactorily restructure its obligations in order to insure that the Company can operate effectively in the future. With that in mind, a strategic decision, albeit a difficult one, was made in February 2011—the Company filed for reorganization under Chapter 11 of the U.S. Bankruptcy Code....

	2011	2010	2009	2008	2007
Revenues:					
Passenger services	$ 141,343	$ 136,057	$354,246	$ 390,080	$ 337,871
Package services	35,199	60,968	145,940	203,675	202,615
Total revenues	176,542	197,025	500,186	593,755	540,486
Operating income	(54,584)	(92,613)	(16,663)	52,137	39,527
Net income (loss)	(182,647)	(340,516)	(67,269)	(14,553)	(22,461)
Current assets	123,553	134,009	183,268	193,943	209,944
Total assets	542,523	678,846	952,623	1,040,903	1,133,498
Current liabilities	698,583	641,645	542,640	129,369	120,960
Long-term debt	116,572	119,481	144,297	576,446	655,383
Stockholders' equity	(272,632)	(82,280)	265,686	335,088	357,155

Required:

1. What trends do you detect in revenues, operating income, and net income for the period 2007–2011?
2. What happened to working capital over the 2007–2011 period? To what do you attribute this result?
3. The price of Wright Brothers stock declined steadily throughout the 2007–2011 period. Do you consider this decline to be a reasonable reaction to the financial results reported? Why or why not?

Case 1-60 Professional Ethics

Professional ethics guide public accountants in their work with financial statements.

Required:

Why is ethical behavior by public accountants important to society? Be sure to describe the incentives that public accountants have to behave *ethically* and *unethically*.

Case 1-61 Ethical Issues

Lola, the CEO of JB Inc., and Frank, the accountant for JB Inc., were recently having a meeting to discuss the upcoming release of the company's financial statements. Following is an excerpt of their conversation:

Lola: These financial statements don't show the hours of hard work that we've put in to restore this company to financial health. In fact, these results may actually prevent us from obtaining loans that are critical to our future.

Frank: Accounting does allow for judgment. Tell me your primary concerns and let's see if we can work something out.

Lola: My first concern is that the company doesn't appear very liquid. As you can see, our current assets are only slightly more than current liabilities. The company has always paid its bills—even when cash was tight. It's not really fair that the financial statements don't reflect this.

Frank: Well, we could reclassify some of the long-term investments as current assets instead of noncurrent assets. Our expectation is that we will hold these investments for several years, but we could sell them at any time; therefore, it's fair to count these as current assets. We could also reclassify some of the accounts payable as noncurrent. Even though we expect to pay them within the next year, no one will ever look close enough to see what we've done. Together these two changes should make us appear more liquid and properly reflect the hard work we've done.

Lola: I agree. However, if we make these changes, our long-term assets will be smaller and our long-term debt will be larger. Many analysts may view this as a sign of financial trouble. Isn't there something we can do?

Frank: Our long-term assets are undervalued. Many were purchased years ago and recorded at historical cost. However, companies that bought similar assets are allowed to record them at an amount closer to their current market values. I've always thought this was misleading. If we increase the value of these long-term assets to their market value, this should provide the users of the financial statements with more relevant information and solve our problem, too.

Lola: Brilliant! Let's implement these actions quickly and get back to work.

Required:

Describe any ethical issues that have arisen as the result of Lola and Frank's conversation.

Case 1-62 Research and Analysis Using the Annual Report

Obtain **Apple Inc.**'s 2009 annual report either through the "Investor Relations" portion of their website (do a web search for Apple investor relations) or go to http://www.sec.gov and click "Search for Company Filings" under "Filings & Forms." Be sure to get the amended annual report filed with the SEC on January 25, 2010.

Required:

Answer the following questions:

1. On what date did Apple's fiscal year end? Was this date different from the previous year? If so, why?
2. How many years of balance sheet and income statement information does Apple present?
3. Why did Apple file an amended annual report?
4. With regard to the balance sheet:

   a. What amounts did Apple report as total assets, liabilities, and stockholders' equity for 2009?
   b. Did the amounts reported as assets, liabilities, and stockholders' equity change over the last year? If so, by how much?
   c. What amounts were reported as current assets and current liabilities for the years presented?
   d. Provide an assessment of Apple's liquidity based on the information obtained in part (b).

5. With regard to the income statement:

   a. What amounts did Apple report as revenues, expenses, and net income for 2009?
   b. Do you detect any trends with regard to revenues, expenses, or net income?

6. With regard to the statement of cash flows:

   a. What amounts did the company report for cash flow from operating activities, cash flow from investing activities, and cash flow from financing activities for 2009?
   b. How much cash did the company spend on purchasing PP&E in 2009?

7. With regard to management's discussion and analysis:

   a. What accounting policies and estimates does Apple consider critical? Where would these policies and estimates be described?
   b. Does management believe that the company performed well during the current year? On what do you base this assessment?

8. Are the financial statements audited? If so, by whom?

Case 1-63 Comparative Analysis: Abercrombie & Fitch versus Aeropostale

Refer to the financial statements of **Abercrombie & Fitch** and **Aeropostale** that are supplied with this text.

Required:

Answer the following questions:

1. a. What is the fiscal year-end of Abercrombie & Fitch? Of Aeropostale? Why would you expect these to be the same?
   b. Why does of the date of the fiscal year end change each year?

2. With regard to the balance sheet:

   a. What amounts did each company report for total assets, liabilities, and stockholders' equity for the year ended January 30, 2010 (fiscal 2009)?
   b. What amounts were reported as current assets and current liabilities for the year ended January 30, 2010 (fiscal 2009)?

   c. Assess the liquidity of each company.

   d. Describe any other similarities and differences that you noticed between the two companies.

3. With regard to the income statement:

   a. What amounts did Abercrombie & Fitch report as revenues, expenses, and net income? What amounts did Aeropostale report as revenues, expenses, and net income for the fiscal year ended January 30, 2010?

   b. Compare any trends that you detect with regard to revenues, expenses, and net income.

4. What were the major sources and uses of cash for each company?

5. What is management's assessment of each company's past performance and future prospects? Where did you find this information?

Case 1-64 Continuing Problem: Front Row Entertainment

Cam Mosley and Anna Newton met during their freshman year of college as they were standing in line to buy tickets to a concert. Over the next several hours, the two shared various aspects of their lives. Cam, whose father was an executive at a major record label, was raised in New York. Some of his favorite memories were meeting popular musical artists—from the Rolling Stones to the Black Eyed Peas—as he accompanied his father on business trips. Anna, on the other hand, was born and raised in a small, rural town in southern Georgia. Her fondest childhood memories involved singing with her family, who often performed at county fairs and other small events. Even though they had different backgrounds, they felt an instant bond through their shared passion for music. Over the course of the next couple of years, this friendship strengthened as they attended numerous concerts and other events together.

While on a road trip to see a new band during their senior year, Cam and Anna started discussing their future career plans. Both had an entrepreneurial spirit and were seeking a way to combine their majors in business with their passion for music. Cam had recently overheard his father discussing how many artists were unhappy with the current concert promoters. Anna had heard similar complaints from her cousin, whose band recently had their first top 25 hit. When Cam suggested that he and Anna form a concert promotion business, they both knew they had found the perfect careers.

Concert promoters sign artists, usually through the artists' agents, to contracts in which the promoter is responsible for organizing live concert tours. Typically, this includes booking the venue, pricing the tour, advertising the tour, and negotiating other services from local vendors. In general, the barriers to entry in the concert promotion industry are relatively low, with one of the more important items being forming a relationship with the various artists. Through their industry contacts (Cam's father, Anna's cousin), they felt that they could develop a client list relatively easily. A second major barrier would be to obtain the up-front cash necessary to promote the tour properly.

Since their friendship had started many years ago as they were trying to get front row seats, they decided to name their business Front Row Entertainment. With their first big decision made, it was time to get to work.

Required:

1. Discuss some of the typical business activities (financing, investing, and operating) that a business like Front Row Entertainment is likely to have. (*Hint*: You may want to perform an Internet search for concert promoters to obtain a better understanding of the industry.) Be sure to list some of the specific account names for assets, liabilities, stockholders' equity, revenues, and expenses that may arise from these activities.

2. Explain the advantages and disadvantages of the forms of business organization that Cam and Anna might choose for Front Row Entertainment. Which form would you recommend?

3. Cam and Anna will need to prepare financial statements to report company performance. What type of information does each financial statement provide? Be sure to describe the insights that each financial statement provides to users.

2

The Accounting Information System

Doug Norman Crystals/Alamy

After studying Chapter 2, you should be able to:

1. Describe the qualitative characteristics, assumptions, and principles that underlie accounting.

2. Explain the relationships among economic events, transactions, and the expanded accounting equation.

3. Analyze the effect of business transactions on the accounting equation.

4. Discuss the role of accounts and how debits and credits are used in the double-entry accounting system.

5. Prepare journal entries for transactions.

6. Explain why transactions are posted to the general ledger.

7. Prepare a trial balance and explain its purpose.

Clynt Garnham Renewable Energy/Alamy

EXPERIENCE FINANCIAL ACCOUNTING

with General Electric

Tracing its roots back to Thomas Edison, the **General Electric Company (GE)** has become one of the largest and most diversified companies in the world, with customers in over 100 countries and more than 300,000 employees worldwide. GE is comprised of five businesses:

- **NBC Universal**—one of the world's leading media and entertainment companies that provides network television services, produces television programs and movies, and operates theme parks.

- Technology Infrastructure—provides essential technologies in the aviation, transportation, enterprise solutions, and healthcare markets. Products include aircraft engines, power generation systems, energy technologies (such as solar and nuclear), water treatment facilities, and medical technologies such as x-rays, MRIs, and patient-monitoring systems.

- Energy—focuses on the development, implementation, and improvement of products and technologies that harness energy resources.

- **GE Capital**—provides financial products and services to consumers and commercial businesses around the world. Products include business loans and leases, as well as home and personal loans, credit cards, and insurance.

- Home & Business Solutions—sells and services consumer products such as home appliances, telephones, and residential water systems as well as industrial products such as switchgear and circuit breakers.

With so many different activities throughout the world, GE faces a difficult task in measuring and reporting its many business activities.

Companies like GE rely on comprehensive accounting systems to capture, record, and report their various business activities. While the type of system depends on many factors such as the company's size and the volume of transactions it processes, most companies will use computerized accounting systems to efficiently provide information that is needed by the users of its financial statements. While GE invests heavily in its accounting system, it recognizes that no system is foolproof. Therefore, financial accounting systems should be based on several key principles, including rigorous oversight by management and dedication to a system of internal controls that are designed to ensure the accuracy and reliability of the accounting records. With such a major emphasis on its accounting system, users of GE's financial statements can feel confident that GE's business activities were recorded and reported properly. In short, it is GE's accounting system that brings "light" to GE's varied business activities.

OBJECTIVE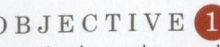
Describe the qualitative characteristics, assumptions, and principles that underlie accounting.

FUNDAMENTAL ACCOUNTING CONCEPTS

In the previous chapter, we described the typical business activities in which companies engage and how accounting systems report these activities through the financial statements. It's also important to understand the underlying concepts behind accounting systems. This chapter will discuss those concepts as well as the procedures that companies use to record information about business activities and how this information ultimately is transformed into financial statements. That is, you will see where the numbers on the financial statements actually come from. An understanding of these procedures is essential if you are to be an effective user of financial statements. As you review the financial statements, you are assessing a company's performance, cash flows, and financial position. To make those assessments, you need to be able to infer the actions of a company from what you see in the financial statements. That inference depends on your understanding of how companies transform the results of their activities into financial statements.

These transforming procedures are called the **accounting cycle**. The accounting cycle is a simple and orderly process, based on a series of steps and conventions. If the financial statements are to present fairly the effects of the company's activities, proper operation of the accounting cycle is essential. For example, if General Electric failed to properly apply accounting procedures, it is likely that many of its business activities would be improperly recorded (if they were even recorded at all) and its financial statements would be seriously misstated.

In this chapter, we will begin the discussion of the accounting cycle and how the completion of each step of the accounting cycle moves the accounting system toward its end product—the financial statements. We will address the following questions:

- What concepts and assumptions underlie accounting information?
- How do companies record business activities?
- What procedures are involved in transforming information about business activities into financial statements?
- How do business activities affect the financial statements?

The Conceptual Framework

IFRS

The conceptual framework is the result of a joint effort of the IASB and the FASB.

Generally accepted accounting principles rest on a conceptual framework of accounting. This framework flows logically from the fundamental objective of financial reporting: to provide information that is useful in making investment and credit decisions. The conceptual framework is designed to support the development of a consistent set of accounting standards and provide a consistent body of thought for financial reporting. An understanding of the conceptual framework should help you in understanding complex accounting standards by providing a logical structure to financial accounting; in other words, the concepts help to explain "why" accountants adopt certain practices. Exhibit 2-1 summarizes the characteristics of useful information as well as the underlying assumptions and principles that make up the conceptual framework and serve as the foundation of GAAP.

Qualitative Characteristics of Useful Information

Given the overall objective of providing useful information, the FASB has identified two fundamental characteristics that useful information should possess—relevance and faithful representation. The application of these criteria determines which economic events should be shown in the financial statements and how best to record these events.

- **Relevance**: Information is relevant if it is capable of making a difference in a business decision by helping users predict future events (*predictive value*) or providing feedback about prior expectations (*confirmatory value*). If the omission or misstatement of information could influence a decision, the information is said to be *material*. Therefore, materiality is also an aspect of relevance.
- **Faithful representation**: Accounting information should be a faithful representation of the real-world economic event that it is intending to portray. Faithfully represented information should be complete (includes all necessary information for the user to understand the economic event), neutral (unbiased), and free from error (as accurate as possible).

The Conceptual Framework

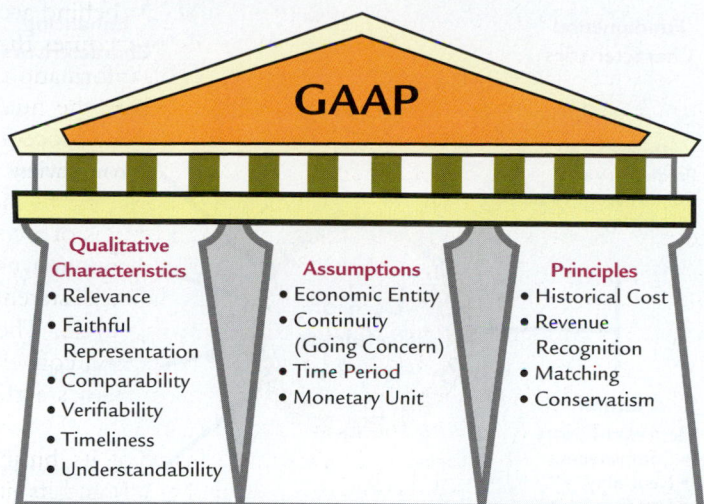

GAAP

Qualitative Characteristics
- Relevance
- Faithful Representation
- Comparability
- Verifiability
- Timeliness
- Understandability

Assumptions
- Economic Entity
- Continuity (Going Concern)
- Time Period
- Monetary Unit

Principles
- Historical Cost
- Revenue Recognition
- Matching
- Conservatism

In applying these fundamental characteristics, the usual process is to identify the most relevant information and then determine if it can be faithfully represented. If so, the fundamental qualitative characteristics have been satisfied. If not, the process should be repeated with the next most relevant type of information.

In addition to the fundamental characteristics, four enhancing characteristics—comparability, verifiability, timeliness, and understandability—have been identified. These enhancing characteristics are considered complementary to the fundamental characteristics, and their presence should help determine the degree of the information's usefulness.

- **Comparability**: Comparable information allows external users to identify similarities and differences between two or more items. Information is useful when it can be compared with similar information about other companies or with similar information about the same company for a different time period. Included within comparability is consistency. **Consistency** can be achieved by a company applying the same accounting principles for the same items over time. Consistency can also be achieved by multiple companies using the same accounting principles in a single time period. Comparability should be viewed as the goal while consistency helps to achieve that goal.
- **Verifiability**: Information is verifiable when independent parties can reach a consensus on the measurement of the activity. When multiple independent observers can reach a general consensus, there is an implication that the information faithfully represents the economic event being measured.
- **Timeliness**: Information is timely if it is available to users before it loses its ability to influence decisions.
- **Understandability**: If users who have a reasonable knowledge of accounting and business can, with reasonable study effort, comprehend the meaning of the information, it is considered understandable.

Enhancing characteristics should be maximized to the extent possible.

These qualitative characteristics are bound by one pervasive constraint—the **cost constraint**. The cost constraint states that the benefit received from accounting information should be greater than the cost of providing that information. If the cost exceeds the benefit, the information is not considered useful. Exhibit 2-2 (p. 56) illustrates the qualitative characteristics of useful financial information.

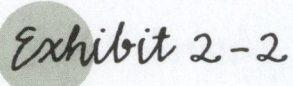

Qualitative Characteristics of Accounting Information

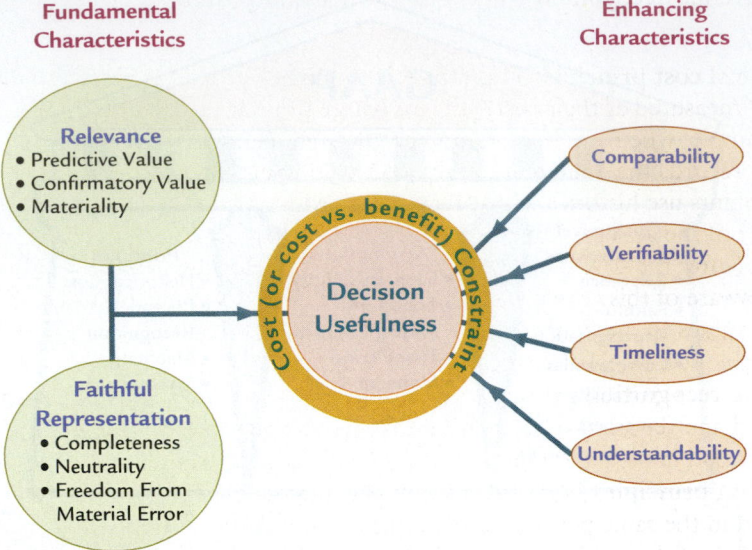

Trade-offs are often necessary in evaluating these criteria. For example, the most relevant information may not be able to be faithfully represented. Similarly, changing economic situations may require a change in the accounting principle used. Such a change may decrease the comparability of the information presented. In these situations, the accountant must exercise judgment in determining the accounting principles that would produce the most useful information for the decision-maker. In all situations, accountants should follow a **full disclosure** policy. That is, any information that would make a difference to financial statement users should be revealed.

Assumptions

The following four basic assumptions underlie accounting:

- **Economic entity assumption**: Under this assumption, each company is accounted for separately from its owners. Steve Jobs' personal transactions, for instance, are not recorded in **Apple**'s financial statements.
- **Continuity** (or **going-concern**) **assumption**: This assumption assumes that a company will continue to operate long enough to carry out its existing commitments. Without this assumption, many of our accounting procedures could not be followed. For example, if **GE** were expected to go bankrupt in the near future, its assets and liabilities would be reported on the balance sheet at an amount the company expects to receive if sold (less any costs of disposal).
- **Time period assumption**: This assumption allows the life of a company to be divided into artificial time periods so net income can be measured for a specific period of time (e.g., monthly, quarterly, annually). Without this assumption, a company's income could only be reported at the end of its life.
- **Monetary unit assumption**: This assumption requires that a company account for and report its financial results in monetary terms (such as U.S. dollar, euro, Japanese yen). This assumption implies that certain nonmonetary items (such as brand loyalty, customer satisfaction) are not reported in a company's financial statements since they can't be measured in monetary terms.

Companies assume they are going concerns. Wouldn't the valuation of a company's assets be more relevant if this assumption were relaxed and the net assets valued at their current selling costs?

Answer: Current selling costs are only relevant if the company intends to sell the assets in the near term. However, many assets (such as machinery, buildings) are used over long periods of time, and in these situations, the use of current selling prices would be of little value to financial statement users. In addition, the cost of obtaining current values for these assets would greatly outweigh the benefits received.

Principles

Principles are general approaches that are used in the measurement and recording of business activities. The four basic principles of accounting are: the historical cost principle, the revenue recognition principle, the matching principle, and the conservatism principle.

- **Historical cost principle**: This principle requires that the activities of a company are initially measured at their cost—the exchange price at the time the activity occurs. For example, when **GE** buys equipment used in manufacturing its products, it initially records the equipment at the cost paid to acquire the equipment. Accountants use historical cost because it provides an objective and verifiable measure of the activity. However, the historical cost principle has been criticized because, after the date of acquisition, it does not reflect changes in market value. The FASB, aware of this criticism, has increasingly been developing standards that use market values to measure certain assets and liabilities (such as investments in marketable securities) after the date of acquisition.
- **Revenue recognition principle**: This principle is used to determine when revenue is recorded and reported. Under this principle, revenue is to be recognized or recorded in the period in which it is earned and the collection of cash is reasonably assured.
- **Matching principle**: This principle requires that an expense be recorded and reported in the same period as the revenue that it helped generate. Together, the application of the revenue recognition and matching principles determine a company's net income. These two principles will be discussed in more detail in Chapter 3.
- **Conservatism principle**: This principle states that accountants should take care to avoid overstating assets or income when they prepare financial statements. The idea behind this principle is that conservatism is a prudent reaction to uncertainty and offsets management's natural optimism about the company's future prospects. However, conservatism should not lead to biased financial information nor should it ever be used to justify the deliberate understatement of assets or income.

The application of these qualitative characteristics, assumptions, and principles is illustrated in **CORNERSTONE 2-1**.

 **CORNERSTONE 2-1**   **Applying the Conceptual Framework**

Concept:
The conceptual framework provides a logical structure and direction to financial accounting and reporting and supports the development of a consistent set of accounting standards.

Information:
Mario is faced with the following questions as he prepares the financial statements of DK Company:

1. Should the purchase of inventory be valued at what DK paid to acquire the inventory or at its estimated selling price?
2. Should information be provided that financial statement users might find helpful in predicting the DK's future income?
3. Faced with a choice between two equally acceptable estimates, should Mario choose the one that results in the higher or the lower amount for net income?
4. Although DK is profitable, should the financial statements be prepared under the assumption that DK will go bankrupt?

(Continued)

5. Should DK's inventory be reported in terms of the number of units on hand or the dollar value of those units?
6. Should equipment leased on a long-term basis be reported as an asset (the economic substance of the transaction) or should it be reported as a rental (the form of the transaction)?
7. Should DK recognize revenue from the sale of its products when the sale is made or when the cash is received?
8. Should DK record the purchase of a vacation home by one of its shareholders?
9. Should DK report income annually to its shareholders, or should it wait until all transactions are complete?
10. Should DK report salary expense in the period that the employees actually worked or when the employees are paid?

Required:

Which qualitative characteristic, assumption, or principle should Mario use in resolving the situation?

Solution:

1. *Historical cost:* The activities of a company (such as purchase of inventory) should be initially measured at the exchange price at the time the activity occurs.
2. *Relevance:* Material information that has predictive or confirmatory value should be provided.
3. *Conservatism:* When faced with a choice, accountants should avoid overstating assets or income.
4. *Continuity (going-concern):* In the absence of information to the contrary, it should be assumed that a company will continue to operate indefinitely.
5. *Monetary unit:* A company should account for and report its financial results in monetary terms.
6. *Faithful representation:* Information should portray the economic event that it is intending to portray completely, accurately, and without bias.
7. *Revenue recognition:* Revenue should be recognized when it is earned and the collection of cash is reasonably assured.
8. *Economic entity:* A company's transactions should be accounted for separately from its owners.
9. *Time period:* The life of a company can be divided into artificial time periods so that income can be measured and reported periodically to interested parties.
10. *Matching:* Expenses should be recorded and reported in the same period as the revenue it helped generate.

Given this conceptual foundation, we will now turn our attention to the process of recording information about business activities in the accounting system.

OBJECTIVE ➋
Explain the relationships among economic events, transactions, and the expanded accounting equation.

MEASURING BUSINESS ACTIVITIES: THE ACCOUNTING CYCLE

The sequence of procedures used by companies to transform the effects of business activities into financial statements is called the accounting cycle. The accounting cycle is shown in Exhibit 2-3.

The steps in the accounting cycle are performed each period and then repeated. Steps 1 through 4 are performed regularly each period as business activities occur. We will discuss these four steps in this chapter. Steps 5 through 7 are performed at the end of a period and are discussed in Chapter 3.

Economic Events

As we discussed in Chapter 1, a company engages in numerous activities that can be categorized as financing, investing, or operating activities. Each of these activities consists of different **events** that affect the company. Some of these events are *external* and result from exchanges between the company and another entity outside of the company. For example, when **GE** issues common stock to investors, purchases equipment used to make an aircraft engine, sells a home appliance at a local retail store, or pays its

Exhibit 2-3

The Accounting Cycle

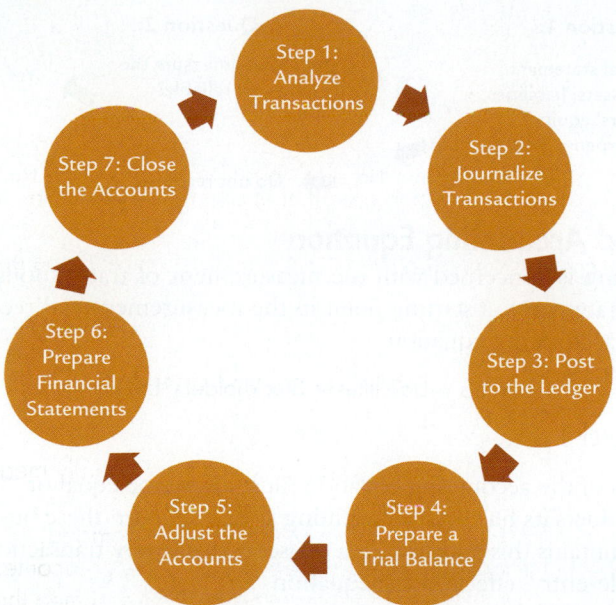

employees a salary, it is engaging in an exchange with another entity. Other events are *internal* and result from the company's own actions. When GE uses equipment to make its products, no other entity is involved; however, the event still has an impact on the company.

Accounting measures the effects of events that influence a company and incorporates these events into the accounting system which, ultimately, produces the financial statements. However, not every event that affects a company is recorded in the accounting records. In order for an event to be recorded, or recognized, in the accounting system, the items making up the event must impact a financial statement element (asset, liability, stockholders' equity, revenue, or expense) and should be a faithful representation of the event.

The first requirement usually is met when at least one party to a contract performs its responsibility according to the contract. For example, assume a buyer and seller agree upon the delivery of an asset and sign a contract. The signing of the contract usually is not recorded in the accounting system because neither party has performed its responsibility. Instead, recognition typically will occur once the buyer receives the asset or pays the seller, whichever comes first.

Even if the event impacts a financial statement element, a faithful representation of the event must be possible if it is to be recorded. A sudden increase in the price of oil or natural gas, for instance, may have an effect on GE's ability to sell its oil and natural gas compressors and turbines. However, the effects of this price increase cannot be faithfully represented, and the event will not be recognized in the financial statements. Providing a measurement that is complete, unbiased, and free from error is important in accounting to avoid misleading users of financial statements. A decision-maker would find it extremely difficult, if not impossible, to use financial statements that include amounts that failed to faithfully represent what has actually occurred. It is very important to pay attention to the recognition criteria as you consider an event for inclusion in the accounting system.

An accounting transaction results from an economic event that causes one of the elements of the financial statements (assets, liabilities, stockholders' equity, revenues, or expenses) to change and that can be faithfully represented. We will use the term **transaction** to refer to any event, external or internal, that is recognized in the financial statements. The process of identifying events to be recorded in the financial statements is illustrated in Exhibit 2-4 (p.60).

Exhibit 2-4

Transaction Identification

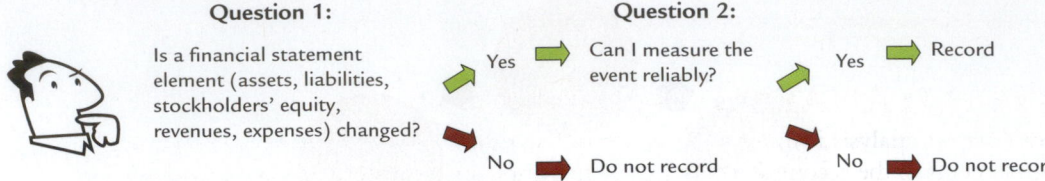

Question 1:

Is a financial statement element (assets, liabilities, stockholders' equity, revenues, expenses) changed? — Yes → Can I measure the event reliably? — Yes → Record

No → Do not record   No → Do not record

The Expanded Accounting Equation

Because accounting is concerned with the measurement of transactions and their effect on the financial statements, a starting point in the measurement and recording process is the fundamental accounting equation:

$$\text{Assets} = \text{Liabilities} + \text{Stockholders' Equity}$$

Recall from Chapter 1 that:

- The two sides of the accounting equation must always be equal or "in balance" as a company conducts its business. Accounting systems record these business activities in a way that maintains this equality. As a consequence, every transaction has a two-part, or double-entry, effect on the equation.
- The balance sheet and the income statement are related through retained earnings. Specifically net income (revenues minus expenses) increases retained earnings. Given this relationship, the fundamental accounting equation can be rewritten to show the elements that make up stockholders' equity.

With the expanded accounting equation shown in Exhibit 2-5, we are now ready to analyze how transactions affect a company's financial statements.

Exhibit 2-5

The Expanded Accounting Equation

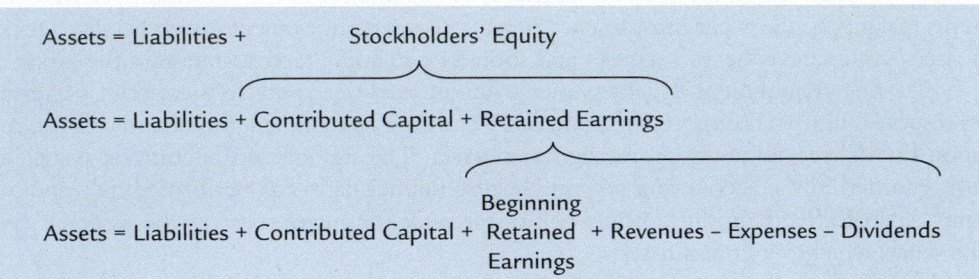

Assets = Liabilities + Stockholders' Equity

Assets = Liabilities + Contributed Capital + Retained Earnings

Assets = Liabilities + Contributed Capital + Beginning Retained Earnings + Revenues – Expenses – Dividends

YOU◆DECIDE   Recognition of Economic Events

As you are analyzing the most recent financial statements of Big Oil (B&O) Company, you question if the company properly recorded an economic event. You know that B&O owns and operates several off-shore oil drilling platforms in the Gulf of Mexico. You also recall from news reports that a hurricane severely damaged two of the platforms, leading to a significant loss in revenue while the platforms were inactive. While you see evidence in the financial statements of the damage and repair to the platforms, you cannot find any evidence of the lost revenue in the financial statements.

Does the loss in revenue from the damaged oil platforms qualify for recognition in the financial statements?

To be recognized in the financial statements, the event must impact a financial statement element and be faithfully represented. While B&O may have been able to measure the loss in revenue, no financial statement element has been affected. While you may argue that this event affected revenue, revenue is an increase in assets resulting from the sale of products. Because the lost sales did not result in an inflow of

(Continued)

assets, it is not considered revenue. In addition, expenses are defined as the cost of resources used to earn revenues. The lost revenue does not represent a use of resources and is therefore not an expense. Therefore the lost revenue cannot be recognized in the financial statements.

Recognition of events in the financial statements requires analysis of whether the event impacted a financial statement element and can be faithfully represented.

STEP 1: ANALYZE TRANSACTIONS

Transaction analysis is the process of determining the economic effects of a transaction on the elements of the accounting equation. Transaction analysis usually begins with the gathering of *source documents* that describe business activities. Source documents can be internally or externally prepared and include items such as purchase orders, cash register tapes, and invoices that describe the transaction and monetary amounts involved. These documents are the beginning of a "trail" of evidence that a transaction was processed by the accounting system.

After gathering the source documents, accountants must analyze these business activities to determine which transactions meet the criteria for recognition in the accounting records. Once it is determined that a transaction should be recorded in the accounting system, the transaction must be analyzed to determine how it will affect the accounting equation. In performing transaction analysis, it is important to remember that the accounting equation must always remain in balance. Therefore, each transaction will have at least two effects on the accounting equation.

In summary, transaction analysis involves the following three steps:

- *Step 1: Write down the accounting equation.* In this chapter, we often use an expanded version of the accounting equation because it provides more information in the analysis. However, the basic accounting equation could also be used.
- *Step 2: Identify the financial statement elements that are affected by the transaction.*
- *Step 3: Determine whether the elements increased or decreased.*

CORNERSTONE 2-2 illustrates the basic process of transaction analysis.

O B J E C T I V E

Analyze the effect of business transactions on the accounting equation.

CORNERSTONE 2-2   Performing Transaction Analysis

Concept:
The economic effect of a transaction will have a two-part, or dual, effect on the accounting equation that results in the equation remaining in balance.

Information:
Luigi Inc. purchases a $3,000 computer from WorstBuy Electronics on credit, with payment due in 60 days.

Required:
Determine the effect of the transaction on the elements on the accounting equation.

Solution:
A computer is an economic resource, or asset, that will be used by Luigi in its business. The purchase of the computer increased assets and also created an obligation, or liability, for Luigi. Therefore, the effect of the transaction on the accounting equation is as follows:

Assets	=	Liabilities	+	Stockholders' Equity	
				Contributed Capital	Retained Earnings
+$3,000		+$3,000			

Note that the transaction analysis in Cornerstone 2-2 conformed to the two underlying principles of transaction analysis:

- There was a dual effect on the accounting equation
- The accounting equation remained in balance after the transaction

All transactions can be analyzed using a similar process.

To provide a further illustration of the effect of transactions on the accounting equation, consider the case of HiTech Communications Inc. HiTech is a newly formed corporation that operates an advertising agency that specializes in promoting computer-related products in the Cincinnati area. We show the effects of thirteen transactions on HiTech's financial position during its first month of operations, March 2011.

Transaction 1: Issuing Common Stock

On March 1, HiTech sold 1,000 shares of common stock to several investors for cash of $12,000. The effect of this transaction on the accounting equation is:

Assets	=	Liabilities	+	Stockholders' Equity	
				Contributed Capital	Retained Earnings
+$12,000				+$12,000	

The sale of stock increases assets, specifically cash, and also increases stockholders' equity (contributed capital or common stock). Notice that there is a dual effect, and although both assets and equity change, the equality of the equation is maintained. The issuance of stock would be considered a financing activity.

Transaction 2: Borrowing Cash

On March 2, HiTech raised additional funds by borrowing $3,000 from First Third Bank of Cincinnati. HiTech promised to pay the amount borrowed plus 8 percent interest to First Third Bank in one year. The financial effect of this transaction is:

Assets	=	Liabilities	+	Stockholders' Equity	
				Contributed Capital	Retained Earnings
+$3,000		+$3,000			

This borrowing has two effects: the asset cash is increased and a liability is created. HiTech has an obligation to repay the cash borrowed according to the terms of the borrowing. Such a liability is termed a note payable. Because this transaction is concerned with obtaining funds to begin and operate a business, it is classified as a financing activity.

Transaction 3: Purchase of Equipment for Cash

On March 3, HiTech purchased office equipment (such as computer equipment) from MicroCenter Inc. for $4,500 in cash. The effect of this transaction on the accounting equation is:

Assets	=	Liabilities	+	Stockholders' Equity	
				Contributed Capital	Retained Earnings
+$4,500					
−$4,500					

There is a reduction in cash (an asset) as it is spent and a corresponding increase in another asset, equipment. The purchased equipment is an asset because HiTech will use it to generate future revenue. Notice that this transaction merely converts one asset (cash) into another (equipment). Total assets remain unchanged and the accounting equation remains in balance. Because transaction 3 is concerned with buying long-term assets that enable HiTech to operate, it is considered an investing activity.

Transaction 4: Purchasing Insurance

On March 4, HiTech purchased a six-month insurance policy for $1,200 cash. The effect of this transaction on the accounting equation is:

Assets	=	Liabilities	+	Stockholders' Equity	
				Contributed Capital	Retained Earnings
+$1,200					
−$1,200					

There is a reduction in cash (an asset) as it is spent and a corresponding increase in another asset, prepaid insurance. The purchased insurance is an asset because the insurance will benefit more than one accounting period. This type of asset is often referred to as a prepaid asset. Notice that like transaction 3, this transaction merely converts one asset (cash) into another (prepaid insurance). Total assets remain unchanged and the accounting equation remains in balance. Because transaction 4 is concerned with the operations of the company, it is classified as an operating activity.

Transaction 5: Purchase of Supplies on Credit

On March 6, HiTech purchased office supplies from Hamilton Office Supply for $6,500. Hamilton Office Supply agreed to accept full payment in 30 days. As a result of this transaction, HiTech received an asset (supplies) but also incurred a liability to pay for these supplies in 30 days. The financial effect of this transaction is:

Assets	=	Liabilities	+	Stockholders' Equity	
				Contributed Capital	Retained Earnings
+$6,500		+$6,500			

A transaction where goods are purchased on credit is often referred to as a purchase "on account" and the liability that is created is referred to as an account payable. Because transaction 5 is concerned with the operations of the company, it is classified as an operating activity.

Transaction 6: Sale of Services for Cash

On March 10, HiTech sold advertising services to Miami Valley Products in exchange for $8,800 in cash. Remember from Chapter 1 that revenue is defined as an increase in assets resulting from the sale of products or services. As an advertising company, the sale of advertising services is HiTech's primary revenue-producing activity. Therefore, this transaction results in an increase in assets (cash) and an increase in revenue.

Assets	=	Liabilities	+	Stockholders' Equity	
				Contributed Capital	Retained Earnings
+$8,800					+$8,800

As shown in the expanded accounting equation discussed earlier, *revenues increase retained earnings*. The dual effects (the increase in assets and the increase in retained earnings) maintain the balance of the accounting equation. Because transaction 6 is concerned with the operations of the company, it is classified as an operating activity.

Transaction 7: Sale of Services for Credit

On March 15, HiTech sold advertising services to the *Cincinnati Enquirer* for $3,300. HiTech agreed to accept full payment in 30 days. When a company performs services for which they will be paid at a later date, this is often referred to as a sale "on account." Instead of receiving cash, HiTech received a promise to pay from the *Cincinnati Enquirer*. This right to collect amounts due from customers creates an asset called an account receivable. Similar to the cash sale in transaction 6, the credit sale represents revenue for HiTech because assets (accounts receivable) were increased as a result of the sale of the advertising service. The financial effect of this transaction is:

Assets	=	Liabilities	+	Stockholders' Equity	
				Contributed Capital	Retained Earnings
+$3,300					+$3,300

Consistent with the revenue recognition principle, *revenue is recorded when earned* (for example, the service is provided) and the collection of cash is reasonably assured, not when the cash is actually received. Because transaction 7 is concerned with the operations of the company, it is classified as an operating activity.

Transaction 8: Receipt of Cash in Advance

On March 19, HiTech received $9,000 from the *OA News* for advertising services to be completed in the next three months. Similar to transaction 6, HiTech received cash for services. However, due to the revenue recognition principle, HiTech cannot recognize revenue until it has performed the advertising service. Therefore, the receipt of cash creates a liability for HiTech for the work that is due in the future. The effect of this transaction on the accounting equation is:

Assets	=	Liabilities	+	Stockholders' Equity	
				Contributed Capital	Retained Earnings
+$9,000		+$9,000			

The liability that is created by the receipt of cash in advance of performing the revenue-generating activities is called an unearned revenue. Because transaction 8 is concerned with the operations of the company, it is classified as an operating activity.

Transaction 9: Payment of a Liability

On March 23, HiTech pays $6,000 cash for the supplies previously purchased from Hamilton Office Supply on credit (transaction 5). The payment results in a reduction of an asset (cash) and the settlement of HiTech's obligation (liability) to Hamilton Office Supply. The financial effect of this transaction is:

Assets	=	Liabilities	+	Stockholders' Equity	
				Contributed Capital	Retained Earnings
−$6,000		−$6,000			

As a result of this cash payment, the liability "Accounts Payable" is reduced to $500 ($6,500 − $6,000). This means that HiTech still owes Hamilton Office Supply $500. Notice that the payment of cash did not result in an expense. The expense related to supplies will be recorded as supplies are used. Because Transaction 9 is concerned with the operations of the company, it is classified as an operating activity.

Transaction 10: Payment of Salaries

On March 26 (a Friday), HiTech paid weekly employee salaries of $1,800. Remember from Chapter 1 that an expense is the cost of an asset consumed in the operation of the business.

Because an asset (cash) is consumed as part of HiTech's normal operations, salaries are an expense. As shown in the expanded accounting equation discussed earlier, *expenses decrease retained earnings*. The effect of this transaction on the accounting equation is:

Assets	=	Liabilities		Stockholders' Equity	
				Contributed Capital	Retained Earnings
−$1,800					−$1,800

Consistent with the matching principle, *expenses are recorded in the same period as the revenue that it helped generate*. Because transaction *10* is concerned with the operations of the company, it is classified as an operating activity.

Transaction 11: Collection of a Receivable

On March 29, HiTech collected $3,000 cash from the *Cincinnati Enquirer* for services sold earlier on credit (transaction *7*). The collection of cash increases assets. In addition, the accounts receivable (an asset) from the *Cincinnati Enquirer* is also reduced. The financial effect of this transaction is:

Assets	=	Liabilities	+	Stockholders' Equity	
				Contributed Capital	Retained Earnings
+$3,000					
−$3,000					

As a result of this cash payment, the *Cincinnati Enquirer* still owes HiTech $300. Notice that the cash collection did not result in the recognition of a revenue. The revenue was recognized as the service was performed (transaction *7*). Because transaction *11* is concerned with the operations of the company, it is classified as an operating activity.

Transaction 12: Payment of Utilities

On March 30, HiTech paid its utility bill of $5,200 for March. Because an asset (cash) is consumed by HiTech as part of the operations of the business, the cost of utilities used during the month is an expense. The effect of this transaction on the accounting equation is:

Assets	=	Liabilities	+	Stockholders' Equity	
				Contributed Capital	Retained Earnings
−$5,200					−$5,200

Similar to the payment of salaries, utility expense is recorded as a decrease in retained earnings in the same period that it helped to generate revenue. Because transaction *12* is concerned with the operations of the company, it is classified as an operating activity.

Transaction 13: Payment of a Dividend

On March 31, HiTech declared and paid a cash dividend of $500 to its stockholders. Dividends are not an expense. Dividends are a distribution of net income and are recorded as a direct reduction of retained earnings. The effect of this transaction on the accounting equation is:

Assets	=	Liabilities	+	Stockholders' Equity	
				Contributed Capital	Retained Earnings
−$500					−$500

The payment of a dividend is classified as a financing activity.

Overview of Transactions for HiTech Communications Inc.

Exhibit 2-6 summarizes HiTech's transactions in order to show their cumulative effect on the accounting equation. The transaction number is shown in the first column on the left. Revenue and expense items are identified on the right. Notice that this summary reinforces the two key principles discussed earlier:

- Each transaction has a dual effect on the elements of the accounting equation.
- The accounting equation always remains in balance—the total change in assets ($29,100) equals the change in liabilities plus stockholders' equity ($29,100).

 *Exhibit 2-6*

Summary of Transactions for HiTech Communications Inc.

	Assets	=	Liabilities +	Stockholders' Equity	
				Contributed Capital	Retained Earnings
(1)	+ $12,000			+ $12,000	
(2)	+ $3,000		+ $3,000		
(3)	+ $4,500				
	– $4,500				
(4)	+ $1,200				
	– $1,200				
(5)	+ $6,500		+ $6,500		
(6)	+ $8,800				+ $8,800 } Revenue
(7)	+ $3,300				+ $3,300 }
(8)	+ $9,000		+ $9,000		
(9)	– $6,000		– $6,000		
(10)	– $1,800				– $1,800 }
(11)	+ $3,000				} Expense
	– $3,000				}
(12)	– $5,200				– $5,200 }
(13)	– $500				– $500 Dividend
	$29,100		$12,500	$12,000	$4,600

$29,100 = $29,100

Transaction analysis can be used to answer many important questions about a company and its activities. Using the information in Exhibit 2-6, we can answer the following questions:

- *What are the amounts of total assets, total liabilities, and total equity at the end of March?* At the end of March, HiTech has total assets of $29,100, total liabilities of $12,500, and total equity of $16,600 ($12,000 of contributed capital plus $4,600 of retained earnings). These amounts for assets, liabilities, and stockholders' equity at the end of March would be carried over as the beginning amounts for April.
- *What is net income for the month?* Net income is $5,100, which represents the excess of revenues of $12,100 ($8,800 + $3,300) over expenses of $7,000 ($5,200 + $1,800). Notice that dividends are not included in income; instead they are included on the retained earnings statement.
- *How much cash was received during the month? How much was spent? How much cash does HiTech have at the end of the month?* During March HiTech received a total of $35,800 in cash ($12,000 + $3,000 + $8,800 + $9,000 + $3,000) and spent a total of $19,200 ($4,500 + $1,200 + $6,000 + $1,800 + $5,200 + $500). At the end of the month, HiTech had cash on hand of $16,600 ($35,800 – $19,200).

The summary in Exhibit 2-6 can become quite cumbersome. For example, in order to determine the amount of cash that HiTech has at the end of the month, you may find it necessary to refer back to the actual transactions to determine which ones involved cash and which did not. In addition, what if an investor or creditor wanted to know not only net income but also the types of expenses that HiTech incurred? (For example, what was the dollar amount spent for salaries?) To answer these questions, more information is needed than the transaction summary provides. For a company like **GE**, a spreadsheet such as the preceding one would prove inadequate to convey its financial information to investors and creditors. A better way to record and track information that is consistent with the preceding model is necessary. The solution is double-entry accounting.

DOUBLE-ENTRY ACCOUNTING

Double-entry accounting describes the system used by companies to record the effects of transactions on the accounting equation. The effects of transactions are recorded in accounts. Under double-entry accounting, each transaction affects at least two accounts. In this section, we will explore accounts and the process by which transactions get reflected in specific accounts.

OBJECTIVE 4

Discuss the role of accounts and how debits and credits are used in the double-entry accounting system.

Accounts

To aid in the recording of transactions, an organizational system consisting of accounts has been developed. An **account** is a record of increases and decreases in each of the basic elements of the financial statements. Each financial statement element is composed of a variety of accounts. All changes in assets, liabilities, stockholders' equity, revenues, or expenses are then recorded in the appropriate account. The list of accounts used by the company is termed a **chart of accounts**.* A typical list of accounts is shown in Exhibit 2-7. These accounts were all discussed in Chapter 1.

Exhibit 2-7

Typical Accounts

Assets	Liabilities	Stockholders' Equity	Revenue	Expense
Cash	Accounts Payable	Common Stock	Sales Revenue	Cost of Goods Sold
Investments	Salaries Payable	Retained Earnings	Interest Income	Salary Expense
Accounts Receivable	Unearned Sales Revenue		Rent Revenue	Rent Expense
Inventory	Interest Payable			Insurance Expense
Land	Income Taxes Payable			Depreciation Expense
Buildings	Notes Payable			Advertising Expense
Equipment	Bonds Payable			Utilities Expense
Patent				Repairs & Maintenance Expense
Copyright				Property Taxes Expense

Every company will have a different chart of accounts depending on the nature of its business activities. However, once a company selects which accounts will be used, all transactions must be recorded into these accounts. As the company engages in transactions, the transaction will either increase or decrease an account. The amount in an account at any time is called the *balance* of the account. For example, the purchase of equipment will increase the balance in the equipment account, whereas the disposal of equipment will decrease the balance of the equipment account. For financial reporting purposes, the balances of related accounts typically are combined and reported as a single amount. For example, **GE** reports a combined, or net, amount of property, plant, and equipment on its balance sheet. However, in its footnotes, GE discloses the amounts of individual accounts such as land, buildings, and machinery.

Although an account can be shown in a variety of ways, transactions are frequently analyzed using a **T-account**. The T-account gets its name because it resembles the capital letter T (see Exhibit 2-8, p. 68). A T-account is a two-column record that consists of an account title and two sides divided by a vertical line—the left and the right side. The left side is referred to as the **debit** side and the right side is referred to as the **credit** side.

Note that the terms debit and credit simply refer to the left and the right side of an account. The left is always the debit side and the right is always the credit side. *Debit and credit do not represent increases or decreases.* (Increases or decreases to accounts are

---

* This textbook uses a simplified and standardized chart of accounts that can be found on the inside cover of the book and on page 107. Account titles for real company financial statements may vary. Common alternate account titles are introduced, as appropriate, when the account is introduced.

Exhibit 2-8

Form of a T-Account

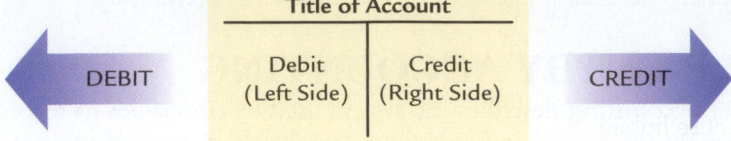

Title of Account	
Debit (Left Side)	Credit (Right Side)

DEBIT ← | → CREDIT

Concept Q&A

On a bank statement, a credit to a person's account means the account has increased. Similarly, a debit means the account has decreased. Why don't credit and debit always mean "add" and "subtract"?

Answer:
From the bank's perspective, a person's account is a liability since the bank must pay cash on demand. Because liabilities have normal credit balances, a credit will increase the account and a debit will decrease the account. However, from an individual's perspective, cash is an asset which has a normal debit balance. Therefore, debits increase cash and credits decrease cash. It is critical to always look at the normal balance of an account before determining if a transaction increases or decreases an account.

discussed in the next section.) Instead, debit and credit simply refer to *where* an entry is made in an account. The terms debit and credit will also be used to refer to the act of entering dollar amounts into an account. For example, entering an amount on the left side of an account will be called debiting the account. Entering an amount on the right side of an account is called crediting the account.

You may be tempted to associate the terms credit and debit with positive or negative events. For example, assume you returned an item that you purchased with a credit card to the local store and the store credited your card. This is generally viewed as a positive event since you now owe less money to the store. Or, if you receive a notice that your bank had debited your account to pay for service charges that you owe, this is viewed negatively because you now have less money in your account. Resist this temptation. In accounting, *debit means the left side of an account and credit means the right side of an account.*

Debit and Credit Procedures

Using the accounting equation, we can incorporate debits and credits in order to determine how balance sheet accounts increase or decrease. There are three steps in determining increases or decreases to a balance sheet account:

- *Step 1: Draw a T-account and label each side of the t-account as either debit (left side) or credit (right side).*
- *Step 2: Determine the normal balance of an account.* All accounts have a **normal balance**. While individual transactions will increase and decrease an account, it would be unusual for an account to have a nonnormal balance.
- *Step 3: Increases or decreases to an account are based on the normal balance of the account.*

This procedure is shown in **CORNERSTONE 2-3**.

CORNERSTONE 2-3   **Determining Increases or Decreases to a Balance Sheet Account**

Concept:
Increases or decreases to an account are based on the normal balance of the account.

Information:
The balance sheet is comprised of three fundamental accounts—assets, liabilities, and stockholders' equity.

(Continued)

Required:
Determine how each of the three balance sheet accounts increases or decreases.

Solution:

- Because assets are located on the left side of the accounting equation, their normal balance is a debit. Therefore, debits will increase assets and credits will decrease assets.
- Because liabilities and stockholders' equity are on the right side of the accounting equation, their normal balance is a credit. Therefore, credits will increase liabilities and stockholders' equity while debits will decrease these accounts.

This is illustrated in the following T-accounts:

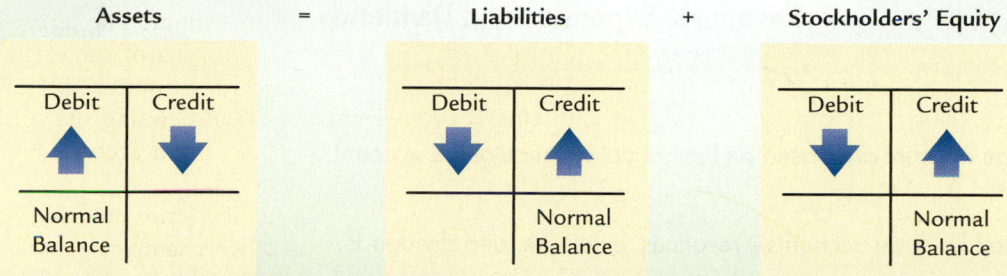

As we illustrated earlier in the chapter, every transaction will increase or decrease the elements of the accounting equation—assets, liabilities, and stockholders' equity. The direction of these increases and decreases must be such that the accounting equation stays in balance—the left side must equal the right side. In other words, *debits must equal credits*. This equality of debits and credits provides the foundation of double-entry accounting in which the two-sided effect of a transaction is recorded in the accounting system.

A similar procedure can be used to determine how increases and decreases are recorded for other financial statement elements. From the expanded accounting equation shown in Exhibit 2-5 (p. 60), we can see that stockholders' equity consists of both contributed capital (such as common stock) and retained earnings. As stockholders' equity accounts, both contributed capital and retained earnings have normal credit balances as shown in Exhibit 2-9. Because these accounts have normal credit balances, they are increased by credits and decreased by debits.

Retained earnings represent a company's accumulated net income (revenues minus expenses) minus any dividends. As we saw from the transaction analysis presented earlier in the chapter:

- Revenues increase retained earnings
- Expenses decrease retained earnings
- Dividends decrease retained earnings

Exhibit 2-9

Normal Balances of Contributed Capital and Retained Earnings

In order to determine increases or decreases in revenues, expenses, and dividends, we can use the following steps:

- *Step 1: Label each side of the t-account as either debit or credit.*
- *Step 2: Determine the normal balance of an account.*
- *Step 3: Increases or decreases to an account are based on the normal balance of the account.*

CORNERSTONE 2-4 demonstrates how increases and decreases in these accounts are recorded.

CORNERSTONE 2-4

Determining Increases or Decreases to Revenues, Expenses, and Dividends

Concept:
Increases or decreases to an account are based on the normal balance of the account.

Information:
Retained earnings is affected by three accounts—revenues, expenses, and dividends.

Required:
Determine how each of these three accounts increases or decreases.

Solution:

- Revenues increase stockholders' equity through retained earnings. Therefore, revenues have a normal credit balance. That means that credits will increase revenues and debits will decrease revenues.
- Expenses decrease stockholders' equity through retained earnings. Therefore, expenses have a normal debit balance. That means that debits will increase expenses and credits will decrease expenses.
- Dividends are defined as a distribution of retained earnings. Because dividends reduce retained earnings and stockholders' equity, dividends have a normal debit balance. That means that debits will increase dividends while credits will decrease dividends.

These procedures are summarized below.

Revenues		Expenses		Dividends	
Debit	Credit	Debit	Credit	Debit	Credit
↓	↑	↑	↓	↑	↓
	Normal Balance	Normal Balance		Normal Balance	

From Cornerstone 2-4, you should notice several items. First, revenues and expenses have opposite effects on retained earnings; therefore, revenues and expenses have opposite normal balances. Second, any change (increase or decrease) in revenue, expense, or dividends effects the balance of stockholders' equity. Specifically,

- an increase in revenue increases stockholders' equity
- a decrease in revenue decreases stockholders' equity
- an increase in expense or dividends decreases stockholders' equity
- a decrease in expense or dividends increases stockholders' equity

Finally, when revenues exceed expenses, a company has reported net income, which increases stockholders' equity. When revenues are less than expenses, a company has reported a net loss, which reduces stockholders' equity. These debit and credit procedures are summarized in Exhibit 2-10.

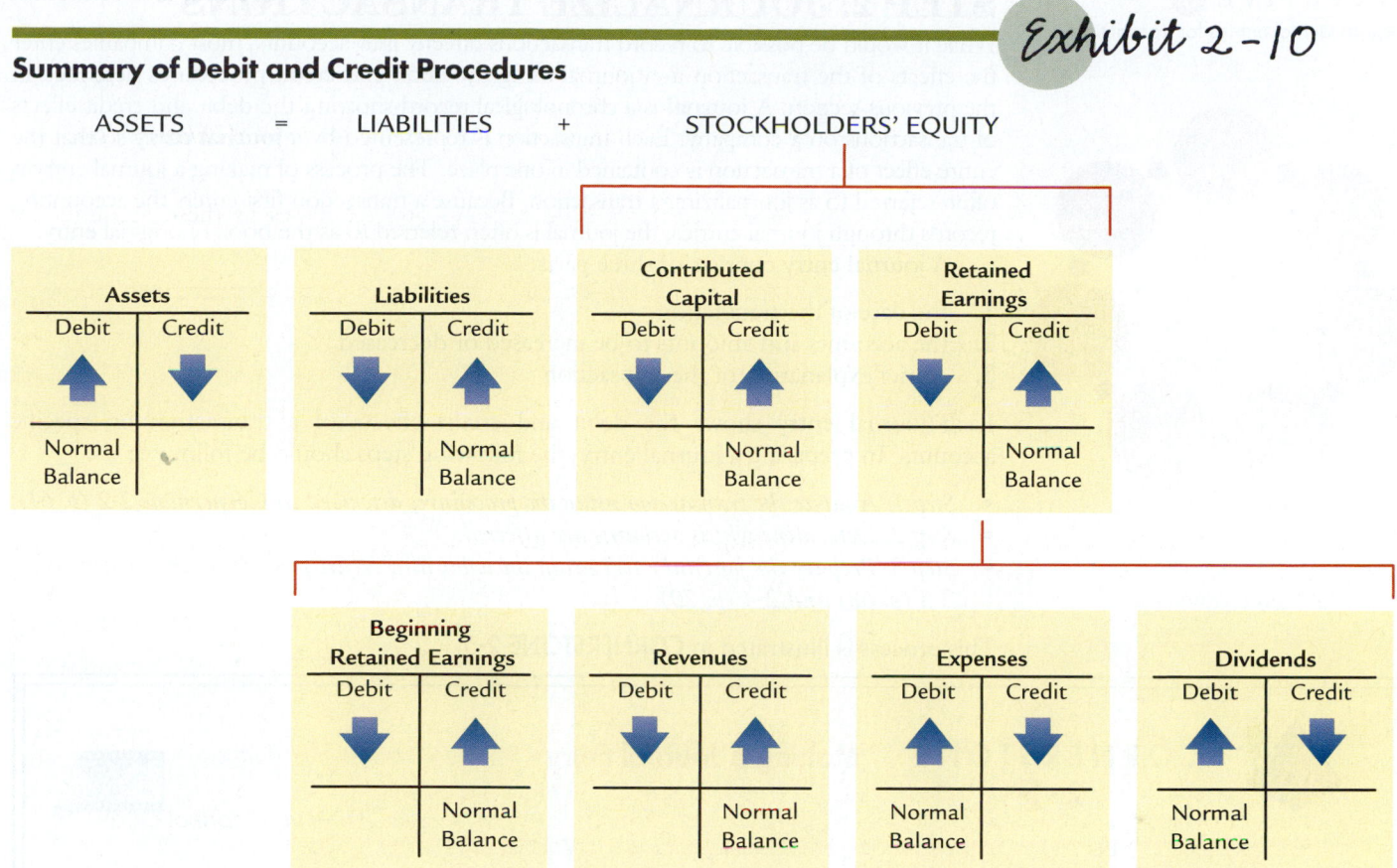

Summary of Debit and Credit Procedures

Exhibit 2-10

The important point from this analysis is that while debits are always on the left and credits are always on the right, the effect of a debit or credit on an account balance depends upon the normal balance of that account.

YOU DECIDE   Inferring Activities from T-accounts

As you examine the accounting records of Newton Inc. you notice that accounts receivable increased from $4,500 to $5,200 during the year and that credit sales were $65,800.

What was the amount of accounts receivable collected?

The primary activities that affect accounts receivable are the sale goods and services on credit (increases in accounts receivable) and the collection of cash related to these credit sales (decreases in accounts receivable). To help visualize the account activity, prepare a T-account as follows:

Accounts Receivable			
Beginning balance	4,500		
Credit sales	65,800	?	Cash collections
Ending balance	5,200		

Because you know the beginning and ending balances of accounts receivable and the amount of credit sales, you can determine the cash collections as:

$$\text{Cash collections} = \$4,500 + \$65,800 - \$5,200 = \mathbf{\$65,100}$$

An understanding of how business activities affect individual accounts can yield valuable insights into the economic events that occurred during a period.

OBJECTIVE 5
Prepare journal entries for transactions.

STEP 2: JOURNALIZE TRANSACTIONS

While it would be possible to record transactions directly into accounts, most companies enter the effects of the transaction in a journal using the debit and credit procedures described in the previous section. A **journal** is a chronological record showing the debit and credit effects of transactions on a company. Each transaction is represented by a **journal entry** so that the entire effect of a transaction is contained in one place. The process of making a journal entry is often referred to as journalizing a transaction. Because a transaction first enters the accounting records through journal entries, the journal is often referred to as the book of original entry.

A journal entry consists of three parts:

1. the date of the transaction
2. the accounts and amounts to be increased or decreased
3. a brief explanation of the transaction

Each journal entry shows the debit and credit effects of a transaction on specific accounts. In preparing a journal entry, the following steps should be followed:

- *Step 1: Analyze the transaction using the procedures described in Cornerstone 2-2 (p. 61).*
- *Step 2: Determine which accounts are affected.*
- *Step 3: Prepare the journal entry using the debit and credit procedures in Cornerstones 2-3 (p. 68) and 2-4 (p. 70).*

This process is illustrated in **CORNERSTONE 2-5**.

 **CORNERSTONE 2-5**   *Making a Journal Entry*

Concept:
A journal entry records the effects of a transaction on accounts using debits and credits.

Information:
On January 1, Luigi Inc. purchases a $3,000 computer from WorstBuy Electronics on credit, with payment due in 60 days.

Required:
Prepare a journal entry to record this transaction.

Solution:
First, analyze the transaction using the procedures described in Cornerstone 2-2 (p. 61):

Assets	=	Liabilities	+	Stockholders' Equity	
				Contributed Capital	Retained Earnings
+$3,000		+$3,000			

The purchase of a computer has increased the asset account "Equipment," which is recorded with a debit. In addition, a liability, "Accounts Payable," was created and the increase in this account is recorded with a credit.

Date	Account and Explanation	Debit	Credit
Jan. 1	Equipment	3,000	
	Accounts Payable		3,000
	(Purchased office equipment on credit)		

From the journal entry in Cornerstone 2-5, notice several items:

- The date of the transaction is entered in the date column
- For each entry in the journal, the debit (the account and amount) is entered first and flush to the left. If there were more than one debit, it would be entered directly

underneath the first debit on the next line. The credit (the account and the amount) is written below the debits and indented to the right. The purpose of this standard format is to make it possible for anyone using the journal to identify debits and credits quickly and correctly.

- *Total debits must equal total credits.*
- An explanation may appear beneath the credit.

In some instances, more than two accounts may be affected by an economic event. For example, assume that Luigi Inc. purchases a $3,000 computer from Worst-Buy Electronics by paying $1,000 cash with the remainder due in 60 days. The purchase of this equipment increased the asset "Equipment," decreased the asset "Cash," and increased the liability "Accounts Payable" as shown in the analysis below:

Assets	=	Liabilities	+	Stockholders' Equity	
				Contributed Capital	Retained Earnings
+$3,000		+$2,000			
−$1,000					

Luigi would make the following journal entry:

Date	Account and Explanation	Debit	Credit
Jan. 1	Equipment	3,000	
	Cash		1,000
	Accounts Payable		2,000
	(Purchased office equipment for cash and on credit)		

This type of entry is called a *compound journal entry* because more than two accounts were affected.

The use of a journal helps prevent the introduction of errors in the recording of business activities. Because all parts of the transaction appear together, it is easy to see whether equal debits and credits have been entered. If debits equal credits for *each* journal entry, then debits equal credits for *all* journal entries. At the end of the period, this fact leads to a useful check on the accuracy of journal entries. However, if the wrong amounts or the wrong accounts are used, debits can still equal credits, yet the journal entries will be incorrect. Additionally, each entry can be examined to see if the accounts that appear together are logically appropriate.

ETHICAL DECISIONS   When an error is discovered in a journal entry, the accountant has an ethical responsibility to correct the error (subject to materiality), even if others would never be able to tell that the error had occurred. For example, if an accountant accidentally records a sale of merchandise by crediting Interest Revenue instead of Sales Revenue, total revenue would be unaffected. However, this error could significantly affect summary performance measures such as gross margin (sales minus cost of goods sold) that are important to many investors. When material errors are discovered, they should be corrected, even if this means embarrassment to the accountant. ●

To provide a further illustration of recording transactions using journal entries, consider the case of HiTech Communications Inc. that was presented earlier in the chapter. For the remainder of the book, we will analyze each transaction and report its effects on the accounting equation in the margin next to the journal entry. Next, we identify the accounts that were affected by incorporating account titles into the transaction analysis model. Finally, we prepare the journal entry based on the analysis. You should always perform these steps as you prepare journal entries.

Concept Q&A

If all journal entries have equal debits and credits, how can mistakes or errors occur?

Answer:
Mistakes or errors could still occur when entire transactions are not recorded, transactions are recorded for the wrong amounts or in the wrong accounts, or transactions are not recorded in the proper accounting period. While journal entries provide a safeguard against errors and mistakes, it will not prevent them all.

Transaction 1: Issuing Common Stock

On March 1, HiTech sold 1,000 shares of common stock to several investors for cash of $12,000.

Assets	= Liabilities +	Stockholders' Equity
+12,000		+12,000

Date	Account and Explanation	Debit	Credit
March 1	Cash	12,000	
	Common Stock		12,000
	(Issued common stock)		

Transaction 2: Borrowing Cash

On March 2, HiTech raised additional funds by borrowing $3,000 on a one-year, 8 percent note payable to First Third Bank of Cincinnati.

Assets	= Liabilities +	Stockholders' Equity
+3,300	+3,300	

Date	Account and Explanation	Debit	Credit
March 2	Cash	3,000	
	Notes Payable		3,000
	(Borrowed cash from bank)		

Transaction 3: Purchase of Equipment for Cash

On March 3, HiTech purchased office equipment (computer equipment) from Micro-Center Inc. for $4,500 in cash.

Assets	= Liabilities +	Stockholders' Equity
+4,500		
−4,500		

Date	Account and Explanation	Debit	Credit
March 3	Equipment	4,500	
	Cash		4,500
	(Purchased equipment)		

Transaction 4: Purchasing Insurance

On March 4, HiTech purchased a six-month insurance policy for $1,200 in cash.

Assets	= Liabilities +	Stockholders' Equity
+1,200		
−1,200		

Date	Account and Explanation	Debit	Credit
March 4	Prepaid Insurance	1,200	
	Cash		1,200
	(Purchased insurance in advance)		

Transaction 5: Purchase of Supplies on Credit

On March 6, HiTech purchased office supplies from Hamilton Office Supply for $6,500. Hamilton Office Supply agreed to accept full payment in 30 days.

Assets	= Liabilities +	Stockholders' Equity
+6,500	+6,500	

Date	Account and Explanation	Debit	Credit
March 6	Supplies	6,500	
	Accounts Payable		6,500
	(Purchased supplies on account)		

Transaction 6: Sale of Services for Cash

On March 10, HiTech sold advertising services to Miami Valley Products in exchange for $8,800 in cash.

Assets	= Liabilities +	Stockholders' Equity
+8,800		+8,800

Date	Account and Explanation	Debit	Credit
March 10	Cash	8,800	
	Service Revenue		8,800
	(Sold advertising services)		

Transaction 7: Sale of Services for Credit

On March 15, HiTech sold advertising services to the *Cincinnati Enquirer* for $3,300. HiTech agreed to accept full payment in 30 days.

Assets	= Liabilities +	Stockholders' Equity
+3,000		+3,000

Date	Account and Explanation	Debit	Credit
March 15	Accounts Receivable	3,300	
	Service Revenue		3,300
	(Sold advertising services)		

Transaction 8: Receipt of Cash in Advance

On March 19, HiTech received $9,000 in advance for advertising services to be completed in the next three months.

Date	Account and Explanation	Debit	Credit
March 19	Cash	9,000	
	Unearned Service Revenue		9,000
	(Sold advertising services in advance)		

Assets	=	Liabilities	+	Stockholders' Equity
+9,000		+9,000		

Transaction 9: Payment of a Liability

On March 23, HiTech pays $6,000 cash for the supplies previously purchased from Hamilton Office Supply (transaction 5).

Date	Account and Explanation	Debit	Credit
March 23	Accounts Payable	6,000	
	Cash		6,000
	(Paid accounts payable)		

Assets	=	Liabilities	+	Stockholders' Equity
−6,000		−6,000		

Transaction 10: Payment of Salaries

On March 26, HiTech paid employees their weekly salary of $1,800 cash.

Date	Account and Explanation	Debit	Credit
March 26	Salaries Expense	1,800	
	Cash		1,800
	(Paid employee salaries)		

Assets	=	Liabilities	+	Stockholders' Equity
−1,800				−1,800

Transaction 11: Collection of a Receivable

On March 29, HiTech collected $3,000 cash from the *Cincinnati Enquirer* for services sold earlier on credit (transaction 7).

Date	Account and Explanation	Debit	Credit
March 29	Cash	3,000	
	Accounts Receivable		3,000
	(Collected accounts receivable)		

Assets	=	Liabilities	+	Stockholders' Equity
+3,000				
−3,000				

Transaction 12: Payment of Utilities

On March 30, HiTech paid its utility bill of $5,200 for March.

Date	Account and Explanation	Debit	Credit
March 30	Utilities Expense	5,200	
	Cash		5,200
	(Paid for utilities used)		

Assets	=	Liabilities	+	Stockholders' Equity
−5,200				−5,200

Transaction 13: Payment of a Dividend

On March 31, HiTech declared and paid a cash dividend of $500 to its stockholders.

Date	Account and Explanation	Debit	Credit
March 31	Dividends	500	
	Cash		500
	(Declared and paid a cash dividend)		

Assets	=	Liabilities	+	Stockholders' Equity
−500				−500

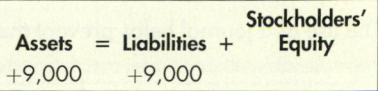 **YOU DECIDE**   Detecting Journal Entry Errors

You have been asked to inspect a delivery company's journal. Upon doing so, you find the following entry:

Date	Account and Explanation	Debit	Credit
June 29	Equipment, Delivery Truck	11,000	
	Prepaid Rent		11,000
	(Purchased delivery truck)		

Is this journal entry correct?

(Continued)

Because delivery trucks cannot be exchanged for prepaid rent, you conclude that an error was made in preparing this journal entry. Given the explanation contained in the journal entry, it's likely that the error was in the credit side of the entry. Instead of prepaid rent, the credit could be either to cash (if the purchase of the truck was for cash) or to note payable (if the purchase were on credit). Had the same data been entered directly into the accounts, this error would have been much more difficult to detect and correct.

The use of a journal helps prevent the introduction of errors in the recording of business activities.

OBJECTIVE
Explain why transactions are posted to the general ledger.

STEP 3: POST TO THE LEDGER

Because the journal lists each transaction in chronological order, it can be quite difficult to use the journal to determine the balance in any specific account. For example, refer to the journal entries shown earlier for HiTech Communications. What is the balance in cash at the end of the month? This relatively simple question is difficult to answer with the use of the journal.

To overcome this difficulty, companies will use a general ledger to keep track of the balances of specific accounts. A **general ledger** is simply a collection of all the individual financial statement accounts that a company uses.[1] In a manual accounting system, a ledger could be as a simple as a notebook with a separate page for each account. Ledger accounts are often shown using the T-account format introduced earlier.

The process of transferring the information from the journalized transaction to the general ledger is called **posting**. Posting is essentially copying the information from the journal into the ledger. Debits in the journal are posted as debits to the specific ledger account, and

Exhibit 2-11

The Posting Process for HiTech Communications Inc.

GENERAL JOURNAL				
				Page: 2
Date	Account and Explanation	Post. Ref.	Debit	Credit
Mar. 31	Dividends	3900	500	
	Cash	1000		500
	(Declared and paid cash dividend)			

GENERAL LEDGER					
Account: CASH				Account Number:	1000
Date	Explanation	Post. Ref.	Debit	Credit	Balance
Mar. 1	Issued stock	1	12,000		12,000
2	Borrowed from bank	1	3,000		15,000
3	Purchased equipment	1		4,500	10,500
4	Purchased insurance	1		1,200	9,300
10	Sold advertising services	1	8,800		18,100
19	Sold advertising services in advance	1	9,000		27,100
23	Paid accounts payable	1		6,000	21,100
28	Paid salaries	1		1,800	19,300
29	Collected receivable	2	3,000		22,300
30	Paid utilities	2		5,200	17,100
31	Paid dividend	2		500	16,600

[1] Most companies supplement the general ledger with subsidiary ledgers that record "subaccounts" that make up the larger general ledger account. For example, a single account such as Accounts Receivable may appear in the general ledger; however, the accounts receivable for individual customers are usually contained in a subsidiary ledger. The general ledger account will equal the total balance of all the accounts in the subsidiary ledger for that account.

credits in the journal are posted as credits in the specific ledger account. To facilitate this process, most journals and ledgers have a column titled "Posting Reference." As the information is copied into the ledger, the number assigned to the account is placed in the "Posting Reference" column of the journal and the journal page number is placed in the "Posting Reference" column of the ledger.

This column provides a link between the ledger and journal that

- helps to prevent errors in the posting process and
- allows you to trace the effects of a transaction through the accounting system.

The posting process is illustrated in Exhibit 2-11 (p. 76) which shows an illustration of a journal page and a ledger page for HiTech Communications.

The ledger for HiTech is shown using T-accounts in Exhibit 2-12. The number in parentheses corresponds to the transaction number.

IFRS

Under IFRS, transactions are analyzed, journalized, and posted in the same manner as under U.S. GAAP.

Exhibit 2-12

General Ledger of HiTech Communications

Assets

Cash			
(T1)	12,000	(T3)	4,500
(T2)	3,000	(T4)	1,200
(T6)	8,800	(T9)	6,000
(T8)	9,000	(T10)	1,800
(T11)	3,000	(T12)	5,200
		(T13)	500
16,600			

Accounts Receivable			
(T7)	3,300	(T11)	3,000
300			

Supplies		
(T5)	6,500	
6,500		

Prepaid Insurance		
(T4)	1,200	
1,200		

Equipment		
(T3)	4,500	
4,500		

Liabilities

Accounts Payable			
(T9)	6,000	(T5)	6,500
		500	

Unearned Service Revenue		
	(T8)	9,000
	9,000	

Notes Payable		
	(T2)	3,000
	3,000	

Stockholders' Equity

Common Stock		
	(T1)	12,000
	12,000	

Service Revenue		
	(T6)	8,800
	(T7)	3,300
	12,100	

Salaries Expense		
(T10)	1,800	
1,800		

Utility Expense		
(T12)	5,200	
5,200		

Dividends		
(T13)	500	
500		

OBJECTIVE 7
Prepare a trial balance and explain its purpose.

STEP 4: PREPARE A TRIAL BALANCE

To aid in the preparation of financial statements, some companies will prepare a trial balance before they prepare financial statements. The **trial balance** is a list of all active accounts and each account's debit or credit balance. The accounts are listed in the order they appear in the ledger—assets first, followed by liabilities, stockholders' equity, revenues, and expenses. By organizing accounts in this manner, the trial balance serves as a useful tool in preparing the financial statements. The preparation of the trial balance for HiTech Communications is shown in **CORNERSTONE 2-6**.

In addition, the trial balance is used to *prove the equality of debits and credits.* If debits did not equal credits, the accountant would quickly know that an error had been made. The error could have been in the journalizing of the transaction, the posting of the transaction, or in the computation of the balance in the ledger. However, a word of caution is necessary: a trial balance whose debits equal credits does *not* mean that all transactions were recorded correctly. A trial balance will not detect errors of analysis or amounts. Sometimes the wrong account is selected for a journal entry or an incorrect amount is recorded for a transaction. In other cases, a journal entry is omitted or entered twice. As long as both the debit and credit portions of the journal entry or posting reflect the incorrect information, the debit and credit totals in a trial balance will be equal.

CORNERSTONE 2-6   Preparing a Trial Balance

Information:
Refer to the general ledger for HiTech in Exhibit 2-12 (p. 77).

Required:
Prepare a trial balance for HiTech Communications Inc. at March 31, 2011.

Solution:

HiTech Communications Inc. Trial Balance March 31, 2011		
Account	**Debit**	**Credit**
Cash	$16,600	
Accounts Receivable	300	
Supplies	6,500	
Prepaid Insurance	1,200	
Equipment	4,500	
Accounts Payable		$ 500
Unearned Service Revenue		9,000
Notes Payable		3,000
Common Stock		12,000
Dividends	500	
Service Revenue		12,100
Salaries Expense	1,800	
Utilities Expense	5,200	
	$36,600	$ 36,600

SUMMARY OF LEARNING OBJECTIVES

LO1. **Describe the qualitative characteristics, assumptions, and principles that underlie accounting.**
- The fundamental qualitative characteristics of accounting information are:
  - Relevance—refers to whether information is capable of making a difference in the decision-making process. Relevant information is material and helps to predict the future or provides feedback about prior expectations.
  - Faithful representation—refers to whether information faithfully represents the economic event that it is intending to portray. Faithfully presented information should be complete, neutral, and free from error.
- The enhancing qualitative characteristics are:
  - Comparability—allows external users to identify similarities and differences between two or more items.
  - Verifiability—results when independent parties can reach a consensus on the measurement of an activity.
  - Timeliness—available to users before the information loses its ability to influence decisions.
  - Understandability—able to be comprehended (with reasonable effort) by users who have a reasonable knowledge of accounting and business.
- The four assumptions are:
  - Economic entity—each company is accounted for separately from its owners
  - Continuity (going-concern)—assumption that a company will continue to operate long enough to carry out its commitments
  - Time-period—allows the life of a company to be divided into artificial time periods
  - Monetary unit—requires financial information to be reported in monetary terms
- The four principles are:
  - Historical cost—requires a business activity to be recorded at the exchange price at the time the activity occurs
  - Revenue recognition—requires revenue to be recognized when it is earned and cash collection is reasonably assured
  - Matching principle—requires that expenses be recognized in the same period as the revenue that it helped generate
  - Conservatism—requires care to be taken to avoid overstating assets or income

LO2. **Explain the relationships among economic events, transactions, and the expanded accounting equation.**
- A company's business activities (operating, investing, and financing) consist of many different economic events that are both external to the company as well as internal to the company. Accounting attempts to measure the economic effect of these events. However, not all events are recognized, or recorded, in the accounting system.
- A transaction is an economic event that is recognized in the financial statements. An accounting transaction causes the elements of the accounting equation (assets, liabilities, contributed capital, retained earnings, revenues, expenses, or dividends) to change in a way that maintains the equality of their relationship.

LO3. **Analyze the effect of business transactions on the accounting equation.**
- This is Step 1 of the accounting cycle.
- Transaction analysis is the process of determining the economic effects of a transaction on the elements of the accounting equation.
- Transaction analysis involves three steps:
  - Step 1: Write down the accounting equation (basic or expanded version).
  - Step 2: Identify the financial statement elements that are affected by the transaction.
  - Step 3: Determine whether the element increased or decreased.
- Each transaction will have a dual-effect on the accounting equation, and the accounting equation will remain in balance after the effects of the transaction are recorded.

LO4. **Discuss the role of accounts and how debits and credits are used in the double-entry accounting system.**
- An account is a record of increases and decreases in each of the basic elements of the financial statements.
- Each financial statement element is made up of a number of different accounts.
- All transactions are recorded into accounts.
- The final account balance, after all changes are recorded, is used in the preparation of the financial statements.
- The left side of an account is referred to as a debit. The right side of an account is referred to as a credit.
- All accounts have a normal balance, which is a positive account balance. Assets, expenses, and dividends have a normal debit balance. Liabilities, stockholders' equity, and revenues have a normal credit balance.
- Increases or decreases to an account are based on the normal balance of an account. Normal debit balance accounts (assets, expenses, and dividends) are increased with debits and decreased with credits. Normal credit balance accounts (liabilities, equity, and stockholders' equity) are increased with credits and decreased with debits.

LO5. **Prepare journal entries for transactions.**
- This is Step 2 of the accounting cycle.
- A journal entry represents the debit and credit effects of a transaction in the accounting records.
- A journal entry is prepared by following three steps:
  - Step 1: Analyzing the transaction.
  - Step 2: Determining which accounts are affected.
  - Step 3: Using the debit and credit procedures to record the effects of the transaction.
- A journal entry is recorded in chronological order and consists of the date of the transaction, the accounts affected, the amount of the transaction, and a brief explanation.

LO6. **Explain why transactions are posted to the general ledger.**
- This is Step 3 of the accounting cycle.
- To overcome the difficulty of determining account balances listed chronologically in the journal, information in the journal is transferred to the general ledger in a process called posting.
- As result of posting, the general ledger accumulates the effects of transactions in individual financial statement accounts.

LO7. **Prepare a trial balance and explain its purpose.**
- This is Step 4 of the accounting cycle.
- The trial balance is a list of all active accounts, in the order they appear in the ledger, and each account's debit or credit balance.
- The trial balance is used to prove the equality of debits and credits and helps to uncover errors in journalizing or posting transactions.
- The trial balance serves as a useful tool in preparing the financial statements.

CORNERSTONES
FOR CHAPTER 2

KEY TERMS

Account (p. 67)
Accounting cycle (p. 54)
Chart of accounts (p. 67)
Comparability (p. 55)
Conservatism principle (p. 57)
Consistency (p. 55)
Continuity (**or** going-concern) assumption
  (p. 56)
Cost constraint (p. 55)
Credit (p. 67)
Debit (p. 67)
Double-entry accounting (p. 67)
Economic entity assumption (p. 56)
Events (p. 58)
Faithful representation (p. 54)
Full disclosure (p. 56)
General ledger (p. 76)

Historical cost principle (p. 57)
Journal (p. 72)
Journal entry (p. 72)
Matching principle (p. 57)
Monetary unit assumption (p. 56)
Normal balance (p. 68)
Posting (p. 76)
Relevance (p. 54)
Revenue recognition principle (p. 57)
T-account (p. 67)
Timeliness (p. 55)
Time period assumption (p. 56)
Transaction (p. 59)
Transaction analysis (p. 61)
Trial balance (p. 78)
Understandability (p. 55)
Verifiability (p. 55)

REVIEW PROBLEM

I. The Accounting Cycle

Concept:

Economic events are recorded in the accounting system through a process of analyzing transactions, journalizing these transactions in a journal, and posting them to the ledger. These activities are the initial steps in the accounting cycle.

Information:

Boonville Delivery Service was recently formed to fill a need for speedy delivery of small packages. In December 2011, its first month of operations, the following transactions occurred.

a.   On December 1, Boonville sells common stock to several investors for $32,000.
b.   On December 2, Boonville borrows $20,000 on a one-year note payable from Warrick National Bank, to be repaid with 8 percent interest on December 7, 2012.
c.   On December 2, Boonville pays rent of $8,000 on its package sorting building for the month of December.
d.   On December 6, Boonville purchases $7,000 worth of office furniture by paying $1,400 in cash and signing a one-year, 12 percent note payable for the balance.
e.   On December 20, Boonville completes a delivery contract for Tornado Corporation and bills its customer $15,000.
f.   On December 24, Boonville makes a rush delivery for $5,300 cash.
g.   On December 28, Tornado pays the $15,000 owed from transaction e.
h.   On December 28, Boonville signs an agreement with BigTime Computers to accept and deliver approximately 400 packages per business day during the next 12 months. Boonville expects to receive $400,000 of revenue for this contract, but the exact amount will depend on the number of packages delivered.
i.   On December 29, Boonville receives a $1,500 bill from Mac's Catering for miscellaneous services performed at a Christmas party Boonville held for its clients. (No previous entry has been made for this activity.)
j.   On December 31, Boonville pays $2,600 cash in salaries to its secretarial staff for work performed in December.
k.   On December 31, Boonville declares and pays dividends of $5,000 on its common stock.

Required:

1.   Analyze and journalize the transactions *a* through *k*.
2.   Post the transactions to the general ledger.
3.   Prepare the December 31, 2011 trial balance for Boonville.

Solution:

1. **Analyzing and Journalizing Transactions**

   Transaction a: Issuing Common Stock.

Assets	=	Liabilities	+	Stockholders' Equity	
				Contributed Capital	Retained Earnings
Cash +$32,000				Common Stock +$32,000	

Date	Account and Explanation	Debit	Credit
Dec. 1	Cash	32,000	
	Common Stock		32,000
	(Issued common stock)		

   Transaction b: Borrowing Cash

Assets	=	Liabilities	+	Stockholders' Equity	
				Contributed Capital	Retained Earnings
Cash +$20,000		Notes Payable +$20,000			

Date	Account and Explanation	Debit	Credit
Dec. 2	Cash	20,000	
	Notes Payable		20,000
	(Borrowed cash from bank)		

   Transaction c: Paying Rent

Assets	=	Liabilities	+	Stockholders' Equity	
				Contributed Capital	Retained Earnings
Cash −$8,000					Rent Expense −$8,000

Date	Account and Explanation	Debit	Credit
Dec. 2	Rent Expense	8,000	
	Cash		8,000
	(Paid rent for December)		

   Transaction d: Purchasing Asset with Cash and Credit

Assets	=	Liabilities	+	Stockholders' Equity	
				Contributed Capital	Retained Earnings
Cash −$1,400		Notes Payable +$5,600			
Furniture +$7,000					

Date	Account and Explanation	Debit	Credit
Dec. 6	Furniture	7,000	
	Cash		1,400
	Notes Payable		5,600
	(Purchased office furniture)		

Transaction e: *Performing Services for Credit*

Assets	=	Liabilities	+	Stockholders' Equity	
				Contributed Capital	Retained Earnings
Accounts Receivable +$15,000					Service Revenue +$15,000

Date	Account and Explanation	Debit	Credit
Dec. 20	Accounts Receivable	15,000	
	Service Revenue		15,000
	(Performed delivery services)		

Transaction f: *Performing Services for Cash*

Assets	=	Liabilities	+	Stockholders' Equity	
				Contributed Capital	Retained Earnings
Cash +$5,300					Service Revenue +$5,300

Date	Account and Explanation	Debit	Credit
Dec. 24	Cash	5,300	
	Service Revenue		5,300
	(Performed delivery services)		

Transaction g: *Collecting an Account Receivable*

Assets	=	Liabilities	+	Stockholders' Equity	
				Contributed Capital	Retained Earnings
Cash +$15,000					
Accounts Receivable −$15,000					

Date	Account and Explanation	Debit	Credit
Dec. 28	Cash	15,000	
	Accounts Receivable		15,000
	(Collected accounts receivable)		

Transaction h: *Signing of an Agreement to Provide Service*

This is an example of an important event that does not produce a journal entry at the time it occurs. There will be no recording of the transaction until one of the companies performs on its part of the contract (so, until Boonville provides the delivery service or BigTime Computers makes a payment to Boonville).

Transaction i: *Using Services*

Assets	=	Liabilities	+	Stockholders' Equity	
				Contributed Capital	Retained Earnings
		Accounts Payable +$1,500			Miscellaneous Expense −$1,500

Date	Account and Explanation	Debit	Credit
Dec. 29	Miscellaneous Expense	1,500	
	Accounts Payable		1,500
	(Used catering service)		

Transaction j: *Payment of Salaries*

Assets	=	Liabilities	+	Stockholders' Equity	
				Contributed Capital	Retained Earnings
Cash					Salaries Expense
−$2,600					−$2,600

Date	Account and Explanation	Debit	Credit
Dec. 31	Salaries Expense	2,600	
	Cash		2,600
	(Paid secretarial staff salaries)		

Transaction k: *Declaring and Paying a Cash Dividend*

Assets	=	Liabilities	+	Stockholders' Equity	
				Contributed Capital	Retained Earnings
Cash					Dividends
−$5,000					−$5,000

Date	Account and Explanation	Debit	Credit
Dec. 31	Dividends	5,000	
	Cash		5,000
	(Declared and paid a cash dividend)		

2. **Posting of Transactions to the Ledger**

General Ledger of Boonville Delivery Service

Assets

Cash

(a)	32,000	(c)	8,000
(b)	20,000	(d)	1,400
(f)	5,300	(j)	2,600
(g)	15,000	(k)	5,000
55,300			

Accounts Receivable

(e)	15,000	(g)	15,000
0			

Furniture

(d)	7,000	
7,000		

Liabilities

Accounts Payable

		(i)	1,500
		1,500	

Notes Payable

		(b)	20,000
		(d)	5,600
		25,600	

Stockholders' Equity

Common Stock

		(a)	32,000
		32,000	

Dividends

(k)	5,000	
5,000		

Service Revenue

		(e)	15,000
		(f)	5,300
		20,300	

Salaries Expense

(j)	2,600	
2,600		

Miscellaneous Expense

(i)	1,500	
1,500		

Rent Expense

(c)	8,000	
8,000		

3. **Preparing a Trial Balance**

Boonville Delivery Service Trial Balance December 31, 2011		
Account	**Debit**	**Credit**
Cash	$55,300	
Accounts Receivable	0	
Furniture	7,000	
Accounts Payable		$ 1,500
Notes Payable		25,600
Common Stock		32,000
Dividends	5,000	
Service Revenue		20,300
Rent Expense	8,000	
Salaries Expense	2,600	
Miscellaneous Expense	1,500	
	$79,400	$ 79,400

DISCUSSION QUESTIONS

1. What is the conceptual framework of accounting?
2. Identify the characteristics of useful information.
3. Discuss the trade-offs that may be necessary between the qualitative characteristics.
4. Distinguish between comparability and consistency.
5. Describe the constraint on providing useful information.
6. Identify the four assumptions that underlie accounting.
7. Discuss the four principles that are used to measure and record business transactions.
8. How are the financial statements related to generally accepted accounting principles?
9. Of all the events that occur each day, how would you describe those that are recorded in a firm's accounting records?
10. In order for a transaction to be recorded in a business' accounting records, the effects of the transaction must be faithfully represented. What is faithful representation, and why is it important?
11. What is the basic process used in transaction analysis?
12. In analyzing a transaction, can a transaction only affect one side of the accounting equation? If so, give an example.
13. How do revenues and expenses affect the accounting equation?
14. What is a T-account? Describe the basic components of any account.
15. Do you agree with the statement that "debits mean increase and credits mean decrease"? If not, what do debit and credit mean?
16. The words *debit* and *credit* are used in two ways in accounting: "to debit an account" and "a debit balance." Explain both usages of the terms *debit and credit*.
17. All accounts have normal balances. What is the normal balance of each of these accounts?

    a. cash
    b. sales
    c. notes payable
    d. inventory

    e. retained earnings
    f. salary expense
    g. equipment
    h. unearned revenue

18. When a journal entry is made, what must be equal? Why?
19. Can accounting transactions be directly recorded in the general ledger? If so, why do most companies initially record transactions in the journal?
20. Why is the term *double-entry* an appropriate expression for describing an accounting system?
21. What are the initial steps in the accounting cycle and what happens in each step?
22. What kinds of errors will a trial balance detect? What kinds of errors will not be detectable by a trial balance?

MULTIPLE-CHOICE EXERCISES

2-1 Which of the following is *not* a benefit derived from the conceptual framework?

a. Supports the objective of providing information useful for making business and economic decisions.
b. Provides a logical structure to aid in the understanding of complex accounting standards.
c. Provides specific guidance on how transactions should be recorded.
d. Supports the development of a consistent set of accounting standards.

2-2 Which of the following is *not* a characteristic of useful information?

a. Conservatism
b. Relevance
c. Faithful representation
d. Comparability

2-3 Information that provides feedback about prior expectations is:

	Relevant	Faithfully Represented
a.	Yes	Yes
b.	No	Yes
c.	Yes	No
d.	No	No

2-4 Relevant information possesses this quality:

	Freedom from Error	Predictive Value
a.	Yes	Yes
b.	No	Yes
c.	Yes	No
d.	No	No

2-5 Which of the following is *not* an assumption that underlies accounting?

a. Economic entity
b. Historical cost
c. Time-period
d. Continuity (going concern)

2-6 Which principle requires that expenses be recorded and reported in the same period as the revenue that it helped generate?

a. Historical cost
b. Revenue recognition
c. Conservatism
d. Matching

2-7 Taylor Company recently purchased a piece of equipment for $2,000 which will be paid within 30 days after delivery. At what point would the event be recorded in Taylor's accounting system?

a. When Taylor signs the agreement with the seller.
b. When Taylor receives an invoice (a bill) from the seller.
c. When Taylor receives the asset from the seller.
d. When Taylor pays $2,000 cash to the seller.

2-8 The effects of purchasing inventory on credit are to:

a. increase assets and increase liabilities.
b. increase assets and increase stockholders' equity.
c. decrease assets and decrease stockholders' equity.
d. decrease assets and decrease liabilities.

2-9 The effects of paying salaries for the current period are to:

a. increase assets and increase stockholders' equity.
b. increase assets and increase liabilities.
c. decrease assets and decrease liabilities.
d. decrease assets and decrease stockholders' equity.

2-10 Which of the following statements is *false*?

a.   Transactions are frequently analyzed using a T-account.
b.   All T-accounts have both a debit and a credit side.
c.   The left side of a T-account is called the credit side.
d.   The amount in an account at any time is called the balance of the account.

2-11 Which of the following statements are true?

  I.   Debits represent decreases and credits represent increases.
 II.   Debits must always equal credits.
III.   Assets have normal debit balances while liabilities and stockholders' equity have normal credit balances.

a.   I
b.   I and II

c.   II and III
d.   All of these are true.

2-12 Debits will:

a.   increase assets, liabilities, revenues, expenses, and dividends.
b.   increase assets, expenses, and dividends.
c.   decrease assets, liabilities, revenues, expenses, and dividends.
d.   decrease liabilities, revenues, and dividends.

2-13 Which of the following statements are true?

  I.   A journal provides a chronological record of a transaction.
 II.   A journal entry contains the complete effect of a transaction.
III.   The first step in preparing a journal entry involves analyzing the transaction.

a.   I and II
b.   II and III

c.   I and III
d.   All of these are true.

2-14 Posting:

a.   involves transferring the information in journal entries to the general ledger.
b.   is an optional step in the accounting cycle.
c.   is performed after a trial balance is prepared.
d.   involves transferring information to the trial balance.

2-15 A trial balance:

a.   lists only revenue and expense accounts.
b.   lists all accounts and their balances.
c.   will help detect omitted journal entries.
d.   detects all errors that could be made during the journalizing or posting steps of the accounting cycle.

CORNERSTONE EXERCISES

Cornerstone Exercise 2-16 Qualitative Characteristics

OBJECTIVE ❶
CORNERSTONE 2-1

Three statements are given below.

a.   When financial information is free from error or bias, the information is said to possess this characteristic.
b.   Griffin Company uses the same depreciation method from period to period.
c.   A trash can that is purchased for $10 is expensed even though it will be used for many years.

Required:
Give the qualitative characteristic or constraint that is most applicable to each of the statements.

OBJECTIVE 1
CORNERSTONE 2-1

Cornerstone Exercise 2-17 Qualitative Characteristics

Three statements are given below.

a. A financial item that may be useful to investors is not required to be reported because the cost of measuring and reporting this information is judged to be too great.

b. Timely information that is used to predict future events or provide feedback about prior events is said to possess this characteristic.

c. A quality of information that enables an analyst to evaluate the financial performance of two different companies in the same industry.

Required:

Give the qualitative characteristic or constraint that is most applicable to each of the statements.

OBJECTIVE 1
CORNERSTONE 2-1

Cornerstone Exercise 2-18 Accounting Assumptions

Four statements are given below.

a. Pewterschmidt Company values its inventory reported in the financial statements in terms of dollars instead of units.

b. Property, plant, and equipment is recorded at cost (less any accumulated depreciation) instead of liquidation value.

c. The accounting records of a company are kept separate from its owners.

d. The accountant assigns revenues and expenses to specific years before preparing the financial statements.

Required:

Give the accounting assumption that is most applicable to each of the statements.

OBJECTIVE 1
CORNERSTONE 2-1

Cornerstone Exercise 2-19 Accounting Principles

Four statements are given below.

a. Quagmire Company recognizes revenue when the goods are delivered to a customer, even though cash will not be collected from the customer for 30 days.

b. Inventory, which was recently damaged by a flood, is reported at the lower of its cost or market value.

c. Land, located in a desirable location, is reported at the original acquisition price, even though its value has increased by over 100 percent since it was purchased.

d. The cost paid for a delivery truck is recorded as an asset and expensed over the next five years as it is used to help generate revenue.

Required:

Give the accounting principle that is most applicable to each of the statements.

OBJECTIVE 3
CORNERSTONE 2-2

Cornerstone Exercise 2-20 Transaction Analysis

Four transactions are listed below.

a. Sold goods to customers on credit
b. Collected amounts due from customers
c. Purchased supplies on account
d. Used supplies in operations of the business

Required:

Prepare three columns labeled assets, liabilities, and stockholders' equity. For each of the transactions, indicate whether the transaction increased (+), decreased (−), or had no effect (NE) on assets, liabilities, or stockholders' equity.

OBJECTIVE 3
CORNERSTONE 2-2

Cornerstone Exercise 2-21 Transaction Analysis

Morgan Inc. entered into the following transactions.

a. Sold common stock to investors in exchange for $50,000 cash
b. Borrowed $15,000 cash from First State Bank
c. Purchased $8,000 of supplies on credit
d. Paid for the purchase in *c*

Required:
Show the effect of each transaction using the following model.

Assets	=	Liabilities	+	Stockholders' Equity	
				Contributed Capital	Retained Earnings

Cornerstone Exercise 2-22 Transaction Analysis

OBJECTIVE 4
CORNERSTONE 2-2

The Mendholm Company entered into the following transactions.

a.   Performed services on account, $18,500
b.   Collected $7,200 from client related to services performed in *a*
c.   Paid $1,500 dividend to stockholders
d.   Paid salaries of $3,500 for the current month

Required:
Show the effect of each transaction using the following model:

Assets	=	Liabilities	+	Stockholders' Equity	
				Contributed Capital	Retained Earnings

Cornerstone Exercise 2-23 Debit and Credit Procedures

OBJECTIVE 4
CORNERSTONE 2-3
CORNERSTONE 2-4

Refer to the accounts listed below.

a.   Accounts Payable
b.   Accounts Receivable
c.   Retained Earnings
d.   Sales

e.   Equipment
f.   Common Stock
g.   Salary Expense
h.   Repair Expense

Required:
For each of the accounts, complete the following table by entering the normal balance of the account (debit or credit) and the word increase or decrease in the debit and credit columns.

Account	Normal Balance	Debit	Credit

Cornerstone Exercise 2-24 Journalize Transactions

OBJECTIVE 5
CORNERSTONE 2-5

Four transactions that occurred during June are listed below.

a.   June 1: Issued common stock to several investors for $83,000
b.   June 8: Purchased equipment for $12,800 cash
c.   June 15: Made cash sales of $21,400 to customers
d.   June 29: Issued a $6,500 dividend to stockholders

Required:
Prepare journal entries for the transactions.

Cornerstone Exercise 2-25 Journalize Transactions

OBJECTIVE 5
CORNERSTONE 2-5

Four transactions that occurred during May are listed below.

a.   May 5: Borrowed cash of $20,000 from Middle State Bank
b.   May 10: Made cash sales of $14,500 to customers
c.   May 19: Paid salaries of $8,600 to employees for services performed
d.   May 22: Purchased and used $4,100 of supplies in operations of the business

Required:
Prepare journal entries for the transactions.

OBJECTIVE **7**
CORNERSTONE 2-6

Cornerstone Exercise 2-26 Preparing a Trial Balance

Listed below are the ledger accounts for Borges Inc. at December 31, 2011. All accounts have normal balances.

Service Revenue	$23,150	Dividends	$ 1,500
Cash	12,850	Salaries Expense	4,300
Accounts Payable	2,825	Equipment	12,725
Common Stock	15,000	Accounts Receivable	5,700
Rent Expense	2,400	Advertising Expense	1,500

Required:
Prepare a trial balance for Borges at December 31, 2011.

EXERCISES

OBJECTIVE **1**

Exercise 2-27 Qualitative Characteristics

Listed below are the fundamental and enhancing qualitative characteristics that make accounting information useful.

a.   Relevance
b.   Faithful representation
c.   Comparability

d.   Verifiability
e.   Timeliness
f.   Understandability

Required:
Match the appropriate qualitative characteristic with the statements below (items can be used more than once).
1.   When information is provided before it loses its ability to influence decisions, it has this characteristic.
2.   When several accountants can agree on the measurement of an activity, the information possesses this characteristic.
3.   If users can comprehend the meaning of the information, the information is said to have this characteristic.
4.   If information confirms prior expectations, it possesses this characteristic.
5.   If information helps to predict future events, it possesses this characteristic.
6.   Freedom from bias is a component of this characteristic.
7.   When several companies in the same industry use the same accounting methods, this qualitative characteristic exists.
8.   Information that accurately portrays an economic event satisfies this characteristic.

OBJECTIVE **1**

Exercise 2-28 Assumptions and Principles

Presented below are the four assumptions and four principles used in measuring and reporting accounting information.

Assumptions	Principles
a. Economic entity	e. Historical cost
b. Continuity (going-concern)	f. Revenue recognition
c. Time-period	g. Matching
d. Monetary unit	h. Conservatism

Required:
Identify the assumption or principle that best describes each situation below.
1.   Requires that an activity be recorded at the exchange price at the time the activity occurred
2.   Allows a company to report financial activities separate from the activities of the owners
3.   Implies that items such as customer satisfaction cannot be reported in the financial statements
4.   Specifies that revenue should only be recognized when earned and the collection of cash is reasonably assured.

5. Justifies why some assets and liabilities are not reported at their value if sold
6. Allows the life of a company to be divided into artificial time periods so accounting reports can be provided on a timely basis
7. Is a prudent reaction to uncertainty
8. Requires that expenses be recorded and reported in the same period as the revenue that it helped generate

Exercise 2-29 Events and Transactions

OBJECTIVE 2

Several events are listed below.

a. Common stock is issued to investors.
b. An agreement is signed with a janitorial service to provide cleaning services over the next 12 months.
c. Inventory is purchased.
d. Inventory is sold to customers.
e. Two investors sell their common stock to another investor.
f. A two-year insurance policy is purchased.

Required:

1. For each of the events, identify which ones qualify for recognition in the financial statements.
2. **Conceptual Connection:** For events that do not qualify for recognition, explain your reasoning.

 YOU DECIDE

Exercise 2-30 Events and Transactions

OBJECTIVE 2

The following economic events that were related to K&B Grocery Store occurred during 2011.

a. On February 7, K&B received a bill from Indianapolis Power and Light indicating that it had used electric power during January 2011 at a cost of $120; the bill need not be paid until February 25, 2011.
b. On February 15, K&B placed an order for a new cash register with NCR, for which $700 would be paid after delivery.
c. On February 21, the cash register ordered on February 15 was delivered. Payment was not due until March.
d. On February 22, the K&B store manager purchased a new passenger car for $15,000 in cash. The car is entirely for personal use and was paid for from the manager's personal assets.
e. On February 24, K&B signed a two-year extension of the lease on the store building occupied by the store. The new lease was effective on April 1, 2011, and required an increase in the monthly rental from $5,750 to $5,900.
f. On March 1, K&B paid $120 to Indianapolis Power and Light.
g. On March 5, K&B paid $5,750 to its landlord for March rent on the store building.

Required:

1. Using the words "qualify" and "does not qualify," indicate whether each of the above events would qualify as a transaction and be recognized and recorded in the accounting system on the date indicated.
2. **Conceptual Connection:** For any events that did not qualify as a transaction to be recognized and recorded, explain why it does not qualify.

YOU DECIDE

Exercise 2-31 Transaction Analysis

OBJECTIVE 3

The following events occurred for Parker Company.

a. Performed consulting services for a client in exchange for $1,200 cash
b. Performed consulting services for a client on account, $700
c. Paid $5,000 cash for land
d. Purchased office supplies on account, $300
e. Paid a $1,000 cash dividend to stockholders
f. Paid $250 on account for supplies purchased in transaction *d*
g. Paid $200 cash for the current month's rent
h. Collected $500 from client in transaction *b*
i. Stockholders invested $12,000 cash in the business

(Continued)
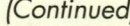

Required:
1. Analyze the effect of each transaction on p. 91 on the accounting equation. For example, if salaries of $500 were paid, the answer would be "Decrease in stockholders' equity (expense) $500 and decrease in assets (cash) $500."
2. **Conceptual Connection:** For *d*, what accounting principle did you use to determine the amount to be recorded for supplies?

OBJECTIVE **3**

Exercise 2-32 Transaction Analysis

Amanda Webb opened a home health care business under the name Home Care Inc. During its first month of operations, the business had the following transactions:

a. Sold common stock to Ms. Webb and other stockholders in exchange for $30,000 cash
b. Paid $18,500 cash for a parcel of land on which the business will eventually build an office building
c. Purchased supplies for $2,750 on credit
d. Used the supplies purchased in part (c).
e. Paid rent for the month on office space and equipment, $800 cash
f. Performed services for clients in exchange for $3,910 cash
g. Paid salaries for the month, $1,100
h. Purchased and used $650 of supplies
i. Paid $1,900 on account for supplies purchased in transaction *c*
j. Performed services for clients on credit in the amount of $1,050
k. Paid a $600 dividend to stockholders

Required:
Prepare an analysis of the effects of these transactions on the accounting equation of the business. Use the format below.

Assets	=	Liabilities	+	Stockholders' Equity	
				Contributed Capital	Retained Earnings

OBJECTIVE **3**

Exercise 2-33 Transaction Analysis and Business Activities

The accountant for Compton Inc. has collected the following information:

a. Compton purchased a tract of land from Jacobsen Real Estate for $925,000 cash.
b. Compton issued 2,000 shares of its common stock to George Micros in exchange for $110,000 cash.
c. Compton purchased a John Deere tractor for $62,000 on credit.
d. Michael Rotunno paid Compton $8,400 cash for services performed. The services had been performed by Compton several months ago for a total price of $10,000 of which Rotunno had previously paid $1,600.
e. Compton paid its monthly payroll by issuing checks totaling $34,750.
f. Compton declared and paid its annual dividend of $10,000 cash.

Required:
1. Prepare an analysis of the effects of these transactions on the accounting equation of the business. Use the format below.

Assets	=	Liabilities	+	Stockholders' Equity	
				Contributed Capital	Retained Earnings

2. Indicate whether the transaction is a financing, investing, or operating activity.

Exercise 2-34 Inferring Transactions from Balance Sheet Changes

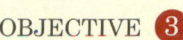

Each of the following balance sheet changes is associated with a particular transaction:

a. Cash decreases by $22,000 and land increases by $22,000.
b. Cash decreases by $9,000 and retained earnings decreases by $9,000.
c. Cash increases by $100,000 and common stock increases by $100,000.
d. Cash increases by $15,000 and notes payable increases by $15,000.

Required:
Describe each transaction listed above.

Exercise 2-35 Transaction Analysis

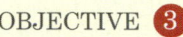

Goal Systems, a business consulting firm, engaged in the following transactions:

a. Sold common stock for $50,000 cash
b. Borrowed $20,000 from a bank
c. Purchased equipment for $7,000 cash
d. Prepaid rent on office space for six months in the amount of $6,600
e. Performed consulting services in exchange for $4,300 cash
f. Performed consulting services on credit in the amount of $16,000
g. Incurred and paid wage expense of $7,500
h. Collected $7,200 of the receivable arising from transaction f
i. Purchased supplies for $1,100 on credit
j. Used $800 of the supplies purchased in transaction i
k. Paid for all of the supplies purchased in transaction i

Required:
For each transaction described above, indicate the effects on assets, liabilities, and stockholders' equity using the format below.

Assets	=	Liabilities	+	Stockholders' Equity	
				Contributed Capital	Retained Earnings

Exercise 2-36 Transaction Analysis

During December, Cynthiana Refrigeration Service engaged in the following transactions:

a. On December 3, Cynthiana sold a one-year service contract to Cub Foods for $12,000 cash.
b. On December 10, Cynthiana repaired equipment of the A&W Root Beer Drive-In. A&W paid $1,100 in cash for the service call.
c. On December 10, Cynthiana purchased a new Chevy truck for business use. The truck cost $36,500. Cynthiana paid $5,500 down and signed a one-year note for the balance.
d. Cynthiana received a $3,200 order of repair parts from Carrier Corporation on December 19. Carrier is expected to bill Cynthiana for $3,200 in early January.
e. On December 23, Cynthiana purchased 20 turkeys from Cub Foods for $300 cash. Cynthiana gave the turkeys to its employees as a Christmas gift.

Required:
For each transaction described above, indicate the effects on assets, liabilities, and stockholders' equity using the format below.

Assets	=	Liabilities	+	Stockholders' Equity	
				Contributed Capital	Retained Earnings

Exercise 2-37 Inferring Transactions from Balance Sheet Changes

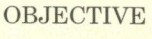

Each of the balance sheet changes below and on p. 94 is associated with a particular transaction:

a. Equipment increases by $5,000 and cash decreases by $5,000.
b. Cash increases by $4,100 and stockholders' equity increases by $4,100.

(Continued)

c. Supplies increases by $400 and accounts payable increases by $400.
d. Supplies decreases by $250 and stockholders' equity decreases by $250.

OBJECTIVE

Required:
Describe each transaction listed above.

Exercise 2-38 Normal Balances and Financial Statements

The following accounts are available for Haubstadt Shoe Works:

Accounts Payable	Utilities Expense
Accounts Receivable	Interest Expense
Accumulated Depreciation (Equipment)	Inventory
Cash	Notes Payable
Common Stock	Retained Earnings
Cost of Goods Sold	Sales Revenue
Depreciation Expense (Equipment)	Advertising Expense
Equipment	

Required:
Using a table like the one below, indicate whether each account normally has a debit or credit balance and indicate on which of the financial statements (income statement, retained earnings statement, or balance sheet) each account appears.

Account	Debit	Credit	Financial Statement

OBJECTIVE

Exercise 2-39 Debit and Credit Effects of Transactions

Lincoln Corporation was involved in the following transactions during the current year:

a. Lincoln borrowed cash from the local bank on a note payable.
b. Lincoln purchased operating assets on credit.
c. Lincoln paid dividends in cash.
d. Lincoln purchased supplies inventory on credit.
e. Lincoln used a portion of the supplies purchased in transaction *d*.
f. Lincoln provided services in exchange for cash from the customer.
g. A customer received services from Lincoln on credit.
h. The owners invested cash in the business in exchange for common stock.
i. The payable from transaction *d* was paid in full.
j. The receivable from transaction *g* was collected in full.
k. Lincoln paid wages in cash.

Required:
Prepare a table like the one shown below and indicate the effect on assets, liabilities, and stockholders' equity. Be sure to enter debits and credits in the appropriate columns for each of the transactions. Transaction *a* is entered as an example:

Assets	=	Liabilities	+	Stockholders' Equity	
				Contributed Capital	Retained Earnings
a. Increase (Debit)		Increase (Credit)			

OBJECTIVE

Exercise 2-40 Debit and Credit Effect on Transactions

Jefferson Framers engaged in the following transactions:

a. Purchased land for $15,200 cash
b. Purchased equipment for $23,600 in exchange for a one-year, 8 percent note payable
c. Purchased office supplies on credit for $1,200 from Office Depot
d. Paid the $10,000 principal plus $700 interest on a note payable
e. Paid an account payable in the amount of $2,600
f. Provided $62,100 of services on credit
g. Provided $11,400 of services for cash
h. Collected $29,800 of accounts receivable

i.   Paid $13,300 of wages in cash
j.   Sold common stock for $21,000 cash

Required:

Using a table like the one below, enter the necessary information for each transaction. Enter the debits before the credits. Transaction *a* is entered as an example.

Transaction	Account	Increase/Decrease	Debit/Credit	Amount
(a)	Land	Increase	Debit	$15,200
	Cash	Decrease	Credit	$15,200

Exercise 2-41 Journalizing Transactions

 OBJECTIVE 5

Kauai Adventures rents and sells surfboards and snorkeling and scuba equipment. During March, Kauai engaged in the following transactions:

March 2   Received $41,200 cash from customers for rental
        3   Purchased on credit five new surfboards (which Kauai classifies as inventory) for $140 each
        6   Paid wages to employees in the amount of $8,500
        9   Paid office rent for the month in the amount of $1,300
       12   Purchased a new Ford truck for $37,800; paid $1,000 down in cash and secured a loan
            from Princeville Bank for the $36,800 balance
       13   Collected a $950 account receivable
       16   Paid an account payable in the amount of $870
       23   Borrowed $15,000 on a six-month, 8 percent note payable
       27   Paid the monthly telephone bill of $145
       30   Paid a monthly advertising bill of $1,260

Required:

Prepare a journal entry for each of these transactions.

Exercise 2-42 Journalizing Transactions

 OBJECTIVE 5

Remington Communications has been providing cellular phone service for several years. During November and December 2011, the following transactions occurred:

Nov. 2   Remington received $2,400 for November phone service from Enrico Company.
       6   Remington purchased $4,750 of supplies from Technology Associates on account.
      10   Remington paid $5,250 to its hourly employees for their weekly wages.
      15   Remington paid $4,750 to Technology Associates in full settlement of their account payable.
      28   Remington paid $2,150 for utilities used during November.
      30   Remington received a bill from Monticello Construction for $1,230 for repairs made to
           Remington's loading dock on November 15. Remington plans to pay the bill in early December.
Dec. 10   Remington paid $1,230 to Monticello Construction to settle the repair bill received on
           November 30.

Required:

1. Prepare a journal entry for each of these transactions.
2. **Conceptual Connection:** What accounting principle did you apply in recording the November 10 transaction?

Exercise 2-43 Transaction Analysis and Journal Entries

 OBJECTIVE 5

Pasta House Inc. was organized in January 2011. During the year, the transactions below and on p. 96 occurred:

a.   On January 14, Pasta House sold Martin Halter, the firm's founder and sole owner, 10,000 shares of its common stock for $8 per share.
b.   On the same day, Bank One loaned Pasta House $45,000 on a 10-year note payable.
c.   On February 22, Pasta House purchased a building and the land on which it stands from Frank Jakubek for $34,000 cash and a 5-year, $56,000 note payable. The land and building had appraised values of $30,000 and $60,000, respectively.
d.   On March 1, Pasta House signed an $15,000 contract with Cosby Renovations to remodel the inside of the building. Pasta House paid $4,000 down and agreed to pay the remainder when Cosby completed its work.

e. On May 3, Cosby completed its work and submitted a bill to Pasta House for the remaining $11,000.

f. On May 20, Pasta House paid $11,000 to Cosby Renovations.

g. On June 4, Pasta House purchased restaurant supplies from Glidden Supply for $650 cash.

Required:

Prepare a journal entry for each of these transactions.

OBJECTIVE

Exercise 2-44 Accounting Cycle

Rosenthal Decorating Inc. is a commercial painting and decorating contractor that began operations in January 2011. The following transactions occurred during the year:

a. On January 15, Rosenthal sold 500 shares of its common stock to William Hensley for $10,000.

b. On January 24, Rosenthal purchased $720 of painting supplies from Westwood Builders' Supply Company on account.

c. On February 20, Rosenthal paid $720 cash to Westwood Builders' Supply Company for the painting supplies purchased on January 24.

d. On April 25, Rosenthal billed Bultman Condominiums $12,500 for painting and decorating services performed in April.

e. On May 12, Rosenthal received $12,500 from Bultman Condominiums for the painting and decorating work billed in April.

f. On June 5, Rosenthal sent Arlington Builders a $9,500 bill for a painting job completed on that day.

g. On June 24, Rosenthal paid wages for work performed during the preceding week in the amount of $6,700.

Required:

1. Prepare a journal entry for each of the transactions.
2. Post the transactions to T-accounts.
3. Prepare a trial balance at June 30, 2011.

OBJECTIVE ⑦

Exercise 2-45 Preparing a Trial Balance Preparation

The following accounts and account balances are available for Badger Auto Parts at December 31, 2011:

Accounts Payable	$ 8,500	Income Taxes Payable	$ 3,600
Accounts Receivable	40,800	Interest Expense	6,650
Accumulated Depreciation (Furniture)	47,300	Interest Payable	1,800
Cash	3,200	Inventory	60,500
Common Stock	100,000	Notes Payable (Long-term)	50,000
Cost of Goods Sold	184,300	Prepaid Rent	15,250
Depreciation Expense (Furniture)	10,400	Retained Earnings, 12/31/2010	15,900
Furniture	128,000	Sales Revenue	264,700
Utilities Expense	9,700	Advertising Expense	29,200
Income Taxes Expense	3,800		

Required:

Prepare a trial balance. Assume that all accounts have normal balances.

OBJECTIVE ⑦

Exercise 2-46 Effect of Errors on a Trial Balance

The bookkeeper for Riley Inc. made the following errors:

a. A cash purchase of supplies of $348 was recorded as a debit to Supplies for $384 and a credit to Cash of $384.

b. A cash sale of $3,128 was recorded as a debit to Cash of $3,128 and a credit to Sales of $3,182.

c. A purchase of equipment was recorded once in the journal and posted twice to the ledger.

d. Cash paid for salaries of $5,270 was recorded as a debit to Salaries Expense of $5,270 and a credit to Accounts Payable of $5,270.

e. A credit sale of $7,600 was recorded as a credit to Sales Revenue of $7,600; however, the debit posting to Accounts Receivable was omitted.

Required:

Indicate whether or not the trial balance will balance after the error. If the trial balance will not balance, indicate the direction of the misstatement for any effected account (such as, Cash will be overstated by $50).

PROBLEM SET A

Problem 2-47A Events and Transactions

OBJECTIVE

The accountant for Boatsman Products Inc. received the following information:

a. Boatsman sent its customers a new price list. Prices were increased an average of 3 percent on all items.

b. Boatsman accepted an offer of $150,000 for land that it had purchased two years ago for $130,000. Cash and the deed for the property are to be exchanged in five days.

c. Boatsman accepted $150,000 cash and gave the purchaser the deed for the property described in item *b*.

d. Boatsman's president purchased 600 shares of the firm's common stock from another stockholder. The president paid $15 per share. The former shareholder had purchased the stock from Boatsman for $4 per share.

e. Boatsman leases its delivery trucks from a local dealer. The dealer also performs maintenance on the trucks for Boatsman. Boatsman received a $1,254 bill for maintenance from the dealer.

Required:

1. Indicate whether or not each item qualifies as a transaction and should be recorded in the accounting system. Explain your reasoning.

2. **Conceptual Connection:** What accounting concept is illustrated by item *d*?

Problem 2-48A Analyzing Transactions

OBJECTIVE

Luis Madero, after working for several years with a large public accounting firm, decided to open his own accounting service. The business is operated as a corporation under the name Madero Accounting Services. The following captions and amounts summarize Madero's balance sheet at July 31, 2011.

Assets			=	Liabilities		+	Equity	
Cash	Accounts Receivable	Supplies		Accounts Payable	Notes Payable		Common Stock	Retained Earnings
8,000	15,900	4,100	=	2,500	4,000	+	12,000	9,500

The following events occurred during August 2011.

a. Sold common stock to Ms. Garriz in exchange for $15,000 cash

b. Paid $850 for first month's rent on office space

c. Purchased supplies of $2,250 on credit

d. Borrowed $8,000 from the bank

e. Paid $1,080 on account for supplies purchased earlier on credit

f. Paid secretary's salary for August of $2,150

g. Performed accounting services for clients who paid cash upon completion of the service in the total amount of $4,700.

h. Used $3,180 of the supplies on hand.

i. Performed accounting services for clients on credit in the total amount of $1,920

j. Purchased $500 in supplies for cash.

k. Collected $1,290 cash from clients for whom services were performed on credit

l. Paid $1,000 dividend to stockholders

Required:

1. Record the effects of the transactions listed above on the accounting equation. Use format given in the problem, starting with the totals at July 31, 2011.

2. Prepare the trial balance at August 31, 2011.

Problem 2-49A Inferring Transactions from T-Accounts

The following T-accounts summarize the operations of Chen Construction Company for July 2011.

Assets	Liabilities	Stockholders' Equity

Assets

Cash

7/1	200		
7/2	1,000	7/5	150
7/7	2,500	7/9	700
7/11	150	7/14	750

Accounts Receivable

7/1	1,400	7/11	150

Supplies

7/1	750	
7/4	250	

Land

7/1	3,000	
7/9	700	

Liabilities

Accounts Payable

		7/1	1,100
7/5	150	7/4	250

Stockholders' Equity

Common Stock

	7/1	4,000
	7/2	1,000

Retained Earnings

		7/1	250
7/14	750	7/7	2,500

Required:

1. Assuming that only one transaction occurred on each day (beginning on July 2) and that no dividends were paid, describe the transactions that most likely took place.
2. Prepare a trial balance at July 31, 2011.

Problem 2-50A Debit and Credit Procedures

A list of accounts for Montgomery Inc. appears below.

Accounts Payable	Interest Expense
Accounts Receivable	Land
Accumulated Depreciation	Notes Payable
Cash	Prepaid Rent
Common Stock	Retained Earnings
Depreciation Expense	Salaries Expense
Equipment	Service Revenue
Income Taxes Expense	Supplies

Required:

Complete the table below for these accounts. The information for the first account has been entered as an example.

Account	Type of Account	Normal Balance	Increase	Decrease
Accounts Payable	Liability	Credit	Credit	Debit

Problem 2-51A Journalizing Transactions

OBJECTIVE 5

Monroe Company rents and sells electronic equipment. During September 2011, Monroe engaged in the transactions described below.

Sept. 5   Purchased a Chevrolet truck for $34,900 cash
   8   Purchased inventory for $3,400 on account
  10   Purchased $1,450 of office supplies on credit
  11   Rented sound equipment to a traveling stage play for $12,800. The producer of the play paid for the service at the time it was provided.
  12   Rented sound equipment and lights to a local student organization for a school dance for $3,600. The student organization will pay for services within 30 days.
  18   Paid employee wages of $4,170 that have been earned during September
  22   Collected the receivable from the September 12 transaction
  23   Borrowed $14,100 cash from a bank on a three-year note payable
  28   Sold common stock to new stockholders for $40,000
  30   Paid a $4,350 cash dividend to stockholders

Required:
Prepare a journal entry for each transaction.

Problem 2-52A Journalizing and Posting Transactions

OBJECTIVE 5 6

Cincinnati Painting Service Inc. specializes in painting houses. During June, its first month of operations, Cincinnati Painting engaged in the following transactions:

June 1   Issued common stock for $10,000
   3   Purchased painting supplies from River City Supply for $1,125 on credit
   8   Purchased a used truck from Hamilton Used Car Sales for $8,700, paying $2,000 down and agreeing to pay the balance in six months
  14   Paid $3,960 to hourly employees for work performed in June
  22   Billed various customers a total of $9,430 for June painting jobs
  26   Received $5,800 cash from James Eaton for a house painting job completed and billed in May
  29   Collected $450 from Albert Montgomery on completion of a one-day painting job. This amount is not included in the June 22 bills.

Required:
1. Prepare a journal entry for each transaction.
2. Post the journal entries to Cincinnati Painting's ledger accounts.

Problem 2-53A The Accounting Cycle

OBJECTIVE 2 3 4 5 6 7

Karleen's Catering Service provides catered meals to individuals and businesses. Karleen's purchases its food ready to serve from Mel's Restaurant. In order to prepare a realistic trial balance, the events described below are aggregations of many individual events during 2011.

a. Common stock was issued for $22,000.
b. During the year, Karleen's paid office rent of $13,500.
c. Utilities expenses incurred and paid were $5,320.
d. Wages of $58,800 were earned by employees and paid during the year.
e. During the year, Karleen's provided catering services:

On credit	$128,200
For cash	18,650

f. Karleen's paid $59,110 for supplies purchased and used during the year.
g. Karleen's paid dividends in the amount of $3,500.
h. Karleen's collected accounts receivable in the amount of $109,400.

Required:
1. Analyze the events for their effect on the accounting equation.
2. Prepare journal entries. (*Note:* Ignore the date because these events are aggregations of individual events.)
3. Post the journal entries to ledger accounts.
4. Prepare a trial balance at December 31, 2011. Assume that all beginning account balances at January 1, 2011, are zero.

OBJECTIVE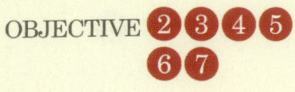

Problem 2-54A   Comprehensive Problem

Western Sound Studios records and masters audio tapes of popular artists in live concerts. The performers use the tapes to prepare "live" albums, CDs, and MP3s. The following account balances were available at the beginning of 2011:

Accounts Payable	$ 11,900
Accounts Receivable	384,000
Cash	16,300
Common Stock	165,000
Interest Payable	11,200
Notes Payable (Long-term)	100,000
Rent Payable (Building)	10,000
Insurance Payable	1,000
Retained Earnings, 12/31/2010	101,200

During 2011, the following transactions occurred (the events described below are aggregations of many individual events):

a.   Taping services in the amount of $994,000 were billed.
b.   The accounts receivable at the beginning of the year were collected.
c.   In addition, cash for $983,000 of the services billed in transaction *a* was collected.
d.   The rent payable for the building was paid. In addition, $48,000 of building rental costs was paid in cash. There was no rent payable or prepaid rent at year-end.
e.   The insurance payable on January 1 was paid. In addition, $4,000 of insurance costs was paid in cash. There was no insurance payable or prepaid insurance at year-end.
f.   Utilities expense of $56,000 was incurred and paid in 2011.
g.   Salaries expense for the year was $702,000. All $702,000 was paid in 2011.
h.   The interest payable at January 1 was paid. During the year, an additional $11,000 of interest was paid. At year-end no interest was payable.
i.   Income taxes for 2011 in the amount of $19,700 were incurred and paid.

Required:

1.   Establish a ledger for the accounts listed above and enter the beginning balances. Use a chart of accounts to order the ledger accounts.
2.   Analyze each transaction. Journalize as appropriate. (*Note:* Ignore the date because these events are aggregations of individual events.)
3.   Post your journal entries to the ledger accounts. Add additional ledger accounts when needed.
4.   Use the ending balances in the ledger accounts to prepare a trial balance.

PROBLEM SET B

OBJECTIVE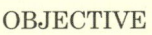

Problem 2-47B   Events and Transactions

The following list contains events that occurred during January 2011 at the local Ford dealer, Malcom Motors:

a.   California Central University (CCU) signed a contract to purchase a fleet of Ford Crown Victoria vehicles from Malcom Motors at a total price of $200,000, payable to Malcom in two equal amounts on August 1, 2011, and September 1, 2011. The cars will be delivered to CCU during August 2011.
b.   The principal stockholder in Malcom Motors sold 10 percent of her stock in the company to John Lewis, the president of Malcom Motors, in exchange for $100,000 in cash.
c.   Malcom Motors issued new stock to John Lewis in exchange for $50,000 in cash.
d.   Malcom Motors owns the building it occupies; the company occupied the building during the entire month of January.
e.   Malcom Motors owns land used for the storage of cars awaiting sale; the land was used by the company during the entire month of January.
f.   Malcom Motors paid its lawyer $1,000 for services rendered in connection with the purchase agreement signed with California Central University.
g.   Maintenance Management Company performed cleaning services for Malcom Motors during January under a contract that does not require payment for those services until March 1, 2011.

Required:
1. Indicate whether each item qualifies as a transaction and should be recorded in the accounting system. Explain your reasoning.
2. **Conceptual Connection:** What concept is illustrated by the event in item *b*?

Problem 2-48B Analyzing Transactions

OBJECTIVE ❸ ❼

Several years ago, Mary Emerson founded Emerson Consulting Inc., a consulting business specializing in financial planning for young professionals. The following captions and amounts summarize Emerson Consulting's balance sheet at December 31, 2010, the beginning of the current year:

Assets			=	Liabilities		+	Equity	
Cash	Accounts Receivable	Supplies		Accounts Payable	Notes Payable		Common Stock	Retained Earnings
3,000	6,600	4,800		500	1,000		10,000	2,900

During January 2011, the following transactions occurred:

a. Sold common stock to a new stockholder in exchange for $12,000 cash
b. Performed advisory services for a client for $3,850 and received the full amount in cash
c. Received $925 on account from a client for whom services had been performed on credit
d. Purchased supplies for $1,140 on credit
e. Paid $875 on accounts payable
f. Performed advisory services for $2,980 on credit
g. Paid cash of $1,350 for secretarial services during January
h. Paid cash of $800 for January's office rent
i. Paid utilities used in January 2011 in the amount of $1,340
j. Paid a dividend of $500

Required:
1. Record the effects of the transactions listed above on the accounting equation for the business. Use the format given in the problem, starting with the totals at December 31, 2010.
2. Prepare the trial balance at January 31, 2011.

Problem 2-49B Inferring Transactions from T-Accounts

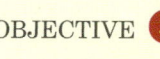

OBJECTIVE ❸ ❹ ❼

The following T-accounts summarize the operations of Brilliant Minds Inc., a tutoring service, for April 2011.

Assets

Cash
4/1	500	4/8	700
4/3	2,000	4/9	325
4/18	1,500	4/15	150
4/24	375		

Accounts Receivable
4/1	700	4/24	375

Supplies
4/1	900	4/11	140
4/15	150		

Equipment
4/1	1,200	
4/8	700	

Liabilities

Accounts Payable
4/9	325	4/1	625

Notes Payable
	4/3	2,000

Stockholders' Equity

Common Stock
	4/1	2,000

Retained Earnings
4/11	140	4/1	675
		4/18	1,500

(Continued)

Required:
1. Assuming that only one transaction occurred on each day (beginning on April 3) and that no dividends were paid, describe the transaction that most likely took place.
2. Prepare a trial balance at April 30, 2011.

OBJECTIVE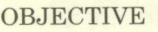

Problem 2-50B Debit and Credit Procedures

A list of accounts for Montgomery Inc. appears below.

Accounts Payable	Copyright
Accounts Receivable	Interest Expense
Bonds Payable	Inventory
Building	Investments
Cash	Retained Earnings
Common Stock	Sales Revenue
Cost of Goods Sold	Unearned Revenue
Depreciation Expense	Utilities Expense
Income Taxes Payable	Income Taxes Expense
Insurance Expense	

Required:
Complete the table below for these accounts. The information for the first account has been entered as an example.

Account	Type of Account	Normal Balance	Increase	Decrease
Accounts Payable	Liability	Credit	Credit	Debit

OBJECTIVE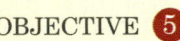

Problem 2-51B Journalizing Transactions

Monilast Chemicals engaged in the following transactions during December 2011:

Dec.	2	Paid rent on office furniture, $900
	3	Borrowed $20,000 on a nine-month, 8 percent note
	7	Provided services on credit, $38,600
	10	Purchased supplies on credit, $3,200 13,200
	13	Collected accounts receivable, $18,800
	19	Sold common stock, $55,000
	22	Paid employee wages for December, $11,650
	23	Paid accounts payable, $6,975
	25	Provided services for cash, $15,430
	30	Paid utility bills for December, $2,180

Required:
Prepare a journal entry for each transaction.

OBJECTIVE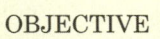

Problem 2-52B Journalizing and Posting Transactions

Findlay Testing Inc. provides water testing and maintenance services for owners of hot tubs and swimming pools. During September the following transactions occurred:

Sept.	1	Issued common stock for $12,000
	2	Purchased chemical supplies for $1,480 cash
	5	Paid office rent for October, November, and December; the rent is $600 per month
	8	Purchased $895 of advertising for September on account
	13	Billed the city of Bellefontaine $4,200 for testing the water in the city's outdoor pools during September
	18	Received $6,850 from Alexander Blanchard upon completion of overhaul of his swimming pool water circulation system. Since the job was completed and collected for on the same day, no bill was sent to Blanchard.
	25	Received $495 from the city of Bellefontaine for water testing that was previously billed
	30	Recorded and paid September salaries of $4,320

Required:
1. Prepare a journal entry for each transaction.
2. Post the journal entries to Findlay Testing's ledger accounts.

Problem 2-53B The Accounting Cycle

OBJECTIVE ② ③ ④ ⑤ ⑥ ⑦

Sweetwater Temporary Clerical Help Service opened for business in June 2011. From the opening until the end of the year, Sweetwater engaged in the activities described below. So that a realistic trial balance can be prepared, the events described below are aggregations of many individual events.

a. Sold 10,000 shares of common stock for $4.50 per share
b. Purchased office equipment from FurnitureMax Inc. for $18,710 cash
c. Received $112,880 from clients for services provided
d. Paid wages of $87,300
e. Borrowed $20,000 from the Bank of America on a three-year note payable
f. Paid office rent of $10,200
g. Purchased office supplies on credit for $2,120 from Office Supply Inc.
h. Paid $1,200 toward the payable established in transaction g
i. Paid utility charges incurred during the year of $3,250

Required:

1. Analyze the events for their effect on the accounting equation.
2. Prepare journal entries. (*Note:* Ignore the date because these events are aggregations of individual events.)
3. Post the journal entries to ledger accounts.
4. Prepare a trial balance at December 31, 2011.

Problem 2-54B Comprehensive Problem

OBJECTIVE ② ③ ④ ⑤ ⑥ ⑦

Mulberry Services sells electronic data processing services to firms too small to own their own computing equipment. Mulberry had the following accounts and account balances as of January 1, 2011:

Accounts Payable	$ 14,000
Accounts Receivable	130,000
Common Stock	114,000
Cash	6,000
Interest Payable	8,000
Notes Payable (Long-term)	80,000
Prepaid Rent (Short-term)	96,000
Retained Earnings, 12/31/2010	16,000

During 2011, the following transactions occurred (the events described below are aggregations of many individual events):

a. During 2011, Mulberry sold $690,000 of computing services, all on credit.
b. Mulberry collected $570,000 from the credit sales in transaction a and an additional $129,000 from the accounts receivable outstanding at the beginning of the year.
c. Mulberry paid the interest payable of $8,000.
d. Wages of $379,000 were paid in cash.
e. Repairs and maintenance of $9,000 were incurred and paid.
f. The prepaid rent at the beginning of the year was used in 2011. In addition, $28,000 of computer rental costs were incurred and paid. There is no prepaid rent or rent payable at year-end.
g. Mulberry purchased computer paper for $13,000 cash in late December. None of the paper was used by year-end.
h. Advertising expense of $26,000 was incurred and paid.
i. Income tax of $10,300 was incurred and paid in 2011.
j. Interest of $5,000 was paid on the long-term loan.

Required:

1. Establish a ledger for the accounts listed above and enter the beginning balances. Use a chart of accounts to order the ledger accounts.
2. Analyze each transaction. Journalize as appropriate. (*Note:* Ignore the date because these events are aggregations of individual events.)
3. Post your journal entries to the ledger accounts. Add additional ledger accounts when needed.
4. Use the ending balances in the ledger accounts to prepare a trial balance.

CASES

Case 2-55 Analysis of the Accounting Cycle

Susan Eel wants to sell you her wholesale fish store. She shows you a balance sheet with total assets of $150,000 and total liabilities of $20,000. According to the income statement, last year's net income was $40,000.

When examining the accounting records, you notice that several accounts receivable in the $10,000 to $15,000 range are not supported by source documents. You also notice that there is no source documentation to support the $30,000 balance in the building account and the $10,000 balance in the equipment account. Susan tells you that she gave the building and refrigeration equipment to the business in exchange for stock. She also says that she has not had time to set up and monitor any paperwork for accounts receivable or accounts payable.

Required:

1. What requirements for transaction recognition appear to have been ignored when the accounts receivable, building, and equipment were recorded?
2. What would be the effect on the financial statements if the values appearing in the balance sheet for accounts receivable, building, and equipment were overstated? What would be the effect if the accounts payable were understated?
3. Assuming that you would like to purchase the company, what would you do to establish a reasonable purchase price?

Case 2-56 Analysis of the Effects of Current Asset and Current Liability Changes on Cash Flows

You have the following data for Cable Company's accounts receivable and accounts payable for 2011:

Accounts receivable, 1/1/2011	$ 4,750
2011 sales on credit	97,400
Accounts receivable, 12/31/2011	8,300
Wages payable, 1/1/2011	5,870
2011 wage expense	38,100
Wages payable, 12/31/2011	3,900

Required:

1. How much cash did Cable collect from customers during 2011?
2. How would you classify cash collected from customers on the statement of cash flows?
3. How much cash did Cable pay for wages during 2011?
4. How would you classify the cash paid for wages on the statement of cash flows?

Case 2-57 Ethical Issues

Kathryn Goldsmith is the chief accountant for Clean Sweep, a national carpet-cleaning service with a December fiscal year-end. As Kathryn was preparing the 2011 financial statements for Clean Sweep, she noticed several odd transactions in the general ledger for December. For example, rent for January 2012, which was paid in December 2011, was recorded by debiting rent expense instead of prepaid rent. In another transaction, Kathryn noticed that the use of supplies was recorded with a debit to insurance expense instead of supplies expense. Upon further investigation, Kathryn discovered that the December ledger contained numerous such mistakes. Even with the mistakes, the trial balance still balanced.

Kathryn traced all of the mistakes back to a recently hired bookkeeper, Ben Goldsmith, Kathryn's son. Kathryn had hired Ben to help out in the accounting department over Christmas break so that he could earn some extra money for school. After discussing the situation with Ben, Kathryn determined that Ben's mistakes were all unintentional.

Required:

1. What ethical issues are involved?
2. What are Kathryn's alternatives? Which would be the most ethical alternative to choose?

Case 2-58 Research and Analysis Using the Annual Report

Obtain **General Electric**'s 2009 annual report either through the "Investor Relations" portion of its Web site (do a web search for GE investor relations) or go to http://www.sec.gov and click "Search for Company Filings" under "Filings and Forms"

Required:

1. Determine the amounts in the accounting equation for the most recent year. Does it balance?

2. What is the normal balance for the following accounts?

    a.   Current Receivables
    b.   Short-Term Borrowings
    c.   Sales of Services
    d.   Property, Plant, and Equipment—Net
    e.   Cost of Goods Sold
    f.   Inventories
    g.   Retained Earnings

3. Identify the additional account that is most likely involved when:

    a.   Accounts Payable is decreased.
    b.   Accounts Receivables is increased.
    c.   Common Stock is increased.
    d.   Wages Payable is increased.

Case 2-59 Comparative Analysis: Abercrombie & Fitch vs. Aeropostale

Refer to the financial statements of **Abercrombie & Fitch** and **Aeropostale** that are supplied with this text.

Required:

1. Determine the amounts in the accounting equation for the year ending January 30, 2010, for each company. Does the accounting equation balance?

2. Set up a T-account for Abercrombie & Fitch's accounts receivable account and include the beginning and ending balances Complete the T-account to reflect the sales and cash collections for the year. Assume all sales are on account.

3. Prepare the journal entry to record the following two events. For simplicity, assume the event was recorded in a single journal entry.

    a.   What journal entry is necessary to record Abercrombie & Fitch's net sales for the year ending January 30, 2010? Assume that all sales were made on account.

    b.   What journal entry is necessary to record Abercrombie & Fitch's cash collections from customers during the year ending January 30, 2010?

4. Where do Abercrombie & Fitch and Aeropostale report credit card receivables? (*Hint:* You may want to refer to the Summary of Significant Accounting Policies in the Notes to the Financial Statements.)

Case 2-60 Accounting for Partially Completed Events: a Prelude to Chapter 3

Ehrlich Smith, the owner of The Shoe Box, has asked you to help him understand the proper way to account for certain accounting items as he prepares his 2011 financial statements. Smith has provided the following information and observations:

a.   A three-year fire insurance policy was purchased on January 1, 2011, for $2,400. Smith believes that a part of the cost of the insurance policy should be allocated to each period that benefits from its coverage.

b.   The store building was purchased for $80,000 in January 2003. Smith expected then (as he does now) that the building will be serviceable as a shoe store for 20 years from the date of purchase. In 2003, Smith estimated that he could sell the property for $6,000 at the end of its serviceable life. He feels that each period should bear some portion of the cost of this long-lived asset that is slowly being consumed.

c.   The Shoe Box borrowed $20,000 on a one-year, 8 percent note that is due on September 1 next year. Smith notes that $21,600 cash will be required to repay the note at maturity. The $1,600 difference is, he feels, a cost of using the loaned funds and should be spread over the periods that benefit from the use of the loan funds.

(Continued)

Required:

1. Explain what Smith is trying to accomplish with the three items on p. 105. Are his objectives supported by the concepts that underlie accounting?
2. Describe how each of the three items should be reflected in the 2011 income statement and the December 31, 2011 balance sheet to accomplish Smith's objectives.

Case 2-61 CONTINUING PROBLEM: FRONT ROW ENTERTAINMENT

After much consideration, Cam and Anna decide to organize their company as a corporation. On January 1, 2011, Front Row Entertainment Inc. begins operations. Due to Cam's family connections in the entertainment industry, Cam assumes the major responsibility for signing artists to a promotion contract. Meanwhile, Anna assumes the financial accounting and reporting responsibilities. The following business activities occurred during January:

Jan.	1	Cam and Anna invest $8,000 each in the company in exchange for common stock.
	1	The company obtains a $25,000 loan from a local bank. Front Row Entertainment agreed to pay annual interest of 9 percent each January 1, starting in 2012. It will repay the amount borrowed in five years.
	1	The company paid $1,200 in legal fees associated with incorporation.
	1	Office equipment was purchased with $7,000 in cash.
	1	The company pays $800 to rent office space for January.
	3	A one year insurance policy was purchased for $3,600.
	3	Office supplies of $2,500 were purchased from Equipment Supply Services. Equipment Supply Services agreed to accept $1,000 in 15 days with the remainder due in 30 days.
	5	The company signs Charm City, a local band with a growing cult following, to a four-city tour that starts on February 15.
	8	Venues for all four Charm City concerts were reserved by paying $10,000 cash.
	12	Advertising costs of $4,500 were paid to promote the concert tour.
	18	Paid $1,000 to Equipment Supply Services for office supplies purchased on January 3.
	25	To aid in the promotion of the upcoming tour, Front Row Entertainment arranged for Charm City to perform a 20-minute set at a local festival. Front Row Entertainment received $1,000 for Charm City's appearance. Of this total amount, $400 was received immediately with the remainder due in 15 days.
	25	Paid Charm City $800 for performing at the festival. Note: Front Row Entertainment records the fees paid to the artist in an operating expense account called Artist Fee Expense.
	28	Due to the success of the marketing efforts, Front Row Entertainment received $3,800 in advance ticket sales for the upcoming tour.
	30	The company collected the $200 of the amount due from the January 25 festival.
	30	Paid salaries of $1,200 each to Cam and Anna.

Required:

1. Analyze and journalize the January transactions.
2. Post the transactions to the general ledger.
3. Prepare a trial balance at January 31, 2011.

TYPICAL CHART OF ACCOUNTS

ASSETS

Accounts Receivable
Accumulated Depletion
Accumulated
    Depreciation
Allowance for Doubtful
    Accounts
Allowance to Adjust
    Available-For-Sale
    Securities to Market
Allowance to Adjust
    Trading Securities to
    Market
Buildings
Cash
Copyright
Equipment
Finished Goods
    Inventory
Franchise
Furniture
Goodwill
Interest Receivable
Inventory
Investments
Investments—Available-
    For-Sale Securities
Investments—Equity
    Method
Investments—Trading
    Securities
Land
Leasehold Improvements
Natural Resources
Notes Receivable
Other Assets
Patent
Petty Cash
Prepaid Advertising
Prepaid Insurance
Prepaid Rent
Prepaid Repairs &
    Maintenance
Prepaid Security Services
Raw Materials Inventory
Rent Receivable
Supplies
Tax Refund Receivable
Trademark
Trucks
Work-in-Process Inventory

LIABILITIES

Accounts Payable
Bonds Payable
Capital Lease Liability
Charitable
    Contributions
Commissions Payable

Discount on Bonds
    Payable
Discount on Notes
    Payable
Dividends Payable
Excise Taxes Payable
Income Taxes Payable
Interest Payable
Lawsuit Payable
Leased Assets
Lease Liability
Medicare Taxes
    Payable
Notes Payable
Premium on Bonds
    Payable
Premium on Notes
    Payable
Property Taxes Payable
Rent Payable
Repair & Maintenance
    Payable
Royalties Payable
Salaries Payable
Sales Taxes Payable
Social Security Taxes
    Payable
Unearned Rent
    Revenue
Unearned Sales
    Revenue
Unearned Service
    Revenue
Unemployment Taxes
    Payable
Union Dues Payable
Utilities Payable
Wages Payable
Warranty Liability

STOCKHOLDERS' EQUITY

Accumulated Other
    Comprehensive
    Income
Additional Paid-In
    Capital—Common
    Stock
Additional Paid-In
    Capital—Preferred
    Stock
Additional Paid-In
    Capital—Treasury
    Stock
Common Stock
Preferred Stock
Retained Earnings
Treasury Stock
Unrealized Gain (Loss)
    on Available-For-Sale
    Securities

EQUITY-RELATED ACCOUNTS

Dividends
Income Summary

REVENUES/GAINS

Dividend Income
Interest Income
Investment Income—
    Equity Method
Rent Revenue
Sales Discounts
Sales Returns and
    Allowances
Sales Revenue
Service Revenue

Gain on Disposal of
    Property, Plant &
    Equipment
Gain on Sale of
    Intangibles
Gain on Sale of
    Investments
Gain on Settlement of
    Lawsuit
Unrealized Gain (Loss) on
    Trading Securities

EXPENSES/LOSSES

Advertising Expense
Amortization Expense
Artist Fee Expense
Bad Debt Expense
Bank Service Charge
    Expense
Cash Over and Short
Commissions Expense
Cost of Goods Sold
Delivery Expense
Depreciation Expense
Income Taxes Expense
Insurance Expense
Interest Expense
Legal Expense
Medicare Taxes Expense
Miscellaneous Expense
Organizational Costs
Other Expense
Postage Expense
Property Taxes Expense

Purchase Allowances
Purchase Discounts
Purchase Returns
Purchases
Rent Expense
Repairs & Maintenance
    Expense
Research and
    Development Expense
Royalties Expense
Salaries Expense
Security Services Expense
Service Charge Expense
Social Security Taxes
    Expense
Supplies Expense
Transportation-In
Unemployment Taxes
    Expense
Utilities Expense
Wages Expense
Warranty Expense

Loss from Impairment
Loss on Disposal of
    Property, Plant &
    Equipment
Loss on Sale of
    Intangibles
Loss on Sales of
    Investments
Loss on Sale of
    Investments

Note:

The Chart of Accounts for this edition of *Cornerstones of Financial Accounting* has been simplified and standardized throughout all hypothetical in-chapter examples and end-of-chapter assignments in order to strengthen the pedagogical structure of the book. Account titles for real company financial statements will vary. Common alternate account titles are given in the textbook where the account is introduced, as appropriate, and real financial statement excerpts are included to help familiarize readers with alternate account titles.

When additional information is needed for an account title, it will be shown in parenthesis after the title [e.g., Accumulated Depreciation (Equipment), Excise Taxes Payable (State), Social Security Taxes Payable (Employer), etc.]

This Chart of Accounts is listed alphabetically by category for ease of reference. However, accounts in the textbook and in real financial statements are listed in order of liquidity.

3 Accrual Accounting

Doug Norman Crystals/Alamy

After studying Chapter 3, you should be able to:

1 Explain the difference between cash-basis and accrual-basis accounting.

2 Explain how the time-period assumption, revenue recognition, and matching principles affect the determination of income.

3 Identify the kinds of transactions that may require adjustments at the end of an accounting period.

4 Prepare adjusting entries for accruals and deferrals.

5 Prepare financial statements from an adjusted trial balance.

6 Explain why and how companies prepare closing entries.

7 Understand the steps in the accounting cycle.

8 *(Appendix 3A)* Understand how to use a worksheet to prepare financial statements.

David Gee1/Alamy

EXPERIENCE FINANCIAL ACCOUNTING

with FedEx®

FedEx began operations in 1973 with 14 jets that connected 25 U.S. cities. Some employees even used their own cars to deliver packages. As a pioneer of the hub and spoke model for overnight package delivery, FedEx is now the world's largest express transportation company with operations in over 220 countries. With approximately 140,000 employees, 654 aircraft, and 51,000 vehicles and trailers, FedEx has the ability to "absolutely, positively" get a package delivered overnight.

The end of the fiscal year, or accounting period, is a busy time as companies like FedEx make adjustments to the accounting information. Adjustments are necessary because a company's business activities often occur over several accounting periods. In its 2009 annual report

shown in Exhibit 3-1, FedEx's financial statements include many expenses that would not have been recognized without adjustments.

This sample of expenses, which doesn't include all the adjustments made, represents almost 13 percent of the total operating expenses that FedEx reported on its 2009 income statement. When FedEx recognized these expenses (except for depreciation and amortization), it also recorded a liability for them. These liabilities represented 55% of FedEx's current liabilities. The adjustment to recognize depreciation and amortization expense resulted in a decrease in assets of $1.975 million. Clearly, the failure to adjust for these expenses would significantly affect FedEx's financial statements.

Excerpt from FedEx's Financial Statements

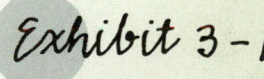

Exhibit 3-1

FedEx Corporation Consolidated Income Statement (partial) For the Year Ended May 31, 2009	
(in millions)	
Revenues	$ 35,497
Operating expenses	(34,750)
Other income (expense)	(70)
Income before income taxes	$ 677
Income taxes	(579)
Net income	$ 98

Sample of expenses resulting from adjustment:	
Salaries	$ 201
Employee benefits and compensated absences	660
Insurance	626
Taxes other than income taxes	338
Depreciation and amortization	1,975
Other	674
Total (13% of Operating expenses)	$4,474

OBJECTIVE
Explain the difference between cash-basis and accrual-basis accounting.

COMPLETING THE ACCOUNTING CYCLE

In the previous chapter, we examined how companies use the double-entry accounting system to record business activities that occur during the accounting period. However, accountants also make numerous adjustments at the end of accounting periods for business activities that occur over several accounting periods—activities like the performance of services for customers, the renting of office space, and the use of equipment. As shown with **FedEx**, these adjustments can be significant.

Why are so many business activities recognized in the accounts through adjustments rather than through the normal journal entry process described in Chapter 2? The illustrations used in Chapter 2 excluded activities that were still underway at the end of the accounting period. However, the recognition of business activities in financial accounting uses the accrual basis of accounting. Accrual accounting requires that any incomplete activities be recognized in the financial statements. This often requires estimates and judgments about the timing of revenue and expense recognition. The result is that accountants must adjust the accounts to properly reflect these partially-completed business activities.

In this chapter, we will review the concepts that form the basis for adjustments and then complete the accounting cycle that was introduced in Chapter 2 by exploring the preparation and effects of adjusting journal entries, preparing financial statements from the adjusted accounts, and closing the accounts in order to prepare for the next accounting period. We will address the following questions:

- What is the difference between the cash basis and the accrual basis of accounting?
- What is the purpose of adjusting entries?
- What types of transactions require adjustment, and how are the adjustments recorded in the accounting system?
- Which accounts are closed at the end of the period, and why is this necessary?

Accrual versus Cash Basis of Accounting

If you were asked what your net income (revenues less expenses) for the month was, what would you do? Most likely, you would go online and look at your bank activity for the month. You would then list the total of the deposits as revenue and the total of the withdrawals as expenses. The difference would be your net income. This method of accounting is called **cash-basis accounting**. Under cash-basis accounting, revenue is recorded when cash is received, regardless of when it is actually earned. Similarly, an expense is recorded when cash is paid, regardless of when it is actually incurred. Therefore, cash-basis accounting does not link recognition of revenues and expenses to the actual business activity but rather the exchange of cash. In addition, by recording only the cash effect of transactions, cash-basis financial statements may not reflect all of the assets and liabilities of a company at a particular date. For this reason, most companies do not use cash-basis accounting.

Accrual-basis accounting (also called *accrual accounting*) is an alternative to cash-basis accounting that is required by generally accepted accounting principles. Under accrual accounting, transactions are recorded when they occur. Accrual accounting is superior to cash-basis because it links income measurement to selling, the principle activity of the company. That is, revenue is recognized as it is earned and expenses are recognized when they are incurred. In contrast to cash-basis accounting, accrual accounting is a more complex system that records both *cash and noncash* transactions.

OBJECTIVE
Explain how the time-period assumption, revenue recognition, and matching principles affect the determination of income.

KEY ELEMENTS OF ACCRUAL ACCOUNTING

As shown in Exhibit 3-2, an accrual accounting system rests on three elements of the conceptual framework that were introduced in Chapter 2—the time-period assumption, the revenue recognition principle, and the matching principle.

Time-Period Assumption

Investors, creditors, and other financial statement users demand timely information from companies. For that reason, companies report their financial results for specific periods of

Exhibit 3-2

Key Elements of Accrual Accounting

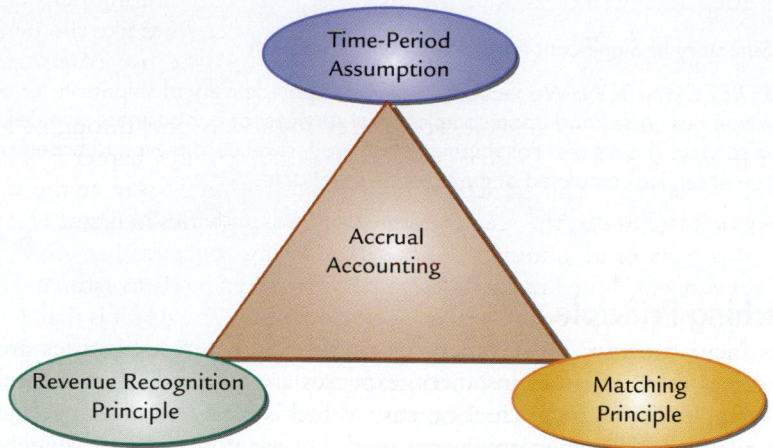

time—a month, a quarter, or a year. The **time-period assumption** allows companies to artificially divide their operations into time periods so they can satisfy users' demands for information.

Companies frequently engage in continuing activities that affect more than one time period. For example, **FedEx** often receives cash from a company to deliver products in one time period, although the actual delivery does not occur until a different time period. In addition, the aircraft and vehicles used by FedEx are purchased at a single point in time but are used over many years. To properly record the use of these aircraft and the providing of its service, accrual accounting requires that FedEx assign the revenue and expenses to the proper time period. This is quite often a difficult task and is guided by the revenue recognition and matching principles.

The Revenue Recognition Principle

The **revenue recognition principle** determines when revenue is recorded and reported. Under this principle, revenue is recognized, or recorded, in the period in which both of the following conditions are met:

IFRS

While revenue recognition concepts under IFRS are similar to U.S. GAAP, U.S. GAAP contains much more specific rules and guidance.

- The revenue has been earned.
- The collection of cash is reasonably assured.

These requirements are usually met when goods have been delivered to a customer or when services have been performed for a customer. At this point, the risks and rewards of ownership usually have been transferred from the seller to the buyer.[1] **Notice that revenue is recorded when these two conditions are met, regardless of when cash is received.**

To illustrate the revenue recognition principle, assume that on March 31, **FedEx** picks up a computer from **Apple**'s distribution center and receives a cash payment of $30 to ship the computer to a customer. FedEx delivers the computer on April 2. Even though cash was received on March 31, FedEx will recognize the $30 of revenue on April 2, the date the computer is delivered to the customer. Notice that revenue is not recognized until it is earned by FedEx (delivery of the computer), and that the receipt of cash prior to the delivery does not affect when revenue is recognized. Exhibit 3-3 (p. 112) shows an excerpt of FedEx's revenue recognition policy that is disclosed in the notes to its financial statements.

---

[1] The Securities and Exchange Commission expanded upon this principle and stated that the revenue recognition criteria are normally met when (1) delivery has occurred or services have been rendered, (2) persuasive evidence of an arrangement exists, (3) the selling price is fixed or determinable, and (4) the collection of cash is reasonably assured.

Exhibit 3-3

Annual Report Excerpt: FedEx's Revenue Recognition Policy

> **Note 1: Summary of Significant Accounting Policies (in part)**
>
> *REVENUE RECOGNITION.* We recognize revenue upon delivery of shipments for our transportation businesses and upon completion of services for our business services, logistics and trade services businesses. For shipments in transit, revenue is recorded based on the percentage of service completed at the balance sheet date.

The Matching Principle

Companies incur expenses for a variety of reasons. Sometimes expenses are incurred when an asset is used. In other instances, expenses are incurred when a liability is created. For example, FedEx incurs fuel expense as fuel is used to deliver packages. FedEx also incurs salary expense when employees work but are not paid immediately. The key idea is that **an expense is recorded when it is incurred, regardless of when cash is paid.**

Expense recognition is the process of identifying an expense with a particular time period. Under accrual accounting, expenses are recognized following the **matching principle**, which requires that expenses be recorded and reported in the same period as the revenue that it helped to generate. Expenses for an accounting period should *include* only those costs used to earn revenue that was recognized in the accounting period. Expenses for an accounting period should *exclude* those costs used to earn revenue in an earlier period and those costs that will be used to earn revenue in a later period. Thus, the key to expense recognition is matching the expense with revenue.

Concept Q&A

Cash-basis accounting seems straightforward. Why complicate matters by introducing accrual accounting?

Answer:
The objective of financial reporting is to provide information that is useful in making business and economic decisions. Most of these decisions involve predicting a company's future cash flows. The use of accrual accounting through the application of the revenue recognition and matching principles links income recognition to the principal activity of the company, selling goods and services. Therefore, accrual accounting provides a better estimate of future cash flows than cash-basis accounting.

ETHICAL DECISIONS   The revenue recognition and matching principles can and have been abused in recent years. As companies strive to meet or exceed Wall Street expectations, management may be tempted to recognize revenue that has not yet been earned or to hide expenses that should be recognized. In recent years, the Securities and Exchange Commission (SEC) has conducted numerous investigations involving the abuse of both revenue and expense recognition. Some notable cases are listed in Exhibit 3-4.

Exhibit 3-4

Instances of Accounting Abuses

Company	Action
Regina Vacuum	Backdated sales invoices, improperly recorded revenue on consignment sales that had not been earned, and hid unpaid bills in a filing cabinet to reduce expenses. Chairman, CEO, and president Donald Sheelen pleaded guilty to fraud, fined $25,000, and sentenced to one year in a work release program in Florida.
Miniscribe	Improperly recognized revenue through a variety of means, including packaging and shipping bricks as finished products. Chief executive Q. T. Wiles fined $250 million.
Sunbeam	Used a variety of techniques to improperly recognize revenue (including bill and hold transactions and channel stuffing). CEO Al Dunlap fined $500,000 and barred from ever serving as an officer or director of a public company.
WorldCom	Improperly reduced operating expenses, which inflated income, by reversing (releasing) accrued liabilities and improperly classifying certain expenses as assets. Chief executive Bernard Ebbers was sentenced to 25 years in jail.
Bally Total Fitness	Recognized revenue on gym membership contracts before it was earned, and improperly delayed the recognition of expenses. In total, more than two dozen improprieties were discovered that caused stockholders' equity to be overstated by $1.8 billion. Bally's auditor paid $8.5 million to settle charges of improper auditing.

While the actions summarized in Exhibit 3-4 were fraudulent and led to severe fines or jail time for many of the company executives, other innocent parties were also affected by these unethical actions. Stockholders, many of whom who had bought the stock at an inflated price, saw a significant drop in the stock's value after these actions were made public. In addition, innocent employees lost their jobs as the companies struggled to deal with the fraud that occurred. When faced with an ethical dilemma to manipulate the recognition of revenue or expenses, make the decision that best portrays the economic reality of your company. ●

Applying the Principles

In order to use the financial statements, it is important to understand how the revenue recognition and matching principles affect the amounts reported. **CORNERSTONE 3-1** compares how the application of these principles results in accrual-basis income that differs from cash-basis income.

CORNERSTONE 3-1

Applying the Revenue Recognition and Matching Principles

Concept:
Under accrual accounting, revenue is recognized when it is earned and the collection of cash is reasonably assured. Expenses are recognized in the same period as the revenue they helped generate.

Information:
The state of Georgia hired Conservation Inc., a consulting company specializing in the conservation of natural resources, to explore options for providing water resources to the Atlanta metropolitan area. In November 2011, Conservation Inc. incurred $60,000 of expenditures, on account, while investigating the water shortage facing the state. Conservation Inc. also delivered its recommendations and billed the state $100,000 for its work. In December 2011, Conservation Inc. paid the $60,000 of expenses. In January 2012, Conservation Inc. received the state's check for $100,000.

Required:
Calculate net income for November 2011, December 2011, and January 2012 using the following methods: (1) the cash-basis of accounting, and (2) the accrual-basis of accounting.

Solution:
1.

November 2011		December 2011		January 2012	
Revenue	$0	Revenue	$ 0	Revenue	$100,000
Expense	0	Expense	60,000	Expense	0
Net income	$0	Net income	$(60,000)	Net income	$100,000
→ Performed Service		→ Paid Expenses		→ Received Payment	

2.

November 2011		December 2011		January 2012	
Revenue	$100,000	Revenue	$0	Revenue	$0
Expense	60,000	Expense	0	Expense	0
Net income	$ 40,000	Net income	$0	Net income	$0
→ Performed Service		→ Paid Expenses		→ Received Payment	

Notice that, under accrual accounting, revenue is recognized when it is earned and expenses are matched with revenues. Even though Conservation Inc. did not receive the payment from the state of Georgia until January 2012, Conservation Inc. had performed services in November 2011 and appropriately recognized the revenue as the service was performed. The $60,000 of expenses were matched with revenues and also recognized in November 2011. If cash-basis accounting would have been used, $60,000 of expense would have been recognized in December 2011 (when the cash was paid) and $100,000 of revenue would have been recognized in January 2012 (when the cash was received). By following the revenue recognition and matching principles, net income was properly recognized in the period that the business activity occurred. In short, the difference between cash-basis and accrual-basis accounting is a matter of timing.

YOU DECIDE   Recognizing a Security Service Contract

You are the chief financial officer of Secure Entry Inc., a security company, and it is your responsibility to develop the company's revenue and expense recognition policies. In April 2010, Secure Entry signed a two-year contract with the Metropolis Stadium Authority (MSA) to provide security services at its stadium gates beginning in January 2011. Under the terms of the contract, MSA agrees to make 24 equal monthly payments to Secure Entry beginning in October 2010.

When should Secure Entry Inc. recognize revenue and expenses associated with the security contract?

To provide investors and creditors with the most useful information and be consistent with GAAP, you decide that Secure Entry should follow accrual accounting principles. Therefore, the contract is initially recognized in October 2010, when MSA makes the first payment. At that time, Secure Entry would record an increase in cash for the payment received and an equal increase in a liability (Unearned Revenue) to recognize that future services are owed. Secure Entry would not record the contract in its accounting system in April 2010 because the event does meet the recognition criteria discussed in Chapter 2.

Consistent with the revenue recognition principle, Secure Entry would recognize revenue each month, as services are performed, beginning in January 2011. Additionally, expenses related to the performance of security services should be matched against revenue from providing the security services and recognized monthly beginning in January 2011.

The proper recognition of revenue and expenses is critical in properly measuring and reporting income in the period that a business activity occurs.

OBJECTIVE 3
Identify the kinds of transactions that may require adjustments at the end of an accounting period.

IFRS

The adjustment process under IFRS is the same as the adjustment process under U.S. GAAP.

ACCRUAL ACCOUNTING AND ADJUSTING ENTRIES

Which Transactions Require Adjustment?

Many business activities continue for a period of time—for example, the use of rented facilities or interest incurred on borrowed money. Because entries in the accounting system are made at particular points in time rather than continuously, adjustments are needed at the end of an accounting period to record partially complete activities.[2] **Adjusting entries** are journal entries made at the end of an accounting period to record the completed portion of partially completed transactions. Adjusting entries are necessary to apply the revenue recognition and matching principles and ensure that a company's financial statements include the proper amount for revenues, expenses, assets, liabilities, and stockholders' equity.

---

[2] The distinction between business activities requiring adjustment and those that do not depends to some extent on our ability and willingness to keep track of activities. Some activities may occur so frequently or are so difficult to measure that no record of individual activities is maintained. In such cases, the sequence of individual activities becomes, for all intents and purposes, a continuous activity. For example, the use of office supplies is often treated as a continuous business activity because it is too costly to maintain a record of each time supplies are used.

In **CORNERSTONE 3-2**, three representative transactions are described. The implications of the "length" of these transactions for recognition in the accounting system and for adjustment is discussed.

CORNERSTONE 3-2

Determining Which Transactions Require Adjustment

Concept:
Adjusting journal entries are required for continuous transactions that are partially complete at the end of an accounting period.

Information:
Computer Town sells computer equipment and provides computer repair service. Sales are typically made in cash or on account. Repairs are provided under service contracts, which customers purchase up front for a specified period of time (two, three, or five years). Customers pay nothing when the computer is brought in for repair.

Required:
1. How should Computer Town account for cash and credit sales of equipment?
2. How should Computer Town account for repair services provided under service contracts?
3. How should Computer Town account for the use of office supplies?

Solution:
1. Cash sales should be recorded as they occur and the equipment is delivered, often at a cash register that tracks total sales for the day. When orders are received from customers who want to purchase equipment on credit, the sale should be recorded when the equipment is delivered to the customer. In both situations, the sale is complete at a single point in time (the delivery of the equipment) and no adjusting entry is needed.
2. Repair service contracts are continuous activities that require an adjustment at the end of the accounting period. Revenue is earned as time passes under the service contract and should be recorded in proportion to the period of time that has passed since the contract became effective. The unexpired portion of the service contract should be recorded as a liability (unearned revenue) until earned. Any expenses associated with the repair services should be recognized in the same period that service revenue is recognized (the matching principle).
3. The use of supplies can be viewed as a sequence of individual activities. However, the preparation of documents required to keep track of each activity individually would be too costly. Instead, the use of supplies can be treated as a continuous transaction and recognized through an adjusting entry. Any supplies used will be reported as an expense, and the unused portion of supplies will be reported as an asset.

Notice that in the second and third situations in Cornerstone 3-2, the preparation of adjusting entries is necessary to get the account balances properly stated and up to date. These end-of-period adjustments can have significant effects on a company's financial statements.

OBJECTIVE 4
Prepare adjusting entries for accruals and deferrals.

STEP 5: ADJUSTING THE ACCOUNTS

Adjustments are often necessary because timing differences exist between when a revenue or expense is recognized and cash is received or paid. These timing differences give rise to two categories of adjusting entries—accruals and deferrals. As shown in Exhibit 3-5 (p. 116), each category has two subcategories, resulting in four possible types of adjustments.

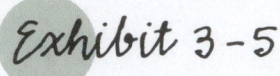

Exhibit 3-5

Types of Adjusting Entries

Accruals:
- **Accrued revenues:** Previously unrecorded revenues that have been earned but for which no cash has yet been received
- **Accrued expenses:** Previously unrecorded expenses that have been incurred but not yet paid in cash

Deferrals:
- **Deferred (unearned) revenues:** Liabilities arising from the receipt of cash for which revenue has not yet been earned
- **Deferred (prepaid) expenses:** Assets arising from the payment of cash which have not been used or consumed by the end of the period

Concept Q&A

Why don't adjusting entries involve cash?

Answer:

Cash receipts and cash payments are recorded when they occur at a specific point in time. Adjusting entries are concerned with applying the revenue recognition and matching principles to continuous activities. Because revenue and expense recognition does not depend on cash receipt or cash payment, adjusting entries for continuous revenue and expense activities will not involve cash.

The purpose of all adjustments is to make sure revenues and expenses get recorded in the proper time period. As the revenue and expense balances are adjusted, asset and liability balances will be adjusted also. Therefore, **all adjusting entries will affect at least one income statement account and one balance sheet account. Note that cash is never affected by adjustments.**

A three-step procedure can be followed for making adjusting journal entries.

Step 1: Identify pairs of income statement and balance sheet accounts that require adjustment.

Step 2: Calculate the amount of the adjustment based on the amount of revenue that was earned or the amount of expense that was incurred during the accounting period.

Step 3: Record the adjusting journal entry.

This process is used for each of the four types of adjusting entries, as we will illustrate in the following sections.

Accrued Revenues

Companies often engage in revenue-producing activities but are not paid until after the activities are complete. For example, **FedEx** has packages in transit at the end of an accounting period, meaning that FedEx has only partially completed its service. These transactions for which FedEx has earned revenue but not received the cash are called **accrued revenues**. Another example of an accrued revenue is interest earned, but not yet received, on a loan. While interest is earned as time passes, the company only receives the cash related to interest periodically (e.g., monthly, semiannually, or annually). Therefore, an adjustment is necessary to record the amount of interest earned but not yet received.

For accrued revenues, an adjustment is necessary to record the revenue and the associated increase in a company's assets, usually a receivable. Exhibit 3-6 demonstrates the process necessary to record accrued revenues. Note that the accrual of revenue is necessary because the revenue was earned prior to the receipt of cash.

Exhibit 3-6

Accrued Revenues

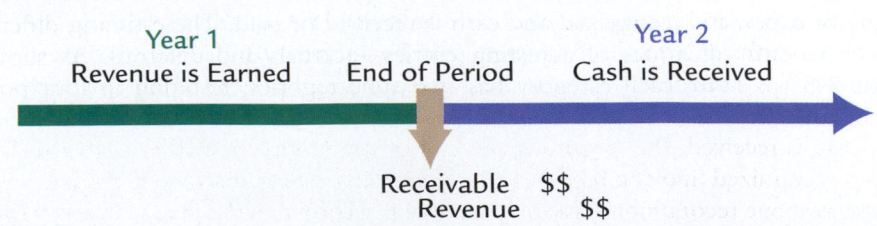

The adjusting entry required to record accrued revenues is shown in **CORNERSTONE 3-3**.

CORNERSTONE 3-3   Recording Accrued Revenues

Concept:
Revenue is recognized when it is earned, regardless of when cash is received. The adjusting entry for an accrued revenue will result in an increase to a revenue account and an increase to an asset account.

Information:
Assume that Porter Properties Inc. a calendar-year company, rented office space, to be occupied immediately, to the Tiger Travel Agency on November 1, 2011, for $5,000 per month. Porter requires Tiger Travel to make a rental payment at the end of every three months. No payment was made on November 1.

Required:
1. Prepare the adjusting journal entry necessary for Porter on December 31, 2011.
2. Prepare the entry necessary on January 31, 2012, to record the receipt of cash.

Solution:
1. **Step 1: Identify the accounts that require adjustment.** Consistent with the revenue recognition principle, Rent Revenue needs to be increased because Porter has earned revenue from providing the office space. Because no payment was received, Porter would need to increase Rent Receivable to reflect their right to receive payment from Tiger Travel.
   Step 2: Calculate the amount of the adjustment. The amount of the adjustment would be calculated as:

   $5,000 per month × 2 months (office space occupied) = $10,000

   Step 3: Record the adjusting journal entry.

Date	Account and Explanation	Debit	Credit
Dec. 31, 2011	Rent Receivable	10,000	
	Rent Revenue		10,000
	(Record rent revenue earned in 2011 but not received)		

Assets	= Liabilities +	Stockholders' Equity
+10,000		+10,000

2. The amount of cash received is calculated as:

   $5,000 per month × 3 months (office space rented) = $15,000

Date	Account and Explanation	Debit	Credit
Jan. 31, 2012	Cash	15,000	
	Rent Revenue		5,000
	Rent Receivable		10,000
	(Record revenue earned in 2012 and the receipt of cash)		

Assets	= Liabilities +	Stockholders' Equity
+15,000		+5,000
−10,000		

The $5,000 of Rent Revenue represents the one month earned in 2012.

If the adjusting entry on December 31, 2011, was not made, assets, stockholders' equity, revenues, and income would be understated. The adjusting journal entry recognizes two months of revenue (November and December 2011) in the accounting period in which it was earned and updates the corresponding balance in Rent Receivable. The revenue has been earned because Porter has provided a service to Tiger Travel. Later, when cash is received, the remaining portion of the revenue that was earned in January 2012 is recognized and the receivable is reduced to reflect that it was paid. Consistent with the revenue recognition principle, revenue is recorded in the period that it is earned.

Accrued Expenses

Similar to the situation with accrued revenues, many companies incur expenses in the current accounting period but do not pay cash for these expenses until a later period. For example, Exhibit 3-1 showed that FedEx reported $201 million of salary expense related to services performed by FedEx employees but not paid as of the end of the year. This situation is quite common for operating costs such as payroll, taxes, utilities, rent, and interest. **Accrued expenses** are previously unrecorded expenses that have been incurred but not yet paid in cash.

For accrued expenses, an adjustment is necessary to record the expense and the associated increase in a company's liabilities, usually a payable. Exhibit 3-7 demonstrates the process necessary to record accrued expenses.

 **Exhibit 3-7**

Accrued Expenses

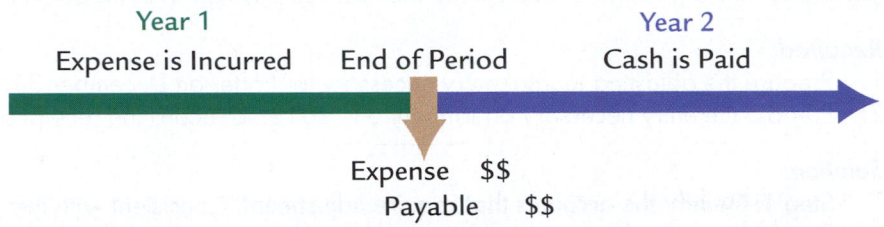

Year 1		Year 2
Expense is Incurred	End of Period	Cash is Paid

Expense $$
Payable $$

Note that the accrual of the expense is necessary because the expense was incurred prior to the payment of cash. The adjusting entry required to record accrued expenses is shown in **CORNERSTONE 3-4**.

 **CORNERSTONE 3-4**   **Recording Accrued Expenses**

Concept:
Expenses are recorded as they are incurred, regardless of when cash is paid. The adjusting entry for an accrued expense will result in an increase to an expense account and an increase to a liability account.

Information:
Assume that Porter Properties Inc. a calendar-year company, paid its clerical employees every two weeks. Employees work five days a week for a total of 10 work days every two weeks. Total wages for 10 days is $50,000. Also assume that December 31, 2011, is four days into a 10-day pay period.

Required:
1. Prepare the adjusting journal entry necessary for Porter on December 31, 2011.
2. Prepare the entry necessary on January 10, 2012, to record the payment of salaries.

Solution:
1. **Step 1: Identify the accounts that require adjustment.** Salaries Expense needs to be increased because Porter has incurred an expense related to its employees working for four days in December. This expense needs to be matched against December revenues (an application of the matching principle). Because no payment to the employees was made, Porter would need to increase Salaries Payable to reflect its obligation to pay its employees.
   Step 2: Calculate the amount of the adjustment. The amount of the adjustment would be calculated as:

   $50,000 bi-weekly salaries × (4 days/10 days) worked in two weeks = $20,000

   (Continued)

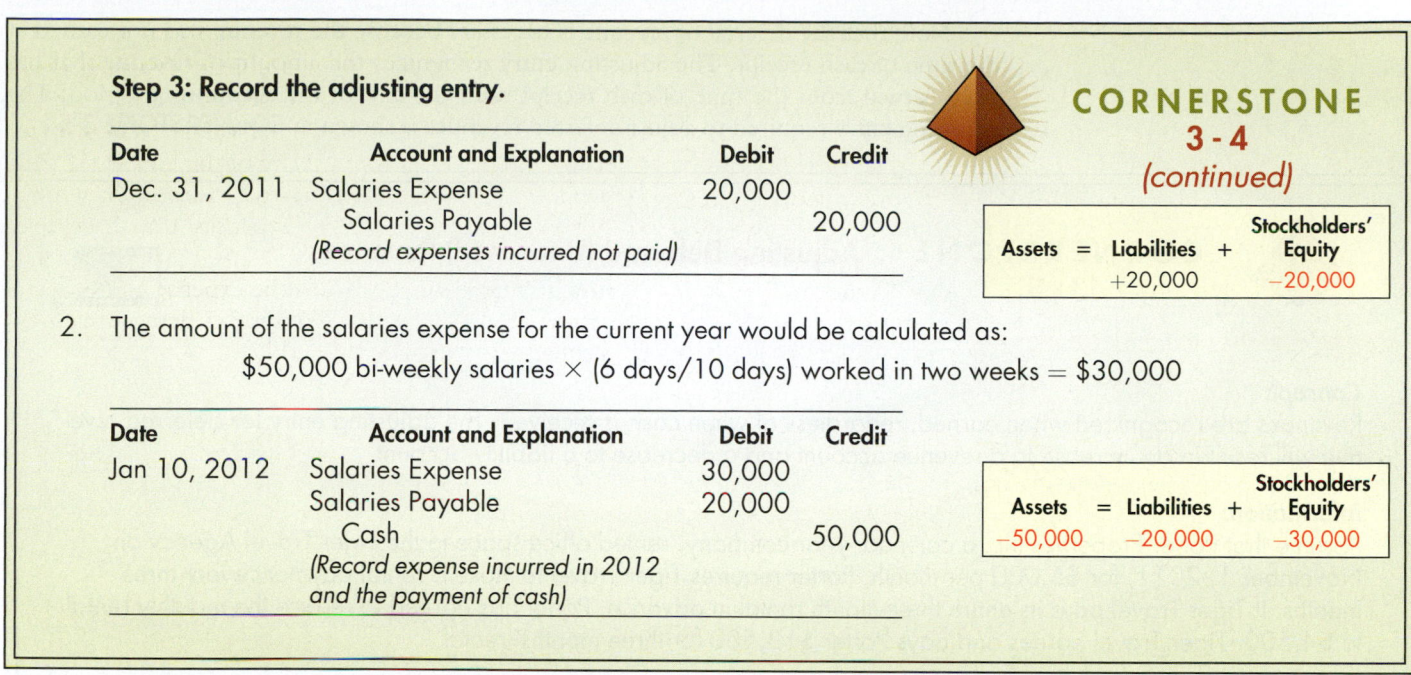

Step 3: Record the adjusting entry.

Date	Account and Explanation	Debit	Credit
Dec. 31, 2011	Salaries Expense	20,000	
	Salaries Payable		20,000
	(Record expenses incurred not paid)		

Assets	=	Liabilities	+	Stockholders' Equity
		+20,000		−20,000

2. The amount of the salaries expense for the current year would be calculated as:

$50,000 bi-weekly salaries × (6 days/10 days) worked in two weeks = $30,000

Date	Account and Explanation	Debit	Credit
Jan 10, 2012	Salaries Expense	30,000	
	Salaries Payable	20,000	
	Cash		50,000
	(Record expense incurred in 2012 and the payment of cash)		

Assets	=	Liabilities	+	Stockholders' Equity
−50,000		−20,000		−30,000

CORNERSTONE 3-4 *(continued)*

If the adjusting journal entry on December 31, 2011, were not made, liabilities and expenses would be understated while income and stockholders' equity would be overstated. The adjusting journal entry recognizes the expense that was incurred during the accounting period and updates the balance in the corresponding liability. Later, when the cash is paid to the employees, the portion of the expense that was incurred in January 2012 is recognized and the previously created liability is reduced. Consistent with the matching principle, expenses are recorded in the period that they were incurred.

Deferred (Unearned) Revenues

Companies may collect payment for goods or services that it sells before it delivers those goods or services. For example, FedEx often collects cash for a package delivery prior to the actual performance of the delivery service. When the cash is collected, the revenue recognition is deferred, or delayed, until the service is performed. Transactions for which a company has received cash but has not yet earned the revenue are called **deferred** (or **unearned**) **revenues**. Other examples of deferred revenues include rent received in advance, magazine or newspaper subscriptions received in advance, and tickets (e.g., for airlines, sporting events, concerts) sold in advance. In all of these situations, the receipt of cash creates a liability for the company to deliver goods or perform services in the future. The unearned revenue account delays, or defers, the recognition of revenue by recording the revenue as a liability until it is earned.

As the goods are delivered or the service is performed, an adjustment is necessary to reduce the previously recorded liability and to recognize the portion of the revenue that has been earned. The portion of revenue that has not been earned remains in the liability account, unearned revenue, until it is earned. Therefore, revenue recognition is delayed, or deferred, until the revenue is earned. Exhibit 3-8 demonstrates the process necessary to record deferred revenues.

Exhibit 3-8

Deferred (Unearned) Revenues

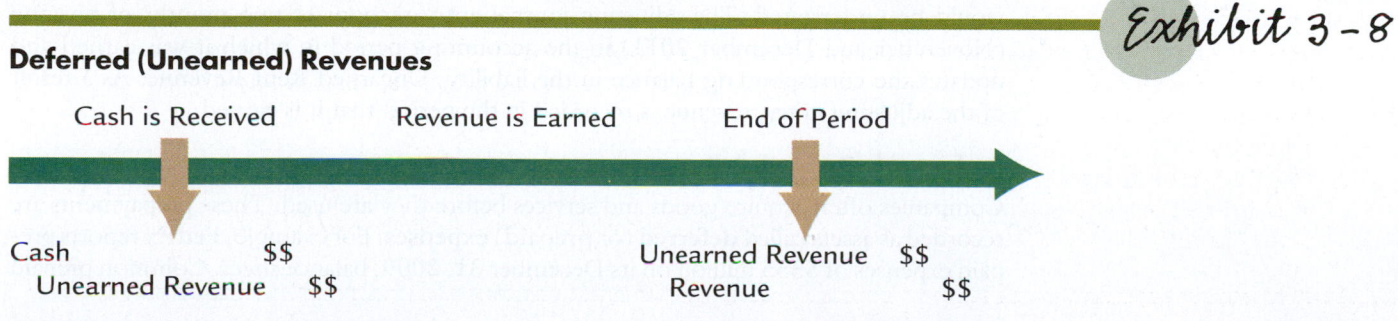

Cash is Received   Revenue is Earned   End of Period

Cash $$
  Unearned Revenue $$

Unearned Revenue $$
  Revenue $$

Note that the deferral of revenue is necessary because the revenue was not earned at the time of cash receipt. The adjusting entry recognizes the amount of revenue that has been earned from the time of cash receipt until the end of the accounting period. The adjusting entry required to adjust deferred revenues is shown in **CORNERSTONE 3-5**.

 ## CORNERSTONE 3-5   Adjusting Deferred (Unearned) Revenues

Concept:
Revenues are recognized when earned, regardless of when cash is received. The adjusting entry for deferred revenue will result in an increase to a revenue account and a decrease to a liability account.

Information:
Assume that Porter Properties Inc. a calendar-year company, rented office space to the Tiger Travel Agency on November 1, 2011, for $5,000 per month. Porter requires Tiger Travel to make a rental payment every three months. If Tiger Travel pays its entire three-month rental in advance, Porter has agreed to reduce the monthly rental to $4,500. Tiger Travel agrees and pays Porter $13,500 for three months' rental.

Required:
1. Prepare the entry on November 1, 2011, to record the receipt of cash.
2. Prepare the adjusting journal entry necessary for Porter on December 31, 2011.

Solution:
1.

Date	Account and Explanation	Debit	Credit
Nov. 1, 2011	Cash	13,500	
	Unearned Rent Revenue		13,500
	(Record receipt of cash for three months' rent)		

Assets	=	Liabilities	+	Stockholders' Equity
+13,500		+13,500		

2. **Step 1: Identify the accounts that require adjustment.** Rent Revenue needs to be increased because Porter has earned revenue from providing the office space. Because a liability was previously recorded, Porter would need to decrease the liability, Unearned Rent Revenue, to reflect the decrease in their obligation to perform the service.
Step 2: Calculate the amount of the adjustment. The amount of the adjustment would be calculated as:

$$\$4,500 \text{ per month} \times 2 \text{ months (office space rented)} = \$9,000$$

Step 3: Record the adjusting entry.

Date	Account and Explanation	Debit	Credit
Dec. 31, 2011	Unearned Rent Revenue	9,000	
	Rent Revenue		9,000
	(Record rent revenue earned in 2011)		

Assets	=	Liabilities	+	Stockholders' Equity
		−9,000		+9,000

If the adjusting entry on December 31, 2011, was not made, liabilities (Unearned Rent Revenue) would be overstated while stockholders' equity, revenue, and net income would be understated. The adjusting journal entry recognizes two months of revenue (November and December 2011) in the accounting period in which it was earned and updates the corresponding balance in the liability, Unearned Rent Revenue. As a result of the adjusting entry, revenue is recorded in the period that it is earned.

Deferred (Prepaid) Expenses

Companies often acquire goods and services before they are used. These prepayments are recorded as assets called **deferred** (or **prepaid**) **expenses**. For example, **FedEx** reports prepaid expenses of $555 million on its December 31, 2009, balance sheet. Common prepaid expenses include items such as supplies, prepaid rent, prepaid advertising, and prepaid insurance. The purchases of buildings and equipment also are considered prepayments.

As the prepaid asset is used to generate revenue, an adjustment is necessary to reduce the previously recorded prepaid asset and recognize the related expense. The portion of the prepaid asset that has not been used represents the unexpired benefits and remains in the asset account until it is used. Therefore, expense recognition is delayed, or deferred, until the expense is incurred. Exhibit 3-9 demonstrates the process necessary to record deferred expenses.

Exhibit 3-9

Deferred (Prepaid) Expenses

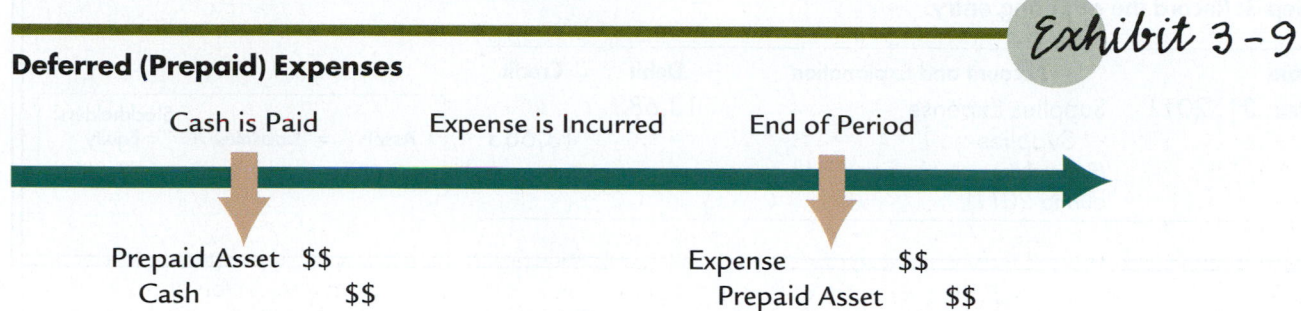

Note that the deferral of the expense is necessary because the initial cash payment did not result in an expense. Instead, an asset that provides future economic benefit was created. The adjusting entry recognizes the amount of expense that has been incurred from the time of the cash payment until the end of the accounting period. The adjusting entry required to adjust deferred expenses is shown in **CORNERSTONE 3-6**.

CORNERSTONE 3-6   Adjusting Deferred (Prepaid) Expenses

Concept:
Expenses are recognized when incurred, regardless of when cash is paid. The adjusting entry for deferred expenses will result in an increase to an expense account and a decrease to an asset account.

Information:
Assume that Porter Properties Inc. a calendar-year company, had $4,581 of office supplies on hand at the beginning of November. On November 10, Porter purchased office supplies totaling $12,365. The amount of the purchase was added to the Supplies account. At the end of the year, the balance in Supplies was $16,946 ($4,581 + $12,365). A count of office supplies on hand indicated that $3,263 of supplies remained.

Required:
1. Prepare the entry on November 10, 2011, to record the purchase of supplies.
2. Prepare the adjusting journal entry necessary for Porter on December 31, 2011.

Solution:
1.

Date	Account and Explanation	Debit	Credit			
				Assets	**= Liabilities +**	**Stockholders' Equity**
Nov. 10, 2011	Supplies	12,365		+12,365		
	Cash		12,365	−12,365		
	(Record purchase of office supplies)					

2. **Step 1: Identify the accounts that require adjustment.** Supplies Expense needs to be increased because Porter has used office supplies during November and December of 2011. The use of the supplies would also decrease the asset, Supplies.

(Continued)

Step 2: Calculate the amount of the adjustment. The amount of the adjustment would be calculated as:

$16,946 (supplies available to be used) − $3,263 (supplies on hand) = $13,683

This amount represents the cost of supplies used during November and December 2011.

Step 3: Record the adjusting entry.

Date	Account and Explanation	Debit	Credit
Dec. 31, 2011	Supplies Expense	13,683	
	Supplies		13,683
	(Record the use of office supplies during 2011)		

Assets	= Liabilities +	Stockholders' Equity
−13,683		−13,683

CORNERSTONE 3-6 (continued)

If the adjusting entry on December 31, 2011, was not made, assets, stockholders' equity, and net income would be overstated and expenses would be understated. The adjusting journal entry recognizes the expense incurred during November and December 2011 and updates the corresponding balance in the asset, Supplies. As a result of the adjusting entry, the expense is recorded in the period that it is incurred.

Depreciation While most deferred (prepaid) expenses are accounted for in a manner similar to that illustrated in Cornerstone 3-6, the purchase of long-lived assets such as buildings and equipment presents a unique situation. Recall from Chapter 1 that these types of assets are classified as property, plant, and equipment on the balance sheet. Because property, plant, and equipment helps to produce revenue over a number of years (instead of just one period), the matching principle requires companies to systematically assign, or allocate, the asset's cost as an expense to each period in which the asset is used. This process is called **depreciation**. This concept and the methods used to compute depreciation expense are discussed in Chapter 7.

The depreciation process requires an adjustment to recognize the expense incurred during the period and reduce the long-lived asset. The unused portion of the asset is reported as property, plant, and equipment on the balance sheet. Therefore, the purchase of a long-lived asset is essentially a long-term prepayment for the service that the asset will provide.

Assume that Porter Properties purchased an office building on January 1, 2009, for $450,000. The depreciation expense on this building is $15,000 per year. Because depreciation is a continuous activity, Porter would need to make the following adjustment at the end of 2011.

Assets	= Liabilities +	Stockholders' Equity
−15,000		−15,000

Date	Account and Explanation	Debit	Credit
Dec. 31, 2011	Depreciation Expense	15,000	
	Accumulated Depreciation		15,000
	(Record depreciation for 2011)		

Depreciation expense represents the portion of the cost of the long-lived asset that is matched against the revenues that the asset helped to generate. In addition, the depreciation process reduces the asset. Accountants normally use a contra account to reduce the amount of a long-lived asset. **Contra accounts** are accounts that have a balance that is opposite of the balance in a related account. In this case, Accumulated Depreciation is a contra account to the building. Therefore, while the asset has a normal debit balance, the contra account has a normal credit balance. Contra accounts are deducted from the balance of the related asset account in the financial statements, and the resulting difference is known as the book value of the asset. Therefore, by increasing the contra account, the above journal entry reduces the book value of the asset. Exhibit 3-10 shows the financial statement presentation of the accumulated depreciation account.

Exhibit 3-10

Financial Statement Presentation of Accumulated Depreciation

Porter Properties Inc.
Balance Sheet
December 31, 2011

Assets:

Current assets	$ 370,000
Property, plant, and equipment (net)	1,450,000
Other assets	80,000
Total assets	$ 1,900,000
Liabilities	$ 825,000
Equity	1,075,000
Total liabilities and equity	$ 1,900,000

Sample of accumulated depreciation presentation:

Building	$ 450,000
Less: Accumulated depreciation	(45,000)
Building (net)	$ 405,000

Notice that accumulated depreciation shows the total amount of depreciation taken in all years of the asset's life ($15,000 per year for 2009, 2010, and 2011). Therefore, the balance in the accumulated depreciation account will increase over the asset's life. The use of the contra account provides more information to users of the financial statements because it preserves both the original cost of the asset and the total cost that has expired to date.

Summary of Financial Statement Effects of Adjusting Entries

The effects of the adjustment process are summarized in Exhibit 3-11.

Adjusting entries are internal events that do not involve another company. The purpose of all adjustments is to make sure that revenues and expenses get recorded in the proper time period. As the revenue and expense balances are adjusted, asset and liability balances will be adjusted also. Therefore, *all adjusting entries will affect at least one income statement account and one balance sheet account.* Remember, *the cash account is never used in an adjusting entry.*

Concept Q&A

What is the relationship between the cash receipt or payment and the recognition of accruals or deferrals?

Answer:

Adjusting entries can be classified as accruals or deferrals depending on the timing of the cash flow relative to when the revenue is earned or the expense is incurred. When the revenue is earned or the expense is incurred **before** the associated cash flow occurs, an accrual adjusting entry is necessary. When the revenue is earned or the expense is incurred **after** the associated cash flow occurs, a deferral adjusting entry is necessary.

Exhibit 3-11

Effects of Adjusting Entries on the Financial Statements

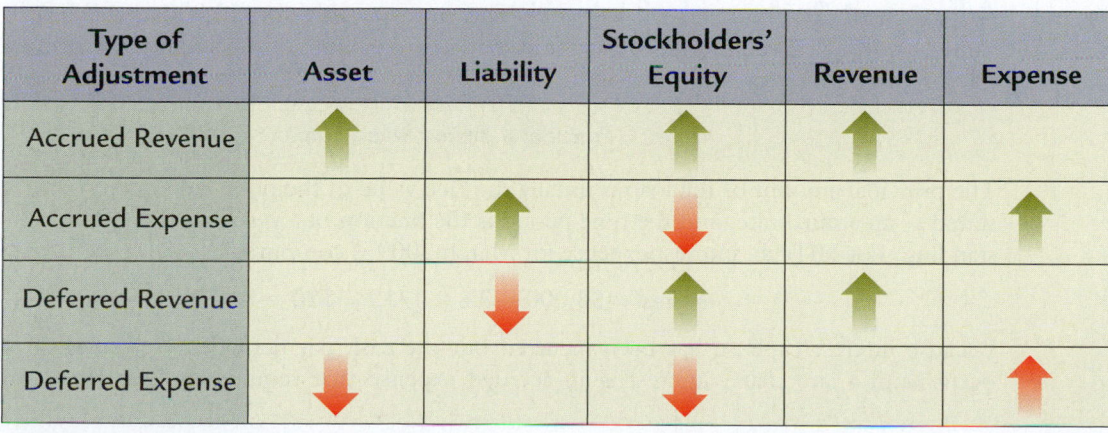

Type of Adjustment	Asset	Liability	Stockholders' Equity	Revenue	Expense
Accrued Revenue	↑		↑	↑	
Accrued Expense		↑	↓		↑
Deferred Revenue		↓	↑	↑	
Deferred Expense	↓		↓		↑

Exhibit 3-12

Trial Balance

HiTech Communications Inc. Trial Balance March 31, 2011		
Account	**Debit**	**Credit**
Cash	$16,600	
Accounts Receivable	300	
Supplies	6,500	
Prepaid Insurance	1,200	
Equipment	4,500	
Accounts Payable		$ 500
Unearned Service Revenue		9,000
Notes Payable		3,000
Common Stock		12,000
Dividends	500	
Service Revenue		12,100
Salaries Expense	1,800	
Utilities Expense	5,200	
	$36,600	$36,600

Comprehensive Example

To provide a comprehensive example of the adjusting process, consider the trial balance of HiTech Communications that was introduced in Chapter 2 (see Exhibit 3-12).

Upon review of the trial balance, the accountant for HiTech noted that the following accounts needed to be adjusted.

Adjustment 1: Accrued Revenue HiTech's accountant noted that HiTech had performed $1,500 of advertising services for which it had not yet billed the customer. Because the services had not yet been billed, no entry was made in the accounting system. However, HiTech must record the revenue that was earned during the accounting period, even though the cash flow will not occur until a later date. The adjusting entry to record this accrued revenue is:

Date	Account and Explanation	Debit	Credit
March 31	Accounts Receivable	1,500	
	Service Revenue		1,500
	(Recognize services earned)		

Assets	= Liabilities +	Stockholders' Equity
+1,500		+1,500

Adjustment 2: Accrual of Interest The note payable for $3,000 that HiTech signed on March 2 required it to pay interest at an annual rate of 8 percent. The formula for computing interest is:

$$\text{Interest} = \text{Principal} \times \text{Interest Rate} \times \text{Time}$$

The principal amount of the loan is usually the face value of the note. The interest rate is stated as an annual rate, and the time period is the fraction of a year that the note is outstanding. For HiTech, interest expense for March 2009 is computed as:

$$\text{Interest} = \$3,000 \times 8\% \times 1/12 = \$20$$

Because interest expense has been incurred but the cash payment for interest will not occur until a later date, interest is an accrued expense that requires an increase to an expense account and an increase to a liability account. The adjusting entry to recognize accrued interest is:

Date	Account and Explanation	Debit	Credit
March 31	Interest Expense	20	
	Interest Payable		20
	(Recognize accrued interest)		

Assets	=	Liabilities	+	Stockholders' Equity
		+20		−20

Adjustment 3: Accrual of Salaries

HiTech paid its weekly salaries on March 26, a Friday, and properly recorded an expense (Transaction 10 from Chapter 2). Salaries for a five-day work week are $1,800, or $360 per day. HiTech will not pay salaries again until April 2. However, employees worked on March 29, March 30, and March 31. Because employees have worked but will not be paid until a later date, an adjustment is necessary to record the salaries incurred in March. Accrued salaries are $1,080 (3 days × $360 per day). The adjusting entry to recognize accrued salaries is:

Date	Account and Explanation	Debit	Credit
March 31	Salaries Expense	1,080	
	Salaries Payable		1,080
	(Recognize accrued salaries)		

Assets	=	Liabilities	+	Stockholders' Equity
		+1,080		−1,080

Adjustment 4: Deferred (Unearned) Revenue

HiTech's trial balance shows that a customer paid $9,000 in advance for services to be performed at a later date. This amount was originally recorded as a liability, Unearned Service Revenue. As HiTech performs services, the liability will be reduced and revenue will be recognized. Based on HiTech's analysis of work performed during March, it is determined that $3,300 of revenue has been earned. The adjusting entry to record this previously unearned revenue is:

Date	Account and Explanation	Debit	Credit
March 31	Unearned Service Revenue	$3,300	
	Service Revenue		$3,300
	(Recognize service revenue earned)		

Assets	=	Liabilities	+	Stockholders' Equity
		−3,300		+3,300

Adjustment 5: Deferred (Prepaid) Expense—Supplies

HiTech's trial balance shows a balance of $6,500 in the Supplies account. However, an inventory count at the close of business on March 31 determined that supplies on hand were $1,200. Because it was not efficient to record supplies expense during the period, HiTech must make an adjustment at the end of the period to record the supplies used during the period. It was determined that HiTech used $5,300 ($6,500 available to be used minus $1,200 not used) of supplies. The adjustment necessary to record the supplies used during March is:

Date	Account and Explanation	Debit	Credit
March 31	Supplies Expense	5,300	
	Supplies		5,300
	(Recognize supplies used)		

Assets	=	Liabilities	+	Stockholders' Equity
−5,300				−5,300

Adjustment 6: Deferred (Prepaid) Expense—Insurance

HiTech's trial balance shows a balance of $1,200 in the Prepaid Insurance account related to a six-month insurance policy purchased at the beginning of March. Because time has passed since the purchase of the insurance policy, the asset, Prepaid Insurance, has partially expired and an expense needs to be recognized. The expired portion of the insurance is $200 ($1,200 × 1/6). The adjustment necessary to record insurance expense is:

Date	Account and Explanation	Debit	Credit
March 31	Insurance Expense	200	
	Prepaid Insurance		200
	(Recognize insurance used)		

Assets	=	Liabilities	+	Stockholders' Equity
−200				−200

Adjustment 7: Depreciation HiTech's trial balance shows that $4,500 of equipment was purchased. Because this equipment is used to generate revenue, a portion of the cost of the equipment must be allocated to expense. For HiTech, assume that depreciation expense is $125 per month. The adjustment necessary to record depreciation expense is:

Date	Account and Explanation	Debit	Credit
March 31	Depreciation Expense	125	
	Accumulated Depreciation—		125
	Equipment		
	(Recognize depreciation on equipment)		

Assets	=	Liabilities	+	Stockholders' Equity
−125				−125

The ledger for HiTech Communications, after posting of the adjusting journal entries, is shown in Exhibit 3-13.

Exhibit 3-13

General Ledger of HiTech Communications

Assets

Cash
16,600	
16,600	

Accounts Receivable
300	
(A1) 1,500	
1,800	

Supplies
6,500	
	5,300 (A5)
1,200	

Prepaid Insurance
1,200	
	200 (A6)
1,000	

Equipment
4,500	
4,500	

Accumulated Depreciation
	125 (A7)
	125

Liabilities

Accounts Payable
	500
	500

Notes Payable
	3,000
	3,000

Interest Payable
	20 (A2)
	20

Salaries Payable
	1,080 (A3)
	1,080

Unearned Service Revenue
	9,000
(A4) 3,300	
	5,700

Stockholders' Equity

Common Stock
	12,000
	12,000

Service Revenue
	12,100
	1,500 (A1)
	3,300 (A4)
	16,900

Salaries Expense
1,800	
(A3) 1,080	
2,880	

Utility Expense
5,200	
5,200	

Depreciation Expense
(A7) 125	
125	

Interest Expense
(A2) 20	
20	

Insurance Expense
(A6) 200	
200	

Supplies Expense
(A5) 5,300	
5,300	

Dividends
500	
500	

Two major items should be apparent:

- Adjusting entries affect one balance sheet account and one income statement account. Without adjusting entries, the balances reported on both the balance sheet and the income statement would have been incorrect. If the adjustments were not recorded, HiTech would have understated revenue by $4,800 and understated expenses by $6,725.
- Adjusting entries do not affect cash.

YOU DECIDE Financial Statement Effects of Adjusting Entries

You are considering investing in Get Fit Inc., a chain of gymnasiums and wellness facilities. As you are analyzing the financial statements to determine if Get Fit is a good investment, three items catch your attention:

- Get Fit requires customers to pay the first six months' membership fees at the time the customer joins one of its facilities. These fees are recorded as revenue at the time of cash receipt since the amount is nonrefundable.
- Get Fit paid for and distributed flyers to advertise its recent membership drive. Because these flyers will circulate and attract customers for approximately a year, Get Fit recorded the expenditures as prepaid advertising that will be expensed over the next year.
- Get Fit provides healthy snacks to its customers by charging their membership account. Get Fit records revenue at the end of the month when it bills customers, although customers do not pay until the next month.

Do you feel that Get Fit is properly recording the above transactions? If not, what is the effect on the financial statements?

First, the membership fees are a continuous activity that Get Fit is incorrectly treating as a point-in-time activity. Because the revenue has not yet been earned, the membership fees should be initially recorded as unearned revenue. As the customers have use of the facility each month, an adjusting entry should be made to reduce unearned revenue and increase revenue. The fact that the fees are nonrefundable is irrelevant in deciding whether revenue should or should not be recognized. Second, because it is difficult to measure any future benefits associated with advertising costs, accountants take a conservative position and these costs should not be deferred; instead they should be expensed as incurred. Finally, Get Fit is appropriately recording an accrued revenue related to providing snacks. The fact that the customers do not pay until a later time period is not relevant in determining when the revenue is recorded.

If the above transactions had been properly recorded, Get Fit would have reported less revenue, higher expenses, and, therefore, lower net income. Financial statement users need to pay close attention to a company's policies with regard to revenue and expense recognition.

Adjusting entries can have a material impact on a company's reported revenues, expenses, and income.

STEP 6: PREPARING THE FINANCIAL STATEMENTS

After a company has journalized and posted all of the adjusting entries, it updates the trial balance to reflect the adjustments that have been made. This trial balance is called an **adjusted trial balance**. Similar to the trial balance, the adjusted trial balance lists all of the active accounts and proves the equality of debits and credits. In addition, the adjusted trial balance is the primary source of information needed to prepare the financial statements. The adjusted trial balance for HiTech Communications is shown in Exhibit 3-14 (p. 128).

The financial statements can now be prepared using the balances obtained from the adjusted trial balance. As discussed in Chapter 1, the financial statements are interrelated. That is, there is a natural progression from one financial statement to another as the numbers in one financial statement flow into another financial statement. Because of this natural progression, financial statements are prepared in a particular order.

OBJECTIVE 5
Prepare financial statements from an adjusted trial balance.

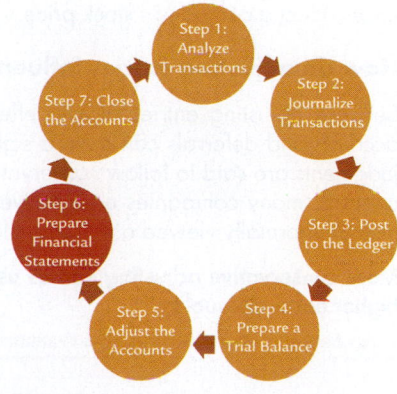

1. The income statement is prepared from the revenue and expense accounts.
2. Net income is used to prepare the retained earnings statement.
3. The balance sheet is prepared using the ending balance of retained earnings from the retained earnings statement.

Exhibit 3-14

Adjusted Trial Balance

HiTech Communications Inc.
Adjusted Trial Balance
March 31, 2011

Account		Debit	Credit
Cash		$16,600	
Accounts Receivable		1,800	
Supplies		1,200	
Prepaid Insurance		1,000	
Equipment	Balance	4,500	
Accumulated Depreciation—Equipment	Sheet		$ 125
Accounts Payable	Accounts		500
Unearned Service Revenue			5,700
Interest Payable			20
Salaries Payable			1,080
Notes Payable			3,000
Common Stock			12,000
Dividends		500	
Service Revenue			16,900
Salaries Expense		2,880	
Utilities Expense	Income	5,200	
Depreciation Expense	Statement	125	
Interest Expense	Accounts	20	
Insurance Expense		200	
Supplies Expense		5,300	
		$39,325	$39,325

YOU DECIDE   Quality of Earnings

Investors and other users often assess the quality of a company's earnings when analyzing companies. The quality of earnings refers to how well a company's reported earnings reflect the company's true earnings. High quality earnings are generally viewed as permanent or persistent earnings that assist financial statement users in predicting future earnings and cash flows. Low quality earnings are temporary or transitory earnings from one-time transactions or events that do not aid in predicting future earnings or cash flows. While there is no consensus on how best to measure earnings quality, research suggests that investors recognize differences in earnings quality and these differences affect a company's stock price.

How do adjusting entries influence the quality of earnings?

Because adjusting entries always effect amounts reported on the income statement, the estimates and judgments involved in making accruals and deferrals can have a significant impact on a company's income. Companies that make relatively pessimistic estimates and judgments are said to follow conservative accounting practices and are generally viewed as having earnings that are of higher quality. In contrast, many companies use relatively optimistic estimates and judgments and employ aggressive accounting practices. These companies are normally viewed as having a lower quality of earnings.

More conservative adjusting entries usually lead to better predictors of future earnings or cash flows and are viewed as contributing to higher earnings quality.

The financial statements and their interrelationship are shown in Exhibit 3-15.

Exhibit 3-15

Relationships Among the Financial Statements

HiTech Communications Inc.
Income Statement
For the Month Ended March 31, 2011

Service revenue		$16,900
Expenses:		
Supplies expense	$5,300	
Utilities expense	5,200	
Salaries expense	2,880	
Insurance expense	200	
Depreciation expense	125	
Interest expense	20	13,725
Net income		$ 3,175

HiTech Communications Inc.
Retained Earnings Statement
For the Month Ended March 31, 2011

Retained earnings, March 1, 2011	$ 0
Add: Net income	3,175
	$3,175
Less: Dividends	(500)
Retained earnings, March 31, 2011	$2,675

HiTech Communications Inc.
Balance Sheet
March 31, 2011

ASSETS			LIABILITIES AND STOCKHOLDERS' EQUITY		
Current assets:			Current liabilities:		
Cash	$16,600		Accounts payable	$ 500	
Accounts receivable	1,800		Unearned service revenue	5,700	
Supplies	1,200		Interest payable	20	
Prepaid insurance	1,000		Salaries payable	1,080	
Total current assets		$20,600	Total current liabilities		$ 7,300
Property, plant, and equipment:			Long-term liabilities:		
Equipment	$ 4,500		Notes payable		3,000
Less: Accumulated depreciation	(125)		Total liabilities		$10,300
Total property, plant, and equipment		4,375	Stockholders' equity:		
			Common stock	$12,000	
			Retained earnings	2,675	
			Total stockholders' equity		14,675
			Total liabilities and stockholders'		
Total assets		$24,975	equity		$24,975

OBJECTIVE 6
Explain why and how companies prepare closing entries.

STEP 7: CLOSING THE ACCOUNTS

When we introduced the fundamental accounting equation in Chapter 1, we identified three kinds of balance sheet accounts: assets, liabilities, and stockholders' equity. These accounts are **permanent accounts** in that their balances are carried forward from the current accounting period to future accounting periods. We also identified three other accounts: revenues, expenses, and dividends. These accounts are used to collect the activities of only one period, so they are considered **temporary accounts**. The final step of the accounting cycle, closing the accounts, is done to:

- Transfer the effects of revenues, expenses, and dividends (the temporary accounts) to the permanent stockholders' equity account, Retained Earnings.
- Clear the revenue, expenses, and dividends (reduce their balances to zero) so they are ready to accumulate the business activities of the next accounting period. Without closing entries, the temporary accounts would accumulate the business activities of *all* accounting periods, not just the current time period.

 **Q&A**

What would happen if we didn't make closing entries?

Answer:
The closing process transfers temporary account balances (revenues, expenses, and dividends) to retained earnings. If the accounts were not closed, these amounts would not get properly reflected in stockholders' equity and the accounting equation wouldn't balance. In addition, the temporary accounts would accumulate amounts from different accounting periods, making it extremely difficult to determine the effect of business activities for a specific accounting period.

The closing process is accomplished through a series of journal entries that are dated as of the last day of the accounting period. Often, another temporary account, called income summary, is used to aid the closing process. The use of the income summary account allows the company to easily identify the net income (or net loss) for the period. The closing process can be completed in a four-step procedure:

Step 1: Close revenues to income summary.
Step 2: Close expenses to income summary. At this point, the balance in the income summary account should be equal to net income.
Step 3: Close income summary to retained earnings.
Step 4: Close dividends to retained earnings.

The closing process is illustrated in **CORNERSTONE 3-7**.

CORNERSTONE 3-7   **Closing the Accounts**

Concept:
The closing process is designed to transfer the balances in the temporary accounts to retained earnings and to prepare the temporary accounts for the next accounting period.

Information:
For 2011, Porter Properties' general ledger shows the following balances: Rent Revenue $2,174,000; Salaries Expense $1,300,000; Supplies Expense $150,000; Interest Expense $15,000; Insurance Expense $20,000; Retained Earnings at the beginning of the year $1,135,000; and Dividends $5,000.

Required:
Prepare the closing entries for Porter at December 31, 2011.

Solution:
Step 1: Close revenues to Income Summary.

Date	Account and Explanation	Debit	Credit
Dec. 31	Rent Revenue	2,174,000	
	Income Summary		2,174,000
	(Close revenue accounts)		

(Continued)

Step 2: Close expenses to Income Summary.

Date	Account and Explanation	Debit	Credit
Dec. 31	Income Summary	1,485,000	
	Salaries Expense		1,300,000
	Supplies Expense		150,000
	Interest Expense		15,000
	Insurance Expense		20,000
	(Close expense accounts)		

Step 3: Close Income Summary to Retained Earnings.

Date	Account and Explanation	Debit	Credit
Dec. 31	Income Summary	689,000	
	Retained Earnings		689,000
	(Close Income Summary)		

Step 4: Close Dividends to Retained Earnings.

Date	Account and Explanation	Debit	Credit
Dec. 31	Retained Earnings	5,000	
	Dividends		5,000
	(Close Dividends)		

CORNERSTONE 3-7 *(continued)*

Notice that revenues, which have a normal credit balance, are closed by debiting the revenue account. Similarly, expenses, which normally have a debit balance, are closed by crediting the expense accounts. Also, after the first two journal entries, the balance in the income summary account is $689,000 ($2,174,000 − $1,485,000), which is the amount of income for the period. This amount is then transferred to retained earnings. Finally, the dividends account is not closed to income summary (because dividends are not part of income) but closed directly to retained earnings. The ending retained earnings account will have a balance of $1,819,000 ($1,135,000 + $689,000 − $5,000). The closing process for Porter is illustrated in Exhibit 3-16.

Exhibit 3-16

The Closing Process

SUMMARY OF THE ACCOUNTING CYCLE

In Chapter 2, we introduced the accounting cycle as a sequence of procedures that transforms business activities into financial statements. The accounting cycle is shown in Exhibit 3-17.

Exhibit 3-17

The Accounting Cycle

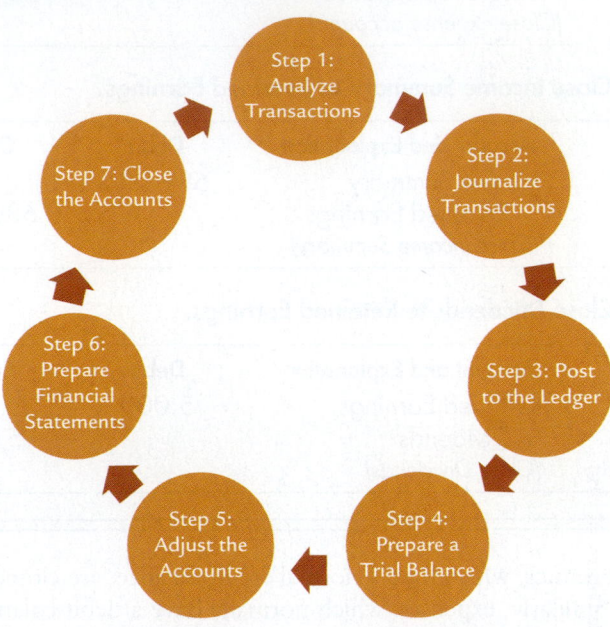

Notice that the accounting cycle begins with the analysis of transactions to determine which business activities are recognized in the accounting records and their effect on the fundamental accounting equation. Those activities that meet the recognition criteria are journalized and posted to the ledger. These three steps are repeated many times during an accounting period. The remaining steps of the accounting cycle are performed only at the end of the accounting period. For those transactions still underway at the end of the accounting period, the completed portion of the transaction is recognized with adjusting entries. Next, the financial statements are prepared. Finally, the temporary accounts—revenues, expenses, and dividends—are closed and their balances transferred to retained earnings. At this point, the income statement accounts have zero balances, and the balance sheet accounts all contain the correct beginning balances for the start of the next accounting period. The accounting cycle can begin again.

APPENDIX 3A: USING A WORKSHEET TO PREPARE FINANCIAL STATEMENTS

Accountants often use an informal schedule called a **worksheet** to assist them in organizing and preparing the information necessary to perform the end-of-period steps in the accounting cycle—namely the preparation of adjusting entries, financial statements, and closing entries. The worksheet is not a financial statement but simply an organizational tool that summarizes the information generated by the accounting system and enables the accountant to check the information for completeness and consistency. While worksheets can be completed manually, most worksheets today are created in computer spreadsheets.

A typical worksheet is shown in Exhibit 3-18. This exhibit uses the information for HiTech Communications that was presented in Chapter 2 and Chapter 3.

Exhibit 3-18 Worksheet

Chapter 3   Accrual Accounting   133

HiTech Communications, Inc.
Work Sheet
For the Month Ended March 31, 2010

Account Titles	Unadjusted Trial Balance Debit	Credit	Adjusting Entries Debit	Credit	Adjusted Trial Balance Debit	Credit	Income Statement Debit	Credit	Statement of Retained Earnings Debit	Credit	Balance Sheet Debit	Credit
Cash	16,600				16,600						16,600	
Accounts Receivable	300		(a) 1,500		1,800						1,800	
Supplies	6,500			(e) 5,300	1,200						1,200	
Prepaid Insurance	1,200			(f) 200	1,000						1,000	
Equipment	4,500				4,500						4,500	
Accounts Payable		500				500						500
Unearned Revenue		9,000	(d) 3,300			5,700						5,700
Notes Payable		3,000				3,000						3,000
Common Stock		12,000				12,000						12,000
Retained Earnings, 3/1/2010		0				0				0		
Dividends	500				500				500			
Service Revenue		12,100		(a) 1,500 / (d) 3,300		16,900		16,900				
Salaries Expense	1,800		(c) 1,080		2,880		2,880					
Utility Expense	5,200				5,200		5,200					
	36,600	36,600										
Interest Expense			(b) 20		20		20					
Interest Payable				(b) 20		20						20
Salaries Payable				(c) 1,080		1,080						1,080
Supplies Expense			(e) 5,300		5,300		5,300					
Insurance Expense			(f) 200		200		200					
Depreciation Expense			(g) 125		125		125					
Accumulated Depreciation— Equipment				(g) 125		125						125
			11,525	11,525	39,325	39,325	13,725	16,900				
Net Income							(h) 3,175			(h) 3,175		
							16,900	16,900	500	3,175		
Retained Earnings, 3/31/2010									(i) 2,675			(i) 2,675
									3,175	3,175	25,100	25,100

The completion of the worksheet requires the following six steps.

Step 1: Unadjusted Trial Balance

The worksheet starts with the unadjusted trial balance. The first column contains the listing of accounts used during the period in the same order as the accounts appear in the trial balance—the balance sheet accounts first followed by the income statement accounts. Note that a retained earnings account was added. Because this is the first month of operations, this account has a zero balance. The next two columns contain the unadjusted balances of these accounts and are totaled to ensure the equality of debits and credits.

Step 2: Adjusting Entry Columns

The next two columns contain the adjustments made to record the completed portion of business activities that remain underway at the end of the accounting period. Rather than take the time to make formal adjusting journal entries, the accountant typically enters the adjustments directly into the worksheet and then makes the formal journal entries after the worksheet has been completed. Two items should be noted:

- Adjustments often require the addition of accounts not included in the unadjusted trial balance. These additional accounts can be added, in no particular order, beneath the previous listing of accounts.
- Letters are typically used on a worksheet to identify the adjusting entries and to allow the accountant to easily match the debit and credit sides of each adjusting entry. The letters (a) through (g) correspond to the adjusting entries (1) through (7) shown earlier in the chapter.

The two columns are totaled to ensure the equality of debits and credits.

Step 3: Adjusted Trial Balance

The next two columns represent an adjusted trial balance. The adjustments entered in columns D and E are added to or subtracted from the unadjusted balances in columns B and C. The two columns are totaled to ensure the equality of debits and credits. The adjusted trial balance is the basis for preparing the financial statements.

Step 4: Income Statement

The income statement balances are transferred to the income statement columns of the worksheet and the columns are totaled. The difference between the two columns is the net income or loss of the period. In Exhibit 3-18, HiTech reports its net income of $3,175 in the debit column of the income statement and the credit column of the retained earnings statement. This entry is made (1) to balance the two income statement columns and (2) to transfer net income to retained earnings.

Step 5: Retained Earnings Statement

The amounts for beginning retained earnings and dividends are transferred from the adjusted trial balance columns (columns F and G) to the retained earnings statement columns (columns J and K). The columns are totaled and the difference is the amount of ending retained earnings. This amount is entered in the debit column of the retained earnings statement (to balance the two columns) and transferred to the credit column of the balance sheet as shown by letter (i).

Step 6: Balance Sheet

The final portion of the worksheet is completed by transferring all the balance sheet account balances from the adjusted trial balance columns (columns F and G) to the balance sheet columns (columns L and M).

At this point, the worksheet provides all the necessary information to prepare the financial statements. The completed financial statements were shown in Exhibit 3-15 (p. 129).

SUMMARY OF LEARNING OBJECTIVES

LO1.   Explain the difference between cash-basis and accrual-basis accounting.
- Cash-basis and accrual-basis accounting are two alternatives for recording business activities in the accounting records.
- Under cash-basis accounting, revenues and expenses are recorded when cash is received or paid, regardless of when the revenues are earned or the expenses are incurred.
- Accrual-basis accounting links income measurement to the selling activities of a company by recognizing revenues and expenses when they occur.

LO2.   Explain how the time-period assumption, revenue recognition, and matching principles affect the determination of income.
- The revenue recognition principle states that revenue is recognized or recorded in the period in which the revenue is earned and the collection of cash is reasonably assured (realized or realizable). These conditions are normally met when goods have been delivered or services have been performed.
- The matching principle requires that expenses be recognized in the same period as the revenue it helped generate.
- The application of these two principles results in income being measured as the business activity occurs, regardless of when cash is received or paid.

LO3.   Identify the kinds of transactions that may require adjustments at the end of an accounting period.
- Many business activities do not occur at a single point in time but continuously over time. Because entries in the accounting system are made at particular points in time, adjustments are needed at the end of an accounting period to record the completed portion of any partially completed activities.
- Adjusting entries apply the revenue recognition and matching principles to ensure that a company's financial statements reflect the proper amount for revenues, expenses, assets, liabilities, and stockholders' equity.
- Adjusting entries are categorized as either accruals (accrued revenues and accrued expenses) or deferrals (deferred revenues and deferred expenses).

LO4.   Prepare adjusting entries for accruals and deferrals.
- Accruals occur when revenues have been earned or expenses have been incurred but no cash has been received or paid.
- The adjusting entry for an accrued revenue will result in an increase to a revenue account and an increase to an asset account. The adjusting entry for an accrued expense account will result in an increase to an expense account and an increase to a liability account.
- Deferrals occur when cash has been received or paid prior to revenue being earned or the expense being incurred.
- The adjusting entry for a deferred (unearned) revenue will result in an increase to a revenue account and a decrease to a liability account. The adjusting entry for a deferred (prepaid) expense will result in an increase to an expense account and a decrease to an asset account.

LO5.   Prepare financial statements from an adjusted trial balance.
- An adjusted trial balance lists all of the active accounts and updates the trial balance to reflect the adjustments that have been made.
- The adjusted trial balance is the primary source of information needed to prepare the financial statements.
- Due to the interrelation between the financial statements, the income statement is prepared first, followed by the retained earnings statement, and finally, the balance sheet.

LO6.   Explain why and how companies prepare closing entries.

- Closing entries transfer the effects of revenues, expenses, and dividends to the stockholders' equity account, Retained Earnings, and clear the balances in revenues, expenses, and dividends (reduce their balances to zero) so that they are ready to accumulate the business activities of the next accounting period.
- To close the accounts, companies make a series of journal entries, dated as of the last day of the accounting period.

LO7.   Understand the steps in the accounting cycle.

- During the accounting period, transactions are analyzed to determine their effect on the accounting equation.
- Transactions that meet the recognition criteria are then journalized and posted to the general ledger.
- A trial balance is prepared to summarize the effects of these transactions.
- At the end of the accounting period, adjusting entries are prepared to recognize the completed portion of any partially completed business activities.
- The financial statements are prepared from the adjusted trial balance and the temporary accounts are closed.
- The accounting cycle repeats for the next accounting period.

LO8.   (Appendix 3A) Understand how to use a worksheet to prepare financial statements.

- A worksheet is an informal schedule that assists accountants in organizing and preparing the information necessary to perform the end-of-period steps in the accounting cycle.
- The worksheet begins with a trial balance and includes columns for adjusting entries, the adjusted trial balance, the income statement, the retained earnings statement, and the balance sheet.

CORNERSTONES
FOR CHAPTER 3

CORNERSTONE 3-1   Applying the revenue recognition and matching principles (p. 113)

CORNERSTONE 3-2   Determining which transactions require adjustment (p. 115)

CORNERSTONE 3-3   Recording accrued revenues (p. 117)

CORNERSTONE 3-4   Recording accrued expenses (p. 118)

CORNERSTONE 3-5   Adjusting deferred (unearned) revenues (p. 120)

CORNERSTONE 3-6   Adjusting deferred (prepaid) expenses (p. 121)

CORNERSTONE 3-7   Closing the accounts (p. 130)

KEY TERMS

REVIEW PROBLEM

I. The Adjustment Process

Concept:

Adjusting journal entries are required for continuous transactions that are partially complete at the end of an accounting period. This often requires estimates and judgments about the timing of revenue and expense recognition. Once the adjustments are made, financial statements can be prepared and the accounts are closed.

Information:

Kenny's Laundry has one laundry plant and uses five rented storefronts on the west side of Indianapolis as its retail locations. At the end of 2011, Kenny's had the following balances in its accounts before adjustment:

Cash	Accounts Receivable	Supplies
4,800	26,000	128,000

Land	Building	Accumulated Depreciation (Building)
124,400	249,000	36,000

Equipment	Accumulated Depreciation (Equipment)	Other Assets
122,000	24,000	16,000

Accounts Payable	Notes Payable (due 2017)	Unearned Service Revenue
8,000	120,000	12,000

Common Stock	Retained Earnings, 12/31/2010	Service Revenue
240,000	69,000	874,200

Rent Expense	Wages Expense	Insurance Expense
168,000	431,000	14,000

Salaries Expense	Interest Expense
92,000	8,000

An examination identified the following items that require adjustment:

a. Kenny's launders shirts for the service staff of a local car dealer. At the end of 2011, the car dealer owes Kenny's $1,040 for laundry services that have been performed but will not be billed until early in 2012.

b. Kenny's supplies inventory on hand at 12/31 was $21,400.

c. Kenny's launders uniforms for a nearby McDonald's franchise. The franchisee pays Kenny's in advance for the laundry service once every three months. After examining the records, Kenny's accountant determines that the laundry has earned $8,400 of the $12,000 of unearned revenue.

d. Salaries in the amount of $1,500 are owed but unpaid and unrecorded.

e. Two months' interest at 8 percent on the note payable (due in 2017) is owed but unpaid and unrecorded.

f. Depreciation expense for the building is $12,000.

g. Depreciation expense for the equipment is $24,000.

h. Income taxes expense of $5,200 is owed but unpaid and unrecorded.

Required:

1. Determine and record the adjusting entries at 12/31/2011 for Kenny's Laundry.
2. Post the effects of the adjustments to the proper accounts, and determine the account balances.
3. Prepare an income statement, retained earnings statement, and a balance sheet for Kenny's using the adjusted account balances.
4. Close the necessary accounts.

Solution:

1. The adjustments for Kenny's are as follows:

   a. The adjustment to record accrued revenue for services already provided is:

Date	Account and Explanation	Debit	Credit
Dec. 31	Accounts Receivable	1,040	
	Service Revenue		1,040
	(Recognize revenue for services performed but not billed)		

Assets	= Liabilities +	Stockholders' Equity
+1,040		+1,040

   b. The before adjustment balance in supplies inventory is $128,000. Supplies actually on hand are $21,400. Supplies expense (used) is $106,600 ($128,000 − $21,400):

Date	Account and Explanation	Debit	Credit
Dec. 31	Supplies Expense	106,600	
	Supplies		106,600
	(Recognize supplies used)		

Assets	= Liabilities +	Stockholders' Equity
−106,600		−106,600

   c. The adjustment to record the amount of deferred (unearned) revenue earned in 2011 is:

Date	Account and Explanation	Debit	Credit
Dec. 31	Unearned Service Revenue	8,400	
	Service Revenue		8,400
	(Recognize revenue earned)		

Assets	= Liabilities +	Stockholders' Equity
	−8,400	+8,400

   d. The entry to record the accrual of salaries is:

Date	Account and Explanation	Debit	Credit
Dec. 31	Salaries Expense	1,500	
	Salaries Payable		1,500
	(Recognize salary expense incurred but not paid)		

Assets	= Liabilities +	Stockholders' Equity
	+1,500	−1,500

   e. Interest expense is $1,600 ($120,000 × 8% × 2/12). The entry to accrue interest expense is:

Date	Account and Explanation	Debit	Credit
Dec. 31	Interest Expense	1,600	
	Interest Payable		1,600
	(Recognize interest expense incurred but not paid)		

Assets	= Liabilities +	Stockholders' Equity
	+1,600	−1,600

   f. The entry to record depreciation expense for the building is:

Date	Account and Explanation	Debit	Credit
Dec. 31	Depreciation Expense (Building)	12,000	
	Accumulated Depreciation (Building)		12,000
	(Record depreciation expense)		

Assets	= Liabilities +	Stockholders' Equity
−12,000		−12,000

   g. The entry to record depreciation expense for the equipment is:

Date	Account and Explanation	Debit	Credit
Dec. 31	Depreciation Expense (Equipment)	24,000	
	Accumulated Depreciation (Equipment)		24,000
	(Record depreciation expense)		

Assets	= Liabilities +	Stockholders' Equity
−24,000		−24,000

   h. The adjustment for income taxes expense is:

Date	Account and Explanation	Debit	Credit
Dec. 31	Income Tax Expense	5,200	
	Income Taxes Payable		5,200
	(Record accrual of income taxes)		

Assets	= Liabilities +	Stockholders' Equity
	+5,200	−5,200

2. The adjusted account balances for Kenny's Laundry are shown in Exhibit 3-19.

Exhibit 3-19

Kenny's Laundry Adjusted Account Balances

Assets	Liabilities	Stockholders' Equity

Assets

Cash

4,800	

Accounts Receivable

26,000	
(a) 1,040	
27,040	

Supplies

128,000	106,600 (b)
21,400	

Land

124,400	

Building

249,000	

Accumulated Depreciation (Building)

	36,000
	12,000 (f)
	48,000

Equipment

122,000	

Accumulated Depreciation (Equipment)

	24,000
	24,000 (g)
	48,000

Other Assets

16,000	

Liabilities

Accounts Payable

	8,000

Notes Payable (due 2017)

	120,000

Interest Payable

	1,600 (e)
	1,600

Salaries Payable

	1,500 (d)
	1,500

Income Taxes Payable

	5,200 (h)
	5,200

Unearned Service Revenue

(c) 8,400	12,000
	3,600

Stockholders' Equity

Common Stock

	240,000

Retained Earnings, 12/31/2010

	69,000

Service Revenue

	874,200
	1,040 (a)
	8,400 (c)
	883,640

Rent Expense

168,000	

Wages Expense

431,000	

Insurance Expense

14,000	

Salaries Expense

92,000	
(d) 1,500	
93,500	

Interest Expense

8,000	
(e) 1,600	
9,600	

Supplies Expense

(b) 106,600	
106,600	

Depreciation Expense (Building)

(f) 12,000	
12,000	

Depreciation Expense (Equipment)

(g) 24,000	
24,000	

Income Taxes Expense

(h) 5,200	
5,200	

3. The income statement, statement of changes in retained earnings, and balance sheet for Kenny's Laundry are prepared from the adjusted account balances and appear in Exhibit 3-20.

Exhibit 3-20

Financial Statements for Kenny's Laundry

Kenny's Laundry
Income Statement
For the Year Ended December 31, 2011

Service revenue		$ 883,640
Less expenses:		
Wages expense	$(431,000)	
Rent expense	(168,000)	
Supplies expense	(106,600)	
Salaries expense	(93,500)	
Depreciation expense (equipment)	(24,000)	
Insurance expense	(14,000)	
Depreciation expense (building)	(12,000)	
Interest expense	(9,600)	
Income taxes expense	(5,200)	(863,900)
Net income		$ 19,740

Kenny's Laundry
Retained Earnings Statement
For the Year Ended December 31, 2011

Retained earnings, 12/31/2010	$69,000
Add: Net income	19,740
	$88,740
Less: Dividends	0
Retained earnings, 12/31/2011	$88,740

Kenny's Laundry
Balance Sheet
December 31, 2011

ASSETS

Current assets:			
Cash		$ 4,800	
Accounts receivable		27,040	
Supplies		21,400	
Total current assets			$ 53,240
Property, plant, and equipment:			
Land		$124,400	
Building	$249,000		
Less: Accumulated depreciation	(48,000)	201,000	
Equipment	$122,000		
Less: Accumulated depreciation	(48,000)	74,000	
Total property, plant, and equipment			399,400
Other assets			16,000
Total assets			$468,640

(Continued)

LIABILITIES AND STOCKHOLDERS' EQUITY

Current liabilities:
Accounts payable	$ 8,000	
Salaries payable	1,500	
Interest payable	1,600	
Income taxes payable	5,200	
Unearned service revenue	3,600	
Total current liabilities		$ 19,900
Long-term liabilities:		
Notes payable (due 2017)		120,000
Total liabilities		$139,900
Stockholders' equity:		
Common stock	$240,000	
Retained earnings	88,740	
Total stockholders' equity		328,740
Total liabilities and stockholders' equity		$468,640

4. The entries to close the accounts are:

Date	Account and Explanation	Debit	Credit
Dec. 31	Service Revenue	883,640	
	Income Summary		883,640
	(Close revenues)		
Dec. 31	Income Summary	863,900	
	Rent Expense		168,000
	Wages Expense		431,000
	Insurance Expense		14,000
	Salaries Expense		93,500
	Supplies Expense		106,600
	Depreciation Expense (Building)		12,000
	Depreciation Expense (Equipment)		24,000
	Interest Expense		9,600
	Income Tax Expense		5,200
	(Close expenses)		
Dec. 31	Income Summary	19,740	
	Retained Earnings		19,740
	(Close Income Summary)		

DISCUSSION QUESTIONS

1. How does accrual-basis net income differ from cash-basis net income?
2. Explain when revenue may be recognized and give an example.
3. What happens during the accounting cycle?
4. Provide two examples of transactions that begin and end at a particular point in time and two examples of continuous transactions.
5. Why are adjusting entries needed?
6. What accounting concepts require that adjusting entries be employed?
7. Describe the recording of transactions that begin and end at a particular point in time and the recording of continuous transactions.
8. For each of the four categories of adjusting entries, describe the business activity that produces circumstances requiring adjustment.

9. What is the difference between an *accrual* and a *deferral*?
10. Which type of adjustment will (a) increase both assets and revenues, (b) increase revenues and decrease liabilities, (c) increase expenses and decrease assets, and (d) increase both expenses and liabilities?
11. How is the amount for an interest expense (or interest revenue) adjustment determined?
12. Describe the effect on the financial statements when an adjustment is prepared that records (a) unrecorded revenue and (b) unrecorded expense.
13. On the basis of what you have learned about adjustments, why do you think that adjusting entries are made on the last day of the accounting period rather than at several times during the accounting period?
14. What is the purpose of closing entries?
15. Describe the four steps in the closing process.
16. Identify each of the following categories of accounts as temporary or permanent: assets, liabilities, equity, revenues, expenses, dividends. How is the distinction between temporary and permanent accounts related to the closing process?
17. Why are only the balance sheet accounts permanent?
18. List the seven steps in the accounting cycle in the order in which they occur and explain what occurs at each step of the accounting cycle.
19. *(Appendix 3A)* What is the relationship between the accounting cycle and the worksheet?
20. *(Appendix 3A)* Describe the structure of the worksheet and the accounting information it contains.

MULTIPLE-CHOICE EXERCISES

3-1 Which of the following statements is true?

a. Under cash-basis accounting, revenues are recorded when earned and expenses are recorded when incurred.
b. Accrual-basis accounting records both cash and noncash transactions when they occur.
c. Generally accepted accounting principles require companies to use cash-basis accounting.
d. The key elements of accrual-basis accounting are the revenue recognition principle, the matching principle, and the historical cost principle.

3-2 In December 2011, Swanstrom Inc. receives a cash payment of $3,000 for services performed in December 2011 and a cash payment of $4,000 for services to be performed in January 2012. Swanstrom also receives the December utility bill for $500 but does not pay this bill until 2012. For December 2011, under the accrual basis of accounting, Swanstrom would recognize:

a. $7,000 of revenue and $500 of expense
b. $7,000 of revenue and $0 of expense
c. $3,000 of revenue and $500 of expense
d. $3,000 of revenue and $0 of expense

3-3 Which transaction would require adjustment at December 31?

a. The sale of merchandise for cash on December 30.
b. Common stock was issued on November 30.
c. Salaries were paid to employees on December 31 for work performed in December.
d. A one-year insurance policy (which took effect immediately) was purchased on December 1.

3-4 Which of the following statements is *false*?

a. Adjusting entries are necessary because timing differences exist between when a revenue or expense is recognized and cash is received or paid.
b. Adjusting entries always affect at least one revenue or expense account and one asset or liability account.
c. The cash account will always be affected by adjusting journal entries.
d. Adjusting entries can be classified as either accruals or deferrals.

3-5 Dallas Company loaned $10,000 to Ewing Company on December 1, 2011. Ewing will pay Dallas $600 of interest ($50 per month) on November 30, 2012. Dallas's adjusting entry at December 31, 2011, is:

a. Interest Expense.............. 50
        Cash........................   50
b. Cash................................ 50
        Interest Revenue   50

c. Interest Receivable 50
        Interest Revenue   50
d. No adjusting entry is required.

3-6 Ron's Diner received the following bills for December 2011 utilities:

- Electricity: $850 on December 29, 2011
- Telephone: $475 on January 5, 2012

Both bills were paid on January 10, 2012. On the December 31, 2011, balance sheet, Ron's Diner will report accrued expenses of:

a. $0
b. $475

c. $850
d. $1,325

3-7 In September 2011, GolfWorld Magazine obtained $12,000 of subscriptions for one year of magazines and credited Unearned Sales Revenue. The magazines will begin to be delivered in October 2011. At December 31, 2011, GolfWorld should make the following adjustment:

a. Debit Sales Revenue by $3,000 and credit Unearned Sales Revenue by $3,000.
b. Debit Unearned Sales Revenue by $3,000 and credit Sales Revenue by $3,000.
c. Debit Sales Revenue by $9,000 and credit Unearned Sales Revenue by $9,000.
d. Debit Unearned Sales Revenue by $9,000 and credit Sales Revenue by $9,000.

3-8 Hurd Inc. prepays rent every three months on March 1, June 1, September 1, and December 1. Rent for the three months totals $3,600. On December 31, 2011, Hurd will report Prepaid Rent of:

a. $0
b. $1,200

c. $2,400
d. $3,600

3-9 Which of the following statements is *incorrect* regarding preparing financial statements?

a. The adjusted trial balance lists only the balance sheet accounts in a "debit" and "credit" format.
b. The adjusted trial balance is the primary source of information needed to prepare the financial statements.
c. The financial statements are prepared in the following order: (1) the income statement, (2) the retained earnings statement, (3) the balance sheet.
d. The income statement and the balance sheet are related through the retained earnings account.

3-10 Reinhardt Company reported revenues of $122,000 and expenses of $83,000 on its 2011 income statement. In addition, Reinhardt paid $4,000 of dividends during 2011. On December 31, 2011, Reinhardt prepared closing entries. The net effect of the closing entries on retained earnings was a(n):

a. Decrease of $4,000
b. Increase of $35,000

c. Increase of $39,000
d. Decrease of $87,000

3-11 Which of the following is true regarding the accounting cycle?

a. The accounts are adjusted after preparing the financial statements.
b. Journal entries are made prior to the transaction being analyzed.
c. The temporary accounts are closed after the financial statements are prepared.
d. An adjusted trial balance is usually prepared after the accounts are closed.

CORNERSTONE EXERCISES

OBJECTIVE
CORNERSTONE 3-1

Cornerstone Exercise 3-12 Accrual- and Cash-Basis Revenue

McDonald Music sells used CDs for $2.00 each. During the month of April, McDonald sold 8,750 CDs for cash and 15,310 CDs on credit. McDonald's cash collections in April included the $17,500 for the CDs sold for cash, $10,300 for CDs sold on credit during the previous month, and $9,850 for CDs sold on credit during April.

Required:

Calculate the amount of revenue recognized in April under (a) the cash-basis of accounting and (b) the accrual-basis of accounting.

OBJECTIVE
CORNERSTONE 3-1

Cornerstone Exercise 3-13 Accrual- and Cash-Basis Expenses

Speedy Delivery Company provides next-day delivery across the southeastern United States. During May, Speedy incurred $132,600 in fuel costs. Speedy paid $95,450 of the fuel cost in May, with the remainder paid in June. In addition, Speedy paid $15,000 in May to another fuel supplier in an effort to build up its supply of fuel.

Required:

Calculate the amount of expense recognized in May under (a) the cash-basis of accounting and (b) the accrual-basis of accounting.

OBJECTIVE
CORNERSTONE 3-1

Cornerstone Exercise 3-14 Revenue and the Recognition Principle

Heartstrings Gift Shoppe sells an assortment of gifts for any occasion. During October, Heartstrings started a Gift-of-the-Month program. Under the terms of this program, beginning in the month of the sale, Heartstrings would select and deliver a random gift each month, over the next 12 months, to the person the customer selects as a recipient. During October, Heartstrings sold 25 of these packages for a total of $11,280 in cash.

Required:

For the month of October, calculate the amount of revenue that Heartstrings will recognize.

OBJECTIVE
CORNERSTONE 3-1

Cornerstone Exercise 3-15 Expenses and the Matching Principle

The following information describes transactions for Morgenstern Advertising Company during July:

a. On July 5, Morgenstern purchased and received $24,300 of supplies on credit from Drexel Supply Inc. During July, Morgenstern paid $20,500 cash to Drexel and used $18,450 of the supplies.
b. Morgenstern paid $9,600 to salespeople for salaries earned during July. An additional $1,610 was owed to salespeople at July 31 for salaries earned during the month.
c. Paid $2,950 to the local utility company for electric service. Electric service in July was $2,300 of the $2,950 total bill.

Required:

Calculate the amount of expense recognized in July under (a) the cash-basis of accounting and (b) the accrual-basis of accounting.

OBJECTIVE
CORNERSTONE 3-2

Cornerstone Exercise 3-16 Identification of Adjusting Entries

Singleton Inc. uses the accrual basis of accounting and had the following transactions during the year.

a. Merchandise was sold to customers on credit.
b. Purchased equipment to be used in the operation of its business.
c. A two-year insurance contract was purchased.
d. Received cash for services to be performed over the next year.
e. Paid monthly employee salaries.
f. Borrowed money from First Bank by signing a note payable due in five years.

Required:

Identify and explain why each transaction may or may not require adjustment.

Cornerstone Exercise 3-17 Accrued Revenue Adjusting Entries

OBJECTIVE ④
CORNERSTONE 3-3

Powers Rental Service had the following items that require adjustment at year-end.

a. Earned $9,880 of revenue from the rental of equipment for which the customer had not yet paid.
b. Interest of $650 on a note receivable has been earned but not yet received.

Required:
1. Prepare the adjusting entries needed at December 31.
2. What is the effect on the financial statements if these adjusting entries are not made?

Cornerstone Exercise 3-18 Accrued Expense Adjusting Entries

OBJECTIVE ④
CORNERSTONE 3-4

Manning Manufacturing Inc. had the following items that require adjustment at year-end.

a. Salaries of $4,980 that were earned in December are unrecorded and unpaid.
b. Used $2,430 of utilities in December, which are unrecorded and unpaid.
c. Interest of $1,575 on a note payable has not been recorded or paid.

Required:
1. Prepare the adjusting entries needed at December 31.
2. What is the effect on the financial statements if these adjusting entries are not made?

Cornerstone Exercise 3-19 Deferred Revenue Adjusting Entries

OBJECTIVE ④
CORNERSTONE 3-5

Olney Cleaning Company had the following items that require adjustment at year-end.

a. For one cleaning contract, $10,500 cash was received in advance. The cash was credited to unearned revenue upon receipt. At year-end, $1,250 of the service revenue was still unearned.
b. For another cleaning contract, $8,300 cash was received in advance and credited to unearned revenue upon receipt. At year-end, $2,700 of the services had been provided.

Required:
1. Prepare the adjusting journal entries needed at December 31.
2. What is the effect on the financial statements if these adjusting entries are not made?
3. What is the balance in unearned revenue at December 31 related to the two cleaning contracts?

Cornerstone Exercise 3-20 Deferred Expense Adjusting Entries

OBJECTIVE ④
CORNERSTONE 3-6

Best Company had the following items that require adjustment at year-end.

a. Cash for equipment rental in the amount of $3,800 was paid in advance. The $3,800 was debited to prepaid rent when paid. At year-end, $2,950 of the prepaid rent had been used.
b. Cash for insurance in the amount of $8,200 was paid in advance. The $8,200 was debited to prepaid insurance when paid. At year-end, $1,850 of the prepaid insurance was still unused.

Required:
1. Prepare the adjusting journal entries needed at December 31.
2. What is the effect on the financial statements if these adjusting entries are not made?
3. What is the balance in prepaid equipment rent and insurance expense at December 31?

Cornerstone Exercise 3-21 Adjustment for Supplies

OBJECTIVE ④
CORNERSTONE 3-6

Pain-Free Dental Group Inc. purchased dental supplies of $12,800 during the year. At the end of the year, a physical count of supplies showed $1,475 of supplies on hand.

Required:
1. Prepare the adjusting entry needed at the end of the year.
2. What is the amount of supplies reported on Pain-Free's balance sheet at the end of the year?

Cornerstone Exercise 3-22 Adjustment for Depreciation

OBJECTIVE ④
CORNERSTONE 3-6

LaGarde Company has a machine that it purchased for $125,000 on January 1. Annual depreciation on the machine is estimated to be $14,500.

(Continued)

Required:
1. Prepare the adjusting entry needed at the end of the year.
2. What is the book value of the machine reported on LaGarde's balance sheet at the end of the year?

OBJECTIVE **4**
CORNERSTONE 3-3
CORNERSTONE 3-4
CORNERSTONE 3-5
CORNERSTONE 3-6

Cornerstone Exercise 3-23 Financial Statement Effects of Adjusting Entries

When adjusting entries were made at the end of the year, the accountant for Parker Company did not make the following adjustments.

a. $2,900 of wages had been earned by employees but were unpaid.
b. $3,750 of revenue had been earned but was uncollected and unrecorded.
c. $2,400 of revenue had been earned. The customer had prepaid for this service and the amount was originally recorded in the Unearned Sales Revenue account.
d. $1,200 of insurance coverage had expired. Insurance had been initially recorded in the Prepaid Insurance account.

Required:
Identify the effect on the financial statements of the adjusting entries that were omitted.

Use the following information for Cornerstone Exercises 3-24 through 3-27:
Sparrow Company had the following adjusted trial balance at December 31, 2011.

Sparrow Company
Adjusted Trial Balance
December 31, 2011

	Debit	Credit
Cash	$ 3,150	
Accounts Receivable	5,650	
Prepaid Insurance	4,480	
Equipment	42,000	
Accumulated Depreciation, Equipment		$ 24,000
Accounts Payable		2,800
Salaries Payable		4,450
Unearned Service Revenue		3,875
Common Stock		8,000
Retained Earnings		2,255
Dividends	10,500	
Service Revenue		99,600
Salaries Expense	49,400	
Rent Expense	17,250	
Insurance Expense	2,200	
Depreciation Expense	4,950	
Income Taxes Expense	5,400	
Total	$144,980	$144,980

OBJECTIVE **5**
CORNERSTONE 1-3

Cornerstone Exercise 3-24 Preparing an Income Statement

Refer to the information for Sparrow Company above.

Required:
Prepare a single-step income statement for Sparrow for 2011.

OBJECTIVE **5**
CORNERSTONE 1-4

Cornerstone Exercise 3-25 Preparing a Retained Earnings Statement

Refer to the information for Sparrow Company above.

Required:
Prepare a retained earnings statement for Sparrow for 2011.

OBJECTIVE **5**
CORNERSTONE 1-2

Cornerstone Exercise 3-26 Preparing a Balance Sheet

Refer to the information for Sparrow Company above.

Required:
Prepare a classified balance sheet for Sparrow at December 31, 2011.

Cornerstone Exercise 3-27 Preparing and Analyzing Closing Entries

Refer to the information for Sparrow Company on the previous page.

OBJECTIVE ⑥
CORNERSTONE 3-7

Required:
1. Prepare the closing entries for Sparrow at December 31, 2011.
2. How does the closing process affect retained earnings?

EXERCISES

Exercise 3-28 Accrual- and Cash-Basis Expense Recognition

The following information is taken from the accrual accounting records of Kroger Sales Company:

OBJECTIVE ①

a. During January, Kroger paid $9,150 for supplies to be used in sales to customers during the next two months (February and March). The supplies will be used evenly over the next two months.

b. Kroger pays its employees at the end of each month for salaries earned during that month. Salaries paid at the end of February and March amounted to $4,925 and $5,100, respectively.

c. Kroger placed an advertisement in the local newspaper during March at a cost of $850. The ad promoted the pre-spring sale during the last week in March. Kroger did not pay for the newspaper ad until mid-April.

Required:
1. Under cash-basis accounting, how much expense should Kroger report for February and March?
2. Under accrual-basis accounting, how much expense should Kroger report for February and March?
3. **Conceptual Connection:** Which basis of accounting provides the most useful information for decision-makers? Why?

Exercise 3-29 Revenue Recognition

Each of the following situations relates to the recognition of revenue:

OBJECTIVE ②

a. A store sells a gift card in December which will be given as a Christmas present. The card is not redeemed until January.

b. A furniture store sells and delivers furniture to a customer in June with no payments and no interest for six months.

c. An airline sells an airline ticket and collects the fare in February for a flight in March to a spring break destination.

d. A theme park sells a season pass and collects the cash in January which allows entrance into the park for an entire year.

e. A package delivery service delivers a package in October but doesn't bill the customer and receive payment until November.

Required:
For each situation, indicate when the company should recognize revenue.

Exercise 3-30 Revenue and Expense Recognition

Electronic Repair Company repaired a high-definition television for Sarah Merrifield in December 2011. Sarah paid $80 at the time of the repair and agreed to pay Electronic Repair $80 each month for five months beginning on January 15, 2012. Electronic Repair used $120 of supplies, which were purchased in November 2011, to repair the television.

OBJECTIVE ②

Required:
1. In what month or months should revenue from this service be recorded by Electronic Repair?
2. In what month or months should the expense related to the repair of the television be recorded by Electronic Repair?
3. **Conceptual Connection:** Describe the accounting principles used to answer the above questions.

Exercise 3-31 Cash-Basis and Accrual-Basis Accounting

The records of Summers Building Company reveal the following information for 2011.

OBJECTIVE ① ②

(Continued)

a. Cash receipts during 2011 (including $50,000 paid by stockholders in exchange for common stock) were $273,500.
b. Cash payments during 2011 (including $8,000 of dividends paid to stockholders) were $164,850.
c. Total selling price of services billed to customers during 2011 was $201,700.
d. Salaries earned by employees during 2011 were $114,250.
e. Cost of supplies used during 2011 in operation of the business was $47,325.

Required:
1. Calculate Summers Building's net income for 2011 on an accrual basis.
2. Calculate Summers Building's net income for 2011 on a cash-basis.
3. **Conceptual Connection:** Explain how the cash-basis of accounting allows for the manipulation of income.

OBJECTIVE ❷

Exercise 3-32 Revenue Recognition and Matching

Omega Transportation Inc., headquartered in Atlanta, Georgia, uses the accrual basis of accounting and engaged in the following transactions:

*   billed customers $2,415,250 for transportation services
*   collected cash from customers in the amount of $1,381,975
*   purchased fuel supplies for $1,333,800 cash
*   used fuel supplies that cost $1,303,490
*   employees earned salaries of $291,500
*   paid employees $280,300 cash for salaries

Required:
Determine the amount of sales revenue and total expenses for Omega's income statement.

OBJECTIVE ❷

Exercise 3-33 Recognizing Expenses

Treadway Dental Services gives each of its patients a toothbrush with the name and phone number of the dentist office and a logo imprinted on the brush. Treadway purchased 15,000 of the toothbrushes in October 2011 for $3,130. The toothbrushes were delivered in November and paid for in December 2011. Treadway began to give the patients the toothbrushes in February 2012. By the end of 2012, 4,500 of the toothbrushes remained in the supplies account.

Required:
1. How much expense should be recorded for the 15,000 toothbrushes in 2011 and 2012 to properly match expenses with revenues?
2. Describe how the 4,500 toothbrushes that remain in the supplies account will be handled in 2013.

OBJECTIVE ❶ ❷

Exercise 3-34 Revenue Recognition and Matching

Carrico Advertising Inc. performs advertising services for several Fortune 500 companies. The following information describes Carrico's activities during 2011.

a. At the beginning of 2011, customers owed Carrico $45,800 for advertising services performed during 2010. During 2011, Carrico performed an additional $695,100 of advertising services on account. Carrico collected $708,700 cash from customers during 2011.
b. At the beginning of 2011, Carrico had $13,350 of supplies on hand for which it owed suppliers $8,150. During 2011, Carrico purchased an additional $14,600 of supplies on account. Carrico also paid $19,300 cash owed to suppliers for goods previously purchased on credit. Carrico had $2,230 of supplies on hand at the end of 2011.
c. Carrico's 2011 operating and interest expenses were $437,600 and $133,400, respectively.

Required:
1. Calculate Carrico's 2011 income before taxes.
2. Calculate the amount of Carrico's accounts receivable, supplies, and accounts payable at December 31, 2011.
3. **Conceptual Connection:** Explain the underlying principles behind why the three accounts computed in part 2 exist.

Exercise 3-35 Identification of Adjusting Entries

OBJECTIVE 3

Conklin Services prepares financial statements only once per year using an annual accounting period ending on December 31. Each of the following statements describes an entry made by Conklin on December 31 of a recent year.

a. On December 31, Conklin completed a service agreement for Pizza Planet and recorded the related revenue. The job started in August.

b. Conklin provides weekly service visits to the local C.J. Nickel department store to check and maintain various pieces of computer printing equipment. On December 31, Conklin recorded revenue for the visits completed during December. The cash will not be received until January.

c. Conklin's salaried employees are paid on the last day of every month. On December 31, Conklin recorded the payment of December salaries.

d. Conklin's hourly wage employees are paid every Friday. On December 31, Conklin recorded as payable the wages for the first three working days of the week in which the year ended.

e. On December 31, Conklin recorded the receipt of a shipment of office supplies from Office Supplies, Inc. to be paid for in January.

f. On December 31, Conklin recorded the estimated use of supplies for the year. The supplies were purchased for cash earlier in the year.

g. Early in December, Conklin was paid in advance by Parker Enterprises for two months of weekly service visits. Conklin recorded the advance payment as a liability. On December 31, Conklin recorded revenue for the service visits to Parker Enterprises that were completed during December.

h. On December 31, Conklin recorded depreciation expense on office equipment for the year.

Required:

Indicate whether each entry is an *adjusting entry* or a *regular journal entry*, and if it is an adjusting entry, identify it as one of the following types: (1) revenue recognized before collection, (2) expense recognized before payment, (3) revenue recognized after collection, or (4) expense recognized after payment.

Exercise 3-36 Identification and Analysis of Adjusting Entries

OBJECTIVE 3

Medina Motor Service is preparing adjusting entries for the year ended December 31, 2011. The following items describe Medina's continuous transactions during 2011:

a. Medina's salaried employees are paid on the last day of every month.

b. Medina's hourly employees are paid every other Friday for the preceding two weeks' work. The next payday falls on January 5, 2012.

c. In November 2011, Medina borrowed $600,000 from Bank One, giving a 9 percent note payable with interest due in January 2012. The note was properly recorded.

d. Medina rents a portion of its parking lot to the neighboring business under a long-term lease agreement that requires payment of rent six months in advance on April 1 and October 1 of each year. The October 1, 2011, payment was made and recorded as prepaid rent.

e. Medina's service department recognizes the entire revenue on every auto service job when the job is complete. At December 31, several service jobs are in process.

f. Medina recognizes depreciation on shop equipment annually at the end of each year.

g. Medina purchases all of its office supplies from Office Supplies Inc. All purchases are recorded in the supplies account. Supplies expense is calculated and recorded annually at the end of each year.

Required:

Indicate whether or not each item requires an adjusting entry at December 31, 2011. If an item requires an adjusting entry, indicate which accounts are increased by the adjustment and which are decreased.

Exercise 3-37 Revenue Adjustments

OBJECTIVE 4

Sentry Transport Inc. of Atlanta provides in-town parcel delivery services in addition to a full range of passenger services. Sentry engaged in the following activities during the current year:

a. Sentry received $3,500 cash in advance from Rich's Department Store for an estimated 175 deliveries during December 2011 and January and February of 2012. The entire amount was

(Continued)

recorded as unearned revenue when received. During December 2011, 60 deliveries were made for Rich's.

b.   Sentry operates several small buses that take commuters from suburban communities to the central downtown area of Atlanta. The commuters purchase, in advance, tickets for 50 one-way trips. Each 50-ride ticket costs $500. At the time of purchase, Sentry credits the cash received to unearned revenue. At year-end, Sentry estimates that revenue from 9,750, one-way rides has been earned.

c.   Sentry operates several buses that provide transportation for the clients of a social service agency in Atlanta. Sentry bills the agency quarterly at the end of January, April, July, and October for the service performed that quarter. The contract price is $9,000 per quarter. Sentry follows the practice of recognizing revenue from this contract in the period in which the service is performed.

d.   On December 23, Delta Airlines chartered a bus to transport its marketing group to a meeting at a resort in southern Georgia. The meeting will be held during the last week in January 2012, and Delta agrees to pay for the entire trip on the day the bus departs. At year-end, none of these arrangements have been recorded by Sentry.

Required:
1.   Prepare adjusting entries at December 31 for these four activities.
2.   What would be the effect on revenue if the adjusting entries were not made?

OBJECTIVE ④

Exercise 3-38 Expense Adjustments

Faraday Electronic Service repairs stereos and DVD players. During a recent year, Faraday engaged in the following activities:

a.   On September 1, Faraday paid Wausau Insurance $4,860 for its liability insurance for the next 12 months. The full amount of the prepayment was debited to prepaid insurance.

b.   At December 31, Faraday estimates that $1,520 of utility costs are unrecorded and unpaid.

c.   Faraday rents its testing equipment from JVC. Equipment rent in the amount of $1,440 is unpaid and unrecorded at December 31.

d.   In late October, Faraday agreed to become the sponsor for the sports segment of the evening news program on a local television station. The station billed Faraday $4,350 for three months' sponsorship—November 2011, December 2011, and January 2012—in advance. When these payments were made, Faraday debited prepaid advertising. At December 31, two months' advertising has been used and one month remains unused.

Required:
1.   Prepare adjusting entries at December 31 for these four activities.
2.   What would be the effect on expenses if the adjusting entries were not made?

OBJECTIVE ④

Exercise 3-39 Prepayments, Collections in Advance

Greensboro Properties Inc. owns a building in which it leases office space to small businesses and professionals. During 2011, Greensboro Properties engaged in the following transactions:

a.   On March 1, Greensboro Properties paid $10,500 in advance to Patterson Insurance Company for one year of insurance beginning March 1, 2011. The full amount of the prepayment was debited to prepaid insurance.

b.   On May 1, Greensboro Properties received $30,000 for one year's rent from Angela Cottrell, a lawyer and new tenant. Greensboro Properties credited unearned rent revenue for the full amount collected from Cottrell.

c.   On July 31, Greensboro Properties received $240,000 for six months' rent on an office building that is occupied by Newnan and Calhoun, a regional accounting firm. The rental period begins on August 1, 2011. The full amount received was credited to unearned rent revenue.

d.   On November 1, Greensboro Properties paid $4,500 to Pinkerton Security for three months' security services beginning on that date. The entire amount was debited to prepaid security services.

Required:
1.   Prepare the journal entry to record the receipt or payment of cash for each of the transactions.
2.   Prepare the adjusting entries you would make at December 31, 2011, for each of these items.

3. What would be the total effect on the income statement and balance sheet if these entries were not recorded?

Exercise 3-40 Prepayment of Expenses

OBJECTIVE 4

JDM Inc. made the following prepayments for expense items during 2011:

a. Prepaid building rent for one year on April 1 by paying $6,600. Prepaid rent was debited for the amount paid.
b. Prepaid twelve months' insurance on October 1 by paying $4,200. Prepaid insurance was debited.
c. Purchased $5,250 of office supplies on October 15, debiting supplies for the full amount. Office supplies costing $1,085 remain unused at December 31, 2011.
d. Paid $600 for a 12-month service contract for repairs and maintenance on a computer. The contract begins November 1. The full amount of the payment was debited to prepaid repairs and maintenance.

Required:
1. Prepare journal entries to record the payment of cash for each transaction.
2. Prepare adjusting entries for the prepayments at December 31, 2011.
3. For all of the above items, assume that the accountant failed to make the adjusting entries. What would be the effect on net income?

Exercise 3-41 Adjustment for Supplies

OBJECTIVE 4

The downtown location of Chicago Clothiers purchases large quantities of supplies, including plastic garment bags and paper bags and boxes. At December 31, 2011, the following information is available concerning these supplies:

ILLUSTRATING
RELATIONSHIPS

Supplies inventory, 1/1/2011	$ 4,150
Supplies inventory, 12/31/2011	5,220
Supplies purchased for cash during 2011	12,690

All purchases of supplies during the year are debited to the supplies inventory.

Required:
1. What is the expense reported on the income statement associated with the use of supplies during 2011?
2. What is the proper adjusting entry at December 31, 2011?
3. By how much would assets and income be overstated or understated if the adjusting entry were not recorded?

Exercise 3-42 Adjusting Entries

OBJECTIVE 4

Allentown Services Inc. is preparing adjusting entries for the year ending December 31, 2011. The following data are available:

a. Interest is owed at December 31, 2011, on a six-month, 8 percent note. Allentown borrowed $120,000 from NBD on September 1, 2011.
b. Allentown provides daily building maintenance services to Mack Trucks for a quarterly fee of $2,700, payable on the fifteenth of the month following the end of each quarter. No entries have been made for the services provided to Mack Trucks during the quarter ended December 31, and the related bill will not be sent until January 15, 2012.
c. At the beginning of 2011, the cost of office supplies on hand was $1,220. During 2011, office supplies with a total cost of $6,480 were purchased from Office Depot and debited to office supplies inventory. On December 31, 2011, Allentown determined the cost of office supplies on hand to be $970.
d. On September 23, 2011, Allentown received a $7,650 payment from Bethlehem Steel for nine months of maintenance services beginning on October 1, 2011. The entire amount was credited to unearned service revenue when received.

Required:
1. Prepare the appropriate adjusting entries at December 31, 2011.
2. What would be the effect on the balance sheet and the income statement if the accountant failed to make the above adjusting entries?

Exercise 3-43 Adjusting Entries

Reynolds Computer Service offers data processing services to retail clothing stores. The following data have been collected to aid in the preparation of adjusting entries for Reynolds Computer Service for 2011:

a. Computer equipment was purchased from IBM in 2008 at a cost of $540,000. Annual depreciation is $132,500.

b. A fire insurance policy for a two-year period beginning September 1, 2011, was purchased from Good Hands Insurance Company for $12,240 cash. The entire amount of the prepayment was debited to prepaid insurance. (Assume that the beginning balance of prepaid insurance was $0 and that there were no other debits or credits to that account during 2011.)

c. Reynolds has a contract to perform the payroll accounting for Dayton's Department Stores. At the end of 2011, $5,450 of services have been performed under this contract but are unbilled.

d. Reynolds rents 12 computer terminals for $65 per month per terminal from Extreme Terminals Inc. At December 31, 2011, Reynolds owes Extreme Terminals for half a month's rent on each terminal. The amount owed is unrecorded.

e. Perry's Tax Service prepays rent for time on Reynolds' computer. When payments are received from Perry's Tax Service, Reynolds credits unearned rent revenue. At December 31, 2011, Reynolds has earned $1,810 for computer time used by Perry's Tax Service during December 2011.

Required:

1. Prepare adjusting entries for each of the transactions.

2. What would be the effect on the balance sheet and the income statement if the accountant failed to make the above adjusting entries?

 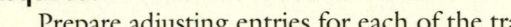
Exercise 3-44 Recreating Adjusting Entries

Selected balance sheet accounts for Gardner Company are presented below:

Prepaid Insurance		Wages Payable	Unearned Sales Revenue		Interest Receivable
May 5 4,300		?		May 10 9,500	?
	?		?		
1,250		5,400		2,250	825

Required:

Analyze each account and recreate the journal entries that were made. For deferrals, be sure to include the original journal entry as well as the adjusting journal entry. Month end is May 31, 2011.

 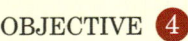
Exercise 3-45 Effect of Adjustments on the Financial Statements

VanBrush Enterprises, a painting contractor, prepared the following adjusting entries at year-end:

a. Wages Expense.................................... 2,550
      Wages Payable............................   2,550
b. Accounts Receivable.......................... 8,110
      Service Revenue   8,110
c. Unearned Service Revenue............... 5,245
      Service Revenue   5,245
d. Rent Expense 3,820
      Prepaid Rent   3,820

Required:

1. Show the effect of these adjustments on (1) assets, liabilities, and equity and (2) revenues, expenses, and net income.

2. If these adjustments were made with estimates that were considered conservative, how would this affect your interpretation of earnings quality?

Exercise 3-46 Preparation of Closing Entries

OBJECTIVE 6

Grand Rapids Consulting Inc. began 2011 with a retained earnings balance of $38,100 and has the following accounts and balances at year-end:

Sales Revenue	$162,820	Supplies Expense	$ 4,348
Salaries Expense	91,660	Income Taxes Expense	13,800
Rent Expense	11,250	Dividends (declared and paid)	8,400
Utilities Expense	8,415		

Required:

1. Prepare the closing entries made by Grand Rapids Consulting at the end of 2011.
2. Prepare Grand Rapids Consulting's retained earnings statement for 2011.

Exercise 3-47 Preparation of Closing Entries

OBJECTIVE 6

James and Susan Morley recently converted a large turn-of-the-century house into a hotel and incorporated the business as Saginaw Enterprises. Their accountant is inexperienced and has made the following closing entries at the end of Saginaw's first year of operations:

	Debit	Credit
Income Summary	210,000	
Service Revenue		177,000
Accumulated Depreciation		33,000
Depreciation Expense	33,000	
Income Taxes Expense	8,200	
Utilities Expense	12,700	
Wages Expense	66,000	
Supplies Expense	31,000	
Accounts Payable	4,500	
Income Summary		155,400
Income Summary	54,600	
Retained Earnings		54,600
Dividends	3,200	
Income Summary		3,200

Required:

1. Indicate what is wrong with the closing entries above.
2. Prepare the correct closing entries. Assume that all necessary accounts are presented above and that the amounts given are correct.
3. **Conceptual Connection:** Explain why closing entries are necessary.

Exercise 3-48 Preparation of a Worksheet *(Appendix 3A)*

OBJECTIVE 8

Unadjusted account balances at December 31, 2011, for Rapisarda Company are as follows:

Rapisarda Company
Unadjusted Trial Balance
December 31, 2011

Account Titles	Debit	Credit
Cash	$ 2,000	
Accounts Receivable	33,000	
Prepaid Rent	26,000	
Equipment	211,000	
Accumulated Depreciation, Equipment		$ 75,000
Other Assets	24,000	
Accounts Payable		12,000
Note Payable (due in 10 years)		40,000
Common Stock		100,000
Retained Earnings, 12/31/2010		11,000
Service Revenue		243,000
Rent Expense	84,000	
Wages Expense	97,000	
Interest Expense	4,000	
Totals	$481,000	$481,000

(Continued)

The following data are not yet recorded:

a. Depreciation on the equipment is $18,350.
b. Unrecorded wages owed at December 31, 2011: $4,680.
c. Prepaid rent at December 31, 2011: $9,240.
d. Income taxes expense: $5,463.

Required:
Prepare a completed worksheet for Rapisarda Company.

PROBLEM SET A

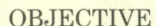

Problem 3-49A Cash-Basis and Accrual-Basis Income

George Hathaway, an electrician, entered into an agreement with a real estate management company to perform all maintenance of basic electrical systems and air-conditioning equipment in the apartment buildings under the company's management. The agreement, which is subject to annual renewal, provides for the payment of a fixed fee of $6,420 on January 1 of each year plus amounts for parts and materials billed separately at the end of each month. Amounts billed at the end of one month are collected in the next month. During the first three months of 2011, George makes the following additional billings and cash collections:

	Billings for Parts and Materials	Cash Collected	Cash Paid for Parts and Materials	Cost of Parts and Materials Used
January	$510	$6,530*	$375	$360
February	0	435	280	270
March	380	0	315	330

*Includes $110 for parts and materials billed in December 2010.

Required:
1. Calculate the amount of cash-basis income reported for each of the first three months.
2. Calculate the amount of accrual-basis income reported for each of the first three months.
3. **Conceptual Connection:** Why do decision-makers prefer the accrual basis of accounting?

Problem 3-50A Revenue Recognition and Matching

Security Specialists performs security services for local businesses. During 2011, Security Specialists performed $915,700 of security services and collected $930,000 cash from customers. Security Specialist's employees earned salaries of $42,350 per month. During 2011, Security Services paid salaries of $491,410 cash for work performed. At the beginning of 2011, Security Specialists had $2,875 of supplies on hand. Supplies of $80,000 were purchased during the year, and $12,150 of supplies were on hand at the end of the year. Other general and administrative expenses incurred during the year were $31,000.

Required:
1. Calculate revenue and expenses for 2011.
2. Prepare the 2011 income statement.
3. **Conceptual Connection:** Describe the accounting principles used to prepare the income statement.

Problem 3-51A Identification and Preparation of Adjusting Entries

Kuepper's Day Care is a large daycare center in South Orange, New Jersey. The daycare center serves several nearby businesses, as well as a number of individual families. The businesses pay $6,180 per child per year for daycare services for their employees' children. The businesses pay in advance on a quarterly basis. For individual families, daycare services are provided monthly and billed at the beginning of the next month. The following transactions describe Kuepper's activities during December 2011:

a. On December 1, Kuepper borrowed $60,000 by issuing a five-year, $60,000, 9 percent note payable.
b. Daycare service in the amount of $12,450 was provided to individual families during December. These families will not be billed until January 2012.

c. At December 1, the balance in unearned service revenue was $43,775. At December 31, Kuepper determined that $3,090 of this revenue was still unearned.

d. On December 31, the daycare center collected $131,325 from businesses for services to be provided in 2012.

e. On December 31, the center recorded depreciation of $2,675 on a bus that it uses for field trips.

f. The daycare center had prepaid insurance at December 1 of $4,200. An examination of the insurance policies indicates that prepaid insurance at December 31 is $2,200.

g. Interest on the $60,000 note payable (see item *a*) is unpaid and unrecorded at December 31.

h. Salaries of $25,320 are owed but unpaid on December 31.

i. Supplies of disposable diapers on December 1 are $4,400. At December 31, the cost of diapers in supplies is $890.

Required:

1. Identify whether each entry is an adjusting entry or a regular journal entry. If the entry is an adjusting entry, identify it as an accrued revenue, accrued expense, deferred revenue, or deferred expense.

2. Prepare the entries necessary to record the transactions above and on the previous page.

Problem 3-52A Preparation of Adjusting Entries

 OBJECTIVE 4

Bartow Photographic Services takes wedding and graduation photographs. At December 31, the end of Bartow's accounting period, the following information is available:

a. All wedding photographs are paid for in advance, and all cash collected for them is credited to unearned service revenue. Except for a year-end adjusting entry, no other entries are made for service revenue from wedding photographs. During the year, Bartow received $42,600 for wedding photographs. At year-end, $37,400 of the $42,600 had been earned. The beginning-of-the-year balance of unearned service revenue was zero.

b. During December, Bartow photographed 225 members of the next year's graduating class of Shaw High School. The school has asked Bartow to print one copy of a photograph of each student for the school files. Bartow delivers these photographs on December 28 and will bill the school $5.00 per student in January of next year. Revenue from photographs ordered by students will be recorded as the orders are received during the early months of next year.

c. Equipment used for developing and printing was rented for $22,500. The rental term was for one year beginning on August 1 and the entire year of rent was paid on August 1. The payment was debited to prepaid rent.

d. Depreciation on the firm's building for the current year is $9,400.

e. Wages of $4,170 are owed but unpaid and unrecorded at December 31.

f. Supplies at the beginning of the year were $2,400. During the year, supplies costing $19,600 were purchased from Kodak. When the purchases were made, their cost was debited to supplies. At year-end a physical inventory indicated that supplies costing $4,100 were on hand.

Required:

1. Prepare the adjusting entries for each of these items.

2. By how much would net income be overstated or understated if the accountant failed to make the adjusting entries?

Problem 3-53A Effects of Adjusting Entries on the Accounting Equation

OBJECTIVE 4

Four adjusting entries are shown below.

		Debit	Credit
a.	Wages Expense	3,410	
	Wages Payable		3,410
b.	Accounts Receivable	8,350	
	Service Revenue		8,350
c.	Rent Expense	2,260	
	Prepaid Rent		2,260
d.	Unearned Service Revenue	5,150	
	Service Revenue		5,150

(Continued)

Required:

Conceptual Connection: Analyze the adjusting entries and identify their effects on the financial statement accounts. (*Note:* Ignore any income tax effects.) Use the following format for your answer:

Transaction	Assets	Liabilities	Beginning Common Stock	Retained Earnings	Revenues	Expenses

OBJECTIVE 4 5

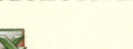

Problem 3-54A Adjusting Entries and Financial Statements

You have the following unadjusted trial balance for Rogers Corporation at December 31, 2011:

Rogers Corporation
Unadjusted Trial Balance
December 31, 2011

Account	Debit	Credit
Cash	$ 3,100	
Accounts Receivable	15,900	
Supplies	4,200	
Prepaid Rent	9,500	
Equipment	625,000	
Accumulated Depreciation (Equipment)		$ 104,000
Other Assets	60,900	
Accounts Payable		9,400
Unearned Service Revenue		11,200
Note Payable (due 2014)		50,000
Common Stock		279,500
Retained Earnings, 12/31/2010		37,000
Service Revenue		598,000
Wages Expense	137,000	
Rent Expense	229,000	
Interest Expense	4,500	
Total	$1,089,100	$1,089,100

At year-end, you have the following data for adjustments:

a. An analysis indicates that prepaid rent on December 31 should be $2,300.
b. A physical inventory shows that $650 of office supplies is on hand.
c. Depreciation for 2011 is $35,250.
d. An analysis indicates that unearned service revenue should be $3,120.
e. Wages in the amount of $3,450 are owed but unpaid and unrecorded at year-end.
f. Six months' interest at 8 percent on the note was paid on September 30. Interest for the period from October 1 to December 31 is unpaid and unrecorded.
g. Income taxes of $55,539 are owed but unrecorded and unpaid.

Required:

1. Prepare the adjusting entries.
2. Prepare an income statement, a retained earnings statement, and a balance sheet using adjusted account balances.
3. **Conceptual Connection:** Why would you not want to prepare financial statements until after the adjusting entries are made?

Problem 3-55A Inferring Adjusting Entries from Account Balance Changes

OBJECTIVE **4**

The following schedule shows all the accounts of Fresno Travel Agency that received year-end adjusting entries:

Account	Unadjusted Account Balance	Adjusted Account Balance
Prepaid Insurance	$ 23,270	$ 6,150
Prepaid Rent	3,600	2,100
Accumulated Depreciation	156,000	(a)
Wages Payable	0	6,750
Unearned Service Revenue	13,620	(b)
Service Revenue	71,600	78,980
Insurance Expense	0	(c)
Rent Expense	29,700	(d)
Depreciation Expense	0	12,500
Wages Expense	44,200	(e)

Required:

1. Calculate the missing amounts identified by the letters (a) through (e).
2. Prepare the five adjusting entries that must have been made to cause the account changes as indicated.

Problem 3-56A Preparation of Closing Entries and an Income Statement

OBJECTIVE **5** **6**

Round Grove Alarm Company provides security services to homes in northwestern Indiana. At year-end 2011, after adjusting entries have been made, the following list of account balances is prepared:

Accounts Receivable	$ 36,800	Prepaid Rent	$ 4,750
Accounts Payable	23,250	Rent Expense	27,600
Accumulated Depreciation (Equipment)	124,000	Retained Earnings, 12/31/2010	29,400
Common Stock	150,000	Salaries Payable	12,600
Depreciation Expense (Equipment)	45,300	Salaries Expense	148,250
Dividends	6,000	Service Revenue	612,900
Equipment	409,500	Supplies Expense	51,900
Income Taxes Expense	30,800	Supplies	12,700
Income Taxes Payable	24,300	Utilities Expense	48,800
Interest Expense	4,800	Wages Expense	183,500
Notes Payable (due in 2014)	34,000	Wages Payable	7,950
Other Assets	7,700		

Required:

1. Prepare closing entries for Round Grove Alarm.
2. Prepare an income statement for Round Grove Alarm.

Problem 3-57A Comprehensive Problem: Reviewing the Accounting Cycle

OBJECTIVE **4** **5** **6** **7**

Tarkington Freight Service provides delivery of merchandise to retail grocery stores in the Northeast. At the beginning of 2011, the following account balances were available:

Cash	$ 92,100	Accumulated Depreciation	
Accounts Receivable	361,500	(Equipment)	$ 580,000
Supplies	24,600	Land	304,975
Prepaid Advertising	2,000	Accounts Payable	17,600
Building (Warehouse)	2,190,000	Wages Payable	30,200
Accumulated Depreciation		Notes Payable (due in 2015)	1,000,000
(Warehouse)	280,000	Common Stock	1,400,000
Equipment	795,000	Retained Earnings, 12/31/2010	462,375

During 2011 the following transactions occurred:

a. Tarkington performed deliveries for customers, all on credit, for $2,256,700. Tarkington also made cash deliveries for $686,838.

b. There remains $286,172 of accounts receivable to be collected at December 31, 2011.

(Continued)

c. Tarkington purchased advertising of $138,100 during 2011 and debited the amount to pre-paid advertising.
d. Supplies of $27,200 were purchased on credit and debited to the supplies account.
e. Accounts payable at the beginning of 2011 were paid early in 2011. There remains $5,600 of accounts payable unpaid at year-end.
f. Wages payable at the beginning of 2011 were paid early in 2011. Wages were earned and paid during 2011 in the amount of $666,142.
g. During the year, Trish Hurd, a principal stockholder, purchased an automobile costing $42,000 for her personal use.
h. One-half year's interest at 6 percent annual rate was paid on the note payable on July 1, 2011.
i. Property taxes were paid on the land and buildings in the amount of $170,000.
j. Dividends were declared and paid in the amount of $25,000.

The following data are available for adjusting entries:

* Supplies in the amount of $13,685 remained unused at year-end.
* Annual depreciation on the warehouse building is $70,000.
* Annual depreciation on the warehouse equipment is $145,000.
* Wages of $60,558 were unrecorded and unpaid at year-end.
* Interest for six months at 6 percent per year on the note is unpaid and unrecorded at year-end.
* Advertising of $14,874 remained unused at the end of 2011.
* Income taxes of $482,549 related to 2011 are unpaid at year end.

Required:
1. Post the 2011 beginning balances to T-accounts. Prepare journal entries for transactions (a) through (j) and post the journal entries to T-accounts adding any new T-accounts you need.
2. Prepare the adjustments and post the adjustments to the T-accounts adding any new T-accounts you need.
3. Prepare an income statement.
4. Prepare a retained earnings statement.
5. Prepare a classified balance sheet
6. Prepare closing entries.
7. **Conceptual Connection:** Did you include transaction (g) among Tarkington's 2011 journal entries? Why or why not?

Problem 3-58A Preparing a Worksheet (Appendix 3A)

Marsteller Properties Inc. owns apartments that it rents to university students. At December 31, 2011, the following unadjusted account balances were available:

Cash	$ 4,600	Notes Payable (due in 2013)	$2,000,000
Rent Receivable	32,500	Common Stock	1,500,000
Supplies	4,700	Retained Earnings, 12/31/2010	39,200
Prepaid Insurance	60,000	Rent Revenue	660,000
Land	274,000	Repairs & Maintenance Expense	73,200
Buildings	4,560,000	Advertising Expense	58,700
Accumulated Depreciation		Wages Expense	84,300
(Buildings)	1,015,000	Utilities Expense	3,400
Other Assets	26,100	Interest Expense	90,000
Accounts Payable	57,300		

The following information is available for adjusting entries:

a. An analysis of apartment rental contracts indicates that $3,800 of apartment rent is unbilled and unrecorded at year-end.
b. A physical count of supplies reveals that $1,400 of supplies are on hand at December 31, 2011.
c. Annual depreciation on the buildings is $204,250
d. An examination of insurance policies indicates that $12,000 of the prepaid insurance applies to coverage for 2011.
e. Six months' interest at 9 percent is unrecorded and unpaid on the notes payable.
f. Wages in the amount of $6,100 are unpaid and unrecorded at December 31.

g. Utilities costs of $300 are unrecorded and unpaid at December 31.
h. Income taxes of $5,738 are unrecorded and unpaid at December 31.

Required:
1. Prepare a worksheet for Marsteller Properties.
2. Prepare an income statement, a retained earnings statement, and a classified balance sheet for Marsteller Properties.
3. Prepare the closing entries.

PROBLEM SET B

Problem 3-49B Cash-Basis and Accrual-Basis Income

OBJECTIVE 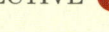 1

Martin Sharp, who repairs lawn mowers, collects cash from his customers when the repair services are completed. He maintains an inventory of repair parts that are purchased from a wholesale supplier. Martin's records show the following information for the first three months of 2011.

	Cash Collected for Repair Work	Cost of Repair Parts Purchased	Cash Payments to Supplier	Cost of Parts Used in Repairs
January	$2,400	$820	$710	$635
February	1,875	0	440	295
March	1,950	695	0	390

Required:
1. Ignoring expenses other than repair parts, calculate net income for each of the three months on a cash basis.
2. Ignoring expenses other than repair parts, calculate net income for each of the three months on an accrual basis.
3. **Conceptual Connection:** Why do decision-makers prefer the accrual basis of accounting?

Problem 3-50B Revenue Recognition and Matching

OBJECTIVE 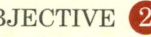 2

Aunt Bea's Catering Service provides catering service for special occasions. During 2011, Aunt Bea performed $128,300 of catering services and collected $118,500 of cash from customers. Salaries earned by Aunt Bea's employees during 2011 were $38,500. Aunt Bea paid employees $35,000 during 2011. Aunt Bea had $1,200 of supplies on hand at the beginning of the year and purchased an additional $8,000 of supplies during the year. Supplies on hand at the end of 2011 were $1,830. Other selling and administrative expenses incurred during 2011 were $5,800.

Required:
1. Calculate revenue and expenses for 2011.
2. Prepare the 2011 income statement.
3. **Conceptual Connection:** Describe the accounting principles used to prepare the income statement.

Problem 3-51B Identification and Preparation of Adjusting Entries

OBJECTIVE  3 4

Morgan Dance Inc. provides ballet, tap, and jazz dancing instruction to promising young dancers. Morgan began operations in January 2012 and is preparing its monthly financial statements. The following items describe Morgan's transactions in January 2012:

a. Morgan requires that dance instruction be paid in advance—either monthly or quarterly. On January 1, Morgan received $3,275 for dance instruction to be provided during 2012.
b. On January 31, Morgan noted that $450 of dance instruction revenue is still unearned.
c. On January 20, Morgan's hourly employees were paid $1,350 for work performed in January.
d. Morgan's insurance policy requires semi-annual premium payments. Morgan paid the $4,500 insurance policy which covered the first half of 2012 in December 2011.
e. When there are no scheduled dance classes, Morgan rents its dance studio for birthday parties for $100 per two-hour party. Three birthday parties were held during January. Morgan will not bill the parents until February.
f. Morgan purchased $250 of office supplies on January 10.

(Continued)

g. On January 31, Morgan determined that office supplies of $75 were unused.

h. Morgan received a January utility bill for $685. The bill will not be paid until it is due in February.

Required:

1. Identify whether each entry is an adjusting entry or a regular journal entry. If the entry is an adjusting entry, identify it as an accrued revenue, accrued expense, deferred revenue, or deferred expense.

2. Prepare the entries necessary to record the transactions above and on the previous page.

OBJECTIVE **4**

Problem 3-52B Preparation of Adjusting Entries

West Beach Resort operates a resort complex that specializes in hosting small business and professional meetings. West Beach closes its fiscal year on January 31, a time when it has few meetings under way. At January 31, 2012, the following data are available:

a. A training meeting is under way for 16 individuals from Fashion Design. Fashion Design paid $4,500 in advance for each person attending the 10-day training session. The meeting began on January 28 and will end on February 6.

b. Twenty-one people from Northern Publishing are attending a sales meeting. The daily fee for each person attending the meeting is $280 (charged for each night a person stays at the resort). The meeting began on January 29, and guests will depart on February 2. Northern will be billed at the end of the meeting.

c. Depreciation on the golf carts used to transport the guests' luggage to and from their rooms is $11,250 for the year. West Beach records depreciation yearly.

d. At January 31, Friedrich Catering is owed $1,795 for food provided for guests through that date. This amount is unrecorded. West Beach classifies the cost of food as an "other expense" on the income statement.

e. An examination indicates that the cost of office supplies on hand at January 31 is $189. During the year, $850 of office supplies was purchased from Supply Depot. The cost of supplies purchased was debited to office supplies inventory. No office supplies were on hand on January 31, 2011.

Required:

1. Prepare adjusting entries at January 31 for each of these items.

2. By how much would net income be overstated or understated if the accountant failed to make the adjusting entries?

OBJECTIVE **4**

Problem 3-53B Effects of Adjusting Entries on the Accounting Equation

Four adjusting entries are shown below:

a. Interest Expense................................ 1,875
  Interest Payable...........................   1,875

b. Interest Receivable 1,150
  Interest Revenue   1,150

c. Insurance Expense............................. 2,560
  Prepaid Insurance.......................   2,560

d. Unearned Rent Revenue 4,680
  Rent Revenue.............................   4,680

Required:

Conceptual Connection: Analyze the adjusting entries and identify their effects on the financial statement accounts. (*Note:* Ignore any income tax effects.) Use the following format for your answer:

Transaction	Assets	Liabilities	Beginning Common Stock	Retained Earnings	Revenues	Expenses

Problem 3-54B Adjusting Entries and Financial Statements

OBJECTIVE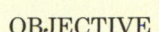

The unadjusted trial balance for Mitchell Pharmacy appears below.

Mitchell Pharmacy
Unadjusted Trial Balance
December 31, 2011

Account	Debit	Credit
Cash	$ 3,400	
Accounts Receivable	64,820	
Inventory	583,400	
Prepaid Insurance	11,200	
Building	230,000	
Accumulated Depreciation (Building)		$ 44,000
Land	31,200	
Other Assets	25,990	
Accounts Payable		47,810
Notes Payable (due 2013)		150,000
Common Stock		600,000
Retained Earnings, 12/31/2010		41,200
Service Revenue		950,420
Wages Expense	871,420	
Interest Expense	12,000	
Total	$1,833,430	$1,833,430

The following information is available at year-end for adjustments:

a. An analysis of insurance policies indicates that $2,180 of the prepaid insurance is coverage for 2012.
b. Depreciation expense for 2011 is $10,130.
c. Four months' interest at 10 percent is owed but unrecorded and unpaid on the note payable.
d. Wages of $4,950 are owed but unpaid and unrecorded at December 31.
e. Income taxes of $11,370 are owed but unrecorded and unpaid at December 31.

Required:
1. Prepare the adjusting entries.
2. Prepare an income statement, a retained earnings statement, and a balance sheet using adjusted account balances.
3. **Conceptual Connection:** Why would you not want to prepare financial statements until after the adjusting entries are made?

Problem 3-55B Inferring Adjusting Entries from Account Balance Changes

OBJECTIVE

The following schedule shows all the accounts of Eagle Imports that received year-end adjusting entries:

Account	Unadjusted Account Balance	Adjusted Account Balance
Prepaid Insurance	$ 15,390	$ (a)
Accumulated Depreciation	92,500	103,000
Interest Payable	0	(b)
Wages Payable	0	(c)
Unearned Service Revenue	12,250	2,620
Service Revenue	122,500	(d)
Insurance Expense	1,500	12,746
Interest Expense	1,125	5,300
Depreciation Expense	0	(e)
Wages Expense	24,200	41,800

(Continued)

Required:

1. Calculate the missing amounts identified by the letters (a) through (e).
2. Prepare the five adjusting entries that must have been made to cause the account changes as indicated.

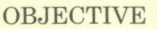

Problem 3-56B Preparation of Closing Entries and an Income Statement

Port Austin Boat Repair Inc. has entered and posted its adjusting entries for 2011. The following are selected account balances after adjustment:

Sales Revenue	$692,500	Insurance Expense	$94,300
Interest Revenue	7,600	Wages Payable	11,700
Accounts Payable	8,330	Utilities Expense	12,300
Wages Expense	405,300	Interest Expense	9,500
Accounts Receivable, 12/31/2011	65,000	Depreciation Expense (Equipment)	20,000
Supplies Expense	68,350	Accumulated Depreciation (Equipment)	75,000
Supplies, 12/31/2011	179,000	Income Taxes Expense	12,300
Prepaid Rent	7,200	Income Taxes Payable	8,300
Rent Expense	28,800	Dividends	7,800
Unearned Sales Revenue	12,200		

Required:

1. Using the accounts and balances above, prepare the closing entries for 2011.
2. Prepare an income statement for Port Austin Boat Repair.

Problem 3-57B Comprehensive Problem: Reviewing the Accounting Cycle

Wilburton Riding Stables provides stables, care for animals, and grounds for riding and showing horses. The account balances at the beginning of 2011 were:

Cash	$ 2,200	Accounts Payable	$ 23,700
Accounts Receivable	4,400	Income Taxes Payable	15,100
Supplies (Feed and Straw)	27,800	Interest Payable	2,700
Land	167,000	Wages Payable	14,200
Buildings	115,000	Notes Payable (due in 2015)	60,000
Accumulated Depreciation (Buildings)	36,000	Common Stock	150,000
Equipment	57,000	Retained Earnings	55,200
Accumulated Depreciation (Equipment)	16,500		

During 2011, the following transactions occurred:

a. Wilburton provided animal care services, all on credit, for $210,300. Wilburton rented stables to customers for $20,500 cash. Wilburton rented its grounds to individual riders, groups, and show organizations for $41,800 cash.
b. There remains $15,600 of accounts receivable to be collected at December 31, 2011.
c. Feed in the amount of $62,900 was purchased on credit and debited to the supplies account.
d. Straw was purchased for $7,400 cash and debited to the supplies account.
e. Wages payable at the beginning of 2011 were paid early in 2011. Wages were earned and paid during 2011 in the amount of $112,000.
f. The income taxes payable at the beginning of 2011 were paid early in 2011.
g. Payments of $73,000 were made to creditors for supplies previously purchased on credit.
h. One year's interest at 9 percent was paid on the note payable on July 1, 2011.
i. During 2011, Jon Wilburton, a principal stockholder, purchased a horse for his wife, Jennifer, to ride. The horse cost $7,000, and Wilburton used his personal credit to purchase it. The horse is stabled at the Wilburtons' home rather than at the riding stables.
j. Property taxes were paid on the land and buildings in the amount of $17,000.
k. Dividends were declared and paid in the amount of $7,200.

The following data are available for adjusting entries:

- Supplies (feed and straw) in the amount of $30,400 remained unused at year-end.
- Annual depreciation on the buildings is $6,000.
- Annual depreciation on the equipment is $5,500.
- Wages of $4,000 were unrecorded and unpaid at year-end.
- Interest for six months at 9 percent per year on the note is unpaid and unrecorded at year-end.
- Income taxes of $16,500 were unpaid and unrecorded at year-end.

Required:

1. Post the 2011 beginning balances to T-accounts. Prepare journal entries for transactions (a) through (k) and post the journal entries to T-accounts adding any new T-accounts you need.
2. Prepare the adjustments and post the adjustments to the T-accounts adding any new T-accounts you need.
3. Prepare an income statement.
4. Prepare a retained earnings statement.
5. Prepare a classified balance sheet.
6. Prepare closing entries.
7. **Conceptual Connection:** Did you include transaction (i) among Wilburton's 2011 journal entries? Why or why not?

Problem 3-58B Preparing a Worksheet *(Appendix 3A)*

Flint Inc. operates a cable television system. At December 31, 2011, the following unadjusted account balances were available:

Cash	$ 2,000	Common Stock	$300,000
Accounts Receivable	89,000	Retained Earnings, 12/31/2010	14,700
Supplies	5,000	Dividends	28,000
Land	37,000	Service Revenue	985,000
Building	209,000	Royalties Expense	398,000
Accumulated Depreciation (Building)	40,000	Property Taxes Expense	10,500
Equipment	794,000	Wages Expense	196,000
Accumulated Depreciation (Equipment)	262,000	Utilities Expense	34,000
Other Assets	19,700	Miscellaneous Expense	44,000
Accounts Payable	29,500	Interest Expense	15,000
Notes Payable (due in 2015)	250,000		

The following data are available for adjusting entries:

a. At year-end $1,500 of office supplies remain unused.
b. Annual depreciation on the building is $20,000.
c. Annual depreciation on the equipment is $150,000.
d. The interest rate on the note is 8 percent. Four months' interest is unpaid and unrecorded at December 31, 2011.
e. At December 31, 2011, service revenue of $94,000 has been earned but is unbilled and unrecorded.
f. Utility bills of $2,800 are unpaid and unrecorded at December 31, 2011.
g. Income taxes of $49,633 were unpaid and unrecorded at year-end.

Required:

1. Prepare a worksheet for Flint.
2. Prepare an income statement, a retained earnings statement, and a classified balance sheet for Flint.
3. Prepare the closing entries.

CASES

Case 3-59 Cash- or Accrual-Basis Accounting

Karen Ragsdale owns a business that rents parking spots to students at the local university. Karen's typical rental contract requires the student to pay the year's rent of $450 ($50 per month) on September 1. When Karen prepares financial statements at the end of December, her accountant requires that Karen spread the $450 over the nine months that each parking spot is rented. Therefore, Karen can recognize only $200 of revenue (four months) from each parking spot rental contract in the year the cash is collected and must defer (delay) recognition of the remaining $250 (five months) to the next year. Karen argues that getting students to agree to rent the parking spot is the most difficult part of the activity so she ought to be able to recognize all $450 as revenue when the cash is received from a student.

(Continued)

Required:

Why do generally accepted accounting principles require the use of accrual accounting rather than cash-basis accounting for transactions like the one described here? (*Hint*: You might find it helpful to read paragraphs 42–48 of *FASB Statement of Financial Accounting Concepts No. 1*, which can be found at http://www.fasb.org, as you formulate your answer.)

Case 3-60 Recognition of Service Contract Revenue

Zac Murphy is president of Blooming Colors Inc., which provides landscaping services in Tallahassee, Florida. On November 20, 2011, Mr. Murphy signed a service contract with Eastern State University. Under the contract, Blooming Colors will provide landscaping services for all of Eastern's buildings for a period of two years, beginning on January 1, 2012, and Eastern will pay Blooming Colors on a monthly basis, beginning on January 31, 2012. Although the same amount of landscaping services will be rendered in every month, the contract provides for higher monthly payments in the first year.

Initially, Mr. Murphy proposed that the revenue from the contract should be recognized in 2011; however, his accountant, Sue Storm, convinced him that this would be inappropriate. Then Mr. Murphy proposed that the revenue should be recognized in an amount equal to the cash collected under the contract in 2011. Again, Ms. Storm argued against his proposal, saying that generally accepted accounting principles (GAAP) required recognition of an equal amount of contract revenue each month.

Required:

1. Give a reason that might explain Mr. Murphy's desire to recognize contract revenue earlier rather than later.
2. Put yourself in the position of Sue Storm. How would you convince Mr. Murphy that his two proposals are unacceptable and that an equal amount of revenue should be recognized every month?
3. If Ms. Storm's proposal is adopted, how would the contract be reflected in the balance sheets at the end of 2011 and at the end of 2012?

Case 3-61 Revenue Recognition

Melaney Parks purchased HealthPlus Fitness in January 2011. Melaney wanted to increase the size of the business by selling three-year memberships for $3,000, payable at the beginning of the membership period. The normal yearly membership fee is $1,500. Since few prospective members were expected to want to spend $3,000 at the beginning of the membership period, Melaney arranged for a local bank to provide a $3,000 installment loan to prospective members. By the end of 2011, 250 customers had purchased the three-year memberships using the loan provided by the bank.

Melaney prepared her income statement for 2011 and included $750,000 ($3,000 × 250 members) as revenue because the club had collected the entire amount in cash. Melaney's accountant objected to the inclusion of the entire $750,000. The accountant argued that the $750,000 should be recognized as revenue as the club provides services for these members during the membership period. Melaney countered with a quotation from generally accepted accounting principles:

Profit is deemed to be realized when a sale in the ordinary course of business is effected, unless the circumstances are such that collection of the sale price is not reasonably assured.

Melaney notes that memberships have been sold and the collection of the selling price has occurred. Therefore, she argues that all $750,000 is revenue in 2011.

Required:

1. Write a short statement supporting either Melaney or the accountant in this dispute.
2. Would your answer change if the $3,000 fee were nonrefundable? Why or why not?

Case 3-62 Applying the Matching Concept

Newman Properties Inc. completed construction of a new shopping center in July 2011. During the first six months of 2011, Newman spent $550,000 for salaries, preparation of documents, travel, and other similar activities associated with securing tenants for the center. Newman was successful (Nordstrom, Best Buy, and Office Depot will be tenants) and the center will open on August 1 with all its stores rented on four-year leases. The rental revenue that Newman expects to receive from the current tenants is $8,500,000 per year for four years. The leases will be renegotiated at the end of the fourth year. The accountant for Newman wonders whether the $550,000 should be expensed in 2011 or whether it should be initially recorded as an asset and matched against revenues over the four-year lease term.

Required:

Write a short statement indicating why you support expensing the $550,000 in the current period or spreading the expense over the four-year lease term.

Case 3-63 Adjusting Entries for Refund Coupons

Cal-Lite Products Inc. manufactures a line of food products that appeals to persons interested in weight loss. To stimulate sales, Cal-Lite includes cash refund coupons in many of its products. Cal-Lite issues the purchaser a check when the coupon is returned to the company, which may be many months after the product is sold to stores and distributors. In addition, a significant number of coupons issued to customers are never returned. As cash distributions are made to customers, they are recorded in an expense account.

Required:

1. Explain the conceptual basis for the determination of the expense in each year. Describe the information and calculations required to estimate the amount of expense for each year.
2. Describe the year-end adjusting entry required at the end of the first year of the program's existence.
3. Describe the adjusting entry at the end of the second year of the program's existence.

Case 3-64 Adjusting Entries for Motion Picture Revenues

Link Pictures Inc. sells (licenses) the rights to exhibit motion pictures to theaters. Under the sales contract, the theater promises to pay a license fee equal to the larger of a guaranteed minimum or a percentage of the box office receipts. In addition, the contract requires the guaranteed minimum to be paid in advance. Consider the following contracts entered by Link during 2011:

a. Contract **A** authorizes a group of theaters in Buffalo, New York, to exhibit a film called Garage for two weeks ending January 7, 2012. Box office statistics indicate that first-week attendance has already generated licensing fees well in excess of the guaranteed minimum.
b. Contract **B** authorizes a chain of theaters in Miami, Florida, to exhibit a film called Blue Denim for a period of two weeks ending January 20, 2012. In most first-run cities, the film has attracted large crowds, and the percentage of box office receipts has far exceeded the minimum.
c. Contract **C** authorizes a chain of theaters in San Francisco to exhibit a film called Toast Points for a period of two weeks ending on December 12, 2011.. The film is a "dog" and the theaters stopped showing it after the first few days. All prints of the film were returned by December 31, 2011.

The guaranteed minimum has been paid on all three contracts and recorded as unearned revenue. No other amounts have been received, and no revenue has been recorded for any of the contracts. Adjusting entries for 2011 are about to be made.

Required:

Describe the adjusting entry you would make at December 31, 2011, to record each contract.

Case 3-65 The Effect of Adjusting Entries on the Financial Statements (A Conceptual Approach)

Don Berthrong, the manager of the local Books-A-Million, is wondering whether adjusting entries will affect his financial statements. Don's business has grown steadily for several years, and Don expects it to continue to grow for the next several years at a rate of 5 to 10 percent per year. Nearly all of Don's sales are for cash. Other than cost of goods sold, which is not affected by

(Continued)

adjusting entries, most of Don's expenses are for items that require cash outflows (e.g., rent on the building, wages, utilities, insurance).

Required:
1. Would Don's financial statement be affected significantly by adjusting entries?
2. Consider all businesses. What kinds of transactions would require adjustments that would have a significant effect on the financial statements? What kinds of businesses would be likely to require these kinds of adjustments?

Case 3-66 Interpreting Closing Entries

Barnes Building Systems made the following closing entries at the end of a recent year:

a.	Income Summary	129,750	
	Retained Earnings		129,750
b.	Retained Earnings	25,000	
	Dividends		25,000
c.	Sales Revenue	495,300	
	Income Summary		495,300
d.	Income Summary	104,100	
	Interest Expense		104,100

Required:
1. What was Barnes's net income?
2. By how much did Barnes's retained earnings change?
3. If the sales revenue identified in entry (c) was Barnes's only revenue, what was the total amount of Barnes's expenses?

Case 3-67 Research and Analysis Using the Annual Report

Obtain **FedEx Corporation**'s 2009 annual report either through the "Investor Relations" portion of their website (do a web search for FedEx investor relations) or go to http://www.sec.gov and click "Search for Company Filings" under "Filings & Forms."

Required:
Answer the following questions:
1. How does FedEx apply the revenue recognition principle?
2. With regard to the balance sheet and the income statement, what accounts may have required adjusting entries? Would these accounts require accruals or deferrals?
3. How much did FedEx owe its employees for services performed at the end of the 2009 fiscal year?
4. How much would FedEx credit to Income Summary for 2009? How much would be debited to Income Summary for 2009?
5. How much did FedEx report as income tax expense for 2009? How much did FedEx report as cash paid for taxes for 2009? Why are the amounts different and where does this difference get reported on FedEx's financial statements?

Case 3-68 Comparative Analysis: Abercrombie & Fitch versus Aeropostale

Refer to the financial statements of **Abercrombie & Fitch** and **Aeropostale** that are supplied with this text.

Required:
Answer the following questions:
1. Does each company apply the revenue recognition principle to sales to customers and to gift cards in the same manner?
2. Which accounts on the balance sheet and income statement of each company may require adjusting entries? Would these accounts require accruals or deferrals?
3. How much would Abercrombie & Fitch credit and debit to Income Summary for the year ending January 30, 2010 (fiscal 2009)? How much would Aeropostale credit and debit to Income Summary for the fiscal year ending January 30, 2010?

4. How much did each company report as an accrued expense for gift cards for the most recent year? Explain why this amount is reported as a liability.

5. Compare how much each company reported as income tax expense and as cash paid for taxes for the most recent year. Why are the amounts different, and where would this difference be reported on the financial statements?

Case 3-69 CONTINUING PROBLEM: FRONT ROW ENTERTAINMENT

Cam and Anna are very satisfied with their first month of operations. Their major effort centered on signing various artists to live performance contracts, and they had more success than they had anticipated. In addition to Charm City, they were able to use their contacts in the music industry to sign twelve other artists. With the tours starting in February, Cam and Anna were eager to hold their first big event. Over the next month, the following transactions occurred.

Feb.	1	Collected advance ticket sales of $28,400 relating to various concerts that were being promoted.
	1	Paid $800 to rent office space in February.
	2	Paid Equipment Supply Services $1,500, the balance remaining from the January 3 purchase of supplies.
	6	Paid $30,150 to secure venues for future concerts.
	9	Received $325 related to the festival held on January 25.
	12	Purchased $475 of supplies on credit from Equipment Supply Services.
	15	Collected $3,400 of ticket sales for the first Charm City concert on the day of the concert.
	15	Paid Charm City $9,000 for performing the Feb. 15 concert. (Remember: Front Row Entertainment records the fees paid to the artist in the Artist Fee Expense account.)
	20	Collected advance ticket sales of $10,125 relating to various concerts that were being promoted.
	21	Collected $5,100 of ticket sales for the second Charm City concert on the day of the concert.
	21	Paid Charm City $12,620 for performing the Feb. 21 concert.

At the end of February, Cam and Anna felt like their business was doing well; however, they decided that they needed to prepare financial statements to better understand the operations of the business. Anna gathered the following information relating to the adjusting entries that needed to be prepared at the end of February.

a. Two months of interest on the note payable is accrued.

b. A count of the supplies revealed that $1,825 of supplies remained on hand at the end of February.

c. Two months of insurance has expired.

d. Depreciation related to the office equipment was $180 per month.

e. The rental of the venues for all four Charm City concerts was paid in advance on January 8. As of the end of February, Charm City has performed two of the four concerts in the contract.

f. An analysis of the unearned sales revenue account reveals that $8,175 of the balance relates to concerts that have not yet been performed.

g. Neither Cam nor Anna has received their salary of $1,200 each for February.

h. A utility bill of $435 relating to utility service on Front Row Entertainment's office for January and February was received but not paid by the end of February.

Required:

1. Analyze and journalize the February transactions.

2. Set up T-accounts for each account, and post the transactions to the T-accounts. Be sure to use the balances computed in Chapter 2 as the beginning balances of the T-accounts.

3. Prepare a trial balance at February 28, 2011.

4. Prepare and post the adjusting entries needed at February 28, 2011.

5. By how much would net income be overstated or understated if the adjusting entries were not made?

6. Prepare an income statement and a retained earnings statement for the two-month period ending February 28, 2011. Prepare a classified balance sheet as of February 28, 2011.

7. Prepare the necessary closing entries.

MAKING THE CONNECTION
INTEGRATIVE EXERCISE

The Accounting Cycle

Begin with the following account balances for University Street Parking Garage (assume all accounts have normal balances) at December 31, 2011:

Accounts payable	$ 16,700
Accounts receivable	39,200
Accumulated depreciation (equipment)	36,800
Common stock (20,000 shares)	100,000
Cash	6,700
Depreciation expense (equipment)	12,300
Dividends	6,300
Equipment	269,500
Income taxes expense	2,700
Income taxes payable	1,100
Interest expense	16,500
Interest payable	0
Interest revenue	4,100
Inventory	4,900
Investments	35,000
Notes payable (due May 2, 2017)	160,000
Prepaid rent (4 months)	36,400
Rent expense	94,400
Retained earnings, 12/31/2010	43,000
Service revenue, parking	224,600
Service revenue, repair	208,100
Supplies expense	36,900
Wages expense	233,600
Wages payable	0

Required:

1. For the following transactions, provide the necessary adjusting entries and update the account balances to appropriately reflect these adjusting entries:

   a. The only lease held by University Street Parking required a lease payment of $9,100 per month. University Street Parking has prepaid rent through March 31, 2012.

   b. At December 31, 2011, University Street Parking owes employees wages of $12,500.

   c. University Street Parking should have total depreciation expense on equipment for 2011 of $14,300.

   d. The note payable of $160,000 has an interest rate of 6.75%. University Street Parking has paid interest through October 31, 2011.

2. Prepare a properly classified income statement for 2011, retained earnings statement for 2011, and a properly classified balance sheet as of December 31, 2011, using the post-adjustment account balances.

4 Internal Control and Cash

Doug Norman Crystals/Alamy

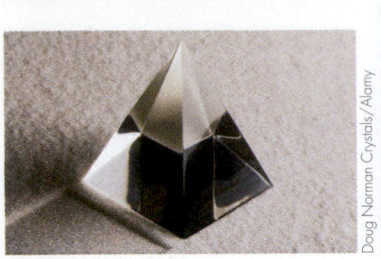

After studying Chapter 4, you should be able to:

1. Discuss the role of internal controls in managing a business.
2. Discuss the five elements of internal control.
3. Describe how businesses account for and report cash.
4. Describe how businesses control cash.
5. Describe the operating cycle and explain the principles of cash management.

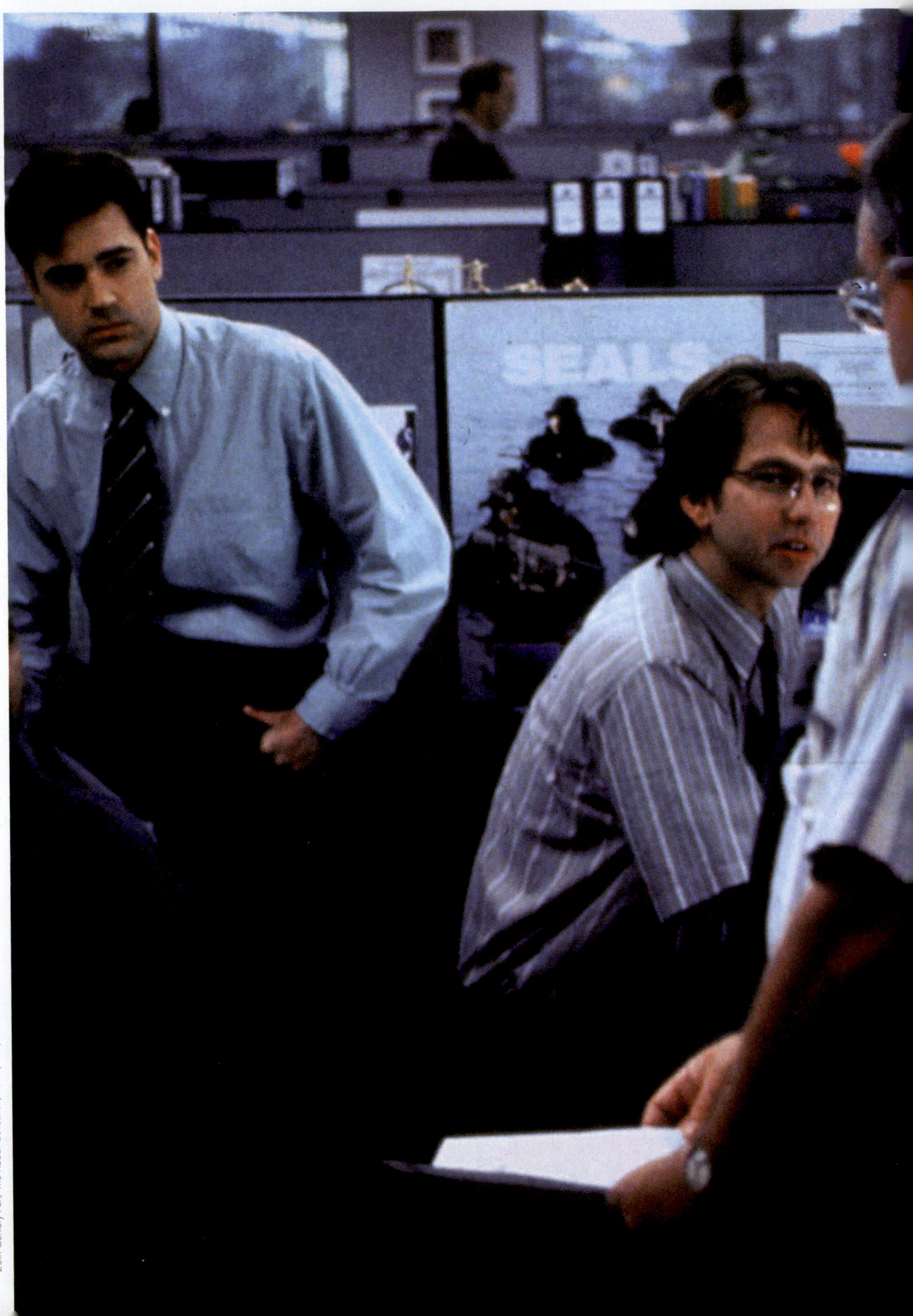

20th Century Fox/The Kobal Collection/Redin, Van/Picture Desk

EXPERIENCE FINANCIAL ACCOUNTING

with Initech

Peter Gibbons is a software engineer at Initech. He has an awful commute, an annoying boss, and a girlfriend he's pretty sure is cheating on him. Of course, Peter is the fictional star of the film *Office Space*. So, what do Peter and Initech have to do with accounting? In the movie, Initech is going through a downsizing and Peter finds out his best friends, Samir and (the unfortunately named) Michael Bolton, are about to be fired. To get back at Initech, the three friends decide to alter the company's software to take the fractions of a penny that are rounded off when calculating interest and deposit them into their personal account. They believe their scheme is undetectable because nobody will notice the gradual theft of these miniscule amounts. However, over time the sheer number of transactions will accumulate to a large sum.

The morning after altering Initech's software, Peter checks the account balance and finds it contains over $300,000. In a panic Peter calls his friends, and Michael Bolton concedes he made a "small" mistake. In the movie the three friends attempt to repay the money and are "saved" by a fire that burns Initech's offices. You may think that this could never happen, but such schemes are real and go by various names such as "penny shaving" or "salami slicing."

In a somewhat related scheme, a hacker noticed that when opening online brokering accounts (such as through **Google** checkout, **PayPal**, and many brokerage houses), it is common practice for the companies to send a confirming payment of a few cents to ensure you have access to the bank account or credit card. He then wrote an automated program (known as a "bot") to open almost 60,000 such accounts, collecting many thousands of these small payments into a few personal bank accounts. This isn't obviously illegal; however, he did run afoul of mail and bank fraud laws because he used false names, addresses, and Social Security numbers when opening the accounts.

In this chapter, we discuss the policies and procedures companies put in place to prevent intentional and unintentional error, theft, and fraud. These policies and procedures are referred to as the internal control system. For example, a commonly seen control that is designed to prevent use of bots to sign up or log in to web functions is a security check where the user must type in the distorted letters seen in a box (**Ticketmaster**, for example, does this to thwart scalpers).

OBJECTIVE
Discuss the role of internal controls in managing a business.

ROLE OF INTERNAL CONTROL

Except in very small businesses, top management delegates responsibility for engaging in business activities and recording their effects in the accounting system to other managers and employees. Management wants to make sure that these employees both:

- operate within the scope of their assigned responsibility and
- act for the good of the business.

To control employees' activities, management puts in place procedures that collectively are called the **internal control system**.

Internal control systems include all the policies and procedures established by top management and the board of directors to provide reasonable assurance that the company's objectives are being met in the following three areas:[1]

- effectiveness and efficiency of operations
- reliability of financial reporting
- compliance with applicable laws and regulations

As such, internal control systems include many elements only indirectly related to our primary concern—the accounting system and financial statements. For example, policies and procedures concerning the extent and nature of research and development or advertising activities may have an important effect on the achievement of an entity's objectives but only indirectly affect its accounting system and financial statements.

Under the Sarbanes-Oxley Act of 2002, top management of publicly-traded corporations have an increased responsibility for a system of internal controls that ensures the reliability of the financial statements. For example, Section 404 of the Act requires management to produce an internal control report. This report must acknowledge that management is responsible for establishing and maintaining an adequate internal control system and procedures for financial reporting and also assess the effectiveness of these controls. Further, Section 302 of the Act requires the principal executive and financial officers to certify that they are responsible for establishing and maintaining the system of internal control over financial reporting (see Exhibit 4-1). This certification was designed to prevent top management from denying knowledge or understanding of deceptive financial reporting as was tried in court by executives of **WorldCom**, among others.

In this chapter, we will examine the elements of internal controls and demonstrate controls over cash, a company's most vulnerable asset. We will address the following questions:

- What are the five elements of internal control?
- How are those controls applied to cash?
- How does the operating cycle affect cash?
- Why is cash management so important to a company?

IFRS
The documentation and assessment requirements of the Sarbanes-Oxley Act imposes a greater burden on U.S. companies relative to international companies.

OBJECTIVE ②
Discuss the five elements of internal control.

ELEMENTS OF INTERNAL CONTROL

The Committee of Sponsoring Organizations of the Treadway Commission (COSO), identified five elements of an internal control system (see Exhibit 4-2). Each element is crucial to meeting the company's objectives.

Control Environment and Ethical Behavior

The foundation of the internal control system is the **control environment**—the collection of environmental factors that influence the effectiveness of control procedures. The control environment includes the following:

- the philosophy and operating style of management
- the personnel policies and practices of the business
- the overall integrity, attitude, awareness, and actions of everyone in the business concerning the importance of control (commonly called the *tone at the top*)

---

[1] The Committee of Sponsoring Organizations of the Treadway Commission (COSO), *Internal Control-Integrated Framework*, 1992.

Exhibit 4-1

Section 302 Certification by Steven P. Jobs (CEO of Apple) Taken from SEC Filings for the Year Ended September 26, 2009

I, Steven P. Jobs, certify that:

1. I have reviewed this annual report on Form 10-K of Apple Inc.;

2. Based on my knowledge, this report does not contain any untrue statement of a material fact or omit to state a material fact necessary to make the statements made, in light of the circumstances under which such statements were made, not misleading with respect to the period covered by this report;

3. Based on my knowledge, the financial statements, and other financial information included in this report, fairly present in all material respects the financial condition, results of operations and cash flows of the registrant as of, and for, the periods presented in this report;

4. The registrant's other certifying officer(s) and I are responsible for establishing and maintaining disclosure controls and procedures and internal control over financial reporting for the registrant . . .

Date: October 27, 2009

By:

Steven P. Jobs

Chief Executive Officer

An important feature of the control environment is recognizing that an individual employee's goals may differ from the goals of other individuals and the goals of the business. For example, when managers receive a bonus based on certain accounting numbers, like sales, they have been known to ship a large quantity of merchandise to customers

Exhibit 4-2

Elements of Internal Control

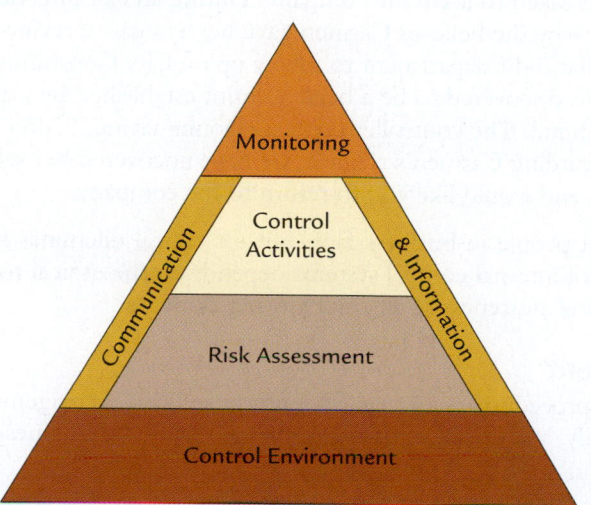

Source: COSO, Internal Control—Integrated Framework, 1992. Used with permission of COSO.

right before year end—even if the merchandise was not ordered (done by such companies as **Bausch and Lomb**, **IBM**, etc.). Although much of the merchandise was returned in the following year, sales targets for the current year were met and bonuses were paid.

Resolving these conflicting incentives in an ethical manner that promotes organizational objectives is highly dependent on the tone at the top. For example, hiring and firing practices that put zero tolerance on unethical behavior are increasingly common. Additionally, the Sarbanes-Oxley Act requires publicly-traded corporations to establish formal procedures to receive, retain, and address any information that may affect the company's accounting or auditing. To comply with this requirement, companies have created ethics hotlines that allow employees to anonymously report unethical behavior. While this was an important step in empowering subordinates to report unethical behavior by their superiors, hotlines only address procedures to receive the information. Companies must also have procedures in place to make sure such information is never destroyed and that it is communicated to those with the power to resolve any issues, such as the board of directors and upper management.

ETHICAL DECISIONS   Donna Jones has just been hired as an accounting clerk. One of her jobs is to summarize invoices presented for payment by various creditors. Once prepared, the summary is first inspected by Carmen Adams, the assistant controller to whom Donna reports, and then presented to Dick Stewart, the controller, for approval. After signing the form, Dick prepares and mails the checks.

During Donna's second week on the job, Carmen tells her that City Consulting Services Inc. will make trouble for the company unless paid immediately. She says, "Dick is rarely at his desk and never looks at signatures anyway. It would cost us at least another day to get the controller's signature. Just put the unsigned summary on Stewart's desk, and the check will be in the mail by the end of the day."

Donna suspects that Carmen will give her a low performance rating if she refuses to follow these instructions, and she wants to do well on her first job. Further, she is quite sure that Dick will not notice the omitted control procedure. On the other hand, Donna knows that the controller's approval is an important control procedure. Consider two possible endings for this story:

1. *Donna goes along with Carmen.* Every month, Carmen tells Donna that City Consulting Services needs to be paid immediately. Donna places the unauthorized summary on Dick's unoccupied desk. All goes well until the internal auditor runs a routine check on the credit ratings of the entities with which the company does business and discovers that City Consulting is nothing more than a bank account established by Carmen. Carmen is charged with fraud, and Donna's role is exposed in the public trial that follows. Donna is not charged in the case, but she loses her job and has great difficulty finding another comparable position.

2. *Donna refuses to go along with Carmen.* Donna receives a negative review from Carmen and is asked to leave the company. During an exit interview, Donna tells the controller why she believes Carmen gave her a negative review. The controller asks the internal audit department to follow up on City Consulting Services, at which time it is discovered to be a bank account established by Carmen. Carmen is charged with fraud. The controller contacts Donna saying, "After investigating your comments regarding Carmen's request, we have uncovered her scheme to defraud the company, and would like you to return to the company.

Like Donna, most people in business face difficult ethical dilemmas from time to time. The effectiveness of internal control systems depends on the ethical tone set by management and the ethical awareness of all company personnel. ●

Risk Assessment

Risk assessment procedures (also called Enterprise Risk Management or ERM) are designed to identify, analyze, and manage **strategic risks** and **business process risks**.

Strategic Risks   Strategic risks are possible threats to the organization's success in accomplishing its objectives and are *external* to the organization. These risks are often classified around industry forces such as competitors, customers, substitute products or services, suppliers, and threat of new competitors (these are known as Porter's Five Forces) or macro factors such as political, economic, social, and technological (also known as PEST factors).

Although entire courses are devoted to management of these strategic risks, the general idea is simple. For example, when **Amazon** was formed, **Barnes & Noble** was in the midst of high growth and was implementing cafes and music shops within supersized bookstores. Barnes & Noble was so deeply rooted in its "bricks-and-mortar" that it failed to respond to a technological factor: the Internet's transformation of the industry. By the time Barnesandnoble.com was launched, Amazon had secured the leading web presence for booksellers—a lead that Barnes & Noble has been unable to erode.

Business Process Risks Business processes are the *internal* processes of the company—specifically, how the company allocates its resources to meet its objectives. There are many business processes, but some of the more common ones are materials acquisition, production, logistics and distribution, branding and marketing, and human resources. The nature and relative importance of the business processes will vary from company to company based on their specific objectives. For example, **Dell** has adopted a low-cost provider objective. As such, it has concentrated on achieving operating efficiencies in order processing, production, and distribution. **Apple**, on the other hand, has adopted a product differentiation objective. This objective has led to an emphasis on product quality and continual research to develop better products with more features. As such, the risk assessment controls for these two companies will differ. Dell will be focused on monitoring inventory levels and production times, while Apple will focus on quality control and product development.

Control Activities

Control activities are the policies and procedures top management establishes to help insure that its objectives are met. The control activities most directly related to the accounting system and financial statements vary widely from one business to another, but generally can be identified with one of the following five categories.

Clearly Defined Authority and Responsibility
The *authority* to perform important duties is delegated to specific individuals, and those individuals should be held *responsible* for the performance of those duties in the evaluation of their performance. Among the designated duties of an individual may be the authority to perform specified types of activities for the business or to authorize others to execute such transactions. The clear delegation of authority and responsibility motivates individuals to perform well because they know they are accountable for their actions. For example, at **Wal-Mart** and other retailers, cashiers enter a code into the cash register and maintain responsibility for cash entering and leaving the register. At the end of their shift, a supervisor counts the money. Should the register have too much or too little cash, the cashier would clearly be responsible for the error.

Segregation of Duties
Accounting and administrative duties should be performed by different individuals, so that no one person prepares all the documents and records for an activity. This **segregation of duties** (also called *separation of duties*) reduces the likelihood that records could be used to conceal *irregularities* (intentional misstatements, theft, or fraud) and increases the likelihood that irregularities will be discovered. Segregation of duties also reduces the likelihood that unintentional record-keeping errors will remain undiscovered.

Although segregation of duties cannot eliminate the possibility of fraud, it does require people to work together. For example, movie theaters like **AMC** and **Showcase** require one employee to collect the cash and another employee to collect the tickets to admit the customer into the theater. If one person was responsible for collecting cash and admitting customers, this person could pocket the cash and let the customer in without issuing a ticket. In this case, the number of tickets issued would match up with the cash collected because no ticket was issued and the cash was pocketed. Instead, movie theaters have one person collect the cash and issue the ticket and a second person admit customers with tickets. Cash can still be pocketed, but the segregation of duties will require both employees to engage in the fraudulent scheme (we call this *collusion*) or the cash collected will not match the tickets collected.

Perhaps the most important aspect of segregation of duties is separating the record-keeping responsibility from the physical control of the assets. For example, if a customer pays $1,000, the employee who collects the $1,000 could easily steal some or all of the money if (s)he has access to the accounting records. In this case, the employee could record that the money was paid and hide the fact that the money was not in the company or record that some or all of the money was not paid and the debt was "bad."

Adequate Documents and Records Accounting records are the basis for the financial statements and other reports prepared for managers, owners, and others both inside and outside the business. Summary records and their underlying documentation must provide information about specific activities and help in the evaluation of individual performance. For example, prenumbered shipping documents provide a basis for monitoring shipments of goods to customers. When warehouse employees receive a shipping document, they ship the goods. If the shipping documents were not prenumbered, a shipping document could be sent to the warehouse and later destroyed. Without the missing number in the sequence to signal a missing document, nobody would realize that the document was missing.

Safeguards over Assets and Records Both assets and records must be secured against theft and destruction. **Safeguarding** requires physical protection of the assets through, for example, fireproof vaults, locked storage facilities, keycard access, and anti-theft tags on merchandise. An increasingly important part of safeguarding assets and records is access controls for computers. Safeguards must be provided for computer programs and data files, which are more fragile and susceptible to unauthorized access than manual record-keeping systems. For example, access controls often mandate use of both alpha and numeric characters and require password changes every few months.

Checks on Recorded Amounts Recorded amounts should be checked by an independent person to determine that amounts are correct and that they correspond to properly authorized activities. These procedures include clerical checks, reconciliations, comparisons of asset inspection reports with recorded amounts, computer-programmed controls, and management review of reports. For example, accounting records should be checked (or reconciled) to the bank statement and any discrepancies should be resolved immediately. Bank reconciliations are illustrated later in the chapter.

Such controls are effective at mitigating unintentional error, theft, and fraud. One of the elements typically cited in discussions of theft and fraud is opportunity. That is, persons committing theft or fraud believe they have the opportunity to "get away with it." Control activities are designed to prevent and detect theft and fraud by reducing employees' opportunity to conceal their actions. Yet, every year billions of dollars are lost to employee theft and fraud because effectively designed control activities are not followed.

Information and Communication

An internal control system will be unable to help a company achieve its objective unless adequate information is identified and gathered on a timely basis. Further, this information must be communicated to the appropriate employees in the organization. For example, consider a company like Mercedes that has a strategy of providing high-quality products. This company may gather information on the percentage of production that is rejected by quality control. If that percentage rises, it signals the possibility of problems in production (such as inferior material being used, poor training of new personnel, etc.). If such information is gathered and communicated, these problems can be addressed before the company's reputation for high quality is harmed; if, on the other hand, such information is not gathered and communicated, then management may not become aware of the problem until returns and complaints are made by dissatisfied customers. At this time, it may be too late to avoid damage to their reputation.

Monitoring

Monitoring is the process of tracking potential and actual problems in the internal control system. Monitoring is accomplished through normal supervising activities such as when a manager asks a subordinate how things are going. However, best practices for larger organizations suggest that an internal audit group help monitor the effectiveness of the internal control system. Monitoring the system of internal controls allows the organization to identify potential and actual weaknesses that could, if uncorrected, produce problems.

In fact, the Sarbanes-Oxley Act requires all publicly-traded corporations to have an internal audit function that reports to the audit committee of the board of directors. The Act allows companies to outsource internal audit, but precludes the business that provides the (external) financial statement audit from performing internal audit services because it may impair the independence of the financial statement audit.

Relationship Between Control Activities and the Accounting System

The **accounting system** consists of the methods and records used to identify, measure, record, and communicate financial information about a business. Although we distinguish between the accounting system and the internal control system, the two are really one integrated system designed to meet the needs of a particular business. It is difficult to generalize the relationship between internal control activities and accounting systems because it directly depends on the objectives of a particular business. Consequently, the relationship is best explored through an example.

Consider Hendrickson Theaters Inc., which operates 10 movie theaters in a single city. All the theaters are rented, as are the projection equipment and concession facilities. Hendrickson's administrative offices, furnishings, and office equipment are also rented. The following chart of accounts indicates the structure of Hendrickson's accounting system:

Chart of Accounts for Hendrickson Theaters Inc.	
Assets	*Revenues*
Cash	Admissions revenue
Concessions inventory	Concessions revenue
Prepaid rent	*Expenses*
Liabilities	Salaries expense
Accounts payable	Wages expense
Salaries payable	Cost of concessions sold
Wages payable	Rent expense, movie
Equity	Rent expense, theater
Capital stock	Rent expense, equipment
Retained earnings	Rent expense, office
	Utilities expense
	Advertising expense
	Office supplies expense

Hendrickson's accountant makes journal entries daily for revenues, biweekly for wages, and monthly for the other expenses using general purpose accounting software. Because Hendrickson has a relatively small number of accounts, its accounting system is quite simple. The portion of Hendrickson's accounting system related to revenues and the associated control activities are described in Exhibit 4-3 (p. 178).

ACCOUNTING AND REPORTING CASH

OBJECTIVE 3
Describe how businesses account for and report cash.

Cash is not only currency and coins, but savings and checking accounts and negotiable instruments like checks and money orders. When cash is received, a cash account is increased by a debit; and when cash is paid out, a cash account is decreased by a credit. Receipt and payment of cash are frequently accomplished by a check sent through the mail, a process that may require several days, and additional time may pass between receipt of the check and its deposit in the bank by the payee. Despite the fact that there may be a time lag between the issuance of a check and the actual transfer of funds, the accounting system treats payment by check in exactly the same way that it treats the transfer of currency. The receipt of either a check or currency is recorded by a debit to cash. Conversely, either the issue of a check or the payment of currency is recorded by a credit to cash.

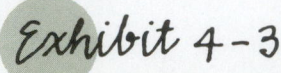

Exhibit 4-3

Relationship Between the Accounting System and Control Procedures

Illustrations from the Internal Control Structure for Revenue and Cash for Hendrickson Theaters Inc.

Accounting System

Entries: Admissions and concessions revenues are recorded daily by increasing both cash and the appropriate revenue accounts.

Documentation: The cash register at each ticket booth and concession stand prepares a detailed list of cash transactions and a daily cash summary report. The daily summary reports from the 10 theaters are electronically transferred to the central office each night and are automatically summarized upon receipt. Each morning, the accountant generates a report and makes revenue entries in the computerized general ledger.

Reports: A variety of revenue analyses can be prepared on the computer system, including analyses by theater, movie, day of the week, and month.

Control Procedures

Authority and responsibility: Each theater manager is responsible for the control of cash in his or her theater, but the central office accountant makes all general ledger entries related to cash.

Segregation of duties: Maintenance of the general ledger is segregated from responsibility for local cash control. Ticket sellers and concession operators may assist in preparation of daily cash deposits, but the manager must check and sign deposit documents.

Documentation: Prenumbered admission tickets are dispensed by machine at each theater. The machine also prepares a report of the tickets issued each day, which is used by the theater manager to reconcile cash collected with the number of tickets sold.

Safeguards: The cash accumulates in each theater until the end of each day. When cash drawers reach a specified level, however, the cash register signals that a fixed amount of cash should be removed by the manager and placed in the theater's safe.

Checks: On an unannounced schedule, Hendrickson's accountant visits each theater and verifies cash receipts reported against the number of tickets issued. On these same visits, the accountant checks concession revenues against the amounts reported by inventorying concession supplies.

Cash is reported on both the balance sheet and the statement of cash flows. The balance sheet typically reports the amount of cash and equivalents available at the balance sheet date, as shown in Exhibit 4-4. The statement of cash flows shows the sources and uses of cash during the year. The statement of cash flows will be discussed in more detail in Chapter 11.

Exhibit 4-4

Balance Sheet Reporting of Cash for Abercrombie & Fitch

Abercrombie & Fitch, Inc. Consolidated Balance Sheet (in thousands)		
	Jan. 30, 2010	**Jan. 31, 2009**
ASSETS **Current assets:**		
Cash and Equivalents*	$680,113	$522,122

*Cash and equivalents include amounts on deposit with financial institutions and investments, primarily held in money market accounts, with original maturities of less than 90 days. Outstanding checks are classified as current liabilities in the Consolidated Balance Sheets and changes in outstanding checks are reported in financing activities on the Consolidated Statements of Cash Flows.

As explained in the notes to **Abercrombie & Fitch**'s financial statements, **cash equivalents** "include amounts on deposit with financial institutions and investments, primarily held in money market accounts, with original maturities of less than 90 days." This is a standard definition and indicates that cash equivalents are both

- easily convertible into known amounts of cash and
- close enough to maturity that they are relatively insensitive to changes in interest rates

But why do companies bother to invest their cash in such short-term investments? The answer is that such investments earn a greater rate of return than cash sitting in a bank account. As shown in Exhibit 4-4, **Abercrombie & Fitch** had over $680,000,000 in cash and equivalents at January 30, 2010. If their investment strategy earns a mere 1 percent more than a bank account, they would earn an extra $6.8 million in interest for the year.

CASH CONTROLS

OBJECTIVE **4**
Describe how businesses control cash.

Internal controls are designed to protect all assets. But the more liquid an asset (the more "liquid" an asset, the more easily it is converted into cash), the more likely it is to be stolen. In fact, an *Association of Certified Fraud Examiners'* fraud study suggested that 80 percent of all workplace frauds involved employee theft of company assets (i.e., embezzlement) and 90 percent of these thefts involved cash.[2] For example, casinos take in huge amounts of cash. At the **Mohegan Sun** casino in Connecticut, while counting cash, employees were required to wear jumpsuits with no pockets while supervisors observed them through one-way mirrors. That sounds good; however, one employee shoved an estimated $600,000 under the elastic wristband of his jumpsuit over the course of his employment. He would take the money out of his sleeve and put it in his pockets during bathroom breaks. On the day he was caught, he had $97,300 in $100 bills. Now the casino uses transparent jumpsuits for its cash counters.

Of course, casinos operate in a particularly difficult environment to control cash, but all companies must use internal control activities. As discussed, the following internal controls help businesses effectively control cash:

- The authority to collect, hold, and pay cash must be clearly assigned to specific individuals. Whenever feasible, cash-handling activities and cash record-keeping activities should be assigned to *different* individuals.
- Cash records should be examined often by an objective party as a basis for evaluating the performance of cash-handling activities.
- Controls should be supported by an appropriately designed record-keeping system.
- Cash should be safeguarded in vaults and banks.

YOU◆DECIDE   Internal Control over Cash in a Student Organization

You are the treasurer of your sorority and have responsibility for collecting dues, depositing cash in the bank, writing all checks, maintaining accounting records, and preparing bank reconciliations and financial statements. After taking your financial accounting course, you realize that this is a clear violation of segregation of duties and mention this to your sorority president. She agrees, but says that segregation of duties is not nearly as important as simply finding someone willing to perform the treasurer's tasks.

What steps can you advise your student organization president to take to strengthen its internal control system?

You can advise the leader of your student organization to look into each of the following areas. A "no" answer to any question indicates a potential internal control weakness.

(Continued)

---

[2] The other 20 percent includes such things as fraudulent financial statements.

- *Is supporting documentation obtained from vendors whenever cash is paid or a liability is incurred?*
  The use of appropriate documentation assures the proper payment of bills and facilitates the appropriate accrual of liabilities on the year end balance sheet.
- *Is every vendor invoice and all supporting documentation cancelled (e.g., by writing "Paid by check number 841 on November 29, 2011") at the time the check is written?*
  This action helps assure that duplicate payments are not made.
- *Does the organization's faculty advisor initial all checks written for amounts greater than some specified minimum (say $500)?*
  This control reduces the possibility of unauthorized payments.
- *Are receipts of members' fees and dues deposited promptly (at least once a week)?*
  Prompt deposits help avoid misplacing receipts.
- *Does the organization have procedures to assist in the collection of membership dues?*
  Despite the mutual trust and friendship that are a part of most student organizations, uncollectible accounts can be a serious problem. The treasurer may need the assistance of formal procedures in collecting overdue accounts (e.g., placing sanctions on members who fail to pay).
- *Does the organization have an accounting policies and procedures manual?*
  Such a manual may be needed to prepare the year-end financial report in conformity with university and/or national governing body requirements.
- *Are complete minutes of all officers' meetings maintained?*
  The minutes should include (a) a listing of all changes in membership and officers, including the names of new members, (b) a schedule of dues that documents all financial obligations of members, (c) approval of payments, and (d) authorization of check signers. Including this information, along with descriptions of important decisions of the organization's governing body, documents all the important activities of the organization.

Businesses can effectively control cash with internal controls, which include guidelines for collecting, holding, and paying cash as well as keeping records and assigning individuals different responsibilities.

Although many of the cash controls with which you are most familiar (e.g., cash registers) might appear to be outside the accounting system, we will highlight three important areas where the accounting system interacts with the internal control system to strengthen cash controls:

- bank reconciliations
- cash over and short
- petty cash

Reconciliation of Accounting Records to Bank Statement

The use of a bank is one of the most important controls over cash. The bank duplicates the company's accounting by keeping their own accounting records of your account. Unfortunately, the bank's accounting records and company's accounting records often disagree because the transactions are not recorded at the same time (for example, a company writes a check on January 18 and credits cash immediately; however, the bank will not debit your account until the check is presented to the bank—typically many days later). Therefore, to ensure that the accounting records are consistent with the bank's accounting records, any differences must be "reconciled." This process is called the **bank reconciliation**.

Periodically—usually once a month—the bank returns all checks processed during the period, together with a detailed record of the activity of the account. The document is a *bank statement*, which shows the beginning and ending account balance and the individual deposits and withdrawals recorded by the bank during the period. Basically, the bank statement is a copy of the bank's accounting records showing each customer the increases and decreases in their balances (see Exhibit 4-5). Remember, a checking account is a liability for the bank (the bank owes you the balance). Therefore, deposits and other events that increase your bank account balance are labeled "credits" on the bank statement (because they increase the bank's liability to you), and withdrawals and other events that decrease your bank account balance are labeled "debits" (because they decrease the bank's liability to you).

Concept Q&A

If a debit increases an asset and decreases a liability and a credit decreases an asset and increases a liability, why does the bank "credit" your account when you make a deposit and "debit" your account when you make a withdrawal?

Answer:
Because the "credit" and "debit" are from the bank's point of view. When you make a deposit, it actually increases the bank's liability to you—the bank now owes you more. When you make a withdrawal, it decreases the bank's liability to you.

Exhibit 4-5

Bank Statement

T N B

THIRD NATIONAL BANK
123 W. Main Street
Batavia, OH 45103

Member FDIC

Account Statement

Statement Date:
August 31, 2011

OHIO ENTERPRISES INC.
519 MAIN STREET
BATAVIA, OH 45103

Account Number:
40056

Previous Balance	Checks and Debits	Deposits and Credits	Current Balance
$7,675.20	$10,685.26	$7,175.10	$4,165.04

Checks and Debits			Deposits and Credits		Daily Balance	
Date	No.	Amount	Date	Amount	Date	Amount
8/3/11	1883	182.00			8/3/11	7,493.20
8/4/11	1884	217.26	8/4/11	2,673.10	8/4/11	9,949.04
8/6/11	1885	1,075.00			8/6/11	8,874.04
8/7/11	1886	37.50	8/7/11	4,500.00	8/7/11	13,336.54
8/10/11	1887	826.00			8/10/11	12,510.54
8/11/11	1888	50.00			8/11/11	12,460.54
8/12/11	1889	2,670.00				
8/12/11	1890	67.90			8/12/11	9,722.64
8/13/11	1891	890.00			8/13/11	8,832.64
8/14/11	1892	27.50			8/14/11	8,805.14
8/17/11	1893	111.00			8/17/11	8,694.14
8/18/11	DM	380.00			8/18/11	8,314.14
8/19/11	1894	60.00				
8/19/11	1895	510.00			8/19/11	7,744.14
8/20/11	1896	30.00			8/20/11	7,714.14
8/21/11	1897	1,600.00			8/21/11	6,114.14
8/24/11	1898	78.00			8/24/11	6,036.14
8/25/11	NSF	200.00			8/25/11	5,836.14
8/26/11	1899	208.80			8/26/11	5,627.34
8/27/11	1900	1,250.00			8/27/11	4,377.34
8/28/11	1902	175.00			8/28/11	4,202.34
8/31/11	1903	25.30	8/31/11 INT	2.00		
8/31/11	SC	14.00			8/31/11	4,165.04

Symbols:	**CM** Credit Memo	**EC** Error Correction	**NSF** Non-sufficient funds
	DM Debit Memo	**INT** Interest Earned	**SC** Service Charge

Reconcile your account immediately

Reconciliation of these separately maintained records serves two purposes:

- It serves a control function by identifying errors and providing an inspection of detailed records that deters theft.
- It serves a transaction detection function by identifying transactions performed by the bank, so the business can make the necessary entries in its records.

In general, differences between the cash account balance (see Exhibit 4-6, p. 182) and the bank statement balance develop from three sources:

- transactions recorded by the business, but not recorded by the bank in time to appear on the current bank statement
- transactions recorded by the bank, but not yet recorded by the business
- errors in recording transactions on either set of records

Exhibit 4 - 6

T-Account for Cash, Prior to Reconciliation

Ohio Enterprises Inc.						
			Cash			
Balance, 7/31/11	$6,200.94					
Date	Amount Deposited	Check Number	Check Amount	Check Number	Check Amount	
8/1	$2,673.10	1886	$ 37.50	1896	$ 30.00	
8/5	4,500.00	1887	826.00	1897	1,600.00	
8/31	300.00	1888	50.00	1898	87.00	
Total deposits	$7,473.10	1889	2,670.00	1899	208.80	
		1890	67.90	1900	1,250.00	
		1891	890.00	1901	93.00	
		1892	27.50	1902	175.00	
		1893	111.00	1903	25.30	
		1894	60.00	1904	72.50	
		1895	510.00	1905	891.00	
			Total disbursements		$9,682.50	
Balance, 8/31/11	$3,991.54					

Transactions Recorded by the Business, but Not Yet Recorded by the Bank

There are generally two types of transactions recorded by the business, but not recorded by the bank in time to appear on the current statement: outstanding checks and deposits in transit.

Outstanding Checks An **outstanding check** is a check issued and recorded by the business that has not been "cashed" by the recipient of the check. The business has (properly) recorded the check as lowering its cash balance and the bank has (properly) not recorded the check as lowering the business's account balance because it has not been cashed. For example, when a check is written during December, but not cashed until January, the business's December 31 cash balance will be lower than its account balance on the December 31 bank statement.

Deposits in Transit A **deposit in transit** is an amount received and recorded by the business, but which has not been recorded by the bank in time to appear on the current bank statement. Deposits in transit cause the bank balance to be smaller than the business's cash account balance. Deposits in transit arise because many banks post any deposit received after 2:00 or 3:00 P.M. into their records on the next business day and because businesses often make deposits on weekends or holidays when the bank is not open for business, which could cause the deposit to appear on the next bank statement.

Transactions Recorded by the Bank, but Not Yet Recorded by the Business

Several types of transactions are recorded by the bank, but not yet recorded by the business, including service charges, non-sufficient funds checks, and debit and credit memos. After the reconciliation process, the business must make adjusting journal entries to record all the transactions that have been recorded by the bank but not yet recorded in the business's ledger cash account.

Service Charges **Service charges** are fees charged by the bank for checking account services. The amount of the fee is not known to the business (and therefore cannot be recorded) until the bank statement is received. Bank service charges unrecorded by the business at the end of a month cause the bank balance to be smaller than the business's cash account balance.

Non-Sufficient Funds Checks A **Non-Sufficient Funds (NSF) check** is a check that has been returned to the depositor because funds in the issuer's account are not sufficient to pay the check (also called a *bounced check*). The amount of the check was added to the depositor's account when the check was deposited; however, since the check cannot be paid, the bank deducts the amount of the NSF check from the account. This deduction is recorded by the bank before it is recorded by the business. NSF checks cause the bank balance to be smaller than the cash account balance.

Debit and Credit Memos A debit memo might result, for example, if the bank makes a prearranged deduction from the business's account to pay a utility bill. Debit memos recorded by the bank but not yet recorded by the business cause the bank balance to be smaller than the cash account balance. A credit memo could result if the bank collected a note receivable for the business and deposited the funds in the business's account. Credit memos recorded by the bank but not recorded by the business cause the bank balance to be larger than the cash account balance.

Errors The previous differences between the accounting records and bank account balances are the result of time lags between the recording of a transaction by the business and its recording by the bank. Errors in recording transactions represent yet another source of difference between a business's cash account balance and the bank balance. Errors are inevitable in any accounting system and should be corrected as soon as discovered. In addition, an effort should be made to determine the cause of any error as a basis for corrective action. Obviously, an intentional error designed to hide misappropriation of funds calls for quite different corrective action than does an error resulting from human fatigue or machine failure.

Performing a Bank Reconciliation To begin the reconciliation, start with the "cash balance from the bank statement" and the "cash balance from company records." These two balances are then adjusted as necessary to produce identical "adjusted cash balances" by following these steps:

Step 1. Compare the deposits on the bank statement to the deposits debited to the cash account. Any deposits debited to the cash account but not on the bank statement are likely deposits in transit, so look at a deposit slip to ensure that these amounts were actually deposited. Deposits in transit should be added to the "cash balance from the bank statement."

Step 2. Compare the paid (often called *cancelled*) checks returned with the bank statement to the amounts credited to the cash account and the list of outstanding checks from prior months. Any checks credited to the cash account but not on the bank statement are likely outstanding checks. These amounts should be subtracted from the "cash balance from the bank statement."

Step 3. Look for items on the bank statement that have not been debited or credited to the cash account. These include bank service charges, interest payments, NSF checks, automatic payments (debit memos), and bank collections on behalf of the company (credit memos). Bank debits should be subtracted from the "cash balance from company records," while bank credits should be added to the "cash balance from company records." Of course, all these amounts should be verified.

Step 4. If the "adjusted cash balances" are still not the same, search for errors. The most common error is a "transposition" error in which, for example, a check is written for $823, but recorded as $283 (the 8 and 2 are transposed). In this case, the accounting records will show a $283 credit to the cash account, but the bank will show a $823 debit to the company's account. All errors made by the company must be added or subtracted from the "cash balance from company records." All errors made by the bank must be added or subtracted from the "cash balance from the bank statement."

This process is illustrated in **CORNERSTONE 4-1** (p. 184).

CORNERSTONE 4-1   Performing a Bank Reconciliation

Concept:
Bank reconciliation is the process of comparing the accounting records and the bank statement, determining where discrepancies occur, and accounting for them.

Information:
Refer to the bank statement in Exhibit 4-5 (p. 181) and the cash account in Exhibit 4-6 (p. 182). Recognize that the beginning balance was reconciled at the end of last month (July). Assume that this was performed correctly and all outstanding checks (numbers 1883, 1884, and 1885) and deposits in transit from July cleared during August.

Required:
1. Determine the adjustments needed by comparing the bank statement to the cash account.
2. Complete the bank reconciliation.

Solution:
1. Four items in the cash account do not appear on the bank statement: the August 31 deposit (in transit), and checks 1901, 1904, and 1905 (outstanding). There is also an error. The amount posted to the cash account for check 1898 does not equal the amount cleared on the bank statement. The cancelled check on record was written for $78.00, not $87.00, so the error is on the company's records.

2.

Cash balance from bank statement		$ 4,165.04	Cash balance from company records			$3,991.54
Add: Deposit in transit (8/31)		300.00	Add:			
Less: Outstanding checks			Error in recording check 1898 (we recorded as $87, should be $78)		$ 9.00	
1901	$ (93.00)		Interest		2.00	11.00
1904	(72.50)		Less:			
1905	(891.00)	(1,056.50)	Service charge		$ 14.00	
Adjusted cash balance		**$ 3,408.54**	NSF check		200.00	
			Electric bill (Debit Memo)		380.00	(594.00)
			Adjusted cash balance			**$ 3,408.54**

Adjusted cash balances should equal.

If the person who writes the checks also performs the reconciliation, it is easier for them to cover up theft and fraud. Therefore, there are additional benefits when the bank reconciliation is performed by someone with no other responsibilities related to cash (the duties of reconciling cash and cash record keeping should be segregated).

Making Adjusting Entries as a Result of the Bank Reconciliation Once the bank reconciliation is completed, some adjustments to the accounting records may be necessary. No adjustments are necessary for outstanding checks or deposits in transit because the accounting records have correctly recorded these amounts. However, as shown in **CORNERSTONE 4-2**, adjustments are necessary for any company errors or items such as bank charges or interest that the company does not find out about until receiving the bank statement.

CORNERSTONE 4-2

Making Adjusting Entries as a Result of the Bank Reconciliation

Concept:
Adjusting journal entries are required for all transactions correctly recorded by the bank that have not yet been included in the accounting records.

Information:
Refer to the bank reconciliation performed in **CORNERSTONE 4-1**. Assume that all checks from this account were written to satisfy accounts payable.

Required:
Prepare the necessary adjusting journal entries.

Solution:

Account and Explanation	Debit	Credit
Cash	9	
Accounts Payable		9
(Correct error in recording check 1898)		
Cash	2	
Interest Income		2
(Record interest)		
Bank Service Charge Expense	14	
Cash		14
(Record bank service charge)		
Accounts Receivable	200	
Cash		200
(Record NSF check)		
Utilities Expense	380	
Cash		380
(Record debit memo for payment of electric bill)		

Assets	=	Liabilities	+	Stockholders' Equity
+9		+9		

Assets	=	Liabilities	+	Stockholders' Equity
+2				+2

Assets	=	Liabilities	+	Stockholders' Equity
−14				−14

Assets	=	Liabilities	+	Stockholders' Equity
+200				
−200				

Assets	=	Liabilities	+	Stockholders' Equity
−380				−380

Cash Over and Short

Another important control activity requires that cash receipts be deposited in a bank daily. At the end of each day, the amount of cash received during the day is debited to the cash accounts to which it has been deposited. The amount deposited should equal the total of cash register tapes. If it does not (and differences will occasionally occur even when cash-handling procedures are carefully designed and executed), the discrepancy is recorded in an account called **cash over and short**, as illustrated in **CORNERSTONE 4-3**.

CORNERSTONE 4-3

Recording Cash Over and Short

Concept:
When the cash in the register does not reconcile with the register tapes, the discrepancy is recorded in cash over and short.

(Continued)

**CORNERSTONE
4-3**
(continued)

Information:
RSA has $20,671.12 prepared for deposit. However, the total of cash register tapes and other documents supporting the receipt of cash on that day is $20,685.14, including collections of accounts receivable of $6,760.50.

Required:
Prepare the necessary adjusting journal entry.

Solution:

Account and Explanation	Debit	Credit
Cash	20,671.12	
Cash Over and Short	14.02	
Sales Revenue*		13,924.64
Accounts Receivable		6,760.50
(Record cash register collections)		

Assets	= Liabilities +	Stockholders' Equity
+20,671.12		−14.02
−6,760.50		+13,924.64

*$20,685.14 − $6,760.50

Observe that a cash *shortage* (as in Cornerstone 4-3) requires a debit to cash over and short, whereas a cash *overage* would require a credit.

One common source of cash over and short is errors in making change for cash sales. Significant amounts of cash over and short signal the need for a careful investigation of the causes and appropriate corrective action. Cash over and short is usually treated as an income statement account and is reported as a part of other expenses or other revenues.

Petty Cash

Cash controls are more effective when companies pay with a check for the following reasons:

- Only certain people have the authority to sign the check. Those authorized to sign do not keep the accounting records and only sign the check with the proper documentation supporting the payment (e.g., evidence that the goods being paid for were properly ordered and received).
- Supporting documents are marked paid to avoid duplicate payment.
- Checks are prenumbered, which makes it easy to identify any missing checks.

However, issuing checks to pay small amounts is usually more costly than paying cash.[3] Therefore, a company may establish a **petty cash** fund to pay for items such as stamps or a cake for an employee birthday party. The petty cash fund is overseen by a petty cash custodian, who both pays for small dollar amounts directly from the fund and reimburses employees who have receipts for items they've bought with their own money. At the end of the month, the custodian submits all receipts (and other supporting documentation) to the company. After company personnel (other than the petty cash custodian) determine that the documents are authentic and that each transaction is supported by appropriate documentation, the custodian is given an amount to replenish the petty cash fund. The company then records the amounts spent in the accounting records. Because the custodian replenishes petty cash at the end of the month, the accounting records are appropriately updated each month. This process is illustrated in **CORNERSTONE 4-4**.

---

[3] Checks cost money to print, mail, and process. Some estimate the cost of processing a check to be over $1. Therefore, banks have developed ways for businesses to transfer money without the use of paper checks. For example, most employees do not see an actual paycheck; instead, money is automatically deposited into their bank account. These are called electronic fund transfers (EFT). Use of EFTs is quite common and has become commonplace at the individual level through the use of debit cards.

CORNERSTONE 4 - 4   Accounting for Petty Cash

Concept:
Companies often establish a petty cash fund account to pay for small dollar amount items.

Information:
On January 1, Oregon Industries establishes a petty cash fund of $500. On January 31, the petty cash custodian presents the following records of the month's transactions, together with related documents, and requests reimbursement:

Jan. 12	Hansen's Grocery (coffee)	$ 30
15	U.S. Post Office (postage)	70
17	Northwest Messenger (package delivery)	25
19	Office Depot (office supplies)	175
25	Mr. Strand, Controller (food for lunch meeting)	63
	Total	$363

After approving the expenses, the company issues a check to the custodian for $363.00 to replenish the fund.

Required:
1. Prepare the journal entry to establish the petty cash fund on January 1.
2. Prepare the journal entry to record the replenishment of the fund on January 31.
3. Assuming the entry from requirement 2 has been made, prepare the journal entry needed to increase the fund balance to $600.

Solution:

	Date	Account and Explanation	Debit	Credit
1.	Jan. 1	Petty Cash	500.00	
		Cash		500.00
		(Establish petty cash fund)		

	Assets	=	Liabilities	+	Stockholders' Equity
	+500				
	−500				

	Date	Account and Explanation	Debit	Credit
2.	Jan. 31	Office Supplies	175.00	
		Postage Expense	70.00	
		Delivery Expense	25.00	
		Miscellaneous Expense	93.00	
		Cash*		363.00
		(Replenish petty cash fund and recognize expenses)		

	Assets	=	Liabilities	+	Stockholders' Equity
	−363				−175
					−70
					−25
					−93

	Date	Account and Explanation	Debit	Credit
3.		Petty Cash	100.00	
		Cash		100.00
		(Increase the fund balance to $600)		

	Assets	=	Liabilities	+	Stockholders' Equity
	−100				
	+100				

*The expenditures of petty cash are not recorded in the accounting records until the fund is replenished. The replenishment does not alter the balance of the petty cash fund on Oregon's records; the balance remains $500.00.

Replenishment of petty cash may also occur during the month if the amount of petty cash available gets too low. However, to assure that all expenses are recorded in the appropriate accounting period, replenishment should occur at the end of the month or accounting period. As an additional control measure, a company should periodically verify its petty cash balances by counting the cash in the hands of custodians and comparing it to the custodian's petty cash record.

We have spent considerable time discussing internal controls both in general and, over cash, in particular, for two reasons. First, internal controls are an integral part of the accounting system and business. Second, the accounting and reporting of cash is not that difficult. We will consider cash management strategies, but first we discuss the operating cycle because this affects the amount of cash needed.

OBJECTIVE 5
Describe the operating cycle and explain the principles of cash management.

OPERATING CYCLE

The **operating cycle** is the elapsed time between the purchase of goods for resale (or the purchase of materials to produce salable goods or services) and the collection of cash from customers (presumably a larger amount of cash than was invested in the goods sold). Although typically a year or less, the operating cycle can be as short as a few days for perishable goods, or as long as many years for the production and sale of products such as timber or wine (see Exhibit 4-7).

Exhibit 4-7

The Operating Cycle

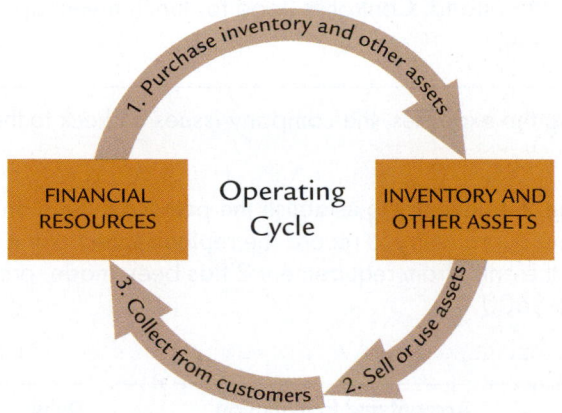

Consider the operating cycle for **H. H. Gregg**, a large appliance retailer that provides long-term financing for customers. Appliances remain in inventory for an average of three months before being sold. Most are sold on credit, and it takes an average of 12 months to collect the full amount of a sale. Thus, Gregg's operating cycle is 15 months, representing the average purchase-to-collection interval (three months to sell plus 12 months to collect).

The length of the operating cycle influences the classification of assets and liabilities on balance sheets. In addition, the operating cycle plays an important role in the measurement of income. The length of the operating cycle also affects the amount of capital a business needs and the policies that govern its sales of goods and services, as the You Decide demonstrates.

YOU DECIDE   Operating Cycle and Capital Requirements

You are the CFO of Tolland Gizmo. You sell, on credit, approximately 1,000 Gizmos per month at $10 per unit. In addition to the accounts receivable, you have an inventory of 200 Gizmos that were purchased at a cost of $6 per unit (a total inventory of $1,200) and $1,000 in cash. Currently, Tolland has one month's sales in accounts receivable and the following balance sheet:

ASSETS	
Cash	$ 1,000
Inventory	1,200
Accounts receivable	10,000
Total	$12,200

(Continued)

LIABILITIES AND STOCKHOLDERS' EQUITY	
Equity	$12,200
Total	$12,200

The sales force wants to lengthen the collection period of the accounts receivable to three months.

How would lengthening the collection period of the accounts receivable effect Tolland's financing requirements?

Tolland will now have interest expense. Presumably, the company would not allow its customers to take three months to pay unless compensated for doing so. Thus, Tolland will probably charge a higher price because of the extended payment terms.

Tolland's higher price to cover the interest expense it pays for a longer collection period will result in higher revenues.

Cash Management

With an understanding of the operating cycle, we now turn our attention to cash management strategies. As discussed, the activities of the operating cycle transform cash into goods and services and then back, through sales, into cash. This sequence of activities includes a continual process of paying and receiving cash. A company can significantly increase its net income through its cash management policies. At a high level, cash management principles entail the following:

- delaying paying suppliers (so a company can earn as much interest on their cash as possible)
- speeding up collection from customers (in order to invest the cash sooner)
- earning the greatest return on any excess cash

We can follow these principles through the operating cycle.

IFRS

The management, control and accounting for cash are the same under IFRS as under U.S. GAAP.

Buying Inventory

The first stage of the operating cycle is buying inventory. Money that is tied up in inventory sitting on the shelves is not earning any return. As such, an important aspect of cash management is to keep inventory levels low. This decreases the need for cash. Companies have made great strides in inventory management over the last few decades. For example, **Dell** went from holding approximately 11 weeks of sales in inventory in 1991 to under one week in 2001, while car companies such as **Toyota** time the delivery of parts such as windows and seats down to the minute.

Paying for Inventory

The second stage of the operating cycle is paying for the inventory. As with all payments, a good cash management principle is to delay payments as long as possible while maintaining a good relationship with the payee. The longer a company keeps cash, the more interest it can collect. This may seem trivial, but consider a company like **Microsoft**. Its 2009 SEC filings reveal approximately $3.3 billion in accounts payable. If Microsoft can earn 5 percent on this money, it will earn close to $450,000 per day in interest. You may practice this in your own lives if you wait until April 15 to pay any income taxes owed or pay your tuition on the last possible day.

Selling Inventory

The third stage is selling the inventory, which often produces receivables. Good cash management suggests increasing the speed of receivable collections. This is an area that has become increasingly sophisticated over the last 20 years. In fact, many companies sell their receivables rather than wait for their customers to pay. Of course, they sell the receivables for less than they will receive (which represents interest and return for the buyer), but it also allows the company to receive the cash sooner and avoid hiring employees to service the receivables.

Short-Term Investments

Beyond delaying payments and speeding up collections, businesses try to keep their bank cash balances to a minimum because most bank accounts earn relatively small amounts of interest. Accordingly, short-term investments are purchased with temporary cash surpluses. The value and composition of short-term investment portfolios change continually in response to seasonal factors and other shifts in the business environment.

These investments will usually be liquidated (converted to cash through selling or maturity) before the business undertakes any significant short-term borrowing because the interest expense on short-term borrowings usually exceeds the return on short-term investments. Nonetheless, temporary shortages can result from the day-to-day ups and downs in the inflows and outflows of cash, as well as unforeseen needs for cash. A business with a good credit rating can borrow funds to resolve a temporary cash shortage. Such borrowings frequently are made under a line of credit, an agreement between the company and its bank in which the bank promises to lend the company funds up to a specified limit and at specified interest rates. The use of short-term investments as part of cash management is illustrated in the following You Decide.

 **Cash Management**

You are the treasurer at Ohio Wire, a medium-size manufacturer of cable and wire used in building and bridge construction. Since most construction is seasonal, Ohio Wire tends to have far more cash inflows during the summer months. Further, during the winter their cash outflows are often greater than their inflows.

How do you manage the excess cash accumulated during the summer months knowing that cash will be needed during the winter?

Ohio Wire will use its excess cash to make short-term investments. These investments should be able to be easily liquidated by winter when the cash will be needed. Some examples of such investments could be certificates of deposit, Treasury Bills, and short-term equity holdings. Further, most companies will have lines of credit at a bank. These arrangements allow the company to borrow any amount up to some limit with a phone call.

Investing excess cash in short-term investments allows companies to have immediate access to cash to cover temporary short falls, while minimizing borrowing costs.

Effective cash management ultimately requires some understanding of future cash flows. For example, if the company is planning to expand or pay off a loan, it must make sure it has the necessary cash on hand. If a company receives most of its cash for the year around the holidays, it must effectively manage the excess until the time it is needed. These projections are made as part of the budgeting process and are an integral part of managerial accounting courses.

SUMMARY OF LEARNING OBJECTIVES

LO1. Discuss the role of internal controls in managing a business.
- Internal control systems provide reasonable assurance that the company's objectives are being met in three areas:
  - effectiveness and efficiency of operations
  - reliability of financial reporting
  - compliance with applicable laws and regulations

LO2. Discuss the five elements of internal control.
- The internal control system includes:
  - the control environment
  - risk assessment

- control activities
- information and communication
- monitoring
- Although we distinguish between the accounting system and the internal controls system, the two are really one integrated system designed to meet the needs of a particular business.

LO3. Describe how businesses account for and report cash.
- A cash account is debited when cash is received and credited when cash is paid out.
- Cash is reported on the balance sheet as the amount of cash and cash equivalents available on the balance sheet date.
- The statement of cash flows shows the sources and uses of cash during the accounting period.
- Cash equivalents are amounts that are easily convertible into known amounts of cash and investments that are close to maturity.

LO4. Describe how businesses control cash.
- Keeping control over cash is extremely difficult.
- It is important to:
  - safeguard cash
  - adequately segregate the custody of cash from the authorization of payments and the accounting records.
- Cash accounts include:
  - Cash in bank
  - Change funds
  - Petty cash
- Controls over these cash accounts include:
  - Bank reconciliations
  - Daily deposits and recording cash over and short amounts
  - Accounting procedures for petty cash funds

LO5. Describe the operating cycle and explain the principles of cash management.
- The operating cycle of the business starts when the business purchases inventory.
- When a business sells goods on credit, creating accounts receivable, cash is not replenished until the receivables are collected, which completes the operating cycle.
- Cash management is an important function at all companies because business is really a continuous cycle of paying and receiving cash.
- Although aspects of cash management have become extremely sophisticated, basic strategies are:
  - keeping inventory levels low
  - delaying payment of liabilities as long as possible
  - speeding up collection of receivables
  - investing idle cash to earn the greatest possible return while still being available when needed

CORNERSTONE 4-1	Performing a bank reconciliation (p. 184)	
CORNERSTONE 4-2	Making adjusting entries as a result of the bank reconciliation (p. 185)	
CORNERSTONE 4-3	Recording cash over and short (p. 185)	
CORNERSTONE 4-4	Accounting for petty cash (p. 187)	**CORNERSTONES** FOR CHAPTER 4

KEY TERMS

Accounting system (p. 177)
Bank reconciliation (p. 180)
Business process risks (p. 174)
Cash equivalents (p. 179)
Cash over and short (p. 185)
Control activities (p. 175)
Control environment (p. 172)
Deposit in transit (p. 182)
Internal control system (p. 172)

Non-Sufficient Funds (NSF) check (p. 183)
Operating cycle (p. 188)
Outstanding check (p. 182)
Petty cash (p. 186)
Safeguarding (p. 176)
Segregation of duties (p. 175)
Service charges (p. 182)
Strategic risks (p. 174)

REVIEW PROBLEM

I. Bank Reconciliation

Fugazi Enterprises has the following information in its accounting records for their primary checking account:

Balance at April 30	$ 18,350
Checks written during May	114,700
Deposits during May	112,200

Fugazi's May bank statement contained the following information:

Balance per bank at April 30		$ 19,800
Credits during May:		
Deposits		109,600
Debits during May:		
Checks paid	$107,400	
Debit memo (May utilities)	8,000	
Bank service charge	80	115,480
Balance per bank at May 31		$ 13,920

The April bank reconciliation had deposits in transit of $850 and outstanding checks of $2,300. All these items cleared during May. These were the only reconciling items in April.

Required:

1. Prepare a bank reconciliation at May 31.

2. Prepare any adjusting entries necessary because of the bank reconciliation.

Solution:

1.

Cash balance from bank statement		$13,920
Add: Deposits in transit	$112,200 − ($109,600 − $850)*	3,450
Less: Outstanding checks	$114,700 − ($107,400 − $2,300)**	(9,600)
Adjusted cash balance		**$ 7,770**
Cash balance from company records	($18,350 + $112,200 − $114,700)	$15,850
Less:		
Debit memo (utilities)	$8,000	
Service charge	80	(8,080)
Adjusted cash balance		**$ 7,770**

*$112,200 was deposited during May, but the account was only credited for $109,600 during May. However, this $109,600 included $850 that was in transit at April 30, so only $108,750 ($109,600 − $850) of the May deposits were credited to the account.

**$114,700 in checks were written in May and $107,400 in checks cleared the bank during May. However, this $107,400 included $2,300 in checks that were outstanding from April, so only $105,100 ($107,400 − $2,300) in checks cleared that were written in May.

2.

Date	Account and Explanation	Debit	Credit
May 31	Utilities Expense	8,000	
	Bank Service Charge Expense	80	
	Cash		8,080

Assets	=	Liabilities	+	Stockholders' Equity
−8,080				−8,000
				−80

DISCUSSION QUESTIONS

1. What is the purpose of an internal control system?
2. Internal control systems include policies and procedures to do what?
3. Section 404 of the Sarbanes-Oxley Act increased top management's responsibility for what?
4. What are the five elements of internal control?
5. What is meant by "tone at the top"? Why is it so important to an effective system of internal controls?
6. What are strategic risks?
7. What are business process risks?
8. What are the five categories of control activities?
9. How do these control activities help protect a company against error, theft, and fraud?
10. How do control activities relate to the accounting system?
11. Why does a company give particular attention to internal controls for cash?
12. Why is it important to segregate the duties for handling cash from the duties for keeping the accounting records for cash?
13. Describe two advantages of performing reconciliations of the cash account to the balances on the bank statements.
14. Describe the potential sources of difference between a cash account and its associated bank statement balance.
15. What kinds of bank reconciliation items require the firm to make adjusting entries?
16. Describe how cash over and short can be used for internal control purposes.
17. Why do most companies have petty cash funds?
18. What are cash equivalents?
19. Why do companies invest their cash in short-term investments?
20. What is the operating cycle?
21. Describe the basic cash management principles.
22. Why do companies hold short-term investments?

MULTIPLE-CHOICE EXERCISES

4-1 What is the primary role of internal controls in managing a business?

a. To prevent cash from being stolen.
b. To constrain subordinates' activities in order to prevent employees from deviating from the scope of their responsibilities and encouraging them to act in the best interest of the business.
c. To ensure that the financial statements are presented in such a manner as to provide relevant and reliable information for financial statement users and the company's creditors.
d. To encourage theft and to ensure that segregation of duties does not take place.

4-2 Which of the following is *not* one of the three areas for which internal control systems are intended to provide reasonable assurance?

a. Certification that the financial statements are without error
b. Compliance with applicable laws and regulations
c. Effectiveness and efficiency of operations
d. Reliability of financial reporting

4-3 Which of the following is *not* one of the five elements of internal control?

a.   Risk assessment
b.   Information and communication

c.   Control environment
d.   Analysis of control procedures

4-4 Which of the following is *not* one of the five categories of control activities?

a.   Defalcation and financial reporting
b.   Checks on recorded amounts

c.   Clearly defined authority and responsibility
d.   Segregation of duties

4-5 The internal audit function is part of what element of the internal control system?

a.   Control Environment
b.   Control Activities

c.   Monitoring
d.   Risk Assessment

4-6 Which of the following is *not* generally an internal control activity?

a.   Establishing clear lines of authority to carry out specific tasks
b.   Physically counting inventory in a perpetual inventory system
c.   Limiting access to computerized accounting records
d.   Reducing the cost of hiring seasonal employees

4-7 Allowing only certain employees to order goods and services for the company is an example of what internal control procedure?

a.   Proper authorizations
b.   Segregation of duties

c.   Safeguarding of assets and records
d.   Independent verifications

4-8 Deposits made by a company but not yet reflected in a bank statement are called

a.   Credit memoranda
b.   Debit memoranda

c.   Deposits in transit
d.   None of the above

4-9 Which one of the following would *not* appear on a bank statement for a checking account?

a.   Interest earned
b.   Deposits

c.   Service charges
d.   Outstanding checks

4-10 Which one of the following is *not* a cash equivalent?

a.   30-day certificate of deposit
b.   60-day corporate commercial paper
c.   90-day U.S. Treasury bill

d.   180-day note issued by a local or state government

4-11 Business activity is best described as:

a.   noncyclical
b.   cyclical

c.   lacking deviation
d.   predictable

4-12 The five primary activities of a business generally consist of:

a.   making a profit, issuing financial statements, repaying debts, issuing dividends to share-holders, and complying with laws and regulations
b.   receiving assets, selling assets, issuing financial statements, collecting cash, and making cash disbursements
c.   receiving cash, disbursing cash, buying assets, issuing dividends, and paying off liabilities
d.   receiving assets, purchasing assets, selling goods or services, collecting cash from customers, and repaying owners and creditors

4-13 Effective cash management and control includes all of the following *except:*

a.   Purchase of stocks and bonds
b.   Bank reconciliations

c.   The use of a petty cash fund
d.   Short-term investments of excess cash

4-14 Cash management principles do *not* include:

a. speeding up collection from customers
b. earning the greatest return possible on excess cash
c. paying suppliers promptly
d. delaying payment of suppliers

4-15 Which one of the following statements is true?

a. Sound internal control practice dictates that cash disbursements should be made by check, unless the disbursement is very small.
b. The person handling the cash should also prepare the bank reconciliation.
c. Good cash management practices dictate that a company should maintain as large a balance as possible in its cash account.
d. Petty cash can be substituted for a checking account to expedite the payment of all disbursements.

CORNERSTONE EXERCISES

Cornerstone Exercise 4-16 Bank Reconciliation

OBJECTIVE ③
CORNERSTONE 4-1

Firebird Corp. prepares monthly bank reconciliations of its checking account balance. The bank statement for May 2011 indicated the following:

Balance, May 31, 2011	$42,600
Service charge for May	50
Interest earned during May	650
NSF check from Valerie Corp. (deposited by Firebird)	870
Note ($7,000) and interest ($250) collected for Firebird from a customer of Firebird's	7,250

An analysis of canceled checks and deposits and the records of Firebird Corp. revealed the following items:

Checking account balance per Firebird's books	$37,205
Outstanding checks as of May 31	4,100
Deposit in transit at May 31	5,640
Error in recording check #4456 issued by Firebird	45

The correct amount of check #4456 is $550. It was recorded as a cash disbursement of $505 by mistake. The check was issued to pay for merchandise purchases. The check appeared on the bank statement correctly.

Required:

1. Prepare a bank reconciliation schedule at May 31, 2011, in proper form.
2. What is the amount of cash that should be reported on the May 31, 2011 balance sheet?

Cornerstone Exercise 4-17 Bank Reconciliation

OBJECTIVE ③
CORNERSTONE 4-1

The accountant for Bellows Corp. was preparing a bank reconciliation as of April 30. The following items were identified:

Bellows' book balance	$28,750
Outstanding checks	900
Interest earned on checking account	75
Customer's NSF check returned by the bank	380

In addition, Bellows made an error in recording a customer's check; the amount was recorded in cash receipts as $370; the bank recorded the amount correctly as $730.

Required:

What amount will Bellows report as its adjusted cash balance at April 30, 2011?

OBJECTIVE
CORNERSTONE 4-2

Cornerstone Exercise 4-18 Adjusting Entry from Bank Reconciliation

A customer of Mutare paid for merchandise originally purchased on account with a check that has been erroneously entered into Mutare's cash account for $570 (it actually has been issued and paid for $750).

Required:

Record the appropriate journal entry to correct the error.

OBJECTIVE
CORNERSTONE 4-2

Cornerstone Exercise 4-19 Adjusting Entry from Bank Reconciliation

Pyramid Corporation is assessed a $20 fee as the result of a $185 NSF check received from a customer for services purchased on account. Neither the fee nor the NSF check has been accounted for on Pyramid's books.

Required:

Record the appropriate journal entry to update Pyramid's books.

OBJECTIVE 3
CORNERSTONE 4-1
CORNERSTONE 4-2

Cornerstone Exercise 4-20 Bank Reconciliation

Tiny Corp. prepares monthly bank reconciliations of its checking account balance. The bank statement indicated the following:

Balance, beginning of the month	$15,640
Service charge for October	65
Interest earned during October	80
NSF check from Green Corp. (deposited by Tiny) for goods purchased on account	615
Note ($2,500) and interest ($75) collected for Tiny from a customer	2,575

An analysis of canceled checks and deposits and the records of Tiny revealed the following items:

Checking account balance per Tiny's books	$12,951
Outstanding checks as of October 31	1,410
Deposit in transit at October 31	750
Error in recording a check issued by Tiny. (Correct amount of the check is $606, but was recorded as a cash disbursement of $660. The check was issued to pay for merchandise originally purchased on account).	54

Required:

1. Prepare a bank reconciliation at October 31, 2011, in proper form.
2. Record any necessary adjusting journal entries.
3. What is the amount of cash that should be reported on the October 31, 2011, balance sheet?

OBJECTIVE 3
CORNERSTONE 4-3

Cornerstone Exercise 4-21 Cash Over and Short

On a recent day, Pence Company obtained the following data from its cash registers:

	Cash Sales per Register Tape	Cash in Register after Removing Opening Change
Register 1	$12,675.12	$12,649.81
Register 2	11,429.57	11,432.16
Register 3	11,591.18	11,590.18

Pence deposits its cash receipts in its bank account daily.

Required:

Prepare a journal entry to record these cash sales.

OBJECTIVE
CORNERSTONE 4-3

Cornerstone Exercise 4-22 Cash Over and Short

Walker Department Store has one cash register. On a recent day, the cash register tape reported sales in the amount of $8,784.17. Actual cash in the register (after deducting and removing the opening change amount of $50) was $8,792.44, which was deposited in the firm's bank account.

Required:

Prepare a journal entry to record these cash collections.

Cornerstone Exercise 4-23 Petty Cash Fund

OBJECTIVE
CORNERSTONE 4-4

Murphy Inc. maintains a balance of $2,500 in its petty cash fund. On December 31, Murphy's petty cash account has a balance of $216. Murphy replenishes the petty cash account to bring it back up to $2,500. Murphy classifies all petty cash transactions as miscellaneous expense.

Required:

What entry is made to record the replenishment of the petty cash fund?

Cornerstone Exercise 4-24 Petty Cash with Change in Fund Balance

OBJECTIVE
CORNERSTONE 4-4

Basque Inc. maintains a petty cash fund with a balance of $800. On December 31, Basque's petty cash account has a balance of $60. Basque replenishes the petty cash account, as it does at the end of every month, but also decides to increase the fund balance to $1,000. Basque classifies all petty cash transactions as miscellaneous expense.

Required:

What entry is made to record this activity?

EXERCISES

Exercise 4-25 Internal Control System

OBJECTIVE 1 2

Required:

A list of terms and another list of definitions and examples are presented below. Make a list numbered 1 through 5 and match the letter of the most directly related definition or example with the number of each term.

Term	Definition or Example
1. Business process risk	a. The internal audit group is testing the operating effectiveness of various internal control activities.
2. Control environment	
3. Information and communication	b. A member of upper management was fired for violating the company's code of conduct.
4. Monitoring	c. Reports documenting problems with production are forwarded to management.
5. Strategic risk	d. Competitors begin offering extended warranty coverage on products.
	e. Problems with our suppliers have resulted in lost sales because our stores were out of stock.

Exercise 4-26 Internal Control Terminology

OBJECTIVE 1 2

Required:

A list of terms and another list of definitions and examples are presented below. Make a list numbered 1 through 7 and match the letter of the most directly related definition or example with the number of each term.

Term	Definition or Example
1. Accounting controls	a. Company policy prevents accountants from handling cash.
2. Adequate documents and records	b. Company policy requires receiving reports to be made for all deliveries by suppliers.
3. Checks on recorded amounts	c. Cash deposits are reconciled with cash register records at the end of every day.
4. Effective personnel policies	d. This includes the accounting system, all policies and procedures of the business, and the environment in which they operate.
5. Internal control structure	e. Every evening, a jewelry store removes all items of merchandise valued at over $100 from its display.
6. Safeguards over assets and records	f. These are policies and procedures that govern the identification, measurement, recording, and communication of economic information.
7. Segregation of duties	g. Every new employee is required to spend two days in training courses to learn company policies.

OBJECTIVE **2**

Exercise 4-27 Classifying Internal Control Procedures

Required:

Match each of the control procedures listed below with the most closely related control procedures type. Your answer should pair each of the numbers 1 through 10 with the appropriate letter.

Control Procedure Types

a. Adequate documents and records
b. Checks on recorded amounts
c. Clearly defined authority and responsibility
d. Safeguards over assets and records
e. Segregation of duties

Control Procedures

1. Only the cashier assigned to the cash register is allowed to perform transactions.
2. Division managers are evaluated annually on the basis of their division's profitability.
3. Invoices received from outside suppliers are filed with purchase orders.
4. Employees with access to the accounting records are not permitted to open the mail because it contains many payments by check from customers.
5. The extent of access to the many segments of the company's computer system is tightly controlled by individual identification cards and passwords that change at regular intervals.
6. Each shipment to customers from inventory is recorded on a specially printed form bearing a sequential number; these forms are the basis for entries into the computer system, which makes entries to inventory records and produces periodic reports of sales and shipments.
7. At regular intervals, internal audit reviews a sample of expenditure transactions to determine that payment has been made to a bona fide supplier and that the related goods or services were received and appropriately used.
8. A construction company stores large steel girders in an open yard surrounded by a 5-foot fence and stores welding supplies in a controlled-access, tightly secured concrete building.
9. Cash registers display the price of each item purchased to the customer as it is recorded and produce a customer receipt that describes each item and gives its price.
10. The person in the controller's office who prepares and mails checks to suppliers cannot make entries in the general ledger system.

OBJECTIVE **2 3**

Exercise 4-28 Internal Control of Cash

Edward Thompson, a longtime employee of a small grocery wholesaler, is responsible for maintaining the company's cash records and for opening the daily mail, through which the company receives about 40 percent of its daily cash receipts. Virtually all cash received by mail is in the form of checks made payable to the company. Thompson is also responsible for preparing deposits of currency and checks for the bank at the end of each day.

Required:

1. **Conceptual Connection:** Explain briefly how Thompson might be able to steal some of the company's cash receipts.
2. What internal control procedures would you recommend to prevent this theft?

OBJECTIVE **3**

Exercise 4-29 Cash Over and Short

Miller Enterprises deposits the cash received during each day at the end of the day. Miller deposited $48,287 on October 3 and $50,116 on October 4. Cash register records and other documents supporting the deposits are summarized as follows:

	10/3	10/4
Cash sales	$36,690	$40,310
Collections on account	10,875	9,813
Total receipts	$47,565	$50,123

Required:

1. Calculate the amount of cash over or cash short for each day.
2. Prepare the journal entry to record the receipt and deposit of cash on October 3.
3. Prepare the journal entry to record the receipt and deposit of cash on October 4.
4. **Conceptual Connection:** If you were the manager with responsibility over the cash registers, how would you use this information?

Exercise 4-30 Bank Reconciliation

OBJECTIVE  3

Johnson Corporation's bank statement for October reports an ending balance of $22,381, whereas Johnson's cash account shows a balance of $22,025 on October 31. The following additional information is available:

a. A $855 deposit made on October 31 was not recorded by the bank until November.
b. At the end of October, outstanding checks total $1,222.
c. The bank statement shows bank service charges of $125 not yet recorded by the company.
d. The company erroneously recorded as $973 a check that it had actually written for $379. It was correctly processed by the bank.
e. A $480 check from a customer, deposited by the company on October 29, was returned with the bank statement for lack of funds.

Required:

1. Prepare the October bank reconciliation for Johnson Corporation.
2. What amount will be reported as cash on the October 31 balance sheet?

Exercise 4-31 Bank Reconciliation (Partial)

OBJECTIVE 3

The cash account for Fleming Company contains the following information for April:

Cash balance, 3/31		$14,685
Cash received during April		55,680
		$70,365
Cash disbursements during April:		
Check 7164	$33,500	
Check 7165	11,250	
Check 7166	18,750	
Check 7167	900	64,400
Cash balance, 4/30		$ 5,965

The bank statement for April contains the following information:

Bank balance, 3/31		$25,285
Add: Deposits during April		55,680
		$80,965
Less: Checks paid during April:		
Check 7162	$ 8,900	
Check 7163	1,700	
Check 7164	33,500	
Check 7165	11,250	55,350
Bank balance, 4/30		$25,615

Required:

Assuming there were no deposits in transit at March 31 and that all outstanding checks at March 31 cleared during April, do the following:

1. Identify the outstanding checks at April 30.
2. Prepare the reconciliation of the bank and cash account balances at April 30.
3. Identify the outstanding checks at March 31.
4. Prepare the reconciliation of the bank and cash account balances at March 31.
5. **Conceptual Connection:** Why could you not perform the bank reconciliations without knowing that there were no deposits in transit on March 31 and that all outstanding checks at March 31 cleared during April?

Exercise 4-32 Bank Reconciliation

OBJECTIVE 3

Valentine Investigations has the following information for its cash account:

Balance, 1/31	$ 7,444
Deposits during February	106,780
Checks written during February	102,341

(Continued)

Valentine's bank statement for February contained the following information:

Balance per bank, 1/31	$ 8,910
Add: February deposits	104,950
	$ 113,860

Less:		
Checks paid in February	$(101,400)	
Bank service charge	(50)	
Debit memo (electric bill)	(800)	(102,250)
Balance per bank, 2/28		$ 11,610

A comparison of company records with the bank statement provided the following data:

	At 1/31	At 2/28
Deposits in transit	$2,750	$4,580
Outstanding checks	4,216	5,157

Required:

1. Prepare a bank reconciliation as of February 28.
2. Prepare adjusting entries for Valentine based on the information developed in the bank reconciliation.
3. What is the amount of cash that should be reported on the February 28 balance sheet?

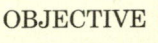

Exercise 4-33 Bank Reconciliation

Conway Company reported the following information:

Cash balance on balance sheet (12/31)	$22,066
Pre-reconciliation cash account balance (12/31)	23,916
Bank Statement (12/31)	23,220
Bank Service Charges	350
Bank Debit Memos (utility payments)	1,500
Deposits in transit (12/31)	9,160

Required:

1. Calculate the amount of outstanding checks as of December 31st.
2. Prepare the adjusting entries that Conway must make at December 31st.

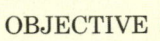

Exercise 4-34 Adjusting Entries from a Bank Reconciliation

Cooper Advisory Services identified the following items on its October reconciliation that may require adjusting entries:

a. A deposit of $670 was recorded in Cooper's accounting records, but not on the October 31 bank statement.
b. A check for $5,444 was outstanding at October 31.
c. Included with the bank statement was a check for $300 written by Hooper Advertising Services. The bank had, in error, deducted this check from Cooper's account.
d. Bank service charges were $250.
e. An NSF check written by one of Cooper's customers in the amount of $987 was returned by the bank with Cooper's bank statement. This customer was paying for merchandise originally purchased on account.

Required:

For each of these five items, prepare an adjusting entry for Cooper's journal, if any is required.

Exercise 4-35 Recording Petty Cash Account Transactions

During March, Anderson Company engaged in the following transactions involving its petty cash fund:

a. On March 1, Anderson Company established the petty cash fund by issuing a check for $1,500 to the fund custodian.
b. On March 4, the custodian paid $85 out of petty cash for freight charges on new equipment. This amount is properly classified as equipment.
c. On March 12, the custodian paid $140 out of petty cash for supplies. Anderson expenses supplies purchases as supplies expense.

d. On March 22, the custodian paid $25 out of petty cash for express mail services for reports sent to the Environmental Protection Agency. This is considered a miscellaneous expense.

e. On March 25, the custodian filed a claim for reimbursement of petty cash expenditures during the month totaling $250.

f. On March 31, Anderson issued a check for $250 to the custodian, replenishing the fund for expenditures during the month.

Required:

Prepare the journal entries required to record the petty cash account transactions that occurred during the month of March.

Exercise 4-36 Cash Reporting

OBJECTIVE 4

Brown Industries has the following items:

Currency	$15,500
Customer checks that have not been deposited	675
Cash in saving and checking accounts	35,000
Certificates of deposits that originally matured in 18 months	44,000
U.S. government bonds that originally matured in 2 months	8,000
U.S. government bonds that originally matured in 12 months	10,000

Required:

How much should Brown report as cash and equivalents on its balance sheet?

Exercise 4-37 Components of Cash

OBJECTIVE 4

The office manager for Bullock Products had accumulated the following information at the end of a recent year:

Item	Amount
Accounts receivable	$16,450
Change for cash registers (currency and coin)	2,500
Amount on deposit in checking account (bank balance)	9,280
Amount on deposit in savings account (bank balance)	25,000
Balance in petty cash	300
Checks received from customers, but not yet deposited in bank	430
Checks sent by Bullock to suppliers, but not yet presented at bank for payment	670
Deposits in transit	1,420
IOU from Gerry Bullock, company president	1,000
Notes receivable	10,000
NSF check written by Johnson Company	320
Prepaid postage	250

Required:

Calculate the total cash amount Bullock will report on its balance sheet.

Exercise 4-38 Operating Cycle

OBJECTIVE 5

Business activity is often described as being cyclical in nature.

Required:

Conceptual Connection: Describe the cyclical nature of business activity.

Exercise 4-39 Operating Cycle

OBJECTIVE 5

Businesses must decide whether to issue credit to customers.

Required:

Conceptual Connection: Describe how selling to customers on credit affects the operating cycle.

Exercise 4-40 Cash Management

OBJECTIVE 5

Effective cash management is very important to the operating performance of a business.

Required:

Conceptual Connection: Explain the principles of cash management. Why might it be advantageous to delay paying suppliers?

OBJECTIVE 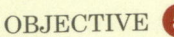 5

Exercise 4-41 Operating Cycle

A list of businesses is presented below:

Business	Operating-Cycle Description
1. Tree nursery 2. Fast food restaurant 3. Appliance store 4. Electric utility 5. Clothing store	a. Very short—customers typically pay cash, and inventory is often held less than one day. b. A few months—merchandise is typically on hand for several weeks, and some customers may use credit. c. More than one year—merchandise may be in inventory for several months, and most customers will pay for purchases after one or two years. d. Several years—a number of years are required to prepare merchandise for sale. Customers probably pay cash for most items. e. A few months—customers pay monthly. The current assets used to provide customer services are consumed within a few months.

Required:

1. Match each business with a description of the operating cycle for that business.
2. How does a longer operating cycle (such as description c or d) change a company's financing needs relative to a shorter operating cycle (such as description a)?

OBJECTIVE 5

Exercise 4-42 Operating Cycle and Current Receivables

a. Dither and Sly are attorneys-at-law who specialize in federal income tax law. They complete their typical case in six months or less and collect from the typical client within one additional month.

b. Johnston's Market specializes in fresh meat and fish. All merchandise must be sold within one week of purchase. Almost all sales are for cash, and any receivables are generally paid by the end of the following month.

c. Mortondo's is a women's clothing store specializing in high-style merchandise. Merchandise spends an average of seven months on the rack following purchase. Most sales are on credit, and the typical customer pays within one month of sale.

d. Trees Inc. grows Christmas trees and sells them to various Christmas tree lots. Most sales are for cash. It takes six years to grow a tree.

Required:

For each of the businesses described above, indicate the length of the operating cycle.

PROBLEM SET A

OBJECTIVE 1 2

Problem 4-43A Role of Internal Control

Internal control systems include policies and procedures designed to provide reasonable assurance that the corporation's objectives are being met in three areas: (a) effectiveness and efficiency of operations, (b) reliability of financial reporting, and (c) compliance with applicable laws and regulations. Like any other business, a grocery store uses internal control activities to meet their objectives in these three areas.

Required:

Attempt to name a control for each area and describe how the control helps accomplish the store's objectives in these areas.

OBJECTIVE 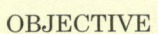 2 3

Problem 4-44A Internal Control Procedures for Cash Receipts

Corey and Dee Post are planning to open and operate a 24-hour convenience store near a university campus. Corey and Dee are concerned that part of the cash that customers pay for merchandise might be kept by some of the store's employees.

Required:

Identify some internal control procedures that could help ensure that all cash paid by customers is remitted to the business.

Problem 4-45A Internal Control for Cash

OBJECTIVE ② ③

After comparing cash register tapes with inventory records, the accountant for Benning Convenience Stores is concerned that someone at one of the stores is not recording some of that store's cash sales and is stealing the cash from the unreported sales.

Required:
1. **Conceptual Connection:** Explain why a comparison of sales and inventory records would reveal a situation in which cash sales are not being recorded and cash from those sales is being stolen.
2. **Conceptual Connection:** Describe how an employee might be able to steal cash from sales.
3. What internal control procedures would you recommend to make the theft you described in requirement 2 more difficult?

Problem 4-46A Bank Reconciliation

OBJECTIVE ③

Shortly after July 31, Morse Corporation received a bank statement containing the following information:

Date		Checks			Deposits	Balance
6/30	Beg. balance					$ 7,958
7/1					$ 1,200	9,158
7/2		$ 620	$ 550	$ 344	12,500	20,144
7/3		35	8,100			12,009
7/5		311	97	4,000	9,100	16,701
7/9		4,500	790	286		11,125
7/12		34	7,100			3,991
7/15		634	1,880		7,000	8,477
7/19		3,780	414			4,283
7/24		1,492	649			2,142
7/29		350	677*		4,620	5,735
7/31		575	18**			5,142

*NSF check
**Bank service charge

July cash transactions and balances on Morse's records are shown in the following T-account:

	Cash					
Balance, 6/30	**$ 7,609**					
Date	Amount Deposited	Check Number	Check Amount	Check Number	Check Amount	
7/1	$12,500	176	$8,100	186	$ 1,880	
7/5	9,100	177	97	187	634	
7/15	7,000	178	4,000	188	3,780	
7/29	4,620	179	311	189	649	
7/30	2,050	180	7,100	190	1,492	
Total deposits	$35,270	181	4,500	191	37	
		182	790	192	350	
		183	34	193	575	
		184	286	194	227	
		185	414	195	1,123	
Balance, 7/31	**$ 6,500**	Total disbursements			$36,379	

Required:
1. Prepare a bank reconciliation for July.
2. Prepare the adjusting entries made by Morse Corporation as a result of this reconciliation process.
3. What amount is reported as cash on the balance sheet at July 31?

OBJECTIVE 3

Problem 4-47A Bank Reconciliation

Raymond Corporation received the following bank statement for the month of October:

Date	Checks			Deposits	Balance
9/30 Beg. balance					$ 4,831.50
10/2	$1,204.50			$2,970.18	6,597.18
10/4	43.80	$ 321.70			6,231.68
10/8	905.36				5,326.32
10/10	100.20	60.00	$38.11		5,128.01
10/13				4,000.00	9,128.01
10/14	290.45*				8,837.56
10/17	516.11	309.24			8,012.21
10/19	106.39	431.15	21.72	2,850.63	10,303.58
10/21	3,108.42				7,195.16
10/23	63.89				7,131.27
10/25	290.00**	111.90			6,729.37
10/27	88.90				6,640.47
10/31	20.00***	1,308.77			5,311.70

  *NSF check
 **Debit memo (Rent Expense)
***Service charge

The cash records of Raymond Corporation provide the following information:

Date	Item	Debit	Credit	Balance
10/1	Balance from 9/30			$ 6,553.38
10/2	Check #1908		$ 321.70	6,231.68
10/5	Check #1909		905.36	5,326.32
10/6	Check #1910		100.20	5,226.12
10/6	Check #1911		60.00	5,166.12
10/7	Check #1912		38.11	5,128.01
10/12	Deposit #411	$4,000.00		9,128.01
10/15	Check #1913		516.11	8,611.90
10/16	Check #1914		309.24	8,302.66
10/17	Check #1915		431.15	7,871.51
10/17	Check #1916		21.72	7,849.79
10/18	Deposit #412	2,850.63		10,700.42
10/18	Check #1917		106.39	10,594.03
10/20	Check #1918		63.89	10,530.14
10/20	Check #1919		3,108.42	7,421.72
10/23	Check #1920		111.90	7,309.82
10/25	Check #1921		88.90	7,220.92
10/29	Check #1922		1,803.77	5,417.15
10/30	Check #1923		284.77	5,132.38
10/31	Check #1924		628.32	4,504.06
10/31	Deposit #413	3,408.20		7,912.26

The items on the bank statement are correct. The debit memo is for the payment by the bank of Raymond's office furniture rent expense for October.

Required:
1. Prepare a bank reconciliation. (*Hint*: There is one transposition error in the cash account.)
2. Prepare adjusting entries based on the bank reconciliation.
3. What amount is reported for cash in bank in the balance sheet at October 31?

OBJECTIVE 3

Problem 4-48A Bank Reconciliation

The cash account of Dixon Products reveals the following information:

Cash			
Balance, 4/30	11,800		
Deposits during May	37,600	Checks written during May	41,620

The bank statement for May contains the following information:

Bank balance, 4/30		$ 11,750
Add: Deposits during May		37,250
		$ 49,000
Less: Checks paid during May	$(40,230)	
NSF check from Frolin Inc.	(190)	
Bank service charges	(40)	(40,460)
Bank balance, 5/31		$ 8,540

A comparison of detailed company records with the bank statement indicates the following information:

	At 4/30	At 5/31
Deposit in transit	$800	$1,150
Outstanding checks	750	2,140

The bank amounts are determined to be correct.

Required:
1. Prepare a bank reconciliation for May.
2. Prepare the adjusting entries made by Dixon as a result of the reconciliation process.
3. What amount is reported for cash on the balance sheet at May 31?

Problem 4-49A Recording Petty Cash Transactions

OBJECTIVE

SCB Inc. had a balance of $400 in cash in its petty cash fund at the beginning of September. The following transactions took place in September:

a. On September 4, the custodian paid $43 out of petty cash for new stationery on which the company president's name appeared prominently. This is considered supplies.
b. On September 11, the custodian paid $75 out of petty cash for maintenance manuals for some equipment. This is a maintenance expense.
c. On September 15, the custodian paid $33 out of petty cash for transportation-in.
d. On September 23, the custodian paid $46 out of petty cash to have documents delivered to the lawyers who were defending the firm in a lawsuit. This is considered an other expense.
e. On September 27, the custodian paid $123 out of petty cash to reimburse the president for costs he had incurred when bad weather prevented the company jet from landing to pick him up after a meeting. This is a travel expense.
f. On September 30, the custodian submitted receipts for the above expenditures and a check was drawn for the amount to replenish the fund.

Required:
Prepare any journal entries made by the corporation to record these transactions.

PROBLEM SET B

Problem 4-43B Role of Internal Control

OBJECTIVE

Internal control systems include policies and procedures designed to provide reasonable assurance that the corporation's objectives are being met in three areas: (a) effectiveness and efficiency of operations, (b) reliability of financial reporting, and (c) compliance with applicable laws and regulations. Like any other business, a bookstore uses internal control activities to meet its objectives in these three areas.

Required:
Attempt to name a control for each area and describe how the control helps accomplish the store's objectives in these areas.

OBJECTIVE ② ③

Problem 4-44B Internal Control Procedures for Cash Receipts

Sean and Liz Kinsella are planning to open and operate a coffee shop on a university campus. Sean and Liz are concerned that part of the cash that customers pay for food might be kept by some of the store's employees.

Required:

Identify some internal control procedures that could help ensure that all cash paid by customers is remitted to the business.

OBJECTIVE ② ③

Problem 4-45B Internal Control for Cash

After comparing cash register tapes with inventory records, the accountant for Good Times Music store is concerned that someone at one of the stores is not recording some of that store's cash sales and is stealing the cash from the unreported sales.

Required:

1. **Conceptual Connection:** Explain why a comparison of sales and inventory records would reveal a situation in which cash sales are not being recorded and cash from those sales is being stolen.
2. **Conceptual Connection:** Describe how an employee might be able to steal cash from sales.

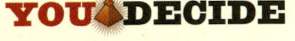

3. What internal control procedures would you recommend to make the theft you described in requirement 2 more difficult?

OBJECTIVE ③

Problem 4-46B Bank Reconciliation

Shortly after July 31, Towanda Corporation received a bank statement containing the following information:

Date		Checks			Deposits	Balance
6/30	Beg. balance					$ 5,550
7/1					$ 300	5,850
7/2		$ 270	$ 150	$ 330	4,500	9,600
7/3		25	7,025			2,550
7/5		150	450	1,400	10,000	10,550
7/9		1,500	25	325		8,700
7/12		500	100			8,100
7/15		1,600	2,700		3,500	7,300
7/19		75	425			6,800
7/24		650	550			5,600
7/29			525*			5,075
7/31			25**			5,050

*NSF check (deposited in previous period, but withdrawn this period)
**Bank service charge

July cash transactions and balances on Towanda's records are shown in the following T-account:

Cash							
Balance, 6/30	$ 5,550						
	Amount		Check	Check		Check	Check
Date	Deposited		Number	Amount		Number	Amount
7/1	$ 300		176	$ 270		186	$ 25
7/5	4,500		177	150		187	100
7/15	10,000		178	330		188	500
7/29	3,500		179	25		189	2,700
7/30	950		180	7,025		190	1,600
Total deposits	$19,250		181	150		191	75
			182	450		192	425
			183	1,400		193	550
			184	1,500		194	650
			185	325		195	275
Balance, 7/31	$ 6,275			Total disbursements			$18,525

Required:

1. Prepare a bank reconciliation for July.
2. Prepare the adjusting entries made by Towanda Corporation as a result of this reconciliation process.
3. What amount is reported as cash on the balance sheet at July 31?

Problem 4-47B Bank Reconciliation

OBJECTIVE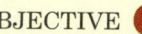

Donald Corporation received the bank statement shown below for the month of October:

Date	Checks			Deposits		Balance
9/30 Beg. balance						$ 5,205
10/2	$1,200			$2,950		6,955
10/4	50	$ 300				6,605
10/8	900					5,705
10/10	100	60	$35			5,510
10/13				4,000		9,510
10/14	300*					9,210
10/17	525	325				8,360
10/19	105	430	20	2,850		10,655
10/21	3,110					7,545
10/23	65					7,480
10/25	250**	110				7,120
10/27	90					7,030
10/31	25***	1,305				5,700

*NSF check
**Debit memo (Rent Expense)
***Service charge

The cash records of Donald Corporation provide the following information:

Date	Item	Debit	Credit	Balance
10/1	Balance from 9/30			$ 6,905
10/2	Check #1908		$ 300	6,605
10/5	Check #1909		900	5,705
10/6	Check #1910		100	5,605
10/6	Check #1911		60	5,545
10/7	Check #1912		35	5,510
10/12	Deposit #411	$4,000		9,510
10/15	Check #1913		525	8,985
10/16	Check #1914		325	8,660
10/17	Check #1915		430	8,230
10/17	Check #1916		20	8,210
10/18	Deposit #412	2,850		11,060
10/18	Check #1917		105	10,955
10/20	Check #1918		65	10,890
10/20	Check #1919		3,110	7,780
10/23	Check #1920		110	7,670
10/25	Check #1921		90	7,580
10/29	Check #1922		1,350	6,230
10/30	Check #1923		250	5,980
10/31	Check #1924		650	5,330
10/31	Deposit #413	3,300		8,630

The items on the bank statement are correct. The debit memo is for the payment by the bank of Donald's office furniture rent expense for October.

Required:

1. Prepare a bank reconciliation. (*Hint:* There is one transposition error in the cash account.)
2. Prepare adjusting entries based on the bank reconciliation.
3. What amount is reported for cash in bank on the balance sheet at October 31?

OBJECTIVE

Problem 4-48B Bank Reconciliation

The cash account of Mason Products reveals the following information:

Cash			
Balance, 4/30	10,100		
Deposits during May	39,600	Checks written during May	40,000

The bank statement for May contains the following information:

Bank balance, 4/30		$ 10,100
Add: Deposits during May		37,400
		$ 47,500
Less: Checks paid during May	$(38,500)	
NSF check from Higgins Inc.	(140)	
Bank service charges	(60)	(38,700)
Bank balance, 5/31		$ 8,800

A comparison of detailed company records with the bank statement indicates the following information:

	At 4/30	At 5/31
Deposit in transit	$900	$2,200
Outstanding checks	550	1,500

The bank amounts are determined to be correct.

Required:

1. Prepare a bank reconciliation for May.
2. Prepare the adjusting entries made by Mason Products as a result of the reconciliation process.
3. What amount is reported for cash on the balance sheet at May 31?

OBJECTIVE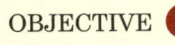

Problem 4-49B Recording Petty Cash Transactions

Chicago Inc. had a balance of $1,200 in cash in its petty cash fund at the beginning of September. The following transactions took place in September:

a. On September 4, the custodian paid $75 out of petty cash for new stationery on which the company president's name appeared prominently. This is considered supplies expense.
b. On September 11, the custodian paid $350 out of petty cash for maintenance manuals for some equipment. This is a maintenance expense.
c. On September 15, the custodian paid $25 out of petty cash for transportation-in.
d. On September 23, the custodian paid $50 out of petty cash to have documents delivered to the lawyers who were defending the firm in a lawsuit. This is considered an other expense.
e. On September 27, the custodian paid $175 out of petty cash to reimburse the president for costs he had incurred when bad weather prevented the company jet from landing to pick him up after a meeting. This is a travel expense.
f. On September 30, the custodian submitted receipts for the above expenditures and a check was drawn for the amount to replenish the fund.

Required:

Prepare any journal entries made by the corporation to record these transactions.

CASES

Case 4-50 Ethics and Cash Controls

Suppose that you have just been hired as a part-time clerk in a large department store. Each week you work three evenings and all day Saturday. Without the income provided by this job, you would be unable to stay in college. Charles Riley, the manager in the clothing department to which you are assigned, has worked for the store for many years. Managers receive both a salary and a commission on their sales.

Late one afternoon, just as you begin work, Mr. Riley is ringing up a purchase. You observe that the purchase consists of two expensive suits, a coat, and several pairs of trousers and that the customer declines Mr. Riley's offer to have the store's tailor do the alterations. After the customer departs with his merchandise and as Mr. Riley is departing for the evening, you say, "See you tomorrow." Mr. Riley gives a brief, barely audible response and departs for the evening.

As you return to the sales counter, you glance at the paper tape displayed through a small opening in the cash register that records all sales on an item-by-item basis. You have just completed the store course in register operation, so you are quite familiar with the register and the tape it produces. To your surprise, you note that the last sale consisted of just a single pair of trousers.

Required:

1. What do you conclude about this transaction?
2. What are the possible consequences for the store, for Mr. Riley, and for you personally of reporting your observations to Mr. Riley's superiors?
3. What are the possible consequences for the store, for Mr. Riley, and for you personally of *not* reporting your observations to Mr. Riley's superiors?
4. What would your decision be?

Case 4-51 The Operating Cycle

There are two retail stores in Millersburgh. One is a full-service store that typically sells on credit to its customers; the other is a smaller discount store that usually sells for cash. Full-service stores typically charge higher prices than do discount stores for identical items.

Required:

1. Does the operating cycle suggest some economic reason for a portion of this price difference? Explain your answer.
2. Can you think of other reasons why a full-service store might charge more than a discount store for the same merchandise?

YOU◆DECIDE

Case 4-52 Internal Controls for Cash Disbursements

Campus Supply Store purchases merchandise on credit from a large number of suppliers. During the past five years, Campus's annual sales have grown from $100,000 to $1,500,000. A recent article in the local newspaper disclosed that an employee of another firm had been arrested for embezzling funds from his employer by diverting payments for purchases to his own bank account. Because of that article, the accountant for Campus has decided to examine Campus's procedures for purchases and payables.

Currently three different employees are authorized to order merchandise for the store. These employees normally complete paperwork provided by the suppliers' sales representatives, keeping a copy for their records. When the ordered merchandise arrives, whomever the delivery person can locate signs for the package. Bills are sent to the store by suppliers and are paid by Campus's accountant when due.

Required:

1. Indicate which general principles of internal control are violated by Campus's procedures for purchases and payables.
2. Recommend procedures that would incorporate the five general categories of internal control where possible.

YOU◆DECIDE

Case 4-53 Internal Controls for Collection of Receivables

Carolyn Furniture Galleries sells traditional furniture from two stores in St. Louis. Carolyn's credit terms allow customers to pay for purchases over three months with no finance charges. Carolyn's accountant has been responsible for approving customers for credit, recording cash received from customers in the accounting records, depositing cash collections in the bank, and following up on customers who are behind in their payments. Each month the accountant has prepared a report for Carolyn's president, indicating the cash collected, outstanding receivables, and uncollectible accounts.

(Continued)

Carolyn's president has been concerned about a significant increase in uncollectible accounts that began about two years ago, shortly after the current accountant was hired. Recently, a personal friend of Carolyn's president called. The caller had moved from St. Louis to Denver about six months ago. A month ago, the caller's new bank had refused a loan because a credit rating bureau in St. Louis had indicated that the caller had left bills unpaid at Carolyn Furniture. Carolyn's president knew that the caller had paid his account before leaving the community.

Carolyn's president called a detective agency and arranged for an investigation. Two weeks later, Carolyn's president was informed that the accountant had been spending much more money than his salary would warrant. Carolyn then called its auditor and arranged to have the accounting records for receivables and uncollectible accounts examined. This examination indicated that about $400,000 of cash had been stolen from the firm by the accountant. The accountant had identified customers who had moved and had recorded cash sales to continuing customers as credit sales in the accounts of the relocated customers. Carolyn's accountant had kept the cash received from the cash sales and had eventually written off the fictitious credit sales as uncollectible accounts. Without the accountant's knowledge, one of Carolyn's new employees had sent the names of the customers who had apparently defaulted on their accounts to the credit bureau.

YOU◆DECIDE

Required:

Identify the internal control weaknesses that permitted the accountant to steal the $400,000. Suggest internal control procedures that would make it difficult for someone else to repeat this theft.

Case 4-54 Cash Management

Hollis Corporation has the following budgeted schedule for expected cash receipts and cash disbursement.

Month	Expected Cash Receipts	Expected Cash Disbursements
July	$210,000	$200,000
August	280,000	210,000
September	230,000	190,000
October	160,000	180,000

Hollis begins July with a cash balance of $20,000, $15,000 of short-term debt, and no short-term investments. Hollis uses the following cash management policy:

a. End-of-month cash should equal $20,000 plus the excess of expected disbursements over receipts for the next month.
b. If receipts are expected to exceed disbursements in the next month, the current month ending cash balance should be $20,000.
c. Excess cash should be invested in short-term investments unless there is short-term debt, in which case excess cash should first be used to reduce the debt.
d. Cash deficiencies are met first by selling short-term investments and second by incurring short-term debt.

Required:

1. Calculate the expected buying and selling of short-term investments and the incurrence and repayment of short-term debt at the end of July, August, and September.
2. Discuss the general considerations that help accountants develop a cash management policy.

Case 4-55 Cash and Internal Controls

Identify a business with which you are familiar.

YOU◆DECIDE

Required:

1. Describe the ways in which it prevents theft of cash.
2. Can you think of a way in which dishonest employees could circumvent the internal controls and steal cash?

Case 4-56 Researching and Analysis Using the Annual Report

Obtain Microsoft's June 30, 2009, 10-K through the "Investor Relations" portion of their website (do a search for Microsoft investor relations) or go to http://www.sec.gov and click "Search for Company Filings" under "Filings & Forms."

Required:

1. How much cash and equivalents and short-term investments did Microsoft hold as a percentage of total assets in 2008 and 2009?
2. What is Microsoft's definition of a cash equivalent (see Note 1)? Does this appear consistent with other companies' definitions?
3. Look at Note 4 and specify how much of Microsoft's cash and equivalent balance is actually cash. What is their largest (in dollar terms) cash equivalent?
4. Locate the certifications required by the CEO and CFO under Section 302 of the Sarbanes-Oxley Act. (*Hint*: It is in Exhibits 31-1 and 31-2 at the end of the 10-K.) Who signed these certifications?

Case 4-57 Comparative Analysis: Abercrombie & Fitch versus Aeropostale

Refer to the financial statements of Abercrombie & Fitch and Aeropostale that are supplied with this text.

Required:

1. How much cash and equivalents and short-term investments (or current marketable securities) did Aeropostale and Abercrombie & Fitch hold as a percentage of total assets at January 30, 2010, and January 31, 2009? Hint: It may help to do a search for "equivalents" in a word or pdf version of the 10-K.
2. Speculate as to differences in cash management policies between the two companies.
3. Describe the change in cash and equivalents and marketable securities as a percentage of total assets for Abercrombie & Fitch between 2009 and 2010.
4. Locate the Audit Opinion and describe the criteria by which Abercrombie & Fitch's and Aeropostale's internal control systems were evaluated.

YOU◆DECIDE

Case 4-58 CONTINUING PROBLEM: FRONT ROW ENTERTAINMENT

Over the next two months, Front Row Entertainment continued to enjoy success in signing artists and promoting their events. However, the increased business has put considerable stress on keeping timely and up-to-date financial records. In particular, both Cam and Anna are concerned with the accounting and management of the company's cash.

The tour promotion industry is a cash-intensive industry, normally requiring large prepayments to secure venues and arrange advertising. When the number of artists under contract were small, Cam and Anna developed a simple system to manage the company's cash. Normally, any cash received was put in a file cabinet in the company's office. If the amount appeared to be getting large, a deposit was made. Similarly, if a large check needed to be written, either Cam or Anna would check the balance in the checkbook. If cash was not sufficient to cover the check, they'd get cash from the file cabinet and deposit the amount necessary to cover the check. However, with the increasing business, they would often forget to make deposits, causing several checks to be returned for nonsufficient funds. In addition, they were in the process of hiring additional office staff who would start work on May 1. They knew that leaving cash in a file cabinet would not be a good idea.

In order to obtain a better understanding of their cash position, Anna decides to perform a bank reconciliation—something she had failed to do since the company was started. According to the accounting records, the cash balance at April 30 was $7,495. Anna obtained the following information from Front Row's April bank statement and an analysis of canceled checks and deposits:

(Continued)

Balance per bank at April 30	$3,250
Deposits in transit at April 30	4,370
Outstanding checks as of April 30	1,160
Debit memo for April utilities	845
Bank service charge for April	50
Interest earned during April	450
NSF check from customer	590

Required:

1. Discuss the purpose of an internal control system. How would the development of an internal control system benefit Front Row Entertainment? In your answer, be sure to highlight any problems that you noted with Front Row Entertainment's current system of accounting for cash.

2. Prepare a bank reconciliation for Front Row Entertainment for the period ending April 30, 2011.

3. Prepare any adjusting entries necessary because of the bank reconciliation.

4. How did the failure to prepare a bank reconciliation affect the amounts reported on the previous financial statements?

5

Sales and Receivables

Doug Norman Crystals/Alamy

After studying Chapter 5, you should be able to:

1. Explain the criteria for revenue recognition.

2. Measure net sales revenue.

3. Describe the principal types of receivables.

4. Measure and interpret bad debt expense and the allowance for doubtful accounts.

5. Describe the cash flow implications of accounts receivable.

6. Account for notes receivable from inception to maturity.

7. Describe internal control procedures for merchandise sales.

8. Analyze profitability and asset management using sales and receivables.

izmostock/Alamy

EXPERIENCE FINANCIAL ACCOUNTING

with Mitsubishi

Mitsubishi's U.S. sales increased from 191,000 cars in 1998 to 322,000 cars in 2001. This 68.5% sales growth made it the fastest growing auto brand in the U.S. Marketed toward Gen Y, Mitsubishi developed an "edgy" image with cross promotions such as Universal Film's *2 Fast 2 Furious*. They also offered a "0-0-0" finance offer—0 percent down, 0 percent interest, and $0 monthly payments for 12 months.

Unfortunately, the economic downturn at the turn of the century hurt Mitsubishi's Gen Y target buyer particularly hard. Consequently, many buyers in the 0-0-0 financing program never made a single payment (some reports put this number as high as 50 or 60 percent of the buyers in this program), leaving Mitsubishi with a year-old used car. This resulted in Mitsubishi taking a loss on bad debts of $454 million during the first half of 2003. Since Mitsubishi operates on a fiscal year of April 1–March 31, this loss was reported in fiscal year 2002.

As you will learn in this chapter, net realizable value is the amount that a company expects to collect from its outstanding accounts receivable. Notice in the graph below, the drop in net realizable value in 2002, due to the loss on bad debts. A loss on bad debts is reported on the income statement, but as you can see here, the loss also impacts the balance sheet. This illustrates an important lesson. You have to be careful to whom you give credit.

In this chapter, we discuss the reporting and analyzing of sales and any related receivables. First, we discuss the timing of revenue recognition. This is followed by accounting for three modifications to sales—sales discounts, sales returns, and sales allowances. We then shift our attention to receivables. When sales are made on credit, the seller recognizes a receivable. Because the collectability of these receivables is uncertain and the balances are often significant, as illustrated in the discussion of Mitsubishi, companies must attempt to appropriately value and manage these assets.

Turning our attention to sales, there are two primary questions in revenue recognition. First, in which period (for example, 2011 or 2012) should the revenue be recognized? Second, what amount of revenue should be recorded?

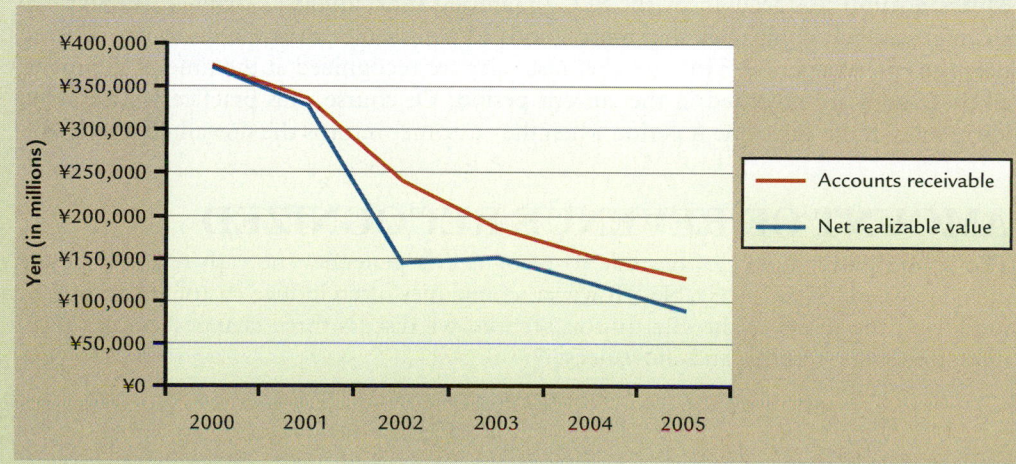

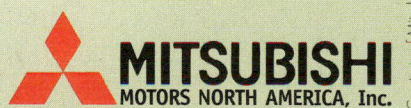

TIMING OF REVENUE RECOGNITION

While cash-basis accounting recognizes revenue in the period payment is received (as on your tax return), accrual-basis accounting recognizes revenue when it is (1) **realized** or **realizable** and (2) **earned**.

The term "realized" means that non-cash resources (such as inventory) have been exchanged for cash or near cash (accounts receivable). This happens, for example, when Foot Locker exchanges a pair of shoes (its inventory and a non-cash resource) for cash or an account receivable. "Realizable" describes a situation where non-cash resources (such as inventory) are readily convertible into known amounts of cash. For example, after a gold mine extracts the gold, the gold (a non-cash resource) is readily convertible into cash because there is an active market for gold. Other examples of non-cash resources readily convertible to cash include wheat, corn, and soybeans.

As for the second criterion, revenues are considered "earned" when the earnings process is substantially complete. For most retail sales, this occurs at the point of sale. That is, the store fulfills its obligation to you when it lets you walk out of the store with the pair of shoes you just bought. For service organizations, the earnings process is substantially complete when the service is performed. For example, if Gold's Gym collects $1,200 for a year-long membership, it should recognize $100 per month. Or, when American Airlines collects $450 in January for a flight to Mexico during spring break, it will recognize the revenue after the flight is provided.

Because sales transactions can be extremely complicated and businesses frequently attempt to recognize revenue too soon, the Securities and Exchange Commission (SEC) has issued further guidance on revenue recognition. Specifically, the SEC maintains that revenue is realized or realizable and earned when the following criteria are met:[1]

- Persuasive evidence of an arrangement exists (e.g., a contract or other proof of the details of the exchange).
- Delivery has occurred or services have been provided.
- The seller's price to the buyer is fixed and determinable.
- Collectability is reasonably assured.

Although these criteria are easy to understand, they can be difficult to apply to complicated sales contracts. Such complicated transactions are best left to more advanced accounting courses. For now, recognize that the vast majority of sales transactions are straightforward and simple—service companies (such as airlines, accountants, lawyers, health clubs, lawn services, etc.) recognize revenue in the period they provide the services to the customer and sellers of goods recognize revenue in the period when title passes (the customer takes possession of the goods).

ETHICAL DECISIONS   Publicly-traded corporations are under tremendous pressure to meet analyst targets for key financial-statement data, such as sales (and earnings per share). Many corporations, when faced with the reality of sales not meeting analysts' targets, resorted to a variety of practices to avoid such shortfalls. For example, Bristol-Myers Squibb was accused by the SEC of, among other things, "channel stuffing." In channel stuffing, companies ship more goods to a customer than the customer ordered near the end of a period. However, because sales are recognized at the time of shipment, all these sales are recorded in the current period. Of course, this practice will result in lower sales in the subsequent period when the customer returns the unwanted goods. ●

AMOUNT OF REVENUE RECOGNIZED

The appropriate amount of revenue to recognize is generally the cash received or the cash equivalent of the receivable. However, companies often induce customers to buy by modifying the terms of the sale. In this section, we discuss three changes to sales revenues: discounts, returns, and allowances.

---

[1] Staff Accounting Bulletin (SAB) 104.

Sales Discounts

To encourage prompt payment, businesses may offer a **sales discount**. This discount is a reduction of the normal selling price and is attractive to both the seller and the buyer. For the buyer, it is a reduction to the cost of the goods and services. For the seller, the cash is more quickly available and collection costs are reduced. For example, when cash is not available quickly, the seller may need to borrow money in order to pay its suppliers, employees, etc. The interest expense associated with borrowing money has a negative effect on net income.

Sales invoices use a standard notation to state discount and credit terms. For example, the invoice of a seller who expects payment in 30 days and offers a 2 percent discount if payment is made within 10 days would bear the notation 2/10, n/30 (which is read "2/10, net 30"). The notation n/30 indicates that the gross amount of the invoice (the full pre-discount amount) must be paid in 30 days. The notation 2/10 indicates that, if payment is made within the 10-day discount period, the amount owed is 2 percent less than the gross (pre-discount) amount of the invoice. Of course, if payment is made within the 20 days following the end of the discount period, then the amount owed is equal to the gross (pre-discount) amount of the invoice.

Most companies record the sale and the associated receivable at the gross (pre-discount) amount of the invoice. This is called the "gross method."[2] If payment is received after the discount period, the cash received equals the associated receivable so no adjustment is needed. But when a discount is taken, the amount of the discount is recorded in a contra-revenue account (i.e., it reduces Gross Sales Revenue to Net Sales Revenue) called *sales discounts*, which balances the entry. This method is illustrated in **CORNERSTONE 5-1**.

 **CORNERSTONE 5-1**   **Recording Receivables Using the Gross Method**

Concept:
Sales discounts offered to encourage prompt payment are recorded at the gross (pre-discount) amount of the invoice. If the discount is taken, a debit is made to Sales Discounts at the time of payment.

Information:
On May 5, 2011, GCD Advisors billed Richardson's Wholesale Hardware $15,000 for consulting services provided during April. GCD offered terms of 2/10, n/30.

Required:
1. Prepare the journal entry to record the sale using the gross method.
2. Prepare the journal entry assuming the payment is received on May 15, 2011 (within the discount period).
3. Prepare the journal entry assuming the payment is received on May 25, 2011 (after the discount period).
4. How would sales revenues be disclosed on the income statement assuming the payment is made within 10 days?

Solution:

Date	Account and Explanation	Debit	Credit
1. May 5, 2011	Accounts Receivable	15,000	
	Sales Revenue		15,000
	(Record sale of merchandise)		

Assets	= Liabilities +	Stockholders' Equity
+15,000		+15,000

(Continued)

[2] GAAP also allows the "net method" of accounting for receivables with sales discounts. This method is demonstrated in intermediate accounting courses.

Date	Account and Explanation	Debit	Credit			
2. May 15, 2011	Cash*	14,700				
	Sales Discounts**	300		**Assets**	**= Liabilities +**	**Stockholders' Equity**
	Accounts Receivable		15,000	+14,700		−300
	(Record collection within the discount period)			−15,000		
3. May 25, 2011	Cash	15,000				
	Accounts Receivable		15,000	**Assets**	**= Liabilities +**	**Stockholders' Equity**
	(Record collection after the discount period)			+15,000		
				−15,000		

*$15,000 × 98%
**$15,000 × 2%

4. Partial income statement:

Sales revenue	$15,000
Less: Sales discounts	(300)
Net sales	$14,700

**CORNERSTONE
5-1**
(continued)

It is also important to monitor changes in how customers use sales discounts. For example, customers who stop taking sales discounts may be experiencing cash flow problems and therefore are potential credit risks. On the other hand, failure of a large number of customers to take discounts may indicate that an increase in the discount percentage is needed.

Finally, sales discounts must be distinguished from both trade and quantity discounts:

- A *trade discount* is a reduction in the selling price granted by the seller to a particular class of customers, for example, to customers who purchase goods for resale rather than for use.
- A *quantity discount* is a reduction in the selling price granted by the seller because selling costs per unit are less when larger quantities are ordered. This is why, for example, a 32-ounce soft drink does not cost double what a 16-ounce one costs at a restaurant.

For accounting purposes, the selling or invoice price is usually assumed to be the price after adjustment for the trade or quantity discounts; accordingly, trade and quantity discounts are not recorded separately in the accounting records.

Sales Returns and Allowances

Occasionally, a customer will return goods as unsatisfactory. In other cases, a customer may agree to keep goods with minor defects if the seller is willing to make an "allowance" by reducing the selling price. The accounting for sales returns and allowances, which is described in the paragraphs that follow, has the effect of reversing all or part of a previously recorded sale.

When goods or services arrive late, or in some other way are rendered less valuable, a customer may be induced to accept the goods/services if a price reduction, called a **sales allowance**, is offered by the seller. A contra-revenue account called *sales returns and allowances* (returns are discussed next) is used to record the price reduction. For example, on November 1, GCD Advisors completed a consulting project for Bolt Manufacturing for which the agreed upon price was $11,400. Because GCD had promised Bolt that the project would be completed by September 15, GCD offered and Bolt accepted, a $1,600 reduction as an allowance for the missed deadline. GCD made the following accounting entries to record these events:

Date	Account and Explanation	Debit	Credit
Nov. 1, 2011	Accounts Receivable	11,400	
	Sales Revenue		11,400
	(Record sale of services)		
Nov. 1, 2011	Sales Returns & Allowances	1,600	
	Accounts Receivable		1,600
	(Record allowance for missed deadline)		

Assets	= Liabilities +	Stockholders' Equity
+11,400		+11,400

Assets	= Liabilities +	Stockholders' Equity
−1,600		−1,600

If the bill has already been paid, the seller can either refund a portion of the purchase price and record a credit to cash or apply the allowance against future purchases by the customer by recording a credit to accounts receivable.

Merchandise or goods returned by the customer to the seller are **sales returns**. Companies also record these returned goods in *sales returns and allowances*. Sales returns will be discussed in Chapter 6 when we introduce inventory.

On the income statement, as indicated in Chapter 2, sales returns and allowances, like sales discounts, are subtracted from gross sales revenue to produce **net sales revenue**, as shown here:

Sales revenue	$752,000
Less: Sales returns and allowances	(1,600)
Net sales	$750,400

In other words, sales returns and allowances is a contra-revenue account. Presenting both gross sales revenue and sales returns and allowances, rather than net sales revenue alone, permits financial-statement users to respond to unusual behavior in either account. Careful users of financial statements look for unusual behavior in both sales revenue and sales returns and allowances in the income statement. Often, significant changes in these accounts help to explain other changes in income statement or balance sheet accounts, as illustrated in the You Decide below.

 **YOU DECIDE**   Sales Returns and Allowances

You are the Controller at Interplains, Inc. Data for the past four years for sales revenue, sales returns and allowances, and net income are shown below.

	2008	2009	2010	2011
Sales revenue	$624,000	$653,000	$671,000	$887,000
Sales returns and allowances	6,100	6,400	6,300	14,800
Net income	30,000	29,000	31,500	12,200

What concerns are raised by the significant changes in sales revenue, sales returns and allowances, and net income in 2011?

Sales revenue, which had been relatively stable, increased by 32 percent in 2011. Often, significant growth in output is accompanied by quality assurance problems, as might be indicated by the 135 percent growth in sales returns and allowances. A check of production data might reveal the use of less highly trained workers or supervisors, or might indicate that the current workforce is being worked heavily on overtime.

Further, notice the significant decrease in net income despite the large increase in sales revenue. When this happens, you must attempt to discover why. For example, when a firm becomes significantly more or less profitable, the attitude of the employees toward their work can change, causing changes in the quality of output. Some key employees may leave a firm with declining profitability, thus causing quality difficulties.

Significant changes in sales revenue, sales returns and allowances, and net income can indicate important changes or trends in the workforce or workflow and should be analyzed so that management can take appropriate action.

OBJECTIVE
Describe the principal types of receivables.

IFRS

The recognition and valuation of receivables under IFRS is generally the same as U.S. GAAP.

TYPES OF RECEIVABLES

Now that we've addressed the timing of revenue recognition and measurement of net sales revenue, we will shift our attention to the accounting and analysis of the related receivables.

A receivable is money due from another business or individual. Receivables are typically categorized along three different dimensions:

- *Accounts Receivable or Notes Receivable:* A "note" is a legal document given by a borrower to a lender stating the timing of repayment and the amount (principal and/or interest) to be repaid. We discuss notes receivable later in the chapter. **Accounts receivable**, on the other hand, do not have a formal note. For example, while you likely signed a formal agreement to rent your apartment, you probably did not sign a formal agreement for your utilities.
- *Current or Noncurrent Receivables:* Although in practice both accounts and notes receivable are typically classified as current, accounts receivable are typically due in 30 to 60 days and do not have interest while notes receivable have interest and typically are due in anywhere from 3 to 12 months. Of course, if the due date is over one year, the note receivable typically will be classified as noncurrent.
- *Trade or Nontrade Receivables:* **Trade receivables** are due from customers purchasing inventory in the ordinary course of business while **nontrade receivables** arise from transactions not involving inventory (such as interest receivable or cash advances to employees).

OBJECTIVE
Measure and interpret bad debt expense and the allowance for doubtful accounts.

ACCOUNTING FOR BAD DEBTS

We discussed the recognition of accounts receivable in the sales section, but an equally important concept is ensuring that the proper amount for accounts receivable is shown on the balance sheet. GAAP requires accounts receivable to be shown at their "net realizable value," which is the amount of cash the company expects to collect. Unfortunately, the amount of cash collected will almost never equal the total amount recognized in accounts receivable because some customers will not pay (for example, a customer declares bankruptcy and ceases operations). When customers do not pay their accounts receivable, bad debts result (also called uncollectible accounts). Although efforts are made to control bad debts, it is an expense of providing credit to customers (the hope is that the increased business associated with providing credit more than makes up for the bad debts).

As we saw in the previous section, when sales revenues are reduced to reflect sales returns and allowances, the reductions are accomplished through a contra-revenue account. Although it might seem logical to reduce sales revenues in the same way when customers default on accounts receivable arising from credit sales, this treatment is inappropriate. Reductions in sales revenue should be recorded only for transactions that result from actions of the seller, such as acceptance of returned merchandise (a sales return) or price reductions offered to purchasers (a sales allowance). Since defaults on credit sales arise from actions of the purchaser rather than the seller, bad debts cannot be recorded as revenue reductions. If bad debts are not treated as negative revenues, then they must be treated as expenses. And if they are expenses, the question then arises as to when the expense should be recorded.

There are two methods to record **bad debt expense**: the direct write off method and the allowance method.

Direct Write-Off Method

The direct write-off method waits until an account is deemed uncollectible before reducing accounts receivable and recording the bad debt expense. As you recall, the matching concept requires that expenses be matched with the related revenues in the period in which the revenues are recognized on the income statement. Since accounts are often determined to be uncollectible in accounting periods subsequent to the sale period, the direct write-off method is inconsistent with the matching concept and can only be used if bad debts are immaterial under GAAP.

Allowance Method

In the allowance method, bad debt expense is recorded in the period of sale, which allows it to be properly matched with revenues according to the matching concept. The result is that bad debt expense is recognized before the actual default. Because defaults for the current period's sales have not actually occurred, the specific accounts receivable are not lowered; instead, an account is established to "store" the estimate until specific accounts are identified as uncollectible. This account is called **Allowance for Doubtful Accounts**.

For example, assume at the end of the first year of operations Hawthorne has an accounts receivable balance of $1,000,000. Although no customers have defaulted, Hawthorne estimates that $25,000 of that balance is uncollectible. At the end of the first year, Hawthorne would make the following adjusting entry:

Date	Account and Explanation	Debit	Credit
Dec. 31, 2010	Bad Debt Expense	25,000	
	Allowance for Doubtful Accounts		25,000
	(Record estimate of uncollectible accounts)		

Assets	= Liabilities +	Stockholders' Equity
−25,000		−25,000

This entry looks very similar to the entry that would be made under the direct write-off method. The major difference is the timing of the entry. The direct write-off method would make the entry in the period the customer defaults, while the allowance method makes the entry in the period of sale. Hawthorne's balance sheet would report accounts receivable as follows:

Accounts receivable	$1,000,000
Less: Allowance for doubtful accounts	(25,000)
Accounts receivable (net)	$ 975,000

However, it is important to recognize that Hawthorne's balance sheet would report the full $1,000,000 as accounts receivable under the direct write-off method at the end of the first year.

When a specific account is ultimately determined to be uncollectible under the allowance method, it is *written off* by a debit to the allowance account and a credit to accounts receivable. This write-off removes the defaulted balance from the accounts receivable balance and also removes it from the estimate "storage" account.

Under the allowance procedure, two methods commonly used to estimate bad debt expense are the *percentage of credit sales method* and the *aging method*.

Percentage of Credit Sales Method The simpler of the two methods for determining bad debt expense is the **percentage of credit sales method**. Using past experience and management's views of how the future may differ from the past (for example, if credit policies change), it is possible to estimate the percentage of the current period's credit sales that will eventually become uncollectible. This percentage is multiplied by the total credit sales for the period to calculate the estimated bad debt expense for the period:

Total Credit Sales × Percentage of Credit Sales Estimated to Default = Estimated Bad Debt Expense

The adjusting entry is then prepared to recognize the bad debt expense as shown in **CORNERSTONE 5-2** (p. 222).

Concept **Q&A**

Why is the direct write-off method not GAAP?

Answer:
Because the direct write-off method fails to "match" the bad debt expense to the sales revenue that it helped generate and does not show accounts receivable at net realizable value on the balance sheet.

CORNERSTONE 5-2

Estimating Bad Debt Expense Using the Percentage of Credit Sales Method

Concept:
The percentage of credit sales method estimates the ending balance in bad debt expense.

Information:
Crimson Company has credit sales of $620,000 during 2011 and estimates at the end of 2011 that 1.43 percent of these credit sales will eventually default. Also, during 2011, a customer defaults on a $524 balance related to goods purchased in 2010. Prior to the adjusting entries, Crimson's accounts receivable and allowance for doubtful accounts balances were $304,000 and $134 (credit), respectively.

Required:
1. Estimate the bad debt expense for the period.
2. Prepare the journal entry to record the write off of the defaulted $524 balance.
3. Prepare the adjusting entry to record the bad debt expense for 2011.
4. What is the net accounts receivable balance at the end of the year? How would this balance have changed if Crimson had not written off the $524 balance during 2011?

Solution:
1. $620,000 × 0.0143 = $8,866
2.

Date	Account and Explanation	Debit	Credit
Dec. 31, 2011	Allowance for Doubtful Accounts	524	
	Accounts Receivable		524
	(Record write-off of defaulted account)		

Assets	=	Liabilities	+	Stockholders' Equity
+524				
−524				

3. *Note:* The calculation in part 1 estimated the *ending* balance of bad debt expense. This amount is also the adjustment because the balance before the adjustment is zero. This is usually the case for income statement accounts because they were closed at the end of the prior year.

Date	Account and Explanation	Debit	Credit
Dec. 31, 2011	Bad Debt Expense	8,866	
	Allowance for Doubtful Accounts		8,866
	(Record adjusting entry for bad debt expense estimate)		

Assets	=	Liabilities	+	Stockholders' Equity
−8,866				−8,866

Bad Debt Expense

Preadjustment balance, 12/31/11	0	
Adjustment	**8,866**	
Ending balance	8,866	

Allowance for Doubtful Accounts

		Beginning balance	134
Write-offs during 2011	524		
Preadjustment balance, 12/31/11	390		
		Adjustment	8,866
		Ending balance	8,476

(Continued)

4.

**CORNERSTONE
5 - 2**
(continued)

	Year End	Assuming No Write-Off
Accounts receivable	$303,476*	$304,000
Less: Allowance for doubtful accounts	(8,476)**	(9,000)***
Net accounts receivable	$295,000	$295,000

*$304,000 − $524 = $303,476
**$134 − $524 + $8,866 = $8,476 (see T-account in part 3.)
***T-account from part 3 without the $524 debit for the write-off.

Note: Under the allowance method the write-off of a specific account does not affect net accounts receivable.

Occasionally, accounts receivable that are written off are later partially or entirely collected. Suppose on February 5, 2012, Crimson receives $25 of the $524 that was written off at the end of the previous year (see part 2 of Cornerstone 5-2). Crimson would make the following entries:

Date	Account and Explanation	Debit	Credit
Feb. 5, 2012	Accounts Receivable	25	
	Allowance for Doubtful Accounts		25
	(Reverse portion of write-off)		
	Cash	25	
	Accounts Receivable		25
	(Record collection of account receivable)		

Assets	=	Liabilities	+	Stockholders' Equity
+25				
−25				
+25				
−25				

Crimson's first entry reverses the appropriate portion of the write-off by restoring the appropriate portion of the accounts receivable and allowance for doubtful accounts balances. The second entry records the cash collection in the typical manner.

Aging Method   Under the **aging method**, bad debt expense is estimated by determining the collectability of the accounts receivable rather than by taking a percentage of total credit sales. At the end of each accounting period, the individual accounts receivable are categorized by age. Then an estimate is made of the amount expected to default in each age category based on past experience and expectations about how the future may differ from the past. As you may expect, the overdue accounts are more likely to default than the currently due accounts, as shown in the example below:

Accounts Receivable Age	Amount	Proportion Expected to Default	Amount Expected to Default
Less than 15 days	$190,000	0.01	$1,900
16–30 days	40,000	0.04	1,600
31–60 days	10,000	0.10	1,000
Over 61 days	9,000	0.30	2,700
	$249,000		$7,200

The total amount expected to default on year-end accounts receivable, $7,200 in the above example, is the amount that should be the ending balance in the allowance for doubtful accounts. Since the objective of the aging method is to estimate the ending balance in the allowance for doubtful accounts, any existing balance in the allowance account must be considered when determining the amount of the adjusting entry as shown in **CORNERSTONE 5-3** (p. 224).

CORNERSTONE 5-3

Estimating the Allowance for Doubtful Accounts Using the Aging Method

Concept:
An aging of the accounts receivable balance estimates the ending balance for the "allowance for doubtful accounts."

Information:
On January 1, 2011, Sullivan, Inc., has the following balances for accounts receivable and allowance for doubtful accounts:

Accounts receivable	$224,000 (debit)
Allowance for doubtful accounts	6,700 (credit)

During 2011, Sullivan had $3,100,000 of credit sales, collected $3,015,000 of accounts receivable, and wrote off $60,000 of accounts receivable as uncollectible.

Required:
1. What is Sullivan's preadjustment balance in accounts receivable on December 31, 2011?
2. What is Sullivan's preadjustment balance in allowance for doubtful accounts on December 31, 2011?
3. Assuming Sullivan's analysis of the accounts receivable balance indicates that $7,200 of the current accounts receivable balance is uncollectible, by what amount will the allowance for doubtful accounts need to be adjusted?
4. What will be the ending balance in bad debt expense?
5. Prepare the necessary adjusting entry for 2011.

Solution:

1.

Accounts Receivable			
Beginning balance	224,000		
Sales	3,100,000	Collections	3,015,000
		Write-offs	60,000
Preadjustment balance	249,000		

2.

Allowance for Doubtful Accounts			
		Beginning balance	6,700
Write-offs	60,000		
Preadjustment balance	53,300		

3.

Allowance for Doubtful Accounts			
Preadjustment balance, 12/31/11	53,300		
		Adjusting entry	**60,500***
		Adjusted balance	7,200**

*Necessary adjustment to end up with an ending balance of $7,200.
**Estimate of ending balance determined by analyzing the receivables aging. This information was given in part 3 of the "Required" section.

4.

Bad Debt Expense		
Preadjustment balance, 12/31/11	0	
Adjustment	**60,500**	
Ending balance	60,500	

(Continued)

5.

Date	Account and Explanation	Debit	Credit
Dec. 31, 2011	Bad Debt Expense	60,500	
	Allowance for Doubtful Accounts		60,500
	(Record adjusting entry for bad debt expense estimate)		

CORNERSTONE 5-3 *(continued)*

Assets	=	Liabilities	+	Stockholders' Equity
−60,500				−60,500

Comparison of Percentage of Credit Sales Method and Aging Method

The underlying difference between the percentage of credit sales method and the aging method is what is being estimated. The percentage of credit sales method is primarily concerned with appropriately estimating bad debt expense on the income statement. Because of the focus on the expense account, any existing balance in the allowance account is ignored when determining the amount of the adjusting entry. The aging method, on the other hand, is a balance sheet approach that analyzes the accounts receivable to estimate its net realizable value. This estimate provides the necessary ending allowance for doubtful accounts balance to report net accounts receivable at net realizable value.

Bad Debts from a Management Perspective

Although bad debts result from actions of the purchaser (nonpayment), the amount of bad debt expense is influenced by the credit policies of the seller, as the You Decide below illustrates.

Concept Q&A

What are the conceptual and practical differences between the percentage of credit sales and aging methods?

Answer:

The percentage of credit sales method estimates the amount to be shown as bad debt expense on the income statement. The aging method estimates the amount to be shown as the allowance for doubtful accounts on the balance sheet. The preadjustment balance in these accounts must be adjusted so that the ending balance equals the respective estimates. However, because bad debt expense is an income statement account that is closed to retained earnings at the end of every period, its preadjustment balance should be zero. As such, the adjustment is equal to the estimate of the ending balance. The allowance for doubtful accounts, on the other hand, is a balance sheet account and will typically have an existing balance.

YOU DECIDE   Are Bad Debts Always Bad?

You are the owner/operator of Mt. Sterling Drug Company, a pharmaceutical wholesaler. In response to Mt. Sterling's "cash only" sales terms, competitors have attempted to lure business away by offering various incentives. Among these are credit terms whereby a customer typically has 30 to 60 days to pay for a purchase and receives a 1 to 2 percent discount for prompt payment (usually within 10 days of sale).

Which is worse —the potential bad debts that come with offering credit or the lost business from not offering credit?

There is no question that the inability to collect an account receivable is a serious problem. However, most wholesalers have come to accept bad debts as just another business expense. Certainly, no company would grant credit knowing that the specific customer will not pay for the goods purchased. Nonetheless, granting credit is a "necessary evil"—something that must be done to generate repeat business and maintain a competitive position.

An existing relationship with customers does not guarantee future business, especially if the customers can get a better deal elsewhere. Further, prudent screening of each customer's credit history should enable you to identify some of those who may have difficulty paying their accounts. Placing such restrictions as relatively low credit limits on these risky accounts or, in some cases, denying credit altogether should help keep bad debts to a minimum.

Suppose Mt. Sterling's gross margin is 30 percent of sales and that, as a result of the more liberal credit policy, sales increase by $100,000 and bad debts are limited to 3 percent of the new credit sales. Then Mt. Sterling's income from operations should increase by $27,000 (increased gross margin of $30,000 less bad debt expense of $3,000), rather than decreasing.

When caution is used, most companies agree that the loss of business for not offering credit is more detrimental than the bad debt expenses incurred in doing so.

CASH MANAGEMENT PRINCIPLES RELATED TO ACCOUNTS RECEIVABLE

We now will focus on the cash management principles associated with accounts receivable.

Factoring Receivables

In Chapter 4, we mentioned that a principle of cash management is increasing the speed of cash collection for receivables. An increasingly common practice is to **factor**, or sell, receivables. When receivables are factored, the seller receives an immediate cash payment reduced by the factor's fees. The factor, the buyer of the receivables, acquires the right to collect the receivables and the risk of uncollectibility. In a typical factoring arrangement, the sellers of the receivables have no continuing responsibility for their collection.

Factoring arrangements vary widely, but typically the factor charges a fee ranging from 1 percent to 3 percent. This fee compensates the factor for the time value of money (i.e., interest), the risk of uncollectability, and the tasks of billing and collection. Large businesses and financial institutions frequently package factored receivables as financial instruments or securities and sell them to investors. This process is known as **securitization**. For example, **General Motors Acceptance Corporation (GMAC)** sells car loans to special financial institutions set up by investment banks. The financial institutions pay GMAC with funds raised from the sale of securities or notes, called certificates for automobile receivables (CARs). Banks use similar arrangements to package their credit card receivables into securities called certificates for amortizing revolving debts (CARDs).

Credit Cards

Bank **credit cards**, such as **Visa** and **MasterCard**, are really just a special form of factoring. The issuer of the credit card (i.e., the bank) pays the seller the amount of each sale less a service charge (on the date of purchase) and then collects the full amount of the sale from the buyer (at some later date).[3] For example, if a retail customer uses a **Citibank** Visa Card to pay $100 for a haircut, the salon would make the following entry assuming Citibank charges a 1.55 percent service charge:

Assets	=	Liabilities	+	Stockholders' Equity
+98.45				−1.55
				+100.00

Account and Explanation	Debit	Credit
Cash	98.45	
Service Charge Expense	1.55	
Sales Revenue		100.00
(Record sales)		

Although a 1.55 percent service charge may seem expensive, credit card sales provide sellers with a number of advantages over supplying credit directly to customers, including the following:

- Sellers receive the money immediately.
- Sellers avoid bad debts because as long as the credit card verification procedures are followed, the credit card company absorbs the cost of customers who do not pay.
- Recordkeeping costs lessen because employees are not needed to manage these accounts.
- Sellers believe that by accepting credit cards, their sales will increase. For example, how many of you have ever driven away from a gas station that does not accept credit cards or even one that merely does not allow you to pay at the pump?

Of course, many large retailers are willing to take on these costs to avoid the credit card service charge. For example, **Sears**, **Kohls**, **Target**, **Macy's**, and most other large retailers have internal credit cards. When these cards are used, the seller records it like any other accounts receivable and no service charge expense is incurred; however, they are accepting the risk of uncollectible accounts and the cost of servicing these accounts.

---

[3] The bank may also pay the full amount of the sale to the seller and then bill the service charge at the end of the period.

Non-bank credit cards, such as **American Express**, also result in a receivable for the seller because the issuer of the credit card (American Express) does not immediately pay the cash to the seller. American Express also charges a higher service charge to the seller. Consequently, sellers find American Express to be more costly than bank cards, such as **Visa** or **MasterCard**, which explains why many businesses do not accept American Express.

Debit Cards

A **debit card** authorizes a bank to make an immediate electronic withdrawal (debit) from the holder's bank account. The debit card is used like a credit card except that a bank electronically reduces (debits) the holder's bank account and increases (credits) the merchant's bank account for the amount of a sale made on a debit card.

Debit cards appear to be somewhat disadvantageous to the card holder as transactions cannot be rescinded by stopping payment. Further, a purchase using a debit card causes an immediate reduction in a bank account balance, while a check written at the same time will require at least one or two days to clear, allowing the depositor to benefit from the additional money in the account until the check is presented at the bank for payment. However, debit cards offer significant advantages to banks and merchants in reduced transaction-processing costs. Thus, banks and merchants have incentive to design debit cards that minimize or eliminate the disadvantages and costs to card users.

NOTES RECEIVABLE

OBJECTIVE 6
Account for notes receivable from inception to maturity.

Notes receivable are receivables that generally specify an interest rate and a maturity date at which any interest and principal must be repaid. Our discussion here is limited to simple notes that specify the repayment of interest and principal in a single payment on a given day (more complicated notes are described in Chapter 10).

The amount lent is the **principal**. The excess of the total amount of money collected over the amount lent is called **interest**. For example, as shown in Exhibit 5-1, if **Caterpillar** lends $500,000 to a customer and is repaid $580,000 at some later date, then $80,000 of interest was collected.

Interest can be considered compensation paid to the lender for giving up the use of resources for the period of a note (the time value of money). The interest rate specified in the note is an annual rate. Therefore, when calculating interest, you must consider the duration of the note using the following formula:

$$\text{Interest} = \text{Principal} \times \text{Annual Interest Rate} \times \text{Fraction of One Year}$$

Exhibit 5-1

Principal and Interest in Loan Repayments

Principal ($500,000)   Interest ($80,000)

Total Amount Borrowed ($580,000)

For example, in the example illustrated in Exhibit 5-1 (p. 227), what was the annual interest rate? The answer is we have no way of knowing because the duration of the loan was not specified. If the duration of the loan was exactly one year, then the annual rate was 16%. If the duration was more (or less) than one year, however, then the annual rate is less (or more) than 16%.

Further, you will recall from Chapter 2 that the matching concept and the revenue recognition concept require that expenses and revenues be identified with specific accounting periods. If only one month of interest has been incurred by year-end, an adjusting entry is required to recognize interest income and a corresponding interest receivable. Any remaining interest is recognized in subsequent periods.[4] The accounting for notes receivable is demonstrated in **CORNERSTONE 5-4**.

CORNERSTONE 5-4   Accounting for Notes Receivable

Concept:
Notes receivable are recognized for the amount of cash loaned or goods/services sold. This is the principal amount of the note receivable. Any excess of the amount received over principal is recognized as interest income in the period the interest was earned.

Information:
Dover Electric Company purchased, on account, $50,000 of consulting services from Thomas, Ltd., on November 1, 2011. The amount is due in full on January 1, 2012. Dover Electric is unable to pay the account by the due date and negotiates an extension with a 10% note in lieu of the unpaid account receivable.

Required:
1. Prepare Thomas's journal entries to record the sale on November 1, 2011, and the modification of payment terms on January 1, 2012.
2. How much interest will be paid if Dover Electric repays the note on (a) July 1, 2012, (b) December 31, 2012, and (c) March 31, 2013?
3. Prepare Thomas's adjusting entry to accrue interest on December 31, 2012, assuming the note is repaid on March 31, 2013.
4. Prepare Thomas's journal entries to record the cash received to pay off the note and interest on each of the three dates specified in part 2.

Solution:
1.

Date	Account and Explanation	Debit	Credit
Nov. 1, 2011	Accounts Receivable	50,000	
	Sales Revenue		50,000
	(Record sale)		
Jan. 1, 2012	Notes Receivable	50,000	
	Accounts Receivable		50,000
	(Record issuance of note receivable)		

Assets	= Liabilities +	Stockholders' Equity
+50,000		+50,000

Assets	= Liabilities +	Stockholders' Equity
+50,000		
−50,000		

(Continued)

---

[4] Interest is, in fact, often computed in terms of days rather than months. Suppose, for example, that the three-month note runs for 92 days (two 31-day months and one 30-day month). The total interest on the 92-day note would be $302.47 [($10,000)(0.12)(92/365)], and the first 31-day month's interest would be $101.92 [($10,000)(0.12)(31/365)]. Observe that daily interest complicates the arithmetic associated with interest calculations but does not alter the basic form of the calculations. To simplify interest computations, we will use monthly interest throughout this chapter.

CORNERSTONE
5-4
(continued)

2. Interest = Principal × Annual Interest Rate × Fraction of One Year

a) July 1, 2012:	b) Dec. 31, 2012:	c) March 31, 2013:
= $50,000 × 10% × (6/12)	= $50,000 × 10% × (12/12)	= $50,000 × 10% × (15/12)
= $2,500	= $5,000	= $6,250

3.

Date	Account and Explanation	Debit	Credit
Dec. 31, 2012	Interest Receivable	5,000	
	Interest Income		5,000
	(Record accrual of interest)		

Assets	= Liabilities +	Stockholders' Equity
+5,000		+5,000

4.

Date	Account and Explanation	Debit	Credit
July 1, 2012	Cash	52,500	
	Notes Receivable		50,000
	Interest Income		2,500
	(Record collection of note receivable)		

Assets	= Liabilities +	Stockholders' Equity
+52,500		+2,500
−50,000		

Date	Account and Explanation	Debit	Credit
Dec. 31, 2012	Cash	55,000	
	Notes Receivable		50,000
	Interest Income		5,000
	(Record collection of note receivable)		

Assets	= Liabilities +	Stockholders' Equity
+55,000		+5,000
−50,000		

Date	Account and Explanation	Debit	Credit
Mar. 31, 2013	Cash	56,250	
	Notes Receivable		50,000
	Interest Receivable		5,000
	Interest Income		1,250
	(Record collection of note receivable)		

Assets	= Liabilities +	Stockholders' Equity
+56,250		+1,250
−50,000		
−5,000		

INTERNAL CONTROL FOR SALES

OBJECTIVE 7
Describe internal control procedures for merchandise sales.

Since sales revenues have a significant effect on a company's net income, internal control procedures must be established to ensure that the amounts reported for these items are correct. For sales revenues, these controls normally involve the following documents and procedures:

- Accounting for a sale begins with the receipt of a purchase order or some similar document from a customer. The order document is necessary for the buyer to be obligated to accept and pay for the ordered goods.
- Shipping and billing documents are prepared based on the order document. Billing documents are usually called *invoices*.
- A sale and its associated receivable are recorded only when the order, shipping, and billing documents are all present.

As illustrated in Exhibit 5-2 (p. 230), sales revenue should be recorded only when these three control documents are completed. When any of these three internal controls is not present, it is possible for valid sales to be unrecorded and for invalid sales to be recorded.

For sales returns and allowances, internal control procedures must be established that identify the conditions and documentation required before a sales return or a sales allowance can be recorded. These controls protect the firm from unwarranted reductions in revenues and receivables.

Exhibit 5-2

Internal Controls for Recording Sales Revenue

PURCHASE ORDER   No. R450
Richardson's Wholesale Hardware
Date: Sept. 1, 2011
To:
Bolt Manufacturing

QTY.	DESCRIPTION	PRICE	AMOUNT
30	Model No. SB100 snowblower	$500	$15,000

Ordered by: Jim Richardson

Jim Richardson

Purchase order number must appear on all shipments and invoice

SHIPPING REPORT   No. B275
Bolt Manufacturing
Date: Sept. 1, 2011
To:
Richardson's Wholesale Hardware

QTY.	DESCRIPTION
30	Model No. SB100 snowblower

Purchase order: R450

INVOICE   No. B100
Bolt Manufacturing
Date: Sept. 1, 2011
Sold to:
Richardson's Wholesale Hardware
Purchase order: R450

QTY.	DESCRIPTION	PRICE	AMOUNT
30	Model No. SB100 snowblower	$500	$15,000
		SUBTOTAL	$15,000
		SALES TAX	0
		SHIPPING & HANDLING	0
		TOTAL DUE	$15,000

Date	Account and Explanation	Debit	Credit
Sept. 1	Accounts Receivable	15,000	
	Sales Revenue		15,000

OBJECTIVE 8
Analyze profitability and asset management using sales and receivables.

ANALYZING SALES AND RECEIVABLES

Analysts of the financial statements are extremely concerned with both sales and receivables.

Sales

Because sales revenue is such a key component of a company's success, analysts are interested in a large number of ratios that incorporate sales. Many of these ratios attempt to measure the return the company is earning on sales. These are called **profitability ratios**. For example, the ratio of income statement subtotals such as gross margin, operating income, and net income to sales are examined, but really any income statement subtotal deemed important can be of interest. The three most common ratios are gross profit margin, operating margin, and net profit margin:

$$\text{Gross Profit Margin} = \frac{\text{Gross Profit}}{\text{Net Sales}}$$

$$\text{Operating Margin} = \frac{\text{Operating Income}}{\text{Net Sales}}$$

$$\text{Net Profit Margin} = \frac{\text{Net Income}}{\text{Net Sales}}$$

Each of these ratios reveals information about a company's strategy and the competition it faces. For example, consider two large players in the retail industry—**Wal-Mart** and **Nordstrom**. Information available indicates that these two stores possess the following five-year averages for these ratios:

	Wal-Mart	Nordstrom
Gross Profit Percentage	24.78%	37.86%
Operating Margin Percentage	5.91%	10.17%
Net Profit Margin Percentage	3.67%	6.53%

Nordstrom's higher gross profit percentage suggests that Nordstrom is able to charge a premium on its merchandise. That is, Nordstrom follows a product differentiation strategy in which it tries to convince customers that its products are superior, distinctive, etc. **Wal-Mart**, on the other hand, is a low-cost provider, who attempts to convince customers that it offers the lowest prices.

Analysts also like to look at the operating margin and net profit margin percentages to see how much is left from a sales dollar after paying for the product and all its operations. For these ratios, **Nordstrom** still retains a larger percentage of each sales dollar than **Wal-Mart**. How is it, then, that Wal-Mart makes so much money? It has a lot of sales dollars—its net sales revenue of $405 billion in 2010 is approximately 47 times greater than Nordstrom's $8.6 billion.

Receivables

Analysts are also concerned with asset management. Asset management refers to how efficiently a company is using the resources at its disposal. One of the most widely-used asset management ratios is accounts receivable turnover:

$$\text{Accounts Receivable Turnover} = \frac{\text{Net Sales}}{\text{Average Net Accounts Receivable}}$$

This ratio provides a measure of how many times average trade receivables are collected during the period. In theory, net credit sales would be a much better numerator, but that figure is not normally disclosed. A higher number is better because it indicates that the company is more quickly collecting cash (through sales) from its inventory. As discussed in Chapter 4's section on cash management, this holds down borrowing costs and allows for a greater investment. Changes in this ratio over time are also very important. For example, a significant reduction in receivables turnover may indicate that management is extending credit to customers who are not paying.

Accounts receivable turnover for **Wal-Mart** and **Nordstrom** is:

	Wal-Mart	Nordstrom
Accounts Receivable Turnover	108.2	4.68

As expected, **Wal-Mart** is extremely efficient with its asset management because effective cash management is necessary for low cost providers. Of course, it is difficult to compare **Nordstrom** to Wal-Mart because they likely engage in different financing practices. For example, a greater proportion of Wal-Mart sales are made using cash or external credit cards (such as **Visa**), while Nordstrom has a larger proportion of sales using internal credit cards (a Nordstrom card). The internal credit cards result in lower accounts receivable turnover. **CORNERSTONE 5-5** illustrates the calculation of these ratios for Wal-Mart.

**CORNERSTONE
5 - 5**

Calculating the Gross Profit Margin, Operating Margin, Net Profit Margin, and Accounts Receivable Turnover Ratios

Concept:
The gross profit margin, operating margin, and net profit margin ratios provide measures of the return the company is earning on sales. The accounts receivable turnover ratio provides a measure of how many times average accounts receivable are collected during the period.

(Continued)

Information:

The following information (in millions) is available for **Wal-Mart** for its fiscal year ending January 31, 2010:

Net sales	$405,046	Accounts receivable, 1/31/10	$4,144
Gross profit	100,389	Accounts receivable, 1/31/09	3,905
Operating income	23,950		
Net income	14,848		

Required:

Compute the (1) gross profit margin, (2) operating margin, (3) net profit margin, and (4) accounts receivable turnover for Wal-Mart for 2010.

CORNERSTONE
5-5
(continued)

Solution:

1.
$$\text{Gross Profit Margin Ratio} = \frac{\text{Gross Profit}}{\text{Net Sales}}$$
$$= \frac{\$100,389}{\$405,046} = 0.2478, \text{ or } 24.78\%$$

2.
$$\text{Operating Margin Ratio} = \frac{\text{Operating Income}}{\text{Net Sales}}$$
$$= \frac{\$23,950}{\$405,046} = 0.0591, \text{ or } 5.91\%$$

3.
$$\text{Net Profit Margin Ratio} = \frac{\text{Net Income}}{\text{Net Sales}}$$
$$= \frac{\$14,848}{\$405,046} = 0.0367, \text{ or } 3.67\%$$

4.
$$\text{Accounts Receivable Turnover Ratio} = \frac{\text{Net Sales}}{\text{Average Net Accounts Receivable}}$$
$$= \frac{\$405,046}{(\$3,905 + \$4,144) \div 2} = 100.65$$

SUMMARY OF LEARNING OBJECTIVES

LO1. Explain the criteria for revenue recognition.
- Revenue is recognized when it is:
  - realized or realizable
  - earned
- The terms "realized" and "realizable" mean that the selling price is fixed and determinable and collectibility is reasonably assured.
- Revenue is considered earned when delivery has occurred or services have been provided.

LO2. Measure net sales revenue.
- The appropriate amount of revenue to recognize is generally the cash received or the cash equivalent of accounts receivable.
- However, companies often induce customers to buy by offering:
  - sales discounts
  - sales returns
  - sales allowances

- Sales discounts are reductions of the normal selling price to encourage prompt payment.
- Sales returns occur when a customer returns goods as unsatisfactory.
- Sales allowances occur when a customer agrees to keep goods with minor defects if the seller reduces the selling price.
- These events are recorded in contra-revenue accounts that reduce gross sales to net sales.

LO3.   **Describe the principal types of receivables.**
- Receivables are classified along three different dimensions:
  - accounts and notes receivable
  - trade and non-trade receivables
  - current and noncurrent receivables

LO4.   **Measure and interpret bad debt expense and the allowance for doubtful accounts.**
- The primary issues in accounting for accounts receivable are when and how to measure bad debts (i.e., accounts that will not be paid).
- GAAP requires receivables to be shown at net realizable value on the balance sheet.
- Further, the matching principle says that an expense should be recognized in the period in which it helps generate revenues.
- Consequently, we must estimate and recognize bad debt expense in the period the sale is made—even though we do not know which accounts will be uncollectible.
- The estimate is made by using either:
  - The percentage of credit sales method or
  - the aging method
- The percentage of credit sales method estimates the bad debt expense directly.
- The aging method estimates the ending balance needed in the allowance for doubtful accounts, and bad debt expense follows.

LO5.   **Describe the cash flow implications of accounts receivable.**
- Companies can increase the speed of cash collection on receivables by factoring, or selling, their receivables.
- The buyer of the receivables will charge a fee to compensate themselves for the time value of money, the risk of uncollectability, and the tasks of billing and collection.
- Receivables may also be packaged as financial instruments or securities and sold to investors. This is referred to as securitization.
- A special case of selling receivables is accepting credit cards like MasterCard and Visa.

LO6.   **Account for notes receivable from inception to maturity.**
- Notes receivable are recognized for the amount of cash borrowed or goods/services purchased.
- This is the principal amount of the note receivable.
- Any excess of amount repaid over principal is recognized as interest income in the period the interest was earned.

LO7.   **Describe internal control procedures for merchandise sales.**
- Since sales revenues have a significant effect on a company's net income, internal control procedures must be established to ensure that the amounts reported are correct.
- Typically sales are not recorded until a three-way match is performed between:
  - the customer purchase order (which indicates that the customer wants the goods)
  - the shipping document (which indicates that the goods have been shipped to the customer)
  - the invoice (which indicates that the customer has been billed)

LO8.   **Analyze profitability and asset management using sales and receivables.**
- Because sales revenue is such a key component of a company's success, analysts are interested in a large number of ratios that incorporate sales.
- Many of these ratios attempt to measure how much the company is making on sales. These are called profitability ratios.
  - Gross profit margin
  - Operating margin
  - Net profit margin

- Analysts are also concerned with asset management. Asset management refers to how efficiently a company is using the resources at its disposal.
- One of the most widely-used asset management ratios is accounts receivable turnover.

CORNERSTONES
FOR CHAPTER 5

CORNERSTONE 5-1   Recording receivables using the gross method (p. 217)

CORNERSTONE 5-2   Estimating bad debt expense using the percentage of credit sales method (p. 222)

CORNERSTONE 5-3   Estimating the allowance for doubtful accounts using the aging method (p. 224)

CORNERSTONE 5-4   Accounting for notes receivable (p. 228)

CORNERSTONE 5-5   Calculating the gross profit margin, operating margin, net profit margin, and accounts receivable turnover ratios (p. 231)

KEY TERMS

Accounts receivable (p. 220)
Aging method (p. 223)
Allowance for Doubtful Accounts (p. 221)
Bad debt expense (p. 220)
Credit cards (p. 226)
Debit card (p. 227)
Earned (p. 216)
Factor (p. 226)
Interest (p. 227)
Net sales revenue (p. 219)
Nontrade receivables (p. 220)

Notes receivable (p. 227)
Percentage of credit sales method (p. 221)
Principal (p. 227)
Profitability ratios (p. 230)
Realizable (p. 216)
Realized (p. 216)
Sales allowance (p. 218)
Sales discount (p. 217)
Sales returns (p. 219)
Securitization (p. 226)
Trade receivables (p. 220)

REVIEW PROBLEM

I. Recording Sales and Receivables

Qwurk Productions performs graphic design services including designing and maintaining websites. The following activities occurred during 2011 and 2012:

11/1/11	Qwurk delivers a new logo to GCD Advisors and submits a bill for $2,000 with terms 2/10, n/30.
11/15/11	Qwurk delivers an overall web concept to Mutare, which Mutare approves. Qwurk submits a bill for $1,000 with terms 2/10, n/30.
11/20/11	Qwurk delivers paper and envelopes incorporating the new logo to GCD Advisors and submits a bill for $200.
11/22/11	Mutare pays for the 11/15 bill related to a new overall web concept.
11/25/11	GCD complains that the printing on much of the paper and envelopes is unacceptable. Qwurk offers to reduce the bill from $200 to $75. GCD accepts.
11/29/11	GCD pays for the 11/1 bill for a new logo and $75 for the 11/20 bill for paper and envelopes.
12/1/11	Qwurk installs a new website incorporating order fulfillment applications for Redbird Enterprises. Redbird signs a note to pay $20,000 plus 6 percent interest due on 7/1/12.
12/15/11	Qwurk writes off a $600 account receivable.
12/31/11	After performing an aging of its accounts receivable, Qwurk estimates that $2,000 of its accounts receivable will be uncollectible on a total balance of $600,000. The allowance for doubtful accounts has a credit balance of $300 prior to adjustment.
7/1/12	Redbird pays the note and interest in full.
12/31/12	For the year ended December 31, 2012, Qwurk has sales of $6,000,000; sales discounts of $15,000; sales returns and allowances of $20,000.

Required:

1. Provide the journal entry for November 1, 2011, assuming Qwurk uses the gross method of recording receivables.

2. Provide the journal entry for November 15, 2011, assuming Qwurk uses the gross method of recording receivables.

3. Provide the journal entry for November 20, 2011, assuming Qwurk uses the gross method of recording receivables.

4. Calculate how much Mutare paid and provide the journal entry for November 22, 2011.

5. Provide the journal entry for November 25, 2011.

6. Calculate how much GCD paid and provide the journal entry for November 29, 2011.

7. Provide the journal entry for December 1, 2011.

8. Provide the journal entry for December 15, 2011.

9. Provide the necessary adjusting entries for December 31, 2011 to accrue interest on the note and adjust the allowance account.

10. What is the net realizable value of Qwurk's accounts receivable at December 31, 2011?

11. Calculate how much interest Redbird paid and provide the journal entry for July 1, 2012.

12. Provide the income statement presentation of Qwurk's 2012 sales.

Solution:

Date	Account and Explanation	Debit	Credit	
2011				
1. Nov. 1	Accounts Receivable	2,000		Stockholders'
	Sales		2,000	Assets = Liabilities + Equity
	(Record sale)			+2,000 +2,000
2. Nov. 15	Accounts Receivable	1,000		Stockholders'
	Sales		1,000	Assets = Liabilities + Equity
	(Record sale)			+1,000 +1,000
3. Nov. 20	Accounts Receivable	200		Stockholders'
	Sales		200	Assets = Liabilities + Equity
	(Record sale)			+200 +200
4. Nov. 22	Cash[a]	980		Stockholders'
	Sales Discounts	20		Assets = Liabilities + Equity
	Accounts Receivable		1,000	+980 −20
	(Record collection within the discount period)			−1,000
5. Nov. 25	Sales Returns & Allowances	125		Stockholders'
	Accounts Receivable		125	Assets = Liabilities + Equity
	(Record allowance for unacceptable merchandise)			−125 −125
6. Nov. 29	Cash[b]	2,075		Stockholders'
	Accounts Receivable		2,075	Assets = Liabilities + Equity
	(Record collection after discount period)			+2,075
				−2,075
7. Dec. 1	Notes Receivable	20,000		Stockholders'
	Sales		20,000	Assets = Liabilities + Equity
	(Record sale)			+20,000 +20,000

[a]

Gross amount	$1,000
Less: Discount ($1,000 × 2%)	(20)
Total paid	$ 980

[b]

Gross amount	$2,000
Less: Discount (not allowed; paid after 10 days)	0
Total paid	$2,000 + 75 = 2,075

Date	Account and Explanation	Debit	Credit
2011			

8.

Date	Account and Explanation	Debit	Credit
Dec. 15	Allowance for Doubtful Accounts	600	
	Accounts Receivable		600
	(Writeoff an accounts receivable)		

Assets	=	Liabilities	+	Stockholders' Equity
+600				
−600				

9.

Date	Account and Explanation	Debit	Credit
Dec. 31	Interest Receivable[c]	100	
	Interest Income		100
	(Record one month's interest on Dec. 1 note receivable)		
	Bad Debt Expense	1,700	
	Allowance for Doubtful Accounts[d]		1,700
	(Record adjusting entry for bad debt expense estimate)		

Assets	=	Liabilities	+	Stockholders' Equity
+100				+100
−1,700				−1,700

[c] $20,000 \times 6\% \times 1/12$

[d] Qwurk's estimate warrants a $2,000 credit balance. Because the account already has a $300 credit balance, a $1,700 credit is needed.

10. December 31, 2011:

Accounts receivable accounts	$600,000
Less: Allowance for doubtful accounts	(2,000)
Net realizable value	$598,000

Net accounts receivable are shown at net realizable value.

11. July 1, 2012:

$$\text{Interest paid} = \$20,000 \times 6\% \times 7/12$$
$$= \$700$$

However, interest income recognized for Qwurk is for the period December 1, 2011, through July 1, 2012. The interest for December 2011 was recognized in 2011 (see journal entry in *9*).

Account and Explanation	Debit	Credit
Cash	20,700	
Interest Income		600
Interest Receivable (from 9)		100
Notes Receivable		20,000
(Record collection of note receivable)		

Assets	=	Liabilities	+	Stockholders' Equity
+20,700				+600
−100				
−20,000				

12.

Gross sales revenue	$6,000,000
Less: Sales discounts	(15,000)
Less: Sales returns and allowances	(20,000)
Net sales revenue	$5,965,000

DISCUSSION QUESTIONS

1. When is revenue recognized?
2. Explain the criteria for revenue recognition.
3. When is revenue generally considered earned?
4. What four criteria has the SEC issued as further guidance for revenue recognition?
5. How is net sales revenue calculated?
6. Why might users of financial statements prefer the separate disclosure of gross sales revenue and sales returns and allowances to the disclosure of a single net sales revenue amount?
7. Why are sales discounts offered?
8. What are sales returns?
9. What are sales allowances? How do sales allowances differ from sales discounts?
10. What are trade discounts and quantity discounts? From an accounting viewpoint, how does the effect of trade and quantity discounts on selling (or invoice) price differ from the effect of sales discounts?

11. What are the principal types of receivables?
12. Under the allowance method, why do we make an entry to record bad debt expense in the period of sale rather than in the period in which an account is determined to be uncollectible?
13. Why is the direct write-off method not GAAP?
14. What is the conceptual difference between the (1) percentage of credit sales and (2) aging methods of estimating bad debts?
15. What kind of account is *allowance for doubtful accounts*? What does it represent?
16. Why do companies issue credit when their past experience indicates that some customers will not pay?
17. How much interest will be due at maturity for each of the following interest-bearing notes?

	Principal	Months to Maturity	Annual Interest Rate
a.	$10,000	2	12%
b.	42,000	5	14
c.	18,000	4	13
d.	37,000	6	11

18. A business borrows $1,000, giving a note that requires repayment of the amount borrowed in two payments of $600 each, one at the end of each of the next two six-month periods. Calculate the total interest on the note. What is the principal amount of the note?
19. A business borrows $1,000, giving a note that requires an interest rate of 12 percent per year and repayment of principal plus interest in a single payment at the end of one year. Calculate the total interest on the note. What is the amount of the single payment?
20. Describe what happens when receivables are factored.
21. Accepting major credit cards requires the seller to pay a service charge. What advantages does the seller obtain by accepting major credit cards?
22. Why is interest typically charged on notes receivable, but not on accounts receivable?
23. What documents must be present to trigger the recording of a sale (and associated receivable) in the accounting records?
24. Describe the documents that underlie the typical accounting system for sales. Give an example of a failure of internal control that might occur if these documents were not properly prepared.
25. How may analyzing sales and receivables provide information about a firm's profitability?
26. How may analyzing sales and receivables provide information about a firm's asset management?

MULTIPLE-CHOICE EXERCISES

5-1 Which of the following is *not* one of the criteria for revenue recognition?

a. Persuasive evidence of an arrangement exists.
b. Collectability is certain.
c. Delivery has occurred or services have been provided.
d. The seller's price to the buyer is fixed and determinable.

5-2 Food To Go is a local catering service. Conceptually, when should Food To Go recognize revenue from its catering service?

a. at the date the invoice is mailed to the customer
b. at the date the customer places the order
c. at the date the customer's payment is received
d. at the date the meals are served

5-3 When is revenue from the sale of merchandise normally recognized?

a. when the customer pays for the merchandise
b. when the customer takes possession of the merchandise
c. either on the date the customer takes possession of the merchandise or the date on which the customer pays
d. when the customer takes possession of the merchandise, if sold for cash, or when payment is received, if sold on credit

5-4 What does the phrase, "Revenue is recognized at the point of sale" mean?

a. Revenue is recorded in the accounting records when the cash is received from a customer, and reported on the income statement when sold to the customer.
b. Revenue is recorded in the accounting records and reported on the income statement when the cash is received from the customer.
c. Revenue is recorded in the accounting records when the goods are sold to a customer, and reported on the income statement when the cash payment is received from the customer.
d. Revenue is recorded in the accounting records and reported on the income statement when goods are sold and delivered to a customer.

5-5 On August 31, 2011, Montana Corporation signed a four-year contract to provide services for Minefield Company at $30,000 per year. Minefield will pay for each year of services on the first day of each service year, starting with September 1, 2011. Using the accrual basis of accounting, when should Montana recognize revenue?

a. only at the end of the entire contract
b. equally throughout the year as services are provided
c. on the first day of each year when the cash is received
d. on the last day of each year after the services have been provided

5-6 Under the gross method, the seller records discounts taken by the buyer

a. in a contra-revenue account
b. never; discounts are irrelevant under the gross method
c. after the receivable is collected
d. at the end of the period in question

5-7 On April 20, McLean Company provides lawn care services to Tazwell Corporation for $3,000 with terms 1/10, n/30. On April 28, Tazwell pays for half of the services provided and on May 19 it pays for the other half. What is the total amount of cash McLean received?

a. $2,700
b. $2,970
c. $2,985
d. $3,000

5-8 Which of the following statements concerning internal control procedures for merchandise sales is *not* correct?

a. A sale and its associated receivable are recorded only when the order, shipping, and billing documents are all present.
b. Shipping and billing documents are prepared based on the order document.
c. The order document is not necessary for the buyer to be obligated to accept and pay for the ordered goods.
d. Accounting for a sale begins with the receipt of a purchase order or some similar document from a customer.

5-9 All of the following are ways in which receivables are commonly distinguished *except*:

a. accounts or notes receivable
b. current or noncurrent
c. collectible or uncollectible
d. trade or nontrade receivable

5-10 Which one of the following best describes the allowance for doubtful accounts?

a. cash flow account
b. contra account
c. income statement account
d. liability account

5-11 If a company uses the direct write-off method of accounting for bad debts,

a. it is applying the matching principle.
b. it will reduce the accounts receivable account at the end of the accounting period for estimated uncollectible accounts.

(Continued)

c.   it will report accounts receivable in the balance sheet at their net realizable value.

d.   it will record bad debt expense only when an account is determined to be uncollectible.

5-12 Which of the following best describes the objective of estimating bad debt expense with the percentage of credit sales method?

a.   to estimate bad debt expense based on a percentage of credit sales made during the period

b.   to estimate the amount of bad debt expense based on an aging of accounts receivable

c.   to determine the amount of uncollectible accounts during a given period

d.   to facilitate the use of the direct write-off method

5-13 Which of the following best describes the concept of the aging method of receivables?

a.   Accounts receivable should be directly written off when the due date arrives and the customers have not paid the bill.

b.   An accurate estimate of bad debt expense may be arrived at by multiplying historical bad debt rates by the amount of credit sales made during a period.

c.   Estimating the appropriate balance for the allowance for doubtful accounts results in the appropriate value for net accounts receivable on the balance sheet.

d.   The precise amount of bad debt expense may be arrived at by multiplying historical bad debt rates by the amount of credit sales made during a period.

5-14 The aging method is closely related to the:

a.   balance sheet

b.   statement of retained earnings

c.   statement of cash flows

d.   income statement

5-15 The percentage of credit sales approach is closely related to the:

a.   balance sheet

b.   statement of retained earnings

c.   statement of cash flows

d.   income statement

5-16 The process by which firms package factored receivables as financial instruments or securities and sell them to investors is known as:

a.   credit extension

b.   aging of accounts receivable

c.   bundling

d.   securitization

5-17 Which one of the following statements is true if a company's collection period for accounts receivable is unacceptably long?

a.   The company should expand operations with its excess cash.

b.   The company may need to borrow to acquire operating cash.

c.   The company may offer trade discounts to lengthen the collection period.

d.   Cash flows from operations may be higher than expected for the company's sales.

5-18 Zenephia Corp. accepted a nine-month note receivable from a customer on October 1, 2011. If Zenephia has an accounting period which ends on December 31, 2011, when would it most likely recognize interest income from the note?

a.   on October 1, 2011

b.   on December 31, 2011, only

c.   on December 31, 2011, and July 1, 2012

d.   on July 1, 2012, only

5-19 The "principal" of a note receivable refers to:

a.   the present value of the note

b.   the amount of cash borrowed

c.   the financing company that is lending the money

d.   the amount of interest due

5-20 Net profit margin percentage is calculated by:

a.   dividing net income by (net) sales

b.   dividing operating income by (net) sales

c.   subtracting operating income from (net) sales

d.   subtracting net income from (net) sales

CORNERSTONE EXERCISES

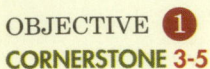

Cornerstone Exercise 5-21 Service Revenue

Kibitz Fitness received $24,000 from customers on August 1, 2011. These payments were advance payments of yearly membership dues.

Required:

At December 31, 2011, calculate what the balances in the Unearned Service Revenue and Service Revenue accounts will be.

Cornerstone Exercise 5-22 Service Revenue

Softball Magazine Company received advance payments of $75,000 from customers during 2011. At December 31, 2011, $20,000 of the advance payments still had not been earned.

Required:

After the adjustments are recorded and posted at December 31, 2011, calculate what the balances will be in the Unearned Magazine Revenue and Magazine Revenue accounts.

> *Use the following information for Cornerstone Exercises 5-23 and 5-24:*
> Bolton sold a customer service contract with a price of $37,000 to Sammy's Wholesale Company. Bolton offered terms of 1/10, n/30 and uses the gross method.

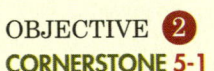

Cornerstone Exercise 5-23 Sales Discounts Taken

Refer to the information for Bolton above.

Required:

Prepare the journal entry to record the sale. Then prepare the journal entry assuming the payment is made within 10 days (within the discount period).

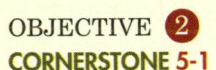

Cornerstone Exercise 5-24 Sales Discounts Not Taken

Refer to the information for Bolton above.

Required:

Prepare the journal entry assuming the payment is made after 10 days (after the discount period).

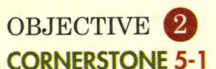

Cornerstone Exercise 5-25 Sales Discounts

Ramsden Inc. provided consulting services with a gross price of $40,000 and terms of 2/10, n/30.

Required:

1. Prepare the necessary journal entries to record the sale under the gross method.
2. Prepare the necessary journal entries to record collection of the receivable assuming the customer pays within 10 days.
3. Prepare the necessary journal entries to record collection of the receivable assuming the customer pays after 10 days.

Cornerstone Exercise 5-26 Percentage of Credit Sales

Clarissa Company has credit sales of $550,000 during 2011 and estimates at the end of 2010 that 2.5 percent of these credit sales will eventually default. Also, during 2011 a customer defaults on a $775 balance related to goods purchased in 2010. Prior to the write off for the $775 default, Clarissa's accounts receivable and allowance for doubtful accounts balances were $402,000 and $129 (credit), respectively.

Required:

1. Prepare the journal entry to record the defaulted account.
2. Prepare the adjusting entry to record the bad debt expense for 2011.

Cornerstone Exercise 5-27 Write-Off of Uncollectible Accounts

OBJECTIVE 4
CORNERSTONE 5-2

The Rock has credit sales of $500,000 during 2011 and estimates at the end of 2011 that 2 percent of these credit sales will eventually default. Also, during 2011 a customer defaults on a $1,800 balance related to goods purchased in 2010.

Required:
1. Prepare the journal entry to record the defaulted balance.
2. Prepare the adjusting entry to record the bad debt expense for 2011.

Cornerstone Exercise 5-28 Aging Method

OBJECTIVE 4
CORNERSTONE 5-3

On January 1, 2011, Hungryman, Inc., has the following balances for accounts receivable and allowance for doubtful accounts:

Accounts Receivable	$1,280,000
Allowance for Doubtful Accounts (a credit balance)	44,000

During 2011, Hungryman had $18,500,000 of credit sales, collected $17,945,000 of accounts receivable, and wrote off $60,000 of accounts receivable as uncollectible. At year end, Hungryman performs an aging of its accounts receivable balance and estimates that $52,000 will be uncollectible.

Required:
1. Calculate Hungryman's preadjustment balance in accounts receivable on December 31, 2011.
2. Calculate Hungryman's preadjustment balance in allowance for doubtful accounts on December 31, 2011.
3. Prepare the necessary adjusting entry for 2011.

Cornerstone Exercise 5-29 Aging Method

OBJECTIVE 4
CORNERSTONE 5-3

On January 1, 2011, Smith, Inc., has the following balances for accounts receivable and allowance for doubtful accounts:

Accounts Receivable	$382,000
Allowance for Doubtful Accounts (a credit balance)	4,200

During 2011, Smith had $2,865,000 of credit sales, collected $2,905,000 of accounts receivable, and wrote off $3,850 of accounts receivable as uncollectible. At year end, Smith performs an aging of its accounts receivable balance and estimates that $3,800 will be uncollectible.

Required:
1. Calculate Smith's preadjustment balance in accounts receivable on December 31, 2011.
2. Calculate Smith's preadjustment balance in allowance for doubtful accounts on December 31, 2011.
3. Prepare the necessary adjusting entry for 2011.

Cornerstone Exercise 5-30 Percentage of Credit Sales Method

OBJECTIVE 4
CORNERSTONE 5-2

At December 31, 2011, Garner has a $10,000 credit balance in its allowance for doubtful accounts. Garner estimates that 3 percent of its 2011 credit sales will eventually default. During 2011, Garner had credit sales of $1,130,000.

Required:
Estimate the bad debt expense under the percentage of credit sales method.

Cornerstone Exercise 5-31 Accounts Receivable Balance

OBJECTIVE 5
CORNERSTONE 5-3

Beginning accounts receivable were $32,350. All sales were on account and totaled $286,480. Cash collected from customers totaled $276,750.

Required:
Calculate the ending accounts receivable balance.

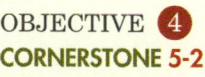

OBJECTIVE ④
CORNERSTONE 5-3

Cornerstone Exercise 5-32 Accounts Receivable Balance

Beginning accounts receivable were $275,500 and ending accounts receivable were $302,300. Cash amounting to $2,965,000 was collected from customers' credit sales.

Required:

Calculate the amount of sales on account during the period.

OBJECTIVE ⑤
CORNERSTONE 5-3

Cornerstone Exercise 5-33 Accounts Receivable Balance

Beginning accounts receivable were $135,720 and ending accounts receivable were $128,640. All sales were on credit and totaled $1,682,480.

Required:

Determine how much cash was collected from customers.

OBJECTIVE ⑤

Cornerstone Exercise 5-34 Accounting for Credit Card Sales

Frank's Tattoos and Body Piercing operates near campus. At the end of a recent day, Frank's cash register included credit card documents for the following sales amounts:

MasterCard	$756
Visa	486

The merchant's charges are 1.8 percent for **MasterCard** and 2.1 percent for **Visa**. Frank's also had cash sales of $375 and $800 of sales on credit to a local business.

Required:

Prepare a journal entry to record these sales.

OBJECTIVE ⑥
CORNERSTONE 5-4

Cornerstone Exercise 5-35 Notes Receivable

Metzler Communications designs and programs a web site for a local business. Metzler charges $33,000 for the project and the local business signs a 7 percent note January 1, 2011.

Required:

1. Prepare the journal entry to record the sale on January 1, 2011.
2. Determine how much interest Metzler will receive if the note is repaid on July 1, 2011.
3. Prepare Metzler's journal entry to record the cash received to pay off the note and interest on July 1, 2011.

OBJECTIVE ⑥
CORNERSTONE 5-4

Cornerstone Exercise 5-36 Notes Receivable

Link Communications programs voicemail systems for businesses. For a recent project they charged $135,000. The customer secured this amount by signing a note bearing 9 percent interest on February 1, 2011.

Required:

1. Prepare the journal entry to record the sale on February 1, 2011.
2. Determine how much interest Link will receive if the note is repaid on December 1, 2011.
3. Prepare Link's journal entry to record the cash received to pay off the note and interest on December 1, 2011.

OBJECTIVE ⑧
CORNERSTONE 5-5

Cornerstone Exercise 5-37 Ratio Analysis

The following information pertains to Cobb Corporation's financial results for the past year.

Net sales	$135,000
Cost of goods sold	48,000
Other expenses	37,000
Net income	50,000

Required:

Calculate Cobb's (1) gross profit margin ratio and (2) net profit margin ratio.

OBJECTIVE ⑧
CORNERSTONE 5-5

Cornerstone Exercise 5-38 Ratio Analysis

Diviney Corporation's net sales and average net trade accounts receivable were $8,750,000 and $630,000, respectively.

Required:

Calculate Diviney's accounts receivable turnover.

Cornerstone Exercise 5-39 Ratio Analysis

OBJECTIVE **8**
CORNERSTONE 5-5

Bo Sports' net sales, average net trade accounts receivable, and net income were $7,300,000, $842,000, and $390,000, respectively.

Required:

Calculate Bo's (1) accounts receivable turnover and (2) net profit margin ratio.

EXERCISES

Exercise 5-40 Calculation of Revenue

OBJECTIVE **1**

Wallace Motors buys and sells used cars. Wallace made the following sales during January and February:

a. Three cars were sold to Russell Taxi for a total of $75,000; the cars were delivered to Russell on January 18. Russell paid Wallace $20,000 on January 18 and the remaining $55,000 on February 12.

b. One car was sold to Hastings Classics for $28,000. The car was delivered to Hastings on January 25. Hastings paid Wallace on February 1.

Required:

Calculate the monthly revenue for Wallace for January and February.

Exercise 5-41 Revenue Recognition

OBJECTIVE **1**

Volume Electronics sold a television to Sarah Merrifield on December 15, 2011. Sarah paid $100 at the time of the purchase and agreed to pay $100 each month for five months beginning January 15, 2012.

Required:

Determine in what month or months revenue from this sale should be recorded by Volume Electronics to ensure proper application of accrual accounting.

Exercise 5-42 Calculation of Revenue from Cash Collection

OBJECTIVE **1**

Anderson Lawn Service provides mowing, weed control, and pest management services for a flat fee of $140 per lawn per month. During July, Anderson collected $6,300 in cash from customers, which included $560 for lawn care provided in June. At the end of July, Anderson had not collected from 11 customers who had promised to pay in August when they returned from vacation.

Required:

Calculate the amount of Anderson's revenue for July.

Exercise 5-43 Effects of Sales Discounts

OBJECTIVE **2**

Citron Mechanical Systems makes all sales on credit, with terms 1/15, n/30. During 2011, the list price (prediscount) of services provided was $687,500. Customers paid $482,000 (list price) of these sales within the discount period and the remaining $205,500 (list price) after the discount period. Citron uses the gross method of recording sales.

Required:

1. Compute the amount of sales that Citron recorded for 2011.
2. Compute the amount of cash that Citron collected from these sales.
3. Prepare a summary journal entry to record these sales and a second summary entry to record the cash collected.

Exercise 5-44 Sales Discount Recorded at Gross

OBJECTIVE **2**

Nevada Company provided services with a list price of $48,500 to Small Enterprises with terms 2/15, n/45. Nevada records sales at gross.

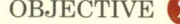

(Continued)

Required:
1. Prepare the entries to record this sale in Nevada's journal.
2. Prepare the entry for Nevada's journal to record receipt of cash in payment for the sale *within* the discount period.
3. Prepare the entry for Nevada's journal to record receipt of cash in payment for the sale *after* the discount period.
4. Assume that Nevada's customer does not have the available cash to pay Nevada within the discount period. How much interest should the customer be willing to pay for a loan to permit them to take advantage of the discount period (assuming no additional costs to the loan)?

Exercise 5-45 Sales and Sales Returns & Allowances

Rubin Enterprises had the following sales-related transactions on a recent day:

a. List price of services provided on credit was $18,150; terms 2/10, n/45.
b. Collected $3,650 in cash for services to be provided in the future.
c. The customer complained about aspects of the services provided in (a). To maintain a good relationship with this customer Rubin granted an allowance of $1,200 off the list price. The customer had not yet paid for the services.
d. Rubin provided the services for the customer in part (b). Additionally, Rubin granted an allowance of $250 because the services were provided after the promised date. Because the customer had already paid, Rubin paid the $250 allowance in cash.

Required:
1. Prepare the necessary journal entry (or entries) for each of these transactions.

2. What concerns would Rubin have assuming that their sales allowances for this period were significantly higher than in previous periods both in absolute turns and as a percentage of gross sales?

Exercise 5-46 Average Uncollectible Account Losses and Bad Debt Expense

The accountant for Porile Company prepared the following data for sales and losses from uncollectible accounts:

Year	Credit Sales	Losses from Uncollectible Accounts*
2007	$ 883,000	$13,125
2008	952,000	14,840
2009	1,083,000	16,790
2010	1,189,000	16,850

*Losses from uncollectible accounts are the actual losses related to sales of that year (rather than write-offs of that year).

Required:
1. Calculate the average percentage of losses from uncollectible accounts for 2007 through 2010.
2. Assume that the credit sales for 2011 are $1,260,000 and that the weighted average percentage calculated in (1) is used as an estimate of losses from uncollectible accounts for 2011 credit sales. Determine the bad debt expense for 2011 using the percentage of credit sales method.
3. **Conceptual Connection:** Do you believe this estimate of bad debt expense is reasonable?
4. **Conceptual Connection:** How would you estimate 2011 bad debt expense if losses from uncollectible accounts for 2010 were $30,000? What other action would management consider?

Exercise 5-47 Bad Debt Expense: Percentage of Credit Sales Method

Gilmore Electronics had the following data for a recent year:

Cash sales	$135,000
Credit sales	512,000
Accounts receivable determined to be uncollectible	9,650

The firm's estimated rate for bad debts is 2.2 percent of credit sales.

Required:

1. Prepare the journal entry to write off the uncollectible accounts.
2. Prepare the journal entry to record the estimate of bad debt expense.
3. By how much would bad debt expense reported on the income statement have changed if Gilmore had written off $3,000 of receivables as uncollectible during the year?
4. Assuming Gilmore's estimate of bad debts is correct (2.2 percent of credit sales) and their gross margin is 20 percent by how much did Gilmore's income from operations increase assuming $150,000 of the sales would have been lost if credit sales were not offered?

Exercise 5-48 Bad Debt Expense: Percentage of Credit Sales Method

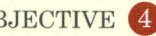 OBJECTIVE 4

Bradford Plumbing had the following data for a recent year:

Credit sales	$873,600
Allowance for doubtful accounts, 1/1 (a credit balance)	19,430
Accounts receivable, 1/1	67,350
Collections on account receivable	846,000
Accounts receivable written off	16,840

Bradford estimates that 2.4 percent of credit sales will eventually default.

Required:

1. Compute bad debt expense for the year (rounding to the nearest whole number).
2. Determine the ending balances in accounts receivable and allowance for doubtful accounts.

Exercise 5-49 Bad Debt Expense: Aging Method

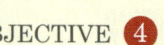 OBJECTIVE 4

Glencoe Supply had the following accounts receivable aging schedule at the end of a recent year.

Accounts Receivable Age	Amount	Proportion Expected to Default	Allowance Required
Current	$310,500	0.005	$ 1,553
1–30 days past due	47,500	0.01	475
31–45 days past due	25,000	0.13	3,250
46–90 days past due	12,800	0.20	2,560
91–135 days past due	6,100	0.25	1,525
Over 135 days past due	4,200	0.60	2,520
			$11,883

The balance in Glencoe's allowance for doubtful accounts at the beginning of the year was $58,620 (credit). During the year, accounts in the total amount of $62,400 were written off.

Required:

1. Determine bad debt expense.
2. Prepare the journal entry to record bad debt expense.
3. By how much would bad debt expense reported on the income statement have changed if Glencoe had written off $90,000 of receivables as uncollectible during the year?

Exercise 5-50 Aging Receivables and Bad Debt Expense

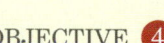 OBJECTIVE 4

Perkinson Corporation sells paper products to a large number of retailers. Perkinson's accountant has prepared the following aging schedule for its accounts receivable at the end of the year.

Accounts Receivable Category	Amount	Proportion Expected to Default
Within discount period	$384,500	0.004
1–30 days past discount period	187,600	0.015
31–60 days past discount period	41,800	0.085
Over 60 days past discount period	21,400	0.200

Before adjusting entries are entered, the balance in the allowance for doubtful accounts is a *debit* of $480.

Required:

1. Calculate the desired postadjustment balance in Perkinson's allowance for doubtful accounts.
2. Determine bad debt expense for the year.

OBJECTIVE 4

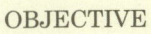

Exercise 5-51 Allowance for Doubtful Accounts

At the beginning of the year, Kullerud Manufacturing had a credit balance in its allowance for doubtful accounts of $6,307 and at the end of the year it was a credit balance of $9,000. During the year Kullerud made credit sales of $890,000, collected receivables in the amount of $812,000, and recorded bad debt expense of $33,750.

Required:

Compute the amount of receivables that Kullerud wrote during the year.

OBJECTIVE 4

Exercise 5-52 Collection of Amounts Previously Written Off

Customer Rob Hufnagel owes Kellman Corp. $1,250. Kellman determines that the total amount is uncollectible and writes off all of Hufnagel's debt. Hufnagel later pays $350 to Kellman.

Required:

Make the appropriate journal entries (if any) to record the receipt of $350 by Kellman.

OBJECTIVE 4

Exercise 5-53 Correcting an Erroneous Write-Off

The new bookkeeper at Karlin Construction Company was asked to write off two accounts totaling $1,710 that had been determined to be uncollectible. Accordingly, he debited accounts receivable for $1,710 and credited bad debt expense for the same amount.

Required:

1. Determine what was wrong with the bookkeeper's entry assuming Karlin uses the allowance method.
2. Give both the entry he should have made and the entry required to correct his error.

OBJECTIVE 6

Exercise 5-54 Accounting for Notes Receivable

On November 30, 2011, Tucker Products performed computer programming services to Thomas, Inc., in exchange for a five-month, $75,000, 10 percent note receivable. Thomas, Inc., paid Tucker the full amount of interest and principal on April 30, 2012.

Required:

Prepare the necessary entries for Tucker to record the transactions described above.

OBJECTIVE 6

Exercise 5-55 Recording Notes Receivable: Issuance, Payment, and Default

Marydale Products permits its customers to defer payment by giving personal notes instead of cash. All the notes bear interest and require the customer to pay the entire note in a single payment six months after issuance. Consider the following transactions, which describe Marydale's experience with two such notes:

a. On October 31, 2011, Marydale accepts a six-month, 9 percent note from customer A in lieu of a $3,600 cash payment for services provided that day.
b. On February 28, 2012, Marydale accepts a six-month, $2,400, 7 percent note from customer B in lieu of a $2,400 cash payment for services provided on that day.
c. On April 30, 2012, customer A pays the entire note plus interest in cash.
d. On August 31, 2012, customer B pays the entire note plus interest in cash.

Required:

Prepare the necessary journal and adjusting entries required to record transactions *a* through *d* in Marydale's records.

OBJECTIVE 7

Exercise 5-56 Internal Control for Sales

Arrow Products is a mail-order computer software sales outlet. Most of Arrow's customers call on its toll-free phone line and order software, paying with a credit card.

Required:

Conceptual Connection: Explain why the shipping and billing documents are important internal controls for Arrow.

Exercise 5-57 Ratio Analysis

OBJECTIVE

The following information was taken from Nash, Inc.'s trial balances as of December 31, 2010, and December 31, 2011.

	12/31/2011	12/31/2010
Accounts receivable	$ 32,000	$ 39,000
Accounts payable	47,000	36,000
Sales	219,000	128,000
Sales returns	4,000	2,300
Retained earnings	47,000	16,000
Dividends	5,000	1,000
Net income	36,000	9,000

Required:

1. Calculate the net profit margin and accounts receivable turnover for 2011. (*Note:* Round answers to two decimal places.)
2. How much does Nash make on each sales dollar?
3. How many days does the average receivable take to be paid (assuming all sales are on account)?

Exercise 5-58 Ratio Analysis

OBJECTIVE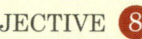

The following information was taken from Logsden Manufacturing's trial balances as of December 31, 2010, and December 31, 2011.

	12/31/2011	12/31/2010
Accounts receivable	$ 13,000	$ 17,000
Accounts payable	22,000	15,000
Cost of goods sold	140,000	119,000
Sales	274,000	239,000
Sales returns	12,000	11,000
Retained earnings	47,000	16,000
Dividends	5,000	1,000
Income from operations	25,000	16,000
Net income	21,000	18,000

Required:

1. Calculate the gross profit margin and operating margin percentage for 2011. (*Note:* Round answers to two decimal places.)
2. Assuming that all of the operating expenses are fixed (or, won't change as sales increase or decrease), what will be the operating margin percentage if sales increase by 25 percent?

PROBLEM SET A

Problem 5-59A Revenue Recognition

OBJECTIVE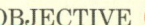

Katie Vote owns a small business that rents computers to students at the local university for the nine-month school year. Katie's typical rental contract requires the student to pay the year's rent of $900 ($100 per month) in advance. When Katie prepares financial statements at the end of December, her accountant requires that Katie spread the $900 over the nine months that a computer is rented. Therefore, Katie can recognize only $400 revenue (four months) from each computer rental contract in the year the cash is collected and must defer recognition of the remaining $500 (five months) to next year. Katie argues that getting students to agree to rent the computer is the most difficult part of the activity so she ought to be able to recognize all $900 as revenue when the cash is received from a student.

Required:

Conceptual Connection: Explain why generally accepted accounting principles require the use of accrual accounting rather than cash-basis accounting for transactions like the one described here.

OBJECTIVE ❷

Problem 5-60A Discount Policy and Gross Profit

Compton Audio sells MP3 players. During 2011, Compton sold 1,000 units at an average of $250 per unit. Each unit cost Compton $100. At present, Compton offers no sales discounts. Compton's controller suggests that a generous sales discount policy would increase annual sales to 1,400 units and also improve cash flow. She proposes 5/10, n/30 and believes that 80 percent of the customers will take advantage of the discount.

Required:
1. If the controller is correct, determine how much the new sales discount policy would add to net sales and gross margin.
2. **Conceptual Connection:** Explain why the sales discount policy might improve cash flow.

OBJECTIVE ❷

Problem 5-61A Effects of Discounts on Sales and Purchases

Helmkamp Products sells golf clubs and accessories to pro shops. Gross sales in 2011 were $2,850,700 (Helmkamp's list price) on terms 2/15, n/45. Customers paid for $2,000,000 (Helmkamp's list price) of the merchandise within the discount period and the remaining $850,700 after the end of the discount period. Helmkamp records purchases and sales using the gross method to account for sales discounts.

Required:
1. Compute the amount of net sales.
2. Determine how much cash was collected from sales.

OBJECTIVE ❷

Problem 5-62A Sales Discounts

Sims Company regularly provides services to Lauber Supply on terms 1/15, n/30 and records sales at gross. During a recent month, the two firms engaged in the following transactions:

a. Sims provided services with a list price of $85,000.
b. Sims provided services with a list price of $30,000.
c. Lauber paid for the purchase in transaction *a* within the discount period.
d. Lauber paid for the purchase in transaction *b* after the discount period.

Required:
1. Prepare the journal entries for Sims to record the sales in *a* and *b* (make separate entries).
2. Prepare the journal entry to record Lauber's payment in *c*.
3. Prepare the journal entry to record Lauber's payment in *d*.
4. **Conceptual Connection:** What implied annual interest rate is Lauber incurring by failing to take the sales discount and, instead, paying the gross amount after 30 days?

OBJECTIVE ❼

Problem 5-63A Internal Control for Sales

Yancy's Hardware has three stores. Each store manager is paid a salary plus a bonus on the sales made by his or her store. On January 5, 2012, Bill Slick, manager of one of the stores, resigned. Bill's store had doubled its expected December 2011 sales, producing a bonus for Bill of $8,000 in December alone. Charles Brook, an assistant manager at another store, was assigned as manager of Bill's store. Upon examination of the store's accounting records, Charles reports that the store's records indicated sales returns and allowances of $110,000 in the first four days of January 2012, an amount equal to about half of December 2011 sales.

Required:
1. **Conceptual Connection:** Explain what the large amount of sales returns and allowances suggest that Bill might have done.
2. **Conceptual Connection:** Determine how Yancy could protect itself from a manager who behaved as Bill did.

OBJECTIVE ❹

Problem 5-64A Bad Debt Expense: Percentage of Credit Sales Method

The Glass House, a glass and china store, sells nearly half its merchandise on credit. During the past four years, the following data were developed for credit sales and losses from uncollectible accounts:

Year of Sales	Credit Sales	Losses from Uncollectible Accounts*
2008	$197,000	$12,608
2009	202,000	13,299
2010	212,000	13,285
2011	273,000	22,274
Total	$884,000	$61,466

*Losses from uncollectible accounts are the actual losses related to sales of that year (rather than write-offs of that year).

Required:
1. Calculate the loss rate for each year from 2008 through 2011. (*Note:* Round answers to three decimal places.)
2. Determine whether there appears to be a significant change in the loss rate over time.
3. **Conceptual Connection:** If credit sales for 2012 are $400,000, determine what loss rate you would recommend to estimate bad debts. (*Note:* Round answers to three decimal places.)
4. Using the rate you recommend, record bad debt expense for 2012.
5. **Conceptual Connection:** Assume that the increase in The Glass House's sales in 2012 was largely due to granting credit to customers who would have been denied credit in previous years. How would this change your answer to part 4? Describe a legitimate business reason why The Glass House would adopt more lenient credit terms.
6. Using the data from 2008 through 2011, estimate the increase in income from operations in total for each of those four years assuming (a) the average gross margin is 25% and (b) 50% of the sales would have been lost if no credit was granted.

Problem 5-65A Aging Method Bad Debt Expense

OBJECTIVE 4

Cindy Bagnal, the manager of Cayce Printing Service, has provided you with the following aging schedule for Cayce's accounts receivable:

Accounts Receivable Category	Amount	Proportion Expected to Default
0–20 days	$ 88,200	0.02
21–40 days	21,500	0.08
41–60 days	11,700	0.15
Over 60 days	5,300	0.30
	$126,700	

Cindy indicates that the $126,700 of accounts receivable identified in the table does not include $8,900 of receivables that should be written off.

Required:
1. Journalize the $8,900 write-off.
2. Determine the desired postadjustment balance in allowance for doubtful accounts.
3. If the balance in allowance for doubtful accounts before the $8,900 write-off was a debit of $450, compute bad debt expense. Prepare the adjusting entry to record bad debt expense.

Problem 5-66A Determining Bad Debt Expense Using the Aging Method

OBJECTIVE 4

At the beginning of the year, Tennyson Auto Parts had an accounts receivable balance of $31,800 and a balance in the allowance for doubtful accounts of $2,980 (credit). During the year Tennyson had credit sales of $624,300, collected accounts receivable in the amount of $602,700, wrote off $18,600 of accounts receivable, and had the following data for accounts receivable at the end of the period:

Accounts Receivable Age	Amount	Proportion Expected to Default
Current	$20,400	0.01
1–15 days past due	5,300	0.02
16–45 days past due	3,100	0.08
46–90 days past due	3,600	0.15
Over 90 days past due	2,400	0.30
	$34,800	

Required:

1. Determine the desired postadjustment balance in allowance for doubtful accounts.
2. Determine the balance in allowance for doubtful accounts before the bad debt expense adjusting entry is posted.
3. Compute bad debt expense.
4. Prepare the adjusting entry to record bad debt expense.

OBJECTIVE 6

Problem 5-67A Accounting for Notes Receivable

Yarnell Electronics sells computer systems to small businesses. Yarnell engaged in the following activities involving notes receivable:

a. On November 1, 2011, Yarnell sold a $5,000 system to Ross Company. Ross gave Yarnell a six-month, 9 percent note as payment.
b. On December 1, 2011, Yarnell sold an $8,000 system to Searfoss Inc. Searfoss gave Yarnell a nine-month, 8 percent note as payment.
c. On May 1, 2012, Ross paid the amount due on its note.
d. On September 1, 2012, Searfoss paid the amount due on its note.

Required:

Prepare the necessary journal and adjusting entries for Yarnell Electronics to record these transactions.

OBJECTIVE 8

Problem 5-68A Ratio Analysis

Selected information from Bigg Company's financial statements follows.

	Fiscal Year Ended December 31		
	2011	2010	2009
	(in thousands)		
Gross sales	$2,004,719	$1,937,021	$1,835,987
Less: Sales discounts	(4,811)	(4,649)	(4,406)
Less: Sales returns and allowances	(2,406)	(2,324)	(2,203)
Net sales	$1,997,502	$1,930,048	$1,829,378
Cost of goods sold	621,463	619,847	660,955
Gross profit	$1,376,039	$1,310,201	$1,168,423
Operating expenses	577,369	595,226	583,555
Operating income	$ 798,670	$ 714,975	$ 584,868
Other income (expenses)	15,973	(5,720)	(8,773)
Net income	$ 814,643	$ 709,255	$ 576,095

	At December 31		
	2011	2010	2009
	(in thousands)		
Accounts receivable	$201,290	$195,427	$182,642
Less: Allowance for doubtful accounts	(2,516)	(2,736)	(2,192)
Net accounts receivable	$198,774	$192,691	$180,450

Required:

1. Calculate the following ratios for 2010 and 2011: (a) gross profit margin, (b) operating margin, (c) net profit margin, and (d) accounts receivable turnover. (*Note:* Round answers to two decimal places.)
2. **Conceptual Connection:** For each of the first three ratios listed above, provide a plausible explanation for any differences that exist. (For example, why is the net profit margin higher or lower than it was the previous year?)
3. **Conceptual Connection:** Explain what each ratio attempts to measure. Make an assessment about Bigg Company based upon the ratios you have calculated. Are operations improving or worsening?

PROBLEM SET B

Problem 5-59B Revenue Recognition

OBJECTIVE ①

Mary Wade owns a small business that rents parking spaces to students at the local university. Mary's typical rental contract requires the student to pay the year's rent of $720 ($60 per month) in advance. When Mary prepares financial statements at the end of December, her accountant requires that Mary spread the $720 over the 12 months that a parking space is rented. Therefore, Mary can recognize only $240 revenue (four months) from each contract in the year the cash is collected and must defer recognition of the remaining $480 (eight months) to next year. Mary argues that getting students to agree to rent the parking space is the most difficult part of the activity so she ought to be able to recognize all $720 as revenue when the cash is received from a student.

Required:

Conceptual Connection: Explain generally accepted accounting principles require the use of accrual accounting rather than cash-basis accounting for transactions like the one described here.

Problem 5-60B Discount Policy and Gross Profit

OBJECTIVE ②

Parker Electronics sells cell phones. During 2011, Parker sold 1,500 units at an average of $500 per unit. Each unit cost Parker $350. At present, Parker offers no sales discounts. Parker's controller suggests that a generous sales discount policy would increase annual sales to 2,000 units and also improve cash flow. She proposes 3/15, n/20 and believes that 75 percent of the customers will take advantage of the discount.

Required:

1. If the controller is correct, determine how much the new sales discount policy would add to net sales and gross margin.
2. **Conceptual Connection:** Explain why the sales discount policy might improve cash flow.

Problem 5-61B Effects of Discounts on Sales and Purchases

OBJECTIVE ②

Smithson Products sells shoes and accessories to retail stores. Gross sales in 2011 were $1,500,250 (Smithson's list price) on terms 4/10, n/30. Customers paid for $1,200,000 (Smithson's list price) of the merchandise within the discount period and the remaining $300,250 after the end of the discount period. Smithson records purchases and sales using the gross method to account for sales discounts.

Required:

1. Compute the amount of net sales.
2. Determine how much cash was collected from sales.

Problem 5-62B Sales Discounts

OBJECTIVE ②

Spartan, Inc., regularly provides services to Grieder Supply on terms 3/10, n/40 and records sales at gross. During a recent month, the two firms engaged in the following transactions:

a. Spartan sold merchandise with a list price of $250,000.
b. Spartan sold merchandise with a list price of $75,000.
c. Grieder paid for the purchase in transaction *a* within the discount period.
d. Grieder paid for the purchase in transaction *b* after the discount period.

Required:

1. Provide the journal entries for Spartan to record the sales in *a* and *b* (make separate entries).
2. Provide the journal entry to record Grieder's payment in *c*.
3. Provide the journal entry to record Grieder's payment in *d*.
4. **Conceptual Connection:** What implied annual interest rate is Grieder incurring by failing to take the sales discount and, instead, paying the gross amount after 40 days?

Problem 5-63B Internal Control for Sales

OBJECTIVE ⑦

Johnson Tires has three stores. Each store manager is paid a salary plus a bonus on the sales made by his or her store. On January 5, 2012, Kevin Sampson, manager of one of the stores, resigned. Kevin's store had doubled its expected December 2011 sales, producing a bonus for Kevin of

$7,000 in December alone. Jason Jones, an assistant manager at another store, was assigned as manager of Kevin's store. Upon examination of the store's accounting records, Jason reports that the store's records indicated sales returns and allowances of $124,000 in the first four days of January 2012, an amount equal to about half of December 2011 sales.

Required:
1. **Conceptual Connection:** Explain what the large amount of sales returns and allowances suggest that Kevin might have done.
2. **Conceptual Connection:** Determine how Johnson could protect itself from a manager who behaved as Kevin did.

OBJECTIVE

Problem 5-64B Bad Debt Expense: Percentage of Credit Sales Method

Kelly's Collectibles sells nearly half its merchandise on credit. During the past four years, the following data were developed for credit sales and losses from uncollectible accounts:

Year of Sales	Credit Sales	Losses from Uncollectible Accounts*
2008	$205,000	$15,527
2009	185,000	11,692
2010	209,000	14,184
2011	253,000	21,933
Total	$852,000	$63,336

*Losses from uncollectible accounts are the actual losses related to sales of that year (rather than write-offs of that year).

Required:
1. Calculate the loss rate for each year from 2008 through 2011. (*Note:* Round answers to three decimal places.)
2. Determine if there appears to be a significant change in the loss rate over time.
3. **Conceptual Connection:** If credit sales for 2012 are $415,000, explain what loss rate you would recommend to estimate bad debts. (*Note:* Round answers to three decimal places.)
4. Using the rate you recommend, record bad debt expense for 2012.
5. **Conceptual Connection:** Assume that the increase in Kelly's sales in 2012 was largely due to granting credit to customers who would have been denied credit in previous years. How would this change your answer to part 4? Describe a legitimate business reason why Kelly's would adopt more lenient credit terms.

 6. Using the data from 2008 through 2011, estimate the increase in income from operations in total for each of those four years assuming (a) the average gross margin is 40% and (b) 20% of the sales would have been lost if no credit was granted.

OBJECTIVE

Problem 5-65B Aging Method Bad Debt Expense

Carol Simon, the manager of Handy Plumbing has provided you with the following aging schedule for Handy's accounts receivable:

Accounts Receivable Category	Amount	Proportion Expected to Default
0–20 days	$ 92,600	0.03
21–40 days	12,700	0.09
41–60 days	17,800	0.14
Over 60 days	2,100	0.30
	$125,200	

Carol indicates that the $125,200 of accounts receivable identified in the table does not include $9,400 of receivables that should be written off.

Required:
1. Journalize the $9,400 write-off.
2. Determine the desired postadjustment balance in allowance for doubtful accounts.
3. If the balance in allowance for doubtful accounts before the $9,400 write-off was a debit of $550, compute bad debt expense. Prepare the adjusting entry to record bad debt expense.

Problem 5-66B Determining Bad Debt Expense Using the Aging Method

At the beginning of the year, Lennon Electronics had an accounts receivable balance of $29,800 and a balance in the allowance for doubtful accounts of $2,425 (credit). During the year, Lennon had credit sales of $752,693, collected accounts receivable in the amount of $653,800, wrote off $20,400 of accounts receivable, and had the following data for accounts receivable at the end of the period:

Accounts Receivable Age	Amount	Proportion Expected to Default
Current	$22,700	0.01
1–15 days past due	8,600	0.04
16–45 days past due	4,900	0.09
46–90 days past due	3,200	0.17
Over 90 days past due	2,100	0.30
	$41,500	

Required:

1. Determine the desired postadjustment balance in allowance for doubtful accounts.
2. Determine the balance in allowance for doubtful accounts before the bad debt expense adjusting entry is posted.
3. Compute bad debt expense.
4. Prepare the adjusting entry to record bad debt expense.

Problem 5-67B Accounting for Notes Receivable

Sloan Systems sells voice mail systems to small businesses. Sloan engaged in the following activities involving notes receivable:

a. On October 1, 2011, Sloan sold an $8,000 system to Majors Company. Majors gave Sloan a seven-month, 10 percent note as payment.
b. On November 1, 2011, Sloan sold a $6,000 system to Hadley Inc. Hadley gave Sloan a ten-month, 12 percent note as payment.
c. On May 1, 2012, Majors paid the amount due on its note.
d. On September 1, 2012, Hadley paid the amount due on its note.

Required:

Prepare the necessary journal and adjusting entries for Sloan Systems to record these transactions.

Problem 5-68B Ratio Analysis

Selected information from Small Company's financial statements follows.

	Fiscal Year Ended December 31		
	2011	2010	2009
	(in thousands)		
Gross sales	$1,663,917	$1,697,195	$1,714,167
Less: Sales discounts	(2,995)	(3,055)	(3,086)
Less: Sales returns and allowances	(2,496)	(2,546)	(2,571)
Net sales	$1,658,426	$1,691,594	$1,708,510
Cost of goods sold	881,876	891,027	860,512
Gross profit	$ 776,550	$ 800,567	$ 847,998
Operating expenses	482,050	496,958	487,214
Operating income	$ 294,500	$ 303,609	$ 360,784
Other income (expenses)	3,534	(3,036)	(1,804)
Net income	$ 298,034	$ 300,573	$ 358,980

	At December 31		
	2011	2010	2009
	(in thousands)		
Accounts receivable	$376,062	$365,109	$341,223
Less: Allowance for doubtful accounts	(8,461)	(71,926)	(5,971)
Net accounts receivable	$367,601	$293,183	$335,252

Required:

1. Calculate the following ratios for 2010 and 2011: (a) gross profit margin, (b) operating margin, (c) net profit margin, and (d) accounts receivable turnover. (*Note:* Round answers to two decimal places.)
2. **Conceptual Connection:** For each of the first three ratios listed above provide a plausible explanation for any differences that exist. (For example, why is the net profit margin higher or lower than it was the previous year?)
3. **Conceptual Connection:** Explain what each ratio attempts to measure. Make an assessment about Small Company based upon the ratios you have calculated. Are operations improving or worsening?

CASES

Case 5-69 Ethics and Revenue Recognition

Alan Spalding is CEO of a large appliance wholesaler. Alan is under pressure from Wall Street Analysts to meet his aggressive sales revenue growth projections. Unfortunately, near the end of the year he realizes that sales must dramatically improve if his projections are going to be met. To accomplish this objective, he orders his sales force to contact their largest customers and offer them price discounts if they buy by the end of the year. Alan also offered to deliver the merchandise to a third-party warehouse with whom the customers could arrange delivery when the merchandise was needed.

Required:

1. Do you believe that revenue from these sales should be recognized in the current year? Why or why not?
2. What are the probable consequences of this behavior for the company in future periods?
3. What are the probable consequences of this behavior for investors analyzing the current year financial statements?

Case 5-70 Recognition of Service Contract Revenues

Jackson Dunlap is president of New Miami Maintenance, Inc., which provides building maintenance services. On October 15, 2011, Jackson signed a service contract with Western College and Western made a down payment of $12,000. Under the contract, New Miami will provide maintenance services for all Western's buildings for a period of two years, beginning on January 1, 2012, and Western will pay New Miami $1,000 per month, beginning on January 31, 2012.

Initially, Jackson proposed that some portion of the revenue from the contract should be recognized in 2011; however, his accountant, Rita McGonigle, convinced him that this would be inappropriate. Then Jackson proposed that the revenue should be recognized in an amount equal to the cash collected under the contract in 2011. Again, Rita argued against his proposal, saying that generally accepted accounting principles required recognition of an equal amount of contract revenue each month.

Required:

1. Give a reason that might explain Jackson's desire to recognize contract revenue earlier rather than later.
2. Put yourself in Rita's position. How would you convince Jackson that his two proposals are unacceptable and that an equal amount of revenue should be recognized every month?
3. If Rita's proposal is adopted, how would the contract be reflected in the balance sheets at the end of 2011 and at the end of 2012?

Case 5-71 Revenue Recognition

Beth Rader purchased North Shore Health Club in June 2011. Beth wanted to increase the size of the business by selling five-year memberships for $2,000, payable at the beginning of the membership period. The normal yearly membership fee is $500. Since few prospective members were expected to have $2,000, Beth arranged for a local bank to provide a $2,000 installment loan to prospective members. By the end of 2011, 250 customers had purchased the five-year memberships using the loan provided by the bank.

Beth prepared her income statement for 2011 and included $500,000 as revenue because the club had collected the entire amount in cash. Beth's accountant objected to the inclusion of the entire $500,000. The accountant argued that the $500,000 should be recognized as revenue as the club provides services for these members during the membership period. Beth countered with a quotation from a part of "Generally Accepted Accounting Principles," *Accounting Research Bulletin 43, Chapter 1, Section A, No. 1*:

> *"Profit is deemed to be realized when a sale in the ordinary course of business is effected, unless the circumstances are such that collection of the sale price is not reasonably assured."*

Beth notes that the memberships have been sold and that collection of the selling price has occurred. Therefore, she argues that all $500,000 is revenue in 2011.

Required:

Write a short statement supporting either Beth or the accountant in this dispute.

Case 5-72 Sales Discount Policies

Consider three businesses, all of which offer price reductions to their customers. The first is an independently owned gas station located at a busy intersection in Cincinnati, Ohio, that offers a 3 percent discount for cash purchases of gasoline. The second is a large home improvement store located near an interstate exit in suburban Cleveland that offers building contractors terms of 3/10, n/45. And third is a clothing manufacturer and catalog retailer located in Columbus. Several times during each year, a catalog is distributed in which men's dress shirts are heavily discounted if purchased in lots of four or more.

Required:

1. What are the main objectives of the discount policies in each of the three businesses?
2. How does accounting information assist each business in achieving its discount policy objectives?

Case 5-73 Financial Analysis of Receivables

A chain of retail stores located in Kansas and Nebraska has requested a loan from the bank at which you work. The balance sheet of the retail chain shows significant accounts receivable related to its in-house credit card. You have been assigned to evaluate these receivables.

Required:

1. What questions concerning the quality of these receivables can you answer by analyzing the retailer's financial statements?
2. What additional questions would you raise, and what information would you request from the retailer to answer these questions?

Case 5-74 Income Effects of Uncollectible Accounts

The credit manager and the accountant for Goldsmith Company are attempting to assess the effect on net income of writing off $100,000 of receivables. Goldsmith uses the aging method of determining bad debt expense and has the following aging schedule for its accounts receivable at December 31, 2011:

Accounts Receivable Category	Amount	Proportion Expected to Default
Current	$2,980,400	0.004
1–30 days past due	722,600	0.035
31–60 days past due	418,500	0.095
Over 60 days past due	322,800	0.250
	$4,444,300	

The receivables being considered for write-off are all over 60 days past due.

Required:

1. Assume that the tax rate is 30 percent. What will be the effect on net income if the $100,000 is written off?

2. What data would you examine to provide some assurance that a company was not holding uncollectible accounts in its accounts receivable rather than writing them off when they are determined to be uncollectible?

Case 5-75 Research and Analysis Using the Annual Report

Obtain **Under Armour**'s 2009 10-K through the "Investor Relations" portion of their website. (Using a search engine, search for: Under Armour investor relations.) Once at the Investor Relations section of the website, look for "SEC Filings." When you see the list of all the filings either filter for the "Annual Filings" or search for "10-K." Another option is to go to http://www.sec.gov and click "Search for Company Filings" under "Filings & Forms."

Required:

1. Look at the "Reserve for Uncollectible Accounts Receivable" heading to Note 2 (Summary of Significant Accounting Policies). Does Under Armour use the percentage of credit sales method or the aging method to estimate bad debt expense?
2. Looking at the same note, what was Under Armour's allowance for doubtful accounts in 2009 and 2008?
3. Was a larger percentage of the gross accounts receivable considered uncollectible at December 31, 2008 or 2009?
4. Calculate Under Armour's receivables turnover for 2008 and 2009 (Accounts Receivable, net, was $71,867 at December 31, 2007). (*Note:* Round answers to two decimal places.) If the industry average for receivables turnover is 24.78, how do you evaluate their efficiency with receivables?
5. Calculate Under Armour's gross profit margin, operating margin, and net profit margin for 2008 and 2009. (*Note:* Round answers to two decimal places.)
6. If the industry average for gross profit ratio is 36.61 percent, what sort of strategy do you think Under Armour is pursuing?
7. Evaluate the trend of Under Armour's operating margin and net profit margin and relate the trend to the industry averages of 10.97 percent and 6.54 percent, respectively.

Case 5-76 Comparative Analysis: Abercrombie & Fitch versus Aeropostale

Refer to the financial statements of **Abercrombie & Fitch** and **Aeropostale** that are supplied with this text.

Required:

1. Look at Abercrombie & Fitch's Note 2 (Summary of Significant Accounting Policies) under the heading Receivables. Based on this disclosure, describe the nature of A&F's receivables reported on the balance sheet. What is the balance in their allowance for doubtful accounts?
2. Look at Aeropostale's Note 1 (Summary of Significant Accounting Policies) under the headings (1) Cash Equivalents and (2) Fair Value of Measurement. Based on these disclosures, how does Aeropostale's receivables differ from Abercrombie & Fitch's receivables? Why isn't there a receivables balance on Aeropostale's balance sheet?
3. Using the balances reported on the balance sheets, what is Abercrombie & Fitch's receivables turnover for the year ended January 30, 2010? (*Note:* Round answer to two decimal places.)
4. Calculate Abercrombie & Fitch's and Aeropostale's gross profit margin for the years ended January 30, 2010, and January 31, 2009. (*Note:* Round answers to two decimal places.) What can you infer about the strategy pursued by these two companies based on these measures assuming the industry average is around 46 percent?
5. Calculate Abercrombie & Fitch's and Aeropostale's operating margin for the years ended January 30, 2010, and January 31, 2009. (*Note:* Round answers to two decimal places.) Comment on these measures assuming the industry average is around 1.5 percent.
6. Calculate Abercrombie & Fitch's and Aeropostale's net profit margin for the years ended January 30, 2010, and January 31, 2009. (*Note:* Round answers to two decimal places.) Comment on these measures assuming the industry average is just under one percent.

Case 5-77 CONTINUING PROBLEM: FRONT ROW ENTERTAINMENT

While Front Row Entertainment has had considerable success in signing artists and promoting concerts, Cam and Anna still had a few ideas to grow their business that they wanted to implement. One idea that they both agreed on was to start an online fan "community" for each of their artists. By providing a more direct connection between the artists and their fans, each artist community would serve as an online fan club that should generate increased interest and attendance in the artists' concerts. In addition to marketing and promoting the artist, Front Row Entertainment could sell advertising space on these fan communities to companies interested in reaching the particular demographic that the artist attracts. Because the summer concert season is one of the busiest and most lucrative times of the year, Cam and Anna felt it was extremely important to get the fan communities in place prior to the beginning of the summer. Therefore, they engaged in the following selected transactions for the months of May and June:

May 1	Paid Web Design Inc. $8,500 to develop the fan websites. The fan websites were operational on May 10. Front Row charged this expenditure to other expense.
May 10	Front Row Entertainment sold $550 worth of advertising to Little John's Restaurant with terms 2/10, n/30. The advertising will randomly appear on the artists' websites throughout the month of May.
May 15	Front Row Entertainment sold $475 worth of advertising to Sherwood Media with terms 2/10, n/30. The advertising related to an in-store DVD promotion that Sherwood was holding later in the month.
May 19	Front Row Entertainment received payment from Little John for the May 8 bill.
May 20	Sherwood Media informed Front Row that an error had been made on its advertisement. Sherwood's promotion was supposed to run from May 20 to May 25; however, the advertisement stated that the promotion would run from May 15 to May 25. Because the error was Front Row's fault, Front Row agreed to reduce the amount owed by $150.
June 1	Front Row Entertainment sold $750 worth of advertising to Big House Entertainment Company with terms 2/10, n/30. The advertising will randomly appear on the artists' websites throughout the month of June.
June 10	Sherwood paid Front Row the amount owed for the May 15 bill less the allowance granted on May 20.
June 20	When Front Row learns that Big House Entertainment has filed for bankruptcy, it writes off the $750 receivable.

Over the next few months, the fan communities continue to grow in popularity, with more and more companies purchasing advertising space. By the end of 2011, Front Row reports the following balances:

Accounts receivable	$17,900
Allowance for doubtful accounts	250 (debit)
Credit sales	45,000

Required:

1. Prepare journal entries for the May and June transactions.
2. Prepare the adjusting entry required at December 31, 2011, with regard to bad debt under each of the following independent assumptions.

   a. Assume that Front Row performed an aging of its accounts receivable. Front Row estimates that $895 of its accounts receivable will be uncollectible.

   b. Assume that Front Row uses the percentage of credit sales method and estimates that 2% of credit sales will be uncollectible.

6 Cost of Goods Sold and Inventory

Doug Norman Crystals/Alamy

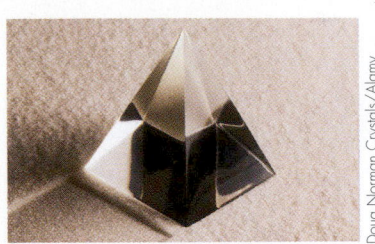

After studying Chapter 6, you should be able to:

1. Describe the types of inventories held by merchandisers and manufacturers, and understand how inventory costs flow through a company.
2. Explain how to record purchases and sales of inventory using a perpetual inventory system.
3. Apply the four inventory costing methods to compute ending inventory and cost of goods sold under a perpetual inventory system.
4. Analyze the financial reporting and tax effects of the various inventory costing methods.
5. Apply the lower of cost or market rule to the valuation of inventory.
6. Evaluate inventory management using the gross profit and inventory turnover ratios.
7. Describe how errors in ending inventory affect income statements and balance sheets.
8. *(Appendix 6A)* Explain how to record purchases of inventory using a periodic inventory system.
9. *(Appendix 6B)* Compute ending inventory and cost of goods sold under a periodic inventory system.

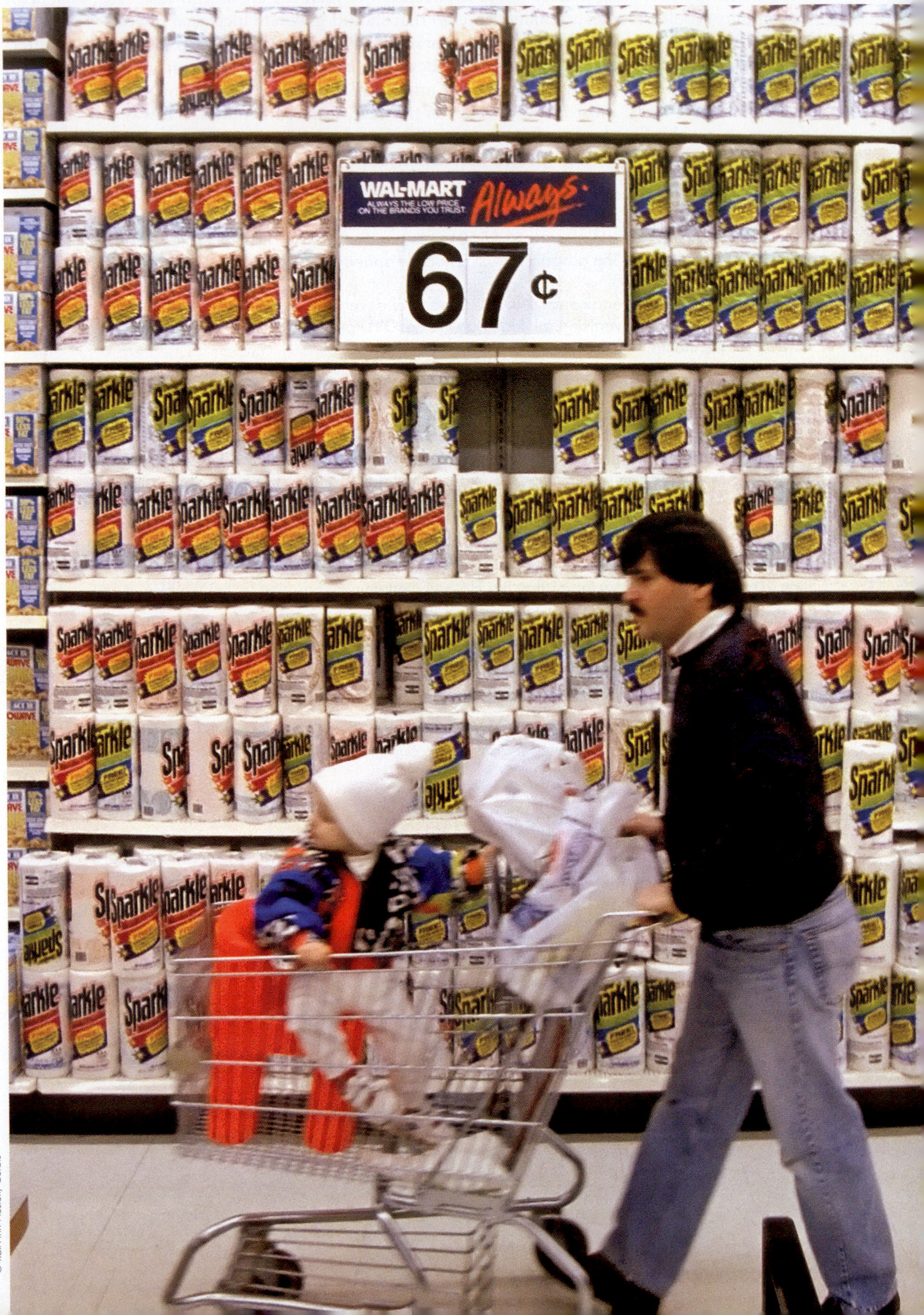

© Ralf-Finn Hestoft/Corbis

EXPERIENCE FINANCIAL ACCOUNTING

with Wal-Mart

Wal-Mart Stores, Inc., based in Bentonville, Arkansas, is America's largest public corporation with $405 billion in sales for its 2010 fiscal year. Wal-Mart serves more than 200 million customers per week through 8,416 retail stores in 15 countries. Given the large volume of merchandise that is sold, Wal-Mart's profits depend heavily on the control and management of its inventory. After all, as shown in Exhibit 6-1, inventory makes up almost 69 percent of Wal-Mart's current assets.

For many companies, inventory is at the heart of the operating cycle and must be carefully managed and controlled. If a company doesn't have enough inventory on its shelves to meet customers' demand, it will lose sales. On the other hand, too much inventory will increase carrying costs such as storage and interest costs as well as increase the risk of obsolescence. Wal-Mart has long been recognized as a world leader in its effective use of technology to manage and control its inventory and distribution.

As you will see in this chapter, even though inventory is an asset, it can have a major impact on net income. That is because all inventory accounting systems allocate the cost of inventory between ending inventory and cost of goods sold. Therefore, the valuation of inventory affects cost of goods sold, which in turn, affects net income. By managing and controlling its inventory, Wal-Mart has been able to tie up less of its money in inventory than its competitors, resulting in greater profits. This focus on inventory allows Wal-Mart to sell its merchandise at "always low prices. Always."

Exhibit 6-1

Composition of Wal-Mart's Current Assets

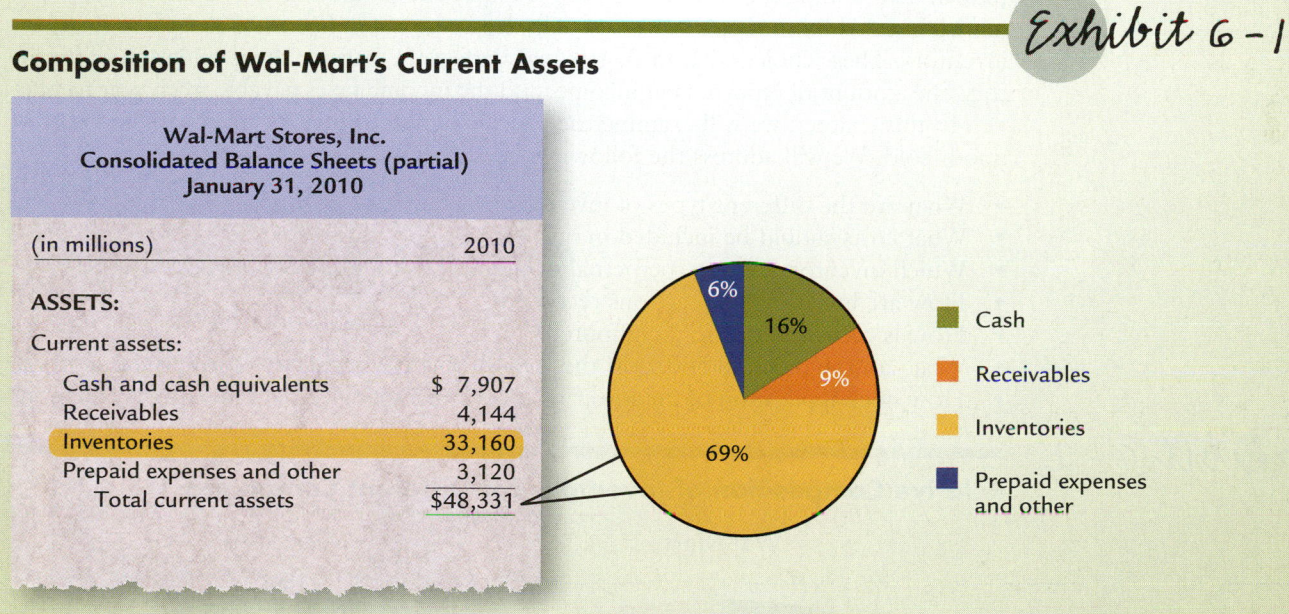

Wal-Mart Stores, Inc. Consolidated Balance Sheets (partial) January 31, 2010	
(in millions)	2010
ASSETS:	
Current assets:	
Cash and cash equivalents	$ 7,907
Receivables	4,144
Inventories	33,160
Prepaid expenses and other	3,120
Total current assets	$48,331

- 6%
- 16% — Cash
- 9% — Receivables
- 69% — Inventories
- Prepaid expenses and other

NATURE OF INVENTORY AND COST OF GOODS SOLD

Inventory represents products held for resale and is classified as a current asset on the balance sheet. The inventories of large companies like General Electric, Procter and Gamble, and Wal-Mart are composed of thousands of different products or materials and millions of individual units that are stored in hundreds of different locations. For other companies, inventories are a much less significant portion of their total assets. Exhibit 6-2 shows the relative composition of inventory for Wal-Mart and Microsoft.

For companies like Wal-Mart, these vast and varied inventories are at the heart of company operations and must be carefully controlled and accounted for. For example, one of Wal-Mart's key performance measures is the comparison of inventory growth to sales growth. In the recessionary economy of 2009, Wal-Mart's sales grew by only 1 percent. In response, it was able to shrink its inventory by 4 percent—an indication that Wal-Mart was effectively managing and controlling its inventory in response to economic pressures.

When companies like Wal-Mart sell their inventory to customers, the cost of the inventory becomes an expense called cost of goods sold. **Cost of goods sold** (or **cost of sales**) represents the outflow of resources caused by the sale of inventory and is the most important expense on the income statement of companies that sell goods instead of services. **Gross margin** (also called **gross profit**), a key performance measure, is defined as sales revenue less cost of goods sold. Thus, gross margin indicates the extent to which the resources generated by sales can be used to pay operating expenses (selling and administrative expenses) and provide for net income. For 2010, Wal-Mart reported a gross margin of $100,389,000,000, calculated as:

$$\text{Revenue} - \text{Cost of Goods Sold} = \text{Gross Margin}$$
$$\$405,046,000,000 - \$304,657,000,000 = \$100,389,000,000 \ (24.8 \text{ percent of revenue})$$

The cost of inventory has a direct effect on cost of goods sold and gross margin. To correctly interpret and analyze financial statements, one must understand inventory accounting. Accounting for inventories requires a matching of costs with revenues based on an appropriate inventory costing method. Management is allowed considerable latitude in determining the cost of inventory and may choose among several different costing methods. In addition, GAAP allows certain departures from historical cost accounting for inventory. These choices that managers make affect the balance sheet valuation of inventory, the amount of reported net income, and the income taxes payable from year to year.

In this chapter, we will examine the process of accounting for inventory and cost of goods sold. We will address the following questions:

- What are the different types of inventory?
- What costs should be included in inventory?
- Which inventory system (perpetual or periodic) should be employed?
- How are inventory transactions recorded?
- How is cost of goods sold computed?
- What are the financial effects of the four alternative inventory costing methods?
- How does application of the lower of cost or market rule affect inventory valuation?

Exhibit 6-2

Relative Composition of Inventory for Different Companies

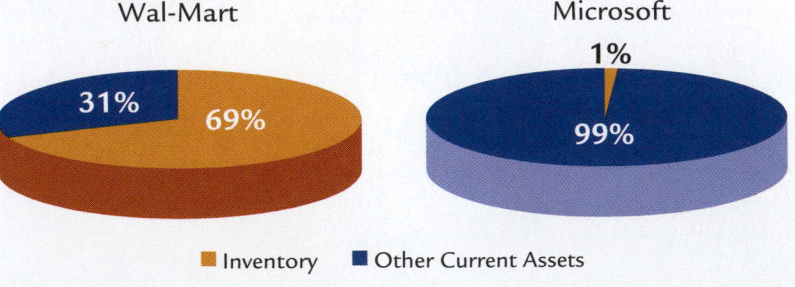

Wal-Mart — Inventory 69%, Other Current Assets 31%

Microsoft — Inventory 1%, Other Current Assets 99%

■ Inventory   ■ Other Current Assets

An understanding of inventory accounting will help in the analysis of financial statements as well as in managing a business.

Types of Inventory and Flow of Costs

In previous chapters, we have generally discussed companies that sell services such as advertising agencies, delivery companies, repair companies, and accounting firms. For these companies, inventory plays a much smaller role. For example, in 2010, Google didn't even report an amount for inventory! Our focus in this chapter will be on companies that sell inventory. These companies are often referred to as either merchandisers or manufacturers.

Merchandisers are companies (either retailers or wholesalers) that purchase inventory in a finished condition and hold it for resale without further processing. **Retailers** such as Wal-Mart, Sears, and Target are merchandisers that sell directly to consumers, while **wholesalers** are merchandisers that sell to other retailers. For example, McKesson and AmerisourceBergen are wholesalers that supply pharmaceutical products to health-care providers; United Natural Foods is a wholesaler that distributes natural, organic, and specialty foods to various retailers. The inventory held by merchandisers is termed **merchandise inventory**. Merchandise inventory is an asset. When that asset is sold to a customer, it becomes an expense called cost of goods sold which appears on the income statement. Wal-Mart's inventory disclosure, shown earlier in Exhibit 6-1 (p. 259), is an example of a typical disclosure made by a merchandising company.

Manufacturers are companies that buy and transform raw materials into a finished product which is then sold. Sony, Toyota, and Eastman Kodak are all manufacturing companies. Manufacturing companies classify inventory into three categories: raw materials, work-in-process, and finished goods.

- **Raw materials inventory** are the basic ingredients used to make a product. When these raw materials are purchased, the raw materials inventory account is increased. As raw materials are used to manufacture a product, they become part of work-in-process inventory.
- **Work-in-process inventory** consists of the raw materials that are used in production as well as other production costs such as labor and utilities. These costs stay in this account until the product is complete. Once the production process is complete, these costs are moved to the finished goods inventory account.
- The **finished goods inventory** account represents the cost of the final product that is available for sale. When the finished goods inventory is sold to a customer, it becomes an expense called cost of goods sold which appears on the income statement.

The inventory disclosure of Eastman Kodak, shown in Exhibit 6-3, is an example of a typical disclosure made by a manufacturing company.

Exhibit 6-3

Inventory Disclosure of Eastman Kodak

(in millions)	December 31 2009	December 31 2008
Current Assets		
Cash and cash equivalents	$2,024	$2,145
Receivables, net	1,395	1,716
Inventories, net	679	948
Other current assets	205	195
Total current assets	$4,303	$5,004

Note 3: Inventories, net

(in millions)	December 31 2009	December 31 2008
Finished goods	$409	$610
Work-in-process	164	193
Raw materials	106	145
Total inventories, net	$679	$948

Exhibit 6-4

Flow of Inventory Costs

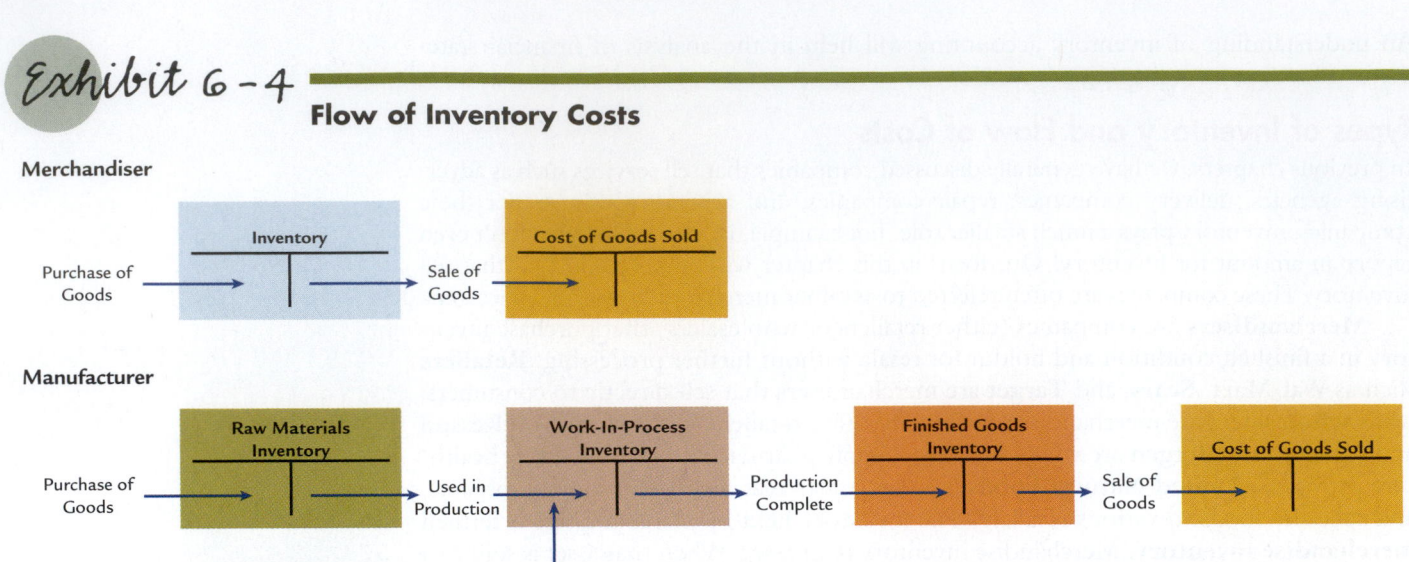

* Work-In-Process Inventory consists of raw materials used in production (also known as direct materials) as well as other production costs. These other production costs are called direct labor and factory overhead. The process by which these costs are converted to a final cost of a product is covered in managerial accounting.

The relationship between the various inventory accounts and cost of goods sold is shown in Exhibit 6-4.

The concepts involved in accounting for inventories of manufacturers and merchandisers are similar. However, due to the additional complexities of accounting for manufacturing inventory, the remainder of this chapter will focus on merchandising companies.

Cost of Goods Sold Model

As shown in Exhibit 6-4, cost of goods sold is the cost to the seller of all goods sold during the accounting period. Recall that the *matching principle* requires that any costs used to generate revenue should be recognized in the same period that the revenue is recognized. Because revenue is recognized as goods are sold, cost of goods sold is an expense.

The relationship between cost of goods sold and inventory is given by the cost of goods sold model:

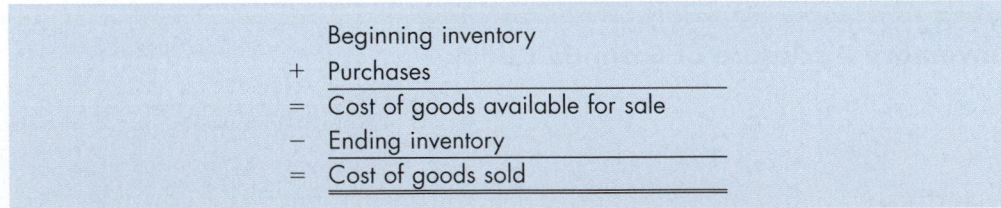

	Beginning inventory
+	Purchases
=	Cost of goods available for sale
−	Ending inventory
=	Cost of goods sold

Except in the case of a new company, merchandisers and manufacturers will start the year with an amount of inventory on hand called *beginning inventory*. During the year, any *purchases* of inventory are added to the inventory account. The sum of beginning inventory and purchases represents the **cost of goods available for sale**. The portion of the cost of goods available for sale that remains unsold at the end of the year is the company's *ending inventory* (the ending inventory for one period becomes the beginning inventory of the next period). The portion of the cost of goods available for sale that is sold becomes *cost of goods sold*. The cost of goods sold model is illustrated in Exhibit 6-5.

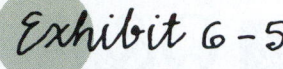

Cost of Goods Sold Model

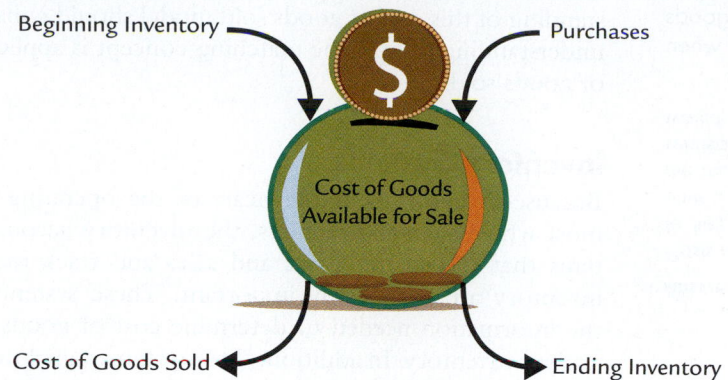

Beginning Inventory → Cost of Goods Available for Sale ← Purchases

Cost of Goods Sold ← → Ending Inventory

The determination of cost of goods sold requires an allocation of the cost of goods available for sale between ending inventory and cost of goods sold. An application of the cost of goods sold model is illustrated in **CORNERSTONE 6-1**.

 **CORNERSTONE 6-1**   **Applying the Cost of Goods Sold Model**

Concept:
The determination of cost of goods sold requires an allocation of the cost of goods available for sale between ending inventory and cost of goods sold.

Information:
Bargain Shops, a retail clothing store, had a beginning inventory of $26,000 on January 1, 2011. During 2011, the company purchased goods from a supplier costing $411,000. At the end of 2011, the cost of the unsold inventory was $38,000.

Required:
Compute cost of goods sold at December 31, 2011.

Solution:

Beginning inventory	$ 26,000
+ Purchases	411,000
= Cost of goods available for sale	$437,000
− Ending inventory	38,000
= Cost of goods sold	$399,000

The general structure of the cost of goods sold model can be rearranged to solve for any missing amount if the other three amounts are known. For example, if Bargain Shops did not know the cost of ending inventory but knew the cost of goods sold was $399,000, the company could determine ending inventory by rearranging the model as follows:

Beginning inventory	$ 26,000
+ Purchases	411,000
= Cost of goods available for sale	$437,000
− Cost of goods sold	399,000
= Ending inventory	$ 38,000

Because all inventories ultimately get expensed as cost of goods sold, why aren't all costs recorded as cost of goods sold when they are incurred?

Answer:
Costs related to inventories are initially recorded in an inventory account to help a company achieve a proper matching of expenses with revenues. By recording costs in an inventory account, a company can delay the recognition of the expense until the goods are sold. If all inventory related costs were expensed when incurred, users of financial statements would see a distorted picture of the company's profitability.

Cornerstone 6-1 reinforces the concept that the computation of cost of goods sold or ending inventory is simply an allocation of the cost of goods available for sale. An understanding of this cost of goods sold model should enhance your understanding of how the matching concept is applied to cost of goods sold.

Inventory Systems

Because inventory is at the heart of the operating cycle for most wholesalers and retailers, the inventory accounting systems that record purchases and sales and track the level of inventory are particularly important. These systems provide the information needed to determine cost of goods sold and analyze inventory. In addition, these systems signal the need to purchase additional inventory or the need to make special efforts to sell existing inventory. They also provide information necessary to safeguard the inventory from misappropriation or theft. In short, these systems provide the information that managers need to manage and control inventory.

Companies use one of two types of inventory accounting systems—a perpetual inventory system or a periodic inventory system.

Perpetual Inventory System In a **perpetual inventory system**, balances for inventory and cost of goods sold are continually (perpetually) updated with each sale or purchase of inventory. This type of system requires that detailed records be maintained on a transaction-by-transaction basis for each purchase and sale of inventory. For example, every time that **Wal-Mart** purchases inventory from a supplier, it records this purchase directly in its inventory records. Similarly, when Wal-Mart makes a sale to a customer, it will not only record the sale (as illustrated in Chapter 5) but will also update its inventory and cost of goods sold balances by decreasing inventory and increasing cost of goods sold. In other words, a perpetual inventory system records both the *revenue* and *cost* side of sales transactions.

With the volume of transactions that **Wal-Mart** has on a daily basis, this task may appear quite daunting. However, with the advent of "point of sale" cash register systems and optical bar code scanners, the implementation of perpetual inventory systems has become quite common. Some companies, such as Wal-Mart, are taking this idea a step further and using radio frequency identification (RFID) technology to track inventory. By attaching RFID tags to its inventory, Wal-Mart is able to more easily track inventory from its suppliers to the final customer, dramatically reducing inventory losses.

In a perpetual inventory system, the accounting system keeps an up-to-date record of both ending inventory and cost of goods sold at any point in time. However, a company that uses a perpetual system should still take a physical count of inventory at least once a year to confirm the balance in the inventory account. Any difference between the physical count of inventory and the inventory balance provided by the accounting system could be the result of errors, waste, breakage, or theft.

Periodic Inventory System A **periodic inventory system** does not require companies to keep detailed, up-to-date inventory records. Instead, a periodic system records the cost of purchases as they occur (in an account separate from the inventory account), takes a physical count of inventory at the end of the period, and applies the cost of goods sold model to determine the balances of ending inventory and cost of goods sold. Thus, a periodic system only produces balances for ending inventory and cost of goods sold at the end of each accounting period (periodically). If a company using the periodic system needs to know the balance of inventory or cost of goods sold during a period, it must do either of the following:

- perform a physical count of inventory or
- estimate the amount of inventory using an acceptable estimation technique.[1]

Comparison of Perpetual and Periodic Inventory Systems Perpetual and periodic systems offer distinct benefits and any choice between the two inventory systems must weigh each system's advantages against its operating costs. The principal advantage of a periodic system is that it is relatively inexpensive to operate. Because perpetual systems require entering and maintaining more data than periodic systems, the additional costs can be quite substantial for a company with thousands of different items in inventory. However, with technological advances, this advantage is rapidly disappearing. The perpetual system has the advantage of making the balances of inventory and cost of goods sold continuously available. This provides management with greater control over inventory than they would have under a periodic inventory system. Providing managers with more timely information can be a significant and extremely valuable advantage in a competitive business environment. For example, much of **Wal-Mart**'s success has been attributed to its sophisticated inventory management and control system.

We will illustrate a perpetual inventory system in this chapter because of its growth and popularity in many different types of companies.

 **Just-In-Time Inventory Management**

As the inventory manager for Goliath Inc., a large national merchandising company, it is your job to balance the costs of carrying inventory (e.g., finance costs, storage costs) against the costs of not meeting customer demand (e.g., the cost of lost sales). If Goliath can rely on its suppliers to deliver inventory on very short notice and in ready-to-use forms, then very low inventory levels can be maintained. This approach to inventory management is called **just in time (JIT)** and is consistent with both minimizing inventory carrying costs and "out-of-stock" costs.

What information would you need to maintain a just-in-time inventory policy?

To synchronize the arrival of new inventory with the selling of the old inventory, you need detailed information about order-to-delivery times, receiving-to-ready-for-sale times, and inventory quantities. Delivery and make-ready times are used to control and minimize time lags between shipment of goods by suppliers and delivery to customers. In some retail stores, for example, merchandise arrives tagged, stacked, and ready for placement on the sales floor while in other retail stores several days may be required to get the merchandise ready for sale. Information on inventory quantities would also be useful as a signal to reorder a particular item of inventory. Perpetual inventory systems, which make inventory balances continuously available, can provide the needed information on inventory quantities.

Inventory management and control can lead to significant cost reductions and improved profitability.

RECORDING INVENTORY TRANSACTIONS— PERPETUAL SYSTEM

The historical cost principle requires that the activities of a company are initially measured at their historical cost—the exchange price at the time the activity occurs. Applied to inventory, this principle implies that *inventory cost includes the purchase price of the merchandise plus any cost of bringing the goods to a salable condition and location.* Therefore, the cost of inventory will include the purchase price plus other "incidental" costs, such as freight charges to deliver the merchandise to the company's warehouse, insurance cost on the inventory while it is in transit, and various taxes.

O B J E C T I V E

Explain how to record purchases and sales of inventory using a perpetual inventory system.

---

[1] More information on the periodic inventory system is provided in Appendices 6A and 6B at the end of this chapter.

In general, a company should stop accumulating costs as a part of inventory once the inventory is ready for sale.[2]

Accounting for Purchases of Inventory

Let's first take a look at how a merchandising company would account for inventory purchases. In a perpetual inventory system, the inventory account is used to record the costs associated with acquiring merchandise.

Purchases **Purchases** refers to the cost of merchandise acquired for resale during the accounting period. The purchase of inventory is recorded by increasing the inventory account. All purchases should be supported by a source document, such as an *invoice*, that provides written evidence of the transaction as well as the relevant details of the purchase. A typical invoice is shown in Exhibit 6-6. Note the various details on the invoice, such as the names of the seller and the purchaser, the invoice date, the credit terms, the freight terms, a description of the goods purchased, and the total invoice amount.

Sample Invoice

Shoes Unlimited					INVOICE

We Care About Your Feet

301 College Street
Irvine, California 92612
Phone 800-555-2389 Fax 949-555-2300

INVOICE #100
DATE: Sept. 1, 2010

TO:

J. Parker Jones, Purchasing Manager
Brandon Shoes
879 University Blvd.
Auburn, Alabama 36830

SALESPERSON	P.O. NUMBER	REQUISITIONER	SHIPPED VIA	F.O.B. POINT	TERMS
E. Higgins	4895721	J. Parker Jones	UPS	Destination	2/10, n/30

QUANTITY	DESCRIPTION	UNIT PRICE	TOTAL
100	Model No. 754 Athletic Running Shoe	$100	$10,000
		SUBTOTAL	$10,000
		SALES TAX	800
		SHIPPING & HANDLING	150
		TOTAL DUE	$10,950

---

[2] For a manufacturing company, costs should be accumulated as raw materials inventory until the goods are ready for use in the manufacturing process.

Relying on the historical cost principle, the cost of purchases must include the effects of purchase discounts, purchase returns, and transportation charges.

Purchase Discounts As noted in Chapter 5, companies that sell goods on credit often offer their customers sales discounts to encourage prompt payment. From the viewpoint of the customer, such price reductions are called **purchase discounts**. The credit terms specify the amount and timing of payments. For example, credit terms of "2/10, n/30" mean that a 2 percent discount may be taken on the invoice price if payment is made within 10 days of the invoice date. This reduced payment period is known as the **discount period**. Otherwise, full payment is due within 30 days of the invoice date. If a purchase discount is taken, the purchaser reduces the inventory account for the amount of the discount taken, resulting in the inventory account reflecting the net cost of the purchase.

Generally, all available discounts should be taken. Failure to pay within the discount period is equivalent to paying interest for the use of money and can be quite expensive. For example, failure to take advantage of the 2 percent discount for credit terms of "2/10, n/30" is equivalent to an annual interest rate of 36.5 percent.[3] Clearly, paying within the discount period is a good cash management policy.

Purchase Returns and Allowances Merchandise is inspected when received and may be tested in various ways before it becomes available for sale. The following issues may result in dissatisfaction with the merchandise:

- The wrong merchandise was delivered.
- The merchandise did not conform to specification.
- The merchandise was damaged or defective.
- The merchandise arrived too late at its destination.

If the purchaser is dissatisfied with the merchandise, it is frequently returned to the seller for credit or for a cash refund. The cost of merchandise returned to suppliers is called **purchase returns**. In some instances, the purchaser may choose to keep the merchandise if the seller is willing to grant a deduction (allowance) from the purchase price. This situation is called a **purchase allowance**. Increases in purchase returns and allowances may signal deteriorating supplier relationships; thus, purchase returns are monitored very closely by purchasing managers. Because inventory was increased when the purchase was initially made, a purchase return or allowance is recorded by decreasing inventory.

Transportation Costs Transportation, or freight, costs are expenditures made to move the inventory from the seller's location to the purchaser's location. The proper recording of transportation costs depends upon whether the buyer or the seller pays for the transportation. Effectively, this question is the same as asking at what point the ownership of the inventory transfers from the seller to the buyer. The point at which ownership, or title, of the inventory changes hands depends on the shipping terms of the contract. The shipping terms can be either F.O.B. (free on board) shipping point or F.O.B. destination as illustrated in Exhibit 6-7 (p. 268).

- *F.O.B. shipping point*: If the shipping terms are **F.O.B. shipping point**, ownership of the inventory passes from the seller to the buyer at the shipping point. Under F.O.B. shipping point terms, the buyer normally pays the transportation costs, commonly termed **freight-in**. These costs are considered part of the total cost of purchases and the inventory account is increased. The seller would normally recognize revenue at the time of the shipment.
- *F.O.B. destination:* When the shipping terms are **F.O.B. destination**, ownership of the inventory passes when the goods are delivered to the buyer. Under F.O.B.

---

[3] This implied interest rate is computed as [365 days ÷ (30 days − 10 days)] × 2%. Notice that this formula uses a 20-day interest period computed as the days until final payment is due (30 days) less the days in the discount period (10 days). This period can be adjusted to fit the specific credit terms of the transaction.

Exhibit 6-7

Shipping Terms

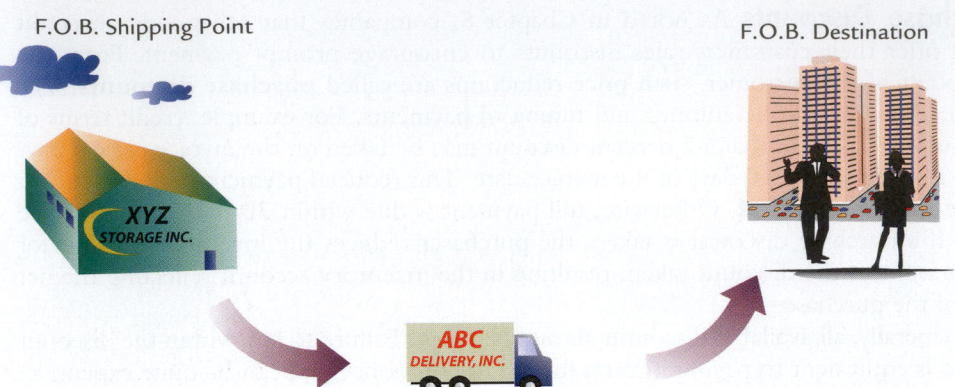

F.O.B. Shipping Point

F.O.B. Destination

➢ Ownership passes from the seller to the buyer when the goods are shipped.
➢ Buyer usually pays freight costs.
➢ Seller recognizes revenue at shipment.

➢ Ownership passes from the seller to the buyer when the goods are received.
➢ Seller usually pays freight costs.
➢ Seller recognizes revenue at delivery.

destination shipping terms, the seller is usually responsible for paying the transportation costs, commonly termed **freight-out**. In this case, the transportation costs are not considered part of inventory; instead, the seller will expense these costs as a selling expense on the income statement. Revenue is not normally recognized until delivery of the goods has occurred.

Consigned Goods Sometimes goods owned by one party are held and offered for sale by another. This arrangement is called a **consignment**. In a consignment, the seller (or *consignee*) earns a fee when the consigned goods are sold, but the original owner (or *consignor*) retains ownership of the goods. Manufacturers often use consignments to encourage large retailers, such as **Wal-Mart** and **Target**, to offer their products for sale. Retailers find these arrangements attractive because it enables them to reduce their investment in inventory. In consignment arrangements, the goods are not included in the seller's inventory.

ETHICAL DECISIONS   The proper determination of whether goods should or should not be considered part of the seller's inventory has created an ethical dilemma for some companies. With shipping terms of F.O.B. shipping point, managers may attempt to encourage customers to take delivery of more goods than are currently needed since such goods would generate revenue when the inventory is shipped. This practice, termed *channel stuffing*, effectively steals sales from the next period and distorts the results of the company's operations. The Securities and Exchange Commission (SEC) has closely examined transactions that were thought to be channel stuffing. For example, **Coca-Cola** recently paid $137.5 million due to channel stuffing allegations that allowed it to report artificially higher sales volumes to maintain a higher stock price. In addition, **Bristol-Myers Squibb** paid $150 million to settle allegations that included channel stuffing. ●

Concept Q&A

The purchase transactions that affect inventory seem complicated. Why go to all that trouble and effort when the periodic inventory system could be used?

Answer:

A perpetual inventory system requires a number of entries that directly affect inventory. While this system is certainly more complex than a periodic inventory system, the numerous entries provide management with up-to-date information that allows them to better manage and control their inventory.

Recording Purchase Transactions To summarize, the purchase price of inventory includes any cost of bringing the goods to a salable condition and location. Therefore, the inventory account is increased for the invoice price of a purchase as well as any transportation costs paid for by the buyer. Any purchase discounts, returns, or allowances reduce the inventory account. **CORNERSTONE 6-2** illustrates the journal entries required to record purchases of merchandise inventory.

CORNERSTONE 6-2

Recording Purchase Transactions in a Perpetual Inventory System

Concept:

The cost of inventory includes the purchase price of the merchandise plus any cost of bringing the goods to a salable condition and location.

Information:

On September 1, Brandon Shoes purchased 50 pairs of hiking boots for $3,750 cash (or $75 a pair) and paid $150 of transportation costs. Also, on September 1, Brandon purchased 100 pairs of running shoes for $10,000; however, the seller paid the transportation costs of $300. The running shoes were purchased on credit with terms of 2/10, n/30. Brandon paid for one-half ($5,000) of the running shoes on September 10, within the discount period. The remaining shoes were paid for on September 30. After inspection, Brandon determined that 10 pairs of the hiking boots were defective and returned them on September 30.

Required:

Prepare the journal entries necessary to record the September transactions for Brandon Shoes.

Solution:

Date	Account and Explanation	Debit	Credit			
Sept. 1	Inventory	3,750		**Assets** = **Liabilities** + **Stockholders' Equity**		
	Cash		3,750	+3,750		
	(Purchased inventory for cash)			−3,750		
1	Inventory	150		**Assets** = **Liabilities** + **Stockholders' Equity**		
	Cash		150	+150		
	(Recorded payment of freight costs)			−150		
1	Inventory	10,000		**Assets** = **Liabilities** + **Stockholders' Equity**		
	Accounts Payable		10,000	+10,000	+10,000	
	(Purchased inventory on credit)					
10	Accounts Payable	5,000		**Assets** = **Liabilities** + **Stockholders' Equity**		
	Cash		4,900	−4,900	−5,000	
	Inventory ($5,000 × 2%)		100	−100		
	(Recorded payment within the discount period)					
30	Accounts Payable	5,000		**Assets** = **Liabilities** + **Stockholders' Equity**		
	Cash		5,000	−5,000	−5,000	
	(Recorded payment outside the discount period)					
30	Cash	750		**Assets** = **Liabilities** + **Stockholders' Equity**		
	Inventory (10 pairs × $75/pair)		750	+750		
	(Returned defective hiking boots)			−750		

Exhibit 6-8

Calculation of Net Purchases

Invoice price of purchase	$13,750
Less: Purchase discounts	(100)
Purchase returns and allowances	(750)
Add: Transportation costs (freight-in)	150
Net cost of purchases	$13,050

Note that the purchase of the hiking boots in Cornerstone 6-2 included the $150 of transportation costs (freight-in) because Brandon paid the freight. However, the purchase of the running shoes did not include freight costs because it was paid by the seller.

These journal entries illustrate that, under a perpetual inventory system, inventory is constantly updated with each purchase so that the net effect of purchases is reflected in the inventory account. The computation of net purchases for Brandon Shoes is summarized in Exhibit 6-8. Although the original invoice price was $13,750, the consideration of purchase discounts, returns, and transportation charges resulted in a much different value in the inventory account.

Accounting for Sales of Inventory

IFRS

The purchase and sale of inventory is generally the same under IFRS as under U.S. GAAP.

In addition to purchase transactions, merchandising companies must also account for the inventory effects of sales and sales returns. Because a perpetual inventory system is being used, the merchandise inventory account is also affected.

Sales As discussed in Chapter 5, companies recognize sales revenue when it is earned and the collection of cash is reasonably assured. The recording of sales revenue involves two journal entries:

- In the first journal entry, sales revenue is recognized.
- The second journal recognizes, consistent with the matching principle, the cost of the goods that are sold. It also reduces the inventory account so that the perpetual inventory system will reflect an up-to-date balance for inventory.

 *Concept* Q&A

Instead of making two entries to record a sale under a perpetual system, why not just make one entry for the net amount? Wouldn't gross margin be the same?

Answer:

A system could be developed that combines the two entries necessary to record a sale of inventory under a perpetual system; however, important information would be lost. If an entry were made to an account such as "Gross Margin" for the difference between sales revenue and cost of goods sold, no information would be provided on the gross amount of revenues or cost of goods sold. This loss of information would be inconsistent with the purpose of financial reporting.

Sales Returns and Allowances If a customer returns an item for some reason, the company will make an adjustment to sales as shown in Chapter 5. In addition, the company must make a second entry to decrease cost of goods sold and increase inventory to reflect the return of the merchandise.

Recording Inventory Effects of Sales Transactions

The use of a perpetual inventory system requires that two journal entries be made for both sales and sales return transactions. These journal entries are illustrated in **CORNERSTONE 6-3**.

CORNERSTONE 6-3   Recording Sales Transactions in a Perpetual Inventory System

Concept:

The sale or return of inventory in a perpetual system requires two journal entries—one to record the revenue portion of the transaction and one to record the expense (and inventory) portion of the transaction.

Information:

On August 1, Brandon Shoes sold 100 pairs of football cleats to the local college football team for $12,000 cash (each pair of cleats was sold for $120 per pair). Brandon paid $10,000 (or $100 per pair) for the cleats from its supplier. On August 15, the local college football team returned 10 pairs of cleats for a cash refund of $1,200.

Required:

1. Prepare the journal entries to record the sale of the football cleats.
2. Prepare the journal entries to record the return of the football cleats.

Solution:

Date		Account and Explanation	Debit	Credit
1. Aug.	1	Cash	12,000	
		Sales Revenue		12,000
		(Recorded sale to customer)		
	1	Cost of Goods Sold	10,000	
		Inventory		10,000
		(Recorded cost of merchandise sold)		
2.	15	Sales Returns and Allowances	1,200	
		Cash		1,200
		(Recorded return of merchandise)		
	15	Inventory	1,000	
		Cost of Goods Sold		1,000
		(Recorded cost of merchandise returned)		

Assets = Liabilities + Stockholders' Equity
+12,000   +12,000

Assets = Liabilities + Stockholders' Equity
−10,000   −10,000

Assets = Liabilities + Stockholders' Equity
−1,200   −1,200

Assets = Liabilities + Stockholders' Equity
+1,000   +1,000

In each of the transactions in Cornerstone 6-3, the external selling price of $120 was recorded as Sales Revenue. The cost of goods sold (or inventory) portion of the transaction was recorded at the cost to Brandon Shoes of $100. Therefore, for each pair of shoes sold, Brandon Shoes made a gross margin of $20 ($120 − $100). The total cost of goods sold recognized by Brandon Shoes is $9,000 ($10,000 − $1,000). *In dealing with sales to customers, it is important to remember to record revenues at the selling price and to record expenses (and inventory) at cost.*

YOU DECIDE   Impact of Shipping Terms on Revenue Recognition

You are a CPA auditing the financial statements of Henderson Electronics, a computer retailer located in Duluth, Georgia. Henderson's policy is to record a sales transaction when the merchandise is shipped to customers (F.O.B. shipping point). During the audit, you notice that 50 computers were sold to the Itasca County School District near the end of the year. Further investigation reveals that these 50 computers are still in Henderson's warehouse. James Henderson, the owner, tells you that the school district wanted to purchase the computers with funds from the district's current fiscal year, but couldn't take delivery because the computer labs at the various schools were under renovation. Therefore, Henderson billed the district and recorded a credit sale in the current year.

(Continued)

Was this transaction accounted for properly?

Because the company has an F.O.B. shipping point policy and the inventory had not been delivered, the computers are not considered sold in the current year. Therefore, the recording of the credit sale should not have been made and the inventory should be included in Henderson's ending inventory. This type of transaction is commonly referred to as a "bill and hold" sale. Although it may be perfectly legal, such transactions have come under scrutiny by the SEC as a means for companies to improperly inflate sales revenue and should be carefully scrutinized.

The proper determination of whether goods should or should not be included in inventory impacts both the balance sheet and the income statement.

OBJECTIVE 3

Apply the four inventory costing methods to compute ending inventory and cost of goods sold under a perpetual inventory system.

COSTING INVENTORY

A key feature of the cost of goods sold model illustrated in Cornerstone 6-1 (p. 263) is that the determination of cost of goods sold requires an allocation of the cost of goods available for sale between ending inventory and cost of goods sold. If the prices paid for goods are constant over time, this allocation is easy to compute—just multiply the cost per unit times the number of units on hand at year-end (to determine the cost of ending inventory) or times the number of units sold (to determine the cost of goods sold). For example, if Speigel Company began operations by purchasing 1,000 units of a single product for $24 each, total goods available for sale would be $24,000, calculated as:

Inventory Available to Be Sold × Cost per Unit = Goods Available for Sale
1,000 units × $24 = $24,000

If 800 units were sold during the period, the cost of the remaining 200-unit ending inventory is $4,800:

Ending Inventory × Cost per Unit = Cost of Ending Inventory
$24 × 200 units = $4,800

Cost of goods sold is $19,200, calculated as:

Units Sold × Cost per Unit = Cost of Goods Sold
800 × $24 = $19,200

It makes no difference which of the 1,000 units remain in ending inventory because all units have the same cost ($24).

On the other hand, if the price paid for a good changes over time, the cost of goods available for sale may include units with different costs per unit. In such cases, the question arises: Which prices should be assigned to the units sold and which assigned to the units in ending inventory? For example, assume that Speigel Company purchased the same total of 1,000 units during a period at different prices as follows:

Jan. 3	300 units purchased at $22 per unit	=	$ 6,600
Jan. 15	400 units purchased at $24 per unit	=	9,600
Jan. 24	300 units purchased at $26 per unit	=	7,800
	Cost of goods available for sale		$24,000

While the cost of goods available for sale is the same ($24,000), the cost of the 200-unit ending inventory depends on which goods remain in ending inventory. As illustrated by the cost of goods sold model discussed earlier, the cost assigned to ending inventory also affects the value of cost of goods sold.

	If ending inventory is made up of $22 per unit goods	If ending inventory is made up of $26 per unit goods
Ending inventory	$4,400 (200 units × $22/unit)	$5,200 (200 units × $26/unit)
Cost of goods sold	$19,600 ($24,000 − $4,400)	$18,800 ($24,000 − $5,200)

The determination of the value of ending inventory and cost of goods sold depends on management's choice of inventory system (perpetual or periodic) and method of allocating inventory costs.

Inventory Costing Methods

The inventory system (perpetual or periodic) determines *when* cost of goods sold is calculated—for every sales transaction or at the end of the period. An *inventory costing method* determines how costs are allocated to cost of goods sold and ending inventory. Although the assumption about how inventory costs flow could take many different forms, accountants typically use one of four inventory costing methods:

- Specific identification
- First-in, first-out (FIFO)
- Last-in, first-out (LIFO)
- Average cost

Each of these four costing methods represents a different procedure for allocating the cost of goods available for sale between ending inventory and cost of goods sold. Only the specific identification method allocates the cost of purchases according to the *physical flow* of specific units through inventory. That is, specific identification is based on a *flow of goods* principle. In contrast, the other three methods—FIFO, LIFO, and average cost—are based on a *flow of cost* principle. When the FIFO, LIFO, or average cost methods are used, the physical flow of goods into inventory and out to the customers is generally unrelated to the flow of unit costs. We make this point here so that you will not be confused in thinking that a cost flow assumption describes the physical flow of goods in a company. *Generally accepted accounting principles do not require that the cost flow assumption be consistent with the physical flow of goods.*

Companies disclose their choice of inventory methods in a note to the financial statements. The 2010 annual report of **Wal-Mart** includes the following statement:

Notes to Consolidated Financial Statements

1. Summary of Significant Accounting Policies
Inventories.
The company values inventories at the lower of cost or market as determined primarily by the retail method of accounting, using the last-in, first-out ("LIFO'") method for substantially all of the Wal-Mart stores segment's merchandise inventories. Sam's Club merchandise and merchandise in our distribution warehouses are valued based on the weighted average cost using the LIFO method. Inventories of International operations are primarily valued by the retail method of accounting, using the first-in, first-out ("FIFO") method. At January 31, 2010 and 2009, our inventories valued at LIFO approximate those inventories as if they were valued at FIFO.

Like many companies, **Wal-Mart** uses more than one method in determining the total cost of inventory. In general, LIFO and FIFO are the most widely used methods. Exhibit 6-9 shows the percentage of companies using each inventory costing method.

Exhibit 6-9

Use of Inventory Costing Methods

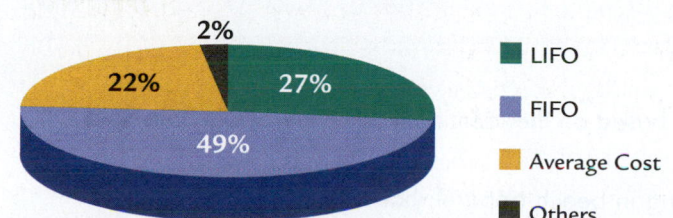

- LIFO
- FIFO
- Average Cost
- Others

Source: AICPA, Accounting Trends & Techniques, 63rd edition, 2009, par. 2.64, p. 165.

With the exception of specific identification, the inventory costing methods allocate cost of goods available for sale between ending inventory and cost of goods sold using the following process.

Step 1: Calculate the cost of goods available for sale *immediately prior* to any sale transaction.

Step 2: Apply the inventory costing method to determine ending inventory and cost of goods sold.

Step 3: Repeat steps 1 and 2 for all inventory transactions during the period. The sum of the cost of goods sold computed in step 2 is the cost of goods sold for the period. Ending inventory is the amount computed during the final application of step 2 for the period.

To understand how inventory costing systems allocate costs (step 2), it is useful to think of inventory as if it were a stack of separate layers, with each stack distinguished by the purchase price. Each time a purchase is made at a unit cost different from that of a previous purchase, a new layer of inventory cost is added to the stack. As inventory is sold, it is removed from the stack according to the cost flow assumption used. This process is illustrated in Exhibit 6-10 for the LIFO and FIFO methods.

Exhibit 6-10

Allocation of Inventory Costs

FIFO		LIFO
Inventory	Purchase 3	Cost of Goods Sold
	Purchase 2	
Cost of Goods Sold	Purchase 1	Inventory

Specific Identification

The **specific identification method** determines the cost of ending inventory and the cost of goods sold based on the identification of the *actual* units sold and in inventory. This method does not require an assumption about the flow of costs but assigns cost based on the specific flow of inventory. It requires that detailed records of each purchase and sale be maintained so that a company knows exactly which items were sold and the cost of those items. Historically, this method was practical only for high-cost items with unique identifiers (e.g., serial numbers) that were sold in low numbers—for example, automobiles. With the introduction of bar coding, electronic scanners, and radio frequency identification, this method has become easier to implement, but its application is still relatively rare. The specific identification method is illustrated in **CORNERSTONE 6-4**.

CORNERSTONE 6-4   **Applying the Specific Identification Method**

Concept:
Cost of goods sold and ending inventory are determined based on the identification of the actual units sold and in inventory.

Information: Tampico Beachwear, a retail store specializing in beach apparel, has the following information related to purchases and sales of one of its more popular products, Crocs brand shoes. (Each inventory layer is a different color.)

(Continued)

Date	Description	Units Purchased at Cost	Units Sold at Retail
Oct. 1	Beginning inventory	300 units @ $16 = $ 4,800	
3	Purchase 1	600 units @ $18 = $10,800	
8	Sale 1		800 units @ $30
Oct. 15	Purchase 2	250 units @ $20 = $5,000	
20	Purchase 3	150 units @ $22 = $3,300	
25	Sale 2		300 units @ $30
		Goods available for sale:	Sales:
		1,300 units = $23,900	1,100 units = $33,000

The following units were sold during the month and remain in ending inventory at the end of the month:

Description	Units Sold	Units in Ending Inventory
Beginning inventory	300	—
Purchase 1	550	50
Purchase 2	170	80
Purchase 3	80	70
Total	1,100	200

CORNERSTONE
6-4
(continued)

Required:
1. Compute the cost of ending inventory at October 31 under the specific identification method.
2. Compute the cost of goods sold at October 31 under the specific identification method.

Solution:

1. Ending Inventory is

50 units @ $18	$ 900
80 units @ $20	1,600
70 units @ $22	1,540
200 units	$4,040

2. Cost of Goods Sold is

300 units @ $16	$ 4,800
550 units @ $18	9,900
170 units @ $20	3,400
80 units @ $22	1,760
1,100 units	$19,860

Three items in Cornerstone 6-4 are of interest.

- *Cost of Goods Available for Sale:* The sum of ending inventory ($4,040) and cost of goods sold ($19,860) equals cost of goods available for sale ($23,900). The specific identification method, like all inventory costing methods, allocates the cost of goods available for sale between ending inventory and cost of goods sold.
- *Cost of Goods Sold:* Because there are usually far fewer units in ending inventory than in cost of goods sold, it is often easier to compute the cost of ending inventory and then find the cost of goods sold by subtracting ending inventory from cost of goods available for sale ($23,900 – $4,040 = $19,860).

- *Financial Statement Effects:* The determination of inventory cost affects both the balance sheet and the income statement. The amount assigned to ending inventory will appear on the balance sheet. The amount assigned to cost of goods sold appears on the income statement and is used in the calculation of a company's gross margin.

First-In, First-Out (FIFO)

The **first-in, first-out (FIFO) method** is based on the assumption that costs move through inventory in an unbroken stream, with the costs entering and leaving the inventory in the same order. In other words, *the earliest purchases (the first in) are assumed to be the first sold (the first out), and the more recent purchases are in ending inventory.* Every time inventory is sold, the cost of the earliest (oldest) purchases that make up cost of goods available for sale is allocated to cost of goods sold, and the cost of the most recent purchases is allocated to ending inventory. In many instances, this cost flow assumption is an accurate representation of the physical flow of goods. **Hewlett-Packard** and restaurant companies such as **Ruby Tuesday** and **Yum Brands** all use FIFO. In addition, grocery stores such as **Publix** use FIFO for their perishable items. **CORNERSTONE 6-5** illustrates the application of the FIFO method.

CORNERSTONE 6-5

Applying the FIFO Inventory Costing Method

Concept:
The cost of the earliest purchases that make up cost of goods available for sale is allocated to cost of goods sold, and the cost of the most recent purchases is allocated to ending inventory.

Information:
Tampico Beachwear, a retail store specializing in beach apparel, has the following information related to purchases and sales of one of its more popular products, Crocs brand shoes. (Each inventory layer is a different color.)

Date		Description	Units Purchased at Cost	Units Sold at Retail
Oct.	1	Beginning inventory	300 units @ $16 = $ 4,800	
	3	Purchase 1	600 units @ $18 = $10,800	
	8	Sale 1		800 units @ $30
	15	Purchase 2	250 units @ $20 = $ 5,000	
	20	Purchase 3	150 units @ $22 = $ 3,300	
	25	Sale 2		300 units @ $30
			Goods available for sale:	Sales:
			1,300 units = $23,900	1,100 units = $33,000

Required:
Compute the cost of ending inventory and the cost of goods sold at October 31 using the FIFO method.

Solution:
Step 1: Compute the cost of goods available for sale immediately prior to the first sale. This produces an inventory balance of $15,600 ($4,800 + $10,800). Notice that this inventory balance is made up of two layers—a $16 layer and an $18 layer.

(Continued)

**CORNERSTONE
6-5**
(continued)

Step 2: Apply FIFO to determine ending inventory and cost of goods sold. The cost of goods available for sale is allocated between inventory (the most recent purchases) and cost of goods sold (the earliest purchases).

Date	Description	Cost of Goods Sold	Inventory Balance	
Oct. 1	Beginning inventory		300 × $16	= $ 4,800
3	Purchase 1 (600 @ $18)		300 × $16 = $ 4,800 } 600 × $18 = $10,800 } = $15,600	
8	Sale 1 (800 @ $30)	300 × $16 = $4,800 } 500 × $18 = $9,000 } = $13,800	100 × $18	= $ 1,800

Step 3: Repeat steps 1 and 2 for the remaining inventory transactions during the period.

Date	Description	Cost of Goods Sold	Inventory Balance	
Oct. 8	Inventory on hand		100 × $18	= $ 1,800
15	Purchase 2 (250 @ $20)		100 × $18 = $ 1,800 } 250 × $20 = $ 5,000 } = $ 6,800	
20	Purchase 3 (150 @ $22)		100 × $18 = $ 1,800 } 250 × $20 = $ 5,000 } 150 × $22 = $ 3,300 } = $10,100	
25	Sale 2 (300 @ $30)	100 × $18 = $1,800 } 200 × $20 = $4,000 } = $5,800	50 × $20 = $ 1,000 } 150 × $22 = $ 3,300 } = $ 4,300	
		Total $19,600		

The application of FIFO in Cornerstone 6-5 resulted in the following:

- Ending inventory reported on the balance sheet is $4,300.
- Cost of goods sold reported on the income statement is $19,600 ($13,800 + $5,800).

Because the sum of ending inventory and cost of goods sold ($4,300 + $19,600) equals cost of goods available for sale ($23,900), Tampico could have also calculated cost of goods sold as the difference between cost of goods available for sale and ending inventory ($23,900 − $4,300).

Last-In, First-Out (LIFO)

The **last-in, first-out (LIFO) method** allocates the cost of goods available for sale between ending inventory and cost of goods sold based on the assumption that the most recent purchases (the last in) are the first to be sold (the first out). Under the LIFO method, *the most recent purchases (newest costs) are allocated to the cost of goods sold and the earliest purchases (oldest costs) are allocated to inventory.* Except for companies that stockpile inventory (e.g., piles of coal, stacks of hay, stacks of rock), this cost flow assumption rarely coincides with the actual physical flow of inventory. Companies such as **General Mills**, **Target**, and **Macy's** all use LIFO. **CORNERSTONE 6-6** (p. 278) illustrates the application of the LIFO method.

IFRS

IFRS do not allow the use of LIFO.

CORNERSTONE
6-6

Applying the LIFO Inventory Costing Method

Concept:
The cost of the most recent purchases that make up cost of goods available for sale is allocated to cost of goods sold, and the cost of the earliest purchases is allocated to ending inventory.

Information:
Tampico Beachwear, a retail store specializing in beach apparel, has the following information related to purchases and sales of one of its more popular products, Crocs brand shoes. (Each inventory layer is a different color.)

Date	Description	Units Purchased at Cost	Units Sold at Retail
Oct. 1	Beginning inventory	300 units @ $16 = $ 4,800	
3	Purchase 1	600 units @ $18 = $10,800	
8	Sale 1		800 units @ $30
15	Purchase 2	250 units @ $20 = $ 5,000	
20	Purchase 3	150 units @ $22 = $ 3,300	
25	Sale 2		300 units @ $30
		Goods available for sale: 1,300 units = $23,900	Sales: 1,100 units = $33,000

Required:
Compute the cost of ending inventory and the cost of goods sold at October 31 using the LIFO method.

Solution:
Step 1: Compute the cost of goods available for sale immediately *prior* to the first sale. This produces an inventory balance of $15,600 ($4,800 + $10,800). Notice that this inventory balance is made up of two layers—a $16 layer and an $18 layer.

Step 2: Apply LIFO to determine ending inventory and cost of goods sold. The cost of goods available for sale is allocated between inventory (the earliest purchases) and cost of goods sold (the most recent purchases).

Date	Description	Cost of Goods Sold	Inventory Balance	
Oct. 1	Beginning inventory		300 × $16	= $ 4,800
3	Purchase 1 (600 @ $18)		300 × $16 = $ 4,800 600 × $18 = $10,800 }	= $15,600
8	Sale 1 (800 @ $30)	600 × $18 = $10,800 200 × $16 = $ 3,200 } = $14,000	100 × $16	= $ 1,600

Step 3: Repeat steps 1 and 2 for the remaining inventory transactions during the period.

Date	Description	Cost of Goods Sold	Inventory Balance	
Oct. 8	Inventory on hand		100 × $16	= $1,600
15	Purchase 2 (250 @ $20)		100 × $16 = $1,600 250 × $20 = $5,000 }	= $6,600
20	Purchase 3 (150 @ $22)		100 × $16 = $1,600 250 × $20 = $5,000 150 × $22 = $3,300 }	= $9,900
25	Sale 2 (300 @ $30)	150 × $22 = $3,300 150 × $20 = $3,000 } = $6,300	100 × $16 = $1,600 100 × $20 = $2,000 }	= $3,600
		Total = **$20,300**		

The application of LIFO in Cornerstone 6-6 resulted in the following:

- Ending inventory reported on the balance sheet is $3,600.
- Cost of goods sold reported on the income statement is $20,300, the sum of cost of goods sold during the period ($14,000 + $6,300).

Because the sum of ending inventory and cost of goods sold ($3,600 + $20,300) equals cost of goods available for sale ($23,900), Tampico could have also calculated cost of goods sold as the difference between cost of goods available for sale and ending inventory ($23,900 – $3,600).

Average Cost

The **average cost method** allocates the cost of goods available for sale between ending inventory and cost of goods sold based on a weighted average cost per unit. This weighted average cost per unit is calculated after each purchase of inventory as follows:

$$\text{Weighted Average Cost per Unit} = \frac{\text{Cost of Goods Available for Sale}}{\text{Units Available for Sale}}$$

Because a new average is computed after each purchase, this method is often called the moving-average method. This weighted average cost per unit is then used to calculate ending inventory and cost of goods sold as follows:

$$\text{Ending Inventory} = \text{Units on Hand} \times \text{Weighted Average Cost per Unit}$$

$$\text{Cost of Goods Sold} = \text{Units Sold} \times \text{Weighted Average Cost per Unit}$$

The average cost method is used by companies such as **Office Depot** and **OfficeMax**. **CORNERSTONE 6-7** illustrates the application of the average cost method.

 **CORNERSTONE 6-7** **Applying the Average Cost Inventory Costing Method**

Concept:
The cost of goods available for sale is allocated between ending inventory and cost of goods sold based on a weighted average cost of the goods available for sale.

Information:
Tampico Beachwear, a retail store specializing in beach apparel, has the following information related to purchases and sales of one of its more popular products, Crocs brand shoes. (Each inventory layer is a different color.)

Date	Description	Units Purchased at Cost	Units Sold at Retail
Oct. 1	Beginning inventory	300 units @ $16 = $ 4,800	
3	Purchase 1	600 units @ $18 = $10,800	
8	Sale 1		800 units @ $30
15	Purchase 2	250 units @ $20 = $ 5,000	
20	Purchase 3	150 units @ $22 = $ 3,300	
25	Sale 2		300 units @ $30
		Goods available for sale: 1,300 units = $23,900	Sales: 1,100 units = $33,000

(Continued)

Required:
Compute the cost of ending inventory and the cost of goods sold at October 31 using the average cost method. (*Note:* Use four decimal places for per unit calculations and round all other numbers to the nearest dollar.)

Solution:
Step 1: Compute the cost of goods available for sale immediately *prior* to the first sale. This produces an inventory balance of $15,600 ($4,800 + $10,800) and inventory units of 900 (300 + 600).

Step 2: Apply the average cost method to determine ending inventory and cost of goods sold. The cost of goods available for sale is allocated between inventory and cost of goods sold using a weighted average cost per unit calculated as:

$$\text{Weighted Average Cost per Unit} = \frac{\text{Cost of Goods Available for Sale}}{\text{Units Available for Sale}}$$

$$= \frac{\$15,600}{900 \text{ units}} = \$17.3333 \text{ per unit}$$

Date	Description	Cost of Goods Sold	Inventory Balance	
Oct. 1	Beginning inventory		300 × $16	= $ 4,800 ($16/unit)
3	Purchase 1 (600 @ $18)		300 × $16 = $ 4,800 600 × $18 = $10,800 }	= $15,600 ($17.3333/unit)[a]
8	Sale 1 (800 @ $30)	800 × $17.3333 = $13,867	100 × $17.3333	= $ 1,733

[a]$15,600 ÷ 900 units = $17.3333/unit

Step 3: Repeat steps 1 and 2 for the remaining inventory transactions during the period.

Date	Description	Cost of Goods Sold	Inventory Balance	
Oct. 8	Inventory on hand		100 × $17.3333	= $ 1,733 ($17.3333/unit)[a]
15	Purchase 2 (250 @ $20)		100 × $17.3333 = $1,733 250 × $20.00 = $5,000 }	= $ 6,733 ($19.2371/unit)[b]
20	Purchase 3 (150 @ $22)		350 × $19.2371 = $6,733 150 × $22.00 = $3,300 }	= $10,033 ($20.0660/unit)[c]
25	Sale 2 (300 @ $30)	300 × $20.0660 = $ 6,020 **Total** = **$19,887**	200 × $20.0660	= $ 4,013

[b]$6,733 ÷ 350 units = $19.2371/unit
[c]$10,033 ÷ 500 units = $20.0660/unit

The application of the average cost method in Cornerstone 6-7 results in the following:

- Ending inventory reported on the balance sheet is $4,013.
- Cost of goods sold reported on the income statement is $19,887, the sum of cost of goods sold during the period ($13,867 + $6,020).

Because the sum of ending inventory and cost of goods sold ($4,013 + $19,887) equals cost of goods available for sale ($23,900), Tampico could have also calculated cost of goods sold as the difference between cost of goods available for sale and ending inventory ($23,900 – $4,013).

The average cost method results in an allocation to ending inventory and cost of goods sold that is somewhere between the allocations produced by FIFO and LIFO.

ANALYSIS OF INVENTORY COSTING METHODS

OBJECTIVE 4

Analyze the financial reporting and tax effects of the various inventory costing methods.

Companies are free to choose among the four inventory costing methods, and the inventory accounting policy decisions that are made can have major effects on the financial statements. Proper management of these decisions, within the bounds of generally accepted accounting principles and good business ethics, can also affect the timing of income tax payments and the judgments of creditors, stockholders, and others. Therefore, it is important to understand the consequences of these accounting choices.

Illustrating Relationships: Financial Statement Effects of Alternative Costing Methods

Financial statement analysts frequently ask the hypothetical question, "How much would inventory and income have been if a different costing method had been used?" If the prices paid for purchased inventory are stable, all inventory costing methods will yield the same amounts for ending inventory and cost of goods sold. However, when purchase prices vary, the FIFO, LIFO and average cost methods will produce different amounts for ending inventory, cost of goods sold and, therefore, income. To properly analyze financial statements, it is necessary to understand the impact of changing prices on inventories and income.

To illustrate, consider the inventory data for Tampico Beachwear, which had revenues for the period of $33,000 (1,100 units sold × $30 per unit) and operating expenses of $4,000 (assumed amount). This information and the related FIFO, LIFO, and average cost inventory calculations in Cornerstones 6-5 through 6-7 produced the income statement amounts shown in Exhibit 6-11.

Notice that sales, purchases, and cost of goods available for sale are the same for each method. However the changing

Concept Q&A

Why doesn't the FASB simply mandate the most conceptually correct inventory costing method instead of giving companies a choice between alternative methods?

Answer:

All inventory costing methods provide an allocation of the total dollar amount of goods available for sale between ending inventory and cost of goods sold. No one cost method is conceptually superior to any other. For example, LIFO actually achieves a better matching of current costs with current revenues on the income statement; however, the resulting balance sheet valuation can be quite misleading about the current market value of inventory on the balance sheet. Companies make the choice between inventory methods for a variety of reasons unique to their own situation. Some companies will adopt LIFO for the tax benefits, while others will adopt FIFO because they want to report higher profits or simply because FIFO is less expensive to implement.

Exhibit 6-11

Financial Statement Effects of Alternative Inventory Costing Methods

Tampico Beachwear Condensed Income Statements For the Month Ending October 31			
	FIFO	**LIFO**	**Average Cost**
Sales	$33,000	$33,000	$33,000
Beginning inventory	$ 4,800	$ 4,800	$ 4,800
Add: Purchases	19,100	19,100	19,100
Cost of goods available for sale	$23,900	$23,900	$23,900
Less: Ending inventory	(4,300)	(3,600)	(4,013)
Cost of goods sold	19,600	20,300	19,887
Gross margin	$13,400	$12,700	$13,113
Operating expenses	4,000	4,000	4,000
Income before taxes	$ 9,400	$ 8,700	$ 9,113
Income tax expense (30%)	2,820	2,610	2,734
Net income	$ 6,580	$ 6,090	$ 6,379

purchase prices of each inventory layer result in different amounts for cost of goods sold, gross margin, and net income.

When purchase prices are rising, as they are in our example (remember that shoes went from $16 to $18 to $20 to $22), the FIFO method produces the highest cost for ending inventory, the lowest cost of goods sold, and, therefore, the highest gross margin (and net income) of the three methods. In contrast, the LIFO method produced the lowest cost for ending inventory, the highest cost of goods sold, and, therefore, the lowest gross margin (and net income) of the three methods. The average cost method produced amounts for inventory, cost of goods sold, and net income that fell between the FIFO and LIFO extremes. *When purchase prices are falling,* the situation is reversed. Exhibit 6-12 summarizes these relationships.

During periods of rising prices, we expect LIFO companies to report lower amounts for inventory cost and higher amounts for cost of goods sold than comparable FIFO companies. And during periods of falling prices, we expect LIFO companies to report higher amounts of inventory cost and lower amounts for cost of goods sold than comparable FIFO companies. Due to these effects, it can be argued that:

- LIFO results in the more realistic amount for income because it matches the most current costs, which are closer to the current market value, against revenue.
- FIFO results in the more realistic amount for inventory because it reports the most current costs, which are closer to the current market value, on the balance sheet.

Income Tax Effects of Alternative Costing Methods

We have seen that in periods of rising prices, LIFO allocates the newest—and therefore highest—inventory purchase prices to cost of goods sold, resulting in a lower gross margin and lower net income. Therefore, in periods of rising prices, companies may choose LIFO because it produces the lowest current taxable income and the lowest current income tax payment. In Exhibit 6-11 (p. 281), LIFO produced income tax expense of $2,610 compared to income tax expense of $2,820 if FIFO had been used.

Of course, in the long run, all inventory costs will find their way to cost of goods sold and the income statement. Therefore, choosing LIFO to minimize current taxes does not avoid the payment of taxes; it merely postpones it, temporarily reducing the company's capital requirements for a period of time. The federal income tax code requires businesses that use LIFO for tax purposes to use LIFO for financial reporting purposes as well. This is known as the LIFO conformity rule.

ETHICAL DECISIONS   When managers select an inventory costing method, it may not always be in the best interest of the company. For example, in a period of rising prices, the owners of the company may prefer that a company use LIFO in order to

Exhibit 6-12

Financial Statement Effects of Alternative Inventory Costing Methods

↑ Rising Purchase Prices	↓ Falling Purchase Prices
FIFO produces:	**FIFO produces:**
• Highest ending inventory	• Lowest ending inventory
• Lowest cost of goods sold	• Highest cost of goods sold
• Highest income	• Lowest income
LIFO produces:	**LIFO produces:**
• Lowest ending inventory	• Highest ending inventory
• Highest cost of goods sold	• Lowest cost of goods sold
• Lowest income	• Highest income

reduce the taxes that must be paid. However, many management bonus plans are based on net income and the use of FIFO would result in larger bonuses. If managers let the choice of inventory costing method be guided solely by its effect on their compensation, the ethics of their behavior can certainly be questioned. ●

Consistency in Application

Companies are free to choose whichever inventory costing method they prefer, regardless of whether the method matches the physical flow of goods. However, once a company adopts a particular costing method for an item, it must continue to use it consistently over time.[4] The consistent application of an accounting principle over time discourages changes in accounting methods from one period to another, even if acceptable alternative methods exist. This enhances the comparability and usefulness of accounting information. A change in accounting method may still be made; however, the effects of the change must be fully disclosed. The consistent application of accounting methods and the required disclosures of any accounting changes permit readers of financial statements to assume that accounting methods do not change over time unless specifically indicated.

YOU◆DECIDE   Choosing Among Inventory Costing Methods

You are the owner and manager of Simply Fresh, a supermarket that specializes in selling fresh, organic food. You know that managing inventory is crucial to the company's success and that generally accepted accounting principles give you the freedom to choose between FIFO, LIFO, and average cost to report inventory and cost of goods sold.

What factors should you consider in selecting among the different inventory costing methods?

Three factors that should be considered are as follows:

- *Actual physical flow of inventory*: Because most companies sell their oldest merchandise first, FIFO will give the closest approximation to the physical flow of inventory. However, GAAP does not require that the choice of inventory costing method be consistent with the physical flow of goods.
- *Financial statement effects*: During periods of rising prices, the use of FIFO will result in the highest cost for ending inventory, the lowest cost of goods sold, and the highest net income. These positive financial results may be desirable to satisfy shareholders who demand higher stock prices or meet lending agreements that are tied to financial performance. In addition, if management's bonus plan is tied to reported income, the use of FIFO may result in higher bonuses for management.
- *Tax benefits*: During periods of rising prices, the use of LIFO will result in lower income and possibly create significant tax savings for the company.

If financial statement users wish to make good decisions, it is important to understand the differences that result from management's choice of inventory method.

LOWER OF COST OR MARKET RULE

OBJECTIVE 5

Apply the lower of cost or market rule to the valuation of inventory.

The inventory accounting procedures described to this point have followed the historical cost principle—inventory is recorded in the firm's records at its historical purchase price (or cost). The price for which inventory items can be sold (their market value) may decline because the goods have become obsolete, have been damaged, or have otherwise diminished in value. For example, clothes that have gone out of style due to changing fashions or seasons have declined in value. Similarly, technology companies experience rapid obsolescence due to quickly changing technologies. In cases where the market value of inventory has dropped below its original cost, generally accepted accounting principles permit a departure from the historical cost concept.

---

[4] All items of inventory need not be accounted for by the same costing method. Many companies use LIFO for a portion of inventory and FIFO or average cost for another portion of their inventory.

IFRS
In applying the LCM rule, IFRS define market value as net realizable value (selling price less cost of completion and disposal) instead of replacement cost.

This departure from the historical cost principle is called the **lower of cost or market (LCM) rule**. Under LCM, if the market value of a company's inventory is lower than its cost, the company reduces the amount recorded for inventory to its market value. To apply LCM, a company must first determine the cost of its inventory using one of the inventory costing methods discussed earlier in the chapter (specific identification, FIFO, LIFO, or average cost). Next, the company will establish the market value of the inventory. Under LCM, market value is defined as current *replacement cost*, the current purchase price for identical goods.[5] Finally, the market value is compared with historical cost (usually on an item-by-item basis), and the lower of market value or historical cost is used as the cost for the inventory on the financial statements. **CORNERSTONE 6-8** illustrates the application of the LCM rule.

CORNERSTONE 6-8

Valuing Inventory at Lower of Cost or Market

Concept:
Inventory should be conservatively valued at the lower of its cost or market value.

Information:
MacKenzie Electronics prepared the following analysis of its inventory at December 31:

Product	Quantity	Historical Cost per Item	Replacement Cost (Market Value) per Item
42" LCD HDTV	12	$1,000	$1,100
50" Plasma HDTV	7	1,300	1,000
DVD Recorders	20	120	100

Required:
1. Determine the lower of cost or market value for each item of inventory.
2. Prepare the journal entry needed on December 31 to value the inventory at LCM.

Solution:
1. The LCM amounts are shown in the last column of the analysis below.

Product	Cost	Market Value	Lower of Cost or Market
42" LCD HDTV	$12,000 (12 × $1,000)	$13,200 (12 × $1,100)	$12,000
50" Plasma HDTV	9,100 (7 × $1,300)	7,000 (7 × $1,000)	7,000
DVD Recorders	2,400 (20 × $120)	2,000 (20 × $100)	2,000
	$23,500	$22,200	$21,000

2. To apply LCM, the inventory must be reduced by $2,500 ($23,500 − $21,000) as follows:

Date	Account and Explanation	Debit	Credit
Dec. 31	Cost of Goods Sold	2,500	
	Inventory		2,500
	(Reduced inventory to market value)		

Assets	=	Liabilities	+	Stockholders' Equity
−2,500				−2,500

[5] In determining the replacement cost (market value) of inventory, a company is subject to two constraints. First, the replacement cost cannot be more than the net realizable value (selling price less costs to sell) of the inventory. Second, replacement cost cannot be less than the net realizable value less a normal profit margin (markup). This concept is discussed more fully in intermediate accounting texts.

Note that, in Cornerstone 6-8, the market value of the LCD HDTVs is greater than its historical cost; however, for the other two products, historical cost is greater than market value. Thus, only the plasma HDTVs and the DVD recorders are reduced to market; the LCD HDTVs remain at historical cost. The journal entry reduces inventory to its market value, and the loss is recorded as an increase to cost of goods sold in the period that the market value of the item dropped.

The LCM rule is an application of the conservatism principle. The *conservatism principle* leads accountants to select the accounting methods or procedures that produce the lowest (most conservative) net income and net assets in the current period. Thus, accountants tend to recognize expenses and losses as early as possible and to recognize gains and revenues as late as possible. By conservatively valuing inventory, the LCM rule is designed to avoid overstating the current earnings and financial strength of a company by recognizing an expense in the period that there is a decline in market value of inventory rather than in the period that the inventory is sold.

Concept Q&A

If the Financial Accounting Standards Board (FASB) allows the value of inventory to be reduced to market value when the market value is less than cost, why can't the value of inventory be increased when the market value is greater than cost?

Answer:
For the same reason that the conservatism principle allows inventory to be written down to market value, it prevents inventory from being written up to market value. Given uncertainty as to the actual future selling price of the inventory, a prudent reaction would be to avoid future overly optimistic about the company's future prospects. Overly optimistic projections of the future usually have far more serious negative consequences for people relying on the financial statements than do understatements.

YOU DECIDE   An Ethical Dilemma Involving Overvalued Inventory

You are the controller for PC Location Inc., a retailer that operates six computer stores in the Chicago area. An analysis of year-end inventory reveals a large number of obsolete laptop computers that require a $180,000 write-down to market value. When you inform the CEO of this issue, she reminds you that PC Location is currently negotiating with Second Chicago Bank to increase its long-term loan and the bank has asked to review PC Location's preliminary financial statements. The CEO asks you to delay recognizing the write-down until Second Chicago has seen the preliminary financial statements. "Let the auditors write down the inventory when they show up in February," she says. "That's what we pay them for."

What should you do in this situation?

If you agree to ignore the required lower of cost or market adjustment, the bank may decide to grant the loan on the basis of the misleading financial statements. But when they receive the audited financial statements several months later, an investigation will no doubt be launched, and you are likely to take the blame. The ethical course of action is for you to refuse to go along with the CEO. You should be prepared to support your adjustment and to argue the disastrous consequences of trying to mislead Second Chicago Bank. In addition, you should be prepared to present alternatives to proceeding with the new loan at this time. Of course, if you refuse to go along with the CEO, you may find yourself unemployed.

The application of judgment in accounting may lead to ethical dilemmas.

ANALYZING INVENTORY

Inventories are at the heart of many companies' operations and must be carefully controlled and accounted for. Two measures of how successful a company is at managing and controlling its inventory are the gross profit ratio and the inventory turnover ratio.

OBJECTIVE 6

Evaluate inventory management using the gross profit and inventory turnover ratios.

Gross Profit Ratio   The **gross profit ratio** is calculated as:

$$\frac{\text{Gross Profit}}{\text{Net Sales}} = \text{Gross Profit Ratio}$$

This ratio is carefully watched by managers, investors, and analysts as a key indicator of a company's ability to sell inventory at a profit. In short, the gross profit ratio tells us how many cents of every dollar are available to cover expenses other than cost of goods sold and to earn a profit. An increasing gross profit ratio could signal that a company is able to charge more for its products due to high demand or has effectively controlled the cost of its inventory. A decrease in this ratio could signal trouble. For example, a company may have reduced its selling price due to increased competition or it is paying more for its inventory.

Inventory Turnover Ratio The **inventory turnover ratio** is calculated as:

$$\frac{\text{Cost of Goods Sold}}{\text{Average Inventory}} = \text{Inventory Turnover Ratio}$$

This ratio describes how quickly inventory is purchased (or produced) and sold. Companies want to satisfy the conflicting goals of having enough inventory on hand to meet customer demand while minimizing the cost of holding inventory (e.g., storage costs, obsolescence). Inventory turnover provides an indicator of how much of the company's funds are tied up in inventory. High inventory turnover ratios indicate that a company is rapidly selling its inventory, thus reducing inventory costs. Low inventory turnover reflects that the company may be holding too much inventory, thereby incurring avoidable costs or signaling that demand for a company's products has fallen. Financial statement users can also compute the **average days to sell inventory** as follows:

$$\frac{365 \text{ days}}{\text{Inventory Turnover}} = \text{Average Days to Sell Inventory}$$

CORNERSTONE 6-9 illustrates the analysis of these performance measures for **Wal-Mart** and **Target**.

CORNERSTONE 6-9

Calculating the Gross Profit and Inventory Turnover Ratios

Concept:

The gross profit and inventory turnover ratios provide measures of how successful a company is at managing and controlling its inventory.

Information:

The following information is available for Wal-Mart and Target for the fiscal year ending January 31, 2010 (all amounts in millions):

Account	Wal-Mart	Target
Net sales	$405,046	$63,435
Cost of goods sold	304,657	44,062
Gross profit	100,389	19,373
Inventory, January 31, 2009	34,511	6,705
Inventory, January 31, 2010	33,160	7,179

Required:

1. Compute the gross profit ratio for Wal-Mart and Target.
2. Compute the inventory turnover ratio and the average days to sell inventory for Wal-Mart and Target.

Solution:

1. $\text{Gross Profit Ratio} = \dfrac{\text{Gross Profit}}{\text{Net Sales}}$

Wal-Mart	Target
$\dfrac{\$100,389}{\$405,046} = 0.248$, or 24.8%	$\dfrac{\$19,373}{\$63,435} = 0.305$, or 30.5%

(Continued)

CORNERSTONE 6-9 *(continued)*

2. Inventory Turnover Ratio = $\dfrac{\text{Cost of Goods Sold}}{\text{Average Inventory}}$

Wal-Mart	Target
$\dfrac{\$304,657}{(\$34,511 + \$33,160) \div 2} = 9.004$	$\dfrac{\$44,062}{(\$6,705 + \$7,179) \div 2} = 6.347$

Average Days to Sell Inventory = $\dfrac{365 \text{ days}}{\text{Inventory Turnover}}$

Wal-Mart	Target
$\dfrac{365}{9.004} = 40.538 \text{ days}$	$\dfrac{365}{6.347} = 57.507 \text{ days}$

As you can see in Cornerstone 6-9, both **Wal-Mart** and **Target** have gross profit ratios below the industry average of 31.28 percent. However, Wal-Mart's gross profit ratio was up 0.6 percent from the previous year, while Target's gross profit ratio improved by 0.7 percent. These trends signal improvements in the management and control over inventory. While Target generates a higher gross profit on each dollar of sales, Wal-Mart is able to more rapidly sell its inventory (approximately 17 days faster) than Target. This higher inventory turnover allows Wal-Mart to lower its cost of carrying inventory which leads to higher income.

LIFO Reserve Adjustments

Analysts and other users often wish to compare companies that use different inventory costing methods. To assist in these comparisons, companies that use LIFO are required to report the amount that inventory would increase (or decrease) if the company had used FIFO. This amount is referred to as the **LIFO reserve**. The LIFO inventory value can be found as follows:

Reported FIFO Inventory – LIFO Reserve = LIFO Inventory Value

In addition, the effect on income can be found by examining the difference in the LIFO reserve.

For example, **General Mills**' disclosure of its LIFO reserve for 2009 is shown in Exhibit 6-13.

Exhibit 6-13

LIFO Reserve Disclosure

General Mills Inc. Notes to Consolidated Financial Statements Note 17: Supplemental Information (in part)		
(in millions)	**May 31, 2009**	**May 25, 2008**
Inventories, at FIFO	$1,496.1	$1,492.6
Excess of FIFO over LIFO	(149.3)	(125.8)
Inventories, at LIFO	$1,346.8	$1,366.8

This disclosure shows that inventories would have been $149.3 million higher under FIFO for the 2009 fiscal year. Analysts can adjust the inventory amount by substituting in the FIFO inventory values ($1,496.1 million and $1,492.6 million for fiscal years 2009 and 2008, respectively) for the LIFO values reported on the balance sheet. In addition, income would have been higher under FIFO by $23.5 million ($149.3 million – $125.8 million)—the difference between the LIFO reserve for fiscal years 2009 and 2008.

YOU ◆ DECIDE   LIFO Liquidations

You are the purchasing manager for Tomlinson Health Management, an aggressively managed new business that provides pharmacy services to retirement communities, nursing homes, and small hospitals in a three-state area. In order to secure tax benefits, Tomlinson uses LIFO for most of its inventories. Tomlinson's business has become increasingly competitive in recent years, and the current year's income has fallen significantly. Avery Tomlinson, the principal stockholder and CEO, has instructed you to hold year-end inventories to the absolute minimum.

What could be Mr. Tomlinson's motivation to reduce inventories?

The LIFO inventory is composed of layers, each one representing a year's contribution to the inventory at the earliest purchase prices of that year. During a period of rising prices, the LIFO inventory will be made up of the relatively older costs trapped in the LIFO layers. If the quantity of inventory falls, some of these older costs, with relatively low unit prices, will be released to cost of goods sold. This produces a lower cost of goods sold, and higher income, than one computed at current FIFO prices.

Mr. Tomlinson may be engaging in the questionable practice of earnings management. Reducing inventories releases old, low-priced LIFO layers to the income statement, lowering cost of goods sold and raising net income. Of course, Tomlinson's act may also raise current income taxes and impair business operations due to insufficient quantities of inventory.

When analyzing inventory, it is important to understand how changing inventory levels affects the financial statements.

OBJECTIVE 7
Describe how errors in ending inventory affect income statements and balance sheets.

EFFECTS OF INVENTORY ERRORS

The cost of goods sold model, illustrated in Cornerstone 6-1 (p. 263), describes the relationship between inventory and cost of goods sold. This relationship implies that the measurement of inventory affects both the balance sheet and the income statement. Even with recent technological advances, it is easy to make errors in determining the cost of the hundreds of items in a typical ending inventory. Incorrect counts, mistakes in costing, or errors in identifying items are common. Because the ending inventory of one period is the beginning inventory of the next period, errors in the measurement of ending inventory affect two accounting periods.

To illustrate the effect of an error in valuing ending inventory on the financial statements, consider the information in Exhibit 6-14. The "Correct" column shows the financial statements for 2011 and 2012 as they would appear if no error were made. The "Erroneous" column shows the financial statements for the two years as they would appear if the firm understated its inventory at December 31, 2011, by $15,000. The "Error" column describes the effect of the error on each line of the statements.

The understatement of the 2011 ending inventory causes an overstatement of 2011 cost of goods sold. Thus, gross margin for 2011 is understated by $15,000. Ignoring income taxes, this error would then flow into both net income and retained earnings for 2011. However, the effect is not limited to 2011. Because the ending inventory for 2011 is the beginning inventory for 2012, the beginning inventory for 2012 is understated by $15,000. Assuming no other errors are made, this would lead to an

Effect of an Inventory Error

Exhibit 6-14

(amounts in thousands)	Correct		Erroneous	Error*
2011 Financial Statements				
Income Statement (partial)				
Sales		$500	$500	
Cost of goods sold:				
Beginning inventory	$ 50		$ 50	
Purchases	250		250	
Cost of goods available for sale	$300		$300	
Less: Ending inventory	(60)		(45)	−$15
Cost of goods sold		240	255	+$15
Gross margin		$260	$245	−$15
Balance Sheet (partial)				
Inventory		$ 60	$ 45	−$15
Retained earnings		$100	$ 85	−$15
2012 Financial Statements				
Income Statement (partial)				
Sales		$600	$600	
Cost of goods sold:				
Beginning inventory	$ 60		$ 45	−$15
Purchases	290		290	
Cost of goods available for sale	$350		$335	−$15
Less: Ending inventory	(50)		50	
Cost of goods sold		300	285	−$15
Gross margin		$300	$315	+$15
Balance Sheet (partial)				
Inventory		$ 50	$ 50	
Retained earnings		180	180	

* A minus sign (−) indicates an understatement and a plus sign (+) indicates an overstatement.

understatement of cost of goods sold and an overstatement of gross margin (and net income) by $15,000. However, notice that when this flows into retained earnings, the understatement in 2011 is offset by the overstatement in 2012 so that retained earnings is correctly stated by the end of 2012. This illustrates the self correcting nature of inventory errors.

CORNERSTONE **6-10** illustrates the analysis of inventory errors.

CORNERSTONE 6-10   **Analyzing Inventory Errors**

Concept:
Errors in the measurement of ending inventory will affect both the current and subsequent period balance sheets as well as the current period income statement.

Information:
Dunn Corporation reported net income of $75,000 for 2011. Early in 2012, Dunn discovers that the December 31, 2011, ending inventory was overstated by $6,000.

Required:
Determine the financial statement effects of the inventory errors for 2011 and 2012.

(Continued)

CORNERSTONE
6-10
(continued)

Solution:

For 2011, assets (ending inventory) are overstated by $6,000. The overstatement of ending inventory causes an understatement of cost of goods sold (an expense) by $6,000. This error flows through to income and retained earnings (equity). Because the ending inventory for 2011 is the beginning inventory for 2012, the error has the opposite effects on income for 2012. Assuming no other errors are made, the inventory error self-corrects and the 2012 balance sheet is correctly stated. These effects are summarized below.

	Assets	Liabilities	Equity	Revenues	Expenses	Income
2011	$6,000 overstated	No effect	$6,000 overstated	No effect	$6,000 understated	$6,000 overstated
2012	No effect	No effect	No effect	No effect	$6,000 overstated	$6,000 understated

Even though inventory errors are self-correcting over two periods, it is still necessary to correct them in order to produce properly stated financial information. If the error is not corrected, both income statements and the 2011 balance sheet will be incorrect.

OBJECTIVE ⑧
Explain how to record purchases of inventory using a periodic inventory system.

APPENDIX 6A: PERIODIC INVENTORY SYSTEM

In a periodic inventory system, the inventory records are not kept continually, or perpetually, up to date. Instead, under a periodic inventory system, the inventory account is updated at the end of the period based on a physical count of the inventory on hand. The balance in the inventory account remains unchanged during the period. As purchase transactions occur, they are recorded in one of four temporary accounts:

- *Purchases:* The purchases account accumvulates the cost of the inventory acquired during the period.
- *Purchase Discounts:* The purchase discounts account accumulates the amount of discounts on purchases taken during the period.
- *Purchase Returns and Allowances:* The purchase returns and allowances account accumulates the cost of any merchandise returned to the supplier or any reductions (allowances) in the purchase price granted by the seller.
- *Transportation-In:* The transportation-in account accumulates the cost paid by the purchaser to transport inventory from suppliers.

The balances in these temporary accounts, along with the beginning and ending inventory balances obtained from the physical count of inventory, are used to compute cost of goods sold using the cost of goods sold model illustrated in Cornerstone 6-1 (p. 263).

CORNERSTONE 6-11 illustrates how to record purchase transactions in a periodic inventory system.

CORNERSTONE
6-11

Recording Purchase Transactions in a Periodic Inventory System

Concept:

The cost of inventory includes the purchase price of the merchandise plus any cost of bringing the goods to a salable condition and location.

(Continued)

**CORNERSTONE
6-11**
(continued)

Information:

On September 1, Brandon Shoes purchased 50 pairs of hiking boots for $3,750 cash (or $75 a pair) and paid $150 of transportation costs. Also, on September 1, Brandon purchased 100 pairs of running shoes for $10,000; however, the seller paid the transportation costs of $300. The running shoes were purchased on credit with credit terms of 2/10, n/30. Brandon paid for one-half ($5,000) of the running shoes on September 10, within the discount period. The remaining shoes were paid for on September 30. After inspection, Brandon determined that 10 pairs of the hiking boots were defective and returned them on September 30.

Required:

Prepare the journal entries necessary to record the September transactions for Brandon Shoes.

Solution:

Date	Account and Explanation	Debit	Credit
Sept. 1	Purchases	3,750	
	Cash		3,750
	(Purchased inventory for cash)		
1	Transportation-In	150	
	Cash		150
	(Recorded payment of freight costs)		
1	Purchases	10,000	
	Accounts Payable		10,000
	(Purchased inventory on credit)		
10	Accounts Payable	5,000	
	Cash		4,900
	Purchase Discounts ($5,000 × 2%)		100
	(Recorded payment within the discount period)		
30	Accounts Payable	5,000	
	Cash		5,000
	(Recorded payment outside of the discount period)		
30	Cash (10 pairs × $75 per pair)	750	
	Purchase Returns and Allowances		750
	(Returned defective hiking boots)		

Assets	=	Liabilities	+	Stockholders' Equity
−3,750				−3,750

Assets	=	Liabilities	+	Stockholders' Equity
−150				−150

Assets	=	Liabilities	+	Stockholders' Equity
		+10,000		−10,000

Assets	=	Liabilities	+	Stockholders' Equity
−4,900		−5,000		+100

Assets	=	Liabilities	+	Stockholders' Equity
−5,000		−5,000		

Assets	=	Liabilities	+	Stockholders' Equity
+750				+750

Under either the periodic or the perpetual inventory system, the net cost of purchases (shown below) is the same.

Purchases	$13,750
Less: Purchase discounts	(100)
Purchase returns and allowances	(750)
Add: Transportation costs (freight-in)	150
Net cost of purchases	$13,050

Additionally, for sales transactions, there is no need to make a second journal entry to record the expense (and inventory) portion of a transaction. Instead, only the revenue portion is recorded as shown earlier in the text.

The differences between a periodic and perpetual inventory system are summarized in Exhibit 6-15 (p. 292).

Perpetual vs. Periodic Inventory Systems

Activity	Perpetual System	Periodic System
Purchase	Inventory purchases are recorded in the *inventory account*.	The costs of inventory purchases are recorded in the *purchases account*.
Sale	When a sale is made, an entry is made to record the amount of sales revenue. *A second entry is made that increases the cost of goods sold account and decreases the inventory account.*	When a sale is made, an entry is made to record the amount of sales revenue only. *No entry is made to cost of goods sold or inventory.*
Costing ending inventory	At the end of the period, the *cost of ending inventory* is the balance in the inventory account (which is verified by a physical count of inventory).	*The amount of ending inventory is determined at the end of the accounting by taking a physical count of inventory,* a procedure by which all items of inventory on a given date are identified and counted.
Determining cost of goods sold	Cost of goods sold for the period is the balance *in the cost of goods sold account* at the end of the period.	Cost of goods sold is determined only at the end of the period by *applying the cost of goods sold model.*

OBJECTIVE ❾
Compute ending inventory and cost of goods sold under a periodic inventory system.

APPENDIX 6B: INVENTORY COSTING METHODS AND THE PERIODIC INVENTORY SYSTEM

Regardless of whether a company uses a perpetual inventory system or a periodic inventory system, inventory costing methods are designed to allocate the cost of goods available for sale between ending inventory and cost of goods sold. Under a periodic inventory system, the inventory costing methods are applied *as if* all purchases during an accounting period take place prior to any sales of the period. While this is not a realistic assumption, it does simplify the computation of the ending inventory and cost of goods sold since only one allocation needs to be made, regardless of the number of purchases and sales. Given this assumption, the following steps can be applied to determine ending inventory and cost of goods sold:

Step 1:   Calculate the cost of goods available for sale for the period.
Step 2:   Apply the inventory costing method to determine ending inventory and cost of goods sold.

First-In, First-Out (FIFO)

Under the FIFO method, *the earliest purchases (the first in) are assumed to be the first sold (the first out) and the more recent purchases are in ending inventory.* **CORNERSTONE 6-12** illustrates the application of the FIFO method. Notice that this is

CORNERSTONE 6-12   Applying the FIFO Inventory Costing Method in a Periodic Inventory System

Concept:
The cost of the earliest purchases that make up cost of goods available for sale is allocated to cost of goods sold, and the cost of the most recent purchases is allocated to ending inventory.

(Continued)

Information:

Tampico Beachwear, a retail store specializing in beach apparel, has the following information related to purchases and sales of one of its more popular products, Crocs brand shoes. (Each inventory layer is a different color.)

**CORNERSTONE
6-12**
(continued)

Date	Description	Units Purchased at Cost	Units Sold at Retail
Oct. 1	Beginning inventory	300 units @ $16 = $ 4,800	
3	Purchase 1	600 units @ $18 = $10,800	
8	Sale 1		800 units @ $30
15	Purchase 2	250 units @ $20 = $ 5,000	
20	Purchase 3	150 units @ $22 = $ 3,300	
25	Sale 2		300 units @ $30
		Goods available for sale: 1,300 units = $23,900	Sales: 1,100 units = $33,000

Ending inventory is made up of 200 units (1,300 units available for sale − 1,100 units sold).

Required:

Compute the cost of ending inventory and the cost of goods sold at October 31 using the FIFO method.

Solution:

Step 1: Compute the cost of goods available for sale for the period ($23,900).

Step 2: Apply FIFO to determine ending inventory and cost of goods sold. The cost of goods available for sale is allocated between inventory (the most recent purchases) and cost of goods sold (the earliest purchases) as follows:

Ending Inventory			Cost of Goods Sold		
150 units × $22	=	$3,300	300 units × $16	=	$ 4,800
50 units × $20	=	1,000	600 units × $18	=	10,800
200 units		$4,300	200 units × $20	=	4,000
			1,100 units		$19,600

the same information used to illustrate the inventory costing methods applied to a perpetual inventory system (Cornerstones 6-5 through 6-7). However, the information on purchases is listed first and the sales can be combined because all purchases are assumed to occur prior to any sales.

Last-In, First-Out (LIFO)

Under the LIFO method, *the most recent purchases (newest costs) are allocated to the cost of goods sold and the earliest purchases (oldest costs) are allocated to ending inventory.* **CORNERSTONE 6-13** (p. 294) illustrates the application of the LIFO method.

CORNERSTONE 6-13
Applying the LIFO Inventory Costing Method in a Periodic Inventory System

Concept:
The cost of the most recent purchases that make up cost of goods available for sale is allocated to cost of goods sold, and the cost of the earliest purchases is allocated to ending inventory.

Information:
Tampico Beachwear, a retail store specializing in beach apparel, has the following information related to purchases and sales of one of its more popular products, Crocs brand shoes. (Each inventory layer is a different color.)

Date	Description	Units Purchased at Cost	Units Sold at Retail
Oct. 1	Beginning inventory	300 units @ $16 = $ 4,800	
3	Purchase 1	600 units @ $18 = $10,800	
8	Sale 1		800 units @ $30
15	Purchase 2	250 units @ $20 = $ 5,000	
20	Purchase 3	150 units @ $22 = $ 3,300	
25	Sale 2		300 units @ $30
		Goods available for sale: 1,300 units = $23,900	Sales: 1,100 units = $33,000

Ending inventory is made up of 200 units (1,300 units available for sale − 1,100 units sold).

Required:
Compute the cost of ending inventory and the cost of goods sold at October 31 using the LIFO method.

Solution:
Step 1: Compute the cost of goods available for sale for the period ($23,900).
Step 2: Apply LIFO to determine ending inventory and cost of goods sold. This cost of goods available for sale is allocated between inventory (the earliest purchases) and cost of goods sold (the most recent purchases) as follows:

Ending Inventory	Cost of Goods Sold		
200 units × $16 = $3,200	100 units × $16	=	$ 1,600
	600 units × $18	=	10,800
	250 units × $20	=	5,000
	150 units × $22	=	3,300
	1,100 units		$20,700

Average Cost Method

Under the average cost method, the weighted average cost per unit is multiplied by:

• the number of units in ending inventory to determine the cost of ending inventory
• the number of units sold to determine cost of goods sold

This method is commonly referred to as the weighted average method. In contrast to the perpetual inventory system, the weighted average cost per unit is not continually calculated. Rather it is calculated based on the total cost of goods available for sale and the total units available for sale. **CORNERSTONE 6-14** illustrates the application of the average cost method.

CORNERSTONE
6-14

Applying the Average Cost Inventory Costing Method in a Periodic Inventory System

Concept:

The cost of goods available for sale is allocated between ending inventory and cost of goods sold based on a weighted average cost of the goods available for sale.

Information:

Tampico Beachwear, a retail store specializing in beach apparel, has the following information related to purchases and sales of one of its more popular products, Crocs brand shoes. (Each inventory layer is a different color.)

Date	Description	Units Purchased at Cost	Units Sold at Retail
Oct. 1	Beginning inventory	300 units @ $16 = $ 4,800	
3	Purchase 1	600 units @ $18 = $10,800	
8	Sale 1		800 units @ $30
15	Purchase 2	250 units @ $20 = $ 5,000	
20	Purchase 3	150 units @ $22 = $ 3,300	
25	Sale 2		300 units @ $30
		Goods available for sale:	Sales:
		1,300 units = $23,900	1,100 units = $33,000

Ending inventory is made up of 200 units (1,300 units available for sale − 1,100 units sold).

Required:

Compute the cost of ending inventory and the cost of goods sold at October 31 using the average cost method.
   (*Note:* Use four decimal places for per unit calculations and round all other numbers to the nearest dollar.)

Solution:

Step 1: Compute the cost of goods available for sale for the period ($23,900).

Step 2: Apply the average cost method to determine ending inventory and cost of goods sold. This method requires you to compute a weighted average cost of the goods available for sale:

$$\text{Weighted Average Cost per Unit} = \frac{\text{Cost of Goods Available for Sale}}{\text{Units Available for Sale}}$$

$$= \$23,900 \div 1,300 \text{ units} = \textbf{\$18.3846 per unit}$$

The cost of goods available for sale ($23,900) is allocated between inventory and cost of goods sold using the average cost of the inventory as follows:

Ending Inventory	**Cost of Goods Sold**
200 units × $18.3846 = $3,677	1,100 units × $18.3846 = **$20,223**

Under all inventory costing methods, periodic inventory systems allocate the cost of purchased goods between cost of goods sold and ending inventory only at the end of the period. In contrast, the perpetual inventory system performs this allocation each time a sale is made. Because of this difference in the timing of cost allocations, the two systems usually yield different amounts for the cost of goods sold and ending inventory under both the LIFO and average cost assumptions. FIFO amounts, however, are always the same under both periodic and perpetual inventory systems.[6]

---

[6] This occurs because FIFO always allocates the earliest items purchased to cost of goods sold, resulting in ending inventory being the latest items purchased. Under both the perpetual and periodic inventory systems, these are the same units of inventory at the same cost. Therefore, the timing of the cost allocation is irrelevant under FIFO.

SUMMARY OF LEARNING OBJECTIVES

LO1. **Describe the types of inventories held by merchandisers and manufacturers, and understand how inventory costs flow through a company.**
- Merchandising companies hold one type of inventory.
- Manufacturing companies have three types of inventory—raw materials, work-in-process, and finished goods.
- When goods are purchased, the cost of the purchase is recorded in inventory (for merchandisers) or raw materials inventory (for manufacturers). During the production process, manufacturers record the cost (raw materials, labor, and overhead) in work-in-process and then transfer the cost to finished goods inventory when the product is complete.
- Once the product is sold, the cost is transferred out of the inventory account (either Inventory or Finished Goods) and into Cost of Goods Sold to match it with Sales Revenue.
- The relationship between inventory and cost of goods sold is described by the cost of goods sold model.

LO2. **Explain how to record purchases and sales of inventory using a perpetual inventory system.**
- In a perpetual inventory system, purchases of inventory are recorded by increasing the inventory account.
- If a purchase discount exists, inventory is reduced by the amount of the discount taken.
- When a purchased item is returned (purchase return) or a price reduction is granted by the seller (purchase allowance), the inventory item is reduced by the amount of the purchase return or allowance given.
- If transportation costs exist and the shipping terms are F.O.B shipping point, the transportation costs are considered part of the total cost of purchases and the inventory account is increased.
- If transportation costs exist and the shipping terms are F.O.B. destination, the seller pays these costs and records them as a selling expense on the income statement.
- In a perpetual inventory system, sales require two entries that (1) record the sales revenue and (2) recognize the expense (cost of goods sold) associated with the decrease in inventory.
- If an item is later returned, two entries must also be made: (1) increase Sales Returns and Allowances (a contra-revenue account) and (2) increase the inventory account and decrease Cost of Goods Sold.

LO3. **Apply the four inventory costing methods to compute ending inventory and cost of goods sold under a perpetual inventory system.**
- The four inventory costing methods are specific identification; first-in, first-out (FIFO); last-in, first-out (LIFO); and average cost.
- The specific identification method determines the cost of ending inventory and the cost of goods sold based on the identification of the actual units sold and the units remaining in inventory.
- The other three inventory costing methods allocate cost of goods available for sale between ending inventory and cost of goods sold using the following process.
  Step 1: Calculate the cost of goods available for sale *immediately prior* to any sales transaction.
  Step 2: Apply the inventory costing method to determine ending inventory and cost of goods sold.
  Step 3: Repeat steps 1 and 2 for all inventory transactions during the period. The sum of the cost of goods sold computed in step 2 is the cost of goods sold for the period. Ending inventory is the amount computed during the final application of step 2 for the period.

LO4.   Analyze the financial reporting and tax effects of the various inventory costing methods.
- If the prices paid for purchased inventory are stable, all inventory costing methods will yield the same amounts for ending inventory and cost of goods sold.
- When purchase prices vary, FIFO, LIFO and the average cost methods will produce different amounts for ending inventory, cost of goods sold, and, therefore, income.
- When prices are rising, the FIFO method produces the highest cost for ending inventory, the lowest cost of goods sold, and the highest gross margin (and net income).
- In contrast, the LIFO method produced the lowest cost for ending inventory, the highest cost of goods sold, and, therefore, the lowest gross margin (and net income) of the three methods. Because LIFO results in lower income, it results in the lowest income taxes.
- When purchase prices are *falling*, the situation is reversed.
- The average cost method produced amounts for inventory, cost of goods sold, and net income that fell between the FIFO and LIFO extremes.

LO5.   Apply the lower of cost or market rule to the valuation of inventory.
- If the market value of inventory has dropped below its original cost, generally accepted accounting principles permit a departure from the historical cost concept.
- A company is allowed to reduce the amount recorded for inventory to its market value, where market value is defined as the current replacement cost.
- This lower of cost or market rule is an application of the conservatism principle.

LO6.   Evaluate inventory management using the gross profit and inventory turnover ratios.
- Two useful measures of how successful a company is at managing and controlling its inventory are the gross profit ratio (gross profit ÷ net sales) and the inventory turnover ratio (cost of goods sold ÷ average inventory).
- The gross profit ratio indicates how many cents of every dollar are available to cover expenses other than cost of goods sold and to earn a profit. The inventory turnover ratio describes how quickly inventory is purchased (or produced) and sold.

LO7.   Describe how errors in ending inventory affect income statements and balance sheets.
- Inventory errors can arise for a number of reasons, including incorrect counts of inventory, mistakes in costing, or errors in identifying items.
- Because the ending inventory of one period is the beginning inventory of the next period, an error in the measurement of ending inventory will affect the cost of goods sold and net income of two consecutive periods.
- Inventory errors are self-correcting; therefore, the assets and stockholders' equity of only the first period are misstated (assuming no other errors are made).

LO8.   *(Appendix 6A)* Explain how to record purchases of inventory using a periodic inventory system.
- In a periodic inventory system, purchases of inventory are recorded by increasing the purchases account.
- If a purchase discount exists, the purchases discount account is increased by the amount of the discount taken.
- When a purchased item is returned (purchase return) or a price reduction is granted by the seller (purchase allowance), the purchase returns and allowances account is increased by the amount of the purchase return or allowance given.
- If transportation costs exist and are paid by the purchaser, the transportation costs are considered part of the total cost of purchases and the purchases account is increased.

LO9.   *(Appendix 6B)* Compute ending inventory and cost of goods sold under a periodic inventory system.
- Under a periodic inventory system, the inventory costing methods are applied as if all purchases during an accounting period take place prior to any sales of the period. Given this assumption, you will then apply the following steps:
  Step 1: Calculate the cost of goods available for sale for the period.
  Step 2: Apply the inventory costing method to determine ending inventory and cost of goods sold.

CORNERSTONES
FOR CHAPTER 6

KEY TERMS

Average cost method (p. 279)
Average days to sell inventory (p. 286)
Consignment (p. 268)
Cost of goods available for sale (p. 262)
Cost of goods sold (p. 260)
Discount period (p. 267)
Finished goods inventory (p. 261)
First-in, first-out (FIFO) method (p. 276)
F.O.B. destination (p. 267)
F.O.B. shipping point (p. 267)
Freight-in (p. 267)
Freight-out (p. 268)
Gross margin (gross profit) (p. 260)
Gross profit ratio (p. 285)
Inventory (p. 260)
Inventory turnover ratio (p. 286)
Last-in, first-out (LIFO) method (p. 277)

LIFO reserve (p. 287)
Lower of cost or market (LCM) rule (p. 284)
Manufacturers (p. 261)
Merchandisers (p. 261)
Merchandise inventory (p. 261)
Periodic inventory system (p. 264)
Perpetual inventory system (p. 264)
Purchase allowance (p. 267)
Purchase discounts (p. 267)
Purchase returns (p. 267)
Purchases (p. 266)
Raw materials inventory (p. 261)
Retailers (p. 261)
Specific identification method (p. 274)
Wholesalers (p. 261)
Work-in-process inventory (p. 261)

REVIEW PROBLEM

Accounting for Inventory

Concept:

The cost of goods available for sale is allocated between ending inventory and cost of goods sold based on the inventory costing method chosen by management. Under a perpetual inventory system, the accounting records are continually (perpetually) updated for each sale or purchase of inventory.

Information:

Sagamore Supplies, an office supply wholesale store, uses a perpetual inventory system. Sagamore recorded the following activity for one of its inventory accounts:

Date	Activity	Number of Units	Cost per Unit
Oct. 1	Beginning inventory	2,500	$16
15	Purchase	5,100	$17
Nov. 3	Sale	5,900	
20	Purchase	4,800	$18
Dec. 10	Sale	5,300	

Additional information on the purchases and sales is as follows:

- All purchases were cash purchases.
- All sales were cash sales and all inventory items were sold for $25 per unit.

Required:

1. Compute the cost of ending inventory and the cost of goods sold using the following methods: (a) FIFO, (b) LIFO, and (c) average cost.

2. Assume that Sagamore uses the FIFO inventory costing method. Prepare the journal entries to record the purchases and sales of inventory.

Solution:

1.

a. Under FIFO, the cost of ending inventory is $21,600 and cost of goods sold is $191,500 ($97,800 + $93,700).

Date	Description	Cost of Goods Sold	Inventory Balance
Oct. 1	Beginning inventory		2,500 × $16 = $ 40,000
15	Purchase (5,100 @ $17)		2,500 × $16 = $40,000 ⎫ = $126,700 5,100 × $17 = $86,700 ⎭
Nov. 3	Sale (5,900 @ $25)	2,500 × $16 = $40,000 ⎫ = **$97,800** 3,400 × $17 = $57,800 ⎭	1,700 × $17 = $ 28,900

This is an interim calculation. Because the period is not over, these steps need to be repeated until the end of the accounting period.

Date	Description	Cost of Goods Sold	Inventory Balance
Nov. 3	Inventory on hand		1,700 × $17 = $ 28,900
20	Purchase (4,800 @ $18)		1,700 × $17 = $28,900 ⎫ = $115,300 4,800 × $18 = $86,400 ⎭
Dec. 10	Sale (5,300 @ $25)	1,700 × $17 = $28,900 ⎫ = **$93,700** 3,600 × $18 = $64,800 ⎭	1,200 × $18 = $ 21,600

b. Under LIFO, the cost of ending inventory is $19,200 and cost of goods sold is $193,900 ($99,500 + $94,400).

Date	Description	Cost of Goods Sold	Inventory Balance
Oct. 1	Beginning inventory		2,500 × $16 = $ 40,000
15	Purchase (5,100 @ $17)		2,500 × $16 = $40,000 ⎫ = $126,700 5,100 × $17 = $86,700 ⎭
Nov. 3	Sale (5,900 @ $25)	5,100 × $17 = $86,700 ⎫ = **$99,500** 800 × $16 = $12,800 ⎭	1,700 × $16 = $ 27,200

This is an interim calculation. Because the period is not over, these steps need to be repeated until the end of the accounting period.

Date	Description	Cost of Goods Sold	Inventory Balance	
Nov. 3	Inventory on hand		$1,700 \times \$16$	$= \$\ 27,200$
20	Purchase (4,800 @ $18)		$\left.\begin{array}{l}1,700 \times \$16 = \$27,200 \\ 4,800 \times \$18 = \$86,400\end{array}\right\}$	$= \$113,600$
Dec. 10	Sale (5,300 @ $25)	$\left.\begin{array}{l}4,800 \times \$18 = \$86,400 \\ 500 \times \$16 = \$8,000\end{array}\right\} = \textbf{\$94,400}$	$1,200 \times \$16$	$= \$\ 19,200$

c.   Under average cost, the cost of ending inventory is $21,183 and cost of goods sold is $191,917 ($98,359 + $93,558).

Date	Description	Cost of Goods Sold	Inventory Balance	
Oct. 1	Beginning inventory		$2,500 \times \$16$	$= \$\ 40,000\ (\$16/\text{unit})$
15	Purchase (5,100 @ $17)		$\left.\begin{array}{l}2,500 \times \$16 = \$40,000 \\ 5,100 \times \$17 = \$86,700\end{array}\right\}$	$= \$126,700\ (\$16.6711/\text{unit})^a$
Nov. 3	Sale (5,900 @ $25)	$5,900 \times \$16.6711 = \textbf{\$98,359}$	$1,700 \times \$16.6711$	$= \$\ 28,341$

[a] $\$126,700 \div 7,600 \text{ units} = \$16.6711/\text{unit}$

This is an interim calculation. Because the period is not over, these steps need to be repeated until the end of the accounting period.

Date	Description	Cost of Goods Sold	Inventory Balance	
Nov. 3	Inventory on hand		$1,700 \times \$16.6711$	$= \$\ 28,341$
20	Purchase (4,800 @ $18)		$\left.\begin{array}{l}1,700 \times \$16.6711 = \$28,341 \\ 4,800 \times \$18\ \ \ \ \ \ = \$86,400\end{array}\right\}$	$= \$114,741\ (\$17.6525/\text{unit})^b$
Dec. 10	Sale 2 (5,300 @ $25)	$5,300 \times \$17.6525 = \textbf{\$93,558}$	$1,200 \times \$17.6525$	$= \$\ 21,183$

[b] $\$114,741 \div 6,500 \text{ units} + \$17.6525/\text{unit}$

2.

Date	Account and Explanation	Debit	Credit	Assets	=	Liabilities	+	Stockholders' Equity
Oct. 15	Inventory	86,700		+86,700	=		+	
	Cash		86,700	−86,700				
	(Purchased inventory for cash)							
Nov. 3	Cash	147,500		+147,500	=		+	+147,500
	Sales Revenue		147,500					
	(Sold 5,900 units @ $25 per unit)							
3	Cost of Goods Sold	97,800		−97,800	=		+	−97,800
	Inventory		97,800					
	(Recorded cost of sale of 5,900 units)							
20	Inventory	86,400		+86,400	=		+	
	Cash		86,400	−86,400				
	(Purchased inventory for cash)							
Dec. 10	Cash	132,500		+132,500	=		+	+132,500
	Sales Revenue		132,500					
	(Sold 5,300 units @ $25 per unit)							
10	Cost of Goods Sold	93,700		−93,700	=		+	−93,700
	Inventory		93,700					
	(Recorded cost of sale of 5,300 units)							

DISCUSSION QUESTIONS

1. What are the differences between merchandisers and manufacturers?
2. Describe the types of inventories used by manufacturers and merchandisers.
3. Compare the flow of inventory costs between merchandisers and manufacturers.
4. What are components of cost of goods available for sale and cost of goods sold?
5. How is cost of goods sold determined?
6. How do the perpetual and periodic inventory accounting systems differ from each other?
7. Why are perpetual inventory systems more expensive to operate than periodic inventory systems? What conditions justify the additional cost of a perpetual inventory system?
8. Why are adjustments made to the invoice price of goods when determining the cost of inventory?
9. Identify the accounting items for which adjustments are made to the invoice price of goods when determining the net cost of purchases.
10. Describe the difference between F.O.B. shipping point and F.O.B. destination.
11. Why do sales transactions under a perpetual inventory system require two journal entries?
12. Why do the four inventory costing methods produce different amounts for the cost of ending inventory and cost of goods sold?
13. The costs of which units of inventory (oldest or newest) are allocated to ending inventory or cost of goods sold using the FIFO, LIFO, and average cost methods?
14. If inventory prices are rising, which inventory costing method should produce the smallest payment for taxes?
15. How would reported income differ if LIFO rather than FIFO were used when purchase prices are rising? When purchase prices are falling?
16. How would the balance sheet accounts be affected if LIFO rather than FIFO were used when purchase prices are rising? When purchase prices are falling?
17. Why are inventories written down to the lower of cost or market?
18. What is the effect on the current period income statement and the balance sheet when inventories are written down using the lower of cost or market method? What is the effect on future period income statements and balance sheets?
19. What do the gross profit and inventory turnover ratios tell company management about inventory?
20. What is the LIFO reserve, and when is it used?
21. How does an error in the determination of ending inventory affect the financial statements of two periods?
22. *(Appendix 6A)* What accounts are used to record inventory purchase transactions under the periodic inventory system? Why aren't these accounts used in a perpetual inventory system?
23. *(Appendix 6B)* "For each inventory costing method, perpetual and periodic systems yield the same amounts for ending inventory and cost of goods sold." Do you agree or disagree with this statement? Explain.

MULTIPLE-CHOICE EXERCISES

6-1 If beginning inventory is $40,000, purchases is $215,000, and ending inventory is $35,000, what is cost of goods sold as determined by the cost of goods sold model?

a. $140,000
b. $210,000
c. $220,000
d. $290,000

6-2 Which of the following transactions would *not* result in an entry to the inventory account in the buyer's accounting records under a perpetual inventory system?

a. The purchase of merchandise on credit.
b. The return of merchandise to the supplier.
c. The payment of a credit purchase of merchandise within the discount period.
d. The payment of freight by the seller for goods received from a supplier.

6-3 Briggs Company purchased $15,000 of inventory on credit with credit terms of 2/10, n/30. Briggs paid for the purchase within the discount period. How much did Briggs pay for the inventory?

a. $14,700   c. $15,000
b. $14,850   d. $15,300

6-4 Which of the following transactions would *not* result in an adjustment to the inventory account under a perpetual inventory system?

a. The sale of merchandise for cash.
b. The sale of merchandise on credit.
c. The receipt of payment from a customer within the discount period.
d. The return of merchandise by a customer.

6-5 U-Save Automotive Group purchased 10 vehicles during the current month. Two trucks were purchased for $20,000 each, two SUVs were purchased for $31,000 each, and six hybrid cars were purchased for $27,000 each. A review of the sales invoices revealed that five of the hybrid cars were sold and both trucks were sold. What is the cost of U-Save's ending inventory if it uses the specific identification method?

a. $89,000   c. $135,000
b. $129,000   d. $175,000

Use the following information for Multiple-Choice Exercises 6-6 through 6-8:

Morgan Inc. has the following units and costs for the month of April:

	Units Purchased at Cost	Units Sold at Retail
Beginning inventory, April 1	1,000 units at $20	
Purchase 1, April 9	1,200 units at $23	
Sale 1, April 12		2,100 units at $40
Purchase 2, April 22	800 units at $25	

6-6 Refer to the information for Morgan Inc. above. If Morgan uses a perpetual inventory system, what is the cost of ending inventory under FIFO at April 30?

a. $18,000   c. $45,300
b. $22,300   d. $49,600

6-7 Refer to the information for Morgan Inc. above. If Morgan uses a perpetual inventory system, what is the cost of goods sold under LIFO at April 30?

a. $22,000   c. $45,300
b. $22,300   d. $45,600

6-8 Refer to the information for Morgan Inc. above. If Morgan uses a perpetual inventory system, what is the cost of ending inventory under average cost at April 30 (*Note:* Use four decimal places for per-unit calculations and round to the nearest dollar)?

a. $20,280   c. $45,436
b. $22,164   d. $47,320

6-9 When purchase prices are rising, which of the following statements is true?

a. LIFO produces a higher cost of goods sold than FIFO.
b. LIFO produces a higher cost for ending inventory than FIFO.
c. FIFO produces a lower amount for net income than LIFO.
d. Average cost produces a higher net income than FIFO or LIFO.

6-10 Which method results in a more realistic amount for income because it matches the most current costs against revenue?

a. FIFO
b. Average cost

c. Specific identification
d. LIFO

6-11 Which of the following statements regarding the lower of cost or market (LCM) rule is true?

a. The LCM rule is an application of the historical cost principle.
b. When the replacement cost of inventory drops below the historical cost of inventory, an adjustment is made to decrease inventory to its market value and decrease income.
c. If a company uses the LCM rule, there is no need to use a cost flow assumption such as FIFO, LIFO, or average cost.
d. When the market value of inventory is above the historical cost of inventory, an adjustment is made to increase inventory to its market value and increase income.

6-12 Which of the following statements is true with regard to the gross profit ratio?

1. An increase in cost of goods sold would increase the gross profit rate (assuming sales remain constant).
2. An increase in the gross profit rate may indicate that a company is efficiently managing its inventory.
3. An increase in selling expenses would lower the gross profit rate.

a. 1
b. 2

c. 1 and 2
d. 2 and 3

6-13 An increasing inventory turnover ratio indicates that:

a. a company has reduced the time it takes to purchase and sell inventory.
b. a company is having trouble selling its inventory.
c. a company may be holding too much inventory.
d. a company has sold inventory at a higher profit.

6-14 Ignoring taxes, if a company understates its ending inventory by $10,000 in the current year:

a. assets for the current year will be overstated by $10,000.
b. net income for the subsequent year will be overstated by $10,000.
c. cost of goods sold for the current year will be understated by $10,000.
d. retained earnings for the current year will be unaffected.

6-15 *(Appendix 6A)* Which of the following statements is true for a company that uses a periodic inventory system?

a. The purchase of inventory requires a debit to Inventory.
b. The return of defective inventory requires a debit to Purchase Returns and Allowances.
c. The payment of a purchase within the discount period requires a credit to Purchase Discounts.
d. Any amounts paid for freight are debited to Inventory.

Use the following information for Multiple-Choice Exercises 6-16 through 6-18:
Morgan Inc. has the following units and costs for the month of April:

	Units Purchased at Cost	Units Sold at Retail
Beginning inventory, April 1	1,000 units at $20	
Purchase 1, April 9	1,200 units at $23	
Sale 1, April 12		2,100 units at $40
Purchase 2, April 22	800 units at $25	

6-16 *(Appendix 6B)* Refer to the information for Morgan Inc. on the previous page. If Morgan uses a periodic inventory system, what is the cost of goods sold under FIFO at April 30?

a. $18,000
b. $22,300

c. $45,300
d. $49,600

6-17 *(Appendix 6B)* Refer to the information for Morgan Inc. on the previous page. If Morgan uses a periodic inventory system, what is the cost of ending inventory under LIFO at April 30?

a. $18,000
b. $22,300

c. $45,300
d. $45,600

6-18 *(Appendix 6B)* Refer to the information for Morgan Inc. on the previous page. If Morgan uses a periodic inventory system, what is the cost of ending inventory under average cost at April 30 (*Note*: Use four decimal places for per-unit calculations and round all other numbers to the nearest dollar)?

a. $20,280
b. $22,164

c. $45,436
d. $47,320

CORNERSTONE EXERCISES

OBJECTIVE ❶
CORNERSTONE 6-1

Cornerstone Exercise 6-19 Applying the Cost of Goods Sold Model

Hempstead Company has the following data for 2011:

Item	Units	Cost
Inventory, 12/31/2010	980	$10,780
Purchases	4,480	49,280
Inventory, 12/31/2011	750	8,250

Required:
1. How many units were sold?
2. Using the cost of goods sold model, determine the cost of goods sold.

Use the following information for Cornerstone Exercises 6-20 and 6-21:
Mathis Company and Reece Company use the perpetual inventory system. The following transactions occurred during the month of April:

a. On April 1, Mathis purchased merchandise on account from Reece with credit terms of 2/10, n/30. The selling price of the merchandise was $3,100, and the cost of the merchandise sold was $2,225.
b. On April 1, Mathis paid freight charges of $250 cash to have the goods delivered to its warehouse.
c. On April 8, Mathis returned $800 of the merchandise. The cost of the merchandise returned was $500.
d. On April 10, Mathis paid Reece the balance due.

OBJECTIVE ❷
CORNERSTONE 6-2

Cornerstone Exercise 6-20 Recording Purchase Transactions

Refer to the information for Mathis and Reece Companies above.

Required:
1. Prepare the journal entry to record the April 1 purchase of merchandise and payment of freight by Mathis.
2. Prepare the journal entry to record the April 8 return of merchandise.
3. Prepare the journal entry to record the April 10 payment to Reece.

OBJECTIVE ❷
CORNERSTONE 6-3

Cornerstone Exercise 6-21 Recording Sales Transactions

Refer to the information for Reece Company above.

Required:
Prepare the journal entries to record these transactions on the books of Reece Company.

Use the following information for Cornerstone Exercises 6-22 through 6-25:
Filimonov Inc. has the following information related to purchases and sales of one of its inventory items:

Date	Description	Units Purchased at Cost	Units Sold at Retail
June 1	Beginning inventory	200 units @ $10 = $2,000	
9	Purchase 1	300 units @ $12 = $3,600	
14	Sale 1		400 units @ $25
22	Purchase 2	250 units @ $14 = $3,500	
29	Sale 2		225 units @ $25

Cornerstone Exercise 6-22 Inventory Costing: FIFO

OBJECTIVE **3**
CORNERSTONE 6-5

Refer to the information for Filimonov Inc. and assume that the company uses a perpetual inventory system.

Required:
Calculate the cost of goods sold and the cost of ending inventory using the FIFO inventory costing method.

Cornerstone Exercise 6-23 Inventory Costing: LIFO

OBJECTIVE **3**
CORNERSTONE 6-6

Refer to the information for Filimonov Inc. and assume that the company uses a perpetual inventory system.

Required:
Calculate the cost of goods sold and the cost of ending inventory using the LIFO inventory costing method.

Cornerstone Exercise 6-24 Inventory Costing: Average Cost

OBJECTIVE **3**
CORNERSTONE 6-7

Refer to the information for Filimonov Inc. and assume that the company uses a perpetual inventory system.

Required:
Calculate the cost of goods sold and the cost of ending inventory using the average cost method. (*Note*: Use four decimal places for per-unit calculations and round all other numbers to the nearest dollar.)

Cornerstone Exercise 6-25 Effects of Inventory Costing Methods

OBJECTIVE **4**
CORNERSTONE 6-5, 6-6, 6-7

Refer to your answers for Filimonov Inc. in **Cornerstone Exercises 6-22** through **6-24.**

Required:
1. In a period of rising prices, which inventory costing method produces the highest amount for ending inventory?
2. In a period of rising prices, which inventory costing method produces the highest net income?
3. In a period of rising prices, which inventory costing method produces the lowest payment for income taxes?
4. In a period of rising prices, which inventory method generally produces the most realistic amount for cost of goods sold? For inventory? Would your answer change if inventory prices were decreasing during the period?

Cornerstone Exercise 6-26 Lower of Cost or Market

OBJECTIVE **5**
CORNERSTONE 6-8

The accountant for Murphy Company prepared the following analysis of its inventory at year-end:

Item	Units	Cost per Unit	Market Value
RSK-89013	500	$36	$44
LKW-91247	329	49	41
QEC-57429	462	29	33

(Continued)

Required:
1. Compute the carrying value of the ending inventory using the lower of cost or market method applied on an item-by-item basis.
2. Prepare the journal entry required to value the inventory at lower of cost or market.

Cornerstone Exercise 6-27 Inventory Analysis

Singleton Inc. reported the following information for the current year:

Net sales	$650,000	Inventory, 1/1	$21,250
Cost of goods sold	495,000	Inventory, 12/31	24,850
Gross profit	$155,000		

Required:
Compute Singleton's (a) gross profit ratio, (b) inventory turnover ratio, and (c) average days to sell inventory (*Note*: Round all answers to two decimal places).

Cornerstone Exercise 6-28 Inventory Errors

McLelland Inc. reported net income of $150,000 for 2011 and $165,000 for 2012. Early in 2012, McLelland discovers that the December 31, 2011, ending inventory was overstated by $15,000. For simplicity, ignore taxes.

Required:
1. What is the correct net income for 2011? For 2012?
2. Assuming the error was not corrected, what is the effect on the balance sheet at December 31, 2011? At December 31, 2012?

Cornerstone Exercise 6-29 *(Appendix 6A)* Recording Purchase Transactions

Refer to the information for Mathis Company (p. 304) and assume that Mathis uses a periodic inventory system.

Required:
1. Prepare the journal entry to record the April 1 purchase of merchandise and payment of freight by Mathis.
2. Prepare the journal entry to record the April 8 return of merchandise.
3. Prepare the journal entry to record the April 10 payment to Reece.

Cornerstone Exercise 6-30 *(Appendix 6B)* Inventory Costing Methods: Periodic FIFO

Refer to the information for Filimonov Inc. (p. 305) and assume that the company uses a periodic inventory system.

Required:
Calculate the cost of goods sold and the cost of ending inventory using the FIFO inventory costing method.

Cornerstone Exercise 6-31 *(Appendix 6B)* Inventory Costing Methods: Periodic LIFO

Refer to the information for Filimonov Inc. (p. 305) and assume that the company uses a periodic inventory system.

Required:
Calculate the cost of goods sold and the cost of ending inventory using the LIFO inventory costing method.

Cornerstone Exercise 6-32 *(Appendix 6B)* Inventory Costing Methods: Periodic Average Cost

OBJECTIVE 9
CORNERSTONE 6-14

Refer to the information for Filimonov Inc. (p. 305) and assume that the company uses a periodic inventory system.

Required:
Calculate the cost of goods sold and the cost of ending inventory using the average cost method. (*Note*: Use four decimal places for per-unit calculations and round all other numbers to the nearest dollar.)

EXERCISES

Exercise 6-33 Applying the Cost of Goods Sold Model

OBJECTIVE 1

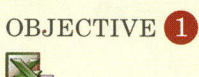

Wilson Company sells a single product. At the beginning of the year, Wilson had 150 units in stock at a cost of $8 each. During the year, Wilson purchased 825 more units at a cost of $8 each and sold 240 units at $13 each, 210 units at $15 each, and 335 units at $14 each.

Required:
1. Using the cost of goods sold model, what is the amount of ending inventory and cost of goods sold?
2. What is Wilson's gross margin for the year?

Exercise 6-34 Applying the Cost of Goods Sold Model

OBJECTIVE 1

ILLUSTRATING
RELATIONSHIPS

The following amounts were obtained from the accounting records of Steed Company:

	2009	2010	2011
Beginning inventory	$10,400	(b)	(d)
Net purchases	(a)	$52,100	$54,600
Ending inventory	9,800	(c)	12,350
Cost of goods sold	46,200	48,700	(e)

Required:
Compute the missing amounts.

Exercise 6-35 Perpetual and Periodic Inventory Systems

OBJECTIVE 2

Below is a list of inventory systems options.
a. Perpetual inventory system
b. Periodic inventory system
c. Both perpetual and periodic inventory systems

Required:
Match each option with one of the following:
1. Only revenue is recorded as sales are made during the period; the cost of goods sold is recorded at the end of the period.
2. Cost of goods sold is determined as each sale is made.
3. Inventory purchases are recorded in an inventory account.
4. Inventory purchases are recorded in a purchases account.
5. Cost of goods sold is determined only at the end of the period by subtracting the cost of ending inventory from the cost of goods available for sale.
6. Both revenue and cost of goods sold are recorded during the period as sales are made.
7. The inventory is verified by a physical count.

OBJECTIVE 2

Exercise 6-36 Recording Purchases

Compass Inc. purchased 1,250 bags of insulation from Glassco Inc. The bags of insulation cost $5.50 each. Compass paid Turner Trucking $320 to have the bags of insulation shipped to its warehouse. Compass returned 50 bags that were defective and paid for the remainder. Assume that Compass uses the perpetual inventory system and that Glassco did not offer a purchase discount.

Required:
1. Prepare a journal entry to record the purchase of the bags of insulation.
2. Prepare the entry to record the payment for shipping.
3. Prepare the entry for the return of the defective bags.
4. Prepare the entry to record the payment for the bags kept by Compass.
5. What is the total cost of this purchase?

OBJECTIVE 2

Exercise 6-37 Recording Purchases

Dawson Enterprises uses the perpetual system to record inventory transactions. In a recent month, Dawson engaged in the following transactions:
a. On April 1, Dawson purchased merchandise on credit for $25,150 with terms 2/10, n/30.
b. On April 2, Dawson purchased merchandise on credit for $28,200 with terms 3/15, n/25.
c. On April 9, Dawson paid for the purchase made on April 1.
d. On April 25, Dawson paid for the merchandise purchased on April 2.

Required:
Prepare journal entries for these four transactions.

OBJECTIVE 2

Exercise 6-38 Recording Purchases and Shipping Terms

On May 12, Digital Distributors received three shipments of merchandise. The first was shipped F.O.B. shipping point, had a total invoice price of $142,500, and was delivered by a trucking company that charged an additional $8,300 for transportation charges from Digital. The second was shipped F.O.B. shipping point and had a total invoice price of $87,250, including transportation charges of $5,700 that were prepaid by the seller. The third shipment was shipped F.O.B. destination and had an invoice price of $21,650, excluding transportation charges of $1,125 paid by the seller. Digital uses a perpetual inventory system. Digital has not paid any of the invoices.

Required:
Prepare journal entries to record these purchases.

OBJECTIVE 2

Exercise 6-39 Recording Sales and Shipping Terms

Stanley Company shipped the following merchandise during the last week of December 2011. All sales were on credit.

Sales Price	Shipping Terms	Date Goods Shipped	Date Goods Received
$5,460	F.O.B. shipping point	December 27	January 3
$3,800	F.O.B. destination	December 29	January 5
$4,250	F.O.B. destination	December 29	December 31

Required:
1. Compute the total amount of sales revenue recognized by Stanley in December 2011.

2. If Stanley included all of the above shipments as revenue, what would be the effect on the financial statements?

OBJECTIVE 2

Exercise 6-40 Recording Purchases and Sales

Printer Supply Company sells computer printers and printer supplies. One of its products is a toner cartridge for laser printers. At the beginning of 2011, there were 225 cartridges on hand that cost $62 each. During 2011, Printer Supply purchased 1,475 cartridges at $62 each. After inspection, Printer Supply determined that 15 cartridges were defective and returned them to the supplier. Printer Supply also sold 830 cartridges at $95 each and sold an additional 710 cartridges at $102 each after a midyear selling price increase. Customers returned 20 of the cartridges that were purchased at $102 to Printer Supply for miscellaneous reasons. Assume that Printer Supply uses a perpetual inventory system.

Required:
1. Prepare summary journal entries to record the purchases, sales, and return of inventory. Assume that all purchases and sales are on credit but no discounts were offered.
2. What is the cost of ending inventory, cost of goods sold, and gross profit for 2011?

Exercise 6-41 Inventory Costing Methods

OBJECTIVE ❸ ❹

Crandall Distributors uses a perpetual inventory system and has the following data available for inventory, purchases, and sales for a recent year:

Activity	Units	Purchase Price (per unit)	Sale Price (per unit)
Beginning inventory	110	$5.90	
Purchase 1, Jan. 18	575	6.00	
Sale 1	380		$8.80
Sale 2	225		9.00
Purchase 2, Mar. 10	680	6.20	
Sale 3	270		9.00
Sale 4	290		9.50
Purchase 3, Sept. 30	230	6.30	
Sale 5	240		9.90

Required:
1. Compute the cost of ending inventory and the cost of goods sold using the specific identification method. Assume the ending inventory is made up of 40 units from beginning inventory, 30 units from purchase 1, 80 units from purchase 2, and 40 units from purchase 3.
2. Compute the cost of ending inventory and cost of goods sold using the FIFO inventory costing method.
3. Compute the cost of ending inventory and cost of goods sold using the LIFO inventory costing method.
4. Compute the cost of ending inventory and cost of goods sold using the average cost inventory costing method. (*Note:* Use four decimal places for per-unit calculations and round all other numbers to the nearest dollar.)
5. **Conceptual Connection:** Compare the ending inventory and cost of goods sold computed under all four methods. What can you conclude about the effects of the inventory costing methods on the balance sheet and the income statement?

Exercise 6-42 Inventory Costing Methods

OBJECTIVE ❸ ❹ ❻

On June 1, Welding Products Company had a beginning inventory of 210 cases of welding rods that had been purchased for $88 per case. Welding Products purchased 1,150 cases at a cost of $95 per case on June 3. On June 19, the company purchased another 950 cases at a cost of $112 per case. Sales data for the welding rods are as follows:

Date	Cases Sold
June 9	990
June 29	975

Welding Products uses a perpetual inventory system, and the sales price of the welding rods was $130 per case.

(Continued)

Required:

1. Compute the cost of ending inventory and cost of goods sold using the FIFO method.
2. Compute the cost of ending inventory and cost of goods sold using the LIFO method.
3. Compute the cost of ending inventory and cost of goods sold using the average cost method. (*Note:* Use four decimal places for per-unit calculations and round all other numbers to the nearest dollar.)
4. **Conceptual Connection:** Assume that operating expenses are $21,600 and Welding Products has a 30 percent tax rate. How much will the cash paid for income taxes differ among the three inventory methods?
5. **Conceptual Connection:** Compute Welding Products' gross profit ratio (rounded to two decimal places) and inventory turnover ratio (rounded to three decimal places) under each of the three inventory costing methods. How would the choice of inventory costing method affect these ratios?

 OBJECTIVE **4**

Exercise 6-43 Financial Statement Effects of FIFO and LIFO

The chart below lists financial statement items that may be affected by the use of either the FIFO or LIFO inventory costing methods.

	FIFO	LIFO
Ending inventory		
Cost of goods sold		
Gross margin		
Income before taxes		
Payments for income taxes		
Net income		

Required:

Assuming that prices are rising, complete the chart by indicating whether the specified item is (a) higher or (b) lower under FIFO and LIFO.

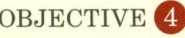 OBJECTIVE **4**

Exercise 6-44 Effects of Inventory Costing Methods

Jefferson Enterprises has the following income statement data available for 2011:

Sales revenue	$737,200
Operating expenses	243,700
Interest expense	39,500
Income tax rate	34%

Jefferson uses a perpetual inventory accounting system and the average cost method. Jefferson is considering adopting the FIFO or LIFO method for costing inventory. Jefferson's accountant prepared the following data:

	If Average Cost Used	If FIFO Used	If LIFO Used
Ending inventory	$ 61,850	$ 80,200	$ 43,400
Cost of goods sold	403,150	384,800	421,600

Required:

1. Compute income before taxes, income taxes expense, and net income for each of the three inventory costing methods (rounded to the nearest dollar).
2. **Conceptual Connection:** Why are the cost of goods sold and ending inventory amounts different for each of the three methods? What do these amounts tell us about the purchase price of inventory during the year?
3. **Conceptual Connection:** Which method produces the most realistic amount for net income? For inventory? Explain your answer.

Exercise 6-45 Inventory Costing Methods

OBJECTIVE 3 4

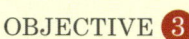

Neyman Inc. has the following data for purchases and sales of inventory:

Date	Units	Cost per Unit
Beginning inventory	22	$400
Purchase 1, Feb. 24	130	370
Sale 1	145	
Purchase 2, July 2	180	330
Purchase 3, Oct. 31	90	250
Sale 2	265	

All sales were made at a sales price of $450 per unit. Assume that Neyman uses a perpetual inventory system.

Required:

1. Compute the cost of goods sold and the cost of ending inventory using the FIFO, LIFO, and average cost methods. (*Note*: Use four decimal places for per-unit calculations and round all other numbers to the nearest dollar.)
2. **Conceptual Connection:** Why is the cost of goods sold lower with LIFO than with FIFO?

Exercise 6-46 Effects of FIFO and LIFO

OBJECTIVE 3 4

Sheepskin Company sells to colleges and universities a special paper that is used for diplomas. Sheepskin typically makes one purchase of the special paper each year on January 1. Assume that Sheepskin uses a perpetual inventory system. You have the following data for the three years ending in 2011:

2009

Beginning inventory	0 pages
Purchases	10,000 pages at $1.60 per page
Sales	8,500 pages

2010

Beginning inventory	1,500 pages
Purchases	16,200 pages at $2.00 per page
Sales	15,000 pages

2011

Beginning inventory	2,700 pages
Purchases	18,000 pages at $2.50 per page
Sales	20,100 pages

Required:

1. What would the ending inventory and cost of goods sold be for each year if FIFO is used?
2. What would the ending inventory and cost of goods sold be for each year if LIFO is used?
3. **Conceptual Connection:** For each year, explain the cause of the differences in cost of goods sold under FIFO and LIFO.

Exercise 6-47 Lower of Cost or Market

OBJECTIVE 5

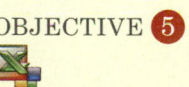

Meredith's Appliance Store has the following data for the items in its inventory at the end of the accounting period:

Item	Number of Units	Historical Cost per Unit	Market Value per Unit
Window air conditioner	18	$194	$110
Dishwasher	30	240	380
Refrigerator	27	415	405
Microwave	19	215	180
Washer (clothing)	32	195	248
Dryer (clothing)	21	197	245

(Continued)

Required:

1. Compute the carrying value of Meredith's ending inventory using the lower of cost or market rule applied on an item-by-item basis.
2. Prepare the journal entry required to value the inventory at lower of cost or market.
3. **Conceptual Connection:** What is the conceptual justification for valuing inventory at the lower of cost or market?

OBJECTIVE 5

Exercise 6-48   Lower of Cost or Market

Shaw Systems sells a limited line of specially made products, using television advertising campaigns in large cities. At year-end, Shaw has the following data for its inventory:

Item	Number of Units	Historical Cost per Unit	Market Value per Unit
Phone	625	$ 24	$ 20
Stereo	180	177	190
Electric shaver	215	30	28
MP3 alarm clock	450	26	25
Handheld game system	570	40	42

Required:

1. Compute the carrying value of the ending inventory using the lower of cost or market rule applied on an item-by-item basis.
2. Prepare the journal entry required to value the inventory at lower of cost or market.
3. **Conceptual Connection:** What is the impact of applying the lower of cost or market rule on the financial statements of the current period? What is the impact on the financial statements of a subsequent period in which the inventory is sold?

OBJECTIVE 6

Exercise 6-49   Analyzing Inventory

The recent financial statements of McLelland Clothing Inc. include the following data:

Sales	$754,690
Cost of goods sold:	
Computed under FIFO	528,600
Computed under LIFO	555,000
Average inventory:	
Computed under FIFO	72,200
Computed under LIFO	45,800

Required:

1. Calculate McLelland's gross profit ratio (rounded to two decimal places), inventory turnover ratio (rounded to three decimal places), and the average days to sell inventory (assume a 365-day year and round to two decimal places) using the FIFO inventory costing method. Be sure to explain what each ratio means.
2. Calculate McLelland's gross profit ratio (rounded to two decimal places), inventory turnover ratio (rounded to three decimal places), and the average days to sell inventory (assume a 365-day year and round to two decimal places) using the LIFO inventory costing method. Be sure to explain what each ratio means.
3. **Conceptual Connection:** Which ratios—the ones computed using FIFO or LIFO inventory values—provide the better indicator of how successful McLelland was at managing and controlling its inventory?

Exercise 6-50 Effects of an Error in Ending Inventory

OBJECTIVE 7

Waymire Company prepared the partial income statements presented below for 2011 and 2010.

	2011		2010	
Sales revenue		$538,200		$483,700
Cost of goods sold:				
Beginning inventory	$ 39,300		$ 32,100	
Purchases	343,200		292,700	
Cost of goods available for sale	$382,500		$324,800	
Ending inventory	(46,800)	335,700	(39,300)	285,500
Gross margin		$202,500		$198,200
Operating expenses		(167,200)		(151,600)
Income before taxes		$ 35,300		$ 46,600

During 2012, Waymire's accountant discovered that ending inventory for 2010 had been overstated by $8,200.

Required:

1. Prepare corrected income statements for 2011 and 2010.
2. Prepare a schedule showing each financial statement item affected by the error and the amount of the error for that item. Indicate whether each error is an overstatement ($+$) or an understatement ($-$).

Exercise 6-51 (Appendix 6A) Recording Purchases

OBJECTIVE 8

Compass Inc. purchased 1,250 bags of insulation from Glassco Inc. The bags of insulation cost $5.50 each. Compass paid Turner Trucking $320 to have the bags of insulation shipped to its warehouse. Compass returned 50 bags that were defective and paid for the remainder. Assume that Compass uses the periodic inventory system.

Required:

1. Prepare a journal entry to record the purchase of the bags of insulation.
2. Prepare the entry to record the payment for shipping.
3. Prepare the entry for the return of the defective bags.
4. Prepare the entry to record the payment for the bags kept by Compass.
5. What is the total cost of this purchase?
6. **Conceptual Connection:** If you have previously worked **Exercise 6-36**, compare your answers. What are the differences? Be sure to explain why the differences occurred.

Exercise 6-52 (Appendices 6A and 6B) Recording Purchases and Sales

OBJECTIVE 8 9

Printer Supply Company sells computer printers and printer supplies. One of its products is a toner cartridge for laser printers. At the beginning of 2011, there were 225 cartridges on hand at a cost of $62 each. During 2011, Printer Supply purchased 1,475 cartridges at $62 each, sold 830 cartridges at $95 each, and sold an additional 710 cartridges at $102 each after a midyear selling price increase. Printer Supply returned 15 defective cartridges to the supplier. In addition, customers returned 20 cartridges that were purchased at $102 to Printer Supply for various reasons. Assume that Printer Supply uses a periodic inventory system.

Required:

1. Prepare journal entries to record the purchases, sales, and return of inventory. Assume that all purchases and sales are on credit but no discounts were offered.
2. What is the cost of inventory, cost of goods sold, and gross profit for 2011?
3. **Conceptual Connection:** If you have previously worked **Exercise 6-40**, compare your answers. What are the differences? Be sure to explain why the differences occurred.

OBJECTIVE 9

Exercise 6-53 (Appendix 6B) Inventory Costing Methods: Periodic Inventory System

Jackson Company had 400 units in beginning inventory at a cost of $24 each. Jackson's 2011 purchases were as follows:

Date	Purchases
Feb. 21	6,100 units at $28 each
July 15	5,700 units at $32 each
Sept. 30	7,800 units at $34 each

Jackson uses a periodic inventory system and sold 19,300 units at $45 each during 2011.

Required:
1. Calculate the cost of ending inventory and the cost of goods sold using the FIFO, LIFO and average cost methods (*Note*: Use four decimal places for per-unit calculations and round all other numbers to the nearest dollar).
2. Prepare income statements through gross margin using each of the costing methods in part (1).
3. **Conceptual Connection:** What is the effect of each inventory costing method on income?

OBJECTIVE 9

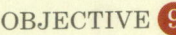

Exercise 6-54 (Appendix 6B) Inventory Costing Methods: Periodic Inventory System

The inventory accounting records for Lee Enterprises contained the following data:

Beginning inventory	1,400 units at $12 each
Purchase 1, Feb. 26	2,400 units at $16 each
Sale 1, March 9	2,300 units at $27 each
Purchase 2, June 14	2,200 units at $20 each
Sale 2, Sept. 22	1,900 units at $29 each

Required:
1. Calculate the cost of ending inventory and the cost of goods sold using the FIFO, LIFO, and average cost methods (*Note*: Use four decimal places for per-unit calculations and round all other numbers to the nearest dollar).
2. **Conceptual Connection:** Compare the ending inventory and cost of goods sold computed under all three methods. What can you conclude about the effects of the inventory costing methods on the balance sheet and the income statement?

OBJECTIVE 9

Exercise 6-55 (Appendix 6B) Inventory Costing Methods: Periodic System

Harrington Company had the following data for inventory during a recent year:

	Units	Cost per Unit	Total Cost
Beginning inventory	500	$ 9.00	$ 4,500
Purchase 1, Jan. 28	1,600	9.40	$15,040
Purchase 2, May 2	1,200	10.20	12,240
Purchase 3, Aug. 13	1,400	10.80	15,120
Purchase 4, Nov. 9	1,100	11.30	12,430
Total purchases	5,300		54,830
Goods available for sale	5,800		$59,330
Less: Sales	(5,240)		
Ending inventory	560		

Assume that Harrington uses a periodic inventory accounting system.

Required:
1. Using the FIFO, LIFO, and average cost methods, compute the ending inventory and cost of goods sold. (*Note*: Use four decimal places for per-unit calculations and round all other numbers to the nearest dollar.)

2. **Conceptual Connection:** Which method will produce the most realistic amount for income? For inventory?
3. **Conceptual Connection:** Which method will produce the lowest amount paid for taxes?

PROBLEM SET A

Problem 6-56A Applying the Cost of Goods Sold Model

OBJECTIVE ❾

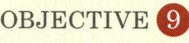

The following amounts were obtained from the accounting records of Rabren Supply Company:

	2010		2011	
Net sales		$359,620		$423,150
Cost of goods sold:				
Beginning inventory	$36,800		(d)	
Purchases	(a)		301,600	
Goods available for sale	(b)		(e)	
Ending inventory	42,780		(f)	
Cost of goods sold		(c)		289,700
Gross margin		$116,450		(g)

Required:

Compute the missing amounts.

Problem 6-57A Recording Sale and Purchase Transactions

OBJECTIVE ❷

Alpharack Company sells a line of tennis equipment to retailers. Alpharack uses the perpetual inventory system and engaged in the following transactions during April 2011, its first month of operations:

a. On April 2, Alpharack purchased, on credit, 360 Wilbur T-100 tennis rackets with credit terms of 2/10, n/30. The rackets were purchased at a cost of $30 each. Alpharack paid Barker Trucking $195 to transport the tennis rackets from the manufacturer to Alpharack's warehouse, shipping terms were F.O.B. shipping point, and the items were shipped on April 2.
b. On April 3, Alpharack purchased, for cash, 115 packs of tennis balls for $10 per pack.
c. On April 4, Alpharack purchased tennis clothing, on credit, from Designer Tennis Wear. The cost of the clothing was $8,250. Credit terms were 2/10, n/25.
d. On April 10, Alpharack paid for the purchase of the tennis rackets in transaction (a).
e. On April 15, Alpharack determined that $325 of the tennis clothing was defective. Alpharack returned the defective merchandise to Designer Tennis Wear.
f. On April 20, Alpharack sold 118 tennis rackets at $90 each, 92 packs of tennis balls at $12 per pack, and $5,380 of tennis clothing.   All sales were for cash. The cost of the merchandise sold was $7,580.
g. On April 23, customers returned $860 of the merchandise purchased on April 20. The cost of the merchandise returned was $450.
h. On April 25, Alpharack sold another 55 tennis rackets, on credit, for $90 each and 15 packs of tennis balls at $12 per pack, for cash. The cost of the merchandise sold was $1,800.
i. On April 29, Alpharack paid Designer Tennis Wear for the clothing purchased on April 4 less the return on April 15.
j. On April 30, Alpharack purchased 20 tennis bags, on credit, from Bag Designs for $320. The bags were shipped F.O.B. destination and arrived at Alpharack on May 3.

Required:

1. Prepare the journal entries to record the sale and purchase transactions for Alpharack during April 2011.
2. Assuming operating expenses of $8,500 and income taxes of $1,180, prepare Alpharack's income statement for April 2011.

OBJECTIVE   **Problem 6-58A   Inventory Costing Methods**

Anderson's Department Store has the following data for inventory, purchases, and sales of merchandise for December:

Activity	Units	Purchase Price (per unit)	Sale Price (per unit)
Beginning inventory	10	$6.00	
Purchase 1, Dec. 2	22	6.80	
Purchase 2, Dec. 5	26	7.50	
Sale 1, Dec. 7	19		$12.00
Sale 2, Dec. 10	25		12.00
Purchase 3, Dec. 12	12	8.00	
Sale 3, Dec. 14	20		12.00

Anderson's uses a perpetual inventory system. All purchases and sales were for cash.

Required:
1. Compute cost of goods sold and the cost of ending inventory using FIFO.
2. Compute cost of goods sold and the cost of ending inventory using LIFO.
3. Compute cost of goods sold and the cost of ending inventory using the average cost method. (*Note*: Use four decimal places for per-unit calculations.)
4. Prepare the journal entries to record these transactions assuming Anderson chooses to use the FIFO method.
5. **Conceptual Connection:** Which method would result in the lowest amount paid for taxes?

OBJECTIVE   **Problem 6-59A   Inventory Costing Methods**

Gavin Products uses a perpetual inventory system. For 2010 and 2011, Gavin has the following data:

Activity	Units	Purchase Price (per unit)	Sale Price (per unit)
2010			
Beginning inventory	200	$ 9	
Purchase 1, Feb. 15	300	11	
Sale 1, Mar. 10	320		$25
Purchase 2, Sept. 15	500	12	
Sale 2, Nov. 3	550		25
Purchase 3, Dec. 20	150	13	
2011			
Sale 3, Apr. 4	200		25
Purchase 4, June 25	200	14	
Sale 4, Dec. 18	150		25

Required:
1. For each year, compute cost of goods sold, the cost of ending inventory, and gross margin using FIFO.
2. For each year, compute cost of goods sold, the cost of ending inventory, and gross margin using LIFO.
3. For each year, compute cost of goods sold, the cost of ending inventory, and gross margin using the average cost method. (*Note*: Use four decimal places for per-unit calculations and round all other numbers to the nearest dollar.)
4. **Conceptual Connection:** Which method would result in the lowest amount paid for taxes?

5. **Conceptual Connection:** Which method produces the most realistic amount for income? For inventory? Explain your answer.
6. **Conceptual Connection:** Compute Gavin's gross profit ratio and inventory turnover ratio under each of the three inventory costing methods. (*Note:* Round answers to two decimal places.) How would the choice of inventory costing method affect these ratios?

Problem 6-60A Lower of Cost or Market

OBJECTIVE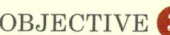

Sue Stone, the president of Tippecanoe Home Products has prepared the following information for the company's television inventory at the end of 2011:

Model	Quantity	Cost per Unit	Market Value per Unit
T-260	15	$250	$445
S-256	28	325	300
R-193	20	210	230
Z-376	15	285	250

Required:

1. Determine the carrying amount of the inventory using lower of cost or market applied on an item-by-item basis.
2. Prepare the journal entry required to value the inventory at lower of cost or market.
3. **Conceptual Connection:** What is the impact of applying the lower of cost or market rule on the financial statements of the current period? What is the impact on the financial statements of a subsequent period in which the inventory is sold?

Problem 6-61A Inventory Costing and LCM

OBJECTIVE 3 5

Ortman Enterprises sells a chemical used in various manufacturing processes. On January 1, 2011, Ortman had 5,000,000 gallons on hand, for which it had paid $0.50 per gallon. During 2011, Ortman made the following purchases:

Date	Gallons	Cost per Gallon	Total Cost
Feb. 20	10,000,000	$0.52	$ 5,200,000
May 15	25,000,000	0.56	14,000,000
Sept. 12	32,000,000	0.60	19,200,000

During 2011, Ortman sold 65,000,000 gallons at $0.75 per gallon (35,000,000 gallons were sold on June 29 and 30,000,000 gallons were sold on Nov. 22), leaving an ending inventory of 7,000,000 gallons. Assume that Ortman uses a perpetual inventory system. Ortman uses the lower of cost or market for its inventories, as required by generally accepted accounting principles.

Required:

1. Assume that the market value of the chemical is $0.76 per gallon on December 31, 2011. Compute the cost of ending inventory using the FIFO, LIFO, and average cost methods and then apply LCM. (*Note:* Use four decimal places for per-unit calculations and round all other numbers to the nearest dollar.)
2. Assume that the market value of the chemical is $0.58 per gallon on December 31, 2011. Compute the cost of ending inventory using the FIFO, LIFO, and average cost methods and then apply LCM. (*Note:* Use four decimal places for per-unit calculations and round all other numbers to the nearest dollar.)

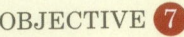 OBJECTIVE

Problem 6-62A Effects of an Inventory Error

The income statements for Graul Corporation for the three years ending in 2011 appear below.

	2011	2010	2009
Sales revenue	$4,643,200	$4,287,500	$3,647,900
Cost of goods sold	(2,475,100)	(2,181,600)	(2,006,100)
Gross margin	$2,168,100	$2,105,900	$1,641,800
Operating expense	(1,548,600)	(1,428,400)	(1,152,800)
Income from operations	$ 619,500	$ 677,500	$ 489,000
Other expenses	(137,300)	(123,600)	(112,900)
Income before taxes	$ 482,200	$ 553,900	$ 376,100
Income tax expense (34%)	(163,948)	(188,326)	(127,874)
Net income	$ 318,252	$ 365,574	$ 248,226

During 2011, Graul discovered that the 2009 ending inventory had been misstated due to the following two transactions being recorded incorrectly.
a. A purchase return of inventory costing $42,000 was recorded twice.
b. A credit purchase of inventory made on December 20 for $28,500 was not recorded. The goods were shipped F.O.B. shipping point and were shipped on December 22, 2009.

Required:
1. Was ending inventory for 2009 overstated or understated? By how much?
2. Prepare correct income statements for all three years.
3. **Conceptual Connection:** Did the error in 2009 affect cumulative net income for the three-year period? Explain your response.
4. **Conceptual Connection:** Why was the 2011 net income unaffected?

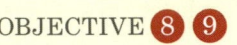 OBJECTIVE

Problem 6-63A *(Appendices 6A and 6B)* Inventory Costing Methods

Spiegel Department Store has the following data for inventory, purchases, and sales of merchandise for December:

Activity	Units	Purchase Price (per unit)	Sale Price (per unit)
Beginning inventory	10	$6.00	
Purchase 1, Dec. 2	22	6.80	
Purchase 2, Dec. 5	26	7.50	
Sale 1, Dec. 7	19		$12.00
Sale 2, Dec. 10	25		12.00
Purchase 3, Dec. 12	12	8.00	
Sale 3, Dec. 14	20		12.00

Spiegel uses a periodic inventory system. All purchases and sales are for cash.

Required:
1. Compute cost of goods sold and the cost of ending inventory using FIFO.
2. Compute cost of goods sold and the cost of ending inventory using LIFO.
3. Compute cost of goods sold and the cost of ending inventory using the average cost method. (*Note:* Use four decimal places for per-unit calculations.)
4. Prepare the journal entries to record these transactions assuming Spiegel chooses to use the FIFO method.
5. **Conceptual Connection:** Which method would result in the lowest amount paid for taxes?
6. **Conceptual Connection:** If you worked **Problem 6-58A**, compare your results. What are the differences? Be sure to explain why the differences occurred.

Problem 6-64A *(Appendix 6B)* Inventory Costing Methods

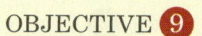

Jet Black Products uses a periodic inventory system. For 2010 and 2011, Jet Black has the following data:

Activity	Units	Purchase Price (per unit)	Sale Price (per unit)
2010			
Beginning inventory	200	$ 9.00	
Purchase 1, Feb. 15	300	11.00	
Sale 1, Mar. 10	320		$25.00
Purchase 2, Sept. 15	500	12.00	
Sale 2, Nov. 3	550		25.00
Purchase 3, Dec. 20	150	13.00	
2011			
Sale 3, Apr. 4	200		25.00
Purchase 4, June 25	200	14.00	
Sale 4, Dec. 18	150		25.00

All purchases and sales are for cash.

Required:

1. Compute cost of goods sold, the cost of ending inventory, and gross margin for each year using FIFO.
2. Compute cost of goods sold, the cost of ending inventory, and gross margin for each year using LIFO.
3. Compute cost of goods sold, the cost of ending inventory, and gross margin for each year using the average cost method. (*Note*: Use four decimal places for per unit calculations and round all other numbers to the nearest dollar).
4. **Conceptual Connection:** Which method would result in the lowest amount paid for taxes?
5. **Conceptual Connection:** Which method produces the most realistic amount for income? For inventory? Explain your answer.
6. What is the effect of purchases made later in the year on the gross margin when LIFO is employed? When FIFO is employed? Be sure to explain why any differences occur.
7. **Conceptual Connection:** If you worked **Problem 6-59A**, compare your answers. What are the differences? Be sure to explain why any differences occurred.

PROBLEM SET B

Problem 6-56B Applying the Cost of Goods Sold Model

ILLUSTRATING RELATIONSHIPS

The following amounts were obtained from the accounting records of Wachter Sports Products Inc.:

	2010	2011
Net sales	(a)	$154,810
Cost of goods sold:		
Beginning inventory	$ (b)	(d)
Purchases	104,250	(e)
Goods available for sale	(c)	$127,500
Ending inventory	6,940	(f)
Cost of goods sold	104,730	(g)
Gross margin	$ 28,600	$ 38,980

Required:

Compute the missing amounts.

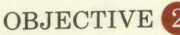

Problem 6-57B Recording Sale and Purchase Transactions

Jordan Footwear sells athletic shoes and uses the perpetual inventory system. During June, Jordan engaged in the following transactions its first month of operations:

a. On June 1, Jordan purchased, on credit, 100 pairs of basketball shoes and 210 pairs of running shoes with credit terms of 2/10, n/30. The basketball shoes were purchased at a cost of $85 per pair, and the running shoes were purchased at a cost of $60 per pair. Jordan paid Mole Trucking $310 cash to transport the shoes from the manufacturer to Jordan's warehouse, shipping terms were F.O.B. shipping point, and the items were shipped on June 1 and arrived on June 4.

b. On June 2, Jordan purchased 88 pairs of cross-training shoes for cash. The shoes cost Jordan $65 per pair.

c. On June 6, Jordan purchased 125 pairs of tennis shoes on credit. Credit terms were 2/10, n/25. The shoes were purchased at a cost of $45 per pair.

d. On June 10, Jordan paid for the purchase of the basketball shoes and the running shoes in transaction (a).

e. On June 12, Jordan determined that $585 of the tennis shoes were defective. Jordan returned the defective merchandise to the manufacturer.

f. On June 18, Jordan sold 50 pairs of basketball shoes at $116 per pair, 92 pairs of running shoes for $85 per pair, 21 pairs of cross-training shoes for $100 per pair, and 48 pairs of tennis shoes for $68 per pair. All sales were for cash. The cost of the merchandise sold was $13,295.

g. On June 21, customers returned 10 pairs of the basketball shoes purchased on June 18. The cost of the merchandise returned was $850.

h. On June 23, Jordan sold another 20 pairs of basketball shoes, on credit, for $116 per pair and 15 pairs of cross-training shoes for $100 cash per pair. The cost of the merchandise sold was $2,675.

i. On June 30, Jordan paid for the June 6 purchase of tennis shoes less the return on June 12.

j. On June 30, Jordan purchased 60 pairs of basketball shoes, on credit, for $85 each. The shoes were shipped F.O.B. destination and arrived at Jordan on July 3.

Required:

1. Prepare the journal entries to record the sale and purchase transactions for Jordan during June 2011.
2. Assuming operating expenses of $5,300 and income taxes of $365, prepare Jordan's income statement for June 2011.

 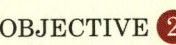

Problem 6-58B Inventory Costing Methods

Ein Company began operations in February 2011. Ein's accounting records provide the following data for the remainder of 2011 for one of the items the company sells:

Activity	Units	Purchase Price (per unit)	Sale Price (per unit)
Beginning inventory	9	$ 88	
Purchase 1, Feb. 15	6	102	
Purchase 2, Mar. 22	8	110	
Sale 1, Apr. 9	10		$180
Purchase 3, May 29	9	123	
Sale 2, July 10	15		180
Purchase 4, Sept. 10	8	135	
Sale 3, Oct. 15	12		180

Ein uses a perpetual inventory system. All purchases and sales were for cash.

Required:

1. Compute cost of goods sold and the cost of ending inventory using FIFO.
2. Compute cost of goods sold and the cost of ending inventory using LIFO.

3. Compute cost of goods sold and the cost of ending inventory using the average cost method. (*Note:* Use four decimal places for per-unit calculations and round all other numbers to the nearest penny.)
4. Prepare the journal entries to record these transactions assuming Ein chooses to use the FIFO method.
5. **Conceptual Connection:** Which method would result in the lowest amount paid for taxes?

Problem 6-59B Inventory Costing Methods

OBJECTIVE 3 4 6

Terpsichore Company uses a perpetual inventory system. For 2010 and 2011, Terpsichore has the following data:

Activity	Units	Purchase Price (per unit)	Sale Price (per unit)
2010			
Beginning inventory	100	$45	
Purchase 1, Feb. 25	700	52	
Sale 1, Apr. 15	600		$90
Purchase 2, Aug. 30	500	56	
Sale 2, Nov. 13	600		90
Purchase 3, Dec. 20	400	58	
2011			
Sale 3, Mar. 8	400		90
Purchase 4, June 28	900	62	
Sale 4, Dec. 18	800		90

Required:

1. For each year, compute cost of goods sold, the cost of ending inventory, and gross margin using FIFO.
2. For each year, compute cost of goods sold, the cost of ending inventory, and gross margin using LIFO.
3. For each year, compute cost of goods sold, the cost of ending inventory, and gross margin using the average cost method. (*Note:* Use four decimal places for per-unit calculations and round all other numbers to the nearest dollar.)
4. **Conceptual Connection:** Which method would result in the lowest amount paid for taxes?
5. **Conceptual Connection:** Which method produces the most realistic amount for income? For inventory? Explain your answer.
6. **Conceptual Connection:** Compute Terpsichore's gross profit ratio and inventory turnover ratio under each of the three inventory costing methods. (*Note:* Round answers to two decimal places.) How would the choice of inventory costing method affect these ratios?

Problem 6-60B Lower of Cost or Market

OBJECTIVE 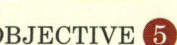 5

Kevin Spears, the accountant of Tyler Electronics Inc. has prepared the following information for the company's inventory at the end of 2011:

Model	Quantity	Cost per Unit	Market Value per Unit
RSQ535	30	$100	$120
JKY942	52	140	125
LLM112	84	85	80
KZG428	63	105	128

(Continued)

Required:
1. Determine the carrying amount of the inventory using lower of cost or market applied on an item-by-item basis.
2. Prepare the journal entry required to value the inventory at lower of cost or market.
3. **Conceptual Connection:** What is the impact of applying the lower of cost or market rule on the financial statements of the current period? What is the impact on the financial statements of a subsequent period in which the inventory is sold?

OBJECTIVE 5

Problem 6-61B Inventory Costing and LCM

J&J Enterprises sells paper cups to fast-food franchises. On January 1, 2011, J&J had 5,000 cups on hand, for which it had paid $0.10 per cup. During 2011, J&J made the following purchases and sales:

Date	Units	Cost per Unit	Total Cost
Feb. 20	100,000	$0.12	$12,000
May 15	57,000	0.14	7,980
Sept. 12	85,000	0.15	12,750

During 2011, J&J sold 240,000 cups at $0.35 per cup (80,000 cups were sold on April 2 and 160,000 cups were sold on October 20), leaving an ending inventory of 7,000 cups. Assume that J&J uses a perpetual inventory system. J&J uses the lower of cost or market for its inventories, as required by generally accepted accounting principles.

Required:
1. Assume that the market value of the cups is $0.38 per cup on December 31, 2011. Compute the cost of ending inventory using the FIFO, LIFO, and average cost methods and then apply LCM. (*Note:* Use four decimal places for per-unit calculations and round all other numbers to the nearest dollar.)
2. Assume that the market value of the cups is $0.12 per cup on December 31, 2011. Compute the cost of ending inventory using the FIFO, LIFO, and average cost methods and then apply LCM. (*Note:* Use four decimal places for per-unit calculations and round all other numbers to the nearest dollar.)

OBJECTIVE 7

Problem 6-62B Effects of an Inventory Error

The income statements for Picard Company for the three years ending in 2011 appear below.

	2011	2010	2009
Sales revenue	$1,168,500	$998,400	$975,300
Cost of goods sold	(785,800)	(675,450)	(659,800)
Gross margin	$ 382,700	$322,950	$315,500
Operating expense	(162,500)	(142,800)	(155,300)
Income from operations	$ 220,200	$180,150	$160,200
Other expenses	(73,500)	(58,150)	(54,500)
Income before taxes	$ 146,700	$122,000	$105,700
Income tax expense (34%)	(49,878)	(41,480)	(35,938)
Net income	$ 96,822	$ 80,520	$ 69,762

During 2011, Picard discovered that the 2009 ending inventory had been misstated due to the following two transactions being recorded incorrectly:
a. Inventory costing $37,000 that was returned to the manufacturer (a purchase return) was not recorded. The items were included in ending inventory.
b. A credit purchase of inventory made on August 30, 2009, for $12,800 was recorded twice. The goods were shipped F.O.B. shipping point and were shipped on September 5, 2009.

Required:
1. Was ending inventory for 2009 overstated or understated? By how much?
2. Prepare correct income statements for all three years.
3. **Conceptual Connection:** Did the error in 2009 affect cumulative net income for the three-year period? Explain your response.
4. **Conceptual Connection:** Why was the 2011 net income unaffected?

Problem 6-63B *(Appendices 6A and 6B)* Inventory Costing Methods

OBJECTIVE 8 9

Edwards Company began operations in February 2011. Edwards accounting records provide the following data for the remainder of 2011 for one of the items the company sells:

Activity	Units	Purchase Price (per unit)	Sale Price (per unit)
Beginning inventory	9	$ 88	
Purchase 1, Feb. 15	6	102	
Purchase 2, Mar. 22	8	110	
Sale 1, Apr. 9	10		$180
Purchase 3, May 29	9	123	
Sale 2, July 10	15		180
Purchase 4, Sept. 10	8	135	
Sale 3, Oct. 15	12		180

Edwards uses a periodic inventory system. All purchases and sales were for cash.

Required:

1. Compute cost of goods sold and the cost of ending inventory using FIFO.
2. Compute cost of goods sold and the cost of ending inventory using LIFO.
3. Compute cost of goods sold and the cost of ending inventory using the average cost method. (*Note:* Use four decimal places for per-unit calculations and round all other numbers to the nearest dollar.)
4. Prepare the journal entries to record these transactions assuming Edwards chooses to use the FIFO method.
5. **Conceptual Connection:** Which method would result in the lowest amount paid for taxes?
6. **Conceptual Connection:** If you worked Problem 6-58B, compare your results. What are the differences? Be sure to explain why the differences occurred.

Problem 6-64B *(Appendix 6B)* Inventory Costing Methods

OBJECTIVE 9

Grencia Company uses a periodic inventory system. For 2010 and 2011, Grencia has the following data (assume all purchases and sales are for cash):

Activity	Units	Purchase Price (per unit)	Sale Price (per unit)
2010			
Beginning inventory	100	$45	
Purchase 1, Feb. 25	700	52	
Sale 1, Apr. 15	600		$90
Purchase 2, Aug. 30	500	56	
Sale 2, Nov. 13	600		90
Purchase 3, Dec. 20	400	58	
2011			
Sale 3, Mar. 8	400		90
Purchase 4, June 28	900	62	
Sale 4, Dec. 18	800		90

Required:

1. Compute cost of goods sold, the cost of ending inventory, and gross margin for each year using FIFO.
2. Compute cost of goods sold, the cost of ending inventory, and gross margin for each year using LIFO.
3. Compute cost of goods sold, the cost of ending inventory, and gross margin for each year using the average cost method. (*Note:* Use four decimal places for per-unit calculations and round all other numbers to the nearest dollar.)
4. **Conceptual Connection:** Which method would result in the lowest amount paid for taxes?

(Continued)

5. **Conceptual Connection:** Which method produces the most realistic amount for income? For inventory? Explain your answer.
6. What is the effect of purchases made later in the year on the gross margin when LIFO is employed? When FIFO is employed? Be sure to explain why any differences occur.
7. **Conceptual Connection:** If you worked **Problem 6-59B**, compare your answers. What are the differences? Be sure to explain why any differences occurred.

CASES

Case 6-65 Inventory Valuation and Ethics

Mary Cravens is an accountant for City Appliance Corporation. One of Mary's responsibilities is developing the ending inventory amount for the calculation of cost of goods sold each month. At the end of September, Mary noticed that the ending inventory for a new brand of televisions was much larger than she had expected. In fact, there had been hardly any change since the end of the previous month when the shipments of televisions arrived. Mary knew that the firm's advertising had featured the new brand's products, so she had expected that a substantial portion of the televisions would have been sold.

Because of these concerns, Mary went to the warehouse to make sure the numbers were correct. While at the warehouse, Mary noticed that 30 of the televisions in question were on the loading dock for delivery to customers and another, larger group, perhaps 200 sets, were in an area set aside for sales returns. Mary asked Barry Tompkins, the returns supervisor, why so many of the televisions had been returned. Barry said that the manufacturer had used a cheap circuit board that failed on many of the sets after they had been in service for a week or two. Mary then asked how the defective televisions had been treated when the inventory was taken at the end of September. Barry said that the warehouse staff had been told to include in the ending inventory any item in the warehouse that was not marked for shipment to customers. Therefore, all returned merchandise was considered part of ending inventory.

Mary asked Barry what would be done with the defective sets. Barry said that they would probably have to be sold to a liquidator for a few cents on the dollar. Mary knew from her examination of the inventory data that all the returned sets had been included in the September inventory at their original cost.

Mary returned to the office and prepared a revised estimate of ending inventory using the information Barry Tompkins had given her to revalue the ending inventory of the television sets. She submitted the revision along with an explanatory note to her boss, Susan Grant. A few days later, Susan stopped by Mary's office to report on a conversation with the chief financial officer, Herb Cobb. Herb told her that the original ending inventory amount would not be revised. Herb said that the television sets in question had been purchased by his brother and adequate documentation existed to support the sale.

Required:
1. What would happen to cost of goods sold, gross margin, income from operations, and net income if the cost of the returned inventory had been reduced to its liquidation price as Mary had proposed?
2. What should Mary do now?

Case 6-66 Inventory Costing When Inventory Quantities are Small

A number of companies have adopted a just-in-time procedure for acquiring inventory. These companies have arrangements with their suppliers that require the supplier to deliver inventory just as the company needs the goods. As a result, just-in-time companies keep very little inventory on hand.

Required:
1. Should the inventory costing method (FIFO or LIFO) have a material effect on cost of goods sold when a company adopts the just-in-time procedure and reduces inventory significantly?
2. Once a company has switched to the just-in-time procedure and has little inventory, should the inventory costing method (LIFO or FIFO) affect cost of goods sold?

Case 6-67 Inventory Purchase Price Volatility

In 2011, Steel Technologies Inc. changed from the LIFO to the FIFO method for its inventory costing. Steel Technologies' annual report indicated that this change had been instituted because the price at which the firm purchased steel was highly volatile.

Required:

Explain how FIFO cost of goods sold and ending inventory would be different from LIFO when prices are volatile.

Case 6-68 The Effect of Reductions in Inventory Quantities

Hill Motor Company, one of the country's largest automobile manufacturers, disclosed the following information about its inventory in the notes to its financial statements:

Inventories are stated generally at cost, which is not in excess of market value. The cost of inventory is determined by the last-in, first-out (LIFO) method. If the first-in, first-out (FIFO) method of inventory valuation had been used, inventory would have been about $2,519 million higher at December 31, 2011, and $2,668 million higher at December 31, 2010. As a result of decreases in inventory, certain inventory quantities carried at lower LIFO costs prevailing in prior years, as compared with costs of current purchases, were liquidated in 2011 and 2010. These inventory adjustments improved pretax operating results by approximately $134 million in 2011 and $294 million in 2010.

Required:

1. Explain why the reduction in inventory quantities increased Hill Motor Company's net income.
2. If Hill Motor Company had used the FIFO inventory costing method, would the reduction in ending inventory quantities have increased net income?

Case 6-69 Errors in Ending Inventory

From time to time, business news will report that the management of a company has misstated its profits by knowingly establishing an incorrect amount for its ending inventory.

Required:

1. Explain how a misstatement of ending inventory can affect profit.
2. Why would a manager intent on misstating profits choose ending inventory to achieve the desired effect?

Case 6-70 Ethics and Inventory

An electronics store has a large number of computers in its inventory that use outdated technology. These computers are reported at their cost. Shortly after the December 31 year-end, the store manager insists that the computers can be sold for well over their cost. But the store's accountant has been told by the sales staff that it will be difficult to sell these computers for more than half of their inventory cost.

Required:

1. Why is the store manager reluctant to admit that these computers have little sales value?
2. What are the consequences for the business of failing to recognize the decline in value?
3. What are the consequences for the accountant of participating in a misrepresentation of the inventory's value?

Case 6-71 Research and Analysis Using the Annual Report

Obtain **Wal-Mart**'s 2010 annual report either through the "Investor Relations" portion of its website (do a web search for Wal-Mart investor relations) or go to http://www.sec.gov and click "Search for company filings" under "Filings and Forms (EDGAR)."

(Continued)

Required:

1. What amount did Wal-Mart report for inventories in its consolidated balance sheets at January 31, 2010? At January 31, 2009?
2. What inventory valuation method does Wal-Mart use to determine the cost of its inventories? (*Hint:* You may need to refer to the notes to the consolidated financial statements.)
3. What amount did Wal-Mart report for cost of goods sold for 2010, 2009, and 2008?
4. Compute the gross profit (rounded to one decimal place) and inventory turnover (rounded to two decimal places) ratios for 2010. What do these ratios tell you?
5. Does Wal-Mart use the lower of cost or market method to account for its inventory? Does it appear that Wal-Mart will write down its inventory to market value?
6. What would be the effect on the financial statements if Wal-Mart were to overstate its inventory by 1 percent?

Case 6-72 Comparative Analysis: Abercrombie & Fitch vs. Aeropostale

Refer to the financial statements of **Abercrombie & Fitch** and **Aeropostale** that are supplied with this text.

Required:

1. What amounts do Abercrombie & Fitch and Aeropostale report for inventories in their consolidated balance sheets at January 30, 2010, and January 31, 2009?
2. Do Abercrombie & Fitch and Aeropostale use the same method to value their inventories?
3. What amount does Abercrombie & Fitch report for cost of goods sold for the years ending January 30, 2010; January 31, 2009; and February 2, 2008? What amount does Aeropostale report for cost of goods sold for the years ending January 30, 2010; January 31, 2009; and February 2, 2008?
4. Compute the gross profit and inventory turnover ratios for fiscal year ending January 30, 2010, for each company. (*Note:* Round answers to two decimal places.) What do these ratios tell you about the success of each company in managing and controlling their inventory?
5. Do Abercrombie & Fitch and Aeropostale use the lower of cost market method to account for their inventories? By what amount have they written inventories down in the fiscal year ending January 30, 2010?

Case 6-73 CONTINUING PROBLEM: FRONT ROW ENTERTAINMENT

In addition to developing online fan communities, Cam and Anna believe that they could increase Front Row Entertainment's revenue by selling live-performance DVDs at the concert. Front Row records the following activity between May and August 2011 for one of its artists:

Date	Activity	Number of Units	Cost per Unit
May 10	Purchase inventory	240	$8.25
25	Sale	180	
June 5	Purchase inventory	300	8.75
12	Sale	150	
July 5	Sale	135	
Aug. 8	Purchase inventory	190	9.25
20	Sale	110	

Front Row sells all of its DVDs for $15 each and uses a perpetual inventory system.

Required:

1. Compute ending inventory and cost of goods sold using the FIFO, LIFO, and average cost methods. (*Note*: Use four decimal places for per-unit calculations and round all other numbers to the nearest penny.)
2. Discuss the advantages and disadvantages of each method.
3. Assume that Front Row decides to use FIFO. Prepare the journal entries necessary to record the above transactions. Assume all purchases and sales were for cash.

7

Operating Assets

Doug Norman Crystals/Alamy

After studying Chapter 7, you should be able to:

1. Define, classify, and describe the accounting for operating assets.

2. Explain how the historical cost principle applies to recording the cost of a fixed asset.

3. Understand the concept of depreciation.

4. Compute depreciation expense using various depreciation methods.

5. Distinguish between capital and revenue expenditures.

6. Understand and account for revisions in depreciation.

7. Describe the process of recording the disposal of a fixed asset.

8. Evaluate the use of fixed assets.

9. Understand the measurement and reporting of intangible assets.

10. Understand the measurement and reporting of natural resources.

11. (Appendix 7A) Describe the process of recording an impairment of a fixed asset.

Adrian Weinbrecht/Jupiter Images

EXPERIENCE FINANCIAL ACCOUNTING

with Verizon

With revenues exceeding $107 billion, **Verizon Communications, Inc.,** is one of the world's leading providers of telecommunications services. Verizon boasts 9.2 million broadband customers as well as 91.2 million subscribers to its wireless voice and data communication services. With users demanding enhanced data-carrying capabilities, higher transmission speeds, and increased multimedia capabilities, Verizon has chosen to use its network to differentiate itself from its competitors. As a result, Verizon has spent over $51 billion between 2007 and 2009 to expand and upgrade its technology infrastructure. This amount includes nearly $20 billion to maintain, upgrade, and expand its wireless network alone. The results of these investments have led Verizon to claim that it operates the most reliable wireless network in the country, which has resulted in impressive growth in the number of subscribers to its wireless services. For a company like Verizon, effective management of its long-term operating assets (e.g., its wireless network) is essential for the generation of revenue and profit.

Verizon's strategy for success rests on two key premises which relate to its network. First, the network must provide reliable access to every location that its customers need to access. For a simple call home or in crises, customers must be able to count on Verizon's network to function effectively. Second, Verizon is committed to investing in new technology in order to maintain a high level of customer satisfaction and remain competitive. Without continual investment, Verizon knows it will lose customers. Consistent with these goals, Verizon spent $17.0 billion in 2009 related to the build-up, expansion, and upgrade of its network. These expenditures represent an asset on Verizon's balance sheet that it hopes will provide a future benefit in terms of growth in market share and profitability. By closely analyzing a company's expenditures on productive assets, you will be able to better assess the company's long-term productivity, profitability, and ability to generate cash flow.

Verizon Wireless Subscribers
(In millions)

Year	Subscribers
2002	32.5
2003	37.5
2004	43.8
2005	51.3
2006	59.1
2007	65.7
2008	72.0
2009	91.2

OBJECTIVE ①
Define, classify, and describe the
accounting for operating assets.

UNDERSTANDING OPERATING ASSETS

In this chapter, we will examine the measurement and reporting issues related to **operating assets**, which are the long-lived assets that are used by the company in the normal course of operations. Unlike inventory, operating assets are not sold to customers. Instead, operating assets are used by a company in the normal course of operations to generate revenue. They are usually held by a company until they are no longer of service to the company. In other words, operating assets are held until their *service potential* has been exhausted. The typical operating asset is used for a period of 4 to 10 years, although some are held for only 2 or 3 years and others for as long as 30 or 40 years. Operating assets are divided into three categories:

- *Property, plant, and equipment (PP&E)*, often called *fixed assets* or *plant assets*, are tangible operating assets that can be seen and touched. They include, among other things, land, buildings, machines, and automobiles.
- *Intangible assets*, which generally result from legal and contractual rights, do not have physical substance. They include patents, copyrights, trademarks, licenses, and goodwill.
- *Natural resources* are naturally occurring materials that have economic value. They include timberlands and deposits such as coal, oil, and gravel.

IFRS

The determination of the cost of operating assets and the accounting for depreciation under IFRS are similar to U.S. GAAP.

Operating assets represent future economic benefits, or service potential, that will be used in the normal course of operations. At acquisition, an operating asset is recorded at its cost, including the cost of acquiring the asset and the cost of preparing the asset for use (historical cost principle). These costs are said to be *capitalized*, which means that they are reported as long-term assets with a service potential of greater than one year. As the service potential of an operating asset declines, the cost of the asset is allocated as an expense among the accounting periods in which the asset is used and benefits are received (the matching principle). This allocation is called *depreciation* for property, plant, and equipment assets, *amortization* for intangible assets, and *depletion* for natural resources.

Operating assets are often the most costly of the various types of assets acquired by an entity. For manufacturing companies, property, plant, and equipment frequently represents a major percentage of a manufacturing company's total assets. However, in other industries, such as computer software, operating assets may be a relatively insignificant portion of a company's assets. For many companies, depreciation, amortization, and depletion are also among the largest items of periodic expense. Exhibit 7-1 shows the percentages of operating assets in relation to total assets for various companies.

Exhibit 7-1

Percentages of Operating Assets in Relation to Total Assets

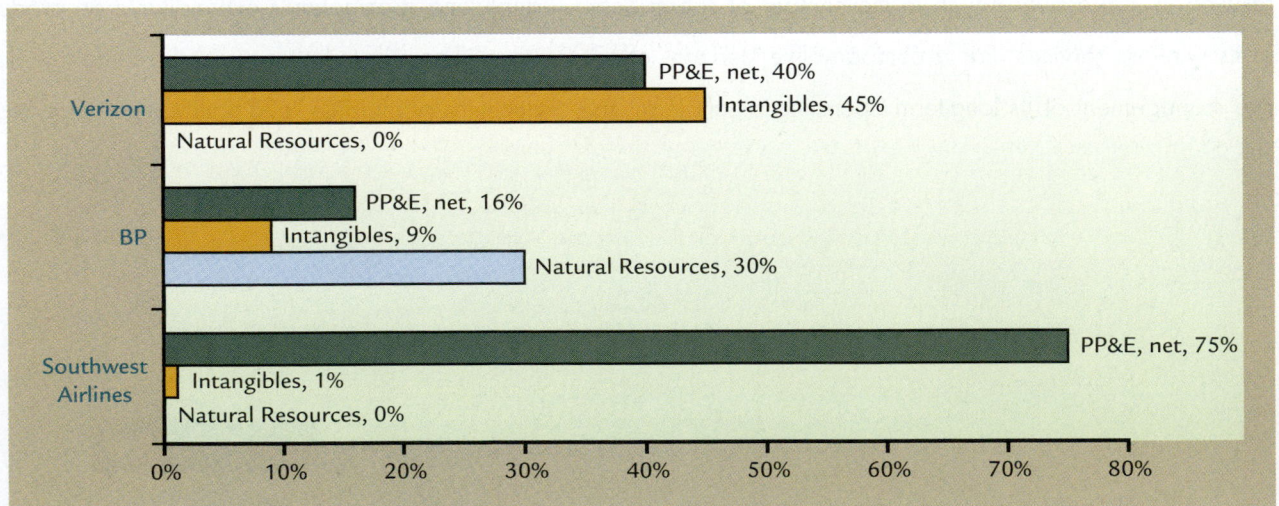

For **Verizon**, operating assets (property, plant, and equipment plus intangible assets) comprise approximately 85 percent of its total assets. Fixed assets include the expenditures required to build, upgrade, and expand its wireless network. However, Verizon has significant investments in intangible operating assets, primarily licenses that provide Verizon with the exclusive right to use certain radio frequencies to provide wireless services. In contrast, companies such as **BP** (one of the largest oil companies in the world) have relatively more natural resources (oil and natural gas properties), while **Southwest Airlines**' operating assets are made up primarily of its airplanes. Information about a company's operating assets gives financial statement users insights into a company's ability to satisfy customer demands (productive capacity) and the effectiveness of management in using the company's assets to generate revenue. While the relative mix of operating assets may vary among companies, it is clear that the management of operating assets is critical to a company's long-term success.

In this chapter, we will discuss the measurement and reporting issues related to the initial acquisition, use, and disposition of operating assets. We will address the following questions:

- What is included in the cost of an operating asset?
- How should an operating asset's cost be allocated to expense?
- How should expenditures after acquisition be treated?
- How is the retirement of an operating asset recorded?

ACQUISITION OF PROPERTY, PLANT, AND EQUIPMENT

OBJECTIVE **2**
Explain how the historical cost principle applies to recording the cost of a fixed asset.

Property, plant, and equipment are the tangible operating assets used in the normal operations of a company. These assets are tangible in the sense that they have a visible, physical presence in the company. Property, plant, and equipment includes:

- Land: The site of a manufacturing facility or office building used in operations[1]
- Land Improvements: Structural additions or improvements to land (such as driveways, parking lots, fences, landscaping, lighting)
- Buildings: Structures used in operations (factory, office, warehouse)
- Equipment: Assets used in operations (machinery, furniture, automobiles)

It is important to note that land has an unlimited life and service potential and is not subject to depreciation. However, land improvements, buildings, and equipment have limited lives and limited service potential. Therefore, the cost of these assets is recorded in separate accounts and depreciated over the periods in which they are used to generate revenue.

Measuring the Cost of a Fixed Asset

The cost of a fixed asset is any expenditure necessary to acquire the asset and to prepare the asset for use. For example, the cost of a machine would be its purchase price (less any discount offered) plus sales taxes, freight, installation costs, and the cost of labor and materials for trial runs that check its performance. Expenditures that are included as part of the cost of the asset are said to be *capitalized*. Exhibit 7-2 (p. 332) shows expenditures that are typically included as part of the cost of various types of property, plant, and equipment.

Expenditures that are *not* included as part of the cost of the asset are expensed immediately. Generally, recurring costs that benefit a period of time, not the asset's life, are expensed instead of capitalized. Careful judgment should be exercised in determining which costs should be capitalized and which costs should be expensed.

ETHICAL DECISION   The distinction between whether an expenditure should be capitalized or expensed can have dramatic consequences for a company's financial statements. **WorldCom**'s handling of this issue triggered one of the largest financial

---

[1] Land purchased for future use or as an investment is not considered part of property, plant, and equipment.

Exhibit 7-2

Typical Costs of Acquiring Property, Plant, and Equipment

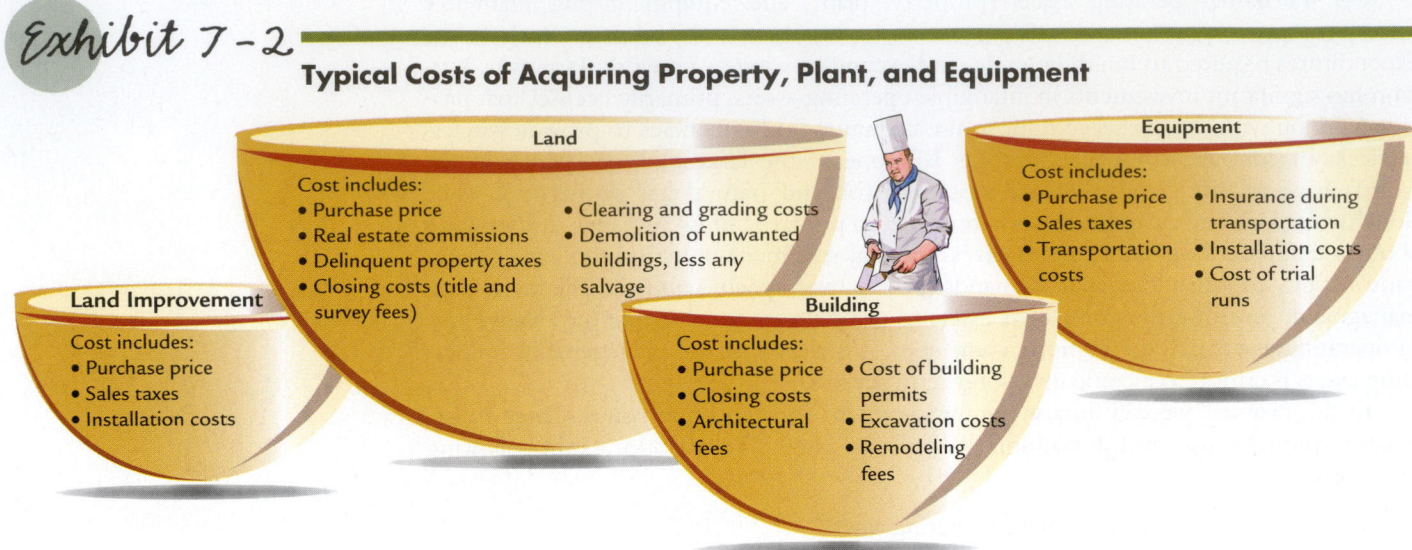

Land

Cost includes:
• Purchase price
• Real estate commissions
• Delinquent property taxes
• Closing costs (title and survey fees)
• Clearing and grading costs
• Demolition of unwanted buildings, less any salvage

Equipment

Cost includes:
• Purchase price
• Sales taxes
• Transportation costs
• Insurance during transportation
• Installation costs
• Cost of trial runs

Land Improvement

Cost includes:
• Purchase price
• Sales taxes
• Installation costs

Building

Cost includes:
• Purchase price
• Closing costs
• Architectural fees
• Cost of building permits
• Excavation costs
• Remodeling fees

restatements in U.S. history. When WorldCom used the telecommunications lines of another company, it paid a fee which should have been expensed in the current period. By improperly capitalizing $3.8 billion of these costs, WorldCom was able to increase its income and its operating cash flow, thereby concealing large losses. ●

Concept Q&A

If a company did not record all of the costs necessary to acquire an asset and prepare it for use, what would be the effect on the financial statements?

Answer:

If costs were not recorded as an asset, these costs would be immediately expensed, which would lower income in the current period. By recording these costs as assets, the company delays the recognition of expense until the service potential of the asset is used.

Recording the Cost of a Fixed Asset

The historical cost principle requires that a company record its fixed assets at the exchange price at the time the asset is purchased. When cash is paid in exchange for an asset, the amount of cash given, plus any other expenditure necessary to prepare the asset for use, becomes part of the historical cost of the acquired asset. In addition to cash purchases, companies often purchase fixed assets by issuing debt. In this situation, the asset is valued at the fair value of the liability on the date the asset is acquired. Interest paid on the debt is generally viewed as resulting from a financing decision rather than from the decision to acquire the asset. Therefore, interest on borrowed funds normally is not added to the purchase price of an asset.[2]

When noncash consideration, such as land or other noncash assets, is given in exchange for an asset, the purchase price of the acquired asset is the fair value of the asset given up or the fair value of the asset received, whichever is more clearly determinable. The fair value of an asset is the estimated amount of cash that would be required to acquire the asset. This cash equivalent cost can be inferred from information about similar assets in comparable transactions.

CORNERSTONE 7-1 illustrates the accounting procedures for the measurement and recording of the cost of a fixed asset. It shows that all costs necessary to acquire the machine and prepare it for use—freight ($2,900) and installation costs ($5,300 + $800 + $1,500)—are included in the machine's historical cost. Interest on the note payable, however, is excluded from the machine's cost and is added to interest expense as it accrues. Finally, note that the cost is capitalized (recorded as an asset), and there is no effect on the income statement.

---

[2] For assets that require a long period of preparation for use, such as ships, large plants, or buildings, GAAP does permit the addition of interest to the cost of the asset.

**CORNERSTONE
7 - 1**

**Measuring and Recording the Cost of
a Fixed Asset**

Concept:
The cost of a fixed asset is any expenditure necessary to acquire the asset and to prepare it for use.

Information:
On June 29, 2011, Drew Company acquired a new automatic milling machine from Dayton Inc. Drew paid $20,000 in cash and signed a one-year, 10 percent note for $80,000. Following the purchase, Drew incurred freight charges, on account, of $2,900 to ship the machine from Dayton's factory to Drew's plant. After the machine arrived, Drew paid J. B. Contractors $5,300 for installation. Drew also used $800 of supplies and $1,500 of labor on trial runs.

Required:
1. Determine the cost of the machine.
2. Prepare the journal entry necessary to record the purchase of the machine.

Solution:
1. $20,000 + $80,000 + $2,900 + $5,300 + $800 + $1,500 = $110,500
2.

Date	Account and Explanation	Debit	Credit
June 29, 2011	Equipment	110,500	
	Cash ($20,000 + $5,300)		25,300
	Notes Payable		80,000
	Accounts Payable (for freight charges)		2,900
	Supplies		800
	Wages Payable		1,500
	(Record purchase of equipment)		

Assets	= Liabilities +	Stockholders' Equity
+110,500	+80,000	
−25,300	+2,900	
−800	+1,500	

Had Drew given 1,600 shares of its own stock, which was selling for $50 per share, instead of the 10 percent note, the acquisition would have been recorded as follows:

Date	Account and Explanation	Debit	Credit
June 29, 2011	Equipment	110,500	
	Cash ($20,000 + $5,300)		25,300
	Common Stock		80,000
	Accounts Payable		2,900
	Supplies		800
	Wages Payable		1,500
	(Record purchase of equipment)		

Assets	= Liabilities +	Stockholders' Equity
+110,500	+2,900	+80,000
−25,300	+1,500	
−800		

Since the fair value of the stock [$50 × 1,600 = $80,000] equals the amount of the note, the cost of the asset is the same in both entries.

The Purchase Decision

You are the controller of Stanley Inc., a struggling manufacturing company that is experiencing cash flow problems. You are reviewing two proposals that would enable the company to obtain a piece of equipment that is critical to its operations. The first proposal would allow the company to purchase the equipment by signing a long-term note payable. The second proposal involves having the company rent the equipment.

(Continued)

What factors should you consider in making the decision of whether to purchase or rent the equipment?

Given the company's financial situation, renting (or leasing) the equipment may provide several advantages.

- Renting often requires little or no down payment, allowing a company with cash flow problems access to fixed assets that it would otherwise not be able to afford while freeing up cash for more immediate needs.
- Renting may allow the company to keep assets and, more importantly, liabilities off of the balance sheet, which increases the perceived borrowing ability of the company. For example, the purchase of the equipment would increase both fixed assets (property, plant, and equipment) and liabilities at the time of the purchase. In contrast, the rental of the equipment would require no entry at the time the agreement is signed. Therefore, the purchase of the asset on credit would cause an immediate increase in the company's debt to equity ratio.
- Renting the equipment may protect the renter against obsolescence since the rented asset can be exchanged for a newer model at the end of the rental agreement.
- Rental agreements may provide the renter with an increased tax benefit.

However, renting also has disadvantages, such as interest rates that may be higher than normal long-term borrowing rates. In short, the decision to purchase or rent is a strategic decision that must be carefully considered.

Managers are often confronted with the decision to purchase or rent fixed assets. In fact, renting assets through leasing arrangements has become one of the more frequently used strategies for acquiring fixed assets.[3]

OBJECTIVE **3**
Understand the concept of depreciation.

DEPRECIATION

We observed earlier that the cost of a fixed asset represents the cost of future benefits or service potential to a company. With the exception of land, this service potential declines over the life of each asset as the asset is used in the operations of the company. **Depreciation** is the process of allocating, in a systematic and rational manner, the cost of a tangible fixed asset (other than land) to expense over the asset's useful life. The matching principle provides the conceptual basis for measuring and recognizing depreciation and requires that the cost of a fixed asset be allocated as an expense among the accounting periods in which the asset is used and revenues are generated by its use.

The amount of depreciation expense is recorded each period by making the following adjusting journal entry:

| Depreciation Expense | xxx | |
| Accumulated Depreciation | | xxx |

The amount of depreciation recorded each period, or **depreciation expense**, is reported on the income statement. **Accumulated depreciation**, which represents the total amount of depreciation expense that has been recorded for an asset since the asset was acquired, is reported on the balance sheet as a contra-asset. That is, accumulated depreciation is deducted from the cost of the asset to get the asset's **book value** (or **carrying value**). Exhibit 7-3 shows the disclosures relating to property, plant, and equipment and depreciation made by **Verizon** in its 2009 annual report.

Before continuing, it is critical to understand the following points:

- Depreciation is a *cost allocation process*. It is *not* an attempt to measure the fair value of the asset or obtain some other measure of the asset's value. In fact, the book value (cost less accumulated depreciation) of an asset that is reported on a company's balance sheet is often quite different from the market value of the asset.
- Depreciation is *not* an attempt to accumulate cash for the replacement of an asset. Depreciation is a cost allocation process that does not involve cash.

Information Required for Measuring Depreciation

The following information is necessary in order to measure depreciation:

- cost of the fixed asset
- useful life (or expected life) of the fixed asset
- residual value (salvage value) of the fixed asset

---

[3] Lease arrangements and their effects are discussed more fully in Chapter 9.

Exhibit 7-3

Excerpt from Verizon's 2009 Annual Report

Notes to Consolidated Financial Statements	
NOTE 5 Plant, Property, and Equipment:	
Land	$ 925
Buildings and equipment	21,492
Network equipment	184,547
Furniture, office, and data processing equipment	9,083
Work in progress	3,331
Leasehold improvements	4,694
Vehicles and other	4,446
	$228,518
Less: Accumulated depreciation	137,052
Property, plant, and equipment, net	$ 91,466

Cost As discussed earlier in the chapter, the **cost** of a fixed asset is any expenditure necessary to acquire the asset and to prepare the asset for use. In addition to cost, we also need to examine two other items—useful life and estimates of residual value—to measure depreciation. Exhibit 7-4 shows the relationship among the factors used to compute depreciation expense.

Exhibit 7-4

Components of Depreciation Expense

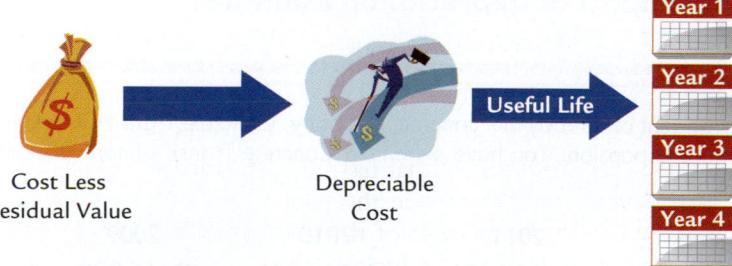

Useful Life The **useful life** of an asset is the period of time over which the company anticipates deriving benefit from the use of the asset.[4] The useful life of any fixed asset reflects both the physical capacities of the asset and the company's plans for its use. Many companies plan to dispose of assets before their entire service potential is exhausted. For example, major automobile rental companies typically use an automobile for only a part of its entire economic life before disposing of it. The useful life also is influenced by technological change. Many assets lose their service potential through obsolescence long before the assets are physically inoperable. As shown in Exhibit 7-5 (p. 336), **Verizon** uses an estimated useful life of 2 to 50 years for its fixed assets.

Residual Value The **residual value** (also called **salvage value**) is the amount of cash or trade-in consideration that the company expects to receive when an asset is retired from service. Accordingly, the residual value reflects the company's plans for the asset and its expectations about the value of the asset once its expected life with the company

---

[4] The useful life can be estimated in *service units* as well as in *units of time*. For example, an airline may choose to measure the useful life of its aircraft in hours of use rather than years.

Exhibit 7-5

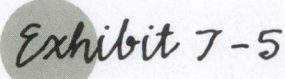

Excerpt from Verizon's 2009 Annual Report

Notes to Consolidated Financial Statements

NOTE 1 Description of Business and Summary of Significant Accounting Policies:

We record plant, property and equipment at cost . . . Plant, property and equipment . . . is generally depreciated on a straight-line basis. The asset lives used by our operations are presented in the following table

Average Useful Lives (in years)

Buildings	15–45
Central office and other network equipment	3–15
Outside communications plant	
Copper cable	15
Fiber cable (including undersea cable)	11–25
Poles, conduit and other	30–50
Furniture, vehicles and other	2–20

is over. A truck used for 2 years may have a substantial residual value, whereas the same truck used for 10 years may have minimal residual value. Residual value is based on projections of some of the same future events that are used to estimate an asset's useful life. Since depreciation expense depends on estimates of both useful life and residual value, depreciation expense itself is an estimate.

The cost of the asset less its residual value gives an asset's **depreciable cost**. The depreciable cost of the asset is the amount that will be depreciated (expensed) over the asset's useful life.

 **Impact of Depreciation Estimates**

You are a loan officer of the Prairie State Bank. The president of a ready-mix concrete company, Concrete Transit Company, has applied for a five-year, $150,000 loan to finance his company's expansion. You have examined Concrete Transit's financial statements for the past three years and found the following:

	2011	2010	2009
Depreciation expense (calculated using the straight-line method)	$ 15,000	$ 15,000	$ 15,000
Income before taxes	$ 15,000	$ 17,000	$ 21,000
Depreciable assets (cost)	$470,000	$470,000	$470,000

Based on other customers in the same business that use the same depreciation method as Concrete Transit, you expected depreciation expense to be approximately 15 percent of the cost of the depreciable assets.

Should you make the loan?

Since Concrete Transit has similar assets and is using a similar depreciation method to its competitors, the most obvious reason for reporting a lower percentage of depreciation expense is that Concrete Transit is using different estimates of residual value and/or useful life than its competitors. As you will see in the next section, if higher estimates of residual value or useful life are used, depreciation expense will be lower and income will be higher. If you adjust Concrete Transit's depreciation expense to 15 percent of the cost of its depreciable assets, depreciation expense will increase from $15,000 to $70,500 ($470,000 × 0.15) for each year. This would cause a decrease in income before taxes of $55,500 each year. These adjusted amounts suggest that Concrete Transit has been increasingly unprofitable. Given the difficulties it would likely have in making the required loan payments, the loan should not be made.

While most companies establish policies for depreciable assets that specify the estimation of useful lives and residual values, the measurement of depreciation expense (and income) ultimately relies on judgment.

DEPRECIATION METHODS

The service potential of a fixed asset is assumed to decline with each period of use, but the pattern of decline is not the same for all assets. Some assets decline at a constant rate each year while others decline sharply in the early years of use and then more gradually as time goes on. For other assets, the pattern of decline depends on how much the asset is used each period. *Depreciation methods* are the standardized calculations required to determine periodic depreciation expense. The most common depreciation methods are:

- straight-line
- declining balance
- units-of-production

For any of these depreciation methods, the total amount of depreciation expense that has been recorded (accumulated depreciation) over the life of the asset will never exceed the depreciable cost (cost less residual value) of the asset.

Exhibit 7-6 shows the methods most commonly used by 500 of the largest U.S. companies.

OBJECTIVE ④

Compute depreciation expense using various depreciation methods.

Concept Q&A

Why does the FASB allow companies to use different depreciation methods instead of requiring the use of a single depreciation method that would improve comparability?

Answer:
The depreciation method chosen by a company should capture the declining service potential of a fixed asset. Because assets are used differently, alternative methods are allowed so that the use of the asset can be better matched with the revenue it helped generate.

The Relative Use of Depreciation Methods

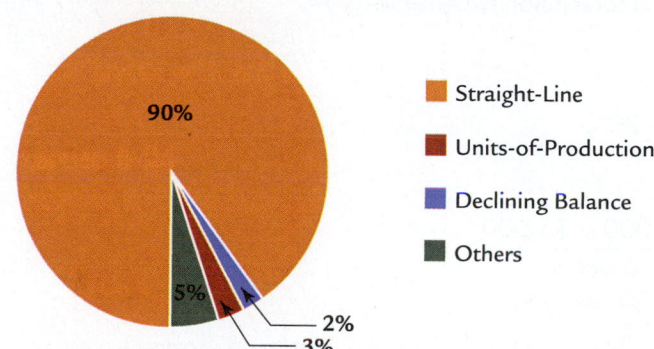

- Straight-Line
- Units-of-Production
- Declining Balance
- Others

90%

5%

2%

3%

Exhibit 7-6

Straight-Line Method

As its name implies, the **straight-line depreciation** method allocates an equal amount of an asset's cost to depreciation expense for each year of the asset's useful life. It is appropriate to apply this method to those assets for which an equal amount of service potential is considered to be used each period. The straight-line method is the most widely used method because it is simple to apply and is based on a pattern of service potential decline that is reasonable for many fixed assets.

The computation of straight-line depreciation expense is based on an asset's depreciable cost, which is the excess of the asset's cost over its residual value. Straight-line depreciation expense for each period is calculated by dividing the depreciable cost of an asset by the asset's useful life:

$$\text{Straight-Line Depreciation} = \frac{(\text{Cost} - \text{Residual Value})}{\text{Expected Useful Life}}$$

Alternatively, some companies will calculate an annual rate at which the asset should be depreciated. The fraction, (1 ÷ Useful Life), is called the *straight-line rate*. Using the straight-line rate, a company would compute depreciation expense by multiplying the straight-line rate by the asset's depreciable cost. **CORNERSTONE 7-2** illustrates the computation of depreciation expense using the straight-line method.

CORNERSTONE
7-2

Computing Depreciation Expense Using the Straight-Line Method

Concept:
As the service potential of a fixed asset declines, the cost of the asset is allocated as an expense among the accounting periods in which the asset is used and benefits are received (the matching principle).

Information:
On January 1, 2011, Morgan Inc. acquired a machine for $50,000. Morgan expects the machine to be worth $5,000 at the end of its five-year useful life. Morgan uses the straight-line method of depreciation.

Required:
1. Compute the straight-line rate of depreciation for the machine.
2. Compute the annual amount of depreciation expense.
3. Prepare a depreciation schedule that shows the amount of depreciation expense for each year of the machine's life.
4. Prepare the journal entry required to record depreciation expense in 2011.

Solution:

1.
$$\text{Straight-Line Rate} = \frac{1}{\text{Useful Life}} = \frac{1}{5 \text{ years}} = 20\%$$

2.
$$\text{Straight-Line Depreciation Expense} = \frac{\$50,000 - \$5,000}{5 \text{ years}}$$
$$= \$9,000 \text{ per year}$$

Note: Depreciation expense may also be found by multiplying the straight-line rate (20%) by the asset's depreciable cost ($45,000).

3.

End of Year	Depreciation Expense	Accumulated Depreciation	Book Value
			$50,000
2011	$ 9,000	$ 9,000	41,000
2012	9,000	18,000	32,000
2013	9,000	27,000	23,000
2014	9,000	36,000	14,000
2015	9,000	45,000	5,000
	$45,000		

4.

Date	Account and Explanation	Debit	Credit
Dec. 31, 2011	Depreciation Expense	9,000	
	Accumulated Depreciation		9,000
	(Record straight-line depreciation expense)		

Assets	=	Liabilities	+	Stockholders' Equity
−9,000				−9,000

Cornerstone 7-2 illustrates three important points:

- The straight-line depreciation method results in the recording of the same amount of depreciation expense ($9,000) each year, as shown in Exhibit 7-7.
- The contra-asset account, accumulated depreciation, increases at a constant rate of $9,000 per year until it equals the depreciable cost ($45,000).
- The book value of the machine (cost less accumulated depreciation) decreases by $9,000 per year until it equals the residual value ($5,000) at the end of the asset's useful life.

Exhibit 7-7

Straight-Line Pattern of Depreciation

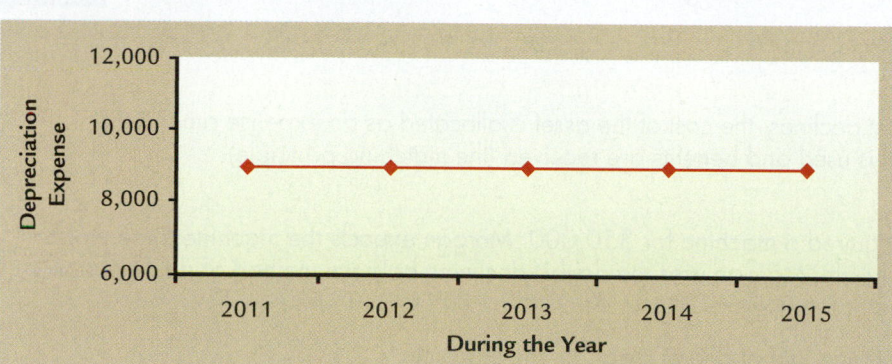

Declining Balance Method

The **declining balance depreciation method** is an accelerated depreciation method that produces a declining amount of depreciation expense each period by multiplying the declining book value of an asset by a constant depreciation rate. It is called an accelerated method because it results in a larger amount of depreciation expense in the early years of an asset's life relative to the straight-line method. However, because the total amount of depreciation expense (the depreciable cost) must be the same under any depreciation method, accelerated methods result in a smaller amount of depreciation expense in the later years of an asset's life. The declining balance method is appropriate for assets that are subject to a rapid decline in service potential due to factors such as rapid obsolescence.

The declining balance depreciation rate is some multiple (m) of the straight-line rate:

$$\text{Declining Balance Rate} = (m) \times \text{Straight-Line Rate}$$

The multiple (m) is often 2, in which case the declining balance method is called the *double-declining-balance method*.[5]

Depreciation expense for each period of an asset's useful life equals the declining balance rate times the asset's book value (cost less accumulated depreciation) at the beginning of the period as shown by the following equation:

$$\text{Declining Balance Depreciation Expense} = \text{Declining Balance Rate} \times \text{Book Value}$$

The calculation of declining balance depreciation expense differs from the calculation of straight-line depreciation expense in two important ways:

- The straight-line method multiplies a depreciation rate by the *depreciable cost* of the asset. However, the declining balance method multiplies a depreciation rate by the *book value* of the asset. Because the book value declines as depreciation expense is recorded, this produces a declining pattern of depreciation expense over time.
- The straight-line method records an equal amount of depreciation expense *each period* of the asset's life. However, it is likely that the computation of depreciation expense under the declining balance method would cause the asset's book value to fall below its residual value. Because an asset's book value cannot be depreciated

[5] In this text, a multiple of 2 is used for the declining balance method unless otherwise noted.

below its residual value, a lower amount of depreciation expense (relative to what is calculated under the declining balance method) must be recorded in the last year of the asset's life so that depreciation stops once the residual value is reached.

CORNERSTONE 7-3 illustrates the computation of depreciation expense using the declining balance method.

CORNERSTONE 7-3   **Computing Depreciation Expense Using the Declining Balance Method**

Concept:
As the service potential of a fixed asset declines, the cost of the asset is allocated as an expense among the accounting periods in which the asset is used and benefits are received (the matching principle).

Information:
On January 1, 2011, Morgan Inc. acquired a machine for $50,000. Morgan expects the machine to be worth $5,000 at the end of its five-year useful life. Morgan uses the double-declining-balance method of depreciation.

Required:
1. Compute the double-declining-balance rate of depreciation for the machine.
2. Prepare a depreciation schedule that shows the amount of depreciation expense for each year of the machine's life.
3. Prepare the journal entry required to record depreciation expense in 2011.

Solution:
1.

$$\frac{1}{\text{Useful Life}} \times 2 = \frac{1}{5} \times 2 = \frac{2}{5} \text{ or } 40\%$$

2.

End of Year	Depreciation Expense (Rate × Book Value)	Accumulated Depreciation	Book Value
			$50,000
2011	40% × $50,000 = $20,000	$20,000	30,000
2012	40% × $30,000 = 12,000	32,000	18,000
2013	40% × $18,000 = 7,200	39,200	10,800
2014	40% × $10,800 = 4,320	43,520	6,480
2015	1,480*	45,000	5,000
	$45,000		

*The computed amount of $2,592 (40% × $6,480) would cause book value to be lower than residual value. Therefore, depreciation expense of $1,480 is taken in 2015 so that the book value equals the residual value.

3.

Date	Account and Explanation	Debit	Credit
Dec. 31, 2011	Depreciation Expense	20,000	
	Accumulated Depreciation		20,000
	(Record declining balance depreciation expense)		

Assets	= Liabilities +	Stockholders' Equity
−20,000		−20,000

Relative to the straight-line method, the double-declining-balance method results in the recognition of higher depreciation expense in the early years of the asset's life and lower depreciation expense in the later years of the asset's life, as shown in Exhibit 7-8.

This pattern of expense is consistent with an asset whose service potential is used more rapidly (and its contribution to revenue is greater) in the early years of the asset's

Exhibit 7 – 8

Declining Balance Pattern of Depreciation

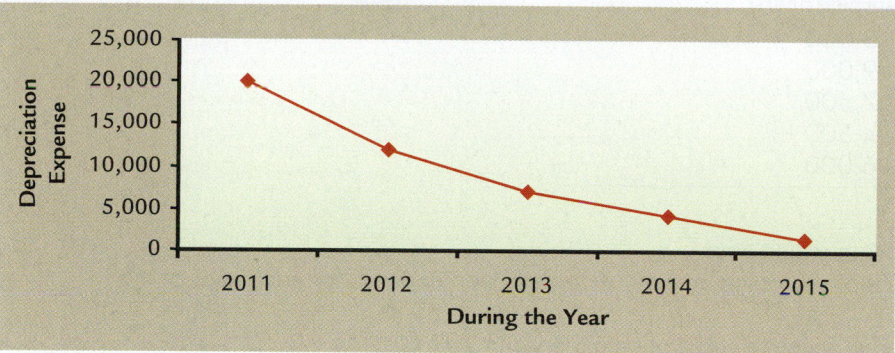

life. For this reason, the declining balance method is often used by companies in industries that experience rapid obsolescence.

Units-of-Production Method

The two previous depreciation methods resulted in a pattern of expense that was related to the passage of time. However, when the decline in an asset's service potential is proportional to the usage of the asset and asset usage can be measured, depreciation expense can be computed using the **units-of-production method**. Usage is typically gauged by a measure of productive capacity (such as units produced, hours worked, or miles driven). An automobile is an example of an asset whose service potential usually declines with use, where usage is measured by the number of miles traveled.

To compute depreciation expense under the units-of-production method, the depreciation cost per unit is determined as shown in the following equation:

$$\text{Depreciation Cost per Unit} = \frac{(\text{Cost} - \text{Residual Value})}{\text{Expected Usage of the Asset}}$$

Next, the depreciation cost per unit is multiplied by the actual usage of the asset:

$$\text{Units-of-Production Depreciation Expense} = \text{Depreciation Cost per Unit} \times \text{Actual Usage of the Asset}$$

An example of depreciation expense computed by the units-of-production method is shown in **CORNERSTONE 7-4**. Depending on the use of the asset during the year, the units-of-production depreciation method can result in a pattern of depreciation expense that may appear accelerated, straight-line, decelerated, or erratic.

CORNERSTONE 7-4   Computing Depreciation Expense Using the Units-of-Production Method

Concept:

As the service potential of a fixed asset declines (as measured by usage), the cost of the asset is allocated as an expense among the accounting periods in which the asset is used and benefits are received (the matching principle).

Information:

On January 1, 2011, Morgan Inc. acquired a machine for $50,000. Morgan expects the machine to be worth $5,000 at the end of its five-year useful life. Morgan expects the machine to run for 30,000 machine hours. Morgan uses the units-of-production method of depreciation. The actual machine hours follow:

(Continued)

CORNERSTONE
7 - 4
(continued)

Year	Actual Usage (in machine hours)
2011	3,000
2012	9,000
2013	7,500
2014	4,500
2015	6,000

Required:
1. Compute the depreciation cost per machine hour.
2. Prepare a depreciation schedule that shows the amount of depreciation expense for each year of the machine's life.
3. Prepare the journal entry required to record depreciation expense in 2011.

Solution:

1.

$$\frac{\text{Depreciable cost}}{\text{Estimated usage}} = \frac{(\$50,000 - \$5,000)}{30,000 \text{ machine hours}} = \$1.50$$

2.

End of Year	Cost per Machine Hour	× Actual Usage	= Depreciation Expense	Accumulated Depreciation	Book Value
					$50,000
2011	$1.50	3,000	$ 4,500	$ 4,500	45,500
2012	1.50	9,000	13,500	18,000	32,000
2013	1.50	7,500	11,250	29,250	20,750
2014	1.50	4,500	6,750	36,000	14,000
2015	1.50	6,000	9,000	45,000	5,000
			$45,000		

3.

Date	Account and Explanation	Debit	Credit
Dec. 31, 2011	Depreciation Expense	4,500	
	Accumulated Depreciation		4,500
	(Record units-of-production depreciation expense)		

Assets	= Liabilities +	Stockholders' Equity
−4,500		−4,500

Note that when production varies widely and irregularly from period to period, the units-of-production method will result in an erratic pattern of depreciation expense, as shown in Exhibit 7-9.

Exhibit 7-9

Units-of-Production Pattern of Depreciation

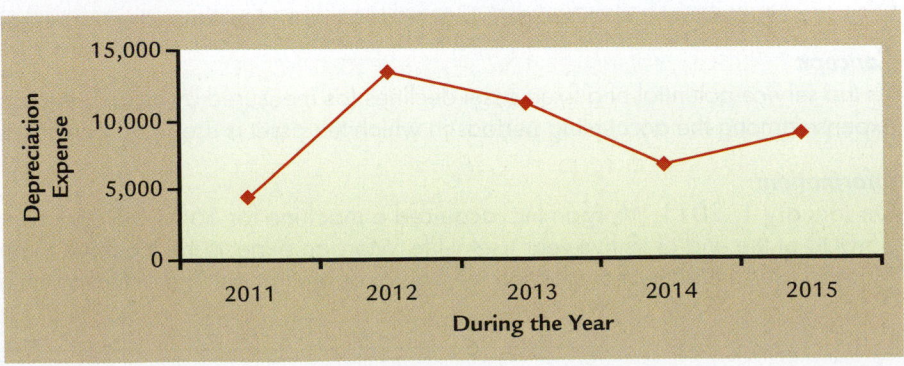

Relative to the prior year, Morgan reported an increase in depreciation expense in 2012 and 2015; depreciation expense decreased in all other years. Thus, the units-of-production method does not produce a predictable pattern of depreciation expense. While this method does an excellent job of matching depreciation expense to usage of the asset, it is difficult to apply because it requires estimation of expected usage (which is a more difficult task than simply estimating useful life in years) and is used less widely than the other two depreciation methods.

Choosing Between Depreciation Methods

The three depreciation methods can be summarized as follows:

- The straight-line depreciation method produces a constant amount of depreciation expense in each period of the asset's life and is consistent with a constant rate of decline in service potential.
- The declining balance depreciation method accelerates the assignment of an asset's cost to depreciation expense by allocating a larger amount of cost to the early years of an asset's life. This is consistent with a decreasing rate of decline in service potential and a decreasing amount for depreciation expense.
- The units-of-production depreciation method is based on a measure of the asset's use in each period, and the periodic depreciation expense rises and falls with the asset's use. In this sense, the units-of-production depreciation method is based not on a standardized pattern of declining service potential but on a pattern tailored to the individual asset and its use.

Exhibit 7-10 compares the depreciation expense recorded by Morgan Inc. under each of the depreciation methods discussed. Note that the total amount of depreciation expense ($45,000) recognized by Morgan Inc. was the same under all three methods. This resulted in the asset having a book value of $5,000 at the end of 2015. At this point, book value is equal to residual value. While the total depreciation expense for each method was the same, the yearly amounts of depreciation expense recognized were different.

IFRS

IFRS allow for companies to increase the value of their property, plant, and equipment up to fair value. This is not permitted under U.S. GAAP.

Exhibit 7-10

Depreciation Patterns over Time

Year	Straight-Line	Double-Declining-Balance	Units-of-Production
2011	$ 9,000	$20,000	$ 4,500
2012	9,000	12,000	13,500
2013	9,000	7,200	11,250
2014	9,000	4,320	6,750
2015	9,000	1,480	9,000
Total	$45,000	$45,000	$45,000

Because each method is acceptable under GAAP, what factors does management use in selecting a depreciation method? Ideally, management should select the method that best matches the pattern of decline in service potential of the asset. This would result in the best matching of depreciation expense to the period in which the asset helped to generate revenue. However, in reality, other factors also help motivate this decision. For example, the simplicity and ease of application of the straight-line method is very appealing to management. In addition, the use of the straight-line method produces a higher reported income in the early years of an asset's life. This higher income may increase management bonuses (which are often based on net income)

Concept Q&A

If all depreciation methods result in the same amount being recorded as an expense over the life of the fixed asset, why would a financial statement user be concerned with the depreciation method chosen?

Answer: The choice of depreciation method affects the amount recognized as an expense during each year of the fixed asset's life. Therefore, the company's reported income each year would be different based on the depreciation method chosen.

and create a favorable impression to outside users which could result in higher stock prices. For these reasons, the straight-line method is the most popular depreciation method. However, once a depreciation method is chosen, that method should be consistently applied over time to enhance the comparability of the financial information.

ETHICAL DECISION   The use of estimates in depreciation calculations presents an ethical issue for accountants. If an estimate is biased upward or downward, it can have significant financial statement impacts. For example, accountants may face pressures to increase the useful life of an asset beyond what is reasonable. This upwardly biased estimate of useful life decreases the amount of depreciation expense recorded and increases the company's net income. Accountants must resist these pressures and provide an unbiased estimate that faithfully portrays the service potential of the asset. ●

Depreciation for Partial Years

Fixed assets are purchased (or disposed of) at various times throughout the year. If the fixed asset is purchased (or disposed of) at the beginning or end of an accounting period, a full year of depreciation is recorded. If, however, the asset is purchased (or disposed of) during the accounting period, the matching principle requires that depreciation be recorded only for the portion of the year that the asset was used to generate revenue.

To illustrate, consider an asset purchased on April 1, 2011, for $100,000, which is being depreciated using the straight-line method over five years with no residual value. For a full year (12 months), depreciation expense would be $20,000, calculated as follows:[6]

$$\frac{\text{(Cost − Residual Value)}}{\text{Expected Useful Life}} = \frac{(\$100,000 − \$0)}{5 \text{ years}}$$

However, this asset was purchased in April, so it was only depreciated for the partial year (9 months) of 2011. Depreciation expense for the partial year would be $15,000, calculated as follows:

$$\$20,000 \times (9/12)$$

A full year of depreciation expense, $20,000, would be recorded for the next four years. Because a full year of depreciation was not taken in 2011, a partial year of depreciation (3 months) of $5,000 would need to be recorded in 2016 to fully depreciate the asset, calculated as follows:

$$\$20,000 \times (3/12)$$

At this point, the asset would be fully depreciated.[7]

Depreciation and Income Taxes

A company can choose between the three depreciation methods discussed earlier as it prepares its financial statements, but the depreciation method used in preparing its tax return does not need to be the same. The Internal Revenue Code specifies which depreciation method a company should use to prepare tax returns. Tax depreciation rules are designed to stimulate investment in operating assets and, therefore, are not guided by the matching concept. Tax depreciation rules provide for the rapid (accelerated) expensing of depreciable assets, which lowers taxes. By bringing forward the bulk of depreciation expense, tax depreciation rules enable companies to save cash by delaying the payment of taxes. Most companies use the Modified Accelerated Cost Recovery System (MACRS) to compute depreciation expense for their tax returns, which is similar to the declining balance method. MACRS is not acceptable for financial reporting purposes.

---

[6] Although acquisitions may occur *during* a month, for purposes of simplifying depreciation calculations, many companies follow the policy of substituting the date of the nearer first of the month for the actual transaction date. Thus, acquisitions on March 25 or April 9 would be treated as acquisitions on April 1 for purposes of calculating depreciation expense.

[7] For the sake of simplicity, most examples, exercises, and problems in this book assume that asset purchases (and disposals) occur at the beginning of the accounting period.

 **Impact of Depreciation Method on Income**

You are a financial analyst trying to assess the earnings performance and profitability of two companies, Cobine Inc. and Stabler Inc., which both began operations within the last year. Both companies report the same amount of income and are comparable in most every respect. However, one item catches your attention. While both companies report the same amount of property, plant, and equipment, Cobine reports a much smaller amount for depreciation expense. In the notes to the financial statements, Cobine indicates that it uses the straight-line depreciation method while Stabler uses the double-declining-balance depreciation method.

How does the difference in depreciation methods affect your assessment of the two companies?

When companies use different depreciation methods, significant variations may result in income although no real economic differences exist. As shown in Exhibit 7-10 (p. 343), all depreciation methods result in the same amount being expensed over the life of the asset; however, the amount expensed each year will differ.

Because its assets are relatively new, Cobine's use of the straight-line depreciation method will result in less expense and higher income compared to Stabler, which uses the double-declining-balance method. However, if the company's fixed assets were relatively older, the situation will be reversed—the use of the accelerated depreciation method will result in lower expense and higher income relative to the straight-line method. In both cases, the differences in expense and income are merely the result of an accounting choice and reflect no real underlying economic differences between the two firms.

Financial statement users must be able to "see through" the financial statement effects of accounting choices and base their decision on the underlying economics of the business.

EXPENDITURES AFTER ACQUISITION

O B J E C T I V E **5**
Distinguish between capital and revenue expenditures.

In addition to expenditures made when property, plant, and equipment is purchased, companies incur costs over the life of the asset that range from ordinary repairs and maintenance to major overhauls, additions, and improvements. Companies must decide whether these expenditures should be capitalized (added to an asset account) or expensed (reported in total on the income statement).

Revenue Expenditures

Expenditures that do not increase the future economic benefits of the asset are called **revenue expenditures** and are expensed in the same period the expenditure is made. Verizon's policy with regard to revenue expenditures, as disclosed in the notes to the financial statements, is shown below:

We charge the cost of maintenance and repairs, including the cost of replacing minor items not constituting substantial betterments, principally to Cost of Services and Sales as these costs are incurred.

These expenditures maintain the level of benefits provided by the asset, relate only to the current period, occur frequently, and typically involve relatively small dollar amounts. An example of a revenue expenditure is the ordinary repair and maintenance of an asset.

Capital Expenditures

Expenditures that extend the life of the asset, expand the productive capacity, increase efficiency, or improve the quality of the product, are called **capital expenditures**. Because these expenditures provide benefits to the company in both current and future periods, capital expenditures are added to an asset account and are subject to depreciation. These expenditures typically involve relatively large dollar amounts. Examples of capital expenditures include extraordinary or major repairs, additions, remodeling of buildings, and improvements (sometimes called betterments). For example, **Verizon** reported capital expenditures of approximately $17 billion related to the build-out, upgrade, and expansion of both its wired and wireless network capacity and the introduction of new technology.

Exhibit 7-11 (p. 346) summarizes different expenditures and how they would be accounted for.

Exhibit 7-11

Types of Expenditures

Type of Expenditure	Description	Examples	Accounting Treatment
Ordinary Repairs and Maintenance	Expenditures that keep an asset in normal operating condition	• Oil change for a truck • Painting of a building • Replacement of a minor part • Normal cleaning costs	*Expense* in the current period
Extraordinary or Major Repairs	Expenditures that extend the asset's useful life	• Overhaul or rebuilding of an engine • Fixing structural damage to a building	*Capitalize and depreciate* over the asset's useful life
Additions	Adding a new or major component to an existing asset	• Adding a new wing to a building • Installing a pollution-control device on a machine	*Capitalize and depreciate* over the shorter of the life of the asset or the addition
Improvements (or Betterments)	The replacement of a component of an asset with a better one that increases efficiency or productivity	• Replacing an old air conditioning unit with a more efficient one • Replacing a manual machine control with computer-controlled controls	*Capitalize and depreciate* over the improved asset's useful life

Because it is often difficult to distinguish capital and revenue expenditures, managers must exercise professional judgment in deciding to capitalize or expense these costs. Many companies develop simple policies to aid them in making this decision. For example, a company may decide to expense all costs under $1,000.

 OBJECTIVE **6**
Understand and account for revisions in depreciation.

REVISION OF DEPRECIATION

Depreciation expense is based on estimates of useful life and residual value. As new or additional information becomes available, a company will often find it necessary to revise its estimates of useful life, residual value, or both. The change of these estimates will result in a recalculation of depreciation expense. In addition, when a capital expenditure is made, it is also necessary for a company to recalculate its depreciation expense. In such situations, the company does not change previously recorded amounts related to depreciation. Instead, any revision of depreciation expense is accounted for in current and future periods.

To revise depreciation expense, the following steps are performed:

Step 1: Obtain the book value of the asset at the date of the revision of depreciation.

Step 2: Compute depreciation expense using the revised amounts for book value, useful life, and/or residual value.

CORNERSTONE 7-5 illustrates the accounting for a revision in depreciation.

 **CORNERSTONE 7-5**   **Revising Depreciation Expense**

Concept:
A revision in depreciation is accounted for in current and future periods.

Information:
On January 1, 2003, Parker Publishing Company bought a printing press for $300,000. Parker estimated that the printing press would have a residual value of $50,000 and a useful life of 10 years. Parker uses the

(Continued)

CORNERSTONE
7-5
(continued)

straight-line depreciation method and the book value of the asset on December 31, 2010, was $100,000. On January 1, 2011, Parker paid $90,000 to add a digital typesetting component to the printing press. After the addition, the printing press is expected to have a remaining useful life of six years and a residual value of $10,000.

Required:
1. What is the book value of the printing press on January 1, 2011?
2. What amount should Parker record for depreciation expense for 2011?

Solution:
1. Because the digital typesetting component is a capital expenditure, the cost of the addition is added to the book value of the asset, resulting in a revised book value of $190,000 ($90,000 + $100,000).
2. Using the revised book value, the revised estimate of residual value, and the revised estimate of useful life, Parker would recognize depreciation expense in 2011 of $30,000, calculated as:

$$\text{Depreciation Expense} = \frac{\$190,000 - \$10,000}{6 \text{ years}} = \$30,000 \text{ per year}$$

Note that only the current and future years are affected by this revision. Parker does not need to adjust the prior years' financial statements based on this new information. However, if the change in estimate is a material amount, it should be disclosed in the notes to the financial statements.

Impairments

Because depreciation is a cost allocation process and does not attempt to measure the fair value of the asset, the book value of an asset and the fair value of an asset may be quite different. When the fair value of the asset falls significantly below the book value of the asset, the asset may be impaired. An *impairment* is a permanent decline in the future benefit or service potential of an asset. The impairment may be due to numerous factors, including too little depreciation expense being recorded in previous years or obsolescence of the asset. Consistent with the principle of conservatism, if a fixed asset is impaired, a company should reduce the asset's book value to its fair value in the year the impairment occurs. The accounting for impairments is discussed more fully in Appendix 7A.

DISPOSAL OF FIXED ASSETS

OBJECTIVE **7**
Describe the process of recording the disposal of a fixed asset.

Although companies usually dispose of fixed assets voluntarily, disposition may also be forced.

- **Voluntary disposal** occurs when the company determines that the asset is no longer useful. The disposal may occur at the end of the asset's useful life or at some other time. For example, obsolescence due to unforeseen technological developments may lead to an earlier than expected disposition of the asset.
- **Involuntary disposal** occurs when assets are lost or destroyed through theft, acts of nature, or by accident.

In either case, disposals rarely occur on the first or last day of an accounting period. Therefore, the disposal of property, plant, and equipment usually requires two journal entries:

1. An entry to record depreciation expense up to the date of disposal.
2. An entry to:
    - Remove the asset's book value (the cost of the asset **and** the related accumulated depreciation).
    - Record a gain or loss on disposal of the asset, which is computed as the difference between the proceeds from the sale and the book value of the asset.

Gains and losses on the disposal of property, plant, and equipment are normally reported as "other revenues or gains" or "other expenses and losses," respectively, and appear immediately after income from operations on a multiple-step income statement.

Verizon's policy for recording disposals, as shown in the notes to its 2009 financial statements is shown below.

When the depreciable assets ... are retired or otherwise disposed of, the related cost and accumulated depreciation are deducted from the plant accounts, and any gains or losses on disposition are recognized in income.

CORNERSTONE 7-6 illustrates the accounting for the disposal of property, plant, and equipment.

CORNERSTONE 7-6
Recording the Disposition of Property, Plant, and Equipment

Concept:
When a company disposes of an asset, the book value at the date of disposition is removed and any related gain or loss is recognized.

Information:
Dickerson Corporation sold a machine on July 1, 2011, for $22,000. The machine had originally cost $100,000. Accumulated depreciation on January 1, 2011, was $80,000. Depreciation expense for the first six months of 2011 was $5,000.

Required:
1. Prepare the journal entry to record depreciation expense up to the date of disposal.
2. Compute the gain or loss on disposal of the machine.
3. Prepare the journal entry to record the disposal of the machine.

Solution:

1.

Date	Account and Explanation	Debit	Credit
July 1, 2011	Depreciation Expense	5,000	
	Accumulated Depreciation		5,000
	(Record depreciation expense)		

Assets	=	Liabilities	+	Stockholders' Equity
−5,000				−5,000

2.

Proceeds from sale		$22,000
Less: Book value of asset sold		
Cost	$100,000	
Accumulated depreciation ($80,000 + $5,000)	(85,000)	15,000
Gain on disposal		$ 7,000

3.

Date	Account and Explanation	Debit	Credit
July 1, 2011	Cash	22,000	
	Accumulated Depreciation	85,000	
	Equipment		100,000
	Gain on Disposal of Property, Plant, and Equipment		7,000
	(Record disposal of machine)		

Assets	=	Liabilities	+	Stockholders' Equity
+22,000				+7,000
+85,000				
−100,000				

Note that Dickerson recorded depreciation expense up to the date of disposal. Once this journal entry is made, the book value is updated to reflect the increased accumulated depreciation. This revised book value is then used to compute the Gain on Disposal of Property, Plant, and Equipment, which appears in the "other revenues and gains" section of the income statement.

If Dickerson had received $12,000 for the asset, the following computation would be made:

Proceeds from sale		$12,000
Less: Book value of asset sold		
Cost	$100,000	
Accumulated depreciation ($80,000 + $5,000)	(85,000)	15,000
Loss on disposal of property, plant, and equipment		$ (3,000)

Because the proceeds from the sale were less than the book value, Dickerson would record a loss as follows:

Date	Account and Explanation	Debit	Credit
July 1, 2011	Cash	12,000	
	Accumulated Depreciation	85,000	
	Loss on Disposal of Property, Plant, and Equipment	3,000	
	Equipment		100,000
	(Record disposal of machine)		

Assets	= Liabilities +	Stockholders' Equity
+12,000		−3,000
+85,000		
−100,000		

Dickerson would report the loss in the "other expenses and losses" section of the income statement.

YOU DECIDE — Future Asset Replacement

You are considering a major investment in one of two long-haul trucking companies. Both companies are about the same size, travel competitive routes, and have similar net incomes. However, the balance sheets reveal a significant difference in the accumulated depreciation for the trucks as shown below:

	Stanley Company	Long Company
Trucks	$ 600,000	$ 550,000
Less: Accumulated depreciation	(138,000)	(477,000)
Book value	$ 462,000	$ 73,000

What conclusions can you make regarding the future cash outflows each company will have to make for future asset replacements?

Assuming that the assets' estimates of useful life are consistent with their economic lives, the closer that accumulated depreciation is to historical cost, the older the assets and the more likely that they will have to be replaced. Long Company's assets are closer to being fully depreciated than those of Stanley Company. Therefore, Long is more likely to make cash outflows for the replacement of its assets. Although more information would be needed about Long in order to know the precise impact of the impending replacement, the comparison of the two accumulated depreciation amounts does provide you with valuable insights. While the recording of depreciation expense does not alter cash flow, accumulated depreciation signals the approaching future replacement of fixed assets, which usually requires cash.

A comparison of accumulated depreciation to historical cost can provide financial statement users with an approximation of the remaining life of the assets.

ANALYZING FIXED ASSETS

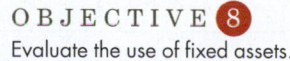

OBJECTIVE **8**

Evaluate the use of fixed assets.

Because fixed assets are a major productive asset of most companies, it is useful to understand if the company is using these assets efficiently. In other words, how well is the company using its fixed assets to generate revenue? One measure of how efficiently a company is using its fixed assets is the **fixed asset turnover ratio**. It is calculated as follows:

$$\text{Fixed Asset Turnover Ratio} = \frac{\text{Net Sales}}{\text{Average Fixed Assets}}$$

The more efficiently a company uses its fixed assets, the higher the ratio will be.

In addition to the fixed asset turnover ratio, investors are also concerned with the condition of a company's fixed assets. Because older assets tend to be less efficient than newer assets, the age of a company's fixed assets can provide useful insights into the company's efficiency. The age of a company's fixed assets also can provide an indication of a company's capital replacement policy and assist managers in estimating future capital expenditures. A rough estimate of the **average age of fixed assets** can be computed as follows:

$$\text{Average Age of Fixed Assets} = \frac{\text{Accumulated Depreciation}}{\text{Depreciation Expense}}$$

CORNERSTONE 7-7 illustrates the calculation of the fixed asset turnover ratio and the average age of fixed assets.

CORNERSTONE 7-7   Analyzing Fixed Asset Ratios

Concept:
The analysis of fixed assets can provide useful information as to how efficiently the assets have been used as well as the condition of the assets.

Information:
The following information was obtained from the financial statements of **Verizon** and **AT&T** (all amounts in millions):

Account	Verizon	AT&T
Property, plant, and equipment, net, 12/31/08	$ 86,546	$ 99,088
Property, plant, and equipment, net, 12/31/09	91,466	100,093
Accumulated depreciation, 12/31/09	137,052	119,491
Net sales	107,808	123,018
Depreciation expense	14,562	15,959

Required:
1. Compute the fixed asset turnover ratio for Verizon and AT&T.
2. Compute the average age of Verizon's and AT&T's fixed assets as of 12/31/2009.

Solution:
1.

$$\text{Fixed Asset Turnover Ratio} = \frac{\text{Net Sales}}{\text{Average Fixed Assets}}$$

Verizon	AT&T
$\dfrac{\$107,808}{\dfrac{(\$86,546 + \$91,466)}{2}} = 1.21$ times	$\dfrac{\$123,018}{\dfrac{(\$99,088 + \$100,093)}{2}} = 1.24$ times

(Continued)

2.

$$\text{Average Age of Fixed Assets} = \frac{\text{Accumulated Depreciation}}{\text{Depreciation Expense}}$$

Verizon	AT&T
$\dfrac{\$137,052}{\$14,562} = 9.41$ years	$\dfrac{\$119,491}{\$15,959} = 7.49$ years

CORNERSTONE 7-7 *(continued)*

In Cornerstone 7-7, the fixed asset ratio tells us that for each dollar invested in fixed assets, **Verizon** generated sales of $1.21 while **AT&T** generated sales of $1.24. In comparison with the industry average of 1.24, it appears that both AT&T and Verizon are efficiently using their fixed assets to generate sales. In addition, Verizon's assets are, on average, 9.41 years old, while AT&T's assets are approximately 7.49 years old. Because Verizon's primary fixed asset is network equipment, which is depreciated between 3 and 15 years (see Exhibit 7-3 and Exhibit 7-5), this signals that Verizon will most likely be making significant capital expenditures over the next several years to replace its network equipment.

In addition to comparing a company's fixed asset turnover ratio with that of prior years and its competitors, it is necessary to gain an understanding of a company's operations to appropriately assess how efficiently a company is using its fixed assets. For example, **Verizon**'s fixed asset turnover may be lower than some of its competitors because it is currently spending large amounts to expand its network in anticipation of future sales. These expansion activities (which are capitalized in the current period) could depress Verizon's fixed asset turnover ratio.

INTANGIBLE ASSETS

Intangible operating assets, like tangible assets, represent future economic benefit to the company, but unlike tangible assets, they lack physical substance. Patents, copyrights, trademarks, leaseholds, organization costs, franchises, and goodwill are all examples of intangible assets. The economic benefits associated with most intangible assets are in the form of legal rights and privileges conferred on the owner of the asset. The economic value of a patent, for example, is the legal right to restrict, control, or charge for the use of the idea or process covered by the patent.

Because intangible assets lack physical substance, it is often easy to overlook their importance to the overall value of a company. Recent research suggests that between 60 percent and 80 percent of a company's market value may be tied to intangible assets. For many companies, intangible assets may be the most important asset it has. A pharmaceutical company such as **GlaxoSmithKline** could easily argue that the true value of the company lies with its intellectual capital and patents, not its tangible property, plant, and equipment. However, due to unique issues with intangibles (such as the highly uncertain nature of future benefits and the possibility of wide fluctuations in value), the value of many intangible assets is not adequately captured by current accounting standards. For example, GlaxoSmithKline's intangible assets only make up approximately 27 percent of its total assets. As the value of intangible assets continues to be a key driver of company value, the measurement and evaluation of intangibles will certainly be a crucial issue.

OBJECTIVE 9
Understand the measurement and reporting of intangible assets.

 **Q&A**

If intangible assets represent a major amount of many companies' value, wouldn't any estimate of the intangible asset's value be better than not recording the asset at all?

Answer:
While intangible assets are certainly relevant to financial statement users, information must be reliably measured to be recorded in the financial statements. For many intangibles, the inability to measure the intangible asset reliably results in the inability to record the intangible asset. This trade-off between the relevance and reliability of information is often a matter of judgment.

Accounting for Intangible Assets

Intangible assets are recorded at cost, consistent with the historical cost principle. Similar to fixed assets, the cost of an intangible asset is any expenditure necessary to acquire the asset

Exhibit 7-12

Common Types of Intangible Assets

Intangible Asset	Description	Cost Includes	Amortization
Patent	Right to manufacture, sell, or use product. The legal life is 20 years from the date of grant.	Purchase price, registration fees, legal costs	Shorter of the economic life or legal life
Copyright	Right to publish, sell, or control a literary or artistic work. The legal life is life of author plus 70 years.	Purchase price, registration fees, legal costs	Shorter of the economic life or legal life
Trademark	Right to the exclusive use of a distinctive name, phrase, or symbol (for example, the iPod name or the Nike "swoosh"). The legal life is 10 years but it can be renewed indefinitely.	Purchase price, registration fees, legal costs	Not amortized since it has an indefinite life; reviewed at least annually for impairment
Franchise	Exclusive right to conduct a certain type of business in some particular geographic area. Life of the franchise depends on specific terms of the franchise contract.	Initial cost paid to acquire the franchise	Shorter of the economic life or legal life
Goodwill	Unidentifiable intangible asset that arises from factors such as customer satisfaction, quality products, skilled employees, and business location. Goodwill is only recognized in business combinations.	The excess of the purchase price over the fair value of the identifiable net assets acquired in a business combination	Not amortized since it has an indefinite life; reviewed at least annually for impairment

IFRS

Under IFRS, research costs are expensed while development costs are capitalized if it is probable that future benefits will be received.

and to prepare the asset for use. For intangible assets purchased from outside the company, the primary element of the cost is the purchase price. Costs such as registration, filing, and legal fees are considered necessary costs and are capitalized as part of the intangible asset.

For internally developed intangible assets, the cost of developing the asset is expensed as incurred and normally recorded as **research and development (R&D) expense**. While expenditures for R&D may lead to intangible assets such as patents and copyrights, R&D is not an intangible asset. While many disagree with this position, current accounting standards require that all R&D be recorded as an expense. Exhibit 7-12 provides a listing of some typical intangible assets.

Companies also incur significant costs such as legal fees, stock issue costs, accounting fees, and promotional fees when they are formed. It can be argued that these **organizational costs** are an intangible asset that provides a benefit to a company indefinitely. However, current accounting standards treat organizational costs as an expense in the period the cost is incurred.

Once an intangible asset is recorded, companies must determine if the asset has a finite life or an indefinite life. The cost of an intangible asset with a *finite life*, like the cost of a tangible asset, is allocated to accounting periods over the life of the asset to reflect the decline in service potential. This process is referred to as **amortization**. Most companies will amortize the cost of an intangible asset on a straight-line basis over the shorter of the economic or legal life of the asset. For example, a patent has a legal life of 20 years from the date it is granted. However, the economic advantage offered by a patent often expires before the end of its legal life as a result of other technological developments. Therefore, the shorter economic life should be used to amortize the cost of the patent.

If an intangible asset is determined to have an *indefinite life*, it is *not* amortized but is reviewed at least annually for impairment. **CORNERSTONE 7-8** illustrates the accounting for the acquisition and amortization of intangible assets.

CORNERSTONE 7-8   Accounting for Intangible Assets

Concept:

Intangible assets are recorded at the cost necessary to acquire the asset and to prepare the asset for use. The cost of the asset is allocated as an expense among the accounting periods in which the asset is used and benefits are received (the matching principle).

Information:

On January 1, 2011, King Company acquired a patent from Queen Inc. for $40,000. The patent was originally granted on January 1, 2005 and has 14 years of its legal life remaining. However, due to technological advancements, King estimates the patent will only provide benefits for 10 years. In addition, King purchased a trademark from Queen for $60,000.

Required:

1. Prepare any journal entries necessary to record the acquisition of the patent and the trademark.
2. Compute the amortization expense for the patent and the trademark.
3. Prepare any adjusting journal entries necessary to record the amortization expense for 2011.

Solution:

1.

Date	Account and Explanation	Debit	Credit
Jan. 1, 2011	Patent	40,000	
	Trademark	60,000	
	Cash		100,000
	(To purchase patent and trademark)		

	Assets	= Liabilities +	Stockholders' Equity
	+40,000		
	+60,000		
	−100,000		

2.

$$\frac{\text{Cost} - \text{Residual Value}}{\text{Useful Life}} = \frac{\$40,000 - \$0}{10 \text{ years}} = \$4,000$$

Note: Because the trademark has an indefinite life, no amortization is necessary.

3.

Date	Account and Explanation	Debit	Credit
Dec. 31, 2011	Amortization Expense	4,000	
	Patent		4,000
	(To record amortization of patent)		

	Assets	= Liabilities +	Stockholders' Equity
	−4,000		−4,000

In Cornerstone 7-8, several items are of note:

- Most intangible assets do not have a residual value. Therefore, the cost that is being amortized is usually the entire cost of the intangible asset.
- King amortized the patent over the shorter of its remaining legal life (14 years) or its economic life (10 years). This is consistent with recognizing amortization expense over the period that the intangible asset is expected to provide benefits.
- King recorded the amortization expense by directly crediting the intangible asset, Patent. After the amortization expense is recorded, the book value of the patent is $36,000 ($40,000 − $4,000).
- Amortization expense is reported as operating expense on the income statement.

YOU◆DECIDE   Measuring and Estimating the Dimensions of a Patent

You are the controller for Marietta Corporation, a research intensive company engaged in the design and sale of ceramic products. For the past year, half of Marietta's research staff has been engaged in designing a process for coating iron and steel with a ceramic material for use in high-temperature areas of automobile engines. The company has secured a patent for its process and is about to begin marketing equipment that uses the patented process. The assistant controller has argued that half of the year's cost of research activities should be assigned to the patent, including the salaries paid to researchers. Additionally, while Marietta expects the patented equipment to be a viable product for only five years, the assistant controller recommends that the patent should be amortized over its legal life of 20 years.

What is the impact of the assistant controller's recommendation, and how should you account for the patent?

If these costs were capitalized as part of the patent as the assistant controller recommended, current period assets and income would be overstated. In future periods, the higher recorded value of the intangible asset would result in an increase in amortization expense. While many analysts agree with the assistant controller that some research and development expenditures create an intangible asset, current accounting standards require that all research activities should be expensed when incurred.

If the patent were amortized over its legal life, the cost of the patent would be spread over 20 years, resulting in lower yearly amounts of amortization expense and higher income. However, accounting standards require that intangible assets be amortized over the shorter of their legal lives or their economic lives. Therefore, a relatively higher amortization expense should be recognized over the five year useful life of the patent.

Current accounting standards should be followed to avoid misstating the financial statements.

OBJECTIVE 10
Understand the measurement and reporting of natural resources.

NATURAL RESOURCES

Natural resources, such as coal deposits, oil reserves, and mineral deposits, make up an important part of the operating assets for many companies. For example, BP has oil and gas properties of over $70 billion, representing approximately 30 percent of its total assets. Like intangible assets, natural resources present difficult estimation and measurement problems. However, natural resources differ from other operating assets in two important ways:

- Unlike fixed assets, natural resources are physically consumed as they are used by a company.
- Natural resources can generally be replaced or restored only by an act of nature. (Timberlands are renewed by replanting and growth, but coal deposits and most mineral deposits are not subject to renewal.)

The accounting for natural resources is quite similar to the accounting for intangible assets and fixed assets. At acquisition, all the costs necessary to ready the natural resource for separation from the earth are capitalized. At the time a company acquires the property on which a natural resource is located (or the property rights to the natural resource itself), only a small portion of the costs necessary to ready the asset for removal are likely to have been incurred. Costs such as sinking a shaft to an underground coal deposit, drilling a well to an oil reserve, or removing the earth over a mineral deposit can be several times greater than the cost of acquiring the property.

As a natural resource is removed from the earth, the cost of the natural resource is allocated to each unit of natural resource removed. This process of allocating the cost of the natural resource to each period in which the resource is used is called **depletion**. Depletion is computed by using a procedure similar to that for the units-of-production method of depreciation. First, a depletion rate is computed as follows:

$$\text{Depletion Rate} = \frac{\text{Cost} - \text{Residual Value}}{\text{Recoverable Units}}$$

Second, depletion is calculated by multiplying the depletion rate by the number of units of the natural resource recovered during the period:

$$\text{Depletion} = \text{Depletion Rate} \times \text{Units Recovered}$$

As the natural resource is extracted, the natural resource is reduced and the amount of depletion computed is added to inventory. As the inventory is sold, the company will recognize an expense (cost of goods sold) related to the natural resource. **CORNERSTONE 7-9** illustrates how to account for depletion of a natural resource.

CORNERSTONE 7-9   Accounting for Depletion of a Natural Resource

Concept:

All costs necessary to acquire the natural resource and prepare it for use are capitalized as part of the natural resource. The depletion of the natural resource is added to inventory as the resource is depleted.

Information:

In 2010, the Miller Mining Company purchased a 4,000-acre tract of land in southern Indiana for $12,000,000, on which it developed an underground coal mine. Miller spent $26,000,000 to sink shafts to the coal seams and otherwise prepare the mine for operation. Miller estimates that there are 10,000,000 tons of recoverable coal and that the mine will be fully depleted eight years after mining begins in early 2011. The land has a residual value of $500,000. During 2011, 800,000 tons of coal were mined.

Required:

1. Compute the cost of the natural resource.
2. Compute the depletion rate.
3. How much depletion is taken in 2011?
4. Prepare the journal entry necessary to record depletion and the related cost of goods sold.

Solution:

1. The cost of the natural resource includes all costs necessary to get the mine ready for use:

Cost	$12,000,000
Development/preparation costs	26,000,000
Cost	$38,000,000

2.

$$\text{Depletion Rate} = \frac{(\$38,000,000 - \$500,000)}{10,000,000 \text{ tons}} = \$3.75 \text{ per ton}$$

3. Depletion = $3.75 × 800,000 = $3,000,000

4.

Date	Account and Explanation	Debit	Credit			Stockholders'
				Assets	= Liabilities +	Equity
Dec. 31, 2011	Inventory	3,000,000		+3,000,000		
	Accumulated Depletion		3,000,000	−3,000,000		
	(Record depletion of coal mine)					

Assuming all of the coal is sold in 2011, the following entry should also be made:

Date	Account and Explanation	Debit	Credit			Stockholders'
				Assets	= Liabilities +	Equity
Dec. 31, 2011	Cost of Goods Sold	3,000,000				
	Inventory		3,000,000	−3,000,000		−3,000,000
	(Record cost of goods sold)					

In Cornerstone 7-9, the following items are of particular importance:

- Miller records depletion initially increasing an inventory account. As the coal is sold, inventory will be reduced and cost of goods sold will be recognized. Thus, the expense related to depletion will be matched with the revenue that is generated from the sale of the natural resource.

- Depletion increases the accumulated depletion account.[8] At December 31, 2011, Miller could present the coal mine among its assets in the balance sheet as shown in Exhibit 7-13.

Exhibit 7-13

Disclosure of Natural Resource

Property, plant, and equipment:	
Land	$ 2,200,000
Equipment and machinery	19,800,000
Coal mine (cost of $38,000,000 less accumulated depletion of $3,000,000)	35,000,000
Total property, plant, and equipment	$57,000,000

Companies will often incur costs for tangible fixed assets in connection with the use of a natural resource (such as buildings, equipment, roads to access the resource). Because the useful life of these assets is often limited by the life of the natural resource, these tangible assets should be depreciated using the units-of-production method on the same basis as the natural resource. However, if the assets have a life shorter than the expected life of the natural resource or will be used for the extraction of other natural resources, the assets should be depreciated over their own useful lives.

OBJECTIVE 11
Describe the process of recording an impairment of a fixed asset.

APPENDIX 7A: IMPAIRMENT OF PROPERTY, PLANT, AND EQUIPMENT

An **impairment** is a permanent decline in the future benefit or service potential of an asset. The impairment may be due to numerous factors, including too little depreciation expense being recorded in previous years or obsolescence of the asset. A company is required to review an asset for impairment if events or circumstances lead the company to believe that an asset may be impaired. Consistent with the principle of conservatism, if a fixed asset is impaired, a company should reduce the asset's book value to its fair value in the year the impairment occurs.

The impairment test consists of two steps:

IFRS

The impairment model under IFRS is a single-step process that measures the impairment as the difference between the book value and the higher of the fair value or value in use.

Step 1. Existence: An impairment exists if the future cash flows expected to be generated by the asset are less than the asset's book value.

Step 2. Measurement: If an impairment exists, the impairment loss is measured as the difference between the book value and the fair value of the asset.

CORNERSTONE 7-10 illustrates the accounting for an impairment.

CORNERSTONE 7-10   **Recording an Impairment of Property, Plant, and Equipment**

Concept:
If there is a permanent decline in the service potential of an operating asset, the asset's book value should be reduced to reflect this reduction in service potential.

(Continued)

[8] An alternative practice allowed by GAAP is to credit depletion directly to the asset account.

**CORNERSTONE
7-10
(continued)**

Information:
Tabor Company acquired a machine on January 1, 2004, for $150,000. On January 3, 2011, when the machine has a book value of $60,000, Tabor believes that recent technological innovations may have led to an impairment in the value of the machine. Tabor estimates the machine will generate future cash flows of $50,000 and its current fair value is $42,000.

Required:
1. Determine if the machine is impaired as of January 2011.
2. If the machine is impaired, compute the loss from impairment.
3. Prepare the journal entry to record the impairment.

Solution:
1. The machine is impaired because the estimated future cash flows expected to be generated by the machine ($50,000) are less than the book value of the machine ($60,000).
2. Fair value − Book value = Loss from impairment

   $42,000 − $60,000 = $18,000
3.

Date	Account and Explanation	Debit	Credit
Jan. 3, 2011	Loss from Impairment	18,000	
	Equipment		18,000
	(Record impairment of asset)		

Assets	=	Liabilities	+	Stockholders' Equity
−18,000				−18,000

SUMMARY OF LEARNING OBJECTIVES

LO1. Define, classify, and describe the accounting for operating assets.
- Operating assets are the long-lived assets used by the company in the normal course of operations to generate revenue.
- Operating assets consist of three categories: property, plant, and equipment, intangible assets, and natural resources.
- Generally, operating assets are recorded at cost.
- As the service potential of the asset is used, the asset's cost is allocated as an expense (called depreciation, amortization, or depletion).

LO2. Explain how the historical cost principle applies to recording the cost of a fixed asset.
- The cost of a fixed asset is any expenditure necessary to acquire the asset and to prepare the asset for use.
- This amount is generally the cash paid.
- If noncash consideration is involved, cost is the fair value of the asset received or the fair value of the asset given up, whichever is more clearly determinable.

LO3. Understand the concept of depreciation.
- Depreciation is the process of allocating the cost of a tangible fixed asset to expense over the asset's useful life.
- Depreciation is not an attempt to measure fair value.
- Instead, depreciation is designed to capture the declining service potential of a fixed asset.
- Three factors are necessary to compute depreciation expense: cost, useful life, and residual value.

LO4. **Compute depreciation expense using various depreciation methods.**
- The straight-line method allocates an equal amount of the asset's cost to each year of the asset's useful life by dividing the asset's depreciable cost (cost less residual value) by the asset's useful life.
- The declining balance method is an accelerated method of depreciation that produces a declining amount of depreciation expense each period by multiplying the declining book value of an asset by a constant depreciation rate (computed as a multiple of the straight-line rate of depreciation).
- The units-of-production method recognizes depreciation expense based on the actual usage of the asset.

LO5. **Distinguish between capital and revenue expenditures.**
- Revenue expenditures are expenditures that do not increase the future benefit of an asset and are expensed as incurred.
- Capital expenditures extend the life of the asset, expand productive capacity, increase efficiency, or improve the quality of the product. Capital expenditures are added to the asset account and are subject to depreciation.

LO6. **Understand and account for revisions in depreciation.**
- When new or additional information becomes available, a company will revise its calculation of depreciation expense.
- A revision in depreciation will be recorded in current and future periods.

LO7. **Describe the process of recording the disposal of a fixed asset.**
- When a fixed asset is disposed of (either voluntarily or involuntarily), a gain or loss is recognized.
- The gain or loss is the difference between the proceeds from the sale and the book value of the asset.
- The gain or loss is reported on the income statement as "other revenues or gains" or "other expenses and losses," respectively.

LO8. **Evaluate the use of fixed assets.**
- The efficiency with which a company uses its fixed assets can be analyzed by using the fixed asset turnover ratio (net sales divided by average fixed assets).
- The condition of a company's assets and insights into the company's capital replacement policy can be examined by computing the average age of fixed assets (accumulated depreciation divided by depreciation expense).

LO9. **Understand the measurement and reporting of intangible assets.**
- Intangible assets are recorded at cost, which is any expenditure necessary to acquire the asset and prepare it for use.
- If the intangible asset has a finite life, it is amortized over the shorter of the economic or legal life of the asset.
- If the intangible asset has an indefinite life, it is not amortized but is reviewed at least annually for impairment.

LO10. **Understand the measurement and reporting of natural resources.**
- The cost of natural resources is any cost necessary to acquire and prepare the resource for separation from the earth.
- As the natural resource is removed, the cost is allocated to each unit of the natural resource that is removed and recorded in an inventory account. This process is called depletion.
- Depletion is calculated using a procedure similar to the units-of-production depreciation method.

LO11. **(Appendix 7A) Describe the process of recording an impairment of a fixed asset.**
- Impairment exists when the future cash flows expected to be generated by an asset are less than the book value of the asset.
- An impairment loss, the difference between the book value and fair value of the asset, is recognized and the asset is reduced.

CORNERSTONE 7-1 Measuring and recording the cost of a fixed asset (p. 333)

CORNERSTONE 7-2 Computing depreciation expense using the straight-line method (p. 338)

CORNERSTONE 7-3 Computing depreciation expense using the declining balance method (p. 340)

CORNERSTONE 7-4 Computing depreciation expense using the units-of-production method (p. 341)

CORNERSTONE 7-5 Revising depreciation expense (p. 346)

CORNERSTONE 7-6 Recording the disposition of property, plant, and equipment (p. 348)

CORNERSTONE 7-7 Analyzing fixed asset ratios (p. 350)

CORNERSTONE 7-8 Accounting for intangible assets (p. 353)

CORNERSTONE 7-9 Accounting for depletion of a natural resource (p. 355)

CORNERSTONE 7-10 *(Appendix 7A)* Recording an impairment of property, plant, and equipment (p. 356)

CORNERSTONES
FOR CHAPTER 7

KEY TERMS

Accumulated depreciation (p. 334)
Amortization (p. 352)
Average age of fixed assets (p. 350)
Book value (Carrying value) (p. 334)
Capital expenditures (p. 345)
Copyright (p. 352)
Cost (p. 335)
Declining balance depreciation method (p. 339)
Depletion (p. 354)
Depreciable cost (p. 336)
Depreciation (p. 334)
Depreciation expense (p. 334)
Franchise (p. 352)
Fixed asset turnover ratio (p. 350)
Goodwill (p. 352)
Impairment (p. 356)

Intangible operating assets (p. 351)
Involuntary disposal (p. 347)
Natural resources (p. 354)
Operating assets (p. 330)
Organizational costs (p. 352)
Patent (p. 352)
Property, plant, and equipment (p. 331)
Research and development (R&D) expense (p. 352)
Residual value (Salvage value) (p. 335)
Revenue expenditures (p. 345)
Straight-line depreciation (p. 337)
Trademark (p. 352)
Units-of-production method (p. 341)
Useful life (p. 335)
Voluntary disposal (p. 347)

REVIEW PROBLEM

I. Accounting for Operating Assets

Concept:

At acquisition, operating assets are capitalized at their historical cost. As the service potential of an operating asset declines, the cost of the asset is allocated as an expense among the accounting periods in which the asset is used and benefits are received.

Information:

The Carroll Company manufactures a line of cranes, shovels, and hoists, all of which are electronically controlled. During 2011, the following transactions occurred:

a. On January 2, Carroll purchased a building by signing a note payable for $702,900. The building is expected to have a useful life of 30 years and a residual value of $3,900.

b. On January 3, Carroll purchased a delivery truck for $34,650 cash. The delivery truck is expected to have a useful life of five years and a $5,000 residual value.

c. Immediately after the acquisition, Carroll spent $5,350 on a new engine for the truck. After installing the engine, Carroll estimated that this expenditure increased the useful life of the truck to eight years. The residual value is still expected to be $5,000.

d. In order to assure a coal supply for its heating plant, Carroll acquired a small operating coal mine for $1,980,000. Carroll estimated that the recoverable coal reserves at acquisition were 495,000 tons. Carroll's mine produced 40,000 tons of coal during 2011.

e. Carroll purchased a patent on January 3 for $100,000. The patent has 12 years remaining on its legal life, but Carroll estimated its economic life to be 8 years. Carroll uses the straight-line amortization method.

Required:

1. Record the acquisition of the building and the delivery truck.

2. Prepare a depreciation schedule and record a full year's depreciation expense for 2011 on the building (use the straight-line depreciation method) and on the truck (use the double-declining-balance depreciation method).

3. Compute and record 2011 depletion for the coal mine.

4. Compute and record the amortization expense on the patent for 2011 on a straight-line basis.

5. Assume Carroll had sales of $8,800,000, fixed assets with an average net book value of $3,200,000, depreciation expense of $375,000, and accumulated depreciation of $2,062,500. Compute the fixed asset turnover ratio and the average age of the fixed assets. Comment on what the ratios mean.

Solution:

1. The cost of the building is $702,900 and is recorded as:

Assets	= Liabilities +	Stockholders' Equity
+702,900	+702,900	

Date	Account and Explanation	Debit	Credit
Jan. 2, 2011	Buildings	702,900	
	Notes Payable		702,900
	(Purchased building by issuing note payable)		

The cost of the truck is $40,000 ($34,650 acquisition price + $5,350 from the overhaul of the engine). The purchase of the truck is recorded as:

Assets	= Liabilities +	Stockholders' Equity
−40,000		
+40,000		

Date	Account and Explanation	Debit	Credit
Jan. 3, 2011	Truck	40,000	
	Cash		40,000
	(Purchase of truck for cash)		

2. Depreciation on the items of property, plant, and equipment:

STRAIGHT-LINE DEPRECIATION ON THE BUILDING

$$\text{Straight-Line Depreciation Expense} = \frac{\text{Cost} - \text{Residual Value}}{\text{Expected Life}}$$

$$= \frac{\$702,900 - \$3,900}{30 \text{ years}} = \$23,300 \text{ per year}$$

Assets	= Liabilities +	Stockholders' Equity
−23,300		−23,300

Date	Account and Explanation	Debit	Credit
Dec. 31, 2011	Depreciation Expense	23,300	
	Accumulated Depreciation		23,300
	(To record depreciation on building)		

DOUBLE-DECLINING-BALANCE DEPRECIATION FOR THE TRUCK

Declining Balance Depreciation Expense = Declining Balance Rate × Book Value

Declining Balance Rate = (1/Useful Life) × 2 = (1/8) × 2 = 2/8, or 25%

Cost = $34,650 (from transaction *b*) + $5,350 overhaul (from transaction *c*)

= $40,000

End of Year	Depreciation Expense	Accumulated Depreciation	Book Value
			$40,000
2011	25% × $40,000 = $10,000	$10,000	30,000
2012	25% × 30,000 = 7,500	17,500	22,500
2013	25% × 22,500 = 5,625	23,125	16,875
2014	25% × 16,875 = 4,219	27,344	12,656
2015	25% × 12,656 = 3,164	30,508	9,492
2016	25% × 9,492 = 2,373	32,881	7,119
2017	25% × 7,119 = 1,780	34,661	5,339
2018	339*	35,000	5,000
	$35,000		

*The amount needed to achieve a $5,000 book value.

Date	Account and Explanation	Debit	Credit
Dec. 31, 2011	Depreciation Expense	10,000	
	Accumulated Depreciation		10,000
	(To record depreciation on truck)		

Assets	= Liabilities +	Stockholders' Equity
−10,000		−10,000

3. Depletion on the coal mine:

$$\text{Depletion Rate} = \frac{\text{Cost} - \text{Residual Value}}{\text{Recoverable Units}}$$

$$= \frac{\$1,980,000}{495,000} = \$4.00 \text{ per ton}$$

Depletion = Depletion Rate × Units Recovered

= $4.00 × 40,000 = $160,000

Date	Account and Explanation	Debit	Credit
Dec. 31, 2011	Inventory	160,000	
	Accumulated Depletion		160,000
	(To record depletion)		

Assets	= Liabilities +	Stockholders' Equity
+160,000		
−160,000		

4. Amortization of the patent:

$$\text{Straight-Line Amortization Expense} = \frac{\text{Cost} - \text{Residual Value}}{\text{Expected Life}}$$

$$= \frac{\$100,000 - \$0}{8 \text{ years}}$$

= $12,500 per year

Date	Account and Explanation	Debit	Credit
Dec. 31, 2011	Amortization Expense	12,500	
	Patent		12,500
	(To record amortization of patent)		

Assets	= Liabilities +	Stockholders' Equity
−12,500		−12,500

5. The fixed asset turnover ratio is computed as its net sales divided by the average of its fixed assets. Carroll Company's fixed asset turnover ratio is 2.75 ($8,800,000/$3,200,000). This ratio describes how efficiently Carroll is using its fixed assets to generate revenue. The average age of fixed assets is computed as accumulated depreciation divided by depreciation expense. Carroll's fixed assets are approximately 5 ½ years old ($2,062,500/$375,000). For every dollar of fixed assets, Carroll is generating $2.75 of sales.

DISCUSSION QUESTIONS

1. How do operating assets differ from nonoperating assets? What benefits do operating assets provide to the company?
2. What are the classifications of operating assets? How do they differ from one another?
3. How does the cost concept affect accounting for operating assets? Under this concept, what is included in the cost of a fixed asset?
4. How is the cost of a fixed asset measured in a cash transaction? In a noncash transaction?
5. What is the effect on the financial statements if a company incorrectly records an expense as an asset?
6. How does the matching concept affect accounting for operating assets?
7. What factors must be known or estimated in order to compute depreciation expense?
8. How do the accelerated and straight-line depreciation methods differ?
9. What objective should guide the selection of a depreciation method for financial reporting purposes?
10. What objective should be of primary importance in the selection of a depreciation method for income tax reporting?
11. What accounting concepts should be considered when evaluating the accounting for expenditures that are made for fixed assets after acquisition? Be sure to distinguish between revenue and capital expenditures.
12. What is the proper accounting for depreciation when new or additional information becomes available that causes a company to change its estimates of useful life or residual value?
13. How is the sale of equipment at an amount greater than its book value recorded? How would your answer change if the equipment is sold at an amount less than its book value?
14. What information does the fixed asset turnover ratio and the average age of fixed assets provide users of financial statements?
15. Describe the benefits that intangible assets provide to a company.
16. What factors should be considered when selecting the amortization period for an intangible asset?
17. What basis underlies the computation of depletion?
18. *(Appendix 7A)* What is an impairment of a fixed asset?

MULTIPLE-CHOICE EXERCISES

7-1 Anniston Company purchased equipment and incurred the following costs:

Purchase price	$52,000
Cost of trial runs	750
Installation costs	250
Sales tax	2,600

What is the cost of the equipment?

a. $52,000
b. $54,600
c. $54,850
d. $55,600

7-2 The cost principle requires that companies record fixed assets at

a. Fair value
b. Book value
c. Historical cost
d. Market value

7-3 When depreciation expense is recorded each period, what account is debited?

a. Depreciation Expense
b. Cash
c. Accumulated Depreciation
d. The fixed asset account involved

> *Use the following information for Multiple-Choice Exercises 7-4 through 7-6:*
> Cox Inc. acquired a machine for $600,000 on January 1, 2011. The machine has a salvage value of $10,000 and a five-year useful life. Cox expects the machine to run for 15,000 machine hours. The machine was actually used for 4,800 hours in 2011 and 3,150 hours in 2012.

7-4 Refer to the information for Cox Inc. above. What would be the balance in the accumulated depreciation account at December 31, 2012, if the straight-line method were used?

a. $216,000
b. $236,000

c. $240,000
d. $250,000

7-5 Refer to the information for Cox Inc. above. What amount would Cox record as depreciation expense at December 31, 2012, if the double-declining-balance method were used?

a. $144,000
b. $145,600

c. $236,000
d. $240,000

7-6 Refer to the information for Cox Inc. above. What amount would Cox record as depreciation expense for 2011 if the units-of-production method were used (*Note:* Round your answer to the nearest dollar)?

a. $123,900
b. $188,800

c. $192,000
d. $195,200

7-7 Which of the following statements is true regarding depreciation methods?

a. The use of a declining balance method of depreciation will produce lower depreciation charges in the early years of an asset's life compared to the straight-line depreciation method.
b. Over the life of an asset, a declining balance depreciation method will recognize more depreciation expense relative to the straight-line method.
c. The use of a declining-balance method instead of the straight-line method will produce higher book values for an asset in the early years of the asset's life.
d. The use of a higher estimated life and a higher residual value will lower the annual amount of depreciation expense recognized on the income statement.

7-8 Normal repair and maintenance of an asset is an example of what?

a. Revenue expenditure
b. Capital expenditure

c. An expenditure that will be depreciated
d. An expenditure that should be avoided

7-9 Chapman Inc. purchased a piece of equipment in 2010. Chapman depreciated the equipment on a straight-line basis over a useful life of 10 years and used a residual value of $12,000. Chapman's depreciation expense for 2011 was $11,000. What was the original cost of the building?

a. $98,000
b. $110,000

c. $122,000
d. $134,000

7-10 Bradley Company purchased a machine for $34,000 on January 1, 2009. It depreciates the machine using the straight-line method over a useful life of 8 years and a $2,000 residual value. On January 1, 2011, Bradley revised its estimate of residual value to $1,000 and shortened the machine's useful life to 4 more years. Depreciation expense for 2011 is:

a. $4,000
b. $5,750

c. $6,000
d. $6,250

7-11 Jerabek Inc. decided to sell one of its fixed assets that had a cost of $55,000 and accumulated depreciation of $35,000 on July 1, 2011. On that date, Jerabek sold the fixed asset for $15,000. What was the resulting gain or loss from the sale of the asset?

a. $5,000 loss
b. $5,000 gain

c. $15,000 loss
d. $15,000 gain

7-12 Which of the following statements is true?

a.   The fixed asset turnover ratio assists managers in determining the estimated future capital expenditures that are needed.
b.   The average age of the fixed assets is computed by dividing accumulated depreciation by depreciation expense.
c.   If net sales increases, the fixed asset turnover ratio will decrease.
d.   A relatively low fixed asset turnover ratio signals that a company is efficiently using its assets.

7-13 Which of the following is *not* an intangible asset?

a.   Patent   c.   Research and development
b.   Trademark   d.   Goodwill

7-14 Heston Company acquired a patent on January 1, 2011, for $75,000. The patent has a remaining legal life of 15 years, but Heston expects to receive benefits from the patent for only five years. What amount of amortization expense does Heston record in 2011 related to the patent?

a. $5,000   d. $0—patents are not amortized.
b. $7,500
c. $15,000

7-15 Howton Paper Company purchased $1,400,000 of timberland in 2010 for its paper operations. Howton estimates that there are 10,000 acres of timberland and it cut 2,000 acres in 2011. The land is expected to have a residual value of $200,000 once all the timber is cut. Which of the following is true with regard to depletion?

a.   Depletion will cause Howton's timber inventory to increase.
b.   Howton will record depletion expense of $280,000 in 2011.
c.   Howton's depletion rate is $140 per acre of timber.
d.   Howton should deplete the timber at a rate of 20% (2,000 acres ÷ 10,000 acres) per year.

7-16 *(Appendix 7A)* Murnane Company purchased a machine on February 1, 2007, for $100,000. In January 2011, when the book value of the machine is $70,000, Murnane believes the machine is impaired due to recent technological advances. Murnane expects the machine to generate future cash flow of $10,000 and has estimated the fair value of the machine to be $55,000. What is the loss from impairment?

a. $5,000   c. $30,000
b. $15,000   d. $45,000

CORNERSTONE EXERCISES

Cornerstone Exercise 7-17 Cost of a Fixed Asset

Borges Inc. recently purchased land to use for the construction of its new manufacturing facility and incurred the following costs: purchase price, $85,000; real estate commissions, $5,100; delinquent property taxes, $1,500; closing costs, $3,500 clearing and grading of the land, $8,100.

Required:
Determine the cost of the land.

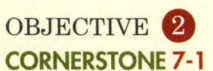

Cornerstone Exercise 7-18 Acquisition Cost

Cox Company recently purchased a machine by paying $8,500 cash and signing a six month, 10% note for $10,000. In addition to the purchase price, Cox incurred the following costs related to the machine: freight charges, $800; interest charges, $500; special foundation for machine, $400; installation costs, $1,100.

Required:
Determine the cost of the machine.

> *Use the following information for Cornerstone Exercises 7-19 through 7-21:*
> Irons Delivery Inc. purchased a new delivery truck for $45,000 on January 1, 2011. The truck is expected to have a $3,000 residual value at the end of its five-year useful life.

Cornerstone Exercise 7-19 Straight-Line Depreciation

Refer to the information for Irons Delivery Inc. above. Irons uses the straight-line method of depreciation.

Required:
Prepare the journal entry to record depreciation expense for 2011 and 2012.

Cornerstone Exercise 7-20 Declining Balance Depreciation

Refer to the information for Irons Delivery Inc. above. Irons uses the double-declining-balance method of depreciation.

Required:
Prepare the journal entry to record depreciation expense for 2011 and 2012.

Cornerstone Exercise 7-21 Units-of-Production Depreciation

Refer to the information for Irons Delivery Inc. above. Irons uses the units-of-production method of depreciation. Irons expects the truck to run for 160,000 miles. The actual miles driven in 2011 and 2012 were 40,000 and 36,000, respectively.

Required:
Prepare the journal entry to record depreciation expense for 2011 and 2012.

Cornerstone Exercise 7-22 Revision of Depreciation

On January 1, 2009, Slade Inc. purchased a machine for $115,000. Slade depreciated the machine with the straight-line depreciation method over a useful life of 10 years, using a residual value of $5,000. At the beginning of 2011, a major overhaul, costing $30,000, was made. After the overhaul, the machine's residual value is estimated to be $7,500, and the machine is expected to have a remaining useful life of eleven years.

Required:
Determine the depreciation expense for 2011.

Cornerstone Exercise 7-23 Disposal of an Operating Asset

On August 30, Williams Manufacturing Company decided to sell one of its fabricating machines that was 15 years old for $6,000. The machine, which originally cost $105,000, had accumulated depreciation of $102,500.

Required:
Prepare the journal entry to record the disposal of the machine.

Cornerstone Exercise 7-24 Analyze Fixed Assets

At December 31, 2011, Clark Corporation reported beginning net fixed assets of $94,150, ending net fixed assets of $103,626, accumulated depreciation of $49,133, net sales of $212,722, and depreciation expense of $12,315.

Required:
Compute Clark Corporation's fixed asset turnover ratio and the average age of its fixed assets. (*Note:* Round answers to two decimal places.)

Cornerstone Exercise 7-25 Cost of Intangible Assets

Advanced Technological Devices Inc. acquired a patent for $120,000. It spent an additional $24,744 defending the patent in legal proceedings.

Required:
Determine the cost of the patent.

Cornerstone Exercise 7-26 Amortization of Intangible Assets

MicroSystems Inc. acquired a patent for $180,000. MicroSystems amortizes the patent on a straight-line basis over its remaining economic life of 12 years.

Required:

Prepare the journal entry to record the amortization expense related to the patent.

Cornerstone Exercise 7-27 Depletion of Natural Resources

Brandon Oil Company recently purchased oil and natural gas reserves in a remote part of Alaska for $1,850,000. Brandon spent $10,000,000 preparing the oil for extraction from the ground. Brandon estimates that 108,000,000 barrels of oil will be extracted from the ground. The land has a residual value of $20,000. During 2011, 15,000,000 barrels are extracted from the ground.

Required:

Calculate the amount of depletion taken in 2011. (*Note*: Use two decimal points for calculations.)

OBJECTIVE 11
CORNERSTONE 7-10

Cornerstone Exercise 7-28 (*Appendix 7A*) Impairment

Brown Industries had two machines that it believes may be impaired. Information on the machines is shown below.

	Book Value	Estimated Future Cash Flows	Fair Value
Machine 1	$42,000	$50,000	$40,000
Machine 2	50,000	40,000	32,000

Required:

For each machine, determine if the machine is impaired. If so, calculate the amount of the impairment loss.

EXERCISES

OBJECTIVE 1

Exercise 7-29 Balance Sheet Presentation

Listed below are items that may appear on a classified balance sheet.

1. Land
2. Amounts due from customers
3. Office building
4. Truck
5. Goods held for resale
6. Amounts owed to suppliers
7. Patent
8. Timberland
9. Land held as investment
10. Goodwill

Required:

Indicate whether each item is included as an operating asset on a classified balance sheet. If the item is an operating asset, indicate whether the item is property, plant, and equipment, an intangible asset, or a natural resource as well as the cost allocation process used (depreciation, amortization, or depletion). If the item is not an operating asset, indicate the proper balance sheet classification.

OBJECTIVE 1

Exercise 7-30 Balance Sheet Classification

Micro-Technologies Inc., a computer manufacturer, has the following items on its balance sheet—office furniture delivery truck, patent, computer assembly machine, building, memory chips.

Required:

Indicate the proper balance sheet classification of each item and the cost allocation process used (depreciation, amortization, depletion).

OBJECTIVE 2

Exercise 7-31 Acquisition Cost

Items that may relate to property, plant, and equipment follow:

1. Purchase price of a machine
2. Delinquent property taxes at the time of purchase
3. Interest on debt used to purchase equipment
4. Sales taxes paid on purchase of equipment
5. Costs to install a machine
6. Ordinary repairs to equipment
7. Cost to remodel a building

(Continued)

8. Architectural fees paid for design of a
    building
9. Cost of training employees to run
    equipment

10. Transportation costs to have furniture
    delivered

Required:

Conceptual Connection: Determine whether each item is included as part of the cost of property, plant, and equipment. For any item excluded from the cost of property, plant, and equipment, explain why the item was excluded.

Exercise 7-32 Cost of a Fixed Asset   OBJECTIVE

Laurel Cleaners purchased an automatic dry cleaning machine for $145,000 from TGF Corporation on April 1, 2011. Laurel paid $45,000 in cash and signed a five-year, 10 percent note for $100,000. Laurel will pay interest on the note each year on March 31, beginning in 2012. Transportation charges of $3,815 for the machine were paid by Laurel. Laurel also paid $2,400 for the living expenses of the TGF installation crew. Solvent, necessary to operate the machine, was acquired for $1,000. Of this amount, $600 of the solvent was used to test and adjust the machine.

Required:

1. Compute the cost of the new dry cleaning machine.
2. **Conceptual Connection:** Explain why you excluded any expenditures from the cost of the dry cleaning machine.

Exercise 7-33 Cost of a Fixed Asset   OBJECTIVE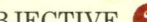

Colson Photography Service purchased a new digital imaging machine on April 15 for $11,200. During installation Colson incurred and paid in cash the following costs:

Rental of drill	$ 150
Electrical contractor	1,300
Plumbing contractor	785

Colson also paid $160 to replace a bracket on the digital imager that was damaged when one of Colson's employees dropped a box on it while it was being installed.

Required:

1. Determine the cost of the digital imaging machine.
2. **Conceptual Connection:** Explain why you included or excluded the $160 bracket replacement cost.

Exercise 7-34 Cost of Fixed Assets   OBJECTIVE

Mooney Sounds, a local stereo retailer, needed a new store because it had outgrown the leased space it had used for several years. Mooney acquired and remodeled a former grocery store. As a part of the acquisition, Mooney incurred the following costs:

Cost of grocery store	$277,400	Wire and electrical supplies	$ 4,290
Cost of land (on which the		New doors	6,400
grocery store is located)	83,580	New windows	3,850
New roof for building	74,000	Wages paid to workers for remodeling	12,500
Lumber used for remodeling	23,200	Additional inventory purchased for	
Paint	515	grand opening sale	45,300

Required:

1. Determine the cost of the land and the building.
2. **Conceptual Connection:** If management misclassified a portion of the building's cost as part of the cost of the land, what would be the effect on the financial statements?

Exercise 7-35 Cost and Depreciation   OBJECTIVE

On January 1, 2011, Quick Stop, a convenience store, purchased a new soft-drink cooler. Quick Stop paid $25,780 cash for the cooler. Quick Stop also paid $1,090 to have the cooler shipped to its location. After the new cooler arrived, Quick Stop paid $1,810 to have the old cooler dismantled and removed. Quick Stop also paid $820 to a contractor to have new wiring and drains

(Continued)

installed for the new cooler. Quick Stop estimated that the cooler would have a useful life of six years and a residual value of $700. Quick Stop uses the straight-line method of depreciation.

Required:
1. Prepare any necessary journal entries to record the cost of the cooler.
2. Prepare the adjusting entry to record 2011 depreciation expense on the new cooler.
3. What is the book value of the cooler at the end of 2011?

4. If Quick Stop had used a useful life of 10 years and a residual value of $1,500, how would this effect depreciation expense for 2011 and the book value of the cooler at the end of 2011?

OBJECTIVE 3

Exercise 7-36 Characteristics of Depreciation Methods

Below is a common list of depreciation methods and characteristics related to depreciation.

Depreciation Methods
a. Straight-line depreciation method
b. Declining balance depreciation method
c. Units-of-production depreciation method when actual units produced increases over the life of the asset

Characteristics
1. Results in depreciation expense that decreases over the life of the asset.
2. Results in depreciation expense that increases over the life of the asset.
3. Allocates the same amount of cost to each period of a depreciable asset's life.
4. Calculated by multiplying a *constant* depreciation rate by depreciable cost.
5. Calculated by applying a *constant* depreciation rate to the asset's book value at the beginning of the period.
6. Results in lowest income taxes in early years of the asset's life.
7. Consistent with the matching concept.

Required:
Match one or more of the depreciation methods with each characteristic.

OBJECTIVE 3 4

Exercise 7-37 Depreciation Methods

Berkshire Corporation purchased a copying machine for $8,700 on January 1, 2011. The machine's residual value was $425 and its expected life was five years or 2,000,000 copies. Actual usage was 480,000 copies the first year and 400,000 the second year.

Required:
1. Compute depreciation expense for 2011 and 2012 using the (a) straight-line method, (b) double-declining-balance method, and (c) units-of-production method.
2. For each depreciation method, what is the book value of the machine at the end 2011? At the end of the 2012?

3. Assume that Berkshire uses the double-declining-balance method of depreciation. What is the effect on assets and income relative to if Berkshire had used the straight-line method of depreciation instead of the double-declining-balance method of depreciation?

OBJECTIVE 3 4

Exercise 7-38 Depreciation Methods

Clearcopy, a printing company, acquired a new press on January 1, 2011. The press cost $173,400 and had an expected life of eight years or 4,500,000 pages and an expected residual value of $15,000. Clearcopy printed 675,000 pages in 2011.

Required:
1. Compute 2011 depreciation expense using the (a) straight-line method, (b) double-declining-balance method, and (c) units-of-production method.
2. What is the book value of the machine at the end of 2011 under each method?

OBJECTIVE 3 4

Exercise 7-39 Depreciation Methods

Quick-as-Lightning, a delivery service, purchased a new delivery truck for $45,000 on January 1, 2011. The truck is expected to have a useful life of ten years or 150,000 miles and an expected residual value of $3,000. The truck was driven 15,000 miles in 2011 and 13,000 miles in 2012.

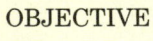

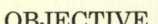

Required:

1. Compute depreciation expense for 2011 and 2012 using the (a) straight-line method, (b) double-declining-balance method, and (c) units-of-production method.
2. For each method, what is the book value of the machine at the end 2011? At the end of 2012?
3. If Quick-as-Lightning used an 8 year useful life or 100,000 miles and a residual value of $1,000, what would be the effect on (a) depreciation expense and (b) book value under each of the depreciation methods?

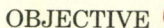

Exercise 7-40 Inferring Original Cost

OBJECTIVE ❸ ❹

Barton Construction Company purchased a piece of heavy equipment on January 1, 2009, which it is depreciating using the straight-line method. The equipment's useful life is five years and its residual value is $5,000. Barton recorded depreciation expense of $44,000 in 2010.

Required:

Determine the original cost of the equipment.

Exercise 7-41 Choice Among Depreciation Methods

OBJECTIVE ❸ ❹

Walnut Ridge Production Inc. purchased a new computerized video editing machine at a cost of $450,000. The system has a residual value of $64,000 and an expected life of five years.

Required:

1. Compute depreciation expense, accumulated depreciation, and book value for the first three years of the machine's life using the (a) straight-line method and (b) double-declining-balance method.
2. Which method would produce the largest income in the first, second, and third years of the asset's life?
3. Why might the controller of Walnut Ridge Production be interested in the effect of choosing a depreciation method? Evaluate the legitimacy of these interests.

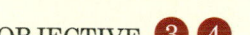

Exercise 7-42 Revision of Depreciation

OBJECTIVE ❸ ❹

On January 1, 2009, Blizzards-R-Us purchased a snow-blowing machine for $73,000. The machine was expected to have a residual value of $5,000 at the end of its five-year useful life. On January 1, 2011, Blizzards-R-Us concluded that the machine would have a remaining useful life of six years with a residual value of $3,800.

Required:

1. Determine the revised annual depreciation expense for 2011 using the straight-line method.
2. **Conceptual Connection:** How does the revision in depreciation affect Blizzards-R-Us's financial statements?

Exercise 7-43 Capital versus Revenue Expenditure

OBJECTIVE ❺

Warrick Water Company, a privately owned business, supplies water to several communities. Warrick has just performed an extensive overhaul on one of its water pumps. The overhaul is expected to extend the life of the pump by 10 years. The residual value of the pump is unchanged. You have been asked to determine which of the following costs should be capitalized as a part of this overhaul. Those costs not capitalized should be expensed.

Element of Cost	Classification and Explanation
New pump motor	
Repacking of bearings (performed monthly)	
New impeller	
Painting of pump housing (performed annually)	
Replacement of pump foundation	
New wiring (needed every five years)	
Installation labor, motor	
Installation labor, impeller	
Installation labor, wiring	
Paint labor (performed annually)	
Placement of fence around pump*	

*A requirement of the Occupational Safety and Health Administration that will add to maintenance costs over the remaining life of the pump.

(Continued)

Required:

Conceptual Connection: Classify each cost as part of the overhaul or as an expense. Be sure to explain your reasoning for each classification.

OBJECTIVE 5

Exercise 7-44 Expenditures After Acquisition

The following expenditures were incurred during the year:

a. Paid $4,000 for an overhaul of an automobile engine.
b. Paid $20,000 to add capacity to a cellular phone company's wireless network.
c. Paid $200 for routine maintenance of a manufacturing machine.
d. Paid $10,000 to remodel an office building.
e. Paid $300 for ordinary repairs

Required:

1. Classify the expenditures as either capital or revenue expenditures.
2. **Conceptual Connection:** If management improperly classified these expenditures, what would be the impact on the financial statements?

OBJECTIVE 5

Exercise 7-45 Expenditures After Acquisition

Roanoke Manufacturing placed a robotic arm on a large assembly machine on January 1, 2011. At the time, the assembly machine, which was acquired on January 1, 2004, was expected to last another three years. The following information is available concerning the assembly machine.

Cost, assembly machine	$750,000
Accumulated depreciation, 1/1/2011	480,000

The robotic arm cost $225,000 and was expected to extend the useful life of the machine by three years. Therefore, the useful life of the assembly machine, after the arm replacement, is six years. The assembly machine is expected to have a residual value of $120,000 at the end of its useful life.

Required:

1. Prepare the journal entry necessary to record the addition of the robotic arm.
2. Compute 2011 depreciation expense for the machine using the straight-line method, and prepare the necessary journal entry.
3. What is the book value of the machine at the end of 2011?
4. **Conceptual Connection:** What would have been the effect on the financial statements if Roanoke had expensed the addition of the robotic arm?

OBJECTIVE 5

Exercise 7-46 Expenditures After Acquisition and Depreciation

Eastern National Bank installed a wireless encryption device in January 2007. The device cost $180,000. At the time the device was installed, Eastern estimated that it would have an expected life of eight years and a residual value of $10,000. By 2010, the bank's business had expanded and modifications to the device were necessary. At the beginning of 2011, Eastern spent $45,000 on modifications for the device. Eastern estimates that the new expected life of the device (from January 2011) is six years and the new residual value is $5,000. Eastern uses the straight-line method of depreciation. Had Eastern not modified the device, it estimates that processing delays would have caused the bank to lose at least $100,000 of business per year.

Required:

1. Compute the accumulated depreciation for the device at the time the modifications were made (four years after acquisition).
2. What is the book value of the device before and after the modification?
3. What will be annual straight-line depreciation expense for the device after the modification?
4. **Conceptual Connection:** The bank's president notes, "Since the after-modification, depreciation expense exceeds the before-modification depreciation expense. This modification was a poor idea." Comment on the president's assertion.

OBJECTIVE 7

Exercise 7-47 Disposal of Fixed Asset

Perfect Auto Rentals sold one of its cars on January 1, 2011. Perfect had acquired the car on January 1, 2009, for $23,400. At acquisition Perfect assumed that the car would have an estimated life of three years and a residual value of $3,000. Assume that Perfect has recorded straight-line depreciation expense for 2009 and 2010.

Required:

1. Prepare the journal entry to record the sale of the car assuming the car sold for (a) $9,800 cash, (b) $7,500 cash, and (c) $11,500 cash.
2. How should the gain or loss on the disposition (if any) be reported on the income statement?

Exercise 7-48 Disposal of Fixed Asset

OBJECTIVE 7

Pacifica Manufacturing retired a computerized metal stamping machine on December 31, 2011. Pacifica sold the machine to another company and did not replace it. The following data are available for the machine:

Cost (installed), 1/1/2006	$920,000
Residual value estimated on 1/1/2006	160,000
Estimated life as of 1/1/2006	10 years

The machine was sold for $188,000 cash. Pacifica uses the straight-line method of depreciation.

Required:

1. Prepare the journal entry to record depreciation expense for 2011.
2. Compute accumulated depreciation at December 31, 2011.
3. Prepare the journal entry to record the sale of the machine.
4. **Conceptual Connection:** Explain how the disposal of the fixed asset would affect the 2011 financial statements.

Exercise 7-49 Depreciation and Disposal of Fixed Assets

OBJECTIVE 3 4 5 7

Stanley Company reported the following information regarding its equipment:

Account	Amount
Equipment, Jan. 1, 2011	$745,120
Equipment, Dec. 31, 2011	831,410
Accumulated depreciation, Jan. 1, 2011	224,350
Accumulated depreciation, Dec. 31, 2011	257,690
Capital expenditures	148,735
Accumulated depreciation on equipment sold	50,320
Cash received for equipment sold	14,150

Required:

1. What journal entry did Stanley make to record depreciation expense for 2011?
2. What journal entry did Stanley make to record the disposal of the equipment?

Exercise 7-50 Analyze Fixed Assets

OBJECTIVE 8

Tabor Industries is a technology company that operates in a highly competitive environment. In 2008, management had significantly curtailed its capital expenditures due to cash flow problems. Tabor reported the following information for 2011:

*   Net fixed assets (beginning of year), $489,000
*   Net fixed assets (end of year), $505,000
*   Net sales, $1,025,000
*   Accumulated depreciation (end of year), $543,000
*   Depreciation expense, $126,000

An analyst reviewing Tabor's financial history noted that Tabor had previously reported fixed asset turnover ratios and average age of its assets as follows:

	2006	2007	2008	2009	2010
Fixed asset turnover	2.48	2.45	2.74	2.57	2.33
Average age of assets (years)	1.81	1.79	1.94	2.81	3.74

During this time frame, the industry average fixed asset turnover ratio is 2.46 and the industry average age of assets is 1.79 years.

(Continued)

Required:
1. Compute Tabor's fixed asset turnover ratio for 2011.
2. Compute the average age of Tabor's fixed assets for 2011.
3. **Conceptual Connection:** Comment on Tabor's fixed asset turnover ratios and the average age of the fixed assets.

OBJECTIVE ❾

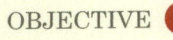

Exercise 7-51 Acquisition and Amortization of Intangible Assets

TLM Technologies had these transactions related to intangible assets during 2011.

Jan. 2	Purchased a patent from Luna Industries for $175,000. The remaining legal life of the patent is 15 years and TLM expects the patent to be useful for 8 years.
Jan. 5	Paid legal fees in a successful legal defense of the patent of $90,000.
June 29	Registered a trademark with the federal government. Registration costs were $4,000. TLM expects to use the trademark indefinitely.
Sept. 2	Paid research and development costs of $478,200.

Required:
1. Prepare the journal entries necessary to record the transactions.
2. Prepare the entries necessary to record amortization expense for the intangible assets.
3. What is the balance of the intangible assets at the end of 2011?

OBJECTIVE ❶❸❹❽ ❾

Exercise 7-52 Balance Sheet Presentation

The following information relates to the assets of Westfield Semiconductors as of December 31, 2011. Westfield uses the straight-line method for depreciation and amortization.

Asset	Acquisition Cost	Expected Life	Residual Value	Time Used
Land	$104,300	Infinite	$100,000	10 years
Building	430,000	25 years	30,000	10 years
Machine	285,000	5 years	10,000	2 years
Patent	80,000	10 years	0	3 years
Truck	21,000	100,000 miles	3,000	44,000 miles

Required:
Use the information above to prepare the property, plant, and equipment and intangible assets portions of a classified balance sheet for Westfield.

OBJECTIVE ❾

Exercise 7-53 Amortization of Intangibles

On January 1, 2011, Boulder Investments Inc. acquired a franchise to operate a Burger Doodle restaurant. Boulder paid $275,000 for a 10-year franchise and incurred organization costs of $8,000.

Required:
1. Prepare the journal entry to record the cash payment for the franchise fee and the organization costs.
2. Prepare the journal entry to record the annual amortization expense at the end of the first year.

OBJECTIVE ❿

Exercise 7-54 Depletion Rate

Oxford Quarries purchased 45 acres of land for $185,000. The land contained stone that Oxford will remove from the ground, finish, and then sell as facing material for buildings. Oxford spent $435,000 preparing the quarry for operation. Oxford estimates that the quarry contains 55,000 tons of usable stone and that it will require six years to remove all the usable stone once quarrying begins. Upon completion of quarrying, Oxford estimates that the land will have a residual value of $11,150. During the current year, Oxford extracted 8,500 tons of stone.

Required:
1. Compute the depletion rate per ton.
2. Prepare the journal entry to record the extraction of the stone.

Exercise 7-55 Depletion of Timber

OBJECTIVE 10

Bedford Ridge Development purchased a 5,000-acre tract of forested land in southern Georgia. The tract contained about 1,440,000 pine trees that, when mature, can be used for utility poles. Bedford paid $900 per acre for the timberland. The land has a residual value of $180 per acre when all the trees are harvested. During 2011, Bedford harvested 150,000 trees.

Required:
1. Compute the depletion per tree.
2. Prepare the journal entry to record the harvesting of the trees for 2011.

Exercise 7-56 (Appendix 7A) Impairment

OBJECTIVE 11

On January 1, 2004, the Key West Company acquired a pie-making machine for $75,000. The machine was expected to have a useful life of 10 years with no residual value. Key West uses the straight-line depreciation method. On January 1, 2011, due to technological changes in the bakery industry, Key West believed that the asset might be impaired. Key West estimates the machine will generate net cash flows of $12,000 and has a current fair value of $10,000.

Required:
1. What is the book value of the machine on January 1, 2011?
2. Compute the loss related to the impairment.
3. Prepare the journal entry necessary to record the impairment of the machine.

PROBLEM SET A

Problem 7-57A Financial Statement Presentation of Operating Assets

OBJECTIVE 1

Olympic Acquisitions Inc. prepared the following post-closing trial balance at December 31, 2011:

	Debit	Credit
Cash	$ 5,400	
Accounts Receivable	16,200	
Supplies	25,800	
Land	42,350	
Buildings	155,900	
Equipment	278,650	
Truck	31,100	
Franchise	49,600	
Goodwill	313,500	
Natural resources	94,600	
Accounts Payable		$ 4,250
Accumulated Depreciation, Buildings		112,000
Accumulated Depreciation, Equipment		153,000
Accumulated Depreciation, Truck		16,300
Wages Payable		6,850
Interest Payable		7,125
Income Taxes Payable		12,125
Notes Payable (due in 8 years)		185,550
Common Stock		304,500
Retained Earnings		211,400
Totals	$1,013,100	$1,013,100

Required:

Prepare a classified balance sheet for Olympic at December 31, 2011. (*Note*: Olympic reports the three categories of operating assets in separate subsections of assets.)

Problem 7-58A Cost of a Fixed Asset

OBJECTIVE 2

Mist City Car Wash purchased a new brushless car-washing machine for one of its bays. The machine cost $32,300. Mist City borrowed the purchase price from its bank on a one-year, 8 percent note payable. Mist City paid $1,250 to have the machine transported to its place of business

(*Continued*)

and an additional $275 in shipping insurance. Mist City incurred the following costs as a part of the installation:

Plumbing	$2,700
Electrical	1,640
Water (for testing the machine)	35
Soap (for testing the machine)	18

During the testing process, one of the motors became defective when soap and water entered the motor because its cover had not been installed properly by Mist City's employees. The motor was replaced at a cost of $450.

Required:
1. Compute the cost of the car-washing machine.
2. **Conceptual Connection:** Explain why any costs were excluded from the cost of the machine.

OBJECTIVE

Problem 7-59A Depreciation Methods

Hansen Supermarkets purchased a radio frequency identification (RFID) system for one of its stores at a cost of $130,000. Hansen determined that the system had an expected life of eight years (or 50,000,000 items scanned) and an expected residual value of $6,000.

Required:
1. Determine the amount of depreciation expense for the first and second years of the system's life using the (a) straight-line and (b) double-declining-balance depreciation methods.
2. If the number of items scanned the first and second years were 7,200,000 and 8,150,000, respectively, compute the amount of depreciation expense for the first and second years of the system's life using the units-of-production depreciation method.
3. Compute the book values for all three depreciation methods as of the end of the first and second years of the system's life.
4. **Conceptual Connection:** What factors might management consider when selecting among depreciation methods?

OBJECTIVE

Problem 7-60A Depreciation Schedules

Wendt Corporation acquired a new depreciable asset for $94,000. The asset has a four-year expected life and a residual value of zero.

Required:
1. Prepare a depreciation schedule for all four years of the asset's expected life using the straight-line depreciation method.
2. Prepare a depreciation schedule for all four years of the asset's expected life using the double-declining-balance depreciation method.
3. **Conceptual Connection:** What questions should be asked about this asset to decide which depreciation method to use?

OBJECTIVE

Problem 7-61A Expenditures After Acquisition

Pasta, a restaurant specializing in fresh pasta, installed a pasta cooker in early 2009 at a cost of $12,400. The cooker had an expected life of five years and a residual value of $900 when installed. As the restaurant's business increased, it became apparent that renovations would be necessary so the cooker's output could be increased. In January 2012, Pasta spent $8,200 to install new heating equipment and $4,100 to add pressure-cooking capability. After these renovations, Pasta estimated that the remaining useful life of the cooker was 10 years and that the residual value was now $1,500.

Required:
1. Compute one year's straight-line depreciation expense on the cooker before the renovations.
2. Assume that three full years of straight-line depreciation expense had been recorded on the cooker before the renovations were made. Compute the book value of the cooker immediately after the renovations were made.
3. Compute one year's straight-line depreciation expense on the renovated cooker.

Problem 7-62A Repair Decision

OBJECTIVE 5

Clermont Transit operates a summer ferry service to islands in the Ohio River. Farmers use the ferry to move farming equipment to and from the islands. Clermont's ferry is in need of repair. A new engine and steering assembly must be installed, or the Coast Guard will not permit the ferry to be used. Because of competition, Clermont will not be able to raise its rates for ferry service if these repairs are made. Costs of providing the ferry service will not be decreased if the repairs are made.

Required:

1. Identify the factors that Clermont should consider when evaluating whether or not to make the repairs.
2. **Conceptual Connection:** Since the revenue rate cannot be increased and costs will not be decreased if the repairs are made, can the cost of the repairs be capitalized? Why or why not?

Problem 7-63A Disposition of Fixed Assets

OBJECTIVE 7

In order to provide capital for new hotel construction in other locations, Wilton Hotel Corporation has decided to sell its hotel in Pierre, South Dakota. Wilton auctions the hotel and its contents on October 1, 2011, with the following results:

Land	$600,000
Building	225,000
Furniture	120,000

Wilton's accounting records reveal the following information about the assets sold:

Asset	Acquisition Cost	Accumulated Depreciation
Land	$ 55,000	
Building	350,000	$155,000
Furniture	285,500	133,000

Required:

1. Prepare a separate journal entry to record the disposition of each of these assets.
2. **Conceptual Connection:** Explain how the disposals of the fixed assets above would affect the current period financial statements.

Problem 7-64A Natural Resource and Intangible Accounting

OBJECTIVE 9 10

McLeansboro Oil Company acquired a small oil company with only three assets during a recent year. The assets were acquired for $1,350,000 cash.

Asset	Fair Value	Expected Life
Oil	$1,125,000	55,000 barrels
Land	78,000	Indefinite
Equipment	62,000	550,000 barrels

Required:

1. Record the entry to record this acquisition in McLeansboro's journal. (*Hint:* Record the cost in excess of fair value as goodwill.)
2. If McLeansboro pumps and sells 11,000 barrels of oil in one year, compute the amount of depletion.
3. Prepare journal entries to record depletion for the 11,000 barrels of oil pumped and sold.
4. **Conceptual Connection:** Is the goodwill amortized? Explain your reasoning.
5. **Conceptual Connection:** Why are the land and the equipment capitalized separately from the oil well?

Problem 7-65A Accounting for Intangible Assets

OBJECTIVE 9

On January 1, 2005, Technocraft Inc. acquired a patent that was used for manufacturing semi-conductor-based electronic circuitry. The patent was originally recorded in Techno-craft's ledger at its cost of $1,596,000. Technocraft has been amortizing the patent using the straight-line method over an expected economic life of 10 years. Residual value was assumed to be zero. Technocraft sued another company for infringing on its patent. On January 1, 2012, Technocraft spent $122,500 on this suit and won a judgment to recover the $122,500 plus damages of $500,000. The sued company paid the $622,500.

(Continued)

Required:

1. Compute and record amortization expense on the patent for 2011 (prior to the lawsuit).
2. Prepare the necessary journal entry on January 1, 2012, to record the expenditure of $122,500 to defend the patent.
3. Prepare the journal entry to record the award of $622,500 on January 1, 2012.
4. Indicate the entry you would have made had Technocraft lost the suit. (*Note:* Assume that the patent would be valueless if Technocraft had lost the suit.)

 5. What are the financial statement effects of capitalizing or expensing the cost of defending the patent?

PROBLEM SET B

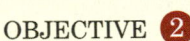

Problem 7-57B Financial Statement Presentation of Operating Assets

Athens Inc. prepared the following post-closing trial balance at December 31, 2011:

	Debit	Credit
Cash	$ 3,325	
Accounts Receivable	27,975	
Prepaid Insurance	8,350	
Land	21,150	
Buildings	305,520	
Equipment	126,310	
Patent	9,970	
Goodwill	42,400	
Natural resources	134,800	
Accounts Payable		$ 7,775
Accumulated Depreciation, Buildings		101,950
Accumulated Depreciation, Equipment		47,875
Unearned Revenue		9,825
Interest Payable		3,625
Income Taxes Payable		17,150
Notes Payable (due in 10 years)		170,000
Common Stock		125,000
Retained Earnings		196,600
Totals	$679,800	$679,800

Required:

Prepare a classified balance sheet for Athens at December 31, 2011. (*Note:* Athens reports the three categories of operating assets in separate subsections of assets.)

Problem 7-58B Cost of a Fixed Asset

Metropolis Country Club purchased a new tractor to be used for golf course maintenance. The tractor cost $53,800. Metropolis borrowed the purchase price from its bank on a one-year, 7 percent note payable. Metropolis incurred the following costs:

Shipping costs	$875
Shipping insurance	150
Calibration of cutting height	83

Required:

1. Compute the cost of the tractor.
2. **Conceptual Connection:** Explain why any costs were excluded from the cost of the tractor.

Problem 7-59B Depreciation Methods

Graphic Design Inc. purchased a state-of-the-art laser engraving machine for $94,500. Parker determined that the system had an expected life of 10 years (or 2,000,000 items engraved) and an expected residual value of $5,400.

Required:

1. Determine the amount of depreciation expense for the first and second years of the machine's life using the (a) straight-line and (b) double-declining-balance depreciation methods.

2. If the number of items engraved the first and second years was 220,000 and 180,000, respectively, compute the amount of depreciation expense for the first and second years of the machine's life using the units-of-production depreciation method.
3. Compute the book values for all three depreciation methods as of the end of the first and second years of the system's life.
4. **Conceptual Connection:** What factors might management consider when selecting among depreciation methods?

Problem 7-60B Depreciation Schedules

OBJECTIVE

Dunn Corporation acquired a new depreciable asset for $135,000. The asset has a five-year expected life and a residual value of zero.

Required:

1. Prepare a depreciation schedule for all five years of the asset's expected life using the straight-line depreciation method.
2. Prepare a depreciation schedule for all five years of the asset's expected life using the double-declining-balance depreciation method.
3. **Conceptual Connection:** What questions should be asked about this asset to decide which depreciation method to use?

Problem 7-61B Expenditures After Acquisition

OBJECTIVE

Murray's Fish Market, a store that specializes in providing fresh fish to the Nashville, Tennessee, area, installed a new refrigeration unit in early 2009 at a cost of $27,500. The refrigeration unit has an expected life of eight years and a residual value of $500 when installed. As the fish market's business increased, it became apparent that renovations were necessary so that the capacity of the refrigeration unit could be increased. In January 2012, Murray's spent $18,785 to install an additional refrigerated display unit (that was connected to the original unit) and replace the refrigeration coils. After this addition and renovation, Murray's Fish Market estimated that the remaining useful life of the original refrigeration unit was 12 years and that the residual value was now $1,000.

Required:

1. Compute one year's straight-line depreciation expense on the refrigeration unit before the addition and renovations.
2. Assume that three full years of straight-line depreciation expense were recorded on the refrigeration unit before the addition and renovations were made. Compute the book value of the refrigeration unit immediately after the renovations were made.
3. Compute one year's straight-line depreciation expense on the renovated refrigeration unit.

Problem 7-62B Remodeling Decision

OBJECTIVE

Ferinni Company operates a travel agency out of a historic building in Smalltown. Ferinni's CEO believes that the building needs to be remodeled in order to reach a wider customer base. The CEO proposes building a new entry that would be adjacent to Main Street in order to attract more foot traffic. The current entry faces a parking deck at the rear of the building and is easily overlooked by customers. The new entry will require the rearrangement of several offices inside the building. Because of competition from Internet travel sites, Ferinni will not be able to raise rates for its travel service after the remodeling is made.

Required:

1. Identify the factors that Ferinni should consider when evaluating whether to remodel the building.
2. **Conceptual Connection:** Since the revenue rate cannot be increased, can the cost of the remodeling be capitalized? Why or why not?

Problem 7-63B Disposition of Operating Assets

OBJECTIVE 7

Salva Pest Control disposed of four assets recently. Salva's accounting records provided the following information about the assets at the time of their disposal:

(Continued)

Asset	Cost	Accumulated Depreciation
Pump	$ 6,200	$ 4,800
Truck	18,600	17,500
Furniture	4,200	3,850
Chemical testing apparatus	6,800	4,000

The truck was sold for $2,450 cash, and the chemical testing apparatus was donated to the local high school. Because the pump was contaminated with pesticides, $500 in cash was paid to a chemical disposal company to decontaminate the pump and dispose of it safely. The furniture was taken to the local landfill.

Required:

1. Prepare a separate journal entry to record the disposition of each of these assets.
2. **Conceptual Connection:** Explain how the disposals of the fixed assets would affect the current period financial statements.

OBJECTIVE

Problem 7-64B Natural Resource and Intangible Accounting

In 2004, the Mudcat Gas Company purchased a small natural gas company with two assets—land and natural gas reserves—for $158,000,000. The fair value of the land was $1,500,000 and the fair value of the natural gas reserves was $155,250,000. At that time, estimated recoverable gas was 105,000,000 cubic feet.

Required:

1. Record the entry to record this acquisition in Mudcat's journal. (*Hint*: Record any cost in excess of fair value as goodwill.)
2. If Mudcat recovers and sells 2,500,000 cubic feet in one year, compute the depletion.
3. Prepare journal entries to record depletion for the 2,500,000 cubic feet of natural gas recovered and sold.
4. **Conceptual Connection:** Is the goodwill amortized? Explain your reasoning.
5. **Conceptual Connection:** Why is the land capitalized separately from the natural gas reserves?

OBJECTIVE

Problem 7-65B Accounting for Intangible Assets

Blackford and Medford Publishing Company own the copyrights on many top authors. In 2012, Blackford and Medford acquired the copyright on the literary works of Susan Monroe, an underground novelist in the 1960s, for $725,000 cash. Due to a recent resurgence of interest in the 1960s, the copyright has an estimated economic life of eight years. The residual value is estimated to be zero.

Required:

1. Prepare a journal entry to record the acquisition of the copyright.
2. Compute and record the 2012 amortization expense for the copyright.

CASES

Case 7-66 Ethics, Internal Controls, and the Capitalization Decision

James Sage, an assistant controller in a large company, has a friend and former classmate, Henry Cactus, who sells computers. Sage agrees to help Cactus get part of the business that has been going to a large national computer manufacturer for many years. Sage knows that the controller would not approve a shift away from the national supplier but believes that he can authorize a number of small orders for equipment that will escape the controller's notice. Company policy requires that all capital expenditures be approved by a management committee; however, expenditures under $2,000 are considered expenses and are subject to much less scrutiny. The assistant controller orders four computers to be used in a distant branch office. In order to keep the size of the order down, he makes four separate orders over a period of several months.

Required:

1. What are the probable consequences of this behavior for the company? For the assistant controller?
2. Describe internal control procedures that would be effective in discouraging and detecting this kind of behavior.

Case 7-67 Management's Depreciation Decision

Great Basin Enterprises, a large holding company, acquired North Spruce Manufacturing, a medium-sized manufacturing business, from its founder, who wishes to retire. Despite great potential for development, North Spruce's income has been dropping in recent years. Great Basin has installed a new management group (including a new controller, Christie Carmichael) at North Spruce and has given the group six years to expand and revitalize the operations. Management compensation includes a bonus based on net income generated by the North Spruce operations. If North Spruce does not show considerable improvement by the end of the sixth year, Great Basin will consider selling it. The new management immediately makes significant investments in new equipment but finds that new revenues develop slowly. Most of the new equipment will be replaced in 8 to 10 years. To defer income taxes to the maximum extent, Ms. Carmichael uses accelerated depreciation methods and the minimum allowable "expected lives" for the new equipment, which average 5 years. In preparing financial statements, Ms. Carmichael uses the straight-line depreciation method and expected lives that average 12 years for the new equipment.

Required:

1. Why did the controller compute depreciation expense on the financial statements as she did?
2. What are the possible consequences of the controller's decision on the amount of depreciation expense shown on the financial statements if this decision goes unchallenged?

Case 7-68 The Effect of Estimates of Life and Residual Value on Depreciation Expense

Hattiesburg Manufacturing purchased a new computer-integrated system to manufacture a group of fabricated metal and plastic products. The equipment was purchased from Bessemer Systems at a cost of $550,000. As a basis for determining annual depreciation expense, Hattiesburg's controller requests estimates of the expected life and residual value for the new equipment. The engineering and production departments submit the following divergent estimates:

	Engineering Department Estimates	Production Department Estimates
Expected life	10 years	8 years
Residual value	$90,000	0

Before considering depreciation expense for the new equipment, Hattiesburg Manufacturing has net income in the amount of $250,000. Hattiesburg uses the straight-line method of depreciation.

Required:

1. Compute a full year's depreciation expense for the new equipment, using each of the two sets of estimates.
2. Ignoring income taxes, what will be the effect on net income of including a full year's depreciation expense based on the engineering estimates? Based on the production estimates?
3. If a business has a significant investment in depreciable assets, the expected life and residual value estimates can materially affect depreciation expense and therefore net income. What might motivate management to use the highest or lowest estimates? How would cash outflows for income taxes be affected by the estimates?

Case 7-69 Research & Analysis Using the Annual Report

Obtain **Verizon Communications, Inc.**'s 2009 annual report either through the "Investor Relations" portion of their website (do a web search for Verizon Communications investor relations) or go to http://www.sec.gov and click "Search for Company Filings" under "Filings & Forms."

Required:

1. What method of depreciation does Verizon use? What are the typical useful lives of Verizon's operating assets?
2. What is the cost of Verizon's property, plant, and equipment on December 31, 2009? List the major components of Verizon's property, plant, and equipment.
3. What amount of accumulated depreciation is associated with property, plant, and equipment as of December 31, 2009?

(Continued)

4. Refer to the statement of cash flows:

    a. What is the amount of depreciation and amortization expense reported for each of the last three years?
    b. How much did Verizon spend on the acquisition of operating assets (capital expenditures) in each of the last three years?
    c. How much property, plant, and equipment was disposed of in 2009? (*Hint:* Also refer to the balance sheet.)
    d. Is the change in depreciation and amortization expense consistent with the pattern of capital expenditures observed? Why or why not? (*Hint:* Also refer to Note 2.)

5. What is the change in accumulated depreciation for the most recent year? Is this change explained by the depreciation and amortization expense reported? If not, what other items might cause accumulated depreciation to change?
6. Describe Verizon's capital expenditure plans for the future. (*Hint:* Refer to the Management Discussion and Analysis section.)
7. Explain Verizon's accounting policy with regard to intangible assets. (*Hint:* Refer to Note 1.)
8. List the types of intangible assets that Verizon possesses. What is Verizon's largest intangible asset?

Case 7-70 Comparative Analysis: Abercrombie & Fitch versus Aeropostale

Refer to the financial statements of **Abercrombie & Fitch** and **Aeropostale** that are supplied with this text.

Required:

1. With regard to depreciation methods:

    a. What depreciation method does Abercrombie & Fitch use? What depreciation method does Aeropostale use?
    b. What are the typical useful lives of each company's operating assets?
    c. What effect will the useful lives have on the company's financial statements?

2. Refer to the statement of cash flows:

    a. What is the amount of depreciation and amortization expense that each company reported for the three years presented?
    b. How much did each company spend on the acquisition of operating assets (capital expenditures) in each of the last three years?
    c. Is the change in depreciation and amortization expense consistent with the pattern of capital expenditures observed? Why or why not?

3. Compute the fixed asset turnover and the average age of fixed assets for each company. What conclusions can you draw from these ratios?

Case 7-71 CONTINUING PROBLEM: FRONT ROW ENTERTAINMENT

After a successful first year, Cam and Anna decide to expand Front Row Entertainment's operations by becoming a venue operator as well as a tour promoter. A venue operator contracts with promoters to rent the venue (which can range from amphitheaters to indoor arenas to nightclubs) for specific events on specific dates. In addition to receiving revenue from renting the venue, venue operators also provide services such as concessions, parking, security, and ushering services. By vertically integrating their business, Cam and Anna can reduce the expense that they pay to rent venues. In addition, they will generate additional revenue by providing services to other tour promoters.

After a little investigation, Cam and Anna locate a small venue operator that owns The Chicago Music House, a small indoor arena with a rich history in the music industry. The current owner has experienced severe health issues and has let the arena fall into a state of disrepair. However, he would like the arena to be preserved and its musical legacy to continue. After a short negotiation, on January 1, 2012, Front Row Entertainment purchases the venue by paying $10,000 in cash and signing a 15-year 10 percent note for $380,000. In addition, Front Row Entertainment purchases the right to use the "Chicago Music House" name for $25,000.

During the month of January 2012, Front Row Entertainment incurred the following expenditures as they renovated the arena and prepared it for the first major event scheduled for February.

Jan. 5 Paid $21,530 to repair damage to the roof of the arena.
    10 Paid $45,720 to remodel the stage area.
    21 Purchased concessions equipment (e.g., popcorn poppers, soda machines) for $12,350.

Renovations were completed on January 28, and the first concert was held in the arena on February 1. The arena is expected to have a useful life of 30 years and a residual value of $35,000. The concessions equipment will have a useful life of 5 years and a residual value of $250.

Required:
1. Prepare the journal entries to record the acquisition of the arena, the concessions equipment, and the trademark.
2. Prepare the journal entries to record the expenditures made in January.
3. Compute and record the depreciation for 2012 (11 months) on the arena (use the straight-line method) and on the concessions equipment (use the double-declining-balance method). Round all answers to the nearest dollar.
4. Would amortization expense be recorded for the trademark? Why or why not?

MAKING THE CONNECTION
INTEGRATIVE EXERCISE

Integrating Asset Accounting

Obtain **Under Armour**'s 2009 10-K (filed February 25, 2010) either through the "Investor Relations" portion of their website (do a web search for "Under Armour Investor Relations") or go to http://www.sec.gov and click "Search for Company Filings" under "Filings & Forms."

Required:
Using Under Armour's 10-K answer the following questions:

1. Looking at Note 2 (*Summary of Significant Accounting Policies*), how does Under Armour define cash equivalents?

2. Looking at the "Report of Independent Registered Public Accounting Firm" (p. 44 of the 10-K), did Under Armour maintain effective internal control over financial reporting? What criteria were used to evaluate the effectiveness of these controls?

3. What was Under Armour's accounts receivable turnover (rounded to two decimal places) in 2008 and 2009? (Accounts receivable were $93,515 at the end of 2007.) Assuming the industry average for 2009 was 4.63, describe Under Armour's relative efficiency with their accounts receivable.

4. What was Under Armour's inventory turnover (rounded to two decimal places) in 2008 and 2009? (Inventories were $166,082 at the end of 2007.) Assuming the industry average for 2009 was 0.89, describe Under Armour's relative efficiency with their inventory.

5. Describe the trend in Under Armour's accounts receivable and inventory turnover.

6. How many days' sales does Under Armour have in receivables and inventory for 2008 and 2009? (When added together this is their operating cycle.) (*Note:* Round all answers to two decimal places.)

7. **Conceptual Connection:** Assuming 10% interest, how much interest expense did Under Armour save by improving their accounts receivable and inventory turnover?

8. What were Under Armour's gross profit, operating margin, and net profit ratios in 2009? (*Note:* Round answers to two decimal places.) Assuming industry averages for 2009 were 15.71%, 4.37%, and 3.17%, respectively, describe Under Armour's profitability.

9. Looking at Note 2 (*Summary of Significant Accounting Policies*) what method of depreciation does Under Armour use? What is the useful life of furniture and office equipment? Do you think this useful life is appropriate?

8

Current and Contingent Liabilities

Doug Norman Crystals/Alamy

After studying Chapter 8, you should be able to:

1. Explain liability recognition and measurement criteria.
2. Identify and record the kinds of activities that produce current liabilities.
3. Describe contingent liabilities and the alternatives for their recognition and measurement.
4. Measure warranty liabilities and warranty expense.
5. Analyze liquidity ratios using information contained in the current liabilities section.

Jamie Richards/Alamy

EXPERIENCE FINANCIAL ACCOUNTING

with Ruth's Chris Steak House

Ruth's Chris Steak House was founded in 1965 when Ruth Fertel mortgaged her home for $33,000 to purchase the "Chris Steak House," a 60-seat restaurant located near the New Orleans Fair Grounds racetrack. Today this brand is considered one of the top restaurants in the world with revenues of over $300 million. Interestingly, in 2009 $43.3 million worth of gift cards were sold. Gift cards have become a popular holiday gift among business professionals. According to the National Retail Federation, gift cards are the most requested holiday item with $23.6 billion spent on holiday gift cards in 2009.

Dan Perelz, 2010/Shutterstock.com

Further, restaurants are the second most popular category.

As you will learn in this chapter, Ruth's Chris has a liability (unearned revenues) related to the sale of gift cards until the meal is provided. That is, gift-card revenue should not be recognized until the services (in this case, a meal) are provided. Gift card revenue should not be recognized until the card is redeemed (for goods or services) and therefore, Ruth's Chris would not expect to see the revenue benefit from this transaction immediately. Generally this would occur within eighteen months after the gift card was purchased.

CURRENT AND CONTINGENT LIABILITIES

Chapters 4, 5, 6, and 7 explained accounting and reporting for assets. Now we will move to the other side of the balance sheet and discuss liabilities and equity, which are the sources of cash and other financial resources used to acquire assets. We begin by examining liabilities.

Finding potential creditors, arranging attractive credit terms, structuring borrowings with lenders, and arranging to have enough cash coming in to pay the liabilities as they come due is one of the most important managerial functions. The result of liability management and the accounting recognition, measurement, and reporting issues for those activities appears in the liabilities portion of the balance sheet. The information provided by **Live Nation Entertainment** in its 2009 balance sheet is typical:

Live Nation Entertainment Consolidated Balance Sheets (Partial) (in thousands) December 31, 2009	
LIABILITIES	
	2009
Current liabilities:	
Accounts payable	$ 50,844
Accrued expenses	357,138
Deferred revenue	284,536
Current portion of long-term debt	41,032
Other current liabilities	18,684
Total current liabilities	$752,234
Long-term debt, net of discount	699,037
Other long-term liabilities	125,047

Naturally, existing and potential creditors also find this information useful as they want to know about the obligations management has assumed.

In this chapter and the next we discuss the three kinds of business obligations: current liabilities, contingent liabilities, and long-term debt. Current liabilities are those obligations that are (1) expected to be retired with existing current assets or creation of new current liabilities, and (2) due within one year or one operating cycle, whichever is longer. All other liabilities are considered long-term. Contingent liabilities can be either current or long-term, but they are "iffy" in two ways. They may or may not turn into actual obligations and, for those contingencies that do become obligations, the timing and amount of the required payment is uncertain. In this chapter we focus on current and contingent liabilities and address the following questions:

- When are liabilities recognized?
- How are liabilities measured?
- What kinds of activities produce current liabilities and how are they recorded in the accounting records?
- What are contingent liabilities and how are they recorded in the accounting records?
- How do you measure and record warranty liabilities?

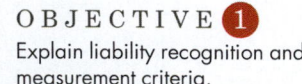

OBJECTIVE 1
Explain liability recognition and measurement criteria.

RECOGNITION AND MEASUREMENT OF LIABILITIES

Liabilities are probable future sacrifices of economic benefits. These commitments, which arise from activities that have already occurred, require the business to transfer assets or provide services to another entity sometime in the future. For example, an account payable arises from a transaction in which the business receives goods or services in return for a cash payment at some future time.

Within this general definition, liabilities have a wide variety of characteristics, as shown in Exhibit 8-1:

Exhibit 8-1

Characteristics of Liabilities

 *Payment of cash*:
Although liabilities frequently require the payment of cash, some may require the transfer of assets other than cash, or the performance of services.

 Certainty:
Although the exact amount and timing of future payments are usually known, for some liabilities they may not be.

 Legal enforceability:
Although many liabilities are legally enforceable claims, some may represent merely *probable* claims.

 Payment recipient:
Although liabilities usually identify the entity to be paid, the definition does not exclude payment to unknown recipients.

Thus, the future outflow associated with a liability may or may not involve the payment of cash; may or may not be known with certainty; may or may not be legally enforceable; and may or may not be payable to a known recipient.

Recognition of Liabilities

Most liabilities are recognized when goods or services are received or money is borrowed (see Exhibit 8-2). When a liability depends on a future event (i.e., a **contingent liability**), such as the outcome of a lawsuit, recognition depends on how likely the occurrence of the event is and whether a good estimate of the payment amount can be made. If the future payment is judged to be less than likely to occur or the payment is not estimable, the obligation should not be recognized. Such obligations may require disclosure in footnotes to the financial statements, as explained later in this chapter.

Measurement of Liabilities

We all know that when you owe money you typically pay interest. That is, if you borrow $100 at 10 percent interest, then when you pay it back one year later you must repay $110:

$$\text{Total payment} = \text{Principal} + (\text{Principal} \times \text{Interest Rate} \times \text{Period})$$
$$= \$100 + (\$100 \times 10\% \times 12/12)$$

Exhibit 8-2

Recognition of Current Liabilities

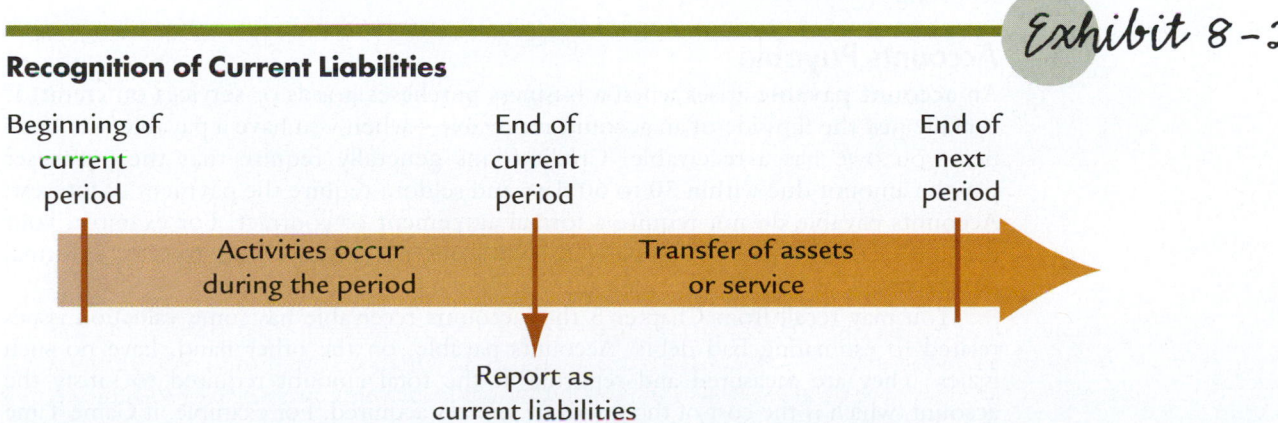

Sometimes companies will appear to give you a zero percent interest loan. For example, furniture and electronics retailers frequently advertise "no interest, no money down for 12 months" or some such terms. Of course, we know this really means that the "interest" is included in the sales price because no business is going to truly provide zero percent interest.

In theory, the amount of the liability reported on the balance sheet should not include any interest that has not yet occurred. For example, on a balance sheet prepared six months after borrowing the $100 at 10 percent interest described above, you should report a liability of $105:

$$\$100 + (\$100 \times 10\% \times 6/12)$$

However, many liabilities are more like your credit card or utilities bill. For example, you might owe your power company $150 for the use of electricity during September. You likely do not receive this bill until sometime during October and you do not have to pay it until near the end of November. Further, there appears to be no interest because you owe $150 whether you pay the bill when you receive it in October or wait until the November due date.

Despite the apparent lack of interest, theoretically interest exists. Consequently, in theory we should calculate the interest on such liabilities. For example, if we made a balance sheet at the end of September, then a liability for the power company should be calculated to exclude the theoretical interest included in the $150 payment at the end of November (i.e., two months interest at the market rate). Fortunately, we ignore the interest for most current liabilities because the amount of interest is relatively small. So most current liabilities are simply recorded and reported at the total amount owed, as we will see in the next section.

OBJECTIVE 2
Identify and record the kinds of activities that produce current liabilities.

IFRS
IFRS commonly reports current liabilities in reverse order relative to U.S. GAAP – from least liquid to most liquid.

CURRENT LIABILITIES

Current liabilities are obligations that require the firm to pay cash or another current asset, create a new current liability, or provide goods or services within the longer of one year or one operating cycle. Since most firms have operating cycles shorter than one year, the one-year rule usually applies.

Some firms combine their current liabilities into a very short list, while others provide considerable detail. Exhibit 8-3 compares the current liabilities sections of the balance sheets for two airlines—**Southwest** and **UAL** (**United Airlines**). Although it's reasonable to assume that both airlines have similar types of current liabilities, Southwest combines theirs into a relatively short list while UAL provides more detail. Further, UAL orders its individual current liabilities from largest to smallest (with "other" at the end), while Southwest appears to order its current liabilities in alphabetical order, or perhaps the order in which the liabilities will be paid (order of liquidity).

In the sections that follow we will briefly describe how various types of current liabilities arise, and the principles that underlie their recognition, measurement, and reporting.

Accounts Payable

An **account payable** arises when a business purchases goods or services on credit. It is really just the flip side of an account receivable—when you have a payable, the business you owe has a receivable. Credit terms generally require that the purchaser pay the amount due within 30 to 60 days and seldom require the payment of interest. Accounts payable do not require a formal agreement or contract. For example, your account with the power company usually does not require you to sign a formal contract.

You may recall from Chapter 5 that accounts receivable has some valuation issues related to estimating bad debts. Accounts payable, on the other hand, have no such issues. They are measured and reported at the total amount required to satisfy the account, which is the cost of the goods or services acquired. For example, if Game Time Sporting Goods buys and receives running shoes on May 15, 2011, for which it pays its supplier $2,000 on June 15, 2011, it would need to make the following journal entries:

Date	Account and Explanation	Debit	Credit
May 15	Inventory	2,000	
	Accounts Payable		2,000
	(Record purchase of inventory)		
June 15	Accounts Payable	2,000	
	Cash		2,000
	(Record payment to supplier)		

	Assets	= Liabilities +	Stockholders' Equity
	+2,000	+2,000	

	Assets	= Liabilities +	Stockholders' Equity
	−2,000	−2,000	

Exhibit 8-3

Current Liability Sections from Two Balance Sheets

Southwest Airlines Co.
Consolidated Balance Sheets
(in millions)

	December 31, 2009	December 31, 2008
Current liabilities:		
Accounts payable	$ 746	$ 668
Accrued liabilities	696	1,012
Air traffic liability	1,044	963
Current maturities of long-term debt	190	163
Total current liabilities	$2,676	$2,806

UAL Corporation
Statement of Consolidated Financial Position
(in millions)

	December 31	
	2009	2008
LIABILITIES AND SHAREHOLDERS' EQUITY		
Current liabilities:		
Mileage Plus deferred revenue	$1,515	$1,414
Advance ticket sales	1,492	1,530
Accounts payable	803	829
Accrued salaries, wages and benefits	701	756
Long-term debt maturing within one year	545	782
Current obligations under capital leases	426	168
Fuel purchase commitments	275	219
Fuel derivative instruments	5	718
Other	711	865
	$6,473	$7,281

Accrued Liabilities

Unlike accounts payable, which are recognized when goods or services change hands, **accrued liabilities** are recognized by adjusting entries. They usually represent the completed portion of activities that are in process at the end of the period. For example, Green's Landscaping pays wages of $10,000 (or $1,000 per work day) to its employees every other Friday. The standard entry is:

Date	Account and Explanation	Debit	Credit
Dec. 20	Wages Expense	10,000	
	Cash		10,000
	(Record payment of wages)		

	Assets	= Liabilities +	Stockholders' Equity
	−10,000		−10,000

What happens, however, when December 31 falls on the Tuesday before the Friday payday? In this case, the expense for the seven days that have already been worked (five days from last week and Monday and Tuesday of this week) must be matched to the proper period. Additionally, because the work has been performed but the employees have not yet been paid, Green's Landscaping has a liability to its employees. As such, on December 31 Green's would make the following adjusting entry:

	Assets	=	Liabilities	+	Stockholders' Equity
			+7,000		−7,000

Date	Account and Explanation	Debit	Credit
Dec. 31	Wages Expense	7,000	
	Wages Payable		7,000
	(Record accrual of wages expense)		

Further, when Green's pays $10,000 to its employees on January 3, three days' pay is an expense of the current year (Wednesday, January 1 through Friday, January 3) and seven days' pay retires the Wages Payable from December 31:

Assets	=	Liabilities	+	Stockholders' Equity
−10,000		−7,000		−3,000

Date	Account and Explanation	Debit	Credit
Jan. 3	Wages Expense	3,000	
	Wages Payable	7,000	
	Cash		10,000
	(Record payment of wages)		

This sort of process is used for a wide variety of activities that are completed over time. For example, taxes are paid on April 15 based on the previous year's net income. As such, on December 31 an adjusting entry will match the appropriate income taxes expense to the current year and set up a liability (income taxes payable) that will be paid off by April 15. The same logic applies to other similar situations, such as property taxes and interest expense.

Notes Payable

A **note payable** typically arises when a business borrows money or purchases goods or services from a company that requires a formal agreement or contract (like when you sign a contract to lease an apartment or buy a car). This formal agreement or contract is what distinguishes the note payable from an account payable. The agreement typically states the timing of repayment and the amount (principal and/or interest) to be repaid. Notes payable typically mature in anywhere from 3 to 12 months, but it can be longer (if it does not mature for over 12 months, it will be classified as a long-term liability). These longer maturities explain why creditors are more likely to impose interest on notes payable than with accounts payable.

Notes Payable from Borrowing from a Bank
Notes payable normally specify the amount to be repaid indirectly, by stating the amount borrowed (the principal) and an interest rate. These notes are called *interest-bearing notes* because they explicitly state an **interest rate**. The maturity amount of an interest-bearing note is not stated explicitly but is determined from the interest rate, the principal amount, and the maturity date.

When a business borrows using a short-term, interest-bearing note, the transaction is recorded at the amount borrowed. This is illustrated in **CORNERSTONE 8-1**.

 **CORNERSTONE 8-1**   **Recording Notes Payable and Accrued Interest**

Concept:
Notes payable are recognized when a business transfers assets (or provides services) to another entity at some point in the future for activities that have already occurred. Interest must be matched to the period in which it helped generate revenues.

Information:
Fitch Auto Parts borrowed $100,000 from a bank on October 1, 2011, at 10 percent interest. The interest and principal are due on October 1, 2012.

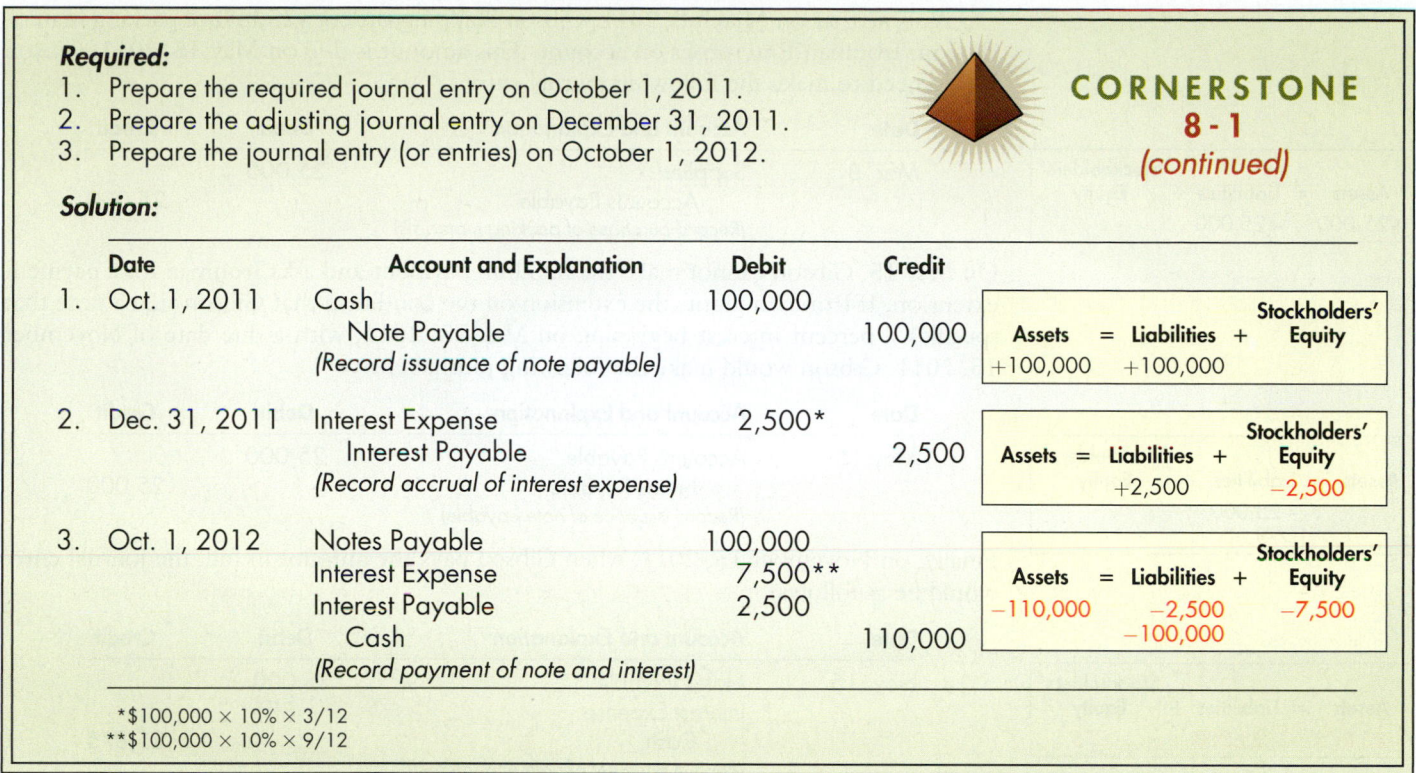

Required:
1. Prepare the required journal entry on October 1, 2011.
2. Prepare the adjusting journal entry on December 31, 2011.
3. Prepare the journal entry (or entries) on October 1, 2012.

CORNERSTONE
8-1
(continued)

Solution:

	Date	Account and Explanation	Debit	Credit
1.	Oct. 1, 2011	Cash	100,000	
		Note Payable		100,000
		(Record issuance of note payable)		
2.	Dec. 31, 2011	Interest Expense	2,500*	
		Interest Payable		2,500
		(Record accrual of interest expense)		
3.	Oct. 1, 2012	Notes Payable	100,000	
		Interest Expense	7,500**	
		Interest Payable	2,500	
		Cash		110,000
		(Record payment of note and interest)		

1.
	Assets	=	Liabilities	+	Stockholders' Equity
	+100,000		+100,000		

2.
	Assets	=	Liabilities	+	Stockholders' Equity
			+2,500		−2,500

3.
	Assets	=	Liabilities	+	Stockholders' Equity
	−110,000		−2,500		−7,500
			−100,000		

*$100,000 × 10% × 3/12
**$100,000 × 10% × 9/12

Exhibit 8-4 illustrates the financial statement effects of the transactions recorded in Cornerstone 8-1. Notice that the interest payment of $10,000 is recorded as interest expense of $2,500 in 2009 and $7,500 in 2010.

Effect of Borrowing Money on the Annual Income Statement and Balance Sheet

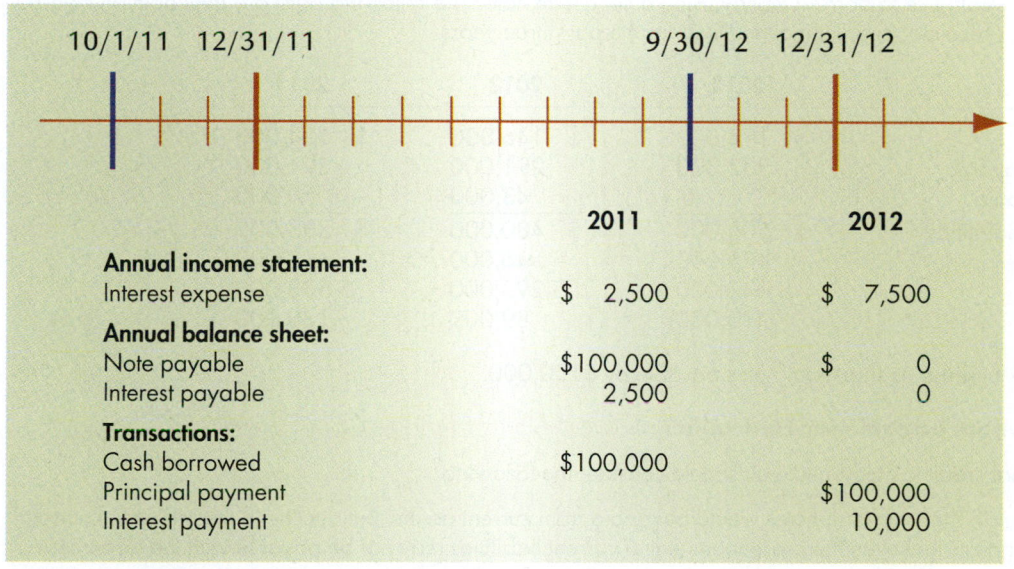

	2011	2012
Annual income statement:		
Interest expense	$ 2,500	$ 7,500
Annual balance sheet:		
Note payable	$100,000	$ 0
Interest payable	2,500	0
Transactions:		
Cash borrowed	$100,000	
Principal payment		$100,000
Interest payment		10,000

Notes Payable from a Payment Extension

In addition to short-term borrowings, notes payable are often created when a borrower is unable to pay an account payable in a timely manner. In this case, the borrower is typically granted a payment extension, but the creditor requires a formal note be signed to impose interest. As discussed, a current liability can be retired through creation of a new current liability. Rolling an account payable into a short-term note payable would be an example of this.

Assume that on March 8, 2011, Gibson Shipping orders $25,000 of packing materials from Ironman Enterprises on account. This amount is due on May 15, 2011. Gibson would need to make the following journal entry:

Date	Account and Explanation	Debit	Credit
Mar. 8	Supplies	25,000	
	Accounts Payable		25,000
	(Record purchase of packing materials)		

Assets	=	Liabilities	+	Stockholders' Equity
+25,000		+25,000		

On May 15, Gibson cannot make the $25,000 payment and asks Ironman for a payment extension. If Ironman grants the extension on the condition that Gibson sign a note that specifies 7 percent interest beginning on May 15, 2011, with a due date of November 15, 2011, Gibson would make the following journal entry:

Date	Account and Explanation	Debit	Credit
May 15	Accounts Payable	25,000	
	Notes Payable		25,000
	(Record issuance of note payable)		

Assets	=	Liabilities	+	Stockholders' Equity
		+25,000		
		−25,000		

Finally, on November 15, 2011, when Gibson pays the amount in full, the journal entry would be as follows:

Date	Account and Explanation	Debit	Credit
Nov. 15	Notes Payable	25,000	
	Interest Expense	875*	
	Cash		25,875
	(Record payment of note and interest)		

Assets	=	Liabilities	+	Stockholders' Equity
−25,875		−25,000		−875

*$25,000 × 7% × 6/12

YOU DECIDE   Making a Short-Term Loan

You are a commercial loan officer at National City Bank. Hydraulic Controls, a local manufacturer of hydraulic clutch assemblies for compact foreign and domestic automobiles, would like to borrow money using a short-term note. The following data are available on Hydraulic's current liabilities, current assets, sales revenue, and net income (loss) for the past three years:

Item	2013	2012	2011
Accounts payable	$ 174,000	$ 146,000	$ 104,000
Short-term notes payable	332,000	291,000	291,000
Income taxes payable	-0-	43,000	50,000
Total current liabilities	$ 506,000	$ 480,000	$ 383,000
Total current assets	485,000	546,000	611,000
Sales revenue	5,047,000	5,293,000	5,538,000
Net income (loss)	(10,000)	89,000	130,000

Hydraulic Controls has asked its bank to increase its short-term notes payable by $100,000.

Should you approve a short-term note payable for Hydraulic?

To determine whether to extend additional credit to Hydraulic, you should consider the following:

- *How will the short-term notes be repaid?* The short-term notes would be repaid from current assets. But decline in the amount of current assets relative to current liabilities suggests that even the present amount of current liabilities may not be payable with the resources currently available.
- *What might be causing the recent increases in current liabilities and decreases in current assets?* Because profitability is declining, the firm may not be able to borrow from outside sources or secure cash from operations. Therefore, it may be drawing down current assets and increasing current liabilities to provide capital.

The decline in profitability, the trend in the ratio of current assets to current liabilities, and the present excess of current liabilities over current assets suggest that it would be unwise to extend additional credit at this time.

Current Portion of Long-Term Debt

The current portion of long-term debt is the amount of long-term debt principal that is due within the next year. At the end of each accounting period, the long-term debt that is due during the next year is reclassified as a current liability (see Exhibit 8-3, p. 389). Since the reclassification of most long-term debt as current does not usually change the accounts or amounts involved, journal entries are not required. In some cases, long-term debt that is due within the next year will be paid with the proceeds of a new long-term debt issue. Remember that current liabilities must be retired with existing current assets or creation of new current liabilities—a new long-term debt issue is creation of a new *long-term*, not current, liability. When such refinancing is expected, the maturing obligation is not transferred to current liabilities but is left as a long-term debt.[1]

Other Payables

So far we have discussed accounts payable, accrued liabilities, and notes payable. However, businesses will have other current liabilities that do not fall into these categories. There are many situations that can give rise to these other payables, but we will restrict our discussion to some of the most common.

Sales Tax   At the time of a sale, most retail businesses collect **sales taxes**, usage taxes, or excise taxes for various state, local, and federal taxing authorities. These taxes, although collected as part of the total selling price, are not additions to revenue. Instead, they are money collected from the customer for the governmental unit levying the tax. These tax collections are liabilities until they are paid to the taxing authority. For example, businesses typically must remit sales tax collected to the state every quarter. **CORNERSTONE 8-2** illustrates the accounting for sales tax.

 **CORNERSTONE 8-2**   **Recording Liabilities at the Point of Sale**

Concept:
The law often requires companies to collect taxes from customers and remit them to a taxing authority.

Information:
During the first quarter of 2012, McLean County Tire sold, on credit, 3,000 truck tires at $75 each plus State of Illinois sales tax of 7 percent and City of Bloomington municipal taxes of 1 percent. These taxes are paid to the appropriate taxing authority each quarter.

Required:
Prepare the journal entry to record (1) first quarter sales and (2) payment of taxes to the appropriate taxing authority.

Solution:

	Date	Account and Explanation	Debit	Credit
1.	Mar. 31	Accounts Receivable	243,000	
		Sales Revenue		225,000*
		Sales Taxes Payable (State)		15,750**
		Sales Taxes Payable (City)		2,250***
		(Record sale of truck tires)		

Assets	=	Liabilities	+	Stockholders' Equity
+243,000		+15,750 +2,250		+225,000

*3,000 tires × $75
**3,000 tires × $75 × 7%
***3,000 tires × $75 × 1%

(Continued)

---

[1] We discuss long-term liabilities in more detail in Chapter 9.

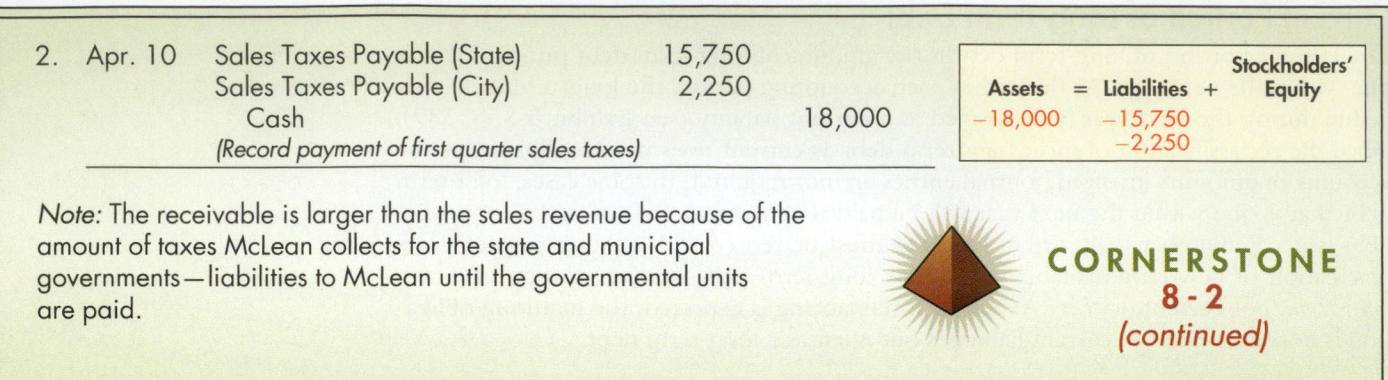

2.	Apr. 10	Sales Taxes Payable (State)	15,750	
		Sales Taxes Payable (City)	2,250	
		Cash		18,000
		(Record payment of first quarter sales taxes)		

Assets	= Liabilities	+ Stockholders' Equity
−18,000	−15,750	
	−2,250	

Note: The receivable is larger than the sales revenue because of the amount of taxes McLean collects for the state and municipal governments—liabilities to McLean until the governmental units are paid.

**CORNERSTONE
8-2
(continued)**

Withholding and Payroll Taxes Businesses are required to withhold taxes from employees' earnings and to pay taxes based on wages and salaries paid to employees. These **withholding** and **payroll taxes** are liabilities until they are paid to the taxing authority. Note that there are really two sources for these taxes: employees and businesses.

Employees Employees must pay certain taxes that are "withheld" from their paycheck. This is the difference between gross pay and net pay. The business does not have any rights to this money; instead, as with sales tax, they must pay these amounts to the proper authority. The standard withholdings are federal, state, and possibly city or county income taxes, as well as Social Security and Medicare. Employees may also have amounts withheld for such things as retirement accounts (e.g., 401-K), parking, and health insurance, among other things, but these are not taxes.

Businesses The business itself must pay certain taxes based on employee payrolls. These amounts are not withheld from employee pay; rather they are additional amounts that must be paid over and above gross pay. For example, employers match your contribution to Social Security and Medicare (together these are called FICA). That is, if you have $400 withheld from your paycheck for Social Security, your employer pays the federal government $800 related to your employment. Employers also pay federal and state unemployment taxes (these are used to fund unemployment benefits) based on their history of firing employees (because fired employees are eligible to collect unemployment benefits). Finally, employers do have other costs—typically called fringe benefits—associated with employees, but these are not taxes. Examples of fringe benefits include employer contributions to retirement accounts and health insurance. Exhibit 8-5 shows the obligations

Exhibit 8-5

Employer Payroll Taxes

Private industry employers (which excludes state and local government employers) break down as follows as of March 10, 2010:

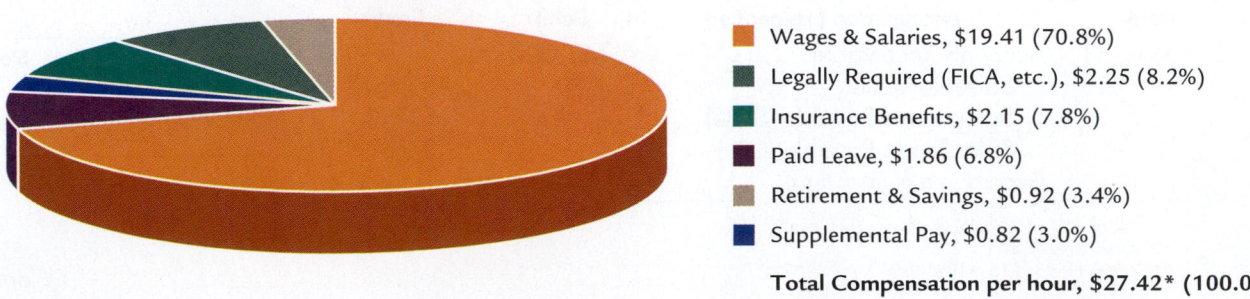

Wages & Salaries, $19.41 (70.8%)
Legally Required (FICA, etc.), $2.25 (8.2%)
Insurance Benefits, $2.15 (7.8%)
Paid Leave, $1.86 (6.8%)
Retirement & Savings, $0.92 (3.4%)
Supplemental Pay, $0.82 (3.0%)

Total Compensation per hour, $27.42* (100.0%)

*Difference from addition of individual expenditures due to rounding.
Source: Bureau of Labor Statistics; news release USDL-10-0283

most U.S. businesses have to pay taxes or withhold them from employee earnings, while
CORNERSTONE 8-3 illustrates the accounting for these obligations.

CORNERSTONE 8-3   Recording Payroll Taxes

Concept:
Employers not only withhold taxes from the employees' gross pay, but also pay amounts over and above gross pay.

Information:
Assume that McLean County Tire's hourly employees earned $48,500 in the pay period ending March 31. Income taxes withheld are $10,185. Additionally, a 3 percent state unemployment tax and a 0.8 percent federal unemployment tax are withheld.

Required:
1. Prepare the journal entry related to the gross pay earned by employees (assume no employees have reached their annual Social Security limit of $106,800).
2. Prepare the journal entry related to the payroll taxes on top of gross pay.

Solution:

Date	Account and Explanation	Debit	Credit
1. Mar. 31	Wages Expense	48,500.00	
	Income Taxes Payable		10,185.00
	Social Security Taxes Payable (Employee)		3,007.00[a]
	Medicare Taxes Payable (Employee)		703.25[b]
	Cash		34,604.75
	(Record wages and liabilities)		

Assets	=	Liabilities	+	Stockholders' Equity
34,604.75		+10,185.00		−48,500.00
		+3,007.00		
		+703.25		

Date	Account and Explanation	Debit	Credit
2.	Unemployment Taxes Expense (Federal)	388.00	
	Unemployment Taxes Expense (State)	1,455.00	
	Social Security Taxes Expense	3,007.00	
	Medicare Taxes Expense	703.25	
	Unemployment Taxes Payable (Federal)		388.00[c]
	Unemployment Taxes Payable (State)		1,455.00[d]
	Social Security Taxes Payable (Employer)		3,007.00[e]
	Medicare Taxes Payable (Employer)		703.25[f]
	(Record employer payroll taxes)		

Assets	=	Liabilities	+	Stockholders' Equity
		+388.00		388.00
		+1,455.00		−1,455.00
		+3,007.00		−3,007.00
		+703.25		−703.25

[a]$48,500 × 6.2%
[b]$48,500 × 1.45%
[c]$48,500 × 0.8%
[d]$48,500 × 3%
[e]$48,500 × 6.2%
[f]$48,500 × 1.45%

Note: The $48,500.00 payroll is (1) smaller than the total expense of $54,053.25 (i.e., the sum of expenses from both journal entries) and (2) larger than the $34,604.75 cash paid (i.e., net pay) to employees. In other words, the actual cost of an employee is more than his or her gross pay.

YOU DECIDE   Full-Time Employee or Consultant?

You are the HR manager of Berndt Chocolates. The marketing department wants to hire a full-time employee at an annual salary of approximately $52,000. They argue that this will save the company money because Berndt will no longer have to pay an outside marketing consultant approximately $60,000 per year to do the same job.

(Continued)

What factors should you consider in deciding whether to hire the full-time employee?

Businesses often must make the decision of whether to hire a full-time employee or pay a consultant. Of course, of primary concern is which person will perform the function better, but there are other factors to consider. Hiring a consultant can provide several advantages. First, a full-time employee will incur costs in addition to salary. For example, assuming federal and state unemployment tax rates totaling 3.5 percent, for a full-time employee earning $52,000, Berndt's payroll taxes will increase as follows:

Employer Payroll Taxes	Cost
OASDI (Social Security at 6.2%)	$3,224
Medicare (at 1.45%)	754
Federal and state unemployment (at 3.5%)	245
Total employer payroll taxes	$4,223

Further, most companies have some fringe benefits such as medical insurance, life insurance, retirement contributions and bonuses. Assuming these fringe benefits are 30 percent of the employee's annual salary, this employee would cost $71,823 [$52,000 + $4,223 + ($52,000 × 30%)] per year. Second, it is much easier and less costly to dramatically decrease or eliminate consultants than full-time employees.

Aside from qualifications, the costs of federal and state taxes and benefits should be considered when deciding whether to hire full-time employees.

Unearned Revenues **Unearned revenue** is the liability created when customers pay for goods or services in advance. In such instances, the amount of the prepayment is a liability for the seller. This liability is discharged either by providing the goods or services purchased (at which time revenue is recognized) or by refunding the amount of the prepayment.[2] **CORNERSTONE 8-4** illustrates the accounting for unearned revenues.

 **CORNERSTONE 8-4**   **Recording Unearned Revenues**

Concept:
When customers pay for goods or services in advance, the business recognizes a liability. The revenue is recognized at the time the goods or services are provided.

Information:
Jim's Steakhouse sells $100,000 of gift cards in December 2011. These gift cards may be redeemed at any time; however, they expire on December 31, 2012. During 2012, $98,875 of gift cards is redeemed.

Required:
1. Prepare the journal entry related to the sale of gift cards.
2. Prepare the journal entry related to redemption of the gift cards.
3. Prepare the journal entry related to the expiration of the remaining gift cards.

Solution:

	Date	Account and Explanation	Debit	Credit
1.	Dec. 2011	Cash	100,000	
		Unearned Sales Revenue		100,000
		(Record sale of gift cards)		

Assets	=	Liabilities	+	Stockholders' Equity
+100,000		+100,000		

(Continued)

---

[2] If the goods or services are not provided, the seller may also be liable for legal damages. The amount of such damages would be recorded as an expense.

						Assets	=	Liabilities	+	Stockholders' Equity

2.*	Dec. 31, 2012	Unearned Sales Revenue	98,875							
		Sales Revenue		98,875						
		(Record redemption of gift cards)						−98,875		+98,875

3.**	Dec. 31, 2012	Unearned Sales Revenue	1,125							
		Sales Revenue		1,125						
		(Record expiration of gift cards)						−1,125		+1,125

*These entries are made individually as each gift card is redeemed.

**When gift cards expire, the sales revenue is recognized because the business does not need to provide any additional goods or services.

CORNERSTONE 8-4
(continued)

A similar *long-term* liability, called *customer deposits*, is recorded when customers make advance payments or security deposits that are not expected to be earned or returned soon enough to qualify as current liabilities.

Cornerstone 8-4 demonstrates that revenue will not be recognized until it is realized (or realizable) and earned. Here, revenue is realized because the cash has been collected, so the first criterion is met; however, it is not earned until the goods or services are provided. Recall the chapter opener discussion of **Ruth's Chris Steak House** and how they sold $43.3 million in gift cards during 2009. This is how Ruth's Chris accounts for these gift cards.

Concept Q&A

Why is a liability recognized when a customer prepays for a good or service (i.e., an unearned revenue)?

Answer:
Liabilities are probable future sacrifices of economic benefits which arise from activities that have already occurred. Because the business here will provide the goods or services purchased by the customer at a future point, the prepayment is a liability.

CONTINGENT LIABILITIES

Measurement of the liabilities described so far was not affected by uncertainties about the amount, timing, or recipient of future asset outflows. However, such uncertainties exist. In financial accounting, a contingency is an "… existing condition, situation, or set of circumstances involving uncertainty" as to possible gain or loss.

A contingent liability is not recognized in the accounts unless

- the event on which it is contingent is probable and
- a reasonable estimate of the loss can be made.

If the contingent event is likely to occur, reliable measurement of the liability is usually possible, so recognition is appropriate. For example, contingent liabilities arising from product warranties and pensions are recognized because previous experience allows for reliable measurements to be made. On the other hand, if occurrence of the contingent event is not probable or reliable measurement of the obligation is impossible, the potential obligation is not recorded as a liability. Instead, as shown in Exhibit 8-6 (p. 398), it may be disclosed in footnotes to the financial statements.

Lawsuits filed against a business are a classic example of contingent liabilities. Most large companies are party to multiple lawsuits at any point in time. Estimating when a loss is probable and determining a reasonable estimate requires information from the attorneys, but businesses rarely record a contingent liability prior to the jury deciding against them. We've probably all heard of such lawsuits as when Stella Liebeck sued **McDonald's** in 1992. Liebeck spilled coffee while removing the lid to add sugar, burning her legs. She suffered third degree burns over 6 percent of her body. McDonald's could have settled the case for $20,000, but they refused. Liebeck ultimately was awarded $200,000 in compensatory damages and $2.7 million in punitive damages.[3]

The accounting question becomes: When is a liability (and corresponding expense) recorded? Proper matching suggests that the expense would be recorded at the time Liebeck spilled the coffee. However, at this time, the loss was contingent. Since the liability and

OBJECTIVE

Describe contingent liabilities and the alternatives for their recognition and measurement.

IFRS

IFRS refers to contingencies as "provisions." In addition, IFRS defines probable as "more likely than not" while U.S. GAAP defines probable as "likely". Therefore, more events will be recognized as provisions under IFRS.

---

[3] Liebek's compensatory damages were reduced to $160,000 because she was found to be 20 percent at fault.

Exhibit 8-6

Recognition of Contingent Liabilities

	A Reasonable Estimate Can Be Made	No Reasonable Estimate Can Be Made
Probable	Make a journal entry to record the liability.	No journal entry is made: disclose information in footnote to the financial statements.
Reasonably Possible	No journal entry is made: disclose information in footnote to the financial statements.	No journal entry is made: disclose information in footnote to the financial statements.
Remote	Neither record as a liability nor disclose in a footnote to the financial statements.	Neither record as a liability nor disclose in a footnote to the financial statements.

Concept Q&A

Accounts receivable have a contingent loss related to bad debts. A group of customers owes money (the accounts receivable); however, there is uncertainty about whether the customers will pay. How do we account for this contingency and why do we account for it in this way?

Answer:

As discussed in Chapter 5, companies typically use an estimate of uncollectible receivables to recognize "bad debt expense" and reduce the accounts receivable valuation through a credit to the "allowance for doubtful accounts." This is done because it is probable that amounts will be uncollectible and this amount is reasonably estimated (generally based on past experience). So, although bad debt expense does not produce a liability (instead, it reduces an asset), the accounting for this contingency is consistent with contingent liabilities.

expense were not recorded until it was deemed probable that McDonald's would lose the lawsuit and a reasonable estimate could be made, McDonald's did not record a liability for this amount until they lost the lawsuit.

Of course, the likelihood that a contingent event will occur may change over time. A contingent liability that should not be recorded or disclosed at one time may need to be recorded or disclosed later because the facts and circumstances change. This frequently happens to contingent liabilities arising from litigation.

ETHICAL DECISIONS   The contingent liability rules create an interesting ethical dilemma in lawsuits. Consider the fictional case of a a class action lawsuit being filed against Giant Pharmaceuticals by patients who used one of Giant's best selling drugs. Further, company attorneys believe it is probable that Giant will settle the lawsuit for approximately $3 billion. However, if Giant were to recognize a $3 billion liability and expense, the plaintiff attorneys would likely refuse to settle for less. After all, what would you think if you were sitting on a jury and the defendants' attorney showed you Giant's financial statements, explained the contingency rule, and said, "See, even Giant thinks it's probable that they will lose this lawsuit and pay damages of $3 billion." As you might expect, companies are extremely reluctant to record expenses and liabilities related to lawsuits for this reason or to even disclose that a loss is probable. Is this ethical? It probably isn't ethical, but it is an area that all parties have seemed to allow. As such, users of the financial statements cannot place too much reliance on the lack of expenses and liabilities related to lawsuits. ●

OBJECTIVE **4**
Measure warranty liabilities and warranty expense.

WARRANTIES

When goods are sold, the customer is often provided with a warranty against certain defects. A **warranty** usually guarantees the repair or replacement of defective goods during a period (ranging from a few days to several years) following the sale.

The use of parts and labor to satisfy warranty claims may occur in the accounting period in which the sale is made, but it is also likely to occur in some subsequent accounting period. The matching concept requires that all expenses required to produce sales revenue for a given period be recorded in that period. Since warranty costs are sales-related, they must be recorded in the sales period. And since all warranty costs probably have not been incurred by the end of the sales period, they must be estimated. Businesses are likely able to make reasonable estimates of their warranty costs based on past experience.

The recognition of warranty expense and (estimated) warranty liability is normally recorded by an adjustment at the end of the accounting period. As warranty claims are paid to customers or related expenditures are made, the liability is reduced. **CORNERSTONE 8-5** illustrates the accounting for warranties.

CORNERSTONE 8-5   Recording Warranty Liabilities

Concept:
Future warranty expenses must be recognized, or matched, in the period of sale.

Information:
Nolan Electronics offers a 12-month warranty on all its computers. Nolan estimates that one computer of each 2,000 sold will require warranty service and that the average warranty claim will cost Nolan $155.

Required:
1. Prepare the journal entry to recognize warranty expense and associated liability, assuming Nolan sells 3,000,000 computers during 2011, for which no warranty work has yet been performed.
2. Prepare the journal entry for warranty repairs, assuming that in January 2012, Nolan sends $10,400 cash and parts costing $8,300 to its dealers for warranty repairs.

Solution:

1.
$$(3{,}000{,}000 \text{ computers sold}) \times \left(\frac{1 \text{ failure}}{2{,}000 \text{ sold}}\right) \times \left(\frac{\$155}{1 \text{ failure}}\right) = \$232{,}500$$

Date	Account and Explanation	Debit	Credit
Dec. 31, 2011	Warranty Expense	232,500	
	Warranty Liability		232,500
	(Record warranty expense for 2011)		

Assets	=	Liabilities	+	Stockholders' Equity
		+232,500		−232,500

2.

Date	Account and Explanation	Debit	Credit
Jan. 2012	Warranty Liability	18,700	
	Cash		10,400
	Inventory		8,300
	(Record payment for warranty repairs for Jan. 2012)		

Assets	=	Liabilities	+	Stockholders' Equity
−10,400 −8,300		−18,700		

Note: The income statement effect of warranties (activity in the equity column) occurs when goods are sold. Payments or other asset outflows associated with the satisfaction of warranty claims do not affect the income statement.

Actual warranty claims are unlikely to exactly equal the business's estimate. Any small overestimate or underestimate is usually combined with the next warranty estimate. However, large overestimates or underestimates must be recognized in the accounts and reported on the income statement as other income or other expenses as soon as they become apparent.

Concept Q&A

Why are warranties expensed at the point of sale when a company often does not incur warranty costs until later periods?

Answer:
Remember, the matching principle says that expenses will be recognized in the periods they helped generate revenues. The presence of the warranty "helped" sell the item. Additionally, warranties are contingencies—if the product fails, then the company will experience a loss. When loss contingencies are probable and a reasonable estimate can be made, a journal entry is made to record the expense and recognize a liability.

ANALYZING CURRENT LIABILITIES

Both investors and creditors are interested in a company's liquidity—that is, its ability to meet its short-term obligations. Failure to pay current liabilities can lead to suppliers refusing to sell to the company and employees leaving. As such, even companies with good business models can be forced into bankruptcy by their inability to pay current liabilities.

The following ratios are often used to analyze a company's ability to meet its current obligations:

$$\text{Current Ratio} = \frac{\text{Current Assets}}{\text{Current Liabilities}}$$

$$\text{Quick Ratio} = \frac{(\text{Cash} + \text{Marketable Securities} + \text{Accounts Receivable})}{\text{Current Liabilities}}$$

$$\text{Cash Ratio} = \frac{(\text{Cash} + \text{Marketable Securities})}{\text{Current Liabilities}}$$

$$\text{Operating Cash Flow Ratio} = \frac{\text{Cash Flows from Operating Activities}}{\text{Current Liabilities}}$$

The first three ratios compare all or parts of current assets to current liabilities. The logic is that current liabilities need to be paid over approximately the same time frame that current assets are turned into cash. "Acceptable" current ratios vary from industry to industry, but the thought is that current assets must exceed current liabilities (which implies a current ratio > 1) to be able to meet current obligations. In fact, the general rule of thumb appears to be that a current ratio greater than two is appropriate.

However, the second and third ratios recognize that some current assets are harder to liquidate. Both the quick and cash ratio exclude inventories because including inventories assumes that sales will be made. The quick ratio assumes that accounts receivable are liquid. This is true when customers have low credit risk and pay in relatively short amounts of time. Of course, such an assumption is not true for all industries. Consequently, the use of the cash ratio may be more appropriate in these cases.

Operating cash flow, on the other hand, looks at the ability of cash generated from operating activities to meet current obligations. As with the current ratio, the operating cash flow ratio assumes that sales will continue into the future. **CORNERSTONE 8-6** illustrates the analysis of current liabilities.

CORNERSTONE 8-6   Calculating Liquidity Ratios

Concept:
Information contained in current liabilities provides investors and creditors with an idea of a company's ability to meet its current obligations.

Information:
Consider the following information from **Standard Pacific**, a large builder of single-family homes, as of December 31, 2006 (in thousands):

Current liabilities	$473,498	Receivables	$ 77,725
Cash & equivalents	17,376	Inventories	3,472,285
Marketable securities	0	Cash flows from operating activities	(360,651)

Required:
Calculate the following: (1) current ratio, (2) quick ratio, (3) cash ratio, and (4) operating cash flow ratio.

Solution:

CORNERSTONE
8 - 6
(continued)

1. current ratio: $\dfrac{(\$17,376 + 0 + \$77,725 + \$3,472,285)}{\$473,498} = 7.53$

2. quick ratio: $\dfrac{(\$17,376 + 0 + \$77,725)}{\$473,498} = 0.20$

3. cash ratio: $\dfrac{(\$17,376 + 0)}{\$473,498} = 0.04$

4. operating cash flow ratio: $\dfrac{-\$360,651}{\$473,498} = -0.76$

Note: Most of the information to calculate these ratios can also be found on the balance sheet (except for cash flows from operating activities, which is on the statement of cash flows).

In isolation, the current ratio in Cornerstone 8-6 appears very strong. For most industries, a current ratio greater than seven is rare. However, a vast majority of the current assets is inventory (unsold homes). In strong real estate markets, new homes can sell quite fast, but when a real estate slump hits, such homes can remain unsold for long periods of time. During the 2007 real estate market slump, for example, home builders experienced much slower sales (Standard Pacific's sales were down approximately 30 percent). A few home builders even resorted to selling homes at a loss to generate needed cash.

The quick ratio and cash ratio in Cornerstone 8-6 show that Standard Pacific must sell homes to generate the necessary cash to meet its current obligations. The highly negative cash flows from operations were due to growing inventory in 2006. Although this growing inventory could be interpreted as expanding operations, it could also signal slowing sales.

SUMMARY OF LEARNING OBJECTIVES

LO1.   Explain liability recognition and measurement criteria.
- Most liabilities are recognized in exchange for goods and services or the borrowing of money.
- In theory, the amount reported on the balance sheet should not include interest that has not yet accrued.
- However, for nearly all current liabilities, unaccrued interest is deemed immaterial, so most current liabilities are simply recorded and reported at the total amount due.

LO2.   Identify and record the kinds of activities that produce current liabilities.
- Current liabilities are obligations to outsiders that require the firm to pay cash or another current asset or provide goods or services within the longer of one year or one operating cycle.
- Such obligations are the result of many common transactions such as:
  - purchasing goods or services on credit (i.e., accounts payable)
  - the completed portion of activities that are in process at the end of the period such as wages or interest (i.e., accrued liabilities)
  - sales tax collected from customers
  - payroll taxes such as income taxes withheld from employees and Social Security
  - notes payable
  - goods or services paid for in advance by customers (i.e., unearned revenues)
  - the portion of long-term debt due within the year

LO3.   Describe contingent liabilities and the alternatives for their recognition and measurement.
- A contingent liability is an obligation whose amount, timing, or recipient depends on future events.
- A contingent liability is not recognized in the accounts unless the event on which it is contingent is probable (likely to occur) and a reasonable estimate of the liability can be made.

- If occurrence of the contingent event is not probable or reliable measurement of the obligation is impossible, the potential obligation is not recorded as a liability, but may be disclosed in the footnotes.

LO4.   Measure warranty liabilities and warranty expense.

- Since warranties help generate sales, the estimated future cost of servicing the warranty must be recorded in the sales period (this is an example of the matching principle).
- This is done by expensing the estimate of the future cost of servicing the warranty and creating a liability.
- As warranty claims are paid to customers or related expenditures are made, the estimated liability is reduced.

LO5.   Analyze liquidity ratios using information contained in the current liabilities section.

- Both investors and creditors are interested in a company's liquidity—that is, its ability to meet its short-term obligations.
- Failure to pay current liabilities can lead to suppliers refusing to sell needed inventory and employees leaving.
- As such, even companies with good business models can be forced into bankruptcy by their inability to pay current liabilities.
- Common ratios used to analyze a company's ability to meet its current obligations are:
  - current ratio
  - quick ratio
  - cash ratio
  - operating cash flow ratio

CORNERSTONES
FOR CHAPTER 8

CORNERSTONE 8-1   Recording notes payable and accrued interest (p. 390)

CORNERSTONE 8-2   Recording liabilities at the point of sale (p. 393)

CORNERSTONE 8-3   Recording payroll taxes (p. 395)

CORNERSTONE 8-4   Recording unearned revenues (p. 396)

CORNERSTONE 8-5   Recording warranty liabilities (p. 399)

CORNERSTONE 8-6   Calculating liquidity ratios (p. 400)

KEY TERMS

Account payable (p. 388)	Note payable (p. 390)
Accrued liabilities (p. 389)	Payroll taxes (p. 394)
Contingent liability (p. 387)	Sales taxes (p. 393)
Current liabilities (p. 388)	Unearned revenue (p. 396)
Interest rate (p. 390)	Warranty (p. 398)
Liabilities (p. 386)	Withholding (p. 394)

REVIEW PROBLEM

I. Recording Current Liabilities and Calculating the Current Ratio

ABC Co. has the following balances in its accounts as of the beginning of the day on December 31 (this is not all of the accounts):

Account	Debit	Credit
Accounts payable		$ 100,000
Accounts receivable	$150,000	
Cash	75,000	
Interest payable		0
Inventory	270,000	
Long-term notes payable		1,000,000
Other current assets	60,000	
Other current liabilities		45,000
Sales taxes payable		10,000
Short-term notes payable		0
Unearned revenues		30,000

The following information is *not* reflected in these balances:

a. On December 1, ABC bought some equipment for $200,000 with a short-term note payable bearing 12 percent interest. ABC has not made any journal entries related to this transaction.

b. On December 31, ABC accepted delivery of $30,000 of inventory. ABC has not yet paid its suppliers.

c. Customers prepaid $10,600 related to services ABC will perform next year. This price included 6 percent state sales tax.

d. Gross salaries and wages in the amount of $20,000 are paid. Assume all employees are below the Social Security maximum; 5.4% of state unemployment taxes and 0.8% of federal unemployment taxes are paid on $3,225.81 of wages; and $2,500 of federal income taxes are withheld from employees.

Required:

1. Prepare the necessary journal entries for a–d.

2. Determine the current ratio before accounting for the additional information.

3. Determine the current ratio after accounting for the additional information.

4. Explain why ABC's current ratio deteriorated so badly.

Solution:

1. The necessary journal entries for each part are as follows:

	Date	Account and Explanation	Debit	Credit	
a.	Dec. 1	Equipment	200,000		
		Short-term Notes Payable		200,000	Stockholders' Assets = Liabilities + Equity +200,000 +200,000
		(Record issue of note for equipment purchase)			
b.	Dec. 31	Inventory	30,000		
		Accounts Payable		30,000	Stockholders' Assets = Liabilities + Equity +30,000 +30,000
		(Record purchase of inventory)			
	ABC must also accrue interest on December 31.				
	31	Interest Expense[a]	2,000		
		Interest Payable		2,000	Stockholders' Assets = Liabilities + Equity +2,000 −2,000
		(Record interest accrued on short-term note)			
c.	31	Cash	10,600		
		Unearned Revenue		10,000	Stockholders' Assets = Liabilities + Equity +10,600 +10,000 +600
		Sales Taxes Payable (State)		600	
		(Record unearned revenue and state sales taxes)			
d.	31	Wages Expense	20,000		
		Social Security Taxes Payable (Employee)[b]		1,240	Stockholders' Assets = Liabilities + Equity −15,970 +1,240 −20,000
		Medicare Taxes Payable (Employee)[c]		290	+290
		Income Taxes Payable (Federal)		2,500	+2,500
		Cash		15,970	
		(Record wages expense and related liabilities)			

[a]$200,000 ×12% × 1/12
[b]$20,000 × 6.2%
[c]$20,000 × 1.45%

(Continued)

Assets =	Liabilities +	Stockholders' Equity
	+174.19	−174.19
	+25.81	−25.81
	+1,240.00	−1,240.00
	+290.00	−290.00

Dec. 31	Social Security Taxes Expense	1,240.00	
	Medicare Taxes Expense	290.00	
	Unemployment Taxes Expense (State)[d]	174.19	
	Unemployment Taxes Expense (Federal)[e]	25.81	
	Social Security Taxes Payable (Employer)		1,240.00
	Medicare Taxes Payable (Employer)		290.00
	Unemployment Taxes Payable (State)[d]		174.19
	Unemployment Taxes Payable (Federal)[e]		25.81
	(Record employer payroll taxes)		

[d]$3,225.81 × 5.4% = $174.19
[e]$3,225.81 × 0.8% = $25.81

2. Before accounting for the additional information:

Current assets:	
Cash	$ 75,000
Accounts receivable	150,000
Inventory	270,000
Other current assets	60,000
Total current assets	$555,000
Current liabilities:	
Accounts payable	$100,000
Interest payable	0
Sales taxes payable	10,000
Short-term notes payable	0
Unearned revenues	30,000
Other current liabilities	45,000
Total current liabilities	$185,000

Current Ratio = $555,000/$185,000 = 3.0

3. After accounting for the additional information:

		Debit	Credit	
Current assets:				
Cash	$ 75,000	$10,600 (c)	$ 15,970 (d)	$ 69,630
Accounts receivable	150,000			150,000
Inventory	270,000	30,000 (a)		300,000
Other current assets	60,000			60,000
Total current assets				$579,630
Current liabilities:				
Accounts payable	100,000		30,000 (a)	$130,000
Interest payable	0		2,000 (b)	2,000
Sales taxes payable	10,000		600 (c)	10,600
Short-term notes payable	0		200,000 (b)	200,000
Unearned revenues	30,000		10,000 (c)	40,000
Other current liabilities	45,000		5,760 (d)*	50,760
Total current liabilities				$433,360

*$1,240 + $290 + $2,500 + $1,240 + $290 + $174.19 + $25.81 = $5,760

Current Ratio = $579,630/$433,360 = 1.34

4. The primary cause of the deterioration of ABC's current ratio is the addition of the short-term note payable related to the equipment. This transaction almost doubled the current liabilities, but current assets were unaffected by the addition of equipment. Another way to think about this is that ABC financed long-term operational assets with short-term financing.

DISCUSSION QUESTIONS

1. What are liabilities?
2. How is the amount of a liability measured?
3. When are most liabilities recognized?
4. What are current liabilities? Provide some common examples.

5. Describe two ways (the book mentions three, but you only need two) in which current liabilities are frequently ordered on the balance sheet.
6. What is the difference between an account payable and a note payable?
7. What sort of transaction typically creates an account payable?
8. What do we mean by accrued liabilities? Provide some common examples.
9. What type of transaction typically creates a note payable?
10. Why is interest ignored when valuing accounts payable?
11. How is interest computed on an interest-bearing short-term note?
12. When would debt that must be repaid within the next year be classified as long-term instead of current?
13. Provide examples of payroll taxes that are paid by the employee through reduction of their gross pay. Provide some examples of payroll taxes that are paid by the employer.
14. Why do unearned revenues and customers' deposits qualify as liabilities?
15. What are contingent liabilities? Provide an example.
16. When is a contingency recognized as a liability?
17. Why is the liability for warranties recognized when products are sold rather than when the warranty services are performed?
18. Describe the circumstances under which the current, quick, and cash ratios, respectively, are more appropriate measures of short-term liquidity than the other ratios.
19. Describe the differences between the current, quick, and cash ratios. Which one is the most conservative measure of short-term liquidity?
20. How does the rationale for the operating cash flow ratio differ from the rationale for the current, quick, and cash ratios?

MULTIPLE-CHOICE EXERCISES

8-1 Liabilities are recognized:

a. in exchange for goods.
b. in exchange for services.
c. in exchange for borrowing money.
d. all of these.

8-2 When reporting liabilities on a balance sheet, in theory, what measurement should be used?

a. future value of the future outflow
b. future value of the present outflow
c. present value of the future outflow
d. present value of the present outflow

> *Use the following information for Multiple-Choice Exercises 8-3 and 8-4:*
> Kinsella Seed borrowed $200,000 on October 1, 2011, at 10 percent interest. The interest and principal are due on October 1, 2012.

8-3 Refer to the information for Kinsella Seed above. What journal entry should be recorded on December 31, 2011?

a. Debit Interest Expense 5,000; credit Interest Payable 5,000.
b. Debit Interest Receivable 20,000; credit Interest Expense 20,000.
c. Debit Interest Payable 5,000; credit Interest Expense 5,000.
d. No entry is necessary.

8-4 Refer to the information for Kinsella Seed above. What journal entry should be made with respect to the interest payment on October 1, 2012?

a. Debit Cash 20,000; credit Interest Expense 15,000; credit Interest Payable 5,000.
b. Debit Interest Expense 15,000; credit Cash 15,000.
c. Debit Interest Expense 20,000; credit Cash 20,000.
d. Debit Interest Expense 15,000; debit Interest Payable 5,000; credit Cash 20,000.

8-5 Which of the following is *not* a current liability?

a. sales taxes payable
b. bonds payable due in five years
c. accounts payable
d. unearned revenue

8-6 Which of the following is *not* an example of an accrued liability?

a. wages payable
b. interest payable

c. accounts payable
d. property taxes payable

8-7 Kramerica, Inc., sold 350 oil drums to Thompson Manufacturing for $75 each. In addition to the $75 sale price per drum, there is a $1 per drum federal excise tax and a 7 percent state sales tax. What journal entry should be made to record this sale?

a. Debit Accounts Receivable 28,438; credit Sales Revenue 28,438.
b. Debit Accounts Receivable 26,250; credit Sales Revenue 26,250.
c. Debit Accounts Receivable 28,438; credit Excise Taxes Payable (Federal) 350; credit Sales Taxes Payable (State) 1,838; credit Sales Revenue 26,250.
d. Debit Accounts Receivable 26,250; debit Taxes Expense 2,188; credit Excise Taxes Payable (Federal) 350; credit Sales Taxes Payable (State) 1,838; credit Sales Revenue 26,250.

8-8 All of the following represent taxes commonly collected by businesses from customers *except*:

a. Unemployment taxes
b. Federal excise taxes

c. State sales taxes
d. City sales taxes

8-9 Payroll taxes typically include all of the following *except:*

a. Medicare taxes
b. Federal unemployment taxes

c. Social Security taxes
d. Federal excise taxes

8-10 When a credit is made to the income taxes payable account related to taxes withheld from an employee, the corresponding debit is made to:

a. Cash
b. Taxes Expense

c. Taxes Payable
d. Wages Expense

8-11 When should a contingent liability be recognized?

a. when the contingent liability is probable
b. when a reasonable estimation can be made

c. neither A nor B
d. A and B

8-12 Which of the following is true?

a. A contingent liability should always be recorded in the footnotes to the financial statements.
b. A contingent liability should always be recorded within the financial statements.
c. A company can choose to record a contingent liability either within its financial statements or in the footnotes to the financial statements.
d. No journal entries or footnotes are necessary if the possibility of a contingent liability is remote.

8-13 ABC Advisors is being sued by a former customer. ABC's lawyers say that it is possible, but not probable, that the company will lose the lawsuit and the trial should last approximately 18 more months. Should ABC lose, they will most likely have to pay approximately $750,000. How should this lawsuit be reported in the financial statements?

a. Current liability of $750,000 and Expense of $750,000.
b. Long-term liability of $750,000 and Expense of $750,000.
c. No effect on the balance sheet or income statement, but described in the footnotes.
d. No disclosure is required.

8-14 Warranty expense is:

a. recorded as it is incurred.
b. capitalized as a warranty asset.

c. recorded in the period of sale.
d. none of these.

8-15 To record warranties, the adjusting journal entry would be:

a.   a debit to Warranty Liability and a credit to Cash.
b.   a debit to Warranty Expense and a credit to Warranty Liability.
c.   a debit to Warranty Expense and a debit to Cash.
d.   a debit to Warranty Liability and a credit to Warranty Expense.

8-16 How is the current ratio calculated?

a.   Cash flows from Operating Activities/Current Liabilities
b.   Current Assets/Current Liabilities
c.   (Cash + Marketable Securities)/Current Liabilities
d.   (Cash + Marketable Securities + Accounts Receivable)/Current Liabilities

8-17 How is the cash ratio calculated?

a.   (Cash + Marketable Securities)/Current Liabilities
b.   Current Assets/Current Liabilities
c.   Cash Flows from Operating Activities/Current Liabilities
d.   (Cash + Marketable Securities + Accounts Receivable)/Current Liabilities

8-18 Which of the following transactions would cause the current ratio to increase (assuming the current ratio is currently greater than 1)?

a.   Receiving money from a customer related to an accounts receivable
b.   Paying off a payable
c.   Purchasing inventory on credit
d.   Purchasing property, plant, and equipment for cash

CORNERSTONE EXERCISES

Cornerstone Exercise 8-19 Issuing Notes Payable

OBJECTIVE ❷
CORNERSTONE 8-1

On June 30, Carmean Inc. borrows $250,000 from 1st National Bank with an 8-month, 7 percent note.

Required:
What journal entry is made on June 30?

Cornerstone Exercise 8-20 Notes Payable

OBJECTIVE ❷
CORNERSTONE 8-1

Rogers Machinery Company borrowed $400,000 on June 1, with a three-month, 7 percent, interest-bearing note.

Required:
1.   Record the borrowing transaction.
2.   Record the repayment transaction.

Cornerstone Exercise 8-21 Accrued Interest

OBJECTIVE ❷
CORNERSTONE 8-1

On August 1, Wilshire Company borrowed $150,000 from People's National Bank on a one-year, 8 percent note.

Required:
What adjusting entry should Wilshire make at December 31?

Cornerstone Exercise 8-22 Accrued Interest

OBJECTIVE ❷
CORNERSTONE 8-1

On March 1, the Garner Corporation borrowed $75,000 from the First Bank of Midlothian on a one-year, 5 percent note.

Required:
If the company keeps its records on a calendar year, what adjusting entry should Garner make on December 31?

OBJECTIVE ❷
CORNERSTONE 8-4

Cornerstone Exercise 8-23 Accrued Wages

Skiles Company's weekly payroll amounts to $10,000 and payday is every Friday. Employees work five days per week, Monday through Friday. The appropriate journal entry was recorded at the end of the accounting period, Wednesday, March 31, 2011.

Required:
What journal entry is made on Friday, April 2, 2011?

OBJECTIVE ❷
CORNERSTONE 8-2

Cornerstone Exercise 8-24 Sales and Excise Tax

Garner's Antique Hot Rods recently sold a 1957 Chevy for $75,000 on account. The state sales tax is 6 percent, and there is a $500-per-car federal excise tax.

Required:
Prepare the journal entry to record the sale.

OBJECTIVE ❷
CORNERSTONE 8-2

Cornerstone Exercise 8-25 Sales Tax

Cobb Baseball Bats sold 60 bats for $70 each, plus an additional state sales tax of 8 percent. The customer paid cash.

Required:
Prepare the journal entry to record the sale.

OBJECTIVE ❷
CORNERSTONE 8-3

Cornerstone Exercise 8-26 Payroll Taxes

Hernandez Builders has a gross payroll for January amounting to $500,000. The following amounts have been withheld:

Income taxes	$63,000
Social Security	31,000
Medicare	7,250
Charitable contributions	1% of gross pay
Union dues	2% of gross pay

Also, the federal unemployment tax rate is 6.2 percent, and applies to all but $50,000 of the gross payroll.

Required:
1. What is the amount of net pay recorded by Hernandez?
2. Prepare the journal entries to record the payroll.

OBJECTIVE ❷
CORNERSTONE 8-3

Cornerstone Exercise 8-27 Payroll Taxes

Kinsella, Inc., has a gross payroll of $10,000 for the pay period. The entire payroll is subject to Social Security and Medicare taxes. Kinsella must also withhold $1,200 in income taxes from the employees and pay state unemployment taxes of $30.

Required:
Prepare the necessary journal entries for Kinsella to record both the gross pay earned by employees and the employer portion of these payroll taxes.

OBJECTIVE ❷
CORNERSTONE 8-3

Cornerstone Exercise 8-28 Payroll Taxes

During October, Seger Insurance employees earned $100,000 in wages. Social Security applied to $86,000 of these wages, while Medicare applies to all $100,000. State and federal unemployment taxes of $1,300 and $650 are owed, respectively.

Required:
Prepare the necessary journal entry for Seger to record the employer portion of these payroll taxes.

OBJECTIVE ❷
CORNERSTONE 8-4

Cornerstone Exercise 8-29 Unearned Sales Revenue

Brand Landscaping offers a promotion where they will mow your lawn 20 times if the customer pays $700 in advance.

Required:
Prepare the journal entry to record (1) the customers' prepayment of $700 and (2) Brand's mowing of the lawn one time.

Cornerstone Exercise 8-30 Unearned Rent Revenue

OBJECTIVE ❷
CORNERSTONE 8-4

EWO Property Management leases commercial properties. A new client signs a 5-year lease and agrees to pay the first 6 months in advance. The monthly rent is $50,000.

Required:

Prepare the journal entry to record (1) the customers' prepayment of six months' rent and (2) the necessary adjusting entry after one month has passed.

Cornerstone Exercise 8-31 Warranties

OBJECTIVE ❹
CORNERSTONE 8-5

In 2011, BMJ Plumbing Company sold 300 water heaters for $850 each. The water heaters carry a two-year warranty for repairs. BMJ Plumbing estimates that repair costs will average 1 percent of the total selling price.

Required:

1. How much is recorded in the warranty liability account as a result of selling the water heaters during 2011, assuming no warranty service has yet been performed?
2. Prepare the necessary adjusting entry at December 31, 2011.

Cornerstone Exercise 8-32 Warranties

OBJECTIVE ❹
CORNERSTONE 8-5

In 2011, Waldo Balloons sold 50 hot air balloons at $25,000 each. The balloons carry a five-year warranty for defects. Waldo estimates that repair costs will average 3 percent of the total selling price. The estimated warranty liability at the beginning of the year was $40,000. Claims of $15,000 were actually incurred during the year to honor their warranties.

Required:

What was the balance in the warranty liability at the end of the year?

Cornerstone Exercise 8-33 Liquidity Ratios

OBJECTIVE ❺
CORNERSTONE 8-6

NWA's financial statements contain the following information:

Cash	$300,000	Accounts payable	$ 500,000
Accounts receivable	650,000	Accrued expenses	150,000
Inventory	800,000	Long-term debt	1,000,000
Marketable securities	100,000		

Note: Round answers to two decimal places.

Required:

1. What is its current ratio?
2. What is its quick ratio?
3. What is its cash ratio?
4. Discuss NWA's liquidity using these ratios.

Cornerstone Exercise 8-34 Liquidity Ratios

OBJECTIVE ❺
CORNERSTONE 8-6

GER's financial statements contain the following information:

Cash	$3,125,000	Accounts payable	$ 3,500,000
Accounts receivable	3,150,000	Accrued expenses	1,800,000
Inventory	4,200,000	Long-term debt	10,000,000
Marketable securities	1,850,000		

Note: Round answers to two decimal places.

Required:

1. What is the current ratio?
2. What is the quick ratio?
3. What is the cash ratio?
4. Discuss GER's liquidity using these ratios.

EXERCISES

Exercise 8-35 Accounts Payable

OBJECTIVE ❷

On May 18 Stanton Electronics purchased, on credit, 1,000 TV sets for $400 each. Stanton plans to resell these TV's in its store. Stanton paid the supplier on June 30.

Required:

Prepare the necessary journal entry (or entries) on May 18 and June 30.

OBJECTIVE ❷

Exercise 8-36 Accounts and Notes Payable

On February 15, Barbour Industries buys $800,000 of inventory on credit. On March 31, Barbour approaches its supplier because it cannot pay the $800,000. The supplier agrees to roll the amount into a note due on September 30 with 10 percent interest.

Required:

Prepare the necessary journal entries from February 15 through payment on September 30.

OBJECTIVE ❷

Exercise 8-37 Accrued Property Taxes

Annual property taxes covering the preceding 12 months are always paid on September 1. Elise Inc. is always assessed $9,000 property taxes.

Required:

Given this information, determine the adjusting journal entry that Elise must make on December 31.

OBJECTIVE ❷

Exercise 8-38 Accrued Income Taxes

Nolan Inc. had taxable income of $400,000 in 2011. Its effective tax rate is 35 percent. Nolan pays its 2011 income taxes on April 15, 2012.

Required:

1. Given this information, determine the adjusting journal entry that Nolan must make on December 31, 2011.
2. Prepare the journal entry to record the tax payment.

OBJECTIVE ❷

Exercise 8-39 Accrued Wages

Rising Stars Gymnastics pays its hourly employees every Saturday. The weekly payroll for hourly employees is $5,000 and the employees' hours are spread evenly from Monday through Saturday. During the current year December 31 falls on a Wednesday.

Required:

Given this information, determine the adjusting journal entry that Rising Stars must make on December 31.

OBJECTIVE ❷

Exercise 8-40 Accrued Wages and Payment of Payroll

GCD Advisors offices are open Monday through Friday and GCD pays employees salaries of $50,000 every other Friday. During the current year December 31 falls on a Thursday and the next payday is January 8.

Required:

Given this information, determine the adjusting journal entry that GCD must make on December 31 as well as the journal entry to record the payment of the payroll on January 8.

OBJECTIVE ❷

Exercise 8-41 Accrued Wages

Employees earn $12,000 per day, work five days per week, Monday through Friday, and get paid every Friday. The previous payday was Friday, January 25 and the accounting period ends on Thursday, January 31.

Required:

What is the ending balance in the wages payable account on January 31?

OBJECTIVE ❷

Exercise 8-42 Recording Various Liabilities

Glenview Hardware had the following transactions that produced liabilities during 2012:

a. Purchased merchandise on credit for $30,000 (*Note:* Assume a periodic inventory system).
b. Year-end wages of $10,000 incurred, but not paid. Related income taxes of $1,200, Social Security of $620 (employee portion), and Medicare taxes of $145 are withheld.
c. Year-end estimated income taxes payable, but unpaid, for the year in the amount of $42,850.

d. Sold merchandise on account for $1,262, including state sales taxes of $48 (*Note:* Assume a periodic inventory system).

e. Employer's share of Social Security and Medicare taxes for the period were $620 and $145, respectively.

f. Borrowed cash under a 90-day, 9 percent, $25,000 note.

Required:
Prepare the entry to record each of these transactions (treat each transaction independently).

Exercise 8-43 Recording Various Liabilities

OBJECTIVE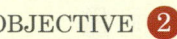

Plymouth Electronics had the following transactions that produced liabilities during 2012:

a. Purchased merchandise on credit for $80,000 (*Note:* Assume a periodic inventory system).

b. Year-end wages of $40,000 incurred, but not paid. Related income taxes of $13,000 and Medicare taxes of $580 are withheld. Employee wages are all above the social security maximum, so only Medicare is paid.

c. Year-end estimated income taxes payable, but unpaid, for the year in the amount of $113,615.

d. Sold merchandise on account for $3,636, including state sales taxes of $180 (*Note:* Assume a periodic inventory system).

e. Employer's share of Medicare taxes for the period was $580. The taxes will be paid at a later date.

f. Borrowed cash under a 180-day, 8 percent, $155,000 note.

Required:
Prepare the entry to record each of these transactions (treat each transaction independently).

Exercise 8-44 Reporting Liabilities

OBJECTIVE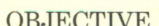

Morton Electronics had the following obligations:

a. A legally enforceable claim against the business to be paid in three months.

b. A guarantee given by a seller to a purchaser to repair or replace defective goods during the first six months following a sale.

c. An amount payable to Bank One in 10 years.

d. An amount to be paid next year to Citibank on a long-term note payable.

Required:
Conceptual Connection: Describe how each of these items should be reported in the balance sheet.

Exercise 8-45 Accounts Payable

OBJECTIVE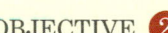

Hammerton Autos, a used-car dealer, has a December 31 year-end date. For Hammerton, the following transactions occurred during the first 10 days of August:

a. Hammerton purchased, on credit, space for classified advertisements in the *Chicago Tribune* for $2,680. The advertising was run the day the space was purchased.

b. Hammerton purchased office supplies from Office Depot on credit in the amount of $250.

c. One of Hammerton's sales staff sold a car. The salesperson's commission is $1,100. The commission will be paid September 10. (*Note:* Concern yourself only with the commission.)

d. The electric bill for July was received. The bill is $6,500 and is due August 15.

e. A $420 bill from Carey Alignment services was received. Carey had repaired 10 cars for Hammerton in late July. The payment is due August 20.

Required:
Prepare journal entries for the above transactions.

Exercise 8-46 Accrued Liabilities

OBJECTIVE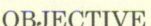

Charger, Inc. had the following items that require adjusting entries at the end of the year.

a. Charger pays its employees $5,000 every Friday for a five-day work week. This year December 31 falls on a Wednesday.

b. Charger earned income of $800,000 for the year for tax purposes. Its effective tax rate is 35 percent. These taxes must be paid by April 15 of next year.

c. Charger borrowed $280,000 with a note payable dated August 1. This note specifies 6 percent. The interest and principal are due on March 31 of the following year.

d. Charger's president earns a bonus equal to 10 percent of income in excess of $650,000. Income for the year was $800,000. This bonus is paid in May of the following year and any expense is charged to wages expense.

Required:

Prepare the adjusting journal entries to record these transactions at the end of the current year.

OBJECTIVE ❷

Exercise 8-47 Accrued Liabilities

Thornwood Tile had the following items that require adjusting entries at the end of the year.

a. Thornwood pays payroll of $180,000 every other Friday for a two-week period. This year the last payday is Friday, December 26. (*Note:* The work week is Monday through Friday.)

b. Thornwood purchased $350,000 of tile on June 1 with a note payable requiring 12 percent interest. The interest and principal on this note are due within one year. As of December 31, Thornwood had not made any principal or interest payments.

c. Thornwood's earned income is $900,000 for the year for tax purposes. Its effective tax rate is 30 percent. These taxes must be paid by April 15 of next year.

Required:

Prepare the adjusting journal entries to record these transactions at the end of the current year.

OBJECTIVE ❷

Exercise 8-48 Sales Tax

Weston Cellular provides wireless phone service. During April 2012, it billed a customer a total of $135,000 before taxes. Weston also must pay the following taxes on these charges:

a. State of Illinois sales tax of 7 percent

b. Federal excise tax of 0.2 percent

c. State of Illinois use tax of 0.3 percent

Required:

Assuming Weston collects these taxes from the customer, what journal entry would Weston make when the customers pay their bills?

OBJECTIVE ❷

Exercise 8-49 Payroll Accounting and Discussion of Labor Costs

Blitzen Marketing Research paid its weekly and monthly payroll on January 31. The following information is available about the payroll:

Item	Amount
Monthly salaries	$237,480
Hourly wages	585,000
FICA:	
Social Security (both Employee & Employer)	6.20%
Medicare (both Employee & Employer)	1.45%
Withholding for income taxes	$108,500
Federal unemployment taxes	1,200
State unemployment taxes	4,000

Blitzen will pay both the employer's taxes and the taxes withheld on April 15.

Required:

1. Prepare the journal entries to record the payroll payment and the incurrence of the associated expenses and liabilities (*Note:* Round to nearest penny).

2. What is the employees' gross pay? What amount does Blitzen pay in excess of gross pay as a result of taxes? (*Note:* Provide both an absolute dollar amount and as a percentage of gross pay, rounding to two decimal places.)

3. How much is the employees' net pay as a percentage of total payroll related expenses? (*Note:* Round answer to two decimal places.)

4. If another employee can be hired for $60,000 per year, what would be the total cost of this employee to Blitzen?

Exercise 8-50 Unearned Revenue

OBJECTIVE 2

Irvine Pest Control signed a $1,500-per-month contract on December 1, 2011, to provide pest control services to rental units owned by Garden Grove Properties. Irvine received six months' service fees in advance on signing the contract.

Required:

1. Prepare Irvine's journal entry to record the cash receipt for the first six months.
2. Prepare Irvine's adjusting entry at December 31, 2011.
3. **Conceptual Connection:** How would the advance payment be reported in Irvine Pest Control's December 31, 2011, balance sheet? How would the advance payment be reported in Garden Grove Properties' December 31, 2011, balance sheet?

Exercise 8-51 Contingent Liabilities

OBJECTIVE 3

Many companies provide warranties with their products. Such warranties typically guarantee the repair or replacement of defective goods for some specified period of time following the sale.

Required:

Conceptual Connection: Why do most warranties require companies to make a journal entry to record a liability for future warranty costs?

Exercise 8-52 Contingent Liabilities

OBJECTIVE 3

SLC Electronics is the plaintiff in a class action lawsuit. Their attorney has written a letter that it is now extremely likely that SLC will lose the lawsuit and be forced to pay $3,000,000 in damages.

Required:

Prepare the necessary journal entry. If no entry is required state "none." Any recognition will be to other expense and lawsuit payable.

Exercise 8-53 Recognition and Reporting of Contingent Liabilities

OBJECTIVE 3

A list of alternative accounting treatments is followed by a list of potential contingent liabilities.

Alternative Accounting Treatments

a. Estimate the amount of liability and record.
b. Do not record as a liability but disclose in a footnote to the financial statements.
c. Neither record as a liability nor disclose in a footnote to the financial statements.

Potential Contingent Liabilities

1. Income taxes related to revenue included in net income this year but taxable in a future year.
2. Potential costs in future periods associated with performing warranty services on products sold this period.
3. Estimated cost of future services under a product warranty related to past sales.
4. Estimated cost of future services under a product warranty related to future sales.
5. Estimated cost of pension benefits related to past employee services that has yet to be funded.
6. Potential loss on environmental cleanup suit against company; a court judgment against the company is considered less than probable but more than remotely likely.
7. Potential loss under class-action suit by a group of customers; during the current year, the likelihood of a judgment against the company has increased from remote to possible but less than probable.
8. Potential loss under an affirmative action suit by a former employee; the likelihood of a judgment against the company is considered to be remote.
9. Potential loss from a downturn in future economic activity.
10. Loss from out-of-court settlement of lawsuit that is likely to occur toward the end of next year.

Required:

Match the appropriate accounting treatment with each of the potential liabilities listed above. Your answer should list the numbers 1 through 10 and, opposite each number, the letter of the appropriate accounting treatment.

OBJECTIVE ❹

Exercise 8-54 Warranties

McKean Entertainment sells televisions and other sound and video equipment. Sales and expected warranty claims for the year are as follows:

Item	Unit Sales	Expected Warranty Claims for Warranty Period	Cost per Claim
Televisions	2,500	2 claims per 100 sold	$45
DVD	360	5 claims per 100 sold	15
Speakers	700	1 claim per 100 sold	25

Required:

1. Prepare the entry to record warranty expense for McKean Entertainment for the year.
2. **Conceptual Connection:** Why does McKean have to record a liability for future warranty claims?

OBJECTIVE ❺

ILLUSTRATING RELATIONSHIPS

Exercise 8-55 Ratio Analysis

Intel Corporation provided the following information on its balance sheet and statement of cash flows:

Current liabilities	$8,514,000,000	Inventories	$ 4,314,000,000
Cash and equivalents	6,598,000,000	Other current assets	2,146,000,000
Marketable securities	3,404,000,000	Cash flows from operating activities	10,620,000,000
Receivables	2,709,000,000		

Required:

1. Calculate the following: (a) current ratio, (b) quick ratio, (c) cash ratio, and (d) operating cash flow ratio. (*Note:* Round answers to two decimal places.)
2. **Conceptual Connection:** Interpret these results.
3. **Conceptual Connection:** Assume that Intel, as a requirement of one of their loans, must maintain a current ratio of at least 2.30. Given their large amount of cash, how could they accomplish this on December 31st (be specific as to dollar amounts)?

PROBLEM SET A

OBJECTIVE ❷

Problem 8-56A Payable Transactions

Richmond Company engaged in the following transactions during 2011:

a. Purchased $16,000 of supplies from ABC Supplies on February 16. Amount due in full on March 31.
b. Paid for 25 percent of the purchased merchandise (transaction *a*) on February 26.
c. On March 31 negotiated a payment extension with ABC for the remainder of the balance from the February 16 purchase by signing a one-year, 10 percent note.
d. Borrowed $300,000 on a 10-month, 8 percent interest-bearing note on April 30.
e. Purchased $78,000 of merchandise on June 4. Amount due in full on June 30.
f. Paid for the purchased merchandise (transaction *e*) on June 24.
g. Received from Haywood, Inc., on August 19, a $22,000 deposit against a total selling price of $220,000 for services to be performed for Haywood.
h. Paid quarterly installments of Social Security and Medicare and individual income tax withholdings, as shown below, on October 15. The Social Security was recorded as an expense during the quarter and the amount paid represents both the employee and employer share:

Social Security taxes	$185,000
Medicare taxes	43,266
Income taxes withheld	319,000

i. On December 15 Richmond completed the services ordered by Haywood on August 19. Haywood's remaining balance of $198,000 is due on January 31.

Required:

1. Prepare journal entries for these transactions.
2. Prepare any adjusting entries necessary at December 31, 2011.

Problem 8-57A Payroll Accounting

Stadium Manufacturing has the following data available for its September 30, 2011, payroll:

Wages earned	$315,000*
Income taxes withheld	79,900

*All subject to Social Security and Medicare matching and withholding of 6.2 percent and 1.45 percent, respectively.

Federal unemployment taxes of 0.80 percent and state unemployment taxes of 1.20 percent are payable on $295,312.50 of the wages earned.

Required:

1. Compute the amounts of taxes payable and the amount of wages that will be paid to employees. Then prepare the journal entries to record the wages earned and the payroll taxes (*Note:* Round to the nearest penny).
2. Stadium Manufacturing would like to hire a new employee at a salary of $50,000. Assuming the payroll taxes are as described above (with unemployment taxes paid on the first $7,000) and fringe benefits (e.g., health insurance, retirement, etc.) are 30% of gross pay, what will be the total cost of this employee for Stadium?

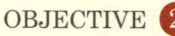

Problem 8-58A Note Payable and Accrued Interest

Fairborne Company borrowed $600,000 on an 8 percent, interest-bearing note on October 1, 2011. Fairborne ends its fiscal year on December 31. The note was paid with interest on May 1, 2012.

Required:

1. Prepare the entry for this note on October 1, 2011.
2. Prepare the adjusting entry for this note on December 31, 2011.
3. Indicate how the note and the accrued interest would appear in the balance sheet at December 31, 2011.
4. Prepare the entry to record the repayment of the note on May 1, 2012.

Problem 8-59A Interest-Bearing Note Replacing an Unpaid Account Payable

Conti Products owed $80,000 on account for inventory purchased on December 1, 2012. Conti uses a perpetual inventory system and has a fiscal year that ends on December 31. Conti was unable to pay the amount owed by the March 1, 2013, due date because of financial difficulties. On March 1, 2013, Conti signed a four-month, $80,000, 6 percent interest-bearing note. This note was repaid with interest on July 1, 2013.

Required:

1. Prepare the entry recorded on December 1, 2012.
2. Prepare the adjusting entry recorded on December 31, 2012.
3. Prepare the entry recorded on March 1, 2013.
4. Prepare the entry recorded on July 1, 2013.

Problem 8-60A Excise Taxes

Clinton Power provides electricity to a wide area of western Kentucky. During October 2011 it billed 20,000 of its residential customers located in the town of Heyworth a total of $2,435,000 for electricity (this is considered revenue). In addition Clinton is required to collect the following taxes:

a. State Excise Tax: A tax of $3.00 per customer plus 2 percent of billing used to fund the Kentucky Energy Commission
b. Federal Excise Tax: A tax of $0.50 per customer plus 0.1 percent of billing used to fund the Federal Energy Commission

Required:

1. Determine how much Clinton will bill these customers in total for the month of October 2011.
2. Prepare the entry to record the billing of these amounts.
3. Prepare the entry to record the collection of these amounts.
4. Prepare the entry to record the payment of the state excise taxes to the appropriate governmental unit.

Problem 8-61A Unearned Revenue and Customer Deposits

On November 20, 2011, Green Bay Electronics agreed to manufacture and supply 750 electronic control units used by Wausau Heating Systems in large commercial and industrial installments. On that date, Wausau deposited $250 per unit upon signing the three-year purchase agreement, which set the selling price of each control unit at $1,000. Green Bay's inventory cost is $225 per unit. No units were delivered during 2011. The first 200 units will be delivered in 2012, 300 units will be delivered during 2013, and the remaining units will be delivered during 2014. Assume Green Bay uses a perpetual inventory system.

Required:

1. **Conceptual Connection:** Prepare the entry by Green Bay to record receipt of the deposit during 2011. How would the deposit be reported in the financial statements at the end of 2011?
2. **Conceptual Connection:** Prepare the entry by Green Bay to record the delivery of 200 units during 2012. How would the deposit be reported in the financial statements at the end of 2012? Wausau pays in cash upon delivery for units not covered by the deposit.
3. Prepare the entry by Green Bay to record the delivery of 300 units during 2013.

Problem 8-62A Warranties

Mason Auto Repair specializes in the repair of foreign car transmissions. To encourage business, Mason offers a six-month warranty on all repairs. The following data are available for 2011:

Transmissions repaired, 2011	6,350
Expected frequency of warranty claims	0.03 per repair
Actual warranty claims, 2011	$63,000
Estimated warranty liability, 1/1/11	$50,000
Estimated cost of each warranty claim	$ 300

Assume that warranty claims are paid in cash.

Required:

1. Compute the warranty expense for 2011.
2. Prepare the entry to record the payment of the 2011 warranty claims.
3. **Conceptual Connection:** What is the December 31, 2011, balance in the estimated warranty liability account? Why has the balance in the warranty liability account changed from January 1, 2011?

Problem 8-63A Ratio Analysis

Consider the following information taken from GER's financial statements:

	September 30 (in thousands)	
	2012	2011
Current assets:		
Cash and cash equivalents	$ 1,274	$ 6,450
Receivables	30,071	16,548
Inventories	31,796	14,072
Other current assets	4,818	2,620
Total current assets	$67,959	$39,690
Current liabilities:		
Current portion of long-term debt	$ 97	$ 3,530
Accounts payable	23,124	11,228
Accrued compensation costs	5,606	1,929
Accrued expenses	9,108	5,054
Other current liabilities	874	777
Total current liabilities	$38,809	$22,518

Also, GER's operating cash flows were $12,829 and $14,874 in 2012 and 2011, respectively.

Note: Round all answers to two decimal places.

Required:
1. Calculate GER's current ratio for 2012 and 2011.
2. Calculate GER's quick ratio for 2012 and 2011.
3. Calculate GER's cash ratio for 2012 and 2011.
4. Calculate GER's operating cash flow ratio for 2012 and 2011.
5. **Conceptual Connection:** Provide some reasons why GER's liquidity may be considered to be improving and some reasons why it may be worsening.

PROBLEM SET B

Problem 8-56B Payable Transactions

OBJECTIVE

Daniels Company engaged in the following transactions during 2012:

a. Purchased $25,000 of merchandise from XYZ Supplies on January 26. Amount due in full on February 28.

b. Paid for 40 percent of the purchased merchandise (transaction *a*) on February 26.

c. On February 28 negotiate a payment extension with XYZ for the remainder of the balance from the January 26 purchase by signing a one-year, 8 percent note.

d. Borrowed $300,000 on an eight-month, 9 percent interest-bearing note on July 31.

e. Purchased $150,000 of merchandise on August 2. Amount due in full on September 30.

f. Paid for the purchased merchandise (transaction *e*) on September 28.

g. Received from Martel, Inc., on October 4, a $40,000 deposit against a total selling price of $400,000 for services to be performed for Martel.

h. Paid quarterly installments of Social Security, Medicare and individual income tax withholdings, as shown below, on October 10. The Social Security and Medicare were recorded as expenses during the quarter and the amount paid represents both the employee and employer share (50 percent each).

Social Security taxes	$280,000
Medicare taxes	65,484
Income taxes withheld	730,000

i. On December 15 Richmond completed the services ordered by Martel on October 4. Martel's remaining balance of $360,000 is due on January 31.

Required:
1. Prepare journal entries for these transactions.
2. Prepare any adjusting entries necessary at December 31, 2012.

Problem 8-57B Payroll Accounting

OBJECTIVE

McLaughlin Manufacturing has the following data available for its March 31, 2011, payroll:

Wages earned	$1,250,000*
Income taxes withheld	180,600

*All subject to Social Security and Medicare matching and withholding at 6.2 percent and 1.45 percent, respectively.

Federal unemployment taxes of 0.50 percent and state unemployment taxes of 0.80 percent are payable on the first $1,000,000.

Required:
1. Compute the taxes payable and wages that will be paid to employees. Then prepare the journal entries to record the wages earned and the payroll taxes (*Note:* Round to the nearest penny).
2. McLaughlin Manufacturing would like to hire a new employee at a salary of $80,000. Assuming the payroll taxes are as described above (with unemployment taxes paid on the first $7,000) and fringe benefits (e.g., health insurance, retirement, etc.) are 28% of gross pay, what will be the total cost of this employee for Stadium?

Problem 8-58B Note Payable and Accrued Interest

OBJECTIVE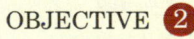

Bordewick Company borrowed $275,000 on a 6 percent, interest-bearing note on November 1, 2012. Bordewick ends its fiscal year on December 31. The note was paid with interest on May 31, 2013.

Required:
1. Prepare the entry for this note on November 1, 2012.
2. Prepare the adjusting entry for this note on December 31, 2012.
3. Indicate how the note and the accrued interest would appear on the balance sheet at December 31, 2012.
4. Prepare the entry to record the repayment of the note on May 31, 2013.

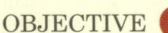

Problem 8-59B Interest-Bearing Note Replacing an Unpaid Account Payable

Monte Cristo Products, which uses a perpetual inventory system, owed $770,000 on account for inventory purchased on November 1, 2012. Monte Cristo's fiscal year ends on December 31. Monte Cristo was unable to pay the amount owed by the February 1 due date because of financial difficulties. On February 1, 2013, Monte Cristo signed a $770,000, 12 percent interest-bearing note. This note was repaid with interest on September 1, 2013.

Required:
1. Prepare the entry recorded on November 1, 2012.
2. Prepare the adjusting entry recorded on December 31, 2012.
3. Prepare the entry recorded on February 1, 2013.
4. Prepare the entry recorded on September 1, 2013.

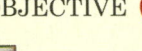

Problem 8-60B Excise Taxes

Yossarian Power Corporation provides electricity to a wide area of eastern Maine. During March 2012 it billed 3,000 of its residential customers located in the town of Maryville a total of $393,000 for electricity. In addition Yossarian Power is required to collect the following taxes:

a. State Excise Tax: A tax of $3.50 per customer plus 2 percent of billing used to fund the Maine Energy Commission
b. Federal Excise Tax: A tax of $0.50 per customer plus 0.15 percent of billing used to fund the Federal Energy Commission

Required:
1. Determine how much Yossarian Power will bill these 3,000 customers in total for the month of March 2012.
2. Prepare the entry to record the billing of these amounts.
3. Prepare the entry to record the collection of these amounts.
4. Prepare the entry to record the payment of the state excise taxes to the appropriate governmental unit.

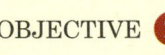

Problem 8-61B Unearned Revenue and Customer Deposits

On November 20, 2011, Billy Pilgrim Technology agreed to manufacture and supply 1,000 centrifuges used by Cathcart Systems to produce chemicals. Cathcart deposited $260 per unit upon signing the three-year purchase agreement, which set the selling price of each centrifuge at $1,300. Billy Pilgrim will record these units at $500 per unit in inventory. No units were delivered during 2011. During 2012, 350 units will be delivered, 400 units will be delivered during 2013, and the remaining units will be delivered during 2014. Assume Billy Pilgrim uses a perpetual inventory system.

Required:
1. **Conceptual Connection:** Prepare the entry by Billy Pilgrim to record receipt of the deposit during 2011. How would the deposit be reported in the financial statements at the end of 2011?
2. **Conceptual Connection:** Prepare the entry by Billy Pilgrim to record the delivery of 350 units during 2012. How would the deposit be reported in the financial statements at the end of 2012?
3. Prepare the entry by Billy Pilgrim to record the delivery of 400 units during 2013. Cathcart pays in cash upon delivery for units not covered by the deposit.

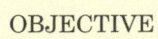

Problem 8-62B Warranties

Montague Auto Repair specializes in the repair of foreign car transmissions. To encourage business, Montague offers a six-month warranty on all repairs. The following data are available for 2011:

Transmissions repaired, 2011	4,500
Expected frequency of warranty claims	0.09 per repair
Actual warranty claims, 2011	$110,000
Estimated warranty liability, 1/1/11	$ 25,000
Estimated cost of each warranty claim	$ 250

Assume that warranty claims are paid in cash.

Required:

1. Compute the warranty expense for 2011.
2. Prepare the entry to record the payment of the 2011 warranty claims.
3. **Conceptual Connection:** What is the December 31, 2011, balance in the warranty liability account? Why has the balance in the warranty liability account changed from January 1, 2011?

Problem 8-63B Ratio Analysis   OBJECTIVE 5

Consider the following information taken from Chicago Water Slide's (CWS's) financial statements:

| | September 30 (in thousands) | |
	2011	2010
Current assets:		
Cash and cash equivalents	$ 2,548	$12,900
Receivables	60,142	33,096
Inventories	63,592	28,144
Other current assets	9,636	5,240
Total current assets	$135,918	$79,380
Current liabilities:		
Current portion of long-term debt	$ 194	$ 7,060
Accounts payable	46,248	22,456
Accrued compensation costs	11,212	3,858
Accrued expenses	18,216	10,108
Other current liabilities	1,748	1,554
Total current liabilities	$ 77,618	$45,036

Also, Chicago Water Slide's Operating Cash Flows were $25,658 and $29,748 in 2011 and 2010, respectively.

Note: Round all answers to two decimal places.

Required:

1. Calculate CWS's current ratio for 2011 and 2010.
2. Calculate CWS's quick ratio for 2011 and 2010.
3. Calculate CWS's cash ratio for 2011 and 2010.
4. Calculate CWS's operating cash flow ratio for 2011 and 2010.
5. **Conceptual Connection:** Provide some reasons why CWS's liquidity may be considered to be improving and some reasons why it may be worsening.

CASES

Case 8-64 Ethics and Current Liabilities

Many long-term loans have contractual restrictions designed to protect the lender from deterioration of the borrower's liquidity or solvency in the future. These restrictions (typically called loan covenants) often take the form of financial-statement ratio values. For example, a lending agreement may state that the loan principal is immediately due and payable if the current ratio falls below 1.2. When borrowers are in danger of violating one or more of these loan covenants, pressure is put on management and the financial accountants to avoid such violations.

Jim is a second year accountant at a large publicly-traded corporation. His boss approaches him and says,

"Jim, I know why we increased our warranty liability, but it puts our current ratio in violation of a loan covenant with our bank loan. I know the bank will pass on it this time, but it's a big hassle to get the waiver. I just don't want to deal with it. I need you to reduce our estimate of warranty liability as far as possible."

Required:

1. How would lowering the estimate of warranty liability affect the current ratio?
2. How should Jim respond to his boss?
3. Given that Jim's employer is a publicly-traded corporation, what safeguards should be at Jim's disposal?

Case 8-65 Short-Term Borrowing with Restrictions

Rocky Mountain Products has a line-of-credit agreement with Norwest Bank that allows it to borrow up to $100,000 at any given time provided that Rocky Mountain's current assets always exceed its current liabilities by the principal amount of the outstanding loan. If this requirement is violated, the entire loan is payable immediately; thus Rocky Mountain is very careful to fulfill the requirement at all times. All loans under this line of credit are due in one month and bear interest at a rate of 1 percent per month. On January 1, 2011, Rocky Mountain has current assets of $150,000 and current liabilities of $92,000; hence, the excess of current assets over current liabilities is $58,000. Rocky Mountain's current liabilities at January 1, 2011, include a short-term loan under the line of credit of $35,000 due on February 1, 2011.

Required:

1. Prepare the journal entry to record the borrowing of $35,000 on January 1, 2011. By how much did this transaction increase or decrease the excess of current assets over current liabilities?
2. Assume that Rocky Mountain used the entire amount of the loan to purchase inventory. Prepare the journal entry to record the purchase. (*Note:* The company uses a perpetual inventory system.) By how much did this purchase increase or decrease the excess of current assets over current liabilities?
3. Without violating the loan restriction, how much more could Rocky Mountain borrow under its line of credit on January 1, 2011, to invest in inventory? To invest in new equipment? Explain.

Case 8-66 Researching and Analysis Using the Annual 10-K

Obtain **Whole Foods**' 2009 annual report (filed November 27, 2009) either through the "Investor Relations" portion of its website (do a web search for Whole Foods investor relations) or go to http://www.sec.gov and click "Search for Company Filings" under "Filings & Forms."

Required:

1. What are Whole Foods' total current liabilities for 2009?
2. How much of their current liabilities is the current portion of all long-term liabilities (including the current portion of capital lease obligations)?
3. Look at Item 3 in the 10-K (this discusses Whole Foods' legal proceedings). Describe Kottaras v. Whole Foods. Based on the information in item 3, do you believe that Whole Foods has recognized a contingent liability related to these current legal proceedings?
4. Calculate Whole Foods' current ratio for 2009 and 2008. (*Note:* Round answers to two decimal places.)
5. Discuss Whole Foods' short-term liquidity based on the values and trends of the current ratio.
6. Calculate Whole Foods' quick ratio and cash ratio for 2009 and 2008. (*Note:* Round answers to two decimal places.)
7. Discuss the implications of these ratios when evaluating Whole Foods' short-term liquidity.
8. Calculate Whole Foods' operating cash flows ratio. (*Note:* Round answer to two decimal places.)
9. Discuss the implications of this ratio when evaluating Whole Foods' short-term liquidity.

Case 8-67 Comparative Analysis: Abercrombie & Fitch versus Aeropostale

Refer to the financial statements of **Abercrombie & Fitch** and **Aeropostale** that are supplied with this text.

Required:

1. Both Aeropostale (Note 14) and Abercrombie & Fitch (Note 16) have notes that discuss contingencies. What contingencies do they disclose? Do you think any of these contingencies are included in the income statement or on the balance sheet? Why or why not?
2. Both companies have notes providing detail on their accrued liabilities. Locate the note and provide the amount of gift card liability for 2009 for both companies.
3. Calculate Abercrombie & Fitch's and Aeropostale's current ratio for the years ended January 30, 2010, and January 31, 2009. (*Note:* Round answers to two decimal places.)
4. Compare Abercrombie & Fitch's and Aeropostale's short-term liquidity based on the values and trends of the current ratio.
5. Calculate Abercrombie & Fitch's and Aeropostale's quick ratio and cash ratio for the years ended January 30, 2010, and January 31, 2009. (*Note:* Round answers to two decimal places.)
6. Compare the values and trends of these ratios when evaluating Abercrombie & Fitch's and Aeropostale's short-term liquidity.
7. Calculate Abercrombie & Fitch's and Aeropostale's operating cash flows ratio for the years ended January 30, 2010, and January 31, 2009. (*Note:* Round answers to two decimal places.)
8. Compare Abercrombie & Fitch's and Aeropostale's short-term liquidity based on the values and trends of the operating cash flows ratio.

Case 8-68 CONTINUING PROBLEM: FRONT ROW ENTERTAINMENT

Front Row has the following selected balances at the February 29, 2012:

Account	Debit	Credit
Cash	$12,480	
Accounts receivable	3,900	
Inventory	20,380	
Other current assets	31,000	
Accounts payable		$ 8,640
Interest payable		375
Sales taxes payable		1,200
Unearned sales revenue		26,100
Other current liabilities		8,300

The following information is *not* reflected in these balances:

a. On February 29, 2012, Front Row Entertainment accepted delivery of $5,325 of live-performance DVDs from their supplier. Front Row has not yet paid the supplier.
b. On February 1, Front Row Entertainment purchased $8,000 of equipment for its Chicago Music House venue by issuing a one-year note payable bearing 10 percent interest. Front Row has not made any journal entries related to this transaction and should accrue for this at month's end. (*Note:* Round any calculations to the nearest dollar.)
c. Front Row Entertainment collected $3,745 of advance ticket sales related to an upcoming concert. This price included 7 percent state sales tax.
d. Amanda Wilson was paid $2,000 in wages to update and monitor the online fan communities. Federal and state unemployment taxes are $16 and $108, respectively. Amanda is below the Social Security minimum. In addition, $375 of income taxes were withheld. (*Note:* Round any calculations to the nearest dollar.)

In addition, several individuals were injured during a concert in February when they pushed past security and rushed the stage. A personal injury lawsuit was filed against Front Row Entertainment in the amount of $250,000. After investigating the incident and consultation with legal counsel, it was determined that the likelihood of a judgment against Front Row was remote.

Required:

1. Prepare the necessary journal entries for *a* through *d* (*Note:* Round all calculations to the nearest dollar).
2. Determine the current ratio before and after the additional information.
3. How should this contingent event be recorded?

9

Long-Term Liabilities

Doug Norman Crystals/Alamy

After studying Chapter 9, you should be able to:

① Describe debt securities and the markets in which they are issued.

② Account for the issuance of long-term debt.

③ Use the straight-line method to account for premium/discount amortization.

④ Use the effective interest rate method to account for premium/discount amortization.

⑤ Determine the after-tax cost of financing with debt and explain financial leverage.

⑥ Compare and contrast operating and capital leases.

⑦ Analyze a company's long-term solvency using information related to long-term liabilities.

⑧ (Appendix 9A) Calculate the market price of long-term debt using present value techniques.

© Javier Larrea/age fotostock/Photolibrary

EXPERIENCE FINANCIAL ACCOUNTING

with American Airlines

AMR Corp is the parent company of **American Airlines**, **AMR Eagle**, and **AmericanConnection** airlines. These airlines serve 250 cities in 40 countries and average more than 3,400 flights per day with approximately 900 airplanes. In 2009, AMR had revenues of just under $20 billion and total assets of $25.4 billion. However, AMR also has long-term debt and lease obligations (including current portions) of $11.7 billion and total stockholders' equity of $3.5 billion.

Companies use long-term debt, along with issuing stock (see Chapter 10), as a way to finance and expand their operations. One measure used to evaluate the mix of debt and equity financing is the long-term debt to equity ratio. A ratio above 1.0 indicates that liabilities are greater than stockholders' equity. According to Reuters Finance, the long-term debt to equity ratio for the airline industry is 3.25. Compare this with the

Monticello, 2010/Shutterstock.com

pharmaceutical industry that has an average long-term debt to equity ratio of 0.19. Why do airlines have so much more debt than pharmaceutical companies?

Industries that use property, plant, and equipment to generate revenues (such as airlines and hotels) typically have higher debt than industries that use intangible assets (such as pharmaceuticals and software). There are a number of reasons for this, but one is that PP&E is readily transferable to creditors in the event of financial distress, so creditors are more receptive to lending at lower rates.

There is a long history of finance research investigating the optimal mix of debt and equity financing because there are advantages and disadvantages for both. Factors affecting the optimal mix are difficult to quantify.

Relatively large amounts of long-term debt are not necessarily bad. Although more long-term debt means more interest expense, interest expense has the advantage of being tax deductible, unlike dividends paid to shareholders. Another advantage is that creditors do not share in the profits of the company, while shareholders do. Thus, if the borrowed money creates a return that is greater than the interest expense on the debt, the shareholders benefit. This is the concept of leverage. We will discuss this concept more in Chapter 12.

Long-term debt generally refers to obligations that extend beyond one year. Bonds, long-term notes, debentures, and capital leases belong in this category of liabilities. Exhibit 9-1 shows **Whirlpool**'s long-term debt obligations.[1]

Exhibit 9-1

Excerpt from Whirlpool's 2009 10-K

	December 31	
	2009	**2008**
	Millions of dollars	
Variable rate notes, maturing through 2009	$ —	$ 200
Senior note—8.6%, maturing 2010	325	325
Senior note—6.125%, maturing 2011	300	300
Senior note—8.0%, maturing 2012	350	—
Medium-term note—5.5%, maturing 2013	499	499
Maytag medium-term note—6.5%, maturing 2014	102	102
Senior note—8.6%, maturing 2014	500	—
Maytag medium-term note—5.0%, maturing 2015	192	190
Senior note—6.5%, maturing 2016	249	249
Debentures—7.75%, maturing 2016	244	243
Other (various maturing through 2016)	119	96
	2,880	2,204
Less current maturities	378	202
Total long-term debt, net of current maturities	$2,502	$2,002

On the balance sheet, long-term debt is typically reported as a single number. The more detailed list, like this one for **Whirlpool**, is usually included in the notes to the financial statements.

Notice that **Whirlpool** subtracted current maturities (just before the bottom line) from the rest of its long-term debt. The difference ($2,502 for 2009) is the amount included as long-term debt on the balance sheet. As we noted in Chapter 8, long-term debt that is due to mature over the next year is reported as a current liability. For simplification, we will disregard the reclassification of long-term debt as current liabilities throughout this chapter.

BONDS PAYABLE AND NOTES PAYABLE

OBJECTIVE 1
Describe debt securities and the markets in which they are issued.

When a company borrows money from a bank, it typically signs a formal agreement or contract called a "note." Frequently, notes are also issued in exchange for a noncash asset such as equipment. Collectively, we refer to these notes as **notes payable**. Larger corporations typically elect to issue bonds instead of notes. A **bond** is a type of note that requires the issuing entity to pay the face value of the bond to the holder when it matures and usually to pay interest periodically at a specified rate.[2] A bond issue essentially breaks down a large debt (large corporations frequently borrow hundreds of millions of dollars) into smaller chunks (usually $1,000) because the total amount borrowed is too large for a single lender. For example, rather than try to find a single

---

[1] We use the term *debt* instead of *liabilities* in this chapter because this is the term used in real financial statements.
[2] Interest is generally paid semiannually. We use both semiannual and annual interest payments in the text to better illustrate interest amortization.

bank willing (and able) to lend $800,000,000 at a reasonable interest rate, corporations typically find it easier and more economical to issue 800,000 bonds with a $1,000 face value. However, the concept behind the way we account for notes and bonds is identical (the only difference is the account title—either "Bonds Payable" or "Notes Payable") and analysts typically do not distinguish between the two. As such, the terms have come to be used somewhat interchangeably.

All such contracts require the borrower to repay the **face value** (also called **par value** or **principal**). Typically the face value is repaid at **maturity**, which is a specified date in the future. However, some contracts require the principal to be repaid in, for example, monthly installments. These contracts typically require equal payments to be made each period. A portion of each payment is interest and a portion is principal. Car, student, and home loans are examples of installment loans.

Most debt contracts also require that the borrower make regular interest payments. Historically, interest payments were made when a bondholder detached a coupon from the debt contract and mailed it to the company on the interest payment date. These obligations are called *coupon notes, coupon debentures*, or *coupon bonds*, and the required interest payments are *coupon payments*. The terminology for coupons is still used today, but now the payments are automatically sent to the registered bondholder.

The amount of each interest payment can be calculated from the face amount, the interest rate, and the number of payments per year, all stated in the debt contract. (The **interest rate** identified in the contract goes by various names, including **stated rate**, **coupon rate**, and **contract rate**.) Recall the formula for calculating interest:

> Face Value × Interest Rate × Time (in years)

To illustrate, consider a contract with a face amount of $1,000, a stated interest rate of 8 percent, and semiannual interest payments. For this $1,000 note, the amount of each semiannual interest payment is $40:

$$\$1,000 \times 8\% \times 6/12 = \$40$$

Types of Bonds

In practice, bonds also differ along a number of other dimensions, as illustrated in Exhibit 9-2 (p. 426).

Secured Bonds A **secured** bond has some collateral pledged against the corporation's ability to pay. For example, **mortgage bonds** are secured by real estate. In this case, should the borrower fail to make the payments required by the bond, the lender can take possession of (repossess) the real estate that secures the bond. The real estate provides "security" for the lender in case the debt is not paid. Bonds are also frequently secured by the stocks or bonds of other corporations and, in theory, can be secured by anything of value.

Unsecured Bonds Most bonds, however, are **unsecured**. These are typically called **debenture bonds**. In this case, there is no collateral; instead, the lender is relying on the general credit of the corporation. What this really means is, should the borrower go bankrupt, any secured bondholders will get their collateral before the unsecured bondholders receive a single penny. That is, unsecured bondholders are the last lenders to be paid in bankruptcy (only the shareholders follow).

You may have heard of the term **junk bonds**. These are unsecured bonds where the risk of the borrower failing to make the interest and/or principal payments is relatively high. Why would anyone lend money under such circumstances? Because they receive a high enough rate of interest to compensate them for the risk.

Callable Bonds **Callable bonds** give the borrower the right to pay off (or call) the bonds prior to their due date. The borrower typically "calls" debt when the interest rate being paid is much higher than the current market conditions. This is similar to home-owners "refinancing" to obtain a lower interest rate on their home mortgage.

Exhibit 9-2

Long-Term Debt Terms

Notes/Bonds	Different names for debt instruments that require borrowers to pay the lender the face value and usually to make periodic interest payments.
Face Value/Par Value/Principal	The amount of money the borrower agrees to repay at maturity.
Maturity Date	The date on which the borrower agrees to pay the creditor the face (or par) value.
Stated/Coupon/Contract Rate	The rate of interest paid on the face (or par) value. The borrower pays the interest to the creditor each period until maturity.
Market/Yield Rate	The market rate of interest demanded by creditors. This is a function of economic factors and the creditworthiness of the borrower. It may differ from the stated rate.
Secured Bonds	Secured debt provides collateral (such as real estate or another asset) for the lender. That is, if the borrower fails to make the payments required by the debt, the lender can "repossess" the collateral.
Unsecured/Debenture Bonds	Debt that does not have collateral is unsecured. Unsecured bonds typically are called debenture bonds.
Junk Bonds	Junk bonds are unsecured bonds that are also very risky, and, therefore, pay a high rate of interest to compensate the lender for the added risk.
Callable Bonds	Callable bonds give the borrower the option to pay off the debt prior to maturity. Borrowers will typically exercise this option when the interest being paid on the debt is substantially greater than the current market rate of interest.
Convertible Bonds	Convertible bonds give the lender the option to convert the bond into other securities—typically shares of common stock. Lenders will typically exercise this option when the value of the shares of common stock is more attractive than the interest and principal payments supplied by the debt instrument.

Convertible Bonds **Convertible bonds** allow the bondholder to convert the bond into another security—typically common stock. Convertible bonds will specify the conversion ratio. For example, each $1,000 bond may be convertible into 20 shares of common stock. In this case, bondholders will convert when the value of the 20 shares becomes more attractive than the interest payments and repayment of the $1,000 principal.

Selling New Debt Securities

Borrowing, through the use of notes or bonds, is attractive to businesses as a source of money because the relative cost of issuing debt (such as the interest payments) is often lower than the cost of issuing equity (such as giving up ownership shares). Businesses may sell bonds directly to institutions such as insurance companies or pension funds. However, bonds are frequently sold to the public through an underwriter. Underwriters generate a profit either by offering a price that is slightly less than the expected market price (thereby producing a profit on resale) or by charging the borrower a fee.

Underwriters examine the provisions of the instrument (secured or unsecured, callable or not callable, convertible or not convertible), the credit standing of the borrowing business, and the current conditions in the credit markets and the economy as a whole to determine the **market rate** of interest (or **yield**) for the bond. The yield may differ from the stated rate because the underwriter disagrees with the borrower as to the correct yield or because of changes in the economy or creditworthiness of the borrower between the setting of the stated rate and the date of issue.

Exhibit 9-3

The Relationships between Stated Interest Rate and Yield

Bonds Sold at	Yield Compared to Stated Rate	Interest Over the Life of the Bonds
Premium (above Par)	Yield < Stated Rate	Interest Expense < Interest Paid
Par	Yield = Stated Rate	Interest Expense = Interest Paid
Discount (below Par)	Yield > Stated Rate	Interest Expense > Interest Paid

As shown in Exhibit 9-3, there are three possible relationships between the stated interest rate and yield: (1) they can be equal, (2) the yield can be less than the stated rate, or (3) the yield can be greater than the stated rate. If the yield is equal to the stated rate, the bonds sell for the face value, or par. If the yield is less than the stated rate, the bonds represent particularly good investments because the interest payments are higher than market. In this case, the demand for such bonds will bid the selling price up above face value. When this happens, bonds are said to sell at a **premium**. On the other hand, if the yield is greater than the stated rate of interest, the below market interest payments will drive the selling price below the face value, in which case, the bond would sell at a **discount**.

Concept Q&A

Why is the market value of bonds not always equal to their face value?

Answer:
If, for example, the stated rate of interest is higher than the market rate of interest, the bonds represent particularly good investments. As such, the demand for such bonds will bid the price up above face value. On the other hand, if the stated rate of interest is lower than the market rate of interest, the lack of demand for such bonds will bid the market price below face value.

YOU DECIDE   Fixed Versus Variable-Rate Debt

You are the CFO of Carmean Corp. Carmean has decided to borrow $100,000,000 to finance expansion plans. One option is to issue 20-year bonds with a fixed rate of 8 percent. Carmean's investment bankers believe these will sell for par. Another option is to issue 20-year bonds with a variable rate of one-year LIBOR (London Interbank Offered Rate) plus 5 percent. For the first year, this will result in a 6.2 percent rate, but the rate will be adjusted annually.

What types of things should you consider in making the decision about which borrowing option is best for Carmean?

Borrowers must trade off the potential benefit of lower rates with the risk of the rate increasing in the future. In fact, risk is what the difference in rates is all about. With a fixed rate, the lender bears all the risk of changing rates. Specifically, if fixed rates increase dramatically, the lender is stuck with a below market return. Admittedly, if rates were to drop, the lender has an above market return, but this uncertainty is the definition of risk. With a variable rate, on the other hand, the borrower bears the risk (and rewards) of changing rates. The shift of risk from the lender to the borrower is why the lender is willing to accept a lower rate initially.

Borrowers must consider terms of the contract, such as how frequently the rate is adjusted, the length of the loan, limits on how much the rate can increase each year or how high the rate can go, etc. Additionally, the borrower must consider its ability to handle increased interest payments should the rate adjust up.

In this case, Carmean should only opt for the lower variable rate if they can absorb the higher interest payments should their rate adjust up.

ACCOUNTING FOR LONG-TERM DEBT

The accounting for notes and bonds is conceptually identical, so keep in mind that, in the bond and note examples that follow, everything would stay the same if we substituted the word note for bond and vice versa.

There are three basic cash flows for which the issuing corporation must account:

- Issuance: the cash received when the bonds are issued (the issue or selling price)
- Interest: the interest payments
- Repayment: the repayment of the principal (or face value)

OBJECTIVE 2
Account for the issuance of long-term debt.

IFRS
The accounting for notes payable and bonds payable is generally the same under IFRS as it is for U.S. GAAP.

Assume that a corporation issues bonds with a total face value of $500,000, with a stated rate of 6.5 percent payable annually, and the principal is due in five years. Exhibit 9-4 depicts all three cash flows.

Exhibit 9-4

Cash Flows for a Bond

Face value:	$500,000	Stated rate:	6.5%
Due:	5 years	Interest payments:	$500,000 × 6.5% × (12/12)

	0	1	2	3	4	5

Issue date:	$500,000					
Interest payments:		($32,500)	($32,500)	($32,500)	($32,500)	($32,500)
Repayment of principal (face value):						($500,000)

Recording Issuance

The market price for debt is typically quoted as a percentage of face value. For example, if $100,000 face value bonds are issued at 103, their selling price is 103 percent of face value, or $103,000. Any amount paid above the face value is called a *premium*. In this case, a $3,000 premium was paid. If the bond is issued below face value, this difference is called a *discount*. For example, if these $100,000 face value bonds were issued at 96, there would be a $4,000 discount.

At the time of issue, the borrower records the face value of the bonds in a bond payable account and records any premium or discount in a separate account called Premium on Bonds Payable or Discount on Bonds Payable. The premium and discount accounts are called "valuation" accounts because they affect the value at which the liability is shown on the balance sheet. That is, as shown in Exhibit 9-5, both the premium and discount accounts are netted with bonds payable on the balance sheet, so on the date of issue the book value of the bonds payable is equal to the market value.

Exhibit 9-5

Balance Sheet Presentation

Long-term liabilities:				Long-term liabilities:	
Bonds payable	$100,000	**OR**		Bonds payable	$100,000
Add: Premium on bonds payable	3,000			Less: Discount on bonds payable	(4,000)
	103,000				96,000

CORNERSTONE 9-1 illustrates recording the issuance of bonds.

CORNERSTONE 9-1   Recording the Issuance of Bonds

Concept:
When bonds are issued, any premium or discount is recorded in a separate valuation account.

Information:
On December 31, 2011, Groening Co. issued $100,000 face value of bonds, with a stated rate of 8 percent, due in five years with interest payable annually on December 31.

Required:
Prepare the journal entries assuming the bonds sell (1) for par, (2) for 103, and (3) for 96.

(Continued)

Solution:

	Date	Account and Explanation	Debit	Credit
1.	Dec. 31, 2011	Cash	100,000	
		Bonds Payable		100,000
		(Record issuance of bonds at par)		
2.	Dec. 31, 2011	Cash (100,000 × 103%)	103,000	
		Bonds Payable		100,000
		Premium on Bonds Payable		3,000
		(Record issuance of bonds at premium)		
3.	Dec. 31, 2011	Cash (100,000 × 96%)	96,000	
		Discount on Bonds Payable	4,000	
		Bonds Payable		100,000
		(Record issuance of bonds at discount)		

CORNERSTONE 9-1 (continued)

Assets	=	Liabilities	+	Stockholders' Equity
+100,000		+100,000		

Assets	=	Liabilities	+	Stockholders' Equity
+103,000		+100,000		
		+3,000		

Assets	=	Liabilities	+	Stockholders' Equity
+96,000		+100,000		
		−4,000		

RECOGNIZING INTEREST EXPENSE AND REPAYMENT OF PRINCIPAL

Repayment of the principal at maturity is trivial. Recall that the principal amount repaid is equal to the face value of the note. This is also the amount that was originally credited to the note or bond payable. As such, you merely need to debit the note or bond payable and credit the cash.

Recognizing the interest expense, on the other hand, is a bit more challenging because any amount paid to the lender in excess of the amount borrowed (face value less any discount or plus any premium) represents interest. In our examples above, when the bonds were issued at par (face value) the amount of cash received when issued was equal to the amount to be repaid at maturity. When the bonds were issued at a premium, the amount of cash received when issued was $103,000 ($3,000 greater than the face value), but only the face value ($100,000) is repaid at maturity. The $3,000 difference represents an effective reduction of the amount of interest paid to the borrower. In contrast, when the bonds were issued at a discount, the amount of cash received was $96,000 ($4,000 less than the face value), but the entire face value ($100,000) must be repaid at maturity. The additional $4,000 effectively represents additional interest.

When an obligation extends over several interest periods, the amount of interest associated with each period also must be determined. **Interest amortization** is the process used to determine the amount of interest to be recorded in each of the periods the liability is outstanding.[3]

This allocation has two parts:

- the actual interest payment made to the lender during the period
- amortizing any premium or discount on the bond.

Interest Amortization Methods

Although the interest payment made to the lender during the period is always a component of the period's interest expense, there are two methods for amortizing any premium or discount:

OBJECTIVE 3
Use the straight-line method to account for premium/discount amortization.

 *Concept* Q&A

Why are premiums and discounts on bonds payable amortized to Interest Expense?

Answer:
Discounts occur when the stated rate of interest is below the market rate of interest. In this case lenders lend less than the face value to the borrower, but are repaid the entire face value at maturity. This difference between the amount lent and the amount repaid conceptually represents an additional interest payment to compensate the lender for accepting a below market interest rate. Similarly, premiums occur when the stated rate of interest is above the market rate of interest. In this case, lenders lend more than the face value to the borrower but are only repaid the face value at maturity. This difference represents a prepayment of interest by the lender to compensate the borrower for providing above market interest payments.

---

[3] The same interest amortization procedures used by borrowers to account for liabilities are also used by lenders to account for the corresponding assets.

- The **effective interest rate method** is based on compound interest calculations. Interest expense for the period is always the yield (the effective interest rate) times the carrying (or book) value of the bonds at the beginning of the period.
- The **straight-line method**, on the other hand, represents a simple approximation of effective interest amortization. Equal amounts of premium or discount are amortized to interest expense each period.

Although the effective interest rate method is GAAP, the straight-line method may be used if it produces approximately the same numerical results as the effective interest rate method. Frequently, the two methods do, in fact, produce quite similar results.

THE STRAIGHT-LINE METHOD

We will now discuss how interest expense is allocated to the various accounting periods using the straight-line method for:

- Debt with regular interest payments sold at their face or par value.
- Debt with regular interest payments sold for more (a premium) or less (a discount) than the face or par value.

Debt with Regular Interest Payments Sold at Par

When debt is sold at par there is no premium or discount to amortize. In this case, the interest expense reported on the income statement is equal to the interest payment(s) made to the creditor during the period. This situation typically happens when a business borrows from a single creditor. In this case, the two parties can easily agree on a stated rate that equals the appropriate yield. **CORNERSTONE 9-2** illustrates how interest expense is recorded in this case.

 **CORNERSTONE 9-2**   **Recording Interest Expense for Bonds Sold at Par**

Concept:
When bonds are issued at par there is no discount or premium to amortize, so the only component of interest expense is the interest paid to the lender for the period.

Information:
On December 31, 2011, Groening Co. issued $100,000 of 8 percent bonds at par. These bonds are due in five years with interest payable annually on December 31.

Required:
1. Calculate the interest payment made on December 31 of each year.
2. Prepare the journal entries necessary to recognize (a) the interest expense on December 31, 2012–2016, and (b) the repayment of the loan principal on December 31, 2016.

Solution:
1. The interest payment on December 31 of each year will be:

$$\$100,000 \times 8\% = \$8,000$$

2.

Date	Account and Explanation	Debit	Credit				
							Stockholders'
				Assets	**= Liabilities**	**+**	**Equity**
a. Dec. 31 2012–2016	Interest Expense	8,000		−8,000			−8,000
	Cash		8,000				
	(Record interest expense)						
							Stockholders'
				Assets	**= Liabilities**	**+**	**Equity**
b. Dec. 31, 2016	Bonds Payable	100,000		−100,000	−100,000		
	Cash		100,000				
	(Record repayment of bond principal)						

Note, from Cornerstone 9-2, that the interest expense recorded is equal to the cash paid to the lender when the bond is issued at par.

Debt with Regular Interest Payments Sold at a Premium or Discount

As mentioned previously, the sale of a bond at a discount or premium affects the borrower's interest expense. This is because total interest expense is the difference between the payments to the lenders and the amount received by the borrowing business. Let us compare a $1,000,000, 10 percent, five-year bond contract with semiannual interest payments that are sold at a $10,000 discount (99 percent of par) with the same issue sold at a $20,000 premium (102 percent of par).

	Bond Sold at a Discount	Bond Sold at a Premium
Face amount payment at maturity	$1,000,000	$ 1,000,000
Interest payments (10 at $50,000 each)	500,000	500,000
Total payments to lenders	$1,500,000	$ 1,500,000
Less: Proceeds at issue	(990,000)	(1,020,000)
Total interest expense over life of bond	$ 510,000	$ 480,000

For the discounted bond, total interest expense ($510,000) exceeds interest payments ($500,000) by $10,000. For the bond issued at a premium, total interest expense ($480,000) is $20,000 less than the cash interest payments ($500,000).

This total interest expense is spread over the life of the bond. For the 10 percent, $1,000,000 bond sold at 99, interest expense would be $51,000 per six-month interest period:

$$\frac{\$510,000}{10} = \$51,000 \text{ per six-month interest period}$$

Another way of calculating this would be as follows:

Interest paid	$50,000
Amortization of discount (10,000/10 periods)	1,000
Total interest expense per period	$51,000

In fact, amortization tables like you see in Cornerstones 9-3 and 9-4 (p. 433) are used to help calculate these amounts. Although such tables aren't really necessary when using the straight-line method for amortizing bond discount or premium, they are extremely helpful when the effective interest rate method is used, as is shown later in the chapter.

CORNERSTONE 9-3 shows how to record interest expense when the bond is issued at a discount.

CORNERSTONE 9-3

Recording Interest Expense for Bonds Sold at a Discount Using the Straight-Line Method

Concept:
When interest-bearing bonds are issued at a discount, the interest expense for the period is the amount of interest payment for the period *plus* the discount amortization for the period. Under the straight-line method, an equal amount of discount is amortized each period.

Information:
On December 31, 2011, Leela Inc. issues five-year, $100,000,000, 8 percent bonds at 99 ($99,000,000). The discount at the time of the sale is $1,000,000. Interest is paid semiannually on June 30 and December 31.

(Continued)

Required:

1. Prepare the journal entry to record the issuance of the bonds on December 31, 2011.
2. Calculate the amount of discount that will be amortized each semiannual period.
3. Calculate the amount of interest expense for each semiannual period.
4. Complete an amortization table for each of the 10 semiannual periods.
5. Prepare the journal entries necessary to (a) recognize the interest expense on June 30 and December 31, 2012–2016 and (b) record the repayment of the loan principal on December 31, 2016.

**CORNERSTONE
9-3**
(continued)

Solution:

1.

Date	Account and Explanation	Debit	Credit
Dec. 31, 2011	Cash	99,000,000	
	Discount on Bonds Payable	1,000,000	
	Bonds Payable		100,000,000
	(Record issuance of bonds at a discount)		

Assets	=	Liabilities	+	Stockholders' Equity
+99,000,000		−1,000,000 +100,000,000		

2. $$\text{Discount Amortization} = \frac{\text{Total Discount}}{\text{Number of Interest Periods}} = \frac{\$1,000,000}{10 \text{ periods}} = \$100,000 \text{ per period}$$

3. Interest Expense = Interest Payment + Discount Amortization
    = ($100,000,000 × 8% × 6/12) + $100,000
    = $4,000,000 + $100,000
    = $4,100,000

4.

Semiannual Period	Cash Payment (Credit)	Interest Expense (Debit)	Discount on Bonds Payable (Credit)	Discount on Bonds Payable Balance	Carrying Value
At issue				$1,000,000	$ 99,000,000
1	$4,000,000	$4,100,000	$100,000	900,000	99,100,000
2	4,000,000	4,100,000	100,000	800,000	99,200,000
3	4,000,000	4,100,000	100,000	700,000	99,300,000
4	4,000,000	4,100,000	100,000	600,000	99,400,000
5	4,000,000	4,100,000	100,000	500,000	99,500,000
6	4,000,000	4,100,000	100,000	400,000	99,600,000
7	4,000,000	4,100,000	100,000	300,000	99,700,000
8	4,000,000	4,100,000	100,000	200,000	99,800,000
9	4,000,000	4,100,000	100,000	100,000	99,900,000
10	4,000,000	4,100,000	100,000	0	100,000,000

Note: The discount on bonds payable is amortized to $0 at maturity.

5.

Date	Account and Explanation	Debit	Credit
a. June 30/Dec. 31	Interest Expense	4,100,000	
	Cash		4,000,000
	Discount on Bonds Payable		100,000
	(Record interest payment on bonds)		

Assets	=	Liabilities	+	Stockholders' Equity
−4,000,000		+100,000		−4,100,000

Date	Account and Explanation	Debit	Credit
b. Dec. 31, 2016	Bonds Payable	100,000,000	
	Cash		100,000,000
	(Record repayment of bond principal)		

Assets	=	Liabilities	+	Stockholders' Equity
−100,000,000		−100,000,000		

Carrying Value over the Life of a Bond Issued at a Discount

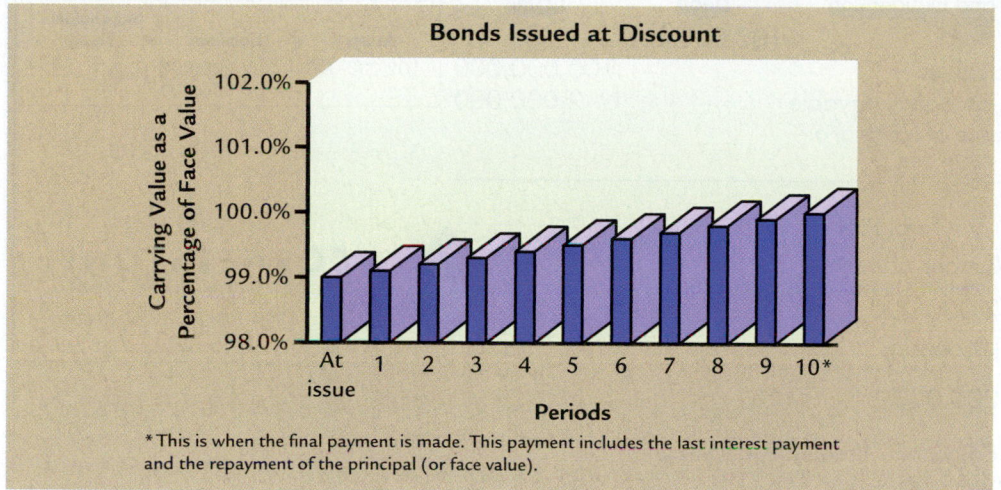

Bonds Issued at Discount

* This is when the final payment is made. This payment includes the last interest payment and the repayment of the principal (or face value).

Exhibit 9-6 illustrates how the carrying value of the bond shown in Cornerstone 9-3 grows over time due to the discount amortization. Notice that the beginning carrying value is 99 percent of the face value. This indicates that although the 8 percent stated rate is below market yield, it is only slightly below. (In fact, the yield would be approximately 8.25 percent.) Further, although the magnitude of the discount and the corresponding amortization is much smaller than it was on the zero-coupon bond, the discount amortization still increases the bond carrying value.

CORNERSTONE 9-4 shows how things change when the bond is issued at a premium.

CORNERSTONE 9-4   Recording Interest Expense for Bonds Sold at a Premium Using the Straight-Line Method

Concept:
When interest-bearing bonds are issued at a premium, the interest expense for the period is the amount of interest payment for the period *less* the premium amortization for the period. Under the straight-line method, an equal amount of premium is amortized each period.

Information:
On December 31, 2011, Farnsworth Inc. issues five-year, $100,000,000, 8 percent bonds at 102 ($102,000,000). The premium at the time of the sale is $2,000,000. Interest is paid semiannually on June 30 and December 31.

Required:
1. Prepare the journal entry to record the issuance of the bonds on December 31, 2011.
2. Calculate the amount of premium that will be amortized each semiannual period.
3. Calculate the amount of interest expense for each semiannual period.
4. Complete an amortization table for the 10 semiannual periods.
5. Prepare the journal entry necessary to (a) recognize the interest expense on June 30 and December 31, 2012–2016, and (b) record the repayment of the loan principal on December 31, 2016.

(Continued)

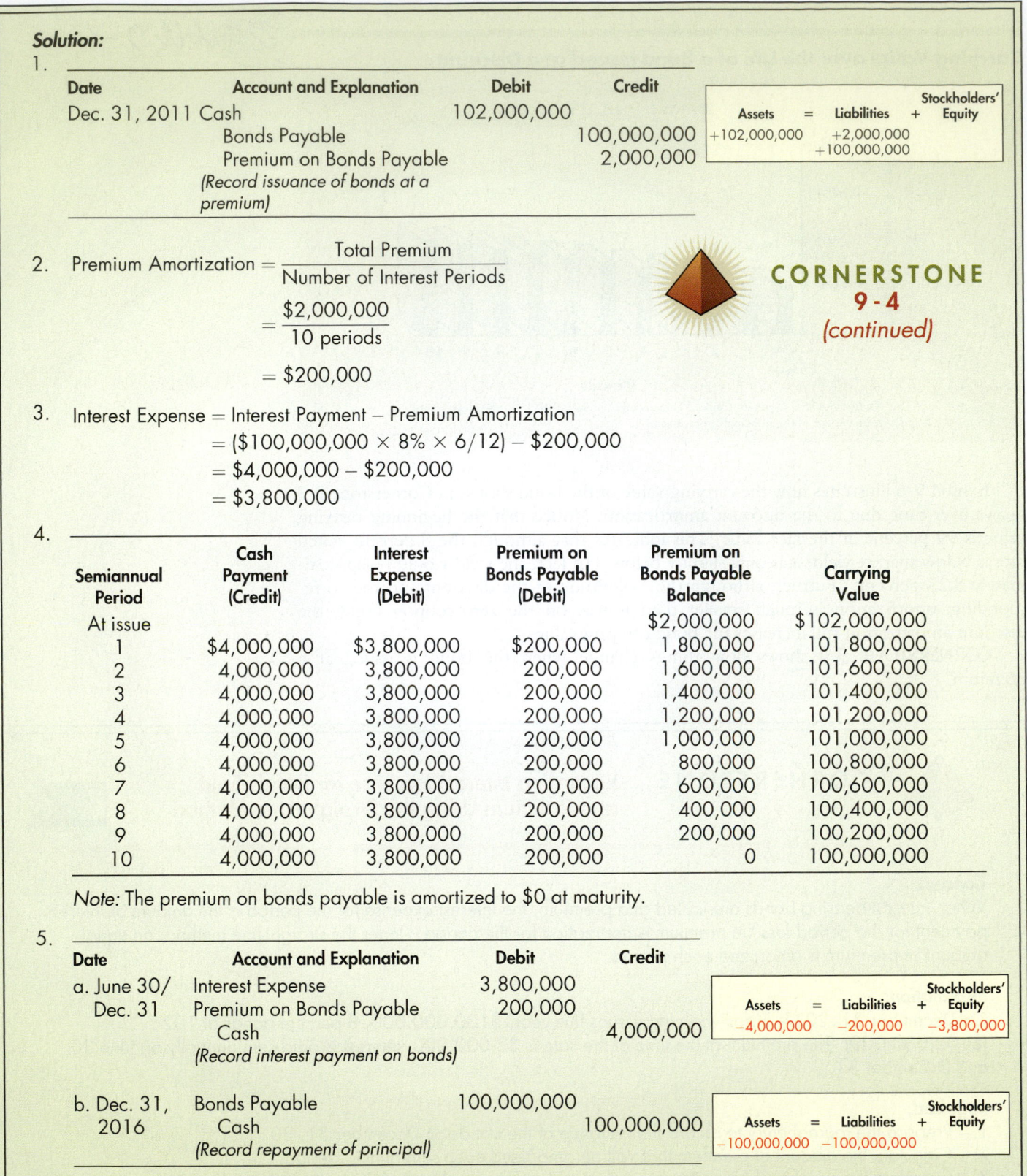

Solution:

1.

Date	Account and Explanation	Debit	Credit
Dec. 31, 2011	Cash	102,000,000	
	Bonds Payable		100,000,000
	Premium on Bonds Payable		2,000,000
	(Record issuance of bonds at a premium)		

	Assets	=	Liabilities	+	Stockholders' Equity
	+102,000,000		+2,000,000 +100,000,000		

CORNERSTONE 9-4
(continued)

2.   Premium Amortization $= \dfrac{\text{Total Premium}}{\text{Number of Interest Periods}}$

$= \dfrac{\$2{,}000{,}000}{10 \text{ periods}}$

$= \$200{,}000$

3.   Interest Expense = Interest Payment − Premium Amortization

$= (\$100{,}000{,}000 \times 8\% \times 6/12) - \$200{,}000$

$= \$4{,}000{,}000 - \$200{,}000$

$= \$3{,}800{,}000$

4.

Semiannual Period	Cash Payment (Credit)	Interest Expense (Debit)	Premium on Bonds Payable (Debit)	Premium on Bonds Payable Balance	Carrying Value
At issue				$2,000,000	$102,000,000
1	$4,000,000	$3,800,000	$200,000	1,800,000	101,800,000
2	4,000,000	3,800,000	200,000	1,600,000	101,600,000
3	4,000,000	3,800,000	200,000	1,400,000	101,400,000
4	4,000,000	3,800,000	200,000	1,200,000	101,200,000
5	4,000,000	3,800,000	200,000	1,000,000	101,000,000
6	4,000,000	3,800,000	200,000	800,000	100,800,000
7	4,000,000	3,800,000	200,000	600,000	100,600,000
8	4,000,000	3,800,000	200,000	400,000	100,400,000
9	4,000,000	3,800,000	200,000	200,000	100,200,000
10	4,000,000	3,800,000	200,000	0	100,000,000

Note: The premium on bonds payable is amortized to $0 at maturity.

5.

Date	Account and Explanation	Debit	Credit
a. June 30/ Dec. 31	Interest Expense	3,800,000	
	Premium on Bonds Payable	200,000	
	Cash		4,000,000
	(Record interest payment on bonds)		

	Assets	=	Liabilities	+	Stockholders' Equity
	−4,000,000		−200,000		−3,800,000

Date	Account and Explanation	Debit	Credit
b. Dec. 31, 2016	Bonds Payable	100,000,000	
	Cash		100,000,000
	(Record repayment of principal)		

	Assets	=	Liabilities	+	Stockholders' Equity
	−100,000,000		−100,000,000		

Exhibit 9-7 illustrates how the carrying value of the bond shown in Cornerstone 9-4 declines over time due to the premium amortization. Notice that the beginning carrying value is 102 percent of the face value. This indicates that the 8 percent stated rate is slightly above market yield. (In fact, the yield would be approximately 7.51 percent.)

Carrying Value over the Life of a Bond Issued at a Premium

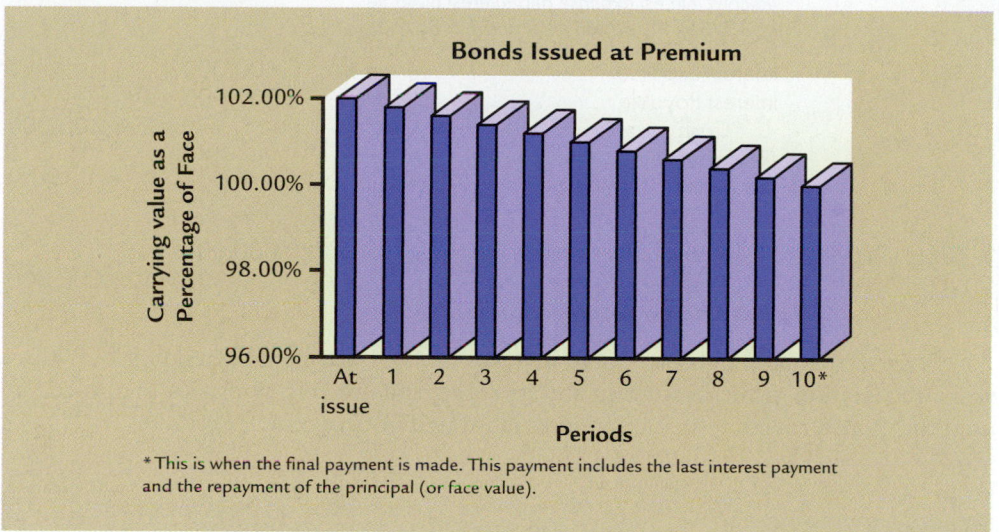

Notice that in this case, the carrying value is the face value of the bond plus the premium because both the bond payable and the premium have credit balances. Further, as the premium is amortized, the premium balance declines and the carrying value moves closer to face value.

Accruing Interest

In the previous discussion, interest payments were made on the last day of the period—December 31. This is frequently not the case in the real world. Assume that on September 1, 2011, Fry Communications borrows $120,000,000 on a three-year, 7 percent note. The note requires annual interest payments (each equal to 7 percent of $120,000,000) and repayment of the principal plus the final year's interest at the end of the third year. This borrowing would be recognized in Fry's accounts as follows:

Date	Account and Explanation	Debit	Credit
Sept. 1, 2011	Cash	120,000,000	
	Notes Payable		120,000,000
	(Record issuance of note)		

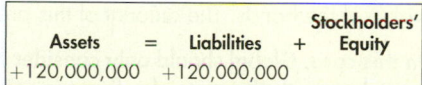

	Assets	=	Liabilities	+	Stockholders' Equity
	+120,000,000		+120,000,000		

Since no interest payment is made at Fry's year end (December 31), interest must be accrued for the period. Interest expense for the four-month period from September through December is $2,800,000 [$120,000,000 × 0.07 × 4/12]. That means interest expense for the eight-month period from January through August is $5,600,000 [$120,000,000 × 0.07 × 8/12]. Fry would recognize interest expense and the payment of interest on this note during 2011 through 2014 as follows:

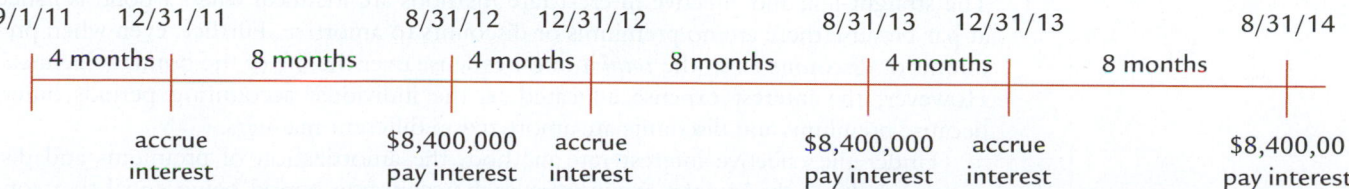

Date	Account and Explanation	Debit	Credit
Dec. 31	Interest Expense	2,800,000	
	Interest Payable		2,800,000
	(Record interest expense and interest payable on 12/31/11, 12/31/12, and 12/31/13)		
Sept. 1	Interest Expense	5,600,000	
	Interest Payable	2,800,000	
	Cash		8,400,000
	(Record interest expense (8 months) and payment of 12 months interest on 9/1/12, 9/1/13 and 9/1/14)		
Sept. 1, 2014	Notes Payable	120,000,000	
	Cash		120,000,000
	(Record repayment of principal on note)		

Assets	=	Liabilities	+	Stockholders' Equity
		+2,800,000		−2,800,000

Assets	=	Liabilities	+	Stockholders' Equity
−8,400,000		−2,800,000		−5,600,000

Assets	=	Liabilities	+	Stockholders' Equity
−120,000,000		−120,000,000		

Observe that although Fry's note involves multiple payments extending over three years, recognition of the borrowing and its repayment are very similar to the procedure used for short-term interest-bearing notes illustrated in Chapter 8.

YOU DECIDE   Financial Statement Effects of Refinancing

You are the CFO of Global Industries. Eight years ago, Global issued $100,000,000 of bonds that yielded 11 percent. Global's borrowing costs are currently 9 percent. If Global were to refinance the debt, interest payments would drop by $2,000,000 per year.

Should Global refinance? How would the refinancing affect net income?

Unlike debt at a bank (such as a car loan or home mortgage), bonds are not paid off by merely repaying the principal; instead, bonds must be repurchased in the market at their fair market value. To illustrate, assume these bonds were issued at par. This means that their fair value was $100,000,000 on the date of issue. However, the fair value is $100,000,000 only when the market rate of interest is 11 percent (such as at issue) and on the maturity date (because no interest payments remain). If market rates fall below the 11-percent yield, the fair value of the debt will increase because the lenders will demand a premium to sell the above market interest payments of 11 percent. Accordingly, to refinance, Global must pay more than $100,000,000. This premium, coupled with the additional costs of refinancing, will more than offset the decrease in interest payments.

As for the effect on net income, because the carrying value of the existing debt is its amortized cost, not its fair market value, refinancing typically results in a gain or loss on refinancing being recognized. In this case, Global will pay more than the $100,000,000 carrying value of the bonds. The amount of this premium will be a loss on Global's income statement, thus lowering net income.

In this case, Global should only consider the cash flow implications. Specifically, Global should refinance if the present value of the interest saved exceeds the costs of refinancing. In reality, however, management also considers the financial-statement effects of the transaction, although any loss on refinancing does not affect the cash flows.

OBJECTIVE
Use the effective interest rate method to account for premium/discount amortization.

THE EFFECTIVE INTEREST RATE METHOD: RECOGNIZING INTEREST EXPENSE AND REPAYMENT OF PRINCIPAL

The straight-line and effective interest rate methods are identical when a bond is issued at par because there are no premiums or discounts to amortize. Further, even when premiums or discounts exist, the *total* interest expense over the life of the bonds is identical. However, the interest expense allocated to the individual accounting periods differs because premiums and discounts are amortized in different manners.

Under the effective interest rate method, the amortization of premiums and discounts results in the interest expense for each accounting period being equal to a constant percentage of the bond book value (also called *carrying value*). That is, the interest expense changes every period, but the effective interest rate on the bond book value is constant. The straight-line method, on the other hand, has a constant interest expense each period, but the effective interest rate on the bond book value changes every period.

To use the effective interest method, you must distinguish between interest payments, which are calculated as follows:

$$\text{Face Value} \times \text{Stated Rate} \times \text{Time (in years)}$$

and effective interest expense, which is calculated as follows:

$$\text{Carrying Value} \times \text{Yield Rate} \times \text{Time (in years)}$$

This difference is so important it bears emphasis. Interest payments are calculated with face value and the stated rate of interest. These payments are the same each period. Interest expense, under the effective rate method, is calculated by using the Carrying Value (Face Value − Discount Balance or Face Value + Premium Balance) and the yield, or market rate, of interest.

CORNERSTONE 9-5 illustrates how discounts are amortized under the effective interest rate method.

Concept Q&A

Is the total amount of interest expense over the life of the bond higher when we use straight-line amortization or the effective interest rate method?

Answer:
Neither—the total amount of interest expense is identical under both methods. What changes is the interest expense allocated to each period (see Exhibit 9-8).

CORNERSTONE 9-5   Recording Interest Expense for Bonds Sold at a Discount Using the Effective Interest Rate Method

Concept:

When interest-bearing bonds are issued at a discount, the interest expense for the period is the amount of interest payment for the period *plus* the discount amortization for the period. Under the effective interest rate method, a constant (or effective) rate of interest on the bond book (or carrying) value is allocated to the period.

Information:

On December 31, 2011, Brannigan Co. issued $1,000,000 of 8 percent bonds, due in five years with interest payable annually on December 31. The market rate of interest is 9 percent. Assume the bond was issued at $961,103. This was calculated using time value of money concepts [see Cornerstone 9-8 (p. 446) in Appendix 9A for the calculation].

Required:

1. Complete an amortization table for each of the five annual periods.
2. Prepare the journal entry necessary to (a) recognize the interest expense on December 31, 2012 and 2013 and (b) record the repayment of the loan principal on December 31, 2016.

Solution:

1.

Annual Period	Cash Payment[a] (Credit)	Interest Expense[b] (Debit)	Discount on Bonds Payable[c] (Credit)	Discount on Bonds Payable Balance	Carrying Value[d]
At issue				$38,897	$ 961,103
12/31/12	$80,000	$86,499	$6,499	32,398	967,602
12/31/13	80,000	87,084	7,084	25,314	974,686
12/31/14	80,000	87,722	7,722	17,592	982,408
12/31/15	80,000	88,417	8,417	9,175	990,825
12/31/16	80,000	89,175	9,175	0	1,000,000

[a]Cash Payment = Face Value × 8% × 12/12 = $80,000
[b]Interest Expense = Carrying Value × 9% × 12/12
[c]Change in Discount Balance = Interest Expense − Cash Payment
[d]New Carrying Value = Previous Carrying Value + Change in Discount on Bonds Payable Balance

(Continued)

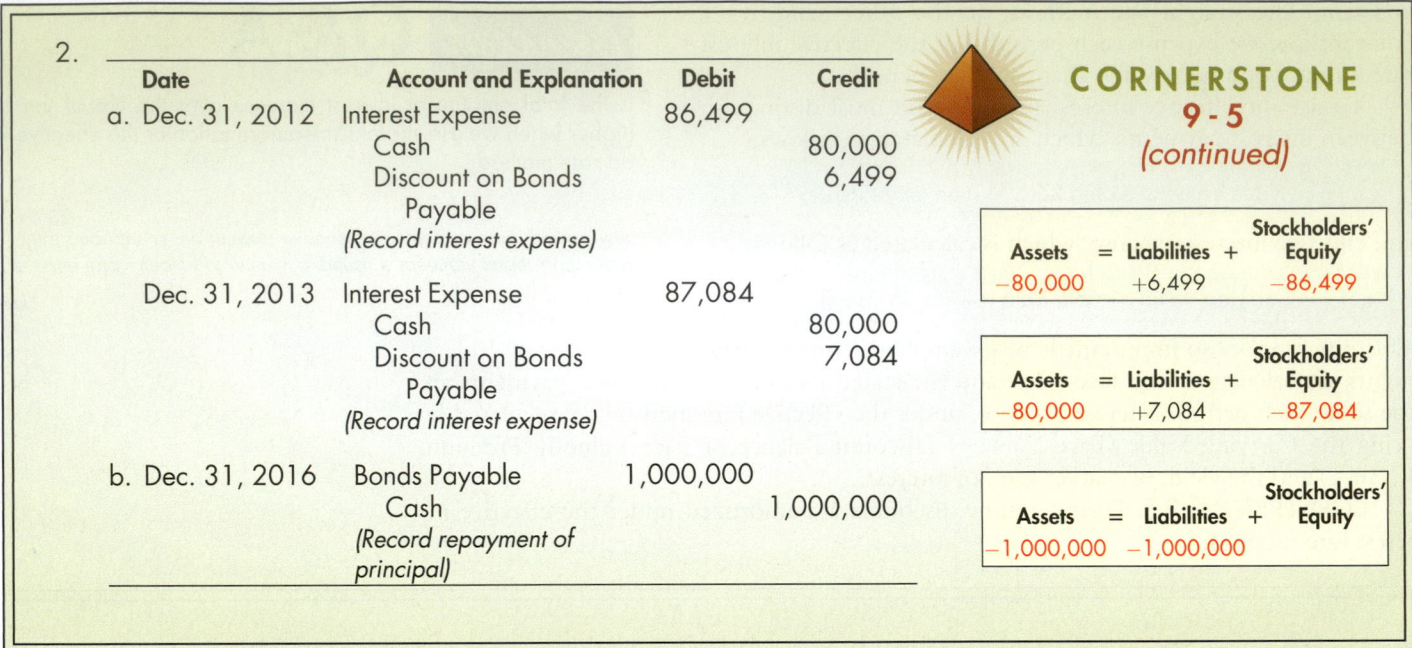

2.

Date	Account and Explanation	Debit	Credit
a. Dec. 31, 2012	Interest Expense	86,499	
	Cash		80,000
	Discount on Bonds Payable		6,499
	(Record interest expense)		
Dec. 31, 2013	Interest Expense	87,084	
	Cash		80,000
	Discount on Bonds Payable		7,084
	(Record interest expense)		
b. Dec. 31, 2016	Bonds Payable	1,000,000	
	Cash		1,000,000
	(Record repayment of principal)		

Assets	=	Liabilities	+	Stockholders' Equity
−80,000		+6,499		−86,499

Assets	=	Liabilities	+	Stockholders' Equity
−80,000		+7,084		−87,084

Assets	=	Liabilities	+	Stockholders' Equity
−1,000,000		−1,000,000		

CORNERSTONE 9-5 (continued)

As in the straight-line method, recording interest expense for bonds issued at a premium is the mirror image of bonds issued at a discount. **CORNERSTONE 9-6** illustrates how premiums are amortized under the effective interest rate method.

CORNERSTONE 9-6

Recording Interest Expense for Bonds Sold at a Premium Using the Effective Interest Rate Method

Concept:
When interest-bearing bonds are issued at a premium, the interest expense for the period is the amount of interest payment for the period *minus* the premium amortization for the period. Under the effective interest rate method, a constant (or effective) rate of interest on the bond book (or carrying) value is allocated to the period.

Information:
On December 31, 2011, Zoidberg Co. issued $1,000,000 of 8 percent bonds, due in five years with interest payable annually on December 31. The market rate of interest is 7 percent. Assume the bond was issued at $1,041,002 [see Cornerstone 9-8 (p. 446) in Appendix 9A for the calculation].

Required:
1. Complete an amortization table for each of the five periods.
2. Prepare the journal entry necessary to (a) recognize the interest expense on December 31, 2012 and 2013 and (b) record the repayment of the loan principal on December 31, 2016.

Solution:
1.

Annual Period	Cash Payment[a] (Credit)	Interest Expense[b] (Debit)	Premium on Bonds Payable[c] (Debit)	Premium on Bonds Payable Balance	Carrying Value[d]
At issue				$41,002	$1,041,002
1	$80,000	$72,870	$7,130	33,872	1,033,872
2	80,000	72,371	7,629	26,243	1,026,243

(Continued)

Annual Period	Cash Payment[a] (Credit)	Interest Expense[b] (Debit)	Premium on Bonds Payable[c] (Debit)	Premium on Bonds Payable Balance	Carrying Value[d]
3	80,000	71,837	8,163	18,080	1,018,080
4	80,000	71,266	8,734	9,346	1,009,346
5	80,000	70,654	9,346	0	1,000,000

[a]Cash Payment = Face Value × 8% × 12/12 = $80,000
[b]Interest Expense = Carrying Value × 7% × 12/12
[c]Change in Premium Balance = Cash Payment − Interest Expense
[d]New Carrying Value = Previous Carrying Value − Change in Premium on Bonds Payable Balance

CORNERSTONE 9-6 *(continued)*

2.

Date	Account and Explanation	Debit	Credit
a. Dec. 31, 2012	Interest Expense	72,870	
	Premium on Bonds Payable	7,130	
	Cash		80,000
	(Record interest expense)		
Dec. 31, 2013	Interest Expense	72,371	
	Premium on Bonds Payable	7,629	
	Cash		80,000
	(Record interest expense)		
b. Dec. 31, 2016	Bonds Payable	1,000,000	
	Cash		1,000,000
	(Record repayment of principal)		

Assets	=	Liabilities	+	Stockholders' Equity
−80,000		−7,130		−72,870

Assets	=	Liabilities	+	Stockholders' Equity
−80,000		−7,629		−72,371

Assets	=	Liabilities	+	Stockholders' Equity
−1,000,000		−1,000,000		

Note that the interest expense using the straight-line method is the same each period. In contrast, the interest expense using the effective interest method results in a different amount each period. This is because the interest expense is based on a constant *rate*. This rate is applied to the remaining carrying value of the bonds each period. Exhibit 9-8 (p. 440) illustrates how the carrying value of the bonds are different between the straight-line and effective interest methods for both a premium and a discount.

Installment Debt

Instead of paying off the principal at maturity, some debt requires a portion of the principal to be paid off each period (usually monthly), along with some interest. Classic installment debt payments are home mortgages or car payments. Installment debt payments are the same each period, but the portion that is considered interest changes because the outstanding principal balance is changing. To illustrate, consider buying a car for $20,000, at 6 percent annual interest, and 48 monthly payments. In this case, each monthly payment would be $469.70. After 48 payments you would have paid a total of $22,545.60 ($469.70 × 48). This means you would have paid $2,545.60 of interest and $20,000 of principal. However, the initial monthly payments would have a relatively high portion allocated to interest because your outstanding loan balance is relatively high. Your last few payments, on the other hand, would have a relatively low portion allocated to interest because your outstanding loan balance is relatively low.

Concept **Q&A**

Why is the effective interest rate method GAAP?

Answer:
The effective interest rate method does a better job allocating, or matching, the time value of money to the proper period. Under the effective interest method, the interest expense is equal to market rate of interest (or yield) at issue on the bond book value. This makes sense because market forces will ensure that the creditor receives the market rate of return on the investment.

Concept **Q&A**

How do credit cards calculate interest?

Answer:
Although terms vary from card to card, they all charge some percentage of our average balance for the period. If your card charges 1.5 percent of the average balance for the month and you have a $5,000 average balance, then interest charge would be $75. Interest of 1.5 percent may not sound that bad, but remember that this is per month. That equates to 18 percent per year (1.5 percent × 12 months). If all you do is pay the interest, you are not lowering your outstanding balance at all.

Exhibit 9-8

Long-Term Debt Carrying Value Using Straight-Line and Effective Interest Methods to Amortize Premium and Discount

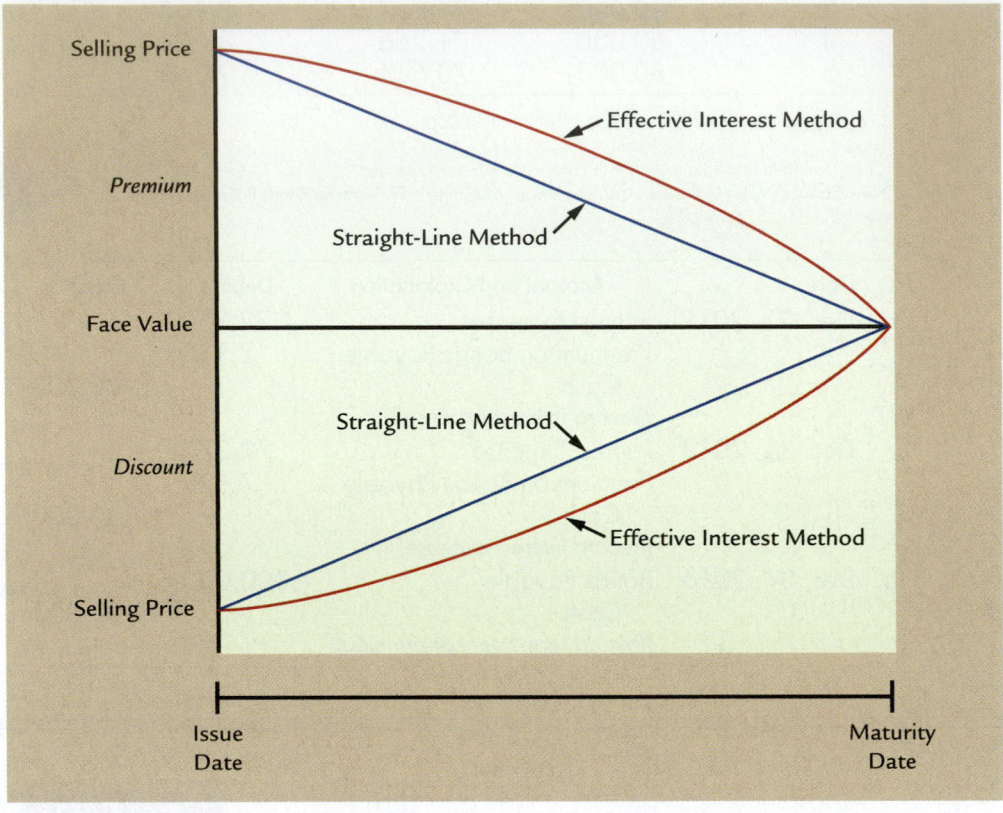

OBJECTIVE ⑤
Determine the after-tax cost of financing with debt and explain financial leverage.

PROS AND CONS OF DEBT FINANCING

A business must weigh both the negative and positive aspects of debt financing in deciding whether or not to take the risk. This extremely complex decision is treated more fully in finance courses, but some general points follow.[4]

Tax Deductible Interest Expense

A significant advantage of financing with debt rather than stock is the fact that the interest expense on debt is deductible for income tax purposes. Consider the case of Carmel Company, which issued $1,000,000 of 8 percent bonds that resulted in interest expense of $80,000 per year. The net cash outflow for Carmel's bonds is significantly less than $80,000, however, because of the effect of interest deductibility.

Since interest expense is deductible, taxable income is $80,000 less than it is without the bond issue. At a rate of 30 percent ($80,000 × 30%), income taxes were reduced by $24,000, yielding a net cash outflow for the bonds of $56,000 ($80,000 − $24,000). In other words, the cost of financing with bonds (or any other form of debt with tax-deductible interest payments) is the interest *net of income taxes*, which is determined using the following formula:

$$\text{Interest Net of Income Taxes} = (1 - \text{Tax Rate})(\text{Interest})$$
$$= (1 - 0.30)(\$80,000)$$
$$= \$56,000$$

[4] The following discussion explains the accounting concepts and procedures for debt used by borrowers. Although the concepts and procedures used by investors in debt securities are based on the same measurements and calculations, the reporting conventions are somewhat different. The most fundamental difference is that investors record debt acquired as assets rather than liabilities and record the interest as revenue rather than expense.

Leverage

Another potential advantage of debt is that it fixes the amount of compensation to the lender. No matter how successful the firm is in using borrowed capital, its creditors receive only the return specified in the debt agreement (interest plus the face amount). Thus, if the borrowed capital generates income in excess of the interest on the debt, the firm's stockholders benefit. The use of borrowed capital to produce more income than needed to pay the interest on the debt is called **leverage**.

Under the right conditions, leverage has significant advantages. However, conditions also exist under which the use of leverage is disadvantageous. Exhibit 9-9 illustrates both conditions in which two companies—Carmel Company and Noblesville Inc.—have identical financial circumstances except that Carmel finances its operations with debt as well as stock; Noblesville carries no debt.

Exhibit 9-9

Effects of Financing with Debt

	2010		2011	
	Carmel Company	Noblesville Inc.	Carmel Company	Noblesville Inc.
Balance sheet:*				
Assets	$3,000,000	$3,000,000	$3,000,000	$3,000,000
Bonds payable	$1,000,000	—	$1,000,000	—
Stockholders' equity	$2,000,000	$3,000,000	$2,000,000	$3,000,000
Number of common stock shares	100,000	150,000	100,000	150,000
Income statement:				
Income from operations	$ 600,000	$ 600,000	$ 200,000	$ 200,000
Interest expense (8%)	80,000	—	80,000	—
Income before taxes	$ 520,000	$ 600,000	$ 120,000	$ 200,000
Income taxes expense (30%)	156,000	180,000	36,000	60,000
Net income	$ 364,000	$ 420,000	$ 84,000	$ 140,000
Earnings per share	$ 3.64	$ 2.80	$ 0.84	$ 0.93

*Annual averages (assume that current liabilities are negligible).

In 2010, favorable economic conditions allow Carmel to make the most of its leverage. Carmel's stockholders earn $3.64 per share, which includes an amount attributable to earnings in excess of the cost of borrowing. In contrast, Noblesville's stockholders earn only $2.80 per share in 2010. However, income from operations falls sharply in 2011. As a result, Carmel's stockholders earn only $0.84 per share compared with $0.93 per share for Noblesville's stockholders. Just as stockholders receive earnings in excess of the interest on debt, so they must bear the burden when the interest on debt exceeds earnings.

Inflation

A third advantage of financing with debt is that in periods of inflation, debt permits the borrower to repay the lender in dollars that have declined in purchasing power. For instance, based on changes in the consumer price index (CPI), $1,000,000 borrowed in 1990 and repaid in 2010 provided the lender with only 59 percent of the purchasing power of the amount loaned in 1990.

Payment Schedule

The primary negative attribute of debt is the inflexibility of the payment schedule. Debt requires specified payments to creditors on specified dates. If a payment is not made as scheduled, the borrower can be forced into bankruptcy. This attribute of debt makes it a more risky source of capital than equity. The larger the proportion of debt an entity uses to finance its capital needs, the greater the risk of default. As risk increases (because of a higher proportion of debt), the cost of the debt increases. At a certain point, the risk becomes so great that additional debt cannot be issued at any cost. For firms whose operational and competitive circumstances produce substantial fluctuations in earnings, even low levels of debt may be considered too risky.

Occasionally, a business finds that it is unable to make the interest or principal payments required by its long-term debt. If there is reason to expect that the firm will eventually be able to secure enough cash to make part of or all the required payments, creditors may permit a restructuring of the cash payment schedule. The amount at which the firm's liabilities are measured may or may not be changed by such a restructuring. In such cases, creditors must analyze the situation to ensure that they are better off than they would be if they forced a bankruptcy.

OBJECTIVE
Compare and contrast operating and capital leases.

LEASES

Many companies choose to **lease**, instead of purchase, some of their assets. For example, **AMR** (the parent of **American Airlines**) reports that of their approximately 900 airplanes, 220 are under operating leases and 80 are under capital leases.

Operating Leases

In an **operating lease**, the **lessor** (the legal owner of the asset) retains substantially all of the risks and obligations of ownership, while the **lessee** uses the asset during the term of the lease. Automobiles, apartments, retail space, and office space are usually rented with operating leases. All discussions of rental arrangements considered earlier in this book have been operating leases.

Under an operating lease, the leased asset does not appear in the records of the lessee because the legal owner of the asset retains the risks and obligations of ownership. Rent paid in advance of the use of the asset is reported as prepaid rent, and rent expense is recognized in the period in which the leased asset is used. However, because many financial statement users view leases as liabilities, the sum of all payments required by noncancelable operating leases for the next five years must be disclosed in a footnote to the lessee's financial statements. Exhibit 9-10 is taken from **AMR**'s 2009 10-K.

To further illustrate, although **AMR** reports the present value of the net minimum lease payments ($689 million) of its capital leases as a liability, no liability is recorded for

Exhibit 9-10

Excerpts from AMR's 2009 10-K

Note 5
Leases
Minimum future rental payments under capital and operating lease obligations as of December 31, 2009, are as follows *(in millions)*:

Year Ending December 31	Capital leases	Operating leases
2010	$ 181	$1,057
2011	184	1,032
2012	134	848
2013	119	755
2014	98	614
2015 and thereafter	436	5,021
	$1,152	$9,327
Less amount representing interest	463	
Present value of net minimum lease payments	$ 689	

the $9.3 billion in future operating lease obligations. For this reason, many companies will intentionally structure the lease to qualify as an operating lease.

Capital Leases

A **capital lease**, on the other hand, is a noncancelable agreement that is in substance a purchase of the leased asset. If a lease has any of the following characteristics, it is essentially a purchase, and is therefore considered a capital lease:

- A transfer of the leased asset to the lessee occurs at the end of the lease at no cost or at a "bargain price."
- The term for the lease is at least 75 percent of the economic life of the leased asset.
- The present value of the lease payments is at least 90 percent of the fair value of the leased asset.

IFRS

IFRS refers to a capital lease as a financial lease.

Although the lessor remains the legal owner of the leased asset, a capital lease transfers virtually all the benefits of ownership to the lessee. Therefore, a capital lease is appropriately shown among the lessee's assets and liabilities. At the beginning of such a lease, a capital lease liability is recorded at the present value of the future lease payments. At this time, an asset is recorded in the same amount. Over the life of the lease the asset is depreciated, using an appropriate depreciation method. The lease liability is reduced and interest expense recorded as lease payments are made.

RATIO ANALYSIS

OBJECTIVE

Analyze a company's long-term solvency using information related to long-term liabilities.

Although long-term creditors are concerned with a company's short-term liquidity, they are primarily concerned with its long-term solvency. As such, long-term creditors focus on ratios that incorporate (1) long-term debt and (2) interest expense/payments.

The following ratios are often used to analyze a company's debt load:

$$\text{Debt to Equity} = \frac{\text{Total Liabilities}}{\text{Total Equity}}$$

$$\text{Debt to Total Assets} = \frac{\text{Total Liabilities}}{\text{Total Assets}}$$

$$\text{Long-Term Debt to Equity} = \frac{\text{Long-Term Debt}}{\text{Total Equity}}$$

The long-term debt to equity ratio is designed to look at the mix of debt and equity financing. For example, if the ratio is 1.00, then 50 percent of the company's financing comes from shareholders while the other 50 percent comes from creditors. However, over the last few decades borrowing arrangements have become much more varied. That is, historically when companies borrowed they locked themselves into long-term debt contracts. Now many companies use short-term borrowing, such as revolving credit, as part of their financing plan. This has the advantage of allowing companies to more frequently adjust their levels of borrowing based on current conditions. The downside is that short-term credit exposes them to greater risk of interest rate changes. For example, when interest rates increase, short-term borrowers may be forced to refinance at these higher rates while long-term borrowers will be locked in at the lower rates. Of course, short-term borrowers can, and do, hedge these interest rate risks, but that is a topic for advanced accounting and finance courses.

Because it is increasingly common to use short-term debt financing, the debt to equity and debt to total asset ratios contain all debt. Although the denominators for these two ratios differ, they both give a sense of the extent to which a company is financed with debt. You can see this more clearly by remembering that Total Assets = Total Liabilities + Total Equity. Both ratios therefore measure the relative size of Total Liabilities in the accounting equation.

Concept Q&A

Is it always better to have lower debt to equity, debt to total assets, and long-term debt to equity ratios?

Answer:
No. Debt provides opportunities for leverage. Think about it in this way—if you're guaranteed a return greater than your interest payments, it would not make sense to avoid borrowing. Of course, the reality is that while no returns are guaranteed, interest payments are unavoidable.

Other ratios focus a company's ability to make interest payments. These ratios are often called coverage ratios because they provide information on the company's ability to meet or cover its interest payments. The most common ratios focus either on accrual basis interest expense or the cash basis interest payment and are typically measured pretax because interest expense is tax deductible.

$$\text{Times Interest Earned (Accrual Basis)} = \frac{\text{Operating Income}}{\text{Interest Expense}}$$

$$\text{Times Interest Earned (Cash Basis)} = \frac{(\text{Cash Flows from Operations} + \text{Taxes Paid} + \text{Interest Paid})}{\text{Interest Payments}}$$

ETHICAL DECISIONS   When evaluating a company's solvency, a major concern is whether all debt was properly recorded. Companies have long engaged in transactions designed to hide debt. Such transactions are typically called *off-balance-sheet financing*. Interestingly, many such transactions are legal and considered to be ethical by most. For example, as discussed previously, many companies structure their lease agreements to avoid meeting the criteria for capital leases that require recording an asset and liability related to the future lease obligation. Because these leases are then treated as operating leases, no asset or liability is recorded on the books.

Because many financial-statement users view operating leases as unavoidable obligations, FASB requires disclosure of operating lease obligations for each of the subsequent five years and in total. This disclosure allows users to adjust ratios. For example, in the footnotes of its 2009 10-K, Delta Airlines reports future minimum lease payments of $11.790 billion related to its operating leases. If we capitalize these amounts, their long-term debt to equity ratio goes from 63.94 (see solution to **CORNERSTONE 9-7**) to 112.06 [($15,665 + $11,790)/$245].

CORNERSTONE 9-7   Calculating and Analyzing Long-Term Debt Ratios

Concept:
Investors and creditors are interested in a company's ability to meet its long-term obligations. Analysis of information about long-term liabilities and interest expense and payments provides such information.

Information:
Consider the following information from the 2009 10-Ks for **Delta Airlines** and **Southwest Airlines** (in millions).

Delta Airlines			
Long-term debt	$15,665	Interest expense	$1,278
Total liabilities	43,294	Operating income	(324)
Total assets	43,539	Interest payments	867
Total equity	245	Cash flows from operations	1,379
		Income tax expense	(344)
		Income tax paid	(15)

Southwest Airlines			
Long-term debt	$ 3,515	Interest expense	$186
Total liabilities	8,803	Operating income	262
Total assets	14,269	Interest payments	152
Total equity	5,466	Cash flows from operations	985
		Income tax expense	65
		Income tax paid	15

(Continued)

Required:

1. Calculate the following ratios for both companies: (a) debt to equity, (b) debt to total assets, (c) long-term debt to equity, (d) times interest earned (accrual basis), and (e) times interest earned (cash basis).
2. Interpret these results.

CORNERSTONE
9-7
(continued)

Solution:

1.

	Delta Airlines	Southwest Airlines
a. debt to equity	$43,294 \div $245 = 176.71	$8,803 \div $5,466 = 1.61
b. debt to total assets	$43,294 \div $43,539 = 0.99	$8,803 \div $14,269 = 0.62
c. long-term debt to equity	$15,665 \div $245 = 63.94	$3,515 \div $5,466 = 0.64
d. times interest earned (accrual basis)	($324) \div $1,278 = -0.25	$262 \div $186 = 1.41
e. times interest earned (cash basis)	[$1,379 + ($15) + $867] \div $867 = 2.57	($985 + $152 + $15) \div $152 = 7.58

2. Southwest's solvency risk is clearly far lower than Delta's. Not only does Delta have an extremely high debt burden, but it has a net operating loss and a huge portion of its operating cash flows are needed to make interest payments. Southwest, on the other hand, has a relatively low debt load and can easily make its interest payments.

   Not surprisingly, Delta is well below industry averages on most ratios while Southwest is an industry leader. These ratios are also reflected in their credit ratings. Delta has typically fluctuated between B and B- (it is currently at CCC) while Southwest has historically ranged between A or A- (although it is currently BBB).

Many companies also create other legal entities (called "special purpose entities" or SPEs) to "hide" debt. As with leases, such transactions are legal when certain rules are met involving outside investors. **Enron**, however, created some SPEs in which the documentation appeared to meet the outside investor rules to keep the debt off Enron's balance sheet. In hindsight, however, either unwritten side-agreements or complicated aspects of some of the contracts indicate that the debt should have been included on Enron's balance sheet. Keeping this debt off their balance sheet was important for Enron in maintaining its credit rating, but these unwritten side-agreements and complicated aspects of the contracts were necessary to attract the outside investors. While virtually nobody considers structuring their leases to allow treatment as an operating lease to be unethical, the side-agreements and subterfuge used by Enron was not only unethical, but in many cases criminal. ●

APPENDIX 9A: PRICING LONG-TERM DEBT

OBJECTIVE

Calculate the market price of long-term debt using present value techniques.

Debt agreements create contractually defined cash flows for the lender. Specifically, lenders typically receive

- periodic interest payments and
- repayment of the loan principal at some future date (loan maturity).

To receive these cash flows, the lender must decide how much to lend. When you borrow from a bank or car dealer, this single lender will set the interest rate to reflect the desired market, or yield, rate. However, there are notable exceptions. For example, if you buy a car for $25,000 at 0.9 percent interest, does that mean the car dealer's yield is 0.9 percent? No, it really means that they would have been happy to sell you the car for something below $25,000, such as $24,250. In this case, the "extra" principal you repay ($750 = $25,000 − $24,250) represents interest.

Of course, similar situations happen to businesses, but by far the most common situation has to do with bonds because the stated rate of interest (e.g., 8 percent) on the bond does not provide the desired yield. As discussed, if the yield is above the stated rate, the bond will sell at a discount (e.g., 98) and if the yield is below the stated rate, it will sell at a premium (e.g., 103). But how are these prices determined?

Bonds are priced at the present value of the two future cash flows—the periodic interest payments provide an annuity, while the repayment of the principal is a lump sum. This calculation is shown in **CORNERSTONE 9-8**.

CORNERSTONE 9-8   Determining the Market Value of a Bond

Concept:
Bonds are issued at the present value of future cash flows. The interest payments and repayment of the bond principal (or face value) are the future cash flows. These amounts must be discounted at the market rate of interest (or yield).

Information:
On December 31, 2011, Kroker Co. issued $1,000,000 of 8 percent bonds, due in five years with interest payable annually on December 31.

Required:
1. Draw the cash flow diagram.
2. What is the market value of these bonds if sold to yield (a) 8 percent, (b) 9 percent, and (c) 7 percent?

Solution:
1. PV = ?

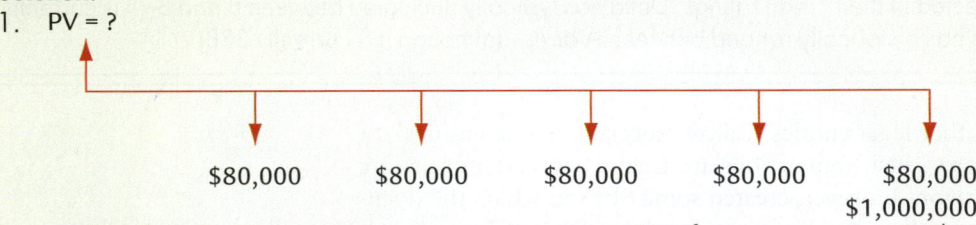

$80,000 $80,000 $80,000 $80,000 $80,000
                                            $1,000,000

2. a. PV of interest payments = Interest payment × PV of an annuity, 5 periods, 8%
                                 = $80,000 × 3.992710* = $319,417
       PV of principal payments = Principal payment × PV of a single sum, 5 periods, 8%
                                 = $1,000,000 × 0.680583* = $680,583

Market price of bonds = $319,417 + $680,583 = $1,000,000

---

*Although present and future value tables provided at the end of Appendix 3 (Exhibits A3-7, A3-8, A3-9, and A3-10) only show five decimal places, we have used factors to six decimal places in these calculations (and those that follow). Use of six decimal places allows the market price of the bond when issued at par to be calculated with no rounding error.

   b. PV of interest payments = Interest payment × PV of an annuity, 5 periods, 9%
                                = $80,000 × 3.889651 = $311,172
      PV of principal payments = Principal payment × PV of a single sum, 5 periods, 9%
                                = $1,000,000 × 0.649931 = $649,931

Market price of bonds = $311,172 + $649,931 = $961,103

---

   c. PV of interest payments = Interest payment × PV of an annuity, 5 periods, 7%
                                = $80,000 × 4.100197 = $328,016
      PV of principal payments = Principal payment × PV of a single sum, 5 periods, 7%
                                = $1,000,000 × 0.712986 = $712,986

Market price of bonds = $328,016 + $712,986 = $1,041,002

SUMMARY OF LEARNING OBJECTIVES

LO1.   **Describe debt securities and the markets in which they are issued.**
- Debt securities are issued in exchange for borrowed cash.
- In return for the borrowed cash, the borrower typically makes periodic interest payments and repays the face, or par, value at maturity.
- These securities may be placed directly with a creditor such as a bank or pension fund or they may be more widely distributed with the help of an underwriter.

LO2.   **Account for the issuance of long-term debt.**
- The issue price of long-term debt is typically quoted as a percentage of face value.
- At the time of issuance the borrower records the face value of the debt in bonds payable (or notes payable).
  - Any amount of cash received over the face value is credited to a premium
  - Any amount of cash received under the face value is debited to a discount
- The bonds payable (or notes payable) is netted with the premium or discount when reported on the balance sheet.

LO3.   **Use the straight-line method to account for premium/discount amortization.**
- In the straight-line method, equal amounts of premium or discount are amortized to interest expense each period.
- This results in a constant interest expense each period.
- Although GAAP requires use of the effective interest rate method, the straight-line method may be used if the results are not materially different from the effective interest rate method.

LO4.   **Use the effective interest rate method to account for premium/discount amortization.**
- GAAP requires the effective interest rate method to be used to amortize any premium or discount, unless the straight-line method is not materially different.
- Under this method, premiums and discounts are amortized in a manner that results in the interest expense for each accounting period being equal to a constant percentage of the bond book, or carrying, value.
- That is, the interest expense changes every period, but the effective interest rate on the bond book value is constant.
- This constant percentage is called the "yield" and represents the market rate of interest at the date of issue.

LO5.   **Determine the after-tax cost of financing with debt and explain financial leverage.**
- Since interest expense is deductible for tax purposes, the presence of interest expense lowers the taxes owed.
- The formula for the after-tax effect of interest expense is $(1 - \text{Tax Rate}) \times \text{Interest Expense}$.

LO6.   **Compare and contrast operating and capital leases.**
- A capital lease is a noncancelable agreement that is, in substance, a purchase of the leased asset.
- If a lease includes one of the following requirements it is considered a capital lease:
  - A transfer of the leased asset to the lessee occurs at the end of the lease at no cost or at a "bargain price," or
  - The term for the lease is at least 75 percent of the economic life of the leased asset, or
  - The present value of the lease payments is at least 90 percent of the fair value of the leased asset.
- If a lease qualifies as a capital lease, an asset and a liability must be recorded.
- If the lease does not meet requirements to be treated as a capital lease, then it is treated as an operating lease.
- Under an operating lease, the leased asset does not appear in the records of the lessee because the legal owner of the asset retains the risks and obligations of ownership.

LO7.   Analyze a company's long-term solvency using information related to long-term liabilities.
- Although long-term creditors are concerned with a company's short-term liquidity, they are primarily concerned with its long-term solvency.
- As such, long-term creditors focus on ratios that incorporate
  - long-term debt and
  - interest expense/payments.

LO8.   (Appendix 9A) Calculate the market price of long-term debt using present value techniques.
- Bonds are issued at the present value of future cash flows.
- The interest payments and repayment of the bond principal (or face value) are the future cash flows.
- These amounts must be discounted at the market rate of interest (or yield).

CORNERSTONES
FOR CHAPTER 9

CORNERSTONE 9-1	Recording the issuance of bonds (p. 428)
CORNERSTONE 9-2	Recording interest expense for bonds sold at par (p. 430)
CORNERSTONE 9-3	Recording interest expense for bonds sold at a discount using the straight-line method (p. 431)
CORNERSTONE 9-4	Recording interest expense for bonds sold at a premium using the straight-line method (p. 433)
CORNERSTONE 9-5	Recording interest expense for bonds sold at a discount using the effective interest rate method (p. 437)
CORNERSTONE 9-6	Recording interest expense for bonds sold at a premium using the effective interest rate method (p. 438)
CORNERSTONE 9-7	Calculating and analyzing long-term debt ratios (p. 444)
CORNERSTONE 9-8	(Appendix 9A) Determining the market value of a bond (p. 446)

KEY TERMS

Bond (p. 424)
Callable bonds (p. 425)
Capital lease (p. 443)
Contract rate (p. 425)
Convertible bonds (p. 426)
Coupon rate (p. 425)
Debenture bonds (p. 425)
Discount (p. 427)
Effective interest rate method (p. 430)
Face value (p. 425)
Interest amortization (p. 429)
Interest rate (p. 425)
Junk bonds (p. 425)
Lease (p. 442)
Lessee (p. 442)
Lessor (p. 442)

Leverage (p. 441)
Long-term debt (p. 424)
Market rate (p. 426)
Maturity (p. 425)
Mortgage bonds (p. 425)
Notes payable (p. 424)
Operating lease (p. 442)
Par value (p. 425)
Premium (p. 427)
Principal (p. 425)
Secured bond (p. 425)
Stated rate (p. 425)
Straight-line method (p. 430)
Unsecured bond (p. 425)
Yield (p. 426)

REVIEW PROBLEM

I. Straight-Line Method

To finance a new hydroelectric plant, Midwest Electric issues $100,000,000 of 9 percent, 15-year bonds on December 31, 2011. The bonds pay interest semiannually on June 30 and December 31. Assume the market rate of interest on December 31, 2011, was above 9 percent.

Required:

1. Will the bonds be issued at par, a premium, or a discount? Why?

2. Describe the cash payments made by Midwest Electric.

3. Prepare the journal entry to record the bond issue assuming the bonds were issued at 91.

4. What is the amount of discount amortization per six month interest period assuming the bonds were issued at 91?

5. Complete an amortization table through June 30, 2014.

6. Prepare the journal entries for December 31, 2013, and June 30, 2014.

7. How will the bonds be shown on the December 31, 2013, balance sheet?

8. Prepare the journal entry to record the repayment of principal at maturity.

Solution:

1. The bonds will be issued at a discount (below par) because the stated rate is below the market rate. Thus, Midwest Electric will have to lower the price below face value to compensate creditors for accepting a below market interest payment.

2. The interest payments are made semiannually, so the interest payments are:

$$\$100,000,000 \times 9\% \times 6/12 = \$4,500,000$$

There are 30 interest payments over the 15-year life of the bonds, so total interest payments are:

$$\$4,500,000 \times 30 = \$135,000,000$$

At maturity, the face value of $100,000,000 is also repaid. Thus, total payments (interest plus principal) of $235,000,000 are made.

3.

Date	Account and Explanation	Debit	Credit
Dec. 31, 2011	Cash	91,000,000	
	Discount on Bonds Payable	9,000,000	
	Bonds Payable		100,000,000
	(Record issuance of bonds)		

Assets	=	Liabilities	+	Stockholders' Equity
+91,000,000		−9,000,000 +100,000,000		

4.

$$\text{Discount Amortization} = \frac{\text{Total Discount}}{\text{Number of Interest Periods}}$$

$$= \frac{\$9,000,000}{30 \text{ periods}}$$

$$= \$300,000$$

5.

Semiannual Period	Cash Payment (Credit)	Interest Expense (Debit)	Discount on Bonds Payable (Credit)	Discount on Bonds Payable Balance	Carrying Value
At issue				$9,000,000	$91,000,000
06/30/12	$4,500,000	$4,800,000	$300,000	8,700,000	91,300,000
12/31/12	4,500,000	4,800,000	300,000	8,400,000	91,600,000
06/30/14	4,500,000	4,800,000	300,000	8,100,000	91,900,000
12/31/13	4,500,000	4,800,000	300,000	7,800,000	92,200,000
06/30/14	4,500,000	4,800,000	300,000	7,500,000	92,500,000

6.

	12/31/13		6/30/14	
Account and Explanation	Debit	Credit	Debit	Credit
Interest Expense	4,800,000		4,800,000	
Cash		4,500,000		4,500,000
Discount on Bonds Payable		300,000		300,00
(Record interest payment on bonds)				

12/31/13

Assets	=	Liabilities	+	Stockholders' Equity
−4,500,000		+300,000		−4,800,000

6/30/14

Assets	=	Liabilities	+	Stockholders' Equity
−4,500,000		+300,000		−4,800,000

7. Long-term liabilities:

Bonds payable	$100,000,000	
Less: Discount on bonds payable	(7,800,000)	92,200,000

8.

	Stockholders'
Assets	=	Liabilities	+	Equity
−100,000,000		−100,000,000		

Date	Account and Explanation	Debit	Credit
Dec. 31, 2026	Bonds Payable	100,000,000	
	Cash		100,000,000
	(Record repayment of bonds)		

II. Effective Interest Method

To finance a new hydroelectric plant, Midwest Electric issues $100,000,000 of 9 percent, 15-year bonds on December 31, 2011. The bonds pay interest semiannually on June 30 and December 31. Assume the market rate of interest on December 31, 2011, was 10 percent.

Required:

1. Will the bonds be issued at par, a premium, or a discount? Why?

2. Describe the cash flows.

3. Using present value techniques, verify the bond issue price of $92,314,025. (*Note*: This requires the use of Appendix 9A and Appendix 3.)

4. Prepare the journal entry to record the bond issue.

5. Complete an amortization table through June 30, 2014 (round to the nearest dollar).

6. Prepare the journal entries for December 31, 2013, and June 30, 2014.

7. How will the bonds be shown on the December 31, 2013, balance sheet?

8. Prepare the journal entry to record the repayment of principal at maturity.

Solution:

1. The bonds will be issued at a discount (below par) because the stated rate is below the market rate. Thus, Midwest Electric will have to lower the price below face value to compensate creditors for accepting a below market interest payment.

2. The interest payments are made semiannually, so the interest payments are:

$$\$100,000,000 \times 9\% \times 6/12 = \$4,500,000$$

There are 30 interest payments over the 15-year life of the bonds, so total interest payments are:

$$\$4,500,000 \times 30 = \$135,000,000$$

At maturity the face value of $100,000,000 is also repaid. Thus, total payments (interest plus principal) of $235,000,000 are made.

3. The issue price is the present value of the cash flows:

PV of interest payments = Interest payment × PV of an annuity, 30 semiannual periods, 5%
$$= \$4,500,000 \times 15.37245 = \$69,176,025$$

PV of principal payments = Principal payment × PV of a single sum, 30 semiannual periods, 5%
$$= \$100,000,000 \times 0.23138 = \$23,138,000$$

Market price of bonds = $69,176,025 + $23,138,000 = $92,314,025

4.

	Stockholders'
Assets	=	Liabilities	+	Equity
+92,314,025		−7,685,975		
		+ 100,000,000		

Date	Account and Explanation	Debit	Credit
Dec. 31, 2011	Cash	92,314,025	
	Discount on Bonds Payable	7,685,975	
	Bonds Payable		100,000,000
	(Record issuance of bonds)		

5.

Annual Period	Cash Payment (Credit)	Interest Expense (Debit)	Discount on Bonds Payable (Credit)	Discount on Bonds Payable Balance	Carrying Value
At issue				$7,685,975	$92,314,025
06/30/12	$4,500,000	$4,615,701	$115,701	7,570,274	92,429,726
12/31/12	4,500,000	4,621,486	121,486	7,448,788	92,551,212
06/30/13	4,500,000	4,627,561	127,561	7,321,227	92,678,773
12/31/13	4,500,000	4,633,939	133,939	7,187,288	92,812,712
06/30/14	4,500,000	4,640,636	140,636	7,046,652	92,953,348

6.

	12/31/13		6/30/14	
Account and Explanation	Debit	Credit	Debit	Credit
Interest Expense	4,633,939		4,640,636	
Cash		4,500,000		4,500,000
Discount on Bonds Payable		133,939		140,636
(Record interest payment on bonds)				

12/31/13

Assets	=	Liabilities	+	Stockholders' Equity
−4,500,000		+133,939		−4,633,939

6/30/14

Assets	=	Liabilities	+	Stockholders' Equity
−4,500,000		+140,636		−4,640,636

7. Long-term liabilities:

Bonds payable	$100,000,000	
Less: Discount on bonds payable	(7,187,288)	(92,812,712)

8.

Date	Account and Explanation	Debit	Credit
Dec. 31, 2026	Bonds Payable	100,000,000	
	Cash		100,000,000
	(Record repayment of bonds)		

Assets	=	Liabilities	+	Stockholders' Equity
−100,000,000		−100,000,000		

DISCUSSION QUESTIONS

1. What is long-term debt?
2. What is the difference between a bond and a note? How do the accounting treatments differ?
3. What does the face (or par) value of a bond represent?
4. What is the maturity date of a bond?
5. What is the stated or coupon rate of a bond?
6. How does a bond's stated rate differ from its yield rate? Which one is used to calculate the interest payment?
7. How does a secured bond differ from an unsecured bond?
8. What does it mean if a bond is "callable"?
9. What does it mean if a bond is "convertible"?
10. What is a junk bond?
11. How is total interest for long-term debt calculated?
12. Describe the process that businesses follow to sell new issues of long-term debt.
13. Describe how the relationship between the stated rate and yield rate affect the price at which bonds are sold.
14. How are premiums and discounts presented on the balance sheet?
15. How do premiums and discounts on long-term debt securities affect interest expense?
16. What is the difference between the straight-line and effective interest rate methods of amortizing premiums and discounts?
17. How can there be interest expense each period for non-interest bearing bonds if there are no interest payments?
18. Under the effective interest rate method, describe the difference in calculating the (a) interest payment and (b) interest expense for the period.
19. How does a firm "leverage" its capital structure? When is leverage advantageous? When is it disadvantageous? Who receives the advantage or bears the disadvantage of leverage?
20. Name and describe two kinds of leases.

21. Which type of lease requires that a long-term debt and an asset be recorded at the inception of the lease?

22. *(Appendix 9A)* Describe how the bond issue price is calculated.

MULTIPLE-CHOICE EXERCISES

9-1 Which of the following statements regarding bonds payable is true?

a. When an issuing company's bonds are traded in the "secondary" market, the company will receive part of the proceeds when the bonds are sold from the first purchaser to the second purchaser.
b. The entire principal amount of most bonds mature on a single date.
c. Generally, bonds are issued in denominations of $100.
d. A debenture bond is backed by specific assets of the issuing company.

9-2 Bonds are sold at a premium if the

a. issuing company has a better reputation than other companies in the same business.
b. market rate of interest was more than the stated rate at the time of issue.
c. company will have to pay a premium to retire the bonds.
d. market rate of interest was less than the stated rate at the time of issue.

9-3 If bonds are issued at 101.25, this means that

a. a $1,000 bond sold for $101.25.
b. a $1,000 bond sold for $1,012.50.
c. the bonds sold at a discount.
d. the bond rate of interest is 10.125 percent of the market rate of interest.

9-4 What best describes the discount on bonds payable account?

a. a liability.
b. a contra liability.
c. an asset.
d. an expense.

9-5 The premium on bonds payable account is shown on the balance sheet as

a. an addition to a long-term liability.
b. a subtraction from a long-term liability.
c. a contra asset.
d. a reduction of an expense.

9-6 When bonds are issued by a company, the accounting entry typically shows an

a. increase in assets and an increase in liabilities.
b. increase in assets and an increase in stockholders' equity.
c. increase in liabilities and an increase in stockholders' equity.
d. increase in liabilities and a decrease in stockholders' equity.

9-7 Bower Company sold $100,000 of 20-year bonds for $95,000. The stated rate on the bonds was 7 percent, and interest is paid annually on December 31. What entry would be made on December 31 when the interest is paid? (Numbers are omitted.)

a. Interest Expense
       Cash
b. Interest Expense
       Bonds Payable
       Cash

c. Interest Expense
       Discount on Bonds Payable
       Cash
d. Interest Expense
       Discount on Bonds Payable
       Cash

9-8 Bonds in the amount of $100,000 with a life of 10 years were issued by the Roundy Company. If the stated rate is 6 percent and interest is paid semiannually, what would be the total amount of interest paid over the life of the bonds?

a. $6,000
b. $30,000
c. $60,000
d. $120,000

9-9 Sean Corp. issued a $40,000, 10-year bond, with a stated rate of 8 percent, paid semiannually. How much cash will the bond investors receive at the end of the first interest period?

a. $4,000
b. $3,200

c. $1,600
d. $800

9-10 When bonds are issued at a discount, the interest expense for the period is

a. the amount of interest payment for the period plus the premium amortization for the period.
b. the amount of interest payment for the period minus the premium amortization for the period.
c. the amount of interest payment for the period minus the discount amortization for the period.
d. the amount of interest payment for the period plus the discount amortization for the period.

9-11 When bonds are issued at a premium, the interest expense for the period is

a. the amount of interest payment for the period plus the premium amortization for the period.
b. the amount of interest payment for the period minus the premium amortization for the period.
c. the amount of interest payment for the period minus the discount amortization for the period.
d. the amount of interest payment for the period plus the discount amortization for the period.

9-12 Installment bonds differ from typical bonds in what way?

a. Essentially they are the same.
b. Installment bonds do not have a stated rate.
c. A portion of each installment bond payment pays down the principal balance.
d. The entire principal balance is paid off at maturity for installment bonds.

9-13 In 2011, Drew Company issued $200,000 of bonds for $189,640. If the stated rate of interest was 6 percent and the yield was 6.73 percent, how would Drew calculate the interest expense for the first year on the bonds using the effective interest method?

a. $189,640 × 6.73%
b. $189,640 × 8%

c. $200,000 × 6.73%
d. $200,000 × 8%

9-14 The result of using the effective interest method of amortization of the discount on bonds is that

a. a constant interest rate is charged against the debt carrying value.
b. the amount of interest expense decreases each period.
c. the interest expense for each amortization period is constant.
d. the cash interest payment is greater than the interest expense.

9-15 Serenity Company issued $100,000 of 6 percent, 10-year bonds when the market rate of interest was 5 percent. The proceeds from this bond issue were $107,732. Using the effective interest method of amortization, which of the following statements is true? Assume interest is paid annually.

a. Interest payments to bondholders each period will be $6,464.
b. Interest payments to bondholders each period will be $5,000.
c. Amortization of the premium for the first interest period will be $613.
d. Amortization of the premium for the first interest period will be $1,464.

9-16 Bonds are a popular source of financing because

a. a company having cash flow problems can postpone payment of interest to bondholders.
b. bond interest expense is deductible for tax purposes, while dividends paid on stock are not.
c. financial analysts tend to downgrade a company that has raised large amounts of cash by frequent issues of stock.
d. the bondholders can always convert their bonds into stock if they choose.

9-17 Which of the following statements regarding leases is *false*?

a. Lease agreements are a popular form of financing the purchase of assets because leases do not require a large initial outlay of cash.
b. Accounting recognizes two types of leases—operating and capital leases.
c. If a lease is classified as a capital lease, the lessee records a lease liability on its balance sheet.
d. If a lease is classified as an operating lease, the lessee records a lease liability on its balance sheet.

9-18 Which of the following lease conditions would result in a capital lease to the lessee?

a. The lessee can purchase the property for $1 at the end of the lease term.
b. The lease term is 70 percent of the property's economic life.
c. The fair market value of the property at the inception of the lease is $18,000; the present value of the minimum lease payments is $15,977.
d. The lessee will return the property to the lessor at the end of the lease term.

9-19 On January 2, 2011, Sylvester Metals Co. leased a mining machine from EDH Leasing Corp. The lease qualifies as an operating lease. The annual payments are $4,000 paid at the end of each year, and the life of the lease is 10 years. What entry would Sylvester make when the machine is delivered by EDH?

a. Leased Assets............   40,000
          Lease Liability.....   40,000

b. Prepaid Rent............   40,000
          Lease Liability.....   40,000

c. Prepaid Rent............   4,000
          Lease Liability.....   4,000

d. No entry is necessary.

9-20 WVA Mining Company has leased a machine from Franklin Machinery Company. The annual payments are $6,000, and the life of the lease is 8 years. It is estimated that the useful life of the machine is 9 years. How would WVA record the acquisition of the machine?

a. The machine would be recorded as an asset with a cost of $54,000.
b. The company would not record the machine as an asset but would record rent expense of $6,000 per year.
c. The machine would be recorded as an asset, at the present value of $6,000 for nine years.
d. The machine would be recorded as an asset, at the present value of $6,000 for eight years.

9-21 Willow Corporation's balance sheet showed the following amounts: current liabilities, $5,000; bonds payable, $1,500; lease obligations, $2,300. Total stockholders' equity was $6,000. The debt to equity ratio is

a. 0.63.   c. 1.42.
b. 0.83.   d. 1.47.

9-22 Kinsella Corporation's balance sheet showed the following amounts: current liabilities, $75,000; total liabilities, $100,000; total assets, $200,000. What is the long-term debt to equity ratio?

a. 0.125   c. 0.375
b. 0.25   d. 0.75

9-23 McLaughlin Corporation's balance sheet showed the following amounts: current liabilities, $75,000; total liabilities, $100,000; total assets, $200,000. What is the debt to total assets ratio?

a. 0.50   c. 1
b. 0.875   d. 2

9-24 *(Appendix 9A)* The bond issue price is determined by calculating the

a. present value of the stream of interest payments and the future value of the maturity amount.
b. future value of the stream of interest payments and the future value of the maturity amount.
c. future value of the stream of interest payments and the present value of the maturity amount.
d. present value of the stream of interest payments and the present value of the maturity amount.

CORNERSTONE EXERCISES

Cornerstone Exercise 9-25 Reporting Long-Term Debt on the Balance Sheet

Dennis Corp. has the following bonds:

a. $1,000,000 in bonds that have $30,000 of unamortized discount associated with them.
b. $2,500,000 in bonds that have $75,000 of unamortized premium associated with them.

Required:

Prepare the balance sheet presentation for these two bonds.

OBJECTIVE ❶
CORNERSTONE 9-1

Cornerstone Exercise 9-26 Issuance of Long-Term Debt

Anne Corp. issued $600,000, 5 percent bonds.

Required:

Prepare the necessary journal entries to record the issuance of these bonds assuming the bonds were issued (a) at par, (b) at 102, and (c) at 92.

OBJECTIVE ❷
CORNERSTONE 9-1

Cornerstone Exercise 9-27 Issuance of Long-Term Debt

EWO Enterprises issues $4,500,000 of bonds payable.

Required:

Prepare the necessary journal entries to record the issuance of the bonds assuming the bonds were issued (a) at par, (b) at 104.5, and (c) at 99.

OBJECTIVE ❷
CORNERSTONE 9-1

Cornerstone Exercise 9-28 Issuance of Long-Term Debt

M. Nickles Company issued $700,000 of bonds for $684,780. Interest is paid semiannually.

Required:

1. Prepare the necessary journal entry to record the issuance of the bonds.
2. Is the yield greater or less than the stated rate? How do you know?

OBJECTIVE ❷
CORNERSTONE 9-1

Cornerstone Exercise 9-29 Debt Issued at Par

On December 31, 2010, Brock & Co. issued a $800,000 of bonds payable at par. The bonds have a 7 percent stated rate, pay interest on June 30 and December 31, and mature on December 31, 2011.

Required:

Prepare the journal entries to record the interest payment on June 30, 2011.

OBJECTIVE ❸
CORNERSTONE 9-2

> *Use the following information for Cornerstone Exercises 9-30 and 9-31:*
> On December 31, 2011, Drew Company issued $350,000, five-year bonds for $320,000. The stated rate of interest was 7 percent and interest is paid annually on December 31.

Cornerstone Exercise 9-30 Debt Issued at a Discount (Straight Line)

Refer to the information for Drew Company above.

Required:

Prepare the necessary journal entry on December 31, 2013, assuming the straight-line method is followed.

OBJECTIVE ❸
CORNERSTONE 9-3

Cornerstone Exercise 9-31 Debt Issued at a Discount (Straight Line)

Refer to the information for Drew Company above.

Required:

Prepare the amortization table for Drew Company's bonds. (*Note:* Round to the nearest dollar.)

OBJECTIVE ❸
CORNERSTONE 9-3

Use the following information for Cornerstone Exercises 9-32 and 9-33:
On December 31, 2011, Ironman Steel issued $800,000, eight-year bonds for $880,000. The stated rate of interest was 6 percent and interest is paid annually on December 31.

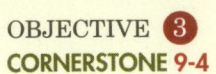

Cornerstone Exercise 9-32 Debt Issued at a Premium (Straight Line)

Refer to the information for Ironman Steel above.

Required:

Prepare the necessary journal entry on December 31, 2015, assuming the straight-line method is followed.

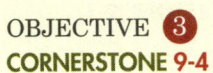

Cornerstone Exercise 9-33 Debt Issued at a Premium (Straight Line)

Refer to the information for Ironman Steel above.

Required:

Prepare the amortization table for Ironman Steel's bonds. (*Note:* Round to the nearest dollar.)

Use the following information for Cornerstone Exercises 9-34 and 9-35:
Sicily Corporation issued $500,000 in 6 percent bonds (payable on December 31, 2021) on December 31, 2011, for $402,440. Interest is paid on June 30 and December 31. The market rate of interest is 9 percent.

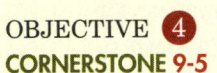

Cornerstone Exercise 9-34 Bonds Issued at a Discount (Effective Interest)

Refer to the information for Sicily Corporation above.

Required:

Prepare the amortization table using the effective interest rate method. (*Note:* Round to the nearest dollar.)

Cornerstone Exercise 9-35 Bonds Issued at a Discount (Effective Interest)

Refer to the information for Sicily Corporation above.

Required:

Prepare the journal entries for December 31, 2013 and 2014.

Use the following information for Cornerstone Exercises 9-36 and 9-37:
Crafty Corporation issued $475,000 of 5 percent, seven-year bonds on December 31, 2011 for $448,484. Interest is paid annually on December 31. The market rate of interest is 6 percent.

Cornerstone Exercise 9-36 Bonds Issued at a Discount (Effective Interest)

Refer to the information for Crafty Corporation above.

Required:

Prepare the amortization table using the effective interest rate method. (*Note:* Round to the nearest dollar.)

Cornerstone Exercise 9-37 Issued at a Discount (Effective Interest)

Refer to the information for Crafty Corporation above.

Required:

Prepare the journal entry for December 31, 2012 and 2013.

> Use the following information for Cornerstone Exercises 9-38 and 9-39:
> Cookie Dough Corporation issued $850,000 in 9 percent, 10-year bonds (payable on December 31, 2022) on December 31, 2012, for $907,759. Interest is paid on June 30 and December 31. The market rate of interest is 8 percent.

Cornerstone Exercise 9-38 Bonds Issued at a Premium (Effective Interest)

Refer to the information for Cookie Dough Corporation above.

Required:

Prepare the amortization table using the effective interest rate method. (*Note:* Round to the nearest dollar.)

Cornerstone Exercise 9-39 Bonds Issued at a Premium (Effective Interest)

Refer to the information for Cookie Dough Corporation above.

Required:

Prepare the journal entries for December 31, 2014 and 2015.

> Use the following information for Cornerstone Exercises 9-40 and 9-41:
> Charger Battery issued $100,000 of 11 percent, seven-year bonds on December 31, 2011 for $104,868. Interest is paid annually on December 31. The market rate of interest is 10 percent.

Cornerstone Exercise 9-40 Bonds Issued at a Premium (Effective Interest)

Refer to the information for Charger Battery above.

Required:

Prepare the amortization table using the effective interest rate method. (*Note:* Round to the nearest dollar.)

Cornerstone Exercise 9-41 Bonds Issued at a Premium (Effective Interest)

Refer to the information for Charger Battery above.

Required:

Prepare the journal entries for December 31, 2013 and 2014.

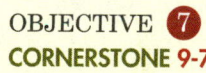

Cornerstone Exercise 9-42 Ratio Analysis

Watterson Corporation's balance sheet showed the following amounts: current liabilities, $70,000; bonds payable, $150,000; and lease obligations, $20,000. Total stockholders' equity was $90,000.

Required:

Calculate the debt to equity ratio. (*Note:* Round answer to three decimal places.)

Cornerstone Exercise 9-43 Ratio Analysis

Blue Corporation has $2,000,000 in total liabilities and $3,500,000 in total assets.

Required:

Calculate Blue's debt to equity ratio. (*Note:* Round answer to three decimal places.)

Cornerstone Exercise 9-44 Ratio Analysis

Red Corporation had $2,000,000 in total liabilities and $3,500,000 in total assets as of December 31, 2012. Of Red's total liabilities, $350,000 is long-term.

Required:

Calculate Red's debt to assets ratio and its long-term debt to equity ratio. (*Note:* Round answers to four decimal places.)

Cornerstone Exercise 9-45 (Appendix 9A) Bond Issue Price

On December 31, 2011, Garner Hot Rods issued $2,000,000 of 6 percent, 10-year bonds. Interest is payable semiannually on June 30 and December 31.

Required:

What is the issue price if the bonds are sold to yield 8 percent? (*Note:* Round to the nearest dollar.)

OBJECTIVE 4
CORNERSTONE 9-6

OBJECTIVE 4
CORNERSTONE 9-6

OBJECTIVE 4
CORNERSTONE 9-6

OBJECTIVE 4
CORNERSTONE 9-6

OBJECTIVE 7
CORNERSTONE 9-7

OBJECTIVE 7
CORNERSTONE 9-7

OBJECTIVE 7
CORNERSTONE 9-7

OBJECTIVE 8
CORNERSTONE 9-8

OBJECTIVE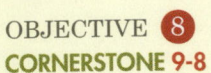
CORNERSTONE 9-8

Cornerstone Exercise 9-46 *(Appendix 9A)* Bond Issue Price

On December 31, 2012, Callahan Auto issued $1,500,000 of 8 percent, 10-year bonds. Interest is payable semiannually on June 30 and December 31.

Required:
What is the issue price if the bonds are sold to yield 6 percent? (*Note:* Round to the nearest dollar.)

EXERCISES

OBJECTIVE

Exercise 9-47 Issuing at par, a Premium, or a Discount

Kartel Company is planning to issue 2,000 bonds, each having a face amount of $1,000.

Required:
1. Prepare the journal entry to record the sale of the bonds at par.
2. Prepare the journal entry to record the sale of the bonds at a premium of $34,000.
3. Prepare the journal entry to record the sale of the bonds at a discount of $41,000.
4. **Conceptual Connection:** In which of the previous three scenarios is the market rate of interest (yield) highest? How do you know?

OBJECTIVE

Exercise 9-48 Bond Premium and Discount

Markway Inc. is contemplating selling bonds. The issue is to be composed of 750 bonds, each with a face amount of $1,000.

Required:
1. Calculate how much Markway is able to borrow if each bond is sold at a premium of $30.
2. Calculate how much Markway is able to borrow if each bond is sold at a discount of $10.
3. Calculate how much Markway is able to borrow if each bond is sold at 92 percent of par.
4. Calculate how much Markway is able to borrow if each bond is sold at 103 percent of par.
5. Assume that the bonds are sold for $975 each. Prepare the entry to recognize the sale of the 750 bonds.
6. Assume that the bonds are sold for $1,015 each. Prepare the entry to recognize the sale of the 750 bonds.

OBJECTIVE

Exercise 9-49 Bonds with Annual Interest Payments

Kiwi Corporation issued at par $350,000, 9 percent bonds on December 31, 2011. Interest is paid annually on December 31. The principal and the final interest payment are due on December 31, 2013.

Required:
1. Prepare the entry to recognize the issuance of the bonds.
2. Prepare the journal entry for December 31, 2012.
3. Prepare the journal entry to record repayment of the principal on December 31, 2013.
4. **Conceptual Connection:** How would the interest expense for 2012 change if the bonds had been issued at a premium?

OBJECTIVE

Exercise 9-50 Issuance and Interest Amortization for Zero Coupon Note (Straight Line)

Kerwin Company borrowed $10,000 on a two-year, zero coupon note. The note was issued on December 31, 2011. The face amount of the note, $12,544, is to be paid at maturity on December 31, 2013.

Required:
1. Allocate the interest of $2,544 to the two one-year interest periods, using straight-line interest amortization.
2. Prepare the entries to recognize the borrowing, the first year's interest expense, and the second year's interest expense plus redemption of the note at maturity.

Exercise 9-51 Interest Payments and Interest Expense for Bonds (Straight Line)

OBJECTIVE ❷ ❸

Klamath Manufacturing sold 20-year bonds with a total face amount of $1,000,000 and a stated rate of 7.5 percent. The bonds sold for $1,080,000 on December 31, 2011, and pay interest semiannually on June 30 and December 31.

Required:
1. Prepare the entry to recognize the sale of the bonds.
2. Determine the amount of the semiannual interest payment required by the bonds.
3. Prepare the journal entry made by Klamath at June 30, 2012, to recognize the interest expense and an interest payment.
4. Determine the amount of interest expense for 2012.
5. **Conceptual Connection:** If Klamath issued bonds with a variable interest rate, would you expect the rate to increase, decrease, or stay the same? Why?
6. **Conceptual Connection:** What should Klamath consider in deciding whether to use a fixed or variable rate?

Exercise 9-52 Interest Payments and Interest Expense for Bonds (Straight Line)

OBJECTIVE ❷ ❸

On December 31, 2011, Harrington Corporation sold $425,000 of 15-year, 11 percent bonds. The bonds sold for $395,000 and pay interest semiannually on June 30 and December 31.

Required:
1. Prepare the journal entry to record the sale of the bonds.
2. Calculate the amount of the semiannual interest payment.
3. Prepare the entry at June 30, 2012, to recognize the payment of interest and interest expense.
4. Calculate the annual interest expense for 2012.

Exercise 9-53 Interest Payments and Interest Expense for Bonds (Straight Line)

OBJECTIVE ❸

On December 31, 2011, Philips Corporation issued bonds with a total face amount of $1,000,000 and a stated rate of 7 percent.

Required:
1. Calculate the interest expense for 2012 if the bonds were sold at par.
2. Calculate the interest expense for 2012 if the bonds were sold at a premium and the straight-line premium amortization for 2012 is $8,000.
3. Calculate the interest expense for 2012 if the bonds were sold at a discount and the straight-line discount amortization for 2012 is $6,000.

Exercise 9-54 Completing a Debt Amortization Table (Straight Line)

OBJECTIVE ❸

Cagney Company sold $200,000 of bonds on December 31, 2011. A portion of the amortization table appears below.

Period	Cash Payment (Credit)	Interest Expense (Debit)	Discount on Bonds Payable (Credit)	Discount on Bonds Payable Balance	Carrying Value
At issue				$8,000	$192,000
06/30/12	$12,000	$12,800	$800	7,200	192,800
12/31/12	12,000	12,800	800	6,400	193,600
06/30/13	?	?	?	?	?

Required:
1. Determine the stated interest rate on these bonds.
2. Calculate the interest expense and the discount amortization for the interest period ending June 30, 2013.
3. Calculate the liability balance shown on a balance sheet after the interest payment is recorded on June 30, 2013.

Exercise 9-55 Using a Premium Amortization Table (Straight Line)

OBJECTIVE ❸

For Dingle Corporation, the following amortization table was prepared when $400,000 of five-year, 7 percent bonds were sold on December 31, 2011, for $420,000.

(Continued)

Period	Cash Payment (Credit)	Interest Expense (Debit)	Premium on Bonds Payable (Debit)	Premium on Bonds Payable Balance	Carrying Value
At issue				$20,000	$420,000
06/30/12	$14,000	$12,000	$2,000	18,000	418,000
12/31/12	14,000	12,000	2,000	16,000	416,000
06/30/13	14,000	12,000	2,000	14,000	414,000
12/31/13	14,000	12,000	2,000	12,000	412,000
06/30/14	14,000	12,000	2,000	10,000	410,000
12/31/14	14,000	12,000	2,000	8,000	408,000
06/30/15	14,000	12,000	2,000	6,000	406,000
12/31/15	14,000	12,000	2,000	4,000	404,000
06/30/16	14,000	12,000	2,000	2,000	402,000
12/31/16	14,000	12,000	2,000	0	400,000

Required:
1. Prepare the entry to recognize the issuance of the bonds on December 31, 2011.
2. Prepare the entry to recognize the first interest payment on June 30, 2012.
3. Determine what interest expense for this bond issue Dingle will report in its 2013 income statement.
4. Indicate how these bonds will appear in Dingle's December 31, 2015, balance sheet.

OBJECTIVE

Exercise 9-56 Using a Discount Amortization Table (Straight Line)

Panamint Candy Company prepared the following amortization table for $300,000 of five-year, 9 percent bonds issued and sold by Panamint on December 31, 2012, for $285,000:

Period	Cash Payment (Credit)	Interest Expense (Debit)	Discount on Bonds Payable (Credit)	Discount on Bonds Payable Balance	Carrying Value
				$15,000	$285,000
06/30/13	$13,500	$15,000	$1,500	13,500	286,500
12/31/13	13,500	15,000	1,500	12,000	288,000
06/30/14	13,500	15,000	1,500	10,500	289,500
12/31/14	13,500	15,000	1,500	9,000	291,000
06/30/15	13,500	15,000	1,500	7,500	292,500
12/31/15	13,500	15,000	1,500	6,000	294,000
06/30/16	13,500	15,000	1,500	4,500	295,500
12/31/16	13,500	15,000	1,500	3,000	297,000
06/30/17	13,500	15,000	1,500	1,500	298,500
12/31/17	13,500	15,000	1,500	0	300,000

Required:
1. Prepare the entry to recognize the sale of the bonds on December 31, 2012.
2. Prepare the entry to recognize the first interest payment on June 30, 2013.
3. Determine the interest expense for these bonds that Panamint will report on its 2015 income statement.
4. Indicate how these bonds will appear in Panamint's December 31, 2016, balance sheet.

OBJECTIVE

Exercise 9-57 Completing an Amortization Table (Straight Line)

Sondrini Corporation sold $1,500,000 face value of bonds at 103 on December 31, 2011. These bonds have an 8 percent stated rate and mature in four years. Interest is payable on June 30 and December 31 of each year.

Required:
1. Prepare a bond amortization table assuming straight-line amortization.
2. Prepare the journal entry for December 31, 2013.
3. Indicate how these bonds will appear in Sondrini's balance sheet at December 31, 2013.

OBJECTIVE

Exercise 9-58 Zero Coupon Bond

Johnson Company sold for $90,000 a $102,400, two-year zero coupon bond on December 31, 2011. The bond matures on December 31, 2013.

Required:
1. Prepare the entry to record the issuance of the bond.
2. Prepare the adjustment to recognize 2012 interest expense.
3. Prepare the entry to recognize the 2013 interest expense and the repayment of the bond on December 31, 2013.

Exercise 9-59 Zero Coupon Note

OBJECTIVE 3

Dodge City Products borrowed $100,000 cash by issuing a 36-month, $120,880 zero coupon note on December 31, 2012. The note matures on December 31, 2015.

Required:
1. Prepare the entry to recognize issuance of the note.
2. Prepare the adjustments to recognize 2013 and 2014 interest.
3. Prepare the entry to recognize 2015 interest and repayment of the note at maturity.

Exercise 9-60 Note Interest Payment and Interest Expense (Effective Interest)

OBJECTIVE 4

Cardinal Company sold $600,000 of 15-year, 6 percent notes for $544,824. The notes were sold December 31, 2011, and pay interest semiannually on June 30 and December 31. The effective interest rate was 7 percent. Assume Cardinal uses the effective interest rate method.

Required:
1. Prepare the entry to record the sale of the notes.
2. Determine the amount of the semiannual interest payments for the notes.
3. Prepare the amortization table through 2013 (*Note:* Round to the nearest dollar).
4. Prepare the entry for Cardinal's journal at June 30, 2012, to record the payment of six months' interest and the related interest expense.
5. Determine interest expense for 2013.

Exercise 9-61 Bond Interest Payments and Interest Expense (Effective Interest)

OBJECTIVE 4

On December 31, 2010, Hawthorne Corporation issued for $155,989, five-year bonds with a face amount of $150,000 and a stated (or coupon) rate of 9 percent. The bonds pay interest annually and have an effective interest rate of 8 percent. Assume Hawthorne uses the effective interest rate method.

Required:
1. Prepare the entry to record the sale of the bonds.
2. Calculate the amount of the interest payments for the bonds.
3. Prepare the amortization table through 2012 (*Note:* Round to the nearest dollar).
4. Prepare the journal entry for December 31, 2011, to record the payment of interest and the related interest expense.
5. Calculate the annual interest expense for 2011 and 2012.

Exercise 9-62 Completing a Bond Amortization Table (Effective Interest Rate Method)

OBJECTIVE 4

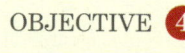

Cagney Company sold $200,000 of bonds on June 30, 2010. A portion of the amortization table appears below.

Period	Cash Payment (Credit)	Interest Expense (Debit)	Discount on Bonds Payable (Credit)	Discount on Bonds Payable Balance	Carrying Value
12/31/11	$9,000	$9,277	$277	$2,340	$197,660
06/30/12	9,000	9,290	290	2,050	197,950
12/31/12	?	?	?	?	?

Required:
1. Indicate the stated interest rate on these bonds.
2. Calculate the effective annual interest rate on these bonds (*Note:* Round to the nearest 0.1 percent).
3. Determine the interest expense and discount amortization for the interest period ending December 31, 2012 (*Note:* Round to the nearest dollar).
4. Determine the liability balance after the interest payment is recorded on December 31, 2012.

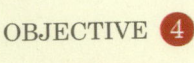

Exercise 9-63 Completing a Bond Amortization Table (Effective Interest Rate Method)

MacBride Enterprises sold $200,000 of bonds on December 31, 2011. These bonds mature on December 31, 2018. A portion of the amortization table appears below.

Period	Cash Payment (Credit)	Interest Expense (Debit)	Premium on Bonds Payable (Debit)	Premium on Bonds Payable Balance	Carrying Value
At issue				$6,457	$206,457
06/30/12	$9,000	$8,465	$535	5,922	205,922
12/31/12	9,000	8,443	557	5,365	205,365
06/30/13	9,000	8,420	580	4,785	204,785
12/31/13	?	?	?	?	?

Required:
1. Indicate the stated annual interest rate on these bonds.
2. Calculate the effective annual interest rate on these bonds (*Note:* Round to the nearest 0.1 percent).
3. Determine the interest expense and premium amortization for the interest period ending December 31, 2013 (*Note:* Round to the nearest dollar).
4. Determine when the bonds will mature.

> *Use the following information for Exercises 9-64 and 9-65:*
> Thornwood Lanes bought a service vehicle for $25,000 by issuing a 6 percent installment note on December 31, 2012. Thornwood will make 12 monthly payments of $2,151.66 at the end of each month.

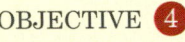

Exercise 9-64 Installment Notes

Refer to the information for Thornwood Lanes above.

Required:
Prepare the amortization table using the effective interest rate method. (*Note:* Round to the nearest cent).

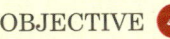

Exercise 9-65 Installment Notes

Refer to the information for Thornwood Lanes above.

Required:
Prepare the journal entries for the end of March and the end of April.

Exercise 9-66 Installment Notes

ABC bank loans $250,000 to Yossarian to purchase a new home. Yossarian will repay the note in equal monthly payments over a period of 30 years. The interest rate is 12 percent.

Required:
If the monthly payment is $2,571.53, how much of the first payment is interest expense and how much is principal repayment (*Note:* Round to the nearest cent)?

Exercise 9-67 Non-Interest Bearing Bonds (Straight Line)

Dean Plumbing issues $1,000,000 face value, noninterest-bearing bonds on December 31, 2012. The bonds are issued at 65 and mature on December 31, 2016.

Required:
Assuming the straight-line amortization method is followed, prepare the journal entry on December 31, 2015.

Exercise 9-68 Cost of Debt Financing

Barney Corporation's cost of debt financing is 7 percent. Its tax rate is 35 percent.

Required:
Calculate the after-tax interest rate. (*Note:* Round answer to three decimal places.)

Exercise 9-69 Cost of Debt Financing

Diamond company's cost of debt financing is 10 percent. Its tax rate is 35 percent. Diamond has $3,000,000 of debt.

Required:

1. Calculate the after-tax cost amount of interest expense.
2. **Conceptual Connection:** How does the tax effect of interest expense affect financial leverage?

Exercise 9-70 Leases

OBJECTIVE **6**

Southern Airlines has leased an aircraft from BAL Aircraft Company. The annual payments are $1,000,000, and the life of the lease is 18 years. It is estimated that the useful life of the aircraft is 20 years. The present value of the future lease payments is $8,755,630.

Required:

Conceptual Connection: Would Southern Airlines record the lease as an operating or capital lease? Why?

Exercise 9-71 Ratio Analysis

OBJECTIVE **7**

Rising Stars Academy provided the following information on its 2011 balance sheet and statement of cash flows:

Long-term debt	$ 4,400	Interest expense	$ 398
Total liabilities	8,972	Net income	559
Total assets	38,775	Interest payments	432
Total equity	29,803	Cash flows from operations	1,015
Operating income	1,223	Income tax expenses	266
		Income taxes paid	150

Required:

1. Calculate the following ratios for Rising Stars: (a) debt to equity, (b) debt to total assets, (c) long-term debt to equity, (d) times interest earned (accrual basis), and (e) times interest earned (cash basis). (*Note:* Round answers to three decimal places.)
2. **Conceptual Connection:** Interpret these results.

Exercise 9-72 *(Appendix 9A)* Calculating Bond Issue Price

OBJECTIVE **8**

On December 31, 2011, University Theatres issued $500,000 face value of bonds. The stated rate is 8 percent, and interest is paid semiannually on June 30 and December 31. The bonds mature in 15 years.

Required:

Calculate at what price the bonds are issued assuming the market rate of interest is (a) 6 percent and (b) 10 percent.

PROBLEM SET A

Problem 9-73A Reporting Long-Term Debt

OBJECTIVE **2**

Fridley Manufacturing's accounting records reveal the following account balances after adjusting entries are made on December 31, 2012:

Accounts payable	$ 62,500	Interest payable	$ 38,700
Bonds payable (9.4%, due in 2019)	800,000	Installment note payable (8%, equal	
Lease liability*	41,500	installments due 2013 to 2016)	120,000
Bonds payable (8.7%, due in 2015)	50,000	Notes payable (7.8%, due in 2017)	400,000
Deferred tax liability*	133,400	Premium on notes payable	
Discount on bonds payable		(7.8%, due in 2017)	6,100
(9.4%, due in 2019)	12,600	Note payable, 4% $50,000 face amount,	
Income taxes payable	26,900	due in 2018 (net of discount)	31,900

*Long-term liability

Required:

Prepare the current liabilities and long-term debt portions of Fridley's balance sheet at December 31, 2012. Provide a separate line item for each issue (do not combine separate bonds or notes payable), but some items may need to be split into more than one item.

OBJECTIVE **2** **3**

Problem 9-74A Entries for and Financial Statement Presentation of a Note

Perez Company borrowed $100,000 from the First National Bank on April 1, 2011, on a three-year, 7.8 percent note. Interest is paid annually on April 1.

Required:
1. Record the borrowing transaction in Perez's journal.
2. Prepare the adjusting entries made at December 31, 2011 and 2012.
3. Prepare the necessary journal entry to recognize the first interest payment on April 1, 2012.
4. Indicate how the note and associated interest would be presented in Perez's December 31, 2012, balance sheet.
5. Prepare the necessary journal entries to record the repayment of the note and the last year's interest payment on April 1, 2014.

OBJECTIVE **2** **3**

Problem 9-75A Preparing a Bond Amortization Table (Straight Line)

On December 31, 2012, Distel Company borrowed $102,700 by issuing three-year, 9 percent bonds with a face amount of $100,000. Interest is paid annually on December 31.

Required:
Prepare an amortization table using the following column headings:

Period	Cash Payment (Credit)	Interest Expense (Debit)	Premium on Bonds Payable (Debit)	Premium on Bonds Payable Balance	Carrying Value

OBJECTIVE **3**

Problem 9-76A Note Computations and Entries (Straight Line)

On December 31, 2011, Sisek Company borrowed $800,000 with a 10-year, 9.75 percent note, interest payable semiannually on June 30 and December 31. Cash in the amount of $792,800 was received when the note was issued.

Required:
1. Prepare the necessary journal entry at December 31, 2011.
2. Prepare the necessary journal entry at June 30, 2012.
3. Prepare the necessary journal entry at December 31, 2012.
4. Determine the carrying amount of these notes at the end of the fifth year (December 31, 2016).

OBJECTIVE **3**

Problem 9-77A Preparing a Bond Amortization Table (Straight Line)

Edmonton-Alston Corporation issued five-year, 9.5 percent bonds with a total face value of $700,000 on December 31, 2011, for $726,000. The bonds pay interest on June 30 and December 31 of each year.

Required:
1. Prepare an amortization table.
2. Prepare the entries to recognize the interest payments made on June 30, 2012, and December 31, 2012.

OBJECTIVE **3**

Problem 9-78A Preparing a Bond Amortization Table (Straight Line)

St. Cloud Manufacturing, Inc., issued five-year, 9.2 percent bonds with a total face value of $500,000 on December 31, 2011, for $484,000. The bonds pay interest on June 30 and December 31 of each year.

Required:
1. Prepare an amortization table.
2. Prepare the entries to recognize the bond issuance and the interest payments made on June 30, 2012, and December 31, 2012.

OBJECTIVE **3**

Problem 9-79A Preparing and Using an Amortization Table (Straight Line)

Girves Development Corporation has agreed to construct a plant in a new industrial park. To finance the construction, the county government issued $5,000,000 of 10-year, 4.75 percent revenue bonds for $5,125,000 on December 31, 2011. Girves will pay the interest and principal on the bonds. When the bonds are repaid, Girves will receive title to the plant. In the interim, Girves will pay property taxes as if it owned the plant. This financing arrangement is attractive to Girves, as state and local government bonds are exempt from federal income taxation and thus carry a lower interest rate. The bonds are attractive to investors, as both Girves and the county are issuers. The bonds pay interest semiannually on June 30 and December 31.

Required:

1. Prepare an amortization table through December 31, 2013, for these revenue bonds assuming straight-line amortization.
2. **Conceptual Connection:** Discuss whether or not Girves should record the plant as an asset after it is constructed.
3. **Conceptual Connection:** Discuss whether or not Girves should record the liability for these revenue bonds.

Problem 9-80A Non-Interest Bearing Note (Straight Line)

OBJECTIVE **3**

On December 31, 2011, Felix Products borrowed $80,000 cash on a $105,800, 24-month zero percent note. Felix uses the straight-line method of amortization.

Required:

1. Record the borrowing in Felix's journal.
2. Prepare the adjusting entry for December 31, 2012.
3. Prepare the entries to recognize the 2013 interest expense and repayment of the note on December 31, 2013.

Problem 9-81A Preparing an Amortization Table for Non-Interest Bearing Bonds (Straight Line)

OBJECTIVE **3**

On December 31, 2012, Georgetown Distributors borrowed $2,180,000 by issuing four-year, zero coupon bonds. The face value of the bonds is $3,000,000. Georgetown uses the straight-line method to amortize any premium or discount.

Required:

Prepare an amortization table for these bonds, using the following column headings:

Period	Cash Payment (Credit)	Interest Expense (Debit)	Discount on Bonds Payable (Credit)	Discount on Bonds Payable Balance	Carrying Value

Problem 9-82A Capital and Operating Leases

OBJECTIVE **6**

Trippler Company has decided to lease its new office building. The following information is available for the lease:

Lease:	
Payments	$100,000 per year*
Length of lease	15 years
Economic life of building	16 years
Appropriate interest rate	8.4%
Cost of building if purchased	$875,000

*The first payment is due at the end of the first year of the lease.

Required:

1. Determine whether this is a capital lease or an operating lease.
2. Regardless of your answer to the preceding question, assume that this is a capital lease and that the present value of the lease payments is $829,500. Record the liability and corresponding asset for this acquisition.
3. Record the interest expense on the capital lease at the end of the first year. Also assume no residual value and a 15-year lease for the building. Record the first year's straight-line depreciation of the cost of the leased asset.

PROBLEM SET B

OBJECTIVE

Problem 9-73B Reporting Long-Term Debt

Craig Corporation's accounting records reveal the following account balances after adjusting entries are made on December 31, 2011:

Accounts payable	$ 73,000	Interest payable	$ 33,400
Bonds payable (9.4%, due in 2016)	900,000	Installment note payable (9%, equal	
Lease liability*	30,000	installments due 2012 to 2022)	110,000
Bonds payable (8.3% due in 2015)	60,000	Notes payable (7.8%, due in 2020)	350,000
Deferred tax liability*	127,600	Premium on notes payable	
Discount on bonds payable		(7.8%, due in 2020)	5,000
(9.4%, due in 2016)	11,900	3% note payable, $50,000 face	
Income taxes payable	28,100	amount, due in 2022	29,800

*Long-term liability

Required:
Prepare the current liabilities and long-term debt portions of Craig's balance sheet at December 31, 2011. Provide a separate line item for each issue (do not combine separate bonds or notes payable), but some items may need to be split into more than one item.

OBJECTIVE

Problem 9-74B Entries for, and Financial Statement Presentation of a Note

Griddley Company borrowed $200,000 from the East Salvador Bank on February 1, 2011, on a three-year, 8.6 percent note. Interest is paid annually on February 1.

Required:
1. Record the borrowing transaction in Griddley's journal.
2. Prepare the adjusting entries made at December 31, 2011 and 2012.
3. Prepare the necessary journal entry to recognize the first interest payment on February 1, 2012 (round to the nearest dollar).
4. Indicate how the note and associated interest would be presented in Griddley's December 31, 2012, balance sheet.
5. Prepare the necessary journal entries to record the repayment of the note and the last year's interest payment on February 1, 2014.

OBJECTIVE

Problem 9-75B Preparing a Bond Amortization Table (Straight Line)

On December 31, 2011, The Rock Restaurant borrowed $254,500 by issuing three-year, 7 percent bonds with a face amount of $250,000. Interest is payable annually on December 31.

Required:
Prepare an amortization table using the following column headings:

Period	Cash Payment (Credit)	Interest Expense (Debit)	Premium on Bonds Payable (Debit)	Premium on Bonds Payable Balance	Carrying Value

OBJECTIVE

Problem 9-76B Note Computations and Entries (Straight Line)

On December 31, 2011, Benton Corporation borrowed $1,000,000 with 10-year, 8.75 percent notes, interest payable semiannually on June 30 and December 31. Cash in the amount of $985,500 was received when the note was issued.

Required:
1. Prepare the necessary journal entry at December 31, 2011.
2. Prepare the necessary journal entry at June 30, 2012.
3. Prepare the necessary journal entry at December 31, 2012.
4. Determine the carrying amount of these notes at the end of the fifth year (December 31, 2016).

Problem 9-77B Preparing a Bond Amortization Table (Straight Line)

OBJECTIVE 3

Dalton Company issued five-year, 7.5 percent bonds with a total face value of $900,000 on December 31, 2011, for $950,000. The bonds pay interest on June 30 and December 31 of each year.

Required:

1. Prepare an amortization table
2. Prepare the entries to recognize the interest payments made on June 30, 2012, and December 31, 2012.

Problem 9-78B Preparing a Bond Amortization Table (Straight Line)

OBJECTIVE 3

Pennington Corporation issued five-year, 8.6 percent bonds with a total face value of $700,000 on December 31, 2012, for $680,000. The bonds pay interest on June 30 and December 31 of each year.

Required:

1. Prepare an amortization table.
2. Prepare the entries to recognize the bond issuance and the interest payments made on June 30, 2013, and December 31, 2013.

Problem 9-79B Preparing a Bond Amortization Table (Straight Line)

OBJECTIVE 3

Dunn-Whitaker Construction has agreed to construct a plant in a new industrial park. To finance the construction, the county government issued $4,000,000 of 10-year, 5.25 percent revenue bonds for $4,100,000 on December 31, 2011. Dunn-Whitaker will pay the interest and principal on the bonds. When the bonds are repaid, Dunn-Whitaker will receive title to the plant. In the interim, Dunn-Whitaker will pay property taxes as if it owned the plant. This financing arrangement is attractive to Dunn-Whitaker, as state and local government bonds are exempt from federal income taxation and thus carry a lower interest rate. The bonds are attractive to investors, as both Dunn-Whitaker and the county are issuers. The bonds pay interest semiannually on June 30 and December 31.

Required:

1. Prepare an amortization table through December 31, 2013, for these revenue bonds assuming straight-line amortization.
2. **Conceptual Connection:** Discuss whether or not Dunn-Whitaker should record the plant as an asset after it is constructed.
3. **Conceptual Connection:** Discuss whether or not Dunn-Whitaker should record the liability for these revenue bonds.

Problem 9-80B Non-Interest Bearing Note (Straight Line)

OBJECTIVE 3

On December 31, 2011, Sorenson Financing Corporation borrowed $90,000 cash on a $110,300, 24-month zero coupon note. Sorenson uses the straight-line method of amortization.

Required:

1. Record the borrowing in Sorenson's journal.
2. Prepare the adjusting entry for December 31, 2012.
3. Prepare the entries to recognize the 2013 interest expense and repayment of the note on December 31, 2013.

Problem 9-81B Preparing an Amortization Table for Non-Interest Bearing Bonds (Straight Line)

OBJECTIVE 3

On December 31, 2011, Beauty Box Company borrowed $3,000,000 by issuing three-year, zero coupon bonds. The face value of the bonds is $3,240,000. Beauty Box uses the straight-line method to amortize any premium or discount.

Required:

Prepare an amortization table for these bonds using the following column headings:

Period	Cash Payment (Credit)	Interest Expense (Debit)	Discount on Bonds Payable (Credit)	Discount on Bonds Payable Balance	Carrying Value

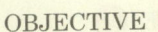

Problem 9-82B Capital and Operating Leases

Kleinfelder Company has decided to lease its new office building. The following information is available for the lease:

Lease:	
Payments	$75,000 per year*
Length of lease	15 years
Economic life of building	16 years
Appropriate interest rate	7.3%
Cost of building if purchased	$750,000

*The first payment is due at the end of the first year of the lease.

Required:
1. Determine whether this is a capital lease or an operating lease.
2. Regardless of your answer to the preceding question, assume that this is a capital lease and that the present value of the lease payments is $740,000. Record the liability and corresponding asset for this acquisition.
3. Record the interest expense on the capital lease at the end of the first year. Also assume no residual value and a 15-year lease for the building. Record the first year's straight-line depreciation of the cost of the leased asset. (*Note:* Round to the nearest dollar.)

CASES

Case 9-83 Long-Term Debt and Ethics

You are the CFO of Diversified Industries. Diversified has suffered through four or five tough years. This has deteriorated their financial condition to a point that they are in danger of violating two loan covenants related to their largest loan, which is not due for 12 more years. The loan contract says that if Diversified violates any of these covenants, the loan principal becomes immediately due and payable. Diversified would be unable to make this payment, and any additional loans taken to repay this loan would likely be at sufficiently higher rates, forcing Diversified into bankruptcy. An investment banker suggests forming another entity (called "special purpose entities" or SPE) and transferring some debt to this SPE. Structuring the SPE very carefully will have the effect of moving enough debt off Diversified's balance sheet to keep the company in compliance with all their loan covenants. The investment banker assures you that accounting rules permit such accounting treatment.

Required:
How do you react to the investment banker?

Case 9-84 Debt Covenants and Financial Reporting Standards

Debtholders receive note contracts, one for each note, that describe the payments promised by the issuer of the debt. In addition, the issuing corporation frequently enters a supplementary agreement, called a *note indenture,* with a trustee who represents the debtholders. The provisions or covenants of the indenture may place restrictions on the issuer for the benefit of the debtholders. For example, an indenture may require that the issuer's ratio of total liabilities to total stockholders' equity never rise above a specified level or that periodic payments be made to the trustee who administers a "sinking fund" to provide for the retirement of debt.

Consider Roswell Manufacturing's debt indenture, which requires Roswell's ratio of total liabilities to total stockholders' equity never to exceed 2:1. If Roswell violates this requirement, the debt indenture specifies very costly penalties, and if the violation continues, the entire debt issue must be retired at a disadvantageous price and refinanced. In recent years, Roswell's ratio has averaged about 1.5:1 ($15 million in total liabilities and $10 million in total stockholders' equity). However, Roswell has an opportunity to purchase one of its major competitors, Ashland Products. The acquisition will require $4.5 million in additional liabilities, but it will double Roswell's net income. Roswell does not believe that a stock issue is feasible in the current environment. The Financial Accounting Standards Board issued a new standard concerning accounting for post employment benefits, which is strongly supported by the Securities and Exchange Commission. Implementation of the new standard will add about $2 million to Roswell's long-term liabilities. Roswell's CEO, Martha Cooper, has written a strong letter of objection to the FASB. The FASB received similar letters from over 300 companies.

Required:
1. Write a paragraph presenting an analysis of the impact of the new standard on Roswell Manufacturing.
2. If you were a member of the FASB and met Martha Cooper at a professional meeting, how would you respond to her objection?

Case 9-85 Evaluating Leverage

Gearing Manufacturing, Inc., is planning a $1,000,000 expansion of its production facilities. The expansion could be financed by the sale of $1,250,000 in 8 percent notes or by the sale of $1,250,000 in common stock, which would raise the number of shares outstanding from 50,000 to 75,000. Gearing pays income taxes at a rate of 30 percent.

Required:
1. Suppose that income from operations is expected to be $550,000 per year for the duration of the proposed debt issue. Should Gearing finance with notes or stock? Explain your answer.
2. Suppose that income from operations is expected to be $275,000 per year for the duration of the proposed debt issue. Should Gearing finance with notes or stock? Explain your answer.
3. Suppose that income from operations varies from year to year but is expected to be above $300,000, 40 percent of the time and below $300,000, 60 percent of the time. Should Gearing finance with notes or stock? Explain your answer.
4. As an investor, how would you use accounting information to evaluate the risk of excessive use of leverage? What additional information would be useful? Explain.

Case 9-86 Leverage

Cook Corporation issued financial statements at December 31, 2011, that include the following information:

Balance sheet at December 31, 2011:

Assets	$8,000,000
Liabilities	$1,200,000
Stockholders' equity (300,000 shares)	$6,800,000

Income statement for 2011:

Income from operations	$1,200,000
Less: Interest expense	(100,000)
Income before taxes	$1,100,000
Less: Income taxes expense (0.30)	(330,000)
Net income	$ 770,000

The levels of assets, liabilities, stockholders' equity, and operating income have been stable in recent years; however, Cook Corporation is planning a $1,800,000 expansion program that will increase income from operations by $350,000 to $1,550,000. Cook is planning to sell 8.5 percent notes at par to finance the expansion.

Required:
1. What earnings per share does Cook report before the expansion?
2. What earnings per share will Cook report if the proposed expansion is undertaken? Would this use of leverage be advantageous to Cook's stockholders? Explain.
3. Suppose income from operations will increase by only $150,000. Would this use of leverage be advantageous to Cook's stockholders? Explain.
4. Suppose that income from operations will increase by $200,000 and that Cook could also raise the required $1,800,000 by issuing an additional 100,000 shares of common stock (assume the additional shares were outstanding for the entire year). Which means of financing would stockholders prefer? Explain.

Case 9-87 Research and Analysis Using the Annual 10-K

Obtain **Marriott**'s 2009 10-K through the "Investor Relations" portion of their website. (Using a search engine, search for: Marriott investor relations.) Once at the Investor Relations part of the website look for "SEC Filings." When you see the list of all the filings, either filter for the "Annual Filings" or search for "10-K" when you find the list of all SEC Filings.

Another option is to go to http://www.sec.gov and click "Search for Company Filings" under "Filings & Forms."

Required:
1. What are Marriott's total liabilities for 2009?
2. How much of these liabilities are classified as long-term debt (not non-current liabilities, but classified as long-term debt)?
3. Look at Marriott's long-term debt footnote and answer the following questions:
   a. When does their debt with the highest stated rate mature?
   b. How much of their debt is maturing in each of the next five years (2010–2014)? How much is maturing in more than five years (2015 and beyond)?
   c. How much debt was repurchased on the open market during 2009? What was the gain or loss recognized on this debt repurchase?
4. Calculate and discuss Marriott's debt to equity and times interest earned (accrual basis) ratios.

Case 9-88 Comparative Analysis: Abercrombie & Fitch versus Aeropostale

Refer to the financial statements of **Abercrombie & Fitch** and **Aeropostale** that are supplied with this text.

Required:
1. Look at Abercrombie & Fitch's and Aeropostale's footnotes. Describe their largest borrowing arrangements and balances at January 30, 2010.
2. Calculate Abercrombie & Fitch's and Aeropostale's times interest earned (accrual basis—in this case interest expense = interest payments for both firms) for the years ended January 31, 2009, and January 30, 2010.
3. Calculate Abercrombie & Fitch's and Aeropostale's long-term debt to equity ratio for the years ended January 31, 2009, and January 30, 2010. (*Note:* Round answers to two decimal places.)
4. Calculate Abercrombie & Fitch's and Aeropostale's debt to equity ratio for the years ended January 31, 2009, and January 30, 2010. (*Note:* Round answers to two decimal places.)
5. Calculate Abercrombie & Fitch's and Aeropostale's long-term debt to total assets ratio for the years ended January 31, 2009, and January 30, 2010. (*Note:* Round answers to two decimal places.)
6. Calculate Abercrombie & Fitch's and Aeropostale's debt to total assets ratio for the years ended January 31, 2009, and January 30, 2010. (*Note:* Round answers to two decimal places.)
7. Comment on Abercrombie & Fitch's and Aeropostale's debt management.

Case 9-89 CONTINUING PROBLEM: FRONT ROW ENTERTAINMENT

In June 2012, Front Row Entertainment had the opportunity to expand its venue operations by purchasing five different venues. To finance this purchase, they issued $1,500,000 of 6 percent, 5-year bonds on July 1, 2012. The bonds were issued for $1,378,300 and pay interest semiannually on June 30 and December 31.

Required:
1. Prepare the journal entry to record the bond issue at July 1, 2012.
2. Assume that Front Row uses the straight-line method of amortization.
   a. Prepare an amortization table through December 31, 2013. (*Note:* Round to the nearest dollar.)
   b. Prepare the journal entry required at December 31, 2012.
   c. How will the bonds be shown on the December 31, 2012 balance sheet?
3. Assume that Front Row uses the effective interest method of amortization and the annual market rate of interest was 8 percent.
   a. Prepare an amortization table through December 31, 2013. (*Note:* Round to the nearest dollar.)
   b. Prepare the journal entry required at December 31, 2012.
   c. How will the bonds be shown on the December 31, 2012 balance sheet?

10 Stockholders' Equity

Doug Norman Crystals/Alamy

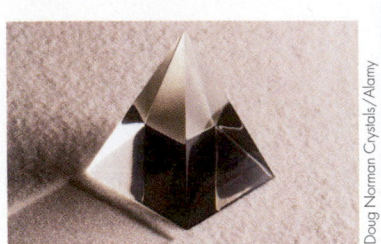

After studying Chapter 10, you should be able to:

1. Distinguish between common and preferred stock and describe their use in raising capital.
2. Record capital stock.
3. Account for the distribution of assets to stockholders.
4. Describe the accounting issues related to retained earnings and accumulated other comprehensive income.
5. Analyze stockholder payout and profitability ratios using information contained in the stockholders' equity section.

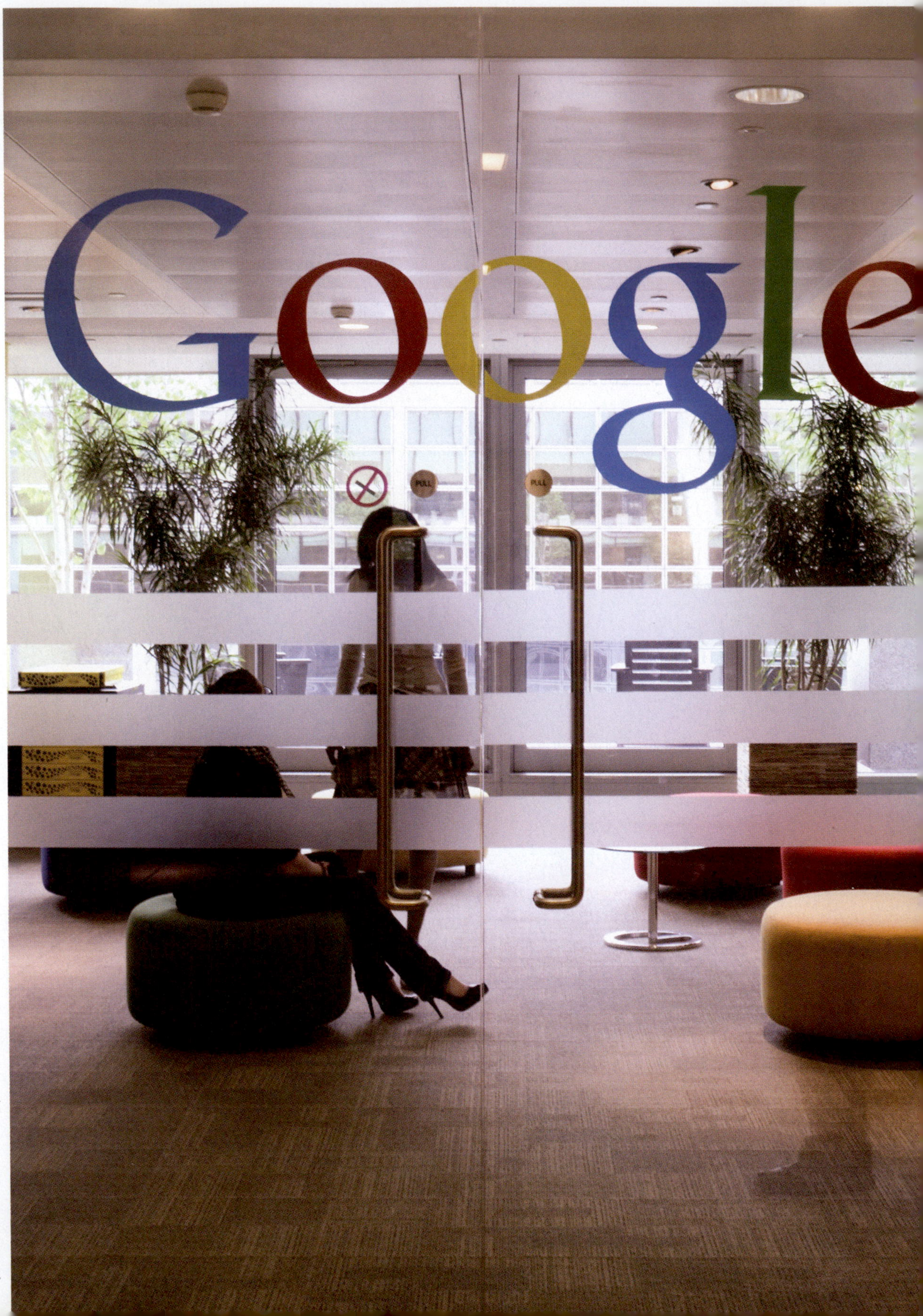

James Brittain/View Pictures/Photolibrary

EXPERIENCE FINANCIAL ACCOUNTING

with Google

In 1998, Sergey Brin and Larry Page, two Ph.D. students at Stanford University, founded **Google**. The incredible growth of Google is evidenced in the fact that, by 2009, Google had revenues in excess of $23.5 billion and net income of over $6.5 billion. These figures are drastically larger than just five years ago. From 2004, revenue was up over 640 percent, while the net income was up over 1,530 percent.

One way that stockholders earn a return on their investment is by receiving dividends yet, despite their profitability, Google has never paid a dividend to stockholders. Instead Google chooses to invest in growth opportunities.

You are likely aware of some of these growth opportunities, like Google's purchases of **YouTube**, **DoubleClick**, and **AdMob**, as well as its roll out of features such as Google Earth and Google Chrome. However, Google's investments do not stop there. In fact, Google's 2009 statement of cash flows shows that Google spent more than $8 billion on investing activities. Since past investment is responsible for Google's large growth in revenues and net income, the hope is that the 2009 investments will fuel profitable growth in the coming years. Review the graph below and notice Google's investing activities over the last five years with very little increase in long-term debt. It is apparent that the investing dollars came from operations.

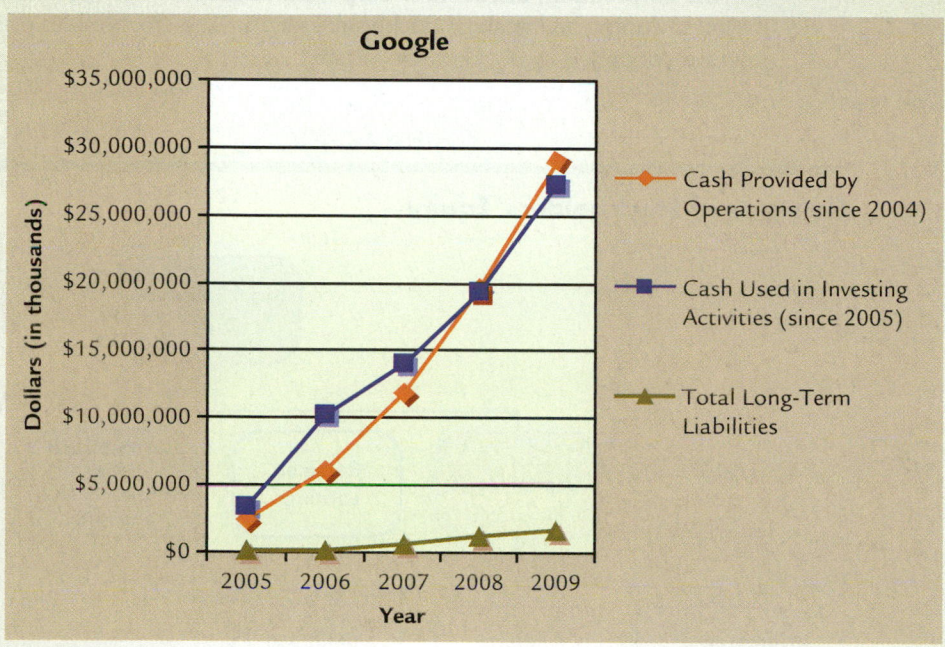

Courtesy of Google, Inc.

Stockholders' equity, which also is called **equity**, represents the owners' claims against the assets of a corporation after all liabilities have been deducted. The stockholders' equity section of the balance sheet clearly identifies various elements of equity according to their source. The most common sources are:

- capital stock—split between (1) preferred and common stock and (2) the associated additional paid-in capital
- retained earnings or deficit
- accumulated other comprehensive income
- treasury stock

In this chapter, we describe how common and preferred stock are used to raise capital for the corporation, discuss how corporations account for the various elements of stockholders' equity, and analyze stockholder payout and stockholder profitability using information contained in stockholders' equity.

Exhibit 10-1

Elements of Stockholders' Equity

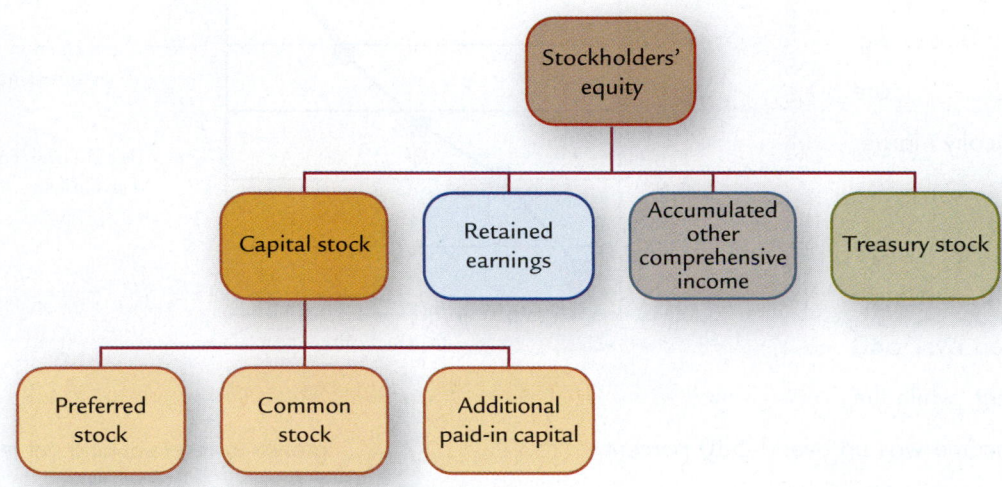

OBJECTIVE

Distinguish between common and preferred stock and describe their use in raising capital.

RAISING CAPITAL WITHIN A CORPORATION

Recall from Chapter 1 that most large businesses are organized as corporations because incorporation increases the company's ability to raise cash (or capital) by easing the transfer of ownership and limiting the liability of owners. Ownership of a corporation is divided into a large number of equal parts or *shares*. Shares are owned in varying numbers by the owners of the corporation called **stockholders** or **shareholders**.

Authorization to Issue Stock

Corporations are authorized, or *chartered*, in accordance with the provisions of state laws that govern the structure and operation of corporations. These laws differ from state to state and a corporation can charter in any state. For instance, although **Google** is headquartered in Mountain View, California, it is chartered in Delaware, as are many corporations due to Delaware's favorable laws.

Although the provisions of incorporation laws vary from state to state, all states require persons who wish to form a corporation to apply to a prescribed state official for the issuance of a charter. The **corporate charter**, which is sometimes called the **articles**

of incorporation, is a document that authorizes the creation of the corporation, setting forth its name and purpose and the names of the incorporators.

The typical corporate charter contains provisions that describe how stock may be issued by the corporation. First, it authorizes the corporation to issue stock in a limited number of classes. It also sets an upper limit on the number of shares that the corporation may issue in each class. And finally, it sets a lower limit on the amount for which each share must be sold.

Shares of stock are sold, or issued, when a corporation is formed. Additional shares may be issued later. The maximum number of shares the business may issue in each class of stock is referred to as the number of **authorized shares**. This must be distinguished from the number of **issued shares**, which is the number of shares actually sold to stockholders. A corporation rarely issues all of its authorized shares.

Corporations can buy back their own stock for reasons explained later in this chapter. Thus, the number of shares issued is further distinguished from the number of **outstanding shares**—which is the number of issued shares actually in the hands of stockholders. When firms reacquire their own stock, the reacquired shares are not considered to be outstanding. Exhibit 10-2 illustrates how the share quantities are determined.

Exhibit 10-2

Determination of Share Quantities

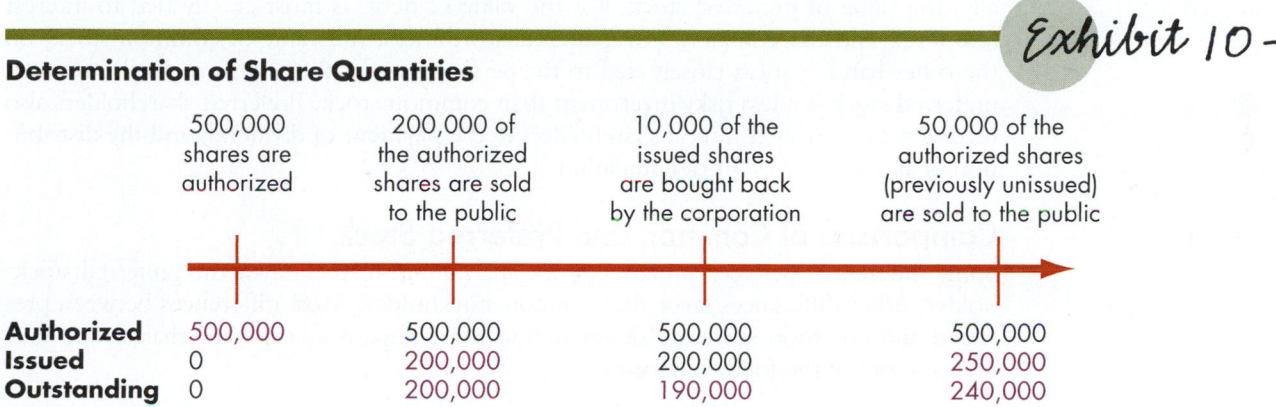

	500,000 shares are authorized	200,000 of the authorized shares are sold to the public	10,000 of the issued shares are bought back by the corporation	50,000 of the authorized shares (previously unissued) are sold to the public
Authorized	500,000	500,000	500,000	500,000
Issued	0	200,000	200,000	250,000
Outstanding	0	200,000	190,000	240,000

These three share quantities—the number of shares authorized, issued, and outstanding—are reported for each class of stock in the balance sheet or its accompanying notes.

Common Stock

All classes of stock are designated as either common stock or preferred stock. These come with different financial benefits and provide different rights regarding the governance of the corporation. The primary rights for owners of **common stock** are:

- Voting in the election of the board of directors. You will recall that the board controls the operating and financial policies of the company.
- Sharing in the profits and dividends of the company. We will talk more about this below.
- Keeping the same percentage of ownership if new stock is issued (preemptive right).
- Sharing in the assets in liquidation in proportion to their holdings. This is referred to as the "residual claim" because common stockholders are only paid after all creditors and preferred stockholders are paid in full (which is very rare in liquidation).

When you hear of someone who "made money by investing in stock" it is almost invariably through an investment in common stock. This is because, although the "residual claim" means common stockholders are only paid after the creditors and preferred stockholders are paid in full, it also means that common stockholders get *everything* that is left over after the creditors and preferred stockholders are paid in full. As such, the common stockholders receive the bulk of the financial gain from a profitable company through stock appreciation and dividends:

- *Stock appreciation*: The value of the stock increases above the price initially paid (of course, it is also possible that the stock's value decreases if the company is unprofitable—this is a risk of owning stock).
- *Dividends*: **Dividends** are payments to a company's shareholders from earnings. These payments are usually in the form of cash, but noncash assets and stock can also be given as dividends. Payment of dividends to common shareholders, however, depends on a company's alternatives. The company may elect to pay down debt or, if the company has growth opportunities, they may elect to keep (or retain) earnings to fund these investment options rather than pay dividends. In fact, many companies do not pay dividends to common shareholders.

Preferred Stock

Preferred stock generally pays a regular dividend. In this regard, preferred stock is similar to debt, with the preferred stock dividend equating to interest payments. Additionally, the value of preferred stock, like the value of debt, is most closely tied to interest rate levels and the company's overall creditworthiness; the value of common stock, on the other hand, is most closely tied to the performance of the company. In this respect, preferred stock is a less risky investment than common stock. Preferred shareholders also receive priority over common shareholders in the payment of dividends and the distribution of assets in the event of liquidation.

Comparison of Common and Preferred Stock

Some differences between preferred stock and common stock favor the preferred stockholder; other differences favor the common stockholder. Most differences between preferred and common stock are designated in the company's corporate charter and take one or more of the following forms:

- *Dividend preferences:* Preferred stock frequently requires that the issuing corporation pay dividends to preferred stockholders before paying dividends to common stockholders. Additionally, preferred dividends may be *cumulative and participating,* as explained on p. 490.
- *Conversion privileges:* Preferred stock may be convertible into common shares if the preferred shareholder elects to do so and certain conditions are satisfied. For example, each share of preferred stock might be convertible into, say, 10 shares of common stock after a certain date.
- *Liquidation preferences:* If and when a corporation is dissolved, liquidating distributions are made to stockholders. Corporate charters frequently require the claims of preferred stockholders to be satisfied before those of common stockholders. Additionally, the charter may specify a liquidating amount for preferred shares.
- *Call provisions (redeemable):* The corporate charter may authorize or even require the corporation to repurchase (or redeem) any preferred shares that are sold. In such cases, the charter usually fixes the *call price* (the amount to be paid to the preferred stockholders) and specifies a date on or after which the shares may or must be repurchased. Note that this feature is similar to the repaying of the principal on a loan at the maturity date—particularly when the charter requires redemption at a specific date.
- *Denial of voting rights:* Most preferred stock does not confer voting rights, which means that preferred stockholders, unlike common stockholders, cannot vote at stockholders' meetings.

The first three characteristics of preferred stock are advantageous for preferred stockholders. The last two characteristics usually work in the interest of common stockholders.

Because of the relative advantages of different forms of stock, corporations are typically authorized by their charters to issue several classes of preferred stock and several classes of common stock, each with a different set of terms and provisions. The 2009 edition of *Accounting Trends & Techniques* (an American Institute of Certified Public Accountants publication that surveys accounting practices followed in 600 sampled financial statements) indicates that only 34 of the 600 companies (a little under 6 percent) had outstanding preferred stock, but all corporations have outstanding common stock.[1] This excerpt from **Procter & Gamble**'s 10-K illustrates how the different classes of stock are shown:

Classes of Stock for Procter & Gamble (amounts in millions)	2009	2008
Convertible Class A preferred stock, stated value $1 per share (600 shares authorized)	$1,324	$1,366
Nonvoting Class B preferred stock, stated value $1 per share (200 shares authorized)	—	—
Common stock, stated value $1 per share (10,000 shares authorized; issued: 2007—4,007.3, 2008—4,001.8)	4,007	4,002

YOU ◆ DECIDE   Issuing Debt or Preferred Stock

You are the CFO of Canova Manufacturing. Your company needs to raise capital to pursue an expansion project, but the company does not want to sell additional common stock.

What factors should you consider in deciding whether to issue debt or preferred stock?

In making your decision, it would be helpful to consider the following differences between debt and preferred stock.

Advantage of debt:
- Interest payments are tax deductible, while preferred dividends are not.

Advantages of preferred stock:
- Preferred stock is historically classified as equity, rather than debt, on the balance sheet. If Canova prefers to, or must, show lower debt totals, preferred stock is advantageous. For example, provisions of existing debt contracts may not allow Canova to issue additional debt.
- Preferred stock is less risky than debt because, unlike interest payments, missing a preferred dividend payment does not trigger bankruptcy. If Canova fears cash flow problems, this will be important.
- Companies with a history of operating losses typically do not pay income taxes. If Canova has these so-called net operating loss carryforwards, then debt no longer has the tax advantage.
- Preferred stock is generally sold to other corporations because these corporations do not pay taxes on the full amount of the dividends (i.e., there is a big tax break relative to receiving interest payments).

Although preferred stock and debt have many similarities, they have some important differences.

ACCOUNTING FOR ISSUANCE OF COMMON AND PREFERRED STOCK

OBJECTIVE 2
Record capital stock.

In examples in previous chapters, we recorded the contributions of stockholders in exchange for stock in a single account. In practice, however, cash or other assets (capital) contributed by stockholders is usually divided between two accounts, on the basis of the par value of the stock. **Par value** is an arbitrary monetary amount printed on each share

IFRS

The accounting for stockholders' equity is generally the same under IFRS as under U.S. GAAP.

---

[1] *Accounting Trends and Techniques for 2009, 63rd edition,* Table 2-272, p. 300.

Concept Q&A

How do we account for stock issued in exchange for noncash assets or services (such as legal services in connection with incorporation)?

Answer:

The amount recorded should be the fair market value of the stock or the fair market value of the asset/service, whichever is more clearly determinable. In the case of a newly organized corporation, the fair market value of the asset/service is usually more clearly determinable. But in the case of established corporations with widely traded stock, the fair market value of the stock is more clearly determinable than the fair market value of the asset/service.

of stock that establishes a minimum price for the stock when issued, but does not determine its market value.[2] When a corporation receives more than par value for newly issued stock, as it usually does (stock rarely sells for exactly its par value), the par value and the excess over par are recorded in separate accounts. The par value multiplied by the number of shares sold is recorded in an account that describes the type of stock—for example, common stock or preferred stock. The amount received in excess of the par value is recorded in an account called **additional paid-in capital**. These accounts are the first accounts shown in the stockholders' equity section of the balance sheet and taken together are known as **capital stock**. **CORNERSTONE 10-1** illustrates the accounting procedures for recording the sale of stock.

CORNERSTONE 10-1   Recording the Sale of Common and Preferred Stock

Concept:

When companies sell common or preferred stock to raise capital, the resulting ownership claims are recorded in the capital stock section of stockholders' equity.

Information:

Spectator Corporation is authorized to issue 1,000 shares of preferred stock with a 9 percent dividend rate and a par value of $20 per share and 50,000 shares of common stock with a par value of $2 per share. On January 2, 2011, Spectator issues 200 shares of preferred stock at $22 per share and 20,000 shares of common stock at $2.50 per share.

Required:

1. How much cash did Spectator raise through their stock issuance?
2. Prepare the journal entries necessary to record the sale of common and preferred stock separately.
3. Provide the stockholders' equity section of Spectator's balance sheet (*Note:* Assume Spectator has yet to engage in any operations).

Solution:

1.

Preferred stock ($22 × 200 shares)	$ 4,400
Common stock ($2.50 × 20,000 shares)	50,000
Total proceeds	**$ 54,400**

2.

Date	Account and Explanation	Debit	Credit
Jan. 2	Cash	4,400	
	Preferred Stock[a]		4,000
	Additional Paid-In Capital—Preferred Stock[b]		400
	(Record sale of preferred stock at $22 per share)		

Assets	= Liabilities +	Stockholders' Equity
+4,400		+4,000
		+400

[a]200 shares × $20 par = $4,000
[b]200 shares × ($22 − $20) = $400

(Continued)

---

[2] The precise meaning of par value is established by securities laws that vary somewhat from state to state.

Date	Account and Explanation	Debit	Credit
Jan. 2	Cash	50,000	
	Common Stock[c]		40,000
	Additional Paid-In Capital—Common		
	Stock[d]		10,000
	(Record sale of common stock at $2.50 per share)		

Assets	= Liabilities +	Stockholders' Equity
+50,000		+40,000
		+10,000

CORNERSTONE 10-1 *(continued)*

[c]20,000 shares $\times$ $2 par = $40,000
[d]20,000 shares $\times$ ($2.50 − $2.00) = $10,000

3.

Stockholders' Equity

Preferred stock, 9 percent, $20 par, 1,000 shares authorized, 200 shares issued and outstanding	$ 4,000	
Common stock, $2 par, 50,000 shares authorized, 20,000 shares issued and outstanding	40,000	
Additional paid-in capital:		
Preferred stock	400	
Common stock	10,000	
Total capital stock		$54,400
Retained earnings*		0
Total stockholders' equity		$54,400

*Note that retained earnings displays a zero balance because Spectator is a newly formed corporation.

Stated Capital and No-Par Stock

The stock issued by Spectator Corporation carried a par value that represents the stated capital of the corporation. **Stated capital** (**legal capital**) is the amount of capital that, under law, cannot be returned to the corporation's owners unless the corporation is liquidated. Even when state law permits the issuance of **no-par stock** (stock without a par value), it frequently requires that no-par stock have a stated (legal) value, set by the corporation, in order to establish the corporation's stated or legal capital. Further, this is a relatively infrequent occurrence.[3]

Stated value, like par value, is recorded separately in the *Common* (or *Preferred*) *Stock* account, while any excess paid over its stated value is recorded in *Additional Paid-In Capital—Common* (or *Preferred*) *Stock*.[4]

Warrants

A **stock warrant** is the right granted by a corporation to purchase a specified number of shares of its common stock at a stated price and within a stated time period. Corporations issue stock warrants in the following two situations:

- First, they may issue warrants along with bonds or preferred stock as an "equity kicker," to make the bonds or preferred stock more attractive. Such warrants often have a duration of five or more years.
- Second, they may issue warrants to existing stockholders who have a legal right to purchase a specified share of a new stock issue, in order to maintain their relative level of ownership in the corporation. Such warrants usually have a duration of less than six months.

[3] *Accounting Trends & Techniques* for 2009 indicated that 47 of the 600 companies surveyed (just under 8 percent) had "no par value" common stock.
[4] In some states, stated value functions exactly as does the par value of stock to identify the legal capital portion of total capital stock. However, in other states, legal capital is defined as the entire capital stock amount associated with the no-par stock. In these states, the entire capital stock amount is recorded in a single common or preferred stock account.

Options

Corporations also grant employees and executives the right to buy stock at a set price as compensation for their services. These "rights" are called *stock options*. Stock options are frequently given to employees and executives as compensation for their services. For example, the employer may give the executive the right to purchase in two years 5,000 shares of the company's stock at $50 per share, today's market price. If in two years the market price of the stock is higher than $50—say, $62—the executive will purchase the 5,000 shares for $50 each and receive effective compensation of $60,000 [($62 − $50) × 5,000 shares]. Of course, if the price is lower than $50, the executive will not exercise the option.

The number of U.S. employees holding stock options increased dramatically through the 1990s and 2000s. The National Center for Employee Ownership estimated that in 1992, approximately 1 million employees held stock options, but by 2006, this number had soared to 10.6 million.

ETHICAL DECISIONS   The compensation expense recorded by a company when they grant stock options depends on many factors including the price at which employees can buy the stock (called the **exercise** or **strike price**) and the market value of the stock on the date of grant. As discussed, the strike price of the options and the market value of the stock are generally the same on the date of grant. However, during 2006, many companies came under investigation for "back dating" stock options. That is, companies waited to announce the granting of options and then picked the date in the past when the stock price was lowest. This maximized the value of each individual option to the employee.

This practice has been curtailed by the Sarbanes-Oxley Act, but in and of itself, this is not illegal. However, if on December 20 a company backdates options to May 1 (the lowest stock price of the year), the value of each option will be greater on December 20 than on May 1. As such, the company should calculate compensation expense using the market value of the stock on December 20. We will never know exactly how widespread the practice of backdating was, but approximately 80 firms were initially the subject of an SEC probe and research estimates that 29.2 percent of firms backdated grants to top executives between 1996 and 2005. ●

Corporations elect to grant stock options for two primary reasons:

- First, stock options allow cash-poor companies to compete for top talent in the employee market. For example, market salary for a manager of systems quality and assurance may be $200,000 per year—well beyond the means of many start-up companies. However, such a person may agree to work for $100,000 per year and a significant number of stock options.

- Second, stock options are believed to better align the incentives of the employee with those of the owners. This concept is easy to understand with a bit of exaggeration. Employees would like to be paid millions of dollars a year to do nothing, while owners would like the employees to work hundreds of hours a week for free. Stock options help align these incentives because now an employee's personal wealth is tied to the success of the company's stock price—just like the owners. Knowledge of these uses of equity is important, but discussion of the complications of accounting for stock warrants and options is left for more advanced accounting courses.

 **Going Public**

You are CEO of Georgian, Inc., a successful manufacturer of electronic components for computer hardware. Georgian wishes to double its scale of operations in order to meet both existing and expected demand for its products. Georgian is a *privately held corporation*. High interest rates preclude Georgian from borrowing the necessary expansion capital, and its current owners are unable to invest significantly more capital at this time.

(Continued)

What effect will going public have on corporate control and expenses?

Raising enough capital to double the scale of operations will likely require giving away a substantial ownership interest. If the new owners are sufficiently well-organized and cohesive, they could elect a majority of directors and control the company. On the other hand, if the new shares were purchased by a large number of investors with no organized interest in controlling Georgian, then effective control would remain in the hands of the original owners. Of course, the risk of losing control at some future time would still exist. Going public will also substantially increase the costs of financial reporting and corporate governance to comply with requirements of the Sarbanes-Oxley Act of 2002.

Going public will most likely require giving up control of the company and will also increase expenses in order to comply with financial reporting standards.

ACCOUNTING FOR DISTRIBUTIONS TO STOCKHOLDERS

OBJECTIVE **3**
Account for the distribution of assets to stockholders.

As discussed, owners invest in corporations through the purchase of stock. Corporations can distribute cash to stockholders in the following ways:

- The corporation can repurchase the shares from owners.
- The corporation can issue dividends.

Historically, dividends were the most common method of distributing cash. Over recent years, however, repurchasing shares has become a more frequent method of cash distribution because it has tax advantages for stockholders relative to dividends.[5] First, dividends are paid to *all* stockholders, thus creating tax consequences for everyone. Stock repurchases, on the other hand, only trigger tax consequences for those stockholders who elect to sell their stock back to the company. Thus, if a stockholder does not want to incur tax consequences in the current year, he or she can elect not to sell the shares back to the company. Second, dividends have usually been taxed at higher rates than gains from selling stock.[6] Dividends do have the advantage of allowing shareholders to receive assets from the corporation without reducing their ownership share.

Stock Repurchases (Treasury Stock)

When a corporation purchases its own previously issued stock, the stock that it buys is called **treasury stock**. Corporations purchase treasury stock for many reasons:

- to buy out the ownership of one or more stockholders
- to reduce the size of corporate operations
- to reduce the number of outstanding shares of stock in an attempt to increase earnings per share and market value per share
- to acquire shares to be transferred to employees under stock bonus, stock option, or stock purchase plans
- to satisfy the terms of a business combination in which the corporation must give a quantity of shares of its stock as part of the acquisition of another business
- to reduce vulnerability to an unfriendly takeover

The stock may be purchased on the open market, by a general offer to the stockholders (called a *tender offer*), or by direct negotiation with a major stockholder. If the objective of acquiring treasury stock is to reduce the size of corporate operations, the treasury shares may be retired after purchase. More frequently, however, repurchased stock is held in the corporation's treasury until circumstances favor its resale, or until it is needed to meet obligations of the corporation that must be satisfied with shares of its stock. Transactions in treasury stock, even very large ones, usually do not require stockholder approval.

---

[5] In fact, one study shows that the number of stock repurchases increased from 87 and $1.4 billion in 1988 to 1,570 and $222 billion in 1998 (Grullon, G. and D. Ikenberry. 2000. "What do we know about stock repurchases?" *Journal of Applied Corporate Finance*. Spring: 31–51).

[6] Dividends were taxed at the same rates as gains from selling stocks from 2003 through 2010 as a result of the *Jobs and Growth Tax Relief Reconciliation Act of 2003*. However, this favorable tax treatment for dividends is scheduled to expire at the end of 2010, unless Congress takes additional measures.

Concept Q&A

If a corporation buys the stock of another corporation and later sells that stock for a different price, a gain or loss is recorded on the income statement. However, when a corporation buys its own stock and later sells it for a different price, the income statement is not affected. Why is this?

Answer:
Transactions with a corporation's owners cannot be included on the income statement.

The 2009 edition of *Accounting Trends & Techniques* indicates that 350 of the 600 companies surveyed hold treasury shares.[7] Interestingly, a few companies hold a relatively large portion of their issued shares in treasury. For example, at the end of 2009 **Coca-Cola Company** held approximately 34.5 percent of its shares in treasury at a repurchase cost of almost $24.4 billion.

Purchase At first thought, one might consider recording the acquisition of treasury stock as an exchange of cash for an investment in stock (an exchange of one asset for another). However, that approach fails to recognize that the treasury stock is already represented by amounts in the corporation's equity accounts. Although the shares would represent an asset to another entity if it acquired them, they cannot represent an asset to the entity that issued them. Thus, the purchase of treasury stock is a reduction of equity rather than the acquisition of an investment. Instead of requiring a debit to an investment account, the reacquisition of treasury stock requires a debit to a contra-equity account, treasury stock. This interpretation is consistent with the provisions of most state incorporation laws, which prohibit the payment of dividends on treasury stock.[8]

Resale If the treasury shares are reissued at some point in the future, the original cost of the shares is removed from the treasury stock account. Any excess of proceeds over the cost of the shares is not considered a gain because a corporation cannot generate income by buying and selling its own stock (income is reserved for transactions with nonowners); instead, a credit is made to a special paid-in capital account—*additional paid-in capital–treasury stock*. If the treasury shares are sold for less than their cost, a debit is first made to "Additional paid-in capital–treasury stock." If the credit balance in Additional paid-in capital–treasury stock is not large enough to absorb the shortfall, then the unabsorbed debit reduces retained earnings. **CORNERSTONE 10-2** illustrates how to account for treasury stock.

CORNERSTONE 10-2   Accounting for Treasury Stock

Concept:
When purchasing its own previously issued stock, corporations record a reduction to stockholders' equity by debiting treasury stock.

Information:
On July 1, 2011, Spectator Corporation repurchases 1,000 shares of its outstanding common stock for $15 per share. On September 15, 2011, Spectator sells 500 shares of treasury stock for $18 per share and on December 1, 2011, Spectator sells 400 shares of treasury stock for $11 per share.

Required:
Prepare the journal entries to record (1) the purchase of treasury stock, (2) the sale of treasury stock on September 15, 2011, and (3) the sale of treasury stock on December 1, 2011.

(Continued)

---

[7] *Accounting Trends and Techniques for 2009, 63rd edition*, Table 2-294, p. 312.
[8] The method of accounting for treasury stock demonstrated here is called the *cost method*. This method is used by approximately 95 percent of the companies engaging in treasury stock transactions. An alternative method, called the *par value method*, is demonstrated in intermediate accounting courses.

**CORNERSTONE
10-2**
(continued)

Solution:

Date	Account and Explanation	Debit	Credit
1. July 1, 2011	Treasury Stock[a]	15,000	
	Cash		15,000
	(Record purchase of treasury shares)		
2. Sept. 15, 2011	Cash[b]	9,000	
	Treasury Stock[c]		7,500
	Additional Paid-in Capital–Treasury Stock[d]		1,500
	(Record reissue of treasury shares)		
3. Dec. 1, 2011	Cash[e]	4,400	
	Additional Paid-in Capital–Treasury Stock[f]	1,500	
	Retained Earnings[g]	100	
	Treasury Stock[h]		6,000
	(Record reissue of treasury shares)		

	Assets	= Liabilities +	Stockholders' Equity
1.	−15,000		−15,000
2.	+9,000		+7,500 +1,500
3.	+4,400		−1,500 −100 +6,000

[a]1,000 shares × $15 = $15,000
[b]500 shares × $18 = $9,000
[c]500 shares × $15 = $7,500
[d]500 shares × ($18 − $15) = $1,500
[e]400 shares × $11 = $4,400
[f]Additional paid-in capital–treasury stock can be debited in a journal entry, but the result of the journal entry cannot be a debit *balance* to the account. Thus, there is a limit of $1,500 due to the credit in part 2.
[g]Retained earnings is debited if there is any remaining debit needed after additional paid-in capital–treasury stock is zeroed out.
[h]400 shares × $15 = $6,000

Transfers Among Shareholders We have been considering the effects on the equity accounts when a corporation buys or sells its own stock. However, treasury stock transactions constitute a special case. In general, the purchase or sale of stock after it is first issued does *not* alter the equity accounts of the issuing corporation, unless that corporation is itself the purchaser or seller. Although the issuing corporation's accounts do not change when shares are sold by one stockholder to another, the corporation's stockholder list must be updated. Large corporations usually retain an independent *stock transfer agent* to maintain their stockholder lists, which include the quantity and serial numbers of the shares held. Stock transfer agents also arrange for the transfer of certificates among stockholders and the issuance of new certificates to stockholders.[9]

Retirement of Treasury Shares Occasionally, treasury shares are permanently retired. That is, these particular shares will no longer be traded. In such cases, the common stock account is debited for the par value of the stock and the additional paid-in capital account is reduced for any excess of the purchase price of the treasury shares over par. If Spectator had retired the 1,000 shares it repurchased for $15/share in Cornerstone 10-2, it would have made the following entry assuming the par value of the stock was $2:

Date	Account and Explanation	Debit	Credit
July 1, 2009	Common Stock*	2,000	
	Additional Paid-In Capital–Common Stock	13,000	
	Cash		15,000
	(Record purchase and retirement of shares)		

	Assets	= Liabilities +	Stockholders' Equity
	−15,000		−2,000 −13,000

*1,000 shares × $2 = $2,000

[9] Although the transfer of shares among stockholders does not affect the accounts of the issuing corporation, such transactions obviously require entries into the accounts of the buyers and sellers of the shares.

Exhibit 10-3

Dividends

Dividends <u>reduce</u> Retained Earnings

| Cash dividends distribute cash to stockholders | Stock dividends distribute additional shares to stockholders | Stock splits transfer additional shares to stockholders without changing equity |

Dividends

A dividend is an amount paid periodically by a corporation to a stockholder as a return on invested capital. Dividends represent distributions of accumulated net income. They are usually paid in cash but may also be paid in the form of noncash assets or even additional shares of a corporation's own stock. All dividends, whatever their form, reduce retained earnings (see Exhibit 10-3).

Cash Dividends Cash dividends are by far the most common form of dividend. The payment of a cash dividend is preceded by an official announcement or declaration by the board of directors of the company's intention to pay a dividend. The dividend declaration specifies:

- the **declaration date**—the date on which a corporation announces its intention to pay a dividend on common or preferred stock
- the dollar amount of the dividend—usually stated as the number of dollars per share
- the **date of record**—the date on which a stockholder must own one or more shares of stock in order to receive the dividend
- the **payment date**—the date on which the dividend will actually be paid

Since the stock of most corporations is continually changing hands, it is necessary to set a date on which the ownership of shares is established as a basis for the payment of dividends. If a share of stock is sold between the date of record and the dividend payment date, the former owner of the share, rather than the new owner, receives the dividend. On the other hand, if a share of stock is sold between the declaration date and the date of record, the new owner, rather than the former owner, receives the dividend. The accounting for cash dividends is illustrated in **CORNERSTONE 10-3**.

CORNERSTONE 10-3   Recording Cash Dividends

Concept:
Dividends are generally paid out of retained earnings.

Information:
The Kingsmill Corporation has issued 3,000 shares of common stock, all of the same class; 2,800 shares are outstanding and 200 shares are held as treasury stock. On November 15, 2011, Kingsmill's board of directors

(Continued)

declares a cash dividend of $2.00 per share payable on December 15, 2011, to stockholders of record on December 1, 2011.

CORNERSTONE 10-3
(continued)

Required:
Prepare the journal entries at (1) the date of declaration, (2) the date of record, and (3) the payment.

Solution:

1. Dividends are not paid on treasury stock. Further, a liability is incurred on the date of declaration because the corporation has the legal obligation to pay after declaring the dividend.

Date	Account and Explanation	Debit	Credit
Nov. 15, 2011	Retained Earnings (or Dividends*)	5,600	
	Dividends Payable		5,600
	(Record liability for dividends)		

Assets	=	Liabilities	+	Stockholders' Equity
		+5,600		−5,600

*Dividends is closed to Retained Earnings at the end of the period (2,800 shares × $2 = $5,600)

2. No journal entry is needed because the date of record is the date at which ownership is recorded to determine who will receive the dividend.

3.

Date	Account and Explanation	Debit	Credit
Dec. 15, 2011	Dividends Payable	5,600	
	Cash		5,600
	(Record payment of dividends)		

Assets	=	Liabilities	+	Stockholders' Equity
−5,600		−5,600		

Dividend Policy The corporation's record of dividends and retained earnings provides useful information to:

- boards of directors and managers who must formulate a dividend policy
- stockholders and potential investors who wish to evaluate past dividend policies and assess prospects for future dividends

Historical records and long-term future projections of earnings and dividends are of particular interest to stockholders because the dividend policies of most large corporations are characterized by long-term stability. In other words, they are designed to produce a smooth pattern of dividends over time. For this reason, directors approach increases in the per-share dividend very cautiously and avoid decreases at all costs.

Liquidating Dividends When retained earnings has been reduced to zero, any additional dividends must come from capital stock. Such dividends are called **liquidating dividends** and must be charged first against additional paid-in capital, then the common (or preferred) stock accounts. The payment of liquidating dividends usually accompanies the dissolution of the corporation and is regulated by various laws designed to protect the interests of creditors and other holders of nonresidual equity. Thus, the presence of significant liabilities will usually prevent, or at least require close monitoring of, liquidating dividends. Since these dividends are a return of paid-in capital, they are not taxed as income to the recipients.

Stock Dividends A cash dividend transfers cash from the corporation to its stockholders. In contrast, a **stock dividend** transfers shares of stock from the corporation to its stockholders—additional shares of the corporation's own stock. For each share outstanding, a fixed number of new shares is issued, and an amount of retained earnings is transferred to contributed capital accounts in a process known as *capitalization of retained* *earnings.* While a cash dividend reduces both total assets and total equity, a stock dividend alters neither total assets nor total equity. A stock dividend merely notifies investors that the equity section of the balance sheet has been rearranged.

The amount of retained earnings capitalized for each new share depends on the size of the stock dividend.

- *Small stock dividends* increase the number of outstanding shares by less than 25 percent; they are capitalized using the stock's market value just before the dividend.
- *Large stock dividends* increase the number of outstanding shares by 25 percent or more and are capitalized at par.

This is illustrated in **CORNERSTONE 10-4**.

CORNERSTONE 10-4   Recording Small and Large Stock Dividends

Concept:
Small stock dividends are capitalized using the stock's market value, while large stock dividends are capitalized at the stock's par value.

Information:
On May 18, 2011, Arlington Corporation has 6,000,000 shares of $10 par common stock outstanding. This stock is currently trading at $12 per share.

Required:
1. Determine how many new shares are issued and prepare the necessary journal entry assuming Arlington declares and pays a 5 percent stock dividend.
2. Determine how many new shares are issued and prepare the necessary journal entry assuming Arlington declares and pays a 30 percent stock dividend.

Solution:
1. 6,000,000 × 0.05 = 300,000 shares

Account and Explanation	Debit	Credit
Retained Earnings*	3,600,000	
Common Stock**		3,000,000
Additional Paid-In Capital—Common Stock		600,000
(Record small stock dividend)		

Assets	=	Liabilities	+	Stockholders' Equity
				−3,600,000
				+3,000,000
				+600,000

  *300,000 shares × $12 = $3,600,000
**300,000 shares × $10 = $3,000,000

2. 6,000,000 × 0.30 = 1,800,000 shares

Account and Explanation	Debit	Credit
Retained Earnings***	18,000,000	
Common Stock***		18,000,000
(Record large stock dividend)		

Assets	=	Liabilities	+	Stockholders' Equity
				−18,000,000
				+18,000,000

***1,800,000 shares × $10 = $18,000,000

Note that the stock dividend merely transfers dollars from retained earnings to the capital stock accounts.

Although a stock dividend increases the *number* of shares held by each stockholder, it does not alter the *proportion* of shares held. For example, if an investor held 100,000 out of

2,000,000 outstanding shares before a 10 percent stock dividend, that investor would hold 110,000 out of 2,200,000 outstanding shares after the dividend. Thus the investor would hold 5 percent of the outstanding shares both before and after the stock dividend and would have a 5 percent claim on earnings and stockholders' equity both before and after:

$$\frac{100,000}{2,000,000} = \frac{110,000}{2,200,000} = 0.05$$

Further, despite the popular belief to the contrary among stockholders and even some financial managers, research shows that neither stock dividends nor stock splits, which we will consider next, enhance the total market value of a corporation's outstanding common stock. Stock dividends should be distinguished from dividend plans that allow stockholders to choose between receiving a cash dividend and a share of stock with equivalent current value. Such plans may enhance a stockholder's proportionate ownership and also avoid brokerage fees.

Stock Splits   A stock split, like a stock dividend, increases the number of outstanding shares without altering the proportionate ownership of a corporation. Unlike a stock dividend, however, a stock split involves a *decrease* in the per-share par value (or stated value), with no capitalization of retained earnings. In other words, a **stock split** is a stock issue that increases the number of outstanding shares of a corporation without changing the balances of its equity accounts.

Consider a corporation that has 10,000 common shares outstanding with a par value of $30 per share. In a two-for-one stock split, stockholders will exchange each of their 10,000 original shares for two new shares; the number of shares will rise from 10,000 to 20,000; and the par value of each share will be reduced to $15 per share. The total par value of all stock will remain $300,000:

$$\$30 \times 10,000 \text{ shares} = \$15 \times 20,000 \text{ shares} = \$300,000$$

The split has the effect of distributing the par value over a larger number of shares.

Stock splits are used to reduce the per-share price of a stock. If nothing else changes, a two-for-one split should cut the market price of a stock in half. A corporation may wish to reduce the per-share price to encourage trading of its stock. The assumption is that a higher per-share price is an obstacle to purchases and sales of stock, particularly for small investors.

No entry is required to record a stock split because no account balances change. The changes in the par value and the number of outstanding shares are merely noted in the corporation's records.

To illustrate how companies use stock splits, look at the **Microsoft** data in Exhibit 10-4. Note that Microsoft stock has split nine times in its history. That means if you had owned 1,000 shares of Microsoft stock prior to September 21, 1987 and you never bought nor sold a single share, you would now have 288,000 shares:

$$1,000 \text{ shares} \times 2 \times 2 \times \left(\frac{3}{2}\right) \times \left(\frac{3}{2}\right) \times 2 \times 2 \times 2 \times 2 \times 2$$

Exhibit 10-4

Microsoft's Stock Price History

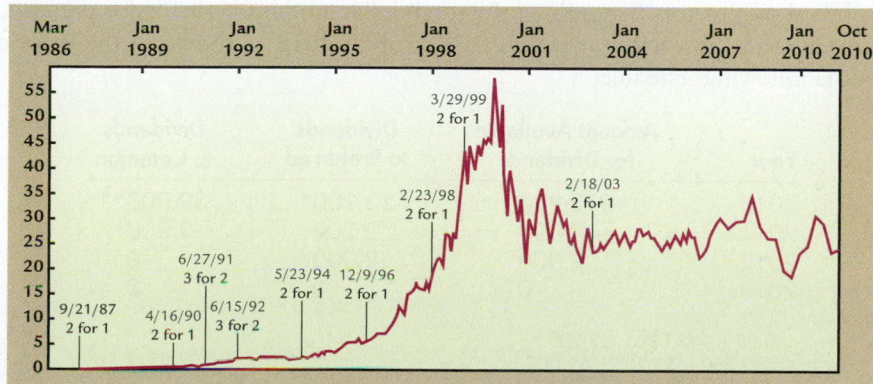

These shares would have been worth approximately $7,100,000 in August 2010. Further, if we assume that splits have no effect on price, the price of a share of Microsoft stock during August 2010 (which was trading slightly below $25 per share), would have been approximately $7,100 per share if there had been no stock splits.

Not many individual investors can pay $8,100 per share, but two notable companies—**Berkshire Hathaway** (Warren Buffet's company) and **Google**—do not issue stock splits. As a consequence, during August 2008, a share of Google stock was selling for approximately $500 per share (down from over $700 in late 2007) while Berkshire Hathaway Class B common was selling for approximately $3,900 per share and its Class A common was selling for approximately $116,000 per share (down from over $150,000 in late 2007). In fact, check to see what Berkshire Hathaway is selling for today by going to **Google Finance** or **Yahoo! Finance** and typing in "Berkshire Hathaway."

Preferred Dividend Preferences While dividends on common stock are set by the corporation's board of directors, dividends on preferred stock are usually established as one of the terms of the issue. Most preferred stock issues fix their dividend rate as a percentage of the par value. For example, an 8 percent preferred share with a $100 par value has an annual dividend of $8 ($100 par $\times$ 8%). Of course, both preferred and common dividends are subject to various restrictions imposed by statute, by corporate charter, by the terms of preferred stock issues, and by contracts with bondholders and others.

Although preferred stockholders have no voting rights, they are "preferred" in the sense that corporations are required to pay dividends to them before paying dividends to common stockholders. Such dividend preferences can take three forms:

- current dividend preference
- cumulative dividend preference
- participating dividend preference

Most preferred stock issues grant a current dividend preference, and some also grant one or both of the other preferences, thereby further enhancing the likelihood of dividend payments.

Current Dividend Preference Preferred stock always has a **current dividend preference**, which provides that current dividends must be paid to preferred stockholders before any dividends are paid to common stockholders. However, the current dividend preference does not guarantee payment of preferred dividends. In lean years, both common and preferred stockholders may fail to receive dividends.

The following illustration demonstrates the impact of the current dividend preference. During the period 2010 through 2013, Cook Corporation maintained the following capital structure:

Preferred stock, 8 percent, $10 par, 5,000 shares authorized, 4,000 shares issued and outstanding	$40,000
Common stock, $5 par, 50,000 shares authorized, 30,000 shares issued and outstanding	150,000
Additional paid-in capital—common stock	60,000
Total capital stock	$250,000

Cook's board of directors determined the total dollar amount available for preferred and common dividends in each year from 2010 through 2013 as shown in the second column of the following schedule:

Year	Amount Available for Dividends	Dividends to Preferred	Dividends to Common
2010	$12,200	$3,200*	$9,000**
2011	7,000	3,200	3,800
2012	2,000	2,000	0
2013	0	0	0

*0.08 $\times$ $40,000 = $3,200
**$12,200 − $3,200 = $9,000

This schedule shows that the common dividend is any positive amount remaining after the full preferred dividend has been paid. If the total amount available for dividends is less than the full preferred dividend, the entire amount is paid to preferred stockholders.

Cumulative Dividend Preference Most preferred stock is cumulative. The **cumulative dividend preference** requires the eventual payment of all preferred dividends—both **dividends in arrears** and current dividends—before any dividends are paid to common stockholders. (Preferred stock dividends remaining unpaid for one or more years are considered to be in arrears.) In other words, no dividends can be paid to common stockholders until all prior and current preferred dividends have been paid. The cumulative dividend preference thus includes the current dividend preference. This is illustrated in **CORNERSTONE 10-5**.

CORNERSTONE 10-5   Calculating Cumulative Preferred Dividends

Concept:
The cumulative feature of preferred stock requires corporations to pay all current and unpaid prior period dividends to preferred stockholders before paying any dividends to common shareholders.

Information:
Jefferson Manufacturing has a single class of common stock and a single class of cumulative preferred stock. The cumulative preferred stock requires the corporation to pay an annual dividend of $6,500 to preferred stockholders. On January 1, 2011, Jefferson's preferred dividends were one year in arrears, which means that Jefferson declared neither preferred nor common dividends in 2010. From 2011 to 2013, Jefferson's board of directors determined they would be able to pay $9,000, $12,000, and $15,000, respectively.

Required:
Show how these anticipated payments will be split between preferred and common stockholders.

Solution:

Year	Amount Available for Dividends	Dividends to Preferred	Dividends to Common
2011	$ 9,000	$ 9,000*	$ 0
2012	12,000	10,500**	1,500**
2013	15,000	6,500	8,500

*The $9,000 dividend paid to preferred stockholders in 2011 removes the $6,500 in arrears from 2010, but leaves dividends in arrears at January 1, 2012, of $4,000—the excess of preferred dividends for 2010 and 2011 over the amount paid in 2011 [(2 × $6,500) − $9,000 = $4,000].

**The $10,500 dividend to preferred stockholders in 2012 pays the current preferred dividend ($6,500), removes the $4,000 in arrears, and leaves $1,500 to be paid to common stockholders [$12,000 − $6,500 − $4,000 = $1,500].

Dividends do not become a liability of a corporation until they have been declared by the board of directors. If preferred dividends in arrears have not been declared, they are not recorded as liabilities but are disclosed in a footnote to the financial statements.

Participating Dividend Preference For some classes of preferred stock, dividends are not restricted to a fixed rate. Preferred stock that pays dividends in excess of its stated dividend rate is called *participating preferred stock*. Preferred stock that cannot pay dividends in excess of the current dividend preference plus cumulative dividends in arrears, if any, is called *nonparticipating preferred stock*.

The **participating dividend preference** provides that stockholders of participating preferred shares receive, in addition to the stated dividend, a share of amounts available for distribution as dividends to other classes of stock. Participating preferred stock may be either fully participating or partially participating:

- Fully participating preferred stock receives a share of *all* amounts available for dividends. Common stock is allocated a dividend at the same rate on par as the current dividend preference, and any remainder is divided between preferred and common stockholders—usually in proportion to the total par value of the two classes of stock.
- Partially participating preferred stock also receives a share of all amounts available for dividends, but the share is limited to a specified percentage of preferred par value.

 **Stock Repurchase or Dividend**

You are the controller at Cohen Industries. The Board of Directors has decided to distribute $5,000,000 in excess cash to common shareholders.

In what ways can this distribution be accomplished? What factors should be considered when determining the best way?

You could either declare and pay a cash dividend or enter a stock repurchase plan. The primary difference between the two methods relates to tax consequences. First, the tax rate for dividends is higher than the rate on gains from selling stock. Second, while all common shareholders participate in dividends and, thus, incur tax consequence, only those shareholders who choose to sell their stock back to Cohen will experience tax consequences. Additionally, you should consider the future of any such distributions to shareholders. Generally, companies do not like to lower dividends. Finally, you should consider the price of the stock. Stock repurchases are most attractive when you believe your stock to be undervalued.

Therefore, if this distribution is a one-time event, a stock repurchase would be the way to go; however, if excess cash is anticipated in future periods, instituting a cash dividend would make sense.

 OBJECTIVE 4

Describe the accounting issues related to retained earnings and accumulated other comprehensive income.

ACCOUNTING FOR RETAINED EARNINGS AND ACCUMULATED OTHER COMPREHENSIVE INCOME

Retained earnings (or **deficit**) is the accumulated earnings (or losses) over the entire life of the corporation that have not been paid out in dividends. Generally, ending retained earnings is calculated with a simple formula:

> Beginning Retained Earnings
> + Net Income
> − Dividends
> = Ending Retained Earnings

Restrictions on Retained Earnings

Under most corporate charters, the balance of a corporation's retained earnings represents an upper limit on the entity's ability to pay dividends. (Dividends cannot reduce retained earnings below zero.) A corporation's capacity to pay dividends may be further restricted by agreements with lenders, by the corporation's board of directors, and by various provisions of state law, as follows:

- An agreement between the corporation and bondholders may require that retained earnings never fall below a specified level so long as the bonds are outstanding.
- The firm's board of directors may set aside a portion of retained earnings and declare it unavailable for the payment of dividends. Such an action may be used to communicate to stockholders changes in dividend policy made necessary by expansion programs or other decisions of the board.
- State law may require that dividends not reduce retained earnings below the cost of treasury stock.

Exhibit 10-5

Information from Deere & Co. 2009 10-K

Deere & Co. 2009 10-K

The following was included in Note 18 of **Deere & Co.**'s 2009 10-K:

The credit agreement also requires the Equipment Operations to maintain a ratio of total debt to total capital (total debt and stockholders' equity excluding accumulated other comprehensive income (loss)) of 65 percent or less at the end of each fiscal quarter according to accounting principles generally accepted in the U.S. in effect at October 31, 2006. Under this provision, the company's excess equity capacity and retained earnings balance free of restriction at October 31, 2009, was $6,494 million.

Although Deere & Co. did not choose to show this restriction in the stockholders' equity portion of their balance sheet, if they had it would have appeared as follows:

STOCKHOLDERS' EQUITY (Partial)

		2009
Common stock, $1 par value (authorized — 1,200,000,000 shares; issued — 536,431,204 shares in 2009, at paid-in amount)		2,996.2
Common stock in treasury, 113,188,823 shares in 2009, at cost		(5,564.7)
Retained earnings:		
Restricted for credit agreement	4,486.5	
Unrestricted	6,494.0	10,980.5

Restrictions of this sort are usually disclosed in footnotes to the financial statements to signify that the restricted amount is unavailable for dividends. In rare cases, a separate "reserve" account is established for the restricted portion of retained earnings. The reserve account is called either *restricted earnings* or *appropriation of retained earnings*. The account title frequently indicates, quite specifically, the nature of the restriction or the appropriation, as, for example, "restricted retained earnings under agreements with bondholders" or "appropriation of retained earnings for plant expansion." When reserve accounts are used, retained earnings is reported on two or more lines in the equity section of the balance sheet (see Exhibit 10-5). One line is devoted to each restriction, and to "unrestricted retained earnings" or "unappropriated retained earnings."

Error Corrections and Prior Period Adjustments

Errors in recording transactions can distort the financial statements. If errors are discovered and corrected before the closing process, then no great harm is done. However, if errors go undetected, then flawed financial statements are issued. No matter when they are discovered, errors should be corrected.

If an error resulted in a misstatement of net income, then correction may require a direct adjustment to retained earnings, called a **prior period adjustment**. To illustrate, suppose that Byrnes Corporation uses a computer program to calculate depreciation expense. In 2010, a programming error caused the 2010 depreciation expense to be understated by $16,000. The error was not discovered until August 2011; consequently, 2010 net income after income taxes (which are paid at a rate of 25 percent) was overstated by $12,000 [$16,000 × (1 − 0.25)]. The error correction would be recorded in 2011 as follows:

Date	Account and Explanation	Debit	Credit
Aug. 31, 2011	Retained Earnings	12,000	
	Tax Refund Receivable	4,000	
	Accumulated Depreciation		16,000
	(Record prior period adjustment)		

Assets	= Liabilities +	Stockholders' Equity
+4,000		−12,000
−16,000		

Byrnes' retained earnings statement for 2011 incorporates the $12,000 prior period adjustment as follows:

Byrnes Corporation Retained Earnings Statement For the Year Ended December 31, 2011		
Retained earnings, January 1, 2011		$157,000
Less: Prior period adjustment:		
Correction of error in calculation of 2010 depreciation expense (net of tax)		(12,000)
Retained earnings as adjusted, December 31, 2010		$145,000
Add: Net income for 2011		65,000
Less: Dividends declared in 2011:		
Cash dividend, preferred stock	$ (4,000)	
Stock dividend, common stock	(20,000)	(24,000)
Retained earnings, December 31, 2011		$186,000

Notice that the adjustment is deducted from the beginning balance of retained earnings to produce an *adjusted* beginning balance.

Financial accounting standards define prior period adjustments in a way that specifically excludes adjustments arising from estimation errors and changes from one accounting principle to another. These changes are corrected by adjusting the related income accounts for the period in which they are discovered.

Accounting for Accumulated Other Comprehensive Income

Financial accounting theory suggests that income represents the changes in the assets and liabilities of the company as a result of transactions with nonowners. However, over time the FASB has allowed the gains and losses from certain nonowner transactions to bypass the income statement and go directly to stockholders' equity. These instances are rare and the transactions that produce them are somewhat complicated, but one example is unrealized gains in losses on investments classified as available-for-sale securities. To illustrate, if a company buys a share of stock for $10 and at the end of the year that share is worth $12, the company has a $2 unrealized gain (a gain or loss is realized when the share is actually sold). It seems logical that this gain would appear on the income statement, but FASB has ruled that these gains and losses, when the investment is available-for-sale, are excluded from net income to reduce volatility due to fluctuations in fair value. At the same time, companies are required to include these gains and losses, along with net income in a measure called comprehensive income.

The FASB currently permits comprehensive income to be reported in one of three methods. Currently, the most popular option is to include a statement of changes in stockholders' equity (see Exhibit 10-6), which includes a column for comprehensive

Exhibit 10-6

Excerpts from Capital One's 2009 10-K

Capital One Financial Corporation Consolidated Balance Sheets		
December 31 (In Thousands, Except Share and Per Share Data)	**2009**	**2008**
Stockholders' Equity:		
Preferred stock, par value $.01 per share; authorized 50,000,000 shares; zero and 3,555,199 issued or outstanding as of December 31, 2009 and 2008, respectively	–	3,096,466
Common stock, par value $.01 per share; authorized 1,000,000,000 shares; 502,394,396 and 438,434,235 issued as of December 31, 2009 and 2008, respectively	5,024	4,384
Paid-in capital, net	18,954,823	17,278,102
Retained earnings	10,727,368	10,621,164
Accumulated other comprehensive income (loss)	82,654	(1,221,796)
Less: Treasury stock, at cost; 47,224,200 and 46,637,241 shares as of December 31, 2009 and 2008, respectively	(3,180,459)	(3,165,887)
Total stockholders' equity	26,589,410	26,612,433

Capital One Financial Corporation
Consolidated Statements of Changes in Stockholders' Equity (Partial)

(In Thousands, Except Per Share Data)	Common Stock		Preferred Stock	Paid-In Capital, Net	Retained Earnings	Accumulated Other Comprehensive Income (Loss)	Treasury Stock	Total Stockholders' Equity
	Shares	Amount						
Balance, December 31, 2008	438,434,235	$4,384	$3,096,466	$17,278,102	$10,621,164	$(1,221,796)	$(3,165,887)	$26,612,433
Comprehensive income:								
Net income (loss)	—	—	—	—	883,781	—	—	883,781
Other comprehensive income (loss), net of income tax:								
Unrealized gains on securities, net of income tax of $520,302	—	—	—	—	—	995,715	—	995,715
Defined benefit pension plans, net of income taxes of $7,307	—	—	—	—	—	13,289	—	13,289
Foreign currency translation adjustments	—	—	—	—	—	201,252	—	201,252
Unrealized gains in cash flow hedging instruments, net of income taxes of $60,904	—	—	—	—	—	94,194	—	94,194
Other comprehensive income (loss)						1,304,450		1,304,450
Comprehensive income (loss)								2,188,231
Cash dividends-Common stock $.53 per share	—	—	—	—	(213,669)	—	—	(213,669)
Cash dividends-Preferred stock 5% per annum	—	—	(22,714)	—	(82,461)	—	—	(105,175)
Purchase of treasury stock	—	—	—	—	—	—	(14,572)	(14,572)
Issuances of common stock and restricted stock, net of forfeitures	61,041,008	610	—	1,535,520	—	—	—	1,536,130
Exercise of stock options and tax benefits of exercises and restricted stock vesting	358,552	4	—	(6,885)	—	—	—	(6,881)
Accretion of preferred stock discount	—	—	33,554	—	(33,554)	—	—	—
Redemption of preferred stock	—	—	(3,107,306)	—	(447,893)	—	—	(3,555,199)
Compensation expense for restricted stock awards and stock options	—	—	—	116,023	—	—	—	116,023
Issuance of common stock for acquisition	2,560,601	26	—	30,830	—	—	—	30,856
Allocation of ESOP shares	—	—	—	1,233	—	—	—	1,233
Balance, December 31, 2009	502,394,396	$5,024	$ —	$18,954,823	$10,727,368	$ 82,654	$(3,180,459)	$26,589,410

Concept Q&A

Assume that a standard condition in a loan contract (called a "loan covenant") requires a borrower to maintain retained earnings of $3,000,000 on a $500,000 loan. The borrower does not like this covenant and asks why it has to be there. What would you say?

Answer:

Loan covenants such as these are there to protect the lender from the borrower removing money from the company, then declaring bankruptcy and never repaying the loan. For example, in the absence of this covenant, an unscrupulous borrower could borrow $500,000 from the bank, then pay out all this cash to shareholders as dividends leaving little (or at least far less) collateral within the company.

income. The FASB also permits a "second" income statement, which begins with net income, then shows items such as unrealized gains and losses on available-for-sale investments and finally totals to comprehensive income. The final option is to present a combined statement of comprehensive income, which includes both net income and comprehensive income on the same statement. Although this method is rarely used currently, the FASB is considering requiring this method. In this option, comprehensive income items will be added to or subtracted from net income to obtain total comprehensive income.

Regardless of which option is used to disclose comprehensive income for the period, **accumulated other comprehensive income** is shown in the stockholders' equity section of the balance sheet. Accumulated other comprehensive income is the total of comprehensive income for all periods. By disclosing this information, companies communicate the changes in assets and liabilities resulting from all transactions with nonowners.

Although it is not a required statement, a vast majority of corporations traded on U.S. stock exchanges also provide a statement of stockholders' equity. This latter statement reconciles the beginning and ending balances for each of the elements of stockholders' equity changes.

OBJECTIVE 5

Analyze stockholder payout and profitability ratios using information contained in the stockholders' equity section.

EQUITY ANALYSIS

Stockholders want to understand the following:

- how the value of their shares of stock will change
- how the company will distribute any excess cash to stockholders

We all know that investors buy stock to increase their personal wealth. But how do stockholders use the financial statements to better understand these two dimensions?

Stockholder Profitability Ratios

A primary driver of an increase in stock price is profitability. Profitability refers to the return that the company earns (in other words, its net income). However, the magnitude of the net income also matters because it shows how much had be to invested to earn the return. That is, would you rather earn $10 on a $100 investment or $20 on a $500 investment? Although the latter return is twice as large as the former, it also took an investment that was five times bigger. Assuming equal risk, etc., most investors would prefer to invest $100 to earn $10 because they then could use the extra $400 to invest somewhere else.

The two most common ratios used to evaluate stockholder profitability are return on common equity and earnings per share (EPS).

Return on Common Equity
Return on common equity shows the growth in equity from operating activities. It is calculated as follows:

$$\text{Return on Common Equity} = \frac{\text{Net Income} - \text{Preferred Dividends}}{\text{Avg. Common Stockholders' Equity}}$$

Common stockholders' equity is calculated by taking total stockholders' equity and subtracting out preferred stock.

Earnings per Share (EPS)
Earnings per share (EPS) measures the net income earned by each share of common stock. It is calculated as follows:

$$\text{EPS} = \frac{\text{Net Income} - \text{Preferred Dividends}}{\text{Avg. Common Shares Outstanding}}$$

CORNERSTONE 10-6 illustrates how to calculate stockholder profitability.

CORNERSTONE 10-6   Calculating Stockholder Profitability Ratios

Concept:
Analysis of information contained in the financial statements, particularly the statement of changes in stockholders' equity, allows stockholders to assess profitability.

Information:
Consider the following information from **Capital One** financial statements (all numbers in thousands other than per share amounts).

Common stock price (12/31/09)	$38.34/share	Avg. common shares outstanding	428,148
Common dividends	$213,669	Dividends per common share	$0.53/share
Preferred dividends*	$563,908	Net income	$883,781
2009 preferred stock	$0	2008 preferred stock	$3,096,466
2009 total stockholders' equity	$26,589,410	2008 total stock-holders' equity	$26,612,433
Purchases of treasury stock	$14,572		

*includes accretion of preferred stock discounts and redemption of preferred stock

Required:
Calculate the following stockholder profitability ratios: (1) return on common equity and (2) EPS.

Solution:
1. Return on Common Equity $= \dfrac{\text{Net Income} - \text{Preferred Dividends}}{\text{Avg. Common Stockholders' Equity}}$

$$= \frac{(\$883,781 - \$563,908)}{[(\$26,589,410 - \$0) + (\$26,612,433 - \$3,096,466)] \div 2} = 1.28\%$$

This information can also be found in the financial statements and statement of stockholders' equity:
*   *Net Income and Preferred Dividends:* Retained earnings column of the statement of changes in stockholders' equity. *Note:* In this case you must also include the "accretion of preferred stock discount" and the "redemption of preferred stock" from the retained earnings column of the statement [see Exhibit 10-6 (p. 492)].
*   *Average Common Stockholders' Equity:* The average is total stockholders' equity less preferred stock at the end and the beginning of the year.
    *   *Total stockholders' equity:* Appropriate balance row of the statement of changes in stockholders' equity
    *   *Total preferred stock:* Preferred stock column of the statement of changes in stockholders' equity and in the stockholders' equity section of the balance sheet.

2. EPS $= \dfrac{\text{Net Income} - \text{Preferred Dividends}}{\text{Avg. Common Shares Outstanding}} = \dfrac{(\$883,781 - \$563,908)}{428,148} = \$0.75$

This information can also be found in the financial statements and statement of stockholders' equity:
*   *Net Income and Preferred Dividends:* Retained earnings column of the statement of changes in stockholders' equity.
*   *Average Common Shares Outstanding:* Notes to the financial statements (or sometimes on the income statement itself).

Stockholder Payout

Stockholders not only experience an increase in wealth through an increasing stock price, but may also receive cash, or a payout, from the company. The most common stockholder payout ratios relate to dividends. Dividend yield considers the ratio of dividends paid to stock price. This ratio is conceptually similar to an interest rate for debt:

$$\text{Dividend Yield} = \frac{\text{Dividends per Common Share}}{\text{Common Stock Price}}$$

Another common dividend ratio calculates the proportion of dividends to earnings:

$$\text{Dividend Payout} = \frac{\text{Common Dividends}}{\text{Net Income}}$$

However, as discussed earlier, payouts to stockholders can also take the form of stock repurchases. As such, the stock repurchase payout ratio is:

$$\text{Stock Repurchase Payout} = \frac{\text{Common Stock Repurchases}}{\text{Net Income}}$$

By using these two ratios, stockholders can easily calculate the total payout:

$$\text{Total Payout} = \text{Dividend Payout} + \text{Stock Repurchase Payout}$$

Or, it can be calculated directly as:

$$\text{Total Payout} = \frac{\text{Common Dividends} + \text{Common Stock Repurchases}}{\text{Net Income (or Comprehensive Income)}}$$

CORNERSTONE 10-7 illustrates how to calculate payout ratios.

 **CORNERSTONE   Calculating Stockholder Payout Ratios**
10-7

Concept:
Analysis of information contained in the financial statements, particularly the statement of changes in stockholders' equity, allows stockholders to assess payout.

Information:
Consider the following information from **Capital One** financial statements (all numbers in thousands other than per share amounts).

Common stock price (12/31/09)	$38.34/share	Avg. common shares outstanding	428,148
Common dividends	$213,669	Dividends per common share	$0.53/share
Preferred dividends*	$563,908	Net income	$883,781
2009 preferred stock	$0	2008 preferred stock	$3,096,466
2009 total stockholders' equity	$26,589,410	2008 total stock-holders' equity	$26,612,433
Purchases of treasury stock	$14,572		

*includes accretion of preferred stock discounts and redemption of preferred stock

Required:
Calculate the following stockholder payout ratios: (1) dividend yield, (2) dividend payout, (3) stock repurchase payout, and (4) total payout.

Solution:
1. $\text{Dividend Yield} = \dfrac{\text{Dividends per Common Share}}{\text{Common Stock Price}} = \dfrac{\$0.53}{\$38.34} = 1.38\%$

(Continued)

**CORNERSTONE
10-7**
(continued)

This information can also be found in the financial statements and statement of stockholders' equity:

- *Dividends per Common Share*: First column of the statement of changes in stockholders equity for Capital One and in the financial press (e.g., Google finance, ticker symbol COF).
- *Common Stock Price*: Any website quoting stock prices.

2. Dividend Payout $= \dfrac{\text{Common Dividends}}{\text{Net Income}} = \dfrac{\$213,669}{\$883,781} = 24.18\%$

- *Common Dividends and Net Income*: Retained earnings column of the statement of changes in stockholders' equity.

3. Stock Repurchase Payout $= \dfrac{\text{Common Stock Repurchases}}{\text{Net Income}} = \dfrac{\$14,572}{\$883,781} = 1.65\%$

- *Stock Repurchases*: Treasury Stock column of the statement of changes in stockholders' equity.

4. Total Payout = Dividend Payout + Stock Repurchase Payout = 24.18% + 1.65% = 25.83%

Note: This can also be calculated directly as (Dividends + Stock Repurchases) ÷ Net Income.

Interpreting Ratios

What do these stockholder profitability and payout ratios mean? The results of these ratios are usually used in two ways:

- *Compared over time to evaluate trends*: For example, in 2009 Capital One's EPS was $0.71. This might be great news if EPS in 2008 were $0.05 or bad news if it were $2.00. In fact, EPS for 2007 and 2008 were $(0.21) and $4.02, respectively, so EPS is down more than 80 percent in two years. This is bad news and not unusual given the time frame of the economic crisis; however, the good news is obviously that 2009 is substantially better than 2008.
- *Compared to results for other companies in the industry*: For example, the 2009 return on common equity for Discover Financial Services was 18.54 percent and for Bank of America Corp it was (1.32) percent. This makes Capital One's return on common equity of 1.28 percent look poor, but at least it's not as bad as Bank of America. You can also look at industry averages. Reuters reports an industry average of 2.14 percent, so Capital One is lagging well behind the industry.

YOU DECIDE   Providing Shares for Employee Stock Options

You are the CFO of DTR Technology, a small, publicly-traded software firm. Your stock price has increased by 120 percent over the last two years and is now at $22 per share. Of course, this is great news. However, one side effect is that DTR employees own approximately 750,000 stock options with an average exercise price of $5 per share.

What factors must be considered in handling the anticipated exercise of these options?

DTR could issue previously unissued shares and take in the exercise price, or $3,750,000 in total (750,000 × $5). Although this seems reasonable, very few companies follow this course of action. Instead, most companies engage in a stock repurchase plan. For example, **Microsoft** repurchased 318 million shares of stock in 2009, at least partly because there were 327 million employee stock options outstanding (and the number is that low because Microsoft has not issued employee stock options other than in mergers since 2004). This despite the fact that Microsoft stock closed fiscal year 2009 at $23.77, while the average exercise price of the options was $9.50. In other words, if Microsoft plans to buy back shares of stock for $23.77 per share while only receiving $9.50 per option exercised, they will lose $14.27 per share (or over $46.5 billion if all options were excised). The reason most companies choose this latter option is because simply issuing previously unissued shares will increase the number of shares outstanding, which will, in turn, decrease (or dilute) earnings per share.

For DTR, repurchasing shares on the open market to cover their 750,000 in options would cost $12,750,000 (750,000 options × ($22 − $5)), but would prevent earnings per share from being diluted.

SUMMARY OF LEARNING OBJECTIVES

LO1. Distinguish between common and preferred stock and describe their use in raising capital.
- Corporations sell both common stock and preferred stock to raise capital.
- Preferred stock generally guarantees a regular dividend and receives priority over common stock in the payment of dividends and distribution of assets in liquidation.
- Common stock has voting rights and receives all benefits not assigned to the preferred stockholders or creditors.
- Selling different classes of stock (with different features) attracts shareholders with diverse risk preferences and tax situations.

LO2. Record capital stock.
- Both preferred and common stock are generally recorded at par or stated value.
- Any extra consideration received is recorded as "additional paid-in capital."

LO3. Account for the distribution of assets to stockholders.
- Assets are distributed to stockholders by:
  - repurchasing their shares of stock, or
  - paying dividends.
- Generally the cost of stock repurchases is recorded as a reduction in stockholders' equity (a debit to treasury stock).
- Typically the corporation pays dividends with cash.
- Stock dividends and stock splits do not represent a payout to stockholders. These transactions have no effect on total stockholders' equity.
- Preferred stock generally has dividend preferences such as being cumulative or participating.

LO4. Describe the accounting issues related to retained earnings and accumulated other comprehensive income.
- Retained earnings represents the earnings that the corporation elects not to pay out in dividends.
- Ending retained earnings is calculated by adding net income and subtracting dividends to beginning retained earnings.
- Retained earnings can be restricted, which communicates to stockholders that this portion of retained earnings is not eligible for dividend payout.
- Certain nonowner transactions are not included on the income statement. These transactions are included in the accumulated other comprehensive income account in the stockholders' equity section of the balance sheet.

LO5. Analyze stockholder payout and profitability ratios using information contained in the stockholders' equity section.
- Stockholders are primarily interested in two things:
  - the creation of value, and
  - the distribution of value.
- Analysis of the stockholders' equity section of the balance sheet in conjunction with the statement of stockholders' equity allows stockholders to separate these concepts.

CORNERSTONES
FOR CHAPTER 10

CORNERSTONE 10-1 Recording the sale of common and preferred stock (p. 478)

CORNERSTONE 10-2 Accounting for treasury stock (p. 482)

CORNERSTONE 10-3 Recording cash dividends (p. 484)

CORNERSTONE 10-4 Recording small and large stock dividends (p. 486)

CORNERSTONE 10-5 Calculating cumulative preferred dividends (p. 489)

CORNERSTONE 10-6 Calculating stockholder profitability ratios (p. 495)

CORNERSTONE 10-7 Calculating stockholder payout ratios (p. 496)

KEY TERMS

Accumulated other comprehensive income (p. 494)

Additional paid-in capital (p. 478)

Articles of incorporation (p. 474)

Authorized shares (p. 475)

Capital stock (p. 478)

Common stock (p. 475)

Corporate charter (p. 474)

Cumulative dividend preference (p. 489)

Current dividend preference (p. 488)

Date of record (p. 484)

Declaration date (p. 484)

Deficit (p. 490)

Dividends in arrears (p. 489)

Dividends (p. 476)

Earnings per share (EPS) (p. 494)

Equity (p. 474)

Exercise (or strike) price (p. 480)

Issued shares (p. 475)

Liquidating dividends (p. 485)

No-par stock (p. 479)

Outstanding shares (p. 475)

Par value (p. 477)

Participating dividend preference (p. 489)

Payment date (p. 484)

Preferred stock (p. 476)

Prior period adjustment (p. 491)

Retained earnings (p. 490)

Return on common equity (p. 494)

Shareholders (p. 474)

Stated capital (legal capital) (p. 479)

Stock dividend (p. 485)

Stock split (p. 487)

Stock warrant (p. 479)

Stockholders (p. 474)

Stockholders' equity (p. 474)

Treasury stock (p. 481)

REVIEW PROBLEM

Stockholders' Equity

Grace Industries, a privately held corporation, has decided to go public. The current ownership group has 10,000,000 common shares (purchased at an average price of $0.50 per share) and the articles of incorporation authorize 50,000,000, $0.10 par, common shares and 1,000,000, 10 percent, $30 par, cumulative, preferred shares. On January 1, 2010, the public offering issues 8,000,000 common shares at $14 per share and 100,000 preferred shares at $33 per share.

On October 3, 2011, Grace Industries repurchases 750,000 common shares at $12 per share. After the repurchase, Grace's board of directors decides to declare dividends totaling $4,050,000 (no dividends were declared or paid in 2010). This dividend will be declared on November 15, 2011, to all shareholders of record on December 8, 2011. This dividend will be paid on December 23, 2011. On December 28, 2011, 100,000 of the treasury shares are reissued for $15 per share.

At December 31, 2011, Grace Industries has $12,000,000 of retained earnings and accumulated other comprehensive income of ($250,000).

Required:

1. Prepare the journal entry to record the January 1, 2010, issuance of the common and preferred stock.

2. Prepare the journal entry to record the October 3, 2011, stock repurchase.

3. Determine how much of the dividend will go to preferred shareholders.

4. Calculate what the dividends per common share will be.

5. Prepare the journal entry for the dividend declaration on November 15, 2011.

6. Prepare the journal entry on the date of record (December 8, 2011).

7. Prepare the journal entry on the dividend payment date (December 23, 2011).

8. Prepare the journal entry for the reissuance of treasury shares on December 28, 2011.

9. Prepare the stockholders' equity section of the balance sheet at December 31, 2011.

Solution:

1.

Assets	= Liabilities +	Stockholders' Equity
+3,300,000		+3,000,000
+112,000,000		+300,000
		+800,000
		+111,200,000

Date	Account and Explanation	Debit	Credit
Jan. 1, 2010	Cash^a	3,300,000	
	Preferred Stock^b		3,000,000
	Additional Paid-In Capital—Preferred Stock^c		300,000
	(Record issuance of preferred stock)		
	Cash^d	112,000,000	
	Common Stock^e		800,000
	Additional Paid-In Capital—Common Stock^f		111,200,000
	(Record issuance of common stock)		

^{a}100,000 shares × $33 = $3,300,000
^{b}100,000 shares × $30 par = $3,000,000
^{c}100,000 shares × ($33 − $30) = $300,000
^{d}8,000,000 shares × $14 = $112,000,000
^{e}8,000,000 shares × $0.10 par = $800,000
^{f}8,000,000 shares × ($14 − $0.10) = $111,200,000

2.

Assets	= Liabilities +	Stockholders' Equity
−9,000,000		−9,000,000

Date	Account and Explanation	Debit	Credit
Oct. 3, 2011	Treasury Stock*	9,000,000	
	Cash		9,000,000
	(Record repurchase of common stock)		

*750,000 shares × $12 = $9,000,000

3. The preferred stock is cumulative, so the preferred shareholders must be paid their annual dividend for 2011 (the current year) and for 2010 (dividends in arrears).

Preferred Dividends* $600,000
*100,000 shares × ($30 par × 10% × 2 years) = $600,000

4. The common stockholders receive any dividend remaining after the preferred dividend has been paid (because the preferred is not participating). Because common dividends are only paid to outstanding stock, the treasury shares must be subtracted from the issued shares. Remember that the ownership group owned 10,000,000 shares then issued 8,000,000 shares in the initial public offering.

Common Dividends $\dfrac{\$4,050,000 - \$600,000}{18,000,000 \text{ issued shares} - 750,000 \text{ treasury shares}}$ $0.20 per share

5.

Assets =	Liabilities +	Stockholders' Equity
	+4,050,000	−4,050,000

Date	Account and Explanation	Debit	Credit
Nov. 15, 2011	Dividends*	4,050,000	
	Cash Dividends Payable		4,050,000
	(Record declaration of cash dividends)		

*Dividends is closed to retained earnings

6. No entry is necessary on the date of record.

7.

Assets	= Liabilities +	Stockholders' Equity
−4,050,000	−4,050,000	

Date	Account and Explanation	Debit	Credit
Dec. 23, 2011	Cash Dividends Payable	4,050,000	
	Cash		4,050,000
	(Record payment of cash dividends)		

8.

Assets	= Liabilities +	Stockholders' Equity
+1,500,000		+1,200,000
		+300,000

Date	Account and Explanation	Debit	Credit
Dec. 28, 2011	Cash*	1,500,000	
	Treasury Stock**		1,200,000
	Additional Paid-in Capital–Treasury Stock		300,000
	(Record reissuance of treasury shares)		

*100,000 shares × $15 = $1,500,000
**100,000 shares × $12 = $1,200,000

9.   **Stockholders' Equity:**

Preferred stock, 10 percent, $30 par, cumulative, 1,000,000 shares authorized, 100,000 shares issued and outstanding	$ 3,000,000[a]
Common stock, $0.10 par, 50,000,000 shares authorized, 18,000,000 shares issued and 17,350,000 outstanding	1,800,000[b]
Additional paid-in capital:	
Preferred stock	300,000[c]
Common stock	115,200,000[d]
Treasury stock	300,000[e]
Total capital stock	$120,600,000
Retained earnings	12,000,000[f]
Less:	
Accumulated other comprehensive income	(250,000)[f]
Treasury stock (650,000 shares at cost)	(7,800,000)[g]
Total stockholders' equity	$124,550,000

[a]100,000 shares issued at $30 par (see journal entry from 1).
[b]18,000,000 shares issued at $0.10 par.
[c]100,000 shares issued at $3 more than par ($33 selling price less $30 par). See journal entry from 1.
[d]10,000,000 shares issued to original ownership group at an average price of $0.50 per share ($0.40 per share in excess of par) plus 8,000,000 shares issued in IPO at $14 ($13.90 per share in excess of par).
[e]100,000 treasury shares issued at $15 per share, which is $3 per share in excess of $12 cost.
[f]Given in information.
[g]750,000 shares repurchased at $12 per share less 100,000 shares reissued.

DISCUSSION QUESTIONS

1.   What does stockholders' equity represent?
2.   What does a share of stock represent?
3.   Why do corporations issue stock?
4.   What is the difference between a privately- and publicly-held corporation?
5.   What are authorized shares?
6.   Why would the number of shares issued be different from the number of shares outstanding?
7.   What are the benefits that common stockholders may receive?
8.   How do common stock and preferred stock differ?
9.   Discuss the similarities between preferred stock and debt.
10.   Why do corporations utilize different forms of equity?
11.   Describe how cumulative preferred stock differs from non-cumulative preferred stock.
12.   How is a preferred stock dividend calculated?
13.   What balance sheet accounts are affected by the issuance of stock?
14.   What is the difference between par value and stated value?
15.   Why might a corporation grant stock options to employees in lieu of a higher salary?
16.   What is a stock warrant? How are they used by corporations?
17.   Describe two ways corporations make payouts to stockholders.
18.   What is treasury stock?
19.   Give four reasons why a company might purchase treasury stock.
20.   How would the purchase of treasury stock affect the stockholders' equity section of a corporation's balance sheet?
21.   A corporation repurchases 10,000 shares of its common stock at $7 per share and later resells it for $11 per share. What is the affect on the income statement of this resell?
22.   What entries are made (if any) at the declaration date, date of record, and date of payment for cash dividends?
23.   Compare and contrast cash dividends and liquidating dividends.
24.   Describe the effect of a cash versus a stock dividend on a company's stockholders' equity.
25.   What is a stock dividend? How does it differ from a stock split?
26.   What is the effect of a stock split on stockholders' equity account balances?
27.   Explain each of the following preferred stock dividend preferences: (1) current dividend preference, (2) cumulative dividend preference, and (3) participating dividend preference.
28.   Are dividends in arrears reported among the liabilities of the dividend-paying firm? If not, how are they reported, and why?

29. What are retained earnings?
30. How may a corporation's retained earnings be restricted?
31. When are prior period adjustments used?
32. Distinguish between retained earnings and accumulated other comprehensive income.
33. Describe the statement of changes in stockholders' equity.
34. How are dividend payout and profitability ratios useful to investors?

MULTIPLE-CHOICE EXERCISES

10-1 Which of the following is *not* a component of stockholders' equity?

a. loss on sale of equipment
b. dividends payable

c. retained earnings
d. net income

10-2 Which of the following statements is true?

a. The shares that are in the hands of the stockholders are said to be outstanding.
b. It is very unlikely that corporations will have more than one class of stock outstanding.
c. Preferred stock is stock that has been retired.
d. The outstanding number of shares is the maximum number of shares that can be issued by a corporation.

10-3 Authorized stock represents the:

a. number of shares that have been sold.
b. number of shares that are currently held by stockholders.
c. number of shares that have been repurchased by the corporation.
d. maximum number of shares that can be issued.

10-4 McKean Corporation authorized 500,000 shares of common stock in its articles of incorporation. On May 1, 2011, 100,000 shares were sold to the company's founders. However, on October 15, 2011, McKean repurchased 20,000 shares to settle a dispute among the founders. At this date, how many shares were issued and outstanding, respectively?

a. 500,000 and 100,000
b. 100,000 and 100,000

c. 100,000 and 80,000
d. 80,000 and 100,000

10-5 Harvey Corporation shows the following in the stockholders' equity section of its balance sheet: The par value of its common stock is $0.25 and the total balance in the common stock account is $50,000. Also noted is that 15,000 shares are currently designated as treasury stock. The number of shares *outstanding* is:

a. 215,000.
b. 200,000.

c. 196,250.
d. 185,000.

10-6 Ames Corporation repurchases 10,000 shares of its common stock for $12 per share. The shares were originally issued at an average price of $10 per share. Later it resells 6,000 of the shares for $15 per share and the remaining 4,000 shares for $17 per share. How much gain or loss should Ames report on its income statement as a result of these transactions?

a. $0
b. $20,000 loss

c. $38,000 gain
d. $20,000 loss and $38,000 gain

10-7 With regard to preferred stock,

a. its issuance provides no flexibility to the issuing company because its terms always require mandatory dividend payments.
b. its stockholders may have the right to participate, along with common stockholders, if an extra dividend is declared.
c. no dividends are expected by the stockholders.
d. there is a legal requirement for a corporation to declare a dividend on preferred stock.

10-8 DAE Parts Shop began business on January 1, 2011. The corporate charter authorized issuance of 20,000 shares of $5 par value common stock and 5,000 shares of $10 par value, 5 percent cumulative preferred stock. DAE issued 12,000 shares of common stock at $25 per share on January 2, 2011. What effect does the entry to record the issuance of stock have on total stockholders' equity?

a. increase of $120,000
b. increase of $150,000

c. increase of $300,000
d. increase of $340,000

10-9 Thornwood Partners began business on January 1, 2011. The corporate charter authorized issuance of 75,000 shares of $1 par value common stock, and 8,000 shares of $3 par value, 10 percent cumulative preferred stock. On July 1, Thornwood issued 20,000 shares of common stock in exchange for two years rent on a retail location. The cash rental price is $3,000 per month and the rental period begins on July 1. What is the correct entry to record the July 1 transaction?

a. Debit to Cash, $72,000; Credit to Prepaid Rent, $57,600
b. Debit to Prepaid Rent, $72,000; Credit to Common Stock, $72,000
c. Debit to Prepaid Rent, $72,000; Credit to Common Stock, $60,000; Credit to Additional Paid-In Capital—Common Stock, $12,000
d. Debit to Prepaid Rent, $72,000; Credit to Common Stock, $20,000; Credit to Additional Paid-In Capital—Common Stock, $52,000

10-10 A company would repurchase its own stock for all of the following reasons *except*:

a. it believes the stock is overvalued.
b. it wishes to increase the earnings per share.
c. it wishes to prevent unwanted takeover attempts.
d. it needs the stock for employee bonuses.

10-11 When a company purchases treasury stock, which of the following statements is true?

a. Dividends continue to be paid on the treasury stock.
b. It is no longer considered to be issued.
c. Treasury stock is considered to be an asset because cash is paid for the stock.
d. The cost of the treasury stock reduces stockholders' equity.

10-12 If a company purchases treasury stock for $6,000 and then reissues it for $5,000, the difference of $1,000 is:

a. an increase in stockholders' equity.
b. a decrease in stockholders' equity.

c. treated as a gain on the sale.
d. treated as a loss on the sale.

10-13 When a company retires its own common stock, the company must:

a. decrease the common stock account balances by the original issue price.
b. record a gain or loss depending on the difference between original selling price and repurchase cost.
c. get the approval of the state to do so.
d. issue a different class of stock to the former stockholders.

10-14 Which of the following should be considered when a company decides to declare a cash dividend on common stock?

a. the retained earnings balance only
b. the amount of authorized shares of common stock
c. the book value of the company's stock
d. the cash available and the retained earnings balance

10-15 When a company declares a cash dividend, which of the following is true?

a. Assets are decreased.
b. Assets are increased.

c. Liabilities are increased.
d. Stockholders' equity is increased.

10-16 What is the effect of a stock dividend on stockholders' equity?

a. Stockholders' equity is decreased.
b. Total stockholders' equity stays the same.

c. Additional paid-in capital is decreased.
d. Retained earnings is increased.

10-17 As a result of a stock split,

a.   stockholders' equity is increased.
b.   the par value of the stock is changed in the reverse proportion as the stock split.
c.   the stockholders have a higher proportionate ownership of the company.
d.   the market price of the outstanding stock is increasing because a split is evidence of a profitable company.

10-18 The balance of the $2.50 par value common stock account for Patriot Company was $240,000,000 before its recent 2-for-1 stock split. The market price of the stock was $50 per share before the stock split. What occurred as a result of the stock split?

a.   The market price of the stock was not affected.
b.   The balance in the common stock account was increased to $480,000.
c.   The market price of the stock dropped to approximately $25 per share.
d.   The balance in the retained earnings account decreased.

10-19 When a company declares a 3-for-1 stock split, the number of outstanding shares:

a.   triples.
b.   stays the same, but the number of issued shares triples.
c.   is reduced by one-third.
d.   is reduced by one-third, and the number of issued shares is tripled.

10-20 Shea Company has 100,000 shares of 6 percent, $50 par value, cumulative preferred stock. In 2010, no dividends were declared on preferred stock. In 2011, Shea had a profitable year and decided to pay dividends to stockholders of both preferred and common stock. If they have $750,000 available for dividends in 2011, how much could it pay to the common stockholders?

a. $0   c. $450,000
b. $150,000   d. $750,000

10-21 RVR Enterprises shows net income of $100,000 for 2011 and retained earnings of $500,000 on its December 31, 2011, balance sheet. During the year RVR declared and paid $60,000 in dividends. What was RVR's retained earnings balance at December 31, 2010?

a. $540,000   c. $440,000
b. $460,000   d. $400,000

10-22 Comprehensive income:

a.   is considered an appropriation of retained earnings.
b.   includes transactions that affect stockholders' equity with the exception of those transactions that involve owners.
c.   includes all transactions that are under management's control.
d.   is the result of all events and transactions reported on the income statement.

10-23 FASB's concept of comprehensive income:

a.   requires that all transactions must be shown on the income statement.
b.   has a primary drawback because it allows management to manipulate the income figure to a certain extent.
c.   excludes the payment of dividends.
d.   allows items that are not necessarily under management's control, such as natural disasters, to be shown as an adjustment of retained earnings.

10-24 Garner Corporation issued $50,000 in common stock dividends. Its net income for the year was $250,000. What is Garner's dividend payout ratio?

a.   0.2   c.   2.5
b.   0.5   d.   5

CORNERSTONE EXERCISES

Cornerstone Exercise 10-25 Recording the Sale of Common and Preferred Stock

Donahue Corporation is authorized by its charter from the State of Illinois to issue 2,000 shares of 7 percent preferred stock with a par value of $30 per share and 125,000 shares of common stock with a par value of $0.01 per share. On January 1, 2011, Donahue issues 1,300 shares of preferred stock at $35 per share and 84,000 shares of common stock at $12.50 per share.

Required:

Prepare the journal entry to record the issuance of the stock.

Cornerstone Exercise 10-26 Recording the Sale of Common Stock

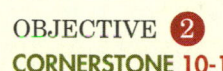

Plymouth Company issues 300,000 shares of common stock (par value $0.05) for $27 per share on June 30, 2011.

Required:

Prepare the journal entry to record this transaction.

Cornerstone Exercise 10-27 Calculating the Number of Shares Issued

Castalia, Inc., has issued shares of its $0.80 par value common stock on September 4, 2011, for $8 per share. The Additional Paid-In Capital—Common Stock account was credited for $612,000 in the journal entry to record this transaction.

Required:

How many shares were issued on September 4, 2011?

Cornerstone Exercise 10-28 Accounting for Treasury Stock

On February 15, 2011, Spring Hope Corporation repurchases 1,200 shares of its outstanding common stock for $7 per share. On March 1, 2011, Spring Hope sells 300 shares of treasury stock for $11 per share. On May 18, 2011, Spring Hope sells the remaining 900 shares of its treasury stock for $4 per share.

Required:

Prepare the journal entries to record these transactions.

Cornerstone Exercise 10-29 Accounting for Treasury Stock

On January 3, 2011, Tommyboy Corporation repurchases 250,000 shares of its outstanding common stock for $18 per share. On May 1, 2011, Tommyboy sells 80,500 shares of treasury stock for $12 per share. On October 1, 2011, Tommyboy sells 40,000 shares of its treasury stock for $31 per share.

Required:

1. Prepare the journal entries to record these transactions.
2. How will these transactions affect Tommyboy's 2011 income statement?

> *Use the following information for Cornerstone Exercises 10-30 and 10-31:*
> Kellman Company purchases 110,000 shares of treasury stock for $8 per share on September 4, 2012.

Cornerstone Exercise 10-30 Treasury Stock

Refer to the information for Kellman Company above.

Required:

1. How will this transaction affect stockholders' equity?
2. How will this transaction affect net income?

Cornerstone Exercise 10-31 Treasury Stock

Refer to the information for Kellman Company above.

Required:

What is the appropriate journal entry to record the transaction?

OBJECTIVE ③
CORNERSTONE 10-3

Cornerstone Exercise 10-32 Cash Dividends

King Tut Corporation has issued 25,000 shares of common stock, all of the same class; 18,000 shares are outstanding and 7,000 shares are held as treasury stock. On December 1, 2011, King Tut's board of directors declares a cash dividend of $0.75 per share payable on December 15, 2011, to stockholders of record on December 10, 2011.

Required:

Prepare the appropriate journal entries for the date of declaration, date of record, and date of payment.

OBJECTIVE ③
CORNERSTONE 10-3

Cornerstone Exercise 10-33 Declaration of Cash Dividend

Wilson Corporation declared a cash dividend of $80,000 on December 31, 2011.

Required:

What is the appropriate journal entry to record this declaration?

OBJECTIVE ③
CORNERSTONE 10-4

Cornerstone Exercise 10-34 Stock Dividend

Bower Corporation reported the following information: common stock, $1 par; 50,000 shares authorized; 35,000 shares issued and outstanding.

Required:

1. What is the appropriate journal entry to record a 10 percent stock dividend if the market price of the common stock is $30 per share when the dividend is declared?
2. What is the appropriate journal entry to record a 30 percent stock dividend if the market price of the common stock is $30 per share when the dividend is declared?
3. How do these transactions affect Bower's total stockholders' equity?

OBJECTIVE ③
CORNERSTONE 10-5

Cornerstone Exercise 10-35 Preferred and Common Stock Dividends

Barstow Corporation has a single class of common stock and a single class of cumulative preferred stock. The cumulative preferred stock requires the corporation to pay an annual dividend of $8,000 to preferred stockholders. On January 1, 2011, Barstow's preferred dividends were one year in arrears, which means that Barstow declared neither preferred nor common dividends in 2010. During the three years (2011–2013), Barstow's board of directors determined they would be able to pay $9,500, $17,000, and $20,000, respectively.

Required:

Show how these anticipated payments will be split between preferred and common stockholders.

OBJECTIVE ③
CORNERSTONE 10-5

Cornerstone Exercise 10-36 Preferred Stock Dividends

Seashell Corporation has 25,000 shares outstanding of 8 percent, $10 par value, cumulative preferred stock. In 2009 and 2010, no dividends were declared on preferred stock. In 2011, Seashell had a profitable year and decided to pay dividends to stockholders of both preferred and common stock.

Required:

If Seashell has $200,000 available for dividends in 2011, how much could it pay to the common stockholders?

OBJECTIVE ⑤
CORNERSTONE 10-6

Cornerstone Exercise 10-37 Stockholder Profitability Ratios

The following information pertains to Montague Corporation:

Net income	$1,420,000
Average common equity	$18,650,000
Preferred dividends	$245,500
Average common shares outstanding	625,000

Required:

Calculate the return on common equity and the earnings per share. (*Note:* Round answers to two decimal places.)

OBJECTIVE ⑤
CORNERSTONE 10-7

Cornerstone Exercise 10-38 Stockholder Payout Ratios

The following information pertains to Milo Mindbender Corporation:

Net income	$123,000
Dividends per common share	$2.00
Common shares	12,000
Purchases of treasury stock	$85,000
Common share price	$20

Required:

Calculate the dividend yield, dividend payout, and total payout. (*Note*: Round answers to two decimal places.)

EXERCISES

Exercise 10-39 Accounting for Shares

OBJECTIVE **1**

Kress Products' corporate charter authorizes the firm to sell 800,000 shares of $10 par common stock. At the beginning of 2011, Kress had sold 318,000 shares and had reacquired 4,500 of those shares. The reacquired shares were held as treasury stock. During 2011, Kress sold an additional 24,350 shares and purchased 8,200 more treasury shares.

Required:

Determine the number of issued and outstanding shares at December 31, 2011.

Exercise 10-40 Outstanding Stock

OBJECTIVE **1**

Ramsden Corporation shows the following information in the stockholders' equity section of its balance sheet: The par value of common stock is $2.50 and the total balance in the common stock account is $175,000. There are 10,000 shares of treasury stock.

Required:

What is the number of shares outstanding?

Use the following information for Exercises 10-41 and 10-42:

Stahl Company was incorporated as a new business on January 1, 2011. The company is authorized to issue 600,000 shares of $2 par value common stock and 80,000 shares of 6 percent, $20 par value, cumulative preferred stock. On January 1, 2011, the company issued 75,000 shares of common stock for $15 per share and 5,000 shares of preferred stock for $25 per share. Net income for the year ended December 31, 2011, was $500,000.

Exercise 10-41 Capital Stock

OBJECTIVE **1**

Refer to the information for Stahl Company above.

Required:

What is the amount of Stahl's total contributed capital at December 31, 2011?

Exercise 10-42 Preparation of Stockholders' Equity Section

OBJECTIVE **1**

Refer to the information for Stahl Company above.

Required:

Prepare the stockholders' equity section of the balance sheet for Stahl Company.

Exercise 10-43 Issuing Common Stock

OBJECTIVE **2**

Carmean Products Inc. sold 49,750 shares of common stock to stockholders at the time of its incorporation. Carmean received $23 per share for the stock.

Required:

1. Assume that the stock has a $18 par value per share. Prepare the journal entry to record the sale and issue of the stock.
2. Assume that the stock has a $10 stated value per share. Prepare the journal entry to record the sale and issue of the stock.
3. Assume that the stock has no par value and no stated value. Prepare the journal entry to record the sale and issue of the stock.
4. **Conceptual Connection:** How do the different par values affect total contributed capital and total stockholders' equity?

OBJECTIVE ②

Exercise 10-44 Issuing and Repurchasing Stock

Redbird Inc. had the following transactions related to its common and preferred stock:

January 15	Sold 350,000 shares of $0.10 par common stock for $15 per share.
	Sold 5,000 shares of $20 par preferred stock at $23 per share.
November 29	Repurchased 30,000 shares of the common stock at $21 per share.

Required:
Prepare the journal entries for these transactions.

OBJECTIVE ②

Exercise 10-45 Prepare the Stockholders' Equity Section

Renee Corporation has the following stockholders' equity information:

	$5 Par Common	$10 Par Preferred
Additional paid-in capital	$2,250,000	$50,000
Shares:		
Authorized	750,000	40,000
Issued	300,000	8,000
Outstanding	250,000	8,000

Retained earnings is $1,837,000, and the cost of treasury shares is $1,200,000.

Required:
Prepare the stockholders' equity portion of Renee's balance sheet.

OBJECTIVE ②

Exercise 10-46 Prepare the Stockholders' Equity Section

Wildcat Drilling has the following accounts on its trial balance.

	Debit	Credit
Retained Earnings		600,000
Cash	825,000	
Additional Paid-In Capital—Common		3,100,000
Additional Paid-In Capital—Preferred		400,000
Accounts Payable		345,000
Accounts Receivable	410,000	
Common Stock, $1 par		600,000
Preferred Stock, $10 par		340,000
Inventory	1,300,000	
Treasury Stock—Common (30,000 shares)	382,000	
Accumulated Other Comprehensive Income		70,000

Required:
Prepare the stockholders' equity portion of Wildcat's balance sheet.

OBJECTIVE ②

Exercise 10-47 Interpret the Stockholders' Equity Section

Medici Inc., has the following stockholders' equity section of the balance sheet:

Medici Inc.
Balance Sheet (Partial)

Stockholders' equity:		
Preferred stock, 100,000 shares authorized;		
30,000 issued and outstanding		$ 300,000
Common stock, 1,000,000 shares authorized;		
600,000 issued; 550,000 outstanding		1,200,000
Additional paid-in capital:		
Preferred stock	$ 90,000	
Common stock	4,800,000	4,890,000
Total capital stock		6,090,000
Retained earnings		450,000
Accumulated other comprehensive income		22,000
Less: Treasury stock, at cost		(800,000)
Total stockholders' equity		$5,762,000

Required:
1. How many shares of preferred stock are authorized?
2. How many shares of common stock are outstanding?
3. What was the average selling price for the common stock when issued?
4. What was the average repurchase price for the treasury shares?
5. If the annual dividends on the preferred stock are $0.80 per share, what is the dividend rate on the preferred stock?

Exercise 10-48 Treasury Stock Transactions

OBJECTIVE 3

Dennison Service Corporation had no treasury stock at the beginning of the year. During January, Dennison purchased 23,500 shares of treasury stock at $18 per share. In April, Dennison sold 6,000 of the treasury shares for $20 per share. In August, Dennison sold the remaining treasury shares for $17 per share.

Required:
Prepare journal entries for the January, April, and August treasury stock transactions.

Exercise 10-49 Cash Dividends on Common Stock

OBJECTIVE 3

Berkwild Company is authorized to issue 2,000,000 shares of common stock. At the beginning of 2011, Berkwild had 248,000 issued and outstanding shares. On July 2, 2011, Berkwild repurchased 4,610 shares of its common stock at $28 per share. On March 1 and September 1, Berkwild declared a cash dividend of $1.10 per share. The dividends were paid on April 1 and October 1.

Required:
1. Prepare the journal entries to record the declaration of the two cash dividends.
2. Prepare the journal entries to record the payment of the two dividends.
3. **Conceptual Connection:** Explain why the amounts of the two dividends are different.

Exercise 10-50 Cash Dividends on Common and Preferred Stock

OBJECTIVE 3

Metzler Design has the following information regarding its preferred and common stock:

Preferred stock, $50 par, 10 percent cumulative; 250,000 shares authorized; 100,000 shares issued and outstanding

Common stock, $2 par; 2,000,000 shares authorized; 1,000,000 shares issued; 800,000 outstanding

As of December 31, 2011, Metzler was two years in arrears on its dividends. During 2012, Metzler declared and paid dividends. As a result, the common shareholders received dividends of $0.60 per share.

Required:
1. What was the total amount of dividends declared and paid?
2. What journal entry was made at the date of declaration?

Exercise 10-51 Distribution to Stockholders

OBJECTIVE 3

Owners invest in corporations through the purchase of stock.

Required:

Describe two ways that corporations distribute assets to stockholders (without liquidating the company). Discuss their relative advantages and disadvantages.

Exercise 10-52 Stock Dividends

OBJECTIVE 3

Crystal Corporation has the following information regarding its common stock:

$10 par, with 500,000 shares authorized, 213,000 shares issued, and 183,700 shares outstanding.

On August 22, 2011, Crystal declared and paid a 15 percent stock dividend when the market price of the common stock was $30 per share.

(Continued)

Required:

1. Prepare the journal entries to record declaration and payment of this stock dividend.
2. Prepare the journal entries to record declaration and payment assuming it was a 30 percent stock dividend.

OBJECTIVE ③

Exercise 10-53 Stock Dividend

The balance sheet of Cohen Enterprises includes the following stockholders' equity section:

Common stock, $1 par, 330,000 shares authorized,	
150,000 shares issued and outstanding	$150,000
Additional paid-in capital —common stock	341,800
Total capital stock	$491,800
Retained earnings	173,000
Total equity	$664,800

Required:

1. On April 15, 2011, when its stock was selling for $18 per share, Cohen Enterprises issued a small stock dividend. After making the journal entry to recognize the stock dividend, Cohen's total capital stock increased by $270,000. In percentage terms, what was the size of the stock dividend?
2. Ignoring the small stock dividend discussed in (1), assume that on June 1, 2011, when its stock was selling for $22 per share, Cohen Enterprises issued a large stock dividend. After making the journal entry to recognize the stock dividend, Cohen's retained earnings decreased by $75,000. In percentage terms, what was the size of the stock dividend?

OBJECTIVE ③

Exercise 10-54 Stock Split

Toy World reported the following information: common stock, $1.50 par; 400,000 shares authorized; 200,000 shares issued and outstanding.

Required:

What is the typical effect of a 3-for-1 stock split on the information Toy World reports above? If the market value of the common stock is $30 per share when the stock split is declared, what would you expect the approximate market value per share to be immediately after the split?

OBJECTIVE ③

Exercise 10-55 Stock Dividends and Stock Splits

The balance sheet of Castle Corporation includes the following stockholders' equity section:

Common stock, $2 par, 80,000 shares authorized,	
60,000 shares issued and outstanding	$120,000
Additional paid-in capital—common stock	371,800
Total capital stock	$491,800
Retained earnings	173,000
Total equity	$664,800

Required:

1. Assume that Castle issued 60,000 shares for cash at the inception of the corporation and that no new shares have been issued since. Determine how much cash was received for the shares issued at inception.
2. Assume that Castle issued 30,000 shares for cash at the inception of the corporation and subsequently declared a 2-for-1 stock split. Determine how much cash was received for the shares issued at inception.
3. Assume that Castle issued 57,000 shares for cash at the inception of the corporation and that the remaining 3,000 shares were issued as the result of stock dividends when the stock was selling for $53 per share. Determine how much cash was received for the shares issued at inception.

OBJECTIVE ③

Exercise 10-56 Preferred Dividends

Nathan Products' equity includes 6.5 percent, $150 par preferred stock. There are 80,000 shares authorized and 30,000 shares outstanding. Assume that Nathan Products declares and pays preferred dividends quarterly.

Required:
1. Prepare the journal entry to record declaration of one quarterly dividend.
2. Prepare the journal entry to record payment of the one quarterly dividend.

Exercise 10-57 Cumulative Preferred Dividends

OBJECTIVE 3

Capital stock of Barr Company includes:

Common stock, $5 par, 650,000 shares outstanding	$3,250,000
Preferred stock, 15 percent cumulative, $60 par, 10,000 shares outstanding	600,000

As of December 31, 2010, two years' dividends are in arrears on the preferred stock. During 2011, Barr plans to pay dividends that total $360,000.

Required:
1. Determine the amount of dividends that will be paid to Barr's common and preferred stockholders in 2011.
2. If Barr paid $280,000 of dividends, determine how much each group of stockholders would receive.

> *Use the following information for Exercises 10-58 and 10-59:*
> Titanic Corporation's net income for the year ended December 31, 2011, is $380,000. On June 30, 2011, a $0.75 per share cash dividend was declared for all common stockholders. Common stock in the amount of 38,000 shares was outstanding at the time. The market price of Titanic's stock at year-end (12/31/11) is $18 per share. Titanic had a $1,100,000 credit balance in retained earnings at December 31, 2010.

Exercise 10-58 Retained Earnings

OBJECTIVE 4

Refer to the information for Titanic Corporation above.

Required:
Calculate the ending balance (12/31/11) of retained earnings.

Exercise 10-59 Retained Earnings

OBJECTIVE 4

Refer to the information for Titanic Corporation above. Assume that on July 31, 2011, Titanic discovered that 2010 depreciation was overstated by $75,000.

Required:
Provide Titanic's retained earnings statement for the year ended December 31, 2011, assuming the 2010 tax rate was 30 percent.

Exercise 10-60 Retained Earnings

OBJECTIVE 4

Gibson Products had beginning retained earnings of $2,000,000. During the year, Gibson paid cash dividends of $120,000 to preferred shareholders and $25,000 to common shareholders. Net income for the year was $600,000.

Required:
1. Reproduce the retained earnings T-account for the year starting with the beginning balance.
2. Determine what Gibson's ending retained earnings is assuming that during the year they discover that net income was overstated by $28,000 in prior years due to an error. The error was corrected and the current year's net income is correct.

Exercise 10-61 Retained Earnings

OBJECTIVE 4

The December 31, 2012, comparative balance sheet of Smith Industries includes the following stockholders' equity section:

(Continued)

	2012	2011
Common stock, $2 par, 80,000 shares authorized, 60,000 shares issued and outstanding	$120,000	$120,000
Additional paid-in capital—common stock	371,800	371,800
Total capital stock	$491,800	$491,800
Retained earnings	173,000	116,000
Total equity	$664,800	$607,800

Required:

During 2012 Smith paid dividends of $0.50 per share. What was Smith's net income for 2012?

OBJECTIVE

Exercise 10-62 Restrictions on Retained Earnings

At December 31, 2010, Longfellow Clothing had $226,700 of retained earnings, all unrestricted. During 2011, Longfellow earned net income of $92,000 and declared and paid cash dividends on common stock of $21,800. During 2011, Longfellow sold a bond issue with a covenant that required Longfellow to transfer from retained earnings to restricted retained earnings an amount equal to the principal of the bond issue, $50,000. At December 31, 2011, Longfellow has 30,000 shares of $5 par common stock issued and outstanding. Additional paid-in capital—common stock is $236,500.

Required:

Prepare the stockholders' equity portion of Longfellow's December 31, 2011, balance sheet.

OBJECTIVE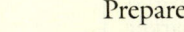

Exercise 10-63 Ratio Analysis

Consider the following information.

Stock price	$24.30/share	Avg. common shares outstanding	28,310,000
Common dividends	$5,662,000	Dividends per common share	$0.20/share
Preferred dividends	$1,444,000	Net income	$69,385,000
2011 preferred stock	$11,464,000	2010 preferred stock	$11,464,000
2011 total stockholders' equity	$954,846,000	2010 total stockholders' equity	$892,567,000
Purchases of treasury stock	$85,840,000		

Required:

1. Calculate the stockholder payout ratios. (*Note:* Round answers to two decimal places.)
2. Calculate the stockholder profitability ratios. (*Note:* Round answers to two decimal places.)

OBJECTIVE

Exercise 10-64 Ratio Analysis

MJO Inc. has the following stockholders' equity section of the balance sheet:

MJO Inc.
Balance Sheet (Partial)

Stockholders' equity:		
Preferred stock, 100,000 shares authorized; 30,000 issued and outstanding		$ 300,000
Common stock, 1,000,000 shares authorized; 600,000 issued; 550,000 outstanding		1,200,000
Additional paid-in capital:		
Preferred stock	$ 90,000	
Common stock	4,800,000	4,890,000
Total capital stock		$6,390,000
Retained earnings		450,000
Accumulated other comprehensive income		22,000
Less: Treasury stock, at cost		(800,000)
Total stockholders' equity		$6,062,000

On this date MJO's stock was selling for $25 per share.

Required:

1. Assuming MJO's dividend yield is 1 percent, what are the dividends per common share?
2. Assuming MJO's dividend yield is 1 percent and its dividend payout is 20 percent, what is MJO's net income?

Exercise 10-65 Stockholders' Equity Terminology

OBJECTIVE ❶❷❸❹

A list of terms and a list of definitions or examples are presented below. Make a list of the numbers 1 through 12 and match the letter of the most directly related definition or example with each number.

Terms

1.	stock warrant	7.	preferred stock
2.	date of record	8.	outstanding shares
3.	par value	9.	authorized shares
4.	stock split	10.	declaration date
5.	treasury stock	11.	comprehensive income
6.	stock dividend	12.	retained earnings

Definitions and Examples

a. Capitalizes retained earnings.
b. Shares issued minus treasury shares.
c. Emerson Electric will pay a dividend to all persons holding shares of its common stock on December 15, 2011, even if they just bought the shares and sell them a few days later.
d. The accumulated earnings over the entire life of the corporation that have not been paid out in dividends.
e. Common stock account balance divided by the number of shares issued.
f. The state of Louisiana set an upper limit of 1,000,000 on the number of shares that Gump's Catch, Inc., can issue.
g. Shares that never earn dividends.
h. Any changes to stockholders' equity from transactions with nonowners.
i. A right to purchase stock at a specified future time and specified price.
j. A stock issue that requires no journal entry.
k. Shares that may earn guaranteed dividends.
l. On October 15, 2011, General Electric announced its intention to pay a dividend on common stock.

PROBLEM SET A

Problem 10-66A Presentation of Stockholders' Equity

OBJECTIVE ❶

Yeager Corporation was organized in January 2011. During 2011, Yeager engaged in the following stockholders' equity activities:

a. Secured approval for a corporate charter that authorizes Yeager to sell 600,000, $8 par common shares and 30,000, $50 par preferred shares
b. Sold 80,000 of the common shares for $13 per share
c. Sold 2,500 of the preferred shares for $57 per share
d. Repurchased 500 shares of the common stock at a cost of $15 per share
e. Earned net income of $48,000
f. Paid dividends of $5,000

Required:

Prepare the stockholders' equity portion of Yeager's balance sheet as of December 31, 2011.

Problem 10-67A Issuing Common and Preferred Stock

OBJECTIVE ❷

Klaus Herrmann, a biochemistry professor, organized Bioproducts, Inc., early this year. The firm will manufacture antibiotics using gene splicing technology. Bioproducts' charter authorizes the firm to issue 10,000 shares of 7 percent, $70 par preferred stock and 150,000 shares of $5 par common stock. During the year, the firm engaged in the transactions listed on the next page:

(Continued)

a.   Issued 50,000 common shares to Klaus Herrmann in exchange for $550,000 cash.
b.   Sold 8,000 common shares to a potential customer for $12 per share.
c.   Issued 4,000 shares of preferred stock to a venture capital firm for $85 per share.
d.   Gave 100 shares of common stock to Margaret Robb, a local attorney, in exchange for Margaret's work in arranging for the firm's incorporation. Margaret usually charges $1,200 for comparable work.

Required:
Prepare a journal entry for each of these transactions.

Problem 10-68A Treasury Stock Transactions

Hansen Inc. engaged in the following transactions during the current year:

a.   Repurchased 13,000 shares of its own $1 par common stock for $14 per share on January 14.
b.   Sold 2,000 treasury shares to employees for $6 per share on January 31.
c.   Repurchased 3,000 more shares of the $1 par common stock for $16 per share on July 24.
d.   Sold the remaining 11,000 shares from the January 14 purchase and 1,200 of the shares from the July 24 purchase to employees for $6.50 per share on August 1.

Required:
1.   Prepare journal entries for each of these transactions.
2.   **Conceptual Connection:** Determine what the effect on total stockholders' equity is for each of the four transactions.

 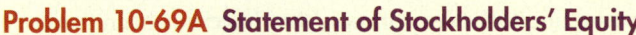

Problem 10-69A Statement of Stockholders' Equity

At the end of 2011, Jeffco Inc. had the following equity accounts and balances:

Common stock, $30 par	$1,400,000
Additional paid-in capital—common stock	526,400
Retained earnings	310,000

During 2012, Jeffco engaged in the following transactions involving its equity accounts:

a.   Sold 8,000 shares of common stock for $35 per share.
b.   Sold 1,000 shares of 9 percent, $120 par preferred stock at $125 per share.
c.   Declared and paid cash dividends of $15,000.
d.   Repurchased 500 shares of treasury stock (common) for $52 per share.
e.   Sold 100 of the treasury shares for $58 per share.

Required:
1.   Prepare the journal entries for a through e.
2.   Assume that 2012 net income was $89,600. Prepare a statement of stockholders' equity at December 31, 2012.

Problem 10-70A Common Dividends

Fusion Payroll Service began 2011 with 1,200,000 authorized and 375,000 issued and outstanding $5 par common shares. During 2011, Fusion entered into the following transactions:

a.   Declared a $0.30 per share cash dividend on March 10.
b.   Paid the $0.30 per share dividend on April 10.
c.   Repurchased 8,000 common shares at a cost of $18 each on May 2.
d.   Sold 1,500 unissued common shares for $23 per share on June 9.
e.   Declared a $0.45 per share cash dividend on August 10.
f.   Paid the $0.45 per share dividend on September 10.
g.   Declared and paid a 5 percent stock dividend on October 15 when the market price of the common stock was $25 per share.
h.   Declared a $0.50 per share cash dividend on November 10.
i.   Paid the $0.50 per share dividend on December 10.

Required:
1.   Prepare journal entries for each of these transactions. (*Note:* Round to the nearest dollar.)
2.   Determine the total dollar amount of dividends (cash and stock) for the year.
3.   **Conceptual Connection:** Determine the effect on total assets and total stockholders' equity of these dividend transactions.

OBJECTIVE 3

OBJECTIVE 1 2

OBJECTIVE 3

Problem 10-71A Stock Dividends and Stock Splits

OBJECTIVE ❸

Lance Products' balance sheet includes total assets of $587,000 and the following equity account balances at December 31, 2011:

Common stock, $2 par, 80,000 shares issued and outstanding	$160,000
Additional paid-in capital—common stock	24,000
Total capital stock	$184,000
Retained earnings	217,000
Total stockholders' equity	$401,000

Lance's common stock is selling for $12 per share on December 31, 2011.

Required:

1. How much would Lance Products have reported for total assets and retained earnings on December 31, 2011, if the firm had declared and paid a $15,000 cash dividend on December 31, 2011? Prepare the journal entry for this cash dividend.
2. How much would Lance have reported for total assets and retained earnings on December 31, 2011, if the firm had issued a 15 percent stock dividend on December 31, 2011? Prepare the journal entry for this stock dividend.
3. **Conceptual Connection:** How much would Lance have reported for total assets and retained earnings on December 31, 2011, if the firm had effected a 2-for-1 stock split on December 31, 2011? Is a journal entry needed to record the stock split? Why or why not?

Problem 10-72A Preferred Dividends

OBJECTIVE ❸

Magic Conglomerates had the following preferred stock outstanding at the end of a recent year:

$25 par, 8 percent	10,000 shares
$30 par, 8 percent, cumulative	8,000 shares
$50 par, 9 percent, cumulative, convertible	5,000 shares
$75 par, 10 percent, nonparticipating	15,000 shares

Required:

1. Determine the amount of annual dividends on each issue of preferred stock and the total annual dividend on all four issues.
2. Calculate what the amount of dividends in arrears would be if the dividends were omitted for one year.

Problem 10-73A Ratio Analysis

OBJECTIVE ❺

Consider the following information taken from the stockholders' equity section:

	(dollar amount in thousands)	
	2012	2011
Preferred stock	$ 1,000	$ 1,000
Common stock, 334,328,193 and 330,961,869 shares issued in 2012 and 2011, respectively	3,343	3,310
Additional paid-in capital—common stock	766,382	596,239
Retained earnings	5,460,629	4,630,390
Accumulated other comprehensive (loss) income	(206,662)	58,653
Treasury stock (76,275,837 and 56,960,213 shares in 2012 and 2011, respectively) at cost	(3,267,955)	(2,205,987)
Total stockholders' equity	$ 2,756,737	$ 3,083,605

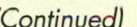

(Continued)

Additional Information (all numbers in thousands other than per share information):	2012
Weighted average common shares outstanding	184,000
Price per share at year end	$105.45
Net income	$1,358,950
Preferred dividends	$100,000
Common dividends	$213,440
Common dividends per share	$1.16
Stock repurchases	$834,975

Required:

1. Calculate the following for 2012 (*Note:* Round answers to two decimal places):

Stockholder Payout	Stockholder Profitability
Dividend yield	Return on common equity
Dividend payout	EPS
Total payout	
Stock repurchase payout	

2. **Conceptual Connection:** Assume 2011 ratios were:

Stockholder Payout	Stockholder Profitability
Dividend yield: 0.85%	Return on common equity: 34.26%
Dividend payout: 9.80%	EPS: $3.51
Total payout: 70.00%	
Stock repurchase payout: 60.20%	

and the current year industry averages are:

Stockholder Payout	Stockholder Profitability
Dividend yield: 0.76%	Return on common equity: 23.81%
Dividend payout: 12.35%	EPS: $1.23
Total payout: 48.37%	
Stock repurchase payout: 36.02%	

How do you interpret the company's payout and profitability performance?

PROBLEM SET B

OBJECTIVE

Problem 10-66B Presentation of Stockholders' Equity

Steven's Restorations was organized in January 2011. During 2011, Steven's engaged in the following stockholders' equity activities:

a. Secured approval for a corporate charter that authorizes Steven's to sell 1,000,000, $10 par common shares and 75,000, $100 par preferred shares.
b. Sold 480,000 of the common shares for $15 per share.
c. Sold 25,000 of the preferred shares for $105 per share.
d. Repurchased 2,000 shares of the common stock at a cost of $18 per share.
e. Earned net income of $107,000.
f. Paid dividends of $13,000.

Required:

Prepare the stockholders' equity portion of Steven's balance sheet as of December 31, 2011.

OBJECTIVE

Problem 10-67B Issuing Common and Preferred Stock

Tom Smith, a biochemistry professor, organized Biointernational, Inc., earlier this year. The firm will manufacture antibiotics using gene splicing technology. Biointernational's charter authorizes the firm to issue 20,000 shares of 10 percent, $50 par preferred stock and 100,000 shares of $3 par common stock. During the year, the firm engaged in the following transactions:

a. Issued 12,000 common shares to Tom Smith in exchange for $170,000 cash.
b. Sold 3,000 common shares to a potential customer for $17 per share.

c.   Issued 1,000 shares of preferred stock to a venture capital firm for $60 per share.
d.   Gave 65 shares of common stock to Susie Thomas, a local attorney, in exchange for Susie's work in arranging for the firm's incorporation. Susie usually charges $1,000 for comparable work.

Required:
Prepare a journal entry for each of these transactions.

Problem 10-68B Treasury Stock Transactions

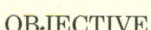

Bentonite Adhesives Inc. engaged in the following transactions during the current year:

a.   Repurchased 8,000 shares of its own $5 par common stock for $13 per share on January 14.
b.   Sold 2,600 of the treasury shares to employees for $8 per share on January 31.
c.   Repurchased 2,000 more shares of the $5 par common stock for $17 each on July 24.
d.   Sold the remaining 5,400 shares from the January 14 purchase and 800 of the shares from the July 24 purchase to employees for $9 per share on August 1.

Required:
1.   Prepare journal entries for each of these transactions.
2.   **Conceptual Connection** Determine the effect on total stockholders' equity for each of the four transactions.

Problem 10-69B Statement of Stockholders' Equity

OBJECTIVE ❶ ❷

At the end of 2011, Stanley Utilities Inc. had the following equity accounts and balances:

Common stock, $1 par	$4,500,000
Additional paid-in capital—common stock	1,375,000
Retained earnings	188,000

During 2012, Stanley Utilities engaged in the following transactions involving its equity accounts:

a.   Sold 3,300 shares of common stock for $15 per share.
b.   Sold 1,000 shares of 12 percent, $100 par preferred stock at $105 per share.
c.   Declared and paid cash dividends of $8,000.
d.   Repurchased 1,000 shares of treasury stock (common) for $38 per share.
e.   Sold 400 of the treasury shares for $42 per share.

Required:
1.   Prepare the journal entries for *a* through *e*.
2.   Assume that 2012 net income was $87,000. Prepare a statement of stockholders' equity at December 31, 2012.

Problem 10-70B Common Dividends

OBJECTIVE ❸

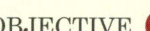

Thompson Payroll Service began in 2011 with 1,500,000 authorized and 820,000 issued and outstanding $8 par common shares. During 2011, Thompson entered into the following transactions:

a.   Declared a $0.20 per share cash dividend on March 24.
b.   Paid the $0.20 per share dividend on April 6.
c.   Repurchased 13,000 common shares for the treasury at a cost of $12 each on May 9.
d.   Sold 2,500 unissued common shares for $15 per share on June 19.
e.   Declared a $0.40 per share cash dividend on August 1.
f.   Paid the $0.40 per share dividend on September 14.
g.   Declared and paid a 10 percent stock dividend on October 25 when the market price of the common stock was $15 per share.
h.   Declared a $0.45 per share cash dividend on November 20.
i.   Paid the $0.45 per share dividend on December 20.

Required:
1.   Prepare journal entries for each of these transactions. (*Note:* Round to the nearest dollar.)
2.   What is the total dollar amount of dividends (cash and stock) for the year?
3.   **Conceptual Connection:** Determine the effect on total assets and total stockholders' equity of these dividend transactions.

OBJECTIVE

Problem 10-71B Stock Dividends and Stock Splits

Murphy Products' balance sheet includes total assets of $1,326,000 and the following equity account balances at December 31, 2011:

Common stock, $3 par, 10,000 shares issued and outstanding	$ 30,000
Additional paid-in capital—common stock	268,000
Total capital stock	$298,000
Retained earnings	206,000
Total stockholders' equity	$504,000

Murphy's common stock is selling for $17 per share on December 31, 2011.

Required:

1. Determine how much Murphy's Products would have reported for total assets and retained earnings on December 31, 2011, if the firm had declared and paid a $5,000 cash dividend on December 31, 2011. Prepare the journal entry for this cash dividend.
2. Determine how much Murphy would have reported for total assets and retained earnings on December 31, 2011, if the firm had issued a 5 percent stock dividend on December 31, 2011. Prepare the journal entry for this stock dividend.
3. **Conceptual Connection:** How much would Murphy have reported for total assets and retained earnings on December 31, 2011, if the firm had effected a 3-for-1 stock split on December 31, 2011? Is a journal entry needed to record the stock split? Why or why not?

OBJECTIVE

Problem 10-72B Preferred Dividends

Steel Corporation had the following preferred stock outstanding at the end of a recent year:

$20 par, 9 percent	30,000 shares
$25 par, 10 percent, cumulative	15,000 shares
$100 par, 6 percent, cumulative, convertible	20,000 shares
$100 par, 8 percent, nonparticipating	8,000 shares

Required:

1. Determine the amount of annual dividends on each issue of preferred stock and the total annual dividend on all four issues.
2. Calculate what the amount of dividends in arrears would be if the dividends were omitted for one year.

OBJECTIVE ⑤

Problem 10-73B Ratio Analysis

Consider the following information taken from the stockholders' equity section:

	(dollar amount in thousands)	
	2012	**2011**
Preferred stock	$ 1,000	$ 2,000
Common stock, 230,000,000 and 176,000,000 shares issued in 2012 and 2011, respectively	2,300	1,760
Additional paid-in capital—common stock	567,000	432,000
Retained earnings	4,604,600	3,700,000
Accumulated other comprehensive (loss) income	(454,600)	147,000
Treasury stock (37,000,000 and 19,000,000 shares in 2012 and 2011, respectively) at cost	(1,750,000)	(975,000)
Total stockholders' equity	$ 2,970,300	$3,307,760

Additional Information (all numbers in thousands other than per share information):	2012
Weighted average common shares outstanding	200,000
Price per share at year end	$58.30
Net income	$1,584,000
Preferred dividends	$50,000
Common dividends	$300,000
Common dividends per share	$1.50
Stock repurchases	$850,000

Required:

1. Calculate the following (*Note:* Round answers to two decimal places):

Stockholder Payout	Stockholder Profitability
Dividend yield	Return on common equity
Dividend payout	EPS
Total payout	
Stock repurchase payout	

2. **Conceptual Connection:** Assume last year's ratios were:

Stockholder Payout	Stockholder Profitability
Dividend yield: 2.31%	Return on common equity: 37.41%
Dividend payout: 13.65%	EPS: $6.12
Total payout: 78.59%	
Stock repurchase payout: 64.94%	

and the current year industry averages are:

Stockholder Payout	Stockholder Profitability
Dividend yield: 2.50%	Return on common equity: 44.44%
Dividend payout: 15.10%	EPS: $6.48
Total payout: 55.10%	
Stock repurchase payout: 40.00%	

How do you interpret the company's payout and profitability performance?

CASES

Case 10-74 Ethics and Equity

Roger and Gordon are middle managers at a large, publicly traded corporation. Roger tells Gordon that the company is about to sign an exclusive product distribution agreement with a small, publicly traded manufacturer. This contract will quadruple the manufacturer's revenue. Roger mentions to Gordon that the manufacturer's stock price will likely go "through the roof." Gordon says, "Maybe we should buy some stock."

Required:

1. Are Roger and Gordon being smart, being unethical but not breaking the law, or breaking the law?
2. How does the SEC monitor such activity?

Case 10-75 Stock Transactions and Ethics

Marilyn Cox is the office manager for DTR, Inc. DTR constructs, owns, and manages apartment complexes. Marilyn has been involved in negotiations between DTR and prospective lenders as DTR attempts to raise $425 million to use to build apartments in a growing area of Tulsa. Based on her experience with past negotiations, Marilyn knows that lenders are concerned about DTR's debt-to-equity ratio. When the negotiations began, DTR had debt of $80 million and equity of $50 million. Marilyn believes that DTR's debt-to-equity ratio of 1.6 is probably the minimum that lenders will accept.

Marilyn is also aware that DTR issued $10 million of common stock to a long-time friend of the corporation's president in exchange for some land just before the negotiations with lenders began. The president's friend constructs and sells single family homes. The land is in an area zoned only for single family housing and would be an attractive site for single family homes. Thus, the land is worth at least $10 million. However, DTR does not intend to build any single family homes.

Required:

1. What would have been DTR's debt-to-equity ratio if the $10 million of stock had not been issued for the land?
2. If Marilyn believes that the $10 million stock issue was undertaken only to improve DTR's debt-to-equity ratio and that it will be reversed whenever the president's friend wants the land back or when DTR's debt-to-equity position improves, what should she do?

Case 10-76 Common and Preferred Stock

Expansion Company now has $2,500,000 of equity (100,000 common shares). Current income is $400,000 and Expansion Company needs $500,000 of additional capital. The firm's bankers insist that this capital be acquired by selling either common or preferred stock. If Expansion sells common stock, the ownership share of the current stockholders will be diluted by 16.7 percent (20,000 more shares will be sold). If preferred stock is sold, the dividend rate will be 15 percent of the $500,000. Furthermore, the preferred stock will have to be cumulative, participating, and convertible into 20,000 shares of common stock.

Required:

Indicate whether Expansion should sell additional common or preferred stock, and explain the reasons for your choice.

Case 10-77 Leverage

Enrietto Aquatic Products' offer to acquire Fiberglass Products for $2,000,000 cash has been accepted. Enrietto has $1,000,000 of liquid assets that can be converted into cash and plans to either sell common stock or issue bonds to raise the remaining $1,000,000. Before this acquisition, Enrietto's condensed balance sheet and condensed income statement were as follows:

**Enrietto Aquatic Products
Preacquisition Condensed Balance Sheet**

Assets		Liabilities and Equity	
Assets	$20,000,000	Liabilities	$ 8,000,000
		Common stock, $10 par	6,000,000
		Retained earnings	6,000,000
		Total liabilities & stockholders' equity	$20,000,000

**Enrietto Aquatic Products
Preacquisition Condensed Income Statement**

Income from operations	$ 6,000,000
Less: Interest expense	(1,000,000)
Income before taxes	$ 5,000,000
Less: Income taxes expense (0.34)	(1,700,000)
Net income	$ 3,300,000

Enrietto's policy is to pay 60 percent of net income to stockholders as dividends. Enrietto expects to be able to raise the $1,000,000 it needs for the acquisition by selling 50,000 shares of common stock at $20 each or by issuing $1,000,000 of 20-year, 12 percent bonds. Enrietto expects income from operations to grow by $700,000 after Fiberglass Products has been acquired. (Interest expense will increase if debt is used to finance the acquisition.)

Required:
1. Determine the return on equity (net income/total equity) before the acquisition and for both financing alternatives.
2. If Enrietto sells additional stock, what will be the cash outflow for dividends?
3. If Enrietto sells bonds, what will be the net cash outflows for new interest and for all dividends? (Remember that interest is tax-deductible.)
4. Assume that Enrietto sells stock and that none of the preacquisition stockholders buy any of the 50,000 new shares. What total amount of dividends will the preacquisition stockholders receive after the acquisition? How does this amount compare with the dividends they receive before the acquisition?
5. Which alternative is better for Enrietto's preacquisition stockholders?

Case 10-78 Researching and Analysis Using the Annual Report

Obtain Priceline.com's 2009 10-K (remember, the 2009 10-K is filed with the SEC in early 2010) through the "Investor Relations" portion of their website (do a web search for Priceline investor relations), or go to http://www.sec.gov and click "Search for Company Filings" under "Filings & Forms."

Required:
1. How many shares of common stock are authorized, issued, and outstanding at December 31, 2009?
2. What is Priceline.com's dividend policy? Why didn't Priceline.com pay dividends to common stockholders in any of the three years shown?
3. What is the common stockholders' equity at December 31, 2009 (in thousands)?
4. How many shares of treasury stock were held at the end of 2009?
5. Calculate the dividend and stock repurchase payouts. (*Note:* Round answers to two decimal places.)
6. Taking the weighted average number of basic common shares outstanding from the EPS information at the bottom of the income statement, calculate the stockholder profitability ratios.

Case 10-79 Comparative Analysis: Abercrombie & Fitch versus Aeropostale

Refer to the financial statements of **Abercrombie & Fitch** and **Aeropostale** that are supplied with this text.

Common Stock Price:		
	January 30, 2010	January 31, 2009
Abercrombie & Fitch	$31.54	$17.85
Aeropostale	$21.93	$14.07

Note: Round all answers to two decimal places. Numbers, other than per share amounts, are in thousands.

Required:
1. What percentage of the total common shares issued have Abercrombie & Fitch and Aeropostale repurchased and retained as treasury shares at January 30, 2010?
2. Calculate Abercrombie & Fitch's and Aeropostale's dividend yield and dividend payout for the years ended January 30, 2010, and January 31, 2009.
3. Calculate Abercrombie & Fitch's and Aeropostale's total payout and stock repurchase payout for the years ended January 30, 2010, and January 31, 2009.
4. Compare Abercrombie & Fitch's and Aeropostale's stockholder payouts based on the values and trends identified in these stockholder payout ratios.
5. Calculate Abercrombie & Fitch's and Aeropostale's return on common equity and earnings per share for the years ended January 30, 2010, and January 31, 2009. Common stockholders' equity for the year ended February 2, 2008, was $1,618,313 and $197,276 for Abercrombie & Fitch and Aeropostale, respectively.
6. Compare the values and trends of these stockholder profitability ratios for Abercrombie & Fitch and Aeropostale.

Case 10-80 CONTINUING PROBLEM: FRONT ROW ENTERTAINMENT

After purchasing the five venues in June 2012, Front Row Entertainment needed additional cash to renovate and operate these venues. While the company had successfully borrowed money before (from bank loans as well as from the issuance of bonds), it could not find a lender willing to invest in the business due to the large amount of debt that the company currently has on its balance sheet.

With debt financing out of the question, Front Row Entertainment considers its other options. The name of an old college friend, Steve Trotter, immediately came to Cam and Anna's mind. Steve had previous work experience in the retail industry and had expressed a desire to manage Front Row Entertainment's current merchandising operations (the sale of DVDs). His vision was to expand the operations to include apparel (t-shirts, hats, etc.) and other items (such as bobble-head dolls of the artists). In addition, several other family members had expressed an interest in investing in the company.

Front Row was authorized to issue 25,000 shares of its $1 par common stock. On January 1, 2011, it had previously issued Cam and Anna 8,000 shares each for $1 per share. Front Row Entertainment was also authorized to issue 20,000 shares of 8 percent, $50 par preferred stock. The following transactions occurred during the remainder of 2012.

June 15	Issued 2,000 shares of $1 par common stock to Steve for $20 per share.
July 1	Issued 3,000 shares of $50 preferred stock to family members for $75 per share.
10	Repurchased 700 common shares at $16 per share.
Aug. 5	The board of directors declared a $25,000 dividend to all shareholders of record on August 31, 2012. The dividend will be paid on Sept. 15, 2012.
Sept. 15	The $25,000 dividend was paid.
Dec. 15	300 of the treasury shares were reissued at $22 per share.

Front Row Entertainment had $53,250 of retained earnings at December 31, 2012.

Required:
1. Prepare the journal entries to record the above transactions.
2. Prepare the stockholders' equity section of the balance sheet at December 31, 2012.

Integrating Accounting for Liabilities and Equity

Obtain **Under Armour**'s 2009 10-K (filed February 25, 2010) either through the "Investor Relations" portion of their website (do a web search for "Under Armour Investor Relations") or go to http://www.sec.gov and click "Search for Company Filings" under "Filings & Forms."

Required:
Using Under Armour's 10-K answer the following questions (*Hint*: It may be easier to use the Word or PDF file and use the search feature within the program):

1. Calculate Under Armour's current, quick, and cash ratios for 2008 and 2009. The industry averages for these ratios for 2009 were 2.62, 1.91, and 0.78, respectively. Comment on Under Armour's short-term liquidity.

2. Calculate Under Armour's debt-to-equity, long-term debt-to-equity, and times interest earned (accrual basis) for 2008 and 2009. The industry averages for these ratios for 2009 were 26.30%, 11.17%, and 0.77, respectively. You will need to read Note 6 (Revolving Credit Facility and Long Term Debt) to find the amount of interest expense. Comment on Under Armour's mix of debt and equity and long-term solvency.

3. Calculate Under Armour's return on equity for 2008 and 2009 (stockholders' equity for 2007 was $280,485). The industry average for 2009 was 8.63%. Comment on Under Armour's profitability.

4. Under Armour did not pay any dividends or repurchase any stock during 2008 or 2009. Why might Under Armour elect not to make any payouts to stockholders?

11

The Statement of Cash Flows

Doug Norman Crystals / Alamy

After studying Chapter 11, you should be able to:

1. Explain the purpose of a statement of cash flows.

2. Identify and classify business activities that produce cash inflows and outflows.

3. Understand the relationship between changes in cash and the changes in the balance sheet accounts.

4. Prepare the cash flows from operating activities section of a statement of cash flows using the indirect method.

5. Prepare the cash flows from the investing activities section of a statement of cash flows.

6. Prepare the cash flows from financing activities section of a statement of cash flows.

7. Analyze information contained in the statement of cash flows.

8. (Appendix 11A) Prepare the cash flows from operating activities section of a statement of cash flows using the direct method.

9. (Appendix 11B) Use a spreadsheet to prepare the statement of cash flows.

Terrance Klassen / age fotostock / Photolibrary

EXPERIENCE FINANCIAL ACCOUNTING

with Deere & Company

Founded in 1837, **Deere & Company** (collectively known as John Deere), is an American success story. From humble beginnings as a blacksmith shop in Illinois, John Deere has grown into one of the world's largest corporations. Not only is John Deere the world's leading manufacturer of farm and forestry equipment, it also sells a broad line of lawn tractors and other outdoor consumer products. John Deere is one of the world's largest equipment finance companies with a managed portfolio of almost $23 billion.

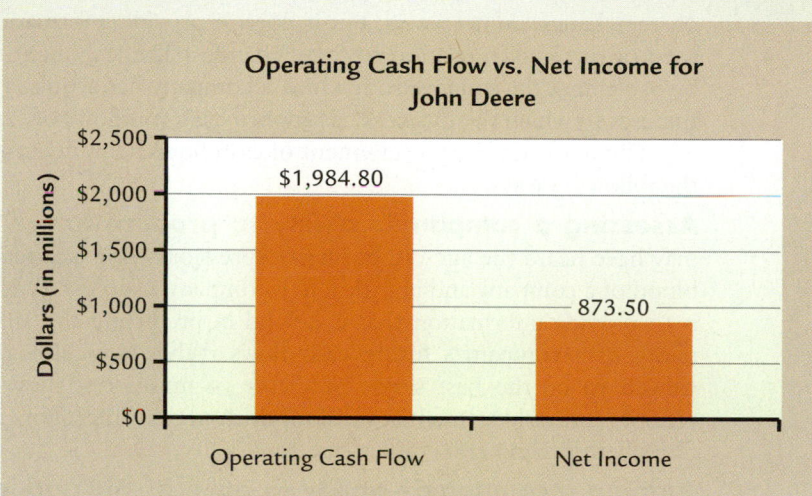

In addition to the income statement, the balance sheet, and the statement of retained earnings, companies are also required to provide a statement of cash flows. The statement of cash flows measures a company's inflows (sources) and outflows (uses) of cash during a period of time. While net income provides important information, the recognition of revenues and expenses can occur at different times than the related cash inflow or outflow. Therefore, a company's net income does not always equal the amount of cash that it received and spent. Because cash is the life-blood of any business, proper cash management is essential for success.

Many financial statement users examine the difference between net income and cash generated from operations to gain valuable insights into a company's operations. With operating cash flow more than $1.1 billion greater than net income, John Deere appears to have no problem in generating cash flow. From this perspective, it is easy to see why some think the color of money is John Deere green!

OBJECTIVE 1

Explain the purpose of a statement of cash flows.

ROLE OF THE STATEMENT OF CASH FLOWS

In addition to being interested in the information in the accrual-basis financial statements, most financial statement users also want to know how a company obtained and used its cash. The purpose of the **statement of cash flows** is to provide relevant information about a company's cash receipts (inflows of cash) and cash payments (outflows of cash) during an accounting period.

The statement of cash flows is one of the primary financial statements. Because the other financial statements—the income statement, the balance sheet, and the statement of retained earnings—provide only limited information about a company's cash flows, the statement of cash flows can be viewed as a complement to these other financial statements. That is, while the income statement provides information about the company's performance on an accrual basis, it does not tell how much cash was generated or used as a result of the company's operations. Similarly, the balance sheet provides information on the changes in net assets, but it doesn't provide information on how much cash was used or received in relation to these changes. The statement of cash flows fills this void by explaining the sources from which a company has acquired cash (inflows of cash) and the uses to which the business has applied cash (outflows of cash).

The information in a statement of cash flows helps investors, creditors, and others in the following ways.

Assessing a company's ability to produce future net cash inflows You may have heard the age-old business expression "cash is king." Cash is certainly the life-blood of a company and is critical to a company's success. One goal of financial reporting is to provide information that is helpful in predicting the amounts, timing, and uncertainty of a company's future cash flows. While accrual-basis net income is generally viewed to be the best single predictor of future cash flows, information about cash receipts and cash payments can, along with net income, allow users to predict future cash flows better than net income alone.

Judging a company's ability to meet its obligations and pay dividends As a company performs its business activities, it will incur various obligations. For example, suppliers want to know if the company can pay for the goods purchased on credit. Employees want to assess the company's ability to pay larger salaries and fringe benefits. Lenders are interested in the company's ability to repay the principal and interest on amounts borrowed. Similarly, investors often wish to know if a company is generating enough cash to be able to pay dividends and expand its productive capacity. In addition, success or failure in business often depends on whether a company has enough cash to meet unexpected obligations and take advantage of unexpected opportunities. Information about cash receipts and cash payments helps financial statement users make these important judgments.

Estimating the company's needs for external financing As companies operate, various expenditures can be financed through either internally generated funds or by external financing (debt or equity). Knowing the amount of cash that a company generates internally helps financial statement users assess whether a company will have to borrow additional funds from creditors or seek additional cash from investors.

Understanding the reasons for the differences between net income and related cash receipts and cash payments As you have already noticed, the amount of a company's net income and the amount of cash generated from operations are often different amounts due to the application of accrual accounting concepts. Because of the judgments and estimates involved in accrual accounting, many financial statement users question the usefulness of reported income. However, when provided with cash flow information, these users can gain insights into the quality and reliability of the reported income amounts.

Evaluating the balance sheet effects of both cash and noncash investing and financing transactions Not all changes in cash are directly related to a company's operations (such as manufacturing a product or selling a good or service). Instead, a company may make investments in productive assets as it expands its operations or upgrades its facilities. In addition, a company may seek sources of cash by issuing debt or equity. These activities can be just as crucial to a company's long-term success as its current operations.

In summary, information about a company's cash receipts and cash payments, along with information contained in the balance sheet and the income statement, is critical to understanding and analyzing a company's operations.

In this chapter, we will explain how a statement of cash flows is prepared from the information contained in the balance sheet and the income statement. We will explore the measurement, presentation, and analysis of cash flow information and address the following questions:

- What are the principal sources and uses of cash?
- How is the statement of cash flows prepared and reported to external users?
- How is the statement of cash flows used by investors, creditors, and others?

CASH FLOW CLASSIFICATIONS

Because our focus is on cash flows, it is important to have a clear understanding of what is included in the term *cash*. For purposes of the statement of cash flows, cash includes both funds on hand (coins and currency) and cash equivalents. Recall from Chapter 4 that cash equivalents are short-term, highly liquid investments that are readily convertible to cash and have original maturities of three months or less. Examples of cash equivalents include money market funds and investments in U.S. government securities (for example, treasury bills). Because of their high liquidity or nearness to cash, cash equivalents are treated as cash in the statement of cash flows.

During an accounting period, a company engages in the three fundamental business activities discussed in Chapter 1—operating activities, investing activities, and financing activities. Each of these activities can contribute to (a cash inflow) or reduce (a cash outflow) a company's cash balance. Therefore, the statement of cash flows reconciles the beginning and ending balances of cash by describing the effects of business activities on a company's cash balance. This relationship is shown in Exhibit 11-1.

Concept Q&A

If we already have the balance sheet and income statement, why is a statement of cash flows so important?

Answer:
The statement of cash flows provides information about a company's sources and uses of cash. Knowing how companies obtain and use cash provides users with a good idea of a company's financial strength and its long-term viability. The decision to invest in a company is much safer if a potential investor—be it a bank or stockholder—knows how much cash is being produced and where it is coming from.

OBJECTIVE 2
Identify and classify business activities that produce cash inflows and outflows.

Exhibit 11-1

How the Statement of Cash Flows Links the Two Balance Sheets

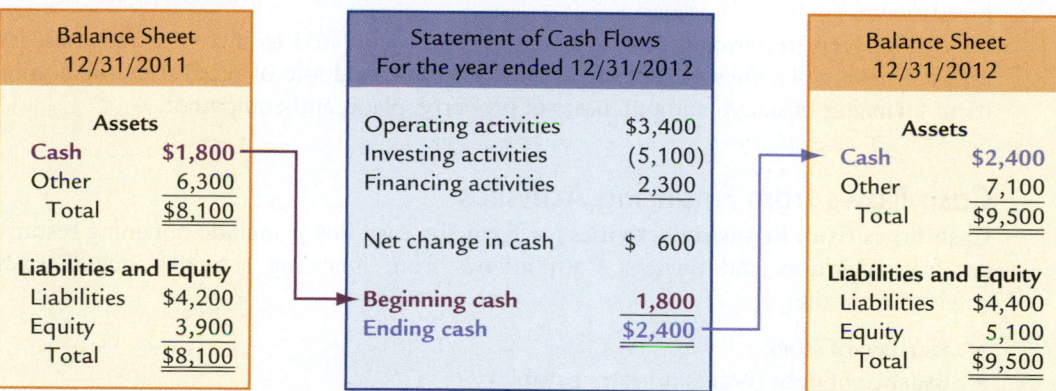

Balance Sheet 12/31/2011		Statement of Cash Flows For the year ended 12/31/2012		Balance Sheet 12/31/2012	
Assets		Operating activities	$3,400	**Assets**	
Cash	$1,800	Investing activities	(5,100)	Cash	$2,400
Other	6,300	Financing activities	2,300	Other	7,100
Total	$8,100			Total	$9,500
		Net change in cash	$ 600		
Liabilities and Equity				**Liabilities and Equity**	
Liabilities	$4,200	Beginning cash	1,800	Liabilities	$4,400
Equity	3,900	Ending cash	$2,400	Equity	5,100
Total	$8,100			Total	$9,500

Cash Flows from Operating Activities

Cash flows from operating activities (or operating cash flows) are the cash inflows and outflows that relate to acquiring (purchasing or manufacturing), selling, and delivering goods or services. Cash inflows from operating activities include:

- cash sales to customers
- collection of accounts receivable arising from credit sales
- cash dividends received
- interest received on investments in equity and debt securities

Cash outflows from operating activities include payments:

- to suppliers for goods and services
- to employees for wages and salaries
- to governments for taxes
- to lenders for interest on debt.

Operating cash flows correspond to the *types* of items that determine net income (revenues and expenses). However, the *amounts* are different because the income statement is accrual-based while the statement of cash flows is cash-based. Therefore, to isolate the current period operating cash flow, companies must adjust the current period income statement items for any related noncash items, which can be determined by examining the changes in the related current assets and current liabilities.

John Deere reported operating cash flow of $1,984.8 million compared to net income of $873.5 million (see Exhibit 11-5, p. 535). While various reasons exist for this difference, two major factors include adjustments for noncash items (such as depreciation and amortization) and accrual accounting adjustments of current assets and liabilities. The adjustments needed to reconcile net income with operating cash flow are discussed later in the chapter.

Cash Flows from Investing Activities

Cash flows from investing activities (or investing cash flows) are the cash inflows and outflows that relate to acquiring and disposing of operating assets and investments in other companies (current and long-term), lending money, and collecting loans. Cash inflows from investing activities include cash received from:

- the sale of property, plant, and equipment
- the collection of the principal amount of a loan (a note receivable)
- the sale of investments in other companies

Cash outflows from investing activities include payments made to:

- acquire property, plant, and equipment
- purchase debt or equity securities of other companies as an investment
- loan money to others (notes receivable)

In general, investing cash flows relate to increases or decreases of long-term assets and investments.

John Deere reported a $57 million cash outflow related to investing activities. Its major investing activities were related to the purchase and sale of receivables (its equipment financing business) and purchases of property, plant, and equipment.

Cash Flows from Financing Activities

Cash flows from financing activities (or financing cash flows) include obtaining resources from creditors and owners. Cash inflows from financing activities include cash received from the:

- issuance of stock
- issuance of debt (bonds or notes payable)

Cash outflows from financing activities include cash payments to:

- repay the principal amount borrowed (bonds or notes payable)
- repurchase a company's own stock (treasury stock)
- pay dividends

In general, financing cash flows involve cash receipts and payments that affect long-term liabilities and stockholders' equity.

John Deere reported a cash inflow of $470 million related to financing activities. Its major source of funds was from long-term debt. It also paid a $473 million dividend to its shareholders.

Noncash Investing and Financing Activities

Occasionally, investing and financing activities take place without affecting cash. For example, a company may choose to acquire an operating asset (such as a building) by issuing long-term debt. Alternatively, a company may acquire one asset by exchanging it for another. These types of activities are referred to as **noncash investing and financing activities**. Because these activities do not involve cash, they are not reported on the statement of cash flows. However, these transactions still provide useful information about a company's overall investing and financing activities. Any significant noncash investing and financing activities are required to be reported in a supplementary schedule that is shown either at the bottom of the statement of cash flows or in the notes to the financial statements. This requirement to disclose any significant noncash investing and financing activities is consistent with the full-disclosure principle—any information that would make a difference to financial statement users should be made known.

Exhibit 11-2 summarizes the classification of business activities as either operating, investing, or financing activities. Two particular activities—interest and dividends—are often misclassified by students. Interest (received or paid) and cash dividends received are classified as operating activities because they go into the determination of income. Cash dividends paid, on the other hand, are not an expense but are a reduction of retained earnings. Therefore, cash dividends paid are classified as a financing activity.

IFRS

IFRS allow companies to report dividends and interest paid as either an operating or a financing activity. Additionally, IFRS allow companies to report dividends and interest received as either an operating or an investing activity.

Classification of Cash Flows

Exhibit 11-2

Cash Inflows

Operating Activities
Cash received from:
- Customers for cash sales
- Collections of accounts receivable
- Dividends
- Interest

Investing Activities
Cash received from:
- The sale of property, plant, and equipment
- The collection of principal on a loan
- The sale or maturity of investments

Financing Activities
Cash received from:
- Issuing stock to owners
- Issuing notes or bonds (debt) to creditors
- Selling treasury stock

Cash Outflows

Operating Activities
Cash paid to:
- Suppliers of goods and services
- Employees for salaries and wages
- Governments for taxes
- Lenders for interest

Investing Activities
Cash paid to:
- Purchase property, plant, and equipment
- Make loans to other companies
- Purchase investments

Financing Activities
Cash paid to:
- Repayment of principal of long-term debt
- Dividends to owners
- Purchase of treasury stock

CORNERSTONE 11-1 shows how business activities can be classified as either operating, investing, financing, or noncash activities.

CORNERSTONE 11-1   Classifying Business Activities

Concept:
Cash flows from operating activities correspond to the cash effects of items that determine net income. Cash flows from investing activities relate to increases or decreases in long-term assets and investments. Cash flows from financing activities involve cash receipts and payments that affect long-term liabilities and stockholders' equity.

Information:
Moore Inc. engaged in the following activities during the current year:

a. Payment of wages to employees
b. Issuance of common stock
c. Purchase of property, plant, and equipment
d. Collection of cash from customers
e. Issuance of bonds
f. Retirement of debt by issuing stock
g. Purchase of inventory
h. Sale of property, plant, and equipment
i. Payment of dividends
j. Payment of interest

Required:
Classify each of the above activities as an operating, investing, or financing activity and indicate whether the activity involved a cash receipt or cash payment. If the transaction does not involve cash, classify it as a noncash investing and financing activity.

Solution:
a. Because wages are an expense on the income statement, the payment of wages is classified as a cash payment for an operating activity.
b. The issuance of common stock results in an increase of stockholders' equity and cash. Therefore, it is classified as a cash receipt from a financing activity.
c. The purchase of property, plant, and equipment results in an increase to a long-term asset and a decrease of cash. Therefore, it is classified as a cash payment for an investing activity.
d. The collection of cash from customers relates to sales revenue on the income statement and is classified as a cash receipt from an operating activity.
e. Issuing bonds results in an increase to long-term liabilities and cash. Therefore, it is classified as a cash receipt from a financing activity.
f. The retirement of debt by issuing stock is a financing activity that does not involve cash. It is classified as a noncash investing and financing activity.
g. Because inventory is a component of cost of goods sold on the income statement, the purchase of inventory is classified as a cash payment for an operating activity.
h. The sale of property, plant, and equipment results in a decrease in a long-term asset and an increase in cash. Therefore, it is classified as a cash receipt from an investing activity.
i. The payment of dividends is a reduction in retained earnings, which is a part of stockholders' equity. Therefore, the payment of dividends is classified as a cash payment for a financing activity.
j. Interest is an expense on the income statement. Therefore, the payment of interest is classified as a cash payment for an operating activity.

Format of the Statement of Cash Flows

Once a company has properly classified its cash inflows and outflows as operating, investing, or financing activities, it reports each of these three categories as shown in Exhibit 11-3. Note that the three cash flow categories are summed to obtain the net increase or decrease in cash. This change in cash reconciles the beginning and ending balances of cash as noted in Exhibit 11-1 (p. 527).

Format of the Statement of Cash Flows

Exhibit 11-3

Brooke Sportswear Inc.
Statement of Cash Flows
For the Year Ended December 31, 2011

Cash flows from operating activities		
Cash inflows	$ xxx	
Cash outflows	(xxx)	
Net cash provided (used) by operating activities		$xxx
Cash flows from investing activities		
Cash inflows	$ xxx	
Cash outflows	(xxx)	
Net cash provided (used) by investing activities		xxx
Cash flows from financing activities		
Cash inflows	$ xxx	
Cash outflows	(xxx)	
Net cash provided (used) by financing activities		xxx
Net increase (decrease) in cash and cash equivalents		$xxx
Cash and cash equivalents at beginning of year		xxx
Cash and cash equivalents at end of year		$xxx

Schedule or note disclosure of noncash investing and financing activities

YOU DECIDE   Statement of Cash Flow Classifications

You are preparing the statement of cash flows for Sienna Corporation and consult the CFO about how to properly classify the cash paid for interest. The CFO states that the company chose to finance its recent expansion activities with large amounts of debt. Because the interest payments resulted from this financing decision, he believes that the cash paid for interest should be classified as a financing activity. In addition, the CFO points out that you shouldn't waste any more time on this since it's simply a classification issue. No matter where the interest payment is reported, the total change in cash will be the same and no one will care.

How should you classify the cash paid for interest?

The CFO certainly makes a good argument to classify interest payments as a financing cash flow. Similar to dividend payments (which are paid for the use of equity capital), interest is paid for the use of debt capital. However, the FASB states that operating cash flows should reflect the cash effects of transactions that enter into the determination of income. Because interest is an expense, it should be classified as an operating activity. While this is a classification issue, the CFO's assertion that the proper classification makes no difference is incorrect. The various classifications on a statement of cash flows provide insights into how a company generated and used its cash.

The proper classification of items in the statement of cash flows is critical for financial statement users.

ANALYZING THE ACCOUNTS FOR CASH FLOW DATA

OBJECTIVE 3
Understand the relationship between changes in cash and the changes in the balance sheet accounts.

Unlike the balance sheet and the income statement, the statement of cash flows cannot be prepared by simply using information obtained from an adjusted trial balance prepared using the accrual basis of accounting. Instead, each item on the balance sheet and the income statement must be analyzed to *explain* why cash changed by the amount that it did. In other words, the accrual-basis numbers in the balance sheet and the income statement must be adjusted to a cash basis. Notice that our concern is not with determining the change in cash but the *reasons why* cash changed.

The recording of any business activity creates two types of financial measures—*balances* and *changes*. Balances measure the dollar amount of an account at a given time. Changes measure the increases or decreases in account balances over a period of time. For example, consider the following T-account:

Accounts Receivable			
Balance, 12/31/2011	11,000		
2012 credit sales	90,000	92,000	Cash collections for 2012
Balance, 12/31/2012	9,000		

Concept Q&A

Why do we analyze changes in the balance sheet accounts to determine the inflows and outflows of cash? Wouldn't it be easier to simply look at the cash account in the general ledger?

Answer:
It is correct that the cash account in the general ledger will contain all cash inflows and cash outflows and a statement of cash flows could be prepared by analyzing this account. However, this would require individuals to identify, understand, and classify every single cash receipt or cash payment. With the large volume of cash transactions, this would be an extremely time-consuming and inefficient task. It is much easier to determine cash flows by analyzing the changes in the balance sheet accounts.

This T-account shows two balances and two changes. The beginning and ending balances ($11,000 and $9,000) measure accounts receivable at December 31, 2011 and 2012, respectively. The credit sales ($90,000) and cash collections ($92,000) are changes that measure the effects of selling goods and collecting cash. Like accounts receivable, every balance sheet account can be described in terms of balances and changes.

To understand a company's cash flows, the relationships between the *changes* in balance sheet accounts and the company's cash flows need to be analyzed. We will begin our analysis with the fundamental accounting equation:

$$\text{Assets} = \text{Liabilities} + \text{Stockholders' Equity}$$

Next, we will restate this equation in terms of changes (Δ):

$$\Delta \text{ Assets} = \Delta \text{ Liabilities} + \Delta \text{ Stockholders' Equity}$$

Separating assets into cash and noncash accounts:

$$\Delta \text{ Cash} + \Delta \text{ Noncash Assets} = \Delta \text{ Liabilities} + \Delta \text{ Stockholders' Equity}$$

Finally, moving the changes in noncash assets to the right-hand side:

$$\Delta \text{ Cash} = \Delta \text{ Liabilities} + \Delta \text{ Stockholders' Equity} - \Delta \text{ Noncash Assets}$$

Where:

> Increases in Cash = Increases in Liabilities + Increases in Stockholders' Equity + Decreases in Noncash Assets

> Decreases in Cash = Decreases in Liabilities + Decreases in Stockholders' Equity + Increases in Noncash Assets

This analysis reveals that **all cash receipts or cash payments are associated with changes in other balance sheet accounts.** CORNERSTONE 11-2 illustrates how to classify specific balance sheet accounts as increases in cash or decreases in cash.

 **CORNERSTONE 11-2**   **Classifying Changes in Balance Sheet Accounts**

Concept:
Increases in cash result from increases in liabilities, increases in stockholders' equity, and decreases in noncash assets. Decreases in cash result from decreases in liabilities, decreases in stockholders' equity, and increases in noncash assets.

Information:

The following changes in the balance sheet accounts have been observed for the current period:

CORNERSTONE
11-2
(continued)

Account	1/1/2011	12/31/2011	Change
a. Accounts receivable	$ 25,000	$ 18,000	$ (7,000)
b. Bonds payable	400,000	300,000	(100,000)
c. Equipment	145,000	175,000	30,000
d. Inventory	15,000	18,000	3,000
e. Common stock	150,000	175,000	25,000
f. Retained earnings	75,000	95,000	20,000
g. Accounts payable	12,000	10,000	(2,000)
h. Unearned revenue	17,000	19,000	2,000

Required:

Classify each change as either an increase in cash or a decrease in cash.

Solution:

a. Increase in cash   e. Increase in cash
b. Decrease in cash   f. Increase in cash
c. Decrease in cash   g. Decrease in cash
d. Decrease in cash   h. Increase in cash

Exhibit 11-4 integrates the analysis of the relationships between the *changes* in balance sheet accounts and the company's cash flows with the cash flow classifications discussed in the previous section. Examining Exhibit 11-4, several items are of interest:

- Cash flows from operating activities generally involve income statement items (which are reflected in retained earnings) and changes in current assets or liabilities.
- Investing activities are related to changes in long-term assets.
- Financing activities are related to changes in long-term liabilities and stockholders' equity.
- Retained earnings affects both cash flows from operating activities (for example, revenues, expenses, net income, or a net loss) and cash flows from financing activities (for example, payment of dividends).
- Each item on the balance sheet and the income statement is analyzed to explain the change in cash.

Exhibit 11-4

Cash Flow Classifications and Changes in Balance Sheet Accounts

Classification	Cash Effect	Balance Sheet Items Affected	Example
Operating	Inflow (+)	Decreases in current assets Increases in current liabilities Increases in retained earnings	Collecting an accounts receivable Receipt of revenue in advance Making a cash sale
	Outflow (−)	Increases in current assets Decreases in current liabilities Decreases in retained earnings	Purchasing inventory Paying an accounts payable Paying interest
Investing	Inflow (+)	Decreases in long-term assets	Selling equipment
	Outflow (−)	Increases in long-term assets	Buying equipment
Financing	Inflow (+)	Increases in long-term liabilities Increases in stockholders' equity	Issuing long-term debt Issuing stock
	Outflow (−)	Decreases in long-term liabilities Decreases in stockholders' equity	Retiring long-term debt Paying dividends

PREPARING A STATEMENT OF CASH FLOWS

After the accounts have been analyzed to identify cash inflows and outflows, a statement of cash flows can be prepared. To prepare a statement of cash flows, you need:

- *Comparative balance sheets:* Used to determine the changes in assets, liabilities, and stockholders' equity during a period
- *A current income statement:* Used to determine cash flows from operating activities
- *Additional information about selected accounts:* Used to determine the reason why cash was received or paid

Using this information, there are five basic steps in preparing the statement of cash flows.

Step 1: **Compute the net cash flow from operating activities.** This involves adjusting the amounts on the income statement for noncash changes reflected in the balance sheet. Two methods, the indirect or direct method (explained in the next section), may be used to determine this amount.

Step 2: **Compute the net cash flow from investing activities.** Information from the balance sheet as well as any additional information provided will need to be analyzed to identify the cash inflows and outflows associated with long-term assets.

Step 3: **Compute the net cash flow from financing activities.** Information from the balance sheet as well as any additional information provided will need to be analyzed to identify the cash inflows and outflows associated with long-term liabilities and stockholders' equity.

Step 4: **Combine the net cash flows from operating, investing, and financing activities to obtain the net increase (decrease) in cash for the period.**

Step 5: **Compute the change in cash for the period and compare this with the change in cash from Step 4.** The change in cash, computed from the beginning balance of cash and the ending balance of cash as shown on the balance sheet, should reconcile with the net cash flow computed in Step 4.

The statement of cash flows for John Deere is shown in Exhibit 11-5.

OBJECTIVE ④

Prepare the cash flows from operating activities section of a statement of cash flows using the indirect method.

PREPARING CASH FLOWS FROM OPERATING ACTIVITIES

The cash flows from operating activities section of the statement of cash flows may be prepared using either of two methods: the direct method or the indirect method. Both methods arrive at an identical amount—the net cash provided (used) by operating activities. The two methods differ only in how this amount is computed.

The Direct Method

In the **direct method**, cash inflows and cash outflows are listed for each type of operating activity that a company performs. These cash flows are generally computed by adjusting *each item* on the income statement by the changes in the related current asset or liability accounts. Typical cash flow categories reported are cash collected from customers, cash paid to suppliers, cash paid to employees, cash paid for interest, and cash paid for taxes. The cash inflows are subtracted from the cash outflows to determine the net cash flow from operating activities. If the direct method is used, companies must also provide a supplementary schedule that shows the reconciliation of net income with operating cash flow. While the FASB prefers the use of the direct method because it is more consistent with the purpose of the statement of cash flows, it is not widely used.

The Indirect Method

The indirect method does not report individual cash inflows and outflows. Instead, it focuses on the *differences* between net income and operating cash flow. The **indirect method** begins with net income and then adjusts it for noncash items to produce net

Statement of Cash Flows for John Deere

Exhibit 11-5

Deere and Company Statement of Consolidated Cash Flows* For the Year Ended October 31, 2009 (in millions of dollars)		
Cash flows from operating activities		
Net income	$ 873.5	
Adjustments to reconcile net income to net cash provided by operating activities:		
Bad debt expense	231.8	
Depreciation and amortization	873.3	
Other noncash items	538.3	
Changes in assets and liabilities:		
Decrease in receivables related to sales	481.8	
Decrease in inventories	452.5	
Decrease in accounts payable and accrued expenses	(1,168.3)	
Net increase (decrease) in accrued income taxes payable/receivable	(234.2)	
Net increase (decrease) in retirement benefit accruals/ prepaid pension costs	(27.9)	
Other	(36.0)	
Net cash provided by operating activities		$1,984.8
Cash flows from investing activities		
Collections of notes receivable	$ 11,252.0	
Proceeds from sales of financing receivables	12.2	
Proceeds from maturities and sales of marketable securities	825.1	
Proceeds from sales of equipment on operating leases	477.3	
Cost of notes receivable acquired	(11,234.2)	
Purchases of marketable securities	(29.5)	
Purchases of property, plant, and equipment	(906.7)	
Cost of equipment on operating leases acquired	(401.4)	
Other	(51.8)	
Net cash used for investing activities		(57.0)
Cash flows from financing activities		
Decrease in short-term borrowings	$ (1,384.8)	
Proceeds from long-term borrowings	6,282.8	
Payments of long-term borrowings	(3,830.3)	
Proceeds from issuance of common stock	16.5	
Repurchases of common stock	(3.2)	
Dividends paid	(473.4)	
Other	(137.3)	
Net cash provided by financing activities		470.3
Effect of exchange rate changes on cash and cash equivalents		42.2
Net increase (decrease) in cash and cash equivalents		$2,440.3
Cash and cash equivalents at beginning of year		2,211.4
Cash and cash equivalents at end of year		$4,651.7

*The statement of cash flows information was taken from the annual report of Deere and Company and has been
   summarized and reformatted by the authors.

cash flow from operating activities. These adjustments to net income are necessary for
two reasons:

- to eliminate income statement items that do not affect cash (such as depreciation and
  gains/losses on sales of assets) and
- to adjust accrual-basis revenues and expenses to cash receipts and cash payments.

Exhibit 11-6

Use of the Indirect and Direct Methods

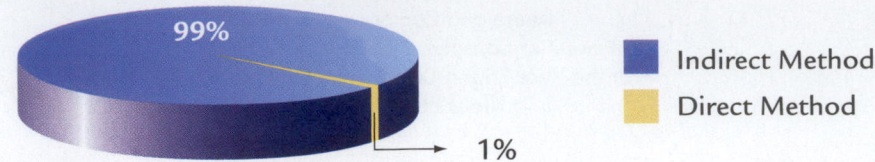

Source: *Accounting Trends and Techniques, 2009.*

The changes in the related current asset and current liability accounts contain the information necessary to make the adjustments to revenue and expense accounts.

Generally, companies prefer the indirect method because it is easier and less costly to prepare. In fact, approximately 99 percent of U.S. companies use the indirect method, as shown in Exhibit 11-6.

ETHICAL DECISIONS   By highlighting the differences between operating cash flows and net income, financial statement users may be able to more easily see attempts at earnings management. If managers try to manage earnings by manipulating the accrual accounting process (for example, increase revenues or decrease expenses on the income statement to increase income), these actions will often have no cash flow effect but will instead reveal themselves through changes in the accrual-basis accounts. When there are growing differences between operating cash flow and net income, the indirect method highlights the changes in the accrual accounts and allows users to judge the cause of these differences. ●

Applying the Indirect Method

We will illustrate the preparation of cash flows from operating activities for Brooke Sportswear using the more popular indirect method. The direct method is illustrated in Appendix 11A. However, remember two important points.

- Cash flow from operating activities is the same under either method.
- The indirect and direct methods only apply to the operating activities section of the statement of cash flows. The investing and financing sections will be prepared the same way regardless of which method is used to prepare the operating activities section.

The income statement and comparative balance sheets for Brooke Sportswear are shown in Exhibit 11-7.

Because income statements are prepared on an accrual basis, the revenues and expenses recognized on the income statement are not necessarily the same as the cash receipts and cash payments for a period. For example, revenues may include credit sales for which the company has not collected cash and exclude collections of cash from credit sales made in a previous period. Similarly, expenses may have been incurred for which no cash has been paid, or cash may have been paid related to expenses incurred in a previous period. Therefore, net income must be adjusted for these timing differences between the recognition of net income and the receipt or payment of cash.

Under the indirect method, four types of adjustments must be made to net income to adjust it to net cash flow from operating activities:

1. Add to net income any noncash expenses and subtract from net income any noncash revenues.
2. Add to net income any losses and subtract from net income any gains.
3. Add to net income any decreases in current assets or increases in current liabilities that are related to operating activities.
4. Subtract from net income any increases in current assets and decreases in current liabilities that are related to operating activities.

Concept Q&A

Why are there differences between net income and net cash flow from operating activities?

Answer:
Net income is prepared under the accrual basis of accounting which records business activities when they occur instead of when cash is received or paid. Therefore, all of the adjustments that are made to net income reflect timing differences between the reporting of revenues and expenses and the related inflow or outflow of cash.

Exhibit 11-7

Financial Statements for Brooke Sportswear

Brooke Sportswear
Balance Sheets
December 31, 2011 and 2010

	2011	2010
ASSETS		
Current assets:		
Cash	$ 15,000	$ 13,000
Accounts receivable	53,000	46,000
Prepaid insurance	1,000	2,000
Inventory	63,000	51,000
Total current assets	$ 132,000	$ 112,000
Long-term investments	53,000	41,000
Property, plant, and equipment:		
Land	325,000	325,000
Equipment	243,000	210,000
Accumulated depreciation	(178,000)	(150,000)
Total assets	$ 575,000	$ 538,000
LIABILITIES AND EQUITY		
Current liabilities:		
Accounts payable	$ 13,000	$ 17,000
Wages payable	3,500	2,000
Interest payable	1,500	1,000
Income taxes payable	3,000	6,000
Total current liabilities	$ 21,000	$ 26,000
Long-term liabilities:		
Notes payable	109,000	115,000
Total liabilities	$130,000	$141,000
Equity:		
Common stock	$165,000	$151,000
Retained earnings	280,000	246,000
Total equity	$445,000	$397,000
Total liabilities and equity	$575,000	$538,000

Brooke Sportswear
Income Statement
For the Year Ended December 31, 2011

Sales revenue	$ 472,000
Less: Cost of goods sold	(232,000)
Gross margin	$ 240,000
Less operating expenses:	
Wages expense	(142,000)
Insurance expense	(15,000)
Depreciation expense	(40,000)
Income from operations	$ 43,000
Other income and expenses:	
Loss on disposal of property, plant, and equipment	(6,000)
Gain on sale of investments	15,000
Interest expense	(5,000)
Income before taxes	$ 47,000
Less: Income taxes expense	(8,000)
Net income	$ 39,000

Additional Information:

1. Equipment with a cost of $20,000 and accumulated depreciation of $12,000 was sold for $2,000 cash. Equipment was purchased for $53,000 cash.
2. Long-term investments with a cost of $16,000 were sold for $31,000 cash. Additional investments were purchased for $28,000 cash.
3. Notes payable in the amount of $35,000 were repaid, and new notes payable in the amount of $29,000 were issued for cash.
4. Common stock was issued for $14,000 cash.
5. Cash dividends of $5,000 were paid (obtained from the retained earnings statement).

These adjustments and the computation of net cash flow from operating activities are illustrated in **CORNERSTONE 11-3**.

CORNERSTONE 11-3
Calculating Net Cash Flow from Operating Activities: Indirect Method

Concept:
The calculation of net cash flow from operating activities requires adjustments to net income for noncash items, gains and losses, and changes in current assets and current liabilities.

(Continued)

Information:
Refer to the income statement and the current assets and current liabilities sections of Brooke Sportswear's balance sheets found in Exhibit 11-7 (p. 537).

CORNERSTONE
11-3
(continued)

Required:
Compute the net cash flow from operating activities using the indirect method.

Solution:

Net income		$39,000
Adjustments to reconcile net income to net cash flow from operating activities:*		
Depreciation expense	$ 40,000	
Loss on disposal of equipment	6,000	
Gain on sale of long-term investments	(15,000)	
Increase in accounts receivable	(7,000)	
Decrease in prepaid insurance	1,000	
Increase in inventory	(12,000)	
Decrease in accounts payable	(4,000)	
Increase in wages payable	1,500	
Increase in interest payable	500	
Decrease in income taxes payable	(3,000)	8,000
Net cash provided by operating activities		$47,000

*The explanation of these adjustments is given in the text of this section

The adjustments made in Cornerstone 11-3 are explained below.

Adjustment of Noncash Revenues and Expenses
The income statement often includes various noncash items such as depreciation expense, amortization expense, and bad debt expense.

- Noncash expenses reduce net income but do not reduce cash. Under the indirect method **noncash expenses are added back to net income.**
- Noncash revenues increase income but do not increase cash. Under the indirect method, **noncash revenues are subtracted from net income.**

Adjustment of Gains and Losses
The sale of a long-term asset or the extinguishment of a long-term liability often produces either a gain or loss that is reported on the income statement. However, the gain or loss does not affect cash flow and should, therefore, not be included as an operating activity. Furthermore, the gain or loss does not reveal the total amount of cash received or paid. Instead, it only gives the amount received or paid in excess of the book value of the asset or liability. The correct procedure is to eliminate the gain or loss from net income and record the full amount of the cash flow as either an investing activity or a financing activity.

- Because gains increase net income, under the indirect method, **gains are subtracted from net income.**
- Because losses decrease net income, under the indirect method, **losses are added back to net income.**

Adjustments for Changes in Current Assets and Current Liabilities
As discussed earlier in the chapter, all cash receipts or cash payments are associated with changes in one or more balance sheet accounts. Generally, current assets and liabilities are related to the operating activities of a company, and changes in these accounts cause a difference between net income and cash flows from operating activities. Based on the earlier analysis of the balance sheet accounts, two general rules emerge.

- **Increases in current assets and decreases in current liabilities are subtracted from net income.**
- **Decreases in current assets and increases in current liabilities are added to net income.**

The adjustments to net income required to calculate cash flow from operating activities are summarized in Exhibit 11-8.

Adjustments Required to Calculate Cash Flow from Operating Activities

Exhibit 11-8

✚ Add to Net Income	━ Subtract from Net Income
• Noncash expenses	• Noncash revenues
• Losses	• Gains
• Decreases in current assets	• Increases in current assets
• Increases in current liabilities	• Decreases in current liabilities

The explanations of these adjustments for Brook Sportswear are shown below.

Accounts Receivable The accounts receivable account increases when credit sales are recorded and decreases when cash is collected from customers.

Accounts Receivable			
Balance, 1/1/2011	46,000		
Credit sales	xxx	Cash collections	xxx
Balance, 12/31/2011	53,000		

The increase of accounts receivable implies that credit sales were $7,000 greater than the cash collected from customers. This is consistent with the results of our earlier analysis indicating that increases in noncash assets are related to decreases in cash. Because cash collections were less than the sales reported on in the income statement, the company would need to subtract the increase in accounts receivable from net income when computing net cash flow from operating activities. (A decrease in accounts receivable would be added to net income when computing net cash flow from operating activities.)

Prepaid Insurance The prepaid insurance account increases when cash prepayments are made and decreases when expenses are incurred.

Prepaid Insurance			
Balance, 1/1/2011	2,000		
Cash prepayments	xxx	Expense incurred	xxx
Balance, 12/31/2011	1,000		

The decrease in prepaid insurance indicates that expenses recorded on the income statement were $1,000 higher than the cash payments. Because more expenses were incurred than were paid in cash, the company actually has more cash available at the end of the period than at the beginning of the period (because less cash was paid). This is consistent with the results of our earlier analysis indicating that decreases in noncash assets are related to increases in cash. The decrease in the prepaid insurance account needs to be added to net income when computing net cash flow from operating activities. (Increases in prepaid insurance would be subtracted from net income.)

Inventory The inventory account increases when inventory is purchased and decreases as inventory is sold.

Inventory			
Balance, 1/1/2011	51,000		
Purchases	xxx	Cost of goods sold	xxx
Balance, 12/31/2011	63,000		

The increase in inventory implies that purchases of inventory exceeded the cost of the inventory sold reported on the income statement by $12,000. Therefore, the company made "extra" cash purchases that were not included in cost of goods sold. To adjust net income to net cash flow from operating activities, the increase in the inventory account, which represents the extra cash purchases, needs to be subtracted from net income. (Decreases in inventory would be added to net income.)

Accounts Payable The accounts payable account increases when credit purchases are made and decreases when cash payments are made to suppliers.

Accounts Payable			
		Balance, 1/1/2011	17,000
Cash payments	xxx	Credit purchases	xxx
		Balance, 12/31/2011	13,000

The decrease in accounts payable indicates that the cash payments to suppliers exceeded the purchases of inventory by $4,000. Because the purchase of inventory is part of cost of goods sold, this implies that more cash was paid than was reflected in expenses. This is consistent with the results of our earlier analysis indicating that decreases in liabilities are related to decreases in cash. Therefore, the decrease in accounts payable needs to be subtracted from net income when computing the net cash flow from operating activities. (Increases of accounts payable are added to net income.)

Wages Payable The wages payable account increases when wages are accrued (incurred but not yet paid) and decreases when wages are paid.

Wages Payable			
		Balance, 1/1/2011	2,000
Cash payments	xxx	Wages expense	xxx
		Balance, 12/31/2011	3,500

The increase in wages payable indicates that wages expense recorded on the income statement was greater than the cash paid for wages by $1,500. Because less cash was paid than expensed, the company actually has more cash available. This is consistent with the results of our earlier analysis indicating that increases in liabilities are related to increases in cash. Therefore, the increase in wages payable is added to net income when computing the net cash flow from operating activities. (Decreases in wages payable are subtracted from net income.)

Interest Payable Interest payable increases when interest expense is recorded and decreases when interest is paid.

Interest Payable			
		Balance, 1/1/2011	1,000
Cash payments	xxx	Interest expense	xxx
		Balance, 12/31/2011	1,500

The increase in interest payable implies that interest expense recorded on the income statement was $500 greater than the cash paid for interest. This is consistent with the results of our earlier analysis indicating that increases in liabilities are related to increases in cash. Therefore, the increase in interest payable is added to net income when computing the net cash flow from operating activities. (Decreases in interest payable are subtracted from net income.)

Income Taxes Payable The income taxes payable account increases when income tax expense is incurred and decreases when income taxes are paid.

Income Taxes Payable			
		Balance, 1/1/2011	6,000
Cash payments	xxx	Income tax expense	xxx
		Balance, 12/31/2011	3,000

The decrease in income taxes payable implies that the cash payments for income taxes were $3,000 greater than the income tax expense reported on the income statement. This is consistent with the results of our earlier analysis indicating that decreases in liabilities are related to decreases in cash. Therefore, less cash is available at the end of the period and the decrease in income taxes payable is subtracted from net income when computing the net cash flow from operating activities. (Increases in income taxes payable are added to net income.)

YOU ◆ DECIDE   Operating Cash Flow and the Quality of Earnings

You are analyzing the financial statements of Slater Inc., a retail company that operates primarily in the southeastern United States. While Slater has reported increasing net income, you notice that its operating cash flow has been declining. Further investigation reveals increasing accounts receivable and inventory balances.

What inferences can you make about the quality of Slater's earnings?

Many analysts will compare net income to operating cash flow as a means of assessing the quality of a company's earnings. All other things equal, the higher a company's operating cash flow relative to its net income, the greater the quality of the company's earnings. In Slater's situation, increasing income with declining operating cash flow is a warning sign that requires closer scrutiny. The increasing accounts receivable balances could simply signal rapidly growing operations. However, it may also signal that a company is attempting to boost sales by allowing customers to take longer to pay or lending to riskier customers. Similarly, increasing inventory balances may be due to seasonal factors (for example, the normal inventory growth during a "slow" quarter), or it could signal that the company was not able to sell its merchandise as it had planned. When differences between net income and operating cash flow are noted, it is critical to fully understand their implications for the company's prospects.

Understanding the differences between net income and operating cash flow can provide useful insights into the quality of a company's earnings.

PREPARING CASH FLOWS FROM INVESTING ACTIVITIES

O B J E C T I V E ⑤
Prepare the cash flows from the investing activities section of a statement of cash flows.

The second major section of the statement of cash flows reports the net cash flow from investing activities. Information for preparing the investing activities portion of the statement of cash flows is obtained from the investment and long-term asset accounts. Because all of these accounts are assets, increases that were financed by cash would be treated as outflows of cash. Decreases in the assets that produced cash receipts would be treated as inflows of cash.

Although the beginning and ending balance sheets are useful sources for identifying changes in these accounts, you must refer to any additional data provided to determine the actual amount of investing cash inflows and outflows. For example, a company might purchase land at a cost of $200,000 and, during the same accounting period, sell land that had a cost of $145,000. If only the beginning and ending amounts for land are examined, one would erroneously conclude that there had been a single cash outflow of $55,000 for land, instead of two separate cash flows—a cash outflow for the purchase of land and a cash inflow related to the sale of land.

Analyzing Investing Activities

To analyze investing activities, follow the three basic steps outlined in Exhibit 11-9.

Analyzing Investing Activities

Exhibit 11-9

Step 1:
Recreate the journal entries to describe the activities that took place during the period.

Step 2:
Record the cash flows as inflows or outflows of cash in the investing activities section of the statement of cash flows.

Step 3:
Analyze the account using all available information to make sure the account activity has been completely explained.

To illustrate the analysis of the relevant accounts and the recreation of the journal entries, consider the information in Brooke Sportswear's financial statements in Exhibit 11-7 (p. 537).

Land Notice that no change occurred in the land account, nor was any additional information given concerning this account. Therefore, there was no cash flow associated with land for the year.

Property, Plant, and Equipment To get a full picture of the equipment account you must examine both the equipment and the related accumulated depreciation account. (For any operating asset that depreciates, you will need to analyze the two related accounts together.) Using the information from the financial statements and the additional information in Exhibit 11-7 (p. 537), you can recreate the activity in these accounts by making the following journal entries:

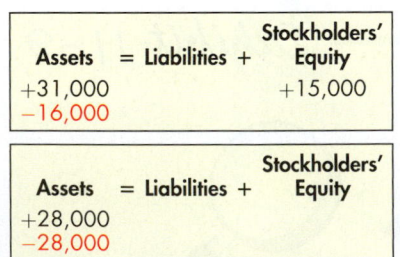

Assets	= Liabilities +	Stockholders' Equity
+2,000		−6,000
+12,000		
−20,000		

	Sale of Equipment	Cash	2,000	
		Accumulated Depreciation	12,000	
		Loss on Disposal of Property, Plant, and Equipment	6,000	
		Equipment		20,000

Assets	= Liabilities +	Stockholders' Equity
+53,000		
−53,000		

	Purchase of Equipment	Equipment	53,000	
		Cash		53,000

Notice that the there are only two cash flows related to investing activities:

- a $2,000 cash inflow associated with the disposal of equipment, and
- a $53,000 cash outflow associated with the purchase of equipment.

The loss on the disposal of equipment does not involve cash and is included as an adjustment in the operating section of the statement of cash flows. The analysis performed above is used to reconcile the change in the equipment and accumulated depreciation accounts as shown in the following T-accounts:

Equipment

Balance, 1/1/2011	210,000		
Purchase	53,000	Disposal	20,000
Balance, 12/31/2011	243,000		

Accumulated Depreciation

		Balance, 1/1/2011	150,000
Disposal	12,000	Dep. exp.	40,000
		Balance, 12/31/2011	178,000

Investments Using the information in Exhibit 11-7 (p. 537), you can recreate the activity in the investment account by making the following journal entries:

Assets	= Liabilities +	Stockholders' Equity
+31,000		+15,000
−16,000		

	Sale of Investment	Cash	31,000	
		Investments		16,000
		Gain on Sale of Investments		15,000

Assets	= Liabilities +	Stockholders' Equity
+28,000		
−28,000		

	Purchase of Investment	Investments	28,000	
		Cash		28,000

Again, notice that two cash flows were related to investing activities:

- a $31,000 inflow of cash related to the sale of an investment, and
- a $28,000 outflow of cash related to the purchase of an investment.

The gain on the sale of the investment does not involve cash and is included as an adjustment in the operating section of the statement of cash flows. The analysis performed above is used to reconcile the change in the investment account as shown in the following T-account.

Investments			
Balance, 1/1/2011	41,000		
Purchase	28,000	Sale	16,000
		Balance, 12/31/2011	53,000

CORNERSTONE 11-4 shows how to compute the investing activities section of the statement of cash flows for Brooke Sportswear.

CORNERSTONE 11-4   Reporting Net Cash Flow from Investing Activities

Concept:
The cash flow effects of changes in long-term assets and investments are reported as investing cash flows.

Information:
Refer to the income statement, the long-term assets sections of Brooke Sportswear's balance sheets, and the first two items of additional information in Exhibit 11-7 (p. 537).

Required:
Compute the net cash flow from investing activities.

Solution:

Cash flows from investing activities:	
Cash received from sale of equipment	$ 2,000
Purchase of equipment	(53,000)
Cash received from sale of investments	31,000
Purchase of investments	(28,000)
Net cash used for investing activities	$(48,000)

PREPARING CASH FLOWS FROM FINANCING ACTIVITIES

OBJECTIVE 6
Prepare the cash flows from financing activities section of a statement of cash flows.

The intent of the financing activities section of the statement of cash flows is to identify inflows and outflows of cash arising from business activities that either produced capital (long-term debt or stockholders' equity) for the company or repaid capital supplied to the company. Information for preparing the financing activities portion of the statement of cash flows is obtained from the long-term debt and stockholders' equity accounts. Increases in these accounts suggest that cash has been received and decreases suggest that cash has been paid. (Because treasury stock is a contra-equity account, increases indicate cash outflows and decreases indicate cash inflows.)

Analyzing Financing Activities

To analyze financing activities, the same basic steps used to analyze investing activities (see Exhibit 11-9, p. 541) are followed:

Step 1: Recreate the journal entries to describe the activities that took place during the period.

Step 2: Record the cash flows as inflows or outflows of cash in the financing activities section of the statement of cash flows.

Step 3: Analyze the account to make sure the account activity has been completely explained.

To illustrate the analysis of the relevant accounts and the recreation of the journal entries, consider the information in Brooke Sportswear's balance sheet.

Notes Payable

Notes Payable Using information in Exhibit 11-7 (p. 537), you can recreate the activity in the notes payable account by making the following journal entries:

Repayment of Principal	Notes Payable	35,000	
	Cash		35,000
Issuance of Note	Cash	29,000	
	Notes Payable		29,000

Assets	= Liabilities +	Stockholders' Equity
−35,000		−35,000

Assets	= Liabilities +	Stockholders' Equity
+29,000		+29,000

Notice that there are two cash flows related to financing activities:

- a $35,000 cash outflow associated with the repayment of principal, and
- a $29,000 cash inflow associated with issuing the note.

The payment of interest is considered an operating activity and is not relevant to this analysis. The analysis performed above is used to reconcile the change in the notes payable account as shown in the following T-account:

Notes Payable

		Balance, 1/1/2011	115,000
Repaid principal	35,000	Issued note	29,000
		Balance, 12/31/2011	109,000

Common Stock

Common Stock Using information in Exhibit 11-7 (p. 537), you can recreate activity in the common stock account by making the following journal entry:

Issuance of Stock	Cash	14,000	
	Common Stock		14,000

Assets	= Liabilities +	Stockholders' Equity
+14,000		+14,000

One cash inflow ($14,000) has caused the change in common stock. The credit entry to the common stock account is used to reconcile the change in the common stock account, as shown in the following T-account:

Common Stock

		Balance, 1/1/2011	151,000
Retired stock	0	Issued stock	14,000
		Balance, 12/31/2011	165,000

Retained Earnings

Retained Earnings Using information in Exhibit 11-7 (p. 537), you can recreate the activity in the retained earnings account by making the following journal entry:

Payment of Dividends	Dividends	5,000	
	Cash		5,000

Assets	= Liabilities +	Stockholders' Equity
−5,000		−5,000

The only cash flow, the payment of dividends, is a financing activity. The following T-account summarizes the activity in the retained earnings account:

Retained Earnings

		Balance, 1/1/2011	246,000
Dividends	5,000	Net income	39,000
		Balance, 12/31/2011	280,000

Note that retained earnings is increased by net income and decreased by the payment of dividends.[1] Net income does not affect cash flow from financing activities but is considered an operating activity.

CORNERSTONE 11-5 shows how to compute the financing activities section of the statement of cash flows for Brooke Sportswear.

---

[1] Dividends declared but not paid also reduce retained earnings but are classified as a noncash activity.

CORNERSTONE 11-5   Reporting Net Cash Flow from Financing Activities

Concept:
The cash flow effects of changes in long-term liabilities and equity are reported as financing cash flows.

Information:
Refer to the income statement, long-term assets, liabilities, and equity sections of Brooke Sportswear's balance sheet, and items 3–5 of additional information in Exhibit 11-7 (p. 537).

Required:
Compute the net cash flow from financing activities.

Solution:

Cash flows from financing activities:	
Cash paid to retire principal on notes payable	$(35,000)
Cash received from issuing notes payable	29,000
Cash received from issuance of common stock	14,000
Cash paid for dividends	(5,000)
Net cash provided by financing activities	$ 3,000

Combining Cornerstones 11-3 through 11-5, a complete statement of cash flows is presented in Exhibit 11-10 (p. 546). This exhibit presents cash flows from operating activities using the indirect method. Notice that the statement of cash flows explains the change in cash shown on the balance sheet of Brooke Sportswear in Exhibit 11-7 (p. 537).

 **YOU DECIDE**   Understanding Patterns in the Statement of Cash Flows

During a recent conference call with analysts, the CEO of Waggoner Inc. said that the company expects future sales growth as it expands into several new geographical markets. To corroborate the CEO's statements, you examine the statement of cash flows and find that the company reported negative operating cash flows, positive investing cash flows, and positive financing cash flows.

Does the statement of cash flows support the CEO's statements?

It does not appear that the CEO's statements are supported by the company's cash flows. An expanding company should exhibit negative investing cash flows as it invests in the long-term assets necessary for expansion. The positive investing cash flows shown by Waggoner indicate that it is a net seller of its fixed assets—not a purchaser. In addition, one would like to see any expansion supported by positive operating cash flows. Instead of being an expanding company, the pattern of cash flows exhibited by Waggoner suggests a company that is experiencing problems in generating operating cash flows. Further, it appears the company may be selling its fixed assets and obtaining capital through borrowing or stockholder contributions in order to cover the operating cash flow shortfall.

Careful analysis of the patterns and interrelationships of a company's cash flows can provide users with insights into a company's operations.

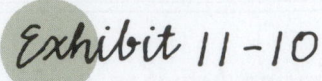
Exhibit 11-10

Statement of Cash Flows for Brooke Sportswear

Brooke Sportswear Statement of Cash Flows For the Year Ended December 31, 2011		
Cash flows from operating activities		
Net income	$ 39,000	
Adjustments to reconcile net income to net cash flow from operating activities:		
Depreciation expense	40,000	
Loss on disposal of equipment	6,000	
Gain on sale of long-term investments	(15,000)	
Increase in accounts receivable	(7,000)	
Decrease in prepaid insurance	1,000	
Increase in inventory	(12,000)	
Decrease in accounts payable	(4,000)	
Increase in wages payable	1,500	
Increase in interest payable	500	
Decrease in income taxes payable	(3,000)	
Net cash provided by operating activities		$ 47,000
Cash flows from investing activities		
Cash received from sale of equipment	$ 2,000	
Purchase of equipment	(53,000)	
Cash received from sale of investments	31,000	
Purchase of investments	(28,000)	
Net cash used for investing activities		(48,000)
Cash flows from financing activities		
Cash paid to retire principal on notes payable	$(35,000)	
Cash received from issuing notes payable	29,000	
Cash received from issuance of common stock	14,000	
Cash paid for dividends	(5,000)	
Net cash provided by financing activities		3,000
Net increase (decrease) in cash		$ 2,000
Cash and cash equivalents, 1/1/2011		13,000
Cash and cash equivalents, 12/31/2011		$ 15,000

OBJECTIVE 7

Analyze information contained in the statement of cash flows.

USING THE STATEMENT OF CASH FLOWS

Effective analysis of the statement of cash flows requires the following:

- an examination of the statement of cash flows itself,
- a comparison of the information on the current statement of cash flows with earlier statements, and
- a comparison of the information in the current statement of cash flows with information from other companies' statements of cash flow.

Examining the Statement of Cash Flows

One of the most important insights that can be gained by inspecting the current period's statement of cash flows is an estimate of how long it will take to recover the cash outflow associated with long-term uses of cash (such as purchase of property, plant, and equipment or payment of dividends). Investments in property, plant, and equipment are likely to require several profitable years before the investment is completely recovered through the sale of goods or services. Therefore, prudent managers will seek long-term sources of cash, such as long-term debt or equity, which will not need to be repaid before the original investment has been recovered through profitable operations.

The sources most frequently used to provide long-term cash inflows are operations, the sale of long-term debt, and the sale of stock. Of these three, operations is generally considered the least risky, or the most controllable. The sale of debt or equity requires that investors or creditors make sizable commitments to the company. Although cash inflows from operations also require that an outsider (the customer) make a commitment, the size and timing of a customer's cash commitments are more flexible. Thus, it is more likely that the company can produce cash inflows from customers on a regular basis. For this reason, most companies attempt to secure a sizable portion of their total cash inflows from operations. Generally, analysts view cash flows from operations as the most important section of the statement of cash flows because, in the long-run, this will be the company's source of cash used to provide a return to investors and creditors.

Because the cost of selling large debt or equity issues in the public capital markets is high, most large companies sell debt or equity in relatively large amounts. They also make smaller long-term or short-term borrowings directly from banks, insurance companies, and other financial intermediaries. Many businesses arrange a "pre-approved" line of credit that can be used, up to some limit, for borrowing whenever cash is needed. Sales of small amounts of stock to employees through stock option and stock bonus plans also help increase cash inflows.

Comparing the Statement of Cash Flows from Several Periods

An analysis of the statement of cash flows also requires a comparison of the company's current statement of cash flows with earlier statements of cash flow. Typically, several consecutive years should be analyzed in order to determine trends in cash inflows and cash outflows. The following questions may be helpful in beginning the analysis of a series of cash flow statements:

- What proportions of cash have come from operating, financing, and investing activities?
- Are there discernible trends in these proportions?
- What proportions of long-term uses of cash are financed by long-term sources of cash?
- How has the company financed any permanent increases in current assets?
- Has the company begun any investment programs that are likely to require significant cash outflows in the future?
- What are the probable sources for the cash inflows the company will need in the near future?
- Are these sources likely to be both able and willing to provide the cash that is needed?
- If the company is unable to secure all the cash it needs, could cash outflows be restricted to the available supply of cash without seriously affecting operations?

Financial statement users will rely on summary cash flow measures to help them make these assessments. Two such measures are a company's free cash flow and its cash flow adequacy ratio.

Free Cash Flow A company's **free cash flow** represents the cash flow that a company is able to generate after considering the maintenance or expansion of its assets (capital expenditures) and the payment of dividends. Free cash flow is computed as:

Free Cash Flow	=	Net Cash Flow from Operating Activities	−	Capital Expenditures	−	Cash Dividends

Having positive free cash flow allows a company to pursue profit-generating opportunities. However, negative free cash flow is not necessarily a bad thing. For example, a company making large investments in productive assets (large capital expenditures) may show negative free cash flow. If these investments provide a high rate of return, this strategy will be good for the company in the long run.

Cash Flow Adequacy Ratio A second useful measure is the **cash flow adequacy ratio**. The cash flow adequacy ratio provides a measure of the company's ability to meet its maturing debt obligations and is calculated as:

$$\text{Cash Flow Adequacy} = \frac{\text{Free Cash Flow}}{\text{Average Amount of Debt Maturing over the Next Five Years}}$$

The cash flow adequacy ratio is also an indicator of whether the company has the capacity to borrow additional debt.

Cornerstone 11-6 illustrates the computation and analysis of these ratios for **John Deere** and **Caterpillar**.

 **CORNERSTONE 11-6**   **Analyzing Free Cash Flow and Cash Flow Adequacy**

Concept:
Cash flow measures can be used to help assess a company's ability to expand its operations, meet its obligations, obtain financing, and pay dividends.

Information:
The following information was obtained from the 2009 annual reports of **John Deere** and **Caterpillar**.

(amounts in millions)	John Deere	Caterpillar
Operating cash flows	$1,984.8	$6,343
Capital expenditures	906.7	1,348
Dividends	473.4	1,029
Average maturities of long-term debt over the next five years	3,043.6	3,623.6

Required:
Compute John Deere's and Caterpillar's free cash flow and cash flow adequacy ratios.

Solution:
Free Cash Flow = Net Cash from Operating Activities − Captial Expenditures − Cash Dividends

John Deere	Caterpillar
$1,984.8 − $906.7 − $473.4 = **$604.7**	$6,343 − $1,348 − $1,029 = **$3,966**

$$\text{Cash Flow Adequacy} = \frac{\text{Free Cash Flow}}{\text{Average Amount of Debt Maturing over the Next Five Years}}$$

John Deere	Caterpillar
$\dfrac{\$604.7}{\$3,043.6} = \mathbf{19.9\%}$	$\dfrac{\$3,966}{\$3,623.6} = \mathbf{109.45\%}$

As you can see in Cornerstone 11-6, with almost $4 billion in free cash flow, **Caterpillar** certainly has the financial flexibility to take advantage of profit-generating opportunities and internally finance its expansion needs. Further, Caterpillar is generating enough free cash flow in one year to repay its average debt obligations. **John Deere**, with approximately $604 million of free cash flow also appears to have a significant amount of free cash flow; however, its cash flow adequacy ratio of 19.9 percent implies that it will take approximately five years to repay the debt that is maturing over the next five years. Overall, John Deere will have a relatively more difficult time in meeting its debt obligations than Caterpillar.

Comparing the Statement of Cash Flows to Similar Companies

Finally, the analysis of the statement of cash flows requires comparing information from similar companies. Such comparisons provide good reference points because similar companies generally secure cash from similar sources and are likely to spend cash for similar activities. Comparative analysis can reveal significant deviations in

- the amounts of cash inflows,
- the source of those inflows, and
- the types of activities to which cash is applied.

When significant differences are found among similar companies, an explanation should be sought in the other financial statements, in the notes accompanying the statements, or from management.

APPENDIX 11A: THE DIRECT METHOD

OBJECTIVE 8

Prepare the cash flows from operating activities section of a statement of cash flows using the direct method.

In the direct method of computing net cash flow from operating activities, inflows and outflows of cash are listed for each type of operating activity that a company performs. This involves adjusting *each item* on the income statement by the changes in the related current asset or liability accounts. Typical operating cash flows and the adjustments necessary to compute them are given below. All numbers are taken from the financial statements for Brooke Sportswear given in Exhibit 11-7 (p. 537).

Cash Collected from Customers

Sales revenue includes both cash sales and credit sales. When all sales are for cash, the cash collected from customers equals sales. However, when credit sales are made, the amount of cash that was collected during a period must be determined by analyzing the sales and accounts receivable accounts. The accounts receivable account increases when credit sales are recorded and decreases when cash is collected from customers.

Accounts Receivable			
Balance, 1/1/2011	46,000		
Credit sales	xxx	Cash collections	xxx
Balance, 12/31/2011	53,000		

The increase of accounts receivable implies that credit sales were $7,000 greater than the cash collected from customers. This is consistent with increases in noncash assets reflecting decreases in cash. Because cash collections were less than reported sales ($472,000), Brooke Sportswear would subtract the increase in accounts receivable from sales when computing cash collected from customers. A general formula to compute cash collections from customers is:

$$\text{Cash Collected from Customers} = \text{Sales} \begin{cases} + \text{ Decrease in Accounts Receivable} \\ - \text{ Increase in Accounts Receivable} \end{cases}$$

Other Cash Collections

If other revenues exist (such as interest or rent), similar adjustments are made to determine the cash collections. For example, interest revenue is adjusted for any change in interest receivable as follows:

$$\text{Cash Collected for Interest} = \text{Interest Revenue} \begin{cases} + \text{ Decrease in Interest Receivable} \\ - \text{ Increase in Interest Receivable} \end{cases}$$

Cash Paid to Suppliers

A company pays its suppliers for inventory which it later sells to customers, as represented by cost of goods sold. These purchases of inventory from suppliers may be either cash purchases or credit purchases, reflected as accounts payable. To compute cash paid to suppliers, it is necessary to analyze two accounts—inventory and accounts payable—and make two adjustments.

Inventory				Accounts Payable		
Balance, 1/1/2011	51,000			Balance, 1/1/2011	17,000
Purchases	xxx	Cost of goods sold	xxx	Cash payments	xxx	Credit purchases	xxx
Balance, 12/31/2011	63,000			Balance, 12/31/2011	13,000

The increase in inventory implies that purchases of inventory exceeded the cost of goods sold by $12,000. (A decrease in inventory would imply that purchases of inventory were less than cost of goods sold.) Therefore, cost of goods sold needs to be increased to reflect the "extra" cash purchases that were not included as an expense. A general formula to capture this relationship is:

$$\text{Cost of Purchases} = \text{Cost of Goods Sold} \begin{cases} + \text{ Increases in Inventory} \\ - \text{ Decreases in Inventory} \end{cases}$$

Next, the cost of purchases must be adjusted by the change in accounts payable to compute the cash paid to suppliers. The decrease in accounts payable implies that the cash payments to suppliers exceeded the purchases of inventory by $4,000. (An increase in accounts payable would imply that cash payments were less than the cost of purchases.) Therefore, Brooke Sportswear would add the increase in accounts payable to the cost of purchases to compute the cash paid to suppliers. A general formula that captures this relationship is:

$$\text{Cash Paid to Suppliers} = \text{Cost of Purchases} \begin{cases} + \text{ Decreases in Accounts Payable} \\ - \text{ Increases in Accounts Payable} \end{cases}$$

Combining this adjustment with the first adjustment, the cash paid to suppliers is computed as follows:

$$\text{Cash Paid to Suppliers} = \begin{cases} + \text{ Increases in Inventory} \\ - \text{ Decreases in Inventory} \end{cases} \begin{cases} + \text{ Decreases in Accounts Payable} \\ - \text{ Increases in Accounts Payable} \end{cases}$$

Cash Paid for Operating Expenses

Recall that operating expenses are the expenses the business incurs in selling goods or providing services and managing the company. These are usually divided into selling and administrative expenses and include items such as advertising expense, salaries and wages, insurance expense, utilities expense, property tax expense, and depreciation. These expenses are recognized when goods and services are used, not when cash is paid. Therefore, the expense amounts reported on the income statement will probably not equal the amount of cash actually paid during the period. Some expenses are paid before they are actually recognized (such as prepaid insurance); other expenses are paid for after they are recognized, creating a payable account at the time of the cash payment (such as salaries payable).

To determine the amount of cash payments for operating expenses, it is necessary to analyze the changes in the balance sheet accounts that are related to operating expenses—prepaid expenses and accrued liabilities. A prepaid expense increases when cash prepayments are made and decreases when expenses are incurred. An accrued liability increases when expenses are accrued (incurred but not yet paid) and decreases when cash payments are made. Brooke Sportswear has two balances that need to be analyzed—prepaid insurance and wages payable.

Prepaid Insurance				Wages Payable		
Balance, 1/1/2011	2,000			Balance, 1/1/2011	2,000
Cash prepayments	xxx	Expense incurred	xxx	Cash payments	xxx	Wages expense	xxx
Balance, 12/31/2011	1,000			Balance, 12/31/2011	3,500

The decrease in prepaid insurance indicates that expenses recorded on the income statement were $1,000 higher than the cash payments. Because more expenses were incurred than were paid in cash, the company actually has more cash available at the end of the period than at the beginning of the period. (An increase in prepaid expenses means that cash payments were higher than the expenses recognized on the income statement and a company would have less cash available at the end of the period.) Therefore, Brooke Sportswear should add the increase in prepaid insurance ($1,000) to insurance expense ($15,000) to compute the cash paid for insurance.

The increase in wages payable indicates that wages expense recorded on the income statement was greater than the cash paid for wages by $1,500. Because less cash was paid than expensed, the company actually has more cash available. (A decrease in wages payable would imply that cash payments were greater than the expense recorded on the income statement.) Therefore, Brooke Sportswear should subtract the increase in wages payable ($1,500) from wages expense to compute cash paid for wages.

Combining these two adjustments, a general formula to compute cash paid for operating expenses is:

$$\text{Cash Paid for Operating Expenses} = \text{Operating Expenses} \begin{cases} + \text{ Increases in Prepaid Expenses} \\ - \text{ Decreases in Prepaid Expenses} \\ + \text{ Decrease in Accrued Liabilities} \\ - \text{ Increase in Accrued Liabilities} \end{cases}$$

Cash Paid for Interest and Income Taxes

Computing cash paid for interest and income taxes is similar to that for operating expenses. Interest payable increases when interest expense is recorded and decreases when interest is paid.

Interest Payable			
		Balance, 1/1/2011	1,000
Cash payments	xxx	Interest expense	xxx
		Balance, 12/31/2011	1,500

The increase in interest payable implies that interest expense recorded on the income statement was $500 greater than the cash paid for interest. (A decrease in interest expense indicates that the cash paid for interest is greater than the interest expense recorded on the income statement.) Therefore, Brooke Sportswear would subtract the $500 increase in interest payable from interest expense ($5,000) to compute the cash paid for interest. A general formula to capture this relationship is:

$$\text{Cash Paid for Interest} = \text{Interest Expense} \begin{cases} + \text{ Decreases in Interest Payable} \\ - \text{ Increases in Interest Payable} \end{cases}$$

The income taxes payable account increases when income tax expense is incurred and decreases when income taxes are paid.

Income Taxes Payable			
		Balance, 1/1/2011	6,000
Cash payments	xxx	Income tax expense	xxx
		Balance, 12/31/2011	3,000

The decrease in income taxes payable implies that the cash payments for income taxes were $3,000 greater than the income tax expense reported on the income statement. (An increase in income taxes payable implies that income tax expense reported on the income statement is greater than the cash paid for income taxes.) Therefore, Brooke Sportswear would add the increase in income taxes payable ($3,000) to income taxes expense ($8,000) to compute cash paid for income taxes. A general formula to capture this relationship is:

$$\text{Cash Paid for Income Taxes} = \text{Income Tax Expense} \begin{cases} + \text{ Decrease in Income Taxes Payable} \\ - \text{ Increase in Income Taxes Payable} \end{cases}$$

Other Items

Noncash Revenues and Expenses The income statement often includes various noncash items such as depreciation expense, amortization expense, and bad debt expense. Noncash items do not affect cash flow. Therefore, under the direct method, **noncash items are not reported on the statement of cash flows**. Sometimes, depreciation expense (or some other noncash expense) is included as part of operating expenses. In this case, depreciation expense must be subtracted from operating expenses to compute the cash paid for operating expenses.

Gains and Losses The sale of a long-term asset or the extinguishment of a long-term liability often produces either a gain or loss that is reported on the income statement. However, the gain or loss does not affect cash flow and should not be included as an operating activity. Furthermore, the gain or loss does not reveal the total amount of cash received or paid. Instead, it only gives the amount received or paid in excess of the book value of the asset or liability. Therefore, **gains and losses are not reported on the statement of cash flows under the direct method.**

Applying the Direct Method

CORNERSTONE 11-7 illustrates and summarizes the computation of the net cash flow from operating activities using the direct method. Because each item on the income statement is adjusted under the direct method, it is common to begin the analysis with

CORNERSTONE 11-7
Calculating Net Cash Flows from Operating Activities: Direct Method

Concept:
To compute net cash flow from operating activities under the direct method, each item on the income statement must be adjusted for changes in the related asset and liability accounts.

Information:
Refer to the financial statements for Brooke Sportswear in Exhibit 11-7 (p. 537).

Required:
Compute the net cash flow from operating activities using the direct method.

Solution:

Cash flows from operating activities		
Cash collected from customers[a]		$ 465,000
Cash paid:		
To suppliers of merchandise[b]	$(248,000)	
For wages[c]	(140,500)	
For insurance[d]	(14,000)	
For interest[e]	(4,500)	
For income taxes[f]	(11,000)	(418,000)
Net cash provided by operating activities		$ 47,000

[a] $472,000 sales − $7,000 change in accounts receivable = $465,000
[b] $232,000 cost of goods sold + $12,000 change in inventory + $4,000 change in accounts payable = $248,000
[c] $142,000 wages expense − $1,500 change in wages payable = $140,500
[d] $15,000 insurance expense − $1,000 change in prepaid insurance = $14,000
[e] $5,000 interest expense − $500 change in interest payable = $4,500
[f] $8,000 income taxes expense + $3,000 change in income taxes payable = $11,000

the first item on the income statement (sales) and proceed down the income statement in the order that the accounts are listed.

It is important to note that both the indirect and direct methods arrive at the identical amount for the net cash provided (used) by operating activities. Therefore, the net cash provided by operating activities of $47,000 computed on the previous page is the same as the net cash flow from operating activities computed under the indirect method shown in Cornerstone 11-3 (p. 537). The two methods differ only in how this amount is computed and the presentation of the details on the statement of cash flows. In addition, if the direct method is used, companies must also provide a supplementary schedule that shows the reconciliation of net income with net cash flow from operating activities. This supplementary schedule is, in effect, the presentation shown under the indirect method in Cornerstone 11-3.

APPENDIX 11B: USING A SPREADSHEET TO PREPARE THE STATEMENT OF CASH FLOWS

OBJECTIVE ❾
Use a spreadsheet to prepare the statement of cash flows.

The use of a spreadsheet provides a means of systematically analyzing changes in the balance sheet amounts, along with the information from the income statement and any additional information, to produce a statement of cash flows. This approach produces spreadsheet entries (made only on the spreadsheet and not in the general ledger) that simultaneously reconstruct and explain the changes in the balance sheet account balances and identify the cash inflows and outflows. The spreadsheet is based on the same underlying principles as discussed in the chapter. Its primary advantage is that it provides a systematic approach to analyze the data, which is helpful in complex situations.

To construct the spreadsheet, follow these steps:

Step 1: Construct five columns. The first column will contain the balance sheet account titles. Immediately beneath the balance sheet accounts, set up the three sections of the statement of cash flows. The second column will contain the beginning balances of the balance sheet accounts (enter the amounts at this time). The third and fourth column will contain the debit and credit adjustments, respectively. The fifth column will contain the ending balances of the balance sheet accounts (enter the amounts at this time).

Step 2: Analyze each change in the balance sheet accounts in terms of debits and credits. Enter the effects in the adjustments column. Note that each entry will adjust both the balance sheet account being considered and either a statement of cash flows section of the spreadsheet or another balance sheet account (other than cash). Note that all inflows of cash are recorded as debits and all outflows of cash are recorded as credits.

Step 3: Prepare the statement of cash flows from the information contained in the statement of cash flows section of the spreadsheet.

Exhibit 11-11 (p. 554) illustrates how to use a spreadsheet to prepare the statement of cash flows for Brooke Sportswear. Refer to the information given earlier in the chapter regarding the logic behind the analysis of the changes in the spreadsheet accounts.

Net Income

a. Net income is listed as a cash inflow in the operating activities section. Because net income flows into retained earnings during the closing process, a credit to retained earnings reflects the effect of the closing entry.

Adjusting for Noncash Items

b. For Brooke Sportswear, the only noncash item was depreciation expense, which is added back to net income in the operating activities section and is reflected as a credit to accumulated depreciation.

Exhibit 11-11

Spreadsheet to Prepare Statement of Cash Flows

	A	B	C	D	E	F	G
1			Brooke Sportswear				
2			Spreadsheet to Prepare the Statement of Cash Flows				
3			For the Year Ended December 31, 2011				
4							
5			Beginning		Adjustments		Ending
6			Balance		Debit	Credit	Balance
7	**Balance Sheet Accounts**						
8	Cash	13,000	(r)	2,000			15,000
9	Accounts receivable	46,000	(g)	7,000			53,000
10	Prepaid insurance	2,000			1,000	(h)	1,000
11	Inventory	51,000	(i)	12,000			63,000
12	Land	325,000					325,000
13	Equipment	210,000	(d)	53,000	20,000	(c)	243,000
14	Accumulated depreciation	150,000	(c)	12,000	40,000	(b)	178,000
15	Investments	41,000	(f)	28,000	16,000	(e)	53,000
16							
17	Accounts payable	17,000	(j)	4,000			13,000
18	Wages payable	2,000			1,500	(k)	3,500
19	Interest payable	1,000			500	(l)	1,500
20	Income taxes payable	6,000	(m)	3,000			3,000
21	Notes payable	115,000	(n)	35,000	29,000	(o)	109,000
22	Common stock	151,000			14,000	(p)	165,000
23	Retained earnings	246,000	(q)	5,000	39,000	(a)	280,000
24							
25	**Statement of Cash Flows**						
26	Cash flow from operating activities						
27	Net income		(a)	39,000			
28	Adjustments to reconcile net						
29	income to net cash flow from						
30	operating activities						
31	Depreciation expense		(b)	40,000			
32	Loss on disposal of equipment		(c)	6,000			
33	Gain on sale of investments				15,000	(e)	
34	Increase in accounts receivable				7,000	(g)	
35	Decrease in prepaid insurance		(h)	1,000			
36	Increase in inventory				12,000	(i)	
37	Decrease in accounts payable				4,000	(j)	
38	Increase in wages payable		(k)	1,500			
39	Increase in interest payable		(l)	500			
40	Decrease in income taxes payable				3,000	(m)	
41							
42	Cash flows from investing activities						
43	Sale of equipment		(c)	2,000			
44	Purchase equipment				53,000	(d)	
45	Sale of investments		(e)	31,000			
46	Purchase of investment				28,000	(f)	
47							
48	Cash flows from financing activities						
49	Repaid note payable				35,000	(n)	
50	Issued note payable		(o)	29,000			
51	Issued common stock		(p)	14,000			
52	Paid dividend				5,000	(q)	
53							
54	Net change in cash				2,000	(r)	
55							
56				325,000	325,000		

Adjusting for Gains and/or Losses Due to Investing and Financing Activities

c. The actual proceeds from the sale of equipment are shown as a cash inflow in the investing activities section. The loss on the disposal of equipment is added back to net income in the operating activities section. In addition, both equipment and accumulated depreciation should be adjusted to reflect the sale.

d. The cash paid to purchase equipment is shown as a cash outflow in the investing activities section. At this point, note that the beginning and ending balances of the equipment and accumulated depreciation accounts are reconciled.

e. The actual proceeds from the sale of the investment are shown as a cash inflow in the investing activities section. The gain on the sale of the investment is subtracted from net income in the operating activities section. In addition, the investment account should be adjusted to reflect the sale.

f. The cash paid to purchase the investment is shown as a cash outflow in the investing activities section. At this point, note that the beginning and ending balances of the investment account are reconciled.

Adjusting for Changes in Current Assets and Current Liabilities

g. The increase in accounts receivable is subtracted from net income and reconciles the change in the accounts receivable account.

h. The decrease in prepaid insurance is added to net income and reconciles the change in the prepaid insurance account.

i. The increase in inventory is subtracted from net income and reconciles the change in the inventory account.

j. The decrease in accounts payable is subtracted from net income and reconciles the change in the accounts payable account.

k. The increase in wages payable is added to net income and reconciles the change in the wages payable account.

l. The increase in interest payable is added to net income and reconciles the change in the interest payable account.

m. The decrease in income taxes payable is subtracted from net income and reconciles the change in the income taxes payable account.

Adjusting for Cash Inflows and Outflows Associated with Financing Activities

n. The repayment of the notes payable is a cash outflow from a financing activity and adjusts the notes payable account.

o. The issuance of a notes payable is a cash inflow from a financing activity and reconciles the change in the notes payable account.

p. The issuance of common stock is a cash inflow from a financing activity and reconciles the change in the common stock account.

q. The payment of dividends is a cash outflow from a financing activity and, together with the first entry, item (a), reconciles the change in retained earnings. The final entry reconciles the cash balance.

r. The summation of the three sections of the statement of cash flows equals the change in cash for the period. This amount can be checked by summing the net cash flows from operating, investing, and financing activities computed in the previous steps.

Completing the Statement of Cash Flows

The statement of cash flows can now be prepared from the information developed in the statement of cash flows portion of the spreadsheet. The statement of cash flows for Brooke Sportswear is shown in Exhibit 11-10 (p. 546).

SUMMARY OF LEARNING OBJECTIVES

LO1.   Explain the purpose of a statement of cash flows.
- The statement of cash flows is one of the primary financial statements whose purpose is to provide information about a company's cash receipts (inflows of cash) and cash payments (outflows of cash) during an accounting period.
- The statement of cash flows is complementary to the information contained in the income statement and the balance sheet and is critical to understanding and analyzing a company's operations.

LO2.   Identify and classify business activities that produce cash inflows and outflows.
- The statement of cash flows is divided into three main sections based on the fundamental business activities that a company engages in during a period:
  - cash flows from operating activities, which encompass the cash inflows and outflows that relate to the determination of net income;
  - cash flows from investing activities, which are related to acquisitions and disposals of long-term assets and investments; and
  - cash flows from financing activities, which are related to the external financing of the company (debt or stockholders' equity).
- Some business activities take place without affecting cash and are referred to as noncash investing and financing activities.

LO3.   Understand the relationship between changes in cash and the changes in the balance sheet accounts.
- Because of timing issues between the recognition of revenues and expenses and the inflows and outflows of cash, information about a company's cash flows can be obtained by examining the changes in the balance sheet account balances over a period.
- Increases in cash result from increases in liabilities, increases in stockholders' equity, and decreases in noncash assets.
- Decreases in cash result from decreases in liabilities, decreases in stockholders' equity, and increases in noncash assets.

LO4.   Prepare the cash flows from operating activities section of a statement of cash flows using the indirect method.
- The indirect method for reporting cash flows from operating activities begins with net income and adjusts it for noncash items to produce net cash flow from operating activities.
- The adjustments to net income are necessary to eliminate income statement items that do not affect cash and to adjust accrual-basis revenues and expenses to cash receipts and cash payments.
- Four types of adjustments are necessary:
  - add to net income any noncash expenses and subtract from net income any noncash revenues;
  - add to net income any losses and subtract from net income any gains;
  - add to net income any decreases in current assets or increases in current liabilities that are related to operating activities; and
  - subtract from net income any increases in current assets and decreases in current liabilities that are related to operating activities.

LO5.   Prepare the cash flows from the investing activities section of a statement of cash flows.
- The cash flows from the investing activities section reports the net cash flow related to buying and selling property, plant, and equipment or other operating assets, purchasing and selling investments in other companies, and lending and collecting the principal amount of loans from borrowers.
- The preparation of the investing activities section of a statement of cash flows involves a careful analysis of the information in the financial statements as well as a recreation of the journal entries that describe the activities that took place during a period.

LO6.   Prepare the cash flows from financing activities section of a statement of cash flows.

- The cash flows from the financing activities section report the net cash flow related to the borrowing and repayment of the principal amount of long-term debt, the sale of common or preferred stock, the payment of dividends, and the purchase and sale of treasury stock.
- The preparation of the financing activities section of a statement of cash flows involves a careful analysis of the information in the financial statements as well as a recreation of the journal entries that describe the activities that took place during a period.

LO7.   Analyze information contained in the statement of cash flows.

- Effective analysis of the statement of cash flows requires an examination of the statement of cash flows itself, a comparison of the information on the current statement of cash flows with earlier statements, and a comparison of the information in the current statement of cash flows with information from other companies' statements of cash flow.
- Financial statement users may also rely on summary cash flow measures such as free cash flow (the cash flow that a company is able to generate after considering the maintenance or expansion of its assets) and the cash flow adequacy ratio (a measure of a company's ability to meet its debt obligations).

LO8.   (Appendix 11A) Prepare the cash flows from operating activities section of a statement of cash flows using the direct method.

- The direct method for reporting cash flows from operating activities lists cash inflows and cash outflows for each type of operating activity that a company performs.
- Cash flows from operating activities are generally computed by adjusting each item on the income statement by the changes in the related current asset or current liability accounts.
- Typical cash flow categories reported under the direct method include cash collected from customers, cash paid to suppliers, cash paid to employees, cash paid for interest, and cash paid for taxes.

LO9.   (Appendix 11B) Use a spreadsheet to prepare the statement of cash flows.

- A spreadsheet provides a means of systematically analyzing changes in the balance sheet amounts, along with the information from the income statement and any additional information, to produce a statement of cash flows.

CORNERSTONE 11-1 Classifying business activities, (p. 530)

CORNERSTONE 11-2 Classifying changes in balance sheet accounts, (p. 532)

CORNERSTONE 11-3 Calculating net cash flow from operating activities: indirect method, (p. 537)

CORNERSTONE 11-4 Reporting net cash flow from investing activities, (p. 543)

CORNERSTONE 11-5 Reporting net cash flow from financing activities, (p. 545)

CORNERSTONE 11-6 Analyzing free cash flow and cash flow adequacy, (p. 548)

CORNERSTONE 11-7 Calculating net cash flows from operating activities: direct method, (p. 552)

CORNERSTONES
FOR CHAPTER 11

KEY TERMS

Cash flow adequacy ratio, (p. 547)
Cash flows from financing activities, (p. 528)
Cash flows from investing activities, (p. 528)
Cash flows from operating activities, (p. 527)
Direct method, (p. 534)

Free cash flow, (p. 547)
indirect method, (p. 534)
Noncash investing and financing activities, (p. 529)
Statement of cash flows, (p. 526)

REVIEW PROBLEM

The Statement of Cash Flows

Concept:

The statement of cash flows measures a company's inflows (sources) and outflows (uses) of cash during a period of time. These cash inflows and cash outflows are classified as operating, investing, and financing activities.

Information:

The income statement and comparative balance sheet for Solar System Company are shown below.

Solar System Company Balance Sheets December 31, 2011 and 2010	2011	2010
ASSETS		
Current assets:		
Cash	$ 56,000	$ 47,000
Accounts receivable	123,000	107,000
Prepaid expenses	10,000	9,000
Inventory	52,000	46,000
Total current assets	$ 241,000	$ 209,000
Property, plant, and equipment:		
Equipment	270,000	262,000
Accumulated depreciation	(118,000)	(109,000)
Total assets	$ 393,000	$ 362,000
LIABILITIES AND EQUITY		
Current liabilities:		
Accounts payable	$ 18,000	$ 11,000
Salaries payable	5,000	9,000
Income taxes payable	7,000	5,000
Total current liabilities	$ 30,000	$ 25,000
Long-term liabilities:		
Notes payable	120,000	130,000
Total liabilities	$150,000	$155,000
Equity:		
Common stock	$213,000	$200,000
Retained earnings	30,000	7,000
Total equity	$243,000	$207,000
Total liabilities and equity	$393,000	$362,000

Solar Systems Company Income Statement For the Year Ended December 31, 2011	
Sales revenue	$1,339,000
Less: Cost of goods sold	(908,000)
Gross margin	$ 431,000
Less operating expenses:	
Salaries expense	(230,000)
Depreciation	(24,000)
Other operating expenses	(116,000)
Income from operations	$ 61,000
Other income and expenses:	
Gain on disposal of equipment	3,000
Interest expense	(14,000)
Income before taxes	$ 50,000
Less: Income taxes expense	(12,000)
Net income	$ 38,000

Additional Information:

1. Equipment with a cost of $24,000 and accumulated depreciation of $15,000 was sold for $12,000 cash. Equipment was purchased for $32,000 cash.
2. Notes payable in the amount of $10,000 were repaid.
3. Common stock was issued for $13,000 cash during 2011.
4. Cash dividends of $15,000 were paid during 2011.

Required:

Prepare a statement of cash flows for Solar Systems Company using the indirect method.

Solution:

Statement of Cash Flows Solar Systems Company For the Year Ended December 31, 2011		
Cash flows from operating activities		
Net income	$ 38,000	
Adjustments to reconcile net income to net cash flow from operating activities:		
Depreciation expense	24,000	
Gain on disposal of equipment	(3,000)	

Increase in accounts receivable	$(16,000)	
Increase in prepaid expenses	(1,000)	
Increase in inventory	(6,000)	
Increase in accounts payable	7,000	
Decrease in salaries payable	(4,000)	
Increase in income taxes payable	2,000	
Net cash provided by operating activities		$ 41,000
Cash flows from investing activities		
Cash received from sale of equipment	$ 12,000	
Purchase of equipment	(32,000)	
Net cash used by investing activities		(20,000)
Cash flows from financing activities		
Cash paid to retire notes payable	$(10,000)	
Cash received from issuance of common stock	13,000	
Cash paid for dividends	(15,000)	
Net cash used by financing activities		(12,000)
Net increase (decrease) in cash		$ 9,000
Cash and cash equivalents, 1/1/2011		47,000
Cash and cash equivalents, 12/31/2011		$ 56,000

DISCUSSION QUESTIONS

1. What is a statement of cash flows?
2. How do investors, creditors, and others typically use the information in the statement of cash flows?
3. How is a statement of cash flows different from an income statement?
4. What are cash equivalents? How are cash equivalents reported on the statement of cash flows?
5. What are the three categories into which inflows and outflows of cash are divided? Be sure to describe what is included in each of these three categories.
6. Why are companies required to report noncash investing and financing activities? How are these activities reported?
7. Why are direct exchanges of long-term debt for items of property, plant, and equipment included in supplementary information for the statement of cash flows even though the exchanges do not affect cash?
8. Describe the relationship between changes in cash and changes in noncash assets, liabilities, and stockholders' equity.
9. What are two ways to report a company's net cash flow from operating activities? Briefly describe each method.
10. Why are depreciation, depletion, and amortization added to net income when the indirect method is used to report net cash flows from operating activities?
11. Where do the components of the changes in retained earnings appear in the statement of cash flows? Assume the indirect method is used to prepare the statement of cash flows.
12. How is the sale of equipment at a loss reported on the statement of cash flows? Assume the indirect method is used to prepare the statement of cash flows.
13. What does an increase in inventory imply? How would this increase in inventory be reported under the indirect method?
14. What does an increase in accounts payable imply? How would this increase in accounts payable be reported under the indirect method?
15. Does the fact that the cash flow from operating activities is normally positive imply that cash and cash equivalents usually increase each year?
16. What are the most common sources of cash inflows from financing and investing activities?
17. What are the most common cash outflows related to investing and financing activities?
18. What balance sheet account changes might you expect to find for a company that must rely on sources other than operations to fund its cash outflows?

19. From what source(s) should most companies secure the majority of cash inflows? Why?
20. Why should companies attempt to secure cash for investment in property, plant, and equipment from long-term or permanent sources?
21. *(Appendix 11A)* When using the direct method, which items usually constitute the largest components of cash inflows from operating activities?
22. *(Appendix 11A)* Describe how to compute each of the cash inflows and cash outflows from operating activities under the direct method.
23. *(Appendix 11A)* Why is depreciation expense not generally reported on the statement of cash flows when using the direct method?
24. *(Appendix 11B)* Why do companies often use a spreadsheet to prepare the statement of cash flows?

MULTIPLE-CHOICE EXERCISES

11-1 Which of the following is *not* a use of the statement of cash flows?

a. Aids in the prediction of future cash flow
b. Provides a measure of the future obligations of the company
c. Helps estimate the amount of funds that will be needed from creditors or stockholders
d. Provides insights into the quality and reliability of reported income

11-2 Which of the following would be classified as a cash outflow from an operating activity?

a. Purchase of an investment
b. Payment of dividends
c. Purchase of equipment
d. Payment of goods purchased from suppliers

11-3 Which of the following is an example of a cash inflow from an operating activity?

a. Collection of cash relating to a note receivable
b. Sale of property, plant, and equipment
c. Collection of an account receivable from a credit sale
d. None of these

11-4 Which of the following is an example of a cash outflow from a financing activity?

a. Payment of cash dividends to stockholders
b. Payment of interest on a note payable
c. Payment of wages to employees
d. Issuance of common stock for cash

11-5 Which of the following is true?

a. An increase in cash may result from an increase in liabilities.
b. An increase in cash may result from a decrease in stockholders' equity.
c. An increase in cash may result from an increase in noncash assets.
d. A decrease in cash may result from an increase in liabilities.

11-6 Which of the following statements is true?

a. Cash flow from operating activities must be prepared using the indirect method.
b. The indirect method adjusts sales for changes in noncash items to produce net cash flow from operating activities.
c. Many companies prefer the indirect method because it is easier and less costly to prepare.
d. The FASB prefers the indirect method.

11-7 Mullinix Inc. reported the following information: net income, $40,000; decrease in accounts receivable, $10,000; decrease in accounts payable, $8,000; and depreciation expense, $6,000. What amount did Mullinix report as cash flow from operating activities on its statement of cash flows?

a. $16,000
b. $36,000
c. $48,000
d. $64,000

11-8 Which item is added to net income when computing cash flows from operating activities?

a. Gain on the disposal of property, plant, and equipment
b. Increase in wages payable
c. Increase in inventory
d. Increase in prepaid rent

Use the following information for Multiple-Choice Exercises 11-9 and 11-10:
Cornett Company reported the following information: cash received from the issuance of common stock, $125,400; cash received from the sale of equipment, $26,500; cash paid to purchase an investment, $12,800; cash paid to retire a note payable, $30,000; cash collected from sales to customers, $248,000.

11-9 Refer to the information for Cornett Company above. What amount should Cornett report on its statement of cash flows as net cash flows provided by investing activities?

a. $13,700
b. $39,300
c. $86,100
d. None of these

11-10 Refer to the information for Cornett Company above. What amount should Cornett report on its statement of cash flows as net cash flows from financing activities?

a. $82,600
b. $95,400
c. $108,200
d. None of these

11-11 Chasse Building Supply Inc. reported net cash provided by operating activities of $243,000, capital expenditures of $112,900, cash dividends of $35,800, and average maturities of long-term debt over the next five years of $122,300. What is Chasse's free cash flow and cash flow adequacy ratio?

a. $94,300 and 0.77, respectively
b. $94,300 and 0.82, respectively
c. $130,100 and 1.06, respectively
d. $165,900 and 1.36, respectively

11-12 Smoltz Company reported the following information for the current year: cost of goods sold, $315,100; increase in inventory, $14,700; and increase in accounts payable, $8,200. What is the amount of cash paid to suppliers that Smoltz would report on its statement of cash flows under the direct method?

a. $292,200
b. $308,600
c. $321,600
d. $338,000

11-13 Romo Inc. reported the following information for the current year: operating expenses, $210,000; increase in prepaid expenses, $4,900; and decrease in accrued liabilities, $6,100. What is the amount of cash paid for operating expenses that Romo would report on its statement of cash flows under the direct method?

a. $199,000
b. $208,800
c. $211,200
d. $221,000

CORNERSTONE EXERCISES

Cornerstone Exercise 11-14 Classification of Cash Flows

OBJECTIVE ②
CORNERSTONE 11-1

Stanfield Inc. reported the following items in its statement of cash flows presented using the indirect method.

a. Decrease in inventory
b. Paid a cash dividend to stockholders
c. Purchased equipment for cash
d. Issued long-term debt
e. Depreciation expense
f. Sold a building for cash

(Continued)

Required:

Indicate whether each item should be classified as a cash flow from operating activities, a cash flow from investing activities, or a cash flow from financing activities.

OBJECTIVE ②
CORNERSTONE 11-1

Cornerstone Exercise 11-15 Classification of Cash Flows

Patel Company reported the following items in its statement of cash flows presented using the indirect method.

a. Issuance of common stock
b. Cash paid for interest
c. Sold equipment for cash

d. Receipt of cash dividend on investment
e. Repayment of principal on long-term debt
f. Loss on disposal of equipment.

Required:

Indicate whether each item should be classified as a cash flow from operating activities, a cash flow from investing activities, or a cash flow from financing activities.

> *Use the following information for Cornerstone Exercises 11-16 and 11-17:*
> A review of the balance sheet of Peterson Inc. revealed the following changes in the account balances:
>
> a. Increase in long-term investment
> b. Increase in accounts receivable
> c. Increase in common stock
> d. Increase in long-term debt
>
> e. Decrease in accounts payable
> f. Decrease in supplies inventory
> g. Increase in prepaid insurance
> h. Decrease in retained earnings

OBJECTIVE ②
CORNERSTONE 11-1

Cornerstone Exercise 11-16 Classification of Cash Flows

Refer to the information for Peterson Inc. above.

Required:

Classify each change in the balance sheet account as a cash flow from operating activities (indirect method), a cash flow from investing activities, a cash flow from financing activities, or a noncash investing and financing activity.

OBJECTIVE ③
CORNERSTONE 11-2

Cornerstone Exercise 11-17 Analyzing the Accounts

Refer to the information for Peterson Inc. above.

Required:

Indicate whether each of the changes above produces a cash inflow, a cash outflow, or is a non-cash activity.

OBJECTIVE ④
CORNERSTONE 11-3

Cornerstone Exercise 11-18 Computing Net Cash Flow from Operating Activities

An analysis of the balance sheet and income statement of Sanchez Company revealed the following: net income, $12,750; depreciation expense, $32,600; decrease in accounts receivable, $21,500; increase in inventory, $18,300; increase in accounts payable, $19,800; and a decrease in interest payable of $1,200.

Required:

Compute the net cash flows from operating activities using the indirect method.

OBJECTIVE ④
CORNERSTONE 11-3

Cornerstone Exercise 11-19 Computing Net Cash Flow from Operating Activities

Brandon Inc. reported the following items in its balance sheet and income statement: net income, $92,600; gain on disposal of equipment, $15,800; increase in accounts receivable, $17,400; decrease in accounts payable, $27,900; and increase in common stock, $50,000.

Required:

Compute the net cash flows from operating activities using the indirect method.

Cornerstone Exercise 11-20 Computing Net Cash Flow from Investing Activities

OBJECTIVE 5
CORNERSTONE 11-4

Davis Inc. reported the following information for equipment:

	12/31/2011	12/31/2010
Equipment	$160,000	$115,000
Accumulated depreciation	(85,000)	(59,000)
Long-term investment	18,610	10,000

In addition, Davis sold equipment costing $12,500 with accumulated depreciation of $8,150 for $3,800 cash, producing a $550 loss. Davis reported net income for 2011 of $122,350.

Required:
Compute net cash flow from investing activities.

Cornerstone Exercise 11-21 Computing Net Cash Flow from Financing Activities

OBJECTIVE 6
CORNERSTONE 11-5

Hebert Company reported the following information for 2011:

Repaid long-term debt	$50,000
Paid interest on note payable	1,320
Issued common stock	25,000
Paid dividends	12,000

Required:
Compute net cash flow from financing activities.

Cornerstone Exercise 11-22 Analyzing the Statement of Cash Flows

OBJECTIVE 7
CORNERSTONE 11-6

Rollins Inc. is considering expanding its operations into different regions of the country; however, this expansion will require significant cash flow as well as additional financing. Rollins reported the following information for 2011: cash provided by operating activities, $387,200; cash provided by investing activities, $108,700; average debt maturing over the next five years, $345,500; capital expenditures, $261,430; dividends, $40,000.

Required:
Compute free cash flow and the cash flow adequacy ratio. (*Note:* Round ratio to two decimal places.) Comment on Rollins' ability to expand its operations.

Cornerstone Exercise 11-23 (Appendix 11A) Cash Receipts from Customers

OBJECTIVE 8
CORNERSTONE 11-7

Singleton Inc. had accounts receivable of $391,400 at January 1, 2011, and $418,650 at December 31, 2011. Net income for 2011 was $550,000 and sales revenue was $925,000.

Required:
Compute the amount of cash collected from customers using the direct method.

Cornerstone Exercise 11-24 (Appendix 11A) Cash Payments to Suppliers

OBJECTIVE 8
CORNERSTONE 11-7

Blackmon Company reported net income of $805,000 and cost of goods sold of $1,525,000 on its 2011 income statement. In addition, Blackmon reported an increase in inventory of $65,410, a decrease in prepaid insurance of $12,800, and a decrease in accounts payable of $43,190.

Required:
Compute the amount of cash payments to suppliers using the direct method.

Cornerstone Exercise 11-25 (Appendix 11A) Cash Payments for Operating Expenses

OBJECTIVE 8
CORNERSTONE 11-7

Luna Inc. reported operating expenses of $174,500, excluding depreciation expense of $36,200 for 2011. During 2011, Luna reported a decrease in prepaid expenses of $8,500 and a decrease in accrued liabilities of $18,200.

Required:
Compute the amount of cash payments for operating expenses using the direct method.

EXERCISES

OBJECTIVE **2**

Exercise 11-26 Classification of Cash Flows

A review of the financial records for Rogers Inc. uncovered the following items:

a. Collected accounts receivable
b. Paid cash to purchase equipment
c. Received cash from the issuance of bonds
d. Paid interest on long-term debt
e. Sold equipment at book value
f. Depreciation on equipment
g. Issued common stock for land
h. Paid rent on building for the current period

i. Paid cash to settle an account payable
j. Declared and paid dividends to stockholders
k. Received cash dividend on investment
l. Repaid the principal amount of long-term debt
m. Amortization of a copyright
n. Sold a long-term investment at a gain

Rogers uses the indirect method to prepare the operating activities of its statement of cash flows.

Required:

Indicate whether each item should be classified as a cash flow from operating activities, a cash flow from investing activities, a cash flow from financing activities, or a noncash investing and financing activity.

OBJECTIVE **2**

Exercise 11-27 Classification of Cash Flows

The following are several items that might be disclosed on a company's statement of cash flows presented using the indirect method.

a. Net income
b. Depreciation expense
c. Issuance of common stock
d. Loss on disposal of equipment
e. Purchase of a building

f. Decrease in accounts payable
g. Converted bonds into common stock
h. Sale of long-term investment
i. Payment of interest
j. Increase in inventory

Required:

1. Indicate whether each item should be classified as a cash flow from operating activities, a cash flow from investing activities, a cash flow from financing activities, or a noncash investing and financing activity.

2. Why is the proper classification of cash flows important?

OBJECTIVE **3**

Exercise 11-28 Analyzing the Accounts

A review of the balance sheet of Mathews Company revealed the following changes in the account balances:

a. Increase in accounts receivable
b. Increase in retained earnings
c. Decrease in salaries payable
d. Increase in common stock

e. Decrease in inventory
f. Increase in accounts payable
g. Decrease in long-term debt
h. Increase in property, plant, and equipment

Required:

1. For each of the above items, indicate whether it produces a cash inflow or a cash outflow.
2. Classify each change as a cash flow from operating activities (indirect method), a cash flow from investing activities, or a cash flow from financing activities.

OBJECTIVE **3**

Exercise 11-29 Analyzing the Accounts

Casey Company engaged in the following transactions:

a. Made credit sales of $615,000. The cost of the merchandise sold was $417,500
b. Collected accounts receivable in the amount of $592,800
c. Purchased goods on credit in the amount of $445,150
d. Paid accounts payable in the amount of $403,200

Required:

Prepare the journal entries necessary to record the transactions. Indicate whether each transaction increased cash, decreased cash, or had no effect on cash.

Exercise 11-30 Analyzing the Accounts

The controller for Summit Sales Inc. provides the following information on transactions that occurred during the year:

a. Purchased supplies on credit, $28,400
b. Paid $24,600 cash toward the purchase in transaction *a*
c. Provided services to customers on credit, $41,800
d. Collected $33,650 cash from accounts receivable
e. Recorded depreciation expense, $10,350
f. Employee salaries accrued, $16,200
g. Paid $16,200 cash to employees for salaries earned
h. Accrued interest expense on long-term debt, $1,400
i. Paid a total of $15,000 on long-term debt, which includes $1,400 interest from transaction *h*

j. Paid $1,850 cash for one year's insurance coverage in advance
k. Recognized insurance expense, $1,125, that was paid in a previous period
l. Sold equipment with a book value of $5,700 for $5,700 cash
m. Declared cash dividend, $10,000
n. Paid cash dividend declared in transaction *m*
o. Purchased new equipment for $24,300 cash
p. Issued common stock for $50,000 cash
q. Used $18,100 of supplies to produce revenues

Summit Sales uses the indirect method to prepare its statement of cash flows.

Required:

1. Construct a table similar to the one shown below. Analyze each transaction and indicate its effect on the fundamental accounting equation. If the transaction increases a financial statement element, write the amount of the increase preceded by a plus sign (+) in the appropriate column. If the transaction decreases a financial statement element, write the amount of the decrease preceded by a minus sign (−) in the appropriate column.
2. Indicate whether each transaction results in a cash inflow or a cash outflow in the "Effect on Cash Flows" column. If the transaction has no effect on cash flow, then indicate this by placing "none" in the "Effect on Cash Flows" column.
3. For each transaction that affected cash flows, indicate whether the cash flow would be classified as a cash flow from operating activities, a cash flow from investing activities, or a cash flow from financing activities. If there is no effect on cash flows, indicate this as a noncash activity.

Effect on Accounting Equation

	Assets		Liabilities and Equity			Effect on Cash
Transaction	Current	Noncurrent	Current Liabilities	Noncurrent Liabilities	Equity	Flows

Exercise 11-31 Reporting Net Cash Flow from Operating Activities

The following information is available for Cornelius Inc.:

Selected Income Statement Information	Amount
Net income	$41,000
Depreciation expense	9,200

Selected Balance Sheet Information	Beginning Balance	Ending Balance
Accounts receivable	$21,200	$27,950
Inventory	45,800	40,125
Accounts payable	23,700	32,600

(Continued)

Required:

1. Compute the net cash flows from operating activities using the indirect method.
2. **Conceptual Connection:** Explain why Cornelius was able to report net cash flow from operating activities that was higher than net income.
3. What could the difference between net income and cash flow from operating activities signal to financial statement users?

OBJECTIVE 4

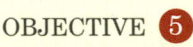

Exercise 11-32 Reporting Net Cash Flow from Operating Activities

The following information is available for Bernard Corporation for 2011:

Net income	$179,200	Decrease in income taxes payable	$ 4,270
Decrease in accounts receivable	7,900	Increase in notes payable (due 2015)	50,000
Increase in inventory	18,300	Depreciation expense	44,700
Decrease in prepaid rent	2,100	Loss on disposal of equipment	11,000
Increase in salaries payable	4,410		

Required:

1. Compute the net cash flows from operating activities using the indirect method.
2. **Conceptual Connection:** What are the causes of the major differences between net income and net cash flow from operating activities?

OBJECTIVE 5

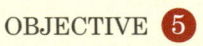

ILLUSTRATING
RELATIONSHIPS

Exercise 11-33 Determining Cash Flows from Investing Activities

Burns Company's 2011 and 2010 balance sheets presented the following data for equipment:

	12/31/2011	12/31/2010
Equipment	$275,000	$225,000
Accumulated depreciation	128,300	92,700
Book value	$146,700	$132,300

During 2011, equipment costing $35,000 with accumulated depreciation of $31,275 was sold for cash, producing a $4,400 gain.

Required:

1. Calculate the amount of depreciation expense for 2011.
2. Calculate the amount of cash spent for equipment during 2011.
3. Calculate the amount that should be included as a cash inflow from the disposal of equipment.

OBJECTIVE 5

ILLUSTRATING
RELATIONSHIPS

Exercise 11-34 Determining Cash Flows from Investing Activities

Airco owns several aircraft and its balance sheet indicated the following amounts for its aircraft accounts at the end of 2011 and 2010:

	12/31/2011	12/31/2010
Equipment, aircraft	$32,700,000	$22,250,000
Accumulated depreciation	13,900,000	13,125,000
Book value	$18,800,000	$ 9,125,000

Required:

1. Assume that Airco did not sell any aircraft during 2011. Determine the amount of depreciation expense for 2011 and the cash spent for aircraft purchases in 2011.
2. If Airco sold for cash aircraft that cost $4,100,000 with accumulated depreciation of $3,825,000, producing a gain of $193,000, determine (a) the amount of depreciation expense, (b) the cash paid for aircraft purchases in 2011, and (c) the cash inflow from the disposal of aircraft.

OBJECTIVE 6

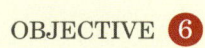

ILLUSTRATING
RELATIONSHIPS

Exercise 11-35 Determining Cash Flows from Financing Activities

Solomon Construction Company reported the following amount on its balance sheet at the end of 2011 and 2010 for notes payable:

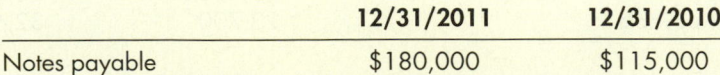

	12/31/2011	12/31/2010
Notes payable	$180,000	$115,000

Required:

1. If Solomon did not repay any notes payable during 2011, determine how much cash Solomon received from the issuance of notes payable.
2. If Solomon repaid $60,000 of notes payable during 2011, determine what amounts Solomon would report in the financing activities section of the statement of cash flows.

Exercise 11-36 Determining Cash Flows from Financing Activities

Nichols Inc. reported the following amounts on its balance sheet at the end of 2011 and 2010 for equity:

	12/31/2011	12/31/2010
Common stock	$164,000	$105,000
Retained earnings	455,490	376,750

Required:

Assume that Nichols did not retire any stock during 2011, it reported $92,630 of net income for 2011, and any dividends declared were paid in cash. Determine the amounts Nichols would report in the financing section of the statement of cash flows.

Exercise 11-37 Partial Statement of Cash Flows

Service Company had net income during the current year of $115,500. The following information was obtained from Service's balance sheet:

Accounts receivable	$22,300 increase
Inventory	28,700 increase
Accounts payable	14,240 decrease
Interest payable	3,180 increase
Accumulated depreciation (equipment)	27,800 increase
Accumulated depreciation (building)	12,340 increase

Additional Information:

1. Equipment with accumulated depreciation of $15,000 was sold during the year.
2. Cash dividends of $36,000 were paid during the year.

Required:

1. Prepare the net cash flows from operating activities using the indirect method.
2. **Conceptual Connection:** How would the cash proceeds from the sale of equipment be reported on the statement of cash flows?
3. **Conceptual Connection:** How would the cash dividends be reported on the statement of cash flows?
4. What could the difference between net income and cash flow from operating activities signal to financial statement users?

Exercise 11-38 Analyzing the Statement of Cash Flows

Information for Ditka Inc. and McMahon Company is given below:

	Ditka Inc.	McMahon Company
Cash provided by operating activities	$2,475,000	$1,639,000
Capital expenditures	1,157,000	748,000
Dividends	285,000	189,000
Average debt maturity over next 5 years	1,988,000	1,212,000

Required:

1. Compute Ditka's and McMahon's free cash flow and cash flow adequacy ratio. (*Note:* Round ratio to two decimal places.)
2. **Conceptual Connection:** What information do these cash-based performance measures provide with regard to the two companies?

OBJECTIVE ④⑤⑥⑦   ## Exercise 11-39 Preparing the Statement of Cash Flows

The comparative balance sheets for Beckwith Products Company are presented below.

	2011	2010
Assets:		
Cash	$ 36,950	$ 25,000
Accounts receivable	75,100	78,000
Inventory	45,300	36,000
Property, plant, and equipment	256,400	153,000
Accumulated depreciation	38,650	20,000
Total assets	$375,100	$272,000
Liabilities and Equity:		
Accounts payable	$ 13,100	$ 11,000
Interest payable	11,500	8,000
Wages payable	8,100	9,000
Notes payable	105,000	90,000
Common stock	100,000	50,000
Retained earnings	137,400	104,000
Total liabilities and equity	$375,100	$272,000

Additional Information:

1. Net income for 2011 was $58,400.
2. Cash dividends of $25,000 were declared and paid during 2011.
3. During 2011, Beckwith issued $50,000 of notes payable and repaid $35,000 principal relating to notes payable.
4. Common stock was issued for $50,000 cash.
5. Depreciation expense was $18,650, and there were no disposals of equipment.

Required:

1. Prepare a statement of cash flows (indirect method) for Beckwith Products for 2011.
2. Compute the following cash-based performance measures: (a) free cash flow, and (b) cash flow adequacy. (*Note:* Assume that the average amount of debt maturing over the next five years is $85,000. Round ratio to two decimal places.)
3. What can you conclude by examining the patterns in Beckwith's cash flows?

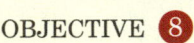

OBJECTIVE ⑧

Exercise 11-40 *(Appendix 11A)* Preparing Net Cash Flows from Operating Activities—Direct Method

Colassard Industries has the following data available for preparation of its statement of cash flows:

Sales revenue	$356,200	Inventory, increase	$ 5,710
Cost of goods sold	182,500	Prepaid insurance, increase	2,100
Wages expense	58,400	Accounts payable, increase	5,680
Insurance expense	8,300	Notes payable, increase	32,000
Interest expense	20,800	Interest payable, increase	3,125
Income taxes expense	16,200	Wages payable, decrease	5,400
Accounts receivable, decrease	14,300		

Required:

Prepare the cash flows from operating activities section of the statement of cash flows, using the direct method.

OBJECTIVE ⑧

Exercise 11-41 *(Appendix 11A)* Preparing a Statement of Cash Flows—Direct Method

The controller of Newstrom Software Inc. provides the following information as the basis for a statement of cash flows:

Cash collected from customers	$785,400	Income taxes paid	$58,300
Cash paid for interest	22,100	Payment of dividends	35,000
Cash paid to employees and other suppliers of goods and services	221,750	Principal payments on mortgage payable	60,000
Cash paid to suppliers of merchandise	395,540	Principal payments on long-term debt	22,000

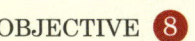

Cash received from the issuance of long-term debt	$ 40,000	Proceeds from the issuance of common stock	$ 85,000
Cash received from disposal of equipment	42,500	Purchase of equipment	120,000
		Purchase of long-term investments	75,800
Cash received from sale of long-term investments	71,400		

Required:

1. Calculate the net cash provided (used) by operating activities.
2. Calculate the net cash provided (used) by investing activities.
3. Calculate the net cash provided (used) by financing activities.

Exercise 11-42 (Appendix 11A) Preparing a Statement of Cash Flows—Direct Method   OBJECTIVE 8

Financial statements for Rowe Publishing Company are presented below.

Rowe Publishing Company
Balance Sheets
December 31, 2011 and 2010

	2011		2010	
ASSETS				
Current assets:				
Cash		$ 85,000		$ 66,000
Accounts receivable		240,000		231,000
Inventory		190,000		170,000
Total current assets		$515,000		$467,000
Property, plant, and equipment:				
Building	$ 400,000		$ 400,000	
Equipment	155,000		130,000	
	$ 555,000		$ 530,000	
Accumulated depreciation	(375,000)		(350,000)	
Net property, plant, and equipment		180,000		180,000
Total assets		$695,000		$647,000

LIABILITIES AND EQUITY				
Current liabilities:				
Accounts payable	$133,000		$121,000	
Salaries payable	15,000		11,000	
Income taxes payable	10,000		17,000	
Total current liabilities		$158,000		$149,000
Long-term liabilities:				
Notes payable	$115,000		$150,000	
Bonds payable	50,000		0	
Total long-term liabilities		165,000		150,000
Total liabilities		$323,000		$299,000
Equity:				
Common stock	$300,000		$300,000	
Retained earnings	72,000		48,000	
Total equity		372,000		348,000
Total liabilities and equity		$695,000		$647,000

Rowe Publishing Company
Income Statement
For the Year Ended
December 31, 2011

Sales		$1,051,000
Less: Cost of goods sold		(578,000)
Gross margin		$ 473,000
Less operating expenses:		
Salaries	$(351,000)	
Depreciation	(25,000)	(376,000)
Income from operations		$ 97,000
Less: Interest expense		(16,000)
Income before taxes		$ 81,000
Less: Income taxes expense		(22,000)
Net income		$ 59,000

Additional information:

1. No buildings nor equipment were sold during 2011. Equipment was purchased for $25,000 cash.
2. Notes payable in the amount of $35,000 were repaid during 2011.
3. Bonds payable of $50,000 were issued for cash during 2011.
4. Rowe Publishing declared and paid dividends of $35,000 during 2011.

Required:

Prepare a statement of cash flows for 2011, using the direct method to determine net cash flow from operating activities.

OBJECTIVE ❾

Exercise 11-43 *(Appendix 11B)* Using a Spreadsheet to Prepare a Statement of Cash Flows

Comparative balance sheets for Cincinnati Health Club are presented below.

Cincinnati Health Club Balance Sheets December 31, 2011 and 2010	2011		2010	
ASSETS				
Current assets:				
Cash		$ 5,300		$ 9,200
Accounts receivable		10,500		8,900
Inventory		19,800		18,600
Total current assets		$ 35,600		$ 36,700
Property, plant, and equipment:				
Building	$ 490,000		$ 490,000	
Equipment	280,000		270,000	
	$ 770,000		$ 760,000	
Accumulated depreciation	(148,000)		(120,000)	
Net property, plant, and equipment		622,000		640,000
Total assets		$657,600		$676,700
LIABILITIES AND EQUITY				
Current liabilities:				
Accounts payable	$ 55,300		$ 36,100	
Salaries payable	9,500		11,700	
Income taxes payable	1,100		9,900	
Total current liabilities		$ 65,900		$ 57,700
Long-term liabilities:				
Bonds payable		350,000		400,000
Total liabilities		$415,900		$457,700
Equity:				
Common stock	$180,000		$150,000	
Retained earnings	61,700		69,000	
Total equity		241,700		219,000
Total liabilities and equity		$657,600		$676,700

Additional information:

1. Cincinnati Health Club reported net income of $2,700 for 2011.
2. No buildings nor equipment were sold during 2011. Equipment was purchased for $10,000 cash.
3. Depreciation expense for 2011 was $28,000.
4. Bonds payable of $50,000 were issued for cash during 2011.
5. Common stock of $30,000 was issued during 2011.
6. Cash dividends of $10,000 were declared and paid during 2011.

Required:

Using a spreadsheet, prepare a statement of cash flows for 2011. Assume Cincinnati Health Club uses the indirect method.

PROBLEM SET A

Problem 11-44A Classifying and Analyzing Business Activities

OBJECTIVE ❷ ❸

CTT Inc. reported the following business activities during 2011:

a. Purchased property, plant, and equipment for cash
b. Purchased merchandise inventory for cash
c. Recorded depreciation on property, plant, and equipment
d. Issued common stock
e. Purchased merchandise inventory on credit
f. Collected cash sales from customers
g. Paid cash dividends
h. Purchased a two-year insurance policy for cash
i. Paid salaries of employees
j. Borrowed cash by issuing a note payable
k. Sold property, plant, and equipment for cash
l. Paid cash for principal amount of mortgage
m. Paid interest on mortgage

Required:

1. Indicate whether each activity should be classified as a cash flow from operating activities, a cash flow from investing activities, a cash flow from financing activities, or a noncash investing and financing activity. Assume that CTT uses the indirect method.
2. For each activity that is reported on the statement of cash flows, indicate whether it produces a cash inflow, a cash outflow, or has no cash effect.

Problem 11-45A Reporting Net Cash Flow from Operating Activities

OBJECTIVE ❹

The income statement for Granville Manufacturing Company is presented below.

Granville Manufacturing Company Income Statement For the Year Ended December 31, 2011		
Sales		$4,199,830
Cost of goods sold		2,787,210
Gross margin		$1,412,620
Operating expenses:		
Salaries expense	$831,800	
Depreciation expense	246,100	
Administrative expense	131,000	
Bad debt expense	51,700	
Other expenses	43,900	1,304,500
Net income		$ 108,120

The following balance sheet changes occurred during the year:

- Accounts receivable increased by $182,400.
- Inventory increased by $98,725.
- Prepaid expenses decreased by $64,100.
- Accounts payable increased by $43,850.
- Salaries payable increased by $54,900.

Required:

1. Prepare the net cash flows from operating activities using the indirect method.
2. **Conceptual Connection:** What are the causes of the major differences between net income and net cash flow from operating activities?

OBJECTIVE

Problem 11-46A Classification of Cash Flows

Rolling Meadows Country Club Inc. is a privately owned corporation that operates a golf club. Rolling Meadows reported the following inflows and outflows of cash during 2011:

Net income	$115,300	Cash received from sale of used golf carts	$ 9,200
Decrease in accounts receivable	5,125	Depreciation expense, buildings	49,100
Increase in pro shop inventory	28,600	Depreciation expense, golf carts	23,700
Increase in prepaid insurance	15,800	Proceeds from issuance of note payable	45,000
Increase in accounts payable	11,400	Payment on mortgage payable	28,000
Decrease in wages payable	9,210	Cash received from issuance of common stock	38,500
Increase in income taxes payable	7,500	Payment of cash dividends	45,000
Cash paid for new golf carts	115,000		

Rolling Meadows had cash on hand at 1/1/11 of $10,300.

Required:

1. Prepare a properly formatted statement of cash flows using the indirect method.
2. What can you conclude by examining the patterns in Rolling Meadow's cash flows?

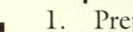

OBJECTIVE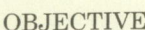

Problem 11-47A Preparing a Statement of Cash Flows

Erie Company reported the following comparative balance sheets:

	2011	2010
Assets:		
Cash	$ 33,200	$ 12,750
Accounts receivable	53,000	44,800
Inventory	29,500	27,500
Prepaid rent	2,200	6,200
Investments (long-term)	17,600	31,800
Property, plant, and equipment	162,000	149,450
Accumulated depreciation	(61,600)	(56,200)
Total assets	$235,900	$216,300
Liabilities and Equity:		
Accounts payable	$ 16,900	$ 19,500
Interest payable	3,500	4,800
Wages payable	9,600	7,100
Income taxes payable	5,500	3,600
Notes payable	28,000	53,000
Common stock	100,000	68,500
Retained earnings	72,400	59,800
Total liabilities and equity	$235,900	$216,300

Additional information:

1. Net income for 2011 was $20,500.
2. Cash dividends of $7,900 were declared and paid during 2011.
3. Long-term investments with a cost of $28,600 were sold for cash at a gain of $4,100. Additional long-term investments were purchased for $14,400 cash.
4. Equipment with a cost of $14,800 and accumulated depreciation of $13,500 was sold for $3,800 cash. New equipment was purchased for $27,350 cash.
5. Depreciation expense was $18,900.
6. A principal payment of $25,000 was made on long-term notes.
7. Common stock was sold for $31,500 cash.

Required:

Prepare a statement of cash flows for Erie, using the indirect method to compute net cash flow from operating activities.

Problem 11-48A Preparing a Statement of Cash Flows

Monon Cable Television Company reported the following financial statements for 2011:

Monon Cable Television Company
Balance Sheets
December 31, 2011 and 2010

	2011	2010
ASSETS		
Current assets:		
Cash	$ 2,000	$ 8,000
Accounts receivable	11,300	6,000
Supplies	1,200	1,700
Total current assets	$ 14,500	$ 15,700
Property, plant, and equipment:		
Equipment (antenna)	$ 60,000	$ 35,000
Buildings	210,000	190,000
Trucks	81,000	75,000
	$ 351,000	$ 300,000
Accumulated depreciation	(125,000)	(131,000)
Net property, plant, and equipment	226,000	169,000
Total assets	$240,500	$184,700
LIABILITIES AND EQUITY		
Current liabilities:		
Accounts payable	$ 6,500	$ 8,000
Rent payable	4,900	13,600
Royalties payable	3,300	3,100
Total current liabilities	$ 14,700	$ 24,700
Long-term liabilities:		
Notes payable (long-term)	40,000	0
Total liabilities	$ 54,700	$ 24,700
Equity:		
Common stock	$100,000	$100,000
Retained earnings	85,800	60,000
Total equity	185,800	160,000
Total liabilities and equity	$240,500	$184,700

Monon Cable Television Company
Income Statement
For the Year Ended December 31, 2011

Sales		$ 519,000
Less operating expenses:		
Royalties expense	$(240,000)	
Salaries expense	(26,000)	
Utilities expense	(83,000)	
Supplies expense	(13,000)	
Rent expense	(79,000)	
Depreciation expense	(28,000)	(469,000)
Income from operations		$ 50,000
Other income (expenses):		
Gain on disposal of property, plant, and equipment	$ 800	
Interest expense	(1,800)	(1,000)
Income before taxes		$ 49,000
Less: Income taxes expense		(9,000)
Net income		$ 40,000

Additional information:

1. Equipment (an old antenna) with a cost of $35,000 and accumulated depreciation of $34,000 was taken down and sold as scrap for $1,800 cash during 2011. A new antenna was purchased for cash at an installed cost of $60,000.
2. A building was purchased for $20,000 cash.
3. Trucks were purchased for $6,000 cash.
4. Depreciation expense for 2011 was $28,000.
5. A long-term note payable was issued for $40,000 cash.
6. Dividends of $14,200 were paid during 2011.

Required:

1. Prepare a statement of cash flows, using the indirect method to compute net cash flow from operating activities.
2. **Conceptual Connection:** Explain what has been responsible for the decrease in cash.

Problem 11-49A (Appendix 11A) Preparing Net Cash Flows from Operating Activities—Direct Method

Yogurt Plus, a restaurant, collected the following information on inflows and outflows for 2011:

Inflows		Outflows	
Sales (all for cash)	$334,500	Cash payments made for merchandise sold	$176,450
Cash received from sale of common stock	72,000	Cash payments for operating expenses	115,210
Proceeds from issuance of long-term notes payable	50,000	Cash payments for interest	24,600
		Cash payments for income taxes	9,475
Proceeds from sale of used restaurant furniture	11,300	Purchase of restaurant furniture for cash	108,800
		Principal payment on mortgage	35,000
Proceeds from issuance of short-term note payable	15,000	Payment of dividends	10,000
Notes payable issued in exchange for kitchen equipment	30,000	Cost of kitchen equipment acquired in exchange for note payable	30,000

Yogurt Plus had a cash balance of $21,800 at 1/1/11.

(Continued)

Required:

1. Prepare a statement of cash flows, using the direct method to determine net cash flow from operating activities.

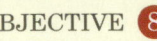

2. What can you conclude by examining the patterns in Yogurt Plus's cash flows?

OBJECTIVE ❽

Problem 11-50A *(Appendix 11A)* Preparing Net Cash Flows from Operating Activities—Direct Method

Refer to the information for Granville Manufacturing Company in **Problem 11-45A**.

Required:

Prepare the cash flows from operating activities section of the statement of cash flows, using the direct method.

OBJECTIVE ❾

Problem 11-51A *(Appendix 11B)* Using a Spreadsheet to Prepare a Statement of Cash Flows

Jane Bahr, a controller of Endicott & Thurston, prepared the following balance sheets at the end of 2011 and 2010:

Endicott & Thurston Associates
Balance Sheets
December 31, 2011 and 2010

	2011	2010
ASSETS		
Current assets:		
Cash	$ 2,000	$ 17,000
Accounts receivable	78,000	219,000
Prepaid rent	29,000	104,000
Total current assets	$109,000	$340,000
Long-term investments	51,000	40,000
Property, plant, and equipment:		
Equipment, computing	$ 488,000	$ 362,000
Furniture	400,000	365,000
	$ 888,000	$ 727,000
Accumulated depreciation	(366,000)	(554,000)
Net property, plant, and equipment	522,000	173,000
Total assets	$682,000	$553,000

	2011	2010
LIABILITIES AND EQUITY		
Current liabilities:		
Accounts payable	$ 56,000	$ 58,000
Salaries payable	89,000	105,000
Total current liabilities	$145,000	$163,000
Long-term liabilities:		
Notes payable, long-term	80,000	105,000
Bonds payable	140,000	0
Total liabilities	$365,000	$268,000
Equity:		
Common stock	$225,000	$225,000
Retained earnings	92,000	60,000
Total equity	317,000	285,000
Total liabilities and equity	$682,000	$553,000

Additional information:

1. Computing equipment with a cost of $250,000 and accumulated depreciation of $230,000 was sold for $5,000. New computing equipment was purchased for $376,000.
2. New office furniture was purchased at a cost of $35,000.
3. Depreciation expense for 2011 was $42,000.
4. Investments costing $20,000 were sold for cash at a loss of $2,000. Additional investments were purchased for $31,000 cash.
5. A $25,000 principal payment on the long-term note was made during 2011.
6. A portion of the cash needed to purchase computing equipment was secured by issuing bonds payable for $140,000 cash.
7. Net income was $70,000 and dividends were $38,000.

Required:

1. Using a spreadsheet, prepare a statement of cash flows for 2011. Assume Endicott & Thurston use the indirect method.
2. **Conceptual Connection:** Discuss whether Endicott & Thurston appear to have matched the timing of inflows and outflows of cash.

PROBLEM SET B

Problem 11-44B Classifying and Analyzing Business Activities

OBJECTIVE

Cowell Company had the following business activities during 2011:

a. Paid cash dividend to shareholders
b. Paid cash for inventory
c. Purchased equipment for cash
d. Paid interest on long-term debt
e. Acquired land in exchange for common stock
f. Issued common stock for cash

g. Paid salaries to employees
h. Received cash from the sale of merchandise
i. Recorded amortization related to an intangible asset
j. Issued bonds payable in exchange for cash
k. Sold equipment for cash
l. Purchased inventory on account

Cowell Company uses the indirect method to prepare its statement of cash flows.

Required:
1. Indicate whether each activity should be classified as a cash flow from operating activities, a cash flow from investing activities, a cash flow from financing activities, or a noncash investing and financing activity.
2. For each activity that is reported on the statement of cash flows, indicate whether each activity produces a cash inflow, a cash outflow, or has no cash effect.

Problem 11-45B Reporting Net Cash Flow from Operating Activities

OBJECTIVE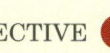

The income statement for Dunn Products Inc. is presented below.

Dunn Products Inc. Income Statement For the Year Ended December 31, 2011		
Sales		$3,584,600
Cost of goods sold		2,557,500
Gross margin		$1,027,100
Other expenses:		
Salaries expense	$455,100	
Administrative expense	247,000	
Depreciation expense	214,500	
Bad debt expense	37,000	
Income taxes expense	28,200	981,800
Net income		$ 45,300

The following balance sheet changes occurred during the year:

- Accounts receivable decreased by $85,150
- Inventory decreased by $138,620
- Prepaid expenses increased by $112,400
- Accounts payable decreased by $67,225
- Salaries payable increased by $18,300

Required:
1. Prepare the net cash flows from operating activities using the indirect method.
2. **Conceptual Connection:** What are the causes of the major differences between net income and net cash flow from operating activities?

OBJECTIVE

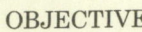

Problem 11-46B Classification of Cash Flows

Fannin Company is a manufacturer of premium athletic equipment. Fannin reported the following inflows and outflows of cash during 2011.

Net income	$574,250	Cash received from sale of investment	$ 12,350
Increase in accounts receivable	34,600	Cash paid for property, plant, and equipment	114,410
Decrease in inventory	59,400	Depreciation expense	103,300
Decrease in prepaid insurance	45,800	Proceeds from issuance of note payable	25,000
Decrease in accounts payable	39,600	Payment on bonds payable	182,000
Decrease in income taxes payable	11,200	Cash received from issuance of common stock	25,000
Increase in wages payable	28,800	Payment of cash dividends	21,000

Fannin had cash on hand at 1/1/11 of $218,500.

Required:
1. Prepare a properly formatted statement of cash flows using the indirect method.
2. What can you conclude by examining the patterns in Fannin's cash flows?

OBJECTIVE

Problem 11-47B Preparing a Statement of Cash Flows

Volusia Company reported the following comparative balance sheets for 2011:

Volusia Company
Balance Sheet
December 31, 2010 and 2011

	2011	2010
ASSETS		
Cash	$ 28,100	$ 16,300
Accounts receivable	26,500	32,725
Inventory	24,100	28,200
Prepaid rent	3,900	1,800
Investments, long-term	37,200	25,500
Property, plant, and equipment	115,000	102,975
Accumulated depreciation	(47,100)	(38,600)
Total assets	$187,700	$168,900
LIABILITIES AND EQUITY		
Accounts payable	$ 24,900	$ 21,200
Interest payable	4,700	3,300
Wages payable	4,600	6,900
Income taxes payable	3,500	5,200
Notes payable	35,000	30,000
Common stock	72,900	65,000
Retained earnings	42,100	37,300
Total liabilities and equity	$187,700	$168,900

Additional information:
1. Net income for 2011 was $18,300.
2. Cash dividends of $13,500 were declared and paid during 2011.
3. Long-term investments with a cost of $21,200 were sold for cash at a loss of $1,500. Additional long-term investments were purchased for $32,900 cash.
4. Equipment with a cost of $25,000 and accumulated depreciation of $16,300 was sold for $4,500 cash. New equipment was purchased for $37,025 cash.
5. Depreciation expense was $24,800.
6. A principal payment of $15,000 was made on long-term notes. Volusia issued notes payable for $20,000 cash.
7. Common stock was sold for $7,900 cash.

Required:
Prepare a statement of cash flows for Volusia, using the indirect method to compute net cash flow from operating activities.

Problem 11-48B Preparing a Statement of Cash Flows

OBJECTIVE

SDPS Inc. provides airport transportation services in southern California. An income statement for 2011 and balance sheets for 2011 and 2010 appear below.

SDPS Inc. Balance Sheets December 31, 2011 and 2010			
		2011	2010
ASSETS			
Current assets:			
Cash		$ 40,000	$ 82,000
Accounts receivable		126,000	109,000
Supplies, fuel		11,000	25,000
Total current assets		$177,000	$216,000
Property, plant, and equipment:			
Equipment, vehicles	$ 524,000		$ 409,000
Accumulated depreciation	(174,000)		(136,000)
Net property, plant, and equipment		350,000	273,000
Total assets		$527,000	$489,000
LIABILITIES AND EQUITY			
Current liabilities:			
Accounts payable	$103,000		$ 58,000
Wages payable	22,000		29,000
Repair and maintenance payable	41,000		34,000
Rent payable	92,000		51,000
Total current liabilities		$258,000	$172,000
Long-term liabilities:			
Notes payable, long-term		100,000	125,000
Total liabilities		$358,000	$297,000
Equity:			
Common stock	$150,000		$150,000
Retained earnings	19,000		42,000
Total equity		169,000	192,000
Total liabilities and equity		$527,000	$489,000

SDPS Inc. Income Statement For the Year Ended December 31, 2011		
Sales		$ 937,000
Less operating expenses:		
Wages expense	$(278,000)	
Rent expense	(229,000)	
Supplies expense	(83,000)	
Maintenance expense	(138,000)	
Depreciation expense	(215,000)	(943,000)
Income (loss) from operations		$ (6,000)
Other income (expenses):		
Loss on disposal of property, plant, and equipment	$ (3,000)	
Interest expense	(14,000)	(17,000)
Net loss		$ (23,000)

Additional information:

1. Vehicles with a cost of $310,000 and accumulated depreciation of $177,000 were sold for $130,000 cash. New vehicles were purchased for $425,000 cash.
2. A $25,000 principal payment on the long-term note was made during 2011.
3. No dividends were paid during 2011.

Required:

1. Prepare a statement of cash flows, using the indirect method to compute net cash flow from operating activities.
2. **Conceptual Connection:** Explain what has been responsible for the decrease in cash.
3. **Conceptual Connection:** Determine how SDPS financed its increase in net property, plant, and equipment during a period in which it had a substantial net loss.

Problem 11-49B (Appendix 11A) Preparing Net Cash Flows from Operating Activities—Direct Method

OBJECTIVE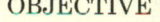

Befuddled Corporation collected the following information on inflows and outflows for 2011:

Inflows

Cash collections from sales	$956,500
Proceeds from disposal of equipment	11,250
Proceeds received from issuance of notes payable	30,000

Outflows

Cash payments for cost of goods sold	$534,900
Cash payments for operating expenses	193,200
Cash payments for interest	36,400
Cash payments for income taxes	21,300
Cash payments for purchases of equipment	217,150
Repayment of short-term notes payable	20,000
Payment of cash dividends	38,000

Befuddled had a cash balance of $89.200 on 1/1/11.

(Continued)

Required:

1. Prepare a statement of cash flows, using the direct method to determine net cash flow from operating activities.

2. What can you conclude by examining the patterns in Befuddled's cash flows?

OBJECTIVE ❽

Problem 11-50B *(Appendix 11A)* Preparing Net Cash Flows from Operating Activities—Direct Method

Refer to the information for Dunn Products Inc. in **Problem 11-45B.**

Required:

Prepare the cash flows from operating activities section of the statement of cash flows, using the direct method.

OBJECTIVE ❾

Problem 11-51B *(Appendix 11B)* Using a Spreadsheet to Prepare a Statement of Cash Flows

Fleet Limousine Service Inc. began operations in late March 2011. At the end of 2011, the following balance sheet was prepared for Fleet.

Fleet Limousine Service Inc.
Balance Sheets
December 31, 2011

	2011	2010
ASSETS		
Current assets:		
Cash	$ 7,200	
Accounts receivable	15,900	
Supplies	3,100	
Total current assets		$ 26,200
Long-term investments		15,000
Property, plant, and equipment:		
Land	$ 11,000	
Building	175,000	
Equipment	233,400	
	$419,400	
Accumulated depreciation	(35,500)	
Net property, plant, and equipment		383,900
Total assets		$425,100
LIABILITIES AND EQUITY		
Current liabilities:		
Accounts payable	$ 12,700	
Unearned service revenue	21,800	
Salaries payable	4,600	
Rent payable	8,200	
Total current liabilities		$ 47,300
Long-term liabilities:		
Notes payable		95,000
Total liabilities		$142,300
Equity:		
Common stock	$300,000	
Retained earnings	(17,200)	
Total equity		282,800
Total liabilities and equity		$425,100

Additional information:

1. During 2011, land was purchased for $11,000, a building was purchased for $175,000, and equipment was purchased for $233,400.
2. Depreciation expense for 2011 was $35,500.
3. The long-term note was issued for $100,000, and a principal payment of $5,000 was made during 2011.
4. Common stock was issued for $300,000 cash during 2011.
5. During 2011, there was a net loss of 17,200 and no dividends were paid.

Required:

1. Using a spreadsheet, prepare a statement of cash flows for 2011. Assume Fleet Limousine uses the indirect method.
2. **Conceptual Connection:** Discuss whether Fleet Limousine appears to have matched the timing of inflows and outflows of cash.

CASES

Case 11-52 The Statement of Cash Flows and Credit Analysis

June's Camera Shop sells cameras and photographic supplies of all types to retail customers. June's also repairs cameras and provides color prints. To compete with other camera
departments, June's offers fast, efficient, and effective repairs and photographic processing.
For fiscal 2011 and 2010, June's accountant prepared the following statements of cash
flows:

June's Camera Shop
Statements of Cash Flows
For the Years Ended January 31, 2011 and 2010

	2011	2010
Cash flows from operating activities		
Net income	$ 87,000	$ 63,000
Adjustments to reconcile net income to net cash provided by operating activities:		
Depreciation expense	$ 41,000	$ 37,000
Increase in accounts receivable	(17,000)	(12,000)
Increase in inventory	(19,000)	(11,000)
Increase in accounts payable	15,000	14,000
Increase in wages payable	11,000	5,000
Increase in income taxes payable	6,000	3,000
Total adjustments	37,000	36,000
Net cash provided by operating activities	$124,000	$ 99,000
Cash flows from investing activities		
Purchase of long-term investments	$(15,000)	$(10,000)
Purchase of equipment	(45,000)	(40,000)
Net cash used by investing activities	(60,000)	(50,000)
Cash flows from financing activities		
Principal payments on mortgage	$(15,000)	$(15,000)
Payment of dividends	(12,000)	(10,000)
Net cash used by financing activities	(27,000)	(25,000)
Net increase in cash and cash equivalents	$ 37,000	$ 24,000
Cash and cash equivalents at beginning of year	158,000	134,000
Cash and cash equivalents at end of year	$195,000	$158,000

Required:

1. Does June's Camera Shop appear to have grown (in terms of property, plant, and
   equipment) during the past two years?
2. June's president, June Smith, would like to open a second store. Smith believes that
   $225,000 is needed to equip the facility properly. The business has $100,000 of cash and liquid investments to apply toward the $225,000 required. Do the data in the 2011 and 2010
   statements of cash flow suggest whether or not June's Camera Shop is likely to be able to
   secure a loan for the remaining $125,000 needed for the expansion?
3. How long should it take June's Camera Shop to pay back the $125,000?

Case 11-53 Profitability Declines and the Statement of Cash Flows

The Bookbarn Inc. is a retail seller of new books in a moderate-sized city. Although initially
very successful, The Bookbarn's sales volume has declined since the opening of two competing bookstores two years ago. The accountant for The Bookbarn prepared the following
statement of cash flows at the end of the current year:

(Continued)

The Bookbarn Inc. Statement of Cash Flows For the Year Ended December 31, 2011		
Cash flows from operating activities		
Net income		$ 26,500
Adjustments to reconcile net income to net cash provided		
by operating activities:		
Depreciation expense	$ 38,500	
Loss on disposal of property, plant, and equipment	2,100	
Increase in accounts receivable	(1,200)	
Increase in inventory	(3,800)	
Increase in accounts payable	6,700	
Decrease in wages payable	(1,200)	
Total adjustments		41,100
Net cash provided by operating activities		$ 67,600
Cash flows from investing activities		
Purchase of equipment	$(12,000)	
Proceeds from disposal of equipment	2,300	
Net cash used by investing activities		(9,700)
Cash flows from financing activities		
Payment of dividends	$ (4,000)	
Repayment of mortgage	(10,000)	
Net cash used by financing activities		(14,000)
Net increase in cash		$ 43,900

Your analysis suggests that The Bookbarn's net income will continue to decline by $8,000 per year to $18,500 as sales continue to fall. Thereafter, you expect sales to stabilize.

Required:
1. What will happen to the amount of cash provided by operations as net income decreases?
2. Assume that equipment is nearly fully depreciated but that it will be fully serviceable for several years. What will happen to cash flows from operations as depreciation declines?
3. Do the operations of businesses experiencing declining sales volumes always consume cash? Explain your answer.
4. Can current assets and current liabilities buffer operating cash flows against the impact of declines in sales volume in the short run? In the long run? Explain your answer.

Case 11-54 Preparing a Prospective Statement of Cash Flows

Jane and Harvey Wentland have decided to open a retail athletic supply store, Fitness Outfitters Inc. They will stock clothing, shoes, and supplies used in running, swimming, bicycling, weight lifting, and other exercise and athletic activities. During their first year of operations, 2011, they expect the following results. (Subsequent years are expected to be more successful.)

Sales revenue	$ 629,000
Less: Cost of goods sold	(291,000)
Gross margin	$ 338,000
Less: Operating expenses	(355,000)
Net loss	$ (17,000)

By the end of 2011, Fitness Outfitters needs to have a cash balance of $5,000 and is expected to have the following partial balance sheet:

ASSETS		
Inventory		$ 53,000
Equipment	$97,000	
Accumulated depreciation, equipment	15,000	82,000
LIABILITIES AND EQUITY		
Accounts payable		$ 37,000
Common stock		100,000
Retained earnings		(17,000)

Assume that all sales will be for cash and that equipment will be acquired for cash.

Required:

1. Prepare as much of the statement of cash flows for 2011 as you can. Use the direct method to determine cash flows from operations.
2. In the statement that you prepared for requirement 1, by how much does the prospective cash balance exceed or fall short of the desired cash balance? If a shortfall occurs, where would you suggest that Jane and Harvey seek additional cash?
3. Does the preparation of a prospective statement of cash flows seem worthwhile for an ongoing business? Why?

Case 11-55 Income, Cash Flow, and Future Losses

On January 1, 2009, Cermack National Bank loaned $5,000,000 under a two-year, zero coupon note to a real estate developer. The bank recognized interest revenue on this note of approximately $400,000 per year. Due to an economic downturn, the developer was unable to pay the $5,800,000 maturity amount on December 31, 2010. The bank convinced the developer to pay $800,000 on December 31, 2010, and agreed to extend $5,000,000 credit to the developer despite the gloomy economic outlook for the next several years. Thus, on December 31, 2010, the bank issued a new two-year, zero coupon note to the developer to mature on December 31, 2012, for $6,000,000. The bank recognized interest revenue on this note of approximately $500,000 per year.

The bank's external auditor insisted that the riskiness of the new loan be recognized by increasing the allowance for uncollectible notes by $1,500,000 on December 31, 2010, and $2,000,000 on December 31, 2011. On December 31, 2012, the bank received $1,200,000 from the developer and learned that the developer was in bankruptcy and that no additional amounts would be recovered.

Required:

1. Prepare a schedule showing annual cash flows for the two notes in each of the four years.
2. Prepare a schedule showing the effect of the notes on net income in each of the four years.
3. Which figure, net income or net cash flow, does the better job of telling the bank's stockholders about the effect of these notes on the bank? Explain by reference to the schedules prepared in requirements 1 and 2.
4. A commonly used method for predicting future cash flows is to predict future income and adjust it for anticipated differences between net income and net cash flow. Does the Cermack National Bank case shed any light on the justification for using net income in this way rather than simply predicting future cash flows by reference to past cash flows?

Case 11-56 Researching Accounting Standards: Dissenting Views and the Statement of Cash Flows

The preparation of cash flow statements is required by generally accepted accounting principles. This accounting standard was initially adopted by a four-to-three vote of the FASB. Several members of the Board took exception to various aspects of the statement, including (1) the classification of interest and dividends received and interest paid as cash flows from operations and (2) the use of the indirect method.

Required:

Obtain a copy of Statement of Financial Accounting Standards No. 95 (FAS 95) from the FASB website. This can be obtained by: (1) entering the following web address in your browser: http://www.fasb.org, (2) highlighting the "Standards" tab at the top of the screen and selecting "Pre-Codification Standards" from the menu, (3) selecting "Statement of Financial Accounting Standards No. 95," and (4) clicking on the "As Issued" link.

1. How did dissenting members of the FASB prefer that interest and dividends received and interest paid be classified? (See the section following paragraph 34 of the full text of Statement No. 95.) How did the FASB justify classifying these items as cash flows from operations? (See paragraph 90 of Statement No. 95.)

(Continued)

2. Why did dissenting members of the FASB take exception to the indirect method? (See the section following paragraph 34 of the full text of Statement No. 95.) How did the FASB justify permitting use of the indirect method? (See paragraphs 108, 109, and 119 of Statement No. 95.)

Case 11-57 Research and Analysis Using the Annual Report

Obtain John Deere's 2009 annual report either through the "Investor Relations" portion of their website (do a web search for John Deere investor relations) or go to http://www.sec.gov and click "Search for Company Filings" under "Filings & Forms."

Required:
1. What method of computing net cash flow from operating activities did John Deere use?
2. What was the amount of net cash provided by operating activities for the two most current years? What were the most significant adjustments that caused a difference between net income and net cash provided by operating activities?
3. What amount did the company pay for interest during the most current year? For taxes during the most current year? (*Hint:* You may need to refer to the notes to the financial statements.)
4. Why was the provision for depreciation and amortization added to net income to compute the net cash provided by operating activities?
5. Refer to John Deere's investing and financing activities. What were some of John Deere's significant uses of cash? What were some of John Deere's significant sources of cash?
6. What was the amount of cash dividends paid by John Deere for the most current year?
7. Are the time commitments of inflows and outflows well matched by John Deere?
8. Are debt and equity likely to be available as inflows of cash in the near future?

Case 11-58 Comparative Analysis: Abercrombie & Fitch versus Aeropostale

Refer to the financial statements of Abercrombie & Fitch and Aeropostale that are supplied with this text.

Required:
1. What method of computing net cash flow from operating activities did Abercrombie & Fitch use? What method of computing net cash flow from operating activities did Aeropostale use? Would you expect these to be the same? Why or why not?
2. Find net cash provided by operating activities for each company:

   a. What was the amount of cash provided by operating activities for the year ending January 30, 2010 (fiscal 2009) for Abercrombie & Fitch? What was the amount of cash provided by operating activities for the year ending January 30, 2010, for Aeropostale?

   b. What was the most significant adjustment that caused a difference between net income and net cash provided by operating activities?

   c. Comparing net income to net cash provided by operating activities, can you draw any conclusions as to the quality of each company's earnings?

3. Refer to each company's investing and financing activities. What were some of the more significant uses of cash? What were some of the more significant sources of cash?
4. Does each company match the time commitments of inflows and outflows of cash well?
5. Are debt and equity likely to be available as inflows of cash in the near future?

Case 11-59 CONTINUING PROBLEM: FRONT ROW ENTERTAINMENT

The income statement and comparative balance sheet for Front Row Entertainment is shown below:

Front Row Entertainment Inc. Balance Sheets December 31, 2012 and 2011		
	2012	**2011**
ASSETS		
Current assets:		
Cash	$ 30,322	$ 9,005
Accounts receivable, net	98,250	17,000
Prepaid expenses	133,400	57,200
Supplies	2,200	3,700
Inventory	61,380	2,850
Total current assets	$ 325,552	$89,755
Property, plant, and equipment:		
Building	1,857,250	0
Equipment	27,350	7,000
Accumulated depreciation	(53,835)	(2,160)
Trademark	25,000	—
Total assets	$2,181,317	$94,595

LIABILITIES AND EQUITY		
Current liabilities:		
Accounts payable	$ 2,450	$12,240
Salaries payable	2,500	3,690
Interest payable	40,917	2,250
Unearned sales revenue	1,780	28,650
Income taxes payable	550	2,180
Notes payable (short-term)	8,000	0
Total current liabilities	$ 56,197	$49,010
Long-term liabilities:		
Notes payable	405,000	25,000
Bonds payable, net	1,500,000	0
Less: Discount on bond payable	(109,530)	
Total long-term liabilities	$1,795,470	$25,000
Equity:		
Preferred stock	$ 150,000	$ 0
Common stock	18,000	16,000
Paid-in capital in excess of par:		
Preferred stock	75,000	0
Common stock	38,000	0
Treasury stock	1,800	0
Retained earnings	53,250	4,585
Less: Treasury stock	(6,400)	0
Total equity	$ 329,650	$20,585
Total liabilities and equity	$2,181,317	$94,595

Front Row Entertainment Inc. Income Statement For the Year Ended December 31, 2012	
Revenues:	
Sales revenue	$3,142,800
Service revenue	636,000
Total revenues	$3,778,800
Expenses:	
Artist fee expense	$2,134,260
Rent expense	952,663
Cost of goods sold	74,800
Salaries and wages expense	345,100
Depreciation expense	51,675
Interest expense	98,087
Income taxes expense	22,000
Other expenses	26,550
Total expenses	$3,705,135
Net income	$ 73,665

Additional Information:

1. Bonds payable of $1,500,000 were issued for $1,378,300 on July 1, 2012. During 2012, $12,170 of the discount on the bonds payable was amortized.
2. In January 2012, a $380,000 long-term note payable was issued in exchange for a building. No buildings were sold during the year.
3. On February 29, an $8,000 short-term note payable was issued in exchange for equipment. No equipment was sold during the year.
4. Cash dividends of $25,000 were declared and paid during 2012.
5. Common stock was issued for $40,000 cash during 2012.
6. Preferred stock was issued for $225,000 cash during 2012.
7. Treasury stock was purchased for $11,200 during 2012. Front Row reissued $4,800 of treasury stock in December 2012 for $6,600.

Required:

1. Prepare a statement of cash flows using the indirect method.
2. What conclusions can you draw about Front Row Entertainment from the observed pattern of cash flows?

12 Financial Statement Analysis

Doug Norman Crystals/Alamy

After studying Chapter 12, you should be able to:

1. Explain how creditors, investors, and others use financial statements in their decisions.

2. Become familiar with the most important SEC filings.

3. Understand the difference between cross sectional and time series analysis.

4. Analyze financial statements using horizontal and vertical analysis.

5. Calculate and use financial statement ratios to evaluate a company.

Kumar Sriskandan/Alamy

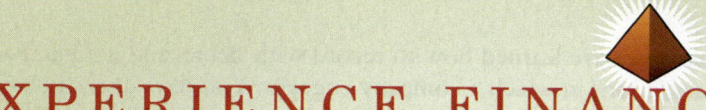

EXPERIENCE FINANCIAL ACCOUNTING

with Abercrombie & Fitch

The **Abercrombie & Fitch (A&F)** brand was established in 1892. Originally an outdoor store, it became well known for supplying Admiral Byrd's expeditions to the North and South Poles and safaris for Teddy Roosevelt and Ernest Hemingway. As such, A&F products gained a reputation for being rugged, high-quality outdoor gear.

One hundred years later, in 1992, A&F was repositioned as a fashion-oriented, casual apparel brand. Marketing was aimed at both male and female college students to reflect East Coast/Ivy League traditions.

Since 1992, the target market has been expanded down to teens and children and now also includes the **abercrombie**, **Hollister**, and **RUEHL** brands. Certainly most of us have seen these brands being worn around our campuses and towns. Yet, how do we know whether A&F would be a good company in which to invest? In reading this chapter, you will learn about a number of tools used by investors and creditors to analyze the financial status of A&F and other companies.

ABERCROMBIE & FITCH CO. CONSOLIDATED STATEMENTS OF OPERATIONS AND COMPREHENSIVE INCOME			
	2009	**2008**	**2007**
	(Thousands, except per share amounts)		
NET SALES	$2,928,626	$3,484,058	$3,699,656
Cost of Goods Sold	1,045,028	1,152,963	1,211,490
GROSS PROFIT	1,883,598	2,331,095	2,488,166
Stores and Distribution Expense	1,425,950	1,436,363	1,344,178
Marketing, General & Administrative Expense	353,269	405,248	376,780
Other Operating Income, Net	(13,533)	(8,778)	(11,702)
OPERATING INCOME	117,912	498,262	778,909
Interest Income, Net	(1,598)	(11,382)	(18,827)

Throughout this book, you have learned how to record with debits and credits many of the most common transactions in which a company engages. You have also studied how these debits and credits are summarized in the financial statements and how this information is useful to those interested in the company. In this chapter, we review, extend, and summarize the role of financial statements in business decision-making. The types of decisions facing customers, suppliers, employees, creditors, and investors are discussed. However, we concentrate primarily on investment and credit decisions and the techniques used for comparison to other companies or previous years.

Reading this chapter will help you answer the following questions:

- What decision-making groups use financial statements and what questions are they able to answer by analyzing the financial statements?
- What information can be found in SEC filings?
- Where can various information be found in the Form 10-K?
- How are financial statements analyzed?

OBJECTIVE
Explain how creditors, investors, and others use financial statements in their decisions.

USE OF FINANCIAL STATEMENTS IN DECISIONS

As we discussed in Chapter 1, the role of financial statements is to provide information that will help creditors, investors, and others make judgments which serve as the foundation for various decisions. While customers, suppliers, employees, creditors, and investors all use financial statement data to make decisions, as shown in Exhibit 12-1, each group uses the accounting information to answer different questions.

Exhibit 12-1

Users of Financial Statements and Typical Questions

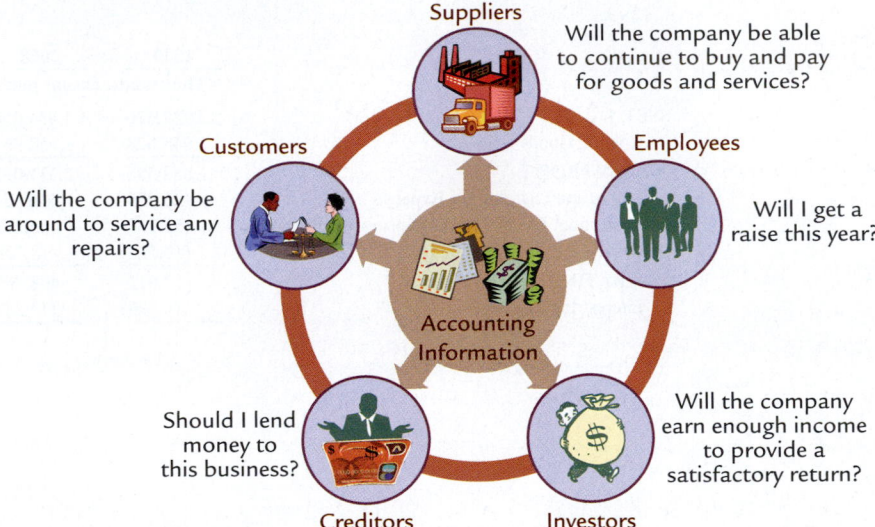

Customer Decisions

Customers want to buy from companies that will

- continue to produce goods or provide services in the future
- provide repair or warranty service if required

The financial statements contain data describing the profitability and efficiency of a company's operations, which customers can use to estimate the likelihood that a supplier will be able to deliver goods or services now and in the future.

Supplier Decisions

A company that is considering selling goods or providing services to another company wants to know whether its customer will

- pay for the purchase as agreed
- be able to continue to purchase and pay for goods and services

Suppliers can use balance sheet data to estimate the likelihood that a customer will be able to pay for current purchases. They can use income statement data to analyze whether a customer will be able to continue purchasing and paying for goods or services in the future.

Employment Decisions

When you select an employer, you want to be sure that the company will provide

- competitive salary and benefits
- experiences that will prepare you to assume increased responsibility
- a secure position for the foreseeable future

Income statement data can help a prospective employee assess the likelihood that a company will provide the growth and profits necessary to support a successful career. For example, examining a company's current assets over the claims against those assets can help prospective employees determine a company's profitability and growth.

In related decisions, unions representing employees use the financial statements. For example, when the employer's income statement suggests the employer is performing very well, the union will seek greater wages and benefits. Conversely, when the income statement suggests the employer is performing poorly (such as in the airline industry), unions may accept lower wages and benefits to help the employer stay in operation.

Credit Decisions

An individual or an organization that is considering making a loan needs to know whether the borrower will be able to repay the loan and its interest. For short-term loans (those of one year or less), the principal and interest will be repaid from current assets—cash on hand and cash that can be secured by selling inventory and collecting accounts receivable. A short-term lender, then, is most interested in the composition and amounts of a borrowing company's current assets and current liabilities. The excess of the current assets over current liabilities, an amount called *working capital*, is particularly important.

For a long-term loan, the principal and interest will be repaid from cash provided by profits earned over the period of the loan. A long-term lender, then, is most interested in estimating

- the future profits of the enterprise
- the amount of other claims against those profits, such as dividends to stockholders, payments to other lenders, and future investments by the firm

Information from three different statements is useful in making credit decisions:

- An analysis of the balance sheet can provide information about the borrower's current liquidity.
- Profitability data developed from current and previous income statements are often helpful in forecasting future profitability.
- Sources and uses of cash presented in the statement of cash flows are helpful in forecasting the amount and timing of future claims against profits.

Investment Decisions

Investors who buy stock in a corporation expect to earn returns on their investment from

- dividends
- an increase in the value of the stock (a capital gain)

Both dividends and increases in the value of the stock depend on the future profitability of the company. The larger the profits, the more resources the company has available for payment of dividends and for investment in new assets to use in creating additional profits.

Although detailed analysis of the corporation is where you find the best information for predicting (or forecasting) future profits, this cannot be done in a vacuum. You must also understand economic and industry factors. For example, if you ignore how economic factors such as rising interest rates affect home construction (it slows it down), then forecasts of corporations whose performances are tied to this industry, such as Lowe's or Home Depot, may be overly optimistic. As such, most analysts take a top-down approach when trying to predict future profits. This approach starts with gathering economic and industry data. In fact, professional analysts typically specialize in certain industries so that their knowledge of how the economy and industry interact will be applicable to all the corporations they analyze (or "follow"). Yet, at some point, you must begin to analyze the corporation itself.

OBJECTIVE 2
Become familiar with the most important SEC filings.

SEC FILINGS

Publicly traded corporations must file a variety of financial information, including audited financial statements, with the Securities and Exchange Commission (SEC) on an ongoing basis. For example, annual reports on **Form 10-K**, quarterly reports on **Form 10-Q**, and current reports for numerous specified events on **Form 8-K**, as well as many other disclosure requirements must be submitted to the SEC in a timely manner. These filings are the most important and complete source of financial information about the corporation and are the major source of information about the business for most investors (and creditors). A summary of the most important SEC filings is provided in Exhibit 12-2. A complete list of mandatory filings with more detailed descriptions is provided at http://www.sec.gov/about/forms/secforms.htm.

 *Exhibit 12-2*

The Most Important SEC Filings

Filing	Description
Form 10-K	The annual report on Form 10-K provides a comprehensive overview of the corporation's business and financial condition and includes *audited* financial statements. Although similarly named, the annual report on Form 10-K is distinct from the "annual report to shareholders," which a corporation must send to its stockholders when it holds an annual meeting to elect directors. For larger filers the 10-K must be filed within 60 days of their fiscal year end.
Form 10-Q	The Form 10-Q includes *unaudited* financial statements and provides a continuing view of the corporation's financial position during the year. The report must be filed for each of the first three fiscal quarters of the corporation's fiscal year. For larger filers this must be done within 40 days of the end of the quarter.
Form 8-K	In addition to filing Forms 10-K and 10-Q, public corporations must report material corporate events on a more current basis. Form 8-K is the "current report" companies must file with the SEC to announce major events that are important to investors and creditors.
Form DEF14A (Proxy Statement)	The Proxy Statement notifies stockholders of issues that will be voted on at the annual stockholders' meeting. For example, stockholders commonly vote on the audit firm, executive compensation issues, and representation on the Board of Directors.
Forms 3, 4, and 5	Corporate officers, directors, and 10+ percent stockholders are collectively known as "insiders." Form 3 must be filed upon becoming an officer, director, or 10+ percent stockholders. Insiders must file Form 4 within two days of buying or selling the corporation's stock. Form 5 is a special annual filing.
Forms S-1 and S-2 (Registration Statements) **Rule 424 (Prospectus)**	Corporations must file these forms to "register" their securities with the SEC prior to offering them to investors. Each form contains information for potential investors related to the sale of stock by the corporation. When the corporation sells stock to the public for the first time it is called an "Initial Public Offering" or IPO. Subsequent offerings are referred to as Secondary Offerings.

*Descriptions taken from the SEC website

Format and Content of Form 10-K

The most useful filing is Form 10-K, which is filed after each fiscal year end. We provide excerpts from **Abercrombie & Fitch**'s and **Aeropostale**'s 10-Ks at the end of the book in Appendices 1 and 2, respectively. The 10-K includes audited financial statements, but there is also a wealth of additional information. As seen in Appendices 4 and 5, 10-Ks are quite long (frequently well over 100 pages; remember these are just excerpts); however, all 10-Ks must follow a format mandated by the SEC. If you familiarize yourself with the mandated format, you will be able to find information of interest more efficiently.

Item 1 outlines the history of the company, discusses recent developments, and provides an overview of its industry and competitors. There is a detailed discussion of such things as major products, major suppliers and sources of raw materials, key customers, seasonalities, government regulations, and risk factors. A thorough read of this section is a good way to better understand the business and determine whether the company has a good strategy for creating profits.

Typically there is little important information in Items 2, 3, and 4. However, you should scan these items for anything of interest. **Item 2** describes the property holdings of the company; **Item 3** discusses lawsuits in which the company is involved; **Item 4** discusses anything brought to a shareholder vote in the fourth quarter (the 10-Qs handle this matter for the first three quarters). Item 3 is likely the most important of these items, as you will want to be aware of any serious litigation facing the company. However, most companies are parties to multiple lawsuits at any point in time, and a vast majority of these lawsuits will not materially affect the company.

Item 5 provides a summary of recent stock price and dividend activity, while **Item 6** summarizes financial data for the last five years. There is not much detail to these sections, but they do provide a nice overview. Further, Item 6 often provides information about key performance indicators, such as sales per square foot in the retail industry or revenues per passenger mile in the airline industry, which are not included in the financial statements. For example, from Item 6 we learn that Aeropostale and Abercrombie & Fitch averaged $624 and $339, respectively, of net sales per square foot of store space for the year ended January 30, 2010.

Item 7 is Management's Discussion and Analysis, more frequently referred to as **MD&A**. This is one of the key parts of the 10-K. In this section, management discusses their views of the financial condition and performance of the company. Management is required to disclose trends, events, or known uncertainties that would materially affect the company. Included in this section are many statements about what will likely happen in the future. Although there is obviously uncertainty about whether these future events will happen, this information is designed to provide investors with information management believes necessary to understand the company and predict, or forecast, future performance. Item 7A is where the effect of market risk factors, such as fluctuating interest rates or currency exchange rates, on the company's financial performance is discussed. It is important to read the MD&A.

Item 8 contains the corporation's balance sheets for the last two years and income statements and statements of cash flows for the last three years. These three financial statements are the primary sources of information for analysts. Specifically, as discussed in other chapters and later in this chapter, financial statement ratio analysis provides analysts with a wealth of information to evaluate such things as the corporation's profitability, asset and debt management, and short-term liquidity. One part of Item 8 that should not be ignored is the footnotes provided as a supplement to the financial statements. This is where you will find information about the corporation's accounting policies (such as, does the company use LIFO or FIFO?), as well as disclosures providing additional detail about various accounts listed on the financial statements.

Finally, Item 8 also includes the auditor's opinions on (1) the effectiveness of the corporation's system of internal controls over financial reporting and (2) the appropriateness of the financial statements and accompanying footnotes. Although these opinions are typically "unqualified," indicating no major problems, you should definitely look at these opinions to ensure this is true. Auditing financial statements is one of the primary services provided by CPAs and is the focus of multiple courses for accounting majors.

Item 9 is reserved for changes in or disagreements with the auditors. This item also rarely indicates a problem, but you should look at it just in case. Item 9A is a recent addition to 10-K's in response to requirements made by the passage of the Sarbanes-Oxley Act. Here management acknowledges their responsibility for establishing and maintaining a system of internal controls over financial reporting, their testing of this system's effectiveness, and their opinion of its effectiveness. It is this system of internal controls on which the auditors provide an opinion, although as discussed in the previous paragraph, the opinion is frequently included in Item 8.

Items 10 through 14 provide information that is usually provided in the proxy statement (see Form DEF 14A in Exhibit 12-2, p. 588) because stockholders typically vote on whether to retain directors, officers, and auditors (or principal accountants). Of course, the names of the parties are disclosed, as are their business experience or any family relationships with other directors or officers. Finally, **Item 15** is a listing of the financial statements (discussed as part of Item 8) and other required filings.

OBJECTIVE ❸

Understand the difference between cross sectional and time series analysis.

ANALYZING FINANCIAL STATEMENTS WITH CROSS SECTIONAL AND TIME SERIES ANALYSIS

As with many things in life, context is all important in financial statement analysis. For example, how well do you believe a corporation with $3.3 billion in net sales is performing? Your answer should be that it depends. That is, if net sales for the previous two years were $4.5 billion and $3.9 billion, respectively, you would say the trend is negative. However, if net sales for the previous two years were $2.0 billion and $2.8 billion, respectively, then you would conclude the trend is positive. Or, you could see how this corporation's sales growth stacks up against a major competitor's.

The context with which we placed our hypothetical corporation's net sales and sales growth demonstrates the two general comparisons we make when analyzing financial statements—cross sectional analysis and time series (or trend) analysis.

Cross Sectional Analysis

Cross sectional analysis compares one corporation to another corporation and to industry averages. Although this method is useful, it is often difficult to find a good comparison corporation, and even corporations classified in the same industry frequently have different aspects to their operations. For example, the Retail (Apparel) Industry in which **Abercrombie & Fitch** and **Aeropostale** are placed also includes **The Shoe Carnival**. Nonetheless, it is useful to highlight similarities, differences, strengths, and weaknesses of the corporation as compared to the competition and the industry as a whole. For example, for the year ended January 30, 2010:

- A&F's gross profit margin percentage was 64.32 percent.
- Aeropostale's gross profit margin percentage was 37.99 percent.
- The Retail—Apparel & Accessories industry had gross profit margin percentages of 6.82 percent.

Along this dimension, A&F outperformed both Aeropostale and the industry. We will discuss more comparisons between A&F, Aeropostale, and the Retail—Apparel and Accessories industry later in the chapter.

Time Series Analysis

Time series (or trend) analysis compares a single corporation across time. For example, if you look at **Abercrombie & Fitch**'s income statement in Appendix 4, you see that its net sales were:

- $3.70 billion in fiscal 2007
- $3.48 billion in fiscal 2008
- $2.93 billion in fiscal 2009

Note that fiscal years end around the end of January of the following year. This shows a negative trend.

Year-to-year comparisons of important accounts and account groups help to identify the causes of changes in a company's income or financial position. Knowing the causes of these changes is helpful in forecasting a company's future profitability and financial position. In fact, the SEC requires comparative financial statements (two years for the balance sheet and three years for both the income statement and statement of cash flows) in the 10-K, which facilitates trend analysis.

Cross Sectional and Time Series Analysis Illustrated

Cross sectional and time series analysis are demonstrated in **CORNERSTONE 12-1**.

CORNERSTONE 12-1

Interpreting Cross Sectional and Time Series (or Trend) Analysis

Concept:

When analyzing a corporation's financial statements, cross sectional analysis, compares the corporation's financial statements to a competitor or industry averages and time series analysis compares specific line items of the financial statements over multiple years.

Information:

Information from **Abercrombie & Fitch**'s and **Aeropostale**'s financial statements follows.

Abercrombie & Fitch (in thousands)

	Fiscal Year Ended		
	1/30/10	1/31/09	2/2/08
Net sales	$2,928,626	$3,484,058	$3,699,656
Cost of goods sold	1,045,028	1,152,963	1,211,490
Gross profit	$1,883,598	$2,331,095	$2,488,166

Aeropostale (in thousands)

	Fiscal Year Ended		
	1/30/10	1/31/09	2/28/08
Net sales	$2,230,105	$1,885,531	$1,590,883
Cost of goods sold	1,382,958	1,231,349	1,037,680
Gross profit	$ 847,147	$ 654,182	$ 553,203

Required:

1. Using time series analysis, comment on the trend of Aeropostale's cost of goods sold and gross profit.
2. What is the primary weakness of using raw financial statement numbers in cross sectional and time series analysis? What can you do about it?
3. Using cross sectional analysis, compare A&F's gross profit to that of Aeropostale's.

Solution:

1. Aeropostale's cost of goods sold increased by $193,669 ($1,231,349 − $1,037,680) from 2008 to 2009 and by $151,609 between 2009 and 2010. In isolation this may seem bad, but the primary reason for this increase is that sales were also increasing. In fact, Aeropostale has a positive trend in gross profit, which increased by $100,979 and $192,965 between 2008 and 2009 and 2009 and 2010, respectively.

(Continued)

**CORNERSTONE
12-1**
(continued)

2. The primary weakness is that raw financial statement numbers can be difficult to compare. For example, Aeropostale's net sales increased by almost $300 million from 2008 to 2009, while their gross profit only increased by about $100 million. However, if you look at the percentage change, both net sales and gross profit increased by between 18 and 19 percent. Further, when comparing two competitors—like A&F and Aeropostale—making comparisons with raw financial statement numbers is difficult because they are often vastly different in size. Using percentage changes from year to year or between two financial statement line items helps overcome the differences in the relative sizes of items of interest.

3. When we look at the percentage change in gross margin from year to year we discover the following:

Growth in Gross Profit:	2009 to 2010*	2008 to 2009**
A&F	−19.20%	−6.31%
Aeropostale	29.50%	18.25%

*(2010 Gross Profit − 2009 Gross Profit) ÷ 2009 Gross Profit
**(2009 Gross Profit − 2008 Gross Profit) ÷ 2008 Gross Profit

This analysis suggests that Aeropostale had a far better year.

OBJECTIVE **4**
Analyze financial statements using horizontal and vertical analysis.

ANALYZING THE FINANCIAL STATEMENTS WITH HORIZONTAL AND VERTICAL ANALYSIS

The comparative financial statements included in the 10-K report the results in dollar amounts. This makes it easy to detect large changes between years in accounts or groups of accounts. These changes may indicate that the corporation is changing or that the conditions under which the corporation operates are changing. However, while comparative financial statements show changes in the amounts of financial statement items, analysts often prefer to restate the financial statements in percentages using common size statements. **Common size statements** express each financial statement line item in percentage terms, which highlights differences. Typically, this conversion from dollar amounts to percentages is done with horizontal or vertical analysis.

Horizontal Analysis

In **horizontal analysis**, each financial statement line item is expressed as a percent of the base year (typically the first year shown). **CORNERSTONE 12-2** shows how to prepare a common size income statement for horizontal analysis.

**CORNERSTONE
12-2**

Preparing Common Size Statements for Horizontal Analysis

Concept:
Horizontal analysis expresses each financial statement line item as a percent of the base year.

Information:
Aeropostale's income statement from its 2010 10-K follows.

Aeropostale, Inc.
Consolidated Statements of Income

	Fiscal Year Ended			
	Jan. 30, 2010	Jan. 31, 2009	Feb. 2, 2008	Feb. 3, 2007
	(In thousands, except per share data)			
Net sales	$2,230,105	$1,885,531	$1,590,883	$1,413,208
Cost of sales (includes certain buying, occupancy and warehousing expenses)	1,382,958	1,231,349	1,037,680	957,791
Gross profit	847,147	654,182	553,203	455,417
Selling, general and administrative expenses	464,462	405,883	345,805	289,736
Jimmy Z asset impairment charges			9,023	
Other operating income			4,078	2,085
Income from operations	382,685	248,299	202,453	167,766
Interest income	121	510	6,550	7,064
Income before income taxes	382,806	248,809	209,003	174,830
Income taxes	153,349	99,387	79,806	68,183
Net income	$ 229,457	$ 149,422	$ 129,197	$ 106,647

Required:

Prepare a common size income statement to be used for horizontal analysis for Aeropostale using 2008 as the base year.

Solution:

Aeropostale, Inc.
Consolidated Statements of Income

	Fiscal Year Ended					
	Jan. 30, 2010		Jan. 31, 2009		Feb. 2, 2008	
	(In thousands, except per share data)					
Net sales	$2,230,105	140.18%	$1,885,531	118.52%	$1,590,883	100.00%
Cost of sales (includes certain buying, occupancy and warehousing expenses)	1,382,958	133.27%	1,231,349	118.66%	1,037,680	100.00%
Gross profit	847,147	153.13%	654,182	118.25%	553,203	100.00%
Selling, general, and administrative expenses	464,462	134.31%	405,883	117.37%	345,805	100.00%
Jimmy Z asset impairment charges					9,023	100.00%
Other operating income					4,078	100.00%
Income from operations	382,685	189.02%	248,299	122.65%	202,453	100.00%
Interest income	121	1.85%	510	7.79%	6,550	100.00%
Income before income taxes	382,806	183.16%	248,809	119.05%	209,003	100.00%
Income taxes	153,349	192.15%	99,387	124.54%	79,806	100.00%
Net income	$ 229,457	177.60%	$ 149,422	115.65%	$ 129,197	100.00%

Horizontal analysis is good for highlighting the growth (or shrinkage) in financial statement line items from year to year and is particularly useful for trend analysis. For example, looking at Aeropostale's common size income statement in Cornerstone 12-3, we see that cost of goods sold has grown slightly faster than sales when comparing 2010 to 2008. This has resulted in the gross profit growth trailing sales growth.

Vertical Analysis

Vertical analysis, on the other hand, expresses each financial statement line item as a percent of the largest amount on the statement. On the income statement, this is net sales and on the balance sheet it is total assets. Vertical analysis helps distinguish between changes in account balances that result from growth and changes that are likely to have arisen from other causes. **CORNERSTONE 12-3** shows how to prepare a common size income statement and balance sheet for vertical analysis.

CORNERSTONE 12-3

Preparing Common Size Statements for Vertical Analysis

Concept:
Vertical analysis expresses each financial statement line item as a percent of the largest amount on the statement.

Information:
Aeropostale's income statements and balance sheets (from the 2010 10-K) follow.

Aeropostale, Inc.
Consolidated Statements of Income

	Fiscal Year Ended			
	Jan. 30, 2010	Jan. 31, 2009	Feb. 2, 2008	Feb. 3, 2007
	(In thousands, except per share data)			
Net sales	$2,230,105	$1,885,531	$1,590,883	$1,413,208
Cost of sales (includes certain buying, occupancy and warehousing expenses)	1,382,958	1,231,349	1,037,680	957,791
Gross profit	847,147	654,182	553,203	455,417
Selling, general and administrative expenses	464,462	405,883	345,805	289,736
Jimmy Z asset impairment charges			9,023	
Other operating income			4,078	2,085
Income from operations	382,685	248,299	202,453	167,766
Interest income	121	510	6,550	7,064
Income before income taxes	382,806	248,809	209,003	174,830
Income taxes	153,349	99,387	79,806	68,183
Net income	$ 229,457	$ 149,422	$ 129,197	$ 106,647

CORNERSTONE
1 2 - 3
(continued)

Aeropostale, Inc.
Consolidated Balance Sheets

	Jan. 30, 2010	Jan. 31, 2009
	(In thousands, except per share data)	
ASSETS		
Current assets:		
Cash and cash equivalents	$346,976	$228,530
Merchandise inventory	132,915	126,360
Prepaid expenses	21,049	17,384
Deferred income taxes	21,683	10,745
Other current assets	7,394	10,862
Total current assets	530,017	393,881
Fixtures, equipment and improvements net	251,558	248,999
Deferred income taxes	6,383	12,509
Other assets	4,351	2,530
Total assets	$792,309	$657,919
LIABILITIES AND STOCKHOLDERS' EQUITY		
Current liabilities:		
Accounts payable	$ 90,850	$ 77,247
Accrued expenses	150,990	98,190
Total current liabilities	241,840	175,437
Tenant allowances	68,174	74,712
Deferred rent	27,559	26,019
Non-current retirement benefit plan liabilities	10,060	22,470
Other non-current liabilities	6,286	1,662
Uncertain tax contingency liabilities	3,901	2,559
Commitments and contingent liabilities		
Stockholders' equity:		
Common stock par value, $0.01 per share; 200,000 shares authorized, 137,090 and 135,708 shares issued	1,371	1,358
Preferred stock par value, $0.01 per share; 5,000 shares authorized, no shares issued or outstanding		
Additional paid-in capital	171,815	145,498
Accumulated other comprehensive loss	(6,993)	(8,998)
Retained earnings	922,790	693,333
Treasury stock at cost 43,095 and 35,313 shares	(654,494)	(476,131)
Total stockholders' equity	434,489	355,060
Total liabilities and stockholders' equity	$ 792,309	$ 657,919

Source: Created by Morningstar Document Research. http://documentresearch.morningstar.com/

(Continued)

**CORNERSTONE
12-3**
(continued)

Required:
Prepare common size income statements and balance sheets to be used in vertical analysis for Aeropostale beginning with the year 2008.

Solution:

**Aeropostale, Inc.
Consolidated Statements of Income**

	Fiscal Year Ended		
	Jan. 30, 2010	Jan. 31, 2009	Feb. 2, 2008
	(In thousands, except per share data)		
Net sales	100.00%	100.00%	100.00%
Cost of sales (includes certain buying, occupancy and warehousing expenses)	62.01%	65.31%	65.23%
Gross profit	37.99%	34.69%	34.77%
Selling, general, and administrative expenses	20.83%	21.53%	21.74%
Jimmy Z asset impairment charges	0.00%	0.00%	0.57%
Other operating income	0.00%	0.00%	0.26%
Income from operations	17.16%	13.17%	12.73%
Interest income	0.01%	0.03%	0.41%
Income before income taxes	17.17%	13.20%	13.14%
Income taxes	6.88%	5.27%	5.02%
Net income	10.29%	7.92%	8.12%

**Aeropostale, Inc.
Consolidated Balance Sheets**

	Jan. 30, 2010	Jan. 31, 2009
	(In thousands, except per share data)	
ASSETS		
Current assets:		
Cash and cash equivalents	43.79%	34.74%
Merchandise inventory	16.78%	19.21%
Prepaid expenses	2.66%	2.64%
Deferred income taxes	2.74%	1.63%
Other current assets	0.93%	1.65%
Total current assets	66.90%	59.87%
Fixtures, equipment and improvements net	31.75%	37.85%
Deferred income taxes	0.81%	1.90%
Other assets	0.55%	0.38%
Total assets	100.00%	100.00%

CORNERSTONE 12-3 *(continued)*

	Jan. 30, 2010	Jan. 31, 2009
	(In thousands, except per share data)	
LIABILITIES AND STOCKHOLDERS' EQUITY		
Current liabilities:		
Accounts payable	11.47%	11.74%
Accrued expenses	19.06%	14.92%
Total current liabilities	30.52%	26.67%
Tenant allowances	8.60%	11.36%
Deferred rent	3.48%	3.95%
Non-current retirement benefit plan liabilities	1.27%	3.42%
Other non-current liabilities	0.79%	0.25%
Uncertain tax contingency liabilities	0.49%	0.39%
Commitments and contingent liabilities		
Stockholders' equity:		
Common stock par value, $0.01 per share; 200,000 shares authorized, 137,090 and 135,708 shares issued	0.17%	0.21%
Preferred stock par value, $0.01 per share; 5,000 shares authorized, no shares issued or outstanding		
Additional paid-in capital	21.69%	22.11%
Accumulated other comprehensive loss	−0.88%	−1.37%
Retained earnings	116.47%	105.38%
Treasury stock at cost 43,095 and 35,313 shares	−82.61%	−72.37%
Total stockholders' equity	54.84%	53.97%
Total liabilities and stockholders' equity	100.00%	100.00%

Identifying nongrowth changes and their causes can help forecast a company's future profitability or its future financial position. For example, in Cornerstone 12-3, **Aeropostle**'s cost of sales decreased from approximately 65.25 percent of net sales in both 2008 and 2009 to 62.01 percent in 2010. This may not seem like much of a change, but if cost of sales had remained near 65.25 percent of net sales, then gross profit would be over $72 million lower. Determining whether this improved cost of sales percentage is sustainable may have a large effect on forecasting the future. Further, vertical analysis of the balance sheet reveals a relatively stable condition; other than cash and cash equivalents, all of the large dollar accounts are about the same percentage of total assets in each year.

Of course, you can, and should, get much more in depth with such analysis. A careful horizontal and vertical analysis serves as a starting point for an inquiry into the causes of these changes, with the objective of forecasting the corporation's future financial statements.

ANALYZING THE FINANCIAL STATEMENTS WITH RATIO ANALYSIS

OBJECTIVE 5
Calculate and use financial statement ratios to evaluate a company.

Ratio analysis is an examination of financial statements conducted by preparing and evaluating a series of ratios. **Ratios** (or **financial ratios**), like other financial analysis data, normally provide meaningful information only when compared with ratios from previous periods for the same firm (i.e., time series, or trend, analysis) or similar firms (i.e., cross sectional analysis). Ratios help by removing most of the effects of size differences. When dollar amounts are used, size differences between firms may make a meaningful comparison impossible. However, properly constructed financial ratios permit the comparison of firms regardless of size.

We discuss six categories of ratio analysis:

- *Short-term liquidity ratios* are particularly helpful to short-term creditors, but all investors and creditors have an interest in these ratios.
- *Debt management ratios* and *profitability ratios* provide information for long-term creditors and stockholders.
- *Asset efficiency (or operating) ratios* help management operate the firm and indicate to outsiders the efficiency with which certain of the company's activities are performed.
- *Stockholder ratios* are of interest to a corporation's stockholders.
- *Dupont analysis* decomposes return on equity into margin, turnover, and leverage.

All these ratios are shown and defined in Exhibit 12-4 at the conclusion of this section (p. 618). We will use data from **Abercrombie & Fitch**'s financial statements in Appendix 4 to illustrate each of these types of financial statement ratios.

Short-Term Liquidity Ratios

Analysts want to know the likelihood that a company will be able to pay its current obligations as they come due. Failure to pay current liabilities can lead to suppliers refusing to sell needed inventory and employees leaving. As such, even companies with good business models can be forced into bankruptcy by their inability to pay current liabilities.

The cash necessary to pay current liabilities will come from existing cash or from receivables and inventory, which should turn into cash approximately at the same time the current liabilities become due. Property, plant, and equipment and other long-lived assets are much more difficult to turn into cash in time to meet current obligations without harming future operations. Accordingly, the **short-term liquidity ratios** compare some combination of current assets or operations to current liabilities.

Current Ratio Since a company must meet its current obligations primarily by using its current assets, the current ratio is especially useful to short-term creditors. The **current ratio** is expressed as follows:

$$\text{Current Ratio} = \frac{\text{Current Assets}}{\text{Current Liabilities}}$$

Using information from **Abercrombie & Fitch**'s 2010 balance sheet, the current ratio for A&F is calculated as follows:

	2010	2009
Total current assets	$1,235,846	$1,072,010
Total current liabilities	449,372	449,797
Current ratio	**2.75**	**2.38**

A&F's current ratio increased because current assets increased more rapidly than current liabilities. In fact, if you look at the details of A&F's current assets you see that increases in cash, marketable securities, and receivables drove the increase in current assets. On the current liabilities side, small increases in accounts payable and accrued expenses were essentially offset by decreases in outstanding checks and income taxes payable.

There are no absolute standards for ratios, so a company's ratios are typically compared to the industry averages and/or competitors. The average for the Retail—Apparel & Accessories is 1.93. By these standards, A&F's current ratio was relatively strong in both years.

Quick Ratio Some analysts believe that the current ratio overstates short-term liquidity. They argue that prepaid expenses (expenses for which payments are made before consumption) often cannot be converted into cash. Further, inventories must be sold and receivables collected from those sales before cash is obtained to pay maturing current liabilities. Both the sale of inventory and collection of receivables can require a lengthy period. Conservative analysts argue that only those current assets that can be turned into cash almost immediately should be used to measure short-term liquidity.

A more conservative measure of short-term liquidity is based on *quick assets* (usually cash, receivables, and short-term investments) and current liabilities. The **quick ratio** (or *acid test ratio*) is expressed as follows:

$$\text{Quick Ratio} = \frac{\text{Cash} + \text{Short-Term Investments} + \text{Receivables}}{\text{Current Liabilities}}$$

Looking at the detail of **Abercrombie & Fitch**'s current assets, the quick ratio is calculated as follows:

	2010	2009
Current Assets:		
Cash and equivalents	$ 680,113	$ 522,122
Marketable securities	32,356	0
Receivables	90,865	53,110
Inventories	310,645	372,422
Deferred income taxes	44,570	43,408
Other current assets	77,297	80,948
Total current assets	$1,235,846	$1,072,010
Quick assets	803,334	575,232
Total current liabilities	$ 449,372	$ 449,797
Quick ratio	**1.79**	**1.28**

Generally, a quick ratio above 1.0 is considered adequate because there are enough liquid assets available to meet current obligations. Using this guideline, we see that A&F had little difficulty meeting its current obligations in 2009 or 2010.

Cash Ratio An even more conservative short-term liquidity ratio is the cash ratio. Specifically, while the current and quick ratios assume that receivables will be collected, the cash ratio does not make this assumption. This ratio may be more appropriate for industries in which collectability is uncertain or for corporations with high credit risk receivables. The **cash ratio** is expressed as follows:

$$\text{Cash Ratio} = \frac{\text{Cash} + \text{Short-Term Investments}}{\text{Current Liabilities}}$$

Although **Abercrombie & Fitch** does not have high credit risk receivables, the cash ratio is calculated as follows:

	2010	2009
Current assets:		
Cash and equivalents	$ 680,113	$ 522,122
Marketable securities	32,356	0
Receivables	90,865	53,110
Inventories	310,645	372,422
Deferred income taxes	44,570	43,408
Other current assets	77,297	80,948
Total current assets	$1,235,846	$1,072,010
Quick assets	712,469	522,122
Total current liabilities	$ 449,372	$ 449,797
Quick ratio	**1.59**	**1.16**

If you questioned the collectability of A&F's receivables, the cash ratio indicates that A&F had more than enough cash and marketable securities to pay off its current liabilities in 2009 and 2010.

Operating Cash Flow Ratio The operating cash flow ratio takes a slightly different approach. This ratio looks at the ability of operations to generate cash, which recognizes the more general concept that current obligations will be paid through operations (after all, selling inventory and collecting receivables is a big part of operations). The **operating cash flow ratio** is expressed as:

$$\text{Operating Cash Flow Ratio} = \frac{\text{Cash Flows from Operating Activities}}{\text{Current Liabilities}}$$

Looking at **Abercrombie & Fitch**'s statement of cash flows and balance sheet, the operating cash flow ratio is calculated as follows:

	2010	2009
Cash flows from operating activities	$402,200	$490,836
Total current liabilities	449,372	449,797
Operating cash flow ratio	**0.90**	**1.09**

In 2010, A&F's operations did not generate enough cash to meet the current obligations due at the end of the year. That means that A&F's operations were going to have to improve in 2011 or A&F will need to use some of their available cash, obtain additional borrowing or sell additional stock.

Overview of Short-Term Liquidity Ratios Most of the short-term liquidity ratios improved in 2010, which indicates an improvement in A&F's short-term liquidity. For creditors, this is clearly good news. Creditors typically prefer all these measures of short-term liquidity be as high as possible. However, because investments in current assets (especially cash, receivables, and inventory) earn very small returns compared with the returns on investments in noncurrent assets, management must minimize the proportion of capital invested in current assets if it is to maximize profit. Using the income statement and balance sheet shown in Exhibit 12-3, **CORNERSTONE 12-4** illustrates how to calculate and interpret short-term liquidity ratios for **Aeropostale**.

Exhibit 12-3

Aeropostale, Inc. Income Statement and Balance Sheet

Aeropostale, Inc.
Consolidated Statements of Income

	Fiscal Year Ended			
	Jan. 30, 2010	Jan. 31, 2009	Feb. 2, 2008	Feb. 3, 2007
		(In thousands, except per share data)		
Net sales	$2,230,105	$1,885,531	$1,590,883	$1,413,208
Cost of sales (includes certain buying, occupancy and warehousing expenses)	1,382,958	1,231,349	1,037,680	957,791
Gross profit	847,147	654,182	553,203	455,417
Selling, general and administrative expenses	464,462	405,883	345,805	289,736
Jimmy Z asset impairment charges			9,023	
Other operating income			4,078	2,085
Income from operations	382,685	248,299	202,453	167,766
Interest income	121	510	6,550	7,064
Income before income taxes	382,806	248,809	209,003	174,830
Income taxes	153,349	99,387	79,806	68,183
Net income	$ 229,457	$ 149,422	$ 129,197	$ 106,647

Exhibit 12-3

Aeropostale, Inc. Income Statement and Balance Sheet (*Continued*)

Aeropostale, Inc.
Consolidated Balance Sheets

	Jan. 30, 2010	Jan. 31, 2009
	(In thousands, except per share data)	
ASSETS		
Current assets:		
Cash and cash equivalents	$346,976	$228,530
Merchandise inventory	132,915	126,360
Prepaid expenses	21,049	17,384
Deferred income taxes	21,683	10,745
Other current assets	7,394	10,862
Total current assets	$530,017	$393,881
Fixtures, equipment and improvements net	251,558	248,999
Deferred income taxes	6,383	12,509
Other assets	4,351	2,530
Total assets	$792,309	$657,919
LIABILITIES AND STOCKHOLDERS' EQUITY		
Current liabilities:		
Accounts payable	$ 90,850	$ 77,247
Accrued expenses	150,990	98,190
Total current liabilities	241,840	175,437
Tenant allowances	68,174	74,712
Deferred rent	27,559	26,019
Non-current retirement benefit plan liabilities	10,060	22,470
Other non-current liabilities	6,286	1,662
Uncertain tax contingency liabilities	3,901	2,559
Commitments and contingent liabilities		
Stockholders' equity:		
Common stock par value, $0.01 per share; 200,000 shares authorized, 137,090 and 135,708 shares issued	1,371	1,358
Preferred stock par value, $0.01 per share; 5,000 shares authorized, no shares issued or outstanding		
Additional paid-in capital	171,815	145,498
Accumulated other comprehensive loss	(6,993)	(8,998)
Retained earnings	922,790	693,333
Treasury stock at cost 43,095 and 35,313 shares	(654,494)	(476,131)
Total stockholders' equity	434,489	355,060
Total liabilities and stockholders' equity	$ 792,309	$ 657,919

Source: Created by Morningstar Document Research. http://documentresearch.morningstar.com/

**CORNERSTONE
12-4**

**Calculating and Interpreting Short-Term
Liquidity Ratios**

Concept:

Short-term liquidity ratios assess the corporation's ability to meet its current obligations.

(*Continued*)

Information:

Refer to the information in **Aeropostale**'s income statement and balance sheet in Exhibit 12-3 (pp. 600–601). Aeropostale's cash flows from operations were (in thousands) $202,135 and $334,440 in 2009 and 2010, respectively.

CORNERSTONE
12-4
(continued)

Required:

Calculate the following short-term liquidity ratios for Aeropostale for 2009 and 2010: (1) current ratio, (2) quick ratio, (3) cash ratio, and (4) operating cash flow ratio (operating cash flows are provided in the Information section).

Solution:

	2010	**2009**
1. $\text{Current Ratio} = \dfrac{\text{Current Assets}}{\text{Current Liabilities}}$	$\dfrac{\$530,017}{\$241,840} = 2.19$	$\dfrac{\$393,881}{\$175,437} = 2.25$

	2010	**2009**
2. $\dfrac{\text{Quick}}{\text{Ratio}} = \dfrac{\text{Cash} + \text{Short-Term Investments} + \text{Receivables}}{\text{Current Liabilities}}$	$\dfrac{(\$346,976 + \$0 + \$0)}{\$241,840} = 1.43$	$\dfrac{(\$228,530 + \$0 + \$0)}{\$175,437} = 1.30$

	2010	**2009**
3. $\text{Cash Ratio} = \dfrac{\text{Cash} + \text{Short-Term Investments}}{\text{Current Liabilities}}$	$\dfrac{(\$346,976 + \$0)}{\$241,840} = 1.43$	$\dfrac{(\$228,530 + \$0)}{\$175,437} = 1.30$

	2010	**2009**
4. $\dfrac{\text{Operating}}{\text{Cash Flow Ratio}} = \dfrac{\text{Cash Flows from Operating Activities}}{\text{Current Liabilities}}$	$\dfrac{\$334,440^*}{\$241,840} = 1.38$	$\dfrac{\$202,135^*}{\$175,437} = 1.15$

*Taken from the statement of cash flows. The numbers were provided in the information section of this Cornerstone.

From Cornerstone 12-4, you can see that **Aeropostale**'s current ratio is well above the industry average of 1.93. Further, its quick and cash ratios are far above the 1.0 threshold considered adequate and its operating cash flow ratio, although weaker than the others, is adequate.

Compared to **Abercrombie and Fitch**'s short term liquidity ratios shown in the body of the text previously, Aeropostale's are generally weaker, albeit adequate. This suggests that Aeropostale's risk of short-term insolvency is higher, although neither corporation is in much danger.

Debt Management Ratios

Debt management ratios provide information on two aspects of debt. First, they provide information on the relative mix of debt and equity financing (often referred to as its capital structure). The primary advantages of debt over equity are as follows:

- Interest payments are tax-deductible.
- Creditors do not share in profits.

Debt, however, is riskier than equity, because unless the interest and principal payments are made when due, the firm may fall into bankruptcy. In most corporations, management attempts to achieve an appropriate balance between the cost advantage of debt and its extra risk.

Second, debt management ratios also try to show the corporation's ability to meet, or cover its debt obligations through operations because interest and principal payments must be made as scheduled, or a company can be declared bankrupt. The times interest earned ratio is an example of the latter type of measurement.

Times Interest Earned Ratio

Times Interest Earned Ratio Some liabilities, like accounts payable, have flexible payment schedules that can be modified when necessary. Other liabilities—primarily short-term and long-term debt—have specific payment schedules that must be met. The cash used to make these payments must come from operations. Analysts use the times interest earned ratio to gauge a firm's ability to repay its debt from recurring operations. This ratio can focus either on accrual basis interest expense or the cash basis interest payments and are typically measured pretax because interest expense is tax deductible. The **times interest earned ratio** is expressed as follows:

$$\text{Times Interest Earned } (Accrual\ Basis) = \frac{\text{Operating Income}}{\text{Interest Expense}}$$

$$\text{Times Interest Earned } (Cash\ Basis) = \frac{(\text{Cash Flows from Operations} + \text{Income Taxes Payable} + \text{Interest Payments})}{\text{Interest Payments}}$$

The times interest earned ratios for **Abercrombie & Fitch** is calculated as follows:

	2010	2009
Cash flows from operating activities	$402,200	$490,836
Operating income	117,912	498,262
Interest payments	6,600*	3,400*
Interest expense	6,600*	3,400*
Income taxes payable	42,301**	191,906**
Times interest earned (cash)	**68.35**	**201.81**
Times interest earned (accrual)	**17.87**	**146.55**

*Taken from Note 12.
**Taken from Note 11.

Note that interest expense is often included in the financial statement footnotes because many corporations, including A&F, net interest income with interest expense on the face of the income statement. A&F appears to have an easy time covering their interest expense/payments.

While times interest earned ratio provides information on the relative mix of debt and equity financing, other debt management ratios assess a company's ability to meet, or cover its debt obligations. We will consider four different ways of measuring the proportion of debt within a corporation's capital structure.

Long-Term Debt-to-Equity Ratio

Long-Term Debt-to-Equity Ratio Despite its apparent misnomer, we prefer to define long-term debt as the sum of long-term debt and the debt-like obligations in current liabilities (notes or short-term loans). It is called the long-term debt-to-equity ratio because historically when corporations borrowed money, they locked themselves into long-term debt contracts. The long-term debt-to-equity ratio provides information on the proportion of capital provided by creditors and by stockholders. Of course, this type of debt also includes any current portion (i.e., long-term debt principal that must be repaid within the next 12 months). Additionally, it can include more flexible borrowing arrangements, such as lines of credit, that may be classified as current liabilities. The **long-term debt-to-equity ratio** is expressed as follows:

$$\text{Long-Term Debt-to-Equity Ratio} = \frac{\text{Long-Term Debt (including current portion)}}{\text{Total Equity}}$$

Abercrombie & Fitch has a long-term debt-to-equity ratio of 0.18 and 0.19 in 2010 and 2009, respectively, based on long-term debt (including both current and long-term deferred lease credits) of $326,862 in 2010 and $354,336 in 2009. This is slightly above the industry average of 0.15 and suggests that A&F's debt burden is not unduly high.

Debt-to-Equity Ratio

Debt-to-Equity Ratio Debt is also occasionally defined as all liabilities. This is a more inclusive view of debt recognizing that if corporations did not have current liabilities such as accounts payable, they would have to take out other borrowings or sell stock to finance its assets. The **debt-to-equity ratio** is expressed as follows:

$$\text{Debt-to-Equity Ratio} = \frac{\text{Total Liabilities}}{\text{Total Equity}}$$

Abercrombie & Fitch's debt-to-equity ratio was 0.54 in both 2010 and 2009, which is well below the industry average of 4.42.

Long-Term Debt or Debt-to-Total Assets   The proportion of total capital provided by creditors is also shown by the **long-term debt-to-total assets ratio** and the **debt-to-total assets ratio**. These measures are more useful when equity is small or subject to substantial changes. These ratios are expressed as follows:

$$\text{Long-Term Debt-to-Total Assets Ratio} = \frac{\text{Long-Term Debt (including current portion)}}{\text{Total Assets}}$$

$$\text{Debt-to-Total Assets Ratio} = \frac{\text{Total Liabilities}}{\text{Total Assets}}$$

Overview of Debt Management Ratios   **CORNERSTONE 12-5** demonstrates how to calculate and interpret debt management ratios.

CORNERSTONE 12-5

Calculating and Interpreting Debt Management Ratios

Concept:
Debt management ratios provide information on the company's ability to meet its debt obligations through operations.

Information:
Information from **Delta Airlines**' 2009 10-K follows.

Delta Airlines Consolidated Balance Sheets	2009	2008
Current Liabilities:		
Current maturities of long-term debt and capital leases	$ 1,533	$ 1,160
Air traffic liability	3,074	3,385
Accounts payable	1,249	1,604
Frequent flyer deferred revenue	1,614	1,624
Accrued salaries and related benefits	1,037	972
Hedge derivatives liability	139	1,247
Taxes payable	525	565
Other accrued liabilities	626	535
Total current liabilities	9,797	11,092
Noncurrent Liabilities:		
Long-term debt and capital leases	15,665	15,411
Pension, postretirement and related benefits	11,745	10,895
Frequent flyer deferred revenue	3,198	3,489
Deferred income taxes, net	1,667	1,981
Other noncurrent liabilities	1,222	1,342
Total noncurrent liabilities	33,497	33,118
Total stockholders' equity	245	874
Total assets	43,539	45,084
Interest expense	1,278	705

	2009	2008
Interest payment	867	742
Income tax expense (benefit)	(344)	(119)
Income tax payment	15	—
Operating income (loss)	(324)	(8,314)
Net income (loss)	(1,237)	(8,922)
Cash flows from operations	1,379	(1,707)

**CORNERSTONE
12-5
*(continued)***

Required:

Calculate the following debt management ratios for Delta Airlines for 2008 and 2009: (1) times interest earned ratio (both cash and accrual), (2) long-term debt-to-equity ratio, (3) debt-to-equity ratio, (4) long-term debt-to-total assets ratio, and (5) debt-to-total assets ratio.

Solution:

		2009	2008
1. Times Interest Earned (*Accrual Basis*) $= \dfrac{\text{Operating Income}}{\text{Interest Expense}}$		$\dfrac{(\$324)}{\$1,278} = -0.25$	$\dfrac{(\$8,314)}{\$705} = -11.79$

		2009	2008
Times Interest Earned (*Cash Basis*) $= \dfrac{(\text{Cash Flows from Operations} + \text{Income Taxes Payable} + \text{Interest Payments})}{\text{Interest Payments*}}$		$\dfrac{(\$1,379 + \$15 + \$867)}{\$867} = 2.61$	$\dfrac{(-\$1,707 + \$0 + \$742)}{\$742} = -1.30$

*Taken from Note 6

		2009	2008
2. Long-Term Debt-to-equity $= \dfrac{\text{Long-Term Debt (including current portion)}}{\text{Total Equity}}$		$\dfrac{[\$15,665 + \$1,533]}{\$245} = 70.20$	$\dfrac{[\$15,411 + \$1,160]}{\$874} = 18.96$

		2009	2008
3. Debt-to-Equity $= \dfrac{\text{Total Liabilities}}{\text{Total Equity}}$		$\dfrac{\$9,797 + \$33,497}{\$245} = 176.71$	$\dfrac{\$11,092 + \$33,118}{\$874} = 50.58$

		2009	2008
4. Long-Term Debt-to-Total Assets $= \dfrac{\text{Long-Term Debt (including current portion)}}{\text{Total Assets}}$		$\dfrac{[\$15,665 + \$1,533]}{\$43,539} = 0.40$	$\dfrac{[\$15,411 + \$1,160]}{\$45,084} = 0.37$

		2009	2008
5. Debt-to-Total Assets $= \dfrac{\text{Total Liabilities}}{\text{Total Assets}}$		$\dfrac{\$9,797 + \$33,497}{\$43,539} = 0.99$	$\dfrac{\$11,092 + \$33,118}{\$45,084} = 0.98$

From the times interest earned ratios in Cornerstone 12-5, you can see that **Delta Airlines** did not produce sufficient operating income to meet their interest expense in either year. Further, even when cash flows from operations were positive in 2009 (they were negative in 2008), over two-thirds of the cash was needed to cover interest payments. Of course, this is a risky situation that must be investigated further.

The long-term debt-to-equity and debt-to-equity ratios paint a similar picture. Delta Airlines obviously has a heavy debt burden, but it is difficult to interpret these numbers because of the low amounts of equity. In this case, a good option is to look at the debt-to-total asset ratios. The long-term debt-to-total asset ratio shows that approximately 40 percent of total assets are financed with long-term debt. The debt-to-total asset ratio being near 1.0 indicates low equity. Further, the trend of these ratios is not improving. It may be wise to consider more years to get a better picture of the trend, especially given the poor economy in 2008 and 2009.

 **Credit Analysis**

You are a loan officer at First National Bank. Your assistant has prepared the following financial statement and debt management ratio information to help you evaluate Carmody Manufacturing's loan application:

	2011	2010	2009	Industry (2009–2011)
Sales	171.2%	131.9%	100%	183.2%
Gross Margin	168.7%	129.4%	100%	184.6%
Operating Expenses	180.3%	134.7%	100%	160.5%
Operating Income	160.5%	124.3%	100%	202.4%
Net Income	162.2%	125.7%	100%	201.7%

You also have the following data for the year ended December 31, 2011:

For the Years 2007–2011	Carmody Manufacturing	Industry
Average current ratio	2.06	1.55
Average debt-to-equity ratio	19.47	80.14
Average long-term debt-to-equity ratio	17.23	49.83
Average times interest earned (accrual)	9.55	3.87

Carmody has asked First National for a long-term loan that will double its long-term debt.

Should you approve the loan for Carmody?

The data you have is somewhat mixed. The debt management ratios are outstanding for the industry. Even after doubling the amount of long-term debt, it is apparent that Carmody will remain better than the industry averages for the debt-to-equity, long-term debt-to-equity, and times interest earned ratios. The operating results, however, are not as encouraging. Carmody's growth is somewhat below industry averages. Further, the growth in operating expenses signals a problem—especially when you consider that many operating expenses are fixed (such as salaries).

Although you probably want to follow up with Carmody regarding their projected results of operations, given their low debt burden, First National should probably grant the loan.

Asset Efficiency Ratios

Asset efficiency ratios (or **operating ratios**) are measures of how efficiently a company uses its assets. The principal asset efficiency ratios are measures of **turnover**, that is, the average length of time required for assets to be consumed or replaced. The faster an asset is turned over, the more efficiently it is being used. These ratios provide managers and other users of a corporation's financial statements with easily interpreted measures of the time required to turn receivables into cash, inventory into cost of goods sold, or total assets into sales.

But managers are not the only people interested in asset efficiency ratios. Since well-managed, efficiently operated companies are usually among the most profitable, and since profits are the sources of cash from which long-term creditors receive their interest and principal payments, creditors seek information about the corporation's profit prospects from asset efficiency ratios. And stockholders find that larger profits are usually followed by increased dividends and higher stock prices, so they, too, are concerned with indicators of efficiency.

Accounts Receivable Turnover Ratio   The length of time required to collect the receivable from a credit sale is the time required to turn over accounts receivable. The accounts receivable turnover ratio indicates how many times accounts receivable is turned over each year. The more times accounts receivable turns over each year, the more efficient are the firm's credit-granting and credit-collection activities. The **accounts receivable turnover ratio** is expressed as follows:

$$\text{Accounts Receivable Turnover Ratio} = \frac{\text{Net Credit Sales or Net Sales}}{\text{Average Accounts Receivable}}$$

In the equation above, "net credit sales" means credit sales less sales returns and allowances. While some firms make all their sales on credit, many also make a substantial proportion of their sales for cash (or on credit cards, which are essentially cash sales). It is unusual for a company making cash and credit sales to report the proportion that is credit sales. For that reason, the accounts receivable turnover ratio is often computed using whatever number the firm reports for sales. In addition, to find the average balance for any financial statement account, like average accounts receivable, divide the sum of the beginning and ending balances by two.

Using net sales, **Abercrombie & Fitch**'s receivables turnover ratios were 65.18 and 40.68 for 2009 and 2010, respectively, so they are very efficient at collecting cash from their sales. This is far better than the industry average of 6.17. This superior ratio probably means that a vast majority of their sales are for cash (or third party credit cards that are collected very quickly). Although their 10-K does not discuss it in detail, A&F also has an in-store credit card, which, as discussed in Chapter 9, will increase receivables balances and reduce third-party credit card fees.

Careful analysts examine quarterly or monthly financial statements, when available, to determine whether the amount of receivables recorded in the annual statements is representative of the receivables carried during the year. For example, retailers like A&F often have much larger receivables after the Christmas selling season than during other parts of the year.

Inventory Turnover Ratio

Inventory turnover is the length of time required to sell inventory to customers. The more efficient a firm, the more times inventory will be turned over. The **inventory turnover ratio** indicates the number of times inventory is sold during the year and is expressed as follows:

$$\text{Inventory Turnover Ratio} = \frac{\text{Cost of Goods Sold}}{\text{Average Inventory}}$$

Average inventory is beginning inventory plus ending inventory divided by 2.

Abercrombie & Fitch's inventory turnover ratios were 3.27 and 3.06 for 2009 and 2010, respectively. This means that A&F turns over its inventory about three times per year or once every four months. Remember that inventory sitting in the warehouse or on the shelf is not earning a return. The weakening inventory turnover deserves some attention. For example, does the slower moving inventory indicate weakening sales? Further, the industry average is 5.33, so A&F is relatively inefficient with its inventory.

Now that we have examined both receivables and inventory turnover, let us combine these measurements to approximate the length of the operating cycle (the length of time required for an investment in inventory to produce cash). **Abercrombie & Fitch**'s 2010 operating cycle can be estimated by adding the number of days needed to turn over both receivables and inventory. The inventory turns over in approximately 119 days (365 days ÷ 3.06 inventory turnover ratio) and the receivables turn over in approximately 9 days (365 days ÷ 40.68 receivables turnover ratio), which gives an operating cycle of approximately 128 days.

The longer the operating cycle, the larger the investment necessary in receivables and inventory. When assets are larger, more liabilities and equity are required to finance them. Large amounts of capital negatively affect net income and cash flows for dividends. Therefore, firms attempt to maintain as short an operating cycle as possible. A&F's operating cycle is relatively long.

Asset Turnover Ratio

Another measure of the efficiency of a corporation's operations is the **asset turnover ratio**. This ratio measures the efficiency with which a corporation's assets are used to produce sales revenues. The more sales dollars produced by each dollar invested in assets, the more efficiently a firm is considered to be operating. The asset turnover ratio is expressed as follows:

$$\text{Asset Turnover Ratio} = \frac{\text{Net Sales}}{\text{Average Total Assets}}$$

Average total assets equals beginning total assets plus ending total assets divided by 2.

Abercrombie & Fitch's asset turnover ratios were 1.29 and 1.03 in 2009 and 2010, respectively, which means about every 354 days (365 ÷ 1.03) in 2010. The asset turnover average for the industry is 1.11, so A&F is below the average. But, it is not as far below on asset turnover as it is on accounts receivable turnover.

Care must be exercised when evaluating the asset turnover ratio. Some industries (such as electric utilities and capital intensive manufacturers) require a substantially larger investment in assets to produce a sales dollar than do other industries (such as fast-food restaurants or footwear and catalog merchants). And obviously, a company's total assets turn over much more slowly than its inventories and receivables.

Overview of Asset Efficiency Ratios CORNERSTONE **12-6** illustrates how to calculate and interpret asset efficiency ratios.

CORNERSTONE 12-6

Calculating and Interpreting Asset Efficiency Ratios

Concept:
Asset efficiency ratios are measures of how efficiently a corporation uses its assets.

Information:
Refer to the information in **Aeropostale**'s income statement and balance sheet in Exhibit 12-3 (pp. 600–601). Additionally, accounts receivable, inventory and total assets for 2008 were $0, $136,488 and $514,169, respectively.

Required:
Calculate the following asset efficiency ratios for Aeropostle for 2009 and 2010: (1) accounts receivable turnover ratio, (2) inventory turnover ratio, and (3) asset turnover ratio.

Solution:

			2010	2009
1.	Accounts Receivable Turnover Ratio	$= \dfrac{\text{Net Sales}}{\text{Average Accounts Receivable*}}$	$\dfrac{\$2,230,105}{\$0} = \text{Infinite}$	$\dfrac{\$1,885,531}{\$0} = \text{Infinite}$
2.	Inventory Turnover Ratio	$= \dfrac{\text{Cost of Goods Sold}}{\text{Average Inventories}}$	$\dfrac{\$1,382,958}{[(\$132,915 + \$126,360) \div 2]} = 10.67$	$\dfrac{\$1,231,349}{[(\$126,360 + \$136,488) \div 2]} = 9.37$
3.	Asset Turnover Ratio	$= \dfrac{\text{Net Sales}}{\text{Average Total Assets}}$	$\dfrac{\$2,230,105}{[(\$792,309 + \$657,919) \div 2]} = 3.08$	$\dfrac{\$1,885,531}{[(\$657,919 + \$514,169) \div 2]} = 3.22$

*Note: Average Balance $= \dfrac{\text{Beginning Balance} + \text{Ending Balance}}{2}$

As you can see in Cornerstone 12-6, **Aeropostale** does not have significant receivables. This is because all its sales are made with cash or third-party credit cards. Although its accounts receivable turnover is obviously stronger than the one calculated earlier for **Abercrombie & Fitch**, A&F does have a strong accounts receivable turnover ratio. Aeropostale's inventory turnover ratios of 9.37 and 10.67 are much stronger than A&F's ratios of 3.27 and 3.06 (and well above the industry averages). These two ratios imply an operating cycle of approximately 34 days for Aeropostale compared to 128 days for A&F. All this information is also consistent with the asset turnover ratio, which is much stronger for Aeropostale.

It is important to note that turnover ratios must be interpreted carefully. A company's ability to increase its receivables turnover is limited by competitive considerations. If competitors allow customers a lengthy period before payment is expected, then the firm must offer similar credit terms or lose customers. In periods of high interest rates, the cost of carrying customers' receivables should not be underestimated. For example, a firm with credit sales of $10,000 per day that collects in 30 rather than 90 days would save $72,000 per year at a 12 percent interest rate (60 days × $10,000 × 12%).

However, a corporation's ability to increase its inventory turnover is also affected by its strategy and what the competition is doing. For example, if its strategy is to offer a wide selection or if its competitors stock large quantities of inventory, a corporation will be forced to keep more inventory on hand. This, of course, leads to lower inventory turnover.

Asset efficiency ratios measure the efficiency of a corporation's operations—a factor ultimately related to the corporation's profits. Let us now examine some direct measures of a corporation's profitability.

Profitability Ratios

Profitability ratios measure two aspects of a corporation's profits:

- elements of operations that contribute to profit
- the relationship of profit to total investment and investment by stockholders

The first group of profitability ratios, which includes gross profit (or gross margin) percentage, operating margin percentage, and net profit margin percentage, expresses income statement elements as percentages of net sales. The second group of profitability ratios, which includes return on assets and return on equity, divides measures of income by measures of investment.

Gross Profit (or Gross Margin) Percentage
Gross profit percentage is a measurement of the proportion of each sales dollar that is available to pay other expenses and provide profit for owners. It indicates the effectiveness of pricing, marketing, purchasing, and production decisions. Gross profit percentage is expressed as follows:

$$\text{Gross Profit Percentage} = \frac{\text{Gross Profit}}{\text{Net Sales}}$$

Abercrombie & Fitch's gross profit percentage was 66.91 percent in 2009 and 64.32 percent in 2010. This means that for every dollar in sales the merchandise cost approximately 35 cents, which results in approximately 65 cents in gross profit. This is far above the industry average of 46.21 percent.

Operating Margin Percentage
The operating margin percentage measures the profitability of a company's operations in relation to its sales. All operating revenues and expenses are included in income from operations, but expenses, revenues, gains, and losses that are unrelated to operations are excluded. For example, a retailer would exclude interest revenues produced by its credit activities from income from operations. The **operating margin percentage** is expressed as follows:

$$\text{Operating Margin Percentage} = \frac{\text{Income from Operations}}{\text{Net Sales}}$$

Abercrombie & Fitch's operating margin percentage was 14.30% percent in 2009 and 4.03% percent in 2010. The difference between the gross profit and operating margin percentage of approximately 60 percent in 2010 (64.32 percent gross margin percentage – 4.03 percent operating margin percentage) means that approximately 60 cents on every dollar of sales were spent on operating expenses in 2010. Although an operating margin of 4.03 percent doesn't sound very good, it is well above the industry average of 1.39 percent for the year.

Net Profit Margin Percentage

The net profit margin percentage measures the proportion of each sales dollar that is profit. The **net profit margin percentage** is expressed as follows:

$$\text{Net Profit Margin Percentage} = \frac{\text{Net Income}}{\text{Net Sales}}$$

Abercrombie & Fitch's net profit margin percentage was 7.81 percent in 2009 and 0.01 percent in 2010. The 2010 figure is below the industry average of 0.89 percent. A closer look at the income statement reveals that the large decline from 2009 to 2010 is primarily the result of an unusually large loss on discontinued operations.

In evaluating the gross profit, operating margin, and net profit margin percentage, it is important to recognize that there is substantial variation in profit margins from industry to industry. For example, retail grocery stores, such as **Kroger** and **Safeway**, earn a relatively small amount of gross profit, operating margin, and net income per sales dollar. Pharmaceutical manufacturers, such as **Pfizer** and **Eli Lilly**, on the other hand, earn much more per sales dollar. Since the magnitude of these percentages is affected by many factors, changes from period to period must be investigated to determine the cause.

Return on Assets

The return on assets ratio measures the profit earned by a corporation through use of all its capital, or the total of the investment by both creditors and owners. The **return on assets ratio** is expressed as:

$$\text{Return on Assets} = \frac{\text{Net Income} + [\text{Interest Expense} \times (1 - \text{Tax Rate})]}{\text{Average Total Assets}}$$

Profit, or return, is determined by adding interest expense net of tax to net income. Interest expense net of tax is expressed as follows:

$$\text{Interest Net of Tax} = \text{Interest Expense} \times (1 - \text{Tax Rate})$$

Interest expense is added to net income because it is a return to creditors for their capital contributions. Because the actual capital contribution made by creditors is included in the denominator (average total assets), the numerator must be computed on a comparable basis.

Abercrombie & Fitch's return on assets was 10.13 percent in 2009 and 0.16 percent in 2010. As with the percentages discussed above, appropriate values for this ratio vary from industry to industry because of differences in risk. Over a several-year period, the average return on assets for an electric utility ought to be smaller than the average return on assets for a company that makes and sells home appliances. Companies in the home appliance industry, such as **Whirlpool Corporation**, have a much larger variability of net income because their operations are more sensitive to economic conditions. The average for the Retail—Apparel industry is 1.50 percent, so A&F is below the mean in 2010 for this ratio.

Return on Equity

The return on equity ratio measures the profit earned by a firm through the use of capital supplied by stockholders. Return on equity is similar to return on assets, except that the payments to creditors are removed from the numerator and the creditors' capital contributions are removed from the denominator. The **return on equity ratio** is expressed as follows:

$$\text{Return on Equity} = \frac{\text{Net Income}}{\text{Average Equity}}$$

One of the primary objectives of the management of a firm is to maximize returns for its stockholders. Although the link between a corporation's net income and increases in dividends and share price return is not perfect, the return on equity ratio is still an effective measure of management's performance for the stockholders. As is the case with return on assets, firms often differ in return on equity because of differences in risk. For example, the average several-year return on equity for a grocery store should be lower than the average return on equity for a retail department store because of the lower sensitivity to economic conditions.

The return on equity for **Abercrombie & Fitch** was 15.72 percent and 0.01 percent in 2009 and 2010, respectively, which is also below the industry average of 3.45 percent in 2010.

Overview of Profitability Ratios   CORNERSTONE 12-7 demonstrates how to calculate and interpret profitability ratios.

CORNERSTONE 12-7   Calculating and Interpreting Profitability Ratios

Concept:
Profitability ratios measure elements of operations that contribute to profit and the relationship of profit to total investment and investment by stockholders.

Information:
Refer to the information in **Aeropostale**'s income statement and balance sheet in Exhibit 12-3 (pp. 600–601). In Aeropostale's income statement, interest expense is netted with interest income. Assume that Aeropostle's interest expense is $100 in both 2009 and 2010. Note that Aeropostale's total assets and equity for 2008 were $514,169 and $197,276, respectively.

Required:
Calculate the following profitability ratios for Aeropostle for 2009 and 2010: (1) gross profit percentage, (2) operating margin percentage, (3) net profit margin percentage, (4) return on assets, and (5) return on equity.

Solution:

		2010	2009
1.	Gross Profit Percentage $= \dfrac{\text{Gross Profit}}{\text{Net Sales}}$	$\dfrac{\$847,147}{\$2,230,105} = 37.99\%$	$\dfrac{\$654,182}{\$1,885,531} = 34.69\%$

		2010	2009
2.	Operating Margin Percentage $= \dfrac{\text{Income from Operations}}{\text{Net Sales}}$	$\dfrac{\$382,685}{\$2,230,105} = 17.16\%$	$\dfrac{\$248,299}{\$1,885,531} = 13.17\%$

		2010	2009
3.	Net Profit Margin Percentage $= \dfrac{\text{Net Income}}{\text{Net Sales}}$	$\dfrac{\$229,457}{\$2,230,105} = 10.29\%$	$\dfrac{\$149,422}{\$1,885,531} = 7.92\%$

4.   Return on Assets $= \dfrac{\text{Net Income} + [\text{Interest Expense} \times (1 - \text{Tax Rate}^{**})]}{\text{Average Total Assets}^{*}}$

2010	2009
$\dfrac{\$229,457 + [100^{***} \times (1 - 40.06\%)]}{[(\$792,309 + \$657,919) \div 2]} = 31.65\%$	$\dfrac{\$149,422 + [100^{***} \times (1 - 39.95\%)]}{[(\$657,919 + \$514,169) \div 2]} = 25.51\%$

*Note: Average Balance $= \dfrac{\text{Beginning Balance} + \text{Ending Balance}}{2}$

**Note: $\left(\text{Tax Rate} = \dfrac{\text{Income Taxes}}{\text{Income before Taxes}}\right)$

***Provided in the part 4 of the *Information* section above.

(Continued)

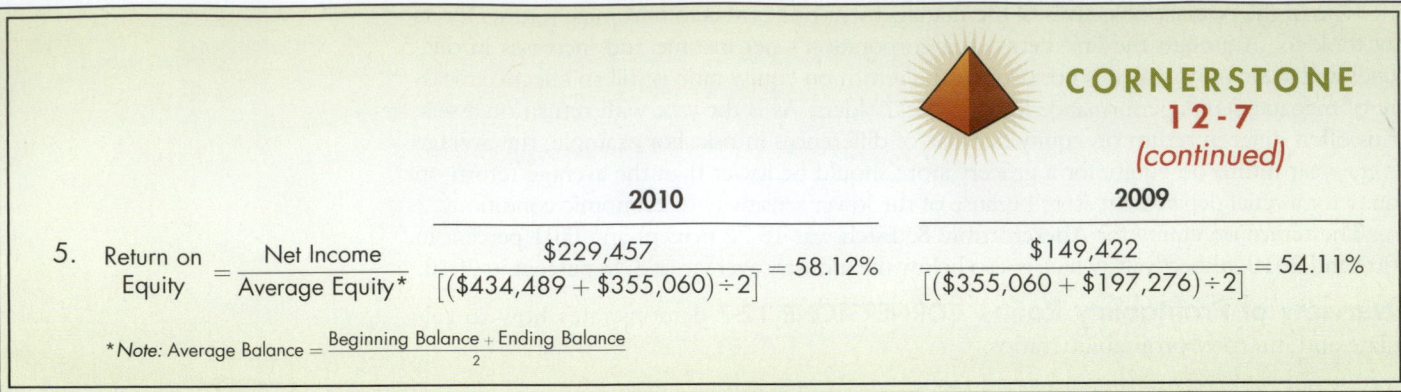

CORNERSTONE 12-7 (continued)

	2010	2009
5. Return on Equity $=\dfrac{\text{Net Income}}{\text{Average Equity*}}$	$\dfrac{\$229,457}{[(\$434,489 + \$355,060) \div 2]} = 58.12\%$	$\dfrac{\$149,422}{[(\$355,060 + \$197,276) \div 2]} = 54.11\%$

*Note: Average Balance $= \dfrac{\text{Beginning Balance} + \text{Ending Balance}}{2}$

As you can see in Cornerstone 12-7, **Abercrombie & Fitch**'s gross profit percentage is 70 percent higher than **Aeropostale**'s. Specifically, A&F makes over 26 cents more in gross profit on every sales dollar than does Aeropostale [(64.32% × $1) − (37.99% × $1)]. However, this advantage is wiped out by the time we reach operating margin, as A&F's operating margin and net profit margin are roughly the same as Aeropostale's in 2009 and substantially below in 2010. Further, Aeropostale has a substantial advantage on the return ratios. Aeropostale has clearly outperformed A&F on profitability measures during 2009 and 2010.

Stockholder Ratios

Stockholders are primarily interested in two things:

- the creation of value
- the distribution of value

Stockholder ratios such as earnings per share and return on common equity provide information about the creation of value for stockholders. As discussed in Chapter 10, value is distributed to stockholders in one of two ways. Either the corporation issues dividends or repurchases stock. The remainder of the stockholder ratios—dividend yield, dividend payout, stock repurchase payout, and total payout—address this distribution of value.

Earnings per Share (EPS) Earnings per share ratio (EPS) measures the income available for common stockholders on a per-share basis and is examined by nearly all statement users. **Earnings per share ratio (EPS)** is expressed as follows:

$$\text{Earnings per Share Ratio} = \frac{\text{Net Income} - \text{Preferred Dividends}}{\text{Average Number of Common Shares Outstanding}}$$

For the average number of common shares outstanding, remember that treasury shares are not considered to be outstanding. Preferred dividends are subtracted from net income because those payments are a return to holders of shares other than common stock. In fact, the numerator, net income less preferred dividends, is often called *income available for common shareholders.*

Although this formula allows you to calculate EPS on your own, corporations are also required to disclose EPS on the income statement. For example, **Abercrombie & Fitch**'s EPS was $3.14 in 2009 and $0.00 in 2010. Obviously, 2010 was not a good year for Abercrombie & Fitch.

Return on Common Equity The return on common equity ratio is arguably the most important ratio for investors. It's similar to the return on equity discussed in the profitability ratio section, but it uses the return on *common* equity rather than equity. Common equity is expressed as follows:

$$\text{Common Equity} = \text{Total Equity} - \text{Preferred Stock}$$

The **return on common equity ratio** is expressed as follows:

$$\text{Return on Common Equity} = \frac{\text{Net Income}}{\text{Average Common Equity}}$$

When there is no preferred stock, as is the case for **Abercrombie & Fitch**, return on common equity will equal traditional return on equity (ROE).

Dividend Yield Ratio   The dividend yield ratio measures the rate at which dividends provide a return to stockholders by comparing dividends with the market price of a share of stock. This ratio is conceptually similar to an interest rate on debt where the dividend is like the interest payment and the cost of the share of stock is the principal. The **dividend yield ratio** is expressed as follows:

$$\text{Dividend Yield Ratio} = \frac{\text{Dividends per Common Share}}{\text{Closing Market Price per Share for the Year}}$$

For the year ended January 30, 2010, **Abercrombie & Fitch** paid dividends of $0.70 per share and the closing market value of their common shares was $31.54. This gives a dividend yield ratio of 2.22 percent, which is slightly below the industry average of 2.56 percent.

Dividend yield is affected by both the corporation's dividend policy and the behavior of its stock price. Because stock prices often change by substantial amounts over short periods, the dividend yield ratio is not stable. In fact, when a stock is traded regularly, the market price is likely to change many times each day. For this reason, some analysts compute dividend yield based on the average stock price for a given period. Others use the highest and the lowest prices for a period and present the dividend yield as a range. For ease, we calculate dividend yield using the closing market price for the year.

Dividend Payout Ratio   The dividend payout ratio measures the proportion of a corporation's profits that are returned to the stockholders immediately as dividends. The **dividend payout ratio** is expressed as follows:

$$\text{Dividend Payout Ratio} = \frac{\text{Common Dividends}}{\text{Net Income}}$$

You could also calculate dividend payout using per share amounts (dividends per share ÷ EPS). You can find the dividends paid in the retained earnings column of the statement of stockholders' equity.

For **Abercrombie & Fitch**, the common dividends paid were $60,769,000 in 2009 and $61,500,000 in 2010. This produces dividend payout ratios of 22.32 percent and 24,212.60 percent in 2009 and 2010, respectively.

The dividend payout ratio varies from corporation to corporation, even within a given industry. Most corporations attempt to pay some stable proportion of earnings as dividends, although A&F pays $0.70 per share every year. Corporations are reluctant to reduce dividends unless absolutely necessary. The result of these two tendencies is that dividends per share are usually increased only when management is confident that higher earnings per share can be sustained. An increase in the dividend payout ratio is usually a signal that management expects future net income to be larger and sustainable.

Stock Repurchase Payout Ratio   The **stock repurchase payout ratio** is expressed as follows:

$$\text{Stock Repurchase Payout Ratio} = \frac{\text{Common Stock Repurchases}}{\text{Net Income}}$$

You can find stock repurchases by looking at the treasury stock column of the statement of stockholders' equity.

Abercrombie & Fitch had $50,000,000 in stock repurchases during 2009 and none in 2010. These repurchases produced stock repurchase payout ratios of 18.37 percent in 2009 and 0 percent in 2010.

Total Payout Ratio The **total payout ratio** is expressed as follows:

$$\text{Total Payout Ratio} = \frac{\text{Common Dividends} + \text{Common Stock Repurchases}}{\text{Net Income}}$$

This ratio can also be calculated indirectly as follows:

$$\text{Total Payout Ratio} = \text{Dividend Payout Ratio} + \text{Stock Repurchase Payout Ratio}$$

Using this latter formula, we see that **Abercrombie & Fitch** had total payout ratios of 40.69 percent (22.32 percent dividend payout + 18.37 percent stock repurchase payout) in 2009 and 24,212.60 percent in 2010.

Overview of Stockholder Ratios **CORNERSTONE 12-8** demonstrates how to calculate and interpret the stockholder ratios.

CORNERSTONE 12-8   Calculating and Interpreting Stockholder Ratios

Concept:
Stockholder ratios measure the creation of value and the distribution of value to stockholders.

Information:
Refer to the information for **Aeropostale**'s income statement and balance sheet in Exhibit 12-3 (pp. 600–601). Aeropostale's average common shares for 2010 and 2009 were 99,629 and 100,248, respectively. They paid no dividends in 2010 or 2009. Aeropostale repurchased $174,257 of common shares in 2010 and $6,681 of common shares in 2009. (Average common shares are typically disclosed on the income statement. Information regarding dividends and stock repurchases can be found in the statement of stockholders' equity.) The price of Aeropostale's stock was $21.92 and $14.07 at the end of 2010 and 2009, respectively.

Required:
Calculate the following stockholder ratios for Aeropostle for 2009 and 2010: (1) earnings per share, (2) return on common equity (assume 2008 total equity, preferred stock and additional paid-in capital from preferred stock were $197,276, $0, and $0, respectively), (3) dividend yield, (4) dividend payout, (5) total payout, and (6) share repurchase payout.

Solution:

		2010	2009
1.	$\text{EPS} = \dfrac{\text{Net Income} - \text{Preferred Dividends}}{\text{Average Number of Common Shares Outstanding}}$	$\dfrac{(\$229,457 - \$0)}{99,629} = \$2.30$	$\dfrac{(\$149,422 - \$0)}{100,248} = \$1.49$

2. $\text{Return on Common Equity} = \dfrac{\text{Net Income}}{\text{Average Common Equity*}}$

2010	2009
$\dfrac{\$229,457}{[(\$434,489 - \$0 - \$0) + (\$355,060 - \$0 - \$0) \div 2]}$	$\dfrac{\$149,422}{[(\$355,060 - \$0 - \$0) + (\$197,276 - \$0 - \$0) \div 2]}$
$= 58.12\%$	$= 54.11\%$

		2010	2009
3.	$\text{Dividend Yield Ratio} = \dfrac{\text{Dividends per Common Share**}}{\text{Closing Market Price per Share for the Year}}$	$\dfrac{\$0}{\$21.92} = 0.00\%$	$\dfrac{\$0}{\$14.07} = 0.00\%$

*Common Equity = Total Equity – Preferred Stock – Additional Paid-In Capital—Preferred Stock

**Dividends per share are taken from the Statement of Stockholders' Equity. Amount is given in the information section of this Cornerstone.

CORNERSTONE 12-8 *(continued)*

		2010	2009
4.	Dividend Payout Ratio $= \dfrac{\text{Common Dividends}}{\text{Net Income}}$	$\dfrac{\$0}{\$229{,}457} = 0.00\%$	$\dfrac{\$0}{\$149{,}422} = 0.00\%$

		2010	2009
5.	Stock Repurchase Payout Ratio $= \dfrac{\text{Common Stock Repurchases}}{\text{Net Income}}$	$\dfrac{\$174{,}257}{\$229{,}457} = 75.94\%$	$\dfrac{\$6{,}681}{\$149{,}422} = 4.47\%$

		2010	2009
6.	Total Payout Ratio $= \dfrac{\text{Common Dividends} + \text{Common Stock Repurchases}}{\text{Net Income}}$	$\dfrac{(\$0 + \$174{,}257)}{\$229{,}457} = 75.94\%$	$\dfrac{(\$0 + \$6{,}681)}{\$149{,}422} = 4.47\%$

As you can see in Cornerstone 12-8, **Aeropostale**'s 2009 EPS of $1.49 is much lower than **Abercrombie & Fitch**'s EPS of $3.14. However, in 2010 Aeropostale's EPS grew by 54.4%, to $2.30, while A&F's dropped by 100% to $0.00.

As for shareholder payout, the firms pursued quite different strategies. Aeropostale did not pay any dividends, but spent approximately 76% percent of net income in 2010 on share repurchases. A&F, on the other hand, paid dividends of $0.70 per share each year. Additionally, in 2009 they spent 18 percent of net income on share repurchases, which resulted in a total payout ratio of approximately 40 percent.

Dupont Analysis

Return on common equity (or return on equity, which is hereafter abbreviated as ROE) is the most important measure of profitability for investors. It represents the amount of income generated per dollar of book value of equity or common equity. In that way, it is conceptually similar to an interest rate. Recall that ROE is calculated as:

$$\text{ROE} = \frac{\text{Net Income}}{\text{Average Equity}}$$

Dupont analysis recognizes that ROE can be broken down into three important aspects of return—net profit margin, asset turnover, and leverage.

$$= \frac{\text{Net Income}}{\text{Sales}} \times \frac{\text{Sales}}{\text{Average Total Assets}} \times \frac{\text{Average Total Assets}}{\text{Average Equity}}$$

Net Profit Margin $\times$ Asset Turnover $\times$ Total Leverage

The logic of this breakdown is compelling. First, profitability requires that the corporation is able to earn an adequate gross profit margin. That is, **Abercrombie & Fitch** and **Aeropostale** must be able to sell their products for more than it costs to buy them. Net profit margin carries this idea down the income statement from gross profit to net income. As we learned earlier in the chapter, the net profit margin represents how many cents of profit there are on every sales dollar.

Second, how efficient is the corporation with its net assets? The desire for asset efficiency is obvious. Everyone knows that you would rather earn $1,000,000 on an investment of $5,000,000 than an investment of $50,000,000. Before discussing leverage, we will focus a little more closely on net profit margin and asset turnover, which taken together give us return on assets (Net Income ÷ Average Total Assets), albeit ignoring the after-tax effect of interest expense in the numerator (see p. 610). To illustrate, consider **Abercrombie & Fitch** and **Aeropostale** for 2009. Their net profit margins and asset turnovers were:

	Net Profit Margin	Asset Turnover	Return on Assets
Abercrombie & Fitch	7.81%	1.29	10.07%
Aeropostale	7.92%	3.22	25.50%*

*This differs from the return on assets shown in part 4 of Cornerstone 12-7 because Dupont analysis does not add back the after tax effect of interest expense to net income (see discussion on p. 610)

Although Abercrombie & Fitch and Aeropostale had similar net profit margins in 2009, their return on assets are quite different because Aeropostale has a much higher asset turnover. This highlights different strategies for achieving profitability. Aeropostale is more efficient with its assets. This is consistent with a corporation that is seeking to compete on price because to keep costs down you must be efficient with net assets. A&F, on the other hand, is a product differentiator. A successful product differentiator can earn higher margins on its products, although A&F didn't in 2009 because customers view their products as sufficiently different from the competition's to warrant paying higher prices. Although not specifically part of the Dupont analysis, this is illustrated by A&F's gross profit margin percentage (66.91 percent) being more than double Aeropostale's (34.69 percent).

Most product differentiators experience lower asset turnover. You can probably think of these distinctions within and between industries. For example, **Wal-Mart** is a cost leader. They have very low margins but make up for it by being extremely efficient with their assets. **Nordstrom's**, on the other hand, has much higher margins, but this is offset by lower turnover. Grocery stores, such as **Trader Joe's** and **Albertson's**, have low margins and high turnover; auto dealers and jewelry stores, such as **Toyota** and **Tiffany & Co.**, have high margins and low turnover. Further, the trade-off between margins and turnover is evident in a number of decisions. For example, if a store puts an item on sale, it sacrifices margins and hopes to make up for it with higher turnover.

Notice that 2009 ROE of 15.72% for **Abercrombie & Fitch** and 54.11% for **Aeropostale** is higher than their respective returns on assets. Return on *equity* can be made larger than return on *assets* by leveraging these assets through the use of debt. The idea of leverage is simple. For example, if you can borrow at 8 percent and earn 10 percent (assuming the same tax rates on the interest and return), then you win. If you could guarantee these two figures after taxes, you should borrow all you can because you are netting 2 percent on every dollar. That is, if you borrow $1,000,000 you will make $20,000 (a $100,000 return less $80,000 in interest). If you can borrow $1,000,000,000, then you will make $20,000,000.

This effect is captured by the total leverage component of the Dupont analysis. Recall that a company can obtain money to finance its business by either selling stock or borrowing. If they choose to sell stock, then stockholders are entitled to their share of the returns. If they borrow the money, on the other hand, the creditors do not share in the returns. So why don't all corporations use debt instead of equity? There are two reasons:

- They may not be able to find a low enough interest rate.
- While interest is guaranteed, returns are not. That is, while the returns may seem better than the interest right now, in a few years it may not be so. For evidence of this, consider stories of people who borrowed money at 15 percent on credit cards to invest in the stock market in the late 1990s.

CORNERSTONE 12-9 illustrates how to perform and interpret Dupont analysis.

CORNERSTONE 12-9   Performing and Interpreting Dupont Analysis

Concept:
Dupont analysis decomposes a corporation's ROE into net profit margin, asset turnover, and total leverage.

Information:

Refer to the information for **Aeropostale**'s income statement and balance sheet in Exhibit 12-3 (pp. 600–601) in addition to the following information for **Abercrombie & Fitch**:

CORNERSTONE
12-9
(continued)

Net income	$ 254	Ending total assets	$2,821,866
Sales	2,928,626	Beginning stockholders' equity	1,845,578
Beginning total assets	2,848,181	Ending stockholders' equity	1,827,917

Required:

Perform Dupont analysis for both corporations for 2010.

Solution:

Aeropostale

$$\text{Dupont Analysis: ROE} = \left(\frac{\text{Net Income}}{\text{Sales}}\right) \times \left(\frac{\text{Sales}}{\text{Average Total Assets}}\right) \times \left(\frac{\text{Average Total Assets}}{\text{Average Equity}}\right)$$

$$= \left(\frac{\$229,457}{\$2,230,105}\right) \times \left\{\frac{\$2,230,105}{(\$657,919 + \$792,309) \div 2}\right\} \times \left\{\frac{(\$657,919 + \$792,309) \div 2}{(\$434,489 + \$355,060) \div 2}\right\}$$

$$= 10.29\% \times 3.08 \times 1.84$$

$$= 58.32\%*$$

*Does not equal the ROE of 58.12% calculated in Cornerstone 12-8 because of rounding in the individual components.

Abercrombie & Fitch

$$= \left(\frac{\$254}{\$2,928,626}\right) \times \left\{\frac{\$2,928,626}{(\$2,848,181 + \$2,821,866) \div 2}\right\} \times \left\{\frac{(\$2,848,181 + \$2,821,866) \div 2}{(\$1,845,578 + \$1,827,917) \div 2}\right\}$$

$$= 0.01\% \times 1.03 \times 1.54$$

$$= 0.02\%*$$

*Does not equal ROE of 0.01% shown on p. 615 because of rounding in the individual components.

The Dupont analysis in Cornerstone 12-9 shows that **Aeropostale** has outperformed **Abercrombie & Fitch** in all aspects of ROE. Aeropostale had far better net profit margin, despite A&F's superior gross profit margin. Further, Aeropostale was much more efficient with its assets as shown by their superior asset turnover. This is consistent with a cost leader (for example, offering the lower prices) because asset efficiency helps contain costs, and cost containment is necessary to compete on price. Finally, Aeropostale has slightly higher leverage (1.84 versus 1.54), which means Aeropostale has a higher proportion of debt financing. This higher proportion of debt financing "leverages" its return on assets to produce an even higher ROE.

Summary of Financial Ratios

Exhibit 12-4 (p. 618) summarizes the financial ratios presented in this chapter. More advanced accounting texts may present additional ratios; however, those introduced here are among the most widely used.

Data for Ratio Comparisons

As we pointed out earlier in the chapter, developing information from financial ratios requires that comparisons be made among the ratios of the following:

- the same corporation over time
- similar corporations over time
- similar corporations at the present time

Analysts rely on several sources to fulfill their need for a broad range of data for individual corporations as well as for industries and the economy.

We believe the best source of information about the corporation starts with the investor relations section of their website. This part of the website should contain links to

Exhibit 12-4

Summary of Financial Ratios

Short-Term Liquidity Ratios

1. $\text{Current Ratio} = \dfrac{\text{Current Assets}}{\text{Current Liabilities}}$

2. $\text{Quick Ratio} = \dfrac{\text{Cash} + \text{Short-Term Investments} + \text{Receivable}}{\text{Current Liabilities}}$

3. $\text{Cash Ratio} = \dfrac{\text{Cash} + \text{Short-Term Investments}}{\text{Current Liabilities}}$

4. $\text{Operating Cash Flow Ratio} = \dfrac{\text{Cash Flows from Operating Activities}}{\text{Current Liabilities}}$

Debt Management Ratios

5a. $\text{Times Interest Earned (\textit{Accrual Basis})} = \dfrac{\text{Operating Income}}{\text{Interest Expense}}$

5b. $\text{Times Interest Earned (\textit{Cash Basis})} = \dfrac{(\text{Cash Flows from Operations} + \text{Income Taxes Payable} + \text{Interest Payments})}{\text{Interest Payments}}$

6. $\text{Long-Term Debt-to-Equity Ratio} = \dfrac{\text{Long-Term Debt (including current portion)}}{\text{Total Equity}}$

7. $\text{Debt-to-Equity Ratio} = \dfrac{\text{Total Liabilities}}{\text{Total Equity}}$

8. $\text{Long-Term Debt-to-Total Assets Ratio} = \dfrac{\text{Long-Term Debt (including current portion)}}{\text{Total Assets}}$

9. $\text{Debt-to-Total Assets Ratio} = \dfrac{\text{Total Liabilities}}{\text{Total Assets}}$

Asset Efficiency Ratios

10. $\text{Accounts Receivable Turnover Ratio} = \dfrac{\text{Net Credit Sales or Net Sales}}{\text{Average Accounts Receivable}}$

11. $\text{Inventory Turnover Ratio} = \dfrac{\text{Cost of Goods Sold}}{\text{Average Inventory}}$

12. $\text{Asset Turnover Ratio} = \dfrac{\text{Net Sales}}{\text{Average Total Assets}}$

Profitability Ratios

13. $\text{Gross Profit Percentage} = \dfrac{\text{Gross Profit}}{\text{Net Sales}}$

14. $\text{Operating Margin Percentage} = \dfrac{\text{Income from Operations}}{\text{Net Sales}}$

15. $\text{Net Profit Margin Percentage} = \dfrac{\text{Net Income}}{\text{Net Sales}}$

16. $\text{Return on Assets} = \dfrac{\text{Net Income} + [\text{Interest Expense} \times (1 - \text{Tax Rate})]}{\text{Average Total Assets}}$

17. $\text{Return on Equity} = \dfrac{\text{Net Income}}{\text{Average Equity}}$

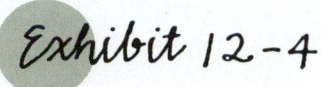
Exhibit 12-4

Summary of Financial Ratios (*Continued*)

Stockholder Ratios

18. Earnings per Share (EPS) $= \dfrac{\text{(Net Income} - \text{Preferred Dividends)}}{\text{Average Number of Common Shares Outstanding}}$

19. Return on Common Equity $= \dfrac{\text{Net Income}}{\text{Average Common Equity}}$

20. Dividend Yield Ratio $= \dfrac{\text{Dividends per Common Share}}{\text{Closing Market Price per Share for the Year}}$

21. Dividend Payout Ratio $= \dfrac{\text{Common Dividends Paid}}{\text{Net Income}}$

22. Total Payout Ratio $= \dfrac{\text{(Common Dividends} + \text{Common Stock Repurchases)}}{\text{Net Income}}$

23. Stock Repurchase Payout $=$ Total Payout Ratio $-$ Dividend Payout Ratio

Dupont Analysis

24. Return on Equity $= \left(\dfrac{\text{Net Income}}{\text{Sales}}\right) \times \left(\dfrac{\text{Sales}}{\text{Average Total Assets}}\right) \times \left(\dfrac{\text{Average Total Assets}}{\text{Average Equity}}\right)$

the corporation's 10-K (and other SEC filings), analyst conference calls, and press releases. However, you can also gain information through the financial press (such as, *The Wall Street Journal*, etc.) and investor discussion boards, although the latter must be evaluated with a critical eye.

Information on the industry can be obtained from industry guides such as **Standard & Poor's** and **IBISWorld**. These are often available through your university library website or in hard copy at the library. We also like websites like **Google** Finance, **Yahoo!** Finance, BizStats, and **MSN**.

SUMMARY OF LEARNING OBJECTIVES

LO1.   **Explain how creditors, investors, and others use financial statements in their decisions.**
   - The role of financial statements is to provide information for
     - Creditors
     - Investors
     - Customers
     - Suppliers
     - Employees
   This information will help these groups form judgments, which will serve as the foundation for various decisions.

LO2.   **Become familiar with the most important SEC filings.**
   - Publicly traded corporations must file a variety of financial information, including audited financial statements, with the Securities and Exchange Commission (SEC) on an ongoing basis. For example,

- annual reports on Form 10-K
- quarterly reports on Form 10-Q
- current reports for numerous specified events on Form 8-K
- The annual report on Form 10-K provides a comprehensive overview of the corporation's business and financial condition and includes *audited* financial statements.
- Although similarly named, the annual report on Form 10-K is distinct from the "annual report to shareholders," which a corporation must send to its stockholders when it holds an annual meeting to elect directors.
- For larger filers, the 10-K must be filed within 60 days of their fiscal year end.

LO3.   Understand the difference between cross sectional and time series analysis.
- Cross sectional analysis entails comparing a corporation's financial statements to its primary competitors and industry averages.
- Time series (or trend) analysis involves comparisons of the current year to previous years.
- Differences may exist in the size of two corporations or even in the same corporation from year to year (perhaps due to the acquisition of another corporation). Analysts address this problem by restating the financial statements in percentage terms.

LO4.   Analyze financial statements using horizontal and vertical analysis.
- In horizontal analysis, each financial statement line item is expressed as a percent of the base year (typically the least recent year shown).
- In vertical analysis, each financial statement line item is expressed as a percent of the largest statement amount—net sales on the income statement and total assets on the balance sheet.

LO5.   Calculate and use financial statement ratios to evaluate a company.
- Ratios help remove the effects of size differences (as measured in dollars).
- Six categories of ratios are discussed:
  - short-term liquidity
  - debt management
  - profitability
  - asset efficiency (or operating)
  - stockholder
  - Dupont
- More advanced accounting and finance texts may present additional ratios; however, those introduced here are among the most widely used.

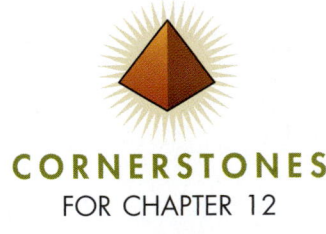

CORNERSTONES
FOR CHAPTER 12

CORNERSTONE 12-1 Interpreting cross sectional and time series (or trend) analysis (p. 591)

CORNERSTONE 12-2 Preparing common size statements for horizontal analysis (p. 592)

CORNERSTONE 12-3 Preparing common size statements for vertical analysis (p. 594)

CORNERSTONE 12-4 Calculating and interpreting short-term liquidity ratios (p. 601)

CORNERSTONE 12-5 Calculating and interpreting debt management ratios (p. 604)

CORNERSTONE 12-6 Calculating and interpreting asset efficiency ratios (p. 608)

CORNERSTONE 12-7 Calculating and interpreting profitability ratios (p. 611)

CORNERSTONE 12-8 Calculating and interpreting stockholder ratios (p. 614)

CORNERSTONE 12-9 Performing and interpreting Dupont analysis (p. 616)

KEY TERMS

Accounts receivable turnover ratio (p. 607)
Asset efficiency ratios (or operating ratios) (p. 606)
Asset turnover ratio (p. 607)
Cash ratio (p. 599)
Common size statements (p. 592)
Cross sectional analysis (p. 590)
Current ratio (p. 598)
Debt management ratios (p. 602)
Debt-to-equity ratio (p. 603)
Debt-to-total assets ratio (p. 604)
Dividend payout ratio (p. 613)
Dividend yield ratio (p. 613)
Dupont analysis (p. 615)
Earnings per share ratio (EPS) (p. 612)
Financial ratios (p. 597)
Form 8-K (p. 588)
Form 10-K (p. 588)
Form 10-Q (p. 588)
Gross profit percentage (p. 609)
Horizontal analysis (p. 592)
Inventory turnover ratio (p. 607)

Long-term debt-to-equity ratio (p. 603)
Long-term debt-to-total assets ratio (p. 604)
MD&A (p. 589)
Net profit margin percentage (p. 610)
Operating cash flow ratio (p. 600)
Operating margin percentage (p. 609)
Profitability ratios (p. 609)
Quick ratio (p. 599)
Ratio analysis (p. 597)
Ratios (financial ratios) (p. 597)
Return on assets ratio (p. 610)
Return on common equity ratio (p. 613)
Return on equity ratio (p. 610)
Short-term liquidity ratios (p. 598)
Stock repurchase payout ratio (p. 613)
Stockholder ratios (p. 612)
Time series (or trend) analysis (p. 590)
Times interest earned ratio (p. 603)
Turnover (p. 606)
Total payout ratio (p. 614)
Vertical analysis (p. 594)

REVIEW PROBLEM

Ratio Analysis

Following are consolidated balance sheets and income statements for Kellman Company:

Kellman Company and Subsidiaries Consolidated Balance Sheets (In thousands)			
	December 31,		
	2010	**2009**	**2008**
ASSETS			
Current assets:			
Cash and cash equivalents	$ 40,588	$ 70,655	$ 62,977
Accounts receivable, net	93,515	71,867	53,132
Inventories	166,082	81,031	53,607
Income taxes receivable	614	4,310	0
Other current assets	11,028	8,944	5,252
Deferred income taxes	10,418	8,145	6,822
Total current assets	**$ 322,245**	**$244,952**	**$181,790**
Property and equipment, net	52,332	29,923	20,865
Intangible assets, net	6,470	7,875	0
Deferred income taxes	8,173	5,180	0
Other noncurrent assets	1,393	1,438	1,032
Total assets	**$ 390,613**	**$289,368**	**$203,687**

LIABILITIES AND STOCKHOLDERS' EQUITY

Current liabilities:			
Accounts payable	$ 55,012	$ 42,718	$ 31,699
Accrued expenses	36,111	25,403	11,449
Income taxes payable	0	0	716
Current maturities of long-term debt	4,111	2,648	1,967
Current maturities of capital lease obligations	465	794	1,841
Total current liabilities	$ 95,699	$ 71,563	$ 47,672
Long-term debt, net of current maturities	9,298	1,893	2,868
Capital lease obligations, net of current maturities	458	922	1,715
Deferred income taxes	0	0	330
Other long-term liabilities	4,673	602	272
Total liabilities	$ 110,128	$ 74,980	$ 52,857
Stockholders' equity:			
Class A common stock	$ 12	$ 12	$ 10
Class B common stock	4	4	5
Additional paid-in capital—common stock	162,362	148,562	124,803
Retained earnings	117,782	66,376	28,067
Unearned compensation	(182)	(463)	(1,889)
Notes receivable from stockholders	0	0	(163)
Accumulated other comprehensive income	507	(103)	(3)
Total stockholders' equity	$ 280,485	$ 214,388	$ 150,830
Total liabilities and stockholders' equity	$ 390,613	$ 289,368	$ 203,687

Kellman Company and Subsidiaries
Consolidated Income Statements
(In thousands)

	December 31,		
	2010	**2009**	**2008**
Net sales	$606,561	$430,689	$281,053
Cost of goods sold	301,517	215,089	145,203
Gross profit	$ 305,044	$ 215,600	$ 135,850
Operating expenses			
Selling, general and administrative expenses	218,779	158,682	100,040
Income from operations	$ 86,265	$ 56,918	$ 35,810
Interest income	1,549	2,231	273
Interest expense	(800)	(774)	(3,188)
Other income, net	2,029	712	79
Income before income taxes	$ 89,043	$ 59,087	$ 32,974
Income tax expense	36,485	20,108	13,255
Net income	$ 52,558	$ 38,979	$ 19,719
Cumulative preferred dividends on preferred stock	0	0	5,307
Net income available to common stockholders	$ 52,558	$ 38,979	$ 14,412

Additionally, you will need the following information:

Weighted average common shares outstanding	48,021	46,983	37,199
Cash flows from operating activities	$(14,628)	$10,701	$15,795
Dividends per share	$0	$0	$0
Dividends	$0	$0	$0
Stock repurchases	$0	$0	$0
Market price per share at year end	$43.67	$50.45	$38.31

Required:
1. Calculate the short-term liquidity ratios for Kellman Company for 2009 and 2010.
2. Calculate the debt management ratios for Kellman Company for 2009 and 2010.
3. Calculate the asset efficiency ratios for Kellman Company for 2009 and 2010.
4. Calculate the profitability ratios for Kellman Company for 2009 and 2010.
5. Calculate the stockholder ratios for Kellman Company for 2009 and 2010.
6. Perform Dupont analysis for Kellman Company for 2009 and 2010.

Solution:
1. Short-term liquidity ratios:

$$\text{Current Ratio} = \frac{\text{Current Assets}}{\text{Current Liabilities}}$$

	2010	2009
Current assets	$322,245	$244,952
Current liabilities	95,699	71,563
Current ratio	**3.37**	**3.42**

$$\text{Quick Ratio} = \frac{\text{Cash} + \text{Short-Term Investments} + \text{Accounts Receivable}}{\text{Current Liabilities}}$$

	2010	2009
Cash	$40,588	$70,655
Short-term investments	0	0
Accounts receivable	93,515	71,867
Current liabilities	95,699	71,563
Quick ratio	**1.40**	**1.99**

$$\text{Cash Ratio} = \frac{\text{Cash} + \text{Short-Term Investments}}{\text{Current Liabilities}}$$

	2010	2009
Cash	$40,588	$70,655
Short-term investments	0	0
Current liabilities	95,699	71,563
Cash ratio	**0.42**	**0.99**

$$\text{Operating Cash Flow Ratio} = \frac{\text{Cash Flows from Operating Activities}}{\text{Current Liabilities}}$$

	2010	2009
Cash flows from operating activities	$(14,628)*	$10,701*
Current liabilities	95,699	71,563
Operating cash flow ratio	**(0.15)**	**0.15**

*Provided in the information section

2. Debt management ratios:

$$\text{Times Interest Earned} = \frac{\text{Operating Income}}{\text{Interest Expense}}$$

	2010	2009
Operating income	$86,265	$56,918
Interest expense	800	774
Times interest earned (accrual)	**107.83**	**73.54**

$$\text{Long-Term Debt-to-Equity Ratio} = \frac{\text{Long-Term Debt (including current portion)}}{\text{Total Equity}}$$

	2010	2009
Long-term debt	$ 9,298	$ 1,893
Current portion of long-term debt	4,111	2,648
Total equity	280,485	214,388
Long-term debt-to-equity	**0.05**	**0.02**

$$\text{Debt-to-equity Ratio} = \frac{\text{Total Liabilities}}{\text{Total Equity}}$$

	2010	2009
Total liabilities	$110,128	$ 74,980
Total equity	280,485	214,388
Debt-to-equity	**0.39**	**0.35**

$$\text{Long-Term Debt-to-Total Assets Ratio} = \frac{\text{Long-Term Debt (including current portion)}}{\text{Total Assets}}$$

	2010	2009
Long-term debt	$ 9,298	$ 1,893
Current portion of long-term debt	4,111	2,648
Total assets	390,613	289,368
Long-term debt-to-total assets	**0.03**	**0.02**

$$\text{Debt-to-Total Assets Ratio} = \frac{\text{Total Liabilities}}{\text{Total Assets}}$$

	2010	2009
Total liabilities	$110,128	$ 74,980
Total assets	390,613	289,368
Debt-to-total assets	**0.28**	**0.26**

3. Asset efficiency ratios:

$$\text{Accounts Receivable Turnover Ratio} = \frac{\text{Net Sales}}{\text{Average Accounts Receivable*}}$$

$$*\text{Average Balance} = \frac{(\text{Beginning Balance} + \text{Ending Balance})}{2}$$

	2010	2009	2008
Net sales	$606,561	$430,689	$281,053
Receivables	93,515	71,867	53,132
Accounts receivable turnover ratio	**7.34**	**6.89**	

$$\text{Inventory Turnover Ratio} = \frac{\text{Cost of Goods Sold}}{\text{Average Inventories}}$$

	2010	2009	2008
Cost of goods sold	$301,517	$215,089	$145,203
Inventories	166,082	81,031	53,607
Inventory turnover ratio	**2.44**	**3.20**	

$$\text{Asset Turnover Ratio} = \frac{\text{Net Sales}}{\text{Average Total Assets}}$$

	2010	2009	2008
Net sales	$606,561	$430,689	$281,053
Total assets	390,613	289,368	203,687
Asset turnover ratio	**1.78**	**1.75**	

4. Profitability ratios:

$$\text{Gross Profit Percentage} = \frac{\text{Gross Profit}}{\text{Net Sales}}$$

	2010	2009
Net sales	$606,561	$430,689
Gross profit	305,044	215,600
Gross profit percentage	**50.29%**	**50.06%**

$$\text{Operating Margin Percentage} = \frac{\text{Income from Operations}}{\text{Net Sales}}$$

	2010	2009
Net sales	$606,561	$430,689
Income from operations	86,265	56,918
Operating margin percentage	**14.22%**	**13.22%**

$$\text{Net Profit Margin Percentage} = \frac{\text{Net Income}}{\text{Net Sales}}$$

	2010	2009
Net sales	$606,561	$430,689
Net income	52,558	38,979
Net profit margin percentage	**8.67%**	**9.05%**

$$\text{Return on Assets} = \frac{\text{Net Income} + [\text{Interest Expense} \times (1 - \text{Tax Rate})]}{\text{Average Total Assets}^*}$$

$$^*\text{Average Balance} = \frac{(\text{Beginning Balance} + \text{Ending Balance})}{2}$$

	2010	2009	2008
Total assets	$390,613	$289,368	$203,687
Income Taxes Expense	36,485	20,108	
Net Income	52,558	38,979	
Interest Expense	800	774	
Income before taxes	89,043	59,087	
Tax rate*	40.97%	34.03%	
Return on assets	**15.60%**	**16.02%**	

*Income Taxes Expense ÷ Income before Taxes

$$\text{Return on Equity} = \frac{\text{Net Income}}{\text{Average Equity}^*}$$

$$^*\text{Average Balance} = \frac{(\text{Beginning Balance} + \text{Ending Balance})}{2}$$

	2010	2009	2008
Net income	$ 52,558	$ 38,979	
Stockholders' equity	280,485	214,388	$150,830
Return on equity	**21.24%**	**21.35%**	

5. Stockholder ratios:

$$\text{Earnings per Share Ratio} = \frac{\text{Net Income} - \text{Preferred Dividends}}{\text{Average Number of Common Shares Outstanding}}$$

	2010	2009
Net income	$52,558	$38,979
Preferred dividends	0	0
Average common shares*	48,021	46,983
EPS	**$ 1.09**	**$ 0.83**

*Provided in the information section.

$$\text{Return on Common Equity} = \frac{\text{Net Income}}{\text{Average Common Equity*}}$$

*Common Equity = Total Equity − Preferred Stock − Additional paid-in capital—preferred stock

	2010	2009	2008
Net income	$ 52,558	$ 38,979	
Stockholders' equity	280,485	214,388	$150,830
Preferred stock	0	0	0
Additional paid-in capital—preferred stock	0	0	0
Return on common equity	**21.24%**	**21.35%**	

$$\text{Dividend Yield Ratio} = \frac{\text{Dividends per Common Share}}{\text{Closing Market Price per Share for the Year}}$$

	2010	2009
Dividends per share*	$ 0	$ 0
Closing market price for year*	43.67	50.45
Dividend yield ratio	**0.0%**	**0.0%**

*Provided in the information section.

$$\text{Dividend Payout Ratio} = \frac{\text{Common Dividends}}{\text{Net Income}}$$

	2010	2009
Common dividends*	$ 0	$ 0
Net income	52,558	38,979
Dividend yield ratio	**0.0%**	**0.0%**

*Provided in the information section.

$$\text{Total Payout Ratio} = \frac{\text{Common Dividends} + \text{Common Stock Repurchases}}{\text{Net Income}}$$

	2010	2009
Common dividends*	$ 0	$ 0
Common stock repurchases*	0	0
Net income	52,558	38,979
Total payout ratio	**0%**	**0%**

*Provided in the information section.

6. Dupont analysis:

$$\text{ROE} = \frac{\text{Net Income}}{\text{Sales}} \times \frac{\text{Sales}}{\text{Average Total Assets}} \times \frac{\text{Average Total Assets}}{\text{Average Equity}}$$

$$= \text{Net Profit Margin} \times \text{Asset Turnover} \times \text{Total Leverage}$$

2010:

$$= \left(\frac{\$52,558}{\$606,561}\right) \times \left\{\frac{\$606,561}{(\$390,613 + \$289,368) \div 2)}\right\} \times \left\{\frac{(\$390,613 + \$289,368) \div 2}{(\$280,485 + \$214,388) \div 2}\right\}$$

$$= 8.67\% \times 1.78 \times 1.37$$

$$= 21.14\%$$

*Does not equal ROE of 21.24% shown in parts 4 and 5 because of rounding in the individual components.

2009:

$$= \left(\frac{\$38,979}{\$430,689}\right) \times \left\{\frac{\$430,689}{(\$289,368 + \$203,687) \div 2}\right\} \times \left\{\frac{(\$289,368 + \$203,687) \div 2}{(\$214,388 + \$150,830) \div 2}\right\}$$

$$= 9.05\% \times 1.75 \times 1.35$$

$$= 21.38\%*$$

*Does not equal ROE of 21.35% shown in parts 4 and 5 because of rounding in the individual components.

DISCUSSION QUESTIONS

1. Describe how some of the primary groups of users use financial statements.
2. What is a 10-K?
3. How does the 10-K differ from the 10-Q?
4. Describe the information provided in Item 1 of the 10-K.
5. Describe the information provided in Item 7 of the 10-K.
6. Describe the information provided in Item 8 of the 10-K.
7. What is the difference between time series and cross sectional analysis?
8. What is the difference between horizontal and vertical analysis?
9. How do the current and quick ratios differ? Which is a more conservative measure of short-term liquidity? Support your answer.
10. How does the operating cash flow ratio differ from the current, quick, and cash ratios?
11. What are you trying to learn by calculating debt management ratios?
12. Why are higher asset turnover ratios considered to be better than lower turnover ratios?
13. What two aspects of a company's profitability are measured by profitability ratios?
14. What are the two major categories of stockholder ratios?
15. Dupont analysis breaks down return on equity into what three components?
16. Why must you analyze the accounting policies of a company when performing financial-statement analysis? Provide an example of how knowledge of accounting policies would affect your analysis of inventory.

MULTIPLE-CHOICE EXERCISES

12-1 Which of the following use financial statement data to make decisions?

a. customers
b. investors
c. suppliers
d. all of these

12-2 Which statement would best provide information about a company's current liquidity?

a. balance sheet
b. income statement
c. statement of cash flows
d. none of these

12-3 A banker is analyzing a company that operates in the petroleum industry. Which of the following might be a major consideration in determining whether the company should receive a loan?

a. The petroleum industry suffers from political pressures concerning the selling price of its products.
b. Inflation has been high for several years in a row.
c. All companies in the petroleum industry use the same accounting principles.
d. The company has a large amount of interest payments related to many outstanding loans.

12-4 Which of the following filings includes unaudited financial statements, provides a continuing view of the corporation's financial position during the year, and must be filed for each of the first three fiscal quarters of the corporation's fiscal year?

a. 8-K
b. 10-K
c. 10-Q
d. Form 13F

12-5 Which of the following filings is known as the "current report" that companies must file with the SEC to announce major events that are important to investors and creditors?

a. 8-K
b. 10-K
c. 10-Q
d. Form 13F

12-6 Which section of the Form 10-K includes an analysis of the company's financial condition and performance of the company?

a. Item 4—Submission of Matters to Vote
b. Item 5—Market for Common Stock
c. Item 6—Selected Financial Data

d. Item 7—Management Discussion and Analysis

12-7 Which of the following are required to be included in the Form 10-K?

a. a list of all financial statements and exhibits required to be filed
b. the name of every person or group who owns more than 5 percent of a class of stock
c. information on the salary and other forms of compensation paid to executive officers and directors
d. all of the above

12-8 Which type of analysis compares a single corporation across time?

a. cross sectional analysis
b. time series analysis

c. timetable analysis
d. company analysis

12-9 Which of the following types of analysis compares one corporation to another corporation and to industry averages?

a. cross sectional analysis
b. time series analysis

c. timetable analysis
d. company analysis

12-10 Which of the following types of analysis is particularly useful for trend analysis?

a. vertical analysis
b. timetable analysis

c. trend-setting analysis
d. horizontal analysis

12-11 Vertical analysis expresses each financial statement line item as a percent of:

a. the average statement amount
b. the smallest statement amount

c. the largest statement amount
d. the mean statement amount

12-12 Horizontal analysis expresses each financial statement line item as a percent of:

a. net income
b. total assets

c. base year
d. stockholders' equity

12-13 How is the current ratio calculated?

a. Current Assets ÷ Current Liabilities
b. (Cash + Marketable Securities + Accounts Receivable) ÷ Current Liabilities
c. (Cash + Marketable Securities) ÷ Current Liabilities
d. Cash Flows from Operating Activities ÷ Current Liabilities

12-14 Partial information from Fabray Company's balance sheet is as follows:

Current Assets:		Current Liabilities:	
Cash	$ 1,200,000	Notes payable	$ 750,000
Marketable securities	3,750,000	Accounts payable	9,750,000
Accounts receivable	28,800,000	Accrued expenses	6,250,000
Inventories	33,150,000	Income taxes payable	250,000
Prepaid expenses	600,000	Total current liabilities	$17,000,000
Total current assets	$67,500,000		

What is Fabray's current ratio?

a. 0.25
b. 3.0

c. 1.8
d. 3.97

12-15 Hummel Inc. has $30,000 in current assets and $15,000 in current liabilities. What is Hummel's current ratio?

a. 0.5   c. 2
b. 1   d. 3

12-16 How is the cash ratio calculated?

a. Current Assets ÷ Current Liabilities
b. (Cash + Marketable Securities + Accounts Receivable) ÷ Current Liabilities
c. (Cash + Marketable Securities) ÷ Current Liabilities
d. Cash Flows from Operating Activities ÷ Current Liabilities

12-17 A firm's quick ratio is typically computed as follows:

a. Total Liabilities ÷ Total Assets   c. Current Liabilities ÷ Current Assets
b. (Cash + Short-Term Investments +   d. Current Assets ÷ Current Liabilities
    Receivables) ÷ Current Liabilities

12-18 Schuester Company has $40,000 in current liabilities, $20,000 in cash, and $25,000 in marketable securities. What Schuester's cash ratio?

a. 1.125   c. 1.6
b. 0.889   d. 0.625

12-19 What ratio is used to measure a firm's liquidity?

a. debt ratio   c. current ratio
b. asset turnover   d. return on equity

12-20 Which of the following transactions could increase a firm's current ratio?

a. purchase of inventory for cash   c. collection of accounts receivable
b. payment of accounts payable   d. purchase of temporary investments for cash

12-21 Total Liabilities ÷ Total Equity equals:

a. Times Interest Earned Ratio   c. Debt-to-Equity Ratio
b. Accounts Payable Turnover Ratio   d. Receivables Turnover Ratio

12-22 Which of the following ratios is *not* a debt management ratio?

a. times interest earned   c. long-term debt-to-equity ratio
b. debt-to-equity ratio   d. return on equity ratio

12-23 The balance sheet for Sylvester Inc. at the end of the first year of operations indicates the following:

	2011		2011
Total current assets	$600,000	Total long-term liabilities	$350,000
Total investments	85,000	Common stock, $10 par	600,000
Total property, plant, and		Additional paid-in capital—common	
equipment	900,000	stock	60,000
Current portion of long-term debt	250,000	Retained earnings	325,000

What is the long-term debt to total assets ratio for 2011 (rounded to one decimal place)?

a. 37.9%   c. 22.1%
b. 40.0%   d. 41.7%

12-24 When analyzing a company's debt-to-equity ratio, if the ratio has a value that is greater than one, then the company has:

a. less debt than equity   c. equal amounts of debt and equity
b. more debt than equity   d. none of these are correct

12-25 Cost of goods sold divided by average inventory is the formula to compute:

a.   accounts receivable turnover
b.   inventory turnover

c.   gross profit percentage
d.   return on sales percentage

12-26 A firm's asset turnover ratio is typically computed as follows:

a.   Net Sales ÷ Average Total Assets
b.   Gross Profit ÷ Net Sales
c.   Operating Income ÷ Net Sales
d.   Net Income + [Interest Expense × (1 − Tax Rate)] ÷ Average Total Assets

12-27 Which of the following ratios is used to measure a firm's efficiency at using its assets?

a.   current ratio
b.   asset turnover ratio

c.   return on sales ratio
d.   return on equity

12-28 Which of the following ratios is used to measure a firm's efficiency?

a.   Net Income ÷ Equity
b.   Net Sales ÷ Average Total Assets

c.   Assets ÷ Equity
d.   Net Income ÷ Sales

12-29 Pillsbury Corporation has $65,000 of cost of goods sold and average inventory of $30,000. What is Pillsbury's inventory turnover ratio?

a.   0.46
b.   1.17

c.   1.46
d.   2.17

12-30 If Abrams Company has an inventory turnover of 7.3 and a receivables turnover of 9.6, approximately how long is its operating cycle?

a.   72 days
b.   88 days
c.   95 days

d.   There is not enough information to calculate the operating cycle.

12-31 Which of the following ratios is used to measure the profit earned on each dollar invested in a firm?

a.   current ratio
b.   asset turnover ratio

c.   return on sales ratio
d.   return on equity

12-32 Which of the following is the formula to compute the net profit margin percentage?

a.   Net Income ÷ Net Sales
b.   Operating Income ÷ Net Sales
c.   Net Income ÷ Average Equity
d.   Net Income + [Interest Expense × (1 − Tax Rate)] ÷ Average Total Assets

12-33 Selected information for Berry Company is as follows:

Average common stock	$600,000
Average additional paid-in capital	250,000
Average retained earnings	370,000
Sales revenue for year	915,000
Net income for year	240,000

Berry's return on equity, rounded to the nearest percentage point, is

a.   20 percent
b.   21 percent

c.   28 percent
d.   40 percent

12-34 Which of the following ratios is used to measure a firm's profitability?

a.   Liabilities ÷ Equity
b.   Sales ÷ Assets

c.   Assets ÷ Equity
d.   Net Income ÷ Net Sales

12-35 Why might an industry group have higher five-year average returns on equity than do other industries?

a.   It is a higher-risk industry.   c.   It is a high-growth industry.
b.   It is a lower-risk industry.   d.   None of these.

12-36 The dividend yield ratio measures:

a.   the income available for common stockholders on a per-share basis
b.   the rate at which dividends provide a return to stockholders
c.   the proportion of a corporation's profits that are returned to the stockholders immediately as dividends
d.   the profit earned by a firm through the use of capital supplied by stockholders

12-37 Corporations are required to disclose earnings per share on which of the following statements?

a.   balance sheet   c.   statement of cash flows
b.   income statement   d.   all of these

12-38 Hudson Company has preferred dividends of $15,000, a net income of $40,000, and average common shares outstanding of 8,000. What is Hudson's earnings per share?

a. $2.67   c. $3.13
b. $5.00   d. $2.13

12-39 Which of the following are *not* part of common equity?

a.   common stock   c.   retained earnings
b.   treasury stock   d.   preferred stock

12-40 Dupont analysis recognizes that return on equity can be broken down into three important aspects of return, which are:

a.   net profit margin, asset turnover, and leverage
b.   net profit margin, asset turnover, and average assets
c.   sales, income, and leverage
d.   sales, income, and equity

12-41 If a company has a higher net profit margin than most of its competitors, this means that:

a.   the company is more efficient with its assets
b.   the company has more loyal customers
c.   the company has a lower proportion of debt financing
d.   the company has a higher proportion of each sales dollar that is profit

12-42 Which of the following ratios is decomposed using the Dupont framework?

a.   return on equity   c.   assets-to-equity ratio
b.   asset turnover   d.   return on sales

12-43 Which of the following is *not* included in the Dupont framework?

a.   a measure of profitability   c.   a measure of market share
b.   a measure of efficiency   d.   a measure of leverage

12-44 When Dupont analysis reveals that a company has much higher than average asset turnover and much lower than average profit margin, what can be concluded about the company's strategy?

a.   It is a product differentiator.   d.   It needs to concentrate on improving its
b.   It is a low-cost provider.   profit margins.
c.   It has no strategy.

12-45 Which of the following questions would be appropriate for an analyst to investigate regarding a company's liabilities?

a. Are all liabilities reported?
b. Are the liabilities properly classified?
c. Are estimated liabilities large enough?
d. All of these

CORNERSTONE EXERCISES

Cornerstone Exercise 12-46 Cross Sectional Analysis

Cross sectional analysis entails comparing a company to its competitors.

Required:

Indicate one of the biggest weaknesses of using cross sectional analysis when analyzing a company.

Cornerstone Exercise 12-47 Time Series Analysis

Time series analysis involves comparing a company's income statement and balance sheet for the current year to its previous years' income statements and balance sheets.

Required:

Explain whether it is always bad if a company's cost of goods sold is increasing from year to year.

OBJECTIVE 4
CORNERSTONE 12-2
CORNERSTONE 12-3

Cornerstone Exercise 12-48 Horizontal and Vertical Analysis

Selected data from the financial statements of Jones Hardware Company follows.

	2011	2010
Accounts receivable	$ 60,000	$ 38,000
Merchandise inventory	12,000	16,000
Total assets	450,000	380,000
Net sales	380,000	270,000
Cost of goods sold	160,000	210,000

Required:

1. Calculate by how much accounts receivable, merchandise inventory, total assets, net sales, and cost of goods sold increased or decreased in dollar terms from 2010 to 2011.
2. Indicate what happened from 2010 to 2011 to accounts receivable and merchandise inventory as a percentage of total assets (rounded to the nearest whole percent). Indicate what happened from 2010 to 2011 to cost of goods sold as a percentage of net sales (rounded to the nearest whole percent).

Cornerstone Exercise 12-49 Short-Term Liquidity Ratios

Three ratios calculated for Puckerman, Cohen, and Chang Companies for 2010 and 2011 follow.

(In millions)		Puckerman	Cohen	Chang
Current ratio	12/31/11	2.8 to 1	2.3 to 1	1.8 to 1
	12/31/10	2.0 to 1	1.5 to 1	2.2 to 1
Inventory turnover ratio	12/31/11	6.9 times	5.8 times	8.0 times
	12/31/10	7.6 times	5.8 times	9.6 times
Quick ratio	12/31/11	2.5 to 1	2.1 to 1	0.5 to 1
	12/31/10	1.0 to 1	1.4 to 1	1.2 to 1

Required:

Explain which company appears to be the most liquid.

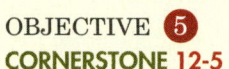

Cornerstone Exercise 12-50 Debt Management Ratios

Selected data from the financial statements of Lopez Company follow.

	2011	2010
Total liabilities	$1,205,000	$952,000
Common stock ($30 par)	250,000	225,000
Additional paid-in capital—common stock	150,000	135,000
Retained earnings	155,000	145,000

Required:

Determine whether the debt-to-equity ratio is increasing or decreasing and whether Lopez should be concerned.

Cornerstone Exercise 12-51 Debt Management and Short-Term Liquidity Ratios

OBJECTIVE ⑤
CORNERSTONE 12-4
CORNERSTONE 12-5

The following items appear on the balance sheet of Figgins Company at the end of 2010 and 2011:

	2011	2010
Current assets	$6,000	$3,000
Long-term assets	7,000	4,000
Current liabilities	2,000	3,000
Long-term liabilities	7,000	0
Stockholders' equity	4,000	4,000

Required:

Between 2010 and 2011, indicate whether Figgins' debt-to-equity ratio increased or decreased. Also, indicate whether Figgins' current ratio increased or decreased. Interpret these ratios.

Cornerstone Exercise 12-52 Asset Efficiency Ratios

OBJECTIVE ⑤
CORNERSTONE 12-6

Selected financial statement numbers for Rutherford Company follow.

Net sales	$277,480	Average inventory	$ 4,145
Cost of goods sold	179,000	Average property, plant, and equipment	75,705
Average accounts receivable	20,730	Average total assets	126,127

Required:

1. Using this information, calculate Rutherford's receivable turnover ratio (rounded to two decimal places.)
2. Using this information, calculate Rutherford's asset turnover ratio (rounded to two decimal places) and also convert the ratio into days (rounded to the nearest whole day).

Cornerstone Exercise 12-53 Profitability Ratios

OBJECTIVE ⑤
CORNERSTONE 12-7

The following data came from the financial statements of Israel Company:

Revenue	$900,000	Assets	$600,000
Expenses	600,000	Liabilities	100,000
Net income	300,000	Average equity	500,000

Required:

Compute Israel's return on equity (in percentage terms, rounded to two decimal places).

Cornerstone Exercise 12-54 Profitability Ratios

OBJECTIVE ⑤
CORNERSTONE 12-7

Tanaka Corporation's balance sheet indicates the following balances as of December 31, 2011.

Cash	$ 70,000	Bonds payable (due in 2015)	$100,000
Accounts receivable	80,000	Common stock (12/31/2010)	275,000
Inventory	55,000	Common stock (12/31/2011)	325,000
Property, plant, and equipment	500,000	Retained earnings (12/31/2010)	200,000
Accounts payable	75,000	Retained earnings (12/31/2011)	260,000

Required:

If Tanaka's 2011 net income is $80,000, determine its return on equity (in percentage terms, rounded to two decimal places).

Cornerstone Exercise 12-55 Profitability Ratios

OBJECTIVE ⑤
CORNERSTONE 12-7

The following data came from the financial statements of St. James Corp. for 2011 and 2010.

	2011	2010
Net income	$150,000	$120,000
Cash dividends paid on preferred stock	$15,000	$15,000
Cash dividends paid on common stock	$42,000	$38,000
Weighted average number of preferred shares outstanding	20,000	20,000
Weighted average number of common shares outstanding	105,000	95,000

(Continued)

Required:

Calculate St. James' earnings per share as it would be reported on the 2011 income statement.

OBJECTIVE 5
CORNERSTONE 12-8

Cornerstone Exercise 12-56 Stockholder Ratios

The following data came from the financial statements of Ryerson Corp. for 2011 and 2010.

	2011	2010
Net income	$110,000	$123,000
Cash dividends paid on common stock	$42,000	$38,000
Market price per share of common stock at the end of the year	$16.00	$13.00
Shares of common stock outstanding	140,000	140,000

Required:

Calculate Ryerson's dividend payout ratio for 2011 (in percentage terms, rounded to two decimal places).

EXERCISES

OBJECTIVE 2

Exercise 12-57 Sec Filings

The SEC requires publicly-traded companies to file many different forms.

Required:
Describe the Form 10-Q.

OBJECTIVE 2

Exercise 12-58 Form 10-K

Form 10-K has many different items.

Required:
1. Indicate what is included in the Management's Discussion and Analysis section of the 10-K.
2. List five important things that are included in the Form 10-K.

OBJECTIVE 2

Exercise 12-59 Getting Familiar with the Format of the 10-K

Refer to Aeropostale's 10-K for the year ended January 30, 2010 (filed March 29, 2010) in Appendix 5. You can also look up the 10-K online (which allows you to search and reference the entire 10-K) by searching for "Aeropostale investor relations." Once at that site click on "SEC Filings," move the "Groupings Filter (View SEC Groupings descriptions)" pull down menu to "Annual Filings," and click the "Search" button.

Required:
Answer the following questions and include in which item number of the 10-K the information was found:
1. Who does Aeropostale principally target with their merchandise?
2. How many stores did Aeropostale plan to open during fiscal 2010 (which will end in January 2011)?
3. Describe the seasonality of Aeropostale's business.
4. Is Aeropostale involved in any litigation that may materially affect its financial position?
5. What are some "key indicators" of financial condition and operational performance that Aeropostale uses to analyze its business?
6. What are three of Aeropostale's most critical accounting estimates?
7. Who audits Aeropostale?

OBJECTIVE 3

Exercise 12-60 Financial Statement Users

Many groups analyze financial statements to make decisions.

Required:
1. **Conceptual Connection:** Explain why a person who is selecting an employer should be sure to view and analyze the company's financial statements.
2. **Conceptual Connection:** Explain why a business that is considering selling goods or providing services to another business should review the company's financial statements.

Exercise 12-61 Horizontal Analysis of Income Statements

OBJECTIVE

Consolidated income statements for Karofsky Computer follow.

Karofsky Computer Inc. Consolidated Income Statements (In thousands except per share amounts)			
	Three fiscal years ended December 31		
	2011	**2010**	**2009**
Sales	$9,188,748	$7,976,954	$7,086,542
Costs and expenses:			
Cost of goods sold	$6,844,915	$5,248,834	$3,991,337
Research and development	564,303	664,564	602,135
Selling, general, and administrative	1,384,111	1,632,362	1,687,262
Restructuring costs and other	(126,855)	320,856	0
	$8,666,474	$7,866,616	$6,280,734
Operating income	$ 522,274	$ 110,338	$ 805,808
Interest and other income, net	(21,988)	29,321	49,634
Income before income taxes	$ 500,286	$ 139,659	$ 855,442
Provision for income taxes	190,108	53,070	325,069
Net income	$ 310,178	$ 86,589	$ 530,373
Earnings per common and common equivalent share	$ 2.61	$ 0.73	$ 4.33
Common and common equivalent shares used in the calculations of earnings per share	118,735	119,125	122,490

Required:

1. Prepare common size income statements for horizontal analysis (in percentage terms, rounded to two decimal places). You do not need to include the actual dollar amounts shown above.
2. **Conceptual Connection:** Explain why net income decreased in 2010 and increased in 2011.

Exercise 12-62 Vertical Analysis of Balance Sheets

OBJECTIVE

Consolidated balance sheets for Karofsky Computer follow.

Karofsky Computer Inc. Consolidated Balance Sheets (Dollars in thousands)		
	December 31	
ASSETS	**2011**	**2010**
Current assets:		
Cash and cash equivalents	$1,203,488	$ 676,413
Short-term investments	54,368	215,890
Accounts receivable, net of allowance for doubtful accounts of $90,992 ($83,776 in 2010)	1,581,347	1,381,946
Inventories	1,088,434	1,506,638
Deferred tax assets	293,048	268,085
Other current assets	255,767	289,383
Total current assets	$4,476,452	$4,338,355
Property, plant, and equipment:		
Land and buildings	$ 484,592	$ 404,688
Machinery and equipment	572,728	578,272
Office furniture and equipment	158,160	167,905
Leasehold improvements	236,708	261,792
	$1,452,188	$1,412,657
Accumulated depreciation and amortization	(785,088)	(753,111)
Net property, plant, and equipment	$ 667,100	$ 659,546
Other assets	159,194	173,511
Total assets	$5,302,746	$5,171,412

(Continued)

LIABILITIES AND STOCKHOLDERS' EQUITY		
Current liabilities:		
Short-term borrowings	$ 292,200	$ 823,182
Accounts payable	881,717	742,622
Accrued compensation and employee benefits	136,895	144,779
Accrued marketing and distribution	178,294	174,547
Accrued restructuring costs	58,238	307,932
Other current liabilities	396,961	315,023
Total current liabilities	$1,944,305	$2,508,085
Long-term debt	304,472	7,117
Deferred tax liabilities	670,668	629,832
Total liabilities	$2,919,445	$3,145,034
Stockholders' equity:		
Common stock, no par value: 320,000,000 shares authorized; 119,542,527 shares issued and outstanding in 2011 (116,147,035 shares in 2010)	$ 297,929	$ 203,613
Retained earnings	2,096,206	1,842,600
Accumulated translation adjustment	(10,834)	(19,835)
Total stockholders' equity	$2,383,301	$2,026,378
Total liabilities and stockholders' equity	$5,302,746	$5,171,412

Required:

1. Prepare common size balance sheets for vertical analysis (in percentage terms, rounded to two decimal places). You do not need to include the actual dollar amounts shown above.
2. Indicate from what sources Karofsky appears to have secured the resources for its asset increase.

OBJECTIVE

Exercise 12-63 Horizontal Analysis Using Income Statements

The consolidated 2011, 2010, and 2009 income statements for Corcoran Inc. and Subsidiaries follow.

Corcoran Inc. and Subsidiaries Consolidated Income Statements (In millions except per share amounts)			
		December 31,	
	2011	**2010**	**2009**
Net sales	$ 25,020.7	$ 21,970.0	$19,292.2
Costs and expenses:			
Cost of goods sold	(11,946.1)	(10,611.7)	(9,366.2)
Selling, general, and administrative expenses	(9,864.4)	(8,721.2)	(7,605.9)
Amortization of intangible assets	(303.7)	(265.9)	(208.3)
Operating profit	$ 2,906.5	$ 2,371.2	$ 2,111.8
Interest expense	(572.7)	(586.1)	(613.7)
Interest income	88.7	113.7	161.6
Income before income taxes	$ 2,422.5	$ 1,898.8	$ 1,659.7
Provision for income taxes	834.6	597.1	597.5
Net income	$ 1,587.9	$ 1,301.7	$ 1,062.2

Required:

1. Prepare common size income statements for horizontal analysis (in percentage terms, rounded to two decimal places). You do not need to include the actual dollar amounts shown above.
2. Indicate what Corcoran's 2011, 2010, and 2009 tax rates were on its income before taxes (in percentage terms, rounded to two decimal places).
3. **Conceptual Connection:** Explain why net income increased by a larger percentage than sales in 2011 and 2010.

Exercise 12-64 Horizontal Analysis Using Balance Sheets

OBJECTIVE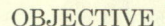

The consolidated 2011 and 2010 balance sheets for Corcoran Inc. and Subsidiaries follow.

Corcoran Inc. and Subsidiaries Consolidated Balance Sheets (In millions except per share amounts)		
	December 31,	
ASSETS	**2011**	**2010**
Current assets:		
Cash and cash equivalents	$ 226.9	$ 169.9
Short-term investments at cost which approximates market	1,629.3	1,888.5
Accounts and notes receivable, less allowance: $128.3 in 2011 and $112.0 in 2010	1,883.4	1,588.5
Inventories	924.7	768.8
Prepaid expenses, taxes, and other current assets	499.8	426.6
Total current assets	$ 5,164.1	$ 4,842.3
Investments in affiliates and other assets	1,756.6	1,707.9
Property, plant, and equipment, net	8,855.6	7,442.0
Intangible assets, net	7,929.5	6,959.0
Total assets	$23,705.8	$20,951.2
LIABILITIES AND STOCKHOLDERS' EQUITY		
Current liabilities:		
Short-term borrowings	$ 2,191.2	$ 706.8
Accounts payable	1,390.0	1,164.8
Income taxes payable	823.7	621.1
Accrued compensation and benefits	726.0	638.9
Accrued marketing	400.9	327.0
Other current liabilities	1,043.1	1,099.0
Total current liabilities	$ 6,574.9	$ 4,557.6
Long-term debt	7,442.6	7,964.8
Other liabilities	1,342.0	1,390.8
Deferred income taxes	2,007.6	1,682.3
Total liabilities	$17,367.1	$15,595.5
Stockholders' equity:		

Capital stock, par value $1 per share: authorized 1,800.0
    million shares, 14.4 million and 7.4 million shares issued at
    December 31, 2011 and 2010, respectively
	$ 14.4	$ 7.4

Capital in excess of par value	879.5	674.6
Retained earnings	6,541.9	5,439.7
Other comprehensive income (loss)	(183.9)	(99.0)
Less: Treasury stock, at cost: 64.3 shares in 2011 and 2010	(913.2)	(667.0)
Total stockholders' equity	$ 6,338.7	$ 5,355.7
Total liabilities and stockholders' equity	$23,705.8	$20,951.2

Required:

1. Calculate the percentage that Corcoran's total assets increased by during 2011 (in percentage terms, rounded to one decimal place). You do not need to include the actual dollar amounts shown above.
2. Determine whether any of the asset categories experienced larger increases than others.
3. Indicate where Corcoran acquired the capital to finance its asset growth.
4. Indicate whether any of the individual liability or equity items increased at a rate different from the rate at which total liabilities and equity increased.

OBJECTIVE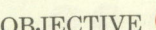

Exercise 12-65 Preparation of Common Size Statements for Vertical Analysis

Financial statements for Remington Inc. follow.

Remington Inc. Consolidated Income Statements (In thousands except per share amounts)			
	2011	2010	2009
Net sales	$ 7,245,088	$ 6,944,296	$ 6,149,218
Cost of goods sold	(5,286,253)	(4,953,556)	(4,355,675)
Gross margin	$ 1,958,835	$ 1,990,740	$ 1,793,543
General and administrative expenses	(1,259,896)	(1,202,042)	(1,080,843)
Special and nonrecurring items	2,617	0	0
Operating income	$ 701,556	$ 788,698	$ 712,700
Interest expense	(63,685)	(62,398)	(63,927)
Other income	7,308	10,080	11,529
Gain on sale of investments	0	9,117	0
Income before income taxes	$ 645,179	$ 745,497	$ 660,302
Provision for income taxes	(254,000)	(290,000)	(257,000)
Net income	$ 391,179	$ 455,497	$ 403,302

Remington Inc. Consolidated Balance Sheets (In thousands)		
ASSETS	Dec. 31, 2011	Dec. 31, 2010
Current assets:		
Cash and equivalents	$ 320,558	$ 41,235
Accounts receivable	1,056,911	837,377
Inventories	733,700	803,707
Other	109,456	101,811
Total current assets	$2,220,625	$1,784,130
Property and equipment, net	1,666,588	1,813,948
Other assets	247,892	248,372
Total assets	$4,135,105	$3,846,450
LIABILITIES AND STOCKHOLDERS' EQUITY		
Current liabilities		
Accounts payable	$ 250,363	$ 309,092
Accrued expenses	347,892	274,220
Other current liabilities	15,700	
Income taxes	93,489	137,466
Total current liabilities	$ 707,444	$ 720,778
Long-term debt	650,000	541,639
Deferred income taxes	275,101	274,844
Other long-term liabilities	61,267	41,572
Total liabilities	$1,693,812	$1,578,833
Stockholders' equity:		
Preferred stock	$ 100,000	$ 100,000
Common stock	89,727	89,727
Additional paid-in capital—common stock	128,906	127,776
Retained earnings	2,397,112	2,136,794
	$2,715,745	$2,454,297
Less: Treasury stock, at cost	(274,452)	(186,680)
Total stockholders' equity	$2,441,293	$2,267,617
Total liabilities and stockholders' equity	$4,135,105	$3,846,450

Required:

1. Prepare common size income statements and balance sheets for Remington to be used in vertical analysis (in percentage terms, rounded to two decimal places). You do not need to include the actual dollar amounts shown above.

2. **Conceptual Connection:** Indicate whether gross margin grew as much as sales between 2009 and 2010 and between 2010 and 2011, and if so, why it grew.

3. **Conceptual Connection:** Indicate whether the relative proportion of Remington's assets changed between 2010 and 2011, and if so, explain the change.

4. **Conceptual Connection:** Indicate whether the relative proportion of Remington's liabilities and equity changed between 2010 and 2011, and if so, explain the change.

5. **Conceptual Connection:** Explain how Remington appears to have financed the 7.5 percent increase in assets that occurred between 2010 and 2011.

Exercise 12-66 Common Size Statements for Vertical Analysis

OBJECTIVE 3 4

The following consolidated income statements and balance sheets are available for Azimio Products:

Azimio Products Consolidated Income Statements						
	Year Ended December 31,					
	2011		**2010**		**2009**	
	Amount	%	Amount	%	Amount	%
Revenues	$901,170	100.0	$728,035	100.0	$661,850	100.0
Costs and expenses:						
Cost of goods sold	$539,801	59.9	$439,005	60.3	$401,743	60.7
Selling and administrative	318,113	35.3	206,034	28.3	176,052	26.6
Interest	17,122	1.9	18,201	2.5	17,208	2.6
Other expenses (income)	9,913	1.1	2,912	0.4	(1,324)	(0.2)
Total costs and expenses	$884,949	98.2	$666,152	91.5	$593,679	89.7
Income before provision for income taxes	$ 16,221	1.8	$ 61,883	8.5	$ 68,171	10.3
Provision for income taxes	4,506	0.5	22,569	3.1	23,827	3.6
Net income	$ 11,715	1.3	$ 39,314	5.4	$ 44,344	6.7

Azimio Products Consolidated Balance Sheets						
	December 31,					
	2011		**2010**		**2009**	
ASSETS	Amount	%	Amount	%	Amount	%
Current assets	$147,129	31.4	$ 62,417	14.3	$ 66,927	16.1
Investment	30,925	6.6	95,589	21.9	91,453	22.0
Property, plant, and equipment (net)	270,831	57.8	261,015	59.8	241,519	58.1
Other assets	19,680	4.2	17,459	4.0	15,796	3.8
Total assets	$468,565	100.0	$436,480	100.0	$415,695	100.0
LIABILITIES AND STOCKHOLDERS' EQUITY						
Current liabilities	$ 68,410	14.6	$ 29,244	6.7	$ 28,683	6.9
Long-term debt	152,284	32.5	162,807	37.3	152,976	36.8
Total liabilities	$220,694	47.1	$192,051	44.0	$181,659	43.7
Common stock	$183,209	39.1	$182,332	41.8	$171,266	41.2
Retained earnings	64,662	13.8	62,097	14.2	62,770	15.1
Total stockholders' equity	$247,871	52.9	$244,429	56.0	$234,036	56.3
Total liabilities and stockholders' equity	$468,565	100.0	$436,480	100.0	$415,695	100.0

(Continued)

Required:

1. **Conceptual Connection:** Explain why income from operations decreased in 2010 and 2011 while sales increased.
2. Determine whether the proportion of resources invested in the various asset categories changed from 2009 to 2011.
3. Determine whether the proportion of capital supplied by creditors changed.
4. Indicate from what sources Azimio secured the capital to finance its increase in current assets in 2011.

OBJECTIVE 5

Exercise 12-67 Short-Term Liquidity Ratios

The financial statements for Giardi Corporation, a retailer, follow.

Giardi Corporation Consolidated Income Statements *(Millions of dollars except per share data)*			
	December 31		
	2011	**2010**	**2009**
Revenues	$19,233	$17,927	$16,115
Costs and expenses:			
Cost of retail sales, buying, and occupancy	$14,164	$13,129	$11,751
Selling, publicity, and administration	3,175	2,978	2,801
Depreciation	498	459	410
Interest expense, net	446	437	398
Taxes other than income taxes	343	313	283
Total costs and expenses	$18,626	$17,316	$15,643
Earnings before income taxes	$ 607	$ 611	$ 472
Provision for income taxes	232	228	171
Net earnings	$ 375	$ 383	$ 301

Giardi Corporation Consolidated Balance Sheets *(Millions of dollars)*		
	December 31,	
ASSETS	**2011**	**2010**
Current assets:		
Cash and cash equivalents	$ 321	$ 117
Accounts receivable	1,536	1,514
Merchandise inventories	2,497	2,618
Other	157	165
Total current assets	$ 4,511	$ 4,414
Property and equipment:		
Land	$ 1,120	$ 998
Buildings and improvements	4,753	4,342
Fixtures and equipment	2,162	2,197
Construction-in-progress	248	223
Accumulated depreciation	(2,336)	(2,197)
Net property and equipment	$ 5,947	$ 5,563
Other	320	360
Total assets	$10,778	$10,337

LIABILITIES AND STOCKHOLDERS' EQUITY		
Current liabilities:		
Notes payable	$ 200	$ 23
Accounts payable	1,654	1,596
Accrued liabilities	903	849
Income taxes payable	145	125
Current portion of long-term debt	173	371
Total current liabilities	$ 3,075	$ 2,964
Long-term debt	4,279	4,330
Deferred income taxes and other	536	450
Loan to ESOP	(217)	(267)
Total liabilities	$ 7,673	$ 7,477
Stockholders' equity:		
Preferred stock	368	374
Common stock	72	71
Additional paid-in capital—common	73	58
Retained earnings	2,592	2,357
Total stockholders' equity	$ 3,105	$ 2,860
Total liabilities and stockholders' equity	$10,778	$10,337

Required:

1. Compute the four short-term liquidity ratios (rounded to two decimal places) for 2010 and 2011, assuming operating cash flows are $281 million and $483 million, respectively.
2. **Conceptual Connection:** Indicate which ratios appear to be most appropriate for a retail organization. Indicate what other information you would like to know to comment on Giardi's short-term liquidity.

Exercise 12-68 Debt Management Ratios

OBJECTIVE **5**

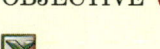

Refer to Remington's financial statements in **Exercise 12-65**.

Required:

1. Compute the five debt management ratios for 2010 and 2011 (rounded to two decimal places).
2. **Conceptual Connection:** Indicate whether the ratios have changed and whether the ratios suggest that Remington is more or less risky for long-term creditors at December 31, 2011, than at December 31, 2010.

Exercise 12-69 Asset Efficiency Ratios

OBJECTIVE **5**

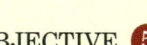

Refer to Remington's financial statements in **Exercise 12-65** and the information below.

Statement Item	January 1, 2010 (In Thousands)
Accounts receivable	$ 752,945
Inventories	698,604
Total assets	3,485,233

Required:

1. Compute the three asset efficiency ratios (rounded to two decimal places) for 2010 and 2011.
2. Indicate the length of Remington's operating cycle in days (rounded to two decimal places) for the years ended December 31, 2011, and December 31, 2010.

Exercise 12-70 Profitability Ratios

OBJECTIVE **5**

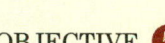

Refer to Remington's financial statements in **Exercise 12-65** and the information below.

Statement Item	January 1, 2010 (In Thousands)
Total assets	$3,485,233
Total stockholders' equity	2,083,122

(Continued)

Required:

1. Compute the five profitability ratios (in percentage terms, rounded to two decimal places) for 2010 and 2011.
2. **Conceptual Connection:** Explain what these ratios suggest about Remington's profitability. Indicate what other information you would like to know to further assess Remington's profitability.

Exercise 12-71 Stockholder Ratios

Refer to Remington's financial statements in **Exercise 12-65** and the information below.

	Year Ended December 31,	
Item	**2011**	**2010**
Average number of common shares outstanding (thousands)	362,202	364,398
Preferred dividends (thousands)	$ 24,000	$ 24,000
Dividends per common share	0.36	1.54
Dividends (thousands)	130,861.00	561,172.30
Common stock repurchases	0	0
Market price per share:		
High	$ 83.25	$ 79.10
Low	63.25	59.00
Close	78.42	66.36

At January 1, 2010, total stockholders' equity was $2,083,122 and there was no preferred stock.

Required:

1. Compute the four stockholder ratios (in percentage terms, rounded to two decimal places except for EPS, which should be rounded to nearest cent) for 2010 and 2011.
2. **Conceptual Connection:** Indicate whether there were significant changes in these ratios between the years ended December 31, 2011, and December 31, 2010. Determine whether the stockholder ratios suggest that Remington was a better investment at December 31, 2011, or December 31, 2010.

Exercise 12-72 Dupont Analysis

Refer to Remington's financial statements in **Exercise 12-65** and the information below.

Statement Item	January 1, 2010 (In Millions)
Total assets	$3,485,233
Total stockholders' equity	2,083,122

	Year Ended December 31,	
Industry Averages	**2011**	**2010**
Return on equity	5.31%	12.54%
Profit margin	4.00	6.21
Asset turnover	0.83	1.96
Leverage	1.60	1.03

Required:

1. Perform Dupont analysis (in percentage terms, rounded to two decimal places) for 2010 and 2011.
2. **Conceptual Connection:** Explain what you learn about Remington's trends from 2010 to 2011 by comparing its performance to the industry averages.

PROBLEM SET A

Problem 12-73A Using Common Size Data for Credit Analysis

OBJECTIVE ③ ④

You are the credit manager for Carmichael Supply Company. One of your sales staff has made a $50,000 credit sale to Zizes Electronics, a manufacturer of small computers. Your responsibility is to decide whether to approve the sale. You have the following data for the computer industry and Zizes:

For the Years 2007–2011	Industry	Zizes Electronics
Average annual sales growth	13.4%	17.6%
Average annual operating income growth	10.8%	9.7%
Average annual net income growth	14.4%	9.9%
Average annual asset growth	10.3%	14.2%
Average debt-to-equity ratio	0.32	0.26
Average current ratio	4.04	3.71
Average inventory turnover ratio	2.53	2.06
Average accounts receivable turnover ratio	3.95	4.18

For Zizes, you have the following data for the year ended December 31, 2011:

Sales revenue	$3,908,000
Net income	$359,000
Total assets	$3,626,000
Current ratio	1.82
Debt-to-equity ratio	0.37
Inventory turnover ratio	1.79
Accounts receivable turnover ratio	3.62

The salesperson believes that Zizes would order about $200,000 per year of materials that would provide a gross margin of $35,000 to Carmichael if reasonable credit terms could be arranged.

Required:

State whether or not you would grant authorization for Zizes to purchase on credit and support your decision.

YOU◆DECIDE

Problem 12-74A Using Common Size Data for Investment Analysis

OBJECTIVE ③ ④

Assume that you are a trust officer for the Wu Bank. You are attempting to select a pharmaceutical manufacturer's stock for a client's portfolio. You have secured the following data:

	Five-Year Averages				
	Industry Average	Hitchens	Rhoades	Castle	Rumba
Sales growth	8.3%	9.8%	7.9%	7.2%	10.1%
Net income growth	13.0	12.0	10.7	4.2	16.1
Asset growth	5.0	6.1	4.6	4.4	6.2
	Current Year				
Return on equity	16.2%	17.5%	17.5%	19.4%	21.6%
Return on assets	8.5	7.8	12.7	8.4	11.4
Dividend payout	43.0	40.0	23.0	31.0	31.0

Required:

Conceptual Connection: Comment on the relative performance of these firms.

Problem 12-75A Using Common Size Income Statement Data

OBJECTIVE ③ ④

The 2011, 2010, and 2009 income statements for Argon Entertainment Enterprises follow.

(Continued)

Argon Entertainment Enterprises Consolidated Income Statements			
	Year Ended December 31,		
	2011	**2010**	**2009**
Revenues			
Theme parks and resorts	$3,440.7	$3,306.9	$2,794.3
Filmed entertainment	3,673.4	3,115.2	2,593.7
Consumer products	1,415.1	1,081.9	724.0
	$8,529.2	$7,504.0	$6,112.0
Costs and Expenses			
Theme parks and resorts	$2,693.8	$2,662.9	$2,247.7
Filmed entertainment	3,051.2	2,606.9	2,275.6
Consumer products	1,059.7	798.9	494.2
	$6,804.7	$6,068.7	$5,017.5
Operating Income			
Theme parks and resorts	$ 746.9	$ 644.0	$ 546.6
Filmed entertainment	622.2	508.3	318.1
Consumer products	355.4	283.0	229.8
	$1,724.5	$1,435.3	$1,094.5
Corporate Activities			
General and administrative expenses	$ 164.2	$ 148.2	$ 160.8
Interest expense	157.7	126.8	105.0
Investment and interest income	(186.1)	(130.3)	(119.4)
	$ 135.8	$ 144.7	$ 146.4
Income (loss) on investment in Asian theme park	$ (514.7)	$ 11.2	$ 63.8
Income before income taxes	$1,074.0	$1,301.8	$1,011.9
Income taxes	402.7	485.1	375.3
Net income	$ 671.3	$ 816.7	$ 636.6

Required:

1. Calculate how much each of the revenues and expenses changed from 2009 through 2011 (in percentage terms, rounded to two decimal places). You do not need to include the actual dollar amounts shown above.

2. **Conceptual Connection:** Explain the primary causes of Argon's increase in net income in 2010 and the decrease in 2011.

OBJECTIVE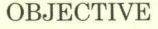

Problem 12-76A Using Common Size Statements

The following income statement and vertical analysis data are available for Colfer Audio Products:

Colfer Audio Products Consolidated Income Statements						
	Year Ended June 30,					
	2011		**2010**		**2009**	
(in thousands)	**Amount**	**%**	**Amount**	**%**	**Amount**	**%**
Sales	$2,970.0	100.0	$3,465.0	100.0	$3,960.0	100.0
Other income, net	23.7	0.8	34.6	1.0	39.6	1.0
Total revenues	$2,993.7	100.8	$3,499.6	101.0	$3,999.6	101.0
Costs and expenses:						
Cost of goods sold	$1,303.8	43.9	$1,566.2	45.2	$1,920.6	48.5
Selling and administrative	1,571.1	52.9	1,593.9	46.0	1,564.2	39.5
Interest	62.4	2.1	65.8	1.9	59.4	1.5
Total costs and expenses	$2,937.3	98.9	$3,225.9	93.1	$3,544.2	89.5
Income before income taxes	$ 56.4	$ 1.9	$ 273.7	$ 7.9	$ 455.4	11.5
Income taxes expense	14.8	0.5	107.4	3.1	182.2	4.6
Net income	$ 41.6	1.4	$ 166.3	4.8	$ 273.2	6.9

Required:

1. **Conceptual Connection:** Suggest why net income declined from $273,200 to $41,600 while the cost of goods sold percentage decreased each year and selling and administrative expenses remained nearly constant.
2. **Conceptual Connection:** Determine what could cause sales to decline while the gross margin percentage increases.

Problem 12-77A Using Common Size Statements

OBJECTIVE ③ ④

Gilsig Inc. owns and operates a small chain of sportswear stores located near colleges and universities. Gilsig has experienced significant growth in recent years. The following data are available for Gilsig:

Gilsig Inc. Consolidated Income Statements (In thousands)			
	Year Ended December 31,		
	2011	2010	2009
Sales	$51,638	$41,310	$34,425
Cost of goods sold	31,050	24,840	20,700
Gross margin	$20,588	$16,470	$13,725
Other income, net	383	426	405
	$20,971	$16,896	$14,130
Costs and expenses:			
Selling and administrative	$16,570	$13,465	$11,350
Interest	1,237	765	554
Total costs and expenses	$17,807	$14,230	$11,904
Income before income taxes	$ 3,164	$ 2,666	$ 2,226
Provision for income taxes	885	746	623
Net income	$ 2,279	$ 1,920	$ 1,603

Gilsig Inc. Consolidated Balance Sheets (In thousands)			
	December 31,		
ASSETS	2011	2010	2009
Current assets:			
Cash	$ 360	$ 293	$ 236
Accounts receivable	4,658	3,690	3,285
Inventories	6,064	4,478	3,442
Total current assets	$11,082	$ 8,461	$ 6,963
Property, plant and equipment (net)	4,860	3,600	2,756
Other assets	574	585	562
Total assets	$16,516	$12,646	$10,281
LIABILITIES AND STOCKHOLDERS' EQUITY			
Current liabilities:			
Short-term notes payable	$ 4,230	$ 1,620	$ 450
Accounts payable	1,147	1,013	720
Total current liabilities	$ 5,377	$ 2,633	$ 1,170
Long-term debt	3,150	3,150	3,150
Total liabilities	$ 8,527	$ 5,783	$ 4,320
Common stock & additional paid-in capital	$ 4,725	$ 4,725	$ 4,725
Retained earnings	3,264	2,138	1,236
Total stockholders' equity	$ 7,989	$ 6,863	$ 5,961
Total liabilities and stockholders' equity	$16,516	$12,646	$10,281

(Continued)

Required:

1. Determine how much Gilsig's sales, net income, and assets have grown during these three years.
2. Explain how Gilsig has financed the increase in assets.
3. Determine whether Gilsig's liquidity is adequate.
4. **Conceptual Connection:** Explain why interest expense is growing.
5. If Gilsig's sales grow by 25 percent in 2012, what would you expect net income to be?
6. If Gilsig's assets must grow by 25 percent to support the 25 percent sales increase and if 50 percent of net income is paid in dividends, how much capital must Gilsig raise in 2012?

OBJECTIVE

Problem 12-78A Preparing Common Size Statements

The financial statements for Lynch Shoes Inc. follow:

Lynch Shoes Inc. Consolidated Income Statements (In thousands, except per share data)			
	Year Ended December 31,		
	2011	**2010**	**2009**
Revenues	$3,930,984	$3,405,211	$3,003,610
Costs and expenses:			
Cost of goods sold	$2,386,993	$2,089,089	$1,850,530
Selling and administrative	922,261	761,498	664,061
Interest	25,739	30,665	27,316
Other expenses (income)	1,475	2,141	(43)
Total costs and expenses	$3,336,468	$2,883,393	$2,541,864
Income before income taxes	$ 594,516	$ 521,818	$ 461,746
Income taxes	229,500	192,600	174,700
Net income	$ 365,016	$ 329,218	$ 287,046

Lynch Shoes Inc. Consolidated Balance Sheets (In thousands)		
	December 31,	
ASSETS	**2011**	**2010**
Current assets:		
Cash and equivalents	$ 291,284	$ 260,050
Accounts receivable, less allowance for doubtful		
accounts of $19,447 and $20,046	667,547	596,018
Inventories	592,986	471,202
Deferred income taxes	26,378	27,511
Prepaid expenses	42,452	32,977
Total current assets	$1,620,647	$1,387,758
Property, plant, and equipment	$ 571,032	$ 497,795
Less accumulated depreciation	(193,037)	(151,758)
Net property, plant, and equipment	$ 377,995	$ 346,037
Goodwill	157,894	110,363
Other assets	30,927	28,703
Total assets	$2,187,463	$1,872,861

LIABILITIES AND STOCKHOLDERS' EQUITY		
Current liabilities:		
Current portion of long-term debt	$ 52,985	$ 3,652
Notes payable	108,165	105,696
Accounts payable	135,701	134,729
Accrued liabilities	138,563	134,089
Income taxes payable	17,150	42,422
Total current liabilities	$ 452,564	$ 420,588
Long-term debt	15,033	77,022
Noncurrent deferred income taxes	29,965	27,074
Other noncurrent liabilities	43,575	23,728
Commitments and contingencies	0	0
Redeemable preferred stock	300	300
Total liabilities	$ 541,437	$ 548,712
Stockholders' equity:		
Common stock at stated value:		
Class A convertible—26,691 and 26,919 shares		
outstanding	$ 159	$ 161
Class B—49,161 and 48,591 shares outstanding	2,720	2,716
Capital in excess of stated value	108,451	93,799
Treasury stock (common at cost)	(7,790)	(6,860)
Retained earnings	1,542,486	1,234,333
Total stockholders' equity	$1,646,026	$1,324,149
Total liabilities and stockholders' equity	$2,187,463	$1,872,861

Required:

1. Prepare common size income statements to be used for horizontal analysis for Lynch for 2009 to 2011 (in percentage terms, rounded to two decimal places). You do not need to include the actual dollar amounts shown above.

2. **Conceptual Connection:** Indicate why Lynch's net income increased between 2009 and 2011.

3. Prepare common size balance sheets to be used for vertical analysis for 2011 and 2010 (in percentage terms, rounded to two decimal places). You do not need to include the actual dollar amounts shown above.

4. Indicate whether the proportion of dollars invested in the various categories of assets has changed significantly between 2010 and 2011.

5. Indicate whether the proportion of capital raised from the various liability categories and common stockholders' equity has changed significantly between 2010 and 2011.

6. **Conceptual Connection:** Describe Lynch's performance and financial position.

Problem 12-79A Preparation of Ratios

OBJECTIVE 5

Refer to the financial statements for Gilsig Inc. in **Problem 12-77A**.

Required:

1. **Conceptual Connection:** Compute the asset efficiency ratios (rounded to two decimal places) for Gilsig for 2011 and 2010 (in percentage terms, rounded to two decimal places). Indicate whether efficiency has changed.

2. **Conceptual Connection:** Compute the profitability ratios (rounded to two decimal places) for Gilsig for 2011 and 2010. Determine by how much Gilsig's profitability ratios have changed (in percentage terms, rounded to two decimal places) for the two-year period.

3. **Conceptual Connection:** Compute the debt management ratios (in percentage terms, rounded to two decimal places) for Gilsig for 2010 and 2011. Discuss whether creditors are as secure in 2011 as they were in 2010.

Problem 12-80A Comparing Financial Ratios

OBJECTIVE 5

Presented below are selected ratios for four firms. Mays is a heavy equipment manufacturer, Riley is a newspaper publisher, Salling is a food manufacturer, and Ushkowitz is a grocery chain.

(Continued)

	Mays	Riley	Salling	Ushkowitz
Short-term liquidity ratio				
Current ratio	1.3	1.7	1.0	1.6
Debt management ratio				
Long-term debt-to-equity	1.81	0.45	0.30	0.09
Asset efficiency ratios				
Accounts receivable turnover	4.66	8.28	11.92	116.15
Inventory turnover	6.26	40.26	7.29	8.43
Profitability ratios				
Operating income	12.6%	25.4%	21.2%	3.8%
Net income	5.9	10.9	10.8	1.9
Return on assets	4.7	10.6	16.8	10.3
Return on equity	36.0	22.6	38.0	21.2

Required:
1. Which firm has the weakest current ratio?
2. **Conceptual Connection:** Explain why the turnover ratios vary so much among the four firms.
3. **Conceptual Connection:** Explain why the return on equity ratio is larger than the return on asset ratio for all four firms.
4. **Conceptual Connection:** Discuss whether the large differences in the return on equity ratios can exist over long periods of time.

OBJECTIVE ## Problem 12-81A Preparation of Ratios

Refer to the financial statements for Lynch Shoes Inc. in **Problem 12-78A** and the following data.

	2011	2010	2009
Average number of common shares outstanding	77,063	76,602	76,067
Accounts receivable	$ 667,547	$ 596,018	$ 521,588
Inventories	592,986	471,202	586,594
Total assets	2,187,463	1,872,861	1,708,430
Stockholders' equity	1,646,026	1,324,149	1,032,789
Stock repurchases	930,111	581,134	288,320
Cash flows from operating activities	190,000	150,000	137,000
Common dividends paid	57,797	45,195	39,555
Dividends per common share	0.75	0.59	0.52
Market price per share:			
High	$ 90.25	$ 77.45	$ 54.50
Low	55.00	35.12	26.00
Close	86.33	71.65	43.22

	Year Ended December 31,	
Industry Averages	2011	2010
Return on equity	25.98%	23.04%
Profit margin	0.05	0.04
Asset turnover	2.24	2.56
Leverage	2.32	2.25

Required:
1. Prepare all the financial ratios for Lynch for 2011 and 2010 (using percentage terms where appropriate and rounding all answers to two decimal places).
2. **Conceptual Connection:** Explain whether Lynch's short-term liquidity is adequate.
3. **Conceptual Connection:** Discuss whether Lynch uses its assets efficiently.
4. **Conceptual Connection:** Determine whether Lynch is profitable.
5. **Conceptual Connection:** Discuss whether long-term creditors should regard Lynch as a high-risk or a low-risk firm.
6. Perform Dupont analysis (rounding to two decimal places) for 2010 and 2011.

OBJECTIVE 6 ## Problem 12-82A Accounting Alternatives and Financial Analysis

Shady Deal Automobile Sales Company has asked your bank for a $100,000 loan to expand its sales facility. Shady Deal provides you with the following data:

	2011	2010	2009
Sales revenue	$6,100,000	$5,800,000	$5,400,000
Net income	119,000	112,000	106,000
Ending inventory (FIFO)*	665,000	600,000	500,000
Purchases	5,370,000	5,105,000	4,860,000
Depreciable assets	1,240,000	1,150,000	1,090,000

*The 2008 ending inventory was $470,000 (FIFO).

Your inspection of the financial statements of other automobiles sales firms indicates that most of these firms adopted the LIFO method in the late 1970s. You further note that Shady Deal has used 5 percent of depreciable asset cost when computing depreciation expense and that other automobile dealers use 10 percent. Assume that Shady Deal's effective tax rate is 25 percent of income before tax. Also assume the following:

	2011	2010	2009
Ending inventory (LIFO)*	$508,000	$495,000	$480,000

*The 2008 ending inventory was $470,000 (LIFO).

Required:

1. Compute cost of goods sold for 2009–2011, using both the FIFO and the LIFO methods.
2. Compute depreciation expense for Shady Deal for 2009–2011, using both 5 percent and 10 percent of the cost of depreciable assets.
3. Recompute Shady Deal's net income for 2009–2011, using LIFO and 10 percent depreciation. (Don't forget the tax impact of the increases in cost of goods sold and depreciation expense.)
4. **Conceptual Connection:** Explain whether Shady Deal appears to have materially changed its financial statements by the selection of FIFO (rather than LIFO) and 5 percent (rather than 10 percent) depreciation.

PROBLEM SET B

Problem 12-73B Using Common Size Data for Credit Analysis

 OBJECTIVE **3 4**

You are the credit manager for McHale Supply Inc. One of your sales staff has made a $60,000 credit sale to Monteith Technology, a manufacturer of small computers. Your responsibility is to decide whether to approve the sale. You have the following data for the computer industry and Monteith:

For the Years 2007–2011	Industry	Monteith
Average annual sales growth	12.6%	16.8%
Average annual operating income growth	11.2%	10.2%
Average annual net income growth	15.3%	10.6%
Average annual asset growth	9.9%	13.9%
Average debt-to-equity ratio	0.36	0.29
Average current ratio	4.12	3.88
Average inventory turnover ratio	2.61	2.19
Average accounts receivable turnover ratio	3.89	4.11

For Montieth, you have the following data for the year ended December 31, 2011:

Sales revenue	$4,120,000
Net income	$367,000
Total assets	$3,752,000
Current ratio	1.79
Debt-to-equity ratio	0.42
Inventory turnover ratio	1.83
Accounts receivable turnover ratio	3.71

The salesperson believes that Monteith would order about $240,000 per year of materials that would provide a gross margin of $40,000 to McHale if reasonable credit terms could be arranged.

Required:

Conceptual Connection: State whether or not you would grant authorization for Monteith to purchase on credit and support your decision.

OBJECTIVE

Problem 12-74B Using Common Size Data for Investment Analysis

Assume that you are a trust officer for Wall Street Bank. You are attempting to select a pharmaceutical manufacturer's stock for a client's portfolio. You have secured the following data:

	Five-Year Averages				
	Industry Average	Morrison	Rivera	O'Malley	Theba
Sales growth	9.3%	8.8%	10.2%	10.0%	7.9%
Net income growth	6.0	15.3	1.9	1.4	1.6
Asset growth	7.0	6.6	8.3	8.9	6.3
	Current Year				
Return on equity	19.5%	18.4%	22.7%	20.8%	17.3%
Return on assets	11.7	10.4	13.7	12.8	11.1
Dividend payout	31.0	30.0	39.0	37.0	29.0

Required:

Conceptual Connection: Comment on the relative performance of these firms.

OBJECTIVE

Problem 12-75B Using Common Size Income Statement Data

The 2011, 2010, and 2009 income statements for Talton Electronics Unlimited follow.

Talton Amusement Ltd. Consolidated Income Statements			
	Year Ended December 31,		
	2011	2010	2009
Revenues			
Theme parks and resorts	$2,723.8	$3,299.9	$3,502.7
Filmed entertainment	2,601.4	3,127.3	3,682.4
Consumer products	752.3	1,121.6	1,493.5
	$6,077.5	$7,548.8	$8,678.6
Costs and expenses			
Theme parks and resorts	$2,263.9	$2,723.4	$2,703.7
Filmed entertainment	2,300.2	2,566.3	3,104.9
Consumer products	503.7	804.5	1,120.6
	$5,067.8	$6,094.2	$6,929.2
Operating income			
Theme parks and resorts	$ 459.9	$ 576.5	$ 799.0
Filmed entertainment	301.2	561.0	577.5
Consumer products	248.6	317.1	372.9
	$1,009.7	$1,454.6	$1,749.4
Corporate activities			
General and administrative expenses	$ 161.2	$ 150.2	$ 165.3
Interest expense	103.7	130.8	158.9
Investment and interest income	(121.1)	(127.4)	(193.6)
	$ 143.8	$ 153.6	$ 130.6
Income (loss) on investment in Asian theme park	$ 62.1	$ 13.6	$ (520.8)
Income before income taxes	$ 928.0	$1,314.6	$1,098.0
Income taxes	376.2	492.3	410.4
Net income	$ 551.8	$ 822.3	$ 687.6

Required:

1. Calculate how much each of the revenues and expenses changed from 2009 through 2011 using horizontal analysis (in percentage terms, rounded to two decimal places). You do not need to include the actual dollar amounts shown above.

2. **Conceptual Connection:** Discuss the primary causes of Talton's increase in net income in 2010 and the decrease in 2011.

Problem 12-76B Using Common Size Statements

OBJECTIVE 3 4

The following income statement and vertical analysis data are available for Sussman Audio Products:

Sussman Audio Products Consolidated Income Statements (in thousands)						
	Year Ended June 30,					
	2011		**2010**		**2009**	
	Amount	%	Amount	%	Amount	%
Sales	$4,122.0	100.0	$3,566.0	100.0	$2,965.0	100.0
Other income, net	39.7	1.0	36.7	1.0	21.3	0.7
Total revenues	$4,161.7	101.0	$3,602.7	101.0	$2,986.3	100.7
Costs and expenses:						
Cost of goods sold	$1,893.6	45.9	$1,610.3	45.2	$1,310.8	44.2
Selling and administrative	1,610.3	39.1	1,603.6	45.0	1,505.3	50.8
Interest	61.4	1.5	69.7	2.0	63.2	2.1
Total costs and expenses	$3,565.3	86.5	$3,283.6	92.2	$2,879.3	97.1
Income before income taxes	$ 596.4	14.5	$ 319.1	8.9*	$ 107.0	3.6
Income taxes expense	181.5	4.4	109.6	3.1	14.5	0.5
Net income	$ 414.9	10.1	$ 209.5	5.9*	$ 92.5	3.1

*Differences due to rounding

Required:

1. **Conceptual Connection:** Suggest why net income increased from $92,500 to $414,900 while the cost of goods sold percentage increased each year and selling and administrative expenses have decreased.
2. **Conceptual Connection:** Explain what could cause sales to increase while the gross margin percentage decreases.

Problem 12-77B Using Common Size Statements

OBJECTIVE   3 4

Groff Graphics Company owns and operates a small chain of sportswear stores located near colleges and universities. Groff has experienced significant growth in recent years. The following data are available for Groff:

Groff Graphics Company Consolidated Income Statements (In thousands)			
	Year Ended December 31,		
	2011	**2010**	**2009**
Sales	$54,922	$42,893	$35,526
Cost of goods sold	32,936	25,682	21,721
Gross margin	$21,986	$17,211	$13,805
Other income, net	397	439	421
	$22,383	$17,650	$14,226
Costs and expenses:			
Selling and administrative	$17,857	$14,665	$12,754
Interest	1,356	863	622
	$19,213	$15,528	$13,376
Income before income taxes	$ 3,170	$ 2,122	$ 850
Provision for income taxes	885	746	623
Net income	$ 2,285	$ 1,376	$ 227

(Continued)

Groff Graphics Company
Consolidated Balance Sheets
(In thousands)

	December 31,		
ASSETS	2011	2010	2009
Current assets:			
Cash	$ 372	$ 301	$ 245
Accounts receivable	4,798	3,546	3,369
Inventories	5,673	4,521	3,389
Total current assets	$10,843	$ 8,368	$ 7,003
Property, plant, and equipment (net)	4,912	3,541	2,937
Other assets	592	592	552
Total assets	$16,347	$12,501	$10,492
LIABILITIES AND STOCKHOLDERS' EQUITY			
Current liabilities:			
Short-term notes payable	$ 4,314	$ 1,731	$ 463
Accounts payable	1,256	987	783
Total current liabilities	$ 5,570	$ 2,718	$ 1,246
Long-term debt	3,241	3,234	3,266
Total liabilities	$ 8,811	$ 5,952	$ 4,512
Common stock & additional paid-in capital	$ 4,367	$ 4,598	$ 4,725
Retained earnings	3,169	1,951	1,255
Total stockholders' equity	$ 7,536	$ 6,549	$ 5,980
Total liabilities and stockholders' equity	$16,347	$12,501	$10,492

Required:

1. Calculate how much Groff's sales, net income, and assets have grown during these three years.
2. Explain how Groff has financed the increase in assets.
3. **Conceptual Connection:** Discuss whether Groff's liquidity is adequate.
4. **Conceptual Connection:** Explain why interest expense is growing.
5. If Groff's sales grow by 25 percent in 2012, what would you expect net income to be?
6. If Groff's assets must grow by 25 percent to support the 25 percent sales increase and if 50 percent of net income is paid in dividends, how much capital must Groff raise in 2012?

OBJECTIVE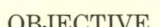

Problem 12-78B Preparing Common Size Statements

The financial statements for Tobolowsky Hats Inc. follow.

Tobolowsky Hats Inc.
Consolidated Income Statements
(In thousands except per share data)

	Year Ended December 31,		
	2011	2010	2009
Revenues	$4,102,721	$3,652,412	$3,178,569
Costs and expenses:			
Cost of goods sold	$2,256,236	$2,234,985	$1,952,123
Selling and administrative	927,412	653,986	598,236
Interest	23,974	32,596	31,853
Other expenses (income)	1,925	2,254	(102)
Total costs and expenses	$3,209,547	$2,923,821	$2,582,110
Income before income taxes	$ 893,174	$ 728,591	$ 596,459
Income taxes	247,692	183,456	163,524
Net income	$ 645,482	545,135	$ 432,935

Tobolowsky Hats Inc. Consolidated Balance Sheets (In thousands)		
	December 31,	
ASSETS	**2011**	**2010**
Current assets:		
Cash and equivalents	$ 301,695	$ 269,648
Accounts receivable, less allowance for doubtful accounts of $20,568 and $18,322	670,469	604,236
Inventories	601,396	469,582
Deferred income taxes	23,415	24,397
Prepaid expenses	43,624	36,478
Total current assets	$1,640,599	$1,404,341
Property, plant, and equipment	$ 583,152	$ 501,239
Less accumulated depreciation	(206,452)	(148,231)
Net property, plant, and equipment	$ 376,700	$ 353,008
Goodwill	162,325	127,695
Other assets	29,158	23,598
Total assets	$2,208,782	$1,908,642
LIABILITIES AND STOCKHOLDERS' EQUITY		
Current liabilities:		
Current portion of long-term debt	$ 63,169	$ 5,665
Notes payable	112,596	110,423
Accounts payable	128,696	139,364
Accrued liabilities	143,874	133,569
Income taxes payable	23,541	38,972
Total current liabilities	$ 471,876	$ 427,993
Long-term debt	16,254	83,456
Noncurrent deferred income taxes	33,489	31,238
Other noncurrent liabilities	46,685	27,434
Commitments and contingencies	0	0
Redeemable preferred stock	200	200
Total liabilities	$ 568,504	$ 570,321
Stockholders' equity:		
Common stock at stated value:		
Class A convertible—27,723 and		
25,832 shares outstanding	$ 164	$ 175
Class B—49,756 and 47,652 shares outstanding	3,152	3,120
Capital in excess of stated value	110,596	96,546
Treasury stock (common at cost)	(8,741)	(7,859)
Retained earnings	1,535,107	1,246,339
Total stockholders' equity	$1,640,278	$1,338,321
Total liabilities and stockholders' equity	$2,208,782	$1,908,642

Required:

1. Prepare common size income statements to be used for horizontal analysis for Tobolowsky for 2009 and 2011 (in percentage terms, rounded to two decimal places). You do not need to include the actual dollar amounts shown above.
2. Indicate why Tobolowsky's net income increased between 2009 and 2011.
3. Prepare common size balance sheets to be used for vertical analysis for 2011 and 2010 (in percentage terms, rounded to two decimal places). You do not need to include the actual dollar amounts shown above.

(Continued)

4. Determine whether the proportion of dollars invested in the various categories of assets has changed significantly between 2010 and 2011.
5. Determine whether the proportion of capital raised from the various liability categories and common stockholders' equity has changed significantly between 2010 and 2011.
6. **Conceptual Connection:** How would you describe Tobolowsky's performance and financial position?

OBJECTIVE

Problem 12-79B Preparation of Ratios

Refer to the financial statements for Groff Graphics Company in **Problem 12-77B**.

Required:

1. **Conceptual Connection:** Compute the asset efficiency ratios for Groff for 2011 and 2010 (in percentage terms, rounded to two decimal places) and determine whether their asset efficiency has changed.
2. **Conceptual Connection:** Compute the profitability ratios (rounded to two decimal places) for Groff for 2011 and 2010. Determine by how much Groff's profitability ratios have changed (in percentage terms, rounded to two decimal places) during the two-year period.
3. **Conceptual Connection:** Compute the debt management ratios for 2010 and 2011. Discuss whether creditors are as secure in 2011 as they were in 2010.

OBJECTIVE

Problem 12-80B Comparing Financial Ratios

Presented below are selected ratios for four firms. Rosemont is a distiller, Adler is a jewelry retailer, Menzel is an airline, and Gallagher is a hotel chain.

	Rosemont	Adler	Menzel	Gallagher
Short-term liquidity ratio				
Current ratio	1.5	3.5	0.9	1.4
Debt management ratio				
Long-term debt-to-equity	0.24	0.20	562.11	209.48
Asset efficiency ratios				
Accounts receivable turnover	7.66	17.07	19.72	11.09
Inventory turnover	2.30	0.95	31.43	7.24
Profitability ratios				
Operating income	17.7%	15.5%	4.2%	9.2%
Net income	13.1	9.6	2.2	5.4
Return on assets	11.9	8.6	1.8	7.9
Return on equity	23.7	14.9	49.2	34.5

Required:

1. **Conceptual Connection:** Explain why the long-term debt-to-equity ratio is so much higher for the airline and hotel chain than it is for the distiller and jewelry retailer.
2. **Conceptual Connection:** Explain why the turnover ratios vary so much among the four firms.
3. **Conceptual Connection:** Explain why the return on equity for the airline and hotel chain is higher than for the distiller and jewelry retailer when their operating income and net income percentages are considerably smaller.

OBJECTIVE

Problem 12-81B Preparation of Ratios

Refer to the financial statements for Tobolowsky Hats Inc. in **Problem 12-78B** and the data below.

	2011	2010	2009
Average number of common shares outstanding	78,273	77,325	77,021
Accounts receivable	$ 670,469	$ 604,236	$ 545,556
Inventories	601,396	469,582	592,524
Total assets	2,208,782	1,908,642	1,699,432
Stockholders' equity	1,640,278	1,338,321	1,075,952
Stock repurchases	990,521	623,259	310,132
Cash flows from operating activities	495,000	380,000	265,000
Common dividends paid	61,836	49,488	37,740
Dividends per common share	0.79	0.64	0.49
Market price per share:			
High	92.17	79.13	56.22
Low	56.59	37.23	27.10
Close	88.47	73.83	44.26

Industry Averages	Year Ended December 31,	
	2011	**2010**
Return on equity	32.71%	27.86%
Profit margin	0.06	0.05
Asset turnover	2.31	2.51
Leverage	2.36	2.22

Required:

1. Prepare all the financial ratios for Tobolowsky for 2011 and 2010 (using percentage terms where appropriate and rounding all answers to two decimal places).
2. **Conceptual Connection:** Indicate whether Tobolowsky's short-term liquidity is adequate.
3. **Conceptual Connection:** Discuss whether Tobolowsky uses its assets efficiently.
4. **Conceptual Connection:** Determine whether Tobolowsky is profitable.
5. **Conceptual Connection:** Discuss whether long-term creditors should regard Tobolowsky as a high-risk or a low-risk firm.
6. Perform Dupont analysis (rounding to two decimal places) for 2011 and 2010.

Problem 12-82B Accounting Alternatives and Financial Analysis

OBJECTIVE **6**

Cheap Auto Inc. has asked your bank for a $100,000 loan to expand its sales facility. Cheap Auto provides you with the following data:

	2011	**2010**	**2009**
Sales revenue	$6,900,000	$6,400,000	$6,100,000
Net income	120,000	113,000	109,000
Ending inventory (FIFO)*	675,000	620,000	510,000
Purchases	5,410,000	5,200,000	4,990,000
Depreciable assets	1,320,000	1,230,000	1,120,000

*The 2008 ending inventory was $420,000 (FIFO).

Your inspection of the financial statements of other automobiles sales firms indicates that most of these firms adopted the LIFO method in the late 1970s. You further note that Cheap Auto has used 10 percent of depreciable asset cost when computing depreciation expense and that other automobile dealers use 20 percent. Assume that Cheap Auto's effective tax rate is 30 percent of income before tax. Also assume the following:

	2011	**2010**	**2009**
Ending inventory (LIFO)*	$518,000	$512,000	$500,000

*The 2008 ending inventory was $420,000 (LIFO).

Required:

1. Compute cost of goods sold for 2009–2011, using both the FIFO and the LIFO methods.
2. Compute depreciation expense for Cheap Auto for 2009–2011, using both 10 percent and 20 percent of the cost of depreciable assets.
3. Recompute Cheap Auto's net income for 2009–2011, using LIFO and 20 percent depreciation. (Don't forget the tax impact of the increases in cost of goods sold and depreciation expense.)
4. **Conceptual Connection:** Does Cheap Auto appear to have materially changed its financial statements by the selection of FIFO (rather than LIFO) and 10 percent (rather than 20 percent) depreciation?

CASES

Case 12-83 Ethics and Equity

Lauren Avenido is employed as a financial analyst at a large brokerage house. Her job is to follow companies in the computer hardware sector and issue reports that will be used by her firm's brokers in making recommendations to the brokerage house's clients. Her reports are

(Continued)

summarized by her ratings of the company—strong buy, buy, hold, sell, or strong sell. She is in frequent contact with the top management of the companies she follows.

After a thorough investigation, she believes she should downgrade Dreamware from a "strong buy" to a "hold." However, when she informs Dreamware's CFO, the CFO threatens to call her boss. Later that week, her boss calls her to request that she reconsider her downgrade and states that her cooperation will be "greatly appreciated."

Required:
How should Lauren respond to her boss? Are there any other steps she should consider taking?

Case 12-84 Assessing the Effects of the "Clean Air" Legislation

Congress is considering legislation that would require significant reductions over a several-year period in the quantity of emissions that electric utilities will be allowed to discharge into the air. Electric utilities that generate their electricity by burning inexpensive, but relatively high-sulfur, coal were most affected by this legislation. Some utilities plan to comply with this legislation by burning coal with a lower sulfur content. Other utilities plan to comply with this legislation by installing devices on power plant smokestacks that would filter emissions before it is discharged into the air.

Required:
1. In what places on the financial statements of coal-dependent electric utilities do you expect to observe the effects of this legislation?
2. In what places on the financial statements of companies that mine coal do you expect to observe the effects of this legislation?

Case 12-85 Changes in the Price of Fuel for Aircraft

The cost of fuel is reported to be about 20 percent of the total operating cost for a major airline. Events in the Middle East caused jet fuel costs to nearly double from 2008 to 2011.

Required:
1. If you were the CEO of a major airline, how would you suggest that the airline respond to the fuel price increase?
2. How would you expect the financial statements of major airlines to be affected by the fuel price increase and the actions that the airlines would take in response?

Case 12-86 Analyzing Growth

Consolidated financial statements for Initech Corporation follow.

Initech Corporation Consolidated Income Statements (In millions except per share amounts)			
	Three Years Ended December 31,		
	2011	**2010**	**2009**
Net revenues	$8,782	$5,844	$4,779
Cost of goods sold	$3,252	$2,557	$2,316
Research and development	970	780	618
Marketing, general and administrative expenses	1,168	1,017	765
Operating costs and expenses	$5,390	$4,354	$3,699
Operating income	$3,392	$1,490	$1,080
Interest expense	(50)	(54)	(82)
Interest income and other, net	188	133	197
Income before taxes	$3,530	$1,569	$1,195
Provision for taxes	1,235	502	376
Net income	$2,295	$1,067	$ 819

Initech Corporation
Consolidated Balance Sheets
(In millions except per share amounts)

	December 31,	
ASSETS	2011	2010
Current assets:		
Cash and cash equivalents	$ 1,659	$ 1,843
Short-term investments	1,477	993
Accounts and notes receivable, net of allowance for doubtful accounts of $22 ($26 in 2010)	1,448	1,069
Inventories	838	535
Deferred tax assets	310	205
Other current assets	70	46
Total current assets	$ 5,802	$ 4,691
Property, plant, and equipment:		
Land and buildings	$ 1,848	$ 1,463
Machinery and equipment	4,148	2,874
Construction in progress	317	311
	$ 6,313	$ 4,648
Less accumulated depreciation	(2,317)	(1,832)
Property, plant, and equipment, net	3,996	2,816
Long-term investments	1,416	496
Other assets	130	86
Total assets	$11,344	$ 8,089

LIABILITIES AND STOCKHOLDERS' EQUITY		
Current liabilities:		
Short-term debt	$ 399	$ 202
Long-term debt redeemable within one year	98	110
Accounts payable	427	281
Deferred income on shipments to distributors	200	149
Accrued compensation and benefits	544	435
Other accrued liabilities	374	306
Income taxes payable	391	359
Total current liabilities	$ 2,433	$ 1,842
Long-term debt	426	249
Deferred tax liabilities	297	180
Other long-term liabilities	688	373
Total liabilities	$ 3,844	$ 2,644
Stockholders' equity:		
Preferred stock, $0.001 par value, 50 shares authorized; none issued	$ 0	$ 0
Common stock, $0.001 par value, 1,400 shares authorized; and issued and outstanding in 2011 and 2010	1	1
Capital in excess of par value	2,193	1,775
Retained earnings	5,306	3,669
Total stockholders' equity	7,500	5,445
Total liabilities and stockholders' equity	$11,344	$ 8,089

Required:

1. Prepare common size income statements to be used for both vertical and horizontal analysis for 2010–2011 (in percentage terms, rounded to two decimal places). You do not need to include the actual dollar amounts shown above.

(Continued)

2. Using the common size income statements for both vertical and horizontal analysis prepared in part 1, indicate why Initech's profits increased more rapidly than sales for 2010 and 2011.

3. Prepare common size balance sheets for vertical analysis for 2010 and 2011 (in percentage terms, rounded to two decimal places). You do not need to include the actual dollar amounts shown above.

4. Did the proportion of assets invested in the various classes of assets change significantly from 2010 to 2011?

5. How has Initech financed its growth in assets?

6. Did the income statement change as much between 2010 and 2011 as the balance sheet?

Case 12-87 Identifying the Causes of Profitability Changes

The consolidated financial statements for Dowsett Shipping Corporation and Subsidiaries follow.

Dowsett Shipping Corporation and Subsidiaries Consolidated Income Statements In thousands, except per share amounts			
	Fiscal Year Ended May 31,		
	2011	2010	2009
Revenues	$7,808,043	$7,550,060	$7,688,296
Operating expenses:			
Salaries and employee benefits	$3,807,493	$3,637,080	$3,438,391
Rentals and landing fees	658,138	672,341	650,001
Depreciation and amortization	579,896	577,157	562,207
Fuel	495,384	508,386	663,327
Maintenance and repairs	404,639	404,311	449,394
Restructuring charges	(12,500)	254,000	121,000
Other	1,497,820	1,473,818	1,551,850
	$7,430,870	$7,527,093	$7,436,170
Operating income	$ 377,173	$ 22,967	$ 252,126
Other income (expenses):			
Interest, net	$(160,923)	$(164,315)	$(181,880)
Gain on disposition of aircraft and related equipment	4,633	2,832	11,375
Other, net	(17,307)	(8,312)	(8,679)
Payroll tax loss	0	0	(32,000)
Other income (expenses), net	$(173,597)	$(169,795)	$(211,184)
Income (loss) before income taxes and extraordinary loss	$ 203,576	$(146,828)	$ 40,942
Provision (credit) for income taxes	93,767	(33,046)	35,044
Income (loss) before extraordinary loss	$ 109,809	$(113,782)	$ 5,898
Extraordinary loss, net of tax benefit of $34,287	(55,943)	0	0
Net income (loss)	$ 53,866	$(113,782)	$ 5,898

Dowsett Shipping Corporation and Subsidiaries
Consolidated Balance Sheets
(In thousands)

	May 31,	
ASSETS	**2011**	**2010**
Current assets:		
Cash and cash equivalents	$ 155,456	$ 78,177
Receivable, less allowance for doubtful accounts of $31,308 and $32,074	922,727	899,773
Spare parts, supplies and fuel	164,087	158,062
Prepaid expenses and other	63,573	69,994
Deferred income taxes	133,875	0
Total current assets	$ 1,439,718	$ 1,206,006
Property and equipment, at cost		
Flight equipment	$ 2,843,253	$ 2,540,350
Package handling and ground support equipment	1,413,793	1,352,659
Computer and electronic equipment	947,913	851,686
Other	1,501,250	1,433,212
	$ 6,706,209	$ 6,177,907
Less accumulated depreciation and amortization	(3,229,941)	(2,766,610)
Net property and equipment	$ 3,476,268	$ 3,411,297
Other assets:		
Goodwill	$ 432,215	$ 487,780
Equipment deposits and other assets	444,863	358,103
Total other assets	$ 877,078	$ 845,883
Total assets	$ 5,793,064	$ 5,463,186
LIABILITIES AND STOCKHOLDERS' EQUITY		
Current liabilities:		
Current portion of long-term debt	$ 133,797	$ 155,257
Accounts payable	554,111	430,130
Accrued expenses	761,357	799,468
Total current liabilities	$ 1,449,265	$ 1,384,855
Long-term debt, less current portion	1,882,279	1,797,844
Deferred income taxes	72,479	123,715
Other liabilities	717,660	577,050
Total liabilities	$ 4,121,683	$ 3,883,464
Common stockholders' equity:		
Common stock, $0.10 par value, 100,000 shares authorized, 54,743 and 54,100 shares issued	$ 5,474	$ 5,410
Additional paid-in capital—common stock	699,385	672,727
Retained earnings	969,515	906,555
	$ 1,674,374	$ 1,584,692
Less treasury stock and deferred compensation related to stock plans	(2,993)	(4,970)
Total common stockholders' equity	1,671,381	1,579,722
Total liabilities and stockholders' equity	$ 5,793,064	$ 5,463,186

Required:

1. Evaluate Dowsett's performance in 2011.
2. What were the primary factors responsible for Dowsett's loss in 2010 and return to profitability in 2011?
3. How did Dowsett finance the $329,878,000 increase in assets in 2011?

Case 12-88 Continuing Problem: Front Row Entertainment

The income statement and consolidated balance sheets for Front Row Entertainment follow.

Front Row Entertainment Inc. Consolidated Balance Sheets		
	December 31	
ASSETS	2012	2011
Current assets:		
Cash	$ 30,322	$ 9,005
Accounts receivable, net	98,250	17,000
Prepaid expenses	133,400	57,200
Supplies	2,200	3,700
Inventory	61,380	2,850
Total current assets	$ 325,552	$89,755
Property, plant, and equipment:		
Building	1,857,250	0
Equipment	27,350	7,000
Accumulated depreciation	(53,835)	(2,160)
Trademark	25,000	0
Total assets	$2,181,317	$94,595
LIABILITIES AND EQUITY		
Current liabilities:		
Accounts payable	$ 2,450	$12,240
Salaries payable	2,500	3,690
Interest payable	40,917	2,250
Unearned sales revenue	1,780	28,650
Income taxes payable	550	2,180
Total current liabilities	$ 56,197	$49,010
Long-term liabilities:		
Notes payable	$ 405,000	$25,000
Bonds payable, net	1,500,000	0
Less: Discount on bond payable	(109,530)	
Total long-term liabilities	$1,795,470	$25,000
Equity:		
Preferred stock	$ 150,000	$ 0
Common stock	18,000	16,000
Additional paid-in capital:		
Preferred stock	75,000	0
Common stock	38,000	0
Treasury stock	1,800	0
Retained earnings	53,250	4,585
Less: Treasury stock	(6,400)	0
Total stockholders' equity	$ 329,650	$20,585
Total liabilities and equity	$2,181,317	$94,595

Front Row Entertainment Inc.
Income Statement
For the Year Ended December 31, 2012

Revenues:	
Sales revenue	$3,142,800
Service revenue	636,000
Total revenues	$3,778,800
Expenses:	
Artist Fee Expense	$2,134,260
Rent expense	952,663
Cost of goods sold	74,800
Salaries and wages expense	345,100
Depreciation expense	51,675
Interest expense	98,087
Income taxes expense	22,000
Other expenses	26,550
Total expenses	$3,705,135
Net income	$ 73,665

Additional information:

- The market price of the common shares at the end of the year is $17.55 per share.
- The average number of common shares outstanding for 2012 is 16,400.
- The dividends per common share for 2012 were approximately $25,000, which is approximately $1.45 per share ($25,000/17,300 common shares). The 17,300 shares can be calculated from information in Chapter 10 (16,000 shares at Jan. 1, 2012 + 2,000 shares issued on June 15, 2012 – 700 shares repurchased on July 10, 2012).
- Common stock repurchases for 2012 were $11,200. This is taken from Chapter 10 as 700 common shares were repurchased as treasury stock at a cost of $16 per share.
- Preferred dividends for 2012 were $0.

Note: Round all answers to two decimal places.

Required:

1. Calculate the short-term liquidity ratios for Front Row Entertainment for 2012.
2. Calculate the debt management ratios for Front Row Entertainment for 2012.
3. Calculate the asset efficiency ratios for Front Row Entertainment for 2012.
4. Calculate the profitability ratios for Front Row Entertainment for 2012.
5. Calculate the stockholder ratios for Front Row Entertainment for 2012.

13 Managerial Accounting Concepts and Decision-Making Support

Doug Norman Crystals/Alamy

After studying Chapter 13, you should be able to:

1. Explain the meaning of managerial accounting and contrast it to financial accounting.

2. Identify and explain the current focus of managerial accounting and the role of managerial accountants in an organization.

3. Explain the meaning of cost and how costs are assigned to products and services.

4. Define the various costs of manufacturing products and providing services as well as selling and administration.

5. Prepare income statements for manufacturing and service organizations.

6. Explain the importance of ethical behavior for managers and managerial accountants.

Jeff Greenberg/PhotoEdit

EXPERIENCE MANAGERIAL DECISIONS

with BuyCostumes.com

The greatest benefit of managerial accounting is also its biggest challenge—to provide managers with information that improves decisions and creates organizational value. This information helps inform managers about the impact of various strategic and operational decisions on key nonfinancial performance measures and their eventual impact on the organization's financial performance. The information is challenging to prepare and analyze because it requires an understanding of all value chain components that affect the organization, including research and development, production, marketing, distribution, and customer service.

Since its inception in 1999, **BuyCostumes.com** has blended the right managerial accounting information and an innovative business model to provide costumes to customers in over 50 countries. Using the Internet and marketing creativity, BuyCostumes.com serves a market of 150 million U.S. consumers that spend $3.6 billion on costumes each year.

GWimages, 2010/Shutterstock.com

According to CEO Jalem Getz, BuyCostumes.com measures key performance indicators to guide its decision making. For example, managerial accountants analyze measures of customer satisfaction, average time between order placement and costume arrival for each shipping method, and the profitability of individual customer types. As customer trends change, competitors emerge, and technological advances occur, BuyCostumes.com's managerial accounting information adapts to provide crucial insight into the company's performance and how its strategy should evolve to remain the world's largest Internet costume retailer.

buycostumes.com©
the web's most popular costume store!

THE MEANING AND PURPOSE OF MANAGERIAL ACCOUNTING

What do we mean by managerial accounting? Quite simply, **managerial accounting** is the provision of accounting information for a company's internal users. Internal users of managerial accounting information include managers of all levels, including the following:

- executives (e.g., chief executive officer, chief financial officer, chief risk officer, etc.)
- members of the company's board of directors, employees (e.g., production floor worker, delivery truck driver, etc.)
- union members
- members of the company's audit committee

The purpose of managerial accounting is to generate information that helps managers and other internal users take actions that create value for the organization. To accomplish its purpose, managerial accounting has three broad objectives:

- To provide information for planning the organization's actions.
- To provide information for controlling the organization's actions.
- To provide information for making effective decisions.

Using recent examples from many companies in both the for-profit and not-for-profit sectors, this textbook explains how all manufacturing (e.g., aircraft producer—**Boeing Corporation**), merchandising (e.g., clothing retailer—**Guess**) and service (e.g., healthcare provider—**The Cleveland Clinic**) organizations use managerial accounting information and concepts. People in all types of positions—from corporate presidents to graphic designers to hospital administrators—can improve their managerial skills by being well-grounded in the basic concepts and use of managerial accounting information for planning, controlling, and decision making.

Furthermore, thousands of companies increasingly release to the public (i.e., suppliers, regulators, employees, human rights organizations, environmental groups, customers, etc.) very large quantities of managerial accounting information that traditionally either did not exist or was released only internally. This information is released through optional reports known as corporate sustainability reports (e.g., **Starbucks**, **McDonald's**), social responsibility reports (e.g., **Apple**, **Chiquita**), or citizenship reports (e.g., **General Electric**). The release of these reports often occurs because firms want to manage their reputation by preparing and releasing such information themselves, rather than having Internet bloggers, newspapers, and cable news networks publish their own estimates of such information. Some leading companies (e.g., **PepsiCo**, **Novo Nordisk**, **British Telecom**) have even moved so far as to combine their sustainability report with their annual report, thereby resulting in a single, integrated report containing both traditional financial accounting information as well as managerial accounting information.[1] The exciting reality is that the importance and scope of managerial accounting information is growing rapidly around the globe. As a result, the demand for business people who possess the ability to create, understand, use and communicate managerial accounting information continues to grow.

Information Needs of Managers and Other Users

Managerial accounting information is needed by a number of individuals. In particular, managers and empowered workers need comprehensive, up-to-date information for the following activities:

- planning
- controlling
- decision making

---

[1] For a more in-depth discussion of the future of sustainability accounting, see Robert Eccles and Michael Krzus, *One Report: Integrated Reporting for a Sustainable Strategy* (John Wiley & Sons, Inc., Hoboken, NJ: 2010) or Brian Ballou and Dan Heitger, "Accounting for the Sustainability Continuum," *Journal of Accountancy* (June 2010).

Planning

The detailed formulation of action to achieve a particular end is the management activity called **planning**. Planning requires setting objectives and identifying methods to achieve those objectives. For example, a firm may set the objective of increasing its short-term and long-term profitability by improving the overall quality of its products. **Daimler-Chrysler** drastically improved the quality and profitability of its **Chrysler** automobile division during the beginning of the 21st century to the point where its quality surpassed that of **Mercedes-Benz** (also owned by DaimlerChrysler).[2] By improving product quality, firms like DaimlerChrysler should be able to reduce scrap and rework, decrease the number of customer complaints and warranty work, reduce the resources currently assigned to inspection, and so on, thus increasing profitability. To realize these benefits, management must develop some specific methods that, when implemented, will lead to the achievement of the desired objective. A plant manager, for example, may start a supplier evaluation program to identify and select suppliers who are willing and able to supply defect-free parts. Empowered workers may be able to identify production causes of defects and to create new methods for producing a product that will reduce scrap and rework and the need for inspection. The new methods should be clearly specified and detailed.

Controlling

Planning is only half the battle. Once a plan is created, it must be implemented and its implementation monitored by managers and workers to ensure that the plan is being carried out as intended. The managerial activity of monitoring a plan's implementation and taking corrective action as needed is referred to as **controlling**. Control is usually achieved by comparing actual performance with expected performance. This information can be used to evaluate or to correct the steps being taken to implement a plan. Based on the feedback, a manager (or worker) may decide to let the plan continue as is, take corrective action of some type to put the actions back in harmony with the original plan, or do some midstream replanning.

The managerial accounting information used for planning and control purposes can be either financial or nonfinancial in nature. For example, **Duffy Tool and Stamping** saved $14,300 per year by redesigning a press operation.[3] In one department, completed parts (made by a press) came down a chute and fell into a parts tub. When the tub became full, press operators had to stop operation while the stock operator removed the full tub and replaced it with an empty one. Workers redesigned the operation so that each press had a chute with two branches—each leading to a different tub. Now when one tub is full, completed parts are routed into the other tub. The $14,300 savings are a financial measure of the success of the redesign. The redesign also eliminated machine downtime and increased the number of units produced per hour (operational feedback), both of which are examples of nonfinancial performance. Both types of measures convey important information. Often financial and nonfinancial feedback is given to managers in the form of performance reports that compare the actual data with planned data or other benchmarks.

Decision Making

The process of choosing among competing alternatives is called **decision making**. This managerial function is intertwined with planning and control in that a manager cannot successfully plan or control the organization's actions without making decisions regarding competing alternatives. For instance, if **BMW** contemplates the possibility of offering a car that runs on gasoline and hydrogen, its ultimate decision would be improved if information about the alternatives (e.g., pertaining to gasoline versus hydrogen versus hybrid combinations of these two automobile fuel options) is gathered and made available to managers. One of the major roles of the managerial accounting information system is to supply information that facilitates decision making.

---

[2] Sarah A. Webster and Joe Guy Collier, "Fixing a Car Company: Zetsche on Mercedes: 'A Lot of Work Is Ahead,'" *Detroit Free Press.* Taken from http://forums.mbworld.org/forums/showthread.php?t=121650 on April 8, 2008.
[3] George F. Hanks, "Excellence Teams in Action," *Management Accounting* (February 1995): 35.

 **What Constitutes Managerial Accounting Information?**

You are the **Costco** executive who has been chosen to decide whether or not the company should continue its policy of sourcing its finest coffee from Rwanda.

What types of information should you consider as you decide how best to structure and analyze this important long-term strategic decision? What challenges do you expect to face in making this decision?

What constitutes managerial accounting information is growing considerably as organizations must make decisions that include the global consequences of their actions, as well as the impact on an increasingly large number of vocal, well-informed, and powerful stakeholders. Stakeholders include the company's customers, suppliers, employees, regulators, politicians, lawmakers, and local community members. Generally speaking, managerial accounting information can be *financial* in nature, such as sales revenue or cost of sales, or *nonfinancial* in nature, such as the number of quality defects or the percentage of manufacturing plants that are inspected for compliance with human rights policies. One of the most exciting—and yet daunting—aspects of managerial accounting is that one can choose to measure *anything*, assuming the resources, information technology, and creativity exist to capture the desired performance measure.

As a Costco executive, one of the first nonfinancial factors you likely would consider measuring is the quality of the Rwandan coffee to ensure that it fulfills Costco's strategic goal of creating a competitive advantage by providing premium coffee to customers. Quality could be defined by the beans' taste, shelf life longevity, or other factors valued by customers. Other important nonfinancial performance measures might include the time required to ship the harvested beans from Rwanda to Costco stores around North America and the presence of a local farming workforce in Rwanda critical to successfully sustaining a long-term supply chain between Rwandan fields and Costco customers.

One of the most important financial items to measure would be the importance to Costco's customers of purchasing premium quality coffee, which could be measured by the additional price they are willing to pay for Rwandan coffee over and above more average quality coffee. Other financial measures might include the cost of harvesting, inspecting, and shipping beans, as well as investments in Rwandan farming communities (e.g., physical infrastructure and schools) that ensure the relationship is sustainable for future generations.

Finally, you should consider how the decision to continue sourcing premium coffee from Rwanda will be perceived by Costco's important stakeholders, including its customers who buy the coffee, suppliers who provide the coffee beans, and government officials in the United States and Rwanda who set trading policies between the two countries. Accurately measuring issues like stakeholder perceptions of such decisions can be difficult because the managerial accountant oftentimes must invent new measures, figure out where the data to create such measures might come from, and estimate how accurate these measures will be once collected.

The managerial accountant's ability to inform executive decision makers by providing innovative, accurate, and timely performance measures can create an important competitive advantage for the organization by improving its key decisions.

FINANCIAL ACCOUNTING AND MANAGERIAL ACCOUNTING

A brief examination of the basic differences between financial accounting and managerial accounting is helpful for understanding the emerging trends and important managerial accounting concepts discussed in the remainder of the chapter. The two basic kinds of accounting information systems are financial accounting and managerial accounting.

Financial Accounting

Financial accounting is primarily concerned with producing information (financial statements) for *external* users, including investors, creditors, customers, suppliers, government agencies (Food and Drug Administration, Federal Communications Commission, etc.), and labor unions. This information has an historical orientation and is used for such things as investment decisions, stewardship evaluation, monitoring activity, and regulatory measures. Financial statements must conform to certain rules and conventions that are defined by various agencies, such as the Securities and Exchange Commission (SEC), the Financial Accounting Standards Board (FASB), and the International Accounting Standards Board (IASB). These rules pertain to issues such as the recognition of revenues; timing of expenses; and recording of assets, liabilities, and stockholders' equity.

Managerial Accounting

The managerial accounting system produces information for *internal* users, such as managers, executives, and workers. Specifically, managerial accounting identifies, collects, measures, classifies, and reports financial and nonfinancial information that is useful to internal users in planning, controlling, and decision making.

Comparison of Financial and Managerial Accounting

While investors look at a firm's overall profitability, managers need to know the profitability of individual products as well. The managerial accounting system should be designed to provide both total profits and profits for individual products and, thus, have a broad audience. Flexibility is crucial—the managerial accounting system should be able to supply forward-looking information for different purposes, as explained throughout this textbook. Unlike financial accounting, managerial accounting is *not* subject to the requirements of generally accepted accounting principles. When comparing financial accounting to managerial accounting, several differences can be identified. Some of the more important differences follow and are summarized in Exhibit 13-1.

- *Targeted users.* Managerial accounting focuses on providing information for internal users, while financial accounting focuses on providing information for external users.
- *Restrictions on inputs and processes.* Managerial accounting is not subject to the requirements of generally accepted accounting principles set by the SEC and the FASB that must be followed for financial reporting. The inputs and processes of financial accounting are well defined. Only certain kinds of economic events qualify as inputs, and processes must follow generally accepted methods. Unlike financial accounting, managerial accounting has no official body that prescribes the format, content, and rules for selecting inputs and processes and preparing reports.
- *Type of information.* The restrictions imposed by financial accounting tend to produce objective and verifiable financial information. For managerial accounting, information may be financial or nonfinancial and may be much more subjective in nature.
- *Time orientation.* Financial accounting has a historical orientation (i.e., looking through the rear view mirror). It records and reports events that have already happened. Although managerial accounting also records and reports events that have already occurred, it strongly emphasizes providing information about future events (i.e., looking through the front windshield). Management, for example, may want to know what it will cost to produce a product next year. This future orientation is necessary for planning and decision making.
- *Degree of aggregation.* Managerial accounting provides measures and internal reports used to evaluate the performance of entities, product lines, departments, and managers. Essentially, detailed information is needed and provided. Financial accounting, on the other hand, focuses on overall firm performance, providing a more aggregated viewpoint.
- *Breadth.* Managerial accounting is much broader than financial accounting. It includes aspects of managerial economics, industrial engineering, and management science as well as numerous other areas.

The accounting system should be designed to provide both financial and managerial accounting information. The key point here is flexibility—the system should be able to supply different information for different purposes.

Exhibit 13-1

Comparison of Financial and Managerial Accounting

Financial Accounting	Managerial Accounting
• Externally focused	• Internally focused
• Must follow externally imposed rules	• No mandatory rules
• Objective financial information	• Financial and nonfinancial information; subjective information possible
• Historical orientation	• Emphasis on the future
• Information about the firm as a whole	• Internal evaluation and decisions based on very detailed information
• More self contained	• Broad, multidisciplinary

OBJECTIVE

Identify and explain the current focus of managerial accounting and the role of managerial accountants in an organization.

CURRENT FOCUS OF MANAGERIAL ACCOUNTING

The business environment in which companies operate has changed dramatically over the past several decades. For instance, advances in technology, the Internet, the opening of markets around the world, increased competitive pressures and increased complexity of strategy (e.g., alliances between **McDonald's** and **The Walt Disney Company** for promotional tie-ins) and operations all have combined to produce a global business environment. Effective managerial accounting systems also have changed in order to provide information that helps improve companies' planning, control, and decision-making activities. Several important uses of managerial accounting resulting from these advances include new methods of estimating product and service cost and profitability, understanding customer orientation, evaluating the business from a cross-functional perspective, and providing information useful in improving total quality.

New Methods of Costing Products and Services

Today's companies need focused, accurate information on the cost of the products and services they produce. In the past, a company might have produced a few products that were roughly similar to one another. Only the cost of materials and labor might have differed from one product to another and figuring out the cost of each unit was relatively easy. Now, with the increase in technology and automation, it is more difficult to generate the costing information needed by management. As Peter Drucker, internationally respected management guru, points out:

> Traditional cost accounting in manufacturing does not record the cost of nonproducing such as the cost of faulty quality, or of a machine being out of order, or of needed parts not being on hand. Yet these unrecorded and uncontrolled costs in some plants run as high as the costs that traditional accounting does record. By contrast, a new method of cost accounting developed in the last 10 years—called "activity-based" accounting—records all costs. And it relates them, as traditional accounting cannot, to value-added.[4]

Activity-based costing (ABC) is a more detailed approach to determining the cost of goods and services. ABC improves costing accuracy by emphasizing the cost of the many activities or tasks that must be done to produce a product or offer a service. **United Parcel Service Inc. (UPS)** used ABC to discover and manage the cost of the activities involved with shipping packages by truck, as opposed to by plane, in order to beat **FedEx** at its overnight delivery business in quick mid-distance (up to 500 miles) overnight deliveries.[5] Process-value analysis focuses on the way in which companies create value for customers. The objective is to find ways to perform necessary activities more efficiently and to eliminate those that do not create customer value.

Customer Orientation

Customer value is a key focus because firms can establish a competitive advantage by creating better customer value for the same or lower cost than competitors or creating equivalent value for lower cost than that of competitors. Customer value is the difference between what a customer receives and what the customer gives up when buying a product or service. When we talk about customer value, we consider the complete range of tangible and intangible benefits that a customer receives from a purchased product. Customers receive basic and special product features, service, quality, instructions for use, reputation, brand name, and other important factors. On the other hand, customers give up the cost of purchasing the product, the time and effort spent acquiring and learning to use the product, and the costs of using, maintaining, and disposing of it.

---

[4] Peter F. Drucker, "We Need to Measure, Not Count," *The Wall Street Journal* (April 13, 1993): A14.
[5] Charles Haddad and Jack Ewing, "Ground Wars: UPS's Rapid Ascent Leaves FedEx Scrambling," *BusinessWeek* (May 21, 2001): 64–68.

Strategic Positioning   Effective cost information can help the company identify strategies that increase customer value and, in so doing, create a sustainable competitive advantage.[6] Generally, firms choose one of two general strategies:

- *Cost leadership*: The objective of the cost leadership strategy is to provide the same or better value to customers at a *lower* cost than competitors.
- *Superior products through differentiation (e.g., highest performance quality, most desired product features, best customer service, etc.)*: A differentiation strategy strives to increase customer value by providing something to customers not provided by competitors. For example, **Best Buy**'s Geek Squad of computer technicians creates a competitive advantage for Best Buy by providing 24-hour in-home technical assistance for its customers. Accurate cost information is important to see whether or not the additional service provided by the Geek Squad adds more to revenue than it does to cost.

The Value Chain   Successful pursuit of cost leadership and/or differentiation strategies requires an understanding of a firm's value chain. The **value chain** is the set of activities required to design, develop, produce, market, and deliver products and services, as well as provide support services to customers. Exhibit 13-2 illustrates the value chain. A managerial accounting system should track information about a wide variety of activities that span the value chain. For example, **Apple** spent considerable effort researching the cost of developing and manufacturing the iPhone, as well as the amount of money potential customers would be willing to spend to purchase it before releasing the most recent version. Also, customer value can be increased by improving the speed of delivery and response, as many customers believe that delivery delayed is delivery denied. **FedEx** exploited this part of the value chain and successfully developed a service that was not being offered by the **U.S. Postal Service**.

The management at **BuyCostumes.com**, for example, focuses on various managerial accounting performance measures to help direct its relationship with customers. BuyCostumes.com typically records over 20 million unique web viewers each year from its more than 150 million customers. Halloween is its biggest season by far, generating $180 million (half of its total sales for the year), each October. Interestingly, since its creation, BuyCostumes.com management has correctly predicted the outcome of each Presidential election based on the sales data from its Presidential candidate mask collection.

Cross-Functional Perspective

In managing the value chain, a managerial accountant must understand and measure many functions of the business. Contemporary approaches to costing may include initial design and engineering costs, as well as manufacturing costs, and the costs of distribution, sales, and service. An individual well-schooled in the various definitions of cost, who understands the shifting definitions of cost from the short-run to the long-run, can be invaluable in determining what information is relevant in decision making. For example,

buycos**tumes**.com©
the web's most popular costume store!

Exhibit 13-2

The Value Chain

Design · Develop · Produce · Market · Deliver

---

[6] C. Rutledge and R. Williams, "A Seat at the Table," *Outlook Journal* (June 2004). Taken from http://www.accenture.com/xd/xd.asp?it=enweb&xd=ideas%5Coutlook%5C2_2004%5Cm on October 6, 2005.

strategic decisions may require a cost definition that assigns the costs of all value chain activities. In a long-run decision environment, the banking industry (e.g., **Chase**) spends an estimated $500 million per year across all functional areas to perform customer profitability analyses that identify their most, and least, profitable customers.[7] However, a short-run decision to determine the profitability of a special order (e.g., an offer made to **Bridgestone Firestone North American Tire** at year-end to use idle machinery to produce 1,000 extra tires for a local tire distributor) may require only the incremental costs of the special order in a single functional area.

Total Quality Management

Continuous improvement is the continual search for ways to increase the overall efficiency and productivity of activities by reducing waste, increasing quality, and managing costs. Managerial accounting information about the costs of products, customers, processes, and other objects of management interest can be the basis for identifying problems and alternative solutions.

Continuous improvement is fundamental for establishing excellence. A philosophy of **total quality management**, in which manufacturers strive to create an environment that will enable workers to manufacture perfect (zero-defect) products, has replaced the "acceptable quality" attitudes of the past. This emphasis on quality has also created a demand for a managerial accounting system that provides information about quality, including quality cost measurement and reporting for both manufacturing and service industries. For example, in response to increasing customer complaints regarding its laptop computer repair process, **Toshiba** formed an alliance with **UPS** in which UPS picks up the broken laptop, Toshiba fixes it, and UPS returns the repaired laptop to the customer. In order for this alliance to work effectively, both Toshiba and UPS require relevant managerial accounting information regarding the cost of existing poor quality and efforts to improve future quality.[8]

Increasingly, companies, such as **DaimlerChrysler**, are using techniques like Six Sigma and Design for Six Sigma (DFSS), together with various types of cost information, to achieve improved quality performance. Chrysler's goal is "to meet customer requirements and improve vehicle and system reliability while reducing development costs and cultivating innovation."[9] On a related note, many companies attempt to increase organizational value by eliminating wasteful activities that exist throughout the value chain. In eliminating such waste, companies usually find that their accounting must also change. This change in accounting, referred to as **lean accounting**, organizes costs according to the value chain and collects both financial and nonfinancial information. The objective is to provide information to managers that supports their waste reduction efforts and to provide financial statements that better reflect overall performance, using both financial and nonfinancial information.

Finally, one of the more recent charges of managerial accountants is to help carry out the company's enterprise risk management (ERM) approach. ERM is a formal way for managerial accountants to identify and respond to the most important threats and business opportunities facing the organization. ERM is becoming increasingly important for long-term success. For example, it is well recognized that **Wal-Mart**'s expert crisis management processes and teams repeatedly responded to the aftermath of Hurricane Katrina throughout Louisiana and Mississippi better and faster than did either local or federal government agencies (e.g., FEMA).[10] The results of many public accounting firm surveys, as well as the *Institute of Management Accountants*, highlight the growing importance that organizations place on conducting effective risk management practices.[11]

---

[7] R. Brooks, "Unequal Treatment: Alienating Customers Isn't Always a Bad Idea, Many Firms Discover," *The Wall Street Journal* (January 7, 1999): A1.

[8] T. Friedman, *The World Is Flat: A Brief History of the Twenty-First Century*, Farrar, Straus and Giroux: New York, New York, 2005.

[9] Kevin Kelly, "Chrysler Continues Quality Push," WardsAuto.Com. Taken from http://wardsauto.com/microsites/newsarticle.asp on September 30, 2005.

[10] A. Zimmerman, and V. Bauerlein, "At Wal-Mart, Emergency Plan Has Big Payoff," *The Wall Street Journal* (September 12, 2005): B1.

[11] *Enterprise Risk Management: Tools and Techniques for Effective Implementation*. Institute of Management Accountants, Montvale, New Jersey, 2007: 1–31.

THE ROLE OF THE MANAGERIAL ACCOUNTANT

Managerial accountants must support management in all phases of business decision making. They must be intelligent, well prepared, up-to-date with new developments, and familiar with the customs and practices of all countries in which their firms operate. They are expected to be knowledgeable about the legal environment of business and, in particular, about the Sarbanes-Oxley Act of 2002.

For example, **Kicker**, a real company that makes car stereo systems, relies heavily on managerial accounting information, as we learned in extensive interviews with their top management. Boxes titled "Here's the Real Kicker," like the one below, detail how the company has used managerial accounting information in its operations.

Here's the Real Kicker

A division of **Stillwater Designs** and **Audio Inc., Kicker** makes car stereo systems. Their signature logo, "Livin' Loud," gives you a hint as to the capabilities of the system. As the company website says, "Livin' Loud has always been the KICKER way—staying one step ahead of the pack—driven to create components that consistently raise the world's expectations for car stereo performance."

Twenty-five years ago, car stereos were underpowered tinny affairs. They could power a radio or an 8-track tape deck. But the in-home listening experience coveted by audio buffs eluded the automobile market. In 1980, Stillwater Designs' founder and president Steve Irby developed the first full-range speaker enclosure designed specifically for automotive use—the Original Kicker®.

Stillwater Designs began in 1973 as a two-person operation, custom designing and building professional sound and musical instrument speaker systems for churches, auditoriums, and entertainers. Building upon the success of the Original Kicker, the company concentrated on the car audio market, applying the same research and design skills that made its first product so successful to the development of a complete line of high-performance components for car audio. What was once a company with two employees in a single-car garage is now a corporation with more than 200 employees in facilities totaling more than 500,000 square feet.

The Kicker brand includes many high-performance car stereo products, including subwoofers, midrange and midbass drivers, tweeters, crossovers, matched component systems, speakers, and power amplifiers. Kicker is proud to have won the prestigious Audio Video International Auto Sound Grand Prix Award, sponsored annually by *Audio-Video International* magazine. Winners are selected by retailers based on fidelity of sound reproduction, design engineering, reliability, craftsmanship and product integrity, and cost/performance ratio. In 2003, seven Kicker products earned Grand Prix awards. Awards emphasizing the performance of the company include the Governor's Award for Excellence in Exporting (2000) and the 1996 Oklahoma City International Trade Association designation as its International Business of the Year.

While Stillwater Designs originally handled research and design (R&D), manufacturing, and sales, it now concentrates primarily on R&D and sales. The bulk of manufacturing has been outsourced (performed by outside firms on a contract basis), although the company still builds some product and plans to build even more as it moves into its new facility for factory-installed audio systems. Engineering and audio research is Kicker president and chief executive officer Steve Irby's first love, and he still heads its design team. The day-to-day involvement of top management, coupled with an energetic workforce of talented individuals in all areas of the company's operations and an innate ability to create truly musical components, has been the reason for the company's remarkable success.

Kicker's organization chart is shown in Exhibit 13-3 (p. 672). The **controller**, or chief accounting officer, for Kicker is located in the administration department. She supervises all accounting functions and reports directly to the general manager and chief operating officer (COO). Because of the critical role that managerial accounting plays in the operation of an organization, the controller is often viewed as a member of the top management team and is encouraged to participate in planning, controlling, and decision-making activities. As the chief accounting officer, the controller has responsibility for both internal and external accounting requirements. In larger firms, this charge may include direct responsibility for internal auditing, cost accounting, financial accounting (including SEC reports and financial statements), systems accounting (including analysis, design, and internal controls), and taxes. In larger companies, the controller is separate from the treasury department. The **treasurer** is responsible for the finance function. Specifically, the treasurer raises capital and manages cash and investments. The treasurer may also be in charge of credit and collection and insurance.

Exhibit 13-3

Kicker Inc. Organizational Chart

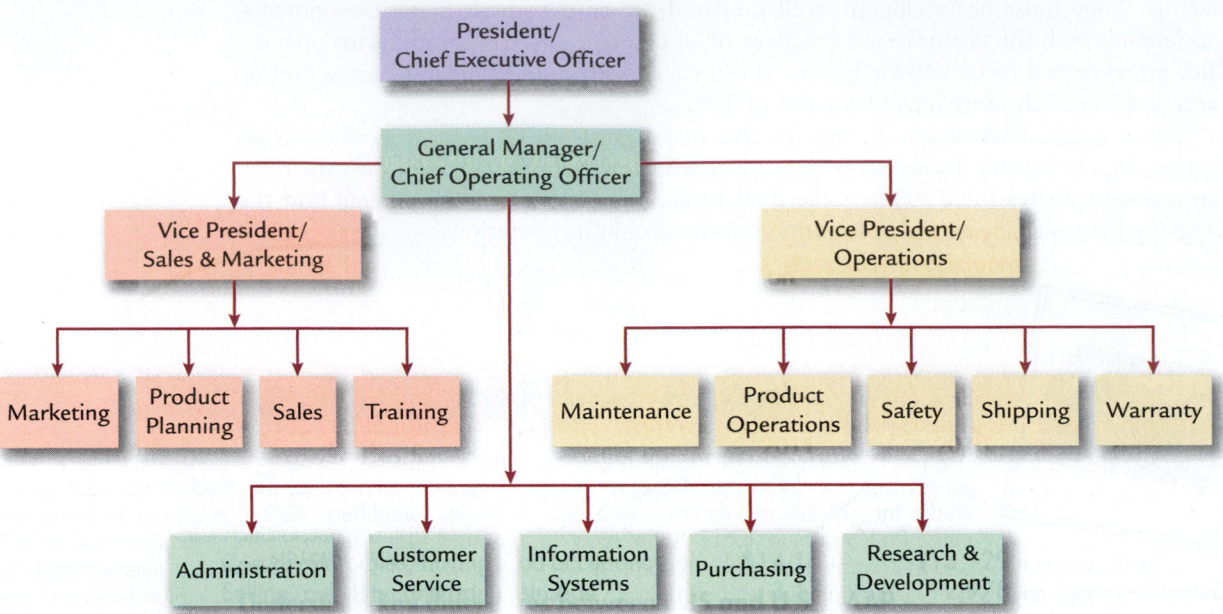

Finally, successful managerial accountants at all levels of the organization must communicate with other personnel—both accounting and nonaccounting—within the organization. Knowing how to "crunch the numbers" is necessary but not sufficient for managerial accounting information to be used successfully. Chief financial officers (CFOs) increasingly expect managerial accountants to be able to help senior executives better understand managerial accounting information in order to analyze complex business decisions.[12] This communications-based challenge for managerial accountants is growing in importance and offers exciting opportunities for well-versed managerial accountants to demonstrate their ability to add value to the organization.

Effectively communicating complex accounting information to interested internal stakeholders (e.g., employees, labor unions, etc.) and external stakeholders (e.g., investors, suppliers, customers, regulators, market analysts, etc.) can be very challenging. In addition, as evidenced by large corporate frauds involving reported accounting information, some executives unfortunately succumb to the pressures placed upon them to report accounting results in line with certain stakeholder expectations, such as meeting analysts' earnings per share forecasts. In 2002 Congress passed the **Sarbanes-Oxley Act (SOX)**, hoping to limit future securities frauds and accounting misconduct scandals like those associated with **Enron**, **WorldCom**, **Adelphia**, and **HealthSouth**. SOX led to increased attention on corporate ethics. While successful on many fronts, SOX has not prevented all subsequent frauds. Evidence is in the Allen Stanford securities fraud and the Bernard Maddoff ponzi scheme, which at the time was the world's biggest fraud, allegedly swindling investors out of a total of $50 billion.

OBJECTIVE **3**

Explain the meaning of cost and how costs are assigned to products and services.

THE MEANING AND USES OF COST

One of the most important tasks of managerial accounting is to determine the cost of products, services, customers, and other items of interest to managers. Therefore, we need to understand the meaning of cost and the ways in which costs can be used to make decisions, both for small entrepreneurial businesses and large international businesses. For example, consider a small gourmet restaurant and its owner Courtney, who

---

[12] C. Rutledge and R. Williams, "A Seat at the Table," *Outlook Journal* (June 2004). Taken from http://www.accenture.com/ Global/Research_and_Insights/Outlook/By_Alphabet/ASeatAtTheTable.htm on September 20, 2010.

also is the head chef. In addition to understanding the complexities of gourmet food preparation, Courtney needs to understand the breakdown of the restaurant's costs into various categories in order to make effective operating decisions. Cost categories of particular interest include:

- direct costs (food and beverages)
- indirect costs (laundry of linens)

On a larger scale, local banks operating in college communities often look at the cost of providing basic checking account services to students. These accounts typically lose money—that is, the accounts cost more to service than they yield in fees and interest revenue. However, the bank finds that students already banking with them are more likely to take out student loans through the bank, and these loans are very profitable. As a result, the bank may actually decide to expand its offerings to students when the related loan business is considered.

Cost

Cost is the amount of cash or cash equivalent sacrificed for goods and/or services that are expected to bring a current or future benefit to the organization. If a furniture manufacturer buys lumber for $10,000, then the cost of that lumber is $10,000 cash. Sometimes, one asset is traded for another asset. Then the cost of the new asset is measured by the value of the asset given up (the cash equivalent). If the same manufacturer trades office equipment valued at $8,000 for a forklift, then the cost of the forklift is the $8,000 value of the office equipment traded for it. Cost is a dollar measure of the resources used to achieve a given benefit. Managers strive to minimize the cost of achieving benefits. Reducing the cost required to achieve a given benefit means that a firm is becoming more efficient.

Costs are incurred to produce future benefits. In a profit-making firm, those benefits usually mean revenues. As costs are used up in the production of revenues, they are said to expire. Expired costs are called **expenses**. On the income statement, expenses are deducted from revenues to determine income (also called *profit*). For a company to remain in business, revenues must be larger than expenses. In addition, the income earned must be large enough to satisfy the owners of the firm.

We can look more closely at the relationship between cost and revenue by focusing on the units sold. The revenue per unit is called **price**. In everyday conversation, we have a tendency to use cost and price as synonyms, because the price of an item (e.g., a CD) is the cost to us. However, accounting courses take the viewpoint of the owner of the company. In that case, cost and price are *not* the same. Instead, for the company, revenue and price are the same. Price must be greater than cost in order for the firm to earn income. Hence, managers need to know cost and trends in cost. For example, the price a consumer pays for a fleece jacket from The North Face might be $200, while the total cost that the company incurs to design, manufacture, deliver, and service that jacket is much lower than the $200 price it charges consumers.

Accumulating and Assigning Costs

Accumulating costs is the way that costs are measured and recorded. The accounting system typically does this job quite well. When the company receives a phone bill, for example, the bookkeeper records an addition to the telephone expense account and an addition to the liability account, Accounts Payable. In this way, the cost is *accumulated*. It would be easy to tell, at the end of the year, the total spending on phone calls. Accumulating costs tells the company what was spent. However, that usually is not enough information. The company also wants to know why the money was spent. In other words, it wants to know how costs were assigned to cost objects.

Assigning costs is the way that a cost is linked to some cost object. A cost object is something for which a company wants to know the cost. For example, of the total phone expense, how much was for the sales department, and how much was for manufacturing? *Assigning* costs tells the company why the money was spent. In this case, cost assignment tells whether the money spent on phone calls was to support the manufacturing or the selling of the product. As we will discuss in later chapters, cost assignment typically is more difficult than cost accumulation.

Here's the Real Kicker

Kicker collects and analyzes many types of costs and breaks cost information into a series of accounts that helps Kicker's management in budgeting and decision making. The sales function, for example, is broken down into three areas: selling, customer service, and marketing. Consider the marketing department, which is responsible for advertising, promotions, and tent shows.

Tent shows are small-scale affairs held several times a year in the central and south-central United States. Kicker brings its semitrailer full of products and sound equipment as well as a couple of show trucks. Then, a large tent is set up to sell Kicker merchandise,

explain products, showcase new models, and sell the previous year's models at greatly reduced prices. The cost of each tent show is carefully tracked and compared with that show's revenue. Sites that don't provide sales revenue greater than cost are not booked for the coming year.

Like many of today's companies, Kicker tracks costs carefully for use in decision making. The general cost categories discussed in this chapter help the company to organize cost information and relate it to decision making.

KICKER
PERFORMANCE AUDIO

Cost Objects

Managerial accounting systems are structured to measure and assign costs to entities called *cost objects*. A **cost object** is any item such as a product, customer, department, project, geographic region, plant, and so on, for which costs are measured and assigned. For example, if **Fifth Third Bank** wants to determine the cost of a platinum credit card, then the cost object is the platinum credit card. All costs related to the platinum card are added in, such as the cost of mailings to potential customers, the cost of telephone lines dedicated to the card, the portion of the computer department that processes platinum card transactions and bills, and so on. In a more personal example, suppose that you are considering taking a course during the summer session. Taking the course is the cost object, and the cost would include tuition, books, fees, transportation, and (possibly) housing. Notice that you could also include the foregone earnings from a summer job (assuming that you cannot work while taking summer classes), which would be an opportunity cost.[13]

YOU DECIDE   **For Which Business Activities Do We Need an Estimate of Cost?**

You are the Chief Financial Officer for a major airline company. Managing the company's numerous costs is critically important in this fiercely competitive industry. Therefore, one of your major tasks is deciding which costs to manage in order to achieve the company's profitability targets. In other words, you must identify the airline's most important cost objects to track, measure, and control.

Which cost objects would you select as critical to the company's success?

Certain airline cost objects are obvious, such as the cost of operating a flight, which includes jet fuel (**Delta** spends over $8 billion annually for jet fuel)[14] and labor costs for pilots, flight crews, and maintenance staffs. However, even the costs of these obvious cost objects can become challenging. For example, when an airline operates multiple types of aircraft, it incurs additional costs to train workers and store spare parts for each aircraft type (i.e., the total cost of training and maintaining 100 aircraft of two different types is greater than the same number of aircraft all of one type). Airlines might be even more specific with certain cost objects, such as when they focus on the cost per available seat mile (or CASM as industry experts refer to it), which typically falls in the 6 to 10 cent range for most airlines.

Other airline cost objects are even more challenging. For example, you likely did not include the cost of managing crises as an important cost object. However, according to the International Air Transit Association, the airline industry took an estimated $1.7 billion hit from disrupted airline travel resulting from the volcanic ash cloud caused by the eruption of the Icelandic volcano Eyjafjallajokull.[15]

(Continued)

---

[13] The concept of opportunity cost will be discussed more later in this chapter, as well as in Chapter 23.
[14] http://images.delta.com.edgesuite.net/delta/pdfs/annual_reports/2009_10K.pdf
[15] http://www.guardian.co.uk/business/2010/apr/21/airline-industry-cost-volcanic-ash (accessed on May 8, 2010).

Finally, you might consider the cost object of processing customers, such as loading and unloading passengers and their baggage on and off of flights. For example, airlines have charged fees for using curbside check-in services, consuming soft drinks during flight, using pillows and blanks while onboard, selecting seats prior to the day of the flight, and checking bags. **Spirit Airlines** raised many customer (and even regulator) eyebrows by being the first airline to charge passengers ($45) for their carry-on bags.[16]

Like any company, an airline can identify and manage any cost objects it so desires. Sometimes the most difficult part of effective cost management is the first step—deciding on the exact items for which one needs to understand the cost. Mistakes in selecting the cost objects almost always lead to poor decisions and subpar performance.

Assigning Costs to Cost Objects

Costs can be assigned to cost objects in a number of ways. Relatively speaking, some methods are more accurate, and others are simpler. The choice of a method depends on a number of factors, such as the need for accuracy. The notion of accuracy is a relative concept and has to do with the reasonableness and logic of the cost assignment methods used. The objective is to measure and assign costs as well as possible, given management objectives. For example, suppose you and three of your friends go out to dinner at a local pizza parlor. When the bill comes, everything has been added together for a total of $36. How much is your share? One easy way to find your share is to divide the bill evenly among you and your friends. In that case, you each owe $9 ($36/4). But suppose that one of you had a small salad and drink (totaling $5), while another had a specialty pizza, appetizer, and beer (totaling $15). Clearly, it is possible to identify what each person had and assign costs that way. The second method is more accurate, but also more work. Which method you choose will depend on how important it is to you to assign the specific meal costs to each individual. It is the same way in accounting. There are a number of ways to assign costs to cost objects. Some methods are quick and easy but may be inaccurate. Other methods are much more accurate, but involve much more work (in business, more work equals more expense).

Direct Costs   **Direct costs** are those costs that can be easily and accurately traced to a cost object. When we say that a cost is easy to trace, we often mean that the relationship between the cost and the object can be physically observed and is easy to track. The more costs that can be traced to the object, the more accurate are the cost assignments. For example, suppose that Chef Courtney, from our earlier discussion, wants to know the cost of emphasizing fresh, in-season fruits and vegetables in her entrees. The purchase cost of the fruits and vegetables would be relatively easy to determine.

Indirect Costs   Some costs, however, are hard to trace. **Indirect costs** are costs that cannot be easily and accurately traced to a cost object. For example, Courtney incurs additional costs in scouting the outlying farms and farmers' markets (as opposed to simply ordering fruits and vegetables from a distributor). She must use her own time and automobile to make the trips. Farmers' markets may not deliver, so Courtney must arrange for a coworker with a van to pick up the produce. By definition, fruits and vegetables that are currently in season will be out of season (i.e., unavailable) in a few weeks. This seasonality means that Courtney must spend more time revising menus and developing new recipes that can be adapted to restaurant conditions. In addition, waste and spoilage may increase until Courtney and the kitchen staff learn just how much to order. These costs are difficult to assign to the meals prepared and sold. Therefore, they are indirect costs. Some businesses refer to indirect costs as overhead costs or support costs. Exhibit 13-4 (p. 676) shows direct and indirect costs being assigned to cost objects.

Assigning Indirect Costs   Even though indirect costs cannot be traced to cost objects, it is still important to assign them. This assignment usually is accomplished by using allocation. **Allocation** means that an indirect cost is assigned to a cost object by using a reasonable and convenient method. Since no clearly observable causal relationship exists, allocating indirect costs is based on convenience or some assumed causal linkage. For example, consider the cost of heating and lighting a plant in which five products are manufactured. Suppose that this utility cost is to be assigned to these five products. It

Exhibit 13-4

Object Costing

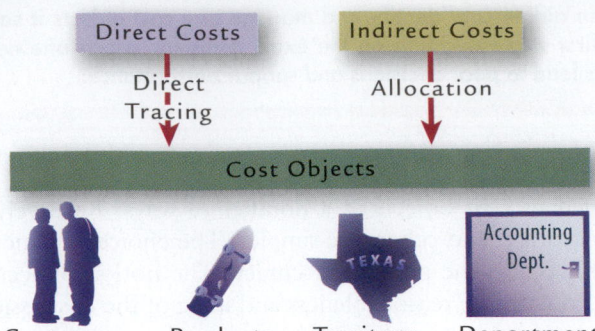

is difficult to see any causal relationship between utility costs and each unit of product manufactured. Therefore, a convenient way to allocate this cost is to assign it in proportion to the direct labor hours used by each product. This method is relatively easy and accomplishes the purpose of ensuring that all costs are assigned to units produced. Allocating indirect costs is important for a variety of reasons. For example, allocating indirect costs to products is needed to determine the value of inventory and of cost of goods sold. Perhaps more importantly, as companies become more complex in the number and types of products and services they offer to customers, the need to understand, allocate, and effectively control indirect costs becomes increasingly important. In addition, indirect costs represent an increasingly large percentage of total costs for many companies.

Direct and indirect costs occur in service businesses as well. For example, a bank's cost of printing and mailing monthly statements to checking account holders is a direct cost of the product—checking accounts. However, the cost of office furniture in the bank is an indirect cost for the checking accounts.

Other Categories of Cost In addition to being categorized as either direct or indirect, costs often are analyzed with respect to their behavior patterns, or the way in which a cost changes when the level of the output changes.

Variable Cost A **variable cost** is one that increases in total as output increases and decreases in total as output decreases. For example, the denim used in making jeans is a variable cost. As the company makes more jeans, it needs more denim.

Fixed Cost A **fixed cost** is a cost that does not increase in total as output increases and does not decrease in total as output decreases. For example, the cost of property taxes on the factory building stays the same no matter how many pairs of jeans the company makes. How can that be, since property taxes can and do change yearly? While the cost changes, it is not because output changes. Rather, it changes because the city or county government decides to raise taxes.

Variable and fixed costs are covered more extensively in Chapter 14.

Opportunity Cost An **opportunity cost** is the benefit given up or sacrificed when one alternative is chosen over another. For example, an opportunity cost of you participating in a summer study abroad program might include the wages you would have earned during that time if you had stayed home to work rather than participating in the overseas program. On the other hand, an opportunity cost of your staying home to work rather than participating in the study abroad program might include the value that future employers would have placed on the knowledge and experience you would have gathered had you participated in the overseas program. Opportunity cost differs from accounting cost in that the opportunity cost is never included in the accounting records because it is the cost of something that did not occur. Opportunity costs are important to decision making, as we will see more clearly in Chapter 23.

We will discuss various methods of assigning costs to cost objects in the succeeding chapters.

PRODUCT AND SERVICE COSTS

OBJECTIVE **4**
Define the various costs of manufacturing products and providing services as well as selling and administration.

Output represents one of the most important cost objects. There are two types of output: products and services.

- **Products** are goods produced by converting raw materials through the use of labor and indirect manufacturing resources, such as the manufacturing plant, land, and machinery. Televisions, hamburgers, automobiles, computers, clothes, and furniture are examples of products.
- **Services** are tasks or activities performed for a customer or an activity performed by a customer using an organization's products or facilities. Insurance coverage, medical care, dental care, funeral care, and accounting are examples of service activities performed for customers. Car rental, video rental, and skiing are examples of services where the customer uses an organization's products or facilities.

Organizations that produce products are called **manufacturing organizations**. Organizations that provide services are called **service organizations**. Managers of both types of organizations need to know how much individual products or services cost. Accurate cost information is vital for profitability analysis and strategic decisions concerning product design, pricing, and product mix. Incidentally, retail organizations, such as **J. Crew**, buy finished products from other organizations, such as manufacturers, and then sell them to customers. The accounting for inventory and cost of goods sold for retail organizations, often referred to as merchandisers, is much simpler than for manufacturing organizations and is usually covered extensively in introductory financial accounting courses. Therefore, the focus here is on manufacturing and service organizations.

Services differ from products in many ways, including the following:

- *Services are intangible:* The buyers of services cannot see, feel, hear, or taste a service before it is bought.
- *Services are perishable:* Services cannot be stored for future use by a consumer but must be consumed when performed. Inventory valuation, so important for products, is not an issue for services. In other words, because service organizations do not produce and sell products as part of their regular operations, they have no inventory asset on the balance sheet.
- *Services require direct contact between providers and buyers:* An eye examination, for example, requires both the patient and the optometrist to be present. However, producers of products need not have direct contact with the buyers of their goods. Thus, buyers of automobiles never need to have contact with the engineers and assembly line workers that produced their automobiles.

The overall way in which a company costs services in terms of classifying related costs as either direct or indirect is very similar to the way in which it costs products. The main difference in costing is that products have inventories, and services do not.

ETHICAL DECISIONS   Tracking costs can also act as an early warning system for unauthorized activity and possible ethical problems. For example, **Metropolitan Life Insurance Company** was dismayed to learn that some of its agents were selling policies as retirement plans. This practice is illegal, and it cost the company more than $20 million in fines as well as $50 million in refunds to policy holders.[17] More accurate and comprehensive data tracking regarding sales, individual agents, types of policies, and policyholders could have alerted Metropolitan Life to a potential problem. Thus, we can see that tracking costs can serve many different and important purposes. ●

Providing Cost Information

Managerial accountants must decide what types of managerial accounting information to provide to managers, how to measure such information, and when and to whom to communicate the information. For example, when making most strategic and operating decisions, managers typically rely on managerial accounting information that is prepared in whatever manner the managerial accountant believes provides the best analysis for the

---

[17] Roush, Chris, "Fields of Green—and Disaster Areas," *BusinessWeek* (January 9, 1995): 94.

decision at hand. Therefore, the majority of the managerial accounting issues explained in this book do not reference a formal set of external rules, but instead consider the context of the given decision (e.g., relevant versus irrelevant cost information for make-or-buy decisions, full cost versus functional cost information for pricing decisions, etc.).

However, there is one major exception. Managerial accountants must follow specific external reporting rules (i.e., generally accepted accounting principles) when their companies provide outside parties with cost information about the amount of ending inventory on the balance sheet and the cost of goods sold on the income statement. In order to calculate these two amounts, managerial accountants must subdivide costs into functional categories: production and period (i.e., nonproduction). The following section describes the process for categorizing costs as either product or period in nature.

Determining Product Cost

Product (manufacturing) costs are those costs, both direct and indirect, of producing a product in a manufacturing firm or of acquiring a product in a merchandising firm and preparing it for sale. Therefore, only costs in the *production* section of the value chain are included in product costs. A key feature of product costs is that they are inventoried. Product costs initially are added to an inventory account and remain in inventory until they are sold, at which time they are transferred to cost of goods sold (COGS). Product costs can be further classified as direct materials, direct labor, and manufacturing overhead, which are the three cost elements that can be assigned to products for external financial reporting (e.g., inventories or COGS). Exhibit 13-5 shows how direct materials, direct labor, and overhead become product costs.

Direct Materials   **Direct materials** are those materials that are a part of the final product and can be directly traced to the goods being produced. The cost of these materials can be directly charged to products because physical observation can be used to measure the quantity used by each product. Materials that become part of a product usually are classified as direct materials. For example, tires on a new **Porsche** automobile, wood in an **Ethan Allen** dining room table, alcohol in an **Estee Lauder** cologne, and denim in a pair of **American Eagle** jeans are all part of direct materials for manufacturers of these products.

A closely related term is raw materials. Often, the inventory of materials is called the raw materials account. Materials in the raw materials account do not become direct materials until they are withdrawn from inventory for use in production. The raw materials inventory account can include indirect materials as well as direct materials. Indirect materials are used in the production process but the amount used by each unit cannot be easily determined and, as a result, these costs are treated as indirect costs (as discussed later).

Direct Labor   **Direct labor** is the labor that can be directly traced to the goods being produced. Physical observation can be used to measure the amount of labor used to produce a product. Those employees who convert direct materials into a product are classified as direct labor. For example, workers on an assembly line at **Dell Computers** are classified as direct labor.

Exhibit 13-5

Product Costs Include Direct Materials, Direct Labor, and Overhead

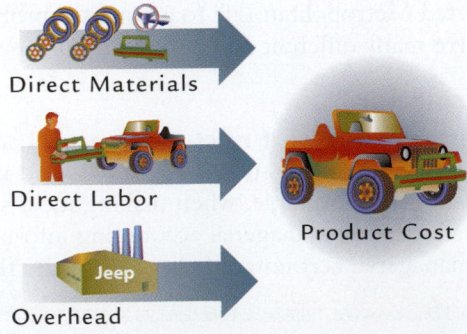

Direct Materials

Direct Labor

Overhead

Product Cost

Just as there were indirect materials in a company, there may also be indirect labor. This labor is not direct labor since these workers do not actually make the product. However, their contribution is necessary to production. An example of indirect labor in a production setting is the maintenance crew who performs regularly scheduled preventative maintenance every other Wednesday morning in **Georgia Pacific**'s plywood manufacturing plants. Indirect labor is included in overhead and, therefore, is an indirect cost rather than a direct cost.

Manufacturing Overhead All product costs other than direct materials and direct labor are put into a category called **manufacturing overhead**. In a manufacturing firm, manufacturing overhead also is known as *factory burden* or *indirect* manufacturing costs. Costs are included as manufacturing overhead if they cannot be traced to the cost object of interest (e.g., unit of product). The manufacturing overhead cost category contains a wide variety of items. Examples of manufacturing overhead costs include depreciation on plant buildings and equipment, janitorial and maintenance labor, plant supervision, materials handling, power for plant utilities, and plant property taxes.

The important thing to remember is that all costs in the factory are classified as direct materials, direct labor, or manufacturing overhead. No product cost can be omitted from classification, no matter how far removed you might think it is from the actual production of a product. Earlier we mentioned that indirect materials and indirect labor are included in overhead. In manufacturing, the glue used in furniture or toys is an example, as is the cost of oil to grease cookie sheets for producing cookies.

Total Product Cost The total product cost equals the sum of direct materials, direct labor, and manufacturing overhead:

Total product cost = Direct materials cost + Direct labor cost + Manufacturing overhead cost

The unit product cost equals total product cost divided by the number of units produced:

$$\text{Per-unit cost} = \frac{\text{Total product cost}}{\text{Number of units produced}}$$

CORNERSTONE 13-1 shows how to calculate total product cost and per unit product cost.

 **CORNERSTONE 13-1**   **Calculating Product Cost in Total and Per Unit**

Information:
BlueDenim Company makes blue jeans. Last week, direct materials (denim, thread, zippers, and rivets) costing $48,000 were put into production. Direct labor of $30,000 (50 workers × 40 hours × $15 per hour) was incurred. Overhead equaled $72,000. By the end of the week, BlueDenium had manufactured 30,000 pairs of jeans.

Required:
1. Calculate the total product cost for last week.
2. Calculate the cost of one pair of jeans that was produced last week.

Solution:
1.

Direct materials	$ 48,000
Direct labor	30,000
Overhead	72,000
Total product cost	$150,000

2. Per-unit product cost = $150,000/30,000 units = $5

Product costs include direct materials, direct labor, and manufacturing overhead. Once the product is finished, no more costs attach to it. That is, any costs associated with storing, selling, and delivering the product are not product costs, but instead are period costs.

Prime and Conversion Costs Product costs of direct materials, direct labor, and manufacturing overhead are sometimes grouped into prime cost and conversion cost:

- **Prime cost** is the sum of direct materials cost and direct labor cost.
- **Conversion cost** is the sum of direct labor cost and manufacturing overhead cost. For a manufacturing firm, conversion cost can be interpreted as the cost of converting raw materials into a final product.

CORNERSTONE 13-2 shows how to calculate prime cost and conversion cost for a manufactured product.

CORNERSTONE
13-2

Calculating Prime Cost and Conversion Cost in Total and Per Unit

Information:
Refer to the information in Cornerstone 13-1 for BlueDenim Company (p. 679).

Required:
1. Calculate the total prime cost for last week.
2. Calculate the per-unit prime cost.
3. Calculate the total conversion cost for last week.
4. Calculate the per-unit conversion cost.

Solution:

1.

Direct materials	$48,000
Direct labor	30,000
Total prime cost	$78,000

2. Per-unit prime cost = $78,000/30,000 units = $2.60

3.

Direct labor	$ 30,000
Overhead	72,000
Total conversion cost	$102,000

4. Per-unit conversion cost = $102,000/30,000 units = $3.40

Note: Remember that prime cost and conversion cost do NOT equal total product cost. This is because direct labor is part of BOTH prime cost and conversion cost.

Period Costs The costs of production are assets that are carried in inventories until the goods are sold. There are other costs of running a company, referred to as *period costs,* that are not carried in inventory. Thus, **period costs** are all costs that are not product costs (i.e., all areas of the value chain except for production). The cost of office supplies, research and development activities, the CEO's salary, and advertising are examples of period costs. For instance, **Victoria's Secret** spent approximately $2.7 million to run a 30-second advertisement during Super Bowl XLII. With the exception of the final episode of M*A*S*H, the Giant's underdog victory over the previously unbeaten Patriots was watched by more viewers (97.5 million) than any television show in history.[18] Despite these record ratings, however, some people considered this $2.7 million period expense to be excessive. Managerial accountants help executives at companies like Victoria's Secret determine whether or not such costly advertising campaigns generate enough additional sales revenue over the long run to make them profitable.

Period costs cannot be assigned to products or appear as part of the reported values of inventories on the balance sheet. Instead, period costs typically are expensed in the period in which they are incurred. However, if a period cost is expected to provide an economic benefit (i.e., revenues) beyond the next year, then it is recorded as an asset (i.e., capitalized) and allocated to expense through depreciation throughout its useful life. The cost associated with the purchase of a delivery truck is an example of a period cost that would be capitalized when incurred and then recognized as an expense over the useful life of the truck. Exhibit 13-6 depicts the distinction between product and period costs and how each type of cost eventually becomes an expense on the income statement. As shown in the exhibit, product costs, which are capitalized as an inventory asset, are expensed on the income statement as cost of goods sold to match against the revenues generated from the sale of the inventory. However, capitalized period costs are depreciated to expense on the income statement over the asset's useful life to match against the revenues generated by the asset over its useful life.

In a manufacturing organization, the level of period costs can be significant (often greater than 25 percent of sales revenue), and controlling them may bring greater cost savings than the same effort exercised in controlling production costs. For example, Nike's period expenses are 37 percent of its revenue ($7,117,700,000/$19,176,100,000).[19] For service organizations, the relative importance of selling and administrative costs depends on the nature of the service produced. Physicians and dentists, for example, do relatively little marketing and thus have very low selling costs. On the other hand, a grocery chain may incur substantial marketing costs. Period costs often are divided into selling costs and administrative costs.

Selling Costs Those costs necessary to market, distribute, and service a product or service are **selling costs**. They are often referred to as *order-getting* and *order-filling* costs. Examples of selling costs include salaries and commissions of sales personnel, advertising, warehousing, shipping, and customer service. The first two items are examples of order-getting costs; the last three are order-filling costs.

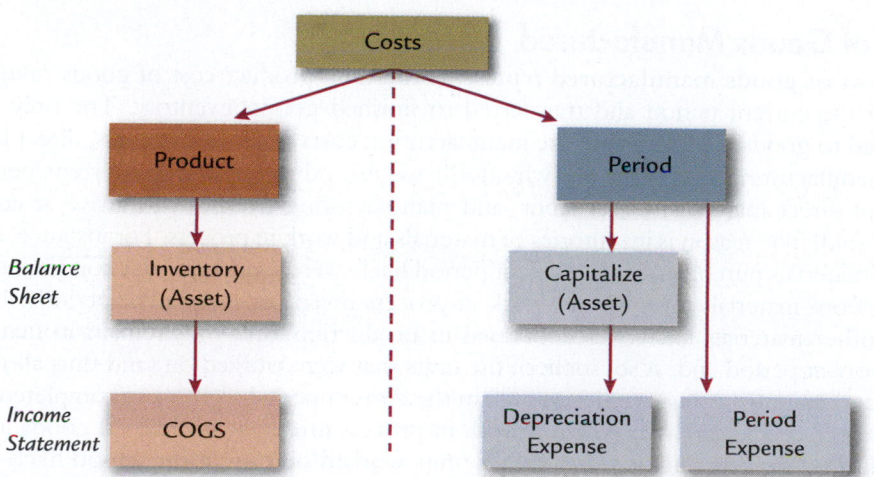

Exhibit 13-6

The Impact of Product versus Period Costs on the Financial Statements

[18] Hiestand, Michael, "Game Attracts Biggest Audience," *USA Today* (February 5, 2008): C1.
[19] From Nike's 2009 Annual Report.

Administrative Costs All costs associated with research, development, and general administration of the organization that cannot reasonably be assigned to either selling or production are **administrative costs**. General administration has the responsibility of ensuring that the various activities of the organization are properly integrated so that the overall mission of the firm is realized. The president of the firm, for example, is concerned with the efficiency of selling, production, and research and development activities. Proper integration of these activities is essential to maximizing the overall profits of a firm. Examples of general administrative costs are executive salaries, legal fees, printing the annual report, and general accounting. Research and development costs are the costs associated with designing and developing new products and must be expensed in the period incurred.

Direct and Indirect Period Costs As with product costs, it is often helpful to distinguish between direct period costs and indirect period costs. Service companies also make this important distinction. For example, a surgical center would show that surgical gauze and anesthesia are direct costs used for an operation because it could be determined how much gauze or anesthesia was used for each procedure or patient. Other examples of direct costs in service industries include the chef in a restaurant, a surgical nurse attending an open heart operation, and a pilot for Southwest Airlines.

Alternately, although shampoo and hair spray are used in a beauty shop, the exact amount used in each individual's hair cut is not easily determinable. As a result, the costs associated with shampoo and hair spray would be considered indirect, or overhead, costs and allocated, rather than traced, to individual hair cuts. Examples of indirect labor costs in a service setting include the surgical assistants in a hospital who clean up the operating room after surgery, dispose of certain used materials, and sterilize the reusable instruments. Indirect labor is included in overhead. The rental of a Santa suit for the annual company Christmas party would be an example of an indirect cost that would be expensed in the period incurred. Although these costs do not affect the calculation of inventories or COGS (i.e., because they are service companies), their correct classification nonetheless affects numerous decisions and planning and control activities for managers, as we will discuss in detail in future chapters.

O B J E C T I V E ❺

Prepare income statements for manufacturing and service organizations.

PREPARING INCOME STATEMENTS

The earlier definitions of product, selling, and administrative costs provide a good conceptual overview of these important costs. However, the actual calculation of these costs in practice is a bit more complicated. Let's take a closer look at just how costs are calculated for purposes of preparing the external financial statements, focusing first on manufacturing firms.

Cost of Goods Manufactured

The **cost of goods manufactured** represents the total product cost of goods *completed* during the current period and transferred to finished goods inventory. The only costs assigned to goods completed are the manufacturing costs of direct materials, direct labor, and manufacturing overhead. So, why don't we just add together the current period's costs of direct materials, direct labor, and manufacturing overhead to arrive at cost of goods sold? The reason is inventories of materials and work in process. For instance, some of the materials purchased in the current period likely were used in production (i.e., transferred from materials inventory to work-in-process inventory during the period). However, other materials likely were not used in production, and thus remain in materials inventory at period end. Also, some of the units that were worked on (and thus allocated labor and manufacturing overhead costs) in the current period likely were completed during the period (i.e., transferred from work-in-process inventory to finished goods inventory during the period). However, other units worked on during the period likely were not completed during the period, and thus remain in work-in-process inventory at period end. In calculating cost of goods sold, we need to distinguish between the total manufacturing cost for the current period and the manufacturing costs associated with the units that were completed during the current period (i.e., cost of goods manufactured).

Let's take a look at direct materials. Suppose a company had no materials on hand at the beginning of the month, then bought $15,000 of direct materials during the month, and used all of them in production. The entire $15,000 would be properly called *direct materials*. Usually, though, the company has some materials on hand at the beginning of the month. These materials are the beginning inventory of materials. Let's say that this beginning inventory of materials cost $2,500. Then during the month, the company would have a total of $17,500 of materials that could be used in production ($2,500 from beginning inventory and $15,000 purchased during the month). Typically, the company would not use the entire amount of materials on hand in production. Perhaps they use only $12,000 of materials. Then, the cost of direct materials used in production this month is $12,000, and the remaining $5,500 of materials is the ending inventory of materials. This reasoning can be easily expressed in a formula:

$$\begin{array}{c} \text{Beginning inventory} \\ \text{of materials} \end{array} + \text{Purchases} - \begin{array}{c} \text{Direct materials} \\ \text{used in production} \end{array} = \begin{array}{c} \text{Ending inventory} \\ \text{of materials} \end{array}$$

While this computation is logical and simple, it does not express the result for which we usually are looking. We are usually trying to figure out the amount of direct materials used in production—not the amount of ending inventory. **CORNERSTONE 13-3** shows how to compute the amount of direct materials used in production.

 **CORNERSTONE 13-3**   **Calculating the Direct Materials Used in Production**

Information:
BlueDenim Company makes blue jeans. On May 1, BlueDenim had $68,000 of materials in inventory. During the month of May, BlueDenim purchased $210,000 of materials. On May 31, materials inventory equaled $22,000.

Required:
Calculate the cost of direct materials used in production for the month of May.

Solution:

Materials inventory, May 1	$ 68,000
Purchases	210,000
Materials inventory, May 31	(22,000)
Direct materials used in production	$256,000

Once the direct materials are calculated, the direct labor and manufacturing overhead *for the time period* can be added to get the total manufacturing cost for the period. Now we need to consider the second type of inventory—work in process. **Work in process (WIP)** is the cost of the partially completed goods that are still on the factory floor at the end of a time period. These are units that have been started, but are not finished. They have value, but not as much as they will when they are completed. Just as there are beginning and ending inventories of materials, there are beginning and ending inventories of WIP. We must adjust the total manufacturing cost for the time period for the inventories of WIP. When that is done, we will have the total cost of the goods that were completed and transferred from work-in-process inventory to finished goods inventory during the time period. **CORNERSTONE 13-4** (p. 684) shows how to calculate the cost of goods manufactured for a particular time period.

CORNERSTONE 13-4   Calculating Cost of Goods Manufactured

Information:
BlueDenim Company makes blue jeans. During the month of May, BlueDenim purchased $210,000 of materials and incurred direct labor cost of $135,000 and manufacturing overhead of $150,000. Inventory information is as follows:

	May 1	May 31
Materials	$68,000	$22,000
Work in process	50,000	16,000

Required:
Calculate the cost of goods manufactured for the month of May.

Solution:

Direct materials used in production*	$256,000
Direct labor	135,000
Manufacturing overhead	150,000
Total manufacturing cost for May	$541,000
WIP, May 1	50,000
WIP, May 31	(16,000)
Cost of goods manufactured	$575,000

*Direct materials = $68,000 + $210,000 – $22,000 = $256,000

Cost of Goods Sold

To meet external reporting requirements, costs must be classified into three categories:

- production
- selling
- administration

Remember that product costs are initially put into inventory. They become expenses only when the products are sold, which matches the expenses of manufacturing the product to the sales revenue generated by the product at the time it is sold. Therefore, the expense of manufacturing is not the cost of goods manufactured; instead it is the cost of the goods that are sold. **Cost of goods sold** represents the cost of goods that were sold during the period and, therefore, transferred from finished goods inventory on the balance sheet to cost of goods sold on the income statement (i.e., as an inventory expense). **CORNERSTONE 13-5** shows how to calculate the cost of goods sold.

CORNERSTONE 13-5   Calculating Cost of Goods Sold

Information:
BlueDenim Company makes blue jeans. During the month of May, 115,000 pairs of jeans were completed at a cost of goods manufactured of $575,000. Suppose that on May 1, BlueDenim had 10,000 units in the finished

(Continued)

goods inventory costing $50,000 and on May 31, the company had 26,000 units in the finished goods inventory costing $130,000.

Required:

1. Prepare a cost of goods sold statement for the month of May.
2. Calculate the number of pairs of jeans that were sold during May.

Solution:

1.

BlueDenim Company Cost of Goods Sold Statement For the Month of May	
Cost of goods manufactured	$ 575,000
Finished goods inventory, May 1	50,000
Finished good inventory, May 31	(130,000)
Cost of goods sold	$ 495,000

2.

Number of units sold:	
Finished goods inventory, May 1	$ 10,000
Units finished during May	115,000
Finished goods inventory, May 31	(26,000)
Units sold during May	$ 99,000

The ending inventories of materials, WIP, and finished goods are important because they are assets and appear on the balance sheet (as current assets). The cost of goods sold is an expense that appears on the income statement. Selling and administrative costs are period costs and also appear on the income statement as an expense. Collectively, Cornerstones 13-3 (p. 683), 13-4, and 13-5 depict the flow of costs through the three inventories (materials, work in process, and finished goods) and finally into cost of goods sold.

Exhibit 13-7 uses the information in Cornerstones 13-3, 13-4, and 13-5 to illustrate how the manufacturing costs—direct materials, direct labor, and manufacturing overhead—flow through the inventories—direct materials, work in process, and finished goods—and eventually into cost of goods sold on the income statement. Exhibit 13-7 also shows the difference between when direct materials are purchased (or incurred and

Exhibit 13-7

Relationship between the Flow of Costs, Inventories, and Cost of Goods Sold

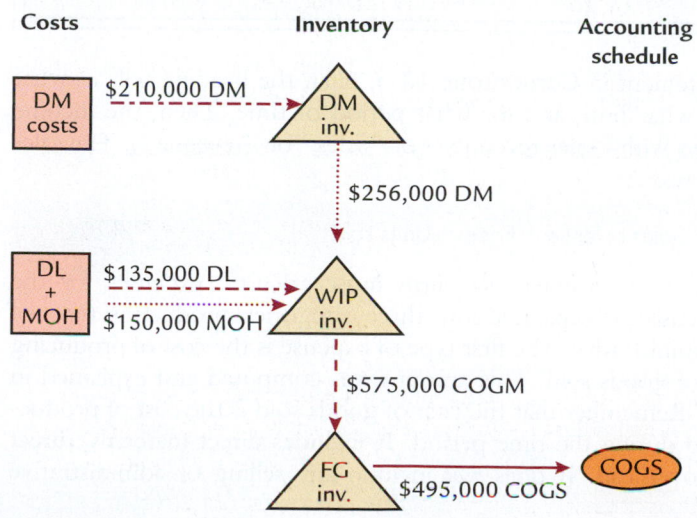

	= Costs (for DM, DL, MOH) incurred
	= Costs of units used in production
	= Costs of units completed this period
	= Impacts cost of good sold schedule

DM: Direct Materials
DL: Direct Labor
MOH: Manufacturing Overhead
WIP: Work in process
FG: Finished Goods
COGS: Cost of Goods Sold

put into direct materials inventory—$210,000) versus when they are used in production (i.e., placed into WIP inventory—$256,000). There is no difference between when direct labor and manufacturing overhead costs are incurred versus when they are used in production because they cannot be stored in inventory before use (as can direct materials).

Income Statement: Manufacturing Firm

The income statement for a manufacturing firm is displayed in **CORNERSTONE 13-6**. This income statement follows the traditional format taught in an introductory financial accounting course. Notice that the income statement covers a certain period of time (i.e., the month of May in Cornerstone 13-6). However, the time period may vary. The key point is that all sales revenue and expenses attached to that period of time appear on the income statement.

CORNERSTONE
13-6

Preparing an Income Statement for a Manufacturing Firm

Information:
Recall that BlueDenim Company sold 99,000 pairs of jeans during the month of May at a total cost of $495,000. Each pair sold at a price of $8. BlueDenim also incurred two types of selling costs: commissions equal to 10 percent of the sales price, and fixed selling expense of $120,000. Administrative expense totaled $85,000.

Required:
Prepare an income statement for BlueDenim for the month of May.

Solution:

BlueDenim Company
Income Statement
For the Month of May

Sales revenue (99,000 × $8)		$792,000
Cost of goods sold		495,000
Gross margin		$297,000
Less:		
Selling expense		
Commissions (0.10 × $792,000)	$ 79,200	
Fixed selling expense	120,000	199,200
Administrative expense		85,000
Operating income		$ 12,800

Look at the income statement in Cornerstone 13-6. First, the heading tells us what type of statement it is, for what firm, and for what period of time. Then, the income statement itself always begins with "sales revenue" (or "sales" or "revenue"). The sales revenue is calculated as follows:

$$\text{Sales revenue} = \text{Price} \times \text{Units sold}$$

After the sales revenue is determined, the firm must calculate expenses for the period. Notice that the expenses are separated into three categories: production (cost of goods sold), selling, and administrative. The first type of expense is the cost of producing the units sold, or the cost of goods sold. This amount was computed and explained in Cornerstone 13-5 (p. 684). Remember that the cost of goods sold is the cost of producing the units that were sold during the time period. It includes direct materials, direct labor, and manufacturing overhead. It does *not* include any selling or administrative expense. In the case of a retail (i.e., a merchandising) firm, the cost of goods sold represents the total cost of the goods sold when they were purchased from an outside supplier. Therefore, the cost of goods sold for a retailer equals the purchase costs adjusted for the beginning and ending balances in its single inventory account. A merchandising firm, such as **Old Navy** or **J. Crew**, has only one inventory account because it does not transform the purchased good into a different form by adding materials, labor, and overhead, as does a manufacturing firm.

Gross margin is the difference between sales revenue and cost of goods sold:

Gross margin = Sales revenue – Cost of goods sold

It shows how much the firm is making over and above the cost of the units sold. Gross margin does *not* equal operating income or profit. Selling and administrative expenses have not yet been subtracted. However, gross margin does provide useful information. If gross margin is positive, the firm at least charges prices that cover the product cost. In addition, the firm can calculate its gross margin percentage (Gross margin/Sales revenue), as shown in **CORNERSTONE 13-7**, and compare it with the average gross margin percentage for the industry to see if its experience is in the ballpark with other firms in the industry.

CORNERSTONE 13-7   **Calculating the Percentage of Sales Revenue for Each Line on the Income Statement**

Information:
Refer to the income statement for BlueDenim Company in Cornerstone 13-6.

Required:
Calculate the percentage of sales revenue represented by each line of the income statement.

Solution:

BlueDenim Company
Income Statement
For the Month of May

			Percent*
Sales revenue (99,000 × $8)		$792,000	100.0
Cost of goods sold		495,000	62.5
Gross margin		$297,000	37.5
Less:			
Selling expense			
Commissions (0.10 × $792,000)	$ 79,200		
Fixed selling expense	120,000	199,200	25.2
Administrative expense		85,000	10.7
Operating income		$ 12,800	1.6

*Steps in calculating the percentages:
1. Sales revenue percent = $792,000/$792,000 = 1.00 or 100% (sales revenue is always 100% of itself)
2. Cost of goods sold percent = $495,000/$792,000 = 0.625 or 62.5%
3. Gross margin percent = $297,000/$792,000 = 0.375 or 37.5%
4. Selling expense percent = $199,200/$792,000 = 0.252 or 25.2% (rounded)
5. Administrative expense percent = $85,000/$792,000 = 0.107 or 10.7% (rounded)
6. Operating income percent = $12,800/$792,000 = 0.016 or 1.6% (rounded)

Finally, selling expense and administrative expense for the period are subtracted from gross margin to arrive at operating income:

Operating income = Gross margin – Selling and administrative expense

Operating income is the key figure from the income statement; it is profit, and shows how much the owners are actually earning from the company. Again, calculating the percentage of operating income (i.e., Operating income/Sales revenue) and comparing it to the average for the industry gives the owners valuable information about relative profitability.

The income statement can be analyzed further by calculating the percentage of sales revenue represented by each line of the statement, as was done in Cornerstone 13-7 (p. 687). How can management use this information? The first thing that jumps out is that operating income is less than 2 percent of sales revenue. That's a very small percentage. Unless this is common for the blue jeans manufacturing business, BlueDenim's management should work hard to increase the percentage. Selling expense is a whopping 25.2 percent of sales. Do commissions really need to be that high? Or is the price too low (compared to competitors' prices)? Can cost of goods sold be reduced? Is 62.5 percent reasonable? These are questions that are suggested by Cornerstone 13-7, but not answered. Answering the questions is the job of management.

Income Statement: Service Firm

In a service organization, there is no product to purchase (e.g., a merchandiser like American Eagle Outfitters) or to manufacture (e.g., Toshiba) and, therefore, there are no beginning or ending inventories. As a result, there is no cost of goods sold or gross margin on the income statement. Instead, the cost of providing services appears along with the other operating expenses of the company. For example, Southwest Airlines' income statement begins with Total Operating Revenues of $10,350,000,000 and subtracts Total Operating Expenses of $10,088,000,000 to arrive at an Operating Income of $262,000,000.[20] An income statement for a service firm is shown in CORNERSTONE 13-8.

 **CORNERSTONE 13-8**   **Preparing an Income Statement for a Service Organization**

Information:
Komala Information Systems designs and installs human resources software for small companies. Last month, Komala had software licensing costs of $5,000, service technicians' costs of $35,000, and research and development costs of $55,000. Selling expenses were $5,000, and administrative expenses equaled $7,000. Sales totaled $130,000.

Required:
Prepare an income statement for Komala Information Systems for the past month.

Solution:

Komala Information Systems
Income Statement
For the Past Month

Sales revenues:		$130,000
Less operating expenses:		
Software licensing	$ 5,000	
Service technicians	35,000	
Research and development	55,000	
Selling expenses	5,000	
Administrative expenses	7,000	107,000
Operating income		$ 23,000

---

[20] Per Southwest Airlines' 2009 Annual Report: http://www.southwest.com/investor_relations/if_sec_filings.html.

MANAGERIAL ACCOUNTING AND ETHICAL CONDUCT

OBJECTIVE ⑥

Explain the importance of ethical behavior for managers and managerial accountants.

Ethical behavior involves choosing actions that are right, proper, and just. Traditionally, actions regarding the economic performance of the firm have been the overriding concern of managerial accounting. Yet managers and managerial accountants should not become so focused on profits that they develop a belief that the only goal of a business is maximizing its net worth. The objective of profit maximization should be constrained by the requirement that profits be achieved through legal and ethical means. While this belief has always been an implicit assumption of managerial accounting, the assumption should be made explicit. To help achieve this objective, many of the problems in this text require explicit consideration of ethical issues.

Many of the well-known accounting scandals, such as those involving **Adelphia**, **WorldCom**, **HealthSouth**, **Parmalat**, and **McKesson**, provide evidence of the pressures faced by top managers and accountants to produce large net income numbers, especially in the short term. Unfortunately, such individuals often give into these pressures when faced with questionable revenue- and cost-related judgments. For example, the scandal at WorldCom was committed because the CEO, Bernie Ebbers, coerced several of the top accountants at WorldCom to wrongfully record journal entries in the company's books that capitalized millions of dollars in costs as assets (i.e., on the balance sheet) rather than as expenses (i.e., on the income statement) that would have dramatically lowered current period net income. Eventually, WorldCom was forced to pay hundreds of millions of dollars to the U.S. government and to shareholders for its illegal and unethical actions. In addition, several of the top executives were sentenced to extensive prison time for their actions. The recent subprime mortgage crisis also highlights the importance of ethical considerations as some banks tried to increase their profits either by lending individuals more money than they could reasonably afford or using terms that were intentionally less clear, or transparent, than many outsiders thought they should be.[21]

Company Codes of Ethical Conduct

To promote ethical behavior by managers and employees, organizations commonly establish standards of conduct referred to as Company Codes of Conduct. **Boeing**'s Code of Conduct[22] states that it will "conduct its business fairly, impartially, in an ethical and proper manner, and in full compliance with all applicable laws and regulations." All employees must sign the code, and the company "requires that they understand the code, and ask questions, seek guidance, report suspected violations, and express concerns regarding compliance with this policy and the related procedures."

Certification

As with the legal and medical professions, the accounting profession relies on certification to help promote ethical behavior, as well as to provide evidence that the certificate holder has achieved a minimum level of professional competence. The accounting profession offers three major forms of certification to managerial accountants:

- Certificate in Management Accounting
- Certificate in Public Accounting
- Certificate in Internal Auditing

In each case, an applicant must meet specific educational and experience requirements and pass a qualifying examination to become certified. These certifying organizations have responded to recent ethics scandals with their own policies. For example, in 2005, the Institute of Management Accountants, which sponsors the Certificate in Management Accounting, revised its Standards of Ethical Conduct for Management Accountants to reflect the impact of the Sarbanes-Oxley Act of 2002. Now called the

---

21 Jane Sasseen, "FBI Widens Net Around Subprime Industry: With 14 Companies Under Investigation, the Bureau's Scope Is the Entire Securitization Process," *BusinessWeek Online* (January 30, 2008). Taken from http://www.businessweek.com/bwdaily/dnflash/content/jan2008/db20080129_728982.htm?chan=search on February 12, 2008.
22 Taken from the Boeing website, http://www.boeing.com/companyoffices/aboutus/ethics/ (accessed May 12, 2004).

Statement of Ethical Professional Practice, the revised code considers global issues and incorporates the principles of the code of the International Federation of Accountants, which is the global association of professional accounting groups.

Perhaps the biggest challenge with ethical dilemmas is that when they arise, employees frequently do not realize either

- that such a dilemma has arisen or
- the "correct" action that should be taken to rectify the dilemma.

SUMMARY OF LEARNING OBJECTIVES

LO1. **Explain the meaning of managerial accounting and contrast it to financial accounting.**
- Managerial accounting information helps managers achieve their objectives of planning, controlling, and decision making. Planning is the detailed formulation of action to achieve a particular end. Controlling is the monitoring of a plan's implementation. Decision making is choosing among competing alternatives.
- Managerial accounting information is intended for internal users and generally is not subject to generally accepted accounting principles (GAAP), whereas financial accounting information is directed toward external users and is subject to GAAP.

LO2. **Identify and explain the current focus of managerial accounting and the role of managerial accountants in an organization.**
- The nature of managerial accounting information depends on the strategic position of the firm—cost leadership strategy, product differentiation strategy, and lean accounting.
- Information about value chain activities and customer satisfaction is collected, including activity-based management information.
- Managerial accountants are responsible for identifying, collecting, measuring, analyzing, preparing, and interpreting information.
- Managerial accountants also must communicate—both orally and in writing—information to individuals inside and outside of the organization, including non-accountants.

LO3. **Explain the meaning of cost and how costs are assigned to products and services.**
- Cost is the cash or cash-equivalent value sacrificed for goods and services that are expected to bring a current or future benefit to the organization.
- Managers use cost information to determine the cost of objects, such as products, plants, geographic regions, and customers.
- Direct costs are traced to cost objects based on cause-and-effect relationships.
- Indirect (i.e., overhead) costs are allocated to cost objects based on assumed relationships and convenience.

LO4. **Define the various costs of manufacturing products and providing services as well as selling and administration.**
- Products are goods that either are purchased or produced by converting raw materials through the use of labor and indirect manufacturing resources, such as plants, land, and machinery. Services are tasks performed for a customer or activities performed by a customer using an organization's products or facilities.
- Product costs are those costs, both direct and indirect, of acquiring a product in a merchandising business and preparing it for sale or of producing a product in a manufacturing business. Product costs are classified as inventory on the balance sheet and then expensed as cost of goods sold on the income statement when the inventory is sold.
- Selling costs are the costs of marketing and distributing goods and services, and administrative costs are the costs of organizing and running a company as well as selling and administration.
- Both selling and administrative costs are period costs as well as selling costs and administration costs.

LO5.   Prepare income statements for manufacturing and service organizations.
- The cost of goods manufactured (COGM) represents the total product cost of goods *completed* during the period and transferred to finished goods inventory. The cost of goods sold (COGS) represents the cost of goods that were sold during the period and, therefore, transferred from finished goods inventory to cost of goods sold. For a retailer, there is no COGM and COGS equals the beginning inventory plus net purchases minus ending inventory.
- For manufacturing and merchandising firms, cost of goods sold is subtracted from sales revenue to arrive at gross margin. In addition, for manufacturing firms, cost of goods manufactured must first be calculated before calculating cost of goods sold.
- Service firms do not calculate gross margin because they do not purchase or produce inventory for sale and, as a result, do not have a cost of goods sold (i.e., inventory expense).
- All firms next subtract selling and administrative expenses to arrive at net income.

LO6.   Explain the importance of ethical behavior for managers and managerial accountants.
- A strong ethical sense is needed to resist pressures to change economic information that may present an untrue picture of firm performance.
- Many firms have a written code of ethics (e.g., IMA) or code of conduct.
- Proper employee training, controls, regulation (e.g., Sarbanes-Oxley Act), and incentive systems can curb ethical problems.

SUMMARY OF IMPORTANT EQUATIONS

1. Total product cost = Direct materials cost + Direct labor cost + Manufacturing overhead cost

2. $\text{Per-unit cost} = \dfrac{\text{Total product cost}}{\text{Number of units produced}}$

3. $\begin{array}{l}\text{Beginning inventory} \\ \text{of materials}\end{array} + \text{Purchases} - \begin{array}{l}\text{Direct materials} \\ \text{used in production}\end{array} = \begin{array}{l}\text{Ending inventory} \\ \text{of materials}\end{array}$

4. Sales revenue = Price × Units sold

5. Gross margin = Sales revenue − Cost of goods sold

6. Operating income = Gross margin − Selling and administrative expense

CORNERSTONE 13-1	Calculating product cost in total and per unit (p. 679)
CORNERSTONE 13-2	Calculating prime cost and conversion cost in total and per unit (p. 680)
CORNERSTONE 13-3	Calculating the direct materials used in production (p. 683)
CORNERSTONE 13-4	Calculating cost of goods manufactured (p. 684)
CORNERSTONE 13-5	Calculating cost of goods sold (p. 684)
CORNERSTONE 13-6	Preparing an income statement for a manufacturing firm (p. 686)
CORNERSTONE 13-7	Calculating the percentage of sales revenue for each line on the income statement (p. 687)
CORNERSTONE 13-8	Preparing an income statement for a service organization (p. 688)

CORNERSTONES
FOR CHAPTER 13

KEY TERMS

Accumulating costs (p. 673)
Administrative costs (p. 682)
Allocation (p. 675)
Assigning costs (p. 673)
Continuous improvement (p. 670)
Controller (p. 671)
Controlling (p. 665)
Conversion cost (p. 680)
Cost (p. 673)
Cost object (p. 674)
Cost of goods manufactured (p. 682)
Cost of goods sold (p. 684)
Decision making (p. 665)
Direct costs (p. 675)
Direct labor (p. 678)
Direct materials (p. 678)
Ethical behavior (p. 689)
Expenses (p. 673)
Financial accounting (p. 666)
Fixed cost (p. 676)
Gross margin (p. 687)

Indirect costs (p. 675)
Lean accounting (p. 670)
Managerial accounting (p. 664)
Manufacturing organizations (p. 677)
Manufacturing overhead (p. 679)
Opportunity cost (p. 676)
Period costs (p. 680)
Planning (p. 665)
Price (p. 673)
Prime cost (p. 680)
Product (manufacturing) costs (p. 678)
Products (p. 677)
Sarbanes-Oxley Act (SOX) (p. 672)
Selling costs (p. 681)
Service organizations (p. 677)
Services (p. 677)
Total quality management (p. 670)
Treasurer (p. 671)
Value chain (p. 669)
Variable cost (p. 676)
Work in process (WIP) (p. 683)

REVIEW PROBLEM

I. Product Costs, Cost of Goods Manufactured Statement, and the Income Statement

Brody Company makes industrial cleaning solvents. Various chemicals, detergent, and water are mixed together and then bottled in 10-gallon drums. Brody provided the following information for last year:

Raw materials purchases	$250,000	Utilities for sales office	$ 1,800
Direct labor	140,000	Administrative salaries	150,000
Depreciation on factory equipment	45,000	Indirect labor salaries	156,000
Depreciation on factory building	30,000	Sales office salaries	90,000
Depreciation on headquarters building	50,000	Beginning balance, Raw materials	124,000
Factory insurance	15,000	Beginning balance, WIP	124,000
Property taxes:		Beginning balance, Finished goods	84,000
Factory	20,000	Ending balance, Raw materials	102,000
Headquarters	18,000	Ending balance, WIP	130,000
Utilities for factory	34,000	Ending balance, Finished goods	82,000

Last year, Brody completed 100,000 units. Sales revenue equaled $1,200,000, and Brody paid a sales commission of 5 percent of sales.

Required:

1. Calculate the direct materials used in production for last year.

2. Calculate total prime cost.

3. Calculate total conversion cost.

4. Prepare a cost of goods manufactured statement for last year. Calculate the unit product cost.

5. Prepare a cost of goods sold statement for last year.

6. Prepare an income statement for last year. Show the percentage of sales that each line item represents.

Solution:

1. Direct materials = $124,000 + $250,000 − $102,000 = $272,000

2. Prime cost = $272,000 + $140,000 = $412,000

3. First, calculate total overhead cost:

Depreciation on factory equipment	$ 45,000
Depreciation on factory building	30,000
Factory insurance	15,000
Factory property taxes	20,000
Factory utilities	34,000
Indirect labor salaries	156,000
Total overhead	$300,000

Conversion cost = $140,000 + $300,000 = $440,000

4.

Direct materials	$272,000
Direct labor	140,000
Overhead	300,000
Total manufacturing cost	$712,000
+ Beginning WIP	124,000
− Ending WIP	130,000
Cost of goods manufactured	$706,000

$$\text{Unit product cost} = \frac{\$706,000}{100,000 \text{ units}} = \$7.06$$

5.

Cost of goods manufactured	$706,000
+ Beginning inventory, Finished goods	84,000
− Ending inventory, Finished goods	82,000
Cost of goods sold	$708,000

6. First, compute selling expense and administrative expense:

Utilities, sales office	$ 1,800
Sales office salaries	90,000
Sales commissions ($1,200,000 × 0.05)	60,000
Total selling expenses	$151,800
Depreciation on headquarters building	$ 50,000
Property taxes, headquarters	18,000
Administrative salaries	150,000
Total administrative expenses	$218,000

Brody Company
Income Statement
For Last Year

		Percent
Sales	$1,200,000	100.00
Cost of goods sold	708,000	59.00
Gross margin	$ 492,000	41.00
Less:		
Selling expenses	151,800	12.65
Administrative expenses	218,000	18.17*
Operating income	$ 122,200	10.18*

*Rounded

DISCUSSION QUESTIONS

1. What is managerial accounting?
2. What are the three broad objectives of managerial accounting?
3. Who are the users of managerial accounting information?
4. What is meant by controlling?
5. Should a managerial accounting system provide both financial and nonfinancial information? Explain.

6. How do managerial accounting and financial accounting differ?
7. Explain the meaning of customer value. How is focusing on customer value changing managerial accounting?
8. What is the value chain? Why is it important?
9. Explain why today's managerial accountant must have a cross-functional perspective.
10. Explain the challenges faced by managerial accountants in effectively communicating managerial accounting information to various interested users.
11. Explain the difference between cost and expense.
12. What is the difference between accumulating cost and assigning cost?
13. What is a cost object? Give some examples.
14. What is a direct cost? An indirect cost? Can the same cost be direct for one purpose and indirect for another? Give an example.
15. Explain the difference between direct materials purchased in a month and direct materials used for the month.
16. Define manufacturing *overhead*.
17. Define *prime cost* and *conversion cost*. Why can't prime cost be added to conversion cost to get total product cost?
18. How does a period cost differ from a product cost?
19. Define *selling cost*. Give five examples of selling cost.
20. What is the difference between cost of goods manufactured and cost of goods sold?
21. Why do firms like to calculate a percentage column on the income statement (in which each line item is expressed as a percentage of sales)?
22. What is the difference between the income statement for a manufacturing firm and the income statement for a service firm?
23. What is ethical behavior? Is it possible to teach ethical behavior in a managerial accounting course?

MULTIPLE-CHOICE EXERCISES

13-1 The provision of accounting information for internal users is known as

a. accounting.
b. financial accounting.
c. managerial accounting.
d. information provision.
e. accounting for planning and control.

13-2 The process of choosing among competing alternatives is called

a. planning.
b. decision making.
c. controlling.
d. performance evaluation.
e. none of these.

13-3 Which of the following is a characteristic of managerial accounting?

a. There is an internal focus.
b. Subjective information may be used.
c. There is an emphasis on the future.
d. It is broad-based and multidisciplinary.
e. All of these.

13-4 In terms of strategic positioning, which two general strategies may be chosen by a company?

a. Revenue production and cost enhancement
b. Activity-based costing and value chain emphasis
c. Increasing customer value and decreasing supplier orientation
d. Cost leadership and product differentiation
e. Product differentiation and cost enhancement

13-5 Accumulating costs means that

a. costs must be summed and entered on the income statement.
b. each cost must be linked to some cost object.
c. costs must be measured and tracked.
d. costs must be allocated to units of production.
e. costs have expired and must be transferred from the balance sheet to the income statement.

13-6 Product (or manufacturing) costs consist of

a. direct materials, direct labor, and selling costs.
b. direct materials, direct labor, overhead, and operating expense.
c. prime costs plus conversion costs.
d. prime costs and overhead.
e. selling and administrative costs.

Use the following information for Multiple-Choice Exercises 13-7 and 13-8:
Wachman Company produces a product with the following per-unit costs:

Direct materials	$15
Direct labor	6
Manufacturing overhead	10

Last year, Wachman produced and sold 1,000 units at a price of $75 each. Total selling and administrative expense was $30,000.

13-7 Refer to the information for Wachman Company above. Conversion cost per unit was

a. $15.
b. $21.
c. $31.
d. $16.
e. none of these.

13-8 Refer to the information for Wachman Company above. Total gross margin for last year was

a. $75,000.
b. $44,000.
c. $61,000.
d. $9,000.
e. $31,000.

13-9 The accountant in a factory that produces biscuits for fast-food restaurants wants to assign costs to boxes of biscuits. Which of the following costs can be traced directly to boxes of biscuits?

a. The cost of flour and baking soda
b. The wages of the mixing labor
c. The cost of the boxes
d. The cost of packing labor
e. All of these

13-10 Which of the following is an indirect cost?

a. The cost of denim in a jeans factory
b. The cost of mixing labor in a factory that makes over-the-counter pain relievers
c. The cost of bottles in a shampoo factory
d. The cost of restriping the parking lot at a perfume factory
e. All of the above

13-11 Bobby Dee's is an owner-operated company that details (thoroughly cleans—inside and out) automobiles. Bobby Dee's is which of the following?

a. Wholesaler
b. Retailer
c. Service firm
d. Manufacturing firm
e. None of these

13-12 Kellogg's makes a variety of breakfast cereals. Kellogg's is which of the following?

a. Wholesaler
b. Retailer
c. Service firm
d. Manufacturing firm
e. None of these

13-13 Target is which of the following?

a. Wholesaler
b. Retailer
c. Service firm
d. Manufacturing firm
e. None of these

13-14 Stone Inc. is a company that purchases goods (e.g., chess sets, pottery) from overseas and resells them to gift shops in the United States. Stone Inc. is which of the following?

a. Wholesaler
b. Retailer
c. Service firm
d. Manufacturing firm
e. None of these

13-15 JackMan Company produces diecast metal bulldozers for toy shops. JackMan estimated the following average costs per bulldozer:

Direct materials	$8.65
Direct labor	1.10
Manufacturing overhead	0.95

Prime cost per unit is

a. $8.65.
b. $1.10.
c. $0.95.
d. $2.05.
e. $9.75.

13-16 Which of the following is a period expense?

a. Factory insurance
b. CEO salary
c. Direct labor
d. Factory maintenance
e. All of these

Use the following information for Multiple-Choice Exercises 13-17 through 13-22:
Last year, Barnard Company incurred the following costs:

Direct materials	$ 50,000
Direct labor	20,000
Manufacturing overhead	130,000
Selling expense	40,000
Administrative expense	36,000

Barnard produced and sold 10,000 units at a price of $31 each.

13-17 Refer to the information for Barnard Company above. Prime cost per unit for is

a. $7.00.
b. $20.00.
c. $15.00.
d. $5.00.
e. $27.60.

13-18 Refer to the information for Barnard Company above. Conversion cost per unit is

a. $7.00.
b. $20.00.
c. $15.00.
d. $5.00.
e. $27.60.

13-19 Refer to the information for Barnard Company above. The cost of goods sold per unit is

a. $7.00.
b. $20.00.
c. $15.00.
d. $5.00.
e. $27.60.

13-20 Refer to the information for Barnard Company above. The gross margin per unit is

a. $24.00.
b. $11.00.
c. $16.00.
d. $26.00.
e. $3.40.

13-21 Refer to the information for Barnard Company above. The total period expense is

a. $276,000.
b. $200,000.
c. $76,000.
d. $40,000.
e. $36,000.

13-22 Refer to the information for Barnard Company on the previous page. Operating income is

a. $34,000.
b. $110,000.
c. $234,000.

d. $270,000.
e. $74,000.

CORNERSTONE EXERCISES

> *Use the following information for Cornerstone Exercises 13-23 and 13-24:*
> Slapshot Company makes ice hockey sticks. Last week, direct materials (wood, paint, Kevlar, and resin) costing $24,000 were put into production. Direct labor of $20,000 (10 workers × 100 hours × $20 per hour) was incurred. Manufacturing overhead equaled $56,000. By the end of the week, the company had manufactured 4,000 hockey sticks.

Cornerstone Exercise 13-23 Total Product Cost and Per-Unit Product Cost

OBJECTIVE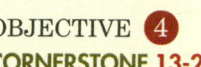
CORNERSTONE 13-1

Refer to the information for Slapshot Company above.

Required:
1. Calculate the total product cost for last week.
2. Calculate the per-unit cost of one hockey stick that was produced last week.

Cornerstone Exercise 13-24 Prime Cost and Conversion Cost

OBJECTIVE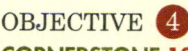
CORNERSTONE 13-2

Refer to the information for Slapshot Company above.

Required:
1. Calculate the total prime cost for last week.
2. Calculate the per-unit prime cost.
3. Calculate the total conversion cost for last week.
4. Calculate the per-unit conversion cost.

Cornerstone Exercise 13-25 Direct Materials Used in Production

OBJECTIVE
CORNERSTONE 13-3

Slapshot Company makes ice hockey sticks. On June 1, Slapshot had $42,000 of materials in inventory. During the month of June, the company purchased $126,000 of materials. On June 30, materials inventory equaled $51,000.

Required:
Calculate the direct materials used in production for the month of June.

Cornerstone Exercise 13-26 Cost of Goods Manufactured

OBJECTIVE 5
CORNERSTONE 13-4

Slapshot Company makes ice hockey sticks. During the month of June, the company purchased $126,000 of materials. Also during the month of June, Slapshot Company incurred direct labor cost of $165,000 and manufacturing overhead of $215,000. Inventory information is as follows:

	June 1	June 30
Materials	$42,000	$51,000
Work in process	60,000	71,000

Required:
1. Calculate the cost of goods manufactured for the month of June.
2. Calculate the cost of one hockey stick assuming that 18,000 sticks were completed during June.

Cornerstone Exercise 13-27 Cost of Goods Sold

OBJECTIVE 5
CORNERSTONE 13-5

Slapshot Company makes ice hockey sticks. During the month of June, 18,000 sticks were completed at a cost of goods manufactured of $486,000. Suppose that on June 1, Slapshot had 5,000 units in finished goods inventory costing $160,000 and on June 30, 7,000 units in finished goods inventory costing $215,000.

Required:
1. Prepare a cost of goods sold statement for the month of June.
2. Calculate the number of sticks that were sold during June.

> *Use the following information for Cornerstone Exercises 13-28 and 13-29:*
> Slapshot Company makes ice hockey sticks and sold 16,000 sticks during the month of June at a total cost of $431,000. Each stick sold at a price of $90. Slapshot also incurred two types of selling costs: commissions equal to 15 percent of the sales price, and other selling expense of $200,000. Administrative expense totaled $115,000.

OBJECTIVE 5
CORNERSTONE 13-6

Cornerstone Exercise 13-28 Manufacturing Firm Income Statement

Refer to the information for Slapshot Company above.

Required:
Prepare an income statement for Slapshot for the month of June.

OBJECTIVE 5
CORNERSTONE 13-7

Cornerstone Exercise 13-29 Income Statement Percentages

Refer to the information for Slapshot Company above.

Required:
Prepare an income statement for Slapshot for the month of June and calculate the percentage of sales revenue represented by each line of the income statement. Round answers to one decimal place.

OBJECTIVE 5
CORNERSTONE 13-8

Cornerstone Exercise 13-30 Service Organization Income Statement

Allstar Exposure designs and sells advertising services to small, relatively unknown companies. Last month, Allstar had sales commissions costs of $50,000, technology costs of $75,000, and research and development costs of $200,000. Selling expenses were $10,000, and administrative expenses equaled $35,000. Sales totaled $410,000.

Required:
1. Prepare an income statement for Allstar for the past month.
2. Briefly explain why Allstar's income statement has no line item for Cost of Goods Sold.

EXERCISES

OBJECTIVE 2

Exercise 13-31 Customer Value, Strategic Positioning

Adriana Alvarado has decided to purchase a personal computer. She has narrowed the choices to two: Drantex and Confiar. Both brands have the same processing speed, 6.4 gigabytes of hard-disk capacity, two USB ports, a DVDRW drive, and each comes with the same basic software support package. Both come from mail-order companies with good reputations. The selling price for each is identical. After some review, Adriana discovers that the cost of operating and maintaining Drantex over a three-year period is estimated to be $300. For Confiar, the operating and maintenance cost is $600. The sales agent for Drantex emphasized the lower operating and maintenance costs. The agent for Confiar, however, emphasized the service reputation of the product and the faster delivery time (Confiar can be purchased and delivered one week sooner than Drantex). Based on all the information, Adriana has decided to buy Confiar.

Required:
1. What is the total product purchased by Adriana?
2. **Conceptual Connection:** How does the strategic positioning differ for the two companies?
3. **Conceptual Connection:** When asked why she decided to buy Confiar, Adriana responded, "I think that Confiar offers more value than Drantex." What are the possible sources of this greater value? What implications does this have for the managerial accounting information system?
4. **Conceptual Connection:** Suppose that Adriana's decision was prompted mostly by the desire to receive the computer quickly. Informed that it was losing sales because of the longer time to produce and deliver its products, the management of the company producing Drantex decided to improve delivery performance by improving its internal processes. These improvements decreased the number of defective units and the time required to produce its product. Consequently, delivery time and costs both decreased, and the company was able to lower its prices on Drantex. Explain how these actions translate into strengthening the competitive position of the Drantex PC relative to the Confiar PC. Also discuss the implications for the managerial accounting information system.

Exercise 13-32 Cost Assignment

OBJECTIVE **3**

The sales staff of Central Media (a locally owned radio and cable television station) consists of two salespeople, Derek and Lawanna. During March, the following salaries and commissions were paid:

	Derek	Lawanna
Salaries	$25,000	$30,000
Commissions	6,000	1,500

Derek spends 100 percent of his time selling advertising. Lawanna spends two-thirds of her time selling advertising and the remaining one-third on administrative work. Commissions are paid only on sales.

Required:

1. Accumulate these costs by account by filling in the following table:

Cost	Salaries	Commissions
Derek		
Lawanna		
Total		

2. Assign the costs of salaries and commissions to selling expense and administrative expense by filling in the following table:

Cost	Selling Costs	Administrative Costs
Derek's salary		
Lawanna's salary		
Derek's commissions		
Lawanna's commissions		
Total		

Exercise 13-33 Products versus Services, Cost Assignment

OBJECTIVE **3**

Holmes Company produces wooden playhouses. When a customer orders a playhouse, it is delivered in pieces with detailed instructions on how to put it together. Some customers prefer that Holmes puts the playhouse together, and they purchase the playhouse plus the installation package. Holmes then pulls two workers off the production line and sends them to construct the playhouse on site.

Required:

1. What two products does Holmes sell? Classify each one as a product or a service.
2. **Conceptual Connection:** Do you think Holmes assigns costs individually to each product or service? Why or why not?
3. **Conceptual Connection:** Describe the opportunity cost of the installation process.

Exercise 13-34 Assigning Costs to a Cost Object, Direct and Indirect Costs

OBJECTIVE **3**

Hummer Company uses manufacturing cells to produce its products (a *cell* is a manufacturing unit dedicated to the production of subassemblies or products). One manufacturing cell produces small motors for lawn mowers. Suppose that the motor manufacturing cell is the cost object. Assume that all or a portion of the following costs must be assigned to the cell.

a. Salary of cell supervisor
b. Power to heat and cool the plant in which the cell is located
c. Materials used to produce the motors
d. Maintenance for the cell's equipment (provided by the maintenance department)
e. Labor used to produce motors
f. Cafeteria that services the plant's employees
g. Depreciation on the plant

h. Depreciation on equipment used to produce the motors
i. Ordering costs for materials used in production
j. Engineering support (provided by the engineering department)
k. Cost of maintaining the plant and grounds
l. Cost of the plant's personnel office
m. Property tax on the plant and land

Required:

Classify each of the costs as a direct cost or an indirect cost to the motor manufacturing cell.

OBJECTIVE ❹

Exercise 13-35 Total and Unit Product Cost

Martinez Manufacturing Inc. showed the following costs for last month:

Direct materials	$7,000
Direct labor	3,000
Manufacturing overhead	2,000
Selling expense	8,000

Last month, 4,000 units were produced and sold.

Required:
1. Classify each of the costs as product cost or period cost.
2. What is total product cost for last month?
3. What is the unit product cost for last month?

OBJECTIVE ❹

Exercise 13-36 Cost Classification

Loring Company incurred the following costs last year:

Direct materials	$216,000	Sales salaries	$ 65,000
Factory rent	24,000	Advertising	37,000
Direct labor	120,000	Depreciation on the headquarters	
Factory utilities	6,300	building	10,000
Supervision in the factory	50,000	Salary of the corporate receptionist	30,000
Indirect labor in the factory	30,000	Other administrative costs	175,000
Depreciation on factory equipment	9,000	Salary of the factory receptionist	28,000
Sales commissions	27,000		

Required:
1. Classify each of the costs using the following table format. Be sure to total the amounts in each column. *Example:* Direct materials, $216,000.

	Product Cost			Period Cost	
Costs	Direct Materials	Direct Labor	Manufact. Overhead	Selling Expense	Administrative Expense
Direct materials	$216,000				

2. What was the total product cost for last year?
3. What was the total period cost for last year?
4. If 30,000 units were produced last year, what was the unit product cost?

OBJECTIVE ❹

Exercise 13-37 Classifying Cost of Production

A factory manufactures jelly. The jars of jelly are packed six to a box, and the boxes are sold to grocery stores. The following types of cost were incurred:

Jars	Receptionist's wages
Sugar	Telephone
Fruit	Utilities
Pectin (thickener used in jams and jellies)	Rental of Santa Claus suit (for the annual
Boxes	Christmas party for factory children)
Depreciation on the factory building	Supervisory labor salaries
Cooking equipment operators' wages	Insurance on factory building
Filling equipment operators' wages	Depreciation on factory equipment
Packers' wages	Oil to lubricate filling equipment
Janitors' wages	

Required:
Classify each of the costs as direct materials, direct labor, or overhead by using the following table. The row for "Jars" is filled in as an example.

Costs	Direct Materials	Direct Labor	Manufact. Overhead
Jars	X		

> *Use the following information for Exercises 13-38 and 13-39:*
> Grin Company manufactures digital cameras. In January, Grin produced 4,000 cameras with the following costs:
>
> | | |
> |---|---:|
> | Direct materials | $400,000 |
> | Direct labor | 80,000 |
> | Manufacturing overhead | 320,000 |
>
> There were no beginning or ending inventories of WIP.

Exercise 13-38 Product Cost in Total and Per Unit

OBJECTIVE 4

Refer to the information for Grin Company above.

Required:
1. What was total product cost in January?
2. What was product cost per unit in January?

Exercise 13-39 Prime Cost and Conversion Cost

OBJECTIVE 4

Refer to the information for Grin Company above.

Required:
1. What was the total prime cost in January?
2. What was the prime cost per unit in January?
3. What was the total conversion cost in January?
4. What was the conversion cost per unit in January?

Exercise 13-40 Direct Materials Used

OBJECTIVE 5

Hannah Banana Bakers makes chocolate chip cookies for cafe restaurants. In June, Hannah Banana purchased $15,500 of materials. On June 1, the materials inventory was $3,700. On June 30, $1,600 of materials remained in materials inventory.

Required:
1. What is the cost of the direct materials used in production during June?
2. **Conceptual Connection:** Briefly explain why there is a difference between the cost of direct materials that were *purchased* during the month and the cost of direct materials that were *used* in production during the month.

Exercise 13-41 Cost of Goods Sold

OBJECTIVE 5

Allyson Ashley makes jet skis. During the year, Allyson manufactured 42,000 jet skis. Finished goods inventory had the following units:

January 1	4,300
December 31	3,900

Required:
1. How many jet skis did Allyson sell during the year?
2. If each jet ski had a product cost of $2,100, what was the cost of goods sold last year?

> *Use the following information for Exercises 13-42 and 13-43:*
> In March, Chilton Company purchased materials costing $12,000 and incurred direct labor cost of $20,000. Overhead totaled $36,000 for the month. Information on inventories was as follows:
>
> | | March 1 | March 31 |
> |---|---|---|
> | Materials | $7,200 | $8,600 |
> | Work in process | 1,700 | 9,000 |
> | Finished goods | 7,000 | 9,500 |

Exercise 13-42 Direct Materials Used, Cost of Goods Manufactured

OBJECTIVE 5

Refer to the information for Chilton Company above.

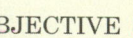

Required:

1. What was the cost of direct materials used in March?
2. What was the total manufacturing cost in March?
3. What was the cost of goods manufactured for March?

OBJECTIVE 5

Exercise 13-43 Cost of Goods Sold

Refer to the information for Chilton Company on the previous page.

Required:

What was the cost of goods sold for March?

Use the following information for Exercises 13-44 through 13-46:
Jasper Company provided the following information for last year:

Sales in units	300,000
Selling price	$ 9
Direct materials	150,000
Direct labor	325,000
Manufacturing overhead	215,000
Selling expense	437,000
Administrative expense	854,000

Last year, beginning and ending inventories of work in process and finished goods equaled zero.

OBJECTIVE 5

Exercise 13-44 Cost of Goods Sold, Sales Revenue, Income Statement

Refer to the information for Jasper Company above.

Required:

Calculate the cost of goods sold for last year.

OBJECTIVE 5

Exercise 13-45 Income Statement

Refer to the information for Jasper Company above.

Required:

1. Calculate the sales revenue for last year.
2. Prepare an income statement for Jasper Company for last year.

OBJECTIVE 5

Exercise 13-46 Income Statement

Refer to the information for Jasper Company above.

Required:

Prepare an income statement for Jasper Company for last year. Calculate the percentage of sales for each line item on the income statement. (*Note:* Round percentages to the nearest tenth of a percent.)

OBJECTIVE 5

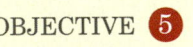

Exercise 13-47 Understanding the Relationship between Cost Flows, Inventories, and Cost of Goods Sold

Ivano Company has collected cost accounting information for the following subset of items for Years 1 and 2.

Item:	Year 1	Year 2
Direct materials used in production	a	$50,000
Direct materials: Beginning inventory	$ 10,000	c
Direct materials purchases	45,000	d
Direct materials: Ending inventory	15,000	17,000
Direct labor used in production	b	53,000
Manufacturing overhead costs used in production	80,000	76,000
Work in process: Beginning inventory	17,000	14,000
Work in process: Ending inventory	14,000	19,000
Finished goods: Beginning inventory	8,000	7,000
Finished goods: Ending inventory	7,000	11,000
Cost of goods sold	169,000	e

Required:

Calculate the values of the missing Items a through e.

Exercise 13-48 Ethical Behavior

OBJECTIVE 6

Manager: If I can reduce my costs by $40,000 during this last quarter, my division will show a profit that is 10 percent above the planned level, and I will receive a $10,000 bonus. However, given the projections for the fourth quarter, it does not look promising. I really need that $10,000. I know of one way that I can qualify. All I have to do is lay off my three most expensive salespeople. After all, most of the orders are in for the fourth quarter, and I can always hire new sales personnel at the beginning of the next year.

Required:

Conceptual Connection: What is the right choice for the manager to make? Why did the ethical dilemma arise? Is there any way to redesign the accounting reporting system to discourage the type of behavior that the manager is contemplating?

Exercise 13-49 Ethical Issues

OBJECTIVE 6

The Bedron Company is a closely held investment service group that has been quite successful over the past five years, consistently providing most members of the top management group with 50 percent bonuses. In addition, both the chief financial officer and the chief executive officer have received 100 percent bonuses. Bedron expects this trend to continue.

Recently, Bedron's top management group, which holds 35 percent of the outstanding shares of common stock, has learned that a major corporation is interested in acquiring Bedron. The other corporation's initial offer is attractive and is several dollars per share higher than Bedron's current share price. One member of management told a group of employees under him about the potential offer. He suggested that they might want to purchase more Bedron stock at the current price in anticipation of the takeover offer.

Required:

Conceptual Connection: Do you think that the employees should take the action suggested by their boss? Suppose the action is prohibited by Bedron's code of ethics. Now suppose that it is not prohibited by Bedron's code of ethics. Is the action acceptable in that case?

Exercise 13-50 Company Codes of Conduct

OBJECTIVE 6

Using the Internet, locate the code of conduct for three different companies.

Required:

Conceptual Connection: Briefly describe each code of conduct. How are they similar? How are they different?

PROBLEMS

Problem 13-51 Manufacturing, Cost Classification, Income Statement Service Firm Product Costs and Selling and Administrative Costs, Income Statement

OBJECTIVE 4 5

Pop's Drive-Thru Burger Heaven produces and sells quarter-pound hamburgers. Each burger is wrapped and put in a "burger bag," which also includes a serving of fries and a soft drink. The price for the burger bag is $3.50. During December, 10,000 burger bags were sold. The restaurant employs college students part-time to cook and fill orders. There is one supervisor (the owner, John Peterson). Pop's maintains a pool of part-time employees so that the number of employees scheduled can be adjusted to the changes in demand. Demand varies on a weekly as well as a monthly basis.

A janitor is hired to clean the building early each morning. Cleaning supplies are used by the janitor, as well as the staff, to wipe counters, wash cooking equipment, and so on. The building is leased from a local real estate company; it has no seating capacity. All orders are filled on a drive-thru basis.

The supervisor schedules work, opens the building, counts the cash, advertises, and is responsible for hiring and firing. The following costs were incurred during December:

Hamburger meat	$4,500	Rent	$1,800
Buns, lettuce, pickles, and onions	800	Depreciation, cooking equipment and	
Frozen potato strips	1,250	fixtures	600
Wrappers, bags, and condiment packages	600	Advertising	500
Other ingredients	660	Janitor's wages	520
Part-time employees' wages	7,250	Janitorial supplies	150
John Peterson's salary	3,000	Accounting fees	1,500
Utilities	1,500	Taxes	4,250

Pop's accountant, Elena DeMarco, does the bookkeeping, handles payroll, and files all necessary taxes. She noted that there were no beginning or ending inventories of materials. To simplify accounting for costs, Elena assumed that all part-time employees are production employees and that John Peterson's salary is selling and administrative expense. She further assumed that all rent and depreciation expense on the building and fixtures are part of product cost. Finally, she decided to put all taxes into one category, taxes, and to treat them as administrative expense.

Required:

1. Classify each of the costs for Pop's December operations using the table format given below. Be sure to total the amounts in each column.
   Example: Hamburger meat, $4,500.

Cost	Direct Materials	Direct Labor	Manufact. Overhead	Selling and Administrative
Hamburger meat	$4,500			
Total				

2. Prepare an income statement for the month of December.
3. **Conceptual Connection:** Elena made some simplifying assumptions. Were those reasonable? Suppose a good case could be made that the portion of the employees' time spent selling the burger bags was really a part of sales. In that case, would it be better to divide their time between production and selling? Should John Peterson's time be divided between marketing and administrative duties? What difference (if any) would that make on the income statement?

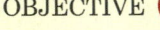 OBJECTIVE 3

Problem 13-52 Cost Assignment, Direct Costs

Harry Whipple, owner of an inkjet printer, has agreed to allow Mary and Natalie, two friends who are pursuing master's degrees, to print several papers for their graduate courses. However, he has imposed two conditions. First, they must supply their own paper. Second, they must pay Harry a fair amount for the usage of the ink cartridge. Harry's printer takes two types of cartridges, a black one and a color one that contains the inks necessary to print in color. Black replacement cartridges cost $25.50 each and print approximately 850 pages. The color cartridge replacement cost $31 and prints approximately 310 color pages. One ream of paper costs $2.50 and contains 500 sheets. Mary's printing requirements are for 500 pages, while Natalie's are for 1,000 pages.

Required:

1. Assuming that both women write papers using text only (i.e., black ink), what is the total amount owed to Harry by Mary? By Natalie?
2. What is the total cost of printing (ink and paper) for Mary? For Natalie?
3. Now suppose that Natalie illustrates her writing with many large colorful pie charts and pictures and that about 20 percent of her total printing is primarily color. Mary uses no color illustrations. What is the total amount owed to Harry by Natalie? What is the total cost of printing (ink and paper) for Natalie?

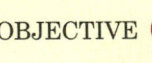 OBJECTIVE 5

Problem 13-53 Cost of Direct Materials, Cost of Goods Manufactured, Cost of Goods Sold

Bisby Company manufactures fishing rods. At the beginning of July, the following information was supplied by its accountant:

Raw materials inventory	$40,000
Work-in-process inventory	21,000
Finished goods inventory	23,200

During July, the direct labor cost was $43,500, raw materials purchases were $64,000, and the total overhead cost was $108,750. The inventories at the end of July were:

Raw materials inventory	$19,800
Work-in-process inventory	32,500
Finished goods inventory	22,100

Required:

1. What is the cost of the direct materials used in production during July?
2. What is the cost of goods manufactured for July?
3. What is the cost of goods sold for July?

Problem 13-54 Preparation of Income Statement: Manufacturing Firm

Laworld Inc. manufactures small camping tents. Last year, 200,000 tents were made and sold for $60 each. Each tent includes the following costs:

Direct materials	$18
Direct labor	12
Manufacturing overhead	16

The only selling expenses were a commission of $2 per unit sold and advertising totaling $100,000. Administrative expenses, all fixed, equaled $300,000. There were no beginning or ending finished goods inventories. There were no beginning or ending work-in-process inventories.

Required:
1. Calculate the product cost for one tent. Calculate the total product cost for last year.
2. **Conceptual Connection:** Prepare an income statement for external users. Did you need to prepare a supporting statement of cost of goods manufactured? Explain.
3. **Conceptual Connection:** Suppose 200,000 tents were produced (and 200,000 sold) but that the company had a beginning finished goods inventory of 10,000 tents produced in the prior year at $40 per unit. The company follows a first-in, first-out policy for its inventory (meaning that the units produced first are sold first for purposes of cost flow). What effect does this have on the income statement? Show the new statement.

Problem 13-55 Cost of Goods Manufactured, Cost of Goods Sold

Hayward Company, a manufacturing firm, has supplied the following information from its accounting records for the month of May:

Direct labor cost	$10,500	Material handling	$ 3,750
Purchases of raw materials	15,000	Materials inventory, May 1	3,475
Supplies used	675	Work-in-process inventory, May 1	12,500
Factory insurance	350	Finished goods inventory, May 1	6,685
Commissions paid	2,500	Materials inventory, May 31	9,500
Factory supervision	2,225	Work-in-process inventory, May 31	14,250
Advertising	800	Finished goods inventory, May 31	4,250

Required:
1. Prepare a statement of cost of goods manufactured.
2. Prepare a statement of cost of goods sold.

Problem 13-56 Cost Identification

Following is a list of cost terms described in the chapter as well as a list of brief descriptive settings for each item.

Cost terms:

a.	Opportunity cost	f.	Conversion cost
b.	Period cost	g.	Prime cost
c.	Product cost	h.	Direct materials cost
d.	Direct labor cost	i.	Manufacturing overhead cost
e.	Selling cost	j.	Administrative cost

Settings:
1. Marcus Armstrong, manager of Timmins Optical, estimated that the cost of plastic, wages of the technician producing the lenses, and overhead totaled $30 per pair of single-vision lenses.
2. Linda was having a hard time deciding whether to return to school. She was concerned about the salary she would have to give up for the next four years.
3. Randy Harris is the finished goods warehouse manager for a medium-sized manufacturing firm. He is paid a salary of $90,000 per year. As he studied the financial statements prepared by the local certified public accounting firm, he wondered how his salary was treated.
4. Jamie Young is in charge of the legal department at company headquarters. Her salary is $95,000 per year. She reports to the chief executive officer.
5. All factory costs that are not classified as direct materials or direct labor.

6. The new product required machining, assembly, and painting. The design engineer asked the accounting department to estimate the labor cost of each of the three operations. The engineer supplied the estimated labor hours for each operation.

7. After obtaining the estimate of direct labor cost, the design engineer estimated the cost of the materials that would be used for the new product.

8. The design engineer totaled the costs of materials and direct labor for the new product.

9. The design engineer also estimated the cost of converting the raw materials into its final form.

10. The auditor for a soft drink bottling plant pointed out that the depreciation on the delivery trucks had been incorrectly assigned to product cost (through overhead). Accordingly, the depreciation charge was reallocated on the income statement.

Required:

Match the cost terms with the settings. More than one cost classification may be associated with each setting; however, select the setting that seems to fit the item best. When you are done, each cost term will be used just once.

OBJECTIVE **5**

Problem 13-57 Cost of Goods Manufactured, Income Statement

W. W. Phillips Company produced 4,000 leather recliners during the year. These recliners sell for $400 each. Phillips had 500 recliners in finished goods inventory at the beginning of the year. At the end of the year, there were 700 recliners in finished goods inventory. Phillips' accounting records provide the following information:

Purchases of raw materials	$320,000	Salary, sales supervisor	$ 90,000
Beginning materials inventory	46,800	Commissions, salespersons	180,000
Ending materials inventory	66,800	General administration	300,000
Direct labor	200,000	Beginning work-in-process inventory	13,040
Indirect labor	40,000	Ending work-in-process inventory	14,940
Rent, factory building	42,000	Beginning finished goods inventory	80,000
Depreciation, factory equipment	60,000	Ending finished goods inventory	114,100
Utilities, factory	11,900		

Required:

1. Prepare a statement of cost of goods manufactured.
2. Compute the average cost of producing one unit of product in the year.
3. Prepare an income statement for external users.

OBJECTIVE **3**

Problem 13-58 Cost Definitions, Income Statement

Luisa Giovanni is a student at New York University. To help pay her way through college, Luisa started a dog walking service. She has 12 client dogs—six are walked on the first shift (6:30 A.M. and 5:00 P.M.), and six are walked on the second shift (7:30 A.M. and 6:00 P.M.).

Last month, Luisa noted the following:

1. Purchase of three leashes at $10 each (she carries these with her in case a leash breaks during a walk).
2. Internet service cost of $40 a month. This enables her to keep in touch with the owners, bill them by email, and so on.
3. Dog treats of $50 to reward each dog at the end of each walk.
4. A heavy-duty raincoat and hat for $100.
5. Partway through the month, Luisa's friend, Jason, offered her a chance to play a bit role in a movie that was shooting on location in New York City. The job paid $100 and would have required Luisa to be on location at 6:00 A.M. and to remain for 12 hours. Regretfully, Luisa turned it down.
6. The dog owners pay Luisa $250 per month per dog for her services.

Required:

1. At the end of the month, how would Luisa classify her Internet payment of $40—as a cost on the balance sheet or as an expense on the income statement?
2. **Conceptual Connection:** Which of the above item is an opportunity cost? Why?
3. What price is charged? What is Luisa's total revenue for a month?

Problem 13-59 Cost Identification and Analysis, Cost Assignment, Income Statement

OBJECTIVE

Melissa Vassar has decided to open a printing shop. She has secured two contracts. One is a five-year contract to print a popular regional magazine. This contract calls for 5,000 copies each month. The second contract is a three-year agreement to print tourist brochures for the state. The state tourist office requires 10,000 brochures per month.

Melissa has rented a building for $1,400 per month. Her printing equipment was purchased for $40,000 and has a life expectancy of 20,000 hours with no salvage value. Depreciation is assigned to a period based on the hours of usage. Melissa has scheduled the delivery of the products so that two production runs are needed. In the first run, the equipment is prepared for the magazine printing. In the second run, the equipment is reconfigured for brochure printing. It takes twice as long to configure the equipment for the magazine setup as it does for the brochure setup. The total setup costs per month are $600.

Insurance costs for the building and equipment are $140 per month. Power to operate the printing equipment is strongly related to machine usage. The printing equipment causes virtually all the power costs. Power costs will run $350 per month. Printing materials will cost $0.40 per copy for the magazine and $0.08 per copy for the brochure. Melissa will hire workers to run the presses as needed (part-time workers are easy to hire). She must pay $10 per hour. Each worker can produce 20 copies of the magazine per printing hour or 100 copies of the brochure. Distribution costs are $500 per month. Melissa will receive a salary of $1,500 per month. She is responsible for personnel, accounting, sales, and production—in effect, she is responsible for administering all aspects of the business.

Required:

1. What are the total monthly manufacturing costs?
2. What are the total monthly prime costs? What are the total monthly prime costs for the regional magazine? For the brochure?
3. What are the total monthly conversion costs? Suppose Melissa wants to determine monthly conversion costs for each product. Assign monthly conversion costs to each product using direct tracing and driver tracing whenever possible. For those costs that cannot be assigned using a tracing approach, you may assign them using direct labor hours.
4. Melissa receives $1.80 per copy of the magazine and $0.45 per brochure. Prepare an income statement for the first month of operations.

Problem 13-60 Cost Analysis, Income Statement

OBJECTIVE

Five to six times a year, Kicker puts on tent sales in various cities throughout Oklahoma and the surrounding states. The tent sales are designed to show Kicker customers new products, engender enthusiasm about those products, and sell soon to be out-of-date products at greatly reduced prices. Each tent sale lasts one day and requires parking lot space to set up the Kicker semitrailer; a couple of show cars; a disc jockey playing music; and a tent to sell Kicker merchandise, distribute brochures, and so on.

Last year, the Austin tent sale was held in a far corner of the parking lot outside the city exhibition hall where the automotive show was in progress. Because most customers were interested more in the new model cars than in the refurbishment of their current cars, foot traffic was low. In addition, customers did not want to carry speakers and amplifiers all the way back to where they had originally parked. Total direct costs for this tent sale were $14,300. Direct costs included gasoline and fuel for three pickup trucks and the semitrailer; wages and per diem for the five Kicker personnel who traveled to the show; rent on the parking lot space; and depreciation on the semitrailer, pickups, tent, tables (in tent), sound equipment; and the like. Revenue was $20,000. Cost of goods sold for the speakers was $7,000.

Required:

1. **Conceptual Connection:** How do you suppose Kicker accounts for the costs of the tent sales? What income statement items are affected by the tent sales?
2. **Conceptual Connection:** What was the profit (loss) from the Austin tent sale? What do you think Kicker might do to make it more profitable in the future?

CASES

OBJECTIVE

Case 13-61 Cost Classification, Income Statement

Gateway Construction Company, run by Jack Gateway, employs 25 to 30 people as subcontractors for laying gas, water, and sewage pipelines. Most of Gateway's work comes from contracts with city and state agencies in Nebraska. The company's sales volume averages $3 million, and profits vary between 0 and 10 percent of sales.

Sales and profits have been somewhat below average for the past three years due to a recession and intense competition. Because of this competition, Jack constantly reviews the prices that other companies bid for jobs. When a bid is lost, he analyzes the reasons for the differences between his bid and that of his competitors and uses this information to increase the competitiveness of future bids.

Jack believes that Gateway's current accounting system is deficient. Currently, all expenses are simply deducted from revenues to arrive at operating income. No effort is made to distinguish among the costs of laying pipe, obtaining contracts, and administering the company. Yet all bids are based on the costs of laying pipe.

With these thoughts in mind, Jack looked more carefully at the income statement for the previous year (see below). First, he noted that jobs were priced on the basis of equipment hours, with an average price of $165 per equipment hour. However, when it came to classifying and assigning costs, he needed some help. One thing that really puzzled him was how to classify his own $114,000 salary. About half of his time was spent in bidding and securing contracts, and the other half was spent in general administrative matters.

Gateway Construction Company
Income Statement
For the Year Ended December 31, 2011

Sales (18,200 equipment hours @ $165 per hour)		$3,003,000
Less expenses:		
Utilities	$ 24,000	
Machine operators	218,000	
Rent, office building	24,000	
CPA fees	20,000	
Other direct labor	265,700	
Administrative salaries	114,000	
Supervisory salaries	70,000	
Pipe	1,401,340	
Tires and fuel	418,600	
Depreciation, equipment	198,000	
Salaries of mechanics	50,000	
Advertising	15,000	
Total expenses		2,818,640
Operating income		$ 184,360

Required:

1. Classify the costs in the income statement as (1) costs of laying pipe (production costs), (2) costs of securing contracts (selling costs), or (3) costs of general administration. For production costs, identify direct materials, direct labor, and overhead costs. The company never has significant work in process (most jobs are started and completed within a day).

2. Assume that a significant driver is equipment hours. Identify the expenses that would likely be traced to jobs using this driver. Explain why you feel these costs are traceable using equipment hours. What is the cost per equipment hour for these traceable costs?

OBJECTIVE

Case 13-62 Cost Information and Ethical Behavior, Service Organization

Jean Erickson, manager and owner of an advertising company in Charlotte, North Carolina, arranged a meeting with Leroy Gee, the chief accountant of a large, local competitor. The two are lifelong friends. They grew up together in a small town and attended the same university. Leroy is a competent, successful accountant but is having some personal financial difficulties after some of his investments turned sour, leaving him with a $15,000 personal loan to pay off—just when his oldest son is starting college.

Jean, on the other hand, is struggling to establish a successful advertising business. She had recently acquired the rights to open a branch office of a large regional advertising firm headquartered in Atlanta, Georgia. During her first two years, she was able to build a small, profitable practice. However, the chance to gain a significant foothold in Charlotte hinged on the success of winning a bid to represent the state of North Carolina in a major campaign to attract new industry and tourism. The meeting she had scheduled with Leroy concerned the bid she planned to submit.

Jean: Leroy, I'm at a critical point in my business venture. If I can win the bid for the state's advertising dollars, I'll be set. Winning the bid will bring $600,000 to $700,000 of revenues into the firm. On top of that, I estimate that the publicity will bring another $200,000 to $300,000 of new business.

Leroy: I understand. My boss is anxious to win that business as well. It would mean a huge increase in profits for my firm. It's a competitive business, though. As new as you are, I doubt that you'll have much chance of winning.

Jean: You're forgetting two very important considerations. First, I have the backing of all the resources and talent of a regional firm. Second, I have some political connections. Last year, I was hired to run the publicity side of the governor's campaign. He was impressed with my work and would like me to have this business. I am confident that the proposals I submit will be very competitive. My only concern is to submit a bid that beats your firm. If I come in with a lower bid and good proposals, the governor can see to it that I get the work.

Leroy: Sounds promising. If you do win, however, there will be a lot of upset people. After all, they are going to claim that the business should have been given to local advertisers, not to some out-of-state firm. Given the size of your office, you'll have to get support from Atlanta. You could take a lot of heat.

Jean: True. But I am the owner of the branch office. That fact alone should blunt most of the criticism. Who can argue that I'm not a local? Listen, with your help, I think I can win this bid. Furthermore, if I do win it, you can reap some direct benefits. With that kind of business, I can afford to hire an accountant, and I'll make it worthwhile for you to transfer jobs. I can offer you an up-front bonus of $15,000. On top of that, I'll increase your annual salary by 20 percent. That should solve most of your financial difficulties. After all, we have been friends since day one—and what are friends for?

Leroy: Jean, my wife would be ecstatic if I were able to improve our financial position as quickly as this opportunity affords. I certainly hope that you win the bid. What kind of help can I provide?

Jean: Simple. To win, all I have to do is beat the bid of your firm. Before I submit my bid, I would like you to review it. With the financial skills you have, it should be easy for you to spot any excessive costs that I may have included. Or perhaps I included the wrong kind of costs. By cutting excessive costs and eliminating costs that may not be directly related to the project, my bid should be competitive enough to meet or beat your firm's bid.

Required:

1. What would you do if you were Leroy? Fully explain the reasons for your choice. What do you suppose the code of conduct for Leroy's company would say about this situation?
2. What is the likely outcome if Leroy agrees to review the bid? Is there much risk to him personally if he reviews the bid? Should the degree of risk have any bearing on his decision?

14 Cost Behavior

Doug Norman Crystals/Alamy

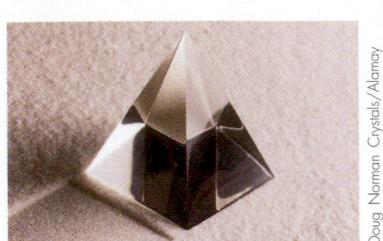

After studying Chapter 14, you should be able to:

1. Explain the meaning of cost behavior, and define and describe fixed and variable costs.
2. Define and describe mixed and step costs.
3. Separate mixed costs into their fixed and variable components using the high-low method, the scattergraph method, and the method of least squares.
4. *(Appendix 14A)* Use a personal computer spreadsheet program to perform the method of least squares.

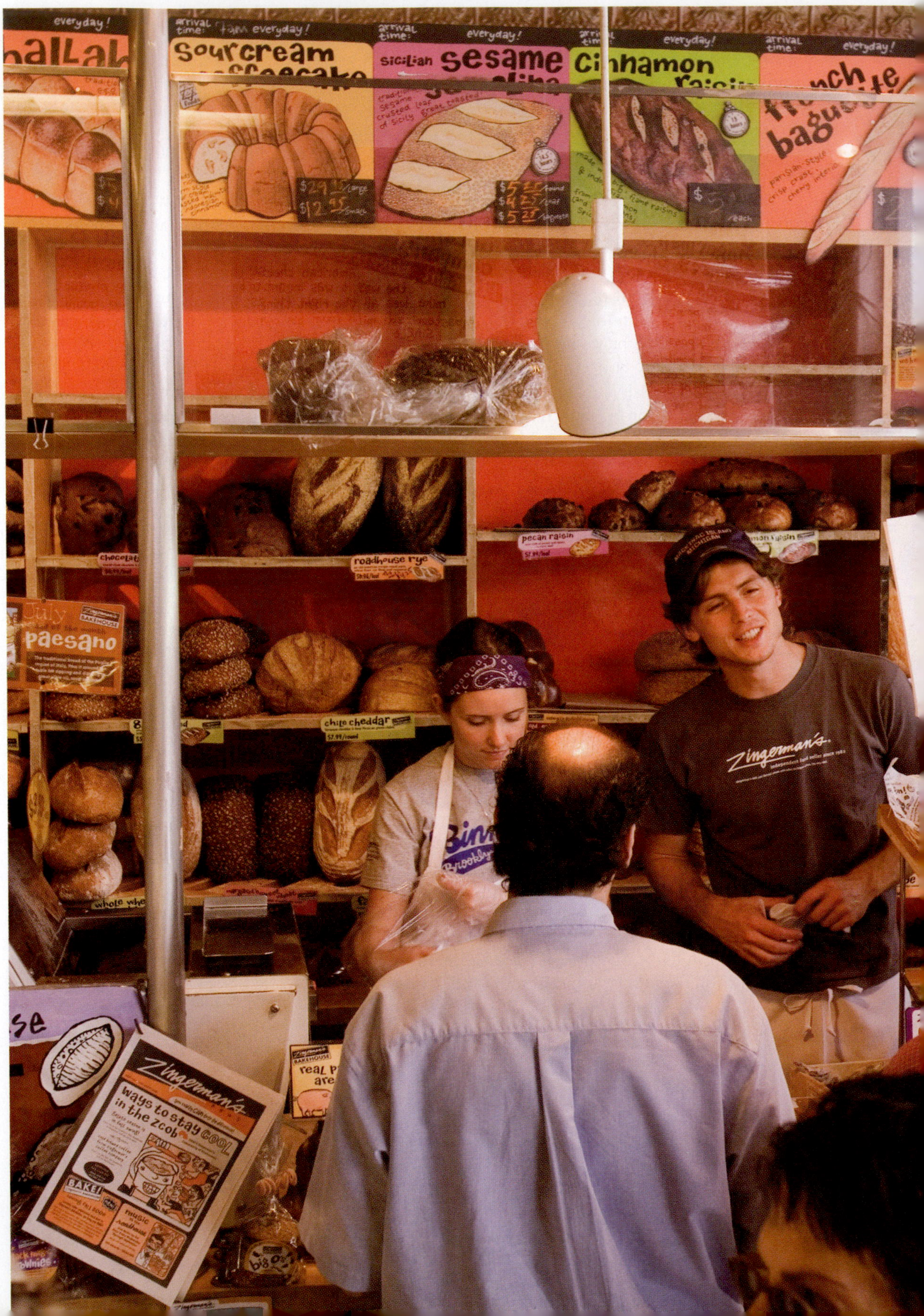

Jim West/Alamy

EXPERIENCE MANAGERIAL DECISIONS

with Zingerman's Deli

Have you ever walked by a bakery counter, or even Mom's kitchen, and been stopped in your tracks by the unmistakable aroma of freshly baked bread or homemade cookies? If so, cost behavior was probably the furthest thing from your mind. However, for the owners of **Zingerman's** deli and bakery, founded in 1982 in Ann Arbor, Michigan, cost behavior is critical in making decisions that improve Zingerman's profitability.

In total, Zingerman's tracks and manages over 3,000 distinct costs! For example, Zingerman's pays close attention to variable costs, such as the all-natural, non-alkalized cocoa powder ingredient used in its signature Hot Cocoa Cake, and the size of its hourly workforce, which varies

Naryashkova Olga, 2010/Shutterstock.com

by season. Zingerman's also closely manages its numerous fixed costs, such as recipe "research and development" creation and ovens, across different production and sales levels to be sure that it doesn't make decisions that increase costs to a greater extent than revenues. Still other costs are mixed in nature, and the variable and fixed components must be disentangled before Zingerman's owners can budget for future periods, set prices, and plan for growth in the businesses. So, the next time you bite into a warm chocolate chip cookie, think about—if only for a brief moment—all of the cost behaviors that went into producing, packaging, selling, and distributing that tasty bite of joy!

Zingerman's

Chapter 13 discussed various types of costs and took a close look at manufacturing and service costs. The primary concern of the chapter was organizing costs into production, selling, and administrative costs and building related schedules of the cost of goods manufactured, cost of goods sold, and income statements. Now let's focus on cost behavior—the way costs change as the related activity changes.

Cost behavior is the foundation upon which managerial accounting is built. In financial accounting, the theoretical pyramid contains critical assumptions (e.g., economic entity assumption) and principles (e.g., matching principle), are necessary for helping financial accountants properly record transactions and prepare financial statements. In much the same way, managers must properly understand cost behavior in order to make wise decisions. In fact, a **Grant Thornton** Survey of 300 U.S. business leaders and senior executives reported that 79 percent of CEOs focus on understanding and managing costs in an attempt to increase company value.[1]

Costs can be variable, fixed, or mixed. Knowing how costs change as output changes is essential to planning, controlling, and decision making. For example, suppose that BlueDenim Company expects demand for its jeans product to increase by 10 percent next year. How will that affect the total costs budgeted for the factory? Clearly, Blue-Denim will need 10 percent more raw materials (denim, thread, zippers, and so on). It will also need more cutting and sewing labor because someone will need to make the additional jeans. These costs are variable. But the factory building will probably not need to be expanded. Neither will the factory need an additional receptionist or plant manager. Those costs are fixed. As long as BlueDenim's accountant understands the behavior of the fixed and variable costs, it will be possible to develop a fairly accurate budget for the next year.

Budgeting, deciding to keep or drop a product line (e.g., **Converse**'s ongoing decision to keep, drop, or alter its Dwyane Wade shoe), and evaluating the performance of a segment (e.g., **Delta Air Lines**' decision to discontinue its low-fare Song Airline business segment) all benefit from knowledge of cost behavior. In fact, failure to know and understand cost behavior can lead to poor—even disastrous—decisions. This chapter discusses cost behavior in depth so that a proper foundation is laid for its use in studying other cost management topics.

OBJECTIVE ❶

Explain the meaning of cost behavior, and define and describe fixed and variable costs.

BASICS OF COST BEHAVIOR

Cost behavior is the general term for describing whether a cost changes when the level of output changes. A cost that does not change in total as output changes is a *fixed cost*. A *variable cost*, on the other hand, increases in total with an increase in output and decreases in total with a decrease in output. Let's first review the basics of cost and output measures. Then we will look at fixed and variable costs.

Measures of Output and the Relevant Range

In order to determine the behavior of a cost, we need to have a good grasp of the cost under consideration and a measure of the output associated with the activity. The terms *fixed cost* and *variable cost* do not exist in a vacuum; they only have meaning when related to some output measure. In other words, a cost is fixed or variable with respect to some output measure or driver. In order to understand the behavior of costs, we must first determine the underlying business activity and ask "What causes the cost of this particular activity to go up (or down)?" A cost **driver** is a causal factor that measures the output of the activity that leads (or causes) costs to change. Identifying and managing drivers helps managers better predict and control costs. For instance, weather is a significant driver in the airline industry, especially when storms concentrate in the country's busiest flight corridors such as the Northeast and Midwest. One analyst estimated that a particularly snowy January through March period cost **US Airways** $30 million and **Continental Airlines** $25 million in terms of lost revenue and extra costs![2]

[1] *Grant Thornton LLP Survey of U.S. Business Leaders*, 12th Edition, 2006.
[2] Elizabeth Strott, "Snowy February Slams Airlines." (March 3, 2010): accessed March 12, 2010, from http://articles.moneycentral.msn.com/Investing/Dispatch/market-dispatches.aspx?post=1673400

Suppose that BlueDenim Company wants to classify its product costs as either variable or fixed with respect to the number of jeans produced. In this case, the number of jeans produced is the driver. Clearly, the use of raw materials (denim, thread, zippers, and buttons) varies with the number of jeans produced. So, materials costs are variable with respect to the number of units produced. How about electricity to run the sewing machines? That, too, is variable with respect to the number of jeans produced because the more jeans that are produced, the more sewing machine time is needed, and the more electricity it takes. Finally, what about the cost of supervision for the sewing department? Whether the company produces many pairs of jeans or fewer pairs of jeans, the cost of supervision is unchanged. So, we would say that supervision is fixed with respect to the number of jeans produced.

How does the relevant range fit into cost relationships? The **relevant range** is the range of output over which the assumed cost relationship is valid for the normal operations of a firm. The relevant range limits the cost relationship to the range of operations that the firm normally expects to occur. Let's consider BlueDenim's cost relationships more carefully. We said that the salary of the supervisor is strictly fixed. But is that true? If the company produced just a few pairs of jeans a year, it would not even need a supervisor. Surely the owner could handle that task (and probably a good number of other tasks as well). On the other hand, suppose that BlueDenim increased its current production by two or three times, perhaps by adding a second and third shift. One supervisor could not possibly handle all three shifts. So, when we talk about supervision cost, we are implicitly talking about it for the range of production that normally occurs. We now take a closer look at fixed, variable, and mixed costs. In each case, the cost is related to only one driver and is defined within the relevant range.

Here's the Real Kicker

Kicker uses information on cost behavior to guide new programs. For example, the variable cost of manufacturing speakers led Kicker to work with its manufacturers to both increase quality and decrease cost. Fixed costs at the **Stillwater** location also received attention. Several years ago Safety Director Terry Williams faced a problem with worker safety. Cost information based on a number of indicators revealed the problem:

- The cost of workmen's compensation insurance was high.
- The workmen's compensation experience rating was high.
- The number of injuries was up.
- The number of injuries requiring time off was up.
- The number of back injuries (the most serious type) was up.
- The average cost per injury was up.

Terry looked for the root cause of the problem and discovered that improper lifting led to the more serious back injuries. He instituted a comprehensive safety program emphasizing 20 minutes of stretching exercises each day (five minutes before work, five minutes after each break, and five minutes after lunch).

Was the program a success? At first, the workers resisted the stretching, so Terry got them weight belts. The workers hated them. They went back to stretching. But this time, any worker who refused to stretch had to wear the weight belt for 30 days. This was a highly visible sign of failure to adhere to the program. In addition, Kicker's president was a big proponent of the safety program. He explained the impact of the increased insurance premiums and lost work time on the Kicker profit-sharing program. The profit-sharing program is an important extra for Kicker employees. Each employee makes it his or her job to contribute to the bottom line whenever possible.

Over several months, workers bought into the program. The indicators decreased dramatically. The cost of workmen's compensation insurance decreased by nearly 50 percent, the average cost per injury is less than 5 percent of the presafety program cost, and there is no lost work time.

Fixed Costs

Fixed costs are costs that *in total* are constant within the relevant range as the level of output increases or decreases. For example, **Southwest Airlines** has a fleet of 737s. The cost of these planes represents a fixed cost to the airline because, within the relevant range, the cost does not change as the number of flights or the number of passengers changes. Similarly, the rental cost of warehouse space by a wholesaler is fixed for the term of the lease. If the wholesaler's sales go up or down, the cost of the leased warehouse stays the same.

To illustrate fixed cost behavior, consider a factory operated by Colley Computers Inc., a company that produces unlabeled personal computers for small computer stores across the Midwest. The assembly department of the factory assembles components into a completed personal computer. Assume that Colley Computers wants to look at the cost relationship between supervision cost and the number of computers processed and has the following information:

- The assembly department can process up to 50,000 computers per year.
- The assemblers (direct labor) are supervised by a production-line manager who is paid $32,000 per year.
- The company was established five years ago.
- Currently, the factory produces 40,000 to 50,000 computers per year.
- Production has never fallen below 20,000 computers in a year.

The cost of supervision for several levels of production is as follows:

Colley Computers Inc.
Cost of Supervision

Number of Computers Produced	Total Cost of Supervision	Unit Cost
20,000	$32,000	$1.60
30,000	32,000	1.07
40,000	32,000	0.80
50,000	32,000	0.64

The cost relationship considered is between supervision cost and the number of computers processed. The number of computers processed is called the *output measure*, or *driver*. Since Colley Computers has been processing between 20,000 and 50,000 computers per year, the relevant range is 20,000 to 50,000. Notice that the *total* cost of supervision remains constant within this range as more computers are processed. Colley Computers pays $32,000 for supervision regardless of whether it processes 20,000, 40,000, or 50,000 computers.

Pay particular attention to the words *in total* in the definition of fixed costs. While the total cost of supervision remains unchanged as more computers are processed, the unit cost does change as the level of output changes. As the example in the table shows, within the relevant range, the unit cost of supervision decreases from $1.60 to $0.64. Because of the behavior of per-unit fixed costs, it is easy to get the impression that the fixed costs themselves are affected by changes in the level of output. But that is not true. Instead, higher output means that the fixed costs can be spread over more units and are thus smaller per unit. Unit fixed costs can often be misleading and may lead to poor decisions. It is often safer to work with total fixed costs.

Let's take a look at the graph of fixed costs given in Exhibit 14-1. For the relevant range, the horizontal line indicates fixed cost behavior. Notice that at 40,000 computers processed, supervision cost is $32,000; at 50,000 computers processed, supervision is also $32,000. This line visually demonstrates that cost remains unchanged as the level of the activity driver varies. For the relevant range, total fixed costs are simply an amount. For Colley Computers, supervision cost amounted to $32,000 for any level of output between 20,000 and 50,000 computers processed. Thus, supervision is a fixed cost and can be expressed as:

$$\text{Supervision cost} = \$32,000$$

Strictly speaking, this equation assumes that the fixed costs are $32,000 for all levels (as if the line extends to the vertical axis as indicated by the dashed portion in Exhibit 14-1). Although this assumption is not true, it is harmless if the operating decisions are confined to the relevant range.

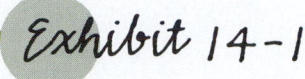

Colley Computers Fixed Cost of Supervision

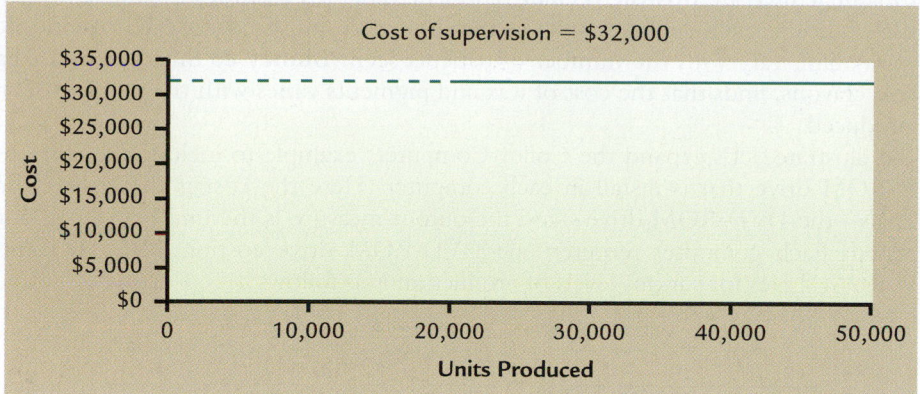

Can fixed costs change? Of course, but this possibility does not make them variable. They are fixed at a new higher (or lower) rate. Going back to Colley Computers, suppose that the company gives a raise to the assembly department supervisor. Instead of being paid $32,000 per year, the salary is $34,000 per year. The cost of supervision within the relevant range is $34,000 per year. However, supervision cost is still *fixed* with respect to the number of computers produced.

Discretionary Fixed Costs and Committed Fixed Costs By their nature, fixed costs are difficult to change quickly—that is why they are considered fixed. Two types of fixed costs are commonly recognized: discretionary fixed costs and committed fixed costs. **Discretionary fixed costs** are fixed costs that can be changed or avoided relatively easily at management discretion. For example, advertising is a discretionary fixed cost. Advertising cost depends on the decision by management to purchase print, radio, or video advertising. This cost might depend on the size of the ad or the number of times it runs, but it does *not* depend on the number of units produced and sold. Management can easily decide to increase or decrease dollars spent on advertising.

As another example, just before a new season, the **National Football League (NFL)** was forced to make a decision involving discretionary costs when they realized that **Wilson Sporting Goods** had already manufactured 500,000 footballs (of the 900,000 footballs needed for the entire season) with the signature of the outgoing NFL Commissioner—Paul Taglibue—instead of the incoming Commissioner—Roger Goodell. The NFL had to decide whether to play the entire season or only half of the season with the incoming Commissioner's signature on the balls. In the end, the NFL decided give the 500,000 existing balls away to high schools. In this case, the $250,000 additional cost to produce another 500,000 balls with the new signature is a discretionary cost because it could be changed (i.e., avoided) relatively easily.[3] The $250,000 is a discretionary cost that is entirely fixed because the NFL needed to purchase the additional footballs regardless of the number of games played (the driver for football cost).

Committed fixed costs, on the other hand, are fixed costs that cannot be easily changed. Often, committed fixed costs are those that involve a long-term contract (e.g., leasing of machinery or warehouse space) or the purchase of property, plant, and equipment. For example, a construction company may lease heavy-duty earth-moving equipment for a period of three years. The lease cost is a committed fixed cost.

Consider the cost of a wedding reception. What costs are fixed? What costs are variable? What output measure did you use in classifying the costs as fixed or variable?

Answer:
Often, the number of guests is the output measure for a wedding reception. The cost of food and drinks varies with the number of guests. The relevant range for a wedding might be the approximate size—perhaps small (less than 100 guests), medium (100–200 guests), and large (200+ guests). Within a relevant range, fixed costs might include rental of the facility, flowers, and the cake.

[3] T. Lowry, "Two-Minute Warning," *BusinessWeek* (September 4, 2006): 12.

Variable Costs

Variable costs are costs that in total vary in direct proportion to changes in output within the relevant range. The costs of producing and assembling the propeller on each boat manufactured by **Boston Whaler** represent variable costs for a manufacturer. In a dentist's office, certain supplies, such as the disposable bib used on each patient, floss, and x-ray film, vary with the number of patients seen. **Binney & Smith**, the maker of Crayola crayons, finds that the cost of wax and pigments varies with the number of crayons produced.

To illustrate, let's expand the Colley Computers example to include the cost of the DVD-ROM drive that is install in each computer. Here the cost is the cost of direct materials—the DVD-ROM drive—and the output measure is the number of computers processed. Each computer requires one DVD-ROM drive costing $40. The cost of DVD-ROM drives for various levels of production is as follows:

Colley Computers Inc.
Cost of DVD-ROM Drives

Number of Computers Produced	Total Cost of DVD-ROM Drives ($)	Unit Cost ($)
20,000	800,000	40
30,000	1,200,000	40
40,000	1,600,000	40
50,000	2,000,000	40

As more computers are produced, the total cost of DVD-ROM drives increases in direct proportion. For example, as production doubles from 20,000 to 40,000 units, the *total* cost of DVD-ROM drives doubles from $800,000 to $1,600,000. Notice also that the unit cost of direct materials is constant.

Variable costs can also be represented by a linear equation. Here, total variable costs depend on the level of output. This relationship can be described by the following equation:

$$\text{Total variable costs} = \text{Variable rate} \times \text{Amount of output}$$

The relationship that describes the cost of disk drives is:

$$\text{Total variable cost} = \$40 \times \text{Number of computers}$$

Applying this to Colley, at 50,000 computers processed, the total cost of disk drives is:

$$\$2,000,000 = \$40 \times 50,000 \text{ computers processed}$$

At 30,000 computers processed, the total cost would be $1,200,000.

Exhibit 14-2 shows graphically that variable cost behavior is represented by a straight line extending out from the origin. Notice that at zero units processed, total variable cost

Colley Computers Variable Cost of DVD-ROM Drives

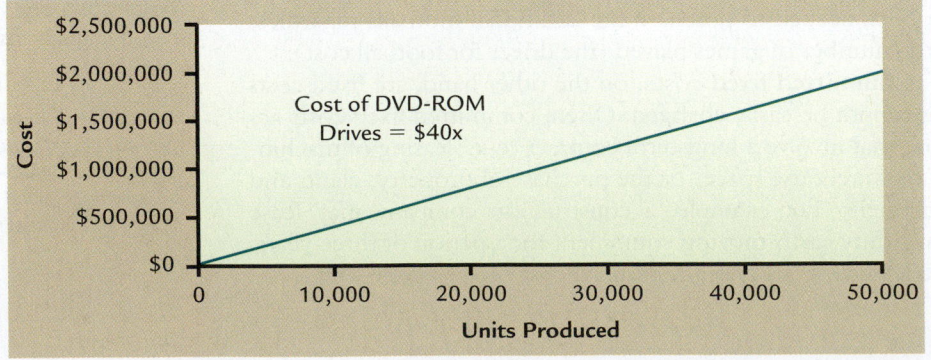

Semi-Variable Cost

Exhibit 14-3

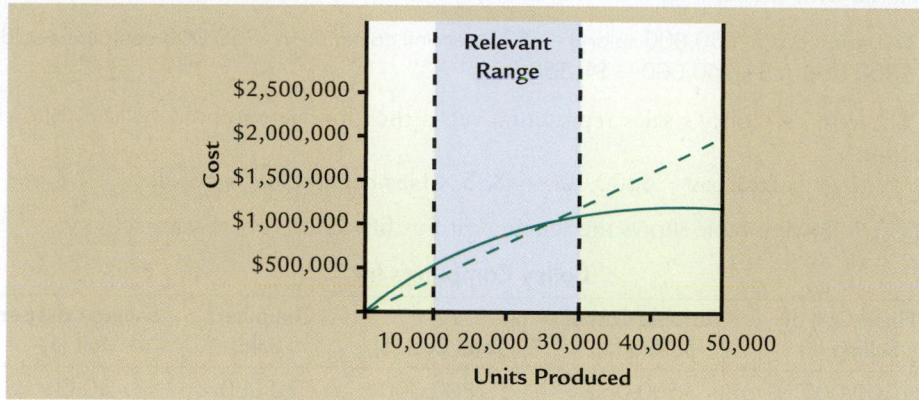

is zero. However, as units produced increase, the total variable cost also increases. Total cost increases in direct proportion to increases in the number of computers processed; the rate of increase is measured by the slope of the line.

The Reasonableness of Straight-Line Cost Relationships

The graphs of fixed and variable costs that were just reviewed show cost relationships that are straight lines. Are real-world cost relationships linear?

For Colley Computers, the DVD-ROM drives cost $40 each—no matter how many were purchased. However, if only a few drives were bought, the per-unit cost would be likely higher. So, there are economies of scale in producing larger quantities of output. For example, at extremely low levels of output workers often use more materials per unit or require more time per unit than they do at higher levels of output. Then, as the level of output increases, workers learn how to use materials and time more efficiently so that the variable cost per unit decreases as more and more output is produced. Therefore, when economies of scale are present, the true total cost function is increasing at a decreasing rate, as shown by the nonlinear cost curve in Exhibit 14-3. Some managers refer to this type of cost behavior as **semi-variable**.

When unit costs change in this way, how do we choose the correct variable rate? Fortunately, the relevant range can help. Recall that *relevant range* is defined as the range of activity for which the assumed cost relationships are valid. Exhibit 14-3 shows how the relevant range can be used to see how well a straight line approximates variable cost. Note that for units of output before 20,000 on the x-axis, the approximation appears to break down. Therefore, managers must be extremely careful in applying cost behavior assumptions to decision making whenever the output level falls outside of the company's relevant range of operations.

MIXED COSTS AND STEP COSTS

While strictly fixed and variable costs are easy to handle, many costs do not fall into those categories. Often, costs are a combination of fixed and variable costs (mixed costs) or have an increased fixed component at specified intervals (step costs).

OBJECTIVE ❷
Define and describe mixed and step costs.

Mixed Costs

Mixed costs are costs that have both a fixed and a variable component. For example, sales representatives are often paid a salary plus a commission on sales. The formula for a mixed cost is as follows:

Total cost = Total fixed cost + Total variable cost

Suppose that Colley Computers has 10 sales representatives, each earning a salary of $30,000 per year plus a commission of $25 per computer sold. The activity is selling, and the output measure is units sold. If 50,000 computers are sold, then the total cost associated with the sales representatives is:

$$= (10 \text{ sales reps} \times \$30,000 \text{ salary}) + (\$25 \text{ per unit commission} \times 50,000 \text{ computers sold})$$
$$= \$300,000 + \$1,250,000 = \$1,550,000$$

The cost of Colley's sales representatives is therefore represented by the following equation:

$$\text{Total cost} = \$300,000 + (\$25 \times \text{Number of computers sold})$$

The following table shows the selling cost for different levels of sales activity:

Colley Computers Inc.

Fixed Cost of Selling ($)	Variable Cost of Selling ($)	Total Cost ($)	Computers Sold	Selling Cost per Unit ($)
300,000	500,000	800,000	20,000	40.00
300,000	750,000	1,050,000	30,000	35.00
300,000	1,000,000	1,300,000	40,000	32.50
300,000	1,250,000	1,550,000	50,000	31.00

The graph for our mixed cost example is given in Exhibit 14-4 (assuming a relevant range of 0 to 50,000 units). Costs are represented in the following ways:

- Mixed costs are represented by a line that intercepts the vertical axis (at $300,000 for this example)
- Fixed costs correspond with the y-intercept
- Variable cost per unit of activity driver is given by the slope of the line ($25 for this example)

Step Cost Behavior

So far, we have assumed that the cost function is continuous. In reality, some cost functions may be discontinuous. These costs are known as *step costs* (or semi-fixed). A **step cost** displays a constant level of cost for a range of output and then jumps to a higher level (or step) of cost at some point, where it remains for a similar range of output. The width of the step defines the range of output for which a particular amount of the resource applies.

Recall the **Zingerman's** deli example at the beginning of the chapter. Zingerman's experiences significant increases in its sales volume during the Christmas holiday season. Because the extra sales demand is temporary, management chooses not to purchase additional freezers, which would permanently increase its fixed costs year-round. Instead,

Exhibit 14-4

Mixed Cost Behavior

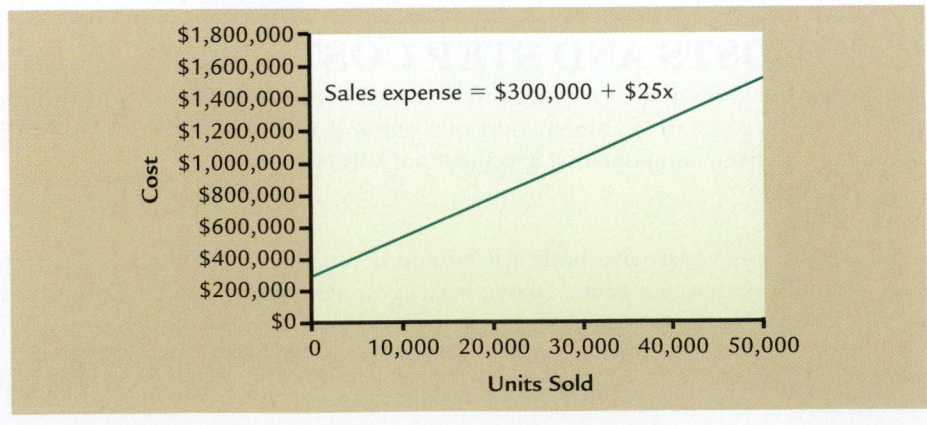

Step Costs: Narrow Steps and Wide Steps

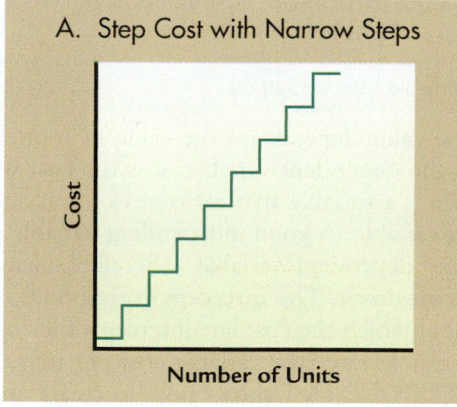

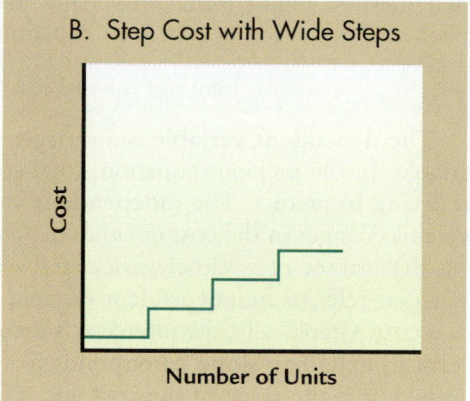

management rents the necessary number of freezer trucks to accommodate its temporary requirements. Renting freezer trucks on an "as needed" basis is an innovative decision for managing Zingerman's fixed costs as they temporarily step up during the holiday season.

Exhibit 14-5 illustrates step costs. Graph A shows a step cost with relatively narrow steps. These narrow steps mean that the cost changes in response to fairly small changes in output. Often, if the steps are very narrow, we can approximate the step cost as a strictly variable cost. For example, Copy-2-Go, a photocopying shop, buys copy paper by the 20-ream box. The shop typically uses three boxes per day. The cost of copy paper is a step cost with very narrow steps. Graph B, however, shows a step cost with relatively wide steps. An example of this type of cost is a factory that leases production machinery. Suppose that each machine can produce 1,000 units per month. If production ranges from 0 to 1,000 units, only one machine is needed. However, if production increases to amounts between 1,001 and 2,000 units, a second machine must be leased. Many so-called fixed costs may be, in reality, step costs.

Accounting Records and Need for Cost Separation

Sometimes it is easy to identify the variable and fixed components of a mixed cost, as in the example given earlier for Colley Computers' sales representatives. Many times, however, the only information available is the total cost and a measure of output. For example, the accounting system will usually record both the total cost of maintenance and the number of maintenance hours provided during a given period of time. How much of the total maintenance cost represents a fixed cost and how much represents a variable cost is not revealed by the accounting records. (In fact, the accounting records may not even reveal the breakdown of costs in the sales representative example.)

Therefore, it is necessary to separate the total cost into its fixed and variable components. Only through a formal effort to separate costs can all costs be classified into the appropriate cost behavior categories.

If mixed costs are a very small percentage of total costs, formal cost separation may be more trouble than it's worth. In this case, mixed costs could be assigned to either the fixed or variable cost category without much concern for the classification error or its effect on decision making. Alternatively, the total mixed cost could be arbitrarily divided between the two cost categories. However, this option is seldom available. Mixed costs for many firms are large enough to call for separation.

METHODS FOR SEPARATING MIXED COSTS INTO FIXED AND VARIABLE COMPONENTS

Three methods of separating a mixed cost into its fixed and variable components are commonly used:

OBJECTIVE
Separate mixed costs into their fixed and variable components using the high-low method, the scattergraph method, and the method of least squares.

- the high-low method
- the scattergraph method
- the method of least squares

Each method requires the simplifying assumption of a linear cost relationship. Let's review the expression of cost as an equation for a straight line.

> Total cost = Fixed cost + (Variable rate × Output)

The **dependent variable** is a variable whose value depends on the value of another variable. In the previous equation, total cost is the dependent variable; it is the cost we are trying to predict. The **independent variable** is a variable that measures output and explains changes in the cost or other dependent variable. A good independent variable is one that causes or is closely associated with the dependent variable. Therefore, many managers refer to an independent variable as a cost driver. The **intercept** corresponds to fixed cost. Graphically, the intercept is the point at which the cost line intercepts the cost (vertical) axis. The **slope** corresponds to the variable rate (the variable cost per unit of output); it is the slope of the cost line. **CORNERSTONE 14-1** shows how to create and use a cost formula.

 **CORNERSTONE 14-1**   **Creating and Using a Cost Formula**

Information:
The art and graphics department of State College decided to equip each faculty office with an inkjet color printer (computers were already in place). Sufficient color printers had monthly depreciation of $250. The department purchased paper in boxes of 10,000 sheets (20 reams of 500 sheets each) for $35 per box. Ink cartridges cost $30 and will print, on average, 300 pages.

Required:
1. Create a formula for the monthly cost of inkjet printing in the department.
2. If the department expects to print 4,400 pages next month, what is the expected total fixed cost? Total variable cost? Total printing cost?

Solution:
1. The cost formula takes the following form:

   > Total cost = Fixed cost + (Variable rate × Number of pages)

   The monthly fixed cost is $250 (the cost of printer depreciation), as it does not vary according to the number of pages printed. The variable costs are paper and ink, as both vary with the number of pages printed.

   Cost of paper per page is $35/10,000 = $0.0035
   Cost of ink per page is $30/300 = $0.10

   Variable rate per page is $0.0035 + $0.10 = $0.1035

   The cost formula is:

   > Total cost of printing = $250 + ($0.1035 × Number of pages)

2. Expected fixed cost for next month is $250.

   Expected variable cost for next month is $0.1035 × 4,400 pages = $455.40
   Expected total printing cost for next month is $250 + $455.40 = $705.40

Since the accounting records reveal only total cost and output, those values must be used to estimate the fixed cost and variable rate. To do so, we'll illustrate the high-low method, the scattergraph method, and the method of least squares (i.e., regression) with the following example. The same data will be used with each method so that comparisons among them can be made. The example focuses on materials handling cost for Anderson Company, a manufacturer of household cleaning products. Materials handling involves moving materials from one area of the factory, say the raw materials storeroom, to another area, such as Workstation 6. Large, complex organizations have found that the cost of moving materials can be quite large. Understanding the behavior of this cost is an important part of deciding how to reduce the cost.

Anderson's controller has accumulated data for the materials handling activity. The plant manager believes that the number of material moves is a good activity driver for the activity. Assume that the accounting records of Anderson Company disclose the following material handling costs and number of material moves for the past 10 months:

Month	Material Handling Cost	Number of Moves
January	$2,000	100
February	3,090	125
March	2,780	175
April	1,990	200
May	7,500	500
June	5,300	300
July	3,800	250
August	6,300	400
September	5,600	475
October	6,240	425

The High-Low Method

From basic geometry, we know that two points are needed to determine a line. Once we know the two points on a line, then its equation can be determined. Recall that the fixed cost is the *intercept* of the total cost line and that the variable rate is the *slope* of the line. Given two points, the slope and the intercept can be determined. The **high-low method** is a method of separating mixed costs into fixed and variable components by using just the high and low data points. Four steps must be taken in the high-low method.

Step 1: Find the high point and the low point for a given data set. The *high point* is defined as the point with the *highest activity* or *output level*. The *low point* is defined as the point with the *lowest activity* or *output level*. It is important to note that the high and low points are identified by looking at the activity levels and not the costs. In some cases the highest (or lowest) activity level might also be associated with the highest (or lowest) cost, whereas in other cases it is not. Therefore, regardless of cost, the managerial accountant must be careful to use the activity level in identifying the high and low data points for the analysis. In the data for maintenance cost, the high output occurred in May, with 500 material moves and total cost of $7,500. The low output was in January with 100 material moves and total cost of $2,000.

Step 2: Using the high and low points, calculate the variable rate. To perform this calculation, we recognize that the variable rate, or slope, is the change in the total cost divided by the change in output.

$$\text{Variable rate} = \frac{\text{High point cost} - \text{Low point cost}}{\text{High point output} - \text{Low point output}}$$

Using the high and low points for our example, the variable rate would be as follows:

$$\text{Variable rate} = \frac{\$7,500 - \$2,000}{500 - 100} = \frac{\$5,500}{400} = \$13.75$$

Step 3: Calculate the fixed cost using the variable rate (from Step 2) and either the high point or low point.

Fixed cost = Total cost at high point − (Variable rate × Output at high point)

OR

Fixed cost = Total cost at low point − (Variable rate × Output at low point)

Let's use the high point to calculate fixed cost.

Fixed cost = $7,500 − ($13.75 × 500) = $625

Step 4: Form the cost formula for materials handling based on the high-low method.

Total cost = $625 + ($13.75 × Number of moves)

CORNERSTONE 14-2 shows how to use the high-low method to construct a cost formula.

CORNERSTONE 14-2

Using the High-Low Method to Calculate Fixed Cost and the Variable Rate and to Construct a Cost Formula

Information:
BlueDenim Company makes blue jeans. The company controller wants to calculate the fixed and variable costs associated with electricity used in the factory. Data for the past eight months were collected:

Month	Electricity Cost	Machine Hours
January	$3,255	460
February	3,485	500
March	4,100	600
April	3,300	470
May	3,312	470
June	2,575	350
July	3,910	570
August	4,200	590

Required:
Using the high-low method, calculate the fixed cost of electricity, calculate the variable rate per machine hour, and construct the cost formula for total electricity cost.

Solution:
Step 1: Find the high and low points: The high number of machine hours is in March, and the low number of machine hours is in June. (*Hint:* Did you notice that the high cost of $4,200 was for August? Yet August is not the high point because its number of machine hours is not the highest activity level. Remember, the high point is associated with the highest activity level; the low point is associated with the lowest activity level.)

Step 2: Calculate the variable rate:

Variable rate = (High cost − Low cost)/(High machine hours − Low machine hours)
= ($4,100 − $2,575)/(600 − 350) = $1,525/250
= $6.10 per machine hour

Step 3: Calculate the fixed cost:

Fixed cost = Total cost − (Variable rate × Machine hours)

Let's choose the high point with cost of $4,100 and machine hours of 600.

Fixed cost = $4,100 − ($6.10 × 600) = $4,100 − $3,660 = $440

(Continued)

**CORNERSTONE
14-2**
(continued)

(*Hint:* Check your work by computing fixed cost using the low point.)

Step 4: *Construct a cost formula*: If the variable rate is $6.10 per machine hour and fixed cost is $440 per month, then the formula for monthly electricity cost is:

$$\text{Total electricity cost} = \$440 + (\$6.10 \times \text{Machine hours})$$

Once we have the cost formula, we can use it in budgeting and in performance control. As we determined earlier, the cost formula for materials handling based on the high-low method is:

$$\text{Total cost} = \$625 + (\$13.75 \times \text{Number of moves})$$

Suppose that the number of moves for November is expected to be 350. Budgeted materials handling cost would be:

$$\$5,437.50 = \$625 + (\$13.75 \times 350)$$

Alternatively, suppose that the controller wondered whether October's materials handling cost of $6,240 was reasonably close to what would have been predicted. Our cost formula would predict October's cost of:

$$\$6,469 \text{ (rounded)} = \$625 + (\$13.75 \times 425)$$

The actual cost is just $229 different from the predicted cost and probably would be judged to be reasonably close to the budgeted cost. **CORNERSTONE 14-3** shows how to use the high-low method to calculate predicted total variable cost and total cost for budgeted output.

**CORNERSTONE
14-3**

Using the High-Low Method to Calculate Predicted Total Variable Cost and Total Cost for Budgeted Output

Information:
Recall that BlueDenim Company constructed the following formula for monthly electricity cost. (Refer to Cornerstone 14-2 to see how the fixed cost per month and the variable rate were computed.)

$$\text{Total electricity cost} = \$440 + (\$6.10 \times \text{Machine hours})$$

Required:
Assume that 550 machine hours are budgeted for the month of October. Use the previous cost formula to calculate (1) total variable electricity cost for October and (2) total electricity cost for October.

Solution:
1. Total variable electricity cost = Variable rate × Machine hours
    = $6.10 × 550
    = $3,355

2. Total electricity cost = Fixed cost + (Variable rate × Machine hours)
    = $440 + ($6.10 × 550)
    = $440 + $3,355
    = $3,795

Let's look at one last point. Notice that monthly data were used to find the high and low points and to calculate the fixed cost and variable rate. This means that the cost formula is the fixed cost *for the month*. Suppose, however, that the company wants to use that formula to predict cost for a different period of time, say a year. In that case, the variable cost rate is just multiplied by the budgeted amount of the independent variable for the year. The intercept, or fixed cost, must be adjusted. To convert monthly fixed cost to yearly fixed cost, simply multiply the monthly fixed cost by 12 (because there are 12 months in a year). If weekly data were used to calculate the fixed and variable costs, one would multiply the weekly fixed cost by 52 to convert it to yearly fixed cost, and so on. **CORNERSTONE 14-4** shows how to use the high-low method to calculate predicted total variable cost and total cost for budgeted output in which the time period differs from the data period.

CORNERSTONE 14-4

Using the High-Low Method to Calculate Predicted Total Variable Cost and Total Cost for a Time Period that Differs from the Data Period

Information:

Recall that BlueDenim Company constructed the following formula for *monthly* electricity cost. (Refer to Cornerstone 14-2 (p. 722) to see how the fixed cost per month and variable rate were computed.)

$$\text{Total electricity cost} = \$440 + (\$6.10 \times \text{Machine hours})$$

Required:

Assume that 6,500 machine hours are budgeted for the coming year. Use the previous cost formula to calculate (1) total variable electricity cost for the year, (2) total fixed electricity cost for the year, and (3) total electricity cost for the coming year.

Solution:

1. Total variable electricity cost = Variable rate × Machine hours
    $$= \$6.10 \times 6,500$$
    $$= \$39,650$$

2. *Note:* The cost formula is for the month, but we need to budget electricity for the year. Thus, we need to multiply the fixed cost for the month by 12 (the number of months in a year).

    Total fixed electricity cost = Fixed cost × 12 months in a year
    $$= \$440 \times 12$$
    $$= \$5,280$$

3. Total electricity cost = 12($440) + ($6.10 × 6,500)
    $$= \$5,280 + \$39,650$$
    $$= \$44,930$$

The high-low method has several important advantages, including the following:

- **Objectivity:** Any two people using the high-low method on a particular data set will arrive at the same answer.
- **Quick overview:** The high-low method allows a manager to get a quick fix on a cost relationship by using only two data points. For example, a manager may have only two months of data. Sometimes this will be enough to get a crude approximation of the cost relationship.
- **Ease of use:** The high-low method is simple, inexpensive, and easily communicated to other individuals, even those who are not comfortable with numerical analyses.

For these reasons, managerial accountants use the high-low method.

However, the high-low method also has several disadvantages that lead some managers to believe that it is not as good as the other methods at separating mixed costs into fixed and variable components.

- **Occurrence of outliers:** The high and low points often can be what are known as outliers. They may represent atypical cost-activity relationships. For instance, if in the Anderson Company example the high output had been 1,000 moves (rather than 500) due to some extremely unusual business activity during a given month, then this high point likely would have fallen outside of the company's relevant range of operations. It would, therefore, represented an outlier. In the case of outliers, the cost formula computed using these two points will not represent what usually takes place. The scattergraph method can help a manager avoid this trap by selecting two points that appear to be representative of the general cost-activity pattern.
- **Potential for misrepresentative data:** Even if the high and low points are not outliers, other pairs of points may be more representative. To stress the likelihood of this possibility, a high-low analysis of 50 weeks of data would ignore 96 percent (i.e., 48 out of the 50 weeks) of the data! Again, the scattergraph method allows the choice of more representative points.

Scattergraph Method

The **scattergraph method** is a way to see the cost relationship by plotting the data points on a graph. The first step in applying the scattergraph method is to plot the data points so that the relationship between materials handling costs and activity output can be seen. This plot is referred to as a scattergraph and is shown in Exhibit 14-6. The vertical axis is total cost (materials handling cost), and the horizontal axis is the driver or output measure (number of moves).

Looking at Graph A, we see that the relationship between materials handling costs and number of moves is reasonably linear. Cost goes up as the number of moves goes up and vice versa.

Now let's examine Graph B to see if the line determined by the high and low points is representative of the overall relationship. Notice that three points lie above the high-low line and five lie below it. This does not give us confidence in the high-low results for fixed and variable costs. In particular, we might wonder if the variable cost (slope) is somewhat higher than it should be and the fixed cost is somewhat lower than it should be.

Thus, one purpose of a scattergraph is to see whether or not a straight line reasonably describes the cost relationship. Additionally, inspecting the scattergraph may reveal one or more points that do not seem to fit the general pattern of behavior. Upon investigation, it may be discovered that these points (the outliers) were due to some irregular

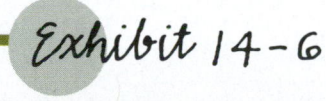

Anderson Company's Materials Handling Cost

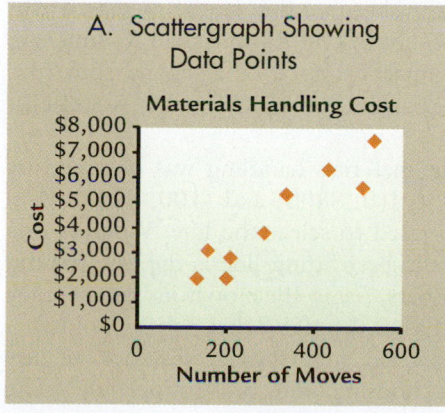

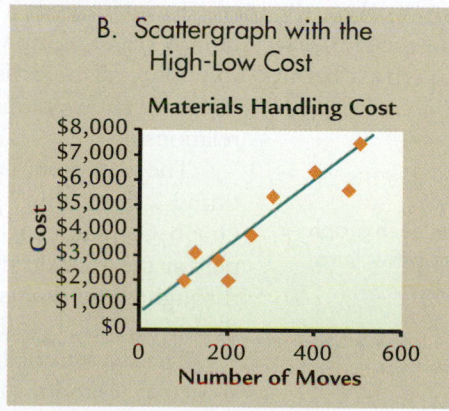

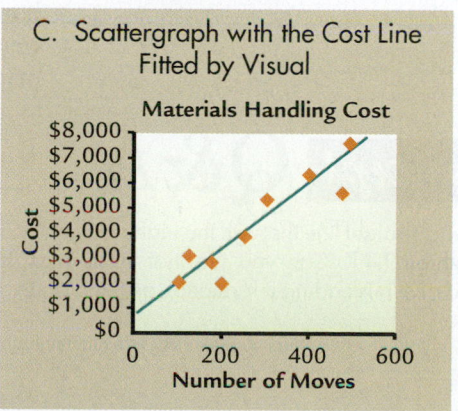

occurrences that are not expected to happen again. This knowledge might justify their elimination and perhaps lead to a better estimate of the underlying cost function.

We can use the scattergraph to visually fit a line to the data points on the graph. Of course, the manager or cost analyst will choose the line that appears to fit the points the best, and perhaps that choice will take into account past experience with the behavior of the cost item. Experience may provide a good intuitive sense of how materials handling costs behave. The scattergraph then becomes a useful tool to quantify this intuition. Fitting a line to the points in this way is how the scattergraph method works. Keep in mind that the scattergraph and other statistical aids are tools that can help managers improve their judgment. Using the tools does not restrict the manager from using judgment to alter any of the estimates produced by formal methods.

Examine Graph A carefully. Based only on the information contained in the graph, how would you fit a line to the points in it? Of course, an infinite number of lines might go through the data, but let's choose one that goes through the point for January (100, $2,000) and intersects the y-axis at $800. This gives us the straight line shown in Graph C. The fixed cost, of course, is $800, the intercept. We can use the high-low method to determine the variable rate.

First, remember that our two points are (100, $2,000) and (0, $800). Next, use these two points to compute the variable rate (the slope):

$$\text{Variable rate} = \frac{\text{High point cost} - \text{Low point cost}}{\text{High point number of moves} - \text{Low point number of moves}}$$

$$= \frac{\$2,000 - \$800}{100 - 0}$$
$$= \$1,200/100$$
$$= \$12$$

Thus, the variable rate is $12 per material move.

The fixed cost and variable rate for materials handling cost have now been identified. The cost formula for the materials handling activity can be expressed as:

$$\text{Total cost} = \$800 + \$12 \times \text{Number of moves}$$

Using this formula, the total cost of materials handling for between 100 and 500 moves can be predicted and then broken down into fixed and variable components. For example, assume that 350 moves are planned for November. Using the cost formula, the predicted cost is:

$$\$5,000 = \$800 + (\$12 \times 350)$$

Of this total cost, $800 is fixed, and $4,200 is variable.

A significant advantage of the scattergraph method is that it allows a cost analyst to inspect the data visually. Exhibit 14-7 illustrates cost behavior situations that are not appropriate for the simple application of the high-low method. Graph A shows a nonlinear relationship between cost and output. An example of this type of relationship is a volume discount given on direct materials or evidence of learning by workers (e.g., as more hours are worked, the total cost increases at a decreasing rate due to the increased efficiency of the workers). Graph B shows an upward shift in cost if more than X_1 units are made—perhaps because an additional supervisor must be hired or a second shift run. Graph C shows outliers that do not represent the overall cost relationship.

The cost formula for materials handling was obtained by fitting a line to two points [(0, $800) and (100, $2,000)] in Graph C. Judgment was used to select the line. Whereas one person may decide that the best-fitting line is the one passing through those points, others, using their own judgment, may decide that the best line passes through other pairs of points.

The scattergraph method suffers from the lack of any objective criterion for choosing the best-fitting line. The

Concept Q&A

Draw a straight line through the high and low points on each graph in Exhibit 14-7. Can you see that these lines, the high-low lines, could give misleading information on fixed and variable costs?

Exhibit 14-7

Scattergraphs with Nonlinear Cost

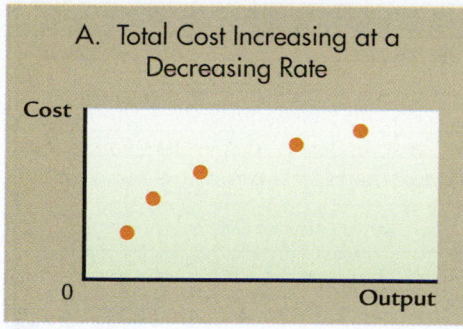

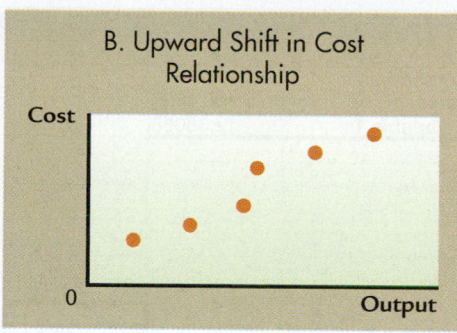

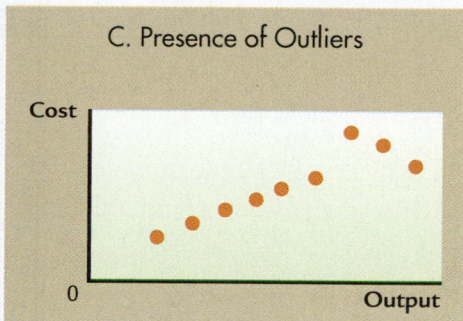

quality of the cost formula depends on the quality of the subjective judgment of the analyst. The high-low method removes the subjectivity in the choice of the line. Regardless of who uses the method, the same line will result.

Looking again at Graphs B and C in Exhibit 14-6 (p. 725), we can compare the results of the scattergraph method with those of the high-low method. There is a difference between the fixed cost components and the variable rates. The predicted materials handling cost for 350 moves is $5,000 according to the scattergraph method and $5,438 according to the high-low method. Which is correct? Since the two methods can produce significantly different cost formulas, the question of which method is the best arises. Ideally, a method that is objective and, at the same time, produces the best-fitting line is needed.

The Method of Least Squares

The **method of least squares (regression)** is a statistical way to find the *best-fitting* line through a set of data points. One advantage of the method of least squares is that for a given set of data, it will always produce the same cost formula. Basically, the best-fitting line is the one in which the data points are closer to the line than to any other line. What do we mean by closest? Let's take a look at Exhibit 14-8. Notice that there are a series of data points and a line—we'll assume that it is the regression line calculated by the method of least squares. The data points do not all lie directly on the line; this is typical. However, the regression line better describes the pattern of the data than other possible lines. This best description results because the squared deviations

Exhibit 14-8

Line Deviations

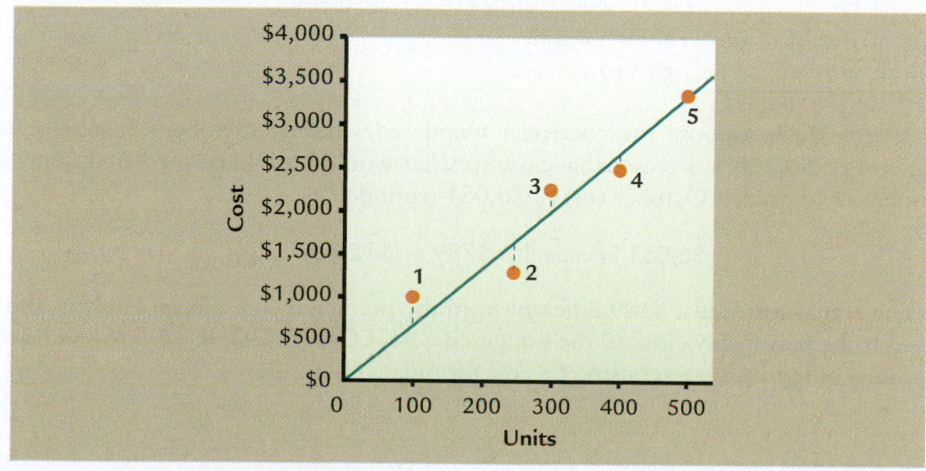

Exhibit 14-9

A Portion of the Summary Output from Excel for Anderson Company

	A	B	C	D	E	F	G	H
1	Coefficients:							
2	Intercept	788.7806						
3	X Variable 1	12.38058						
4								
5								
6								
7								
8								
9								
10								
11								
12								
13								
14								
15								

Anderson Company.xls — Sheet1 / Sheet2 / Sheet3

between the regression line and each data point are, in total, smaller than the sum of the squared deviations of the data points and any other line. The least squares statistical formulas can find the one line with the smallest sum of squared deviations. In other words, this method identifies the regression line that minimizes the cost prediction errors or differences between predicted costs (i.e., on the regression line) and actual costs (i.e., the actual data points). Given that the method of least squares generates the smallest possible cost prediction errors, many managers refer to it as the most accurate method.

Formerly, the method of least squares had to be calculated by hand. It was a complicated and lengthy process. Today, spreadsheet programs for personal computers have regression packages. It is easy to use them to input data and to let the programs calculate the fixed cost and variable rate.[4] Exhibit 14-9 shows a printout from a Microsoft Excel® spreadsheet regression that was run on the data from Anderson Company. Notice that the intercept term is the fixed cost, which is $789 (rounded). The variable rate is shown as "X Variable 1." In other words, it is the first independent variable. So, the variable rate is $12.38 (rounded). We can use the output of regression in budgeting and control the same way that we used the results of the high-low and scattergraph methods.

Suppose that Anderson Company expects the number of moves for November to be 350. Budgeted materials handling cost would be:

$$\text{Total cost} = \text{Fixed cost} + (\text{Variable rate} \times \text{Output})$$
$$= \$789 \text{ (rounded)} + [\$12.38 \text{ (rounded)} \times 350 \text{ moves}]$$
$$= \$789 + 4{,}333$$
$$= \$5{,}122$$

Alternatively, suppose the controller wondered whether October's materials handling cost of $6,240 was reasonably close to what would have been predicted. Our cost formula would predict October cost of $6,051 (rounded):

$$\$6{,}051 \text{ (rounded)} = \$789 + (\$12.38 \times 425)$$

The actual cost is just $189 different from the predicted cost and probably would be judged to be reasonably close to the budgeted cost. **CORNERSTONE 14-5** shows how to use results of regression to construct a cost formula.

---

[4] See Appendix 14A at the end of this chapter for more information on how to use regression programs in Excel.

CORNERSTONE 14-5

Using the Regression Method to Calculate Fixed Cost and the Variable Rate and to Construct a Cost Formula and to Determine Budgeted Cost

Information:

BlueDenim Company makes blue jeans. The company controller wanted to calculate the fixed and variable costs associated with electricity used in the factory. Data for the past eight months were collected:

Month	Electricity Cost	Machine Hours
January	$3,255	460
February	3,485	500
March	4,100	600
April	3,300	470
May	3,312	470
June	2,575	350
July	3,910	570
August	4,200	590

Coefficients shown by a regression program are:

Intercept	321
X Variable 1	6.38

Required:

Use the results of regression to perform the following:

1. Calculate the fixed cost of electricity and the variable rate per machine hour.
2. Construct the cost formula for total electricity cost.
3. Calculate the budgeted cost for next month, assuming that 550 machine hours are budgeted.

Solution:

1. The fixed cost and the variable rate are given directly by regression.

$$\text{Fixed cost} = \$321$$
$$\text{Variable rate} = \$6.38$$

2. The cost formula is:

Total electricity cost = $321 + ($6.38 × Machine hours)

3. Budgeted electricity cost = $321 + ($6.38 × 550) = $3,830

Comparison of Methods

Knowing how costs change in relation to changes in output is essential to planning, controlling, and decision making. Each of the methods for separating mixed costs into fixed and variable components help managers understand cost behavior and consequently make good business decisions. Exhibit 14-10 (p. 730) provides an overview of each of these methods, along with the advantages and disadvantages of each.

Managerial Judgment

Managerial judgment is critically important in determining cost behavior and is by far the most widely used method in practice. Many managers simply use their experience and past observation of cost relationships to determine fixed and variable costs. This method, however, may take a number of forms. Some managers simply assign some costs to the fixed

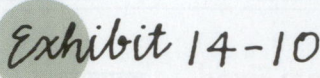

Exhibit 14-10

Overview of Methods for Separating Mixed Costs into Fixed and Variable Components

Method	Overview	Advantages	Disadvantages
High-low method	A method for separating mixed costs into fixed and variable components by using just the low and high data points	• Objective • Quick • Simple • Inexpensive • Easily communicated to others	• Occurrence of outliers • Potential for misrepresentative data
Scattergraph method	A method for separating mixed costs into fixed and variable components by fitting a line to a set of data using two points that are selected by judgment	• Simple • Visual representation of the data	• Subjective (choosing the best-fitting line)
Method of least squares (regression)	A method for separating mixed costs into fixed and variable components by statistically finding the best-fitting line through a set of data points	• Objective • Regression packages can quickly and easily calculate the fixed cost and variable rate	• Complicated, lengthy process if done by hand

category and others to the variable category. They ignore the possibility of mixed costs. Thus, a chemical firm may regard materials and utilities as strictly variable, with respect to pounds of chemical produced, and all other costs as fixed. Even labor, the textbook example of a strictly variable cost, may be fixed for this firm. The appeal of using a managerial judgment method is simplicity. Before opting for this method, management would do well to make sure that each cost is predominantly fixed or variable and that the decisions being made are not highly sensitive to errors in classifying costs as fixed or variable.

To illustrate the use of judgment in assessing cost behavior, consider companies like **Honda** that use large quantities of manufacturing labor hours in China. Some companies might assume that hourly manufacturing labor cost is strictly variable and, therefore, not worthy of careful cost analysis. However, as workers in China begin to demand significantly higher wages and more lucrative labor deals, some resulting labor costs might (1) increase significantly in amount and (2) change their behavior pattern to become more similar to other countries in which labor unions can guarantee that workers receive certain wages even when manufacturing levels fall dramatically (i.e., labor becomes a mixed, semi-fixed, or even fixed cost).[5] Or more specifically, consider **Elgin Sweeper Company**, a leading manufacturer of motorized street sweepers. Using production volume as the measure of activity output, Elgin revised its chart of accounts to organize costs into fixed and variable components. Elgin's accountants used their knowledge of the company to assign expenses to either a fixed or variable category, using a decision rule that categorized an expense as fixed if it were fixed 75 percent of the time and as variable if it were variable 75 percent of the time.[6]

Management may instead identify mixed costs and divide these costs into fixed and variable components by deciding what the fixed and variable parts are. That is, they may use

Concept Q&A

Suppose that you own a small business with a photocopier that a neighboring business owner asks to use occasionally. What is the average cost of copying one page? What cost items would you include? Now consider **Kinko's**: What cost items do you think that it would include?

Answer:

If a neighboring business owner only needed a copy rarely, you might consider it a favor and not charge at all. If it happened several times a month, you might charge the variable cost of paper and toner. Finally, if the neighboring business owner used your copier frequently, you might charge 10¢ to 20¢ per page—a price similar to that of an outside photocopying shop. Alternatively, the neighbor might buy you a ream a paper from time to time. **Kinko's** must include all costs in determining the cost of copies, including paper, toner, depreciation on equipment, cost of electricity and utilities, wages of staff, and so on.

5 Courtney Rubin. "In China, the Cost of Doing Business Rises: Recent Wage Hikes Combined with Rising Prices Mean China Isn't as Cheap an Option as It Once Was" (June 8, 2010): http://www.inc.com/news/articles/2010/06/rising-cost-of-business-in-china.html (accessed on July 12, 2010).

6 John P. Callan, Wesley N. Tredup, and Randy S. Wissinger, "Elgin Sweeper Company's Journey Toward Cost Management," *Management Accounting* (July 1991): 24–27.

experience to say that a certain amount of a cost is fixed and that the rest therefore must be variable. Suppose that a small business had a photocopier with a fixed cost of $3,000 per year. The variable component could be computed by using one or more cost/volume data points. This approach has the advantage of accounting for mixed costs but is subject to a similar type of error as the strict fixed/variable dichotomy. That is, management may be wrong in its assessment.

Finally, management may use experience and judgment to refine statistical estimation results. Perhaps the experienced manager might "eyeball" the data and throw out several points as being highly unusual or revise the results of estimation account for projected changes in cost structure or technology. For example, **Tecnol Medical Products Inc.** radically changed its method of manufacturing medical face masks. Traditionally, face-mask production was labor intensive, requiring hand stitching. Tecnol developed its own highly automated equipment and became the industry's low cost supplier—beating both **Johnson & Johnson** and **3M**. Tecnol's rapid expansion into new product lines and European markets means that historical data on costs and revenues are for the most part irrelevant. Tecnol's management must look forward, not back, to predict the impact of changes on profit.[7] Statistical techniques are highly accurate in depicting the past, but they cannot foresee the future, which, of course, is what management really wants.

The advantage of using managerial judgment to separate fixed and variable costs is its simplicity. In situations in which the manager has a deep understanding of the firm and its cost patterns, this method can give good results. However, if the manager does not have good judgment, errors will occur. Therefore, it is important to consider the experience of the manager, the potential for error, and the effect that error could have on related decisions.

ETHICAL DECISIONS   There are ethical implications to the use of managerial judgment. Managers use their knowledge of fixed and variable costs to make important decisions, such as whether to switch suppliers, expand or contract production, or lay off workers. These decisions affect the lives of workers, suppliers, and customers. Ethical managers will make sure that they have the best information possible when making these decisions. In addition, managers will not let personal factors affect the use of cost information. For example, suppose that the purchasing department manager has a good friend who wants to supply some materials for production. The price of the friend's materials is slightly lower than that of the current supplier. However, the friend's company will not ensure 100 percent quality control—and that will lead to additional costs for rework and warranty repair. The ethical manager will include these additional costs along with the purchase price to calculate the full cost of purchasing from the friend's company. ●

YOU◆DECIDE   Choosing a Cost Estimation Method

Assume that you work as a financial analyst for **Royal Caribbean Cruises Ltd.** The company operates some of the world's biggest cruise ships, such as The Allure of the Seas, which weighs 222,000 tons and carries 5,400 guests, as well as 1,650 crew members. As an internal financial analyst, one of your most important tasks is to estimate the costs that Royal will incur on the many cruises it offers to customers each year. The accuracy with which you predict Royal's most important cruise-related costs will affect many of the strategic and operating decisions made by management. You are familiar with several common cost estimation methods, including scattergraph, high-low, and regression. However, you also are aware that each method has its advantages and disadvantages.

Which cost estimation method should you employ?

If the scattergraph method were used, the analysis would be quite easy as you could employ Excel to quickly create a plot of the important costs against various potential cost drivers. However, this method does not involve quantitative analysis, which some individuals believe is a significant weakness. If the high-low method were adopted, the analysis would be quantitative in nature and relatively easy to conduct and explain to management. However, this method can be subject to considerable inaccuracy if one or both of the two data points used to

(Continued)

[7] Stephanie Anderson Forest, "Who's Afraid of J&J and 3M," *BusinessWeek* (December 5, 1994): 66, 68.

construct the cost formula is an outlier. Finally, regression overcomes many of the weaknesses of high-low because it incorporates all of the data into its estimate of the cost formula. Nevertheless, regression can require considerably more time than other methods to collect the necessary input data, ensure their accuracy, and explain the results to the ultimate users of the results.

To determine which method to employ, you would be wise to consult the managers who will be using your analysis. For example, does management need a general "ball park" estimate or does it need the most accurate estimate possible? The results from your cost analysis, along with the competitive pressures facing Royal, will affect important decisions such as how much to pay cruise ship employees to ensure a high quality customer experience, the prices to charge customers to ensure affordability yet exclusivity, and the types and quantities of food, beverages, and shopping to offer onboard the ships.

There is no obvious, one-size-fits-all answer as to the best cost estimation method to employ. Regardless of the cost estimation method ultimately selected, you likely will supplement the results with a dose of managerial judgment to help management make the best decisions possible.

OBJECTIVE 4
Use a personal computer spreadsheet program to perform the method of least squares.

APPENDIX 14A: USING THE REGRESSION PROGRAMS

Computing the regression formula manually is tedious, even with only a few data points. As the number of data points increases, manual computation becomes impractical. Fortunately, spreadsheet packages such as Microsoft Excel® have regression routines that will perform the computations. All you need to do is input the data. The spreadsheet regression program supplies more than the estimates of the coefficients. It also provides information that can be used to see how reliable the cost equation is—a feature that is not available for the scattergraph and high-low methods.

The first step in using the computer to calculate regression coefficients is to enter the data. Exhibit 14-11 shows the computer screen that you would see if you entered the Anderson Company data on material moves into a spreadsheet. It is a good idea to label your variables as is done in the exhibit. The months are labeled, as are column B for moving costs and column C for number of moves. The next step is to run the regression. In Excel, if the regression feature needs to be installed, press the Office button, click the Excel Options button at the bottom of the drop down menu, and click Add-Ins from the menu at the left. Click the Go button to the right of the Manage list box at the bottom of the dialog box, click to add a check mark beside Analysis ToolPak, and click OK. Click Yes to install. When the data analysis tools have been added, Data Analysis will appear in the Analysis group on the Data tab. Click on Data Analysis and then choose Regression.

When the regression screen pops up, you can tell the program where the dependent and independent variables are located. Place the cursor at the beginning of the independent rectangle and then (again using the cursor) drag down to select the values under the independent variable column—in this case, cells C2 through C10. Then, move the cursor

Exhibit 14-11

Spreadsheet Data for Anderson Company

	A	B	C	D	E	F	G	H
1	Month	Cost	# Moves					
2	January	$2,000	100					
3	February	3,090	125					
4	March	2,780	175					
5	April	1,990	200					
6	May	7,500	500					
7	June	5,300	300					
8	July	3,800	250					
9	August	6,300	400					
10	September	5,600	475					
11								
12								
13								
14								

Spreadsheet Data for Anderson Company.xls

Sheet1 / Sheet2 / Sheet3

to the beginning of the dependent rectangle, and select the values in cells B2 through B10. Finally, you need to tell the computer where to place the output. Block a nice-size rectangle, say cells A13 through F20, and click OK. In less than the blink of an eye, the regression output is complete. The regression output is shown in Exhibit 14-12.

Now, let's take a look at the output in Exhibit 14-12. First, let's locate the fixed cost and variable rate coefficients. At the bottom of the exhibit, the intercept and X Variable 1 are shown, and the next column gives their coefficients. Rounding, the fixed cost is 789 and the variable rate is 12.38. Now we can construct the cost formula for materials handling cost. It is:

Materials handling cost = $789 + ($12.38 × Number of moves)

We can use this formula to predict the materials handling cost for future months as we did with the formulas for the high-low and scattergraph methods.

Since the regression cost formula is the best-fitting line, it should produce better predictions of materials handling costs. For 350 moves, the total materials handling cost predicted by the least squares line is:

$5,122 = $789 + ($12.38 × 350)

Of the total materials handling cost, $789 is fixed and $4,333 is variable. Using this prediction as a standard, the scattergraph line most closely approximates the least squares line.

While the computer output in Exhibit 14-12 can give us the fixed and variable cost coefficients, its major usefulness lies in its ability to provide information about reliability of the estimated cost formula. This is a feature not provided by either the scattergraph or high-low methods.

Goodness of Fit

Regression routines provide information on goodness of fit. Goodness of fit tells us how well the independent variable predicts the dependent variable. This information can be used to assess reliability of the estimated cost formula, a feature not provided by either the scattergraph or high-low methods. The summary output in Exhibit 14-12 provides a wealth of statistical information. However, we will look at just one more feature—the coefficient of determination, or R^2. (The remaining information is discussed in statistics classes and higher-level accounting classes.)

The Anderson Company example suggests that the number of moves can explain changes in materials handling costs. The scattergraph shown in Graph A in Exhibit 14-6 (p. 725) confirms this belief because it reveals that materials handling costs and activity output (as measured by number of moves) seem to move together. It is quite likely that a significant percentage of the total variability in cost is explained by our output variable.

Regression Output for Anderson Company

Exhibit 14-12

	A	B	C	D	E	F	G	H
	Regression Output for Anderson Company.xls							
1	SUMMARY OUTPUT							
2								
3	*Regression Statistics*							
4	Multiple R	0.92436						
5	R Square	0.854442						
6	Standard Error	810.1969						
7	Observations	9						
8								
9								
10		*Coefficients*						
11	Intercept	788.7806						
12	X Variable 1	12.38058						
13								
14								
15								

We can determine statistically just how much variability is explained by looking at the coefficient of determination. The percentage of variability in the dependent variable explained by an independent variable (in this case, a measure of activity output) is called the **coefficient of determination (R^2)**. The higher the percentage of cost variability explained, the better job the independent variable does of explaining the dependent variable. Since R^2 is the percentage of variability explained, it always has a value between 0 and 1.00. In the summary output in Exhibit 14-12 (p. 733), the coefficient of determination is labeled R Square (R^2). The value given is 0.85 (rounded), which means that 85 percent of the variability in the materials handling cost is explained by the number of moves.

How good is this result? There is no cutoff point for a good versus bad coefficient of determination. Clearly, the closer R^2 is to 1.00, the better. Is 85 percent good enough? How about 73 percent? Or even 46 percent? The answer is that it depends. If your cost equation yields a coefficient of determination of 75 percent, you know that your independent variable explains three-fourths of the variability in cost. You also know that some other factor or combination of factors explains the remaining one-fourth. Depending on your tolerance for error, you may want to improve the equation by trying different independent variables (e.g., materials handling hours worked rather than number of moves) or by trying multiple regressions. (Multiple regressions use two or more independent variables. This topic is saved for later courses.)

We note from the summary output in Exhibit 14-12 that the R^2 for materials handling cost is 0.85. In other words, material moves explain about 85 percent of the variability in the materials handling cost. This is not bad. However, something else explains the remaining 15 percent. Anderson Company's controller may want to keep this in mind when using the regression results.

SUMMARY OF LEARNING OBJECTIVES

LO1. Explain the meaning of cost behavior, and define and describe fixed and variable costs.
- Cost behavior is the way a cost changes in relation to changes in activity output.
- Time horizon is important because costs can change from fixed to variable depending on whether the decision takes place over the short run or the long run.
- Variable costs change *in total* as the driver, or output measure, changes. Usually, we assume that variable costs increase in direct proportion to increases in activity output.
- Fixed costs do not change *in total* as activity output changes.

LO2. Define and describe mixed and step costs.
- Mixed costs have both a variable and a fixed component.
- Step costs remain at a constant level of cost for a range of output and then jump to a higher level of cost at some point, where they remain for a similar range of output.
- Cost objects that display a step cost behavior must be purchased in chunks.
- The width of the step defines the range of output for which a particular amount of the resource applies.

LO3. Separate mixed costs into their fixed and variable components using the high-low method, the scattergraph method, and the method of least squares.
- In the high-low method, only two data points are used—the high point and the low point with respect to activity level. These two points then are used to compute the intercept and the slope of the line on which they lie.
- The high-low method is objective and easy, but a nonrepresentative high or low point will lead to an incorrectly estimated cost relationship.
- The scattergraph method involves inspecting a graph showing total mixed cost at various output levels and selecting two points that seem to best represent the relationship between cost and output, and drawing a straight line. The intercept gives an estimate of the fixed cost component and the slope an estimate of the variable cost per unit of activity.

- The scattergraph method is a good way to identify nonlinearity, the presence of outliers, and the presence of a shift in the cost relationship. Its disadvantage is that it is subjective.
- The method of least squares uses all of the data points (except outliers) on the scattergraph and produces a line that best fits all of the points.
- The method of least squares offers ways to assess the reliability of cost equations.
- Managers use their experience and knowledge of cost and activity-level relationships to identify outliers, understand structural shifts, and adjust parameters due to anticipated changing conditions.

LO4. *(Appendix 14A)* **Use a personal computer spreadsheet program to perform the method of least squares.**

SUMMARY OF IMPORTANT EQUATIONS

1. Total variable costs = Variable rate × Amount of output
2. Total cost = Total fixed cost + Total variable cost
3. Total cost = Fixed cost + (Variable rate × Output)

4. $\text{Variable rate} = \dfrac{\text{High point cost} - \text{Low point cost}}{\text{High point output} - \text{Low point output}}$

5. Fixed cost = Total cost at high point − (Variable rate × Output at high point)
6. Fixed cost = Total cost at low point − (Variable rate × Output at low point)

7. $\text{Variable rate} = \dfrac{\text{High point cost} - \text{Low point cost}}{\text{High point number of moves} - \text{Low point number of moves}}$

CORNERSTONE 14-1	Creating and using a cost formula (p. 720)
CORNERSTONE 14-2	Using the high-low method to calculate fixed cost and the variable rate and to construct a cost formula (p. 722)
CORNERSTONE 14-3	Using the high-low method to calculate predicted total variable cost and total cost for budgeted output (p. 723)
CORNERSTONE 14-4	Using the high-low method to calculate predicted total variable cost and total cost for a time period that differs from the data period (p. 724)
CORNERSTONE 14-5	Using the regression method to calculate fixed cost and the variable rate and to construct a cost formula and to determine budgeted cost (p. 729)

CORNERSTONES
FOR CHAPTER 14

KEY TERMS

Committed fixed costs (p. 715)
Cost behavior (p. 712)
Dependent variable (p. 720)
Discretionary fixed costs (p. 715)
Driver (p. 712)
Fixed costs (p. 713)
High-low method (p. 721)
Independent variable (p. 720)
Intercept (p. 720)
Method of least squares (regression) (p. 727)

Mixed costs (p. 717)
Relevant range (p. 713)
Scattergraph method (p. 725)
Semi-variable (p. 717)
Slope (p. 720)
Step cost (p. 718)
Variable costs (p. 716)
Coefficient of determination
    (R^2) (p. 734)(*Appendix 14A*)

REVIEW PROBLEM

Kim Wilson, controller for Max Enterprises, has decided to estimate the fixed and variable components associated with the company's shipping activity. She has collected the following data for the past six months:

Packages Shipped	Total Shipping Costs
10	$ 800
20	1,100
15	900
12	900
18	1,050
25	1,250

Required:

1. Estimate the fixed and variable components for the shipping costs using the high-low method. Using the cost formula, predict the total cost of shipping if 14 packages are shipped.

2. Estimate the fixed and variable components using the method of least squares. Using the cost formula, predict the total cost of shipping if 14 packages are shipped.

3. *(Appendix 14A)* For the method of least squares, explain what the coefficient of determination tells us.

Solution:

1. The estimate of fixed and variable costs using the high-low method is as follows:

$$\text{Variable rate} = \frac{\$1{,}250 - \$800}{25 - 10}$$
$$= \$450/15 \text{ packages}$$
$$= \$30 \text{ per package}$$
$$\text{Fixed amount} = \$1{,}250 - \$30(25) = \$500$$
$$\text{Total cost} = \$500 + \$30X$$
$$= \$500 + \$30(14)$$
$$= \$920$$

2. The output of a spreadsheet regression routine is as follows: Regression output:

Constant	509.911894273125
Std Err of Y Est	32.1965672507378
R Squared	0.96928536465981
4	
No. of Observations	6
Degrees of Freedom	4
X Coefficient(s)	29.4052863436125
Std Err of Coef	2.61723229918858

$$Y = \$509.91 + \$29.41(14) = \$921.65$$

3. The coefficient of determination (R^2) tells us that about 96.9 percent of total shipping cost is explained by the number of packages shipped.

DISCUSSION QUESTIONS

1. Why is knowledge of cost behavior important for managerial decision making? Give an example to illustrate your answer.

2. What is a driver? Give an example of a cost and its corresponding output measure or driver.

3. Suppose a company finds that shipping cost is $3,560 each month plus $6.70 per package shipped. What is the cost formula for monthly shipping cost? Identify the independent variable, the dependent variable, the fixed cost per month, and the variable rate.

4. Some firms assign mixed costs to either the fixed or variable cost categories without using any formal methodology to separate them. Explain how this practice can be defended.
5. Explain the difference between committed and discretionary fixed costs. Give examples of each.
6. Explain why the concept of relevant range is important when dealing with step costs.
7. Why do mixed costs pose a problem when it comes to classifying costs into fixed and variable categories?
8. Describe the cost formula for a strictly fixed cost such as depreciation of $15,000 per year.
9. Describe the cost formula for a strictly variable cost such as electrical power cost of $1.15 per machine hour (i.e., every hour the machinery is run, electrical power cost goes up by $1.15).
10. What is the scattergraph method, and why is it used? Why is a scattergraph a good first step in separating mixed costs into their fixed and variable components?
11. Describe how the scattergraph method breaks out the fixed and variable costs from a mixed cost. Now describe how the high-low method works. How do the two methods differ?
12. What are the advantages of the scattergraph method over the high-low method? The high-low method over the scattergraph method?
13. Describe the method of least squares. Why is this method better than either the high-low method or the scattergraph method?
14. What is meant by the best-fitting line?
15. Explain the meaning of the coefficient of determination.

MULTIPLE-CHOICE EXERCISES

14-1 A factor that causes or leads to a change in a cost or activity is a(n)

a. slope.
b. intercept.
c. driver.

d. variable term.
e. cost object.

14-2 Which of the following would probably be a variable cost in a soda bottling plant?

a. Direct labor
b. Bottles
c. Carbonated water

d. Power to run the bottling machine
e. All of these

14-3 Which of the following would probably be a fixed cost in an automobile insurance company?

a. Application forms
b. The salary of customer service representatives
c. Time spent by adjusters to evaluate accidents

d. All of these
e. None of these

> *Use the following information for Multiple-Choice Exercises 14-4 though 14-7:*
> The following cost formula was developed by using monthly data for a hospital.
>
> Total cost = $51,400 + ($125 × Number of patient days)

14-4 In the cost formula, the term $51,400

a. is the dependent variable.
b. is the variable rate.
c. is the intercept.

d. is the independent variable.
e. cannot be determined from the above formula.

14-5 In the cost formula, the term $125

a. is the dependent variable.
b. is the variable rate.
c. is the intercept.

d. is the independent variable.
e. cannot be determined from the above formula.

14-6 In the cost formula, the term "Number of patient days"

a. is the variable rate.
b. is the intercept.
c. is the dependent variable.

d. is the independent variable.
e. cannot be determined from the formula on the previous page.

14-7 In the cost formula, the term "Total cost"

a. is the variable rate.
b. is the intercept.
c. is the dependent variable.

d. is the independent variable.
e. cannot be determined from the formula on the previous page.

14-8 The following cost formula for total purchasing cost in a factory was developed using monthly data.

$$\text{Purchasing cost} = \$123{,}800 + (\$15 \times \text{Number of purchase orders})$$

Next month, 2,000 purchase orders are predicted. The total cost predicted for the purchasing department next month

a. is $2,000.
b. is $153,800.
c. is $30,000.

d. is $123,800.
e. cannot be determined from the above formula.

14-9 An advantage of the high-low method is that it

a. is subjective.
b. is objective.
c. is the most accurate method.

d. removes outliers.
e. is descriptive of nonlinear data.

Use the following information for Multiple-Choice Exercises 14-10 and 14-11:
The following six months of data were collected on maintenance cost and the number of machine hours in a factory:

Month	Maintenance Cost	Machine Hours
January	$16,900	5,600
February	13,900	4,500
March	10,900	3,800
April	11,450	3,700
May	13,050	4,215
June	16,990	4,980

14-10 Select the independent and dependent variables.

	Independent Variable	Dependent Variable
a.	Maintenance cost	Machine hours
b.	Machine hours	Maintenance cost
c.	Maintenance cost	Month
d.	Machine hours	Month
e.	Month	Maintenance cost

14-11 Select the correct set of high and low months.

	High	Low
a.	January	April
b.	January	March
c.	June	March
d.	June	April

14-12 An advantage of the scattergraph method is that it

a. is objective.
b. is easier to use than the high-low method.
c. is the most accurate method.

d. removes outliers.
e. is descriptive of nonlinear data.

14-13 The total cost for monthly supervisory cost in a factory is $4,500. This cost

a. is strictly variable.
b. is strictly fixed.
c. is a mixed cost.

d. is a step cost.
e. cannot be determined from this information.

14-14 (*Appendix 14A*) In the method of least squares, the coefficient that tells the percentage of variation in the dependent variable that is explained by the independent variable is

a. the intercept term.
b. the x-coefficient.
c. the coefficient of correlation.

d. the coefficient of determination.
e. none of these.

CORNERSTONE EXERCISES

Cornerstone Exercise 14-15 Creating and Using a Cost Formula

OBJECTIVE ③
CORNERSTONE 14-1

Big Thumbs Company manufactures portable flash drives for computers. Big Thumbs incurs monthly depreciation costs of $15,000 on its plant equipment. Also, each drive requires materials and manufacturing overhead resources. On average, the company uses 10,000 ounces of materials to manufacture 5,000 flash drives per month. Each ounce of material costs $3.00. In addition, manufacturing overhead resources are driven by machine hours. On average, the company incurs $22,500 of variable manufacturing overhead resources to produce 5,000 flash drives per month.

Required:
1. Create a formula for the monthly cost of flash drives for Big Thumbs.
2. If the department expects to manufacture 6,000 flash drives next month, what is the expected fixed cost (assume that 6,000 units is within the company's current relevant range)? Total variable cost? Total manufacturing cost (i.e., both fixed and variable)?

Use the following information for Cornerstone Exercises 14-16 through 14-19:
Pizza Vesuvio makes specialty pizzas. Data for the past eight months were collected:

Month	Labor Cost	Employee Hours
January	$ 7,000	360
February	8,140	550
March	9,899	630
April	9,787	610
May	8,490	480
June	7,450	350
July	9,490	570
August	7,531	310

Cornerstone Exercise 14-16 Using High-Low to Calculate Fixed Cost, Calculate the Variable Rate, and Construct a Cost Function

OBJECTIVE ③
CORNERSTONE 14-2

Refer to the information for Pizza Vesuvio above. Pizza Vesuvio's controller wants to calculate the fixed and variable costs associated with labor used in the restaurant.

Required:
Using the high-low method, calculate the fixed cost of labor, calculate the variable rate per employee hour, and construct the cost formula for total labor cost.

OBJECTIVE ❸
CORNERSTONE 14-3

Cornerstone Exercise 14-17 Using High-Low to Calculate Predicted Total Variable Cost and Total Cost for Budgeted Output

Refer to the information for Pizza Vesuvio on the previous page. Assume that this information was used to construct the following formula for monthly labor cost.

$$\text{Total labor cost} = \$5{,}237 + (\$7.40 \times \text{Employee hours})$$

Required:

Assume that 675 employee hours are budgeted for the month of September. Use the total labor cost formula for the following calculations:

1. Calculate total variable labor cost for September.
2. Calculate total labor cost for September.

OBJECTIVE ❸
CORNERSTONE 14-4

Cornerstone Exercise 14-18 Using High-Low to Calculate Predicted Total Variable Cost and Total Cost for a Time Period that Differs from the Data Period

Refer to the information for Pizza Vesuvio on the previous page. Assume that this information was used to construct the following formula for monthly labor cost.

$$\text{Total labor cost} = \$5{,}237 + (\$7.40 \times \text{Employee hours})$$

Required:

Assume that 4,000 employee hours are budgeted for the coming year. Use the total labor cost formula to make the following calculations:

1. Calculate total variable labor cost for the year.
2. Calculate total fixed labor cost for the year.
3. Calculate total labor cost for the coming year.

OBJECTIVE ❸
CORNERSTONE 14-5

Cornerstone Exercise 14-19 Using Regression to Calculate Fixed Cost, Calculate the Variable Rate, Construct a Cost Formula, and Determine Budgeted Cost

Refer to the information for Pizza Vesuvio on the previous page. Coefficients shown by a regression program for Pizza Vesuvio's data are:

Intercept	4,764
X Variable	7.55

Required:

Use the results of regression to make the following calculations:

1. Calculate the fixed cost of labor and the variable rate per employee hour.
2. Construct the cost formula for total labor cost.
3. Calculate the budgeted cost for next month, assuming that 675 employee hours are budgeted. (*Note:* Round answers to the nearest dollar.)

EXERCISES

OBJECTIVE ❶

Exercise 14-20 Variable and Fixed Costs

What follows are a number of resources that are used by a manufacturer of futons. Assume that the output measure or cost driver is the number of futons produced. All direct labor is paid on an hourly basis, and hours worked can be easily changed by management. All other factory workers are salaried.

a. Power to operate a drill (to drill holes in the wooden frames of the futons)
b. Cloth to cover the futon mattress
c. Salary of the factory receptionist *fixed*
d. Cost of food and decorations for the annual Fourth of July party for all factory employees
e. Fuel for a forklift used to move materials in a factory
f. Depreciation on the factory
g. Depreciation on a forklift used to move partially completed goods
h. Wages paid to workers who assemble the futon frame
i. Wages paid to workers who maintain the factory equipment
j. Cloth rags used to wipe the excess stain off the wooden frames

Required:

Classify the resource costs as variable or fixed.

Exercise 14-21 Cost Behavior, Classification

OBJECTIVE ▸ 1

Smith Concrete Company owns enough ready-mix trucks to deliver up to 100,000 cubic yards of concrete per year (considering each truck's capacity, weather, and distance to each job). Total truck depreciation is $200,000 per year. Raw materials (cement, gravel, and so on) cost about $25 per cubic yard of cement.

Required:

1. Prepare a graph for truck depreciation. Use the vertical axis for cost and the horizontal axis for cubic yards of cement.
2. Prepare a graph for raw materials. Use the vertical axis for cost and the horizontal axis for cubic yards of cement.
3. Assume that the normal operating range for the company is 90,000 to 96,000 cubic yards per year. Classify truck depreciation and raw materials as variable or fixed costs.
4. **Conceptual Connection:** Briefly describe actions that Smith management could take to reduce the truck depreciation cost from year to year.
5. **Conceptual Connection:** Briefly describe actions that Smith management could take to reduce the total raw material cost from year to year.

Exercise 14-22 Classifying Costs as Fixed and Variable in a Service Organization

OBJECTIVE ▸ 1

Alva Community Hospital has five laboratory technicians who are responsible for doing a series of standard blood tests. Each technician is paid a salary of $30,000. The lab facility represents a recent addition to the hospital and cost $300,000. It is expected to last 20 years. Equipment used for the testing cost $10,000 and has a life expectancy of five years. In addition to the salaries, facility, and equipment, Alva expects to spend $200,000 for chemicals, forms, power, and other supplies. This $200,000 is enough for 200,000 blood tests.

Required:

Assuming that the driver (measure of output) for each type of cost is the number of blood tests run, classify the costs by completing the following table. Put an X in the appropriate box for variable cost, discretionary fixed cost, or committed fixed cost.

Cost Category	Variable Cost	Discretionary Fixed Cost	Committed Fixed Cost
Technician salaries			
Laboratory facility			
Laboratory equipment			
Chemicals and other supplies			

> *Use the following information for Exercises 14-23 and 14-24:*
> Alisha Incorporated manufactures medical stints for use in heart bypass surgery. Based on past experience, Alisha has found that its total maintenance costs can be represented by the following formula: Maintenance cost = $310,000 + $16.50X, where X = Number of heart stints. Last year, Alisha produced 150,000 stints. Actual maintenance costs for the year were as expected. (*Note:* Round all answers to two decimal places.)

Exercise 14-23 Cost Behavior

OBJECTIVE ▸ 1

Refer to the information for Alisha Incorporated above.

Required:

1. What is the total maintenance cost incurred by Alisha last year?
2. What is the total fixed maintenance cost incurred by Alisha last year?
3. What is the total variable maintenance cost incurred by Alisha last year?

(Continued)

4.   What is the maintenance cost per unit produced?
5.   What is the fixed maintenance cost per unit?
6.   What is the variable maintenance cost per unit?
7.   **Conceptual Connection:** Briefly explain how Alisha management could improve its cost function to better understand past maintenance costs and predict future maintenance costs.

OBJECTIVE

Exercise 14-24 Cost Behavior

Refer to the information for Alisha Incorporated on the previous page. However, now assume that Alisha produced 80,000 medical stints (rather than 150,000). (*Note:* Round all answers to two decimal places.)

Required:
1.   What is the total maintenance cost incurred by Alisha last year?
2.   What is the total fixed maintenance cost incurred by Alisha last year?
3.   What is the total variable maintenance cost incurred by Alisha last year?
4.   What is the maintenance cost per unit produced?
5.   What is the fixed maintenance cost per unit?
6.   What is the variable maintenance cost per unit?

OBJECTIVE

Exercise 14-25 Step Costs, Relevant Range

Bellati Inc. produces large industrial machinery. Bellati has a machining department and a group of direct laborers called machinists. Each machinist can machine up to 500 units per year. Bellati also hires supervisor develop machine specification plans and to oversee production within the machining department. Given the planning and supervisory work, a supervisor can oversee, at most, three machinists. Bellati's accounting and production history shows the following relationships between number of units produced and the costs of supervision and materials handling (by machinists), measured on an annual basis:

Units Produced	Direct Labor	Supervision
0–500	$ 36,000	$ 40,000
501–1,000	72,000	40,000
1,001–1,500	108,000	40,000
1,501–2,000	144,000	80,000
2,001–2,500	180,000	80,000
2,501–3,000	216,000	80,000
3,001–3,500	252,000	120,000
3,501–4,000	288,000	120,000

Required:
1.   Prepare a graph that illustrates the relationship between direct labor cost and number of units produced in the machining department. (Let cost be the vertical axis and number of units produced be the horizontal axis.) Would you classify this cost as a strictly variable cost, a fixed cost, or a step cost?
2.   Prepare a graph that illustrates the relationship between the cost of supervision and the number of units produced. (Let cost be the vertical axis and number of units produced be the horizontal axis.) Would you classify this cost as a strictly variable cost, a fixed cost, or a step cost?
3.   Suppose that the normal range of production is between 1,400 and 1,500 units and that the exact number of machinists are currently hired to support this level of activity. Further suppose that production for the next year is expected to increase by an additional 500 units. What is the increase in the cost of direct labor? Cost of supervision?

OBJECTIVE

Exercise 14-26 Matching Cost Behavior Descriptions to Cost Behavior Graphs

Select the graph (A through K) that best matches the numbered (1 through 6) descriptions of various cost behavior. For each graph, the vertical (y) axis represents total dollars of cost, and the horizontal (x) axis represents output units during the period. The graphs may be used more than once.

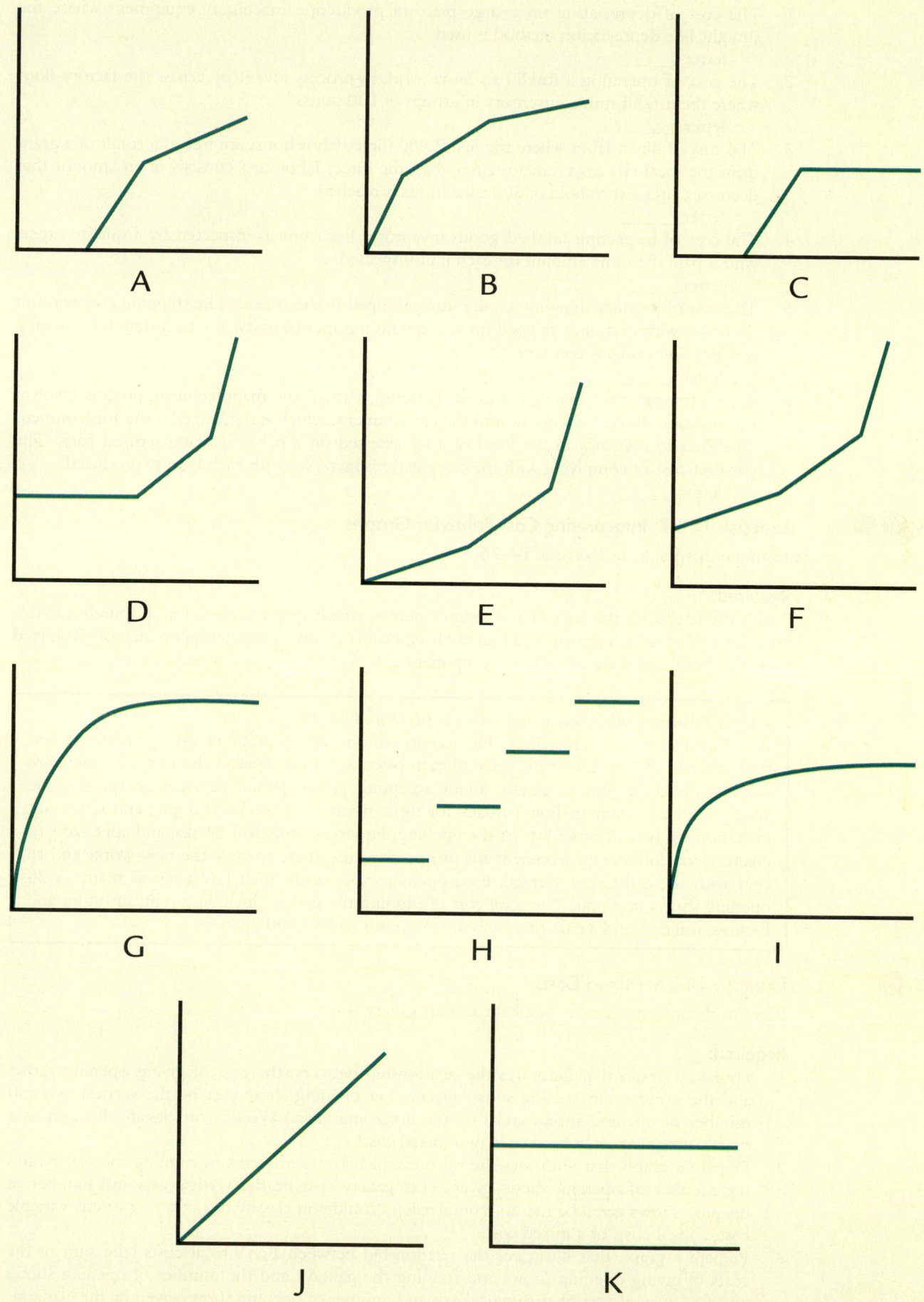

1. The cost of depreciation on a large piece of production machinery equipment where the straight-line depreciation method is used.

    letter _____

2. The cost of operating a forklift to move work-in-process inventory across the factory floor where the forklift moves inventory in groups of 100 units.

    letter _____

3. The cost of direct labor where the first 2,000 direct labor hours are free as a result of a grant from the local city government. After that, the direct labor cost consists of an amount that decreases after a threshold of 500 total hours is reached.

    letter _____

4. The cost of inspecting finished goods inventory. Each unit is inspected by a quality expert who is paid the same amount for each unit inspected.

    letter _____

5. The cost of product shipping for all output shipped in the period. The shipping cost per unit decreases with each unit shipped up to a certain number of units, at which time the shipping cost per unit remains constant.

    letter _____

6. An electric car plant manufactures car batteries. Part of the manufacturing process involves the emission of toxic chemicals into the environment, which is regulated by the Environmental Protection Agency in the form of a fee assessed on a per-unit manufactured basis. The per-unit cost of complying with these regulations increases with each battery produced.

    letter _____

OBJECTIVE

Exercise 14-27 Interpreting Cost Behavior Graphs

Examine the graphs in **Exercise 14-26**.

Required:

Using the letters (A through J) as reference points, which graph(s) depict a (1) purely variable cost (i.e., no fixed component), (2) purely fixed cost (i.e., no variable component), or (3) mixed cost (i.e., both a variable and a fixed component).

Use the following information for Exercises 14-28 and 14-29:
Ben Palman owns an art gallery. He accepts paintings and sculpture on consignment and then receives 20 percent of the price of each piece as his fee. Space is limited, and there are costs involved, so Ben is careful about accepting artists. When he does accept one, he arranges for an opening show (usually for three hours on a weekend night) and sends out invitations to his customer list. At the opening, he serves wine, soft drinks, and appetizers to create a comfortable environment for prospective customers to view the new works and to chat with the artist. On average, each opening costs $500. Ben has given as many as 20 opening shows in a year. The total cost of running the gallery, including rent, furniture and fixtures, utilities, and a part-time assistant, amounts to $80,000 per year.

OBJECTIVE

Exercise 14-28 Mixed Costs

Refer to the information for Ben Palman's art gallery above.

Required:

1. Prepare a graph that illustrates the relationship between the cost of giving opening shows and the number of opening shows given. (Let opening show cost be the vertical axis and number of opening shows given be the horizontal axis.) Would you classify this cost as a strictly variable cost, a fixed cost, or a mixed cost?

2. Prepare a graph that illustrates the relationship between the cost of running the gallery and the number of opening shows given. (Let gallery cost be the vertical axis and number of opening shows given be the horizontal axis.) Would you classify this cost as a strictly variable cost, a fixed cost, or a mixed cost?

3. Prepare a graph that illustrates the relationship between Ben's total costs (the sum of the costs of giving opening shows and running the gallery) and the number of opening shows given. (Let total cost be the vertical axis and number of opening shows given be the horizontal axis.) Would you classify this cost as a strictly variable cost, a fixed cost, or a mixed cost?

Exercise 14-29 Mixed Costs and Cost Formula

OBJECTIVE 3

Refer to the information for Ben Palman's art gallery on the previous page.

Required:

1. Assume that the cost driver is number of opening shows. Develop the cost formula for the gallery's costs for a year.
2. Using the formula developed in Requirement 1, what is the total cost for Ben in a year with 12 opening shows? With 14 opening shows?

Use the following information for Exercises 14-30 through 14-32:

Luisa Crimini has been operating a beauty shop in a college town for the past 10 years. Recently, Luisa rented space next to her shop and opened a tanning salon. She anticipated that the costs for the tanning service would primarily be fixed but found that tanning salon costs increased with the number of appointments. Costs for this service over the past eight months are as follows:

Month	Tanning Appointments	Total Cost
January	700	$1,754
February	2,000	2,140
March	3,500	2,790
April	2,500	2,400
May	1,500	1,790
June	2,300	2,275
July	2,150	2,200
August	3,000	2,640

Exercise 14-30 High-Low Method

OBJECTIVE 3

Refer to the information for Luisa Crimini above.

Required:

1. Which month represents the high point? The low point?
2. Using the high-low method, compute the variable rate for tanning. Compute the fixed cost per month.
3. Using your answers to Requirement 2, write the cost formula for tanning services.
4. Calculate the total predicted cost of tanning services for September for 2,500 appointments using the formula found in Requirement 3. Of that total cost, how much is the total fixed cost for September? How much is the total predicted variable cost for September?
5. **Conceptual Connection:** Identify and briefly explain any additional issues that Luisa might be wise to consider when using the high-low method to estimate the costs of her tanning salon.

Exercise 14-31 Scattergraph Method

OBJECTIVE 3

Refer to the information for Luisa Crimini above.

Required:

Conceptual Connection: Prepare a scattergraph based on Luisa's data. Use cost for the vertical axis and number of tanning appointments for the horizontal. Based on an examination of the scattergraph, does there appear to be a linear relationship between the cost of tanning services and the number of appointments?

Exercise 14-32 Method of Least Squares

OBJECTIVE 3

Refer to the information for Luisa Crimini above.

Required:
1. Using a computer spreadsheet program such as Excel, run a regression on these data. Based on the regression output, write the cost formula for tanning. (*Note*: Round the fixed cost to the nearest dollar and the variable rate to the nearest cent.)
2. Using the formula computed in Requirement 1, what is the predicted cost of tanning services for September for 2,500 appointments?

Use the following information for Exercises 14-33 and 14-34:

During the past year, the high and low use of three different resources for Fly High Airlines occurred in July and April. The resources are airplane depreciation, fuel, and airplane maintenance. The number of airplane flight hours is the driver. The total costs of the three resources and the related number of airplane flight hours are as follows:

Resource	Airplane Flight Hours	Total Cost
Airplane depreciation:		
High	44,000	$ 18,000,000
Low	28,000	18,000,000
Fuel:		
High	44,000	445,896,000
Low	28,000	283,752,000
Airplane maintenance:		
High	44,000	15,792,000
Low	28,000	11,504,000

OBJECTIVE 3

Exercise 14-33 High-Low Method, Cost Formulas

Refer to the information for Fly High Airlines above.

Required:
Use the high-low method to answer the following questions.
1. What is the variable rate for airplane depreciation? The fixed cost?
2. What is the cost formula for airplane depreciation?
3. What is the variable rate for fuel? The fixed cost?
4. What is the cost formula for fuel?
5. What is the variable rate for airplane maintenance? The fixed cost?
6. What is the cost formula for airplane maintenance?
7. Using the three cost formulas that you developed, predict the cost of each resource in a month with 36,000 airplane flight hours.

OBJECTIVE 3

Exercise 14-34 Changing the Cost Formula for a Month to the Cost Formula for a Year

Refer to the information for Fly High Airlines above.

Required:
1. Develop annual cost formulas for airplane depreciation, fuel, and airplane maintenance.
2. Using the three annual cost formulas that you developed, predict the cost of each resource in a year with 480,000 airline flight hours.

OBJECTIVE 3

Exercise 14-35 Method of Least Squares, Developing and Using the Cost Formula

The method of least squares was used to develop a cost equation to predict the cost of receiving. Ninety-six data points from monthly data were used for the regression. The following computer output was received:

Intercept	23,100
Slope	316

The driver used was number of parts inspected.

Required:
1. What is the cost formula?
2. Using the cost formula from Requirement 1, identify each of the following: independent variable, dependent variable, variable rate, and fixed cost per month.
3. Using the cost formula, predict the cost of receiving for a month in which 2,500 parts are inspected.

Exercise 14-36 Method of Least Squares, Budgeted Time Period Is Different from Time Period Used to Generate Results

OBJECTIVE ③

Refer to the company information in **Exercise 14-35**.

Required:
1. What is the cost formula for a year?
2. Using the cost formula from Requirement 1, predict the cost of parts inspection for a year in which 29,000 parts are inspected.

Exercise 14-37 Identifying the Parts of the Cost Formula; Calculating Monthly, Quarterly, and Yearly Costs Using a Cost Formula Based on Monthly Data

OBJECTIVE ③

Gordon Company's controller, Eric Junior, estimated the following formula, based on monthly data, for overhead cost:

$$\text{Overhead cost} = \$150,000 + (\$52 \times \text{Direct labor hours})$$

Required:
1. Link each term in column A to the corresponding term in column B.

Column A	Column B
Overhead cost	Fixed cost (intercept)
$150,000	Dependent variable
$52	Independent variable
Direct labor hours	Variable rate (slope)

2. If next month's budgeted direct labor hours equal 8,000, what is the budgeted overhead cost?
3. If next quarter's budgeted direct labor hours equal 23,000, what is the budgeted overhead cost?
4. If next year's budgeted direct labor hours equal 99,000, what is the budgeted overhead cost?

Exercise 14-38 *(Appendix 14A)* Method of Least Squares Using Computer Spreadsheet Program

OBJECTIVE ④

The controller for Beckham Company believes that the number of direct labor hours is associated with overhead cost. He collected the following data on the number of direct labor hours and associated factory overhead cost for the months of January through August.

Month	Number of Direct Labor Hours	Overhead Cost
January	689	$5,550
February	700	5,590
March	720	5,650
April	690	5,570
May	680	5,570
June	590	5,410
July	750	5,720
August	675	5,608

Required:
1. Using a computer spreadsheet program such as Excel, run a regression on these data. Print out your results.
2. Using your results from Requirement 1, write the cost formula for overhead cost. (*Note*: Round the fixed cost to the nearest dollar and the variable rate to the nearest cent.)

(Continued)

3. **Conceptual Connection:** What is R^2 based on your results? Do you think that the number of direct labor hours is a good predictor of factory overhead cost?

4. Assuming that expected September direct labor hours are 700, what is expected factory overhead cost using the cost formula in Requirement 2?

OBJECTIVE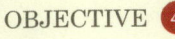

Exercise 14-39 *(Appendix 14A)* Method of Least Squares Using Computer Spreadsheet Program

Susan Lewis, owner of a florist shop, is interested in predicting the cost of delivering floral arrangements. She collected monthly data on the number of deliveries and the total monthly delivery cost (depreciation on the van, wages of the driver, and fuel) for the past year.

Month	Number of Deliveries	Delivery Cost
January	100	$1,200
February	550	1,800
March	85	1,100
April	115	1,050
May	160	1,190
June	590	1,980
July	500	1,800
August	520	1,700
September	100	1,100
October	200	1,275
November	260	1,400
December	450	2,200

Required:

1. Using a computer spreadsheet program such as Excel, run a regression on these data. Print out your results.

2. Using your results from Requirement 1, write the cost formula for delivery cost. (*Note:* Round the fixed cost to the nearest dollar and the variable rate to the nearest cent.)

3. **Conceptual Connection:** What is R^2 based on your results? Do you think that the number of direct labor hours is a good predictor of delivery cost?

4. Using the cost formula in Requirement 2, what would predicted delivery cost be for a month with 300 deliveries?

PROBLEMS

OBJECTIVE

Problem 14-40 Identifying Fixed, Variable, Mixed, and Step Costs

Consider each of the following independent situations:

a. A computer service agreement in which a company pays $150 per month and $15 per hour of technical time

b. Fuel cost of the company's fleet of motor vehicles

c. The cost of beer for a bar

d. The cost of computer printers and copiers in your college

e. Rent for a dental office

f. The salary of a receptionist in a law firm

g. The wages of counter help in a fast-food restaurant

h. The salaries of dental hygienists in a three-dentist office. One hygienist can take care of 120 cleanings per month

i. Electricity cost which includes a $15 per month billing charge and an additional amount depending on the number of kilowatt-hours used

Required:

1. For each situation, describe the cost as one of the following: fixed cost, variable cost, mixed cost, or step cost. (*Hint:* First, consider what the driver or output measure is. If additional assumptions are necessary to support your cost type decision, be sure to write them down.)
   Example: Raw materials used in production—Variable cost

2. **Conceptual Connection:** Change your assumption(s) for each situation so that the cost type changes to a different cost type. List the new cost type and the changed assumption(s) that gave rise to it.

Example: Raw materials used in production. Changed assumption—the materials are difficult to obtain, and a year's worth must be contracted for in advance. Now, this is a fixed cost. (This is the case with diamond sales by **DeBeers Inc.** to its sightholders. See the following website for information: http://www.keyguide.net/sightholders/.)

Problem 14-41 Identifying Use of the High-Low, Scattergraph, and Least Squares Methods

OBJECTIVE ❸

Consider each of the following independent situations:

a. Shaniqua Boyer just started her new job as controller for St. Matthias General Hospital. She wants to get a feel for the cost behavior of various departments of the hospital. Shaniqua first looks at the radiology department. She has annual data on total cost and the number of procedures that have been run for the past 15 years. However, she knows that the department upgraded its equipment substantially two years ago and is doing a wider variety of tests. So, Shaniqua decides to use data for just the past two years.

b. Francis Hidalgo is a summer intern in the accounting department of a manufacturing firm. His boss assigned him a special project to determine the cost of manufacturing a special order. Francis needs information on variable and fixed overhead, so he gathers monthly data on overhead cost and machine hours for the past 60 months and enters them into his personal computer. A few keystrokes later, he has information on fixed and variable overhead costs.

c. Ron Wickstead sighed and studied his computer printout again. The results made no sense to him. He seemed to recall that sometimes it helped to visualize the cost relationships. He reached for some graph paper and a pencil.

d. Lois March had hoped that she could find information on the actual cost of promoting new products. Unfortunately, she had spent the weekend going through the files and was only able to find data on the total cost of the sales department by month for the past three years. She was also able to figure out the number of new product launches by month for the same time period. Now, she had just 15 minutes before a staff meeting in which she needed to give the vice president of sales an expected cost of the average new product launch. A light bulb went off in her head, and she reached for paper, pencil, and a calculator.

Required:

Determine which of the following cost separation methods is being used: the high-low method, the scattergraph method, or the method of least squares.

Problem 14-42 Identifying Variable Costs, Committed Fixed Costs, and Discretionary Fixed Costs

OBJECTIVE ❶

Required:

Classify each of the following costs for a jeans manufacturing company as a variable cost, committed fixed cost, or discretionary fixed cost.

a. The cost of buttons
b. The cost to lease warehouse space for completed jeans—the lease contract runs for two years at $5,000 per year
c. The salary of a summer intern
d. The cost of landscaping and mowing the grass—the contract with a local mowing company runs from month to month
e. Advertising in a national magazine for teenage girls
f. Electricity to run the sewing machines
g. Oil and spare needles for the sewing machines
h. Quality training for employees—typically given for four hours at a time, every six months
i. Food and beverages for the company Fourth of July picnic
j. Natural gas to heat the factory during the winter

(Continued)

Use the following information for Problems 14-43 and 14-44:

Farnsworth Company has gathered data on its overhead activities and associated costs for the past 10 months. Tracy Heppler, a member of the controller's department, has convinced management that overhead costs can be better estimated and controlled if the fixed and variable components of each overhead activity are known. One such activity is receiving raw materials (unloading incoming goods, counting goods, and inspecting goods), which she believes is driven by the number of receiving orders. Ten months of data have been gathered for the receiving activity and are as follows:

Month	Receiving Orders	Receiving Cost
1	1,000	$18,000
2	700	15,000
3	1,500	28,000
4	1,200	17,000
5	1,300	25,000
6	1,100	21,000
7	1,600	29,000
8	1,400	24,000
9	1,700	27,000
10	900	16,000

OBJECTIVE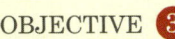

Problem 14-43 Scattergraph, High-Low Method, and Predicting Cost for a Different Time Period from the One Used to Develop a Cost Formula

Refer the the information for Farnsworth Company above.

Required:

1. Prepare a scattergraph based on the 10 months of data. Does the relationship appear to be linear?
2. Using the high-low method, prepare a cost formula for the receiving activity. Using this formula, what is the predicted cost of receiving for a month in which 1,450 receiving orders are processed?
3. Prepare a cost formula for the receiving activity for a quarter. Based on this formula, what is the predicted cost of receiving for a quarter in which 4,650 receiving orders are anticipated? Prepare a cost formula for the receiving activity for a year. Based on this formula, what is the predicted cost of receiving for a year in which 18,000 receiving orders are anticipated?

OBJECTIVE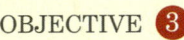

Problem 14-44 Method of Least Squares, Predicting Cost for Different Time Periods from the One Used to Develop a Cost Formula

Refer to the information for Farnsworth Company above. However, assume that Tracy has used the method of least squares on the receiving data and has gotten the following results:

Intercept	3,212
Slope	15.15

Required:

1. Using the results from the method of least squares, prepare a cost formula for the receiving activity.
2. Using the formula from Requirement 1, what is the predicted cost of receiving for a month in which 1,450 receiving orders are processed? (*Note:* Round your answer to the nearest dollar.)
3. Prepare a cost formula for the receiving activity for a quarter. Based on this formula, what is the predicted cost of receiving for a quarter in which 4,650 receiving orders are anticipated? Prepare a cost formula for the receiving activity for a year. Based on this formula, what is the predicted cost of receiving for a year in which 18,000 receiving orders are anticipated?

OBJECTIVE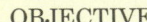

Problem 14-45 Cost Behavior, High-Low Method, Pricing Decision

Fonseca, Ruiz, and Dunn is a large, local accounting firm located in a southwestern city. Carlos Ruiz, one of the firm's founders, appreciates the success his firm has enjoyed and wants to give something back to his community. He believes that an inexpensive accounting services clinic could provide basic accounting services for small businesses located in the barrio. He wants to price the services at cost.

Since the clinic is brand new, it has no experience to go on. Carlos decided to operate the clinic for two months before determining how much to charge per hour on an ongoing basis. As a temporary measure, the clinic adopted an hourly charge of $25, half the amount charged by Fonseca, Ruiz, and Dunn for professional services.

The accounting services clinic opened on January 1. During January, the clinic had 120 hours of professional service. During February, the activity was 150 hours. Costs for these two levels of activity usage are as follows:

	120 Professional Hours	150 Professional Hours
Salaries:		
Senior accountant	$2,500	$2,500
Office assistant	1,200	1,200
Internet and software subscriptions	700	850
Consulting by senior partner	1,200	1,500
Depreciation (equipment)	2,400	2,400
Supplies	905	1,100
Administration	500	500
Rent (offices)	2,000	2,000
Utilities	332	365

Required:

1. Classify each cost as fixed, variable, or mixed, using hours of professional service as the activity driver.
2. Use the high-low method to separate the mixed costs into their fixed and variable components.
3. Luz Mondragon, the chief paraprofessional of the clinic, has estimated that the clinic will average 140 professional hours per month. If the clinic is to be operated as a nonprofit organization, how much will it need to charge per professional hour? How much of this charge is variable? How much is fixed?
4. **Conceptual Connection:** Suppose the accounting center averages 170 professional hours per month. How much would need to be charged per hour for the center to cover its costs? Explain why the per-hour charge decreased as the activity output increased.

Problem 14-46 Flexible and Committed Resources, Capacity Usage for a Service

OBJECTIVE ❶ ❷ ❸

Jana Morgan is about to sign up for cellular telephone service. She is primarily interested in the safety aspect of the phone; she wants to have one available for emergencies. She does not want to use it as her primary phone. Jana has narrowed her options down to two plans:

	Plan 1	Plan 2
Monthly fee	$ 20	$ 30
Free local minutes	60	120
Additional charges per minute:		
Airtime	$ 0.40	$ 0.30
Long distance	0.15	—
Regional roaming	0.60	—
National roaming	0.60	0.60

Both plans are subject to a $25 activation fee and a $120 cancellation fee if the service is cancelled before one year. Jana's brother will give her a cell phone that he no longer needs. It is not the latest version (and is not Internet capable) but will work well with both plans.

Required:

1. Classify the charges associated with the cellular phone service as (a) committed resources or (b) flexible resources.
2. **Conceptual Connection:** Assume that Jana will use, on average, 45 minutes per month in local calling. For each plan, split her minute allotment into used and unused capacity. Which plan will be most cost effective? Why?

(Continued)

3. **Conceptual Connection:** Assume that Jana loves her cell phone and ends up talking frequently with friends while traveling within her region. On average, she uses 60 local minutes a month and 30 regional minutes. For each plan, split her minute allotment into used and unused capacity. Which plan will be most cost effective? Why?

4. **Conceptual Connection:** Analyze your own cellular phone plan by comparing it with other possible options.

OBJECTIVE

Problem 14-47 Variable and Fixed Costs, Cost Formula, High-Low Method

Li Ming Yuan and Tiffany Shaden are the department heads for the accounting department and human resources department, respectively, at a large textile firm in the southern United States. They have just returned from an executive meeting at which the necessity of cutting costs and gaining efficiency has been stressed. After talking with Tiffany and some of her staff members, as well as his own staff members, Li Ming discovered that there were a number of costs associated with the claims processing activity. These costs included the salaries of the two paralegals who worked full-time on claims processing; the salary of the accountant who cut the checks; the cost of claims forms, checks, envelopes, and postage; and depreciation on the office equipment dedicated to the processing. Some of the paralegals' time is spent in the routine processing of uncontested claims, but much time is spent on the claims that have incomplete documentation or are contested. The accountant's time appears to vary with the number of claims processed.

Li Ming was able to separate the costs of processing claims from the costs of running the departments of accounting and human resources. He gathered the data on claims processing cost and the number of claims processed per month for the past six months. These data are as follows:

Month	Claims Processing Cost	Number of Claims Processed
February	$34,907	5,700
March	31,260	4,900
April	37,950	6,100
May	38,250	6,500
June	44,895	7,930
July	44,055	7,514

Required:

1. Classify the claims processing costs that Li Ming identified as variable and fixed.
2. What is the independent variable? The dependent variable?
3. Use the high-low method to find the fixed cost per month and the variable rate. What is the cost formula?
4. **Conceptual Connection:** Suppose that an outside company bids on the claims processing business. The bid price is $4.60 per claim. If Tiffany expects 75,600 claims next year, should she outsource the claims processing or continue to do it in house?

OBJECTIVE

Problem 14-48 Cost Separation

About eight years ago, **Kicker** faced the problem of rapidly increasing costs associated with workplace accidents. The costs included the following:

State unemployment insurance premiums	$100,000
Average cost per injury	$ 1,500
Number of injuries per year	15
Number of serious injuries	4
Number of workdays lost	30

A safety program was implemented with the following features: hiring a safety director, new employee orientation, stretching required four times a day, and systematic monitoring of adherence to the program by directors and supervisors. A year later, the indicators were as follows:

State unemployment insurance premiums	$50,000
Average cost per injury	$ 50
Number of injuries per year	10
Number of serious injuries	0
Number of workdays lost	0
Safety director's starting salary	$60,000

Required:
1. **Conceptual Connection:** Discuss the safety-related costs listed. Are they variable or fixed with respect to speakers sold? With respect to other independent variables (describe)?
2. **Conceptual Connection:** Did the safety program pay for itself? Discuss your reasoning.

Problem 14-49 *(Appendix 14A)* Method of Least Squares

OBJECTIVE ④

Refer to the information for Farnsworth Company (p. 750) for the first 10 months of data on receiving orders and receiving cost. Now suppose that Tracy has gathered two more months of data:

Month	Receiving Orders	Receiving Cost
11	1,200	$28,000
12	950	17,500

Note: For the following requirements, round the intercept terms to the nearest dollar and round the variable rates to the nearest cent.

Required:
1. Run two regressions using a computer spreadsheet program such as Excel. First, use the method of least squares on the first 10 months of data. Then, use the method of least squares on all 12 months of data. Write down the results for the intercept, slope, and R^2 for each regression. Compare the results.
2. **Conceptual Connection:** Prepare a scattergraph using all 12 months of data. Do any points appear to be outliers? Suppose Tracy has learned that the factory suffered severe storm damage during Month 11 that required extensive repairs to the receiving area—including major repairs on a forklift. These expenses, included in Month 11 receiving costs, are not expected to recur. What step might Tracy, using her judgment, take to amend the results from the method of least squares?
3. **Conceptual Connection:** Rerun the method of least squares, using all the data except for Month 11. (You should now have 11 months of data.) Prepare a cost formula for receiving based on these results, and calculate the predicted receiving cost for a month with 1,450 receiving orders. Discuss the results from this regression versus those from the regression for 12 months of data.

Problem 14-50 *(Appendix 14A)* Scattergraph, High-Low Method, Method of Least Squares, Use of Judgment

OBJECTIVE ③ ④

The management of Wheeler Company has decided to develop cost formulas for its major overhead activities. Wheeler uses a highly automated manufacturing process, and power costs are a significant manufacturing cost. Cost analysts have decided that power costs are mixed. The costs must be broken into their fixed and variable elements so that the cost behavior of the power usage activity can be properly described. Machine hours have been selected as the activity driver for power costs. The following data for the past eight quarters have been collected:

Quarter	Machine Hours	Power Cost
1	20,000	$26,000
2	25,000	38,000
3	30,000	42,500
4	22,000	37,000
5	21,000	34,000
6	18,000	29,000
7	24,000	36,000
8	28,000	40,000

Note: For the following requirements, round the fixed cost to the nearest dollar and round the variable rates to the nearest cent.

Required:
1. Prepare a scattergraph by plotting power costs against machine hours. Does the scattergraph show a linear relationship between machine hours and power cost?
2. Using the high and low points, compute a power cost formula.

(Continued)

3. Use the method of least squares to compute a power cost formula. Evaluate the coefficient of determination.

4. **Conceptual Connection:** Rerun the regression, and drop the point (20,000, $26,000) as an outlier. Compare the results from this regression to those for the regression in Requirement 3. Which is better?

OBJECTIVE **3 4**

Problem 14-51 *(Appendix 14A)* Separating Fixed and Variable Costs, Service Setting

Louise McDermott, controller for the Galvin plant of Veromar Inc., wanted to determine the cost behavior of moving materials throughout the plant. She accumulated the following data on the number of moves (from 100 to 800 in increments of 100) and the total cost of moving materials at those levels of moves:

Number of Moves	Total Cost
100	$ 3,000
200	4,650
300	3,400
400	8,500
500	10,000
600	12,600
700	13,600
800	14,560

Note: For the following requirements, round the fixed costs to the nearest dollar and round the variable cost to the nearest cent.

Required:

1. Prepare a scattergraph based on these data. Use cost for the vertical axis and number of moves for the horizontal. Based on an examination of the scattergraph, does there appear to be a linear relationship between the total cost of moving materials and the number of moves?

2. Compute the cost formula for moving materials by using the high-low method. Calculate the predicted cost for a month with 550 moves by using the high-low formula.

3. **Conceptual Connection:** Compute the cost formula for moving materials using the method of least squares. Using the regression cost formula, what is the predicted cost for a month with 550 moves? What does the coefficient of determination tell you about the cost formula computed by regression?

4. **Conceptual Connection:** Evaluate the cost formula using the least squares coefficients. Could it be improved? Try dropping the third data point (300, $3,400), and rerun the regression.

CASES

OBJECTIVE **1 2 3 4**

Case 14-52 Cost Formulas, Single and Multiple Cost Drivers

For the past five years, Garner Company has had a policy of producing to meet customer demand. As a result, finished goods inventory is minimal, and for the most part, units produced equal units sold.

Recently, Garner's industry entered a recession, and the company is producing well below capacity (and expects to continue doing so for the coming year). The president is willing to accept orders that at least cover their variable costs so that the company can keep its employees and avoid layoffs. Also, any orders above variable costs will increase overall profitability of the company. Toward that end, the president of Garner Company implemented a policy that any special orders will be accepted if they cover the costs that the orders cause.

To help implement the policy, Garner's controller developed the following cost formulas:

$$\text{Direct material usage} = \$94X, \quad R^2 = 0.90$$

$$\text{Direct labor usage} = \$16X, \quad R^2 = 0.92$$

$$\text{Overhead} = \$350,000 + \$80X, \quad R^2 = 0.56$$

$$\text{Selling costs} = \$50,000 + \$7X, \quad R^2 = 0.86$$

where X = direct labor hours

Required:

1. Compute the total unit variable cost. Suppose that Garner has an opportunity to accept an order for 20,000 units at $212 per unit. Each unit uses one direct labor hour for production. Should Garner accept the order? (The order would not displace any of Garner's regular orders.)

2. *(Appendix 14A)* Explain the significance of the coefficient of determination measures for the cost formulas. Did these measures have a bearing on your answer in Requirement 1? Should they have a bearing? Why?

3. *(Appendix 14A)* Suppose that a multiple regression equation is developed for overhead costs: Y = $100,000 + $85X1 + $5,000X2 + $300X3, where X1 = Direct labor hours, X2 = Number of setups, and X3 = Engineering hours. The coefficient of determination for the equation is 0.89. Assume that the order of 20,000 units requires 12 setups and 600 engineering hours. Given this new information, should the company accept the special order referred to in Requirement 1? Is there any other information about cost behavior that you would like to have? Explain.

Case 14-53 Suspicious Acquisition of Data, Ethical Issues

OBJECTIVE

Bill Lewis, manager of the Thomas Electronics Division, called a meeting with his controller, Brindon Peterson, and his marketing manager, Patty Fritz. The following is a transcript of the conversation that took place during the meeting:

Bill: Brindon, the variable costing system that you developed has proved to be a big plus for our division. Our success in winning bids has increased, and as a result our revenues have increased by 25 percent. However, if we intend to meet this year's profit targets, we are going to need something extra—am I right, Patty?

Patty: Absolutely. While we have been able to win more bids, we still are losing too many, particularly to our major competitor, Kilborn Electronics. If we knew more about their bidding strategy, we could be more successful at competing with them.

Brindon: Would knowing their variable costs help?

Patty: Certainly. It would give me their minimum price. With that knowledge, I'm sure that we could find a way to beat them on several jobs, particularly on those jobs where we are at least as efficient. It would also help us to identify where we are not cost competitive. With this information, we might be able to find ways to increase our efficiency.

Brindon: Well, I have good news. I've been talking with Carl Penobscot, Kilborn's assistant controller. Carl doesn't feel appreciated by Kilborn and wants to make a change. He could easily fit into our team here. Plus, Carl has been preparing for a job switch by quietly copying Kilborn's accounting files and records. He's already given me some data that reveal bids that Kilborn made on several jobs. If we can come to a satisfactory agreement with Carl, he'll bring the rest of the information with him. We'll easily be able to figure out Kilborn's prospective bids and find ways to beat them. Besides, I could use another accountant on my staff. Bill, would you authorize my immediate hiring of Carl with a favorable compensation package?

Bill: I know that you need more staff, Brindon, but is this the right thing to do? It sounds like Carl is stealing those files, and surely Kilborn considers this information confidential. I have real ethical and legal concerns about this. Why don't we meet with Laurie, our attorney, and determine any legal problems?

Required:

1. Is Carl's behavior ethical? What would Kilborn think?

2. Is Bill correct in supposing that there are ethical and/or legal problems involved with the hiring of Carl? (Reread the section on corporate codes of conduct in Chapter 13.) What would you do if you were Bill? Explain.

15

Cost-Volume-Profit Analysis: A Managerial Planning Tool

Doug Norman Crystals/Alamy

After studying Chapter 15, you should be able to:

1. Determine the break-even point in number of units and in total sales dollars.

2. Determine the number of units that must be sold, and the amount of revenue required, to earn a targeted profit.

3. Prepare a profit-volume graph and a cost-volume-profit graph, and explain the meaning of each.

4. Apply cost-volume-profit analysis in a multiple-product setting.

5. Explain the impact of risk, uncertainty, and changing variables on cost-volume-profit analysis.

Paul Burns, Fancy/Fancy/Jupiter Images

EXPERIENCE MANAGERIAL DECISIONS

with Boyne Resorts

Boyne USA Resorts owns and operates ski resorts in British Columbia, Washington, Montana, and Michigan. Boyne earns a significant portion of its revenue from winter skiing. However, winter ski volume depends heavily on natural snowfall, which varies significantly from year to year. As a result, Boyne uses creative thinking along with cost-volume-profit (CVP) analyses to develop activities that generate additional profit. Consider ski lifts at Boyne Highlands, an important source of revenue for the company. What other revenue-generating activities might Boyne develop that revolve around such ski lifts? What additional variable and fixed costs might be involved with these activities, and what are the profit implications?

Boyne develops a variety of lift ticket packages to accommodate as many snow skiers and snow boarders as possible. Lift tickets are interchangeable between multiple Boyne properties and can be used during night skiing in certain areas. Like many ski resorts, Boyne markets spring, summer, and fall activities as well. For instance, many resorts promote mountain biking and hiking where participants purchase lift tickets for enclosed lifts, called gondolas, that carry them and their gear to the top of the mountain to begin their descent. Other ski resorts, such as Aspen, build elaborate children's playgrounds and bungee trampolines at the top of the lifts to generate additional summer business in ski areas that might otherwise be dormant during the off-season. Still other resorts build elaborate mountaintop restaurants and entertainment areas that can be reached only via ski lifts or gondolas, thereby increasing revenues and profits. Using CVP equations and contribution margin formulas, as well as cost-volume-profit and profit-volume graphs, Boyne spends considerable effort analyzing the revenue, cost, volume, and profit implications of these varied activities. With careful CVP analysis and sound judgment, Boyne attempts to make the best decisions possible to continue its profitability and reputation for fun.

BOYNE RESORTS

EXPERIENCE THE LIFESTYLE

BREAK-EVEN POINT IN UNITS AND IN SALES DOLLARS

Cost-volume-profit (CVP) analysis estimates how changes in costs (both variable and fixed), sales volume, and price affect a company's profit. CVP is a powerful tool for planning and decision making. In fact, CVP is one of the most versatile and widely applicable tools used by managerial accountants to help managers make better decisions.

Companies use CVP analysis to reach important benchmarks, such as their break-even point. The **break-even point** is the point where total revenue equals total cost (i.e., the point of zero profit). New companies typically experience losses (negative operating income) initially and view their first break-even period as a significant milestone. For example, online retail pioneer **Amazon.com** was founded in 1994 but did not break even until the fourth quarter of 2001. Also, managers become very interested in CVP analysis during times of economic trouble. For example, to the dismay of many of its shareholders, **Sirius Satellite Radio** signed shock-jock Howard Stern to a five-year, $500 million employment contract for joining the young company. As a result of Stern's huge contract cost, some analysts estimated that Sirius would need an additional 2.4 million subscribers (i.e., customers) to reach breakeven. Therefore, CVP analysis helps managers pinpoint problems and find solutions.

CVP analysis can address many other issues as well, including:

- the number of units that must be sold to break even
- the impact of a given reduction in fixed costs on the break-even point
- the impact of an increase in price on profit

Additionally, CVP analysis allows managers to do sensitivity analysis by examining the impact of various price or cost levels on profit.

Since CVP analysis shows how revenues, expenses, and profits behave as volume changes, it is natural to begin by finding the firm's break-even point in units sold.

Here's The Real Kicker

Kicker separates cost into fixed and variable components by using judgment. Because the bulk of manufacturing is outsourced, the cost of a set of speakers starts with the purchase price from the manufacturer. This cost is strictly variable in nature. Additional variable costs include duty (ranging from 9 to 30 percent—electronics are at the high end) and freight (all units are shipped to Stillwater, Oklahoma, for distribution). In-house labor may be needed at Kicker's Stillwater facilities, and that cost has both fixed (salaried workers) and variable (temporary workers) components.

The salaried staff in Stillwater, research and development, depreciation on property, plant and equipment, utilities, and so on, are all fixed.

These fixed and variable costs are used in monthly cost-volume-profit analysis and in management decision making. For example, the monthly cost-volume-profit figures can be used to monitor the effect of changing volume on profit and spotlight increases in fixed and variable costs. If costs are going up, management finds out about the problem early and can make adjustments.

Using Operating Income in Cost-Volume-Profit Analysis

In CVP analysis, the terms "cost" and "expense" are often used interchangeably. This is because the conceptual foundation of CVP analysis is the economics of breakeven analysis in the short run. For this, it is assumed that all units produced are sold. Therefore, all product and period costs do end up as expenses on the income statement. We will look more closely at the assumptions of CVP later in this chapter. Remember from Chapter 13 that operating income is total revenue minus total expense:

$$\text{Operating income} = \text{Total revenue} - \text{Total expense}$$

For the income statement, expenses are classified according to function; that is, the manufacturing (or service provision) function, the selling function, and the administrative function. For CVP analysis, however, it is much more useful to organize costs into fixed and variable components. The focus is on the firm as a whole. Therefore, the costs refer

The Contribution Margin Income Statement

Exhibit 15-1

Sales	$ XXX
Total variable cost	(XXX)
Total contribution margin	$ XXX
Total fixed cost	(XXX)
Operating income	$ XXX

to all costs of the company—production, selling, and administration. So variable costs are all costs that increase as more units are sold, including:

- direct materials
- direct labor
- variable overhead
- variable selling and administrative costs

Similarly, fixed costs include:

- fixed overhead
- fixed selling and administrative expenses

The income statement format that is based on the separation of costs into fixed and variable components is called the **contribution margin income statement**. Exhibit 15-1 shows the format for the contribution margin income statement.

Contribution margin is the difference between sales and variable expense. It is the amount of sales revenue left over after all the variable expenses are covered that can be used to contribute to fixed expense and operating income. The contribution margin can be calculated in total (as it was in Exhibit 15-1) or per unit.

Let's use Whittier Company, a manufacturer of mulching lawn mowers, as an example. **CORNERSTONE 15-1** illustrates how to calculate the variable and fixed expenses and prepare the contribution margin statement for Whittier.

 **CORNERSTONE 15-1** **Preparing a Contribution Margin Income Statement**

Information:

Whittier Company plans to sell 1,000 mowers at $400 each in the coming year. Product costs include:

Direct materials per mower	$ 180
Direct labor per mower	100
Variable factory overhead per mower	25
Total fixed factory overhead	15,000

Variable selling expense is a commission of $20 per mower; fixed selling and administrative expense totals $30,000.

Required:

1. Calculate the total variable expense per unit.
2. Calculate the total fixed expense for the year.
3. Prepare a contribution margin income statement for Whittier for the coming year.

Solution:

1. Total variable expense per unit
   = Direct materials + Direct labor + Variable factory overhead + Variable selling expense
   = $180   + $100   + $25   + $20
   = $325

(Continued)

CORNERSTONE 15-1
(continued)

2. Total fixed expense = Fixed factory overhead
   + Fixed selling and administrative expense
   = $15,000 + $30,000 = $45,000

3.

Whittier Company
Contribution Margin Income Statement
For the Coming Year

	Total	Per Unit
Sales ($400 × 1,000 mowers)	$400,000	$400
Total variable expense ($325 × 1,000)	325,000	325
Total contribution margin	$ 75,000	$ 75
Total fixed expense	45,000	
Operating income	$ 30,000	

Notice that the contribution margin income statement in Cornerstone 15-1 shows a total contribution margin of $75,000. The per-unit contribution margin is $75 ($400 − $325). That is, every mower sold contributes $75 toward fixed expense and operating income.

What does Whittier's contribution margin income statement show? First, we see that Whittier will more than break even at sales of 1,000 mowers, since operating income is $30,000. Clearly, Whittier would just break even if total contribution margin equaled the total fixed cost. Let's see how to calculate the break-even point.

Break-Even Point in Units

If the contribution margin income statement is recast as an equation, it becomes more useful for solving CVP problems. The operating income equation is:

> Operating income = Sales − Total variable expenses − Total fixed expenses

Notice that all we have done is remove the total contribution margin line from Exhibit 15-1, since it is identical to sales minus total variable expense. This equation is the basis of all the coming work on CVP. We can think of it as the basic CVP equation.

We can expand the operating income equation by expressing sales revenues and variable expenses in terms of unit dollar amounts and the number of units sold. Specifically, sales revenue equals the unit selling price times the number of units sold, and total variable costs equal the unit variable cost times the number of units sold. With these expressions, the operating income equation becomes:

> Operating income = (Price × Number of units sold) − (Variable cost per unit × Number of units sold) − Total fixed cost

At the break-even point, operating income equals $0. **CORNERSTONE 15-2** shows how to use the operating income equation to find the break-even point in units for Whittier Company.

CORNERSTONE 15-2   **Calculating the Break-Even Point in Units**

Information:
Refer to the Whittier Company information in Cornerstone 15-1. Recall that mowers sell for $400 each, and variable cost per mower is $325. Total fixed cost equals $45,000.

(Continued)

CORNERSTONE
15-2
(continued)

Required:
1. Calculate the number of mowers that Whittier must sell to break even.
2. Check your answer by preparing a contribution margin income statement based on the break-even point.

Solution:
1. Break-even number of mowers = $\dfrac{\text{Total fixed cost}}{\text{Price} - \text{Variable cost per unit}}$

   $= \dfrac{\$45,000}{\$400 - \$325} = 600$

2. Contribution margin income statement based on 600 mowers.

Sales ($400 × 600 mowers)	$240,000
Total variable expense ($325 × 600)	195,000
Total contribution margin	$ 45,000
Total fixed expense	45,000
Operating income	$ 0

Indeed, selling 600 units does yield a zero profit.

When Whittier breaks even, total contribution margin equals total fixed cost. Exhibit 15-2 illustrates this important observation.

The operating income equation can be rearranged as follows to show the number of units at breakeven:

$$\text{Break-even units} = \dfrac{\text{Total fixed cost}}{\text{Price} - \text{Variable cost per unit}}$$

In other words, the break-even units are equal to the fixed cost divided by the contribution margin per unit. So, if a company sells enough units for the contribution margin to just cover fixed costs, it will earn zero operating income: it will break even. It is quicker to solve break-even problems using this break-even version of the operating income equation than it is using the original operating income equation.

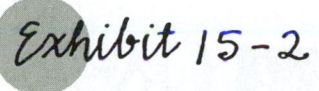

Contribution Margin and Fixed Cost at Breakeven for Whittier Company

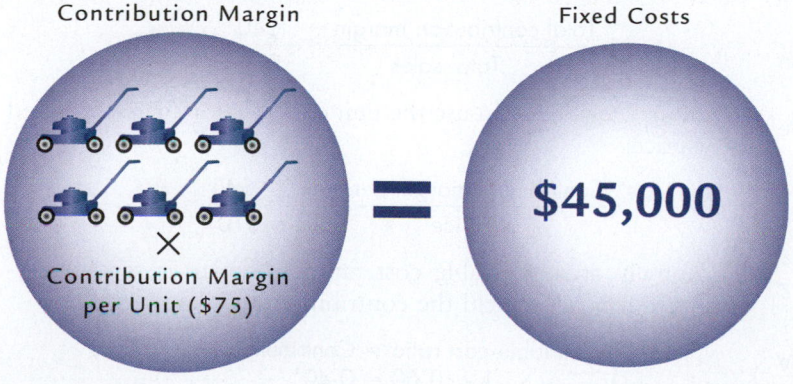

Contribution Margin

Fixed Costs

× Contribution Margin per Unit ($75)

= $45,000

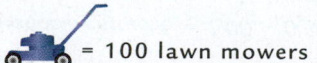

= 100 lawn mowers

Break-Even Point in Sales Dollars

Sometimes, managers using CVP analysis may prefer to use sales revenue as the measure of sales activity instead of units sold. A units sold measure can be converted to a sales revenue measure by multiplying the unit selling price by the units sold:

> Sales revenue = Unit selling price × Units sold

For example, the break-even point for Whittier is 600 mulching mowers. Since the selling price for each lawn mower is $400, the break-even volume in sales revenue is $240,000 ($400 × 600).

Any answer expressed in units sold can be easily converted to one expressed in sales revenues, but the answer can be computed more directly by developing a separate formula for the sales revenue case. Here, the important variable is sales dollars, so both the revenue and the variable costs must be expressed in dollars instead of units. Since sales revenue is always expressed in dollars, measuring that variable is no problem. Let's look more closely at variable costs and see how they can be expressed in terms of sales dollars.

Variable Cost Ratio

To calculate the break-even point in sales dollars, total variable costs are defined as a percentage of sales rather than as an amount per unit sold. Suppose that a company sells a product for $10 per unit and incurs a variable cost of $6 per unit. The contribution margin would be $4:

> Price − Variable cost per unit = $10 − $6 = $4

If 10 units are sold, total variable costs are $60:

> Variable cost × Units sold = $6 × 10 units = $60

Alternatively, since each unit sold earns $10 of revenue and has $6 of variable cost, one could say that 60 percent of each dollar of revenue earned is attributable to variable cost:

$$\frac{\text{Variable cost per unit}}{\text{Price}} = \frac{\$6}{\$10} = 60\%$$

Thus, sales revenues of $100 would result in total variable costs of $60 (0.60 × $100). This 60 percent is the variable cost ratio.

The **variable cost ratio** is the proportion of each sales dollar that must be used to cover variable costs. The variable cost ratio can be computed using either total data or unit data.

Contribution Margin Ratio

The percentage of sales dollars remaining after variable costs are covered is the contribution margin ratio. The **contribution margin ratio** is the proportion of each sales dollar available to cover fixed costs and provide for profit. For Whittier, if the variable cost ratio is 60 percent of sales, then the contribution margin ratio must be the remaining 40 percent of sales. It makes sense that the complement of the variable cost ratio is the contribution margin ratio. After all, total variable costs and total contribution margin sum to sales revenue.

Just as the variable cost ratio can be computed using total or unit figures, the contribution margin ratio, 40 percent in our example, can also be computed in these two ways. So, one can divide the total contribution margin by total sales:

$$\frac{\text{Total contribution margin}}{\text{Total sales}} = \frac{\$40}{\$100} = 40\%$$

Alternatively, one can use the unit contribution margin divided by price:

$$\frac{\text{Contribution margin per unit}}{\text{Price}} = \frac{\$4}{\$10} = 40\%$$

Naturally, if the variable cost ratio is known, it can be subtracted from 1 to yield the contribution margin ratio:

> 1 − Variable cost ratio = Contribution margin ratio
> 1 − 0.60 = 0.40

CORNERSTONE 15-3 shows how the income statement can be expanded to yield the variable cost ratio and the contribution margin ratio.

CORNERSTONE 15-3

Calculating the Variable Cost Ratio and the Contribution Margin Ratio

Information:

Whittier Company plans to sell 1,000 mowers at $400 each in the coming year. Variable cost per unit is $325. Total fixed cost is $45,000.

Required:

1. Calculate the variable cost ratio.
2. Calculate the contribution margin ratio using unit figures.
3. Prepare a contribution margin income statement based on the budgeted figures for next year. In a column next to the income statement, show the percentages based on sales for sales, total variable expense, and total contribution margin.

Solution:

1. $\text{Variable cost ratio} = \dfrac{\text{Variable cost per unit}}{\text{Price}}$

$\qquad = \dfrac{\$325}{\$400} = 0.8125, \text{ or } 81.25\%$

2. $\text{Contribution margin per unit} = \text{Price} - \text{Variable cost per unit}$
$\qquad\qquad\qquad\qquad\qquad\quad = \$400 - \$325 = \$75$

$\text{Contribution margin ratio} = \dfrac{\text{Contribution margin per unit}}{\text{Price}}$

$\qquad\qquad\qquad\qquad\quad = \dfrac{\$75}{\$400} = 0.1875, \text{ or } 18.75\%$

3. Contribution margin income statement based on budgeted figures:

		Percent of Sales
Sales ($400 × 1,000 mowers)	$400,000	100.00
Total variable expense (0.8125 × $400,000)	325,000	81.25
Total contribution margin	$ 75,000	18.75
Total fixed expense	45,000	
Operating income	$ 30,000	

Notice in Cornerstone 15-3, Requirement 3, that sales revenue, variable costs, and contribution margin have been expressed as a percent of sales. The variable cost ratio is 0.8125 ($325,000/$400,000); the contribution margin ratio is 0.1875 (computed either as 1 − 0.8125, or $75,000/$400,000).

How do fixed costs relate to the variable cost ratio and contribution margin ratio? Since the total contribution margin is the revenue remaining after total variable costs are covered, it must be the revenue available to cover fixed costs and contribute to profit. How does the relationship of fixed cost to contribution margin affect operating income? There are three possibilities:

- Fixed cost equals contribution margin; operating income is zero; the company breaks even.
- Fixed cost is less than contribution margin; operating income is greater than zero; the company makes a profit.
- Fixed cost is greater than contribution margin; operating income is less than zero; the company makes a loss.

Calculating Break-Even Point in Sales Dollars Now, let's turn to the equation for calculating the break-even point in sales dollars. One way of calculating break-even sales revenue is to multiply the break-even units by the price. However, often the company is a multiple-product firm, and it can be difficult to figure the break-even point for each product sold. The operating income equation can be used to solve for break-even sales for Whittier as follows:

$$\text{Operating income} = \text{Sales} - \text{Total variable expenses} - \text{Total fixed expenses}$$
$$\$0 = \text{Break-even sales} - (0.8125 \times \text{Break-even sales}) - \$45,000$$
$$\$0 = \text{Break-even sales} \, (1.00 - 0.8125) - \$45,000$$
$$\text{Break-even sales} = \frac{\$45,000}{(1.00 - 0.8125)}$$
$$\text{Break-even sales} = \$240,000$$

So, Whittier Company has sales of $240,000 at the break-even point.

Just as it was quicker to use an equation to calculate the break-even units directly, it is helpful to have an equation to figure the break-even sales dollars. This equation is:

$$\text{Break-even sales} = \frac{\text{Total fixed expenses}}{\text{Contribution margin ratio}}$$

CORNERSTONE 15-4 shows how to obtain the break-even point in sales dollars for Whittier Company.

CORNERSTONE 15-4

Calculating the Break-Even Point in Sales Dollars

Information:
Whittier Company plans to sell 1,000 mowers at $400 each in the coming year. Total variable expense per unit is $325. Total fixed expense is $45,000.

Required:
1. Calculate the contribution margin ratio.
2. Calculate the sales revenue that Whittier must make to break even by using the break-even point in sales equation.
3. Check your answer by preparing a contribution margin income statement based on the break-even point in sales dollars.

Solution:
1. Contribution margin per unit = Price − Variable cost per unit
   $$= \$400 - \$325 = \$75$$

   $$\text{Contribution margin ratio} = \frac{\text{Contribution margin per unit}}{\text{Price}}$$

   $$= \frac{\$75}{\$400} = 0.1875, \text{ or } 18.75\%$$

   [*Hint:* The contribution margin ratio comes out cleanly to four decimal places. Don't round it, and your break-even point in sales dollars will yield an operating income of $0 (rather than being a few dollars off due to rounding).]

   Notice that the variable cost ratio equals 0.8125, or the difference between 1.0000 and the contribution margin ratio.

2. Calculate the break-even point in sales dollars:

   $$\text{Break-even sales dollars} = \frac{\text{Total fixed cost}}{\text{Contribution margin ratio}}$$

   $$= \frac{\$45,000}{0.1875} = \$240,000$$

   (Continued)

3. Contribution margin income statement based on sales of $240,000:

Sales	$240,000
Total variable expense (0.8125 × $240,000)	195,000
Total contribution margin	$ 45,000
Total fixed expense	45,000
Operating income	$ 0

CORNERSTONE 15-4 *(continued)*

Indeed, sales equal to $240,000 does yield a zero profit.

Accountants for the snowsports division of **Boyne USA Resorts** analyze their fixed and variable costs each month as they work to anticipate their break-even point and potential operating income. The contribution margin income statement is a powerful tool to help them with this. They pay close attention to the week between Christmas and New Years, as this is their peak revenue opportunity. Depending on what occurs that week, pricing and cost management for the rest of the season are adjusted.

BOYNE RESORTS
EXPERIENCE THE LIFESTYLE

UNITS AND SALES DOLLARS NEEDED TO ACHIEVE A TARGET INCOME

OBJECTIVE ❷
Determine the number of units that must be sold, and the amount of revenue required, to earn a targeted profit.

While the break-even point is useful information and an important benchmark for relatively young companies, most companies would like to earn operating income greater than $0. CVP analysis gives us a way to determine how many units must be sold, or how much sales revenue must be generated, to earn a particular target income. Let's look first at the number of units that must be sold to earn a targeted operating income.

Units to Be Sold to Achieve a Target Income

Remember that at the break-even point, operating income is $0. How can the equations used in our earlier break-even analyses be adjusted to find the number of units that must be sold to earn a target income? The answer is to add the target income amount to the fixed costs. Let's try it two different ways—with the operating income equation and with the basic break-even equation.

Remember that the equation for the operating income is:

Operating income = (Price × Units sold) − (Unit variable cost × Units sold) − Fixed cost

To solve for positive operating income, replace the operating income term with the target income. Recall that Whittier sells mowers at $400 each, incurs variable cost per unit of $325, and has total fixed expense of $45,000. Suppose that Whittier wants to make a target operating income of $37,500. The number of units that must be sold to achieve that target income is calculated as follows:

$37,500 = ($400 × Number of units) − ($325 × Number of units) − $45,000

$$\text{Number of units} = \frac{\$37,500 + \$45,000}{\$400 - \$325} = 1,100$$

Does the sale of 1,100 units really result in operating income of $37,500? The contribution margin income statement provides a good check.

Sales ($400 × 1,100)	$440,000
Total variable expense ($325 × 1,100)	357,500
Total contribution margin	$ 82,500
Total fixed expense	45,000
Operating income	$ 37,500

Indeed, selling 1,100 units does yield operating income of $37,500.

The operating income equation can be used to find the number of units to sell to earn a targeted income. However, it is quicker to adjust the break-even units equation by adding target income to the fixed cost. This adjustment results in the following equation:

$$\text{Number of units to earn target income} = \frac{\text{Total fixed cost} + \text{Target income}}{\text{Price} - \text{Variable cost per unit}}$$

This equation was used when calculating the 1,100 units needed to earn operating income of $37,500. **CORNERSTONE 15-5** shows how Whittier Company can use this approach.

 **CORNERSTONE 15-5**   **Calculating the Number of Units to Be Sold to Earn a Target Operating Income**

Information:
Whittier Company sells mowers at $400 each. Variable cost per unit is $325, and total fixed cost is $45,000.

Required:
1. Calculate the number of units that Whittier must sell to earn operating income of $37,500.
2. Check your answer by preparing a contribution margin income statement based on the number of units calculated.

Solution:
1. $$\text{Number of units} = \frac{\text{Target income} + \text{Total fixed cost}}{\text{Price} - \text{Variable cost per unit}}$$

$$= \frac{\$37,500 + \$45,000}{\$400 - \$325} = 1,100$$

2. Contribution margin income statement based on sales of 1,100 units:

Sales ($400 × 1,100)	$440,000
Total variable expense ($325 × 1,100)	357,500
Total contribution margin	$ 82,500
Total fixed expense	45,000
Operating income	$ 37,500

Indeed, selling 1,100 units does yield operating income of $37,500.

Another way to check the number of units to be sold to yield a target operating income is to use the break-even point. As shown in Cornerstone 15-5, Whittier must sell 1,100 lawn mowers, or 500 more than the break-even volume of 600 units, to earn a profit of $37,500. The contribution margin per lawn mower is $75. Multiplying $75 by the 500 lawn mowers above breakeven produces the operating income of $37,500 ($75 × 500). This outcome demonstrates that contribution margin per unit for each unit above breakeven is equivalent to operating income per unit. Since the break-even point had already been computed, the number of lawn mowers to be sold to yield a $37,500 operating income could have been calculated by dividing the unit contribution margin into the target income and adding the resulting amount to the break-even volume:

$$\text{Operating income} = \frac{\text{Target income}}{\text{Unit contribution margin}} + \text{Break-even volume}$$

In general, assuming that fixed costs remain the same, the impact on a firm's income resulting from a change in the number of units sold can be assessed by multiplying the unit contribution margin by the change in units sold:

> Operating income = Unit contribution margin × Change in units sold

For example, if 1,400 lawn mowers instead of 1,100 are sold, how much more operating income will be earned? The change in units sold is an increase of 300 lawn mowers, and the unit contribution margin is $75. Thus, operating income will increase by $22,500 ($75 × 300) over the $37,500 initially calculated, and total operating income will be $60,000.

Sales Revenue to Achieve a Target Income

Consider the following question: How much sales revenue must Whittier generate to earn an operating income of $37,500? This question is similar to the one we asked earlier in terms of units but phrases the question directly in terms of sales revenue. To answer the question, add the targeted operating income of $37,500 to the $45,000 of fixed cost and divide by the contribution margin ratio. This equation is:

$$\text{Sales dollars to earn target income} = \frac{\text{Fixed cost} + \text{Target income}}{\text{Contribution margin ratio}}$$

CORNERSTONE 15-6 shows how to calculate the sales revenue needed to earn a target operating income of $37,500.

 **CORNERSTONE 15-6**   **Calculating Sales Needed to Earn a Target Operating Income**

Information:
Whittier Company sells mowers at $400 each. Variable cost per unit is $325, and total fixed cost is $45,000.

Required:
1. Calculate the contribution margin ratio.
2. Calculate the sales that Whittier must make to earn an operating income of $37,500.
3. Check your answer by preparing a contribution margin income statement based on the sales dollars calculated.

Solution:

1. Contribution margin ratio $= \dfrac{\$400 - \$325}{\$400} = 0.1875$

2. Sales dollars $= \dfrac{\text{Target income} + \text{Total fixed cost}}{\text{Contribution margin ratio}}$

   $= \dfrac{\$37,500 + \$45,000}{0.1875} = \$440,000$

3. Contribution margin income statement based on sales revenue of $440,000:

Sales	$440,000
Total variable expense (0.8125 × $440,000)	357,500
Total contribution margin	$ 82,500
Total fixed expense	45,000
Operating income	$ 37,500

Indeed, sales revenue of $440,000 does yield operating income of $37,500.

Concept Q&A

Lorna makes and sells decorative candles through gift shops. She knows she must sell 200 candles a month to break even. Every candle has a contribution margin of $1.50. So far this month, Lorna has sold 320 candles. How much has Lorna earned so far this month in operating income? If she sells 10 more candles, by how much will income increase?

Answer:

320 candles sold − 200 candles at breakeven = 120 candles above breakeven. 120 × $1.50 = $180. Lorna has earned operating income of $180 so far during the month. An additional 10 candles contribute $15 to operating income ($1.50 × 10).

Whittier must earn revenues equal to $440,000 to achieve a profit target of $37,500. Since break-even sales equals $240,000, additional sales of $200,000 ($440,000 − $240,000) must be earned above breakeven. Notice that multiplying the contribution margin ratio by revenues above breakeven yields the profit of $37,500 (0.1875 × $200,000). Above break even, the contribution margin ratio is a profit ratio; therefore, it represents the proportion of each sales dollar attributable to profit. For Whittier, every sales dollar earned above breakeven increases profits by $0.1875.

In general, assuming that fixed costs remain unchanged, the contribution margin ratio can be used to find the profit impact of a change in sales revenue. To obtain the total change in profits from a change in revenues, multiply the contribution margin ratio times the change in sales:

> Change in profits = Contribution margin ratio × Change in sales

For example, if sales revenues are $400,000 instead of $440,000, how will the expected profits be affected? A decrease in sales revenues of $40,000 will cause a decrease in profits of $7,500 (0.1875 × $40,000).

OBJECTIVE ③
Prepare a profit-volume graph and a cost-volume-profit graph, and explain the meaning of each.

GRAPHS OF COST-VOLUME-PROFIT RELATIONSHIPS

Graphical representations of CVP relationships can help managers clearly see the difference between variable cost and revenue. It may also help them understand quickly what impact an increase or decrease in sales will have on the break-even point. Two basic graphs are the profit-volume graph and the cost-volume-profit graph.

The Profit-Volume Graph

A **profit-volume graph** visually portrays the relationship between profits (operating income) and units sold. The profit-volume graph is the graph of the operating income equation:

> Operating income = (Price × Units) − (Unit variable cost × Units) − Total fixed cost

In this graph, operating income is the dependent variable, and units is the independent variable. Usually, values of the independent variable are measured along the horizontal axis, and values of the dependent variable are measured along the vertical axis.

Assume that Tyson Company produces a single product with the following cost and price data:

Total fixed costs	$10
Variable costs per unit	5
Selling price per unit	10

Using these data, operating income can be expressed as:

> Operating income = ($10 × Units) − ($5 × Units) − $100
> = ($5 × Units) − $100

This relationship can be graphed by plotting units along the horizontal axis and operating income (or loss) along the vertical axis. Two points are needed to graph a linear equation. While any two points will do, the two points often chosen are those that correspond to zero units sold and zero profits. When units sold are 0, Tyson experiences an operating loss of $100 (or an operating income of –$100). The point corresponding to zero sales volume, therefore, is (0, –$100). When no sales take place, the company suffers a loss equal to its total fixed costs. When operating income is $0, the units sold are equal to 20. The point corresponding to zero profits (breakeven) is (20, $0). These two points, plotted in Exhibit 15-3, define the profit graph.

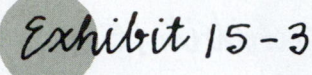

Profit-Volume Graph

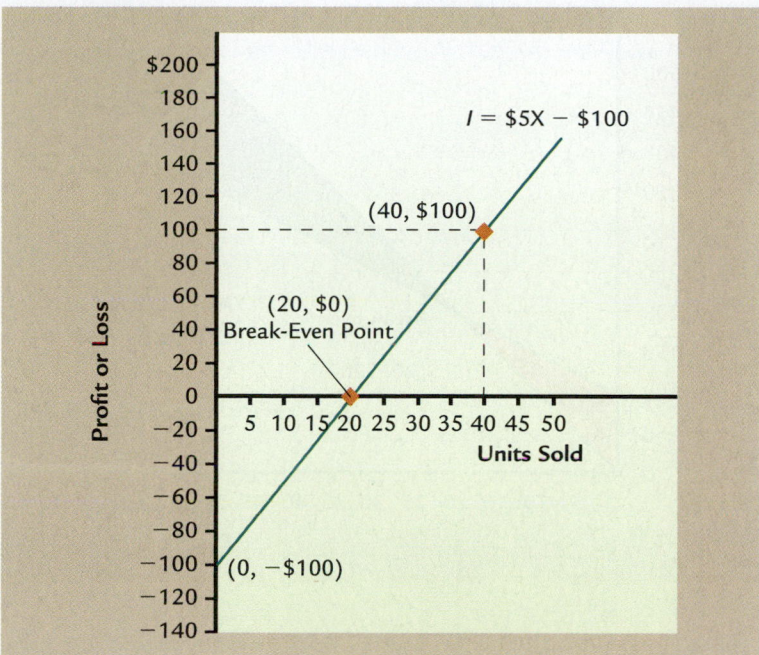

The graph in Exhibit 15-3 can be used to assess Tyson's profit (or loss) at any level of sales activity. For example, the profit associated with the sale of 40 units can be read from the graph by:

1. drawing a vertical line from the horizontal axis to the profit line and
2. drawing a horizontal line from the profit line to the vertical axis.

As illustrated in Exhibit 15-3, the profit associated with sales of 40 units is $100. The profit-volume graph, while easy to interpret, fails to reveal how costs change as sales volume changes. An alternative approach to graphing can provide this detail.

The Cost-Volume-Profit Graph

The **cost-volume-profit graph** depicts the relationships among cost, volume, and profits (operating income) by plotting the total revenue line and the total cost line on a graph. To obtain the more detailed relationships, it is necessary to graph two separate lines—the total revenue line and the total cost line. These two lines are represented by the following two equations:

> Revenue = Price × Units

> Total cost = (Unit variable cost × Units) + Fixed cost

Using the Tyson example, the revenue and cost equations are:

$$Revenue = \$10 \times Units$$
$$Total\ cost = (\$5 \times Units) + \$100$$

To portray both equations in the same graph, the vertical axis is measured in dollars, and the horizontal axis is measured in units sold.

Again, two points are needed to graph each equation. For the revenue equation, setting number of units equal to 0 results in revenue of $0, and setting number of units equal to 20 results in revenue of $200. Therefore, the two points for the revenue equation are (0, $0) and (20, $200). For the cost equation, units sold of 0 and units sold of 20 produce the points (0, $100) and (20, $200). The graph of each equation appears in Exhibit 15-4 (p. 770).

Exhibit 15-4

Cost-Volume-Profit Graph

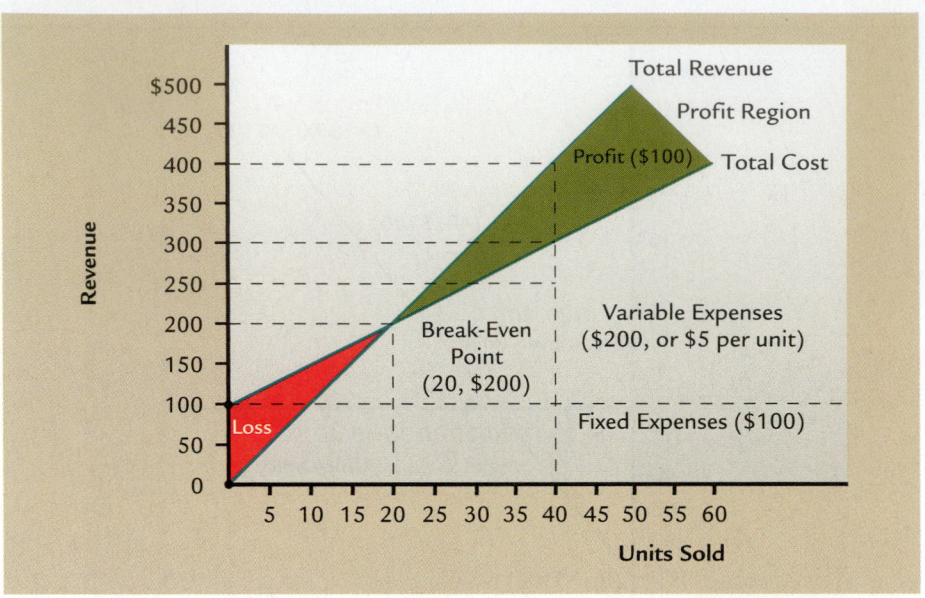

Concept Q&A

Suppose that the revenue line in Exhibit 15-4 had a steeper slope due to a higher price. What would that imply for the break-even point? For the amount of operating income (profit) for units sold above breakeven? Now suppose that the revenue line remains unchanged, but that variable cost per unit increases. How would this increase affect the total cost line? What would this increase imply for the break-even point? For the amount of operating income (profit) for units sold above breakeven?

Answer:

A steeper revenue line would intersect the total cost line sooner. Thus, the break-even point would be lower; operating income above breakeven would be higher. (Hint: Draw a steeper total revenue line on Exhibit 15-4 to check this reasoning. Remember, revenue still starts at the origin; zero units sold means zero total revenue.) Increased variable cost per unit means a steep slope for the total cost line. Thus, the break-even point would be higher, and the operating income above breakeven would be lower.

Notice that the total revenue line begins at the origin and rises with a slope equal to the selling price per unit (a slope of 10). The total cost line intercepts the vertical axis at a point equal to total fixed costs and rises with a slope equal to the variable cost per unit (a slope of 5). When the total revenue line lies below the total cost line, a loss region is defined. Similarly, when the total revenue line lies above the total cost line, a profit region is defined. The point where the total revenue line and the total cost line intersect is the break-even point. To break even, Tyson must sell 20 units and, thus, receive $200 in total revenues.

Now, let's compare the information available from the CVP graph with that available from the profit-volume graph. Consider the sale of 40 units. The profit-volume graph showed that 40 units produced profits of $100. Examine Exhibit 15-4 again. The CVP graph also shows profits of $100, but it reveals more. The CVP graph discloses that total revenues of $400 and total costs of $300 are associated with the sale of 40 units. Furthermore, the total costs can be broken down into fixed costs of $100 and variable costs of $200. The CVP graph provides revenue and cost information not provided by the profit-volume graph. Unlike the profit-volume graph, some computation is needed to determine the profit associated with a given sales volume. However, the greater information content means that managers are likely to find the CVP graph more useful.

Assumptions of Cost-Volume-Profit Analysis

The profit-volume and cost-volume-profit graphs rely on important assumptions. Some of these assumptions are as follows:

- There are identifiable linear revenue and linear cost functions that remain constant over the relevant range.
- Selling prices and costs are known with certainty.
- Units produced are sold—there are no finished goods inventories.
- Sales mix is known with certainty for multiple-product break-even settings (explained later in this chapter).

Linear Cost and Revenue Functions   CVP assumes that cost and revenue functions are linear; that is, they are straight lines. But, as was discussed in Chapter 14 on cost behavior, these functions are often not linear. They may be curved or step functions. Fortunately, it is not necessary to consider all possible ranges of production and sales for a firm. Remember that CVP analysis is a short-run decision-making tool. (We know that it is short run in orientation because some costs are fixed.) It is only necessary for us to determine the current operating range, or relevant range, for which the linear cost and revenue relationships are valid. Once a relevant range has been identified, then the cost and price relationships are assumed to be known and constant.

Prices and Costs Known with Certainty   In reality, firms seldom know prices, variable costs, and fixed costs with certainty. A change in one variable usually affects the value of others. Often, there is a probability distribution to consider. There are formal ways of explicitly building uncertainty into the CVP model. These issues are explored in the section on incorporating risk and uncertainty into CVP analysis.

Production Equal to Sales   CVP assumes that all units produced are sold. There is no change in inventory over the period. The idea that inventory has no impact on break-even analysis makes sense. Break-even analysis is a short-run decision-making technique, so we are looking to cover all costs of a particular period of time. Inventory embodies costs of a previous period and is not considered in CVP analyses.

Constant Sales Mix   In single-product analysis, the sales mix is obviously constant—the one product accounts for 100 percent of sales. Multiple-product break-even analysis requires a constant sales mix. However, it is virtually impossible to predict with certainty the sales mix. Typically, this constraint is handled in practice through sensitivity analysis. By using the capabilities of spreadsheet analysis, the sensitivity of variables to a variety of sales mixes can be readily assessed.

ILLUSTRATING RELATIONSHIPS AMONG CVP VARIABLES

It is critically important to understand the relationships among the CVP variables of price, unit variable cost, and total fixed costs. Consider Lotts Company, which produces and sells a product with the following costs.

Unit sales price	$ 10.00
Unit costs	5.00
Fixed costs	10,000

$$\text{Contribution margin} = \$10 - \$5 = \$5$$
$$\text{Break-even units} = \$10{,}000/(\$10 - \$5) = 2{,}000$$

This is illustrated in Panel A of Exhibit 15-5 (p. 772). The total revenue line, shown in blue, has a slope of 10 and the total cost line, shown in red, has a slope of 5. The point of intersection is 2,000 units, which is the break-even point. Units sold above breakeven yield a profit; units sold below breakeven result in a loss. What happens if changes occur in the price, unit variable cost, and fixed costs?

Impact of Changing Sales Price   In Panel B, price increases to $12, but unit variable cost and total fixed cost are the same. The new unit contribution margin is $7 ($12 − $5). Compare the new, steeper revenue, with a slope of 12, to the original revenue line shown in blue. The total cost line remains unchanged. The intersection of the revenue and total cost lines has moved toward the left, resulting in a new, lower break-even point of 1,429 units (rounded).

$$\text{Break-even units} = \frac{\$10{,}000}{\$12 - \$5} = 1{,}429 \text{ (rounded)}$$

Any increase in price will mean a higher contribution margin and, thus, a lower break-even point.

Exhibit 15-5

Cost-Volume-Profit Relationships

Panel A.

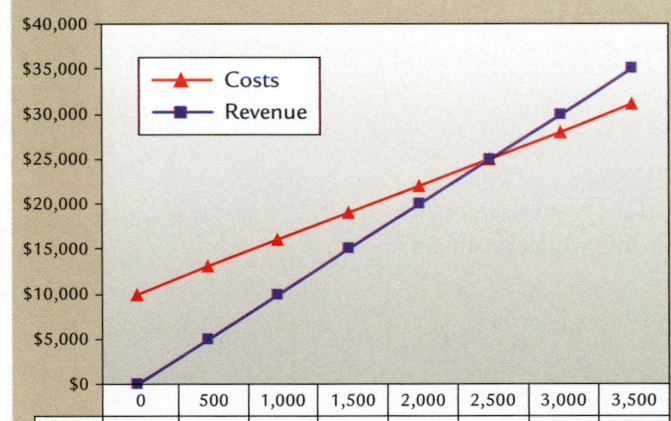

	0	500	1,000	1,500	2,000	2,500	3,000	3,500
Costs	$10,000	$12,500	$15,000	$17,500	$20,000	$22,500	$25,000	$27,500
Revenue	$0	$5,000	$10,000	$15,000	$20,000	$25,000	$30,000	$35,000

Unit sales price	$10.00
Cost per unit	$5.00
Fixed costs	$10,000
Break-even point (in units)	2,000 units

Panel B.

	0	500	1,000	1,500	2,000	2,500	3,000	3,500
Costs	$10,000	$12,500	$15,000	$17,500	$20,000	$22,500	$25,000	$27,500
Revenue	$0	$6,000	$12,000	$18,000	$24,000	$30,000	$36,000	$42,000

Unit sales price	$12.00
Cost per unit	$5.00
Fixed costs	$10,000
Break-even point (in units)	1,429 units (rounded)

Panel C.

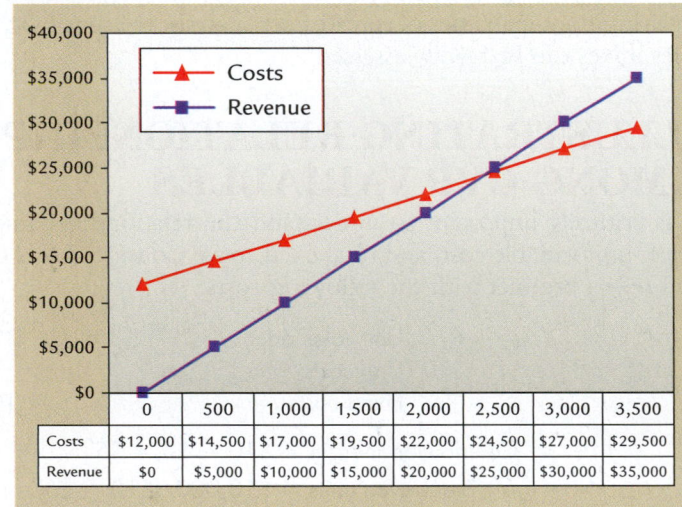

	0	500	1,000	1,500	2,000	2,500	3,000	3,500
Costs	$10,000	$13,000	$16,000	$19,000	$22,000	$25,000	$28,000	$31,000
Revenue	$0	$5,000	$10,000	$15,000	$20,000	$25,000	$30,000	$35,000

Unit sales price	$10.00
Cost per unit	$6.00
Fixed costs	$10,000
Break-even point (in units)	2,500 units

Panel D.

	0	500	1,000	1,500	2,000	2,500	3,000	3,500
Costs	$12,000	$14,500	$17,000	$19,500	$22,000	$24,500	$27,000	$29,500
Revenue	$0	$5,000	$10,000	$15,000	$20,000	$25,000	$30,000	$35,000

Unit sales price	$10.00
Cost per unit	$5.00
Fixed costs	$12,000
Break-even point (in units)	2,400 units

Impact of Changing Unit Variable Costs   In Panel C, unit variable cost increases to $6, but price and total fixed costs are the same. The new contribution margin is lower at $4 ($10 − $6). The total revenue line is the same as in Panel A. However, the total cost line has a steeper slope of 6, and it intersects the total revenue line further out to the right, resulting in a higher break-even point. Compare the new total cost line to the original line shown in blue.

$$\text{Break-even units} = \frac{\$10,000}{\$10 - \$6} = 2,500$$

Thus, any increase in unit variable costs will mean a lower contribution margin and a higher break-even point.

Impact of Changing Fixed Costs   Finally, in Panel D, total fixed costs increase to $12,000, but price and unit variable cost are the same. The new total cost line is red and can be compared to the original total cost line in gray. Since price and unit variable cost remain unchanged, the contribution margin stays at $5 per unit and the total revenue line is unchanged from Panel A. However, the total cost line has shifted upward, reflecting the increase in fixed costs. The new break-even point occurs farther out to the right from what it was in Panel A and shows break-even units of 2,400.

$$\text{Break-even units} = \frac{\$12,000}{\$10 - \$5} = 2,400$$

Thus, any increase in fixed costs will mean a higher break-even point.

Of course, many changes can be made to this simple data set for Lott Company to see how the contribution margin and break-even point are affected. You can make these changes yourself by going to www.cengage.com/accounting/cornerstones and working with the interactive graph there.

MULTIPLE-PRODUCT ANALYSIS

OBJECTIVE 4
Apply cost-volume-profit analysis in a multiple-product setting.

Cost-volume-profit analysis is fairly simple in the single-product setting. However, most firms produce and sell a number of products or services. Even though CVP analysis becomes more complex with multiple products, the operation is reasonably straightforward. Let's see how we can adapt the formulas used in a single-product setting to a multiple-product setting by expanding the Whittier example.

Whittier has decided to offer two models of lawn mowers: a mulching mower that sells for $400 and a riding mower that sells for $800. The marketing department is convinced that 1,200 mulching mowers and 800 riding mowers can be sold during the coming year. The controller has prepared the following projected income statement based on the sales forecast:

	Mulching Mower	Riding Mower	Total
Sales	$480,000	$640,000	$1,120,000
Total variable cost	390,000	480,000	870,000
Contribution margin	$ 90,000	$160,000	$ 250,000
Direct fixed cost	30,000	40,000	70,000
Product margin	$ 60,000	$120,000	$ 180,000
Common fixed cost			26,250
Operating income			$ 153,750

Note that the controller has separated *direct fixed expenses* from *common fixed expenses*. The **direct fixed expenses** are those fixed costs that can be traced to each segment and would be avoided if the segment did not exist. The **common fixed expenses** are the fixed costs that are not traceable to the segments and would remain even if one of the segments was eliminated.

Break-Even Point in Units

The owner of Whittier is a bit concerned about adding a new product line and wants to know how many units of each model must be sold to break even. If you were responsible for answering this question, how would you respond? One possibility is to use the equation developed earlier in which fixed costs were divided by the contribution margin. However, this equation was developed for single-product analysis. For two products, there are two prices and two variable costs per unit, calculated as follows:

	Equation	Mulching Mower	Riding Mower
Total variable costs	$\dfrac{\text{Variable cost per unit}}{\text{Price}}$	$\dfrac{\$390,000}{1,200} = \$325$	$\dfrac{\$480,000}{800} = \$600$
Contribution margin	$\dfrac{\text{Total contribution margin}}{\text{Sales}}$	$\$400 - \$325$ $= \$75$	$\$800 - \$600$ $= \$200$

One possible solution is to apply the analysis separately to each product line. It is possible to obtain individual break-even points when income is defined as product margin. Breakeven for the mulching mower is as follows:

$$\text{Mulching mower break-even units} = \frac{\text{Fixed cost}}{\text{Price} - \text{Unit variable cost}}$$

$$= \frac{\$30,000}{\$75}$$

$$= 400 \text{ units}$$

Breakeven for the riding mower can be computed as well:

$$\text{Riding mower break-even units} = \frac{\text{Fixed cost}}{\text{Price} - \text{Unit variable cost}}$$

$$= \frac{\$40,000}{\$200}$$

$$= 200 \text{ units}$$

Thus, 400 mulching mowers and 200 riding mowers must be sold to achieve a break-even product margin. But a break-even product margin covers only direct fixed costs; the common fixed costs remain to be covered. Selling these numbers of lawn mowers would result in a loss equal to the common fixed costs. This level of sales is not the break-even point for the firm as a whole; somehow the common fixed costs must be factored into the analysis.

We could allocate the common fixed costs to each product line before computing a break-even point. However, the allocation of the common fixed costs is arbitrary. Thus, no meaningful break-even volume is readily apparent.

Another possible solution is to convert the multiple-product problem into a single-product problem. If this can be done, then all of the single-product CVP methodology can be applied directly. The key to this conversion is to identify the expected sales mix, in units, of the products being marketed. **Sales mix** is the relative combination of products being sold by a firm.

Determining the Sales Mix
The sales mix is measured in units sold. For example, if Whittier plans on selling 1,200 mulching mowers and 800 riding mowers, then the sales mix in units is 1,200:800. Usually, the sales mix is reduced to the smallest possible whole numbers. Thus, the relative mix, 1,200:800, can be reduced to 12:8, and further reduced to 3:2. That is, Whittier expects that for every three mulching mowers sold, two riding mowers will be sold.

An endless number of different sales mixes can be used to define the break-even volume in a multiple-product setting. For example, a sales mix of 2:1 will define a break-even point of 550 mulching mowers and 275 riding mowers. The total contribution margin produced by this mix is $96,250:

(Mulching mower price × Break-even quantity) + (Riding mower price × Break-even quantity)

($75 × 550) + ($200 × 275)

Similarly, if 350 mulching mowers and 350 riding mowers are sold (corresponding to a 1:1 sales mix), then the total contribution margin is also $96,250:

($75 × 350) + ($200 × 350)

Since total fixed costs are $96,250, both sales mixes define break-even points. Fortunately, every sales mix need not be considered. According to Whittier's marketing study, a sales mix of 3:2 can be expected. This is the ratio that should be used; all others can be ignored. The sales mix that is expected to prevail should be used for CVP analysis.

Sales Mix and Cost-Volume-Profit Analysis

Sales Mix and Cost-Volume-Profit Analysis Defining a particular sales mix allows the conversion of a multiple-product problem into a single-product CVP format. Since Whittier expects to sell three mulching mowers for every two riding mowers, it can define the single product it sells as a package containing three mulching mowers and two riding mowers. By defining the product as a package, the multiple-product problem is converted into a single-product one. To use the approach of break-even point in units, the package selling price and the variable cost per package must be known. To compute these package values, the sales mix, individual product prices, and individual variable costs are needed. **CORNERSTONE 15-7** shows how to determine the overall break-even point for each product.

CORNERSTONE 15-7   Calculating the Break-Even Units for a Multiple-Product Firm

Information:

Recall that Whittier sells two products: mulching mowers priced at $400 and riding mowers priced at $800. The variable cost per unit is $325 per mulching mower and $600 per riding mower. Total fixed cost is $96,250. Whittier's expected sales mix is three mulching mowers to two riding mowers.

Required:

1. Form a package of mulching and riding mowers based on the sales mix and calculate the package contribution margin.
2. Calculate the break-even point in units for mulching mowers and for riding mowers.
3. Check your answers by preparing a contribution margin income statement.

Solution:

1. Each package consists of three mulching mowers and two riding mowers:

Product	Price	Unit Variable Cost	Unit Contribution Margin	Sales Mix	Package Contribution Margin
Mulching	$400	$325	$ 75	3	$225
Riding	800	600	200	2	400
Package total					$625

The three mulching mowers in the package yield $225 (3 × $75) in contribution margin. The two riding mowers in the package yield $400 (2 × $200) in contribution margin. Thus, a package of five mowers (three mulching and two riding) has a total contribution margin of $625.

2. $$\text{Break-even packages} = \frac{\text{Total fixed cost}}{\text{Package contribution margin}}$$

$$= \frac{\$96,250}{\$625}$$

$$= 154 \text{ packages}$$

Mulching mower break-even units = 154 × 3 = 462
Riding mower break-even units = 154 × 2 = 308

3. Income statement—break-even solution:

	Mulching Mower	Riding Mower	Total
Sales	$184,800	$246,400	$431,200
Total variable cost	150,150	184,800	334,950
Contribution margin	$ 34,650	$ 61,600	$ 96,250
Total fixed cost			96,250
Operating income			$ 0

Concept Q&A

Suppose a men's clothing store sells two brands of suits: designer suits with a contribution margin of $600 each and regular suits with a contribution margin of $500 each. At breakeven, the store must sell a total of 100 suits a month. Last month, the store sold 100 suits in total but incurred an operating loss. There was no change in fixed cost, variable cost, or price. What happened?

Answer:
Probably, the sales mix shifted toward the relatively lower contribution margin suits. For example, suppose that the break-even point for regular suits was 80, and the break-even point for designer suits was 20. If the mix shifted to 90 regular and 10 designer, it is easy to see that less total contribution margin (and, hence, operating income) would be realized.

The complexity of determining the break-even point in units increases dramatically as the number of products increases. Imagine performing this analysis for a firm with several hundred products. Luckily, computers can easily handle a problem with so much data. Furthermore, many firms simplify the problem by analyzing product groups rather than individual products. Another way to handle the increased complexity is to switch from the units sold to the sales revenue approach. This approach can accomplish a multiple-product CVP analysis using only the summary data found in an organization's income statement.

Break-Even Point in Sales Dollars

To illustrate the break-even point in sales dollars, the same examples will be used. However, the only information needed is the projected income statement for Whittier Company as a whole.

Sales	$1,120,000
Total variable cost	870,000
Contribution margin	$ 250,000
Total fixed cost	96,250
Operating income	$ 153,750

Notice that this income statement corresponds to the total column of the more detailed income statement examined previously. The projected income statement rests on the assumption that 1,200 mulching mowers and 800 riding mowers will be sold (a 3:2 sales mix). The break-even point in sales revenue also rests on the expected sales mix. (As with the units sold approach, different sales mixes will produce different results.)

With the income statement, the usual CVP questions can be addressed. For example, how much sales revenue must be earned to break even? **CORNERSTONE 15-8** shows how to calculate the break-even point in sales dollars for a multiple-product firm.

 **CORNERSTONE 15-8** **Calculating the Break-Even Sales Dollars for a Multiple-Product Firm**

Information:
Recall that Whittier Company sells two products that are expected to produce total revenue next year of $1,120,000 and total variable cost of $870,000. Total fixed cost is expected to equal $96,250.

Required:
1. Calculate the break-even point in sales dollars for Whittier.
2. Check your answer by preparing a contribution margin income statement.

Solution:
1. Contribution margin ratio $= \dfrac{\$250,000}{\$1,120,000}$

$= 0.2232$

(Continued)

**CORNERSTONE
15-8**
(continued)

$$\text{Break-even sales} = \frac{\text{Fixed cost}}{\text{Contribution margin ratio}}$$

$$= \frac{\$96,250}{0.2232}$$

$$= \$431,228$$

[*Note:* Total break-even sales differ slightly between Cornerstones 15-7 and 15-8 ($431,200 vs. $431,228) due to the rounding of the contribution margin ratio to only four decimal places (0.2232).]

2. Income statement—break-even solution:

Sales	$431,228
Total variable cost (0.7768 × $431,228)	334,978
Contribution margin	$ 96,250
Total fixed cost	96,250
Operating income	$ 0

The break-even point in sales dollars implicitly uses the assumed sales mix but avoids the requirement of building a package contribution margin. No knowledge of individual product data is needed. The computational effort is similar to that used in the single-product setting. Unlike the break-even point in units, the answer to CVP questions using sales dollars is still expressed in a single summary measure. The sales revenue approach, however, does sacrifice information concerning individual product performance.

 **Finding the Break-Even Point for a New Business**

You are an accountant in private practice. A friend of yours, Linda, recently started a novelty greeting card business. Linda designs greeting cards that allow the sender to write in his or her own message. She uses heavy card stock, cut to size, and decorates the front of each card with bits of fabric, lace, and ribbon in seasonal motifs (e.g., a heart for Valentine's Day, a pine tree for Christmas). Linda hired several friends to make the cards, according to Linda's instructions, on a piece-work basis. (In piece work, the worker is paid on the basis of number of units produced.) The workers could make the cards at their homes, meaning that no factory facilities were involved. Linda designs the cards and travels around her four-state region to sell the completed cards on consignment. For the few months the company has been in existence, the cards have been selling well, but Linda is operating at a loss.

What types of information do you need to find the break-even point? How can the business owner use this information to make decisions?

In order to determine the break-even point, you need to determine the prices and variable costs for the cards. Since creating a multi-product break-even analysis could be complex, it may be easier to determine the average price and the average variable cost for the cards, then find the total fixed cost, and tell Linda how many cards she would need to sell to break even.

Suppose that the break-even number of cards is 250 per month, and that the average contribution margin per card is $0.80. Then, as soon as Linda sells the 250th card, she knows she is in the black. From then on, every card sold adds $0.80 to her profit. This was very important information for Linda—whose business losses are coming right out of her family's checking account. Not only does Linda have a sales goal for each month, she also knows at any point in time how much income she has made.

Owners of small businesses find break-even analysis and concepts to be very helpful. A knowledge of contribution margin helps owners know how they are doing at any point in time.

OBJECTIVE ❺

Explain the impact of risk, uncertainty, and changing variables on cost-volume-profit analysis.

COST-VOLUME-PROFIT ANALYSIS AND RISK AND UNCERTAINTY

Because firms operate in a dynamic world, they must be aware of changes in prices, variable costs, and fixed costs. They must also account for the effect of risk and uncertainty. The break-even point can be affected by changes in price, unit contribution margin, and fixed cost. Managers can use CVP analysis to handle risk and uncertainty.

For example, France-based **Airbus** reported its first ever loss in 2006. The loss resulted from a decreased sales volume and costly production delays in the redesign of its "extra wide-body" passenger jet to compete with **Boeing**'s 787 Dreamliner. In response to this loss, Airbus used CVP analysis to estimate how a $2.6 billion reduction in its annual variable and fixed costs, as well as various reductions in its $144 million unit jet price, would affect its annual profit.[1] Shipping giant **Maersk** added capacity just before the recession of 2008 hit. As a result, shipping rates were so low that Maersk had a more than $2 billion loss in 2009. Improved economic conditions and an increase in demand above that originally predicted allowed the company to announce that it would break even in 2010.[2]

For a given sales mix, CVP analysis can be used as if the firm were selling a single product. However, when the prices of individual products change, the sales mix can be affected because consumers may buy relatively more or less of the product. Keep in mind that a new sales mix will affect the units of each product that need to be sold in order to achieve a desired profit target. If the sales mix for the coming period is uncertain, it may be necessary to look at several different mixes. In this way, a manager gains insight into the possible outcomes facing the firm.

Suppose that Whittier recently conducted a market study of the mulching lawn mower that revealed three different alternatives:

- *Alternative 1:* If advertising expenditures increase by $8,000, then sales will increase from 1,600 units to 1,725 units.
- *Alternative 2:* A price decrease from $400 to $375 per lawn mower will increase sales from 1,600 units to 1,900 units.
- *Alternative 3:* Decreasing price to $375 *and* increasing advertising expenditures by $8,000 will increase sales from 1,600 units to 2,600 units.

Should Whittier maintain its current price and advertising policies, or should it select one of the three alternatives described by the marketing study?

The first alternative, increasing advertising costs by $8,000 with a resulting sales increase of 125 units, is summarized in Exhibit 15-6. This alternative can be analyzed by using the contribution margin per unit of $75. Since units sold increase by 125, the increase in total contribution margin is $9,375 ($75 × 125 units). However, since fixed costs increase by $8,000, profits only increase by $1,375 ($9,375 − $8,000). Notice that we need to look only at the incremental increase in total contribution margin and fixed expenses to compute the increase in total operating income.

For the second alternative, the price is dropped to $375 (from $400), and the units sold increase to 1,900 (from 1,600). The effects of this alternative are summarized in Exhibit 15-7. Here, fixed expenses do not change, so only the change in total contribution margin is relevant. For the current price of $400, the contribution margin per unit is $75 ($400 − $325), and the total contribution margin is $120,000 ($75 × 1,600). For the new price, the contribution margin drops to $50 per unit ($375 − $325). If 1,900 units are sold at the new price, then the new total contribution margin is $95,000 ($50 × 1,900). Dropping the price results in a profit decline of $25,000 ($120,000 − $95,000).

The third alternative calls for a decrease in the unit selling price and an increase in advertising costs. Like the first alternative, the profit impact can be assessed by looking

---

[1] "Planemaker Airbus to Report Its First Annual Loss," *USA Today* (January 18, 2007): 3B.
[2] Peter T. Leach. "Maersk Line Close to Break Even, CEO Says." *The Journal of Commerce Online* (March 29, 2010). http://www.joc.com/maritime/maersk-line-close-break-even-says-ceo.

Exhibit 15-6

Summary of the Effects of Alternative 1

	Before the Increased Advertising	With the Increased Advertising
Units sold	1,600	1,725
Unit contribution margin	× $75	× $75
Total contribution margin	$120,000	$129,375
Less: Fixed expenses	45,000	53,000
Operating income	$ 75,000	$ 76,375

	Difference in Profit
Change in sales volume	125
Unit contribution margin	× $75
Change in contribution margin	$9,375
Less: Change in fixed expenses	8,000
Increase in operating income	$1,375

Exhibit 15-7

Summary of the Effects of Alternative 2

	Before the Proposed Price Decrease	With the Proposed Price Decrease
Units sold	1,600	1,900
Unit contribution margin	× $75	× $50
Total contribution margin	$120,000	$ 95,000
Less: Fixed expenses	45,000	45,000
Operating income	$ 75,000	$ 50,000

	Difference in Profit
Change in contribution margin ($95,000 – $120,000)	$(25,000)
Less: Change in fixed expenses	—
Decrease in operating income	$(25,000)

at the incremental effects on contribution margin and fixed expenses. The incremental profit change can be found by:

1. computing the incremental change in total contribution margin
2. computing the incremental change in fixed expenses
3. adding the two results

As shown in Exhibit 15-8 (p. 780), the current total contribution margin (for 1,600 units sold) is $120,000. Since the new unit contribution margin is $50, the new total contribution margin is $130,000 ($50 × 2,600 units). Thus, the incremental increase in total contribution margin is $10,000 ($130,000 – $120,000). However, to achieve this incremental increase in contribution margin, an incremental increase of $8,000 in fixed costs is needed. The net effect is an incremental increase in operating income of $2,000.

Of the three alternatives identified by the marketing study, the third alternative promises the most benefit. It increases total operating income by $2,000. The first alternative increases operating income by only $1,375, and the second *decreases* operating income by $25,000.

These examples are all based on a units sold approach. However, we could just as easily have applied a sales revenue approach. The answers would be the same.

Exhibit 15-8

Summary of the Effects of Alternative 3

	Before the Proposed Price and Advertising Changes	With the Proposed Price Decrease and Advertising Increase
Units sold	1,600	2,600
Unit contribution margin	× $75	× $50
Total contribution margin	$120,000	$130,000
Less: Fixed expenses	45,000	53,000
Profit	$ 75,000	$ 77,000

	Difference in Profit
Change in contribution margin ($130,000 – $120,000)	$10,000
Less: Change in fixed expenses ($53,000 – $45,000)	8,000
Increase in profit	$ 2,000

Introducing Risk and Uncertainty

An important assumption of CVP analysis is that prices and costs are known with certainty. This assumption is seldom accurate. Risk and uncertainty are a part of business decision making and must be dealt with somehow. Formally, risk differs from uncertainty in that under risk, the probability distributions of the variables are known; under uncertainty, they are not known. For purposes of CVP analysis, however, the terms will be used interchangeably.

How do managers deal with risk and uncertainty? There are a variety of methods.

- First, of course, is that management must realize the uncertain nature of future prices, costs, and quantities.
- Next, managers move from consideration of a break-even point to what might be called a "break-even band." In other words, given the uncertain nature of the data, perhaps a firm might break even when 1,800 to 2,000 units are sold instead of at the point estimate of 1,900 units.
- Further, managers may engage in sensitivity or what-if analysis. In this instance, a computer spreadsheet is helpful because managers can set up the break-even (or targeted profit) relationships and then check to see the impact that varying costs and prices have on quantity sold.

Two concepts useful to management are *margin of safety* and *operating leverage*. Both of these concepts may be considered measures of risk. Each requires knowledge of fixed and variable costs.

Margin of Safety

The **margin of safety** is the units sold or the revenue earned above the break-even volume. For example, if the break-even volume for a company is 200 units and the company is currently selling 500 units, then the margin of safety is 300 units:

$$\text{Sales} - \text{Break-even units} = 500 - 200$$

The margin of safety can be expressed in sales revenue as well. If the break-even volume is $200,000 and current revenues are $500,000, then the margin of safety is $300,000:

$$\text{Revenues} - \text{Margin of safety} = \$500,000 - \$200,000$$

In addition, margin of safety sales revenue can be expressed as a percentage of total sales dollars, which some managers refer to as the margin of safety ratio. In this example, the margin of safety ratio would be 60 percent:

$$\frac{\text{Margin of safety}}{\text{Revenues}} = \frac{\$300,000}{\$500,000}$$

Exhibit 15-9 shows the calculation of the margin of safety and the margin of safety ratio.

Summary of the Effects of Alternative 1

Exhibit 15-9

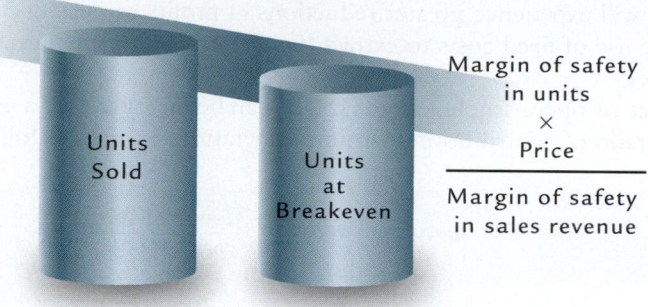

Margin of safety
in units
×
Price
—————————————
Margin of safety
in sales revenue

CORNERSTONE 15-9 shows the expected margin of safety for Whittier.

CORNERSTONE 15-9   Computing the Margin of Safety

Information:
Recall that Whittier plans to sell 1,000 mowers at $400 each in the coming year. Whittier has unit variable cost of $325 and total fixed cost of $45,000. Break-even units were previously calculated as 600.

Required:
1. Calculate the margin of safety for Whittier in terms of the number of units.
2. Calculate the margin of safety for Whittier in terms of sales revenue.

Solution:
1. Margin of safety in units = 1,000 − 600 = 400
2. Margin of safety in sales revenue = $400(1,000) − $400(600) = $160,000

The margin of safety can be viewed as a crude measure of risk. There are always events, unknown when plans are made, that can lower sales below the original expected level. In the event that sales take a downward turn, the risk of suffering losses is less if a firm's expected margin of safety is large than if the margin of safety is small. Managers who face a low margin of safety may wish to consider actions to increase sales or decrease costs. These steps will increase the margin of safety and lower the risk of incurring losses.

Operating Leverage

In physics, a lever is a simple machine used to multiply force. Basically, the lever multiplies the effort applied to create more work. The larger the load moved by a given amount of effort, the greater is the mechanical advantage. In financial terms, operating leverage is concerned with the relative mix of fixed costs and variable costs in an organization. Sometimes fixed costs can be traded off for variable costs. As variable costs decrease, the unit contribution margin increases, making the contribution of each unit sold that much greater. In such a case, fluctuations in sales have an increased effect on profitability. Thus, firms that have realized lower variable costs by increasing

Concept Q&A

Two companies have identical sales revenue of $15 million. Is it true that both have the same operating income and the same margin of safety? Is it possible that one company has a higher margin of safety?

Answer:
It is not necessarily true that the two companies make the same operating income. If one company has lower variable costs per unit and/or a lower total fixed cost, then its operating income would be higher. The differences in variable cost per unit and total fixed cost would lead to different break-even revenues. Of course, the company with the lower break-even sales would have a higher margin of safety.

the proportion of fixed costs will benefit with greater increases in profits as sales increase than will firms with a lower proportion of fixed costs. Fixed costs are being used as leverage to increase profits. Unfortunately, it is also true that firms with a higher operating leverage will experience greater reductions in profits as sales decrease. **Operating leverage** is the use of fixed costs to extract higher percentage changes in profits as sales activity changes.

The **degree of operating leverage (DOL)** can be measured for a given level of sales by taking the ratio of contribution margin to operating income, as follows:

$$\text{Degree of operating leverage} = \frac{\text{Contribution margin}}{\text{Operating income}}$$

If fixed costs are used to lower variable costs such that contribution margin increases and operating income decreases, then the degree of operating leverage increases—signaling an increase in risk. **CORNERSTONE 15-10** shows how to compute the degree of operating leverage for Whittier.

CORNERSTONE 15-10   **Computing the Degree of Operating Leverage**

Information:
Recall that Whittier plans to sell 1,000 mowers at $400 each in the coming year. Whittier has unit variable cost per unit of $325 and total fixed cost of $45,000. Operating income at that level of sales was previously computed as $30,000.

Required:
Calculate the degree of operating leverage for Whittier.

Solution:

$$\text{Degree of operating leverage} = \frac{\text{Total contribution margin}}{\text{Operating income}}$$

$$= \frac{(\$400 - \$325)(1,000 \text{ units})}{\$30,000}$$

$$= 2.5$$

The greater the degree of operating leverage, the more that changes in sales will affect operating income. Because of this phenomenon, the mix of costs that an organization chooses influences its operating risk and profit level. A company's mix of fixed costs relative to variable costs is referred to as its **cost structure**. Often, a company changes its cost structure by taking on more of one type of cost in exchange for reducing its amount of the other type of cost. For example, as U.S. companies try to compete more effectively with foreign competitors' significantly lower hourly labor costs (a variable cost), many are altering their cost structures by taking on more plant machine automation (a fixed cost) in exchange for using less labor.

To illustrate the impact of these concepts on management decision making, consider a firm that is planning to add a new product line. In adding the line, the firm can choose to rely heavily on automation or on labor. If the firm chooses to emphasize automation rather than labor, fixed costs will be higher, and unit variable costs will be lower. Relevant data for a sales level of 10,000 units follow:

	Automated System	Manual System
Sales	$1,000,000	$1,000,000
Total variable cost	500,000	800,000
Contribution margin	$ 500,000	$ 200,000
Total fixed cost	375,000	100,000
Operating income	$ 125,000	$ 100,000
Unit selling price	$ 100	$ 100
Unit variable cost	50	80
Unit contribution margin	50	20

The degree of operating leverage for the automated system is 4.0 ($500,000/ $125,000). The degree of operating leverage for the manual system is 2.0 ($200,000/$100,000). What happens to profit in each system if sales increase by 40 percent? We can generate the following income statements to see the following:

	Automated System	Manual System
Sales	$1,400,000	$1,400,000
Total variable cost	700,000	1,120,000
Contribution margin	$ 700,000	$ 280,000
Total fixed cost	375,000	100,000
Operating income	$ 325,000	$ 180,000

Profits for the automated system would increase by $200,000 ($325,000 − $125,000) for a 160 percent increase. In the manual system, profits increase by only $80,000 ($180,000 − $100,000) for an 80 percent increase. The automated system has a greater percentage increase because it has a higher degree of operating leverage.

The degree of operating leverage can be used directly to calculate the change in operating income that would result from a given percentage change in sales.

> Percentage change in operating income = DOL × Percent change in sales

Since sales are predicted to increase by 40 percent, and the DOL for the automated system is 4.0, operating income increases by 160 percent. Since operating income based on the original sales level is $125,000, the operating income based on the increased sales level would be $325,000:

> Operating income + (Operating income × Percent change in sales)
> = $125,000 + ($125,000 × 1.6)

Similarly, for the manual system, increased sales of 40 percent and DOL of 2.0 imply increased operating income of 80 percent. Therefore, operating income based on the increased sales level would be $180,000:

> $100,000 + ($100,000 × 0.8)

CORNERSTONE 15-11 (p. 784) illustrates the impact of increased sales on operating income using the degree of operating leverage.

In choosing between the two systems, the effect of operating leverage is a valuable piece of information. Higher operating leverage multiplies the impact of increased sales on income. However, the effect is a two-edged sword. As sales decrease, the automated system will also show much higher percentage decreases. The increased operating leverage is available under the automated system because of the presence of increased fixed costs. The break-even point for the automated system is 7,500 units ($375,000/$50), whereas the break-even point for the manual system is 5,000 units ($100,000/$20).

CORNERSTONE 15-11 — Calculating the Impact of Increased Sales on Operating Income Using the Degree of Operating Leverage

Information:
Recall that Whittier had expected to sell 1,000 mowers and earn operating income equal to $30,000 next year. Whittier's degree of operating leverage is equal to 2.5. The company plans to increase sales by 20 percent next year.

Required:
1. Calculate the percent change in operating income expected by Whittier for next year using the degree of operating leverage.
2. Calculate the operating income expected by Whittier next year using the percent change in operating income calculated in Requirement 1.

Solution:
1. Percent change in operating income = DOL × Percent change in sales
   = 2.5 × 20% = 50%
2. Expected operating income = $30,000 + (0.5 × $30,000) = $45,000

Thus, the automated system has greater operating risk. The increased risk, of course, provides a potentially higher profit level as long as units sold exceed 9,167. Why 9,167? Because that is the quantity for which the operating income for the automated system equals the operating income for the manual system. The quantity at which two systems produce the same operating income is referred to as the **indifference point**. This number of units is computed by setting the operating income equations of the two systems equal and solving for number of units:

$$\$50 \text{ (Units)} - \$375,000 = \$20 \text{ (Units)} - \$100,000$$
$$\text{Units} = 9,167$$

In choosing between the automated and manual systems, the manager must consider the likelihood that sales will exceed 9,167 units. If there is a strong belief that sales will easily exceed this level, then the choice is obviously the automated system. On the other hand, if sales are unlikely to exceed 9,167 units, then the manual system is preferable. Exhibit 15-10 summarizes the relative differences between the manual and automated systems in terms of some of the CVP concepts.

Sensitivity Analysis and Cost-Volume-Profit

The widespread use of personal computers and spreadsheets has placed sensitivity analysis within reach of most managers. An important tool, **sensitivity analysis** is a "what-if" technique that examines the impact of changes in underlying assumptions on an answer. It is relatively simple to input data on prices, variable costs, fixed costs, and sales mix and

Exhibit 15-10

Differences between a Manual and an Automated System

	Manual System	Automated System
Price	Same	Same
Variable cost	▲ Relatively higher	▼ Relatively lower
Fixed cost	▼ Relatively lower	▲ Relatively higher
Contribution margin	▼ Relatively lower	▲ Relatively higher
Break-even point	▼ Relatively lower	▲ Relatively higher
Margin of safety	▲ Relatively higher	▼ Relatively lower
Degree of operating leverage	▼ Relatively lower	▲ Relatively higher
Down-side risk	▼ Relatively lower	▲ Relatively higher
Up-side potential	▼ Relatively lower	▲ Relatively higher

to set up formulas to calculate break-even points and expected profits. Then, the data can be varied as desired to see how changes impact the expected profit.

In the example on operating leverage, a company analyzed the impact on profit of using an automated versus a manual system. The computations were essentially done by hand, and too much variation is cumbersome. Using the power of a computer, it would be an easy matter to change the sales price in $1 increments between $75 and $125, with related assumptions about quantity sold. At the same time, variable and fixed costs could be adjusted. For example, suppose that the automated system has fixed costs of $375,000 but that those costs could easily double in the first year and come back down in the second and third years as bugs are worked out of the system and workers learn to use it. Again, the spreadsheet can effortlessly handle the many computations.

A spreadsheet, while wonderful for cranking out numerical answers, cannot do the most difficult job in CVP analysis. That job is determining the data to be entered in the first place. The managerial accountant must be aware of the cost and price distributions of the firm as well as of the impact of changing economic conditions on these variables. The fact that variables are seldom known with certainty is no excuse for ignoring the impact of uncertainty on CVP analysis. Fortunately, sensitivity analysis can also give managers a feel for the degree to which a poorly forecast variable will affect an answer. That is also an advantage.

ETHICAL DECISIONS   It is important to note that the CVP results are only one input into business decisions. There are many other factors that may bear on decisions to choose one type of process over another, for example, or whether or not to delete certain costs. Businesses and nonprofit entities often face trade-offs involving safety. Ethical concerns also have an important place in CVP analysis. When one company buys another one, it bases its decision in part on the information presented by the to-be-acquired firm. For example, China's Geely purchased Volvo from Ford in 2010. As the head of Geely stated, "As far as I know, Volvo is in good operating condition and it's possible it could break even in the fourth quarter of this year."[3] Often, however, the costs and probabilities are not known with sufficient certainty. In that case, these factors are included in the ultimate decision-making process. Chapter 23, on short-run decision making, covers this topic in more detail. ●

Despite the fact that future conditions cannot be known with certainty, there are various ways of incorporating risk and uncertainty into the analysis. One possibility is that cost of potential problems can be estimated and included in the CVP results. Another is that various scenarios can be considered by running sensitivity analysis—varying costs and prices to see what happens.

BOYNE RESORTS
EXPERIENCE THE LIFESTYLE

YOU◆DECIDE   Using Contribution Margin Income Statements to Consider Varying Scenarios

You are the chief accountant for Boyne Resorts winter sports. Early in the year, you had budgeted sales prices (lift tickets, restaurant prices), costs, and expected quantity to be sold. However, once the season starts, you will know from week to week more about the actual weather conditions.

How can you use this information about current weather conditions to better predict budgets for Boyne?

You can recast the budgeted statements according to how the weather will affect skiing. If the snow is good, some costs will go down. For example, you will lower the predicted cost of running the snow-making machines. However, good weather and more skiers will require additional seasonal hiring as more direct labor will be needed to run the lifts, operate ski equipment rental shops, restaurants, and so on. You can put together contribution margin income statements under various scenarios, increasing volume with good ski weather, decreasing it with poor weather.

Having the ability to recast budgets will help managers respond quickly to the changing conditions and be able to raise or lower some prices as needed.

[3] Drew Johnson, "Geely: Volvo Could Breakeven by Year's End." *Left Lane News* (March 13, 2010). http://www.leftlanenews.com/geely-volvo-could-break-even-by-years-end.html.

SUMMARY OF LEARNING OBJECTIVES

LO1.   Determine the break-even point in number of units and in total sales dollars.
- At breakeven, total costs (variable and fixed) equal total sales revenue.
- Break-even units equal total fixed costs divided by the contribution margin (price minus variable cost per unit).
- Break-even revenue equals total fixed costs divided by the contribution margin ratio.

LO2.   Determine the number of units that must be sold, and the amount of revenue required, to earn a targeted profit.
- To earn a target (desired) profit, total costs (variable and fixed) plus the amount of target profit must equal total sales revenue.
- Units to earn target profit equal total fixed costs plus target profit divided by the contribution margin.
- Sales revenue to earn target profit equals total fixed costs plus target profit divided by the contribution margin ratio.

LO3.   Prepare a profit-volume graph and a cost-volume-profit graph, and explain the meaning of each.
- CVP assumes linear revenue and cost functions, no finished goods ending inventories, constant sales mix, and selling prices and fixed and variable costs that are known with certainty.
- Profit-volume graphs plot the relationship between profit (operating income) and units sold. Break-even units are shown where the profit line crosses the horizontal axis.
- CVP graphs plot a line for total costs and a line for total sales revenue. The intersection of these two lines is the break-even point in units.

LO4.   Apply cost-volume-profit analysis in a multiple-product setting.
- Multiple-product analysis requires the expected sales mix.
- Break-even units for each product will change as the sales mix changes.
- Increased sales of high contribution margin products decrease the break-even point.
- Increased sales of low contribution margin products increase the break-even point.

LO5.   Explain the impact of risk, uncertainty, and changing variables on cost-volume-profit analysis.
- Uncertainty regarding costs, prices, and sales mix affect the break-even point.
- Sensitivity analysis allows managers to vary costs, prices, and sales mix to show various possible break-even points.
- Margin of safety shows how far the company's actual sales and/or units are above or below the break-even point.
- Operating leverage is the use of fixed costs to increase the percentage changes in profits as sales activity changes.

SUMMARY OF IMPORTANT EQUATIONS

1. Operating income = Total revenue − Total expense

2. Operating income = Sales − Total variable expenses − Total fixed expenses

3. Operating income = (Price × Number of units sold) − (Variable cost per unit × Number of units sold) − Total fixed cost

4. Break-even units = $\dfrac{\text{Total fixed cost}}{\text{Price} - \text{Variable cost per unit}}$

5. Sales revenue = Unit selling price × Units sold

6. Break-even sales $= \dfrac{\text{Total fixed expenses}}{\text{Contribution margin ratio}}$

7. Operating income = (Price × Units sold) − (Unit variable cost × Units sold) − Fixed cost

8. Number of units to earn target income $= \dfrac{\text{Total fixed cost} + \text{Target income}}{\text{Price} - \text{Variable cost per unit}}$

9. Operating income $= \dfrac{\text{Target income}}{\text{Unit contribution margin}} + \text{Break-even volume}$

10. Operating income = Unit contribution margin × Change in units sold

11. Sales dollars to earn target income $= \dfrac{\text{Total fixed cost} + \text{Target income}}{\text{Contribution margin ratio}}$

12. Change in profits = Contribution margin ratio × Change in sales

13. Operating income = (Price × Units) − (Unit variable cost × Units) − Total fixed cost

14. Revenue = Price × Units

15. Total cost = (Unit variable cost × Units) + Fixed cost

16. Degree of operating leverage $= \dfrac{\text{Contribution margin}}{\text{Operating income}}$

17. Percentage change in operating income = DOL × Percent change in sales

---

CORNERSTONE 15-1   Preparing a contribution margin income statement (p. 759)

CORNERSTONE 15-2   Calculating the break-even point in units (p. 760)

CORNERSTONE 15-3   Calculating the variable cost ratio and the contribution margin ratio (p. 763)

CORNERSTONE 15-4   Calculating the break-even point in sales dollars (p. 764)

CORNERSTONE 15-5   Calculating the number of units to be sold to earn a target operating income (p. 766)

CORNERSTONE 15-6   Calculating sales needed to earn a target operating income (p. 767)

CORNERSTONE 15-7   Calculating the break-even units for a multiple-product firm (p. 775)

CORNERSTONE 15-8   Calculating the break-even sales dollars for a multiple-product firm (p. 776)

CORNERSTONE 15-9   Computing the margin of safety (p. 781)

CORNERSTONE 15-10   Computing the degree of operating leverage (p. 782)

CORNERSTONE 15-11   Calculating the impact of increased sales on operating income using the degree of operating leverage (p. 784)

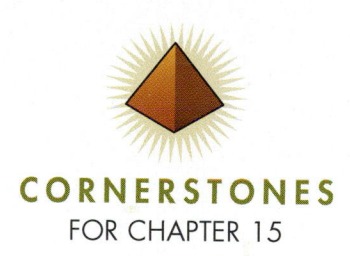

CORNERSTONES
FOR CHAPTER 15

KEY TERMS

Break-even point (p. 758)
Common fixed expenses (p. 773)
Contribution margin (p. 759)
Contribution margin income statement (p. 759)
Contribution margin ratio (p. 762)
Cost-volume-profit (CVP) analysis (p. 758)
Cost structure (p. 782)
Cost-volume-profit graph (p. 769)
Degree of operating leverage (DOL) (p. 782)

Direct fixed expenses (p. 773)
Indifference point (p. 784)
Margin of safety (p. 780)
Operating leverage (p. 782)
Profit-volume graph (p. 768)
Sales mix (p. 774)
Sensitivity analysis (p. 784)
Variable cost ratio (p. 762)

REVIEW PROBLEMS

I. Single-Product Cost-Volume-Profit Analysis

Cutlass Company's projected profit for the coming year is as follows:

	Total	Per Unit
Sales	$200,000	$20
Total variable cost	120,000	12
Contribution margin	$ 80,000	$ 8
Total fixed cost	64,000	
Operating income	$ 16,000	

Required:

1. Compute the variable cost ratio. Compute the contribution margin ratio.
2. Compute the break-even point in units.
3. Compute the break-even point in sales dollars.
4. How many units must be sold to earn a profit of $30,000?
5. Using the contribution margin ratio computed in step 1, compute the additional profit that Cutlass would earn if sales were $25,000 more than expected.
6. For the projected level of sales, compute the margin of safety in units and in sales dollars.
7. Calculate the degree of operating leverage. Now suppose that Cutlass revises the forecast to show a 30 percent increase in sales over the original forecast. What is the percent change in operating income expected for the revised forecast? What is the total operating income expected by Cutlass after revising the sales forecast?

Solution:

1. $$\text{Variable cost ratio} = \frac{\text{Total variable cost}}{\text{Sales}}$$

   $$= \frac{\$120,000}{\$200,000}$$

   $$= 0.60, \text{ or } 60\%$$

   $$\text{Contribution margin ratio} = \frac{\text{Contribution margin}}{\text{Sales}}$$

   $$= \frac{\$80,000}{\$200,000}$$

   $$= 0.40, \text{ or } 40\%$$

2. The break-even point is computed as follows:

   $$\text{Units} = \frac{\text{Total fixed cost}}{(\text{Price} - \text{Variable cost per unit})}$$

   $$= \frac{\$64,000}{(\$20 - \$12)}$$

   $$= \frac{\$64,000}{\$8} = 8,000$$

3. The break-even point in sales dollars is computed as follows:

   $$\text{Break-even sales dollars} = \frac{\text{Total fixed cost}}{\text{Contribution margin ratio}}$$

   $$= \frac{\$64,000}{0.40}$$

   $$= \$160,000$$

4. The number of units that must be sold to earn a profit of $30,000 is calculated as follows:

   $$\text{Units} = \frac{(\$64,000 + \$30,000)}{\$8}$$

   $$= \frac{\$94,000}{\$8}$$

   $$= 11,750$$

5. The additional contribution margin on additional sales of $25,000 would be 0.40 × $25,000 = $10,000.

6. Margin of safety in units = Projected units − Break-even units

$$= 10,000 - 8,000 = 2,000$$

Margin of safety in sales dollars = $200,000 − $160,000 = $40,000

7. Degree of operating leverage $= \dfrac{\text{Contribution margin}}{\text{Operating income}}$

$$= \frac{\$80,000}{\$16,000} = 5.0$$

Percentage change in operating income = Degree of operating leverage
$$\times \text{ Percent change in sales}$$
$$= 5.0 \times 30\%$$
$$= 150\%$$

Expected operating income = $16,000 + (1.5 × $16,000)
$$= \$40,000$$

II. Multiple-Product Cost-Volume-Profit Analysis

Alpha Company produces and sells two products: Alpha-Basic and Alpha-Deluxe. In the coming year, Alpha expects to sell 3,000 units of Alpha-Basic and 1,500 units of Alpha-Deluxe. Information on the two products is as follows:

	Alpha-Basic	Alpha-Deluxe
Price	$120	$200
Variable cost per unit	40	80

Total fixed cost is $140,000.

Required:
1. What is the sales mix of Alpha-Basic to Alpha-Deluxe?
2. Compute the break-even quantity of each product.

Solution:
1. The sales mix of Alpha-Basic to Alpha-Deluxe is 3,000:1,500 or 2:1.
2. Each package consists of two Alpha-Basic and one Alpha-Deluxe:

Product	Price	Unit Variable Cost	Unit Contribution Margin	Sales Mix	Package Unit Contribution Margin
Alpha-Basic	$120	$40	$ 80	2	$160
Alpha-Deluxe	200	80	120	1	120
Package total					$280

Break-even packages $= \dfrac{\text{Total fixed cost}}{\text{Package contribution margin}}$

$$= \frac{\$140,000}{\$280}$$

$$= 500$$

Alpha-Basic break-even units = 500 × 2 = 1,000
Alpha-Deluxe break-even units = 500 × 1 = 500

DISCUSSION QUESTIONS

1. Explain how CVP analysis can be used for managerial planning.
2. Describe the difference between the units sold approach to CVP analysis and the sales revenue approach.
3. Define the term *break-even point*.
4. Explain why contribution margin per unit becomes profit per unit above the break-even point.
5. What is the variable cost ratio? The contribution margin ratio? How are the two ratios related?
6. Suppose a firm with a contribution margin ratio of 0.3 increased its advertising expenses by $10,000 and found that sales increased by $30,000. Was it a good decision to increase advertising expenses? Suppose that the contribution margin ratio is now 0.4. Would it be a good decision to increase advertising expenses?
7. Define the term *sales mix*. Give an example to support your definition.
8. Explain how CVP analysis developed for single products can be used in a multiple-product setting.
9. Since break-even analysis focuses on making zero profit, it is of no value in determining the units a firm must sell to earn a targeted profit. Do you agree or disagree with this statement? Why?
10. How does targeted profit enter into the break-even units equation?
11. Explain how a change in sales mix can change a company's break-even point.
12. Define the term *margin of safety*. Explain how it can be used as a crude measure of operating risk.
13. Explain what is meant by the term *operating leverage*. What impact does increased leverage have on risk?
14. How can sensitivity analysis be used in conjunction with CVP analysis?
15. Why is a declining margin of safety over a period of time an issue of concern to managers?

MULTIPLE-CHOICE EXERCISES

15-1 If the variable cost per unit goes down,

	Contribution margin	Break-even point
a.	increases	increases.
b.	increases	decreases.
c.	decreases	decreases.
d.	decreases	increases.
e.	decreases	remains unchanged.

15-2 The amount of revenue required to earn a targeted profit is equal to

a. total fixed cost divided by contribution margin.
b. total fixed cost divided by the contribution margin ratio.
c. targeted profit divided by the contribution margin ratio.
d. total fixed cost plus targeted profit divided by contribution margin ratio.
e. targeted profit divided by the variable cost ratio.

15-3 Break-even revenue for the multiple-product firm can

a. be calculated by dividing total fixed cost by the overall contribution margin ratio.
b. be calculated by dividing segment fixed cost by the overall contribution margin ratio.
c. be calculated by dividing total fixed cost by the overall variable cost ratio.
d. be calculated by multiplying total fixed cost by the contribution margin ratio.
e. not be calculated; break-even revenue can only be computed for a single-product firm.

15-4 In the cost-volume-profit graph,

a.   the break-even point is found where the total revenue curve crosses the x-axis.
b.   the area of profit is to the left of the break-even point.
c.   the area of loss cannot be determined.
d.   both the total revenue curve and the total cost curve appear.
e.   neither the total revenue curve nor the total cost curve appear.

15-5 An important assumption of cost-volume-profit analysis is that

a.   both costs and revenues are linear functions.
b.   all cost and revenue relationships are analyzed within the relevant range.
c.   there is no change in inventories.
d.   the sales mix remains constant.
e.   all of the above are assumptions of cost-volume-profit analysis.

15-6 The use of fixed costs to extract higher percentage changes in profits as sales activity changes involves

a.   margin of safety.   d.   sensitivity analysis.
b.   operating leverage.   e.   variable cost reduction.
c.   degree of operating leverage.

15-7 If the margin of safety is 0, then

a.   the company is precisely breaking even.
b.   the company is operating at a loss.
c.   the company is earning a small profit.
d.   the margin of safety cannot be less than or equal to 0; it must be positive.
e.   none of the above is true.

15-8 The contribution margin is the

a.   amount by which sales exceed total fixed cost.
b.   difference between sales and total cost.
c.   difference between sales and operating income.
d.   difference between sales and total variable cost.
e.   difference between variable cost and fixed cost.

Use the following information for Multiple-Choice Exercises 15-9 and 15-10:
Dartmouth Company produces a single product with a price of $10, variable cost per unit of $3, and total fixed cost of $8,400.

15-9 Refer to the information for Dartmouth above. Dartmouth's break-even point in units

a.   is 840.
b.   is 1,200.
c.   is 2,800.
d.   is 3,000.
e.   cannot be determined from the information given.

15-10 Refer to the information for Dartmouth above. The variable cost ratio and the contribution margin ratio for Dartmouth are

	Variable cost ratio	**Contribution margin ratio**
a.	70%	70%.
b.	30%	30%.
c.	30%	70%.
d.	70%	30%.
e.	The contribution margin ratio cannot be determined from the information given.	

15-11 If a company's total fixed cost rises by $10,000, which of the following will be true?

a.   The break-even point will decrease.
b.   The variable cost ratio will increase.
c.   The break-even point will be unchanged.
d.   The variable cost ratio will decrease.
e.   The contribution margin ratio will be unchanged.

15-12 Solemon Company has total fixed cost of $15,000, variable cost per unit of $6, and a price of $8. If Solemon wants to earn a targeted profit of $3,600, how many units must be sold?

a.   2,500
b.   7,500
c.   9,300
d.   18,600
e.   18,750

CORNERSTONE EXERCISES

OBJECTIVE ❶
CORNERSTONE 15-1

Cornerstone Exercise 15-13 Variable Cost, Fixed Cost, Contribution Margin Income Statement

Head-First Company plans to sell 5,000 bicycle helmets at $75 each in the coming year. Product costs include:

Direct materials per helmet	$ 30
Direct labor per helmet	8
Variable factory overhead per helmet	4
Total fixed factory overhead	20,000

Variable selling expense is a commission of $3 per helmet; fixed selling and administrative expense totals $29,500.

Required:
1.   Calculate the total variable cost per unit.
2.   Calculate the total fixed expense for the year.
3.   Prepare a contribution margin income statement for Head-First Company for the coming year.

OBJECTIVE ❶
CORNERSTONE 15-2

Cornerstone Exercise 15-14 Break-Even Point in Units

Head-First Company plans to sell 5,000 bicycle helmets at $75 each in the coming year. Unit variable cost is $45 (includes direct materials, direct labor, variable factory overhead, and variable selling expense). Total fixed cost equals $49,500 (includes fixed factory overhead and fixed selling and administrative expense).

Required:
1.   Calculate the break-even number of helmets.
2.   Check your answer by preparing a contribution margin income statement based on the break-even units.

OBJECTIVE ❶
CORNERSTONE 15-3

Cornerstone Exercise 15-15 Variable Cost Ratio, Contribution Margin Ratio

Head-First Company plans to sell 5,000 bicycle helmets at $75 each in the coming year. Unit variable cost is $45 (includes direct materials, direct labor, variable factory overhead, and variable selling expense). Fixed factory overhead is $20,000 and fixed selling and administrative expense is $29,500.

Required:
1.   Calculate the variable cost ratio.
2.   Calculate the contribution margin ratio.
3.   Prepare a contribution margin income statement based on the budgeted figures for next year. In a column next to the income statement, show the percentages based on sales for sales, total variable cost, and total contribution margin.

Cornerstone Exercise 15-16   Break-Even Point in Sales Dollars

OBJECTIVE ①
CORNERSTONE 15-4

Head-First Company plans to sell 5,000 bicycle helmets at $75 each in the coming year. Variable cost is 60 percent of the sales price; contribution margin is 40 percent of the sales price. Total fixed cost equals $49,500 (includes fixed factory overhead and fixed selling and administrative expense).

Required:

1. Calculate the sales revenue that Head-First must make to break even by using the break-even point in sales equation.
2. Check your answer by preparing a contribution margin income statement based on the break-even point in sales dollars.

Cornerstone Exercise 15-17   Units to Earn Target Income

OBJECTIVE ②
CORNERSTONE 15-5

Head-First Company plans to sell 5,000 bicycle helmets at $75 each in the coming year. Unit variable cost is $45 (includes direct materials, direct labor, variable factory overhead, and variable selling expense). Total fixed cost equals $49,500 (includes fixed factory overhead and fixed selling and administrative expense).

Required:

1. Calculate the number of helmets Head-First must sell to earn operating income of $81,900.
2. Check your answer by preparing a contribution margin income statement based on the number of units calculated.

Cornerstone Exercise 15-18   Sales Needed to Earn Target Income

OBJECTIVE ②
CORNERSTONE 15-6

Head-First Company plans to sell 5,000 bicycle helmets at $75 each in the coming year. Variable cost is 60 percent of the sales price; contribution margin is 40 percent of the sales price. Total fixed cost equals $49,500 (includes fixed factory overhead and fixed selling and administrative expense).

Required:

1. Calculate the sales revenue that Head-First must make to earn operating income of $81,900.
2. Check your answer by preparing a contribution margin income statement based on the sales dollars calculated in Requirement 1.

Cornerstone Exercise 15-19   Break-Even Point in Units for a Multiple-Product Firm

OBJECTIVE ④
CORNERSTONE 15-7

Suppose that Head-First Company now sells both bicycle helmets and motorcycle helmets. The bicycle helmets are priced at $75 and have variable costs of $45 each. The motorcycle helmets are priced at $220 and have variable costs of $140 each. Total fixed cost for Head-First as a whole equals $58,900 (includes all fixed factory overhead and fixed selling and administrative expense). Next year, Head-First expects to sell 5,000 bicycle helmets and 2,000 motorcycle helmets.

Required:

1. Form a package of bicycle and motorcycle helmets based on the sales mix expected for the coming year.
2. Calculate the break-even point in units for bicycle helmets and for motorcycle helmets.
3. Check your answer by preparing a contribution margin income statement.

Cornerstone Exercise 15-20   Break-Even Sales Dollars for a Multiple-Product Firm

OBJECTIVE ④
CORNERSTONE 15-8

Head-First Company now sells both bicycle helmets and motorcycle helmets. Next year, Head-First expects to produce total revenue of $570,000 and incur total variable cost of $388,000. Total fixed cost is expected to be $58,900.

Required:

1. Calculate the break-even point in sales dollars for Head-First. (*Note:* Round the contribution margin ratio to four decimal places.)
2. Check your answer by preparing a contribution margin income statement.

Cornerstone Exercise 15-21 Margin of Safety

Head-First Company plans to sell 5,000 bicycle helmets at $75 each in the coming year. Unit variable cost is $45 (includes direct materials, direct labor, variable factory overhead, and variable selling expense). Total fixed cost equals $49,500 (includes fixed factory overhead and fixed selling and administrative expense). Break-even units equal 1,650.

Required:
1. Calculate the margin of safety in terms of the number of units.
2. Calculate the margin of safety in terms of sales revenue.

Cornerstone Exercise 15-22 Degree of Operating Leverage

Head-First Company plans to sell 5,000 bicycle helmets at $75 each in the coming year. Unit variable cost is $45 (includes direct materials, direct labor, variable factory overhead, and variable selling expense). Total fixed cost equals $49,500 (includes fixed factory overhead and fixed selling and administrative expense). Operating income at 5,000 units sold is $100,500.

Required:
Calculate the degree of operating leverage. (*Note:* Round answer to the nearest tenth.)

Cornerstone Exercise 15-23 Impact of Increased Sales on Operating Income Using the Degree of Operating Leverage

Head-First Company had planned to sell 5,000 bicycle helmets at $75 each in the coming year. Unit variable cost is $45 (includes direct materials, direct labor, variable factory overhead, and variable selling expense). Total fixed cost equals $49,500 (includes fixed factory overhead and fixed selling and administrative expense). Operating income at 5,000 units sold is $100,500. The degree of operating leverage is 1.5. Now Head-First expects to increase sales by 10 percent next year.

Required:
1. Calculate the percent change in operating income expected.
2. Calculate the operating income expected next year using the percent change in operating income calculated in Requirement 1.

EXERCISES

Exercise 15-24 Basic Break-Even Calculations

Suppose that Adams Company sells a product for $20. Unit costs are as follows:

Direct materials	$3.90
Direct labor	1.40
Variable factory overhead	2.10
Variable selling and administrative expense	1.60

Total fixed factory overhead is $52,000 per year, and total fixed selling and administrative expense is $38,530.

Required:
1. Calculate the variable cost per unit and the contribution margin per unit.
2. Calculate the contribution margin ratio and the variable cost ratio.
3. Calculate the break-even units.
4. Prepare a contribution margin income statement at the break-even number of units.

Exercise 15-25 Price, Variable Cost per Unit, Contribution Margin, Contribution Margin Ratio, Fixed Expense

For each of the following independent situations, calculate the amount(s) required.

Required:

1. At the break-even point, Jefferson Company sells 115,000 units and has fixed cost of $349,600. The variable cost per unit is $4.56. What price does Jefferson charge per unit?
2. Sooner Industries charges a price of $120 and has fixed cost of $458,000. Next year, Sooner expects to sell 15,600 units and make operating income of $166,000. What is the variable cost per unit? What is the contribution margin ratio (*Note:* Round answer to four decimal places)?
3. Last year, Jasper Company earned operating income of $22,500 with a contribution margin ratio of 0.25. Actual revenue was $235,000. Calculate the total fixed cost.
4. Laramie Company has variable cost ratio of 0.56. The fixed cost is $103,840 and 23,600 units are sold at breakeven. What is the price? What is the variable cost per unit? The contribution margin per unit?

Exercise 15-26 Contribution Margin Ratio, Variable Cost Ratio, Break-Even Sales Revenue

OBJECTIVE ❶

The controller of Andreston Company prepared the following projected income statement:

Sales	$93,000
Total variable cost	70,680
Contribution margin	$22,320
Total fixed cost	12,000
Operating income	$10,320

Required:

1. Calculate the contribution margin ratio.
2. Calculate the variable cost ratio.
3. Calculate the break-even sales revenue for Andreston.
4. **Conceptual Connection:** How could Andreston increase projected operating income without increasing the total sales revenue?

Exercise 15-27 Income Statement, Break-Even Units, Units to Earn Target Income

OBJECTIVE ❷

Melford Company sold 26,800 units last year at $16.00 each. Variable cost was $11.50, and total fixed cost was $126,000.

Required:

1. Prepare an income statement for Melford for last year.
2. Calculate the break-even point in units.
3. Calculate the units that Melford must sell to earn operating income of $12,150 next year.

Exercise 15-28 Units Sold to Break Even, Unit Variable Cost, Unit Manufacturing Cost, Units to Earn Target Income

OBJECTIVE ❶

Werner Company produces and sells disposable foil baking pans to retailers for $2.75 per pan. The variable cost per pan is as follows:

Direct materials	$0.37
Direct labor	0.63
Variable factory overhead	0.53
Variable selling expense	0.12

Fixed manufacturing cost totals $111,425 per year. Administrative cost (all fixed) totals $48,350.

Required:

1. Compute the number of pans that must be sold for Werner to break even.
2. **Conceptual Connection:** What is the unit variable cost? What is the unit variable manufacturing cost? Which is used in cost-volume-profit analysis and why?
3. How many pans must be sold for Werner to earn operating income of $13,530?
4. How much sales revenue must Werner have to earn operating income of $13,530?

Exercise 15-29 Margin of Safety

Yuan Company produces and sells strings of colorful indoor/outdoor lights for holiday display to retailers for $8.42 per string. The variable costs per string are as follows:

Direct materials	$1.87
Direct labor	1.70
Variable factory overhead	0.57
Variable selling expense	0.42

Fixed manufacturing cost totals $245,650 per year. Administrative cost (all fixed) totals $301,505. Yuan expects to sell 225,000 strings of light next year.

Required:

1. Calculate the break-even point in units.
2. Calculate the margin of safety in units.
3. Calculate the margin of safety in dollars.
4. **Conceptual Connection:** Suppose Yuan actually experiences a price decrease next year while all other costs and the number of units sold remain the same. Would this increase or decrease risk for the company? (*Hint*: Consider what would happen to the number of break-even units and to the margin of safety.)

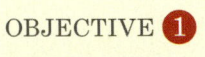

Exercise 15-30 Contribution Margin, Unit Amounts, Break-Even Units

Information on four independent companies follows. Calculate the correct amount for each question mark. (*Note*: Round answers to two decimal places.)

	Laertes	Ophelia	Fortinbras	Claudius
Sales	$15,000	$?	$?	$10,600
Total variable cost	5,000	11,700	9,750	?
Total contribution margin	$10,000	$ 3,900	$?	$?
Total fixed cost	?	4,000	?	4,452
Operating income (loss)	$ 500	$?	$ 364	$ 848
Units sold	?	1,300	125	1,000
Price per unit	$ 5.00	?	$ 130	?
Variable cost per unit	$?	$ 9	$?	$?
Contribution margin per unit	$?	$ 3	$?	$?
Contribution margin ratio	?	?	40%	?
Break-even units	?	?	?	?

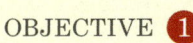

Exercise 15-31 Sales Revenue Approach, Variable Cost Ratio, Contribution Margin Ratio

Silberg Company's controller prepared the following budgeted income statement for the coming year:

Sales	$415,000
Total variable cost	282,200
Contribution margin	$132,800
Total fixed cost	63,000
Operating income	$ 69,800

Required:

1. What is Silberg's variable cost ratio? What is its contribution margin ratio?
2. Suppose Silberg's actual revenues are $30,000 more than budgeted. By how much will operating income increase? Give the answer without preparing a new income statement.
3. How much sales revenue must Silberg earn to break even? Prepare a contribution margin income statement to verify the accuracy of your answer.
4. What is Silberg's expected margin of safety?
5. What is Silberg's margin of safety if sales revenue is $380,000?

Use the following information for Exercises 15-32 and 15-33:

Peace River Products Inc. produces and sells yoga-training products: how-to DVDs and a basic equipment set (blocks, strap, and small pillows). Last year, Peace River Products sold 18,000 DVDs and 4,500 equipment sets. Information on the two products is as follows:

	DVDs	Equipment Sets
Price	$8	$25
Variable cost per unit	4	16

Total fixed cost is $85,000.

Exercise 15-32 Multiple-Product Breakeven

OBJECTIVE 4

Refer to the information for Peace River Products above.

Required:
1. What is the sales mix of DVDs and equipment sets?
2. Compute the break-even quantity of each product.

Exercise 15-33 Multiple-Product Breakeven, Break-Even Sales Revenue

OBJECTIVE 1 5

Refer to the information for Peace River Products above. Suppose that in the coming year, the company plans to produce an extra-thick yoga mat for sale to health clubs. The company estimates that 9,000 mats can be sold at a price of $18 and a variable cost per unit of $13. Total fixed cost must be increased by $29,100 (making total fixed cost $114,100). Assume that anticipated sales of the other products, as well as their prices and variable costs, remain the same.

Required:
1. What is the sales mix of DVDs, equipment sets, and yoga mats?
2. Compute the break-even quantity of each product.
3. Prepare an income statement for Peace River Products for the coming year. What is the overall contribution margin ratio? The overall break-even sales revenue?
4. Compute the margin of safety for the coming year in sales dollars. (*Note*: Round the contribution margin ratio to three decimal places; round the break-even sales revenue to the nearest dollar.)

Exercise 15-34 Contribution Margin Ratio, Break-Even Sales Revenue, and Margin of Safety for Multiple-Product Firm

OBJECTIVE 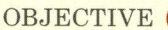 1 4 5

Texas-Q Company produces and sells barbeque grills. Texas-Q sells three models: a small portable gas grill, a larger stationary gas grill, and the specialty smoker. In the coming year, Texas-Q expects to sell 20,000 portable grills, 50,000 stationary grills, and 5,000 smokers. Information on the three models is as follows:

	Portable	Stationary	Smokers
Price	$90	$200	$250
Variable cost per unit	45	130	140

Total fixed cost is $2,128,500.

Required:
1. What is the sales mix of portable grills to stationary grills to smokers?
2. Compute the break-even quantity of each product.
3. Prepare an income statement for Texas-Q for the coming year. What is the overall contribution margin ratio? The overall break-even sales revenue? (*Note*: Round the contribution margin ratio to four decimal places; round the break-even sales revenue to the nearest dollar.)
4. Compute the margin of safety for the coming year.

OBJECTIVE ➌

Exercise 15-35 Cost-Volume-Profit Graphs

Lotts Company produces and sells one product. The selling price is $10, and the unit variable cost is $6. Total fixed cost is $10,000.

Required:
1. Prepare a CVP graph with "Units Sold" as the horizontal axis and "$ Profit" as the vertical axis. Label the break-even point on the horizontal axis.
2. Prepare CVP graphs for each of the following independent scenarios: (a) Fixed cost increases by $5,000, (b) Unit variable cost increases to $7, (c) Unit selling price increases to $12, and (d) Fixed cost increases by $5,000 and unit variable cost is $7.

OBJECTIVE ➊

Exercise 15-36 Basic Cost-Volume-Profit Concepts

Naismith Company produces a single product. The projected income statement for the coming year is as follows:

Sales (53,000 units @ $36)	$1,908,000
Total variable cost	1,030,320
Contribution margin	$ 877,680
Total fixed cost	898,380
Operating income	$ (20,700)

Required:
1. Compute the unit contribution margin and the units that must be sold to break even.
2. Suppose 10,000 units are sold above breakeven. What is the operating income?
3. Compute the contribution margin ratio and the break-even point in sales revenue. Suppose that revenues are $200,000 more than expected *for the coming year*. What would the total operating income be?

OBJECTIVE ➊ ➎

Exercise 15-37 Margin of Safety and Operating Leverage

Espanola Company produces a single product. The projected income statement for the coming year is as follows:

Sales (50,000 units @ $45)	$2,250,000
Total variable cost	1,305,000
Contribution margin	$ 945,000
Total fixed cost	916,650
Operating income	$ 28,350

(*Note*: Round all dollar answers to the nearest dollar. Round fractional answers to two decimal places.)

Required:
1. Compute the break-even sales dollars.
2. Compute the margin of safety in sales dollars.
3. Compute the degree of operating leverage (*Note:* Round answer to two decimal places).
4. Compute the new operating income if sales are 20 percent higher than expected. (*Note*: Round answer to the nearest dollar.)

OBJECTIVE ➊ ➍

Exercise 15-38 Multiple-Product Breakeven

Parker Pottery produces a line of vases and a line of ceramic figurines. Each line uses the same equipment and labor; hence, there are no traceable fixed costs. Common fixed cost equals $30,000. Parker's accountant has begun to assess the profitability of the two lines and has gathered the following data for last year:

	Vases	Figurines
Price	$40	$70
Variable cost	30	42
Contribution margin	$10	$28
Number of units	1,000	500

Required:

1. Compute the number of vases and the number of figurines that must be sold for the company to break even.
2. Parker Pottery is considering upgrading its factory to improve the quality of its products. The upgrade will add $5,260 per year to total fixed cost. If the upgrade is successful, the projected sales of vases will be 1,500, and figurine sales will increase to 1,000 units. What is the new break-even point in units for each of the products?

Exercise 15-39 Break-Even Units, Contribution Margin Ratio, Multiple-Product Breakeven, Margin of Safety, Degree of Operating Leverage

OBJECTIVE ❶❷❹❺

Jellico Inc.'s projected operating income (based on sales of 450,000 units) for the coming year is as follows:

	Total
Sales	$11,700,000
Total variable cost	8,190,000
Contribution margin	$ 3,510,000
Total fixed cost	2,254,200
Operating income	$ 1,255,800

Required:

1. Compute: (a) variable cost per unit, (b) contribution margin per unit, (c) contribution margin ratio, (d) break-even point in units, and (e) break-even point in sales dollars.
2. How many units must be sold to earn operating income of $296,400?
3. Compute the additional operating income that Jellico would earn if sales were $50,000 more than expected.
4. For the projected level of sales, compute the margin of safety in units, and then in sales dollars.
5. Compute the degree of operating leverage. (*Note*: Round answer to two decimal places.)
6. Compute the new operating income if sales are 10 percent higher than expected.

PROBLEMS

Problem 15-40 Break-Even Units, Contribution Margin Ratio, Margin of Safety

OBJECTIVE ❶❷❺

Tensing Company's projected profit for the coming year is as follows:

	Total	Per Unit
Sales	$2,480,000	$20
Total variable cost	1,488,000	12
Contribution margin	$ 992,000	$ 8
Total fixed cost	626,400	
Operating income	$ 365,600	

Required:

1. Compute the break-even point in units.
2. How many units must be sold to earn a profit of $450,000?
3. Compute the contribution margin ratio. Using that ratio, compute the additional profit that Tensing would earn if sales were $37,000 more than expected.
4. For the projected level of sales, compute the margin of safety in units.

OBJECTIVE

Problem 15-41 Break-Even Units, Operating Income, Margin of Safety

Kallard Manufacturing Company produces T-shirts screen-printed with the logos of various sports teams. Each shirt is priced at $13.50 and has a unit variable cost of $9.85. Total fixed cost is $197,600.

Required:

1. Compute the break-even point in units. (*Note*: Round answer to the nearest whole unit.)
2. Suppose that Kallard could reduce its fixed costs by $23,500 by reducing the amount of setup and engineering time needed. How many units must be sold to break even in this case? (*Note*: Round answer to the nearest whole unit.)
3. **Conceptual Connection:** How does the reduction in fixed cost affect the break-even point? Operating income? The margin of safety?

OBJECTIVE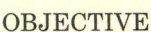

Problem 15-42 Contribution Margin, Break-Even Units, Break-Even Sales, Margin of Safety, Degree of Operating Leverage

Cerling Company produces a variety of chemicals. One division makes reagents for laboratories. The division's projected income statement for the coming year is:

Sales (218,000 units @ $60)	$13,080,000
Total variable cost	7,630,000
Contribution margin	$ 5,450,000
Total fixed cost	4,250,000
Operating income	$ 1,200,000

Required:

1. Compute the contribution margin per unit, and calculate the break-even point in units (*Note*: Round answer to the nearest unit.) Calculate the contribution margin ratio and the break-even sales revenue.
2. The divisional manager has decided to increase the advertising budget by $250,000. This will increase sales revenues by $1 million. By how much will operating income increase or decrease as a result of this action?
3. Suppose sales revenues exceed the estimated amount on the income statement by $1,500,000. Without preparing a new income statement, by how much are profits underestimated?
4. Compute the margin of safety based on the original income statement.
5. Compute the degree of operating leverage based on the original income statement. If sales revenues are 8 percent greater than expected, what is the percentage increase in operating income? (*Note*: Round operating leverage to two decimal places.)

OBJECTIVE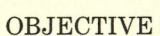

Problem 15-43 Multiple-Product Analysis, Changes in Sales Mix, Sales to Earn Target Operating Income

Basu Company produces two types of sleds for playing in the snow: basic sled and aerosled. The projected income for the coming year, segmented by product line, follows:

	Basic Sled	Aerosled	Total
Sales	$3,000,000	$2,400,000	$5,400,000
Total variable cost	1,000,000	1,000,000	2,000,000
Contribution margin	$2,000,000	$1,400,000	$3,400,000
Direct fixed cost	778,000	650,000	1,428,000
Product margin	$1,222,000	$ 750,000	$1,972,000
Common fixed cost			198,900
Operating income			$1,773,100

The selling prices are $30 for the basic sled and $60 for the aerosled.

Required:

1. Compute the number of units of each product that must be sold for Basu to break even.
2. Assume that the marketing manager changes the sales mix of the two products so that the ratio is five basic sleds to three aerosleds. Repeat Requirement 1.

3. **Conceptual Connection:** Refer to the original data. Suppose that Basu can increase the sales of aerosleds with increased advertising. The extra advertising would cost an additional $195,000, and some of the potential purchasers of basic sleds would switch to aerosleds. In total, sales of aerosleds would increase by 12,000 units, and sales of basic sleds would decrease by 5,000 units. Would Basu be better off with this strategy?

Problem 15-44   Cost-Volume-Profit Equation, Basic Concepts, Solving for Unknowns

OBJECTIVE ❶❷❸❺

Legrand Company produces hand cream in plastic jars. Each jar sells for $3.40. The variable cost for each jar (materials, labor, and overhead) totals $2.55. The total fixed cost is $58,140. During the most recent year, 81,600 jars were sold.

Required:

1. What is the break-even point in units for Legrand? What is the margin of safety in units for the most recent year?
2. Prepare an income statement for Legrand's most recent year.
3. How many units must be sold for Legrand to earn a profit of $25,500?
4. What is the level of sales dollars needed for Legrand to earn operating income of 10 percent of sales?

Problem 15-45   Contribution Margin Ratio, Break-Even Sales, Operating Leverage

OBJECTIVE ❶❺

Elgart Company produces plastic mailboxes. The projected income statement for the coming year follows:

Sales	$460,300
Total variable cost	165,708
Contribution margin	$294,592
Total fixed cost	150,000
Operating income	$144,592

Required:

1. Compute the contribution margin ratio for the mailboxes.
2. How much revenue must Elgart earn in order to break even?
3. What is the effect on the contribution margin ratio if the unit selling price and unit variable cost each increase by 15 percent?
4. **Conceptual Connection:** Suppose that management has decided to give a 4 percent commission on all sales. The projected income statement does not reflect this commission. Recompute the contribution margin ratio, assuming that the commission will be paid. What effect does this have on the break-even point?
5. **Conceptual Connection:** If the commission is paid as described in Requirement 4, management expects sales revenues to increase by $80,000. How will this affect operating leverage? Is it a sound decision to implement the commission? Support your answer with appropriate computations.

Problem 15-46   Multiple Products, Break-Even Analysis, Operating Leverage

OBJECTIVE ❹❺

Carlyle Lighting Products produces two different types of lamps: a floor lamp and a desk lamp. Floor lamps sell for $30, and desk lamps sell for $20. The projected income statement for the coming year follows:

Sales	$600,000
Total variable cost	400,000
Contribution margin	$200,000
Total fixed cost	150,000
Operating income	$ 50,000

The owner of Carlyle estimates that 60 percent of the sales revenues will be produced by floor lamps and the remaining 40 percent by desk lamps. Floor lamps are also responsible for 60 percent of the variable cost. Of the fixed cost, one-third is common to both products, and one-half is directly traceable to the floor lamp product line.

(Continued)

Required:
1. Compute the sales revenue that must be earned for Carlyle to break even.
2. Compute the number of floor lamps and desk lamps that must be sold for Carlyle to break even.
3. Compute the degree of operating leverage for Carlyle. Now assume that the actual revenues will be 40 percent higher than the projected revenues. By what percentage will profits increase with this change in sales volume?

 OBJECTIVE ❶ ❹

Problem 15-47 Multiple-Product Breakeven

Polaris Inc. manufactures two types of metal stampings for the automobile industry: door handles and trim kits. Fixed cost equals $146,000. Each door handle sells for $12 and has variable cost of $9; each trim kit sells for $8 and has variable cost of $5.

Required:
1. What are the contribution margin per unit and the contribution margin ratio for door handles and for trim kits?
2. If Polaris sells 20,000 door handles and 40,000 trim kits, what is the operating income?
3. How many door handles and how many trim kits must be sold for Polaris to break even?
4. **Conceptual Connection:** Assume that Polaris has the opportunity to rearrange its plant to produce only trim kits. If this is done, fixed costs will decrease by $35,000, and 70,000 trim kits can be produced and sold. Is this a good idea? Explain.

 OBJECTIVE ❶ ❺

Problem 15-48 Cost-Volume-Profit, Margin of Safety

Victoria Company produces a single product. Last year's income statement is as follows:

Sales (29,000 units)	$1,218,000
Total variable cost	812,000
Contribution margin	$ 406,000
Total fixed cost	300,000
Operating income	$ 106,000

Required:
1. Compute the break-even point in units and sales dollars.
2. What was the margin of safety for Victoria last year?
3. Suppose that Victoria is considering an investment in new technology that will increase fixed cost by $250,000 per year but will lower variable costs to 45 percent of sales. Units sold will remain unchanged. Prepare a budgeted income statement assuming that Victoria makes this investment. What is the new break-even point in units and sales dollars, assuming that the investment is made?

 OBJECTIVE ❶ ❺

Problem 15-49 Cost-Volume-Profit, Margin of Safety

Abraham Company had revenues of $830,000 last year with total variable costs of $647,400 and fixed costs of $110,000.

Required:
1. What is the variable cost ratio for Abraham? What is the contribution margin ratio?
2. What is the break-even point in sales revenue?
3. What was the margin of safety for Abraham last year?
4. **Conceptual Connection:** Abraham is considering starting a multimedia advertising campaign that is supposed to increase sales by $12,000 per year. The campaign will cost $4,500. Is the advertising campaign a good idea? Explain.

OBJECTIVE ❶

Problem 15-50 Using the Break-Even Equations to Solve for Price and Variable Cost per Unit

Solve the following independent problems.

ILLUSTRATING
RELATIONSHIPS

Required:

1. Andromeda Company's break-even point is 2,400 units. Variable cost per unit is $42; total fixed costs are $67,200 per year. What price does Andromeda charge?
2. Immelt Company charges a price of $6.50; total fixed cost is $314,400 per year, and the break-even point is 131,000 units. What is the variable cost per unit?

Problem 15-51 Contribution Margin, Cost-Volume-Profit, Margin of Safety

 OBJECTIVE **1 2 5**

Candyland Inc. produces a particularly rich praline fudge. Each 10-ounce box sells for $5.60. Variable unit costs are as follows:

Pecans	$0.70
Sugar	0.35
Butter	1.85
Other ingredients	0.34
Box, packing material	0.76
Selling commission	0.20

Fixed overhead cost is $32,300 per year. Fixed selling and administrative costs are $12,500 per year. Candyland sold 35,000 boxes last year.

Required:

1. What is the contribution margin per unit for a box of praline fudge? What is the contribution margin ratio?
2. How many boxes must be sold to break even? What is the break-even sales revenue?
3. What was Candyland's operating income last year?
4. What was the margin of safety?
5. **Conceptual Connection:** Suppose that Candyland Inc. raises the price to $6.20 per box but anticipates a sales drop to 31,500 boxes. What will be the new break-even point in units? Should Candyland raise the price? Explain.

Problem 15-52 Break-Even Sales, Operating Leverage, Change in Income

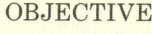 OBJECTIVE **1 5**

Income statements for two different companies in the same industry are as follows:

	Duncan	Macduff
Sales	$375,000	$375,000
Total variable cost	300,000	150,000
Contribution margin	$ 75,000	$225,000
Total fixed cost	50,000	200,000
Operating income	$ 25,000	$ 25,000

Required:

1. Compute the degree of operating leverage for each company.
2. **Conceptual Connection:** Compute the break-even point for each company. Explain why the break-even point for Macduff is higher.
3. **Conceptual Connection:** Suppose that both companies experience a 30 percent increase in revenues. Compute the percentage change in profits for each company. Explain why the percentage increase in Macduff's profits is so much larger than that of Duncan.

Problem 15-53 Contribution Margin, Break-Even Sales, Margin of Safety

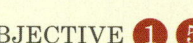 OBJECTIVE **1 5**

Suppose that Kicker had the following sales and cost experience (in thousands of dollars) for May of the current year and for May of the prior year:

(Continued)

	May, Current Year	May, Prior Year
Total sales	$ 43,560	$ 41,700
Less:		
Purchase price paid	(17,000)	(16,000)
Additional labor and supplies	(1,400)	(1,200)
Commissions	(1,250)	(1,100)
Contribution margin	$ 23,910	$ 23,400
Less:		
Fixed warehouse cost	(680)	(500)
Fixed administrative cost	(4,300)	(4,300)
Fixed selling cost	(5,600)	(5,000)
Research and development	(9,750)	(4,000)
Operating income	$ 3,580	$ 9,600

In May of the prior year, **Kicker** started an intensive quality program designed to enable it to build original equipment manufacture (OEM) speaker systems for a major automobile company. The program was housed in research and development. In the beginning of the current year, Kicker's accounting department exercised tighter control over sales commissions, ensuring that no dubious (e.g., double) payments were made. The increased sales in the current year required additional warehouse space that Kicker rented in town.

Required:
1. Calculate the contribution margin ratio for May of both years.
2. Calculate the break-even point in sales dollars for both years.
3. Calculate the margin of safety in sales dollars for both years.
4. **Conceptual Connection:** Analyze the differences shown by your calculations in Requirements 1, 2, and 3.

CASES

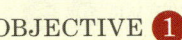

Case 15-54 Cost-Volume-Profit with Multiple Products, Sales Mix Changes, Changes in Fixed and Variable Costs

Artistic Woodcrafting Inc. began several years ago as a one-person, cabinet-making operation. Employees were added as the business expanded. Last year, sales volume totaled $850,000. Volume for the first five months of the current year totaled $600,000, and sales were expected to be $1.6 million for the entire year. Unfortunately, the cabinet business in the region where Artistic is located is highly competitive. More than 200 cabinet shops are all competing for the same business.

Artistic currently offers two different quality grades of cabinets: Grade I and Grade II, with Grade I being the higher quality. The average unit selling prices, unit variable costs, and direct fixed costs are as follows:

	Unit Price	Unit Variable Cost	Direct Fixed Cost
Grade I	$3,400	$2,686	$95,000
Grade II	1,600	1,328	95,000

Common fixed costs (fixed costs not traceable to either cabinet) are $35,000. Currently, for every three Grade I cabinets sold, seven Grade II cabinets are sold.

Required:
1. Calculate the number of Grade I and Grade II cabinets that are expected to be sold during the current year.
2. Calculate the number of Grade I and Grade II cabinets that must be sold for Artistic to break even.
3. Artistic can buy computer-controlled machines that will make doors, drawers, and frames. If the machines are purchased, the variable costs for each type of cabinet will decrease by 9 percent, but common fixed cost will increase by $44,000. Compute the effect on operating

income, and also calculate the new break-even point. Assume the machines are purchased at the beginning of the sixth month. Fixed costs for the company are incurred uniformly throughout the year.

4. Refer to the original data. Artistic is considering adding a retail outlet. This will increase common fixed cost by $70,000 per year. As a result of adding the retail outlet, the additional publicity and emphasis on quality will allow the firm to change the sales mix to 1:1. The retail outlet is also expected to increase sales by 30 percent. Assume that the outlet is opened at the beginning of the sixth month. Calculate the effect on the company's expected profits for the current year, and calculate the new break-even point. Assume that fixed costs are incurred uniformly throughout the year.

Case 15-55 Ethics and a Cost-Volume-Profit Application

OBJECTIVE ❶

Danna Lumus, the marketing manager for a division that produces a variety of paper products, is considering the divisional manager's request for a sales forecast for a new line of paper napkins. The divisional manager has been gathering data so that he can choose between two different production processes. The first process would have a variable cost of $10 per case produced and total fixed cost of $100,000. The second process would have a variable cost of $6 per case and total fixed cost of $200,000. The selling price would be $30 per case. Danna had just completed a marketing analysis that projects annual sales of 30,000 cases.

Danna is reluctant to report the 30,000 forecast to the divisional manager. She knows that the first process would be labor intensive, whereas the second would be largely automated with little labor and no requirement for an additional production supervisor. If the first process is chosen, Jerry Johnson, a good friend, will be appointed as the line supervisor. If the second process is chosen, Jerry and an entire line of laborers will be laid off. After some consideration, Danna revises the projected sales downward to 22,000 cases.

She believes that the revision downward is justified. Since it will lead the divisional manager to choose the manual system, it shows a sensitivity to the needs of current employees—a sensitivity that she is afraid her divisional manager does not possess. He is too focused on quantitative factors in his decision making and usually ignores the qualitative aspects.

Required:

1. Compute the break-even point in units for each process.
2. Compute the sales volume for which the two processes are equally profitable. Identify the range of sales for which the manual process is more profitable than the automated process. Identify the range of sales for which the automated process is more profitable than the manual process. Why does the divisional manager want the sales forecast?
3. Discuss Danna's decision to alter the sales forecast. Do you agree with it? Is she acting ethically? Is her decision justified since it helps a number of employees retain their employment? Should the impact on employees be factored into decisions? In fact, is it unethical not to consider the impact of decisions on employees?

Cost Behavior and Cost-Volume-Profit Analysis for Many Glacier Hotel

Chapters	Objectives	Cornerstones
13-15	13-2	14-2
	14-3	15-2
	15-1	15-5
	15-2	15-7
	15-4	15-9
	15-5	

The purpose of this integrated exercise is to demonstrate the interrelationship between cost estimation techniques and subsequent uses of cost information. In particular, this exercise illustrates how the variable and fixed cost information estimated from a high-low analysis can be used in a single- and multiple-product CVP analysis.

Using the High-Low Method to Estimate Variable and Fixed Costs

Located on Swiftcurrent Lake in Glacier National Park, **Many Glacier Hotel** was built in 1915 by the Great Northern Railway. In an effort to supplement its lodging revenue, the hotel decided in 1998 to begin manufacturing and selling small wooden canoes decorated with symbols hand painted by Native Americans living near the park. Due to the great success of the canoes, the hotel began manufacturing and selling paddles as well in 2001. Many hotel guests purchase a canoe and paddles for use in self-guided tours of Swiftcurrent Lake. Because production of the two products began in different years, the canoes and paddles are produced in separate production facilities and employ different laborers. Each canoe sells for $500, and each paddle sells for $50. A 2001 fire destroyed the hotel's accounting records. However, a new system put into place before the 2002 season provides the following aggregated data for the hotel's canoe and paddle manufacturing and marketing activities:

Manufacturing Data:

Year	Number of Canoes Manufactured	Total Canoe Manufacturing Costs	Year	Number of Paddles Manufactured	Total Paddle Manufacturing Costs
2007	250	$106,000	2007	900	$38,500
2006	275	115,000	2006	1,200	49,000
2005	240	108,000	2005	1,000	42,000
2004	310	122,000	2004	1,100	45,500
2003	350	130,000	2003	1,400	56,000
2002	400	140,000	2002	1,700	66,500

Marketing Data:

Year	Number of Canoes Sold	Total Canoe Marketing Costs	Year	Number of Paddles Sold	Total Paddle Marketing Costs
2007	250	$45,000	2007	900	$ 7,500
2006	275	47,500	2006	1,200	9,000
2005	240	44,000	2005	1,000	8,000
2004	310	51,000	2004	1,100	8,500
2003	350	55,000	2003	1,400	10,000
2002	400	60,000	2002	1,700	11,500

Required:

1. High-Low Cost Estimation Method

   a. Use the high-low method to estimate the per-unit variable costs and total fixed costs for the *canoe* product line.

   b. Use the high-low method to estimate the per-unit variable costs and total fixed costs for the *paddle* product line.

2. Cost-Volume-Profit Analysis, Single-Product Setting

   Use CVP analysis to calculate the break-even point in units for

   a. The *canoe* product line *only* (i.e., single-product setting)

   b. The *paddle* product line *only* (i.e., single-product setting)

3. Cost-Volume-Profit Analysis, Multiple-Product Setting

   The hotel's accounting system data show an average sales mix of approximately 300 canoes and 1,200 paddles each season. Significantly more paddles are sold relative to canoes because some inexperienced canoe guests accidentally break one or more paddles, while other guests purchase additional paddles as presents for friends and relatives. In addition, for this multiple-product CVP analysis, assume the existence of an additional $30,000 of common fixed costs for a customer service hotline used for both canoe and paddle customers. Use CVP analysis to calculate the break-even point in units for both the canoe and paddle product lines combined (i.e., the multiple-product setting).

4. Cost Classification

   a. Classify the manufacturing costs, marketing costs, and customer service hotline costs either as production expenses or period expenses.

   b. For the period expenses, further classify them into either selling expenses or general and administrative expenses.

5. Sensitivity Cost-Volume-Profit Analysis and Production Versus Period Expenses, Multiple-Product Setting

   If both the variable and fixed *production* expenses (refer to your answer to Requirement 1) associated with the *canoe* product line increased by 5 percent (beyond the estimate from the high-low analysis), how many canoes and paddles would need to be sold in order to earn a target income of $96,000? Assume the same sales mix and additional fixed costs as in Requirement 3.

6. Margin of Safety

   Calculate the hotel's margin of safety (both in units and in sales dollars) for Many Glacier Hotel, assuming the same facts as in Requirement 3, and it sells 700 canoes and 2,500 paddles next year.

16 Job-Order Costing

Doug Norman Crystals/Alamy

After studying Chapter 16, you should be able to:

1. Describe the differences between job-order costing and process costing, and identify the types of firms that would use each method.

2. Compute the predetermined overhead rate, and use the rate to assign overhead to units or services produced.

3. Identify and set up the source documents used in job-order costing.

4. Describe the cost flows associated with job-order costing.

5. (Appendix 16A) Prepare the journal entries associated with job-order costing.

6. (Appendix 16B) Allocate support department costs to producing departments.

Kemter/iStockphoto.com

EXPERIENCE MANAGERIAL DECISIONS

with Washburn Guitars

Since 1883, **Washburn Guitars** has manufactured high-quality acoustic and electric guitars. Washburn's guitar buyers include musicians ranging from garage bands to some of the world's most famous bands.

Washburn produces many guitar series. Each series has many different models that require the use of varied resources.[1] For example, in 2006 Washburn introduced the Damen Idol, retailing for $2,249. The Damen, named after Damen Avenue in Chicago's Wicker Park—a known hot spot for alternative, pop, and punk musicians, illustrates the complexity and individuality of specialized guitars. It featured a mahogany body, flame maple top, mahogany neck with cream binding, rosewood fingerboard, Seymour Duncan Custom pickups in the bridge and a Seymour Duncan '59 in the neck, a Tone Pros Bridge and Tailpiece, and numerous other options for frets, scaling, finishing, and tuning. Joe Trohman from Fall Out Boy, Aaron Dugan of Matisyahu, Mike Kennerty from The All American Rejects, Shaun Glass from

Thomas Sztanek, 2010/Shutterstock.com

Soil, and Marty Casey from the Lovehammers and INXS all played the Damen Idol at one time or another.

Many guitar buyers, including most professionals, request various product customizations. For example, Washburn's Custom Shop Pilsen guitar was made especially for Billy Sawilchik to play the National Anthem at Game 2 of the 2005 American League Championship Series between the White Sox and Angels. While customization created great publicity for Washburn, it also created significant design and product differences between guitars, even those within the same model line of a given series. This variability led to differences in the use of materials and labor, which required Washburn to estimate the cost of each guitar job according to the desired degree of customization. Washburn managers relied heavily on their effective job-order costing system to help them understand the costs associated with such product alterations. This ensured that the particular customizations provided a profit after all costs were covered.

---

[1] By 2009, Washburn stopped making the customized guitars favored by top rock musicians. It now concentrates on guitars for a mass audience. While the Damen Idol is no longer in production, it is still an excellent example of job-order production.

OBJECTIVE ①
Describe the differences between job-order costing and process costing, and identify the types of firms that would use each method.

CHARACTERISTICS OF THE JOB-ORDER ENVIRONMENT

Companies can be divided into two major types, depending on whether their products/services are unique. Manufacturing and service firms producing unique products or services require a job-order accounting system. When Washburn Guitars was producing its custom guitars, it fell into this category. On the other hand, those firms producing similar products or services can use a process-costing accounting system. **Ben & Jerry's Homemade, Inc.**, a producer of premium ice creams with the whimsical flavor names, falls into this latter category. Each pint of a particular flavor of ice cream, say Cherry Garcia or Triple Caramel Chunk, is indistinguishable from the other pints. The characteristics of a company's actual production process determine whether it needs a job-order or a process-costing accounting system.

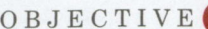

Here's the Real Kicker

In the 1970s, **Kicker** began operations in Steve Irby's garage. Steve was an engineering student at Oklahoma State University and a keyboard player with a local band. The band needed speakers but couldn't afford new ones. Steve and his father built wooden boxes and fitted them with secondhand components. Word spread, and other bands asked for speakers. Steve partnered with a friend to fill the orders. Then, an oil-field worker asked if Steve could rig up speakers for his pickup truck. Long days bouncing over rough fields went more smoothly with music, but the built-in audio systems at the time were awful. Steve designed and built a speaker to fit behind the driver's seat, and Kicker was born.

At first, each job was made to order to fit a particular truck or car. The price Steve charged depended heavily on the cost of the job. Since each job was different, the various costs had to be computed individually. Clearly, the costs of wood, fabric, glue, and components were traceable to each job. Steve could also trace labor time. But the other costs of design time, use of power tools, and space were combined to create an overhead rate. To the extent that the price of a job was greater than its costs, Steve earned a profit.

Job-Order Production and Costing

Firms operating in job-order industries produce a wide variety of services or products that are quite distinct from each other. Customized or built-to-order products fit into this category, as do services that vary from customer to customer, like **Sky Limo Corporation**, which provides air charter services. A **job** is one distinct unit or set of units. For example, a job might be a kitchen remodel for the Ruiz family, or a set of 12 tables for the children's reading room at the local library. Common job-order processes include:

- printing
- construction
- furniture making
- medical and dental services
- automobile repair
- beautician services

Often, a job is associated with a particular customer order. The key feature of job-order costing is that the cost of one job differs from that of another and must be kept track of separately.

For job-order production systems, costs are accumulated by job. This approach to assigning costs is called a **job-order costing system**. In a job-order firm, collecting costs by job provides vital information for management. For example, prices frequently are based on costs in a job-order environment.

Process Production and Costing

Firms in process industries mass-produce large quantities of similar or homogeneous products. Examples of process manufacturers include:

- food canning and manufacturing
- cement
- petroleum
- pharmaceutical and chemical manufacturing

One gallon of paint is the same as another gallon; one bottle of aspirin is the same as another bottle. The important point is that the cost of one unit of a product is identical to the cost of another. Service firms can also use a process-costing approach. For example, check-clearing departments of banks incur a uniform cost to clear a check, no matter the size of the check or the name of the payee.

Process firms accumulate production costs by process or by department for a given period of time. The output for the process for that period of time is measured. Unit costs are computed by dividing the process costs for the given period by the output of the period:

$$\text{Unit costs} = \frac{\text{Process costs}}{\text{Output}}$$

This approach to cost accumulation is known as a **process-costing system** and is examined in detail in Chapter 17. A comparison of job-order costing and process costing is given in Exhibit 16-1.

Concept **Q&A**

Give examples of businesses in your community that would use job-order costing and process costing, and tell why each would be appropriate.

Answer: Answers will vary. One possible example: A tax accounting firm would keep track of costs by job because some tax returns are relatively simple while others are complex and require time to fill out additional forms and to do necessary research. A "while you wait" oil change shop would use process costing (but cost the oil required separately) since each car would take about the same amount of time and supplies to perform the oil change.

Production Costs in Job-Order Costing

While the variety of product-costing definitions discussed in Chapter 13 applies to both job-order and process costing, we will use the traditional definition to illustrate job-order costing procedures. That is, production costs consist of direct materials, direct labor, and overhead. Direct materials and direct labor are typically fairly easy to trace to individual jobs, while overhead, because it consists of all production costs other than direct materials and direct labor, is not always as simple.

NORMAL COSTING AND OVERHEAD APPLICATION

Unit costs are very important because managers need accurate cost information on materials, labor, and overhead when making decisions. For example, Bechtel Construction, whose projects include the Channel Tunnel connecting England and France and Boston's "Big Dig," typically bills its clients at set points throughout construction. As a result, it is important that the unit cost be generated in a timely fashion. Job-order costing using a normal cost system will give the company the unit cost information it needs.

OBJECTIVE **2**

Compute the predetermined overhead rate, and use the rate to assign overhead to units or services produced.

Actual Costing versus Normal Costing

Two ways are commonly used to measure the costs associated with production: actual costing and normal costing.

Exhibit 16-1

Comparison of Job-Order and Process Costing

Job-Order Costing	Process Costing
• Wide variety of distinct products	• Homogeneous products
• Costs accumulated by job	• Costs accumulated by process or department
• Unit cost = Total job costs/Output	• Unit cost = Process costs/Output

Actual Costing In an **actual cost system**, only *actual* costs of direct materials, direct labor, and overhead are used to determine unit cost. However, there are several issues involved in using actual costing.

Defining Overhead Costs Per-unit computation of the direct materials and direct labor costs is relatively easy to determine. However, defining overhead is much more difficult. Overhead items do not have the direct relationship with units produced that direct materials and direct labor do. For example, how much of a security guard's salary should be assigned to a unit of product or service? Even if the firm averages overhead cost by totaling manufacturing overhead costs for a given period and then divides this total by the number of units produced, distorted costs can occur. The distortion can be traced to uneven incurrence of overhead costs and uneven production from period to period.

Uneven Overhead Costs Many overhead costs are not incurred uniformly throughout the year. For example, actual repair cost occurs whenever a machine breakdown occurs. This timing can make overhead costs in the month of a machine breakdown higher than in other months. The second problem, nonuniform production levels, can mean that low production in one month would give rise to high unit overhead costs, and high production in another month would give rise to low unit overhead costs. Yet the production process and total overhead costs may remain unchanged. One solution would be to wait until the end of the year to total the actual overhead costs and divide by the total actual production, an option that is not realistic for most companies.

Uneven Production Strict actual cost systems are rarely used because they cannot provide accurate unit cost information on a timely basis. A company needs unit cost information throughout the year. This information is needed to prepare interim financial statements and to help managers make decisions such as pricing. Managers must react to day-to-day conditions in the marketplace in order to maintain a sound competitive position. Therefore, they need timely information.

Normal Costing Normal costing solves the problems associated with actual costing. A **normal cost system** determines unit cost by adding actual direct materials, actual direct labor, and estimated overhead. Overhead can be estimated by approximating the year's actual overhead at the *beginning* of the year and then using a predetermined rate throughout the year to obtain the needed unit cost information. Virtually all firms use normal costing.

Importance of Unit Costs to Manufacturing Firms

Unit cost is a critical piece of information for a manufacturer. Unit costs are essential for valuing inventory, determining income, and making numerous important decisions.

Disclosing the cost of inventories and determining income are financial reporting requirements that a firm faces at the end of each period. In order to report the cost of its inventories, a firm must know the number of units on hand and the unit cost. The cost of goods sold (COGS), used to determine income, requires knowledge of the units sold and their unit cost.

Note that full cost information is useful as an input for a number of important internal decisions as well as for financial reporting. In the long run, for any product to be viable, its price must cover its full cost. Decisions to introduce a new product, to continue a current product, and to analyze long-run prices are examples of important internal decisions that rely on full unit cost information.

Importance of Unit Costs to Service Firms

Like manufacturing firms, service and nonprofit firms also require unit cost information. Conceptually, the way companies accumulate and assign costs is the same whether or not the firm is a manufacturer. The service firm must first identify

Concept Q&A

The TV reality series *Trading Spaces* involves two pairs of homeowners who, with the guidance of an interior designer and the help of a professional carpenter, redo one room in each other's house. Each pair has 48 hours and $1,000 to accomplish the renovation. At the end of each show, the host and interior designer total up the "costs" of the redecoration project, which typically comes in at pennies under $1,000. What costs are included in the $1,000? What costs are not? Does each redecoration really cost under $1,000? (*Hint:* Think about direct materials, direct labor, and overhead in your answer.)

Answer:
The $1,000 is used to cover the cost of furniture, fabrics, and materials. It does not cover the services of the designer or carpenter. There is clearly a good deal of overhead involved that includes the power tools, carpentry supplies (nails, glue), hand tools, sewing machine(s), and so on. The completed room costs considerably more than $1,000.

the service "unit" being provided. A hospital would accumulate costs by patient, patient day, and type of procedure (e.g., X-ray, complete blood count test). A governmental agency must also identify the service provided. For example, city government might provide household trash collection and calculate the cost by truck run or number of houses served.

Service firms use cost data in much the same way that manufacturing firms do. They use costs to determine profitability, the feasibility of introducing new services, and so on. However, because service firms do not produce physical products, they do not need to value work-in-process and finished goods inventories. (Inventories of supplies are simply valued at historical cost.)

ETHICAL DECISIONS   Nonprofit firms must track costs to be sure that they provide their services in a cost-efficient way. Governmental agencies have a fiduciary responsibility to taxpayers to use funds wisely, and that requires accurate accounting for costs. Without such responsibility, questionable results can occur, such as the alleged overcharges by several pharmaceutical firms for common prescription drugs used by Medicaid patients. Under Medicaid rules, the government reimburses companies for the average wholesale price of the drugs used. **Sandoz Pharmaceuticals**, among others, allegedly inflated the prices charged by up to 60,000%. (See Chapter 23 for additional discussion of ethics involving cost-plus pricing).[2] ●

A cost accounting system measures and assigns costs so that the unit cost of a product or service can be determined. Unit cost is a critical piece of information for both manufacturing and service firms. Bidding is a common requirement in the markets for specialized products and services (e.g., bids for special tools, audits, legal services, and medical tests and procedures). For example, it would be virtually impossible for **KPMG** to submit a meaningful bid to one of its large audit clients without knowing the unit costs of its services.

Normal Costing and Estimating Overhead

In normal costing, overhead is estimated and applied to production. The basics of overhead application can be described in three steps:

Step 1: Calculate the predetermined overhead rate.
Step 2: Apply overhead to production throughout the year.
Step 3: Reconcile the difference between the total actual overhead incurred during the year and the total overhead applied to production.

Step 1: Calculating the Predetermined Overhead Rate   The **predetermined overhead rate** is calculated at the beginning of the year by dividing the total estimated annual overhead by the total estimated level of associated activity or cost driver:

$$\text{Predetermined overhead rate} = \frac{\text{Estimated annual overhead}}{\text{Estimated annual activity level}}$$

Notice that the predetermined overhead rate includes estimated amounts in *both* the numerator and the denominator. This estimation is necessary because the predetermined overhead rate is calculated in advance, usually at the beginning of the year. It is impossible to use actual overhead or actual activity level for the year because at that time, the company does not know what the actual levels will be.

Estimated overhead is the firm's best estimate of the amount of overhead (utilities, indirect labor, depreciation, etc.) to be incurred in the coming year. The estimate is often based on last year's figures and is adjusted for anticipated changes in the coming year.

The associated activity level depends on which activity is best associated with overhead. Often, the activity chosen is the number of direct labor hours or the direct labor cost. This makes sense when much of overhead cost is associated with direct labor

[2] Jim Edwards, "Sandoz Overcharged Medicaid by 60,000% in $13B Pricing Scam, Says Judge," *BNET.* (January 28, 2010): http://industry.bnet.com/pharma/10006357/sandoz-overcharged-medicaid-by-60000-in-13b-pricing-scam-says-judge/.

(e.g., fringe benefits, worker safety training programs, the cost of running the personnel department). The number of machine hours could be a good choice for a company with automated production. Then, much of the overhead cost might consist of equipment maintenance, depreciation on machinery, electricity to run the machinery, and so on. The estimated activity level is the number of direct labor hours, or machine hours, expected for the coming year. **Washburn Guitars** found that much of its overhead was connected to the use of direct labor (e.g., body and neck sanding, fret board assembly, neck joint sanding, taping and painting, wiring and assembly) and of machinery (e.g., CNC body and neck roughing, fret board inlay programming and cutting). Therefore, direct labor and machine hours were good activity choices for overhead application.

Step 2: Applying Overhead to Production

Once the overhead rate has been computed, the company can begin to apply overhead to production. **Applied overhead** is found by multiplying the predetermined overhead rate by the actual use of the associated activity for the period:

> Applied overhead = Predetermined overhead rate × Actual activity level

Suppose that a company has an overhead rate of $5 per machine hour. In the first week of January, the company used 9,000 hours of machine time. The overhead applied to the week's production is computed as:

$$\$5 \times 9{,}000 = \$45{,}000$$

The concept is the same for any time period. So, if the company runs its machines for 50,000 hours in the month of January, applied overhead for January would be $250,000 ($5 × 50,000).

The total cost of product for the period is the actual direct materials and direct labor, plus the applied overhead:

> Total product costs = Actual direct materials + Actual direct labor + Applied overhead

CORNERSTONE 16-1 shows how to calculate the predetermined overhead rate and how to use that rate to apply overhead to production.

CORNERSTONE 16-1

Calculating the Predetermined Overhead Rate and Applying Overhead to Production

Information:

At the beginning of the year, Argus Company estimated the following costs:

Overhead	$360,000
Direct labor cost	720,000

Argus uses normal costing and applies overhead on the basis of direct labor cost. (Direct labor cost equals total direct labor hours worked multiplied by the wage rate.) For the month of February, direct labor cost was $56,000.

Required:
1. Calculate the predetermined overhead rate for the year.
2. Calculate the overhead applied to production in February.

Solution:

1. Predetermined overhead rate $= \dfrac{\$360{,}000}{\$720{,}000}$

   $= 0.50$, or 50 percent of direct labor cost

2. Overhead applied to February production $= 0.50 \times \$56{,}000 = \$28{,}000$

Step 3: Reconciling Actual Overhead with Applied Overhead Recall that two types of overhead are recorded:

- *Actual overhead*: Costs are tracked throughout the year in the overhead account.
- *Applied overhead*: Costs are computed throughout the year and added to actual direct materials and actual direct labor to get total product cost.

At the end of the year, any difference between actual and applied overhead must be recognized and closed to the cost of goods sold account so that it reflects actual overhead spending.

Suppose that Proto Company had actual overhead of $400,000 for the year but had applied $390,000 to production. Proto Company has *underapplied* overhead by $10,000. If applied overhead had been $410,000, too much overhead would have been applied to production. The firm would have *overapplied* overhead by $10,000. The difference between actual overhead and applied overhead is called an **overhead variance**:

> Overhead variance = Actual overhead − Applied overhead

If actual overhead is greater than applied overhead, then the variance is called **underapplied overhead**. If actual overhead is less than applied overhead, then the variance is called **overapplied overhead**. If overhead has been underapplied, then product cost has been understated. In this case, the cost appears lower than it really is. Conversely, if overhead has been overapplied, then product cost has been overstated. In this case, the cost appears higher than it really is. Exhibit 16-2 illustrates the concepts of over- and underapplied overhead.

Because it is impossible to perfectly estimate future overhead costs and production activity, overhead variances are virtually inevitable. However, at year-end, costs reported on the financial statements must be actual amounts. Thus, something must be done with the overhead variance. Usually, the entire overhead variance is assigned to Cost of Goods Sold. This practice is justified on the basis of materiality, the same principle used to justify expensing the entire cost of a stapler in the period acquired rather than depreciating its cost over the life of the stapler. Since the overhead variance is usually relatively small, and all production costs should appear in cost of goods sold eventually, the method of disposition is not a critical matter. Thus,

- Underapplied overhead is added to Cost of Goods Sold.
- Overapplied overhead is subtracted from Cost of Goods Sold.

> Adjusted cost of goods sold = Unadjusted cost of goods sold ± Overhead variance

Suppose Proto Company has an ending balance in its cost of goods sold account equal to $607,000. The underapplied overhead variance of $10,000 would be added to produce a new adjusted balance of $617,000. (Since applied overhead was $390,000, and actual overhead was $400,000, production costs were *understated* by $10,000. Cost

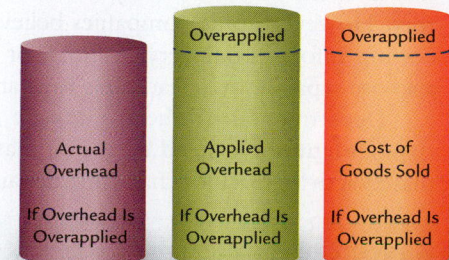

Exhibit 16-2

Actual and Applied Overhead

of Goods Sold must be increased to correct the problem.) If the variance had been over-applied, it would have been subtracted from Cost of Goods Sold to produce a new balance of $597,000. **CORNERSTONE 16-2** shows how to reconcile actual overhead with applied overhead for Argus Company.

CORNERSTONE 16-2   Reconciling Actual Overhead with Applied Overhead

Information:
Recall that Argus Company's predetermined overhead rate was 0.50 or 50 percent of direct labor cost. By the end of the year, actual data are:

Overhead	$375,400
Direct labor cost	750,000

Cost of Goods Sold (before adjusting for any overhead variance) is $632,000.

Required:
1. Calculate the overhead variance for the year.
2. Dispose of the overhead variance by adjusting Cost of Goods Sold.

Solution:
1. Overhead applied for the year = 0.50 × $750,000 = $375,000

Actual overhead	$375,400
Applied overhead	375,000
Overhead variance—underapplied	$ 400

2.

Unadjusted cost of goods sold	$632,000
Add: Overhead variance—underapplied	400
Adjusted cost of goods sold	$632,400

If the overhead variance is material, or large, another approach would be taken. That approach, allocating the variance among the ending balances of Work in Process, Finished Goods, and Cost of Goods Sold, is discussed in more detail in later accounting courses.

Departmental Overhead Rates

The description of overhead application so far has emphasized the plantwide overhead rate. A **plantwide overhead rate** is a single overhead rate calculated by using all estimated overhead for a factory divided by the estimated activity level across the entire factory. However, some companies believe that multiple overhead rates give more accurate costing information. Service firms, or service departments of manufacturing firms, can also use separate overhead rates to charge out their services.

Departmental overhead rates are a widely used type of multiple overhead rate. A **departmental overhead rate** is estimated overhead for a department divided by the estimated activity level for that same department:

$$\text{Departmental overhead rate} = \frac{\text{Estimated department overhead}}{\text{Estimated departmental activity level}}$$

The steps involved in calculating and applying overhead are the same as those involved for one plantwide overhead rate. The company has as many overhead rates as it has departments. **CORNERSTONE 16-3** shows how to calculate and apply departmental overhead rates.

CORNERSTONE 16-3

Calculating Predetermined Departmental Overhead Rates and Applying Overhead to Production

Information:

At the beginning of the year, Sorrel Company estimated the following:

	Machining Department	Assembly Department	Total
Overhead	$240,000	$360,000	$600,000
Direct labor hours	135,000	240,000	375,000
Machine hours	200,000	—	200,000

Sorrel uses departmental overhead rates. In the machining department, overhead is applied on the basis of machine hours. In the assembly department, overhead is applied on the basis of direct labor hours. Actual data for the month of June are as follows:

	Machining Department	Assembly Department	Total
Overhead	$22,500	$30,750	$53,250
Direct labor hours	11,000	20,000	31,000
Machine hours	17,000	—	17,000

Required:

1. Calculate the predetermined overhead rates for the machining and assembly departments.
2. Calculate the overhead applied to production in each department for the month of June.
3. By how much has each department's overhead been overapplied? Underapplied?

Solution:

1. Machining department overhead rate $= \dfrac{\$240,000}{200,000 \text{ mhrs}}$

   $= \$1.20$ per machine hour

   Assembly department overhead rate $= \dfrac{\$360,000}{240,000 \text{ DLH}}$

   $= \$1.50$ per direct labor hour

2. Overhead applied to machining in June $= \$1.20 \times 17,000 = \$20,400$

   Overhead applied to assembly in June $= \$1.50 \times 20,000 = \$30,000$

	Machining Department	Assembly Department
Actual overhead	$22,500	$30,750
Applied overhead	20,400	30,000
Underapplied overhead	$ 2,100	$ 750

It is important to realize that departmental overhead rates simply carve total overhead into two or more parts. The departments can be added back to get plantwide overhead, as illustrated in **CORNERSTONE 16-4** (p. 818).

CORNERSTONE 16-4

Converting Departmental Data to Plantwide Data to Calculate the Overhead Rate and Apply Overhead to Production

Information:

At the beginning of the year, Sorrel Company estimated the following:

	Machining Department	Assembly Department	Total
Overhead	$240,000	$360,000	$600,000
Direct labor hours	135,000	240,000	375,000
Machine hours	200,000	—	200,000

Sorrel has decided to use a plantwide overhead rate based on direct labor hours. Actual data for the month of June are as follows:

	Machining Department	Assembly Department	Total
Overhead	$22,500	$30,750	$53,250
Direct labor hours	11,000	20,000	31,000
Machine hours	17,000	—	17,000

Required:

1. Calculate the predetermined plantwide overhead rate.
2. Calculate the overhead applied to production for the month of June.
3. Calculate the overhead variance for the month of June.

Solution:

1. Predetermined plantwide overhead rate $= \dfrac{\$600,000}{375,000 \text{ DLH}}$

   $= \$1.60$ per direct labor hour

2. Overhead applied in June $= \$1.60 \times 31,000 = \$49,600$

3. Overhead variance $=$ Actual overhead $-$ Applied overhead

   $= \$53,250 - \$49,600$

   $= \$3,650$ underapplied

Considerable emphasis has been placed on describing how overhead costs are treated because this is the key to normal costing. Now, it is time to see how normal costing is used to develop unit costs in the job-order costing system.

Unit Costs in the Job-Order System

In a job-order environment, predetermined overhead rates are always used because the completion of a job rarely coincides with the completion of a fiscal year. Therefore, in the remainder of this chapter, normal costing is used.

The unit cost of a job is the total cost of the job (materials used on the job, labor worked on the job, and applied overhead) divided by the number of units in the job:

$$\text{Unit product cost} = \frac{\text{Total product cost}}{\text{Number of units}}$$

Although the concept is simple, the practical reality of the computation can be somewhat more complex because of the recordkeeping involved.

For example, suppose that Stan Johnson forms a new company, Johnson Leathergoods, which produces custom leather products. Stan believes that there is a market for one-of-a-kind leather purses, briefcases, and backpacks. In January, its first month of operation, he obtains two orders. The first order is for 20 leather backpacks for a local sporting goods store. The second order is for 10 distinctively tooled briefcases for the coaches of a local college. The price of each order is cost plus 50 percent of cost. The first order, the backpacks, requires direct materials (leather, thread, buckles), direct labor (cutting, sewing, assembling), and overhead. Assume that overhead is applied using direct labor hours. Suppose that the materials cost $1,000 and the direct labor costs $1,080 (60 hours at $18 per hour). If the predetermined overhead rate is $4 per direct labor hour, then the overhead applied to this job is $240 (60 hours at $4 per hour). The total cost of the backpacks is $2,320, and the unit cost is $116, computed as follows:

Direct materials	$1,000
Direct labor	1,080
Overhead	240
Total cost	$2,320
÷ Number of units	÷ 20
Unit cost	$ 116

Since cost is so closely linked to price in this case, it is easy to see that Stan will charge the sporting goods store $3,480 (cost of $2,320 plus 50 percent of $2,320), or $174 per backpack.

KEEPING TRACK OF JOB COSTS WITH SOURCE DOCUMENTS

OBJECTIVE 3
Identify and set up the source documents used in job-order costing.

Accounting for job-order production begins by preparing the source documents that are used to keep track of the costs of jobs. In a job-order firm, where price is so often based on cost, it is critically important to keep careful track of the costs of a job.

ETHICAL DECISIONS   Ethical issues arise when a firm adds costs from one job to the job-order sheet of another job. The first job is undercosted and underpriced, while the second job is overcosted and overpriced. Customers rely on the professionalism and honesty of the job-order firm in recordkeeping. ●

Job-Order Cost Sheet

How does Stan know that actual materials will cost $1,000 or that actual direct labor for this particular job will come to $1,080? In order to determine those figures, Stan will need to keep track of costs. One way to do so is to prepare a job-order cost sheet every time a new job is started. The earlier computation for Stan's backpack job, which lists the total cost of materials, labor, and overhead for a single job, is the simplest example of a job-order cost sheet. The **job-order cost sheet** is prepared for every job; it is subsidiary to the work-in-process account and is the primary document for accumulating all costs related to a particular job. Exhibit 16-3 illustrates a simple job-order cost sheet.

Job-Order Cost Sheet

Exhibit 16-3

Johnson Leathergoods
Job-Order Cost Sheet

Job Name: Backpacks   Date Started: Jan. 3, 20XX   Date Completed: Jan. 29, 20XX

Direct materials	$1,000
Direct labor	1,080
Applied overhead	240
Total cost	$2,320
÷ Number of units	÷ 20
Unit cost	$ 116

Concept Q&A

Job-order cost sheets are subsidiary to the work-in-process account. Can you think of other accounts that have subsidiary accounts? (*Hint:* Consider Accounts Receivable or Accounts Payable. What might their respective subsidiary accounts be?)

Answer:

Accounts Receivable is a control account; its subsidiary accounts are named (or numbered) by customers having an account with the company. Similarly, Accounts Payable has subsidiary accounts for each person/company to whom money is owed.

The job-order cost sheet contains all information pertinent to a job. For a simple job, the job-order cost sheet is quite brief, containing only the job description (backpacks) and cost of materials, labor, and overhead added during the month.

Johnson Leathergoods had only two jobs in January. These could be easily identified by calling them "Backpacks" and "Briefcases." Some companies may find that the customer's name is sufficient to identify a job. For example, a construction company may identify its custom houses as the "Kumar Residence" or the "Malkovich House."

As more and more jobs are produced, a company will usually find it more convenient to number them. For example, it may number them as Job 13, Job 5776, or Job ALM67. Perhaps the job number starts with the year so that the first job of 2012 is 2012-001, the second is 2012-002, and so on. The key point is that each job is unique and must have a uniquely identifiable name. This name, or job-order number, heads the job-order cost sheet.

Work in process consists of all incomplete work. In a job-order system, this will be all of the unfinished jobs. The balance in Work in Process at the end of the month will be the total of all the job-order cost sheets for the incomplete jobs.

A job-order costing system must have the ability to identify the quantity of direct materials, direct labor, and overhead consumed by each job. That is, documentation and procedures are needed to associate the manufacturing inputs used by a job with the job itself. This need is satisfied through the use of materials requisitions for direct materials, time tickets for direct labor, and source documents for other activity drivers that might be used in applying overhead.

Materials Requisitions

The cost of direct materials is assigned to a job by the use of a source document known as a **materials requisition form**, which is illustrated in Exhibit 16-4. Notice that the form asks for the type, quantity, and unit price of the direct materials issued and, most importantly, the number of the job. Using this form, the cost accounting department can enter the cost of direct materials onto the correct job-order cost sheet.

If the accounting system is automated, this posting may entail directly entering the data at a computer terminal, using the materials requisition forms as source documents. A program enters the cost of direct materials into the record for each job. In addition to providing essential information for assigning direct materials costs to jobs, the materials

Exhibit 16-4

Materials Requisition Form

Materials Requisition Number: 012

Date: January 11, 20XX
Department: Assembly
Job: Briefcases

Description	Quantity	Cost/Unit	Total Cost
Buckles	10	$3	$30

Authorized Signature *Jim Lawson*

Time Ticket

Exhibit 16–5

Job Time Ticket #: 008

Employee Name: Ed Wilson
Date: January 12, 20XX

Start Time	Stop Time	Total Time	Hourly Rate	Amount	Job Number
8:00	10:00	2	$18	$36	Backpacks
10:00	11:00	1	18	18	Briefcases
11:00	12:00	1	18	18	Backpacks
1:00	5:00	4	18	72	Backpacks

Approved by: ___*Jim Lawson*___
(Department Supervisor)

requisition form may also include other data items, such as a requisition number, a date, and a signature. These items are useful for maintaining proper control over a firm's inventory of direct materials. The signature, for example, transfers responsibility for the materials from the storage area to the person receiving the materials, usually a production supervisor.

No attempt is made to trace the cost of other materials, such as supplies, lubricants, and the like, to a particular job. These indirect materials are assigned to jobs through the predetermined overhead rate.

Time Tickets

Direct labor must be associated with each particular job. The means by which direct labor costs are assigned to individual jobs is the source document known as a **time ticket** (Exhibit 16-5). Each day, the employee fills out a time ticket that identifies his or her name, wage rate, and the hours worked on each job. These time tickets are collected and transferred to the cost accounting department where the information is used to post the cost of direct labor to individual jobs. Again, in an automated system, posting involves entering the data into the computer.

Time tickets are used only for direct laborers. Since indirect labor is common to all jobs, these costs belong to overhead and are allocated using one or more predetermined overhead rates.

All completed job-order cost sheets of a firm can serve as a subsidiary ledger for the finished goods inventory. Then, the work-in-process account consists of all of the job-order cost sheets for the unfinished jobs. The finished goods inventory account consists of all the job-order cost sheets for jobs that are complete but not yet sold. As finished goods are sold and shipped, the cost records will be pulled (or deleted) from the finished goods inventory file. These records then form the basis for calculating a period's cost of goods sold. We will examine the flow of costs through these accounts next.

 **DECIDE**   **Creating Source Documents for Other Activities**

You are the cost accounting manager for a company that provides photography services for special events, such as weddings, bar mitzvahs, anniversary parties, and corporate functions. The cost of the services varies from job to job. The time of the photographers assigned to the job is already kept track of using labor time tickets. However, your company now wants to reimburse the photographers for mileage and may want to include an additional charge to clients for mileage.

(Continued)

What type of source document could serve to accumulate miles driven?

In this case, your company needs to know not only the number of miles each photographer drives, but also to which job the mileage pertains. A relatively simple mileage log, listing the date, starting mileage, ending mileage, and purpose of the trip should suffice. This will allow you to compute the miles driven (ending mileage minus beginning mileage) and assign it to the specific photographic job. In addition, total miles for each photographer can be computed on a monthly basis and multiplied by your company's mileage reimbursement rate for purposes of reimbursing each photographer for automotive operating costs.

Some companies might have other specific needs. For example, perhaps the company has a fleet of different vehicles and wants to compute different rates depending on the vehicle. Using a van might require a higher rate than using a small automobile. In this case, an additional column to record the type of vehicle or vehicle's license plate would be necessary.

Still other companies may use an overhead application base other than direct labor hours. Perhaps machine hours may be used to apply overhead. Then, a new document must be developed. A source document that will track the machine hours used by each job can be modeled on job time tickets.

As a result, different firms may have different source documents to support their specialized needs for accounting information.

OBJECTIVE
Describe the cost flows associated with job-order costing.

THE FLOW OF COSTS THROUGH THE ACCOUNTS

Cost flow describes the way costs are accounted for from the point at which they are incurred to the point at which they are recognized as an expense on the income statement. The principal interest in a job-order costing system is the flow of manufacturing costs. Accordingly, we begin with a description of exactly how the three manufacturing cost elements—direct materials, direct labor, and overhead—flow through Work in Process, into Finished Foods, and, finally, into Cost of Goods Sold. Exhibit 16-6 illustrates the flow of costs through the accounts of a job-order costing firm.

The simplified job-shop environment provided by Johnson Leathergoods continues to serve as an example. To start the business, Stan leased a small building and bought the necessary production equipment. Recall that he obtained two orders for January: one for 20 backpacks for a local sporting goods store and a second for 10 briefcases for the coaches of a local college. Both orders will be sold for manufacturing costs plus 50 percent. Stan expects to average two orders per month for the first year of operation.

Stan created two job-order cost sheets, the first of which is for the backpacks; the second is for the briefcases.

Accounting for Materials

Since the company is just starting business, it has no beginning inventories. To produce the backpacks and briefcases in January and to have a supply of materials on hand at the

Exhibit 16-6

Flow of Costs through the Accounts of a Job-Order Costing Firm

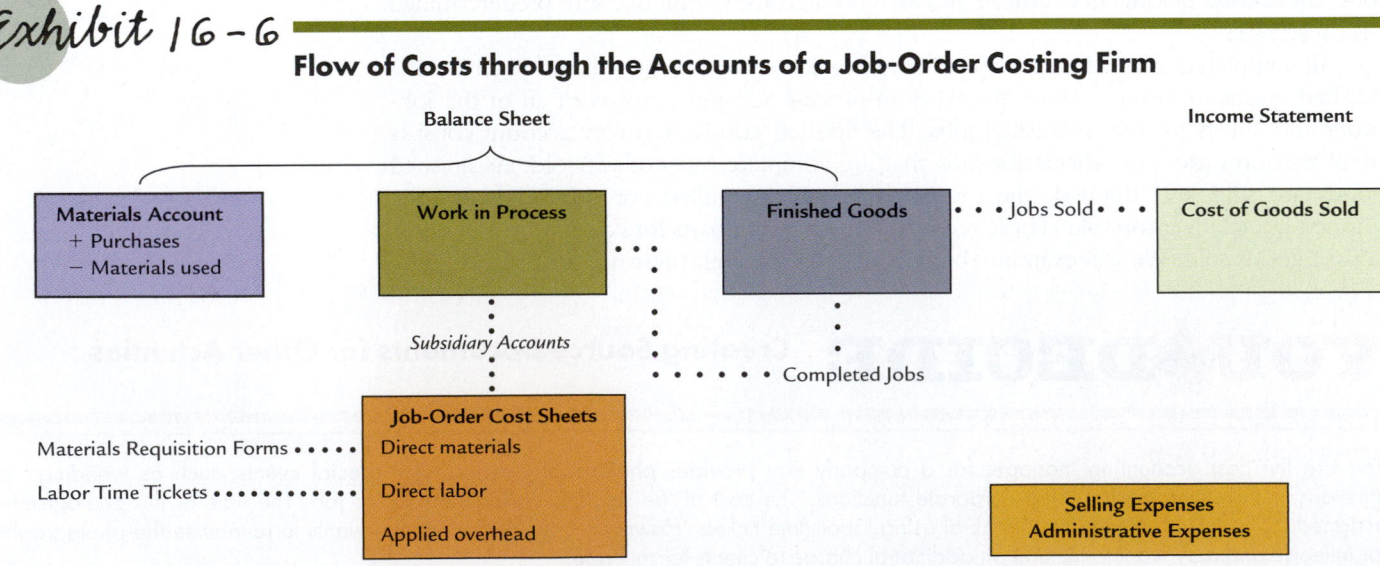

beginning of February, Stan purchases, on account, $2,500 of raw materials (leather, webbing for backpack straps, heavy-duty thread, buckles). Physically, the materials are put in a materials storeroom. In the accounting records, the raw materials and the accounts payable accounts are each increased by $2,500. Raw Materials is an inventory account (it appears on the balance sheet under current assets). It also is the controlling account for all raw materials. Any purchase increases the raw materials account.

When the production supervisor needs materials for a job, materials are removed from the storeroom. The cost of the materials is removed from the raw materials account and added to the work-in-process account. Of course, in a job-order environment, the materials moved from the storeroom to work stations on the factory floor must be "tagged" with the appropriate job name. Suppose that Stan needs $1,000 of materials for the backpacks and $500 for the briefcases. Then the job-order cost sheet for the backpacks would show $1,000 for direct materials, and the job-order cost sheet for the briefcases would show $500 for direct materials. Exhibit 16-7 summarizes the raw materials cost flow into these two jobs.

Summary of Materials Cost Flows

Exhibit 16-7

	A	B	C	D	E	F	G	H
1	Raw Materials Account							
2	Beginning balance		$ 0					
3	Add: Purchases		2,500					
4	Less: Direct materials charged to jobs		1,500					
5	Ending balance		$1,000					
6								
7	Work-in-Process Account							
8	Job: Backpacks				Job: Briefcases			
9	Direct materials		$1,000		Direct materials		$500	
10	Direct labor				Direct labor			
11	Applied overhead				Applied overhead			
12	Total cost				Total cost			
13	Number of units		÷ 20		Number of units		÷ 10	
14	Unit cost				Unit cost			
15								

The raw materials account increased by $2,500 due to purchases and decreased by $1,500 as materials were withdrawn for use in production. So, the balance in the raw materials account after these two transactions would be:

Raw materials beginning balance + Purchases − Materials used = Raw materials balance

$$\$0 + \$2{,}500 - \$1{,}500 = \$1{,}000$$

Accounting for Direct Labor Cost

Since two jobs were in process during January, Stan must determine not only the total number of direct labor hours worked but also the time worked on each job. The back-packs required 60 hours at an average wage rate of $18 per hour, for a total direct labor cost of $1,080. For the briefcases, the total was $450, based on 25 hours at an average hourly wage of $18. These amounts are posted to each job's cost sheet. The summary of the labor cost flows is given in Exhibit 16-8 (p. 824). Notice that the direct labor costs assigned to the two jobs exactly equal the total labor costs assigned to Work in Process. Remember that the labor cost flows reflect only direct labor cost. Indirect labor is assigned as part of overhead.

More accounts are involved in this transaction than meet the eye in Exhibit 16-8. Accounting for labor cost is a complex process because the company must keep track of FICA, Medicare, federal and state unemployment taxes, vacation time, and so on. We will concentrate on the concept that direct labor adds to the cost of the product or service and not on the details of the various labor-related accounts.

Exhibit 16-8

Summary of Direct Labor Cost Flows

	A	B	C	D	E	F	G	H
1	**Wages Payable Account**							
2	Direct labor hours for backpacks		60					
3	Direct labor hours for briefcases		25					
4	Total direct labor hours		85					
5	Wage rate		× $18					
6	Total direct labor		$1,530					
7								
8				**Work-in-Process Account**				
9	**Job: Backpacks**				**Job: Briefcases**			
10	Direct materials		$1,000		Direct materials		$500	
11	Direct labor		1,080		Direct labor		450	
12	Applied overhead				Applied overhead			
13	Total cost				Total cost			
14	Number of units		÷ 20		Number of units		÷ 10	
15	Unit cost				Unit cost			
16								

Accounting for Overhead

The use of normal costing means that overhead is applied to each job by using a predetermined rate. Actual overhead costs incurred must be accounted for as well, but on an overall (not a job-specific) basis.

Overhead costs can be assigned using a single plantwide overhead rate or departmental rates. Typically, direct labor hours is the measure used to calculate a plantwide overhead rate, and departmental rates are based on drivers such as direct labor hours, machine hours, or direct materials dollars. The use of a plantwide rate has the virtue of being simple and reduces data collection requirements. To illustrate these two features, assume that total estimated overhead cost for Johnson Leathergoods is $9,600, and the estimated direct labor hours total 2,400 hours. Accordingly, the predetermined overhead rate is:

$$\text{Overhead rate} = \frac{\$9,600}{2,400} = \$4 \text{ per direct labor hour}$$

For the backpacks, with a total of 60 hours worked, the amount of applied overhead cost posted to the job-order cost sheet is $240 ($4 × 60). For the briefcases, the applied overhead cost is $100 ($4 × 25). Note that assigning overhead to jobs only requires a rate and the direct labor hours used by the job. Since direct labor hours are already being collected to assign direct labor costs to jobs, overhead assignment will not demand any additional data collection.

Accounting for Actual Overhead Costs

Overhead has been applied to the jobs, but what about the actual overhead incurred? To illustrate how actual overhead costs are recorded, assume that Johnson Leathergoods incurred the following indirect costs for January:

Lease payment	$200
Utilities	50
Equipment depreciation	100
Indirect labor	65
Total overhead costs	$415

It is important to understand that the actual overhead costs never enter the work-in-process account. The usual procedure is to record actual overhead to the overhead control account. Then, at the end of a period (typically a year), actual overhead is reconciled with applied overhead, and, if the overhead variance is immaterial, it is closed to Cost of Goods Sold.

For Johnson Leathergoods at the end of January, actual overhead incurred is $415, while applied overhead is $340. Therefore, the overhead variance of $75 ($415 – $340) means that overhead is underapplied for the month of January.

The flow of overhead costs is summarized in Exhibit 16-9. Notice that the total overhead applied from all jobs is entered in the work-in-process account.

Let's take a moment to recap. The cost of a job includes direct materials, direct labor, and applied overhead. These costs are entered on the job-order cost sheet. Work in Process, at any point in time, is the total of the costs on all open job-order cost sheets. When the job is complete, it must leave Work in Process and be entered into Finished Goods or Cost of Goods Sold.

Exhibit 16-9

Summary of Overhead Cost Flows

	A	B	C	D	E	F	G	H
1	**Actual Overhead Account**				**Applied Overhead Account**			
2	Lease		$200		Direct labor hours		85	
3	Utilities		50		Overhead rate		× $4	
4	Equipment depreciation		100		Total applied overhead		340	
5	Indirect labor		65					
6	Total actual overhead		$415					
7								
8	Work-in-Process Account							
9	Job: Backpacks				Job: Briefcases			
10	Direct materials		$1,000		Direct materials		$500	
11	Direct labor		1,080		Direct labor		450	
12	Applied overhead		240		Applied overhead		100	
13	Total cost				Total cost			
14	Number of units		÷ 20		Number of units		÷ 10	
15	Unit cost				Unit cost			
16								

Accounting for Finished Goods

When a job is complete, direct materials, direct labor, and applied overhead amounts are totaled to yield the manufacturing cost of the job. Simultaneously, the costs of the completed job are transferred from the work-in-process account to the finished goods account.

For example, assume that the backpacks were finished in January with the completed cost sheet shown in Exhibit 16-9. Since the backpacks are finished, the total manufacturing costs of $2,320 must be transferred from the work-in-process account to the finished goods account. A summary of the cost flows occurring when a job is finished is shown in Exhibit 16-10 (p. 826).

The completion of a job is an important step in the flow of manufacturing costs. The cost of the finished job is removed from Work in Process, added to Finished Goods, and, eventually, added to cost of goods sold on the income statement. To ensure accuracy in computing these costs, a cost of goods manufactured statement is prepared. Exhibit 16-11 (p. 826) shows the schedule of cost of goods manufactured for Johnson Leathergoods for January. Notice that applied overhead is used to obtain the cost of goods manufactured. Both work-in-process and finished goods inventories are carried at normal cost rather than actual cost.

The balance of ending work in process is $1,050. Where did this figure come from? Of the two jobs, the backpacks were finished and transferred to finished goods. The

Exhibit 16-10

Summary of Cost Flows from Work in Process to Finished Goods

	A	B	C	D	E	F	G	H
1	**Work-in-Process Account BEFORE Transfer of Backpacks to Finished Goods**							
2	Job: Backpacks				Job: Briefcases			
3	Direct materials		$1,000		Direct materials		$500	
4	Direct labor		1,080		Direct labor		450	
5	Applied overhead		240		Applied overhead		100	
6	Total cost		$2,320		Total cost		$1,050	
7	Number of units		÷ 20		Number of units			
8	Unit cost*		$ 116		Unit cost*			
9								
10	**Work-in-Process Account AFTER Transfer of Backpacks to Finished Goods**							
11	Job: Briefcases							
12	Direct materials		$ 500					
13	Direct labor		450					
14	Applied overhead		100					
15	Total cost		$1,050					
16	Number of units							
17	Unit cost							
18								
19	Finished Goods Account							
20	Beginning balance		$ 0					
21	Add: Completed backpacks		2,320					
22	Less: Jobs sold		0					
23	Ending balance		$2,320					
24								

*Unit cost information is included for backpacks because they are finished. The briefcases are still in process, so no unit cost is calculated.

Exhibit 16-11

Schedule of Cost of Goods Manufactured

Johnson Leathergoods Schedule of Cost of Goods Manufactured For the Month of January		
Direct materials:		
Beginning raw materials inventory	$ 0	
Purchases of raw materials	2,500	
Total raw materials available	$2,500	
Ending raw materials	1,000	
Total raw materials used		$1,500
Direct labor		1,530
Overhead:		
Lease	$ 200	
Utilities	50	
Depreciation	100	
Indirect labor	65	
	$ 415	
Less: Underapplied overhead	75	
Overhead applied		340
Current manufacturing costs		$3,370
Add: Beginning work in process		0
Total manufacturing costs		$3,370
Less: Ending work in process		1,050
Cost of goods manufactured		$2,320

Statement of Cost of Goods Sold

Exhibit 16-12

Statement of Cost of Goods Sold	
Beginning finished goods inventory	$ 0
Cost of goods manufactured	2,320
Goods available for sale	$2,320
Less: Ending finished goods inventory	0
Normal cost of goods sold	$2,320
Add: Underapplied overhead	75
Adjusted cost of goods sold	$2,395

briefcases are still in process, however, and the manufacturing costs assigned thus far are direct materials, $500; direct labor, $450; and overhead applied, $100. The total of these costs gives the cost of ending work in process. Check these figures against the job-order cost sheet for briefcases shown at the top right of Exhibit 16-10.

Accounting for Cost of Goods Sold

In a job-order firm, units can be produced for a particular customer, or they can be produced with the expectation of selling the units later. If a job is produced especially for a customer (as with the backpacks) and then shipped to the customer, then the cost of the finished job becomes the cost of goods sold. When the backpacks are finished, Cost of Goods Sold increases by $2,320, while Work in Process decreases by the same amount (the job is no longer incomplete, so its costs cannot stay in Work in Process). Then, the sale is recognized by increasing both Sales Revenue and Accounts Receivable by $3,480 (cost plus 50 percent of cost, or $2,320 + $1,160).

A schedule of cost of goods sold usually is prepared at the end of each reporting period (e.g., monthly and quarterly), as shown in Exhibit 16-12 for Johnson Leathergoods for January. Typically, the overhead variance is not material and, therefore, is closed to the cost of goods sold account. The cost of goods sold before an adjustment for an overhead variance is called **normal cost of goods sold**. After the adjustment for the period's overhead variance takes place, the result is called the **adjusted cost of goods sold**. This latter figure appears as an expense on the income statement.

Typically, the overhead variance is closed to the cost of goods sold account at the end of the year. Variances occur each month because of nonuniform production and nonuniform actual overhead costs. As the year unfolds, these monthly variances should about offset each other so that the year-end variance is small. However, to illustrate how the year-end overhead variance would be treated, we will close out the overhead variance for Johnson Leathergoods in January.

Notice that there are two cost of goods sold figures in Exhibit 16-12. The first is normal cost of goods sold and is equal to actual direct materials, actual direct labor, and applied overhead for the jobs that were sold. The second figure is adjusted cost of goods sold. The adjusted cost of goods sold is equal to normal cost of goods sold plus or minus the overhead variance. In this case, overhead has been underapplied (actual overhead of $415 is $75 higher than the applied overhead of $340), so this amount is added to normal cost of goods sold. If the overhead variance shows overapplied overhead, then that amount will be subtracted from normal cost of goods sold.

Suppose that the backpacks had not been ordered by a customer but had been produced with the expectation that they could be sold through a subsequent marketing effort. Then, all 20 units might not be sold at the same time. Assume that on January 31, there were 15 backpacks sold. In this case, the cost of goods sold figure is the unit cost times the number of units sold ($116 × 15, or $1,740). The unit cost figure is found on the cost sheet in Exhibit 16-10.

Sometimes it is simpler to use a briefer version of the job-order cost sheet in order to calculate ending Work in Process, Finished Goods, and Cost of Goods Sold. (This is particularly true when working homework and test questions.) **CORNERSTONE 16-5** shows how to set up such a version to calculate account balances (p. 828).

CORNERSTONE 16-5

Preparing Brief Job-Order Cost Sheets

Information:

At the beginning of June, Galway Company had two jobs in process, Job 78 and Job 79, with the following accumulated cost information:

	Job 78	Job 79
Direct materials	$1,000	$ 800
Direct labor	600	1,000
Applied overhead	750	1,250
Balance, June 1	$2,350	$3,050

During June, two more jobs (80 and 81) were started. The following direct materials and direct labor costs were added to the four jobs during the month of June:

	Job 78	Job 79	Job 80	Job 81
Direct materials	$500	$1,110	$ 900	$100
Direct labor	400	1,400	2,000	320

At the end of June, Jobs 78, 79, and 80 were completed. Only Job 79 was sold. On June 1, the balance in Finished Goods was zero.

Required:

1. Calculate the overhead rate based on direct labor cost.
2. Prepare a brief job-order cost sheet for the four jobs. Show the balance as of June 1 as well as direct materials and direct labor added in June. Apply overhead to the four jobs for the month of June, and show the ending balances.
3. Calculate the ending balances of Work in Process and Finished Goods as of June 30.
4. Calculate Cost of Goods Sold for June.

Solution:

1. While the predetermined overhead rate is calculated using estimated overhead and estimated direct labor cost, those figures were not given. However, we can work backward from the applied overhead and direct labor cost given in the June 1 balance for Job 78.

$$\text{Applied overhead} = \text{Predetermined overhead rate} \times \text{Actual activity level for Job 78,}$$
$$\$750 = \text{Predetermined overhead rate} \times \$600$$
$$\text{Predetermined overhead rate} = \frac{\$750}{\$600}$$
$$= 1.25, \text{ or } 125 \text{ percent of direct labor cost}$$

(The predetermined overhead rate using Job 79 is identical.)

2.

	Job 78	Job 79	Job 80	Job 81
Beginning balance, June 1	$2,350	$3,050	$ 0	$ 0
Direct materials	500	1,110	900	100
Direct labor	400	1,400	2,000	320
Applied overhead	500*	1,750*	2,500*	400*
Total, June 30	$3,750	$7,310	$5,400	$820

*$500 = $400 × 1.25; $1,750 = $1,400 × 1.25; $2,500 = $2,000 × 1.25; $400 = $320 × 1.25

(Continued)

CORNERSTONE
16-5
(continued)

3. By the end of June, Jobs 78, 79, and 80 have been transferred out of Work in Process. Thus, the ending balance in Work in Process consists only of Job 81.

Work in process, June 30	$820

While three jobs (78, 79, and 80) were transferred out of Work in Process and into Finished Goods during June, only two jobs remain (Jobs 78 and 80).

Finished goods, June 1	$ 0
Job 78	3,750
Job 80	5,400
Finished goods, June 30	$9,150

4. One job, Job 79, was sold during June.

Cost of Goods Sold	$7,310

Accounting for Nonmanufacturing Costs

Manufacturing costs are not the only costs experienced by a firm. Nonmanufacturing, or period, costs are also incurred. These include selling and general administrative costs, which are never assigned to the product; they are not part of the manufacturing cost flows.

To illustrate how these costs are accounted for, assume Johnson Leathergoods had the following additional transactions in January:

Advertising circulars	$ 75
Sales commission	125
Office salaries	500
Depreciation, office equipment	50

The first two transactions are selling expenses and the last two are administrative expenses. Therefore, the selling expense account would increase by $200 ($75 + $125), and the administrative expense account would increase by $550 ($500 + $50).

Controlling accounts accumulate all of the selling and administrative expenses for a period. At the end of the period, all of these costs flow to the period's income statement. An income statement for Johnson Leathergoods is shown in Exhibit 16-13.

Exhibit 16-13

Income Statement

Johnson Leathergoods Income Statement For the Month Ended January 31, 20XX		
Sales		$3,480
Less: Cost of goods sold		2,395
Gross margin		$1,085
Less selling and administrative expenses:		
Selling expenses	$200	
Administrative expenses	550	750
Net operating income		$ 335

With the preparation of the income statement, the flow of costs through the manufacturing, selling, and administrative expense accounts is complete. A more detailed look at the actual accounting for these cost flows is undertaken in Appendix 16A.

OBJECTIVE 5
Prepare the journal entries associated with job-order costing.

APPENDIX 16A: JOURNAL ENTRIES ASSOCIATED WITH JOB-ORDER COSTING

The transactions that flow through the accounts in job-order costing are entered into the accounting system by making journal entries and posting them to the accounts. Let's complete this process for the various transactions that occurred during the month of January for Johnson Leathergoods.

1. Purchased raw materials costing $2,500 on account.

Raw Materials	2,500	
Accounts Payable		2,500

This journal entry shows that the purchase of materials increases the raw materials account as well as the accounts payable account. In other words, the company has increased both assets (materials on hand) and liabilities (through Accounts Payable).

2. Requisitioned materials costing $1,500 for use in production.

Work in Process	1,500	
Raw Materials		1,500

This entry shows the transfer from the materials storeroom to the factory floor. That is, the materials are no longer awaiting requisition; they are being used. So, the work-in-process account goes up, but the raw materials account goes down.

3. Recognized direct labor costing $1,530 (that is, it was not paid in cash but was shown as a liability in the wages payable account).

Work in Process	1,530	
Wages Payable		1,530

This entry recognizes the cost of direct labor. The amount of direct labor wages is added to Work in Process and is added to the liability account, Wages Payable.

4. Applied overhead to production at the rate of $4 per direct labor hour. A total of 85 direct labor hours were worked.

Work in Process	340	
Overhead Control		340

This entry recognizes the application of overhead to the jobs. Since 85 hours of direct labor were worked, and the overhead rate is $4 per direct labor hour, then $340 has been applied to overhead. The application of overhead increases the work-in-process account and is credited to Overhead Control.

5. Incurred actual overhead costs of $415.

Overhead Control	415	
Lease Payable		200
Utilities Payable		50
Accumulated Depreciation		100
Wages Payable		65

This entry shows that the actual overhead incurred is debited to Overhead Control. The credit is to the various payable accounts.

6. Completed the backpack job and transferred it to Finished Goods.

Finished Goods	2,320	
Work in Process		2,320

This entry shows the transfer of the backpack job from Work in Process to Finished Goods. We find the appropriate cost by referring to the job-order cost sheet in Exhibit 16-10 (p. 826).

7. Sold the backpack job at cost plus 50 percent.

Cost of Goods Sold	2,320	
Finished Goods		2,320
Accounts Receivable	3,480	
Sales Revenue		3,480

First, we recognize the cost of the backpack job by debiting Cost of Goods Sold for the cost and crediting Finished Goods. This entry mirrors the physical movement of the backpacks out of the warehouse and to the customer. Second, the sales price is shown. It is very important to separate the cost of the job from the sale. This always requires two entries.

8. Closed underapplied overhead to Cost of Goods Sold.

Cost of Goods Sold	75	
Overhead Control		75

Finally, we check the overhead control account. It has a debit balance of $75, indicating that the overhead variance is $75 underapplied. To bring the balance to zero, then, Overhead Control must be credited $75, and Cost of Goods Sold must be debited $75.

Exhibit 16-14 summarizes theses journal entries and posts them to the appropriate accounts.

Exhibit 16-14

Posting of Journal Entries to the Accounts

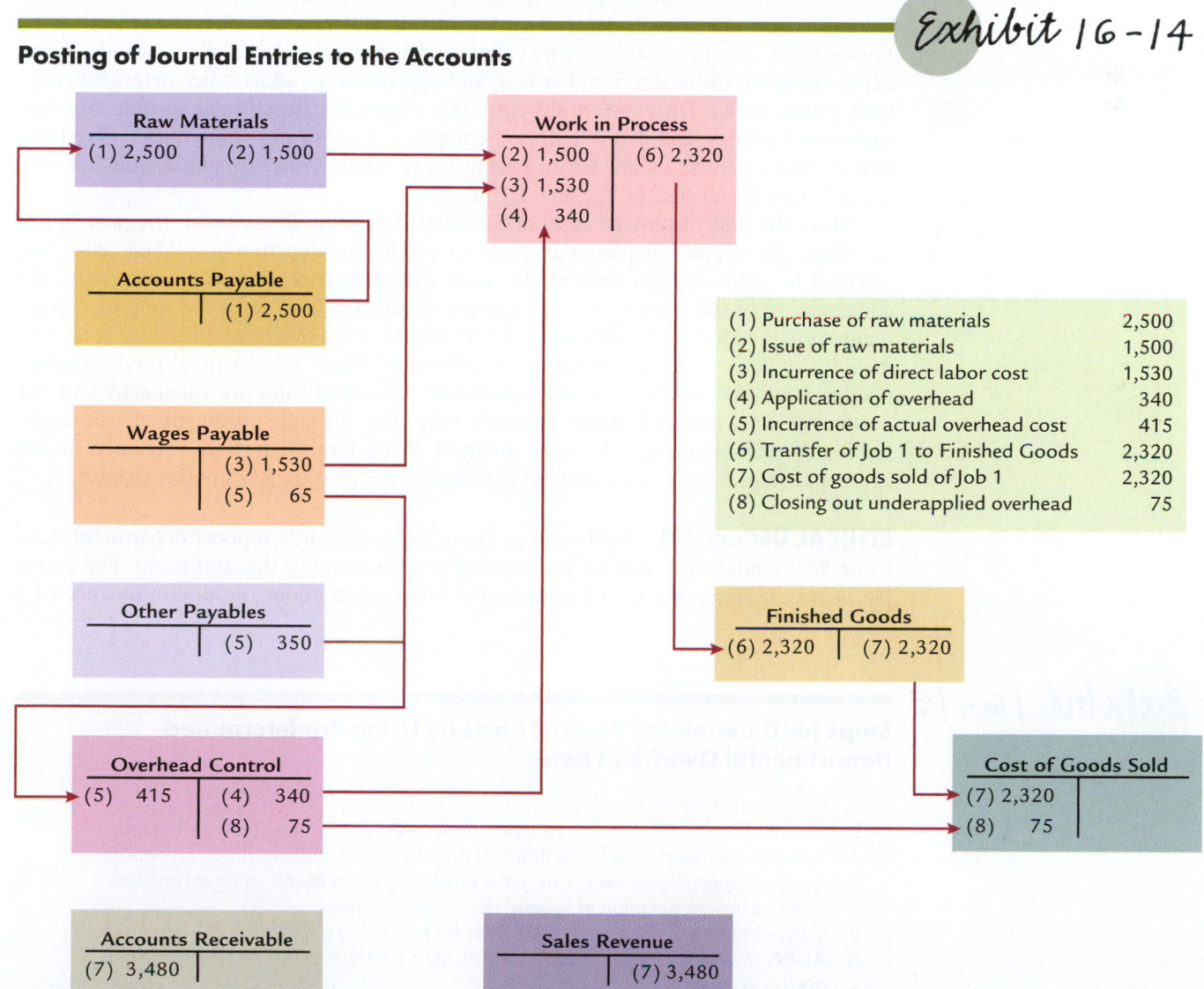

(1) Purchase of raw materials	2,500
(2) Issue of raw materials	1,500
(3) Incurrence of direct labor cost	1,530
(4) Application of overhead	340
(5) Incurrence of actual overhead cost	415
(6) Transfer of Job 1 to Finished Goods	2,320
(7) Cost of goods sold of Job 1	2,320
(8) Closing out underapplied overhead	75

APPENDIX 16B: SUPPORT DEPARTMENT COST ALLOCATION

The costs of resources shared by two or more services or products are referred to as **common costs**. For example, the cost of a maintenance department is shared by producing departments that use these services. How to assign these shared costs to individual producing departments is the focus of this appendix.

Types of Departments

Nearly every company or factory has producing departments and support departments.

- **Producing departments** are directly responsible for creating the products or services sold to customers. For example, a public accounting firm might have producing departments devoted to auditing, tax, and management advisory services. In a factory, producing departments are those that work directly on the products being manufactured, such as the grinding and assembly departments.
- **Support departments** provide essential services for producing departments, but they do not actually make the product or service being sold. Examples include the maintenance, grounds, engineering, housekeeping, personnel, and photocopying departments.

Once producing and support departments have been identified, overhead costs that belong exclusively to each department are identified—these are direct overhead costs. For example, direct costs of a factory cafeteria include food, salaries of cooks and servers, depreciation on dishwashers and stoves, and supplies (e.g., dishwasher detergent, napkins, plastic forks). Direct overhead costs of a producing department include supplies, supervisory salaries, and depreciation on equipment used in that department. Overhead that cannot easily be assigned to a producing or support department is assigned to a catchall department such as "general factory."

Once the direct overhead costs of each department are determined, the next step is to assign the support department costs to producing departments. These costs are assigned to producing departments by using **causal factors** (drivers) that measure the consumption of the services. Each producing department's share of the support department costs is added to the producing department's direct overhead cost. This total estimated overhead is then divided by a unit-level driver to obtain a predetermined overhead rate for each producing department. Overhead rates are calculated only for producing departments because products only pass through producing departments. Exhibit 16-15 summarizes the steps involved. Steps 1 through 4 are explained in this appendix; Steps 5 and 6 are explained in Cornerstone 16-3 (p. 817) of this chapter.

ETHICAL DECISIONS   Deliberations about discontinuing a support department need to be kept confidential. Ethical professional practice requires this and more. For example, it may be tempting to use confidential information about the discontinuance of a

Exhibit 16-15

Steps for Determining Product Costs by Using Predetermined Departmental Overhead Rates

1. Departmentalize the firm.
2. Classify each department as a support department or a producing department.
3. Trace all overhead costs in the firm to a support department or producing department.
4. Assign support department costs to the producing departments using drivers that measure the consumption of support department services.
5. Calculate predetermined overhead rates for producing departments.
6. Assign overhead costs to the units of individual products using the predetermined overhead rates.

support department to provide an unfair advantage to a friend or relative who may be the owner of an outside service firm that essentially would be replacing the support department. ●

Methods of Support Department Cost Allocation

In order to calculate departmental overhead rates (as opposed to plantwide overhead rates), it is necessary to allocate support department costs to the producing departments. The three methods of assigning costs of multiple support departments to producing departments are the *direct method*, the *sequential method*, and the *reciprocal method*. In determining which support department cost allocation method to use, companies must determine the extent of support department interaction and weigh the individual costs and benefits of each method. In the next three sections, the direct, sequential, and reciprocal methods are discussed.

Direct Method   The direct method is the simplest and most straightforward way to

assign support department costs. The **direct method** ignores support department interactions and assigns support department costs *only* to the producing departments. No cost from one support department is given to another support department. Thus, no support department interaction is recognized. Exhibit 16-16 illustrates the way support department costs are allocated to producing departments using the direct method.

Exhibit 16-16

Illustration of the Direct Method

Suppose there are two support departments, Power and Maintenance, and two producing departments, Grinding and Assembly, each with a "bucket" of directly traceable overhead cost.

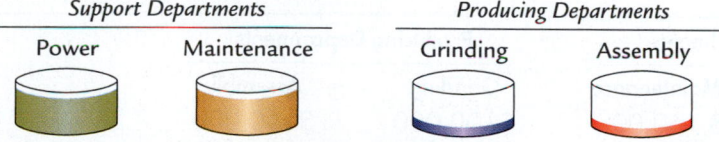

Objective: Distribute all maintenance and power costs to Grinding and Assembly using the direct method.

Direct method—Allocate maintenance and power costs only to Grinding and Assembly.

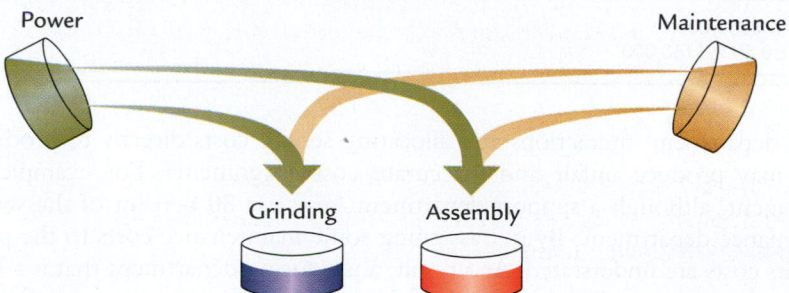

After allocation—Zero cost in Maintenance and Power; all overhead cost is in Grinding and Assembly.

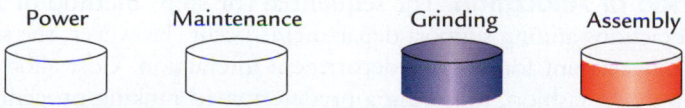

CORNERSTONE 16-6 shows how the direct method is used to assign the costs of two support departments to two producing departments.

CORNERSTONE 16-6   Assigning Support Department Costs by Using the Direct Method

Information:
Departmental data:

	Support Departments		Producing Departments	
	Power	**Maintenance**	**Grinding**	**Assembly**
Direct overhead costs*	$250,000	$160,000	$100,000	$ 60,000
Expected activity:				
Kilowatt-hours	—	200,000	600,000	200,000
Maintenance hours	1,000	—	4,500	4,500

*Overhead costs that are directly traceable to the department.

Required:
Using the direct method, assign the support department costs to the producing departments.

Solution:
Calculate usage or allocation ratios:

	Grinding	**Assembly**
Power: 600,000/(600,000 + 200,000)	0.75	—
200,000/(600,000 + 200,000)	—	0.25
Maintenance: 4,500/(4,500 + 4,500)	0.50	—
4,500/(4,500 + 4,500)	—	0.50

	Support Departments		Producing Departments	
	Power	**Maintenance**	**Grinding**	**Assembly**
Direct costs	$ 250,000	$ 160,000	$100,000	$ 60,000
Power[a]	(250,000)	—	187,500	62,500
Maintenance[b]	—	(160,000)	80,000	80,000
Total	$ 0	$ 0	$367,500	$202,500

[a]Using the allocation ratios for Power: 0.75 × $250,000; 0.25 × $250,000.
[b]Using the allocation ratios for Maintenance: 0.50 × $160,000; 0.50 × $160,000.

Ignoring department interactions and allocating service costs directly to producing departments may produce unfair and inaccurate cost assignments. For example, the power department, although a support department, may use 30 percent of the services of the maintenance department. By not assigning some maintenance costs to the power department, its costs are understated. As a result, a producing department that is a heavy user of power and an average or below-average user of maintenance may then receive, under the direct method, a cost allocation that is understated.

Sequential Method of Allocation The **sequential (or step) method** of allocation recognizes that interactions among support departments occur. However, the sequential method does not fully account for support department interaction. Cost allocations are performed in a step-down fashion, following a predetermined ranking procedure. Usually, the sequence is defined by ranking the support departments in order of the amount of service rendered, from the greatest to the least, where degree of service is measured by the direct costs of each support department.

Exhibit 16-17 provides a visual portrayal of the sequential method. First, the support departments are ranked, usually in accordance with direct costs; here, the power department is first, then the maintenance department. Next, power costs are allocated to the maintenance department and the two producing departments. Finally, the costs of the maintenance department are allocated only to producing departments.

The costs of the support department rendering the greatest service are assigned to all support departments below it in the sequence and to all producing departments. The costs of the support department next in sequence are similarly allocated, and so on. *In the sequential method, once a support department's costs are allocated, it never receives a subsequent allocation from another support department.* In other words, costs of a support department are never allocated to support departments above it in the sequence. *Note that the costs allocated from a support department are its direct costs plus any costs it receives in allocations from other support departments.*

Exhibit 16-17

Illustration of the Sequential Method

Suppose there are two support departments, Power and Maintenance, and two producing departments, Grinding and Assembly, each with a "bucket" of directly traceable overhead cost.

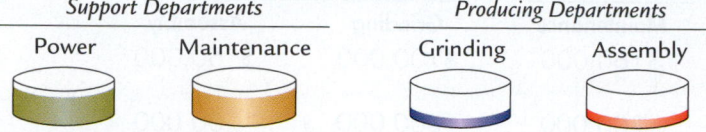

Objective: Distribute all maintenance and power costs to Grinding and Assembly using the sequential method.

Sequential—Step 1: Rank service departments—#1 Power, #2 Maintenance.
      Step 2: Distribute power to Maintenance, Grinding, and Assembly.

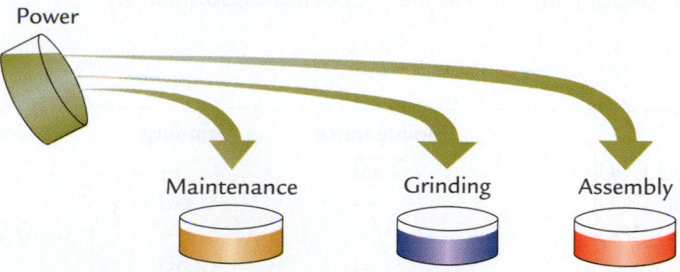

Then, distribute maintenance to Grinding and Assembly.

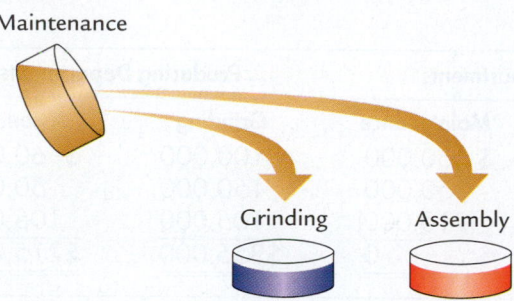

After allocation—Zero cost in Maintenance and Power; all overhead cost is in Grinding and Assembly.

Concept Q&A

Why is the sequential method considered to be more accurate than the direct method?

Answer:

The sequential method considers some of the interactions among service departments, whereas the direct method ignores these interactions.

CORNERSTONE 16-7 shows how to assign support department costs to producing departments by using the sequential method. The power department will be allocated first since its direct cost is higher, followed by the maintenance department. Note that the allocation ratios for the maintenance department ignore the usage by the power department because Power is above Maintenance in the allocation sequence. Unlike the direct method, the sequential method recognizes some interactions among the support departments.

 **CORNERSTONE 16-7** **Assigning Support Department Costs by Using the Sequential Method**

Information:
Departmental data:

	Support Departments		Producing Departments	
	Power	**Maintenance**	**Grinding**	**Assembly**
Direct costs*	$250,000	$160,000	$100,000	$ 60,000
Expected activity:				
Kilowatt-hours	—	200,000	600,000	200,000
Maintenance hours	1,000	—	4,500	4,500

*Overhead costs that are directly traceable to the department.

Required:
Using the sequential method, assign the support department costs to the producing departments.

Solution:
Calculate usage ratios:

	Maintenance	Grinding	Assembly
Power: 200,000/(200,000 + 600,000 + 200,000)	0.20	—	—
600,000/(200,000 + 600,000 + 200,000)	—	0.60	—
200,000/(200,000 + 600,000 + 200,000)	—	—	0.20
Maintenance: 4,500/(4,500 + 4,500)	—	0.50	—
4,500/(4,500 + 4,500)	—	—	0.50

	Support Departments		Producing Departments	
	Power	**Maintenance**	**Grinding**	**Assembly**
Direct costs	$ 250,000	$ 160,000	$100,000	$ 60,000
Power[a]	(250,000)	50,000	150,000	50,000
Maintenance[b]	—	(210,000)	105,000	105,000
	$ 0	$ 0	$355,000	$215,000

[a]Using the usage ratios for Power: 0.20 × $250,000; 0.60 × $250,000; 0.20 × $250,000.
[b]Using the usage ratios for Maintenance: 0.50 × $210,000; 0.50 × $210,000.

Reciprocal Method of Allocation The **reciprocal method** of allocation recognizes all interactions among support departments. Under the reciprocal method, one support department's use by another figures in determining the total cost of each support department, where the total cost reflects interactions among the support departments. Then, the new total of support department costs is allocated to the producing departments. This method fully accounts for support department interaction by using a system of simultaneous linear equations. The reciprocal method is not widely used due to its complexity. This method will not be illustrated. Rather, its complete description is left to a more advanced course.

Technology and Support Department Cost Allocation Another factor in allocating support department cost is the rapid change in technology. Many firms currently find that support department cost allocation is useful for them. However, the move toward activity-based costing and just-in-time manufacturing can virtually eliminate the need for support department cost allocation.

SUMMARY OF LEARNING OBJECTIVES

LO1.   Describe the differences between job-order costing and process costing, and identify the types of firms that would use each method.
- Job-order firms collect costs by job.
- Job-order firms produce heterogeneous products/services—each unit or batch has a different total cost.
- Job-order firms include construction, custom cabinetry, dentistry, medical services, and automotive repair.
- Process firms produce homogeneous products.
- In process firms, the cost of one batch or unit is the same as another batch or unit.
- Process firms include paint manufacturing, check clearing, and toy manufacturing.

LO2.   Compute the predetermined overhead rate, and use the rate to assign overhead to units or services produced.
- Predetermined overhead is total budgeted overhead divided by total budgeted activity level.
- Overhead is applied by multiplying the rate by the actual activity usage.
- Applied overhead is added to total actual direct materials and direct labor cost, which is divided by number of units to yield unit cost.

LO3.   Identify and set up the source documents used in job-order costing.
- Job-order cost sheets summarize all costs associated with a job.
- Materials requisition forms are used to request direct materials for a job.
- Time tickets show the number of labor hours worked on a job.

LO4.   Describe the cost flows associated with job-order costing.
- The job-order cost sheet is subsidiary to the work-in-process account.
- The balance in Work in Process consists of the balances of all incomplete jobs.
- The cost of a finished job is transferred out of Work in Process and into Finished Goods.
- The cost of jobs sold is transferred out of Finished Goods and into Cost of Goods Sold.

LO5.   (Appendix 16A) Prepare the journal entries associated with job-order costing.
- Direct materials and direct labor are charged to Work in Process.
- Applied overhead costs are charged to Work in Process. Actual overhead costs are charged to Overhead Control.
- When units are completed, their total cost is debited to Finished Goods and credited to Work in Process.
- When units are sold, their total cost is debited to Cost of Goods Sold and credited to Finished Goods.

LO6.   (Appendix 16B) Allocate support department costs to producing departments.
- Producing departments actually make the products or services. Support departments provide service to the producing departments.

- When departmental overhead rates are used, the costs of support departments must be allocated to the producing departments.
- Three methods of support department cost allocation are direct method, sequential method, and reciprocal method.

SUMMARY OF IMPORTANT EQUATIONS

1. $\text{Predetermined overhead rate} = \dfrac{\text{Estimated annual overhead}}{\text{Estimated annual activity level}}$

2. Applied overhead = Predetermined overhead rate × Actual activity level
3. Total product costs = Actual direct materials + Actual direct labor + Applied overhead
4. Overhead variance = Applied overhead − Actual overhead
5. Adjusted COGS = Unadjusted COGS ± Overhead variance
   (*Note:* Applied overhead > Actual overhead *means* Overapplied overhead; subtract from COGS
   Applied overhead < Actual overhead *means* Underapplied overhead; add to COGS)

6. $\text{Departmental overhead rate} = \dfrac{\text{Estimated department overhead}}{\text{Estimated departmental activity level}}$

7. $\text{Unit product cost} = \dfrac{\text{Total product cost}}{\text{Number of units}}$

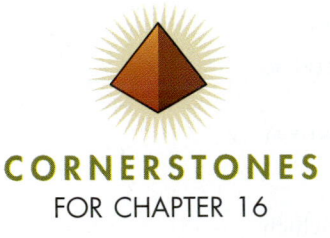

CORNERSTONES FOR CHAPTER 16

CORNERSTONE 16-1   Calculating the predetermined overhead rate and applying overhead to production (p. 814)

CORNERSTONE 16-2   Reconciling actual overhead with applied overhead (p. 816)

CORNERSTONE 16-3   Calculating predetermined departmental overhead rates and applying overhead to production (p. 817)

CORNERSTONE 16-4   Converting departmental data to plantwide data to calculate the overhead rate and apply overhead to production (p. 818)

CORNERSTONE 16-5   Preparing brief job-order cost sheets (p. 828)

CORNERSTONE 16-6   *(Appendix 16B)* Assigning support department costs by using the direct method (p. 834)

CORNERSTONE 16-7   *(Appendix 16B)* Assigning support department costs by using the sequential method (p. 836)

KEY TERMS

Actual cost system (p. 812)
Adjusted cost of goods sold (p. 827)
Applied overhead (p. 814)
Causal factors (p. 832) *(Appendix 16B)*
Common costs (p. 832) *(Appendix 16B)*
Departmental overhead rate (p. 816)
Direct method (p. 833) *(Appendix 16B)*
Job (p. 810)
Job-order cost sheet (p. 819)
Job-order costing system (p. 810)
Materials requisition form (p. 820)
Normal cost of goods sold (p. 827)

Normal cost system (p. 812)
Overapplied overhead (p. 815)
Overhead variance (p. 815)
Plantwide overhead rate (p. 816)
Predetermined overhead rate (p. 813)
Process-costing system (p. 811)
Producing departments (p. 832) *(Appendix 16B)*
Reciprocal method (p. 836) *(Appendix 16B)*
Sequential (or step) method (p. 834) *(Appendix 16B)*
Support departments (p. 832) *(Appendix 16B)*
Time ticket (p. 821)
Underapplied overhead (p. 815)

REVIEW PROBLEMS

I. Job Cost Using Plantwide and Departmental Overhead Rates

Lindberg Company uses a normal job-order costing system. There are two departments, Assembly and Finishing, through which most jobs pass. Selected budgeted and actual data for the past year follow:

	Assembly	Finishing
Budgeted overhead	$330,000	$1,000,000
Actual overhead	110,000	520,000
Expected activity (direct labor hours)	150,000	25,000
Expected machine hours	25,000	125,000

During the year, several jobs were completed. Data pertaining to one such job, Job 330, follow:

Direct materials	$730,000
Direct labor cost:	
Assembly (5,000 hours @ $12 per hr.)	$60,000
Finishing (400 hours @ $12 per hr.)	$4,800
Machine hours used:	
Assembly	100
Finishing	1,200
Units produced	10,000

Lindberg uses a plantwide predetermined overhead rate based on direct labor hours (DLH) to assign overhead to jobs.

Required:

1. Compute the predetermined overhead rate.

2. Using the predetermined rate, compute the per-unit manufacturing cost for Job 330. (*Note:* Round the unit cost to the nearest cent.)

3. Recalculate the unit manufacturing cost for Job 330 using departmental overhead rates. Use direct labor hours for Assembly and machine hours for Finishing.

Solution:

1. Predetermined overhead rate = $1,330,000/175,000 DLH = $7.60 per DLH. Add the budgeted overhead for the two departments, and divide by the total expected direct labor hours (DLH = 150,000 + 25,000).

2.

Direct materials	$730,000
Direct labor ($12 × 5,400 DLH)	64,800
Overhead ($7.60 × 5,400 DLH)	41,040
Total manufacturing costs	$835,840
Unit cost ($835,840/10,000 units)	$ 83.58

3. Predetermined rate for Assembly = $\dfrac{\$330,000}{150,000}$ = $2.20 per DLH

Predetermined rate for Finishing = $\dfrac{\$1,000,000}{125,000}$ = $8 per machine hour

Direct materials	$730,000
Direct labor	64,800
Overhead:	
Assembly ($2.20 × 5,000 DLH)	11,000
Finishing ($8 × 1,200 mhrs)	9,600
Total manufacturing costs	$815,400
Unit cost ($815,400/10,000 units)	$ 81.54

II. Calculation of Work in Process and Cost of Goods Sold with Multiple Jobs

Kennedy Kitchen and Bath (KKB) Company designs and installs upscale kitchens and bathrooms. On May 1, there were three jobs in process, Jobs 77, 78, and 79. During May, two more jobs

(Continued)

were started, Jobs 80 and 81. By May 31, Jobs 77, 78, and 80 were completed. The following data were gathered:

	Job 77	Job 78	Job 79	Job 80	Job 81
May 1 balance	$875	$1,140	$410	$ 0	$ 0
Direct materials	690	320	500	3,500	2,750
Direct labor	450	420	80	1,800	1,300

Overhead is applied at the rate of 150 percent of direct labor cost. Jobs are sold at cost plus 30 percent. Operating expenses for May totaled $2,700.

Required:

1. Prepare job-order cost sheets for each job as of May 31.

2. Calculate the ending balance in Work in Process (as of May 31) and Cost of Goods Sold for May.

3. Construct an income statement for KKB for the month of May.

Solution:

1.

	Job 77	Job 78	Job 79	Job 80	Job 81
May 1 balance	$ 875	$1,140	$ 410	$ 0	$ 0
Direct materials	690	320	500	3,500	2,750
Direct labor	450	420	80	1,800	1,300
Applied overhead	675	630	120	2,700	1,950
Totals	$2,690	$2,510	$1,110	$8,000	$6,000

2. Ending balance in Work in Process = Job 79 + Job 81

$$= \$1,110 + \$6,000$$

$$= \$7,110$$

Cost of Goods Sold for May = Job 77 + Job 78 + Job 80

$$= \$2,690 + \$2,510 + \$8,000$$

$$= \$13,200$$

3.

Kennedy Kitchen and Bath Company
Income Statement
For the Month Ended May 31, 20XX

Sales*	$17,160
Cost of goods sold	13,200
Gross margin	$ 3,960
Less: Operating expenses	2,700
Operating income	$ 1,260

*Sales = $13,200 + 0.30($13,200) = $17,160

III. Allocation: Direct and Sequential Methods

Barok Manufacturing produces machine parts on a job-order basis. Most business is obtained through bidding. Most firms competing with Barok bid full cost plus a 20 percent markup. Recently, with the expectation of gaining more sales, Barok reduced its markup from 25 percent to 20 percent. The company operates two service departments and two producing departments. The budgeted costs and the normal activity levels for each department are given below.

	Service Departments		Producing Departments	
	A	B	C	D
Direct overhead costs	$100,000	$200,000	$100,000	$50,000
Number of employees	8	7	30	30
Maintenance hours	2,000	200	6,400	1,600
Machine hours	—	—	10,000	1,000
Labor hours	—	—	1,000	10,000

The direct costs of Department A are allocated on the basis of employees. The direct costs of Department B are allocated on the basis of maintenance hours. Departmental overhead rates are used to assign costs to products. Department C uses machine hours, and Department D uses labor hours.

The firm is preparing to bid on a job (Job K) that requires three machine hours per unit produced in Department C and no time in Department D. The expected prime costs per unit are $67.

Required:

1. Allocate the service costs to the producing departments by using the direct method.

2. What will the bid be for Job K if the direct method of allocation is used?

3. Allocate the service costs to the producing departments by using the sequential method.

4. What will the bid be for Job K if the sequential method is used?

Solution:

1.

	Service Departments		Producing Departments	
	A	B	C	D
Direct overhead costs	$ 100,000	$ 200,000	$100,000	$ 50,000
Department A^a	(100,000)	—	50,000	50,000
Department B^b	—	(200,000)	160,000	40,000
Total	$ 0	$ 0	$310,000	$140,000

^{a}Department A costs are allocated on the basis of the number of employees in the producing departments, Departments C and D. The percentage of Department A cost allocated to Department C = 30/(30 + 30) = 0.50. Cost of Department A allocated to Department C = 0.50 × $100,000 = $50,000. The percentage of Department A cost allocated to Department D = 30/(30 + 30) = 0.50. Cost of Department A allocated to Department D = 0.50 × $100,000 = $50,000.
^{b}Department B costs are allocated on the basis of maintenance hours used in the producing departments, Departments C and D. The percentage of Department B cost allocated to Department C = 6,400/(6,400 + 1,600) = 0.80. Cost of Department B allocated to Department C = 0.80 × $200,000 = $160,000. The percentage of Department B cost allocated to Department D = 1,600/(6,400 + 1,600) = 0.20. Cost of Department B allocated to Department D = 0.20 × $200,000 = $40,000.

2. Department C: Overhead rate = $310,000/10,000 mhrs = $31 per machine hour. Product cost and bid price:

Prime cost	$ 67
Overhead (3 × $31)	93
Total unit cost	$160

Bid price = $160 × 1.20 = $192

3.

	Service Departments		Producing Departments	
	A	B	C	D
Direct overhead costs	$ 100,000	$ 200,000	$100,000	$ 50,000
Department B^a	40,000	(200,000)	128,000	32,000
Department A^b	(140,000)	—	70,000	70,000
Total	$ 0	$ 0	$298,000	$152,000

^{a}Department B ranks first because its direct costs are higher than those of Department A. Department B costs are allocated on the basis of maintenance hours used in Department A, and producing Departments C and D. Percent of Department B cost allocated to Department A is 0.20 [2,000/(2,000 + 6,400 + 1,600)]; cost of Department B allocated to Department A = 0.20 × $200,000 = $40,000. The percentage of Department B cost allocated to Department C = 6,400/(2,000 + 6,400 + 1,600) = 0.64. Cost of Department B allocated to Department C = 0.64 × $200,000 = $128,000. The percentage of Department B cost allocated to Department D = 1,600/(2,000 + 6,400 + 1,600) = 0.16. Cost of Department B allocated to Department D = 0.16 × $200,000 = $32,000.
^{b}Department A costs are allocated on the basis of number of employees in the producing departments, Departments C and D. The percentage of Department A cost allocated to Department C = 30/(30 + 30) = 0.50. Cost of Department A allocated to Department C = 0.50 × $140,000 = $70,000. The percentage of Department A cost allocated to Department D = 30/(30 + 30) = 0.50. Cost of Department A allocated to Department D = 0.50 × $140,000 = $70,000. (Note: Department A cost is no longer $100,000. It is $140,000 due to the $40,000 that was allocated from Department B.)

4. Department C: Overhead rate = $298,000/10,000 mhrs = $29.80 per machine hour. Product cost and bid price:

Prime cost	$ 67.00
Overhead (3 × $29.80)	89.40
Total unit cost	$156.40

Bid price = $156.40 × 1.20 = $187.68

DISCUSSION QUESTIONS

1. What are job-order costing and process costing? What types of firms use job-order costing? Process costing?
2. Give some examples of service firms that might use job-order costing, and explain why it is used in those firms.
3. What is normal costing? How does it differ from actual costing?
4. Why are actual overhead rates seldom used in practice?
5. Explain how overhead is assigned to production when a predetermined overhead rate is used.
6. What is underapplied overhead? When Cost of Goods Sold is adjusted for underapplied overhead, will the cost increase or decrease? Why?
7. What is overapplied overhead? When Cost of Goods Sold is adjusted for overapplied overhead, will the cost increase or decrease? Why?
8. Suppose that you and a friend decide to set up a lawn mowing service next summer. Describe the source documents that you would need to account for your activities.
9. Why might a company decide to use departmental overhead rates instead of a plantwide overhead rate?
10. What is the role of materials requisition forms in a job-order costing system? Time tickets? Predetermined overhead rates?
11. Carver Company uses a plantwide overhead rate based on direct labor cost. Suppose that during the year, Carver raises its wage rate for direct labor. How would that affect overhead applied? The total cost of jobs?
12. What is an overhead variance? How is it accounted for typically?
13. Is the cost of a job related to the price charged? Explain.
14. If a company decides to increase advertising expense by $25,000, how will that affect the predetermined overhead rate? Eventual cost of goods sold?
15. How can a departmental overhead system be converted to a plantwide overhead system?
16. *(Appendix 16B)* Describe the difference between producing and support departments.
17. *(Appendix 16B)* Assume that a company has decided not to allocate any support department costs to producing departments. Describe the likely behavior of the managers of the producing departments. Would this be good or bad? Explain why allocation would correct this type of behavior.
18. *(Appendix 16B)* Why is it important to identify and use causal factors to allocate support department costs?
19. *(Appendix 16B)* Identify some possible causal factors for the following support departments:
    a. Cafeteria
    b. Custodial services
    c. Laundry
    d. Receiving, shipping, and storage
    e. Maintenance
    f. Personnel
    g. Accounting
20. *(Appendix 16B)* Explain the difference between the direct method and the sequential method.

MULTIPLE-CHOICE EXERCISES

16-1 Which of the following statements is true?

a. Job-order costing is used only in manufacturing firms.
b. Process costing is used only for services.
c. Job-order costing is simpler to use than process costing because the recordkeeping requirements are less.
d. The job cost sheet is subsidiary to the work-in-process account.
e. All of the above are true.

16-2 The ending balance of which of the following accounts is calculated by summing the totals of the open (unfinished) job-order cost sheets?

a. Raw Materials
b. Overhead Control
c. Work in Process
d. Finished Goods
e. Cost of Goods Sold

16-3 In a normal costing system, the cost of a job includes

a. actual direct materials, actual direct labor, and estimated (applied) overhead.
b. estimated direct materials, estimated direct labor, and estimated overhead.
c. actual direct materials, actual direct labor, actual overhead, and actual selling cost.
d. actual direct materials, actual direct labor, and actual overhead.
e. none of the above. Job-order costing requires the use of actual, not normal, costing.

16-4 The predetermined overhead rate equals

a. actual overhead divided by actual activity level for a period.
b. estimated overhead divided by estimated activity level for a period.
c. actual overhead minus estimated overhead.
d. actual overhead multiplied by actual activity level for a period.
e. one-twelfth of estimated overhead.

16-5 The predetermined overhead rate is

a. calculated at the end of each month.
b. calculated at the end of the year.
c. equal to actual overhead divided by actual activity level for a period.
d. equal to estimated overhead divided by actual activity level for a period.
e. calculated at the beginning of the year.

16-6 Applied overhead is

a. an important part of normal costing.
b. never used in normal costing.
c. an important part of actual costing.
d. the predetermined overhead rate multiplied by estimated activity level.
e. the predetermined overhead rate multiplied by estimated activity level for the month.

16-7 The overhead variance is underapplied if

a. actual overhead is less than applied overhead.
b. actual overhead is more than applied overhead.
c. applied overhead is more than actual overhead.
d. estimated overhead is less than applied overhead.
e. estimated overhead is more than applied overhead.

16-8 Which of the following is typically a job-order costing firm?

a. Paint manufacturer
b. Pharmaceutical manufacturer
c. Large regional medical center
d. Cement manufacturer
e. Cleaning products manufacturer

16-9 Which of the following is typically a process-costing firm?

a. Paint manufacturer
b. Custom cabinetmaker
c. Large regional medical center
d. Law office
e. Custom framing shop

16-10 When materials are requisitioned for use in production in a job-order costing firm, the cost of materials is added to the

a. raw materials account.
b. work-in-process account.
c. finished goods account.
d. accounts payable account.
e. cost of goods sold account.

16-11 When a job is completed, the total cost of the job is

a. subtracted from the raw materials account.
b. added to the work-in-process account.
c. added to the finished goods account.
d. added to the accounts payable account.
e. subtracted from the cost of goods sold account.

16-12 The costs of a job are accounted for on the

a. materials requisition sheet.
b. time ticket.
c. requisition for overhead application.
d. sales invoice.
e. job-order cost sheet.

16-13 Wilson Company has a predetermined overhead rate of $5 per direct labor hour. The job-order cost sheet for Job 145 shows 500 direct labor hours costing $10,000 and materials requisitions totaling $7,500. Job 145 had 1,000 units completed and transferred to Finished Goods. What is the cost per unit for Job 145?

a. $20
b. $17.50
c. $25
d. $30
e. $22,500

16-14 *(Appendix 16A)* When a job costing $2,000 is finished but not sold, the following journal entry is made:

a. Cost of Goods Sold   2,000
      Finished Goods   2,000
b. Finished Goods   2,000
      Cost of Goods Sold   2,000
c. Finished Goods   2,000
      Work in Process   2,000
d. Work in Process   2,000
      Finished Goods   2,000
e. Cost of Goods Sold   2,000
      Sales   2,000

16-15 *(Appendix 16B)* Those departments responsible for creating products or services that are sold to customers are referred to as

a. profit making departments.
b. production departments.
c. cost centers.
d. support departments.
e. none of these.

16-16 *(Appendix 16B)* Those departments that provide essential services to producing departments are referred to as

a. revenue generating departments.
b. support departments.
c. profit centers.
d. production departments.
e. none of these.

16-17 *(Appendix 16B)* An example of a producing department is

a. a materials storeroom.
b. the maintenance department.
c. engineering design.
d. assembly.
e. all of these.

16-18 *(Appendix 16B)* An example of a support department is

a. data processing.
b. personnel.
c. a materials storeroom.
d. payroll.
e. all of these.

16-19 *(Appendix 16B)* The method that assigns support department costs only to producing departments in proportion to each department's usage of the service is known as

a.   the sequential method.   d.   the direct method.
b.   the proportional method.   e.   none of these.
c.   the reciprocal method.

16-20 *(Appendix 16B)* The method that assigns support department costs by giving partial recognition to support department interactions is known as

a.   the sequential method.   d.   the direct method.
b.   the proportional method.   e.   none of these.
c.   the reciprocal method.

16-21 *(Appendix 16B)* The method that assigns support department costs by giving full recognition to support department interactions is known as

a.   the sequential method.   d.   the direct method.
b.   the proportional method.   e.   none of these.
c.   the reciprocal method.

CORNERSTONE EXERCISES

Cornerstone Exercise 16-22 Predetermined Overhead Rate, Overhead Application

OBJECTIVE **2**
CORNERSTONE 16-1

At the beginning of the year, Ilberg Company estimated the following costs:

Overhead	$416,000
Direct labor cost	520,000

Ilberg uses normal costing and applies overhead on the basis of direct labor cost. (Direct labor cost is equal to total direct labor hours worked multiplied by the wage rate.) For the month of December, direct labor cost was $43,700.

Required:
1. Calculate the predetermined overhead rate for the year.
2. Calculate the overhead applied to production in December.

Cornerstone Exercise 16-23 Overhead Variance (Over- or Underapplied), Closing to Cost of Goods Sold

OBJECTIVE **2**
CORNERSTONE 16-2

At the end of the year, Ilberg Company provided the following actual information:

Overhead	$423,600
Direct labor cost	532,000

Ilberg uses normal costing and applies overhead at the rate of 80 percent of direct labor cost. At the end of the year, Cost of Goods Sold (before adjusting for any overhead variance) was $1,890,000.

Required:
1. Calculate the overhead variance for the year.
2. Dispose of the overhead variance by adjusting Cost of Goods Sold.

Use the following information for Cornerstone Exercises 16-24 and 16-25:
At the beginning of the year, Hallett Company estimated the following:

	Cutting Department	Sewing Department	Total
Overhead	$240,000	$350,000	$590,000
Direct labor hours	31,200	100,000	131,200
Machine hours	150,000	—	150,000

(Continued)

OBJECTIVE
CORNERSTONE 16-3

Cornerstone Exercise 16-24 Predetermined Departmental Overhead Rates, Applying Overhead to Production

Refer to the information for Hallett Company on the previous page. Hallett uses departmental overhead rates. In the cutting department, overhead is applied on the basis of machine hours. In the sewing department, overhead is applied on the basis of direct labor hours. Actual data for the month of June are as follows:

	Cutting Department	Sewing Department	Total
Overhead	$20,610	$35,750	$56,360
Direct labor hours	2,800	8,600	11,400
Machine hours	13,640	—	13,640

Required:

1. Calculate the predetermined overhead rates for the cutting and sewing departments.
2. Calculate the overhead applied to production in each department for the month of June.
3. By how much has each department's overhead been overapplied? Underapplied?

OBJECTIVE
CORNERSTONE 16-4

Cornerstone Exercise 16-25 Convert Departmental Data to Plantwide Data, Plantwide Overhead Rate, Apply Overhead to Production

Refer to the information in **Cornerstone Exercise 16-24** for data. Now, assume that Hallett has decided to use a plantwide overhead rate based on direct labor hours.

Required:

1. Calculate the predetermined plantwide overhead rate. (*Note:* Round to the nearest cent.)
2. Calculate the overhead applied to production for the month of June.
3. Calculate the overhead variance for the month of June.

OBJECTIVE
CORNERSTONE 16-5

Cornerstone Exercise 16-26 Prepare Job-Order Cost Sheets, Predetermined Overhead Rate, Ending Balance of WIP, Finished Goods, and COGS

At the beginning of June, Rhone Company had two jobs in process, Job 44 and Job 45, with the following accumulated cost information:

	Job 44	Job 45
Direct materials	$5,100	$1,500
Direct labor	1,200	3,000
Applied overhead	780	1,950
Balance, June 1	$7,080	$6,450

During June, two more jobs (46 and 47) were started. The following direct materials and direct labor costs were added to the four jobs during the month of June:

	Job 44	Job 45	Job 46	Job 47
Direct materials	$2,500	$7,110	$1,800	$1,700
Direct labor	800	6,400	900	560

At the end of June, Jobs 44, 45, and 47 were completed. Only Job 45 was sold. On June 1, the balance in Finished Goods was zero.

Required:

1. Calculate the overhead rate based on direct labor cost. (*Note:* Round to four decimal places.)
2. Prepare a brief job-order cost sheet for the four jobs. Show the balance as of June 1 as well as direct materials and direct labor added in June. Apply overhead to the four jobs for the month of June, and show the ending balances. (*Note:* Round all amounts to the nearest dollar.)
3. Calculate the ending balances of Work in Process and Finished Goods as of June 30.
4. Calculate the Cost of Goods Sold for June.

Use the following information for Cornerstone Exercises 16-27 and 16-28:

Quillen Company manufactures a product in a factory that has two producing departments, Cutting and Sewing, and two support departments, S1 and S2. The activity driver for S1 is number of employees, and the activity driver for S2 is number of maintenance hours. The following data pertain to Quillen:

	Support Departments		Producing Departments	
	S1	S2	Cutting	Sewing
Direct costs	$180,000	$150,000	$122,000	$90,500
Normal activity:				
Number of employees	—	30	63	147
Maintenance hours	1,200	—	16,000	4,000

Cornerstone Exercise 16-27 *(Appendix 16B)* Assigning Support Department Costs by Using The Direct Method

OBJECTIVE 6
CORNERSTONE 16-6

Refer to the information for Quillen Company above.

Required:

1. Calculate the cost assignment ratios to be used under the direct method for Departments S1 and S2. (*Note:* Each support department will have two ratios—one for Cutting and the other for Sewing.)
2. Allocate the support department costs to the producing departments by using the direct method.

Cornerstone Exercise 16-28 *(Appendix 16B)* Sequential Method

OBJECTIVE 6
CORNERSTONE 16-7

Refer to the information for Quillen Company above. Now assume that Quillen uses the sequential method to allocate support department costs. S1 is allocated first, then S2.

Required:

1. Calculate the cost assignment ratios to be used under the sequential method for S2, Cutting, and Sewing. Carry out your answers to four decimal places.
2. Allocate the overhead costs to the producing departments by using the sequential method.

EXERCISES

Exercise 16-29 Job-Order Costing versus Process Costing

OBJECTIVE 1

a. Hospital services
b. Custom cabinet making
c. Toy manufacturing
d. Soft-drink bottling
e. Airplane manufacturing (e.g., 767s)
f. Personal computer assembly
g. Furniture making (e.g., computer desks sold at discount stores)
h. Custom furniture making
i. Dental services
j. Paper manufacturing
k. Nut and bolt manufacturing
l. Auto repair
m. Architectural services
n. Landscape design services
o. Flashlight manufacturing

Required:

Identify each of these preceding types of businesses as either job-order or process costing.

Exercise 16-30 Job-Order Costing versus Process Costing

OBJECTIVE 1

a. Auto manufacturing
b. Dental services
c. Auto repair
d. Costume making

Required:

Conceptual Connection: For each of the given types of industries, give an example of a firm that would use job-order costing. Then, give an example of a firm that would use process costing.

OBJECTIVE ②

Exercise 16-31 Calculating the Predetermined Overhead Rate, Applying Overhead to Production

At the beginning of the year, Kester Company estimated the following:

Overhead	$621,600
Direct labor hours	84,000

Kester uses normal costing and applies overhead on the basis of direct labor hours. For the month of March, direct labor hours were 7,400.

Required:
1. Calculate the predetermined overhead rate for Kester.
2. Calculate the overhead applied to production in March.

OBJECTIVE ②

Exercise 16-32 Calculating the Predetermined Overhead Rate, Applying Overhead to Production, Reconciling Overhead at the End of the Year, Adjusting Cost of Goods Sold for Under- and Overapplied Overhead

At the beginning of the year, Gaudi Company estimated the following:

Overhead	$432,000
Direct labor hours	90,000

Gaudi uses normal costing and applies overhead on the basis of direct labor hours. For the month of January, direct labor hours were 7,650. By the end of the year, Gaudi showed the following actual amounts:

Overhead	$436,000
Direct labor hours	89,600

Assume that unadjusted Cost of Goods Sold for Gaudi was $707,000.

Required:
1. Calculate the predetermined overhead rate for Gaudi.
2. Calculate the overhead applied to production in January.
3. Calculate the total applied overhead for the year. Was overhead over- or underapplied? By how much?
4. Calculate adjusted Cost of Goods Sold after adjusting for the overhead variance.

OBJECTIVE ②

Exercise 16-33 Calculating Departmental Overhead Rates and Applying Overhead to Production

At the beginning of the year, Tecknik Company estimated the following:

	Assembly Department	Testing Department	Total
Overhead	$435,000	$720,000	$1,155,000
Direct labor hours	145,000	30,000	175,000
Machine hours	80,000	120,000	200,000

Tecknik uses departmental overhead rates. In the assembly department, overhead is applied on the basis of direct labor hours. In the testing department, overhead is applied on the basis of machine hours. Actual data for the month of March are as follows:

	Assembly Department	Testing Department	Total
Overhead	$38,500	$76,500	$115,000
Direct labor hours	13,000	1,680	14,680
Machine hours	6,800	13,050	19,850

Required:
1. Calculate the predetermined overhead rates for the assembly and testing departments.
2. Calculate the overhead applied to production in each department for the month of March.
3. By how much has each department's overhead been overapplied? Underapplied?

Exercise 16-34 Job-Order Costing Variables

On July 1, Job 88 had a beginning balance of $710. During July, prime costs added to the job totaled $640. Of that amount, direct materials were three times as much as direct labor. The ending balance of the job was $1,550.

Required:

1. What was overhead applied to the job during July?
2. What was direct materials for Job 88 for July? Direct labor?
3. Assuming that overhead is applied on the basis of direct labor cost, what is the overhead rate for the company? (*Note:* Round your answer to four decimal places.)

Exercise 16-35 Source Documents

For each of the following independent situations, give the source document that would be referred to for the necessary information.

Required:

1. Direct materials costing $460 are requisitioned for use on a job.
2. Greiner's Garage uses a job-order costing system. Overhead is applied to jobs based on direct labor hours. Which source document gives the number of direct labor hours worked on Job 2005-276?
3. Pasilla Investigative Services bills clients on a monthly basis for costs to date. Job 3-48 involved an investigator following the client's business partner for a week by automobile. Mileage is billed at number of miles times $0.75.
4. The foreman on the Jackson job wonders what the actual direct materials cost was for that job.

Exercise 16-36 Applying Overhead to Jobs, Costing Jobs

Rector Company designs and builds retaining walls for individual customers. On August 1, there were two jobs in process: Job 547 with a beginning balance of $9,300, and Job 548 with a beginning balance of $7,800. Rector applies overhead at the rate of $9 per direct labor hour. Direct labor wages average $15 per hour.

Data on August costs for all jobs are as follows:

	Job 547	Job 548	Job 549	Job 550
Direct materials	$ 950	$4,500	$3,300	$1,300
Direct labor cost	2,700	6,000	2,100	900

During August, Jobs 549 and 550 were started. Job 547 was completed on August 17, and the client was billed at cost plus 30 percent. All other jobs remained in process.

Required:

1. Calculate the number of direct labor hours that were worked on each job in August.
2. Calculate the overhead applied to each job during the month of August.
3. Prepare job-order cost sheets for each job as of the end of August.
4. Calculate the balance in Work in Process on August 31.
5. What is the price of Job 547?
6. **Conceptual Connection:** Partway though the year, Rector bought a bulldozer to handle larger jobs. The bulldozer cost $38,000 and is needed for larger commercial jobs. Smaller residential jobs can still be done with the smaller bobcat tractor. How could Rector apply the bulldozer cost to only those jobs that need the larger equipment?

Exercise 16-37 Applying Overhead to Jobs, Costing Jobs

Gorman Company builds internal conveyor equipment to client specifications. On October 1, Job 877 was in process with a cost of $18,640 to date.

During October, Jobs 878, 879, and 880 were started. Data on costs added during October for all jobs are as follows:

	Job 877	Job 878	Job 879	Job 880
Direct materials	$14,460	$6,000	$3,500	$1,800
Direct labor	14,800	8,500	1,750	2,150

(Continued)

Overhead is applied to production at the rate of 80 percent of direct labor cost. Job 877 was completed on October 28, and the client was billed at cost plus 50 percent. All other jobs remained in process.

Required:
1. Prepare a brief job-order cost sheet showing the October 1 balances of all four jobs, plus the direct materials and direct labor costs during October. (*Note:* There is no need to calculate applied overhead at this point or to total the costs.)
2. Calculate the overhead applied during October.
3. Calculate the balance in Work in Process on October 31.
4. What is the price of Job 877?

OBJECTIVE 4

Exercise 16-38 Balance of Work in Process and Finished Goods, Cost of Goods Sold

Zanthum Company uses job-order costing. At the end of the month, the following information was gathered:

Job #	Total Cost	Complete?	Sold?
301	$ 730	Yes	No
302	1,560	Yes	Yes
303	550	No	No
304	2,300	Yes	No
305	4,560	Yes	No
306	280	No	No
307	360	Yes	Yes
308	780	No	No
309	1,200	No	No
310	260	No	No

The beginning balance of Finished Goods was $300, consisting of Job 300 which was not sold by the end of the month.

Required:
1. Calculate the balance in Work in Process at the end of the month.
2. Calculate the balance in Finished Goods at the end of the month.
3. Calculate Cost of Goods Sold for the month.

OBJECTIVE 4

Exercise 16-39 Job-Order Cost Sheets, Balance in Work in Process and Finished Goods

Schulberg Company, a job-order costing firm, worked on three jobs in July. Data are as follows:

	Job 94	Job 95	Job 96
Balance, July 1	$18,450	$0	$0
Direct materials	$10,450	$12,300	$16,150
Direct labor	$16,000	$12,200	$24,000
Machine hours	500	300	1,000

Overhead is applied to jobs at the rate of $20 per machine hour. By July 31, Jobs 94 and 96 were completed. Jobs 90 and 94 were sold. Job 95 remained in process. On July 1, the balance in Finished Goods was $49,000 (consisting of Job 90 for $25,600 and Job 92 for $23,400).

Schulberg prices its jobs at cost plus 20 percent. During July, variable marketing expenses were 5 percent of sales, and fixed marketing expenses were $2,000; administrative expenses were $4,800.

Required:
1. Prepare job-order cost sheets for all jobs in process during July, showing all costs through July 31.
2. Calculate the balance in Work in Process on July 31.
3. Calculate the balance in Finished Goods on July 31.
4. Calculate Cost of Goods Sold for July.
5. Calculate operating income for Schulberg Company for the month of July.

OBJECTIVE 4

ILLUSTRATING
RELATIONSHIPS

Exercise 16-40 Cost Flows

Consider the following independent jobs. Overhead is applied in Department 1 at the rate of $6 per direct labor hour. Overhead is applied in Department 2 at the rate of $8 per machine hour. Direct labor wages average $10 per hour in each department.

	Job 213	Job 214	Job 217	Job 225
Total sales revenue	$?	$4,375	$5,600	$1,150
Price per unit	$12	$?	$14	$5
Materials used in production	$365	$?	$488	$207
Department 1, direct labor cost	$?	$700	$2,000	$230
Department 1, machine hours	15	35	50	12
Department 2, direct labor cost	$50	$100	$?	$0
Department 2, machine hours	25	50	?	?
Department 1, overhead applied	$90	$?	$1,200	$138
Department 2, overhead applied	$?	$400	$160	$0
Total manufacturing cost	$855	$3,073	$?	$575
Number of units	?	350	400	?
Unit cost	$8.55	$?	$9.87	$?

Required:

Fill in the missing data for each job.

Exercise 16-41 Job Cost Flows

OBJECTIVE 4

Roseler Company uses a normal job-order costing system. The company has two departments through which most jobs pass. Overhead is applied using a plantwide overhead rate of $10 per direct labor hour. During the year, several jobs were completed. Data pertaining to one such job, Job 9-601, follow:

Direct materials	$12,000
Direct labor cost:	
Department A (450 hours @ $18)	$8,100
Department B (120 hours @ $18)	$2,160
Machine hours used:	
Department A	200
Department B	800
Units produced	1,000

Required:

1. Compute the total cost of Job 9-601.
2. Compute the per-unit manufacturing cost for Job 9-601.

> *For Requirements 3 and 4, assume that Roseler uses departmental overhead rates. In Department A, overhead is applied at the rate of $3 per direct labor hour. In Department B, overhead is applied at the rate of $7 per machine hour.*

3. Compute the total cost of Job 9-601.
4. Compute the per-unit manufacturing cost for Job 9-601.

Exercise 16-42 Calculation of Work in Process and Cost of Goods Sold with Multiple Jobs

OBJECTIVE 4

Ensign Landscape Design designs landscape plans and plants the material for clients. On April 1, there were three jobs in process, Jobs 39, 40, and 41. During April, two more jobs were started, Jobs 42 and 43. By April 30, Jobs 40, 41, and 43 were completed and sold. The following data were gathered:

	Job 39	Job 40	Job 41	Job 42	Job 43
Balance, April 1	$540	$3,400	$2,990	—	—
Direct materials	700	560	375	$3,500	$6,900
Direct labor	500	600	490	2,500	3,000

Overhead is applied at the rate of 110 percent of direct labor cost. Jobs are sold at cost plus 30 percent. Selling and administrative expenses for April totaled $4,575.

(Continued)

Required:
1. Prepare job-order cost sheets for each job as of April 30.
2. Calculate the ending balance in Work in Process (as of April 30) and Cost of Goods Sold for April.
3. Construct an income statement for Ensign Landscape Design for the month of April.

OBJECTIVE 5

Exercise 16-43 (Appendix 16A) Journal Entries

Olduvai Inc. uses a job-order costing system. During the month of May, the following transactions occurred:

a. Purchased materials on account for $24,550.
b. Requisitioned materials totaling $23,130 for use in production. Of the total, $8,900 was for Job 58, $8,800 for Job 59, and the remainder for Job 60.
c. Incurred direct labor for the month of $36,000, with an average wage of $20 per hour. Job 58 used 800 hours; Job 59, 600 hours; and Job 60, 400 hours.
d. Incurred and paid actual overhead of $17,880 (credit Various Payables).
e. Charged overhead to production at the rate of $4.80 per direct labor hour.
f. Completed and transferred Jobs 58 and 59 to Finished Goods.
g. Sold Job 57 (see beginning balance of Finished Goods) and Job 58 to their respective clients on account for a price of cost plus 40 percent.

Beginning balances as of May 1 were:

Materials	$ 2,500
Work in Process	0
Finished Goods (Job 57)	27,400

Required:
1. Prepare the journal entries for transactions (a) through (g).
2. Prepare brief job-order cost sheets for Jobs 58, 59, and 60.
3. Calculate the ending balance of Raw Materials.
4. Calculate the ending balance of Work in Process.
5. Calculate the ending balance of Finished Goods.

OBJECTIVE 6

Exercise 16-44 (Appendix 16B) Direct Method of Support Department Cost Allocation

Jekyll Company is divided into two operating divisions: Battery and Small Motors. The company allocates power and human resources costs to each operating division using the direct method. Power costs are allocated on the basis of the number of machine hours and human resources costs on the basis of the number of employees. Support department cost allocations using the direct method are based on the following data:

	Support Departments		Operating Divisions	
	Power	Human Resources	Battery	Small Motors
Overhead costs	$160,000	$205,000	$176,000	$93,500
Machine hours	2,000	2,000	7,000	1,000
Number of employees	10	15	10	30
Direct labor hours			18,000	60,000

Required:
1. Calculate the allocation ratios for Power and Human Resources. (*Note:* Carry these calculations out to four decimal places.)
2. Allocate the support service costs to the operating divisions. (*Note:* Round all amounts to the nearest dollar.)
3. Assume divisional overhead rates are based on direct labor hours. Calculate the overhead rate for the Battery Division and for the Small Motors Division. (*Note:* Round overhead rates to the nearest cent.)

OBJECTIVE 6

Exercise 16-45 (Appendix 16B) Sequential Method of Support Department Cost Allocation

Refer to **Exercise 16-44** for data. Now assume that Jekyll uses the sequential method to allocate support department costs to the operating divisions. Human Resources is allocated first in the sequential method for Jekyll.

Required:

1. Calculate the allocation ratios for Power and Human Resources. (*Note:* Carry these calculations out to four decimal places.)
2. Allocate the support service costs to the operating divisions. (*Note:* Round all amounts to the nearest dollar.)
3. Assume divisional overhead rates are based on direct labor hours. Calculate the overhead rate for the Battery Division and for the Small Motors Division. (*Note:* Round overhead rates to the nearest cent.)

PROBLEMS

Problem 16-46 Overhead Application and Job-Order Costing

Heurion Company is a job-order costing firm that uses a plantwide overhead rate based on direct labor hours. Estimated information for the year is as follows:

Overhead	$789,000
Direct labor hours	100,000

Heurion worked on five jobs in July. Data are as follows:

	Job 741	Job 742	Job 743	Job 744	Job 745
Balance, July 1	$29,870	$55,215	$27,880	$0	$0
Direct materials	$25,500	$39,800	$14,450	$13,600	$ 8,420
Direct labor cost	$61,300	$48,500	$28,700	$24,500	$21,300
Direct labor hours	4,000	3,400	1,980	1,600	1,400

By July 31, Jobs 741 and 743 were completed and sold. The remaining jobs were in process.

Required:

1. Calculate the plantwide overhead rate for Heurion Company. (*Note:* Round to the nearest cent.)
2. Prepare job-order cost sheets for each job showing all costs through July 31.
3. Calculate the balance in Work in Process on July 31.
4. Calculate Cost of Goods Sold for July.

OBJECTIVE

Problem 16-47 Job Cost, Source Documents

Spade Millhone Detective Agency performs investigative work for a variety of clients. Recently, Alban Insurance Company asked Spade Millhone to investigate a series of suspicious claims for whiplash. In each case, the claimant was driving on a freeway and was suddenly rear-ended by an Alban-insured client. The claimants were all driving old, uninsured automobiles. The Alban clients reported that the claimants suddenly changed lanes in front of them, and the accidents were unavoidable. Alban suspected that these "accidents" were the result of insurance fraud. Basically, the claimants cruised the freeways in virtually worthless cars, attempting to cut in front of expensive late-model cars that would surely be insured. Alban believed that the injuries were faked.

Rex Spade spent 37 hours shadowing the claimants and taking pictures as necessary. His surveillance methods located the office of a doctor used by all claimants. He also took pictures of claimants performing tasks that they had sworn were now impossible to perform due to whiplash injuries. Victoria Millhone spent 48 hours using the Internet to research court records in surrounding states to locate the names of the claimants and their doctor. She found a pattern of similar insurance claims for each of the claimants.

Spade Millhone Detective Agency bills clients for detective time at $120 per hour. Mileage is charged at $0.50 per mile. The agency logged in 510 miles on the Alban job. The film and developing amounted to $120.

OBJECTIVE

Required:

1. Prepare a job-order cost sheet for the Alban job.
2. **Conceptual Connection:** Why is overhead not specified in the charges? How does Spade Millhone charge clients for the use of overhead (e.g., the ongoing costs of their office—supplies, paper for notes and reports, telephone, utilities)?

(Continued)

3. The mileage is tallied from a source document. Design a source document for this use, and make up data for it that would total the 510 miles driven on the Alban job.

OBJECTIVE 4

Problem 16-48 Calculating Ending Work in Process, Income Statement

Pavlovich Prosthetics Company produces artificial limbs for individuals. Each prosthetic is unique. On January 1, three jobs, identified by the name of the person being fitted with the prosthetic, were in process with the following costs:

	Carter	Pelham	Tillson
Direct materials	$ 210	$ 615	$1,290
Direct labor	440	700	1,260
Applied overhead	374	595	1,071
Total	$1,024	$1,910	$3,621

During the month of January, two more jobs were started, Jasper and Dashell. Materials and labor costs incurred by each job in January are as follows:

	Materials	Direct Labor
Carter	$ 600	$ 300
Pelham	550	200
Tillson	770	240
Jasper	2,310	2,100
Dashell	190	240

Tillson and Jasper's prosthetics were completed and sold by January 31.

Required:

1. If overhead is applied on the basis of direct labor dollars, what is the overhead rate? (*Note:* Round your answer to four decimal places.)
2. Prepare simple job-order cost sheets for each of the five jobs in process during January. (*Note:* Round all amounts to the nearest dollar.)
3. What is the ending balance of Work in Process on January 31? What is the Cost of Goods Sold in January?
4. Suppose that Pavlovich Prosthetics Company prices its jobs at cost plus 30 percent. In addition, during January, marketing and administrative expenses of $2,635 were incurred. Prepare an income statement for the month of January.

OBJECTIVE 2

Problem 16-49 Overhead Applied to Jobs, Departmental Overhead Rates

Xania Inc. uses a normal job-order costing system. Currently, a plantwide overhead rate based on machine hours is used. Xania's plant manager has heard that departmental overhead rates can offer significantly better cost assignments than a plantwide rate can offer. Xania has the following data for its two departments for the coming year:

	Department A	Department B
Overhead costs (expected)	$75,000	$33,000
Normal activity (machine hours)	10,000	8,000

Required:

1. Compute a predetermined overhead rate for the plant as a whole based on machine hours.
2. Compute predetermined overhead rates for each department using machine hours. (*Note:* Carry your calculations out to three decimal places.)
3. **Conceptual Connection:** Job 73 used 20 machine hours from Department A and 50 machine hours from Department B. Job 74 used 50 machine hours from Department A and 20 machine hours from Department B. Compute the overhead cost assigned to each job using the plantwide rate computed in Requirement 1. Repeat the computation using the departmental rates found in Requirement 2. Which of the two approaches gives the fairer assignment? Why?
4. **Conceptual Connection:** Repeat Requirement 3, assuming the expected overhead cost for Department B is $60,000 (not $33,000). For this company, would you recommend departmental rates over a plantwide rate? (*Note:* Round overhead rates to the nearest cent.)

Problem 16-50 Overhead Rates, Unit Costs

OBJECTIVE ②

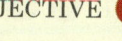

Folsom Company manufactures specialty tools to customer order. There are three producing departments. Departmental information on budgeted overhead and various activity measures for the coming year is as follows:

	Welding	Assembly	Finishing
Estimated overhead	$220,000	$62,000	$150,000
Direct labor hours	4,500	10,000	6,000
Direct labor cost	$90,000	$150,000	$120,000
Machine hours	5,000	1,000	2,000

Currently, overhead is applied on the basis of machine hours using a plantwide rate. However, Janine, the controller, has been wondering whether it might be worthwhile to use departmental overhead rates. She has analyzed the overhead costs and drivers for the various departments and decided that Welding and Finishing should base their overhead rates on machine hours and that Assembly should base its overhead rate on direct labor hours.

Janine has been asked to prepare bids for two jobs with the following information:

	Job 1	Job 2
Direct materials	$6,725	$9,340
Direct labor cost	$1,800	$3,100
Direct labor hours:		
Welding	20	10
Assembly	60	20
Finishing	20	70
Number of machine hours:		
Welding	50	50
Assembly	60	25
Finishing	90	125

The typical bid price includes a 35 percent markup over full manufacturing cost. Round all overhead rates to the nearest cent. Round all bid prices to the nearest dollar.

Required:

1. Calculate a plantwide rate for Folsom Company based on machine hours. What is the bid price of each job using this rate? (*Note:* Round to the nearest cent.)
2. Calculate departmental overhead rates for the producing departments. What is the bid price of each job using these rates? (*Note:* Round overhead rates to the nearest cent.)

Problem 16-51 Calculate Job Cost and Use It to Calculate Price

OBJECTIVE ② ④

Suppose that back in the 1970s, Steve was asked to build speakers for two friends. The first friend, Jan, needed a speaker for her band. The second friend, Ed, needed a speaker built into the back of his hatchback automobile. Steve figured the following costs for each:

	Jan's Job	Ed's Job
Materials	$50	$75
Labor hours	10	20

Steve knew that Jan's job would be easier, since he had experience in building the type of speaker she needed. Her job would not require any special equipment or specialized fitting. Ed's job, on the other hand, required specialized design and precise fitting. Steve thought he might need to build a mock-up of the speaker first, to fit it into the space. In addition, he might have to add to his tool collection to complete the job. Normally, Steve figured a wage rate of $6 per hour and charged 20 percent of labor and materials as an overhead rate.

Required:

1. Prepare job-order cost sheets for the two jobs, showing total cost.
2. **Conceptual Connection:** Which cost do you think is more likely to be accurate? How might Steve build in some of the uncertainty of Ed's job into a budgeted cost?

OBJECTIVE ④ ⑤

Problem 16-52 *(Appendix 16A)* Unit Cost, Ending Work in Process, Journal Entries

During August, Leming Inc. worked on two jobs. Data relating to these two jobs follow:

	Job 64	Job 65
Units in each order	50	80
Units sold	50	—
Materials requisitioned	$3,560	$785
Direct labor hours	410	583
Direct labor cost	$6,720	$9,328

Overhead is assigned on the basis of direct labor hours at a rate of $11. During August, Job 64 was completed and transferred to Finished Goods. Job 65 was the only unfinished job at the end of the month.

Required:
1. Calculate the per-unit cost of Job 64. (*Note:* Round per-unit cost to the nearest cent.)
2. Compute the ending balance in the work-in-process account.
3. Prepare the journal entries reflecting the completion and sale on account of Job 64. The selling price is 175 percent of cost. (*Note:* Round all journal entry amounts to the nearest dollar.)

OBJECTIVE ④ ⑤

Problem 16-53 *(Appendix 16A)* Journal Entries, Job Costs

The following transactions occurred during the month of April for Nelson Company:

a. Purchased materials costing $4,610 on account.
b. Requisitioned materials totaling $4,800 for use in production, $3,170 for Job 518 and the remainder for Job 519.
c. Recorded 65 hours of direct labor on Job 518 and 90 hours on Job 519 for the month. Direct laborers are paid at the rate of $14 per hour.
d. Applied overhead using a plantwide rate of $6.20 per direct labor hour.
e. Incurred and paid in cash actual overhead for the month of $973.
f. Completed and transferred Job 518 to Finished Goods.
g. Sold on account Job 517, which had been completed and transferred to Finished Goods in March, for cost ($2,770) plus 25 percent.

Required:
1. Prepare journal entries for transactions (a) through (e).
2. Prepare job-order cost sheets for Jobs 518 and 519. Prepare journal entries for transactions (f) and (g). (*Note:* Round to the nearest dollar.)
3. Prepare a schedule of cost of goods manufactured for April. Assume that the beginning balance in the raw materials account was $1,025 and that the beginning balance in the work-in-process account was zero.

OBJECTIVE ② ④ ⑤

Problem 16-54 *(Appendix 16A)* Predetermined Overhead Rates, Variances, Cost Flows

Barrymore Costume Company, located in New York City, sews costumes for plays and musicals. Barrymore considers itself primarily a service firm, as it never produces costumes without a pre-existing order and only purchases materials to the specifications of the particular job. Any finished goods ending inventory is temporary and is zeroed out as soon as the show producer pays for the order. Overhead is applied on the basis of direct labor cost. During the first quarter of the year, the following activity took place in each of the accounts listed:

Work in Process					Finished Goods			
Bal.	17,000	Complete	245,000		Bal.	40,000	Sold	210,000
DL	80,000				Complete	245,000		
OH	140,000				Bal.	75,000		
DM	40,000							
Bal.	32,000							

Overhead					Cost of Goods Sold		
	138,500		140,000		210,000		
		Bal.	1,500				

Job 32 was the only job in process at the end of the first quarter. A total of 1,000 direct labor hours at $10 per hour were charged to Job 32.

Required:

1. Assuming that overhead is applied on the basis of direct labor cost, what was the overhead rate used during the first quarter of the year?
2. What was the applied overhead for the first quarter? The actual overhead? The under- or overapplied overhead?
3. What was the cost of the goods manufactured for the quarter?
4. Assume that the overhead variance is closed to the cost of goods sold account. Prepare the journal entry to close out the overhead control account. What is the adjusted balance in Cost of Goods Sold?
5. For Job 32, identify the costs incurred for direct materials, direct labor, and overhead.

Problem 16-55 *(Appendix 16A)* Overhead Application, Journal Entries, Job Cost

OBJECTIVE

At the beginning of the year, Smith Company budgeted overhead of $129,600 as well as 13,500 direct labor hours. During the year, Job K456 was completed with the following information: direct materials cost, $2,750; direct labor cost, $5,355. The average wage for Smith Company employees is $17 per hour.

By the end of the year, 18,100 direct labor hours had actually been worked, and Smith incurred the following actual overhead costs for the year:

Equipment lease	$ 6,800
Depreciation on building	19,340
Indirect labor	90,400
Utilities	14,560
Other overhead	41,400

Required:

1. Calculate the overhead rate for the year. (*Note:* Round to the nearest cent.)
2. Calculate the total cost of Job K456. (*Note:* Round to the nearest dollar.)
3. Prepare the journal entries to record actual overhead and to apply overhead to production for the year.
4. Is overhead overapplied or underapplied? By how much?
5. Assuming that the normal cost of goods sold for the year is $635,600, what is the adjusted cost of goods sold?

Problem 16-56 *(Appendix 16A)* Journal Entries, T-Accounts

OBJECTIVE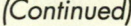

Lowder Inc. builds custom conveyor systems for warehouses and distribution centers. During the month of July, the following occurred:

a. Purchased materials on account for $42,630.
b. Requisitioned materials totaling $27,000 for use in production: $12,500 for Job 703 and the remainder for Job 704.
c. Recorded direct labor payroll for the month of $26,320 with an average wage of $14 per hour. Job 703 required 780 direct labor hours; Job 704 required 1,100 direct labor hours.
d. Incurred and paid actual overhead of $19,950.
e. Charged overhead to production at the rate of $10 per direct labor hour.
f. Completed Job 703 and transferred it to Finished Goods.
g. Kept Job 704, which was started during July, in process at the end of the month.
h. Sold Job 700, which had been completed in May, on account for cost plus 30 percent.

Beginning balances as of July 1 were:

Raw Materials	$ 6,070
Work in Process (for Job 703)	10,000
Finished Goods (for Job 700)	6,240

Required:

1. Prepare the journal entries for events (a) through (e).
2. Prepare simple job-order cost sheets for Jobs 703 and 704.

(Continued)

3. Prepare the journal entries for events (f) and (h).
4. Calculate the ending balances of the following: (a) Raw Materials, (b) Work in Process, and (c) Finished Goods.

OBJECTIVE ❻

Problem 16-57 (Appendix 16B) Support Department Cost Allocation

MedServices Inc. is divided into two operating departments: Laboratory and Tissue Pathology. The company allocates delivery and accounting costs to each operating department. Delivery costs include the costs of a fleet of vans and drivers that drive throughout the state each day to clinics and doctors' offices to pick up samples and deliver them to the centrally located laboratory and tissue pathology offices. Delivery costs are allocated on the basis of number of samples. Accounting costs are allocated on the basis of the number of transactions processed. No effort is made to separate fixed and variable costs; however, only budgeted costs are allocated. Allocations for the coming year are based on the following data:

	Support Departments		Operating Departments	
	Delivery	Accounting	Laboratory	Pathology
Overhead costs	$240,000	$270,000	$345,000	$456,000
Number of samples	—	—	70,200	46,800
Transactions processed	2,000	—	24,700	13,300

Required:

1. Assign the support department costs by using the direct method. (*Note:* Round allocation ratios to four decimal places.)
2. Assign the support department costs by using the sequential method, allocating accounting costs first. (*Note:* Round allocation ratios to four decimal places.)

OBJECTIVE ❻

Problem 16-58 (Appendix 16B) Support Department Cost Allocation: Comparison of Methods of Allocation

Bender Automotive Works Inc. manufactures a variety of front-end assemblies for automobiles. A front-end assembly is the unified front of an automobile that includes the headlamps, fender, and surrounding metal/plastic. Bender has two producing departments: Drilling and Assembly. Usually, the front-end assemblies are ordered in batches of 100.

Two support departments provide support for Bender's producing departments: Maintenance and Power. Budgeted data for the coming quarter follow. The company does not separate fixed and variable costs.

	Support Departments		Producing Departments	
	Maintenance	Power	Drilling	Assembly
Overhead costs	$320,000	$400,000	$163,000	$ 90,000
Machine hours	—	22,500	30,000	7,500
Kilowatt-hours	40,000	—	36,000	324,000
Direct labor hours	—	—	5,000	40,000

The predetermined overhead rate for Drilling is computed on the basis of machine hours. Direct labor hours are used for Assembly.

Recently, a truck manufacturer requested a bid on a three-year contract that would supply front-end assemblies to a nearby factory. The prime costs for a batch of 100 front-end assemblies are $1,817. It takes two machine hours to produce a batch in the drilling department and 50 direct labor hours to assemble the 100 front-end assemblies in the assembly department.

Bender's policy is to bid full manufacturing cost, plus 15 percent. (*Note:* Round allocation ratios to four decimal places, allocated support department cost to the nearest dollar, and the job cost components to the nearest cent.)

Required:

1. Prepare bids for Bender by using each of the following allocation methods: (a) direct method and (b) sequential method, allocating power costs first. (*Note:* Round allocation ratios to four decimal places, allocated support department cost to the nearest dollar, and the job cost components to the nearest cent.)
2. **Conceptual Connection:** Which method most accurately reflects the cost of producing the front-end assemblies? Why?

CASES

Case 16-59 Overhead Assignment: Actual and Normal Activity Compared

OBJECTIVE

Reynolds Printing Company specializes in wedding announcements. Reynolds uses an actual job-order costing system. An actual overhead rate is calculated at the end of each month using actual direct labor hours and overhead for the month. Once the actual cost of a job is determined, the customer is billed at actual cost plus 50 percent.

During April, Mrs. Lucky, a good friend of owner Jane Reynolds, ordered three sets of wedding announcements to be delivered May 10, June 10, and July 10, respectively. Reynolds scheduled production for each order on May 7, June 7, and July 7, respectively. The orders were assigned job numbers 115, 116, and 117, respectively.

Reynolds assured Mrs. Lucky that she would attend each of her daughters' weddings. Out of sympathy and friendship, she also offered a lower price. Instead of cost plus 50 percent, she gave her a special price of cost plus 25 percent. Additionally, she agreed to wait until the final wedding to bill for the three jobs.

On August 15, Reynolds asked her accountant to bring her the completed job-order cost sheets for Jobs 115, 116, and 117. She also gave instructions to lower the price as had been agreed upon. The cost sheets revealed the following information:

	Job 115	Job 116	Job 117
Cost of direct materials	$250.00	$250.00	$250.00
Cost of direct labor (5 hours)	25.00	25.00	25.00
Cost of overhead	200.00	400.00	400.00
Total cost	$475.00	$675.00	$675.00
Total price	$593.75	$843.75	$843.75
Number of announcements	500	500	500

Reynolds could not understand why the overhead costs assigned to Jobs 116 and 117 were so much higher than those for Job 115. She asked for an overhead cost summary sheet for the months of May, June, and July, which showed that actual overhead costs were $20,000 each month. She also discovered that direct labor hours worked on all jobs were 500 hours in May and 250 hours each in June and July.

Required:

1. How do you think Mrs. Lucky will feel when she receives the bill for the three sets of wedding announcements?
2. Explain how the overhead costs were assigned to each job.
3. Assume that Reynolds's average activity is 500 hours per month and that the company usually experiences overhead costs of $240,000 each year. Can you recommend a better way to assign overhead costs to jobs? Recompute the cost of each job and its price given your method of overhead cost assignment. Which method do you think is best? Why?

Case 16-60 Assigning Overhead to Jobs—Ethical Issues

OBJECTIVE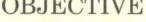

Tonya Martin, CMA and controller of the Parts Division of Gunderson Inc., was meeting with Doug Adams, manager of the division. The topic of discussion was the assignment of overhead costs to jobs and their impact on the division's pricing decisions. Their conversation was as follows:

Tonya: Doug, as you know, about 25 percent of our business is based on government contracts, with the other 75 percent based on jobs from private sources won through bidding. During the last several years, our private business has declined. We have been losing more bids than usual. After some careful investigation, I have concluded that we are overpricing some jobs because of improper assignment of overhead costs. Some jobs are also being underpriced. Unfortunately, the jobs being overpriced are coming from our higher-volume, labor-intensive products, so we are losing business.

Doug: I think I understand. Jobs associated with our high-volume products are being assigned more overhead than they should be receiving. Then when we add our standard 40 percent markup, we end up with a higher price than our competitors, who assign costs more accurately.

(Continued)

Tonya: Exactly. We have two producing departments, one labor-intensive and the other machine-intensive. The labor-intensive department generates much less overhead than the machine-intensive department. Furthermore, virtually all of our high-volume jobs are labor-intensive. We have been using a plantwide rate based on direct labor hours to assign overhead to all jobs. As a result, the high-volume, labor-intensive jobs receive a greater share of the machine-intensive department's overhead than they deserve. This problem can be greatly alleviated by switching to departmental overhead rates. For example, an average high-volume job would be assigned $100,000 of overhead using a plantwide rate and only $70,000 using departmental rates. The change would lower our bidding price on high-volume jobs by an average of $42,000 per job. By increasing the accuracy of our product costing, we can make better pricing decisions and win back much of our private-sector business.

Doug: Sounds good. When can you implement the change in overhead rates?

Tonya: It won't take long. I can have the new system working within four to six weeks—certainly by the start of the new fiscal year.

Doug: Hold it. I just thought of a possible complication. As I recall, most of our government contract work is done in the labor-intensive department. This new overhead assignment scheme will push down the cost on the government jobs, and we will lose revenues. They pay us full cost plus our standard markup. This business is not threatened by our current costing procedures, but we can't switch our rates for only the private business. Government auditors would question the lack of consistency in our costing procedures.

Tonya: You do have a point. I thought of this issue also. According to my estimates, we will gain more revenues from the private sector than we will lose from our government contracts. Besides, the costs of our government jobs are distorted. In effect, we are overcharging the government.

Doug: They don't know that and never would unless we switch our overhead assignment procedures. I think I have the solution. Officially, let's keep our plantwide overhead rate. All of the official records will reflect this overhead costing approach for both our private and government business. Unofficially, I want you to develop a separate set of books that can be used to generate the information we need to prepare competitive bids for our private-sector business.

Required:
1. Do you believe that the solution proposed by Doug is ethical? Explain.
2. Suppose that Tonya decides that Doug's solution is not right and objects strongly. Further suppose that, despite Tonya's objections, Doug insists strongly on implementing the action. What should Tonya do?

17 Process Costing

Doug Norman Crystals/Alamy

After studying Chapter 17, you should be able to:

1. Describe the basic characteristics and cost flows associated with process manufacturing.

2. Define *equivalent units* and explain their role in process costing. Explain the differences between the weighted average method and the FIFO method of accounting for process costs.

3. Prepare a departmental production report using the weighted average method.

4. Explain how nonuniform inputs and multiple processing departments affect process costing.

5. *(Appendix 17A)* Prepare a departmental production report using the FIFO method.

JENS WOLF/DPA/landov

EXPERIENCE MANAGERIAL DECISIONS

with BP

The only consideration that most people give to gasoline is the price charged at the local pump. However, BP, one of the largest energy companies in the world, has been thinking about this issue and a lot more for quite a long time. BP was founded in 1901 after William D'Arcy obtained permission from the shah of Persia to dig for oil in what is now the Iranian desert. BP drastically expanded its reach and, as of the early 21st century, had active excavation and production occurring in 22 countries. BP runs its processes nonstop—24 hours a day, 365 days a year—to produce to full capacity, which represents 2.6 million barrels of oil each day or approximately 30 barrels every second. Producing that much of anything is a bit mind-boggling, which hints at the importance of BP's effective process-costing system in determining the costs associated with its numerous products, which include gasoline, heating fuel, greases, and asphalt.

Picsfive, 2010/Shutterstock.com

In order to determine costs for a particular process, BP needs to know the total costs of production and the total number of units processed in a specified period of time. The costs include raw crude oil, which varies widely from sweet West Texas crude to heavier Canadian crude, plus labor and management overhead. Other costs include catalysts, which enhance the reactivity to make a molecule turn into something else, and chemicals, which become part of the final product. BP goes to a lot of trouble to combine its process-costing system outputs, current market prices, and a linear programming model in order to calculate the most profitable mix of products to produce from a given mix of raw crude materials. Determining the costs associated with running a refinery with a continuous production process is complex. However, by calculating process costs and carefully setting production levels and product mixes, BP is able to manage this complex process at its facilities around the globe, thereby providing significant profits for use in future energy discovery, distribution efforts, and unexpected and costly events such as the 2010 oil gusher in the Gulf of Mexico.

The recent oil rig explosion and subsequent oil gusher in the Gulf of Mexico have caused tremendous political and financial stress for BP and will continue to do so for some time. The costs associated with stopping the oil from gushing, subsequent cleanup, and ultimate reparations to businesses affected by the gusher are already huge and likely to continue increasing. The image and goodwill of BP have also been negatively impacted. The ultimate effect on BP is not yet known, but BP's ability to deal with these issues is certainly related to the company's significant profitability.

Courtesy of BP (British Petroleum)

CHARACTERISTICS OF PROCESS MANUFACTURING

As illustrated by **BP**, production processes help determine the best way of accounting for its costs. For example, BP's refinery in Whiting, Indiana can process up to 400,000 barrels of crude oil per day. A barrel of crude oil is refined into a number of different products such as gasoline, heating oil, greases, and asphalts. In this setting, a large number of similar products pass through an identical set of processes. Since each product within a product line passing through the processes would receive similar "doses" of materials, labor, and overhead, there is no need to accumulate costs by batches (as a job-order costing system does). Instead, costs are accumulated by process. Process costing works well whenever relatively homogeneous products pass through a series of processes and receive similar amounts of manufacturing costs.

Consider the process-costing environment of Healthblend Nutritional Supplements, a company which manufactures minerals, herbs, and vitamins. Healthblend uses the following three processes:

- *Mixing or Picking*: In the mixing or picking department for a given product, the appropriate herbs, vitamins, minerals, and inert materials (typically some binder such as cornstarch) are selected, measured in the prescribed proportions, and then combined in a mixer to blend them thoroughly. When the mix is complete, the resulting mixture is sent to the encapsulation department.
- *Encapsulation*: In encapsulating, the vitamin, mineral, or herb blend is loaded into a machine that fills one-half of a gelatin capsule. The filled half is matched to another half of the capsule, and a safety seal is applied. This process is entirely mechanized. Overhead in this department consists of depreciation on machinery, maintenance of machinery, supervision, fringe benefits, lights, and power. Finally, the filled capsules are transferred to the bottling department.
- *Bottling*: In the bottling department, the capsules are loaded into a hopper, automatically counted into bottles, which are then mechanically capped. Workers then manually pack the correct number of bottles into boxes to ship to retailers.

Types of Processes

Production at Healthblend is an example of sequential processing. **Sequential processing** requires that units pass through one process before they can be worked on in the next process in the sequence. Exhibit 17-1 shows the sequential pattern of the manufacture of Healthblend's minerals, herbs, and vitamins.

Thus, in a process firm, units typically pass through a series of producing departments where each department or process brings a product one step closer to completion. In each department, materials, labor, and overhead may be needed. Upon completion of a particular process, the partially completed goods are transferred to the next

Exhibit 17-1

Sequential Processing Illustrated

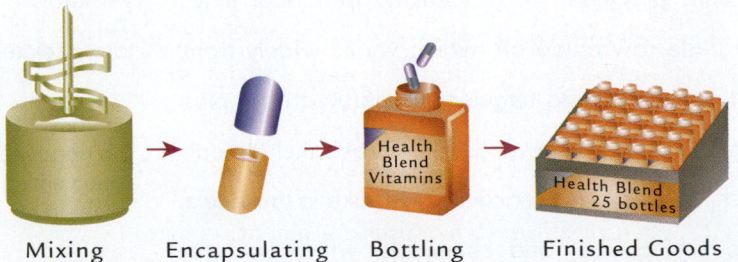

Mixing   Encapsulating   Bottling   Finished Goods

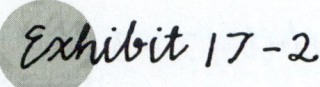

Parallel Processing Illustrated

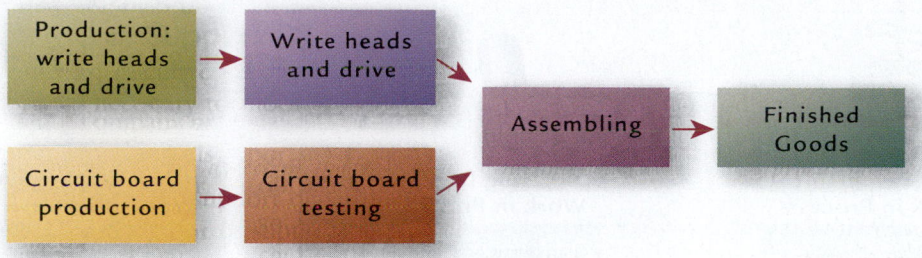

department. After passing through the final department, the goods are completed and transferred to the warehouse.

Parallel processing is another processing pattern that requires two or more sequential processes to produce a finished good. Partially completed units (e.g., two subcomponents) can be worked on simultaneously in different processes and then brought together in a final process for completion. Consider, for example, the manufacture of hard disk drives for personal computers. In one series of processes, write heads and cartridge disk drives are produced, assembled, and tested. In a second series of processes, printed circuit boards are produced and tested. These two major subcomponents then come together for assembly in the final process. Exhibit 17-2 portrays this type of process pattern. Notice that the write head and drive processes can occur independently of (or parallel to) the circuit board production and testing processes.

Other forms of parallel processes also exist. However, regardless of which processing pattern exists within a firm, all units produced share a common property. Since units are homogeneous and subjected to the same operations for a given process, each unit produced in a period should receive the same unit cost. Understanding how unit costs are computed requires an understanding of the manufacturing cost flows that take place in a process-costing firm.

How Costs Flow through the Accounts in Process Costing

The manufacturing cost flows for a process-costing system are generally the same as those for a job-order system. As raw materials are purchased, the cost of these materials flows into a raw materials inventory account. Similarly, raw materials, direct labor, and applied overhead costs flow into a work-in-process (WIP) account. When goods are completed, the cost of the completed goods is transferred from WIP to the finished goods account. Finally, as goods are sold, the cost of the finished goods is transferred to the cost of goods sold account. The journal entries generally parallel those described in a job-order costing system.

Although job-order and process cost flows are generally similar, some differences exist. In process costing, each producing department has its own WIP account. As goods are completed in one department, they are transferred to the next department. The costs attached to the goods transferred out are also transferred to the next department. Exhibit 17-3 (p. 866) illustrates this process for Healthblend. By the end of the process, all manufacturing costs end up in the final department (here, bottling) with the final product.

Will process costing be the same for sequential and parallel processing systems?

Answer:
Yes. Process-costing procedures are the same for both process settings. Costs are collected by process and are assigned to units produced by the process. Each process undergoes this costing action regardless of whether it is a member of a sequential or a parallel process system. Once goods are costed, they are transferred out to the next process.

Exhibit 17-3

Flow of Manufacturing Costs through the Accounts of a Process-Costing Firm

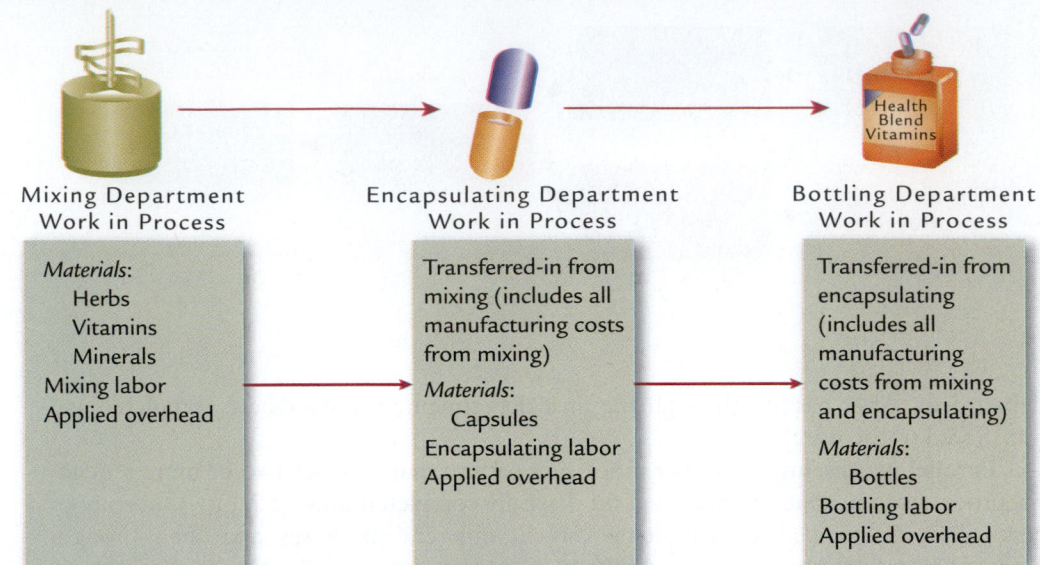

Mixing Department Work in Process	Encapsulating Department Work in Process	Bottling Department Work in Process

Materials:
   Herbs
   Vitamins
   Minerals
 Mixing labor
 Applied overhead
	Transferred-in from mixing (includes all manufacturing costs from mixing)
	 Materials:
	   Capsules
	 Encapsulating labor
	 Applied overhead
		Transferred-in from encapsulating (includes all manufacturing costs from mixing and encapsulating)
		 Materials:
		   Bottles
		 Bottling labor
		 Applied overhead

CORNERSTONE 17-1 attaches costs to the various departments and shows how the costs flow from one department to the next.

 ### CORNERSTONE 17-1   Calculating Cost Flows without Work in Process

Information:

Suppose that Healthblend decides to produce 2,000 bottles of multivitamins with the following costs (there is no beginning or ending work in process for each department):

	Mixing Department	Encapsulating Department	Bottling Department
Direct materials	$1,700	$1,000	$800
Direct labor	50	60	300
Applied overhead	450	500	600

Required:

1. Calculate the costs transferred out of each department.
2. Prepare journal entries that reflect these cost transfers.

Solution:

1.

	Mixing Department	Encapsulating Department	Bottling Department
Direct materials	$1,700	$1,000	$ 800
Direct labor	50	60	300
Applied overhead	450	500	600
Costs added	$2,200	$1,560	$1,700
Costs transferred in	0	2,200	3,760
Costs transferred out	$2,200	$3,760	$5,460

(Continued)

**CORNERSTONE
17-1**
(continued)

2. Work in Process (Encapsulating)	2,200	
Work in Process (Mixing)		2,200
Work in Process (Bottling)	3,760	
Work in Process (Encapsulating)		3,760
Finished Goods	5,460	
Work in Process (Bottling)		5,460

Cornerstone 17-1 shows that when the multivitamin mixture is transferred from the mixing department to the encapsulating department, it takes $2,200 of cost along with it. **Transferred-in costs** are costs transferred from a prior process to a subsequent process. For the subsequent process, transferred-in costs are a type of raw material cost. The same relationship exists between the encapsulating and bottling departments. The completed bottles of multivitamins are transferred to the finished goods warehouse at a total cost of $5,460.

Accumulating Costs in the Production Report

In process costing, costs are accumulated by department for a period of time. The **production report** is the document that summarizes the manufacturing activity that takes place in a process department for a given period of time. A production report contains information on costs transferred in from prior departments as well as costs added in the department such as direct materials, direct labor, and overhead; similar to the job-order cost sheet, it is subsidiary to the WIP account.

A production report provides information about the physical units processed in a department and their associated manufacturing costs. Thus, a production report is divided into the following sections and subdivisions:

- *Unit information section*: The unit information section has two major subdivisions:
  - units to account for
  - units accounted for
- *Cost information section*: The cost information section has two major subdivisions:
  - costs to account for
  - costs accounted for

A production report traces the flow of units through a department, identifies the costs charged to the department, shows the computation of unit costs, and reveals the disposition of the department's costs for the reporting period.

Service and Manufacturing Firms

Any product or service that is basically homogeneous and repetitively produced can take advantage of a process-costing approach. Let's look at three possibilities: services, manufacturing firms with a just-in-time (JIT) orientation, and traditional manufacturing firms.

Service Firms Check processing in a bank, teeth cleaning by a hygienist, air travel between Dallas and Los Angeles, and sorting mail by zip code are examples of homogeneous services that are repetitively produced. It is possible for firms engaged in service production to have WIP inventories. For example, a batch of tax returns can be partially completed at the end of a period. However, many services are provided so quickly that there are no WIP inventories. Teeth cleaning, funerals, surgical operations, and carpet cleaning are a few examples where WIP inventories virtually would be nonexistent. Therefore, process costing for services is relatively simple. The total costs for the period are divided by the number of services provided to compute unit cost:

$$\text{Unit cost} = \frac{\text{Total costs for the period}}{\text{Number of services provided}}$$

Manufacturing Firms Using JIT   Manufacturing firms may also operate without significant WIP inventories. Specifically, firms that have adopted a JIT approach try to reduce WIP inventories to very low levels. Furthermore, JIT firms usually structure their manufacturing so that process costing can be used to determine product costs.

In many JIT firms, work cells are created that produce a product or subassembly from start to finish. Costs are collected by cell for a period of time, and output for the cell is measured for the same period. Unit cost is computed by dividing the costs of the period by output of the period:

$$\text{Unit cost} = \frac{\text{Total costs for the period}}{\text{Total output of the period}}$$

There is no ambiguity concerning what costs belong to the period and how output is measured. This simplification illustrates one of the significant benefits of JIT.

Traditional Manufacturing Firms   On the other hand, traditional manufacturing firms may have significant beginning and ending WIP inventories. This causes complications in process costing due to several factors such as the presence of beginning and ending WIP inventories and different approaches to the treatment of beginning inventory cost. These complicating factors are discussed in the following sections.

OBJECTIVE **2**
Define *equivalent units* and explain their role in process costing. Explain the differences between the weighted average method and the FIFO method of accounting for process costs.

THE IMPACT OF WORK-IN-PROCESS INVENTORIES ON PROCESS COSTING

The computation of unit cost for the work performed during a period is a key part of the production report. This unit cost is needed both to compute the cost of goods transferred out of a department and to value **ending work-in-process (EWIP)** inventory. Conceptually, calculating the unit cost is easy—just divide total cost by the number of units produced. However, the presence of WIP inventories causes two problems:

- Defining the units produced can be difficult, given that some units produced during a period are complete, while those in ending inventory are not. This is handled through the concept of equivalent units of production.
- How should the costs and work of **beginning work-in-process (BWIP)** be treated? Should they be counted with the current period work and costs or treated separately? Two methods have been developed to solve this problem: the weighted average method and the FIFO method.

Equivalent Units of Production

By definition, EWIP is not complete. Thus, a unit completed and transferred out during the period is not identical (or equivalent) to one in EWIP inventory, and the cost attached to the two units should not be the same. In computing the unit cost, the output of the period must be defined, a significant issue for process costing.

To illustrate, assume that Department A had the following data for October:

Units in BWIP	—
Units completed	1,000
Units in EWIP (25 percent complete)	600
Total manufacturing costs	$11,500

What is the output in October for this department? 1,000? 1,600? If the answer is 1,000 units, the effort expended on the units in EWIP is ignored. The manufacturing costs incurred in October belong to both the units completed and to the partially completed units in EWIP. Yet, if the answer is 1,600 units, the fact that the 600 units in EWIP are only partially completed is ignored. Therefore, output must be measured so that it reflects the effort expended on both completed and partially completed units.

The solution is to calculate equivalent units of output. **Equivalent units of output** are the complete units that could have been produced given the total amount of manufacturing effort expended for the period under consideration. Determining equivalent units of output for transferred-out units is easy; a unit would not be transferred out unless it was complete. Thus, every transferred-out unit is an equivalent unit. Units remaining in EWIP inventory, however, are not complete. Thus, someone in production must "eyeball" EWIP to estimate its degree of completion. **CORNERSTONE 17-2** illustrates how to calculate equivalent units of production.

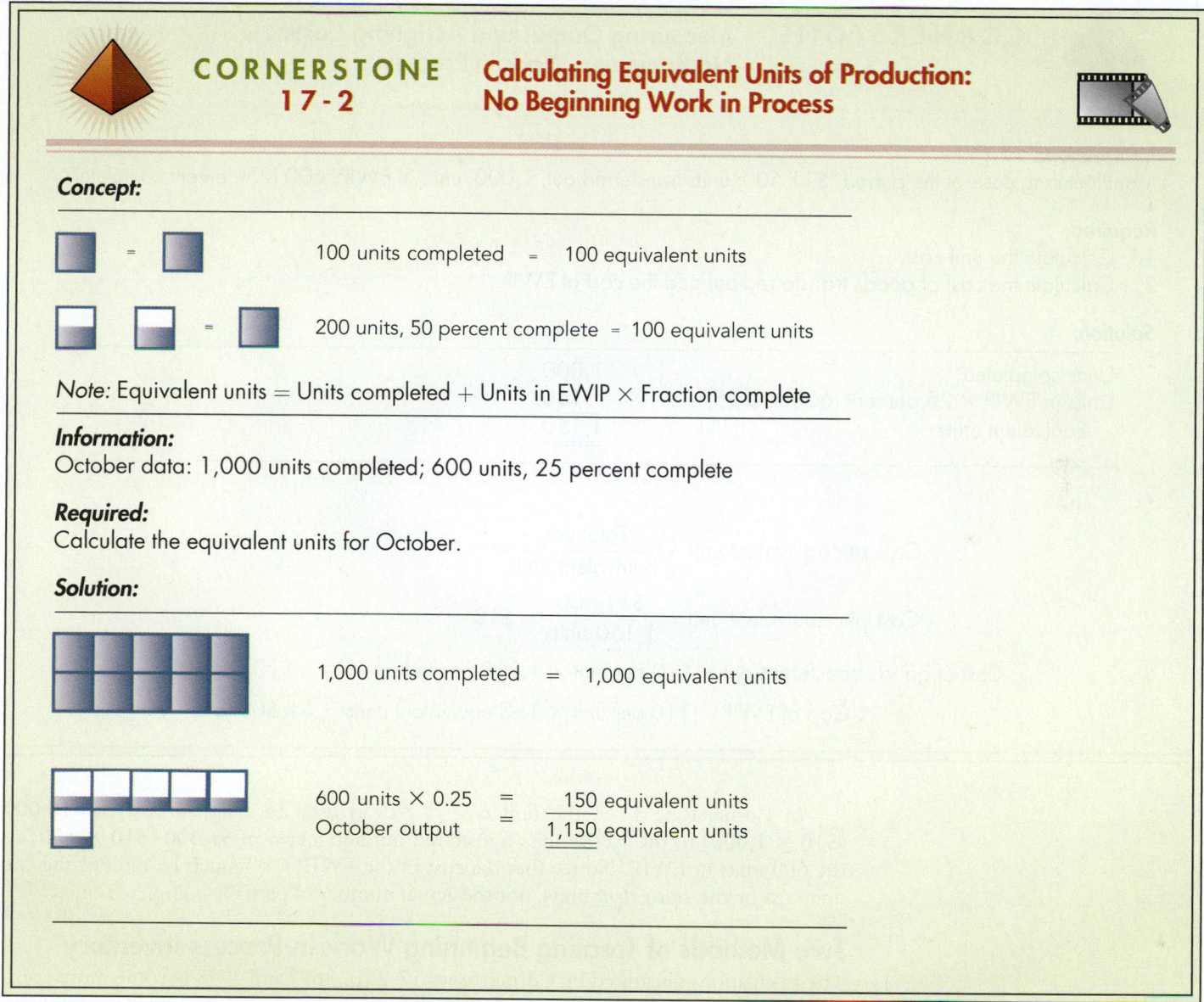

CORNERSTONE 17-2   Calculating Equivalent Units of Production: No Beginning Work in Process

Concept:

100 units completed = 100 equivalent units

200 units, 50 percent complete = 100 equivalent units

Note: Equivalent units = Units completed + Units in EWIP × Fraction complete

Information:
October data: 1,000 units completed; 600 units, 25 percent complete

Required:
Calculate the equivalent units for October.

Solution:

1,000 units completed = 1,000 equivalent units

600 units × 0.25 = 150 equivalent units
October output = 1,150 equivalent units

ETHICAL DECISIONS   Estimating the degree of completion is an act that requires judgment and ethical behavior. Overestimating the degree of completion will increase the equivalent units of output and decrease per-unit costs. This outcome, in turn, would cause an increase in both income (cost of goods sold will be less) and in assets (WIP cost will increase). Deliberately overestimating the degree of completion would clearly be in violation of ethical professional practice. ●

Knowing the output for a period and the manufacturing costs for the department for that period, a unit cost can be calculated as:

$$\text{Unit cost} = \frac{\text{Total cost}}{\text{Equivalent units}}$$

The unit cost can then be used to determine the cost of units transferred out and the cost of the units in EWIP. **CORNERSTONE 17-3** shows how the calculations are done when there is no BWIP.

CORNERSTONE 17-3

Measuring Output and Assigning Costs: No Beginning Work in Process

Information:
Manufacturing costs of the period, $11,500; units transferred out, 1,000; units in EWIP, 600 (25 percent complete).

Required:
1. Calculate the unit cost.
2. Calculate the cost of goods transferred out and the cost of EWIP.

Solution:
1.

Units completed	1,000
Units in EWIP × 25 percent (600 × 0.25)	150
Equivalent units	1,150

2.

$$\text{Cost per equivalent unit} = \frac{\text{Total cost}}{\text{Equivalent units}}$$

$$\text{Cost per equivalent unit} = \frac{\$11,500}{1,150 \text{ units}} = \$10$$

Cost of goods transferred out = $10 per unit × 1,000 equivalent units = $10,000

Cost of EWIP = $10 per unit × 150 equivalent units = $1,500

In Cornerstone 17-3, the unit cost of $10 is used to assign a cost of $10,000 ($10 × 1,000) to the 1,000 units transferred out and a cost of $1,500 ($10 × 150) to the 600 units in EWIP. Notice that the cost of the EWIP is obtained by multiplying the unit cost by the *equivalent* units, not the actual number of partially completed units.

Two Methods of Treating Beginning Work-in-Process Inventory

The calculations illustrated by Cornerstones 17-2 (p. 869) and 17-3 become more complicated when there are BWIP inventories. The work done on these partially completed units represents prior-period work, and the costs assigned to them are prior-period costs. In computing a current-period unit cost for a department, two approaches have evolved for dealing with the prior-period output and prior-period costs found in BWIP:

*   The **weighted average costing method** combines beginning inventory costs and work done with current-period costs and work to calculate this period's unit cost. In essence, the costs and work carried over from the prior period are counted as if they belong to the current period. Thus, beginning inventory work and costs are pooled with current work and costs, and an average unit cost is computed and applied to both units transferred out and units remaining in ending inventory.
*   The **FIFO costing method** separates work and costs of the equivalent units in beginning inventory from work and costs of the equivalent units produced during the current period. Only current work and costs are used to calculate this period's unit cost. It is assumed that units from beginning inventory are completed first and

transferred out. The costs of these units include the costs of the work done in the prior period as well as the current-period costs necessary to complete the units. Units started in the current period are divided into two categories: units started and completed and units started but not finished (EWIP). Units in both of these categories are valued using the current period's cost per equivalent unit.

If product costs do not change from period to period, or if there is no BWIP inventory, the FIFO and weighted average methods yield the same results. The weighted average method is discussed in more detail in the next section. Further discussion of the FIFO method is found in Appendix 17A.

Concept Q&A

What is the key difference between FIFO and the weighted average costing methods?

Answer:

FIFO treats work and costs in BWIP separately from the work and costs of the current period. Weighted average rolls back and picks up the work and costs of BWIP and counts them as if they belong to the current period's work and costs.

YOU DECIDE   Estimating the Degree of Completion

You are the cost accounting manager for a plant that produces riding lawn mowers. The plant manager receives a bonus at the end of each quarter if the plant's income meets or exceeds the quarter's budgeted income. The plant had no work in process at the beginning of the quarter; however, it had 2,500 partially completed units at the end of the quarter. During the quarter, 4,000 units were completed and sold. Manufacturing costs for the quarter totaled $2,750,000. The production line supervisors estimated that the units in process at the end of the quarter were 40 percent finished. Using this initial estimate, the income for the quarter was $190,000 less than the quarter's budgeted profit. After seeing this tentative result, the plant manager approaches you and argues that the degree of the completion is underestimated and that it should be 60 percent and not 40 percent. He explains that he personally examined the partially completed work and that 60 percent is his best guess. He would prefer that this new estimate be used.

What effect does the estimated degree of completion have on the quarter's income? Should you use the new estimate?

The two estimates produce significantly different unit costs, as illustrated below:

Measure	Equation	40% degree of completion	60% degree of completion
Total equivalent units	Equivalent units = Units completed + (Units in EWIP × Fraction complete)	4,000 + (0.40 × 2,500) = 5,000 equivalent units	4,000 + (0.60 × 2,500) = 5,500 equivalent units
Unit cost	Unit cost = Total cost/Equivalent units	$2,750,000/5,000 = $550	$2,750,000/5,500 = $500
Cost of goods sold	Cost of goods sold = Units sold × Unit cost	4,000 × $550 = $2,200,000	4,000 × $500 = $2,000,000

Compared to the 40 percent estimate, the 60 percent estimate increases income by $200,000.

Whether or not, as the cost accounting manager, you would feel comfortable using the new estimate depends on several factors. First, is the 60 percent estimate better than the 40 percent estimate? (Suppose the line supervisors insist that their estimate is correct?) Second, does the plant manager regularly participate in estimating degree of completion? If not, what are the motives for doing so this time? Answers to these questions are important. The estimate by the plant manager allows income to increase by a sufficient amount to qualify him for a bonus. If evidence favors the 40 percent estimate and the plant manager's motive is the bonus, then an ethical dilemma exists. In this case, you would need to follow the organization's established policies on the resolution of such conflicts.

Estimating the degree of completion is a vital and important part of process costing and needs to be done with care and honesty.

WEIGHTED AVERAGE COSTING

 OBJECTIVE 3
Prepare a departmental production report using the weighted average method.

The weighted average costing method treats beginning inventory costs and the accompanying equivalent output as if they belong to the current period. This is done for costs by adding the manufacturing costs in BWIP to the manufacturing costs incurred during the current period. The total cost is treated as if it were the current period's total manufacturing cost. Similarly, beginning inventory output and current period output are merged in the calculation of equivalent units. Under the weighted average method, equivalent units of output are computed by adding units completed to equivalent units in EWIP. Notice that the equivalent units in BWIP are included in the computation. Consequently, these units are counted as part of the current period's equivalent units of output.

Overview of the Weighted Average Method

The essential conceptual and computational features of the weighted average method are illustrated in **CORNERSTONE 17-4**, which uses production data for Healthblend's mixing department for July. The objective is to calculate a unit cost for July and to use this unit cost to value goods transferred out and EWIP.

 **CORNERSTONE 17-4**   **Measuring Output and Assigning Costs: Weighted Average Method**

Information:

Production:

Units in process, July 1, 75 percent complete	20,000 gallons
Units completed and transferred out	50,000 gallons
Units in process, July 31, 25 percent complete	10,000 gallons

Costs:

Work in process, July 1	$3,525
Costs added during July	$10,125

Required:

1. Calculate an output measure for July.
2. Assign costs to units transferred out and EWIP using the weighted average method.

Solution:

1. *Key:*   = 10,000 units completed   = 10,000 units, 25% complete

   Output for July:

   60,000 total units ⟶ Become 52,500 equivalent units

   Units completed:
   BWIP:

                      = 20,000

   Units Started and Completed:

                  = 30,000   50,000

   + EWIP, 25% complete:

   ▢   =   2,500
                                      52,500

(Continued)

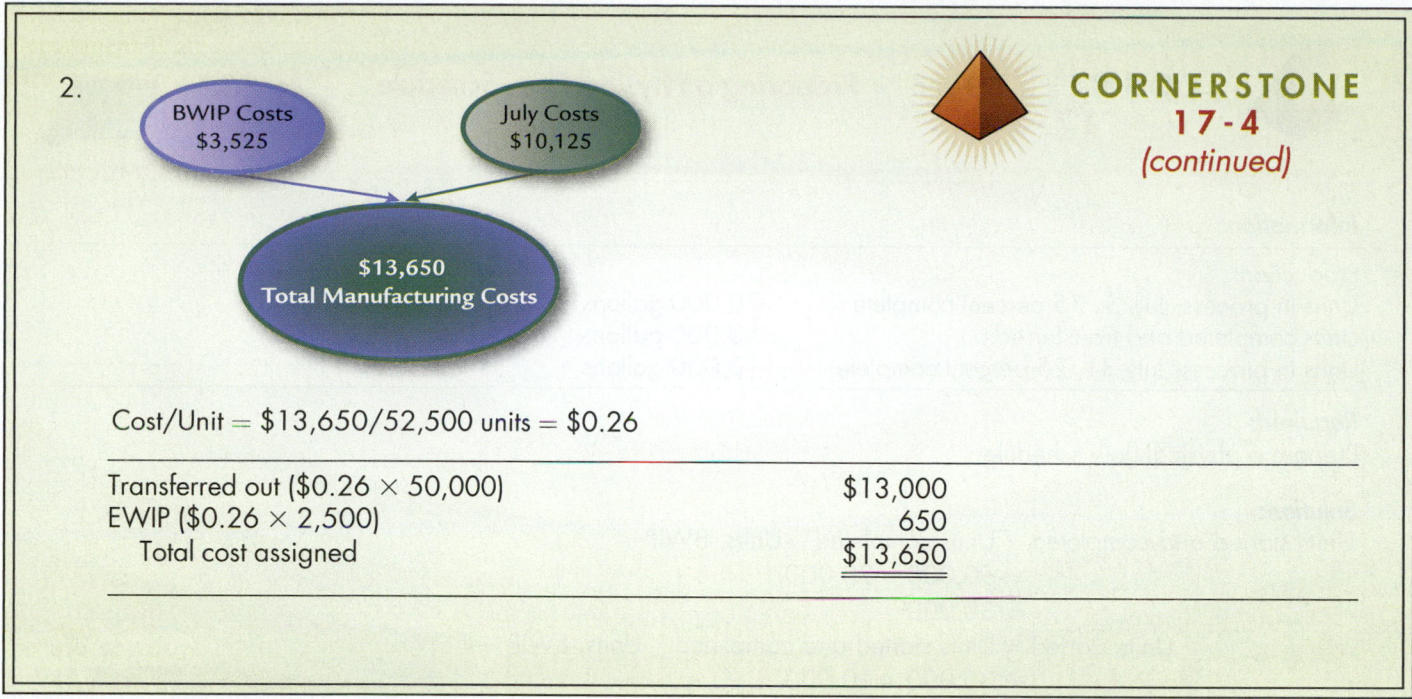

2.

Cost/Unit = $13,650/52,500 units = $0.26

Transferred out ($0.26 × 50,000)	$13,000
EWIP ($0.26 × 2,500)	650
Total cost assigned	$13,650

CORNERSTONE
17-4
(continued)

Cornerstone 17-4 illustrates that costs from BWIP are pooled with costs added to production during July. These total pooled costs ($13,650) are divided by output to obtain a unit cost which is then used to assign costs to units transferred out and to units in EWIP. On the output side, it is necessary to concentrate on the degree of completion of all units at the *end* of the period. There is no need to be concerned with the percentage of completion of BWIP inventory. The only issue is whether these units are complete or not by the end of July. Thus, equivalent units are computed by pooling manufacturing efforts from June and July.

Five Steps in Preparing a Production Report

The elements of Cornerstone 17-4 are used to prepare a production report. Recall that the production report summarizes cost and manufacturing activity for a producing department for a given period of time. The production report is subsidiary to the WIP account for a department. The following five steps describe the general pattern of a process-costing production report:

Step 1. physical flow analysis
Step 2. calculation of equivalent units
Step 3. computation of unit cost
Step 4. valuation of inventories (goods transferred out and EWIP)
Step 5. cost reconciliation

These five steps provide structure to the method of accounting for process costs.

Step 1: Physical Flow Analysis   The purpose of Step 1 is to trace the physical units of production. Physical units are not equivalent units. They are units that may be in any stage of completion. The **physical flow schedule**, like the one shown by **CORNERSTONE 17-5** (p. 874) for Healthblend's mixing department, provides an analysis of the physical flow of units. To construct the schedule from the information given, the following two calculations are needed:

Units started and completed = Total units completed − Units in BWIP
Units started = Units started and completed + Units in EWIP

CORNERSTONE 17-5   Preparing a Physical Flow Schedule

Information:

Production:
Units in process, July 1, 75 percent complete	20,000 gallons
Units completed and transferred out	50,000 gallons
Units in process, July 31, 25 percent complete	10,000 gallons

Required:
Prepare a physical flow schedule.

Solution:

Units started and completed = Units completed − Units, BWIP
$$= 50,000 - 20,000$$
$$= 30,000$$

Units started = Units started and completed + Units, EWIP
$$= 30,000 + 10,000$$
$$= 40,000$$

Physical flow schedule:

Units to account for:
Units in BWIP (75 percent complete)	20,000	
Units started during the period	40,000	
Total units to account for	60,000	

Units accounted for:
Units completed and transferred out:		
Started and completed	30,000	
From beginning work in process	20,000	50,000
Units in EWIP (25 percent complete)		10,000
Total units accounted for		60,000

Notice from Cornerstone 17-5 that the "Total units to account for" must equal the "Total units accounted for." The physical flow schedule is important because it contains the information needed to calculate equivalent units (Step 2).

Step 2: Calculation of Equivalent Units Given the information in the physical flow schedule, the weighted average equivalent units for July can be calculated as follows:

Notice that July's output is measured as 52,500 units, 50,000 units completed and transferred out and 2,500 equivalent units from ending inventory (10,000 × 25 percent). What about beginning inventory? There were 20,000 units in beginning inventory, 75 percent complete. These units are included in the 50,000 units completed and transferred out during the month. Thus, the weighted average method treats beginning inventory units as if they were started and completed during the current period. Because of this, the equivalent unit schedule shown in Step 2 shows only the total units completed. There is no need to show whether the units completed are from July or from BWIP as was done by Cornerstone 17-4 (p. 872).

Step 3: Computation of Unit Cost In addition to July output, July manufacturing costs are needed to compute a unit cost. The weighted average method rolls back and includes the manufacturing costs associated with the units in BWIP and counts these costs as if they belong to July. Thus, as Cornerstone 17-4 illustrated, these costs are pooled to define total manufacturing costs for July:

$$\text{Total manufacturing costs for July} = \text{WIP, July} + \text{Costs added in July}$$
$$\$13,650 = \$3,525 + \$10,125$$

The manufacturing costs carried over from the prior period ($3,525) are treated as if they were current period costs. The unit cost for July is computed as follows:

$$\text{Unit cost} = \text{Total costs/Equivalent units for July}$$
$$\$0.26 = \$13,650/52,500$$

Step 4: Valuation of Inventories Cornerstone 17-4 also showed how to value goods transferred out and EWIP. Using the unit cost of $0.26, we value the two inventories as follows:

- Cost of goods transferred to the encapsulating department is $13,000 (50,000 units × $0.26 per unit)
- Cost of EWIP is $650 (2,500 equivalent units × $0.26 per unit).

Units completed (from Step 1), equivalent units in EWIP (from Step 2), and the unit cost (from Step 3) are all needed to value both goods transferred out and EWIP.

Step 5: Cost Reconciliation The total manufacturing costs assigned to inventories are as follows:

Goods transferred out	$13,000
Goods in EWIP	650
Total costs accounted for	$13,650

The manufacturing costs to account for are also $13,650.

BWIP	$ 3,525
Incurred during the period	10,125
Total costs to account for	$13,650

Thus, **cost reconciliation** checks to see if the costs to account for are exactly assigned to inventories. Remember, the total costs assigned to goods transferred out and to EWIP must agree with the total costs in BWIP and the manufacturing costs incurred during the current period.

Production Report

Steps 1 through 5 provide all of the information needed to prepare a production report for the mixing department for July. The method for preparing this report is shown in **CORNERSTONE 17-6**.

CORNERSTONE 17-6

Preparing a Production Report: Weighted Average Method

Information:
Refer to Steps 1 to 5 of the Healthblend Company example.

Required:
Prepare a production report.

(Continued)

Solution:

CORNERSTONE
17-6
(continued)

Healthblend Company
Mixing Department
Production Report For July 2011
(Weighted Average Method)

UNIT INFORMATION

Physical Flow

Units to account for:		Units accounted for:	
Units in beginning work in process	20,000	Units completed	50,000
Units started	40,000	Units in ending work in process	10,000
Total units to account for	60,000	Total units accounted for	60,000

Equivalent Units

Units completed	50,000
Units in ending work in process	2,500
Total equivalent units	52,500

COST INFORMATION

Costs to account for:	
Beginning work in process	$ 3,525
Incurred during the period	10,125
Total costs to account for	$13,650
Cost per equivalent unit	$ 0.26

	Transferred Out	Ending Work in Process	Total
Costs accounted for:			
Goods transferred out ($0.26 × 50,000)	$13,000	—	$13,000
Goods in ending work in process ($0.26 × 2,500)	—	$650	650
Total costs accounted for	$13,000	$650	$13,650

Evaluation of the Weighted Average Method

The major benefit of the weighted average method is simplicity. By treating units in BWIP as belonging to the current period, all equivalent units belong to the same category when it comes to calculating unit costs. Thus, unit cost computations are simplified. The main disadvantage of this method is reduced accuracy in computing unit costs for current period output and for units in BWIP. If the unit cost in a process is relatively stable from one period to the next, the weighted average method is reasonably accurate. However, if the price of manufacturing inputs increases significantly from one period to the next, the unit cost of current output is understated, and the unit cost of BWIP units is overstated. If greater accuracy in computing unit costs is desired, a company should use the FIFO method to determine unit costs.

OBJECTIVE 4
Explain how nonuniform inputs and multiple processing departments affect process costing.

MULTIPLE INPUTS AND MULTIPLE DEPARTMENTS

Accounting for production under process costing is complicated by nonuniform application of manufacturing inputs and the presence of multiple processing departments. How process-costing methods address these complications will now be discussed.

Nonuniform Application of Manufacturing Inputs

Up to this point, we have assumed that WIP being 60 percent complete meant that 60 percent of materials, labor, and overhead needed to complete the process have been used and that another 40 percent are needed to finish the units. In other words, we have assumed that manufacturing inputs are applied uniformly as the manufacturing process unfolds.

risteski goce, 2010/Shutterstock.com

Here's the Real Kicker

Stillwater Designs builds a limited number of items on site. The manufacturing activities include designing and building prototypes and rebuilding of warranty returns (only of certain models such as the square L7s). Rebuilding of warranty returns follows a process manufacturing structure. All units are alike and go through the same steps.

- The woofers are removed from the cabinet, and the cabinet is stripped and cleaned.
- The speaker is torn down to its structures with all chemicals and glues removed.
- The speaker is passed through a demagnetizing process so that all metal pieces and shavings can be removed.
- The speaker is rebuilt using a recone kit to replace damaged and defective parts.

Once the cabinets and speakers are ready, they are assembled, tested, and boxed. Assembly involves placing the speakers in the cabinets and connecting the wire harnesses. There are two tests:

- In-phase test: The in-phase test is to make sure that the power is hooked up correctly.
- Air leak test: The product must be properly sealed because an air leak can damage the woofer.

Notice that the rebuilding and assembly processes are sequential. When finished, the rebuilt speakers and cabinets are transferred from the rebuilding process to the assembly process. Also, note that the cost of the final product is the cost of the materials transferred in from the rebuilding process, plus the cost of the other components and materials added, plus the assembly conversion cost. For example, at the end of the assembly process, the assembled product is packaged for delivery. In this simple process application, it is easy to see that some materials are added at the beginning of the assembly process (the cabinet and components) and some at the end of the process (packaging). The **Kicker** example also shows how process costing handles multiple departments.

Courtesy of Kicker

Assuming uniform application of conversion costs (direct labor and overhead) is not unreasonable. Direct labor input is usually needed throughout the process, and overhead is normally assigned on the basis of direct labor hours. Direct materials, on the other hand, are not as likely to be applied uniformly. In many instances, materials are added at either the beginning or the end of the process.

For example, look at the differences in Healthblend's three departments. In the mixing and encapsulating departments, all materials are added at the beginning of the process. However, in the bottling department, materials are added both at the beginning (filled capsules and bottles) and at the end (bottle caps and boxes).

WIP in the mixing department that is 50 percent complete with respect to conversion inputs would be 100 percent complete with respect to the material inputs. But WIP in bottling that is 50 percent complete with respect to conversion would be 100 percent complete with respect to bottles and transferred-in capsules, but 0 percent complete with respect to bottle caps and boxes.

Different percentage completion figures for manufacturing inputs pose a problem for the calculation of equivalent units, unit cost, and valuation of EWIP (Steps 2–4). In such cases, equivalent unit calculations are done for each category of manufacturing input. Thus, equivalent units are calculated for each category of materials and for conversion cost. Next, a unit cost for each category is computed. The individual category costs are then used in Step 4 to cost out EWIP. The total unit cost is used to calculate the cost of goods transferred out in the same way as when there was only one input category. **CORNERSTONE 17-7** (p. 878) shows how to calculate Steps 2 through 4 with nonuniform inputs, using the weighted average method.

CORNERSTONE 17-7

Calculating Equivalent Units, Unit Costs, and Valuing Inventories with Nonuniform Inputs

Information:
The mixing department of Healthblend has the following data for September:

Production:
Units in process, September 1, 50 percent complete*	10,000
Units completed and transferred out	60,000
Units in process, September 30, 40 percent complete*	20,000

Costs:
WIP, September 1:
Materials	$ 1,600
Conversion costs	200
Total	$ 1,800

Current costs:
Materials	$12,000
Conversion costs	3,200
Total	$15,200

*With respect to conversion costs, all materials are added at the beginning of the process.

Required:
Calculate Steps 2 through 4 using the weighted average method.

Solution:
1. **Step 2:** Calculation of equivalent units, nonuniform application:

	Materials	Conversion
Units completed	60,000	60,000
Add: Units in ending work in process × Fraction complete:		
20,000 × 100 percent	20,000	—
20,000 × 40 percent	—	8,000
Equivalent units of output	80,000	68,000

2. **Step 3:** Calculation of unit costs:

   Unit materials cost = ($1,600 + $12,000)/80,000 = $0.17

   Unit conversion cost = ($200 + $3,200)/68,000 = $0.05

   Total unit cost = Unit materials cost + Unit conversion cost

   = $0.17 + $0.05

   = $0.22 per completed unit

3. **Step 4:** Valuation of EWIP and goods transferred out:
   The cost of EWIP is as follows:

Materials: $0.17 × 20,000	$3,400
Conversion: $0.05 × 8,000	400
Total cost	$3,800

Valuation of goods transferred out:

$$\text{Cost of goods transferred out} = \$0.22 \times 60,000 = \$13,200$$

Production Report: Weighted Average Method

Exhibit 17-4

Healthblend Company
Mixing Department
Production Report for September 2011
(Weighted Average Method)

UNIT INFORMATION

Units to account for:		Units accounted for:	
Units in beginning work in process	10,000	Units completed	60,000
Units started during the period	70,000	Units in ending work in process	20,000
Total units to account for	80,000	Total units accounted for	80,000

Equivalent Units

	Materials	Conversion
Units completed	60,000	60,000
Units in ending work in process	20,000	8,000
Total equivalent units	80,000	68,000

COST INFORMATION

	Materials	Conversion	Total
Costs to account for:			
Beginning work in process	$ 1,600	$ 200	$ 1,800
Incurred during the period	12,000	3,200	15,200
Total costs to account for	$13,600	$3,400	$17,000
Cost per equivalent unit	$ 0.17	$ 0.05	$ 0.22

	Transferred Out	Ending Work in Process	Total
Costs accounted for:			
Goods transferred out ($0.22 × 60,000)	$13,200	—	$13,200
Goods in ending work in process:			
Materials ($0.17 × 20,000)	—	$3,400	3,400
Conversion ($0.05 × 8,000)	—	400	400
Total costs accounted for	$13,200	$3,800	$17,000

For illustrative purposes, a production report, based on Cornerstone 17-7, is shown in Exhibit 17-4. As the example shows, applying manufacturing inputs at different stages of a process poses no serious problems, though it requires more effort.

Multiple Departments

In process manufacturing, some departments receive partially completed goods from prior departments. The usual approach is to treat transferred-in goods as a separate material category when calculating equivalent units. Thus, the department receiving transferred-in goods would have *three* input categories:

- one for the transferred-in materials
- one for materials added
- one for conversion costs

In dealing with transferred-in goods, two important points should be remembered.

- The cost of this material is the cost of the goods transferred out as computed in the prior department.

Concept Q&A

How are transferred-in goods viewed and treated by the department receiving them?

- The units started in the subsequent department correspond to the units transferred out from the prior department (assuming that there is a one-to-one relationship between the output measures of both departments).

CORNERSTONE 17-8 shows how to calculate the first three process-costing steps when there are transferred-in goods, where Steps 2 and 3 are restricted to the transferred-in category.

 **CORNERSTONE 17-8**   **Calculating the Physical Flow Schedule, Equivalent Units, and Unit Costs with Transferred-In Goods**

Information:

For September, Healthblend's encapsulating department had 15,000 units in beginning inventory (with transferred-in costs of $3,000) and completed 70,000 units during the month. Further, the mixing department completed and transferred out 60,000 units at a cost of $13,200 in September.

Required:

1. Prepare a physical flow schedule with transferred-in goods.
2. Calculate equivalent units for the transferred-in category.
3. Calculate unit cost for the transferred-in category.

Solution:

1. In constructing a physical flow schedule for the encapsulating department, its dependence on the mixing department must be considered:

Units to account for:	
Units in BWIP	15,000
Units transferred in during September	60,000
Total units to account for	75,000
Units accounted for:	
Units completed and transferred out:	
Started and completed	55,000
From BWIP	15,000
Units in EWIP	5,000
Total units accounted for	75,000

2. Equivalent units for the transferred-in category only:

Transferred in:	
Units completed	70,000
Add: Units in EWIP × Fraction complete (5,000 × 100 percent)*	5,000
Equivalent units of output	75,000

*Remember that the EWIP is 100 percent complete with respect to transferred-in costs, not to all costs of the encapsulating department.

3. To find the unit cost for the transferred-in category, we add the cost of the units transferred in from mixing in September to the transferred-in costs in BWIP and divide by transferred-in equivalent units:

$$\text{Unit cost (transferred-in category)} = (\$13,200 + \$3,000)/75,000 \text{ units}$$
$$= \$16,200/75,000 \text{ units} = \$0.216$$

The only additional complication introduced in the analysis for a subsequent department is the presence of the transferred-in category. As shown, dealing with this category is similar to handling any other category. However, it must be remembered that the current cost of this special type of raw material is the cost of the units transferred in from the prior process and that the units transferred in are the units started.

APPENDIX 17A: PRODUCTION REPORT— FIRST-IN, FIRST-OUT COSTING

O B J E C T I V E ⑤
Prepare a departmental production report using the FIFO method.

Under the FIFO costing method, the equivalent units and manufacturing costs in BWIP are excluded from the current period unit cost calculation. This method recognizes that the work and costs carried over from the prior period legitimately belong to that period.

Differences between the First-In, First-Out and Weighted Average Methods

If changes occur in the prices of the manufacturing inputs from one period to the next, then FIFO produces a more accurate (i.e., more current) unit cost than does the weighted average method. A more accurate unit cost means better cost control, better pricing decisions, and so on. Keep in mind that if the period is as short as a week or a month, however, the unit costs calculated under the two methods will not likely differ much. In that case, the FIFO method has little, if anything, to offer over the weighted average method. Perhaps for this reason, many firms use the weighted average method.

Since FIFO excludes prior-period work and costs, it is necessary to create two categories of completed units:

- BWIP units (FIFO assumes that units in BWIP are completed first, before any new units are started)
- Units started and completed during the current period

For example, assume that a department had 20,000 units in BWIP and completed and transferred out a total of 50,000 units. Of the 50,000 completed units, 20,000 are the units initially found in WIP. The remaining 30,000 were started and completed during the current period.

These two categories of completed units are needed in the FIFO method so that each category can be costed correctly. For the units started and completed, the unit cost is obtained by dividing total current manufacturing costs by the current period equivalent output. However, for the BWIP units, the total associated manufacturing costs are the sum of the prior period costs plus the costs incurred in the current period to finish the units.

Example of the First-In, First-Out Method

CORNERSTONE 17-9 shows how FIFO handles output and cost calculations using the same Healthblend data used for the weighted average method (Cornerstone 17-4) to highlight the differences between the two methods. Cornerstone 17-9 shows that the equivalent unit calculation measures only the output for the current period.

 **C O R N E R S T O N E   17-9**   Calculating Output and Cost Assignments: First-In, First-Out Method

Information:

Production:

Units in process, July 1, 75 percent complete	20,000 gallons
Units completed and transferred out	50,000 gallons
Units in process, July 31, 25 percent complete	10,000 gallons

(Continued)

**CORNERSTONE
17-9**
(continued)

Costs:
Work in process, July 1	$ 3,525
Costs added during July	$10,125

Required:
1. Calculate the output measure for July.
2. Assign costs to units transferred out and EWIP using the FIFO method.

Solution:
1.

Key: = 10,000 units completed   = 10,000 units, 25% complete

Output for July:
60,000 total units ———→ Become 37,500 equivalent units

BWIP: To be completed (20,000 × 25%):

   =   5,000

+ Units started and completed:

   =   30,000

+ EWIP: Started but not completed (10,000 × 0.25)

        =   2,500
                             =   37,500

2. Costs for July:

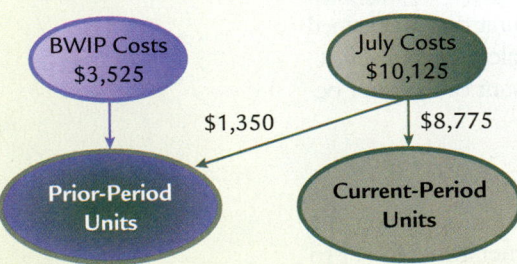

Cost/Unit = $10,125/37,500 units = $0.27

Transferred out:	
Cost from BWIP (prior period carryover)	$ 3,525
To complete BWIP ($0.27 × 5,000)	1,350
Started and completed ($0.27 × 30,000)	8,100
Total	$12,975
EWIP ($0.27 × 2,500)	675
Total cost assigned	$13,650

Cornerstone 17-9 reveals that costs from the current period and costs carried over from June (beginning inventory costs) are not pooled to calculate July's unit cost. The unit cost calculation uses only July (current period) costs. The five steps to cost out production follow.

Step 1: Physical Flow Analysis The purpose of Step 1 is to trace the physical units of production. As with the weighted average method, in the FIFO method, a physical flow schedule is prepared. This schedule is identical for both methods and is presented again in Exhibit 17-5. (See Cornerstone 17-5, p. 874 for details on how to prepare this schedule.)

Exhibit 17-5

Physical Flow Schedule

Units to account for:		
Units in beginning work in process (75 percent complete)		20,000
Units started during the period		40,000
Total units to account for		60,000
Units accounted for:		
Units completed:		
Started and completed	30,000	
From beginning work in process	20,000	50,000
Units in ending work in process (25 percent complete)		10,000
Total units accounted for		60,000

Step 2: Calculation of Equivalent Units From the equivalent unit computation, one difference between weighted average and FIFO becomes immediately apparent. Under FIFO, the equivalent units in BWIP (work done in the prior period) are not counted as part of the total equivalent work. Only the equivalent work to be completed this period is counted. The equivalent work to be completed for the units from the prior period is computed by multiplying the number of units in BWIP by the percentage of work remaining. Since in this example the percentage of work done in the prior period is 75 percent, the percentage left to be completed this period is 25 percent, or an equivalent of 5,000 additional units of work.

The effect of excluding prior period effort is to produce the current period equivalent output. Recall that under the weighted average method, 52,500 equivalent units were computed for this month. Under FIFO, only 37,500 units are calculated for the same month. These 37,500 units represent current period output. The difference, of course, is explained by the fact that the weighted average method rolls back and counts the 15,000 equivalent units of prior period work (20,000 units BWIP × 75 percent) as belonging to this period.

Step 3: Computation of Unit Cost The additional manufacturing costs incurred in the current period are $10,125. Thus, the current period unit manufacturing cost is $10,125/37,500, or $0.27. Notice that the costs of beginning inventory are excluded from this calculation. Only current period manufacturing costs are used.

Step 4: Valuation of Inventories Cornerstone 17-9 shows FIFO values for EWIP and goods transferred out. Since all equivalent units in ending work in process are current period units, the cost of EWIP is simply $0.27 × 2,500, or $675, the same value that the weighted average method would produce. However, when it comes to valuing goods transferred out, a significant difference emerges between the weighted average method and FIFO.

Under weighted average, the cost of goods transferred out is simply the unit cost times the units completed. Under FIFO, however, there are two categories of completed units:

- Units started and completed (30,000)
- Units from beginning inventory (20,000)

The cost of each category must be calculated separately and then summed to obtain the total cost of goods transferred out. The cost of the first category is calculated as follows:

$$\text{Cost of units started and completed} = \text{Unit cost} \times \text{Units started and completed}$$
$$= \$0.27 \times 30,000$$
$$= \$8,100$$

For these units, the use of the current period unit cost is entirely appropriate. However, the cost of BWIP units that were transferred out is another matter. These units started the period with $3,525 of manufacturing costs already incurred and 15,000 units of equivalent output already completed. To finish these units, the equivalent of 5,000 units were needed. Thus, the cost of these units being transferred out is:

$$\text{Cost of units in BWIP} = \text{Prior period costs} + (\text{Unit cost} \times \text{Equivalent units to complete})$$
$$= \$3,525 + (\$0.27 \times 5,000)$$
$$= \$4,875$$

The unit cost of these 20,000 units, then, is about $0.244 ($4,875/20,000), a blend of prior period and current manufacturing costs.

Step 5: Cost Reconciliation The total costs assigned to production are as follows:

Goods transferred out:	
Units in BWIP	$ 4,875
Units started and completed	8,100
Goods in EWIP	675
Total costs accounted for	$13,650

The total manufacturing costs to account for during the period are:

BWIP	$ 3,525
Incurred during the period	10,125
Total costs to account for	$13,650

The costs assigned, thus, equal the costs to account for. With the completion of Step 5, the production report can be prepared. **CORNERSTONE 17-10** shows how to prepare this report for FIFO.

CORNERSTONE 17-10

Preparing a Production Report: First-In, First-Out Method

Information:
Refer to the five steps for the Healthblend Company.

Required:
Prepare a production report for July 2011 (FIFO method).

Solution:

Healthblend Company
Mixing Department
Production Report For July 2011
(FIFO Method)

UNIT INFORMATION

Units to account for:

Units in beginning work in process	20,000
Units started during the period	40,000
Total units to account for	60,000

	Physical Flow	Equivalent Units
Units accounted for:		
Units started and completed	30,000	30,000
Units completed from beginning work in process	20,000	5,000
Units in ending work in process	10,000	2,500
Total units accounted for	60,000	37,500

COST INFORMATION

Costs to account for:

Beginning work in process	$ 3,525
Incurred during the period	10,125
Total costs to account for	$13,650
Cost per equivalent unit	$ 0.27

	Transferred Out	Ending Work in Process	Total
Costs accounted for:			
Units in beginning work in process:			
From prior period	$ 3,525	—	$ 3,525
From current period ($0.27 × 5,000)	1,350	—	1,350
Units started and completed ($0.27 × 30,000)	8,100	—	8,100
Goods in ending work in process ($0.27 × 2,500)	—	$675	675
Total costs accounted for	$12,975	$675	$13,650

SUMMARY OF LEARNING OBJECTIVES

LO1.   **Describe the basic characteristics and cost flows associated with process manufacturing.**
- Cost flows under process costing are similar to those under job-order costing.
- Raw materials are purchased and debited to the raw materials account.
- Direct materials used in production, direct labor, and applied overhead are charged to the WIP account.
- In a production process with several processes, there is a WIP account for each department or process. Goods completed in one department are transferred out to the next department.
- When units are completed in the final department or process, their cost is credited to Work in Process and is debited to Finished Goods.

LO2.   **Define *equivalent units* and explain their role in process costing. Explain the differences between the weighted average method and the FIFO method of accounting for process costs.**
- Equivalent units of production are the complete units that could have been produced given the total amount of manufacturing effort expended during the period.
- The number of physical units is multiplied by the percentage of completion to calculate equivalent units.
- The weighted average costing method combines beginning inventory costs to compute unit costs.
- The FIFO costing method separates units in beginning inventory from those produced during the current period.

LO3.   **Prepare a departmental production report using the weighted average method.**
- The production report summarizes the manufacturing activity occurring in a department for a given period.
- It discloses information concerning the physical flow of units, equivalent units, unit costs, and the disposition of the manufacturing costs associated with the period.

LO4.   **Explain how nonuniform inputs and multiple processing departments affect process costing.**
- Nonuniform inputs and multiple departments are easily handled by process-costing methods.
- When inputs are added nonuniformly, equivalent units and unit cost are calculated for each separate input category.
- The adjustment for multiple departments is also relatively simple.
- The goods transferred from a prior department to a subsequent department are treated as a material added at the beginning of the process. Thus, there is a separate transferred-in materials category, where the equivalent units and unit cost are calculated.

LO5.   ***(Appendix 17A)* Prepare a departmental production report using the FIFO method.**
- A production report prepared according to the FIFO method separates the cost of BWIP from the cost of the current period.
- BWIP is assumed to be completed and transferred out first.
- Costs from BWIP are not pooled with the current period costs in computing unit cost. Additionally, equivalent units of production exclude work done in the prior period.
- When calculating the cost of goods transferred out, the prior period costs are added to the costs of completing the units in BWIP, and then these costs are added to the costs of units started and completed.

SUMMARY OF IMPORTANT EQUATIONS

1. Unit cost $= \dfrac{\text{Total cost}}{\text{Equivalent units}}$

2. Units started and completed = Total units completed − Units in BWIP

   Units started = Units started and completed + Units in EWIP

CORNERSTONE 17-1	Calculating cost flows without work in process (p. 866)
CORNERSTONE 17-2	Calculating equivalent units of production: no beginning work in process (p. 869)
CORNERSTONE 17-3	Measuring output and assigning costs: no beginning work in process (p. 870)
CORNERSTONE 17-4	Measuring output and assigning costs: weighted average method (p. 872)
CORNERSTONE 17-5	Preparing a physical flow schedule (p. 874)
CORNERSTONE 17-6	Preparing a production report: weighted average method (p. 875)
CORNERSTONE 17-7	Calculating equivalent units, unit costs, and valuing inventories with nonuniform inputs (p. 878)
CORNERSTONE 17-8	Calculating the physical flow schedule, equivalent units, and unit costs with transferred-in goods (p. 880)
CORNERSTONE 17-9	*(Appendix 17A)* Calculating output and cost assignments: first-in, first-out method (p. 881)
CORNERSTONE 17-10	*(Appendix 17A)* Preparing a production report: first-in, first-out method (p. 885)

CORNERSTONES FOR CHAPTER 17

KEY TERMS

Beginning work-in-process (BWIP) (p. 868)
Cost reconciliation (p. 875)
Ending work-in-process (EWIP) (p. 868)
Equivalent units of output (p. 868)
FIFO costing method (p. 870)
Parallel processing (p. 865)

Physical flow schedule (p. 873)
Production report (p. 867)
Sequential processing (p. 864)
Transferred-in costs (p. 867)
Weighted average costing method (p. 870)

REVIEW PROBLEMS

I. Process Costing

Springville Company, which uses the weighted average method, produces a product that passes through two departments: Blending and Cooking. In the blending department, all materials are added at the beginning of the process. All other manufacturing inputs are added uniformly. The following information pertains to the blending department for February:

a. BWIP, February 1: 100,000 pounds, 40 percent complete with respect to conversion costs. The costs assigned to this work are as follows:

Materials	$20,000
Labor	10,000
Overhead	30,000

(Continued)

b. EWIP, February 28: 50,000 pounds, 60 percent complete with respect to conversion costs.

c. Units completed and transferred out: 370,000 pounds. The following costs were added during the month:

Materials	$211,000
Labor	100,000
Overhead	270,000

Required:

1. Prepare a physical flow schedule.

2. Prepare a schedule of equivalent units.

3. Compute the cost per equivalent unit.

4. Compute the cost of goods transferred out and the cost of EWIP.

5. Prepare a cost reconciliation.

Solution:

1. Physical flow schedule:

Units to account for:		
Units in BWIP	100,000	
Units started	320,000	
Total units to account for	420,000	
Units accounted for:		
Units completed and transferred out:		
Started and completed	270,000	
From BWIP	100,000	370,000
Units in EWIP		50,000
Total units accounted for		420,000

2. Schedule of equivalent units:

	Materials	Conversion
Units completed	370,000	370,000
Units in EWIP × Fraction complete:		
Materials (50,000 × 100 percent)	50,000	—
Conversion (50,000 × 60 percent)	—	30,000
Equivalent units of output	420,000	400,000

3. Cost per equivalent unit:

Materials unit cost = ($20,000 + $211,000)/420,000 units

= $0.550

Conversion unit cost = ($40,000 + $370,000)/400,000 units

= $1.025

Total unit cost = $1.575 per equivalent unit

4. Cost of goods transferred out and cost of EWIP:

Cost of goods transferred out = $1.575 × 370,000

= $582,750

Cost of EWIP = ($0.550 × 50,000) + ($1.025 × 30,000)

= $58,250

5. Cost reconciliation:

Costs to account for:		
BWIP		$ 60,000
Incurred during the period		581,000
Total costs to account for		$641,000
Costs accounted for:		
Goods transferred out		$582,750
WIP		58,250
Total costs accounted for		$641,000

II. Process Costing

Now suppose that Springville Company uses the FIFO method for inventory valuations. Springville produces a product that passes through two departments: Blending and Cooking. In the blending department, all materials are added at the beginning of the process. All other manufacturing inputs are added uniformly. The following information pertains to the blending department for February:

a. BWIP, February 1: 100,000 pounds, 40 percent complete with respect to conversion costs. The costs assigned to this work are as follows:

Materials	$20,000
Labor	10,000
Overhead	30,000

b. EWIP, February 28: 50,000 pounds, 60 percent complete with respect to conversion costs.
c. Units completed and transferred out: 370,000 pounds. The following costs were added during the month:

Materials	$211,000
Labor	100,000
Overhead	270,000

Required:

1. Prepare a physical flow schedule.
2. Prepare a schedule of equivalent units.
3. Compute the cost per equivalent unit.
4. Compute the cost of goods transferred out and the cost of EWIP.

Solution:

1. Physical flow schedule:

Units to account for:		
Units in BWIP	100,000	
Units started	320,000	
Total units to account for	420,000	
Units accounted for:		
Units completed and transferred out:		
Started and completed	270,000	
From BWIP	100,000	370,000
Units in EWIP		50,000
Total units accounted for		420,000

2. Schedule of equivalent units:

	Materials	Conversion
Units started and completed	270,000	270,000
Units, BWIP × Percentage complete	—	60,000
Units, EWIP × Percentage complete:		
Direct materials (50,000 × 100 percent)	50,000	—
Conversion costs (50,000 × 60 percent)	—	30,000
Equivalent units of output	320,000	360,000

3. Cost per equivalent unit:

DM unit cost $211,000/320,000 units	$0.659*
CC unit cost $370,000/360,000 units	1.028*
Total cost per equivalent unit	$1.687

*Rounded.

(Continued)

4. Cost of goods transferred out and cost of EWIP:

$$\text{Cost of goods transferred out} = (\$1.687 \times 270{,}000) + (\$1.028 \times 60{,}000) + \$60{,}000 = \$577{,}170$$
$$\text{Cost of EWIP} = (\$0.659 \times 50{,}000) + (\$1.028 \times 30{,}000) = \$63{,}790$$

DISCUSSION QUESTIONS

1. Describe the differences between process costing and job-order costing.
2. Distinguish between sequential processing and parallel processing.
3. What are the similarities in and differences between the manufacturing cost flows for job-order firms and process firms?
4. What journal entry would be made as goods are transferred out from one department to another department? From the final department to the warehouse?
5. How would process costing for services differ from process costing for manufactured goods?
6. How does the adoption of a JIT approach to manufacturing affect process costing?
7. What are equivalent units? Why are they needed in a process-costing system?
8. Under the weighted average method, how are prior period costs and output treated? How are they treated under the FIFO method?
9. Under what conditions will the weighted average and FIFO methods give the same results?
10. Describe the five steps in accounting for the manufacturing activity of a processing department, and explain how they interrelate.
11. What is a production report? What purpose does this report serve?
12. How is the equivalent unit calculation affected when materials are added at the beginning or end of the process rather than uniformly throughout the process?
13. Explain why transferred-in costs are a special type of raw material for the receiving department.
14. In assigning costs to goods transferred out, how do the weighted average and FIFO methods differ?

MULTIPLE-CHOICE EXERCISES

17-1 Process costing works well whenever

a. heterogeneous products pass through a series of processes and receive different doses of materials, labor, and overhead.
b. material cost is accumulated by process and conversion cost is accumulated by process.
c. homogeneous products pass through a series of processes and receive similar doses of conversion inputs and different doses of material inputs.
d. homogeneous products pass through a series of processes and receive similar amounts of materials, labor, and overhead.
e. none of the above.

17-2 Job-order costing works well whenever

a. homogeneous products pass through a series of processes and receive similar doses of conversion inputs and different doses of material inputs.
b. homogeneous products pass through a series of processes and receive similar doses of materials, labor, and overhead.
c. heterogeneous products pass through a series of processes and receive different doses of materials, labor, and overhead.
d. material cost is accumulated by process and conversion cost is accumulated by process.

17-3 Sequential processing is characterized by

a. a pattern where partially completed units are worked on simultaneously.
b. a pattern where partially completed units must pass through one process before they can be worked on in later processes.
c. a pattern where different partially completed units must pass through parallel processes before being brought together in a final process.

d. a pattern where partially completed units must be purchased from outside suppliers and delivered to the final process in a sequential time mode.
e. none of these.

17-4 To record the transfer of costs from a prior process to a subsequent process, the following entry would be made:

a. debit Finished Goods and credit Work in Process.
b. debit Work in Process (subsequent department) and credit Transferred-In Materials.
c. debit Work in Process (prior department) and credit Work in Process (subsequent department).
d. debit Work in Process (subsequent department) and credit Work in Process (prior department)
e. none of the above.

17-5 The costs transferred from a prior process to a subsequent process are

a. treated as another type of conversion cost.
b. referred to as transferred-out costs (for the receiving department).
c. referred to as the cost of goods transferred in (for the transferring department).
d. all of the above.
e. none of the above.

17-6 During the month of May, the grinding department produced and transferred out 2,000 units. EWIP had 500 units, 40 percent complete. There was no BWIP. The equivalent units of output for May are

a. 2,000.
b. 2,500.
c. 2,300.
d. 2,200.
e. none of these.

Use the following information for Multiple-Choice Exercises 17-7 through 17-9:
The mixing department incurred $30,000 of manufacturing costs during the month of September. The department transferred out 2,000 units and had 500 equivalent units in EWIP. There was no BWIP.

17-7 The unit cost for the month of September is

a. $12.
b. $10.
c. $24.
d. $120.
e. $100.

17-8 The cost of goods transferred out is

a. $20,000.
b. $24,000.
c. $28,800.
d. $18,000.
e. none of these.

17-9 The cost of EWIP is

a. $600.
b. $4,800.
c. $4,000.
d. $8,800.
e. none of these.

17-10 During May, Kimbrell Manufacturing completed and transferred out 100,000 units. In EWIP, there were 25,000 units, 40 percent complete. Using the weighted average method, the equivalent units are

a. 100,000 units.
b. 125,000 units.
c. 105,000 units.
d. 110,000 units.
e. 120,000 units.

17-11 During June, Kimbrell Manufacturing completed and transferred out 100,000 units. In EWIP, there were 25,000 units, 80 percent complete. Using the weighted average method, the equivalent units are

a. 100,000 units.
b. 125,000 units.
c. 105,000 units.
d. 110,000 units.
e. 120,000 units.

17-12 For August, Kimbrell Manufacturing has costs in BWIP equal to $112,500. During August, the cost incurred was $450,000. Using the weighted average method, Kimbrell had 125,000 equivalent units for August. There were 100,000 units transferred out during the month. The cost of goods transferred out is

a. $500,000.
b. $400,000.
c. $450,000.
d. $360,000.
e. $50,000.

17-13 For September, Murphy Company has manufacturing costs in BWIP equal to $100,000. During September, the manufacturing costs incurred were $550,000. Using the weighted average method, Murphy had 100,000 equivalent units for September. The equivalent unit cost for September is

a. $1.00.
b. $7.50.
c. $6.50.
d. $6.00.
e. $6.62.

17-14 During June, Faust Manufacturing started and completed 80,000 units. In BWIP, there were 25,000 units, 80 percent complete. In EWIP, there were 25,000 units, 60 percent complete. Using FIFO, the equivalent units are

a. 80,000 units.
b. 95,000 units.
c. 85,000 units.
d. 115,000 units.
e. 100,000 units.

17-15 During July, Faust Manufacturing started and completed 80,000 units. In BWIP, there were 25,000 units, 20 percent complete. In EWIP, there were 25,000 units, 80 percent complete. Using FIFO, the equivalent units are

a. 80,000 units.
b. 120,000 units.
c. 65,000 units.
d. 85,000 units.
e. 100,000 units.

17-16 Assume for August that Faust Manufacturing has manufacturing costs in BWIP equal to $80,000. During August, the cost incurred was $720,000. Using the FIFO method, Faust had 120,000 equivalent units for August. The cost per equivalent unit for August is

a. $6.12.
b. $6.50.
c. $5.60.
d. $6.00.
e. $6.67.

17-17 For August, Lanny Company had 25,000 units in BWIP, 40 percent complete, with costs equal to $36,000. During August, the cost incurred was $450,000. Using the FIFO method, Lanny had 125,000 equivalent units for August. There were 100,000 units transferred out during the month. The cost of goods transferred out is

a. $500,000.
b. $360,000.
c. $450,000.
d. $400,000.
e. $50,000.

17-18 When materials are added either at the beginning or the end of the process, a unit cost should be calculated for the

a. materials and conversion categories.
b. materials category only.
c. materials and labor categories.
d. conversion category only.
e. labor category only.

17-19 With nonuniform inputs, the cost of EWIP is calculated by

a. adding the materials cost to the conversion cost.
b. subtracting the cost of goods transferred out from the total cost of materials.
c. multiplying the unit cost in each input category by the equivalent units of each input found in EWIP.
d. multiplying the total unit cost by the units in EWIP.
e. none of the above.

17-20 Transferred-in goods are treated by the receiving department as

a. units started for the period.
b. a material added at the beginning of the process.
c. a category of materials separate from conversion costs.
d. all of these.
e. none of these.

CORNERSTONE EXERCISES

Cornerstone Exercise 17-21 Basic Cost Flows

OBJECTIVE 1
CORNERSTONE 17-1

Grano Company produces 18-ounce boxes of a wheat cereal in three departments: Mixing, Cooking, and Packaging. During August, Grano produced 150,000 boxes with the following costs:

	Mixing Department	Cooking Department	Packaging Department
Direct materials	$275,000	$125,000	$110,000
Direct labor	40,000	25,000	60,000
Applied overhead	50,000	27,500	77,500

Required:
1. Calculate the costs transferred out of each department.
2. Prepare journal entries that reflect these cost transfers.

Cornerstone Exercise 17-22 Equivalent Units, No Beginning Work in Process

OBJECTIVE 2
CORNERSTONE 17-2

Hromas Manufacturing produces cylinders used in internal combustion engines. During June, Hromas' welding department had the following data:

Units in BWIP	—
Units completed	50,000
Units in EWIP (40 percent complete)	7,500

Required:
Calculate June's output for the welding department in equivalent units of production.

Cornerstone Exercise 17-23 Unit Cost, Valuing Goods Transferred Out and EWIP

OBJECTIVE 2
CORNERSTONE 17-3

During May, the molding department of Lawler Foundry completed and transferred out 42,000 units. At the end of May, there were 15,000 units in process, 60 percent complete. Paterson incurred manufacturing costs totaling $612,000.

Required:
1. Calculate the unit cost.
2. Calculate the cost of goods transferred out and the cost of EWIP.

Cornerstone Exercise 17-24 Weighted Average Method, Unit Cost, Valuing Inventories

OBJECTIVE 3
CORNERSTONE 17-4

Manzer Enterprises produces premier raspberry jam. Output is measured in pints. Manzer uses the weighted average method. During January, Manzer had the following production data:

Units in process, January 1, 60 percent complete	36,000 pints
Units completed and transferred out	240,000 pints
Units in process, January 31, 40 percent complete	75,000 pints

(Continued)

Costs:	
Work in process, January 1	$ 54,000
Costs added during January	351,000

Required:
1. Using the weighted average method, calculate the equivalent units for January.
2. Calculate the unit cost for January.
3. Assign costs to units transferred out and EWIP.

OBJECTIVE **3**
CORNERSTONE 17-5

Cornerstone Exercise 17-25 Physical Flow Schedule

Buckner Inc. just finished its second month of operations. Buckner mass produces integrated circuits. The following production information is provided for December:

Units in process, December 1, 80 percent complete	100,000
Units completed and transferred out	475,000
Units in process, December 31, 60 percent complete	75,000

Required:
Prepare a physical flow schedule.

OBJECTIVE **3**
CORNERSTONE 17-6

Cornerstone Exercise 17-26 Production Report, Weighted Average

Murray Inc. manufactures bicycle frames in two departments: Cutting and Welding. Murray uses the weighted average method. Manufacturing costs are added uniformly throughout the process. The following are cost and production data for the cutting department for October:

Production:	
Units in process, October 1, 40 percent complete	10,000
Units completed and transferred out	68,000
Units in process, October 31, 60 percent complete	20,000
Costs:	
WIP, October 1	$ 80,000
Costs added during October	1,520,000

Required:
Prepare a production report for the cutting department.

OBJECTIVE **4**
CORNERSTONE 17-7

Cornerstone Exercise 17-27 Nonuniform Inputs, Weighted Average

Integer Inc. had the following production and cost information for its fabrication department during April (materials are added at the beginning of the fabrication process):

Production:	
Units in process, April 1, 50 percent complete with respect to conversion	5,000
Units completed	32,600
Units in process, April 30, 60 percent complete	6,000
Costs:	
Work in process, April 1:	
Materials	$ 20,000
Conversion costs	15,000
Total	$ 35,000
Current costs:	
Materials	$ 62,500
Conversion costs	105,000
Total	$167,500

Integer uses the weighted average method.

Required:
1. Prepare an equivalent units schedule.
2. Calculate the unit cost. (*Note:* Round answers to two decimal places).
3. Calculate the cost of units transferred out and the cost of EWIP.

Cornerstone Exercise 17-28 Transferred-In Cost

OBJECTIVE **4**
CORNERSTONE 17-8

Fuerza Inc. produces a protein drink. The product is sold by the gallon. The company has two departments: Mixing and Bottling. For August, the bottling department had 60,000 gallons in beginning inventory (with transferred-in costs of $213,000) and completed 262,500 gallons during the month. Further, the mixing department completed and transferred out 240,000 gallons at a cost of $687,000 in August.

Required:

1. Prepare a physical flow schedule for the bottling department.
2. Calculate equivalent units for the transferred-in category.
3. Calculate the unit cost for the transferred-in category.

Use the following information for Cornerstone Exercises 17-29 and 17-30:

Inca Inc. produces soft drinks. Mixing is the first department and its output is measured in gallons. Inca uses the FIFO method. All manufacturing costs are added uniformly. For July, the mixing department provided the following information:

Production:	
Units in process, July 1, 80 percent complete	24,000 gallons
Units completed and transferred out	138,000 gallons
Units in process, July 31, 75 percent complete	16,000 gallons
Costs:	
Work in process, July 1	$ 24,000
Costs added during July	301,000

Cornerstone Exercise 17-29 *(Appendix 17A)* First-In, First-Out Method; Equivalent Units

OBJECTIVE **5**
CORNERSTONE 17-9

Refer to the information for Inca Inc. above.

Required:

1. Calculate the equivalent units for August.
2. Calculate the unit cost. (*Note:* Round to two decimal places).
3. Assign costs to units transferred out and EWIP using the FIFO method.

Cornerstone Exercise 17-30 *(Appendix 17A)* FIFO; Production Report

OBJECTIVE **5**
CORNERSTONE 17-10

Refer to the information for Inca Inc. above.

Required:

Prepare a production report.

EXERCISES

Exercise 17-31 Basic Cost Flows

OBJECTIVE **1**

Curtis Company produces a common machine component for industrial equipment in three departments: molding, grinding, and finishing. The following data are available for October:

	Molding Department	Grinding Department	Finishing Department
Direct materials	$71,600	$ 7,600	$4,900
Direct labor	4,600	11,200	7,600
Applied overhead	7,000	54,400	7,600

During October, 6,000 components were completed. There is no beginning or ending WIP in any department.

(Continued)

Required:
1. Prepare a schedule showing, for each department, the cost of direct materials, direct labor, applied overhead, product transferred in from a prior department, and total manufacturing cost.
2. Calculate the unit cost.

OBJECTIVE 1

Exercise 17-32 Journal Entries, Basic Cost Flows

In November, Curtis Company had the following cost flows:

	Molding Department	Grinding Department	Finishing Department
Direct materials	$55,800	$ 15,000	$ 8,600
Direct labor	4,000	6,800	5,800
Applied overhead	4,200	30,200	5,600
Transferred-in cost:			
From Molding		64,000	
From Grinding			116,000
Total cost	$64,000	$116,000	$136,000

Required:
1. Prepare the journal entries to transfer costs from (a) Molding to Grinding, (b) Grinding to Finishing, and (c) Finishing to Finished Goods.
2. **Conceptual Connection:** Explain how the journal entries differ from a job-order cost system.

OBJECTIVE 2

Exercise 17-33 Equivalent Units, Unit Cost, Valuation of Goods Transferred Out and Ending Work in Process

The cooking department had the following data for the month of March:

Units in BWIP	—
Units completed	4,800
Units in EWIP (40 percent complete)	500
Total manufacturing costs	$9,000

Required:
1. What is the output in equivalent units for March?
2. What is the unit manufacturing cost for March?
3. Compute the cost of goods transferred out for March.
4. Calculate the value of March's EWIP.

OBJECTIVE 3

Exercise 17-34 Weighted Average Method, Equivalent Units

Lambert Company produces a product where all manufacturing inputs are applied uniformly. Lambert produced the following physical flow schedule for April:

Units to account for:	
Units in BWIP (40 percent complete)	45,000
Units started	105,000
Total units to account for	150,000
Units accounted for:	
Units completed:	
From BWIP	30,000
Started and completed	96,000
	126,000
Units, EWIP (75 percent complete)	24,000
Total units accounted for	150,000

Required:
Prepare a schedule of equivalent units using the weighted average method.

Exercise 17-35 Weighted Average Method, Unit Cost, Valuing Inventories

OBJECTIVE 3

Lorenen Inc. manufactures products that pass through two or more processes. During June, equivalent units were computed using the weighted average method:

Units completed	35,600
Units in EWIP × Fraction complete (24,000 × 60 percent)	14,400
Equivalent units of output	50,000

April's costs to account for are as follows:

BWIP (10,000 units, 80 percent complete)	$ 32,000
Materials	60,000
Conversion costs	24,000
Total	$116,000

Required:

1. Calculate the unit cost for June using the weighted average method.
2. Using the weighted average method, determine the cost of EWIP and the cost of the goods transferred out.
3. **Conceptual Connection:** Lorenen had just finished implementing a series of measures designed to reduce the unit cost to $2.00 and was assured that this had been achieved and should be realized for June's production; yet upon seeing the unit cost for June, the president of the company was disappointed. Can you explain why the full effect of the cost reductions may not show up in June? What can you suggest to overcome this problem?

Exercise 17-36 Weighted Average Method, Unit Costs, Valuing Inventories

OBJECTIVE 3

Byford Inc. produces a product that passes through two processes. During November, equivalent units were calculated using the weighted average method:

Units completed	196,000
Add: Units in EWIP × Fraction complete	
(60,000 × 40 percent)	24,000
Equivalent units of output (weighted average)	220,000
Less: Units in BWIP × Fraction complete	
(50,000 × 70 percent)	35,000
Equivalent units of output (FIFO)	185,000

The costs that Byford had to account for during the month of November were as follows:

BWIP	$ 107 000
Costs added	993,000
Total	$1,100,000

Required:

1. Using the weighted average method, determine unit cost.
2. Under the weighted average method, what is the total cost of units transferred out? What is the cost assigned to units in ending inventory?
3. **Conceptual Connection:** Bill Johnson, the manager of Byford, is considering switching from Weighted Average to FIFO. Explain the key differences between the two approaches and make a recommendation to Bill about which method should be used.

Exercise 17-37 Physical Flow Schedule

OBJECTIVE 3

The following information was obtained for the grinding department of Harlan Company for May:

a. BWIP had 91,500 units, 30 percent complete with respect to manufacturing costs.
b. EWIP had 25,200 units, 25 percent complete with respect to manufacturing costs.
c. Started 99,000 units in May.

Required:

Prepare a physical flow schedule.

OBJECTIVE ③

Exercise 17-38 Physical Flow Schedule

Nelrok Company manufactures fertilizer. Department 1 mixes the chemicals required for the fertilizer. The following data are for the year:

BWIP (40 percent complete)	25,000
Units started	142,500
Units in EWIP (60 percent complete)	35,000

Required:

Prepare a physical flow schedule.

OBJECTIVE ③

Exercise 17-39 Production Report, Weighted Average

Mino Inc. manufactures chocolate syrup in three departments: Cooking, Mixing, and Bottling. Mino uses the weighted average method. The following are cost and production data for the cooking department for April (*Note:* Assume that units are measured in gallons):

Production:	
Units in process, April 1, 60 percent complete	20,000
Units completed and transferred out	50,000
Units in process, April 30, 20 percent complete	10,000
Costs:	
WIP, April 1	$ 93,600
Costs added during April	314,600

Required:

Prepare a production report for the cooking department.

OBJECTIVE ④

Exercise 17-40 Nonuniform Inputs, Equivalent Units

Terry Linens Inc. manufactures bed and bath linens. The bath linens department sews terry cloth into towels of various sizes. Terry uses the weighted average method. All materials are added at the beginning of the process. The following data are for the bath linens department for August:

Production:	
Units in process, August 1, 25 percent complete*	10,000
Units completed and transferred out	60,000
Units in process, August 31, 60 percent complete	20,000

*With respect to conversion costs.

Required:

Calculate equivalent units of production for the bath linens department for August.

OBJECTIVE ④

Exercise 17-41 Unit Cost and Cost Assignment, Nonuniform Inputs

Loran Inc. had the following equivalent units schedule and cost for its fabrication department during September:

	Materials	Conversion
Units completed	180,000	180,000
Add: Units in ending WIP × Fraction complete (60,000 × 60%)	60,000	36,000
Equivalent units of output	240,000	216,000
Costs:		
Work in process, September 1:		
Materials	$ 147,000	
Conversion costs	7,875	
Total	$ 154,875	
Current costs:		
Materials	$1,053,000	
Conversion costs	236,205	
Total	$1,289,205	

Required:

1. Calculate the unit cost for materials, for conversion, and in total for the fabrication department for September.
2. Calculate the cost of units transferred out and the cost of EWIP.

Exercise 17-42 Nonuniform Inputs, Transferred-In Cost

OBJECTIVE ❹

Drysdale Dairy produces a variety of dairy products. In Department 12, cream (transferred in from Department 6) and other materials (sugar and flavorings) are mixed at the beginning of the process and churned to make ice cream. The following data are for Department 12 for August:

ILLUSTRATING
RELATIONSHIPS

Production:	
Units in process, August 1, 25 percent complete*	40,000
Units completed and transferred out	120,000
Units in process, August 31, 60 percent complete*	30,000

*With respect to conversion costs.

Required:

1. Prepare a physical flow schedule for the month.
2. Using the Weighted Average Method, calculate equivalent units for the following categories: transferred-in, materials, and conversion.

Exercise 17-43 Transferred-In Cost

OBJECTIVE ❹

Golding's finishing department had the following data for July:

	Transferred-In	Materials	Conversion
Units transferred out	60,000	60,000	60,000
Units in EWIP	15,000	15,000	9,000
Equivalent units	75,000	75,000	69,000

Costs:	
Work in process, July 1:	
Transferred-in from fabricating	$ 2,100
Materials	1,500
Conversion costs	3,000
Total	$ 6,600
Current costs:	
Transferred-in from fabricating	$30,900
Materials	22,500
Conversion costs	45,300
Total	$98,700

Required:

1. Calculate unit costs for the following categories: transferred-in, materials, and conversion.
2. Calculate total unit cost.

Exercise 17-44 (Appendix 17A) First-In, First-Out Method; Equivalent Units

OBJECTIVE ❺

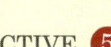

Lawson Company produces a product where all manufacturing inputs are applied uniformly. Lawson produced the following physical flow schedule for March:

Units to account for:	
Units in BWIP (40 percent complete)	15,000
Units started	35,000
Total units to account for	50,000
Units accounted for:	
Units completed:	
From BWIP	10,000
Started and completed	32,000
	42,000
Units, EWIP (75 percent complete)	8,000
Total units accounted for	50,000

Required:

Prepare a schedule of equivalent units using the FIFO method.

OBJECTIVE

Exercise 17-45 *(Appendix 17A)* First-In, First-Out Method; Unit Cost; Valuing Inventories

Loren Inc. manufactures products that pass through two or more processes. During April, equivalent units were computed using the FIFO method:

Units started and completed	4,600
Units in BWIP × Fraction to complete (60 percent)	840
Units in EWIP × Fraction complete (4,000 × 60 percent)	2,400
Equivalent units of output (FIFO)	7,840
April's costs to account for are as follows:	
BWIP (40 percent complete)	$ 1,120
Materials	10,000
Conversion cost	4,000
Total	$15,120

Required:

1. Calculate the unit cost for April using the FIFO method. (*Note:* Round to two decimal places.)
2. Using the FIFO method, determine the cost of EWIP and the cost of the goods transferred out.

PROBLEMS

OBJECTIVE

Problem 17-46 Basic FLows, Equivalent Units

Bowman Company produces an arthritis medication that passes through two departments: Mixing and Tableting. Bowman uses the weighted average method. Data for February for Mixing is as follows: BWIP was zero; EWIP had 7,200 units, 50 percent complete; and 84,000 units were started. Tableting's data for February is as follows: BWIP was 4,800 units, 20 percent complete; and 2,400 units were in EWIP, 40 percent complete.

Required:

1. For Mixing, calculate the (a) number of units transferred to Tableting, and (b) equivalent units of production.
2. For Tableting, calculate the number of units transferred out to Finished Goods.
3. **Conceptual Connection:** Suppose that the units in the mixing department are measured in ounces, while the units in Tableting are measured in bottles of 100 tablets, with a total weight of eight ounces (excluding the bottle). Decide how you would treat units that are measured differently, and then repeat Requirement 2 using this approach.

OBJECTIVE

Problem 17-47 Steps in Preparing a Production Report

Several years ago, **Stillwater Designs** expanded its market by becoming an original equipment supplier to **DaimlerChrysler**. At the time, DaimlerChrysler wanted to offer a high-end **Kicker** audio package for its Dodge Neon SRT4 line. As part of this effort, Stillwater Designs produced the plastic cabinet prototypes that housed the Kicker speakers and amplifiers. After producing the prototype cabinets, the production was outsourced while assembly remained in-house. Stillwater Designs assembled the product by placing the speakers and amplifiers (produced according to specifications by outside manufacturers) in the plastic cabinets. Plastic cabinets and Kicker speaker and amplifier components are added at the beginning of the assembly process.

Assume that **Stillwater Designs** uses the weighted average method to cost out the audio package. The following are cost and production data for the assembly process for April:

Production:	
Units in process, April 1, 60 percent complete	60,000
Units completed and transferred out	150,000
Units in process, April 30, 20 percent complete	30,000
Costs:	
WIP, April 1:	
Plastic cabinets	$ 1,200,000
Kicker components	12,600,000
Conversion costs	5,400,000
Costs added during April:	
Plastic cabinets	$ 2,400,000
Kicker components	25,200,000
Conversion costs	8,640,000

Required:

1. Prepare a physical flow analysis for the assembly department for the month of April.
2. Calculate equivalent units of production for the assembly department for the month of April.
3. Calculate unit cost for the assembly department for the month of April.
4. Calculate the cost of units transferred out and the cost of EWIP inventory.
5. Prepare a cost reconciliation for the assembly department for the month of April.

Problem 17-48 Steps for a Production Report

OBJECTIVE **1 3**

Refer to the data of **Problem 17-47**.

Required:

1. Prepare a production report for the assembly department for the month of April.
2. **Conceptual Connection:** Write a one-page report that compares the purpose and content of the production report with the job-order cost sheet.

Use the following information for Problems 17-49 and 17-50:
Alfombra Inc. manufactures throw rugs. The throw rugs department weaves cloth and yarn into throw rugs of various sizes. Alfombra uses the weighted average method. Materials are added uniformly throughout the weaving process. In August, Alfombra switched from FIFO to the weighted average method. The following data are for the throw-rug department for August:

Production:
Units in process, August 1, 60 percent complete	50,000
Units completed and transferred out	150,000
Units in process, August 31, 60 percent complete	50,000

Costs:
WIP, August 1	$180,000
Current costs	756,000
Total	$936,000

Problem 17-49 Equivalent Units, Unit Cost, Weighted Average

OBJECTIVE **1 2 3 4**

Refer to the information for Alfombra Inc. above.

Required:

1. Prepare a physical flow analysis for the throw-rug department for August.
2. Calculate equivalent units of production for the throw-rug department for August.
3. Calculate the unit cost for the throw-rug department for August.
4. Show that the cost per unit calculated in Requirement 3 is a weighted average of the FIFO cost per equivalent unit in BWIP and the FIFO cost per equivalent unit for August. (*Hint:* The weights are in proportion to the number of units from each source.)

Problem 17-50 Production Report

OBJECTIVE **3**

Refer to the information for Alfombra Inc. above. The owner of Alfombra insisted on a formal report that provided all the details of the weighted average method. In the manufacturing process, all materials are added uniformly throughout the process.

Required:

Prepare a production report for the bath linens department for August using the weighted average method.

Problem 17-51 Weighted Average Method, Physical Flow, Equivalent Units, Unit Costs, Cost Assignment

OBJECTIVE

Mimasca Inc. manufactures various holiday masks. Each mask is shaped from a piece of rubber in the molding department. The masks are then transferred to the finishing department, where they are painted and have elastic bands attached. Mimasca uses the weighted average method. In May, the molding department reported the following data:

a. BWIP consisted of 15,000 units, 20 percent complete. Cost in beginning inventory totaled $1,656.
b. Costs added to production during the month were $26,094.

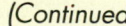
(Continued)

c. At the end of the month, 45,000 units were transferred out to Finishing. Then, 5,000 units remained in EWIP, 25 percent complete.

Required:
1. Prepare a physical flow schedule.
2. Calculate equivalent units of production.
3. Compute unit cost.
4. Calculate the cost of goods transferred to Finishing at the end of the month. Calculate the cost of ending inventory.
5. **Conceptual Connection:** Assume that the masks are inspected at the end of the molding process. Of the 45,000 units inspected, 2,500 are rejected as faulty and are discarded. Thus, only 42,500 units are transferred to the finishing department. The manager of Mimasca considers all such spoilage as abnormal and does not want to assign any of this cost to the 42,500 good units produced and transferred to finishing. Your task is to determine the cost of this spoilage of 2,500 units and then to discuss how you would account for this spoilage cost. Now suppose that the manager feels that this spoilage cost is just part of the cost of producing the good units transferred out. Therefore, he wants to assign this cost to the good production. Explain how this would be handled. (*Hint:* Spoiled units are a type of output, and equivalent units of spoilage can be calculated.)

Use the following information for Problems 17-52 and 17-53:
Millie Company produces a product that passes through an assembly process and a finishing process. All manufacturing costs are added uniformly for both processes. The following information was obtained for the assembly department for June:

a. WIP, June 1, had 24,000 units (60 percent completed) and the following costs:

Direct materials	$186,256
Direct labor	64,864
Overhead applied	34,400

b. During June, 70,000 units were completed and transferred to the finishing department, and the following costs were added to production:

Direct materials	$267,880
Direct labor	253,000
Overhead applied	117,600

c. On June 30, there were 10,000 partially completed units in process. These units were 70 percent complete.

OBJECTIVE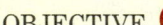

Problem 17-52 Weighted Average Method, Single-Department Analysis

Refer to the information for Millie Company above.

Required:
Prepare a production report for the assembly department for June using the weighted average method of costing. The report should disclose the physical flow of units, equivalent units, and unit costs and should track the disposition of manufacturing costs.

OBJECTIVE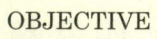

Problem 17-53 First-In, First-Out Method; Single-Department Analysis; One Cost Category

Refer to the information for Millie Company above.

Required:
Prepare a production report for the assembly department for June using the FIFO method of costing. The report should disclose the physical flow of units, equivalent units, and unit costs and should track the disposition of manufacturing costs. (*Note:* Carry the unit cost computation to four decimal places.)

Problem 17-54 Weighted Average Method, Separate Materials Cost

OBJECTIVE ❶ ❷ ❸

Janbo Company produces a variety of stationery products. One product, sealing wax sticks, passes through two processes: blending and molding. The weighted average method is used to account for the costs of production. After blending, the resulting product is sent to the molding department, where it is poured into molds and cooled. The following information relates to the blending process for August:

a. WIP, August 1, had 30,000 pounds, 20 percent complete. Costs associated with partially completed units were:

Materials	$220,000
Direct labor	30,000
Overhead applied	20,000

b. WIP, August 31, had 50,000 pounds, 40 percent complete.
c. Units completed and transferred out totaled 480,000 pounds. Costs added during the month were (all inputs are added uniformly):

Materials	$5,800,000
Direct labor	4,250,000
Overhead applied	1,292,500

Required:

1. Prepare (a) a physical flow schedule and (b) an equivalent unit schedule.
2. Calculate the unit cost. (*Note:* Round to three decimal places.)
3. Compute the cost of EWIP and the cost of goods transferred out.
4. Prepare a cost reconciliation.
5. Suppose that the materials added uniformly in blending are paraffin and pigment and that the manager of the company wants to know how much each of these materials costs per equivalent unit produced. The costs of the materials in BWIP are as follows:

Paraffin	$120,000
Pigment	100,000

The costs of the materials added during the month are also given:

Paraffin	$3,060,000
Pigment	2,550,000

Prepare an equivalent unit schedule with cost categories for each material. Calculate the cost per unit for each type of material.

Problem 17-55 Weighted Average Method, Journal Entries

OBJECTIVE ❶ ❷ ❸ ❹

Seacrest Company uses a process costing system. The company manufactures a product that is processed in two departments: A and B. As work is completed, it is transferred out. The following summarizes the production activity and costs for November:

	Department A	Department B
Beginning inventories:		
Physical units	5,000	8,000
Costs:		
Transferred in	—	$ 45,320
Direct materials	$10,000	—
Conversion costs	$ 6,900	$ 16,800
Current production:		
Units started	25,000	?
Units transferred out	28,000	33,000
Costs:		
Transferred in	—	?
Direct materials	$57,800	$ 37,950
Conversion costs	$95,220	$128,100
Percentage completion:		
Beginning inventory	40%	50%
Ending inventory	80%	50%

(Continued)

Required:

1. Using the weighted average method, prepare the following for Department A: (a) a physical flow schedule, (b) an equivalent unit calculation, (c) calculation of unit costs (*Note:* Round to two decimal places), (d) cost of EWIP and cost of goods transferred out, and (e) a cost reconciliation.

2. **Conceptual Connection:** Prepare journal entries that show the flow of manufacturing costs for Department A. Use a conversion cost control account for conversion costs. Many firms are now combining direct labor and overhead costs into one category. They are not tracking direct labor separately. Offer some reasons for this practice.

OBJECTIVE ❶❷❸❹   **Problem 17-56** *(Appendix 17A)* **First-In, First-Out Method; Journal Entries**

Refer to **Problem 17-55.**

Required:

1. Using the FIFO method, prepare the following for Department A: (a) a physical flow schedule, (b) an equivalent unit calculation, (c) calculation of unit costs (*Note:* Round to two decimal places), (d) cost of EWIP and cost of goods transferred out, and (e) a cost reconciliation.

2. **Conceptual Connection:** Prepare journal entries that show the flow of manufacturing costs for Department A. Use a conversion cost control account for conversion costs. Many firms are now combining direct labor and overhead costs into one category. They are not tracking direct labor separately. Offer some reasons for this practice.

OBJECTIVE ❶❷❹❺   **Problem 17-57** **Weighted Average Method, Nonuniform Inputs, Multiple Departments**

Benson Pharmaceuticals uses a process-costing system to compute the unit costs of the over-the-counter cold remedies that it produces. It has three departments: Mixing, Encapsulating, and Bottling. In Mixing, the ingredients for the cold capsules are measured, sifted, and blended (materials are thus assumed to be uniformly added throughout the process). The mix is transferred out in gallon containers. The encapsulating department takes the powdered mix and places it in capsules (capsules are necessarily added at the beginning of the process). One gallon of powdered mix converts into 1,500 capsules. After the capsules are filled and polished, they are transferred to Bottling, where they are placed in bottles that are then affixed with a safety seal, lid, and label. Each bottle receives 50 capsules.

During March, the following results are available for the first two departments:

	Mixing	Encapsulating
Beginning inventories:		
Physical units	10 gallons	4,000
Costs:		
Materials	$ 252	$ 32
Labor	$ 282	$ 20
Overhead	?	?
Transferred in		$ 140
Current production:		
Transferred out	140 gallons	208,000
Ending inventory	20 gallons	6,000
Costs:		
Materials	$3,636	$ 1,573
Transferred in	—	?
Labor	$4,618	$ 1,944
Overhead	?	?
Percentage of completion:		
Beginning inventory	40%	50%
Ending inventory	50%	40%

Overhead in both departments is applied as a percentage of direct labor costs. In the mixing department, overhead is 200 percent of direct labor. In the encapsulating department, the overhead rate is 150 percent of direct labor.

Required:

1. Prepare a production report for the mixing department using the weighted average method. Follow the five steps outlined in the chapter. (*Note*: Round to two decimal places for the unit cost.)
2. Prepare a production report for the encapsulating department using the weighted average method. Follow the five steps outlined in the chapter. (*Note:* Round to four decimal places for the unit cost.)
3. **Conceptual Connection:** Explain why the weighted average method is easier to use than FIFO. Explain when weighted average will give about the same results as FIFO.

Problem 17-58 *(Appendix 17A)* First-In, First-Out Method

OBJECTIVE ⑤

Refer to **Problem 17-57.**

Required:

Prepare a production report for the mixing and encapsulating departments using the FIFO method. (*Note*: Round the unit cost to four decimal places.) (*Hint:* For the second department, you must convert gallons to capsules.)

CASES

Case 17-59 Process Costing versus Alternative Costing Methods, Impact on Resource Allocation Decision

OBJECTIVE ①②③④

Golding Manufacturing, a division of Farnsworth Sporting Inc., produces two different models of bows and eight models of knives. The bow-manufacturing process involves the production of two major subassemblies: the limbs and the handles. The limbs pass through four sequential processes before reaching final assembly: layup, molding, fabricating, and finishing. In the layup department, limbs are created by laminating layers of wood. In the molding department, the limbs are heat-treated, under pressure, to form strong resilient limbs. In the fabricating department, any protruding glue or other processing residue is removed. Finally, in the finishing department, the limbs are cleaned with acetone, dried, and sprayed with the final finishes.

The handles pass through two processes before reaching final assembly: pattern and finishing. In the pattern department, blocks of wood are fed into a machine that is set to shape the handles. Different patterns are possible, depending on the machine's setting. After coming out of the machine, the handles are cleaned and smoothed. They then pass to the finishing department, where they are sprayed with the final finishes. In final assembly, the limbs and handles are assembled into different models using purchased parts such as pulley assemblies, weight-adjustment bolts, side plates, and string.

Golding, since its inception, has been using process costing to assign product costs. A predetermined overhead rate is used based on direct labor dollars (80 percent of direct labor dollars). Recently, Golding has hired a new controller, Karen Jenkins. After reviewing the product-costing procedures, Karen requested a meeting with the divisional manager, Aaron Suhr. The following is a transcript of their conversation:

Karen: Aaron, I have some concerns about our cost accounting system. We make two different models of bows and are treating them as if they were the same product. Now I know that the only real difference between the models is the handle. The processing of the handles is the same, but the handles differ significantly in the amount and quality of wood used. Our current costing does not reflect this difference in material input.

Aaron: Your predecessor is responsible. He believed that tracking the difference in material cost wasn't worth the effort. He simply didn't believe that it would make much difference in the unit cost of either model.

Karen: Well, he may have been right, but I have my doubts. If there is a significant difference, it could affect our views of which model is more important to the company. The additional bookkeeping isn't very stringent. All we have to worry about is the pattern department. The other departments fit what I view as a process-costing pattern.

Aaron: Why don't you look into it? If there is a significant difference, go ahead and adjust the costing system.

(Continued)

After the meeting, Karen decided to collect cost data on the two models: the Deluxe model and the Econo model. She decided to track the costs for one week. At the end of the week, she had collected the following data from the pattern department:

a. There were a total of 2,500 bows completed: 1,000 Deluxe models and 1,500 Econo models.

b. There was no BWIP; however, there were 300 units in EWIP: 200 Deluxe and 100 Econo models. Both models were 80 percent complete with respect to conversion costs and 100 percent complete with respect to materials.

c. The pattern department experienced the following costs:

Direct materials	$114,000
Direct labor	45,667

d. On an experimental basis, the requisition forms for materials were modified to identify the dollar value of the materials used by the Econo and Deluxe models:

Econo model	$30,000
Deluxe model	84,000

Required:

1. Compute the unit cost for the handles produced by the pattern department assuming that process costing is totally appropriate. Round unit cost to two decimal places.

2. Compute the unit cost of each handle using the separate cost information provided on materials. Round unit cost to two decimal places.

3. Compare the unit costs computed in Requirements 1 and 2. Is Karen justified in her belief that a pure process-costing relationship is not appropriate? Describe the costing system that you would recommend.

4. In the past, the marketing manager has requested more money for advertising the Econo line. Aaron has repeatedly refused to grant any increase in this product's advertising budget because its per-unit profit (selling price minus manufacturing cost) is so low. Given the results in Requirements 1 through 3, was Aaron justified in his position?

OBJECTIVE  **Case 17-60 Equivalent Units; Valuation of Work-in-Process Inventories; First-In, First-Out versus Weighted Average**

AKL Foundry manufactures metal components for different kinds of equipment used by the aerospace, commercial aircraft, medical equipment, and electronic industries. The company uses investment casting to produce the required components. Investment casting consists of creating, in wax, a replica of the final product and pouring a hard shell around it. After removing the wax, molten metal is poured into the resulting cavity. What remains after the shell is broken is the desired metal object ready to be put to its designated use.

Metal components pass through eight processes: gating, shell creating, foundry work, cutoff, grinding, finishing, welding, and strengthening. Gating creates the wax mold and clusters the wax pattern around a sprue (a hole through which the molten metal will be poured through the gates into the mold in the foundry process), which is joined and supported by gates (flow channels) to form a tree of patterns. In the shell-creating process, the wax molds are alternately dipped in a ceramic slurry and a fluidized bed of progressively coarser refractory grain until a sufficiently thick shell (or mold) completely encases the wax pattern. After drying, the mold is sent to the foundry process. Here, the wax is melted out of the mold, and the shell is fired, strengthened, and brought to the proper temperature. Molten metal is then poured into the dewaxed shell. Finally, the ceramic shell is removed, and the finished product is sent to the cutoff process, where the parts are separated from the tree by the use of a band saw. The parts are then sent to the grinding process, where the gates that allowed the molten metal to flow into the ceramic cavities are ground off using large abrasive grinders. In the finishing process, rough edges caused by the grinders are removed by small handheld pneumatic tools. Parts that are flawed at this point are sent to welding for corrective treatment. The last process uses heat to treat the parts to bring them to the desired strength.

In 2011, the two partners who owned AKL Foundry decided to split up and divide the business. In dissolving their business relationship, they were faced with the problem of dividing the business assets equitably. Since the company had two plants—one in Arizona and one in New Mexico—a suggestion was made to split the business on the basis of geographic location. One partner would assume ownership of the plant in New Mexico, and the other would assume ownership of the plant in Arizona. However, this arrangement had one major complication: the amount of WIP inventory located in the Arizona plant.

The Arizona facilities had been in operation for more than a decade and were full of WIP. The New Mexico facility had been operational for only two years and had much smaller WIP inventories. The partner located in New Mexico argued that to disregard the unequal value of the WIP inventories would be grossly unfair.

Unfortunately, during the entire business history of AKL Foundry, WIP inventories had never been assigned any value. In computing the cost of goods sold each year, the company had followed the policy of adding depreciation to the out-of-pocket costs of direct labor, direct materials, and overhead. Accruals for the company are nearly nonexistent, and there are hardly ever any ending inventories of materials.

During 2011, the Arizona plant had sales of $2,028,670. The cost of goods sold is itemized as follows:

Direct materials	$378,000
Direct labor	530,300
Overhead	643,518

Upon request, the owners of AKL provided the following supplementary information (percentages are cumulative):

Costs Used by Each Process as a Percentage of Total Cost

	Direct Materials (%)	Direct Total Labor Cost (%)
Gating	23	35
Shell creating	70	50
Foundry work	100	70
Cutoff	100	72
Grinding	100	80
Finishing	100	90
Welding	100	93
Strengthening	100	100

Gating had 10,000 units in BWIP, 60 percent complete. Assume that all materials are added at the beginning of each process. During the year, 50,000 units were completed and transferred out. The ending inventory had 11,000 unfinished units, 60 percent complete.

Required:

1. The partners of AKL want a reasonable estimate of the cost of WIP inventories. Using the gating department's inventory as an example, prepare an estimate of the cost of the EWIP. What assumptions did you make? Did you use the FIFO or weighted average method? Why? (*Note*: Round unit cost to two decimal places.)

2. Assume that the shell-creating process has 8,000 units in BWIP, 20 percent complete. During the year, 50,000 units were completed and transferred out. (*Note*: All 50,000 units were sold; no other units were sold.) The EWIP inventory had 8,000 units, 30 percent complete. Compute the value of the shell-creating department's EWIP. What additional assumptions had to be made?

Case 17-61 Production Report, Ethical Behavior

OBJECTIVE 3

Consider the following conversation between Gary Means, manager of a division that produces industrial machinery, and his controller, Donna Simpson, a certified management accountant and certified public accountant:

Gary: Donna, we have a real problem. Our operating cash is too low, and we are in desperate need of a loan. As you know, our financial position is marginal, and we need to show as much income as possible—and our assets need bolstering as well.

Donna: I understand the problem, but I don't see what can be done at this point. This is the last week of the fiscal year, and it looks like we'll report income just slightly above breakeven.

Gary: I know all this. What we need is some creative accounting. I have an idea that might help us, and I wanted to see if you would go along with it. We have 200 partially finished machines in process, about 20 percent complete. That compares with the 1,000 units that we completed and sold during the year. When you computed the per-unit cost, you used 1,040 equivalent units, giving us a manufacturing cost of $1,500 per unit. That per-unit cost gives us cost of goods sold equal to $1.5 million and ending work in process worth $60,000. The presence of the work in process gives us a chance to improve our financial position. If we report the units in work in process as 80 percent complete, this will increase our equivalent units to 1,160. This, in turn, will decrease our unit cost to about $1,345 and cost of goods sold to $1.345 million. The value of our work in process will increase to $215,200. With those financial stats, the loan would be a cinch.

Donna: Gary, I don't know. What you're suggesting is risky. It wouldn't take much auditing skill to catch this one.

Gary: You don't have to worry about that. The auditors won't be here for at least six to eight more weeks. By that time, we can have those partially completed units completed and sold. I can bury the labor cost by having some of our more loyal workers work overtime for some bonuses. The overtime will never be reported. And, as you know, bonuses come out of the corporate budget and are assigned to overhead—next year's overhead. Donna, this will work. If we look good and get the loan to boot, corporate headquarters will treat us well. If we don't do this, we could lose our jobs.

Required:

1. Should Donna agree to Gary's proposal? Why or why not? To assist in deciding, review the corporate code of ethics standards described in Chapter 13. Do any apply?
2. Assume that Donna refuses to cooperate and that Gary accepts this decision and drops the matter. Does Donna have any obligation to report the divisional manager's behavior to a superior? Explain.
3. Assume that Donna refuses to cooperate; however, Gary insists that the changes be made. Now what should she do? What would you do?
4. Suppose that Donna is 63 and that the prospects for employment elsewhere are bleak. Assume again that Gary insists that the changes be made. Donna also knows that his supervisor, the owner of the company, is his father-in-law. Under these circumstances, would your recommendations for Donna differ?

18 Activity-Based Costing and Management

Doug Norman Crystals/Alamy

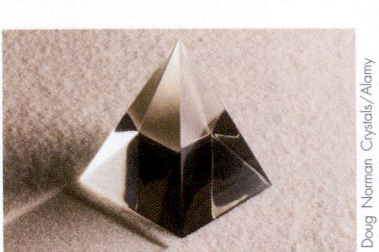

After studying Chapter 18, you should be able to:

1. Explain why functional (or volume)-based costing approaches may produce distorted costs.
2. Explain how an activity-based costing system works for product costing.
3. Describe activity-based customer costing and activity-based supplier costing.
4. Explain how activity-based management can be used for cost reduction.

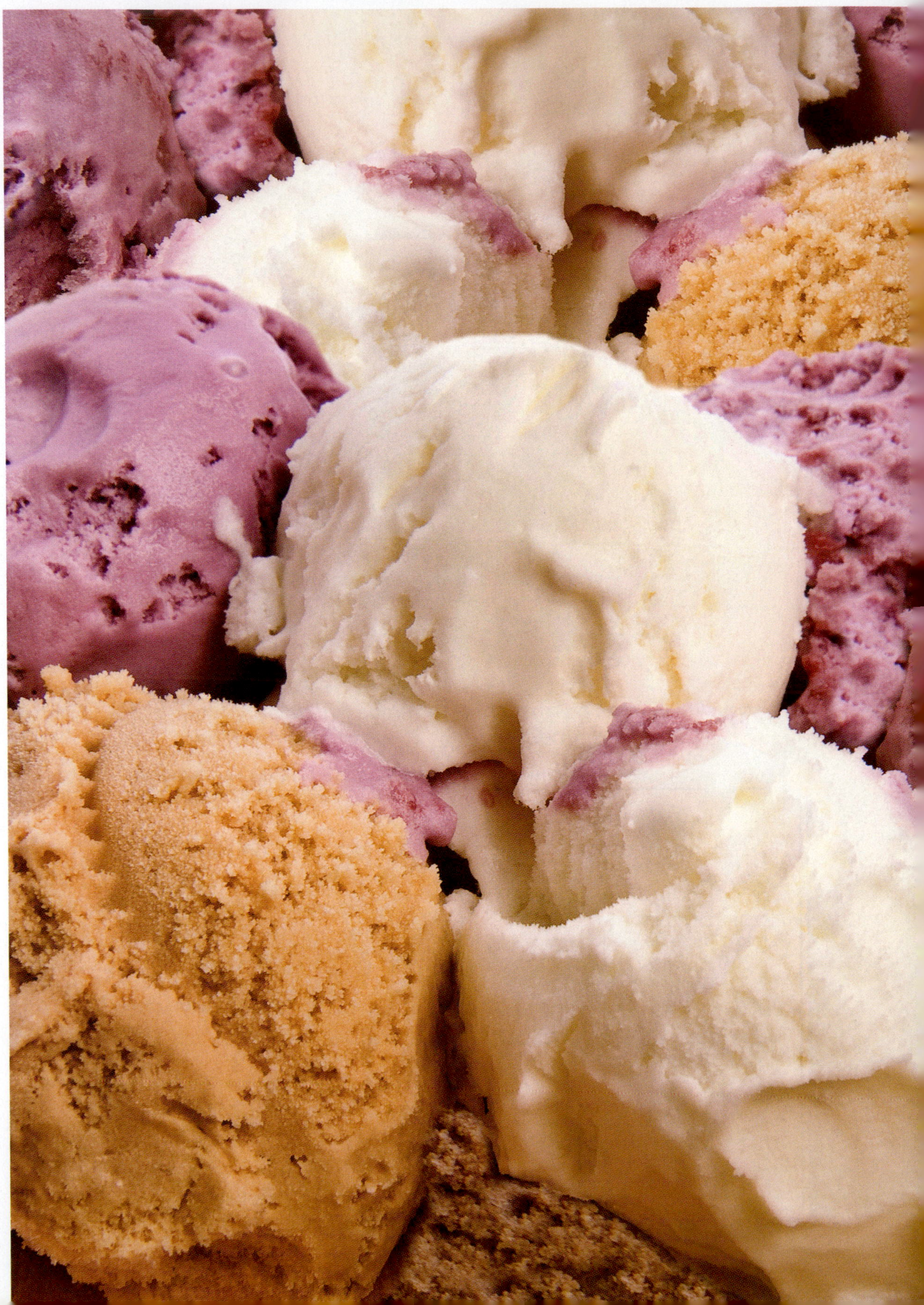

Image Copyright Madlen. Shutterstock.com

EXPERIENCE MANAGERIAL DECISIONS

with Cold Stone Creamery

Experts believe that ice cream as we know it was invented in the 1600s and was popularized in part by Charles I of England, who made it a staple of the royal table. Ice cream remains as popular as ever today, but trips to the local ice cream parlor have changed dramatically.

Cold Stone Creamery, founded in 1988 in Tempe, Arizona, has helped to lead this change with its innovative business model focused on making the ice cream trip an entertainment experience for the entire family. Cold Stone operates nearly 1,500 stores worldwide. Cold Stone executives must understand and control the company's complex cost structure in order to profitably manage its ice cream empire. For example, its most popular product line—ice cream with "mix in" ingredients—boasts 16 basic ice cream flavors with 30 different ingredients and three sizes, which represent thousands of possible ice cream product options! These options are great for customers with varied tastes, but are challenging for Cold Stone to manage given the different types of activities associated with different types of product orders. Therefore, Cold Stone adopted activity-based costing (ABC) to identify the activity drivers associated with each type of ice cream order and to estimate the costs of these activities.

Vladimir Stefanovic/Shutterstock.com

Two important drivers of costs for Cold Stone include ingredients and time, both of which vary significantly across different ice cream product orders. With the insights gained from its ABC analysis, Cold Stone understands the cost of various orders' preparation time, which is measured in seconds. In addition to labor, Cold Stone's ABC system considers the costs associated with training, uniforms, and employee benefits when estimating the cost of each second required in making each product. When combined with other costs, the ABC analysis provides an estimate of profit margin by product type. If a particular product is not making its expected margin, Cold Stone managers know to look at the activities involved in creating the product and to fine-tune that activity. This understanding of Cold Stone's complex cost structure has provided the company with a valuable competitive advantage to become one of the most profitable and fastest-growing franchises in America.

LIMITATIONS OF FUNCTIONAL-BASED COST ACCOUNTING SYSTEMS

Plantwide and departmental rates based on direct labor hours, machine hours, or other volume-based measures have been used for decades to assign overhead costs to products and continue to be used successfully by many organizations. However, for many settings, this approach to costing is equivalent to an averaging approach and may produce distorted, or inaccurate, costs. For example, assume two friends, Lisa and Jessie, go to **Cold Stone Creamery** for dessert. Lisa orders a small chocolate ice cream in a plastic cup with no mix-ins, costing $3.00, and Jessie orders a medium strawberry banana rendezvous in a waffle dish (which has four mix-ins: graham cracker pie crust, white chocolate chips, strawberries, and bananas), costing $10. If the total bill is split evenly between the two, each individual would pay $6.50, which doesn't accurately represent the actual cost of each dessert. Lisa's dessert is overstated by $3.50, and Jessie's is understated by $3.50. If it is important to know the cost of each dessert, the averaging approach is not suitable.

In the same way, plantwide and departmental rates can produce average costs that severely understate or overstate individual product costs. Thus, **Cold Stone Creamery** would be very interested in knowing the cost of its numerous products and likely would not be satisfied with an averaging approach. Without accurate costing, Cold Stone would not be able to properly price its various products. Product cost distortions can be damaging, particularly for those firms whose business environment is characterized by the following:

- intense or increasing competitive pressures (often on a worldwide level)
- small profit margins
- continuous improvement
- total quality management
- total customer satisfaction
- sophisticated technology

Firms operating in theses types of business environments in particular need accurate cost information in order to make effective decisions.

In order for accurate cost information to be produced, it is important that the firm's cost system accurately reflect the firm's underlying business, or economic, reality. Thus, it is important that the managerial accountant continually ask the question, "How well does the cost system's *representation* of my business match the economic *reality* of my business?" If the answer is "not very well," then the cost system needs to be changed. Therefore, in much the same way that financial statements must be transparent for external users, the cost system must be transparent in its assignment of costs for internal users.

The need for more accurate product costs has forced many companies to take a serious look at their costing procedures. Two major factors impair the ability of unit-based plantwide and departmental rates to assign overhead costs accurately:

- The proportion of nonunit-related overhead costs to total overhead costs is large.
- The degree of product diversity is great.

Nonunit-Related Overhead Costs

The use of either plantwide rates or departmental rates assumes that a product's consumption of overhead resources is related strictly to the units produced. For **unit-level activities**—activities that are performed each time a unit is produced—this assumption makes sense. Traditional, volume-based cost systems label the costs associated with these activities as variable in nature, because they increase or decrease in direct proportion to increases or decreases in the levels of these unit-level activities. All other costs (i.e., ones that are not unit-level) are considered fixed by volume-based cost systems.

But what if there are *nonunit-level activities*—activities that are not performed each time a unit of product is produced? The costs associated with these nonunit-level activities are unlikely to vary (i.e., increase or decrease) with units produced. These costs vary with other factor(s), besides units, and identifying such factor(s) is helpful in predicting

Exhibit 18-1

ABC Hierarchy

Type of Cost	Description of Cost Driver	Example
Unit-level	Varies with output volume (e.g., units); traditional variable costs	Cost of indirect materials for labeling each bottle of **Victoria's Secret** perfume
Batch-level	Varies with the number of batches produced	Cost of setting up laser engraving equipment for each batch of **Epilog** key chains
Product-sustaining	Varies with the number of product lines	Cost of inventory handling and warranty servicing of different brands carried by **Best Buy** electronics store
Facility-sustaining	Necessary to operate the plant facility but does not vary with units, batches, or product lines	Cost of **General Motors** plant manager salary

and managing these costs. Proponents of activity-based costing (ABC) refer to the ABC cost hierarchy that categorizes costs either as *unit-level* (i.e., vary with output volume), *batch-level* (i.e., vary with the number of groups or batches that are run), *product-sustaining* (i.e., vary with the diversity of the product or service line), or *facility-sustaining* (i.e., do not vary with any factor but are necessary in operating the plant).[1] Exhibit 18-1 shows the activity-based costing hierarchy.

Nonunit-Level Activity Drivers   Setting up equipment is one example of a nonunit-level activity because, often, the same equipment is used to produce different products. Setting up equipment means preparing it for the particular type of product being made. For example, a vat may be used to dye t-shirts. After completing a batch of 1,000 red t-shirts, the vat must be carefully cleaned before a batch of 3,000 green t-shirts is produced. Thus, setup costs are incurred each time a batch of products is produced. A batch may consist of 1,000 or 3,000 units, and the cost of setup is the same. Yet as more setups are done, setup costs increase. The number of setups (a batch-level cost), not the number of units produced (a unit-level cost), is a much better measure of the consumption of the setup activity.

Another example of a nonunit-level activity is reengineering products. At times, based on customer feedback, firms face the necessity of redesigning their products. This product reengineering activity is authorized by a document called an *engineering work order*. For example, **Multibras S.A. Electrodomesticos**, a Brazilian appliance manufacturer (and subsidiary of Whirlpool), may issue engineering work orders to correct design flaws of its refrigerators, freezers, and washers. Product reengineering costs may depend on the number of different engineering work orders (a product-sustaining cost) rather than the units produced of any given product.

Similarly, **JetBlue**'s decision to add a second type of jet, the Embraer 190, to its existing fleet of Airbus A320s, caused it to incur significant additional product-sustaining costs that it would not have incurred had it stayed with only one type of plane. These additional product-sustaining costs included the costs for doubling the spare parts inventory, maintenance programs, and separate pilot-training tracks.[2]

---

[1] R. Cooper, Cost Classification in Unit-Based and Activity-Based Manufacturing Cost Systems, *Journal of Cost Management for the Manufacturing Industry* (Fall 1990): 4–14.
[2] S. Carey, "Balancing Act: Amid JetBlue's Rapid Ascent, CEO Adopts Big Rivals' Traits," *The Wall Street Journal* (August 25, 2005).

Therefore, **nonunit-level activity drivers** (i.e., batch, product-sustaining, and facility-sustaining) are factors that measure the consumption of nonunit-level activities by products and other cost objects, whereas **unit-level activity drivers** measure the consumption of unit-level activities. **Activity drivers**, then, are factors that measure the consumption of activities by products and other cost objects and can be classified as either *unit-level* or *nonunit-level*.

Using only unit-based activity drivers to assign nonunit-related overhead costs can create distorted product costs. The severity of this distortion depends on what proportion of total overhead costs these nonunit-based costs represent. For many companies, this percentage can be significant, so care should be exercised in assigning nonunit-based overhead costs. If nonunit-based overhead costs are only a small percentage of total overhead costs, then the distortion of product costs will be quite small. In such a case, using unit-based activity drivers to assign overhead costs is acceptable.

Product Diversity

The presence of significant nonunit overhead costs is a necessary but not sufficient condition for plantwide and departmental rate failure (i.e., distorted costs). For example, if products consume the nonunit-level overhead activities in the same proportion as the unit-level overhead activities, then no product-costing distortion will occur (with the use of traditional overhead assignment methods). The presence of product diversity is also necessary for product cost distortion to occur. **Product diversity** means that products consume overhead activities in systematically different proportions. This may occur for several reasons, including differences in:

- product size
- product complexity
- setup time
- size of batches

Illustrating the Failure of Unit-Based Overhead Rates

To illustrate how traditional unit-based overhead rates can distort product costs, refer to the data for Rio Novo's Porto Behlo plant in Exhibit 18-2 (assume that the measures are expected and actual outcomes). The Porto Behlo plant produces two models of washers: a deluxe and a regular model. Because the quantity of regular models produced is 10 times greater than that of the deluxe, the regular model is a high-volume product and the deluxe model is a low-volume product. The models are produced in batches.

Remember that prime costs represent direct materials and direct labor. Given that these costs are direct in nature, they can be traced to each individual unit produced. It is the indirect, or overhead, costs that typically are treated differently by different types of cost systems. Usually, activity-based cost systems generate more accurate cost data than unit-based cost systems because of their more appropriate treatment of overhead costs. For simplicity, only four types of overhead activities, performed by four distinct support departments, are assumed:

- setting up the equipment for each batch (different configurations are needed for the electronic components associated with each model)
- moving a batch
- machining
- assembly (performed after each department's operations)

Problems with Costing Accuracy The activity usage data in Exhibit 18-2 reveal some serious problems with either plantwide or departmental rates for assigning overhead costs. The main problem with either procedure is the assumption that unit-level drivers such as machine hours or direct labor hours drive or cause all overhead costs.

Product-Costing Data for Rio Novo's Porto Behlo Plant

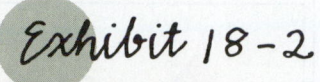
Exhibit 18-2

	Activity Usage Measures			Activity Cost Data (Overhead Activities)	
	Deluxe	Regular	Total	Activity	Activity Cost
Units produced	10	100	110	Setting up equipment	$1,000
Prime costs	$800	$8,000	$8,800	Moving goods	1,000
Direct labor hours	20	80	100	Machining	1,500
Machine hours	10	40	50	Assembly	500
Setup hours	3	1	4	Total	$4,000
Number of moves	6	4	10		

From Exhibit 18-2, it can be seen that regular models, the high-volume product, use four times as many direct labor hours as deluxe models, the low-volume product (80 hours vs. 20 hours). Thus, if a plantwide rate is used, the regular models will be assigned four times more overhead cost than the deluxe models. But is this reasonable? Do unit-based drivers explain the consumption of all overhead activities? In particular, is it reasonable to assume that each product's consumption of overhead increases in direct proportion to the direct labor hours used? Now consider the four overhead activities to see if the unit-level drivers accurately reflect the demands of regular and deluxe model production.

Examination of the data in Exhibit 18-2 suggests that a significant portion of overhead costs is not driven or caused by direct labor hours. Each product's demands for setup and material-moving activities are more logically related to the setup hours and the number of moves, respectively. These nonunit activities represent 50 percent ($2,000/$4,000) of the total overhead costs—a significant percentage. Notice that the low-volume product, deluxe models, uses three times more setup hours than the regular models (3/1) and one and a half as many moves (6/4). However, using a plantwide rate based on direct labor hours, a unit-based activity driver assigns four times more setup and material moving costs to the regular models than to the deluxe. Thus, product diversity exists, and we should expect product cost distortion because the quantity of unit-based overhead that each product consumes does not vary in direct proportion to the quantity consumed of nonunit-based overhead.

Regardless of the nature of the product diversity, product cost will be distorted whenever the quantity of unit-based overhead that a product consumes does not vary in direct proportion to the quantity consumed of nonunit-based overhead. The proportion of each activity consumed by a product is defined as the **consumption ratio** and is calculated as:

$$\text{Consumption ratio} = \frac{\text{Amount of activity driver per product}}{\text{Total driver quantity}}$$

CORNERSTONE 18-1 (p. 916) illustrates how to calculate the consumption ratios for the two products.

CORNERSTONE
18-1

Calculating Consumption Ratios

Information:
Refer to the activity usage information for Rio Novo's Porto Behlo plant in Exhibit 18-2 (p. 915).

Required:
Calculate the consumption ratios for each product.

Solution:
Step 1:   Identify the activity driver for each activity.
Step 2:   Divide the amount of driver used for each product by the total driver quantity.

	Consumption Ratios		
Overhea Activity	**Deluxe Model**	**Regular Model**	**Activity Driver**
Setting up equipment	0.75[a]	0.25[a]	Setup hours
Moving goods	0.60[b]	0.40[b]	Number of moves
Machining	0.20[c]	0.80[c]	Machine hours
Assembly	0.20[d]	0.80[d]	Direct labor hours

[a]3/4 (deluxe) and 1/4 (regular).   [c]10/50 (deluxe) and 40/50 (regular).
[b]6/10 (deluxe) and 4/10 (regular).   [d]20/100 (deluxe) and 80/100 (regular).

The consumption ratios in Cornerstone 18-1 suggest that a plantwide rate based on direct labor hours will overcost the regular models and undercost the deluxe models.

Solving the Problem of Cost Distortion   This cost distortion can be solved using activity rates. Instead of assigning the overhead costs using a single, plantwide rate, a rate for each overhead activity can be calculated and used to assign overhead costs. **CORNERSTONE 18-2** shows how to calculate these rates.

CORNERSTONE
18-2

Calculating Activity Rates

Information:
Rio Novo's Porto Behlo plant activity cost and driver data follow:

Activity	Activity Cost ($)	Driver	Driver Quantity
Setting up equipment	1,000	Setup hours	4
Moving goods	1,000	Number of moves	10
Machining	1,500	Machine hours	50
Assembly	500	Direct labor hours	100

Required:
Calculate the activity rates.

Solution:
Divide the activity cost by the total driver quantity:

Setup rate:	$1,000/4 setup hours = $250 per setup hour
Materials handling rate:	$1,000/10 moves = $100 per move
Machining rate:	$1,500/50 machine hours = $30 per machine hour
Assembly rate:	$500/100 direct labor hours = $5 per direct labor hour

To assign overhead costs, the amount of activity consumed by each product is needed along with the activity rates. **CORNERSTONE 18-3** shows how to calculate the unit cost for each product by using activity rates.

CORNERSTONE 18-3   Calculating Activity-Based Unit Costs

Information:
Rio Novo's Porto Behlo plant activity rate data for deluxe and regular models follows:

	Deluxe	Regular	Activity Rate
Units produced per year	10	100	
Prime costs	$800	$8,000	
Setup hours	3	1	$250
Number of moves	6	4	$100
Machine hours	10	40	$ 30
Direct labor hours	20	80	$ 5

Required:
Calculate the unit cost for deluxe and regular models.

Solution:

	Deluxe	Regular
Prime costs	$ 800	$ 8,000
Overhead costs:		
Setups:		
$250 × 3 setup hours	750	
$250 × 1 setup hour		250
Moving materials:		
$100 × 6 moves	600	
$100 × 4 moves		400
Machining:		
$30 × 10 machine hours	300	
$30 × 40 machine hours		1,200
Assembly:		
$5 × 20 direct labor hours	100	
$5 × 80 direct labor hours		400
Total manufacturing costs	$2,550	$10,250
Units produced	÷10	÷100
Unit cost (Total costs/Units)	$ 255	$102.50

Exhibit 18-3 (p. 918) visually summarizes the calculations in Cornerstones 18-2 and 18-3.

Comparison of Functional-Based and Activity-Based Product Costs   A plant-wide rate based on direct labor hours is calculated as follows:

$$\text{Overhead rate} = \frac{\text{Total overhead costs}}{\text{Total direct labor hours}}$$

$$\frac{\$4,000}{100} = \$40 \text{ per direct labor hour}$$

Exhibit 18-3

Activity Rates and Activity-Based Unit Costs for Rio Novo's Porto Behlo Plant

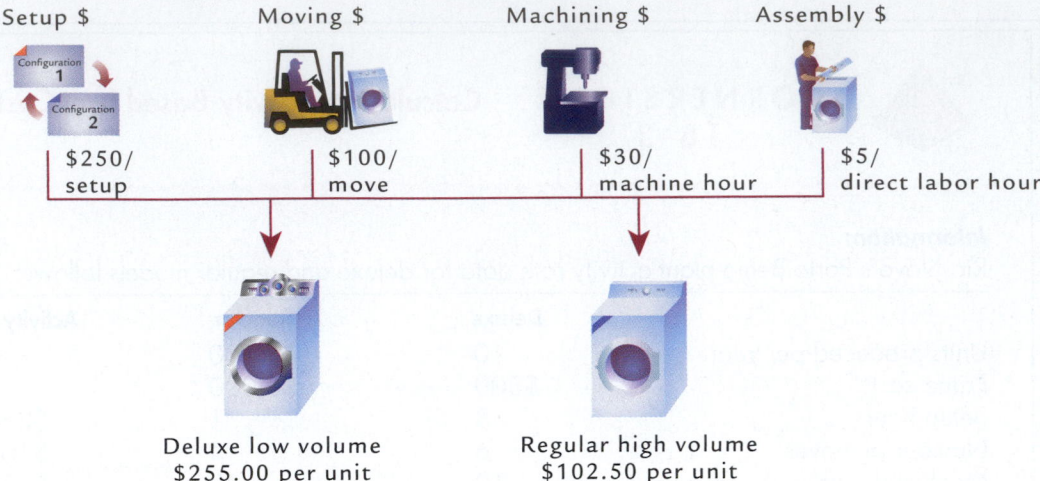

	Setup $	Moving $	Machining $	Assembly $
	$250/ setup	$100/ move	$30/ machine hour	$5/ direct labor hour

Deluxe low volume
$255.00 per unit

Regular high volume
$102.50 per unit

The product cost for each product using this single unit-level overhead rate is calculated as follows:

	Deluxe	Regular
Prime costs	$ 800	$ 8,000
Overhead costs:		
$40 × 20	800	
$40 × 80		3,200
Total cost	$1,600	$11,200
Units produced	÷10	÷100
Unit cost	$ 160	$ 112

Now compare these product costs with the activity-based cost of Cornerstone 18-3 (p. 917). This comparison clearly illustrates the effects of using only unit-based activity drivers to assign overhead costs. The activity-based cost assignment reflects the pattern of overhead consumption and is, therefore, the most accurate. Activity-based product costing reveals that functional-based costing undercosts the low volume deluxe models and overcosts the high volume regular models. In fact, the ABC assignment increases the reported cost of the deluxe models by $95 per unit and decreases the reported cost of the regular models by $9.50 per unit—a movement in the right direction given the pattern of overhead consumption.

ILLUSTRATING RELATIONSHIPS

Illustrating Relationships: Product Diversity and Product Costing Accuracy

For unit-level overhead rates to fail, products must consume the non-unit-level activities in proportions significantly different than the unit-level activities. The greater the difference in this consumption pattern, the greater the potential product cost distortion. For example, the Regular model of Rio Novo consumes activities in the following proportions:

- 25 percent of the setup hours
- 40 percent of the number of moves
- 80 percent of the machine hours
- 80 percent of the direct labor hours

Since the plantwide overhead rate uses direct labor hours, a unit-level driver, 80 percent of the total overhead would be assigned to the Regular model. However, the Regular model consumes only an average of 32.5 percent of the nonunit-level overhead

[(0.25 + 0.40)/2] and so we would expect a significant cost distortion. Intuitively, if the *average* consumption ratio of the nonunit-level activities differs markedly from the unit-level consumption ratio, as 32.5 percent differs from 80 percent, then there is greater product diversity and greater product cost distortion. As expected, the distortion is significant because the plantwide rate assigns $3,200 of overhead while the ABC approach assigns only $2,250. Alternatively, if there is little or no product diversity, then products consume unit-level activities and nonunit-level activities in the same (or close to the same) proportion and a plantwide rate works well.

This diversity-accuracy relationship can be seen in the Rio Novo example in Cornerstones 18-2 (p. 916) and 18-3 (p. 917), by allowing the average nonunit-level consumption ratio to vary. We see a special structure characterized by the following features:

- The Deluxe and Regular products have the same consumption ratios (0.20 and 0.80, respectively) for the unit-level activities (machining and assembly).
- The cost of the nonunit-level activities, setting up and moving, is the same ($1,000 for each activity).
- The total cost of the unit-level (nonunit-level) activities is $2,000.

This special structure means that the average consumption ratio for the two unit-level (nonunit-level) activities can be used to assign the activity costs to each product, achieving the same assignment as when done for each individual activity. This can be calculated as follows:

$$\text{Overhead cost} = \text{Average consumption ratio} \times \text{Total cost of each set of activities}$$

The average consumption ratios for the Regular product are:

$$\text{Unit-level activities} = (0.80 + 0.80)/2$$
$$= 0.80$$
$$\text{Nonunit-level activities} = (0.25 + 0.40)/2$$
$$= 0.325$$

Thus, for the Regular product:

$$\text{Overhead cost} = (0.80 \times \$2,000) + (0.325 \times \$2,000)$$
$$= \$1,600 + \$650$$
$$= \$2,250$$

This is the same as the assignments using individual activities and activity rates.

To explore the effect of product diversity on accuracy, hold the unit-level consumption ratios constant and allow the average nonunit-level consumption ratio to vary. This produces the following overhead cost assignment equation for the Regular product:

$$\text{Overhead cost} = \$1,600 + \text{Average nonunit consumption ratio} \times \$2,000$$

Using this equation, Exhibit 18-4 (p. 920) shows the overhead cost assigned to the Regular model as the average nonunit-level consumption ratio varies. The blue line represents the average nonunit consumption ratio function. The red horizontal line is the overhead cost assignment using the plantwide rate. Notice that when it intersects $3,200 the overhead cost assignment is the same for both ABC and plantwide assignments (the average consumption ratio is 0.80, which is the same as the consumption ratio for the plantwide rate). As the average consumption ratio decreases, the difference between the ABC and plantwide assignments increases. The vertical lines indicate the difference between the ABC and plantwide rate overhead assignments. Clearly, some values can occur that would produce little difference between the plantwide and ABC assignments, and thus it would be cheaper and simpler to use a single-rate costing system. For example, the vertical lines are small between 0.70 and 1.00, indicating that when the average nonunit consumption ratio is in this range, then a plantwide rate would provide good accuracy. The purple vertical line represents the accuracy loss when the product diversity corresponds to the original example data.

Exhibit 18-4

Diversity and Product Costing Accuracy

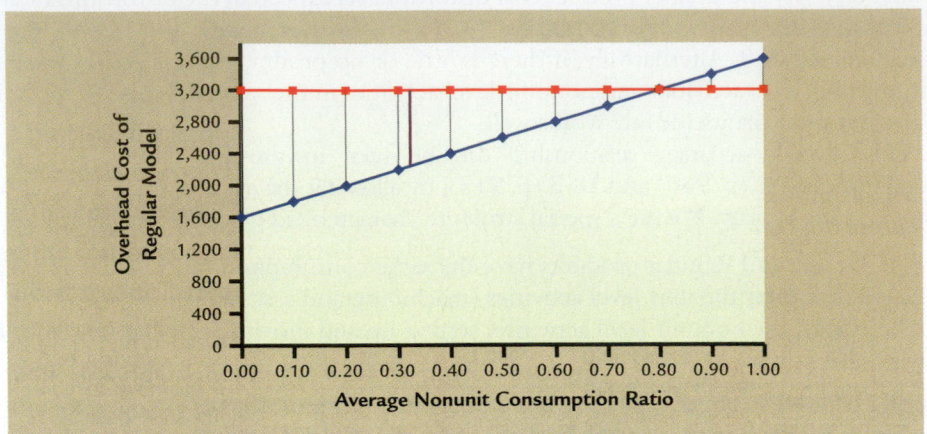

The key message of the relationship analysis is that in a diverse product environment, activity-based costing promises greater accuracy. Given the importance of making decisions based on accurate facts, a detailed look at activity-based costing is certainly merited.

ETHICAL DECISIONS   One of the ethical standards of the Institute of Management Accountants (IMA) requires that its members maintain professional expertise by continually developing knowledge and skills. An interesting issue is whether accounting professionals who resist learning different cost management methods are exhibiting ethical behavior. At the very least, cost accounting professionals should learn about different approaches and assess whether the benefit-cost trade-offs justify their use. ●

OBJECTIVE ②
Explain how an activity-based costing system works for product costing.

ACTIVITY-BASED PRODUCT COSTING

Functional-based overhead costing involves two major stages:

1. Overhead costs are assigned to an organizational unit (plant or department).
2. Overhead costs are then assigned to cost objects.

As Exhibit 18-5 illustrates, an **activity-based costing (ABC) system** is also a two-stage process:

1. Trace costs to activities.
2. Trace costs to cost objects.

The underlying assumption is that activities consume resources, and cost objects, in turn, consume activities. An ABC system, however, emphasizes direct tracing and driver tracing (exploiting cause-and-effect relationships), while a volume-based costing system tends to be allocation-intensive (largely ignoring cause-and-effect relationships). Since the focus of ABC is activities, identifying activities must be the first step in designing an ABC system.

Concept Q&A

What are some key differences between ABC and volume-based costing?

Answer:

ABC uses cause-and-effect relationships to assign overhead costs. Volume-based costing uses unit-based drivers such as direct labor hours, which often have nothing to do with the actual overhead resources consumed by a product.

Identifying Activities and Their Attributes

An **activity** is action taken or work performed by equipment or people for other people. Identifying activities usually is accomplished by interviewing managers or representatives of functional work areas (departments). A set of key questions is asked in which answers provide much of the data needed for an ABC system.

Set of Key Questions   Interview questions can be used to identify activities and activity attributes needed for costing purposes. The information derived from these questions provides data helpful for assigning resource costs to individual activities. To prevent the number of activities from becoming unmanageably large, a common rule of thumb

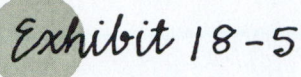

Activity-Based Costing: Assigning Cost of Overhead

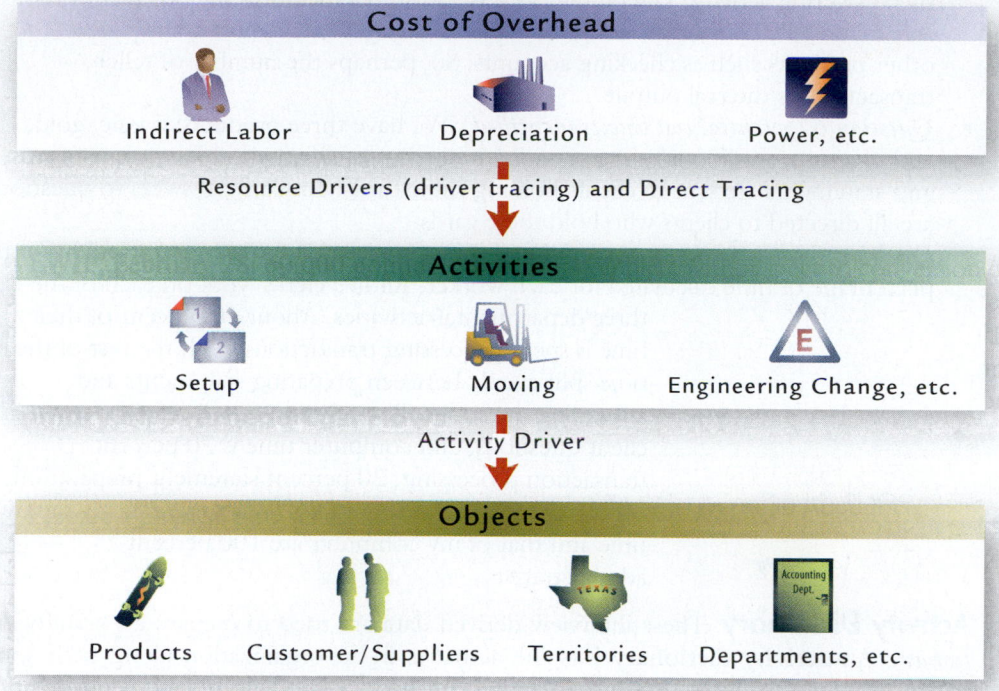

employed by the interviewer is to tell the interviewee to ignore activities that require less than 5 percent of an individual's time. Examples of questions that interviewers might ask to gather information include the following:

1. How many employees are in your department? (Activities consume labor.)
2. What do they do (please describe)? (Activities are people doing things for other people.)
3. Do customers outside your department use any equipment? (Activities also can be equipment working for other people. In other words, the equipment provides the service for someone by itself).
4. What resources are used by each activity (equipment, materials, energy)? (Activities consume resources in addition to labor.)
5. What are the outputs of each activity? (Helps to identify activity drivers.)
6. Who or what uses the activity output? (Identifies the cost object: products, other activities, customers, etc.)
7. How much time do workers spend on each activity? Time on each activity by equipment? (Information assigns the cost of labor and equipment to activities.)

Illustrative Example: Hemingway Bank Suppose that the manager of Hemingway Bank's credit card department is interviewed and presented with the seven questions just listed. Consider the purpose and response to each question in the order indicated.

- *Question 1 (labor resource):* There are five employees.
- *Question 2 (activity identification):* There are three major activities: processing credit card transactions, issuing customer statements, and answering customer questions.
- *Question 3 (activity identification):* Yes. Automatic bank tellers service customers who require cash advances.
- *Question 4 (resource identification):* Each employee has his or her own computer, printer, and desk. Paper and other supplies are needed to operate the printers. Each employee has a telephone as well.

- *Question 5 (potential activity drivers):* Processing transactions produces a posting for each transaction in our computer system and serves as a source for preparing the monthly statements. The number of monthly customer statements has to be the product for the issuing activity, and I suppose that customers served is the output for the answering activity. The number of cash advances measures the product of the automatic teller activity, although the teller really generates more transactions for other products such as checking accounts. So, perhaps the number of teller transactions is the real output.
- *Question 6 (potential cost objects identified):* We have three products: classic, gold, and platinum credit cards. Transactions are processed for these three types of cards, and statements are sent to clients holding these cards. Similarly, answers to questions are all directed to clients who hold these cards.
- *Question 7 (identifying resource drivers):* I just completed a work survey and have the percentage of time calculated for each worker. All five clerks work on each of the three departmental activities. About 40 percent of their time is spent processing transactions, with the rest of their time split evenly between preparing statements and answering questions. Phone time is used only for answering client questions, and computer time is 70 percent transaction processing, 20 percent statement preparation, and 10 percent answering questions. Furthermore, my own time and that of my computer are 100 percent administrative.

Concept Q&A

What is the purpose of the interview questions?

Answer:
The purpose is to identify activities, drivers, and other important attributes essential for ABC.

Activity Dictionary These interview-derived data are used to prepare an *activity dictionary*. An **activity dictionary** lists the activities in an organization along with some critical activity attributes. Activity attributes are financial and nonfinancial information items that describe individual activities. What attributes are used depends on the purpose. Examples of activity attributes associated with a costing objective include the following:

- types of resources consumed
- amount (percentage) of time spent on an activity by workers
- cost objects that consume the activity output (reason for performing the activity)
- measure of the activity output (activity driver)
- activity name

Illustrative Example: Hemingway Bank Exhibit 18-6 illustrates the activity dictionary for Hemingway's credit card department. The three products, classic, gold, and platinum credit cards, in turn, consume the activities. It is not unusual for a typical organization to produce an activity dictionary containing 200 to 300 activities.

Activity Dictionary for Hemingway Bank's Credit Card Department

Activity Name	Activity Description	Cost Object(s)	Activity Driver
Processing	Sorting, keying, and transactions verifying	Credit cards	Number of transactions
Preparing statements	Reviewing, printing, stuffing, and mailing	Credit cards	Number of statements
Answering questions	Answering, logging, reviewing database, and making call backs	Credit cards	Number of cards
Providing automatic tellers	Accessing accounts, withdrawing funds	Credit cards, checking and savings accounts	Number of teller transactions

Assigning Costs to Activities

Once activities are identified and described, the next task is to determine how much it costs to perform each activity. This determination requires identification of the resources being consumed by each activity. Some cost system experts consider this task to be the most difficult one in creating an accurate cost system. Activities consume resources such as labor, materials, energy, and capital. The cost of these resources is found in the general ledger, but the money spent on each activity is not revealed. Thus, it becomes necessary to assign the resource costs to activities by using direct and driver tracing. For labor resources, a *work distribution matrix* often is used. A **work distribution matrix** identifies the amount of labor consumed by each activity and is derived from the interview process (or a written survey).

Illustrative Example: Hemingway Bank Exhibit 18-7 (p. 924) provides an example of a work distribution matrix supplied by the manager of Hemingway's credit card department for individual activities (refer to Question 7).

From Exhibit 18-5 (p. 921), we know that both direct tracing and driver tracing are used to assign resource costs to activities. For this example, the time spent on each activity is the basis for assigning the labor costs to the activity. If the time is 100 percent, then labor is exclusive to the activity, and the assignment method is direct tracing. If the resource is shared by several activities (as is the case of the clerical resource), then the assignment is driver tracing, and the drivers are called *resource drivers*. **Resource drivers** are factors that measure the consumption of resources by activities. Once resource drivers are identified, then the costs of the resource can be assigned to the activity. **CORNERSTONE 18-4** shows how resource drivers and direct tracing are used to assign labor cost to the credit department activities.

CORNERSTONE 18-4

Assigning Resource Costs to Activities by Using Direct Tracing and Resource Drivers

Information:
Refer to the work distribution matrix for Hemingway Bank's credit card department in Exhibit 18-7 (p. 924). Assume that each clerk is paid a salary of $30,000 ($150,000 total clerical cost for five clerks).

Required:
Assign the cost of labor to each of the activities in the credit department.

Solution:
The amount of labor cost assigned to each activity is given below. (*Note*: The percentages come from the work distribution matrix.)

Processing transactions	$60,000 (0.40 × $150,000)
Preparing statements	$45,000 (0.30 × $150,000)
Answering questions	$45,000 (0.30 × $150,000)

Labor, of course, is not the only resource consumed by activities. Activities also consume materials, capital, and energy. The interview, for example, reveals that the activities within the credit card department use computers (capital), phones (capital), desks (capital), and paper (materials). The automatic teller activity uses the automatic teller (capital) and energy. The cost of these other resources must also be assigned to the various activities. They are assigned in the same way as was described for labor (using direct tracing and resource drivers). The cost of computers could be assigned by using direct tracing (for the supervising activity) and hours of usage for the remaining activities. From the

Exhibit 18-7

Work Distribution Matrix for Hemingway Bank's Credit Card Department

Activity	Percentage of Time per Activity
Processing transactions	40%
Preparing statements	30%
Answering questions	30%

interview, we know the relative usage of computers by each activity. The general ledger reveals that the cost per computer is $1,200 per year. Thus, an additional $6,000 (5 × $1,200) would be assigned to three activities based on relative usage:

- 70 percent to processing transactions ($4,200)
- 20 percent to preparing statements ($1,200)
- 10 percent to answering questions ($600)

Repeating this process for all resources, the total cost of each activity can be calculated. Exhibit 18-8 gives the cost of the activities associated with Hemingway's credit card department under the assumption that all resource costs have been assigned (these numbers are assumed because all resource data are not given for their calculation).

Assigning Costs to Products

From Cornerstone 18-3 (p. 917), we know that activity costs are assigned to products by multiplying a predetermined activity rate by the usage of the activity, as measured by activity drivers. Exhibit 18-6 (p. 922) identified the activity drivers for each of the four credit card activities:

- number of transactions for processing transactions
- number of statements for preparing statements
- number of calls for answering questions
- number of teller transactions for the activity of providing automatic tellers

To calculate an activity rate, the practical capacity of each activity must be determined. To assign costs, the amount of each activity consumed by each product must also be known.

Illustrative Example: Hemingway Bank Assuming that the practical activity capacity is equal to the total activity usage by all products, the following actual data have been collected for Hemingway's credit card department:

	Classic Card	Gold Card	Platinum Card	Total
Number of cards	5,000	3,000	2,000	10,000
Transactions processed	600,000	300,000	100,000	1,000,000
Number of statements	60,000	36,000	24,000	120,000
Number of calls	10,000	12,000	8,000	30,000
Number of teller transactions*	15,000	3,000	2,000	20,000

*The number of teller transactions for the cards is 10 percent of the total transactions from all sources. Thus, teller transactions total 20,000 (0.10 × 200,000).

Exhibit 18-8

Activity Costs for Hemingway Bank's Credit Card Department

Processing transactions	$130,000
Preparing statements	102,000
Answering questions	92,400
Providing automatic tellers	250,000

Exhibit 18-9

Assigning Costs for Hemingway Bank's Credit Card Department

	Gold	Classic	Platinum
Processing transactions:			
$0.13 × 600,000	$ 78,000		
$0.13 × 300,000		$ 39,000	
$0.13 × 100,000			$13,000
Preparing statements:			
$0.85 × 60,000	51,000		
$0.85 × 36,000		30,600	
$0.85 × 24,000			20,400
Answering questions:			
$3.08 × 10,000	30,800		
$3.08 × 12,000		36,960	
$3.08 × 8,000			24,640
Providing automatic tellers:			
$1.25 × 15,000	18,750		
$1.25 × 3,000		3,750	
$1.25 × 2,000			2,500
Total costs	$178,550	$110,310	$60,540
Units	÷5,000	÷3,000	÷2,000
Unit cost	$ 35.71	$ 36.77	$ 30.27

Applying Cornerstone 18-2 (p. 916) by using the data and costs from Exhibit 18-8, the activity rates are calculated as follows:

Rate calculations:

Processing transactions:	$130,000/1,000,000 = $0.13 per transaction
Preparing statements:	$102,000/120,000 = $0.85 per statement
Answering questions:	$92,400/30,000 = $3.08 per call
Providing automatic tellers:	$250,000/200,000 = $1.25 per transaction

These rates provide the cost of each activity usage. Using these rates, costs are assigned as shown in Exhibit 18-9. However, we now know the whole story behind the development of the activity rates and usage measures. Furthermore, the banking example emphasizes the utility of ABC in service organizations.

ACTIVITY-BASED CUSTOMER COSTING AND ACTIVITY-BASED SUPPLIER COSTING

OBJECTIVE 3
Describe activity-based customer costing and activity-based supplier costing.

ABC systems originally became popular for their ability to improve product-costing accuracy by tracing activity costs to the products that consume the activities. However, since the beginning of the 21st century, the use of ABC has expanded into areas upstream (i.e., before the production section of the value chain—research and development, prototyping, etc.) and downstream (i.e., after the production section of the value chain—marketing, distribution, customer service, etc.) from production. Specifically, ABC often is used to more accurately determine the upstream costs of suppliers and the downstream costs of customers. Knowing the costs of suppliers and customers can be vital information for improving a company's profitability.

LSI Logic, a high-tech producer of semiconductors, implemented ABC customer costing and discovered that 10 percent of its customers were responsible for about 90 percent of its profits. LSI also discovered that it was actually losing money on about 50 percent of its customers. It worked to convert its unprofitable customers into profitable ones and invited those who would not provide a fair return to take their

Exhibit 18-10

The Whale Curve of Cumulative Customer Profitability

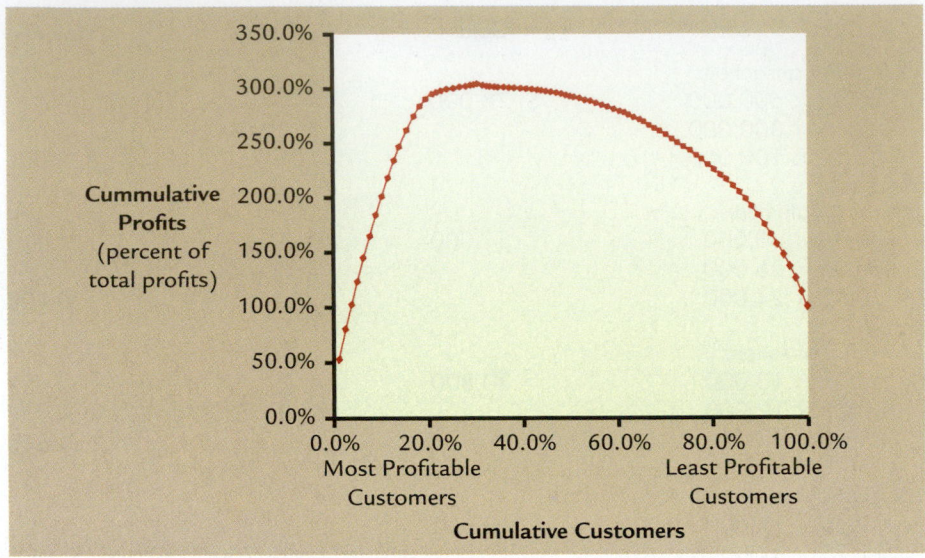

business elsewhere. As a consequence, LSI's sales decreased, but its profit tripled.[3] Exhibit 18-10 depicts this interesting yet common relationship between customers and their contribution to company profitability. Some managers refer to this graph as the "whale curve" of customer profitability, likely because of its resemblance to the shape of whale cresting at the water's surface. The important observation from the curve is that the customers to the left of the hump, or peak, increase the company's profitability, while the customers to the right decrease the company's profitability. Therefore, activity-based customer costing is helpful in determining where each customer falls on the curve and, subsequently, how each customer should therefore be treated given its position on the curve. Of particular interest are those customers to the far right because they severely decrease the company's profitability and need to be terminated as unacceptably bad customers or altered in some way so as to become profitable customers for the company.

Activity-Based Customer Costing

Customers are cost objects of fundamental interest. As the **LSI Logic** experience illustrates, customer management can produce significant gains in profit. It is possible to have customer diversity, just as it is possible to have product diversity. Customers can consume customer-driven activities in different proportions. Sources of customer diversity include order frequency, delivery frequency, geographic distance, sales and promotional support, and engineering support requirements. Knowing how much it costs to service different customers can be vital information for the following purposes:

- setting pricing
- determining customer mix
- improving profitability

Furthermore, because of diversity of customers, multiple drivers are needed to trace costs accurately. This outcome means that ABC can be useful to organizations that have only one product, homogeneous products, or a just-in-time (JIT) structure where direct tracing diminishes the value of ABC for product costing.

Customer Costing versus Product Costing Assigning the costs of customer service to customers is done in the same way that manufacturing costs are assigned to

---

[3] Gary Cokins, "Are All of Your Customers Profitable (To You)?" (June 14, 2001): http://www.bettermanagment.com/Library (accessed May 2010).

products. Customer-driven activities such as order entry, order picking, shipping, making sales calls, and evaluating a client's credit are identified and listed in an activity dictionary. The cost of the resources consumed is assigned to activities, and the cost of the activities is assigned to individual customers. The same model and procedures that apply to products apply to customers as well. **CORNERSTONE 18-5** illustrates how ABC assigns costs to customers.

Concept Q&A

How are costs assigned to customers by using the ABC approach?

Answer:
Costs are traced to activities and then assigned to customers based on their usage of these activities.

CORNERSTONE 18-5   Calculating Activity-Based Customer Costs

Information:

Milan Company produces precision parts for 11 major buyers. Of the 11 customers, one accounts for 50 percent of the sales, with the remaining 10 accounting for the rest of the sales. The 10 smaller customers purchase parts in roughly equal quantities. Orders placed by the smaller customers are about the same size. Data concerning Milan's customer activity follow:

	Large Customer	Ten Smaller Customers
Units purchased	500,000	500,000
Orders placed	2	200
Number of sales calls	10	210
Manufacturing costs	$3,000,000	$3,000,000
Order filling costs allocated*	$202,000	$202,000
Sales force costs allocated*	$110,000	$110,000

*Allocated based on sales volume.

Currently, customer-driven costs are assigned to customers based on units sold, a unit-level driver.

Required:

Assign costs to customers using an ABC approach.

Solution:

The appropriate drivers are orders placed and number of sales calls.
The activity rates are:

$$\$404{,}000/202 \text{ orders} = \$2{,}000 \text{ per order}$$
$$\$220{,}000/220 \text{ calls} = \$1{,}000 \text{ per call}$$

Using this information, the customer-driven costs can be assigned to each group of customers as follows:

	Large Customer	Ten Smaller Customers
Order filling costs:		
($2,000 × 2)	$ 4,000	
($2,000 × 200)		$400,000
Sales force costs:		
($1,000 × 10)	10,000	
($1,000 × 210)		210,000
	$14,000	$610,000

The activity-based cost assignments reveal a much different picture of the cost of servicing each type of customer. The smaller customer is costing more due to its smaller, more frequent orders and the need of the sales force to engage in more negotiations to make a sale.

What does this analysis tell management that it didn't know before? First, the large customer costs much less to service than the smaller customers and perhaps should be charged less. Second, it raises some significant questions relative to the smaller customers. For example, is it possible to encourage larger, less frequent orders? Perhaps offering discounts for larger orders would be appropriate. Why is it more difficult to sell to the smaller customers? Why are more calls needed? Are they less informed than the larger customer about the products? Can we improve profits by influencing our customers to change their buying behavior?

Activity-Based Supplier Costing

ABC can also help managers identify the true cost of a firm's suppliers. The cost of a supplier is much more than the purchase price of the components or materials acquired. Just like customers, suppliers can affect many internal activities of a firm and significantly increase the cost of purchasing. A more correct view is one where the costs associated with quality, reliability, and late deliveries are added to the purchase costs. Managers are then required to evaluate suppliers based on total cost, not just purchase price. ABC is the key to tracing costs relating to these factors.

Supplier Costing Methodology
Assigning the costs of supplier-related activities to suppliers follows the same pattern as ABC product and customer costing. Supplier-driven activities are identified and listed in an activity dictionary. Some examples of supplier-driven activities include the following:

- purchasing
- receiving
- inspection of incoming components
- reworking products (because of defective components)
- expediting products (because of late deliveries of suppliers)
- warranty work (due to defective supplier components)

The cost of the resources consumed is assigned to these activities, and the cost of the activities is assigned to individual suppliers. **CORNERSTONE 18-6** illustrates how to use ABC for supplier costing.

Concept Q&A

How are costs assigned to suppliers by using the ABC approach?

Answer:
Costs are traced to activities and are then assigned to suppliers based on a cause-and-effect relationship.

CORNERSTONE 18-6   Calculating Activity-Based Supplier Costs

Information:
Assume that a purchasing manager uses two suppliers, Murray Inc. and Plata Associates, as the source of two machine parts: Part A1 and Part B2. Consider two activities: repairing products (under warranty) and expediting products. Repairing products occurs because of part failure (bought from suppliers). Expediting products occurs because suppliers are late in delivering needed parts. Activity cost information and other data needed for supplier costing follow:

I. Activity Costs Caused by Suppliers (e.g., failed parts or late delivery)

Activity	Costs
Repairing products	$800,000
Expediting products	$200,000

(Continued)

II. Supplier Data

CORNERSTONE
18-6
(continued)

	Murray Inc.		Plata Associates	
	Part A1	Part B2	Part A1	Part B2
Unit purchase price	$ 20	$ 52	$ 24	$ 56
Units purchased	80,000	40,000	10,000	10,000
Failed units	1,600	380	10	10
Late shipments	60	40	0	0

Required:
Determine the cost of each supplier by using ABC.

Solution:
Using the above data, the activity rates for assigning costs to suppliers are computed as follows:

Repair rate = $800,000/2,000* unit
$\qquad$ = $400 per failed unit

*(1,600 + 380 + 10 + 10)

Expediting rate = $200,000/100** late shipment
$\qquad$ = $2,000 per late shipment

**(60 + 40)

Using these rates and the activity data, the total purchasing cost per unit of each component is computed:

	Murray Inc.		Plata Associates	
	Part A1	Part B2	Part A1	Part B2
Purchase cost:				
$20 × 80,000	$1,600,000			
$52 × 40,000		$2,080,000		
$24 × 10,000			$240,000	
$56 × 10,000				$560,000
Repairing products:				
$400 × 1,600	$ 640,000			
$400 × 380		$ 152,000		
$400 × 10			$ 4,000	
$400 × 10				$ 4,000
Expediting products:				
$2,000 × 60	120,000			
$2,000 × 40		80,000		
Total costs	$2,360,000	$2,312,000	$244,000	$564,000
Units	÷80,000	÷40,000	÷10,000	÷10,000
Total unit cost	$ 29.50	$ 57.80	$ 24.40	$ 56.40

The example in Cornerstone 18-6 shows that Murray, the "low-cost" supplier (as measured by the purchase price of the two parts), actually costs more when the supplier-related activities of repairing and expediting are considered. If all costs are considered, then the choice becomes clear: Plata Associates is the better supplier with a higher-quality product, more on-time deliveries, and, consequently, a lower overall cost per unit.

YOU DECIDE   Managing Customer Profitability

As a consultant, you recently implemented an activity-based customer-profitability system. In your written report to management, you classified the customers of the company into one of four categories based on current profitability and the potential for future profitability[4]:

High Profitability, Substantial Future Potential   High Profitability, Limited Future Potential
Low Profitability, Substantial Future Potential   Low Profitability, Limited Future Potential

After discussing the report with the CEO, he asks you to answer the following question:

How would you manage the customers in each of the four categories?

For highly profitable customers, and especially those with long-term potential, special efforts should be made to retain these customers as it is much more expensive to attract new customers. Offering these customers special discounts and new products and service lines coupled with managing their costs-to-serve to a lower level and improving business processes are ways to increase customer satisfaction while at the same time maintaining or increasing profitability. For customers with low profitability but substantial potential, the goal is to move these customers up to a high profitability state. Pricing policies or initiatives related to both the order and the transactions caused by the order is one way to increase profitability (e.g., activity-based pricing is based on the costs-to-serve, something clearly revealed by the ABC customer model). Another way is to lower the costs to serve by improving activity efficiency and eliminating nonvalue-added activities. The final category of customers (low-profitability and limited potential) is managed up or out—these customers need to be made profitable quickly or simply dropped.

Knowing customer profitability is important because not every revenue dollar contributes equally to overall profitability. Thus, it is critical for a manager to understand the net profit contribution that each customer makes to the company. Understanding individual customer profitability and the associated drivers allows managers to take actions to sustain and maintain profitable customers and transform unprofitable customers into profitable customers.[5]

OBJECTIVE 4
Explain how activity-based management can be used for cost reduction.

PROCESS-VALUE ANALYSIS

Process-value analysis is fundamental to *activity-based management*. **Activity-based management** is a system-wide, integrated approach that focuses management's attention on activities with the objective of improving customer value and profit achieved by providing this value. **Process value analysis** focuses on cost reduction instead of cost assignment and emphasizes the maximization of systemwide performance. As Exhibit 18-11 illustrates, process-value analysis is concerned with:

- driver analysis
- activity analysis
- performance measurement

Driver Analysis: The Search for Root Causes

Managing activities requires an understanding of what causes activity costs. Every activity has inputs and outputs. **Activity inputs** are the resources consumed by the activity in

Exhibit 18-11

Process-Value Analysis Model

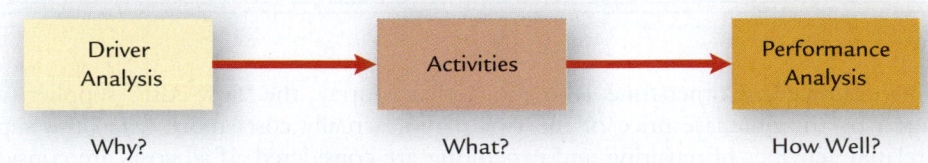

Driver Analysis → Activities → Performance Analysis

Why?   What?   How Well?

4 Based on a classification in Cokins, Gary, *Performance Management: Finding the Missing Pieces (to Close the Intelligence Gap)*. Wiley and SAS Business Series, March 29, 2004.
5 Kaplan, Robert S. and V. G. Narayanan, "Measuring and Managing Customer Profitability," *Journal of Cost Management*, (September/October 2001) 5–15.

producing its output. **Activity output** is the result or product of an activity. For example, if the activity is moving materials, the inputs would be such things as a forklift, a forklift driver, fuel (for the forklift), and crates. The output would be moved goods and materials. An **activity output measure** is the number of times the activity is performed. It is the quantifiable measure of the output. For example, the number of moves or distance moved are possible output measures for the material moving activity.

The output measure effectively is a measure of the demands placed on an activity and is what we have been calling an *activity driver*. As the demands for an activity change, the cost of the activity can change. For example, as the number of programs written increases, the activity of writing programs may need to consume more inputs (labor, CD-ROMs, paper, and so on). However, output measures, such as the number of programs, may not (and usually do not) correspond to the root causes of activity costs. They are the consequences of the activity being performed. The purpose of driver analysis is to reveal root causes. Thus, **driver analysis** is the effort expended to identify those factors that are the root causes of activity costs. For example, an analysis may reveal that the root cause of the cost of moving materials is plant layout. Once the root cause is known, then action can be taken to improve the activity. Specifically, reorganizing plant layout can reduce the cost of moving materials.

Often, the root cause of the cost of an activity is also the root cause of other related activities. For example, the costs of inspecting purchased parts and reordering may both be caused by poor supplier quality. By working with suppliers to reduce the number of defective components supplied (or choosing suppliers that have fewer defects), the demand for both activities may then decrease, allowing the company to save money.

Activity Analysis: Identifying and Assessing Value Content

The heart of process-value analysis is activity analysis. **Activity analysis** is the process of identifying, describing, and evaluating the activities that an organization performs. Activity analysis produces four outcomes:

1. what activities are done
2. how many people perform the activities
3. the time and resources required to perform the activities
4. an assessment of the value of the activities to the organization, including a recommendation to select and keep only those that add value.

Steps 1 through 3 have been described earlier and are common to the information needed for determining and assigning activity costs. Knowing how much an activity costs is clearly an important part of activity-based management. Step 4, determining the value-added content of activities, is concerned with cost reduction rather than cost assignment. Thus, some managerial accountants feel that this is the most important part of activity analysis. Activities can be classified as *value-added* or *nonvalue-added*.

Value-Added Activities   Those activities necessary to remain in business are called **value-added activities**. Some activities—required activities—are necessary to comply with legal mandates. Activities needed to comply with the reporting requirements of the Securities and Exchange Commission (SEC) and the filing requirements of the Internal Revenue Service (IRS) are examples. These activities are value-added by *mandate*. The remaining activities in the firm are *discretionary*. A discretionary activity is classified as value-added provided it simultaneously satisfies all of the following conditions:

- The activity produces a change of state.
- The change of state was not achievable by preceding activities.
- The activity enables other activities to be performed.

For example, consider the production of rods used in hydraulic cylinders. The first activity, cutting rods, cuts long rods into the correct lengths for the cylinders.

Next, the cut rods are welded to cut plates. The cutting rods activity is value-added because:

- It causes a change of state—uncut rods become cut rods.
- No prior activity was supposed to create this change of state.
- It enables the welding activity to be performed.

Though the value-added properties are easy to see for an operational activity like cutting rods, what about a more general activity like supervising production workers? A managerial activity is specifically designed to manage other value-added activities—to ensure that they are performed in an efficient and timely manner. Supervision certainly satisfies the enabling condition. Is there a change in state? There are two ways of answering affirmatively:

- First, supervising can be viewed as an enabling resource that is consumed by the operational activities that do produce a change of state. Thus, supervising is a secondary activity that serves as an input that is needed to help bring about the change of state expected for value-added primary activities.
- Second, it could be argued that the supervision brings order by changing the state from uncoordinated activities to coordinated activities.

Once value-added activities are identified, we can define value-added costs. **Value-added costs** are the costs to perform value-added activities with perfect efficiency.

Nonvalue-Added Activities

Nonvalue-Added Activities All activities other than those that are absolutely essential to remain in business, and therefore considered unnecessary, are referred to as **nonvalue-added activities**. A nonvalue-added activity can be identified by its failure to satisfy any one of the three previous defining conditions for adding value. Violation of the first two conditions is the usual case for nonvalue-added activities. Inspecting cut rods (for correct length), for example, is a nonvalue-added activity. Inspection is a state-detection activity, not a state-changing activity. (It tells us the state of the cut rod—whether it is the right length.) Thus, it fails the first condition (activity produced a change of state). Consider the activity of reworking goods or subassemblies. Rework is designed to bring a good from a non-conforming state to a conforming state. Thus, a change of state occurs. Yet the activity is nonvalue-added because it repeats work; it is doing something that should have been done by preceding activities Condition 2 (change of state was not achievable by preceding activities) is violated.

Nonvalue-added costs are costs that are caused either by nonvalue-added activities or the inefficient performance of valued-added activities. For nonvalue-added activities, the nonvalue-added cost is the cost of the activity itself. For inefficient value-added activities, the activity cost must be broken into its value-added and nonvalue-added components. For example, if Receiving should use 10,000 receiving orders but uses 20,000, then half of the cost of Receiving is value-added and half is nonvalue-added. The value-added component is the waste-free component of the value-added activity and is, therefore, the *value-added standard*. Due to increased competition, many firms are attempting to eliminate nonvalue-added activities because they add unnecessary cost and impede performance. Firms are also striving to optimize value-added activities. Thus activity analysis identifies and eventually eliminates all unnecessary activities and, simultaneously, increases the efficiency of necessary activities.

The theme of activity analysis is waste elimination. As waste is eliminated, costs are reduced. The cost reduction *follows* the elimination of waste. Note the value of managing the causes of the costs rather than the costs themselves. Though managing costs may increase the efficiency of an activity, if the activity is unnecessary, what does it matter if it's performed efficiently? An unnecessary activity is wasteful and should be eliminated. For example, moving raw materials and partially finished goods is often cited as a nonvalue-added activity. Installing an automated materials handling system may increase the efficiency of this activity, but changing to cellular manufacturing with on-site, just-in-time delivery of raw materials could virtually eliminate the activity. It's easy to see which is preferable.

Examples of Nonvalue-Added Activities Reordering parts, expediting production, and rework because of defective parts are all examples of nonvalue-added activities. Other examples include warranty work, handling customer complaints, and reporting defects. Nonvalue-added activities can exist anywhere in the organization. In the manufacturing operation, the following major activities are often cited as wasteful and unnecessary:

- *Scheduling:* An activity that uses time and resources to determine when different products have access to processes (or when and how many setups must be done) and how much will be produced.
- *Moving:* An activity that uses time and resources to move raw materials, work in process, and finished goods from one department to another.
- *Waiting:* An activity in which raw materials or work in process use time and resources by waiting on the next process.
- *Inspecting:* An activity in which time and resources are spent ensuring that the product meets specifications.
- *Storing:* An activity that uses time and resources while a good or raw material is held in inventory.

None of these activities adds any value for the customer. (Note that inspection would not be necessary if the product were produced correctly the first time and, therefore, adds no value for the customer.) The challenge of activity analysis is to find ways to produce the good without using any of these activities.

risteski goce,2010/Shutterstock.com

Here's the Real Kicker

For **Stillwater Designs**, warranty work is a significant cost. Warranty work associated with defective products is typically labeled a nonvalue-added cost. Stillwater Designs recognizes the nonvalue-added nature of this activity and takes measures to eliminate the causes of the defective units. The company tracks return failures (over time) and provides this information to its research and development (R&D) department. R&D then uses this information to make design improvements on existing models (running changes) as well as to change the design on future models. The objective of the design changes is to reduce the demand for the warranty activity, thus reducing warranty cost.

However, not all **Kicker** warranty costs can be classified as nonvalue-added. When products are returned, customer service decides whether or not the problem is covered under warranty. Sometimes, problems are covered even though they are not attributable to a defective product. When the company decides to replace a nondefective product, it is making a conscious decision to increase customer satisfaction and brand loyalty. This part of the warranty cost is a "marketing warranty cost" and could be classified as a value-added cost. For example, customers sometimes buy amplifiers that are more powerful than the subwoofers can handle, resulting in burnt voice coils. By replacing the product (even though technically it's the customer's fault), the customer will be more likely to buy again and to provide good word-of-mouth advertising for Kicker products.

KICKER

Courtesy of Kicker

Cost Reduction Activity management carries with it the objective of cost reduction. Competitive conditions dictate that companies must deliver customer desired products on time and at the lowest possible cost. These conditions mean that an organization must continually strive for cost improvement. Activity management can reduce costs in four ways:[6]

- activity elimination
- activity selection
- activity reduction
- activity sharing

Activity Elimination Activity elimination focuses on nonvalue-added activities. Once activities that fail to add value are identified, measures must be taken to rid the

[6] Peter B. B. Turney, "How Activity-Based Costing Helps Reduce Cost," *Journal of Cost Management* (Winter 1991): 29–35.

organization of these activities. For example, the activity of inspecting incoming parts seems necessary to ensure that the product using the parts functions according to specifications. Use of a bad part can produce a bad final product. Yet this activity is necessary only because of the poor quality performance of the supplying firms. Selecting suppliers who are able to supply high-quality parts or who are willing to improve their quality performance to achieve this objective will eventually allow the elimination of incoming inspection. Cost reduction then follows.

Activity Selection Activity selection involves choosing among different sets of activities that are caused by competing strategies. Different strategies cause different activities. Different product design strategies, for example, can require significantly different activities. Activities, in turn, cause costs. Each product design strategy has its own set of activities and associated costs. All other things being equal, the lowest-cost design strategy should be chosen. In a continual-improvement environment, redesign of existing products and processes can lead to a different, cheaper set of activities. Thus activity selection can have a significant effect on cost reduction.

Activity Reduction Activity reduction decreases the time and resources required by an activity. This approach to cost reduction should be primarily aimed at improving the efficiency of necessary activities or a short-term strategy for improving nonvalue-added activities until they can be eliminated. Setup activity is a necessary activity that is often cited as an example for which less time and fewer resources need to be used. Finding ways to reduce setup time—and thus lower the cost of setups—is another example of the concept of gradual reductions in activity costs.

Activity Sharing Activity sharing increases the efficiency of necessary activities by using economies of scale. Specifically, the quantity of the cost driver is increased without increasing the total cost of the activity itself. This lowers the per-unit cost of the cost driver and the amount of cost traceable to the products that consume the activity. For example, a new product can be designed to use components already being used by other products. By using existing components, the activities associated with these components already exist, and the company avoids the creation of a whole new set of activities.

Assessing Nonvalue-Added Costs CORNERSTONE 18-7 shows how to determine the nonvalue-added cost of activities. Determining the cost is followed by a root-cause analysis and then by the selection of an approach to reduce the waste found in the activity. For example, defective products cause warranty work. Defective products, in turn, are caused by such factors as defective internal processes, poor product design, and defective supplier components. Correcting the causes will lead to the elimination of the warranty activity. Inefficient purchasing could be attributable to such root causes as poor product design (too many components), orders that are incorrectly filled out, and defective supplier components (producing additional orders). Correcting the causes will reduce the demand for the purchasing activity, and as the activity is reduced, cost reduction will follow.

 **CORNERSTONE 18-7**   **Assessing Nonvalue-Added Costs**

Information:
Consider the following two activities: (1) Performing warranty work, cost: $120,000. The warranty cost of the most efficient competitor is $20,000. (2) Purchasing components, cost: $200,000 (10,000 purchase orders). A benchmarking study reveals that the most efficient level will use 5,000 purchase orders and entail a cost of $100,000.

(Continued)

CORNERSTONE
18-7
(continued)

Required:
Determine the nonvalue-added cost of each activity.

Solution:
Determine the value content of each activity: Is the activity nonvalue-added or value-added?

1. Performing warranty work is nonvalue-added; it is done to correct something that wasn't done right the first time. Thus, the nonvalue-added cost of performing warranty work is $120,000. The cost of the competitor has no bearing on the analysis. Root causes for warranty work are defective products.

2. Purchasing components is necessary so that materials are available to produce products and, thus, is value-added. However, the activity is not performed efficiently, as revealed by the benchmarking study. The cost per purchase order is $20 ($100,000/5,000). The nonvalue-added cost is calculated as:

$$(\text{Actual quantity} - \text{Value-added quantity}) \times \text{Cost per purchase order}$$
$$(10,000 - 5,000) \times \$20 = \$100,000$$
$$(\text{or simply, } \$200,000 - \$100,000)$$

Activity Performance Measurement

Assessing how well activities (and processes) are performed is fundamental to management's efforts to improve profitability. Activity performance measures exist in both financial and nonfinancial forms. These measures are designed to assess how well an activity was performed and the results achieved. They are also designed to reveal if constant improvement is being realized. Measures of activity performance center on three major dimensions:

- efficiency
- time
- quality

Efficiency *Efficiency* focuses on the relationship of activity inputs to activity outputs. For example, one way to improve activity efficiency is to produce the same activity output with lower cost for the inputs used. Thus cost and trends in cost become important measures of efficiency.

Time The *time* required to perform an activity is also critical. Longer times usually mean more resource consumption and less ability to respond to customer demands. Time measures of performance tend to be nonfinancial, whereas efficiency and quality measures are both financial and nonfinancial.

Cycle time and velocity are two operational measures of time-based performance. Cycle time can be applied to any activity or process that produces an output, and it measures how long it takes to produce an output from start to finish. In a manufacturing process, **cycle time** is the length of time that it takes to produce a unit of output from the time raw materials are received (starting point of the cycle) until the good is delivered to finished goods inventory (finishing point of the cycle). Thus, cycle time is the time required to produce one unit of a product (Time/Units produced). **Velocity** is the number of units of output that can be produced in a given period of time (Units produced/Time). Notice that velocity is the reciprocal of cycle time. For the cycle time example, the velocity is two units per hour. **CORNERSTONE 18-8** demonstrates how to compute cycle time and velocity.

CORNERSTONE 18-8   Calculating Cycle Time and Velocity

Information:
Assume that Frost Company takes 10,000 hours to produce 20,000 units of a product.

Required:
What is the velocity in hours? Cycle time in hours? Cycle time in minutes?

Solution:

Velocity = 20,000/10,000 = 2 units per hour
Cycle time = 10,000/20,000 = 1/2 hour
= 10,000(60 minutes)/20,000 = 30 minutes

Quality *Quality* is concerned with doing the activity right the first time it is performed. If the activity output is defective, then the activity may need to be repeated, causing unnecessary cost and reduction in efficiency. Quality cost management is a major topic and is discussed in more detail next.

 **Q&A**

What are the three dimensions of performance for activities? Explain why they are important.

Answer:
Efficiency, time, and quality are the three performance dimensions. All three relate to the ability of a manager to reduce activity cost.

Quality Cost Management

Activity-based management also is useful for understanding how quality costs can be managed. Quality costs can be substantial *in size* and a source of significant savings *if managed effectively.* Improving quality can produce significant improvements in profitability and overall efficiency. Quality improvement can increase profitability in two ways:

- by increasing customer demand *and thus sales revenues*
- by decreasing costs

For example, when Toyota sold more cars and trucks than General Motors for the first time ever in 2007, some automotive industry experts attributed this crowning achievement to Toyota's long-time commitment to quality-related issues, such as quality cost management.[7]

Quality-Related Activities Quality-linked activities are those activities performed because poor quality may or does exist. The costs of performing these activities are referred to as **costs of quality**. The definitions of *quality-related activities* imply four categories of quality costs:

- prevention costs
- appraisal costs
- internal failure costs
- external failure costs

Thus, the costs of quality are associated with two subcategories of quality-related activities: *control activities and failure activities.*

Control Activities **Control activities** are performed by an organization to prevent or detect poor quality (because poor quality may exist). **Control costs** are the costs of performing control activities. Control activities are made up of prevention and appraisal activities.

  Prevention costs are incurred to prevent poor quality in the products or services being produced. As prevention costs increase, we would expect the costs of failure to decrease. Examples of prevention costs are quality engineering, quality training programs, quality planning, quality reporting, supplier evaluation and selection, quality audits, quality circles, field trials, and design reviews.

  Appraisal costs are incurred to determine whether products and services are conforming to their requirements or customer needs. Examples include inspecting and

[7] D. Jones, "Toyota's Success Pleases Proponents of 'Lean'," *USA Today* (May 3, 2007): 2B.

testing raw materials, packaging inspection, supervising appraisal activities, product acceptance, process acceptance, measurement (inspection and test) equipment, and outside endorsements. The main objective of the appraisal function is to prevent nonconforming goods from being shipped to customers.

Failure Activities **Failure activities** are performed by an organization or its customers in response to poor quality (poor quality does exist). **Failure costs** are the costs incurred by an organization because failure activities are performed. Notice that the definitions of *failure activities* and *failure costs* imply that customer response to poor quality can impose costs on an organization.

Internal failure costs are incurred when products and services do not conform to specifications or customer needs. This nonconformance is detected *before* the bad products or services (nonconforming, unreliable, not durable, and so on) are shipped or delivered to outside parties. These are the failures detected by appraisal activities. Examples of internal failure costs are scrap, rework, downtime (due to defects), reinspection, retesting, and design changes. These costs disappear if no defects exist.

External failure costs are incurred when products and services fail to conform to requirements or satisfy customer needs *after* being delivered to customers. Of all the costs of quality, this category can be the most devastating. For example, costs of recalls can run into the hundreds of millions of dollars. Other examples include lost sales because of poor product performance, returns and allowances because of poor quality, warranties, repairs, product liability, customer dissatisfaction, lost market share, and complaint adjustment. **Northwest Airlines** is notorious for placing near the bottom of customer satisfaction rankings, which some analysts believe consistently hurts its ticket sales. External failure costs, like internal failure costs, disappear if no defects exist.

Environmental Cost Management

For many organizations, management of environmental costs is becoming a matter of high priority and a significant competitive issue. Many executives now believe that improving environmental quality may actually reduce environmental costs rather than increase them. For example, between 2002 and 2008, **Baxter International Inc.**, a producer of medical products, reduced toxic wastes emitted to air, water, and soil; increased recycling activity; and, as a consequence, reported environmental income, savings, and cost avoidance for the seven-year period of $91.9 million.[8]

Before environmental cost information can be provided to management, environmental costs must be defined. Various possibilities exist; however, an appealing approach is to adopt a definition consistent with a total environmental quality model. Accordingly, environmental costs can be referred to as *environmental quality costs*. Similar to product quality, environmentally linked activities are those activities performed because poor environmental quality may or does exist. The costs of performing these activities are referred to as *environmental costs*. **Environmental costs** are associated with the creation, detection, remediation, and prevention of environmental degradation. With this definition, environmental costs, like quality costs, are classified into four analogous categories:

- prevention costs
- detection costs
- internal failure costs
- external failure costs

External failure costs, in turn, can be subdivided into realized and unrealized categories. As with quality costs, environmental costs are associated with two subcategories of environmentally related activities: *control activities* and *failure activities*.

Control Activities **Environmental prevention costs** are the costs of activities carried out to prevent the production of contaminants and/or waste that could cause damage to the environment. Examples of prevention activities include evaluating and selecting suppliers, evaluating and selecting equipment to control pollution, designing processes and products to reduce or eliminate contaminants, training employees, studying environmental impacts, auditing environmental risks, undertaking environmental research, developing environmental management systems, and recycling products.

[8] Baxter Environmental Financial Statement, 2008, at http://www.baxter.com/sustainability (accessed May 2010).

Environmental detection costs are the costs of activities executed to determine if products, processes, and other activities within the firm are in compliance with appropriate environmental standards. The environmental standards and procedures that a firm seeks to follow are defined in three ways:

- regulatory laws of governments
- voluntary standards developed by private organizations
- environmental policies developed by management

Examples of detection activities are auditing environmental activities, inspecting products and processes (for environmental compliance), developing environmental performance measures, carrying out contamination tests, verifying supplier environmental performance, and measuring levels of contamination.

Failure Activities **Environmental internal failure costs** are costs of activities performed because contaminants and waste have been produced but not discharged into the environment. Thus, internal failure costs are incurred to eliminate and manage contaminants or waste once produced. Internal failure activities have one of two goals:

- to ensure that the contaminants and waste produced are not released to the environment
- to reduce the level of contaminants released to an amount that complies with environmental standards

Examples of internal failure activities include operating equipment to minimize or eliminate pollution, treating and disposing of toxic materials, maintaining pollution equipment, licensing facilities for producing contaminants, and recycling scrap.

Environmental external failure costs are the costs of activities performed after discharging contaminants and waste into the environment. **Realized external failure costs** are those incurred and paid for by the firm. Examples of realized external failure activities are cleaning up a polluted lake, cleaning up oil spills, cleaning up contaminated soil, using materials and energy inefficiently, settling personal injury claims from environmentally unsound practices, settling property damage claims, restoring land to its natural state, and losing sales from a bad environmental reputation. **Unrealized external failure costs**, or **societal costs**, are caused by the firm but are incurred and paid for by parties outside the firm. Examples of societal costs include receiving medical care because of polluted air (individual welfare), losing a lake for recreational use because of contamination (degradation), losing employment because of contamination (individual welfare), and damaging ecosystems from solid waste disposal (degradation).

Why are there two categories of external failure costs?

Answer:
One category represents those external environmental costs that the firm causes and pays for, and the other category is those external environmental costs caused by the firm but paid for by parties outside the firm.

SUMMARY OF LEARNING OBJECTIVES

LO1.   Explain why functional (or volume)-based costing approaches may produce distorted costs.
- Overhead costs have increased in significance over time and in many firms represent a much higher percentage of product costs than direct labor.
- Many overhead activities are unrelated to the units produced.
- Functional-based costing systems are not able to assign the costs of these nonunit-based overhead activities properly.
- Nonunit-based overhead activities often are consumed by products in different proportions than are unit-based overhead activities. Because of this nonproportionality, assigning overhead by using only unit-based drivers can distort product costs.
- If the nonunit-based overhead costs are a significant proportion of total overhead costs, the inaccuracy in cost assignments can be a serious matter.

LO2.   Explain how an activity-based costing system works for product costing.
- Activities are identified and defined through the use of interviews and surveys. This information allows an activity dictionary to be constructed.
- The activity dictionary lists activities and potential activity drivers, classifies activities as primary or secondary, and provides any other attributes deemed to be important.

- Resource costs are assigned to activities by using direct tracing and resource drivers.
- The costs of secondary activities are ultimately assigned to primary activities by using activity drivers.
- Finally, the costs of primary activities are assigned to products, customers, and other cost objects.
- The cost assignment process is described by the following general steps: (1) identifying the major activities and building an activity dictionary, (2) determining the cost of those activities, (3) identifying a measure of consumption for activity costs (activity drivers), (4) calculating an activity rate, (5) measuring the demands placed on activities by each product, and (6) calculating product costs.

LO3.   Describe activity-based customer costing and activity-based supplier costing.
- Tracing customer-driven costs to customers can provide significant information to managers.
- Accurate customer costs allow managers to make better pricing decisions, customer-mix decisions, and other customer-related decisions that improve profitability.
- Tracing supplier-driven costs to suppliers can enable managers to choose the true low-cost suppliers, producing a stronger competitive position and increased profitability.

LO4.   Explain how activity-based management can be used for cost reduction.
- Assigning costs accurately is vital for good decision making.
- Assigning the costs of an activity accurately does not address the issue of whether or not the activity should be performed or whether it is being performed efficiently.
- Activity-based management focuses on process-value analysis.
- Process-value analysis has three components: driver analysis, activity analysis, and performance evaluation. These three steps determine what activities are being done, why they are being done, and how well they are done.
- Understanding the root causes of activities provides the opportunities to manage activities so that costs can be reduced.
- Quality and environmental activities are particularly susceptible to activity-based management.
- Quality costs are costs that are incurred because poor product quality exists or may exist.
- Environmental costs are costs that are incurred because environmental degradation exists or may exist.

SUMMARY OF IMPORTANT EQUATIONS

1. Consumption ratio $= \dfrac{\text{Amount of activity driver per product}}{\text{Total driver quantity}}$

2. Overhead rate $= \dfrac{\text{Total overhead costs}}{\text{Total direct labor hours}}$

3. Overhead cost $=$ Average consumption ratio $\times$ Total cost of each set of activities

CORNERSTONE 18-1 Calculating consumption ratios (p. 916)	
CORNERSTONE 18-2 Calculating activity rates (p. 916)	
CORNERSTONE 18-3 Calculating activity-based unit costs (p. 917)	
CORNERSTONE 18-4 Assigning resource costs to activities by using direct tracing and resource drivers (p. 923)	**CORNERSTONES**
CORNERSTONE 18-5 Calculating activity-based customer costs (p. 927)	FOR CHAPTER 18
CORNERSTONE 18-6 Calculating activity-based supplier costs (p. 928)	
CORNERSTONE 18-7 Assessing nonvalue-added costs (p. 934)	
CORNERSTONE 18-8 Calculating cycle time and velocity (p. 936)	

KEY TERMS

Activity (p. 920)
Activity analysis (p. 931)
Activity-based costing (ABC) system (p. 920)
Activity-based management (p. 930)
Activity dictionary (p. 922)
Activity drivers (p. 914)
Activity elimination (p. 933)
Activity inputs (p. 930)
Activity output measure (p. 931)
Activity output (p. 931)
Activity reduction (p. 934)
Activity selection (p. 934)
Activity sharing (p. 934)
Appraisal costs (p. 936)
Consumption ratio (p. 915)
Control activities (p. 936)
Control costs (p. 936)
Costs of quality (p. 936)
Cycle time (p. 935)
Driver analysis (p. 931)
Environmental costs (p. 937)
Environmental detection costs (p. 938)
Environmental external failure costs (p. 938)

Environmental internal failure costs (p. 938)
Environmental prevention costs (p. 937)
External failure costs (p. 937)
Failure activities (p. 937)
Failure costs (p. 937)
Internal failure costs (p. 937)
Nonunit-level activity drivers (p. 914)
Nonvalue-added activities (p. 932)
Nonvalue-added costs (p. 932)
Prevention costs (p. 936)
Process value analysis (p. 930)
Product diversity (p. 914)
Realized external failure costs (p. 938)
Resource drivers (p. 923)
Societal costs (p. 938)
Unit-level activities (p. 912)
Unit-level activity drivers (p. 914)
Unrealized external failure costs (p. 938)
Value-added activities (p. 931)
Value-added costs (p. 932)
Velocity (p. 935)
Work distribution matrix (p. 923)

REVIEW PROBLEMS

I. Plantwide Rates

Gee Company produces two types of stereo units: deluxe and regular. For the most recent year, Gee reports the following data:

Budgeted overhead	$180,000
Expected activity (in direct labor hours)	50,000
Actual activity (in direct labor hours)	51,000
Actual overhead	$200,000

	Deluxe	Regular
Units produced	5,000	50,000
Prime costs	$40,000	$300,000
Direct labor hours	5,000	46,000

Required:

1. Calculate a predetermined overhead rate based on direct labor hours.

2. What is the applied overhead?

3. What is the under- or overapplied overhead?

4. Calculate the unit cost of each stereo unit.

Solution:

1. Rate = $180,000/50,000 = $3.60 per direct labor hour

2. Applied overhead = $3.60 × 51,000 = $183,600

3. Overhead variance = $200,000 − $183,600 = $16,400 underapplied

4.   Unit cost:

	Deluxe	Regular
Prime costs	$40,000	$300,000
Overhead costs:		
$3.60 × 5,000	18,000	
$3.60 × 46,000		165,600
Total manufacturing costs	$58,000	$465,600
Units produced	÷5,000	÷50,000
Unit cost (Total costs/Units)	$ 11.60	$ 9.31*

*Rounded.

II. Departmental Rates

Gee Company gathers the following departmental data for a second year. Two types of stereo units are produced: deluxe and regular.

	Fabrication	Assembly
Budgeted overhead	$120,000	$60,000
Expected and actual usage (direct labor hours):		
Deluxe	3,000	2,000
Regular	3,000	43,000
	6,000	45,000
Expected and actual usage (machine hours):		
Deluxe	2,000	5,000
Regular	18,000	5,000
	20,000	10,000

In addition to the departmental data, the following information is provided:

	Deluxe	Regular
Units produced	5,000	50,000
Prime costs	$40,000	$300,000

Required:
1.   Calculate departmental overhead rates by using machine hours for fabrication and direct labor hours for assembly.
2.   Calculate the applied overhead by department.
3.   Calculate the applied overhead by product.
4.   Calculate unit costs.

Solution:
1.   Departmental rates

Fabrication: $120,000/20,000 machine hours = $6.00 per machine hour
Assembly: $60,000/45,000 direct labor hours = $1.33* per direct labor hour

*Rounded.

2.   Applied overhead (by department):

Fabrication: $6.00 × 20,000 = $120,000
Assembly: $1.33 × 45,000 = $59,850

3.   Applied overhead (by product):

Deluxe: ($6.00 × 2,000) + ($1.33 × 2,000) = $14,660
Regular: ($6.00 × 18,000) + ($1.33 × 43,000) = $165,190

4.   Unit cost:

Deluxe: ($40,000 + $14,660)/5,000 = $10.93*
Regular: ($300,000 + $165,190)/50,000 = $9.30*

*Rounded to nearest cent.

III. Activity-Based Rates

Gee Company produces two types of stereo units: deluxe and regular. Activity data follow:

	Product-Costing Data		
Activity Usage Measures	Deluxe	Regular	Total
Units produced per year	5,000	50,000	55,000
Prime costs	$39,000	$369,000	$408,000
Direct labor hours	5,000	45,000	50,000
Machine hours	10,000	90,000	100,000
Production runs	10	5	15
Number of moves	120	60	180

Activity Cost Data (Overhead Activities)

Activity	Cost
Setups	$ 60,000
Material handling	30,000
Power	50,000
Testing	40,000
Total	$180,000

Required:

1. Calculate the consumption ratios for each activity.

2. Group activities based on the consumption ratios.

3. Calculate a rate for each pooled group of activities.

4. Using the pool rates, calculate unit product costs.

Solution:

1. Consumption ratios:

Overhead Activity	Deluxe	Regular	Activity Driver
Setups	0.67[a]	0.33[a]	Production runs
Material handling	0.67[b]	0.33[b]	Number of moves
Power	0.10[c]	0.90[c]	Machine hours
Testing	0.10[d]	0.90[d]	Direct labor hours

[a] 10/15 (deluxe) and 5/15 (regular)
[b] 120/180 (deluxe) and 60/180 (regular)
[c] 10,000/100,000 (deluxe) and 90,000/100,000 (regular)
[d] 5,000/50,000 (deluxe) and 45,000/50,000 (regular)

2. Batch-level: Setups and Material handling
   Unit-level: Power and Testing

3.

Batch-Level Pool			Unit-Level Pool	
Setups	$60,000		Power	$ 50,000
Material handling	30,000		Testing	40,000
Total	$90,000		Total	$ 90,000
Runs	÷15		Machine hours	÷100,000
Pool rate	$ 6,000 per run		Pool rate	$ 0.90 per machine hour

4. Unit costs: Activity-based costing

	Deluxe	Regular
Prime costs	$ 39,000	$369,000
Overhead costs:		
Batch-level pool:		
($6,000 × 10)	60,000	
($6,000 × 5)		30,000

(Continued)

	Deluxe	Regular
Unit-level pool:		
($0.90 × 10,000)	9,000	
($0.90 × 90,000)		81,000
Total manufacturing costs	$108,000	$480,000
Units produced	÷5,000	÷50,000
Unit cost (Total costs/Units)	$ 21.60	$ 9.60

IV. Environmental Costs

At the beginning of 2012, Kleaner Company initiated a program to improve its environmental performance. Efforts were made to reduce the production and emission of contaminating gaseous, solid, and liquid residues. By the end of the year, in an executive meeting, the environmental manager indicated that the company had made significant improvement in its environmental performance, reducing the emission of contaminating residues of all types. The president of the company was pleased with the reported success but wanted an assessment of the financial consequences of the environmental improvements. To satisfy this request, the following financial data were collected for 2011 and 2012 (all changes in costs are a result of environmental improvements):

	2011	2012
Sales	$20,000,000	$20,000,000
Evaluating and selecting suppliers	0	600,000
Treating and disposing of toxic materials	1,200,000	800,000
Inspecting processes (environmental objective)	200,000	300,000
Land restoration (annual fund contribution)	1,600,000	1,200,000
Maintaining pollution equipment	400,000	300,000
Testing for contaminants	150,000	100,000

Required:
Classify the costs as prevention, detection, internal failure, or external failure.

Solution:
Prevention costs: evaluating and selecting suppliers
Detection costs: testing for contaminants and inspecting processes
Internal failure: maintaining pollution equipment and treating and disposing of toxic materials
External failure: land restoration

DISCUSSION QUESTIONS

1. Describe the two-stage process associated with plantwide overhead rates.
2. Describe the two-stage process for departmental overhead rates.
3. What are nonunit-level overhead activities? Nonunit-based cost drivers? Give some examples.
4. What is meant by "product diversity"?
5. What is an overhead consumption ratio?
6. What is activity-based product costing?
7. What is an activity dictionary?
8. Explain how costs are assigned to activities.
9. Describe the value of activity-based customer costing.
10. Explain how ABC can help a firm identify its true low-cost suppliers.
11. What is driver analysis? What role does it play in process-value analysis?
12. What are value-added activities? Value-added costs?
13. What are nonvalue-added activities? Nonvalue-added costs? Give an example of each.
14. Identify and define four different ways to manage activities so that costs can be reduced.
15. What is cycle time? Velocity?

MULTIPLE-CHOICE EXERCISES

18-1 A unit-level driver is consumed by a product each and every time that

a. a batch of products is produced.
b. a unit is produced.
c. a purchase order is issued.
d. a customer complains.
e. none of these.

18-2 Which of the following is a nonunit-level driver?

a. Direct labor hours
b. Machine hours
c. Direct materials
d. Setup hours
e. Assembly hours

Use the following information for Multiple-Choice Exercises 18-3 and 18-4:
Consider the information given on two products and their activity usage:

	Laser Printer	Inkjet Printer
Units produced	1,000	4,000
Setup hours	800	400
Inspection hours	500	500
Machine hours	200	1,000

18-3 Refer to the information above. The consumption ratios for the setup activity for each product are

a. 0.167; 0.833.
b. 0.333; 0.667.
c. 0.500; 0.500.
d. 0.667; 0.333.
e. none of these.

18-4 Refer to the information above. Suppose that machine hours are used to assign all overhead costs to the two products. Select the best answer from the following:

a. Laser printers are overcosted, and inkjet printers are undercosted.
b. Laser printers and inkjet printers are accurately costed.
c. Laser printers are undercosted, and inkjet printers are overcosted.
d. Using inspection hours to assign overhead costs is the most accurate approach.
e. None of the above.

18-5 The first stage of ABC entails the assignment of

a. resource costs to departments.
b. activity costs to products or customers.
c. resource costs to a plantwide pool.
d. resource costs to distribution channels.
e. resource costs to individual activities.

18-6 The second stage of ABC entails the assignment of

a. activity costs to products or customers.
b. resource costs to departments.
c. resource costs to a plantwide pool.
d. resource costs to individual activities.
e. resource costs to distribution channels.

18-7 Interview questions are asked to determine

a. what activities are being performed.
b. who performs the activities.
c. the relative amount of time spent on each activity by individual workers.
d. possible activity drivers for assigning costs to products.
e. all of these.

18-8 The receiving department employs one worker, who spends 25 percent of his time on the receiving activity and 75 percent of his time on inspecting products. His salary is $40,000. The amount of cost assigned to the receiving activity is

a. $34,000.
b. $40,000.
c. $10,000.

d. $30,000.
e. none of these.

18-9 Assume that the moving activity has an expected cost of $80,000. Expected direct labor hours are 40,000, and expected number of moves is 20,000. The best activity rate for moving is

a. $4 per move.
b. $1.33 per hour-move.
c. $4 per hour.

d. $2 per move.
e. none of these.

18-10 Which of the following is a true statement about activity-based customer costing?

a. Customer diversity does not require multiple drivers to trace costs accurately to customers.
b. Customers consume customer-driven activities in the same proportions.
c. It seldom produces changes in the company's customer mix.
d. It never improves profitability.
e. None of the above are true.

18-11 Which of the following is a true statement about activity-based supplier costing?

a. The cost of a supplier is the purchase price of the components or materials acquired.
b. It encourages managers to increase the number of suppliers.
c. It encourages managers to evaluate suppliers based on purchase cost.
d. Suppliers can affect many internal activities of a firm and significantly increase the cost of purchasing.
e. All of the above are true.

18-12 This year, Lambert Company will ship 1,500,000 pounds of goods to customers at a cost of $1,200,000. If a customer orders 10,000 pounds and produces $200,000 of revenue (total revenue is $20 million), the amount of shipping cost assigned to the customer by using ABC would be

a. unable to be determined.
b. $8,000 ($0.80 per pound shipped).
c. $24,000 (2 percent of the shipping cost).

d. $12,000 (1 percent of the shipping cost).
e. none of these.

18-13 Lambert Company has two suppliers: Deming and Leming. The cost of warranty work due to defective components is $2,000,000. The total units repaired under warranty average 100,000, of which 90,000 have components from Deming and 10,000 have components from Leming. Select the items below that represent true statements.

a. Components purchased from Leming cost $200,000 more than their purchase price.
b. Components purchased from Deming cost $1,800,000 more than their purchase price.
c. Components from Leming appear to be of higher quality.
d. All of the above are true.
e. None of the above is true.

18-14 A forklift and its driver used for moving materials are examples of

a. activity inputs.
b. activity output measures.
c. resource drivers.

d. activity outputs.
e. root causes.

18-15 Which of the following are nonvalue-added activities?

a. Moving goods
b. Storing goods
c. Inspecting finished goods

d. Reworking a defective product
e. All of these

18-16 Suppose that a company is spending $50,000 per year for inspecting, $40,000 for purchasing, and $40,000 for reworking products. A good estimate of nonvalue-added costs would be

a. $110,000.
b. $50,000.
c. $60,000.

d. $90,000.
e. $100,000.

18-17 The cost of inspecting incoming parts is most likely to be reduced by

a. activity sharing.
b. activity elimination.
c. activity reduction.

d. activity selection.
e. none of these.

18-18 Thom Company produces 100 units in 10 hours. The cycle time for Thom

a. is 10 units per hour.
b. is 10 hours per unit.
c. is 10 minutes per unit.

d. is 6 minutes per unit.
e. cannot be calculated.

18-19 Thom Company produces 100 units in 10 hours. The velocity for Thom

a. is 6 minutes per unit.
b. is 10 minutes per units.
c. is 10 units per hour.

d. is 1 hour per 10 units.
e. cannot be calculated.

18-20 Striving to produce the same activity output with lower costs for the input used is concerned with which of the following dimensions of activity performance?

a. Quality
b. Time
c. Activity sharing

d. Effectiveness
e. Efficiency

18-21 Which of the following is a quality prevention cost?

a. Quality planning
b. Supplier evaluation and selection
c. Quality audits

d. Field trials
e. All of these

18-22 Which of the following is an appraisal cost (quality)?

a. Manager of an inspection team
b. Quality reporting
c. Design reviews

d. Warranties
e. Retesting

18-23 Which of the following is an internal failure cost (quality)?

a. Supplier evaluation and selection
b. Packaging inspection
c. Retesting

d. Product liability
e. Complaint adjustment

18-24 Which of the following is an external failure cost (quality)?

a. Design reviews
b. Retesting
c. Rework

d. Lost sales
e. All of these

18-25 Which of the following represents environmental detection costs?

a. Depreciation on scrubbers
b. Recycling products
c. Disposing of toxic materials

d. Carrying out contamination tests
e. None of these

18-26 An example of an environmental internal failure cost is

a. cleaning up oil spills.
b. damaging ecosystems from solid waste disposal.
c. cost of operating scrubbers.

d. measuring levels of contamination.
e. none of these.

18-27 An example of a societal cost is

a. medical care due to polluted air.
b. recycling scrap.
c. disposing of toxic materials.

d. maintaining pollution equipment.
e. all of these.

18-28 An example of an environmental prevention cost is

a. restoring land to its natural state.
b. auditing environmental activities.
c. licensing facilities for producing contaminants.

d. developing environmental management systems.
e. treating toxic materials.

CORNERSTONE EXERCISES

Use the following information for Cornerstone Exercises 18-29 and 18-30:
Zapato Company produces two types of boots: cowboy and cowgirl. There are four activities associated with the two products. Drivers for the four activities are as follows:

	Cowboy	Cowgirl
Cutting hours	2,100	3,900
Assembly hours	1,500	2,250
Inspection hours	675	1,575
Rework hours	75	225

Cornerstone Exercise 18-29 Consumption Ratios

OBJECTIVE ❶
CORNERSTONE 18-1

Refer to the information for Zapato Company above.

Required:
1. Calculate the consumption ratios for the four drivers.
2. Is there evidence of product diversity? Explain.

Cornerstone Exercise 18-30 Activity Rates

OBJECTIVE ❶
CORNERSTONE 18-2

Refer to the information for Zapato Company above. The following activity data have been collected:

Cutting	$60,000
Assembling	75,000
Inspecting	18,000
Reworking	9,000

Required:
Calculate the activity rates that would be used to assign costs to each product.

Cornerstone Exercise 18-31 Calculating ABC Unit Costs

Perry National Bank has collected the following information for four activities and two types of credit cards:

Activity	Driver	Classic	Gold	Activity Rate
Processing transactions	Transactions processed	8,000	4,800	$0.15
Preparing statements	Number of statements	8,000	4,800	0.90
Answering questions	Number of calls	16,000	24,000	3.00
Providing ATMs	ATM transactions	32,000	9,600	1.20

There are 5,000 holders of Classic cards and 20,000 holders of the Gold cards.

Required:
Calculate the unit cost for Classic and Gold credit cards.

Cornerstone Exercise 18-32 Assigning Costs to Activities

Golding produces small engines for lawnmower producers. The accounts payable department at Golding has five clerks who process and pay supplier invoices. The total cost of their salaries is $275,000. The work distribution for the activities that they perform is as follows:

Activity	Percentage of Time on Each Activity
Comparing source documents	20%
Resolving discrepancies	55%
Processing payment	25%

Required:
Assign the cost of labor to each of the three activities in the accounts payable department.

Cornerstone Exercise 18-33 Activity-Based Customer Costing

Dormirbien Company produces mattresses for 20 retail outlets. Of the 20 retail outlets, 19 are small, separately owned furniture stores and one is a retail chain. The retail chain buys 60 percent of the mattresses produced. The 19 smaller customers purchase mattresses in approximately equal quantities, where the orders are about the same size. Data concerning Dormirbien's customer activity are as follows:

	Large Retailer	Smaller Retailers
Units purchased	36,000	24,000
Orders placed	12	1,200
Number of sales calls	6	294
Manufacturing costs	$14,400,000	$9,600,000
Order filling costs allocated*	$484,800	$323,200
Sales force costs allocated*	$240,000	$160,000

*Currently allocated on sales volume (units sold).

Currently, customer-driven costs are assigned to customers based on units sold, a unit-level driver.

Required:
Assign costs to customers by using an ABC approach. Round activity rates to two decimal places and the activity costs to the nearest dollar.

Cornerstone Exercise 18-34 Activity-Based Supplier Costing

LissenPhones uses Alpha Electronics and La Paz Company to buy two electronic components used in the manufacture of its cell phones: Component 125X and Component 30Y. Consider two activities: testing and reordering components. After the two components are inserted, testing is done to ensure that the two components in the phones are working properly. Reordering occurs because one or both of the components have failed the test and it is necessary to replenish component inventories. Activity cost information and other data needed for supplier costing are as follows:

I. Activity Costs Caused by Suppliers (testing failures and reordering as a result)

Activity	Costs
Testing components	$1,500,000
Reordering components	375,000

II. Supplier Data

	Alpha Electronics		La Paz Company	
	125X	30Y	125X	30Y
Unit purchase price	$10	$26	$12	$28
Units purchased	150,000	75,000	18,750	18,750
Failed tests	1,500	975	13	12
Number of reorders	75	50	0	0

Required:

Determine the cost of each supplier by using ABC.

Cornerstone Exercise 18-35 Nonvalue-Added Costs

OBJECTIVE ④
CORNERSTONE 18-7

Boothe Inc. has the following two activities: (1) Retesting reworked products, cost: $480,000. The retesting cost of the most efficient competitor is $150,000. (2) Welding subassemblies, cost: $900,000 (45,000 welding hours). A benchmarking study reveals that the most efficient level for Boothe would use 36,000 welding hours and entail a cost of $720,000.

Required:

Determine the nonvalue-added cost of each activity.

Cornerstone Exercise 18-36 Velocity and Cycle Time

OBJECTIVE ④
CORNERSTONE 18-8

Karsen Company takes 7,200 hours to produce 28,800 units of a product.

Required:

What is the velocity? Cycle time?

EXERCISES

Exercise 18-37 Consumption Ratios; Activity Rates

OBJECTIVE ①

Felicidad Company produces two types of get-well cards: scented and regular. Drivers for the four activities are as follows:

ILLUSTRATING
RELATIONSHIPS

	Scented Cards	Regular Cards
Inspection hours	120	80
Setup hours	80	20
Machine hours	200	600
Number of moves	225	75

The following activity data have been collected:

Inspecting products	$5,000
Setting up equipment	4,750
Machining	6,400
Moving materials	1,350

Required:

1. Calculate the consumption ratios for the four drivers.
2. **Conceptual Connection:** Is there evidence of product diversity? Explain the significance of product diversity for decision making if the company chooses to use machine hours to assign all overhead.
3. Calculate the activity rates that would be used to assign costs to each product.
4. Suppose that the activity rate for inspecting products is $20 per inspection hour. How many hours of inspection are expected for the coming year?

OBJECTIVE ❷

Exercise 18-38 Activity Rates

Pratt Company uses activity-based costing (ABC). Pratt manufactures toy cars using two activities: plastic injection molding and decal application. Pratt's 2011 total budgeted overhead costs for these two activities are $450,000 (80 percent for injection molding and 20 percent for decal application). Molding overhead costs are driven by the number of pounds of plastic that are molded together. Decal application overhead costs are driven by the number of decals applied to toys. The budgeted activity data for 2010 are as follows:

Pounds of plastic molded	2,000,000
Number of decals applied	250,000

Required:
1. Calculate the activity rate for the plastic injection molding activity.
2. Calculate the activity rate for the decal application activity.

OBJECTIVE ❷

Exercise 18-39 Comparing ABC and Plantwide Overhead Cost Assignments

The Oscuro Chocolate Company uses activity-based costing (ABC). The controller identified two activities and their budgeted costs:

Setting up equipment	$108,000
Other overhead	$360,000

Setting up equipment is based on setup hours, and other overhead is based on oven hours.
    Oscuro produces two products, Fudge and Cookies. Information on each product is as follows:

	Fudge	Cookies
Units produced	2,000	10,000
Setup hours	1,600	400
Oven hours	400	2,000

Required:
(*Note:* Round answers to two decimal places.)
1. Calculate the activity rate for (a) setting up equipment and (b) other overhead.
2. How much total overhead is assigned to Fudge using ABC?
3. What is the unit overhead assigned to Fudge using ABC?
4. Now, ignoring the ABC results, calculate the plantwide overhead rate, based on oven hours.
5. How much total overhead is assigned to Fudge using the plantwide overhead rate?
6. **Conceptual Connection:** Explain why the total overhead assigned to Fudge is different under the ABC system (i.e., using the activity rates) than under the non-ABC system (i.e., using the plantwide rate).

OBJECTIVE ❶❷

Exercise 18-40 Activity-Based Product Costing

Suppose that a surgical ward has gathered the following information for four nursing activities and two types of patients:

		Patient Category		
	Driver	Normal	Intensive	Activity Rate
Treating patients	Treatments	8,000	10,000	$4.00
Providing hygienic care	Hygienic hours	6,000	22,000	5.00
Responding to requests	Requests	40,000	100,000	2.00
Monitoring patients	Monitoring hours	7,500	90,000	3.00

Required:
1. Determine the total nursing costs assigned to each patient category.
2. Output is measured in patient days. Assuming that the normal patient category uses 10,000 patient days and the intensive patient category uses 8,000 patient days, calculate the nursing cost per patient day for each type of patient.
3. **Conceptual Connection:** The supervisor of the surgical ward has suggested that patient days is the only driver needed to assign nursing costs to each type of patient. Calculate the charge per patient day using this approach and then explain to the supervisor why this would be a bad decision.

Exercise 18-41 Assigning Costs to Activities, Resource Drivers

OBJECTIVE ❷

The Receiving Department has three activities: unloading, counting goods, and inspecting. Unloading uses a forklift that is leased for $15,000 per year. The forklift is used only for unloading. The fuel for the forklift is $3,600 per year. Other operating costs (maintenance) for the forklift total $1,500 per year. Inspection uses some special testing equipment that has a depreciation of $1,200 per year and an operating cost of $750. Receiving has three employees who have an average salary of $50,000 per year. The work distribution matrix for the receiving personnel is as follows:

Activity	Percentage of Time on Each Activity
Unloading	40%
Counting	25%
Inspecting	35%

No other resources are used for these activities.

Required:

1. Calculate the cost of each activity.
2. **Conceptual Connection:** Explain the two methods used to assign costs to activities.

Exercise 18-42 Activity-Based Customer-Driven Costs

OBJECTIVE ❷

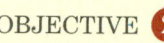

Suppose that **Stillwater Designs** has two classes of distributors: JIT distributors and non-JIT distributors. The JIT distributor places small, frequent orders, and the non-JIT distributor tends to place larger, less frequent orders. Both types of distributors are buying the same product. Stillwater Designs provides the following information about customer-related activities and costs for the most recent quarter:

	JIT Distributors	Non-JIT Distributors
Sales orders	700	70
Sales calls	70	70
Service calls	350	175
Average order size	750	7,500
Manufacturing cost/unit	$125	$125
Customer costs:		
Processing sales orders	$3,080,000	
Selling goods	1,120,000	
Servicing goods	1,050,000	
Total	$5,250,000	

Required:

1. Calculate the total revenues per distributor category, and assign the customer costs to each distributor type by using revenues as the allocation base. Selling price for one unit is $150.
2. **Conceptual Connection:** Calculate the customer cost per distributor type using activity-based cost assignments. Discuss the merits of offering the non-JIT distributors a $3 price decrease (assume that they are agitating for a price concession).
3. **Conceptual Connection:** Assume that the JIT distributors are simply imposing the frequent orders on **Stillwater Designs**. No formal discussion has taken place between JIT customers and Stillwater Designs regarding the supply of goods on a JIT basis. The sales pattern has evolved over time. As an independent consultant, what would you suggest to Stillwater Designs' management?

Exercise 18-43 Activity-Based Supplier Costing

OBJECTIVE ❸

Bowman Company manufactures cooling systems. Bowman produces all the parts necessary for its product except for one electronic component, which is purchased from two local suppliers: Manzer Inc. and Buckner Company. Both suppliers are reliable and seldom deliver late; however, Manzer sells the component for $89 per unit, while Buckner sells the same component for $86. Bowman purchases 80 percent of its components from Buckner because of its lower price. The total annual demand is 4,000,000 components.

To help assess the cost effect of the two components, the following data were collected for supplier-related activities and suppliers:

(Continued)

I. Activity Data

	Activity Cost
Inspecting components (sampling only)	480,000
Reworking products (due to failed component)	6,084,000
Warranty work (due to failed component)	9,600,000

II. Supplier Data

	Manzer Inc.	Buckner Company
Unit purchase price	$89	$86
Units purchased	800,000	3,200,000
Sampling hours*	80	3,920
Rework hours	360	5,640
Warranty hours	800	15,200

*Sampling inspection for Manzer's product has been reduced because the reject rate is so low.

Required:

1. Calculate the cost per component for each supplier, taking into consideration the costs of the supplier-related activities and using the current prices and sales volume. (*Note*: Round the unit cost to two decimal places.)

2. Suppose that Bowman loses $4,000,000 in sales per year because it develops a poor reputation due to defective units attributable to failed components. Using warranty hours, assign the cost of lost sales to each supplier. By how much would this change the cost of each supplier's component?

3. **Conceptual Connection:** Based on the analysis in Requirements 1 and 2, discuss the importance of activity-based supplier costing for internal decision making.

Use the following information for Exercises 18-44 through 18-46:
The following six situations at Diviney Manufacturing Inc. are independent.

a. A manual insertion process takes 30 minutes and 8 pounds of material to produce a product. Automating the insertion process requires 15 minutes of machine time and 7.5 pounds of material. The cost per labor hour is $12, the cost per machine hour is $8, and the cost per pound of materials is $10.

b. With its original design, a gear requires 8 hours of setup time. By redesigning the gear so that the number of different groves needed is reduced by 50 percent, the setup time is reduced by 75 percent. The cost per setup hour is $50.

c. A product currently requires 6 moves. By redesigning the manufacturing layout, the number of moves can be reduced from 6 to 0. The cost per move is $20.

d. Inspection time for a plant is 16,000 hours per year. The cost of inspection consists of salaries of 8 inspectors, totaling $320,000. Inspection also uses supplies costing $5 per inspection hour. The company eliminated most defective components by eliminating low-quality suppliers. The number of production errors was reduced dramatically by installing a system of statistical process control. Further quality improvements were realized by redesigning the products, making them easier to manufacture. The net effect was to achieve a close to zero-defect state and eliminate the need for any inspection activity.

e. Each unit of a product requires 6 components. The average number of components is 6.5 due to component failure, requiring rework and extra components. Developing relations with the right suppliers and increasing the quality of the purchased component can reduce the average number of components to 6 components per unit. The cost per component is $500.

f. A plant produces 100 different electronic products. Each product requires an average of 8 components that are purchased externally. The components are different for each part. By redesigning the products, it is possible to produce the 100 products so that they all have 4 components in common. This will reduce the demand for purchasing, receiving, and paying bills. Estimated savings from the reduced demand are $900,000 per year.

Exercise 18-44 Nonvalue-Added Costs

OBJECTIVE **4**

Refer to the information for Diviney Manufacturing on the previous page.

Required:

Estimate the nonvalue-added cost for each situation.

Exercise 18-45 Driver Analysis

OBJECTIVE **4**

Refer to the information for Diviney Manufacturing on the previous page.

Required:

Conceptual Connection: For each situation, identify the possible root cause(s) of the activity cost (such as plant layout, process design, and product design).

Exercise 18-46 Type of Activity Management

OBJECTIVE **4**

Refer to the information for Diviney Manufacturing on the previous page.

Required:

For each situation, identify the cost reduction measure: activity elimination, activity reduction, activity sharing, or activity selection.

Exercise 18-47 Cycle Time and Velocity

OBJECTIVE **1 2 4**

In the first quarter of operations, a manufacturing cell produced 80,000 stereo speakers, using 20,000 production hours. In the second quarter, the cycle time was 10 minutes per unit with the same number of production hours as were used in the first quarter.

ILLUSTRATING RELATIONSHIPS

Required:

1. Compute the velocity (per hour) for the first quarter.
2. Compute the cycle time for the first quarter (minutes per unit produced).
3. How many units were produced in the second quarter?

Exercise 18-48 Product-Costing Accuracy, Consumption Ratios

OBJECTIVE **4**

Plata Company produces two products: a mostly handcrafted soft leather briefcase sold under the label Maletin Elegant and a leather briefcase produced largely through automation and sold under the label Maletin Fina. The two products use two overhead activities, with the following costs:

Setting up equipment	$ 3,000
Machining	18,000

The controller has collected the expected annual prime costs for each briefcase, the machine hours, the setup hours, and the expected production.

	Elegant	Fina
Direct labor	$9,000	$3,000
Direct materials	$3,000	$3,000
Units	3,000	3,000
Machine hours	500	4,500
Setup hours	100	100

Required:

1. **Conceptual Connection:** Do you think that the direct labor costs and direct materials costs are accurately traced to each briefcase? Explain.
2. Calculate the consumption ratios for each activity.
3. Calculate the overhead cost per unit for each briefcase by using a plantwide rate based on direct labor costs. Comment on this approach to assigning overhead.
4. **Conceptual Connection:** Calculate the overhead cost per unit for each briefcase by using overhead rates based on machine hours and setup hours. Explain why these assignments are more accurate than using the direct labor costs.

Exercise 18-49 Product-Costing Accuracy, Consumption Ratios, Activity Rates, Activity Costing

OBJECTIVE **1 2**

Tristar Manufacturing produces two types of battery-operated toy soldiers: infantry and special forces. The soldiers are produced by using one continuous process. Four activities have been

(Continued)

identified: machining, setups, receiving, and packing. Resource drivers have been used to assign costs to each activity. The overhead activities, their costs, and the other related data are as follows:

Product	Machine Hours	Setups	Receiving Orders	Packing Orders
Infantry	20,000	300	900	1,600
Special forces	20,000	100	100	800
Costs	$80,000	$24,000	$18,000	$30,000

Required:
1. Calculate the total overhead assigned to each product by using only machine hours to calculate a plantwide rate.
2. Calculate consumption ratios for each activity.
3. Calculate a rate for each activity by using the associated driver.
4. Assign the overhead costs to each product by using the activity rates computed in Requirement 3.
5. **Conceptual Connection:** Comment on the difference between the assignment in Requirement 1 and the activity-based assignment.

Exercise 18-50 Formation of an Activity Dictionary

A hospital is in the process of implementing an ABC system. A pilot study is being done to assess the effects of the costing changes on specific products. Of particular interest is the cost of caring for patients who receive in-patient recovery treatment for illness, surgery (noncardiac), and injury. These patients are housed on the third and fourth floors of the hospital (the floors are dedicated to patient care and have only nursing stations and patient rooms). A partial transcript of an interview with the hospital's nursing supervisor is as follows:

1. How many nurses are in the hospital?
   There are 101 nurses, including me.
2. Of these 100 nurses, how many are assigned to the third and fourth floors?
   Fifty nurses are assigned to these two floors.
3. What do these nurses do (please describe)?
   Provide nursing care for patients, which, as you know, means answering questions, changing bandages, administering medicine, changing clothes, etc.
4. And what do you do?
   I supervise and coordinate all the nursing activity in the hospital. This includes surgery, maternity, the emergency room, and the two floors you mentioned.
5. What other lodging and care activities are done for the third and fourth floors by persons other than the nurses?
   The patients must be fed. The hospital cafeteria delivers meals. The laundry department picks up dirty clothing and bedding once each shift. The floors also have a physical therapist assigned to provide care on a physician-directed basis.
6. Do patients use any equipment?
   Yes. Mostly monitoring equipment.
7. Who or what uses the activity output?
   Patients. But there are different kinds of patients. On these two floors, we classify patients into three categories according to severity: intensive care, intermediate care, and normal care. The more severe the illness, the more activity is used. Nurses spend much more time with intermediate care patients than with normal care. The more severe patients tend to use more of the laundry service as well. Their clothing and bedding need to be changed more frequently. On the other hand, severe patients use less food. They eat fewer meals. Typically, we measure each patient type by the number of days of hospital stay. And you have to realize that the same patient contributes to each type of product.

Required:
Prepare an activity dictionary with three categories: activity name, activity description, and activity driver.

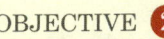

Exercise 18-51 Activity Rates and Activity-Based Product Costing

Hammer Company produces a variety of electronic equipment. One of its plants produces two laser printers: the deluxe and the regular. At the beginning of the year, the following data were prepared for this plant:

	Deluxe	Regular
Quantity	100,000	800,000
Selling price	$900	$750
Unit prime cost	$529	$483

In addition, the following information was provided so that overhead costs could be assigned to each product:

Activity Name	Activity Driver	Activity Cost	Deluxe	Regular
Setups	Number of setups	$ 2,000,000	300	200
Machining	Machine hours	80,000,000	100,000	300,000
Engineering	Engineering hours	6,000,000	50,000	100,000
Packing	Packing orders	100,000	100,000	400,000

Required:

1. Calculate the overhead rates for each activity.
2. Calculate the per-unit product cost for each product.

Exercise 18-52 Value- and Nonvalue-Added Costs

 OBJECTIVE 4

Waterfun Technology produces engines for recreational boats. Because of competitive pressures, the company was making an effort to reduce costs. As part of this effort, management implemented an activity-based management system and began focusing its attention on processes and activities. Purchasing was among the processes (activities) that were carefully studied. The study revealed that the number of purchase orders was a good driver for purchasing costs. During the last year, the company incurred fixed receiving costs of $630,000 (salaries of 15 employees). These fixed costs provide a capacity of processing 72,000 receiving orders (7,200 per employee at practical capacity). Management decided that the efficient level for purchasing should use 36,000 receiving orders.

Required:

1. **Conceptual Connection:** Explain why receiving would be viewed as a value-added activity. List all possible reasons. Also, list some possible reasons that explain why the demand for purchasing is more than the efficient level of 36,000 orders.
2. Break the cost of receiving into its value-added and nonvalue-added components.

PROBLEMS

Problem 18-53 Functional-Based versus Activity-Based Costing

 OBJECTIVE 1 2

For years, Tamarindo Company produced only one product: backpacks. Recently, Tamarindo added a line of duffel bags. With this addition, the company began assigning overhead costs by using departmental rates. (Prior to this, the company used a predetermined plantwide rate based on units produced.) Surprisingly, after the addition of the duffel-bag line and the switch to departmental rates, the costs to produce the backpacks increased, and their profitability dropped.

Josie, the marketing manager, and Steve, the production manager, both complained about the increase in the production cost of backpacks. Josie was concerned because the increase in unit costs led to pressure to increase the unit price of backpacks. She was resisting this pressure because she was certain that the increase would harm the company's market share. Steve was receiving pressure to cut costs also, yet he was convinced that nothing different was being done in the way the backpacks were produced. After some discussion, the two managers decided that the problem had to be connected to the addition of the duffel-bag line.

Upon investigation, they were informed that the only real change in product costing procedures was in the way overhead costs are assigned. A two-stage procedure was now in use. First, overhead costs are assigned to the two producing departments, Patterns and Finishing. Second, the costs accumulated in the producing departments are assigned to the two products by using direct labor hours as a driver (the rate in each department is based on direct labor hours). The managers were assured that great care was taken to associate overhead costs with individual products. So that they could construct their own example of overhead cost assignment, the controller provided them with the information necessary to show how accounting costs are assigned to products:

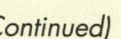 *(Continued)*

| | Department | | |
	Patterns	Finishing	Total
Accounting cost	$48,000	$72,000	$120,000
Transactions processed	32,000	48,000	80,000
Total direct labor hours	10,000	20,000	30,000
Direct labor hours per backpack*	0.10	0.20	0.30
Direct labor hours per duffel bag*	0.40	0.80	1.20

*Hours required to produce one unit of each product.

The controller remarked that the cost of operating the accounting department had doubled with the addition of the new product line. The increase came because of the need to process additional transactions, which had also doubled in number.

During the first year of producing duffel bags, the company produced and sold 100,000 backpacks and 25,000 duffel bags. The 100,000 backpacks matched the prior year's output for that product.

Required:
1. **Conceptual Connection:** Compute the amount of accounting cost assigned to a backpack before the duffel-bag line was added by using a plantwide rate approach based on units produced. Is this assignment accurate? Explain.
2. Suppose that the company decided to assign the accounting costs directly to the product lines by using the number of transactions as the activity driver. What is the accounting cost per unit of backpacks? Per unit of duffel bags?
3. Compute the amount of accounting cost assigned to each backpack and duffel bag by using departmental rates based on direct labor hours.
4. **Conceptual Connection:** Which way of assigning overhead does the best job—the functional-based approach by using departmental rates or the activity-based approach by using transactions processed for each product? Explain. Discuss the value of ABC before the duffel-bag line was added.

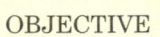

Problem 18-54 Plantwide versus Departmental Rates, Product-Costing Accuracy: Activity-Based Costing

Ramsey Company produces speakers (Model A and Model B). Both products pass through two producing departments. Model A's production is much more labor-intensive than that of Model B. Model B is also the more popular of the two speakers. The following data have been gathered for the two products:

| | Product Data | |
	Model A	Model B
Units produced per year	10,000	100,000
Prime costs	$150,000	$1,500,000
Direct labor hours	140,000	300,000
Machine hours	20,000	200,000
Production runs	40	60
Inspection hours	800	1,200
Maintenance hours	10,000	90,000
Overhead costs:		
Setup costs	$270,000	
Inspection costs	210,000	
Machining	240,000	
Maintenance	270,000	
Total	$990,000	

Required:
1. Compute the overhead cost per unit for each product by using a plantwide rate based on direct labor hours. (*Note:* Round to two decimal places.)
2. Compute the overhead cost per unit for each product by using ABC. (*Note:* Round to two decimal places.)

3. Suppose that Ramsey decides to use departmental overhead rates. There are two departments: Department 1 (machine intensive) with a rate of $3.50 per machine hour and Department 2 (labor intensive) with a rate of $0.90 per direct labor hour. The consumption of these two drivers is as follows:

	Department 1 Machine Hours	Department 2 Direct Labor Hours
Model A	10,000	130,000
Model B	170,000	270,000

Compute the overhead cost per unit for each product by using departmental rates. (*Note:* Round to two decimal places.)

4. **Conceptual Connection:** Using the activity-based product costs as the standard, comment on the ability of departmental rates to improve the accuracy of product costing. Did the departmental rates do better than the plantwide rate?

Problem 18-55 Production-Based Costing versus Activity-Based Costing, Assigning Costs to Activities, Resource Drivers

OBJECTIVE 1 2

Willow Company produces lawn mowers. One of its plants produces two versions of mowers: a basic model and a deluxe model. The deluxe model has a sturdier frame, a higher horsepower engine, a wider blade, and mulching capability. At the beginning of the year, the following data were prepared for this plant:

	Basic Model	Deluxe Model
Expected quantity	40,000	20,000
Selling price	$180	$360
Prime costs	$80	$160
Machine hours	5,000	5,000
Direct labor hours	10,000	10,000
Engineering support (hours)	1,500	4,500
Receiving (orders processed)	250	500
Materials handling (number of moves)	1,200	4,800
Purchasing (number of requisitions)	100	200
Maintenance (hours used)	1,000	3,000
Paying suppliers (invoices processed)	250	500
Setting up equipment (number of setups)	16	64

Additionally, the following overhead activity costs are reported:

Maintaining equipment	$114,000
Engineering support	120,000
Materials handling	?
Setting up equipment	96,000
Purchasing materials	60,000
Receiving goods	40,000
Paying suppliers	30,000
Providing space	20,000
Total	$?

Facility-level costs are allocated in proportion to machine hours (provides a measure of time the facility is used by each product). Materials handling uses three inputs: two forklifts, gasoline to operate the forklift, and three operators. The three operators are paid a salary of $40,000 each. The operators spend 25 percent of their time on the receiving activity and 75 percent on moving goods (materials handling). Gasoline costs $3 per move. Depreciation amounts to $6,000 per forklift per year.

Required:

(*Note:* Round answers to two decimal places.)
1. Calculate the cost of the materials handling activity. Label the cost assignments as driver tracing or direct tracing. Identify the resource drivers.
2. Calculate the cost per unit for each product by using direct labor hours to assign all overhead costs.

(Continued)

3. Calculate activity rates, and assign costs to each product. Calculate a unit cost for each product, and compare these costs with those calculated in Requirement 2.
4. Calculate consumption ratios for each activity.
5. **Conceptual Connection:** Explain how the consumption ratios calculated in Requirement 4 can be used to reduce the number of rates. Calculate the rates that would apply under this approach.

OBJECTIVE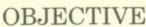

Problem 18-56 Activity Costing, Assigning Resource Costs, Primary and Secondary Activities

Trinity Clinic has identified three activities for daily maternity care: occupancy and feeding, nursing, and nursing supervision. The nursing supervisor oversees 150 nurses, 25 of whom are maternity nurses (the other nurses are located in other care areas such as the emergency room and intensive care). The nursing supervisor has three assistants, a secretary, several offices, computers, phones, and furniture. The three assistants spend 75 percent of their time on the supervising activity and 25 percent of their time as surgical nurses. They each receive a salary of $52,000. The nursing supervisor has a salary of $80,000. She spends 100 percent of her time supervising. The secretary receives a salary of $28,000 per year. Other costs directly traceable to the supervisory activity (depreciation, utilities, phone, etc.) average $135,000 per year.

Daily care output is measured as "patient days." The clinic has traditionally assigned the cost of daily care by using a daily rate (a rate per patient day). Daily rates can differ between units, but within units the daily rates are the same for all patients. Under the traditional approach, the daily rate is computed by dividing the annual costs of occupancy and feeding, nursing, and a share of supervision by the unit's capacity expressed in patient days. The cost of supervision is assigned to each care area based on the number of nurses. A single driver (patient days) is used to assign the costs of daily care to each patient.

A pilot study has revealed that the demands for nursing care vary within the maternity unit, depending on the severity of a patient's case. Assume that the maternity unit has three levels of increasing severity: normal patients, cesarean patients, and patients with complications. The pilot study provided the following activity and cost information:

Activity	Annual Cost	Activity Driver	Annual Quantity
Occupancy and feeding	$1,200,000	Patient days	10,000
Nursing care (maternity)	1,000,000	Hours of nursing care	50,000
Nursing supervision	?	Number of nurses	150

The pilot study also revealed the following information concerning the three types of patients and their annual demands:

Patient Type	Patient Days Demanded	Nursing Hours Demanded
Normal	7,000	17,500
Cesarean	2,000	12,500
Complications	1,000	20,000
Total	10,000	50,000

Required:
1. Calculate the cost per patient day by using a functional-based approach.
2. Calculate the cost per patient day by using an activity-based approach.
3. **Conceptual Connection:** The hospital processes 1,000,000 pounds of laundry per year. The cost for the laundering activity is $500,000 per year. In a functional-based cost system, the cost of the laundry department is assigned to each user department in proportion to the pounds of laundry produced. Typically, maternity produces 200,000 pounds per year. How much would this change the cost per patient day calculated in Requirement 1? Now, describe what information you would need to modify the calculation made in Requirement 2. Under what conditions would this activity calculation provide a more accurate cost assignment?

Problem 18-57 Customers as a Cost Object

OBJECTIVE   ❸

Morrisom National Bank has requested an analysis of checking account profitability by customer type. Customers are categorized according to the size of their account: low balances, medium balances, and high balances. The activities associated with the three different customer categories and their associated annual costs are as follows:

Opening and closing accounts	$ 300,000
Issuing monthly statements	450,000
Processing transactions	3,075,000
Customer inquiries	600,000
Providing automatic teller machine (ATM) services	1,680,000
Total cost	$6,105,000

Additional data concerning the usage of the activities by the various customers are also provided:

	Account Balance		
	Low	Medium	High
Number of accounts opened/closed	22,500	4,500	3,000
Number of statements issued	675,000	150,000	75,000
Processing transactions	27,000,000	3,000,000	750,000
Number of telephone minutes	1,500,000	900,000	600,000
Number of ATM transactions	2,025,000	300,000	75,000
Number of checking accounts	57,000	12,000	6,000

Required:

(*Note:* Round answers to two decimal places.)

1. Calculate a cost per account per year by dividing the total cost of processing and maintaining checking accounts by the total number of accounts. What is the average fee per month that the bank should charge to cover the costs incurred because of checking accounts?
2. Calculate a cost per account by customer category by using activity rates.
3. Currently, the bank offers free checking to all of its customers. The interest revenues average $90 per account; however, the interest revenues earned per account by category are $80, $100, and $165 for the low-, medium-, and high-balance accounts, respectively. Calculate the average profit per account (average revenue minus average cost from Requirement 1). Then calculate the profit per account by using the revenue per customer type and the unit cost per customer type calculated in Requirement 2.
4. **Conceptual Connection:** After the analysis in Requirement 3, a vice president recommended eliminating the free checking feature for low-balance customers. The bank president expressed reluctance to do so, arguing that the low-balance customers more than made up for the loss through cross-sales. He presented a survey that showed that 50 percent of the customers would switch banks if a checking fee were imposed. Explain how you could verify the president's argument by using ABC.

Problem 18-58 Activity-Based Costing and Customer-Driven Costs

OBJECTIVE

Sorensen Manufacturing produces several types of bolts used in aircrafts. The bolts are produced in batches and grouped into three product families. Because the product families are used in different kinds of aircraft, customers also can be grouped into three categories, corresponding to the product family that they purchase. The number of units sold to each customer class is the same. The selling prices for the three product families range from $0.50 to $0.80 per unit. Historically, the costs of order entry, processing, and handling were expensed and not traced to individual customer groups. These costs are not trivial and totaled $4,500,000 for the most recent year. Recently, the company started emphasizing a cost reduction strategy with an emphasis on creating a competitive advantage.

Upon investigation, management discovered that order-filling costs were driven by the number of customer orders processed with the following cost behavior:

Step-fixed cost component: $50,000 per step (2,000 orders define a step)*
Variable cost component: $20 per order

*Sorensen currently has sufficient steps to process 100,000 orders.

(Continued)

The expected customer orders for the year total 100,000. The expected usage of the order-filling activity and the average size of an order by customer category follow:

	Category I	Category II	Category III
Number of orders	50,000	30,000	20,000
Average order size	600	1,000	1,500

As a result of cost behavior analysis, the marketing manager recommended the imposition of a charge per customer order. The charge was implemented by adding the cost per order to the price of each order (computed by using the projected ordering costs and expected orders). This ordering cost was then reduced as the size of the order increased and was eliminated as the order size reached 2,000 units. Within a short period of communicating this new price information to customers, the average order size for all three product families increased to 2,000 units.

Required:

1. **Conceptual Connection:** Sorensen traditionally has expensed order-filling costs. What is the most likely reason for this practice?
2. Calculate the cost per order for each customer category. (*Note:* Round to two decimal places.)
3. **Conceptual Connection:** Calculate the reduction in order-filling costs produced by the change in pricing strategy (assume that resource spending is reduced as much as possible and that the total units sold remain unchanged). Explain how exploiting customer activity information produced this cost reduction. Would any other internal activities benefit from this pricing strategy?

OBJECTIVE

Problem 18-59 Activity-Based Supplier Costing

Levy Inc. manufactures tractors for agricultural usage. Levy purchases the engines needed for its tractors from two sources: Johnson Engines and Watson Company. The Johnson engine has a price of $1,000. The Watson engine is $900 per unit. Levy produces and sells 22,000 tractors. Of the 22,000 engines needed for the tractors, 4,000 are purchased from Johnson Engines, and 18,000 are purchased from Watson Company. The production manager, Jamie Murray, prefers the Johnson engine. However, Jan Booth, purchasing manager, maintains that the price difference is too great to buy more than the 4,000 units currently purchased. Booth also wants to maintain a significant connection with the Johnson source just in case the less expensive source cannot supply the needed quantities. Jamie, however, is convinced that the quality of the Johnson engine is worth the price difference.

Frank Wallace, the controller, has decided to use activity costing to resolve the issue. The following activity cost and supplier data have been collected:

Activity	Cost
Replacing engines[a]	$ 800,000
Expediting orders[b]	1,000,000
Repairing engines[c]	1,800,000

[a] All units are tested after assembly, and some are rejected because of engine failure. The failed engines are removed and replaced, with the supplier replacing any failed engine. The replaced engine is retested before being sold. Engine failure often causes collateral damage, and other parts often need to be replaced.
[b] Due to late or failed delivery of engines.
[c] Repair work is for units under warranty and almost invariably is due to engine failure. Repair usually means replacing the engine. This cost plus labor, transportation, and other costs make warranty work very expensive.

	Watson	Johnson
Engines replaced by source	1,980	20
Late or failed shipments	198	2
Warranty repairs (by source)	2,440	60

Required:

1. **Conceptual Connection:** Calculate the activity-based supplier cost per engine (acquisition cost plus supplier-related activity costs). Which of the two suppliers is the low-cost supplier? Explain why this is a better measure of engine cost than the usual purchase costs assigned to the engines.
2. **Conceptual Connection:** Consider the supplier cost information obtained in Requirement 1. Suppose further that Johnson can only supply a total of 20,000 units. What actions would you advise Levy to undertake with its suppliers?

Problem 18-60 Activity-Based Management, Nonvalue-Added Costs

OBJECTIVE 4

Danna Martin, president of Mays Electronics, was concerned about the end-of-the year marketing report that she had just received. According to Larry Savage, marketing manager, a price decrease for the coming year was again needed to maintain the company's annual sales volume of integrated circuit boards (CBs). This would make a bad situation worse. The current selling price of $18 per unit was producing a $2-per-unit profit—half the customary $4-per-unit profit. Foreign competitors kept reducing their prices. To match the latest reduction would reduce the price from $18 to $14. This would put the price below the cost to produce and sell it. How could these firms sell for such a low price? Determined to find out if there were problems with the company's operations, Danna decided to hire a consultant to evaluate the way in which the CBs were produced and sold. After two weeks, the consultant had identified the following activities and costs:

Setting up equipment	$ 125,000
Materials handling	180,000
Inspecting products	122,000
Engineering support	120,000
Handling customer complaints	100,000
Filling warranties	170,000
Storing goods	80,000
Expediting goods	75,000
Using materials	500,000
Using power	48,000
Manual insertion labor[a]	250,000
Other direct labor	150,000
Total costs	$1,920,000[b]

[a]Diodes, resistors, and integrated circuits are inserted manually into the circuit board.
[b]This total cost produces a unit cost of $16 for last year's sales volume.

The consultant indicated that some preliminary activity analysis shows that per-unit costs can be reduced by at least $7. Since the marketing manager had indicated that the market share (sales volume) for the boards could be increased by 50 percent if the price could be reduced to $12, Danna became quite excited.

Required:

1. **Conceptual Connection:** What is activity-based management? What phases of activity analysis did the consultant provide? What else remains to be done?

2. **Conceptual Connection:** Identify as many nonvalue-added costs as possible. Compute the cost savings per unit that would be realized if these costs were eliminated. Was the consultant correct in the preliminary cost reduction assessment? Discuss actions that the company can take to reduce or eliminate the nonvalue-added activities.

3. Compute the unit cost required to maintain current market share, while earning a profit of $4 per unit. Now compute the unit cost required to expand sales by 50 percent, assuming a per unit profit of $4. How much cost reduction would be required to achieve each unit cost?

4. Assume that further activity analysis revealed the following: switching to automated insertion would save $60,000 of engineering support and $90,000 of direct labor. Now, what is the total potential cost reduction per unit available from activity analysis? With these additional reductions, can Mays achieve the unit cost to maintain current sales? To increase it by 50 percent? What form of activity analysis is this: reduction, sharing, elimination, or selection?

5. **Conceptual Connection:** Calculate income based on current sales, prices, and costs. Then calculate the income by using a $14 price and a $12 price, assuming that the maximum cost reduction possible is achieved (including Requirement 4's reduction). What price should be selected?

Problem 18-61 Nonvalue-Added Costs, Activity Costs, Activity Cost Reduction

OBJECTIVE 3 4

John Thomas, vice president of Mallett Company (a producer of a variety of plastic products), has been supervising the implementation of an ABC management system. John wants to improve process efficiency by improving the activities that define the processes. To illustrate the potential of the new system to the president, John has decided to focus on two processes: production and customer service.

(Continued)

Within each process, one activity will be selected for improvement: materials usage for production and sustaining engineering for customer service (sustaining engineers are responsible for redesigning products based on customer needs and feedback). Value-added standards are identified for each activity. For materials usage, the value-added standard calls for six pounds per unit of output (the products differ in shape and function, but their weight—is uniform). The value-added standard is based on the elimination of all waste due to defective molds. The standard price of materials is $5 per pound. For sustaining engineering, the standard is 58 percent of current practical activity capacity. This standard is based on the fact that about 42 percent of the complaints have to do with design features that could have been avoided or anticipated by the company.

Current practical capacity (at the end of 2011) is defined by the following requirements: 6,000 engineering hours for each product group that has been on the market or in development for five years or less and 2,400 hours per product group of more than five years. Four product groups have less than five years' experience, and 10 product groups have more. Each of the 24 engineers is paid a salary of $60,000. Each engineer can provide 2,000 hours of service per year. No other significant costs are incurred for the engineering activity.

Actual materials usage for 2011 was 25 percent above the level called for by the value-added standard; engineering usage was 46,000 hours. A total of 80,000 units of output were produced. John and the operational managers have selected some improvement measures that promise to reduce nonvalue-added activity usage by 40 percent in 2012. Selected actual results achieved for 2012 are as follows:

Units produced	80,000
Materials used	584,800
Engineering hours	35,400

The actual prices paid for materials and engineering hours are identical to the standard or budgeted prices.

Required:

1. For 2011, calculate the nonvalue-added usage and costs for materials usage and sustaining engineering.
2. **Conceptual Connection:** Using the budgeted improvements, calculate the expected activity usage levels for 2012. Now, compute the 2012 usage variances (the difference between the expected and actual values), expressed in both physical and financial measures, for materials and engineering. Comment on the company's ability to achieve its targeted reductions. In particular, discuss what measures the company must take to capture any realized reductions in resource usage.

Problem 18-62 Cycle Time, Velocity, Product Costing

Goldman Company has a JIT system in place. Each manufacturing cell is dedicated to the production of a single product or major subassembly. One cell, dedicated to the production of telescopes, has four operations: machining, finishing, assembly, and qualifying (testing).

For the coming year, the telescope cell has the following budgeted costs and cell time (both at theoretical capacity):

Budgeted conversion costs	$7,500,000
Budgeted raw materials	$9,000,000
Cell time	12,000 hours
Theoretical output	90,000 telescopes

During the year, the following actual results were obtained:

Actual conversion costs	$7,500,000
Actual materials	$7,800,000
Actual cell time	12,000 hours
Actual output	75,000 telescopes

Required:

Round answers to two decimal places.

1. Compute the velocity (number of telescopes per hour) that the cell can theoretically achieve. Now, compute the theoretical cycle time (number of hours or minutes per telescope) that it takes to produce one telescope.

2. Compute the actual velocity and the actual cycle time.
3. **Conceptual Connection:** Compute the budgeted conversion costs per minute. Using this rate, compute the conversion costs per telescope if theoretical output is achieved. Using this measure, compute the conversion costs per telescope for actual output. Does this product costing approach provide an incentive for the cell manager to reduce cycle time? Explain.

Problem 18-63 Classification of Environmental Costs

Consider the following independent environmental activities:

a. A company takes actions to reduce the amount of material in its packages.
b. After its useful life, a soft-drink producer returns the activated carbon used for purifying water for its beverages to the supplier. The supplier reactivates the carbon for a second use in nonfood applications. As a consequence, many tons of material are prevented from entering landfills.
c. An evaporator system is installed to treat wastewater and to collect usable solids for other uses.
d. The inks used to print snack packages (for chips) contain heavy metals.
e. Processes are inspected to ensure compliance with environmental standards.
f. Delivery boxes are used five times and then recycled. This prevents 112 million pounds of cardboard from entering landfills and saves two million trees per year.
g. Scrubber equipment is installed to ensure that air emissions are less than the level permitted by law.
h. Local residents are incurring medical costs from illnesses caused by air pollution from automobile exhaust pollution.
i. As part of implementing an environmental perspective for a balanced performance measurement system, environmental performance measures are developed.
j. Because of liquid and solid residues being discharged into a local lake, it is no longer fit for swimming, fishing, and other recreational activities.
k. To reduce energy consumption, magnetic ballasts are replaced with electronic ballasts, and more efficient light bulbs and lighting sensors are installed. As a result, 2.3 million kilowatt-hours of electricity are saved per year.
l. Because of a legal settlement, a chemical company must spend $20,000,000 to clean up contaminated soil.
m. A soft-drink company uses the following practice: In all bottling plants, packages damaged during filling are collected and recycled (glass, plastic, and aluminum).
n. Products are inspected to ensure that the gaseous emissions produced during operation follow legal and company guidelines.
o. Costs are incurred to operate pollution-control equipment.
p. An internal audit is conducted to verify that environmental policies are being followed.

Required:

Classify these environmental activities as prevention, detection, internal failure, or external failure costs. For external failure costs, classify the costs as societal or private. Also, label those activities that are compatible with sustainable development with "SD."

CASES

OBJECTIVE

Case 18-64 Activity-Based Costing, Distorted Product Costs

Sharp Paper Inc. has three paper mills, one of which is located in Memphis, Tennessee. The Memphis mill produces 300 different types of coated and uncoated specialty printing papers. Management was convinced that the value of the large variety of products more than offset the extra costs of the increased complexity.

During 2011, the Memphis mill produced 120,000 tons of coated paper and 80,000 tons of uncoated paper. Of the 200,000 tons produced, 180,000 were sold. Sixty products account for 80 percent of the tons sold. Thus, 240 products are classified as low-volume products.

Lightweight lime hopsack in cartons (LLHC) is one of the low-volume products. LLHC is produced in rolls, converted into sheets of paper, and then sold in cartons. In 2011 the cost to produce and sell one ton of LLHC was as follows:

Direct materials:		
Furnish (3 different pulps)	2,225 pounds	$ 450
Additives (11 different items)	200 pounds	500
Tub size	75 pounds	10
Recycled scrap paper	(296 pounds)	(20)
Total direct materials		$ 940
Direct labor		$ 450
Overhead:		
Paper machine ($100 per ton × 2,500 pounds)		$ 125
Finishing machine ($120 per ton × 2,500 pounds)		150
Total overhead		$ 275
Shipping and warehousing		$ 30
Total manufacturing and selling cost		$1,695

Overhead is applied by using a two-stage process. First, overhead is allocated to the paper and finishing machines by using the direct method of allocation with carefully selected cost drivers. Second, the overhead assigned to each machine is divided by the budgeted tons of output. These rates are then multiplied by the number of pounds required to produce one good ton.

In 2011, LLHC sold for $2,400 per ton, making it one of the most profitable products. A similar examination of some of the other low-volume products revealed that they also had very respectable profit margins. Unfortunately, the performance of the high volume products was less impressive, with many showing losses or very low profit margins. This situation led Ryan Chesser to call a meeting with his marketing vice president, Jennifer Woodruff, and his controller, Kaylin Penn.

Ryan: The above-average profitability of our low-volume specialty products and the poor profit performance of our high-volume products make me believe that we should switch our marketing emphasis to the low-volume line. Perhaps we should drop some of our high-volume products, particularly those showing a loss.

Jennifer: I'm not convinced that solution is the right one. I know our high-volume products are of high quality, and I'm convinced that we are as efficient in our production as other firms. I think that somehow our costs are not being assigned correctly. For example, the shipping and warehousing costs are assigned by dividing these costs by the total tons of paper sold. Yet …

Kaylin: Jennifer, I hate to disagree, but the $30-per-ton charge for shipping and warehousing seems reasonable. I know that our method to assign these costs is identical to a number of other paper companies.

Jennifer: Well, that may be true, but do these other companies have the variety of products that we have? Our low-volume products require special handling and processing, but when we assign shipping and warehousing costs, we average these special costs across our entire product line. Every ton produced in our mill passes through our mill shipping department and is either sent directly to the customer or to our distribution center and then eventually to customers. My records indicate quite clearly that virtually all of the high-volume products are sent directly to customers, whereas most of the low-volume products are sent to the distribution center. Now, all of the products passing through the mill shipping department should receive a share of the $2,000,000 annual shipping costs. I'm not convinced, however, that all products should receive a share of the receiving and shipping costs of the distribution center as currently practiced.

Ryan: Kaylin, is this true? Does our system allocate our shipping and warehousing costs in this way?

Kaylin: Yes, I'm afraid it does. Jennifer may have a point. Perhaps we need to reevaluate our method to assign these costs to the product lines.

Ryan: Jennifer, do you have any suggestions concerning how the shipping and warehousing costs should be assigned?

Jennifer: It seems reasonable to make a distinction between products that spend time in the distribution center and those that do not. We should also distinguish between the receiving and shipping activities at the distribution center. All incoming shipments are packed on pallets and weigh one ton each (there are 14 cartons of paper per pallet). In 2011, the receiving department processed 56,000 tons of paper. Receiving employs 15 people at an annual cost of $600,000. Other receiving costs total about $500,000. I would recommend that these costs be assigned by using tons processed.

Shipping, however, is different. There are two activities associated with shipping: picking the order from inventory and loading the paper. We employ 30 people for picking and 10 for loading, at an annual cost of $1,200,000. Other shipping costs total $1,100,000. Picking and loading are more concerned with the number of shipping items than with tonnage. That is, a shipping item may consist of two or three cartons instead of pallets. Accordingly, the shipping costs of the distribution center should be assigned by using the number of items shipped. In 2011, for example, we handled 190,000 shipping items.

Ryan: These suggestions have merit. Kaylin, I would like to see what effect Jennifer's suggestions have on the per-unit assignment of shipping and warehousing for LLHC. If the effect is significant, then we will expand the analysis to include all products.

Kaylin: I'm willing to compute the effect, but I'd like to suggest one additional feature. Currently, we have a policy to carry about 25 tons of LLHC in inventory. Our current costing system totally ignores the cost of carrying this inventory. Since it costs us $1,665 to produce each ton of this product, we are tying up a lot of money in inventory—money that could be invested in other productive opportunities. In fact, the return lost is about 16 percent per year. This cost should also be assigned to the units sold.

Ryan: Kaylin, this also sounds good to me. Go ahead and include the carrying cost in your computation.

To help in the analysis, Kaylin gathered the following data for LLHC for 2011:

Tons sold	10
Average cartons per shipment	2
Average shipments per ton	7

Required:

1. Identify the flaws associated with the current method of assigning shipping and warehousing costs to Sharp's products.

2. Compute the shipping and warehousing cost per ton of LLHC sold by using the new method suggested by Jennifer and Kaylin.

3. Using the new costs computed in Requirement 2, compute the profit per ton of LLHC. Compare this with the profit per ton computed by using the old method. Do you think that this same effect would be realized for other low-volume products? Explain.

4. Comment on Ryan's proposal to drop some high-volume products and place more emphasis on low-volume products. Discuss the role of the accounting system in supporting this type of decision making.

5. After receiving the analysis of LLHC, Ryan decided to expand the analysis to all products. He also had Kaylin reevaluate the way in which mill overhead was assigned to products. After the restructuring was completed, Ryan took the following actions: (a) the prices of most low-volume products were increased, (b) the prices of several high-volume products were decreased, and (c) some low-volume products were dropped. Explain why his strategy changed so dramatically.

OBJECTIVE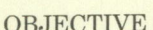

Case 18-65 Activity-Based Product Costing and Ethical Behavior

Consider the following conversation between Leonard Bryner, president and manager of a firm engaged in job manufacturing, and Chuck Davis, certified management accountant, the firm's controller.

Leonard: Chuck, as you know, our firm has been losing market share over the past three years. We have been losing more and more bids, and I don't understand why. At first, I thought that other firms were undercutting simply to gain business, but after examining some of the public financial reports, I believe that they are making a reasonable rate of return. I am beginning to believe that our costs and costing methods are at fault.

Chuck: I can't agree with that. We have good control over our costs. Like most firms in our industry, we use a normal job-costing system. I really don't see any significant waste in the plant.

Leonard: After talking with some other managers at a recent industrial convention, I'm not so sure that waste by itself is the issue. They talked about activity-based management, activity-based costing, and continuous improvement. They mentioned the use of something called "activity drivers" to assign overhead. They claimed that these new procedures can help to produce more efficiency in manufacturing, better control of overhead, and more accurate product costing. A big deal was made of eliminating activities that added no value. Maybe our bids are too high because these other firms have found ways to decrease their overhead costs and to increase the accuracy of their product costing.

Chuck: I doubt it. For one thing, I don't see how we can increase product costing accuracy. So many of our costs are indirect costs. Furthermore, everyone uses some measure of production activity to assign overhead costs. I imagine that what they are calling "activity drivers" is just some new buzzword for measures of production volume. Fads in costing come and go. I wouldn't worry about it. I'll bet that our problems with decreasing sales are temporary. You might recall that we experienced a similar problem about 12 years ago—it was 2 years before it straightened out.

Required:

1. Do you agree or disagree with Chuck Davis and the advice that he gave Leonard Bryner? Explain.
2. Was there anything wrong or unethical in the behavior that Chuck Davis displayed? Explain your reasoning.
3. Do you think that Chuck was well informed—that he was aware of the accounting implications of ABC and that he knew what was meant by cost drivers? Should he have been well informed? Review (in Chapter 13) the first category of the standards of ethical conduct for management accountants. Do any of these standards apply in Chuck's case?

19 Profit Planning

Doug Norman Crystals/Alamy

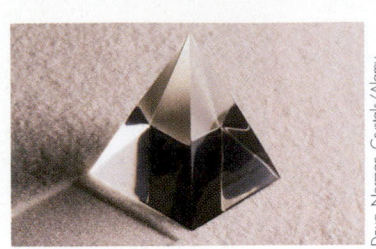

After studying Chapter 19, you should be able to:

1. Define budgeting and discuss its role in planning, control, and decision making.
2. Define and prepare the operating budget, identify its major components, and explain the interrelationships of its various components.
3. Define and prepare the financial budget, identify its major components, and explain the interrelationships of its various components.
4. Describe the behavioral dimension of budgeting.

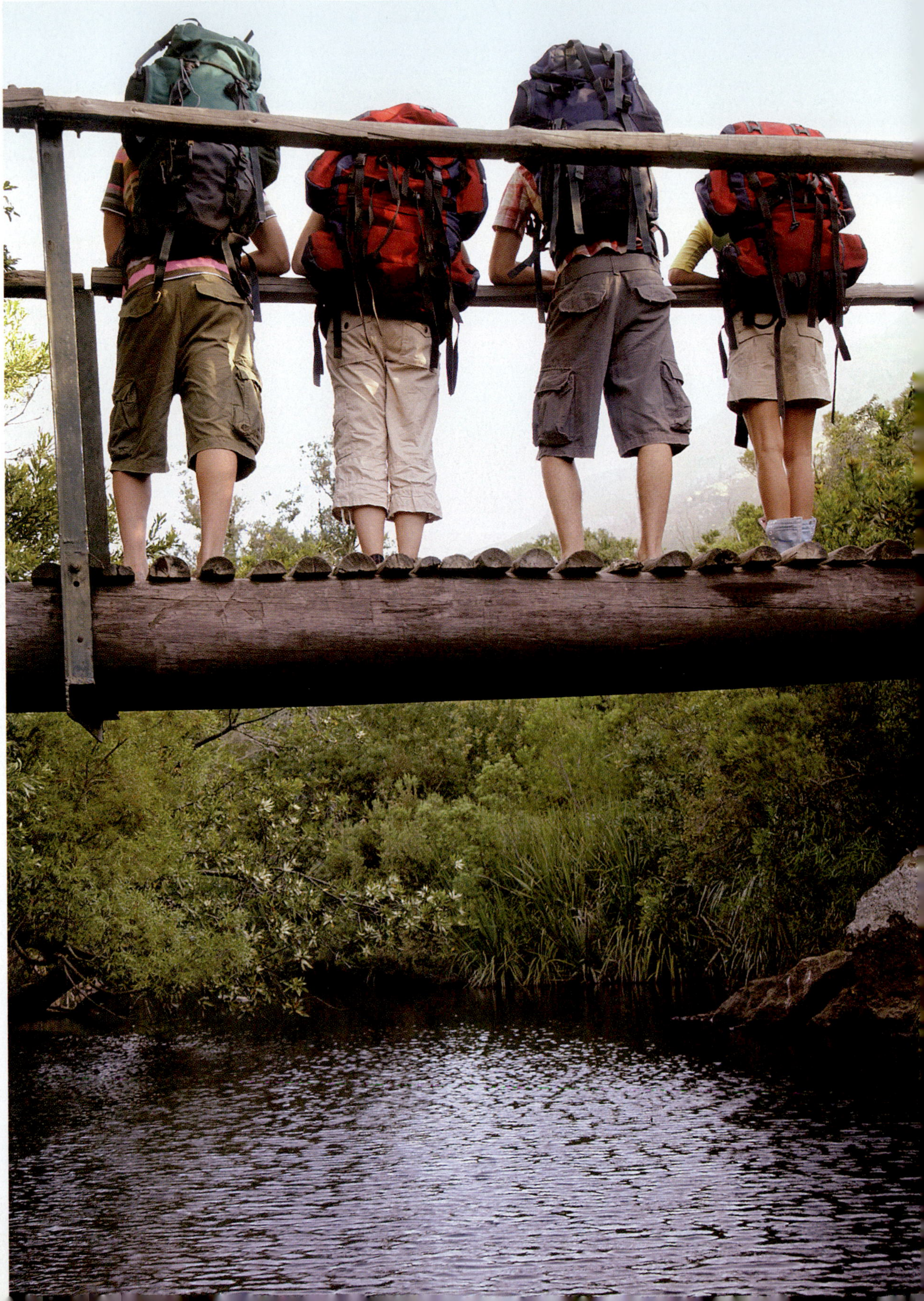

Mike Watson Images/moodboard/Jupiter Images

EXPERIENCE MANAGERIAL DECISIONS

with High Sierra

Have you ever wondered where that huge backpack you use to lug 50 pounds of books all over campus originated? If so, you might be surprised by the history behind the company. After World War II, Army and Navy Surplus stores supplied consumers with tents, canteens, and canvas bags. One of these stores was Seaway Importing, a company founded in 1978 by Harry Bernbaum. Harry and his son Hank recognized the need to develop more durable products and founded the **High Sierra Sport Company**.

Budgeting plays an important role in High Sierra's decision making process. Throughout the 1980s, High Sierra developed its brand reputation as a manufacturer and supplier of numerous types of quality outdoor and foul

Quang Ho, 2010/Shutterstock.com

weather gear, including backpacks, duffel bags, book bags, and hydration gear. During the mid-1990s, budgeting played a key role in helping High Sierra realize it needed to streamline its brand identity in order to keep its competitive edge in quality and price. High Sierra's management used its budgeting process to eliminate poor performing products and to analyze new products, such as a winter sports product line that focused more directly on the company's brand and target market (e.g., alliances with the U.S. Ski and Snowboard Association). During the early 2000s, High Sierra's budgeting process showed management that it needed to expand operations by outsourcing some of its production overseas in order to remain cost competitive. To ensure that its budgeting process continues to provide useful insights, High Sierra frequently adopts new and evolving techniques, such as participative budgeting and continuous budgeting. In summary, High Sierra uses budgeting as an effective planning and control tool to promote successful new product development that creates value for the company and keeps students buying those huge backpacks every year.

▲ **HIGH SIERRA**®

DESCRIPTION OF BUDGETING

All businesses should prepare budgets. Budgets help business owners and managers to plan ahead, and later, exercise control by comparing what actually happened to what was expected in the budget. Budgets formalize managers' expectations regarding sales, prices, and costs. Even small businesses and nonprofit entities can benefit from the planning and control provided by budgets.

Budgeting and Planning and Control

Planning and control are linked. *Planning* is looking ahead to see what actions should be taken to realize particular goals. *Control* is looking backward, determining what actually happened and comparing it with the previously planned outcomes. This comparison can then be used to adjust the budget, looking forward once more. Exhibit 19-1 illustrates the cycle of planning and control using budgets.

Budgets are financial plans for the future and are a key component of planning. They identify objectives and the actions needed to achieve them. Before preparing a budget, an organization should develop a strategic plan. The **strategic plan** plots a direction for an organization's future activities and operations; it generally covers at least five years. The overall strategy is then translated into the long- and short-term objectives that form the basis of the budget. The budget and the strategic plan should be tightly linked. Since budgets, especially one-year plans, are short run in nature, this linkage is important because it helps management to ensure that not all attention is focused on the short run. For example, in early 2009 **Home Depot Inc.** planned to open 12 new stores in that year. By November, however, the economic situation had deteriorated badly. The number of transactions was down as was the size of the average sale. Home Depot slashed its capital expenditure by 52 percent and its administrative expenses by 8.4 percent. When the economy improves and sales increase, the company will be better positioned to return to the earlier budgeted amounts.[1]

Exhibit 19-1

Planning, Control, and Budgets

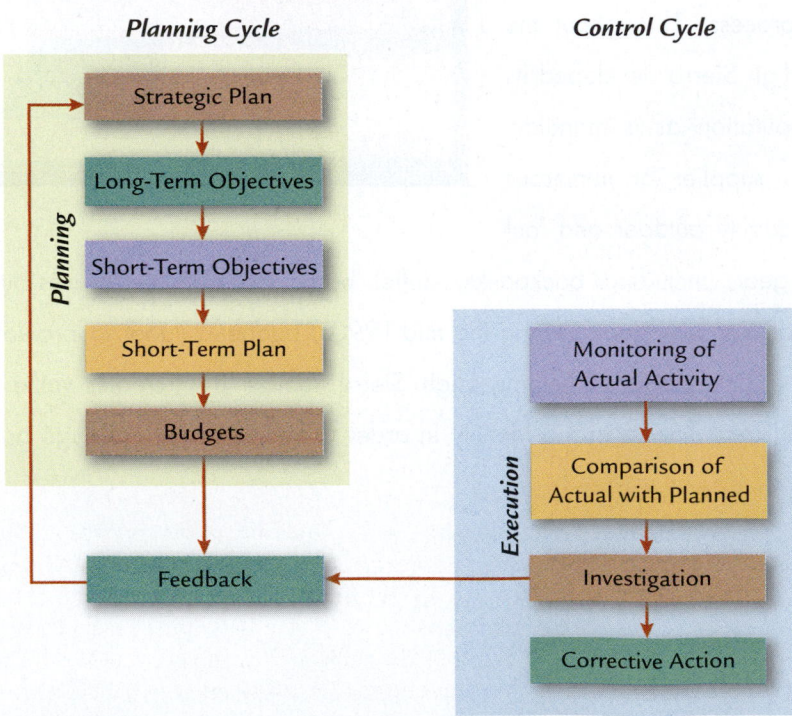

[1] Chris Burritt, "Home Depot Says Profit Fell as Shoppers Spent Less." November 17, 2009. Bloomberg.Com. http://www.bloomberg.com/apps/news?pid=20601103&sid=au1udfheLWj0

Advantages of Budgeting

A budgetary system gives an organization several advantages.

Planning Budgeting forces management to plan for the future. It encourages managers to develop an overall direction for the organization, foresee problems, and develop future policies.

Information for Decision Making Budgets improve decision making. For example, a restaurant owner who knows the expected revenues and the costs of meat, vegetables, cheeses, and so on might make menu changes that play up the less expensive items and reduce the use of more expensive ingredients. These better decisions, in turn, may keep customers happy while still providing a profitable living for the chefs, waiters, and others who work at the restaurant.

Standards for Performance Evaluation Budgets set standards that can control the use of a company's resources and motivate employees. A vital part of the budgetary system, **control** is achieved by comparing actual results with budgeted results on a periodic basis (e.g., monthly). A large difference between actual and planned results is feedback that prompts managers to take corrective action. For example, High Sierra, Inc. saw that sales of certain items were not meeting the budgeted amounts. Further market research showed that few customers needed the features of those particular products. As a result, the company could reduce its budgeted production in units and phase out the products.

Improved Communication and Coordination Budgets also serve to communicate and coordinate the plans of the organization to each employee. Accordingly, employees can be aware of their particular role in achieving those objectives. Since budgets for the various areas and activities of the organization must all work together to achieve organizational objectives, coordination is promoted. Managers can see the needs of other areas and are encouraged to subordinate their individual interests to those of the organization. The role of communication and coordination becomes more even more important as an organization grows.

Concept Q&A

How can a budget help in planning and control?

Answer:
A budget requires a plan. It also sets benchmarks that can be used to evaluate performance.

The Master Budget

The **master budget** is the comprehensive financial plan for the organization as a whole. Typically, the master budget is for a one-year period, corresponding to the fiscal year of the company. Yearly budgets are broken down into quarterly and monthly budgets. The use of smaller time periods allows managers to compare actual data with budgeted data more frequently, so problems may be noticed and resolved sooner.

Some organizations have developed a continuous budgeting philosophy. A **continuous budget** is a moving 12-month budget. As a month expires in the budget, an additional month in the future is added so that the company always has a 12-month plan on hand. Proponents of continuous budgeting maintain that it forces managers to plan ahead constantly.

Concept Q&A

What is the main objective of continuous budgeting?

Answer:
It forces managers to plan ahead constantly—something needed when firms operate in rapidly changing environments.

Directing and Coordinating Most organizations prepare the master budget for the coming year during the last four or five months of the current year. The **budget committee** reviews the budget, provides policy guidelines and budgetary goals, resolves differences that arise as the budget is prepared, approves the final budget, and monitors the actual performance of the organization as the year unfolds. The president of the organization appoints the members of the committee, who are usually the president, vice president of marketing, vice president of manufacturing, other vice presidents, and the controller. The controller usually serves as the **budget director**, the person responsible for directing and coordinating the organization's overall budgeting process.

Exhibit 19-2

The Master Budget and Its Interrelationships

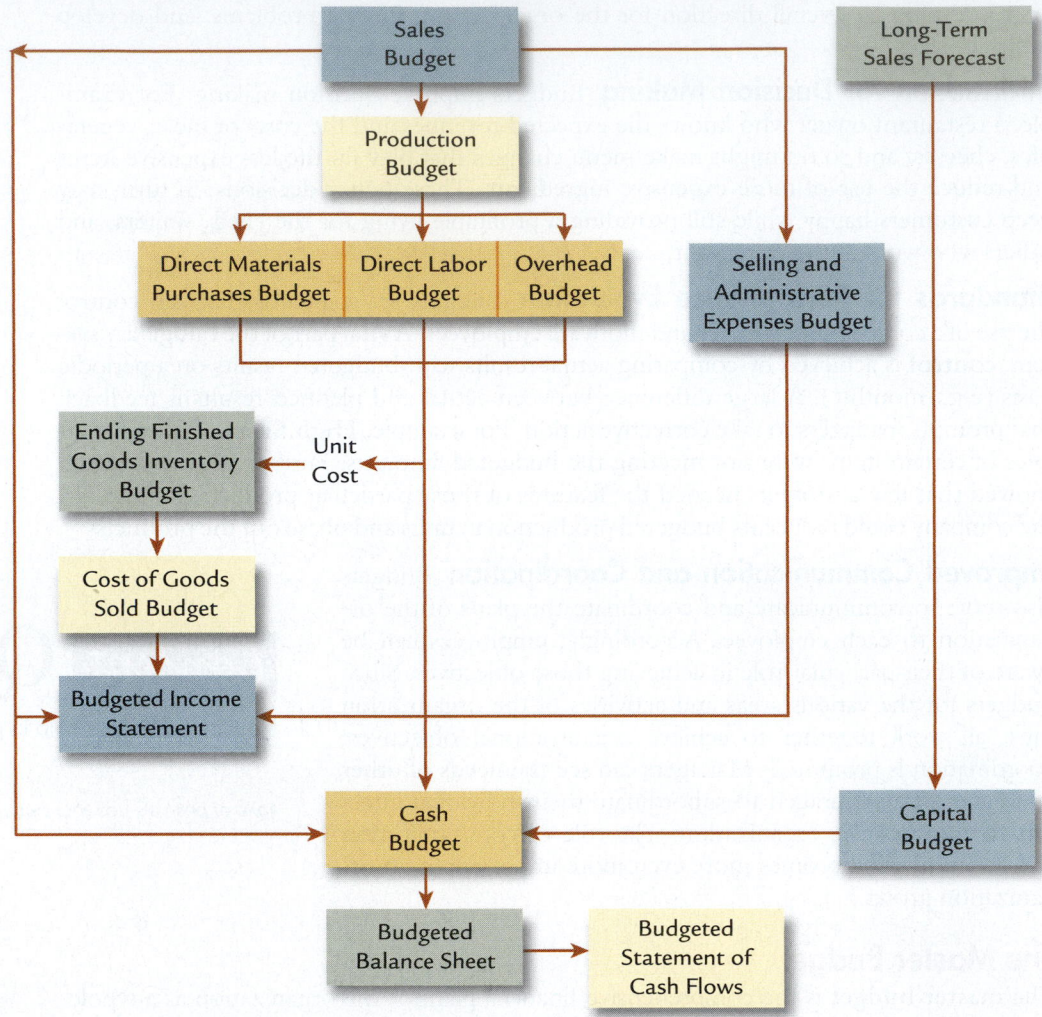

Major Components of the Master Budget A master budget can be divided into operating and financial budgets:

- **Operating budgets** describe the income-generating activities of a firm: sales, production, and finished goods inventories. The ultimate outcome of the operating budgets is a pro forma or budgeted income statement.
- **Financial budgets** detail the inflows and outflows of cash and the overall financial position. Planned cash inflows and outflows appear in the cash budget. The expected financial position at the end of the budget period is shown in a budgeted, or pro forma, balance sheet.

Since many of the financing activities are not known until the operating budgets are known, the operating budget is prepared first. Describing and illustrating the individual budgets that make up the master budget will reveal the interdependencies of the component budgets. A diagram displaying these interrelationships is shown in Exhibit 19-2. Details of the capital budget are covered in a separate chapter.

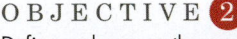

OBJECTIVE **2**

Define and prepare the operating budget, identify its major components, and explain the interrelationships of its various components.

PREPARING THE OPERATING BUDGET

The operating budget consists of a budgeted income statement accompanied by the following supporting schedules:

- sales budget
- production budget
- direct materials purchases budget
- direct labor budget
- overhead budget
- selling and administrative expenses budget
- ending finished goods inventory budget
- cost of goods sold budget

We illustrate the master budgeting process with an example based on the activities of Texas Rex Inc., a trendy restaurant in the Southwest that sells t-shirts with the Texas Rex logo (a dinosaur that engages in a variety of adventures while eating the Mexican food for which the restaurant is known). The example focuses on the Texas Rex clothing manufacturing plant.

Sales Budget

The **sales budget** is approved by the budget committee and describes expected sales in units and dollars. Because the sales budget is the basis for all of the other operating budgets and most of the financial budgets, it is important that it be as accurate as possible.

The first step in creating a sales budget is to develop the sales forecast. This is usually the responsibility of the marketing department. One approach to forecasting sales is the *bottom-up approach*, which requires individual salespeople to submit sales predictions. These are aggregated to form a total sales forecast. The accuracy of this sales forecast may be improved by considering other factors such as the general economic climate, competition, advertising, pricing policies, and so on. Some companies use more formal approaches, such as time-series analysis, correlation analysis, and econometric modeling. For example, the regression technique studied in the Appendix of Chapter 14 can be applied to forecasting sales, in addition to costs.

The sales forecast is just the initial estimate, and it is often adjusted by the budget committee. The budget committee may decide that the forecast is too pessimistic or too optimistic and revise it appropriately. For example, **Nintendo** set very conservative sales estimates for 2008 and later had to increase its sales forecast. Wii hardware sales alone were so robust that sales were expected to increase by one million units more than the company's original forecast.[2]

Concept Q&A

Why is the sales budget not necessarily the same as the sales forecast?

Answer:
The sales forecast is a starting point and an important input to the budgetary process. However, it is usually adjusted up or down, depending on the strategic objectives and plans of management.

Here's the Real Kicker

Stillwater Designs has 14 departments. Each department is given a budget for the coming fiscal year. The budgeting process begins with a sales forecast prepared by the president and vice presidents. The fiscal year for the company is October 1 through September 30, which is driven by the seasonal nature of the business. In January of each year, there is a consumer electronics show in Las Vegas, Nevada. New products are introduced, and initial orders from distributors are taken. The sales season starts earnestly in March, reaches its peak in June or July, and drops to its lowest level in the fall. The sales season is driven by the anticipation of warm weather. The young men buying the Kicker speakers and amplifiers want to drive with windows down—with the apparent hope of impressing young women. The budget is therefore prepared during August and September, the last two months of the fiscal year.

Each department is given a percentage of sales as its budget. The amount ultimately decided upon is not simply a top-down decision. Department managers submit a request for their desired budget. Negotiation takes place between the department managers and their associated vice presidents (each departmental manager is answerable to a specific vice president). Whether or not

(Continued)

2 "Pachter finds Nintendo's Sales Forecast Too Humble." Posted January 31, 2008 at 02:57 pm by Pulkit Chandna: http://www.gamertell.com/gaming/comment/analyst-nintendos-forecasts-remain-too-low/, accessed March 16, 2008.

the desired levels are provided depends on how well the departmental manager can justify the expenditures. An important criterion is the notion that resources are expended to make profits.

The budget is reviewed monthly. Any large deviations from the budget (usually more than a 10 percent deviation) are investigated. However, no formal incentive system is tied to budgetary performance. The budget is viewed as a guideline. If more resources are needed, then they can be obtained provided the request is backed up with a good idea and a promising payout.

CORNERSTONE 19-1 shows how to prepare the sales budget for Texas Rex's standard t-shirt line. For simplicity, assume that Texas Rex has only one product: a standard short-sleeved t-shirt with the Texas Rex logo screen printed on the back. (For a multiple-product firm, the sales budget reflects sales for each product in units and sales dollars.)

CORNERSTONE 19-1   Preparing a Sales Budget

Information:
Budgeted units to be sold for each quarter of the year 2012: 1,000, 1,200, 1,500, and 2,000. Selling price is $10 per t-shirt.

Required:
Prepare a sales budget for each quarter and for the year.

Solution:

Texas Rex Inc.
Sales Budget
For the Year Ended December 31, 2012

	Quarter				
	1	2	3	4	Year
Units	1,000	1,200	1,500	2,000	5,700
Unit selling price	×$10	×$10	×$10	×$10	×$10
Budgeted sales	$10,000	$12,000	$15,000	$20,000	$57,000

Notice that the sales budget in Cornerstone 19-1 reveals that Texas Rex's sales fluctuate seasonally. Most sales take place in the summer and fall quarters. This is due to the popularity of the t-shirts in the summer and the sales promotions that Texas Rex puts on for "back to school" and Christmas.

 **Budgeting in a Service Industry**

You are the controller for a large, regional medical center. The chief of cardiology has been pushing to have a free-standing heart hospital built on the medical center campus. However, you are concerned that taking the heart cases away from the main hospital will hurt its bottom line. While the medical center is nonprofit, it does need to cover all of its costs to stay in business. You also wonder whether the heart hospital will break even.

What information do you need to forecast revenues and costs of the heart hospital?

This is a two part problem. The first question, what impact will the heart hospital have on the main hospital's revenues, requires knowledge of the number and types of heart cases seen at the main hospital each year. This information could come from the sales revenue budget

(Continued)

from the previous year, assuming that the total number of patient days and procedures are broken out by type of case and procedure. Since so many of the costs of a hospital are fixed, there will probably be little decrease in costs as those heart patients leave for the free-standing heart hospital. The second question requires a forecast of the number of patients and probably reimbursement rates expected for procedures to be performed by the heart hospital. This information can be compared with budgeted operating costs to see if the heart hospital's revenues can cover its costs.

Forecasts of sales revenues and costs are dependent on detailed information provided by sources like the marketing or sales department and past accounting information and need to be revised and updates as new information or circumstances dictate.

Production Budget

The **production budget** tells how many units must be produced to meet sales needs and to satisfy ending inventory requirements. The Texas Rex production budget would show how many t-shirts are needed to satisfy sales demand for each quarter and for the year. If there were no beginning or ending inventories, the t-shirts to be produced would exactly equal the units to be sold. This would be the case in a just-in-time (JIT) firm. However, many firms use inventories as a buffer against uncertainties in demand or production. Thus, they need to plan for inventory levels as well as sales.

To compute the units to be produced, both unit sales and units of beginning and ending finished goods inventory are needed:

> Units to be produced = Expected unit sales + Units in desired ending inventory (EI)
> − Units in beginning inventory (BI)

CORNERSTONE 19-2 shows how to prepare a production budget using this formula. Consider the first column (Quarter 1) of the budget in Cornerstone 19-2. Texas Rex anticipates sales of 1,000 t-shirts. In addition, the company wants 240 t-shirts in ending inventory at the end of the first quarter ($0.20 \times 1,200$). Thus, 1,240 t-shirts are needed during the first quarter. Where will these 1,240 t-shirts come from? Beginning inventory can provide 180 of them, leaving 1,060 to be produced during the quarter. Notice that the production budget is expressed in terms of units.

**CORNERSTONE
19-2**   **Preparing a Production Budget**

Information:
Budgeted units to be sold for each quarter: 1,000, 1,200, 1,500, and 2,000. Assume that company policy requires 20 percent of the next quarter's sales in ending inventory and that beginning inventory of t-shirts for the first quarter of the year was 180. Assume also that sales for the first quarter of 2013 are estimated at 1,000 units.

Required:
1. Calculate the desired ending inventory in units for the each quarter of the year. What is the ending inventory in units for the year?
2. Prepare a production budget for each quarter and for the year.

Solution:
1. Ending inventory, Quarter 1 = $0.20 \times 1,200$ units = 240
    Ending inventory, Quarter 2 = $0.20 \times 1,500$ units = 300
    Ending inventory, Quarter 3 = $0.20 \times 2,000$ units = 400
    Ending inventory, Quarter 4 = $0.20 \times 1,000$ units = 200
    Ending inventory for the year = Ending inventory for Quarter 4 = 200 units

(Continued)

2.

Texas Rex Inc.
Production Budget
For the Year Ended December 31, 2012

	Quarter				
	1	2	3	4	Year
Sales in units	1,000	1,200	1,500	2,000	5,700
Desired ending inventory	240	300	400	200	200
Total needs	1,240	1,500	1,900	2,200	5,900
Less: Beginning inventory*	(180)	(240)	(300)	(400)	(180)
Units to be produced	1,060	1,260	1,600	1,800	5,720

*Beginning inventory for Quarter 1 is given in information. Beginning inventory for the remaining quarters is equal to ending inventory for the previous quarter.

CORNERSTONE
19-2
(continued)

Two important points regarding Cornerstone 19-2 should be emphasized:

- The beginning inventory for one quarter is always equal to the ending inventory of the previous quarter. For Quarter 2, the beginning inventory is 240 t-shirts, which is identical to the desired ending inventory for Quarter 1.
- The column for the year is not simply the addition of the amounts for the four quarters. Notice that the desired ending inventory for the year is 200 t-shirts, which is, of course, equal to the desired ending inventory for the fourth quarter.

Direct Materials Purchases Budget

After the production budget is completed, the budgets for direct materials, direct labor, and overhead can be prepared. The **direct materials purchases budget** tells the amount and cost of raw materials to be purchased in each time period. It depends on the expected use of materials in production and the raw materials inventory needs of the firm. The company needs to prepare a separate direct materials purchases budget for every type of raw material used. The formula used for calculating purchases is as follows:

> Purchases = Direct materials needed for production
> + Direct materials in desired ending inventory
> − Direct materials in beginning inventory

The quantity of direct materials in inventory is determined by the firm's inventory policy.

Texas Rex uses two types of raw materials: plain t-shirts and ink. The direct materials purchases budgets for these two materials are presented in **CORNERSTONE 19-3**.

CORNERSTONE
19-3

Preparing a Direct Materials Purchases Budget

Information:
Budgeted units to be produced for each quarter: 1,060, 1,260, 1,600, and 1,800. Plain t-shirts cost $3 each, and ink (for the screen printing) costs $0.20 per ounce. On a per-unit basis, the factory needs one plain t-shirt and five ounces of ink for each logoed t-shirt that it produces. Texas Rex's policy is to have 10 percent of the following quarter's production needs in ending inventory. The factory has 58 plain t-shirts and 390 ounces of ink on hand on January 1. At the end of the year, the desired ending inventory is 106 plain t-shirts and 530 ounces of ink.

(Continued)

Required:
1. Calculate the ending inventory of plain t-shirts and of ink for Quarters 2 and 3.
2. Prepare a direct materials purchases budget for plain t-shirts and one for ink.

**CORNERSTONE
19-3**
(continued)

Solution:
1. Ending inventory plain t-shirts, Quarter 2 = 0.10 × (1,600 units × 1 t-shirt) = 160
   Ending inventory plain t-shirts, Quarter 3 = 0.10 × (1,800 units × 1 t-shirt) = 180
   Ending inventory ink, Quarter 2 = 0.10 × (1,600 units × 5 ounces) = 800
   Ending inventory ink, Quarter 3 = 0.10 × (1,800 units × 5 ounces) = 900

2.

Texas Rex Inc.
Direct Materials Purchases Budget
For the Year Ended December 31, 2012

Plain t-shirts

	Quarter				
	1	2	3	4	Year
Units to be produced	1,060	1,260	1,600	1,800	5,720
Direct materials per unit	×1	×1	×1	×1	×1
Production needs	1,060	1,260	1,600	1,800	5,720
Desired ending inventory	126	160	180	106	106
Total needs	1,186	1,420	1,780	1,906	5,826
Less: Beginning inventory	(58)	(126)	(160)	(180)	(58)
Direct materials to be purchased	1,128	1,294	1,620	1,726	5,768
Cost per t-shirt	×$3	×$3	×$3	×$3	×$3
Total purchase cost plain t-shirts	$3,384	$3,882	$4,860	$5,178	$17,304

Ink

	Quarter				
	1	2	3	4	Year
Units to be produced	1,060	1,260	1,600	1,800	5,720
Direct materials per unit	×5	×5	×5	×5	×5
Production needs	5,300	6,300	8,000	9,000	28,600
Desired ending inventory	630	800	900	530	530
Total needs	5,930	7,100	8,900	9,530	29,130
Less: Beginning inventory	(390)	(630)	(800)	(900)	(390)
Direct materials to be purchased	5,540	6,470	8,100	8,630	28,740
Cost per ounce	×$0.20	×$0.20	×$0.20	×$0.20	×$0.20
Total purchase cost of ink	$1,108	$1,294	$1,620	$1,726	$5,748
Total direct materials purchase cost	$4,492	$5,176	$6,480	$6,904	$23,052

Notice how similar the direct materials purchases budget is to the production budget. Consider the first quarter, starting with the plain t-shirts. It takes one plain t-shirt for every logo t-shirt, so the 1,060 logo t-shirts to be produced are multiplied by one to obtain the number of plain t-shirts needed for production. Next, the desired ending inventory of 126 (10 percent of the next quarter's production needs) is added. Thus, 1,186 plain t-shirts are needed during the first quarter. Of this total, 58 are already in beginning inventory, meaning that the remaining 1,128 must be purchased. Multiplying the 1,128 plain t-shirts by the cost of $3 each gives Texas Rex the $3,384 expected cost of plain t-shirt purchases for the first quarter of the year. The direct materials purchases budget for ink is done in the same way as t-shirts except that each unit produced requires 5 ounces of ink. So the total units to be produced must be multiplied by 5 to get the production needs of ink.

Direct Labor Budget

The **direct labor budget** shows the total direct labor hours and the direct labor cost needed for the number of units in the production budget. As with direct materials, the budgeted hours of direct labor are determined by the relationship between labor and output. The direct labor budget for Texas Rex is shown in **CORNERSTONE 19-4**.

CORNERSTONE 19-4   Preparing a Direct Labor Budget

Information:
Recall from Cornerstone 19-2 (p. 975) that budgeted units to be produced for each quarter are: 1,060, 1,260, 1,600, and 1,800. It takes 0.12 hour to produce one t-shirt. The average wage cost per hour is $10.

Required:
Prepare a direct labor budget.

Solution:

Texas Rex Inc.
Direct Labor Budget
For the Year Ended December 31, 2012

	Quarter				
	1	**2**	**3**	**4**	**Year**
Units to be produced	1,060	1,260	1,600	1,800	5,720
Direct labor time per unit in hours	×0.12	×0.12	×0.12	×0.12	×0.12
Total hours needed	127.2	151.2	192.0	216.0	686.4
Average wage per hour	×$10	×$10	×$10	×$10	×$10
Total direct labor cost	$1,272	$1,512	$1,920	$2,160	$6,864

Overhead Budget

The **overhead budget** shows the expected cost of all production costs other than direct materials and direct labor. Many companies use direct labor hours as the driver for overhead. Then costs that vary with direct labor hours are pooled and called variable overhead. The remaining overhead items are pooled into fixed overhead. The method for preparing an overhead budget using this approach to cost behavior is shown in **CORNERSTONE 19-5**.

CORNERSTONE 19-5   Preparing an Overhead Budget

Information:
Refer to Cornerstone 19-4 for the direct labor budget. The variable overhead rate is $5 per direct labor hour. Fixed overhead is budgeted at $1,645 per quarter (this amount includes $540 per quarter for depreciation).

(Continued)

CORNERSTONE 19-5 (continued)

Required:
Prepare an overhead budget.

Solution:

Texas Rex Inc.
Overhead Budget
For the Year Ended December 31, 2012

	Quarter				
	1	2	3	4	Year
Budgeted direct labor hours	127.2	151.2	192.0	216.0	686.4
Variable overhead rate	×$ 5	×$ 5	×$ 5	×$ 5	×$ 5
Budgeted variable overhead	$ 636	$ 756	$ 960	$1,080	$ 3,432
Budgeted fixed overhead*	1,645	1,645	1,645	1,645	6,580
Total overhead	$2,281	$2,401	$2,605	$2,725	$10,012

*Includes $540 of depreciation in each quarter.

Ending Finished Goods Inventory Budget

The **ending finished goods inventory budget** supplies information needed for the balance sheet and also serves as an important input for the preparation of the cost of goods sold budget. To prepare this budget, the unit cost of producing each t-shirt must be calculated by using information from the direct materials, direct labor, and overhead budgets. The way to calculate the unit cost of a t-shirt and the cost of the planned ending inventory is shown in **CORNERSTONE 19-6**.

Concept Q&A

What operating budgets are needed to calculate a budgeted unit cost?

Answer:
Materials, labor, and overhead budgets. It could be argued that sales and production budgets are needed also because the three budgets listed cannot be developed until the sales and production budgets are known.

CORNERSTONE 19-6

Preparing an Ending Finished Goods Inventory Budget

Information:
Refer to Cornerstones 19-3 (p. 976), 19-4, and 19-5 for the direct materials, direct labor, and overhead budgets.

Required:
1. Calculate the unit product cost.
2. Prepare an ending finished goods inventory budget.

Solution:
1.

Direct materials:		
Plain t-shirt	$3	
Ink (5 oz. @ $0.20)	1	$4.00
Direct labor (0.12 hr. @ $10)		1.20
Overhead:		
Variable (0.12 hr. @ $5)		0.60
Fixed (0.12 hr. @ $9.59*)		1.15**
Total unit cost		$6.95

*Budgeted fixed overhead/Budgeted direct labor hours = $6,580/686.4 – $9.59
**Rounded

(Continued)

2.

Texas Rex Inc.	
Ending Finished Goods Inventory Budget	
For the Year Ended December 31, 2012	
Logo t-shirts	200
Unit cost	×$6.95
Total ending inventory	$1,390

CORNERSTONE
19-6
(continued)

Notice that the Ending Finished Goods Inventory Budget brings together information from the production, direct labor, and overhead budgets to compute the unit product cost for the year.

Cost of Goods Sold Budget

Assuming that the beginning finished goods inventory is valued at $1,251, the budgeted cost of goods sold schedule can be prepared using information from Cornerstones 19-3 to 19-6. The **cost of goods sold budget** reveals the expected cost of the goods to be sold and is shown in **CORNERSTONE 19-7**.

**CORNERSTONE
19-7**

Preparing a Cost of Goods Sold Budget

Information:
Refer to Cornerstones 19-3 through 19-6 (beginning p. 976) for the direct materials, direct labor, overhead, and ending finished goods budgets. The cost of beginning finished goods inventory is $1,251.

Required:
Prepare a cost of goods sold budget.

Solution:

Texas Rex Inc.	
Cost of Goods Sold Budget	
For the Year Ended December 31, 2012	
Direct materials used (Cornerstone 19-3)*	$22,880
Direct labor used (Cornerstone 19-4)	6,864
Overhead (Cornerstone 19-5)	10,012
Budgeted manufacturing costs	$39,756
Beginning finished goods	1,251
Cost of goods available for sale	$41,007
Less: Ending finished goods (Cornerstone 19-6)	(1,390)
Budgeted cost of goods sold	$39,617

*Production needs = (5,720 plain t-shirts × $3) + (28,600 oz. ink × $0.20)

The output of the Cost of Goods Sold Budget, the budgeted cost of goods sold, will appear in the budgeted income statement.

Selling and Administrative Expenses Budget

The next budget to be prepared, the **selling and administrative expenses budget**, outlines planned expenditures for nonmanufacturing activities. As with overhead, selling and administrative expenses can be broken down into fixed and variable components. Such items as sales commissions, freight, and supplies vary with sales activity. The selling and administrative expenses budget is illustrated in **CORNERSTONE 19-8**.

CORNERSTONE 19-8   Preparing a Selling and Administrative Expenses Budget

Information:

Refer to Cornerstone 19-1 (p. 974) for the sales budget. Variable expenses are $0.10 per unit sold. Salaries average $1,420 per quarter; utilities, $50 per quarter; and depreciation, $150 per quarter. Advertising for Quarters 1 through 4 is $100, $200, $800, and $500, respectively.

Required:

Prepare a selling and administrative expenses budget.

Solution:

Texas Rex Inc.
Selling and Administrative Expenses Budget
For the Year Ended December 31, 2012

	Quarter				
	1	2	3	4	Year
Planned sales in units (Cornerstone 19-1)	1,000	1,200	1,500	2,000	5,700
Variable selling and administrative expenses per unit	×$ 0.10	×$ 0.10	×$ 0.10	×$ 0.10	×$ 0.10
Total variable expenses	$ 100	$ 120	$ 150	$ 200	$ 570
Fixed selling and administrative expenses:					
Salaries	$1,420	$1,420	$1,420	$1,420	$5,680
Utilities	50	50	50	50	200
Advertising	100	200	800	500	1,600
Depreciation	150	150	150	150	600
Total fixed expenses	$1,720	$1,820	$2,420	$2,120	$8,080
Total selling and administrative expenses	$1,820	$1,940	$2,570	$2,320	$8,650

Notice how the selling and administrative expenses budget follows a very similar format as that of the overhead budget. In both cases, variable and fixed expenses are calculated. Notice also that depreciation, a noncash expense, is shown separately. This will be important later on when the company prepares the cash budget.

Budgeted Income Statement

With the completion of the budgeted cost of goods sold schedule and the budgeted selling and administrative expenses budget, Texas Rex has all the operating budgets needed to prepare an estimate of *operating* income. The way to prepare this budgeted income statement is shown in **CORNERSTONE 19-9** (p. 982). The eight budgets already prepared, along with the budgeted operating income statement, define the operating budget for Texas Rex.

CORNERSTONE 19-9   Preparing a Budgeted Income Statement

Information:
Refer to Cornerstones 19-1 (p. 974), 19-7 (p. 980), 19-8 (p. 981), and 19-12 (p. 986) for the sales budget, the cost of goods sold budget, the selling and administrative expenses budget, and the cash budget. Assume that the tax rate is 40 percent.

Required:
Prepare a budgeted income statement.

Solution:

Texas Rex Inc.
Budgeted Income Statement
For the Year Ended December 31, 2012

Sales (Cornerstone 19-1)	$ 57,000
Less: Cost of goods sold (Cornerstone 19-7)	(39,617)
Gross margin	$ 17,383
Less: Selling and administrative expenses (Cornerstone 19-8)	(8,650)
Operating income	$ 8,733
Less: Interest expense (Cornerstone 19-12)	(60)
Income before income taxes	$ 8,673
Less: Income taxes (0.40 × $8,673)	(3,469)*
Net income	$ 5,204

*Rounded

Concept Q&A

Why is it not possible to prepare a budgeted income statement by using only operating budgets?

Answer:
Interest expense comes from the financial budgets. Only operating income can be computed by using operating budgets.

Operating income is *not* equivalent to the net income of a firm. To yield net income, interest expense and taxes must be subtracted from operating income. The interest expense deduction is taken from the cash budget for Texas Rex (Cornerstone 19-12, p. 986), a budget discussed in the section on financial budgets. The taxes owed depend on the current federal and state tax laws. For simplicity, a combined rate of 40 percent is assumed.

OBJECTIVE ❸

Define and prepare the financial budget, identify its major components, and explain the interrelationships of its various components.

PREPARING THE FINANCIAL BUDGET

The remaining budgets found in the master budget are the financial budgets. The usual financial budgets prepared are:

- cash budget
- budgeted balance sheet
- budget for capital expenditures

The master budget also contains a plan for acquiring long-term assets—assets that have a time horizon that extends beyond the one-year operating period. Some of these assets may be purchased during the coming year. Plans to purchase others may be detailed for future periods. This part of the master budget is typically referred to as the *capital budget*. Decision making for capital expenditures is considered in Chapter 24. Accordingly, only the cash budget and the budgeted balance sheet will be illustrated here.

The Cash Budget

Exhibit 19-3

Expected beginning balance	$ 3,000
Add cash receipts	45,000
Cash available	$48,000
Less disbursements	39,000
Expected ending balance	$ 9,000

Cash Budget

Understanding cash flows is critical in managing a business. Often, a business successfully produces and sells products but fails because of timing problems associated with cash inflows and outflows. Examples include the smallest entrepreneurs, who are required by suppliers to pay cash up front but must sell to their customers on credit, as well large corporations like **Sears**. In early 2008, Sears acknowledged that available cash had dropped by nearly 60 percent over 2007. A cash crunch was leading Sears to consider selling assets.[3] By the end of 2009, Sears had closed more than 60 stores, liquidating inventory and realizing cash from the closings.[4]

By knowing when cash inflows and outflows are likely to occur, a manager can plan to borrow cash when needed and to repay the loans during periods of excess cash. Because cash flow is the lifeblood of an organization, the cash budget is one of the most important budgets in the master budget. The basic structure of a **cash budget** includes cash receipts, disbursements, any excess or deficiency of cash, and financing. At its simplest, a cash budget is cash inflows minus cash outflows. Suppose, for example, that a company expects $3,000 in the cash account on June 1. During June, cash sales of $45,000 are predicted, as are cash disbursements of $39,000. The company wants to have a $2,500 minimum cash balance. The resulting cash budget for June is illustrated in Exhibit 19-3.

Cash Available

Cash available consists of the beginning cash balance and the expected cash receipts. Expected cash receipts include all sources of cash for the period being considered. The principal source of cash is from sales. Since a large proportion of sales is usually on account, a major task of an organization is to determine the pattern of collection for its accounts receivable. If a company has been in business for a while, it can use past experience to determine what percentage of credit sales are paid in the month of and months following sales. This is used to create a schedule of cash collections on accounts receivable. **CORNERSTONE 19-10** shows how to create a schedule for cash collections on accounts receivable for Texas Rex.

CORNERSTONE 19-10   **Preparing a Schedule for Cash Collections on Accounts Receivable**

Information:

From past experience, Texas Rex expects that, on average, 25 percent of total sales are cash and 75 percent of total sales are on credit. Of the credit sales, Texas Rex expects that 90 percent will be paid in cash during the quarter of sale, and the remaining 10 percent will be paid in the following quarter. Recall from Cornerstone 19-1 (p. 974) that Texas Rex expects the following total sales:

(Continued)

---

[3] Gary McWilliams, "Profit Down, Sears May Hold Yard Sale," *The Wall Street Journal* (February 29, 2008): A13.
[4] Edward S. Lampert Chairman's Letter, February 23, 2010. http://www.searsholdings.com/invest/

Quarter 1	$10,000
Quarter 2	$12,000
Quarter 3	$15,000
Quarter 4	$20,000

The balance in accounts receivable as of the last quarter of 2011 was $1,350. This will be collected in cash during the first quarter of 2012.

Required:
1. Calculate cash sales expected in each quarter of 2012.
2. Prepare a schedule showing cash receipts from sales expected in each quarter of 2012.

Solution:
1. Cash sales expected in Quarter 1 = $10,000 × 0.25 = $2,500

   Cash sales expected in Quarter 2 = $12,000 × 0.25 = $3,000

   Cash sales expected in Quarter 3 = $15,000 × 0.25 = $3,750

   Cash sales expected in Quarter 4 = $20,000 × 0.25 = $5,000

2.

| | Quarter | | | |
Source	1	2	3	4
Cash sales	$ 2,500	$ 3,000	$ 3,750	$ 5,000
Received on account from:				
Quarter 4, 2011	1,350			
Quarter 1, 2012	6,750[a]	750[b]		
Quarter 2, 2012		8,100[c]	900[d]	
Quarter 3, 2012			10,125[e]	1,125[f]
Quarter 4, 2012				13,500[g]
Total cash receipts	$10,600	$11,850	$14,775	$19,625

[a]($10,000 × 0.75)(0.9)
[b]($10,000 × 0.75)(0.1)
[c]($12,000 × 0.75)(0.9)
[d]($12,000 × 0.75)(0.1)
[e]($15,000 × 0.75)(0.9)
[f]($15,000 × 0.75)(0.1)
[g]($20,000 × 0.75)(0.9)

Concept Q&A

Sales for a month totaled $10,000. Cash receipts for the same month were $15,000. How is it possible for cash receipts to be more than sales?

Answer:
Money can be collected from credit sales of prior month(s).

While Texas Rex expects no bad debts expense, that may not be the case for all firms. If a firm expects less than 100 percent of the credit sales to be received in cash, then it expects some bad debts. For example, if a firm expected to be repaid 98 percent of credit sales, then it expects 2 percent bad debts. In other words, not everyone pays for their credit sales. This 2 percent is ignored for purposes of cash budgeting since it will not be received in cash. Different firms have different accounts receivable repayment experiences.

Cash Disbursements The cash disbursements section lists all planned cash outlays for the period. All expenses that do not require a cash outlay are *excluded* from the list (e.g., depreciation is never included in the disbursements section). Just as sources of cash may require a schedule of cash collections on accounts receivable to calculate cash expected from credit sales, the disbursements section may require care in handling payments on account. **CORNERSTONE 19-11** shows how to handle timing differences arising from paying for items on account.

CORNERSTONE
19-11

Determining Cash Payments on Accounts Payable

Information:

Texas Rex purchases all raw materials on account. 80 percent of purchases are paid for in the quarter of purchase; the remaining 20 percent are paid for in the following quarter. The purchases for the fourth quarter of 2011 were $5,000. Recall from Cornerstone 19-3 (p. 976) that Texas Rex expects the following purchases of raw materials:

Quarter 1	$4,492
Quarter 2	$5,176
Quarter 3	$6,480
Quarter 4	$6,904

Required:

Prepare a schedule showing anticipated payments for accounts payable for materials.

Solution:

Cash needed for payments on account:

	Quarter			
Source	**1**	**2**	**3**	**4**
Quarter 4, 2011	$1,000[a]			
Quarter 1, 2012	3,594[b]	$ 898[c]		
Quarter 2, 2012		4,141[d]	$1,035[e]	
Quarter 3, 2012			5,184[f]	$1,296[g]
Quarter 4, 2012				5,523[h]
Total cash needed	$4,594	$5,039	$6,219	$6,819

(*Note:* All footnote calculations are rounded.)
[a]($5,000 × 0.20)
[b]($4,492 × 0.80)
[c]($4,492 × 0.20)
[d]($5,176 × 0.80)
[e]($5,176 × 0.20)
[f]($6,480 × 0.80)
[g]($6,480 × 0.20)
[h]($6,904 × 0.80)

Note that Cornerstone 19-11 does not allow for less than 100 percent repayment of accounts payable. The ethical firm always intends to repay its debts.

A disbursement that is typically not included in the disbursements section is interest on short-term borrowing. This interest expenditure is reserved for the section on loan repayments.

Cash Excess or Deficiency The cash budget shown in Exhibit 19-3 (p. 983) is a very simple one. Sometimes companies expand this format, as is done for the cash budget for Texas Rex in Cornerstone 19-12 (p. 986), by adding lines to show any borrowing or repayment necessary to achieve a minimum desired cash amount. When this is done, the preliminary ending cash balance is called *cash excess or deficiency*. The cash excess or deficiency line is compared to the minimum cash balance required by company policy. The minimum cash balance is simply the lowest amount of cash on hand that the firm finds acceptable. Consider your own checking account. You probably try to keep at least some cash in the account, perhaps because by having a minimum balance you avoid service charges, or because a minimum balance allows you to make an unplanned purchase. Similarly, companies also require minimum cash balances. The amount varies from

Concept Q&A

Why would a company want a minimum cash balance? Suppose that the minimum cash balance is $1,000 and that the projected cash surplus is $500. What would a company have to do to achieve the desired minimum?

Answer:

A minimum cash balance is needed to reduce the risk of insufficient funds and satisfy account agreements with the banks. In the event of a shortage, it is necessary to borrow the difference.

firm to firm and is determined by each company's particular needs and policies. If there is a cash deficiency, then the cash on hand is less than the cash needed. In such a case, a short-term loan will be needed. On the other hand, with a cash excess (cash available is greater than the firm's cash needs), the firm has the ability to repay loans and perhaps to make some temporary investments. For example, in mid-2010, **Target** raised its dividend from $0.17 to $0.25, reasoning that its surplus of cash was above what was needed for reinvestment in its core business. **Pep Boys** (automotive parts supplier) announced that its cash balance was up by four times what it had been the year before and was considering additional capital investment.[5]

Borrowings and Repayments If a company converts its preliminary cash balance line to a cash excess (deficiency) line, it may be borrowing or repaying money. If there is a deficiency, this section shows the necessary amount to be borrowed. When excess cash is available, this section shows planned repayments, including interest expense.

Ending Cash Balance The last line of the cash budget is the ending cash balance. This is the planned amount of cash to be on hand at the end of the period after all receipts and disbursements, as well as borrowings and repayments, are considered.

Preparing a Cash Budget The way to prepare a cash budget is illustrated in **CORNERSTONE 19-12**.

CORNERSTONE 19-12   Preparing a Cash Budget

Information:

Refer to Cornerstones 19-1 (p. 974), 19-3 (p. 976), 19-4 (p. 978), 19-5 (p. 978), 19-8 (p. 981), 19-9 (p. 982), 19-10 (p. 983) and 19-11 (p. 985) as well as the following details:

a. A $1,000 minimum cash balance is required for the end of each quarter. Money can be borrowed and repaid in multiples of $1,000. Interest is 12 percent per year. Interest payments are made only for the amount of the principal being repaid. All borrowing takes place at the beginning of a quarter, and all repayment takes place at the end of a quarter.

b. Budgeted depreciation is $540 per quarter for overhead and $150 per quarter for selling and administrative expenses (Cornerstones 19-5 and 19-8).

c. The capital budget for 2012 revealed plans to purchase additional screen printing equipment. The cash outlay for the equipment, $6,500, will take place in the first quarter. The company plans to finance the acquisition of the equipment with operating cash, supplementing it with short-term loans as necessary.

d. Corporate income taxes are approximately $3,469 and will be paid at the end of the fourth quarter (Cornerstone 19-9).

e. Beginning cash balance equals $5,200.

f. All amounts in the budget are rounded to the nearest dollar.

Required:

Prepare a cash budget for Texas Rex.

(Continued)

Solution:

CORNERSTONE 19-12 (continued)

Texas Rex Inc.
Cash Budget
For the Year Ended December 31, 2012

	Quarter					
	1	2	3	4	Year	Source*
Beginning cash balance	$ 5,200	$ 1,023	$ 1,611	$ 3,762	$ 5,200	e
Cash sales and collections on account:	10,600	11,850	14,775	19,625	56,850	10
Total cash available	$ 15,800	$ 12,873	$ 16,386	$ 23,387	$ 62,050	
Less disbursements:						
Payments for:						
Raw materials	$ (4,594)	$ (5,039)	$ (6,219)	$ (6,819)	$(22,671)	11
Direct labor	(1,272)	(1,512)	(1,920)	(2,160)	(6,864)	4
Overhead	(1,741)	(1,861)	(2,065)	(2,185)	(7,852)	b,5
Selling and administrative expenses	(1,670)	(1,790)	(2,420)	(2,170)	(8,050)	b,8
Income taxes	—	—	—	(3,469)	(3,469)	d,9
Equipment	(6,500)	—	—	—	(6,500)	c
Total disbursements	$(15,777)	$(10,202)	$(12,624)	$(16,803)	$(55,406)	
Excess (deficiency) of cash available over needs	$ 23	$ 2,671	$ 3,762	$ 6,584	$ 6,644	
Financing:						
Borrowings	1,000	—	—	—	1,000	
Repayments	—	(1,000)	—	—	(1,000)	a
Interest**	—	(60)	—	—	(60)	a
Total financing	$ 1,000	$ (1,060)	—	—	$ (60)	
Ending cash balance***	$ 1,023	$ 1,611	$ 3,762	$ 6,584	$ 6,584	

*Letters refer to the detailed information above. Numbers refer to Cornerstone schedules.

**Interest payment is 6/12 × 0.12 × $1,000. Since borrowings occur at the beginning of the quarter and repayments at the end of the quarter, the principal repayment takes place after six months.

***Total cash available minus total disbursements plus (or minus) total financing.

Cornerstone 19-12 reveals that much of the information needed to prepare the cash budget comes from the operating budgets and from the schedules for cash receipts on accounts receivable and cash payments on accounts payable. It is important to recall that only cash expenditures are included in the cash budget. The operating budgets for overhead and selling and administrative expenses included depreciation expense, which is a noncash expense. Therefore, depreciation expense was subtracted from the totals to yield the cash expenditures for overhead and for selling and administrative expense.

The cash budget underscores the importance of breaking down the annual budget into smaller time periods. The cash budget for the year gives the impression that sufficient operating cash will be available to finance the acquisition of the new equipment. Quarterly information, however, shows the need for short-term borrowing ($1,000) because of both the acquisition of the new equipment and the timing of the firm's cash flows. Most firms prepare monthly cash budgets, and some even prepare weekly and daily budgets.

Texas Rex's cash budget provides another piece of useful information. By the end of the third quarter, the firm has more cash ($3,762) than needed to meet operating needs. Management should consider investing the excess cash in an interest-bearing account.

Once plans are finalized for use of the excess cash, the cash budget should be revised to reflect those plans. Budgeting is a dynamic process. As the budget is developed, new information becomes available, and better plans can be formulated.

Budgeted Balance Sheet

The budgeted balance sheet depends on information contained in the current balance sheet and in the other budgets in the master budget. Exhibit 19-4 shows the budgeted balance sheets as of December 31, 2011 and December 31, 2012. Explanations for the budgeted figures are provided in the footnotes.

YOU DECIDE   Cash Budgeting for a Small Painting Company

You are the accountant for a number of small businesses in your town, one of which is Ramon's Paint and Plaster. Ramon has been through a tough year as construction in the town has been down. However, new home construction is picking up and Ramon has been asked to bid on twice as many jobs in the past month as he was last year at this time. Ramon needs to know what his cash flow will be for the coming year. You are starting to amass information to help you forecast monthly cash inflows and outflows for the next six months.

What information do you need to forecast cash inflows and outflows for the paint and plaster business for the next six months?

This is a two part problem. The first question, what inflows of cash are expected, depends on the number and size of the jobs Ramon can successfully bid on. Ramon's business has been primarily residential, so you'll need to know the number of housing starts (or the number of building permits applied for) and the number of remodeling jobs expected. You will also need to consider the price Ramon charges as well as the probability of prompt payment. Some builders have a good reputation for paying promptly in the first ten days of the month following work by Ramon's crew. Others lag behind. While you can encourage Ramon to work primarily with the better builders, he may be forced to accept some jobs with contractors who frequently pay later.

The second question requires a forecast of the potential cash outflows. Ramon has a crew of six workers and the hourly rate is known. He also can figure out the cost of the paint and plaster materials fairly accurately, once the size of the job is known. It will be difficult to forecast the cash inflows and outflows too far in advance. As a result, you will probably want to set up the cash budget for one to three months in advance and then update the forecasted numbers as the year progresses.

Forecasts of cash inflows and outflows depend on the economic conditions, the reputation of the payment patterns of the customers, and the prices charged both for the jobs obtained as well as for the supplies used. Information from the past year can be used as a baseline, however, changing economic conditions will affect future amounts.

OBJECTIVE 4
Describe the behavioral dimension of budgeting.

USING BUDGETS FOR PERFORMANCE EVALUATION

Budgets are often used to judge the performance of managers. Bonuses, salary increases, and promotions are all affected by a manager's ability to achieve or beat budgeted goals. Since a manager's financial status and career can be affected, budgets can have a significant behavioral effect. Whether that effect is positive or negative depends in large part on how budgets are used.

Positive behavior occurs when the goals of each manager are aligned with the goals of the organization and each manager has the drive to achieve them. The alignment of managerial and organizational goals is often referred to as **goal congruence**. If the budget is improperly administered, subordinate managers may subvert the organization's goals. **Dysfunctional behavior** is individual behavior that is in basic conflict with the goals of the organization.

An ideal budgetary system is one that achieves complete goal congruence and, simultaneously, creates a drive in managers to achieve the organization's goals in an ethical manner. While an ideal budgetary system probably does not exist,

In the last quarter of the fiscal year, a divisional manager chose to delay budgeted preventive maintenance expenditures so that the budgeted income goals could be achieved. Is this an example of goal congruent behavior or dysfunctional behavior?

Answer:
Assuming that the budgeted maintenance expenditures were well specified, the manager is sacrificing the long-run well-being of the division to achieve a short-run benefit (dysfunctional behavior).

Exhibit 19-4

Budgeted Balance Sheet

Texas Rex Inc.
Balance Sheet
December 31, 2011

Assets

Current assets:		
Cash	$ 5,200	
Accounts receivable	1,350	
Raw materials inventory	252	
Finished goods inventory	1,251	
Total current assets		$ 8,053
Property, plant, and equipment (PP&E):		
Land	$ 1,100	
Building and equipment	30,000	
Accumulated depreciation	(5,000)	
Total PP&E		26,100
Total assets		$34,153

Liabilities and Owner's Equity

Current liabilities:	
Accounts payable	$ 1,000
Owner's equity:	
Retained earnings	33,153
Total liabilities and owner's equity	$34,153

Texas Rex Inc.
Budgeted Balance Sheet
December 31, 2012

Assets

Current assets:		
Cash	$ 6,584[a]	
Accounts receivable	1,500[b]	
Raw materials inventory	424[c]	
Finished goods inventory	1,390[d]	
Total current assets		$ 9,898
Property, plant, and equipment (PP&E):		
Land	$ 1,100[e]	
Building and equipment	36,500[f]	
Accumulated depreciation	(7,760)[g]	
Total PP&E		29,840
Total assets		$39,738

Liabilities and Owner's Equity

Current liabilities:	
Accounts payable	$ 1,381[h]
Owner's equity:	
Retained earnings	38,357[i]
Total liabilities and owner's equity	$39,738

[a]Ending balance from Cornerstone 19-12.
[b]Ten percent of fourth-quarter credit sales (0.75 × $20,000)—see Cornerstones 19-1 and 19-12.
[c]From Cornerstone 19-3 [(106 × $3) + (530 × $0.20)].
[d]From Cornerstone 19-6.
[e]From the December 31, 2011, balance sheet.
[f]December 31, 2011, balance ($30,000) plus new equipment acquisition of $6,500 (see the 2011 ending balance sheet and Cornerstone 19-12).
[g]From the December 31, 2011, balance sheet, Cornerstone 19-5, and Cornerstone 19-8 ($5,000 + $2,160 + $600).
[h]Twenty percent of fourth-quarter purchases (0.20 × $6,904)—see Cornerstones 19-3 and 19-12.
[i]$33,153 + $5,204 (December 31, 2011, balance plus net income from Cornerstone 19-9).

research and practice have identified some key features that promote a reasonable degree of positive behavior. These features include:

- frequent feedback on performance
- monetary and nonmonetary incentives
- participative budgeting
- realistic standards
- controllability of costs
- multiple measures of performance

Frequent Feedback on Performance

Managers need to know how they are doing as the year progresses. Frequent, timely performance reports allow managers to know how successful their efforts have been, to take corrective actions, and to change plans as necessary.

Monetary and Nonmonetary Incentives

A sound budgetary system encourages goal-congruent behavior. **Incentives** are the means an organization uses to influence a manager to exert effort to achieve an organization's goal Traditional organizational theory assumes that employees are primarily motivated by monetary rewards, they resist work, and they are inefficient and wasteful. Thus, **monetary incentives** are used to control a manager's tendency to shirk and waste resources by relating budgetary performance to salary increases, bonuses, and promotions. The threat of dismissal is the ultimate economic sanction for poor performance. In reality, employees are motivated by more than economic factors. Employees are also motivated by intrinsic psychological and social factors, such as the satisfaction of a job well done, recognition, responsibility, self-esteem, and the nature of the work itself. Thus **nonmonetary incentives**, including job enrichment, increased responsibility and autonomy, recognition programs, and so on, can be used to enhance a budgetary control system.

Participative Budgeting

Rather than imposing budgets on subordinate managers, **participative budgeting** allows subordinate managers considerable say in how the budgets are established. Typically, overall objectives are communicated to the manager, who helps develop a budget that will accomplish these objectives. Participative budgeting communicates a sense of responsibility to subordinate managers and fosters creativity. Since the subordinate manager creates the budget, the budget's goals will more likely become the manager's personal goals, resulting in greater goal congruence. The increased responsibility and challenge inherent in the process provide nonmonetary incentives that lead to a higher level of performance.

Participative budgeting has three potential problems:

- setting standards that are either too high or too low
- building slack into the budget (often referred to as padding the budget)
- pseudoparticipation

Concept Q&A

Assume that a company evaluates and rewards its managers based on their ability to achieve budgeted goals. Why would the same company ask its managers to participate in setting their budgeted standards?

Answer:
Participation encourages managers to internalize the goals and make them their own, leading to improved performance.

Standard Setting Some managers may tend to set the budget either too loose or too tight. Since budgeted goals tend to become the manager's goals when participation is allowed, making this mistake in setting the budget can result in decreased performance levels. If goals are too easily achieved, a manager may lose interest, and performance may actually drop. Feeling challenged is important to aggressive and creative individuals. Similarly, setting the budget too tight ensures failure to achieve the standards and frustrates the manager. This frustration, too, can lead to poorer performance (see Exhibit 19-5). The trick is to get managers in a participative setting to set high but achievable goals.

Exhibit 19-5

The Art of Standard Setting

Standard Set Too Loose
Goals Too Easily Achieved

Standard Set Too Tight
Frustration

Budgetary Slack The second problem with participative budgeting is the opportunity for managers to build slack into the budget. **Budgetary slack** (or *padding the budget*) exists when a manager deliberately underestimates revenues or overestimates costs in an effort to make the future period appear less attractive in the budget than they think it will be in reality. Either approach increases the likelihood that the manager will achieve the budget and consequently reduces the risk that the manager faces. Top management should carefully review budgets proposed by subordinate managers and provide input, where needed, in order to decrease the effects of building slack into the budget.

ETHICAL DECISIONS The act of padding the budget is questionable when considering what is viewed as ethical professional practice. Padding the budget is a deliberate misrepresentation of costs and/or revenues. It is certainly not communicating information fairly and objectively and constitutes a violation of the credibility standard. The motive for such behavior is also not consistent with the professional responsibility to exhibit integrity. While it might be useful to estimate some costs at a little higher amount than expected to factor in uncertainty, excessive padding is misrepresentation and can lead to failure to spend resources in other areas that may need them. •

Pseudoparticipation The third problem with participation occurs when top management assumes total control of the budgeting process, seeking only superficial participation from lower-level managers. This practice is termed **pseudoparticipation**. Top management is simply obtaining formal acceptance of the budget from subordinate managers, not seeking real input. Accordingly, none of the behavioral benefits of participation will be realized.

Realistic Standards

Budgeted objectives are used to gauge performance. Accordingly, they should be based on realistic conditions and expectations. Budgets should reflect operating realities, including the following:

- *Actual Levels of Activity*: Flexible budgets are used to ensure that budgeted costs can be realistically compared with costs for actual levels of activity.
- *Seasonal Variations*: Interim budgets should reflect seasonal effects. **Toys "R" Us**, for example, would expect much higher sales in the quarter that includes Christmas than in other quarters.
- *Efficiencies*: Budgetary cuts should be based on *planned* increases in efficiency and not simply arbitrary across-the-board reductions. Across-the-board cuts without any formal evaluation may impair the ability of some units to carry out their missions.
- *General Economic Trends*: General economic conditions also need to be considered. Budgeting for a significant increase in sales when a recession is projected is not only foolish but also potentially dangerous.

Controllability of Costs

Ideally, managers are held accountable only for costs that they can control. **Controllable costs** are costs whose level a manager can influence. For example, divisional managers have no power to authorize such corporate-level costs as research and development and salaries of top managers. Therefore, they should not be held accountable for the incurrence of those costs. If noncontrollable costs are put in the budgets of subordinate managers to help them understand that these costs also need to be covered, then they should be separated from controllable costs and labeled as *noncontrollable*.

Multiple Measures of Performance

Often, organizations make the mistake of using budgets as their only measure of managerial performance. While financial measures of performance are important, overemphasis can lead to a form of dysfunctional behavior called *milking the firm* or *myopia*. **Myopic behavior** occurs when a manager takes actions that improve budgetary performance in the short run but bring long-run harm to the firm. For example, to meet budgeted cost objectives or profits, managers can delay promoting deserving employees or reducing expenditures for preventive maintenance, advertising, and new product development. Using measures that are both financial and nonfinancial and that are long term and short term can alleviate this problem. For example, Starwood Hotels incurs considerable costs every year to research consumer trends and to train its hotel staff members to help ensure sustainable growth in room revenue for its luxury St. Regis brand. Budgetary measures alone cannot prevent myopic behavior.

SUMMARY OF LEARNING OBJECTIVES

LO1.   Define budgeting and discuss its role in planning, control, and decision making.
- Budgeting is the creation of a plan of action expressed in financial terms.
- Budgeting plays a key role in planning, control, and decision making.
- Budgets serve to improve communication and coordination, a role that becomes increasingly important as organizations grow in size.
- The master budget, which is the comprehensive financial plan of an organization, is made up of the operating and financial budgets.

LO2.   Define and prepare the operating budget, identify its major components, and explain the interrelationships of its various components.
- The operating budget is the budgeted income statement and all supporting budgets.
- The sales budget consists of the anticipated quantity and price of all products to be sold. It is done first, and the results feed directly into the production budget.
- The production budget gives the expected production in units to meet forecasted sales and desired ending inventory goals. Expected production is supplemented by beginning inventory. The results of the production budget are needed for the direct materials purchases budget and the direct labor budget.
- The direct materials purchases budget gives the necessary purchases during the year for every type of raw material to meet production and desired ending inventory goals.
- The direct labor budget shows the number of direct labor hours, and the direct labor cost needed to support production. The resulting direct labor hours are needed to prepare the overhead budget.
- The overhead budget may be broken down into fixed and variable components to facilitate preparation of the budget.
- The selling and administrative expenses budget gives the forecasted costs for these functions.
- The finished goods inventory budget and the cost of goods sold budget detail production costs for the expected ending inventory and the units sold, respectively.
- The budgeted income statement outlines the net income to be realized if budgeted plans come to fruition.

LO3. **Define and prepare the financial budget, identify its major components, and explain the interrelationships of its various components.**
- The financial budget includes the cash budget, the capital expenditures budget, and the budgeted balance sheet.
- The cash budget is the beginning balance in the cash account, plus anticipated receipts, minus anticipated disbursements, plus or minus any necessary borrowing.
- The budgeted (or pro forma) balance sheet gives the anticipated ending balances of the asset, liability, and equity accounts if budgeted plans hold.

LO4. **Describe the behavioral dimension of budgeting.**
- The success of a budgetary system depends on how seriously human factors are considered.
- To discourage dysfunctional behavior, organizations should avoid overemphasizing budgets as a control mechanism.
- Budgets can be improved as performance measures by using participative budgeting and other nonmonetary incentives, providing frequent feedback on performance, using flexible budgeting, ensuring that the budgetary objectives reflect reality, and holding managers accountable for only controllable costs.

SUMMARY OF IMPORTANT EQUATIONS

1. Units to be produced = Expected unit sales + Units in desired ending inventory (EI)
   − Units in beginning inventory (BI)

2. Purchases = Direct materials needed for production
   + Direct materials in desired ending inventory
   − Direct materials in beginning inventory

CORNERSTONE 19-1 Preparing a sales budget (p. 974)	
CORNERSTONE 19-2 Preparing a production budget (p. 975)	
CORNERSTONE 19-3 Preparing a direct materials purchases budget (p. 976)	
CORNERSTONE 19-4 Preparing a direct labor budget (p. 978)	
CORNERSTONE 19-5 Preparing an overhead budget (p. 978)	
CORNERSTONE 19-6 Preparing an ending finished goods inventory budget (p. 979)	**CORNERSTONES**
CORNERSTONE 19-7 Preparing a cost of goods sold budget (p. 980)	FOR CHAPTER 19
CORNERSTONE 19-8 Preparing a selling and administrative expenses budget (p. 981)	
CORNERSTONE 19-9 Preparing a budgeted income statement (p. 982)	
CORNERSTONE 19-10 Preparing a schedule for cash collections on accounts receivable (p. 983)	
CORNERSTONE 19-11 Determining cash payments on accounts payable (p. 985)	
CORNERSTONE 19-12 Preparing a cash budget (p. 986)	

KEY TERMS

Budget committee (p. 971)
Budget director (p. 971)
Budgetary slack (p. 991)
Budgets (p. 970)

Cash budget (p. 983)
Continuous budget (p. 971)
Control (p. 971)
Controllable costs (p. 992)

REVIEW PROBLEMS

I. Select Operational Budgets

Joven Products produces coat racks. The projected sales for the first quarter of the coming year and the beginning and ending inventory data are as follows:

Unit sales	100,000
Unit price	$15
Units in beginning inventory	8,000
Units in targeted ending inventory	12,000

The coat racks are molded and then painted. Each rack requires four pounds of metal, which costs $2.50 per pound. The beginning inventory of materials is 4,000 pounds. Joven Products wants to have 6,000 pounds of metal in inventory at the end of the quarter. Each rack produced requires 30 minutes of direct labor time, which is billed at $9 per hour.

Required:

1. Prepare a sales budget for the first quarter.
2. Prepare a production budget for the first quarter.
3. Prepare a direct materials purchases budget for the first quarter.
4. Prepare a direct labor budget for the first quarter.

Solution:

1.

Joven Products
Sales Budget
For the First Quarter

Units	100,000
Unit price	×$15
Sales	$1,500,000

2.

Joven Products
Production Budget
For the First Quarter

Sales (in units)	100,000
Desired ending inventory	12,000
Total needs	112,000
Less: Beginning inventory	8,000
Units to be produced	104,000

3.

Joven Products
Direct Materials Purchases Budget
For the First Quarter

Units to be produced	104,000
Direct materials per unit (lb.)	×4
Production needs (lb.)	416,000
Desired ending inventory (lb.)	6,000
Total needs (lb.)	422,000
Less: Beginning inventory (lb.)	4,000
Materials to be purchased (lb.)	418,000
Cost per pound	×$2.50
Total purchase cost	$1,045,000

4.

Joven Products
Direct Labor Budget
For the First Quarter

Units to be produced	104,000
Labor hours per unit	×0.5
Total hours needed	52,000
Cost per hour	×$9
Total direct labor cost	$468,000

II. Cash Budgeting

Kylles Inc. expects to receive cash from sales of $45,000 in March. In addition, Kylles expects to sell property worth $3,500. Payments for materials and supplies are expected to total $10,000, direct labor payroll will be $12,500, and other expenditures are budgeted at $14,900. On March 1, the cash account balance is $1,230.

Required:

1. Prepare a cash budget for Kylles Inc. for the month of March.

2. Assume that Kylles Inc. wanted a minimum cash balance of $15,000 and that it could borrow from the bank in multiples of $1,000 at an interest rate of 12 percent per year. What would the adjusted ending balance for March be for Kylles? How much interest would Kylles owe in April, assuming that the entire amount borrowed in March would be paid back?

Solution:

1.

Kylles Inc.
Cash Budget for the Month of March

Beginning cash balance	$ 1,230
Cash sales	45,000
Sale of property	3,500
Total cash available	$49,730
Less disbursements:	
Materials and supplies	$10,000
Direct labor payroll	12,500
Other expenditures	14,900
Total disbursements	$37,400
Ending cash balance	$12,330

2.

Unadjusted ending balance	$12,330
Plus borrowing	3,000
Adjusted ending balance	$15,330

In April, interest owed would be $(1/12 \times 0.12 \times \$3,000) = \$30$.

DISCUSSION QUESTIONS

1. Define the term *budget*. How are budgets used in planning?
2. Define *control*. How are budgets used to control?
3. Explain how both small and large organizations can benefit from budgeting.
4. Discuss some reasons for budgeting.
5. What is a master budget? An operating budget? A financial budget?
6. Explain the role of a sales forecast in budgeting. What is the difference between a sales forecast and a sales budget?
7. All budgets depend on the sales budget. Is this true? Explain.
8. Why is goal congruence important?
9. Why is it important for a manager to receive frequent feedback on his or her performance?
10. Discuss the roles of monetary and nonmonetary incentives. Do you believe that nonmonetary incentives are needed? Why?
11. What is participative budgeting? Discuss some of its advantages.
12. A budget too easily achieved will lead to diminished performance. Do you agree? Explain.
13. What is the role of top management in participative budgeting?
14. Explain why a manager has an incentive to build slack into the budget.
15. Explain how a manager can milk the firm to improve budgetary performance.

MULTIPLE-CHOICE EXERCISES

19-1 A budget

a. is a long-term plan.
b. covers at least two years.
c. is only a control tool.
d. is a short-term financial plan.
e. is necessary only for large firms.

19-2 Which of the following is part of the control process?

a. Monitoring of actual activity
b. Comparison of actual with planned activity
c. Investigating
d. Taking corrective action
e. All of these

19-3 Which of the following is *not* an advantage of budgeting?

a. It forces managers to plan.
b. It provides information for decision making.
c. It guarantees an improvement in organizational efficiency.
d. It provides a standard for performance evaluation.
e. It improves communication and coordination.

19-4 The budget committee

a. reviews the budget.
b. resolves differences that arise as the budget is prepared.
c. approves the final budget.
d. is directed (typically) by the controller.
e. does all of these.

19-5 A moving, 12-month budget that is updated monthly is

a. a continuous budget.
b. waste of time and effort.
c. a master budget.
d. not used by industrial firms.
e. always used by firms that prepare a master budget.

19-6 Which of the following is *not* part of the operating budget?

a. The direct labor budget
b. The cost of goods sold budget
c. The production budget
d. The capital budget
e. The selling and administrative expenses budget

19-7 Before a direct materials purchases budget can be prepared, you should first

a. prepare a sales budget.
b. prepare a production budget.
c. decide on the desired ending inventory of materials.
d. obtain the expected price of each type of material.
e. do all of these.

19-8 The first step in preparing the sales budget is to

a. prepare a sales forecast.
b. review the production budget carefully.
c. assess the desired ending inventory of finished goods.
d. talk with past customers.
e. increase sales beyond the forecast level.

19-9 Which of the following is needed to prepare the production budget?

a. Direct materials needed for production
b. Direct labor needed for production
c. Expected unit sales
d. Units of materials in ending inventory
e. None of these

19-10 A company requires 100 pounds of plastic to meet the production needs of a small toy. It currently has 30 pounds of plastic inventory. The desired ending inventory of plastic is 10 pounds. How many pounds of plastic should be budgeted for purchasing during the coming period?

a. 80 pounds
b. 110 pounds
c. 120 pounds
d. 130 pounds
e. None of these

19-11 A company plans on selling 220 units. The selling price per unit is $24. There are 20 units in beginning inventory, and the company would like to have 50 units in ending inventory. How many units should be produced for the coming period?

a. 250
b. 200
c. 230
d. 220
e. None of these

19-12 Which of the following is needed to prepare a budgeted income statement?

a. The production budget
b. Budgeted selling and administrative expenses
c. The budgeted balance sheet
d. The capital expenditures budget
e. Last year's income statement

19-13 Select the one budget below that is *not* an operating budget.

a. Cost of goods sold budget
b. Cash budget
c. Production budget
d. Overhead budget
e. All of these are operating budgets.

19-14 The cash budget serves which of the following purposes?

a. Documents the need for liberal inventory policies
b. Reveals the amount of depreciation expense
c. Reveals the amount lost due to uncollectible accounts
d. Provides information about the ability to repay loans
e. None of the above

19-15 Assume that a company has the following accounts receivable collection pattern:

Month of sale	40%
Month following sale	60%

All sales are on credit. If credit sales for January and February are $200,000 and $100,000, respectively, the cash collections for February are

a. $140,000.
b. $300,000.
c. $120,000.
d. $160,000.
e. $80,000.

19-16 The percentage of accounts receivable that are uncollectible can be ignored for cash budgeting because

a. no cash is received from an account that defaults.
b. it is included in cash sales.
c. it appears on the budgeted income statement.
d. for most companies, it is not a material amount.
e. none of the above is correct.

19-17 An ideal budgetary system is one that

a. encourages dysfunctional behavior.
b. encourages goal-congruent behavior.
c. encourages myopic behavior.
d. encourages subversion of an organization's goals.
e. does none of these.

19-18 Some key budgetary features that tend to promote positive managerial behavior are

a. frequent feedback on performance.
b. participative budgeting.
c. realistic standards.
d. well-designed monetary and nonmonetary incentives.
e. all of these.

19-19 Which of the following is *not* an advantage of participative budgeting?

a. It fosters a sense of creativity in managers.
b. It tends to lead to a higher level of performance.
c. It fosters a sense of responsibility.
d. It encourages greater goal congruence.
e. It encourages budgetary slack.

19-20 Which of the following items is a possible example of myopic behavior?

a. Failure to promote deserving employees
b. Reducing expenditures on preventive maintenance
c. Cutting back on new product development
d. Buying cheaper, lower-quality materials so that the company does not exceed the materials purchases budget
e. All of these.

CORNERSTONE EXERCISES

OBJECTIVE ❷
CORNERSTONE 19-1

Cornerstone Exercise 19-21 Preparing a Sales Budget

Patrick Inc. sells industrial solvents in five-gallon drums. Patrick expects the following units to be sold in the first three months of the coming year:

January	41,000
February	38,000
March	50,000

The average price for a drum is $35.

Required:
Prepare a sales budget for the first three months of the coming year, showing units and sales revenue by month and in total for the quarter.

Cornerstone Exercise 19-22 Preparing a Production Budget

OBJECTIVE **2**
CORNERSTONE 19-2

Patrick Inc. makes industrial solvents. In the first four months of the coming year, Patrick expects the following unit sales:

January	41,000
February	38,000
March	50,000
April	51,000

Patrick's policy is to have 25 percent of next month's sales in ending inventory. On January 1, it is expected that there will be 6,700 drums of solvent on hand.

Required:

Prepare a production budget for the first quarter of the year. Show the number of drums that should be produced each month as well as for the quarter in total.

Cornerstone Exercise 19-23 Preparing a Direct Materials Purchases Budget

OBJECTIVE **2**
CORNERSTONE 19-3

Patrick Inc. makes industrial solvents sold in five-gallon drums. Planned production in units for the first three months of the coming year is:

January	43,800
February	41,000
March	50,250

Each drum requires 5.5 gallons of chemicals and one plastic drum. Company policy requires that ending inventories of raw materials for each month be 15 percent of the next month's production needs. That policy was met for the ending inventory of December in the prior year. The cost of one gallon of chemicals is $2.00. The cost of one drum is $1.60. (*Note:* Round all unit amounts to the nearest unit. Round all dollar amounts to the nearest dollar.)

Required:

1. Calculate the ending inventory of chemicals in gallons for December of the prior year, and for January and February. What is the beginning inventory of chemicals for January?
2. Prepare a direct materials purchases budgets for chemicals for the months of January and February.
3. Calculate the ending inventory of drums for December of the prior year, and for January and February.
4. Prepare a direct materials purchases budgets for drums for the months of January and February.

Cornerstone Exercise 19-24 Preparing a Direct Labor Budget

OBJECTIVE **2**
CORNERSTONE 19-4

Patrick Inc. makes industrial solvents. Planned production in units for the first three months of the coming year is:

January	43,800
February	41,000
March	50,250

Each drum of industrial solvent takes 0.3 direct labor hours. The average wage is $18 per hour.

Required:

Prepare a direct labor budget for the months of January, February, and March, as well as the total for the first quarter.

Cornerstone Exercise 19-25 Preparing an Overhead Budget

OBJECTIVE **2**
CORNERSTONE 19-5

Patrick Inc. makes industrial solvents. Budgeted direct labor hours for the first three months of the coming year are:

January	13,140
February	12,300
March	15,075

The variable overhead rate is $0.70 per direct labor hour. Fixed overhead is budgeted at $2,750 per month.

(Continued)

Required:

Prepare an overhead budget for the months of January, February, and March, as well as the total for the first quarter.

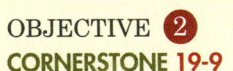

OBJECTIVE ② CORNERSTONE 19-6

Cornerstone Exercise 19-26 Preparing an Ending Finished Goods Inventory Budget

Andrews Company manufactures a line of office chairs. Each chair takes $14 of direct materials and uses 1.9 direct labor hours at $16 per direct labor hour. The variable overhead rate is $1.20 per direct labor hour and the fixed overhead rate is $1.60 per direct labor hour. Andrews expects to have 675 chairs in ending inventory. There is no beginning inventory of office chairs.

Required:

1. Calculate the unit product cost. (*Note:* Round to the nearest cent.)
2. Calculate the cost of budgeted ending inventory. (*Note:* Round to the nearest dollar.)

OBJECTIVE ② CORNERSTONE 19-7

Cornerstone Exercise 19-27 Preparing a Cost of Goods Sold Budget

Andrews Company manufactures a line of office chairs. Each chair takes $14 of direct materials and uses 1.9 direct labor hours at $16 per direct labor hour. The variable overhead rate is $1.20 per direct labor hour and the fixed overhead rate is $1.60 per direct labor hour. Andrews expects to produce 20,000 chairs next year and expects to have 675 chairs in ending inventory. There is no beginning inventory of office chairs.

Required:

Prepare a cost of goods sold budget for Andrews Company.

OBJECTIVE ② CORNERSTONE 19-8

Cornerstone Exercise 19-28 Preparing a Selling and Administrative Expenses Budget

Fazel Company makes and sells paper products. In the coming year, Fazel expects total sales of $19,730,000. There is a 3 percent commission on sales. In addition, fixed expenses of the sales and administrative offices include the following:

Salaries	$ 960,000
Utilities	365,000
Office space	230,000
Advertising	1,200,000

Required:

Prepare a selling and administrative expenses budget for Fazel Company for the coming year.

OBJECTIVE ② CORNERSTONE 19-9

Cornerstone Exercise 19-29 Preparing a Budgeted Income Statement

Oliver Company provided the following information for the coming year:

Units produced and sold	160,000
Cost of goods sold per unit	$ 6.30
Selling price	$ 10.80
Variable selling and administrative expenses per unit	$ 1.10
Fixed selling and administrative expenses	$423,000
Tax rate	35%

Required:

Prepare a budgeted income statement for Oliver Company for the coming year. (*Note:* Round all income statement amounts to the nearest dollar.)

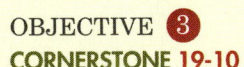

OBJECTIVE ③ CORNERSTONE 19-10

Cornerstone Exercise 19-30 Preparing a Schedule of Cash Collections on Accounts Receivable

Kailua and Company is a legal services firm. All sales of legal services are billed to the client (there are no cash sales). Kailua expects that, on average, 20 percent will be paid in the month of billing, 50 percent will be paid in the month following billing, and 25 percent will be paid in the second month following billing. For the next five months, the following sales billings are expected:

May	$ 84,000
June	100,800
July	77,000
August	86,800
September	91,000

Required:

Prepare a schedule showing the cash expected in payments on accounts receivable in August and in September.

Cornerstone Exercise 19-31 Preparing an Accounts Payable Schedule

OBJECTIVE

CORNERSTONE 19-11

Wight Inc. purchases raw materials on account for use in production. The direct materials purchases budget shows the following expected purchases on account:

April	$374,400
May	411,200
June	416,000

Wight typically pays 20 percent on account in the month of billing and 80 percent the next month.

Required:

1. How much cash is required for payments on account in May?
2. How much cash is expected for payments on account in June?

Cornerstone Exercise 19-32 Preparing a Cash Budget

OBJECTIVE 3

CORNERSTONE 19-12

La Famiglia Pizzeria provided the following information for the month of October:

a. Sales are budgeted to be $157,000. About 85 percent of sales are cash; the remainder are on account.

b. La Famiglia expects that, on average, 70 percent of credit sales will be paid in the month of sale, and 28 percent will be paid in the following month.

c. Food and supplies purchases, all on account, are expected to be $116,000. La Famiglia pays 25 percent in the month of purchase and 75 percent in the month following purchase.

d. Most of the work is done by the owners, who typically withdraw $6,000 a month from the business as their salary. (*Note:* The $6,000 is a payment in total to the two owners, not per person.) Various part-time workers cost $7,300 per month. They are paid for their work weekly, so on average 90 percent of their wages are paid in the month incurred and the remaining 10 percent in the next month.

e. Utilities average $5,950 per month. Rent on the building is $4,100 per month.

f. Insurance is paid quarterly; the next payment of $1,200 is due in October.

g. September sales were $181,500 and purchases of food and supplies in September equaled $130,000.

h. The cash balance on October 1 is $2,147.

Required:

1. Calculate the cash receipts expected in October. (*Hint:* Remember to include both cash sales and payments from credit sales.)
2. Calculate the cash needed in October to pay for food purchases.
3. Prepare a cash budget for the month of October.

EXERCISES

OBJECTIVE ①

Exercise 19-33 Planning and Control

a. Dr. Jones, a dentist, wants to increase the size and profitability of his business by building a reputation for quality and timely service.

b. To achieve this, he plans on adding a dental laboratory to his building so that crowns, bridges, and dentures can be made in-house.

c. To add the laboratory, he needs additional money, which he decides must be obtained by increasing revenues. After some careful calculation, Dr. Jones concludes that annual revenues must be increased by 10 percent.

d. Dr. Jones finds that his fees for fillings and crowns are below the average in his community and decides that the 10 percent increase can be achieved by increasing these fees.

e. He then identifies the quantity of fillings and crowns expected for the coming year, the new per-unit fee, and the total fees expected.

f. As the year unfolds (on a month-by-month basis), Dr. Jones compares the actual revenues received with the budgeted revenues. For the first three months, actual revenues were less than planned.

g. Upon investigating, he discovered that he had some reduction in the number of patients because he had also changed his available hours of operation.

h. He returned to his old schedule and found out that the number of patients was restored to the original expected levels.

i. However, to make up the shortfall, he also increased the price of some of his other services.

Required:

Match each statement with the following planning and control elements (*Note:* A letter may be matched to more than one item):

1.	Corrective action	6.	Comparison of actual with planned
2.	Budgets	7.	Monitoring of actual activity
3.	Feedback	8.	Strategic plan
4.	Investigation	9.	Short-term objectives
5.	Short-term plan	10.	Long-term objectives

Use the following information for Exercises 19-34 and 19-35:

Assume that **Stillwater Designs** produces two automotive subwoofers: S12L7 and S12L5. The S12L7 sells for $475, and the S12L5 sells for $300. Projected sales (number of speakers) for the coming five quarters are as follows:

	S12L7	S12L5
First quarter, 2012	800	1,300
Second quarter, 2012	2,200	1,400
Third quarter, 2012	5,600	5,300
Fourth quarter, 2012	4,600	3,900
First quarter, 2013	900	1,200

The vice president of sales believes that the projected sales are realistic and can be achieved by the company.

OBJECTIVE ① ②

Exercise 19-34 Sales Budget

Refer to the information regarding **Stillwater Designs** above.

Required:

1. Prepare a sales budget for each quarter of 2012 and for the year in total. Show sales by product and in total for each time period.

2. **Conceptual Connection:** How will Stillwater Designs use this sales budget?

Exercise 19-35 Production Budget

OBJECTIVE 2

Refer to the information regarding **Stillwater Designs** on the previous page. Stillwater Designs needs a production budget for each product (representing the amount that must be outsourced to manufacturers located in Asia). Beginning inventory of S12L7 for the first quarter of 2012 was 340 boxes. The company's policy is to have 20 percent of the next quarter's sales of S12L7 in ending inventory. Beginning inventory of S12L5 was 170 boxes. The company's policy is to have 30 percent of the next quarter's sales of S12L5 in ending inventory.

Required:

Prepare a production budget for each quarter for 2012 and for the year in total.

Exercise 19-36 Production Budget and Direct Materials Purchases Budgets

OBJECTIVE 2

Smee Inc. produces all-natural organic peanut butter. The peanut butter is sold in 12-ounce jars. The sales budget for the first four months of the year is as follows:

	Unit Sales	Dollar Sales ($)
January	50,000	105,000
February	55,000	115,500
March	60,000	126,000
April	58,000	121,800

Company policy requires that ending inventories for each month be 15 percent of next month's sales. At the beginning of January, the inventory of peanut butter is 36,000 jars.

Each jar of peanut butter needs two raw materials: 24 ounces of peanuts and one jar. Company policy requires that ending inventories of raw materials for each month be 20 percent of the next month's production needs. That policy was met on January 1.

Required:

1. Prepare a production budget for the first quarter of the year. Show the number of cans that should be produced each month as well as for the quarter in total.
2. Prepare separate direct materials purchases budgets for jars and for peanuts for the months of January and February.

Exercise 19-37 Production Budget

OBJECTIVE 2

Pumpro Inc. produces submersible water pumps for ponds and cisterns. The unit sales for selected months of the year are as follows:

	Unit Sales
April	200,000
May	240,000
June	220,000
July	260,000

Company policy requires that ending inventories for each month be 30 percent of next month's sales. However, at the beginning of April, due to greater sales in March than anticipated, the beginning inventory of water pumps is only 40,000.

Required:

Prepare a production budget for the second quarter of the year. Show the number of units that should be produced each month as well as for the quarter in total.

Exercise 19-38 Direct Materials Purchases Budget

OBJECTIVE 2

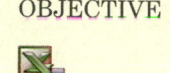

Fang Company produces decorative plastic items, including hollow plastic pumpkins often used by trick-or-treaters for Halloween. Each pumpkin requires about 5 ounces of plastic costing $0.08 per ounce. Fang molds the plastic into a pumpkin shape and applies decoration to the outside of each pumpkin. Fang has budgeted production of the pumpkins for the next four months as follows:

	Units
July	2,800
August	20,000
September	30,000
October	2,000

(Continued)

Inventory policy requires that sufficient plastic be in ending monthly inventory to satisfy 20 percent of the following month's production needs. The inventory of plastic at the beginning of July equals exactly the amount needed to satisfy the inventory policy.

Required:
Prepare a direct materials purchases budget for July, August, and September, showing purchases in units and in dollars for each month and in total.

OBJECTIVE 2

Exercise 19-39 Direct Labor Budget

Joaquin Company produces asphalt roofing materials. The production budget in bundles for Joaquin's most popular weight of asphalt shingle is shown for the following months:

	Units
March	2,000
April	12,000
May	13,000
June	17,000

Each bundle produced requires (on average) 0.30 direct labor hours. The average cost of direct labor is $20 per hour.

Required:
Prepare a direct labor budget for March, April, and May, showing the hours needed and the direct labor cost for each month and in total.

OBJECTIVE 2

Exercise 19-40 Sales Budget

Alger Inc. manufactures six models of leaf blowers and weed eaters. Alger's budgeting team is finalizing the sales budget for the coming year. Sales in units and dollars for last year follow:

Product	Number Sold	Price ($)	Revenue
LB-1	14,700	32	$ 470,400
LB-2	18,000	20	360,000
WE-6	25,200	15	378,000
WE-7	16,200	10	162,000
WE-8	6,900	18	124,200
WE-9	4,000	22	88,000
Total			$1,582,600

In looking over the previous year's sales figures, Alger's sales budgeting team recalled the following:

a. Model LB-1 is a newer version of the leaf blower with a gasoline engine. The LB-1 is mounted on wheels instead of being carried. This model is designed for the commercial market and did better than expected in its first year. As a result, the number of units of Model LB-1 to be sold was forecast at 250 percent of the previous year's units.

b. Models WE-8 and WE-9 were introduced on July 1 of last year. They are lighter versions of the traditional weed eater and are designed for smaller households or condo units. Alger estimates that demand for both models will continue at the previous year's rate.

c. A competitor has announced plans to introduce an improved version of model WE-6, Alger's traditional weed eater. Alger believes that the model WE-6 price must be cut 30 percent to maintain unit sales at the previous year's level.

d. It was assumed that unit sales of all other models would increase by 5 percent, prices remaining constant.

Required:
Prepare a sales budget by product and in total for Alger Inc. for the coming year.

OBJECTIVE 2

Exercise 19-41 Production Budget and Direct Materials Purchases Budget

Jani Subramanian, owner of Jani's Flowers and Gifts, produces gift baskets for various special occasions. Each gift basket includes fruit or assorted small gifts (e.g., a coffee mug, deck of cards, novelty cocoa mixes, scented soap) in a basket that is wrapped in colorful cellophane. Jani has estimated the following unit sales of the standard gift basket for the rest of the year and for January of next year.

September	250
October	200
November	230
December	380
January	100

Jani likes to have 5 percent of the next month's sales needs on hand at the end of each month. This requirement was met on August 31.

Two materials are needed for each fruit basket:

Fruit	1 pound
Small gifts	6 items

The materials inventory policy is to have 5 percent of the next month's fruit needs on hand and 30 percent of the next month's production needs of small gifts. (The relatively low inventory amount for fruit is designed to prevent spoilage.) Materials inventory on September 1 met this company policy.

Required:
1. Prepare a production budget for September, October, November, and December for gift baskets. (*Note*: Round all answers to the nearest whole unit.)
2. Prepare a direct materials purchases budget for the two types of materials used in the production of gift baskets for the months of September, October, and November. (*Note*: Round answers to the nearest whole unit.)
3. **Conceptual Connection:** Why do you think there is such a big difference in budgeted units from November to December? Why did Jani budget fewer units in January than in December?

Exercise 19-42 Schedule of Cash Collections on Accounts Receivable and Cash Budget   OBJECTIVE ③

Lopez Inc. found that about 35 percent of its sales during the month were for cash. Lopez has the following accounts receivable payment experience:

Percent paid in the month of sale	25
Percent paid in the month after the sale	68
Percent paid in the second month after the sale	5

Lopez's anticipated sales for the next few months are as follows:

April	$200,000
May	240,000
June	230,000
July	240,000
August	250,000

Required:
1. Calculate credit sales for May, June, July, and August.
2. Prepare a schedule of cash receipts for July and August.

Exercise 19-43 Schedule of Cash Collections on Accounts Receivable and Cash Budget   OBJECTIVE ③

Fahrad Inc. sells all of its product on account. Fahrad has the following accounts receivable payment experience:

Percent paid in the month of sale	10
Percent paid in the month after the sale	64
Percent paid in the second month after the sale	22

To encourage payment in the month of sale, Fahrad gives a 2 percent cash discount. Fahrad's anticipated sales for the next few months are as follows:

April	$220,000
May	242,000
June	253,000
July	231,000
August	275,000

(Continued)

Required:
1. Prepare a schedule of cash receipts for July.
2. Prepare a schedule of cash receipts for August.

OBJECTIVE **3**

Exercise 19-44 Cash Payments Schedule

Draper Company provided the following information relating to cash payments:

a. Draper purchased direct materials on account in the following amounts:

June	$76,000
July	82,000
August	69,000

b. Draper pays 15 percent of accounts payable in the month of purchase and the remaining 85 percent in the following month.

c. In July, direct labor cost was $34,500. August direct labor cost was $36,700. The company finds that typically 90 percent of direct labor cost is paid in cash during the month, with the remainder paid in the following month.

d. August overhead amounted to $83,200, including $5,900 of depreciation.

e. Draper had taken out a loan of $15,000 on May 1. Interest, due with payment of principal, accrued at the rate of 9 percent per year. The loan and all interest were repaid on August 31.

Required:

Prepare a schedule of cash payments for Draper Company for the month of August.

OBJECTIVE **3**

Exercise 19-45 Cash Budget

The owner of a small mining supply company has requested a cash budget for June. After examining the records of the company, you find the following:

a. Cash balance on June 1 is $1,230.

b. Actual sales for April and May are as follows:

	April	May
Cash sales	$10,000	$18,000
Credit sales	28,900	35,000
Total sales	$38,900	$53,000

c. Credit sales are collected over a three-month period: 40 percent in the month of sale, 35 percent in the second month, and 20 percent in the third month. The sales collected in the third month are subject to a 2 percent late fee, which is paid by those customers in addition to what they owe. The remaining sales are uncollectible.

d. Inventory purchases average 65 percent of a month's total sales. Of those purchases, 20 percent are paid for in the month of purchase. The remaining 80 percent are paid for in the following month.

e. Salaries and wages total $12,500 per month, including a $4,500 salary paid to the owner.

f. Rent is $4,340 per month.

g. Taxes to be paid in June are $6,780.

The owner also tells you that he expects cash sales of $19,500 and credit sales of $52,000 for June. No minimum cash balance is required. The owner of the company doesn't have access to short-term loans.

Required:

1. Prepare a cash budget for June. Include supporting schedules for cash collections and cash payments.

2. **Conceptual Connection:** Did the business show a negative cash balance for June? Suppose that the owner has no hope of establishing a line of credit for the business, what recommendations would you give the owner for dealing with a negative cash balance?

PROBLEMS

Problem 19-46 Cash Budget

OBJECTIVE ③

Morrissey Law Firm has found from past experience that 20 percent of its services are for cash. The remaining 80 percent are on credit. An aging schedule for accounts receivable reveals the following pattern:

a. Ten percent of fees on credit are paid in the month that service is rendered.
b. Seventy percent of fees on credit are paid in the month following legal service.
c. Seventeen percent of fees on credit are paid in the second month following the legal service.
d. Three percent of fees on credit are never collected.

Fees (on credit) that have not been paid until the second month following performance of the legal service are considered overdue and are subject to a 3 percent late charge. Morrissey has developed the following forecast of fees:

May	$230,000
June	250,000
July	240,000
August	240,000
September	290,000

Required:

Prepare a schedule of cash receipts for August and September.

Problem 19-47 Operating Budget, Comprehensive Analysis

OBJECTIVE ① ② ③ ④

Allison Manufacturing produces a subassembly used in the production of jet aircraft engines. The assembly is sold to engine manufacturers and aircraft maintenance facilities. Projected sales in units for the coming five months follow:

January	40,000
February	50,000
March	60,000
April	60,000
May	62,000

The following data pertain to production policies and manufacturing specifications followed by Allison Manufacturing:

a. Finished goods inventory on January 1 is 32,000 units, each costing $166.06. The desired *Prod. Budget* ending inventory for each month is 80 percent of the next month's sales.
b. The data on materials used are as follows:

Direct Material	Per-Unit Usage	Unit Cost ($)
Metal	10 lbs.	8
Components	6	5

Inventory policy dictates that sufficient materials be on hand at the end of the month to produce 50 percent of the next month's production needs. This is exactly the amount of material on hand on December 31 of the prior year.

c. The direct labor used per unit of output is three hours. The average direct labor cost per hour is $14.25.
d. Overhead each month is estimated using a flexible budget formula. (*Note:* Activity is measured in direct labor hours.)

	Fixed-Cost Component ($)	Variable-Cost Component ($)
Supplies	—	1.00
Power	—	0.50
Maintenance	30,000	0.40
Supervision	16,000	—
Depreciation	200,000	—
Taxes	12,000	—
Other	80,000	0.50

(Continued)

sell and adm budget exp.

Sales budget 1

Cash Budget

e. Monthly selling and administrative expenses are also estimated using a flexible budgeting formula. (*Note:* Activity is measured in units sold.)

	Fixed Costs ($)	Variable Costs ($)
Salaries	50,000	—
Commissions	—	2.00
Depreciation	40,000	—
Shipping	—	1.00
Other	20,000	0.60

f. The unit selling price of the subassembly is $205.
g. All sales and purchases are for cash. The cash balance on January 1 equals $400,000. The firm requires a minimum ending balance of $50,000. If the firm develops a cash shortage by the end of the month, sufficient cash is borrowed to cover the shortage. Any cash borrowed is repaid at the end of the quarter, as is the interest due (cash borrowed at the end of the quarter is repaid at the end of the following quarter). The interest rate is 12 percent per annum. No money is owed at the beginning of January.

Required:

1. Prepare a monthly operating budget for the first quarter with the following schedules. (*Note:* Assume that there is no change in work-in-process inventories.)

a. Sales budget
b. Production budget
c. Direct materials purchases budget
d. Direct labor budget
e. Overhead budget

f. Selling and administrative expenses budget
g. Ending finished goods inventory budget
h. Cost of goods sold budget
i. Budgeted income statement
j. Cash budget

2. **Conceptual Connection:** Form a group with two or three other students. Locate a manufacturing plant in your community that has headquarters elsewhere. Interview the controller for the plant regarding the master budgeting process. Ask when the process starts each year, what schedules and budgets are prepared at the plant level, how the controller forecasts the amounts, and how those schedules and budgets fit in with the overall corporate budget. Is the budgetary process participative? Also, find out how budgets are used for performance analysis. Write a summary of the interview.

OBJECTIVE ❸

ILLUSTRATING
RELATIONSHIPS

Problem 19-48 Understanding Relationships, Cash Budget, Pro Forma Balance Sheet

Ryan Richards, controller for Grange Retailers, has assembled the following data to assist in the preparation of a cash budget for the third quarter of 2012:

a. Sales:

May (actual)	$100,000
June (actual)	120,000
July (estimated)	90,000
August (estimated)	100,000
September (estimated)	135,000
October (estimated)	110,000

b. Each month, 30 percent of sales are for cash and 70 percent are on credit. The collection pattern for credit sales is 20 percent in the month of sale, 50 percent in the following month, and 30 percent in the second month following the sale.
c. Each month, the ending inventory exactly equals 50 percent of the cost of next month's sales. The markup on goods is 25 percent of cost.
d. Inventory purchases are paid for in the month following the purchase.
e. Recurring monthly expenses are as follows:

Salaries and wages	$10,000
Depreciation on plant and equipment	4,000
Utilities	1,000
Other	1,700

f. Property taxes of $15,000 are due and payable on July 15, 2012.
g. Advertising fees of $6,000 must be paid on August 20, 2012.
h. A lease on a new storage facility is scheduled to begin on September 2, 2012. Monthly payments are $5,000.
i. The company has a policy to maintain a minimum cash balance of $10,000. If necessary, it will borrow to meet its short-term needs. All borrowing is done at the beginning of the month. All payments on principal and interest are made at the end of a month. The annual interest rate is 9 percent. The company must borrow in multiples of $1,000.
j. A partially completed balance sheet as of June 30, 2012, follows. (*Note:* Accounts payable is for inventory purchases only.)

Cash	$?		
Accounts receivable	?		
Inventory	?		
Plant and equipment, net	425,000		
Accounts payable		$	?
Common stock			210,000
Retained earnings			268,750
Total	$?	$	?

Required:

1. Complete the balance sheet given in Item j.
2. Prepare a cash budget for each month in the third quarter and for the quarter in total (the third quarter begins on July 1). Provide a supporting schedule of cash collections.
3. Prepare a pro forma balance sheet as of September 30, 2012.
4. **Conceptual Connection:** Form a group with two or three other students. Discuss why a bank might require a cash budget for businesses that are seeking short-term loans. Determine what other financial reports might be useful for a loan decision. Also, discuss how the reliability of cash budgets and other financial information can be determined.

Problem 19-49 Participative Budgeting, Not-for-Profit Setting

OBJECTIVE

Dwight D. Eisenhower was the 34th president of the United States and the Supreme Commander of the Allied Forces during World War II. Much of his army career was spent in planning. He once said that "planning is everything; the plan is nothing."

Required:

Conceptual Connection: What do you think he meant by this? Consider his comment with respect to the master budget. Do you agree or disagree? Be sure to include the impact of the master budget on planning and control.

Problem 19-50 Cash Budget

OBJECTIVE

The controller of Feinberg Company is gathering data to prepare the cash budget for July. He plans to develop the budget from the following information:

a. Of all sales, 40 percent are cash sales.
b. Of credit sales, 45 percent are collected within the month of sale. Half of the credit sales collected within the month receive a 2 percent cash discount (for accounts paid within 10 days). Thirty percent of credit sales are collected in the following month; remaining credit sales are collected the month thereafter. There are virtually no bad debts.
c. Sales for the second two quarters of the year follow. (*Note:* The first three months are actual sales, and the last three months are estimated sales.)

	Sales
April	$ 450,000
May	580,000
June	900,000
July	1,140,000
August	1,200,000
September	1,134,000

d. The company sells all that it produces each month. The cost of raw materials equals 26 percent of each sales dollar. The company requires a monthly ending inventory of raw materials

(Continued)

equal to the coming month's production requirements. Of raw materials purchases, 50 percent are paid for in the month of purchase. The remaining 50 percent is paid for in the following month.

e. Wages total $105,000 each month and are paid in the month incurred.

f. Budgeted monthly operating expenses total $376,000, of which $45,000 is depreciation and $6,000 is expiration of prepaid insurance (the annual premium of $72,000 is paid on January 1).

g. Dividends of $130,000, declared on June 30, will be paid on July 15.

h. Old equipment will be sold for $25,200 on July 4.

i. On July 13, new equipment will be purchased for $173,000.

j. The company maintains a minimum cash balance of $20,000.

k. The cash balance on July 1 is $27,000.

Required:

Prepare a cash budget for July. Give a supporting schedule that details the cash collections from sales.

OBJECTIVE ❶ ❷ ❸

Problem 19-51 Understanding Relationships, Master Budget, Comprehensive Review

Optima Company is a high-technology organization that produces a mass-storage system. The design of Optima's system is unique and represents a breakthrough in the industry. The units Optima produces combine positive features of both compact and hard disks. The company is completing its fifth year of operations and is preparing to build its master budget for the coming year (2012). The budget will detail each quarter's activity and the activity for the year in total. The master budget will be based on the following information:

a. Fourth-quarter sales for 2011 are 55,000 units.

b. Unit sales by quarter (for 2012) are projected as follows:

First quarter	65,000
Second quarter	70,000
Third quarter	75,000
Fourth quarter	90,000

The selling price is $400 per unit. All sales are credit sales. Optima collects 85 percent of all sales within the quarter in which they are realized; the other 15 percent is collected in the following quarter. There are no bad debts.

c. There is no beginning inventory of finished goods. Optima is planning the following ending finished goods inventories for each quarter:

First quarter	13,000 units
Second quarter	15,000 units
Third quarter	20,000 units
Fourth quarter	10,000 units

d. Each mass-storage unit uses five hours of direct labor and three units of direct materials. Laborers are paid $10 per hour, and one unit of direct materials costs $80.

e. There are 65,700 units of direct materials in beginning inventory as of January 1, 2012. At the end of each quarter, Optima plans to have 30 percent of the direct materials needed for next quarter's unit sales. Optima will end the year with the same level of direct materials found in this year's beginning inventory.

f. Optima buys direct materials on account. Half of the purchases are paid for in the quarter of acquisition, and the remaining half are paid for in the following quarter. Wages and salaries are paid on the 15th and 30th of each month.

g. Fixed overhead totals $1 million each quarter. Of this total, $350,000 represents depreciation. All other fixed expenses are paid for in cash in the quarter incurred. The fixed overhead rate is computed by dividing the year's total fixed overhead by the year's budgeted production in units.

h. Variable overhead is budgeted at $6 per direct labor hour. All variable overhead expenses are paid for in the quarter incurred.

i. Fixed selling and administrative expenses total $250,000 per quarter, including $50,000 depreciation.

j. Variable selling and administrative expenses are budgeted at $10 per unit sold. All selling and administrative expenses are paid for in the quarter incurred.

k.   The balance sheet as of December 31, 2011, is as follows:

Assets

Cash	$ 250,000
Direct materials inventory	5,256,000
Accounts receivable	3,300,000
Plant and equipment, net	33,500,000
Total assets	$42,306,000

Liabilities and Stockholders' Equity

Accounts payable	$ 7,248,000*
Capital stock	27,000,000
Retained earnings	8,058,000
Total liabilities and stockholders' equity	$42,306,000

*For purchase of direct materials only.

l.   Optima will pay quarterly dividends of $300,000. At the end of the fourth quarter, $2 million of equipment will be purchased.

Required:

Prepare a master budget for Optima Company for each quarter of 2012 and for the year in total. The following component budgets must be included:

1.   Sales budget
2.   Production budget
3.   Direct materials purchases budget
4.   Direct labor budget
5.   Overhead budget
6.   Selling and administrative expenses budget
7.   Ending finished goods inventory budget
8.   Cost of goods sold budget (*Note:* Assume that there is no change in work-in-process inventories.)
9.   Cash budget
10. Pro forma income statement (using absorption costing) (*Note:* Ignore income taxes.)
11. Pro forma balance sheet (*Note:* Ignore income taxes.)

Problem 19-52 Direct Materials and Direct Labor Budgets

OBJECTIVE 2

Willison Company produces stuffed toy animals; one of these is Betty Rabbit. Each rabbit takes 0.2 yards of fabric and six ounces of polyfiberfill. Fabric costs $3.50 per yard, and polyfiberfill is $0.05 per ounce. Willison has budgeted production of stuffed rabbits for the next four months as follows:

	Units
October	20,000
November	40,000
December	25,000
January	30,000

Inventory policy requires that sufficient fabric be in ending monthly inventory to satisfy 15 percent of the following month's production needs and sufficient polyfiberfill be in inventory to satisfy 30 percent of the following month's production needs. Inventory of fabric and polyfiberfill at the beginning of October equals exactly the amount needed to satisfy the inventory policy.

Each rabbit produced requires (on average) 0.10 direct labor per hour. The average cost of direct labor is $15.50 per hour.

Required:

1.   Prepare a direct materials purchases budget of fabric for the last quarter of the year, showing purchases in units and in dollars for each month and for the quarter in total.
2.   Prepare a direct materials purchases budget of polyfiberfill for the last quarter of the year, showing purchases in units and in dollars for each month and for the quarter in total.
3.   Prepare a direct labor budget for the last quarter of the year, showing the hours needed and the direct labor cost for each month and for the quarter in total.

OBJECTIVE ❸

Problem 19-53 Cash Budgeting

Jordana Krull owns The Eatery in Miami, Florida. The Eatery is an affordable restaurant located near tourist attractions. Jordana accepts cash and checks. Checks are deposited immediately. The bank charges $0.50 per check; the amount per check averages $65. Bad checks that Jordana cannot collect make up 2 percent of check revenue.

During a typical month, The Eatery has sales of $75,000. About 75 percent are cash sales. Estimated sales for the next three months are as follows:

July	$60,000
August	75,000
September	80,000

Jordana thinks that it may be time to refuse to accept checks and to start accepting credit cards. She is negotiating with a credit card processing service that will allow her to accept all major credit cards. She would start the new policy on May 1. Jordana estimates that with the drop in sales from the no-checks policy and the increase in sales from the acceptance of credit cards, the net increase in sales will be 20 percent. The credit card processing service will charge no setup fee, however the following fees and conditions apply:

- Monthly gateway and statement fee totaling $19, paid on the first day of the month.
- Discount fee of 2 percent of the total sale. This is not paid separately, instead, the amount that Jordana receives from each credit sale is reduced by 2 percent. For example, on a credit card sale of $150, the processing company would take $3 and remit a net amount of $147 to Jordana's account.
- Transaction fee of $0.25 per transaction paid at the time of the transaction.

There will be a two-day delay between the date of the transaction and the date on which the net amount will be deposited into Jordana's account. On average, 94 percent of a month's net credit card sales will be deposited into her account that month. The remaining 6 percent will be deposited the next month.

If Jordana adds credit cards, she believes that cash sales will average just 5 percent of total sales, and that the average credit card transaction will be $50.

Required:

1. Prepare a schedule of cash receipts for August and September under the current policy of accepting checks.
2. Assuming that Jordana decides to accept credit cards,
   a. Calculate revised total sales, cash sales, and credit card sales by month for August and September.
   b. Calculate the total estimated credit card transactions for August and September.

3. Prepare a schedule of cash receipts for August and September that incorporates the changes in policy.

CASES

Case 19-54 Budgeting in the Government Sector, Internet Research

OBJECTIVE

Similar to companies, the U.S. government must prepare a budget each year. However, unlike private, for-profit companies, the budget and its details are available to the public. The entire budgetary process is established by law. The government makes available a considerable amount of information concerning the federal budget. Most of this information can be found on the Internet. Using Internet resources (e.g., consider accessing the Office of Management and Budget at http://www.whitehouse.gov/omb), answer the following questions:

Required:

1. When is the federal budget prepared?
2. Who is responsible for preparing the federal budget?
3. How is the final federal budget determined? Explain in detail how the government creates its budget.
4. What percentage of the gross domestic product (GDP) is represented by the federal budget?
5. What are the revenue sources for the federal budget? Indicate the percentage contribution of each of the major sources.
6. How does U.S. spending as a percentage of GDP compare with spending of other countries?
7. How are deficits financed?

Case 19-55 Cash Budget

OBJECTIVE

Dr. Roger Jones is a successful dentist but is experiencing recurring financial difficulties. For example, Jones owns his office building, which he leased to the professional corporation that housed his dental practice (he owns all shares in the corporation). After the corporation's failure to pay payroll taxes for the past six months, however, the Internal Revenue Service is threatening to impound the business and sell its assets. Also, the corporation has had difficulty paying its suppliers, owing one of them over $200,000 plus interest. In the past, Jones had borrowed money on the equity in either his personal residence or his office building, but he has grown weary of these recurring problems and has hired a local consultant for advice.

According to the consultant, the financial difficulties facing Jones have been caused by the absence of proper planning and control. Budgetary control is sorely needed. The following financial information is available for a typical month:

Revenues

	Average Fee ($)	Quantity
Fillings	50	90
Crowns	300	19
Root canals	170	8
Bridges	500	7
Extractions	45	30
Cleaning	25	108
X-rays	15	150

Costs

Salaries:		
Two dental assistants	$1,900	
Receptionist/bookkeeper	1,500	
Hygienist	1,800	
Public relations (Mrs. Jones)	1,000	
Personal salary	6,500	
Total salaries		$12,700
Benefits		1,344
Building lease		1,500
Dental supplies		1,200
Janitorial		300
Utilities		400

(Continued)

Costs	
Phone	150
Office supplies	100
Lab fees	5,000
Loan payments	570
Interest payments	500
Miscellaneous	500
Depreciation	700
Total costs	$24,964

Benefits include Jones's share of social security and a health insurance premium for all employees. Although all revenues billed in a month are not collected, the cash flowing into the business is approximately equal to the month's billings because of collections from prior months. The office is open Monday through Thursday from 9:00 A.M. to 4:00 P.M. and on Friday from 9:00 A.M. to 12:30 P.M. A total of 32 hours are worked each week. Additional hours could be worked, but Jones is reluctant to do so because of other personal endeavors that he enjoys.

Jones has noted that the two dental assistants and receptionist are not fully utilized. He estimates that they are busy about 65 to 70 percent of the time. Jones's wife spends about five hours each week on a monthly newsletter that is sent to all patients. She also maintains a birthday list and sends cards to patients on their birthdays.

Jones recently attended an informational seminar designed to teach dentists how to increase their revenues. An idea from that seminar persuaded Jones to invest in promotion and public relations (the newsletter and the birthday list).

Required:
1. Prepare a monthly cash budget for Dr. Jones. Does Jones have a significant cash flow problem? How would you use the budget to show Jones why he is having financial difficulties?
2. Using the cash budget prepared in Requirement 1 and the information given in the case, recommend actions to solve Dr. Jones's financial problems. Prepare a cash budget that reflects these recommendations and demonstrates to Jones that the problems can be corrected. Do you think that Jones will accept your recommendations? Do any of the behavioral principles discussed in the chapter have a role in this type of setting? Explain.

OBJECTIVE

Case 19-56 Budgetary Performance, Rewards, Ethical Behavior

Linda Ellis, division manager, is evaluated and rewarded on the basis of budgetary performance. Linda, her assistants, and the plant managers are all eligible to receive a bonus if actual divisional profits are between budgeted profits and 120 percent of budgeted profits. The bonuses are based on a fixed percentage of actual profits. Profits above 120 percent of budgeted profits earn a bonus at the 120 percent level (in other words, there is an upper limit on possible bonus payments). If the actual profits are less than budgeted profits, no bonuses are awarded. Consider the following actions taken by Linda:

a. Linda tends to overestimate expenses and underestimate revenues. This approach facilitates the ability of the division to attain budgeted profits. Linda believes that the action is justified because it increases the likelihood of receiving bonuses and helps to keep the morale of the managers high.

b. Suppose that toward the end of the fiscal year, Linda saw that the division would not achieve budgeted profits. Accordingly, she instructed the sales department to defer the closing of a number of sales agreements to the following fiscal year. She also decided to write off some inventory that was nearly worthless. Deferring revenues to next year and writing off the inventory in a no-bonus year increased the chances of a bonus for next year.

c. Assume that toward the end of the year, Linda saw that actual profits would likely exceed the 120 percent limit and that she took actions similar to those described in Item b.

Required:
1. Comment on the ethics of Linda's behavior. Are her actions right or wrong? What role does the company play in encouraging her actions?
2. Suppose that you are the marketing manager for the division, and you receive instructions to defer the closing of sales until the next fiscal year. What would you do?

3. Suppose that you are a plant manager, and you know that your budget has been padded by the division manager. Further, suppose that the padding is common knowledge among the plant managers, who support it because it increases the ability to achieve the budget and receive a bonus. What would you do?

4. Suppose that you are the division controller, and you receive instructions from the division manager to accelerate the recognition of some expenses that legitimately belong to a future period. What would you do?

20 Standard Costing: A Managerial Control Tool

Doug Norman Crystals/Alamy

After studying Chapter 20, you should be able to:

1. Explain how unit standards are set and why standard cost systems are adopted.
2. Explain the purpose of a standard cost sheet.
3. Describe the basic concepts underlying variance analysis, and explain when variances should be investigated.
4. Compute the materials variances, and explain how they are used for control.
5. Compute the labor variances, and explain how they are used for control.
6. *(Appendix 20A)* Prepare journal entries for materials and labor variances.

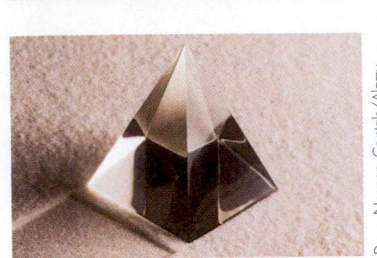

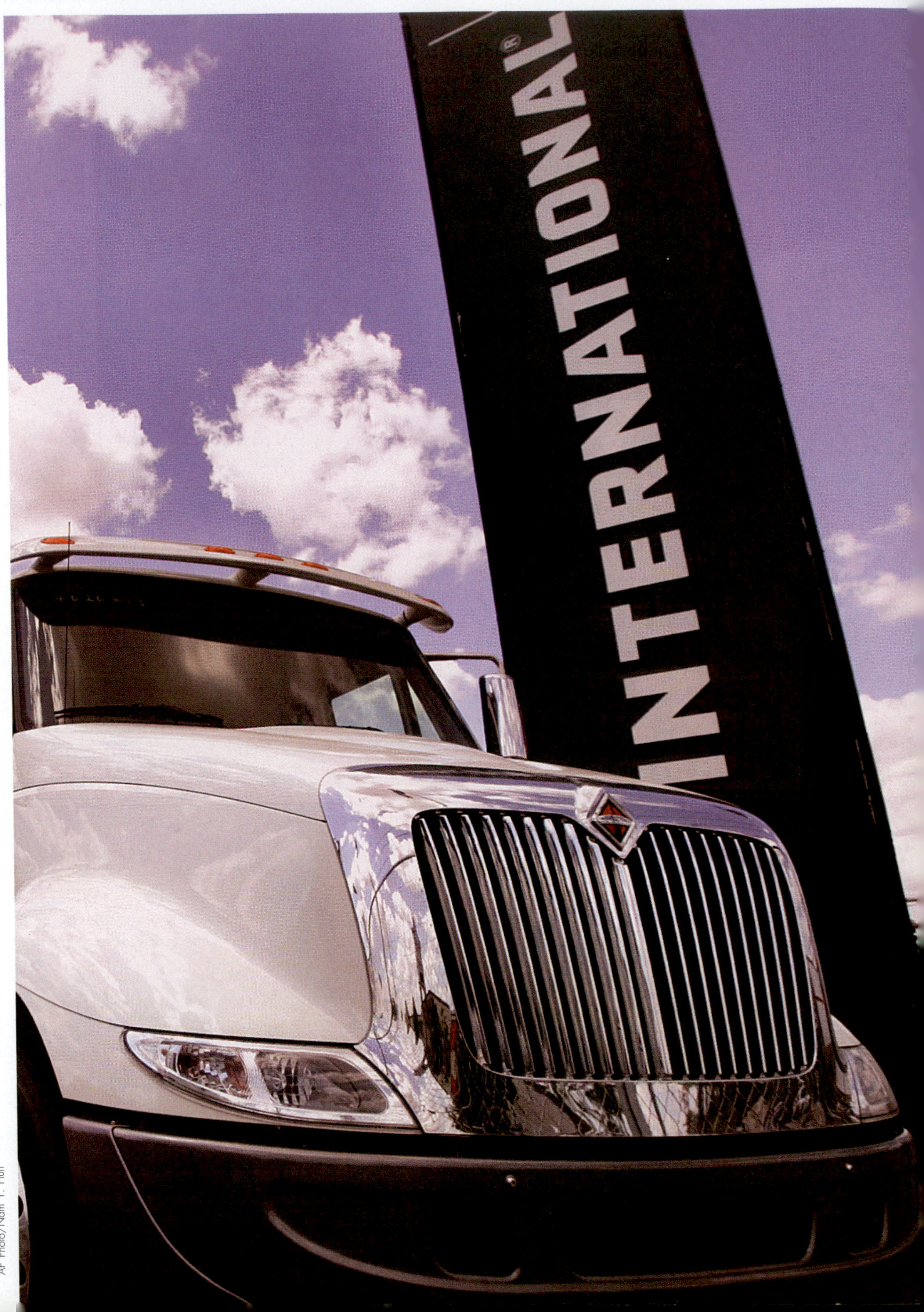

AP Photo/Nam Y. Huh

EXPERIENCE MANAGERIAL DECISIONS

with Navistar, Inc.

Understanding an income statement is a relatively easy task. However, understanding the causes underlying net income represents a far more challenging task, especially for Fortune 300 companies like **Navistar, Inc.**, whose annual net income typically falls in the neighborhood of several hundred million dollars. Navistar, Inc. uses variance analysis to learn which parts of the company are contributing to net income as expected and which parts are not contributing to net income as expected and, as such, will require careful attention to improve in the future.

Bruce Works, 2010/Shutterstock.com

For example, Navistar, Inc. recently reported that its monthly production cost was $48 million to manufacture 1,129 actual units—considerably higher than its budgeted production cost of only $41 million to produce 883 expected units. If you were the manager in charge of Navistar, Inc.'s production, what would you do after receiving the news that actual costs were $7 million greater (or approximately 17 percent more than the budgeted total production cost) than expected?

Before Navistar, Inc.'s management took any rash actions, it performed an in-depth variance analysis on all of its key production factors to try and understand what had caused the unfavorable static budget variance between its actual costs at month-end and its budgeted costs at the beginning of the month. These key production factors included direct and indirect materials, direct and indirect labor, benefits, utilities, depreciation, and information technology expense.

Variance analysis revealed that the $7 million unfavorable static budget variance was comprised of numerous smaller variances, some favorable and others unfavorable, involving many of Navistar, Inc.'s key production factors. Most importantly, Navistar, Inc.'s managers were happy to learn that when adjusting the total budgeted costs for the higher production volume, total production costs should have increased by over $11 million, much more than the actual cost increase of $7 million. In fact, effective management of labor and materials purchasing—both of which had large favorable flexible budget variances—actually helped Navistar, Inc. to save $4 million. Without variance analysis, Navistar, Inc. would have a much harder time understanding the causes of its net income and taking the appropriate action when components of income are different than expected.

OBJECTIVE ❶

Explain how unit standards are set and why standard cost systems are adopted.

UNIT STANDARDS

Most operating managers recognize the need to control costs. Cost control often means the difference between success and failure or between above-average profits and lesser profits. For example, Navistar, Inc. had a specific plan to produce 883 trucks for a given month at a cost of $41 million. In reality, they produced 1,228 units at a cost of $48 million. Clearly, in total they spent more than planned but also produced more than they planned. The key question is whether the $48 million associated with the 1,228 trucks was consistent with the original plan or not. Were production costs in control or not? Did the manager do well or not?

In order to answer these questions, information about the budgeted and actual costs must be compared. The total cost per unit is computed as follows:

Cost per unit = Total cost / Total units

Therefore, cost per unit for both scenarios can be calculated as follows:

	Budgeted	**Actual**
Cost per unit =	$46,433 cost per unit	$39,088 per unit
Total cost/Total units	($41 million/883 units)	($48 million/1,228 units)

Comparing the actual cost per vehicle with the standard cost produces a favorable variance of $7,345 per truck ($46,433 − $39,088), about a 16 percent savings. This outcome reveals that the Navistar, Inc. managers were cost conscious and able to increase overall production efficiency.

In Chapter 19, we learned that budgets set standards that are used to control and evaluate managerial performance. However, budgets are aggregate measures of performance; they identify the revenues and costs in total that an organization should experience if plans are executed as expected. By comparing the actual costs and actual revenues with the corresponding budgeted amounts at the same level of activity, a measure of managerial efficiency emerges.

Although this process provides significant information for control, developing standards for unit amounts, as well as for total amounts, can further enhance control.

To determine the unit standard cost for a particular input, two decisions must be made:

- *The quantity decision*: The amount of input that *should be used* per unit of output
- *The pricing decision*: The amount that *should be paid* for the quantity of the input to be used

The quantity decision produces **quantity standards**, and the pricing decision produces **price standards**. The unit standard cost can be computed by multiplying these two standards:

Standard cost per unit = Quantity standard × Price standard

For example, a soft-drink bottling company may decide that five ounces of fructose should be used for every 16-ounce bottle of cola (the quantity standard), and the price of the fructose should be $0.05 per ounce (the price standard). The standard cost of the fructose per bottle of cola would be:

$$\$0.25 = 5 \times \$0.05$$

The standard cost per unit of fructose can be used to predict what the total cost of fructose should be as the activity level varies; thus, it becomes a flexible budget formula. If 10,000 bottles of cola are produced, then the total expected cost of fructose is $2,500 ($0.25 × 10,000); if 15,000 bottles are produced, then the total expected cost of fructose is $3,750 ($0.25 × 15,000).

How Standards Are Developed

Three potential sources of quantitative standards are as follows:

- *Historical experience*: Historical experience can provide an initial guideline for setting standards, but should be used with caution because they can perpetuate existing inefficiencies.

- *Engineering studies*: Engineering studies can identify efficient approaches and can provide rigorous guidelines, but engineered standards often are too rigorous.
- *Input from operating personnel*: Since operating personnel are accountable for meeting standards, they should have significant input in setting standards.

Price standards are the joint responsibility of operations, purchasing, personnel, and accounting. Operating personnel determine the quality of the inputs required; personnel and purchasing have the responsibility of acquiring the labor and materials quality requested at the lowest price. Market forces limit the range of choices for price standards. In setting price standards, purchasing must consider discounts, freight, and quality. Personnel, on the other hand, must consider payroll taxes, fringe benefits, and qualifications. Accounting is responsible for recording the price standards as well as for preparing reports that compare actual performance with the standard.

Types of Standards

Standards are generally classified as either ideal or currently attainable.

- *Ideal standards* demand maximum efficiency and can be achieved only if everything operates perfectly. No machine breakdowns, slack, or lack of skill (even momentarily) are allowed.
- *Currently attainable standards* can be achieved under efficient operating conditions. Allowance is made for normal breakdowns, interruptions, less than perfect skill, and so on. These standards are demanding but achievable.

Exhibit 20-1 provides a visual and conceptual portrayal of the two standards.

Of the two types, currently attainable standards offer the most behavioral benefits. If standards are too tight and never achievable, workers become frustrated and performance levels decline. However, challenging but achievable standards tend to extract higher performance levels—particularly when the individuals subject to the standards have participated in their creation.

Concept Q&A

What is the difference between an ideal standard and a currently attainable standard?

Answer:
An ideal standard is a standard of perfection—absolute efficiency is required. A currently attainable standard is rigorous but achievable and reflects a reasonable level of efficiency.

Why Standard Cost Systems Are Adopted

Two reasons for adopting a standard cost system are frequently mentioned: to improve planning and control and to facilitate product costing.

Planning and Control   Standard costing systems enhance planning and control and improve performance measurement. A flexible budgeting system is a key feature of standard costing systems. Comparing actual costs with budgeted costs identifies

Exhibit 20-1

Types of Standards

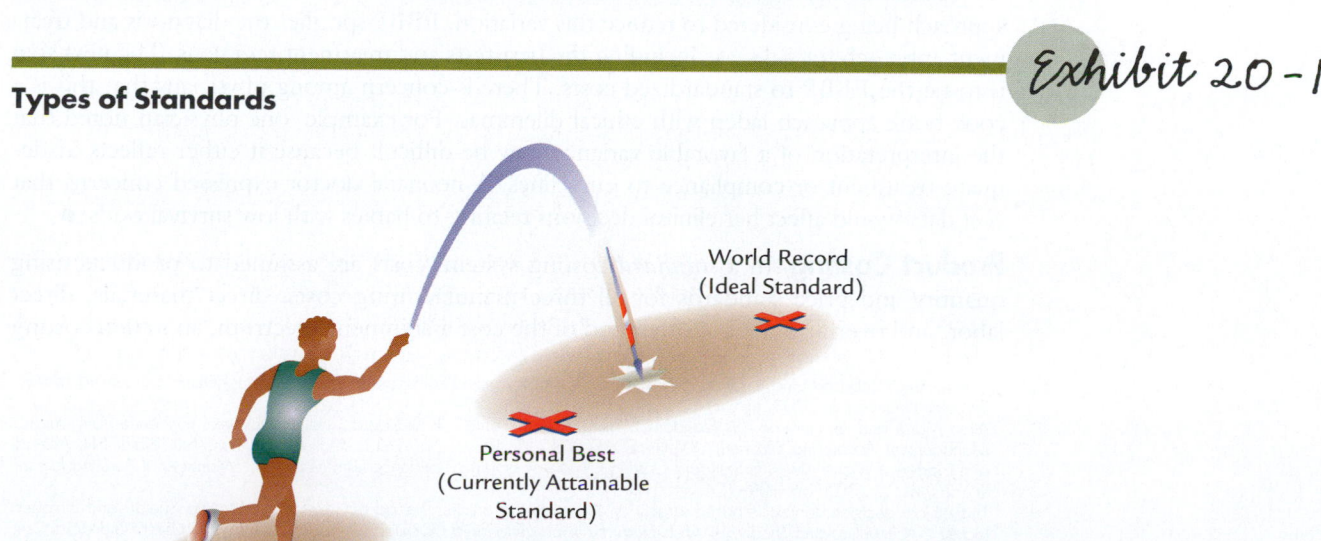

World Record
(Ideal Standard)

Personal Best
(Currently Attainable
Standard)

variances, the difference between the actual and planned costs for the actual level of activity. Overall variances can be further broken down into a price variance or a usage or efficiency variance if unit price or quantity standards have been developed. This additional information is very helpful for managers. For example, if the variance is unfavorable, this decomposition can inform a manager whether it is attributable to discrepancies between planned prices and actual prices, to discrepancies between planned usage and actual usage, or to both. Since managers have more control over the usage of inputs than over their prices, efficiency variances provide specific signals regarding the need for corrective action and where that action should be focused. Thus, in principle, the use of efficiency variances enhances operational control. Additionally, by breaking out the price variance, over which managers potentially have less control, the system provides an improved measure of managerial efficiency.

The benefits of operational control, however, may not extend to the manufacturing environments that are emphasizing continuous improvement and just-in-time (JIT) purchasing and manufacturing. The use of a standard cost system for operational control in these settings can produce dysfunctional behavior. For example, materials price variance reporting may encourage the purchasing department to buy in large quantities in order to take advantage of discounts. Yet this practice might lead to holding significant inventories, something not desired by JIT firms. Therefore, the detailed computation of variances—at least at the operational level—is discouraged for JIT firms. Nonetheless, standards in this newer manufacturing environment are still useful for planning, such as in the creation of bids. Also, variances may still be computed and presented in reports to higher-level managers so that the financial dimension can be monitored. In addition, other incentives, such as a fee charged to managers for holding excessive inventories, can be created to discourage managers from allowing inventories to grow beyond the level desired by JIT systems.

Finally, many U.S. firms operate with conventional product costing systems (about 76 percent of those surveyed).[1] Surveys in countries such as Dubai and Malaysia also indicate that standard costing systems specifically continue to be used by well over 70 percent of the firms responding.[2] Thus, there is evidence that standard costing continues to be an important management accounting tool.

ETHICAL DECISIONS   Standard costing and variance analysis for controlling cost and evaluating performance can have strong ethical implications.[3] For example, standard costing methods have been proposed for medicine as a means for controlling costs and enhancing performance. Research has revealed wide variations in how physicians diagnose and treat patients with similar conditions. Some of these clinical variations are attributable to unwarranted tests and treatments stemming from the perceived need to practice defensive medicine against malpractice law suits. Others may be motivated by the desire to increase revenues.

Standardization of medicine, called Evidence Based Best Practices (EBBP), is one approach being considered to reduce this variation. EBBP specifies the diagnosis and treatment approach for a disease including the best tests and treatment regimens. The next step is to tie the EBBP to standardized costs. There is concern among physicians that this is a cook-book approach laden with ethical dilemmas. For example, one physician noted that the interpretation of a favorable variance may be difficult because it either reflects inadequate treatment or compliance to guidelines. A neonatal doctor expressed concerns that cost data would affect her clinical decisions relating to babies with low survival odds. ●

Product Costing   In a *standard* costing system, costs are assigned to products using quantity and price standards for all three manufacturing costs: direct materials, direct labor, and overhead. At the other end of the cost assignment spectrum, an *actual* costing

---

[1] Ashish Garg, Debashis Ghosh, James Hudick, and Chuen Nowacki, "Roles and Practices in Management Accounting Today," *Strategic Finance*, July 2003, pp. 30–35.

[2] Atiea Marie and Ananth Rao, "Is Standard Costing Still Relevant?" "Is Standard Costing Obsolete? Evidence from Dubai," *Management Accounting Quarterly*, Winter 2010, Vol. 11, Iss. 2, pp. 1–11; Maliah Sulaiman, Nik Nazli Nik Ahmad, and Norhayati Mohd Alwi, "Is Standard Costing Obsolete? Empirical Evidence from Malaysia," *Managerial Auditing Journal*, Vol. 20, Iss. 2, 2005, pp. 109–124.

[3] This ethical decision context is based largely on the following article: Thebadouix, Greg M., Marsha Sheidt, and Elizabeth Luckey, "Accounting and Medicine: An Exploratory Investigation into Physician's Attitudes, Toward the Use of Standard Cost-Accounting Methods in Medicine," *Journal of Business Ethics*, (2007): 75:137–149.

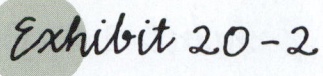

Cost Assignment Approaches

	Standard Costing System	Normal Costing System	Actual Costing System
Direct materials	Standard	Actual	Actual
Direct labor	Standard	Actual	Actual
Overhead	Standard	Budgeted	Actual

system assigns the actual costs of all three manufacturing inputs to products. In the middle of this spectrum is a *normal* costing system, which predetermines overhead costs for the purpose of product costing but assigns direct materials and direct labor to products by using actual costs. Thus, a normal costing system assigns actual direct costs to products but allocates budgeted indirect costs to products using a budgeted rate and actual activity. Exhibit 20-2 summarizes these three cost assignment approaches.

Standard product costing has several advantages over normal costing and actual costing. One, of course, is the greater capacity for control. Standard costing systems also provide readily available unit cost information that can be used for pricing decisions at any time throughout the period because actual costs (either direct or indirect) do not need to be known. This ability is particularly helpful for companies that do a significant amount of bidding and that are paid on a cost-plus basis. Other simplifications also are possible. For example, if a process-costing system uses standard costing to assign product costs, there is no need to compute a unit cost for each equivalent unit cost category. A standard unit cost would exist for each category. Additionally, there is no need to distinguish between the first-in, first-out (FIFO) and weighted average methods of accounting for beginning inventory costs. Usually, a standard process-costing system will follow the equivalent unit calculation of the FIFO approach. That is, current equivalent units of work are calculated. By calculating current equivalent work, current actual production costs can be compared with standard costs for control purposes.

Why would a firm adopt a standard costing system?

Answer:

Standard costing enhances planning and control and improves performance evaluation. It also simplifies product costing. Having a readily available product cost facilitates pricing decisions.

STANDARD PRODUCT COSTS

In manufacturing firms, standard costs are developed for direct materials, direct labor, and overhead. Using these costs, the **standard cost per unit** is computed. The **standard cost sheet** provides the production data needed to calculate the standard unit cost. To illustrate, a standard cost sheet will be developed for a 16-ounce bag of corn chips produced by Crunchy Chips Inc. The production of corn chips begins by steaming and soaking corn kernels overnight in a lime solution. This process softens the kernels so that they can be shaped into a sheet of dough. The dough is then cut into small triangular chips. Next, the chips are toasted in an oven and are dropped into a deep fryer. After cooking, the chips pass under a salting device and are inspected for quality. Substandard chips are sorted and discarded; the chips that pass inspection are bagged by a packaging machine. The bagged chips are manually packed into boxes for shipping.

Four materials are used to process corn chips: yellow corn, cooking oil, salt, and lime. The package in which the chips are placed is also classified as a direct material. Crunchy Chips has two types of direct laborers: machine operators and inspectors (or sorters). Variable overhead is made up of three costs: gas, electricity, and water. Both variable and fixed overhead are applied by using direct labor hours. The standard cost sheet is given in Exhibit 20-3 (p. 1022).

OBJECTIVE

Explain the purpose of a standard cost sheet.

Exhibit 20-3

Standard Cost Sheet for Corn Chips

Description	Standard Price	Standard Usage	Standard Cost*	Subtotal
Direct materials:				
Yellow corn	$ 0.01	18 oz.	$0.18	
Cooking oil	0.03	2 oz.	0.06	
Salt	0.01	1 oz.	0.01	
Lime	0.50	0.04 oz.	0.02	
Bags	0.05	1 bag	0.05	
Total direct materials				$0.32
Direct labor:				
Inspection	8.00	0.01 hr.	$0.08	
Machine operators	10.00	0.01 hr.	0.10	
Total direct labor				0.18
Overhead:				
Variable overhead	4.00	0.02 hr.	$0.08	
Fixed overhead	15.00	0.02 hr.	0.30	
Total overhead				0.38
Total standard unit cost				$0.88

*Calculated by multiplying price times usage.

Exhibit 20-3 shows the company should use 18 ounces of corn to produce a 16-ounce package of chips. There are two reasons for this two-ounce difference:

- *Waste*: Some chips are discarded during the inspection process. The company plans on a normal amount of waste.
- *Packaging*: The company wants to have more than 16 ounces in each package to increase customer satisfaction with its product and to avoid any problems with fair packaging laws.

Exhibit 20-3 also reveals that the standard usage for variable and fixed overhead is tied to the direct labor standards. For variable overhead, the rate is $4.00 per direct labor hour. Since one package of corn chips should use 0.02 hours of direct labor per unit, the variable overhead cost assigned to a package of corn chips is $0.08 ($4.00 × 0.02). For fixed overhead, the rate is $15.00 per direct labor hour, making the fixed overhead cost per package of corn chips $0.30 ($15.00 × 0.02). About one-third of the cost of production is fixed, indicating a capital-intensive production effort. Indeed, much of the operation is mechanized.

The standard cost sheet also shows the quantity of each input that should be used to produce one unit of output. The unit quantity standards can be used to compute the total amount of inputs allowed for the actual output. This computation is an essential component in computing efficiency variances. A manager should be able to compute the **standard quantity of materials allowed (*SQ*)** and the **standard hours allowed (*SH*)** for the actual output, where

$$SQ = \text{Unit quantity standard} \times \text{Actual output}$$

and

$$SH = \text{Unit labor standard} \times \text{Actual output}$$

This computation must be done for every class of direct material and every class of direct labor. **CORNERSTONE 20-1** shows how to compute these quantities by using one type of material and one class of labor.

CORNERSTONE 20-1

Computing Standard Quantities Allowed (*SQ* and *SH*)

Information:

Assume that 100,000 packages of corn chips are produced during the first week of March. Recall from Exhibit 20-3 that the unit quantity standard is 18 ounces of yellow corn per package and the unit quantity standard for machine operators is 0.01 hour per package produced.

Required:

How much yellow corn and how many operator hours should be used for the actual output of 100,000 packages?

Solution:

Corn allowed:

$$SQ = \text{Unit quantity standard} \times \text{Actual output}$$
$$= 18 \times 100,000$$
$$= 1,800,000 \text{ ounces}$$

Operator hours allowed:

$$SH = \text{Unit labor standard} \times \text{Actual output}$$
$$= 0.01 \times 100,000$$
$$= 1,000 \text{ direct labor hours}$$

Here's the Real Kicker

About 15 percent of the defective **Kicker** speakers returned to **Stillwater Designs** can be rebuilt. The other 85 percent are sold as metal scrap. Speakers are candidates for rebuilding if the cost of direct materials and labor is less than the sum of the speaker's purchase cost, shipping cost, and duty (the production of Kicker speakers is outsourced to mostly Asian producers). This is true, for example, of the square S12L7 speakers.

To rebuild a square S12L7, the returned speaker is torn down to its basic structures, chemical and glue residues are removed, and the speaker is demagnetized in order to get rid of metal shavings and pieces. After this preparatory work, recone kits are used to replace the stripped-out components. The rebuilt woofer is then placed in a cabinet and sealed. The completed unit undergoes two tests—one to ensure that the power is hooked up correctly and a second that checks for air leaks.

Every two years, standard costs for materials and labor are set. Time studies are used to determine the time required for rebuilding, and, thus, the labor content. The cost of the recone kit is the major material cost. These standard costs are used for two purposes: (1) to determine if rebuilding is feasible for a given model and (2) to assign costs to the rebuilt product on an ongoing basis if rebuilding is the decision.

VARIANCE ANALYSIS: GENERAL DESCRIPTION

OBJECTIVE 3
Describe the basic concepts underlying variance analysis, and explain when variances should be investigated.

Actual input cost can be calculated as:

$$\text{Actual cost} = AP \times AQ$$

where

AP = Actual price per unit

AQ = Actual quantity of input used

It is also possible to calculate the costs that should have been incurred for the actual level of activity. This figure is obtained by multiplying the amount of input allowed (either materials or labor) for the actual output by the standard price of the input, as follows:

$$\text{Planned cost} = SP \times SQ$$

where

SP = Standard price per unit

SQ = Standard quantity of input allowed for the actual output

The **total budget variance** is the difference between the actual cost of the input and its planned cost:

$$\text{Total variance} = \text{Actual cost} - \text{Planned cost}$$
$$= (AP \times AQ) - (SP \times SQ)$$

As will be explained in Chapter 21, this budget is formally called the static budget variance. However, for now, the total budget variance will simply be called the *total variance*.

Because responsibility for deviations from planned prices tends to be located in the purchasing or personnel department and responsibility for deviations from planned usage of inputs tends to be located in the production department, it is important to separate the total variance into price and usage (quantity) variances.

Price and Usage Variances

Exhibit 20-4 provides a general model for calculating price and quantity variances for materials and labor.[4] For labor, the price variance is usually called a *rate variance*. **Price (rate) variance** is the difference between the actual and standard unit price of an input multiplied by the number of inputs used:

$$\text{Price variance} = (AP - SP) \times AQ$$

 **Exhibit 20-4**

Variance Analysis: General Description

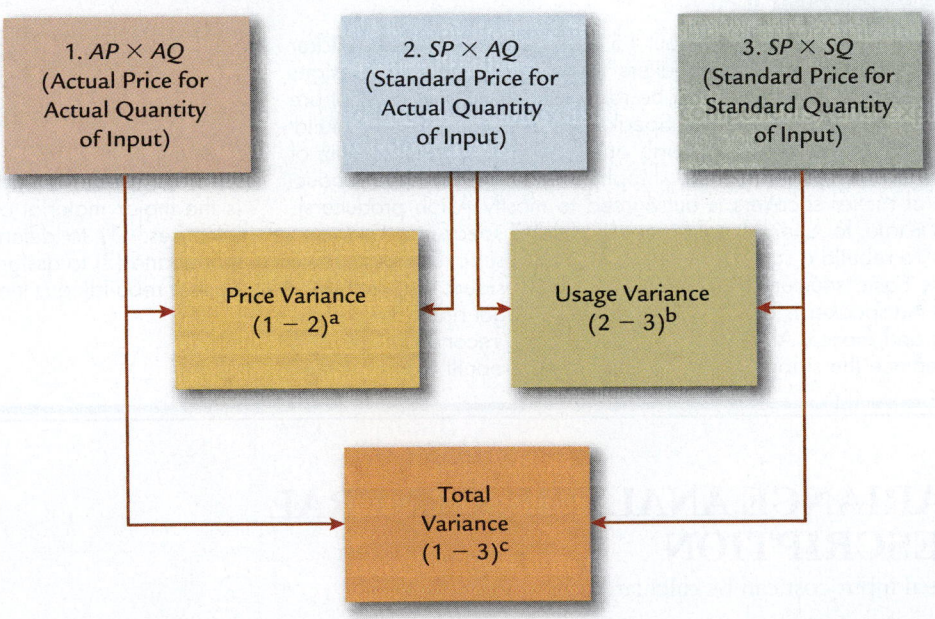

| 1. $AP \times AQ$ (Actual Price for Actual Quantity of Input) | 2. $SP \times AQ$ (Standard Price for Actual Quantity of Input) | 3. $SP \times SQ$ (Standard Price for Standard Quantity of Input) |

Price Variance $(1 - 2)^{a}$

Usage Variance $(2 - 3)^{b}$

Total Variance $(1 - 3)^{c}$

[a]Price variance = $(AP \times AQ) - (SP \times AQ) = (AP - SP) \times AQ$
[b]Usage variance = $(SP \times AQ) (SP \times SQ) (AQ - SQ) \times SP$
[c]Total variance = $(AP \times AQ) (SP \times SQ)$

---

[4] Overhead variance analysis is discussed in Chapter 21.

The usage (quantity) variance is called an *efficiency variance*. **Usage (efficiency) variance** is the difference between the actual and standard quantity of inputs multiplied by the standard unit price of the input:

$$\text{Usage variance} = (AQ - SQ) \times SP$$

Unfavorable (U) variances occur whenever actual prices or actual usage of inputs are greater than standard prices or standard usage. When the opposite occurs, **favorable (F) variances** are obtained. Favorable and unfavorable variances are not equivalent to good and bad variances. The terms merely indicate the relationship of the actual prices (or quantities) to the standard prices (or quantities). Whether or not the variances are good or bad depends on why they occurred. Determining the cause of a variance requires managers to do some investigation.

Concept Q&A

Suppose that the actual labor rate paid is $12 per hour, while the standard labor rate is $11.50. Will the labor rate variance be favorable or unfavorable?

Answer:
It will be unfavorable because the rate actually paid is more than the rate allowed.

The Decision to Investigate

Rarely will actual performance exactly meet the established standards, and management does not expect it to do so. Instead, it is important to understand when further investigate is necessary. Investigating the cause of variances and taking corrective action, like all activities, have a cost associated with them. As a general principle, an investigation should be undertaken only if the expected benefits are greater than the expected costs. Assessing the costs and benefits of a variance investigation is not an easy task, however. A manager must consider whether a variance will recur. If so, the process may be permanently out of control, meaning that periodic savings may be achieved if corrective action is taken. But how is it possible to know if the variance is going to recur unless an investigation is conducted? And how is it possible to know the cost of corrective action unless the cause of the variance is known?

Because it is difficult to assess the costs and benefits of variance analysis on a case-by-case basis, many firms adopt the general guideline of investigating variances only if they fall outside of an acceptable range. They are not investigated unless they are large enough to be of concern. They must be large enough to be caused by something other than random factors and large enough (on average) to justify the costs of investigating and taking corrective action.

How do managers determine whether variances are significant? How is the acceptable range established? The acceptable range is the standard, plus or minus an allowable deviation. The top and bottom measures of the allowable range are called the **control limits**. The upper control limit is the standard plus the allowable deviation, and the lower control limit is the standard minus the allowable deviation. Current practice sets the control limits subjectively: Based on past experience, intuition, and judgment, management determines the allowable deviation from standard.[5] The actual deviations from standard often are plotted over time against the upper and lower limits to allow managers to see the significance of the variance. **CORNERSTONE 20-2** shows how control limits are used to trigger an investigation.

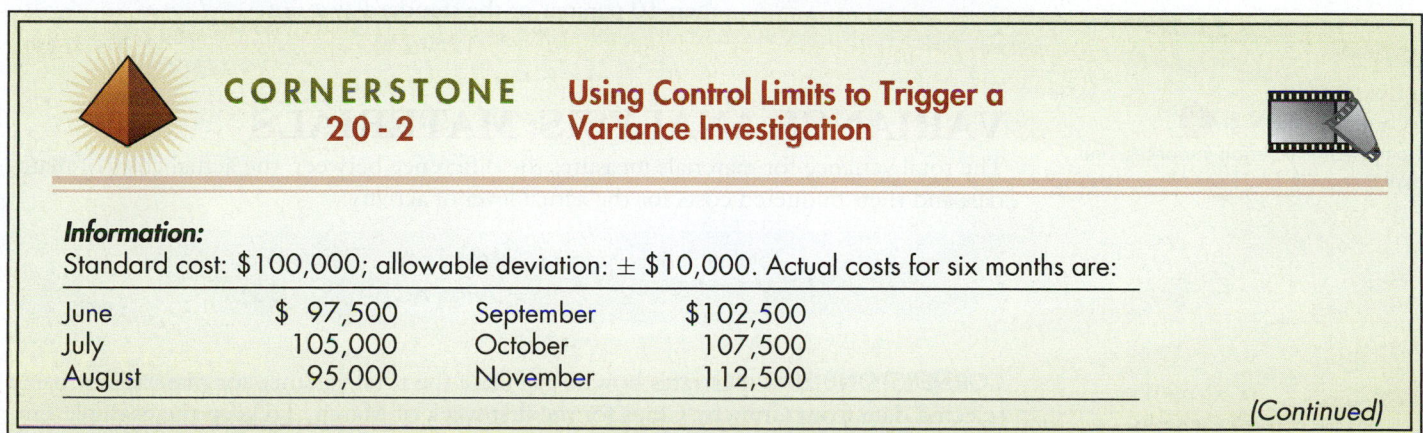

CORNERSTONE 20-2 — Using Control Limits to Trigger a Variance Investigation

Information:
Standard cost: $100,000; allowable deviation: ± $10,000. Actual costs for six months are:

June	$ 97,500	September	$102,500
July	105,000	October	107,500
August	95,000	November	112,500

(Continued)

---

[5] Gaumnitz and Kollaritsch, "Manufacturing Variances: Current Practices and Trends," reports that about 45 to 47 percent of the firms use dollar or percentage control limits. Most of the remaining firms use judgment rather than any formal identification of limits.

Required:
Plot the actual costs over time against the upper and lower control limits. Determine when a variance should be investigated.

CORNERSTONE 20-2 *(continued)*

Solution:

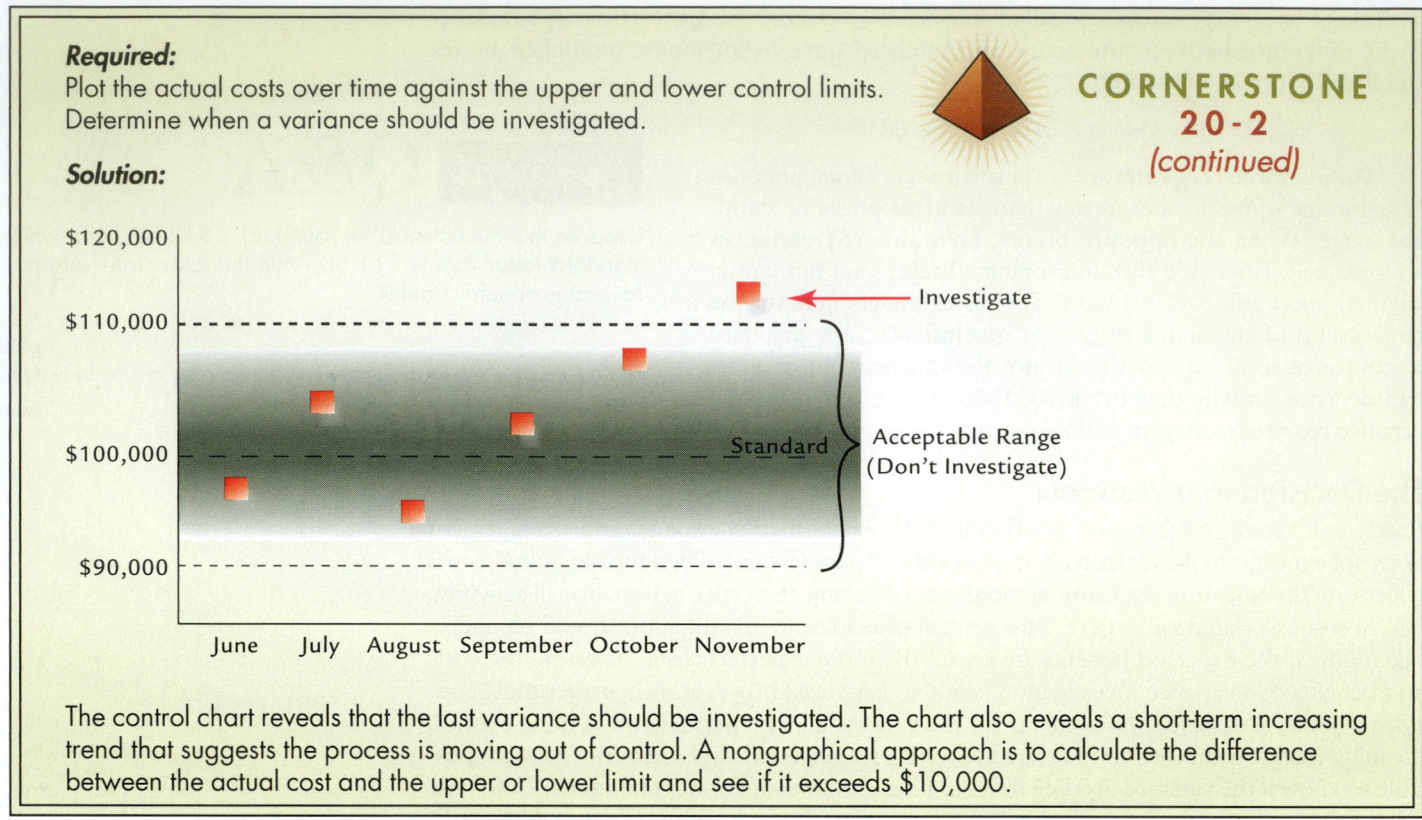

The control chart reveals that the last variance should be investigated. The chart also reveals a short-term increasing trend that suggests the process is moving out of control. A nongraphical approach is to calculate the difference between the actual cost and the upper or lower limit and see if it exceeds $10,000.

The control chart in Cornerstone 20-2 graphically illustrates the concept of control limits. The assumed standard is $100,000, and the allowable deviation is plus or minus $10,000. The upper limit is $110,000, and the lower limit is $90,000. Investigation occurs whenever an observation falls outside of these limits (as would be the case for the sixth observation). Trends can also be important.

The control limits often are expressed both as a percentage of the standard and as an absolute dollar amount. For example, the allowable deviation may be expressed as the lesser of 10 percent of the standard amount, or $10,000. In other words, management will not accept a deviation of more than $10,000 even if that deviation is less than 10 percent of the standard. Alternatively, even if the dollar amount is less than $10,000, an investigation is required if the deviation is more than 10 percent of the standard amount.

Concept **Q&A**

Refer to the control chart in Cornerstone 20-2. What action would you take for an actual value of $89,750?

Answer:
This would produce a value below the lower control limit, so there should be an investigation to find the cause or causes of the deviation. Corrective action could then be taken.

OBJECTIVE ❹
Compute the materials variances, and explain how they are used for control.

VARIANCE ANALYSIS: MATERIALS

The total variance for materials measures the difference between the actual costs of materials and their budgeted costs for the actual level of activity:

$$\text{Total materials variance} = \text{Actual cost} - \text{Planned cost}$$
$$= (AP \times AQ) - (SP \times SQ)$$

CORNERSTONE 20-3 illustrates how to calculate the total variance for materials by using selected data from Crunchy Chips for the first week of March. To keep the example simple, only one material (corn) is illustrated.

CORNERSTONE 20-3 — Calculating the Total Variance for Materials

Information:
Refer to the unit standards from Exhibit 20-3 (p. 1022). The actual results for the first week in March are:

Actual production	48,500 bags of corn chips
Actual cost of corn	780,000 ounces at $0.015 = $11,700
Actual cost of inspection labor	360 hours at $8.35 = $3,006

Required:
Calculate the total variance for corn for the first week in March.

Solution:

	Actual Costs $AP \times AQ$	Budgeted Costs* $SP \times SQ$	Total Variance $(AP \times AQ) - (SP \times SQ)$
Corn	$11,700	$8,730	$2,970 U

*The standard quantities for materials and labor are computed as unit quantity standards from Exhibit 20-3:
Corn: $SQ = 18 \times 48,500 = 873,000$ ounces
Multiplying these standard quantities by the unit standard prices given in Exhibit 20-3 produces the budgeted amounts appearing in this column:
Corn: $0.01 \times 873,000 = $8,730

Direct Materials Variances

To help control the cost of materials, price and usage variances are calculated. However, the sum of the price and usage variances will add up to the total materials variance calculated in Cornerstone 20-3 *only if the materials purchased equal the materials used*. The materials price variance is computed by using the actual quantity of materials purchased, and the materials usage variance is computed by using the actual quantity of materials used, calculated as:

$$MPV = (AP - SP) \times AQ$$
$$MUV = (AQ - SQ) \times SP$$

Since it is better to have information on variances earlier rather than later, the materials price variance uses the actual quantity of materials purchased rather than the actual quantity of materials used. Old information often is useless information. Materials may sit in inventory for weeks or months before they are needed in production. By the time the materials price variance is computed, signaling a problem, it may be too late to take corrective action. Or, even if corrective action is still possible, the delay may cost the company thousands of dollars. For example, suppose a new purchasing agent is unaware of the availability of a quantity discount on a raw material. If the materials price variance that ignores the discount is computed when a new purchase is made, the resulting unfavorable signal would lead to quick corrective action. (In this case, the action would be to use the discount for future purchases.) If the materials price variance is not computed until the material is issued to production, it may be several weeks or even months before the problem is discovered. The more timely the information, the more likely that proper managerial action can be taken.

Materials price and usage variances normally should be calculated using variance formulas. However, the three-pronged (columnar) approach is used when the materials purchased equal the materials used. **CORNERSTONE 20-4** shows how to calculate the

When is the total materials variance the sum of the price variance and the usage variance?

Answer:
When the materials purchased equal the materials used.

materials price and usage variances using either a columnar approach or a formula approach for the Crunchy Chips example (for corn only).

 **CORNERSTONE 20-4**   **Calculating Materials Variances: Formula and Columnar Approaches**

Information:
Refer to the unit standards from Exhibit 20-3 (p. 1022). The actual results for the first week in March are:

Actual production	48,500 bags of corn chips
Actual cost of corn	780,000 ounces @ $0.015

Required:
Calculate the materials price and usage variances by using the three-pronged (columnar) and formula approaches.

Solution:
1. Formulas (recommended approach for materials variances because materials purchased may differ from materials used):

$$MPV = (AP - SP) \times AQ$$
$$= (\$0.015 - \$0.01) \times 780,000$$
$$= \$3,900 \ U$$
$$MUV = (AQ - SQ) \times SP$$
$$= (780,000 - 873,000) \times \$0.01$$
$$= \$930 \ F$$

2. Columnar (this approach is possible only if the materials purchased equal materials used):

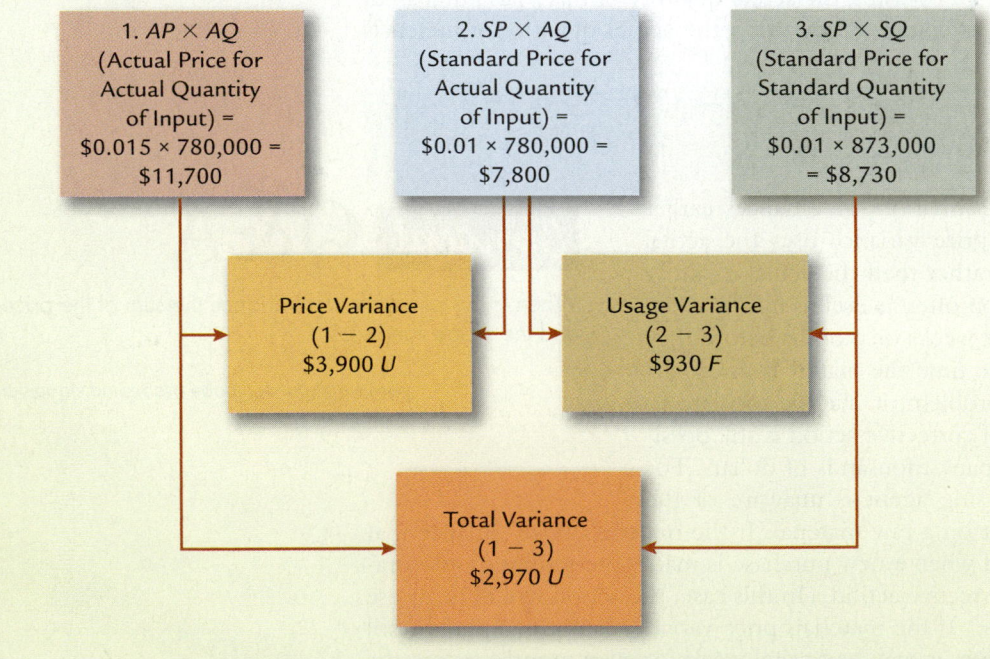

The **materials price variance (MPV)** measures the difference between what should have been paid for raw materials and what was actually paid and is calculated as:

$$MPV = (AP \times AQ) - (SP \times AQ)$$

or, factoring, we have:

$$MPV = (AP - SP) \times AQ$$

where

AP = Actual price per unit

SP = Standard price per unit

AQ = Actual quantity of material purchased

It should be noted that the *MPV* formula uses the *actual* quantity purchased, rather than the standard amount that should have been purchased, because purchasing managers typically influence the amount of materials actually purchased. Likewise, the *MPV* uses material *purchased*, rather than used, because purchasing managers typically do not control the amount of material actually used in production. Thus, the *MPV* contains items over which purchasing managers likely have control, which is helpful given that their bonuses often are affected by the *MPV*.

The **materials usage variance (*MUV*)** measures the difference between the direct materials actually used and the direct materials that should have been used for the actual output. The formula for computing this variance is:

$$MUV = (SP \times AQ) - (SP \times SQ)$$

or, factoring:

$$MUV = (AQ - SQ) \times SP$$

where

AQ = Actual quantity of materials used

SQ = Standard quantity of materials allowed for the actual output

SP = Standard price per unit

The *MUV* formula uses the *standard* price that should have been paid, rather than the actual price that was paid, because production managers typically do not influence the actual price paid for materials. Using the standard price in the *MUV*—a variance for which production managers typically are held accountable—prevents them from unfairly being affected by the actual price.

Using Materials Variance Information

Calculating materials variances is only the first step. Using the variance information to exercise control is fundamental to a standard cost system. Responsibility must be assigned, variance significance must be assessed, and the variances must be accounted for and disposed of at the end of the year.

Responsibility for the Materials Price Variance

The responsibility for controlling the materials price variance usually belongs to the purchasing agent. Admittedly, the price of materials is largely beyond the agent's control; however, the price variance can be influenced by such factors as quality, quantity discounts, distance of the source from the plant, and so on. These factors often are under the control of the agent.

Using the price variance to evaluate the performance of purchasing has some limitations. Emphasis on meeting or beating the standard can produce some undesirable outcomes. For example, if the purchasing agent feels pressured to produce favorable variances, materials of lower quality than desired may be purchased or too much inventory may be acquired to take advantage of quantity discounts.

Analysis of the Materials Price Variance

The first step in variance analysis is deciding whether or not the variance is significant. If it is judged insignificant, no further steps are needed. The materials price variance is $3,900 unfavorable, which is about 45 percent of standard cost ($3,900/$8,730). Most managers would judge this variance to be significant. The next step is to find out why it occurred.

For Crunchy Chips, the investigation revealed that a higher-quality corn was purchased because of a shortage of the usual grade in the market. Once the reason is known, corrective action can be taken if necessary—and if possible. In this case, no corrective action is needed. The firm has no control over the supply shortage; it will simply have to wait until market conditions improve.

Responsibility for the Materials Usage Variance The production manager is generally responsible for materials usage. Minimizing scrap, waste, and rework are all ways in which the manager can ensure that the standard is met. However, at times, the cause of the variance is attributable to others outside of the production area, as the next section shows.

As with the price variance, using the usage variance to evaluate performance can lead to undesirable behavior. For example, a production manager feeling pressure to produce a favorable variance might allow a defective unit to be transferred to finished goods. While this transfer avoids the problem of wasted materials, it may create customer relation problems.

Analysis of the Materials Usage Variance The materials usage variance is approximately 11 percent of standard cost ($930/$8,730). A deviation greater than 10 percent likely is to be judged significant. Thus, investigation is needed. Investigation revealed that the favorable materials usage variance was the result of the higher-quality corn acquired by the purchasing department. In this case, the favorable variance is essentially assignable to purchasing. Since the materials usage variance is favorable—but smaller than the unfavorable price variance—the overall result of the change in purchasing is unfavorable. In the future, management should try to resume purchasing of the normal-quality corn.

If the overall variance had been favorable, a different response would be expected. If the favorable variance were expected to persist, the higher-quality corn should be purchased regularly and the price and quantity standards revised to reflect it. In other words, standards are not static. As improvements in production take place and conditions change, standards may need to be revised to reflect the new operating environment. The importance of evaluating current business conditions and updating standards to reflect any changes in these conditions cannot be overemphasized.

Accounting and Disposition of Materials Variances Recognizing the price variance for materials at the point of purchase also means that the raw materials inventory is carried at standard cost. In general, materials variances are not inventoried. Typically, materials variances are added to cost of goods sold if unfavorable and are subtracted from cost of goods sold if favorable. The journal entries associated with the purchase and usage of raw materials for a standard cost system are illustrated in Appendix 20A.

YOU◆DECIDE   Relationship between *MPV* and *MUV*

As plant manager, you have been approached by the purchasing manager and the production manager and provided the following input. Kent Bowman, the purchasing manager is unhappy with the quality of the electronic components being purchased. He claims that the quality of the component from the current supplier makes it impossible to meet the materials usage standard of 1.05 components per unit produced (one component out of every hundred must be replaced before a good product is obtained). Laura Shorts, the purchasing agent, on the other hand, claims that the only supplier available that will sell the needed component for $2.00, which exactly meets the current price standard. There are two alternative suppliers that sell higher quality components, but the prices are higher.

To obtain more information, you ask Laura to buy the component from each of the alternative suppliers, one week at a time. That way, the *MPV* and *MUV* can be compared for all three suppliers. Laura provides the following results (there are no beginning or ending inventories of the component for any of the three suppliers):

Supplier	AP	SP	AQ	SQ*	MPV	MUV
Current	$2.00	$2.00	11,000	10,500	$ 0	$1,000 U
Alternative 1	$2.05	$2.00	10,500	10,500	$ 500 U	$ 0
Alternative 2	$2.10	$2.00	10,010	10,400	$1,000 U	$ 980 F

*$1.05 × 10,000

(Continued)

As plant manager, how would you interpret these results? If they are expected to continue, what actions would you take?

There is a definite relationship between the *MPV* and *MUV*. Since the quality of materials purchased can affect the usage through rejects and waste, it is important to look at the tradeoffs for the two variances. Relative to the current standard, higher quality improves the materials usage variance but causes the materials price variance to deteriorate. Adding the two together reveals the best outcome for the company:

Supplier	MPV + MUV
Current	$1,000 U
Alternative 1	500 U
Alternative 2	20 U

The best outcome is for the Alternative 2 supplier. Thus, the purchasing manager should be instructed to buy from this supplier and the price standard should be changed to $2.10 and the unit materials standard to 1.001.

Managers often have to consider the perspectives of both the purchasing and production departments. It's important to understand how each department measures success (*MPV* versus *MUV*) in order make the best decision for the company.

VARIANCE ANALYSIS: DIRECT LABOR

OBJECTIVE 5
Compute the labor variances, and explain how they are used for control.

The total labor variance measures the difference between the actual costs of labor and their budgeted costs for the actual level of activity:

$$\text{Total labor variance} = (AR \times AH) - (SR \times SH)$$

where

AH = Actual direct labor hours used
SH = Standard hours allowed
AR = Actual hourly wage rate
SR = Standard hourly wage rate

CORNERSTONE 20-5 illustrates how to calculate the total variance for labor by using selected data from Crunchy Chips for the first week of March. To keep the example simple, only inspection labor is illustrated.

CORNERSTONE 20-5   **Calculating the Total Variance for Labor**

Information:
Refer to the unit standards from Exhibit 20-3 (p. 1022). The actual results for the first week in March are:

Actual production	48,500 bags of corn chips
Actual cost of inspection labor	360 hours @ $8.35 = $3,006

Required:
Calculate the total labor variance for inspection labor for the first week in March.

Solution:

	Actual Costs	Budgeted Costs*	Total Variance
	AR × AH	SR × SH	(AR × AH) − (SR × SH)
Inspection labor	$3,006	$3,880	$874 F

*The standard quantities for inspection labor are computed as unit quantity standards from Exhibit 20-3:
Labor: $SH = 0.01 \times 48,500 = 485$ hours
Multiplying these standard quantities by the unit standard prices given in Exhibit 20-3 produces the budgeted amounts appearing in this column:
Labor: $8.00 × 485 = $3,880

Direct Labor Variances

Labor hours cannot be purchased and stored for future use as can be done with materials (i.e., there can be no difference between the amount of labor purchased and the amount of labor used). Therefore, unlike the total materials variance, the labor rate and labor efficiency variances always will add up to the total labor variance, as calculated in Cornerstone 20-5 (p. 1031):

$$\text{Total labor variance} = \text{Labor rate variance} + \text{Labor efficiency variance}$$

Thus, the rate (price) and efficiency (usage) variances for labor can be calculated by using either the columnar approach or the associated formulas. Which technique to use is a matter of preference. The formulas are adapted to reflect the specific terms used for labor prices (rates) and usage (efficiency).

The **labor rate variance (*LRV*)** computes the difference between what was paid to direct laborers and what should have been paid:

$$LRV = (AR \times AH) - (SR \times AH)$$

or, factoring:

$$LRV = (AR - SR) \times AH$$

The **labor efficiency variance (*LEV*)** measures the difference between the labor hours that were actually used and the labor hours that should have been used:

$$LEV = (SR \times AH) - (SR \times SH)$$

or, factoring:

$$LEV = (AH - SH) \times SR$$

CORNERSTONE 20-6 shows how to calculate the labor rate and efficiency variances for Crunchy Chips (for inspection labor only) using either a columnar approach or a formula approach.

C O R N E R S T O N E 20-6

Calculating Labor Variances: Formula and Columnar Approaches

Information:
Refer to the unit standards from Exhibit 20-3 (p. 1022). The actual results for the first week in March are:

Actual production	48,500 bags of corn chips
Actual cost of inspection labor	360 hours @ $8.35

Required:
Calculate the labor rate and efficiency variances by using the three-pronged (columnar) and formula approaches.

Solution:
Formulas:

$LRV = (AR - SR) \times AH$
     $= (\$8.35 - \$8.00) \times 360$
     $= \$126\ U$

$LEV = (AH - SH) \times SR$
     $= (360 - 485) \times \$8.00$
     $= \$1,000\ F$

(Continued)

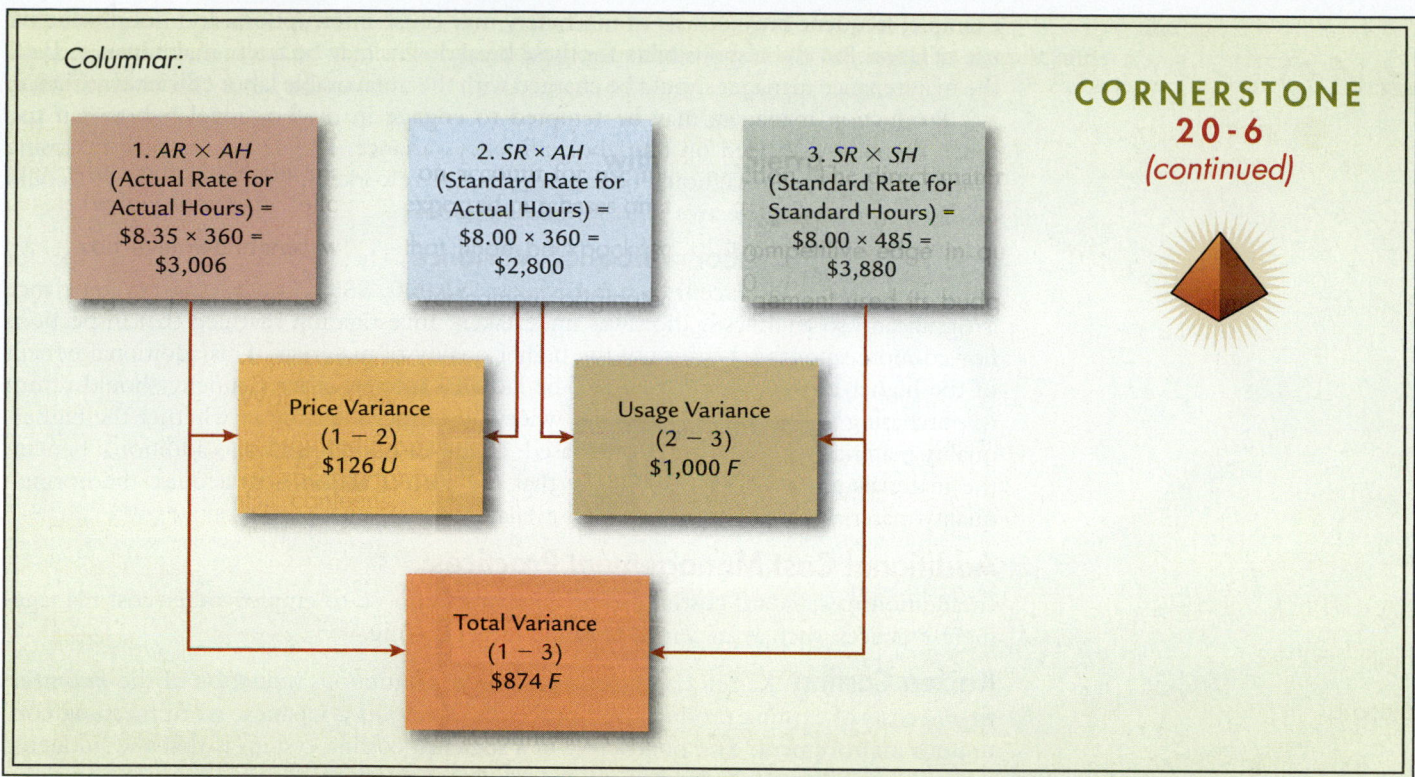

Columnar:

CORNERSTONE
20-6
(continued)

Using Labor Variance Information

As with materials variances, calculating labor variances initiates the feedback process. Using the labor variance information to exercise control is fundamental. Responsibility must be assigned, variance significance must be assessed, and the variances must be accounted for and disposed of at the end of the year.

Responsibility for the Labor Rate Variance Labor rates are largely determined by such external forces as labor markets and union contracts. The actual wage rate rarely departs from the standard rate. When labor rate variances do occur, they usually do so because an average wage rate is used for the rate standard and because more skilled and more highly paid laborers are used for less skilled tasks. Unexpected overtime also can be the cause of a labor rate variance.

Wage rates for a particular labor activity often differ among workers because of differing levels of seniority. Rather than selecting labor rate standards reflecting those different levels, an average wage rate often is chosen. As the seniority mix of workers changes, the average rate changes. This rate change will give rise to a labor rate variance; it also calls for a new standard to reflect the new seniority mix. Controllability is not assignable for this cause of a labor rate variance.

However, the use of labor is controllable by the production manager. The use of more skilled workers to perform less skilled tasks (or vice versa) is a decision that a production manager consciously makes. For this reason, responsibility for the labor rate variance generally is assigned to the individuals who decide how labor will be used.

Analysis of the Labor Rate Variance The labor rate variance for Crunchy Chips is only 3 percent of the standard cost ($126/$3,880). Although a 3 percent variance is not likely to be judged significant, for illustrative purposes, assume that an investigation is conducted. The cause of the variance is found to be the use of more highly paid and skilled machine operators as inspectors, which occurred because two inspectors quit without formal notice. The corrective action is to hire and train two new inspectors.

Responsibility for the Labor Efficiency Variance Generally speaking, production managers are responsible for the productive use of direct labor. However, as is true of all variances, once the cause is discovered, responsibility may be assigned elsewhere. For example, frequent breakdowns of machinery may cause interruptions and nonproductive use of labor. But the responsibility for these breakdowns may be faulty maintenance. If so, the maintenance manager should be charged with the unfavorable labor efficiency variance.

Production managers may be tempted to engage in dysfunctional behavior if too much emphasis is placed on the labor efficiency variance. For example, to avoid losing hours or using additional hours because of possible rework, a production manager could deliberately transfer defective units to finished goods.

Analysis of the Labor Efficiency Variance The labor efficiency variance for Crunchy Chips is 26 percent of standard cost ($1,000/$3,880). This favorable variance is significant, so an investigation was undertaken. Investigation revealed that inspections flowed more smoothly because of the higher quality of materials. This additional benefit of the higher-quality materials should be factored into whether Crunchy should return to purchasing the normal-quality corn when it becomes available or whether the higher-quality material should again be purchased. In this case, even with this additional benefit, the materials price variance is so large that the correct action is to acquire the normal-quality material when it again becomes available.

Additional Cost Management Practices

In addition to standard costing, some companies choose to employ other cost management practices, such as kaizen costing and target costing.

Kaizen Costing Kaizen costing focuses on the continuous reduction of the *manufacturing* costs of existing products and processes. *Kaizen* is a Japanese word meaning continuous improvement. The philosophy in a standard costing system is that the budgeted expectation, or standard, should be met each period. However, as the phrase "continuous improvement" suggests, the philosophy in a kaizen costing system is that the budgeted expectation, or kaizen standard, of the current period should exceed the improvement accomplished the previous period. Using this philosophy, each period's kaizen standard is set based on prior periods' improvements, thereby locking in these improvements to push for even greater improvements in the future. Typically, continuous cost improvements are achieved by identifying a large number of relatively small cost-reducing opportunities (e.g., repositioning factory work space, placing or transporting work-in-process inventory in such a way that the next worker can immediately access the inventory and begin working on it, etc.). For example, **Honda** uses kaizen costing practices to help its engineers implement the product design improvements identified by its shop floor workers.

Target Costing Target costing focuses on the reduction of the *design* costs of existing and future products and processes. Increasingly, companies such as **Toyota, Boeing**, and **Olympus** are emphasizing cost management in the design stage as they begin to recognize that an astonishingly large percentage (somewhere between 75 to 90 percent) of a product's total costs are "locked in" or "committed to" by the time it finishes the design stage and moves into the manufacturing stage.[6] A **target cost** is the difference between the sales price needed to capture a predetermined market share and the desired per-unit profit:

Target cost per unit = Expected sales price per unit − Desired profit per unit

The sales price reflects the product specifications or functions valued by the customer. If the target cost is *less* than the current actual cost, then management must find cost reductions that decrease the actual cost to the target cost. Some managers refer to this process as closing the cost gap, which is the difference between current actual cost and the necessary target cost.

Closing this cost gap is the principal challenge of target costing and usually requires the participation of suppliers and other business partners outside of the company over a period of several years. If this cost gap is not closed to zero (i.e., the actual cost is not reduced to the target cost) by the date the new product is planned to launch, then most target costing proponents will follow the cardinal rule of target costing and delay the product launch date until the gap is closed. The reason for the delay is that many

[6] See Julie H. Hertenstein and Marjorie B. Platt. *Management Accounting.* Apr. 1998. Vol. 79, Iss. 10; p. 50 (6 pages).

managers feel that once the product launches, the incentive to reduce the actual cost falls significantly and, thus, the likelihood of the actual cost eventually decreasing to the target cost level necessary to generate the desired profit margin becomes unacceptably small. **Caterpillar** is famous for adhering to this rule even though the launch delay means that the company must forego significant sales revenues during the delay period.

As you might have noticed, target costing is more than just cost control, because it includes expected sales revenues and desired profit margins in the calculation of the target cost. For this reason, target costing often is referred to as a profit planning technique. In addition, target costing is more of a long-term approach to cost reduction, whereas kaizen costing is more of a continuous, short-term approach to cost reduction. Finally, given that target and kaizen costing practices focus on different segments of the value chain, they can serve as effective complements as an organization strives to reduce its costs along the entire value chain.

APPENDIX 20A: ACCOUNTING FOR VARIANCES

OBJECTIVE **6**
Prepare journal entries for materials and labor variances.

To illustrate recording variances, we will assume that the materials price variance is computed at the time materials are purchased. With this assumption, we can state a general rule for a firm's inventory accounts: All inventories are carried at standard cost. As a result, actual costs are not entered into an inventory account. Instead, applied standard costs flow through inventory and eventually to cost of goods sold. As illustrated in this appendix, the accounts containing the variances between applied standard costs and actual costs are closed, which allows the amount of actual costs to ultimately impact the final cost of goods sold number that appears in the financial statements. In recording variances, unfavorable variances always are debits, and favorable variances always are credits.

Entries for Direct Materials Variances

Materials Price Variance The entry to record the purchase of materials follows (assuming an unfavorable *MPV* and that *AQ* is materials purchased):

Materials	$SP \times AQ$	
Materials Price Variance	$(AP - SP) \times AQ$	
Accounts Payable		$AP \times AQ$

For example, if *AP* is $0.0069 per ounce of corn, *SP* is $0.0060 per ounce, and 780,000 ounces of corn are purchased, the entry would be:

Materials	4,680	
Materials Price Variance	702	
Accounts Payable		5,382

Notice that the raw materials are carried in the inventory account at standard cost.

Materials Usage Variance The general form for the entry to record the issuance and usage of materials, assuming a favorable *MUV*, is as follows:

Work in Process	$SP \times SQ$	
Materials Usage Variance		$(AQ - SQ) \times SP$
Materials		$SP \times AQ$

Here, *AQ* is the materials issued and used, not necessarily equal to the materials purchased. Notice that only standard quantities and standard prices are used to assign costs to Work in Process. No actual costs enter this account.

For example, if *AQ* is 780,000 ounces of corn, *SQ* is 873,000 ounces, and SP is $0.006, then the entry would be:

Work in Process	5,238	
Materials Usage Variance		558
Materials		4,680

Notice that the favorable usage variance appears as a credit entry.

Entries for Direct Labor Variances

Unlike the materials variances, the entry to record both types of labor variances is made simultaneously. The general form of this entry follows (assuming an unfavorable labor rate variance and an unfavorable labor efficiency variance).

Work in Process	$SR \times SH$	
Labor Efficiency Variance	$(AH - SH) \times SR$	
Labor Rate Variance	$(AR - SR) \times AH$	
Accrued Payroll		$AR \times AH$

Again, notice that only standard hours and standard rates are used to assign costs to Work in Process. Actual prices or quantities are not used.

To give a specific example, assume that AR is $7.35 per hour, SR is $7.00 per hour, AH is 360 hours of inspection, and SH is 339.5 hours. The following journal entry would be made:

Work in Process	2,376.50	
Labor Efficiency Variance	143.50	
Labor Rate Variance	126.00	
Accrued Payroll		2,646.00

Disposition of Materials and Labor Variances

At the end of the year, the variances for materials and labor usually are closed to Cost of Goods Sold. (This practice is acceptable provided that variances are not material in amount.) Using the previous data, the entries would take the following form:

Cost of Goods Sold	971.50	
Materials Price Variance		702.00
Labor Efficiency Variance		143.50
Labor Rate Variance		126.00
Materials Usage Variance	558.00	
Cost of Goods Sold		558.00

If the variances are material, they must be prorated among various accounts. For the materials price variance, it is prorated among Materials Inventory, Materials Usage Variance, Work in Process, Finished Goods, and Cost of Goods Sold. The remaining materials and labor variances are prorated among Work in Process, Finished Goods, and Cost of Goods Sold. Typically, materials variances are prorated on the basis of the materials balances in each of these accounts and the labor variances on the basis of the labor balances in the accounts.

SUMMARY OF LEARNING OBJECTIVES

LO1.   Explain how unit standards are set and why standard cost systems are adopted.

- A standard cost system budgets quantities and costs on a unit basis. These unit budgets are for labor, materials, and overhead. Standard costs, therefore, are the amount that should be expended to produce a product or service.
- Standards are set by using historical experience, engineering studies, and input from operating personnel, marketing, and accounting.
- Currently attainable standards are those that can be achieved under efficient operating conditions.
- Ideal standards are those achievable under maximum efficiency, or ideal operating conditions.
- Standard cost systems are adopted to improve planning and control and to facilitate product costing. By comparing actual outcomes with standards and breaking the variance into price and quantity components, detailed feedback is provided to managers. This information allows managers to exercise a greater degree of cost control than that found in a normal or actual cost system.

LO2.   Explain the purpose of a standard cost sheet.

- The standard cost sheet provides the details for computing the standard cost per unit. It shows the standard costs for materials, labor, and variable and fixed overhead.
- The standard cost sheet reveals the quantity of each input that should be used to produce one unit of output. By using these unit quantity standards, the standard quantity of materials allowed and the standard hours allowed can be computed for the actual output.

LO3.   Describe the basic concepts underlying variance analysis, and explain when variances should be investigated.

- The total variance is the difference between actual costs and planned costs.
- In a standard costing system, the total variance is broken down into price and usage variances. By breaking the total variances into price and usage variances, managers are better able to analyze and control the total variance.
- Variances should be investigated if they are material (i.e., significant) and if the benefits of corrective action are greater than the costs of investigation. Because of the difficulty of assessing cost and benefits on a case-by-case basis, many firms set up formal control limits—either a dollar amount, a percentage, or both. Other firms use judgment to assess the need to investigate.

LO4.   Compute the materials variances, and explain how they are used for control.

- The materials price and usage variances are computed by using either a three-pronged (columnar) approach or formulas.
- The materials price variance is the difference between what was actually paid for materials (generally associated with the purchasing activity) and what should have been paid.
- The materials usage variance is the difference between the actual amount of materials used (generally associated with the production activity) and the amount of materials that should have been used.
- When a significant variance is signaled, an investigation is undertaken to find the cause. Corrective action is taken, if possible, to put the system back in control.

LO5.   Compute the labor variances, and explain how they are used for control.

- The labor variances are computed by using either a three-pronged approach or formulas.
- The labor rate variance is caused by the actual wage rate differing from the standard wage rate. It is the difference between the wages that were paid and those that should have been paid.
- The labor efficiency variance is the difference between the actual amount of labor that was used and the amount of labor that should have been used.
- When a significant variance is signaled, investigation is called for, and corrective action should be taken, if possible, to put the system back in control.
- Kaizen costing focuses on continuous short-term improvements in manufacturing costs, while target costing focuses on long-term improvements in design costs. Target cost is the difference between the targeted revenue and the targeted profit.

LO6.   (Appendix 20A) Prepare journal entries for materials and labor variances.

- Assuming that the materials price variance is computed at the point of purchase, all inventories are carried at standard cost.
- Actual costs are not entered into an inventory account. Instead, standard costs are applied to inventory and eventually flow through to cost of goods sold.
- Accounts are created for materials price and usage variances and for labor rate and efficiency variances.
- Unfavorable variances are always debits; favorable variances are always credits.
- The closing of the variance accounts, which contain the difference between applied standard costs and actual costs, results in the amount of actual costs ultimately impacting cost of goods sold.

SUMMARY OF IMPORTANT EQUATIONS

1. Cost per unit = Total cost/Total units
2. Standard cost per unit = Quantity standard × Price standard
3. SQ = Unit quantity standard × Actual output
4. SH = Unit labor standard × Actual output
5. Total variance = Actual cost − Planned cost = $(AP \times AQ) - (SP \times SQ)$
6. Total materials variance = Actual cost − Planned cost = $(AP \times AQ) - (SP \times SQ)$
7. $MPV = (AP - SP) \times AQ$
8. $MUV = (AQ - SQ) \times SP$
9. $MPV = (AP \times AQ) - (SP \times AQ)$
10. $MPV = (AP - SP) \times AQ$
11. $MUV = (SP \times AQ) - (SP \times SQ)$
12. $MUV = (AQ - SQ) \times SP$
13. Total labor variance = $(AR \times AH) - (SR \times SH)$
14. Total labor variance = Labor rate variance + Labor efficiency variance
15. $LRV = (AR \times AH) - (SR \times AH)$
16. $LEV = (SR \times AH) - (SR \times SH)$
17. Target cost per unit = Expected sales price per unit − Desired profit per unit

---

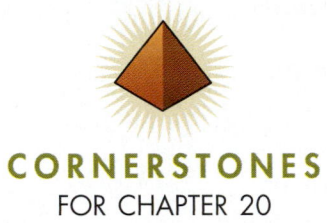

CORNERSTONES FOR CHAPTER 20

CORNERSTONE 20-1 Computing standard quantities allowed (SQ and SH) (p. 1023)

CORNERSTONE 20-2 Using control limits to trigger a variance investigation (p. 1025)

CORNERSTONE 20-3 Calculating the total variance for materials (p. 1027)

CORNERSTONE 20-4 Calculating materials variances: Formula and Columnar Approaches (p. 1028)

CORNERSTONE 20-5 Calculating the total variance for labor (p. 1031)

CORNERSTONE 20-6 Calculating labor variances: Formula and Columnar Approaches (p. 1032)

KEY TERMS

Control limits (p. 1025)
Favorable *(F)* variances (p. 1025)
Labor efficiency variance *(LEV)* (p. 1032)
Labor rate variance *(LRV)* (p. 1032)
Materials price variance *(MPV)* (p. 1028)
Materials usage variance *(MUV)* (p. 1029)
Price (rate) variance (p. 1024)
Price standards (p. 1018)
Quantity standards (p. 1018)

Standard cost per unit (p. 1021)
Standard cost sheet (p. 1021)
Standard hours allowed *(SH)* (p. 1022)
Standard quantity of materials
  allowed *(SQ)* (p. 1022)
Target cost (p. 1034)
Total budget variance (p. 1024)
Unfavorable *(U)* variances (p. 1025)
Usage (efficiency) variance (p. 1025)

REVIEW PROBLEMS

I. Materials, Labor, and Overhead Variances

Willhelm Manufacturing has the following standards for one of its products:

Direct materials (2 ft. @ $5)	$10
Direct labor (0.5 hr. @ $10)	5

During the most recent year, the following actual results were recorded:

Production	6,000 units
Direct materials (11,750 ft. purchased and used)	$61,100
Direct labor (2,900 hrs.)	29,580

Required:

Compute the following variances:

1. Materials price and usage variances.

2. Labor rate and efficiency variances.

Solution:

1. Materials variances:

$$MPV = (AP - SP) \times AQ$$
$$= (\$5.20 - \$5.00) \times 11{,}750 = \$2{,}350 \ U$$
$$MUV = (AQ - SQ) \times SP$$
$$= (11{,}750 - 12{,}000) \times \$5.00 = \$1{,}250 \ F$$

2. Labor variances:

$$LRV = (AR - SR) \times AH$$
$$= (\$10.20 - \$10.00) \times 2{,}900 = \$580 \ U$$
$$LEV = (AH - SH) \times SR$$
$$= (2{,}900 - 3{,}000) \times \$10.00 = \$1{,}000 \ F$$

DISCUSSION QUESTIONS

1. Discuss the difference between budgets and standard costs.
2. Describe the relationship that unit standards have with flexible budgeting.
3. Why is historical experience often a poor basis for establishing standards?
4. What are ideal standards? Currently attainable standards? Of the two, which is usually adopted? Why?
5. Explain why standard costing systems are adopted.
6. How does standard costing improve the control function?
7. Discuss the differences among actual costing, normal costing, and standard costing.
8. What is the purpose of a standard cost sheet?
9. The budget variance for variable production costs is broken down into quantity and price variances. Explain why the quantity variance is more useful for control purposes than the price variance.
10. When should a standard cost variance be investigated?
11. What are control limits, and how are they set?
12. Explain why the materials price variance is often computed at the point of purchase rather than at the point of issuance.
13. The materials usage variance is always the responsibility of the production supervisor. Do you agree or disagree? Why?
14. The labor rate variance is never controllable. Do you agree or disagree? Why?
15. Suggest some possible causes of an unfavorable labor efficiency variance.
16. What is kaizen costing? On which part of the value chain does kaizen costing focus?
17. What is target costing? Describe how costs are reduced so that the target cost can be met.

MULTIPLE-CHOICE EXERCISES

20-1 Historical experience should be used with caution in setting standards because

a. they may perpetuate operating inefficiencies.
b. ideal standards are always better than historical standards.
c. they may not be achievable by operating personnel.
d. most companies keep poor records.
e. none of the above.

20-2 Standards set by engineering studies

a.   can determine the most efficient way of operating.
b.   can provide rigorous guidelines.
c.   may not be achievable by operating personnel.
d.   often do not allow operating personnel to have much input.
e.   all of these.

20-3 The standard cost per unit of output for a particular input is calculated as

a.   Actual input price per unit × Actual input used per unit.
b.   Standard input price × Inputs allowed for the actual output.
c.   Standard input price × Standard input allowed per unit of output produced.
d.   Standard price per unit × Standard units produced.
e.   Standard input price × Actual inputs.

20-4 A currently attainable standard is one that

a.   relies on maximum efficiency.
b.   uses only historical experience.
c.   is based on ideal operating conditions.
d.   can be achieved under efficient operating conditions.
e.   none of these.

20-5 An ideal standard is one that

a.   uses only historical experience.
b.   relies on maximum efficiency.
c.   can be achieved under efficient operating conditions.
d.   makes allowances for normal breakdowns, interruptions, less than perfect skill, and so on.
e.   none of these.

20-6 Reasons for adopting a standard costing system include

a.   to encourage purchasing managers to purchase cheap materials.
b.   to imitate most other firms.
c.   to enhance operational control.
d.   that the weighted average method can be used for process manufacturers.
e.   none of these.

20-7 Standard costs are developed for

a.   indirect materials.
b.   indirect labor.
c.   variable selling cost.
d.   fixed overhead.
e.   all of these.

20-8 The underlying details for the standard cost per unit are provided in

a.   the standard work-in-process account.
b.   the standard production budget.
c.   the standard cost sheet.
d.   the balance sheet.
e.   none of these.

20-9 The standard quantity of materials allowed is computed as

a.   Unit quantity standard × Standard output.
b.   Unit quantity standard × Normal output.
c.   Unit quantity standard × Practical output.
d.   Unit quantity standard × Actual output.
e.   none of these.

20-10 The standard direct labor hours allowed is computed as

a.   Unit labor standard × Actual output.
b.   Unit labor standard × Practical output.
c.   Unit labor standard × Standard output.
d.   Unit labor standard × Normal output.
e.   Unit labor standard × Theoretical output.

20-11 The total (budget) variance is computed as

a. $(SP \times AQ) - (AP \times SQ)$.
b. $(AP \times AQ) - (SP \times SQ)$.
c. $(SP \times AQ) - (SP \times SQ)$.
d. $(AP \times SP) - (AQ \times SQ)$.
e.   none of these.

20-12 Investigating variances from standard is

a. always done.
b. done if the variance is inside an acceptable range.
c. not done if the variance is expected to recur.
d. done if the variance is outside the control limits.
e. none of these.

20-13 Responsibility for the materials price variance typically belongs to

a. production.
b. purchasing.
c. marketing.
d. personnel.
e. the chief executive officer (CEO).

20-14 The materials price variance is usually computed

a. when goods are finished.
b. when materials are issued to production.
c. when materials are purchased.
d. after suppliers are paid.
e. none of these.

20-15 Responsibility for the materials usage variance is usually assigned to

a. the chief executive officer (CEO).
b. marketing.
c. purchasing.
d. personnel.
e. production.

20-16 Responsibility for the labor rate variance typically is assigned to

a. production.
b. labor markets.
c. personnel.
d. labor unions.
e. engineering.

20-17 Responsibility for the labor efficiency variance typically is assigned to

a. labor unions.
b. personnel.
c. engineering.
d. production.
e. outside trainers.

20-18 *(Appendix 20A)* Which of the following items describes practices surrounding the recording of variances?

a. All inventories are typically carried at standard.
b. Unfavorable variances appear as debits.
c. Favorable variances appear as credits.
d. Immaterial variances are typically closed to Cost of Goods Sold.
e. All of these.

20-19 *(Appendix 20A)* Which of the following is true concerning significantly large labor variances?

a. They are closed to Cost of Goods Sold.
b. They are prorated among Work in Process, Finished Goods, and Cost of Goods Sold.
c. They are prorated among Materials, Work in Process, Finished Goods, and Cost of Goods Sold.
d. They are reported on the balance sheet at the end of the year.
e. All of the above.

CORNERSTONE EXERCISES

Cornerstone Exercise 20-20 Standard Quantities Allowed of Labor and Materials

CORNERSTONE 20-1
OBJECTIVE ❷

Packard Company produces ready-to-cook oatmeal. Each carton of oatmeal requires 16 ounces of rolled oats per carton (the unit quantity standard) and 0.04 labor hours (the unit labor standard). During the year, 700,000 cartons of oatmeal were produced.

Required:
1. Calculate the total amount of oats allowed for the actual output.
2. Calculate the total amount of labor hours allowed for the actual output.

CORNERSTONE 20-2
OBJECTIVE 3

Cornerstone Exercise 20-21 Control Limits

During the last six weeks, the actual costs of materials for Mandarin Company were as follows:

Week 1	$48,000	Week 4	$57,000
Week 2	$50,000	Week 5	$60,000
Week 3	$52,500	Week 6	$65,000

The standard materials cost for each week was $50,000 with an allowable deviation of ±5,000.

Required:
Plot the actual costs over time against the upper and lower limits. Comment on whether or not there is a need to investigate any of the variances.

> *Use the following information to complete Cornerstone Exercises 20-22 and 20-23:*
> Lata Inc., produces aluminum cans. Production of 12-ounce cans has a standard unit quantity of 4.5 ounces of aluminum per can. During the month of April, 300,000 cans were produced using 1,250,000 ounces of aluminum. The actual cost of aluminum was $0.09 per ounce and the standard price was $0.08 per ounce. There are no beginning or ending inventories of aluminum.

CORNERSTONE 20-3
OBJECTIVE 4

Cornerstone Exercise 20-22 Total Materials Variance

Refer to the information for Lata Inc. above.

Required:
Calculate the total variance for aluminum for the month of April.

CORNERSTONE 20-4
OBJECTIVE 4

Cornerstone Exercise 20-23 Materials Variances

Refer to the information for Lata Inc. above.

Required:
Calculate the materials price and usage variances using the columnar and formula approaches.

> *Use the following information to complete Cornerstone Exercises 20-24 and 20-25:*
> Botella, Inc. produces plastic bottles. Each bottle has a standard labor requirement of 0.025 hours. During the month of April, 500,000 bottles were produced using 14,000 labor hours @ $9.00. The standard wage rate is $8.50 per hour.

CORNERSTONE 20-5
OBJECTIVE 5

Cornerstone Exercise 20-24 Total Labor Variance

Refer to the information for Botella Inc. above.

Required:
Calculate the total variance for production labor for the month of April.

CORNERSTONE 20-6
OBJECTIVE 5

Cornerstone Exercise 20-25 Labor Rate and Efficiency Variances

Refer to the information for Botella Inc. above.

Required:
Calculate the labor rate and efficiency variances using the columnar and formula approaches.

EXERCISES

OBJECTIVE 2

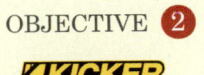

Exercise 20-26 Standard Quantities of Labor and Materials

Stillwater Designs rebuilds defective units of its S12L7 **Kicker** speaker model. During the year, Stillwater rebuilt 7,500 units. Materials and labor standards for performing the repairs are as follows:

Direct materials (1 recon kit @ $150)	$150.00
Direct materials (1 cabinet @ $50)	50.00
Direct labor (5 hrs. @ $12)	60.00

Required:

1. Compute the standard hours allowed for a volume of 7,500 rebuilt units.
2. Compute the standard number of kits and cabinets allowed for a volume of 7,500 rebuilt units.
3. Suppose that during the first month of the year, 3,750 standard hours were allowed for the units rebuilt. How many units were rebuilt during the first month?

Exercise 20-27 Investigation of Variances

OBJECTIVE ❸

Sommers Company uses the following rule to determine whether materials usage variances should be investigated: A materials usage variance will be investigated anytime the amount exceeds the lesser of $12,000 or 10 percent of the standard cost. Reports for the past five weeks provided the following information:

Week	MUV	Standard Materials Cost
1	$10,500 F	$120,000
2	10,700 U	100,500
3	9,000 F	120,000
4	13,500 U	127,500
5	10,500 U	103,500

Required:

1. Using the rule provided, identify the cases that will be investigated.
2. **Conceptual Connection:** Suppose investigation reveals that the cause of an unfavorable materials usage variance is the use of lower-quality materials than are normally used. Who is responsible? What corrective action would likely be taken?
3. **Conceptual Connection:** Suppose investigation reveals that the cause of a significant unfavorable materials usage variance is attributable to a new approach to manufacturing that takes less labor time but causes more material waste. Examination of the labor efficiency variance reveals that it is favorable and larger than the unfavorable materials usage variance. Who is responsible? What action should be taken?

Use the following information for Exercises 20-28 through 20-30:
Bolsa Corporation produces high-quality leather belts. The company's plant in Boise uses a standard costing system and has set the following standards for materials and labor:

Leather (3 strips @ $4)	$12.00
Direct labor (0.75 hr. @ $12)	9.00
Total prime cost	$21.00

During the first month of the year, Boise plant produced 40,000 belts. Actual leather purchased was 125,000 strips at $3.60 per strip. There were no beginning or ending inventories of leather. Actual direct labor was 34,000 hours at $12.50 per hour.

Exercise 20-28 Budget Variances, Materials and Labor

OBJECTIVE ❹ ❺

Refer to the information for Bolsa Corporation above.

Required:

1. Compute the costs of leather and direct labor that should be incurred for the production of 40,000 leather belts.
2. Compute the total budget variances for materials and labor.
3. **Conceptual Connection:** Would you consider these variances material with a need for investigation? Explain.

Exercise 20-29 Materials Variances

OBJECTIVE ❹

Refer to the information for Bolsa Corporation above.

Required:

1. Break down the total variance for materials into a price variance and a usage variance using the columnar and formula approaches.
2. **Conceptual Connection:** Suppose the Boise plant manager investigates the materials variances and is told by the purchasing manager that a cheaper source of leather strips had been

(Continued)

discovered and that this is the reason for the favorable materials price variance. Quite pleased, the purchasing manager suggests that the materials price standard be updated to reflect this new, less expensive source of leather strips. Should the plant manager update the materials price standard as suggested? Why or why not?

OBJECTIVE ❺

Exercise 20-30 Labor Variances

Refer to the information for Bolsa Corporation (p. 1043).

Required:

1. Break down the total variance for labor into a rate variance and an efficiency variance using the columnar and formula approaches.
2. **Conceptual Connection:** As part of the investigation of the unfavorable variances, the plant manager interviews the production manager. The production manager complains strongly about the quality of the leather strips. He indicates that the strips are of lower quality than usual and that workers have to be more careful to avoid a belt with cracks and more time is required. Also, even with extra care, many belts have to be discarded and new ones produced to replace the rejects. This replacement work has also produced some overtime demands. What corrective action should the plant manager take?

OBJECTIVE ❹

ILLUSTRATING RELATIONSHIPS

Exercise 20-31 Materials Variances

Manzana Company produces apple juice sold in gallons. Recently, the company adopted the following material standard for one gallon of its apple juice:

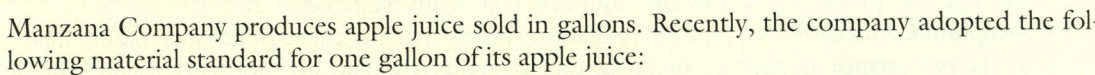

Direct materials 128 oz. @ $0.05 = $6.40

During the first week of operation, the company experienced the following results:

a. Gallon units produced: 20,000.
b. Ounces of materials purchased and used: 2,650,000 ounces at $0.045.
c. No beginning or ending inventories of raw materials.

Required:

1. Compute the materials price variance.
2. Compute the materials usage variance.
3. During the second week, the materials usage variance was $4,000 unfavorable and the materials price variance was $20,000 unfavorable. The company purchased and used 2,000,000 ounces of material during this week. How many gallons of juice were produced and what was the actual price paid per ounce of materials?

OBJECTIVE ❺

Exercise 20-32 Labor Variances

Verde Company produces wheels for bicycles. During the year, 660,000 wheels were produced. The actual labor used was 360,000 hours at $9.50 per hour. Verde has the following labor standard: 0.5 hour at $10.

Required:

1. Compute the labor rate variance.
2. Compute the labor efficiency variance.

OBJECTIVE ❹ ❺

Exercise 20-33 Materials and Labor Variances

At the beginning of the year, Shults Company had the following standard cost sheet for one of its plastic products:

Direct materials (6 lbs. @ $5)	$30.00
Direct labor (2 hrs. @ $12)	24.00
Standard prime cost per unit	$54.00

The actual results for the year are as follows:

a. Units produced: 350,000.
b. Materials purchased: 1,860,000 pounds @ $5.10.
c. Materials used: 1,850,000 pounds.
d. Direct labor: 725,000 hours @ $11.85.

Required:
1. Compute price and usage variances for materials.
2. Compute the labor rate and labor efficiency variances.

Exercise 20-34 Variances, Evaluation, and Behavior

OBJECTIVE ❶

Jackie Iverson was furious. She was about ready to fire Tom Rich, her purchasing agent. Just a month ago, she had given him a salary increase and a bonus for his performance. She had been especially pleased with his ability to meet or beat the price standards. But now, she found out that it was because of a huge purchase of raw materials. It would take months to use that inventory, and there was hardly space to store it. In the meantime, space had to be found for the other materials supplies that would be ordered and processed on a regular basis. Additionally, it was a lot of capital to tie up in inventory—money that could have been used to help finance the cash needs of the new product just coming online.

Her interview with Tom was frustrating. He was defensive, arguing that he thought she wanted those standards met and that the means were not that important. He also pointed out that quantity purchases were the only way to meet the price standards. Otherwise, an unfavorable variance would have been realized.

Required:
1. **Conceptual Connection:** Why did Tom Rich purchase the large quantity of raw materials? Do you think that this behavior was the objective of the price standard? If not, what is the objective(s)?
2. **Conceptual Connection:** Suppose that Tom is right and that the only way to meet the price standards is through the use of quantity discounts. Also, assume that using quantity discounts is not a desirable practice for this company. What would you do to solve this dilemma?
3. **Conceptual Connection:** Should Tom be fired? Explain.

Use the following information for Exercises 20-35 and 20-36:

Deporte Company produces single-colored t-shirts. Materials for the shirts are dyed in large vats. After dying the materials for a given color, the vats must be cleaned and prepared for the next batch of materials to be colored. The following standards for changeover for a given batch have been established:

Direct materials (2.4 lbs. @ $0.95)	$2.28
Direct labor (0.75 hr. @ $7.40)	5.55
Standard prime cost	$7.83

During the year, 79,500 pounds of material were purchased and used for the changeover activity. There were 30,000 batches produced, with the following actual prime costs:

Direct materials	$ 63,000
Direct labor	$153,000 (for 22,450 hrs.)

Exercise 20-35 Materials and Labor Variances

OBJECTIVE ❹ ❺

Refer to the information for Deporte Company above.

Required:
Compute the materials and labor variances associated with the changeover activity, labeling each variance as favorable or unfavorable.

Exercise 20-36 *(Appendix 20A)* Journal Entries

OBJECTIVE ❻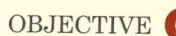

Refer to the information for Deporte Company above.

Required:
1. Prepare a journal entry for the purchase of raw materials.
2. Prepare a journal entry for the issuance of raw materials.
3. Prepare a journal entry for the addition of labor to Work in Process.
4. Prepare a journal entry for the closing of variances to Cost of Goods Sold.

OBJECTIVE ④ ⑥

Exercise 20-37 *(Appendix 20A)* Materials Variances, Journal Entries

Esteban Products produces instructional aids, including white boards, which use colored markers instead of chalk. These are particularly popular for conference rooms in educational institutions and executive offices of large corporations. The standard cost of materials for this product is 12 pounds at $8.25 per pound.

During the first month of the year, 3,200 boards were produced. Information concerning actual costs and usage of materials follows:

Materials purchased	38,000 lbs. @ $8.35
Materials used	37,500 lbs.

Required:
1. Compute the materials price and usage variances.
2. Prepare journal entries for all activity relating to materials.

OBJECTIVE ⑤ ⑥

Exercise 20-38 *(Appendix 20A)* Labor Variances, Journal Entries

Escuchar Products, a producer of DVD players, has established a labor standard for its product—direct labor: 2 hrs at $9.65 per hour. During January, Escuchar produced 12,800 DVD players. The actual direct labor used was 25,040 hours at a total cost of $245,392.

Required:
1. Compute the labor rate and efficiency variances.
2. Prepare journal entries for all activities relating to labor.

PROBLEMS

OBJECTIVE ①

Problem 20-39 Setting Standards and Assigning Responsibility

Cabanarama Inc. designs and manufactures easy-to-set-up beach cabanas that families can set up for picnicking, protection from the sun, and so on. The cabanas come in a kit that includes canvas, lacing, and aluminum support poles. Cabanarama has expanded rapidly from a two-person operation to one involving over a hundred employees. Cabanarama's founder and owner, Frank Love, understands that a more formal approach to standard setting and control is needed to ensure that the consistent quality for which the company is known continues.

Frank and Annette Wilson, his financial vice president, divided the company into departments and designated each department as a cost center. Sales, Quality Control, and Design report directly to Frank. Production, Shipping, Finance, and Accounting report to Annette. In the production department, one of the supervisors was assigned the materials purchasing function. The job included purchasing all raw materials, overseeing inventory handling (receiving, storage, etc.), and tracking materials purchases and use.

Frank felt that control would be better achieved if there were a way for his employees to continue to perform in such a way that quality was maintained and cost reduction was achieved. Annette suggested that Cabanarama institute a standard costing system. Variances for materials and labor could then be calculated and reported directly to her, and she could alert Frank to any problems or opportunities for improvement.

Required:
1. a. **Conceptual Connection:** When Annette designs the standard costing system for Cabanarama, who should be involved in setting the standards for each cost component?
    b. **Conceptual Connection:** What factors should be considered in establishing the standards for each cost component?
2. **Conceptual Connection:** Assume that Cabanarama develops the standards for materials use, materials price, labor use, and labor wages. Who will be assigned responsibility for each and for any resulting variances? Why?

OBJECTIVE ③ ④ ⑤

Problem 20-40 Basics of Variance Analysis, Variable Inputs

Basuras Waste Disposal Company has a long-term contract with several large cities to collect garbage and trash from residential customers. To facilitate the collection, Basuras places a large plastic container with each household. Because of wear and tear, growth, and other factors, Basuras places about 200,000 new containers each year (about 20 percent of the total households). Several years ago, Basuras decided to manufacture its own containers as a cost-saving measure. A strategically located plant involved in this type of manufacturing was acquired. To help ensure cost efficiency, a standard cost system was installed in the plant. The following standards have been established for the product's variable inputs:

	Standard Quantity	Standard Price (rate in $)	Standard Cost
Direct materials	12 lbs.	$ 3.50	$42.00
Direct labor	1.70 hrs.	11.00	18.70
Variable overhead	1.70 hrs.	3.00	5.10
Total			$65.80

During the first week, Basuras had the following actual results:

Units produced	6,000
Actual labor costs	$118,800
Actual labor hours	10,800
Materials purchased and used	69,000 lbs. @ $3.55
Actual variable overhead costs	$39,750

The purchasing agent located a new source of slightly higher-quality plastic, and this material was used during the first week in January. Also, a new manufacturing process was implemented on a trial basis. The new process required a slightly higher level of skilled labor. The higher-quality material has no effect on labor utilization. However, the new manufacturing process was expected to reduce materials usage by 0.25 pound per can.

Required:

1. **Conceptual Connection:** Compute the materials price and usage variances. Assume that the 0.25 pound per can reduction of materials occurred as expected and that the remaining effects are all attributable to the higher-quality material. Would you recommend that the purchasing agent continue to buy this quality, or should the usual quality be purchased? Assume that the quality of the end product is not affected significantly.

2. **Conceptual Connection:** Compute the labor rate and efficiency variances. Assuming that the labor variances are attributable to the new manufacturing process, should it be continued or discontinued? In answering, consider the new process's materials reduction effect as well. Explain.

3. **Conceptual Connection:** Refer to Requirement 2. Suppose that the industrial engineer argued that the new process should not be evaluated after only one week. His reasoning was that it would take at least a week for the workers to become efficient with the new approach. Suppose that the production is the same the second week and that the actual labor hours were 9,000 and the labor cost was $99,000. Should the new process be adopted? Assume the variances are attributable to the new process. Assuming production of 6,000 units per week, what would be the projected annual savings? (Include the materials reduction effect.)

Problem 20-41 Setting Standards, Materials and Labor Variances

OBJECTIVE   5

Tom Belford and Tony Sorrentino own a small business devoted to kitchen and bath granite installations. Recently, building contractors have insisted on up-front bid prices for a house rather than the cost-plus system that Tom and Tony were used to. They worry because natural flaws in the granite make it impossible to tell in advance exactly how much granite will be used on a particular job. In addition, granite can be easily broken, meaning that Tom or Tony could ruin a slab and would need to start over with a new one. Sometimes the improperly cut pieces could be used for smaller installations, sometimes not. All their accounting is done by a local certified public accounting firm headed by Charlene Davenport. Charlene listened to their concerns and suggested that it might be time to implement tighter controls by setting up a standard costing system.

Charlene reviewed the invoices pertaining to a number of Tom and Tony's previous jobs to determine the average amount of granite and glue needed per square foot. She then updated prices on both materials to reflect current conditions. The standards she developed for one square foot of counter installed were as follows:

(Continued)

Granite, per square foot	$50.00
Glue (10 oz. @ $0.15)	1.50
Direct labor hours:	
Cutting labor (0.10 hr. @ $15)	1.50
Installation labor (0.25 hr. @ $25)	6.25

These standards assumed that one seamless counter requires one sink cut (the space into which the sink will fit) as well as cutting the counter to fit the space available.

Charlene tracked the actual costs incurred by Tom and Tony for granite installation for the next six months. She found that they completed 50 jobs with an average of 32 square feet of granite installed in each one. The following information on actual amounts used and cost was gathered:

Granite purchased and used (1,640 sq. ft.)	$79,048
Glue purchased and used (16,000 oz.)	$2,560
Actual hours cutting labor	180
Actual hours installation labor	390

The actual wage rate for cutting and installation labor remained unchanged from the standard rate.

Required:

1. Calculate the materials price variances and materials usage variances for granite and for glue for the past six months.
2. Calculate the labor rate variances and labor efficiency variances for cutting labor and for installation labor for the past six months.
3. **Conceptual Connection:** Would it be worthwhile for Charlene to establish standards for atypical jobs (such as those with more than one sink cut or wider than normal)?

OBJECTIVE ❶ ❷ ❺

Problem 20-42 Setting a Direct Labor Standard, Learning Curve Effects, Service Company

Mantenga Company provides routine maintenance services for heavy moving and transportation vehicles. Although the vehicles vary, the maintenance services provided follow a fairly standard pattern. Recently, a potential customer has approached the company, requesting a new maintenance service for a radically different type of vehicle. New servicing equipment and some new labor skills will be needed to provide the maintenance service. The customer is placing an initial order to service 150 vehicles and has indicated that if the service is satisfactory, several additional orders of the same size will be placed every three months over the next three to five years.

Mantenga uses a standard costing system and wants to develop a set of standards for the new vehicle. The usage standards for direct materials such as oil, lubricants, and transmission fluids were easily established. The usage standard is 25 quarts per servicing, with a standard cost of $4 per quart. Management has also decided on standard rates for labor and overhead: The standard labor rate is $15 per direct labor hour, the standard variable overhead rate is $8 per direct labor hour, and the standard fixed overhead rate is $12 per direct labor hour. The only remaining decision is the standard for labor usage. To assist in developing this standard, the engineering department has estimated the following relationship between units serviced and average direct labor hours used:

Units Serviced	Cumulative Average Time per Unit (hours)
40	2.500
80	2.000
160	1.600
320	1.280
640	1.024

As the workers learn more about servicing the new vehicles, they become more efficient, and the average time needed to service one unit declines. Engineering estimates that all of the learning effects will be achieved by the time that 320 units are produced. No further improvement will be realized past this level.

Required:

1. Assume that the average labor time is 0.768 hour per unit after the learning effects are achieved. Using this information, prepare a standard cost sheet that details the standard service cost per unit. (*Note:* Round costs to two decimal places.)

2. **Conceptual Connection:** Given the per-unit labor standard set, would you expect a favorable or an unfavorable labor efficiency? Explain. Calculate the labor efficiency variance for servicing the first 320 units.

3. **Conceptual Connection:** Assuming no further improvement in labor time per unit is possible past 320 units, explain why the cumulative average time per unit at 640 is lower than the time at 320 units. Show that the standard labor time should be 0.768 hour per unit. Explain why this value is a good choice for the per-unit labor standard.

Problem 20-43 Unit Costs, Multiple Products, Variance Analysis, Service Setting

OBJECTIVE

The maternity wing of the city hospital has two types of patients: normal and cesarean. The standard quantities of labor and materials per delivery for 2011 are:

	Normal	Cesarean
Direct materials (lbs.)	9.0	21
Nursing labor (hrs.)	2.5	5

The standard price paid per pound of direct materials is $10. The standard rate for labor is $16. Overhead is applied on the basis of direct labor hours. The variable overhead rate for maternity is $30 per hour, and the fixed overhead rate is $40 per hour.

Actual operating data for 2011 are as follows:

a. Deliveries produced: normal, 4,000; cesarean, 8,000.

b. Direct materials purchased and used: 200,000 pounds at $9.50—35,000 for normal maternity patients and 165,000 for the cesarean patients; no beginning or ending raw materials inventories.

c. Nursing labor: 50,700 hours—10,200 hours for normal patients and 40,500 hours for the cesarean; total cost of labor, $580,350.

Required:

1. Prepare a standard cost sheet showing the unit cost per delivery for each type of patient.
2. Compute the materials price and usage variances for each type of patient.
3. Compute the labor rate and efficiency variances.
4. **Conceptual Connection:** Assume that you know only the total direct materials used for both products and the total direct labor hours used for both products. Can you compute the total materials usage and labor efficiency variances? Explain.
5. **Conceptual Connection:** Standard costing concepts have been applied in the healthcare industry. For example, diagnostic-related groups (DRGs) are used for prospective payments for Medicare patients. Select a search engine (such as Yahoo! or Google), and conduct a search to see what information you can obtain about DRGs. You might try "Medicare DRGs" as a possible search topic. Write a memo that answers the following questions:

   a. What is a DRG?
   b. How are DRGs established?
   c. How many DRGs are used?
   d. How does the DRG concept relate to standard costing concepts discussed in the chapter? Can hospitals use DRGs to control their costs? Explain.

Problem 20-44 Control Limits, Variance Investigation

OBJECTIVE

Buenolorl Company produces a well-known cologne. The standard manufacturing cost of the cologne is described by the following standard cost sheet:

Direct materials:	
Liquids (4.5 oz. @ $0.40)	$1.80
Bottles (1 @ $0.05)	0.05
Direct labor (0.2 hr. @ $15.00)	3.00
Variable overhead (0.2 hr. @ $5.00)	1.00
Fixed overhead (0.2 hr. @ $1.50)	0.30
Standard cost per unit	$6.15

Management has decided to investigate only those variances that exceed the lesser of 10 percent of the standard cost for each category or $20,000.

(Continued)

During the past quarter, 250,000 four-ounce bottles of cologne were produced. Descriptions of actual activity for the quarter follow:

a. A total of 1.35 million ounces of liquids was purchased, mixed, and processed. Evaporation was higher than expected (no inventories of liquids are maintained). The price paid per ounce averaged $0.42.

b. Exactly 250,000 bottles were used. The price paid for each bottle was $0.048.

c. Direct labor hours totaled 48,250, with a total cost of $733,000.

Normal production volume for Buenolorl is 250,000 bottles per quarter. The standard overhead rates are computed by using normal volume. All overhead costs are incurred uniformly throughout the year.

Required:

1. Calculate the upper and lower control limits for materials and labor.
2. Compute the total materials variance, and break it into price and usage variances. Would these variances be investigated?
3. Compute the total labor variance, and break it into rate and efficiency variances. Would these variances be investigated?

OBJECTIVE

Problem 20-45 Control Limits, Variance Investigation

The management of Golding Company has determined that the cost to investigate a variance produced by its standard cost system ranges from $2,000 to $3,000. If a problem is discovered, the average benefit from taking corrective action usually outweighs the cost of investigation. Past experience from the investigation of variances has revealed that corrective action is rarely needed for deviations within 8 percent of the standard cost. Golding produces a single product, which has the following standards for materials and labor:

Direct materials (8 lbs. @ $0.25)	$2
Direct labor (0.4 hr. @ $7.50)	3

Actual production for the past three months with the associated actual usage and costs for materials and labor follow. There were no beginning or ending raw materials inventories.

	April	May	June
Production (units)	90,000	100,000	110,000
Direct materials:			
Cost	$189,000	$218,000	$230,000
Usage (lbs.)	723,000	870,000	885,000
Direct labor:			
Cost	$270,000	$323,000	$360,000
Usage (hrs.)	36,000	44,000	46,000

Required:

1. What upper and lower control limits would you use for materials variances? For labor variances?
2. Compute the materials and labor variances for April, May, and June. Identify those that would require investigation.
3. **Conceptual Connection:** Let the horizontal axis be time and the vertical axis be variances measured as a percentage deviation from standard. Draw horizontal lines that identify upper and lower control limits. Plot the labor and material variances for April, May, and June. Prepare a separate graph for each type of variance. Explain how you would use these graphs (called *control charts*) to assist your analysis of variances.

OBJECTIVE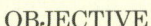

Problem 20-46 Standard Costing, Planned Variances

Juguette Company manufactures a plastic toy cell phone. The following standards have been established for the toy's materials and labor inputs:

	Standard Quantity	Standard Price (rate in $)	Standard Cost
Direct materials	0.5 lb.	$ 1.50	$0.75
Direct labor	0.15 hr.	10.00	1.50

During the first week of July, the company had the following results:

Units produced	60,000
Actual labor costs	$92,000
Actual labor hours	7,000
Materials purchased and used	29,500 lbs. @ $1.55 per lb

Other information: The purchasing agent located a new source of slightly higher-quality plastic, and this material was used during the first week in July. Also, a new manufacturing layout was implemented on a trial basis. The new layout required a slightly higher level of skilled labor. The higher-quality material has no effect on labor utilization. Similarly, the new manufacturing approach has no effect on material usage.

Required:

1. **Conceptual Connection:** Compute the materials price and usage variances. Assuming that the materials variances are essentially attributable to the higher quality of materials, would you recommend that the purchasing agent continue to buy this quality, or should the usual quality be purchased? Assume that the quality of the end product is not affected significantly.

2. **Conceptual Connection:** Compute the labor rate and efficiency variances. Assuming that the labor variances are attributable to the new manufacturing layout, should it be continued or discontinued? Explain.

3. **Conceptual Connection:** Refer to Requirement 2. Suppose that the industrial engineer argued that the new layout should not be evaluated after only one week. His reasoning was that it would take at least a week for the workers to become efficient with the new approach. Suppose that the production is the same the second week and that the actual labor hours were 8,800 and the labor cost was $88,000. Should the new layout be adopted? Assume the variances are attributable to the new layout. If so, what would be the projected annual savings?

Problem 20-47 Standard Costing

OBJECTIVE

Claro Company produces plastic bottles. The unit for costing purposes is a case of 18 bottles. The following standards for producing one case of bottles have been established:

Direct materials (5 lbs. @ $0.90)	$ 4.50
Direct labor (1.5 hours @ $14.00)	21.00
Standard prime cost	$25.50

During December, 78,000 pounds of material were purchased and used in production. There were 15,000 cases produced, with the following actual prime costs:

Direct materials	$ 74,000
Direct labor	$315,000 (for 22,500 hrs.)

Required:

1. Compute the materials variances.
2. Compute the labor variances.
3. **Conceptual Connection:** What are the advantages and disadvantages that can result from the use of a standard costing system?

Problem 20-48 *(Appendix 20A)* Variance Analysis, Revision of Standards, Journal Entries

OBJECTIVE

The Lubbock plant of Morril's Small Motor Division produces a major subassembly for a 6.0 horsepower motor for lawn mowers. The plant uses a standard costing system for production costing and control. The standard cost sheet for the subassembly follows:

Direct materials (6.0 lbs. @ $5)	$30.00
Direct labor (1.6 hrs. @ $12)	19.20

During the year, the Lubbock plant had the following actual production activity:

a. Production of subassemblies totaled 50,000 units.
b. A total of 260,000 pounds of raw materials was purchased at $4.70 per pound.
c. There were 60,000 pounds of raw materials in beginning inventory (carried at $5 per lb.). There was no ending inventory.
d. The company used 82,000 direct labor hours at a total cost of $1,066,000.

(Continued)

The Lubbock plant's practical activity is 60,000 units per year. Standard overhead rates are computed based on practical activity measured in standard direct labor hours.

Required:

1. **Conceptual Connection:** Complete the materials price and usage variances. Of the two materials variances, which is viewed as the most controllable? To whom would you assign responsibility for the usage variance in this case? Explain.

2. **Conceptual Connection:** Compute the labor rate and efficiency variances. Who is usually responsible for the labor efficiency variance? What are some possible causes for this variance?

3. **Conceptual Connection:** Assume that the purchasing agent for the small motors plant purchased a lower-quality raw material from a new supplier. Would you recommend that the plant continue to use this cheaper raw material? If so, what standards would likely need revision to reflect this decision? Assume that the end product's quality is not significantly affected.

4. Prepare all possible journal entries.

CASES

OBJECTIVE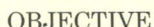

Case 20-49 Establishment of Standards, Variance Analysis

Paul Golding and his wife, Nancy, established Crunchy Chips in 1938. Over the past 60 years, the company has established distribution channels in 11 western states, with production facilities in Utah, New Mexico, and Colorado. In 1980, Paul's son, Edward, took control of the business. By 2011, it was clear that the company's plants needed to gain better control over production costs to stay competitive. Edward hired a consultant to install a standard costing system. To help the consultant establish the necessary standards, Edward sent her the following memo:

To:	Diana Craig, Certified Management Accountant
From:	Edward Golding, President, Crunchy Chips
Subject:	Description and Data Relating to the Production of Our Plain Potato Chips
Date:	September 28, 2011

The manufacturing process for potato chips begins when the potatoes are placed into a large vat in which they are automatically washed. After washing, the potatoes flow directly to an automatic peeler. The peeled potatoes then pass by inspectors, who manually cut out deep eyes or other blemishes. After inspection, the potatoes are automatically sliced and are dropped into the cooking oil. The frying process is closely monitored by an employee. After the chips are cooked, they pass under a salting device and then pass by more inspectors, who sort out the unacceptable finished chips (those that are discolored or too small). The chips then continue on the conveyor belt to a bagging machine that bags them in one-pound bags. After bagging, the bags are placed in a box and shipped. The box holds 15 bags.

The raw potato pieces (eyes and blemishes), peelings, and rejected finished chips are sold to animal feed producers for $0.16 per pound. The company uses this revenue to reduce the cost of potatoes; we would like this reflected in the price standard relating to potatoes.

Crunchy Chips purchases high-quality potatoes at a cost of $0.245 per pound. Each potato averages 4.25 ounces. Under efficient operating conditions, it takes four potatoes to produce one 16-ounce bag of plain chips. Although we label bags as containing 16 ounces, we actually place 16.3 ounces in each bag. We plan to continue this policy to ensure customer satisfaction. In addition to potatoes, other raw materials are the cooking oil, salt, bags, and boxes. Cooking oil costs $0.04 per ounce, and we use 3.3 ounces of oil per bag of chips. The cost of salt is so small that we add it to overhead. Bags cost $0.11 each and boxes $0.52 each.

Our plant produces 8.8 million bags of chips per year. A recent engineering study revealed that we would need the following direct labor hours to produce this quantity if our plant operates at peak efficiency:

Raw potato inspection	3,200
Finished chip inspection	12,000
Frying monitor	6,300
Boxing	16,600
Machine operators	6,300

I'm not sure that we can achieve the level of efficiency advocated by the study. In my opinion, the plant is operating efficiently for the level of output indicated if the hours allowed are about 10 percent higher.

The hourly labor rates agreed upon with the union are:

Raw potato inspectors	$15.20
Finished chip inspectors	10.30
Frying monitor	14.00
Boxing	11.00
Machine operators	13.00

Overhead is applied on the basis of direct labor dollars. We have found that variable overhead averages about 116 percent of our direct labor cost. Our fixed overhead is budgeted at $1,135,216 for the coming year.

Required:
1. Discuss the benefits of a standard costing system for Crunchy Chips.
2. Discuss the president's concern about using the result of the engineering study to set the labor standards. What standard would you recommend?
3. Form a group with two or three other students. Develop a standard cost sheet for Crunchy Chips' plain potato chips.
4. Suppose that the level of production was 8.8 million bags of potato chips for the year as planned. If 9.5 million pounds of potatoes were used, compute the materials usage variance for potatoes.

Case 20-50 Standard Costing, Ethical Behavior, Usefulness of Costing

OBJECTIVE

Pat James, the purchasing agent for a local plant of the Oakden Electronics Division, was considering the possible purchase of a component from a new supplier. The component's purchase price, $0.90, compared favorably with the standard price of $1.10. Given the quantity that would be purchased, Pat knew that the favorable price variance would help to offset an unfavorable variance for another component. By offsetting the unfavorable variance, his overall performance report would be impressive and good enough to help him qualify for the annual bonus. More importantly, a good performance rating this year would help him to secure a position at division headquarters at a significant salary increase.

Purchase of the part, however, presented Pat with a dilemma. Consistent with his past behavior, Pat made inquiries regarding the reliability of the new supplier and the part's quality. Reports were basically negative. The supplier had a reputation for making the first two or three deliveries on schedule but being unreliable from then on. Worse, the part itself was of questionable quality. The number of defective units was only slightly higher than that for other suppliers, but the life of the component was 25 percent less than what normal sources provided.

If the part were purchased, no problems with deliveries would surface for several months. The problem of shorter life would cause eventual customer dissatisfaction and perhaps some loss of sales, but the part would last at least 18 months after the final product began to be used. If all went well, Pat expected to be at headquarters within six months. He saw little personal risk associated with a decision to purchase the part from the new supplier. By the time any problems surfaced, they would belong to his successor. With this rationalization, Pat decided to purchase the component from the new supplier.

Required:
1. Do you agree with Pat's decision? Why or why not? How important was Pat's assessment of his personal risk in the decision? Should it be a factor?
2. Do you think that the use of standards and the practice of holding individuals accountable for their achievement played major roles in Pat's decision?
3. Review the discussion on corporate ethical standards in Chapter 13. Identify the standards that might apply to Pat's situation. Should every company adopt a set of ethical standards that apply to its employees, regardless of their specialty?
4. The usefulness of standard costing has been challenged in recent years. Some claim that its use is an impediment to the objective of continuous improvement (an objective that many feel is vital in today's competitive environment). Write a short paper (individually or in a

(Continued)

small group with two or three other students) that analyzes the role and value of standard costing in today's manufacturing environment. Address the following questions:

a. What are the major criticisms of standard costing?
b. Will standard costing disappear, or is there still a role for it in the new manufacturing environment? If so, what is the role?
c. Given the criticisms, can you explain why its use continues to be so prevalent? Will this use eventually change?

In preparing your paper, the following references may be useful; however, do not restrict your literature search to these references. They are simply to help you get started.

- Robin Cooper and Robert S. Kaplan, "Activity-Based Systems: Measuring the Costs of Resource Usage," *Accounting Horizons* (September 1992): 1–13.
- Forrest B. Green and Felix E. Amenkhienan, "Accounting Innovations: A Cross-Sectional Survey of Manufacturing Firms," *Journal of Cost Management* (Spring 1992): 59–64.
- Bruce R. Gaumnitz and Felix P. Kollaritsch, "Manufacturing Variances: Current Practice and Trends," *Journal of Cost Management* (Spring 1991): 59–64.
- Chris Guilding, Dane Lamminmaki, and Colin Drury, "Budgeting and Standard Costing Practices in New Zealand and the United Kingdom," *Journal of International Accounting, Vol.* 33, No. 5 (1998): 569–588.

MAKING THE CONNECTION

INTEGRATIVE EXERCISE

Cost System Choices, Budgeting, and Variance Analyses for Sacred Heart Hospital

Chapters	Objectives	Cornerstones
18	18-1	18-2
19	18-2	18-3
20	18-4	20-1
	19-1	20-3
	20-1	20-4
	20-3	20-5
	20-4	20-6
	20-5	

The purpose of this integrated exercise is to demonstrate how a change in the cost system's allocation base can result in significantly different reported costs for control purposes (e.g., the cost of various service lines), as well as significantly different budgeted costs for planning purposes (e.g., flexible budgets and variance analyses).

The Two Cost Systems

Sacred Heart Hospital (SHH) faces skyrocketing nursing costs, all of which relate to its two biggest nursing service lines—the Emergency Room (ER) and the Operating Room (OR). SHH's current cost system assigns total nursing costs to the ER and OR based on the number of patients serviced by each line. Total hospital annual nursing costs for these two lines are expected to equal $300,000. The table below shows expected patient volume for both lines.

Measure	ER	OR	Total
Number of patients (ER visits or OR surgeries)	1,000	1,000	2,000
Number of vital signs checks	2,000	4,000	6,000
Number of nursing hours	10,000	5,000	15,000

Required:

1. Using the current cost system, calculate the hospital-wide rate based on number of patients.

2. Calculate the amount of nursing costs that the current cost system assigns to the ER and to the OR.

3. Using the results from Requirement 2, calculate the cost per OR nursing hour under the current cost system.

After discussion with several experienced nurses, Jack Bauer (SHH's accountant) decided that assigning nursing costs to the two service lines based on the number of times that nurses must check patients' vital signs might more closely match the underlying use of costly hospital resources. Therefore, for comparative purposes, Jack decided to develop a second cost system on his computer that assigns total nursing costs to the ER and OR based on the number of times nurses check patients' vital signs. This system is referred to as the "vital-signs costing system." The earlier table also shows data for vital sign checks for lines.

4. Using the vital-signs costing system, calculate the hospital-wide rate based on the number of vital sign checks.

5. Calculate the amount of nursing costs that the vital-signs costing system assigns to the ER and to the OR.

6. Using the results from Requirement 5, calculate the cost per OR nursing hour under the vital-signs costing system.

Budgeting and Variance Analysis

In an effort to better plan for and control OR costs, SHH management asked Jack to calculate the flexible budget variance (i.e., flexible budget costs-actual costs) for OR nursing costs, including the price variance and efficiency variance that make up the flexible budget variance for OR nursing costs. Given that Jack is interested in comparing the reported costs of both systems, he decided to prepare the requested OR variance analysis for both the current cost system and the vital signs costing system. In addition, Jack chose to use each cost system's estimate of the cost per OR nursing hour as the standard cost per OR nursing hour. Jack collected the following additional information for use in preparing the flexible budget variance for both systems:

Actual number of surgeries performed = 950

Standard number of nursing hours allowed for each OR surgery = 5

Actual number of OR nursing hours used = 5,000

Actual OR nursing costs = $190,000

7. For the OR service line, use the information above and the cost per OR nursing hour under the current cost system to calculate the

   a. flexible budget variance (*Hint:* Use your answer to Requirement 3 as the standard cost per OR nursing hour for the current cost system.)
   b. price variance
   c. efficiency variance

8. For the OR service line, use the information above and the cost per OR nursing hour under the vital signs cost system to calculate the

   a. flexible budget variance (*Hint:* Use your answer to Requirement 6 as the standard cost per OR nursing hour for the vital signs cost system.)
   b. price variance
   c. efficiency variance

Discussion of Reported Costs and Variances from the Two Systems

9. Consider SHH's need to control its skyrocketing costs, Jack's discussion with experienced nurses regarding their use of hospital resources, and the reported costs that you calculated from each cost system. Based on these considerations, which cost system (current or vital signs) should Jack choose? Briefly explain the reasoning behind your choice.

10. What does each of the calculated variances suggest to Jack regarding actions that he should or should not take with respect to investigating and improving each variance? Also, briefly explain why the variances differ between the two cost systems.

21

Flexible Budgets and Overhead Analysis

Doug Norman Crystals/Alamy

After studying Chapter 21, you should be able to:

1 Prepare a flexible budget, and use it for performance reporting.

2 Calculate the variable overhead variances, and explain their meaning.

3 Calculate the fixed overhead variances, and explain their meaning.

4 Prepare an activity-based flexible budget.

© Steve Skjold/Alamy

EXPERIENCE MANAGERIAL DECISIONS

with The Second City

The Second City has been North America's premiere live improvisational and sketch comedy theater company for the past 50 years. Many famous stars began their careers at The Second City, including John Candy, Tina Fey, Mike Myers, Eugene Levy, and Bill Murray. More than just The Second City Television (SCTV), The Second City includes training centers, national touring companies, media and entertainment offshoots, and a corporate communication division. The Second City is an entrepreneurial organization, as evidenced most recently by its decision to provide comedy theater aboard Norwegian Cruise Line ships.

Given the nature of its businesses, The Second City is extremely dependent on overhead costs. These overhead costs must be allocated to each business to create accurate budgets, which is followed by variance analyses when actual overhead costs differ significantly from budgeted overhead costs. Its fixed overhead costs are associated with capacity and relate primarily to its home and resident stages in Chicago, Toronto, Las Vegas, Denver, and Detroit, rather than to its traveling shows. Examples of The Second City's fixed overhead costs include salaries, stage and other facilities rent, facilities maintenance, depreciation, taxes, and insurance. These overhead costs then are

roadk, 2010/Shutterstock.com

assigned to individual business budgets by using allocation bases such as square footage, number of employees, and percentage of earnings. The Second City then uses overhead cost variances to "red flag" potential problems that might need managerial attention.

For example, The Second City Theatricals might have a slow year because the producers are too busy with other ventures to mount a new production, while at the same time, The Second City Training Center might have a surge in enrollment. Such a scenario likely would lead The Second City financial executives to shift some assigned overhead costs from the theatrical business to the training center business. The Second City uses flexible budgets for planning and control of its businesses that experience fluctuating volumes, such as the seasonality present in some of its traveling and cruise activities. While the managerial accountants likely do not provide too many jokes, they do provide the critical function of budgeting and examining variances for overhead costs. That allows the comic talent of The Second City to continue to do what it does best—make us laugh.

The Second City

OBJECTIVE ①
Prepare a flexible budget, and use it for performance reporting.

USING BUDGETS FOR PERFORMANCE EVALUATION

Budgets are useful for both planning and control, where they are used as benchmarks for performance evaluation. Determining how budgeted amounts should be compared with actual results is a major consideration that must be addressed.

Static Budgets versus Flexible Budgets

In Chapter 19, we learned how companies prepare a master budget based on their best estimate of the level of sales and production activity for the coming year. We also discussed some behavioral issues associated with performance reporting. However, no detailed discussion was provided on how to prepare budgetary *performance reports*. A **performance report** compares actual costs with budgeted costs. There are two ways to make this comparison:

- Compare actual costs with the budgeted costs for the budgeted level of activity.
- Compare actual costs with the actual level of activity.

The first choice is a report based on *static budgets,* whereas the second choice is for a report based on *flexible budgets.* The two approaches for variance calculation are illustrated in Exhibit 21-1. Notice the relationship between the actual number of units produced (10,000) and the two types of budgets. The static budget compares actual costs for production of 10,000 units with the budgeted costs for 8,000 units. Unsurprisingly, the variance is unfavorable. The flexible budget, on the other hand, compares actual costs for production of 10,000 units with the budgeted costs for 10,000 units. This is a much more meaningful comparison.

Static Budgets and Performance Reports

A **static budget** is a budget created in advance that is based on a particular level of activity. Master budgets are generally created for a particular level of activity. Thus, one way to prepare a performance report is to compare the actual costs with the budgeted costs from the master budget. As an example, the production of Cool-U screen-printed t-shirts will be considered. In setting up the master budget for the first quarter of the year, Cool-U expected to produce 1,060 t-shirts. When the quarter had ended, Cool-U found that it had actually produced 1,200 t-shirts. **CORNERSTONE 21-1** shows how to prepare a performance report based on a static budget for the first quarter of operations for Cool-U's clothing manufacturing plant. For simplicity, the report only considers production costs.

Exhibit 21-1

The Relationship between Static and Flexible Budget Variances for the Actual Quantity Produced

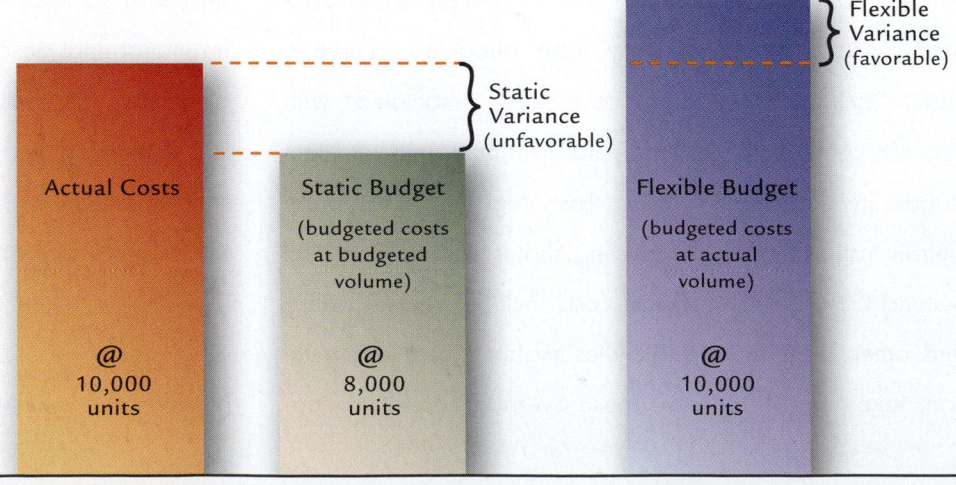

CORNERSTONE 21-1

Preparing a Performance Report Based on a Static Budget (Using Budgeted Production)

Information:

Relationships from the Master Budget	Actual Data for Quarter 1
Budgeted production for Quarter 1: 1,060	Production: 1,200 units
Materials:	
1 plain t-shirt @ $3.00	Materials cost: $4,830
5 ounces of ink @ $0.20	
Labor:	
0.12 hr. @ $10.00	Labor cost: $1,500
Variable overhead (*VOH*):	
Maintenance:	
0.12 hr. @ $3.75	Maintenance cost: $535
Power:	
0.12 hr. @ $1.25	Power cost: $170
Fixed overhead (*FOH*):	
Grounds keeping: $1,200 per quarter	Grounds keeping: $1,050
Depreciation: $600 per quarter	Depreciation: $600

Required:

Prepare a performance report using a budget based on expected production.

Solution:

	Actual	Budgeted	Variance
Units produced	1,200	1,060	140 *F*[a]
Direct materials cost	$4,830	$4,240[b]	$ 590 *U*[c]
Direct labor cost	1,500	1,272[d]	228 *U*
VOH:			
Maintenance	535	477[e]	58 *U*
Power	170	159[f]	11 *U*
FOH:			
Grounds keeping	1,050	1,200	(150) *F*
Depreciation	600	600	0
Total	$8,685	$7,948	$ 737 *U*

[a]*F* means the variance is favorable.
[b]Budgeted units (T-shirt cost + Ink cost) = 1,060[($3 + (5 oz. × $0.20)].
[c]*U* means the variance is unfavorable.
[d]Budgeted units (Number of direct labor hours × Cost per hour) + 1,060 (0.12 × $10.00).
[e]Budgeted units (Number of direct labor hours × Variable maintenance rate) = 1,060 (0.12 × $3.75).
[f]Budgeted units (Number of direct labor hours × Variable power rate) = 1,060 (0.12 × $1.25).

According to Cornerstone 21-1, there were unfavorable variances for direct materials, direct labor, maintenance, and power. However, actual costs for production of 1,200 t-shirts are being compared with planned costs for production of 1,060. Because direct materials, direct labor, and *VOH* are variable costs, they should be higher at higher production levels. Thus, even if cost control were perfect for the production of 1,200 units, unfavorable variances would be produced for at least some of the variable costs. To create a meaningful performance report, actual costs and expected costs must be compared at the *same* level of activity. Since actual output often differs from planned output, a

Concept Q&A

Why are static budgets usually not a good choice for benchmarks in preparing a performance report?

Answer:
The actual output may differ from the budgeted output, thus causing significant differences in cost. Comparing planned costs for one level of activity with the actual costs of a different level of activity does not provide good control information.

method is needed to compute what the costs should have been for the actual output level.

ETHICAL DECISIONS Companies that use static budgets as the benchmark for performance evaluation invite potential abuse by managers. Although unethical, a manager could deliberately produce less than the planned output—producing, for example, 1,000 t-shirts instead of the planned 1,060. By producing less, the actual costs will be less than the budgeted amounts, creating a favorable performance outcome. Using flexible budgeting allows the benchmark to be adjusted to reflect the expected costs for the actual level of output. ●

Flexible Budgets A **flexible budget** enables a firm to compute expected costs for a range of activity levels. The key to flexible budgeting is knowledge of fixed and variable costs. The two types of flexible budgets are:

- before-the-fact, in which the budget gives expected outcomes for a range of activity levels
- after-the-fact, in which a budget is based on the actual level of activity

A before-the-fact flexible budget allows managers to generate financial results for a number of potential scenarios. The after-the-fact flexible budget is used to compute what costs should have been for the actual level of activity. Those expected costs are then compared with the actual costs in order to assess performance. Flexible budgeting is the key to providing the frequent feedback that managers need to exercise control and effectively carry out the plans of an organization.

To illustrate a before-the-fact flexible budget, suppose that the management of Cool-U wants to know the cost of producing 1,000 t-shirts, 1,200 t-shirts, and 1,400 t-shirts. To compute the expected cost for these different levels of output, managers need to know the cost behavior pattern of each item in the budget. Knowing the variable cost per unit and the total fixed costs allows the calculation of the expected costs for any level of activity within the relevant range. **CORNERSTONE 21-2** shows how budgets can be prepared for different levels of activity, using cost formulas for each item.

CORNERSTONE 21-2

Preparing a Before-the-Fact Flexible Production Budget

Information:
Levels of output: 1,000, 1,200, and 1,400.

Materials:
    1 plain t-shirt @ $3.00
    5 ounces of ink @ $0.20 per oz.:
Labor:
    0.12 hr. @ $10.00

VOH:
    Maintenance: 0.12 hr. @ $3.75
    Power: 0.12 hr. @ $1.25
FOH:
    Grounds keeping: $1,200 per quarter
    Depreciation: $600 per quarter

Required:
Prepare a budget for three levels of output: 1,000, 1,200, and 1,400 units.

(Continued)

Solution:

CORNERSTONE 21-2 *(continued)*

Production Costs	Variable Cost per Unit	Range of Production (units) 1,000	1,200	1,400
Variable:				
Direct materials	$4.00[a]	$4,000[b]	$4,800	$5,600
Direct labor	1.20[c]	1,200[d]	1,440	1,680
VOH:				
Maintenance	0.45[e]	450[f]	540	630
Power	0.15[g]	150[h]	180	210
Total variable costs	$5.80	$5,800	$6,960	$8,120
FOH:				
Grounds keeping		$1,200	$1,200	$1,200
Depreciation		600	600	600
Total fixed costs		$1,800	$1,800	$1,800
Total production costs		$7,600	$8,760	$9,920

[a]T-shirt cost + Ink cost = [($3.00 × 1 t-shirt) × ($0.20 × 5 oz.)]
[b]($4 × 1,000 units)
[c]($10.00 per direct labor hour × 0.12 direct labor hours per unit)
[d]($1.20 × 1,000 units)
[e]($3.75 per direct labor hour × 0.12 direct labor hours per unit)
[f]($0.45 × 1,000 units)
[g]($1.25 per direct labor hour × 0.12 direct labor hours per unit)
[h]($0.15 × 1,000 units)

Cornerstone 21-2 shows that total budgeted production costs increase as the production level increases. Budgeted costs change because total variable costs go up as output increases. Because of this, flexible budgets are sometimes referred to as **variable budgets**. Since Cool-U has a mix of variable and fixed costs, the overall average cost of producing one t-shirt goes *down* as production goes *up*. This makes sense. As production increases, there are more units over which to spread the fixed production costs.

Often, the flexible budget formulas are based on direct labor hours instead of units. This is easy to do because direct labor hours are correlated with units produced. For example, the variable cost formulas for *VOH* are $3.75 and $1.25 per direct labor hour ($5.00 per direct labor hour in total) for maintenance and power, respectively. When standard hours are used, we need to convert units into direct labor hours. For Cool-U, the production of 1,000 budgeted units means that 120 direct labor hours will be needed (0.12 direct labor hours per unit × 1,000 budgeted units).

Here's the Real Kicker

Stillwater Designs has a Product Steering Committee that decides on the timing for upgrades and redesigns for its various **Kicker** speaker models. About every four years, a complete redesign is done for a Kicker speaker. A complete redesign takes about 16 to 18 months. A specification workshop is held that identifies features, benefits, customers, and competitors. Additionally, the costs of the new model, including the design costs (research and development), acquisition costs, freight, and duties, are estimated for various sales volumes. During this phase, the company will work closely with the manufacturers to control the design so that manufacturing costs are carefully set. A financial analysis is run over the expected life cycle of the new product (two to three years) to see what the profit potential is. Thus, both expected revenues and costs for various levels of activity are assessed. This before-the-fact flexible budgeting analysis is especially important for those products with which the company has less experience. At times, a new product may be produced even if at the most likely volume the product is not expected to be profitable. The reason? The new product may complete a line or may enhance the overall image of the Kicker speakers.

Flexible budgets are powerful control tools because they allow management to compute what the costs should be for the level of *output that actually occurred*. Recall that Cool-U thought that 1,060 units would be produced, and budgeted for that amount. However, actual production was 1,200 units. It does not make sense to compare the actual costs for 1,200 t-shirts to the budgeted costs for 1,060 t-shirts. Management needs a performance report that compares actual and budgeted costs for the actual level of activity. This is the second type of flexible budget and preparation of this report is shown in **CORNERSTONE 21-3**.

CORNERSTONE 21-3
Preparing a Performance Report Using a Flexible Budget

Information:
From Cornerstones 21-1 (p. 1061) and 21-2 (p. 1062), the actual costs for 1,200 units and the budgeted costs for the actual level of activity are as follows:

	Actual Costs	Budgeted Costs
Units produced	1,200	1,200
Direct materials cost	$4,830	$4,800
Direct labor cost	1,500	1,440
VOH:		
Maintenance	535	540
Power	170	180
FOH:		
Grounds keeping	1,050	1,200
Depreciation	600	600

Required:
Prepare a performance report using budgeted costs for the actual level of activity.

Solution:

	Actual	Budget	Variance
Units produced	1,200	1,200	—
Production costs:			
Direct materials	$4,830	$4,800	$ 30 U
Direct labor	1,500	1,440	60 U
VOH:			
Maintenance	535	540	(5) F
Power	170	180	(10) F
Total variable costs	$7,035	$6,960	$ 75 U
FOH:			
Grounds keeping	$1,050	$1,200	$(150) F
Depreciation	600	600	(0)
Total fixed costs	$1,650	$1,800	$(150) F
Total production costs	$8,685	$8,760	$ (75) F

The revised performance report in Cornerstone 21-3 paints a much different picture than the one in Cornerstone 21-1 (p. 1061). All of the variances are fairly small. Had they been larger, management should search for the cause and try to correct the problems.

A difference between the actual amount and the flexible budget amount is the **flexible budget variance**. The flexible budget provides a measure of the efficiency of a manager. That is, how well did the manager control costs for the actual level of production? To measure whether or not a manager accomplishes his or her goals, the static budget is used. The static budget represents certain goals that the firm wants to achieve. A manager is effective if the goals described by the static budget are achieved or exceeded. In the Cool-U example, production volume was 140 units greater than the original budgeted amount; the manager exceeded the original budgeted goal. Therefore, the effectiveness of the manager is not in question.

YOU◆DECIDE   Flexible Budgeting for Entertainment

You are the chief accountant for **The Second City**, the company described in the chapter opener. Your job includes budgeting for the live performances, including the national touring companies and the customized comedy shows put on by the company. (See http://www.secondcity.com/ for examples of the live performances.) At the beginning of each year, you must put together budgets for these performances based on projected demand for the shows and projected costs. As the year unfolds, you want to update the budgets in accordance with new information and create performance reports that compare the actual costs with projected costs.

What information will you need to create flexible budgets for the live performances?

You will need to consider the fixed and variable costs associated with putting on live performances away from **The Second City**'s Chicago base. The variable costs will include travel and salary costs for the performers, stage and facilities rent for each venue, and other variable costs associated with the shows (e.g., costs of hiring ticket sellers and ushers, supplies such as programs and tickets). Clearly, the variable costs will increase with an increase in the number of shows and venues. Some fixed costs must also be determined. These include the salaries of the writers, insurance, costs of props and costumes, costs of marketing the shows to prospective customers including corporations and regional theatres.

Knowing the difference between the fixed and variable costs will enable you to create budgets that are useful to management in planning for the year ahead, as well as controlling costs as the year unfolds.

VARIABLE OVERHEAD ANALYSIS

OBJECTIVE **2**
Calculate the variable overhead variances, and explain their meaning.

In Chapter 20, total variances for direct materials and direct labor were broken down into price and efficiency variances. In a standard cost system, the total overhead variance, or the difference between applied and actual overhead, is also broken down into component variances. There are several methods of overhead variance analysis; the four-variance method is described in this chapter. First, overhead is divided into fixed and variable categories. Next, two variances are calculated for each category.

- Variable overhead variances
  - Variable overhead spending variance
  - Variable overhead efficiency variance
- Fixed overhead variances
  - Fixed overhead spending variance
  - Fixed overhead volume variance

Total Variable Overhead Variance

The total variable overhead variance is simply the difference between the *actual variable overhead* and *applied variable overhead*. *VOH* is applied by using hours allowed in a standard cost system. The total variable overhead variance can be divided into spending and efficiency variances. Variable overhead spending and efficiency variances can be calculated by using either the three-pronged (columnar) approach or formulas. The best approach is a matter of preference. However, the formulas first need to be expressed specifically for *VOH*.

   Because the equations for variable overhead variances can be long if expressed in words, abbreviations are often used. Here are some common abbreviations that you will find in the rest of this section:

> FOH = fixed overhead
> VOH = variable overhead
> AH = actual direct labor hours
> SH = standard direct labor hours that *should have been worked* for actual units produced
> $AVOR$ = actual variable overhead rate
> $SVOR$ = standard variable overhead rate

CORNERSTONE 21-4 illustrates how to calculate the total variable overhead variance using the first quarter data for Cool-U. The unit prices and quantities used for the flexible budget are assumed to be the standards associated with Cool-U's standard cost system.

 **CORNERSTONE 21-4**   **Calculating the Total Variable Overhead Variance**

Information:

Standard variable overhead rate ($SVOR$)	$5.00 per direct labor hour
Actual variable overhead costs (AH)	$705
Standard hours allowed per unit	0.12 hour
Actual direct labor hours worked (AH)	150 hours
Actual production	1,200 units

Required:
Calculate (1) the actual variable overhead rate and (2) the total variable overhead variance.

Solution:
1. Actual variable overhead rate = Actual variable overhead cost/Actual direct labor hours
$$AVOR = \$705/150 \text{ hours}$$
$$AVOR = \$4.70$$

2.

Actual variable overhead ($AH \times AVOR$)	$705
Applied variable overhead ($SH \times SVOR$)*	720
Total variable overhead variance [($AH \times AVOR$) − ($SH \times SVOR$)]	$ (15)

*$SH \times SVOR$ = (0.12 hours per unit × 1,200 units) × $5.

Variable Overhead Spending Variance The **variable overhead spending variance** measures the aggregate effect of differences between the actual variable overhead rate ($AVOR$) and the standard variable overhead rate ($SVOR$). The actual variable overhead rate is computed as follows:

$$AVOR = \frac{\text{Actual variable overhead}}{\text{Actual hours}}$$

As shown by Cornerstone 21-4, this rate is $4.70 per hour ($705/150 AH). The formula for computing the variable overhead spending variance is:

$$\text{Variable overhead spending variance} = (AH \times AVOR) - (AH \times SVOR)$$
$$= (AVOR - SVOR) \times AH$$

Variable Overhead Efficiency Variance

VOH is assumed to vary in proportion to changes in the direct labor hours used. The **variable overhead efficiency variance** measures the change in the actual variable overhead cost (*VOH*) that occurs because of efficient (or inefficient) use of direct labor. The variable overhead efficiency variance is computed by using the following formula:

$$\text{Variable overhead efficiency variance} = (AH - SH) \times SVOR$$

CORNERSTONE 21-5 shows how to calculate the variable overhead variances for Cool-U using both a columnar and a formula approach.

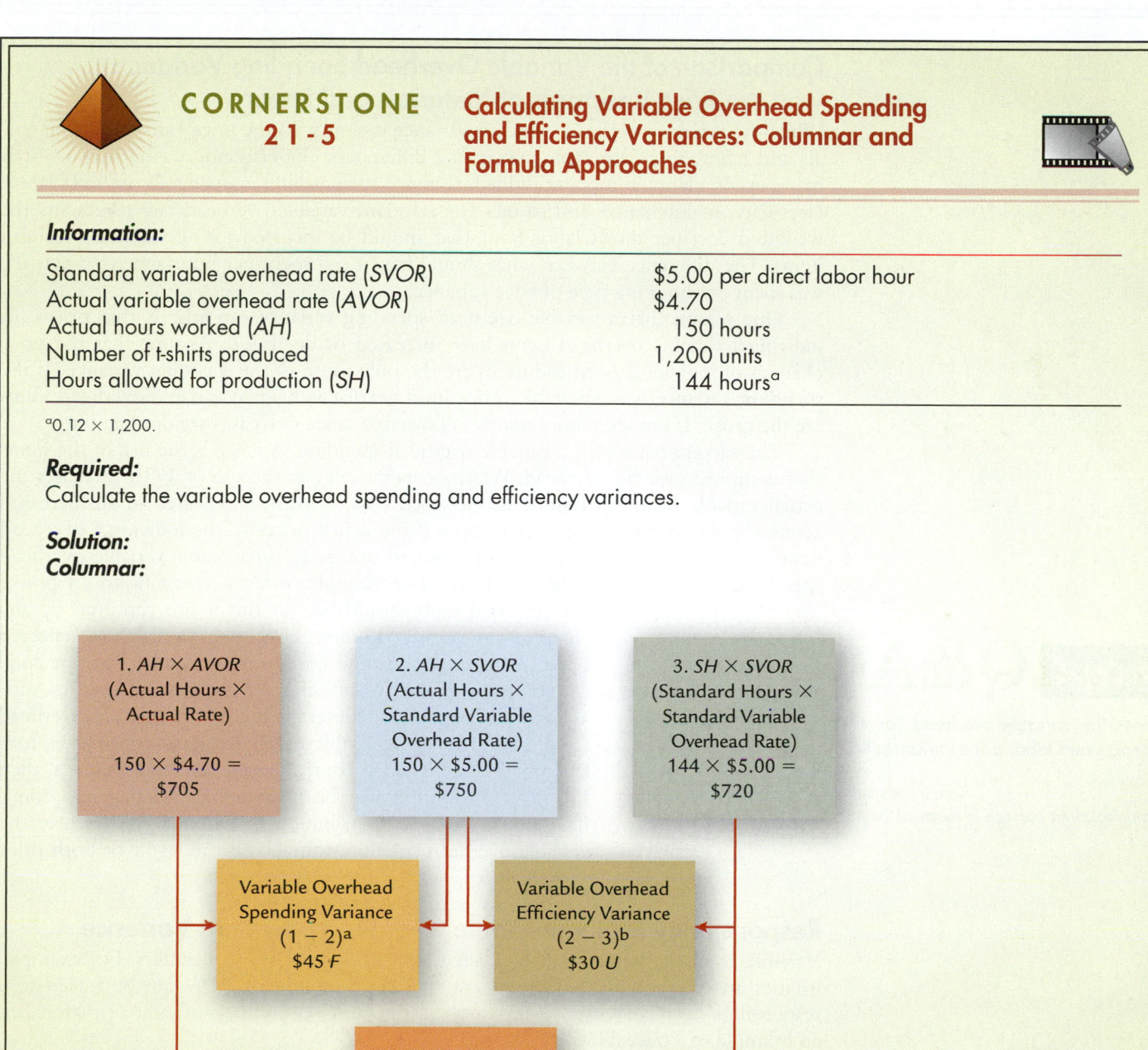

CORNERSTONE 21-5   **Calculating Variable Overhead Spending and Efficiency Variances: Columnar and Formula Approaches**

Information:

Standard variable overhead rate (*SVOR*)	$5.00 per direct labor hour
Actual variable overhead rate (*AVOR*)	$4.70
Actual hours worked (*AH*)	150 hours
Number of t-shirts produced	1,200 units
Hours allowed for production (*SH*)	144 hours[a]

[a]0.12 × 1,200.

Required:

Calculate the variable overhead spending and efficiency variances.

Solution:
Columnar:

1. *AH* × *AVOR* (Actual Hours × Actual Rate)	2. *AH* × *SVOR* (Actual Hours × Standard Variable Overhead Rate)	3. *SH* × *SVOR* (Standard Hours × Standard Variable Overhead Rate)
150 × $4.70 = $705	150 × $5.00 = $750	144 × $5.00 = $720

Variable Overhead Spending Variance (1 − 2)[a] $45 F	Variable Overhead Efficiency Variance (2 − 3)[b] $30 U

Total Variance (1 − 3) $15 F

(Continued)

Formulas:

[a]VOH spending variance $= (AVOR - SVOR) \times AH$
$= (\$4.70 - \$5.00) \times 150$
$= \$45\ F$

[b]VOH efficiency variance $= (AH - SH) \times SVOR$
$= (150 - 144) \times \$5.00$
$= \$30\ U$

CORNERSTONE 21-5
(continued)

Comparison of the Variable Overhead Spending Variance with the Price Variances of Materials and Labor

While the variable overhead spending variance is similar to the price variances of materials and labor, there are some conceptual differences. *VOH* is not a single input—it is made up of a large number of individual items, such as indirect materials, indirect labor, electricity, maintenance, and so on. The standard variable overhead rate represents the weighted cost per direct labor hour that should be incurred for all variable overhead items. The difference between what should have been spent per hour and what actually was spent per hour is a type of price variance.

One reason that a variable overhead spending variance can arise is that prices for individual variable overhead items have increased or decreased. Assume that the price changes of individual overhead items are the only cause of the spending variance. If the spending variance is unfavorable, price increases for individual variable overhead items are the cause. If the spending variance is favorable, price decreases are dominating.

The second reason for a variable overhead spending variance is the use of the items that comprise variable overhead. Waste or inefficiency in the use of *VOH* increases the actual variable overhead cost. This increased cost, in turn, is reflected in an increased actual variable overhead rate. Thus, even if the actual prices of the individual overhead items were equal to the budgeted or standard prices, an unfavorable variable overhead spending variance could still take place. For example, more kilowatt-hours of power may be used than should be, yet this is not captured by any change in direct labor hours. However, the effect is reflected by an increase in the total cost of power and, thus, the total cost of *VOH*. Similarly, efficiency can decrease the actual variable overhead cost and decrease the actual variable overhead rate. Efficient use of variable overhead items contributes to a favorable spending variance. If the waste effect dominates, then the net contribution will be unfavorable. If efficiency dominates, then the net contribution is favorable. Therefore, the variable overhead spending variance is the result of both price and efficiency.

Concept Q&A

How does the variable overhead spending variance differ from the materials and labor price variances?

Answer:
The variable overhead spending variance is affected by price changes of individual items as well as efficiency issues.

Responsibility for the Variable Overhead Spending Variance

Variable overhead items may be affected by several responsibility centers. For example, utilities are a joint cost. To the extent that consumption of *VOH* can be traced to a responsibility center, responsibility can be assigned. Consumption of indirect materials is an example of a traceable variable overhead cost.

Controllability is a prerequisite for assigning responsibility. Price changes of variable overhead items are essentially beyond the control of supervisors. If price changes are small (as they often are), then the spending variance is primarily a matter of the efficient use of overhead in production. This is controllable by production supervisors. Accordingly, responsibility for the variable overhead spending variance is generally assigned to production departments.

Responsibility for the Variable Overhead Efficiency Variance

The variable overhead efficiency variance is directly related to the direct labor efficiency or usage variance. If *VOH* is truly proportional to direct labor consumption, then like the labor usage variance, the variable overhead efficiency variance is caused by efficient or inefficient use of direct labor. If more (or fewer) direct labor hours are used than the standard calls for, then the total variable overhead cost will increase (or decrease). The validity of the measure depends on the validity of the relationship between variable overhead costs and direct labor hours. In other words, do variable overhead costs really change in proportion to changes in direct labor hours? If so, responsibility for the variable overhead efficiency variance should be assigned to the individual who has responsibility for the use of direct labor: the production manager.

Why are the labor efficiency and variable overhead efficiency variances similar in nature?

Answer:
Both depend on the difference between actual and standard direct labor hours.

A Performance Report for the Variable Overhead Spending and Efficiency Variances

Cornerstone 21-5 (p. 1067) showed a favorable $45 variable overhead spending variance and an unfavorable $30 variable overhead efficiency variance. The $45 *F* spending variance means that overall Cool-U spent less than expected on variable overhead. The reasons for the $30 unfavorable variable overhead efficiency variance are the same as those offered for an unfavorable labor usage variance. An unfavorable variance means that more hours were used than called for by the standard. Even if the total variable overhead spending and efficiency variances are insignificant, they reveal nothing about how well costs of *individual* variable overhead items were controlled. It is possible for two large variances of opposite sign to cancel each other out. Control of *VOH* requires line-by-line analysis for each item. **CORNERSTONE 21-6** shows how to prepare a performance report that supplies the line-by-line information essential for detailed analysis of the variable overhead variances.

CORNERSTONE 21-6

Preparing a Performance Report for the Variable Overhead Variances

Information:

Standard variable overhead rate (*SVOR*)	$5.00 per direct labor hour
Actual costs:	
Maintenance	$535
Power	$170
Actual hours worked (*AH*)	150 hours
Number of t-shirts produced	1,200 units
Hours allowed for production (*SH*)	144 hours[a]
Variable overhead (*VOH*):	
Maintenance	0.12 hr. @ $3.75
Power	0.12 hr. @ $1.25

[a] 0.12 × 1,200

Required:

Prepare a performance report that shows the variances on an item-by-item basis.

(Continued)

CORNERSTONE
21-6
(continued)

Solution:

Performance Report for the Quarter Ended March 31, 2011

Cost	Cost Formula[a]	Actual Costs	Budget for Actual Hours[b]	Spending Variance[c]	Budget for Standard Hours[d]	Efficiency Variance[e]
Maintenance	$3.75	$535	$562.50	$27.50 F	$540	$22.50 U
Power	1.25	170	187.50	17.50 F	180	7.50 U
Total	$5.00	$705	$750.00	$45.00 F	$720	$30.00 U

[a]Per direct labor hour.
[b]Computed using the cost formula and 150 actual hours.
[c]Spending variance = Actual costs − Budget for actual hours.
[d]Computed using the cost formula and an activity level of 144 standard hours.
[e]Efficiency variance = Budget for actual hours − Budget for standard hours.

The analysis on a line-by-line basis reveals no unusual problems such as two large individual item variances with opposite signs. No individual item variance is more than 10 percent of its budgeted amount. Thus, no single variance appears large enough to be of concern.

OBJECTIVE ❸
Calculate the fixed overhead variances, and explain their meaning.

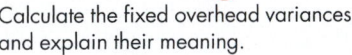

FIXED OVERHEAD ANALYSIS

Fixed overhead costs are capacity costs acquired in advance of usage. For example, **The Second City**, described in the chapter opener, has fixed overhead costs that include salaries, stage and facilities rent, depreciation, and taxes. Recall from Chapter 16 that the predetermined overhead rate is calculated at the beginning of the year by dividing budgeted overhead by the budgeted amount of the base (e.g., direct labor hours). Now, however, we need to divide that predetermined overhead rate into variable and fixed overhead rates. It was easy to find the variable overhead rate since that rate is unchanged even though the number of units produced, and thus direct labor hours, changes. However, the fixed overhead rate changes as the underlying production level changes. To keep a stable fixed overhead rate throughout the year, companies typically use practical capacity to determine the number of direct labor hours in the denominator of the fixed overhead rate.

Suppose that Cool-U can produce 1,500 t-shirts per quarter under efficient operating conditions. Practical capacity measured in standard hours (SH_p) is calculated by the following formula:

$$SH_p = \text{Unit standard} \times \text{Units of practical capacity}$$

$$= 0.12 \times 1,500$$
$$= 180 \text{ hours}$$

Recall from Cornerstone 21-2 (p. 1062) that Cool-U's total fixed costs per quarter equal $1,800. The standard fixed overhead rate ($SFOR$) is calculated as follows:

$$SFOR = \frac{\text{Budgeted fixed overhead costs}}{\text{Practical capacity}}$$

$$SFOR = \frac{\$1,800}{180}$$
$$= \$10 \text{ per direct labor hour}$$

Some firms use average or expected capacity instead of practical capacity to calculate fixed overhead rates. In this case, the standard hours used to calculate the fixed overhead rate typically will be less than the standard direct labor hours at practical capacity.

Total Fixed Overhead Variances

The total fixed overhead variance is the difference between actual fixed overhead and applied fixed overhead, when applied fixed overhead is obtained by multiplying the standard fixed overhead rate (SFOR) times the standard hours allowed for the actual output (SH). Thus, the applied fixed overhead is:

$$\text{Applied fixed overhead} = SH \times SFOR$$

The total fixed overhead variance is the difference between the actual fixed overhead and the applied fixed overhead:

$$\text{Total variance} = \text{Actual fixed overhead} - \text{Applied fixed overhead}$$

The total fixed overhead variance can be divided into spending and volume variances. Spending and volume variances can be calculated by using either the three-pronged (columnar) approach or formulas. The best approach to use is a matter of preference. However, the formulas first need to be expressed specifically for *FOH*. **CORNERSTONE 21-7** illustrates how to calculate the total fixed overhead variance for Cool-U.

CORNERSTONE 21-7   Calculating the Total Fixed Overhead Variance

Information:

Standard fixed overhead rate (SFOR)	$10.00 per direct labor hour
Actual fixed overhead costs	$1,650
Standard hours allowed per unit	0.12 hour
Actual production	1,200 units

Required:

Calculate the (1) standard hours for actual units produced, (2) total applied fixed overhead, and (3) total fixed overhead variance.

Solution:

1. SH = Actual units × Standard hours allowed per unit
    $= 1{,}200 \text{ units } \times 0.12 \text{ hour}$
    $= 144 \text{ hours}$

2. Applied fixed overhead = $SH \times SFOR$
    $= 144 \times \$10$
    $= \$1{,}440$

3.

Actual fixed overhead cost	$1,650
Applied fixed overhead	1,440
Total variance	$ 210 U

Fixed Overhead Spending Variance

The fixed overhead spending variance is defined as the difference between the actual fixed overhead (*AFOH*) and the budgeted fixed overhead (*BFOH*):

$$\text{Fixed overhead spending variance} = AFOH - BFOH$$

Fixed Overhead Volume Variance   The fixed overhead volume variance is the difference between budgeted fixed overhead ($BFOH$) and applied fixed overhead:

$$\text{Volume variance} = \text{Budgeted fixed overhead} - \text{Applied fixed overhead}$$
$$= BFOH - (SH \times SFOR)$$

The volume variance measures the effect of the actual output differing from the output used at the beginning of the year to compute the predetermined standard fixed overhead rate. If you think of the output used to calculate the fixed overhead rate as the capacity acquired (practical capacity) and the actual output as the capacity used, then the volume variance is the cost of unused capacity. **CORNERSTONE 21-8** illustrates how to calculate the fixed overhead variances using either a columnar or a formula approach.

CORNERSTONE 21-8

Calculating Fixed Overhead Variances: Columnar and Formula Approaches

Information:

Actual fixed overhead (*AH*)	$1,650
Standard fixed overhead rate (*SFOR*)	$10.00 per direct labor hour
Budgeted fixed overhead (*BFOH*)	$1,800
Number of t-shirts produced	1,200 units
Hours allowed for production (*SH*)	144 hours[a]

[a] 0.12 × 1,200.

Required:

Calculate the fixed overhead spending and volume variances.

Solution:
Columnar:

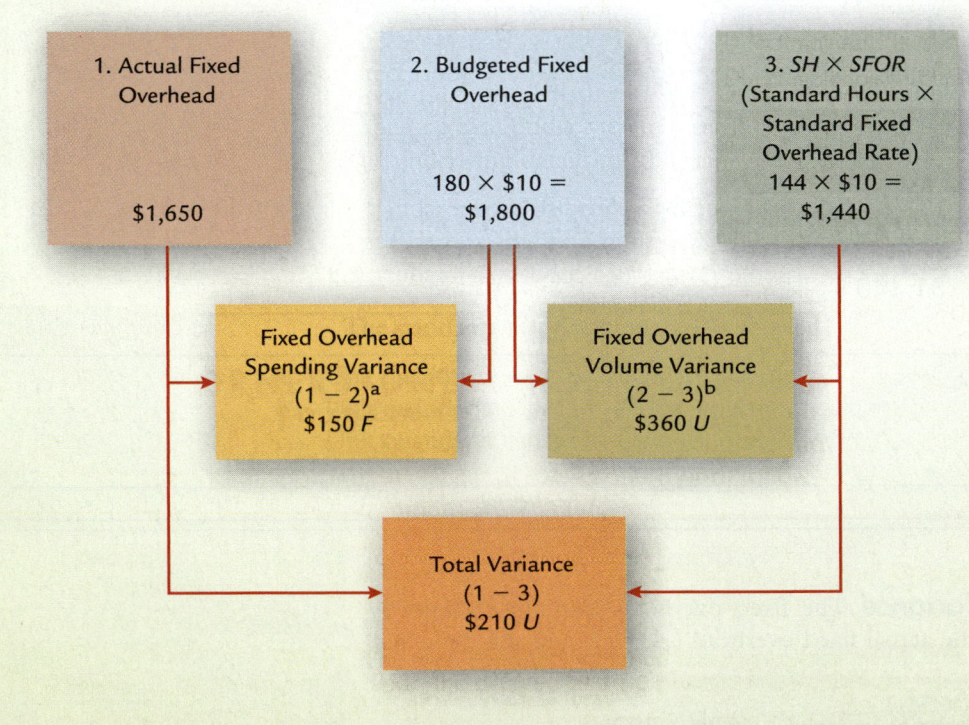

(Continued)

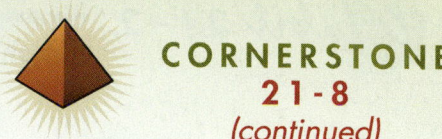

Formulas:

[a]FOH spending variance = Actual fixed overhead − Budgeted
$$\text{fixed overhead}$$
$$= \$1,650 - \$1,800$$
$$= \$150 \ F$$

[b]FOH volume variance = Budgeted fixed overhead − Applied fixed overhead
$$= BFOH - (SH \times SFOR)$$
$$= \$1,800 - (144 \times \$10)$$
$$= \$1,800 - \$1,440$$
$$= \$360 \ U$$

**CORNERSTONE
21-8
(continued)**

Responsibility for the Fixed Overhead Spending Variance

FOH is made up of items such as salaries, depreciation, taxes, and insurance. Many fixed overhead items—long-run investments, for instance—cannot be changed in the short run. Consequently, fixed overhead costs are often beyond the immediate control of management. Since many fixed overhead costs are affected primarily by long-run decisions, and not by changes in production levels, the budget variance is usually small. For example, actual depreciation, salaries, taxes, and insurance costs are not likely to be much different from planned costs.

Analysis of the Fixed Overhead Spending Variance

Because *FOH* is made up of many individual items, a line-by-line comparison of budgeted costs with actual costs provides more information concerning the causes of the spending variance. The *FOH* section of Cornerstone 21-3 (p. 1064) provides such a report. The report reveals that the fixed overhead spending variance is out of line with expectations. Less was spent on grounds keeping than expected. In fact, the entire spending variance is attributable to this one item. Since the amount is more than 10 percent of budget, it merits investigation. An investigation, for example, might reveal that the weather was especially wet and thus reduced the cost of watering for the period involved. In this case, no action is needed, as a natural correction would be forthcoming.

Responsibility for the Fixed Overhead Volume Variance

Assuming that volume variance measures capacity utilization implies that the general responsibility for this variance should be assigned to the production department. At times, however, a significant volume variance may be due to factors beyond the control of production. For example, if the purchasing department buys lower-quality raw materials than usual, significant rework time may result. This will cause lower production and an unfavorable volume variance. In this case, responsibility for the variance rests with purchasing, not production.

Analysis of the Volume Variance

The $360 *U* variance (Cornerstone 21-8) occurs because the production capacity is 180 hours and only 144 hours should have been used. Why the company failed to use all of its capacity is not known. Given that unused capacity is about 20 percent of the total, investigation seems merited. Exhibit 21-2 graphically illustrates the volume variance. Notice that the volume variance occurs because fixed overhead is treated as if it were a variable cost. In reality, fixed costs do not change as activity changes, as a predetermined fixed overhead rate allows.

Exhibit 21-2

Graphical Analysis of the Volume Variance

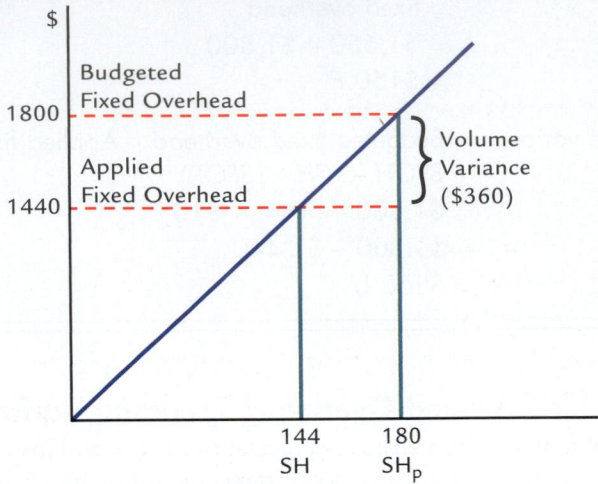

OBJECTIVE 4

Prepare an activity-based flexible budget.

ACTIVITY-BASED BUDGETING

The traditional approach to budgeting (explained in Chapter 19) emphasizes:

- estimation of revenues and costs by organizational units (e.g., departments, plants)
- use of a single unit-based driver such as direct labor hours

Companies that have implemented an activity-based costing (ABC) system may also wish to install an *activity-based budgeting system*. An **activity-based budgeting (ABB) system** focuses on:

- estimation of the costs of activities rather than the costs of departments and plants
- use of multiple drivers, both unit-based and nonunit-based

The ABB approach supports continuous improvement and process management. Because activities consume resources (which cause cost), ABB can be used to reduce cost through the elimination of wasteful activities and improving the efficiency of necessary activities.

Static Activity Budgets

Assuming that activity-based costing (ABC) has been implemented, the major emphasis for ABB is estimating the workload (demand) for each activity and then determining the resources required for this workload. The workload for each activity must be set to support the sales and production activities expected for the coming period.

As with traditional budgeting, ABB begins with sales and production budgets. Direct materials and direct labor budgets are also compatible with an activity-based costing framework because these inputs can be directly traced to the individual products. The major differences between traditional and ABB are found in the overhead and selling and administration categories. In a traditional-based approach, budgets within these categories are typically detailed by cost categories. These cost categories are classified as variable or fixed, using production or sales output measures as the basis for determining cost behavior. Furthermore, traditional budgets are usually constructed by budgeting for a cost item within a department and then rolling these items up into the master overhead budget. For example, the cost of supervision in an overhead budget is the sum of all the supervision costs of the various departments. ABB, on the other hand, identifies the overhead, selling, and administrative *activities* and then builds a budget for each activity, based on the resources needed to provide the required output levels. Costs are classified as variable or fixed with respect to the *activity* output measure or driver.

Concept Q&A

What are the main differences between ABB and traditional budgeting?

Answer:
ABB differs primarily with overhead and selling and administrative budgets. ABB builds a budget for each activity based on the demands of the activity for resources. Traditional budgeting focuses on cost items required by organizational units such as departments.

Consider, for example, purchasing materials. The demand for this activity is based on the materials requirements for the various products and services produced. An activity driver, such as number of purchase orders, measures the output demanded. **CORNERSTONE 21-9** illustrates how to prepare a budget at the activity level for the purchasing activity.

CORNERSTONE 21-9   Preparing a Static Budget for an Activity

Information:

1. Demand for purchase orders based on materials requirements: 15,000 purchase orders.
2. Resources needed:
    a. Five purchasing agents, each capable of processing 3,000 orders per year; salary, $40,000 each
    b. Supplies (forms, paper, stamps, envelopes, etc.); projected to cost $1.00 per purchase order
    c. Desks and computers; depreciation $5,000 per year
    d. Office space, rent, and utilities, $6,000

Required:
Prepare a budget for the purchasing activity.

Solution:
Purchasing budget:

Salaries	$200,000
Supplies	15,000
Depreciation	5,000
Occupancy	6,000
Total	$226,000

For the purchasing activity in Cornerstone 21-9, Supplies is a variable cost, and the other resources are fixed costs (a step-fixed cost behavior in the case of salaries and depreciation). However, one important difference should be mentioned: Fixed and variable purchasing costs are defined with respect to the *number of purchase orders* and not direct labor hours or units produced or other measures of production output. In budgeting at the activity level, the cost behavior of each activity is defined with respect to *its own* output measure. Knowing the output measure helps control activity costs by controlling the underlying activities. For example, by redesigning products so that they use more common components, the number of purchase orders can be decreased. Decreasing the number of purchase orders reduces the use of resources used by the Purchasing Department. Furthermore, decreasing the number of purchase orders demanded reduces the activity capacity needed. Thus, activity costs will decrease.

Activity Flexible Budgeting

Understanding the relationship between changes in activity costs and changes in activity drivers allows managers to more carefully plan and monitor activity improvements. **Activity flexible budgeting** is the prediction of what activity costs will be as related output changes. Variance analysis within an activity framework makes it possible to improve traditional budgetary performance reporting, and enhances the ability to manage activities.

Why does activity-based flexible budgeting provide a more accurate prediction of costs?

In a traditional-based approach, budgeted costs for the actual level of activity are obtained by assuming that a single unit-based driver (e.g., units of product or direct labor hours) drives all costs. A cost formula is developed for each cost item as a function of units produced or direct labor hours. Cornerstone 21-2 (p. 1062) illustrated a traditional flexible budget for production based on direct labor hours. If, however, costs vary with respect to more than one driver, and the drivers are not highly correlated with direct labor hours, then the predicted costs can be misleading.

The solution is to build flexible budget formulas for more than one driver. Cost estimation procedures (high-low method, the method of least squares, and so on) can be used to estimate cost formulas for each activity. This multiple-formula approach allows managers to predict more accurately what costs should be for different levels of activity, as measured by the drivers. These costs can then be compared with the actual costs to help assess budgetary performance. **CORNERSTONE 21-10** illustrates how to prepare an activity flexible budget. Notice that flexible budgets are computed for *each driver*.

CORNERSTONE 21-10   Preparing an Activity Flexible Budget

Information:
Information on four overhead activities for Kellman Company is given below.

Activity	Driver	Fixed Cost	Variable Rate
Maintenance	Machine hours	$ 20,000	$ 5.50
Machining	Machine hours	15,000	2.00
Setting up	Setups	—	1,800
Inspection	Setups	80,000	2,100
Purchasing	Purchase Orders	211,000	1.00

Required:
Prepare an activity-based flexible budget for the following production levels:

Driver	32,000 units	64,000 units
Machine hours	8,000	16,000
Setups	25	30
Purchase orders	15,000	25,000

Solution:
Steps in forming the activity-based flexible budget include:

1. Set up a table showing the activities under their related driver.
2. Calculate total activity cost by multiplying the variable rate times the driver level and adding the fixed amount. For example, at 8,000 machine hours,

$$\text{Maintenance} = \$20,000 + (\$5.50 \times 8,000 \text{ machine hours}) = \$64,000$$

And at 16,000 machine hours,

$$\text{Maintenance} = \$20,000 + (\$5.50 \times 16,000 \text{ machine hours}) = \$108,000$$

(Continued)

			Required for	
			32,000 units	64,000 units
Driver: Machine Hours				
	Fixed	Variable	8,000	16,000
Maintenance	$20,000	$5.50	$64,000	$108,000
Machining	15,000	2.00	31,000	47,000
Subtotal	$35,000	$7.50	$95,000	$155,000
Driver: Number of Setups				
	Fixed	Variable	25	30
Setups	$ —	$1,800	$ 45,000	$ 54,000
Inspections	80,000	2,100	132,500	143,000
Subtotal	$80,000	$3,900	$177,500	$197,000
Driver: Number of Purchase Orders				
	Fixed	Variable	15,000	25,000
Purchasing	$211,000	$1.00	$226,000	$236,000
Total			$498,500	$588,000

CORNERSTONE 21-10 (continued)

The flexible budget shown in Cornerstone 21-10 will be more accurate than one based on just a single unit-based driver. This will also give managers information that can be used in cost control because they can see what effect an increase or decrease in each driver has on total cost.

An activity-based performance report is shown in **CORNERSTONE 21-11**. It compares the budgeted costs for the actual activity usage levels with the actual costs.

CORNERSTONE 21-11   Preparing an Activity-Based Performance Report

Information:
Actual activity level is the first one for each activity listed in Cornerstone 21-10. For example, budgeted costs for maintenance would be based on 8,000 machine hours and would equal $64,000.

Actual costs:

Maintenance	$ 55,000	Setups	$ 46,500
Machining	29,000	Purchasing	220,000
Inspections	125,500		

Required:
Prepare an activity-based performance report.

Solution:
Note: For this performance report, just input the actual costs as given above. Then input the budgeted costs for the activity levels required. The budget variance is the difference between the actual costs and the budgeted costs. If actual costs are greater than budgeted costs, the budget variance is unfavorable (U). If actual costs are less than budgeted costs, the budget variance is favorable (F).

(Continued)

	Actual Costs	Budgeted Costs	Budget Variance	
Maintenance	$ 55,000	$ 64,000	$ 9,000 F	**CORNERSTONE 21-11** (continued)
Machining	29,000	31,000	2,000 F	
Inspections	125,500	132,500	7,000 F	
Setups	46,500	45,000	1,500 U	
Purchases	220,000	226,000	6,000 F	
Total	$476,000	$498,500	$22,500 F	

Looking at Cornerstone 21-11, we see that the variances for the five items are mixed. The net outcome is a favorable variance of $22,500. The preparation of the activity-based performance report follows the pattern and approach of the traditional report shown in Cornerstone 21-3 (p. 1064). The difference is that the comparison is for *each* activity.

One can also compare the actual fixed activity costs with the budgeted fixed activity costs and the actual variable activity costs with the budgeted variable costs. For example, assume that the actual fixed inspection costs are $82,000 (due to a midyear salary adjustment, reflecting a more favorable union agreement than anticipated) and that the actual variable inspection costs are $43,500. The variable and fixed budget variances for the inspection activity are computed as follows:

Activity	Actual Cost	Budgeted Cost	Variance
Inspection			
Fixed	$ 82,000	$ 80,000	$2,000 U
Variable	43,500	52,500	9,000 F
Total	$125,500	$132,500	$7,000 F

Breaking each variance into fixed and variable components provides more insight into the source of the variation in planned and actual expenditures.

YOU◆DECIDE   Activity Flexible Budgeting for Museums

Museums do much more than simply present art to the public. Today's art museums put on shows, provide access to the public to view the collections, sell art-related merchandise in the museum store and online, and may put on special events and performances. The annual budget for a museum can easily run into millions of dollars, so cost understanding and control are crucial.[1] As an accountant for a large metropolitan museum, you would be responsible for budgeting and controlling costs. Splitting costs into fixed and variable components would be a first step in budgeting. However, what driver would you use? Number of patrons going through the museum? That would be a good driver for a few costs, especially those related to printing tickets and explanatory materials (such as maps of the museum to help people navigate through the collections). However, the vast majority of costs would be fixed with respect to the number of people going through the museum. ABC and budgeting would give a much richer view of the costs of running the various activities of the museum.

What type of information would you need to create activity-based budgets?

Your first step would be to determine the various activities of the museum. These might include: providing access to the public, selling merchandise through the museum store, putting on special events (e.g., concerts, lectures, benefits), acquiring and cataloging pieces of art, and so on. For example, the activity of cataloguing new art pieces would include the salaries of staff who catalog the pieces, or clean and restore them, insurance on the art, and so on. Many of these costs vary with the number of newly donated or purchased pieces. The activity of selling merchandise would have costs of staff to run the store, cost of the items purchased for sale, advertising, and so on. Those costs might vary with the number of items sold or with the revenue earned. Putting on special events would have a different set of costs attached and those might vary with the number of events and the number of attendees.

Recognizing the different activities associated with the museum and relating the costs to specific activity drivers will give you a much better idea of what costs to expect. This understanding can help the museum director exercise good stewardship of the funds donated and provide important services to the public.

[1] The newly opened National Museum of 21st Century Arts in Rome (dubbed the ''Maxxi'') has an annual operating budget of 9 million euros (about $11 million). Kelly Crow, ''Rome turns to the art of today,'' *The Wall Street Journal*, May 21, 2010. http://online.wsj.com/article/SB10001424052748703691804575254362971810080.html

SUMMARY OF LEARNING OBJECTIVES

LO1.   Prepare a flexible budget, and use it for performance reporting.
- Static budgets provide expected cost for a given level of activity. If the actual level of activity differs from the static budget level, then comparing actual costs with budgeted costs does not make sense. The solution is flexible budgeting.
- Flexible budgets divide costs into those that vary with units of production (or direct labor hours) and those that are fixed with respect to unit-level drivers. These relationships allow the identification of a cost formula for each item in the budget.
- Cost formulas calculate expected costs for various levels of activity. There are two applications of flexible budgets: before-the-fact and after-the-fact.
  - Before-the-fact applications allow managers to see what costs will be for different levels of activity, thus helping in planning.
  - After-the-fact applications allow managers to see what the cost should have been for the actual level of activity. Knowing these after-the-fact expected or budgeted costs provides the opportunity to evaluate efficiency by comparing actual costs with budgeted costs.

LO2.   Calculate the variable overhead variances, and explain their meaning.
- Overhead costs are often a significant proportion of budget costs.
- Comparing actual variable and fixed overhead costs with applied overhead costs yields a total overhead variance.
- In a standard cost system, it is possible to break down overhead variances into component variances.
- For variable overhead, the two component variances are the spending variance and the efficiency variance.
- The spending variance is the result of comparing the actual costs with budgeted costs.
- The variable overhead efficiency variance is the result of efficient or inefficient use of labor because variable overhead is assumed to vary with direct labor hours.

LO3.   Calculate the fixed overhead variances, and explain their meaning.
- For fixed overhead, the two component variances are the spending variance and the volume variance.
- The spending variance is the result of comparing the actual costs with budgeted costs.
- The fixed overhead volume variance is the result of producing a level different than that used to calculate the predetermined fixed overhead rate. It can be interpreted as a measure of capacity utilization.

LO4.   Prepare an activity-based flexible budget.
- Activity-based budgeting is done at the activity level.
  - First, demand for products is assessed.
  - Next, the level of activity output needed to support the expected production level is estimated.
  - Finally, the resources needed to support the required activity output are estimated. This then becomes the activity budget.
- Activity flexible budgets differ from traditional flexible budgets because the cost formulas are based on the activity drivers for the respective activities rather than being based only on a single unit-based driver, such as direct labor hours.

SUMMARY OF IMPORTANT EQUATIONS

Abbreviations:

FOH = fixed overhead
VOH = variable overhead
AH = actual direct labor hours
SH = standard direct labor hours that *should have been worked* for actual units produced
$AVOR$ = actual variable overhead rate
$SVOR$ = standard variable overhead rate

1. $AVOR = \dfrac{\text{Actual variable overhead}}{\text{Actual hours}}$

2. Variable overhead spending variance $= (AH \times AVOR) - (AH \times SVOR)$
$$= (AVOR - SVOR) \times AH$$

3. Variable overhead efficiency variance $= (AH - SH) \times SVOR$

4. SH_p = Unit standard $\times$ Units of practical capacity

5. $SFOR = \dfrac{\text{Budgeted fixed overhead costs}}{\text{Practical capacity}}$

6. Applied fixed overhead $= SH \times SFOR$

7. Total variance = Actual fixed overhead − Applied fixed overhead

8. Fixed overhead spending variance $= AFOH - BFOH$

9. Volume variance = Budgeted fixed overhead − Applied fixed overhead
$$= BFOH - (SH \times SFOR)$$

CORNERSTONES FOR CHAPTER 21

KEY TERMS

REVIEW PROBLEMS

I. Flexible Budgeting

Trina Hoyt, controller of Ferrel Company wants to prepare a quarterly budget for three different levels of output (measured in units): 2,000, 2,500, and 3,000.

The product uses the following inputs:

Materials:
   Three pounds of plastic @ $6.00
   4 ounces of metal @ $2.00
Labor:
   0.5 hr. @ $10.00

VOH:
   Inspection: 0.2 hr. @ $10
   Machining: 0.3 hr. @ $5
FOH:
   Rent: $15,000 per quarter
   Utilities: $3,000 per quarter

Required:
Prepare a budget for three levels of output: 2,000, 2,500, and 3,000 units.

Solution:

Production Costs	Variable Cost per Unit	Range of Production (units)		
		2,000	2,500	3,000
Variable:				
Direct materials	$26.00ª	$52,000ᵇ	$ 65,000	$ 78,000
Direct labor	5.00ᶜ	10,000ᵈ	12,500	15,000
VOH:				
Inspection	2.00ᵉ	4,000ᶠ	5,000	6,000
Machining	1.50ᵍ	3,000ʰ	3,750	4,500
Total variable costs	$34.50	$69,000	$ 86,250	$103,500
FOH:				
Rent		$15,000	$ 15,000	$ 15,000
Utilities		3,000	3,000	3,000
Total fixed costs		$18,000	$ 18,000	$ 18,000
Total production costs		$87,000	$104,250	$121,500

ª(3 × $6.00) + (4 × $2.00)
ᵇ($26 × 2,000)
ᶜ(0.50 × $10.00)
ᵈ($5 × 2,000)
ᵉ(0.20 × $10)
ᶠ($2 × 2,000)
ᵍ(0.30 × $5.00)
ʰ($1.50 × 2,000)

II. Overhead Variances

Klemmens Manufacturing has the following standard cost sheet for one of its products:

Direct materials (2 ft. @ $5)	$10
Direct labor (0.5 hr. @ $10)	5
Fixed overhead (0.5 hr. @ $2)*	1
Variable overhead (0.5 hr. @ $4)	2
Standard unit cost	$18

*Rate based on budgeted fixed overhead of $5,000 and expected activity of 2,500 direct labor hours.

During the most recent year, the following actual results were recorded:

Production	6,000 units
Direct materials (11,750 ft. purchased and used)	$61,100
Direct labor (2,900 hrs.)	29,580
FOH	6,000
VOH	10,500

Required:
Compute the following variances for Klemmens Manufacturing:
1. Variable overhead spending and efficiency variances
2. Fixed overhead spending and volume variances

(Continued)

Solution:

1. Variable overhead variances:

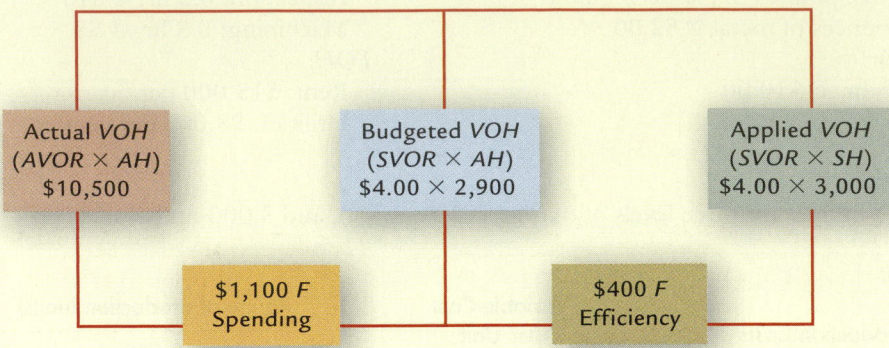

2. Fixed overhead variances:

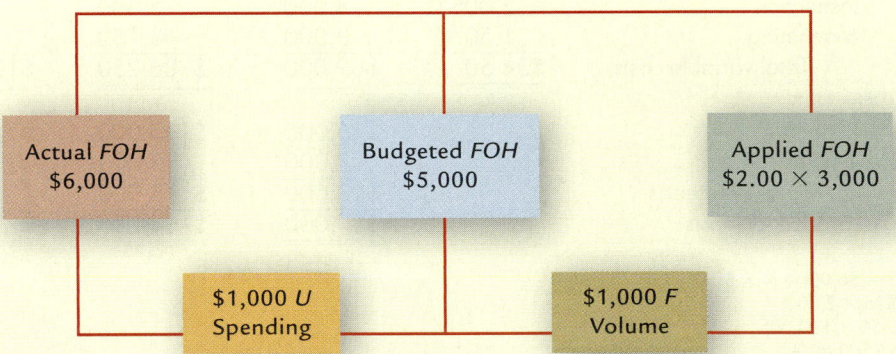

DISCUSSION QUESTIONS

1. Discuss the differences between static and flexible budgets.
2. Why are flexible budgets superior to static budgets for performance reporting?
3. Explain why mixed costs must be broken down into their fixed and variable components before a flexible budget can be developed.
4. What is the purpose of a before-the-fact flexible budget?
5. What is the purpose of an after-the-fact flexible budget?
6. Explain why the variable overhead spending variance is not a pure price variance.
7. The variable overhead efficiency variance has nothing to do with efficient use of variable overhead. Do you agree or disagree? Why?
8. Describe the difference between the variable overhead efficiency variance and the labor efficiency variance.
9. Explain why the fixed overhead spending variance is usually very small.
10. What is the cause of an unfavorable volume variance?
11. Does the volume variance convey any meaningful information to managers?
12. Which do you think is more important for control of fixed overhead costs: the spending variance or the volume variance? Explain.
13. Explain how an activity-based budget is prepared.
14. What is the difference between an activity flexible budget and a traditional-based flexible budget?
15. Why would an activity-based performance report be more accurate than a report based on a traditional flexible budget?

MULTIPLE-CHOICE EXERCISES

21-1 For performance reporting, it is best to compare actual costs with budgeted costs using

a. short-term budgets.
b. static budgets.
c. master budgets.
d. flexible budgets.
e. none of these.

21-2 To create a meaningful performance report, actual costs and expected costs should be compared

a. at the actual level of activity.
b. weekly.
c. at the budgeted level of activity.
d. at the average level of activity.
e. hourly.

21-3 To help deal with uncertainty, managers should use

a. an after-the-fact flexible budget.
b. a before-the-fact flexible budget.
c. a static budget.
d. a master budget.
e. none of these.

21-4 To help assess performance, managers should use

a. a static budget.
b. a master budget.
c. a continuous budget.
d. a before-the-fact flexible budget.
e. none of these.

21-5 A firm comparing the actual variable costs of producing 10,000 units with the total variable costs of a static budget based on 9,000 units would probably see

a. no variances.
b. small favorable variances.
c. large unfavorable variances.
d. large favorable variances.
e. small unfavorable variances.

21-6 The total variable overhead variance is the difference between

a. the budgeted variable overhead and the actual variable overhead.
b. the actual variable overhead and the applied variable overhead.
c. the budgeted variable overhead and the applied variable overhead.
d. the applied variable overhead and the budgeted total overhead.
e. none of the above.

21-7 A variable overhead spending variance can occur because

a. prices for individual overhead items have increased.
b. prices for individual overhead items have decreased.
c. more of an individual overhead item was used than expected.
d. less of an individual overhead item was used than expected.
e. of all of the above.

21-8 Because the calculation of both variances is based on direct labor hours, an unfavorable labor efficiency variance implies that

a. the variable overhead efficiency variance will be favorable.
b. the variable overhead efficiency variance will also be unfavorable.
c. there will be no variable overhead efficiency variance.
d. the variable overhead spending variance will be unfavorable.
e. the variable overhead is overapplied.

21-9 The total variable overhead variance can be expressed as the sum of

a. the underapplied variable overhead and the spending variance.
b. the efficiency variance and the overapplied variable overhead.
c. the spending, efficiency, and volume variances.
d. the spending and efficiency variances.
e. none of these.

21-10 In a performance report that details the spending and efficiency variances, which of the following columns will be found?

a. A cost formula for each item
b. A budget for actual hours for each item
c. A budget of standard hours for each item
d. All of these
e. Only a and b

21-11 The total fixed overhead variance is

a. the difference between actual and applied fixed overhead costs.
b. the difference between budgeted and applied fixed overhead costs.
c. the difference between budgeted fixed and variable overhead costs.
d. the difference between actual and budgeted fixed overhead costs.
e. none of the above.

21-12 The total fixed overhead variance can be expressed as the sum of

a. the spending and efficiency variances.
b. the efficiency and volume variances.
c. the spending and volume variances.
d. the flexible budget and the volume variances.
e. none of these.

21-13 Because of the nature of fixed overhead items, the difference between the actual fixed overhead cost and the budgeted fixed overhead is

a. likely to be small.
b. likely to be large.
c. usually a major concern.
d. often attributable to labor inefficiency.
e. none of these.

21-14 A favorable volume variance can occur because

a. too much finished goods inventory was held.
b. the company overproduced.
c. the actual output was less than expected or practical capacity.
d. the actual output was greater than expected or practical capacity.
e. of all of the above.

21-15 Responsibility for the volume variance usually is assigned to

a. the manufacturing department.
b. the receiving department.
c. the shipping department.
d. the purchasing department.
e. none of these.

21-16 In activity-based budgeting, costs are classified as variable or fixed with respect to

a. only the units budgeted.
b. only the units produced.
c. only the units sold.
d. only the direct labor hours.
e. none of these.

21-17 Activity flexible budgeting makes it possible to

a. predict what activity costs will be as activity output changes.
b. improve traditional budgetary performance reporting.
c. enhance the ability to manage activities.
d. do all these.
e. do only a and c.

21-18 In activity-based budgeting, flexible budget formulas are created using

a. only unit-level drivers.
b. only nonunit-level drivers.
c. both unit-level and nonunit-level drivers.
d. only direct labor hours.
e. all of these.

CORNERSTONE EXERCISES

Cornerstone Exercise 21-19 Performance Report

OBJECTIVE ▶ 1
CORNERSTONE 21-1

Bowling Company provided the following information for last year.

	Master Budget	Actual Data
Budgeted production 4,000		3,800 units
Direct materials:		
3 pounds @ $0.60 per pound		$ 6,800
Direct labor:		
0.5 hr. @ $16.00 per hour		30,500
VOH:		
0.5 hr. @ $2.20		4,200
FOH:		
Materials handling, $6,200		6,300
Depreciation, $2,600		2,600

Required:

1. Calculate the budgeted amounts for each cost category listed above for the 4,000 budgeted units.
2. Prepare a performance report using a budget based on expected production.

Cornerstone Exercise 21-20 Flexible Budget with Different Levels of Production

OBJECTIVE ▶ 1
CORNERSTONE 21-2

Bowling Company budgeted the following amounts:

Variable costs of production:	
Direct materials	3 pounds @ $0.60 per pound
Direct labor	0.5 hr. @ $16.00 per hour
VOH	0.5 hr. @ $2.20
FOH:	
Materials handling	$6,200
Depreciation	$2,600

Required:

Prepare a flexible budget for 2,500 units, 3,000 units, and 3,500 units.

Cornerstone Exercise 21-21 Performance Report

OBJECTIVE ▶ 1
CORNERSTONE 21-3

Bowling Company budgeted the following amounts:

Variable costs of production:	
Direct materials	3 pounds @ $0.60 per pound
Direct labor	0.5 hr. @ $16.00 per hour
VOH	0.5 hr. @ $2.20
FOH:	
Materials handling	$6,200
Depreciation	$2,600

At the end of the year, Bowling had the following actual costs for production of 3,800 units:

Direct materials	$ 6,800
Direct labor	30,500
VOH	4,200
FOH:	
Materials handling	6,300
Depreciation	2,600

Required:

Prepare a performance report using a budget based on the actual level of production.

OBJECTIVE ❷
CORNERSTONE 21-4

Cornerstone Exercise 21-22 Total Variable Overhead Variance

Aretha Company showed the following information for the year:

Standard variable overhead rate (*SVOR*) per direct labor hour	$3.70
Standard hours (*SH*) allowed per unit	4
Actual production	14,000
Actual variable overhead costs	$206,816
Actual direct labor hours	56,200

Required:
1. Calculate the actual variable overhead rate (*AVOR*).
2. Calculate the applied variable overhead.
3. Calculate the total variable overhead variance.

OBJECTIVE ❷
CORNERSTONE 21-5

Cornerstone Exercise 21-23 Variable Overhead Spending and Efficiency Variances, Columnar and Formula Approaches

Gladys Company provided the following information:

Standard variable overhead rate (*SVOR*) per direct labor hour	$3.70
Actual variable overhead rate (*AVOR*) per direct labor hour	$3.68
Actual direct labor hours worked (*AH*)	56,200
Actual production in units	14,000
Standard hours (*SH*) allowed for actual units produced	56,000

Required:
1. Using the columnar approach, calculate the variable overhead spending and efficiency variances.
2. Using the formula approach, calculate the variable overhead spending variance.
3. Using the formula approach, calculate the variable overhead efficiency variance.
4. Calculate the total variable overhead variance.

OBJECTIVE ❷
CORNERSTONE 21-6

Cornerstone Exercise 21-24 Performance Report for Variable Variances

Smokey Company provided the following information:

Standard variable overhead rate (*SVOR*) per direct labor hour	$3.70
Actual variable overhead costs:	
Inspection	$112,300
Power	$95,600
Actual direct labor hours worked (*AH*)	56,200
Actual production in units	14,000
Standard hours (*SH*) allowed for actual units produced	56,000
VOH:	
Inspection	4 hours @ $2.00
Power	4 hours @ $1.70

Required:
Prepare a performance report that shows the variances for each variable overhead item (inspection and power).

OBJECTIVE ❸
CORNERSTONE 21-7

Cornerstone Exercise 21-25 Total Fixed Overhead Variance

Ross Company provided the following data:

Standard fixed overhead rate (*SFOR*)	$5 per direct labor hour
Actual fixed overhead costs	$281,680
Standard hours allowed per unit	4 hours
Actual production	14,000 units

Required:
1. Calculate the standard hours allowed for actual production.
2. Calculate the applied fixed overhead.
3. Calculate the total fixed overhead variance.

Cornerstone Exercise 21-26 Fixed Overhead Spending and Volume Variances, Columnar and Formula Approaches

OBJECTIVE 3
CORNERSTONE 21-8

Marvelettes Company provided the following information:

Standard fixed overhead rate (SFOR) per direct labor hour	$5.00
Actual fixed overhead rate (AFOR) per direct labor hour	$5.03
Actual direct labor hours worked (AH)	56,200
Actual production in units	14,000
Standard hours allowed for actual units produced (SH)	56,000

Required:
1. Using the columnar approach, calculate the fixed overhead spending and efficiency variances.
2. Using the formula approach, calculate the fixed overhead spending variance.
3. Using the formula approach, calculate the fixed overhead efficiency variance.
4. Calculate the total fixed overhead variance.

Cornerstone Exercise 21-27 Static Budget for an Activity

OBJECTIVE 4
CORNERSTONE 21-9

Madison Company decided to look more closely at the inspection activity in its factory. The following information for a year was collected:

Demand for inspections: 170,000
Resources needed:

a. 6 inspectors, capable of inspecting 30,000 units per year; salary is $32,000 each
b. Supplies (small tools, oil, rags) expected to cost $0.70 per inspection
c. Workbenches, computers, etc.; depreciation $18,300 per year
d. Factory space for the inspection station, utilities; $12,600 per year

Required:
Prepare a static budget for the inspection activity for the year.

Cornerstone Exercise 21-28 Activity Flexible Budget

OBJECTIVE 4
CORNERSTONE 21-10

Jarend Company provided information on the following four overhead activities.

Activity	Driver	Fixed Cost	Variable Rate
Maintenance	Machine hours	$50,000	$ 1.80
Machining	Machine hours	25,000	3.00
Setting up	Setups	—	2,100
Purchasing	Purchase Orders	75,000	7.00

Jarend has found that the following driver levels are associated with two different levels of production.

Driver	40,000 units	60,000 units
Machine hours	60,000	90,000
Setups	50	70
Purchase orders	12,000	18,000

Required:
Prepare an activity-based flexible budget for 40,000 units and 60,000 units.

Cornerstone Exercise 21-29 Activity-Based Performance Report

OBJECTIVE 4
CORNERSTONE 21-11

Jarend Company produced 40,000 units last year. The information on the actual costs and budgeted costs at actual production of four activities is provided below.

Activity	Actual Cost	Budgeted Cost for Actual Production
Maintenance	$158,300	$158,000
Machining	205,400	205,000
Setting up	106,700	105,000
Purchasing	158,800	159,000

Required:
Prepare an activity-based performance report for the four activities for the past year.

EXERCISES

OBJECTIVE ❶

Exercise 21-30 Performance Report

Master Budget	Actual Data
Budgeted production: 4,000	Actual production: 4,100 units
Materials:	
2 leather strips @ $6.00	Materials cost: $48,700
Labor:	
0.5 hr. @ $18.00	Labor cost: $35,800

Required:
1. Prepare a performance report using a budget based on expected production.
2. **Conceptual Connection:** Comment on the limitations of this report.

OBJECTIVE ❶

Exercise 21-31 Flexible Budget for Various Levels of Production

Budgeted amounts for the year:

Materials	2 leather strips @ $6.00
Labor	0.5 hr. @ $18.00
VOH	0.5 hr. @ $1.20
FOH	$6,800

Required:
1. Prepare a flexible budget for 3,500, 4,000, and 4,500 units.
2. **Conceptual Connection:** Calculate the unit cost at 3,500, 4,000, and 4,500 units. (*Note:* Round unit costs to the nearest cent.) What happens to unit cost as the number of units produced increases?

Use the following information for Exercises 21-32 and 21-33:

Ionia Inc. produces a variety of shampoos, conditioners, and hair care products. Ionia's controller has developed standard costs for the following four overhead items:

Overhead Item	Total Fixed Cost	Variable Rate per Direct Labor Hour
Maintenance	$173,000	$0.20
Power		0.45
Indirect labor	128,000	2.10
Rent	30,000	

Next year, Ionia expects production to require 140,000 direct labor hours.

OBJECTIVE ❶

Exercise 21-32 Flexible Budget for Various Levels of Activity

Refer to the information for Ionia Inc. above.

Required:
1. Prepare an overhead budget for the expected level of direct labor hours for the coming year.
2. Prepare an overhead budget that reflects production that is 15 percent higher than expected, and for production that is 15 percent lower than expected.

OBJECTIVE ❶

Exercise 21-33 Performance Report Based on Actual Production

Refer to the information for Ionia Inc. above. Assume that Ionia's actual production required 142,000 direct labor hours at standard. The actual overhead costs incurred were as follows:

Maintenance	$202,000	Indirect labor	$426,100
Power	63,000	Rent	30,000

Required:
Prepare a performance report for the period based on actual production.

> *Use the following information for Exercises 21-34 and 21-35:*
> Rostand Inc. operates a delivery service for over 70 restaurants. The corporation has a fleet of vehicles and has invested in a sophisticated, computerized communications system to coordinate its deliveries. Rostand has gathered the following actual data on last year's delivery operations:
>
> | | |
> |---|---|
> | Deliveries made | 38,600 |
> | Direct labor | 31,000 direct labor hours @ $9.00 |
> | Actual variable overhead | $157,700 |
>
> Rostand employs a standard costing system. During the year, a variable overhead rate of $5.10 per hour was used. The labor standard requires 0.80 hour per delivery.

Exercise 21-34 Variable Overhead Variances, Service Company

OBJECTIVE **2**

Refer to the information for Rostand Inc. above.

Required:
1. Compute the standard hours allowed for actual deliveries made last year.
2. Compute the variable overhead spending and efficiency variances.

Exercise 21-35 Fixed Overhead Variances

OBJECTIVE **3**

Refer to the information for Rostand Inc. above. Assume that the actual fixed overhead was $403,400. Budgeted fixed overhead was $400,000, based on practical capacity of 32,000 direct labor hours.

Required:
1. Calculate the standard fixed overhead rate based on budgeted fixed overhead and practical capacity.
2. Compute the fixed overhead spending and volume variances.

Exercise 21-36 Overhead Variances

OBJECTIVE **2 3**

At the beginning of the year, Gaillard Company had the following standard cost sheet for one of its chemical products:

Direct materials (5 lbs. @ $3.20)	$16.00
Direct labor (2 hrs. @ $18.00)	36.00
FOH (2 hrs. @ $4.30)	8.60
VOH (2 hrs. @ $0.90)	1.80
Standard cost per unit	$62.40

Gaillard computes its overhead rates using practical volume, which is 144,000 units. The actual results for the year are as follows: (a) Units produced: 143,400; (b) Direct labor: 286,400 hours at $18.10; (c) *FOH*: $1,235,900; and (d) *VOH*: $259,300.

Required:
1. Compute the variable overhead spending and efficiency variances.
2. Compute the fixed overhead spending and volume variances.

Exercise 21-37 Overhead Application, Fixed and Variable Overhead Variances

OBJECTIVE **2 3**

Chesley Company is planning to produce 2,600,000 power drills for the coming year. The company uses direct labor hours to assign overhead to products. Each drill requires 0.6 standard hour of labor for completion. The total budgeted overhead was $1,981,200. The total fixed overhead budgeted for the coming year is $1,326,000. Predetermined overhead rates are calculated using expected production, measured in direct labor hours. Actual results for the year are:

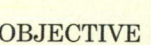

Actual production (units)	2,560,000	Actual variable overhead	$ 644,100
Actual direct labor hours (*AH*)	1,535,400	Actual fixed overhead	$1,330,000

Required:
1. Compute the applied fixed overhead.
2. Compute the fixed overhead spending and volume variances.

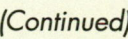

(Continued)

3.   Compute the applied variable overhead.
4.   Compute the variable overhead spending and efficiency variances.

OBJECTIVE ❷ ❸

ILLUSTRATING RELATIONSHIPS

Exercise 21-38 Understanding Relationships between Overhead Variances, Budgeted Amounts, and Actual Units Produced and Direct Labor Hours Worked

Last year, Gladner Company had planned to produce 140,000 units. However, 143,000 units were actually produced. The company uses direct labor hours to assign overhead to products. Each unit requires 0.9 standard hour of labor for completion. The fixed overhead rate was $11 per direct labor hour and the variable overhead rate was $6.36 per direct labor hour.

The following variances were computed:

Fixed overhead spending variance	$24,000 *U*	Variable overhead spending variance	$9,196 *U*
Fixed overhead volume variance	29,700 *F*	Variable overhead efficiency variance	1,272 *U*

Required:
1.   Calculate the total applied fixed overhead.
2.   Calculate the budgeted fixed overhead.
3.   Calculate the actual fixed overhead.
4.   Calculate the total applied variable overhead.
5.   Calculate the number of actual direct labor hours.
6.   Calculate the actual variable overhead.

OBJECTIVE ❶

Exercise 21-39 Performance Report for Variable Overhead Variances

Bansker Company had the data below for its most recent year, ended December 31:

Actual costs:		Variable overhead standards:	
Indirect labor	$30,100	Indirect labor	0.25 hr. @ $20.00
Supplies	$4,400	Supplies	0.25 hr. @ $2.40
Actual hours worked	1,530 hours	Standard variable	$22.40 per direct
Units produced	6,000 units	overhead rate	labor hour
Hours allowed for production	1,500 hours		

Required:
Prepare a performance report that shows the variances on an item-by-item basis.

OBJECTIVE ❹

Exercise 21-40 Activity-Based Budgeting

Fermi Company decided to look more closely at the materials receiving activity in its factory. The driver for receiving is the number of receiving orders. The following information for a year was collected:

Demand for receiving orders: 130,000
Resources needed:

   a.   6 workers capable of completing 25,000 receiving orders per year. (The completion of a receiving order requires unloading the materials onto the receiving dock, checking the receiving order against the purchase order and invoice, and carrying the materials to the materials storeroom.) Salary is $27,000 for each worker
   b.   Supplies (paper, grease markers, small tools, rags) expected to cost $0.80 per receiving order
   c.   Workbenches, dollies, computers, etc.; depreciation $14,400 per year
   d.   Space for the receiving dock, utilities; $9,800 per year

Required:
1.   Prepare a static budget for the receiving activity for the year.
2.   Calculate the cost per receiving order based on annual demand for receiving orders. (*Note:* Round to the nearest cent.)

Exercise 21-41 Activity Flexible Budget

OBJECTIVE 4

Healder Company provided information on the following three overhead activities.

Activity	Driver	Fixed Cost	Variable Rate
Engineering	Engineering hours	$67,000	$5.50
Machining	Machine hours	36,000	1.40
Receiving	Receiving orders	51,000	3.75

Healder has found that the following driver levels are associated with two different levels of production.

Driver	40,000 units	50,000 units
Engineering hours	500	750
Machine hours	30,000	37,500
Receiving orders	9,000	12,000

Required:

Prepare an activity-based flexible budget for the two levels of activity.

Exercise 21-42 Activity-Based Performance Report

OBJECTIVE 4

Inchon produced 312,000 units last year. The information on the actual costs and budgeted costs at actual production of four activities follows.

Activity	Actual Cost	Budgeted Cost for Actual Production
Maintenance	$179,600	$176,700
Machining	90,500	89,800
Setting up	119,500	121,000
Purchasing	75,750	74,600

Required:

Prepare an activity-based performance report for the four activities for the past year.

PROBLEMS

Use the following information for Problems 21-43 through 21-45:

Ladan Suriman, controller for Healthy Pet Company, has been instructed to develop a flexible budget for overhead costs. The company produces two types of dog food. BasicDiet is a standard mixture for healthy dogs. SpecialDiet is a reduced protein formulation for older dogs with health problems. The two dog foods use common raw materials in different proportions. The company expects to produce 100,000 bags of each product during the coming year. BasicDiet requires 0.30 direct labor hours per bag, and SpecialDiet requires 0.40 direct labor hours per bag. Ladan has developed the following fixed and variable costs for each of the four overhead items:

Overhead Item	Fixed Cost	Variable Rate per Direct Labor Hour
Maintenance	$21,000	$0.50
Power		0.70
Indirect labor	38,500	1.60
Rent	42,000	

Problem 21-43 Overhead Budget for a Particular Level of Activity

OBJECTIVE 1

Refer to the information for Healthy Pet Company above.

Required:

1. Calculate the total direct labor hours required for the production of 100,000 bags of Basic-Diet and 100,000 bags of SpecialDiet.

2. Prepare an overhead budget for the expected activity level (calculated in Requirement 1) for the coming year.

Problem 21-44 Flexible Budget for Various Production Levels

Refer to the information for Healthy Pet Company on the previous page.

Required:

1. Calculate the direct labor hours required for production that is 10 percent higher than expected. Calculate the direct labor hours required for production that is 20 percent lower than expected.
2. Prepare an overhead budget that reflects production that is 10 percent higher than expected, and for production that is 20 percent lower than expected. (*Hint*: Use total direct labor hours calculated in Requirement 1.)

Problem 21-45 Performance Report Based on Actual Production

Refer to the information for Healthy Pet Company on the previous page. Assume that Healthy Pet actually produced 120,000 bags of BasicDiet and 100,000 bags of SpecialDiet. The actual overhead costs incurred were as follows:

Maintenance	$58,760	Indirect labor	$161,000
Power	54,150	Rent	42,000

Required:

1. Calculate the number of direct labor hours budgeted for actual production of the two products.
2. Prepare a performance report for the period based on actual production.
3. **Conceptual Connection:** Based on the report, would you judge any of the variances to be significant? Can you think of some possible reasons for the variances?

Problem 21-46 Overhead Budget, Flexible Budget

Spelzig Company manufactures radio-controlled toy cars. Spelzig has developed the following flexible budget for overhead for the coming year. Activity level is measured in direct labor hours.

	Variable Cost Formula	Activity Level (hours)		
		15,000	20,000	25,000
Variable costs:				
Maintenance	$3.80	$ 57,000	$ 76,000	$ 95,000
Supplies	4.25	63,750	85,000	106,250
Power	0.08	1,200	1,600	2,000
Total variable costs	$8.13	$121,950	$162,600	$203,250
Fixed costs:				
Depreciation		$144,700	$144,700	$144,700
Salaries		188,900	188,900	188,900
Total fixed costs		$333,600	$333,600	$333,600
Total overhead costs		$455,550	$496,200	$536,850

The factory produces two different toy cars. The production budget for November is 30,000 units for Car W23 and 60,000 units for Car Z280. Car W23 requires 12 minutes of direct labor time, and Car Z280 requires 24 minutes. Fixed overhead costs are incurred uniformly throughout the year.

Required:

1. Calculate the number of direct labor hours needed in November to produce Car W23 and the number of direct labor hours needed in November to produce Car Z280. What are the total direct labor hours budgeted for November?
2. Prepare an overhead budget for November. Round all amounts to the nearest dollar. (*Hint*: The budgeted fixed costs given are for the year.)

Problem 21-47 Kicker Speakers, Before-The-Fact Flexible Budgeting, Flexible Budgeting for the New Solo X18 Model

Stillwater Designs is considering a new **Kicker** speaker model: Solo X18, which is a large and expensive subwoofer (projected price is $760 to distributors). The company controls the design specifications of the model and contracts with manufacturers in mainland China to produce the model. Stillwater Designs pays the freight and custom duties. The product is shipped to Stillwater and then sold to distributors throughout the United States.

The market for this type of subwoofer is small and competitive. It is expected to have a 3-year life cycle. Market test reviews were encouraging. One potential customer noted that the speaker could make a deaf person hear again. Another remarked that the bass could be heard two miles away. Another customer was simply impressed by the size and watts of the subwoofer (a maximum of 10,000 watts capability). Encouraged by the results of market tests, the Product Steering Committee also wanted to review the financial analysis. The projected revenues and costs at three levels of sales volume are as follows (for the 3-year life cycle):

	Pessimistic	Most Likely	Optimistic
Sales volume (units)	72,000	150,000	250,000
Variable costs (total):			
Acquisition cost	$43,200,000	$ 90,000,000	$150,000,000
Freight	4,320,000	9,000,000	15,000,000
Duties	1,800,000	3,750,000	6,250,000
Total	$49,320,000	$102,750,000	$171,250,000
Fixed costs (total):			
Engineering (R&D)	$10,000,000	$ 10,000,000	$ 10,000,000
Overhead	3,000,000	3,000,000	3,000,000
Total	$13,000,000	$ 13,000,000	$ 13,000,000

Required:
1. Prepare flexible budget formulas for the cost items listed for the Solo X18 model. Also, provide a flexible budget formula for total costs.
2. **Conceptual Connection:** Prepare an income statement for each of the three levels of sales volume. Discuss the value of before-the-fact flexible budgeting and relate this to the current example.
3. **Conceptual Connection:** Form a group with two to four other students. Assume that the group is acting as a Product Steering Committee. Evaluate the feasibility of producing the Solo X18 model (using the given financial data and the results of Requirements 1 and 2.) If the financial performance of the model is questionable, discuss possible courses of action that the company might take to improve the financial performance of the product. Also, discuss some reasons why the company might wish to produce the model even if it does not promise a good financial return.

Problem 21-48 Flexible Budgeting

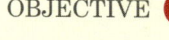

OBJECTIVE **1**

ILLUSTRATING RELATIONSHIPS

Quarterly budgeted overhead costs for two different levels of activity follow. The 2,000 level was the expected level from the master budget.

	Cost Formula ($)		Direct Labor Hours	
	Fixed	Variable	1,000 Hours	2,000 Hours
Maintenance	7,500	5.00	$12,500	$17,500
Depreciation	5,600	—	5,600	5,600
Supervision	22,000	—	22,000	22,000
Supplies	—	2.30	2,300	4,600
Power	—	0.60	600	1,200
Other	18,000	1.25	19,250	20,500

The actual activity level was 1,700 hours.

Required:
1. Prepare a flexible budget for an activity level of 1,700 direct labor hours.
2. Suppose that all of the formulas for each item are missing. You only have the budgeted costs for each level of activity. Show how you can obtain the formulas for each item by using the information given for the budgeted costs for the two levels.

OBJECTIVE ❶

Problem 21-49 Flexible Budgeting

Orchard Fresh Inc. purchases fruit from numerous growers and packs fruit boxes and fruit baskets for sale. Orchard Fresh has developed the following flexible budget for overhead for the coming year. Activity level is measured in direct labor hours.

| | | Activity Level (hours) | | |
		2,000	2,500	3,000
Variable costs:				
Maintenance	$0.76	$ 1,520	$ 1,900	$ 2,280
Supplies	0.45	900	1,125	1,350
Power	0.20	400	500	600
Total variable costs	$1.41	$ 2,820	$ 3,525	$ 4,230
Fixed costs:				
Depreciation		$ 4,800	$ 4,800	$ 4,800
Salaries		24,500	24,500	24,500
Total fixed costs		$29,300	$29,300	$29,300
Total overhead costs		$32,120	$32,825	$33,530

Required:
1. Prepare a flexible budget for May, using 200, 240, and 280 direct labor hours.
2. The Cushing High School Parent-Teacher Organization ordered 200 gift baskets from Orchard Fresh to be given to high school teachers and support staff as a thank you for a successful school year. These gift baskets must be ready by May 31 and were not included in the original production budget for May. Without preparing a new overhead budget, what is the new total budgeted overhead for May for Orchard Fresh?

OBJECTIVE ❶

Problem 21-50 Performance Reporting

Fernando's is a tiny sandwich shop just off the State University campus. Customers enter and place their orders at a small counter area. All orders are take-out because there is no space for dining in.

The owner of Fernando's, Luis Azaria, is attempting to construct a series of budgets. He has accumulated the following information:

a. The average sandwich (which sells for $4.50) requires 1 roll, 4 ounces of meat, 2 ounces of cheese, 0.05 head of lettuce, 0.25 of a tomato, and a healthy squirt (1 ounce) of secret sauce.

b. Each customer typically orders one soft drink (average price $1.50) consisting of a cup and 12 ounces of soda. Refills are free, but this offer is seldom taken advantage of because the typical customer carries out his/her sandwich and soda.

c. Use of paper supplies (napkins, bag, sandwich wrap, cups) averages $1,650 per month.

d. Fernando's is open for two 4-hour shifts. The noon shift on Monday through Friday requires two workers earning $10 per hour. The evening shift is only worked on Friday, Saturday, and Sunday nights. The two evening shift employees also earn $10 per hour. There are 4.3 weeks in a month.

e. Rent is $575 per month. Other monthly cash expenses average $1,800.

f. Food costs are:

Meat	$7.00/lb	Tomatoes (a box contains about 20	
Cheese	$6.00/lb	tomatoes)	$4/box
Rolls	$28.80/gross	Secret sauce	$6.40/gallon
Lettuce (a box contains		Soda (syrup and carbonated water)	$2.56/gallon
24 heads)	$12.00/box		

In a normal month when school is in session, Fernando's sells 5,000 sandwiches and 5,000 sodas. In October, State U holds its homecoming celebration. Luis figures that if he adds a noon shift on Saturday and Sunday of homecoming weekend, October sales will be 30 percent higher than normal. To advertise his noon shifts during homecoming weekend, Luis will buy cups emblazoned with the State U Homecoming schedule. This will add $200 to paper costs for the month. Last year, he added two additional shifts, and his sales goal was realized.

Required:
1. Prepare a flexible budget for a normal school month.
2. Prepare a flexible budget for October.
3. **Conceptual Connection:** Do you think it was worthwhile for Luis to add the additional shifts for homecoming weekend last October?

Problem 21-51 Traditional versus Activity Flexible Budgeting

OBJECTIVE 1 4

Carly Davis, production manager, was upset and puzzled by the latest performance report, which indicated that she was $100,000 over budget. She and her staff had worked hard to beat the budget. Now she saw that three items—direct labor, power, and setups—were over budget. The actual costs for these three items were as follows:

Direct labor	$210,000
Power	135,000
Setups	140,000
Total	$485,000

Carly felt that the additional labor and power cost were due to the fact that her team produced more units than originally budgeted. Uncertainty in scheduling had led to more setups than planned. She asked Sean Carpenter, the controller, why the performance report did not take the additional production into account. Sean assured Carly that he did adjust the report for increased production and showed her the budget formulas he used to predict the costs for different levels of activity. The formulas were based on direct labor hours as follows:

$$\text{Direct labor cost} = \$10X$$
$$\text{Power cost} = \$5,000 + \$4X$$
$$\text{Setup cost} = \$100,000$$

Carly pointed out that power costs were unrelated to direct labor hours, but that they seemed to vary with machine hours instead. She also pointed out that setup costs were not fixed. They varied with the number of setups—which had increased due to scheduling changes. The increase in setups required her team to work overtime, adding to the costs. Each setup also took supplies that added significantly to overhead costs.

Sean agreed that the formulas did not adequately take care of Carly's concerns. He agreed to develop a new set of cost formulas based on better explanatory variables. After a few days, Sean shared the following cost formulas with Carly:

$$\text{Direct labor cost} = \$10X, \text{ where } X = \text{Direct labor hours}$$
$$\text{Power cost} = \$68,000 + 0.9Y, \text{ where } Y = \text{Machine hours}$$
$$\text{Setup cost} = \$98,000 + \$400Z, \text{ where } Z \text{ Number of setups}$$

The actual measure of each activity driver is as follows:

Direct labor hours	20,000
Machine hours	90,000
Number of setups	110

Required:
1. Prepare a performance report for direct labor, power, and setups using the direct labor-based formulas.
2. Prepare a performance report for direct labor, power, and setups using the multiple cost driver formulas that Sean developed.
3. **Conceptual Connection:** Of the two approaches, which provides the more accurate picture of Carly's performance? Why?

OBJECTIVE

Problem 21-52 Activity Flexible Budgeting

Billy Adams, controller for Westcott Inc., prepared the following budget for manufacturing costs at two different levels of activity for 2012:

DIRECT LABOR HOURS				MACHINE HOURS		
	Level of Activity				**Level of Activity**	
	50,000	100,000			200,000	300,000
Direct materials	$300,000	$ 600,000	Maintenance		$360,000	$510,000
Direct labor	200,000	400,000	equipment			
Depreciation (plant)	100,000	100,000	Machining		112,000	162,000
Subtotal	$600,000	$1,100,000	Subtotal		$472,000	$672,000

MATERIAL MOVES				NUMBER OF BATCHES INSPECTED		
	Level of Activity				**Level of Activity**	
	20,000	40,000			100	200
Materials handling	$165,000	$290,000	Inspecting products		$ 125,000	$ 225,000
			Total		$1,362,000	$2,287,000

During 2012, Westcott employees worked a total of 80,000 direct labor hours, used 250,000 machine hours, made 32,000 moves, and performed 120 batch inspections. The following actual costs were incurred:

Direct materials	$440,000	Machining	$142,000
Direct labor	355,000	Materials handling	232,500
Depreciation	100,000	Inspecting products	160,000
Maintenance	425,000		

Westcott applies overhead using rates based on direct labor hours, machine hours, number of moves, and number of batches. The second level of activity (the far right column in the preceding table) is the practical level of activity (the available activity for resources acquired in advance of usage) and is used to compute predetermined overhead pool rates.

Required:

1. Prepare a performance report for Westcott's manufacturing costs in 2012.
2. Assume that one of the products produced by Westcott is budgeted to use 10,000 direct labor hours, 15,000 machine hours, and 500 moves and will be produced in 5 batches. A total of 10,000 units will be produced during the year. Calculate the budgeted unit manufacturing cost.
3. **Conceptual Connection:** One of Westcott's managers said: "Budgeting at the activity level makes a lot of sense, but this budget needs to provide more detailed information. For example, the materials handling activity requires forklifts and operators, and this information is lost with simply reporting the total cost of the activity for various levels of output. We have four forklifts; each is rented for $10,000 per year and can provide 10,000 moves per year. Furthermore, for our two shifts, we need up to eight operators if we run all four forklifts. Each operator is paid a salary of $30,000 per year. Fuel costs us about $0.25 per move."

    Based on these comments, explain how this additional information may help Westcott to better manage its costs. Also, assuming that these are the only three items, expand the detail of the flexible budget for materials handling to reveal the cost of these three resource items for 20,000 moves and 40,000 moves, respectively. (*Note*: You may wish to review the concepts of flexible, committed, and discretionary resources found in Chapter 14.)

Problem 21-53 Flexible Budgeting

OBJECTIVE ①

At the beginning of last year, Jean Bingham, controller for Thorpe Inc., prepared the following budget for conversion costs at two levels of activity for the coming year:

	Direct Labor Hours	
	100,000	120,000
Direct labor	$1,000,000	$1,200,000
Supervision	180,000	180,000
Utilities	18,000	21,000
Depreciation	225,000	225,000
Supplies	25,000	30,000
Maintenance	240,000	284,000
Rent	120,000	120,000
Other	60,000	70,000
Total manufacturing cost	$1,868,000	$2,130,000

During the year, the company worked a total of 112,000 direct labor hours and incurred the following actual costs:

Direct labor	$963,200	Supplies	$ 24,640
Supervision	190,000	Maintenance	237,000
Utilities	20,500	Rent	120,000
Depreciation	225,000	Other	60,500

Thorpe applied overhead on the basis of direct labor hours. Normal volume of 120,000 direct labor hours is the activity level to be used to compute the predetermined overhead rate.

Required:

1. Determine the cost formula for each of Thorpe's conversion costs. (*Hint*: Use the high-low method.)
2. **Conceptual Connection:** Prepare a performance report for Thorpe's conversion costs for last year. Should any cost item be given special attention? Explain.

Problem 21-54 Overhead Application, Overhead Variances

OBJECTIVE ② ③

Moleno Company produces a single product and uses a standard cost system. The normal production volume is 120,000 units; each unit requires five direct labor hours at standard. Overhead is applied on the basis of direct labor hours. The budgeted overhead for the coming year is as follows:

FOH	$2,160,000*
VOH	1,440,000

*At normal volume.

During the year, Moleno produced 118,600 units, worked 592,300 direct labor hours, and incurred actual fixed overhead costs of $2,150,400 and actual variable overhead costs of $1,422,800.

Required:

1. Calculate the standard fixed overhead rate and the standard variable overhead rate.
2. Compute the applied fixed overhead and the applied variable overhead. What is the total fixed overhead variance? Total variable overhead variance?
3. **Conceptual Connection:** Break down the total fixed overhead variance into a spending variance and a volume variance. Discuss the significance of each.
4. **Conceptual Connection:** Compute the variable overhead spending and efficiency variances. Discuss the significance of each.

(Continued)

5. Journal entries for overhead variances were not discussed in this chapter. Typically, the over-head variance entries happen at the end of the year. Assume that applied fixed (variable) overhead is accumulated on the credit side of the fixed (variable) overhead control account. Actual fixed (variable) overhead costs are accumulated on the debit side of the respective control accounts. At the end of the year, the balance in each control account is the total fixed (variable) variance. Create accounts for each of the four overhead variances and close out the total variances to each of these four variance accounts. These four variance accounts are then usually closed to Cost of Goods Sold.

Form a group with two to four other students, and prepare the journal entries that isolate the four variances. Finally, prepare the journal entries that close these variances to Cost of Goods Sold.

OBJECTIVE

Problem 21-55 Overhead Variance Analysis

The Lubbock plant of Morril's Small Motor Division produces a major subassembly for a 6.0 horsepower motor for lawn mowers. The plant uses a standard costing system for production costing and control. The standard cost sheet for the subassembly follows:

Direct materials (6.0 lbs. @ $5.00)	$30.00
Direct labor (1.6 hrs. @ $12.00)	19.20
VOH (1.6 hrs. @ $10.00)	16.00
FOH (1.6 hrs. @ $6.00)	9.60
Standard unit cost	$74.80

During the year, the Lubbock plant had the following actual production activity: (a) Production of motors totaled 50,000 units; (b) The company used 82,000 direct labor hours at a total cost of $1,066,000; (c) Actual fixed overhead totaled $556,000; and (d) Actual variable overhead totaled $860,000.

The Lubbock plant's practical activity is 60,000 units per year. Standard overhead rates are computed based on practical activity measured in standard direct labor hours.

Required:
1. Compute the variable overhead spending and efficiency variances.
2. **Conceptual Connection:** Compute the fixed overhead spending and volume variances. Interpret the volume variance. What can be done to reduce this variance?

OBJECTIVE

Problem 21-56 Overhead Variances

Extrim Company produces monitors. Extrim's plant in San Antonio uses a standard costing system. The standard costing system relies on direct labor hours to assign overhead costs to production. The direct labor standard indicates that four direct labor hours should be used for every microwave unit produced. (The San Antonio plant produces only one model.) The normal production volume is 120,000 units. The budgeted overhead for the coming year is as follows:

FOH	$1,286,400
VOH	888,000*

*At normal volume.

Extrim applies overhead on the basis of direct labor hours.

During the year, Extrim produced 119,000 units, worked 487,900 direct labor hours, and incurred actual fixed overhead costs of $1.3 million and actual variable overhead costs of $927,010.

Required:
1. Calculate the standard fixed overhead rate and the standard variable overhead rate.
2. Compute the applied fixed overhead and the applied variable overhead. What is the total fixed overhead variance? Total variable overhead variance?
3. **Conceptual Connection:** Break down the total fixed overhead variance into a spending variance and a volume variance. Discuss the significance of each.
4. **Conceptual Connection:** Compute the variable overhead spending and efficiency variances. Discuss the significance of each.

Problem 21-57 Understanding Relationships, Incomplete Data, Overhead Analysis

OBJECTIVE ② ③

ILLUSTRATING
RELATIONSHIPS

Lynwood Company produces surge protectors. To help control costs, Lynwood employs a standard costing system and uses a flexible budget to predict overhead costs at various levels of activity. For the most recent year, Lynwood used a standard overhead rate of $18 per direct labor hour. The rate was computed using practical activity. Budgeted overhead costs are $396,000 for 18,000 direct labor hours and $540,000 for 30,000 direct labor hours. During the past year, Lynwood generated the following data: (a) Actual production: 100,000 units; (b) Fixed overhead volume variance: $20,000 *U*; (c) Variable overhead efficiency variance: $18,000 *F*; (d) Actual fixed overhead costs: $200,000; and (e) Actual variable overhead costs: $310,000.

Required:
1. Calculate the fixed overhead rate.
2. Determine the fixed overhead spending variance.
3. Determine the variable overhead spending variance.
4. Determine the standard hours allowed per unit of product

Problem 21-58 Flexible Budget, Overhead Variances

OBJECTIVE ① ② ③

Shumaker Company manufactures a line of high-top basketball shoes. At the beginning of the year, the following plans for production and costs were revealed:

Pairs of shoes to be produced and sold	55,000
Standard cost per unit:	
Direct materials	$15
Direct labor	12
VOH	6
FOH	3
Total unit cost	$36

During the year, a total of 50,000 units were produced and sold. The following actual costs were incurred:

Direct materials	$775,000	VOH	$310,000
Direct labor	590,000	FOH	180,000

There were no beginning or ending inventories of raw materials. In producing the 50,000 units, 63,000 hours were worked, 5 percent more hours than the standard allowed for the actual output. Overhead costs are applied to production using direct labor hours.

Required:
1. Using a flexible budget, prepare a performance report comparing expected costs for the actual production with actual costs.
2. Determine the following: (a) Fixed overhead spending and volume variances and (b) Variable overhead spending and efficiency variances.

CASES

 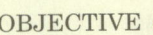
Case 21-59 Fixed Overhead Spending and Volume Variances, Capacity Management

Lorale Company, a producer of recreational vehicles, recently decided to begin producing a major subassembly for jet skis. The subassembly would be used by Lorale's jet ski plants and also would be sold to other producers. The decision was made to lease two large buildings in two different locations: Little Rock, Arkansas, and Athens, Georgia. The company agreed to a 11-year, renewable lease contract. The plants were of the same size, and each had 10 production lines. New equipment was purchased for each line and workers were hired to operate the equipment. The company also hired production line supervisors for each plant. A supervisor is capable of directing up to two production lines per shift. Two shifts are run for each plant. The practical production capacity of each plant is 300,000 subassemblies per year. Two standard direct labor hours are allowed for each subassembly. The costs for leasing, equipment depreciation, and supervision for a single plant are as follows (the costs are assumed to be the same for each plant):

Supervision (10 supervisors @ $50,000)	$ 500,000
Building lease (annual payment)	800,000
Equipment depreciation (annual)	1,100,000
Total fixed overhead costs*	$2,400,000

*For simplicity, assume these are the only fixed overhead costs.

After beginning operations, Lorale discovered that demand for the product in the region covered by the Little Rock plant was less than anticipated. At the end of the first year, only 240,000 units were sold. The Athens plant sold 300,000 units as expected. The actual fixed overhead costs at the end of the first year were $2,500,000 (for each plant).

Required:
1. Calculate a fixed overhead rate based on standard direct labor hours.
2. Calculate the fixed overhead spending and volume variances for the Little Rock and Athens plants. What is the most likely cause of the spending variance? Why are the volume variances different for the two plants?
3. Suppose that from now on the sales for the Little Rock plant are expected to be no more than 240,000 units. What actions would you take to manage the capacity costs (fixed overhead costs)?
4. Calculate the fixed overhead cost per subassembly for each plant. Do they differ? Should they differ? Explain. Do ABC concepts help in analyzing this issue?

Case 21-60 Ethical Considerations; Flexible Budgeting and the Environment

Harry Johnson, the chief financial officer of Ur Thrift, Inc, a large retailer, had just finished a meeting with the Roger Swasey, the chief financial officer of the large retailer, and Connie Baker, its environmental officer. Over the years, Harry had overseen the development of a number of cost formulas that allowed Ur Thrift to budget the variable costs of a variety of items. For example, packaging for one of its private line of dolls had a cost formula of Y = $2.20X, where X represented the number of dolls sold. The formula was used to calculate the expected packaging costs which were then compared with the actual packaging costs. Over the last several years, the actual costs and budgeted costs were virtually on target, prompting Harry to claim that packaging costs were well controlled.

Connie Baker, however, argued that the packaging costs were not well controlled. In fact, she was adamant in her view that the packaging was excessive and that by reducing the packaging, costs could be reduced and the environmental impacts reduced as well. She argued that the company had an ethical obligation to reduce environmental impacts and that cost savings would also be captured, improving the profitability of the company. As another example, Connie discussed the fleet of semitrailer trucks used by Ur Thrift to move goods from its warehouses to retail outlets. The fuel cost formula was $3X, where X represented gallons of fuel consumed. She pointed out that the performance data also revealed that fuel costs were in control. Yet her office had recently recommended the installation of an auxiliary power unit to heat and cool the cabs of the trucks during the mandatory ten-hour breaks required of its drivers. This avoided the need to have the engine idle during this rest period. She claimed that this would significantly reduce fuel costs and easily pay for the new auxiliary units in a short period of time.

Connie had also made some comments that caused Harry to pause and do some soul searching. She noted that the financial officers of the company should be more concerned about reducing costs than simply predicting what they should be. Thus (according to her view), cost formulas are useful only to tell us where we currently are so that they can be used to assess how to reduce costs. The so-called flexible budgets are simply a means of enforcing static standards. She also said that the company's managers had an ethical obligation to not overconsume the resources of the planet. She urged both Harry and Roger to help position the company so that it could reduce its environmental impacts.

Required:

1. Do financial officers have an ethical obligation to help in reducing negative environmental impacts? Identify and discuss which of the Institute of Management Accountant's ethical standards might be used to sustain this point of view. Also, describe the role that flexible budgeting may play in reducing environmental impacts.

2. Suppose that Harry and Connie embark on a cooperative effort to eliminate any excessive packaging. The projected results are impressive. The expected reductions will save $3 million in shipping costs ($0.50 per package), $1.5 million in packaging materials ($0.40 per package), 5,000 trees, and 1.25 million barrels of oil. Are there any ethical issues associated with these actions? What standards might apply?

3. Identify two potential ethical dilemmas that might surface in the use of flexible budgeting for performance evaluation (the dilemmas do not need to be connected with environmental activities).

22

Performance Evaluation, Variable Costing, and Decentralization

Doug Norman Crystals/Alamy

After studying Chapter 22, you should be able to:

1. Explain how and why firms choose to decentralize.

2. Explain the difference between absorption and variable costing, and prepare segmented income statements.

3. Compute and explain return on investment.

4. Compute and explain residual income and economic value added.

5. Explain the uses of the Balanced Scorecard and the role of transfer pricing in a decentralized firm.

Carlos Caetano, 2010/Shutterstock.com

EXPERIENCE MANAGERIAL DECISIONS

with Herman Miller

The goal of performance evaluation is to provide information useful for assessing the effectiveness of past decisions so that future decisions can be improved. As you might guess, this goal is difficult to achieve because of the sheer quantity of information present in organizations and the complexity of the business environment in which most decisions are made. However, **Herman Miller, Inc.**, a large furniture manufacturer headquartered in western Michigan with business activities in over 100 countries, uses an increasingly popular performance evaluation technique—economic value added (EVA)—to help it make better decisions. For example, the entire office furniture market experienced a devastating slump in the early 2000s as a result of the dot-com bust and the 9/11 disaster. EVA measures provided Herman Miller with information beyond traditional accounting performance metrics that was critical to its dramatic and quick recovery from the

NatashaBo, 2010/Shutterstock.com

negative operating margins it experienced during the slump to the near double-digit positive margins it enjoyed only a few years later. EVA identifies the return generated by the company's assets and then subtracts the cost of all capital, both debt (e.g., money raised from loans, leases, and bonds) and equity (e.g., money raised from investors), used by the company to finance those assets in order to determine whether value is being created or destroyed. More specifically, EVA helps Herman Miller to quantify the long-term financial benefits of carrying less inventory and employing fewer fixed assets in its business. As a result of such EVA analyses, Herman Miller makes fundamentally different strategic and operating decisions involving its furniture production processes than it would if it relied solely on traditional accounting metrics. The ability to impact decisions in such a positive fashion has catapulted EVA into a position of prominence in Herman Miller's successful performance evaluation system.

⌂HermanMiller

OBJECTIVE ❶
Explain how and why firms choose to decentralize.

DECENTRALIZATION AND RESPONSIBILITY CENTERS

In general, a company is organized along lines of responsibility. Traditional organizational charts illustrate the flow of responsibilities from the chief executive officer down through the vice presidents to middle- and lower-level managers. Today, most companies use a flattened hierarchy—emphasizing teams. This structure is consistent with decentralization. GE Capital, for example, is essentially a group of smaller businesses. Ideally, the responsibility accounting system mirrors and supports the structure of an organization.

Firms with multiple responsibility centers usually choose one of two decision-making approaches to manage their diverse and complex activities: *centralized* or *decentralized*.

- In centralized decision making, decisions are made at the very top level, and lower-level managers are charged with implementing these decisions.
- Decentralized decision making allows managers at lower levels to make and implement key decisions pertaining to their areas of responsibility. This practice of delegating decision-making authority to the lower levels of management in a company is called **decentralization**.

Exhibit 22-1 illustrates the difference between centralized and decentralized companies.

Organizations range from highly centralized to strongly decentralized. Most firms fall somewhere in between, with the majority tending toward decentralization. The reasons for the popularity of decentralization and the ways in which a company may choose to decentralize are discussed next.

Reasons for Decentralization

Firms decide to decentralize for several reasons, including the following:

- ease of gathering and using local information
- focusing of central management
- training and motivating of segment managers
- enhanced competition, exposing segments to market forces

Gathering and Using Local Information   The quality of decisions is affected by the quality of information available. As a firm grows in size and operates in different markets and regions, central management may not understand local conditions. Lower-level managers, however, are in contact with immediate operating conditions (such as the strength and nature of local competition, the nature of the local labor force, and so on). As a result, they often are better positioned to make local decisions. For example,

Exhibit 22-1

Centralization and Decentralization

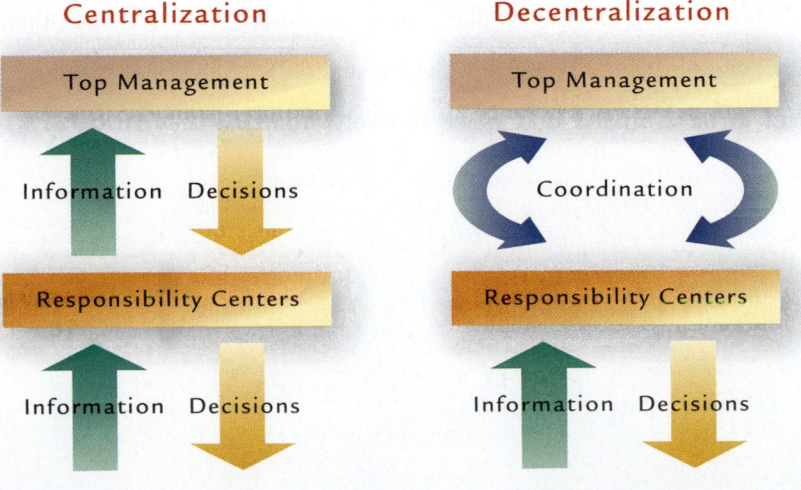

McDonald's has restaurants around the world. The tastes of people in China or France differ from those of people in the United States. So, McDonald's tailors its menu to different countries. The result is that the McDonald's in each country can differentiate to meet the needs of its local market.

Focusing of Central Management

By decentralizing the operating decisions, central management is free to engage in strategic planning and decision making. The long-run survival of the organization should be of more importance to central management than day-to-day operations.

Training and Motivating of Managers

Organizations always need well-trained managers to replace higher-level managers who leave to take advantage of other opportunities. What better way to prepare a future generation of higher-level managers than by providing them the opportunity to make significant decisions? These opportunities also enable top managers to evaluate local managers' capabilities and promote those who make the best decisions.

Enhanced Competition

In a highly centralized company, overall profit margins can mask inefficiencies within the various subdivisions. Large companies now find that they cannot afford to keep a noncompetitive division. One of the best ways to improve performance of a division or factory is to expose it more fully to market forces. At **Koch Industries Inc.**, each unit is expected to act as an autonomous business unit and to set prices both externally and internally. Units whose services are not required by other Koch units may face possible elimination.

Divisions in the Decentralized Firm

Decentralization involves a cost-benefit trade-off. As a firm becomes more decentralized, it passes more decision authority down the managerial hierarchy. As a result, managers in a decentralized firm make and implement more decisions than do managers in a centralized firm. The benefit of decentralization is that decisions are more likely to be made by managers who possess the specific local knowledge—not possessed by high level managers—to use the firm's resources in the best way possible to maximize firm value. However, the cost of decentralization is that lower-level managers who have the knowledge to make the best decisions with the firm's resources are less likely to possess the same incentive as high-level managers to maximize firm value. Stated differently, as compared to high-level managers, lower-level managers are more likely to use the firm's resources for personal gain than for increasing the firm's stock value.

Decentralization usually is achieved by creating units called *divisions*. Divisions can be differentiated a number of different ways, including the following:

- types of goods or services
- geographic lines
- responsibility centers

Types of Goods or Services

One way in which divisions are differentiated is by the types of goods or services produced. For example, divisions of **PepsiCo** include the Snack Ventures Europe Division (a joint venture with **General Mills**), **Frito-Lay Inc.**, and **Tropicana**, as well as its flagship soft-drink division. Exhibit 22-2 (p. 1106) shows decentralized divisions of PepsiCo. These divisions are organized on the basis of product lines. Notice that some divisions depend on other divisions. For example, PepsiCo spun off its restaurant divisions to **YUM! Brands**. As a result, the cola you drink at **Pizza Hut**, **Taco Bell**, and **KFC** will be Pepsi—not Coke. In a decentralized setting, some interdependencies usually exist; otherwise, a company would merely be a collection of totally separate entities.

Concept **Q&A**

Think about summer jobs that you and your friends have held. To what extent did you or your friends work in a centralized or decentralized decision-making environment?

Answer:

If you worked at a *Taco Bell* or *Pizza Hut*, you were working for a decentralized company: **YUM**. This company owns many Taco Bells and Pizza Huts. Some decision making is pushed down to lower-level managers. On the other hand, suppose you worked for a small law or accounting firm that has only the local office. Then you were working for a centralized company, and the owner probably made all important operating and strategic decisions.

Exhibit 22-2

Decentralized Divisions

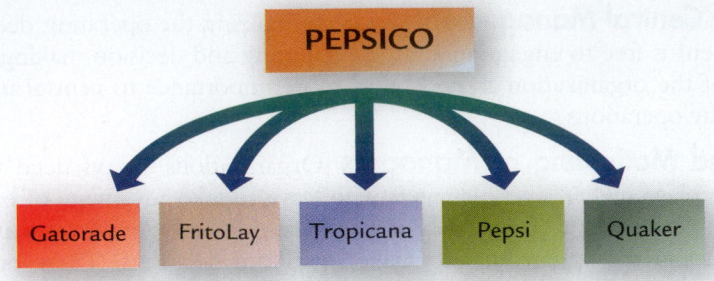

Geographic Lines

Divisions may also be created along geographic lines. For example, **UAL Inc.** (parent of **United Airlines**) has a number of regional divisions: Asian/Pacific, Caribbean, European, Latin American, and North American. The presence of divisions spanning one or more regions creates the need for performance evaluation that can take into account differences in divisional environments.

Responsibility Centers

A third way divisions differ is by the type of responsibility given to the divisional manager. As a firm grows, top management typically creates areas of responsibility, known as responsibility centers, and assigns subordinate managers to those areas. A **responsibility center** is a segment of the business whose manager is accountable for specified sets of activities. The results of each responsibility center can be measured according to the information that managers need to operate their centers. The four major types of responsibility centers are as follows:

- **Cost center:** Manager is responsible only for costs.
- **Revenue center:** Manager is responsible only for sales, or revenue.
- **Profit center:** Manager is responsible for both revenues and costs.
- **Investment center:** Manager is responsible for revenues, costs, and investments.

The choice of responsibility center typically mirrors the actual situation and the type of information available to the manager. Information is the key to appropriately holding managers responsible for outcomes. For example, a production department manager is held responsible for departmental *costs* but not for sales. This responsibility choice occurs because the production department manager understands and directly controls some production costs but does not set prices. Any difference between actual and expected costs can best be explained at this level.

The marketing department manager sets the price and projected sales *revenue*. Therefore, the marketing department may be evaluated as a revenue center. Direct costs of the marketing department and overall sales are the responsibility of the sales manager.

In some companies, plant managers are given the responsibility for manufacturing and marketing their products. These plant managers control both *costs and revenues*, putting them in control of a profit center. Operating income is an important performance measure for profit center managers.

Finally, divisions sometimes are cited as examples of investment centers. In addition to having control over cost and pricing decisions, divisional managers have the power to make *investment* decisions such as plant closings and openings and decisions to keep or drop a product line. As a result, both operating income and some type of return on investment are important performance measures for investment center

Exhibit 22-3

Types of Responsibility Centers and Accounting Information Used to Measure Performance

	Cost	Sales	Capital Investment	Other
Cost center	X			
Revenue center		X		
Profit center	X	X		
Investment center	X	X	X	X

managers. Exhibit 22-3 displays these centers along with the type of information that managers need to manage their operations. As the exhibit shows, investment centers represent the greatest degree of decentralization (followed by profit centers and finally by cost and revenue centers) because their managers have the freedom to make the greatest variety of decisions.

It is important to realize that while the responsibility center manager has responsibility only for the activities of that center, decisions made by that manager can affect other responsibility centers. For example, the sales force at a floor care products firm routinely offers customers price discounts at the end of the month. Sales increase dramatically, which is good for revenue and the sales force. However, the factory is forced to institute overtime shifts to keep up with demand. These overtime shifts increase the costs of the factory as well as the cost per unit of product.

Organizing divisions as responsibility centers creates the opportunity to control the divisions through the use of responsibility accounting. Revenue center control is achieved by evaluating the efficiency and the effectiveness of divisional managers on the basis of sales revenue. Cost center control is based on control of costs and frequently employs variance analysis, as described in Chapters 20 and 21. This chapter focuses on the evaluation of profit centers and investment centers.

YOU DECIDE   Organizational Structure

You have been chosen as the CEO of a new hospital. One important decision you face early is determining the optimal level of decentralization for your various levels of supporting management.

What factors should you consider as you decide how best to structure the hospital management?

There is no easy, one-size-fits all answer. However, some of the top ranked hospitals in the world, such as the **Cleveland Clinic**, recognize that much of the specific knowledge critically important for making the best patient care decisions resides with the hospital's physicians, surgeons, and nurses rather than with the Chief Executive Officer or other "C-Suite" executives (e.g., Chief Financial Officer, Chief Operations Officer, Chief Integrity Officer, etc.). Such hospitals choose a highly decentralized organizational structure so that many important decisions that affect patient treatment are made by individuals far removed from top management. The biggest challenge to effectively managing a highly decentralized decision making structure like this one is to create quantitative performance measures for the decision makers—in this case the physicians, surgeons, and nurses—to assess the quality of their decisions. Furthermore, these performance measures need to be used as part of the decision makers' compensation packages to reward (or punish) their wise (or unwise) decisions that hopefully are taken in the best interest of the patients and, ultimately, the hospital. A growing number of publicly-traded companies, such as **Starbucks**, offer lower level employees—even part-time employees—incentives such as healthcare benefits and stock options to motivate them to take actions that are in the companies' best long-term interests.

In decentralized organizations, managerial accounting is important in designing effective performance measures and incentive systems to help ensure that lower-level managers use their decision-making authority to improve the organization's performance.

MEASURING THE PERFORMANCE OF PROFIT CENTERS BY USING VARIABLE AND ABSORPTION INCOME STATEMENTS

Profit centers are evaluated based on income statements. However, the overall income statement for the company would be of little use for this purpose. Instead, it is important to develop a segmented income statement for each profit center. Two methods of computing income have been developed: one based on variable costing and the other based on full or absorption costing. These are costing methods because they refer to the way in which product costs are determined. Recall from Chapter 13 that *product costs* are inventoried; they include direct materials, direct labor, and overhead. *Period costs*, such as selling and administrative expense, are expensed in the period incurred. The difference between variable and absorption costing hinges on the treatment of one particular cost: fixed factory overhead.

Absorption Costing

Absorption costing assigns *all* manufacturing costs to the product. Direct materials, direct labor, variable overhead, and fixed overhead define the cost of a product. Thus, under absorption costing, fixed overhead is viewed as a product cost, not a period cost. Under this method, fixed overhead is assigned to the product through the use of a predetermined fixed overhead rate and is not expensed until the product is sold. In other words, fixed overhead is an inventoriable cost.

Variable Costing

Variable costing stresses the difference between fixed and variable manufacturing costs. **Variable costing** assigns only variable manufacturing costs to the product; these costs include direct materials, direct labor, and variable overhead. Fixed overhead is treated as a period expense and is *excluded* from the product cost. The rationale for this is that fixed overhead is a cost of capacity, or staying in business. Once the period is over, any benefits provided by capacity have expired and should not be inventoried. Under variable costing, fixed overhead of a period is seen as expiring that period and is charged in total against the revenues of the period.

Comparison of Variable and Absorption Costing Methods

Exhibit 22-4 illustrates the classification of costs as product or period costs under absorption and variable costing.

Generally accepted accounting principles (GAAP) require absorption costing for external reporting. The Financial Accounting Standards Board (FASB), the Internal Revenue Service (IRS), and other regulatory bodies do not accept variable costing as a product-costing method for external reporting. Yet variable costing can supply vital cost information for decision making and control, information not supplied by absorption costing. For *internal* application, variable costing is an important managerial tool.

Exhibit 22-4

Classification of Costs under Absorption and Variable Costing as Product or Period Costs

	Absorption Costing	Variable Costing
Product costs	Direct materials Direct labor Variable overhead Fixed overhead	Direct materials Direct labor Variable overhead
Period costs	Selling expenses Administrative expenses	Fixed overhead Selling expenses Administrative expenses

Inventory Valuation

Inventory is valued at product or manufacturing cost. (Recall that inventory cost *never* includes the period costs of selling or administration.) Under absorption costing, that product cost includes direct materials, direct labor, variable overhead, and fixed overhead. Under variable costing, the product cost includes only direct materials, direct labor, and variable overhead. **CORNERSTONE 22-1** shows how to compute inventory cost under absorption and variable costing.

CORNERSTONE 22-1   Computing Inventory Cost under Absorption and Variable Costing

Information:

During the most recent year, Fairchild Company had the following data associated with the product it makes:

Units in beginning inventory	—
Units produced	10,000
Units sold ($300 per unit)	8,000
Variable costs per unit:	
Direct materials	$50
Direct labor	$100
Variable overhead	$50
Fixed costs:	
Fixed overhead per unit produced	$25
Fixed selling and administrative	$100,000

Required:

1. How many units are in ending inventory?
2. Using absorption costing, calculate the per-unit product cost. What is the value of ending inventory?
3. Using variable costing, calculate the per-unit product cost. What is the value of ending inventory?

Solution:

1. Units in ending inventory = Units in beginning inventory + Units produced − Units sold
   $$= 0 + 10,000 − 8,000 = 2,000$$

2. Absorption costing unit cost:

Direct materials	$ 50
Direct labor	100
Variable overhead	50
Fixed overhead	25
Unit product cost	$225

   Value of ending inventory = Units ending inventory × Absorption unit product cost
   $$= 2,000 \text{ units} × \$225 = \$450,000$$

3. Variable costing unit cost:

Direct materials	$ 50
Direct labor	100
Variable overhead	50
Unit product cost	$200

   Value of ending inventory = Units ending inventory × Variable unit product cost
   $$= 2,000 \text{ units} × \$200 = \$400,000$$

Income Statements Using Variable and Absorption Costing

Because unit product costs are the basis for cost of goods sold, the variable- and absorption-costing methods can lead to different operating income figures. The difference arises because of the amount of fixed overhead recognized as an expense under the two methods. **CORNERSTONE 22-2** shows how to develop cost of goods sold and income statements for absorption and variable costing.

CORNERSTONE 22-2

Preparing Income Statements under Absorption and Variable Costing

Information:

During the most recent year, Fairchild Company had the following data associated with the product it makes:

Units in beginning inventory	—
Units produced	10,000
Units sold ($300 per unit)	8,000
Variable costs per unit:	
Direct materials	$50
Direct labor	$100
Variable overhead	$50
Fixed costs:	
Fixed overhead per unit produced	$25
Fixed selling and administrative	$100,000

Required:

1. Calculate the cost of goods sold under absorption costing.
2. Calculate the cost of goods sold under variable costing.
3. Prepare an income statement using absorption costing.
4. Prepare an income statement using variable costing.

Solution:

1. Cost of goods sold = Absorption unit product cost × Units sold
   = $225 × 8,000 = $1,800,000

   Note: Cornerstone 22-1 (p. 1109) shows the detailed calculation of the $225 unit product cost under absorption costing.

2. Cost of goods sold = Variable unit product cost × Units sold
   = $200 × 8,000 = $1,600,000

   Note: Cornerstone 22-1 shows the detailed calculation of the $200 unit product cost under variable costing.

3.
Fairchild Company
Absorption-Costing Income Statement
For Most Recent Year

Sales ($300 × 8,000)	$ 2,400,000
Less: Cost of goods sold	(1,800,000)
Gross margin	$ 600,000
Less: Selling and administrative expenses	(100,000)
Operating income	$ 500,000

(Continued)

4.

Fairchild Company
Variable-Costing Income Statement
For Most Recent Year

Sales ($300 × 8,000)		$ 2,400,000
Less variable expenses:		
Variable cost of goods sold		(1,600,000)
Contribution margin		$ 800,000
Less fixed expenses:		
Fixed overhead	$(250,000)*	
Fixed selling and administrative	(100,000)	(350,000)
Operating income		$ 450,000

*$25/unit × 10,000 units = $250,000

CORNERSTONE
22-2
(continued)

Cornerstone 22-2 demonstrates that absorption-costing income is $50,000 higher than variable-costing income. This difference is due to some of the period's fixed overhead flowing into inventory when absorption costing is used. As a result, less fixed overhead cost flowed into the absorption-costing cost of goods sold, thereby increasing net income by $50,000 relative to variable costing operating income. In fact, only $200,000 ($25 × 8,000) of fixed overhead was included in cost of goods sold for absorption costing; the remaining $50,000 ($25 × 2,000) was added to inventory. Under variable costing, however, all of the $250,000 of fixed overhead cost for the period was added to expense on the income statement.

Notice that selling and administrative expenses are never included in product cost. They always are expensed on the income statement and never appear on the balance sheet.

Production, Sales, and Income Relationships

The relationship between variable-costing income and absorption-costing income changes as the relationship between production and sales changes. If more is sold than was produced, variable-costing income is greater than absorption-costing income. This situation is just the opposite of the Fairchild example. Selling more than was produced means that beginning inventory and units produced are being sold. Under absorption costing, units coming out of inventory have attached to them fixed overhead from a prior period. In addition, units produced and sold have all of the current period's fixed overhead attached. Thus, the amount of fixed overhead expensed by absorption costing is greater than the current period's fixed overhead by the amount of fixed overhead flowing out of inventory. Accordingly, variable-costing income is greater than absorption-costing income by the amount of fixed overhead flowing out of beginning inventory.

If production and sales are equal, of course, no difference exists between the two reported incomes. Since the units produced are all sold, absorption costing, like variable costing, will recognize the total fixed overhead of the period as an expense. No fixed overhead flows into or out of inventory.

The relationships between production, sales, and the two reported incomes are summarized in Exhibit 22-5 (p. 1112). Note that if production is greater than sales, then inventory has increased. If production is less than sales, then inventory must have decreased. If production is equal to sales, then the number of units in beginning inventory is equal to the number of units in ending inventory.

The difference between absorption and variable costing centers on the recognition of expense associated with fixed factory overhead. Under absorption costing, fixed factory overhead must be assigned to units produced. This presents two problems that we have not explicitly considered.

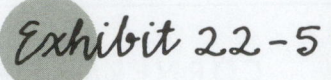
Exhibit 22-5

Production, Sales, and Income Relationships

If	Then
1. Production > Sales	Absorption income > Variable income
2. Production < Sales	Absorption income < Variable income
3. Production = Sales	Absorption income = Variable income

- First, how do we convert factory overhead applied on the basis of direct labor hours or machine hours into factory overhead applied to units produced?
- Second, what is done when actual factory overhead does not equal applied factory overhead?

The solution to these problems is reserved for a more advanced accounting course.

Evaluating Profit-Center Managers

The evaluation of managers is often tied to the profitability of the units that they control. How income changes from one period to the next and how actual income compares with planned income are frequently used as signals of managerial ability. To be meaningful signals, however, income should reflect managerial effort. For example, if a manager has worked hard and increased sales while holding costs in check, income should increase over the prior period, signaling success. In general terms, if income performance is expected to reflect managerial performance, then managers have the right to expect the following:

- As sales revenue increases from one period to the next, all other things being equal, income should increase.
- As sales revenue decreases from one period to the next, all other things being equal, income should decrease.
- As sales revenue remains unchanged from one period to the next, all other things being equal, income should remain unchanged.

Variable costing ensures that the above relationships hold; however, absorption costing may not.

SEGMENTED INCOME STATEMENTS USING VARIABLE COSTING

Variable costing is useful in preparing segmented income statements because it gives useful information on variable and fixed expenses. A **segment** is a subunit of a company of sufficient importance to warrant the production of performance reports. Segments can be divisions, departments, product lines, customer classes, and so on. In segmented income statements, fixed expenses are broken down into two categories: *direct fixed expenses* and *common fixed expenses*. This additional subdivision highlights controllable versus noncontrollable costs and enhances the manager's ability to evaluate each segment's contribution to overall firm performance.

Direct Fixed Expenses

Direct fixed expenses are fixed expenses that are directly traceable to a segment. These are sometimes referred to as *avoidable fixed expenses* or *traceable fixed expenses* because they vanish if the segment is eliminated. For example, if the segments were sales regions, a direct fixed expense for each region would be the rent for the sales office, salary of the sales manager of each region, and so on. If one region were to be eliminated, then those fixed expenses would disappear. For instance, if **United Airlines** were to vacate the $515 million, 85-acre "Terminal for Tomorrow" at Chicago's O'Hare International Airport, it would avoid the substantial costs it incurs each year to operate and maintain that terminal.

Common Fixed Expenses

Common fixed expenses are jointly caused by two or more segments. These expenses persist even if one of the segments to which they are common is eliminated. For example, depreciation on the corporate headquarters building, the salary of the CEO, and the cost of printing and distributing the annual report to shareholders are common fixed expenses for **Walt Disney Company**. If Walt Disney Company were to sell a theme park or open a new one, those common expenses would not be affected.

Preparing Segmented Income Statements

CORNERSTONE 22-3 shows how to prepare a segmented income statement where the segments are product lines. In the example, Audiomatronics produces both MP3 players and DVD players.

CORNERSTONE
22-3

Preparing a Segmented Income Statement

Information:

Audiomatronics Inc. produces MP3 players and DVD players in a single factory. The following information was provided for the coming year.

	MP3 Players	DVD Players
Sales	$400,000	$290,000
Variable cost of goods sold	200,000	150,000
Direct fixed overhead	30,000	20,000

A 5 percent sales commission is paid for each of the product lines. Direct fixed selling and administrative expense was estimated to be $10,000 for the MP3 line and $15,000 for the DVD line. Common fixed overhead for the factory was estimated to be $100,000. Common selling and administrative expense was estimated to be $20,000.

Required:

Prepare a segmented income statement for Audiomatronics Inc. for the coming year, using variable costing.

Solution:

Audiomatronics Inc.
Segmented Income Statement
For the Coming Year

	MP3 Players	DVD Players	Total
Sales	$ 400,000	$ 290,000	$ 690,000
Variable cost of goods sold	(200,000)	(150,000)	(350,000)
Variable selling expense*	(20,000)	(14,500)	(34,500)
Contribution margin	$ 180,000	$ 125,500	$ 305,500
Less direct fixed expenses:			
Direct fixed overhead	(30,000)	(20,000)	(50,000)
Direct selling and administrative	(10,000)	(15,000)	(25,000)
Segment margin	$ 140,000	$ 90,500	$ 230,500
Less common fixed expenses:			
Common fixed overhead			(100,000)
Common selling and administrative			(20,000)
Operating income			$ 110,500

*Variable selling expense for MP3 players = 0.05 × Sales = 0.05 × $400,000 = $20,000
 Variable selling expense for DVD players = 0.05 × Sales = 0.05 × $290,000 = $14,500

Notice that Cornerstone 22-3 (p. 1113) shows that both products have large positive contribution margins ($180,000 for MP3 players and $125,500 for DVD players). Both products are providing revenue above variable costs that can be used to help cover the firm's fixed costs. However, some of the firm's fixed costs are caused by the segments themselves. Thus, the real measure of the profit contribution of each segment is what is left over after these direct fixed costs are covered.

The profit contribution each segment makes toward covering a firm's common fixed costs is called the **segment margin**. A segment should at least be able to cover both its own variable costs and direct fixed costs. A negative segment margin drags down the firm's total profit, making it time to consider dropping the product. Ignoring any effect a segment may have on the sales of other segments, the segment margin measures the change in a firm's profits that would occur if the segment were eliminated.

OBJECTIVE ③
Compute and explain return on investment.

MEASURING THE PERFORMANCE OF INVESTMENT CENTERS BY USING RETURN ON INVESTMENT

Typically, investment centers are evaluated on the basis of return on investment (ROI). Other common measures include residual income and economic value added (EVA).

Return on Investment

Divisions that are investment centers will have an income statement and a balance sheet. So, could those divisions be ranked on the basis of income? Suppose, for example, that a company has two divisions—Alpha and Beta. Alpha's income is $100,000, and Beta's income is $200,000. Did Beta perform better than Alpha? What if Alpha used an investment of $500,000 to produce the contribution of $100,000, while Beta used an investment of $2 million to produce the $200,000 contribution? Does your response change? Clearly, it does. Relating the reported operating profits to the assets used to produce them is a more meaningful measure of performance.

One way to relate operating profits to assets employed is to compute the **return on investment (ROI)**, which is the profit earned per dollar of investment. ROI is the most common measure of performance for an investment center. It can be defined as follows:

$$ROI = \frac{\text{Operating income}}{\text{Average operating assets}}$$

Operating income refers to earnings before interest and taxes. **Operating assets** are all assets acquired to generate operating income, including cash, receivables, inventories, land, buildings, and equipment. Average operating assets is computed as follows:

$$\text{Average operating assets} = \frac{(\text{Beginning assets} + \text{Ending assets})}{2}$$

Opinions vary regarding how long-term assets (plant and equipment) should be valued (e.g., gross book value vs. net book value or historical cost vs. current cost). Most firms use historical cost and net book value.[1]

Going back to our example, Alpha's ROI is 0.20, calculated as:

$$\frac{\text{Operating income}}{\text{Average operating assets}} = \frac{\$100,000}{\$500,000}$$

Beta's ROI is only 0.10 ($200,000/$2,000,000). The formula for ROI is quick and easy to use. However, the decomposition of ROI into margin and turnover ratios gives additional information. **CORNERSTONE 22-4** shows how to calculate these ratios.

---

[1] There is no one correct way to calculate ROI. The important thing is to be sure that one method is applied consistently, which allows the company to compare the ROIs among divisions and over time.

CORNERSTONE 22-4
Calculating Average Operating Assets, Margin, Turnover, and Return on Investment

Information:

Celimar Company's Western Division earned operating income last year as shown in the following income statement:

Sales	$ 480,000
Cost of goods sold	(222,000)
Gross margin	$ 258,000
Selling and administrative expense	(210,000)
Operating income	$ 48,000

At the beginning of the year, the value of operating assets was $277,000. At the end of the year, the value of operating assets was $323,000.

Required:

For the Western Division, calculate the following: (1) average operating assets, (2) margin, (3) turnover, and (4) return on investment.

Solution:

1. Average operating assets = (Beginning assets + Ending assets)/2
    = ($277,000 + $323,000)/2
    = $300,000

2. Margin = Operating income/Sales = $48,000/$480,000
    = 0.10 or 10 percent

3. Turnover = Sales/Average operating assets = $480,000/$300,000 = 1.6

4. ROI = Operating income/Average operating assets = $480,000/$300,000 = 0.16 or 16 percent

    Note: As will be discussed in the section that follows, ROI can also be calculated as
    ROI = Margin × Turnover
    = 0.10 × 1.6
    = 0.16, or 16 percent

Margin and Turnover

A second way to calculate ROI is to separate the formula (Operating income/Average operating assets) into margin and turnover. **Margin** is the ratio of operating income to sales. It tells how many cents of operating income result from each dollar of sales. It expresses the portion of sales that is available for interest, taxes, and profit. Some managers also refer to margin as return on sales. **Turnover** is a different measure; it is found by dividing sales by average operating assets. Turnover tells how many dollars of sales result from every dollar invested in operating assets. It shows how productively assets are being used to generate sales.

$$\text{ROI} = \underbrace{\frac{\text{Operating income}}{\text{Sales}}}_{\text{Margin}} \times \underbrace{\frac{\text{Sales}}{\text{Average operating assets}}}_{\text{Turnover}}$$

Notice that "Sales" in the above formula can be cancelled out to yield the original ROI formula of Operating income/Average operating assets.

Suppose, for example, that Alpha had sales of $400,000. Then, margin would be 0.25, calculated as

$$\frac{\text{Operating income}}{\text{Sales}} = \frac{\$100,000}{\$400,000}$$

Turnover would be 0.80, calculated as

$$\frac{\text{Sales}}{\text{Average operating assets}} = \frac{\$400,000}{\$500,000}$$

While both approaches yield the same ROI, the calculation of margin and turnover gives a manager valuable information. To illustrate this additional information, consider the data presented in Exhibit 22-6. The Electronics Division improved its ROI from 18 percent in Year 1 to 20 percent in Year 2. The Medical Supplies Division's ROI, however, dropped from 18 to 15 percent. Computing the margin and turnover ratios for each division gives a better picture of what caused the change in rates. As with variance analysis, understanding the causes of managerial accounting measures (i.e., variances, margins, turnover, etc.) helps managers take actions to improve the division. These ratios also are presented in Exhibit 22-6.

Notice that the margins for both divisions dropped from Year 1 to Year 2. In fact, the divisions experienced the *same* percentage of decline (16.67 percent). A declining margin could be explained by increasing expenses, competitive pressures (forcing a decrease in selling prices), or both.

Despite the declining margin, the Electronics Division was able to increase its rate of return. The reason is that the increase in turnover more than compensated for the decline in margin. One explanation for the increased turnover could be a deliberate policy to reduce inventories.

(Notice that the average assets employed remained the same for the Electronics Division even though sales increased by $10 million.)

Exhibit 22-6

Comparison of Divisional Performance

	Comparison of ROI	
	Electronics Division	**Medical Supplies Division**
Year 1:		
Sales	$30,000,000	$117,000,000
Operating income	1,800,000	3,510,000
Average operating assets	10,000,000	19,510,000
ROI[a]	18%	18%
Year 2:		
Sales	$40,000,000	$117,000,000
Operating income	2,000,000	2,925,000
Average operating assets	10,000,000	19,500,000
ROI[a]	20%	15%

	Margin and Turnover Comparisons			
	Electronics Division		**Medical Supplies Division**	
	Year 1	**Year 2**	**Year 1**	**Year 2**
Margin[b]	6.0%	5.0%	3.0%	2.5%
Turnover[c]	×3.0	×4.0	×6.0	×6.0
ROI	18.0%	20.0%	18.0%	15.0%

[a]Operating income/Average operating assets
[b]Operating income/Sales
[c]Sales/Average operating assets

The experience of the Medical Supplies Division was less favorable. Because its turnover rate remained unchanged, its ROI dropped. This division, unlike the Electronics Division, could not overcome the decline in margin.

Advantages of Return on Investment

At least three positive results stem from the use of ROI:

- It encourages managers to focus on the relationship among sales, expenses, and investment, as should be the case for a manager of an investment center.
- It encourages managers to focus on cost efficiency.
- It encourages managers to focus on operating asset efficiency.

These advantages are illustrated by the following three scenarios.

Concept Q&A

Think about some stores in your town, such as a jewelry store, fast-food outlet, and grocery store. How do you suppose their margins and turnover ratios compare with each other? Explain your thinking.

Answer:

Fast-food outlets and grocery stores probably have low margins and high turnover. These financial characteristics exist because they deal in perishables and must have continual turnover or the food will go bad. A jewelry store, on the other hand, has high margin and relatively low turnover. These financial characteristics exist because the goods are not perishable and there is relatively less competition in this market. (The existence of competition, of course, changes as more jewelry stores enter a market and as consumers become more confident about buying jewelry online.)

Illustrating Relationships: Focus on Return on Investment Relationships

Della Barnes, manager of the Plastics Division, is mulling over a suggestion from her marketing vice president to increase the advertising budget by $100,000. The marketing vice president is confident that this increase will boost sales by $200,000. Della realizes that the increased sales will also raise expenses. She finds that the increased variable cost will be $80,000.

The division also will need to purchase additional machinery to handle the increased production. The equipment will cost $50,000 and will add $10,000 of depreciation expense. As a result, the proposal will add $10,000 ($200,000 − $80,000 − $10,000 − $100,000) to operating income. Currently, the division has sales of $2 million, total expenses of $1,850,000, and operating income of $150,000. Operating assets equal $1 million.

	Without Increased Advertising	With Increased Advertising
Sales	$2,000,000	$2,200,000
Less: Expenses	1,850,000	2,040,000
Operating income	$ 150,000	$ 160,000
Average operating assets	$1,000,000	$1,050,000

ROI:

$150,000/$1,000,000 = 0.15, or 15 percent

$160,000/$1,050,000 = 0.1524, or 15.24 percent

The ROI without the additional advertising is 15 percent. The ROI with the additional advertising and $50,000 investment in assets is 15.24 percent. Since ROI is increased by the proposal, Della decides to authorize the increased advertising. In effect, the current ROI, without the proposal, is the hurdle rate. **Hurdle rate** indicate the minimum ROI necessary to accept an investment.

Focus on Cost Efficiency

Kyle Chugg, manager of Turner's Battery Division, groaned as he reviewed the projections for the last half of the current fiscal year. The recession was hurting his division's performance. Adding the projected operating income of $200,000 to the actual operating income of the first half produced expected annual earnings of $425,000. Kyle then divided the expected operating income by the division's average operating assets to obtain an expected ROI of 12.15 percent. "This is awful," muttered Kyle. "Last year our ROI was 16 percent. And I'm looking at a couple more bad years before business returns to normal. Something has to be done to improve our performance."

Kyle directed all operating managers to identify and eliminate nonvalue-added activities. As a result, lower-level managers found ways to reduce costs by $150,000 for the remaining half of the year. This reduction increased the annual operating income from

$425,000 to $575,000, increasing ROI from 12.15 percent to 16.43 percent as a result. Interestingly, Kyle found that some of the reductions could be maintained after business returned to normal.

Focus on Operating Asset Efficiency The Electronic Storage Division prospered during its early years. In the beginning, the division developed portable external disk drives for storing data; sales and ROI were extraordinarily high. However, during the past several years, competitors had developed similar technology, and the division's ROI had plunged from 30 to 15 percent. Cost cutting had helped initially, but all of the fat had been removed, making further improvements from cost reductions impossible. Moreover, any increase in sales was unlikely—competition was too stiff. The divisional manager searched for some way to increase the ROI by at least 3 to 5 percent. Only by raising the ROI so that it compared favorably with that of the other divisions, could the division expect to receive additional capital for research and development (R&D).

The divisional manager initiated an intensive program to reduce operating assets. Most of the gains were made in the area of inventory reductions. However, one plant was closed because of a long-term reduction in market share. By installing a just-in-time purchasing and manufacturing system, the division was able to reduce its asset base without threatening its remaining market share. Finally, the reduction in operating assets meant that operating costs could be decreased still further. The end result was a 50 percent increase in the division's ROI, from 15 percent to more than 22 percent.

Disadvantages of the Return on Investment Measure

Overemphasis on ROI can produce myopic behavior. Two negative aspects associated with ROI frequently are:

- It can produce a narrow focus on divisional profitability at the expense of profitability for the overall firm.
- It encourages managers to focus on the short run at the expense of the long run.

These disadvantages are illustrated by the following two scenarios.

Narrow Focus on Divisional Profitability A Cleaning Products Division has the opportunity to invest in two projects for the coming year. The outlay required for each investment, the dollar returns, and the ROI are as follows:

	Project I	Project II
Investment	$10,000,000	$4,000,000
Operating income	1,300,000	640,000
ROI	13%	16%

The division currently earns ROI of 15 percent, with operating assets of $50 million and operating income on current investments of $7.5 million. The division has approval to request up to $15 million in new investment capital. Corporate headquarters requires that all investments earn at least 10 percent (this rate represents the corporation's cost of acquiring the capital). Any capital not used by a division is invested by headquarters, and it earns exactly 10 percent.

The division manager has four alternatives: (1) invest in Project I, (2) invest in Project II, (3) invest in both Projects I and II, or (4) invest in neither project. The divisional ROI was computed for each alternative.

	Alternatives			
	Select Project I	Select Project II	Select Both Projects	Select Neither Project
Operating income	$8,800,000	$8,140,000	$9,440,000	$7,500,000
Operating assets	$60,000,000	$54,000,000	$64,000,000	$50,000,000
ROI	14.67%	15.07%	14.75%	15.00%

The divisional manager chose to invest only in Project II, since it would boost ROI from 15.00 percent to 15.07 percent.

While the manager's choice maximized divisional ROI, it did not maximize the profit the company could have earned. If Project I had been selected, the company would have earned $1.3 million in profits. By not selecting Project I, the $10 million in capital is invested at 10 percent, earning only $1 million (0.10 × $10,000,000). The single-minded focus on divisional ROI, then, cost the company $300,000 in profits ($1,300,000 − $1,000,000).

Encourages Short-Run Optimization Ruth Lunsford, manager of a Small Tools Division, was displeased with her division's performance during the first three quarters. Given the expected income for the fourth quarter, the ROI for the year would be 13 percent, at least two percentage points below where she had hoped to be. Such an ROI might not be strong enough to justify the early promotion she wanted. With only three months left, drastic action was needed. Increasing sales for the last quarter was unlikely. Most sales were booked at least two to three months in advance. Emphasizing extra sales activity would benefit next year's performance. What was needed were some ways to improve this year's performance.

After careful thought, Ruth decided to take the following actions:

- Lay off five of the highest paid salespeople.
- Cut the advertising budget for the fourth quarter by 50 percent.
- Delay all promotions within the division for three months.
- Reduce the preventive maintenance budget by 75 percent.
- Use cheaper raw materials for fourth-quarter production.

In the aggregate, these steps would reduce expenses, increase income, and raise the ROI to about 15.2 percent for the current year.

While Ruth's actions increase the profits and ROI in the short run, they have some long-run negative consequences. Laying off the highest paid (and possibly the best) salespeople may harm the division's future sales-generating capabilities. Future sales could also be hurt by cutting back on advertising and using cheaper raw materials. Delaying promotions could hurt employee morale, which could, in turn, lower productivity and future sales. Finally, reducing preventive maintenance will likely increase downtime and decrease the life of the productive equipment.

ETHICAL DECISION Ethical considerations also come into play when managers attempt to "game" ROI. Ruth's five top-earning salespeople probably were her best salespeople. Letting them go meant that sales probably would decrease, an outcome not in the best interest of the firm. Thus, her action is directly contrary to her obligation to take actions in the best interests of the company. The layoffs also might violate the implicit contract a company has with workers that outstanding work will lead to continued employment. ●

MEASURING THE PERFORMANCE OF INVESTMENT CENTERS BY USING RESIDUAL INCOME AND ECONOMIC VALUE ADDED

OBJECTIVE 4
Compute and explain residual income and economic value added.

To compensate for the tendency of ROI to discourage investments that are profitable for the company but that lower a division's ROI, some companies have adopted alternative performance measures such as residual income. EVA is an alternate way to calculate residual income that is being used in a number of companies, such as **Herman Miller**.

 HermanMiller

Residual Income

Residual income is the difference between operating income and the minimum dollar return required on a company's operating assets:

Residual income = Operating income − (Minimum rate of return × Average operating assets)

CORNERSTONE 22-5 shows how to calculate residual income.

CORNERSTONE 22-5

Calculating Residual Income

Information:
Celimar Company's Western Division earned operating income last year as shown in the following income statement:

Sales	$480,000
Cost of goods sold	222,000
Gross margin	$258,000
Selling and administrative expense	210,000
Operating income	$ 48,000

At the beginning of the year, the value of operating assets was $277,000. At the end of the year, the value of operating assets was $323,000. Celimar Company requires a minimum rate of return of 12 percent.

Required:
For the Western Division, calculate (1) average operating assets and (2) residual income.

Solution:
1. Average operating assets = (Beginning assets + Ending assets)/2
    = ($277,000 + $323,000)/2
    = $300,000

2. Residual income = Operating income − (Minimum rate of return × Average operating assets)
    = $48,000 − (0.12 × $300,000)
    = $48,000 − $36,000
    = $12,000

The minimum rate of return is set by the company and is the same as the hurdle rate (see the section on ROI). If residual income is greater than zero, then the division is earning more than the minimum required rate of return (or hurdle rate). If residual income is less than zero, then the division is earning less than the minimum required rate of return. Finally, if residual income equals zero, then the division is earning precisely the minimum required rate of return.

Advantage of Residual Income Recall that the manager of the Cleaning Products Division rejected Project I because it would have reduced divisional ROI. However, that decision cost the company $300,000 in profits. The use of residual income as the performance measure would have prevented this loss. The residual income for each project is computed as follows:

Project I
Residual income = Operating income − (Minimum rate of return × Average operating assets)
    = $1,300,000 − (0.10 × $10,000,000)
    = $1,300,000 − $1,000,000
    = $300,000

Project II
Residual income = $640,000 − (0.10 × $4,000,000)
    = $640,000 − $400,000
    = $240,000

Notice that both projects have positive residual income. For comparative purposes, the divisional residual income for each of the four alternatives identified is as follows:

	Alternatives			
	Select Only Project I	Select Only Project II	Select Both Projects	Select Neither Project
Operating assets	$60,000,000	$54,000,000	$64,000,000	$50,000,000
Operating income	$ 8,800,000	$ 8,140,000	$ 9,440,000	$ 7,500,000
Minimum return*	6,000,000	5,400,000	6,400,000	5,000,000
Residual income	$ 2,800,000	$ 2,740,000	$ 3,040,000	$ 2,500,000

*0.10 × Operating assets

As shown in the table, selecting both projects produces the greatest increase in residual income. The use of residual income encourages managers to accept any project that earns a return that is above the minimum rate.

Disadvantages of Residual Income Residual income, like ROI, can encourage a short-run orientation. If Ruth Lunsford were being evaluated on the basis of residual income, she could have taken the same actions.

Another problem with residual income is that, unlike ROI, it is an absolute measure of profitability. Thus, direct comparison of the performance of two different investment centers becomes difficult, as the level of investment may differ. For example, consider the residual income computations for Division A and Division B where the minimum required rate of return is 8 percent.

	Division A	Division B
Average operating assets	$15,000,000	$2,500,000
Operating income	$ 1,500,000	$ 300,000
Minimum return[a]	(1,200,000)	(200,000)
Residual income	$ 300,000	$ 100,000
Residual return[b]	2%	4%

[a]0.08 × Operating assets
[b]Residual income/Operating assets

It is tempting to claim that Division A is outperforming Division B since its residual income is three times higher. Notice, however, that Division A is considerably larger than Division B and has six times as many assets. One possible way to correct this disadvantage is to compute both ROI and residual income and to use both measures for performance evaluation. ROI could then be used for interdivisional comparisons.

Economic Value Added (EVA)

Another financial performance measure that is similar to residual income is *economic value added*. **Economic value added (EVA)**[2] is after tax operating income minus the dollar cost of capital employed. The dollar cost of capital employed is the actual percentage cost of capital[3] multiplied by the total capital employed, expressed as follows:

EVA = After-tax operating income − (Actual percentage cost of capital × Total capital employed)

[2] EVA was developed by Stern Stewart & Co. in the 1990s. More information can be found on the firm's website, http://www.sternstewart.com/evaabout/whatis.php.
[3] The computation of a company's actual cost of capital is reserved for advanced accounting courses.

CORNERSTONE **22-6** shows how to calculate EVA.

CORNERSTONE 22-6

Calculating Economic Value Added

Information:

Celimar Company's Western Division earned net income last year as shown in the following income statement:

Sales	$480,000
Cost of goods sold	222,000
Gross margin	$258,000
Selling and administrative expense	210,000
Operating income	$ 48,000
Less: Income taxes (@ 30%)	14,400
Net income	$ 33,600

Total capital employed equaled $300,000. Celimar Company's actual cost of capital is 10 percent.

Required:

Calculate EVA for the Western Division.

Solution:

EVA = After-tax operating income − (Actual percentage cost of capital × Total capital employed)

$\quad$ = $33,600 − (0.10 × $300,000)

$\quad$ = $33,600 − $30,000

$\quad$ = $3,600

Basically, EVA is residual income with the minimum rate of return equal to the actual cost of capital for the firm (as opposed to some minimum rate of return desired by the company for other reasons). If EVA is positive, then the company has increased its wealth during the period. If EVA is negative, then the company has decreased its wealth during the period. Consider the old saying, "It takes money to make money." EVA helps the company to determine whether the money it makes is more than the money it takes to make it. Over the long term, only those companies creating capital, or wealth, can survive.

As a form of residual income, EVA is a dollar figure, not a percentage rate of return. However, it does bear a resemblance to rates of return such as ROI because it links net income (return) to capital employed. The key feature of EVA is its emphasis on *after-tax* operating profit and the *actual* cost of capital. Residual income, on the other hand, uses a minimum expected rate of return.

Investors like EVA because it relates profit to the amount of resources needed to achieve it. A number of companies are evaluated on the basis of EVA. For example, the annual economic value added for **General Electric**, **Wal-Mart**, and **Merck & Co.** was reported to be $5.98 billion, $2.93 billion, and $3.87 billion, respectively.[4] Among large companies showing negative EVA were **IBM** at ($8.03) billion, **Verizon Communications** at ($5.61) billion, and **Disney Company** at ($2.07) billion. Smaller companies also differed in terms of their economic value added. **Pixar**'s was positive at $31 million

Concept Q&A

What are the differences and similarities between the basic residual income calculation and EVA?

Answer:

Residual income can use either before-tax income (operating income) or after-tax income. In addition, residual income uses a minimum required rate of return set by upper management. EVA, on the other hand, uses after-tax income and requires the company to compute its actual cost of capital.

[4] Stephen Taub, "MVPs of MVA," *CFO Magazine* (July 1, 2003), http://www.cfo.com/article/1,5309,9854%7C22%7CA%7C14%7C,00.html (accessed December 13, 2006).

while **JetBlue Airways Corp.** came in at $15 million. One important caveat for EVA metrics is that their calculation is not based on Generally Accepted Accounting Principles (GAAP), which means that ten different organizations likely will calculate EVA in ten different ways, unlike GAAP metrics that must be calculated in the same manner by all organizations.

Behavioral Aspects of Economic Value Added A number of companies have discovered that EVA helps to encourage the right kind of behavior from their divisions in a way that emphasis on operating income alone cannot. The underlying reason is EVA's reliance on the true cost of capital. In some companies, the responsibility for investment decisions rests with corporate management. As a result, the cost of capital is considered a corporate expense rather than an expense attributable to particular divisions. If a division builds inventories and investment, the cost of financing that investment is passed along to the overall income statement and does not show up as a reduction from that division's operating income as it would under an EVA analysis. Without an EVA analysis, the result is to make investment seem free to the divisions, and of course, they want more.

Let's return briefly to **Herman Miller**'s use of EVA that was introduced at the beginning of the chapter. Before developing its EVA metrics (as part of its lean manufacturing initiative), Herman Miller would purchase or build in large batches to capture savings resulting from bulk transactions. For example, managers often would order a batch of 1,000 parts when only 200 actually were needed for custom orders. However, with the introduction of EVA, a capital charge was assessed on the fixed warehousing- and equipment-related assets required to process, transport, store, replace (in the event of obsolescence), and repair (if damaged) these large quantities of excess inventory. In so doing, EVA helped managers quickly realize that the costs of processing excess inventory often outweigh any benefits of purchasing or building in unnecessarily large quantities. Manager behavior at Herman Miller has changed dramatically as a result of EVA, as each part in the production process now is produced or purchased to match the customer order and that part moves through the entire process without significant delay, usually going out the door within a single day.

Not surprisingly, research indicates that more firms continue to adopt EVA measures as part of their overall performance evaluation package.[5] It should be cautioned, however, that research also shows that some firms that collect EVA measures struggle to integrate these relatively complex measures into managerial decision making without considerable training for the managers.[6]

THE BALANCED SCORECARD— BASIC CONCEPTS

OBJECTIVE **5**

Explain the uses of the Balanced Scorecard and the role of transfer pricing in a decentralized firm.

Segment income, ROI, residual income, and EVA are important measures of managerial performance, but they lead managers to focus only on dollar figures, which may not tell the whole story for the company. In addition, lower-level managers and employees may feel helpless to affect income or investment. As a result, nonfinancial operating measures that look at such factors as market share, customer complaints, personnel turnover ratios, and personnel development have been developed. Letting lower-level managers know that attention to long-run factors is also vital reduces the tendency to overemphasize financial measures.

Managers in an advanced manufacturing environment are especially likely to use multiple measures of performance and to include nonfinancial as well as financial measures. For example, **General Motors** evaluated Robert Lutz, then head of product development, on the basis of 12 criteria. These criteria include how well he used existing parts in new vehicles and how many engineering hours he cut from the development process.[7]

[5] Stern Stewart Research, "Stern Stewart's EVA Clients Outperform the Market and Their Peers," *EVAluation: Special Report* (October 2002).

[6] Alexander Mersereau, "Pushing the Art of Management Accounting," *CMA Management*, Volume 79, Issue 9 (February 1, 2006).

[7] David Welch and Kathleen Kerwin, "Rick Wagoner's Game Plan," *BusinessWeek* (February 10, 2003): 52–60.

The **Balanced Scorecard** is a strategic management system that defines a strategic-based responsibility accounting system. The Balanced Scorecard *translates* an organization's mission and strategy into operational objectives and performance measures for the following four perspectives:

- The **financial perspective** describes the economic consequences of actions taken in the other three perspectives.
- The **customer perspective** defines the customer and market segments in which the business unit will compete.
- The **internal business process perspective** describes the internal processes needed to provide value for customers and owners.
- The **learning and growth (infrastructure) perspective** defines the capabilities that an organization needs to create long-term growth and improvement. This perspective is concerned with three major *enabling factors:* employee capabilities, information systems capabilities, and employee attitudes (motivation, empowerment, and alignment).

Exhibit 22-7 shows a Balanced Scorecard for a typical hotel based on questionnaire data provided by a research survey of three- and four-star hotels.[8] The scorecard includes the four basic scorecard categories and objectives with key measures for each category.

Exhibit 22-7

Balanced Scorecard for Ashley Hotel*

Objective	Measure
Financial Perspective	
Operating Revenues	• Total daily operating revenue • Revenue per available room
Operating Costs	• Operating expenses relative to budget • Cost per occupant
Customer Perspective	
Customer Satisfaction	• Customer satisfaction ratings • Number of monthly complaints
Customer Loyalty	• Number of new reward club members • Percent of returning guests
Internal Perspective	
Employee Turnover	• Employee turnover rate • Number of employee complaints
Response to Customer Complaint	• Percentage of complaints receiving response • Average response time
Learning and Growth	
New Market Identification	• Growth in reward club membership for new demographic segments
Employee Training and Advancement	• Percentage of employees participating in training courses • Survey scores pre- and post-training sessions

*Measures are based on survey data reported from actual hotels—N. Evans, Assessing the Balanced Scorecard as a Management Tool for Hotels, *International Journal of Contemporary Hospitality Management.* Vol. 17 (Issue 4/5): 376–390.

---

[8] N. Evans, "Assessing the Balanced Scorecard as a Management Tool for Hotels," *International Journal of Contemporary Hospitality Management*, Vol. 17 (Issue 4/5, 2005): 376–390.

The Role of Performance Measures   The Balanced Scorecard is not simply a collection of critical performance measures. The performance measures are derived from a company's vision, strategy, and objectives. These measures must be *balanced* between the following measures:

- performance driver measures (i.e., lead indicators of future financial performance) and outcome measures (i.e., lagged indicators of financial performance)
- objective and subjective measures
- external and internal measures
- financial and nonfinancial measures

The performance measures must also be carefully *linked* to the organization's strategy. Doing so creates significant advantages for an organization. For example, each quarter, **Analog Devices**' senior managers discuss Balanced Scorecard results for the various divisions. On one occasion, managers noted problems with their new-product ratios—used to measure the effectiveness of R&D spending. They quickly discovered that one division lagged in developing new products. The division's manager focused heavily on R&D by investing more money and exploring new market segments, new product sales, and marketing strategies. Analog Devices' corporate vice president for marketing, quality, and planning noted that they wouldn't have been able to catch the problem so early if they just looked at financials.[9] Other companies, such as **Bank of Montreal**, **Hilton Hotels Corporation**, and **Duke University Children's Hospital** have had similar success.

The rapid and widespread adoption of this strategic management system is a strong testimonial of its worth. For example, companies like **General Electric**, **Verizon**, and **Microsoft** have adapted their initial Balanced Scorecards into risk dashboards that contain key financial and nonfinancial measures pertaining to the important risks that threaten organizational success.[10] In addition, other organizations, like **Wal-Mart**, adapt their Balanced Scorecards to include measures that help their suppliers focus on increasingly important sustainability issues like using less packaging materials and more effective packaging techniques.[11]

TRANSFER PRICING

One final issue that affects the performance measurement and evaluation of divisions within a decentralized organization is that of transfer pricing. In many decentralized organizations, the output of one division is used as the input of another. For example, assume that one division of **Sony** manufactures batteries for its VAIO computers, which in turn sells the batteries to another Sony division that uses them to complete the computer manufacturing process. This internal transfer between two divisions within Sony raises an accounting issue. How is the transferred good valued? When divisions are treated as responsibility centers, they are evaluated on the basis of their contribution to costs, revenues, operating income, ROI, and residual income or EVA, depending on the particular center type. As a result, the value of the transferred good is revenue to the selling division and cost to the buying division. This value, or internal price, is called the *transfer price*. In other words, a **transfer price** is the price charged for a component by the selling division to the buying division of the same company. Transfer pricing is a complex issue and has an impact on divisions and the company as a whole.

Impact of Transfer Pricing on Divisions and the Firm as a Whole

When one division of a company sells to another division, both divisions as well as the company as a whole are affected. The price charged for the transferred good affects both

- the costs of the buying division
- the revenues of the selling division

[9] Joel Kurtzman, "Is Your Company Off Course: Now You Can Find Out Why," *Fortune* (February 17, 1997), http://money.cnn.com/magazines/fortune/fortune_archive/1997/02/17/222180/index.htm (accessed December 13, 2006).
[10] Ante Spencer, "Giving the Boss the Big Picture," *BusinessWeek* (February 13, 2006).
[11] "Getting Leaner—Ahead of the Pack: Suppliers Adjust to New Packaging Priorities," *Retailing Today* (2006): 16–18.

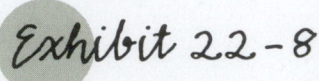

Exhibit 22-8

Impact of Transfer Price on Transferring Divisions and the Company, ABC Inc., as a Whole

Division A	Division C
Produces component and transfers it to C for transfer price of $30 per unit.	Purchases component from A at transfer price of $30 per unit and uses it in production of final product.
Transfer price = $30 per unit	Transfer price = $30 per unit
Revenue to A	Cost to C
Increases income	Decreases income
Increases ROI	Decreases ROI

Note: Transfer price revenue = Transfer price cost; zero dollar impact on ABC Inc.

Thus, the profits of both divisions, as well as the evaluation and compensation of their managers, are affected by the transfer price. Since profit-based performance measures of the two divisions are affected (for example, ROI and residual income), transfer pricing often can be an emotionally charged issue. Exhibit 22-8 illustrates the effect of the transfer price on two divisions of ABC Inc. Division A produces a component and sells it to another division of the same company, Division C. The $30 transfer price is revenue to Division A; clearly, Division A wants the price to be as high as possible. Conversely, the $30 transfer price is cost to Division C, just like the cost of any raw material. Division C prefers as low a transfer price as possible.

The actual transfer price nets out for the company *as a whole* in that total *pretax* income for the company is the same regardless of the transfer price. However, transfer pricing can affect the level of *after-tax* profits earned by the multinational company that operates in multiple countries with different corporate tax rates and other legal requirements set by the countries in which the various divisions generate income. For example, if the selling division operates in a low-tax country and the buying division operates in a high-tax country, the transfer price may be set quite high. Then, the high transfer price (a revenue for A) would increase profit in the division in the low-tax country, and the high transfer price (a cost for B) would decrease profit in the division in the high-tax country. This transfer pricing strategy reduces overall corporate income taxes. The international transfer pricing situation is examined in detail in more advanced courses.

Transfer Pricing Policies

Recall that a decentralized company allows much more authority for decision making at lower management levels. It would be counterproductive for the decentralized company to then decide on the actual transfer prices between two divisions. As a result, top management usually sets the transfer pricing policy.

Several transfer pricing policies are used in practice, including the following:

- market price
- cost-based transfer prices
- negotiated transfer prices

Market Price   If there is a competitive outside market for the transferred product, then the best transfer price is the market price. In such a case, divisional managers' actions will simultaneously optimize divisional profits and firmwide profits. Furthermore, no division can benefit at the expense of another. In this setting, top management will not be tempted to intervene.

Suppose that the Furniture Division of a corporation produces hide-a-beds. The Mattress Division of that same corporation produces mattresses, including a mattress model that fits into the hide-a-bed. If mattresses are transferred from the Mattress Division to the Furniture Division, a transfer pricing opportunity exists. Suppose that the mattresses can be sold to outside buyers at $50 each; this $50 is the market price and likely would serve as the transfer price.

Cost-Based Transfer Prices

Frequently, there is no good outside market price. The lack of a market price might occur because the transferred product uses patented designs owned by the parent company. Then, a company might use a *cost-based* transfer pricing approach. For example, suppose that the mattress company uses a high-density foam padding in the hide-a-bed mattress and that outside companies do not produce this type of mattress in the appropriate size. If the company has set a cost-based transfer pricing policy, then the Mattress Division will charge some measure of cost as the transfer price, such as the $28 mattress production cost.

Negotiated Transfer Prices

Finally, top management may allow the selling and buying division managers to *negotiate* a transfer price. This approach is particularly useful in cases with market imperfections, such as the ability of an in-house division to avoid selling and distribution costs that external market participants would have to incur. Using a negotiated transfer price then allows the two divisions to share any cost savings resulting from avoided costs.

Using the example of the Mattress and Furniture divisions, suppose that the hide-a-bed mattress typically sells for $50 and has product cost of $28. Normally, a sales commission of $5 is paid to the salesperson, but that cost will not be incurred for any internal transfers. Now, a bargaining range exists. That range goes from the minimum transfer price to the maximum. The two divisions will negotiate the transfer price deciding how much of the cost savings will go to each division.

Here's the Real Kicker

Kicker's top management is closely involved in all aspects of the company, from design and development through production, sales, delivery, and aftermarket activities. Profit performance, as measured by periodic income statements, is an important measure, but Kicker also keeps track of a number of other measures of performance.

For example, financial information is very important. Financial statements are presented to the president and vice presidents every month. These are reviewed carefully for trends and are compared with the budgeted amounts. Worrisome increases in expenses or decreases in revenue are analyzed to see what the underlying factors might be.

Customer satisfaction is also continually measured. Kicker has two major types of customers—dealers who sell Kicker products and end users who have Kicker car speakers installed. Each customer type has specific needs. For example, dealers have the exclusive right to sell Kicker products and Kicker offers a one-year warranty on speakers sold through a dealer. However, end users want as low a price as possible and will occasionally find speakers available on the Internet (called "gray market" speakers because the seller is not authorized to sell them). In the past, no warranty was available on non-dealer-sold speakers, but problems arose when customers purchased obviously new products through the Internet, and they were not covered under warranty when something went wrong. Kicker therefore decided to offer a shorter warranty for new products sold by unauthorized sellers in order to keep the customer base happy and increase satisfaction.

Kicker focuses on strategic objectives for the long term. For example, engineers in R&D take continuing education to stay current in their fields. When Kicker approached producing and selling original equipment manufacture (OEM) speakers to a major automobile maker, a number of employees had to learn International Organization for Standardization (ISO) quality concepts quickly. They took classes, met with consultants, and traveled to the site of other ISO-qualified firms to learn how to meet quality standards.

SUMMARY OF LEARNING OBJECTIVES

LO1.   Explain how and why firms choose to decentralize.
- In a decentralized organization, lower-level managers make and implement decisions. In a centralized organization, lower-level managers are responsible only for implementing decisions.
- Reasons why companies decentralize:
  - Local managers can make better decisions using local information.
  - Local managers can provide a more timely response.
  - It is impossible for any one central manager to be fully knowledgeable about all products and markets.
- Decentralization can train and motivate local managers and free top management from day-to-day operating conditions so that they can spend time on more long-range activities, such as strategic planning. Managerial accounting plays an important role in designing effective performance measures and incentive systems to help ensure that managers in a decentralized organization use their decision-making authority in a way that improves the organization's performance.
- Four types of responsibility centers are:
  - Cost centers—manager is responsible for costs.
  - Revenue centers—manager is responsible for price and quantity sold.
  - Profit centers—manager is responsible for costs and revenues.
  - Investment centers—manager is responsible for costs, revenues, and investment.

LO2.   Explain the difference between absorption and variable costing, and prepare segmented income statements.
- Absorption costing treats fixed factory overhead as a product cost. Unit product cost consists of direct materials, direct labor, variable factory overhead, and fixed factory overhead.
- Absorption-costing income statement groups expenses according to function:
  - Production cost—cost of goods sold, including variable and fixed product cost.
  - Selling expense—variable and fixed cost of selling and distributing product.
  - Administrative expense—variable and fixed cost of administration.
- Variable costing treats fixed factory overhead as a period expense. Unit product cost consists of direct materials, direct labor, and variable factory overhead.
- Variable-costing income statement groups expenses according to cost behavior:
  - Variable expenses of manufacturing, selling, and administration.
  - Fixed expenses of manufacturing (fixed factory overhead), selling, and administration.
- Impact of units produced and units sold on absorption-costing income and variable-costing income:
  - If units produced > units sold, then absorption-costing income > variable-costing income.
  - If units produced < units sold, then absorption-costing income < variable-costing income.
  - If units produced = units sold, then absorption-costing income = variable-costing income.

LO3.   Compute and explain return on investment.
- ROI is the ratio of operating income to average operating assets.
- Margin is operating income divided by sales.
- Turnover is sales divided by average operating assets.
- Advantage: ROI encourages managers to focus on improving sales, controlling costs, and using assets efficiently.
- Disadvantage: ROI can encourage managers to sacrifice long-run benefits for short-run benefits.

LO4.   **Compute and explain residual income and economic value added.**
- Residual income is operating income minus a minimum percentage cost of capital times capital employed.
  - If residual income > 0, then the division is earning more than the minimum cost of capital.
  - If residual income < 0, then the division is earning less than the minimum cost of capital.
  - If residual income = 0, then the division is earning just the minimum cost of capital.
- Economic value added is *after-tax* operating profit minus the *actual* total annual cost of capital.
  - If EVA > 0, then the company is creating wealth (or value).
  - If EVA < 0, then the company is destroying wealth.

LO5.   **Explain the uses of the Balanced Scorecard and the role of transfer pricing in a decentralized firm.**
- Balanced Scorecard is a strategic management system.
- Objectives and measures are developed for four perspectives:
  - Financial perspective
  - Customer perspective
  - Internal perspective
  - Learning and growth perspective
- Transfer price is charged by the selling division of a company to a buying division of the same company.
  - Increases revenue to the selling division.
  - Increases cost to the buying division.
- Common transfer pricing policies are:
  - Cost based (e.g., total product cost)
  - Market based (price charged in the outside market)
  - Negotiated (between the buying and selling divisions' managers).

SUMMARY OF IMPORTANT EQUATIONS

1. $\text{ROI} = \dfrac{\text{Operating income}}{\text{Average operating assets}}$

2. $\text{Average operating assets} = \dfrac{(\text{Beginning assets} + \text{Ending assets})}{2}$

3.

$$\text{ROI} = \underbrace{\dfrac{\text{Operating income}}{\text{Sales}}}_{\textbf{Margin}} \times \underbrace{\dfrac{\text{Sales}}{\text{Average operating assets}}}_{\textbf{Turnover}}$$

4. Residual income = Operating income − (Minimum rate of return × Average operating assets)

5. EVA = After-tax operating income − (Actual percentage cost of capital × Total capital employed)

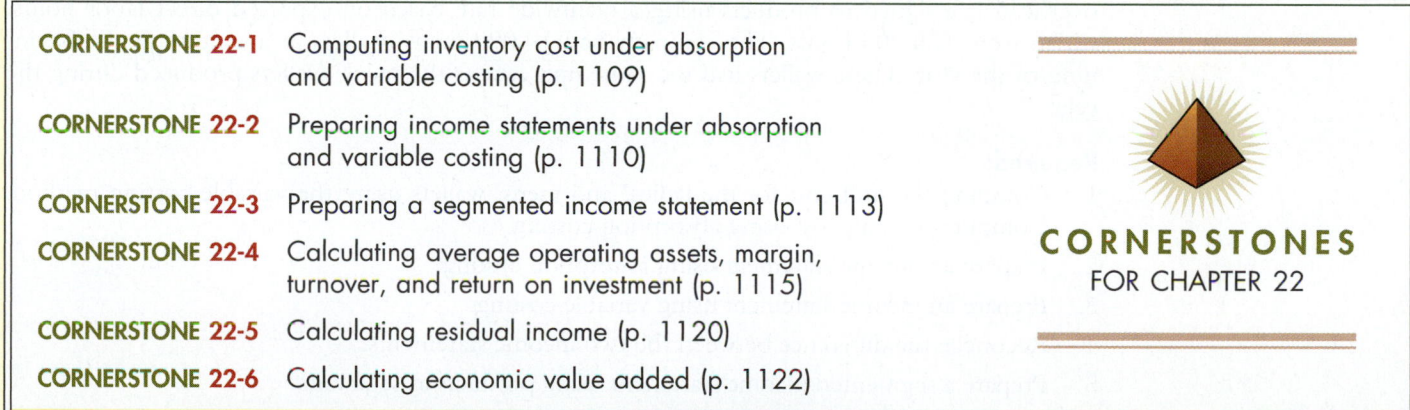

CORNERSTONE 22-1	Computing inventory cost under absorption and variable costing (p. 1109)
CORNERSTONE 22-2	Preparing income statements under absorption and variable costing (p. 1110)
CORNERSTONE 22-3	Preparing a segmented income statement (p. 1113)
CORNERSTONE 22-4	Calculating average operating assets, margin, turnover, and return on investment (p. 1115)
CORNERSTONE 22-5	Calculating residual income (p. 1120)
CORNERSTONE 22-6	Calculating economic value added (p. 1122)

CORNERSTONES
FOR CHAPTER 22

KEY TERMS

Absorption costing (p. 1108)
Balanced Scorecard (p. 1124)
Common fixed expenses (p. 1113)
Cost center (p. 1106)
Customer perspective (p. 1124)
Decentralization (p. 1104)
Direct fixed expenses (p. 1112)
Economic value added (EVA) (p. 1121)
Financial perspective (p. 1124)
Hurdle rate (p. 1117)
Internal business process perspective (p. 1124)
Investment center (p. 1106)
Learning and growth (infrastructure) perspective (p. 1124)

Margin (p. 1115)
Operating assets (p. 1114)
Operating income (p. 1114)
Profit center (p. 1106)
Residual income (p. 1119)
Responsibility center (p. 1106)
Return on investment (ROI) (p. 1114)
Revenue center (p. 1106)
Segment (p. 1112)
Segment margin (p. 1114)
Transfer price (p. 1125)
Turnover (p. 1115)
Variable costing (p. 1108)

REVIEW PROBLEMS

I. Absorption and Variable Costing; Segmented Income Statements

Fine Leathers Company produces a ladies' wallet and a mens' wallet. Selected data for the past year follow:

	Ladies' Wallet	Mens' Wallet
Production (units)	100,000	200,000
Sales (units)	90,000	210,000
Selling price	$5.50	$4.50
Direct labor hours	50,000	80,000
Manufacturing costs:		
Direct materials	$ 75,000	$100,000
Direct labor	250,000	400,000
Variable overhead	20,000	24,000
Fixed overhead:		
Direct	50,000	40,000
Common[a]	20,000	20,000
Nonmanufacturing costs:		
Variable selling	30,000	60,000
Direct fixed selling	35,000	40,000
Common fixed selling[b]	25,000	25,000

[a] Common overhead totals $40,000 and is divided equally between the two products.
[b] Common fixed selling costs total $50,000 and are divided equally between the two products.

Budgeted fixed overhead for the year, $130,000, equaled the actual fixed overhead. Fixed overhead is assigned to products using a plantwide rate based on expected direct labor hours, which were 130,000 hours. The company had 10,000 mens' wallets in inventory at the beginning of the year. These wallets had the same unit cost as the mens' wallets produced during the year.

Required:

1. Compute the unit cost for the ladies' and mens' wallets using the variable-costing method. Compute the unit cost using absorption costing.

2. Prepare an income statement using absorption costing.

3. Prepare an income statement using variable costing.

4. Reconcile the difference between the two income statements.

5. Prepare a segmented income statement using products as segments.

Solution:

1. The unit cost for the ladies' wallet is as follows:

Direct materials ($75,000/100,000)	$0.75
Direct labor ($250,000/100,000)	2.50
Variable overhead ($20,000/100,000)	0.20
Variable cost per unit ($0.75 + $2.50 + $0.20)	$3.45
Fixed overhead [(50,000 × $1.00)/100,000]	0.50
Absorption cost per unit	$3.95

The unit cost for the mens' wallet is as follows:

Direct materials ($100,000/200,000)	$0.50
Direct labor ($400,000/200,000)	2.00
Variable overhead ($24,000/200,000)	0.12
Variable cost per unit ($0.50 + $2.00 + $0.12)	$2.62
Fixed overhead [(80,000 × $1.00)/200,000]	0.40
Absorption cost per unit	$3.02

Notice that the only difference between the two unit costs is the assignment of the fixed overhead cost. Notice also that the fixed overhead unit cost is assigned using the predetermined fixed overhead rate ($130,000/130,000 hours = $1 per hour).

For example, the ladies' wallets used 50,000 direct labor hours and so receive $1 × 50,000, or $50,000, of fixed overhead. This total, when divided by the units produced, gives the $0.50 per-unit fixed overhead cost. Finally, observe that variable nonmanufacturing costs are not part of the unit cost under variable costing. For both approaches, only manufacturing costs are used to compute the unit costs.

2. The income statement under absorption costing is as follows:

Sales [($5.50 × 90,000) + ($4.50 × 210,000)]	$1,440,000
Less: Cost of goods sold [($3.95 × 90,000) + ($3.02 × 210,000)]	989,700
Gross margin	$ 450,300
Less: Selling expenses*	215,000
Operating income	$ 235,300

*The sum of selling expenses for both products.

3. The income statement under variable costing is as follows:

Sales [($5.50 × 90,000) + ($4.50 × 210,000)]	$1,440,000
Less variable expenses:	
Variable cost of goods sold [($3.45 × 90,000) + ($2.62 × 210,000)]	(860,700)
Variable selling expenses	(90,000)
Contribution margin	$ 489,300
Less fixed expenses:	
Fixed overhead	(130,000)
Fixed selling	(125,000)
Operating income	$ 234,300

4. Reconciliation is as follows:

$$I_A - I_V = \$235,300 - \$234,300 = \$1,000$$

Thus, variable-costing income is $1,000 less than absorption-costing income. This difference can be explained by the net change of fixed overhead found in inventory under absorption costing.

Ladies' wallet:	
Units produced	100,000
Units sold	90,000
Increase in inventory	10,000
Unit fixed overhead	× $0.50
Increase in fixed overhead	$5,000

Mens' wallet:

Units produced	200,000
Units sold	210,000
Decrease in inventory	(10,000)
Unit fixed overhead	× $0.40
Decrease in fixed overhead	$(4,000)

The net change is a $1,000 ($5,000 − $4,000) increase in fixed overhead in inventories. Thus, under absorption costing, there is a net flow of $1,000 of the current period's fixed overhead into inventory. Since variable costing recognized all of the current period's fixed overhead as an expense, variable-costing income should be $1,000 lower than absorption costing, as it is.

5. Segmented income statement:

	Ladies' Wallet	Mens' Wallet	Total
Sales	$ 495,000	$ 945,000	$1,440,000
Less variable expenses:			
Variable cost of goods sold	(310,500)	(550,200)	(860,700)
Variable selling expenses	(30,000)	(60,000)	(90,000)
Contribution margin	$ 154,500	$ 334,800	$ 489,300
Less direct fixed expenses:			
Direct fixed overhead	(50,000)	(40,000)	(90,000)
Direct selling expenses	(35,000)	(40,000)	(75,000)
Segment margin	$ 69,500	$ 254,800	$ 324,300
Less common fixed expenses:			
Common fixed overhead			(40,000)
Common selling expenses			(50,000)
Operating income			$ 234,300

II. ROI

Flip Flop Politics Inc. had gross margin of $550,000 and selling and administrative expense of $300,000 last year. Also, Flip Flop began last year with $1,400,000 of operating assets and ended the year with $1,100,000 of operating assets.

Required:
Calculate return on investment for Flip Flop Politics.

Solution:

$$\text{Return on investment} = \frac{\text{Operating income}}{\text{Average operating assets}}$$

Gross margin	$550,000
Selling and administrative expense	300,000
Operating income	$250,000

$$\text{Average operating assets} = \frac{(\text{Beginning operating assets} + \text{Ending operating assets})}{2}$$

$$= \frac{(\$1,400,000 + \$1,100,000)}{2}$$

$$= \frac{\$2,500,000}{2}$$

$$= \$1,250,000$$

$$\text{Therefore, Return on investment} = \frac{\text{Operating income}}{\text{Average operating assets}}$$

$$= \frac{\$250,000}{\$1,250,000}$$

$$= 0.20, \text{ or } 20 \text{ percent}$$

III. Economic Value Added

El Suezo Inc. had sales of $5,000,000, cost of goods sold of $3,500,000, and selling and administrative expense of $500,000 for its most recent year of operations. El Suezo faces a tax rate of 40 percent. Also, El Suezo employed $2,000,000 of debt capital and $4,000,000 of equity capital in generating its return. Finally, the company's actual cost of capital is 8 percent.

Required:

1.   Calculate after-tax operating income for El Suezo.

2.   Calculate EVA for El Suezo.

Solution:

1.
Sales	$5,000,000
Cost of goods sold	3,500,000
Gross margin	$1,500,000
Selling and administrative expense	500,000
Operating income	$1,000,000
Income taxes (@ 40%)	400,000
Net income	$ 600,000

2. EVA = After-tax operating income − (Actual percentage cost of capital × Total capital employed)

   = $600,000 − [0.08 × ($2,000,000 + $4,000,000)]

   = $600,000 − (0.08 × $6,000,000)

   = $600,000 − $480,000

   = $120,000

DISCUSSION QUESTIONS

1.   Discuss the differences between centralized and decentralized decision making.
2.   What is decentralization?
3.   Explain why firms choose to decentralize.
4.   What is the difference between the unit cost of a product under absorption costing and under variable costing?
5.   If a company produces 10,000 units and sells 8,000 units during a period, which method of computing operating income (absorption costing or variable costing) will result in the higher operating income? Why?
6.   What is a segment?
7.   What is the difference between contribution margin and segment margin?
8.   What are margin and turnover? Explain how these concepts can improve the evaluation of an investment center.
9.   What are the three benefits of ROI? Explain how each benefit can lead to improved profitability.
10.   What is residual income? What is EVA? How does EVA differ from the general definition of residual income?
11.   Can residual income or EVA ever be negative? What is the meaning of negative residual income or EVA?
12.   What is the Balanced Scorecard?
13.   Describe the four perspectives of the Balanced Scorecard.
14.   What is a transfer price?
15.   Briefly explain three common transfer pricing policies used by organizations.

MULTIPLE-CHOICE EXERCISES

22-1 The practice of delegating authority to division-level managers by top management is

a.   decentralization.

b.   good business practice.

c.   centralization.

d.   autonomy.

e.   never done in business today.

22-2 Which of the following is *not* a reason for decentralizing?

a. Training and motivating managers
b. Unmasking inefficiencies in subdivisions of an overall profitable company
c. Allowing top management to focus on strategic decision making
d. Allowing top management to make all key operating decisions throughout the company
e. All of the above are reasons for decentralizing.

22-3 A responsibility center in which a manager is responsible for both revenues and costs is a(n)

a. investment center.   c. profit center.
b. revenue center.   d. cost center.

22-4 A responsibility center in which a manager is responsible for revenues, costs, and investments is a(n)

a. investment center.   c. profit center.
b. revenue center.   d. cost center.

22-5 If sales and average operating assets for Year 2 are identical to their values in Year 1, yet operating income is higher, Year 2 return on investment (compared with Year 1 ROI) will

a. decrease.   d. The direction of change in ROI cannot be
b. increase.   determined by this information.
c. stay the same.

22-6 If sales and average operating assets for Year 2 are identical to their values in Year 1, yet operating income is higher, Year 2 turnover (compared with Year 1 turnover) will

a. decrease.   d. The direction of change in turnover can-
b. increase.   not be determined by this information.
c. stay the same.

22-7 The key difference between residual income and EVA is that EVA

a. uses the actual cost of capital for the company rather than a minimum required cost of capital.
b. uses the minimum required cost of capital for a company rather than the actual percentage cost of capital.
c. is a ratio rather than an absolute dollar amount.
d. cannot be negative.
e. There is no difference between residual income and EVA.

22-8 Assume that a division has residual income of $6,500,000, operating income of $8,500,000, beginning operating assets of $45,000,000, and minimum rate of return requirement of 4 percent. What is the amount of the division's ending operating assets?

a. $6,700,000
b. $45,000,000
c. $50,000,000
d. $55,000,000
e. Impossible to determine

22-9 Which of the following is a common transfer pricing policy?

a. Negotiated between buyer and seller   d. All of these are correct
b. Cost based   e. None of these are correct
c. Market based

22-10 HD Television is a multinational corporation that operates two divisions, A and B, in two different countries. Division A operates in a country with a 20 percent corporate tax rate while Division B operates in a country with a 40 percent corporate tax rate. Division A manufactures an electrical component that its sells to Division B, which in turn uses the electrical component to complete final construction of the televisions. Therefore, the internal sale between the two divisions requires that a transfer price be established. Which of the following transfer prices would result in the smallest after-tax profit for HD Television as a whole?

a. $26
b. $40
c. $33

d. $38
e. $44

22-11 Kellman Company shows the following unit costs for its product:

Direct materials	$40
Direct labor	30
Variable overhead	2
Fixed overhead	5

Kellman started the year with 8,000 units in inventory, produced 50,000 units during the year, and sold 55,000 units. The value of ending inventory is

a. greater under absorption costing than variable costing.
b. greater under variable costing than absorption costing.
c. the same under both variable and absorption costing.
d. There is no ending inventory.
e. This situation cannot happen.

22-12 In a segmented income statement, which of the following statements is true?

a. Segment margin is greater than contribution margin.
b. Common fixed expenses must be allocated to each segment.
c. Contribution margin is equal to sales less all variable and direct fixed expenses of a segment.
d. Segment margin is equal to contribution margin less direct fixed expenses.
e. Segment margin is equal to contribution margin less direct and common fixed expenses.

22-13 Which of the following is *not* a perspective of the Balanced Scorecard?

a. Learning and growth (infrastructure)
b. Internal business process
c. Customer

d. Nonfinancial
e. All of these are perspectives of the Balanced Scorecard.

CORNERSTONE EXERCISES

Cornerstone Exercise 22-14 Computing Inventory Cost under Absorption and Variable Costing

OBJECTIVE
CORNERSTONE 22-1

During the most recent year, Morgancafé Company had the following data associated with the items it makes:

Units in beginning inventory	—
Units produced	18,000
Units sold ($200 per unit)	16,000
Variable costs per unit:	
Direct materials	$23
Direct labor	$46
Variable overhead	$15
Fixed costs:	
Fixed manufacturing overhead per unit produced	$30
Fixed selling and administrative	$165,000

Required:
1. How many units are in ending inventory?
2. Using absorption costing, calculate the per-unit product cost. What is the value of ending inventory?
3. Using variable costing, calculate the per-unit product cost. What is the value of ending inventory?

OBJECTIVE  ②
CORNERSTONE 22-2

Cornerstone Exercise 22-15 Preparing Income Statements under Absorption and Variable Costing

During the most recent year, Morgan Company had the following data associated with the items it makes:

Units in beginning inventory	—
Units produced	18,000
Units sold ($140 per unit)	16,000
Variable costs per unit:	
Direct materials	$23
Direct labor	$46
Variable overhead	$15
Fixed costs:	
Fixed overhead per unit produced	$30
Fixed selling and administrative	$165,000

Required:

1. Calculate the cost of goods sold under absorption costing.
2. Calculate the cost of goods sold under variable costing.
3. Prepare an income statement using absorption costing.
4. Prepare an income statement using variable costing.

OBJECTIVE ②
CORNERSTONE 22-3

Cornerstone Exercise 22-16 Preparing a Segmented Income Statement

Cazmir Inc. produces high-end sweaters and jackets in a single factory. The following information was provided for the coming year.

	Sweaters	Jackets
Sales	$540,000	$470,000
Variable cost of goods sold	297,000	175,000
Direct fixed overhead	124,000	40,000

A sales commission of 4 percent of sales is paid for each of the two product lines. Direct fixed selling and administrative expense was estimated to be $50,000 for the sweater line and $23,000 for the jacket line.

Common fixed overhead for the factory was estimated to be $63,000. Common selling and administrative expense was estimated to be $75,000.

Required:

Prepare a segmented income statement for Cazmir Inc. for the coming year, using variable costing.

Use the following information for Cornerstone Exercises 22-17 through 22-19:

East Mullett Manufacturing earned operating income last year as shown in the following income statement:

Sales	$630,000
Cost of goods sold	380,000
Gross margin	$250,000
Selling and administrative expense	174,400
Operating income	$ 75,600
Less: Income taxes (@ 40%)	30,240
Net income	$ 45,360

At the beginning of the year, the value of operating assets was $345,000. At the end of the year, the value of operating assets was $405,000.

OBJECTIVE  ③
CORNERSTONE 22-4

Cornerstone Exercise 22-17 Calculating Average Operating Assets, Margin, Turnover, and Return on Investment

Refer to the information for East Mullett Manufacturing above.

Required:

Calculate (1) average operating assets, (2) margin, (3) turnover and (4) return on investment.

Cornerstone Exercise 22-18 Calculating Residual Income

OBJECTIVE **4**
CORNERSTONE 22-5

Refer to the information for East Mullett Manufacturing on the previous page. East Mullett requires a minimum rate of return of 10 percent.

Required:

Calculate (1) average operating assets and (2) residual income.

Cornerstone Exercise 22-19 Calculating Economic Value Added

OBJECTIVE **4**
CORNERSTONE 22-6

Refer to the information for East Mullett Manufacturing on the previous page. Total capital employed equaled $400,000. East Mullett's actual cost of capital is 8 percent.

Required:

Calculate the EVA for East Mullett Manufacturing.

EXERCISES

Exercise 22-20 Types of Responsibility Centers

OBJECTIVE **1**

Consider each of the following independent scenarios:

a. Terrin Belson, plant manager for the laser printer factory of Compugear Inc., brushed his hair back and sighed. December had been a bad month. Two machines had broken down, and some factory production workers (all on salary) were idled for part of the month. Materials prices increased, and insurance premiums on the factory increased. No way out of it; costs were going up. He hoped that the marketing vice president would be able to push through some price increases, but that really wasn't his department.

b. Joanna Pauly was delighted to see that her ROI figures had increased for the third straight year. She was sure that her campaign to lower costs and use machinery more efficiently (enabling her factories to sell several older machines) was the reason why. Joanna planned to take full credit for the improvements at her semiannual performance review.

c. Gil Rodriguez, sales manager for ComputerWorks, was not pleased with a memo from headquarters detailing the recent cost increases for the laser printer line. Headquarters suggested raising prices. "Great," thought Gil, "an increase in price will kill sales and revenue will go down. Why can't the plant shape up and cut costs like every other company in America is doing? Why turn this into my problem?"

d. Susan Whitehorse looked at the quarterly profit and loss statement with disgust. Revenue was down, and cost was up—what a combination! Then she had an idea. If she cut back on maintenance of equipment and let a product engineer go, expenses would decrease—perhaps enough to reverse the trend in income.

e. Shonna Lowry had just been hired to improve the fortunes of the Southern Division of ABC Inc. She met with top staff and hammered out a three-year plan to improve the situation. A centerpiece of the plan is the retiring of obsolete equipment and the purchasing of state-of-the-art, computer-assisted machinery. The new machinery would take time for the workers to learn to use, but once that was done, waste would be virtually eliminated.

Required:

For each of the above independent scenarios, indicate the type of responsibility center involved (cost, revenue, profit, or investment).

Use the following information for Exercises 22-21 and 22-22:
Romer Company produced 14,000 units during its first year of operations and sold 13,800 at $22 per unit. The company chose practical activity—at 14,000 units—to compute its predetermined overhead rate. Manufacturing costs are as follows:

Direct materials	$ 88,200
Direct labor	105,000
Variable overhead	15,820
Fixed overhead	49,000

(Continued)

OBJECTIVE ❷

Exercise 22-21 Inventory Valuation under Absorption Costing

Refer to the information for Romer Company on the previous page.

Required:
1. Calculate the unit cost for each of these four costs.
2. Calculate the cost of one unit of product under absorption costing.
3. How many units are in ending inventory?
4. Calculate the cost of ending inventory under absorption costing.

OBJECTIVE ❷

Exercise 22-22 Inventory Valuation under Variable Costing

Refer to the information for Romer Company on the previous page.

Required:
1. Calculate the cost of one unit of product under variable costing.
2. Calculate the cost of ending inventory under variable costing.

Use the following information for Exercises 22-23 and 22-24:
The following information pertains to Berting Inc. for last year:

Beginning inventory in units	—
Units produced	25,000
Units sold	23,600
Costs per unit:	
Direct materials	$4.00
Direct labor	$1.60
Variable overhead	$0.75
Fixed overhead*	$3.80
Variable selling expenses	$3.00
Fixed selling and administrative costs	$24,300

*Fixed overhead totals $95,000 per year.

OBJECTIVE ❷

Exercise 22-23 Inventory Valuation under Absorption and Variable Costing

Refer to the information for Berting Inc. above.

Required:
1. Calculate the cost of one unit of product under absorption costing.
2. Calculate the cost of one unit of product under variable costing.
3. How many units are in ending inventory?
4. Calculate the cost of ending inventory under absorption costing.
5. Calculate the cost of ending inventory under variable costing.

OBJECTIVE ❷

Exercise 22-24 Income Statements under Absorption and Variable Costing

Refer to the information for Berting Inc. above. Assume that the selling price is $16 per unit.

Required:
1. Prepare an income statement using absorption costing.
2. Prepare an income statement using variable costing.

OBJECTIVE ❸

Exercise 22-25 Margin, Turnover, Return on Investment

Pelak Company had sales of $30,000,000, expenses of $27,600,000, and average operating assets of $6,000,000.

Required:
Compute the (1) operating income, (2) margin and turnover ratios, and (3) ROI.

Exercise 22-26 Margin, Turnover, Return on Investment, Average Operating Assets

OBJECTIVE 3

Elway Company provided the following income statement for the last year:

Sales	$980,000
Less: Variable expenses	670,000
Contribution margin	$310,000
Less: Fixed expenses	172,800
Operating income	$137,200

At the beginning of last year, Elway had $44,500 in operating assets. At the end of the year, Elway had $33,900 in operating assets.

Required:
1. Compute average operating assets.
2. Compute the margin and turnover ratios for last year.
3. Compute ROI.
4. **Conceptual Connection:** Briefly explain the meaning of ROI.
5. **Conceptual Connection:** Comment on why the ROI for Elway Company is relatively high (as compared to the lower ROI of a typical manufacturing company).

Exercise 22-27 Return on Investment, Margin, Turnover

OBJECTIVE 3

Data follow for the Construction Division of D. Jack Inc.:

	Year 1	Year 2
Sales	$ 52,000,000	$ 57,750,000
Operating income	7,280,000	7,507,500
Average operating assets	200,000,000	262,500,000

(*Note:* Round all answers to two decimal places.)

Required:
1. Compute the margin and turnover ratios for each year.
2. Compute the ROI for the Construction Division for each year.

Exercise 22-28 Residual Income

OBJECTIVE 4

The Tuxedo Division of Shamus O'Toole Company had operating income last year of $340,000 and average operating assets of $3,500,000. O'Toole's minimum acceptable rate of return is 7 percent. (*Note:* Round all answers to two decimal places.)

Required:
1. Calculate the residual income for the Tuxedo Division.
2. Was the ROI for the Tuxedo Division greater than, less than, or equal to 7 percent?

Exercise 22-29 Economic Value Added

OBJECTIVE 4

Falconer Company had net (after-tax) income last year of $1,125,000 and total capital employed of $3,500,000. Falconer's actual cost of capital was 11 percent.

Required:
1. Calculate the EVA for Falconer Company.
2. **Conceptual Connection:** Is Falconer creating or destroying wealth?

Use the following information for Exercises 22-30 and 22-31:

Washington Company has two divisions: the Adams Division and the Jefferson Division. The following information pertains to last year's results:

	Adams Division	Jefferson Division
Net (after-tax) income	$ 605,000	$ 315,000
Total capital employed	4,000,000	3,250,000

Washington's actual cost of capital was 12 percent.

(Continued)

OBJECTIVE **4**

Exercise 22-30 Economic Value Added

Refer to the information for Washington Company on the previous page.

Required:
1. Calculate the EVA for the Adams Division.
2. Calculate the EVA for the Jefferson Division.
3. **Conceptual Connection:** Is each division creating or destroying wealth?
4. **Conceptual Connection:** Describe generally the types of actions that Washington's management team could take to increase Jefferson Division's EVA?

OBJECTIVE **4**

Exercise 22-31 Residual Income

Refer to the information for Washington Company on the previous page. In addition, Washington Company's top management has set a minimum acceptable rate of return equal to 8 percent.

Required:
1. Calculate the residual income for the Adams Division.
2. Calculate the residual income for the Jefferson Division.

PROBLEMS

OBJECTIVE **2**

Problem 22-32 Variable- and Absorption-Costing Income

Spicer Company produces and sells wooden pallets that are used for moving and stacking materials. The operating costs for the past year were as follows:

Variable costs per unit:		
Direct materials	$	2.45
Direct labor		2.10
Variable overhead		0.25
Variable selling		0.30
Fixed costs per year:		
Fixed overhead		180,000
Selling and administrative		56,000

During the year, Spicer produced 200,000 wooden pallets and sold 208,000 at $9 each. Spicer had 11,300 pallets in beginning finished goods inventory; costs have not changed from last year to this year. An actual costing system is used for product costing.

Required
1. What is the per-unit inventory cost that will be reported on Spicer's balance sheet at the end of the year? How many units are in ending inventory? What is the total cost of ending inventory?
2. Calculate absorption-costing operating income.
3. **Conceptual Connection:** What would the per-unit inventory cost be under variable costing? Does this differ from the unit cost computed in Requirement 1? Why or why not?
4. Calculate variable-costing operating income.
5. Suppose that Spicer Company had sold 196,700 pallets during the year. What would absorption-costing operating income have been? Variable-costing operating income?

OBJECTIVE **2**

Problem 22-33 Variable Costing, Absorption Costing, Segmented Income Statements, Inventory Valuation

During its first year of operations, Sugarsmooth Inc. produced 55,000 jars of hand cream based on a formula containing 10 percent glycolic acid. Unit sales were 52,300 jars. Fixed overhead totaled $27,500 and was applied at the rate of $0.50 per unit produced. The results of the year's operations are as follows (on an absorption-costing basis):

Sales (52,300 units @ $8.70)	$455,010
Less: Cost of goods sold	222,275
Gross margin	$232,735
Less: Selling and administrative (all fixed)	145,000
Operating income	$ 87,735

At the end of the first year of operations, Sugarsmooth is considering expanding its customer base. In its first year, it sold to small drugstores and supermarkets. Now, Sugarsmooth wants to add large discount stores and small beauty shops. Working together, the company controller and marketing manager have accumulated the following information:

a. Anticipated sales to discount stores would be 20,000 units at a discounted price of $5.80. Higher costs of shipping and return penalties would be incurred. Shipping would amount to $8,500 per year, and return penalties would average 4 percent of sales. In addition, a clerk would need to be hired solely to handle the discount stores' accounts. The clerk's salary and benefits would be $28,000 per year.

b. Anticipated sales to beauty shops would be 10,000 units at a price of $9. A commission of 10 percent of sales would be paid to independent jobbers who sell to the shops. In addition, an extra packing expense of $0.50 per unit would be incurred because the shops require fewer bottles per carton.

c. The sales to small drugstores and supermarkets will remain the same.

d. The fixed overhead and selling and administrative expenses would remain unchanged and are treated as common costs.

Required:

1. Calculate the cost of Sugarsmooth's ending inventory at the end of the first year under absorption costing.

2. Calculate the cost of Sugarsmooth's ending inventory at the end of the first year under variable costing. What is operating income for the first year using variable costing?

3. Prepare a segmented variable-costing income statement for next year. The segments correspond to customer groups: drugstores and supermarkets, discount stores, and beauty shops.

4. **Conceptual Connection:** Are all three customer groups profitable? Should Sugarsmooth expand its marketing base?

Problem 22-34 Return on Investment and Investment Decisions

OBJECTIVE

Leslie Blandings, division manager of Audiotech Inc., was debating the merits of a new product—a weather radio that would put out a warning if the county in which the listener lived were under a severe thunderstorm or tornado alert.

The budgeted income of the division was $725,000 with operating assets of $3,625,000. The proposed investment would add income of $640,000 and would require an additional investment in equipment of $4,000,000. The minimum required return on investment for the company is 12 percent. Round all numbers to two decimal places.

Required:

1. Compute the ROI of the:

    a. division if the radio project is *not* undertaken.
    b. radio project alone.
    c. division if the radio project is undertaken.

2. Compute the residual income of the:

    a. division if the radio project is *not* undertaken.
    b. radio project alone.
    c. division if the radio project is undertaken.

3. **Conceptual Connection:** Do you suppose that Leslie will decide to invest in the new radio? Why or why not?

OBJECTIVE

Problem 22-35 Return on Investment, Margin, Turnover

Ready Electronics is facing stiff competition from imported goods. Its operating income margin has been declining steadily for the past several years. The company has been forced to lower prices so that it can maintain its market share. The operating results for the past three years are as follows:

	Year 1	Year 2	Year 3
Sales	$10,000,000	$ 9,500,000	$ 9,000,000
Operating income	1,200,000	1,045,000	945,000
Average assets	15,000,000	15,000,000	15,000,000

For the coming year, Ready's president plans to install a JIT purchasing and manufacturing system. She estimates that inventories will be reduced by 70 percent during the first year of operations, producing a 20 percent reduction in the average operating assets of the company, which would remain unchanged without the JIT system. She also estimates that sales and operating income will be restored to Year 1 levels because of simultaneous reductions in operating expenses and selling prices. Lower selling prices will allow Ready to expand its market share. (*Note:* Round all numbers to two decimal places.)

Required:

1. Compute the ROI, margin, and turnover for Years 1, 2, and 3.
2. **Conceptual Connection:** Suppose that in Year 4 the sales and operating income were achieved as expected, but inventories remained at the same level as in Year 3. Compute the expected ROI, margin, and turnover. Explain why the ROI increased over the Year 3 level.
3. **Conceptual Connection:** Suppose that the sales and net operating income for Year 4 remained the same as in Year 3 but inventory reductions were achieved as projected. Compute the ROI, margin, and turnover. Explain why the ROI exceeded the Year 3 level.
4. **Conceptual Connection:** Assume that all expectations for Year 4 were realized. Compute the expected ROI, margin, and turnover. Explain why the ROI increased over the Year 3 level.

OBJECTIVE 3 4

Problem 22-36 Return on Investment for Multiple Investments, Residual Income

The manager of a division that produces add-on products for the automobile industry has just been presented the opportunity to invest in two independent projects. The first is an air conditioner for the back seats of vans and minivans. The second is a turbocharger. Without the investments, the division will have average assets for the coming year of $28.9 million and expected operating income of $4.335 million. The outlay required for each investment and the expected operating incomes are as follows:

	Air Conditioner	Turbocharger
Outlay	$750,000	$540,000
Operating income	90,000	82,080

(*Note:* Round all numbers to two decimal places.)

Required:

1. Compute the ROI for each investment project.
2. Compute the budgeted divisional ROI for each of the following four alternatives:
   a. The air conditioner investment is made.
   b. The turbocharger investment is made.
   c. Both investments are made.
   d. Neither additional investment is made.
3. **Conceptual Connection:** Assuming that divisional managers are evaluated and rewarded on the basis of ROI performance, which alternative do you think the divisional manager will choose?
4. **Conceptual Connection:** Suppose that the company sets a minimum required rate of return equal to 14 percent. Calculate the residual income for each of the following four alternatives:
   a. The air conditioner investment is made.
   b. The turbocharger investment is made.

c. Both investments are made.
d. Neither additional investment is made.

Which option will the manager choose based on residual income? Explain.

5. **Conceptual Connection:** Suppose that the company sets a minimum required rate of return equal to 10 percent. Calculate the residual income for each of the following four alternatives:

a. The air conditioner investment is made.
b. The turbocharger investment is made.
c. Both investments are made.
d. Neither additional investment is made.

Based on residual income, are the investments profitable? Why does your answer differ from your answer in Requirement 3?

Problem 22-37 Return on Investment and Economic Value Added Calculations with Varying Assumptions

OBJECTIVE 3 4

Knitpix Products is a division of Parker Textiles Inc. During the coming year, it expects to earn operating income of $310,000 based on sales of $3.45 million. Without any new investments, the division will have average operating assets of $3 million. The division is considering a capital investment project—adding knitting machines to produce gaiters—that requires an additional investment of $600,000 and increases operating income by $57,500 (sales would increase by $575,000). If made, the investment would increase beginning operating assets by $600,000 and ending operating assets by $400,000. Assume that the actual cost of capital for the company is 7 percent. (*Note:* Round all numbers to four decimal places.)

Required:
1. Compute the ROI for the division without the investment.
2. Compute the margin and turnover ratios without the investment. Show that the product of the margin and turnover ratios equals the ROI computed in Requirement 1.
3. **Conceptual Connection:** Compute the ROI for the division with the new investment. Do you think the divisional manager will approve the investment?
4. **Conceptual Connection:** Compute the margin and turnover ratios for the division with the new investment. How do these compare with the old ratios?
5. **Conceptual Connection:** Compute the EVA of the division with and without the investment. Should the manager decide to make the knitting machine investment?

Problem 22-38 Balanced Scorecard

OBJECTIVE 5

The following list gives a number of measures associated with the Balanced Scorecard:

a. number of new customers
b. percentage of customer complaints resolved with one contact
c. unit product cost
d. cost per distribution channel
e. suggestions per employee

f. warranty repair costs
g. consumer satisfaction (from surveys)
h. cycle time for solving a customer problem
i. strategic job coverage ratio
j. on-time delivery percentage
k. percentage of revenues from new products

Required:
1. Classify each performance measure as belonging to one of the following perspectives: financial, customer, internal business process, or learning and growth.
2. Suggest an additional measure for each of the four perspectives.

CASES

OBJECTIVE **3**

Case 22-39 Return on Investment Ethical Considerations

Jason Kemp was torn between conflicting emotions. On the one hand, things were going so well. He had just completed six months as the assistant financial manager in the Electronics Division of Med-Products Inc. The pay was good, he enjoyed his coworkers, and he felt that he was part of a team that was making a difference in American health care. On the other hand, his latest assignment was causing some sleepless nights. Mel Cravens, his boss, had asked him to "refine" the figures on the division's latest project—a portable imaging device code—named ZM. The original estimates called for investment of $15.6 million and projected annual income of $1.87 million. Med-Products required an ROI of at least 15 percent for new project approval. So far, ZM's rate of return was nowhere near that hurdle rate. Mel encouraged him to show increased sales and decreased expenses in order to get the projected income above $2.34 million. Jason asked for a meeting with Mel to voice his concerns.

Jason: Mel, I've gone over the figures for the new project and can't find any way to get the income above $1.9 million. The salespeople have given me the most likely revenue figures, and production feels that the expense figures are solid.

Mel: Jason, those figures are just projections. Sales doesn't really know what the revenue will be. In fact, when I talked with Sue Harris, our sales vice president, she said that sales could range from $1.5 million to $2.5 million. Use the higher figure. I'm sure this product will justify our confidence in it!

Jason: I know the range of sales was that broad, but Sue felt the $2.5 million estimate was pretty unlikely. She thought that during the first five years or so that ZM sales would stay in the lower end of the range.

Mel: Again, Sue doesn't know for sure. She's just estimating. Let's go with the higher estimate. We really need this product to expand our line and to give our division a chance to qualify for sales-based bonuses. If ZM sells at all, our revenue will go up, and we'll all share in the bonus pool!

Jason: I don't know, Mel. I feel pretty bad signing off on ROI projections that I have so little confidence in.

Mel: (frustrated) Look, Jason, just prepare the report. I'll back you up.

Required:

1. What is the ROI of project ZM based on the initial estimates? What would ROI be if the income rose to $2.34 million?
2. Do you agree that Jason has an ethical dilemma? Explain. Is there any way that Mel could ethically justify raising the sales estimates and/or lowering expense estimates?
3. What do you think Jason should do? Explain.

OBJECTIVE **1** **2**

Case 22-40 Ethical Issues, Absorption Costing, Performance Measurement

Ruth Swazey, divisional controller and certified management accountant, was upset by a recent memo she received from the divisional manager, Paul Chesser. Ruth was scheduled to present the division's financial performance at headquarters in one week. In the memo, Paul had given Ruth some instructions for this upcoming report. In particular, she had been told to emphasize the significant improvement in the division's profits over last year. Ruth, however, didn't believe that there was any real underlying improvement in the division's performance and was reluctant to say otherwise. She knew that the increase in profits was because of Paul's conscious decision to produce for inventory.

In an earlier meeting, Paul had convinced his plant managers to produce more than they knew they could sell. By doing so, more of the fixed factory overhead could be moved into inventory with the extra units produced. He argued that by deferring some of this period's fixed costs, reported profits would jump. He pointed out two significant benefits. First, by increasing profits, the division could exceed the minimum level needed so that all the managers would qualify for the annual bonus. Second, by meeting the budgeted profit level, the division would be better able to compete for much needed capital. Ruth had objected but had been overruled. The most persuasive counterargument was that the increase in inventory could be liquidated in the coming year as the economy improved. However, Ruth considered this event unlikely. Based on past experience, she believed that it would take at least two years of improved market demand before the productive capacity of the division was exceeded.

Required:

1. Discuss the behavior of Paul, the divisional manager. Was the decision to produce for inventory an ethical one?

2. What should Ruth do? Should she comply with the directive to emphasize the increase in profits? If not, what options does she have?

3. Review the Institute of Management Accountants "Statement of Ethical Professional Practice" found at http://www.imanet.org/PDFs/StatementofEthics_web.pdf. Identify any standards that apply in this situation.

23

Short-Run Decision Making: Relevant Costing and Inventory Management

Doug Norman Crystals/Alamy

After studying Chapter 23, you should be able to:

1. Describe the short-run decision-making model, and explain how cost behavior affects the information used to make decisions.

2. Apply relevant costing and decision-making concepts in a variety of business situations.

3. Choose the optimal product mix when faced with one constrained resource.

4. Explain the impact of cost on pricing decisions.

5. Discuss inventory management and just-in-time (JIT) models.

Dave Martin/Getty Images Sport/Getty Images

EXPERIENCE MANAGERIAL DECISIONS

with Navistar, Inc.

Relevant decision analysis represents one of the most exciting and widely applicable managerial accounting tools in existence. One big proponent of relevant analysis is **Navistar, Inc.**, a multibillion Fortune 300 company founded in 1902. More than 100 years later, the company has grown to manufacture components and electronics for a wide variety of vehicles, including buses, tractor trailers, military vehicles, and trucks, to its diverse customers all around the world.

Faced with important, long-term growth issues, Navistar, Inc. used relevant analysis to decide whether to expand axle production at its truck assembly plant in Ontario or to outsource its extra axle production requirements to an outside supplier company. Before the analysis could be conducted, Navistar, Inc.'s managerial accountants first had to identify all relevant factors, both quantitative and qualitative, as well as the short-term and long-term impacts of these factors. Some factors were relatively easy to identify and measure, such as the labor cost that would be required if the additional axles were made in-house or the cost of acquiring the extra factory space needed to produce the additional axles in-house. However, other factors, such as the need to eliminate bottlenecks that would be created from producing the additional axles in-house, complicated the in-house analysis for Navistar, Inc.

In addition, if Navistar, Inc. decided to make the additional axles in-house, it would require significant capacity-related capital expenditures. That carried a risk associated with the possibility that the current demand for additional axles might not persist in the long term. In this case, Navistar, Inc. would be stuck with the cost of the additional capacity without the business to generate additional revenues to cover those costs. On the other hand, if the additional axle production were outsourced, Navistar, Inc. would have to ensure that its new axle supplier partnered with the Canadian Auto Workers union to minimize the outsourcing effect on Navistar, Inc.'s existing workforce labor agreements. Furthermore, suppliers would have to be trained to deliver parts and subassemblies in sequence with Navistar, Inc.'s demanding schedule. This training represented a considerable outsourcing cost to Navistar, Inc.

In the end, the relevant costing analysis helped Navistar, Inc.'s executives decide to outsource its additional axle production. As a result, Navistar, Inc.'s Ontario plant has enjoyed annual cost savings of over $3 million! A careful analysis of all relevant factors helped the company make the right decision and avoid being burdened in the long run by the costs of excess capacity that occur in the always cyclical truck assembly business.

OBJECTIVE ①

Describe the short-run decision-making model, and explain how cost behavior affects the information used to make decisions.

SHORT-RUN DECISION MAKING

Short-run decision-making consists of choosing among alternatives with an immediate or limited end in view. Short-term decisions sometimes are referred to as *tactical* decisions because they involve choosing between alternatives with an immediate or limited time frame in mind. Strategic decisions, on the other hand, usually are long-term in nature because they involve choosing between different strategies that attempt to provide a competitive advantage over a long time frame. Accepting a special order for less than the normal selling price to utilize idle capacity and to increase this year's profits is an example of a tactical decision. While such decisions tend to be *short run* in nature, it should be emphasized that they often have long-run consequences. Consider a second example. Suppose that a company is thinking about producing a component instead of buying it from suppliers. The immediate objective may be to lower the cost of making the main product. Yet this decision may be a small part of the overall strategy of establishing a cost leadership position for the firm. Therefore, short-run decisions are often *small-scale actions* that serve a larger purpose.

The Decision-Making Model

How does a company go about making good short-run decisions? A **decision model**, a specific set of procedures that produces a decision, can be used to structure the decision maker's thinking and to organize the information to make a good decision. The following is an outline of one decision-making model.

Step 1. Recognize and define the problem.

Step 2. Identify alternatives as possible solutions to the problem. Eliminate alternatives that clearly are not feasible.

Step 3. Identify the costs and benefits associated with each feasible alternative. Classify costs and benefits as relevant or irrelevant, and eliminate irrelevant ones from consideration.

Step 4. Estimate the relevant costs and benefits for each feasible alternative.

Step 5. Assess qualitative factors.

Step 6. Make the decision by selecting the alternative with the greatest overall net benefit.

The decision-making model just described has six steps. Nothing is special about this particular listing. You may find it more useful to break the steps into 8 or 10 segments. Alternatively, you may find it useful to aggregate them into a shorter list. For example, you could use a three-step model:

Step 1. Identify the problem.

Step 2. Identify alternatives and their associated relevant costs

Step 3. Make the decision.

The key point is to find a comfortable way for you to remember the important steps in the decision-making model.

Here's the Real Kicker

Two years ago, the loan officer at **Kicker**'s bank left for another job out of state. This was an excellent time for Kicker to reevaluate its banking relationship. The company took a number of bids from the four major banks in town. In the process, Kicker executives learned a great deal about various banking services and the way that banks charged for them. Some examples include Internet service, loan rates, credit card transactions, returned check fees, and wire fees. Qualitative factors played a role in the ultimate decision. For example, how quickly does the bank respond? Does Kicker feel comfortable with its banking officer (is she or he knowledgeable about the speaker and electronics industry and attuned to Kicker's special needs)? After weighing both the monetary and nonmonetary factors, Kicker switched banks.

To illustrate the decision-making model, consider Audio-Blast Inc., a company that manufactures speaker systems for new automobiles. Recently, Audio-Blast was approached by a major automobile manufacturer about the possibility of installing Audio-Blast's main product—the mega-blast speaker system—into its new sports car. Audio-Blast speakers would be installed at the factory. Suppose that Audio-Blast decides to pursue the speaker order from the automobile manufacturer. Currently, the company does not have sufficient productive and storage capacity to fulfill the order. How might the decision-making model help Audio-Blast find the best way of obtaining that capacity?

Step 1: Recognize and Define the Problem

The first step is to recognize and define a specific problem. For example, the members of Audio-Blast's management team recognized the need for additional productive capacity as well as increased space for raw materials and finished goods inventories. The number of workers and the amount of space needed, the reasons for the need, and how the additional space would be used are all important dimensions of the problem. However, the central question is *how* to acquire the additional capacity.

Step 2: Identify Alternatives as Possible Solutions

The second step is to list and consider possible solutions. Suppose that the production head and the consulting engineer identified the following possible solutions:

1. Build a new factory with sufficient capacity to handle current and foreseeable needs.
2. Lease a larger facility, and sublease its current facility.
3. Lease an additional, similar facility.
4. Institute a second shift in the main factory, and lease an additional building that would be used for storage of raw materials and finished goods inventories only, thereby freeing up space for expanded production.
5. Outsource production to another company, and resell the speakers to the auto manufacturer.

As part of this step, Audio-Blast's upper management team met to discuss and eliminate alternatives that clearly were not feasible. The first alternative was eliminated because it carried too much risk for the company. The order had not even been secured, and the popularity of the new sports car model was not proven. Audio-Blast's president refused to "bet the company" on such a risky proposition. The second alternative was rejected because the economy in Audio-Blast's small town was such that subleasing a facility of its size was not possible. The third alternative was eliminated because it went too far in solving the space problem and, presumably, was too expensive. The fourth and fifth alternatives were feasible; they were within the cost and risk constraints and solved the needs of the company. Notice that the president linked the short-run decision (increase productive capacity) to the company's overall growth strategy by rejecting alternatives that involved too much risk at this stage of the company's development.

Step 3: Identify the Costs and Benefits Associated with Each Feasible Alternative

In the third step, the costs and benefits associated with each feasible alternative are identified. At this point, clearly irrelevant costs can be eliminated from consideration. (It is fine to include irrelevant costs and benefits in the analysis as long as they are included for *all* alternatives. We usually do not include them because focusing only on the relevant costs and benefits reduces the amount of data to be collected.) Typically, the controller is responsible for gathering necessary data.

Assume that Audio-Blast determines that the costs of making 20,000 speakers include the following:

Direct materials	$ 60,000
Direct labor	110,000
Variable overhead	10,000
Total variable production cost	$180,000

In addition, a second shift must be put in place and a warehouse must be leased to store raw materials and finished goods inventories if Audio-Blast continues to manufacture the speakers internally. Additional costs of the second shift, including a production supervisor and part-time maintenance and engineering, amount to $90,000 per year. A building that could serve as a warehouse is sitting empty across the street and can be rented for $20,000 per year. Costs of operating the building for inventory storage, including telephone and Internet access as well as salaries of materials handlers, would amount to $80,000 per year. The second alternative is to purchase the speakers externally and use the freed-up production space for inventory. An outside supplier has offered to supply sufficient volume for $360,000 per year.

Note that when the cash flow patterns become complicated for competing alternatives, it is difficult to produce a stream of equal cash flows for each alternative. In such a case, more sophisticated procedures can and should be used for the analysis. These procedures are discussed in Chapter 24, which deals with the long-run investment decisions referred to as *capital expenditure decisions*.

Step 4: Estimate the Relevant Costs and Benefits for Each Feasible Alternative

We now see that the fourth alternative—continuing to produce internally and leasing more space—costs $370,000. The fifth alternative—purchasing outside and using internal space—costs $360,000. The comparison follows:

Alternative 4		Alternative 5	
Variable cost of production	$180,000	Purchase price	$360,000
Added second shift costs	90,000		
Building lease and operating costs	100,000		
Total	$370,000		

The **differential cost** is the difference between the summed costs of two alternatives in a decision. Notice that the differential cost is $10,000 in favor of the fifth alternative. Typically, a differential cost compares the sum of each alternative's *relevant* costs only, as in the differential cost comparison of Alternatives 4 and 5. Emphasis on differential cost allows decision makers to occasionally include irrelevant costs in the alternatives if they choose to do so. However, the inclusion of irrelevant costs is acceptable *only if all irrelevant costs are included for each alternative*. For example, suppose that the controller had included fixed manufacturing cost that must be paid whether or not the speakers are made internally or externally. Then, the total cost of each alternative would increase, but the differential cost would still be $10,000. Again, as noted earlier in the chapter, it is recommended to compare only relevant costs because the inclusion of irrelevant costs often adds unnecessary data collection expenses and confusion in communicating additional information that is not relevant to the given analysis.

Step 5: Assess Qualitative Factors

While the costs and revenues associated with the alternatives are important, they do not tell the whole story. Qualitative factors can significantly affect the manager's decision. Qualitative factors are simply those factors that are hard to put a number on, including things like political pressure and product safety.

- *Political Pressure:* Companies like **Levi's** that relocate some or all of their U.S. manufacturing facilities to countries outside of the United States with cheaper labor often face stiff political pressure in the United States as a result of such offshoring decisions. Some managers worry that such political pressure from customers can have long-term negative effects on sales that more than offset the labor cost savings that spurred the decision to offshore.
- *Product Safety:* Product safety represents another key qualitative factor for outsourcing organizations, as illustrated by the trouble **Toyota** faced when it appeared to let its product quality slip by postponing safety recalls to save money in

the short-term. **Mattel** also discovered the importance of safety as a key qualitative factor when it discovered that its Chinese suppliers used illegal lead paint on thousands of its toys, which lead to an onslaught of toy recalls and a decrease in parents' trust of Mattel's products.

Returning to Audio-Blast, its president likely would be concerned with qualitative considerations such as the quality of the speakers purchased externally, the reliability of supply sources, the expected stability of prices over the next several years, labor relations, community image, and so on. To illustrate the possible impact of qualitative factors on Audio-Blast's decision, consider the first two factors, quality and reliability of supply:

- *Quality:* If the quality of speakers is significantly less when purchased externally from what is available internally, then the quantitative advantage from purchasing may be more fictitious than real. Reselling lower-quality speakers to such a high-profile buyer could permanently damage Audio-Blast's reputation. Because of this possibility, Audio-Blast may choose to continue to produce the speakers internally.
- *Reliability of Supply:* If supply sources are not reliable, production schedules could be interrupted, and customer orders could arrive late. These factors can increase labor costs and overhead and hurt sales. Again, depending on the perceived trade-offs, Audio-Blast may decide that producing the speakers internally is better than purchasing them, even if relevant cost analysis gives the initial advantage to purchasing.

How should qualitative factors be handled in the decision-making process? First, they must be identified. Second, the decision maker should try to quantify them. Often, qualitative factors are simply more difficult to quantify, not impossible. For example, possible unreliability of the outside supplier might be quantified as the probable number of late delivery days multiplied by the penalty Audio-Blast would be charged by the auto manufacturer for later delivery. More difficult measurement challenges exist. For example, **Mobil Corporation** decided to implement a strategic change of focusing on a new target audience, including "road warriors" (employees who drive a lot), "true blues" (affluent, loyal customers), and generation F3 (yuppies on the go who want fuel, want food, and want them fast).[1] However, successful implementation required that the company find a way to measure the experience of new target customers at newly designed Mobil gas pumps and convenience stores. After considerable thought, an innovative manager developed one of the first recognized "secret shopper" programs in which Mobil employees secretly dressed as customers in order to live the Mobil gas station "experience." These secret shoppers then recorded numerous aspects of their experience on quantitative scales for feedback to station managers. Without such evaluative data, it would have been extremely difficult for Mobil managers to assess the causes of success or failure of the new strategy implementation. Finally, truly qualitative factors, such as the impact of late orders on customer relations, must be taken into consideration in the final step of the decision-making model—the selection of the alternative with the greatest overall benefit.

Step 6: Make the Decision

Once all relevant costs and benefits for each alternative have been assessed and the qualitative factors weighed, a decision can be made.

ETHICAL DECISIONS Ethical concerns revolve around the way in which decisions are implemented and the possible sacrifice of long-run objectives for short-run gain. Relevant costs are used in making short-run decisions. However, decision makers should always maintain an ethical framework. Reaching objectives is important, but how you get there is perhaps more

Concept Q&A

Apply the decision-making model outlined in this section to a problem you have faced. For example, the problem might be whether or not to go to college or which car to buy. Include all of the steps. Will the application of the decision-making model help you to make the decision? Why or why not?

Answer:
List the six steps of the decision-making model, and briefly explain how each one applies to your decision. Answers will vary.

---

[1] Marc Epstein and Bill Birchard, *Counting What Counts: Turning Corporate Accountability to Competitive Advantage*. Perseus Books, New York, NY. 2000.

important. Unfortunately, many managers have the opposite view. Part of the reason for the problem is the extreme pressure to perform that many managers face. Often, the individual who is not a top performer may be laid off or demoted. Under such conditions, there is great temptation to engage in questionable behavior today and to let the future take care of itself. Unfortunately, as the historic banking regulatory upheaval of the late 2000s demonstrates, many financial services institutions in the mid-2000s yielded to unethical temptations to lend excessive amounts of money to prospective homeowners who in the end could not afford such loans. Whenever relevant costing is used, it is important to include all costs that are relevant—including those involving ethical ramifications. ●

Relevant Costs Defined

The decision-making approach just described emphasized the importance of identifying and using relevant costs. **Relevant costs** possess two characteristics: (1) they are *future* costs AND (2) they *differ* across alternatives. All pending decisions relate to the future. Accordingly, only future costs can be relevant to decisions. However, to be relevant, a cost must not only be a future cost but must also differ from one alternative to another. If a future cost is the same for more than one alternative, then it has no effect on the decision. Such a cost is *irrelevant*. The same relevance characteristics also apply to benefits. One alternative may produce an amount of future benefits different from another alternative (e.g., differences in future revenues). If future benefits differ across alternatives, then they are relevant and should be included in the analysis. The ability to identify relevant and irrelevant costs (and revenues) is a very important decision-making skill.

Relevant Costs Illustrated Consider Audio-Blast's make-or-buy alternatives. The cost of direct labor to produce the additional 20,000 speakers is $110,000. In order to determine if this $110,000 is a relevant cost, we need to ask the following:

1. *Is the direct labor cost a future cost?*
    It is certainly a future cost. Producing the speakers for the auto manufacturer requires the services of direct laborers who must be paid.
2. *Does it differ across the two alternatives?*
    If the speakers are purchased from an external supplier, then a second shift, with its direct labor, will not be needed. Thus, the cost of direct labor differs across alternatives ($110,000 for the make alternative and $0 for the buy alternative).

Therefore, it is a relevant cost.

Implicit in this analysis is the use of a past cost to estimate a future cost. The most recent cost of direct labor has averaged $5.50 per speaker; for 20,000 speakers, the direct labor will cost $110,000. This past cost was used as the estimate of next year's cost. Although past costs are not relevant, they often are used to predict what future costs will be.

Opportunity Costs Another type of relevant cost is opportunity cost. **Opportunity cost** is the benefit sacrificed or foregone when one alternative is chosen over another. Therefore, an opportunity cost is relevant because it is both a future cost and one that differs across alternatives. While an opportunity cost is not an accounting cost, because accountants do not record the cost of what might happen in the future (i.e., they do not appear in financial statements), it is an important consideration in relevant decision making.

For example, if you are deciding whether to work full time or to go to school full time, the opportunity cost of going to school would be the wages you give up by not working. Companies also include opportunity costs in many of their decision analyses. When **Ernst & Young** estimates the net benefit of sending thousands of its accountants to week-long training courses, it includes the opportunity cost of the tens of millions of dollars in lost revenue that it foregoes by not being able to bill clients for the time accountants spend in training. Oftentimes, opportunity costs are quite challenging to estimate. However, their inclusion can change the final result of the analysis, such as whether to accept or reject a special sales opportunity or to outsource a product rather than make it in-house. Therefore, managerial accountants have the ability to add significant value to relevant decision making by finding ways to measure particularly challenging opportunity costs.

Irrelevant Past Cost Illustrated Audio-Blast uses large power saws to cut the lumber that forms the housings for speakers. These saws were purchased three years ago and are being depreciated at an annual rate of $25,000. In order to determine if this $25,000 is a relevant cost, we need to ask the following:

1. *Is the direct labor cost a future cost?*
   Depreciation represents an allocation of a cost already incurred. It is a **sunk cost,** a cost that cannot be affected by any future action. Although we allocate this sunk cost to future periods and call that allocation depreciation, none of the original cost is avoidable.
2. *Does it differ across the two alternatives?*
   Sunk costs are always the same across alternatives and, therefore, always irrelevant.

Thus, depreciation costs, like all sunk costs, fail to possess the two characteristics required of relevant costs and, therefore, always are irrelevant.

In choosing between the two alternatives, the original cost of the power saws and their associated depreciation are not relevant factors. However, it should be noted that salvage value of the machinery is a relevant cost for certain decisions. For example, if Audio-Blast decides to transform itself into a distributor, not a producer, of speakers, the amount that can be realized from the sale of the power equipment will be relevant and will be included as a benefit of the switch to distributor status.

Sunk Costs It is important to note the psychology behind managers' treatment of sunk costs. Although managers *should ignore* sunk costs for relevant decisions, such as whether or not to continue funding a particular product in the future, it unfortunately is human nature to allow sunk costs to affect these decisions. For example, Toshiba and its HD DVD product team engaged in a fierce, multiyear battle with Sony and its Blu-ray product team for recognition as the universally accepted format in the growing next-generation high-definition DVD market. Throughout the battle, both sides spent millions of dollars developing, manufacturing, and advertising its own format. However, Sony's Blu-ray sales trounced Toshiba's HD DVD sales one Christmas shopping season, which prompted Hollywood giant Warner Bros. to decide to release its films only on Sony's Blu-ray format, rather than on both formats as it had done previously (the other major production companies had already sided with Sony as well). Around the same time, Blockbuster Video announced that it would only carry DVDs with the Blu-ray format. To objective entertainment business experts outside of Toshiba, these decisions by Warner Bros. and Blockbuster were the final blow to Toshiba's format and it was obvious that the HD DVD product line should be discontinued immediately to cut its losses and stop the financial bleeding. However, rather than ignore its significant sunk costs by cutting its future losses, Toshiba announced that it was "unwilling to concede defeat in the next-generation-DVD battle" and decided to launch an "aggressive advertising campaign to promote its [Toshiba's] HD DVD players and slash prices about 50 percent."[2] Therefore, not only did Toshiba continue to spend money developing, manufacturing, and marketing its failed product, it expected to earn only about half of the regular sales revenue per unit sold. Eventually, even Toshiba recognized the handwriting on the wall and dropped its HD DVD format, but only after throwing away a considerable amount of money on a product that most experts believed should have been dropped much earlier.

Another classic example of inappropriately honoring sunk costs is Coca-Cola's New Coke debacle in the mid-1980s. The development and launching of New Coke was very costly and also an undeniably huge failure. However, Coca-Cola unwisely elected to continue to spend money to advertise and maintain its failed new product simply because

---

[2] Michelle Kessler, "Toshiba Turns Up Heat in DVD War," *USA Today* (January 15, 2008): 4B.

it had already spent so much money on the product in the past. As business experts repeatedly noted, no amount of advertising cost was going to change the company's past expenditures to develop and launch New Coke and the company would have been far better off to scrap New Coke as soon as its failure was apparent.

The **XFL** football league and the **Concorde** supersonic jet over a period of 20 years are additional examples of companies that failed to cut their losses and drop their product or service and instead continued to pour money into past failed ideas because of their large associated sunk costs.

Irrelevant Future Cost Illustrated Suppose that Audio-Blast currently pays an Internet provider $5,000 per year to store its website on the server. Since Audio-Blast intends to keep the web page no matter what is decided regarding the potential speaker order, that cost is not relevant to the decision.

The same concepts apply to benefits. One alternative may produce an amount of future benefits different from another alternative (e.g., differences in future revenues). If future benefits differ across alternatives, then they are relevant and should be included in the analysis.

Cost Behavior and Relevant Costs

Most short-run decisions require extensive consideration of cost behavior. It is easy to fall into the trap of believing that variable costs are relevant and fixed costs are not. But this assumption is not true. For example, the variable costs of production *were* relevant to Audio-Blast's decision. The fixed costs associated with the existing factory *were not* relevant. However, the additional fixed cost of the supervisor for a second shift *was* relevant to the decision.

The key point is that changes in supply and demand for resources must be considered when assessing relevance. If changes in demand and supply for resources across alternatives bring about changes in spending, then the changes in resource spending are the relevant costs that should be used in assessing the relative desirability of the two alternatives.

Flexible resources can be easily purchased in the amount needed and at the time of use. For example, electricity used to run stoves that boil fruit in the production of jelly is a resource that can be acquired and used as needed. Thus, if the jelly manufacturer wants to increase production of jelly, electricity will increase just enough to satisfy that demand. This type of resource is typically referred to as a strictly variable cost.

Some resources are purchased before they are used. Clearly, investment in a factory of a particular size falls into this category; so does a year-to-year lease of office space or equipment. These costs usually are treated as fixed costs. If the decision covers a situation shorter than the time period for which the resource is fixed, then this cost usually is irrelevant.

Still other resources are acquired in advance of usage through implicit contracting; they are usually acquired in lumpy amounts. In Chapter 14, these costs were shown as step costs. This category may include an organization's salaried and hourly employees. The implicit understanding is that the organization will maintain employment levels even though there may be temporary downturns in the quantity of an activity used. This understanding means that an activity may have unused capacity available. Recall that the relevant range is important in considering step costs. As long as a company remains within the relevant range, it will not go up or down a step, so the cost is fixed for all intents and purposes.

For example, assume that a company has three purchasing agents each of whom can process 15,000 purchase orders a year. This assumption means that the existing staff can handle 45,000 purchase orders a year. If the company is processing only 40,000 purchase orders, then there is some unused capacity in purchasing. If the company is considering a special order that will require an additional 2,000 purchase orders, then there is no increased cost to purchasing. However, if the company considers an expansion that will require an additional 8,000 purchase orders per year, then an additional staffing cost will need to be incurred in purchasing.

SOME COMMON RELEVANT COST APPLICATIONS

Relevant costing is of value in solving many different types of problems. Traditionally, these applications include decisions:

- to make or buy a component.
- to keep or drop a segment or product line.
- to accept a special order at less than the usual price.
- to further process joint products or sell them at the split-off point.

Though by no means an exhaustive list, many of the same decision-making principles apply to a variety of problems.

Make-or-Buy Decisions

Managers often face the decision of whether to make a particular product (or provide a service) or to purchase it from an outside supplier. A manufacturer may need to consider whether to make or buy components used in manufacturing. A manager of a service firm may need to decide whether to provide a service in-house or to out-source it. For example, many large accounting firms increasingly are sending certain accounting service tasks overseas in an effort to reduce their U.S. staff accountant labor costs, as well as to free up U.S. staff accountants' time for more challenging, value-adding service tasks. **Make-or-buy decisions** are those decisions involving a choice between internal and external production. Exhibit 23-1 illustrates the make-or-buy decision.

Let's return briefly to **Navistar, Inc.**'s use of relevant analysis in making the make-or-buy decision for its additional axle needs. In question was whether it should manufacture (i.e., "make") the additional axles it needed or purchase (i.e., "buy") them from an external vendor. After a careful discussion with a cross functional team representing personnel from Human Resources, Accounting, Purchasing, and Finance, managers decided that the key costs of on the "make" side included one-time capital and start-up expenditures on machines and ongoing expenditures for labor, repairs and maintenance, utilities, depreciation, and insurance. Key costs on the "buy" side included one-time vendor tooling expenditures and ongoing expenditures for freight, logistics, inventory storage and movement, and training. In addition, managers considered important qualitative characteristics such as ensuring high quality, which was particularly relevant for the training costs because Navistar, Inc. wanted to be sure that any purchased axles were of a high quality and delivered to the right place at the appropriate time. After these relevant costs were identified, quantified, and analyzed, Navistar, Inc. confidently elected to outsource its additional axle production.

Make or Buy Decision Illustrated   Assume that Swasey Manufacturing currently produces an electronic component used in one of its printers. In one year, Swasey will switch production to another type of printer, and the electronic component will not be

---

Make or Buy Decisions

OR

Exhibit 23-1

used. However, for the coming year, Swasey must produce 10,000 of these parts to support the production requirements for the old printer.

A potential supplier has approached Swasey about the component. The supplier will build the electronic component to Swasey's specifications for $4.75 per unit. The offer sounds very attractive since the full manufacturing cost per unit is $8.20. Should Swasey Manufacturing make or buy the component?

Recall the steps involved in short-run decision making (p. 1148). The problem (Step 1) and the feasible alternatives (Step 2) are both readily identifiable. Since the horizon for the decision is only one period, there is no need to be concerned about periodically recurring costs (Step 3). Relevant costing is particularly useful for short-run analysis. We simply need to identify the relevant costs (Step 4), total them, and make a choice (Step 6) [assuming no overriding qualitative concerns (Step 5)].

The full absorption cost of the component is computed as follows:

	Total Cost	Unit Cost
Direct materials	$10,000	$1.00
Direct labor	20,000	2.00
Variable overhead	8,000	0.80
Fixed overhead	44,000	4.40
Total	$82,000	$8.20

Fixed overhead consists of common factory costs that are allocated to each product line. No matter what happens to the component line, overall fixed overhead will not be affected. As a result, the fixed overhead is irrelevant; it can be ignored in structuring the problem.

All other costs in this example are relevant. The costs of direct materials and direct labor are relevant because they will not be needed if the part is purchased externally. Similarly, variable overhead is relevant, because its cost would not be incurred if the component were purchased externally.

Now, what about the purchase of the component? Of course, the purchase price is relevant. If the component were made, this cost would not be incurred. Are there any other costs associated with an outside purchase? A check with the purchasing department and receiving dock confirmed that there was sufficient slack in the system to easily handle the additional purchase, suggesting that there are no additional relevant costs of purchasing the component. **CORNERSTONE 23-1** shows how to structure this make-or-buy problem.

 **CORNERSTONE 23-1**   **Structuring a Make-or-Buy Problem**

Information:

Swasey Manufacturing needed to determine if it would be cheaper to make 10,000 units of a component in-house or to purchase them from an outside supplier for $4.75 each. Cost information on internal production includes the following:

	Total Cost	Unit Cost
Direct materials	$10,000	$1.00
Direct labor	20,000	2.00
Variable overhead	8,000	0.80
Fixed overhead	44,000	4.40
Total	$82,000	$8.20

(Continued)

Fixed overhead will continue whether the component is produced internally or externally. No additional costs of purchasing will be incurred beyond the purchase price.

Required:

1. What are the alternatives for Swasey Manufacturing?
2. List the relevant cost(s) of internal production and of external purchase.
3. Which alternative is more cost effective and by how much?
4. Now assume that the fixed overhead includes $10,000 of cost that can be avoided if the component is purchased externally. Which alternative is more cost effective and by how much?

Solution:

1. There are two alternatives: make the component in-house or purchase it externally.
2. Relevant costs of making the component in-house include direct materials, direct labor, and variable overhead. Relevant costs of purchasing the component externally include the purchase price.

| | Alternatives | | Differential |
	Make	Buy	Cost to Make
Direct materials	$10 000	—	$ 10,000
Direct labor	20,000	—	20,000
Variable overhead	8,000	—	8,000
Purchase cost	—	$47,500	(47,500)
Total relevant cost	$38,000	$47,500	$ (9,500)

3. It is cheaper (by $9,500) to make the component in-house.

4.

| | Alternatives | | Differential |
	Make	Buy	Cost to Make
Direct materials	$10,000	—	$ 10,000
Direct labor	20,000	—	20,000
Variable overhead	8,000	—	8,000
Avoidable fixed overhead	10,000	—	10,000
Purchase cost	—	$47,500	(47,500)
Total relevant cost	$48,000	$47,500	$ 500

Now it is cheaper (by $500) to purchase the component.

Be sure to read the analysis in Cornerstone 23-1 carefully. At first, the fixed overhead remains whether or not the component is made internally. In this case, fixed overhead is not relevant, and making the product is $9,500 cheaper than buying it. Later, in Requirement 4, part of the fixed overhead is avoidable. This condition means that purchasing the component externally will save $10,000 in fixed cost (i.e., Swasey can avoid $10,000 of fixed overhead if it buys the component). Now, the $10,000 of fixed cost is relevant—it is a future cost and it differs between the two alternatives—and the offer of the supplier should be accepted; it is $500 cheaper to buy the component.

The same analysis can be performed on a unit-cost basis. Once the relevant costs are identified, relevant unit costs can be compared. For this example, these costs are $3.80 ($38,000/10,000) for the make alternative and $4.75 ($47,500/10,000) for the buy alternative.

One type of relevant cost that is becoming increasingly large due to globalization and the green environmental movement concerns the disposal costs associated with

Concept Q&A

You also have make-or-buy decisions to make. For example, do you change the oil in your car yourself, or do you take it to the shop? Choose one such decision, and explain why you have chosen to "make it" or "buy it." What factors could influence you to change your mind?

Answer:

Suppose that you choose the oil-change decision. You might decide to change it yourself because (1) you know how to, (2) you have the appropriate tools to do the job, (3) you have the time, and (4) you don't mind messing around under the hood. Alternatively, you might decide to have it done because (1) you don't have confidence in your ability to do it, (2) you don't own the equipment (nozzle, pan to hold oil), (3) you are unsure which oil to choose, or (4) you don't want to do the job. A factor that could influence your decision from changing your own oil to taking it to a shop might be that you have graduated from college and are working full time and really don't want to mess with oil changes in the few hours of free time that you do have.

electronic waste (or e-waste). Increasingly government agencies are assessing manufacturers of computers, televisions, digital music devices, etc., a costly fee at production to cover product disposal costs that public landfills eventually incur once the products reach the end of their life cycle, become obsolete, and are thrown out to pollute the environment. **Hewlett-Packard Co.** has taken a strategic leadership position by recycling approximately 10 percent of its sales as a more cost effective means than incurring the aforementioned governmental fees at production.[3] The failure to include relevant life cycle costs can cause the make side of the make-or-buy analysis to appear more attractive (i.e., less costly) than it is in reality.

Special-Order Decisions

From time to time, a company may consider offering a product or service at a price different from the usual price. Prices can vary to customers in the same market, and firms often have the opportunity to consider special orders from potential customers in markets not ordinarily served. For example, **General Motors** contracted with the Pentagon to use excess production capacity to manufacture its popular 4-wheel drive pickup truck for use by U.S. troops in desert combat situations, except that these trucks were altered to include bulletproof windows, mounts for machine guns, and night vision capability. A potentially important qualitative factor in this example is that certain customer segments might hold strong opinions about General Motors' association with combat activities. Such opinions might help or hurt regular sales, but their effect should be estimated and included in the relevant analysis if they are deemed to be significant. **Special-order decisions** focus on whether a specially priced order should be accepted or rejected. These orders often can be attractive, especially when the firm is operating below its maximum productive capacity. Exhibit 23-2 illustrates the special-order decision.

Exhibit 23-2

Accept or Reject a Special Order

Capacity: **20** million units

Special Order Decision Illustrated Suppose that an ice cream company produces only premium ice cream. Its factory has a capacity of 20 million half-gallon units but only plans to produce 16 million units. The total costs associated with producing and selling 16 million units are as follows (in thousands of dollars):

	Total	Unit Cost
Variable costs:		
Ingredients	$15,200	$0.95
Packaging	3,200	0.20
Direct labor	4,000	0.25
Variable overhead	1,280	0.08
Selling commission	320	0.02
Total variable costs	$24,000	$1.50
Total fixed costs	1,552	0.097
Total costs	$25,552	$1.597
Selling price		$2.00

An ice cream distributor from a geographic region not normally served by the company has offered to buy 2 million units at $1.55 per unit, provided its own label can be attached to the product. Since the distributor approached the company directly, there is no sales commission. As the manager of the ice cream company, would you accept or reject this order?

The offer of $1.55 is well below the normal selling price of $2.00. In fact, it is even below the total unit cost. Even so, accepting the order may be profitable. The company has idle capacity, and the order will not replace, or cannibalize, other units being produced to sell at the normal price. Additionally, many of the costs are not relevant; fixed costs will continue regardless of whether the order is accepted or rejected.

If the order is accepted, a benefit of $1.55 per unit will be realized that otherwise wouldn't be. However, all of the variable costs except for commissions ($0.02) also will be incurred, producing a cost of $1.48 per unit. The net benefit is $0.07 ($1.55 – $1.48) per unit. The relevant cost analysis can be summarized as follows:

	Accept	Reject	Differential Benefit to Accept
Revenues	$ 3,100,000	$—	$ 3,100,000
Ingredients	(1,900,000)	—	(1,900,000)
Packaging	(400,000)	—	(400,000)
Direct labor	(500,000)	—	(500,000)
Variable overhead	(160,000)	—	(160,000)
Profit	$ 140,000	$ 0	$ 140,000

We see that for this company, accepting the special order will increase profits by $140,000 ($0.07 × 2,000,000).

CORNERSTONE 23-2 shows how to apply relevant costing to a special-order problem.

CORNERSTONE 23-2   Structuring a Special-Order Problem

Information:

Leibnitz Company has been approached by a new customer with an offer to purchase 20,000 units of model TR8 at a price of $9 each. The new customer is geographically separated from the company's other customers, and existing sales would not be affected. Leibnitz normally produces 100,000 units of TR8 per year but only plans to produce and sell 75,000 in the coming year. The normal sales price is $14 per unit. Unit cost information for the normal level of activity is as follows:

(Continued)

**CORNERSTONE
23-2**
(continued)

Direct materials	$3.00
Direct labor	2.80
Variable overhead	1.50
Fixed overhead	2.00
Total	$9.30

Fixed overhead will not be affected by whether or not the special order is accepted.

Required:
1. What are the relevant costs and benefits of the two alternatives (accept or reject the special order)?
2. By how much will operating income increase or decrease if the order is accepted?

Solution:
1. Relevant costs and benefits of accepting the special order include the sales price of $9, direct materials, direct labor, and variable overhead. No relevant costs or benefits are attached to rejecting the order.
2. If the problem is analyzed on a unit basis:

	Accept	Reject	Differential Benefit to Accept
Price	$ 9.00	$—	$ 9.00
Direct materials	(3.00)	—	(3.00)
Direct labor	(2.80)	—	(2.80)
Variable overhead	(1.50)	—	(1.50)
Increase in operating income	$ 1.70	$ 0	$ 1.70

Operating income will increase by $34,000 ($1.70 × 20,000 units) if the special order is accepted.

Keep-or-Drop Decisions

Often, a manager needs to determine whether a segment, such as a product line, should be kept or dropped. Keep-or-drop decisions can be relatively small scale in nature, such as when **Nike** decides what to do with particular existing celebrity- and athlete-sponsored clothing or equipment lines. On the other hand, these decisions can be very large scale in nature, such as when **Ford Motor Company** contemplated the sale of its luxury Jaguar and Land Rover automobile lines. Segmented reports prepared on a variable-costing basis provide valuable information for these **keep-or-drop decisions.** Both the segment's contribution margin and its segment margin are useful in evaluating the performance of segments. However, while segmented reports provide useful information for keep-or-drop decisions, relevant costing describes how the information should be used to arrive at a decision.

Keep-or-Drop Decision Illustrated Consider Norton Materials Inc., which produces concrete blocks, bricks, and roofing tile. The controller has prepared the following estimated segment income statement for next year (in thousands of dollars):

	Blocks	Bricks	Tile	Total
Sales revenue	$ 500	$ 800	$ 150	$1,450
Less: Variable expenses	(250)	(480)	(140)	(870)
Contribution margin	$ 250	$ 320	$ 10	$ 580
Less: Direct fixed expenses:				
Advertising	(10)	(10)	(10)	(30)
Salaries	(37)	(40)	(35)	(112)
Depreciation	(53)	(40)	(10)	(103)
Segment margin	$ 150	$ 230	$ (45)	$ 335

The projected performance of the roofing tile line shows a negative segment margin. This occurrence would be the third consecutive year of poor performance for that line. The president of Norton Materials, Tom Blackburn—concerned about this poor performance—is trying to decide whether to keep or drop the roofing tile line.

His first reaction is to try to increase the sales revenue of roofing tiles, possibly through an aggressive sales promotion coupled with an increase in the selling price. The marketing manager thinks that this approach would be fruitless; the market is saturated, and the level of competition is too keen to hold out any hope for increasing the firm's market share.

Increasing the product line's profits through cost cutting is not feasible either. Costs were cut the past two years to reduce the loss to its present anticipated level. Any further reductions would lower the quality of the product and adversely affect sales.

With no hope for improving the profit performance of the line beyond its projected level, Tom has decided to drop it. He reasons that the firm will lose a total of $10,000 in contribution margin but will save $45,000 by dismissing the line's supervisor and eliminating its advertising budget. (The depreciation cost of $10,000 is not relevant because it represents an allocation of a sunk cost.) Thus, dropping the product line has a $35,000 advantage over keeping it. **CORNERSTONE 23-3** shows how to structure this information as a keep-or-drop product line problem.

 **CORNERSTONE 23-3**   **Structuring a Keep-or-Drop Product Line Problem**

Information:
Shown below is a segmented income statement for Norton Materials Inc.'s three product lines:

	Blocks	Bricks	Tile	Total
Sales revenue	$ 500,000	$ 800,000	$ 150,000	$1,450,000
Less: Variable expenses	(250,000)	(480,000)	(140,000)	(870,000)
Contribution margin	$ 250,000	$ 320,000	$ 10,000	$ 580,000
Less: Direct fixed expenses:				
Advertising	(10,000)	(10,000)	(10,000)	(30,000)
Salaries	(37,000)	(40,000)	(35,000)	(112,000)
Depreciation	(53,000)	(40,000)	(10,000)	(103,000)
Segment margin	$ 150,000	$ 230,000	$ (45,000)	$ 335,000

The roofing tile line has a contribution margin of $10,000 (sales of $150,000 less total variable costs of $140,000). All variable costs are relevant. Relevant fixed costs associated with this line include $10,000 in advertising and $35,000 in supervision salaries.

Required:
1. List the alternatives being considered with respect to the roofing tile line.
2. List the relevant benefits and costs for each alternative.
3. Which alternative is more cost effective and by how much?

Solution:
1. The two alternatives are to keep the roofing tile line or to drop it.
2. The relevant benefits and costs of keeping the roofing tile line include sales of $150,000, variable costs of $140,000, advertising cost of $10,000, and supervision cost of $35,000.
    None of the relevant benefits and costs of keeping the roofing tile line would occur under the drop alternative.

(Continued)

3.

	Keep	Drop	Differential Amount to Keep
Sales	$ 150,000	$—	$ 150,000
Less: Variable expenses	(140,000)	—	(140,000)
Contribution margin	$ 10,000	$—	$ 10,000
Less: Advertising	(10,000)	—	(10,000)
Cost of supervision	(35,000)	—	(35,000)
Total relevant benefit (loss)	$ (35,000)	$ 0	$ (35,000)

CORNERSTONE 23-3 (continued)

The difference is $35,000 in favor of dropping the roofing tile line.

A merger between companies is another type of keep-or-drop decision that requires managerial accountants to estimate relevant costs, such as which costs would go away when two companies merge and which costs would remain. For example, when **XM Satellite Radio** and **Sirius Satellite Radio** first considered merging into one giant satellite radio company, proponents argued that the merger would create significant cost savings to the new company that could be passed along to consumers in the form of lower prices.[4] They reasoned that many of the costs that XM and Sirius incurred as separate companies would either decrease or be eliminated because the new combined company would need only one research and development group, one marketing department, etc. Any costs that would decrease or go away after the merger would be relevant costs for the merger analysis, while any costs that would remain unchanged after the merger would be irrelevant.

Keep or Drop with Complementary Effects Suppose that dropping Norton's roofing tile line would lower sales of blocks by 10 percent and bricks by 8 percent, as many customers buy roofing tile at the same time that they purchase blocks or bricks. Some customers will go elsewhere if they cannot buy both products at the same location. How does this information affect the keep-or-drop decision? **CORNERSTONE 23-4** shows the impact on all product lines.

CORNERSTONE 23-4

Structuring a Keep-or-Drop Product Line Problem with Complementary Effects

Information:
Refer to Norton Materials' segmented income statement in Cornerstone 23-3. Assume that dropping the product line reduces sales of blocks by 10 percent and sales of bricks by 8 percent. All other information remains the same.

Required:
1. If the roofing tile line is dropped, what is the contribution margin for the block line? For the brick line?
2. Which alternative (keep or drop the roofing tile line) is now more cost effective and by how much?

(Continued)

[4] Kim Peterson, "XM Plus Sirius Doesn't Equal Monopoly?" (March 24, 2008): accessed April 5, 2008, from http://blogs.money central.msn.com/topstocks/archive/2008/03/24/xm-plus-sirius-doesn-t-equal-monopoly-feds-say.aspx.

Solution:

1. Previous contribution margin of blocks was $250,000. A 10 percent decrease in sales implies a 10 percent decrease in total variable costs, so the contribution margin decreases by 10 percent.

CORNERSTONE 23-4 *(continued)*

New contribution margin for blocks = $250,000 − 0.10($250,000) = $225,000

The reasoning is the same for the brick line, but the decrease is 8 percent.

New contribution margin for bricks = $320,000 − 0.08($320,000) = $294,400.

Therefore, if the roofing tile product line were dropped, the resulting total contribution margin for Norton Materials would equal $519,400 ($225,000 + $294,400).

2.

	Keep	Drop	Differential Amount to Keep
Contribution margin	$ 580,000	$519,400	$ 60,600
Less: Advertising	(30,000)	(20,000)	(10,000)
Cost of supervision	(112,000)	(77,000)	(35,000)
Total	$ 438,000	$422,400	$ 15,600

Notice that the contribution margin for the drop alternative equals the new contribution margins of the block and brick lines ($225,000 + $294,400).

Also, advertising and supervision remain relevant across these alternatives.

Now the analysis favors keeping the roofing tile line. In fact, company income will be $15,600 higher if all three lines are kept as opposed to dropping the roofing tile line.

The example provides some insights beyond the simple application of the decision model. The initial analysis, which focused on two feasible alternatives, led to a tentative decision to drop the product line. Additional information provided by the marketing manager led to a reversal of the first decision. Perhaps other feasible alternatives exist as well. These additional alternatives would require still more analyses.

YOU DECIDE   Relevant Decision Making

You are an elected official in a major city that is considering whether to move forward with a proposed plan to demolish the city's existing professional sports stadium and build an elaborate new stadium. One of the most difficult aspects of this decision is estimating the new stadium's incremental revenues and costs that would result if it were built.

What specific types of relevant revenues and costs would you consider in making this important decision?

There are many stadium events for which the associated relevant revenues and costs must be estimated accurately if the correct decision is to be made. These stadium events (and their relevant revenues and costs) include:

- Main attraction sporting events (e.g., ticket revenues from baseball, basketball, and/or football games for which the stadium would be built; additional staffing, cleanup, and insurance costs)
- Concessions and other sales (e.g., contribution margins or fees earned from product and service sales—most new stadiums boast as many high-end shopping opportunities as an upscale mall!)
- Television contract terms (e.g., the amount and percentage of revenue brought in by *additional* games being televised in the new stadium, perhaps in primetime slots)
- Offseason events (e.g., the ticket revenue from boxing matches, music concerts, etc.).

For this relevant stadium decision, estimating the relevant revenues might be even more difficult than estimating the relevant costs. For instance, projecting how many *more* people will want to attend games in a new stadium can be unclear, as well as how much money they would be willing to spend for various seats located around the stadium.

Several New York City area stadiums experienced tremendous difficulty in accurately estimating these same items. For example, the **New York Yankees** and **New York Mets** organizations built new stadiums with price tags of over $1.2 billion and $800 million,

(Continued)

respectively! However, in the new Yankee stadium, many of the more expensive seats—the ones behind the batter and, thus, most visible on television—remained empty because of their hefty $2,500 per seat price tag. In fact, the Yankee organization decreased some of its highest ticket prices by 50 percent during the stadium's first season in an attempt to fill these high profile empty seats. In other words, decision makers struggled to estimate the amount of incremental revenue that would result from some of the more important seats in a new Yankee stadium. Undaunted by such challenging relevant analyses, however, the New York area also built a $1.6 billion new Meadowlands Stadium to be shared by the New York Jets and New York Giants.

In addition to the previously mentioned relevant items, some citizens raise objections to such large amounts of money being spent on replacing existing fully functional sporting facilities with gargantuan sports palaces. They argue that $1 billion could be better spent on different causes. Such sentiments, whether you agree or disagree with them, represent potentially important qualitative factors that effective managerial accountants should take into account when performing relevant analyses for proposed new stadiums, especially when these citizens represent tax payers or potential fans the stadium builders count on for purchasing expensive tickets in the future.

When making such an important decisions, relevant costs for things like sporting events, concessions, television contracts, and off-season events must be considered in addition to qualitative factors like citizen sentiment.

Further Processing of Joint Products

Joint products have common processes and costs of production up to a split-off point. At that point, they become distinguishable as separately identifiable products. For example, certain minerals such as copper and gold may both be found in a given ore. The ore must be mined, crushed, and treated before the copper and gold are separated. The point of separation is called the **split-off point**. The costs of mining, crushing, and treatment are common to both products and, therefore, are incurred regardless of whether the ore is sold at the split-off point or further processed into copper, gold and any other substances that exist in the ore. As a result, joint costs are irrelevant to the decision of whether to sell at the split-off point or to process further.

Many joint products are sold at the split-off point. However, sometimes it is more profitable to process a joint product further, beyond the split-off point, prior to selling it. A **sell-or-process-further decision** is an important relevant decision that a manager must make.

Sell-or-Process-Further Decision Illustrated
Consider Appletime Corporation, a large corporate farm that specializes in growing apples. Each plot produces approximately one ton of apples. The trees in each plot must be sprayed, fertilized, watered, and pruned. When the apples are ripened, workers are hired to pick them. The apples are then transported to a warehouse, where they are washed and sorted. The approximate cost of all these activities (including processing) is $300 per ton per year.

Apples are sorted into three grades (A, B, and C), determined by size and blemishes. Large apples without blemishes (bruises, cuts, wormholes, and so on) are sorted into one bin and classified as Grade A. Small apples without blemishes are sorted into a second bin and classified as Grade B. All remaining apples are placed in a third bin and classified as Grade C. Every ton of apples produces 800 pounds of Grade A, 600 pounds of Grade B, and 600 pounds of Grade C.

Grade A apples are sold to large supermarkets for $0.40 per pound. Grade B apples are packaged in five-pound bags and sold to supermarkets for $1.30 per bag. (The cost of each bag is $0.05.) Grade C apples are processed further and made into applesauce. The sauce is sold in 16-ounce cans for $0.75 each. The cost of processing is $0.10 per pound of apples. The final output is 500 sixteen-ounce cans.

A large supermarket chain recently requested that Appletime supply 16-ounce cans of apple pie filling for which the chain is willing to pay $0.90 per can. Appletime determined that the Grade B apples would be suitable for this purpose and estimated that it would cost $0.24 per pound to process the apples into pie filling. The output would be 500 cans. Exhibit 23-3 illustrates the decision to sell Grade B apples at the split-off point or to process them further into pie filling.

In deciding whether to sell Grade B apples at split-off or to process them further and sell them as pie filling, the common costs of spraying, pruning, and so on are not relevant. The company must pay the $300 per ton for these activities regardless of whether

Further Processing of Joint Products

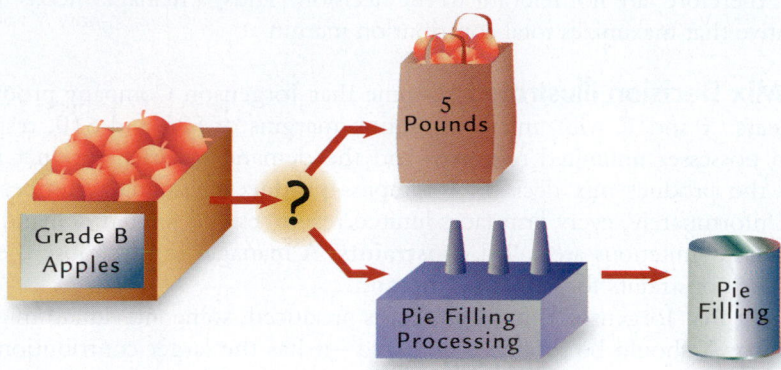

it sells at split-off or processes further. However, the revenues earned at split-off are likely to differ from the revenues that would be received if the Grade B apples were further processed and sold as pie filling. Therefore, revenues are a relevant consideration. Similarly, the processing costs occur only if further processing takes place. Hence, processing costs are relevant. **CORNERSTONE 23-5** shows how to structure the sell-or-process-further decision for the Grade B apples.

CORNERSTONE 23-5   Structuring the Sell-or-Process-Further Decision

Information:

Appletime grows apples and then sorts them into one of three grades, A, B, or C, based on their condition. Appletime must decide whether to sell the Grade B apples at split-off or to process them into apple pie filling. The company normally sells the Grade B apples in 120 five-pound bags at a per-unit price of $1.25. If the apples are processed into pie filling, the result will be 500 cans of filling with additional costs of $0.24 per can. The buyer will pay $0.90 per can.

Required:

1. What is the contribution to income from selling the Grade B apples in five-pound bags?
2. What is the contribution to income from processing the Grade B apples into pie filling?
3. Should Appletime continue to sell the Grade B apples in bags or process them further into pie filling?

Solution:

1. Revenue from apples in bags = $1.25 × 120 = $150
2. Revenue from further processing = $0.90 × 500 = $450
   Further processing cost = $0.24 × 500 = $120
   Income from further processing = $450 − $120 = $330
3. Appletime should process the Grade B apples into pie filling because the company will make $330 versus the $150 it would make by selling the apples in bags.

PRODUCT MIX DECISIONS

Most of the time, organizations have wide flexibility in choosing their product mix. Product mix refers to the relative amount of each product manufactured (or service provided) by a company. Decisions about product mix can have a significant impact on an organization's profitability.

OBJECTIVE 3
Choose the optimal product mix when faced with one constrained resource.

Each mix represents an alternative that carries with it an associated profit level. A manager should choose the alternative that maximizes total profits. Since fixed costs do not vary with activity level, the total fixed costs of a firm will be the same for all possible mixes and, therefore, are not relevant to the decision. Thus, a manager needs to choose the alternative that maximizes total contribution margin.

Product Mix Decision Illustrated   Assume that Jorgenson Company produces two types of gears: X and Y, with unit contribution margins of $25 and $10, respectively. If the firm possesses unlimited resources and the demand for each product is unlimited, then the product mix decision is simple—produce an infinite number of each product. Unfortunately, every firm faces limited resources and limited demand for each product. These limitations are called **constraints**. A manager must choose the optimal mix given the constraints found within the firm.

Assuming that Jorgenson can sell all that is produced, some individuals might argue that only Gear X should be produced and sold—it has the larger contribution margin. However, this solution is not necessarily the best choice. The selection of the optimal mix can be significantly affected by the relationships of the constrained, or scarce, resources to the individual products. These relationships affect the quantity of each product that can be produced and, consequently, the total contribution margin that can be earned. This point is most vividly illustrated when faced with one resource constraint. **CORNERSTONE 23-6** shows how to determine the optimal product mix with one constrained resource.

CORNERSTONE 23-6   Determining the Optimal Product Mix with One Constrained Resource

Information:

Jorgenson Company produces two types of gears, X and Y, with unit contribution margins of $25 and $10, respectively. Each gear must be notched by a special machine. The firm owns eight machines that together provide 40,000 hours of machine time per year. Gear X requires two hours of machine time, and Gear Y requires 0.5 hour of machine time. There are no other constraints.

Required:

1. What is the contribution margin per hour of machine time for each gear?
2. What is the optimal mix of gears?
3. What is the total contribution margin earned for the optimal mix?

Solution:

1.

	Gear X	Gear Y
Contribution margin per unit	$25.00	$10.00
Required machine time per unit	÷ 2	÷ 0.5
Contribution margin per hour of machine time	$12.50	$20.00

2. Since Gear Y yields $20 of contribution margin per hour of machine time, all machine time should be devoted to the production of Gear Y.

Units Gear Y = 40,000 total hours/0.5 hour per Gear Y = 80,000 units

The optimal mix is Gear Y = 80,000 units and Gear X = 0 units.

3. Total contribution margin of optimal mix = (80,000 units Gear Y)$10

= $800,000

Cornerstone 23-6 clearly illustrates a fundamentally important point involving relevant decision making with a constrained resource. This point is that the contribution margin *per unit* of each product is not the critical concern when deciding how much of each product type to produce and sell. Instead, the contribution margin *per unit of the scarce resource* is the deciding factor, which means that the product yielding the highest contribution margin per unit of the scarce resource should be selected. Returning to Cornerstone 23-6, Gear X earns contribution margin per unit of $25, which is 2.5 times greater than the $10 contribution margin per unit earned by Gear Y. However, each Gear X unit requires *more* than 2.5 times as much machine time (the constrained factor) to produce than does each Gear Y unit, thereby making Gear Y more attractive financially than Gear X. Specifically, Gear X earns $12.50 of contribution margin per machine hour ($25/2), but Gear Y earns $20 of contribution margin per machine hour ($10/0.5). Thus, Gear Y is the more attractive product and the optimal mix is 80,000 units of Gear Y and no units of Gear X.

$$\text{Contribution margin per unit of the scarce resource} = \frac{\text{Selling price per unit} - \text{Variable cost per unit}}{\text{Required amount of scarce resource per unit}}$$

Suppose, however, that there is also a demand constraint. Only 60,000 units of Gear Y can be sold. **CORNERSTONE 23-7** shows how to incorporate this additional constraint.

Coffee chain **Caribou Coffee**, as well as other retail businesses, pay careful attention to profitability and sales per square foot of cafe floor space, which often is the most

CORNERSTONE 23-7   Determining the Optimal Product Mix with One Constrained Resource and a Sales Constraint

Information:

Jorgenson Company produces two types of gears, X and Y, with unit contribution margins of $25 and $10, respectively. Each gear must be notched by a special machine. The firm owns eight machines that together provide 40,000 hours of machine time per year. Gear X requires two hours of machine time, and Gear Y requires 0.5 hour of machine time. A maximum of 60,000 units of each gear can be sold.

Required:

1. What is the contribution margin per hour of machine time for each gear?
2. What is the optimal mix of gears?
3. What is the total contribution margin earned for the optimal mix?

Solution:

1.

	Gear X	Gear Y
Contribution margin per unit	$25.00	$10.00
Required machine time per unit	÷ 2	÷ 0.5
Contribution margin per hour of machine time	$12.50	$20.00

2. Since Gear Y yields $20 of contribution margin per hour of machine time, the first priority is to produce all of Gear Y that the market will take (i.e., demands).

Machine time required for maximum amount of Gear Y = 60,000 units × 0.5 machine hours
required for each Gear Y unit
= 30,000 hours needed to manufacture 60,000 Gear Y units

(Continued)

CORNERSTONE
23-7
(continued)

Remaining machine time for Gear X = 40,000 hours − 30,000 hours
$$= 10,000 \text{ hours}$$

Units of Gear X to be produced in remaining 10,000 hours
$$= 10,000 \text{ hours}/2 \text{ hours per unit} = 5,000 \text{ units}$$

Now the optimal mix is 60,000 units of Gear Y and 5,000 units of Gear X. This mix will precisely exhaust the machine time available.

3. Total contribution margin of optimal mix = (60,000 units Gear Y × $10)
$$+ (5,000 \text{ units Gear X} \times \$25)$$
$$= \$725,000$$

important constrained resource. The importance of this metric explains why fast-food restaurants like **McDonald's** push their drive-through service—customers using the drive-through option do not require any internal store floor space. In fact, some restaurants generate more than 80 percent of sales from this service.

Multiple Constrained Resources

The presence of only one constrained resource might not be realistic. Organizations often face multiple constraints: limitations of raw materials, limitations of skilled labor, limited demand for each product, and so on. The solution of the product mix problem in the presence of multiple constraints is considerably more complicated and requires the use of a specialized mathematical technique known as *linear programming*, which is reserved for advanced cost management courses.

OBJECTIVE 4
Explain the impact of cost on pricing decisions.

THE USE OF COSTS IN PRICING DECISIONS

One of the more difficult decisions faced by a company is pricing. This section examines the impact of cost on price and the role of the accountant in gathering the needed information.

Cost-Based Pricing

Demand is one side of the pricing equation; supply is the other side. Since revenue must cover all costs for the firm to make a profit, many companies start with cost to determine price. That is, they calculate product cost and add the desired profit. The mechanics of this approach are straightforward. Usually, there is a cost base and a markup. The **markup** is a percentage applied to the base cost and is calculated as follows:

> Price using markup = Cost per unit + (Cost per unit × Markup percentage)

It includes desired profit and any costs not included in the base cost. Companies that bid for jobs routinely base bid price on cost. Law firms and public accounting firms are service organizations that use cost-plus pricing to bid for clients. **CORNERSTONE 23-8** shows how to apply a markup percentage to cost to obtain price.

CORNERSTONE
23-8

Calculating Price by Applying a Markup Percentage to Cost

Information:
Elvin Company assembles and installs computers to customer specifications. Elvin has decided to price its jobs at the cost of direct materials and direct labor plus 20 percent. The job for a local vocational-technical school included the following costs:

(Continued)

CORNERSTONE
23-8
(continued)

| Direct materials | $65,000 |
| Direct labor (assembly and installation) | 4,000 |

Required:

Calculate the price charged by Elvin Company to the vocational-technical school.

Solution:

Price = Cost + (Markup percentage × Cost)

= $69,000 + 0.20($69,000)

= $69,000 + $13,800

= $82,800

Notice in Cornerstone 23-8 that the markup of 20 percent is not pure profit. Instead, it includes other costs not specified, such as overhead (including Elvin's offices and management salaries) as well as any marketing and administrative expenses. The markup percentage can be calculated using a variety of bases.

Retail stores often use markup pricing, and typical markup is 100 percent of cost. Thus, if Graham Department Store purchases a sweater for $24, the retail price marked is $48 [$24 + (1.00 × $24)]. Again, the 100 percent markup is not pure profit—it goes toward the salaries of the clerks, payment for space and equipment (cash registers, furniture, and fixtures), utilities, advertising, and so on. A major advantage of markup pricing is that standard markups are easy to apply. Consider the difficulty of setting a price for every piece of merchandise in a hardware or department store. It is much simpler to apply a uniform markup to cost and then to adjust prices upward (downward) if demand is more (less) than anticipated.

Several important observations are in order at this point concerning the relationship between the base cost, the markup percentage, and the firm's cost system. First, when the firm includes relatively few costs in the base cost (rather than a large number of costs), it usually becomes very important that the firm selects a large enough markup percentage to ensure that the markup covers all of the remaining costs not included in the base cost. Determining a price that is large enough to cover significant other costs with the markup requires considerable judgment and cost estimation. Second, on a related note, the effectiveness of cost-plus pricing relies heavily on the accuracy of the cost system and pricing managers' understanding of the firm's cost structure. For example, assume that a firm marks up only its direct manufacturing costs and does not understand well the behavior of its indirect manufacturing costs or its nonmanufacturing costs (e.g., research and development costs, distribution costs, customer service costs, etc.). In this case, it is likely that the firm will encounter problems in setting prices either too high—and will be undercut by competitors with more appropriate lower prices—or too low—and will not cover all costs, thereby resulting in a net loss.

Target Costing and Pricing

Many American and European firms set the price of a new product as the sum of the costs and the desired profit. The rationale is that the company must earn sufficient revenues to cover all costs and yield a profit. Peter Drucker writes, "This is true but irrelevant: Customers do not see it as their job to ensure manufacturers a profit. The only sound way to price is to start out with what the market is willing to pay."[5]

Consider a situation in which you want to buy something, but it is quite expensive. Suppose the salesperson says that the price of the item is high because the cost to the store is high. (That is, price is related to cost.) Suppose, on the other hand, that the salesperson says the price is high because the demand for the item is strong. (That is, price is not related to cost.) Which explanation would make you happier to buy the item?

Answer:

You would probably be more likely to buy the item when the reason for the high price is high cost to the store. This situation makes the high price seem "fairer" to you, since the store is not gouging you but simply is trying to make a normal profit.

---

[5] Peter Drucker, "The Five Deadly Business Sins," *The Wall Street Journal* (October 21, 1993): A22.

Target costing is a method of determining the cost of a product or service based on the price (target price) that customers are willing to pay. The marketing department determines what characteristics and price for a product are most acceptable to consumers. Then, it is the job of the company's engineers to design and develop the product such that cost and profit can be covered by that price. Japanese firms have practiced this approach for years; American companies increasingly use target costing. For example, **Olympus**, **Toyota**, **Boeing**, **Nissan**, and **Caterpillar** have used a value chain perspective to implement target costing. Target costing recognizes that between 75 and 90 percent of a product's cost becomes "committed" or "locked into" by the time it finishes the design stage.[6] Therefore, it is most effective to make such large changes in the design and development stage of the product life cycle because at this point the features of the product, as well as its costs, still are fairly easy to adjust. Typical target costing efforts to reduce costs focus on redesigning the product to require fewer or less costly materials, labor, and processes during production, delivery and customer service. **Mercedes**, for instance, used target costing extensively in the design of its popular M-class sports utility vehicle series, which made its public debut in the blockbuster movie *Jurassic Park*.

Target Costing Illustrated

Consider the target costing experience used by Digitime Company in developing a wristwatch that incorporates a PDA (personal digital assistant). The "cool factor" on this item is high, but actually inputting data on the watch is difficult. So, the company expects to be able to charge a premium price to a relatively small number of early adopters. The marketing vice president's price estimate is $200. Digitime's management requires a 15 percent profit on new products. Therefore, target cost is calculated using the following equation:

$$\text{Target cost} = \text{Target price} - \text{Desired profit}$$

CORNERSTONE 23-9 shows how to calculate a target cost.

CORNERSTONE 23-9   Calculating a Target Cost

Information:
Digitime manufactures wristwatches and is designing a new watch model that incorporates a PDA (personal digital assistant), which Digitime hopes consumers will view as a cool and valuable design feature. As such, the new PDA watch has a target price of $200. Management requires a 15 percent profit on new product revenues.

Required:
1. Calculate the amount of desired profit.
2. Calculate the target cost.

Solution:
1. Desired profit = 0.15 × Target price
   = 0.15 × $200
   = $30

2. Target cost = Target price − Desired profit
   = $200 − $30
   = $170

Target costing involves much more up front work than cost-based pricing. If Digitime can't make the watch for $170, then the engineers and designers will have to go back to the drawing board and find a way to get it done on budget. However, let's not forget the additional work that must be done if the cost-based price turns out to be higher than what customers will accept. Then, the arduous task of bringing costs into line to support a lower price, or the opportunity cost of missing the market altogether, begins. For example, in the 1980s, the U.S. consumer electronics market became virtually nonexistent because cost-based pricing led to increasingly higher prices. Japanese (and later Korean) firms practicing target costing offered lower prices and just the features wanted by consumers to win the market.

Target costing can be used most effectively in the design and development stage of the product life cycle. At that point, the features of the product, as well as its costs, still are relatively easy to adjust.

DECISION MAKING FOR INVENTORY MANAGEMENT

OBJECTIVE **5**
Discuss inventory management and just-in-time (JIT) models.

Other types of short-run decisions relate to inventories of raw materials, work in process, and finished goods. For example, companies sometimes experience problems with raw materials and finished goods inventories, such as a lack of storage for these inventories that then has a spill-over effect on productive capacity and warehouse costs.

Inventory-Related Costs

When the demand for a product or material is known with near certainty for a given period of time (usually a year), two major costs are associated with inventory. If the inventory is a material or good purchased from an outside source, then these inventory-related costs are known as *ordering costs* and *carrying costs*. (If the material or good is produced internally, then the costs are called *setup costs* and *carrying costs*.)

- **Ordering costs** are the costs of placing and receiving an order. Examples include order processing costs (clerical costs and documents), the cost of insurance for shipment, and unloading and receiving costs.
- **Carrying costs** are the costs of keeping and storing inventory. Examples include insurance, inventory taxes, obsolescence, the opportunity cost of funds tied up in inventory, handling costs, and storage space.

If demand is not known with certainty, then a third category of inventory costs—called *stockout costs*—exists.

- **Stockout costs** are the costs of not having a product available when demanded by a customer or the cost of not having a raw material available when needed for production. Examples are lost sales (both current and future), the costs of expediting (increased transportation charges, overtime, and so on), and the costs of interrupted production (e.g., idled workers).

It is important to realize that the purchase price of raw materials is not a part of the total cost associated with carrying inventory. That price must be paid anyway. Similarly, the product cost of units produced is not an inventory-related cost.

Exhibit 23-4 (p. 1172) summarizes the reasons typically offered for carrying inventory. It's important to realize that these reasons are given to *justify* carrying inventories. A host of other reasons can be offered that *encourage* the carrying of inventories. For example, performance measures such as measures of machine and labor efficiency may promote the buildup of inventories.

Concept **Q&A**

Has a store ever been out of an item that you wanted to buy? What did you do? What is the impact of the stockout on the store?

Answer:
You might have gone to another store or tried to buy the item online. The stockout cost for the first store is not only the profit to be made from selling to you, but also, potentially, your future business.

Just-in-Time Approach to Inventory Management

The economic environment for many traditional, large-batch, high setup cost firms has changed dramatically in the past few decades. Advances in transportation and communication have contributed significantly to the creation of global competition. Advances in

Exhibit 23-4

Traditional Reasons for Carrying Inventory

- To balance ordering or setup costs and carrying costs.
- To satisfy customer demand (for example, meet delivery dates).
- To avoid shutting down manufacturing facilities because of:
  - Machine failure.
  - Defective parts.
  - Unavailable parts.
  - Late delivery of parts.
- To buffer against unreliable production processes.
- To take advantage of discounts.
- To hedge against future price increases.

technology have contributed to shorter life cycles for products, and product diversity has increased. These competitive pressures have led many firms to abandon the EOQ model in favor of a just-in-time (JIT) approach.

The **just-in-time (JIT)** approach maintains that goods should be pulled through the system by present demand rather than being pushed through on a fixed schedule based on anticipated demand. Many fast-food restaurants, like **McDonald's**, use a pull system to control their finished goods inventory. When a customer orders a hamburger, it is taken from the warming rack. When the number of hamburgers gets too low, the cooks cook more hamburgers. Customer demand pulls the materials through the system. This same principle is used in manufacturing settings. Each operation produces only what is necessary to satisfy the demand of the succeeding operation. The material or subassembly arrives just in time for production to occur so that demand can be met.

Comparing Just-in-Time and Traditional Inventory Approaches The hallmark of JIT is to reduce all inventories to very low levels. This idea of maintaining smaller inventories, however, challenges the traditional reasons for holding inventories illustrated in Exhibit 23-4. JIT inventory management offers alternative solutions that do not require high inventories.

Ordering Costs For example, in a traditional system, inventory resolves the conflict between ordering or setup costs and carrying costs by selecting an inventory level that minimizes the sum of these costs. If demand is greater than expected or if production is reduced by breakdowns and production inefficiencies, then inventories serve as buffers, providing products to customers that may otherwise not have been available. In a JIT environment, however, ordering costs are reduced by developing close relationships with suppliers. Negotiating long-term contracts for the supply of outside materials will obviously reduce the number of orders and the associated ordering costs. Some retailers have reduced ordering costs by allowing the manufacturer to handle inventory management for the retailer. The manufacturer tells the retailer when and how much stock to reorder. The retailer reviews the recommendation and approves the order if it makes sense. **Wal-Mart** and **Procter & Gamble**, for example, use this arrangement to reduce inventories as well as stockout problems.

Uncertainty in Demand According to the traditional view, inventories prevent shutdowns caused by machine failure, defective material or subassembly, and unavailability of a raw material or subassembly. Those espousing the JIT approach claim that inventories do not solve these problems but rather cover up or hide them. JIT solves the three problems by emphasizing total preventive maintenance and total quality control and by building the right kind of relationship with suppliers. In JIT, reduced setup times allow manufacturers to literally produce to order.

Lower Cost of Inventory Traditionally, inventories are carried so that a firm can take advantage of quantity discounts and hedge against future price increases of the items purchased. The objective is to lower the cost of inventory. JIT achieves the same objective without carrying inventories. The JIT solution is to negotiate long-term contracts with a few chosen suppliers located as close to the production facility as possible and to establish more extensive supplier involvement. Suppliers are not selected on the basis of price alone. Performance—the quality of the component and the ability to deliver as needed—and commitment to JIT purchasing are vital considerations. Other benefits of long-term contracts exist. They stipulate prices and acceptable quality levels. Long-term contracts also reduce dramatically the number of orders placed, which helps to drive down the ordering cost.

Limitations of the Just-in-Time Approach JIT does have limitations. It is often referred to as a program of simplification—yet this does not imply that JIT is simple or easy to implement. Time is required, for example, to build sound relationships with suppliers. Insisting on immediate changes in delivery times and quality may not be realistic and may cause difficult confrontations between a company and its suppliers. Workers also may be affected by JIT. Studies have shown that sharp reductions in inventory buffers may cause a regimented workflow and high levels of stress among production workers. If the workers perceive JIT as a way of simply squeezing more out of them, then JIT efforts may be doomed. Perhaps a better strategy for JIT implementation is one where inventory reductions follow the process improvements that JIT offers. It requires careful and thorough planning and preparation. Companies should expect some struggle and frustration.

The most glaring deficiency of JIT is the absence of inventory to buffer production interruptions. Current sales are constantly being threatened by an unexpected interruption in production. In fact, if a problem occurs, JIT's approach consists of trying to find and solve the problem before any further production activity occurs. Retailers who use JIT tactics also face the possibility of shortages. (JIT retailers order what they need now, not what they expect to sell. The idea is to flow goods through the channel as late as possible, keeping inventories low and decreasing the need for markdowns.) If demand increases well beyond the retailer's supply of inventory, then the retailer may be unable to make order adjustments quickly enough to avoid lost sales and irritated customers. The JIT manufacturing company is also willing to place current sales at risk to achieve assurance of future sales. This assurance comes from higher quality, quicker response time, and less operating costs. Even so, we must recognize that a sale lost today is a sale lost forever. Installing a JIT system so that it operates with little interruption is not a short-run project. Thus, losing sales is a real cost of installing a JIT system.

SUMMARY OF LEARNING OBJECTIVES

LO1.   Describe the short-run decision-making model, and explain how cost behavior affects the information used to make decisions.
- Six steps of the decision making model are:
  - Recognize and define the problem.
  - Identify feasible alternatives.
  - Identify costs and benefits with each feasible alternative.
  - Estimate the relevant costs and benefits for each feasible alternative.
  - Assess qualitative factors.
  - Make the decision by selecting the alternative with the greatest overall net benefit.
- Relevant costs:
  - These are future costs that differ across alternatives.
  - They frequently are variable costs—called flexible resources.

LO2.   Apply relevant costing and decision-making concepts in a variety of business situations.
- Make-or-buy decision
- Special-order decision
- Keep-or-drop decision
- Further processing of joint products

LO3. **Choose the optimal product mix when faced with one constrained resource.**
- Single constraint leads to production of product with the greatest contribution margin per unit of scarce resource.
- Multiple constraints require linear programming.

LO4. **Explain the impact of cost on pricing decisions.**
- Markup costing applies markup to cost to determine price.
- Target costing works backward from desired price to find allowable cost.

LO5. **Discuss inventory management and just-in-time (JIT) models.**
- JIT models solve problems of uneven demand, production failures, and so on, without using inventory.
  - Long-term contracts
  - Supplier relationships
  - Reduce setup times to produce on demand
  - Creation of manufacturing cells
  - Maximizing quality and productivity

SUMMARY OF IMPORTANT EQUATIONS

1. $\text{Contribution margin per unit of the scarce resource} = \dfrac{\text{Selling price per unit} - \text{Variable cost per unit}}{\text{Required amount of scarce resource per unit}}$

2. Price using markup = Cost per unit + (Cost per unit × Markup percentage)

3. Target cost = Target price − Desired profit

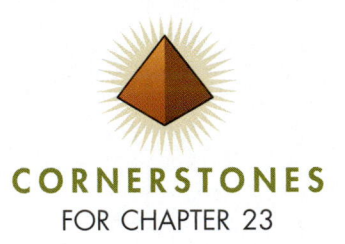

CORNERSTONES
FOR CHAPTER 23

CORNERSTONE 23-1   Structuring a make-or-buy problem (p. 1156)

CORNERSTONE 23-2   Structuring a special-order problem (p. 1159)

CORNERSTONE 23-3   Structuring a keep-or-drop product line problem (p. 1161)

CORNERSTONE 23-4   Structuring a keep-or-drop product line problem with complementary effects (p. 1162)

CORNERSTONE 23-5   Structuring the sell-or-process-further decision (p. 1165)

CORNERSTONE 23-6   Determining the optimal product mix with one constrained resource (p. 1166)

CORNERSTONE 23-7   Determining the optimal product mix with one constrained resource and a sales constraint (p. 1167)

CORNERSTONE 23-8   Calculating price by applying a markup percentage to cost (p. 1168)

CORNERSTONE 23-9   Calculating a target cost (p. 1170)

KEY TERMS

REVIEW PROBLEMS

I. Special-Order Decision

Pastin Company produces a light-weight travel raincoat with the following unit cost:

Direct materials	$4.00
Direct labor	1.00
Variable overhead	1.75
Fixed overhead	2.00
Unit cost	$8.75

While production capacity is 200,000 units per year, Pastin expects to produce only 170,000 raincoats for the coming year. The fixed selling costs total $85,000 per year, and variable selling costs are $0.50 per unit sold. The raincoats normally sell for $12 each.

At the beginning of the year, a customer from a geographic region outside the area normally served by the company offered to buy 20,000 raincoats for $8 each. The customer would pay all transportation costs, and there would be no variable selling costs.

Required:

Should the company accept the order? Provide both qualitative and quantitative justification for your decision. Assume that no other orders are expected beyond the regular business and the special order.

Solution:

The company expects idle capacity. Accepting the special order would bring production up to near capacity. The two options are to accept or reject the order. If the order is accepted, then the company could avoid laying off employees and would enhance and maintain its community image. However, the order is considerably below the normal selling price of $12. Because the price is so low, the company needs to assess the potential impact of the sale on its regular customers and on the profitability of the firm. Considering the fact that the customer is located in a region not usually served by the company, the likelihood of an adverse impact on regular business is not high. Thus, the qualitative factors seem to favor acceptance.

To assess profitability, the firm should identify the relevant costs and benefits of each alternative. This analysis is as follows:

	Accept	Reject
Revenues	$160,000	$—
Direct materials	(80,000)	—
Direct labor	(20,000)	—
Variable overhead	(35,000)	—
Total benefits	$ 25,000	$ 0

Accepting the order would increase profits by $25,000. (The fixed overhead and selling costs are all irrelevant because they are the same across both alternatives.) *Conclusion:* The order should be accepted because both qualitative and quantitative factors favor it.

II. Optimal Mix

Two types of gears are produced: A and B. Gear A has a unit contribution margin of $200, and Gear B has a unit contribution margin of $400. Gear A uses two hours of grinding time, and Gear B uses five hours of grinding time. There are 200 hours of grinding time available per week. This is the only constraint.

Required:

1. Is the grinding constraint an internal constraint or an external constraint?

2. Determine the optimal mix. What is the total contribution margin?

3. .Suppose that there is an additional demand constraint: Market conditions will allow the sale of only 80 units of each gear. Now, what is the optimal mix? The total contribution margin per week?

(Continued)

Solution:

1. It's an internal constraint.

2. Gear A: $200/2 hours = $100 per grinding hour
    Gear B: $400/5 hours = $80 per grinding hour
    Since Gear A earns more contribution margin per unit of scarce resource than Gear B, only Gear A should be produced and sold (this is based on the fact that we can sell all we want of each product).
    Optical mix: Gear A = 100 units* and Gear B = 0

    Total contribution margin = $200 × 100 units = $20,000 per week

    *200 hours/2 hours per unit = 100 units of A can be produced per week

3. Now, we should sell 80 units of Gear A using 160 hours (2 × 80) and 8 units of Gear B (40 hours/5 hours per unit).

    Total contribution margin = (80 × $200) + (8 × $400) = $19,200 per week

DISCUSSION QUESTIONS

1. What is the difference between tactical and strategic decisions?
2. What are some ways that a manager can identify a feasible set of decision alternatives?
3. Explain why depreciation on an existing asset is always irrelevant.
4. Give an example of a future cost that is not relevant.
5. What role do past costs play in relevant costing decisions?
6. Can direct materials ever be irrelevant in a make-or-buy decision? Explain.
7. Why would a firm ever offer a price on a product that is below its full cost?
8. Discuss the importance of complementary effects in a keep-or-drop decision.
9. Should joint costs be considered in a sell-or-process-further decision? Explain.
10. Suppose that a product can be sold at split-off for $5,000 or processed further at a cost of $1,000 and then sold for $6,400. Should the product be processed further?
11. Suppose that a firm produces two products. Should the firm always place the most emphasis on the product with the largest contribution margin per unit? Explain.
12. What are ordering costs? Carrying costs? Give examples of each.
13. What are the reasons for carrying inventory?

MULTIPLE-CHOICE EXERCISES

23-1 Which of the following is *not* a step in the short-run decision-making model?

a. Define the problem.
b. Identify alternatives.
c. Identify the costs and benefits of feasible alternatives.
d. Assess qualitative factors.
e. All of these are steps in the short-run decision-making model.

23-2 Costs that *cannot* be affected by any future action are called

a. differential costs.
b. sunk costs.
c. inventory costs.
d. relevant costs.
e. joint costs.

Use the following information for Multiple-Choice Exercises 23-3 through 23-5:
Sandy is considering moving from her apartment into a small house with a fenced yard. The apartment is noisy, and she has difficulty studying. In addition, the fenced yard would be great for her dog. The distance from school is about the same from the house and from the apartment. The apartment costs $750 per month, and she has two months remaining on her lease. The lease cannot be broken, so Sandy must pay the last two months of rent whether she lives there or not. The rent for the house is $450 per month, plus utilities, which should

> average $100 per month. The apartment is furnished; the house is not. If Sandy moves into the house, she will need to buy a bed, dresser, desk, and chair immediately. She thinks that she can pick up some used furniture for a good price.

23-3 Refer to the information for Sandy on the previous page and above. Which of the following costs is *irrelevant* to Sandy's decision to stay in the apartment or move to the house?

a. House rent of $450 per month
b. Utilities for the house of $100 per month
c. The noise in the apartment house
d. The cost of the used furniture
e. The last two months of rent in the apartment

23-4 Refer to the information for Sandy on the previous page and above. Which of the following is a qualitative factor?

a. House rent of $450 per month
b. Utilities for the house of $100 per month
c. The noise in the apartment house
d. The cost of the used furniture
e. The last two months of rent in the apartment

23-5 Refer to the information for Sandy on the previous page and above. Suppose that the apartment building was within walking distance to campus and the house was five miles away. Sandy does not own a car. How would that affect her decision?

a. It would make the house more desirable.
b. It would make the apartment more desirable.
c. It would make both choices less desirable.
d. It would make both choices more desirable.
e. It would have no effect on the decision; buying or not buying a car is a separate decision.

23-6 Which of the following is a true statement?

a. Fixed costs are always irrelevant.
b. Variable costs are always relevant.
c. Usually, variable costs are irrelevant.
d. Step costs may be relevant if an alternative requires moving outside the existing relevant range.
e. All of the above.

23-7 In a make-or-buy decision, the company

a. must choose between expanding or dropping a product line.
b. must choose between accepting or rejecting a special order.
c. would consider the purchase price of the externally provided good to be relevant.
d. would consider all fixed overhead to be irrelevant.
e. none of the above.

23-8 Carroll Company, a manufacturer of vitamins and minerals, has been asked by a large drugstore chain to provide bottles of vitamin E. The bottles would be labeled with the name of the drugstore chain, and the chain would pay Carroll $2.30 per bottle rather than the $3.00 regular price. Which type of a decision is this?

a. Make-or-buy
b. Special-order
c. Keep-or-drop
d. Economic order quantity
e. Markup pricing

23-9 Jennings Hardware Store marks up its merchandise by 80 percent. If a part costs $1.50, which of the following is true?

a. The price is $1.20.
b. The markup is $2.70.
c. The price is $2.70.
d. The markup is pure profit.
e. All of these.

23-10 When a company faces a production constraint or scarce resource (e.g., only a certain number of machine hours is available), it is important to

a. produce the product with the highest contribution margin in total.
b. produce the product with the lowest full manufacturing cost.
c. produce the product with the highest contribution margin per unit of scarce resource.
d. produce the product with the highest contribution margin per unit.
e. The constraint is not relevant to the production problem.

23-11 In the keep-or-drop decision, the company will find which of the following income statement formats most useful?

a. A segmented income statement in the contribution margin format
b. A segmented income statement in the full costing format that is used for financial reporting
c. An overall income statement in the contribution margin format
d. An overall income statement in the full costing format that is used for financial reporting
e. Income statements are of no use in making this type of decision.

23-12 In the sell-or-process-further decision,

a. joint costs are always relevant.
b. total costs of joint processing and further processing are relevant.
c. all costs incurred prior to the split-off point are relevant.
d. the most profitable outcome can be to further process some separately identifiable products beyond the split-off point, but sell others at the split-off point.
e. none of the above.

23-13 Which of the following is a reason for carrying inventory?

a. To balance setup and carrying costs
b. To satisfy customer demand
c. To avoid shutting down manufacturing facilities

d. To take advantage of discounts
e. All of these

CORNERSTONE EXERCISES

OBJECTIVE ❷
CORNERSTONE 23-1

Cornerstone Exercise 23-14 Structuring a Make-or-Buy Problem

Fresh Foods, a large restaurant chain, needed to determine if it would be cheaper to produce 5,000 units of its main food ingredient for use in its restaurants or to purchase them from an outside supplier for $12 each. Cost information on internal production includes the following:

	Total Cost	Unit Cost
Direct materials	$25,000	$ 5.00
Direct labor	15,000	3.00
Variable manufacturing overhead	7,500	1.50
Variable marketing overhead	10,000	2.00
Fixed plant overhead	30,000	6.00
Total	$87,500	$17.50

Fixed overhead will continue whether the ingredient is produced internally or externally. No additional costs of purchasing will be incurred beyond the purchase price.

Required:
1. What are the alternatives for Fresh Foods?
2. List the relevant cost(s) of internal production and of external purchase.
3. Which alternative is more cost effective and by how much?
4. Now assume that 20 percent of the fixed overhead can be avoided if the ingredient is purchased externally. Which alternative is more cost effective and by how much?

OBJECTIVE ❷
CORNERSTONE 23-2

Cornerstone Exercise 23-15 Structuring a Special-Order Problem

Harrison Ford Company has been approached by a new customer with an offer to purchase 10,000 units of its model IJ4 at a price of $4 each. The new customer is geographically separated from the company's other customers, and existing sales would not be affected. Harrison normally produces 75,000 units of IJ4 per year but only plans to produce and sell 60,000 in the coming year. The normal sales price is $12 per unit. Unit cost information for the normal level of activity is as follows:

Direct materials	$1.50
Direct labor	2.00
Variable overhead	1.00
Fixed overhead	3.25
Total	$7.75

Fixed overhead will not be affected by whether or not the special order is accepted.

Required:
1. What are the relevant costs and benefits of the two alternatives (accept or reject the special order)?
2. By how much will operating income increase or decrease if the order is accepted?

Use the following information for Cornerstone Exercises 23-16 and 23-17:
Shown below is a segmented income statement for Hickory Company's three wooden flooring product lines:

	Strip	Plank	Parquet	Total
Sales revenue	$ 400,000	$ 200,000	$ 300,000	$ 900,000
Less: Variable expenses	(225,000)	(120,000)	(250,000)	(595,000)
Contribution margin	$ 175,000	$ 80,000	$ 50,000	$ 305,000
Less: Direct fixed expenses:				
Machine rent	(5,000)	(20,000)	(30,000)	(55,000)
Supervision	(15,000)	(10,000)	(5,000)	(30,000)
Depreciation	(35,000)	(10,000)	(25,000)	(70,000)
Segment margin	$ 120,000	$ 40,000	$ (10,000)	$ 150,000

Cornerstone Exercise 23-16 Structuring a Keep-or-Drop Product Line Problem

OBJECTIVE **2**
CORNERSTONE 23-3

Refer to the information for Hickory Company above. Hickory's management is deciding whether to keep or drop the Parquet product line. Hickory's parquet flooring product line has a contribution margin of $50,000 (sales of $300,000 less total variable costs of $250,000). All variable costs are relevant. Relevant fixed costs associated with this line include $30,000 in machine rent and $5,000 in supervision salaries.

Required:
1. List the alternatives being considered with respect to the parquet flooring line.
2. List the relevant benefits and costs for each alternative.
3. Which alternative is more cost effective and by how much?

Cornerstone Exercise 23-17 Structuring a Keep-or-Drop Product Line Problem with Complementary Effects

OBJECTIVE **2**
CORNERSTONE 23-4

Refer to the information for Hickory Company above. Assume that dropping the parquet product line would reduce sales of the strip line by 25 percent and sales of the plank line by 20 percent. All other information remains the same.

Required:
1. If the parquet product line is dropped, what is the contribution margin for the strip line? For the plank line?
2. Which alternative (keep or drop the parquet product line) is now more cost effective and by how much?

Cornerstone Exercise 23-18 Structuring the Sell-or-Process-Further Decision

OBJECTIVE **2**
CORNERSTONE 23-5

Jack's Lumber Yard receives 8,000 large trees each period that it subsequently processes into rough logs by stripping off the tree bark and leaves (i.e., one tree equals one log). Jack's then

(Continued)

must decide whether to sell its rough logs (for use in log cabin construction) at split-off or to process them further into refined lumber (for use in regular construction framing). Jack's normally sells logs for a per-unit price of $500. Alternately, each log can be processed further into 800 feet of lumber at an additional cost of $0.15 per board foot. Also, lumber can be sold for $0.75 per board foot.

Required:

1. What is the contribution to income from selling the logs for log cabin construction?
2. What is the contribution to income from processing the logs into lumber?
3. Should Jack's continue to sell the logs or process them further into lumber?

Use the following information for Cornerstone Exercises 23-19 and 23-20:

Comfy Fit Company manufactures two types of university sweatshirts, the Swoop and the Rufus, with unit contribution margins of $5 and $15, respectively. Regardless of type, each sweatshirt must be fed through a stitching machine to affix the appropriate university logo. The firm leases seven machines that each provides 1,000 hours of machine time per year. Each Swoop sweatshirt requires 6 minutes of machine time, and each Rufus sweatshirt requires 20 minutes of machine time.

OBJECTIVE ③
CORNERSTONE 23-6

Cornerstone Exercise 23-19 Determining the Optimal Product Mix with One Constrained Resource

Refer to the information for Comfy Fit Company above. Assume that there are no other constraints.

Required:

1. What is the contribution margin per hour of machine time for each type of sweatshirt?
2. What is the optimal mix of sweatshirts?
3. What is the total contribution margin earned for the optimal mix?

OBJECTIVE ③
CORNERSTONE 23-7

Cornerstone Exercise 23-20 Determining the Optimal Product Mix with One Constrained Resource and a Sales Constraint

Refer to the information for Comfy Fit Company above. Assume that a maximum of 40,000 units of each sweatshirt can be sold.

Required:

1. What is the contribution margin per hour of machine time for each type of sweat shirt?
2. What is the optimal mix of sweatshirts?
3. What is the total contribution margin earned for the optimal mix?

OBJECTIVE ④
CORNERSTONE 23-8

Cornerstone Exercise 23-21 Calculating Price by Applying a Markup Percentage to Cost

Integrity Accounting Firm provides various financial services to organizations. Integrity has decided to price its jobs at the total variable costs of the job plus 10 percent. The job for a medium-sized dance club client included the following costs:

Direct materials	$ 5,000
Direct labor (partners and staff accountants)	90,000
Depreciation (using straight-line method) on Integrity's office building	50,000

Required:

Calculate the price charged by Integrity Accounting to the dance club.

OBJECTIVE ④
CORNERSTONE 23-9

Cornerstone Exercise 23-22 Calculating a Target Cost

Yuhu manufactures cell phones and is developing a new model with a feature (aptly named Don't Drink and Dial) that prevents the phone from dialing an owner-defined list of phone numbers between the hours of midnight and 6:00 A.M. The new phone model has a target price of $350. Management requires a 20 percent profit on new product revenues.

Required:
1. Calculate the amount of desired profit.
2. Calculate the target cost.

EXERCISES

Exercise 23-23 Model for Making Tactical Decisions

OBJECTIVE

The model for making tactical decisions described in the text has six steps. These steps are listed, out of order, below.

Required:
Put the steps in the correct order, starting with the step that should be taken first.
1. Select the alternative with the greatest overall benefit.
2. Identify the costs and benefits associated with each feasible alternative.
3. Assess qualitative factors.
4. Recognize and define the problem.
5. Identify alternatives as possible solutions to the problem.
6. Total the relevant costs and benefits for each alternative.

Exercise 23-24 Model for Making Tactical Decisions

OBJECTIVE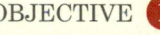

Austin Porter is a sophomore at a small Midwestern university (SMWU). He is considering whether to continue at this university or to transfer to one with a nationally recognized engineering program. Austin's decision-making process included the following:

a. He surfed the web to check out the sites of a number of colleges and universities with engineering programs.
b. Austin wrote to five of the universities to obtain information on their engineering colleges, tuition and room and board costs, the likelihood of being accepted, and so on.
c. Austin compared costs of the five other schools with the cost of his present school. He totaled the balance in his checking and savings accounts, estimated the earnings from his work-study job, and asked his parents whether or not they would be able to help him out.
d. Austin's high-school sweetheart had a long heart-to-heart talk with him about their future—specifically, that there might be no future if he left town.
e. Austin thought that while he enjoyed his present college, its engineering program did not have the national reputation that would enable him to get a good job on either the East or West Coast. Working for a large company on the coast was an important dream of his.
f. Austin's major advisor agreed that a school with a national reputation would make job hunting easier. However, he reminded Austin that small college graduates had occasionally gotten the kind of jobs that Austin wanted.
g. Austin had a number of good friends at SMWU, and they were encouraging him to stay.
h. A friend of Austin's from high school returned home for a long weekend. She attends a prestigious university and told Austin of the fun and opportunities available at her school. She encouraged Austin to check out the possibilities elsewhere.
i. A friendly professor outside of Austin's major area ran into him at the student union. She listened to his thinking and reminded him that a degree from SMWU would easily get him into a good graduate program. Perhaps he should consider postponing the job hunt until he had his master's degree in hand.
j. Two of the three prestigious universities accepted Austin and offered financial aid. The third one rejected his application.
k. Austin made his decision.

Required:
Classify the events a through k under one of the six steps of the model for making tactical decisions described in your text.

> *Use the following information for Exercises 23-25 and 23-26:*
> Zion Manufacturing had always made its components in-house. However, Bryce Component Works had recently offered to supply one component, K2, at a price of $25 each. Zion uses 10,000 units of Component K2 each year. The cost per unit of this component is as follows:
>
> | | |
> |---|---:|
> | Direct materials | $12.00 |
> | Direct labor | 8.25 |
> | Variable overhead | 4.50 |
> | Fixed overhead | 2.00 |
> | Total | $26.75 |

OBJECTIVE

Exercise 23-25 Make-or-Buy Decision

Refer to the information for Zion Manufacturing above. The fixed overhead is an allocated expense; none of it would be eliminated if production of Component K2 stopped.

Required:

1. What are the alternatives facing Zion Manufacturing with respect to production of Component K2?
2. List the relevant costs for each alternative.
3. **Conceptual Connection:** If Zion decides to purchase the component from Bryce, by how much will operating income increase or decrease? Which alternative is better?

OBJECTIVE

Exercise 23-26 Make-or-Buy Decision

Refer to the information for Zion Manufacturing above. Assume that 75 percent of Zion Manufacturing's fixed overhead for Component K2 would be eliminated if that component were no longer produced.

Required:

1. **Conceptual Connection:** If Zion decides to purchase the component from Bryce, by how much will operating income increase or decrease? Which alternative is better?
2. **Conceptual Connection:** Briefly explain how increasing or decreasing the 75 percent figure affects Zion's final decision to make or purchase the component.
3. **Conceptual Connection:** By how much would the 75 percent figure have to decrease before Zion would be indifferent (i.e., incur the same cost) between "making" versus "purchasing" the component? Show and briefly explain your calculations.

> *Use the following information for Exercises 23-27 and 23-28:*
> Smooth Move Company manufactures professional paperweights and has been approached by a new customer with an offer to purchase 15,000 units at a per-unit price of $7.00. The new customer is geographically separated from Smooth Move's other customers, and existing sales will not be affected. Smooth Move normally produces 82,000 units but plans to produce and sell only 65,000 in the coming year. The normal sales price is $12 per unit. Unit cost information is as follows:
>
> | | |
> |---|---:|
> | Direct materials | $3.00 |
> | Direct labor | 2.25 |
> | Variable overhead | 1.15 |
> | Fixed overhead | 1.80 |
> | Total | $8.20 |

OBJECTIVE

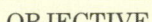

Exercise 23-27 Special-Order Decision

Refer to the information for Smooth Move Company above. If Smooth Move accepts the order, no fixed manufacturing activities will be affected because there is sufficient excess capacity.

Required:
1. What are the alternatives for Smooth Move?
2. **Conceptual Connection:** Should Smooth Move accept the special order? By how much will profit increase or decrease if the order is accepted?

Exercise 23-28 Special Order

OBJECTIVE 2

Refer to the information for Smooth Move Company on the previous page. Suppose a customer wants to have its company logo affixed to each paperweight using a label. Smooth Move would have to purchase a special logo labeling machine that will cost $14,000. The machine will be able to label the 15,000 units and then it will be scrapped (with no further value). No other fixed overhead activities will be incurred.

Required:
Conceptual Connection: Should Smooth Move accept the special order? By how much will profit increase or decrease if the order is accepted?

Use the following information for Exercises 23-29 through 23-31:
Petoskey Company produces three products: Alanson, Boyne, and Conway. A segmented income statement, with amounts given in thousands, follows:

	Alanson	Boyne	Conway	Total
Sales revenue	$ 1,280	$185	$ 300	$ 1,765
Less: Variable expenses	(1,115)	(45)	(225)	(1,385)
Contribution margin	$ 165	$140	$ 75	$ 380
Less: Direct fixed expenses:				
Depreciation	(50)	(15)	(10)	(75)
Salaries	(95)	(85)	(80)	(260)
Segment margin	$ 20	$ 40	$ (15)	$ 45

Direct fixed expenses consist of depreciation and plant supervisory salaries. All depreciation on the equipment is dedicated to the product lines. None of the equipment can be sold.

Exercise 23-29 Keep-or-Drop Decision

OBJECTIVE 2

Refer to the information for Petoskey Company above. Assume that each of the three products has a different supervisor whose position would *remain* if the associated product were dropped.

Required:
Conceptual Connection: Estimate the impact on profit that would result from dropping Conway. Explain why Petoskey should keep or drop Conway.

Exercise 23-30 Keep-or-Drop Decision

OBJECTIVE 2

Refer to the information for Petoskey Company above. Assume that, each of the three products has a different supervisor whose position would *be eliminated* if the associated product were dropped.

Required:
Conceptual Connection: Estimate the impact on profit that would result from dropping Conway. Explain why Petoskey should keep or drop Conway.

Exercise 23-31 Keep-or-Drop Decision

OBJECTIVE 2

Refer to the information for Petoskey Company from **Exercise 23-30**. Assume that 20 percent of the Alanson customers choose to buy from Petoskey because it offers a full range of products, including Conway. If Conway were no longer available from Petoskey, these customers would go elsewhere to purchase Alanson.

Required:
Conceptual Connection: Estimate the impact on profit that would result from dropping Conway. Explain why Petoskey should keep or drop Conway.

OBJECTIVE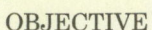

Exercise 23-32 Keep or Buy, Sunk Costs

Heather Alburty purchased a previously owned, two-year-old Grand Am for $8,900. Since purchasing the car, she has spent the following amounts on parts and labor:

New stereo system	$1,200
Trick paint	400
New wide racing tires	800
Total	$2,400

Unfortunately, the new stereo doesn't completely drown out the sounds of a grinding transmission. Apparently, the Grand Am needs a considerable amount of work to make it reliable transportation. Heather estimates that the needed repairs include the following:

Transmission overhaul	$2,000
Water pump	400
Master cylinder work	1,100
Total	$3,500

In a visit to a used car dealer, Heather has found a one-year-old Neon in mint condition for $9,400. Heather has advertised and found that she can sell the Grand Am for only $6,400. If she buys the Neon, she will pay cash, but she would need to sell the Grand Am.

Required:

1. **Conceptual Connection:** In trying to decide whether to restore the Grand Am or to buy the Neon, Heather is distressed because she already has spent $11,300 on the Grand Am. The investment seems too much to give up. How would you react to her concern?
2. **Conceptual Connection:** Assuming that Heather would be equally happy with the Grand Am or the Neon, should she buy the Neon, or should she restore the Grand Am?

Use the following information for Exercises 23-33 and 13-34:
Blasingham Company is currently manufacturing Part Q108, producing 35,000 units annually. The part is used in the production of several products made by Blasingham. The cost per unit for Q108 is as follows:

Direct materials	$ 6.00
Direct labor	2.00
Variable overhead	1.50
Fixed overhead	3.50
Total	$13.00

OBJECTIVE

Exercise 23-33 Make or Buy

Refer to the information for Blasingham Company above. Of the total fixed overhead assigned to Q108, $77,000 is direct fixed overhead (the lease of production machinery and salary of a production line supervisor—neither of which will be needed if the line is dropped). The remaining fixed overhead is common fixed overhead. An outside supplier has offered to sell the part to Blasingham for $11. There is no alternative use for the facilities currently used to produce the part.

Required:

1. **Conceptual Connection:** Should Blasingham make or buy Part Q108?
2. What is the most that Blasingham would be willing to pay an outside supplier?
3. If Blasingham buys the part, by how much will income increase or decrease?

OBJECTIVE

Exercise 23-34 Make or Buy

Refer to the information for Blasingham Company above. All of the fixed overhead is common fixed overhead. An outside supplier has offered to sell the part to Blasingham for $11. There is no alternative use for the facilities currently used to produce the part.

Required:

1. **Conceptual Connection:** Should Blasingham make or buy Part Q108?
2. What is the most Blasingham would be willing to pay an outside supplier?
3. If Blasingham buys the part, by how much will income increase or decrease?

Exercise 23-35 Sell at Split-Off or Process Further

OBJECTIVE ❷

Bozo Inc. manufactures two products from a joint production process. The joint process costs $110,000 and yields 6,000 pounds of LTE compound and 20,000 pounds of HS compound. LTE can be sold at split-off for $55 per pound. HS can be sold at split-off for $8 per pound. A buyer of HS asked Bozo to process HS further into CS compound. If HS were processed further, it would cost $34,000 to turn 20,000 pounds of HS into 4,000 pounds of CS. The CS would sell for $45 per pound.

Required:

1. What is the contribution to income from selling the 20,000 pounds of HS at split-off?
2. **Conceptual Connection:** What is the contribution to income from processing the 20,000 pounds of HS into 4,000 pounds of CS? Should Bozo continue to sell the HS at split-off or process it further into CS?

> *Use the following information for Exercises 23-36 and 23-37:*
> Billings Company produces two products, Product Reno and Product Tahoe. Each product goes through its own assembly and finishing departments. However, both of them must go through the painting department. The painting department has capacity of 2,460 hours per year. Product Reno has a unit contribution margin of $120 and requires five hours of painting department time. Product Tahoe has a unit contribution margin of $75 and requires three hours of painting department time. There are no other constraints.

Exercise 23-36 Choosing the Optimal Product Mix with One Constrained Resource

OBJECTIVE ❸

Refer to the information for Billings Company above.

Required:

1. What is the contribution margin per hour of painting department time for each product?
2. What is the optimal mix of products?
3. What is the total contribution margin earned for the optimal mix?

Exercise 23-37 Choosing the Optimal Product Mix with a Constrained Resource and a Demand Constraint

OBJECTIVE ❸

Refer to the information for Billings Company above. Assume that only 500 units of each product can be sold.

Required:

1. What is the optimal mix of products?
2. What is the total contribution margin earned for the optimal mix?

Exercise 23-38 Calculating Price Using a Markup Percentage of Cost

OBJECTIVE ❹

Grinnell Lake Gift Shop has decided to price the candles that it sells at cost plus 80 percent. One type of carved bear-shaped candle costs $12, and huckleberry-scented votive candles cost $1.10 each.

Required:

1. What price will Grinnell Lake Gift Shop charge for the carved bear candle?
2. What price will Grinnell Lake Gift Shop charge for each scented votive candle?
3. **Conceptual Connection:** Briefly explain two specific challenges that the financial manager of Grinnell Lake Gift Shop might encounter in employing this cost-plus pricing approach.

Exercise 23-39 Target Costing

OBJECTIVE ❹

H. Banks Company would like to design, produce, and sell versatile toasters for the home kitchen market. The toaster will have four slots that adjust in thickness to accommodate both slim slices of bread and oversized bagels. The target price is $75. Banks requires that new products be priced such that 20 percent of the price is profit.

(Continued)

Required:
1. Calculate the amount of desired profit per unit of the new toaster.
2. Calculate the target cost per unit of the new toaster.

Exercise 23-40 Ordering Cost, Carrying Cost, and Total Inventory-Related Cost

Aravan Company purchases 4,000 units of Product Beta each year in lots of 400 units per order. The cost of placing one order is $20, and the cost of carrying one unit of product in inventory for a year is $4.

Required:
1. How many orders for Product Beta does Aravan place per year?
2. What is the total ordering cost of Beta per year?
3. What is the total carrying cost of Beta per year?
4. What is the total cost of Aravan's inventory policy for Beta per year?

PROBLEMS

Problem 23-41 Special-Order Decision

Rianne Company produces a light fixture with the following unit cost:

Direct materials	$2
Direct labor	1
Variable overhead	3
Fixed overhead	2
Unit cost	$8

The production capacity is 300,000 units per year. Because of a depressed housing market, the company expects to produce only 180,000 fixtures for the coming year. The company also has fixed selling costs totaling $500,000 per year and variable selling costs of $1 per unit sold. The fixtures normally sell for $12 each.

At the beginning of the year, a customer from a geographic region outside the area normally served by the company offered to buy 100,000 fixtures for $7 each. The customer also offered to pay all transportation costs. Since there would be no sales commissions involved, this order would not have any variable selling costs.

Required:
1. **Conceptual Connection:** Based on a quantitative (numerical) analysis, should the company accept the order?
2. **Conceptual Connection:** What qualitative factors might impact the decision? Assume that no other orders are expected beyond the regular business and the special order.

Problem 23-42 Make or Buy, Qualitative Considerations

Hetrick Dentistry Services operates in a large metropolitan area. Currently, Hetrick has its own dental laboratory to produce porcelain and gold crowns. The unit costs to produce the crowns are as follows:

	Porcelain	Gold
Raw materials	$ 70	$130
Direct labor	27	27
Variable overhead	8	8
Fixed overhead	22	22
Total	$127	$187

Fixed overhead is detailed as follows:

Salary (supervisor)	$26,000
Depreciation	5,000
Rent (lab facility)	32,000

Overhead is applied on the basis of direct labor hours. These rates were computed by using 5,500 direct labor hours.

A local dental laboratory has offered to supply Hetrick all the crowns it needs. Its price is $125 for porcelain crowns and $150 for gold crowns; however, the offer is conditional on supplying both types of crowns—it will not supply just one type for the price indicated. If the offer is accepted, the equipment used by Hetrick's laboratory would be scrapped (it is old and has no market value), and the lab facility would be closed. Hetrick uses 2,000 porcelain crowns and 600 gold crowns per year.

Required:

1. **Conceptual Connection:** Should Hetrick continue to make its own crowns, or should they be purchased from the external supplier? What is the dollar effect of purchasing?
2. **Conceptual Connection:** What qualitative factors should Hetrick consider in making this decision?
3. **Conceptual Connection:** Suppose that the lab facility is owned rather than rented and that the $32,000 is depreciation rather than rent. What effect does this have on the analysis in Requirement 1?
4. **Conceptual Connection:** Refer to the original data. Assume that the volume of crowns used is 3,400 porcelain and 600 gold. Should Hetrick make or buy the crowns? Explain the outcome.

Problem 23-43 Sell or Process Further

OBJECTIVE 2

Zanda Drug Corporation buys three chemicals that are processed to produce two types of analgesics used as ingredients for popular over-the-counter drugs. The purchased chemicals are blended for two to three hours and then heated for 15 minutes. The results of the process are two separate analgesics, depryl and pencol, which are sent to a drying room until their moisture content is reduced to 6 to 8 percent. For every 1,300 pounds of chemicals used, 600 pounds of depryl and 600 pounds of pencol are produced. After drying, depryl and pencol are sold to companies that process them into their final form. The selling prices are $12 per pound for depryl and $30 per pound for pencol. The costs to produce 600 pounds of each analgesic are as follows:

Chemicals	$8,500
Direct labor	6,735
Overhead	9,900

The analgesics are packaged in 20-pound bags and shipped. The cost of each bag is $1.30. Shipping costs $0.10 per pound.

Zanda could process depryl further by grinding it into a fine powder and then molding the powder into tablets. The tablets can be sold directly to retail drug stores as a generic brand. If this route were taken, the revenue received per bottle of tablets would be $4.00, with 10 bottles produced by every pound of depryl. The costs of grinding and tableting total $2.50 per pound of depryl. Bottles cost $0.40 each. Bottles are shipped in boxes that hold 25 bottles at a shipping cost of $1.60 per box.

Required:

1. **Conceptual Connection:** Should Zanda sell depryl at split-off, or should depryl be processed and sold as tablets?
2. If Zanda normally sells 265,000 pounds of depryl per year, what will be the difference in profits if depryl is processed further?

Problem 23-44 Keep or Drop

OBJECTIVE

AudioMart is a retailer of radios, stereos, and televisions. The store carries two portable sound systems that have radios, tape players, and speakers. System A, of slightly higher quality than System B, costs $20 more. With rare exceptions, the store also sells a headset when a system is sold. The headset can be used with either system. Variable-costing income statements for the three products follow:

(Continued)

	System A	System B	Headset
Sales	$ 45,000	$ 32,500	$ 8,000
Less: Variable expenses	(20,000)	(25,500)	(3,200)
Contribution margin	$ 25,000	$ 7,000	$ 4,800
Less: Fixed costs*	(10,000)	(18,000)	(2,700)
Operating income	$ 15,000	$(11,000)	$ 2,100

*This includes common fixed costs totaling $18,000, allocated to each product in proportion to its revenues.

The owner of the store is concerned about the profit performance of System B and is considering dropping it. If the product is dropped, sales of System A will increase by 30 percent, and sales of headsets will drop by 25 percent. (*Note:* Round all answers to the nearest whole number.)

Required:
1. Prepare segmented income statements for the three products using a better format.
2. **Conceptual Connection:** Prepare segmented income statements for System A and the headsets assuming that System B is dropped. Should B be dropped?
3. **Conceptual Connection:** Suppose that a third system, System C, with a similar quality to System B, could be acquired. Assume that with C the sales of A would remain unchanged. However, C would produce only 80 percent of the revenues of B, and sales of the headsets would drop by 10 percent. The contribution margin ratio of C is 50 percent, and its direct fixed costs would be identical to those of B. Should System B be dropped and replaced with System C?

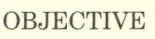
OBJECTIVE ❶ ❷

Problem 23-45 Accept or Reject a Special Order

Steve Murningham, manager of an electronics division, was considering an offer by Pat Sellers, manager of a sister division. Pat's division was operating below capacity and had just been given an opportunity to produce 8,000 units of one of its products for a customer in a market not normally served. The opportunity involves a product that uses an electrical component produced by Steve's division. Each unit that Pat's division produces requires two of the components. However, the price that the customer is willing to pay is well below the price that is usually charged. To make a reasonable profit on the order, Pat needs a price concession from Steve's division. Pat had offered to pay full manufacturing cost for the parts. So Steve would know that everything was above board, Pat supplied the following unit cost and price information concerning the special order, excluding the cost of the electrical component:

Selling price	$ 32
Less costs:	
Direct materials	(17)
Direct labor	(7)
Variable overhead	(2)
Fixed overhead	(3)
Operating profit	$ 3

The normal selling price of the electrical component is $2.30 per unit. Its full manufacturing cost is $1.85 ($1.05 variable and $0.80 fixed). Pat argued that paying $2.30 per component would wipe out the operating profit and result in her division showing a loss. Steve was interested in the offer because his division was also operating below capacity (the order would not use all the excess capacity).

Required:
1. **Conceptual Connection:** Should Steve accept the order at a selling price of $1.85 per unit? By how much will his division's profits be changed if the order is accepted? By how much will the profits of Pat's division change if Steve agrees to supply the part at full cost?
2. **Conceptual Connection:** Suppose that Steve offers to supply the component at $2. In offering this price, Steve says that it is a firm offer, not subject to negotiation. Should Pat accept this price and produce the special order? If Pat accepts the price, what is the change in profits for Steve's division?
3. **Conceptual Connection:** Assume that Steve's division is operating at full capacity and that Steve refuses to supply the part for less than the full price. Should Pat still accept the special order? Explain.

Problem 23-46 Cost-Based Pricing Decision

OBJECTIVE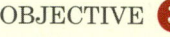

Jeremy Costa, owner of Costa Cabinets Inc., is preparing a bid on a job that requires $1,800 of direct materials, $1,600 of direct labor, and $800 of overhead. Jeremy normally applies a standard markup based on cost of goods sold to arrive at an initial bid price. He then adjusts the price as necessary in light of other factors (e.g., competitive pressure). Last year's income statement is as follows:

Sales	$130,000
Cost of goods sold	(48,100)
Gross margin	$ 81,900
Selling and administrative expenses	(46,300)
Operating income	$ 35,600

Required:

1. Calculate the markup that Jeremy will use.
2. What is Jeremy's initial bid price?

Problem 23-47 Product Mix Decision, Single Constraint

OBJECTIVE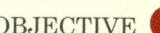

Sealing Company manufactures three types of DVD storage units. Each of the three types requires the use of a special machine that has a total operating capacity of 15,000 hours per year. Information on the three types of storage units is as follows:

	Basic	Standard	Deluxe
Selling price	$9.00	$30.00	$35.00
Variable cost	$6.00	$20.00	$10.00
Machine hours required	0.10	0.50	0.75

Sealing's marketing director has assessed demand for the three types of storage units and believes that the firm can sell as many units as it can produce.

Required:

1. How many of each type of unit should be produced and sold to maximize the company's contribution margin? What is the total contribution margin for your selection?
2. **Conceptual Connection:** Now suppose that Sealing Company believes that it can sell no more than 12,000 of the deluxe model but up to 50,000 each of the basic and standard models at the selling prices estimated. What product mix would you recommend, and what would be the total contribution margin?

Problem 23-48 Special-Order Decision, Qualitative Aspects

OBJECTIVE

Randy Stone, manager of Specialty Paper Products Company, was agonizing over an offer for an order requesting 5,000 boxes of calendars. Specialty Paper Products was operating at 70 percent of its capacity and could use the extra business. Unfortunately, the order's offering price of $4.20 per box was below the cost to produce the calendars. The controller, Louis Barns, was opposed to taking a loss on the deal. However, the personnel manager, Yatika Blaine, argued in favor of accepting the order even though a loss would be incurred. It would avoid the problem of layoffs and would help to maintain the company's community image. The full cost to produce a box of calendars follows:

Direct materials	$1.15
Direct labor	2.00
Variable overhead	1.10
Fixed overhead	1.00
Total	$5.25

Later that day, Louis and Yatika met over coffee. Louis sympathized with Yatika's concerns and suggested that the two of them rethink the special-order decision. He offered to determine relevant costs if Yatika would list the activities that would be affected by a layoff. Yatika eagerly agreed and came up with the following activities: an increase in the state unemployment insurance rate from 1 percent to 2 percent of total payroll, notification costs to lay off approximately 20 employees, and increased costs of rehiring and retraining workers when the downturn was over. Louis determined that these activities would cost the following amounts:

(Continued)

- Total payroll is $1,460,000 per year.
- Layoff paperwork is $25 per laid-off employee.
- Rehiring and retraining is $150 per new employee.

Required:

1. **Conceptual Connection:** Assume that the company will accept the order only if it increases total profits. Should the company accept or reject the order? Provide supporting computations.
2. **Conceptual Connection:** Consider the new information on activity costs associated with the layoff. Should the company accept or reject the order? Provide supporting computations.

OBJECTIVE ❶ ❷

Problem 23-49 Sell or Process Further, Basic Analysis

Shenista Inc. produces four products (Alpha, Beta, Gamma, and Delta) from a common input. The joint costs for a typical quarter follow:

Direct materials	$95,000
Direct labor	43,000
Overhead	85,000

The revenues from each product are as follows: Alpha, $100,000; Beta, $93,000; Gamma, $30,000; and Delta, $40,000.

Management is considering processing Delta beyond the split-off point, which would increase the sales value of Delta to $75,000. However, to process Delta further means that the company must rent some special equipment that costs $15,400 per quarter. Additional materials and labor also needed will cost $8,500 per quarter.

Required:

1. What is the operating profit earned by the four products for one quarter?
2. **Conceptual Connection:** Should the division process Delta further or sell it at split-off? What is the effect of the decision on quarterly operating profit?

OBJECTIVE ❸

Problem 23-50 Product Mix Decision, Single Constraint

Norton Company produces two products (Juno and Hera) that use the same material input. Juno uses two pounds of the material for every unit produced, and Hera uses five pounds. Currently, Norton has 16,000 pounds of the material in inventory. All of the material is imported. For the coming year, Norton plans to import an additional 8,000 pounds to produce 2,000 units of Juno and 4,000 units of Hera. The unit contribution margin is $30 for Juno and $60 for Hera. Also, assume that Norton's marketing department estimates that the company can sell a maximum of 2,000 units of Juno and 4,000 of Hera.

Norton has received word that the source of the material has been shut down by embargo. Consequently, the company will not be able to import the 8,000 pounds it planned to use in the coming year's production. There is no other source of the material.

Required:

1. Compute the total contribution margin that the company would earn if it could manufacture 2,000 units of Juno and 4,000 units of Hera.
2. Determine the optimal usage of the company's inventory of 16,000 pounds of the material. Compute the total contribution margin for the product mix that you recommend.

OBJECTIVE ❷

Problem 23-51 Sell at Split-Off or Process Further

Eunice Company produces two products from a joint process. Joint costs are $70,000 for one batch, which yields 1,000 liters of Germain and 4,000 liters of Hastain. Germain can be sold at the split-off point for $24 or be processed further, into Geraiten, at a manufacturing cost of $4,100 (for the 1,000 liters) and sold for $33 per liter.

If Geraiten is sold, additional distribution costs of $0.80 per liter and sales commissions of 10 percent of sales will be incurred. In addition, Eunice's legal department is concerned about potential liability issues with Geraiten—issues that do not arise with Germain.

Required:

1. **Conceptual Connection:** Considering only gross profit, should Germain be sold at the split-off point or processed further?
2. **Conceptual Connection:** Taking a value-chain approach (by considering distribution, marketing, and after-the-sale costs), determine whether or not Germain should be processed into Geraiten.

Problem 23-52 Differential Costing

As pointed out earlier in "Here's the Real Kicker," Kicker changed banks a couple of years ago because the loan officer at its bank moved out of state. Kicker saw that as an opportunity to take bids for its banking business and to fine-tune the banking services it was using. This problem uses that situation as the underlying scenario but uses three banks: FirstBank, Community Bank, and RegionalOne Bank. A set of representative data was presented to each bank for the purpose of preparing a bid. The data are as follows:

Checking accounts needed: 6
Checks per month:* 2,000
Foreign debits/credits on checking accounts per month: 200
Deposits per month:* 300
Returned checks:* 25 per month
Credit card charges per month: 4,000
Wire transfers per month: 100, of which 60 are to foreign bank accounts
Monthly credit needs (line of credit availability and cost): $100,000 average monthly usage

*These are overall totals for the six accounts during a month.

Internet banking services?
Knowledgeable loan officer?
Responsiveness of bank?

FirstBank Bid:
Checking accounts: $5 monthly maintenance fee per account
$0.10 foreign debit/credit
$0.50 earned for each deposit
$3 per returned check

Credit card fees: $0.50 per item

Wire transfers: $15 to domestic bank accounts, $50 to foreign bank accounts

Line of credit: Yes, this amount is available,
interest charged at prime plus 2 percent,
subject to a 6 percent minimum interest rate

Internet banking services? Yes, full online banking available:
$15 one-time setup fee for each account,
$20 monthly fee for software module

The loan officer assigned to the potential Kicker account had 10 years of experience with medium to large business banking and showed an understanding of the audio industry.

Community Bank Bid:
Checking accounts: No fees for the accounts, and no credits earned on deposits;
$2.00 per returned check

Credit card fees: $0.50 per item, $7 per batch processed.
Only manual processing was available, and
Kicker estimated 20 batches per month

Wire transfers: $30 per wire transfer

Line of credit: Yes, this amount is available,
interest charged at prime plus 2 percent,
subject to a 7 percent minimum interest rate

Internet banking services? Not currently, but within the next six months

The loan officer assigned to the potential Kicker account had four years of experience with medium to large business banking, none of which pertained to the audio industry.

(Continued)

RegionalOne Bank Bid:

Checking accounts: $5 monthly maintenance fee per account to be waived for Kicker
$0.20 foreign debit/credit
$0.30 earned for each deposit
$3.80 per returned check

Credit card fees: $0.50 per item

Wire transfers: $10 to domestic bank accounts, $55 to foreign bank accounts

Line of credit: Yes, this amount is available,
interest charged at prime plus 2 percent,
subject to a 6.5 percent minimum interest rate

Internet banking services? Yes, full online banking available,
one-time setup fee for each account waived for Kicker
$20 monthly fee for software module

The loan officer assigned to the potential **Kicker** account had two years of experience with large business banking. Another branch of the bank had expertise in the audio industry and would be willing to help as needed. This bank was the first one to submit a bid.

Required:
1. Calculate the predicted monthly cost of banking with each bank.
2. **Conceptual Connection:** Suppose **Kicker** felt that full online Internet banking was critical. How would that affect your analysis from Requirement 1? How would you incorporate the subjective factors (e.g., experience, access to expertise)?

CASES

OBJECTIVE

Case 23-53 Make or Buy: Ethical Considerations

Pamela McDonald, chief management accountant and controller for Murray Manufacturing Inc., was having lunch with Roger Branch, manager of the company's power department. Over the past six months, Pamela and Roger had developed a romantic relationship and were making plans for marriage. To keep company gossip at a minimum, Pamela and Roger had kept the relationship very quiet, and no one in the company was aware of it. The topic of the luncheon conversation centered on a decision concerning the company's power department that Larry Johnson, president of the company, was about to make.

Pamela: Roger, in our last executive meeting, we were told that a local utility company offered to supply power and quoted a price per kilowatt-hour that they said would hold for the next three years. They even offered to enter into a contractual agreement with us.

Roger: This is news to me. Is the bid price a threat to my area? Can they sell us power cheaper than we make it? And why wasn't I informed about this matter? I should have some input. This burns me. I think I should give Larry a call this afternoon and lodge a strong complaint.

Pamela: Calm down, Roger. The last thing I want you to do is call Larry. Larry made us all promise to keep this whole deal quiet until a decision had been made. He did not want you involved because he wanted to make an unbiased decision. You know that the company is struggling somewhat, and they are looking for ways to save money.

Roger: Yeah, but at my expense? And at the expense of my department's workers? At my age, I doubt that I could find a job that pays as well and has the same benefits. How much of a threat is this offer?

Pamela: Jack Lacy, my assistant controller, prepared an analysis while I was on vacation. It showed that internal production is cheaper than buying, but not by much. Larry asked me to review the findings and submit a final recommendation for next Wednesday's meeting. I've reviewed Jack's analysis, and it's faulty. He overlooked the interactions of your department with other service departments. When these are considered, the analysis is overwhelmingly in favor of purchasing the power. The savings are about $300,000 per year.

Roger: If Larry hears that, my department's gone. Pam, you can't let this happen. I'm three years away from having a vested retirement. And my workers—they have home mortgages, kids in college, families to support. No, it's not right. Pam, just tell him that your assistant's analysis is on target. He'll never know the difference.

Pamela: Roger, what you're suggesting doesn't sound right either. Would it be ethical for me to fail to disclose this information?

Roger: Ethical? Do you think it's right to lay off employees that have been loyal, faithful workers simply to fatten the pockets of the owners of this company? The Murrays already are so rich that they don't know what to do with their money. I think that it's even more unethical to penalize me and my workers. Why should we have to bear the consequences of some bad marketing decisions? Anyway, the effects of those decisions are about gone, and the company should be back to normal within a year or so.

Pamela: You may be right. Perhaps the well-being of you and your workers is more important than saving $300,000 for the Murrays.

Required:

1. Should Pamela have told Roger about the impending decision concerning the power department? What do you think most corporate codes of ethics would say about this?
2. Should Pamela provide Larry with the correct data concerning the power department? Or should she protect its workers? What would you do if you were Pamela?

Case 23-54 Keep or Drop a Division

OBJECTIVE

Jan Shumard, president and general manager of Danbury Company, was concerned about the future of one of the company's largest divisions. The division's most recent quarterly income statement follows:

Sales	$ 3,751,500
Less: Cost of goods sold	(2,722,400)
Gross profit	$ 1,029,100
Less: Selling and administrative expenses	(1,100,000)
Operating (loss)	$ (70,900)

Jan is giving serious consideration to shutting down the division because this is the ninth consecutive quarter that it has shown a loss. To help him in his decision, the following additional information has been gathered:

- The division produces one product at a selling price of $100 to outside parties. The division sells 50 percent of its output to another division within the company for $83 per unit (full manufacturing cost plus 25 percent). The internal price is set by company policy. If the division is shut down, the user division will buy the part externally for $100 per unit.
- The fixed overhead assigned per unit is $20.
- There is no alternative use for the facilities if shut down. The facilities and equipment will be sold and the proceeds invested to produce an annuity of $100,000 per year. Of the fixed selling and administrative expenses, 30 percent represent allocated expenses from corporate headquarters. Variable selling expenses are $5 per unit sold for units sold externally. These expenses are avoided for internal sales. No variable administrative expenses are incurred.

Required:

1. Prepare an income statement that more accurately reflects the division's profit performance.
2. Should the president shut down the division? What will be the effect on the company's profits if the division is closed?

Case 23-55 Internet Research, Group Case

OBJECTIVE

Often, websites for major airlines contain news of current special fares and flights. A decision to run a brief "fare special" is an example of a tactical decision. Form a group with one to three other students. Have each member of the group choose one or two airlines and check their websites for recent examples of fare specials. Have the group collaborate in preparing a presentation to the class discussing the types of cost and revenue information that would go into making this type of tactical decision.

24 Capital Investment Decisions

Doug Norman Crystals/Alamy

After studying Chapter 24, you should be able to:

1. Explain the meaning of *capital investment decisions*, and distinguish between independent and mutually exclusive capital investment decisions.

2. Compute the payback period and accounting rate of return for a proposed investment, and explain their roles in capital investment decisions.

3. Use net present value analysis for capital investment decisions involving independent projects.

4. Use the internal rate of return to assess the acceptability of independent projects.

5. Explain the role and value of postaudits.

6. Explain why net present value is better than internal rate of return for capital investment decisions involving mutually exclusive projects.

7. *(Appendix 24A)* Explain the relationship between current and future dollars.

Wesley Hitt/Tips Italia/Photolibrary

EXPERIENCE MANAGERIAL DECISIONS

with Hard Rock International

Launched in 1971 in London, England, nearly everyone has visited, or at least seen t-shirts for, one of **Hard Rock International**'s world-famous cafe restaurants located around the globe, from the U.S. to Europe to Asia and Australia. What visitors likely appreciate most is Hard Rock's impressive collection of rock 'n' roll memorabilia and its tasty fare. However, for Hard Rock's managerial accountants and the readers of this textbook, what is most likely to be appreciated is Hard Rock's masterful use of effective capital budgeting techniques to make decisions on a very big scale that are critical to the company's continued success. One of those decisions concerns the opening of new cafes all over the world from Mumbai, India, to Louisville, Kentucky.

Svetlana_Lukienko_2010_/Shutterstock.com

New cafes require advanced planning concerning anticipated cash flows, both for future costs and revenues. Future cost-related cash flow projections include items such as labor and materials from different countries, licensing laws, utilities, kitchen and bar equipment, computers, construction, and audio-visual equipment. Future cash flows for food and beverage sales are even more difficult to project than costs because of uncertainties involving demographics, economic conditions, and competition. Another complicating factor is the challenge of estimating local awareness of the Hard Rock brand. Brand awareness is important because it drives Hard Rock's merchandise sales. Estimates of future cash flows for revenues and expenses are combined to calculate a proposed cafe's payback period and net present value (NPV). These metrics then are compared with Hard Rock's decision model requirements to help determine whether or not the proposed cafe is a wise decision.

Another capital investment decision for Hard Rock surrounds the acquisition of its rock 'n' roll memorabilia. Hard Rock uses its memorabilia to generate food and merchandise revenues by attracting more customers into the cafe. The collection has grown from a single Eric Clapton guitar to more than 72,000 instruments, stage outfits, platinum and gold LPs, music and lyric sheets, and photographs.

All of these decisions require effective capital budgeting practices.

TYPES OF CAPITAL INVESTMENT DECISIONS

Organizations, like **Hard Rock**, often are faced with the opportunity (or need) to invest in assets or projects that represent long-term commitments. New production systems, new plants, new equipment, new product development, and, in the case of Hard Rock, new cafes are examples of assets and projects that fit this category. Usually, many alternatives are available. Hard Rock, for example, may be faced with the decision of whether or not to develop a new cafe in a certain location. Manufacturing firms, on the other hand, may need to decide whether to invest in a flexible manufacturing system or to continue with an existing traditional manufacturing system. These long-range decisions are examples of *capital investment decisions*.

Capital investment decisions are concerned with the process of planning, setting goals and priorities, arranging financing, and using certain criteria to select long-term assets. Because capital investment decisions place large amounts of resources at risk for long periods of time and simultaneously affect the future development of the firm, they are among the most important decisions made by managers. Poor capital investment decisions can be disastrous. For example, a failure to invest in automated manufacturing when other competitors do so may result in significant losses in market share because of the inability to compete on the basis of quality, cost, and delivery time. Making the right capital investment decisions is absolutely essential for long-term survival.

Independent and Mutually Exclusive Projects

The process of making capital investment decisions often is referred to as **capital budgeting**. Two types of capital budgeting projects will be considered: *independent projects* and *mutually exclusive projects*.

- **Independent projects** are projects that, if accepted or rejected, do not affect the cash flows of other projects. For example, a decision by **Hard Rock** to develop a cafe in Argentina is not affected by its decision to build a new cafe in Singapore. These are independent capital investment decisions.
- **Mutually exclusive projects** are those projects that, if accepted, preclude the acceptance of all other competing projects. For example, each time **Hard Rock** develops a new cafe, it installs kitchen and bar equipment. Some equipment uses standard technology while other options offer advanced technology for energy efficiency. Once one type of equipment is chosen the other type is excluded; they are mutually exclusive.

Concept Q&A

What is the difference between independent and mutually exclusive investments?

Answer:
Acceptance or rejection of an independent investment does not affect the cash flows of other investments. Acceptance of a mutually exclusive investment precludes the acceptance of any competing project.

Making Capital Investment Decisions

In general terms, a sound capital investment will earn back its original capital outlay over its life and, at the same time, provide a reasonable return on the original investment. After making this assessment, managers must decide on the acceptability of independent projects and compare competing projects on the basis of their economic merits.

But what is meant by reasonable return? Generally, any new project must cover the opportunity cost of the funds invested. For example, if a company takes money from a money market fund that is earning 4 percent and invests it in a new project, then the project must provide at least a 4 percent return (the return that could have been earned had the money been left in the money market fund). In reality, funds for investment often come from different sources—each representing a different opportunity cost. The return that must be earned is a blend of the opportunity costs of the different sources. Thus, if a company uses two sources of funds, one with an opportunity cost of 4 percent and the other with an opportunity cost of 6 percent, then the return that must be earned is somewhere between 4 and 6 percent, depending on the relative amounts used from each source. Furthermore, it is usually assumed that managers should select projects that maximize the wealth of the firm's owners.

To make a capital investment decision, a manager must

- estimate the quantity and timing of cash flows
- assess the risk of the investment
- consider the impact of the project on the firm's profits

Hard Rock has little difficulty estimating what a new cafe will cost (the investment required). However, estimating future cash flows is much more challenging. For example, Hard Rock projects sales for a new cafe by first looking at sales from existing cafes with a similar size and location. Next, local factors such as demographics, economic conditions, competition, and awareness of the Hard Rock brand are considered. After taking all these factors into account, two sets of sales estimates are made for a ten-year horizon: (1) a likely scenario, and (2) a worst case scenario. Sales are also broken out into four sources: Restaurant, Catering, Bar, and Retail. This breakout is important because each revenue area has a different labor and materials cost structure. This facilitates the estimating of operating costs. Given the estimated revenues and costs, the future cash flows can then calculated. Obviously, as the accuracy of cash flow forecasts increases, the reliability of the decision improves.

Managers must set goals and priorities for capital investments. They also must identify some basic criteria for the acceptance or rejection of proposed investments. In this chapter, we will study four basic methods to guide managers in accepting or rejecting potential investments. The methods include both nondiscounting and discounting decision approaches (two methods are discussed for each approach). The discounting methods are applied to investment decisions involving both independent and mutually exclusive projects.

Note that, for simplicity, although forecasting future cash flows is a critical part of the capital investment process, we will reserve discussions of forecasting methodologies for more advanced courses. Furthermore, the cash flows projected must be *after-tax cash flows*. Taxes have an important role in developing cash flow assessments. Here, however, tax effects either are assumed away or the cash flows can be thought of as after-tax cash flows. Consequently, after-tax cash flows are assumed to be known and the focus in this chapter will be on making capital investment decisions *given* these cash flows.

NONDISCOUNTING MODELS: PAYBACK PERIOD AND ACCOUNTING RATE OF RETURN

The basic capital investment decision models can be classified into two major categories: *nondiscounting models* and *discounting models*:

- **Nondiscounting models** ignore the time value of money.
- **Discounting models** explicitly consider the time value of money.

OBJECTIVE 2
Compute the payback period and accounting rate of return for a proposed investment, and explain their roles in capital investment decisions.

Although many accounting theorists disparage the nondiscounting models because they ignore the time value of money, many firms continue to use these models in making capital investment decisions. However, the use of discounting models has increased over the years, and few firms use only one model. Indeed, most firms seem to use both types.[1] This pattern suggests that both categories—nondiscounted and discounted—supply useful information to managers as they struggle to make a capital investment decision.

Payback Period

One type of nondiscounting model is the *payback period*. The **payback period** is the time required for a firm to recover its original investment. If the cash flows of a project are an equal amount each period, then the following formula can be used to compute its payback period:

---

[1] From the mid-1950s to 1988, surveys reveal that the use of discounting models as the primary evaluation method for capital projects went from about 9 to 80 percent. See A. Robichek and J. G. McDonald, "Financial Planning in Transition, Long Range Planning Service," Report No. 268 (Stanford Research Institute, Menlo Park, CA: January 1966); and T. Klammer, B. Koch, and N. Wilner, "Capital Budgeting Practices—A Survey of Corporate Use," published in the Proceedings of Decision Sciences National Meeting, November 21-24, 1988, North Texas State University.

$$\text{Payback period} = \frac{\text{Original investment}}{\text{Annual cash flow}}$$

If, however, the cash flows are unequal, the payback period is computed by adding the annual cash flows until such time as the original investment is recovered. If a fraction of a year is needed, it is assumed that cash flows occur evenly within each year. **CORNERSTONE 24-1** shows how payback analysis is done for both even and uneven cash flows.

CORNERSTONE 24-1   Calculating Payback

Information:

Suppose that a new car wash facility requires an investment of $100,000 and either has: (a) even cash flows of $50,000 per year or (b) the following expected annual cash flows: $30,000, $40,000, $50,000, $60,000, and $70,000.

Required:

Calculate the payback period for each case.

Solution:

a. Payback period = Original investment/Annual cash flow
    = $100,000/$50,000 = 2 years

b.

Year	Unrecovered Investment (beginning of year)	Annual Cash Flow	Time Needed for Payback (years)
1	$ 100,000	$ 30,000	1.0
2	70,000	40,000	1.0
3	30,000	50,000	0.6*
4	0	60,000	0.0
5	0	70,000	0.0
			2.6

*At the beginning of Year 3, $30,000 is needed to recover the investment. Since a net cash flow of $50,000 is expected, only 0.6 year ($30,000/$50,000) is needed to recover the remaining $30,000, assuming a uniform cash inflow throughout the year.

Using the Payback Period to Assess Risk One way to use the payback period is to set a maximum payback period for all projects and to reject any project that exceeds this level. Why would a firm use the payback period in this way? Some analysts suggest that the payback period can be used as a rough measure of risk, with the notion that the longer it takes for a project to pay for itself, the riskier it is. Also, firms with riskier cash flows in general could require a shorter payback period than normal. Additionally, firms with liquidity problems would be more interested in projects with quick paybacks. Another critical concern is obsolescence. In some industries, the risk of obsolescence is high. Firms within these industries, such as computer and MP3 player manufacturers, would be interested in recovering funds rapidly.

ETHICAL DECISIONS Another reason, less beneficial to the firm, may also be involved. Many managers in a position to make capital investment decisions may choose investments with quick payback periods out of self-interest. If a manager's performance is measured using such short-run criteria as annual net income, projects with quick paybacks may be chosen to show improved net income and cash flow as quickly as possible. Consider that divisional managers often are responsible for making capital investment decisions and are evaluated on divisional profit. The tenure of divisional managers, however, is typically short—three to five years on average. Consequently, an incentive exists for self-interested managers to shy away from investments that promise healthy long-run returns but relatively meager returns in the short run. New products and services that require time to develop a consumer following fit this description. However, ethical managers would avoid responding to these types of incentives. Corporate budgeting policies and a budget review committee can mitigate these problems by clearly communicating expected behaviors. ●

Using the Payback Period to Choose Among Alternatives The payback period can be used to choose among competing alternatives. Under this approach, the investment with the shortest payback period is preferred over investments with longer payback periods. However, this use of the payback period is less defensible because this measure suffers from two major deficiencies:

- It ignores the cash flow performance of the investments beyond the payback period.
- It ignores the time value of money.

These two significant deficiencies are easily illustrated. Assume that an engineering firm is considering two different types of computer-aided design (CAD) systems: CAD-A and CAD-B. Each system requires an initial outlay of $150,000, has a five-year life, and displays the following annual cash flows:

Investment	Year 1	Year 2	Year 3	Year 4	Year 5
CAD-A	$90,000	$ 60,000	$50,000	$50,000	$50,000
CAD-B	40,000	110,000	25,000	25,000	25,000

Both investments have payback periods of two years. In other words, if a manager uses the payback period to choose among competing investments, the two investments would be equally desirable. In reality, however, the CAD-A system should be preferred over the CAD-B system for two reasons:

- The CAD-A system provides a much larger dollar return for the Years 3, 4, and 5 beyond the payback period ($150,000 vs. $75,000).
- The CAD-A system returns $90,000 in the first year, while B returns only $40,000. The extra $50,000 that the CAD-A system provides in the first year could be put to productive use, such as investing in another project. It is better to have a dollar now than to have it one year from now, because the dollar on hand can be invested to provide a return one year from now.

In summary, the payback period provides information to managers that can be used as follows:

- To help control the risks associated with the uncertainty of future cash flows.
- To help minimize the impact of an investment on a firm's liquidity problems.
- To help control the risk of obsolescence.
- To help control the effect of the investment on performance measures.

However, the method suffers significant deficiencies: It ignores a project's total profitability and the time value of money. While the computation of the payback period may be useful to a manager, relying on it solely for a capital investment decision would be foolish.

Accounting Rate of Return

The *accounting rate of return* is the second commonly used nondiscounting model. The **accounting rate of return (ARR)** measures the return on a project in terms of income, as opposed to using a project's cash flow. The accounting rate of return is computed by the following formula:

$$\text{Accounting rate of return} = \frac{\text{Average income}}{\text{Initial investment}}$$

Income is not equivalent to cash flows because of accruals and deferrals used in its computation. The average income of a project is obtained by adding the net income for each year of the project and then dividing this total by the number of years. **CORNERSTONE 24-2** shows how to calculate the accounting rate of return.

CORNERSTONE 24-2

Calculating the Accounting Rate of Return

Information:
An investment requires an initial outlay of $100,000 and has a five-year life with no salvage value. The yearly cash flows are $50,000, $50,000, $60,000, $50,000 and $70,000.

Required:
1. Calculate the annual net income for each of the five years.
2. Calculate the accounting rate of return.

Solution:
1. Yearly depreciation expense = ($100,000 − $0)/5 years = $20,000
   Annual net income = Net cash flow − depreciation expense
   Year 1 net income = $50,000 − $20,000 = $30,000
   Year 2 net income = $50,000 − $20,000 = $30,000
   Year 3 net income = $60,000 − $20,000 = $40,000
   Year 4 net income = $50,000 − $20,000 = $30,000
   Year 5 net income = $70,000 − $20,000 = $50,000

2. Total net income (five years) = $180,000
   Average net income = $180,000/5 = $36,000
   $$\text{Accounting rate of return} = \frac{\$36,000}{\$100,000} = 0.36$$

Limitations of Accounting Rate of Return Unlike the payback period, the ARR does consider a project's profitability. However, the ARR has other potential drawbacks, including the following.

- *Ignoring Time Value of Money:* Like the payback period, it ignores the time value of money. Ignoring the time value of money is a critical deficiency in this method as well. It can lead a manager to choose investments that do not maximize profits. The ARR and payback model are referred to as *nondiscounting models* because they ignore the time value of money.
- *Dependency on Net Income:* ARR is dependent upon net income, which is the financial measure most likely to be manipulated by managers. Some of the reasons for manipulating net income include debt contracts (i.e., debt covenants) and bonuses. Often, debt contracts require that a firm maintain certain financial accounting ratios, which can be affected by the income reported and by the level of long-term assets. Accordingly, the ARR may be used as a screening measure to ensure that any new investment will not adversely affect these ratios.
- *Managers' Incentive:* Additionally, because bonuses to managers often are based on accounting income or return on assets, managers may have a personal interest in seeing that any new investment contributes significantly to net income. A manager seeking to maximize personal income is likely to select investments that return the

highest net income per dollar invested, even if the selected investments are not the ones that produce the greatest cash flows and return to the firm in the long-run.

DISCOUNTING MODELS: THE NET PRESENT VALUE METHOD

Discounting models use **discounted cash flows** which are future cash flows expressed in terms of their present value. The use of discounting models requires an understanding of the present value concepts. Present value concepts are reviewed in Appendix 24A (p. 1213). Review these concepts and make sure that you understand them before studying capital investment discount models. Present value tables [Exhibits 24B-1 (p. 1216) and 24B-2 (p. 1217)] are presented in Appendix 24B (p. 1215). These tables are referred to and used throughout the rest of this chapter. Two discounting models will be considered: *net present value* and *internal rate of return*.

Concept Q&A

Why would a manager choose only investments that return the highest income per dollar invested?

O B J E C T I V E 3

Use net present value analysis for capital investment decisions involving independent projects.

Net Present Value Defined

Net present value (NPV) is the difference between the present value of the cash inflows and outflows associated with a project:

$$NPV = \left[\sum CF_t/(1+i)^t\right] - I$$
$$= \left[\sum CF_t df_t\right]$$
$$= P - I$$

where

I = The present value of the project's cost (usually the initial cash outlay)

CF_t = The cash inflow to be received in period t, with $t = 1 \ldots n$

i = The required rate of return

t = The time period

P = The present value of the project's future cash inflows

df_t = $1/(1 = i)^t$, the discount factor

NPV measures the profitability of an investment. A positive NPV indicates that the investment increases the firm's wealth. To use the NPV method, a *required rate of return* must be defined. The **required rate of return** is the minimum acceptable rate of return. It also is referred to as the *discount rate, hurdle rate*, and *cost of capital*. In theory, if future cash flows are known with certainty, then the correct required rate of return is the firm's **cost of capital**. In practice, future cash flows are uncertain, and managers often choose a discount rate higher than the cost of capital to deal with the uncertainty. However, if the rate chosen is excessively high, it will bias the selection process toward short-term investments. Because of the risk of being overly conservative, it may be better to use the cost of capital as the discount rate and find other approaches to deal with uncertainty.

Once the NPV for a project is computed, it can be used to determine whether or not to accept and investment:

- If the NPV is greater than zero the investment is profitable and, therefore, acceptable. A positive NPV signals that (1) the initial investment has been recovered, (2) the required rate of return has been recovered, and (3) a return in excess of (1) and (2) has been received.
- If the NPV equals zero, the decision maker will find acceptance or rejection of the investment equal.
- If the NPV is less than zero, the investment should be rejected. In this case, it is earning less than the required rate of return.

Concept Q&A

Suppose that the NPV of an investment is $2,000. Why does this mean that the investment should be accepted?

Answer:
NPV greater than zero means that the investment recovers its capital while simultaneously earning a return in excess of the required rate.

Net Present Value Illustrated

Brannon Company has developed new earphones for portable MP3 players that it believes are superior to anything on the market. The earphones have a projected product life cycle of five years. Although the marketing manager is excited about the new product's prospects, a decision to manufacture the new product depends on whether it can earn a positive NPV given the company's required rate of return of 12 percent. In order to make a decision regarding the earphones, two steps must be taken:

Step 1: The cash flows for each year must be identified.
Step 2: The NPV must be computed using the cash flows from Step 1.

CORNERSTONE 24-3 shows how to calculate the NPV.

CORNERSTONE 24-3   Assessing Cash Flows and Calculating Net Present Value

Information:
A detailed market study revealed expected annual revenues of $300,000 for new earphones. Equipment to produce the earphones will cost $320,000. After five years, the equipment can be sold for $40,000. In addition to equipment, working capital is expected to increase by $40,000 because of increases in inventories and receivables. The firm expects to recover the investment in working capital at the end of the project's life. Annual cash operating expenses are estimated at $180,000. The required rate of return is 12 percent.

Required:
Estimate the annual cash flows, and calculate the NPV.

Solution:

STEP 1. CASH FLOW IDENTIFICATION

Year	Item	Cash Flow
0	Equipment	$(320,000)
	Working capital	(40,000)
	Total	$(360,000)
1–4	Revenues	$ 300,000
	Operating expenses	(180,000)
	Total	$ 120,000
5	Revenues	$ 300,000
	Operating expenses	(180,000)
	Salvage	40,000
	Recovery of working capital	40,000
	Total	$ 200,000

STEP 2A. NPV ANALYSIS

Year	Cash Flow[a]	Discount Factor[b]	Present Value
0	$(360,000)	1.00000	$(360,000)
1	120,000	0.89286	107,143
2	120,000	0.79719	95,663
3	120,000	0.71178	85,414
4	120,000	0.63552	76,262
5	200,000	0.56743	113,486
Net present value			$ 117,968

(Continued)

STEP 2B. NPV ANALYSIS

Year	Cash Flow	Discount Factor[c]	Present Value
0	$(360,000)	1.00000	$(360,000)
1–4	120,000	3.03735	364,482
5	200,000	0.56743	113,486
Net present value			$ 117,968

[a]From Step 1.
[b]From Exhibit 24B-1.
[c]Years 1–4 from Exhibit 24B-2; Year 5 from Exhibit 24B-1.

CORNERSTONE 24-3 *(continued)*

In Cornerstone 24-3, notice that Step 2 offers two approaches for computing NPV. Step 2A computes NPV by using discount factors from Exhibit 24B-1. Step 2B simplifies the computation by using a single discount factor from Exhibit 24B-2 for the even cash flows occurring in Years 1 through 4.

Illustrating Relationships: NPV, Discount Rates, and Cash Flows

Estimating cash flows is often difficult and certainly a major source of risk for capital budgeting decisions. The discount rate is the minimum acceptable required rate of return and, under certainty, would correspond to the firm's cost of capital. Because of uncertain future cash flows, firms may use a higher discount rate than its cost of capital. It is also common to provide pessimistic and most likely cash flow scenarios to help assess a project's risk (as **Hard Rock** does). As the discount rate increases, the present value of future cash flows decreases, making it harder for a project to achieve a positive NPV. Alternatively, providing pessimistic and likely assessments of cash flows also allows managers to see the effect of differences in cash flow estimates on project viability as measured by NPV. Illustrating the relationship between the discount rate and cash flows affords rich insight about the economic feasibility of a project.

For purposes of illustration, suppose that an amusement park is considering an investment in a new ride that has the following data:

Investment:	$3,500,000
Likely annual cash flow:	$1,200,000
Pessimistic annual cash flow:	$800,000
Discount rate range:	.08 to .18, increments of 0.02
Expected cost of capital:	0.10
Project life:	6 years

Using this information, the NPV is calculated and plotted as the discount rate varies (increasing by increments of 0.02 for the range indicated) for each series of cash flows. Exhibit 24-1 illustrates the relationships. For the likely cash flow scenario, the project

NPV, Discount Rates and Cash Flow

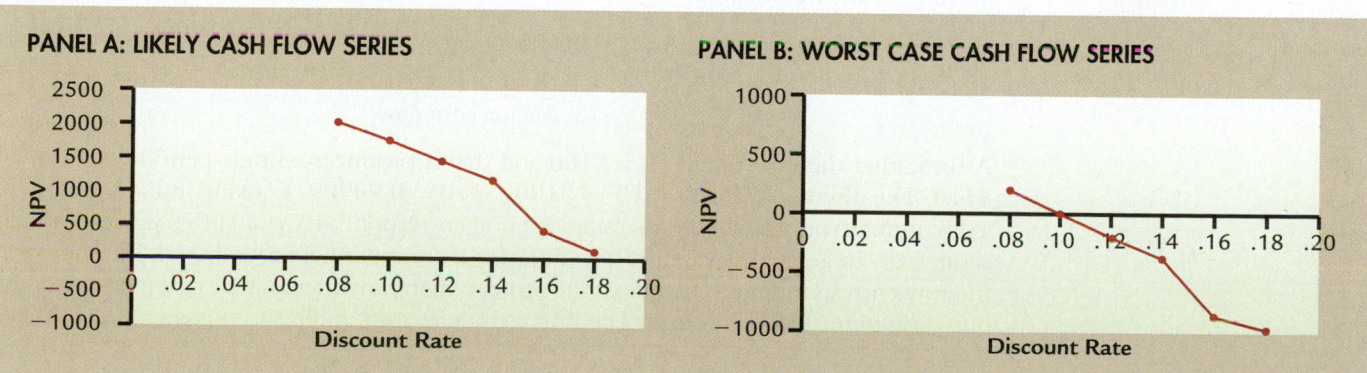

has a positive NPV for all discount rates. For the worst case scenario, the NPV is negative for the four highest discount rates, about zero (actually slightly negative) for the 10 percent rate and positive only for the 8 percent rate.

Knowing these relationships, what decision should be made? For the expected cost of capital of 10 percent, the worst prediction is a NPV of about zero (−$16,000). Thus, it appears to be a fairly safe investment since there seems to be very little likelihood of losing on the project. Using both Panels A and B provides good insight into the risk and economic viability of the proposed project.

OBJECTIVE 4
Use the internal rate of return to assess the acceptability of independent projects.

INTERNAL RATE OF RETURN

Another discounting model is the *internal rate of return* method.

Internal Rate of Return Defined

The **internal rate of return (IRR)** is defined as the interest rate that sets the present value of a project's cash inflows equal to the present value of the project's cost. In other words, it is the interest rate that sets the project's NPV at zero. The following equation can be used to determine a project's IRR:

$$I = \sum[CF_t/(1 + i)^t]$$

where $t = 1, …, n$

The right side of this equation is the present value of future cash flows, and the left side is the investment. I, CF_t, and t are known. Thus, the IRR (the interest rate, i, in the equation) can be found using trial and error. Once the IRR for a project is computed, it is compared with the firm's required rate of return:

- If the IRR is greater than the required rate, the project is deemed acceptable.
- If the IRR is less than the required rate of return, the project is rejected.
- If the IRR is equal to the required rate of return, the firm is indifferent between accepting or rejecting the investment proposal.

The IRR is the most widely used of the capital investment techniques. One reason for its popularity may be that it is a rate of return, a concept that managers are comfortable with using. Another possibility is that managers may believe (in most cases, incorrectly) that the IRR is the true or actual compounded rate of return being earned by the initial investment. Whatever the reasons for its popularity, a basic understanding of the IRR is necessary.

Internal Rate of Return Illustrated: Multiple-Period Setting with Uniform Cash Flows

Assume initially that the investment produces a series of uniform cash flows. Since the series of cash flows is uniform, a single discount factor from the present value table in Exhibit 24B-2 (p. 1217) can be used to compute the present value of the annuity. Letting *df* be this discount factor and *CF* be the annual cash flow, the IRR equation assumes the following form:

$$I = CF(df)$$

Solving for *df*, we obtain:

$$df = I/CF$$
$$= \frac{\text{Investment}}{\text{Annual cash flow}}$$

Assume that the investment (I) is $100 and that it produces a single-period cash flow of $110. The discount factor is I/CF = $100/$110 = 0.90909. Looking in Exhibit 24B-2, a discount factor of 0.90909 for a single period corresponds to a rate of 10 percent, which is the IRR. In general, once the discount factor is computed, go to Exhibit 24B-2 and find the row corresponding to the life of the project, then move across that row until the computed discount factor is found. The interest rate corresponding to this discount factor is the IRR. **CORNERSTONE 24-4** illustrates how to calculate the IRR for multiple-period uniform cash flows.

CORNERSTONE 24-4   Calculating Internal Rate of Return with Uniform Cash Flows

Information:
Assume that a hospital has the opportunity to invest $205,570.50 in a new ultrasound system that will produce net cash inflows of $50,000 at the end of each of the next six years.

Required:
Calculate the IRR for the ultrasound system.

Solution:

$df = I/CF$

$\quad = \$205,570.50/\$50,000$

$\quad = 4.11141$

Since the life of the investment is six years, find the sixth row in Exhibit 24B-2 and then move across this row until $df = 4.11141$ is found. The interest rate corresponding to 4.11141 is 12 percent, which is the IRR.

Exhibit 24B-2 (p. 1217) does not provide discount factors for every possible interest rate. To illustrate, assume that the annual cash inflows expected by the hospital (in Cornerstone 24-4) are $51,000 instead of $50,000. The new discount factor is 4.03079 ($205,570.50/$51,000). Going once again to the sixth row in Exhibit 24B-2, it is clear that the discount factor—and thus the IRR—lies between 12 and 14 percent. Although it is possible to approximate the IRR by interpolation, for simplicity, we can identify the range for the IRR as indicated by the table values. In practice, business calculators or spreadsheet programs like Excel can provide the values of IRR without the use of tables such as Exhibit 24B-2.

Internal Rate of Return Illustrated: Multiple-Period Setting with Uneven Cash Flows

If the cash flows are not uniform, then the IRR equation must be used. For a multiple-period setting, this equation can be solved by trial and error or by using a business calculator or a spreadsheet program. To illustrate the solution by trial and error, assume that a $10,000 investment in a PC system produces clerical savings of $6,000 and $7,200, respectively, for the two years. The IRR is the interest rate that sets the present value of these two cash inflows equal to $10,000:

$$P = \left[\frac{\$6,000}{(1+i)}\right] + \left[\frac{\$7,200}{(1+i)^2}\right]$$

$$= \$10,000$$

To solve this equation by trial and error, start by selecting a possible value for i. Given this first guess, the present value of the future cash flows is computed and then compared with the initial investment. If the present value is greater than the initial investment, then the interest rate is too low. If the present value is less than the initial investment, then the interest rate is too high. The next guess is adjusted accordingly.

Assume that the first guess is 18 percent. Using i equal to 0.18, the present value table in Exhibit 24B-1 (p. 1216) yields the following discount factors: 0.84746 and 0.71818. These discount factors produce the following present value for the two cash inflows:

$$P = (0.84746 \times \$6,000) + (0.71818 \times \$7,200)$$
$$= \$10,256$$

Since P is greater than $10,000, the interest rate selected is too low. A higher guess is needed. If the next guess is 20 percent, we obtain the following:

$$P = (0.83333 \times \$6,000) + (0.69444 \times \$7,200)$$
$$= \$9,999.95$$

Since this value is very close to $10,000, we can say that the IRR is 20 percent. (The IRR is, in fact, exactly 20 percent. The present value is slightly less than the investment because the discount factors found in Exhibit 24B-1 (p. 1216) have been rounded to 5 decimal places.)

YOU DECIDE   IRR and Uncertainty in Estimates of Cash Savings and Project Life

As a manager of a plant producing cooking oils and margarines, you are concerned about the emission of contaminated water effluents. On a regular basis, your plant violates its discharge permit and dumps many times the allowable waste (organic solids) into a local river. This practice is beginning to draw increased attention and criticism from the state environmental agency. You are considering the acquisition and installation of a zero-discharge system, closed-loop system with an expected life of ten years and a required investment of $250,000. The closed-loop system is expected to produce the following expected annual savings:

Water (from the ability to recycle the water):	$20,000
Materials (from the ability to use extracted materials):	5,000
Avoidance of fines and penalties:	15,000
Reduction in demand for laboratory analysis:	10,000
Total Savings	$50,000

To accept any project, the IRR must be greater than the cost of capital, which is 10 percent.

Upon calculating the IRR, you find that it is about 15 percent, significantly greater than the 10 percent benchmark rate. However, upon seeking approval for the project from the divisional manager, he asks you how certain you are about the projected cash savings. He also questions the estimated life, arguing that based on his experience the expected life of the particular closed-loop system is usually closer to eight years than ten.

How would you address the divisional manager's concerns about projected cash savings and estimated life?

The concerns of the divisional manager relate to the uncertainty surrounding both the cash flow and project life estimates. The savings from recycling water and the fines and penalties probably have very little uncertainty attached to them. The same may also be true of the lab costs, especially if the analysis is outsourced. The major source of uncertainty probably is attached to the quantity of organic solids that once extracted can be used to produce additional margarines and cooking oils. Assuming that the extraction process does not produce any usable organic solids, the annual savings would be $45,000 ($50,000 − $45,000), yielding the worst case scenario for cash flows. This uncertainty in the cash flows can be dealt with by first calculating the minimum annual cash savings that must be realized to earn a rate equal to the firm's cost of capital and then comparing this minimum cash savings with the cash flows of the worst case scenario ($45,000). Calculating this minimum cash flow for an eight year life simultaneously addresses the project life issue.

The minimum cash flow is calculated as follows (where df is the discount factor for eight years and 10 percent, from Exhibit 24B-2, p. 1217):

$$I = CF(df)$$
$$CF = I/df$$
$$= \$250,000/5.33493$$
$$= \$48,861 \text{ (rounded)}$$

In the worst case scenario, the project will not meet the minimum cash savings requirement. The cash savings from the extraction of organic solids can only be off by about 20 percent to retain project viability. As a plant manager, you might argue that there is a likely *underestimation* of future fines and penalties resulting from the increased political attention to polluting of the local river. Also, there may be a positive benefit, not included in the savings, of a more favorable public image (e.g., increased sales because of the favorable environmental action). Taken together, you should have a strong position for winning approval of the project.

Sensitivity analysis thus provides a powerful tool for assessing the impact of uncertainty in capital investment analysis.

POSTAUDIT OF CAPITAL PROJECTS

A key element in the capital investment process is a follow-up analysis of a capital project once it is implemented. This analysis is called a *postaudit*. A **postaudit** compares the actual benefits with the estimated benefits and actual operating costs with estimated operating costs. It evaluates the overall outcome of the investment and proposes corrective action if needed. The following real-world case illustrates the usefulness of a postaudit activity.

Postaudit Illustrated

Allen Manesfield and Jenny Winters were discussing a persistent and irritating problem present in the process of producing intravenous (IV) needles. Allen and Jenny are employed by Honley Medical, which specializes in the production of medical products and has three divisions: the IV Products Division, the Critical Care Monitoring Division, and the Specialty Products Division. Allen and Jenny are associated with the IV Products Division—Allen as the senior production engineer and Jenny as the marketing manager.

The IV Products Division produces needles of five different sizes. During one stage of the manufacturing process, the needle itself is inserted into a plastic hub and is bonded by using epoxy glue. According to Jenny, the use of epoxy to bond the needles was causing the division all kinds of problems. In many cases, the epoxy wasn't bonding correctly. The rejects were high and the division was receiving a large number of complaints from its customers. Corrective action was needed to avoid losing sales. After some discussion and analysis, a recommendation was made to use induction welding in lieu of epoxy bonding. In induction welding, the needles are inserted into the plastic hub, and an RF generator is used to heat the needles. The RF generator works on the same principle as a microwave oven. As the needles get hot, the plastic melts and the needles are bonded.

Switching to induction welding required an investment in RF generators and the associated tooling. The investment was justified by the IV Products Division based on the savings associated with the new system. Induction welding promised to reduce the cost of direct materials by eliminating the need to buy and use epoxy. Savings of direct labor costs also were predicted because the welding process is more automated. Adding to these savings were the avoidance of daily cleanup costs and the reduction in rejects. Allen presented a formal NPV analysis showing that the welding system was superior to the epoxy system. Headquarters approved its purchase.

One year later, Allen and Jenny had the following conversation regarding the induction welding decision.

Jenny: Allen, I'm quite pleased with induction welding for bonding needles. In the year since the new process was implemented, we've had virtually no complaints from our customers. The needles are firmly bonded.

Allen: I wish that positive experience were true for all other areas as well. Unfortunately, implementing the process has uncovered some rather sticky and expensive problems that I didn't anticipate. The Internal Audit Department recently completed a postaudit of the project, and now my feet are being held to the fire.

Jenny: That's too bad. What's the problem?

Allen: You mean problems. Let me list a few for you. One is that the RF generators interfered with the operation of other equipment. To eliminate this interference, we had to install filtering equipment. But that's not all. We also discovered that the average maintenance person doesn't know how to maintain the new equipment. Now we're faced with the need to initiate a training program to upgrade the skills of our maintenance people. Upgrading skills implies higher wages. Although the RF bonding process is less messy, it is more complex. The manufacturing people complained to the internal auditors about that. They maintain that a simple process, even if messy, is preferred—especially now that demand for the product is increasing by leaps and bounds.

Jenny: What did the internal auditors conclude?

Allen: They concluded that many of the predicted savings did take place but that significant costs were not foreseen. Because of these unforeseen problems, they recommended that I look carefully at the possibility of moving back to using epoxy. They indicated that NPV analysis using actual data appears to favor that process. With production expanding, the acquisition of additional RF generators and filtering equipment plus the necessary training is simply not as attractive as returning to epoxy bonding. This conclusion is reinforced by the fact that the epoxy process is simpler and by the auditors' conclusion that the mixing of the epoxy can be automated, avoiding the quality problem we had in the first place.

Jenny: Well, Allen, you can't really blame yourself. You had a real problem and took action to solve it. It's difficult to foresee all the problems and hidden costs of a new process.

Allen: Unfortunately, the internal auditors don't agree. In fact, neither do I. I probably jumped too quickly. In the future, I intend to think through new projects more carefully.

In the case of the RF bonding decision for Honley Medical, some of the estimated capital investment benefits did materialize: complaints from customers decreased, rejects were fewer, and direct labor and materials costs decreased. However, the investment was greater than expected because filtering equipment was needed, and actual operating costs were much higher because of the increased maintenance cost and the increased complexity of the process. Overall, the internal auditors concluded that the investment was a poor decision. The corrective action that they recommended was to abandon the new process and return to epoxy bonding. Based on this recommendation, the firm abandoned inductive welding and returned to epoxy bonding, which was improved by automating the mix.

Postaudit Benefits

Firms that perform postaudits of capital projects experience a number of benefits, including the following.

- *Resource Allocation:* By evaluating profitability, postaudits ensure that resources are used wisely. If the project is doing well, it may call for additional funds and additional attention. If the project is not doing well, corrective action may be needed to improve performance or abandon the project.

- *Positive Impact on Managers' Behavior:* If managers are held accountable for the results of a capital investment decision, they are more likely to make such decisions in the best interests of the firm. Additionally, postaudits supply feedback to managers that should help to improve future decision making. Consider Allen's reaction to the postaudit of the RF bonding process. Certainly, we would expect him to be more careful and more thorough in making future investment recommendations. In the future, Allen will probably consider more than one alternative, such as automating the mixing of the epoxy. Also, for those alternatives being considered, he will probably be especially alert to the possibility of hidden costs, such as increased training requirements for a new process.

- *Independent Perspective:* For Honley Medical, the postaudit was performed by the internal audit staff. Generally, more objective results are obtainable if the postaudit is done by an independent party. Since considerable effort is expended to ensure as much independence as possible for the internal audit staff, that group is usually the best choice for this task.

Concept Q&A

Why do a postaudit?

Answer:
Postaudits allow a company to assess the quality of capital investment decisions and also produce corrective actions where some of the initial assumptions prove to be wrong. They also encourage managerial accountability and provide useful information for improving future capital budgeting decisions.

Postaudit Limitations

Postaudits, however, are costly. Moreover, even though they may provide significant benefits, they have other limitations. Most obvious is the fact that the assumptions driving the original analysis may often be invalidated by changes in the actual operating environment. Accountability must be qualified to some extent by the impossibility of foreseeing every possible eventuality.

MUTUALLY EXCLUSIVE PROJECTS

OBJECTIVE 6
Explain why net present value is better than internal rate of return for capital investment decisions involving mutually exclusive projects.

Up to this point, we have focused on independent projects. Many capital investment decisions deal with mutually exclusive projects. How NPV analysis and IRR are used to choose among competing projects is an interesting question. An even more interesting question to consider is whether NPV and IRR differ in their ability to help managers make wealth-maximizing decisions in the presence of competing alternatives. For example, we already know that the nondiscounting models can produce erroneous choices because they ignore the time value of money. Because of this deficiency, the discounting models are judged superior. Similarly, it can be shown that the NPV model is generally preferred to the IRR model when choosing among mutually exclusive alternatives.

Net Present Value Compared with Internal Rate of Return

NPV and IRR both yield the same decision for independent projects. For example, if the NPV is greater than zero, then the IRR is also greater than the required rate of return. Both models signal the correct decision. However, for competing projects, the two methods can produce different results. Intuitively, we believe that for mutually exclusive projects, the project with the highest NPV or the highest IRR should be chosen. Since it is possible for the two methods to produce different rankings of mutually exclusive projects, the method that consistently reveals the wealth-maximizing project is preferred.

NPV differs from IRR in two major ways:

- The NPV method assumes that each cash inflow received is reinvested at the required rate of return, whereas the IRR method assumes that each cash inflow is reinvested at the computed IRR. Reinvesting at the required rate of return is more realistic and produces more reliable results when comparing mutually exclusive projects.
- The NPV method measures profitability in absolute terms, whereas the IRR method measures it in relative terms. NPV measures the amount by which the value of the firm changes.

These differences are summarized in Exhibit 24-2.

Since NPV measures the impact that competing projects have on the value of the firm, choosing the project with the largest NPV is consistent with maximizing the wealth of shareholders. On the other hand, IRR does not consistently result in choices that maximize wealth. IRR, as a relative measure of profitability, has the virtue of measuring accurately the rate of return of funds that remain internally invested. However, maximizing IRR will not necessarily maximize the wealth of firm owners because it cannot, by nature, consider the absolute dollar contributions of projects. In the final analysis, what counts are the total dollars earned—the absolute profits—not the relative profits. Accordingly, NPV, not IRR, should be used for choosing among competing, mutually exclusive projects or competing projects when capital funds are limited.

Concept Q&A

Why is NPV better than IRR for choosing among competing projects?

Answer:
NPV uses a more realistic reinvestment assumption, and its signal is consistent with maximizing the wealth of firm owners (IRR does not measure absolute profits).

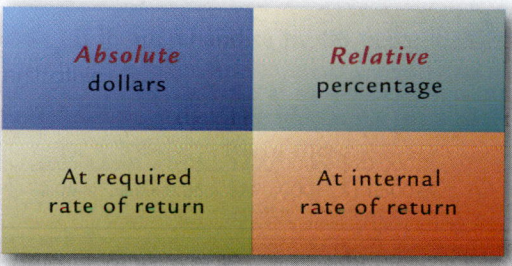

Exhibit 24-2

Net Present Value Compared with Internal Rate of Return

	NPV	IRR
Type of measure	*Absolute* dollars	*Relative* percentage
Cash flow reinvestment assumption	At required rate of return	At internal rate of return

An independent project is acceptable if its NPV is positive. For mutually exclusive projects, the project with the largest NPV is chosen. There are three steps in selecting the best project from several competing projects:

Step 1: Assess the cash flow pattern for each project.
Step 2: Compute the NPV for each project.
Step 3: Identify the project with the greatest NPV.

NPV Analysis for Mutually Exclusive Projects Illustrated

Bintley Corporation has committed to improving its environmental performance. One environmental project identified a manufacturing process as being the source of both liquid and gaseous residues. After six months of research activity, the engineering department announced that it is possible to redesign the process to prevent the production of contaminating residues. Two different process designs (A and B) that prevent the production of contaminants are being considered. Both process designs are more expensive to operate than the current process. However, because the designs prevent production of contaminants, significant annual benefits are created. These benefits stem from eliminating the need to operate and maintain expensive pollution control equipment, treat and dispose of toxic liquid wastes, and pay the annual fines for exceeding allowable contaminant releases. Increased sales to environmentally conscious customers also are factored into the benefit estimates. **CORNERSTONE 24-5** shows how NPV and IRR analyses are carried out for this setting.

 **CORNERSTONE 24-5**   **Calculating Net Present Value and Internal Rate of Return for Mutually Exclusive Projects**

Information:

Consider two pollution prevention designs: Design A and Design B. Both designs have a project life of five years. Design A requires an initial outlay of $180,000 and has a net annual after-tax cash inflow of $60,000 (revenues of $180,000 minus costs of $120,000). Design B, with an initial outlay of $210,000, has a net annual cash inflow of $70,000 ($240,000 − $170,000). The after-tax cash flows are summarized as follows:

	CASH FLOW PATTERN	
Year	**Design A**	**Design B**
0	$(180,000)	$(210,000)
1	60,000	70,000
2	60,000	70,000
3	60,000	70,000
4	60,000	70,000
5	60,000	70,000

The cost of capital for the company is 12 percent.

Required:

Calculate the NPV and the IRR for each project.

Solution:

	DESIGN A: NPV ANALYSIS		
Year	**Cash Flow**	**Discount Factor***	**Present Value**
0	$(180,000)	1.00000	$(180,000)
1–5	60,000	3.60478	216,287
Net present value			$ 36,287

(Continued)

**CORNERSTONE
24-5**
(continued)

DESIGN A: IRR ANALYSIS

Discount factor = Initial investment/Annual cash flow
= $180,000/$60,000
= 3.00000

From Exhibit 24B-2 (p. 1217), *df* = 3.00000 for five years implies that IRR ≈ 20 percent.

DESIGN B: NPV ANALYSIS

Year	Cash Flow	Discount Factor*	Present Value
0	$(210,000)	1.00000	$(210,000)
1–5	70,000	3.60478	252,335
Net present value			$ 42,335

DESIGN B: IRR ANALYSIS

Discount factor = Initial investment/Annual cash flow
= $210,000/$70,000
= 3.00000

From Exhibit 24B-2, *df* = 3.00000 for five years implies that IRR ≈ 20 percent.

*From Exhibit 24B-2.

Based on the NPV analysis in Cornerstone 24-5, Design B is more profitable; it has the larger NPV. Accordingly, the company should select Design B over Design A. Interestingly, Designs A and B have identical internal rates of return. As shown by Cornerstone 24-5, both designs have a discount factor of 3.00000. From Exhibit 24B-2, it is seen that a discount factor of 3.00000 and a life of five years yields an IRR of about 20 percent. Even though both projects have an IRR of 20 percent, the firm should not consider the two designs to be equally desirable. The analysis demonstrates that Design B produces a larger NPV and, therefore, will increase the value of the firm more than Design A. Design B should be chosen. This illustrates the conceptual superiority of NPV over IRR for analysis of competing projects.

Here's the Real Kicker

During the period of 2001–2003, **Stillwater Designs** experienced high sales of their Kicker products. As a result, the levels of inventory filled all storage areas to capacity. Consequently, Stillwater Designs began plans to add another building on existing property with 50,000 square feet of capacity. This new facility had an estimated construction cost between $1 and $1.5 million. During this preliminary planning phase, a shipping strike placed extra storage demands on existing facilities, and Stillwater Designs began looking for a warehousing facility that could be leased on a short-term basis.

They identified a 250,000-square-foot facility on 22 acres that was owned by Moore Business Forms. This facility was an attractive leasing option, and it quickly became a competing alternative to adding the 50,000-square-foot facility to Stillwater's current complex. In fact, the company began looking at the possibility of buying and renovating the Moore facility and moving all of its operations into the one facility. Renovation required such actions as installing a new HVAC system, bringing the building up to current fire codes, painting and resealing the floor, and adding a large number of offices. After careful financial analysis, Stillwater Designs decided that the buy-and-renovate option was more profitable than adding the 50,000-square-foot building to its current complex. Two economic factors affecting the decision were (1) selling the current complex of five buildings would help pay for the needed renovations, and (2) the purchase cost of the nonrenovated Moore facility was less than the cost of building the 50,000-square-foot facility.

KICKER

Special Considerations for Advanced Manufacturing Environment

For advanced manufacturing environments, like those using automated systems, capital investment decisions can be more complex because they must take special considerations into account.

How Investment Differs Investment in automated manufacturing processes is much more complex than investment in the standard manufacturing equipment of the past. For standard equipment, the direct costs of acquisition represent virtually the entire investment. For automated manufacturing, the direct costs can represent as little as 50 or 60 percent of the total investment. Software, engineering, training, and implementation are a significant percentage of the total costs. Thus, great care must be exercised to assess the actual cost of an automated system. It is easy to overlook the peripheral costs, which can be substantial.

How Estimates of Operating Cash Flows Differ Estimates of operating cash flows from investments in standard equipment typically have relied on directly identifiable tangible benefits, such as direct savings from labor, power, and scrap. However, when investing in automated systems, the intangible and indirect benefits can be material and critical to the viability of the project. Greater quality, more reliability, reduced lead time, improved customer satisfaction, and an enhanced ability to maintain market share all are important intangible benefits of an advanced manufacturing system. Reduction of labor in support areas such as production scheduling and stores are indirect benefits. More effort is needed to measure these intangible and indirect benefits in order to assess more accurately the potential value of investments.

Consider, for example, Zielesch Manufacturing, which is evaluating a potential investment in a flexible manufacturing system (FMS). The choice facing the company is to continue producing with its traditional equipment, expected to last 10 years, or to switch to the new system, which also is expected to have a useful life of 10 years. Zielesch's discount rate is 12 percent. The data pertaining to the investment are presented in Exhibit 24-3. Notice that for Zielesch, the *incremental cash flows* are used to

Exhibit 24-3

Investment Data; Direct, Intangible, and Indirect Benefits

	FMS	Status Quo
Investment (current outlay):		
Direct costs	$10,000,000	—
Software, engineering	8,000,000	—
Total current outlay	$18,000,000	—
Net after-tax cash flow	$ 5,000,000	$1,000,000
Less: After-tax cash flows for status quo	1,000,000	n/a
Incremental benefit	$ 4,000,000 ←	n/a
Incremental Benefit Explained		
Direct benefits:		
Direct labor	$ 1,500,000	
Scrap reduction	500,000	
Setups	200,000	
	$ 2,200,000	
Intangible benefits (quality savings):		
Rework	$ 200,000	
Warranties	400,000	
Maintenance of competitive position	1,000,000	
	1,600,000	
Indirect benefits:		
Production scheduling	$ 110,000	
Payroll	90,000	
	200,000	
Total	$ 4,000,000 ←	

compare the new project with the old. Instead of calculating the NPV for each alternative and comparing, an equivalent approach is to calculate the NPV of the incremental cash flows of the new system (cash flows of new system minus cash flows of old system). If the NPV for the incremental cash flows is positive, then the new equipment is preferred to the old.

Using the incremental data in Exhibit 24-3, the NPV of the proposed system can be computed as follows:

Present value ($4,000,000 × 5.65022*)	$22,600,880
Investment	18,000,000
NPV	$ 4,600,880

*This number is the discount factor for an interest rate of 12 percent and a life of 10 years (see Exhibit 24B-2, p. 1217).

The NPV is positive and large in magnitude, and it clearly signals the acceptability of the FMS. This outcome, however, is strongly dependent on explicit recognition of both intangible and indirect benefits. If those benefits are eliminated, then the direct savings total $2.2 million, and the NPV is negative:

Present value ($2,200,000 × 5.65022)	$12,430,484
Investment	18,000,000
NPV	$ (5,569,516)

The rise of activity-based costing has made identifying indirect benefits easier with the use of cost drivers. Once they are identified, they can be included in the analysis if they are material.

Examination of Exhibit 24-3 reveals the importance of intangible benefits. One of the most important intangible benefits is maintaining or improving a firm's competitive position. A key question is what will happen to the cash flows of the firm if the investment is not made. That is, if Zielesch chooses to forego an investment in technologically advanced equipment, will it be able to continue to compete with other firms on the basis of quality, delivery, and cost? (The question becomes especially relevant if competitors choose to invest in advanced equipment.) If the competitive position deteriorates, Zielesch's current cash flows will decrease.

If cash flows will decrease if the investment is not made, this decrease should show up as an incremental benefit for the advanced technology. In Exhibit 24-3, Zielesch estimates this competitive benefit as $1,000,000. Estimating this benefit requires some serious strategic planning and analysis, but its effect can be critical. If this benefit had been ignored or overlooked, then the NPV would have been negative and the investment alternative rejected:

Present value ($3,000,000 × 5.65022)	$16,950,660
Investment	18,000,000
NPV	$ (1,049,340)

APPENDIX 24A: PRESENT VALUE CONCEPTS

OBJECTIVE **7**
Explain the relationship between current and future dollars.

An important feature of money is that it can be invested and can earn interest. A dollar today is not the same as a dollar tomorrow. This fundamental principle is the backbone of discounting methods. Discounting methods rely on the relationships between current and future dollars. Thus, to use discounting methods, we must understand these relationships.

Future Value

Suppose that a bank advertises a 4 percent annual interest rate. If a customer invests $100, he or she would receive, after one year, the original $100 plus $4 interest $[\$100 + (0.04)(\$100)] = (1 + 0.04)\$100 = (1.04)(\$100) = \$104$. This result can be expressed by the following equation, where F is the future amount, P is the initial or current outlay, and i is the interest rate:

$$F = P(1 + i)$$

For the example, $F = \$100(1 + 0.04) = \$100(1.04) = \$104$.

Now suppose that the same bank offers a 5 percent rate if the customer leaves the original deposit, plus any interest, on deposit for a total of two years. How much will the customer receive at the end of two years? Again assume that a customer invests $100. Using the future value equation, the customer will earn $105 at the end of Year 1:

$$F = \$100(1 + 0.05) = \$100(1.05) = \$105$$

If this amount is left in the account for a second year, this equation is used again with P now assumed to be $105. At the end of the second year, then, the total is $110.25:

$$F = \$105(1 + 0.05) = \$105(1.05) = \$110.25$$

In the second year, interest is earned on both the original deposit and the interest earned in the first year. The earning of interest on interest is referred to as **compounding of interest**. The value that will accumulate by the end of an investment's life, assuming a specified compound return, is the **future value**. The future value of the $100 deposit in the second example is $110.25.

A more direct way to compute the future value is possible. Since the first application of the future value equation can be expressed as $F = \$105 = \$100(1.05)$, the second application can be expressed as $F = \$105(1.05) = \$100(1.05)(1.05) = \$100(1.05)^2 = P(1 + i)^2$. This suggests the following compounding interest formula for computing amounts for n periods into the future:

$$F = P(1 + i)^n$$

Present Value

Often, a manager needs to compute not the future value but the amount that must be invested now in order to yield some given future value. The amount that must be invested now to produce the future value is known as the **present value** of the future amount. For example, how much must be invested now in order to yield $363 two years from now, assuming that the interest rate is 10 percent? Or, put another way, what is the present value of $363 to be received two years from now?

In this example, the future value, the years, and the interest rate are all known. We want to know the current outlay that will produce that future amount. In the compounding interest equation, the variable representing the current outlay (the present value of F) is P. Thus, to compute the present value of a future outlay, all we need to do is solve the compounding interest equation for P:

$$P = F/(1 + i)^n$$

Using this present value equation, we can compute the present value of $363:

$$P = \frac{\$363}{(1 + 0.1)^2}$$
$$= \$363/1.21$$
$$= \$300$$

The present value, $300, is what the future amount of $363 is worth today. All other things being equal, having $300 today is the same as having $363 two years from now. Put another way, if a firm requires a 10 percent rate of return, the most the firm would be willing to pay today is $300 for any investment that yields $363 two years from now.

The process of computing the present value of future cash flows is often referred to as **discounting**. Thus, we say that we have discounted the future value of $363 to its present value of $300. The interest rate used to discount the future cash flow is the **discount rate**. The expression $1/(1 + i)^n$ in the present value equation is the **discount factor**. By letting the discount factor, called df, equal $1/(1 + i)^n$, the present value equation can be expressed as $P = F(df)$. To simplify the computation of present value, a table of discount factors is given for various combinations of i and n [refer to Exhibit 24B-1 (p. 1216) in Appendix 24B]. For example, the discount factor for $i = 10$ percent and $n = 2$ is 0.82645 (go to the 10 percent column of the table and move down to the second row). With the discount factor, the present value of $363 is computed as follows:

$$P = F(df)$$
$$= \$363 \times 0.82645$$
$$= \$300 \text{ (rounded)}$$

Present Value of an Uneven Series of Cash Flows

Exhibit 24B-1 (p. 1216) can be used to compute the present value of any future cash flow or series of future cash flows. A series of future cash flows is called an **annuity**. The present value of an annuity is found by computing the present value of each future cash flow and then summing these values. For example, suppose that an investment is expected to produce the following annual cash flows: $110, $121, and $133.10. Assuming a discount rate of 10 percent, the present value of this series of cash flows is computed in Exhibit 24A-1.

Exhibit 24A-1

Present Value of an Uneven Series of Cash Flows

Year	Cash Receipt	Discount Factor	Present Value*
1	$110.00	0.90909	$100.00
2	121.00	0.82645	100.00
3	133.10	0.75131	100.00
		2.48685	$300.00

*Rounded.

Present Value of a Uniform Series of Cash Flows

If the series of cash flows is even, the computation of the annuity's present value is simplified. For example, assume that an investment is expected to return $100 per year for three years. Using Exhibit 24B-1 and assuming a discount rate of 10 percent, the present value of the annuity is computed in Exhibit 24A-2.

Exhibit 24A-2

Present Value of an Annuity

Year	Cash Receipt*	Discount Factor	Present Value*
1	$100	0.90909	$ 90.91
2	100	0.82645	82.65
3	100	0.75131	75.13
		2.48685	$248.69

*The annual cash flow of $100 can be multiplied by the sum of the discount factors (2.48685) to obtain the present value of the uniform series ($248.69).

As with the uneven series of cash flows, the present value in Exhibit 24A-2 was computed by calculating the present value of each cash flow separately and then summing them. However, in the case of an annuity displaying uniform cash flows, the computations can be reduced from three to one as described in the footnote to the exhibit. The sum of the individual discount factors can be thought of as a discount factor for an annuity of uniform cash flows. A table of discount factors that can be used for an annuity of uniform cash flows is available in Exhibit 24B-2.

APPENDIX 24B: PRESENT VALUE TABLES

The present value tables are found on pages 1216 and 1217.

Exhibit 24B-1
Present Value of a Single Amount*

n/i	1%	2%	3%	4%	5%	6%	7%	8%	9%	10%	12%	14%	16%	18%	20%	25%	30%
1	0.99010	0.98039	0.97087	0.96154	0.95238	0.94340	0.93458	0.92593	0.91743	0.90909	0.89286	0.87719	0.86207	0.84746	0.83333	0.80000	0.76923
2	0.98030	0.96117	0.94260	0.92456	0.90703	0.89000	0.87344	0.85734	0.84168	0.82645	0.79719	0.76947	0.74316	0.71818	0.69444	0.64000	0.59172
3	0.97059	0.94232	0.91514	0.88900	0.86384	0.83962	0.81630	0.79383	0.77218	0.75131	0.71178	0.67497	0.64066	0.60863	0.57870	0.51200	0.45517
4	0.96098	0.92385	0.88849	0.85480	0.82270	0.79209	0.76290	0.73503	0.70843	0.68301	0.63552	0.59208	0.55229	0.51579	0.48225	0.40960	0.35013
5	0.95147	0.90573	0.86261	0.82193	0.78353	0.74726	0.71299	0.68058	0.64993	0.62092	0.56743	0.51937	0.47611	0.43711	0.40188	0.32768	0.26933
6	0.94205	0.88797	0.83748	0.79031	0.74622	0.70496	0.66634	0.63017	0.59627	0.56447	0.50663	0.45559	0.41044	0.37043	0.33490	0.26214	0.20718
7	0.93272	0.87056	0.81309	0.75992	0.71068	0.66506	0.62275	0.58349	0.54703	0.51316	0.45235	0.39964	0.35383	0.31393	0.27908	0.20972	0.15937
8	0.92348	0.85349	0.78941	0.73069	0.67684	0.62741	0.58201	0.54027	0.50187	0.46651	0.40388	0.35056	0.30503	0.26604	0.23257	0.16777	0.12259
9	0.91434	0.83676	0.76642	0.70259	0.64461	0.59190	0.54393	0.50025	0.46043	0.42410	0.36061	0.30751	0.26295	0.22546	0.19381	0.13422	0.09430
10	0.90529	0.82035	0.74409	0.67556	0.61391	0.55839	0.50835	0.46319	0.42241	0.38554	0.32197	0.26974	0.22668	0.19106	0.16151	0.10737	0.07254
11	0.89632	0.80426	0.72242	0.64958	0.58468	0.52679	0.47509	0.42888	0.38753	0.35049	0.28748	0.23662	0.19542	0.16192	0.13459	0.08590	0.05580
12	0.88745	0.78849	0.70138	0.62460	0.55684	0.49697	0.44401	0.39711	0.35553	0.31863	0.25668	0.20756	0.16846	0.13722	0.11216	0.06872	0.04292
13	0.87866	0.77303	0.68095	0.60057	0.53032	0.46884	0.41496	0.36770	0.32618	0.28966	0.22917	0.18207	0.14523	0.11629	0.09346	0.05498	0.03302
14	0.86996	0.75788	0.66112	0.57748	0.50507	0.44230	0.38782	0.34046	0.29925	0.26333	0.20462	0.15971	0.12520	0.09855	0.07789	0.04398	0.02540
15	0.86135	0.74301	0.64186	0.55526	0.48102	0.41727	0.36245	0.31524	0.27454	0.23939	0.18270	0.14010	0.10793	0.08352	0.06491	0.03518	0.01954
16	0.85282	0.72845	0.62317	0.53391	0.45811	0.39365	0.33873	0.29189	0.25187	0.21763	0.16312	0.12289	0.09304	0.07078	0.05409	0.02815	0.01503
17	0.84438	0.71416	0.60502	0.51337	0.43630	0.37136	0.31657	0.27027	0.23107	0.19784	0.14564	0.10780	0.08021	0.05998	0.04507	0.02252	0.01156
18	0.83602	0.70016	0.58739	0.49363	0.41552	0.35034	0.29586	0.25025	0.21199	0.17986	0.13004	0.09456	0.06914	0.05083	0.03756	0.01801	0.00889
19	0.82774	0.68643	0.57029	0.47464	0.39573	0.33051	0.27651	0.23171	0.19449	0.16351	0.11611	0.08295	0.05961	0.04308	0.03130	0.01441	0.00684
20	0.81954	0.67297	0.55368	0.45639	0.37689	0.31180	0.25842	0.21455	0.17843	0.14864	0.10367	0.07276	0.05139	0.03651	0.02608	0.01153	0.00526
21	0.81143	0.65978	0.53755	0.43883	0.35894	0.29416	0.24151	0.19866	0.16370	0.13513	0.09256	0.06383	0.04430	0.03094	0.02174	0.00922	0.00405
22	0.80340	0.64684	0.52189	0.42196	0.34185	0.27751	0.22571	0.18394	0.15018	0.12285	0.08264	0.05599	0.03819	0.02622	0.01811	0.00738	0.00311
23	0.79544	0.63416	0.50669	0.40573	0.32557	0.26180	0.21095	0.17032	0.13778	0.11168	0.07379	0.04911	0.03292	0.02222	0.01509	0.00590	0.00239
24	0.78757	0.62172	0.49193	0.39012	0.31007	0.24698	0.19715	0.15770	0.12640	0.10153	0.06588	0.04308	0.02838	0.01883	0.01258	0.00472	0.00184
25	0.77977	0.60953	0.47761	0.37512	0.29530	0.23300	0.18425	0.14602	0.11597	0.09230	0.05882	0.03779	0.02447	0.01596	0.01048	0.00378	0.00142
26	0.77205	0.59758	0.46369	0.36069	0.28124	0.21981	0.17220	0.13520	0.10639	0.08391	0.05252	0.03315	0.02109	0.01352	0.00874	0.00302	0.00109
27	0.76440	0.58586	0.45019	0.34682	0.26785	0.20737	0.16093	0.12519	0.09761	0.07628	0.04689	0.02908	0.01818	0.01146	0.00728	0.00242	0.00084
28	0.75684	0.57437	0.43708	0.33348	0.25509	0.19563	0.15040	0.11591	0.08955	0.06934	0.04187	0.02551	0.01567	0.00971	0.00607	0.00193	0.00065
29	0.74934	0.56311	0.42435	0.32065	0.24295	0.18456	0.14056	0.10733	0.08215	0.06304	0.03738	0.02237	0.01351	0.00823	0.00506	0.00155	0.00050
30	0.74192	0.55207	0.41199	0.30832	0.23138	0.17411	0.13137	0.09938	0.07537	0.05731	0.03338	0.01963	0.01165	0.00697	0.00421	0.00124	0.00038

*$P_n = A/(1 + i)^n$

Exhibit 24B-2   Present Value of an Annuity*

n/i	1%	2%	3%	4%	5%	6%	7%	8%	9%	10%	12%	14%	16%	18%	20%	25%	30%
1	0.99010	0.98039	0.97087	0.96154	0.95238	0.94340	0.93458	0.92593	0.91743	0.90909	0.89286	0.87719	0.86207	0.84746	0.83333	0.80000	0.76923
2	1.97040	1.94156	1.91347	1.88609	1.85941	1.83339	1.80802	1.78326	1.75911	1.73554	1.69005	1.64666	1.60523	1.56564	1.52778	1.44000	1.36095
3	2.94099	2.88388	2.82861	2.77509	2.72325	2.67301	2.62432	2.57710	2.53129	2.48685	2.40183	2.32163	2.24589	2.17427	2.10648	1.95200	1.81611
4	3.90197	3.80773	3.71710	3.62990	3.54595	3.46511	3.38721	3.31213	3.23972	3.16987	3.03735	2.91371	2.79818	2.69006	2.58873	2.36160	2.16624
5	4.85343	4.71346	4.57971	4.45182	4.32948	4.21236	4.10020	3.99271	3.88965	3.79079	3.60478	3.43308	3.27429	3.12717	2.99061	2.68928	2.43557
6	5.79548	5.60143	5.41719	5.24214	5.07569	4.91732	4.76654	4.62288	4.48592	4.35526	4.11141	3.88867	3.68474	3.49760	3.32551	2.95142	2.64275
7	6.72819	6.47199	6.23028	6.00205	5.78637	5.58238	5.38929	5.20637	5.03295	4.86842	4.56376	4.28830	4.03857	3.81153	3.60459	3.16114	2.80211
8	7.65168	7.32548	7.01969	6.73274	6.46321	6.20979	5.97130	5.74664	5.53482	5.33493	4.96764	4.63886	4.34359	4.07757	3.83716	3.32891	2.92470
9	8.56602	8.16224	7.78611	7.43533	7.10782	6.80169	6.51523	6.24689	5.99525	5.75902	5.32825	4.94637	4.60654	4.30302	4.03097	3.46313	3.01900
10	9.47130	8.98259	8.53020	8.11090	7.72173	7.36009	7.02358	6.71008	6.41766	6.14457	5.65022	5.21612	4.83323	4.49409	4.19247	3.57050	3.09154
11	10.36763	9.78685	9.25262	8.76048	8.30641	7.88687	7.49867	7.13896	6.80519	6.49506	5.93770	5.45273	5.02864	4.65601	4.32706	3.65640	3.14734
12	11.25508	10.57534	9.95400	9.38507	8.86325	8.38384	7.94269	7.53608	7.16073	6.81369	6.19437	5.66029	5.19711	4.79322	4.43922	3.72512	3.19026
13	12.13374	11.34837	10.63496	9.98565	9.39357	8.85268	8.35765	7.90378	7.48690	7.10336	6.42355	5.84236	5.34233	4.90951	4.53268	3.78010	3.22328
14	13.00370	12.10625	11.29607	10.56312	9.89864	9.29498	8.74547	8.24424	7.78615	7.36669	6.62817	6.00207	5.46753	5.00806	4.61057	3.82408	3.24867
15	13.86505	12.84926	11.93794	11.11839	10.37966	9.71225	9.10791	8.55948	8.06069	7.60608	6.81086	6.14217	5.57546	5.09158	4.67547	3.85926	3.26821
16	14.71787	13.57771	12.56110	11.65230	10.83777	10.10590	9.44665	8.85137	8.31256	7.82371	6.97399	6.26506	5.66850	5.16235	4.72956	3.88741	3.28324
17	15.56225	14.29187	13.16612	12.16567	11.27407	10.47726	9.76322	9.12164	8.54363	8.02155	7.11963	6.37286	5.74870	5.22233	4.77463	3.90993	3.29480
18	16.39827	14.99203	13.75351	12.65930	11.68959	10.82760	10.05909	9.37189	8.75563	8.20141	7.24967	6.46742	5.81785	5.27316	4.81219	3.92794	3.30369
19	17.22601	15.67846	14.32380	13.13394	12.08532	11.15812	10.33560	9.60360	8.95011	8.36492	7.36578	6.55037	5.87746	5.31624	4.84350	3.94235	3.31053
20	18.04555	16.35143	14.87747	13.59033	12.46221	11.46992	10.59401	9.81815	9.12855	8.51356	7.46944	6.62313	5.92884	5.35275	4.86958	3.95388	3.31579
21	18.85698	17.01121	15.41502	14.02916	12.82115	11.76408	10.83553	10.01680	9.29224	8.64869	7.56200	6.68696	5.97314	5.38368	4.89132	3.96311	3.31984
22	19.66038	17.65805	15.93692	14.45112	13.16300	12.04158	11.06124	10.20074	9.44243	8.77154	7.64465	6.74294	6.01133	5.40990	4.90943	3.97049	3.32296
23	20.45582	18.29220	16.44361	14.85684	13.48857	12.30338	11.27219	10.37106	9.58021	8.88322	7.71843	6.79206	6.04425	5.43212	4.92453	3.97639	3.32535
24	21.24339	18.91393	16.93554	15.24696	13.79864	12.55036	11.46933	10.52876	9.70661	8.98474	7.78432	6.83514	6.07263	5.45095	4.93710	3.98111	3.32719
25	22.02316	19.52346	17.41315	15.62208	14.09394	12.78336	11.65358	10.67478	9.82258	9.07704	7.84314	6.87293	6.09709	5.46691	4.94759	3.98489	3.32861
26	22.79520	20.12104	17.87684	15.98277	14.37519	13.00317	11.82578	10.80998	9.92897	9.16095	7.89566	6.90608	6.11818	5.48043	4.95632	3.98791	3.32970
27	23.55961	20.70690	18.32703	16.32959	14.64303	13.21053	11.98671	10.93516	10.02658	9.23722	7.94255	6.93515	6.13636	5.49189	4.96360	3.99033	3.33054
28	24.31644	21.28127	18.76411	16.66306	14.89813	13.40616	12.13711	11.05108	10.11613	9.30657	7.98442	6.96066	6.15204	5.50160	4.96967	3.99226	3.33118
29	25.06579	21.84438	19.18845	16.98371	15.14107	13.59072	12.27767	11.15841	10.19828	9.36961	8.02181	6.98304	6.16555	5.50983	4.97472	3.99381	3.33168
30	25.80771	22.39646	19.60044	17.29203	15.37245	13.76483	12.40904	11.25778	10.27365	9.42691	8.05518	7.00266	6.17720	5.51681	4.97894	3.99505	3.33206

*$P_n = [1/i][1 - 1/(1 + i)^n]$

SUMMARY OF LEARNING OBJECTIVES

LO1. Explain the meaning of *capital investment decisions*, and distinguish between independent and mutually exclusive capital investment decisions.

- Capital investment decisions are concerned with the acquisition of long-term assets and usually involve a significant outlay of funds.
- The two types of capital investment projects are independent and mutually exclusive.
- Independent projects are projects that, whether accepted or rejected, do not affect the cash flows of other projects.
- Mutually exclusive projects are projects that, if accepted, preclude the acceptance of all other competing projects.

LO2. Compute the payback period and accounting rate of return for a proposed investment, and explain their roles in capital investment decisions.

- Managers make capital investment decisions by using formal models to decide whether to accept or reject proposed projects.
- These decision models are classified as nondiscounting and discounting, depending on whether they address the question of the time value of money.
- The two nondiscounting models are the payback period and the ARR.
- The payback period is the time required for a firm to recover its initial investment. For even cash flows, it is calculated by dividing the investment by the annual cash flow. For uneven cash flows, the cash flows are summed until the investment is recovered. If only a fraction of a year is needed, then it is assumed that the cash flows occur evenly within each year.
- The payback period ignores the time value of money and the profitability of projects because it does not consider the cash inflows available beyond the payback period. The payback period is useful for assessing and controlling risk, minimizing the impact of an investment on a firm's liquidity, and controlling the risk of obsolescence.
- The ARR is computed by dividing the average income expected from an investment by either the original or average investment.
- Unlike the payback period, the ARR does consider the profitability of a project; however, it ignores the time value of money.
- The ARR may be useful to managers for screening new investments to ensure that certain accounting ratios are not adversely affected (specifically, accounting ratios that may be monitored to ensure compliance with debt covenants).

LO3. Use net present value analysis for capital investment decisions involving independent projects.

- NPV is the difference between the present value of future cash flows and the initial investment outlay.
- To use the NPV model, a required rate of return must be identified (usually the cost of capital). The NPV method uses the required rate of return to compute the present value of a project's cash inflows and outflows.
- If the present value of the inflows is greater than the present value of the outflows, then the NPV is greater than zero, and the project is profitable. If the NPV is less than zero, then the project is not profitable and should be rejected.

LO4. Use the internal rate of return to assess the acceptability of independent projects.

- The IRR is computed by finding the interest rate that equates the present value of a project's cash inflows with the present value of its cash outflows.
- If the IRR is greater than the required rate of return (cost of capital), then the project is acceptable; if the IRR is less than the required rate of return, then the project should be rejected.

LO5.   Explain the role and value of postaudits.

- Postauditing of capital projects is an important step in capital investment.
- Postaudits evaluate the actual performance of a project in relation to its expected performance.
- A postaudit may lead to corrective action to improve the performance of the project or to abandon it.
- Postaudits also serve as an incentive for managers to make capital investment decisions prudently.

LO6.   Explain why net present value is better than internal rate of return for capital investment decisions involving mutually exclusive projects.

- In evaluating mutually exclusive or competing projects, managers have a choice of using NPV or IRR.
- When choosing among competing projects, the NPV model correctly identifies the best investment alternative.
- IRR may choose an inferior project. Thus, since NPV always provides the correct signal, it should be used.

LO7.   (Appendix 24A) Explain the relationship between current and future dollars.

- The value of an investment at the end of its life is called its future value.
- Present value is the amount that must be invested now to yield some future value.
- Present value is computed by discounting the future value using a discount rate. The discount rate is the interest rate used to discount the future amount.
- An annuity is a series of future cash flows. If the annuity is uneven, then each future cash flow must be discounted using individual discount rates (the present value for each cash flow is calculated separately and then summed). For even cash flows, a single discount rate, which is the sum of each discount rate for each cash flow, can be used.

SUMMARY OF IMPORTANT EQUATIONS

1. $\text{Payback period} = \dfrac{\text{Original investment}}{\text{Annual cash flow}}$

2. $\text{Accounting rate of return} = \dfrac{\text{Average income}}{\text{Initial investment}}$

3. $NPV = \left[\sum CF_t / (1+i)^t\right] - I$

   $ = \left[\sum CF_t df_t\right]$

   $ = P - I$

4. $I = \sum [CF_t / (1+i)^t]$

5. $I = CF(df)$

6. $df = I/CF$

   $ = \dfrac{\text{Investment}}{\text{Annual cash flow}}$

Appendix 24A:

7. $F = P(1+i)$

8. $F = P(1+i)^n$

9. $P = F/(1+i)^n$

CORNERSTONES
FOR CHAPTER 24

CORNERSTONE 24-1   Calculating payback (p. 1198)

CORNERSTONE 24-2   Calculating the accounting rate of return (p. 1200)

CORNERSTONE 24-3   Assessing cash flows and calculating net present value (p. 1202)

CORNERSTONE 24-4   Calculating internal rate of return with uniform cash flows (p. 1205)

CORNERSTONE 24-5   Calculating net present value and internal rate of return for mutually exclusive projects (p. 1210)

KEY TERMS

Accounting rate of return (ARR) (p. 1199)
Annuity (p. 1215)
Capital budgeting (p. 1196)
Capital investment decisions (p. 1196)
Compounding of interest (p. 1214)
Cost of capital (p. 1201)
Discount factor (p. 1214)
Discount rate (p. 1214)
Discounted cash flows (p. 1201)
Discounting models (p. 1197)
Discounting (p. 1214)

Future value (p. 1214)
Independent projects (p. 1196)
Internal rate of return (IRR) (p. 1204)
Mutually exclusive projects (p. 1196)
Net present value (NPV) (p. 1201)
Nondiscounting models (p. 1197)
Payback period (p. 1197)
Postaudit (p. 1207)
Present value (p. 1214)
Required rate of return (p. 1201)

REVIEW PROBLEMS

I. Basics of Capital Investment

Kenn Day, manager of Day Laboratory, is investigating the possibility of acquiring some new test equipment. The equipment requires an initial outlay of $300,000. To raise the capital, Kenn will sell stock valued at $200,000 (the stock pays dividends of $24,000 per year) and borrow $100,000. The loan for $100,000 would carry an interest rate of 6 percent. Kenn figures that his weighted average cost of capital is 10 percent $[(2/3 \times 0.12) + (1/3 \times 0.06)]$. This weighted cost of capital is the discount rate that will be used for capital investment decisions.

Kenn estimates that the new test equipment will produce a cash inflow of $50,000 per year. Kenn expects the equipment to last for 20 years.

Required:

1. Compute the payback period.

2. Assuming that depreciation is $14,000 per year, compute the ARR (on total investment).

3. Compute the NPV of the test equipment.

4. Compute the IRR of the test equipment.

5. Should Kenn buy the equipment?

Solution:

1. The payback period is $300,000/$50,000, or six years.

2. The ARR is ($50,000 − $14,000)/$300,000, or 12 percent.

3. From Exhibit 24B-2 (p. 1217), the discount factor for an annuity with i at 10 percent and n at 20 years is 8.51356. Thus, the NPV is (8.51356 × $50,000) − $300,000, or $125,678.

4. The discount factor associated with the IRR is 6.00000 ($300,000/$50,000). From Exhibit 24B-2, the IRR is between 14 and 16 percent (using the row corresponding to Period 20).

5. Since the NPV is positive and the IRR is greater than Kenn's cost of capital, the test equipment is a sound investment. This, of course, assumes that the cash flow projections are accurate.

II. Capital Investments with Competing Projects

A hospital is considering the possibility of two new purchases: new x-ray equipment and new biopsy equipment. Each project would require an investment of $750,000. The expected life for each is five years with no expected salvage value. The net cash inflows associated with the two independent projects are as follows:

Year	X-Ray Equipment	Biopsy Equipment
1	$375,000	$ 75,000
2	150,000	75,000
3	300,000	525,000
4	150,000	600,000
5	75,000	675,000

Required:

1. Compute the net present value of each project, assuming a required rate of 12 percent.

2. Compute the payback period for each project. Assume that the manager of the hospital accepts only projects with a payback period of three years or less. Offer some reasons why this may be a rational strategy even though the NPV computed in Requirement 1 may indicate otherwise.

Solution:

1. X-ray equipment:

Year	Cash Flow	Discount Factor	Present Value
0	$(750,000)	1.00000	$(750,000)
1	375,000	0.89286	334,823
2	150,000	0.79719	119,579
3	300,000	0.71178	213,534
4	150,000	0.63552	95,328
5	75,000	0.56743	42,557
NPV			$ 55,821

Biopsy equipment:

Year	Cash Flow	Discount Factor	Present Value
0	$(750,000)	1.00000	$(750,000)
1	75,000	0.89286	66,965
2	75,000	0.79719	59,789
3	525,000	0.71178	373,685
4	600,000	0.63552	381,312
5	675,000	0.56743	383,015
NPV			$ 514,766

2. X-ray equipment:

Payback period =	$375,000	1.00 year
	150,000	1.00
	225,000	0.75 ($225,000/$300,000)
	$750,000	2.75 years

Biopsy equipment:

Payback period =	$ 75,000	1.00 year
	75,000	1.00
	525,000	1.00
	75,000	0.13 ($75,000/$600,000)
	$750,000	3.13 years

This might be a reasonable strategy because payback is a rough measure of risk. The assumption is that the longer it takes a project to pay for itself, the riskier the project is. Other reasons might be that the firm might have liquidity problems, the cash flows might be risky, or there might be a high risk of obsolescence.

DISCUSSION QUESTIONS

1. Explain the difference between independent projects and mutually exclusive projects.
2. Explain why the timing and quantity of cash flows are important in capital investment decisions.
3. The time value of money is ignored by the payback period and the ARR. Explain why this is a major deficiency in these two models.
4. What is the payback period? Compute the payback period for an investment requiring an initial outlay of $80,000 with expected annual cash inflows of $30,000.
5. Name and discuss three possible reasons that the payback period is used to help make capital investment decisions.
6. What is the accounting rate of return? Compute the ARR for an investment that requires an initial outlay of $300,000 and promises an average net income of $100,000.
7. The NPV is the same as the profit of a project expressed in present dollars. Do you agree? Explain.
8. Explain the relationship between NPV and a firm's value.
9. What is the cost of capital? What role does it play in capital investment decisions?
10. What is the role that the required rate of return plays in the NPV model? In the IRR model?
11. Explain how the NPV is used to determine whether a project should be accepted or rejected.
12. The IRR is the true or actual rate of return being earned by the project. Do you agree or disagree? Discuss.
13. Explain what a postaudit is and how it can provide useful input for future capital investment decisions, especially those involving advanced technology.
14. Explain why NPV is generally preferred over IRR when choosing among competing or mutually exclusive projects. Why would managers continue to use IRR to choose among mutually exclusive projects?
15. Suppose that a firm must choose between two mutually exclusive projects, both of which have negative NPVs. Explain how a firm can legitimately choose between two such projects.

MULTIPLE-CHOICE EXERCISES

24-1 Capital investments should

a. always produce an increase in market share.
b. only be analyzed using the ARR.
c. earn back their original capital outlay.
d. always be done using a payback criterion.
e. do none of these.

24-2 To make a capital investment decision, a manager must

a. estimate the quantity and timing of cash flows.
b. assess the risk of the investment.
c. consider the impact of the investment on the firm's profits.
d. choose a decision criterion to assess viability of the investment (such as payback period or NPV).
e. do all of these.

24-3 Mutually exclusive capital budgeting projects are those that

a. if accepted or rejected do not affect the cash flows of other projects.
b. if accepted will produce a negative NPV.
c. if rejected preclude the acceptance of all other competing projects.
d. if accepted preclude the acceptance of all other competing projects.
e. if rejected imply that all other competing projects have a positive NPV.

24-4 An investment of $1,000 produces a net annual cash inflow of $2,000 for each of five years. What is the payback period?

a. Two years
b. One-half year
c. Unacceptable
d. Three years
e. Cannot be determined

24-5 An investment of $1,000 produces a net cash inflow of $500 in the first year and $750 in the second year. What is the payback period?

a. 1.67 years
b. 0.50 year
c. 2.00 years

d. 1.20 years
e. Cannot be determined

24-6 The payback period suffers from which of the following deficiencies?

a. It is a rough measure of the uncertainty of future cash flows.
b. It helps control the risk of obsolescence.
c. It ignores the uncertainty of future cash flows.
d. It ignores the financial performance of a project beyond the payback period.
e. Both c and d.

24-7 The ARR has one specific advantage *not* possessed by the payback period in that it

a. considers the time value of money.
b. measures the value added by a project.
c. is always an accurate measure of profitability.
d. is more widely accepted by financial managers.
e. considers the profitability of a project beyond the payback period.

24-8 An investment of $1,000 provides an average net income of $400. Depreciation is $40 per year with zero salvage value. The ARR using the original investment is

a. 44 percent.
b. 22 percent.
c. 20 percent.

d. 40 percent.
e. none of these.

24-9 If the NPV is positive, it signals

a. that the initial investment has been recovered.
b. that the required rate of return has been earned.

c. that the value of the firm has decreased.
d. all of these.
e. both a and b.

24-10 NPV measures

a. the profitability of an investment.
b. the change in wealth.
c. the change in firm value.

d. the difference in present value of cash inflows and outflows.
e. all of these.

24-11 NPV is calculated by using

a. the required rate of return.
b. accounting income.
c. the IRR.

d. the future value of cash flows.
e. none of these.

24-12 Using NPV, a project is rejected if it is

a. equal to zero.
b. negative.
c. positive.

d. equal to the required rate of return.
e. greater than the cost of capital.

24-13 If the present value of future cash flows is $4,200 for an investment that requires an outlay of $2,000, the NPV

a. is $200.
b. is $1,000.
c. is $1,200.

d. is $2,200.
e. cannot be determined.

24-14 Assume that an investment of $1,000 produces a future cash flow of $1,000. The discount factor for this future cash flow is 0.80. The NPV is

a. $0.
b. $110.
c. ($200).
d. $911.
e. none of these.

24-15 Which of the following is *not* true regarding the IRR?

a. The IRR is the interest rate that sets the present value of a project's cash inflows equal to the present value of the project's cost.
b. The IRR is the interest rate that sets the NPV equal to zero.
c. The popularity of IRR may be attributable to the fact that it is a rate of return, a concept that is comfortably used by managers.
d. If the IRR is greater than the required rate of return, then the project is acceptable.
e. The IRR is the most reliable of the capital budgeting methods.

24-16 Using IRR, a project is rejected if the IRR

a. is equal to the required rate of return.
b. is less than the required rate of return.
c. is greater than the cost of capital.
d. is greater than the required rate of return.
e. produces an NPV equal to zero.

24-17 A postaudit

a. is a follow-up analysis of a capital project, once implemented.
b. compares the actual benefits with the estimated benefits.
c. evaluates the overall outcome of the investment.
d. proposes corrective action, if needed.
e. does all of these.

24-18 Postaudits of capital projects are useful because

a. they are not very costly.
b. they have no significant limitations.
c. the assumptions underlying the original analyses are often invalidated by changes in the actual working environment.
d. they help to ensure that resources are used wisely.
e. of all of these.

24-19 For competing projects, NPV is preferred to IRR because

a. maximizing IRR maximizes the wealth of the owners.
b. in the final analysis, relative profitability is what counts.
c. choosing the project with the largest NPV maximizes the wealth of the shareholders.
d. assuming that cash flows are reinvested at the computed IRR is more realistic than assuming that cash flows are reinvested at the required rate of return.
e. of all of the above.

24-20 Assume that there are two competing projects, A and B. Project A has a NPV of $1,000 and an IRR of 15 percent. Project B has an NPV of $800 and an IRR of 20 percent. Which of the following is true?

a. Project A should be chosen because it has a higher NPV.
b. Project B should be chosen because it has a higher IRR.
c. It is not possible to use NPV or IRR to choose between the two projects.
d. Neither project should be chosen.
e. None of these.

CORNERSTONE EXERCISES

OBJECTIVE ❷
CORNERSTONE 24-1

Cornerstone Exercise 24-21 Payback Period

Ventura Manufacturing is considering an investment in a new automated manufacturing system. The new system requires an investment of $3,000,000 and either has (a) even cash flows of $750,000 per year or (b) the following expected annual cash flows: $375,000, $375,000, $1,000,000, $1,000,000, and $250,000.

Required:
Calculate the payback period for each case.

Cornerstone Exercise 24-22 Accounting Rate of Return

OBJECTIVE ❷
CORNERSTONE 24-2

Monson Company invested $15,000,000 in a new product line. The life cycle of the product is projected to be seven years with the following net income stream: $300,000, $900,000, $1,000,000, $1,800,000, $2,400,000, $3,800,000, and $2,400,000.

Required:
Calculate the ARR.

Cornerstone Exercise 24-23 Net Present Value

OBJECTIVE ❸
CORNERSTONE 24-3

Holland, Inc., has just completed development of a new cell phone. The new product is expected to produce annual revenues of $1,350,000. Producing the cell phone requires an investment in new equipment, costing $1,440,000. The cell phone has a projected life cycle of five years. After five years, the equipment can be sold for $180,000. Working capital is also expected to increase by $180,000, which Holland will recover by the end of the new product's life cycle. Annual cash operating expenses are estimated at $810,000. The required rate of return is 8 percent.

Required:
1. Prepare a schedule of the projected annual cash flows.
2. Calculate the NPV using only discount factors from Exhibit 24B-1 (p. 1216).
3. Calculate the NPV using discount factors from both Exhibit 24B-1 and 24B-2 (p. 1217).

Cornerstone Exercise 24-24 Internal Rate of Return

OBJECTIVE ❹
CORNERSTONE 24-4

Jardin Company produces a variety of gardening tools and aids. The company is examining the possibility of investing in a new production system that will reduce the costs of the current system. The new system will require a cash investment of $2,303,600 and will produce net cash savings of $400,000 per year. The system has a projected life of nine years.

Required:
Calculate the IRR for the new production system.

Cornerstone Exercise 24-25 NPV and IRR, Mutually Exclusive Projects

OBJECTIVE ❻
CORNERSTONE 24-5

Hardy Inc. intends to invest in one of two competing types of computer-aided manufacturing equipment: CAM X and CAM Y. Both CAM X and CAM Y models have a project life of 10 years. The purchase price of the CAM X model is $3,000,000, and it has a net annual after-tax cash inflow of $750,000. The CAM Y model is more expensive, selling for $3,500,000, but it will produce a net annual after-tax cash inflow of $875,000. The cost of capital for the company is 10 percent.

Required:
1. Calculate the NPV for each project. Which model would you recommend?
2. Calculate the IRR for each project. Which model would you recommend?

EXERCISES

Exercise 24-26 Payback Period

OBJECTIVE ❶ ❷

Each of the following scenarios is independent. Assume that all cash flows are after-tax cash flows.

a. Colby Hepworth has just invested $400,000 in a book and video store. She expects to receive a cash income of $120,000 per year from the investment.
b. Kylie Sorensen has just invested $1,400,000 in a new biomedical technology. She expects to receive the following cash flows over the next five years: $350,000, $490,000, $700,000, $420,000, and $280,000.
c. Carsen Nabors invested in a project that has a payback period of four years. The project brings in $960,000 per year.
d. Rahn Booth invested $1,300,000 in a project that pays him an even amount per year for five years. The payback period is 2.5 years.

(Continued)

Required:
1. What is the payback period for Colby?
2. What is the payback period for Kylie?
3. How much did Carsen invest in the project?
4. How much cash does Rahn receive each year?

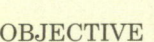

Exercise 24-27 Accounting Rate of Return

Each of the following scenarios is independent. Assume that all cash flows are after-tax cash flows.

a. Cobre Company is considering the purchase of new equipment that will speed up the process for extracting copper. The equipment will cost $3,600,000 and have a life of five years with no expected salvage value. The expected cash flows associated with the project are as follows:

Year	Cash Revenues	Cash Expenses
1	$6,000,000	$4,800,000
2	6,000,000	4,800,000
3	6,000,000	4,800,000
4	6,000,000	4,800,000
5	6,000,000	4,800,000

b. Emily Hansen is considering investing in one of the following two projects. Either project will require an investment of $75,000. The expected cash revenues minus cash expenses for the two projects follow. Assume each project is depreciable.

Year	Project A	Project B
1	$22,500	$22,500
2	30,000	30,000
3	45,000	45,000
4	75,000	22,500
5	75,000	22,500

c. Suppose that a project has an ARR of 30 percent (based on initial investment) and that the average net income of the project is $120,000.

d. Suppose that a project has an ARR of 50 percent and that the investment is $150,000.

Required:
1. Compute the ARR on the new equipment that Cobre Company is considering.
2. **Conceptual Connection:** Which project should Emily Hansen choose based on the ARR? Notice that the payback period is the same for both investments (thus equally preferred). Unlike the payback period, explain why ARR correctly signals that one project should be preferred over the other.
3. How much did the company in Scenario c invest in the project?
4. What is the average net income earned by the project in Scenario d?

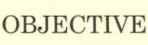

Exercise 24-28 Net Present Value

Each of the following scenarios is independent. Assume that all cash flows are after-tax cash flows.

a. Southward Manufacturing is considering the purchase of a new welding system. The cash benefits will be $400,000 per year. The system costs $2,250,000 and will last 10 years.

b. Kaylin Day is interested in investing in a women's specialty shop. The cost of the investment is $180,000. She estimates that the return from owning her own shop will be $35,000 per year. She estimates that the shop will have a useful life of six years.

c. Goates Company calculated the NPV of a project and found it to be $21,300. The project's life was estimated to be eight years. The required rate of return used for the NPV calculation was 10 percent. The project was expected to produce annual after-tax cash flows of $45,000.

Required:
1. Compute the NPV for Southward Manufacturing, assuming a discount rate of 12 percent. Should the company buy the new welding system?

2. **Conceptual Connection:** Assuming a required rate of return of 8 percent, calculate the NPV for Kaylin Day's investment. Should she invest? What if the estimated return was $45,000 per year? Would this affect the decision? What does this tell you about your analysis?

3. What was the required investment for Goates Company's project?

Exercise 24-29 Internal Rate of Return

OBJECTIVE ❶ ❹

ILLUSTRATING
RELATIONSHIPS

Each of the following scenarios is independent. Assume that all cash flows are after-tax cash flows.

a. Cuenca Company is considering the purchase of new equipment that will speed up the process for producing flash drives. The equipment will cost $7,200,000 and have a life of five years with no expected salvage value. The expected cash flows associated with the project follow:

Year	Cash Revenues	Cash Expenses
1	$8,000,000	$6,000,000
2	8,000,000	6,000,000
3	8,000,000	6,000,000
4	8,000,000	6,000,000
5	8,000,000	6,000,000

b. Kathy Shorts is evaluating an investment in an information system that will save $240,000 per year. She estimates that the system will last 10 years. The system will cost $1,248,000. Her company's cost of capital is 10 percent.

c. Elmo Enterprises just announced that a new plant would be built in Helper, Utah. Elmo told its shareholders that the plant has an expected life of 15 years and an expected IRR equal to 25 percent. The cost of building the plant is expected to be $2,880,000.

Required:

1. Calculate the IRR for Cuenca Company. The company's cost of capital is 16 percent. Should the new equipment be purchased?

2. Calculate Kathy Short's IRR. Should she acquire the new system?

3. What should be Elmo Enterprises' expected annual cash flow from the plant?

Exercise 24-30 Net Present Value and Competing Projects

OBJECTIVE ❶ ❻

ILLUSTRATING
RELATIONSHIPS

Wilburton Hospital is investigating the possibility of investing in new dialysis equipment. Two local manufacturers of this equipment are being considered as sources of the equipment. After-tax cash inflows for the two competing projects are as follows:

Year	Puro Equipment	Briggs Equipment
1	$400,000	$150,000
2	350,000	150,000
3	300,000	400,000
4	200,000	500,000
5	150,000	550,000

Both projects require an initial investment of $700,000. In both cases, assume that the equipment has a life of five years with no salvage value.

Required:

1. Assuming a discount rate of 12 percent, compute the net present value of each piece of equipment.

2. A third option has surfaced for equipment purchased from an out-of-state supplier. The cost is also $700,000, but this equipment will produce even cash flows over its five-year life. What must the annual cash flow be for this equipment to be selected over the other two? Assume a 12 percent discount rate.

Exercise 24-31 Payback, Accounting Rate of Return, Net Present Value, Internal Rate of Return

OBJECTIVE ❶❷❸❹

Craig Company wants to buy a numerically controlled (NC) machine to be used in producing specially machined parts for manufacturers of tractors. The outlay required is $640,000. The NC equipment will last five years with no expected salvage value. The expected after-tax cash flows associated with the project follow:

(Continued)

Year	Cash Revenues	Cash Expenses
1	$850,000	$600,000
2	850,000	600,000
3	850,000	600,000
4	850,000	600,000
5	850,000	600,000

Required:
1. Compute the payback period for the NC equipment.
2. Compute the NC equipment's ARR.
3. Compute the investment's NPV, assuming a required rate of return of 10 percent.
4. Compute the investment's IRR.

OBJECTIVE  **Exercise 24-32 Payback, Accounting Rate of Return, Present Value, Net Present Value, Internal Rate of Return**

All scenarios are independent of all other scenarios. Assume that all cash flows are after-tax cash flows.

a. Kambry Day is considering investing in one of the following two projects. Either project will require an investment of $20,000. The expected cash flows for the two projects follow. Assume that each project is depreciable.

Year	Project A	Project B
1	$ 6,000	$ 6,000
2	8,000	8,000
3	10,000	10,000
4	10,000	3,000
5	10,000	3,000

b. Wilma Golding is retiring and has the option to take her retirement as a lump sum of $450,000 or to receive $30,000 per year for 20 years. Wilma's required rate of return is 6 percent.

c. David Booth is interested in investing in some tools and equipment so that he can do independent drywalling. The cost of the tools and equipment is $30,000. He estimates that the return from owning his own equipment will be $9,000 per year. The tools and equipment will last six years.

d. Patsy Folson is evaluating what appears to be an attractive opportunity. She is currently the owner of a small manufacturing company and has the opportunity to acquire another small company's equipment that would provide production of a part currently purchased externally. She estimates that the savings from internal production will be $75,000 per year. She estimates that the equipment will last 10 years. The owner is asking $400,000 for the equipment. Her company's cost of capital is 8 percent.

Required:
1. **Conceptual Connection:** What is the payback period for each of Kambry Day's projects? If rapid payback is important, which project should be chosen? Which would you choose?
2. **Conceptual Connection:** Which of Kambry's projects should be chosen based on the ARR? Explain why the ARR performs better than the payback period in this setting.
3. Assuming that Wilma Golding will live for another 20 years, should she take the lump sum or the annuity?
4. Assuming a required rate of return of 8 percent for David Booth, calculate the NPV of the investment. Should David invest?
5. Calculate the IRR for Patsy Folson's project. Should Patsy acquire the equipment?

OBJECTIVE ❸ **Exercise 24-33 Net Present Value, Basic Concepts**

Tree Company is considering an investment that requires an outlay of $240,000 and promises an after-tax cash inflow one year from now of $277,200. The company's cost of capital is 10 percent.

Required:

1. Break the $277,200 future cash inflow into three components: (a) the return of the original investment, (b) the cost of capital, and (c) the profit earned on the investment. Now compute the present value of the profit earned on the investment.
2. **Conceptual Connection:** Compute the NPV of the investment. Compare this with the present value of the profit computed in Requirement 1. What does this tell you about the meaning of NPV?

Exercise 24-34 Solving for Unknowns

OBJECTIVE

Each of the following scenarios are independent. Assume that all cash flows are after-tax cash flows.

a. Thomas Company is investing $120,000 in a project that will yield a uniform series of cash inflows over the next four years.
b. Video Repair has decided to invest in some new electronic equipment. The equipment will have a three-year life and will produce a uniform series of cash savings. The NPV of the equipment is $1,750, using a discount rate of 8 percent. The IRR is 12 percent.
c. A new lathe costing $60,096 will produce savings of $12,000 per year.
d. The NPV of a project is $3,927. The project has a life of four years and produces the following cash flows:

Year 1	$10,000	Year 3	$15,000
Year 2	$12,000	Year 4	?

The cost of the project is two times the cash flow produced in Year 4. The discount rate is 10 percent.

Required:

1. If the internal rate of return is 14 percent for Thomas Company, how much cash inflow per year can be expected?
2. Determine the investment and the amount of cash savings realized each year for Video Repair.
3. For Scenario c, how many years must the lathe last if an IRR of 18 percent is realized?
4. For Scenario d, find the cost of the project and the cash flow for Year 4.

Exercise 24-35 Net Present Value versus Internal Rate of Return

OBJECTIVE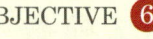

Skiba Company is thinking about two different modifications to its current manufacturing process. The after-tax cash flows associated with the two investments follow:

Year	Project I	Project II
0	$(100,000)	$(100,000)
1	—	63,857
2	134,560	63,857

Skiba's cost of capital is 10 percent.

Required:

1. Compute the NPV and the IRR for each investment.
2. **Conceptual Connection:** Explain why the project with the larger NPV is the correct choice for Skiba.

PROBLEMS

Problem 24-36 Basic Net Present Value Analysis

OBJECTIVE

James Chesser, process engineer, knows that the acceptance of a new process design will depend on its economic feasibility. The new process is designed to improve environmental performance. On the negative side, the process design requires new equipment and an infusion of working capital. The equipment will cost $400,000, and its cash operating expenses will total $90,000 per year. The equipment will last for seven years but will need a major overhaul costing $40,000 at

(Continued)

the end of the fifth year. At the end of seven years, the equipment will be sold for $32,000. An increase in working capital totaling $40,000 will also be needed at the beginning. This will be recovered at the end of the seven years.

On the positive side, James estimates that the new process will save $180,000 per year in environmental costs (fines and cleanup costs avoided). The cost of capital is 10 percent.

Required:
1. Prepare a schedule of cash flows for the proposed project. (*Note:* Assume that there are no income taxes.)
2. Compute the NPV of the project. Should the new process design be accepted?

OBJECTIVE

Problem 24-37 Net Present Value Analysis

Vernal Communications Company is considering the production and marketing of a communications system that will increase the efficiency of messaging for small businesses or branch offices of large companies. Each unit hooked into the system is assigned a mailbox number, which can be matched to a telephone extension number, providing access to messages 24 hours a day. Up to 20 units can be hooked into the system, allowing the delivery of the same message to as many as 20 people. Personal codes can be used to make messages confidential. Furthermore, messages can be reviewed, recorded, cancelled, replied to, or deleted all during the same message playback. Indicators wired to the telephone blink whenever new messages are present.

To produce this product, a $1.5 million investment in new equipment is required. The equipment will last 10 years but will need major maintenance costing $125,000 at the end of its sixth year. The salvage value of the equipment at the end of 10 years is estimated to be $80,000. If this new system is produced, working capital must also be increased by $75,000. This capital will be restored at the end of the product's 10 year life cycle. Revenues from the sale of the product are estimated at $1.6 million per year. Cash operating expenses are estimated at $1.3 million per year.

Required:
1. Prepare a schedule of cash flows for the proposed project. (*Note:* Assume that there are no income taxes.)
2. Assuming that Vernal's cost of capital is 12 percent, compute the project's NPV. Should the product be produced?

OBJECTIVE

Problem 24-38 Basic Internal Rate of Return Analysis

Megan Murray, owner of Golding Company, was approached by a local dealer of air-conditioning units. The dealer proposed replacing Golding's old cooling system with a modern, more efficient system. The cost of the new system was quoted at $226,000, but it would save $40,000 per year in energy costs. The estimated life of the new system is 10 years, with no salvage value expected. Excited over the possibility of saving $40,000 per year and having a more reliable unit, Megan requested an analysis of the project's economic viability. All capital projects are required to earn at least the firm's cost of capital, which is 8 percent. There are no income taxes.

Required:
1. Calculate the project's IRR. Should the company acquire the new cooling system?
2. Suppose that energy savings are less than claimed. Calculate the minimum annual cash savings that must be realized for the project to earn a rate equal to the firm's cost of capital.
3. Suppose that the life of the new system is overestimated by two years. Repeat Requirements 1 and 2 under this assumption.
4. **Conceptual Connection:** Explain the implications of the answers from Requirements 1, 2, and 3.

OBJECTIVE

Problem 24-39 Net Present Value, Uncertainty

Ondi Airlines is interested in acquiring a new aircraft to service a new route. The route will be from Tulsa to Denver. The aircraft will fly one round-trip daily except for scheduled maintenance days. There are 15 maintenance days scheduled each year. The seating capacity of the aircraft is

150. Flights are expected to be fully booked. The average revenue per passenger per flight (one-way) is $235. Annual operating costs of the aircraft follow:

Fuel	$1,750,000
Flight personnel	750,000
Food and beverages	100,000
Maintenance	550,000
Other	100,000
Total	$3,250,000

The aircraft will cost $120,000,000 and has an expected life of 20 years. The company requires a 12 percent return. Assume there are no income taxes.

Required:

1. Calculate the NPV for the aircraft. Should the company buy it?
2. In discussing the proposal, the marketing manager for the airline believes that the assumption of 100 percent booking is unrealistic. He believes that the booking rate will be somewhere between 70 and 90 percent, with the most likely rate being 80 percent. Recalculate the NPV by using an 80 percent seating capacity. Should the aircraft be purchased?
3. Calculate the average seating rate that would be needed so that NPV will equal zero.
4. **Conceptual Connection:** Suppose that the price per passenger could be increased by 10 percent without any effect on demand. What is the average seating rate now needed to achieve a NPV equal to zero? What would you now recommend?

Problem 24-40 Review of Basic Capital Budgeting Procedures

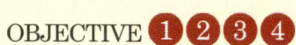

Dr. Whitley Avard, a plastic surgeon, had just returned from a conference in which she learned of a new surgical procedure for removing wrinkles around eyes, reducing the time to perform the normal procedure by 50 percent. Given her patient-load pressures, Dr. Avard is excited to try out the new technique. By decreasing the time spent on eye treatments or procedures, she can increase her total revenues by performing more services within a work period. In order to implement the new procedure, special equipment costing $74,000 is needed. The equipment has an expected life of four years, with a salvage value of $6,000. Dr. Avard estimates that her cash revenues will increase by the following amounts:

Year	Revenue Increases
1	$19,800
2	27,000
3	32,400
4	32,400

She also expects additional cash expenses amounting to $3,000 per year. The cost of capital is 12 percent. Assume that there are no income taxes.

Required:

1. Compute the payback period for the new equipment.
2. Compute the ARR.
3. **Conceptual Connection:** Compute the NPV and IRR for the project. Should Dr. Avard purchase the new equipment? Should she be concerned about payback or the ARR in making this decision?
4. **Conceptual Connection:** Before finalizing her decision, Dr. Avard decided to call two plastic surgeons who have been using the new procedure for the past six months. The conversations revealed a somewhat less glowing report than she received at the conference. The new procedure reduced the time required by about 25 percent rather than the advertised 50 percent. Dr. Avard estimated that the net operating cash flows of the procedure would be cut by one-third because of the extra time and cost involved (salvage value would be unaffected). Using this information, recompute the NPV of the project. What would you now recommend?

Problem 24-41 Net Present Value and Competing Alternatives

Stillwater Designs has been rebuilding Model 100, Model 120, and Model 150 Kicker subwoofers that were returned for warranty action. Customers returning the subwoofers receive a new replacement. The warranty returns are then rebuilt and resold (as seconds). Tent sales are

(Continued)

often used to sell the rebuilt speakers. As part of the rebuilding process, the speakers are demagnetized so that metal pieces and shavings can be removed. A demagnetizing (demag) machine is used to achieve this objective. A product design change has made the most recent Model 150 speakers too tall for the demag machine. They no longer fit in the demag machine.

Stillwater Designs has two alternatives that it is currently considering. First, a new demag machine can be bought that has a different design, eliminating the fit problem. The cost of this machine is $600,000, and it will last five years. Second, Stillwater can keep the current machine and sell the 150 speakers for scrap, using the old demag machine for the Model 100 and 120 speakers only. A rebuilt speaker sells for $295 and costs $274.65 to rebuild (for materials, labor, and overhead cash outlays). The $274.65 outlay includes the annual operating cash effects of the new demag machine. If not rebuilt, the Model 150 speakers can be sold for $4 each as scrap. There are 10,000 Model 150 warranty returns per year. Assume that the required rate of return is 10 percent.

Required:
1. Determine which alternative is the best for Stillwater Designs by using NPV analysis.
2. **Conceptual Connection:** Determine which alternative is best for Stillwater Designs by using an IRR analysis. Explain why NPV analysis is a better approach.

OBJECTIVE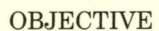

Problem 24-42 Basic Net Present Value Analysis, Competing Projects

Kildare Medical Center, a for-profit hospital, has three investment opportunities: (1) adding a wing for in-patient treatment of substance abuse, (2) adding a pathology laboratory, and (3) expanding the outpatient surgery wing. The initial investments and the net present value for the three alternatives are as follows:

	Substance Abuse	Laboratory	Outpatient Surgery
Investment	$1,500,000	$500,000	$1,000,000
NPV	150,000	140,000	135,000

Although the hospital would like to invest in all three alternatives, only $1.5 million is available.

Required:
1. Rank the projects on the basis of NPV, and allocate the funds in order of this ranking. What project or projects were selected? What is the total NPV realized by the medical center using this approach?
2. **Conceptual Connection:** Assume that the size of the lot on which the hospital is located makes the substance abuse wing and the outpatient surgery wing mutually exclusive. With unlimited capital, which of those two projects would be chosen? With limited capital and the three projects being considered, which projects would be chosen?
3. **Conceptual Connection:** Form a group with two to four other students, and discuss qualitative considerations that should be considered in capital budgeting evaluations. Identify three such considerations.

OBJECTIVE

Problem 24-43 Payback, Net Present Value, Internal Rate of Return, Intangible Benefits, Inflation Adjustment

Foster Company wants to buy a numerically controlled (NC) machine to be used in producing specially machined parts for manufacturers of trenching machines (to replace an existing manual system). The outlay required is $3,500,000. The NC equipment will last five years with no expected salvage value. The expected incremental after-tax cash flows (cash flows of the NC equipment minus cash flows of the old equipment) associated with the project follow:

Year	Cash Benefits	Cash Expenses
1	$3,900,000	$3,000,000
2	3,900,000	3,000,000
3	3,900,000	3,000,000
4	3,900,000	3,000,000
5	3,900,000	3,000,000

Foster has a cost of capital equal to 10 percent. The above cash flows are expressed without any consideration of inflation.

Required:
1. Compute the payback period.
2. Calculate the NPV and IRR of the proposed project.
3. **Conceptual Connection:** Inflation is expected to be 5 percent per year for the next five years. The discount rate of 10 percent is composed of two elements: the real rate and the inflationary element. Since the discount rate has an inflationary component, the projected cash flows should also be adjusted to account for inflation. Make this adjustment, and recalculate the NPV. Comment on the importance of adjusting cash flows for inflationary effects.

Problem 24-44   Cost of Capital, Net Present Value   OBJECTIVE ❸

Leakam Company's product engineering department has developed a new product that has a three-year life cycle. Production of the product requires development of a new process that requires a current $100,000 capital outlay. The $100,000 will be raised by issuing $60,000 of bonds and by selling new stock for $40,000. The $60,000 in bonds will have net (after-tax) interest payments of $3,000 at the end of each of the three years, with the principal being repaid at the end of Year 3. The stock issue carries with it an expectation of a 17.5 percent return, expressed in the form of dividends at the end of each year ($7,000 in dividends is expected for each of the next three years). The sources of capital for this investment represent the same proportion and costs that the company typically has. Finally, the project will produce after-tax cash inflows of $50,000 per year for the next three years.

Required:
1. Compute the cost of capital for the project. (*Hint*: The cost of capital is a weighted average of the two sources of capital where the weights are the proportion of capital from each source.)
2. **Conceptual Connection:** Compute the NPV for the project. Explain why it is not necessary to subtract the interest payments and the dividend payments and appreciation from the inflow of $50,000 in carrying out this computation.

Problem 24-45   Capital Investment, Advanced Manufacturing Environment   OBJECTIVE ❶

"I know that it's the thing to do," insisted Pamela Kincaid, vice president of finance for Colgate Manufacturing. "If we are going to be competitive, we need to build this completely automated plant."

"I'm not so sure," replied Bill Thomas, CEO of Colgate. "The savings from labor reductions and increased productivity are only $4 million per year. The price tag for this factory—and it's a small one—is $45 million. That gives a payback period of more than 11 years. That's a long time to put the company's money at risk."

"Yeah, but you're overlooking the savings that we'll get from the increase in quality," interjected John Simpson, production manager. "With this system, we can decrease our waste and our rework time significantly. Those savings are worth another million dollars per year."

"Another million will only cut the payback to about nine years," retorted Bill. "Ron, you're the marketing manager—do you have any insights?"

"Well, there are other factors to consider, such as service quality and market share. I think that increasing our product quality and improving our delivery service will make us a lot more competitive. I know for a fact that two of our competitors have decided against automation. That'll give us a shot at their customers, provided our product is of higher quality and we can deliver it faster. I estimate that it'll increase our net cash benefits by another $2.4 million."

"Wow! Now that's impressive," Bill exclaimed, nearly convinced. "The payback is now getting down to a reasonable level."

"I agree," said Pamela, "but we do need to be sure that it's a sound investment. I know that estimates for construction of the facility have gone as high as $48 million. I also know that the expected residual value, after the 20 years of service we expect to get, is $5 million. I think I had better see if this project can cover our 14 percent cost of capital."

"Now wait a minute, Pamela," Bill demanded. "You know that I usually insist on a 20 percent rate of return, especially for a project of this magnitude."

Required:
1. Compute the NPV of the project by using the original savings and investment figures. Calculate by using discount rates of 14 percent and 20 percent. Include salvage value in the computation.

(Continued)

2. Compute the NPV of the project using the additional benefits noted by the production and marketing managers. Also, use the original cost estimate of $45 million. Again, calculate for both possible discount rates.
3. Compute the NPV of the project using all estimates of cash flows, including the possible initial outlay of $48 million. Calculate by using discount rates of 14 percent and 20 percent.
4. **Conceptual Connection:** If you were making the decision, what would you do? Explain.

OBJECTIVE **Problem 24-46 Postaudit, Sensitivity Analysis**

Newmarge Products Inc. is evaluating a new design for one of its manufacturing processes. The new design will eliminate the production of a toxic solid residue. The initial cost of the system is estimated at $860,000 and includes computerized equipment, software, and installation. There is no expected salvage value. The new system has a useful life of eight years and is projected to produce cash operating savings of $225,000 per year over the old system (reducing labor costs and costs of processing and disposing of toxic waste). The cost of capital is 16 percent.

Required:
1. Compute the NPV of the new system.
2. One year after implementation, the internal audit staff noted the following about the new system: (1) the cost of acquiring the system was $60,000 more than expected due to higher installation costs, and (2) the annual cost savings were $20,000 less than expected because more labor cost was needed than anticipated. Using the changes in expected costs and benefits, compute the NPV as if this information had been available one year ago. Did the company make the right decision?
3. **Conceptual Connection:** Upon reporting the results mentioned in the postaudit, the marketing manager responded in a memo to the internal auditing department indicating that revenues had increased by $60,000 per year because of increased purchases by environmentally sensitive customers. Describe the effect that this has on the analysis in Requirement 2.
4. **Conceptual Connection:** Why is a postaudit beneficial to a firm?

OBJECTIVE **Problem 24-47 Discount Rates, Automated Manufacturing, Competing Investments**

Patterson Company is considering two competing investments. The first is for a standard piece of production equipment. The second is for computer-aided manufacturing (CAM) equipment. The investment and after-tax operating cash flows follow:

Year	Standard Equipment	CAM Equipment
0	$(500,000)	$(2,000,000)
1	300,000	100,000
2	200,000	200,000
3	100,000	300,000
4	100,000	400,000
5	100,000	400,000
6	100,000	400,000
7	100,000	500,000
8	100,000	1,000,000
9	100,000	1,000,000
10	100,000	1,000,000

Patterson uses a discount rate of 18 percent for all of its investments. Patterson's cost of capital is 10 percent.

Required:
1. Calculate the NPV for each investment by using a discount rate of 18 percent.
2. Calculate the NPV for each investment by using a discount rate of 10 percent.
3. **Conceptual Connection:** Which rate should Patterson use to compute the NPV? Explain.

OBJECTIVE 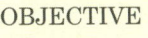 **Problem 24-48 Quality, Market Share, Automated Manufacturing Environment**

Fabre Company, Patterson Company's competitor, is considering the same investments as Patterson. Refer to the data above. Assume that Fabre's cost of capital is 14 percent.

Required:
1. Calculate the NPV of each alternative by using the 14 percent rate.
2. **Conceptual Connection:** Now assume that if the standard equipment is purchased, the competitive position of the firm will deteriorate because of lower quality (relative to competitors who did automate). Marketing estimates that the loss in market share will decrease the projected net cash inflows by 50 percent for years 3 through 10. Recalculate the NPV of the standard equipment given this outcome. What is the decision now? Discuss the importance of assessing the effect of intangible benefits.

CASES

Case 24-49 Capital Investment and Ethical Behavior

OBJECTIVE ❸

Manny Carson, certified management accountant and controller of Wakeman Enterprises, has been given permission to acquire a new computer and software for the company's accounting system. The capital investment analysis showed an NPV of $100,000. However, the initial estimates of acquisition and installation costs were made on the basis of tentative costs without any formal bids. Manny now has two formal bids, one that would allow the firm to meet or beat the original projected NPV and one that would reduce the projected NPV by $50,000. The second bid involves a system that would increase both the initial cost and the operating cost.

Normally, Manny would take the first bid without hesitation. However, Todd Downing, the owner of the firm presenting the second bid, is a close friend. Manny called Todd and explained the situation, offering Todd an opportunity to alter his bid and win the job. Todd thanked Manny and then made a counteroffer.

Todd: Listen, Manny, this job at the original price is the key to a successful year for me. The revenues will help me gain approval for the loan I need for renovation and expansion. If I don't get that loan, I see hard times ahead. The financial stats for loan approval are so marginal that reducing the bid price may blow my chances.

Manny: Losing the bid altogether would be even worse, don't you think?

Todd: True. However, if you award me the job, I'll be able to add personnel. I know that your son is looking for a job, and I can offer him a good salary and a promising future. Additionally, I'll be able to take you and your wife on that vacation to Hawaii that we've been talking about.

Manny: Well, you have a point. My son is having an awful time finding a job, and he has a wife and three kids to support. My wife is tired of having them live with us. She and I could use a vacation. I doubt that the other bidder would make any fuss if we turned it down. Its offices are out of state, after all.

Todd: Out of state? All the more reason to turn it down. Given the state's economy, it seems almost criminal to take business outside. Those are the kind of business decisions that cause problems for people like your son.

Required:

Evaluate the ethical behavior of Manny. Should Manny have called Todd in the first place? What if Todd had agreed to meet the lower bid price—would there have been any problems? Identify the standards of ethical conduct (listed in Chapter 13) that Manny may be violating, if any.

Case 24-50 Payback, Net Present Value, Internal Rate of Return, Effects of Differences in Sales on Project Viability

OBJECTIVE

Shaftel Ready Mix is a processor and supplier of concrete, aggregate, and rock products. The company operates in the intermountain western United States. Currently, Shaftel has 14 cement-processing plants and a labor force of more than 375 employees. With the exception of cement powder, all materials (e.g., aggregates and sand) are produced internally by the company. The demand for concrete and aggregates has been growing steadily nationally. In the West, the growth rate has been above the national average. Because of this growth, Shaftel has more than tripled its gross revenues over the past 10 years.

Of the intermountain states, Arizona has been experiencing the most growth. Processing plants have been added over the past several years, and the company is considering the addition of yet another plant to be located in Scottsdale. A major advantage of another plant in Arizona is the ability to operate year round, a feature not found in states such as Utah and Wyoming.

In setting up the new plant, land would have to be purchased and a small building constructed. Equipment and furniture would not need to be purchased; these items would be transferred from a plant that opened in Wyoming during the oil boom period and closed a few years after the end of that boom. However, the equipment needs some repair and modifications before it can be used. The equipment has a book value of $200,000, and the furniture has a book value of $30,000. Neither has any outside market value. Other costs, such as the installation of a silo, well, electrical hookups, and so on, will be incurred. No salvage value is expected. The summary of the initial investment costs by category is as follows:

Land	$ 20,000
Building	135,000
Equipment:	
Book value	200,000
Modifications	20,000
Furniture (book value)	30,000
Silo	20,000
Well	80,000
Electrical hookups	27,000
General setup	50,000
Total	$582,000

Estimates concerning the operation of the Scottsdale plant follow:

Life of plant and equipment	10 years
Expected annual sales (in cubic yards of cement)	35,000
Selling price (per cubic yard of cement)	$ 45.00
Variable costs (per cubic yard of cement):	
Cement	$ 12.94
Sand/gravel	6.42
Fly ash	1.13
Admixture	1.53
Driver labor	3.24
Mechanics	1.43
Plant operations (batching and cleanup)	1.39
Loader operator	0.50
Truck parts	1.75
Fuel	1.48
Other	3.27
Total variable costs	$ 35.08
Fixed costs (annual):	
Salaries	$135,000
Insurance	75,000
Telephone	5,000
Depreciation	58,200*
Utilities	25,000
Total fixed costs	$298,200

*Straight-line depreciation is calculated by using all initial investment costs over a 10-year period assuming no salvage value.

After reviewing these data, Karl Flemming, vice president of operations, argued against the proposed plant. Karl was concerned because the plant would earn significantly less than the normal 8.3 percent return on sales. All other plants in the company were earning between 7.5 and 8.5 percent on sales. Karl also noted that it would take more than five years to recover the total initial outlay of $582,000. In the past, the company had always insisted that payback be no more than four years. The company's cost of capital is 10 percent. Assume that there are no income taxes.

Required:

1. Prepare a variable-costing income statement for the proposed plant. Compute the ratio of net income to sales. Is Karl correct that the return on sales is significantly lower than the company average?

2. Compute the payback period for the proposed plant. Is Karl right that the payback period is greater than four years? Explain. Suppose you were told that the equipment being transferred from Wyoming could be sold for its book value. Would this affect your answer?

3. Compute the NPV and the IRR for the proposed plant. Would your answer be affected if you were told that the furniture and equipment could be sold for their book values? If so, repeat the analysis with this effect considered.

4. Compute the cubic yards of cement that must be sold for the new plant to break even. Using this break-even volume, compute the NPV and the IRR. Would the investment be acceptable? If so, explain why an investment that promises to do nothing more than break even can be viewed as acceptable.

5. Compute the volume of cement that must be sold for the IRR to equal the firm's cost of capital. Using this volume, compute the firm's expected annual income. Explain this result.

MAKING THE CONNECTION
INTEGRATIVE EXERCISE

Relevant Costing, Cost-Based Pricing, Cost Behavior, and Net Present Value Analysis for NoFat

Chapters	Objectives	Cornerstones
14	14-1	18-2
18	18-1	23-2
23	23-2	23-8
24	23-4	24-3
	24-1	24-5
	24-3	
	24-6	

The purpose of this integrated exercise is to demonstrate how a special sales-relevant decision analysis relies on knowledge of cost behavior (including variable, fixed, and batch costs) and how the adoption of a long-term time horizon can affect the final decision.

Special Sales Offer Relevant Analysis

NoFat manufactures one product, olestra, and sells it to large potato chip manufacturers as the key ingredient in nonfat snack foods, including Ruffles, Lays, Doritos, and Tostitos brand products.[1] For each of the past three years, sales of olestra have been far less than the expected annual volume of 125,000 pounds. Therefore, the company has ended each year with significant unused capacity. Due to a short shelf life, NoFat must sell every pound of olestra that it produces each year. As a result, NoFat's controller, Allyson Ashley, has decided to seek out potential special sales offers from other companies. One company, Patterson Union (PU)—a toxic waste cleanup company—offered to buy 10,000 pounds of olestra from NoFat during December for a price of $2.20 per pound. PU discovered through its research that olestra has proven to be very effective in cleaning up toxic waste locations designated as Superfund Sites by the U.S. Environmental Protection Agency.[2] Allyson was excited, noting that "This is another way to use our expensive olestra plant!"

The annual costs incurred by NoFat to produce and sell 100,000 pounds of olestra are as follows:

Variable costs per pound:	
Direct materials	$1.00
Variable manufacturing overhead	0.75
Sales commissions	0.50
Direct manufacturing labor	0.25
Total fixed costs:	
Advertising	$ 3,000
Customer hotline service	4,000
Machine set-ups	40,000
Plant machinery lease	12,000

In addition, Allyson met with several of NoFat's key production managers and discovered the following information:

- The special order could be produced without incurring any additional marketing or customer service costs.

---

[1] Over 6 billion servings of Olean (the Procter & Gamble brand name for olestra) have been consumed. See further information at the Procter & Gamble website: http://www.olean.com/default.asp?p=products&id=fll.

[2] This exercise is based on facts reported in the business press (e.g., Nanci Hellmich and Bruce Horovitz, "Fat Substitute Olestra Eyed as Hazardous Waste Cleaner: Potato Chips Sales Fall Short," *USA TODAY* (May 31, 2001): 1A).

- NoFat owns the aging plant facility that it uses to manufacture olestra.
- NoFat incurs costs to set up and clean its machines for each production run, or batch, of olestra that it produces. The total set-up costs shown in the previous table represent the production of 20 batches during the year.
- NoFat leases its plant machinery. The lease agreement is negotiated and signed on the first day of each year. NoFat currently leases enough machinery to produce 125,000 pounds of olestra.
- PU requires that an independent quality team inspects any facility from which it makes purchases. The terms of the special sales offer would require NoFat to bear the $1,000 cost of the inspection team.

Required:

1. Conduct a relevant analysis of the special sales offer by calculating the following:

    a. The relevant revenues associated with the special sales offer
    b. The relevant costs associated with the special sales offer
    c. The relevant profit associated with the special sales offer

2. Based solely on financial factors, explain why NoFat should accept or reject PU's special sales offer.

3. Describe at least one qualitative factor that NoFat should consider, in addition to the financial factors, in making its final decision regarding the acceptance or rejection of the special sales offer.

Cost-Based Pricing

Assume for this question that NoFat rejected PU's special sales offer because the $2.20 price suggested by PU was too low. In response to the rejection, PU asked NoFat to determine the price at which it would be willing to accept the special sales offer. For its regular sales, NoFat sets prices by marking up *variable costs* by 10 percent.

4. If Allyson decides to use NoFat's 10 percent mark-up pricing method to set the price for PU's special sales offer,

    a. Calculate the price that NoFat would charge PU for each pound of olestra.
    b. Calculate the relevant profit that NoFat would earn if it set the special sales price by using its mark-up pricing method. (*Hint:* Use the estimate of relevant costs that you calculated in response to Requirement 1b.)
    c. Explain why NoFat should accept or reject the special sales offer if it uses its mark-up pricing method to set the special sales price.

Incorporating a Long-Term Horizon into the Decision Analysis

Assume for this question that Allyson's relevant analysis reveals that NoFat would earn a positive relevant profit of $10,000 from the special sale (i.e., the special sales alternative). However, after conducting this traditional, short-term relevant analysis, Allyson wonders whether it might be more profitable over the long-term to downsize the company by reducing its manufacturing capacity (i.e., its plant machinery and plant facility). She is aware that downsizing requires a multiyear time horizon because companies usually cannot increase or decrease fixed plant assets every year. Therefore, Allyson has decided to use a five-year time horizon in her long-term decision analysis. She has identified the following information regarding capacity downsizing (i.e., the downsizing alternative):

- The plant facility consists of several buildings. If it chooses to downsize its capacity, NoFat can immediately sell one of the buildings to an adjacent business for $30,000.
- If it chooses to downsize its capacity, NoFat's annual lease cost for plant machinery will decrease to $9,000.

Therefore, Allyson must choose between these two alternatives: Accept the special sales offer each year and earn a $10,000 relevant profit for each of the next five years *or* reject the special sales offer and downsize as described above.

5. Assume that NoFat pays for all costs with cash. Also, assume a 10-percent discount rate, a five-year time horizon, and all cash flows occur at the end of the year. Using an NPV approach to discount future cash flows to present value,

   a. Calculate the NPV of accepting the special sale with the assumed positive relevant profit of $10,000 per year (i.e., the special sales alternative).

   b. Calculate the NPV of downsizing capacity as previously described (i.e., the down sizing alternative).

   c. Based on the NPV of Calculations a and b, identify and explain which of these two alternatives is best for NoFat to pursue in the long term.

1

Appendix

International Financial Reporting Standards

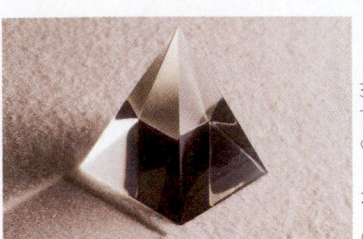

Doug Norman Crystals/Alamy

After studying Appendix 1, you should be able to:

1. Understand and describe some of the important aspects of international financial reporting standards.
2. Understand key differences between IFRS and U.S. GAAP.

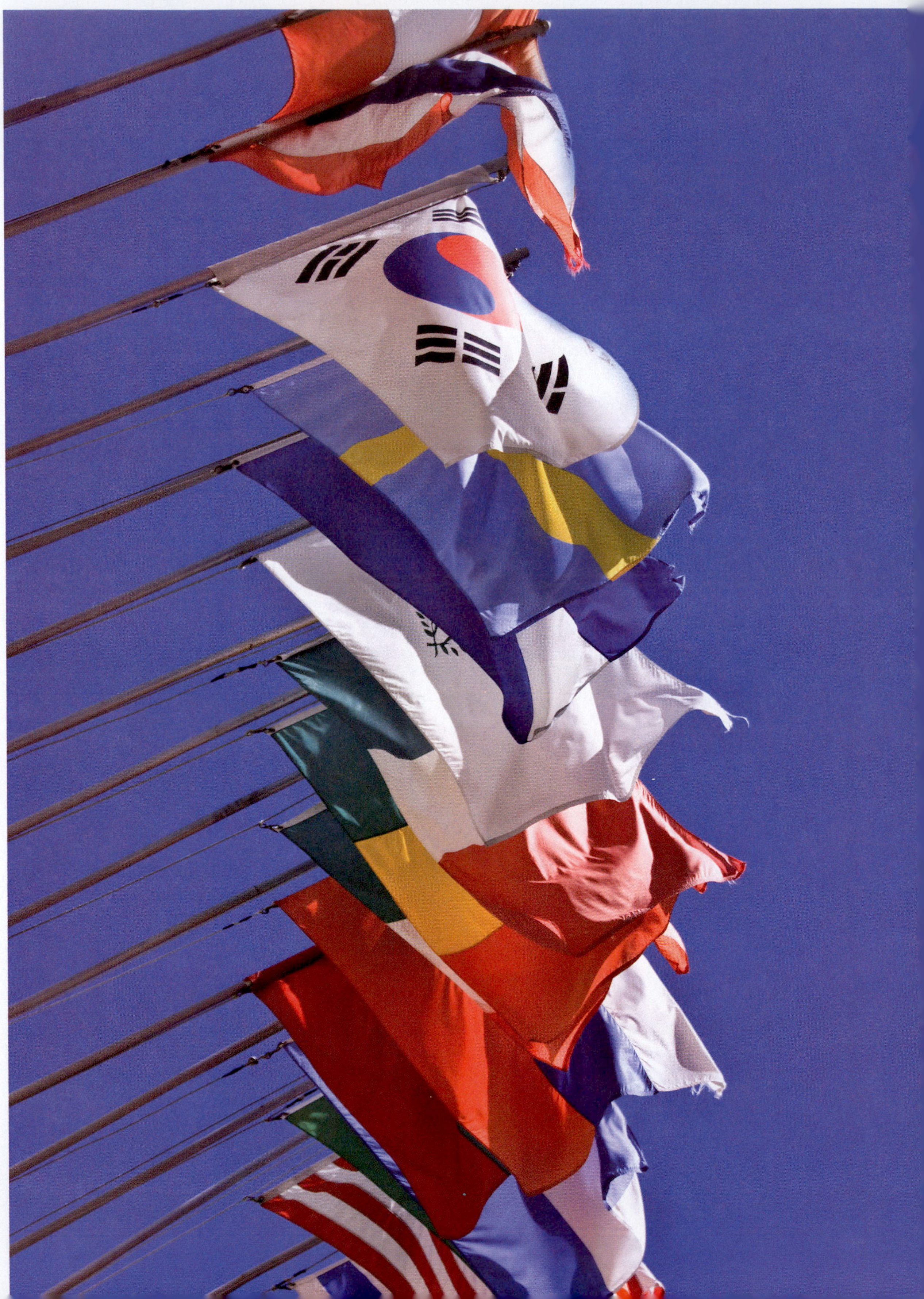

CAN BALCIOGLU, 2009/Shutterstock.com

INTERNATIONAL FINANCIAL REPORTING

Business is becoming an increasingly global activity as companies conduct operations across national boundaries. Not only are more and more companies engaging in international transactions, they are also seeking capital from foreign stock exchanges. Due to a variety of factors (such as cultural differences, differences in legal systems, differences in business environments), the historical development of accounting standards on a country-by-country basis has led to considerable diversity in financial accounting practices. To facilitate the conduct of business in an international environment, there has been heightened interest in the development of international accounting standards. The purpose of this appendix is to address some of the more frequently asked questions with regard to **international financial reporting standards (IFRS)**.

O B J E C T I V E ❶
Understand and describe some of the important aspects of international financial reporting standards.

What Are IFRS?

IFRS is a general term that describes an international set of generally accepted accounting standards. IFRS encompasses:

- international accounting standards (IAS) issued prior to 2001
- international financial reporting standards (IFRS) issued after 2001
- interpretations of these standards

IFRS are generally considered less detailed and more concept-based than U.S. GAAP. Over the last several years, IFRS have assumed the role as the common language of financial reporting in much of the world.

Who Develops IFRS?

The following bodies play an instrumental role in the development of IFRS.

International Accounting Standards Board (IASB) IFRS are developed by the **International Accounting Standards Board (IASB)**, which is headquartered in London. The IASB is an independent, privately-funded accounting standard-setting body which consists of 16 members from nine countries. To ensure geographical diversity, members of the IASB normally include four members from the Asia/Oceania region, four members from Europe, four members from North America, one each from Africa and South America, and two members from any area. The goal of the IASB is to develop a single set of high-quality accounting standards that result in transparent and comparable information reported in general purpose financial statements. The general structure of the IASB is shown in Exhibit A1-1.

Exhibit A1-1

Structure of the IASB

Source: Adapted from www.iasplus.com

International Financial Reporting Standards (IFRS) Foundation The IASB is overseen by the International Financial Reporting Standards Foundation. The IFRS Foundation funds, appoints the members of, and oversees the IASB. The IFRS Foundation is composed of 22 trustees who possess a wide degree of professional experience—including auditors, preparers, users, academics, and others.

IFRS Interpretations Committee The IFRS Interpretations Committee interprets the application of and provides guidance on financial reporting issues not specifically addressed in IFRS. Any interpretations must be reported to the IASB for approval.

IFRS Advisory Council The IFRS Advisory Council advises the IASB on a number of issues, such as items that should be on the IASB agenda, input on the timetable of the various IASB projects, and advice on various aspects of these projects.

How Long Has the IASB Been Issuing Standards?

International standard setting began in 1973 with the formation of the International Accounting Standards Committee (IASC). Between 1973 and 1988, the IASC completed a set of core standards, which began to gain global acceptance. In all, the IASC issued 41 International Accounting Standards (IAS).

In 2001, the IASB was established as the successor organization of the IASC and assumed the standard-setting responsibilities from the IASC. The IASB endorsed the standards of the IASC and began issuing its own standards, which are called International Financial Reporting Standards (IFRS). At this point, with support from the Securities and Exchange Commission (SEC), the Financial Accounting Standards Board (FASB), the European Union (EU), and others, the movement to a single set of high-quality international accounting standards began to pick up considerable momentum. Therefore, IFRS represent a relatively young body of accounting literature. Exhibit A1-2 outlines key dates in the development of IFRS.

Exhibit A1-2

Key Dates in the Development of IFRS

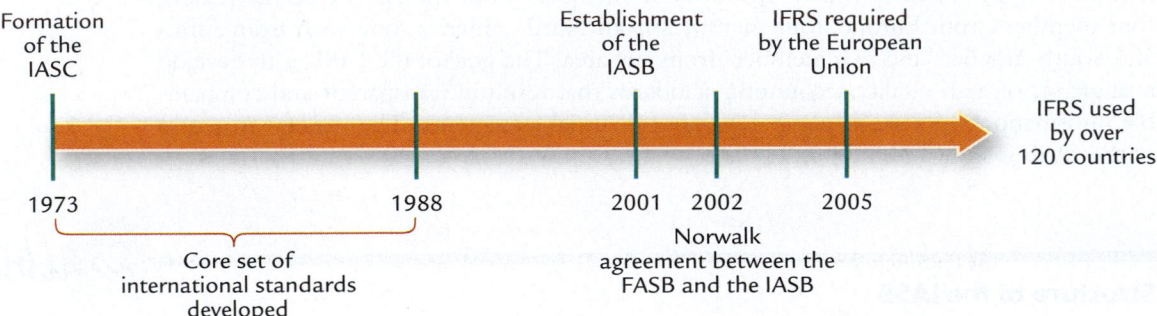

What Organizations Have Played a Role in the Development of IFRS?

In 2002, the FASB and the IASB reached an agreement, known as the Norwalk Agreement, in which both standard setters formalized their commitment to develop "as quickly as practicable" a common set of accounting standards. This process, commonly referred to as **convergence** or **harmonization** of U.S. GAAP and IFRS, involves removing existing differences between the two sets of accounting standards and working together on future accounting standards. The FASB and the IASB are currently involved in several joint standard setting projects aimed at reducing the differences between U.S. GAAP and IFRS.

The Securities and Exchange Commission (SEC) has long supported (as early as 1988) the development of an internationally acceptable set of accounting standards, and it publicly supported the Norwalk Agreement. Current statements by the SEC have reiterated its support for a single set of high-quality globally accepted accounting standards and encouraged continued convergence of U.S. GAAP and IFRS. The SEC plans to make a determination in 2011 regarding the use of IFRS for publicly traded U.S. companies.

The EU has been instrumental to the global acceptance of IFRS. In a pivotal event for the use of IFRS, the EU, in 2002, required its member countries to use IFRS by 2005. With the EU adoption of IFRS, the number of countries using IFRS more than doubled between 2003 and 2006.

Who Uses IFRS?

IFRS are quickly gaining global acceptance and are currently used by over 120 countries, including over 30 member-states of the European Union, Australia, and Israel. Exhibit A1-3 highlights the use of IFRS around the world. Countries such as Canada, India, Mexico, Japan, and Taiwan are expected to transition to IFRS in the near future.

IFRS Around the World

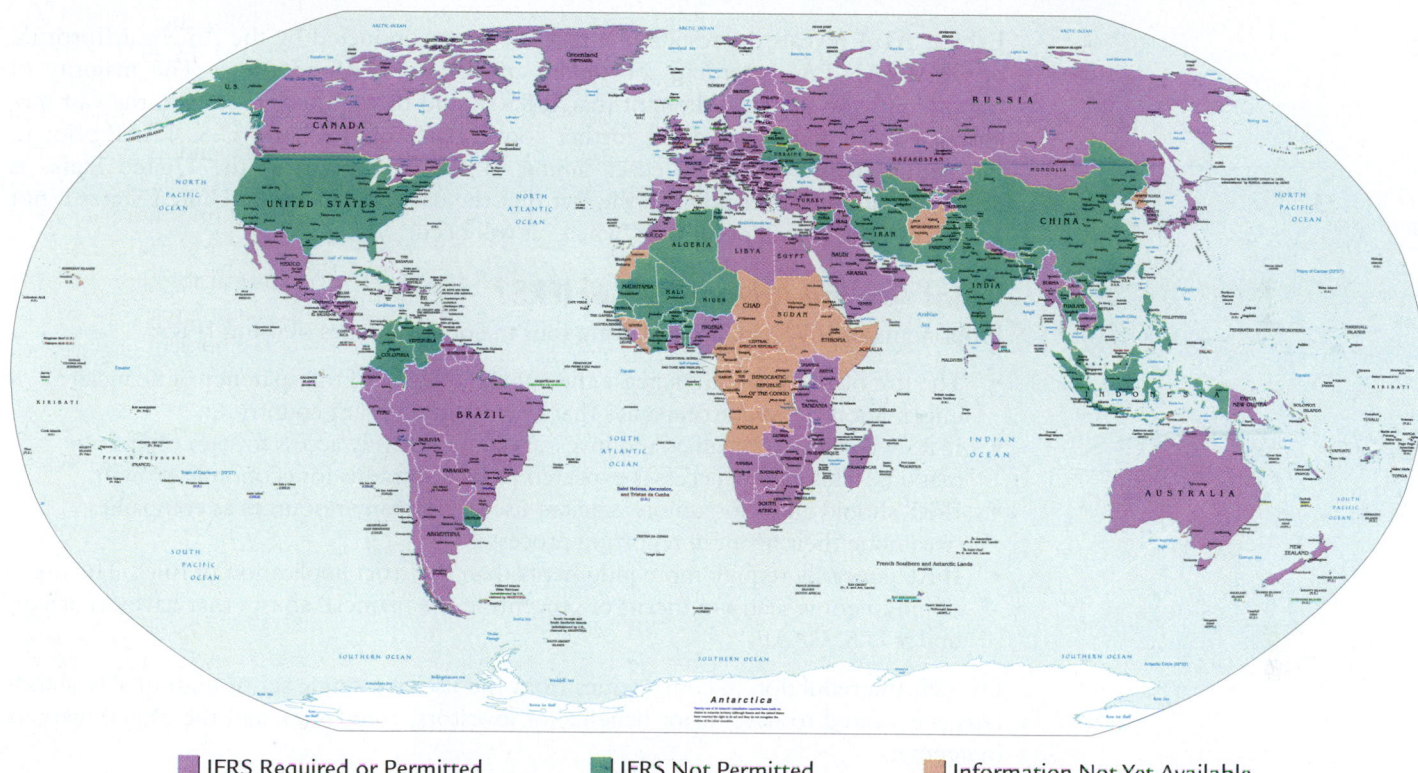

| IFRS Required or Permitted | IFRS Not Permitted | Information Not Yet Available |

When Are IFRS Expected to Be Used in the United States?

With the majority of companies throughout the world following IFRS, there is considerable pressure for the United States to adopt IFRS. The United States currently allows foreign companies who trade on U.S. stock exchanges to use IFRS without reconciliation to U.S. GAAP. In addition, the SEC has proposed a timeline that envisions 2015 as the earliest possible date for the mandatory adoption of IFRS by U.S. companies. In considering the adoption of IFRS, the SEC has identified several key issues that will be considered in transitioning to IFRS, including:

- determining whether IFRS is sufficiently developed and applied consistently enough to be used in the United States
- understanding the impact of IFRS adoption on companies
- evaluating whether the financial statement preparers and auditors are sufficiently prepared to convert to IFRS
- determining if investors have adequate preparation and understanding of IFRS and how it differs from U.S. GAAP

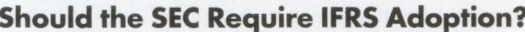

Should the SEC Require IFRS Adoption?

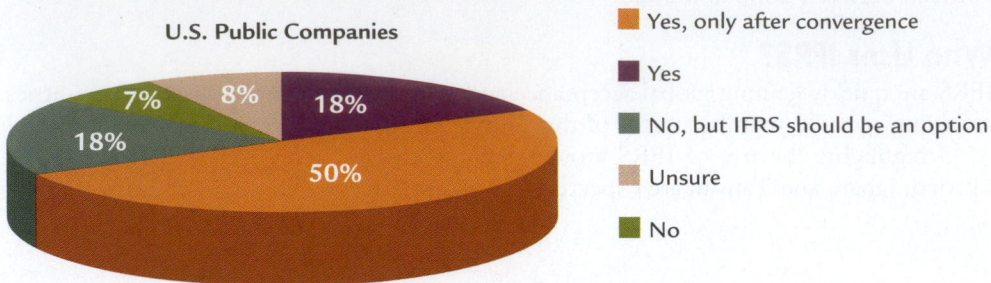

U.S. Public Companies

- Yes, only after convergence
- Yes
- No, but IFRS should be an option
- Unsure
- No

Source: Adapted from AICPA's IFRS Readiness Tracking Survey (May 2010).

Exhibit A1-4 reveals the results of a recent survey conducted by the American Institute of CPAs (AICPA) regarding the public attitude to IFRS adoption. The majority of respondents (68 percent) thought that IFRS should be required. However, the vast majority of these companies desire further convergence of IFRS and U.S. GAAP prior to this requirement. While the exact timing of IFRS adoption in the United States is unknown, all indicators point to the fact that the use of IFRS in the United States is not a matter of "if" it will occur but "when" it will occur.

What Are the Advantages of IFRS?

Proponents of IFRS cite the following four major advantages of using IFRS:

- The use of IFRS should increase the comparability and transparency of financial information between companies that operate in different countries.
- IFRS will allow companies and investors to more easily access foreign capital markets. This ease of access is expected to be a stimulus for economic growth.
- IFRS should allow for a more efficient use of company resources as companies streamline their financial reporting processes.
- IFRS generally require more judgments than the strict application of rules. The use of judgment is seen as a means of preventing the financial abuses that have occurred under U.S. GAAP.

Overall, the reduction in complexities from the use of a single set of high-quality standards is expected to have major benefits for investors, companies, and the capital markets in general.

Are There Potential Problems with Adopting IFRS?

The movement toward IFRS presents many challenges as well as opportunities, including the following:

- IFRS, which are relatively young, may be viewed by some as a lower quality set of standards compared to U.S. GAAP, which has stood the test of time.
- There are inherent difficulties involved with integrating worldwide cultural differences to ensure that IFRS are applied and interpreted consistently.
- IFRS generally require more judgment and less reliance on rules than U.S. GAAP. While this exercise of judgment can be a positive aspect of IFRS, many see the potential abuses of judgment as a key problem with IFRS.
- Not all countries will use the same version of IFRS. Many countries that currently use IFRS have selectively modified (or carved out) certain standards with which they do not agree. Such modification will reduce comparability and increase complexity in financial reporting.
- Companies will incur significant transition costs in creating new accounting policies, modifying their accounting systems, and training their employees with regard to IFRS.

IFRS Implementation Challenges

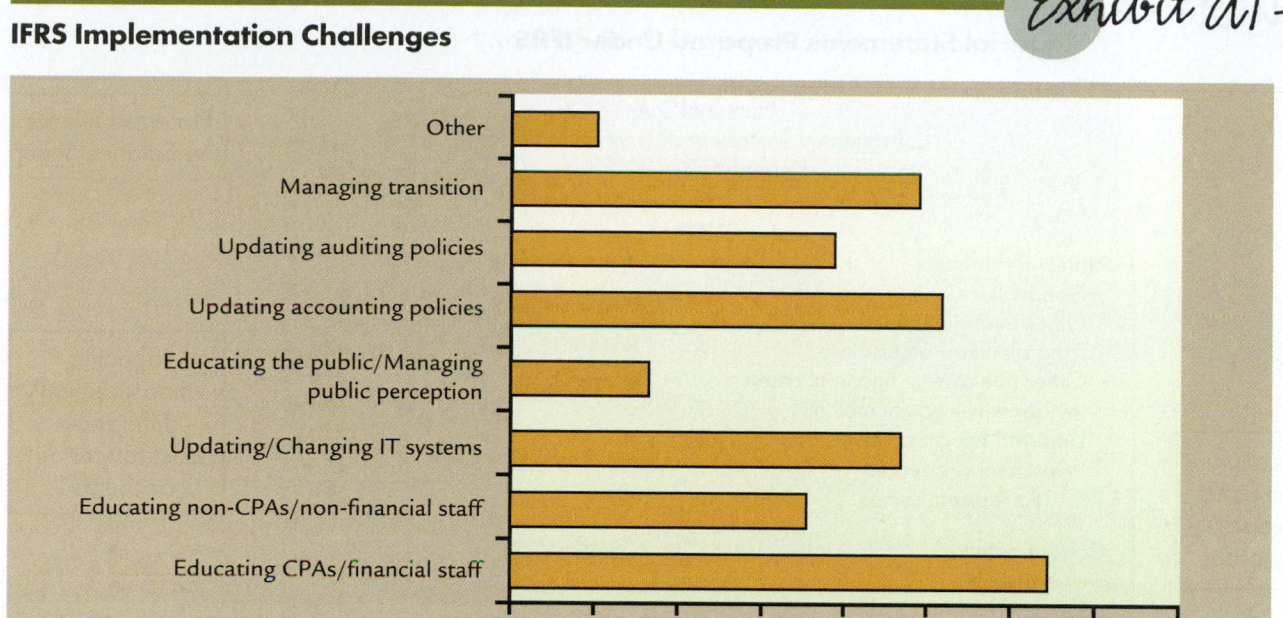

Exhibit A1-5

Source: Adapted from AICPA's IFRS Readiness Tracking Survey (May 2010).

Exhibit A1-5 lists the major challenges that companies foresee in implementing IFRS.

What Do Financial Statements Look Like Under IFRS?

While the details of preparing financial statements under IFRS is a topic more appropriately covered in intermediate accounting courses, it is helpful to identify a few of the major differences between financial statements prepared under U.S. GAAP and those prepared under IFRS. As an example of financial statements prepared according to IFRS, Exhibit A1-6 (p. 1248–1249) shows the income statement and balance sheet of **Carrefour S.A.**, a French retailer that operates in Europe, South America, North Africa, and parts of Asia.[1] Carrefour is the second largest retailer in the world in terms of revenue, trailing only **Wal-Mart**.

---

[1] The differences between the retained earnings statement and the statement of cash flows under U.S. GAAP and IFRS are relatively minor, so we will focus on the balance sheet and income statement here.

Financial Statements Prepared Under IFRS

Carrefour S.A.
Consolidated Statement of Financial Position
December 31, 2009

Preferred title for the Balance Sheet

Assets

Non-current assets

Goodwill	€	11,473
Other intangible fixed assets		1,083
Tangible fixed assets		15,044
Other non-current financial assets		3,319
Investments—equity method		201
Deferred tax on assets		712
Investment properties		455
Non-current assets	€	32,286

Current assets

Inventories		6,670
Commerical receivables	€	2,238
Consumer credit from financial companies—short-term		5,266
Tax receivables		563
Other assets		1,230
Cash and cash equivalents		3,301
Current assets	€	19,267

Total assets € **51,553**

Specific measurement differences exist for certain accounts*

Classifications are often listed in reverse liquidity order

Shareholders' Equity

Equity capital	€	1,762
Consolidated reserves (including income)		8,552
Minority interests		800
Shareholders' equity	€	11,115

Equities are listed before liabilities

Note terminology differences for common stock and retained earnings

Liabilities

Non-current liabilities

Borrowing—long-term	€	9,974
Provisions		2,520
Deferred tax liabilities		496
Other non-current liabilities		592
Non-current liabilities	€	13,402

Current liabilities

Borrowing—short-term	€	2,018
Suppliers and other creditors		16,800
Tax payables		1,324
Other liabilities		6,894
Current liabilities	€	27,036

Total shareholders' equity and liabilties € **51,553**

Provisions refers to contingent and other liabilities (e.g. retirement costs)

Noncurrent assets listed before current assets

*IFRS differs from U.S. GAAP in many respects. For example, IFRS allows companies to increase the value of their property, plant, and equipment to fair value and does not permit the use of LIFO for valuing inventories. See Exhibit A1-7 for a listing of some of these specific differences.

(Continued)

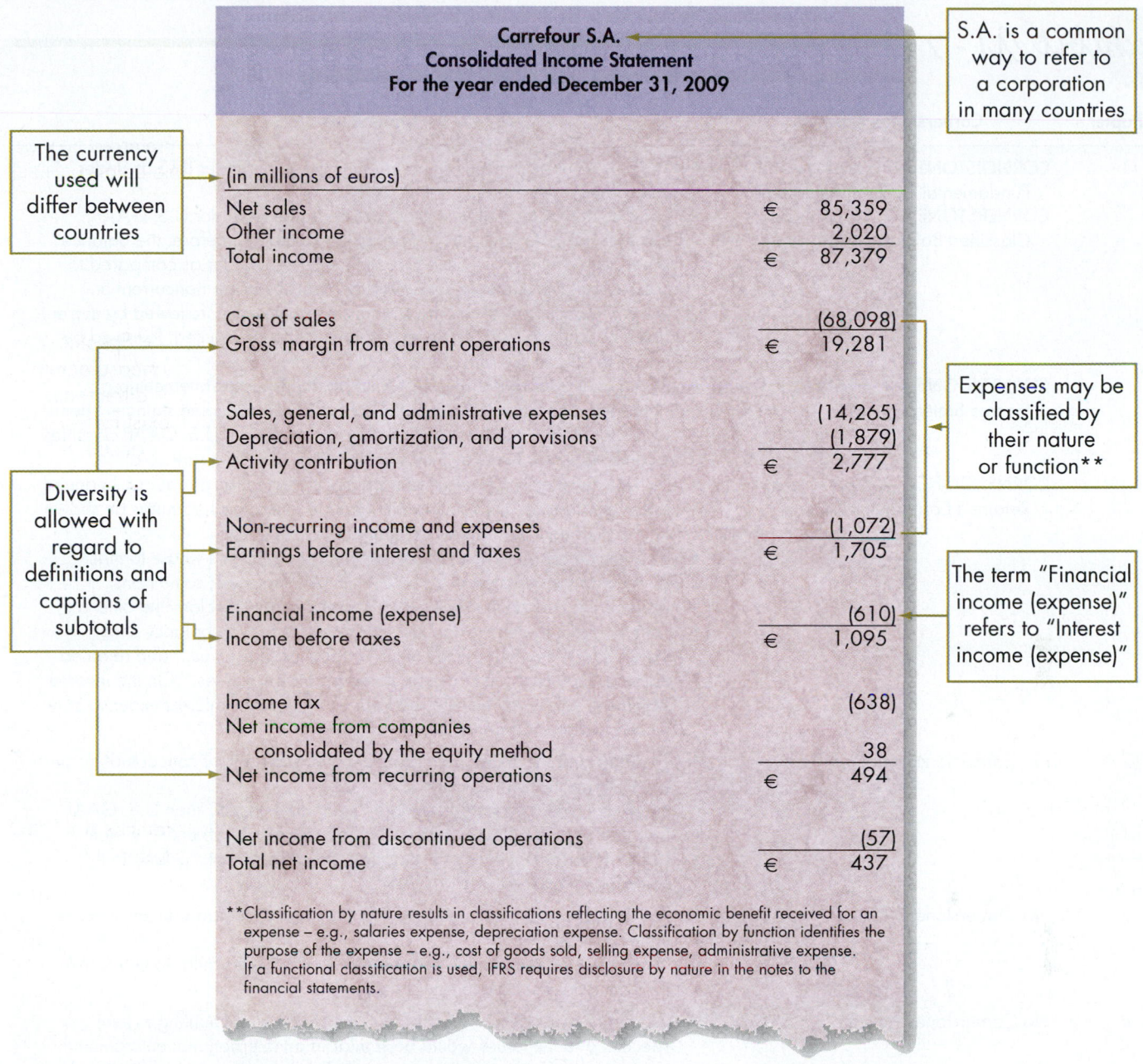

The currency used will differ between countries

S.A. is a common way to refer to a corporation in many countries

Diversity is allowed with regard to definitions and captions of subtotals

Expenses may be classified by their nature or function**

The term "Financial income (expense)" refers to "Interest income (expense)"

Carrefour S.A.
Consolidated Income Statement
For the year ended December 31, 2009

(in millions of euros)

Net sales	€	85,359
Other income		2,020
Total income	€	87,379
Cost of sales		(68,098)
Gross margin from current operations	€	19,281
Sales, general, and administrative expenses		(14,265)
Depreciation, amortization, and provisions		(1,879)
Activity contribution	€	2,777
Non-recurring income and expenses		(1,072)
Earnings before interest and taxes	€	1,705
Financial income (expense)		(610)
Income before taxes	€	1,095
Income tax		(638)
Net income from companies consolidated by the equity method		38
Net income from recurring operations	€	494
Net income from discontinued operations		(57)
Total net income	€	437

**Classification by nature results in classifications reflecting the economic benefit received for an expense – e.g., salaries expense, depreciation expense. Classification by function identifies the purpose of the expense – e.g., cost of goods sold, selling expense, administrative expense. If a functional classification is used, IFRS requires disclosure by nature in the notes to the financial statements.

KEY DIFFERENCES BETWEEN IFRS AND U.S. GAAP

OBJECTIVE 2
Understand key differences between IFRS and U.S. GAAP.

While IFRS is expected to have far-reaching impacts on financial accounting, there are more similarities than differences between IFRS and U.S. GAAP.

How Will IFRS Impact My Study of Accounting?

To aid in understanding the impact of IFRS on the cornerstones of financial accounting, review Exhibit A1-7 (p. 1250). As you can see, the Cornerstones of accounting covered in this text will still provide you with a solid foundation for your study of accounting.

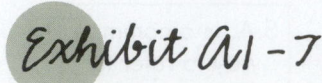

Effect of IFRS on Cornerstones of Financial Accounting

Chapter	Cornerstones Affected	Comments
1	**CORNERSTONE 1-1**: Using the Fundamental Accounting Equation **CORNERSTONE 1-2**: Preparing a Classified Balance Sheet **CORNERSTONE 1-3**: Preparing an Income Statement **CORNERSTONE 1-4**: Preparing a Retained Earnings Statement	• The fundamental accounting equation is the same under IFRS as under U.S. GAAP. • The elements of the balance sheet are the same as under U.S. GAAP; however, IFRS do not specify a particular format. Therefore, the balance sheet classifications are often listed in the reverse order as compared to U.S. GAAP. For example, IFRS classify assets as either noncurrent or current. Noncurrent assets are typically presented first, followed by current assets. Additionally, stockholders' equity is often presented, followed by noncurrent liabilities and then current liabilities. • IFRS do not prescribe a specific format for the income statement (e.g., single-step or multiple-step). In addition, IFRS allow income statement items to be classified either by their nature or their function. U.S. GAAP classifies income statement items by their function (e.g., cost of goods sold). • IFRS do not specify the retained earnings statement as a required financial statement. Instead, IFRS require the change in retained earnings be shown on the statement of changes in equity. • IFRS require the presentation of a statement of cash flows whose format is similar to the one prescribed by U.S. GAAP. However, some items (as described on the next page for Chapter 11) may be classified differently. • Terminology differences do exist. For example, on the balance sheet, stockholders' equity may be called "capital and reserves," and retained earnings may be called "accumulated profits and losses." On the income statement, sales may be referred to as "turnover" or interest expense may be referred to as "finance costs."
2	No Cornerstones Affected	• The IASB and the FASB are currently working on a joint conceptual framework as described in Chapter 2. • In general, IFRS is considered more "principles-based" than U.S. GAAP • IFRS and U.S. GAAP use the identical double-entry accounting system. • Under IFRS, transactions are analyzed, journalized, and posted in the same manner as under U.S. GAAP.
3	No Cornerstones Affected	• The adjustment process under IFRS is the same as the adjustment process under U.S. GAAP. • While revenue recognition concepts under IFRS are similar to U.S. GAAP, IFRS contains less detailed guidance.
4	No Cornerstones Affected	• Internal control issues are company and financial accounting system-specific, and the issues would be similar in an international environment. However, the documentation and assessment requirements of Section 404 of the Sarbanes-Oxley Act (SOX) impose a much greater burden on U.S. companies compared to international companies. • The management, control, and accounting for cash are the same under IFRS as under U.S. GAAP.
5	No Cornerstones Affected	• The recognition of sales revenue under IFRS is generally similar to U.S. GAAP. However, the amount of guidance provided by IFRS as to when revenue should be recognized is considerably less and more principles-based than the amount of guidance provided by U.S. GAAP. • The recognition and valuation of receivables under IFRS is generally the same as U.S. GAAP.
6	**CORNERSTONE 6-6**: Applying the LIFO Inventory Costing Method **CORNERSTONE 6-8**: Valuing Inventory at Lower of Cost or Market	• The purchase and sale of inventory is generally the same under IFRS as under U.S. GAAP. • IFRS do not allow the use of LIFO for determining the cost of inventory. • IFRS require the use of the lower of cost or market method, but it defines market value as net realizable value (the estimated selling price less costs of completion and disposal) instead of replacement cost. IFRS also permits reversal of inventory write-downs.

(Continued)

Chapter	Cornerstones Affected	Comments
7	**CORNERSTONE 7-1**: Measuring and Recording the Cost of a Fixed Asset	• While the accounting for an asset's initial cost is similar under IFRS and U.S. GAAP, IFRS allow for companies to increase the value of their property, plant, equipment, and intangible assets up to fair value. This is not permitted under U.S. GAAP.
	CORNERSTONES 7-2, 7-3, and **7-4**: Depreciation	• While similar depreciation methods are used, IFRS requires depreciating each component of an asset separately (component depreciation); this is permitted, but not required, by U.S. GAAP.
	CORNERSTONE 7-8: Accounting for Intangible Assets	• Generally the accounting for intangible assets under IFRS is similar to U.S. GAAP. However, under IFRS, research costs are expensed while development costs are capitalized as an intangible asset if it is probable that future benefits will be generated.
	CORNERSTONE 7-10: Recording an Impairment of Property, Plant, and Equipment	• The impairment model under IFRS is a single-step process rather than the two-step process that is used in U.S. GAAP. In addition, IFRS allows recovery of impairment losses, which is not allowed under U.S. GAAP.
8	No Cornerstones Affected	• While the accounting for current liabilities is generally the same under IFRS and U.S. GAAP, IFRS commonly reports liabilities in reverse order relative to U.S. GAAP—from least liquid to most liquid. • IFRS refer to loss contingencies that are recognized in the financial statements as "provisions." Loss contingencies that are not recognized in the financial statements are referred to as "contingencies." • Similar to U.S. GAAP, IFRS recognize provisions when the contingent event is probable. However, IFRS define probable as "more likely than not" while U.S. GAAP defines probable as "likely." Therefore, more events will be recognized as provisions under IFRS.
9	No Cornerstones Affected	• The accounting for bonds and notes payable is generally the same under IFRS as under U.S. GAAP. • A capital lease under U.S. GAAP is referred to as a finance lease under IFRS.
10	No Cornerstones Affected	• The accounting for equity is generally the same under IFRS as under U.S. GAAP. However, some terminology differences exist. For example, under IFRS, stockholders' equity is typically called "capital and reserves." The use of the term "reserves" has generally been discouraged under U.S. GAAP.
11	**CORNERSTONE 11-1**: Classifying Business Activities	• The classification of certain business activities does differ under IFRS relative to U.S. GAAP. For example, IFRS allow companies to report the payment of dividends and interest as either an operating cash outflow or a financing cash outflow. In addition, the payment of income taxes can be reported as an investing or financing transaction if it can be identified with an investing or financing activity. Finally, interest or dividends received may be reported as either operating or investing cash inflows.
12	No Cornerstones Affected	• The analysis of financial statements is the same under IFRS as it is under U.S. GAAP.

Where Can I Go to Find Out More About IFRS?

IFRS Foundation website:
www.ifrs.org

American Institute of Certified Public Accountants' (AICPA) website for IFRS Resources:
www.IFRS.com

Ernst & Young IFRS page:
http://www.ey.com/GL/en/Issues/IFRS

Deloitte IFRS page:
www.iasplus.com

International Association for Accounting Education & Research:
www.iaaer.org/resources

PricewaterhouseCoopers IFRS page:
http://www.pwc.com/gx/en/ifrs-reporting/index.jhtml

KPMG IFRS page:
http://www.kpmginstitutes.com/ifrs-institute/

SUMMARY OF LEARNING OBJECTIVES

LO1. **Understand and describe some of the important aspects of international financial reporting standards.**

- International financial reporting standards (IFRS) are an international set of generally accepted accounting standards.
- IFRS are developed by the International Accounting Standards Board (IASB), an independent, privately-funded standard-setting body consisting of 16 members from nine countries.
- International standard setting began in 1973; however, the development of a single-set of high quality international accounting standards accelerated in 2001 with the establishment of the IASB and the European Union's requirement of the use of IFRS.
- IFRS are currently used in more than 120 countries and are currently being considered in the United States.
- The reduction in complexities from the use of a single set of high-quality standards is expected to have major benefits for investors, companies and capital markets in general. However, the movement toward IFRS presents many challenges as well.
- A familiarity with financial statements prepared under IFRS is useful for financial statement users.

LO2. **Understand key differences between IFRS and U.S. GAAP.**

- IFRS is expected to have far-reaching impacts on financial accounting; however, the cornerstones of accounting will provide a strong foundation for the study of accounting.
- Within each topical area of accounting, financial statement users need to be able to identify key differences between U.S. GAAP and IFRS.

KEY TERMS

Convergence (Harmonization) (p. 1244)
International Accounting Standards Board
  (IASB) (p. 1243)

International financial reporting standards
  (IFRS) (p. 1243)

MULTIPLE-CHOICE EXERCISES

A1-1 Which of the following best describes international financial reporting standards?

a. IFRS describes the generally accepted accounting principles that are currently used by all companies in the United States.
b. IFRS consist only of standards that have been issued since the IASB was formed in 2001.
c. IFRS are considered to be more concept-based than U.S. GAAP.
d. IFRS will be required to be used in the United States beginning in 2015.

A1-2 Which of the following statements is true?

a. The FASB has consistently resisted the adoption of IFRS in the United States for fear that it will lose its standard-setting authority.
b. The requirement to use IFRS by the European Union led to a significant increase in the global acceptance of IFRS.
c. IFRS has existed for nearly as long as U.S. GAAP; however, it only recently began to gain acceptance as a body of high-quality accounting standards.
d. The SEC is considering allowing foreign companies who trade stock on the U.S. stock exchanges to use IFRS.

A1-3 Convergence of U.S. GAAP and IFRS is best described as:

a. the replacement of U.S. GAAP by IFRS.
b. the replacement of IFRS by U.S. GAAP.
c. changing existing U.S. GAAP so that any differences in IFRS will be insignificant.
d. changing both existing U.S. GAAP and IFRS to reduce differences and developing new GAAP through a joint standard-setting process.

A1-4 Which of the following organizations has the responsibility to create IFRS?

a. Financial Accounting Standards Board
b. International Financial Reporting Standards Foundation
c. International Accounting Standards Board
d. Securities and Exchange Commission

A1-5 Which of the following is *not* an advantage of IFRS?

a. The use of IFRS should increase the comparability and transparency of financial information.
b. The use of IFRS will make it easier to access foreign capital markets.
c. IFRS requires more judgments than U.S. GAAP.
d. IFRS is less conservative than U.S. GAAP, so net income under IFRS will generally be higher than net income under U.S. GAAP.

A1-6 Which of the following is *not* a disadvantage of IFRS?

a. The use of IFRS will lead to an outflow of capital from the U.S. to foreign countries.
b. The use of IFRS could be viewed as adopting a lower quality standard.
c. Due to cultural differences among countries, it will be difficult to ensure consistent application and interpretation of IFRS.
d. Different versions of IFRS exist that may cause confusion for users of financial statements.

A1-7 With regard to the presentation of financial information under IFRS, which of the following is true?

a. The terminology on the balance sheet and the income statement is the same under IFRS and U.S. GAAP.
b. Under IFRS, the elements of the balance sheet are often presented in reverse order relative to U.S. GAAP, with noncurrent assets presented before current assets and stockholders' equity presented before liabilities.
c. Under IFRS, the elements of the income statement are often presented in reverse order, with expenses presented first followed by revenues.
d. IFRS do not require the presentation of a statement of cash flows.

A1-8 Which of the following inventory costing methods is *not* allowed under IFRS?

a. FIFO
b. specific identification
c. average cost
d. LIFO

A1-9 Which of the following is true?

a. IFRS allows property, plant, and equipment to be revalued upward if fair value is higher than historical cost.
b. IFRS contains more extensive guidance on revenue recognition than U.S. GAAP.
c. IFRS has a much more broad definition of cash than U.S. GAAP.
d. The accounting for research and development costs is identical under IFRS and U.S. GAAP.

A1-10 Which of the following is true with regard to contingent liabilities?

a. IFRS and U.S. GAAP use the same terminology to refer to contingent liabilities.
b. A contingent liability is recognized under IFRS when it is more likely than not that the contingent event will occur.
c. Fewer events will be recognized as contingent liabilities under IFRS than under U.S. GAAP.
d. Provisions are contingent liabilities that are not recognized in the financial statements.

2
Appendix

Investments

Doug Norman Crystals/Alamy

After studying Appendix 2, you should be able to:

1. Choose between and use the amortized cost, fair value, and equity methods for reporting investments.
2. Describe the consolidated balance sheet and income statement.
3. Describe accounting for business combinations.

Amanda Rohde/iStockphoto.com

Although companies can invest in virtually any asset (such as land), here we will concentrate on the most common investments—buying equity or debt securities.

- *Equity Securities*: An **equity security** represents an ownership interest in a corporation. Although most equity securities are common stock, preferred stock is also an equity security.
- *Debt Securities*: A **debt security** exists when another entity owes the security holder some combination of interest and principal. Debt securities include corporate bonds, U.S. treasury securities, and municipal bonds.

A company buys debt or equity securities with either short- or long-term investment horizons. As discussed in Chapter 4, short-term investment horizons are typically attempts to earn greater returns with cash that is not immediately needed for operations. Such "excess cash" results when cash inflows are not evenly distributed throughout the year. For example, many retail businesses, such as **Abercrombie & Fitch**, **Aeropostale**, and **Toys "R" Us**, collect significantly more cash around Christmas than in the summer. Consequently, they may need to save some of the cash collected at Christmas to meet operational needs during the summer. Other companies, such as banks, mutual funds, and insurance companies, buy and sell securities to profit from day-to-day changes in security prices.

Companies also attempt to maximize returns over long-term investment horizons. For insurance companies, such as **State Farm**, and mutual funds, such as **Fidelity**, for example, long-term investment income generated from debt and equity securities is a core part of operations. Or, companies may accumulate capital for future expansion to avoid having to borrow or sell additional stock. Companies may also invest in equity securities to establish long-term relationships, obtain significant influence, or control the other company. For example, to assure itself of access to high quality raw materials, a company may purchase the common stock of a supplier—the more common stock purchased, the more influence that can be exerted.

OVERVIEW OF ACCOUNTING FOR INVESTMENTS IN DEBT AND EQUITY

OBJECTIVE
Choose between and use the amortized cost, fair value, and equity methods for reporting investments.

Accounting for investments in equity securities differs depending upon the amount of common stock owned. The difference exists because of the nature of the ownership interest.

- *Passive:* If an investor owns less than 20 percent of the common stock, the investment is generally considered to be passive; that is, the investor is not attempting to exert influence over the operating and financial policies of the investee. In this case, the *fair value method* is used.
- *Significant Influence*: Because owning stock entitles the investor to vote for members of the board of directors, if the investor owns 20 to 50 percent of the outstanding common stock, then the investor is assumed to possess significant influence over the operating and financial policies of the investee. In this case, the *equity method* is used to account for the investment.
- *Control*: If the investor owns over 50 percent of the outstanding common stock, the investor is deemed to have control over the operating and financial policies of the investee. The investor is then called the **parent** and the investee is called a **subsidiary**. In these cases, the subsidiary's financial statements are combined with the parent's into a single set of **consolidated financial statements**.

Each of the methods for accounting for investments in debt and equity will be discussed in the sections that follow.

Classifying and Accounting for Equity Securities

When an investor owns less than 20 percent of the outstanding common stock of a corporation, the equity securities are classified as either *trading securities* or *available-for-sale securities.* Debt securities are also classified as trading or available-for-sale, but debt securities may also be classified in a third category—*held-to-maturity*. The distinction between these classifications is as follows:

- **Trading securities** are equity or debt investments that management intends to sell in the near term. Trading securities are bought and sold frequently and typically are owned for under one month. Trading securities are always classified as current assets on the balance sheet.
- **Available-for-sale securities** are equity and debt investments that management intends to sell in the future, but not necessarily in the near term. In reality, they are all investments that don't warrant inclusion as trading securities or held-to-maturity securities. On the balance sheet, available-for-sale securities are classified as current or noncurrent assets depending on whether they will be sold within one year or one operating cycle, whichever is longer.
- **Held-to-maturity securities** are debt investments (not equity, because stock does not mature) that management intends to hold until the debt contract requires the borrower to repay the debt in its entirety. On the balance sheet, held-to-maturity securities are classified as noncurrent assets unless the date of maturity is within one year or one operating cycle, whichever is longer.

Debt securities that are classified as "held-to-maturity" are valued at an amortized cost basis. Securities (both debt and equity) that are classified as trading or available-for-sale are valued at fair market value. An overview of the accounting for investments in debt and equity securities is shown in Exhibit A2-1. We will illustrate these different methods of accounting for investments using Redbird Corporation.

 *Exhibit A2-1*

Accounting for Investments in Debt and Equity Securities

Investments in Equity Securities	Method	Reporting of Dividends	Reporting of Unrealized Gains and Losses
1. Passive investment (own <20% of the stock)			
a. Trading	Fair value	Net income	Net income
b. Available-for-sale	Fair value	Net income	Other comprehensive income
2. Significant influence (own 20% to 50% of the stock)	Equity	Reduces investment account	Not recognized
3. Control (own >50% of the stock)	Equity plus consolidation	Eliminated	Not recognized

Investments in Debt Securities	Method	Reporting of Interest Income	Reporting of Unrealized Gains and Losses
1. Trading	Fair value	Net income	Net income
2. Available-for-sale	Fair value	Net income	Other comprehensive income
3. Held-to-maturity	Amortized cost	Net income	Not recognized

Amortized Cost Method

All investments in debt securities that are classified as held-to-maturity are accounted for by the **amortized cost method** (also called *the cost method*). Investments are recorded at cost when acquired and interest income is recognized with appropriate amortization of premiums and discounts. In other words, the amortized cost method closely parallels accounting for long-term liabilities, which is described in Chapter 9.

Purchase of Bonds

On December 31, 2011, Redbird Corporation purchases 10-year, 5-percent bonds with a face value of $100,000 for $96,000 cash. Redbird would record the purchase with the following journal entry:

Dec. 31, 2011	Investments—Held to Maturity	96,000	
	Cash		96,000
	(Record issuance of bonds at discount)		

Assets	= Liabilities +	Stockholders' Equity
+96,000		
−96,000		

Receipt of Interest Payment

These bonds pay interest of $2,500 ($100,000 × 5% × 6/12) every six months. Additionally, you will recall from Chapter 9 that any premium or discount must be amortized over the life of the bond. For simplicity, we will amortize the discount on a straight-line basis. This results in discount amortization of $200 {[($100,000 − $96,000)/10 years] × 6/12} every six months. The following entries would therefore need to be made to record receipt of the interest payments during 2012:

June 30, 2012	Cash	2,500	
	Investments—Held-to-Maturity	200	
	Interest Income		2,700
	(Record receipt of interest payment)		

Assets	= Liabilities +	Stockholders' Equity
+2,500		+2,700
+200		

Dec. 31, 2012	Cash	2,500	
	Investments—Held-to-Maturity	200	
	Interest Income		2,700
	(Record receipt of interest payment)		

Assets	= Liabilities +	Stockholders' Equity
+2,500		
+200		+2,700

The same entries would be made each year to record receipt of the interest payments.

Reporting in the Financial Statements

As shown in the preceding entries, at December 31, 2012, $400 of the discount has been amortized to the investment account. This means the book value of the held-to-maturity investments is $96,400 ($96,000 + $400). However, assume that the fair market value of these bonds is $98,000 at December 31, 2012. The 2012 financial statements would report this investment as follows:

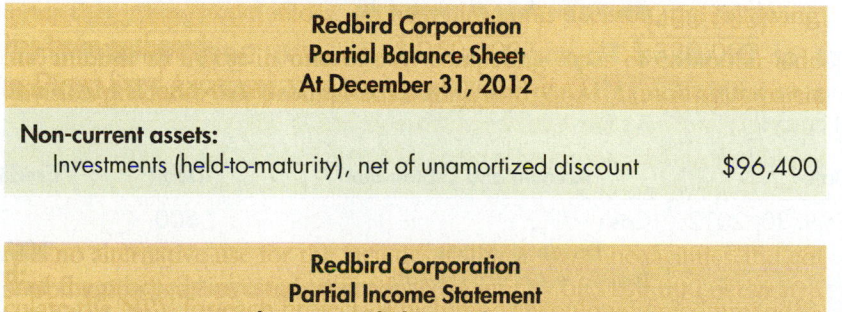

Redbird Corporation
Partial Balance Sheet
At December 31, 2012

Non-current assets:
Investments (held-to-maturity), net of unamortized discount $96,400

Redbird Corporation
Partial Income Statement
For the Year Ended December 31, 2012

Interest income $5,400

Because the market value of Redbird's investment is $1,600 ($98,000 − $96,400) more than its book value, there is an unrealized gain of $1,600. The rationale for not recognizing unrealized gains or losses on held-to-maturity investments is that changes in market value do not affect the amount that is realized from such investments. If securities are held to maturity, the amount that is realized is the face value—as determined by the debt agreement.

Receipt of Principal Payment

When the bonds mature on December 31, 2021, the following journal entry is made:

Dec. 31, 2021	Cash	100,000	
	Investments—Held-to-Maturity		100,000
	(Record receipt of principal payment)		

Assets	= Liabilities +	Stockholders' Equity
+100,000		
−100,000		

Note that this entry zeros out the investment account because, at maturity, the discount has been fully amortized, which makes the balance in the investment account equal to the face value of the bonds.

Fair Value Method

Recall that when an investment is considered passive (less than 20 percent common stock ownership), the investor usually cannot significantly influence the investee. These investments are classified as trading or available-for-sale securities. In such cases, the investor must use the **fair value method** to account for the investment. This means the investment is valued at the price for which the investor could sell the asset in an orderly transaction between market participants. For most securities, this price is a quoted price in an active market, but if no active market exists, other techniques are used to estimate the fair market value.

Purchase of Securities   Like other assets, trading and available-for-sale securities are recorded at cost, which is also fair value on the date of purchase. To illustrate, on August 1, 2012, Redbird Corporation made the following purchases of securities:

Security	Type	Classification	Amount
Illinois Enterprises	Equity	Trading	$10,000
Metzler Design	Debt	Trading	6,000
IMG	Equity	Trading	4,100
Total Trading Securities			**$ 20,100**
Alabama Co.	Debt	AFS	$ 8,100
Mutare, Inc.	Debt	AFS	6,300
ABC	Equity	AFS	12,000
Total Available-for-Sale Securities			**$ 26,400**

These acquisitions are recorded by the following journal entry:

Date	Account and Explanation	Debit	Credit
Aug. 1, 2012	Investments—Trading Securities	20,100	
	Investments—Available-for-Sale		
	Securities	26,400	
	Cash		46,500
	(Record purchase of investments)		

Assets	= Liabilities +	Stockholders' Equity
+20,100		
+26,400		
−46,500		

Receipt of Dividend Payment   On September 30, 2012, Redbird received cash dividends of $300 from IMG and $200 from ABC, which are recorded by the following journal entry:[1]

Date	Account and Explanation	Debit	Credit
Sept. 30, 2012	Cash	500	
	Dividend Income		500
	(Record receipt of dividends)		

Assets	= Liabilities +	Stockholders' Equity
+500		+500

Selling Securities   On December 20, 2012, the market price of IMG stock had climbed to $4,900, and Redbird decided to sell its entire holding. The following journal entry records the sale:

Date	Account and Explanation	Debit	Credit
Dec. 20, 2012	Cash	4,900	
	Investments—Trading Securities		4,100
	Gain on Sale of Investments		800
	(Record sale of security)		

Assets	= Liabilities +	Stockholders' Equity
+4,900		+800
−4,100		

The $800 gain will be included in Redbird's year-end net income, as will the $500 of dividends received on September 30.

---

[1] Dividend income should be recognized by investors at the dividend declaration date rather than the dividend payment date. When a cash dividend is declared in one year and paid in the following year, the investor should record the dividend declaration at year-end by a debit to dividends receivable and a credit to dividend income. In the following year, when the related cash is received, the investor should debit cash and credit dividends receivable.

In summary, this investment yielded two forms of income—dividends ($500) and a gain on sale ($800)—giving Redbird additional net income of $1,300.

Receipt of Interest Payments In addition, Mutare, Metzler Design, and Alabama Co. (the three debt securities) pay interest totaling $1,500 on December 31, 2012, which is recorded with the following journal entry:

Date	Account and Explanation	Debit	Credit
Dec. 31, 2012	Cash	1,500	
	Interest Income		1,500
	(Record receipt of interest payment)		

Assets	=	Liabilities	+	Stockholders' Equity
+1,500				+1,500

Reporting on the Financial Statements On the balance sheet, both trading and available-for-sale securities are recorded at fair value. Use of the fair value method results in **unrealized gains** and/or **unrealized losses** because the value of the securities must be written up or down to fair market value at the balance sheet date (this is often called "marking to market"). For example, consider the securities shown in Exhibit A2-2.

Exhibit A2-2

Investment Portfolio Data

	Redbird Corporation Investment Portfolio December 31, 2012		
Security	**Classification**	**Acquisition Cost**	**Market Value at 12/31**
Illinois Enterprises	Trading	$10,000	$ 8,800
Metzler Design	Trading	6,000	6,400
Total Trading Securities		**$ 16,000**	**$ 15,200**
Alabama Co.	AFS	$ 8,100	$ 8,600
Mutare, Inc.	AFS	6,300	6,500
ABC	AFS	12,000	13,500
Total Available-for-Sale Securities		**$ 26,400**	**$ 28,600**

On December 31, Redbird Corporation would make the following entries to "mark the investments to market":

Date	Account and Explanation	Debit	Credit
Dec. 31, 2012	Allowance to Adjust Available-for-Sale Securities to Market	2,200	
	Unrealized Gain (Loss) on Available-for-Sale Securities*		2,200
	(Record available-for-sale securities at fair value)		

Assets	=	Liabilities	+	Stockholders' Equity
+2,200				+2,200

*Recognize that for Available-for-Sale Securities, any unrealized gain or loss goes to the "accumulated other comprehensive income" portion of stockholders' equity—not to the income statement.

Date	Account and Explanation	Debit	Credit
Dec. 31, 2012	Unrealized Gain (Loss) on Trading Securities**	800	
	Allowance to Adjust Trading Securities to Market		800
	(Record trading securities at fair value)		

Assets	=	Liabilities	+	Stockholders' Equity
−800				−800

**Recognize that for Trading Securities, any unrealized gain or loss goes to the income statement.

The allowance accounts (both Available-for-Sale and Trading) are valuation accounts containing the unrealized gains and losses for the Available-for-Sale and Trading investment portfolios, respectively. Valuation accounts are used to record changes in the fair values of the investments so that the investment accounts (both Available-for-Sale and Trading) reflect the original cost. At the balance sheet date, the allowance accounts are adjusted to reflect the current amount of unrealized gain or loss in the investment portfolio. On the balance sheet, the allowance accounts are netted with the respective investment accounts (added if the allowance has a debit balance and subtracted if it has a credit balance) to report the investments at fair value as follows:

Redbird Corporation Partial Balance Sheet December 31, 2012		
Current assets:		
Trading securities, at cost	$16,000	
Less: Allowance to adjust trading securities to market	(800)	
Trading securities, at market*		$15,200
Noncurrent assets:		
Available-for-sale securities, at cost	$26,400	
Add: Allowance to adjust available-for-sale securities to market	2,200	
Available-for-sale securities, at market*		$28,600
Stockholders' equity:		
Accumulated other comprehensive income		$ 2,200

*While trading securities will always be classified as current assets, available-for-sale securities are classified as current or noncurrent assets depending on whether they will be sold within one year or one operating cycle, whichever is longer.

Redbird Corporation Partial Income Statement For the Year Ended December 31, 2012		
Other income:		
Interest income	$1,500	
Dividend income	500	
Other loss:		
Unrealized loss on trading securities	$ 800	

To summarize, the debits and credits for trading securities and available-for-sale securities are identical. The only difference is that unrealized gains and losses affect the financial statements differently:

- Unrealized gains and losses for trading securities are included on the income statement and thus, flow into retained earnings.
- Unrealized gains and losses for available-for-sale securities, on the other hand, are *not* included on the income statement. Instead, they are included as part of "accumulated other comprehensive income," a separate account in stockholders' equity.

Equity Method

The fair value method should be used when investors are considered passive. But when the investor possesses significant influence over the operating and financial policies of the investee (20 to 50 percent common stock ownership), the investor must use the *equity method* to account for the investment. The **equity method** requires an investor to recognize income when it is reported as earned by the investee, rather than when dividends accrue. The earlier recognition of investment income and loss under the equity method is consistent with the close relationship between the investor and investee.

Purchase of Stock   On January 1, 2012, Redbird purchases 25 percent of the common stock of one of its major suppliers—Korsgard Mining, a newly formed corporation—for $4,000,000 cash. Redbird would record the purchase with the following journal entry:

Date	Account and Explanation	Debit	Credit
Jan. 1, 2012	Investments—Equity Method	4,000,000	
	Cash		4,000,000
	(Record purchase of Korsgard stock)		

Assets	= Liabilities +	Stockholders' Equity
+4,000,000		
−4,000,000		

Note that the investment is recorded at cost, just as it is in the amortized cost and fair value methods. In addition, the investment is recorded in a separate account, not with the trading or available-for-sale securities.

Investee Income and Dividends On November 1, 2012, Korsgard declared and paid a cash dividend of $60,000. Further, for the year ended December 31, 2012, Korsgard reported net income of $440,000. Under the equity method, these events would have the following effect on Redbird's accounts:

Date	Account and Explanation	Debit	Credit
Nov. 1, 2012	Cash*	15,000	
	Investments—Equity Method		15,000
	(Record receipt of dividends)		

Assets	= Liabilities +	Stockholders' Equity
+15,000		
−15,000		

Date	Account and Explanation	Debit	Credit
Dec. 31, 2012	Investments—Equity Method**	110,000	
	Investment Income—Equity Method		110,000
	(Record Redbird's share of Korsgard net income)		

Assets	= Liabilities +	Stockholders' Equity
+110,000		+110,000

*25% × $60,000 = $15,000
**25% × $440,000 = $110,000

Unlike the fair value method, the equity method recognizes income when income is earned by the investee, not when a dividend is declared and paid. Instead, the dividend paid by Korsgard is a distribution to owners and therefore reduces the amount of Redbird's investment.

Reporting on the Financial Statements Equity method investments are carried on the balance sheet as follows:

$$\text{Acquisition cost} + \text{Investor's share of the investee's income (loss)} \\ - \text{Investor's share of the investee's dividends}$$

This means the investment account is not adjusted for changes in the fair market value of the common stock. Redbird would account for its investment in Korsgard as follows:

Investments—Equity Method (Korsgard Mining)

Purchase of Korsgard stock, 1/1/12	4,000,000	Receipt of Korsgard dividends, 11/1/12	15,000
Redbird's share of Korsgard net income, 12/31/12	110,000		
	4,095,000		

Redbird Corporation
Partial Balance Sheet
At December 31, 2012

Non-current assets:
Investments—Equity Method (Korsgard Mining) $4,095,000

Redbird Corporation
Partial Income Statement
For the Year Ended December 31, 2012

Investment Income—Equity Method (Korsgard) $110,000

One advantage of the equity method over the fair value method is that it prevents an investor from manipulating its own income by exerting influence over the amount and timing of investee dividends.

CONSOLIDATED FINANCIAL STATEMENTS

If the investor holds enough common stock to control the investee (50 percent or more common stock ownership), then the two corporations are no longer separate accounting entities. In such cases, in addition to using the equity method, the investor must prepare consolidated financial statements, which combine information about the two corporations as if they were a single company. In this case the investor is referred to as the parent and the investee is called the subsidiary. Of course, the parent and subsidiary continue to maintain separate accounting records.

Preparing Consolidated Statements

Consolidated financial statements are prepared from information contained in the separate financial statements of the parent and subsidiary:

- The consolidated balance sheet is essentially the same as the parent's balance sheet, except the parent's "investment in subsidiary" account is replaced by the subsidiary's assets and liabilities.
- The consolidated income statement is essentially the parent's income statement, except the parent's "income from subsidiary" is replaced by the sub's revenues and expenses.

Consolidated Balance Sheet
To illustrate the preparation of consolidated balance sheets, consider the following situation in which a parent owns all the outstanding stock of its subsidiary.[2]

On January 1, 2012, Parent, Inc., purchases all the outstanding common stock of Sub Corporation for $2,750,000. In this case, since Parent has control over Sub, a consolidated balance sheet needs to be prepared from the individual balance sheets of both companies. To do so, a **consolidation worksheet** must be prepared. Exhibit A2-3 presents the worksheet that is used to prepare the consolidated income statement for Parent and Sub at acquisition. The corporate balance sheets for Parent and Sub are listed in the two left-hand columns of the worksheet. Consolidation adjustments are entered into the third column. The amounts in the fourth column can be computed by adding the first two columns and the adjustments.

As you can see in Exhibit A2-3, the consolidation of these two balance sheets requires a credit adjustment that eliminates Parent's Investment in Sub account. This is

Worksheet for Preparing the Consolidated Balance Sheet on January 1, 2012

| | Parent | Sub | Adjustments | | Consolidated |
			Debit	Credit	
Assets:					
Current assets	$ 9,250,000	$ 700,000			$ 9,950,000
Investment—equity method	2,750,000			2,750,000	—
Property, plant, and equipment	68,000,000	2,300,000			70,300,000
Total assets	$80,000,000	$3,000,000			$80,250,000
Liabilities	$10,000,000	$ 250,000			$10,250,000
Stockholders' equity					
Common stock	40,000,000	1,000,000	1,000,000		40,000,000
Retained earnings	30,000,000	1,750,000	1,750,000		30,000,000
Total liabilities and stockholders' equity	$80,000,000	$3,000,000			$80,250,000

[2] Many large corporations have a complex network of many subsidiaries. However, for the sake of simplicity, the examples here discuss a two-corporation structure involving one parent and one subsidiary.

offset by debits to the Common Stock and Retained Earnings accounts, which eliminates the related stockholders' equity of Sub. These worksheet adjustments are not entered on the accounting records of either Parent or Sub.

Consolidated Income Statement Just as a consolidation worksheet was used to prepare the consolidated balance sheet for Parent and Sub, a similar worksheet must be prepared for the consolidated income statement. Exhibit A2-4 presents the worksheet that is used to prepare the consolidated income statement for Parent and Sub one year after acquisition.

Exhibit A2-4

Worksheet for Preparing the Consolidated Income Statement on December 31, 2012

	Parent	Sub	Adjustments Debit	Adjustments Credit	Consolidated
Revenue	$9,000,000	$2,000,000			$11,000,000
Cost of goods sold	3,200,000	950,000			4,150,000
Depreciation expense	2,100,000	220,000			2,320,000
Other expenses	1,600,000	230,000			1,830,000
Investment income—equity method	600,000		600,000		
Net income	$2,700,000	$ 600,000			$ 2,700,000

Notice that the consolidated net income is exactly the same as Parent's net income. From Parent's viewpoint, the consolidation procedure does not change net income, only the revenues and expenses on which net income is based. The credit needed to offset the $600,000 debit adjustment (and keep everything in balance) occurs on the balance sheet—against the Investment in Sub account. Preparation of the consolidated balance sheet on December 31, 2012, one year after the acquisition, follows the same principles. However, it is complicated by Parent's equity method journal entries. Further, adjustments are required to eliminate any transactions between Parent and Sub (such as the sale or other transfer of assets). Because you cannot make a sale to yourself, such transactions between the two corporations must be eliminated to present the two corporations as a single accounting entity.

Reporting a Minority or Noncontrolling Interest

Consolidation is required when a parent acquires between 50 and 100 percent of the subsidiary's stock. Any voting stock not held by the parent is called the **minority interest** or **noncontrolling interest**, and the holders of such shares are called minority stockholders. However, even when the parent owns less than 100 percent of the subsidiary's stock, 100 percent of the subsidiary's assets and liabilities are included in the consolidated balance sheet. In other words, if the parent controls the subsidiary, it controls *all* of the subsidiary's assets and liabilities.

For example, assume Parent had acquired only 80 percent of Sub. The consolidated total assets would have still been $80,250,000 because Parent controls all of the assets of Sub. However, the minority interest would have been $550,000 [20% × ($1,000,000 + $1,750,000)] and this amount must be shown as a component of stockholders' equity on the consolidated balance sheet. Further, the consolidated income statement would show 100 percent of Sub's revenues and expenses, but 20 percent of net income would be deducted as belonging to the minority interest.

BUSINESS COMBINATIONS

Any transaction or set of transactions that brings together two or more previously separate entities to form a single accounting entity is called a **business combination**. Business combinations take many forms. Some, like Parent–Sub described in the previous section, involve the acquisition of another corporation's stock in exchange for cash.

OBJECTIVE **3**
Describe accounting for business combinations.

Others involve the acquisition of another corporation's stock with the parent's own common stock. In either case, these are called **stock acquisitions** because the stock of the other corporation is being acquired. The parent could also purchase some or all of the assets of the other corporation. This is referred to as an **asset acquisition**. In this case, the two entities actually become a single legal entity.

Business combinations usually, but not always, transfer ownership of the acquired business entity from one stockholder group to another. In general, purchased assets are recorded at current cost, which is measured as the fair value of the cash and other consideration given up to acquire the asset. Thus, a purchased asset is recorded at its current value to the purchaser, without regard to its recorded value to the seller. Applying this logic to a business combination, a purchased company must be recorded at the value of the cash and other consideration given by the acquiring company.

To illustrate, consider the acquisition of all the assets and liabilities (i.e., an asset acquisition) of Landron Bottling Works by CactusCo for $12,000,000. With the approval of Landron's stockholders and creditors, Landron transfers all of its assets and liabilities to CactusCo and distributes the cash to Landron's stockholders. On the acquisition date, Landron's stockholders' equity was $6,500,000. CactusCo determines that Landron's liabilities of $1,000,000 are correctly valued, but its identifiable assets have a fair value of $3,800,000 more than their book value of $7,500,000. Thus, the acquisition cost exceeds the fair value of the net assets (assets minus liabilities) acquired by $1,700,000:

Acquisition cost			$ 12,000,000
Current value of identifiable net assets acquired:			
Book value of assets acquired	$ 7,500,000		
Adjustment to current value	$ 3,800,000	$11,300,000	
Less:			
Book value of liabilities acquired	$(1,000,000)		
Adjustment to current value	0	$ (1,000,000)	$ (10,300,000)
Excess of acquisition cost over current value (goodwill)			$ 1,700,000

The excess of acquisition cost over the fair value of Landron's identifiable net assets is recorded as goodwill. **Goodwill** is an intangible asset arising from attributes that are not separable from the business—such as customer satisfaction, product quality, skilled employees, and business location. CactusCo's recording of the acquisition would be recorded with following journal entry:

Account and Explanation	Debit	Credit
Assets (various accounts)	11,300,000	
Goodwill	1,700,000	
Liabilities (various accounts)		1,000,000
Cash		12,000,000
(Record the acquisition of Landron's net assets)		

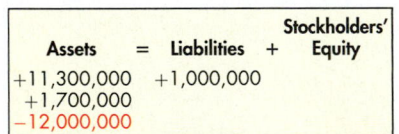

Assets	=	Liabilities	+	Stockholders' Equity
+11,300,000		+1,000,000		
+1,700,000				
−12,000,000				

This entry assumes that Landron goes out of existence as a corporation. If, instead of selling its net assets to CactusCo, Landron stockholders sell all their stock (as in a stock acquisition) to CactusCo, Landron will continue as a legal entity and the journal entry would be as follows:

Account and Explanation	Debit	Credit
Investments—Equity Method	12,000,000	
Cash		12,000,000
(Record the acquisition of Landron's stock)		

Assets	=	Liabilities	+	Stockholders' Equity
+12,000,000				
−12,000,000				

In this case, CactusCo must also consolidate Landron's financial statements, substituting the detailed assets (including goodwill) and liabilities for the investment account. The financial statements for a 100 percent asset acquisition will be identical to the consolidated financial statements for a 100 percent stock acquisition.

SUMMARY OF LEARNING OBJECTIVES

LO1.   Choose between and use the amortized cost, fair value, and equity methods for reporting investments.
- There are three methods of accounting for investments.
  - The amortized cost method is used only for debt securities that the business plans to hold until maturity.
  - The fair value method is used for both debt and equity securities that are classified as either trading securities or available-for-sale securities (less than 20 percent common stock ownership).
  - The equity method is used for equity securities in which 20 percent or more of the outstanding common stock is owned.
- Investments in equity securities in which more than 50 percent of the outstanding common stock is owned are also required to issue consolidated financial statements.

LO2.   Describe the consolidated balance sheet and income statement.
- When a company owns more than 50 percent of the outstanding common stock of another corporation, the investor (parent) is deemed to control the other corporation (subsidiary).
- In this case, the parent is required to issue consolidated financial statements in which the parent's and subsidiary's financial statements are combined.
- Minority (or noncontrolling) interest is disclosed when the parent owns more than 50 percent, but less than 100 percent of the outstanding common stock.

LO3.   Describe accounting for business combinations.
- Business combinations can occur through either an asset or stock acquisition.
- The business combination is recorded at the cost of acquisition, without regard to the seller's book value.
- The excess of acquisition cost over the current value of identifiable net assets is recorded as goodwill.

KEY TERMS

Amortized cost method (p. 1256)
Asset acquisition (p. 1264)
Available-for-sale securities (p. 1256)
Business combination (p. 1263)
Consolidated financial statements (p. 1255)
Consolidation worksheet (p. 1262)
Debt security (p. 1255)
Equity method (p. 1260)
Equity security (p. 1255)
Fair value method (p. 1258)

Goodwill (p. 1264)
Held-to-maturity securities (p. 1256)
Minority interest (p. 1263)
Noncontrolling interest (p. 1263)
Parent (p. 1255)
Stock acquisitions (p. 1264)
Subsidiary (p. 1255)
Trading securities (p. 1256)
Unrealized gains (p. 1259)
Unrealized losses (p. 1259)

DISCUSSION QUESTIONS

1. How do long-term investments differ from short-term investments?
2. Describe the three classifications that are possible for investments in debt securities.
3. Describe the amortized cost method of accounting for investments. Under which circumstances should it be used?
4. Describe the fair value method of accounting for investments. Under which circumstances should it be used?
5. Describe the equity method of accounting for investments. Under which circumstances should it be used?
6. How do available-for-sale securities differ from trading securities?

7. What event triggers the recognition of investment income under the amortized cost method? Under the fair value method? Under the equity method?
8. How does the equity method discourage the manipulation of net income by investors?
9. Define the terms *parent* and *subsidiary*.
10. What is minority interest and where is it reported on the consolidated balance sheet?
11. How does the consolidated balance sheet differ from the balance sheet of the parent?
12. What is the allowance to adjust short-term investments to market, and why is it used?
13. Why is it necessary to eliminate transactions between the parent and subsidiary in consolidation?
14. What is the difference between an asset acquisition and a stock acquisition?
15. What is goodwill, and how is it calculated?

MULTIPLE-CHOICE EXERCISES

A2-1 Investments in equity securities are deemed to be "passive" if:

a. 100 percent of the firm's stock is owned.
b. between 50 percent and 100 percent of the firm's stock is owned.
c. between 20 percent and 50 percent of the firm's stock is owned.
d. less than 20 percent of the firm's stock is owned.

A2-2 Equity and debt investments that management intends to sell in the future, but not necessarily in the near term, are called:

a. Trading securities
b. Available-for-sale securities
c. Debt securities
d. Stock securities

A2-3 Which of the following is a reason businesses purchase securities?

a. To profit from changes in day-to-day security prices.
b. To diversify risk.
c. To save (and earn returns on) money from uneven cash flows.
d. All of the above are reasons to purchase securities.

A2-4 Which of the following terms is not used for debt securities?

a. Trading Securities
b. Fair Value Securities
c. Available-for-Sale Securities
d. Held to Maturity Securities

A2-5 How are held-to-maturity securities valued?

a. Historical Cost
b. Fair Market Value
c. Amortized Cost
d. Amortized Fair Value

A2-6 The Boss Inc. reported an unrealized gain *on its income statement* due to appreciation in the stock price of AMW Corp. How much of AMW does The Boss own, and how have they classified this investment?

a. Owns 35%, trading security
b. Owns 18%, available-for-sale security
c. The Boss owns over half of AMW and has consolidated the companies' income statement information.
d. Owns 9%, trading security

A2-7 EMK Corp. is holding two bonds to maturity, both of which have a book value of $132,000. At the end of the fiscal year, the fair market value of bond A is $118,000, and the fair market value of bond B is $136,000. What is the unrealized gain or loss for EMK on these two bonds?

a. Unrealized loss of $14,000
b. Unrealized loss of $10,000
c. Unrealized gain of $4,000
d. No unrealized gain or loss

Refer to the following information for Multiple-Choice Exercises A2-8 and A2-9:
Shackley Inc. owns three available-for-sale equity securities, which have yielded the following fiscal year-end results:

A. Dividend income: $350
B. Gain on sale: $2,000
C. Unrealized loss: $600

A2-8 Refer to the information for Shackley above. Which of these are reported on Shackley's income statement?

a. A & B
b. B only
c. A & C
d. B & C

A2-9 Refer to the information for Shackley above. Assume that one of the securities was solely responsible for the $600 unrealized loss and was responsible for $150 of the dividend income. If Shackley bought that security for $3,500, what is the value of the security on the year-end balance sheet?

a. $3,500
b. $3,050
c. $3,650
d. $2,900

A2-10 JFK Inc. buys 30 percent of the shares outstanding for KLN Company. What account will JFK debit?

a. Trading Securities
b. Available-for-Sale Securities
c. Investments – Equity Method
d. Investments

A2-11 Whopper Corporation owns a 40 percent interest in BigMac Corporation, which it purchased for $2.5 million. During fiscal year 2012, BigMac paid cash dividends of $50,000 and reported net income of $700,000. What is the value of Whopper's investment in BigMac reported on its 2012 balance sheet?

a. $3,150,000
b. $2,500,000
c. $2,760,000
d. $2,450,000

A2-12 When the market value of a company's available-for-sale securities is lower than its cost, the difference should be:

a. shown as a liability.
b. shown as a valuation allowance subtracted from the historical cost of the investments.
c. shown as a valuation allowance added to the historical cost of the investments.
d. No entry is made, the securities are shown at historical cost.

A2-13 What account title will *not* appear on consolidated financial statements?

a. Inventory
b. Investment in EBL Corporation (80% ownership)
c. Investment in MJK Corporation (35% ownership)
d. Common stock

A2-14 Consolidated financial statements are required:

a. whenever the common stock of another corporation is owned.
b. only when significant influence or control can be exerted over another company.
c. when over 50 percent of the common stock of another corporation is owned.
d. only when 100 percent of the common stock of another corporation is owned.

A2-15 Assume a parent has total assets of $6,000,000 and a subsidiary has total assets of $4,000,000. If the parent owns 70 percent of the subsidiary's common stock, what amount of total assets will be reported on the consolidated balance sheet?

a. $0, consolidation is not necessary
b. $6,000,000

c. $7,000,000
d. $10,000,000

A2-16 Goodwill is calculated as the excess of the cost of an acquired company over the:

a. book value of net assets acquired.
b. fair value of assets acquired.
c. fair value of identifiable net assets acquired.
d. book value of identifiable net assets acquired.

EXERCISES

OBJECTIVE 1

Exercise A2-17 Matching Accounting Methods and Investments

Consider the following accounting methods for long-term investments:

a. Amortized cost method
b. Fair value method

c. Equity method
d. Consolidation of parent and sub

Required:
Match one or more of these methods with each of the investments described below:

1. Mueller Inc. owns 75 percent of Johnston Corporation's outstanding common stock.
2. Anderson Inc. owns 25 percent of Peterson Corporation's outstanding common stock.
3. Wixon Corporation owns 12 percent of the outstanding common stock of Gilman, Inc., which is classified as available-for-sale.
4. Kohler Corporation holds a $40,000 long-term note receivable from Bennett, Inc., a major customer. Kohler expects to sell the note within the next two or three years.
5. Janis Products Inc. holds $200,000 in Gibson Manufacturing bonds. Janis plans to hold these until they mature.

OBJECTIVE 1

Exercise A2-18 Trading Securities

Franzen Finance began operations in 2012 and invests in securities classified as trading securities. During 2012, it entered into the following trading security transactions:

Purchased 20,000 shares of ABC common stock at $38 per share
Purchased 32,000 shares of XYZ common stock at $17 per share

At December 31, 2012, ABC common stock was trading at $39.50 per share and XYZ common stock was trading at $16.50 per share.

Required:
1. Prepare the necessary adjusting entry to value the trading securities at fair market value.
2. **Conceptual Connection:** What is the income statement effect of this adjusting entry?

OBJECTIVE 1

Exercise A2-19 Available-for-Sale Securities

Tolland Financial began operators in 2012 and invests in securities classified as available-for-sale. During 2012, it entered into the following available-for-sale security transactions:

Purchased 10,000 shares of DTR common stock at $50 per share
Purchased 44,000 shares of MJO common stock at $22 per share

At December 31, 2012, DTR common stock was trading at $62 per share and MJO common stock was trading at $21 per share.

Required:
1. Prepare the necessary adjusting entry to value the available-for-sale securities at fair market value.
2. **Conceptual Connection:** What is the income statement effect of this adjusting entry?

Exercise A2-20   Allowance for Available-for-Sale Securities

OBJECTIVE ❶

McCarthy Corporation's allowance to reduce available-for-sale securities to market has a $7,200 credit balance on December 31, 2012, before the lower-of-cost-or-market adjustment. The cost and market value of the available-for-sale portfolio at December 31, 2012 are $120,000 and $117,000, respectively.

Required:

Prepare the adjusting entry, if any, to adjust the allowance at year-end.

Exercise A2-21   Adjusting the Allowance to Adjust Trading Securities to Market

OBJECTIVE ❶

Perry Corporation has the following information for its portfolio of trading securities at the end of the past four years:

Date	Portfolio Cost	Portfolio Market Value
12/31/09	$162,300	$153,800
12/31/10	109,600	106,200
12/31/11	148,900	151,300
12/31/12	139,000	138,700

Required:

1. Prepare the journal entries, if necessary, to adjust the allowance account at the end of 2010, 2011, and 2012.
2. **Conceptual Connection:** What is the income statement effect of the 2012 entry?
3. **Conceptual Connection:** How would your answer to 2 change if this was an available-for-sale portfolio?

Exercise A2-22   Investments in Available-for-Sale Securities

OBJECTIVE ❶

Williams Corporation acquired the following equity securities during 2012:

200 shares of Southwestern Company capital stock	$14,600
500 shares of Montgomery Products capital stock	14,500

Williams's investment in both of these companies is passive and Williams classifies these securities as available-for-sale. During 2012, Southwestern paid a dividend of $1.20 per share, and Montgomery paid a dividend of $1.80 per share. At December 31, 2012, the Southwestern stock has a market value of $75 per share, and the Montgomery stock has a market value of $25 per share.

Required:

1. Prepare entries for Williams's journal to record these two investments and the receipt of the dividends.
2. Calculate the market value of Williams's short-term investment portfolio at December 31, 2012.
3. Prepare the necessary adjusting entry at December 31, 2012.
4. How would these securities be disclosed on the December 31, 2012, balance sheet?

Exercise A2-23   Fair Value and Equity Methods

OBJECTIVE ❶

Nadal Corporation purchased the 10,000 shares of Cutler Inc.'s common stock, on January 1, 2011, for $100,000. During 2011, Cutler declared and paid cash dividends to Nadal in the amount of $8,000. Nadal's share of Cutler's net income for 2011 was $12,400. At December 31, 2011, the fair value of 10,000 shares of Cutler's common stock was $120,000. This is Nadal's only investment.

Required:

1. Assume that Cutler has 75,000 shares of common stock outstanding. What journal entries will Nadal make during 2011 relative to this investment?
2. Assume that Cutler has 40,000 shares of common stock outstanding. What journal entries will Nadal make during 2011 relative to this investment?

OBJECTIVE ❶

Exercise A2-24 Fair Value Method

On January 1, 2011, Reduction Products Inc. acquired 1,500 shares of the outstanding common stock of Tupper Corp. for $24,000. On that date, Tupper had 10,000 shares of common stock outstanding. On October 1, 2011, Tupper declared and paid a cash dividend of $2 per share. On November 13, 2011, Reduction sold 300 shares of Tupper for $5,000. Tupper reported 2011 net income of $36,000. Tupper's stock sold for $15 per share at December 31, 2011. This is Reduction's only investment and they plan on remaining invested in Tupper for a number of years.

Required:

1. Prepare Reduction's journal entries to record the transactions related to its investment in Tupper.
2. Give the title and amount of each item (except cash) on the December 31, 2011, balance sheet related to this investment. Name the balance sheet section in which each item appears.

OBJECTIVE ❶

Exercise A2-25 Equity Method

On January 1, 2011, Hill Corporation acquired 40 percent of the outstanding common stock (400 of 1,000 outstanding shares) of Valley Manufacturing Inc. for $60,000, which equals the book value of Valley. On December 31, 2011, Valley reported net income of $30,000 and declared and paid a cash dividend of $11,500.

Required:

1. Prepare the journal entries made by Hill to record the transactions related to its investment in Valley.
2. Give the title and amount of each item (except cash) on the December 31, 2011, balance sheet related to the investment. Name the balance sheet section in which each item appears.

OBJECTIVE ❶

Exercise A2-26 Accounting for Investments in Equity Securities

On January 1, 2011, Stern Corporation purchased 100 shares of common stock issued by Milstein, Inc. (representing 12 percent of the total shares outstanding) for $6,000 and 500 shares of Heifetz Inc. (representing 25 percent of the total shares outstanding) for $20,000. Assume that the acquisition cost of each investment equals the book value of the related stockholders' equity on the records of the investee. During 2011, Milstein declared and paid cash dividends to Stern of $500 and Heifetz declared and paid cash dividends to Stern of $1,700. Milstein reported 2011 net income of $12,000 and Heifetz reported 2011 net income of $15,000. On December 31, 2011, the market value of 100 shares of Milstein was $6,450 and the market value of 500 shares of Heifetz was $19,720.

Required:

Answer the following questions for both investments:

	Milstein	Heifetz
1. Which accounting method is applicable?		
2. What amount is recorded in the investment account on the date of acquisition?		
3. What amount is recorded in Stern's net income from the investment?		
4. What amount is reported for the investment on the balance sheet at December 31, 2011?		

OBJECTIVE ❶

Exercise A2-27 Investments in Trading Securities

Maxwell Company engaged in the following transactions involving short-term investments:

a. Purchased 200 shares of Bartco stock for $12,800.
b. Received a $1.60-per-share dividend on the Bartco stock.
c. Sold 40 shares of the Bartco stock for $61 per share.
d. Purchased 380 shares of Newton stock for $20,900.
e. Received a dividend of $1.00 per share on the Newton stock.

At December 31, the Bartco stock has a market value of $60 per share, and the Newton stock has a market value of $59 per share.

Required:

1. Prepare entries for Maxwell's journal to record these transactions assuming they are trading securities.
2. Calculate the market value of Maxwell's short-term investment portfolio at December 31.
3. Prepare the necessary adjusting entry at December 31.
4. **Conceptual Connection:** What is the income statement effect of the adjusting entry?
5. How would these investments be reported on the December 31 balance sheet?

Exercise A2-28 Consolidated Balance Sheet

OBJECTIVE

Peachtree Corporation acquired 100 percent of the outstanding common stock of Standard Company in a business combination. Immediately before the business combination, the two businesses had the following balance sheets:

Peachtree		Standard	
Cash	$ 3,100	Cash	$ 180
Equipment (net)	9,500	Equipment (net)	930
Total assets	$12,600	Total assets	$1,110
Common stock	9,100	Common stock	700
Retained earnings	3,500	Retained earnings	410
Total liabilities & equity	$12,600	Total liabilities & equity	$1,110

Peachtree agreed to give Standard's shareholders $1,500 cash in exchange for all their Standard common stock. Standard's equipment has a fair value of $1,100.

Required:

1. Prepare the entries for Peachtree and Standard to record the business combination.
2. Prepare the balance sheet of Peachtree immediately after the business combination.
3. Prepare the balance sheet of Standard immediately after the business combination.
4. Calculate the amount of the adjustment to the book value of Standard's equity and the amount of goodwill.
5. Prepare a consolidated balance sheet immediately after the combination.

Exercise A2-29 Consolidated Income Statement

OBJECTIVE

Johnson Inc. is the wholly owned subsidiary of Stuart Corporation. The 2012 income statements for the two corporations are as follows:

Stuart			Johnson		
Sales revenue		$3,200	Sales revenue		$500
Income from investment in Johnson		?			
Total revenue		?	Total revenue		$500
Cost of goods sold	$920		Cost of goods sold	$160	
Depreciation expense	410		Depreciation expense	95	
Other expenses	680	$2,010	Other expenses	135	$390
Net income		?	Net income		$110

The acquisition cost of Stuart's 100 percent ownership interest in Johnson equaled its book value on Johnson's records. During 2012, Johnson pays a cash dividend of $25 to Stuart.

Required:

1. Calculate the income from investment in Johnson as reported on Stuart's income statement.
2. Calculate the 2012 net income reported by the parent company (Stuart) on its income statement.
3. Prepare the 2012 consolidated income statement for Stuart and Johnson.

OBJECTIVE

Exercise A2-30 Goodwill

Pindar Corporation acquired all the outstanding stock of Strauss Company for $23,000,000 on January 1, 2012. On the date of acquisition, Strauss had the following balance sheet:

Strauss Company
Balance Sheet
January 1, 2012

Assets		Liabilities	
Accounts receivable	$ 6,800,000	Accounts payable	$ 2,000,000
Inventory	4,700,000	Notes payable	8,000,000
Property, plant & equipment (net)	16,300,000	Total liabilities	$10,000,000
		Stockholders' Equity	
		Common stock	$ 2,000,000
		Additional paid-in capital— common stock	8,000,000
		Retained earnings	7,800,000
		Total stockholders' equity	$17,800,000
Total assets	$27,800,000	Total liabilities & stockholders' equity	$27,800,000

All Strauss' assets and liabilities have book values equal to their fair values except for equipment, which has a fair value of $20,700,000.

Required:
1. Calculate the amount of goodwill.
2. Prepare the journal entry by Pindar to record the acquisition.
3. Assume that instead of acquiring all the outstanding common stock of Strauss, Pindar acquired 100 percent of Strauss' net assets. What would Pindar's journal entry be in this case?

Time Value of Money

3
Appendix

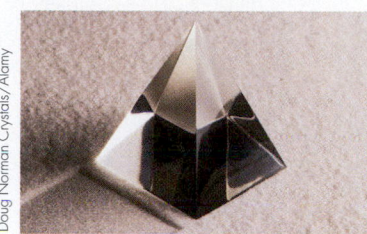

Doug Norman Crystals/Alamy

After studying Appendix 3, you should be able to:

1. Explain how compound interest works.
2. Use future value and present value tables to apply compound interest to accounting transactions.

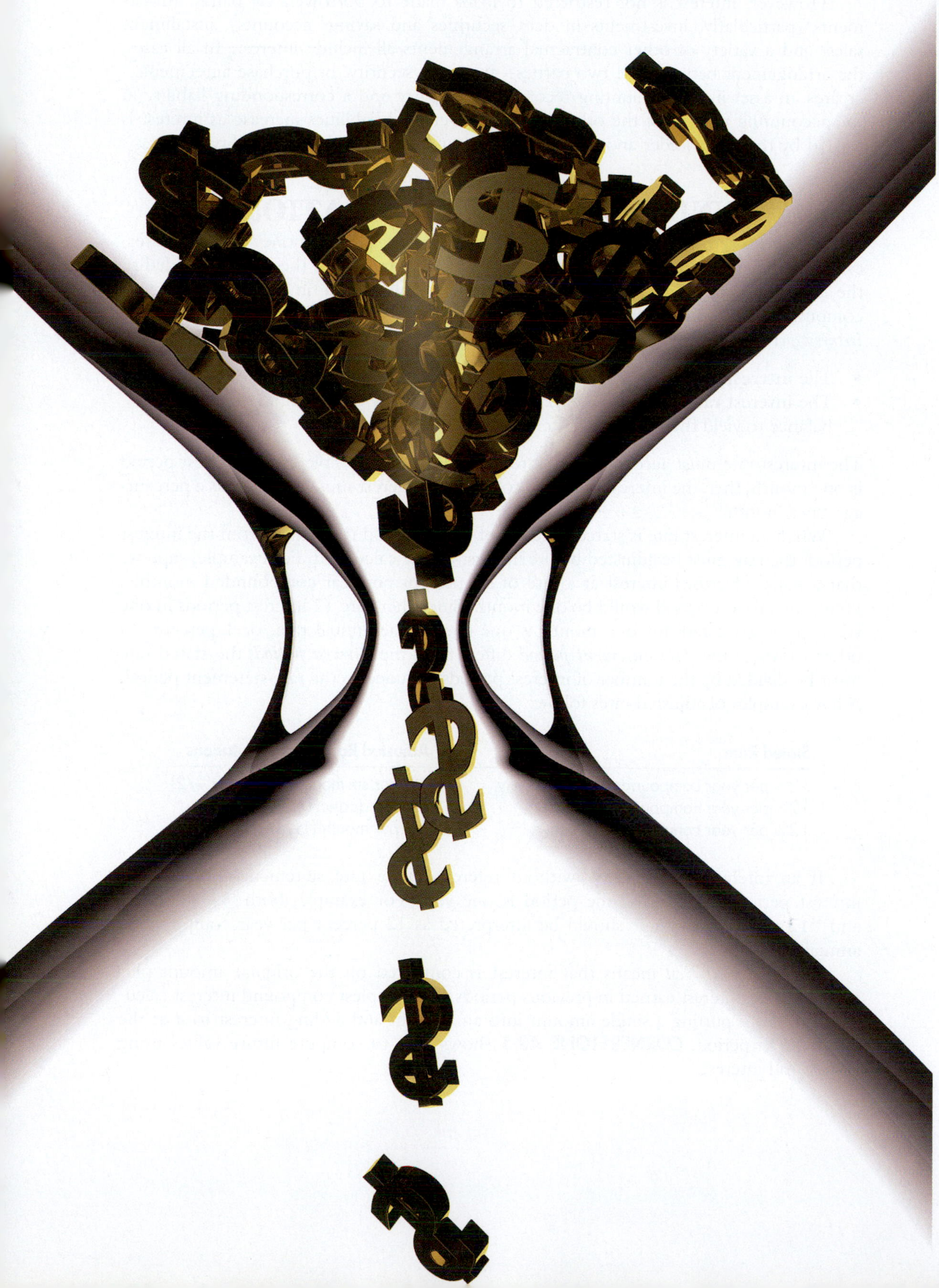

BrooksElliott/iStockphoto

Time value of money is widely used in business to measure today's value of future cash outflows or inflows and the amount to which liabilities (or assets) will grow when compound interest accumulates.

In transactions involving the borrowing and lending of money, the borrower usually pays *interest*. In effect, interest is the **time value of money**. The amount of interest paid is determined by the length of the loan and the interest rate.

However, interest is not restricted to loans made to borrowers by banks. Investments (particularly, investments in debt securities and savings accounts), installment sales, and a variety of other contractual arrangements all include interest. In all cases, the arrangement between the two parties—the note, security, or purchase agreement—creates an asset in the accounting records of one party and a corresponding liability in the accounting records of the other. All such assets and liabilities increase as interest is earned by the asset holder and decrease as payments are made by the liability holder.

OBJECTIVE ❶
Explain how compound interest works.

COMPOUND INTEREST CALCULATIONS

Compound interest is a method of calculating the time value of money in which interest is earned on the previous periods' interest. That is, interest for the period is added to the account balance and interest is earned on this new balance in the next period. In computing compound interest, it's important to understand the difference between the *interest period* and the *interest rate*:

- The **interest period** is the time interval between interest calculations.
- The **interest rate** is the percentage that is multiplied by the beginning-of-period balance to yield the amount of interest for that period.

The interest rate must agree with the interest period. For example, if the interest period is one month, then the interest rate used to calculate interest must be stated as a percentage "per month."

When an interest rate is stated in terms of a time period that differs from the interest period, the rate must be adjusted before interest can be calculated. For example, suppose that a bank advertises interest at a rate of 12 percent per year compounded monthly. Here, the interest period would be one month. Since there are 12 interest periods in one year, the interest rate for one month is one-twelfth the annual rate, or 1 percent. In other words, if the *rate statement period* differs from the *interest period*, the stated rate must be divided by the number of interest periods included in the rate statement period. A few examples of adjusted rates follow:

Stated Rate	Adjusted Rate for Computations
12% per year compounded semiannually	6% per six-month period (12%/2)
12% per year compounded quarterly	3% per quarter (12%/4)
12% per year compounded monthly	1% per month (12%/12)

If an interest rate is stated without reference to a rate statement period or an interest period, assume that the period is one year. For example, both "12 percent" and "12 percent per year" should be interpreted as 12 percent per year compounded annually.

Compound interest means that interest is computed on the original amount plus undistributed interest earned in previous periods. The simplest compound interest calculation involves putting a single amount into an account and adding interest to it at the end of each period. **CORNERSTONE A3-1** shows how to compute future values using compound interest.

CORNERSTONE
A3-1

Computing Future Values Using Compound Interest

Concept:
When deposits earn compound interest, interest is earned on the interest.

Information:
An investor deposits $20,000 in a savings account on January 1, 2012. The bank pays interest of 6 percent per year compounded monthly.

Required:
Assuming that the only activity to the account is the deposit of interest at the end of each month, how much money will be in the account after the interest payment on March 31, 2012?

Solution:
Monthly interest will be ½% (6% per year/12 months).

Account balance, 1/1/12	$20,000.00
January interest ($20,000.00 × ½%)	100.00
Account balance, 1/31/12	$20,100.00
February interest ($20,100.00 × ½%)	100.50
Account balance, 2/28/12	$20,200.50
March interest ($20,200.50 × ½%)	101.00
Account balance, 3/31/12	$20,301.50

Note: Here, interest was the only factor that altered the account balance after the initial deposit. In more complex situations, the account balance is changed by subsequent deposits and withdrawals as well as by interest. Withdrawals reduce the balance and therefore, the amount of interest in subsequent periods. Additional deposits have the opposite effect, increasing the balance and the amount of interest earned.

As you can see in Cornerstone A3-1, the balance in the account continues to grow each month by an increasing amount of interest. The amount of monthly interest increases because interest is *compounded*. In other words, interest is computed on accumulated interest as well as on principal. For example, February interest of $100.50 consists of $100 interest on the $20,000 principal and 50¢ interest on the $100 January interest ($100 × 0.005 = 50¢).

In Cornerstone A3-1, the compound interest only amounts to 25¢. That might seem relatively insignificant, but if the investment period is sufficiently long, the amount of compound interest grows large even at relatively small interest rates. For example, suppose your parents invested $1,000 at ½ percent per month when you were born with the objective of giving you a college graduation present at age 21. How much would that investment be worth after 21 years? The answer is $3,514. In 21 years, the compound interest is $2,514—more than 2½ times the original principal. Without compounding, interest over the same period would have been only $1,260.

The amount to which an account will grow when interest is compounded is the **future value** of the account. Compound interest calculations can assume two fundamentally different forms:

- calculations of future values
- calculations of present values

As shown, calculations of future values are projections of future balances based on *past and future* cash flows and interest payments. In contrast, calculations of present values are determinations of present amounts based on *expected* future cash flows.

PRESENT VALUE OF FUTURE CASH FLOWS

Whenever a contract establishes a relationship between an initial amount borrowed or loaned and one or more future cash flows, the initial amount borrowed or loaned is the **present value** of those future cash flows. The present value can be interpreted in two ways:

- From the borrower's viewpoint, it is the liability that will be exactly paid by the future payments.
- From the lender's viewpoint, it is the receivable balance that will be exactly satisfied by the future receipts.

In understanding cash flows, cash flow diagrams that display both the amounts and the times of the cash flows specified by a contract can be quite help helpful. In these diagrams, a time line runs from left to right. Inflows are represented as arrows pointing upward and outflows as arrows pointing downward. For example, suppose that the Hilliard Corporation borrows $100,000 from Citizens Bank of New Hope on January 1, 2013. The note requires three $38,803.35 payments, one each at the end of 2013, 2014, and 2015, and includes interest at 8 percent per year. The cash flows for Hilliard are shown in Exhibit A3-1.

Exhibit A3-1

Cash Flow Diagram

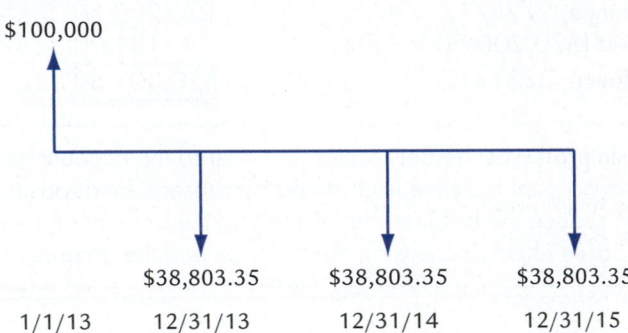

The calculation that follows shows, from the borrower's perspective, the relationship between the amount borrowed (*the present value*) and the future payments (*future cash flows*) required by Hilliard's note.

Amount borrowed, 1/1/13	$100,000.00
Add: 2013 interest ($100,000.00 × 0.08)	8,000.00
Subtract payment on 12/31/13	(38,803.35)
Liability at 12/31/13	$ 69,196.65
Add: 2014 interest ($69,196.65 × 0.08)	5,535.73
Subtract payment on 12/31/14	(38,803.35)
Liability at 12/31/14	$ 35,929.03
Add: 2015 interest ($35,929.03 × 0.08)	2,874.32
Subtract payment on 12/31/15	(38,803.35)
Liability at 12/31/15	$ 0.00

Present value calculations like this one are future value calculations in reverse. Here, the three payments of $38,803.35 exactly pay off the liability created by the note. Because the reversal of future value calculations can present a burdensome and sometimes difficult algebraic problem, shortcut methods using tables have been developed (see Exhibits A3-7, A3-8, A3-9, and A3-10, discussed later in this appendix).

Exhibit A3-2

Effect of Interest Periods on Compound Interest

Investment	Interest Period	I	N	Calculation of Future Amount In One Year*
A	1 year	12%	1	($10,000 × 1.12000) = $11,200
B	6 months	6%	2	($10,000 × 1.12360) = 11,236
C	1 quarter	3%	4	($10,000 × 1.12551) = 11,255
D	1 month	1%	12	($10,000 × 1.12683) = 11,268

*The multipliers (1.12 for Investment A, 1.12360 for investment B, etc.) are taken from the present and future value tables in Exhibit A3-7 (p. 1292).

Interest and the Frequency of Compounding

The number of interest periods into which a compound interest problem is divided can make a significant difference in the amount of compound interest. For example, assume that you are evaluating four 1-year investments, each of which requires an initial $10,000 deposit. All four investments earn interest at a rate of 12 percent per year, but they have different compounding periods. The data in Exhibit A3-2 show the impact of compounding frequency on future value. Investment D, which offers monthly compounding, accumulates $68 more interest by the end of the year than investment A, which offers only annual compounding.

FOUR BASIC COMPOUND INTEREST PROBLEMS

Any present value or future value problems can be broken down into one or more of the following four basic problems:

- computing the future value of a single amount
- computing the present value of a single amount
- computing the value of an annuity
- computing the present value of an annuity

OBJECTIVE **2**

Use future value and present value tables to apply compound interest to accounting transactions.

Computing the Future Value of a Single Amount

In computing the future value of a single amount, the following elements are used:

- f: the cash flow
- FV: the future value
- n: the number of periods between the cash flow and the future value
- i: the interest rate per period

To find the future value of a single amount, establish an account for f dollars and add compound interest at i percent to that account for n periods:

$$FV = (f)(1 + i)^n$$

The balance of the account after n periods is the future value.

Because people frequently need to compute the future value of a single amount, tables have been developed to make it easier. Therefore, instead of using the formula above, you could use the future value table in Exhibit A3-7 (p. 1292), where M_1 is the multiple that corresponds to the appropriate values of n and i:

$$FV = (f)(M_1)$$

For example, suppose Allied Financial loans $200,000 at a rate of 6 percent per year compounded annually to an auto dealership dealer for four years. Exhibit A3-3 shows

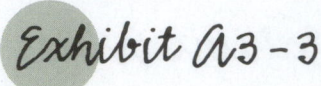

Exhibit A3-3

Future Value of a Single Amount: An Example

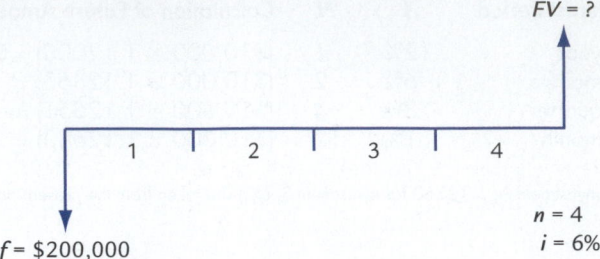

$FV = ?$

| | 1 | 2 | 3 | 4 |

$n = 4$
$i = 6\%$

$f = \$200,000$

how to compute the future value (FV) at the end of the four years—the amount that will be repaid. Assuming Allied's viewpoint (the lender's), using a compound interest calculation, the unknown future value (FV) would be found as follows:

Amount loaned	$200,000.00
First year's interest ($200,000.00 × 0.06)	12,000.00
Loan receivable at end of first year	$212,000.00
Second year's interest ($212,000.00 × 0.06)	12,720.00
Loan receivable at end of second year	$224,720.00
Third year's interest ($224,720.00 × 0.06)	13,483.20
Loan receivable at end of third year	$238,203.20
Fourth year's interest ($238,203.20 × 0.06)	14,292.19
Loan receivable at end of the fourth year	$252,495.39

As you can see, the amount of interest increases each year. This growth is the effect of computing interest for each year based on an amount that includes the interest earned in prior years.

The shortcut calculation, using the future value table (Exhibit A3-7, p. 1292), would be as follows:

$$FV = (f)(M_1)$$
$$= (\$200,000)(1.26248)$$
$$= \$252,496$$

You can find M_1 at the intersection of the 6 percent column ($i = 6\%$) and the fourth row ($n = 4$) or by calculating 1.06^4. This multiple is the future value of the single amount after having been borrowed (or invested) for four years at 6 percent interest. The future value of $200,000 is 200,000 times the multiple.

Note that there is a difference between the answer ($252,495.39) developed in the compound interest calculation and the answer ($252,496) determined using the future value table. This is because the numbers in the table have been rounded to five decimal places. If they were taken to eight digits ($1.06^4 = 1.26247696$), the two answers would be equal. **CORNERSTONE A3-2** shows how to compute the future value of a single amount.

CORNERSTONE
A3-2

Computing Future Value of a Single Amount

Concept:
The future value of a single amount is the original cash flow plus compound interest as of a specific future date.

Information:
The Kitchner Company sells an unneeded factory site for $200,000 on July 1, 2012. Kitchner expects to purchase a different site in 18 months so that it can expand into a new market. Meanwhile, Kitchner decides to invest the

(Continued)

$200,000 in a money market fund that is guaranteed to earn 6 percent per year compounded semiannually (3 percent per six-month period).

**CORNERSTONE
A3-2**
(continued)

Required:
1. Draw a cash flow diagram for this investment from Kitchner's perspective.
2. Calculate the amount of money in the money market fund on December 31, 2012, and prepare the journal entry necessary to recognize interest income.
3. Calculate the amount of money in the money market fund on December 31, 2013, and prepare the journal entry necessary to recognize interest *i*.

Solution:

1.

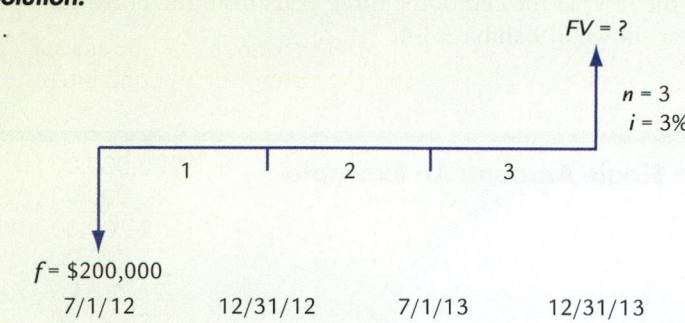

2. Because we are calculating the value at 12/31/12, there is only one period:

$$FV = (f)(FV \text{ of a Single Amount, 1 period, 3\%})$$
$$= (\$200,000)(1.03)$$
$$= \$206,000$$

The excess of the amount of money over the original deposit is the interest earned from July 1 through December 31, 2012.

Dec. 31, 2012	Cash	6,000	
	Interest Income		6,000
	(Record interest income)		

		Stockholders'
Assets	= Liabilities +	Equity
+6,000		+6,000

3. $$FV = (f)(FV \text{ of a Single Amount, 1 period, 3\%})$$
$$= (\$200,000)(1.03)$$
$$= \$206,000$$

The interest income for the year is the increase in the amount of money during 2012, which is $12,546 ($218,546 − $206,000). The journal entry to record interest income would be as follows:

Dec. 31, 2013	Cash	12,546	
	Interest income		12,546
	(Record interest income)		

		Stockholders'
Assets	= Liabilities +	Equity
+12,546		+12,546

Computing the Present Value of a Single Amount

In computing the present value of a single amount, the following elements are used:

- *f*: the future cash flow
- *PV*: the present value
- *n*: the number of periods between the present time and the future cash flow
- *i*: the interest rate per period

In present value problems, the interest rate is sometimes called the *discount rate*.

To find the present value of a single amount, use the following equation:

$$PV = \frac{f}{(1 + i)^n}$$

You could use the present value table in Exhibit A3-8 (p. 1293), where M_2 is the multiple from Exhibit A3-8 that corresponds to the appropriate values of n and i:

$$PV = (f)(M_2)$$

Suppose **Marathon Oil** has purchased property on which it plans to develop oil wells. The seller has agreed to accept a single $150,000,000 payment three years from now, when Marathon expects to be selling oil from the field. Assuming an interest rate of 7 percent per year, the (PV) at the end of the three years from the borrower's perspective can be calculated as shown in Exhibit A3-4.

Exhibit A3-4

Present Value of a Single Amount: An Example

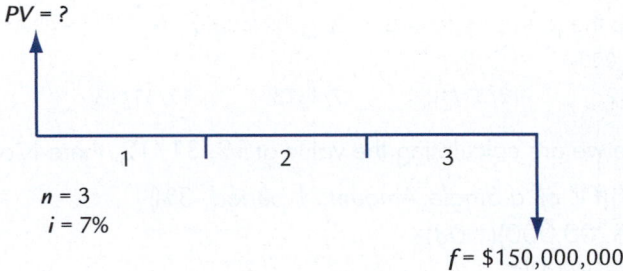

PV = ?

1   2   3

$n = 3$
$i = 7\%$

f = $150,000,000

The shortcut calculation, using the present value table (Exhibit A3-8, p. 1293), would be as follows:

$$PV = (f)(M_2)$$
$$= (\$150,000,000)(0.81630)$$
$$= \$122,445,000$$

You can find M_2 at the intersection of the 7 percent column $(i = 7\%)$ and the third row $(n = 3)$ in Exhibit A3-8 or by calculating $[1/(1.07)^3]$. This multiple is the present value of a $1 cash inflow or outflow in three years at 7 percent. Thus, the present value of $150,000,000 is 150,000,000 times as much as the multiple.

Although the future value calculation cannot be used to determine the present value, it can be used to verify that the present value calculated by using the table is correct. The following calculation is proof for the present value problem:

Calculated present value *(PV)*	$122,445,000
First year's interest ($122,445,000 × 0.07)	8,571,150
Loan payable at end of first year	$131,016,150
Second year's interest ($131,016,150 × 0.07)	9,171,131
Loan payable at end of second year	$140,187,281
Third year's interest ($140,187,281 × 0.07)	9,813,110
Loan payable at end of the third year *(f)*	$150,000,391

Again, the $391 difference between the amount here and the assumed $150,000,000 cash flow is due to rounding.

When interest is compounded on the calculated present value of $122,445,000, then the present value calculation is reversed and we return to the future cash flow of $150,000,000. This reversal proves that $122,445,000 is the correct present value. **CORNERSTONE A3-3** shows how to compute the present value of a single amount.

CORNERSTONE A3-3   Computing Present Value of a Single Amount

Concept:
The present value of a single cash flow is the original cash flow that must be invested to produce a known value at a specific future date.

Information:
On October 1, 2012, Adelsman Manufacturing Company sold a new machine to Randell, Inc. The machine represented a new design that Randell was eager to place in service. Since Randell was unable to pay for the machine on the date of purchase, Adelsman agreed to defer the $60,000 payment for 15 months. The appropriate rate of interest in such transactions is 8 percent per year compounded quarterly (2 percent per three-month period).

Required:
1. Draw the cash flow diagram for this deferred-payment purchase from Randell's (the borrower's) perspective.
2. Calculate the present value of this deferred-payment purchase.
3. Prepare the journal entry necessary to record the acquisition of the machine.

Solution:
1.

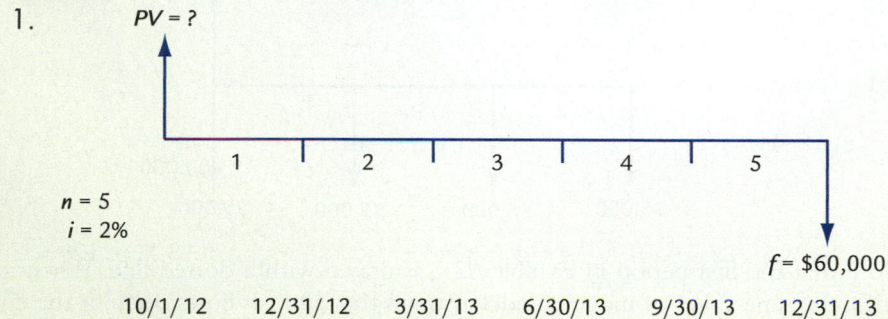

2. $FV = (f)(FV \text{ of a Single Amount, 1 period, 3\%})$
   $= (\$60,000)(0.90573)$
   $= \$54,344$

3.

Oct. 1, 2012	Equipment	54,344	
	Note Payable		54,344
	(Record purchase of equipment)		

Assets	=	Liabilities	+	Stockholders' Equity
+54,344		+54,344		

Computing the Future Value of an Annuity

So far, we have been discussing problems that involve a single cash flow. However, there are also instances of multiple cash flows one period apart. An **annuity** is a number of equal cash flows; one to each interest period. For example, an investment in a security that pays $1,000 to an investor every December 31 for 10 consecutive years is an annuity. A loan repayment schedule that calls for a payment of $367.29 on the first day of each month can also be considered an annuity. (Although the number of days in a month varies from 28 to 31, the interest period is defined as one month without regard to the number of days in each month.)

In computing the future value of an annuity, the following elements are used:

- f: the amount of each repeating cash flow
- FV: the future value after the last (n^{th}) cash flow
- n: the number of cash flows
- i: the interest rate per period

To find the future value of an annuity, use the following equation:

$$FV = (f)\left[\frac{(1 + i)^n - 1}{i}\right]$$

Alternatively, you could use the future value table in Exhibit A3-9 (p. 1294), where M_3 is the multiple from Exhibit A3-9 that corresponds to the appropriate values of n and i compound interest calculations:

$$FV = (f)(M_3)$$

Assume that **Chase** wants to advertise a new savings program to its customers. The savings program requires the customers to make four annual payments of $5,000 each, with the first payment due three years before the program ends. Chase advertises a 6 percent interest rate compounded annually. The future value of this annuity immediately after the fourth cash payment from the investor's perspective is shown in Exhibit A3-5.

Future Value of an Annuity: An Example

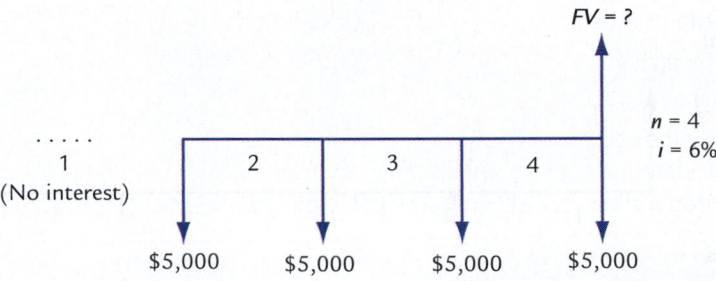

Note that the first period in Exhibit A3-5 is drawn with a dotted line. When using annuities, the time-value-of-money model assumes that all cash flows occur at the end of a period. Therefore, the first cash flow in the future value of an annuity occurs at the end of the first period. However, since interest cannot be earned until the first deposit has been made, the first period is identified as a no-interest period.

The future value (*FV*) can be computed as follows:

Interest for first period ($0 × 6%)	$ 0.00
First deposit	5,000.00
Investment balance at end of first year	$ 5,000.00
Second year's interest ($5,000.00 × 0.06)	300.00
Second deposit	5,000.00
Investment balance at end of second year	$10,300.00
Third year's interest ($10,300.00 × 0.06)	618.00
Third deposit	5,000.00
Investment balance at end of third year	$15,918.00
Fourth year's interest ($15,918.00 × 0.06)	955.08
Fourth deposit	5,000.00
Investment at end of the fourth year	$21,873.08

This calculation shows that the lender has accumulated a future value (*FV*) of $21,873.08 by the end of the fourth period, immediately after the fourth cash investment.

The shortcut calculation, using the future value table (Exhibit A3-9, p. 1294), would be as follows:

$$
\begin{aligned}
FV &= (f)(M_3) \\
&= (\$5,000)(4.37462) \\
&= \$21,873
\end{aligned}
$$

You can find M_3 at the intersection of the 6 percent column ($i = 6\%$) and the fourth row ($n = 4$) in the Exhibit A3-9 (p. 1294) or by calculating $(1.06^4 - 1)/0.06$. This multiple is the future value of an annuity of four cash flows of $1 each at 6 percent. The future value of an annuity of $5,000 cash flows is 5,000 times the multiple. Thus, the table allows us to calculate the future value of an annuity by a single multiplication, no matter how many cash flows are involved. **CORNERSTONE A3-4** shows how to compute the future value of an annuity.

 **CORNERSTONE** **Computing Future Value of an Annuity**
A 3 - 4

Concept:
The future value of an annuity is the value of a series of equal cash flows made at regular intervals with compound interest at some specific future date.

Information:
Greg Smith is a lawyer and CPA specializing in retirement and estate planning. One of Greg's clients, the owner of a large farm, wants to retire in five years. To provide funds to purchase a retirement annuity from New York Life at the date of retirement, Greg asks the client to give him annual payments of $170,000, which Greg will deposit in a special fund that will earn 7 percent per year.

Required:
1. Draw the cash flow diagram for the fund from Greg's client's perspective.
2. Calculate the future value of the fund immediately after the fifth deposit.
3. If Greg's client needs $1,000,000 to purchase the annuity, how much must be deposited every year?

Solution:
1.

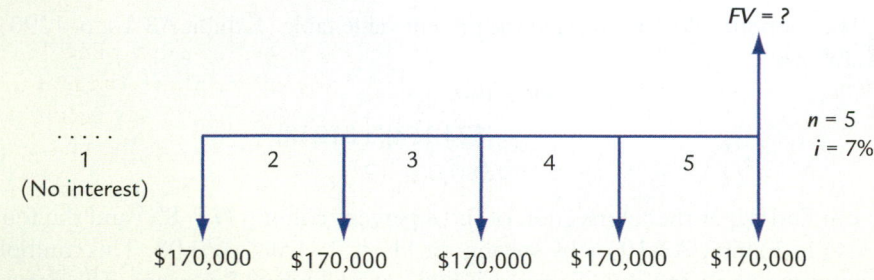

2. FV = (f)(FV of an Annuity, 5 periods, 7%)
   = ($170,000)(5,75074)
   = $977,626

3. In this case, the future value is known, but the annuity amount (f) is not:

   1,000,000 = (f)(FV of an Annuity, 5 periods, 7%)
   1,000,000 = (f)(5.75074)
       f = 1,000,000/5.75074
       f = $173,890.66

Present Value of an Annuity
In computing the present value of an annuity, the following elements are used:

- *f*: the amount of each repeating cash flow
- *PV*: the present value of the *n* future cash flows
- *n*: the number of cash flows and periods
- *i*: the interest (or discount) rate per period

To find the present value of an annuity, use the following equation:

$$PV = (f)\,\frac{1 - \dfrac{1}{(1+i)^n}}{i}$$

You could also use the present value table in Exhibit A3-10 (p. 1295), where M_4 is the multiple from Exhibit A3-10 that corresponds to the appropriate values of n and i:

$$PV = (f)(M_4)$$

For example, assume that **Xerox Corporation** purchased a new machine for its manufacturing operations. The purchase agreement requires Xerox to make four equally-spaced payments of $24,154 each. The interest rate is 8 percent compounded annually and the first cash flow occurs one year after the purchase. Exhibit A3-6 shows how to determine the present value of this annuity from Xerox's (the borrower's) perspective. Note that the same concept applies to both the lender's and borrower's perspectives.

Exhibit A3-6

Present Value of An Annuity: An Example

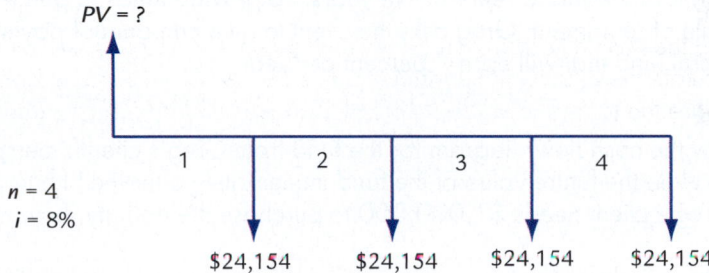

The shortcut calculation, using the present value table (Exhibit A3-10, p. 1295), would be as follows:

$$
\begin{aligned}
PV &= (f)(M_4) \\
&= (\$24{,}154)(3.31213) \\
&= \$80{,}001.19
\end{aligned}
$$

You can find M_4 at the intersection of the 8 percent column ($i = 8\%$) and the fourth row ($n = 4$) in Exhibit A3-10 or by solving for $[1 - (1/1.08^4)]/0.08$. This multiple is the present value of an annuity of four cash flows of $1 each at 8 percent. The present value of an annuity of four $24,154 cash flows is 24,154 times the multiple.

Again, although the compound interest calculation is not used to determine the present value, it can be used to prove that the present value found using the table is correct. The following calculation verifies the present value in the problem:

Calculated present value (PV)	$ 80,001.19
Interest for first year ($80,001.19 × 0.08)	6,400.10
Less: First cash flow	(24,154.00)
Balance at end of first year	$ 62,247.29
Interest for second year ($62,247.29 × 0.08)	4,979.78
Less: Second cash flow	(24,154.00)
Balance at end of second year	$ 43,073.07
Interest for third year ($43,073.07 × 0.08)	3,445.85
Less: Third cash flow	(24,154.00)
Balance at end of third year	$ 22,364.92
Interest for fourth year ($22,364.92 × 0.08)	1,789.19
Less: Fourth cash flow	(24,154.00)
Balance at end of fourth year	$ 0.11

This proof uses a compound interest calculation that is the reverse of the present value formula. If the present value (*PV*) calculated with the formula is correct, then the proof should end with a balance of zero immediately after the last cash flow. This proof ends with a balance of $0.11 because of rounding in the proof itself and in the table in Exhibit A3-10 (p. 1295).

CORNERSTONE A3-5 shows how to compute the present value of an annuity.

CORNERSTONE A3-5   Computing Present Value of an Annuity

Concept:
The present value of an annuity is the value of a series of equal future cash flows made at regular intervals with compound interest discounted back to today.

Information:
Bates Builders purchased a subdivision site from the Second National Bank and Trust Co. on January 1, 2012. Bates gave the bank an installment note. The note requires Bates to make four annual payments of $600,000 each on December 31 of each year, beginning in 2012. Interest is computed at 9 percent.

Required:
1. Draw the cash flow diagram for this purchase from Bates' perspective.
2. Calculate the cost of the land as recorded by Bates on January 1, 2012.
3. Prepare the journal entry that Bates will make to record the purchase of the land.

Solution:
1.

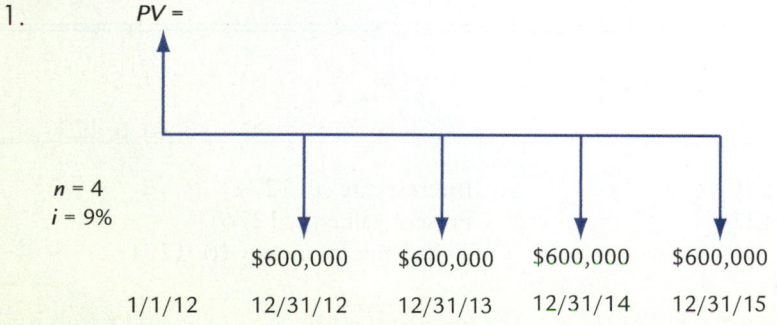

$n = 4$
$i = 9\%$

	$600,000	$600,000	$600,000	$600,000
1/1/12	12/31/12	12/31/13	12/31/14	12/31/15

2. $PV = (f)(PV \text{ of an Annuity, 4 periods, 9\%})$
   $= (\$600{,}000)(3.23972)$
   $= \$1{,}943{,}832$

3.

Jan. 1, 2012	Land	1,943,832	
	Notes Payable		1,943,832
	(Record purchase of land)		

			Stockholders'
Assets	=	**Liabilities** +	**Equity**
+1,943,832		+1,943,832	

SUMMARY OF LEARNING OBJECTIVES

LO1.   Explain how compound interest works.
- In transactions involving the borrowing and lending of money, it is customary for the borrower to pay interest.
- With compound interest, interest for the period is added to the account and interest is earned on the total balance in the next period.
- Compound interest calculations require careful specification of the interest period and the interest rate.

LO2. **Use future value and present value tables to apply compound interest to accounting transactions.**
- Cash flows are described as either
  - single cash flows, or
  - annuities.
- An annuity is a number of equal cash flows made at regular intervals.
- All other cash flows are a series of one or more single cash flows.
- Accounting for such cash flows may require
  - calculation of the amount to which a series of cash flows will grow when interest is compounded (i.e., the future value) or
  - the amount a series of future cash flows is worth today after taking into account compound interest (i.e., the present value).

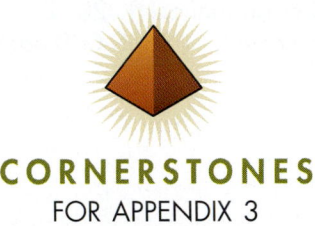

CORNERSTONES
FOR APPENDIX 3

CORNERSTONE A3-1 Computing future values using compound interest (p. 1275)

CORNERSTONE A3-2 Computing future value of a single amount (p. 1278)

CORNERSTONE A3-3 Computing present value of a single amount (p. 1281)

CORNERSTONE A3-4 Computing future value of an annuity (p. 1283)

CORNERSTONE A3-5 Computing present value of an annuity (p. 1285)

KEY TERMS

Annuity (p. 1281)
Compound interest (p. 1274)
Future value (p. 1275)
Interest period (p. 1274)

Interest rate (p. 1274)
Present value (p. 1276)
Time value of money (p. 1274)

DISCUSSION QUESTIONS

1. Why does money have a time value?
2. Describe the four basic time-value-of-money problems.
3. How is compound interest computed? What is a future value? What is a present value?
4. Define an annuity in general terms. Describe the cash flows related to an annuity from the viewpoint of the lender in terms of receipts and payments.
5. Explain how to use time-value-of-money calculations to measure an installment note liability.

CORNERSTONE EXERCISES

OBJECTIVE ➊
CORNERSTONE A3-1

Cornerstone Exercise A3-1 Explain How Compound Interest Works

Jim Emig has $6,000.

Required:
Calculate the future value of the $6,000 at 12 percent compounded quarterly for five years. (*Note:* Round answers to two decimal places.)

OBJECTIVE ➋
CORNERSTONE A3-2

Cornerstone Exercise A3-2 Use Future Value and Present Value Tables to Apply Compound Interest to Accounting Transactions

Cathy Lumbattis inherited $140,000 from an aunt.

(Continued)

Required:

If Cathy decides not to spend her inheritance but to leave the money in her savings account until she retires in 15 years, how much money will she have, assuming an annual interest rate of 8 percent, compounded semiannually? (*Note:* Round answers to two decimal places.)

Cornerstone Exercise A3-3 Use Future Value and Present Value Tables to Apply Compound Interest to Accounting Transactions

OBJECTIVE ❷
CORNERSTONE A3-3

LuAnn Bean will receive $7,000 in seven years.

Required:

What is the present value at 7 percent compounded annually? (*Note:* Round answers to two decimal places.)

Cornerstone Exercise A3-4 Use Future Value and Present Value Tables to Apply Compound Interest to Accounting Transactions

OBJECTIVE ❷
CORNERSTONE A3-3

A bank is willing to lend money at 6 percent interest, compounded annually.

Required:

How much would the bank be willing to loan you in exchange for a payment of $600 four years from now? (*Note:* Round answers to two decimal places.)

Cornerstone Exercise A3-5 Use Future Value and Present Value Tables to Apply Compound Interest to Accounting Transactions

OBJECTIVE ❷
CORNERSTONE A3-4

Ed Walker wants to save some money so that he can make a down payment of $3,000 on a car when he graduates from college in four years.

Required:

If Ed opens a savings account and earns 3 percent on his money, compounded annually, how much will he have to invest now? (*Note:* Round answers to two decimal places.)

Cornerstone Exercise A3-6 Use Future Value and Present Value Tables to Apply Compound Interest to Accounting Transactions

OBJECTIVE ❷
CORNERSTONE A3-4

Kristen Quinn makes equal deposits of $500 semiannually for four years.

Required:
What is the future value at 8 percent? (*Note:* Round answers to two decimal places.)

Cornerstone Exercise A3-7 Use Future Value and Present Value Tables to Apply Compound Interest to Accounting Transactions

OBJECTIVE ❷
CORNERSTONE A3-4

Chuck Russo, a high school math teacher, wants to set up an IRA account into which he will deposit $2,000 per year. He plans to teach for 20 more years and then retire.

Required:

If the interest on his account is 7 percent compounded annually, how much will be in his account when he retires? (*Note:* Round answers to two decimal places.)

Cornerstone Exercise A3-8 Use Future Value Tables to Apply Compound Interest to Accounting Transactions

OBJECTIVE ❷
CORNERSTONE A3-4

Larson Lumber makes annual deposits of $500 at 6 percent compounded annually for three years.

Required:
What is the future value of these deposits? (*Note:* Round answers to two decimal places.)

Cornerstone Exercise A3-9 Use Future Value and Present Value Tables to Apply Compound Interest to Accounting Transactions

OBJECTIVE ❷
CORNERSTONE A3-5

Michelle McFeaters can earn 6 percent.

Required:

How much would have to be deposited in a savings account in order for Michelle to be able to make equal annual withdrawals of $200 at the end of each of 10 years? (*Note:* Round answers to two decimal places.) The balance at the end of the last year would be zero.

OBJECTIVE ②
CORNERSTONE A3-5

Cornerstone Exercise A3-10 Use Future Value and Present Value Tables to Apply Compound Interest to Accounting Transactions

Barb Muller wins the lottery. She wins $20,000 per year to be paid for 10 years. The state offers her the choice of a cash settlement now instead of the annual payments for 10 years.

Required:

If the interest rate is 6 percent, what is the amount the state will offer for a settlement today? (*Note:* Round answers to two decimal places.)

EXERCISES

OBJECTIVE ②

Exercise A3-11 Practice with Tables

Refer to the appropriate tables in the text.

Required:

Note: Round answers to two decimal places. Determine:

a. the future value of a single cash flow of $5,000 that earns 7 percent interest compounded annually for 10 years.
b. the future value of an annual annuity of 10 cash flows of $500 each that earns 7 percent compounded annually.
c. the present value of $5,000 to be received 10 years from now, assuming that the interest (discount) rate is 7 percent per year.
d. the present value of an annuity of $500 per year for 10 years for which the interest (discount) rate is 7 percent per year and the first cash flow occurs one year from now.

OBJECTIVE ②

Exercise A3-12 Practice with Tables

Refer to the appropriate tables in the text.

Required:

Note: Round answers to two decimal places. Determine:

a. the present value of $1,200 to be received in seven years, assuming that the interest (discount) rate is 8 percent per year.
b. the present value of an annuity of seven cash flows of $1,200 each (one at the end of each of the next seven years) for which the interest (discount) rate is 8 percent per year.
c. the future value of a single cash flow of $1,200 that earns 8 percent per year for seven years.
d. the future value of an annuity of seven cash flows of $1,200 each (one at the end of each of the next seven years), assuming that the interest rate is 8 percent per year.

OBJECTIVE ②

Exercise A3-13 Future Values

Refer to the appropriate tables in the text.

Required:

Note: Round answers to two decimal places. Determine:

a. the future value of a single deposit of $15,000 that earns compound interest for four years at an interest rate of 10 percent per year.
b. the annual interest rate that will produce a future value of $13,416.80 in six years from a single deposit of $8,000.
c. the size of annual cash flows for an annuity of nine cash flows that will produce a future value of $79,428.10 at an interest rate of 9 percent per year.
d. the number of periods required to produce a future value of $17,755.50 from an initial deposit of $7,500 if the annual interest rate is 9 percent.

OBJECTIVE ②

Exercise A3-14 Future Values and Long-Term Investments

Fired Up Pottery, Inc., engaged in the following transactions during 2012:

a. On January 1, 2012, Fired Up deposited $12,000 in a certificate of deposit paying 6 percent interest compounded semiannually (3 percent per six-month period). The certificate will mature on December 31, 2015.

(Continued)

b.   On January 1, 2012, Fired Up established an account with Rookwood Investment Management. Fired Up will make quarterly payments of $2,500 to Rookwood beginning on March 31, 2012, and ending on December 31, 2013. Rookwood guarantees an interest rate of 8 percent compounded quarterly (2 percent per three-month period).

Required:
1.   Prepare the cash flow diagram for each of these two investments.
2.   Calculate the amount to which each of these investments will accumulate at maturity. (*Note:* Round answers to two decimal places.)

Exercise A3-15 Future Values

OBJECTIVE 2

On January 1, Beth Woods made a single deposit of $8,000 in an investment account that earns 8 percent interest.

Required:

Note: Round answers to two decimal places.

1.   Calculate the balance in the account in five years assuming the interest is compounded annually.
2.   Determine how much interest will be earned on the account in seven years if interest is compounded annually.
3.   Calculate the balance in the account in five years assuming the 8 percent interest is compounded quarterly.

Exercise A3-16 Future Values

OBJECTIVE 2

Palmer Transit Company invested $70,000 in a tax-anticipation note on June 30, 2012. The note earns 12 percent interest compounded monthly (1 percent per month) and matures on March 31, 2013.

Required:

Note: Round answers to two decimal places.

1.   Prepare the cash flow diagram for this investment.
2.   Determine the amount Palmer will receive when the note matures.
3.   Determine how much interest Palmer will earn on this investment from June 30, 2012, through December 31, 2012.

Exercise A3-17 Present Values

OBJECTIVE 2

Refer to the appropriate tables in the text.

Required:

Note: Round answers to two decimal places. Determine:

a.   the present value of a single $14,000 cash flow in seven years if the interest (discount) rate is 8 percent per year.
b.   the number of periods for which $5,820 must be invested at an annual interest (discount) rate of 7 percent to produce an investment balance of $10,000.
c.   the size of the annual cash flow for a 25-year annuity with a present value of $49,113 and an annual interest rate of 9 percent. One payment is made at the end of each year.
d.   the annual interest rate at which an investment of $2,542 will provide for a single $4,000 cash flow in four years.
e.   the annual interest rate earned by an annuity that costs $17,119 and provides 15 payments of $2,000 each, one at the end of each of the next 15 years.

Exercise A3-18 Present Values

OBJECTIVE 2

Wilson Company signed notes to make the following two purchases on January 1, 2012:

a.   a new piece of equipment for $60,000, with payment deferred until December 31, 2013. The appropriate interest rate is 9 percent compounded annually.
b.   a small building from Johnston Builders. The terms of the purchase require a $75,000 payment at the end of each quarter, beginning March 31, 2012, and ending June 30, 2014. The appropriate interest rate is 2 percent per quarter.

Required:

Note: Round answers to two decimal places.

1.   Prepare the cash flow diagrams for these two purchases.
2.   Prepare the entries to record these purchases in Wilson's journal.

3. Prepare the cash payment and interest expense entries for purchase *b* at March 31, 2012, and June 30, 2012.
4. Prepare the adjusting entry for purchase *a* at December 31, 2012.

OBJECTIVE

Exercise A3-19 Present Values

Krista Kellman has an opportunity to purchase a government security that will pay $200,000 in five years.

Required:

Note: Round answers to two decimal places.

1. Calculate what Krista would pay for the security if the appropriate interest (discount) rate is 6 percent compounded annually.
2. Calculate what Krista would pay for the security if the appropriate interest (discount) rate is 10 percent compounded annually.
3. Calculate what Krista would pay for the security if the appropriate interest (discount) rate is 6 percent compounded semiannually.

OBJECTIVE

Exercise A3-20 Future Values of an Annuity

On December 31, 2012, Natalie Livingston signs a contract to make annual deposits of $4,200 in an investment account that earns 10 percent. The first deposit is made on December 31, 2012.

Required:

Note: Round answers to two decimal places.

1. Calculate what the balance in this investment account will be just after the seventh deposit has been made if interest is compounded annually.
2. Determine how much interest will have been earned on this investment account just after the seventh deposit has been made if interest is compounded annually.

OBJECTIVE

Exercise A3-21 Future Values of an Annuity

Filimonov Savings Bank pays 8 percent interest compounded weekly (0.154 percent per week) on savings accounts. The bank has asked your help in preparing a table to show potential customers the number of dollars that will be available at the end of 10-, 20-, 30-, and 40-week periods during which there are weekly deposits of $1, $5, $10, or $50. The following data are available:

Length of Annuity	Future Value of Annuity at an Interest Rate of 0.154% per Week
10 weeks	10.0696
20 weeks	20.2953
30 weeks	30.6796
40 weeks	41.2250

Required:

Complete a table similar to the one below. (*Note:* Round answers to two decimal places.)

	Amount of Each Deposit			
Number of Deposits	$1	$5	$10	$50
10				
20				
30				
40				

OBJECTIVE

Exercise A3-22 Future Value of a Single Cash Flow

Jenkins Products has just been paid $25,000 by Shirley Enterprises, which has owed Jenkins this amount for 30 months but been unable to pay because of financial difficulties. Had it been able to invest this cash, Jenkins assumes that it would have earned an interest rate of 12 percent compounded monthly (1 percent per month).

(Continued)

Required:

Note: Round answers to two decimal places.

1. Prepare a cash flow diagram for the investment that could have been made if Shirley had paid 30 months ago.
2. Determine how much Jenkins has lost by not receiving the $25,000 when it was due 30 months ago.
3. **Conceptual Connection:** Indicate whether Jenkins would make an entry to account for this loss. Why, or why not?

Exercise A3-23   Installment Sale

OBJECTIVE **2**

Wilke Properties owns land on which natural gas wells are located. Cincinnati Gas Company signs a note to buy this land from Wilke on January 1, 2012. The note requires Cincinnati to pay Wilke $775,000 per year for 25 years. The first payment is to be made on December 31, 2012. The appropriate interest rate is 9 percent compounded annually.

Required:

Note: Round answers to two decimal places.

1. Prepare a diagram of the appropriate cash flows from Cincinnati Gas's perspective.
2. Determine the present value of the payments.
3. Indicate what entry Cincinnati Gas should make at January 1, 2012.

Exercise A3-24   Installment Sale

OBJECTIVE **2**

Bailey's Billiards sold a pool table to Sheri Sipka on October 31, 2012. The terms of the sale are no money down and payments of $50 per month for 30 months, with the first payment due on November 30, 2012. The table they sold to Sipka cost Bailey's $800, and Bailey uses a perpetual inventory system. Bailey's uses an interest rate of 12 percent compounded monthly (1 percent per month).

Required:

Note: Round answers to two decimal places.

1. Prepare the cash flow diagram for this sale.
2. Calculate the amount of revenue Bailey's should record on October 31, 2012.
3. Prepare the journal entry to record the sale on October 31. Assume that Bailey's records cost of goods sold at the time of the sale (perpetual inventory accounting).
4. Determine how much interest income Bailey's will record from October 31, 2012, through December 31, 2012.
5. Determine how much Bailey's 2012 income before taxes increased by this sale.

Exhibit A3–7

Future Value of a Single Amount

$FV = 1(1 + i)^n$

n/i	1%	2%	3%	4%	5%	6%	7%	8%	9%	10%	12%	14%	16%	18%	20%	25%	30%
1	1.01000	1.02000	1.03000	1.04000	1.05000	1.06000	1.07000	1.08000	1.09000	1.10000	1.12000	1.14000	1.16000	1.18000	1.20000	1.25000	1.30000
2	1.02010	1.04040	1.06090	1.08160	1.10250	1.12360	1.14490	1.16640	1.18810	1.21000	1.25440	1.29960	1.34560	1.39240	1.44000	1.56250	1.69000
3	1.03030	1.06121	1.09273	1.12486	1.15763	1.19102	1.22504	1.25971	1.29503	1.33100	1.40493	1.48154	1.56090	1.64303	1.72800	1.95313	2.19700
4	1.04060	1.08243	1.12551	1.16986	1.21551	1.26248	1.31080	1.36049	1.41159	1.46410	1.57352	1.68896	1.81064	1.93878	2.07360	2.44141	2.85610
5	1.05101	1.10408	1.15927	1.21665	1.27628	1.33823	1.40255	1.46933	1.53862	1.61051	1.76234	1.92541	2.10034	2.28776	2.48832	3.05176	3.71293
6	1.06152	1.12616	1.19405	1.26532	1.34010	1.41852	1.50073	1.58687	1.67710	1.77156	1.97382	2.19497	2.43640	2.69955	2.98598	3.81470	4.82681
7	1.07214	1.14869	1.22987	1.31593	1.40710	1.50363	1.60578	1.71382	1.82804	1.94872	2.21068	2.50227	2.82622	3.18547	3.58318	4.76837	6.27485
8	1.08286	1.17166	1.26677	1.36857	1.47746	1.59385	1.71819	1.85093	1.99256	2.14359	2.47596	2.85259	3.27841	3.75886	4.29982	5.96046	8.15731
9	1.09369	1.19509	1.30477	1.42331	1.55133	1.68948	1.83846	1.99900	2.17189	2.35795	2.77308	3.25195	3.80296	4.43545	5.15978	7.45058	10.60450
10	1.10462	1.21899	1.34392	1.48024	1.62889	1.79085	1.96715	2.15892	2.36736	2.59374	3.10585	3.70722	4.41144	5.23384	6.19174	9.31323	13.78585
11	1.11567	1.24337	1.38423	1.53945	1.71034	1.89830	2.10485	2.33164	2.58043	2.85312	3.47855	4.22623	5.11726	6.17593	7.43008	11.64153	17.92160
12	1.12683	1.26824	1.42576	1.60103	1.79586	2.01220	2.25219	2.51817	2.81266	3.13843	3.89598	4.81790	5.93603	7.28759	8.91610	14.55192	23.29809
13	1.13809	1.29361	1.46853	1.66507	1.88565	2.13293	2.40985	2.71962	3.06580	3.45227	4.36349	5.49241	6.88579	8.59936	10.69932	18.18989	30.28751
14	1.14947	1.31948	1.51259	1.73168	1.97993	2.26090	2.57853	2.93719	3.34173	3.79750	4.88711	6.26135	7.98752	10.14724	12.83918	22.73737	39.37376
15	1.16097	1.34587	1.55797	1.80094	2.07893	2.39656	2.75903	3.17217	3.64248	4.17725	5.47357	7.13794	9.26552	11.97375	15.40702	28.42171	51.18589
16	1.17258	1.37279	1.60471	1.87298	2.18287	2.54035	2.95216	3.42594	3.97031	4.59497	6.13039	8.13725	10.74800	14.12902	18.48843	35.52714	66.54166
17	1.18430	1.40024	1.65285	1.94790	2.29202	2.69277	3.15882	3.70002	4.32763	5.05447	6.86604	9.27646	12.46768	16.67225	22.18611	44.40892	86.50416
18	1.19615	1.42825	1.70243	2.02582	2.40662	2.85434	3.37993	3.99602	4.71712	5.55992	7.68997	10.57517	14.46251	19.67325	26.62333	55.51115	112.45541
19	1.20811	1.45681	1.75351	2.10685	2.52695	3.02560	3.61653	4.31570	5.14166	6.11591	8.61276	12.05569	16.77652	23.21444	31.94800	69.38894	146.19203
20	1.22019	1.48595	1.80611	2.19112	2.65330	3.20714	3.86968	4.66096	5.60441	6.72750	9.64629	13.74349	19.46076	27.39303	38.33760	86.73617	190.04946
21	1.23239	1.51567	1.86029	2.27877	2.78596	3.39956	4.14056	5.03383	6.10881	7.40025	10.80385	15.66758	22.57448	32.32378	46.00512	108.42022	247.06453
22	1.24472	1.54598	1.91610	2.36992	2.92526	3.60354	4.43040	5.43654	6.65860	8.14027	12.10031	17.86104	26.18640	38.14206	55.20614	135.52527	321.18389
23	1.25716	1.57690	1.97359	2.46472	3.07152	3.81975	4.74053	5.87146	7.25787	8.95430	13.55235	20.36158	30.37622	45.00763	66.24737	169.40659	417.53905
24	1.26973	1.60844	2.03279	2.56330	3.22510	4.04893	5.07237	6.34118	7.91108	9.84973	15.17863	23.21221	35.23642	53.10901	79.49685	211.75824	542.80077
25	1.28243	1.64061	2.09378	2.66584	3.38635	4.29187	5.42743	6.84848	8.62308	10.83471	17.00006	26.46192	40.87424	62.66863	95.39622	264.69780	705.64100
26	1.29526	1.67342	2.15659	2.77247	3.55567	4.54938	5.80735	7.39635	9.39916	11.91818	19.04007	30.16658	47.41412	73.94898	114.47546	330.87225	917.33330
27	1.30821	1.70689	2.22129	2.88337	3.73346	4.82235	6.21387	7.98806	10.24508	13.10999	21.32488	34.38991	55.00038	87.25980	137.37055	413.59031	1192.53329
28	1.32129	1.74102	2.28793	2.99870	3.92013	5.11169	6.64884	8.62711	11.16714	14.42099	23.88387	39.20449	63.80044	102.96656	164.84466	516.98788	1550.29328
29	1.33450	1.77584	2.35657	3.11865	4.11614	5.41839	7.11426	9.31727	12.17218	15.86309	26.74993	44.69312	74.00851	121.50054	197.81359	646.23485	2015.38126
30	1.34785	1.81136	2.42726	3.24340	4.32194	5.74349	7.61226	10.06266	13.26768	17.44940	29.95992	50.95016	85.84988	143.37064	237.37631	807.79357	2619.99564

Exhibit A3–8

Present Value of a Single Amount

$$PV = \frac{1}{(1+i)^n}$$

n/i	1%	2%	3%	4%	5%	6%	7%	8%	9%	10%	12%	14%	16%	18%	20%	25%	30%
1	0.99010	0.98039	0.97087	0.96154	0.95238	0.94340	0.93458	0.92593	0.91743	0.90909	0.89286	0.87719	0.86207	0.84746	0.83333	0.80000	0.76923
2	0.98030	0.96117	0.94260	0.92456	0.90703	0.89000	0.87344	0.85734	0.84168	0.82645	0.79719	0.76947	0.74316	0.71818	0.69444	0.64000	0.59172
3	0.97059	0.94232	0.91514	0.88900	0.86384	0.83962	0.81630	0.79383	0.77218	0.75131	0.71178	0.67497	0.64066	0.60863	0.57870	0.51200	0.45517
4	0.96098	0.92385	0.88849	0.85480	0.82270	0.79209	0.76290	0.73503	0.70843	0.68301	0.63552	0.59208	0.55229	0.51579	0.48225	0.40960	0.35013
5	0.95147	0.90573	0.86261	0.82193	0.78353	0.74726	0.71299	0.68058	0.64993	0.62092	0.56743	0.51937	0.47611	0.43711	0.40188	0.32768	0.26933
6	0.94205	0.88797	0.83748	0.79031	0.74622	0.70496	0.66634	0.63017	0.59627	0.56447	0.50663	0.45559	0.41044	0.37043	0.33490	0.26214	0.20718
7	0.93272	0.87056	0.81309	0.75992	0.71068	0.66506	0.62275	0.58349	0.54703	0.51316	0.45235	0.39964	0.35383	0.31393	0.27908	0.20972	0.15937
8	0.92348	0.85349	0.78941	0.73069	0.67684	0.62741	0.58201	0.54027	0.50187	0.46651	0.40388	0.35056	0.30503	0.26604	0.23257	0.16777	0.12259
9	0.91434	0.83676	0.76642	0.70259	0.64461	0.59190	0.54393	0.50025	0.46043	0.42410	0.36061	0.30751	0.26295	0.22546	0.19381	0.13422	0.09430
10	0.90529	0.82035	0.74409	0.67556	0.61391	0.55839	0.50835	0.46319	0.42241	0.38554	0.32197	0.26974	0.22668	0.19106	0.16151	0.10737	0.07254
11	0.89632	0.80426	0.72242	0.64958	0.58468	0.52679	0.47509	0.42888	0.38753	0.35049	0.28748	0.23662	0.19542	0.16192	0.13459	0.08590	0.05580
12	0.88745	0.78849	0.70138	0.62460	0.55684	0.49697	0.44401	0.39711	0.35553	0.31863	0.25668	0.20756	0.16846	0.13722	0.11216	0.06872	0.04292
13	0.87866	0.77303	0.68095	0.60057	0.53032	0.46884	0.41496	0.36770	0.32618	0.28966	0.22917	0.18207	0.14523	0.11629	0.09346	0.05498	0.03302
14	0.86996	0.75788	0.66112	0.57748	0.50507	0.44230	0.38782	0.34046	0.29925	0.26333	0.20462	0.15971	0.12520	0.09855	0.07789	0.04398	0.02540
15	0.86135	0.74301	0.64186	0.55526	0.48102	0.41727	0.36245	0.31524	0.27454	0.23939	0.18270	0.14010	0.10793	0.08352	0.06491	0.03518	0.01954
16	0.85282	0.72845	0.62317	0.53391	0.45811	0.39365	0.33873	0.29189	0.25187	0.21763	0.16312	0.12289	0.09304	0.07078	0.05409	0.02815	0.01503
17	0.84438	0.71416	0.60502	0.51337	0.43630	0.37136	0.31657	0.27027	0.23107	0.19784	0.14564	0.10780	0.08021	0.05998	0.04507	0.02252	0.01156
18	0.83602	0.70016	0.58739	0.49363	0.41552	0.35034	0.29586	0.25025	0.21199	0.17986	0.13004	0.09456	0.06914	0.05083	0.03756	0.01801	0.00889
19	0.82774	0.68643	0.57029	0.47464	0.39573	0.33051	0.27651	0.23171	0.19449	0.16351	0.11611	0.08295	0.05961	0.04308	0.03130	0.01441	0.00684
20	0.81954	0.67297	0.55368	0.45639	0.37689	0.31180	0.25842	0.21455	0.17843	0.14864	0.10367	0.07276	0.05139	0.03651	0.02608	0.01153	0.00526
21	0.81143	0.65978	0.53755	0.43883	0.35894	0.29416	0.24151	0.19866	0.16370	0.13513	0.09256	0.06383	0.04430	0.03094	0.02174	0.00922	0.00405
22	0.80340	0.64684	0.52189	0.42196	0.34185	0.27751	0.22571	0.18394	0.15018	0.12285	0.08264	0.05599	0.03819	0.02622	0.01811	0.00738	0.00311
23	0.79544	0.63416	0.50669	0.40573	0.32557	0.26180	0.21095	0.17032	0.13778	0.11168	0.07379	0.04911	0.03292	0.02222	0.01509	0.00590	0.00239
24	0.78757	0.62172	0.49193	0.39012	0.31007	0.24698	0.19715	0.15770	0.12640	0.10153	0.06588	0.04308	0.02838	0.01883	0.01258	0.00472	0.00184
25	0.77977	0.60953	0.47761	0.37512	0.29530	0.23300	0.18425	0.14602	0.11597	0.09230	0.05882	0.03779	0.02447	0.01596	0.01048	0.00378	0.00142
26	0.77205	0.59758	0.46369	0.36069	0.28124	0.21981	0.17220	0.13520	0.10639	0.08391	0.05252	0.03315	0.02109	0.01352	0.00874	0.00302	0.00109
27	0.76440	0.58586	0.45019	0.34682	0.26785	0.20737	0.16093	0.12519	0.09761	0.07628	0.04689	0.02908	0.01818	0.01146	0.00728	0.00242	0.00084
28	0.75684	0.57437	0.43708	0.33348	0.25509	0.19563	0.15040	0.11591	0.08955	0.06934	0.04187	0.02551	0.01567	0.00971	0.00607	0.00193	0.00065
29	0.74934	0.56311	0.42435	0.32065	0.24295	0.18456	0.14056	0.10733	0.08215	0.06304	0.03738	0.02237	0.01351	0.00823	0.00506	0.00155	0.00050
30	0.74192	0.55207	0.41199	0.30832	0.23138	0.17411	0.13137	0.09938	0.07537	0.05731	0.03338	0.01963	0.01165	0.00697	0.00421	0.00124	0.00038

Exhibit A3-9

Future Value of an Annuity

$$FVA = \frac{(1+i)^n - 1}{i}$$

n/i	1%	2%	3%	4%	5%	6%	7%	8%	9%	10%	12%	14%	16%	18%	20%	25%	30%
1	1.00000	1.00000	1.00000	1.00000	1.00000	1.00000	1.00000	1.00000	1.00000	1.00000	1.00000	1.00000	1.00000	1.00000	1.00000	1.00000	1.00000
2	2.01000	2.02000	2.03000	2.04000	2.05000	2.06000	2.07000	2.08000	2.09000	2.10000	2.12000	2.14000	2.16000	2.18000	2.20000	2.25000	2.30000
3	3.03010	3.06040	3.09090	3.12160	3.15250	3.18360	3.21490	3.24640	3.27810	3.31000	3.37440	3.43960	3.50560	3.57240	3.64000	3.81250	3.99000
4	4.06040	4.12161	4.18363	4.24646	4.31013	4.37462	4.43994	4.50611	4.57313	4.64100	4.77933	4.92114	5.06650	5.21543	5.36800	5.76563	6.18700
5	5.10101	5.20404	5.30914	5.41632	5.52563	5.63709	5.75074	5.86660	5.98471	6.10510	6.35285	6.61010	6.87714	7.15421	7.44160	8.20703	9.04310
6	6.15202	6.30812	6.46841	6.63298	6.80191	6.97532	7.15329	7.33593	7.52000	7.71561	8.11519	8.53552	8.97748	9.44197	9.92992	11.25879	12.75603
7	7.21354	7.43428	7.66246	7.89829	8.14201	8.39384	8.65402	8.92280	9.20043	9.48717	10.08901	10.73049	11.41387	12.14152	12.91590	15.07349	17.58284
8	8.28567	8.58297	8.89234	9.21423	9.54911	9.89747	10.25980	10.63663	11.02847	11.43589	12.29969	13.23276	14.24009	15.32700	16.49908	19.84186	23.85769
9	9.36853	9.75463	10.15911	10.58280	11.02656	11.49132	11.97799	12.48756	13.02104	13.57948	14.77566	16.08535	17.51851	19.08585	20.79890	25.80232	32.01500
10	10.46221	10.94972	11.46388	12.00611	12.57789	13.18079	13.81645	14.48656	15.19293	15.93742	17.54874	19.33730	21.32147	23.52131	25.95868	33.25290	42.61950
11	11.56683	12.16872	12.80780	13.48635	14.20679	14.97164	15.78360	16.64549	17.56029	18.53117	20.65458	23.04452	25.73290	28.75514	32.15042	42.56613	56.40535
12	12.68250	13.41209	14.19203	15.02581	15.91713	16.86994	17.88845	18.97713	20.14072	21.38428	24.13313	27.27075	30.85017	34.93107	39.58050	54.20766	74.32695
13	13.80933	14.68033	15.61779	16.62684	17.71298	18.88214	20.14064	21.49530	22.95338	24.52271	28.02911	32.08865	36.78620	42.21866	48.49660	68.75958	97.62504
14	14.94742	15.97394	17.08632	18.29191	19.59863	21.01507	22.55049	24.21492	26.01919	27.97498	32.39260	37.58107	43.67199	50.81802	59.19592	86.94947	127.91255
15	16.09690	17.29342	18.59891	20.02359	21.57856	23.27597	25.12902	27.15211	29.36092	31.77248	37.27971	43.84241	51.65951	60.96527	72.03511	109.68684	167.28631
16	17.25786	18.63929	20.15688	21.82453	23.65749	25.67253	27.88805	30.32428	33.00340	35.94973	42.75328	50.98035	60.92503	72.93901	87.44213	138.10855	218.47220
17	18.43044	20.01207	21.76159	23.69751	25.84037	28.21288	30.84022	33.75023	36.97370	40.54470	48.88367	59.11760	71.67303	87.06804	105.93056	173.63568	285.01386
18	19.61475	21.41231	23.41444	25.64541	28.13238	30.90565	33.99903	37.45024	41.30134	45.59917	55.74971	68.39407	84.14072	103.74028	128.11667	218.04460	371.51802
19	20.81090	22.84056	25.11687	27.67123	30.53900	33.75999	37.37896	41.44626	46.01846	51.15909	63.43968	78.96923	98.60323	123.41353	154.74000	273.55576	483.97343
20	22.01900	24.29737	26.87037	29.77808	33.06595	36.78559	40.99549	45.76196	51.16012	57.27500	72.05244	91.02493	115.37975	146.62797	186.68800	342.94470	630.16546
21	23.23919	25.78332	28.67649	31.96920	35.71925	39.99273	44.86518	50.42292	56.76453	64.00250	81.69874	104.76842	134.84051	174.02100	225.02560	429.68087	820.21510
22	24.47159	27.29898	30.53678	34.24797	38.50521	43.39229	49.00574	55.45676	62.87334	71.40275	92.50258	120.43600	157.41499	206.34479	271.03072	538.10109	1067.27963
23	25.71630	28.84496	32.45288	36.61789	41.43048	46.99583	53.43614	60.89330	66.17394	79.54302	104.60289	138.29704	183.60138	244.48685	326.23686	673.62636	1388.46351
24	26.97346	30.42186	34.42647	39.08260	44.50200	50.81558	58.17667	66.76476	76.78981	88.49733	118.15524	158.65862	213.97761	289.49448	392.48424	843.03295	1806.00257
25	28.24320	32.03030	36.45926	41.64591	47.72710	54.86451	63.24904	73.10594	84.70090	98.34706	133.33387	181.87083	249.21402	342.60349	471.98108	1054.79118	2348.80334
26	29.52563	33.67091	38.55304	44.31174	51.11345	59.15638	68.67647	79.95442	93.32398	109.18177	150.33393	208.33274	290.08827	405.27211	567.37730	1319.48898	3054.44434
27	30.82089	35.34432	40.70963	47.08421	54.66913	63.70577	74.48382	87.35077	102.72313	121.09994	169.37401	238.49933	337.50239	479.22109	681.85276	1650.36123	3971.77764
28	32.12910	37.05121	42.93092	49.96758	58.40258	68.52811	80.69769	95.33883	112.96822	134.20994	190.69889	272.88923	392.50277	566.48089	819.22331	2063.95153	5164.31093
29	33.45039	38.79223	45.21885	52.96629	62.32271	73.63980	87.34653	103.96594	124.13536	148.63093	214.58275	312.09373	456.30322	669.44745	984.06797	2580.93941	6714.60421
30	34.78489	40.56808	47.57542	56.08494	66.43885	79.05819	94.46079	113.28321	136.30754	164.49402	241.33268	356.78685	530.31173	790.94799	1181.88157	3227.17427	8729.98548

Exhibit A3-10

Present Value of an Annuity

$$PVA = \frac{1 - \frac{1}{(1+i)^n}}{i}$$

n/i	1%	2%	3%	4%	5%	6%	7%	8%	9%	10%	12%	14%	16%	18%	20%	25%	30%
1	0.99010	0.98039	0.97087	0.96154	0.95238	0.94340	0.93458	0.92593	0.91743	0.90909	0.89286	0.87719	0.86207	0.84746	0.83333	0.80000	0.76923
2	1.97040	1.94156	1.91347	1.88609	1.85941	1.83339	1.80802	1.78326	1.75911	1.73554	1.69005	1.64666	1.60523	1.56564	1.52778	1.44000	1.36095
3	2.94099	2.88388	2.82861	2.77509	2.72325	2.67301	2.62432	2.57710	2.53129	2.48685	2.40183	2.32163	2.24589	2.17427	2.10648	1.95200	1.81611
4	3.90197	3.80773	3.71710	3.62990	3.54595	3.46511	3.38721	3.31213	3.23972	3.16987	3.03735	2.91371	2.79818	2.69006	2.58873	2.36160	2.16624
5	4.85343	4.71346	4.57971	4.45182	4.32948	4.21236	4.10020	3.99271	3.88965	3.79079	3.60478	3.43308	3.27429	3.12717	2.99061	2.68928	2.43557
6	5.79548	5.60143	5.41719	5.24214	5.07569	4.91732	4.76654	4.62288	4.48592	4.35526	4.11141	3.88867	3.68474	3.49760	3.32551	2.95142	2.64275
7	6.72819	6.47199	6.23028	6.00205	5.78637	5.58238	5.38929	5.20637	5.03295	4.86842	4.56376	4.28830	4.03857	3.81153	3.60459	3.16114	2.80211
8	7.65168	7.32548	7.01969	6.73274	6.46321	6.20979	5.97130	5.74664	5.53482	5.33493	4.96764	4.63886	4.34359	4.07757	3.83716	3.32891	2.92470
9	8.56602	8.16224	7.78611	7.43533	7.10782	6.80169	6.51523	6.24689	5.99525	5.75902	5.32825	4.94637	4.60654	4.30302	4.03097	3.46313	3.01900
10	9.47130	8.98259	8.53020	8.11090	7.72173	7.36009	7.02358	6.71008	6.41766	6.14457	5.65022	5.21612	4.83323	4.49409	4.19247	3.57050	3.09154
11	10.36763	9.78685	9.25262	8.76048	8.30641	7.88687	7.49867	7.13896	6.80519	6.49506	5.93770	5.45273	5.02864	4.65601	4.32706	3.65640	3.14734
12	11.25508	10.57534	9.95400	9.38507	8.86325	8.38384	7.94269	7.53608	7.16073	6.81369	6.19437	5.66029	5.19711	4.79322	4.43922	3.72512	3.19026
13	12.13374	11.34837	10.63496	9.98565	9.39357	8.85268	8.35765	7.90378	7.48690	7.10336	6.42355	5.84236	5.34233	4.90951	4.53268	3.78010	3.22328
14	13.00370	12.10625	11.29607	10.56312	9.89864	9.29498	8.74547	8.24424	7.78615	7.36669	6.62817	6.00207	5.46753	5.00806	4.61057	3.82408	3.24867
15	13.86505	12.84926	11.93794	11.11839	10.37966	9.71225	9.10791	8.55948	8.06069	7.60608	6.81086	6.14217	5.57546	5.09158	4.67547	3.85926	3.26821
16	14.71787	13.57771	12.56110	11.65230	10.83777	10.10590	9.44665	8.85137	8.31256	7.82371	6.97399	6.26506	5.66850	5.16235	4.72956	3.88741	3.28324
17	15.56225	14.29187	13.16612	12.16567	11.27407	10.47726	9.76322	9.12164	8.54363	8.02155	7.11963	6.37286	5.74870	5.22233	4.77463	3.90993	3.29480
18	16.39827	14.99203	13.75351	12.65930	11.68959	10.82760	10.05909	9.37189	8.75563	8.20141	7.24967	6.46742	5.81785	5.27316	4.81219	3.92794	3.30369
19	17.22601	15.67846	14.32380	13.13394	12.08532	11.15812	10.33560	9.60360	8.95011	8.36492	7.36578	6.55037	5.87746	5.31624	4.84350	3.94235	3.31053
20	18.04555	16.35143	14.87747	13.59033	12.46221	11.46992	10.59401	9.81815	9.12855	8.51356	7.46944	6.62313	5.92884	5.35275	4.86958	3.95288	3.31579
21	18.85698	17.01121	15.41502	14.02916	12.82115	11.76408	10.83553	10.01680	9.29224	8.64869	7.56200	6.68696	5.97314	5.38368	4.89132	3.96311	3.31984
22	19.66038	17.65805	15.93692	14.45112	13.16300	12.04158	11.06124	10.20074	9.44243	8.77154	7.64465	6.74294	6.01133	5.40990	4.90943	3.97049	3.32296
23	20.45582	18.29220	16.44361	14.85684	13.48857	12.30338	11.27219	10.37106	9.58021	8.88322	7.71843	6.79206	6.04425	5.43212	4.92453	3.97639	3.32535
24	21.24339	18.91393	16.93554	15.24696	13.79864	12.55036	11.46933	10.52876	9.70661	8.98474	7.78432	6.83514	6.07263	5.45095	4.93710	3.98111	3.32719
25	22.02316	19.52346	17.41315	15.62208	14.09394	12.78336	11.65358	10.67478	9.82258	9.07704	7.84314	6.87293	6.09709	5.46691	4.94759	3.98489	3.32861
26	22.79520	20.12104	17.87684	15.98277	14.37519	13.00317	11.82578	10.80998	9.92897	9.16095	7.89566	6.90608	6.11818	5.48043	4.95632	3.98791	3.32970
27	23.55961	20.70690	18.32703	16.32959	14.64303	13.21053	11.98671	10.93516	10.02658	9.23722	7.94255	6.93515	6.13636	5.49189	4.96360	3.99033	3.33054
28	24.31644	21.28127	18.76411	16.66306	14.89813	13.40616	12.13711	11.05108	10.11613	9.30657	7.98442	6.96066	6.15204	5.50160	4.96967	3.99226	3.33118
29	25.06579	21.84438	19.18845	16.98371	15.14107	13.59072	12.27767	11.15841	10.19828	9.36961	8.02181	6.98304	6.16555	5.50983	4.97472	3.99381	3.33168
30	25.80771	22.39646	19.60044	17.29203	15.37245	13.76483	12.40904	11.25778	10.27365	9.42691	8.05518	7.00266	6.17720	5.51681	4.97894	3.99505	3.33206

Financial Statement Information: Abercrombie & Fitch

ITEM 8. *FINANCIAL STATEMENTS AND SUPPLEMENTARY DATA.*

ABERCROMBIE & FITCH CO.

CONSOLIDATED STATEMENTS OF OPERATIONS AND COMPREHENSIVE INCOME

	2009	2008	2007
	(Thousands, except per share amounts)		
NET SALES	$ 2,928,626	$ 3,484,058	$ 3,699,656
Cost of Goods Sold	1,045,028	1,152,963	1,211,490
GROSS PROFIT	1,883,598	2,331,095	2,488,166
Stores and Distribution Expense	1,425,950	1,436,363	1,344,178
Marketing, General & Administrative Expense	353,269	405,248	376,780
Other Operating Income, Net	(13,533)	(8,778)	(11,702)
OPERATING INCOME	117,912	498,262	778,909
Interest Income, Net	(1,598)	(11,382)	(18,827)
INCOME FROM CONTINUING OPERATIONS BEFORE INCOME TAXES	119,510	509,644	797,737
Income Tax Expense from Continuing Operations	40,557	201,475	298,610
NET INCOME FROM CONTINUING OPERATIONS	$ 78,953	$ 308,169	$ 499,127
NET LOSS FROM DISCONTINUED OPERATIONS (net of taxes)	$ (78,699)	$ (35,914)	$ (23,430)
NET INCOME	$ 254	$ 272,255	$ 475,697
NET INCOME PER SHARE FROM CONTINUING OPERATIONS:			
BASIC	$ 0.90	$ 3.55	$ 5.72
DILUTED	$ 0.89	$ 3.45	$ 5.45
NET LOSS PER SHARE FROM DISCONTINUED OPERATIONS:			
BASIC	$ (0.90)	$ (0.41)	$ (0.27)
DILUTED	$ (0.89)	$ (0.40)	$ (0.26)
NET INCOME PER SHARE:			
BASIC	$ 0.00	$ 3.14	$ 5.45
DILUTED	$ 0.00	$ 3.05	$ 5.20
WEIGHTED-AVERAGE SHARES OUTSTANDING:			
BASIC	87,874	86,816	87,248
DILUTED	88,609	89,291	91,523
DIVIDENDS DECLARED PER SHARE	$ 0.70	$ 0.70	$ 0.70
OTHER COMPREHENSIVE INCOME			
Foreign Currency Translation Adjustments	$ 5,942	$ (13,173)	$ 7,328
Unrealized Gains (Losses) on Marketable Securities, net of taxes of $(4,826), $10,312 and $(584) for Fiscal 2009, Fiscal 2008 and Fiscal 2007, respectively	8,217	(17,518)	912
Unrealized (Loss) Gain on Derivative Financial Instruments, net of taxes of $265, $(621) and $82 for Fiscal 2009, Fiscal 2008 and Fiscal 2007, respectively	(451)	892	(128)
Other Comprehensive Income (Loss)	$ 13,708	$ (29,799)	$ 8,112
COMPREHENSIVE INCOME	$ 13,962	$ 242,456	$ 483,809

The accompanying Notes are an integral part of these Consolidated Financial Statements.

ABERCROMBIE & FITCH CO.

CONSOLIDATED BALANCE SHEETS

	January 30, 2010	January 31, 2009
	(Thousands, except share amounts)	

ASSETS

CURRENT ASSETS:		
Cash and Equivalents	$ 680,113	$ 522,122
Marketable Securities	32,356	—
Receivables	90,865	53,110
Inventories	310,645	372,422
Deferred Income Taxes	44,570	43,408
Other Current Assets	77,297	80,948
TOTAL CURRENT ASSETS	1,235,846	1,072,010
PROPERTY AND EQUIPMENT, NET	1,244,019	1,398,655
NON-CURRENT MARKETABLE SECURITIES	141,794	229,081
OTHER ASSETS	200,207	148,435
TOTAL ASSETS	$ 2,821,866	$ 2,848,181

LIABILITIES AND SHAREHOLDERS' EQUITY

CURRENT LIABILITIES:		
Accounts Payable	$ 110,212	$ 92,814
Outstanding Checks	39,922	56,939
Accrued Expenses	246,289	241,231
Deferred Lease Credits	43,597	42,358
Income Taxes Payable	9,352	16,455
TOTAL CURRENT LIABILITIES	449,372	449,797
LONG-TERM LIABILITIES:		
Deferred Income Taxes	47,142	34,085
Deferred Lease Credits	212,052	211,978
Long-term Debt	71,213	100,000
Other Liabilities	214,170	206,743
TOTAL LONG-TERM LIABILITIES	544,577	552,806
SHAREHOLDERS' EQUITY:		
Class A Common Stock — $.01 par value: 150,000,000 shares authorized and 103,300,000 shares issued at January 30, 2010 and January 31, 2009, respectively	1,033	1,033
Paid-In Capital	339,453	328,488
Retained Earnings	2,183,690	2,244,936
Accumulated Other Comprehensive Loss, net of tax	(8,973)	(22,681)
Treasury Stock, at Average Cost 15,314,481 and 15,664,385 shares at January 30, 2010 and January 31, 2009, respectively	(687,286)	(706,198)
TOTAL SHAREHOLDERS' EQUITY	1,827,917	1,845,578
TOTAL LIABILITIES AND SHAREHOLDERS' EQUITY	$ 2,821,866	$ 2,848,181

The accompanying Notes are an integral part of these Consolidated Financial Statements.

ABERCROMBIE & FITCH CO.

CONSOLIDATED STATEMENTS OF SHAREHOLDERS' EQUITY

(Thousands)	Common Stock		Paid-In Capital	Retained Earnings	Other Comprehensive (Loss) Income	Treasury Stock		Total Shareholders' Equity
	Shares Outstanding	Par Value				Shares	At Average Cost	
Balance, February 3, 2007	88,300	$ 1,033	$289,732	$1,646,290	$ (994)	15,000	$ (530,764)	$ 1,405,297
FIN 48 Impact	—	—	—	(2,786)	—	—	—	(2,786)
Net Income	—	—	—	475,697	—	—	—	475,697
Purchase of Treasury Stock	(3,654)	—	—	—	—	3,654	(287,916)	(287,916)
Dividends ($0.70 per share)	—	—	—	(61,330)	—	—	—	(61,330)
Share-based Compensation Issuances and Exercises	1,513	—	(19,051)	(6,408)	—	(1,513)	57,928	32,469
Tax Benefit from Share-based Compensation Issuances and Exercises	—	—	17,600	—	—	—	—	17,600
Share-based Compensation Expense	—	—	31,170	—	—	—	—	31,170
Unrealized Gains on Marketable Securities	—	—	—	—	912	—	—	912
Net Change in Unrealized Gains or Losses on Derivative Financial Instruments	—	—	—	—	(128)	—	—	(128)
Foreign Currency Translation Adjustments	—	—	—	—	7,328	—	—	7,328
Balance, February 2, 2008	86,159	$ 1,033	$319,451	$2,051,463	$ 7,118	17,141	$ (760,752)	$ 1,618,313
Net Income	—	—	—	272,255	—	—	—	272,255
Purchase of Treasury Stock	(682)	—	—	—	—	682	(50,000)	(50,000)
Dividends ($0.70 per share)	—	—	—	(60,769)	—	—	—	(60,769)
Share-based Compensation Issuances and Exercises	2,159	—	(49,844)	(18,013)	—	(2,159)	104,554	36,697
Tax Benefit from Share-based Compensation Issuances and Exercises	—	—	16,839	—	—	—	—	16,839
Share-based Compensation Expense	—	—	42,042	—	—	—	—	42,042
Unrealized Losses on Marketable Securities	—	—	—	—	(17,518)	—	—	(17,518)
Net Change in Unrealized Gains or Losses on Derivative Financial Instruments	—	—	—	—	892	—	—	892
Foreign Currency Translation Adjustments	—	—	—	—	(13,173)	—	—	(13,173)
Balance, January 31, 2009	87,636	$ 1,033	$328,488	$2,244,936	$ (22,681)	15,664	$ (706,198)	$ 1,845,578

(Continued)

ABERCROMBIE & FITCH CO.

CONSOLIDATED STATEMENTS OF SHAREHOLDERS' EQUITY—(Continued)

(Thousands)	Common Stock Shares Outstanding	Par Value	Paid-In Capital	Retained Earnings	Other Comprehensive (Loss) Income	Treasury Stock Shares	At Average Cost	Total Shareholders' Equity
Balance, January 31, 2009	87,636	$ 1,033	$328,488	$2,244,936	$ (22,681)	15,664	$ (706,198)	$ 1,845,578
Net Income	—	—	—	254	—	—	—	254
Purchase of Treasury Stock	—	—	—	—	—	—	—	—
Dividends ($0.70 per share)	—	—	—	(61,500)	—	—	—	(61,500)
Share-based Compensation Issuances and Exercises	350	—	(19,690)	—	—	(350)	18,912	(778)
Tax Deficiency from Share-based Compensation Issuances and Exercises	—	—	(5,454)	—	—	—	—	(5,454)
Share-based Compensation Expense	—	—	36,109	—	—	—	—	36,109
Unrealized Gains on Marketable Securities	—	—	—	—	8,217	—	—	8,217
Net Change in Unrealized Gains or Losses on Derivative Financial Instruments	—	—	—	—	(451)	—	—	(451)
Foreign Currency Translation Adjustments	—	—	—	—	5,942	—	—	5,942
Balance, January 30, 2010	87,986	$ 1,033	$339,453	$2,183,690	$ (8,973)	15,314	$ (687,286)	$ 1,827,917

The accompanying Notes are an integral part of these Consolidated Financial Statements.

ABERCROMBIE & FITCH CO.

CONSOLIDATED STATEMENTS OF CASH FLOWS

	2009	2008	2007
		(Thousands)	
OPERATING ACTIVITIES:			
Net Income	$ 254	$ 272,255	$ 475,697
Impact of Other Operating Activities on Cash Flows:			
Depreciation and Amortization	238,752	225,334	183,716
Non-Cash Charge for Asset Impairment	84,754	30,574	2,312
Amortization of Deferred Lease Credits	(47,182)	(43,194)	(37,418)
Share-Based Compensation	36,109	42,042	31,170
Tax (Deficiency) Benefit from Share-Based Compensation	(5,454)	16,839	17,600
Excess Tax Benefit from Share-Based Compensation	—	(5,791)	(14,205)
Deferred Taxes	7,605	14,005	1,342
Loss on Disposal / Write-off of Assets	10,646	7,607	7,205
Lessor Construction Allowances	47,329	55,415	43,391
Changes in Assets and Liabilities:			
Inventories	62,720	(40,521)	87,657
Accounts Payable and Accrued Expenses	39,394	(23,875)	22,375
Income Taxes Payable	(7,386)	(55,565)	(13,922)
Other Assets and Liabilities	(65,341)	(4,289)	10,604
NET CASH PROVIDED BY OPERATING ACTIVITIES	402,200	490,836	817,524
INVESTING ACTIVITIES:			
Capital Expenditures	(175,472)	(367,602)	(403,345)
Purchases of Marketable Securities	—	(49,411)	(1,444,736)
Proceeds from Sales of Marketable Securities	77,450	308,673	1,362,911
Purchases of Trust-Owned Life Insurance Policies	(13,539)	(4,877)	(15,000)
NET CASH USED FOR INVESTING ACTIVITIES	(111,561)	(113,217)	(500,170)
FINANCING ACTIVITIES:			
Proceeds from Borrowings under Credit Agreement	48,056	100,000	—
Repayment of Borrowings under Credit Agreement	(100,000)	—	—
Dividends Paid	(61,500)	(60,769)	(61,330)
Proceeds from Share-Based Compensation	2,048	55,194	38,750
Excess Tax Benefit from Share-Based Compensation	—	5,791	14,205
Purchase of Treasury Stock	—	(50,000)	(287,916)
Change in Outstanding Checks and Other	(24,654)	(19,747)	13,536
NET CASH (USED FOR) PROVIDED BY FINANCING ACTIVITIES	(136,050)	30,469	(282,755)
EFFECT OF EXCHANGE RATES ON CASH	3,402	(4,010)	1,486
NET INCREASE IN CASH AND EQUIVALENTS	157,991	404,078	36,085
Cash and Equivalents, Beginning of Year	522,122	118,044	81,959
CASH AND EQUIVALENTS, END OF YEAR	$ 680,113	$ 522,122	$ 118,044
SIGNIFICANT NON-CASH INVESTING ACTIVITIES:			
Change in Accrual for Construction in Progress	$ (21,882)	$ (27,913)	$ 8,791

The accompanying Notes are an integral part of these Consolidated Financial Statements.

ABERCROMBIE & FITCH CO.

NOTES TO CONSOLIDATED FINANCIAL STATEMENTS

1.   BASIS OF PRESENTATION

Abercrombie & Fitch Co. ("A&F"), through its wholly-owned subsidiaries (collectively, A&F and its wholly-owned subsidiaries are referred to as "Abercrombie & Fitch" or the "Company"), is a specialty retailer of high-quality, casual apparel for men, women and kids with an active, youthful lifestyle.

The accompanying consolidated financial statements include the historical financial statements of, and transactions applicable to, the Company and reflect its assets, liabilities, results of operations and cash flows.

On June 16, 2009, A&F's Board of Directors approved the closure of the Company's 29 RUEHL branded stores and related direct-to-consumer operations. The determination to take this action was based on a comprehensive review and evaluation of the performance of the RUEHL branded stores and related direct-to-consumer operations, as well as the related real estate portfolio. The Company completed the closure of the RUEHL branded stores and related direct-to-consumer operations during the fourth quarter of Fiscal 2009. Accordingly, the results of operations of RUEHL are reflected in Net Loss from Discontinued Operations for all periods presented on the Consolidated Statements of Operations and Comprehensive Income.

FISCAL YEAR

The Company's fiscal year ends on the Saturday closest to January 31, typically resulting in a fifty-two week year, but occasionally giving rise to an additional week, resulting in a fifty-three week year. Fiscal years are designated in the consolidated financial statements and notes by the calendar year in which the fiscal year commences. All references herein to "Fiscal 2009" represent the results of the 52-week fiscal year ended January 30, 2010; to "Fiscal 2008" represent the results of the 52-week fiscal year ended January 31, 2009; and to "Fiscal 2007" represent the results of the 52-week fiscal year ended February 2, 2008. In addition, all references herein to "Fiscal 2010" represent the 52-week fiscal year that will end on January 29, 2011.

RECLASSIFICATIONS

Certain prior period amounts have been reclassified to conform to the current year presentation.

SEGMENT REPORTING

The Company determines its operating segments on the same basis that it uses to evaluate performance internally. The operating segments identified by the Company are Abercrombie & Fitch, abercrombie kids, Hollister and Gilly Hicks. The operating segments have been aggregated and are reported as one reportable segment because they have similar economic characteristics and meet the required aggregation criteria. The Company believes its operating segments may be aggregated for financial reporting purposes because they are similar in each of the following areas: class of consumer, economic characteristics, nature of products, nature of production processes, and distribution methods.

Geographic Information

Financial information relating to the Company's operations by geographic area is as follows:

Net Sales:

Net sales includes net merchandise sales through stores and direct-to-consumer operations, including shipping and handling revenue. Net sales are reported by geographic area based on the location of the customer.

	Fifty-Two Weeks Ended	
	January 30, 2010	January 31, 2009
	(In thousands):	
United States	$ 2,566,118	$ 3,219,624
International	362,508	264,434
Total	$ 2,928,626	$ 3,484,058

ABERCROMBIE & FITCH CO.

NOTES TO CONSOLIDATED FINANCIAL STATEMENTS—(Continued)

Long-Lived Assets:

	January 30, 2010	January 31, 2009
	(In thousands):	
United States	$ 1,137,844	$ 1,371,734
International	194,461	80,341
Total	$ 1,332,305	$ 1,452,075

Long-lived assets included in the table above include primarily property and equipment, net, store supplies, and lease deposits.

2.   SUMMARY OF SIGNIFICANT ACCOUNTING POLICIES

PRINCIPLES OF CONSOLIDATION

The consolidated financial statements include the accounts of A&F and its subsidiaries. All intercompany balances and transactions have been eliminated in consolidation.

CASH AND EQUIVALENTS

Cash and equivalents include amounts on deposit with financial institutions and investments, primarily held in money market accounts, with original maturities of less than 90 days. Outstanding checks are classified as current liabilities in the Consolidated Balance Sheets and changes in outstanding checks are reported in financing activities on the Consolidated Statements of Cash Flows.

INVESTMENTS

See Note 4, *"Cash and Equivalents and Investments"*.

RECEIVABLES

Receivables include credit card receivables, construction allowances, value added tax ("VAT") receivables and other tax receivable balances.

As part of the normal course of business, the Company has approximately three to four days of sales transactions outstanding with its third-party credit card vendors at any point. The Company classifies these outstanding balances as credit card receivables. Construction allowances are recorded for certain store lease agreements for improvements completed by the Company. VAT receivables are payments the Company has made on purchases of goods and services that will be recovered as sales are made to customers.

INVENTORIES

Inventories are principally valued at the lower of average cost or market utilizing the retail method. The Company determines market value as the anticipated future selling price of merchandise less a normal margin. An initial markup is applied to inventory at cost in order to establish a cost-to-retail ratio. Permanent markdowns, when taken, reduce both the retail and cost components of inventory on hand so as to maintain the already established cost-to-retail relationship. At first and third fiscal quarter end, the Company reduces inventory value by recording a valuation reserve that represents the estimated future anticipated selling price decreases necessary to sell-through the current season inventory. At second and fourth fiscal quarter end, the Company reduces inventory value by recording a valuation reserve that represents the estimated future selling price decreases necessary to sell-through any remaining carryover inventory from the season then ending. The valuation reserve was $11.4 million, $9.1 million and $5.4 million at January 30, 2010, January 31, 2009 and February 2, 2008, respectively.

Additionally, as part of inventory valuation, inventory shrinkage estimates based on historical trends from actual physical inventories are made each period that reduce the inventory value for lost or stolen items. The Company performs physical inventories on a periodic basis and adjusts the shrink reserve accordingly. The shrink reserve was $8.1 million, $10.8 million and $11.5 million at January 30, 2010, January 31, 2009 and February 2, 2008, respectively.

ABERCROMBIE & FITCH CO.

NOTES TO CONSOLIDATED FINANCIAL STATEMENTS—(Continued)

STORE SUPPLIES

Store supplies include in-store supplies and packaging, as well as replenishment inventory held on the Company's behalf by a third party. The initial inventory of supplies for new stores including, but not limited to, hangers, frames, security tags and point-of-sale supplies are capitalized at the store opening date. In lieu of amortizing the initial balances over their estimated useful lives, the Company expenses all subsequent replacements and adjusts the initial balance, as appropriate, for changes in store quantities or replacement cost. The Company believes this policy approximates the expense that would have been recognized under accounting principles generally accepted in the United States of America ("GAAP"). Packaging and consumable store supplies are expensed as used. Current store supplies, including packaging and consumable store supplies held at a third party replenishment center, were $11.1 million and $19.7 million at January 30, 2010 and January 31, 2009, respectively, and were classified as Other Current Assets on the Consolidated Balance Sheets. Non-current store supplies were $32.4 million and $35.7 million at January 30, 2010 and January 31, 2009, respectively, and were classified as Other Assets on the Consolidated Balance Sheets.

PROPERTY AND EQUIPMENT

Depreciation and amortization of property and equipment are computed for financial reporting purposes on a straight-line basis, using service lives ranging principally from 30 years for buildings; the lesser of the useful life of the asset, which ranges from three to 15 years, or the term of the lease for leasehold improvements; the lesser of the useful life of the asset, which ranges from three to seven years, or the term of the lease when applicable for information technology; and from three to 20 years for other property and equipment. The cost of assets sold or retired and the related accumulated depreciation or amortization are removed from the accounts with any resulting gain or loss included in net income. Maintenance and repairs are charged to expense as incurred. Major remodels and improvements that extend service lives of the assets are capitalized.

Long-lived assets, primarily comprised of property and equipment, are reviewed periodically for impairment or whenever events or changes in circumstances indicate that full recoverability of net asset balances through future cash flows is in question. Factors used in the evaluation include, but are not limited to, management's plans for future operations, recent operating results and projected cash flows. During Fiscal 2009, as a result of a strategic review of the RUEHL business, the Company determined that a triggering event occurred. As a result of that assessment, the Company incurred non-cash pre-tax impairment charges of $51.5 million, reported in Net Loss from Discontinued Operations on the Consolidated Statement of Operations and Comprehensive Income for the fifty-two weeks ended January 30, 2010. There was no remaining fair value of RUEHL long-lived assets as of January 30, 2010.

In the fourth quarter of Fiscal 2009, as part of the Company's year-end review of assets, the Company incurred a non-cash pre-tax impairment charge of $33.2 million, reported in Stores and Distribution Expense on the Consolidated Statement of Operations and Comprehensive Income for the fifty-two weeks ended January 30, 2010. The charge was associated with 34 Abercrombie & Fitch stores, 46 abercrombie kids stores and 19 Hollister stores. In Fiscal 2008, the Company incurred a non-cash pre-tax impairment charge of approximately $8.3 million related to long-lived assets. The charge was associated with 11 Abercrombie & Fitch stores, six abercrombie kids stores and three Hollister stores and was reported in Stores and Distribution Expense on the Consolidated Statement of Operations and Comprehensive Income for the fifty-two weeks ended January 31, 2009.

The Company also incurred a non-cash pre-tax impairment charge of approximately $22.3 million related to long-lived assets associated with nine RUEHL stores which is reported in Net Loss from Discontinued Operations on the Consolidated Statement of Operations and Comprehensive Loss for the fifty-two weeks ended January 31, 2009.

The Company expenses all internal-use software costs incurred in the preliminary project stage and capitalizes certain direct costs associated with the development and purchase of internal-use software within property and equipment. Capitalized costs are amortized on a straight-line basis over the estimated useful lives of the software, generally not exceeding seven years.

OTHER ASSETS

Other assets include lease deposits, assets held in the rabbi trust, long-term store supplies, pre-paid foreign income tax and other miscellaneous non-current assets.

ABERCROMBIE & FITCH CO.

NOTES TO CONSOLIDATED FINANCIAL STATEMENTS—(Continued)

INCOME TAXES

Income taxes are calculated using the asset and liability method. Deferred tax assets and liabilities are recognized based on the difference between the financial statement carrying amounts of existing assets and liabilities and their respective tax bases. Deferred tax assets and liabilities are measured using current enacted tax rates in effect for the years in which those temporary differences are expected to reverse. Inherent in the measurement of deferred balances are certain judgments and interpretations of enacted tax law and published guidance with respect to applicability to the Company's operations. A valuation allowance is established against deferred tax assets when it is more likely than not that some portion or all of the deferred tax assets will not be realized. The Company has recorded a valuation allowance against the deferred tax asset arising from the net operating loss of certain foreign subsidiaries, for capital loss carryovers related to sales of securities and for unrealized losses on certain securities. No other valuation allowances have been provided for deferred tax assets. The effective tax rate utilized by the Company reflects management's judgment of expected tax liabilities within the various tax jurisdictions.

See Note 11, "*Income Taxes*" for a discussion regarding the Company's policies for uncertain tax positions.

FOREIGN CURRENCY TRANSLATION

Some of the Company's international operations use local currencies as the functional currency. Assets and liabilities denominated in foreign currencies were translated into U.S. dollars (the reporting currency) at the exchange rate prevailing at the balance sheet date. Equity accounts denominated in foreign currencies were translated into U.S. dollars at historical exchange rates. Revenues and expenses denominated in foreign currencies were translated into U.S. dollars at the monthly average exchange rate for the period. Gains and losses resulting from foreign currency transactions are included in the results of operations; whereas, related translation adjustments and inter-company loans of a long-term investment nature are reported as an element of Other Comprehensive Income. Gains and losses resulting from foreign currency transactions included in the results of operations were immaterial for the fifty-two weeks ended January 30, 2010 and January 31, 2009.

DERIVATIVES

See Note 13, "*Derivatives*" for further discussion.

CONTINGENCIES

In the normal course of business, the Company must make continuing estimates of potential future legal obligations and liabilities, which requires the use of management's judgment on the outcome of various issues. Management may also use outside legal advice to assist in the estimating process. However, the ultimate outcome of various legal issues could be different than management estimates, and adjustments may be required.

SHAREHOLDERS' EQUITY

At January 30, 2010 and January 31, 2009, there were 150 million shares of A&F's $.01 par value Class A Common Stock authorized, of which 88.0 million and 87.6 million shares were outstanding at January 30, 2010 and January 31, 2009, respectively, and 106.4 million shares of $.01 par value Class B Common Stock authorized, none of which were outstanding at January 30, 2010 and January 31, 2009. In addition, 15 million shares of A&F's $.01 par value Preferred Stock were authorized, none of which have been issued. See Note 17, "*Preferred Stock Purchase Rights*" for information about Preferred Stock Purchase Rights.

Holders of Class A Common Stock generally have identical rights to holders of Class B Common Stock, except holders of Class A Common Stock are entitled to one vote per share while holders of Class B Common Stock are entitled to three votes per share on all matters submitted to a vote of shareholders.

REVENUE RECOGNITION

The Company recognizes retail sales at the time the customer takes possession of the merchandise. Direct-to-consumer sales are recorded based on an estimated date for customer receipt of merchandise. Amounts relating to shipping and handling billed to customers in a sale transaction are classified as revenue and the related direct shipping and handling costs are classified as Stores and Distribution Expense. Associate discounts are classified as a reduction of revenue. The Company reserves for sales returns through estimates based on historical experience and various other assumptions that management believes to be reasonable. The sales return reserve was $11.7 million, $9.1 million and $10.7 million at January 30, 2010, January 31, 2009 and February 2, 2008, respectively.

ABERCROMBIE & FITCH CO.

NOTES TO CONSOLIDATED FINANCIAL STATEMENTS—(Continued)

The Company sells gift cards in its stores and through direct-to-consumer operations. The Company accounts for gift cards sold to customers by recognizing a liability at the time of sale. Gift cards sold to customers do not expire or lose value over periods of inactivity. The liability remains on the Company's books until the earlier of redemption (recognized as revenue) or when the Company determines the likelihood of redemption is remote (recognized as other operating income). The Company determines the probability of the gift card being redeemed to be remote based on historical redemption patterns. At January 30, 2010 and January 31, 2009, the gift card liabilities on the Company's Consolidated Balance Sheets were $49.8 million and $57.5 million, respectively.

The Company is not required by law to escheat the value of unredeemed gift cards to the states in which it operates. During Fiscal 2009, Fiscal 2008 and Fiscal 2007, the Company recognized other operating income for adjustments to the gift card liability of $9.0 million, $8.2 million and $10.8 million, respectively.

The Company does not include tax amounts collected as part of the sales transaction in its net sales results.

COST OF GOODS SOLD

Cost of goods sold is primarily comprised of the following: cost of merchandise, markdowns, inventory shrink, valuation reserves and freight expenses.

STORES AND DISTRIBUTION EXPENSE

Stores and distribution expense includes store payroll, store management, rent, utilities and other landlord expenses, depreciation and amortization, repairs and maintenance and other store support functions, as well as Direct-to-Consumer and Distribution Center ("DC") expenses.

MARKETING, GENERAL & ADMINISTRATIVE EXPENSE

Marketing, general and administrative expense includes photography and media ads; store marketing; home office payroll, except for those departments included in stores and distribution expense; information technology; outside services such as legal and consulting; relocation, as well as recruiting, samples and travel expenses.

OTHER OPERATING INCOME, NET

Other operating income consists primarily of: income related to gift card balances whose likelihood of redemption has been determined to be remote; gains and losses on foreign currency transactions; and the net impact of the change in valuation on other-than-temporary gains and losses on auction rate securities; and changes in the value of the UBS Put Option. See Note 4, "*Cash and Equivalents and Investments*".

WEBSITE AND ADVERTISING COSTS

Website costs, including photography, mail list expense and other production and miscellaneous expenses, are expensed as incurred as a component of Stores and Distribution Expense on the Consolidated Statements of Operations and Comprehensive Income. Fiscal 2007 also included costs related to catalogue production and mailing costs of catalogues. Advertising costs consist of in-store photographs and advertising in selected national publications and billboards, and are expensed as incurred as a component of Marketing, General and Administrative Expense on the Consolidated Statements of Operations and Comprehensive Income. Direct-to-consumer and advertising costs, including photo shoot costs, amounted to $17.7 million, $28.7 million and $31.3 million in Fiscal 2009, Fiscal 2008 and Fiscal 2007, respectively.

LEASES

The Company leases property for its stores under operating leases. Most lease agreements contain construction allowances, rent escalation clauses and/or contingent rent provisions.

For construction allowances, the Company records a deferred lease credit on the Consolidated Balance Sheets and amortizes the deferred lease credit as a reduction of rent expense on the Consolidated Statements of Operations and Comprehensive Income over the terms of the leases. For scheduled rent escalation clauses during the lease terms, the Company records minimum rental expenses on a straight-line basis over the terms of the leases on the Consolidated Statements of Operations and Comprehensive Income. The term of the lease over which the Company amortizes construction allowances and minimum rental expenses on a straight-line basis begins on the date of initial possession, which is generally when the Company enters the space and begins to make improvements in preparation for intended use.

Certain leases provide for contingent rents, which are determined as a percentage of gross sales. The Company records a contingent rent liability in accrued expenses on the Consolidated Balance Sheets and the corresponding rent expense on the Consolidated Statements of Operations and Comprehensive Income when management determines that achieving the specified levels during the fiscal year is probable.

ABERCROMBIE & FITCH CO.

NOTES TO CONSOLIDATED FINANCIAL STATEMENTS—(Continued)

Under U.S. generally accepted accounting principles, the Company is considered to be the owner of certain store locations, primarily related to flagships, in which the Company is deemed to be involved in structural construction and has substantially all of the risks of ownership during construction of the leased property. Accordingly, the Company records a construction-in-progress asset which is included in Property and Equipment, Net and a related lease financing obligation which is included in Long-Term Debt on the Consolidated Balance Sheets. Once construction is complete, the Company determines if the asset qualifies for sale-leaseback accounting treatment. If the arrangement does not qualify for sale lease-back treatment, the Company continues to amortize the obligation over the lease term and depreciates the asset over its useful life.

STORE PRE-OPENING EXPENSES

Pre-opening expenses related to new store openings are charged to operations as incurred.

DESIGN AND DEVELOPMENT COSTS

Costs to design and develop the Company's merchandise are expensed as incurred and are reflected as a component of "Marketing, General and Administrative Expense."

NET INCOME PER SHARE

Net income per basic share is computed based on the weighted-average number of outstanding shares of Class A Common Stock ("Common Stock"). Net income per diluted share includes the weighted-average effect of dilutive stock options, stock appreciation rights and restricted stock units.

Weighted-Average Shares Outstanding and Anti-dilutive Shares (in thousands):

	2009	2008	2007
Shares of Common Stock issued	103,300	103,300	103,300
Treasury shares	(15,426)	(16,484)	(16,052)
Weighted-Average — basic shares	87,874	86,816	87,248
Dilutive effect of stock options, stock appreciation rights and restricted stock units	735	2,475	4,275
Weighted-Average — diluted shares	88,609	89,291	91,523
Anti-dilutive shares(1)	6,698	3,746	404

(1) Reflects the number of stock options, stock appreciation rights, and restricted stock units ousanding, but is excluded from the computation of net income per diluted share because the impact would be anti-dilutive.

SHARE-BASED COMPENSATION

See Note 3, "Share-Based Compensation".

USE OF ESTIMATES IN THE PREPARATION OF FINANCIAL STATEMENTS

The preparation of financial statements in accordance with generally accepted accounting principles requires management to make estimates and assumptions that affect the reported amounts of assets and liabilities as of the date of the financial statements and the reported amounts of revenues and expenses during the reporting period. Since actual results may differ from those estimates, the Company revises its estimates and assumptions as new information becomes available.

3.   SHARE-BASED COMPENSATION

Financial Statement Impact

The Company recognized share-based compensation expense, including expense for RUEHL associates, of $36.1 million, $42.0 million and $31.2 million for the fifty-two week periods ended January 30, 2010, January 31, 2009 and February 2, 2008, respectively. The Company also recognized $12.8 million, $15.4 million and $11.5 million in tax benefits related to share-based compensation, including benefit for RUEHL associates, for the fifty-two week periods ended January 30, 2010, January 31, 2009 and February 2, 2008, respectively.

ABERCROMBIE & FITCH CO.

NOTES TO CONSOLIDATED FINANCIAL STATEMENTS—(Continued)

A deferred tax asset is recorded on the compensation expense required to be accrued under the accounting rules. A current income tax deduction arises at the time the restricted stock unit vests or stock option/stock appreciation right is exercised. In the event the current income tax deduction is greater or less than the associated deferred tax asset, the difference is required under the accounting rules to be charged first to the "windfall tax benefit" account. In the event there is not a balance in the "windfall tax benefit" account, the shortfall is charged to tax expense. The amount of the Company's "windfall tax benefit" account, which is recorded as a component of additional paid in capital, was approximately $86.0 million as of January 30, 2010. Based upon outstanding awards, the "windfall tax benefit" account is sufficient to fully absorb any shortfall which may develop.

Additionally, during Fiscal 2008, the Company recognized $9.9 million of non-deductible tax expense as a result of the execution of the Chairman and Chief Executive Officer's new employment agreement on December 19, 2008, which pursuant to Section 162(m) of the Internal Revenue Code resulted in the exclusion of previously recognized tax benefits on share-based compensation.

Share-based compensation expense is recognized, net of estimated forfeitures, over the requisite service period on a straight-line basis. The Company adjusts share-based compensation expense on a quarterly basis for actual forfeitures and for changes to the estimate of expected award forfeitures based on actual forfeiture experience. The effect of adjusting the forfeiture rate is recognized in the period the forfeiture estimate is changed. The effect of adjustments for forfeitures during the fifty-two week period ended January 30, 2010 was $6.7 million. The effect of adjustments for forfeitures during the fifty-two week period ended January 31, 2009 was immaterial.

A&F issues shares of Common Stock for stock option and stock appreciation right exercises and restricted stock unit vestings from treasury stock. As of January 30, 2010, A&F had sufficient treasury stock available to settle stock options, stock appreciation rights and restricted stock units outstanding without having to repurchase additional shares of Common Stock. Settlement of stock awards in Common Stock also requires that the Company has sufficient shares available in shareholder-approved plans at the applicable time.

Plans

As of January 30, 2010, A&F had two primary share-based compensation plans: the 2005 Long-Term Incentive Plan (the "2005 LTIP"), under which A&F grants stock options, stock appreciation rights and restricted stock units to associates of the Company and non-associate members of the A&F Board of Directors, and the 2007 Long-Term Incentive Plan (the "2007 LTIP"), under which A&F grants stock options, stock appreciation rights and restricted stock units to associates of the Company. A&F also has four other share-based compensation plans under which it granted stock options and restricted stock units to associates of the Company and non-associate members of the A&F Board of Directors in prior years.

The 2007 LTIP, a shareholder-approved plan, permits A&F to grant up to 2.0 million shares annually, plus any unused eligibility from prior years, of A&F's Common Stock to any associate of the Company eligible to receive awards under the 2007 LTIP. The 2005 LTIP, a shareholder-approved plan, permits A&F to grant up to approximately 250,000 shares of A&F's Common Stock to any associate of the Company (other than Michael S. Jeffries) who is subject to Section 16 of the Securities Exchange Act of 1934, as amended, at the time of the grant. In addition, any non-associate director of A&F is eligible to receive awards under the 2005 LTIP. Under both plans, stock options, stock appreciation rights and restricted stock units vest primarily over four years for associates. Under the 2005 LTIP, restricted stock units typically vest over one year for non-associate directors of A&F. Stock options have a ten-year term and stock appreciation rights have up to a ten-year term, subject to forfeiture under the terms of the plans. The plans provide for accelerated vesting if there is a change of control as defined in the plans.

Fair Value Estimates

The Company estimates the fair value of stock options and stock appreciation rights granted using the Black-Scholes option-pricing model, which requires the Company to estimate the expected term of the stock options and stock appreciation rights and expected future stock price volatility over the expected term. Estimates of expected terms, which represent the expected periods of time the Company believes stock options and stock appreciation rights will be outstanding, are based on historical experience. Estimates of expected future stock price volatility are based on the volatility of A&F's Common Stock price for the most recent historical period equal to the expected term of the stock option or stock appreciation right, as appropriate. The Company calculates the volatility as the annualized standard deviation of the differences in the natural logarithms of the weekly stock closing price, adjusted for stock splits and dividends.

In the case of restricted stock units, the Company calculates the fair value of the restricted stock units granted as the market price of the underlying Common Stock on the date of grant adjusted for anticipated dividend payments during the vesting period.

ABERCROMBIE & FITCH CO.

NOTES TO CONSOLIDATED FINANCIAL STATEMENTS—(Continued)

Stock Options

The weighted-average estimated fair values of stock options granted during the fifty-two week periods ended January 30, 2010, January 31, 2009 and February 2, 2008, and the weighted-average assumptions used in calculating such fair values, on the date of grant, were as follows:

| | Fifty-Two Weeks Ended | | |
	January 30, 2010	January 31, 2009	February 2, 2008
Grant date market price	$ 22.87	$ 67.63	$ 74.05
Exercise price	$ 22.87	$ 67.63	$ 74.05
Fair value	$ 8.26	$ 18.03	$ 22.56
Assumptions:			
Price volatility	50%	33%	34%
Expected term (Years)	4.1	4.0	4.0
Risk-free interest rate	1.6%	2.3%	4.5%
Dividend yield	1.7%	1.0%	1.0%

Below is a summary of stock option activity for the fifty-two weeks ended January 30, 2010:

| | Fifty-Two Weeks Ended January 30, 2010 | | | |
Stock Options	Number of Shares	Weighted-Average Exercise Price	Aggregate Intrinsic Value	Weighted-Average Remaining Contractual Life
Outstanding at January 31, 2009	6,675,990	$ 41.70		
Granted	4,000	22.87		
Exercised	(79,552)	24.51		
Forfeited or expired	(3,630,577)	44.73		
Outstanding at January 30, 2010	2,969,861	$ 38.36	$10,644,614	3.6
Stock options expected to become exercisable at January 30, 2010	411,921	$ 66.59	$ 685,266	7.7
Stock options exercisable at January 30, 2010	2,527,786	$ 33.47	$ 9,868,334	2.9

The total intrinsic value of stock options exercised during the fifty-two week periods ended January 30, 2010, January 31, 2009 and February 2, 2008 was $0.6 million, $40.3 million and $64.2 million, respectively.

The grant date fair value of stock options vested during the fifty-two week periods ended January 30, 2010, January 31, 2009 and February 2, 2008 was $5.0 million, $5.1 million and $5.1 million, respectively.

As of January 30, 2010, there was $5.0 million of total unrecognized compensation cost, net of estimated forfeitures, related to stock options. The unrecognized cost is expected to be recognized over a weighted-average period of 1.0 years.

ABERCROMBIE & FITCH CO.

NOTES TO CONSOLIDATED FINANCIAL STATEMENTS—(Continued)

Stock Appreciation Rights

The weighted-average estimated fair value of stock appreciation rights granted during the fifty-two week periods ended January 30, 2010 and January 31, 2009, as well as the weighted-average assumptions used in calculating such values, on the date of grant, were as follows. There were no stock appreciation rights granted in Fiscal 2007.

| | Fifty-Two Weeks Ended | | | Fifty-Two Weeks Ended |
| | January 30, 2010 | | | January 31, 2009 |
	Chairman and Chief Executive Officer	Executive Officers (excluding Chairman and Chief Executive Officer)	All Other Associates	Chairman and Chief Executive Officer
Grant date market price	$ 28.42	$ 25.77	$ 26.43	$ 22.84
Exercise price	$ 32.99	$ 25.77	$ 26.43	$ 28.55
Fair value	$ 9.67	$ 10.06	$ 10.00	$ 8.06
Assumptions:				
Price volatility	47%	52%	53%	45%
Expected term (Years)	5.6	4.5	4.1	6.4
Risk-free interest rate	2.5%	1.6%	1.6%	1.6%
Dividend yield	2.4%	1.7%	1.7%	1.3%

Below is a summary of stock appreciation rights activity for the fifty-two weeks ended January 30, 2010:

| | Fifty-Two Weeks Ended January 30, 2010 | | | |
Stock Appreciation Rights	Number of Shares	Weighted-Average Exercise Price	Aggregate Intrinsic Value	Weighted-Average Remaining Contractual Life
Outstanding at January 31, 2009	1,600,000	$ 28.55		
Granted	4,236,367	31.70		
Exercised	—	—		
Forfeited or expired	(47,500)	25.77		
Outstanding at January 30, 2010	5,788,867	$ 30.88	$19,853,605	6.4
Stock appreciation rights expected to become exercisable at January 30, 2010	5,705,376	$ 31.00	$19,389,978	6.4
Stock appreciation rights exercisable at January 30, 2010	—	—	—	—

As of January 30, 2010, there was $45.5 million of total unrecognized compensation cost, net of estimated forfeitures, related to stock appreciation rights. The unrecognized cost is expected to be recognized over a weighted-average period of 1.9 years.

Restricted Stock Activity

Below is a summary of restricted stock unit activity for the fifty-two weeks ended January 30, 2010:

Restricted Stock Units	Number of Shares	Weighted-Average Grant Date Fair Value
Non-vested at January 31, 2009	1,498,355	$ 64.18
Granted	473,197	24.29
Vested	(411,308)	64.26
Forfeited	(229,196)	55.94
Non-vested at January 30, 2010	1,331,048	$ 55.45

ABERCROMBIE & FITCH CO.

NOTES TO CONSOLIDATED FINANCIAL STATEMENTS—(Continued)

The total fair value of restricted stock units granted during the fifty-two week periods ended January 30, 2010, January 31, 2009 and February 2, 2008 was $11.5 million, $51.3 million and $53.9 million, respectively.

The total grant date fair value of restricted stock units vested during the fifty-two week periods ended January 30, 2010, January 31, 2009 and February 2, 2008 was $26.4 million, $54.8 million and $14.2 million, respectively.

As of January 30, 2010, there was $41.1 million of total unrecognized compensation cost, net of estimated forfeitures, related to non-vested restricted stock units. The unrecognized cost is expected to be recognized over a weighted-average period of 1.1 years.

4.   CASH AND EQUIVALENTS AND INVESTMENTS

Cash and equivalents and investments consisted of (in thousands):

	January 30, 2010	January 31, 2009
Cash and equivalents:		
Cash	$ 196,496	$ 137,383
Money market funds	483,617	384,739
Total cash and equivalents	680,113	522,122
Marketable securities—Current:		
Trading securities:		
Auction rate securities—UBS—student loan backed	20,049	—
Auction rate securities—UBS—municipal authority bonds	12,307	—
Total trading securities	32,356	—
Marketable securities—Non-Current:		
Trading securities:		
Auction rate securities—UBS—student loan backed	—	50,589
Auction rate securities—UBS—municipal authority bonds	—	11,959
Total trading securities	—	62,548
Available-for-sale securities:		
Auction rate securities—student loan backed	118,390	139,239
Auction rate securities—municipal authority bonds	23,404	27,294
Total available-for-sale securities	141,794	166,533
Total non-current marketable securities	141,794	229,081
Rabbi Trust assets:(1)		
Money market funds	1,316	473
Municipal notes and bonds	18,537	18,804
Trust-owned life insurance policies (at cash surrender value)	51,391	32,549
Total Rabbi Trust assets	71,244	51,826
Total cash and equivalents and investments	$ 925,507	$ 803,029

(1) Rabbi Trust assets are included in Other Assets on the Consolidated Balance Sheets and are restricted as to their use.

At January 30, 2010 and January 31, 2009, the Company's marketable securities consisted of investment grade auction rate securities ("ARS") invested in insured student loan backed securities and insured municipal authority bonds, with maturities ranging from 17 to 33 years. Each investment in student loans is insured by (1) the U.S. government under the Federal Family Education Loan Program, (2) a private insurer, or (3) a combination of both. The percentage coverage of the outstanding principal and interest of the ARS varies by security.

ABERCROMBIE & FITCH CO.

NOTES TO CONSOLIDATED FINANCIAL STATEMENTS—(Continued)

The par and fair values, and related cumulative impairment charges for the Company's marketable securities as of January 30, 2010 were as follows:

(In thousands)	Par Value	Temporary Impairment	Other-Than-Temporary Impairment ("OTTI")	Fair Value
Trading securities:				
Auction rate securities—UBS—student loan backed	$ 22,100	$ —	$ (2,051)	$ 20,049
Auction rate securities—UBS—municipal authority bonds	15,000	—	(2,693)	12,307
Total trading securities	37,100	—	(4,744)	32,356
Available-for-sale securities:				
Auction rate securities—student loan backed	128,099	(9,709)	—	118,390
Auction rate securities—municipal authority bonds	28,575	(5,171)	—	23,404
Total available-for-sale securities	156,674	(14,880)	—	141,794
Total	$ 193,774	$ (14,880)	$ (4,744)	$ 174,150

See Note 5, "*Fair Value*," for further discussion on the valuation of the ARS.

The temporary impairment related to available-for-sale ARS was reduced by $13.3 million for the fifty-two weeks ended January 30, 2010 due to redemptions and changes in fair value. An impairment is considered to be other-than-temporary if an entity (i) intends to sell the security, (ii) more likely than not will be required to sell the security before recovering its amortized cost basis, or (iii) does not expect to recover the security's entire amortized cost basis, even if there is no intent to sell the security. As of January 30, 2010, the Company had not incurred any credit-related losses on available-for-sale ARS. Furthermore, as of January 30, 2010, the issuers continued to perform under the obligations, including making scheduled interest payments, and the Company expects that this will continue going forward.

On November 13, 2008, the Company entered into an agreement (the "UBS Agreement") with UBS AG ("UBS"), a Swiss corporation, relating to ARS ("UBS ARS") with a par value of $76.5 million, of which $37.1 million, at par value, are still held as of January 30, 2010. By entering into the UBS Agreement, UBS received the right to purchase these UBS ARS at par, at any time, commencing on November 13, 2008 and the Company received the right to sell ("Put Option") the UBS ARS back to UBS at par, commencing on June 30, 2010. Upon acceptance of the UBS Agreement, the Company no longer had the intent to hold the UBS ARS until maturity. Therefore, the impairment could no longer be considered temporary. As a result, the Company transferred the UBS ARS from available-for-sale securities to trading securities and recognized an other-than-temporary impairment of $14.0 million in Other Operating (Income) Expense, Net in the Consolidated Statements of Operations and Comprehensive Income in the fourth quarter of Fiscal 2008. In addition, and simultaneously, the Company elected to apply fair value accounting for the related Put Option and recognized an asset of $12.3 million in Other Current Assets and a gain in Other Operating (Income) Expense, Net in the Consolidated Statements of Operations and Comprehensive Income in the fourth quarter of Fiscal 2008. During the fifty-two weeks ended January 30, 2010, the Company recognized, as a result of redemptions and changes in fair value of the UBS ARS, a reduction of the other-than-temporary impairment related to the UBS ARS of $9.2 million, and recognized a corresponding loss of $7.7 million related to the Put Option. As the Company has the right to sell the UBS ARS back to UBS on June 30, 2010, the remaining UBS ARS are classified as Current Assets on the Consolidated Balance Sheet as of January 30, 2010.

The irrevocable rabbi trust (the "Rabbi Trust") is intended to be used as a source of funds to match respective funding obligations to participants in the Abercrombie & Fitch Co. Nonqualified Savings and Supplemental Retirement Plan I, the Abercrombie & Fitch Co. Nonqualified Savings and Supplemental Retirement Plan II and the Chief Executive Officer Supplemental Executive Retirement Plan. The Rabbi Trust assets are consolidated and recorded at fair value, with the exception of the trust-owned life insurance policies which are recorded at cash surrender value. The Rabbi Trust assets are included in Other Assets on the Consolidated Balance Sheets and are restricted to their use as noted above. Net unrealized gains and losses related to the available-for-sale securities held in the Rabbi Trust were not material for fifty-two week periods ended January 30, 2010 and January 31, 2009. The change in cash surrender value of the trust-owned life insurance policies held in the Rabbi Trust resulted in a realized gain of $5.3 million and a realized loss of $3.6 million for the fifty-two weeks ended January 30, 2010 and January 31, 2009, respectively, recorded in Interest Income, Net on the Consolidated Statements of Operations and Comprehensive Income.

ABERCROMBIE & FITCH CO.

NOTES TO CONSOLIDATED FINANCIAL STATEMENTS—(Continued)

5.   FAIR VALUE

Fair value is the price that would be received to sell an asset or paid to transfer a liability in an orderly transaction between market participants at the measurement date. The inputs used to measure fair value are prioritized based on a three-level hierarchy. The three levels of inputs to measure fair value are as follows:

- Level 1— inputs are unadjusted quoted prices for identical assets or liabilities that are available in active markets.
- Level 2— inputs are other than quoted market prices included within Level 1 that are observable for assets or liabilities, directly or indirectly.
- Level 3— inputs to the valuation methodology are unobservable.

The lowest level of significant input determines the placement of the entire fair value measurement in the hierarchy. The three levels of the hierarchy and the distribution of the Company's assets, measured at fair value, within it were as follows:

	Assets Fair Value as of January 30, 2010			
	Level 1	Level 2	Level 3	Total
ASSETS:				
Money market funds (1)	$ 484,933	$ —	$ —	$ 484,933
ARS— trading— student loan backed	—	—	20,049	20,049
ARS— trading— municipal authority bonds	—	—	12,307	12,307
ARS— available-for-sale— student loan backed	—	—	118,390	118,390
ARS— available-for-sale— municipal authority bonds	—	—	23,404	23,404
UBS put option	—	—	4,640	4,640
Municipal bonds held in the Rabbi Trust	18,537	—	—	18,537
Derivative financial instruments	—	1,348	—	1,348
Total assets measured at fair value	$ 503,470	$ 1,348	$ 178,790	$ 683,608

(1) Includes $483.6 million in money market funds included in Cash and Equivalents and $1.3 million of money market funds held in the Rabbi Trust which are included in Other Assets on the Consolidated Balance Sheet.

The level 2 assets consist of derivative financial instruments, primarily forward foreign exchange contracts. The fair value of forward foreign exchange contracts is determined by using quoted market prices of the same or similar instruments, adjusted for counterparty risk.

The level 3 assets primarily include investments in insured student loan backed ARS and insured municipal authority bonds ARS, which include both the available-for-sale and trading ARS. Additionally, level 3 assets include the Put Option related to the UBS Agreement.

As a result of the market failure and lack of liquidity in the current ARS market, the Company measured the fair value of its ARS primarily using a discounted cash flow model as of January 30, 2010. Certain significant inputs into the model are unobservable in the market including the periodic coupon rate adjusted for the marketability discount, market required rate of return and expected term. The coupon rate is estimated using the results of a regression analysis factoring in historical data on the par swap rate and the maximum coupon rate paid in the event of an auction failure. In making the assumption of the market required rate of return, the Company considered the risk-free interest rate and an appropriate credit spread, depending on the type of security and the credit rating of the issuer. The expected term is identified as the time the Company believes the principal will become available to the investor. The Company utilized a term of five years to value its securities. The Company also included a marketability discount which takes into account the lack of activity in the current ARS market.

As of January 30, 2010, approximately 70% of the Company's ARS were "AAA" rated and approximately 14% of the Company's ARS were "AA" or "A" rated with the remaining ARS having an "A−" or "BBB+" rating, in each case as rated by one or more of the major credit rating agencies.

ABERCROMBIE & FITCH CO.

NOTES TO CONSOLIDATED FINANCIAL STATEMENTS—(Continued)

In Fiscal 2008, the Company elected to apply fair value accounting for the Put Option related to the Company's UBS ARS. The fair value of the Put Option was determined by calculating the present value of the difference between the par value and the fair value of the UBS ARS as of January 30, 2010, adjusted for counterparty risk. The present value was calculated using a discount rate that incorporates an investment grade corporate bond index rate and the credit default swap rate for UBS. The Put Option is recognized as an asset within Other Current Assets on the accompanying Consolidated Balance Sheets and the corresponding gains and losses within Other Operating Income, Net on the accompanying Consolidated Statements of Operations and Comprehensive Income.

The table below includes a roll forward of the Company's level 3 assets from January 31, 2009 to January 30, 2010. When a determination is made to classify an asset or liability within level 3, the determination is based upon the lack of significance of the observable parameters to the overall fair value measurement. However, the fair value determination for level 3 financial assets and liabilities may include observable components.

	Trading ARS - Student Loans	Trading ARS - Muni Bonds	Available-for-sale ARS - Student Loans	Available-for-sale ARS - Muni Bonds	Put Option	Total
			(In thousands)			
Fair value, January 31, 2009	$ 50,589	$ 11,959	$ 139,239	$ 27,294	$ 12,309	$ 241,390
Redemptions	(39,400)	—	(31,650)	(6,400)	—	(77,450)
Transfers (out)/in	—	—	—	—	—	—
Gains and (losses), net:						
Reported in Net Income	8,860	348	—	—	(7,669)	1,539
Reported in Other Comprehensive Income (Loss)	—	—	10,801	2,510	—	13,311
Fair value, January 30, 2010	$ 20,049	$ 12,307	$ 118,390	$ 23,404	$ 4,640	$ 178,790

6.   PROPERTY AND EQUIPMENT

Property and equipment, at cost, consisted of (thousands):

	2009	2008
Land	$ 32,877	$ 32,302
Building	223,532	235,738
Furniture, fixtures and equipment	593,984	628,195
Information technology	211,461	138,096
Leasehold improvements	1,205,276	1,143,656
Construction in progress	48,352	114,280
Other	47,010	47,017
Total	$ 2,362,492	$ 2,339,284
Less: Accumulated depreciation and amortization	1,118,473	940,629
Property and equipment, net	$ 1,244,019	$ 1,398,655

Long-lived assets, primarily comprised of property and equipment, are reviewed periodically for impairment or whenever events or changes in circumstances indicate that full recoverability of net asset balances through future cash flows is in question. Factors used in the evaluation include, but are not limited to, management's plans for future operations, recent operating results and projected cash flows. During Fiscal 2009, as a result of a strategic review of the RUEHL business, the Company determined that a triggering event occurred. As a result of that assessment, the Company incurred non-cash pre-tax impairment charges of $51.5 million, reported in Net Loss from Discontinued Operations on the Consolidated Statement of Operations and Comprehensive Income for the fifty-two weeks ended January 30, 2010. There was no remaining fair value of RUEHL long-lived assets as of January 30, 2010.

ABERCROMBIE & FITCH CO.

NOTES TO CONSOLIDATED FINANCIAL STATEMENTS—(Continued)

In the fourth quarter of Fiscal 2009, as a part of the Company's year-end review for impairment of store related assets, the Company incurred a non-cash pre-tax impairment charge of $33.2 million, reported in Stores and Distribution Expense on the Consolidated Statements of Operations and Comprehensive Income for the fifty-two weeks ended January 30, 2010. The charge was associated with 34 Abercrombie & Fitch stores, 46 abercrombie kids stores and 19 Hollister stores. In Fiscal 2008, the Company incurred a non-cash pre-tax impairment charge of approximately $8.3 million related to long-lived assets. The charge was associated with 11 Abercrombie & Fitch stores, six abercrombie kids stores and three Hollister stores and was reported in Stores and Distribution Expense on the Consolidated Statement of Operations and Comprehensive Income for the fifty-two weeks ended January 31, 2009.

The Company also incurred a non-cash pre-tax impairment charge of approximately $22.3 million related to long-lived assets associated with nine RUEHL stores, which was reported in Net Loss from Discontinued Operations on the Consolidated Statement of Operations and Comprehensive Income for the fifty-two weeks ended January 31, 2009.

Store related assets are considered Level 3 assets in the fair value hierarchy and the fair values were determined at the store level primarily using a discounted cash flow model. The estimation of future cash flows from operating activities requires significant estimates of factors that include future sales, gross margin performance and operating expenses. In instances where the discounted cash flow analysis indicated a negative value at the store level, the market exit price based on historical experience was used to determine the fair value by asset type. The Company had store related assets measured at fair value of $19.3 million on the Consolidated Balance Sheet at January 30, 2010.

7.   DEFERRED LEASE CREDITS, NET

Deferred lease credits are derived from payments received from landlords to partially offset store construction costs and are reclassified between current and long-term liabilities. The amounts, which are amortized over the life of the related leases, consisted of the following (thousands):

	2009	2008
Deferred lease credits	$ 546,191	$ 514,041
Amortization of deferred lease credits	(290,542)	(259,705)
Total deferred lease credits, net	$ 255,649	$ 254,336

8.   LEASED FACILITIES AND COMMITMENTS

Annual store rent is comprised of a fixed minimum amount, plus contingent rent based on a percentage of sales. Store lease terms generally require additional payments covering taxes, common area costs and certain other expenses.

A summary of rent expense follows (thousands):

	2009	2008	2007
Store rent:			
Fixed minimum	$ 301,138	$ 267,108	$ 221,651
Contingent	6,136	14,289	21,453
Total store rent	307,274	281,397	243,104
Buildings, equipment and other	5,071	5,905	6,066
Total rent expense	$ 312,345	$ 287,302	$ 249,170

At January 30, 2010, the Company was committed to non-cancelable leases with remaining terms of one to 19 years. A summary of operating lease commitments under non-cancelable leases follows (thousands):

Fiscal 2010	$	324,280
Fiscal 2011	$	315,696
Fiscal 2012	$	290,573
Fiscal 2013	$	270,335
Fiscal 2014	$	251,404
Thereafter	$	1,146,587

ABERCROMBIE & FITCH CO.

NOTES TO CONSOLIDATED FINANCIAL STATEMENTS—(Continued)

9. ACCRUED EXPENSES

Accrued expenses consisted of (thousands):

	2009	2008
Gift card liability	$ 49,778	$ 57,459
Construction in progress	5,838	27,329
Accrued payroll and related costs	45,476	46,248
Accrued taxes	32,784	20,328
RUEHL lease termination costs	29,595	—
Other	82,818	89,867
Accrued expenses	$ 246,289	$ 241,231

Accrued payroll and related costs include salaries, benefits, withholdings and other payroll related costs.

10. OTHER LIABILITIES

Other liabilities consisted of (thousands):

	2009	2008
Accrued straight-line rent	$ 87,147	$ 77,312
RUEHL lease termination costs	16,391	—
Unrecognized tax benefits, including interest and penalties	39,314	53,419
Deferred compensation	66,053	71,288
Other	5,265	4,724
Other liabilities	$ 214,170	$ 206,743

Deferred compensation includes the Chief Executive Officer Supplemental Executive Retirement Plan (the "SERP"), the Abercrombie & Fitch Co. Savings and Retirement Plan and the Abercrombie & Fitch Nonqualified Savings and Supplemental Retirement Plan, all further discussed in Note 15, *Retirement Benefits*", as well as deferred Board of Directors compensation and other accrued retirement benefits.

11. INCOME TAXES

Earnings from continuing operations before taxes (in thousands):

	2009	2008	2007
Domestic	$ 119,358	$ 501,125	$ 802,494
Foreign	152	8,519	(4,757)
Total	$ 119,510	$ 509,644	$ 797,737

ABERCROMBIE & FITCH CO.

NOTES TO CONSOLIDATED FINANCIAL STATEMENTS—(Continued)

The provision for income taxes from continuing operations consisted of (thousands):

	2009	2008	2007
Currently Payable:			
Federal	$ 33,212	$ 166,327	$ 254,089
State	4,003	17,467	38,649
Foreign	5,086	8,112	2,805
	$ 42,301	$ 191,906	$ 295,543
Deferred:			
Federal	$ 10,055	$ 14,028	$ 4,611
State	(147)	2,480	459
Foreign	(11,652)	(6,939)	(2,003)
	$ (1,744)	$ 9,569	$ 3,067
Total provision	$ 40,557	$ 201,475	$ 298,610

Reconciliation between the statutory federal income tax rate and the effective tax rate for continuing operations is as follows:

	2009	2008	2007
Federal income tax rate	35.0%	35.0%	35.0%
State income tax, net of federal income tax effect	2.1	2.5	3.2
Tax effect of foreign earnings	(4.4)	(0.1)	0.4
Internal Revenue Code ("IRC") Section 162(m)	1.5	2.5	0.2
Other items, net	(0.3)	(0.4)	(1.4)
Total	33.9%	39.5%	37.4%

Amounts paid directly to taxing authorities were $27.1 million, $198.2 million and $259.0 million in Fiscal 2009, Fiscal 2008, and Fiscal 2007, respectively.

The effect of temporary differences which give rise to deferred income tax assets (liabilities) were as follows (thousands):

	2009	2008
Deferred tax assets:		
Deferred compensation	$ 48,476	$ 37,635
Rent	40,585	59,809
Accrued expenses	15,464	17,023
Foreign net operating losses	11,329	1,692
Reserves	8,757	11,020
Inventory	7,829	10,347
Other	2,223	—
Realized and unrealized investment losses	1,152	560
Valuation allowance	(1,369)	(1,275)
Total deferred tax assets	$ 134,446	$ 136,811
Deferred tax liabilities:		
Store supplies	(12,128)	(12,844)
Property and equipment	(127,983)	(123,813)
Total deferred tax liabilities	$ (140,111)	$ (136,657)
Net deferred income tax (liabilities) assets	$ (5,665)	$ 154

ABERCROMBIE & FITCH CO.

NOTES TO CONSOLIDATED FINANCIAL STATEMENTS—(Continued)

Accumulated other comprehensive income is shown net of deferred tax assets and deferred tax liabilities, resulting in a deferred tax asset of $4.6 million and $9.2 million for Fiscal 2009 and Fiscal 2008, respectively. Accordingly, these deferred taxes are not reflected in the table on the previous page.

The Company has recorded a valuation allowance against the deferred tax assets arising from the net operating loss of certain foreign subsidiaries and for realized and unrealized domestic operations' investment losses.

As of January 30, 2010 and January 31, 2009, the net operating foreign subsidiaries' valuation allowance totaled $0.2 million and $1.3 million, respectively. A portion of these net operating loss carryovers begin expiring in Fiscal 2013 and some have an indefinite carry-forward period.

As of January 30, 2010, the valuation allowance for realized and unrealized investment losses totaled approximately $1.1 million. Realized losses begin expiring in Fiscal 2011. There was no valuation allowance as of January 31, 2009.

No other valuation allowances have been provided for deferred tax assets because management believes that it is more likely than not that the full amount of the net deferred tax assets will be realized in the future.

A reconciliation of the beginning and ending amounts of unrecognized tax benefits is as follows:

	2009	2008
Unrecognized tax benefits, beginning of year	$ 43,684	$ 38,894
Gross addition for tax positions of the current year	222	5,539
Gross addition for tax positions of prior years	2,167	8,754
Reductions of tax positions of prior years for:		
Changes in judgment/excess reserve	(10,744)	(4,206)
Settlements during the period	(5,444)	(1,608)
Lapses of applicable statutes of limitations	(448)	(3,689)
Unrecognized tax benefits, end of year	$ 29,437	$ 43,684

The amount of the above unrecognized tax benefits at January 30, 2010 and January 31, 2009 which would impact the Company's effective tax rate, if recognized is $29.4 million and $33.3 million, respectively.

The Company recognizes accrued interest and penalties related to unrecognized tax benefits as a component of income tax expense. Tax expense for Fiscal 2009 includes $1.2 million of net accrued interest, compared to $0.5 million of net accrued interest for Fiscal 2008. Interest and penalties of $9.9 million have been accrued as of the end of Fiscal 2009, compared to $9.7 million accrued as of the end of Fiscal 2008.

The Internal Revenue Service ("IRS") is currently conducting an examination of the Company's U.S. federal income tax return for Fiscal 2009 as part of the IRS's Compliance Assurance Process program. IRS examinations for Fiscal 2008 and prior years have been completed and settled, except for a transfer pricing matter that is the subject of an ongoing Advanced Pricing Agreement negotiation that is before the U.S. Competent Authority. State and foreign returns are generally subject to examination for a period of 3-5 years after the filing of the respective return. The Company has various state income tax returns in the process of examination or administrative appeals.

The Company does not expect material adjustments to the total amount of unrecognized tax benefits within the next 12 months, but the outcome of tax matters is uncertain and unforeseen results can occur.

As of January 30, 2010, the Company had undistributed earnings of approximately $18.9 million from certain non-U.S. subsidiaries that are intended to be permanently reinvested in non-U.S. operations. Because these earnings are considered permanently reinvested, no U.S. tax provision has been accrued related to the repatriation of these earnings. It is not practicable to estimate the amount of U.S. tax that might be payable on the eventual remittance of such earnings.

12.   LONG-TERM DEBT

On April 15, 2008, the Company entered into a syndicated unsecured credit agreement (as previously amended by Amendment No.1 to Credit Agreement made as of December 29, 2008, the "Credit Agreement") under which up to $450 million was available. On June 16, 2009, the Company amended the Credit Agreement and, as a result, revised the ratio requirements, as further discussed below, and also reduced the amount available from $450 million to $350 million (as amended, the "Amended Credit Agreement"). The primary purposes of the Amended Credit Agreement are for trade and stand-by letters of credit in the ordinary course of business, as well as to fund working capital, capital expenditures, acquisitions and investments, and other general corporate purposes.

ABERCROMBIE & FITCH CO.

NOTES TO CONSOLIDATED FINANCIAL STATEMENTS—(Continued)

The Amended Credit Agreement has several borrowing options, including interest rates that are based on: (i) a Base Rate, plus a margin based on the Leverage Ratio, payable quarterly; (ii) an Adjusted Eurodollar Rate (as defined in the Amended Credit Agreement) plus a margin based on the Leverage Ratio, payable at the end of the applicable interest period for the borrowing; or (iii) an Adjusted Foreign Currency Rate (as defined in the Amended Credit Agreement) plus a margin based on the Coverage Ratio, payable at the end of the applicable interest period for the borrowing and, for interest periods in excess of three months, on the date that is three months after the commencement of the interest period. The Base Rate represents a rate per annum equal to the higher of (a) PNC Bank's then publicly announced prime rate or (b) the Federal Funds Effective Rate (as defined in the Amended Credit Agreement) as then in effect plus 1/2 of 1.0%. The facility fees payable under the Amended Credit Agreement are based on the Company's Leverage Ratio (i.e., the ratio, on a consolidated basis, of (a) the sum of total debt (excluding trade letters of credit) plus 600% of forward minimum rent commitments to (b) consolidated earnings before interest, taxes, depreciation, amortization and rent with the further adjustments to be discussed in the following paragraphs ("Consolidated EBITDAR") for the trailing four-consecutive-fiscal-quarter periods. The facility fees accrue at a rate of 0.25% to 0.625% per annum based on the Leverage Ratio for the most recent determination date. The Amended Credit Agreement did not have a utilization fee as of January 30, 2010. The Amended Credit Agreement requires that the Leverage Ratio not be greater than 3.75 to 1.00 at the end of each testing period. The Company's Leverage Ratio was 2.95 as of January 30, 2010. The Amended Credit Agreement also required that the Coverage Ratio for A&F and its subsidiaries on a consolidated basis of (i) Consolidated EBITDAR for the trailing four-consecutive-fiscal-quarter period to (ii) the sum of, without duplication, (x) net interest expense for such period, (y) scheduled payments of long-term debt due within twelve months of the date of determination and (z) the sum of minimum rent and contingent store rent, not be less than 1.65 to 1.00 at January 30, 2010. The minimum Coverage Ratio varies over time based on the terms set forth in the Amended Credit Agreement. The Amended Credit Agreement amended the definition of Consolidated EBITDAR to add back the following items, among others: (a) recognized losses arising from investments in certain ARS to the extent such losses do not exceed a defined level of impairments for those investments; (b) non-cash charges in an amount not to exceed $50 million related to the closure of RUEHL branded stores and related direct-to-consumer operations; (c) non-recurring cash charges in an aggregate amount not to exceed $61 million related to the closure of RUEHL branded stores and related direct-to-consumer operations; (d) additional non-recurring non-cash charges in an amount not to exceed $20 million in the aggregate over the trailing four fiscal quarter period; and (e) other non-recurring cash charges in an amount not to exceed $10 million in the aggregate over the trailing four fiscal quarter period. The Company's Coverage Ratio was 2.10 as of January 30, 2010. The Amended Credit Agreement also limits the Company's consolidated capital expenditures to $275 million in Fiscal 2009, and to $325 million in Fiscal 2010 plus any unused portion from Fiscal 2009. The Company was in compliance with the applicable ratio requirements and other covenants at January 30, 2010.

The terms of the Amended Credit Agreement include customary events of default such as payment defaults, cross-defaults to other material indebtedness, bankruptcy and insolvency, the occurrence of a defined change in control, or the failure to observe the negative covenants and other covenants related to the operation and conduct of the business of A&F and its subsidiaries. Upon an event of default, the lenders will not be obligated to make loans or other extensions of credit and may, among other things, terminate their commitments to the Company, and declare any then outstanding loans due and payable immediately.

The Amended Credit Agreement will mature on April 12, 2013. Trade letters of credit totaling approximately $35.9 million and $21.1 million were outstanding on January 30, 2010 and January 31, 2009, respectively. Stand-by letters of credit totaling approximately $14.1 million and $16.9 million were outstanding on January 30, 2010 and January 31, 2009, respectively. The stand-by letters of credit are set to expire primarily during the fourth quarter of Fiscal 2010. To date, no beneficiary has drawn upon the stand-by letters of credit.

The Company had $50.9 million and $100.0 million outstanding under the Amended Credit Agreement as of January 30, 2010, and January 31, 2009, respectively. The $50.9 million outstanding under the Amended Credit Agreement as of January 30, 2010 was denominated in Japanese Yen. At January 30, 2010, the Company also had $20.3 million of long-term debt related to the landlord financing obligation for certain leases where the Company is deemed the owner of the project for accounting purposes, as substantially all of the risk of ownership during construction of a leased property is held by the Company. The landlord financing obligation is amortized over the life of the related lease.

As of January 30, 2010, the carrying value of the Company's long-term debt approximated fair value. Total interest expense was $6.6 million and $3.4 million for Fiscal 2009 and Fiscal 2008, respectively. The average interest rate for the long-term debt recorded under the Amended Credit Agreement was 2.0% for the fifty-two week period ended January 30, 2010.

On March 6, 2009, the Company entered a secured, uncommitted demand line of credit ("UBS Credit Line") under which up to $26.3 million was available at January 30, 2010. The amount available under the UBS Credit Line is subject to adjustment from time-to-time based on the market value of the Company's UBS ARS as determined by UBS. The UBS Credit Line is to be used for general corporate purposes. Being a demand line of credit, the UBS Credit Line does not have a stated maturity date.

ABERCROMBIE & FITCH CO.

NOTES TO CONSOLIDATED FINANCIAL STATEMENTS—(Continued)

As security for the payment and performance of the Company's obligations under the UBS Credit Line, the UBS Credit Line provides that the Company grants a security interest to UBS Bank USA, as lender, in each account of the Company at UBS Financial Services Inc. that is identified as a Collateral Account (as defined in the UBS Credit Line), as well as any and all money, credit balances, securities, financial assets and other investment property and other property maintained from time-to-time in any Collateral Account, any over-the-counter options, futures, foreign exchange, swap or similar contracts between the Company and UBS Financial Services Inc. or any of its affiliates, any and all accounts of the Company at UBS Bank USA or any of its affiliates, any and all supporting obligations and other rights relating to the foregoing property, and any and all interest, dividends, distributions and other proceeds of any of the foregoing property, including proceeds of proceeds.

Because certain of the Collateral consists of ARS (as defined in the UBS Credit Line), the UBS Credit Line provides further that the interest rate payable by the Company will reflect any changes in the composition of such ARS Collateral (as defined in the UBS Credit Line) as may be necessary to cause the interest payable by the Company under the UBS Credit Line to equal the interest or dividend rate payable to the Company by the issuer of any ARS Collateral.

The terms of the UBS Credit Line include customary events of default such as payment defaults, the failure to maintain sufficient collateral, the failure to observe any covenant or material representation, bankruptcy and insolvency, cross-defaults to other indebtedness and other stated events of default. Upon an event of default, the obligations under the UBS Credit Line will become immediately due and payable. No borrowings were outstanding under the UBS Credit Line as of January 30, 2010.

13. DERIVATIVES

All derivative instruments are recorded at fair value on the Consolidated Balance Sheets as either Other Assets or Accrued Expenses. The accounting for changes in the fair value of a derivative instrument depends on whether it has been designated as a hedge and qualifies for hedge accounting treatment. Refer to Note 5, "*Fair Value*" for further discussion of the determination of the fair value of derivatives. As of January 30, 2010, all outstanding derivative instruments were designated as hedges and qualified for hedge accounting treatment. There were no outstanding derivative instruments as of January 31, 2009.

In order to qualify for hedge accounting, a derivative must be considered highly effective at offsetting changes in either the hedged item's cash flows or fair value. Additionally, the hedge relationship must be documented to include the risk management objective and strategy, the hedging instrument, the hedged item, the risk exposure, and how hedge effectiveness will be assessed prospectively and retrospectively. The extent to which a hedging instrument has been and is expected to continue to be effective at achieving offsetting changes in fair value or cash flows is assessed and documented at least quarterly. Any hedge ineffectiveness is reported in current period earnings and hedge accounting is discontinued if it is determined that the derivative is not highly effective.

For derivatives that either do not qualify for hedge accounting or are not designated as hedges, all changes in the fair value of the derivative are recognized in earnings. For qualifying cash flow hedges, the effective portion of the change in the fair value of the derivative is recorded as a component of Other Comprehensive Income (Loss) ("OCI") and recognized in earnings when the hedged cash flows affect earnings. The ineffective portion of the derivative gain or loss, as well as changes in the fair value of the derivative's time value are recognized in current period earnings. The effectiveness of the hedge is assessed based on changes in fair value attributable to changes in spot prices. The changes in the fair value of the derivative contract related to the changes in the difference between the spot price and the forward price are excluded from the assessment of hedge effectiveness and are also recognized in current period earnings. If the cash flow hedge relationship is terminated, the derivative gains or losses that are deferred in OCI will be recognized in earnings when the hedged cash flows occur. However, for cash flow hedges that are terminated because the forecasted transaction is not expected to occur in the original specified time period, or a two-month period thereafter, the derivative gains or losses are immediately recognized in earnings. There were no gains or losses reclassified into earnings as a result of the discontinuance of cash flow hedges as of January 30, 2010.

The Company uses derivative instruments, primarily forward contracts designated as cash flow hedges, to hedge the foreign currency exposure associated with forecasted foreign-currency-denominated inter-company inventory sales to foreign subsidiaries and the related settlement of the foreign-currency-denominated inter-company receivable. Fluctuations in exchange rates will either increase or decrease the Company's U.S. dollar equivalent cash flows and affect the Company's U.S. dollar earnings. Gains or losses on the foreign exchange forward contracts that are used to hedge these exposures are expected to partially offset this variability. Foreign exchange forward contracts represent agreements to exchange the currency of one country for the currency of another country at an agreed-upon settlement date. As of January 30, 2010, the maximum length of time over which forecasted foreign denominated inter-company inventory sales were hedged was twelve months. The sale of the inventory to the Company's customers will result in the reclassification of related derivative gains and losses that are reported in Accumulated Other Comprehensive Loss. Substantially all of the remaining unrealized gains or losses related to foreign denominated inter-company inventory sales that have occurred as of January 30, 2010 will be recognized in costs of goods sold over the following two months at the values at the date the inventory was sold to the respective subsidiary.

ABERCROMBIE & FITCH CO.

NOTES TO CONSOLIDATED FINANCIAL STATEMENTS—(Continued)

The Company nets derivative assets and liabilities on the Consolidated Balance Sheet to the extent that master netting arrangements meet the specific accounting requirements set forth by U.S. generally accepted accounting principles.

As of January 30, 2010, the Company had the following outstanding foreign exchange forward contracts that were entered into to hedge forecasted foreign denominated inter-company inventory sales and the resulting settlement of the foreign denominated inter-company accounts receivable:

	Notional Amount(1)
Canada	$ 24,641
Europe	$ 45,703

(1) Amounts are reported in thousands and in U.S. Dollars. The notional amount of derivatives related to Europe are denominated primarily in Sterling Pound.

The location and amounts of derivative fair values on the Consolidated Balance Sheets as of January 30, 2010 and January 31, 2009 were as follows:

	Asset Derivatives			Liability Derivatives		
	Balance Sheet Location	January 30, 2010	January 31, 2009	Balance Sheet Location	January 30, 2010	January 31, 2009
			(In thousands)			
Derivatives Designated as Hedging Instruments:						
Foreign Exchange Forward Contracts	Other Current Assets	$ 1,348	$ —	Accrued Expenses	$ —	$ —

The location and amounts of derivative gains and losses for the fifty-two weeks ended January 30, 2010 and January 31, 2009 on the Consolidated Statements of Operations and Comprehensive Income are as follows:

	Amount of (Loss) Gain Recognized in OCI on Derivative Contracts (Effective Portion) (a)		Location of (Gain) Loss Reclassified from Accumulated OCI into Earnings (Effective Portion)	Amount of (Gain) Loss Reclassified from Accumulated OCI into Earnings (Effective Portion) (b)		Location of Gain Recognized in Earnings on Derivative (Ineffective Portion and Amount Excluded from Effectiveness Testing)	Amount of Gain Recognized in Earnings on Derivative (Ineffective Portion and Amount Excluded from Effectiveness Testing) (c)	
	For the Fifty-Two Weeks Ended							
	January 30, 2010	January 31, 2009		January 30, 2010	January 31, 2009		January 30, 2010	January 31, 2009
				(In thousands)				
Derivatives in Cash Flow Hedging Relationships								
Foreign Exchange Forward Contracts	$ (3,790)	$3,406	Cost of Goods Sold	$ (3,074)	$ 1,893	Other Operating (Income) Loss, Net	$ (74)	$ (219)

(a) The amount represents the change in fair value of derivative contracts due to changes in spot rates.

(b) The amount represents reclassification from OCI to earnings that occurs when the hedged item affects earnings, which is when merchandise is sold to the Company's customers.

(c) The amount represents the change in fair value of derivative contracts due to changes in the difference between the spot price and forward price that is excluded from the assessment of hedge effectiveness and therefore recognized in earnings. There were no ineffective portions recorded in earnings for the fifty-two weeks ended January 30, 2010 and January 31, 2009.

The Company does not use forward contracts to engage in currency speculation and does not enter into derivative financial instruments for trading purposes.

ABERCROMBIE & FITCH CO.

NOTES TO CONSOLIDATED FINANCIAL STATEMENTS—(Continued)

14.   DISCONTINUED OPERATIONS

On June 16, 2009, A&F's Board of Directors approved the closure of the Company's 29 RUEHL branded stores and related direct-to-consumer operations. The determination to take this action was based on a comprehensive review and evaluation of the performance of the RUEHL branded stores and related direct-to-consumer operations, as well as the related real estate portfolio. The Company completed the closure of the RUEHL branded stores and related direct-to-consumer operations during the fourth quarter of Fiscal 2009. Accordingly, the results of operations of RUEHL are reflected in Net Loss from Discontinued Operations for all periods presented on the Consolidated Statements of Operations and Comprehensive Income.

Costs associated with exit or disposal activities are recorded when the liability is incurred. Below is a roll forward of the liabilities recognized on the Consolidated Balance Sheet as of January 30, 2010 related to the closure of the RUEHL branded stores and related direct-to-consumer operations (in thousands):

	Fifty-Two Weeks Ended January 30, 2010
Beginning Balance	$ —
Cash Charges	68,363
Interest Accretion	358
Cash Payments	(22,635)
Ending Balance(1)	$ 46,086

(1)   Ending balance primarily reflects the net present value of obligations due under signed lease termination agreements and obligations due under a lease, for which no agreement exists, less estimated sublease income. As of January 30, 2010, there were $29.6 million of lease termination charges and $0.1 million of severance charges recorded as a current liability in Accrued Expenses and $16.4 million of lease termination charges recorded as a long-term liability in Other Liabilities on the Consolidated Balance Sheet.

Below is a summary of charges related to the closure of the RUEHL branded stores and related direct-to-consumer operations (in thousands):

	Fifty-Two Weeks Ended January 30, 2010
Asset Impairments(1)	$ 51,536
Lease Terminations, net(2)	53,916
Severance and Other(3)	2,189
Total Charges	$ 107,641

(1)   Asset impairment charges primarily related to store furniture, fixtures and leasehold improvements.

(2)   Lease terminations reflect the net present value of obligations due under signed lease termination agreements and obligations due under a lease, for which no agreement exists, less estimated sublease income. The charges are presented net of the reversal of non-cash credits.

(3)   Severance and other reflects charges primarily related to severance and merchandise and store supply inventory.

The table on the next page presents the significant components of RUEHL's results included in Net Loss from Discontinued Operations on the Consolidated Statements of Operations and Comprehensive Income for fiscal years ended January 30, 2010, January 31, 2009 and February 2, 2008.

ABERCROMBIE & FITCH CO.

NOTES TO CONSOLIDATED FINANCIAL STATEMENTS—(Continued)

	2009	2008	2007
NET SALES	$ 48,393	$ 56,218	$ 50,192
Cost of Goods Sold	22,037	25,621	26,990
GROSS PROFIT	26,356	30,597	23,202
Stores and Distribution Expense	146,826	75,148	42,668
Marketing, General and Administrative Expense	8,556	14,411	18,978
Other Operating Income, Net	(11)	(86)	(28)
NET LOSS BEFORE INCOME TAXES(1)	$ (129,016)	$ (58,876)	$ (38,416)
Income Tax Benefit	(50,316)	(22,962)	(14,982)
NET LOSS FROM DISCONTINUED OPERATIONS, NET OF TAX	$ (78,699)	$ (35,914)	$ (23,434)
NET LOSS PER SHARE FROM DISCONTINUED OPERATIONS:			
BASIC	$ (0.90)	$ (0.41)	$ (0.27)
DILUTED	$ (0.89)	$ (0.40)	$ (0.26)

(1) Includes non-cash pre-tax asset impairment charges of approximately $51.5 million and $22.3 million during the fifty-two weeks ended January 30, 2010 and January 31, 2009, respectively, and net costs associated with the closure of the RUEHL business, primarily net lease termination costs of approximately $53.9 million and severance and other charges of $2.2 million during the fifty-two weeks ended January 30, 2010.

15. RETIREMENT BENEFITS

The Company maintains the Abercrombie & Fitch Co. Savings & Retirement Plan, a qualified plan. All U.S. associates are eligible to participate in this plan if they are at least 21 years of age and have completed a year of employment with 1,000 or more hours of service. In addition, the Company maintains the Abercrombie & Fitch Nonqualified Savings and Supplemental Retirement Plan. Participation in this plan is based on service and compensation. The Company's contributions are based on a percentage of associates' eligible annual compensation. The cost of the Company's contributions to these plans was $17.8 million in Fiscal 2009, $24.7 million in Fiscal 2008 and $21.0 million in Fiscal 2007.

Effective February 2, 2003, the Company established a Chief Executive Officer Supplemental Executive Retirement Plan (the "SERP") to provide additional retirement income to its Chairman and Chief Executive Officer ("CEO"). Subject to service requirements, the CEO will receive a monthly benefit equal to 50% of his final average compensation (as defined in the SERP) for life. The final average compensation used for the calculation is based on actual compensation, base salary and cash incentive compensation for the past three fiscal years. In Fiscal 2009 and Fiscal 2008, the Company recorded income of $1.0 million and $2.5 million associated to the SERP, respectively. The amounts recognized in Fiscal 2009 and Fiscal 2008 were primarily the result of a reduction in average compensation, partially offset by a reduction in the discount rate. The expense associated with the SERP was $1.4 million in Fiscal 2007.

16. CONTINGENCIES

A&F is a defendant in lawsuits and other adversary proceedings arising in the ordinary course of business.

On June 23, 2006, Lisa Hashimoto, et al. v. Abercrombie & Fitch Co. and Abercrombie & Fitch Stores, Inc., was filed in the Superior Court of the State of California for the County of Los Angeles. In that action, plaintiffs alleged, on behalf of a putative class of California store managers employed in Hollister and abercrombie kids stores, that they were entitled to receive overtime pay as "non-exempt" employees under California wage and hour laws. The complaint seeks injunctive relief, equitable relief, unpaid overtime compensation, unpaid benefits, penalties, interest and attorneys' fees and costs. The defendants answered the complaint on August 21, 2006, denying liability. On June 23, 2008, the defendants settled all claims of Hollister and abercrombie kids store managers who served in stores from June 23, 2002 through April 30, 2004, but continued to oppose the plaintiffs' remaining claims. On January 29, 2009, the Court certified a class consisting of all store managers who served at Hollister and abercrombie kids stores in California from May 1, 2004 through the future date upon which the action concludes. The parties are continuing to litigate the claims of that putative class.

ABERCROMBIE & FITCH CO.

NOTES TO CONSOLIDATED FINANCIAL STATEMENTS—(Continued)

On September 2, 2005, a purported class action, styled Robert Ross v. Abercrombie & Fitch Company, et al., was filed against A&F and certain of its officers in the United States District Court for the Southern District of Ohio on behalf of a purported class of all persons who purchased or acquired shares of A&F's Common Stock between June 2, 2005 and August 16, 2005. In September and October of 2005, five other purported class actions were subsequently filed against A&F and other defendants in the same Court. All six securities cases allege claims under the federal securities laws related to sales of Common Stock by certain defendants and to a decline in the price of A&F's Common Stock during the summer of 2005, allegedly as a result of misstatements attributable to A&F. Plaintiffs seek unspecified monetary damages. On November 1, 2005, a motion to consolidate all of these purported class actions into the first-filed case was filed by some of the plaintiffs. A&F joined in that motion. On March 22, 2006, the motions to consolidate were granted, and these actions (together with the federal court derivative cases described in the following paragraph) were consolidated for purposes of motion practice, discovery and pretrial proceedings. A consolidated amended securities class action complaint (the "Complaint") was filed on August 14, 2006. On October 13, 2006, all defendants moved to dismiss that Complaint. On August 9, 2007, the Court denied the motions to dismiss. On September 14, 2007, defendants filed answers denying the material allegations of the Complaint and asserting affirmative defenses. On October 26, 2007, plaintiffs moved to certify their purported class. After briefing and argument, the motion was submitted on March 24, 2009, and granted on May 21, 2009. On June 5, 2009, defendants petitioned the Sixth Circuit for permission to appeal the class certification order and on August 24, 2009, the Sixth Circuit granted leave to appeal.

On September 16, 2005, a derivative action, styled The Booth Family Trust v. Michael S. Jeffries, et al., was filed in the United States District Court for the Southern District of Ohio, naming A&F as a nominal defendant and seeking to assert claims for unspecified damages against nine of A&F's present and former directors, alleging various breaches of the directors' fiduciary duty and seeking equitable and monetary relief. In the following three months, four similar derivative actions were filed (three in the United States District Court for the Southern District of Ohio and one in the Court of Common Pleas for Franklin County, Ohio) against present and former directors of A&F alleging various breaches of the directors' fiduciary duty allegedly arising out of the same matters alleged in the Ross case and seeking equitable and monetary relief on behalf of A&F. In March of 2006, the federal court derivative actions were consolidated with the Ross actions for purposes of motion practice, discovery and pretrial proceedings. A consolidated amended derivative complaint was filed in the federal proceeding on July 10, 2006. On February 16, 2007, A&F announced that its Board of Directors had received a report of the Special Litigation Committee established by the Board to investigate and act with respect to claims asserted in the derivative lawsuit, which concluded that there was no evidence to support the asserted claims and directed the Company to seek dismissal of the derivative cases. On September 10, 2007, the Company moved to dismiss the federal derivative cases on the authority of the Special Litigation Committee report. On March 12, 2009, the Company's motion was granted and, on April 10, 2009, plaintiffs filed an appeal from the order of dismissal. The state court has stayed further proceedings in the state-court derivative action until resolution of the consolidated federal derivative cases.

Management intends to defend the aforesaid matters vigorously, as appropriate. Management is unable to quantify the potential exposure of the aforesaid matters. However, management's assessment of the Company's current exposure could change in the event of the discovery of additional facts with respect to legal matters pending against the Company or determinations by judges, juries, administrative agencies or other finders of fact that are not in accordance with management's evaluation of the claims.

17. PREFERRED STOCK PURCHASE RIGHTS

On July 16, 1998, A&F's Board of Directors declared a dividend of one Series A Participating Cumulative Preferred Stock Purchase Right (the "Rights") for each outstanding share of Class A Common Stock (the "Common Stock"), par value $.01 per share, of A&F. The dividend was paid on July 28, 1998 to stockholders of record on that date. Shares of Common Stock issued after July 28, 1998 and prior to May 25, 1999 were issued with one Right attached. A&F's Board of Directors declared a two-for-one stock split (the "Stock Split") on the Common Stock, payable on June 15, 1999 to the holders of record at the close of business on May 25, 1999. In connection with the Stock Split, the number of Rights associated with each share of Common Stock outstanding as of the close of business on May 25, 1999, or issued or delivered after May 25, 1999 and prior to the "Distribution Date" (as defined below), was proportionately adjusted from one Right to 0.50 Right. Each share of Common Stock issued after May 25, 1999 and prior to the Distribution Date has been, and will be issued, with 0.50 Right attached so that all shares of Common Stock outstanding prior to the Distribution Date will have 0.50 Right attached.

ABERCROMBIE & FITCH CO.

NOTES TO CONSOLIDATED FINANCIAL STATEMENTS—(Continued)

The Rights are initially attached to the shares of Common Stock. The Rights will separate from the Common Stock after a Distribution Date occurs. The "Distribution Date" generally means the earlier of (i) the close of business on the 10th day after the date (the "Share Acquisition Date") of the first public announcement that a person or group (other than A&F or any of A&F's subsidiaries or any employee benefit plan of A&F or of any of A&F's subsidiaries) has acquired beneficial ownership of 20% or more of A&F's outstanding shares of Common Stock (an "Acquiring Person"), or (ii) the close of business on the 10th business day (or such later date as A&F's Board of Directors may designate before any person has become an Acquiring Person) after the date of the commencement of a tender or exchange offer by any person which would, if consummated, result in such person becoming an Acquiring Person. The Rights are not exercisable until the Distribution Date. After the Distribution Date, each whole Right may be exercised to purchase, at an initial exercise price of $250, one one-thousandth of a share of Series A Participating Cumulative Preferred Stock.

At any time after any person becomes an Acquiring Person, but before the occurrence of any of the events described in the immediately following paragraph, each holder of a Right, other than the Acquiring Person and certain affiliated persons, will be entitled to purchase, upon exercise of the Right, shares of Common Stock having a market value of twice the exercise price of the Right. At any time after any person becomes an Acquiring Person, but before any person becomes the beneficial owner of 50% or more of the outstanding shares of Common Stock or the occurrence of any of the events described in the immediately following paragraph, A&F's Board of Directors may exchange all or part of the Rights, other than Rights beneficially owned by an Acquiring Person and certain affiliated persons, for shares of Common Stock at an exchange ratio of one share of Common Stock per 0.50 Right.

If, after any person has become an Acquiring Person, (i) A&F is involved in a merger or other business combination transaction in which A&F is not the surviving corporation or A&F's Common Stock is exchanged for other securities or assets, or (ii) A&F and/or one or more of A&F's subsidiaries sell or otherwise transfer 50% or more of the assets or earning power of A&F and its subsidiaries, taken as a whole, each holder of a Right, other than the Acquiring Person and certain affiliated persons, will be entitled to buy, for the exercise price of the Rights, the number of shares of common stock of the other party to the business combination or sale, or in certain circumstances, an affiliate, which at the time of such transaction will have a market value of twice the exercise price of the Right.

The Rights will expire on July 16, 2018, unless earlier exchanged or redeemed. A&F may redeem all of the Rights at a price of $.01 per whole Right at any time before any person becomes an Acquiring Person.

Rights holders have no rights as a stockholder of A&F, including the right to vote and to receive dividends.

18. QUARTERLY FINANCIAL DATA (UNAUDITED)

Summarized unaudited quarterly financial results for Fiscal 2009 and Fiscal 2008 follows (thousands, except per share amounts):

Fiscal 2009 Quarter[1]	First	Second	Third	Fourth
Net sales	$ 601,729	$ 637,221	$ 753,684	$ 935,991
Gross profit	$ 381,453	$ 424,516	$ 483,087	$ 594,542
Net (loss) income from continuing operations	$ (23,104)	$ (8,191)	$ 49,222	$ 61,025
Net loss from discontinued operations, net of tax	$ (36,135)	$ (18,557)	$ (10,439)	$ (13,566)
Net (loss) income	$ (59,239)	$ (26,747)	$ 38,784	$ 47,459
Net (loss) income per diluted share from continuing operations	$ (0.26)	$ (0.09)	$ 0.55	$ 0.68
Net loss per diluted share from discontinued operations	$ (0.41)	$ (0.21)	$ (0.12)	$ (0.15)
Net (loss) income per diluted share	$ (0.68)	$ (0.30)	$ 0.44	$ 0.53

(*Continued*)

(1) Results of operations of RUEHL are reflected as discontinued operations for all periods presented. Refer to Note 14, "*Discontinued Operations*" for further discussion.

ABERCROMBIE & FITCH CO.

NOTES TO CONSOLIDATED FINANCIAL STATEMENTS—(Continued)

Fiscal 2008 Quarter[1]	First	Second	Third	Fourth
Net sales	$ 787,139	$ 833,298	$ 882,811	$ 980,809
Gross profit	$ 526,734	$ 585,547	$ 584,965	$ 633,849
Net income from continuing operations	$ 67,167	$ 83,236	$ 69,743	$ 88,021
Net loss from discontinued operations, net of tax	$ (5,051)	$ (5,404)	$ (5,844)	$ (19,614)
Net income	$ 62,116	$ 77,832	$ 63,900	$ 68,407
Net income per diluted share from continuing operations	$ 0.75	$ 0.93	$ 0.79	$ 1.00
Net loss per diluted share from discontinued operations	$ (0.06)	$ (0.06)	$ (0.07)	$ (0.22)
Net income per diluted share	$ 0.69	$ 0.87	$ 0.72	$ 0.78

(1) Results of operations of RUEHL are reflected as discontinued operations for all periods presented. Refer to Note 14, "*Discontinued Operations*" for further discussion.

Report of Independent Registered Public Accounting Firm

To the Board of Directors and Shareholders of
Abercrombie & Fitch Co.:

In our opinion, the consolidated financial statements listed in the accompanying index appearing under item 15(a)(1) present fairly, in all material respects, the financial position of Abercrombie & Fitch Co. and its subsidiaries at January 30, 2010 and January 31, 2009, and the results of their operations and their cash flows for each of the three years in the period ended January 30, 2010 in conformity with accounting principles generally accepted in the United States of America. Also in our opinion, the Company maintained, in all material respects, effective internal control over financial reporting as of January 30, 2010, based on criteria established in *Internal Control - Integrated Framework* issued by the Committee of Sponsoring Organizations of the Treadway Commission (COSO). The Company's management is responsible for these financial statements, for maintaining effective internal control over financial reporting and for its assessment of the effectiveness of internal control over financial reporting, included in the accompanying Management's Report on Internal Control over Financial Reporting. Our responsibility is to express opinions on these financial statements and on the Company's internal control over financial reporting based on our integrated audits. We conducted our audits in accordance with the standards of the Public Company Accounting Oversight Board (United States). Those standards require that we plan and perform the audits to obtain reasonable assurance about whether the financial statements are free of material misstatement and whether effective internal control over financial reporting was maintained in all material respects. Our audits of the financial statements included examining, on a test basis, evidence supporting the amounts and disclosures in the financial statements, assessing the accounting principles used and significant estimates made by management, and evaluating the overall financial statement presentation. Our audit of internal control over financial reporting included obtaining an understanding of internal control over financial reporting, assessing the risk that a material weakness exists, and testing and evaluating the design and operating effectiveness of internal control based on the assessed risk. Our audits also included performing such other procedures as we considered necessary in the circumstances. We believe that our audits provide a reasonable basis for our opinions.

A company's internal control over financial reporting is a process designed to provide reasonable assurance regarding the reliability of financial reporting and the preparation of financial statements for external purposes in accordance with generally accepted accounting principles. A company's internal control over financial reporting includes those policies and procedures that (i) pertain to the maintenance of records that, in reasonable detail, accurately and fairly reflect the transactions and dispositions of the assets of the company; (ii) provide reasonable assurance that transactions are recorded as necessary to permit preparation of financial statements in accordance with generally accepted accounting principles, and that receipts and expenditures of the company are being made only in accordance with authorizations of management and directors of the company; and (iii) provide reasonable assurance regarding prevention or timely detection of unauthorized acquisition, use, or disposition of the company's assets that could have a material effect on the financial statements.

Because of its inherent limitations, internal control over financial reporting may not prevent or detect misstatements. Also, projections of any evaluation of effectiveness to future periods are subject to the risk that controls may become inadequate because of changes in conditions, or that the degree of compliance with the policies or procedures may deteriorate.

/s/PricewaterhouseCoopers LLP

Columbus, Ohio
March 29, 2010

5 Appendix

Financial Statement Information: Aeropostale

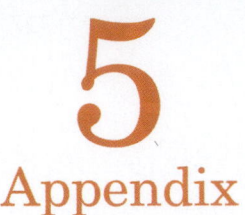

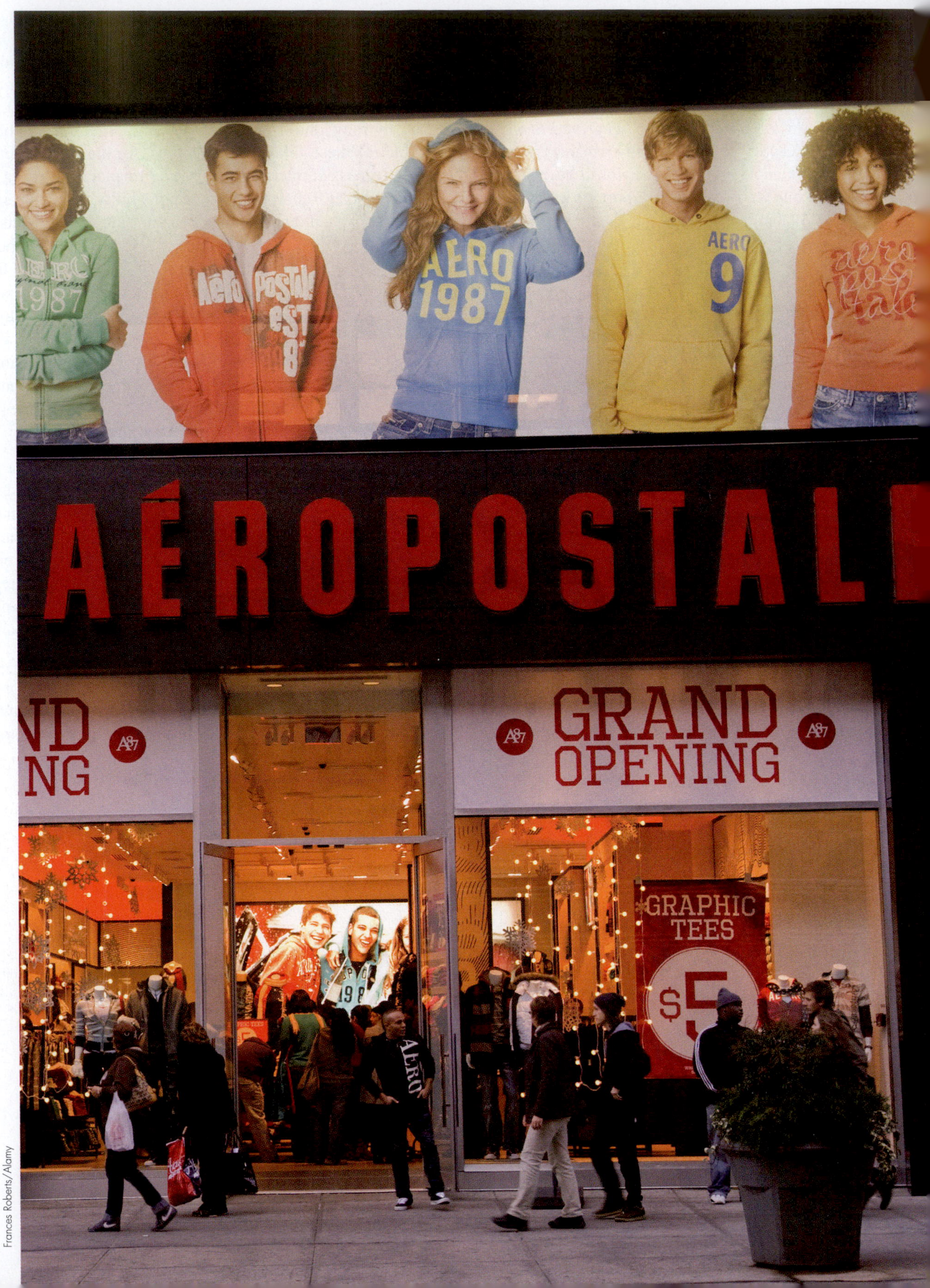

Frances Roberts/Alamy

REPORT OF INDEPENDENT REGISTERED PUBLIC ACCOUNTING FIRM

To the Board of Directors and Stockholders of Aéropostale, Inc.
New York, New York

We have audited the internal control over financial reporting of Aéropostale, Inc. and subsidiaries (the "Company") as of January 30, 2010, based on criteria established in Internal Control — Integrated Framework issued by the Committee of Sponsoring Organizations of the Treadway Commission. The Company's management is responsible for maintaining effective internal control over financial reporting and for its assessment of the effectiveness of internal control over financial reporting, included in the accompanying Management's Report on Internal Control over Financial Reporting. Our responsibility is to express an opinion on the Company's internal control over financial reporting based on our audit.

We conducted our audit in accordance with the standards of the Public Company Accounting Oversight Board (United States). Those standards require that we plan and perform the audit to obtain reasonable assurance about whether effective internal control over financial reporting was maintained in all material respects. Our audit included obtaining an understanding of internal control over financial reporting, assessing the risk that a material weakness exists, testing and evaluating the design and operating effectiveness of internal control based on the assessed risk, and performing such other procedures as we considered necessary in the circumstances. We believe that our audit provides a reasonable basis for our opinion.

A company's internal control over financial reporting is a process designed by, or under the supervision of, the company's principal executive and principal financial officers, or persons performing similar functions, and effected by the company's board of directors, management, and other personnel to provide reasonable assurance regarding the reliability of financial reporting and the preparation of financial statements for external purposes in accordance with generally accepted accounting principles. A company's internal control over financial reporting includes those policies and procedures that (1) pertain to the maintenance of records that, in reasonable detail, accurately and fairly reflect the transactions and dispositions of the assets of the company; (2) provide reasonable assurance that transactions are recorded as necessary to permit preparation of financial statements in accordance with generally accepted accounting principles, and that receipts and expenditures of the company are being made only in accordance with authorizations of management and directors of the company; and (3) provide reasonable assurance regarding prevention or timely detection of unauthorized acquisition, use, or disposition of the company's assets that could have a material effect on the financial statements.

Because of the inherent limitations of internal control over financial reporting, including the possibility of collusion or improper management override of controls, material misstatements due to error or fraud may not be prevented or detected on a timely basis. Also, projections of any evaluation of the effectiveness of the internal control over financial reporting to future periods are subject to the risk that the controls may become inadequate because of changes in conditions, or that the degree of compliance with the policies or procedures may deteriorate.

In our opinion, the Company maintained, in all material respects, effective internal control over financial reporting as of January 30, 2010, based on the criteria established in Internal Control — Integrated Framework issued by the Committee of Sponsoring Organizations of the Treadway Commission.

We have also audited, in accordance with the standards of the Public Company Accounting Oversight Board (United States), the consolidated financial statements and financial statement schedule as of and for the year ended January 30, 2010, of the Company and our report dated March 29, 2010 expressed an unqualified opinion on those financial statements and financial statement schedule.

/s/ Deloitte and Touche LLP

New York, New York

March 29, 2010

AÉROPOSTALE, INC. AND SUBSIDIARIES

CONSOLIDATED BALANCE SHEETS

	January 30, 2010	January 31, 2009
	(In thousands, except per share data)	
ASSETS		
Current assets:		
Cash and cash equivalents	$ 346,976	$ 228,530
Merchandise inventory	132,915	126,360
Prepaid expenses	21,049	17,384
Deferred income taxes	21,683	10,745
Other current assets	7,394	10,862
Total current assets	530,017	393,881
Fixtures, equipment and improvements— net	251,558	248,999
Deferred income taxes	6,383	12,509
Other assets	4,351	2,530
Total assets	$ 792,309	$ 657,919
LIABILITIES AND STOCKHOLDERS' EQUITY		
Current liabilities:		
Accounts payable	$ 90,850	$ 77,247
Accrued expenses	150,990	98,190
Total current liabilities	241,840	175,437
Tenant allowances	68,174	74,712
Deferred rent	27,559	26,019
Non-current retirement benefit plan liabilities	10,060	22,470
Other non-current liabilities	6,286	1,662
Uncertain tax contingency liabilities	3,901	2,559
Commitments and contingent liabilities		
Stockholders' equity Common stock — par value, $0.01 per share; 200,000 shares authorized, 137,090 and 135,708 shares issued	1,371	1,358
Preferred stock — par value, $0.01 per share; 5,000 shares authorized, no shares issued or outstanding	—	—
Additional paid-in capital	171,815	145,498
Accumulated other comprehensive loss	(6,993)	(8,998)
Retained earnings	922,790	693,333
Treasury stock at cost — 43,095 and 35,313 shares	(654,494)	(476,131)
Total stockholders' equity	434,489	355,060
Total liabilities and stockholders' equity	$ 792,309	$ 657,919

See Notes to Consolidated Financial Statements.

AÉROPOSTALE, INC. AND SUBSIDIARIES
CONSOLIDATED STATEMENTS OF INCOME

	Fiscal Year Ended		
	January 30, 2010	January 31, 2009	February 2, 2008
	(In thousands, except per share data)		
Net sales	$ 2,230,105	$ 1,885,531	$ 1,590,883
Cost of sales (includes certain buying, occupancy and warehousing expenses)	1,382,958	1,231,349	1,037,680
Gross profit	847,147	654,182	553,203
Selling, general and administrative expenses	464,462	405,883	345,805
Jimmy'Z asset impairment charges	—	—	9,023
Other operating income	—	—	4,078
Income from operations	382,685	248,299	202,453
Interest income	121	510	6,550
Income before income taxes	382,806	248,809	209,003
Income taxes	153,349	99,387	79,806
Net income	$ 229,457	$ 149,422	$ 129,197
Basic earnings per common share	$ 2.30	$ 1.49	$ 1.16
Diluted earnings per common share	$ 2.27	$ 1.47	$ 1.15
Weighted average basic shares	99,629	100,248	111,473
Weighted average diluted shares	101,025	101,364	112,269

CONSOLIDATED STATEMENTS OF COMPREHENSIVE INCOME

	Fiscal Year Ended		
	January 30, 2010	January 31, 2009	February 2, 2008
	(In thousands)		
Net income	$ 229,457	$ 149,422	$ 129,197
Pension liability (net of tax of $598, $321, and $229)	(712)	(474)	(582)
Foreign currency translation adjustment	2,717	(3,874)	1,206
Comprehensive income	$ 231,462	$ 145,074	$ 129,821

See Notes to Consolidated Financial Statements.

AÉROPOSTALE, INC. AND SUBSIDIARIES
CONSOLIDATED STATEMENTS OF STOCKHOLDERS' EQUITY

	Common Stock Shares	Common Stock Amount	Additional Paid-in Capital	Treasury Stock, at Cost Shares	Treasury Stock, at Cost Amount	Accumulated Other Comprehensive Loss	Retained Earnings	Total
					(In thousands)			
BALANCE, FEBRUARY 4, 2007	133,497	$ 1,335	$ 100,687	(17,297)	$ (199,548)	$	$ 414,916	$ 312,116
Net income	—	—	—	—	—	—	129,197	129,197
Stock options exercised	1,208	12	8,016	—	—	—	—	8,028
Pension liability (net of tax of $229)	—	—	—	—	—	(582)	—	(582)
Excess tax benefit from stock-based compensation	—	—	5,519	—	—	—	—	5,519
Adoption of ASC 740-10	—	—	—	—	—	—	(202)	(202)
Repurchase of common stock	—	—	—	(17,498)	(266,692)	—	—	(266,692)
Stock-based compensation	—	—	9,381	—	—	—	—	9,381
Foreign currency translation adjustment	—	—	—	—	—	1,206	—	1,206
Vesting of stock	157	2	(1)	(41)	(696)	—	—	(695)
BALANCE, FEBRUARY 2, 2008	134,862	1,349	123,602	(34,836)	(466,936)	(4,650)	543,911	197,276
Net income	—	—	—	—	—	—	149,422	149,422
Stock options exercised	378	4	3,750	—	—	—	—	3,754
Pension liability (net of tax of $321)	—	—	—	—	—	(474)	—	(474)
Excess tax benefit from stock-based compensation	—	—	1,482	—	—	—	—	1,482
Repurchase of common stock	—	—	—	(312)	(6,681)	—	—	(6,681)
Stock-based compensation	—	—	16,666	—	—	—	—	16,666
Foreign currency translation adjustment	—	—	—	—	—	(3,874)	—	(3,874)
Vesting of stock	468	5	(2)	(165)	(2,514)	—	—	(2,511)

(Continued)

BALANCE, JANUARY 31, 2009	135,708	1,358	145,498	(35,313)	(476,131)	(8,998)	693,333	355,060
Net income	—	—	—	—	—	—	229,457	229,457
Stock options exercised	845	8	10,461	—	—	—	—	10,469
Pension liability (net of tax of $598)	—	—	—	—	—	(712)	—	(712)
Excess tax benefit from stock-based compensation	—	—	1,184	—	—	—	—	1,184
Repurchase of common stock	—	—	—	(7,583)	(174,257)	—	—	(174,257)
Stock-based compensation	—	—	14,673	—	—	—	—	14,673
Foreign currency translation adjustment	—	—	—	—	—	2,717	—	2,717
Vesting of stock	537	5	(1)	(199)	(4,106)	—	—	(4,102)
BALANCE, JANUARY 30, 2010	137,090	$ 1,371	$ 171,815	(43,095)	$ (654,494)	(6,993)	$ 922,790	$ 434,489

See Notes to Consolidated Financial Statements.

AÉROPOSTALE, INC. AND SUBSIDIARIES

CONSOLIDATED STATEMENTS OF CASH FLOWS

	Fiscal Year Ended		
	January 30, 2010	January 31, 2009	February 2, 2008
	(In thousands)		
Cash Flows Provided by Operating Activities			
Net income	$ 229,457	$ 149,422	$ 129,197
Adjustments to reconcile net income to net cash provided by operating activities:			
Depreciation and amortization	52,851	45,773	36,756
Stock-based compensation	14,673	16,666	9,381
Amortization of tenant allowances	(12,348)	(11,745)	(10,315)
Amortization of deferred rent expense	1,366	2,357	2,427
Pension expense	3,361	2,757	2,202
Deferred income taxes	(4,170)	3,022	(12,990)
Jimmy'Z asset impairment charges	—	—	9,023
Excess tax benefits from stock-based compensation	(1,184)	(1,482)	(5,519)
Other	—	—	1,217
Changes in operating assets and liabilities:			
Merchandise inventory	(5,599)	9,063	(35,002)
Prepaid expenses and other assets	(1,308)	(5,202)	(4,447)
Accounts payable	13,210	(21,717)	35,451
Accrued expenses and other liabilities	44,131	13,221	13,700
Net cash provided by operating activities	334,440	202,135	171,081
Cash Flows Used for Investing Activities			
Capital expenditures	(53,883)	(83,035)	(82,306)
Purchase of short-term investments	—	—	(313,572)
Proceeds from sale of short-term investments	—	—	389,795
Net cash used for investing activities	(53,883)	(83,035)	(6,083)
Cash Flows Used for Financing Activities			
Purchase of treasury stock	(174,257)	(6,681)	(266,692)
Proceeds from stock options exercised	10,469	3,754	8,020
Excess tax benefits from stock-based compensation	1,184	1,482	5,519
Borrowings under revolving credit facility	—	—	31,300
Repayments under revolving credit facility	—	—	(31,300)
Net cash used for financing activities	(162,604)	(1,445)	(253,153)
Effect of exchange rate changes	493	(1,052)	18
Net Increase (Decrease) in Cash and Cash Equivalents	118,446	116,603	(88,137)
Cash and Cash Equivalents, Beginning of Year	228,530	111,927	200,064
Cash and Cash Equivalents, End of Year	$ 346,976	$ 228,530	$ 111,927
Supplemental Disclosures of Cash Flow Information:			
Interest paid	$ —	$ —	$ 110
Income taxes paid	$ 139,019	$ 112,469	$ 102,051
Accruals related to purchases of property and equipment	$ 696	$ 785	$ 313

See Notes to Consolidated Financial Statements.

AÉROPOSTALE, INC. AND SUBSIDIARIES

NOTES TO CONSOLIDATED FINANCIAL STATEMENTS

1.   Summary of Significant Accounting Policies

Organization

References to the "Company," "we," "us," or "our" means Aéropostale, Inc. and its subsidiaries, except as expressly indicated or unless the context otherwise requires. We are a mall-based specialty retailer of casual apparel and accessories for young women and men. As of January 30, 2010, we operated 938 Aéropostale stores consisting of 894 stores in 49 states and Puerto Rico and 44 stores in Canada. In addition, our new concept, P.S. from Aéropostale, offers casual clothing and accessories focusing on elementary school children between the ages of 7 and 12. As of January 30, 2010, we operated 14 P.S. from Aéropostale stores in five states. In addition, pursuant to a Licensing Agreement, our international licensee operated five Aéropostale stores in the United Arab Emirates as of January 30, 2010.

Basis of Consolidation and Presentation

The accompanying consolidated financial statements have been prepared in accordance with accounting principles generally accepted in the United States of America ("U.S."). The consolidated financial statements include the accounts of Aéropostale, Inc. and its subsidiaries. All inter-company accounts and transactions have been eliminated in consolidation.

Fiscal Year

Our fiscal year ends on the Saturday nearest to January 31. Fiscal 2009 was the 52-week period ended January 30, 2010, fiscal 2008 was the 52-week period ended January 31, 2009 and fiscal 2007 was the 52-week period ended February 2, 2008. Fiscal 2010 will be the 52-week period ending January 29, 2011.

Use of Estimates

The preparation of the consolidated financial statements in conformity with accounting principles generally accepted in the United States requires us to make estimates and assumptions that affect the amounts reported in our consolidated financial statements and accompanying notes. Actual results could differ materially from those estimated.

The most significant estimates made by management include those made in the areas of merchandise inventory, defined benefit retirement plans, long-lived assets, and income taxes. Management periodically evaluates estimates used in the preparation of the consolidated financial statements for continued reasonableness. Appropriate adjustments, if any, to the estimates used are made prospectively based on such periodic evaluations.

Concentration of Credit Risk

Financial instruments that potentially subject the Company to concentrations of credit risk consist of cash and cash equivalents. The Company invests its excess cash in demand deposits and money market funds that are classified as cash equivalents. The Company has established guidelines that relate to credit quality, diversification and maturity and that limit exposure to any one issuer of securities.

Seasonality

Our business is highly seasonal, and historically we have realized a significant portion of our sales, net income, and cash flow in the second half of the fiscal year, attributable to the impact of the back-to-school selling season in the third quarter and the holiday selling season in the fourth quarter. Additionally, working capital requirements fluctuate during the year, increasing in mid-summer in anticipation of the third and fourth quarters.

Translation of Foreign Currency Financial Statements and Foreign Currency Transactions

The financial statements of our Canadian subsidiary have been translated into United States dollars by translating balance sheet accounts at the year-end exchange rate and statement of income accounts at the average exchange rates for the year. Foreign currency translation gains and losses are reflected in the equity section of our consolidated balance sheet in accumulated other comprehensive loss and are not adjusted for income taxes as they relate to a permanent investment in our subsidiary in Canada. The balance of the unrealized foreign currency translation adjustment included in accumulated other comprehensive loss was income of approximately $49,000 as of January 30, 2010 compared to a loss of $2.7 million as of January 31, 2009. Foreign currency transaction gains and losses are charged or credited to earnings as incurred.

Cash Equivalents

We include credit card receivables and all short-term investments that qualify as cash equivalents with an original maturity of three months or less in cash and cash equivalents.

Fair Value Measurements

We follow the guidance in Financial Accounting Standards Board ("FASB") Accounting Standards Codification ("ASC") Topic 820, "Fair Value Measurement Disclosures" ("ASC 820") as it relates to financial and nonfinancial assets and liabilities. We currently have no financial assets or liabilities that are measured at fair value. Our non-financial assets, which include property and equipment, are not required to be measured at fair value on a recurring basis. However, if certain triggering events occur, or if an annual impairment test is required and we are required to evaluate the non-financial asset for impairment, a resulting asset impairment would require that the non-financial asset be recorded at the fair value. ASC 820 prioritizes inputs used in measuring fair value into a hierarchy of three levels: Level 1—quoted prices (unadjusted) in active markets for identical assets or liabilities; Level 2—inputs other than quoted prices included within Level 1 that are either directly or indirectly observable; and Level 3—unobservable inputs in which little or no market activity exists, therefore requiring an entity to develop its own assumptions about the assumptions that market participants would use in pricing.

The fair value of cash and cash equivalents, receivables, and accounts payable approximates their carrying value due to their short-term maturities.

Merchandise Inventory

Merchandise inventory consists of finished goods and is valued utilizing the cost method at the lower of cost or market determined on a weighted-average basis. Merchandise inventory includes warehousing, freight, merchandise and design costs as an inventory product cost. We make certain assumptions regarding future demand and net realizable selling price in order to assess that our inventory is recorded properly at the lower of cost or market. These assumptions are based on both historical experience and current information. We recorded adjustments to inventory and cost of sales for lower of cost or market of $9.3 million as of January 30, 2010 and $9.5 million as of January 31, 2009.

Vendor Rebates

We receive vendor rebates from certain merchandise suppliers. The vendor rebates are earned as we receive merchandise from the suppliers and are computed at an agreed upon percentage of the purchase amount. Vendor rebates are recorded as a reduction of merchandise inventory, and are then recognized as a reduction of cost of sales when the related inventory is sold. Vendor rebates recorded as a reduction of merchandise inventory were $1.5 million as of January 30, 2010 and $0.9 million as of January 31, 2009. Vendor rebates recorded as a reduction of cost of sales were $8.8 million for fiscal 2009, $8.3 million for fiscal 2008, and $7.4 million for fiscal 2007.

Fixtures, Equipment and Improvements

Fixtures, equipment and improvements are stated at cost. Depreciation and amortization are provided for by the straight-line method over the following estimated useful lives:

Fixtures and equipment	10 years
Leasehold improvements	Lesser of 10 years or lease term
Computer equipment	5 years
Software	3 years

Evaluation for Long-Lived Asset Impairment

We periodically evaluate the need to recognize impairment losses relating to long-lived assets in accordance with FASB ASC Topic 360, "Property, Plant and Equipment" ("ASC 360"). Long-lived assets are evaluated for recoverability whenever events or changes in circumstances indicate that an asset may have been impaired. In evaluating an asset for recoverability, we estimate the future undiscounted cash flows expected to result from the use of the asset and eventual disposition. If the sum of the expected future cash flows is less than the carrying amount of the asset, we write the asset down to fair value and we record impairment charges, accordingly. The estimation of fair value is measured by discounting expected future cash flows. The recoverability assessment related to store-level assets requires judgments and estimates of future revenues, gross margin rates and store expenses. The Company bases these estimates upon its past and expected future performance. The Company believes its estimates are appropriate in light of current market conditions. However, future impairment charges could be required for certain store locations if the Company does not achieve its current revenue or cash flow projections (see note 4 for a further discussion).

Pre-Opening Expenses

New store pre-opening costs are expensed as they are incurred.

Leases

Our store operating leases typically provide for fixed non-contingent rent escalations. Rent payments under our store leases typically commence when the store opens. These leases include a pre-opening period that allows us to take possession of the property to construct the store. We recognize rent expense on a straight-line basis over the non-cancelable term of each individual underlying lease, commencing when we take possession of the property (see note 14 for a further discussion).

In addition, our store leases require us to pay additional rent based on specified percentages of sales, after we achieve specified annual sales thresholds. We use store sales trends to estimate and record liabilities for these additional rent obligations during interim periods. Most of our store leases entitle us to receive tenant allowances from our landlords. We record these tenant allowances as a deferred rent liability, which we amortize as a reduction of rent expense over the non-cancelable term of each underlying lease.

Revenue Recognition

Sales revenue is recognized at the "point of sale" in our stores, and at the time our e-commerce customers take possession of merchandise. Allowances for sales returns are recorded as a reduction of net sales in the periods in which the related sales are recognized. Also included in sales revenue is shipping revenue from our e-commerce customers. Revenue from licensing arrangements is recognized when earned in accordance with the terms of the underlying agreement, generally based upon the greater of the contractually earned or guaranteed minimum royalty levels.

Gift Cards

We sell gift cards to our customers in our retail stores, through our Web site, and through select third parties. We do not charge administrative fees on unused gift cards and our gift cards do not have an expiration date. We recognize income from gift cards when the gift card is redeemed by the customer. In addition, in the fourth quarter of fiscal 2007, we relieved our legal obligation to escheat the value of unredeemed gift cards to the relevant jurisdiction. We therefore determined that the likelihood of certain gift cards being redeemed by the customer was remote, based upon historical redemption patterns of gift cards. For those gift cards that we determined redemption to be remote, we reversed our liability, and recorded gift card breakage income. In fiscal 2009, we recorded $4.0 million in net sales related to gift card breakage income. In fiscal 2008, we recorded $2.9 million in net sales related to gift card breakage income compared to the initial recognition of $7.7 million in the fourth quarter of fiscal 2007, of which, $5.9 million was related to gift cards issued prior to fiscal 2007 (see note 7 for a further discussion).

Cost of Sales

Cost of sales includes costs related to merchandise sold, including inventory valuation adjustments, distribution and warehousing, freight from the distribution center to the stores, shipping and handling costs, payroll for our design, buying and merchandising departments, and occupancy costs. Occupancy costs include rent, contingent rent, common area maintenance, real estate taxes, utilities, repairs, maintenance, depreciation and amortization and impairment charges.

Selling, General and Administrative Expenses

Selling, general and administrative expenses, or SG&A, include costs related to selling expenses, store management and corporate expenses such as payroll and employee benefits, marketing expenses, employment taxes, information technology maintenance costs and expenses, insurance and legal expenses, store pre-opening and other corporate level expenses. Store pre-opening expenses include store level payroll, grand opening event marketing, travel, supplies and other store preopening expenses.

Self-Insurance

We self-insure our workers compensation claims and our employee medical benefits. The recorded liabilities for these risks are calculated primarily using historical experience and current information. The liabilities include amounts for actual claims and estimated claims incurred but not yet reported. Self-insurance liabilities were $4.8 million at January 30, 2010 and $4.3 million at January 31, 2009. We paid workers compensation claims of $0.7 million in fiscal 2009, $0.4 million in fiscal 2008 and $0.3 million in fiscal 2007. In addition, we paid employee medical claims of $11.8 million in fiscal 2009, $9.0 million in fiscal 2008 and $7.1 million in fiscal 2007.

Retirement Benefit Plans

Our retirement benefit plan costs are accounted for using actuarial valuations required by FASB ASC Topic 715 "Compensation – Retirement Benefits" ("ASC 715") . ASC 715 requires an entity to recognize the funded status of its defined pension plans on the balance sheet and to recognize changes in the funded status that arise during the period but are not recognized as components of net periodic benefit cost, within other comprehensive loss, net of income taxes (see note 11 for a further discussion).

Marketing Costs

Marketing costs, which include e-commerce, print, radio and other media advertising and collegiate athletic conference sponsorships, are expensed at the point of first broadcast or distribution, and were $8.5 million in fiscal 2009, $9.5 million in fiscal 2008, and $7.6 million in fiscal 2007.

Stock-Based Compensation

We follow the provisions from the FASB ASC Topic 718 "Compensation – Stock Compensation" ("ASC 718"). Under such guidance, all forms of share-based payment to employees and directors, including stock options, must be treated as compensation and recognized in the income statement.

Segment Reporting

FASB ASC Topic 280, "Segment Reporting" ("ASC 280"), establishes standards for reporting information about a company's operating segments. It also establishes standards for related disclosures about products and services, geographic areas and major customers. We operate in and report as a single aggregated operating segment, which includes the operations of our Aéropostale retail stores, P.S. from Aéropostale retail stores, our Aéropostale e-commerce site, and licensing revenue. We do not rely on any major customers as a source of revenue. Licensing revenue was less than 1% of total net sales for each period presented.

The following tables present summarized geographical information (in thousands):

	Fiscal		
	2009	2008	2007
Net sales:			
United States[1]	$ 2,141,247	$ 1,840,238	$ 1,577,189
Canada	88,858	45,293	13,694
Total net sales	$ 2,230,105	$ 1,885,531	$ 1,590,883

[1] Amounts represent sales from Aéropostale U.S. retail stores, as well as e-commerce sales, that are billed to and/or shipped to foreign countries and licensing revenue.

	January 30, 2010	January 31, 2009
Long-lived assets, net:		
United States	$ 228,491	$ 234,367
Canada	23,067	14,632
Total long-lived assets, net	$ 251,558	$ 248,999

Our consolidated net sales mix by merchandise category was as follows:

	Fiscal		
Merchandise Categories	2009	2008	2007
Young Women's	70%	71%	72%
Young Men's	30	29	28
Total Merchandise Sales	100%	100%	100%

During fiscal 2009, we sourced approximately 81% of our merchandise from our top five merchandise vendors. During fiscal 2008, we sourced approximately 76% of our merchandise from our top five merchandise vendors. The loss of any of these sources could adversely impact our ability to operate our business. We ceased doing business with South Bay Apparel Inc., one of our largest suppliers of graphic T-shirts and fleece, in July 2007 (see note 14 for a further discussion). We have replaced this business both with new vendors and our existing vendor base.

Income Taxes

Income taxes are accounted for in accordance with FASB ASC Topic 740, "Income Taxes" ("ASC 740") . Under ASC 740, income taxes are recognized for the amount of taxes payable for the current year and deferred tax assets and liabilities for the future tax consequence of events that have been recognized differently in the financial statements than for tax purposes. Deferred tax assets and liabilities are established using statutory tax rates and are adjusted for tax rate changes. ASC 740 clarifies the accounting for uncertainty in income taxes recognized in an entity's financial statements and requires companies to determine whether it is "more likely than not" that a tax position will be sustained upon examination by the appropriate taxing authorities before any part of the benefit can be recorded in the financial statements. For those tax positions where it is not "more likely than not" that a tax benefit will be sustained, no tax benefit is recognized. Where applicable, associated interest and penalties are also recorded. Interest and penalties, if any, are recorded within the provision for income taxes in the Company's Consolidated Statements of Income and are classified on the Consolidated Balance Sheets with the related liability for uncertain tax contingency liabilities.

Subsequent Events

For the fiscal year ended January 30, 2010, the Company has evaluated subsequent events for potential recognition and disclosure through the date of financial statement issuance (see notes 2 and 3 for a further discussion).

Recent Accounting Developments

In June 2009, the FASB issued authoritative guidance which established the FASB Accounting Standards Codification ("Codification"). The Codification became the source of authoritative generally accepted accounting principles in the United States of America. It changed the referencing of financial standards but was not intended to change or alter existing U.S. GAAP. The Codification was effective for interim or annual financial periods ending after September 15, 2009 and was effective for us in the third quarter of 2009. This new guidance applies only to financial statement disclosures and therefore we have updated our references for the accounting guidance.

In May 2009, the FASB issued authoritative guidance now codified as FASB ASC Topic 855, "Subsequent Events". The objective of this guidance is to establish general standards of accounting for and disclosure of events that occur after the balance sheet date but before financial statements are issued or are available to be issued. In particular, this guidance sets forth: a) the period after the balance sheet date during which management of a reporting entity should evaluate events or transactions that may occur for potential recognition or disclosure in the financial statements; b) the circumstances under which an entity should recognize events or transactions occurring after the balance sheet date in its financial statements; and c) the disclosures that an entity should make about events or transactions that occurred after the balance sheet date. In accordance with this guidance, an entity should apply the requirements to interim or annual financial periods ending after June 15, 2009. We adopted the new guidance in the second quarter of 2009. The adoption did not have an impact on our consolidated financial statements.

In December 2008, the FASB issued authoritative guidance now codified as FASB ASC Topic 715, "Compensation – Retirement Benefits" ("ASC 715"). The guidance requires more detailed disclosures about employers' plan assets, including employers' investment strategies, major categories of plan assets, concentrations of risk within plan assets, and valuation techniques used to measure the fair value of plan assets. The new guidance was effective for fiscal years ending after December 15, 2009 and the adoption did not have a material impact on our consolidated financial statements.

In September 2006, the FASB issued authoritative guidance now codified as FASB ASC Topic 820, "Fair Value Measurements and Disclosures" ("ASC 820"). The guidance defines fair value, establishes a framework for measuring fair value in generally accepted accounting principles, and expands disclosures about fair value measurements. This guidance applies under other accounting pronouncements that require or permit fair value measurements, the FASB having concluded in those other accounting pronouncements that fair value is the relevant measurement attribute. It is effective in financial statements issued for fiscal years beginning after November 15, 2007. However, in February 2008, the FASB issued additional ASC 820 guidance which delayed application of certain guidance related to nonrecurring fair value measurements of non-financial assets and non-financial liabilities until fiscal years beginning after November 15, 2008. We adopted the provisions of ASC 820 as it related to nonrecurring fair value measurements of non-financial assets and liabilities at the beginning of fiscal 2009. The adoption did not have a material impact on our consolidated financial statements.

2.   Stock Split

On February 3, 2010, we announced a three-for-two stock split on all shares of our common stock. The stock split was consummated and distributed on March 5, 2010 in the form of a stock dividend to all shareholders of record on February 24, 2010. All share and per share amounts presented in this report were retroactively adjusted for the common stock split, as were all previously reported periods contained herein. This stock split resulted in the issuance of 31.3 million additional shares of common stock and was accounted for in accordance with FASB ASC Topic 260, "Earnings Per Share" ("ASC 260") by the transfer of $0.3 million from additional paid-in capital to common stock, which is the amount equal to the par value of the additional shares issued to effect the stock split on March 5, 2010.

3.   Executive Transition

On February 1, 2010, Julian R. Geiger, our Chairman and former Chief Executive Officer, provided us with formal notice of election in accordance with the terms of his employment agreement, thereby ending his service as Chief Executive Officer effective February 12, 2010. Mr. Geiger has served as our Chairman and CEO since 1996. Mr. Geiger continues to serve as Chairman of our Board of Directors and as a part-time advisor to the Company. Effective February 12, 2010, Mindy C. Meads and Thomas P. Johnson were each promoted to the position of Co-Chief Executive Officer. In addition, also effective February 12, 2010, Michael J. Cunningham was promoted to the position of President and Chief Financial Officer. On February 12, 2010, Ms. Meads and Mr. Johnson each received a grant of 43,092 shares of restricted stock, 50% of which will vest one year from the grant date, and 50% two years from the grant date. Additionally, Mr. Cunningham received a grant of 19,103 shares of restricted stock in September 2009, 50% of which will vest in September 2010 and 50% in September 2011.

In connection with his advisory role, Mr. Geiger will receive an annual advisory fee of $250,000 and an annual grant of not less than 30,000 shares, or more than 60,000 shares of restricted stock, depending upon Company performance during that fiscal year. As a result of the election by Mr. Geiger, we expect to make a payment to Mr. Geiger, in August 2010, of approximately $16.5 million from our Supplemental Executive Retirement Plan ("SERP"). Accordingly, the SERP liability related to Mr. Geiger has been classified as a current liability in our consolidated balance sheet as of January 30, 2010 (see note 11 for a further discussion). Such amount will be paid from our cash flows from operations. At the date of payment to Mr. Geiger, we will record a charge of approximately $5.7 million in selling, general and administrative expenses, with a corresponding amount recorded to relieve accumulated other comprehensive loss included in our stockholder's equity. This accounting treatment is in accordance with settlement accounting procedures under the provisions of ASC 715-30-35-79. In February 2010, we recorded a charge of $0.5 million in selling, general and administrative expenses for the accelerated amortization of stock compensation expense in connection with the accelerated vesting of Mr. Geiger's remaining stock awards.

4.   Asset Impairment and Jimmy'Z Store Concept Closing

Asset Impairment

We have recorded Aéropostale store impairments of $3.0 million in fiscal 2009 for six stores, $3.7 million in fiscal 2008 for 11 stores and $1.7 million in fiscal 2007 for five stores. These charges were included in depreciation and amortization expense, which is included as a component of cost of sales. These amounts include the write-down of long-lived assets at stores that were assessed for impairment because of changes in circumstances that indicated the carrying value of an asset may not be recoverable or management's intention to relocate or close the stores. The 2009 impairment charges were primarily related to revenues not meeting targeted levels of the respective stores as a result of the macroeconomic conditions, location related conditions and other factors that are negatively impacting the sales and cash flows of these locations.

Long-lived assets are measured at fair value on a nonrecurring basis for purposes of calculating impairment using Level 3 inputs as defined in the fair value hierarchy as described in note 1. The fair value of long-lived assets is determined by estimating the amount and timing of net future discounted cash flows. We estimate future cash flows based on our experience, current trends and local market conditions.

The table below sets forth by level within the fair value hierarchy the long-lived assets as of January 30, 2010 for which an impairment assessment was performed.

	Quoted Prices in Active Markets for Identical Assets (Level 1)	Significant Other Observable Inputs (Level 2)	Significant Unobservable Inputs (Level 3)	Total Fair Value	Total Losses
			(In thousands)		
Long-lived assets held and used	$ —	$ —	$ —	$ —	$ 2,988

In accordance with the provisions of the Impairment or Disposal of Long-Lived Assets Subsections of ASC 360, long-lived assets held and used with a carrying amount of $3.0 million were written down to zero, which is their fair value, resulting in an impairment charge of $3.0 million, which was included in earnings for the period.

Jimmy'Z Store Concept Closing

During the second quarter of fiscal 2009, we closed all 11 Jimmy'Z stores. During the first twenty-six weeks of fiscal 2009, we recorded inventory related charges of $1.3 million, severance charges of $1.1 million, and net lease termination charges of $0.7 million. Of these costs, $2.8 million was recorded in cost of sales and $0.3 million was recorded in selling, general and administrative expenses. All of the above costs were paid as of January 30, 2010 and there are no remaining costs to be incurred in connection with the closings.

5.   Accumulated Other Comprehensive Loss

The following table sets forth the components of accumulated other comprehensive loss:

	January 30, 2010	January 31, 2009	February 2, 2008
Pension liability, net of tax	$ (7,042)	$ (6,330)	$ (5,856)
Cumulative foreign currency translation adjustment[1]	49	(2,668)	1,206
Total accumulated other comprehensive loss	$ (6,993)	$ (8,998)	$ (4,650)

[1] Foreign currency translation adjustments are not adjusted for income taxes as they relate to a permanent investment in our subsidiary in Canada.

6.   Fixtures, Equipment and Improvements

Fixtures, equipment and improvements consist of the following (in thousands):

	January 30, 2010	January 31, 2009
Leasehold improvements	$ 269,809	$ 248,724
Fixtures and equipment	118,591	109,158
Computer equipment and software	68,561	55,503
Construction in progress	696	1,339
	457,657	414,724
Less accumulated depreciation and amortization	206,099	165,725
	$ 251,558	$ 248,999

Depreciation and amortization expense was $52.9 million in fiscal 2009, $45.8 million in fiscal 2008, and $36.8 million in fiscal 2007. Included in depreciation and amortization expense are Aéropostale store impairment charges of $3.0 million in fiscal 2009, $3.7 million in fiscal 2008 and $1.7 million in fiscal 2007.

7.   Accrued Expenses

Accrued expenses consist of the following (in thousands):

	January 30, 2010	January 31, 2009
Accrued compensation	$ 32,682	$ 30,043
Income taxes payable	26,867	10,862
Accrued gift cards	24,559	19,349
Current portion of SERP liability	17,080	—
Accrued rent	16,804	13,748
Other	32,998	24,188
	$ 150,990	$ 98,190

8.   Revolving Credit Facility

We have an amended and restated revolving credit facility with Bank of America, N.A. (the "Credit Facility"). The Credit Facility provides for a $150.0 million revolving credit line. The Credit Facility is available for working capital and general corporate purposes, including the repurchase of the Company's capital stock and for its capital expenditures. The Credit Facility is scheduled to expire on November 13, 2012 and is guaranteed by all of our domestic subsidiaries (the "Guarantors").

Loans under the Credit Facility are secured by all our assets and are guaranteed by the Guarantors. Upon the occurrence of a Cash Dominion Event (as defined in the Credit Facility) among other limitations, our ability to borrow funds, make investments, pay dividends and repurchase shares of our common stock would be limited. Direct borrowings under the Credit Facility bear interest at a margin over either LIBOR or a Base Rate (as each such term is defined in the Credit Facility).

The Credit Facility also contains covenants that, subject to specified exceptions, restrict our ability to, among other things:

* incur additional debt or encumber assets of the Company;
* merge with or acquire other companies, liquidate or dissolve;
* sell, transfer, lease or dispose of assets; and
* make loans or guarantees.

Events of default under the Credit Facility include, subject to grace periods and notice provisions in certain circumstances, failure to pay principal amounts when due, breaches of covenants, misrepresentation, default of leases or other indebtedness, excess uninsured casualty loss, excess uninsured judgment or restraint of business, business failure or application for bankruptcy, institution of legal process or proceedings under federal, state or civil statutes, legal challenges to loan documents, and a change in control. If an event of default occurs, the Lender will be entitled to take various actions, including the acceleration of amounts due thereunder and requiring that all such amounts be immediately paid in full as well as possession and sale of all assets that have been used as collateral. Upon the occurrence of an event of default under the Credit Facility, the lenders may cease making loans, terminate the Credit Facility, and declare all amounts outstanding to be immediately due and payable. As of January 30, 2010, we are not aware of any instances of noncompliance with any covenants or any other event of default under the Credit Facility. As of January 30, 2010, we had no outstanding balances or stand-by or commercial letters of credit issued under the Credit Facility.

9.   Earnings Per Share

In accordance with ASC 260, basic earnings per share has been computed based upon the weighted average of common shares during the applicable fiscal year. Diluted net income per share includes the additional dilutive effect of our potentially dilutive securities, which include certain stock options, restricted stock units and performance shares.

Earnings per common share has been computed as follows (in thousands, except per share data):

	Fiscal		
	2009	2008	2007
Net income	$ 229,457	$ 149,422	$ 129,197
Weighted average basic shares	99,629	100,248	111,473
Impact of dilutive securities	1,396	1,116	796
Weighted average diluted shares	101,025	101,364	112,269
Per common share:			
Basic earnings per share	$ 2.30	$ 1.49	$ 1.16
Diluted earnings per share	$ 2.27	$ 1.47	$ 1.15

Options to purchase 6,000 shares in fiscal 2009, 1,572,764 shares in fiscal 2008, and 766,500 in fiscal 2007 were excluded from the computation of diluted earnings per share because the exercise prices of the options were greater than the average market price of the common shares.

10.   Stock-Based Compensation

Under the provisions of ASC 718, all forms of share-based payment to employees and directors, including stock options, must be treated as compensation and recognized in the income statement.

Stock Options

We have stock option plans under which we may grant qualified and non-qualified stock options to purchase shares of our common stock to executives, consultants, directors, or other key employees. As of January 30, 2010, a total of 4,296,008 shares were available for future grant under our plans compared to a total of 5,150,118 shares as of January 31, 2009. Stock options may not be granted at less than the fair market value at the date of grant. Stock options generally vest over four years on a pro rata basis and expire after eight years. All outstanding stock options and restricted stock immediately vest upon (i) a change in control of the company and (ii) termination of the employee within one year of such change of control. We did not grant any stock options during fiscal 2009.

The fair value of options was estimated on the date of grant using the Black-Scholes option-pricing model. The Black-Scholes model requires certain assumptions, including estimating the length of time employees will retain their vested stock options before exercising them ("expected term"), the estimated volatility of our common stock price over the expected term and the number of options that will ultimately not complete their vesting requirements ("forfeitures"). Changes in the subjective assumptions can materially affect the estimate of fair value of stock-based compensation and consequently, the related amount recognized in the consolidated statements of income.

In accordance with the provisions of ASC 718, the fair value of each option grant is estimated on the date of grant using the Black-Scholes option-pricing model based on certain assumptions for the grants in the respective periods. For fiscal 2008, our expected volatility was 43%, expected term was 5.25 years, risk-free interest rate was 2.68% and expected forfeiture rate was 25%. For fiscal 2007, our expected volatility was 45%, expected term was 5.25 years, risk-free interest rate was 4.49% and expected forfeiture rate was 25%.

We have elected to adopt the simplified method to establish the beginning balance of the additional paid-in capital pool ("APIC Pool") related to the tax effects of employee share-based compensation, and to determine the subsequent impact on the APIC Pool and condensed consolidated statements of cash flows of the tax effects of employee and director share-based awards that were outstanding.

The effects of applying the provisions of ASC 718 and the results obtained through the use of the Black-Scholes option-pricing model are not necessarily indicative of future values.

The following tables summarize stock option transactions for common stock for fiscal 2009:

	Shares	Weighted Average Exercise Price	Weighted-Average Remaining Contractual Term	Aggregate Intrinsic Value
	(In thousands)		(In years)	(In millions)
Outstanding as of February 1, 2009	2,175	$ 13.91		
Granted	—	$ —		
Exercised	(844)	$ 12.40		
Cancelled	(20)	$ 16.65		
Outstanding as of January 30, 2010	1,311	$ 14.85	4.31	$ 9.3
Options vested and expected to vest [1] at January 30, 2010	1,214	$ 14.67	4.31	$ 8.8
Exercisable as of January 30, 2010	700	$ 13.03	3.55	$ 6.2

[1] The number of options expected to vest takes into consideration estimated expected forfeitures.

We recognized $2.7 million in compensation expense related to stock options in fiscal 2009, $3.7 million in fiscal 2008 and $4.7 million in fiscal 2007. The weighted-average grant-date fair value of options granted was $8.07 during fiscal 2008, and $8.23 during fiscal 2007. The intrinsic value of options exercised was $8.0 million in fiscal 2009, $1.7 million in fiscal 2008, and $15.4 million in fiscal 2007.

The following tables summarize information regarding non-vested outstanding stock options as of January 30, 2010:

	Shares	Weighted Average Grant-Date Fair Value
	(In thousands)	
Non-vested as of February 1, 2009	1,100	$ 7.54
Granted	—	$ —
Vested	(472)	$ 7.15
Cancelled	(17)	$ 7.98
Non-vested as of January 30, 2010	611	$ 7.83

As of January 30, 2010, there was $2.6 million of total unrecognized compensation cost related to non-vested options that we expect to be recognized over the remaining weighted-average vesting period of one year. We expect to recognize $1.9 million of this cost in fiscal 2010, $0.6 million in fiscal 2011 and $0.1 million in fiscal 2012.

Non-Vested Stock

Certain of our employees and all of our directors have been awarded non-vested stock, pursuant to non-vested stock agreements. The non-vested stock awarded to employees cliff vest after up to three years of continuous service with us. Initial grants of non-vested stock awarded to directors vest, pro-rata, over a three-year period, based upon continuous service. Subsequent grants of non-vested stock awarded to directors vest in full one year after the grant-date.

The following table summarizes non-vested shares of stock outstanding at January 30, 2010:

	Shares	Weighted-Average Grant-Date Fair Value
	(In thousands)	
Outstanding as of February 1, 2009	1,092	$ 16.75
Granted	449	$ 19.52
Vested	(537)	$ 15.31
Cancelled	(24)	$ 18.74
Outstanding as of January 30, 2010	980	$ 18.76

Total compensation expense is being amortized over the vesting period. Compensation expense was $8.1 million for fiscal 2009, $11.4 million for fiscal 2008 and $4.1 million for fiscal 2007. As of January 30, 2010, there was $7.2 million of unrecognized compensation cost related to non-vested stock awards that is expected to be recognized over the weighted average period of one year. The total fair value of shares vested were $8.2 million during fiscal 2009, $7.7 million during fiscal 2008 and $1.3 million during fiscal 2007.

Performance Shares

Certain of our executives have been awarded performance shares, pursuant to performance shares agreements. The performance shares vest at the end of three years of continuous service with us, and the number of shares ultimately awarded is contingent upon meeting various cumulative consolidated earnings targets. Compensation cost for the performance shares are periodically reviewed and adjusted based upon the probability of achieving certain performance goals targets. If the probability of achieving targets changes, compensation cost will be adjusted in the period that the probability of achievement changes.

The following table summarizes performance shares of stock outstanding at January 30, 2010:

	Shares	Weighted-Average Grant-Date Fair Value
	(In thousands)	
Outstanding as of February 1, 2009	239	$ 18.20
Granted	440	$ 16.85
Vested	—	—
Cancelled	(15)	$ 16.65
Outstanding as of January 30, 2010	664	$ 17.35

Total compensation expense is being amortized over the vesting period. Compensation expense was $3.9 million for fiscal 2009, $1.5 million for fiscal 2008 and $0.6 million in fiscal 2007. As of January 30, 2010, there was $5.6 million of unrecognized compensation cost related to performance shares awards that is expected to be recognized over the weighted average period of two years.

11. Retirement Benefit Plans

Retirement benefit plan liabilities consisted of the following (in thousands):

	January 30, 2010	January 31, 2009
Supplemental Executive Retirement Plan ("SERP")	$ 25,282	$ 21,224
Long-term incentive deferred compensation plan	935	591
Postretirement benefit plan	923	655
Total	27,140	22,470
Less amount classified in accrued expenses related to SERP	17,080	—
Long-term retirement benefit plan liabilities	$ 10,060	$ 22,470

401(k) Plan

We maintain a qualified, defined contribution retirement plan with a 401(k) salary deferral feature that covers substantially all of our employees who meet certain requirements. Under the terms of the plan, employees may contribute, subject to statutory limitations, up to 14% of gross earnings and we will provide a matching contribution of 50% of the first 5% of gross earnings contributed by the participants. We also have the option to make additional contributions. The terms of the plan provide for vesting in our matching contributions to the plan over a five-year service period with 20% vesting after two years and 50% vesting after year three. Vesting increases thereafter at a rate of 25% per year so that participants will be fully vested after year five. Contribution expense was $1.1 million in fiscal 2009, $0.8 million in fiscal 2008 and $0.7 million in fiscal 2007.

Supplemental Executive Retirement Plan

Our SERP is a non-qualified defined benefit plan for certain officers. The plan is non-contributory and not funded and provides benefits based on years of service and compensation during employment. Participants are fully vested upon entrance in the plan. Pension expense is determined using the projected unit credit cost method to estimate the total benefits ultimately payable to officers and this cost is allocated to service periods. The actuarial assumptions used to calculate pension costs are reviewed annually.

The following information about the SERP is provided below (in thousands):

	January 30, 2010	January 31, 2009
CHANGE IN BENEFIT OBLIGATION:		
Benefit obligation at beginning of period	$ 21,224	$ 17,830
Service cost	686	655
Interest cost	1,514	1,146
Plan amendments	—	—
Actuarial loss	1,858	1,593
Benefits paid	—	—
Settlements	—	—
Special termination benefits	—	—
Benefit obligation at end of period	$ 25,282	$ 21,224
CHANGE IN PLAN ASSETS:		
Fair value of plan assets at beginning of period	$ —	$ —
Actual return on plan assets	—	—
Employer contributions	—	—
Benefits paid	—	—
Settlements	—	—
Fair value of plan assets at end of period	$ —	$ —
Funded status at end of period	$ (25,282)	$ (21,224)
AMOUNTS RECOGNIZED IN THE STATEMENT OF FINANCIAL POSITION:		
Noncurrent assets	$ —	$ —
Current liabilities	(17,080)	—
Noncurrent liabilities	(8,202)	(21,224)
	$ (25,282)	$ (21,224)
AMOUNTS RECOGNIZED IN ACCUMULATED OTHER COMPREHENSIVE LOSS:		
Net loss	$ 10,337	$ 9,107
Prior service cost	759	833
Total	$ 11,096	$ 9,940
INFORMATION FOR PENSION PLANS WITH AN ACCUMULATED BENEFIT OBLIGATION IN EXCESS OF PLAN ASSETS:		
Projected benefit obligation	$ 25,282	$ 21,224
Accumulated benefit obligation	20,609	17,240
Fair value of plan assets	—	—

Pension expense includes the following components (in thousands):

		Fiscal				
		2009		**2008**		**2007**
COMPONENTS OF NET PERIODIC BENEFIT COST:						
Service cost	$	686	$	655	$	534
Interest cost		1,514		1,146		901
Expected return on plan assets		—		—		—
Amortization of prior service cost		74		74		74
Amortization of net loss		628		594		421
Net periodic benefit cost	$	2,902	$	2,469	$	1,930
OTHER CHANGES IN PLAN ASSETS AND BENEFIT OBLIGATIONS RECOGNIZED IN OTHER COMPREHENSIVE LOSS:						
Net actuarial loss	$	1,858	$	1,593	$	1,248
Prior service cost		—		—		—
Amortization of net loss		(628)		(594)		(421)
Amortization of prior service cost		(74)		(74)		(74)
Total recognized in other comprehensive loss	$	1,156	$	925	$	753
Total recognized in net periodic benefit cost and other comprehensive loss	$	4,058	$	3,394	$	2,683
WEIGHTED-AVERAGE ASSUMPTIONS USED:						
Discount rate to determine benefit obligations		5.60%		6.75%		5.75%
Discount rate to determine net periodic pension cost		6.75%		5.75%		5.75%
Rate of compensation increase[1]		4.50%		4.50%		4.50%

[1] Rate of compensation is used for determining the benefit obligation and net periodic pension cost.

The estimated net loss and prior service cost for the defined benefit pension plan that will be amortized from accumulated other comprehensive loss into net periodic benefit cost over the next fiscal year are $544,000 and $74,000, respectively. The estimated net loss and prior service cost for the other postretirement plan that will be amortized from accumulated other comprehensive loss into net periodic benefit cost over the next fiscal year are $14,000 and $17,000, respectively.

The discount rates were determined by matching a published set of zero coupon yields and associated durations to expected plan benefit payment streams to obtain an implicit internal rate of return.

Long-term Incentive Deferred Compensation Plan

We have a long-term incentive deferred compensation plan established for the purpose of providing long-term incentives to a select group of management, with liabilities of $0.9 million as of January 30, 2010 and $0.6 million at January 31, 2009. The plan is a non-qualified, defined contribution plan and is not funded. Participants in this plan include all employees designated by us as Vice President, or other higher-ranking positions that are not participants in the SERP. We record annual monetary credits to each participant's account based on compensation levels and years as a participant in the plan. Annual interest credits are applied to the balance of each participant's account based upon established benchmarks. Each annual credit is subject to a three-year cliff-vesting schedule, and participants' accounts will be fully vested upon retirement after completing five years of service and attaining age 55.

Postretirement Benefit Plan

We have a postretirement benefit plan for certain executives that provides retiree medical and dental benefits. The plan is an other post-employment benefit plan and is not funded. We have recorded non-current liabilities of $0.9 million as of January 30, 2010 and $0.7 million as of January 31, 2009 for the accumulated postretirement benefit obligation. Pension expense and the liability related to this plan was not material to our consolidated financial statements for any period presented.

We expect to contribute approximately $17.6 million to the SERP and $19,000 to the Postretirement Benefit Plan in fiscal 2010. The amount of cash contributions we are required to make to the plans could increase or decrease depending on when employees make retirement elections and other factors which are not in the control of the Company. Our expected cash contributions to the plans are equal to the expected benefit payments as shown in the table below.

Future benefit payments are expected to be (in thousands):

	SERP Plan	Postretirement Benefit Plan
2010	$ 17,598	$ 19
2011	—	21
2012	—	23
2013	—	22
2014	—	20
Years 2015-2019	5,162	182

12. Stock Repurchase Program

We repurchase our common stock from time to time under a stock repurchase program. The repurchase program may be modified or terminated by the Board of Directors at any time, and there is no expiration date for the program. The extent and timing of repurchases will depend upon general business and market conditions, stock prices, opening and closing of the stock trading window, and liquidity and capital resource requirements going forward. During fiscal 2009, we repurchased 7.6 million shares for $174.3 million, as compared to repurchases of 0.3 million shares for $6.7 million during fiscal 2008 and 17.5 million shares for $266.7 million during fiscal 2007. On December 7, 2009, our Board of Directors approved a $250.0 million increase in repurchase availability under the program, bringing total repurchase authorization, since inception of the program, to $850.0 million. As of January 30, 2010, we have approximately $202.8 million of repurchase authorization remaining under our $850.0 million share repurchase program.

13. Income Taxes

Domestic and foreign pretax income are as follows (in thousands):

	Fiscal		
	2009	2008	2007
Domestic	$ 376,773	$ 249,726	$ 210,016
Foreign	6,033	(917)	(1,013)
Total income before provision for income taxes	$ 382,806	$ 248,809	$ 209,003

The provision for income taxes consists of the following (in thousands):

	Fiscal		
	2009	2008	2007
Current:			
Federal	$ 127,119	$ 78,823	$ 77,489
State and local	28,865	17,376	15,227
Foreign	1,535	166	80
	157,519	96,365	92,796
Deferred:			
Federal	(3,204)	4,012	(8,831)
State and local	(1,479)	(756)	(3,775)
Foreign	513	(234)	(384)
	(4,170)	3,022	(12,990)
	$ 153,349	$ 99,387	$ 79,806

Reconciliation of the U.S. statutory tax rate with our effective tax rate is summarized as follows:

	Fiscal		
	2009	2008	2007
Federal statutory rate	35.0%	35.0%	35.0%
Increase (decrease) in tax resulting from:			
State income taxes, net of federal tax benefits	4.5	4.2	3.6
Other	0.6	0.7	(0.4)
Effective rate	40.1%	39.9%	38.2%

The components of the net deferred income tax assets are as follows (in thousands):

	January 30, 2010	January 31, 2009
Current:		
Inventory	$ 1,889	$ 1,212
Unredeemed gift cards	1,119	1,261
Accrued compensation	9,766	7,597
Retirement benefit plan liabilities	6,985	—
Other	1,924	675
	$ 21,683	$ 10,745
Non-current:		
Furniture, equipment and improvements	$ (12,686)	$ (11,813)
Retirement benefit plan liabilities	3,844	8,901
Stock-based compensation	9,810	6,887
Deferred rent and tenant allowances	1,925	3,720
Net operating loss carry-forwards ("NOL's")	2,147	2,364
Valuation allowances for NOL's	(281)	(551)
Other	1,624	3,001
	6,383	12,509
Net deferred income tax assets	$ 28,066	$ 23,254

As of January 30, 2010, we had approximately $40.5 million of NOL's from certain states that were generated principally by our Jimmy'Z subsidiary that will expire between 2011 and 2030. We have recorded valuation allowances against certain of these NOL's. Subsequent recognition of these deferred tax assets that were previously reduced by valuation allowances would result in an income tax benefit in the period of such recognition.

We have not recognized any United States ("U.S.") tax expense on undistributed foreign earnings as they are intended to be indefinitely reinvested outside of the U.S.

We follow the provisions of FASB ASC Topic 740, "Income Taxes" ("ASC 740"), which clarifies the accounting and disclosure for uncertainty in income taxes. On February 4, 2007, the first day of our 2007 fiscal year, we recorded a decrease to beginning retained earnings of approximately $0.2 million and correspondingly increased our liabilities for uncertain tax positions and related interest and penalties. In addition, we recorded liabilities of $10.7 million for uncertain tax positions inclusive of interest and penalties. Also as of February 4, 2007, we recorded deferred tax assets of $7.9 million for federal and state benefits related to the uncertain tax positions. Net uncertain tax positions inclusive of interest and penalties of $2.8 million as of the adoption date, $2.4 million as of February 2, 2008, $2.6 million as of January 31, 2009 and $4.9 million as of January 30, 2010, would favorably impact our effective tax rate if these net liabilities were reversed. As of January 30, 2010, $1.0 million of uncertain tax positions were classified in accrued expenses.

We recognize interest and, if applicable, penalties, which could be assessed, related to uncertain tax positions in income tax expense. As of February 4, 2007, the total amount of accrued interest and penalties was $1.7 million before federal and, if applicable, state effect. We recorded approximately $0.9 million, $0.3 million and $0.2 million in additional interest and penalties, before federal and, if applicable, state tax effect in fiscal 2009, 2008 and 2007, respectively. We had liabilities for accrued interest and penalties of $1.6 million as of January 30, 2010 and $0.7 million as of January 31, 2009.

Below is a reconciliation of the beginning and ending amount of the gross unrecognized tax benefits relating to uncertain tax positions, which are recorded in our Consolidated Balance Sheets.

	Unrecognized Tax Benefits (In thousands)
Balance at February 4, 2007	$ 8,956
Increases due to tax positions related to prior years	94
Increases due to tax positions related to current year	448
Increases due to settlements with taxing authorities	286
Decreases due to tax positions related to prior years	(78)
Decreases due to expiration of statute of limitations	(112)
Balance at February 2, 2008	9,594
Increases due to tax positions related to prior years	485
Increases due to tax positions related to current year	316
Increases due to settlements with taxing authorities	229
Decreases due to settlements with taxing authorities	(8,487)
Decreases due to tax positions related to prior years	(180)
Decreases due to expiration of statute of limitations	(20)
Balance at January 31, 2009	1,937
Increases due to tax positions related to prior years	1,312
Increases due to tax positions related to current year	139
Decreases due to tax positions related to prior years	(20)
Decreases due to expiration of statute of limitations	(84)
Balance at January 30, 2010	$ 3,284

We file U.S. and Canadian federal, various state and provincial income tax returns. Our U.S. federal filings for the years 2002 through 2005 were examined by the IRS and were settled in the fourth quarter of fiscal 2007. We paid approximately $7.7 million relating to this settlement in the first quarter of fiscal 2008. This liability was included in the above balance of uncertain tax position liabilities at February 2, 2008. The examination liability related to the timing of taxable revenue from unredeemed gift cards. Our 2006 and 2007 returns are currently under audit by the IRS. Currently, no significant issues have been identified and we expect the audit to be completed by the end of 2010. All tax returns remain open for examination generally for our 2005 through 2007 tax years by various taxing authorities. However, certain states may keep their statute open for six to ten years.

14. Commitments and Contingencies

Leases — We are committed under non-cancelable leases for our entire store, distribution centers and office space locations, which generally provide for minimum rent plus additional increases in real estate taxes, certain operating expenses, etc. Certain leases also require contingent rent based on sales.

The aggregate minimum annual real estate rent commitments as of January 30, 2010 are as follows (in thousands):

Due in Fiscal Year	Total
2010	$ 106,736
2011	106,437
2012	100,441
2013	93,678
2014	83,712
Thereafter	235,844
Total	$ 726,848

Additionally, as of January 30, 2010, we were committed to equipment leases in aggregate of $6.6 million through fiscal 2013.

Rental expense consists of the following (in thousands):

	Fiscal		
	2009	2008	2007
Minimum rentals for stores	$ 97,889	$ 88,040	$ 77,640
Contingent rentals	23,809	18,793	13,384
Office space rentals	3,921	3,914	2,819
Distribution centers rentals	3,181	3,181	3,080
Equipment rentals	3,070	1,981	1,234

Employment Agreements — As of January 30, 2010, we had outstanding employment agreements with certain members of our senior management totaling $7.0 million. These employment agreements expire at February 12, 2012, except for the advisory role agreement with our Chairman and former Chief Executive Officer, which expires at the end of fiscal 2010.

Legal Proceedings — In January 2008, we learned that the SEC had issued a formal order of investigation with respect to matters arising from the activities of Christopher L. Finazzo, our former Executive Vice President and Chief Merchandising Officer. The SEC's investigation is a non-public, fact-finding inquiry to determine whether any violations of law have occurred. We are cooperating fully with the SEC in its investigation.

In November 2007, we entered into an agreement (the "Agreement") with Mr. Finazzo settling disputes between us. In the fourth quarter of fiscal 2007, pursuant to the terms of the Agreement, Mr. Finazzo paid us $5.0 million, and in turn, we paid Mr. Finazzo, simultaneously with his payment to us, approximately $0.9 million, which represented the value of Mr. Finazzo's benefits under our Supplemental Executive Retirement Plan. We recorded net other operating income of approximately $4.1 million in the fourth quarter of fiscal 2007.

In November 2006, we announced that Mr. Finazzo had been terminated for cause, based upon information uncovered by management and after an independent investigation was conducted at the direction, and under the supervision, of a special committee of our Board of Directors. The investigation revealed that Mr. Finazzo:

- concealed from management and our Board of Directors, and failed to disclose in corporate disclosure documents, his personal ownership interests in, and officer positions of, certain corporate entities affiliated with one of our primary vendors at the time, South Bay Apparel, Inc.,

- without the knowledge or authorization of our management, executed a corporate Guaranty Agreement in March 1999, that, had it been enforceable, would have obligated us to guarantee any payments due from South Bay Apparel, Inc. to Tricot Richelieu, Inc., an apparel manufacturer and vendor to South Bay Apparel, Inc., and

- failed to disclose unauthorized business relationships and transactions between immediate and extended family members of Mr. Finazzo and certain other of our vendors.

In December 2006, we entered into an agreement with South Bay Apparel, Inc. and Douglas Dey, South Bay Apparel, Inc.'s President, whereby the parties resolved certain outstanding matters between them. As such, South Bay Apparel, Inc. paid us $8.0 million, representing (i) a concession of $7.1 million by South Bay Apparel, Inc. and Mr. Dey concerning prior purchases of merchandise by us, which was reflected as a reduction in the cost of merchandise in fiscal 2006, and (ii) reimbursement by South Bay Apparel, Inc. of $0.9 million, which offset professional fees that we incurred associated with the negotiation of the Agreement and the investigation of the underlying facts associated with those outstanding matters. In addition, South Bay Apparel, Inc. and Mr. Dey reduced the price of merchandise sold to us to a price that we believed represented fair value, based on costs of comparable merchandise. We also agreed to purchase excess merchandise held at the time by South Bay Apparel, Inc. Once the excess inventory was fully depleted during the third quarter of fiscal 2007, we ceased doing business with South Bay Apparel Inc.

We are also party to various litigation matters and proceedings in the ordinary course of business. In the opinion of our management, dispositions of these matters are not expected to have a material adverse affect on our financial position, results of operations or cash flows.

Guarantees — We had no financial guarantees outstanding at January 30, 2010. We had no commercial commitments outstanding as of January 30, 2010.

15.   Selected Quarterly Financial Data (Unaudited)

The following table sets forth certain unaudited quarterly financial information (in thousands, except per share amounts):

	13 Weeks Ended			
	May 2, 2009	August 1, 2009	October 31, 2009	January 30, 2010
Fiscal 2009				
Net sales	$ 408,024	$ 453,020	$ 567,838	$ 801,223
Gross profit	147,890	165,692	222,917	310,648
Net income	31,675	38,589	62,629	96,564
Basic earnings per share	0.31	0.38	0.62	1.00
Diluted earnings per share	0.31	0.38	0.61	0.99

	13 Weeks Ended			
	May 3, 2008	August 2, 2008	November 1, 2008	January 31, 2009
Fiscal 2008				
Net sales	$ 336,332	$ 377,145	$ 482,037	$ 690,017
Gross profit	111,278	125,936	173,451	243,517
Net income	17,498	21,053	42,646	68,225
Basic earnings per share	0.17	0.21	0.43	0.68
Diluted earnings per share	0.17	0.21	0.42	0.67

GLOSSARY

A

absorption costing – a product-costing method that assigns all manufacturing costs to units of product: direct materials, direct labor, variable overhead, and fixed overhead.

account – a record of increases and decreases in each of the basic elements of the financial statements (each of the company's asset, liability, stockholders' equity, revenue, expense, gain, and loss items).

account payable – an obligation that arises when a business purchases goods or services on credit.

account receivable – money due from another business or individual as payment for services performed or goods delivered. Payment is typically due in 30 to 60 days and does not involve a formal note between the parties nor does it include interest.

accounting – the process of identifying, measuring, recording, and communicating financial information about a company's activities so decision makers can make informed decisions.

accounting cycle – the procedures that a company uses to transform the results of its business activities into financial statements.

accounting rate of return – the rate of return obtained by dividing the average accounting net income by the original investment (or by average investment).

accounting system – the methods and records used to identify, measure, record, and communicate financial information about a business.

accounts receivable turnover ratio – a ratio that measures the liquidity of receivables. It is computed by dividing net sales by average accounts receivable.

accrual accounting – see *accrual-basis accounting*

accrual-basis accounting – a method of accounting in which revenues are generally recorded when earned (rather than when cash is received) and expenses are matched to the periods in which they help produce revenues (rather than when cash is paid).

accrued expenses – previously unrecorded expenses that have been incurred, but not yet paid in cash.

accrued liabilities – liabilities that usually represent the completed portion of activities that are in process at the end of the period.

accrued revenues – previously unrecorded revenues that have been earned but for which no cash has yet been received.

accumulated depreciation – the total amount of depreciation expense that has been recorded for an asset since the asset was acquired. It is reported on the balance sheet as a contra-asset.

accumulated other comprehensive income – the total of comprehensive income for all periods and conveys the changes in assets and liabilities resulting from all transactions with nonowners.

accumulating costs – the way that costs are measured and recorded.

activity – action taken or work performed by equipment or people for other people.

activity analysis – the process of identifying, describing, and evaluating the activities an organization performs.

activity attributes – nonfinancial and financial information items that describe individual activities.

activity-based budgeting system (ABB) – a budget system that focuses on estimating the costs of activities rather than the costs of departments and plants and the use of multiple drivers, both unit-based and nonunit-based.

activity-based costing (ABC) system – a cost assignment approach that first uses direct and driver tracing to assign costs to activities and then uses drivers to assign costs to cost objects.

activity-based management – a systemwide, integrated approach that focuses management's attention on activities with the objective of improving customer value and the profit achieved by providing this value. It includes driver analysis, activity analysis, and performance evaluation, and draws on activity-based costing as a major source of information.

activity dictionary – a list of activities described by specific attributes such as name, definition, classification as primary or secondary, and activity driver.

activity drivers – factors that measure the consumption of activities by products and other cost objects.

activity elimination – the process of eliminating nonvalue-added activities.

activity flexible budgeting – predicting what activity costs will be as activity usage changes.

activity inputs – the resources consumed by an activity in producing its output (they are the factors that enable the activity to be performed).

activity output – the result or product of an activity.

activity output measure – the number of times an activity is performed. It is the quantifiable measure of the output.

activity reduction – decreasing the time and resources required by an activity.

activity selection – the process of choosing among sets of activities caused by competing strategies.

activity sharing – increasing the efficiency of necessary activities by using economies of scale.

actual cost system – an approach that assigns actual costs of direct materials, direct labor, and overhead to products.

additional paid-in capital – the amount received in excess of the par value.

adjusted cost of goods sold – the cost of goods sold after all adjustments for overhead variances are made.

adjusted trial balance – an updated trial balance that reflects the changes to account balances as the result of adjusting entries.

adjusting entries – journal entries that are made at the end of an accounting period to record the completed portion of partially completed transactions.

administrative costs – all costs associated with research, development, and general administration of the organization that cannot reasonably be assigned to either selling or production.

aging method – a method in which bad debt expense is estimated indirectly by determining the ending balance desired in the allowance for doubtful accounts and then computing the necessary adjusting entry to achieve this balance; the amount of this adjusting entry is also the amount of bad debt expense.

allocation – when an indirect cost is assigned to a cost object using a reasonable and convenient method.

allowance for doubtful accounts – a contra-asset account that is established to "store" the estimate of uncollectible accounts until specific accounts are identified as uncollectible.

amortization – the process whereby companies systematically allocate the cost of their intangible operating assets as an expense among the accounting periods in which the asset is used and the benefits are received.

annuity – a series of equal cash flows at regular intervals.

applied overhead – overhead assigned to production using predetermined rates.

appraisal costs – cost incurred to determine whether products and services are conforming to requirements.

articles of incorporation – a document that authorizes the creation of the corporation, setting forth its name, purpose, and the names of the incorporators.

asset efficiency ratios (operating ratios) – ratios that measure how efficiently a company uses its assets.

asset turnover ratio – a ratio that measures the efficiency with which a corporation's assets (usually accounts receivable or inventory) are used to produce sales revenues.

assets – economic resources representing expected future economic benefits controlled by the business (e.g., cash, accounts receivable, inventory, land, buildings, equipment, and intangible assets).

assigning costs – the way that a cost is linked to some cost object.

audit report – the auditor's opinion as to whether the company's financial statements are fairly stated in accordance with generally accepted accounting principles (GAAP).

authorized shares – the maximum number of shares a company may issue in each class of stock.

average age of fixed assets – a rough estimate of the age of fixed assets that can be computed by dividing accumulated depreciation by depreciation expense.

average cost method – an inventory costing method that allocates the cost of goods available for sale between ending inventory and cost of goods sold based on a weighted average cost per unit.

average days to sell inventory – an estimate of the number of days it takes a company to sell its inventory. It is found by dividing 365 days by the inventory turnover ratio.

B

bad debt expense – the expense that results from receivables that are not paid.

balance sheet – a financial statement that reports the resources (assets) owned by a company and the claims against those resources (liabilities and stockholders' equity) at a specific point in time.

balanced scorecard – a strategic management system that defines a strategic-based responsibility accounting system. The Balanced Score-card translates an organization's mission and strategy into operational objectives and performance measures for four different perspectives: the financial perspective, the customer perspective, the internal business process perspective, and the learning and growth (infrastructure) perspective.

bank reconciliation – the process of reconciling any differences between a company's accounting records and the bank's accounting records.

beginning work-in-process (BWIP) – consists of work done on partially completed units that represents prior-period work with the costs assigned to them being prior-period costs. Uses two approaches for dealing with the prior-period output and costs found in BWIP: the weighted average method and the FIFO method.

bond – a type of note that requires the issuing entity to pay the face value of the bond to the holder when it matures and, usually, periodic interest at a specified rate.

book value (carrying value) – the value of an asset or liability as it appears on the balance sheet. Book value is calculated as the cost of the asset or liability minus the balance in its related contra-account (e.g., cost of equipment less accumulated depreciation; notes payable less discount on notes payable).

break-even point – the point where total sales revenue equals total cost; at this point, neither profit nor loss is earned.

budget committee – a committee responsible for setting budgetary policies and goals, reviewing and approving the budget, and resolving any differences that may arise in the budgetary process.

budget director – the individual responsible for coordination and directing the overall budgeting process.

budgetary slack – the process of padding the budget by overestimating costs and underestimating revenues.

budgets – plans of action expressed in financial terms.

business process risks – threats to the internal processes of a company.

C

callable bonds – bonds that give the borrower the right to pay off (or call) the bonds prior to their due date. The borrower typically "calls" debt when the interest rate being paid is much higher than the current market conditions.

capital – a company's assets less its liabilities. Capital is also known as stockholders' equity.

capital budgeting – the process of making capital investment decisions.

capital expenditures – expenditures to acquire long-term assets or extend the life, expand the productive capacity, increase the efficiency, or improve the quality of existing long-term assets.

capital investment decisions – the process of planning, setting goals and priorities, arranging financing, and identifying criteria for making long-term investments.

capital lease – a noncancelable agreement that is in substance a purchase of the leased asset.

capital stock – the portion of a corporation's stockholders' equity contributed by investors (owners) in exchange for shares of stock.

carrying costs – the costs of holding inventory.

cash-basis accounting – a method of accounting in which revenue is recorded when cash is received, regardless of when it is actually earned. Similarly, an expense is recorded when cash is paid, regardless of when it is actually incurred. Cash-basis accounting does not tie recognition of revenues and expenses to the actual business activity but rather to the exchange of cash.

cash budget – a detailed plan that outlines all sources and uses of cash.

cash equivalents – highly liquid investments such as treasury bills, money market funds, and commercial paper.

cash flow adequacy ratio – the cash flow adequacy ratio provides a measure of the company's ability to meet its debt obligations and is calculated as: Cash Flow Adequacy = Free Cash Flow ÷ Average Amount of Debt Maturing over the Next Five Years.

cash flows from financing activities – any cash flow related to obtaining resources from creditors or owners, which includes the issuance and repayment of debt, common and preferred stock transactions, and the payment of dividends.

cash flows from investing activities – the cash inflows and outflows that relate to acquiring and disposing of operating assets, acquiring and selling investments (current and long-term), and lending money and collecting loans.

cash flows from operating activities – any cash flows directly related to earning income, including cash sales and collections of accounts receivable as well as cash payments for goods, services, salaries, and interest.

cash over and short – an account that records the discrepancies between deposited amounts of actual cash received and the total of the cash register tape.

cash ratio – a short-term liquidity ratio that is calculated as: (Cash + Short-Term Investments) ÷ Current Liabilities.

causal factors – activities or variables that invoke service costs. Generally, it is desirable to use causal factors as the basis for allocating service costs.

certified internal auditor (CIA) – the CIA has passed a comprehensive examination designed to ensure technical competence and has two years' experience.

certified management accountant (CMA) – a certified management accountant has passed a rigorous qualifying examination, met an experience requirement, and participates in continuing education.

certified public accountant (CPA) – a certified accountant who is permitted (by law) to serve as an external auditor. CPAs must pass a national examination and be licensed by the state in which they practice.

chart of accounts – the list of accounts used by a company.

coefficient of determination (R^2) – the percentage of total variability in a dependent variable that is explained by an independent variable. It assumes a value between 0 and 1.

committed fixed cost – a fixed cost that cannot be easily changed.

common costs – the costs of resources used in the output of two or more services or products.

common fixed expenses – fixed expenses that cannot be directly traced to individual segments and that are unaffected by the elimination of any one segment.

common stock – the basic ownership interest in a corporation. Owners of common stock have the right to vote in the election of the board of directors, share in the profits and dividends of the company, keep the same percentage of ownership if new stock is issued (preemptive right), and share in the assets in liquidation in proportion to their holdings.

common-size statements – financial statements that express each financial statement line item in percentage terms.

comparability – one of the four qualitative characteristics that useful information should possess. Information has comparability if it allows comparisons to be made between companies.

compound interest – a method of calculating the time value of money in which interest is earned on the previous periods' interest.

compounding of interest – paying interest on interest.

conservatism principle – a principle which states that when more than one equally acceptable accounting method exists, the method that results in the lower assets and revenues or higher liabilities and expenses should be selected.

consignment – an arrangement where goods owned by one party are held and offered for sale by another.

consistency – one of the four qualitative characteristics that useful information should possess. Consistency refers to the application of the same accounting principles by a single company over time.

constraints – mathematical expressions that express resource limitations.

consumption ratio – the proportion of an overhead activity consumed by a product.

contingent liability – an obligation whose amount or timing is uncertain and depends on future events. For example, a firm may be contingently liable for damages under a lawsuit that has yet to be decided by the courts.

continuity (or going concern) assumption – one of the four basic assumptions that underlie accounting that assumes a company will continue to operate long enough to carry out its existing commitments.

continuous budget – a moving 12-month budget with a future month added as the current month expires.

continuous improvement – searching for ways to increase the overall efficiency and productivity of activities by reducing waste, increasing quality, and reducing costs.

contra accounts – accounts that have a balance that is opposite of the balance in the related account.

contract rate – see *interest rate*

contribution margin – sales revenue minus total variable cost or price minus unit variable cost.

contribution margin income statement – the income statement format that is based on the separation of costs into fixed and variable components.

contribution margin ratio – contribution margin divided by sales revenue. It is the proportion of each sales dollar available to cover fixed costs and provide for profit.

control – the process of setting standards, receiving feedback on actual performance, and taking corrective action whenever actual performance deviates significantly from planned performance.

control activities – activities performed by an organization to prevent or detect poor quality (because poor quality may exist).

control costs – costs incurred from performing control activities.

control environment – the collection of environmental factors that influence the effectiveness of control procedures such as the philosophy and operating style of management, the personnel policies and practices of the business, and the overall integrity, attitude, awareness, and actions of everyone in the business concerning the importance of control.

control limits – the maximum allowable deviation from a standard.

controllable costs – costs that managers have the power to influence.

controller – the chief accounting officer in an organization.

controlling – the managerial activity of monitoring a plan's implementation and taking corrective action as needed.

conversion cost – the sum of direct labor cost and overhead cost.

convertible bonds – bonds that allow the bondholder to convert the bond into another security—typically common stock.

copyright – an intangible asset that grants the holder the right to publish, sell, or control a literary or artistic work. The legal life is the life of author plus 70 years.

core objectives and measures – those objectives and measures common to most organizations.

corporate charter – see *articles of incorporation*

corporation – a company chartered by the state to conduct business as an "artificial person" and owned by one or more stockholders.

cost – the amount of cash or cash equivalent sacrificed for goods and/ or services that are expected to bring a current or future benefit to the organization.

cost behavior – the way in which a cost changes when the level of output changes.

cost center – a division of a company that is evaluated on the basis of cost.

cost constraint – qualitative characteristic of useful information that states that the benefit received from accounting information should be greater than the cost of providing that information.

cost object – any item such as products, customers, departments, projects, and so on, for which costs are measured and assigned.

cost of capital – the cost of investment funds, usually viewed as a weighted average of the costs of funds from all sources.

cost of goods available for sale – the sum of the cost of beginning inventory and the cost of purchases.

cost of goods manufactured – the total product cost of goods completed during the current period.

cost of goods sold – an expense that represents the outflow of resources caused by the sale of inventory. This is often computed as the cost of goods available for sale less the cost of ending inventory.

cost of goods sold budget – the estimated costs for the units sold.

cost reconciliation – the final section of the production report that compares the costs to account for with the costs accounted for to ensure that they are equal.

cost structure – a company's mix of fixed costs relative to variable costs.

cost-volume-profit (CVP) analysis – a decision-making and planning tool that estimates how changes in costs (both variable and fixed), sales volume, and prices affect a company's profit.

cost-volume-profit graph – a graph that depicts the relationships among costs, volume, and profits. It consists of a total revenue line and a total cost line.

costs of quality – costs incurred because poor quality may exist or because poor quality does exist.

coupon rate – see *interest rate*

credit – the right side of a T account; alternatively, credit may refer to the act of entering an amount on the right side of an account.

credit cards – a card that authorizes the holder to make purchases up to some limit from specified retailers. Credits cards are a special form of factoring in which the issuer of the credit card pays the seller the amount of each sale less a service charge and then collects the full amount of the sale from the buyer at some later date.

creditor – the person to whom money is owed.

cross sectional analysis – a type of analysis that compares one corporation to another corporation and to industry averages.

cumulative dividend preference – a provision that requires the eventual payment of all preferred dividends–both dividends in arrears and current dividends–to preferred stockholders before any dividends are paid to common stockholders.

current assets – cash and other assets that are reasonably expected to be converted into cash within one year or one operating cycle, whichever is longer.

current dividend preference – a provision that requires that current dividends must be paid to preferred stockholders before any dividends are paid to common stockholders.

current liabilities – obligations that require a firm to pay cash or another current asset, create a new current liability, or provide goods or services within one year or one operating cycle, whichever is longer.

current ratio – a measure of liquidity that is computed as: Current Assets – Current Liabilities.

customer perspective – a balanced scorecard viewpoint that defines the customer and market segments in which the business will compete.

D

date of record – the date on which a stockholder must own one or more shares of stock in order to receive the dividend.

debenture bonds – another name for unsecured bonds.

debit – the left side of a T account; alternatively, debit may refer to the act of entering an amount on the left side of an account.

debit card – a card that authorizes a bank to make an immediate electronic withdrawal (debit) from the holder's bank account and a corresponding deposit to another party's account.

debt management ratios – a type of ratio that provides information on two aspects of debt: (1) the relative mix of debt and equity financing (often referred to as its capital structure) and (2) the corporation's ability to meet its debt obligations through operations because interest and principal payments must be made as scheduled, or a company can be declared bankrupt.

debt-to-equity ratio – a measure of the proportion of capital provided by creditors relative to that provided by stockholders. This ratio is calculated as: Total Liabilities ÷ Total Equity.

debt-to-total assets ratio – a measure of the proportion of capital provided by creditors. This ratio is calculated as: Total Liabilities ÷ Total Assets.

decentralization – the granting of decision-making freedom to lower operating levels.

decision making – the process of choosing among competing alternatives.

decision model – a specific set of procedures that, when followed, produces a decision.

declaration date – the date on which a corporation announces its intention to pay a dividend on common stock.

declining balance depreciation method – an accelerated depreciation method that produces a declining amount of depreciation expense each period by multiplying the declining book value of an asset by a constant depreciation rate. Declining balance depreciation expense for each period of an asset's useful life equals the declining balance rate times the asset's book value (cost less accumulated depreciation) at the beginning of the period.

deferred (or prepaid) expenses – asset arising from the payment of cash which has not been used or consumed by the end of the period.

deferred (or unearned) revenues – liability arising from the receipt of cash for which revenue has not yet been earned.

deficit – the accumulated losses over the entire life of a corporation that have not been paid out in dividends.

degree of operating leverage (DOL) – a measure of the sensitivity of profit changes to changes in sales volume. It measures the percentage change in profits resulting from a percentage change in sales.

departmental overhead rate – estimated overhead for a single department divided by the estimated activity level for that same department.

dependent variable – a variable whose value depends on the value of another variable.

depletion – the process of allocating the cost of a natural resource to each period in which the resource is removed from the earth.

deposit in transit – an amount received and recorded by a company, but which has not been recorded by the bank in time to appear on the current bank statement.

depreciable cost – depreciable cost is calculated as the cost of the asset less its residual (or salvage) value. This amount will be depreciated (expensed) over the asset's useful life.

depreciation – the process whereby companies systematically allocate the cost of their tangible operating assets (other than land) as an expense in each period in which the asset is used.

depreciation expense – the amount of depreciation recorded on the income statement.

differential cost – the difference in total cost between the alternatives in a decision.

direct costs – costs that can be easily and accurately traced to a cost object.

direct fixed expenses – fixed costs that are directly traceable to a given segment and, consequently, disappear if the segment is eliminated.

direct labor – the labor that can be directly traced to the goods or services being produced.

direct labor budget – a budget showing the total direct labor hours needed and the associated cost for the number of units in the production budget.

direct materials – materials that are a part of the final product and can be directly traced to the goods or services being produced.

direct materials purchases budget – a budget that outlines the expected usage of materials production and purchases of the direct materials required.

direct method – a method of computing net cash flow from operating activities by adjusting each item on the income statement by the changes in the related current asset or liability accounts. Typical cash flow categories reported are cash collected from customers, cash paid to suppliers, cash paid to employees, cash paid for interest, and cash paid for taxes.

discount – when a bond sells at a price below face value, due to the yield being greater than the stated rate of interest.

discount factor – the factor used to convert a future cash flow to its present value.

discount period – the reduced payment period associated with purchase discounts.

discount rate – the rate of return used to compute the present value of future cash flows.

discounted cash flows – future cash flows expressed in present-value terms.

discounting – the act of finding the present value of future cash flows.

discounting models – capital investment models that explicitly consider the time value of money in identifying criteria for accepting and rejecting proposed projects.

discretionary fixed costs – fixed costs that can be changed relatively easily at management discretion.

dividend – amounts paid periodically by a corporation to its stockholders as a return of their invested capital. Dividends represent a distribution of retained earnings, not an expense.

dividend payout ratio – a ratio that measures the proportion of a corporation's profits that are returned to the stockholders immediately as dividends. It is calculated as: Common Dividends ÷ Net Income.

dividend yield ratio – a ratio that measures the rate at which dividends provide a return to stockholders, by comparing dividends with the market price of a share of stock. It is calculated as: Dividends per Common Share ÷ Closing Market Price per Share for the Year.

dividends in arrears – cumulative preferred stock dividends remaining unpaid for one or more years are considered to be in arrears.

double-entry accounting – a type of accounting in which the two-sided effect that every transaction has on the accounting equation is recorded in the accounting system.

driver – a factor that causes or leads to a change in a cost or an activity; a driver is an output measure.

driver analysis – the effort expended to identify those factors that are the root causes of activity costs.

dupont analysis – a type of analysis that recognizes that ROE can be broken down into three important components—net profit margin, asset turnover, and leverage.

dysfunctional behavior – individual behavior that conflicts with the goals of the organization.

E

earned – one of two requirements for the recognition of revenue. Revenues are considered "earned" when the earnings process is substantially complete. This typically happens when the goods are delivered or the service is provided.

earnings per share (EPS) – a ratio that measures the income available for common stockholders on a per-share basis. EPS is calculated as net income less preferred dividends divided by the average number of common shares outstanding.

economic entity assumption – one of the four basic assumptions that underlie accounting that assumes each company is accounted for separately from its owners.

economic value added (EVA) – a performance measure that is calculated by taking the after-tax operating profit minus the total annual cost of capital.

effective interest rate method – a method of interest amortization that is based on compound interest calculations.

ending finished goods inventory budget – a budget that describes planned ending inventory of finished goods in units and dollars.

ending work-in–process (EWIP) – inventory that is not complete and attaching a unit cost to it requires defining the output of the period. A unit completed and transferred out during the period is not identical (or equivalent) to one in EWIP inventory, and the cost attached to the two units should not be the same.

environmental costs – costs that are incurred because poor environmental quality exists or may exist.

environmental detection costs – costs incurred to detect poor environmental performance.

environmental external failure costs – costs incurred after contaminants are introduced into the environment.

environmental internal failure costs – costs incurred after contaminants are produced but before they are introduced into the environment.

environmental prevention costs – costs incurred to prevent damage to the environment.

equity – see *stockholders' equity*

equivalent units of output – complete units that could have been produced given the total amount of manufacturing effort expended during the period.

ethical behavior – choosing actions that are right, proper, and just.

events – events make up the multitude of activities in which companies engage. External events result from exchange between the company and another outside entity, and internal events result from a company's own actions that do not involve other companies.

exercise (or strike) price – the price at which employees can buy stock when their employer when it grants stock options.

expenses – costs that are used up (expired) in the production of revenue.

external failure costs – costs incurred because products fail to conform to requirements after being sold to outside parties.

F

F.O.B. destination – a shipping arrangement in which ownership of inventory passes when the goods are delivered to the buyer.

F.O.B. shipping point – a shipping arrangement in which ownership of inventory passes from the seller to the buyer at the shipping point.

face value – the amount of money that a borrower must repay at maturity; also called par value or principal.

factor – a method of handling receivables in which the seller receives an immediate cash payment reduced by the factor's fees. The factor, the buyer of the receivables, acquires the right to collect the receivables and the risk of uncollectibility. In a typical factoring arrangement, the sellers of the receivables have no continuing responsibility for their collection.

failure activities – activities performed by an organization or its customers in response to poor quality (poor quality does exist).

failure costs – the costs incurred by an organization because failure activities are performed.

faithful representation – qualitative characteristic of information stipulating it should be complete, neutral, and free from error.

favorable (F) variances – variances produced whenever the actual amounts are less than the budgeted or standard allowances.

FIFO costing method – a process-costing method that separates units in beginning inventory from those produced during the current period. Unit costs include only current–period costs and production.

financial accounting – accounting and reporting to satisfy the outside demand (primarily investors and creditors) for accounting information.

Financial Accounting Standards Board (FASB) – the primary accounting standard-setter in the United States which has been granted this power to set standards by the Securities and Exchange Commission.

financial budgets – financial plans for the future that detail the inflows and outflows of cash and the overall financial position of a company. Include the cash budget, budgeted balance sheet, and budget for capital expenditures.

financial perspective – a balanced scorecard viewpoint that describes the financial consequences of actions taken in the other three perspectives.

financial statements – a set of standardized reports in which the detailed transactions of a company's activities are reported and summarized so they can be communicated to decision-makers.

finished goods inventory – the account in manufacturing firms that represents the cost of the final product that is available for sale.

first-in, first-out (FIFO) method – an inventory costing system in which the earliest (oldest) purchases (the first in) are assumed to be the first sold (the first out) and the more recent purchases are in ending inventory.

fiscal year – an accounting period that runs for one year.

fixed asset turnover ratio – a ratio that indicates how efficiently a company uses its fixed assets. This ratio is calculated by dividing net sales by average fixed assets.

fixed costs – costs that, in total, are constant within the relevant range as the level of output increases or decreases.

flexible budget – a budget that can specify costs for a range of activity.

flexible budget variance – the sum of price variances and efficiency variances in a performance report comparing actual costs to expected costs predicted by a flexible budget.

footnotes – notes to the financial statements that help clarify and expand upon the information presented in those statements.

Form 10-K – the annual report on Form 10-K provides a comprehensive overview of the corporation's business and financial condition and includes *audited* financial statements. Although similarly named, the annual report on Form 10-K is distinct from the "annual report to shareholders," which a corporation must send to its shareholders when it holds an annual meeting to elect directors. For larger filers the 10-K must be filed within 60 days of their fiscal year end.

Form 10-Q – the Form 10-Q includes *unaudited* financial statements and provides a continuing view of the corporation's financial position during the year. The report must be filed for each of the first three fiscal quarters of the corporation's fiscal year. For larger filers this must be done within 40 days of the end of the quarter.

Form 8-K – the "current report" companies must file with the SEC to announce major events that are important to investors and creditors.

franchise – an exclusive right to conduct a certain type of business in some particular geographic area.

free cash flow – the cash flow that a company is able to generate after considering the maintenance or expansion of its assets (capital expenditures) and the payment of dividends. Free cash flow is calculated as Net Cash Flow from Operating Activities – Capital Expenditures – Cash Dividends.

freight-in – the transportation costs that are normally paid by the buyer under F.O.B. shipping point terms.

freight-out – the transportation costs that the seller is usually responsible for paying under F.O.B. destination shipping terms.

full disclosure – a policy that requires any information that would make a difference to financial statement users to be revealed.

fundamental accounting equation – Assets = Liabilities + Stockholders' Equity. The left side of the accounting equation shows the assets, or economic resources of a company. The right side of the accounting equation indicates who has a claim on the company's assets.

future value – the value that will accumulate by the end of an investment's life if the investment earns a specified compounded return.

G

GAAP – see *generally accepted accounting principles*

general ledger – a collection of all the individual financial statement accounts that a company uses in its financial statements.

goal congruence – the alignment of a manager's personal goals with those of the organization.

goodwill – an unidentifiable intangible asset that arises from factors such as customer satisfaction, quality products, skilled employees, and business location.

gross margin (gross profit) – a key performance measure that is computed as sales revenue less cost of goods sold.

gross profit percentage – a measurement of the proportion of each sales dollar that is available to pay other expenses and provide profit for owners.

gross profit ratio – a measurement of the proportion of each sales dollar that is available to pay other expenses and provide profit for owners; it is computed by dividing gross margin by net sales.

H

high-low method – a method for separating mixed costs into fixed and variable components by using just the high and low data points. [*Note:* The high (low) data point corresponds to the high (low) output level.]

historical cost principle – a principle that requires the activities of a company to be initially measured at their cost—the exchange price at the time the activity occurs.

horizontal analysis – a type of analysis in which each financial statement line item is expressed as a percent of the base year (typically the first year shown).

hurdle rate – the rate that indicates the minimum ROI necessary to accept an investment.

I

impairment – a permanent decline in the future benefits or service potential of an asset.

incentives – the positive or negative measures taken by an organization to induce a manager to exert effort toward achieving the organization's goals.

income from operations – gross margin less operating expenses. This represents the results of the core operations of the business.

income statement – a financial statement that reports the profitability of a business over a specific period of time.

independent projects – projects that, if accepted or rejected, will not affect the cash flows of another project.

independent variable – a variable whose value does not depend on the value of another variable.

indifference point – the quantity at which two systems produce the same operating income.

indirect costs – costs that cannot be easily and accurately traced to a cost object.

indirect method – a method that computes operating cash flows by adjusting net income for items that do not affect cash flows.

intangible operating assets – assets that provide a benefit to a company over a number of years but lack physical substance. Examples of intangible assets include patents, copyrights, trademarks, and goodwill.

intercept – the fixed cost, representing the point where the cost formula intercepts the vertical axis.

interest – the excess of the total amount of money paid to a lender over the amount borrowed.

interest amortization – the process used to determine the amount of interest to be recorded in each of the periods a liability is outstanding.

interest period – is the time interval between interest calculations.

interest rate – a percentage of the principal that must be paid in order to have use of the principal. It is multiplied by the beginning-of-period balance to yield the amount of interest for the period.

internal business process perspective – a balanced scorecard viewpoint that describes the internal processes needed to provide value for customers and owners.

internal control system – the policies and procedures established by top management and the board of directors to provide reasonable assurance that the company's objectives are being met in three areas: (1) effectiveness and efficiency of operations, (2) reliability of financial reporting, and (3) compliance with applicable laws and regulations.

internal failure costs – costs incurred because products and services fail to conform to requirements where lack of conformity is discovered prior to external sale.

internal rate of return – the rate of return that equates the present value of a project's cash inflows with the present value of its cash outflows (i.e., it sets the NPV equal to zero). Also, the rate of return being earned on funds that remain internally invested in a project.

international accounting standards board (IASB) – an independent, privately-funded accounting standard-setting body with the goal of developing a single set of high-quality accounting standards that result in transparent and comparable information reported in general purpose financial statements.

international financial reporting standards (IFRS) – a general term that describes an international set of generally accepted accounting standards.

inventory – products held for resale that are classified as current assets on the balance sheet.

inventory turnover ratio – a ratio that describes how quickly inventory is purchased (or produced) and sold. It is calculated as cost of goods sold divided by average inventory.

investment center – a division of a company that is evaluated on the basis of return on investment.

involuntary disposal – a type of disposal that occurs when assets are lost or destroyed through theft, acts of nature, or by accident.

issued shares – the number of shares actually sold to stockholders.

J

job – one distinct unit or set of units for which the costs of production must be assigned.

job-order cost sheet – a subsidiary account to the work-in-process account on which the total costs of materials, labor, and overhead for a single job are accumulated.

job-order costing system – a costing system in which costs are collected and assigned to units of production for each individual job.

joint products – products that are inseparable prior to a split-off point. All manufacturing costs up to the split-off point are joint costs.

journal – a chronological record showing the debit and credit effects of transactions on a company.

journal entry – a record of a transaction that is made in a journal so that the entire effect of the transaction is contained in one place.

junk bonds – unsecured bonds where the risk of the borrower failing to make the payments is relatively high.

just-in-time (JIT) – a demand-pull system whose objective is to eliminate waste by producing a product only when it is needed and only in the quantities demanded by customers.

K

keep-or-drop decisions – relevant costing analyses that focus on keeping or dropping a segment of a business.

L

labor efficiency variance (LEV) – the difference between the actual direct labor hours used and the standard direct labor hours allowed multiplied by the standard hourly wage rate.

labor rate variance (LRV) – the difference between the actual hourly rate paid and the standard hourly rate multiplied by the actual hours worked.

last-in, first-out (LIFO) method – an inventory costing system that allocates the cost of goods available for sale between ending inventory and cost of goods sold based on the assumption that the most recent purchases (the last in) are the first to be sold (the first out).

lean accounting – an accounting practice that organizes costs according to the value chain by focusing primarily on the elimination of waste. The objective is to provide information to managers that support this effort and to provide financial statements that better reflect overall performance, using financial and nonfinancial information.

learning and growth (infrastructure) perspective – a balanced scorecard viewpoint that defines the capabilities that an organization needs to create long-term growth and improvement.

lease – an agreement that enables a company to use property without legally owning it.

lessee – one who uses an asset during the term of the lease.

lessor – the legal owner of an asset and retains substantially all of the risks and obligations of ownership.

leverage – the use of borrowed capital to produce more income than needed to pay the interest on a debt.

liabilities – probable future sacrifices of economic benefits; liabilities usually require the payment of cash, the transfer of assets other than cash, or the performance of services.

LIFO reserve – the amount that inventory would increase (or decrease) if the company had used FIFO.

line positions – positions that have direct responsibility for the basic objectives of an organization.

liquidating dividends – dividends that return paid-in capital to stockholders; liquidating dividends occur when retained earnings has been reduced to zero.

liquidity – a company's ability to pay obligations as they become due.

long-term debt – obligations that extend beyond one year.

long-term debt-to-equity ratio – a ratio that provides information on the proportion of capital provided by this type of debt and by stockholders. It is calculated as: Long-Term Debt (including current portion) ÷ Total Equity.

long-term debt-to-total assets ratio – a measure of the proportion of capital provided by long-term creditors which is calculated as: Long-Term Debt (including current portion) ÷ Total Assets.

long-term investments – investments that the company expects to hold for longer than one year. This includes land or buildings that a company is not currently using in operations, as well as debt and equity securities.

long-term liabilities – the obligations of the company that will require payment beyond one year or the operating cycle, whichever is longer.

lower of cost or market (LCM) rule – a rule that requires a company to reduce the carrying value of its inventory to its market value if the market value is lower than its cost.

M

make-or-buy decisions – relevant costing analyses that focus on whether a component should be made internally or purchased externally.

management's discussion and analysis (MD&A) – a section of the annual report that provides a discussion and explanation of various items reported in the financial statements. Management uses this section to highlight favorable and unfavorable trends and significant risks facing the company.

managerial accounting – the provision of accounting information for a company's internal users.

manufacturers – companies that buy and transform raw materials into a finished product which is then sold.

manufacturing organization – an organization that produces tangible products.

manufacturing overhead – all product costs other than direct materials and direct labor. In a manufacturing firm, manufacturing overhead also is known as *factory burden* or *indirect* manufacturing costs. Costs are included as manufacturing overhead if they cannot be traced to the cost object of interest (e.g., unit of product).

margin – the ratio of net operating income to sales.

margin of safety – the units sold, or expected to be sold, or sales revenue earned, or expected to be earned, above the break-even volume.

market rate – the market rate of interest demanded by creditors.

markup – the percentage applied to a base cost; it includes desired profit and any costs not included in the base cost.

master budget – the collection of all area and activity budgets representing a firm's comprehensive plan of action.

matching principle – a principle that requires an expense to be recorded and reported in the same period as the revenue that it helped generate.

materials price variance (MPV) – the difference between the actual price paid per unit of materials and the standard price allowed per unit multiplied by the actual quantity of materials purchased.

materials requisition form – a source document that records the type, quantity, and unit price of the direct materials issued to each job.

materials usage variance (MUV) – the difference between the direct materials actually used and the direct materials allowed for the actual output multiplied by the standard price.

maturity – the date on which a borrower agrees to pay the creditor the face (or par) value.

merchandise inventory – the inventory held by merchandisers.

merchandisers – companies, either retailers or wholesalers, that purchase inventory in a finished condition and hold it for resale without further processing.

method of least squares (regression) – a statistical method to find the best-fitting line through a set of data points. It is used to break out the fixed and variable components of a mixed cost.

mixed costs – costs that have both a fixed and a variable component.

monetary incentives – the use of economic rewards to motivate managers.

monetary unit assumption – one of the four basic assumptions that underlie accounting that requires that a company account for and report its financial results in monetary terms (e.g., U.S. dollar, euro, Japanese yen).

mortgage bonds – bonds that are secured by real estate.

mutually exclusive projects – projects that, if accepted, preclude the acceptance of competing projects.

myopic behavior – behavior that occurs when a manager takes actions that improve budgetary performance in the short run but bring long-run harm to the firm.

N

natural resources – resources, such as coal deposits, oil reserves, and mineral deposits, that are physically consumed as they are used by a company and that can generally be replaced or restored only by an act of nature.

net income – the excess of a company's revenue over its expenses during a period of time.

net loss – the excess of a company's expenses over its revenues during a period of time.

net present value – the difference between the present value of a project's cash inflows and the present value of its cash outflows.

net profit margin percentage – a measure of the proportion of each sales dollar that is profit, determined by dividing net income by net sales.

net sales revenue – computed as gross sales revenue minus sales returns and allowances, as well as sales discounts.

noncash investing and financing activities – investing and financing activities that take place without affecting cash. For example, a company may choose to acquire an operating asset (e.g., building) by issuing long-term debt.

nondiscounting models – capital investment models that identify criteria for accepting or rejecting projects without considering the time value of money.

nonmonetary incentives – the use of psychological and social rewards to motivate managers.

non-sufficient funds (NSF) check – a check that has been returned to the depositor because funds in the issuer's account are not sufficient to pay the check (also called a "bounced" check).

nontrade receivables – receivables that arise from transactions not involving inventory (e.g., interest receivable or cash advances to employees).

nonunit-level activity drivers – factors that measure the consumption of nonunit-level activities by products and other cost objects.

nonvalue-added activities – all activities other than those that are absolutely essential to remain in business.

nonvalue-added costs – costs that are caused either by nonvalue-added activities or by the inefficient performance of value-added activities.

no-par stock – stock without a par value.

normal balance – the type of balance expected of an account based on its effect on the fundamental accounting equation. Assets, expenses and dividends have normal debit balances while liabilities, stockholders' equity, and revenues have normal credit balances.

normal cost of goods sold – the cost of goods sold before adjustment for any overhead variance.

normal cost system – an approach that assigns the actual costs of direct materials and direct labor to products but uses a predetermined rate to assign overhead costs.

note(s) payable – a payable that arises when a business borrows money or purchases goods or services from a company that requires a formal agreement or contract.

notes receivable – receivables that generally specify an interest rate and a maturity date at which any interest and principal must be repaid.

notes to the financial statements (or footnotes) – notes that clarify and expand upon the information presented in the financial statements.

O

operating assets – assets used to generate operating income, consisting usually of cash, inventories, receivables, and property, plant, and equipment. Average operating assets are found by adding together beginning operating assets and ending operating assets, and dividing the result by 2.

operating budgets – budgets associated with the income-producing activities of an organization.

operating cash flow ratio – a ratio that looks at the ability of operations to generate cash, which recognizes the more general concept that current obligations will be paid through operations (after all, selling inventory and collecting receivables is a big part of operations). This ratio is calculated as Cash Flows from Operating Activities ÷ Current Liabilities.

operating cycle – the average time that it takes a company to purchase goods, resell the goods, and collect the cash from customers.

operating income – revenues minus operating expenses from the firm's normal operations. Operating income is before-tax income.

operating lease – the most common form of lease in which the lessor (the legal owner of the asset) retains the risks and obligations of ownership, while the lessee uses the asset during the term of the lease.

operating leverage – the use of fixed costs to extract higher percentage changes in profits as sales activity changes. Leverage is achieved by increasing fixed costs while lowering variable costs.

operating margin percentage – a measure of the profitability of a company's operations in relation to its sales that is calculated as Income from Operations ÷ Net Sales.

opportunity cost – the benefit given up or sacrificed when one alternative is chosen over another.

ordering costs – the costs of placing and receiving an order.

organizational costs – significant costs such as legal fees, stock issue costs, accounting fees, and promotional fees that a company may incur when it is formed.

outstanding check – a check that has been issued and recorded by the business but that has not been "cashed" by the recipient of the check.

outstanding shares – the number of issued shares actually in the hands of stockholders.

overapplied overhead – the amount by which applied overhead exceeds actual overhead.

overhead budget – a budget that reveals the planned expenditures for all indirect manufacturing items.

overhead variance – the difference between actual overhead and applied overhead.

P

par value – for stock, it is an arbitrary monetary amount printed on each share of stock that establishes a minimum price for the stock when issued, but does not determine its market value. For debt, par value is the amount of money the borrower agrees to repay at maturity.

parallel processing – a processing pattern in which two or more sequential processes are required to produce a finished good.

participating dividend preference – a provision that stockholders of participating preferred shares receive, in addition to the stated dividend, a share of amounts available for distribution as dividends to other classes of stock.

participative budgeting – an approach to budgeting that allows managers who will be held accountable for budgetary performance to participate in the budget's development.

partnership – a business owned jointly by two or more individuals.

patent – a type of intangible asset that grants the holder the right to manufacture, sell, or use a product. The legal life is 20 years from the date of the grant.

payback period – the time required for a project to return its investment.

payment date – the date on which the dividend will actually be paid.

payroll taxes – taxes that businesses must pay based on employee payrolls; these amounts are not withheld from employee pay, rather they are additional amounts that must be paid over and above gross pay.

percentage of credit sales method – a method of determining bad debt expense whereby past experience and management's view of how the future may differ from the past are used to estimate the percentage of the current period's credit sales that will eventually become uncollectible.

performance report – a report that compares the actual data with planned data.

period costs – costs that are expensed in the period in which they are incurred; they are not inventoried.

periodic inventory system – an inventory system that records the cost of purchases as they occur (in an account separate from the inventory account), takes a physical count of inventory at the end of the period, and applies the cost of goods sold model to determine the balances of ending inventory and cost of goods sold. The inventory account reflects the correct inventory balance only at the end of each accounting period.

permanent accounts – accounts of asset, liability, and stockholders' equity items whose balances are carried forward from the current accounting period to future accounting periods.

perpetual inventory system – an inventory system in which balances for inventory and cost of goods sold are continually (perpetually) updated with each sale or purchase of inventory. The accounts reflect the correct inventory and cost of goods sold balances throughout the period.

petty cash – a fund used to pay for small dollar amounts.

physical flow schedule – a schedule that reconciles units to account for with units accounted for. The physical units are not adjusted for percent of completion.

planning – a management activity that involves the detailed formulation of action to achieve a particular end.

plantwide overhead rate – a single overhead rate calculated using all estimated overhead for a factory divided by the estimated activity level across the entire factory.

postaudit – a follow-up analysis of an investment decision, comparing actual benefits and costs with expected benefits and costs.

posting – the process of transferring information from journalized transactions to the general ledger.

predetermined overhead rate – an overhead rate computed using estimated data.

preferred stock – a class of stock that generally does not give voting rights, but grants specific guarantees and dividend preferences.

premium – when a bond's selling price is above face value.

present value – determinations of present amounts based on expected future cash flows.

present value – the current value of a future cash flow. It represents the amount that must be invested now if the future cash flow is to be received assuming compounding at a given rate of interest.

prevention costs – cost incurred to prevent defects in products or services being produced.

price – the revenue per unit.

price (rate) variance – the difference between standard price and actual price multiplied by the actual quantity of inputs used.

price standards – the price that should be paid per unit of input.

prime cost – the sum of direct materials cost and direct labor cost.

principal – the amount of money borrowed and promised to be repaid (usually with interest).

prior period adjustment – the correction of an error made in the financial statements of a prior period. The adjustment is entered as a direct adjustment to retained earnings.

process-costing system – a costing system that accumulates production costs by process or by department for a given period of time.

process-value analysis – an approach that focuses on processes and activities and emphasizes systemwide performance instead of individual performance.

producing departments – units within an organization responsible for producing the products or services that are sold to customers.

product diversity – the situation present when products consume overhead in different proportions.

product (manufacturing) costs – costs associated with the manufacture of goods or the provision of services. Product costs include direct materials, direct labor, and overhead.

products – goods produced by converting raw materials through the use of labor and indirect manufacturing resources, such as the manufacturing plant, land, and machinery.

production budget – a budget that shows how many units must be produced to meet sales needs and satisfy ending inventory requirements.

production report – a document that summarizes the manufacturing activity that takes place in a process department for a given period of time.

profit center – a division of a company that is evaluated on the basis of operating income or profit.

profit-volume graph – a graphical portrayal of the relationship between profits and sales activity in units.

profitability ratios – ratios that measure two aspects of a corporation's profits: (1) those elements of operations that contribute to profit and (2) the relationship of profit to total investment and investment by stockholders.

property, plant, and equipment – the tangible, long-lived, productive assets used by a company in its operations to produce revenue. This includes land, buildings, machinery, manufacturing equipment, office equipment, and furniture.

pseudoparticipation – a budgetary system in which top management solicits inputs from lower-level managers and then ignores those inputs. Thus, in reality, budgets are dictated from above.

publicly traded companies – companies that issue stock traded on U.S. stock exchanges to which the Sarbanes-Oxley Act applies.

purchase allowance – a situation in which the purchaser chooses to keep the merchandise if the seller is willing to grant a deduction (allowance) from the purchase price.

purchase discounts – price reductions (usually expressed as a percentage of the purchase price) that companies offer their customers to encourage prompt payment.

purchase returns – the cost of merchandise returned to suppliers.

purchases – the cost of merchandise acquired for resale during the accounting period.

Q

quantity standards – the amount of input that should be used per unit of output.

quick ratio – a measure of a company's short-term liquidity that is calculated as follows: (Cash + Short-Term Investments + Receivables) ÷ Current Liabilities.

R

ratio analysis – an examination of financial statements conducted by preparing and evaluating a series of ratios.

ratios (financial ratios) – data that provide meaningful information only when compared with ratios from previous periods for the same firm or similar firms; they help by removing most of the effects of size differences.

raw materials inventory – the account in manufacturing firms that includes the basic ingredients to make a product.

realized external failure costs – environmental costs caused by environmental degradation and paid for by the responsible organization.

realized/realizable – one of two requirements for revenue to be recognized. An item is realized, or realizable, if noncash resources (i.e., inventory) have been exchanged for cash or near cash (e.g., accounts receivable).

reciprocal method – a method that simultaneously allocates service costs to all user departments. It gives full consideration to interactions among support departments.

relevance – one of the four qualitative characteristics that useful information should possess. Accounting information is said to be relevant if it is capable of making a difference in a business decision by helping users users predict future events or by providing feedback about prior expectations. Relevant information must also be provided in a timely manner.

relevant costs – future costs that change across alternatives.

relevant range – the range of output over which an assumed cost relationship is valid for the normal operations of a firm.

required rate of return – the minimum rate of return that a project must earn in order to be acceptable. Usually corresponds to the cost of capital.

research and development (R&D) expense – the cost of internal development of intangible assets that is expensed as incurred.

residual income – the difference between operating income and the minimum dollar return required on a company's operating assets.

residual value (salvage value) – the amount of cash or trade-in consideration that the company expects to receive when an asset is retired from service.

responsibility center – a segment of the business whose manager is accountable for specified sets of activities.

resource drivers – factors that measure the consumption of resources by activities.

retailers – merchandisers that sell directly to consumers.

retained earnings (or deficit) – the accumulated earnings (or losses) over the entire life of the corporation that have not been paid out in dividends.

return on assets – a ratio that measures the profit earned by a corporation through use of all its capital, or the total of the investment by both creditors and owners. Return on assets is calculated as: [Net Income + Interest (1 – Tax Rate)]/Average Total Assets.

return on common equity ratio – a ratio that is basically the same as the return on equity ratio. It is calculated as: Net Income/(Total Equity + Preferred Stock + Paid-In Capital – Preferred Stock).

return on equity – a ratio that measures the profit earned by a firm through the use of capital supplied by stockholders. Return on equity is computed as net income divided by average equity.

return on investment (ROI) – the ratio of operating income to average operating assets.

revenue – the increase in assets that results from the sale of products or services.

revenue center – a segment of the business that is evaluated on the basis of sales.

revenue expenditures – expenditures that do not increase the future economic benefits of the asset. These expenditures are expensed as they are incurred.

revenue recognition principle – a principle that requires revenue to be recognized or recorded in the period in which it is earned and the collection of cash is reasonably assured.

S

safeguarding – the physical protection of assets through, for example, fireproof vaults, locked storage facilities, keycard access, and anti-theft tags on merchandise.

sales allowance – a price reduction offered by the seller to induce the buyer to keep the goods when the goods are only slightly defective, are shipped late, or in some other way are rendered less valuable.

sales budget – a budget that describes expected sales in units and dollars for the coming period.

sales discount – a price reduction (usually expressed as a percentage of the selling price) that companies may offer to encourage prompt payment.

sales mix – the relative combination of products (or services) being sold by an organization.

sales returns – merchandise or goods returned by the customer to the seller.

sales taxes – money collected from the customer for the governmental unit levying the tax.

Sarbanes-Oxley Act (SOX) – passed in 2002 in response to revelations of misconduct and fraud by several well-known firms, this legislation established stronger governmental control and regulation of public companies in the United States, from enhanced oversight (PCAOB), to increased auditor independence and tightened regulation of corporate governance.

scattergraph method – a method to fit a line to a set of data using two points that are selected by judgment. It is used to break out the fixed and variable components of a mixed cost.

secured – a term used for a bond that has some collateral pledged against the corporation's ability to pay.

Securities and Exchange Commission (SEC) – the federal agency established by Congress to regulate securities markets and ensure effective public disclosure of accounting information. The SEC has the power to set accounting rules for publicly traded companies.

securitization – a process in which large businesses and financial institutions frequently package factored receivables as financial instruments or securities and sell them to investors.

segment – a subunit of a company of sufficient importance to warrant the production of performance reports.

segment margin – the contribution a segment makes to cover common fixed costs and provide for profit after direct fixed costs and variable costs are deducted from the segment's sales revenue.

segregation of duties – the idea that accounting and administrative duties should be performed by different individuals, so that no one person has access to the asset and prepares all the documents and records for an activity.

sell-or-process-further decision – relevant costing analysis that focuses on whether a product should be processed beyond the split-off point.

selling and administrative expenses budget – a budget that outlines planned expenditures for nonmanufacturing activities.

selling costs – those costs necessary to market, distribute, and service a product or service.

semi-variable – a type of cost behavior where the true total cost function is increasing at a decreasing rate.

sensitivity analysis – the "what-if" process of altering certain key variables to assess the effect on the original outcome.

sequential (or step) method – a method that allocates service costs to user departments in a sequential manner. It gives partial consideration to interactions among support departments.

sequential processing – a processing pattern in which units pass from one process to another in a set order.

service charges – fees charged by the bank for checking account services.

service organization – an organization that produces intangible products.

services – tasks or activities performed for a customer or an activity performed by a customer using an organization's products or facilities.

shareholders – see *stockholders*

short-term liquidity ratios – a type of ratio that compares some combination of current assets or operations to current liabilities.

slope – the variable cost per unit of activity usage.

societal costs – see *unrealized external failure costs*

sole proprietorship – a business owned by one person.

special-order decisions – relevant costing analyses that focus on whether a specially priced order should be accepted or rejected.

specific identification method – an inventory costing method that determines the cost of ending inventory and the cost of goods sold based on the identification of the actual units sold and in inventory. This method does not require an assumption about the flow of costs but actually assigns cost based on the specific flow of inventory.

split-off point – the point at which products become distinguishable after passing through a common process.

staff positions – positions that are supportive in nature and have only indirect responsibility for an organization's basic objectives.

standard cost per unit – the per-unit cost that should be achieved given materials, labor, and overhead standards.

standard cost sheet – a listing of the standard costs and standard quantities of direct materials, direct labor, and overhead that should apply to a single product.

standard hours allowed (SH) – the direct labor hours that should have been used to produce the actual output (Unit labor standard × Actual output).

standard quantity of materials allowed (*SQ*) – the quantity of materials that should have been used to produce the actual output (Unit materials standard × Actual output).

stated capital (legal capital) – the amount of capital that, under law, cannot be returned to the corporation's owners unless the corporation is liquidated.

stated rate – see *interest rate*

statement of cash flows – a financial statement that provides relevant information about a company's cash receipts (inflows of cash) and cash payments (outflows of cash) during an accounting period.

statement of retained earnings – a financial statement that reports how much of the company's income was retained in the business and how much was distributed to owners for a period of time.

static budget – a budget for a particular level of activity.

step cost – a cost that displays a constant level of cost for a range of output and then jumps to a higher level of cost at some point, where it remains for a similar range of output.

stock dividend – a dividend paid to stockholders in the form of additional shares of stock (instead of cash).

stock repurchase payout ratio – a ratio that addresses the distribution of company value and can be calculated directly as Common Stock Repurchase ÷ Net Income, or indirectly as Stock Repurchase Payout Ratio = Total Payout Ratio – Dividend Payout Ratio.

stock split – a stock issue that increases the number of outstanding shares of a corporation without changing the balances of its equity accounts.

stock warrant – the right granted by a corporation to purchase a specified number of shares of its capital stock at a stated price and within a stated time period.

stockholder ratios – ratios such as earnings per share and return on common equity that provide information about the creation of value for shareholders.

stockholders – the owners of a corporation who own its shares in varying numbers.

stockholders' equity – the owners' claims against the assets of a corporation after all liabilities have been deducted.

stockout costs – the costs of insufficient inventory.

straight-line depreciation – a depreciation method that allocates an equal amount of an asset's cost to depreciation expense for each year of the asset's useful life. Straight-line depreciation expense for each period is calculated by dividing the depreciable cost of an asset by the asset's useful life.

strategic plan – the long–term plan for future activities and operations, usually involving at least five years.

strategic risks – possible threats to the organization's success in accomplishing its objectives that are external to the organization.

sunk costs – costs for which the outlay has already been made and that cannot be affected by a future decision.

support departments – units within an organization that provide essential support services for producing departments.

T

T-account – a graphical representation of an account that gets its name because it resembles the capital letter T. A T-account is a two-column record that consists of an account title and two sides divided by a vertical line—the left side is called the debit side and the right side is called the credit side.

target cost – the difference between the sales price needed to achieve a projected market share and the desired per-unit profit.

target costing – a method of determining the cost of a product or service based on the price (target price) that customers are willing to pay.

temporary accounts – the accounts of revenue, expense, and dividend items that are used to collect the activities of only one period.

time period assumption – one of the four basic assumptions that underlie accounting that allows the life of a company to be divided into artificial time periods so net income can be measured for a specific period of time (e.g., monthly, quarterly, annually).

time series (or trend) analysis – a type of analysis that compares a single corporation across time.

time ticket – a source document by which direct labor costs are assigned to individual jobs.

time value of money – the idea that a cash flow in the future is less valuable than a cash flow at present.

timeliness – quality of information where it is available to users before it loses its ability to influence decisions.

times-interest-earned ratio – a leverage ratio that uses the income statement to assess a company's ability to service its debt. It is computed by dividing net income before taxes and interest by interest expense.

total budget variance – the difference between the actual cost of an input and its planned cost.

total payout ratio – a ratio that adds stock repurchases to common dividends and compares this to net income. It is calculated as: Total Payout Ratio = (Common Dividends + Common Stock Repurchases)/ Net Income.

total quality management – a management philosophy in which manufacturers strive to create an environment that will enable workers to manufacture perfect (zero-defect) products.

trade receivable – an account receivable that is due from a customer purchasing inventory in the ordinary course of business.

trademark – an intangible asset that grants the holder the right to the exclusive use of a distinctive name, phrase, or symbol. The legal life is 20 years but it can be renewed indefinitely.

transaction – any event, external or internal, that is recognized in the financial statements.

transaction analysis – the process of determining the economic effects of a transaction on the elements of the accounting equation.

transfer price – the price charged for goods transferred from one division to another.

transferred–in costs – costs transferred from a prior process to a subsequent process.

transportation-in – see *freight-in*

treasurer – the individual responsible for the finance function; raises capital and manages cash and investments.

treasury stock – previously issued stock that is repurchased by the issuing corporation.

trial balance – a list of all active accounts and each account's debit or credit balance.

turnover – the ratio of sales to average operating assets.

U

underapplied overhead – the amount by which actual overhead exceeds applied overhead.

understandability – quality of information whereby users with a reasonable knowledge of accounting and business can comprehend the meaning of that information.

unearned revenue – a liability that occurs when a company receives payment for goods that will be delivered or services that will be performed in the future.

unfavorable (*U*) variances – variances produced whenever the actual input amounts are greater than the budgeted or standard allowances.

unit-level activities – activities that are performed each time a unit is produced.

unit-level activity drivers – factors that measure the consumption of unit-level activities by products and other cost objects.

units-of-production method – a depreciation method that allocates the cost of an asset over its expected life in direct proportion to the actual use of the asset; depreciation expense is computed by multiplying an asset's depreciable cost by a usage ratio.

unrealized external failure costs – environmental costs caused by an organization but paid for by society.

unsecured – a term used for bonds in which the lender is relying on the general credit of the borrowing corporation rather than on collateral.

usage (efficiency) variance – the difference between standard quantities and actual quantities multiplied by standard price.

useful life – the period of time over which the company anticipates deriving benefit from the use of the asset.

V

value-added activities – activities that are necessary for a business to achieve corporate objectives and remain in business.

value-added costs – costs caused by value-added activities.

value chain – the set of activities required to design, develop, produce, market, and deliver products and services to customers.

variable budgets – see *flexible budget*

variable cost ratio – variable costs divided by sales revenues. It is the proportion of each sales dollar needed to cover variable costs.

variable costing – a product-costing method that assigns only variable manufacturing costs to production: direct materials, direct labor, and variable overhead. Fixed overhead is treated as a period cost.

variable costs – costs that, in total, vary in direct proportion to changes in output within the relevant range.

variable overhead efficiency variance – the difference between the actual direct labor hours used and the standard hours allowed multiplied by the standard variable overhead rate.

variable overhead spending variance – the difference between the actual variable overhead and the budgeted variable overhead based on actual hours used to produce the actual output.

verifiability – quality of information indicating the information is verifiable when independent parties can reach a consensus on the measurement of the activity.

vertical analysis – a type of analysis that expresses each financial statement line item as a percent of the largest amount on the statement.

voluntary disposal – a type of disposal that occurs when a company determines that the asset is no longer useful; the disposal may occur at the end of the asset's useful life or at some other time.

W

warranty – a warranty is a guarantee to repair or replace defective goods during a period (ranging from a few days to several years) following the sale.

weighted average costing method – a process-costing method that combines beginning inventory costs with current-period costs to compute unit costs. Costs and output from the current period and the previous period are averaged to compute unit costs.

wholesalers – merchandisers that sell to other retailers.

withholding – businesses are required to withhold taxes from employees' earnings; standard withholdings include federal, state, and possibly city or county income taxes, as well as Social Security and Medicare. Employees may also have amounts withheld for such things as retirement accounts and health insurance.

work distribution matrix – identifies the amount of labor consumed by each activity and is derived from the interview process (or a written survey).

work in process (WIP) – the cost of the partially completed goods that are still being worked on at the end of a time period.

work-in-process inventory – the account in manufacturing firms that consists of the raw materials that are used in production as well as other production costs such as labor and utilities.

working capital – a measure of liquidity computed as: Current Assets – Current Liabilities.

worksheet – an informal schedule that accountants use to assist them in organizing and preparing the information necessary to perform the end-of-period steps in the accounting cycle–namely the preparation of adjusting entries, financial statements, and closing entries.

Y

yield – the market rate of interest demanded by creditors; yield may differ from stated rate because the underwriter disagrees with the borrower as to the correct yield or because of changes in the economy or creditworthiness of the borrower between the setting of the stated rate and the date of issue.

CHECK FIGURES

Check figures are given for selected problems here. For the complete Check Figures for all applicable Cornerstone Exercises, Exercises, Problems, and Cases, please visit the companion website at www.cengagebrain.com.

Chapter 1

1-45A		2011 ending retained earnings = $93,450
1-46A	(b)	Equity at the beginning of the year = $52,600
	(d)	Expenses = $477,300
1-47A		Net income = $102,450
1-48A	(d)	Total liabilities = $1,165
	(e)	Total revenue = $72
1-49A		Net income = $30,100
		Retained earnings = $135,710
1-50A		2011 ending retained earnings = $41,850
1-51A	(d)	2011 dividends = $3,700
1-52A	1.	Net income = $36,000
		Ending retained earnings = $90,000
		Total current liabilities = $35,990
1-53A	(f)	Manning Company 2011 ending retained earnings = $7,500
	(m)	Corey Company 2011 net income = $7,100
1-54A	2.	Net loss = $(11,450)
	4.	Net income = $9,550
1-45B		2011 ending retained earnings = $303,700
1-46B	(b)	Total liabilities at the end of the year = $426,630
	(d)	Net income for the year = $94,120
1-47B		Net income = $143,425
1-48B	(d)	Total liabilities = $860
	(e)	Total revenue = $503
1-49B		Net income = $12,250
		Retained earnings = $48,200
1-50B		2011 ending retained earnings = $93,500
1-51B	(c)	Net income = $12,400
1-52B		Net income = $76,500
		Ending retained earnings = $179,800
		Total current liabilities = $68,400
1-53B	(f)	Compton Company total equity = $60,600
	(m)	Merlotte Company total equity = $34,400
1-54B	2.	Net income = $63,250
	4.	Net income = $71,250

Chapter 2

2-48A	1.	Cash column total = $31,410
		Retained Earnings column total = $8,940
	2.	Trial balance total = $58,790
2-49A	2.	Trial balance total = $8,200
2-52A	2.	Ending Cash balance = $10,290
2-53A	3.	Ending Cash balance = $9,820
	4.	Trial balance total = $168,850
2-54A	3.	Ending Cash balance = $520,400

		Ending Accounts Receivable balance = $11,000
	4.	Trial balance total = $1,372,100
2-48B	1.	Cash column total = $14,910
		Retained Earnings column total = $5,740
	2.	Trial balance total = $33,495
2-49B	2.	Trial balance total = $6,335
2-52B	2.	Ending Cash balance = $11,745
2-53B	3.	Ending Cash balance = $57,220
	4.	Trial balance total = $178,800
2-54B	3.	Ending Cash balance = $226,700
		Ending Accounts Receivable balance = $121,000
	4.	Trial balance total = $914,000

Chapter 3

3-57A	1. b.	Credit to Accounts Receivable = $2,332,028
	e.	Debit to Accounts Payable = $39,200
	h.	Debit to Interest Expense = $30,000
	2.	Ending Cash balance = $2,012,324
		Ending Interest Payable balance = $30,000
	3.	Net income = $1,125,948
	4.	Ending retained earnings = $1,563,323
	5.	Total current liabilities = $578,707
3-58A	1.	Adjusted Trial Balance columns totals = $5,581,688
		Net income = $32,512
		Ending retained earnings = $71,712
	2.	Total current liabilities = $159,438
3-49B	1.	Cash-basis March income = $1,950
	2.	Accrual-basis March income = $1,560
3-50B	1 and 2.	2011 total expenses = $51,670
3-51B	2. b.	Credit to Service Revenue = $2,825
	d.	Credit to Prepaid Insurance = $750
	g.	Debit to Supplies Expense = $175
3-52B	1. b.	Debit to Accounts Receivable = $17,640
	e.	Debit to Supplies Expense = $661
	2.	Net understatement of income would be $32,734
3-54B	2.	Total operating expenses = $923,890
		Ending retained earnings = $67,730
		Total current liabilities = $69,130
3-55B	1. (a)	Adjusted Prepaid Insurance = $4,144
	(d)	Adjusted Service Revenue = $132,130
	(e)	Adjusted Depreciation Expense = $10,500
	2. (b)	Credit to Interest Payable = $4,175
	(c)	Credit to Wages Payable = $17,600
3-56B	1.	Credit to Retained Earnings = $49,250
	2.	Net income = $49,250
3-57B	1. b.	Credit to Accounts Receivable = $199,100
	g.	Debit to Accounts Payable = $73,000
	h.	Debit to Interest Expense = $2,700
	2.	Ending Cash balance = $12,300
		Ending Interest Payable balance = $2,700

3. Net income = $38,500
4. Ending retained earnings = $86,500
5. Total current liabilities = $36,800
3-58B 1. Adjusted Trial Balance columns totals = $2,204,300
Net income = $148,900
Ending retained earnings = $135,600
2. Total current liabilities = $88,600

Chapter 4

4-46A 1. Adjusted cash balance = $5,805
4-47A 1. Adjusted cash balance = $7,806.81
4-48A 1. Adjusted cash balance = $7,550
4-49A f. Credit to Cash = $320
4-46B 1. Adjusted cash balance = $5,725
4-47B 1. Adjusted cash balance = $8,100
4-48B 1. Adjusted cash balance = $9,500
4-49B f. Credit to Cash = $675

Chapter 5

5-60A 1. Expected gross margin with discount policy = $196,000
5-61A 2. Cash collected = $2,810,700
5-62A 2. Debit to Cash = $84,150
4. Implied interest rate = 24% (approximate)
5-64A 1. 2011 loss rate = 0.082
6. Increase in income from operations = $49,034
5-65A 3. Credit to Allowance for Doubtful Accounts = $16,179
5-66A 4. Credit to Allowance for Doubtful Accounts = $17,438
5-67A May 1, 2012 credit to Interest Income = $150
Sept. 1, 2012 credit to Interest Receivable = $53.33
5-68A 1. b. 2010 operating margin = 37.04%
d. 2010 accounts receivable turnover = 10.34
5-60B 1. Expected gross margin with discount policy = $277,500
5-61B 2. Cash collected = $1,452,250
5-62B 2. Debit to Cash = $242,500
4. Implied interest rate = 36+% (approximate)
5-64B 1. 2011 loss rate = 0.087
6. Increase in income from operations = $4,824
5-65B 3. Credit to Allowance for Doubtful Accounts = $16,993
5-66B 4. Credit to Allowance for Doubtful Accounts = $20,161
5-67B May 1, 2012 credit to Interest Income = $267
Sept. 1, 2012 credit to Interest Receivable = $120
5-68B 1. b. 2010 operating margin = 17.95%
d. 2010 accounts receivable turnover = 5.38

Chapter 6

6-56A (c) 2010 cost of goods sold = $243,170
(f) 2011 ending inventory = $54,680
6-57A 2. Gross margin = $12,444
6-58A 1. FIFO cost of goods sold = $452.60
2. LIFO ending inventory = $36

3. Average cost method cost of goods sold = $455.91
6-59A 1. FIFO 2010 cost of goods sold = $9,540
2. LIFO 2011 ending inventory = $1,420
3. Average cost 2011 cost of goods sold = $4,491
6. Weighted average 2011 inventory turnover = 1.73
6-60A 2. Credit to inventory = $1,225
6-61A 1. FIFO cost of goods sold = $36,700,000
LIFO cost of goods sold = $37,200,000
Average cost method cost of goods sold = $36,753,500
2. FIFO final inventory valuation = $4,060,000
6-62A 2. 2010 gross margin = $2,035,400
6-63A 1. FIFO ending inventory = $48
2. LIFO ending inventory = $36
3. Weighted average cost per unit = $7.1514
6-64A 1. FIFO 2010 gross margin = $12,210
2. LIFO 2010 gross margin = $11,380
3. Weighted average 2010 cost per unit = $11.3478
6-56B (c) 2010 goods available for sale = $111,670
(f) 2011 ending inventory = $11,670
6-57B 2. Gross margin = $6,524
6-58B 1. FIFO cost of goods sold = $4,066
2. LIFO ending inventory = $264
3. Average cost method cost of goods sold = $4,102.40
6-59B 1. FIFO 2010 cost of goods sold = $63,300
2. LIFO 2011 ending inventory = $10,700
3. Average cost 2011 cost of goods sold = $72,155
6. Weighted average 2011 inventory turnover = 3.52
6-60B 2. Credit to Inventory = $1,200
6-61B 1. FIFO cost of goods sold = $32,180
LIFO cost of goods sold = $32,490
Average cost method cost of goods sold = $32,224
2. LIFO final inventory valuation = $740
6-62B 2. 2010 gross margin = $372,750
6-63B 1. FIFO ending inventory = $405
2. LIFO ending inventory = $264
3. Weighted average cost per unit = $111.7750
6-64B 1. FIFO 2010 gross margin = $44,700
2. LIFO 2010 gross margin = $41,200
3. Weighted average 2010 cost per unit = $54.1765

Chapter 7

7-57A Total property, plant, and equipment = $226,700
7-58A 1. Acquisition cost = $38,218
2. Two items were expensed.
7-59A 3. Straight-line year 2 book value = $99,000
Double-declining year 2 book value = $73,125
Units-of-production year 2 book value = $91,932
7-60A 2. Year 3 ending book value = $11,750
7-61A 2. Book value after renovation = $17,800
3. Revised yearly depreciation = $1,630
7-63A 1. Gain on building = $30,000
Loss on furniture and fixtures = $32,500
7-64A 1. Debit to Goodwill = $85,000
3. Credit to Accumulated Depletion = $225,000
7-65A 1. Credit to Patent = $159,600
2. Debit to Patent = $122,500
4. Debit to Loss from Impairment = $478,800

7-57B		Total property, plant, and equipment = $303,155
7-58B	1.	Acquisition cost = $54,908
	2.	One item is expensed.
7-59B	3.	Straight-line year 2 book value = $76,680
		Double-declining year 2 book value = $60,480
		Units-of-production year 2 book value = $76,680
7-60B	2.	Year 3 ending book value = $29,160
7-61B	2.	Book value after renovation = $36,160
	3.	Revised yearly depreciation = $2,930
7-63B	1.	Gain on truck = $1,350
		Loss on furniture = $350
7-64B	1.	Debit to Goodwill = $1,250,000
	3.	Credit to Accumulated Depletion = $3,696,429
7-65B	2.	Credit to Copyright = $90,625

Chapter 8

8-56A	1. h.	Credit to Cash = $547,266
	i.	Debit to Unearned Sales Revenue = $22,000
	2.	Debit to Interest Expense = $25,000
8-57A	1.	Credit to Cash = $211,002.50
	2.	Total cost = 138.6% of gross pay
8-58A	2.	Credit to Interest Payable = $12,000
	4.	Debit to Interest Expense = $16,000
8-59A	2.	No journal entry necessary.
	4.	Credit to Cash = $81,600
8-60A	1.	Total billing = $2,556,135
8-61A	1.	Reported as current liability = $50,000
	2.	Debit to Cash = $150,000
		Reported as noncurrent liability = $62,500
	3.	Debit to Unearned Sales Revenue = $75,000
8-62A	1.	2011 warranty expense = $57,300
	3.	Balance 12/31/11 = $44,300
8-63A	2.	2012 quick ratio = 0.81
	3.	2011 cash ratio = .29
	4.	2012 operating cash flows ratio = 0.33
8-56B	1. h.	Credit to Cash = $1,075,484
	i.	Debit to Unearned Sales Revenue = $40,000
	2.	Debit to Interest Expense = $21,250
8-57B	1.	Credit to Cash = $973,775
	2.	Total cost = 136.95% of gross pay
8-58B	2.	Credit to Interest Payable = $2,750
	4.	Debit to Interest Expense = $6,875
8-59B	2.	No journal entry necessary.
	4.	Credit to Cash = $823,900
8-60B	1.	Total billing = $415,099.50
8-61B	1.	Reported as current liability = $91,000
	2.	Debit to Cash = $364,000
		Reported as noncurrent liability = $65,000
	3.	Debit to Unearned Sales Revenue = $104,000
8-62B	1.	2011 warranty expense = $101,250
	3.	Balance 12/31/11 = $16,250
8-63B	2.	2011 quick ratio = 0.81
	3.	2010 cash ratio = .29
	4.	2011 operating cash flows ratio = 0.33

Chapter 9

9-73A		Current liabilities = $158,100
9-74A	2.	Credit to Interest Payable = $5,850
	3.	Debit to Interest Expense = $1,950
9-75A		Carrying value 12/31/13 = $101,800
9-76A	2.	Credit to Discount on Notes Payable = $360
	4.	Carrying value = $796,400

9-77A	1.	Carrying value 12/31/14 = $710,400
	2.	Debit to Interest Expense = $30,650
9-78A	1.	Carrying value, 06/30/15 = $495,200
	2.	06/30/12 credit to Discount on Bonds Payable = $1,600
9-79A	1.	Carrying value, 12/31/13 = $5,100,000
9-80A	2.	Debit to Interest Expense = $12,900
9-81A		Carrying value, 12/31/14 = $2,590,000
9-82A	3.	Debit to Capital Lease Liability = $30,322
9-73B		Current liabilities = $144,500
9-74B	2.	Credit to Interest Payable = $15,767
	3.	Debit to Interest Expense = $1,433
9-75B		Carrying value 12/31/13 = $251,500
9-76B	2.	Credit to Discount on Notes Payable = $725
	4.	Carrying value = $992,750
9-77B	1.	Carrying value 12/31/14 = $920,000
	2.	Debit to Interest Expense = $28,750
9-78B	1.	Carrying value, 06/30/16 = $694,000
	2.	06/30/13 credit to Discount on Bonds Payable = $2,000
9-79B	1.	Carrying value, 12/31/13 = $4,080,000
9-80B	2.	Debit to Interest Expense = $10,150
9-81B		Carrying value, 12/31/13 = $3,160,000
9-82B	3.	Debit to Capital Lease Liability = $20,980

Chapter 10

10-66A		Total stockholders' equity = $1,218,000
10-67A	b.	Credit to Additional Paid-In Capital—Common Stock = $56,000
	c.	Credit to Additional Paid-In Capital—Preferred Stock = $60,000
10-68A	1. b.	Debit to Retained Earnings = $16,000
	d.	Credit to Treasury Stock = $173,200
	2.	Cumulative effect on equity = $(138,700)
10-69A	1. e.	Credit to Treasury Stock = $5,200
	2.	Total stockholders' equity = $2,695,800
10-70A	1. e.	Credit to Dividends Payable = $165,825
	g.	Debit to Retained Earnings = $460,625
	h.	Credit to Dividends Payable = $193,463
	2.	Total dividends for the year = $932,413
	3.	Cumulative effect on assets = $(471,788)
10-71A	2.	Retained earnings reported = $73,000
		Credit to Additional Paid-In Capital—Common Stock = $120,000
10-72A	1.	Total annual dividends = $174,200
	2.	Total dividends in arrears = $41,700
10-73A		Stock repurchase payout = 61.44%
		Return on common equity = 43.13%
10-66B		Total stockholders' equity = $9,883,000
10-67B	b.	Credit to Additional Paid-In Capital—Common Stock = $42,000
	c.	Credit to Additional Paid-In Capital—Preferred Stock = $10,000
10-68B	1. b.	Debit to Retained Earnings = $13,000
	d.	Credit to Treasury Stock = $83,800
	2.	Cumulative effect on equity = $(61,400)
10-69B	1. e.	Credit to Treasury Stock = $15,200
	2.	Total stockholders' equity = $6,275,300
10-70B	1. e.	Credit to Dividends Payable = $323,800
	g.	Debit to Retained Earnings = $1,214,250
	h.	Credit to Dividends Payable = $400,703

2.   Total dividends for the year = $2,102,753
3.   Cumulative effect on assets = $(888,503)

10-71B 2.   Retained earnings reported = $197,500
      Credit to Additional Paid-In Capital—Common
      Stock = $7,000

10-72B 1.   Total annual dividends = $275,500
     2.   Total dividends in arrears = $157,500

10-73B 1.   Stock repurchase payout = 53.66%
      Return on common equity = 48.89%

Chapter 11

11-44A 1.   Financing = 4 items
     2.   No cash effect = 2 items

11-45A 1.   Total adjustments = $179,525

11-46A 1.   Total adjustments = $43,215
      Net cash used for investing activities = $(105,800)

11-47A   Gain on disposal of equipment = $(2,500)
      Gain on sale of investments = $(4,100)
      Net cash provided by operating activities =
      $27,100
      Net cash used for investing activities = $(5,250)

11-48A 1.   Total adjustments = $12,400
      Net cash used for investing activities = $(84,200)

11-49A 1.   Net cash provided by operating activities = $8,765
      Net cash provided by financing activities = $92,000

11-50A   Cash paid for operating expenses = $(887,700)
      Net cash provided by operating activities =
      $287,645

11-51A 1.   Total of Adjustments columns = $1,276,000
      Total adjustments to net income = $257,000
      Net cash used for investing activities = $(419,000)

11-44B 1.   Financing = 3 items
     2.   No cash effect = 3 items

11-45B 1.   Total adjustments = $313,945

11-46B 1.   Total adjustments = $151,900
      Net cash used for investing activities = $(102,060)

11-47B   Loss on disposal of PP&E = $4,200
      Loss on sale of investments = $1,500
      Net cash provided by operating activities =
      $58,125
      Net cash used for investing activities = $(45,725)

11-48B 1.   Total adjustments = $301,000
      Net cash used for investing activities = $(295,000)

11-49B 1.   Net cash provided by operating activities =
      $170,700
      Net cash used for financing activities = $(28,000)

11-50B   Cash paid for operating expenses = $(824,400)
      Net cash provided by operating activities =
      $359,245

11-51B 1.   Purchase of investments = $15,000
      Total of Adjustments columns = $965,600
      Total adjustments to net income = $63,800
      Net cash used for investing activities = $(434,400)

Chapter 12

12-75A   2011 total revenues = 139.55%
      2010 total costs and expenses = 120.95%
      2011 total operating income = 157.56%
      2010 net income = 128.29%

12-77A 1.   Net income growth = 42%
     3.   Quick ratio = 0.93

5.   2012 expected net income = $2,849
6.   Capital to be raised = $2,704.50

12-78A 1.   2011 revenues = 130.88%
      2011 total costs and expenses = 131.26%
      2011 net income = 127.16%
      2010 revenues = 113.37%
      2010 total costs and expenses = 113.44%
      2010 net income = 114.69%
     3.   2011 current assets = 74.09%
      2011 total liabilities = 24.75%
      2011 shareholders' equity = 75.25%
      2010 current assets = 74.10%
      2010 total liabilities = 29.30%
      2010 shareholders' equity = 70.70%

12-79A 1.   2011 average accounts receivable = $4,174
      2010 accounts receivable turnover ratio = 11.85
      2011 average inventories = $5,271
      2010 inventory turnover ratio = 6.27
      2011 average total assets = $14,581
      2010 asset turnover ratio = 3.60
     2.   2010 gross profit percentage = 39.87
      2010 operating margin percentage = 7.27%
      2010 net profit margin percentage = 4.65%
      2011 interest expense net of tax = $890.60
      2011 average total assets = $14,581
      2010 return on assets = 21.55%
      2011 average equity = $7,426
      2010 return on equity = 29.94%
     3.   2011 EBIT = $4,401
      2010 EBIT = $3,431
      2010 long-term debt-to-equity ratio = 0.46
      2010 long-term debt-to-total assets ratio = 0.25

12-81A 1.   2011 quick assets = $958,831
      2010 quick assets = $856,068
      2010 cash ratio = 0.62
      2010 operating cash flow ratio = 0.36
      2011 EBIT = $620,255
      2010 times interest earned ratio = 18.02
      2010 long-term debt-to-equity ratio = 0.06
      2010 long-term debt-to-total assets ratio = 0.04
      2011 average accounts receivable = $631,782.50
      2010 accounts receivable turnover ratio = 6.09
      2011 average inventory = $532,094
      2010 inventory turnover ratio = 3.95
      2011 average total assets = $2,030,162
      2010 asset turnover ratio = 1.90
      2011 income from operations = $621,730
      2010 income from operations = $554,624
      2011 net income + interest net of
      tax = $380,819.75
      2010 average total assets = $1,790,646
      2011 average common equity = $1,485,087.50
      2010 return on common equity = 27.94%
      2010 total payout ratio = 190.25%
      2011 stock repurchase payout = 254.82%

12-82A 1.   2010 LIFO cost of goods sold = $5,090,000
      2010 FIFO cost of goods sold = $5,005,000
     2.   2010 depreciation at 10% = $115,000

12-75B   2011 total revenues = 70.03%
      2010 total costs and expenses = 87.95%
      2011 total operating income = 57.72%
      2010 net income = 119.59%

12-77B 1. Net income growth = 906%
3. Quick ratio = 0.93
5. 2012 expected net income = $2,856
6. Capital to be raised = $2,658.75

12-78B 1. 2011 revenues = 129.07%
2011 total costs and expenses = 124.30%
2011 net income = 149.09%
2010 revenues = 114.91%
2010 total costs and expenses = 113.23%
2010 net income = 125.92%
3. 2011 current assets = 74.28%
2011 total liabilities = 25.74%
2011 shareholders' equity = 74.26%
2010 current assets = 73.58%
2010 total liabilities = 29.88%
2010 shareholders' equity = 70.12%

12-79B 1. 2011 average accounts receivable = $4,172
2010 accounts receivable turnover ratio = 12.41
2011 average inventories = $5,097
2010 inventory turnover ratio = 6.49
2011 average total assets = $14,424
2010 asset turnover ratio = 3.73
2. 2010 gross profit percentage = 40.13
2010 operating margin percentage = 5.94%
2010 net profit margin percentage = 3.21%
2011 interest expense net of tax = $976.30
2011 average total assets = $14,424
2010 return on assets = 16.85%
2011 average equity = $7,043
2010 return on equity = 21.96%
3. 2011 EBIT = $4,526
2010 EBIT = $2,985
2010 long-term debt-to-equity ratio = 0.49
2010 long-term debt-to-total assets ratio = 0.26

12-81B 1. 2011 quick assets = $972,164
2010 quick assets = $873,884
2010 cash ratio = 0.63
2010 operating cash flow = 0.89
2011 EBIT = $917,148
2010 times interest earned ratio = 23.35
2010 long-term debt-to-equity ratio = 0.07
2010 long-term debt-to-total assets ratio = 0.05
2011 average accounts receivable = $637,352.50
2010 accounts receivable turnover ratio = 6.35
2011 average inventory = $535,489
2010 inventory turnover ratio = 4.21
2011 average total assets = $2,058,712
2010 asset turnover ratio = 2.02
2011 income from operations = $919,073
2010 income from operations = $763,441
2011 net income + interest net of tax = $662,815.20
2010 average total assets = $1,804,037
2011 average equity = $1,489,299.50
2010 return on equity = 45.16%
2010 total payout ratio = 123.41%
2011 stock repurchase payout = 153.45%

12-82B 1. 2010 LIFO cost of goods sold = $5,188,000
2010 FIFO cost of goods sold = $5,090,000
2010 depreciation at 20% = $246,000
3. 2011 total current assets = 51.15%

2010 total current assets = 57.99%
2011 total liabilities = 33.89%
2010 total liabilities = 32.69%

Chapter 13

13-51 1. Total direct materials = $7,810
2. Net income = $6,120
13-52 1. Total owed by Natalie = $30
2. Total cost for Mary = $17.50
13-53 2. Cost of goods manufactured = $224,950
3. Cost of goods sold = $226,050
13-54 1. Total product cost = $9,200,000
2. Operating income = $2,000,000
3. Gross margin = $2,860,000
13-55 1. Cost of goods manufactured = $24,725
2. Cost of goods sold = $27,160
13-57 3. Operating income = $332,100
13-59 2. Magazine total prime costs = $4,500
4. Income before taxes = $2,010
13-60 2. Tent sale loss = ($1,300)

Chapter 14

14-43 2. Fixed receiving cost = $6,600
3. Receiving cost for the year = $295,200
14-44 2. Receiving cost = $25,180
14-45 2. Supplies variable rate = $6.50
4. Charge per hour = $75.69
14-46 2. Plan 2 unused minutes = 75
3. Plan 2 minutes used = 90
14-47 3. Variable rate = $4.50
14-49 1. 10 months' data intercept = 3,212.12
14-50 2. Variable power cost = $1.13 (rounded)
14-51 2. Fixed rate = $1,349

Chapter 15

15-40 1. Break-even units = 78,300
2. Units for target profit = 134,550
4. Margin of safety in units = 45,700
15-41 2. Break-even units = 47,699
15-42 1. Break-even sales = $10,199,184 (rounded) or $10,200,000
3. Profits underestimated = $625,050
5. Operating leverage = 4.54
15-43 2. Break-even basic sleds = 39,680
3. Increase in total contribution margin = $320,000
15-44 1. Margin of safety in units = 13,200
2. Operating income = $11,220
3. Units for target profit = 98,400
15-45 2. Revenue = $234,375
4. Break-even point = $250,000
15-46 1. Revenue = $450,000
2. Desk lamps = 8,998
3. Operating leverage = 4.0
15-47 2. Operating income = $34,000
3. Trim kits = 32,444
15-48 1. Breakeven units = 21,429
3. Operating income = $119,900
15-49 1. Contribution margin ratio = 0.22

	3.	Margin of safety = $330,000
	4.	Contribution margin from increased sales = $2,640
15-50	1.	Price = $70
15-51	1.	Contribution margin ratio = 0.25
	2.	Break-even units = 32,000
	4.	Margin of safety = $16,800
	5.	New operating income = $18,200
15-52	1.	Macduff degree of operating leverage = 9
	2.	Duncan break-even point = $250,000
	3.	Macduff increase in profits = 270%
15-53	1.	May current year contribution margin ratio = 0.549
	2.	May prior year breakeven sales = $24,599
	3.	May current year margin of safety = $6,529
15-54	1.	Grade I sales = 224 units
	2.	Grade II breakeven in units = 392
	3.	Additional contribution margin = $73,602
	4.	Increase in operating income = $25,365
15-55	1.	First process break even = 5,000 cases
	2.	Units for equal profit = 25,000 cases

Chapter 16

16-46	2.	Total cost Job 741 = $148,230
	4.	Cost of goods sold = $234,882
16-47	1.	Total = $10,575
16-48	2.	Total cost of Carter job = $2,179
	4.	Gross margin = $3,309
16-49	1.	Overhead rate = $6
	2.	Department B overhead rate = $4.125
16-50	2.	Finishing overhead rate = $75 per machine hour
	2.	Total manufacturing cost Job 2 = $24,170
16-51	1.	Total Ed's Job = $234
16-52	2.	Ending Work in Process = $16,526
16-53	2.	Total Job 519 = $3,448
16-54	1.	Overhead rate = 175%
	3.	Cost of goods manufactured = $245,000
16-55	2.	Applied overhead = $3,024
	5.	Adjusted cost of goods sold = $634,340
16-56	2.	Total Job 703 = $41,220
	4.	Ending balance Work in Process = $40,900
16-57	1.	Direct (lab) = $664,500
	2.	Sequential (lab) = $663,825
16-58	1.	Drilling rate = $15.30 per machine hour (direct); $16.23 (sequential)
16-59	2.	May overhead assigned = $200
	3.	Total cost = $475

Chapter 17

17-46	1.	Equivalent units of output = 80,400
	2.	Units transferred out = 79,200
	3.	Units transferred out = 9,900
17-47	1.	Total units to account for = 180,000
	2.	Equivalent units, conversion = 156,000
	3.	Total equivalent unit cost = $320
	4.	Cost of EWIP = $7,440,000
17-48	1.	Total equivalent unit cost = $320
17-49	1.	Total units to account for = 200,000
	2.	Equivalent units = 180,000
	3.	Unit cost = $5.20
17-50	1.	Cost per equivalent unit = $5.20

17-51	1.	Units to account for = 50,000
	2.	Equivalent units = 46,250
	3.	Unit cost = $0.60
	4.	Cost of EWIP = $750
	5.	Spoilage cost = $1,500
17-52	1.	Cost per equivalent unit = $12.00
17-53	1.	Cost per equivalent unit = $10.1994
17-54	1.	Total equivalent units = 500,000
	2.	Unit cost = $23.23
	3.	Cost of goods transferred out = $11,148,000
	5.	Unit paraffin cost = $6.36
17-55	1.	Unit cost = $5.74
17-56	1.	Cost of goods transferred out = $160,940
17-57	1.	Cost of goods transferred out = $17,349
	2.	Cost of units transferred out = $23,400
17-58	1.	Cost of units started and completed = $15,573
	2.	Cost of units started and completed = $23,174

Chapter 18

18-53	1.	Unit cost = $0.60
	2.	Duffel bags = $2.40 per unit
	3.	Backpacks = $1.20 per unit
18-54	1.	Model B overhead cost per unit = $6.75
	2.	Model B overhead per unit = $7.49
	3.	Model B overhead cost per unit = $8.38
18-55	1.	Total cost = $120,000
	2.	Basic unit cost = $87.50
18-56	1.	Cost per patient day = $226
	2.	Cost per patient day (complications) = $544
18-57	1.	Average monthly fee = $6.78
	2.	Cost per account (low) = $87.37
	3.	Profit (high balance) = $112.50
18-58	2.	Category 1 per-unit ordering cost = $0.08
	3.	Reduction = $2,450,000
18-59	1.	Watson unit cost = $1,096.60
18-60	2.	Potential reduction per unit = $7.10
	4.	Total potential unit reduction = $8.35
	5.	Greatest benefit = $12 price
18-61	1.	Total nonvalue cost = $1,204,800
	2.	Materials nonvalue-added cost = $164,000 U
18-62	1.	Theoretical cycle time = 8 minutes
	2.	Actual cycle time = 9.6 minutes
	3.	Reduction = $16.67 per telescope

Chapter 19

19-46	1.	Total cash, September = $249,219
19-47	1.	i. Budgeted income before taxes = $4,971,260
		j. Cash budget ending balance (March) = $2,686,004
19-48	1.	Total assets = $562,750
	2.	Cash budget ending cash balance (Sept.) = $12,005
	3.	Total assets = $565,605
19-50	1.	Ending cash balance = $24,722
19-51	10.	Income before taxes = $16,129,000
19-52	1.	December materials to be purchased = 5,150 yards
19-53	1.	September total cash = $79,446

Chapter 20

20-40	1.	MUV = $10,500 F
	2.	LRV = $0
	3.	LEV = $13,200 F
20-41	2.	LEV, Cutting = $300 U
20-42	1.	Standard cost per unit = $126.88
	2.	LEV = $2,457.60 U
	3.	Average time = 0.768 per unit
20-43	1.	Standard cost (normal) = $305 per patient day
	2.	MUV (cesarean) = $30,000 F
	3.	LEV (normal) = $3,200 U
	4.	LEV = $11,200 U
20-44	1.	UCL (labor) = $770,000
	2.	Total liquid variance = $117,000 U
	3.	LEV = $26,250 F
20-45	1.	June UCL (labor) = $26,400 (quantity standard)
	2.	May LRV = $6,996 F (2.12%)
20-46	1.	MPV = $1,475 U
	2.	LEV = $20,000 F
	3.	LRV = $0
20-47	1.	MUV = $2,700 U
	2.	LEV = $0
20-48	1.	MUV = $100,000 U
	2.	LEV = $24,000 U
	3.	Net effect = $46,000 U

Chapter 21

21-43	1.	Direct labor hours = 70,000 hours
	2.	Total variable costs = $196,000
21-44	1.	Direct labor hours for 20% lower = 56,000
	2.	Total overhead for 10% higher = $317,100
21-45	2.	Total cost variance = $1,610 U
21-46	1.	Total direct labor hours = 30,000
	2.	Total overhead costs = $271,700
21-47	1.	Variable = $685; Fixed = $13,000,000
	2.	Optimistic income = $5,750,000
21-48	1.	Total = $68,655
	2.	Supplies, variable = $2.30
21-49	1.	Total overhead costs (Formula 280) = $2,836.47
21-50	1.	Total cost = $22,127
21-51	1.	Total variance = $100,000 U
	2.	Total variance = $6,000 F
21-52	1.	Total variance = $2,500 F
	2.	Unit cost = $15.29
	3.	Total (20,000 moves) = $165,000
21-53	2.	Total variance = $184,360 F
21-54	1.	SFOR = $3.60; SVOR = $2.40
	2.	Total FOH variance = $15,600 U
	3.	Volume variance = $25,200 U
	4.	VOH efficiency variance = $1,680 F
21-55	1.	VOH efficiency = $20,000 U
	2.	FOH spending = $20,000 F
21-56	1.	Standard variable overhead rate = $1.85
	3.	Volume variance = $10,720 U
	4.	Efficiency variance = $22,015 U
21-57	3.	VOH spending variance = $7,996 U
	4.	0.26667 hour per unit
21-58	1.	Total variance = $40,000 U
	2.	Volume variance = $15,000 U; Efficiency variance = $15,000 U

Chapter 22

22-34	1.	ROI of radio project = 0.16
	2.	Residual income of division with radio = $450,000
22-35	1.	ROI Year 3 = 6.30%
	3.	Turnover = 0.75
	4.	Turnover = 0.83
22-36	1.	Turbocharger ROI = 15%
	4.	Residual income with neither = $289,000
22-37	2.	ROI = 10.34% (rounded)
	4.	Margin = 0.0913
	5.	EVA with investment = $122,500

Chapter 23

23-41	1.	Total net benefit = $100,000
23-42	1.	Cost to make = $367,000
	4.	Cost to make = $514,000
23-43	2.	Additional income per pound = $21.025
23-44	1.	Operating income = $6,100
	2.	Operating income = $16,558
	3.	Total segment margin = $29,620
23-45	1.	Increase Pat's profit = $18,400
	2.	Increase Steve's profit = $15,200
23-46	2.	Markup = $2,646
23-47	1.	Standard contribution margin per machine hour = $20
23-48	1.	Loss per box = ($0.05)
23-49	1.	Operating profit = $40,000
23-50	1.	$300,000
23-51	1.	Differential amount to process further = $4,900
23-52	1.	Monthly cost for Community Bank = $5,773

Chapter 24

24-36	2.	NPV = $10,269
24-37	2.	NPV = $106,642
24-38	1.	IRR = 12%
	2.	Cash flow = $33,681
	3.	Minimum CF = $39,327
24-39	1.	NPV = $40,032,752
	2.	NPV = $3,171,066
	3.	Seating rate = 78%
	4.	Seating rate = 71%
24-40	1.	Payback = 3.13 years
	2.	ARR = 10.68%
	3.	IRR = 14% (approximately)
	4.	NPV = $(21,025)
24-41	1.	NPV (scrap alternative) = $151,632
24-43	1.	Payback = 3.89 years
	2.	NPV = $(88,298)
	3.	NPV = $422,302
24-44	1.	Cost of capital = 0.10
	2.	NPV = $24,344
24-45	1.	NPV (20% rate) = $(25,391,280)
	2.	NPV (14%) = $4,374,962
	3.	NPV (14%) = $1,374,962
24-46	1.	NPV = $117,308
	2.	NPV = $(29,564)
	3.	NPV = $231,051
24-47	1.	NPV (standard) = $190,719
	2.	NPV (CAM) = $761,682
24-48	1.	NPV (CAM) = $198,550
	2.	NPV (Standard) = $95,524

INDEX

Summary of Managerial Equations

Chapter 13

1. Total product cost = Direct materials cost + Direct labor cost + Manufacturing overhead cost

2. $\text{Per-unit cost} = \dfrac{\text{Total product cost}}{\text{Number of units produced}}$

3. Beginning inventory of materials + Purchases − Direct materials used in production = Ending inventory of materials

4. Sales revenue = Price × Units sold

5. Gross margin = Sales revenue − Cost of goods sold

6. Operating income = Gross margin − Selling and administrative expense

Chapter 14

1. Total variable costs = Variable rate × Amount of output

2. Total cost = Total fixed cost + Total variable cost

3. Total cost = Fixed cost + (Variable rate × Output)

4. $\text{Variable rate} = \dfrac{\text{High point cost} - \text{Low point cost}}{\text{High point output} - \text{Low point output}}$

5. Fixed cost = Total cost at high point − (Variable rate × Output at high point)

6. Fixed cost = Total cost at low point − (Variable rate × Output at low point)

7. Variable rate
   $= \dfrac{\text{High point cost} - \text{Low point cost}}{\text{High point number of moves} - \text{Low point number of moves}}$

Chapter 15

1. Operating income = Total revenue − Total expense

2. Operating income = Sales − Total variable expenses − Total fixed expenses

3. Operating income = (Price × Number of units sold) − (Variable cost per unit × Number of units sold) − Total fixed cost

4. $\text{Break-even units} = \dfrac{\text{Total fixed cost}}{\text{Price} - \text{Variable cost per unit}}$

5. Sales revenue = Unit selling price × Units sold

6. $\text{Break-even sales} = \dfrac{\text{Total fixed expenses}}{\text{Contribution margin ratio}}$

7. Operating income = (Price × Units sold) − (Unit variable cost × Units sold) − Fixed cost

8. Number of units to earn target income
   $= \dfrac{\text{Fixed cost} + \text{Target income}}{\text{Price} - \text{Variable cost per unit}}$

9. $\text{Operating income} = \dfrac{\text{Target income}}{\text{Unit contribution margin}} + \text{Break-even volume}$

10. Operating income = Unit contribution margin × Change in units sold

11. $\text{Sales dollars to earn target income} = \dfrac{\text{Total fixed cost} + \text{Target income}}{\text{Contribution margin ratio}}$

12. Change in profits = Contribution margin ratio × Change in sales

13. Operating income = (Price × Units) − (Unit variable cost × Units) − Total fixed cost

14. Revenue = Price × Units

15. Total cost = (Unit variable cost × Units) + Fixed cost

16. $\text{Degree of operating leverage} = \dfrac{\text{Contribution margin}}{\text{Operating income}}$

17. Percentage change in operating income = DOL × Percent change in sales

Chapter 16

1. $\text{Predetermined overhead rate} = \dfrac{\text{Estimated annual overhead}}{\text{Estimated annual activity level}}$

2. Applied overhead = Predetermined overhead rate × Actual activity level

3. Total product costs = Actual direct materials + Actual direct labor + Applied overhead

4. Overhead variance = Applied overhead − Actual overhead

5. Adjusted COGS = Unadjusted COGS ± Overhead variance
   (*Note:* Applied overhead > Actual overhead *means* Overapplied overhead; subtract from COGS
   Applied overhead < Actual overhead *means* Underapplied overhead; add to COGS)

6. $\text{Departmental overhead rate} = \dfrac{\text{Estimated department overhead}}{\text{Estimated departmental activity level}}$

7. $\text{Unit product cost} = \dfrac{\text{Total product cost}}{\text{Number of units}}$

Chapter 17

1. $\text{Unit cost} = \dfrac{\text{Total cost}}{\text{Equivalent units}}$

2. Units started and completed = Total units completed − Units in BWIP
   Units started = Units started and completed + Units in EWIP

Chapter 18

1. $\text{Consumption ratio} = \dfrac{\text{Amount of activity driver per product}}{\text{Total driver quantity}}$

2. $\text{Overhead rate} = \dfrac{\text{Total overhead costs}}{\text{Total direct labor hours}}$

3. Overhead cost = Average consumption ratio × Total cost of each set of activities

Chapter 19

1. Units to be produced = Expected unit sales + Units in desired ending inventory (EI) − Units in beginning inventory (BI)

2. Purchases = Direct materials needed for production + Direct materials in desired ending inventory − Direct materials in beginning inventory

Chapter 20

1. Cost per unit = Total cost/Total units

2. Standard cost per unit = Quantity standard × Price standard

3. SQ = Unit quantity standard × Actual output

4. SH = Unit labor standard × Actual output

5. Total variance = Actual cost − Planned cost
   $= (AP \times AQ) - (SP \times SQ)$

6. Total materials variance = Actual cost − Planned cost
   $= (AP \times AQ) - (SP \times SQ)$

7. $MPV = (AP - SP) \times AQ$

8. $MUV = (AQ - SQ) \times SP$

9. $MPV = (AP \times AQ) - (SP \times AQ)$

10. $MPV = (AP - SP) \times AQ$

11. $MUV = (SP \times AQ) - (SP \times SQ)$

12. $MUV = (AQ - SQ) \times SP$

13. Total labor variance $= (AR \times AH) - (SR \times SH)$

14. Total labor variance = Labor rate variance + Labor efficiency variance

15. $LRV = (AR \times AH) - (SR \times AH)$

16. $LRV = (AR - SR) \times AH$
17. $LEV = (SR \times AH) - (SR \times SH)$
18. $LEV = (AH - SH) \times SR$
19. Target cost per unit = Expected sales price per unit − Desired profit per unit

Chapter 21

Abbrevations:

FOH = fixed overhead
VOH = variable overhead
AH = actual direct labor hours
SH = standard direct labor hours that *should have been worked* for actual units produced
$AVOR$ = actual variable overhead rate
$SVOR$ = standard variable overhead rate

1. $AVOR = \dfrac{\text{Actual variable overhead}}{\text{Actual hours}}$

2. Variable overhead spending variance $= (AH \times AVOR) - (AH \times SVOR)$
$= (AVOR - SVOR) \times AH$

3. Variable overhead efficiency variance $= (AH - SH) \times SVOR$

4. SH_p = Unit standard × Units of practical capacity

5. $SFOR = \dfrac{\text{Budgeted fixed overhead costs}}{\text{Practical capacity}}$

6. Applied fixed overhead $= SH \times SFOR$

7. Total variance = Actual fixed overhead − Applied fixed overhead

8. Fixed overhead spending variance $= AFOH - BFOH$

9. Volume variance = Budgeted fixed overhead − Applied fixed overhead
$= BFOH - (SH \times SFOR)$

Chapter 22

1. $ROI = \dfrac{\text{Operating income}}{\text{Average operating assets}}$

2. Average operating assets $= \dfrac{\text{(Beginning assets + Ending assets)}}{2}$

3.
$$ROI = \frac{\text{Operating income}}{\text{Sales}} \underset{\text{Margin}}{} \times \frac{\text{Sales}}{\text{Average operating assets}} \underset{\text{Turnover}}{}$$

4. Residual income = Operating income − (Minimum rate of return × Average operating assets)

5. EVA = After-tax operating income − (Actual percentage cost of capital × Total capital employed)

Chapter 23

1. Contribution margin per unit of the scare resource
$= \dfrac{\text{Selling price per unit} - \text{Variable cost per unit}}{\text{Required amount of scare resource per unit}}$

2. Price using markup = Cost per unit + (Cost per unit × Markup percentage)

3. Target cost = Target price − Desired profit

Chapter 24

1. Payback period $= \dfrac{\text{Original investment}}{\text{Annual cash flow}}$

2. Accounting rate of return $= \dfrac{\text{Average income}}{\text{Initial investment}}$

3. $NPV = \left[\sum CF_t/(1+i)^t\right] - I$
$= \left[\sum CF_t df_t\right]$
$= P - I$

4. $I = \sum [CF_t/(1+i)^t]$

5. $I = CF(df)$

6. $df = I/CF = \dfrac{\text{Investment}}{\text{Annual cash flow}}$

7. $F = P(1+i)$

8. $F = P(1+i)^n$

9. $P = F/(1+i)^n$

Cornerstones